Format for Bank Reconciliation:

Cash balance according to bank statement		$XXX
Add: Additions by company not on bank		
statement	$XXX	
Bank errors	XXX	XXX
		$XXX
Deduct: Deductions by company not on bank		
statement	$XXX	
Bank errors	XXX	XXX
Adjusted balance		$XXX

Cash balance according to company's records		$XXX
Add: Additions by bank not recorded by company	$XXX	
Company errors	XXX	XXX
		$XXX
Deduct: Deductions by bank not recorded		
by company	$XXX	
Company errors	XXX	XXX
Adjusted balance		$XXX

Inventory Costing Methods:

- First-in, First-out (FIFO)
- Last-in, First-out (LIFO)
- Average Cost

Interest Computations:

$$\text{Interest} = \text{Face Amount (or Principal)} \times \text{Rate} \times \text{Time}$$

Methods of Determining Annual Depreciation:

Straight-Line: $\dfrac{\text{Cost} - \text{Estimated Residual Value}}{\text{Estimated Life}}$

Double-Declining-Balance: Rate* × Book Value at Beginning of Period

*Rate is commonly twice the straight-line rate (1 ÷ Estimated Life).

Units-of-Activity Method:

Depreciation per Unit $= \dfrac{\text{Cost} - \text{Residual Value}}{\text{Total Estimated Units of Activity}}$

Depreciation Expense = Depreciation per Unit × Units of Activity for Period

Adjustments to Net Income (Loss) Using the Indirect Method:

	Increase (Decrease)
Net income (loss)	$ XXX
Adjustments to reconcile net income to	
net cash flow from operating activities:	
Depreciation of fixed assets	XXX
Amortization of intangible assets	XXX
Losses on disposal of assets	XXX
Gains on disposal of assets	(XXX)
Changes in current operating assets and liabilities:	
Increases in noncash current operating assets	(XXX)
Decreases in noncash current operating assets	XXX
Increases in current operating liabilities	XXX
Decreases in current operating liabilities	(XXX)
Net cash flow from operating activities	$ XXX
	or
	$(XXX)

Contribution Margin Ratio $= \dfrac{\text{Sales} - \text{Variable Costs}}{\text{Sales}}$

Break-Even Sales (Units) $= \dfrac{\text{Fixed Costs}}{\text{Unit Contribution Margin}}$

Sales (Units) $= \dfrac{\text{Fixed Costs} + \text{Target Profit}}{\text{Unit Contribution Margin}}$

Margin of Safety $= \dfrac{\text{Sales} - \text{Sales at Break-Even Point}}{\text{Sales}}$

Operating Leverage $= \dfrac{\text{Contribution Margin}}{\text{Income from Operations}}$

Variances:

$$\text{Direct Materials Price Variance} = \left(\text{Actual Price} - \text{Standard Price} \right) \times \text{Actual Quantity}$$

$$\text{Direct Materials Quantity Variance} = \left(\text{Actual Quantity} - \text{Standard Quantity} \right) \times \text{Standard Price}$$

$$\text{Direct Labor Rate Variance} = \left(\text{Actual Rate per Hour} - \text{Standard Rate per Hour} \right) \times \text{Actual Hours}$$

$$\text{Direct Labor Time Variance} = \left(\text{Actual Direct Labor Hours} - \text{Standard Direct Labor Hours} \right) \times \text{Standard Rate per Hour}$$

$$\text{Variable Factory Overhead Controllable Variance} = \text{Actual Variable Factory Overhead} - \text{Budgeted Variable Factory Overhead}$$

$$\text{Fixed Factory Overhead Volume Variance} = \left(\begin{array}{c} \text{Standard Hours for} \\ \text{100\% of Normal} \\ \text{Capacity} \end{array} - \begin{array}{c} \text{Standard} \\ \text{Hours for} \\ \text{Actual Units} \\ \text{Produced} \end{array} \right) \times \begin{array}{c} \text{Fixed Factory} \\ \text{Overhead} \\ \text{Rate} \end{array}$$

Return on Investment (ROI) $= \dfrac{\text{Income from Operations}}{\text{Invested Assets}}$

Alternative ROI Computation:

$$\text{ROI} = \dfrac{\text{Income from Operations}}{\text{Sales}} \times \dfrac{\text{Sales}}{\text{Invested Assets}}$$

Capital Investment Analysis Methods:

Methods That Ignore Present Values:

- Average Rate of Return Method
- Cash Payback Method

Methods That Use Present Values:

- Net Present Value Method
- Internal Rate of Return Method

Average Rate of Return $= \dfrac{\text{Estimated Average Annual Income}}{\text{Average Investment}}$

Present Value Index $= \dfrac{\text{Total Present Value of Net Cash Flow}}{\text{Amount to Be Invested}}$

Present Value Factor for an Annuity of $1 $= \dfrac{\text{Amount to Be Invested}}{\text{Equal Annual Net Cash Flows}}$

The Warren/Reeve/Duchac Family

The Warren/Reeve/Duchac Family of solutions provides a host of options to fit your exact teaching style—all with an integrated technology solution.

Sole Proprietorship Approach

- 26 Chapters
- 65% Financial Accounting/
  35% Managerial Accounting

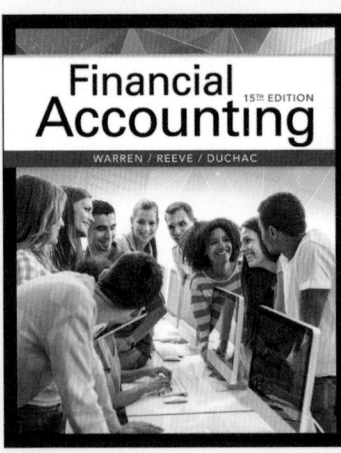

- Financial Chapters 1–17 from
  Accounting, 27e

Corporate Approach

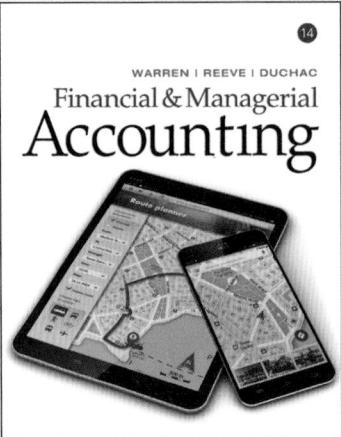

- 26 Chapters
- 50% Financial Accounting/
  50% Managerial Accounting

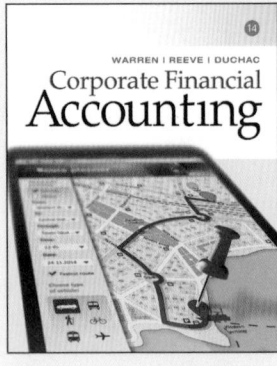

- Chapters 1–14
  from *Financial &
  Managerial
  Accounting, 14e*

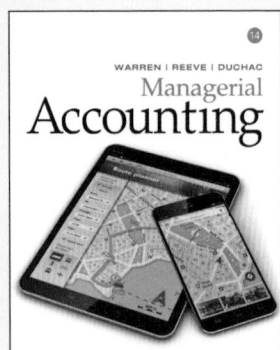

- Chapters 13–26
  from *Financial &
  Managerial
  Accounting, 14e*

Financial and Managerial
Accounting 14e

Carl S. Warren
Professor Emeritus of Accounting
University of Georgia, Athens

James M. Reeve
Professor Emeritus of Accounting
University of Tennessee, Knoxville

Jonathan E. Duchac
Professor of Accounting
Wake Forest University

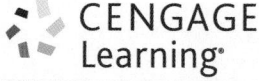
CENGAGE
Learning

Australia • Brazil • Japan • Korea • Mexico • Singapore • Spain • United Kingdom • United States

CENGAGE
Learning®

Financial and Managerial Accounting, 14e

Carl S. Warren
James M. Reeve
Jonathan E. Duchac

Senior Vice President, General Manager, Social Sciences, Humanities, and Business: Erin Joyner

Executive Product Director: Mike Schenk

Product Director: Jason Fremder

Senior Product Manager: Matt Filimonov

Content Development Manager: Daniel Celenza

Senior Content Developer: Diane Bowdler

Product Assistant: Audrey Jacobs

Executive Marketing Manager: Robin LeFevre

Marketing Program Manager: Eileen Corcoran

Senior Digital Production Project Manager: Jessica Robbe

Senior Digital Content Specialist: Tim Ross

Senior Content Project Manager: Tim Bailey

Manufacturing Planner: Doug Wilke

Production Service: Cenveo Publisher Services, Inc.

Senior Art Director: Michelle Kunkler

Cover Designer: cmillerdesign

Internal Designer: Ke Design

Intellectual Property
   Analyst: Brittani Morgan
   Project Manager: Betsy Hathaway

Library of Congress Control Number: 2016949721

Student Edition ISBN: 978-1-337-11920-7
Loose-Leaf Edition ISBN: 978-1-337-27070-0

Cengage Learning
20 Channel Center Street
Boston, MA 02210
USA

Cengage Learning is a leading provider of customized learning solutions with employees residing in nearly 40 different countries and sales in more than 125 countries around the world. Find your local representative at **www.cengage.com**.

Cengage Learning products are represented in Canada by Nelson Education, Ltd.

To learn more about Cengage Learning Solutions, visit **www.cengage.com**

Purchase any of our products at your local college store or at our preferred online store **www.cengagebrain.com**

Printed in the United States of America
Print Number: 03   Print Year: 2017

Roadmap for Success

Warren/Reeve/Duchac *Financial and Managerial Accounting, 14e*, makes it easy for you to give students a solid foundation in business and accounting. Warren/Reeve/Duchac covers the fundamentals AND motivates students to learn by showing how accounting is important to a business.

Warren/Reeve/Duchac is successful because it reaches students with a combination of new and tried-and-tested pedagogy.

This revision includes a range of exciting new and existing features that help Warren/Reeve/Duchac provide students with the context to see how accounting is valuable to business. These include:

- New! Schema
- New! Links to Business
- New! Why It Matters
- New! Analysis for Decision Making and Make a Decision
- New! Accounting Equation Impacts added beside journal entries

Warren/Reeve/Duchac also includes a thorough grounding in the fundamentals that any business student will need to be successful. These key features include:

- Stepwise approach to accounting cycle
- Presentation style designed around the way students learn
- New! Check Up Corner
- New! Let's Review

Hallmarks of the revision include:

- At the start of each chapter, **a schema, or roadmap, shows students what they are going to learn and how it is connected to the larger picture**. In the early chapters, the schema shows how the steps in the accounting cycle are interrelated. In later financial chapters, the schema shows how each chapter's topics are connected to the financial statements.

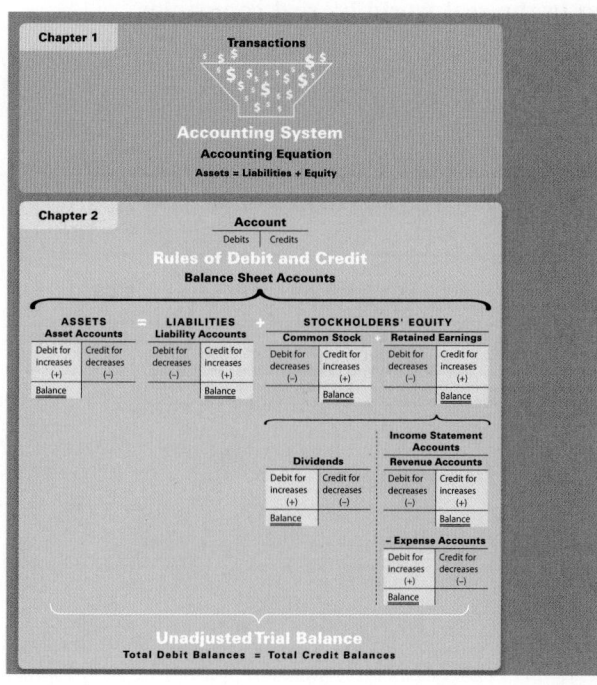

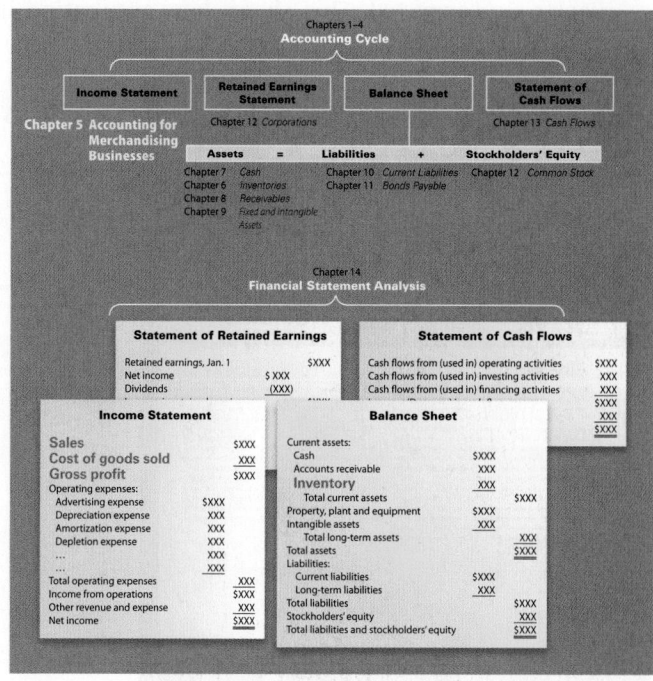

The schema in the managerial accounting chapters emphasizes the role of managerial accounting in developing and providing information for decision making.

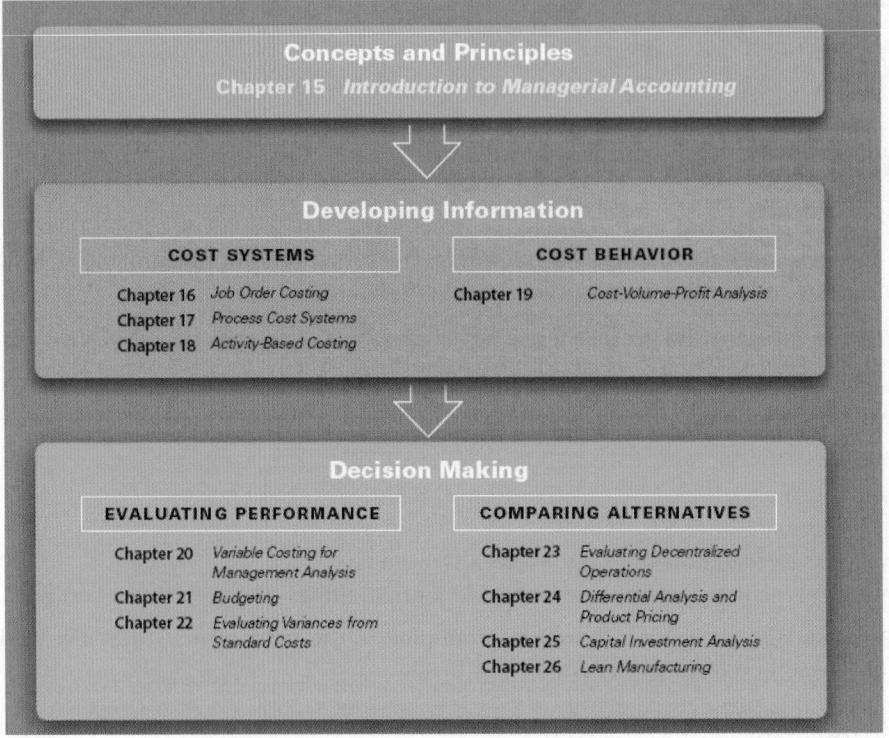

> *"The schema shows the 'big picture.' It connects all the chapters. Students need help seeing the big picture and the connection."*
>
> — Gloria Sanchez, Mt. San Jacinto College

- **Link to the "opening company" of each chapter** calls out examples of how the concepts introduced in the chapter are connected. **This shows how accounting is used in the real world by real companies**.

McDonald's

McDonald's began in 1940 in San Bernardino, California, as a Bar-B-Q restaurant operated by two brothers, Dick and Mac McDonald. In 1954, Ray Kroc visited the restaurant and convinced the McDonald brothers to let him franchise its operations nationwide. Ray Kroc opened his first McDonald's in Des Plaines, Illinois, in 1955, with its distinguishing, newly designed Golden Arches. Today, McDonald's operates in more than 100 countries, has more than 30,000 restaurants, employs more than 400,000 people, has sold billions of hamburgers, and generates yearly revenues in excess of $27 billion.

Would you like to own and operate a McDonald's restaurant? McDonald's grants 20-year franchises to individuals who want to become owner/operators of a restaurant. When opening a new restaurant, the owner must invest in the store equipment, signs, seating, and décor. The company normally owns the land and the building. McDonald's also provides training for its owner/operators. In return, the company is paid a monthly service charge, which is either a fixed amount or a percent of sales. The total cost of opening a new restaurant may exceed several million dollars.

Obviously, the decision to open a McDonald's restaurant is a major commitment with long-lasting implications. This chapter discusses the accounting for investments in long-term, fixed assets such as a new restaurant. This accounting addresses such issues as how much of the investment should be recorded as an asset, how much should be written off as an expense each year, and how the disposal of a fixed asset should be recorded. Finally, accounting for natural resources, such as mineral deposits, and intangible assets, such as patents and copyrights, are discussed.

Source: www.aboutmcdonalds.com

> **McDonald's** recently reported that it is the lessee in over 14,000 locations. The leases are normally for 20 years with an option to renew.
>
> *Link to McDonald's*

The accounting for leases is currently the focus of a joint project by the Financial Accounting Standards (FASB) and the International Accounting Standards Board (IASB) to merge U.S. and international standards.[2] Under the proposed standard lessors and lessees would be required to record assets and liabilities related to certain long-term lease contracts.

For purposes of this text, we assume that leases are short-term and not extending beyond one year. Thus, lease payments are recorded as rent by debiting Rent Expense and crediting Cash. The lease terms, such as a renewal option, may be disclosed in the notes to the financial statements. The asset rentals described in the earlier chapters of this text were accounted for in this manner.

IFRS
See Appendix C for more information.

- NEW! Located early in each chapter, **Why It Matters** shows students how accounting is important to businesses with which they are familiar.

Why It Matters

Fixed Assets

Fixed assets often represent a significant portion of a company's total assets. The table that follows shows the fixed assets as a percent of total assets for some select companies across a variety of industries.

As can be seen, the type of industry will impact the proportion of fixed assets to total assets. Retail has the highest percent of fixed assets to total assets, while social media and software are on the lower end of the scale. High-tech service companies often use fewer fixed assets to deliver their services than will companies that use stores, equipment, planes, cell towers, or theme parks.

Company	Industry	Percent of Fixed Assets to Total Assets
McDonald's Corporation	Food Retail	72%
Target Corporation	Merchandise Retail	63%
Alcoa Inc.	Heavy Industry	44%
Delta Air Lines, Inc.	Transportation	41%
Verizon Communications Inc.	Communications	39%
The Walt Disney Company	Entertainment	28%
Facebook, Inc.	Social Media	10%
Microsoft Corporation	Software	8%

Fixed assets have important properties that require management attention:

- Fixed assets require a long-term commitment. Mistakes in acquiring fixed assets can be very costly and difficult to reverse, thus managers must take special care in acquiring fixed assets.
- Fixed assets wear out over time and need to be replaced. Managers must monitor fixed assets and know when to replace fixed assets due to wear and tear, and obsolescence.

- Fixed assets need to be maintained during use. Managers need to develop maintenance programs to keep the investment in fixed assets productive.
- Fixed assets often require significant acquisition funds. Managers need to acquire funding internally or by other sources to finance the purchase of fixed assets.

"These features show students the relevance to the business world of what they are learning and so should help motivate them to learn."

— *Steven J. LaFave, Augsburg College*

"It does a good job of bringing the materials into a 'real world' environment."

— *Bob Urell, Irvine Valley College*

- To aid comprehension and to demonstrate the impact of transactions, **journal entries include the net effect of the transaction on the accounting equation**.

2019				
Jan. 3	Inventory	2,510		A = L + E
	Cash		2,510	+ −
	Purchased inventory from Bowen Co.			

Purchases of inventory on account are recorded as follows:

Jan. 4	Inventory	9,250		A = L + E
	Accounts Payable—Thomas Corporation		9,250	+ +
	Purchased inventory on account.			

The terms of purchases on account are normally indicated on the **invoice** or bill that the seller sends the buyer. An example of an invoice sent to NetSolutions by Alpha Technologies is shown in Exhibit 2.

■ To aid learning and problem solving, throughout each chapter new **Check Up Corners** provide students with step-by-step guidance on how to solve problems. Problem-solving tips help students avoid common errors.

Check Up Corner 9-1   Fixed Assets

On the first day of the year, Firefall Company acquired equipment for use in operations at a cost of $340,000. The equipment was expected to have a useful life of four years or 1,000 hours, and a residual value of $20,000. The equipment was used for 280 hours during the first year, 260 hours during the second year, 240 hours during the third year, and 220 hours during the fourth year.

A. Determine the annual depreciation expense in each year and the book value of the equipment at the end of each year under the:
  1. straight-line method
  2. units-of-activity method
  3. double-declining-balance method

B. Assuming the equipment was sold for $95,000 on the first day of the fourth year of operations, journalize the entry to record the sale if the equipment was depreciated under the:
  1. straight-line method
  2. units-of-activity method
  3. double-declining-balance method

Solution:

A. 1. Straight-Line Method:

$$\frac{\text{Annual}}{\text{Depreciation Expense}} = \frac{\text{Cost} - \text{Residual Value}}{\text{Useful Life}} = \frac{\$340,000 - \$20,000}{4\ \text{Years}} = \$80,000$$

The straight-line percentage is computed as follows:

$$\text{Straight-Line Percentage} = \frac{100\%}{4\ \text{Years}} = 25\%$$

Annual depreciation expense and end-of-year book value are computed as follows:

| | Calculation of Depreciation | | | | End of Year | |
Year	Straight-Line Percentage	×	Depreciable Cost	=	Annual Depreciation Expense	Accumulated Depreciation	Book Value
1	25%	×	$320,000	=	$80,000	$ 80,000	$260,000
2	25%	×	320,000	=	80,000	160,000	180,000
3	25%	×	320,000	=	80,000	240,000	100,000
4	25%	×	320,000	=	80,000	320,000	20,000

Book Value = Asset Cost ($340,000) − Accumulated Depreciation

Ending Book Value = Residual Value

2. Units-of-Activity Method:

$$\frac{\text{Depreciation per}}{\text{Hour of Use}} = \frac{\text{Cost} - \text{Residual Value}}{\text{Total Number of Hours}} = \frac{\$340,000 - \$20,000}{1,000\ \text{Hours}} = \$320\ \text{per Hour}$$

Annual depreciation expense and end-of-year book value are computed as follows:

| | Calculation of Depreciation | | | | End of Year | |
Year	Depreciation per Hour of Use	×	Total Hours of Activity Used	=	Annual Depreciation Expense	Accumulated Depreciation	Book Value
1	$320	×	280	=	$89,600	$ 89,600	$250,400
2	320	×	260	=	83,200	172,800	167,200
3	320	×	240	=	76,800	249,600	90,400
4	320	×	220	=	70,400	320,000	20,000

Book Value = Asset Cost ($340,000) − Accumulated Depreciation

Ending Book Value = Residual Value

"These are good, I like the step-by-step approach. I also like it when it reinforces concepts before the solution begins."

— *Pam Neely, The College at Brockport, SUNY*

■ In each chapter, **Analysis for Decision Making** highlights how businesses use accounting information to make decisions and evaluate the health of a business. This provides students with context of why accounting is important to a business.

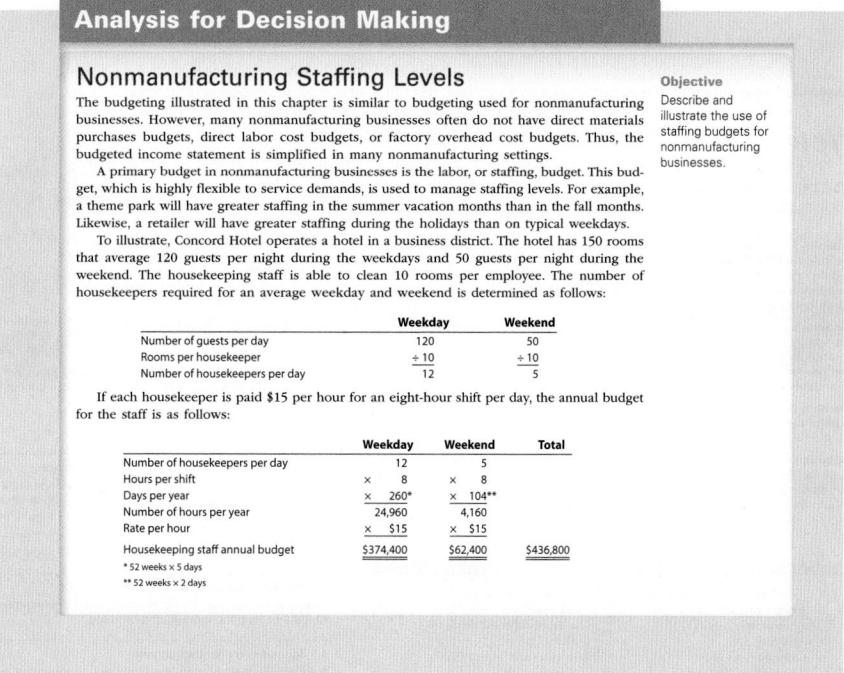

■ Following the Analysis for Decision Making segment, students have an opportunity to apply their knowledge in making decisions.

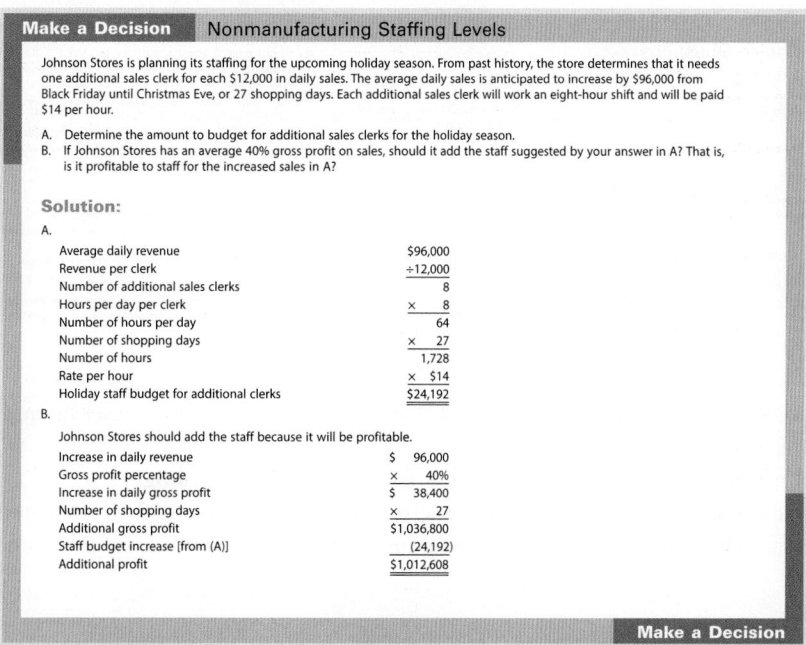

> "I like the explanation of how to calculate the ratio and the way it's demonstrated how to calculate McDonald's – the presentation is clear and concise. Then, I really like the clear and concise answer to 'Is 1.1 efficient?' Ex 14 is great. I like the Make a Decision feature so students get to practice right away. Overall, a great section."
>
> — *Barbara Muller, Arizona State University*

- At the end of each chapter, **Let's Review** is a new chapter summary and self-assessment feature that is designed to help busy students prepare for an exam. It includes a summary of each learning objective's key points, key terms, multiple-choice questions, exercises, and a sample problem that students may use to practice.

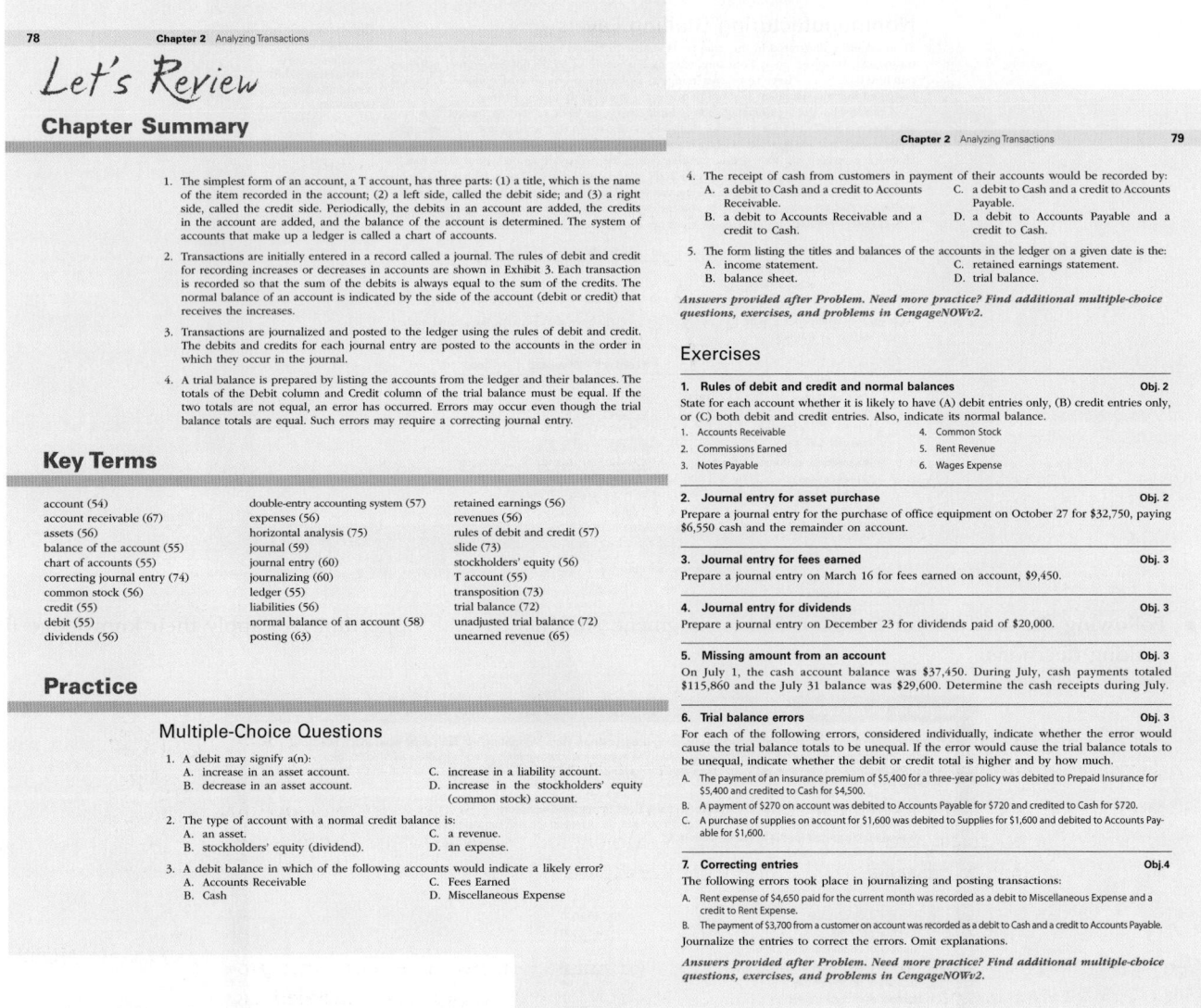

- Sample multiple-choice questions allow students to practice with the type of assessments they are likely to see on an exam.
- Short exercises and a longer problem allow students to apply their knowledge.
- **Answers** provided at the end of the Let's Review section let students check their knowledge immediately.
- Algorithmic practice activities in the accompanying CengageNOWv2 allow students to regenerate a practice activity at will.

> "I like the idea that they're within the chapter and immediately after the specific chapter topic. Also, they're easy and promote a sense of accomplishment and understanding in the student."
>
> — John Seilo, Irvine Valley College

- **Take It Further** in the end-of-chapter activities allows instructors to assign other special activities related to ethics, communication, and teamwork.

Take It Further

TIF 11-1   Ethics in Action

CEG Capital Inc. is a large holding company that uses long-term debt extensively to fund its operations. At December 31, the company reported total assets of $100 million, total debt of $55 million, and total equity of $45 million. In January, the company issued $11 billion in long-term bonds to investors at par value. This was the largest debt issuance in the company's history, and it significantly increased the company's ratio of total debt to total equity. Five days after the debt issuance, CEG filed legal documents to prepare for an additional $50 billion long-term bond issue. As a result of this filing, the price of the $11 billion in bonds that the company issued earlier in the week dropped to 94 because of the increased risk associated with the company's debt. The investors in the original $11 billion bond issuance were not informed of the company's plans to issue additional debt so quickly after the initial bond issue.

➤ Did CEG Capital act unethically by not disclosing to initial bond investors its immediate plans to issue an additional $50 billion debt offering?

TIF 11-2   Team Activity

In teams, select a public company that interests you. Obtain the company's most recent annual report on Form 10-K. The Form 10-K is a company's annually required filing with the Securities and Exchange Commission (SEC). It includes the company's financial statements and accompanying notes. The Form 10-K can be obtained either (A) from the investor relations section of the company's Web site or (B) by using the company search feature of the SEC's EDGAR database service found at www.sec.gov/edgar/searchedgar/companysearch.html.

1. Based on the information in the company's most recent annual report, answer the following questions:
   A. How much long-term debt does the company report at the end of the most recent year presented?
   B. Does the company have any bonds outstanding at the end of the most recent year? If so, read the supporting notes to the financial statements and determine:
      (1) The contract rate of interest on the bond issue(s).
      (2) The discount or premium on the bond issue(s).
      (3) The due date of the bond issue(s).
      (4) The total amount of any bonds that will mature within one year of the balance sheet date.
2. ➤ Based on your answers to the questions in requirement 1, evaluate the company's debt position.

Other Icons

- IFRS icon directs students to content specific to the International Financial Reporting Standards. More information about IFRS can be found in Appendix C.

IFRS

- Mornin' Joe is a fictitious coffeehouse chain whose financial statements are provided to illustrate the complete financial statements of a corporation. Excerpts of the Mornin' Joe financial statements are used to illustrate topics discussed in Chapters 6–13.

Mornin' Joe

CengageNOWv2

CengageNOWv2 is a powerful course management and online homework resource that provides control and customization to optimize the student learning experience. Included are many proven resources, including algorithmic activities, a test bank, course management tools, reporting and assessment options, and much more.

Closing the Gap between Homework and Exam Performance

Many students perform well on homework but struggle when it comes to exams. Now, with the new Blank Sheet of Paper Experience, students must problem-solve on their own, just as they would if taking a test on a blank sheet of paper.

Blank Sheet of Paper Experience

A less-leading Blank Sheet of Paper Experience discourages overreliance on the system.

- Instructors may choose between Learning Problems that guide student learning via drop-down menus, or they may use Blank Sheet of Paper problems.
- In Blank Sheet of Paper items, students must refer to the Chart of Accounts and decide for themselves which account is impacted.
- The number of accounts in each transaction is not given away.
- Whether the account should be debited or credited is not given away.

- Transactions may be entered in any order (as long as the entries are correct).
- Check My Work feedback only reports on what students have actually attempted, which prevents students from "guessing" their way through the assignment.

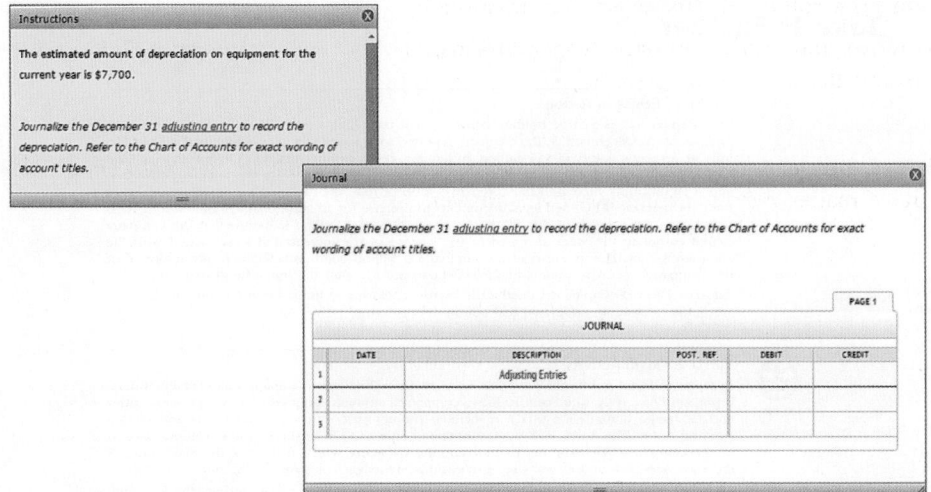

- New! **The link between the journal entry and the accounting equation is also included in the accompanying CengageNOWv2 course** in the accounting cycle chapters, automatically reminding students of the link—but not requiring them to actively make the link.

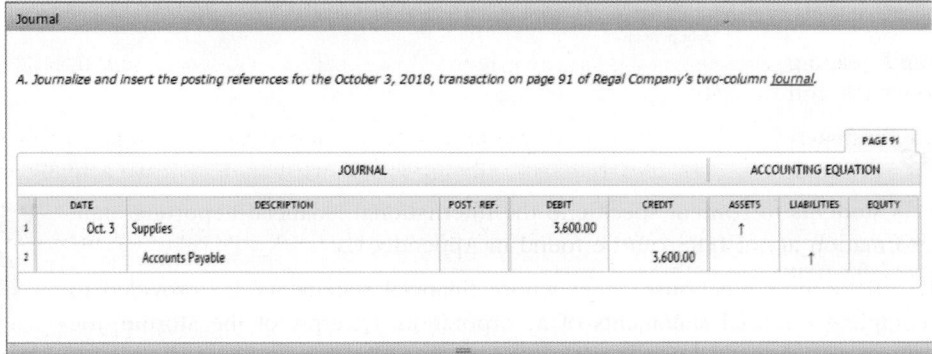

"As they are creating their journal entry, this will allow them to see when they debit or credit an account the effect it has on the accounting equation. If they are not sure of the debit or credit, this might help them to figure it out."

— Cecile Roberti, Community College of Rhode Island

"With the Accounting Equation impact automatically recorded, the student sees the impact, which I think is a better learning tool than having an additional step to completing the journal entry. The student sees the cause and effect, which for a beginning accounting student would help to increase understanding."

— Sally Whitney, Colorado State University

Multi-Panel View

The new Multi-Panel View in CengageNOWv2 enables students to see all the elements of a problem on one screen.

- Students make connections and see the tasks as connected components in the accounting process.
- Dramatically reduced scrolling eliminates student frustration.

With the ability to move and resize journals, ledgers, forms, and financial statements, it is easier to navigate the problem and understand the accounting system.

Adaptive Feedback

Adaptive Feedback in CengageNOWv2 responds to students based upon their unique answers and alerts them to the type of error they have made without giving away the answer.

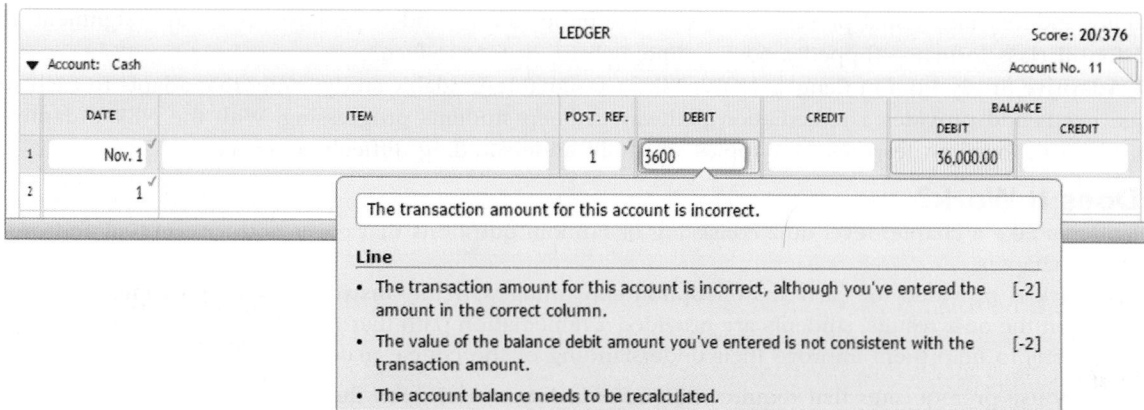

In addition to groundbreaking, adaptive feedback, CengageNOWv2 continues to provide multiple layers of guidance to keep students on track and progressing.

- **Check My Work Feedback** provides general guidance and hints as students work through homework assignments.
- **Check My Work Feedback** in CengageNOWv2 now only reports on what students have actually attempted, which prevents them from "guessing" their way through assignments.
- **Explanations** are available after the assignment has been submitted and provide a detailed description of how the student should have arrived at the solution.

Motivation: Set Expectations and Prepare Students for the Course

CengageNOWv2 helps motivate students and get them ready to learn by reshaping their misconceptions about the introductory accounting course and providing a powerful tool to engage students.

CengageNOWv2 Start-Up Center

Students are often surprised by the amount of time they need to spend outside of class working through homework assignments in order to succeed. The CengageNOWv2 Start-Up Center will help students identify what they need to do and where they need to focus in order to be successful with a variety of new resources.

- What Is Accounting? Module ensures students understand course expectations and how to be successful in the introductory accounting course. This module consists of two assignable videos: *Introduction to Accounting* and *Success Strategies*. The Student Advice Videos offer advice from real students about what it takes to do well in the course.
- Math Review Module, designed to help students get up to speed with necessary math skills, includes math review assignments and Show Me How math review videos to ensure that students have an understanding of basic math skills, including:
  - Whole number operations
  - Decimal operations and rounding
  - Percentage operations and conversion

- Fraction operations
- Converting numbers expressed in one form to a different form
- Positive and negative numbers
- Ratios and averages

■ How to Use CengageNOWv2 Module focuses on learning accounting, not on a particular software system. Quickly familiarize your students with CengageNOWv2 and direct them to all of its built-in student resources.

Motivation: Prepare Them for Class

With all the outside obligations accounting students have, finding time to read the textbook before class can be a struggle. Point students to the key concepts they need to know before they attend class.

■ **Video: Tell Me More.** Short Tell Me More lecture activities explain the core concepts of the chapter through an engaging auditory and visual presentation. Available either on a stand-alone basis or as an assignment, they are ideal for all class formats—flipped model, online, hybrid, or face-to-face.

■ **NEW Adaptive Study Plan** in CengageNOWv2 is an assignable/gradable study center that adapts to each student's unique needs and provides a remediation pathway to keep students progressing. With the NEW Adaptive Study Plan, they can focus on learning new topics and fully understanding difficult concepts.

How Does It Work?

Step 1: Students take a chapter-level quiz consisting of random questions that cover both conceptual and procedural aspects of the chapter.

Step 2: Feedback is provided for each answer option explaining why the answer is right or wrong.

Step 3: Based on the quiz results, students are provided a remediation path that includes media assets and algorithmic practice problems to help them improve their understanding of the course material.

Instructors may use prerequisites that require students to achieve mastery in the Adaptive Study Plan before moving on to new material.

Using the Adaptive Study Plan, students may also review and check their knowledge with the new Practice! Activities. These items (generally one per learning objective) build application skills by allowing students to complete practice problems and "Try Another Version."

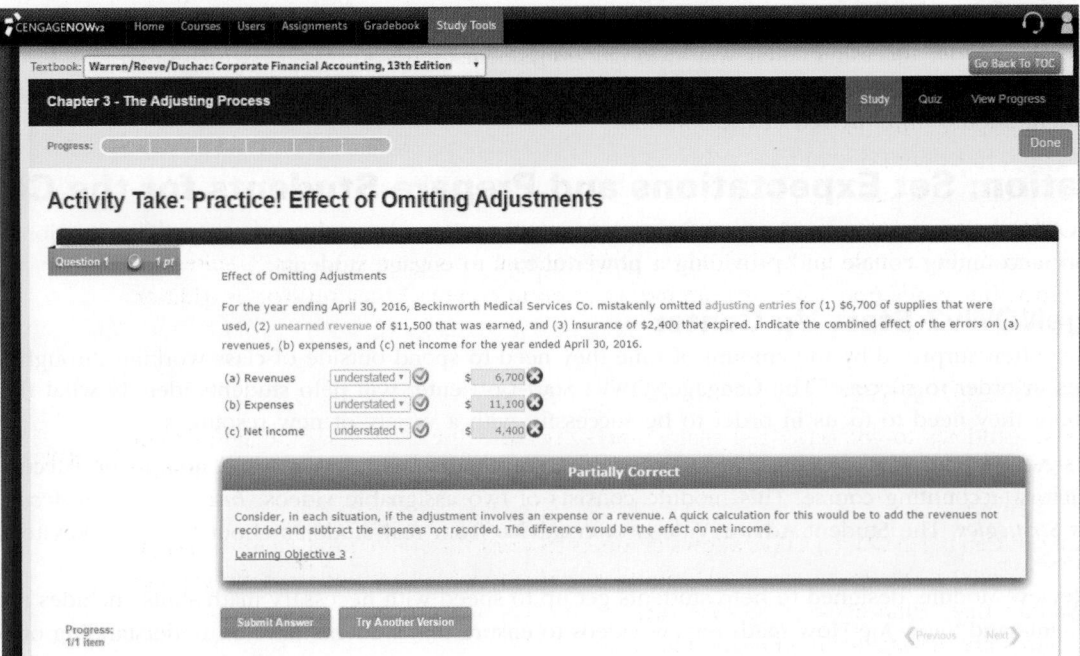

Provide Help Right When Students Need It

The best way to learn accounting is through practice, but students often get stuck when attempting homework assignments on their own.

SHOW ME HOW

- **Video: Show Me How.** Created for the most frequently assigned end-of-chapter items, NEW Show Me How problem demonstration videos provide a step-by-step model of a similar problem. Embedded tips and warnings help students avoid common mistakes and pitfalls.

Help Students Go Beyond Memorization to True Understanding

Students often struggle to understand how concepts relate to one another. For most students, an introductory accounting course is their first exposure to both business transactions and the accounting system. While these concepts are already difficult to master individually, their combination and interdependency in the introductory accounting course often pose a challenge for students.

- **Mastery Problems.** New Mastery Problems enable you to assign problems and activities designed to test students' comprehension and mastery of difficult concepts.
- **Dynamic Exhibits.** To overcome this gap, the authors have created a series of interactive Dynamic Exhibits that allow students to change the variables in a scenario and see how a change ripples through the accounting system. Dynamic Exhibits allow students to see connections and relationships like never before.

DYNAMIC EXHIBIT

Other features of Gradebook Analytics include:

- Ability to drill into both aggregate class performance and individual student performance.
- Preview items and view score distribution on that item.
- View at a glance summary information for a particular class, assignment, or item.

MindTap eReader

The MindTap eReader for Warren/Reeve/Duchac's *Financial and Managerial Accounting* is the most robust digital reading experience available. Hallmark features include:

- Fully optimized for the iPad.
- Note taking, highlighting, and more.
- Embedded digital media.
- The MindTap eReader also features ReadSpeaker®, an online text-to-speech application that vocalizes, or "speech-enables," online educational content. This feature is ideally suited for both instructors and learners who would like to listen to content instead of (or in addition to) reading it.

Cengage Learning General Ledger Software (CLGL)

GENERAL LEDGER

CLGL exposes students to computerized accounting software without teaching the specifics of a certain software system—preparing students for *any* software program they might encounter in the real world.

- Available in CengageNOWv2, CLGL allows students to work through end-of-chapter assignments and practice sets in a format that emulates commercial general ledger software, but in a manner that is more forgiving of errors.
- Assignments are automatically graded online.
- Selected problems that can be solved using CLGL are designated by an icon in the textbook and are listed in the assignment preparation grid in the Instructor's Manual.

New to This Edition

In this edition, we have reorganized the sequence of the financial chapters so that they follow the order of the balance sheet. Installment Notes (Chapter 10) and Bonds Payable (Chapter 11) now precede Corporations (Chapters 12). We have also reorganized the sequence of the managerial chapters. Additionally, in all chapters, the following improvements have been made:

- Added schema at beginning of each chapter linking material to the accounting cycle or the financial statements
- Updated dates and real company information for currency
- Added "Link to" for the opening company to interweave real-world references throughout each chapter
- Added margin accounting equation impact for journal entries
- Refreshed end-of-chapter assignments with different numerical values and updated information
- Replaced the following:
  - "Financial Analysis and Interpretation" with "Analysis for Decision Making" followed by an exercise "Make a Decision"
  - "Business Connection" articles with "Why It Matters"
  - "Integrity, Objectivity, and Ethics in Business" articles with "Ethics: (Don't) Do It!"
  - "Example Exercises" with "Check Up Corner" boxes throughout chapter
  - "At a Glance" summaries with "Let's Review" while retaining key points
  - "Illustrative Problems" with "Practice" which includes multiple-choice questions, exercises, problems, and related answers
  - "Practice Exercises" with "Basic Exercises"
  - "Cases & Projects" with "Take It Further"

Chapter 1

- Added Characteristics of Financial Information section
- Updated sections on Assumptions and Principles
- Added "Why It Matters" article on Round-Tripping, which describes commercial substance
- Added "Check Up Corner" boxes on:
  - Business Transactions and the Accounting Equation
  - Financial Statements
- Introduced the "report" form of balance sheet so that one form is used throughout the text

Chapter 2

- Refreshed exhibit Rules of Debit and Credit, Normal Balances of Accounts
- Added "Why It Matters" on Debits and Credits at the Bank and refreshed the Why It Matters on Computerized Accounting Systems
- Added "Check Up Corner" boxes on:
  - Balance Sheet Accounts
  - Preparing Journal Entries
  - Trial Balance

- When appropriate, account numbers are included in the trial balance

Chapter 3

- Added Revenue and Expense Recognition section
- Added new Exhibits 1 and 2 that illustrate why adjustments are required for accruals and deferrals
- Reorganized/streamlined Accruals and Deferrals
- Added "Check Up Corner" boxes on:
  - Adjusting Entries for Accruals
  - Adjusting Entries for Deferrals
  - Depreciation
- Added "Why It Matters" on Sports Signing Bonus
- When given in end-of-chapter items, account numbers are included in the trial balance

Chapter 4

- Added "Check Up Corner" boxes on:
  - Prepare Financial Statements from Adjusted Trial Balance
  - Closing Entries
- Added a "Why It Matters" on Temporary Accounts on Your Pay Stub
- Modified exhibit on Accounting Cycle so that it is consistent with the schema presented at the beginning of Chapters 1–4
- When appropriate, account numbers are included in the trial balance
- Added Appendix 2 Reversing Entries with exhibits on Accrued Wages, Wages Expense and Wages Payable after adjustment, and Wages Expense and Wages Payable after reversing entry

Chapter 5

- Added "Why It Matters" on:
  - Comcast Versus Lowe's
  - Apple's Credit Terms
  - E-commerce Shopping Carts
- Changed account titles of "Cost of Merchandise Sold" to "Cost of Goods Sold" and "Merchandise Inventory" to "Inventory"
- Added "Check Up Corner" boxes on:
  - Purchases Transactions
  - Sales Transactions
  - Multiple-Step Income Statement
- Revised the illustration for NetSolutions, including the chart of accounts, to include customer returns and allowances
- Revised the discussion of customer returns and allowances so that the adjusting entries for returns and allowances are presented with the adjusting entry for inventory shrinkage near the end of the chapter
- Expanded and refreshed exhibits on Illustration of Inventory Transactions for Seller and Buyer, Multiple-Step Income Statement, Single-Step Income Statement, Retained Earnings Statement for Merchandising Business, and Balance Sheet for Merchandising Business

- Revised Appendix on the Periodic Inventory System to include customer returns and allowances

Chapter 6

- Added "Why It Matters" on:
  - Pawn Stars and Specific Identification
  - Good Samaritan
- Added "Check Up Corner" boxes on:
  - Perpetual Inventory Costing
  - Periodic Inventory
  - Lower of Cost or Market
  - Effects of Inventory Errors

Chapter 7

- Revised chapter title
- Added new exhibit on eBay's Report of Compliance with Sarbanes-Oxley
- Added "Why It Matters" on:
  - Mobile Payments
  - Bank Error in Your Favor (or Maybe Not)
  - Apple's Hedge Fund
- Updated "Why It Matters" on Employee Fraud
- Added "Check Up Corner" boxes on:
  - Internal Controls
  - Bank Reconciliation
- Revised the form of the bank reconciliation to be consistent with CengageNOWv2
- Added calculation of Days' Cash on Hand in Analysis for Decision Making

Chapter 8

- New chapter opener on Keurig Green Mountain, Inc.
- Added "Why It Matters" on:
  - Warning Signs
  - Failure to Collect
- Refreshed "Why It Matters" on Allowance Percentages Across Companies
- Added "Ethics: Don't Do It!" on extending credit to financially distressed companies
- Added "Check Up Corner" boxes on:
  - Percent of Sales Method
  - Analysis of Receivables Method
  - Notes Receivable

Chapter 9

- Revised chapter title
- Changed "units-of-output method" to "units-of-activity method"
- Added new sections on Partial-Year Depreciation and Repair and Improvements
- Modified existing exhibits and added several new exhibits
- Added "Why It Matters" on:
  - Selling a Fixed Asset
  - Depreciation under IRS MACRS
  - Percent of Fixed Assets to Total Assets
  - Market Value versus Book Value
- Added "Check Up Corner" boxes on:
  - Fixed Assets

- Natural Resources
- Intangible Assets

Chapter 10

- Revised chapter title
- Revamped and simplified discussion of Payroll and added new topic on Installment Notes (from Chapter 12 in previous edition)
- Added "Check Up Corner" boxes on:
  - Short-Term Note Payable
  - Payroll Entries
  - Installment Note
  - Contingent Liabilities
- Added "Why It Matters" on:
  - State Pension Obligations
  - Installment Credit
- Added new exhibits on Note Transactions: Borrower and Creditor and on Allocation of Periodic Payments

Chapter 11

- Chapter 12 in the previous edition
- Moved topic of Installment Notes to Chapter 10
- New chapter opener on PepsiCo, Inc.
- Added a "Why It Matters" on Investor Bond Price Risk
- Added "Check Up Corner" boxes on:
  - Nature of Bonds Payable
  - Bond Issued at a Discount
  - Bond Issued at a Premium
- Updated "Ethics: Don't Do It!" article on The Ratings Game

Chapter 12

- Chapter 11 in the previous edition
- Added "Why It Matters" on:
  - Red Tape and Starting a Business
  - You Have No Vote
  - Treasury Stock vs. Dividends
- Added "Check Up Corner" boxes on:
  - Classes of Stock
  - Dividends
  - Treasury Stock Transactions
- Refreshed exhibits on Stockholders' Equity Section of a Balance Sheet and on Retained Earnings Statement

Chapter 13

- Chapter 14 in the previous edition
- Added "Check Up Corner" boxes on:
  - Cash Flows from Operating Activities
  - Cash Flows from Investing Activities
  - Classify Cash Flows
- Added "Why It Matters" on:
  - Growing Pains
  - Twenty Years After
- Refreshed exhibits on Statement of Cash Flows—Indirect Method and Statement of Cash Flows—Direct Method
- Moved the discussion of the direct method to Appendix 2

Chapter 14

- Chapter 15 in the previous edition
- Revamped sections on Analyzing Liquidity and Analyzing Solvency
- Name changes to several ratios:
  - "Number of Times Interest Charges Are Earned" to "Times Interest Earned"
  - "Ratio of Sales to Assets" to "Asset Turnover"
  - "Rate Earned on Total Assets" to "Return on Total Assets"
  - "Rate Earned on Stockholders' Equity" to "Return on Stockholders' Equity"
  - "Rate Earned on Common Stockholders' Equity" to "Return on Common Stockholders' Equity"
- Refreshed exhibit on Summary of Analytical Measures
- Added Appendix 2 on Fair Value and Comprehensive Income (from Chapter 13 in previous edition)
- Added "Check Up Corner" boxes on:
  - Horizontal and Vertical Analysis
  - Liquidity Analysis
  - Solvency Analysis
  - Profitability Analysis
- Added "Why It Matters" on:
  - Flying Off the Shelves
  - Economic Success
  - Investing for Yield

Chapter 15

- Chapter 16 in the previous edition
- Revised chapter title
- New chapter opener on Gibson Guitars
- Added Links to Gibson Guitars throughout chapter
- Added new Learning Objective on Sustainability and Accounting Information
- Added "Why It Matters" on:
  - Line and Staff for Service Companies
  - Not According to Plan: Contract Clauses
  - Overhead Costs
  - Service Companies and Product Costs
- Added "Check Up Corner" boxes on:
  - Management Process
  - Manufacturing Operations
  - Manufacturing Financial Statements
- Added Analysis for Decision Making section on measuring utilization for a service company with related end-of-chapter assignments
- Added Take It Further section with assignments involving ethics, teams, and communication

Chapter 16

- Chapter 17 in the previous edition
- New chapter opener on Gibson Guitars
- Added Links to Gibson Guitars throughout chapter
- Added in the margin the impact of each journal entry on the accounting equation
- Added "Why It Matters" on:
  - 3D Printing

- Advanced Robotics
- Job Order Costing in Hollywood
- Added "Check Up Corner" boxes on:
  - Direct Materials, Direct Labor, and Factory Overhead Costs
  - Applying Overhead and Determining Job Cost
  - Job Order Costing for a Service Business
- Added Analysis for Decision Making section on using job order costs in a service company with related end-of-chapter assignments
- Added Take It Further section with assignments involving ethics, teams, and communication

Chapter 17

- Chapter 18 in the previous edition
- Added Links to Dreyer's Ice Cream throughout chapter
- Added "Why It Matters" on:
  - Sustainable Papermaking
  - Cost of Gasoline
- Added "Check Up Corner" boxes on:
  - Equivalent Units
  - Cost per Equivalent Unit
  - Process Costing Journal Entries
- Added Analysis for Decision Making section on using cost of production reports with related end-of-chapter assignments
- Added Take It Further section with assignments involving ethics, teams, and communication

Chapter 18

- Chapter 26 in the previous edition
- Revised chapter title
- Added Links to Cold Stone Creamery throughout chapter
- Added "Why It Matters" on:
  - Activity-Based Costing in the Public Sector
  - $600 Hammer (Cost Allocation Distortion)
- Added "Check Up Corner" boxes on:
  - Single Plantwide Factory Overhead Rate
  - Multiple Production Department Factory Overhead Rates
  - Activity-Based Costing: Factory Overhead Costs
  - Activity-Based Costing for a Service Business
- Added Analysis for Decision Making section on using ABC to reduce costs with related end-of-chapter assignments
- Added Take It Further section with assignments involving ethics, teams, and communication

Chapter 19

- Revised chapter title
- Added Links to Ford Motor Company throughout chapter
- Added "Why It Matters" on:
  - Variable Cost for Home and Business
  - Booking Fees
- Added "Check Up Corner" boxes on:
  - Cost Behavior
  - Contribution Margin

- Break-Even Sales and Target Profit
- Special Cost-Volume-Profit Relationships
- Added Analysis for Decision Making section on using cost-volume-profit for service companies with related end-of-chapter assignments
- Removed the Variable Costing Appendix
- Added Take It Further section with assignments involving ethics, teams, and communication

Chapter 20

- Added Links to Adobe Systems, Incorporated throughout chapter
- Added "Why It Matters" on:
  - Business Segments
  - Eastman Revenue Price and Volume Effects
- Added "Check Up Corner" boxes on:
  - Absorption and Variable Costing Income Statements: Production Greater than Sales
  - Absorption and Variable Costing Income Statements: Different Levels of Production
  - Contribution Margin by Segment
  - Contribution Margin Analysis
- Added Analysis for Decision Making section on using segment analysis and EBITDA with related end-of-chapter assignments
- Added Take It Further section with assignments involving ethics, teams, and communication

Chapter 21

- Added Links to Hendrick Motorsports throughout chapter
- Added "Why It Matters" on Advertising Budget
- Added "Check Up Corner" boxes on:
  - Flexible Budget
  - Direct Materials, Direct Labor, and Cost of Goods Sold Budget
  - Cash Budget
- Added Analysis for Decision Making section on using staffing budgets for nonmanufacturing businesses with related end-of-chapter assignments
- Added Take It Further section with assignments involving ethics, teams, and communication

Chapter 22

- Revised chapter title
- Added Links to BMW Group throughout chapter
- Added "Why It Matters" on The Lesson of Moneyball
- Added "Check Up Corner" boxes on:
  - Direct Materials and Direct Labor Cost Variances
  - Factory Overhead Cost Variances
  - Income Statement with Variances
- Added Analysis for Decision Making section on using direct labor time variance in evaluating staff in a service business with related end-of-chapter assignments
- Added Take It Further section with assignments involving ethics, teams, and communication

Chapter 23

- Revised chapter title
- Added Links to Caterpillar Inc. throughout chapter
- Added "Why It Matters" on:
  - Dover Corporation: Many Pieces, One Picture
  - Coca-Cola Company Expansion
- Added "Check Up Corner" boxes on:
  - Cost Center Responsibility Measures
  - Profit Center Responsibility Reporting
  - Investment Center Performance Measures
  - Transfer Pricing
- Added Analysis for Decision Making section on whether a company should franchise its operations with related end-of-chapter assignments
- Added Take It Further section with assignments involving ethics, teams, and communication

Chapter 24

- Added Links to Facebook Inc. throughout chapter
- Added a "Why It Matters" on Dynamic Pricing
- Added "Check Up Corner" boxes on:
  - Differential Analysis
  - Setting Product Selling Prices
- Added Analysis for Decision Making section on the use of yield pricing in service businesses with related end-of-chapter assignments
- Added Take It Further section with assignments involving ethics, teams, and communication

Chapter 25

- Added Links to Vail Resorts Inc. throughout chapter
- Added "Check Up Corner" boxes on:
  - Capital Investment Analysis Not Using Present Value
  - Net Present Value and Internal Rate of Return Analyses
  - Net Present Value—Unequal Lives
- Added Analysis for Decision Making section on using capital investment analysis in evaluating sustainability with related end-of-chapter assignments
- Added Take It Further section with assignments involving ethics, teams, and communication

Chapter 26

- Chapter 27 in previous edition
- Revised chapter title
- Added Links to Precor Incorporated throughout chapter
- Added a "Why It Matters" on External Failure Costs: Lululemon Stretched Thin
- Added "Check Up Corner" boxes on:
  - Lean Principles
  - Lean Accounting
  - Cost of Quality Report
- Added Analysis for Decision Making section on using lean principles in service or administrative settings with related end-of-chapter assignments
- Added Take It Further section with assignments involving ethics, teams, and communication

Instructor Resources

Solutions Manual

Author-written and carefully verified multiple times to ensure accuracy and consistency with the text, the Solutions Manual contains answers to the Discussion Questions, Basic Exercises, Exercises, Problems (Series A and Series B), Continuing Problems, Comprehensive Problems, Analysis for Decision Making, and Take It Further activities that appear in the text. These solutions help you easily plan, assign, and efficiently grade assignments.

Test Bank

Test Bank content is delivered via Cengage Learning Testing, powered by Cognero® a flexible, online system that allows you to:

- Author, edit, and manage test bank content from multiple Cengage Learning solutions
- Create multiple test versions in an instant
- Deliver tests from your LMS, your classroom, or through CengageNOWv2

Companion Web Site

This robust companion web site provides immediate access to a rich array of teaching and learning resources—including the Instructor's Manual, PowerPoint slides, and Excel Template Solutions. Easily download the instructor resources you need from the password-protected, instructor-only section of the site.

Instructor's Manual Discover new ways to engage your students by utilizing the Instructor's Manual ideas for class discussion, group learning activities, writing exercises, and Internet activities. Moreover, simplify class preparation by reviewing a brief summary of each chapter, a detailed chapter synopsis, teaching tips regarding a suggested approach to the material, questions students frequently ask in the classroom, lecture aids, and demonstration problems in the Instructor's Manual. Transparency Masters and Handouts (with solutions) are also included.

Quickly identify the assignments that best align with your course with the assignment preparation grid that includes information about learning objective coverage, difficulty level and Bloom's taxonomy categorization, time estimates, and accrediting standard alignment for business programs, AICPA, ACBSP, and IMA.

PowerPoint Slides Bring your lectures to life with slides designed to clarify difficult concepts for your students. The lecture PowerPoints include key terms and definitions, equations, examples, and exhibits from the textbook. Descriptions for all graphics in the PowerPoints are included to enhance PowerPoint usability for students with disabilities.

A separate PowerPoint deck that includes just the Exhibits from the textbook is ideal for instructors who create their own PowerPoint decks and just want to refresh them.

Excel Template Solutions Excel Templates are provided for selected long or complicated end-of-chapter exercises and problems to assist students as they set up and work the problems. Certain cells are coded to display a red asterisk when an incorrect answer is entered, which helps students stay on track. Selected problems that can be solved using these templates are designated by an icon in the textbook and are listed in the assignment preparation grid in the Instructor's Manual. The Excel Template Solutions provide answers to these templates.

Practice Set Solutions Establish a fundamental understanding of the accounting cycle for your students with Practice Sets, which require students to complete one month of transactions for a fictional company. Brief descriptions of each Practice Set are provided in the Table of Contents. The Practice Set Solutions provide answers to these practice sets.

Student Resources

Study Guide

Now available free in CengageNOWv2, the Study Guide allows students to easily assess what they know with a "Do You Know" checklist covering the key points in each chapter. To further test their comprehension, students can work through Practice Exercises, which include a "strategy" hint and solution so they can continue to practice applying key accounting concepts.

Working Papers

Students will find the tools they need to help work through end-of-chapter assignments with the Working Papers. The preformatted templates provide a starting point by giving students a basic structure for problems and journal entries. Working Papers are available in a printed format as a bundle option.

Practice Sets

For more in-depth application of accounting practices, instructors may choose from among six different Practice Sets for long-term assignments. Each Practice Set requires students to complete one month of transactions for a fictional company. Practice Sets can be solved manually or with the Cengage Learning General Ledger software.

GENERAL LEDGER

Web Site

Designed specifically for your students' accounting needs, this web site features student PowerPoint slides, Excel Templates, learning games, and flashcards.

- **PowerPoint Slides:** Students can easily take notes or review difficult concepts with the student version of this edition's PowerPoint slides.
- **Excel Templates:** These Excel Templates help students stay on track. If students enter an incorrect answer in certain cells, a red asterisk will appear to let them know something is wrong. Problems that can be solved using these templates are designated by an icon.

EXCEL TEMPLATE

- **Crossword Puzzles:** Students can focus on learning the key terms and definitions for each chapter in a different way by completing these crossword puzzles.
- **Flashcards:** Students can prepare with these flashcards, which cover the key terms and definitions they need to know for each chapter.

Acknowledgements

The many enhancements to this edition of *Financial and Managerial Accounting* are the direct result of one-on-one interviews, surveys, and focus groups with over 250 instructors at institutions across the country over the past year. We would like to take this opportunity to thank those who helped us better understand the challenges of the financial accounting course and provided valuable feedback on our content and digital assets.

Instructors:

Deborah S. Adkins, Remington Online
Deborah S. Adkins, University of Phoenix
Sol Ahiarah, SUNY Buffalo State
Dave Alldredge, Salt Lake Community College
Lynn Almond, Virginia Tech
Elizabeth Ammann, Lindenwood University
Sean Andre, York College of Pennsylvania
Rick Andrews, Sinclair Community College
Leah Arrington, Northwest Mississippi Community College
Christopher Ashley, Everest College
John Babich, Kankakee Community College
Benjamin Bae, California State University, Bakersfield
Felicia Baldwin, Richard J. Daley College
Laura K. Bantz, McHenry County College
Geoffrey Bartlett, Drake University
Elise Bartley, Westminster College
Jan Barton, Emory University
Progyan Basu, University of Maryland—College Park
Robert E. Bates, Glendale Community College
Jason Bergner, University of Nevada
Eric Blazer, Millersville University
Janell Blazovich, University of St. Thomas
Cindy Bleasdale, hilbert college
Cynthia E. Bolt-Lee, The Citadel
John Borke, University of Wisconsin—Platteville
Anna M. Boulware, St. Charles Community College
Amy Bourne, Oregon State University
Gary R. Bower, Community College of Rhode Island

Tom Branton, Alvin Community College
Robert L. Braun, Southeastern Louisiana University
Darryl L. Brown, Illinois Wesleyan University
Amy Browning, Monmouth College
Tracy L. Bundy, University of Louisiana at Lafayette
Esther Bunn, Stephen F. Austin State University
Lisa Busto, Harper College
Thane Butt, Champlain College
Marci L. Butterfield, University of Utah
Edward J. Bysiek, St. Bonaventure University
Magan Calhoun, Austin Peay State University
Julia Camp, Providence College
David Candelaria, Mt San Jacinto College
Brenda Canning, Springfield College
Kirk Canzano, Long Beach City College
Cassandra H. Catlett, Carson Newman University
David Centers, Grand Valley State University
Machiavelli Chao, University of California, Irvine
Bea Chiang, The College of New Jersey
C. Catherine Chiang, Elon University
Linda Christiansen, Indiana University Southeast
Lawrence Chui, University of St. Thomas
Bob Churchman, Harding University
Tony Cioffi, Lorain County Community College
George Cooper, Lakeland Community College
Sandra Copa, North Hennepin Community College
Leonard Cronin, Rochester Community and Technical College
Alyson Crow, Temple College

Louann Hofheins Cummings, The University of Findlay
Rick Cummings, University of Wisconsin—Whitewater
Sue Cunningham, Rowan-Cabarrus Community College
Dori Danko, Grand Valley State University
Bruce L. Darling, University of Oregon
Rebecca G. Davis, East Mississippi Community College
Julie Dawson, Carthage College
Laurence DeGaetano, Montclair State University
Peggy DeJong, Kirkwood Community College
Robert Derstine, West Chester University
Joel M. DiCicco, Florida Atlantic University
Carol Dickerson, Chaffey College
Julie Dilling, Moraine Park Technical College
Michael P. Dole, Marquette University
Patricia Dorris-Crenny, Villanova University
G. Seth Dunn, Tennessee Temple University
Gertrude A. Eguae-Obazee, Albright College
Karen C. Elsom, Fayetteville Technical Community College
James M. Emig, Villanova University
Sharif Erik-Soussi, Charter Oak State College
Mary Ewanechko, Monroe Community College
Farima Fakoor, Golden Gate University
Alan Falcon, Loyola Marymount University
Lucile Faurel, University of California, Irvine
Robert Foster, Pierce College
Corey Frad, Eastern Iowa Community Colleges

Kimberly Franklin, St. Louis Community College

Alan S. Fudge, Linn-Benton Community College

Michael J. Gallagher, DeSales University

Regan Garey, Lock Haven University

Alex Gialanella, Manhattanville College

John Giles, North Carolina State University

Michael Goeken, Northwest Vista College

Lynn P. Gonzalez, Concordia College

Saturnino (Nino) Gonzalez, Jr., El Paso Community College

Charles Goodman, University of Illinois at Chicago

Doug Gordon, University of California, Irvine

Carol Graham, The University of San Francisco

Thomas Grant, Kutztown University

Marina Grau, Houston Community College

Gloria Grayless, Sam Houston State University

Sheila Guillot, Lamar State College—Port Arthur

Hongtao Guo, Salem State University

Bob Gutschick, College of Southern Nevada

Joohyung Ha, University of San Francisco

Marcye S. Hampton, University of Central Florida

Becky Hancock, El Paso Community College

Martin Hart, Manchester Community College

Sueann Hely, West Kentucky Community & Technical College

Joshua Herbold, University of Montana

Len Heritage, Tacoma Community College

Katherine Sue Hewitt, Klamath Community College

Merrily Hoffman, San Jacinto College—Central

Jana Hosmer, Blue Ridge Community College

Jeff Hsu, St. Louis Community College at Meramec

Marianne James, California State University, Los Angeles

Ching-Lih Jan, California State University, East Bay

Cynthia Johnson, University of Arkansas, Little Rock

Lori Johnson, Minnesota State University, Moorhead

Jeffrey Jones, The College of Southern Nevada

Odessa Jordan, Calhoun Community College

Edward H. Julius, California Lutheran University

Brad Van Kalsbeek, University of Sioux Falls

Stani Kantcheva, Cincinnati State Technical and Community College

Stephen Keels, Everest University at Jacksonville

Taylor Klett, Sam Houston State University

Stacy Kline, Drexel University

William J. Knight, Flagler College

Satoshi Kojima, East Los Angeles College

Stephen Kolenda, Hartwick College

Lynn Krausse, Bakersfield College

Barbara Kren, Marquette University

Jeffrey T. Kunz, Carroll University

Steven J. LaFave, Augsburg College

Tara Laken, Joliet Junior College

Meg Costello Lambert, Oakland Community College—Auburn Hills Campus

Margie Ness LaShaw, Whitworth University

Richard Lau, California State University, Los Angeles

Greg Lauer, North Iowa Area Community College

David Laurel, South Texas College

G. Suzanne Lay, Colorado Mesa University

Rose Layton, University of Southern California

Charles J. F. Leflar, University of Arkansas

Annette M. Leps, Johns Hopkins University

Jennifer LeSure, Ivy Tech Community College

Erik H. Lindquist, Lansing Community College

Danny S. Litt, University of California, Los Angeles

Harold Little, Western Kentucky University

Katy Long, Hill College

Dawn Lopez, Johnson & Wales University

Ming Lu, Santa Monica College

Debra Luna, El Paso Community College

Jennifer A. Mack, Lindenwood University

Suneel Maheshwari, Indiana University of Pennsylvania

Lois S. Mahoney, Eastern Michigan University

Richard Mandau, Piedmont Technical College

Ken Marc, Johnson & Wales University

Michele Martinez, Hillsborough Community College

Anthony Masino, East Tennessee State University

Dawn L. Mason, Western Michigan University

Karen McDougal, St. Joseph's University

Robert W. McGee, Fayetteville State University

Noel McKeon, Florida State College Jacksonville

Allison McLeod, University of North Texas

Chris McNamara, Finger Lakes Community College

Glenn (Mel) McQueary, Houston Community College

Brenda J. McVey, University of Mississippi

Jean A. Meyer, Loyola University of New Orleans

Pam Meyer, University of Louisiana at Lafayette

Paul A. San Miguel, Western Michigan University

Linda Miller, Northeast Community College

Timothy Miller, El Camino College

Barbara J. Muller, Arizona State University

Johnna Murray, University of Missouri—St. Louis

Adam Myers, Texas A&M University

John Nader, Davenport University

Araks Navasartian, Everest University, Tampa Campus

Pam Neely, The College at Brockport, SUNY

Joseph Malino Nicassio, Westmoreland County Community College

Lisa Novak, Mott Community College

Christopher O'Byrne, Cuyamaca College

Joseph Onyeocha, South Carolina State University

Edwin Pagan, Passaic County Community College

Kalpana Pai, Texas Wesleyan University

Susanna Pendergast, Western Illinois University

Rachel Pernia, Essex County College

Dawn Peters, Southwestern Illinois College

Vickie Petritz, Highlands College of Montana Tech

Cynthia Phipps, Lake Land College

April Poe, University of the Incarnate Word

Sharon Price, Southwestern Assemblies of God University

Michael P. Prockton, Finger Lakes Community College

Craig Reeder, Florida A&M University

Barbara Rice, Gateway Community and Technical College

Renee Richard, Pima Community College

Laurie Hays Rivera, Western Michigan University

Cecile M. Roberti, Community College of Rhode Island

Shani N. Robinson, Sam Houston State University

Constance Rodriguez, SUNY Brockport

Patrick Rogan, Cosumnes River College

Lawrence A. Roman, Cuyahoga Community College

Debbie Rose, Northeast Wisconsin Technical College

Brent Russ, The University of Montana

Gloria Sanchez, Mt. San Jacinto College

Lynn K. Saubert, Radford University

Jennifer Schneider, University of North Georgia

Darlene Schnuck, Waukesha County Technical College

John Seilo, Irvine Valley College

Mon Sellers, Lone Star College—North Harris

Perry Sellers, Louisiana State University in Shreveport

Lewis Shaw, Suffolk University

James G. Shelton, Harding University

Eileen Shifflett, James Madison University

Ercan Sinmaz, Houston Community College

Lee G. Smart, Southwest Tennessee Community College

Gerald Smith, University of Northern Iowa

Nancy L. Snow, University of Toledo

Kristen Sohlberg, The University of Montana

Leslie "Andy" Speck, Embry-Riddle Aeronautical University

Marilyn Stansbury, Calvin College

Catherine L. Staples, Randolph-Macon College

Larry G. Stephens, Austin Community College District

Dawn W. Stevens, Northwest Mississippi Community College—Desoto Center

Jeff Strawser, Sam Houston State University

Ronald Strittmater, North Hennepin Community College

Joel Strong, St. Cloud State University

Gracelyn Stuart-Tuggle, Palm Beach State College—Boca

Mary Sykes, University of Houston

Linda H. Tarrago, Hillsborough Community College

Denise Teixeira, Chemeketa Community College

Theresa Tiggeman, University of the Incarnate Word

Patricia Hart Timm, Northwood University

Anthony L. Tocco, Rockhurst University

Lana Tuss, Chemeketa Community College

Mark M. Ulrich, St. John's University

Robert Urell, Irvine Valley College

Jeff Varblow, College of Lake County

Lynne Velie, College of Coastal Georgia

Drakopoulou Veliota, Ashford University

John Verani, White Mountains Community College

Marcia M. Vinci, Johnson & Wales University

Dale A. Walker, Arkansas State University

Robert J. Walsh, University of Dallas

Doris Warmflash, SUNY Westchester Community College

James Webb, University of the Pacific

Eric Weinstein, Suffolk County Community College

Robert J. Wesoloskie, Eastern University

Micheline West, Manchester Community College

Nancy L. Wilburn, Northern Arizona University

Patricia Worsham, California State Polytechnic University Pomona

Patricia Worsham, Norco College

Judith Zander, Grossmont College

Athena Zhang, Ithaca College

About the Authors

Carl S. Warren

Dr. Carl S. Warren is Professor Emeritus of Accounting at the University of Georgia, Athens. Dr. Warren has taught classes at the University of Georgia, University of Iowa, Michigan State University, and University of Chicago. He focused his teaching efforts on principles of accounting and auditing. Dr. Warren received his PhD from Michigan State University and his BBA and MA from the University of Iowa. During his career, Dr. Warren published numerous articles in professional journals, including *The Accounting Review*, *Journal of Accounting Research*, *Journal of Accountancy*, *The CPA Journal*, and *Auditing: A Journal of Practice and Theory*. Dr. Warren has served on numerous committees of the American Accounting Association, the American Institute of Certified Public Accountants, and the Institute of Internal Auditors. He also has consulted with numerous companies and public accounting firms. His outside interests include handball, golfing, skiing, backpacking, motorcycling, and fly-fishing.

Terry R. Spray InHisImage Studios

James M. Reeve

Dr. James M. Reeve is Professor Emeritus of Accounting and Information Management at the University of Tennessee. Professor Reeve taught full time as part of the accounting faculty for twenty-five years after graduating with his PhD from Oklahoma State University. He presently teaches part time at UT. His teaching efforts focused on Senior Executive MBA programs. Beyond this, Professor Reeve is very active in the Supply Chain Certification program, which is a major executive education and research effort of the college. His research interests are varied and include work in managerial accounting, supply chain management, lean manufacturing, and information management. He has published over forty articles in academic and professional journals, including *Journal of Cost Management*, *Journal of Management Accounting Research*, *Accounting Review*, *Management Accounting Quarterly*, *Supply Chain Management Review*, and *Accounting Horizons*. He has consulted or provided training around the world for a variety of organizations, including Boeing, Procter & Gamble, Norfolk Southern, Hershey Foods, Coca-Cola, and Sony. When not writing books, Professor Reeve plays golf and is involved in faith-based activities.

Charles J. Garvey III / Garvey Photography

Jonathan Duchac

Dr. Jonathan Duchac is the Wayne Calloway Professor of Accounting and Acting Associate Dean of Accounting Programs at Wake Forest University. He earned his PhD in accounting from the University of Georgia and currently teaches introductory and advanced courses in financial accounting. Dr. Duchac has received a number of awards during his career, including the Wake Forest University Outstanding Graduate Professor Award, the T.B. Rose Award for Instructional Innovation, and the University of Georgia Outstanding Teaching Assistant Award. In addition to his teaching responsibilities, Dr. Duchac has served as Accounting Advisor to Merrill Lynch Equity Research, where he worked with research analysts in reviewing and evaluating the financial reporting practices of public companies. He has testified before the U.S. House of Representatives, the Financial Accounting Standards Board, and the Securities and Exchange Commission and has worked with a number of major public companies on financial reporting and accounting policy issues. In addition to his professional interests, Dr. Duchac is an avid runner, mountain biker, and snow skier.

© Ken Bennett

Brief Contents

Contents

5 Accounting for Merchandising Businesses 226

Practice Set: Lawn Ranger Landscaping
This set is a service business operated as a proprietorship. It includes a narrative of transactions and instructions for an optional solution with no debits and credits. This set can be solved manually or with the General Ledger software.

---

6 Inventories 286

7 Internal Control and Cash 334

8 Receivables 380

9 Long-Term Assets: Fixed and Intangible 424

10 Liabilities: Current, Installment Notes, Contingencies 476

11 Liabilities: Bonds Payable 522

12 Corporations: Organization, Stock Transactions, and Dividends 560

Practice Set: My Place, House of Décor
This set is a service and merchandising business operated as a corporation. It includes narrative for six months of transactions, which are to be recorded in a general journal. The set can be solved manually or with the General Ledger software.

Practice Set: JP's Tech Solutions
This set is a departmentalized merchandising business operated as a corporation. It includes a narrative of transactions, which are to be recorded in special journals. The set can be solved manually or with the General Ledger software.

13 Statement of Cash Flows 606

14 Financial Statement Analysis 664

Mornin' Joe 727

15 Introduction to Managerial Accounting 740

16 Job Order Costing 784

17 Process Cost Systems 830

18 Activity-Based Costing 886

19 Cost-Volume-Profit Analysis 940

20 Variable Costing for Management Analysis 994

21 Budgeting 1052

22 Evaluating Variances from Standard Costs 1106

23 Evaluating Decentralized Operations 1156

Introduction to Accounting and Business

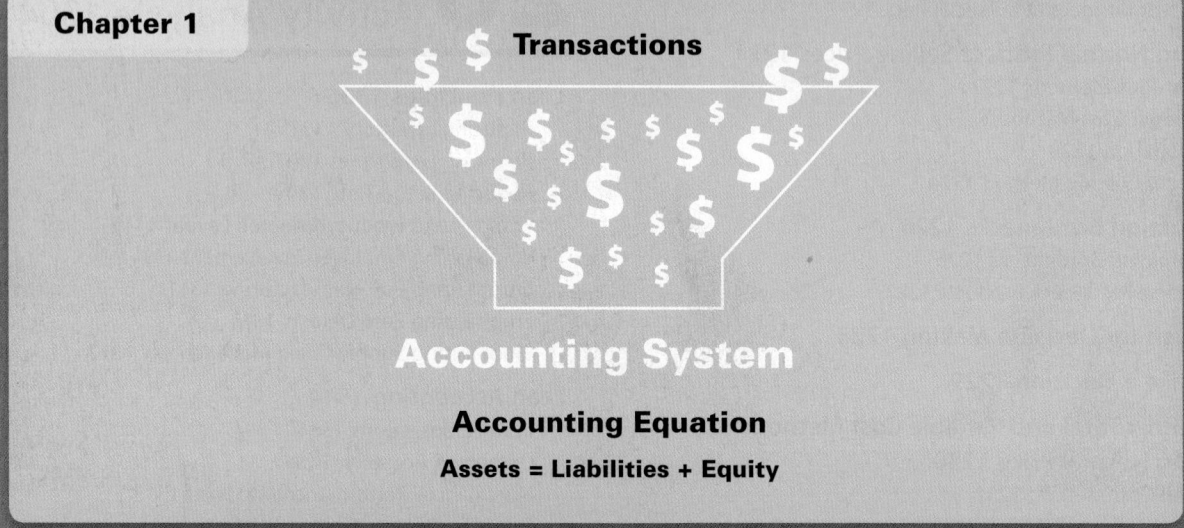

Chapter 1

Transactions

Accounting System

Accounting Equation

Assets = Liabilities + Equity

Twitter

When two teams pair up for a game of football, there is often a lot of noise. The band plays, the fans cheer, and fireworks light up the scoreboard. Obviously, the fans are committed and care about the outcome of the game. Just like fans at a football game, the owners of a business want their business to "win" against their competitors in the marketplace. While having your football team win can be a source of pride, winning in the marketplace goes beyond pride and has many tangible benefits. Companies that are winners are better able to serve customers, provide good jobs for employees, and make money for their owners.

Twitter is one of the most visible companies on the Internet. It provides a real-time information network where members can post messages, called Tweets, for free. Millions post Tweets every day throughout the world.

Do you think Twitter is a successful company? Does it make money? How would you know? Accounting helps to answer these questions.

This textbook introduces you to accounting, the language of business. Chapter 1 begins by discussing what a business is, how it operates, and the role that accounting plays.

Introduction to Accounting and Business

Nature of Business	**Nature of Accounting**	**Analyzing Business Transactions**	**Financial Statements**
■ Types (Obj. 1)	■ Types (Obj. 1)	■ Accounting Equation (Obj. 3)	■ Income Statement (Obj. 5)
■ Role of Accounting (Obj. 1)	■ Opportunities (Obj. 1)	■ Transactions (Obj. 4)	■ Retained Earnings Statement (Obj. 5)
■ Ethics (Obj. 1)	■ Generally Accepted Accounting Principles (Obj. 2)		■ Balance Sheet (Obj. 5)
			■ Statement of Cash Flows (Obj. 5)

Learning Objectives

Obj. 1 Describe the nature of business and the role of accounting and ethics in business.

Obj. 2 Describe generally accepted accounting principles, including the underlying assumptions and principles.

Obj. 3 State the accounting equation and define each element of the equation.

Obj. 4 Describe and illustrate how business transactions can be recorded in terms of the resulting change in the elements of the accounting equation.

Obj. 5 Describe the financial statements of a corporation and explain how they interrelate.

Analysis for Decision Making

Describe and illustrate the use of the ratio of liabilities to stockholders' equity in evaluating a company's financial condition.

Objective 1

Describe the nature of business and the role of accounting and ethics in business.

Nature of Business and Accounting

A **business**[1] is an organization in which basic resources (inputs), such as materials and labor, are assembled and processed to provide goods or services (outputs) to customers. Businesses come in all sizes, from a local coffee house to **Starbucks**, which sells over $10 billion of coffee and related products each year.

The objective of most businesses is to earn a **profit**. Profit is the difference between the amounts received from customers for goods or services and the amounts paid for the inputs used to provide the goods or services. This text focuses on businesses operating to earn a profit. However, many of the same concepts and principles also apply to not-for-profit organizations such as hospitals, churches, and government agencies.

Types of Businesses

Three types of businesses operating for profit include service, merchandising, and manufacturing businesses. Some examples of each type of business follow:

■ **Service businesses** provide services rather than products to customers.
     Delta Air Lines (transportation services)
     The Walt Disney Company (entertainment services)

■ **Merchandising businesses** sell products they purchase from other businesses to customers.
     Walmart (general merchandise)
     Amazon.com (Internet books, music, videos, ...)

■ **Manufacturing businesses** change basic inputs into products that are sold to customers.
     Ford Motor Co. (cars, trucks, vans)
     Dell Inc. (personal computers)

Link to Twitter   **Twitter** is a service company that provides a platform for individuals to send text messages called tweets.

---

[1] A complete glossary of terms appears at the end of the text.

Role of Accounting in Business

The role of accounting in business is to provide information for managers to use in operating the business. In addition, accounting provides information to other users in assessing the economic performance and condition of the business.

Thus, **accounting** can be defined as an information system that provides reports to users about the economic activities and condition of a business. You could think of accounting as the "language of business." This is because accounting is the means by which businesses' financial information is communicated to users.

Twitter communicates to investors in an annual report that includes accounting information.

Link to Twitter

The process by which accounting provides information to users is as follows:

1. Identify users.
2. Assess users' information needs.
3. Design the accounting information system to meet users' needs.
4. Record economic data about business activities and events.
5. Prepare accounting reports for users.

As illustrated in Exhibit 1, users of accounting information can be divided into two groups: internal users and external users.

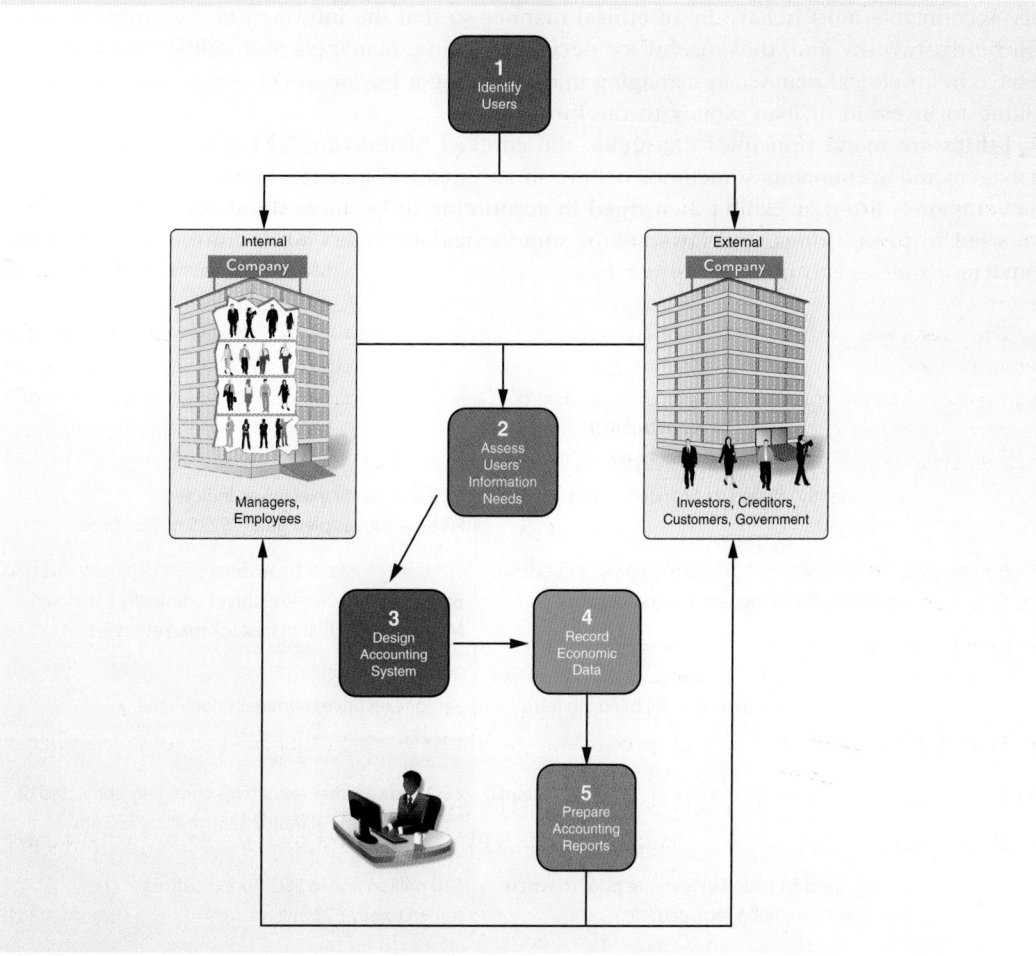

Exhibit 1

Accounting as an Information System

Managerial Accounting Internal users of accounting information include managers and employees. These users are directly involved in managing and operating the business. The area of accounting that provides internal users with information is called **managerial accounting**, or **management accounting**.

The objective of managerial accounting is to provide relevant and timely information for managers' and employees' decision-making needs. Often, such information is sensitive and is not distributed outside the business. Examples of sensitive information might include information about customers, prices, and plans to expand the business. Managerial accountants employed by a business are employed in **private accounting**.

Financial Accounting External users of accounting information include investors, creditors, customers, and the government. These users are not directly involved in managing and operating the business. The area of accounting that provides external users with information is called **financial accounting**.

The objective of financial accounting is to provide relevant and timely information for the decision-making needs of users outside of the business. For example, financial reports on the operations and condition of the business are useful for banks and other creditors in deciding whether to lend money to the business. **General-purpose financial statements** are one type of financial accounting report that is distributed to external users. The term *general-purpose* refers to the wide range of decision-making needs that these reports are designed to serve. Later in this chapter, general-purpose financial statements are described and illustrated.

Link to Twitter **Twitter** publishes general-purpose financial statements in its annual report to investors.

Role of Ethics in Accounting and Business

ETHICS

The objective of accounting is to provide relevant, timely information for user decision making. Accountants must behave in an ethical manner so that the information they provide users will be trustworthy and, thus, useful for decision making. Managers and employees must also behave in an ethical manner in managing and operating a business. Otherwise, no one will be willing to invest in or loan money to the business.

Ethics are moral principles that guide the conduct of individuals. Unfortunately, business managers and accountants sometimes behave in an unethical manner. Many of the managers of the companies listed in Exhibit 2 engaged in accounting or business fraud. These ethical violations led to fines, firings, and lawsuits. In some cases, managers were criminally prosecuted, convicted, and sent to prison.

Exhibit 2 Accounting and Business Frauds

Company	Nature of Accounting or Business Fraud	Result
Computer Associates International, Inc.	Fraudulently inflated its financial results.	CEO and senior executives indicted. Five executives pled guilty. $225 million fine.
Enron	Fraudulently inflated its financial results.	Bankrupcty. Senior executives criminally convicted. More than $60 billion in stock market losses.
HealthSouth	Overstated performance by $4 billion in false entries.	Senior executives criminally convicted.
Qwest Communications International, Inc.	Improperly recognized $3 billion in false receipts.	CEO and six other executives criminally convicted of "massive financial fraud." $250 million SEC fine.
Xerox Corporation	Recognized $3 billion in revenue prior to when it should have been recorded.	$10 million fine to SEC. Six executives forced to pay $22 million.

What went wrong for the managers and companies listed in Exhibit 2? The answer normally involved one or both of the following two factors:

■ **Failure of Individual Character:** Ethical managers and accountants are honest and fair. However, managers and accountants often face pressures from supervisors to meet company and investor expectations. In many of the cases in Exhibit 2, managers and accountants justified small ethical violations to avoid such pressures. However, these small violations became big violations as the company's financial problems became worse.

- **Culture of Greed and Ethical Indifference:** By their behavior and attitude, senior managers set the company culture. In most of the companies listed in Exhibit 2, the senior managers created a culture of greed and indifference to the truth.

As a result of the accounting and business frauds shown in Exhibit 2, Congress passed laws to monitor the behavior of accounting and business. For example, the **Sarbanes-Oxley Act (SOX)** was enacted. SOX established a new oversight body for the accounting profession called the **Public Company Accounting Oversight Board (PCAOB)**. In addition, SOX established standards for independence, corporate responsibility, and disclosure.

How does one behave ethically when faced with financial or other types of pressure? Guidelines for behaving ethically follow:[2]

1. Identify an ethical decision by using your personal ethical standards of honesty and fairness.
2. Identify the consequences of the decision and its effect on others.
3. Consider your obligations and responsibilities to those who will be affected by your decision.
4. Make a decision that is ethical and fair to those affected by it.

Twitter's "Code of Business Conduct and Ethics" can be found at https://investor.twitterinc.com/corporate-governance.cfm.   *Link to Twitter*

Opportunities for Accountants

Numerous career opportunities are available for students majoring in accounting. Currently, the demand for accountants exceeds the number of new graduates entering the job market. This is partly due to the increased regulation of business caused by the accounting and business frauds shown in Exhibit 2. Also, more and more businesses have come to recognize the importance and value of accounting information.

As indicated earlier, accountants employed by a business are employed in private accounting. Private accountants have a variety of possible career options within a company. Some of these career options are shown in Exhibit 3 along with their starting salaries. As shown in Exhibit 3, several private accounting careers have certification options. Accountants who provide audit services, called *auditors*, verify the accuracy of financial records, accounts, and systems.

 Ethics: Don't Do It!

Bernie Madoff

Bernard L. "Bernie" Madoff was sentenced to 150 years in prison for defrauding thousands of investors in one of the biggest frauds in American history. Madoff's fraud started several decades earlier when he began a "Ponzi scheme" in his investment management firm, Bernard L. Madoff Investment Securities LLC.

In a Ponzi scheme, the investment manager uses funds received from new investors to pay a return to existing investors, rather than basing investment returns on the fund's actual performance. As long as the investment manager is able to attract new investors, he or she will have new funds to pay existing investors and continue the fraud. While most Ponzi schemes collapse quickly when the investment manager runs out of new investors, Madoff's reputation, popularity, and personal contacts provided a steady stream of investors, which allowed the fraud to survive for decades.

Source: Bernie Madoff

[2] Many companies have ethical standards of conduct for managers and employees. In addition, the Institute of Management Accountants and the American Institute of Certified Public Accountants have professional codes of conduct, which can be obtained from their Web sites at www.imanet.org and www.aicpa.org, respectively.

Exhibit 3 Accounting Career Paths and Salaries

Accounting Career Track	Description	Career Options	Annual Starting Salaries*	Certification
Private Accounting	Accountants employed by companies, government, and not-for-profit entities.	Bookkeeper	$45,000	
		Payroll clerk	$41,000	Certified Payroll Professional (CPP)
		General accountant	$49,000	
		Budget analyst	$52,000	
		Cost accountant	$53,000	Certified Management Accountant (CMA)
		Internal auditor	$60,000	Certified Internal Auditor (CIA)
		Information technology auditor	$68,000	Certified Information Systems Auditor (CISA)
Public Accounting	Accountants employed individually or within a public accounting firm in audit, tax, or management advisory services.	Large firms (over $250 million in revenue)	$65,000	Certified Public Accountant (CPA)
		Mid-size firms ($25–$250 million in revenue)	$58,000	Certified Public Accountant (CPA)
		Small firms (less than $25 million in revenue)	$54,000	Certified Public Accountant (CPA)

*Average salaries rounded to the nearest thousand. Salaries may vary by size of company and region.
Source: Robert Half *2016 U.S. Salary Guide (Finance and Accounting)*, Robert Half International, Inc. (www.roberthalf.com/workplace-research/salary-guides)

Accountants and their staff who provide services on a fee basis are said to be employed in **public accounting**. In public accounting, an accountant may practice as an individual or as a member of a public accounting firm. Public accountants who have met a state's education, experience, and examination requirements may become **Certified Public Accountants (CPAs)**. CPAs typically perform general accounting, audit, or tax services. As can be seen in Exhibit 3, CPAs have slightly better starting salaries than private accountants. Career statistics indicate, however, that these salary differences tend to disappear over time. The American Institute of Certified Public Accountants (AICPA) provides information and resources for students interested in accounting at www.startheregoplaces.com.

Because all functions within a business use accounting information, experience in private or public accounting provides a solid foundation for a career. Many positions in industry and in government agencies are held by individuals with accounting backgrounds.

Why It Matters

Pathways Commission

The Pathways Commission recently issued its study titled *Charting a National Strategy for the Next Generation of Accountants*. The Commission was made up of diverse members and was jointly sponsored by the American Institute of Certified Public Accountants (AICPA) and the American Accounting Association (AAA). The Commission emphasized the importance of accounting for a prosperous society and good decision making. The Commission also emphasized that accountants must be critical thinkers who are comfortable addressing the shades of gray required by accounting judgments.

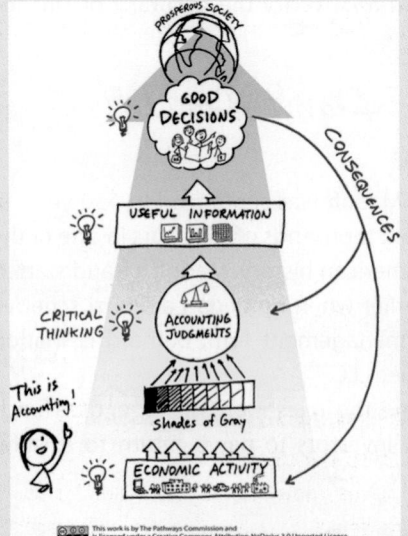

Source: *Charting a National Strategy for the Next Generation of Accountants*, The Pathways Commission, July 2012.

Generally Accepted Accounting Principles (GAAP)

Objective 2
Describe generally accepted accounting principles, including the underlying assumptions and principles.

Financial information in the United States is based on **generally accepted accounting principles (GAAP)**. GAAP is a collection of *accounting standards*, *principles*, and *assumptions* that define how financial information will be reported.

- **Accounting standards** are the rules that determine the accounting for individual business transactions.
- **Accounting principles** and **assumptions** provide the framework upon which accounting standards are constructed.

Within the United States, the **Financial Accounting Standards Board (FASB)** has the primary responsibility for developing accounting standards. The FASB publishes *Statements of Financial Accounting Standards*, *Statements of Financial Accounting Concepts*, and *Interpretations*, which make up GAAP. The **Securities and Exchange Commission (SEC)**, an agency of the U.S. government, has authority over the accounting and financial disclosures for companies whose shares of ownership (stock) are traded and sold to the public. The SEC normally accepts the accounting standards set forth by the FASB. However, the SEC may issue *Staff Accounting Bulletins* on accounting matters that may not have been addressed by the FASB.

Outside the United States, most countries use accounting standards and principles adopted by the **International Accounting Standards Board (IASB)**. The IASB issues *International Financial Reporting Standards* (IFRS). Differences currently exist between FASB and IASB accounting principles.

Characteristics of Financial Information

The primary goal of financial accounting is to provide information that is useful for decision making. To be useful, financial reports must possess two important characteristics: *relevance* and *faithful representation*.

- **Relevant** information has the potential to impact decision making.
- **Faithful representation** means that the information accurately reflects an entity's economic activity or condition.

In addition to the preceding characteristics, GAAP has evolved based upon assumptions and principles.

Assumptions

Financial accounting and generally accepted accounting principles are based upon the following assumptions:

- Monetary unit
- Time period
- Business entity
- Going concern

International Connection

IFRS **International Financial Reporting Standards (IFRS)**

IFRS are considered to be more "principles-based" than U.S. GAAP, which is considered to be more "rules-based." For example, U.S. GAAP consists of approximately 17,000 pages, which include numerous industry-specific accounting rules. In contrast, IFRS allow more judgment in deciding how business transactions are recorded. Many believe that the strong regulatory and litigation environment in the United States is the cause for the more rules-based GAAP approach. Regardless, IFRS and GAAP share many common principles.*

*Differences between U.S. GAAP and IFRS are further discussed and illustrated in Appendix C.

The **monetary unit assumption** requires that financial reports be expressed in a single money unit, or currency. This provides a common measurement of the effects of economic events and transactions on an entity. The monetary unit used is normally determined by the country in which the company operates. For example, in the United States, the U.S. dollar is used as the monetary unit.

The **time period assumption** allows a company to report its economic activities on a regular basis for a specific period of time. In doing so, financial condition and changes in financial condition are reported periodically on a consistent basis. In the United States, reports are normally required on a yearly basis supplemented with quarterly reports.

Link to Twitter **Twitter** publishes quarterly as well as yearly financial reports that are available at https://investor.twitterinc.com.

The **business entity assumption** limits the economic data in financial reports to that directly related to the activities of the business. In other words, the business is viewed as an entity separate from its owners, creditors, or other businesses. For example, the accountant for a business with one owner would record the activities of the business only and would not record the personal activities, property, or debts of the owner.

A business entity may take the form of a proprietorship, partnership, corporation, or limited liability company (LLC). Each of these forms and their major characteristics are listed in Exhibit 4.

Exhibit 4 Forms of Business Entities

Form of Business Entity	Characteristics	Examples
Proprietorship is owned by one individual.	• 70% of business entities in the United States. • Easy and inexpensive to organize. • Resources are limited to those of the owner. • Used by small businesses.	• A & B Painting
Partnership is owned by two or more individuals.	• 10% of business organizations in the United States (combined with limited liability companies). • Combines the skills and resources of more than one person.	• Jones & Smith, Architects
Corporation is organized under state or federal statutes as a separate legal taxable entity.	• Generates 90% of business revenues. • 20% of the business organizations in the United States. • Ownership is divided into shares called stock. • Can obtain large amounts of resources by issuing stock. • Used by large businesses.	• Apple • Google • Ford Motor Company
Limited liability company (LLC) combines the attributes of a partnership and a corporation.	• 10% of business organizations in the United States (combined with partnerships). • Often used as an alternative to a partnership. • Has tax and legal liability advantages for owners.	• Boston Basketball Partners, LLC

Link to Twitter Although **Twitter** is organized as a corporation in Delaware, its principal offices are in San Francisco.

The three types of businesses discussed earlier—service, merchandising, and manufacturing—may be organized as proprietorships, partnerships, corporations, or limited liability companies.

Because of the large amount of resources required to operate a manufacturing business, most manufacturers such as **Ford Motor Company** are corporations. Most large retailers such as **Walmart** and **The Home Depot** are also corporations. Companies organized as corporations often include Inc. as part of their name to indicate that they are incorporated. For example, Twitter's legal name is Twitter, Inc.

The **going concern assumption** requires that financial reports be prepared assuming that the entity will continue operating into the future. This assumption justifies reporting items such as equipment, buildings, and land at their initial or historical cost rather than liquidation or forced sale values.

Principles

In addition to the preceding assumptions, the following four principles are an integral part of financial accounting:

- Measurement
- Historical cost
- Revenue recognition
- Expense recognition

The **measurement principle** determines the amount that will be recorded and reported. The measurement principle requires that amounts be *objective* and verifiable. An amount is objective if it is based upon independent, unbiased evidence. An amount is *verifiable* if it can be confirmed by a third party. Transactions between two independent parties, called **arm's-length transactions**, provide amounts that are objective and verifiable.

To illustrate, assume that Aaron Publishers purchased the following building from Schenk Enterprises on February 20, 2018, for $150,000:

Price listed by Schenk Enterprises on January 1, 2018	$160,000
Aaron Publishers' initial offer to buy on January 31, 2018	140,000
Aaron Publishers' purchase price on February 20, 2018	150,000
Estimated selling price on December 31, 2020	220,000
Assessed value for property taxes, December 31, 2020	190,000

Aaron Publishers would record the building at the February 20, 2018, purchase price of $150,000. This amount is both objective and verifiable, as it was the result of a transaction between two independent parties. Recording an item at its initial transaction price is called the **historical cost principle** or **cost principle**. Under the historical cost principle, amounts do not normally change until another transaction occurs.

To illustrate, the fact that the preceding building has an estimated selling price of $220,000 on December 31, 2020, indicates that the building's value has increased. However, the $220,000 is not recorded in the accounting records because Aaron Publishers has not sold the building. If, however, Aaron sells the building on January 9, 2021, for $240,000, a profit of $90,000 ($240,000 − $150,000) would be recorded by Aaron Publishers.

Revenue is the amount earned for selling goods or services to customers. The **revenue recognition principle** determines when revenue is recorded in the accounting records. Normally, revenue is recorded when the services have been performed or goods are delivered to the customer.

Expenses are amounts used to generate revenue. The **expense recognition principle**, sometimes called the *matching principle*, requires expenses to be recorded in the same period as the related revenue. Doing so allows the reporting of a profit or loss for the period.

The Accounting Equation

The resources owned by a business are its **assets**. Examples of assets include cash, land, buildings, and equipment. The rights or claims to the assets are divided into two types: (1) the rights of creditors and (2) the rights of owners. The rights of creditors are the debts of the business and are called **liabilities**. The rights of owners are called **equity**. Since stockholders own a corporation, equity is called **stockholders' equity**. For a proprietorship, partnership, or limited liability company, equity is called **owner's equity**.

Objective 3

State the accounting equation and define each element of the equation.

Why It Matters

The Accounting Equation

The accounting equation serves as the basic foundation for the accounting systems of all companies. The accounting equation is used by the smallest business, such as the local convenience store, to the largest business, such as The Coca-Cola Company. Some examples taken from recent financial reports of well-known companies follow:

Company	Assets*	=	Liabilities	+	Stockholders' Equity
The Coca-Cola Company	$92,023	=	$61,462	+	$30,561
DuPont	$49,876	=	$36,498	+	$13,378
eBay	$45,132	=	$25,226	+	$19,906
Google	$110,920	=	$23,611	+	$87,309
McDonald's	$34,281	=	$21,428	+	$12,853
Microsoft Corporation	$172,384	=	$82,600	+	$89,784
Southwest Airlines	$20,200	=	$13,425	+	$6,775
Walmart	$203,706	=	$117,769	+	$85,937

*Amounts are shown in millions of dollars.

The following equation shows the relationship among assets, liabilities, and equity:

$$\text{Assets} = \text{Liabilities} + \text{Equity}$$

This equation is called the **accounting equation**. Liabilities usually are shown before equity in the accounting equation because creditors have first rights to the assets.

Throughout this text, we use the corporate form of business. However, most of the concepts and principles described and illustrated also apply to proprietorships, partnerships, and limited liability companies.

Given any two amounts, the accounting equation may be solved for the third unknown amount. To illustrate, if the assets owned by a corporation amount to $100,000 and the liabilities amount to $30,000, the stockholders' equity is equal to $70,000, computed as follows:

Assets	−	Liabilities	=	Stockholders' Equity
$100,000	−	$30,000	=	$70,000

Link to Twitter

Twitter's accounting equation for a recent year is: Assets ($3,366 million) = Liabilities ($416 million) + Stockholders' Equity ($2,950 million).

Objective 4

Describe and illustrate how business transactions can be recorded in terms of the resulting change in the elements of the accounting equation.

Business Transactions and the Accounting Equation

Paying a monthly bill, such as a telephone bill of $168, affects a business's financial condition because it now has less cash on hand. Such an economic event or condition that directly changes an entity's financial condition or its results of operations is a **business transaction**. For example, purchasing land for $50,000 is a business transaction. In contrast, a change in a business's credit rating does not directly affect cash or any other asset, liability, or stockholders' equity amount.

All business transactions can be stated in terms of changes in the elements of the accounting equation. How business transactions affect the accounting equation can be illustrated by using some typical transactions. As a basis for illustration, a business organized by Chris Clark is used.

Assume that on November 1, 2017, Chris Clark organizes a corporation that will be known as **NetSolutions**. The first phase of Chris's business plan is to operate NetSolutions as a service business assisting individuals and small businesses in developing Web pages and installing computer software. Chris expects this initial phase of the business to last one to two years. During this period, Chris plans on gathering information on the software and hardware needs of customers. During the second phase of the business plan, Chris plans to expand NetSolutions into a personalized retailer of software and hardware for individuals and small businesses.

Each transaction during NetSolutions' first month of operations is described in the following paragraphs. The effect of each transaction on the accounting equation is then shown.

note:
All business transactions can be stated in terms of changes in the elements of the accounting equation.

		Transaction A
Nov. 1, 2017	*Chris Clark deposited $25,000 in a bank account in the name of NetSolutions in exchange for shares of common stock in the corporation.*	

A corporation issues **common stock** to investors as proof of their ownership rights.[3]

This transaction increases Cash under Assets (on the left side of the equation) by $25,000. To balance the equation, Common Stock under Stockholders' Equity (on the right side of the equation) increases by the same amount.

The effect of this transaction on NetSolutions' accounting equation is as follows:

Assets	=	**Stockholders' Equity**
Cash		Common Stock
A. 25,000	=	25,000

The preceding accounting equation is only for the business, NetSolutions. Under the business entity assumption, Chris's personal assets, such as a home or personal bank account, and personal liabilities are excluded from the equation.

		Transaction B
Nov. 5, 2017	*NetSolutions paid $20,000 for the purchase of land as a future building site.*	

The land is located in a business park with access to transportation facilities. Chris Clark plans to rent office space and equipment during the first phase of the business plan. During the second phase, Chris plans to build an office and a warehouse for NetSolutions on the land.

The purchase of the land changes the makeup of the assets, but it does not change the total assets. The items in the equation prior to this transaction and the effect of the transaction follow. The new amounts are called *balances*.

	Assets		=	**Stockholders' Equity**
	Cash	+ Land		Common Stock
Bal.	25,000		=	25,000
B.	−20,000	+20,000		
Bal.	5,000	20,000		25,000
		25,000	=	25,000

		Transaction C
Nov. 10, 2017	*NetSolutions purchased supplies for $1,350 and agreed to pay the supplier in the near future.*	

You have probably used a credit card to buy clothing or other merchandise. In this type of transaction, you received clothing for a promise to pay your credit card bill in the future. That is, you received an asset and incurred a liability to pay a future bill. NetSolutions entered into a similar transaction

---

[3] To simplify, we assume that NetSolutions issued no-par stock. Types of stock as well as par and stated values are discussed in Chapter 12.

by purchasing supplies for $1,350 and agreeing to pay the supplier in the near future. This type of transaction is called a purchase *on account* and is often described as follows: *Purchased supplies on account, $1,350.*

The liability created by a purchase on account is called an **account payable**. Items such as supplies that will be used in the business in the future are called **prepaid expenses**, which are assets. Thus, the effect of this transaction is to increase assets (Supplies) and liabilities (Accounts Payable) by $1,350, as follows:

	Assets			**=**	**Liabilities + Stockholders' Equity**	
					Accounts +	Common Stock
	Cash	+ Supplies +	Land		Payable	
Bal.	5,000		20,000	=		25,000
C.		+1,350			+1,350	
Bal.	5,000	1,350	20,000		1,350	25,000

26,350 = 26,350

Transaction D   *Nov. 18, 2017   NetSolutions received cash of $7,500 for providing services to customers.*

You may have earned money by painting houses or mowing lawns. If so, you received money for rendering services to a customer. Likewise, a business earns money by selling goods or services to its customers. This amount is called **revenue**.

During its first month of operations, NetSolutions received cash of $7,500 for providing services to customers. The receipt of cash increases NetSolutions' assets and also increases stockholders' equity in the business. The revenues of $7,500 are recorded in a Fees Earned column to the right of Common Stock. The effect of this transaction is to increase Cash and Fees Earned by $7,500, as follows:

	Assets			**=**	**Liabilities +**	**Stockholders' Equity**	
					Accounts	Common	Fees
	Cash	+ Supplies +	Land		Payable +	Stock +	Earned
Bal.	5,000	1,350	20,000	=	1,350	25,000	
D.	+7,500						+7,500
Bal.	12,500	1,350	20,000		1,350	25,000	7,500

33,850 = 33,850

Different terms are used for the various types of revenues. As illustrated for NetSolutions, revenue from providing services is recorded as **fees earned**. Revenue from the sale of merchandise is recorded as **sales**. Other examples of revenue include rent, which is recorded as **rent revenue**, and interest, which is recorded as **interest revenue**.

Instead of receiving cash at the time services are provided or goods are sold, a business may accept payment at a later date. Such revenues are described as *fees earned on account* or *sales on account*. For example, if NetSolutions had provided services on account instead of for cash, transaction (D) would have been described as follows: *Fees earned on account, $7,500.*

In such cases, the firm has an asset, called an **account receivable**, which is a claim against the customer. The effect of the transaction increases Accounts Receivable and Fees Earned. When customers pay their accounts, Cash increases and Accounts Receivable decreases.

Why It Matters

Round-Tripping

Accounting principles require that a transaction have *commercial substance*. Commercial substance means that the transaction has an economic impact on the entity. An example of a transaction lacking commercial substance is round-tripping. Round-tripping is a situation whereby a company "sells" goods and services to another company and then, under a prearranged agreement, the customer resells the exact same goods and services back to the original company. Round-tripping has been used by companies to artificially inflate their sales. However, such agreements do not have commercial substance, since there is no economic change to either company after the round-trip. Thus, round-tripped sales are not transactions from an accounting perspective.

Transaction E

Nov. 30, 2017 NetSolutions paid the following expenses during the month: wages, $2,125; rent, $800; utilities, $450; and miscellaneous, $275.

During the month, NetSolutions spent cash or used up other assets in earning revenue. Assets used in this process of earning revenue are called **expenses**. Expenses include supplies used and payments for employee wages, utilities, and other services.

NetSolutions paid the following expenses during the month: wages, $2,125; rent, $800; utilities, $450; and miscellaneous, $275. Miscellaneous expenses include small amounts paid for such items as postage, coffee, and newspapers. The effect of expenses is the opposite of revenues in that expenses reduce assets and stockholders' equity. Like fees earned, the expenses are recorded in columns to the right of Common Stock. However, since expenses reduce stockholders' equity, the expenses are entered as negative amounts. The effect of this transaction is as follows:

	Assets			=	Liabilities +		Stockholders' Equity				
					Accounts	Common	Fees	Wages	Rent	Utilities	Misc.
	Cash +	Supplies +	Land		Payable +	Stock	+ Earned −	Exp. −	Exp. −	Exp. −	Exp.
Bal.	12,500	1,350	20,000	=	1,350	25,000	7,500				
E.	−3,650							−2,125	−800	−450	−275
Bal.	8,850	1,350	20,000		1,350	25,000	7,500	−2,125	−800	−450	−275

30,200 = 30,200

Businesses usually record each revenue and expense transaction as it occurs. However, to simplify, NetSolutions' revenues and expenses are summarized for the month in transactions (D) and (E).

Transaction F

Nov. 30, 2017 NetSolutions paid creditors on account, $950.

When you pay your monthly credit card bill, you decrease the cash and decrease the amount you owe to the credit card company. Likewise, when NetSolutions pays $950 to creditors during the month, it reduces assets and liabilities, as follows:

	Assets			=	Liabilities +		Stockholders' Equity				
					Accounts	Common	Fees	Wages	Rent	Utilities	Misc.
	Cash +	Supplies +	Land		Payable +	Stock	+ Earned −	Exp. −	Exp. −	Exp. −	Exp.
Bal.	8,850	1,350	20,000	=	1,350	25,000	7,500	−2,125	−800	−450	−275
F.	−950				−950						
Bal.	7,900	1,350	20,000		400	25,000	7,500	−2,125	−800	−450	−275

29,250 = 29,250

Paying an amount on account is different from paying an expense. The paying of an expense reduces stockholders' equity, as illustrated in transaction (E). Paying an amount on account reduces the amount owed on a liability.

Transaction G

Nov. 30, 2017 Chris Clark determined that the cost of supplies on hand at the end of the month was $550.

The cost of the supplies on hand (not yet used) at the end of the month is $550. Thus, $800 ($1,350 − $550) of supplies must have been used during the month. This decrease in supplies is recorded as an expense, as follows:

	Assets			=	Liabilities +		Stockholders' Equity					
					Accounts	Common	Fees	Wages	Rent	Supplies	Utilities	Misc.
	Cash +	Supplies +	Land		Payable +	Stock	+ Earned −	Exp. −	Exp. −	Exp. −	Exp. −	Exp.
Bal.	7,900	1,350	20,000	=	400	25,000	7,500	−2,125	−800		−450	−275
G.		−800								−800		
Bal.	7,900	550	20,000		400	25,000	7,500	−2,125	−800	−800	−450	−275

28,450 = 28,450

Transaction H   *Nov. 30, 2017   Paid dividends, $2,000.*

Dividends are distributions of earnings to stockholders. The payment of dividends decreases cash and stockholders' equity. Like expenses, dividends are recorded in a separate column to the right of Common Stock as a negative amount. The effect of the payment of dividends of $2,000 is as follows:

	Assets			=	Liabilities +			Stockholders' Equity					
	Cash +	Supp. +	Land	=	Accounts Payable +	Common Stock -	Dividends +	Fees Earned -	Wages Exp. -	Rent Exp. -	Supplies Exp. -	Utilities Exp. -	Misc. Exp.
Bal.	7,900	550	20,000	=	400	25,000		7,500	-2,125	-800	-800	-450	-275
H.	-2,000						-2,000						
Bal.	5,900	550	20,000		400	25,000	-2,000	7,500	-2,125	-800	-800	-450	-275

26,450   =   26,450

Dividends should not be confused with expenses. Dividends do not represent assets or services used in the process of earning revenues. Instead, dividends are considered a distribution of earnings to stockholders.

DYNAMIC EXHIBIT

Summary

The transactions of **NetSolutions** are summarized in Exhibit 5. Each transaction is identified by letter, and the balance of each accounting equation element is shown after every transaction.

Exhibit 5   Summary of Transactions for NetSolutions

	Assets			= Liabilities +			Stockholders' Equity					
	Cash +	Supp. +	Land =	Accounts Payable +	Common Stock -	Dividends +	Fees Earned -	Wages Exp. -	Rent Exp. -	Supplies Exp. -	Utilities Exp. -	Misc. Exp.
A.	+25,000				+25,000							
B.	-20,000		+20,000									
Bal.	5,000		20,000		25,000							
C.		+1,350		+1,350								
Bal.	5,000	+1,350	20,000	+1,350	25,000							
D.	+7,500						+7,500					
Bal.	12,500	1,350	20,000	1,350	25,000		7,500					
E.	-3,650							-2,125	-800		-450	-275
Bal.	8,850	1,350	20,000	1,350	25,000		7,500	-2,125	-800		-450	-275
F.	-950			-950								
Bal.	7,900	1,350	20,000	400	25,000		7,500	-2,125	-800		-450	-275
G.		-800								-800		
Bal.	7,900	550	20,000	400	25,000		7,500	-2,125	-800	-800	-450	-275
H.	-2,000					-2,000						
Bal.	5,900	550	20,000	400	25,000	-2,000	7,500	-2,125	-800	-800	-450	-275

26,450   =   26,450

You should note the following:

- The effect of every transaction *is an increase or a decrease in one or more of the accounting equation elements.*
- The two sides of the accounting equation are *always equal.*
- The stockholders' equity is *increased by amounts invested by stockholders (common stock).*
- The stockholders' equity is *increased by revenues and decreased by expenses.*
- The stockholders' equity is *decreased by dividends paid to stockholders.*

Classifications of Stockholders' Equity

Stockholders' equity is classified as:

- Common Stock
- Retained Earnings

Common stock is shares of ownership distributed to investors of a corporation. It represents the portion of stockholders' equity contributed by investors. For NetSolutions, shares of common stock of $25,000 were distributed to Chris Clark in exchange for investing in the business.

Retained earnings is the stockholders' equity created from business operations through revenue and expense transactions. For NetSolutions, retained earnings of $3,050 were created by its November operations (revenue and expense transactions), computed as follows:

**NetSolutions Retained Earnings
November Operations
(Revenue and Expense Transactions)**

	Fees Earned	−	Wages Exp.	−	Rent Exp.	−	Supplies Exp.	−	Utilities Exp.	−	Misc. Exp.
Transaction D.	+7,500										
Transaction E.			−2,125		−800				−450		−275
Transaction G.							−800				
Balance, Nov. 30	7,500		−2,125		−800		−800		−450		−275

$3,050

Stockholders' equity created by investments by stockholders (common stock) and by business operations (retained earnings) are reported separately. Since dividends are distributions of earnings to stockholders, dividends reduce retained earnings. NetSolutions paid $2,000 in dividends during November, thus reducing retained earnings to $1,050 ($3,050 − $2,000).

The effects of investments by stockholders, dividends, revenues, and expenses on stockholders' equity are illustrated in Exhibit 6.

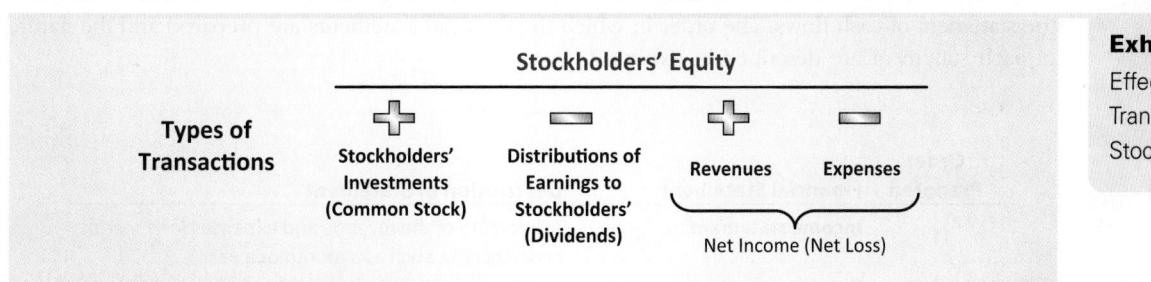

Stockholders' Equity

Types of Transactions + Stockholders' Investments (Common Stock) − Distributions of Earnings to Stockholders' (Dividends) + Revenues − Expenses

Net Income (Net Loss)

Exhibit 6

Effects of Transactions on Stockholders' Equity

Check Up Corner 1-1 Business Transactions and the Accounting Equation

Drive Time Delivery is a local delivery service operating in Cleveland, Ohio. At the beginning of the month, February 1, Drive Time has the following account balances: Cash, $32,500; Accounts Receivable, $5,000; Accounts Payable, $2,500; Common Stock, $32,500; Fees Earned, $5,000; Wages Expense, $2,500.

The following selected transactions were completed by the company during the month of February:

A.   Received cash from owner as an additional investment in common stock, $20,000.

B.   Paid creditors on account, $2,000.

C.   Received cash from customers on account, $5,000.

D.   Billed customers for delivery services on account, $18,000.

E.   Paid wages expense, $10,000.

F.   Paid utilities expense, $3,000.

G.   Paid dividends, $4,500.

Prepare a table to indicate the effect that each of these transactions has on the following asset, liability, and stockholders' equity accounts: Cash, Accounts Receivable, Accounts Payable, Common Stock, Dividends, Fees Earned, Wages Expense, Utilities Expense.

Solution:

The change in an asset account is accompanied by a change in another asset, liability, or stockholders' equity account.

		Assets		=	Liabilities	+			Stockholders' Equity		
	Cash	+	Accounts Receivable	=	Accounts Payable	+	Common Stock	− Dividends +	Fees Earned	− Wages Expense	− Utilities Expense
Bal.	32,500		5,000		2,500		32,500		5,000	−2,500	
A.	20,000						20,000				
B.	−2,000				−2,000						
C.	5,000		−5,000								
D.			18,000						18,000		
E.	−10,000									−10,000	
F.	−3,000										−3,000
G.	−4,500							−4,500			
Bal.	38,000		18,000	=	500	+	52,500	−4,500	23,000	−12,500	−3,000
		56,000		=					56,000		

Check Up Corner

Objective 5

Describe the financial statements of a corporation and explain how they interrelate.

Financial Statements

After transactions have been recorded and summarized, reports are prepared for users. The accounting reports providing this information are called **financial statements**. The primary financial statements of a corporation are the income statement, the retained earnings statement, the balance sheet, and the statement of cash flows. The order in which the financial statements are prepared and the nature of each statement are described in Exhibit 7.

Exhibit 7

Financial Statements

Order Prepared	Financial Statement	Description of Statement
1.	Income statement	A summary of the revenue and expenses *for a specific period of time,* such as a month or a year.
2.	Retained earnings statement	A summary of the changes in the retained earnings that have occurred *during a specific period of time,* such as a month or a year.
3.	Balance sheet	A list of the assets, liabilities, and stockholders' equity *as of a specific date,* usually at the close of the last day of a month or a year.
4.	Statement of cash flows	A summary of the cash receipts and cash payments for a *specific period of time,* such as a month or a year.

The four financial statements and their interrelationships are illustrated in Exhibit 8, The data for the statements are taken from the summary of **NetSolutions**' transactions in Exhibit 5.

All financial statements are identified by the name of the business, the title of the statement, and the *date* or *period of time.* The data presented in the income statement, the retained earnings statement, and the statement of cash flows are for a period of time. The data presented in the balance sheet are for a specific date.

NetSolutions
Income Statement
For the Month Ended November 30, 2017

Fees earned...		$7,500
Expenses:		
Wages expense	$2,125	
Rent expense	800	
Supplies expense...	800	
Utilities expense	450	
Miscellaneous expense	275	
Total expenses		4,450
Net income		$3,050

NetSolutions
Retained Earnings Statement
For the Month Ended November 30, 2017

Retained earnings, November 1, 2017............................		$ 0
Net income	$ 3,050	
Dividends	(2,000)	
Change in retained earnings		1,050
Retained earnings, November 30, 2017		$1,050

NetSolutions
Balance Sheet
November 30, 2017

Assets

Cash		$ 5,900
Supplies		550
Land		20,000
Total assets		$26,450

Liabilities

Accounts payable		$ 400

Stockholders' Equity

Common stock...	$25,000	
Retained earnings..	1,050	
Total stockholders' equity		26,050
Total liabilities and stockholders' equity		$26,450

NetSolutions
Statement of Cash Flows
For the Month Ended November 30, 2017

Cash flows from operating activities:		
Cash received from customers	$ 7,500	
Cash payments for expenses and payments to creditors	(4,600)	
Net cash flow from operating activities		$ 2,900
Cash flows used for investing activities:		
Cash payments for purchase of land............................		(20,000)
Cash flows from financing activities:		
Cash received from issuing common stock.......................	$25,000	
Cash dividends	(2,000)	
Net cash flows from financing activities		23,000
Net increase in cash and November 30, 2017, cash balance		$ 5,900

Exhibit 8
Financial Statements for NetSolutions

DYNAMIC EXHIBIT

note:
When revenues exceed expenses, it is referred to as *net income, net profit,* or *earnings*. When expenses exceed revenues, it is referred to as *net loss*.

Income Statement

The income statement reports the revenues and expenses for a period of time, based on the revenue and expense recognition principles. These principles match revenues and their related expenses so that they are reported in the same period. The excess of the revenue over the expenses is called **net income**, **net profit**, or **earnings**. If the expenses exceed the revenue, the excess is a **net loss**.

Link to Twitter   For a recent year, **Twitter** reported a net loss of $645 million.

The revenue and expenses for **NetSolutions** were shown in Exhibit 5 as separate increases and decreases. Net income for a period increases the stockholders' equity (retained earnings) for the period. A net loss decreases stockholders' equity (retained earnings) for the period.

The revenue, expenses, and net income of $3,050 for NetSolutions are reported in the income statement in Exhibit 8. The order in which the expenses are listed in the income statement varies among businesses. Most businesses list expenses in order of size, beginning with the larger items. Miscellaneous expense is usually shown as the last item, regardless of the amount.

Retained Earnings Statement

The retained earnings statement reports the changes in the retained earnings for a period of time. It is prepared *after* the income statement because the net income or net loss for the period must be reported in this statement. Similarly, it is prepared *before* the balance sheet, since the amount of retained earnings at the end of the period must be reported on the balance sheet. Because of this, the retained earnings statement is often viewed as the connecting link between the income statement and balance sheet.

The following two types of transactions affected NetSolutions' retained earnings during November:

- Revenues and expenses, which resulted in net income of $3,050.
- Dividends of $2,000 paid to stockholders (Chris Clark).

These transactions are summarized in the retained earnings statement for **NetSolutions** shown in Exhibit 8.

Since NetSolutions has been in operation for only one month, it has no retained earnings at the beginning of November. For December, however, there is a beginning balance—the balance at the end of November. This balance of $1,050 is reported on the retained earnings statement.

To illustrate, assume that NetSolutions earned net income of $4,155 and paid dividends of $2,000 during December. The retained earnings statement for NetSolutions for December follows:

NetSolutions
Retained Earnings Statement
For the Month Ended December 31, 2017

Retained earnings, December 1, 2017		$1,050
Net income...	$ 4,155	
Dividends...	(2,000)	
Change in retained earnings.................................		2,155
Retained earnings, December 31, 2017		$3,205

Balance Sheet

The balance sheet in Exhibit 8 reports the amounts of **NetSolutions**' assets, liabilities, and stockholders' equity as of November 30, 2017, in a vertical format. This form of balance sheet is commonly used and is called the **report form**.[4]

The asset and liability amounts are taken from the last line of the summary of transactions in Exhibit 5. Retained earnings as of November 30, 2017, is taken from the retained earnings statement.

---

[4] An alternative form of balance sheet reports assets, liabilities, and stockholders' equity in a horizontal format, called the account form.

The assets section of the balance sheet presents assets in the order that they will be converted into cash or used in operations. Cash is presented first, followed by receivables, supplies, prepaid insurance, and other assets. The assets of a more permanent nature are shown next, such as land, buildings, and equipment.

In the liabilities section of the balance sheet in Exhibit 8, accounts payable is the only liability. When there are two or more liabilities, each should be listed and the total amount of liabilities presented as follows:

	Liabilities	
Accounts payable	$12,900	
Wages payable	2,570	
Total liabilities		$15,470

Statement of Cash Flows

The statement of cash flows consists of the following three sections, as shown in Exhibit 8:

1. operating activities
2. investing activities
3. financing activities

Cash Flows from Operating Activities This section reports a summary of cash receipts and cash payments from operations. The net cash flow from operating activities normally differs from the amount of net income for the period. In Exhibit 8, **NetSolutions** reported net cash flows from operating activities of $2,900 and net income of $3,050. This difference occurs because revenues and expenses may not be recorded at the same time that cash is received from customers or paid to creditors.

Cash Flows from Investing Activities This section reports the cash transactions for the acquisition and sale of relatively permanent assets. Exhibit 8 reports that **NetSolutions** paid $20,000 for the purchase of land during November.

Cash Flows from Financing Activities This section reports the cash transactions related to cash investments by stockholders, borrowings, and dividends. Exhibit 8 shows that Chris Clark invested $25,000 in exchange for common stock of **NetSolutions**. NetSolutions also paid $2,000 of dividends during November.

For a recent year, **Twitter** reported $1.4 million of cash inflows from operating activities, $1,306.1 million of cash used for investing activities, $1,942.2 million of cash from financing activities, and net increase in cash of $637.5 million.

Link to Twitter

Preparing NetSolutions' Statement of Cash Flows Preparing the statement of cash flows requires that each of the November cash transactions for **NetSolutions** be classified as an operating, investing, or financing activity. Using the summary of transactions shown in Exhibit 5, the November cash transactions for NetSolutions are classified as follows:

Transaction	Amount	Cash Flow Activity
A.	$25,000	Financing (Issued common stock)
B.	−20,000	Investing (Purchase of land)
D.	7,500	Operating (Fees earned)
E.	−3,650	Operating (Payment of expenses)
F.	−950	Operating (Payment of account payable)
H.	−2,000	Financing (Paid dividends)

Transactions (C) and (G) are not listed since they did not involve a cash receipt or payment. In addition, the payment of accounts payable in transaction (F) is classified as an operating activity because the account payable arose from the purchase of supplies, which are used in operations. Using the preceding classifications of November cash transactions, the statement of cash flows is prepared as shown in Exhibit 8.[5]

The ending cash balance shown on the statement of cash flows is also reported on the balance sheet as of the end of the period. To illustrate, the ending cash of $5,900 reported on the November statement of cash flows in Exhibit 8 is also reported as the amount of cash on hand in the November 30, 2017, balance sheet.

Since November is NetSolutions' first period of operations, the net cash flow for November and the November 30, 2017, cash balance are the same amount, $5,900, as shown in Exhibit 8. In later periods, NetSolutions will report in its statement of cash flows a beginning cash balance, an increase or a decrease in cash for the period, and an ending cash balance. For example, assume that for December NetSolutions has a decrease in cash of $3,835. The last three lines of NetSolutions' statement of cash flows for December would be as follows:

Decrease in cash	$(3,835)
Cash as of December 1, 2017	5,900
Cash as of December 31, 2017	$ 2,065

Interrelationships Among Financial Statements

Financial statements are prepared in the order of the income statement, retained earnings statement, balance sheet, and statement of cash flows. This order is important because the financial statements are interrelated. These interrelationships for **NetSolutions** are shown in Exhibit 8 and are described in Exhibit 9.[6]

Exhibit 9 Financial Statement Interrelationships

Financial Statements	Interrelationship	NetSolutions Example (Exhibit 8)
Income Statement *and* Retained Earnings Statement	Net income or net loss reported on the income statement is also reported on the retained earnings statement as either an addition (net income) to or deduction (net loss) from the beginning retained earnings.	NetSolutions' net income of $3,050 for November is added to the beginning retained earnings on November 1, 2017, on the retained earnings statement.
Retained Earnings Statement *and* Balance Sheet	Retained earnings at the end of the period reported on the retained earnings statement is also reported on the balance sheet as retained earnings.	NetSolutions' retained earnings of $1,050 as of November 30, 2017, on the retained earnings statement also appears on the November 30, 2017, balance sheet as retained earnings.
Balance Sheet *and* Statement of Cash Flows	The cash reported on the balance sheet is also reported as the end-of-period cash on the statement of cash flows.	Cash of $5,900 reported on the balance sheet as of November 30, 2017, is also reported on the November statement of cash flows as the end-of-period cash.

The preceding interrelationships are important in analyzing financial statements and the impact of transactions on a business. In addition, these interrelationships serve as a check on whether the financial statements are prepared correctly. For example, if the ending cash on the statement of cash flows does not agree with the balance sheet cash, then an error has occurred.

---

[5] This method of preparing the statement of cash flows is called the "direct method." This method and the indirect method are discussed further in Chapter 13.
[6] Depending on the method of preparing the cash flows from operating activities section of the statement of cash flows, net income (or net loss) may also appear on the statement of cash flows. This interrelationship or method of preparing the statement of cash flows, called the "indirect method," is described and illustrated in Chapter 13.

Check Up Corner 1-2 Financial Statements

Levart Travel Service's assets and liabilities at December 31, 2018, the end of the year, and its revenue and expenses for the year follow.

Accounts payable	$ 12,200	Land	$ 90,000
Accounts receivable	31,350	Miscellaneous expense	12,950
Cash	53,050	Office expense	63,000
Common stock	100,000	Supplies	3,350
Fees earned	263,200	Wages expense	131,700

The retained earnings were $30,000 on January 1, 2018, the beginning of the year. During the year, dividends of $20,000 were paid.

A. Prepare an income statement for the year ended December 31, 2018.

B. Prepare a retained earnings statement for the year ended December 31, 2018.

C. Prepare a balance sheet as of December 31, 2018.

D. Show the interrelationships of these three financial statements.

Solution:

The income statement reports revenues and expenses **for the period.**

The retained earnings statement **connects** the income statement to the balance sheet.

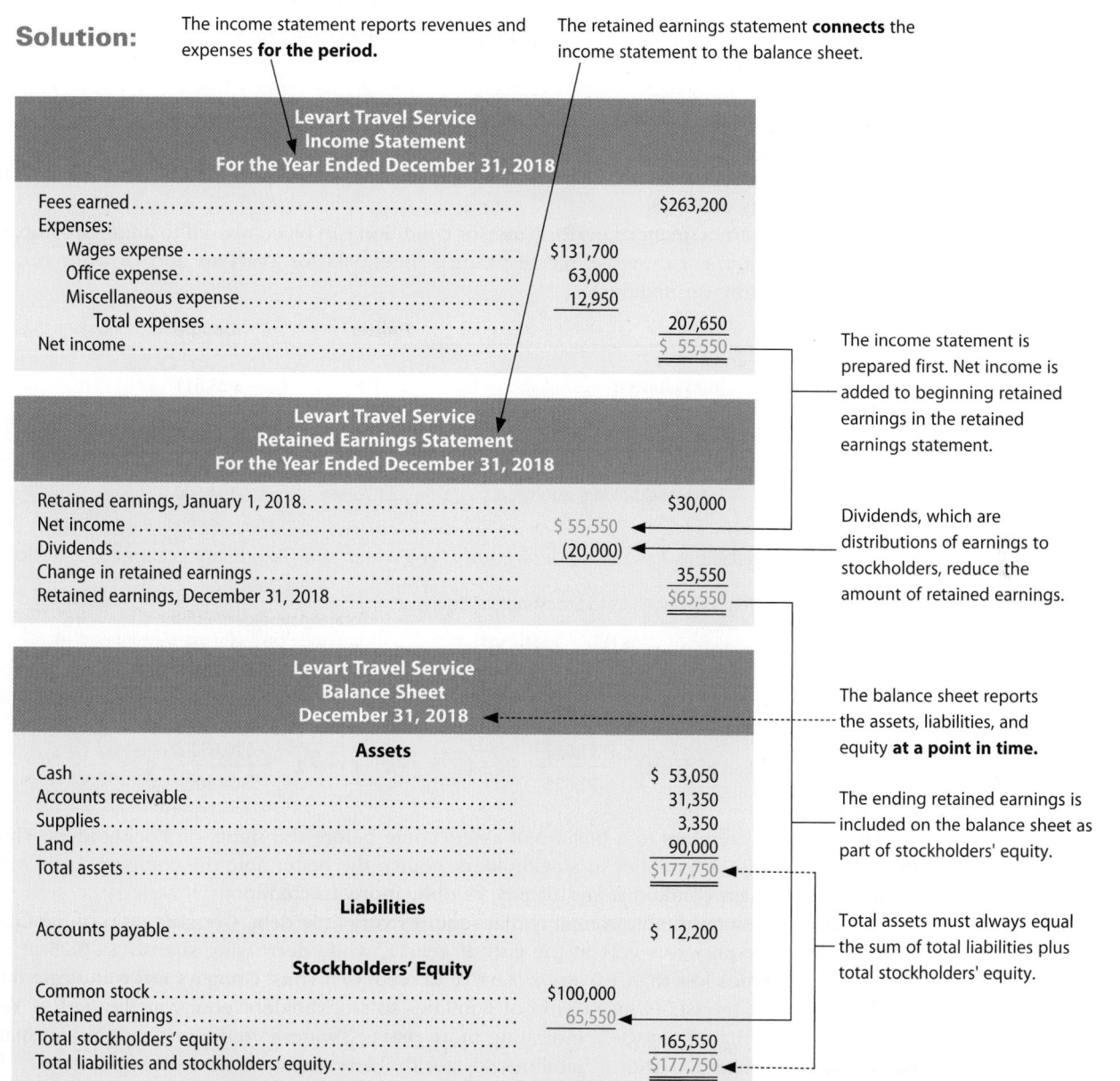

Levart Travel Service
Income Statement
For the Year Ended December 31, 2018

Fees earned		$263,200
Expenses:		
Wages expense	$131,700	
Office expense	63,000	
Miscellaneous expense	12,950	
Total expenses		207,650
Net income		$ 55,550

The income statement is prepared first. Net income is added to beginning retained earnings in the retained earnings statement.

Levart Travel Service
Retained Earnings Statement
For the Year Ended December 31, 2018

Retained earnings, January 1, 2018		$30,000
Net income	$ 55,550	
Dividends	(20,000)	
Change in retained earnings		35,550
Retained earnings, December 31, 2018		$65,550

Dividends, which are distributions of earnings to stockholders, reduce the amount of retained earnings.

Levart Travel Service
Balance Sheet
December 31, 2018

Assets

Cash	$ 53,050
Accounts receivable	31,350
Supplies	3,350
Land	90,000
Total assets	$177,750

Liabilities

Accounts payable	$ 12,200

Stockholders' Equity

Common stock	$100,000	
Retained earnings	65,550	
Total stockholders' equity		165,550
Total liabilities and stockholders' equity		$177,750

The balance sheet reports the assets, liabilities, and equity **at a point in time.**

The ending retained earnings is included on the balance sheet as part of stockholders' equity.

Total assets must always equal the sum of total liabilities plus total stockholders' equity.

Analysis for Decision Making

Objective

Describe and illustrate the use of the ratio of liabilities to stockholders' equity in evaluating a company's financial condition.

Ratio of Liabilities to Stockholders' Equity

The basic financial statements illustrated in this chapter are useful to bankers, creditors, stockholders, and others in analyzing and interpreting the financial performance and condition of a company. Various tools and techniques that are often used to analyze and interpret a company's financial performance and condition are described and illustrated in the Analysis for Decision Making section at the end of selected chapters. We begin with a method for analyzing the ability of a company to pay its creditors.

The relationship between liabilities and stockholders' equity can be expressed as a **ratio of liabilities to stockholders' equity**, as follows:

$$\text{Ratio of Liabilities to Stockholders' Equity} = \frac{\text{Total Liabilities}}{\text{Total Stockholders' Equity}}$$

NetSolutions' ratio of liabilities to stockholders' equity at the end of November is 0.015 (1.5%), computed as follows:

$$\text{Ratio of Liabilities to Stockholders' Equity} = \frac{\$400}{\$26,050} = 0.015 \text{ (rounded)}$$

Since the total liabilities are only 1.5% of the total stockholders' equity, **NetSolutions** is in a solid position to pay its creditors.

Often, a company's financial performance or condition can be compared to another company in a similar industry. For example, recent balance sheet data for **Twitter** and **Google Inc.** at December 31 follow (in millions):

	Twitter	**Google**
End of Year 1		
Total liabilities	$ 416	$ 23,611
Total stockholders' equity	2,950	87,309
End of Year 2		
Total liabilities	$1,957	$ 26,633
Total stockholders' equity	3,626	104,500

The ratios of liabilities to stockholders' equity for Twitter and Google are computed as follows:

$$\text{Ratio of Liabilities to Stockholders' Equity} = \frac{\text{Total Liabilities}}{\text{Total Stockholders' Equity}}$$

Twitter:

End of Year 1: $\dfrac{\$416}{\$2,950} = 0.14$

End of Year 2: $\dfrac{\$1,957}{\$3,626} = 0.54$

Google:

End of Year 1: $\dfrac{\$23,611}{\$87,309} = 0.27$

End of Year 2: $\dfrac{\$26,633}{\$104,500} = 0.25$

The rights of creditors to a business's assets come before the rights of stockholders. Thus, the lower the ratio of liabilities to stockholders' equity, the better able the company is to withstand poor business conditions and to pay its obligations to creditors.

Google is a very profitable company that requires very little debt. Google's ratio of liabilities to stockholders' equity was 0.27 at the end of Year 1, while decreasing slightly to 0.25 at the end of Year 2. Ratios less than 1.0 are protective to creditors. Thus, Google's ratios indicate little creditor risk. In contrast, Twitter's ratio of liabilities to stockholders' equity at the end of Year 2 is nearly twice that of Google's, indicating more risk to Twitter's creditors. Creditors normally would not be concerned with a liabilities to stockholders' equity ratio of 0.54. However, the growth in this ratio from 0.14 to 0.54 within one year indicates that Twitter is increasing its debt. This increase in the use of debt should be monitored.

| **Make a Decision** | Ratio of Liabilities to Stockholders' Equity |

Apple Inc. and **Hewlett-Packard Co (HP)** compete in the electronics industry. The liabilities and stockholders' equity at the end of two recent years for both companies follow:

	Apple	HP
End of Year 1		
Liabilities	$ 83,451	$78,020
Stockholders' equity	123,549	27,269
End of Year 2		
Liabilities	$120,292	$76,079
Stockholders' equity	111,547	26,731

A. Compute the ratio of liabilities to stockholders' equity for each company for each year. (Round to two decimal places.)

B. On a line chart, plot each company's end-of-year ratios of liabilities to stockholders' equity. Use a separate line to connect the two ratios for each company.

C. If you were a creditor, to which company would you prefer to loan money?

D. Which company has shown the larger change in creditor risk between the two years?

Solution:

A.

$$\text{Ratio of Liabilities to Stockholders' Equity} = \frac{\text{Total Liabilities}}{\text{Total Stockholders' Equity}}$$

Apple:

Year 1: $\dfrac{\$83,451}{\$123,549} = 0.7$

Year 2: $\dfrac{\$120,292}{\$111,547} = 1.1$

HP:

Year 1: $\dfrac{\$78,020}{\$27,269} = 2.9$

Year 2: $\dfrac{\$76,079}{\$26,731} = 2.8$

B.

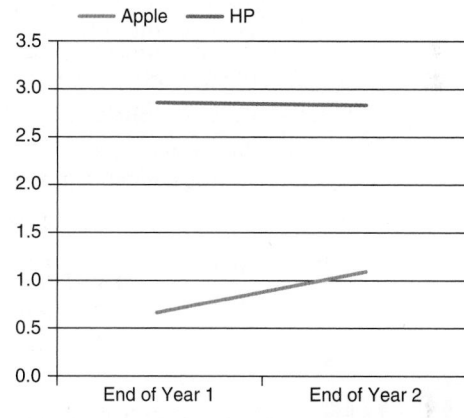

C. HP's ratio of liabilities to stockholders' equity is more than twice as large as Apple's ratio at the end of each year. Thus, HP is more risky to creditors. You should prefer to lend money to Apple over HP.

D. Apple has the larger change in creditor risk between the two years. Its ratio of liabilities to stockholders' equity increased from 0.7 to 1.1, or approximately 57% [(1.1 − 0.7) ÷ 0.7]. In contrast, HP's ratio changed little between the end of the two years. The change in Apple's ratio is due to using debt to finance the purchase of its own common stock. As a result, its stockholders' equity decreased, while its long-term debt increased, causing an increase in its ratio.

Make a Decision

Let's Review

Chapter Summary

1. A business provides goods or services (outputs) to customers with the objective of earning a profit. Three types of businesses include service, merchandising, and manufacturing businesses. Accounting is an information system that provides reports to users about the economic activities and condition of a business. Ethics are moral principles that guide the conduct of individuals. Good ethical conduct depends on individual character and company culture. Accountants are engaged in private accounting or public accounting.

2. Generally accepted accounting principles (GAAP) are used in preparing financial statements. To be useful, financial reports should provide information that is relevant and a faithful representation of the economic activity or condition. GAAP is based upon the assumptions of monetary unit, time period, business entity, and going concern. The principles of measurement, historical cost, revenue recognition, and expense recognition are an integral part of GAAP. The Financial Standards Board (FASB), Security and Exchange Commission (SEC), and International Accounting Standards Board (IASB) develop standards that are incorporated into GAAP.

3. The resources owned by a business and the rights or claims to these resources may be stated in the form of an equation, as follows: Assets = Liabilities + Equity

4. All business transactions can be stated in terms of the change in one or more of the three elements of the accounting equation.

5. The primary financial statements of a corporation are the income statement, the retained earnings statement, the balance sheet, and the statement of cash flows. The income statement reports a period's net income or net loss, which is also reported on the retained earnings statement. The ending retained earnings reported on the retained earnings statement is also reported on the balance sheet. The ending cash balance is reported on the balance sheet and the statement of cash flows.

Key Terms

account payable (14)
account receivable (14)
accounting (5)
accounting assumptions (9)
accounting equation (12)
accounting principles (9)
accounting standards (9)
arm's-length transactions (11)
assets (11)
balance sheet (18)
business (4)
business entity assumption (10)
business transaction (12)
Certified Public Accountant (CPA) (8)
common stock (13)
corporation (10)
cost principle (11)
dividends (16)
earnings (20)
equity (11)

ethics (6)
expense recognition principle (11)
expenses (11)
faithful representation (9)
fees earned (14)
financial accounting (6)
Financial Accounting Standards Board (FASB) (9)
financial statements (18)
generally accepted accounting principles (GAAP) (9)
general-purpose financial statements (6)
going concern assumption (11)
historical cost principle (11)
income statement (18)
interest revenue (14)
International Accounting Standards Board (IASB) (9)
liabilities (11)

limited liability company (LLC) (10)
management (or managerial) accounting (5)
manufacturing business (4)
measurement principle (11)
merchandising business (4)
monetary unit assumption (10)
net income (or net profit) (20)
net loss (20)
owner's equity (11)
partnership (10)
prepaid expenses (14)
private accounting (6)
profit (4)
proprietorship (10)
public accounting (8)
Public Company Accounting Oversight Board (PCAOB) (7)

ratio of liabilities to stockholders'
   equity (24)
relevant (9)
rent revenue (14)
report form (20)
retained earnings (17)

retained earnings statement (18)
revenue (11)
revenue recognition
   principle (11)
sales (14)
Sarbanes-Oxley Act (SOX) (7)

Securities and Exchange
   Commission (SEC) (9)
service business (4)
statement of cash flows (18)
stockholders' equity (11)
time period assumption (10)

Practice

Multiple-Choice Questions

1. A profit-making business operating as a separate legal entity and in which ownership is divided into shares of stock is known as a:
   - A. proprietorship.
   - B. service business.
   - C. partnership.
   - D. corporation.

2. The resources owned by a business are called:
   - A. assets.
   - B. liabilities.
   - C. retained earnings.
   - D. common stock.

3. A listing of a business entity's assets, liabilities, and stockholders' equity as of a specific date is a(n):
   - A. balance sheet.
   - B. income statement.
   - C. retained earnings statement.
   - D. statement of cash flows.

4. If total assets increased $20,000 during a period and total liabilities increased $12,000 during the same period, the amount and direction (increase or decrease) of the change in stockholders' equity for that period is a(n):
   - A. $32,000 increase.
   - B. $32,000 decrease.
   - C. $8,000 increase.
   - D. $8,000 decrease.

5. If revenue was $45,000, expenses were $37,500, and dividends were $10,000, the amount of net income or net loss would be:
   - A. $45,000 net income.
   - B. $7,500 net income.
   - C. $37,500 net loss.
   - D. $2,500 net loss.

Answers provided after Problem. Need more practice? Find additional multiple-choice questions, exercises, and problems in CengageNOWv2.

Exercises

SHOW ME HOW

1. Cost principle

Obj. 2

On February 22, Kountry Repair Service extended an offer of $200,000 for land that had been priced for sale at $250,000. On April 3, Kountry Repair accepted the seller's counteroffer of $230,000 and bought the land for this amount. On September 15, the land was assessed at a value of $185,000 for property tax purposes. On January 9 of the next year, Kountry Repair was offered $300,000 for the land by a national retail chain. At what value should the land be recorded in Kountry Repair Service's records?

SHOW ME HOW

2. Accounting equation

Obj. 3

Dream-It LLC is a motivational consulting business. At the end of its accounting period, December 31, 2017, Dream-It has assets of $780,000 and liabilities of $150,000. Using the accounting equation, determine the following amounts:

A. Stockholders' equity as of December 31, 2017.

B. Stockholders' equity as of December 31, 2018, assuming that assets increased by $90,000 and liabilities increased by $25,000 during 2018.

SHOW ME HOW

3. Transactions

Obj. 4

Arrowhead Delivery Service is owned and operated by Gates Deeter. The following selected transactions were completed by Arrowhead Delivery during August:

1. Received cash in exchange for common stock, $25,000.
2. Paid creditors on account, $3,750.
3. Billed customers for delivery services on account, $22,400.
4. Received cash from customers on account, $11,300.
5. Paid dividends, $6,000.

Indicate the effect of each transaction on the following accounting equation elements: Assets, Liabilities, Common Stock, Dividends, Revenue, and Expense. To illustrate, the answer to (1) follows:

(1) Asset (Cash) increases by $25,000; Common Stock increases by $25,000.

SHOW ME HOW

4. Income statement

Obj. 5

The revenues and expenses of Ousel Travel Service for the year ended November 30, 2018, follow:

Fees earned	$1,475,000
Office expense	320,000
Miscellaneous expense	28,000
Wages expense	885,000

Prepare an income statement for the year ended November 30, 2018.

SHOW ME HOW

5. Retained earnings statement

Obj. 5

Using the income statement for Ousel Travel Service shown in Exercise 4, prepare a retained earnings statement for the year ended November 30, 2018. Shane Ousel invested an additional $50,000 in the business in exchange for common stock during the year and cash dividends of $30,000 were paid. Retained earnings as of December 1, 2017, was $566,000.

SHOW ME HOW

6. Balance sheet

Obj. 5

Using the following data for Ousel Travel Service as well as the retained earnings statement shown in Exercise 5, prepare a balance sheet as of November 30, 2018:

Accounts payable	$ 62,500
Accounts receivable	186,000
Cash	308,000
Common stock	150,000
Land	480,000
Supplies	16,500

SHOW ME HOW

7. Statement of cash flows

Obj. 5

A summary of cash flows for Ousel Travel Service for the year ended November 30, 2018, follows:

Cash receipts:	
Cash received from customers	$1,465,000
Cash received from issuing common stock	50,000
Cash payments:	
Cash paid for operating expenses	1,230,000
Cash paid for land	150,000
Cash paid as dividends	30,000

The cash balance as of December 1, 2017, was $203,000.

Prepare a statement of cash flows for Ousel Travel Service for the year ended November 30, 2018.

Answers provided after Problem. Need more practice? Find additional multiple-choice questions, exercises, and problems in CengageNOWv2.

Problem

Cecil Jameson, Attorney-at-Law, is organized as a corporation and operated by Cecil Jameson. On July 1, 2018, the company has the following assets, liabilities, and common stock: cash, $1,000; accounts receivable, $3,200; supplies, $850; land, $10,000; accounts payable, $1,530; common stock, $10,000. Office space and office equipment are currently being rented, pending the construction of an office complex on land purchased last year. Business transactions during July are summarized as follows:

A. Received cash from clients for services, $3,928.

B. Paid creditors on account, $1,055.

C. Received cash from Cecil Jameson as an additional investment in exchange for common stock, $3,700.

D. Paid office rent for the month, $1,200.

E. Charged clients for legal services on account, $2,025.

F. Purchased supplies on account, $245.

G. Received cash from clients on account, $3,000.

H. Received invoice for paralegal services from Legal Aid Inc. for July (to be paid on August 10), $1,635.

I. Paid the following: wages expense, $850; utilities expense, $325; answering service expense, $250; and miscellaneous expense, $75.

J. Determined that the cost of supplies on hand was $980; therefore, the cost of supplies used during the month was $115.

K. Paid dividends, $1,000.

Instructions

1. Determine the amount of retained earnings as of July 1, 2018.

2. State the assets, liabilities, and stockholders' equity as of July 1 in equation form similar to that shown in this chapter. In tabular form below the equation, indicate the increases and decreases resulting from each transaction and the new balances after each transaction.

3. Prepare an income statement for July, a retained earnings statement for July, and a balance sheet as of July 31, 2018.

4. (*Optional*) Prepare a statement of cash flows for July.

Need more practice? Find additional multiple-choice questions, exercises, and problems in CengageNOWv2.

Answers

Multiple-Choice Questions

1. **D** A corporation, organized in accordance with state or federal statutes, is a separate legal entity in which ownership is divided into shares of stock (answer D). A proprietorship (answer A) is an unincorporated business owned by one individual. A service business (answer B) provides services to its customers. It can be organized as a proprietorship, partnership, corporation, or limited liability company. A partnership (answer C) is an unincorporated business owned by two or more individuals.

2. **A** The resources owned by a business are called assets (answer A). The debts of the business are called liabilities (answer B), the stockholders' equity created from business operations through revenue and expense transactions is retained earnings (answer C), and shares of ownership in a corporation are common stock (answer D).

3. **A** The balance sheet is a listing of the assets, liabilities, and stockholders' equity of a business at a specific date (answer A). The income statement (answer B) is a summary of the revenue and expenses of a business for a specific period of time. The retained earnings statement (answer C) summarizes the changes in retained earnings during a specific period of time. The statement of cash flows (answer D) summarizes the cash receipts and cash payments for a specific period of time.

4. **C** The accounting equation is:

Assets = Liabilities + Stockholders' Equity

Therefore, if assets increased by $20,000 and liabilities increased by $12,000, stockholders' equity must have increased by $8,000 (answer C), as indicated in the following computation:

Assets	=	Liabilities	+	Stockholders' Equity
+$20,000	=	+$12,000	+	Stockholders' Equity
+$20,000 – $12,000	=			Stockholders' Equity
+$8,000	=			Stockholders' Equity

5. **B** Net income is the excess of revenue over expenses, or $7,500 (answer B). If expenses exceed revenue, the difference is a net loss. Dividends are the opposite of investing in the business and do not affect the amount of net income or net loss.

Exercises

1. $230,000. Under the cost concept, the land should be recorded at the cost to Kountry Repair Service.

2. A.   A = L + SE
   $780,000 = $150,000 + SE
         SE = $630,000

   B.   A = L + SE
   +$90,000 = +$25,000 + SE
         SE = +$65,000
   SE on December 31, 2018 = $630,000 + $65,000
   SE on December 31, 2018 = $695,000

3. (1) Asset (Cash) increases by $25,000;
   Common Stock increases by $25,000.
   (2) Asset (Cash) decreases by $3,750;
   Liability (Accounts Payable) decreases by $3,750.
   (3) Asset (Accounts Receivable) increases by $22,400;
   Revenue (Delivery Service Fees) increases by $22,400.
   (4) Asset (Cash) increases by $11,300;
   Asset (Accounts Receivable) decreases by $11,300.
   (5) Asset (Cash) decreases by $6,000;
   Dividends increases by $6,000.

4.

Ousel Travel Service Income Statement For the Year Ended November 30, 2018		
Fees earned..		$ 1,475,000
Expenses:		
Wages expense..	$885,000	
Office expense	320,000	
Miscellaneous expense......................................	28,000	
Total expenses...		1,233,000
Net income...		$ 242,000

5.

Ousel Travel Service Retained Earnings Statement For the Year Ended November 30, 2018		
Retained earnings, December 1, 2017		$ 566,000
Net income	$242,000	
Dividends	(30,000)	
Change in retained earnings		212,000
Retained earnings, November 30, 2018		$778,000

6.

Ousel Travel Service Balance Sheet November 30, 2018		
Assets		
Cash		$308,000
Accounts receivable		186,000
Supplies		16,500
Land		480,000
Total assets		$990,500
Liabilities		
Accounts payable		$ 62,500
Stockholders' Equity		
Common stock	$150,000	
Retained earnings	778,000	
Total stockholders' equity		928,000
Total liabilities and stockholders' equity		$990,500

7.

Ousel Travel Service Statement of Cash Flows For the Year Ended November 30, 2018		
Cash flows from operating activities:		
Cash received from customers	$ 1,465,000	
Cash payments for operating expenses	(1,230,000)	
Net cash flows from operating activities		$235,000
Cash flows used for investing activities:		
Cash payments for purchase of land		(150,000)
Cash flows from financing activities:		
Cash received from issuing common stock	$ 50,000	
Cash dividends	(30,000)	
Net cash flows from financing activities		20,000
Net increase in cash		$105,000
Cash as of December 1, 2017		203,000
Cash as of November 30, 2018		$308,000

Need more help? Watch step-by-step videos of how to compute answers to these Exercises in CengageNOWv2.

Problem

1.

$$\text{Assets} - \text{Liabilities} = \text{Stockholders' Equity}$$
$$(\$1,000 + \$3,200 + \$ 850 + \$10,000) - \$1,530 = \text{Common Stock} + \text{Retained Earnings}$$
$$\$15,050 - \$1,530 = \$10,000 + \text{Retained Earnings}$$
$$\$3,520 = \text{Retained Earnings}$$

2.

	Assets			=	Liabilities +		Stockholders' Equity								Answering		
		Accts.				Accts.	Common	Retained		Fees	Paralegal	Rent	Wages	Utilities	Service	Supp.	Misc.
	Cash +	Rec. +	Supp. +	Land =		Pay. +	Stock	Earnings	− Dividends +	Earned −	Exp. −	Exp. −	Exp. −	Exp. −	Exp. −	Exp. −	Exp.
Bal.	1,000	3,200	850	10,000		1,530	10,000	3,520									
A.	+3,928									3,928							
Bal.	4,928	3,200	850	10,000		1,530	10,000	3,520		3,928							
B.	−1,055					−1,055											
Bal.	3,873	3,200	850	10,000		475	10,000	3,520		3,928							
C.	+3,700						+3,700										
Bal.	7,573	3,200	850	10,000		475	13,700	3,520		3,928							
D.	−1,200											−1,200					
Bal.	6,373	3,200	850	10,000		475	13,700	3,520		3,928		−1,200					
E.		+ 2,025								+ 2,025							
Bal.	6,373	5,225	850	10,000		475	13,700	3,520		5,953		−1,200					
F.			+245			+245											
Bal.	6,373	5,225	1,095	10,000		720	13,700	3,520		5,953		−1,200					
G.	+3,000	−3,000															
Bal.	9,373	2,225	1,095	10,000		720	13,700	3,520		5,953		−1,200					
H.						+1,635					−1,635						
Bal.	9,373	2,225	1,095	10,000		2,355	13,700	3,520		5,953	−1,635	−1,200					
I.	−1,500												−850	−325	−250		−75
Bal.	7,873	2,225	1,095	10,000		2,355	13,700	3,520		5,953	−1,635	−1,200	−850	−325	−250		−75
J.			−115													−115	
Bal.	7,873	2,225	980	10,000		2,355	13,700	3,520		5,953	−1,635	−1,200	−850	−325	−250	−115	−75
K.	−1,000								−1,000								
Bal.	6,873	2,225	980	10,000		2,355	13,700	3,520	−1,000	5,953	−1,635	−1,200	−850	−325	−250	−115	−75

3.

Cecil Jameson, Attorney-at-Law
Income Statement
For the Month Ended July 31, 2018

Fees earned..		$5,953
Expenses:		
Paralegal expense..	$1,635	
Rent expense	1,200	
Wages expense	850	
Utilities expense	325	
Answering service expense	250	
Supplies expense	115	
Miscellaneous expense	75	
Total expenses..		4,450
Net income		$1,503

Cecil Jameson, Attorney-at-Law
Retained Earnings Statement
For the Month Ended July 31, 2018

Retained earnings, July 1, 2018.......................................		$3,520
Net income..	$ 1,503	
Dividends	(1,000)	
Change in retained earnings		503
Retained earnings, July 31, 2018		$4,023

Cecil Jameson, Attorney-at-Law Balance Sheet July 31, 2018		
Assets		
Cash		$ 6,873
Accounts receivable		2,225
Supplies		980
Land		10,000
Total assets		$20,078
Liabilities		
Accounts payable		$ 2,355
Stockholders' Equity		
Common stock	$13,700	
Retained earnings	4,023	
Total stockholders' equity		17,723
Total liabilities and stockholders' equity		$20,078

4. *(Optional)*

Cecil Jameson, Attorney-at-Law Statement of Cash Flows For the Month Ended July 31, 2018		
Cash flows from operating activities:		
Cash received from customers	$ 6,928*	
Cash payments for operating expenses	(3,755)**	
Net cash flows from operating activities		$3,173
Cash flows from investing activities		—
Cash flows from financing activities:		
Cash received from issuing common stock	$ 3,700	
Cash dividends	(1,000)	
Net cash flows from financing activities		2,700
Net increase in cash		$5,873
Cash as of July 1, 2018		1,000
Cash as of July 31, 2018		$6,873

*$6,928 = $3,928 + $3,000
**$3,755 = $1,055 + $1,200 + $1,500

Discussion Questions

1. Name some users of accounting information.

2. What is the role of accounting in business?

3. Why are most large companies like **Microsoft, PepsiCo, Caterpillar**, and **AutoZone** REAL WORLD organized as corporations?

4. Josh Reilly is the owner of Dispatch Delivery Service. Recently Josh paid interest of $4,500 on a personal loan of $75,000 that he used to begin the business. Should Dispatch Delivery Service record the interest payment? Explain.

5. On July 12, Reliable Repair Service extended an offer of $150,000 for land that had been priced for sale at $185,000. On September 3, Reliable Repair accepted the seller's counteroffer of $167,500. Describe how Reliable Repair Service should record the land.

6. A. Land with an assessed value of $750,000 for property tax purposes is acquired by a business for $900,000. Ten years later, the plot of land has an assessed value of $1,200,000 and the business receives an offer of $2,000,000 for it. Should the monetary amount assigned to the land in the business records now be increased?

   B. Assuming that the land acquired in (A) was sold for $2,125,000, how would the various elements of the accounting equation be affected?

7. Describe the difference between an account receivable and an account payable.

8. A business had revenues of $679,000 and operating expenses of $588,000. What was the amount of (A) net loss or (B) net income?

9. A business had revenues of $640,000 and operating expenses of $715,000. What was the amount of (A) net loss or (B) net income?

10. The financial statements are interrelated. (A) What item of financial or operating data appears on both the income statement and the retained earnings statement? (B) What item appears on both the balance sheet and the retained earnings statement? (C) What item appears on both the balance sheet and the statement of cash flows?

Basic Exercises

SHOW ME HOW

BE 1-1   Cost principle   Obj. 2

On June 25, Ritts Roofing extended an offer of $250,000 for land that had been priced for sale at $300,000. On July 9, Ritts accepted the seller's counteroffer of $275,000. On October 1, the land was assessed at a value of $280,000 for property tax purposes. On December 22, Ritts was offered $305,000 for the land by a national retail chain. At what value should the land be recorded in Ritts Roofing's records?

SHOW ME HOW

BE 1-2   Accounting equation   Obj. 3

Be-The-One is a motivational consulting business. At the end of its accounting period, December 31, 2017, Be-The-One has assets of $395,000 and liabilities of $97,000. Using the accounting equation, determine the following amounts:

A.   Stockholders' equity as of December 31, 2017.

B.   Stockholders' equity as of December 31, 2018, assuming that assets decreased by $65,000 and liabilities increased by $36,000 during 2018.

SHOW ME HOW

BE 1-3   Transactions   Obj. 4

Interstate Delivery Service is owned and operated by Katie Wyer. The following selected transactions were completed by Interstate Delivery during May:

1.   Received cash in exchange for common stock, $18,000.
2.   Paid advertising expense, $4,850.
3.   Purchased supplies on account, $2,100.
4.   Billed customers for delivery services on account, $14,700.
5.   Received cash from customers on account, $8,200.

Indicate the effect of each transaction on the following accounting equation elements: Assets, Liabilities, Common Stock, Dividends, Revenue, and Expense. To illustrate, the answer to (1) follows:

(1) Asset (Cash) increases by $18,000; Common Stock increases by $18,000.

SHOW ME HOW

BE 1-4   Income statement   Obj. 5

The revenues and expenses of Paradise Travel Service for the year ended May 31, 2018, follow:

Fees earned	$900,000
Office expense	300,000
Miscellaneous expense	15,000
Wages expense	450,000

Prepare an income statement for the year ended May 31, 2018.

SHOW ME HOW

BE 1-5 Retained earnings statement

Obj. 5

Using the income statement for Paradise Travel Service shown in Basic Exercise 1-4, prepare a retained earnings statement for the year ended May 31, 2018. Everett McCauley invested an additional $40,000 in the business in exchange for common stock, and $10,000 of dividends were paid during the year. Retained earnings as of June 1, 2017, were $300,000.

SHOW ME HOW

BE 1-6 Balance sheet

Obj. 5

Using the following data for Paradise Travel Service as well as the retained earnings statement shown in Basic Exercise 1-5, prepare a balance sheet as of May 31, 2018:

Accounts payable	$ 18,000
Accounts receivable	38,000
Cash	52,000
Common stock	100,000
Land	450,000
Supplies	3,000

SHOW ME HOW

BE 1-7 Statement of cash flows

Obj. 5

A summary of cash flows for Paradise Travel Service for the year ended May 31, 2018, follows:

Cash receipts:	
Cash received from customers	$880,000
Cash received from issuing common stock	40,000
Cash payments:	
Cash paid for operating expenses	758,000
Cash paid for land	150,000
Cash paid as dividends	10,000

The cash balance as of June 1, 2017, was $50,000.

Prepare a statement of cash flows for Paradise Travel Service for the year ended May 31, 2018.

Exercises

REAL WORLD

Internet Project

EX 1-1 Types of businesses

Obj. 1

The following is a list of well-known companies:

1. Alcoa Inc.
2. Boeing
3. Caterpillar
4. Citigroup Inc.
5. CVS
6. Dow Chemical Company
7. eBay Inc.
8. FedEx
9. Ford Motor Company
10. Gap Inc.
11. H&R Block
12. Hilton Hospitality, Inc.
13. Procter & Gamble
14. SunTrust
15. Walmart Stores, Inc.

A. Indicate whether each of these companies is primarily a service, merchandise, or manufacturing business. If you are unfamiliar with the company, use the Internet to locate the company's home page or use the finance Web site of Yahoo (finance.yahoo.com).

B. For which of the preceding companies is the accounting equation relevant?

ETHICS

EX 1-2   Professional ethics   Obj. 1

A fertilizer manufacturing company wants to relocate to Yellowstone County. A report from a fired researcher at the company indicates the company's product is releasing toxic by-products. The company suppressed that report. A later report commissioned by the company shows there is no problem with the fertilizer.

➤ Should the company's chief executive officer reveal the content of the unfavorable report in discussions with Yellowstone County representatives? Discuss.

EX 1-3   Business entity assumption   Obj. 2

Ozark Sports sells hunting and fishing equipment and provides guided hunting and fishing trips. Ozark is owned and operated by Eric Griffith, a well-known sports enthusiast and hunter. Eric's wife, Linda, owns and operates Lake Boutique, a women's clothing store. Eric and Linda have established a trust fund to finance their children's college education. The trust fund is maintained by Missouri State Bank in the name of the children, Mark and Steffy.

A.   For each of the following transactions, identify which of the entities listed should record the transaction in its records:

Entities	
L	Lake Boutique
M	Missouri State Bank
O	Ozark Sports
X	None of the above

1. Linda authorized the trust fund to purchase mutual fund shares.
2. Linda purchased two dozen spring dresses from a St. Louis designer for a special spring sale.
3. Eric paid a breeder's fee for an English springer spaniel to be used as a hunting guide dog.
4. Linda deposited a $2,000 personal check in the trust fund at Missouri State Bank.
5. Eric paid a local doctor for his annual physical, which was required by the workers' compensation insurance policy carried by Ozark Sports.
6. Eric received a cash advance from customers for a guided hunting trip.
7. Linda paid her dues to the YWCA.
8. Linda donated several dresses from inventory for a local charity auction for the benefit of a women's abuse shelter.
9. Eric paid for dinner and a movie to celebrate their twelfth wedding anniversary.
10. Eric paid for an advertisement in a hunters' magazine.

B.   ➤ What is a business transaction?

EX 1-4   Accounting equation   Obj. 3

✔ Starbucks, $5,272

SHOW ME HOW   REAL WORLD

The total assets and total liabilities (in millions) of **Keurig Green Mountain Coffee, Inc.** and **Starbucks Corporation** follow:

	Keurig	Starbucks
Assets	$4.797	$10,753
Liabilities	1,338	5,481

Determine the stockholders' equity of each company.

EX 1-5   Accounting equation   Obj. 3

✔ Dollar Tree, $1,171

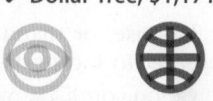

SHOW ME HOW   REAL WORLD

The total assets and total liabilities (in millions) of **Dollar Tree Inc.** and **Target Corporation** follow:

	Dollar Tree	Target
Assets	$2,772	$44,553
Liabilities	1,601	28,322

Determine the stockholders' equity of each company.

EX 1-6 Accounting equation

Obj. 3

✔ A. $1,895,000

SHOW ME HOW

Determine the missing amount for each of the following:

	Assets	=	Liabilities	+	Stockholders' Equity
A.	X	=	$550,000	+	$1,345,000
B.	$776,500	=	X	+	$588,800
C.	$14,750,000	=	$4,455,000	+	X

EX 1-7 Accounting equation

Obj. 3, 4

✔ B. $4,120,000

SHOW ME HOW

Inspirational Inc. is a motivational consulting business. At the end of its accounting period, October 31, 2017, Inspirational has assets of $5,250,000 and liabilities of $1,600,000. Using the accounting equation and considering each case independently, determine the following amounts:

A. Stockholders' equity as of October 31, 2017.

B. Stockholders' equity as of October 31, 2018, assuming that assets increased by $800,000 and liabilities increased by $330,000 during 2018.

C. Stockholders' equity as of October 31, 2018, assuming that assets decreased by $600,000 and liabilities increased by $140,000 during 2018.

D. Stockholders' equity as of October 31, 2018, assuming that assets increased by $440,000 and liabilities decreased by $90,000 during 2018.

E. Net income (or net loss) during 2018, assuming that as of October 31, 2018, assets were $6,140,000, liabilities were $1,950,000, and no additional common stock was issued or dividends paid.

EX 1-8 Asset, liability, and stockholders' equity items

Obj. 3

Indicate whether each of the following is identified with (1) an asset, (2) a liability, or (3) stockholders' equity:

A. accounts payable

B. cash

C. fees earned

D. land

E. supplies

F. wages expense

EX 1-9 Effect of transactions on accounting equation

Obj. 4

What is the effect of each of the following transactions on the three elements (assets, liabilities, and stockholders' equity) of the accounting equation?

A. Invested cash in business.

B. Paid for utilities used in the business.

C. Purchased supplies for cash.

D. Purchased supplies on account.

E. Received cash for services performed.

EX 1-10 Effect of transactions on accounting equation

Obj. 4

✔ A. (1) increase $183,000

SHOW ME HOW

A. A vacant lot acquired for $115,000 is sold for $298,000 in cash. What is the effect of the sale on the total amount of the seller's (1) assets, (2) liabilities, and (3) stockholders' equity?

B. Assume that the seller owes $80,000 on a loan for the land. After receiving the $298,000 cash in (A), the seller pays the $80,000 owed. What is the effect of the payment on the total amount of the seller's (1) assets, (2) liabilities, and (3) stockholders' equity?

C. ▬▬▶ Is it true that a transaction always affects at least two elements (Assets, Liabilities, or Stockholders' Equity) of the accounting equation? Explain.

EX 1-11 Effect of transactions on stockholders' equity

Obj. 4

Indicate whether each of the following types of transactions will either (A) increase stockholders' equity or (B) decrease stockholders' equity:

1. expenses

2. issuing common stock in exchange for cash

3. dividends

4. revenues

EX 1-12   Transactions   Obj. 4

The following selected transactions were completed by Cota Delivery Service during July:

1. Received cash in exchange for common stock, $35,000.
2. Purchased supplies for cash, $1,100.
3. Paid rent for October, $4,500.
4. Paid advertising expense, $900.
5. Received cash for providing delivery services, $33,000.
6. Billed customers for delivery services on account, $58,000.
7. Paid creditors on account, $2,900.
8. Received cash from customers on account, $27,500.
9. Determined that the cost of supplies on hand was $300 and $8,600 of supplies had been used during the month.
10. Paid cash dividends, $2,500.

Indicate the effect of each transaction on the accounting equation by listing the numbers identifying the transactions, (1) through (10), in a column, and inserting at the right of each number the appropriate letter from the following list:

A.   Increase in an asset, decrease in another asset.
B.   Increase in an asset, increase in a liability.
C.   Increase in an asset, increase in stockholders' equity.
D.   Decrease in an asset, decrease in a liability.
E.   Decrease in an asset, decrease in stockholders' equity.

EX 1-13   Nature of transactions   Obj. 4

✔ D. $22,800

SHOW ME HOW

Teri West operates her own catering service. Summary financial data for July are presented in equation form as follows. Each line designated by a number indicates the effect of a transaction on the equation. Each increase and decrease in stockholders' equity, except transaction (5), affects net income.

	Assets			= Liabilities +		Stockholders' Equity			
				Accounts	**Common**	**Retained**		**Fees**	
	Cash +	**Supplies +**	**Land**	**= Payable +**	**Stock**	**Earnings –**	**Dividends +**	**Earned –**	**Expenses**
Bal.	40,000	3,000	82,000	7,500	50,000	67,500			
1.	+71,800							+71,800	
2.	−15,000		+15,000						
3.	−47,500								−47,500
4.		+1,100		+1,100					
5.	−5,000						−5,000		
6.	−4,000			−4,000					
7.		−1,500							−1,500
Bal.	40,300	2,600	97,000	4,600	50,000	67,500	−5,000	71,800	−49,000

A.   ▬▬▶ Describe each transaction.
B.   What is the amount of the net increase in cash during the month?
C.   What is the amount of the net increase in stockholders' equity during the month?
D.   What is the amount of the net income for the month?
E.   How much of the net income for the month was retained in the business?

EX 1-14   Net income and dividends   Obj. 5

The income statement for the month of February indicates a net income of $17,500. During the same period, $25,500 in cash dividends were paid.

▬▬▶ Would it be correct to say that the business incurred a net loss of $8,000 during the month? Discuss.

EX 1-15 Net income and stockholders' equity for four businesses Obj. 5

SHOW ME HOW

Four different corporations, Amber, Blue, Coral, and Daffodil, show the same balance sheet data at the beginning and end of a year. These data, exclusive of the amount of stockholders' equity, are summarized as follows:

	Total Assets	Total Liabilities
Beginning of the year	$1,220,000	$ 990,000
End of the year	1,730,000	1,150,000

On the basis of the preceding data and the following additional information for the year, determine the net income (or loss) of each company for the year. (*Hint*: First determine the amount of increase or decrease in stockholders' equity during the year.)

Amber: No additional common stock was issued and no dividends were paid.

Blue: No additional common stock was issued, but dividends of $60,000 were paid.

Coral: Additional common stock of $140,000 was issued, but no dividends were paid.

Daffodil: Additional common stock of $140,000 was issued and dividends of $60,000 were paid.

EX 1-16 Balance sheet items Obj. 5

From the following list of selected items taken from the records of Bobcat Appliance Service as of a specific date, identify those that would appear on the balance sheet:

1. Accounts Receivable
2. Cash
3. Common Stock
4. Fees Earned
5. Land
6. Supplies
7. Supplies Expense
8. Utilities Expense
9. Wages Expense
10. Wages Payable

EX 1-17 Income statement items Obj. 5

Based on the data presented in Exercise 1-16, identify those items that would appear on the income statement.

SHOW ME HOW   EXCEL TEMPLATE

EX 1-18 Retained earnings statement Obj. 5

Financial information related to Healthy Products Company for the month ended November 30, 2018, is as follows:

Net income for November	$ 93,500
Cash dividends paid during November	7,000
Retained earnings, November 1, 2018	2,940,000

A. Prepare a retained earnings statement for the month ended November 30, 2018.

B. ➤ Why is the retained earnings statement prepared before the November 30, 2018, balance sheet?

SHOW ME HOW   EXCEL TEMPLATE

EX 1-19 Income statement Obj. 5

Imaging Services was organized on March 1, 2018. A summary of the revenue and expense transactions for March follows:

Fees earned	$482,000
Wages expense	300,000
Rent expense	41,500
Supplies expense	3,600
Miscellaneous expense	1,900

Prepare an income statement for the month ended March 31.

EX 1-20 Missing amounts from balance sheet and income statement data   Obj. 5

SHOW ME HOW

One item is omitted in each of the following summaries of balance sheet and income statement data for the following four different corporations:

	Freeman	Heyward	Jones	Ramirez
Beginning of the year:				
Assets	$ 900,000	$490,000	$115,000	D
Liabilities	360,000	260,000	81,000	$120,000
End of the year:				
Assets	1,260,000	675,000	100,000	270,000
Liabilities	330,000	220,000	80,000	136,000
During the year:				
Additional common stock issued	A	150,000	10,000	55,000
Dividends	75,000	32,000	C	39,000
Revenue	570,000	B	115,000	115,000
Expenses	240,000	128,000	122,500	128,000

Determine the missing amounts, identifying them by letter. (*Hint:* First determine the amount of increase or decrease in stockholders' equity during the year.)

EX 1-21 Balance sheets, net income   Obj. 5

SHOW ME HOW   EXCEL TEMPLATE

Financial information related to Ebony Interiors for February and March 2018 is as follows:

	February 28, 2018	March 31, 2018
Cash	320,000	380,000
Accounts receivable	800,000	960,000
Supplies	30,000	35,000
Accounts payable	310,000	400,000
Common stock	200,000	200,000
Retained earnings	?	?

A. Prepare balance sheets for Ebony Interiors as of February 28 and March 31, 2018.

B. Determine the amount of net income for March, assuming that no additional common stock was issued and no dividends were paid during the month.

C. Determine the amount of net income for March, assuming that no additional common stock was issued, but dividends of $50,000 were paid during the month.

EX 1-22 Financial statements   Obj. 5

REAL WORLD

Each of the following items is shown in the financial statements of **Exxon Mobil Corporation**:

1. Accounts payable
2. Cash equivalents
3. Crude oil inventory
4. Equipment
5. Exploration expenses
6. Income taxes payable
7. Investments
8. Long-term debt
9. Marketable securities
10. Notes and loans payable
11. Notes receivable
12. Operating expenses
13. Prepaid taxes
14. Sales
15. Selling expenses

A. Identify the financial statement (balance sheet or income statement) in which each item would appear.

B. Can an item appear on more than one financial statement?

C. Is the accounting equation relevant for Exxon Mobil Corporation? Explain.

EX 1-23 Statement of cash flows   Obj. 5

Indicate whether each of the following activities would be reported on the statement of cash flows as (A) an operating activity, (B) an investing activity, or (C) a financing activity:

1. Cash received from fees earned.
2. Cash paid for expenses.
3. Cash paid for land.
4. Cash paid for dividends.

SHOW ME HOW

EX 1-24 Statement of cash flows

Obj. 5

A summary of cash flows for Ethos Consulting Group for the year ended May 31, 2018, follows:

Cash receipts:	
Cash received from customers	$637,500
Cash received from issuing common stock	62,500
Cash payments:	
Cash paid for operating expenses	475,000
Cash paid for land	90,000
Cash paid for dividends	17,500

The cash balance as of June 1, 2017, was $58,000.

Prepare a statement of cash flows for Ethos Consulting Group for the year ended May 31, 2018.

EX 1-25 Financial statements

Obj. 5

✔ Correct amount
of total assets is
$51,500.

We-Sell Realty, organized as a corporation on August 1, 2018, is owned and operated by Omar Farah, the sole stockholder. How many errors can you find in the following statements for We-Sell Realty, prepared after its first month of operations?

We-Sell Realty
Income Statement
August 31, 2018

Sales commissions		$140,000
Expenses:		
Office salaries expense	$87,000	
Rent expense	18,000	
Automobile expense	7,500	
Miscellaneous expense	2,200	
Supplies expense	1,150	
Total expenses		115,850
Net income		$ 25,000

Omar Farah
Retained Earnings Statement
August 31, 2017

Retained earnings, August 1, 2018	$ 0
Dividends	(10,000)
	$(10,000)
Issued additional common stock August 1, 2018	15,000
	$ 5,000
Net income	25,000
Retained earnings, August 31, 2018	$ 30,000

Balance Sheet
For the Month Ended August 31, 2018

Assets

Cash	$ 8,900
Accounts payable	22,350
Total assets	$31,250

Liabilities

Accounts receivable	$38,600
Supplies	4,000

Stockholders' Equity

Retained earnings	30,000
Total liabilities and stockholders' equity	$72,600

Problems: Series A

PR 1-1A Transactions

Obj. 4

✔ Cash bal. at end of
September: $27,975

SHOW ME HOW

On September 1 of the current year, Joy Tucker established a business to manage rental property. She completed the following transactions during September:

A. Opened a business bank account with a deposit of $36,000 in exchange for common stock.
B. Purchased office supplies on account, $1,800.
C. Received cash from fees earned for managing rental property, $6,750.
D. Paid rent on office and equipment for the month, $5,000.
E. Paid creditors on account, $1,375.
F. Billed customers for fees earned for managing rental property, $9,500.
G. Paid automobile expenses for month, $840, and miscellaneous expenses, $960.
H. Paid office salaries, $3,600.
I. Determined that the cost of supplies on hand was $350; therefore, the cost of supplies used was $1,450.
J. Paid dividends, $3,000.

Instructions

1. Indicate the effect of each transaction and the balances after each transaction, using the following tabular headings:

Assets			= Liabilities +		Stockholders' Equity						
Cash +	Accounts Receivable +	Supplies =	Accounts Payable +	Common Stock −	Dividends +	Fees Earned −	Rent Expense −	Salaries Expense −	Supplies Expense −	Auto Expense −	Misc. Expense

2. ➡ Briefly explain why issuing common stock and revenues increased stockholders' equity, while dividends and expenses decreased stockholders' equity.
3. Determine the net income for September.
4. How much did September's transactions increase or decrease retained earnings?

PR 1-2A Financial statements

Obj. 5

✔ 1. Net income:
$148,500

SHOW ME HOW   EXCEL TEMPLATE

The amounts of the assets and liabilities of Journey Travel Agency at December 31, 2018, the end of the year, and its revenue and expenses for the year follow. The retained earnings were $1,341,000 on January 1, 2018, the beginning of the year. During the year, dividends of $75,000 were paid.

Accounts payable	$ 69,500	Miscellaneous expense	$ 14,500
Accounts receivable	236,500	Rent expense	22,500
Cash	190,500	Supplies	7,000
Common stock	450,000	Supplies expense	11,300
Fees earned	383,500	Utilities expense	16,700
Land	1,500,000	Wages expense	170,000

Instructions

1. Prepare an income statement for the year ended December 31, 2018.
2. Prepare a retained earnings statement for the year ended December 31, 2018.
3. Prepare a balance sheet as of December 31, 2018.
4. What item appears on both the retained earnings statement and the balance sheet?

PR 1-3A Financial statements

Obj. 5

✔ 1. Net income:
$31,200

EXCEL TEMPLATE

Seth Feye established Reliance Financial Services on July 1, 2018. Reliance Financial Services offers financial planning advice to its clients. The effect of each transaction and the balances after each transaction for July follow:

	Assets			= Liabilities +				Stockholders' Equity					
	Cash	+ Accounts Receivable	+ Supplies =	Accounts Payable +	Common Stock	− Dividends +	Fees Earned	− Salaries Expense	− Rent Expense	− Auto Expense	− Supplies Expense	− Misc. Expense
A.	+50,000				+50,000							
B.			+7,000	+7,000								
Bal.	50,000		7,000	7,000	50,000							
C.	−3,600			−3,600								
Bal.	46,400		7,000	3,400	50,000							
D.	+110,000						+110,000					
Bal.	156,400		7,000	3,400	50,000		110,000					
E.	−33,000								−33,000			
Bal.	123,400		7,000	3,400	50,000		110,000		−33,000			
F.	−20,800									−16,000		−4,800
Bal.	102,600		7,000	3,400	50,000		110,000		−33,000	−16,000		−4,800
G.	−55,000							−55,000				
Bal.	47,600		7,000	3,400	50,000		110,000	−55,000	−33,000	−16,000		−4,800
H.			−4,500								−4,500	
Bal.	47,600		2,500	3,400	50,000		110,000	−55,000	−33,000	−16,000	−4,500	−4,800
I.		+34,500					+ 34,500					
Bal.	47,600	34,500	2,500	3,400	50,000		144,500	−55,000	−33,000	−16,000	−4,500	−4,800
J.	−15,000					−15,000						
Bal.	32,600	34,500	2,500	3,400	50,000	−15,000	144,500	−55,000	−33,000	−16,000	−4,500	−4,800

Instructions

1. Prepare an income statement for the month ended July 31, 2018.
2. Prepare a retained earnings statement for the month ended July 31, 2018.
3. Prepare a balance sheet as of July 31, 2018.
4. (*Optional*) Prepare a statement of cash flows for the month ending July 31, 2018.

PR 1-4A Transactions; financial statements

Obj. 4, 5

✔ 2. Net income: $39,750

On August 1, 2018, Brooke Kline established Western Realty. Brooke completed the following transactions during the month of August:

A. Opened a business bank account with a deposit of $35,000 in exchange for common stock.
B. Purchased supplies on account, $2,750.
C. Paid creditor on account, $1,800.
D. Earned sales commissions, receiving cash, $52,800.
E. Paid rent on office and equipment for the month, $4,500.
F. Paid dividends, $3,000.
G. Paid automobile expenses for month, $1,100, and miscellaneous expenses, $1,200.
H. Paid office salaries, $5,250.
I. Determined that the cost of supplies on hand was $1,750; therefore, the cost of supplies used was $1,000.

Instructions

1. Indicate the effect of each transaction and the balances after each transaction, using the following tabular headings:

Assets		= Liabilities +			Stockholders' Equity					
Cash + Supplies =		Accounts Payable +	Common Stock	− Dividends +	Sales Commissions	− Salaries Expense	− Rent Expense	− Auto Expense	− Supplies Expense	− Misc. Expense

2. Prepare an income statement for August, a retained earnings statement for August, and a balance sheet as of August 31.

PR 1-5A   Transactions; financial statements

Obj. 4, 5

✔ 3. Net income:
$63,775

EXCEL TEMPLATE

D'Lite Dry Cleaners is owned and operated by Joel Palk. A building and equipment are currently being rented, pending expansion to new facilities. The actual work of dry cleaning is done by another company at wholesale rates. The assets, liabilities, and common stock of the business on July 1, 2018, are as follows: Cash, $45,000; Accounts Receivable, $93,000; Supplies, $7,000; Land, $75,000; Accounts Payable, $40,000; Common Stock, $60,000. Business transactions during July are summarized as follows:

A.   Joel Palk invested additional cash in exchange for common stock with a deposit of $35,000 in the business bank account.

B.   Paid $50,000 for the purchase of land adjacent to land currently owned by D'Lite Dry Cleaners as a future building site.

C.   Received cash from customers for dry cleaning revenue, $32,125.

D.   Paid rent for the month, $6,000.

E.   Purchased supplies on account, $2,500.

F.   Paid creditors on account, $22,800.

G.   Charged customers for dry cleaning revenue on account, $84,750.

H.   Received monthly invoice for dry cleaning expense for July (to be paid on August 10), $29,500.

I.   Paid the following: wages expense, $7,500; truck expense, $2,500; utilities expense, $1,300; miscellaneous expense, $2,700.

J.   Received cash from customers on account, $88,000.

K.   Determined that the cost of supplies on hand was $5,900; therefore, the cost of supplies used during the month was $3,600.

L.   Paid dividends, $12,000.

Instructions

1.   Determine the amount of retained earnings as of July 1, 2018.

2.   State the assets, liabilities, and stockholders' equity as of July 1 in equation form similar to that shown in this chapter. In tabular form below the equation, indicate increases and decreases resulting from each transaction and the new balances after each transaction.

3.   Prepare an income statement for July, a retained earnings statement for July, and a balance sheet as of July 31.

4.   (*Optional*) Prepare a statement of cash flows for July.

PR 1-6A   Missing amounts from financial statements

Obj. 5

✔ K. $750,000

The financial statements at the end of Wolverine Realty's first month of operations are as follows:

Wolverine Realty
Income Statement
For the Month Ended April 30, 2018

Fees earned..		$ A
Expenses:		
Wages expense	$300,000	
Rent expense	100,000	
Supplies expense	B	
Utilities expense	20,000	
Miscellaneous expense	25,000	
Total expenses..		475,000
Net income		$275,000

Wolverine Realty
Retained Earnings Statement
For the Month Ended April 30, 2018

Retained earnings, April 1, 2018		$ C
Net income	$ D	
Dividends	(125,000)	
Change in retained earnings		E
Retained earnings, April 30, 2018..................................		$ F

Wolverine Realty
Balance Sheet
April 30, 2018

Assets

Cash	$462,500
Supplies	12,500
Land	150,000
Total assets	$ G

Liabilities

Accounts payable	$ 100,000

Stockholders' Equity

Common stock..	$375,000	
Retained earnings...	H	
Total stockholders' equity		I
Total liabilities and stockholders' equity...................		$ J

Wolverine Realty
Statement of Cash Flows
For the Month Ended April 30, 2018

Cash flows from operating activities:		
Cash received from customers.....................................	$ K	
Cash payments for expenses and payments to creditors............	(387,500)	
Net cash flows from operating activities		$ L
Cash flows used for investing activities:		
Cash payments for acquisition of land		M
Cash flows from financing activities:		
Cash received from issuing common stock	$ N	
Cash dividends..	(O)	
Net cash flows from financing activities.......................		P
Net increase (decrease) in cash and April 30, 2018, cash balance		$ Q

Instructions

By analyzing the interrelationships among the four financial statements, determine the proper amounts for A through Q.

Problems: Series B

PR 1-1B Transactions

Obj. 4

✔ Cash bal. at end of March: $48,650

SHOW ME HOW

Amy Austin established an insurance agency on March 1 of the current year and completed the following transactions during March:

A. Opened a business bank account with a deposit of $50,000 in exchange for common stock.
B. Purchased supplies on account, $4,000.
C. Paid creditors on account, $2,300.
D. Received cash from fees earned on insurance commissions, $13,800.
E. Paid rent on office and equipment for the month, $5,000.
F. Paid automobile expenses for month, $1,150, and miscellaneous expenses, $300.
G. Paid office salaries, $2,500.
H. Determined that the cost of supplies on hand was $2,700; therefore, the cost of supplies used was $1,300.
I. Billed insurance companies for sales commissions earned, $12,500.
J. Paid dividends, $3,900.

Instructions

1. Indicate the effect of each transaction and the balances after each transaction, using the following tabular headings:

Assets			= Liabilities +		Stockholders' Equity						
Cash +	Accounts Receivable +	Supplies =	Accounts Payable +	Common Stock	− Dividends	+ Fees Earned	− Rent Expense	− Salaries Expense	− Supplies Expense	− Auto Expense	− Misc. Expense

2. ▬▬▶ Briefly explain why issuing common stock and revenues increased stockholders' equity, while dividends and expenses decreased stockholders' equity.
3. Determine the net income for March.
4. How much did March's transactions increase or decrease retained earnings?

PR 1-2B Financial statements

Obj. 5

✔ 1. Net income: $200,000

SHOW ME HOW   EXCEL TEMPLATE

The amounts of the assets and liabilities of Wilderness Travel Service at April 30, 2018, the end of the year, and its revenue and expenses for the year follow. The retained earnings were $145,000 at May 1, 2017, the beginning of the year, and dividends of $40,000 were paid during the year.

Accounts payable	$ 25,000	Rent expense	$ 75,000
Accounts receivable	210,000	Supplies	9,000
Cash	146,000	Supplies expense	12,000
Common stock	35,000	Taxes expense	10,000
Fees earned	875,000	Utilities expense	38,000
Miscellaneous expense	15,000	Wages expense	525,000

Instructions
1. Prepare an income statement for the year ended April 30, 2018.
2. Prepare a retained earnings statement for the year ended April 30, 2018.
3. Prepare a balance sheet as of April 30, 2018.
4. What item appears on both the income statement and retained earnings statement?

PR 1-3B Financial statements

Obj. 5

✔ 1. Net income: $10,900

Jose Loder established Bronco Consulting on August 1, 2018. The effect of each transaction and the balances after each transaction for August follow:

		Assets			=Liabilities+		Stockholders' Equity						
	Cash	+ Accounts Receivable	+ Supplies	=	Accounts Payable +	Common Stock	– Dividends +	Fees Earned	– Salaries Expense	– Rent Expense	– Auto Expense	– Supplies Expense	– Misc. Expense
A.	+75,000					+75,000							
B.			+9,000		+9,000								
Bal.	75,000		9,000		9,000	75,000							
C.	+92,000							+92,000					
Bal.	167,000		9,000		9,000	75,000		92,000					
D.	–27,000									–27,000			
Bal.	140,000		9,000		9,000	75,000		92,000		–27,000			
E.	–6,000				–6,000								
Bal.	134,000		9,000		3,000	75,000		92,000		–27,000			
F.		+33,000						+33,000					
Bal.	134,000	33,000	9,000		3,000	75,000		125,000		–27,000			
G.	–23,000										–15,500		–7,500
Bal.	111,000	33,000	9,000		3,000	75,000		125,000		–27,000	–15,500		–7,500
H.	–58,000								–58,000				
Bal.	53,000	33,000	9,000		3,000	75,000		125,000	–58,000	–27,000	–15,500		–7,500
I.			–6,100									–6,100	
Bal.	53,000	33,000	2,900		3,000	75,000		125,000	–58,000	–27,000	–15,500	–6,100	–7,500
J.	–5,000						–5,000						
Bal.	48,000	33,000	2,900		3,000	75,000	–5,000	125,000	–58,000	–27,000	–15,500	–6,100	–7,500

EXCEL TEMPLATE

Instructions
1. Prepare an income statement for the month ended August 31, 2018.
2. Prepare a retained earnings statement for the month ended August 31, 2018.
3. Prepare a balance sheet as of August 31, 2018.
4. (*Optional*) Prepare a statement of cash flows for the month ending August 31, 2018.

PR 1-4B Transactions; financial statements

Obj. 4, 5

✔ 2. Net income: $10,850

On April 1, 2018, Maria Adams established Custom Realty. Maria completed the following transactions during the month of April:

A. Opened a business bank account with a deposit of $24,000 in exchange for common stock.
B. Paid rent on office and equipment for the month, $3,600.
C. Paid automobile expenses for month, $1,350, and miscellaneous expenses, $600.
D. Purchased supplies on account, $1,200.
E. Earned sales commissions, receiving cash, $19,800.
F. Paid creditor on account, $750.
G. Paid office salaries, $2,500.
H. Paid dividends, $3,500.
I. Determined that the cost of supplies on hand was $300; therefore, the cost of supplies used was $900.

Instructions

1. Indicate the effect of each transaction and the balances after each transaction, using the following tabular headings:

Assets		= Liabilities +			Stockholders' Equity					
Cash + Supplies	=	Accounts Payable +	Common Stock	– Dividends +	Sales Commissions	Rent – Expense	Salaries – Expense	Auto – Expense	Supplies – Expense	Misc. – Expense

2. Prepare an income statement for April, a retained earnings statement for April, and a balance sheet as of April 30.

PR 1-5B Transactions; financial statements

Obj. 4, 5

✔ 3. Net income: $40,150

EXCEL TEMPLATE

Bev's Dry Cleaners is owned and operated by Beverly Zahn. A building and equipment are currently being rented, pending expansion to new facilities. The actual work of dry cleaning is done by another company at wholesale rates. The assets, liabilities, and common stock of the business on November 1, 2018, are as follows: Cash, $39,000; Accounts Receivable, $80,000; Supplies, $11,000; Land, $50,000; Accounts Payable, $31,500; Common Stock, $50,000. Business transactions during November are summarized as follows:

A. Beverly Zahn invested additional cash in exchange for common stock with a deposit of $21,000 in the business bank account.
B. Purchased land adjacent to land currently owned by Bev's Dry Cleaners to use in the future as a parking lot, paying cash of $35,000.
C. Paid rent for the month, $4,000.
D. Charged customers for dry cleaning revenue on account, $72,000.
E. Paid creditors on account, $20,000.
F. Purchased supplies on account, $8,000.
G. Received cash from customers for dry cleaning revenue, $38,000.
H. Received cash from customers on account, $77,000.
I. Received monthly invoice for dry cleaning expense for November (to be paid on December 10), $29,450.
J. Paid the following: wages expense, $24,000; truck expense, $2,100; utilities expense, $1,800; miscellaneous expense, $1,300.
K. Determined that the cost of supplies on hand was $11,800; therefore, the cost of supplies used during the month was $7,200.
L. Paid dividends, $5,000.

Instructions

1. Determine the amount of retained earnings as of November 1.
2. State the assets, liabilities, and stockholders' equity as of November 1 in equation form similar to that shown in this chapter. In tabular form below the equation, indicate increases and decreases resulting from each transaction and the new balances after each transaction.
3. Prepare an income statement for November, a retained earnings statement for November, and a balance sheet as of November 30.
4. (*Optional*) Prepare a statement of cash flows for November.

PR 1-6B   Missing amounts from financial statements   Obj. 5

✔ I. $208,000   The financial statements at the end of Atlas Realty's first month of operations follow:

Atlas Realty
Income Statement
For the Month Ended May 31, 2018

Fees earned..		$400,000
Expenses:		
Wages expense	$ A	
Rent expense	48,000	
Supplies expense	17,600	
Utilities expense	14,400	
Miscellaneous expense	4,800	
Total expenses...		288,000
Net income		$ B

Atlas Realty
Retained Earnings Statement
For the Month Ended May 31, 2018

Retained earnings, May 1, 2018.....................................		$ C
Net income	$ D	
Dividends	(E)	
Change in retained earnings		F
Retained earnings, May 31, 2018		$ G

Atlas Realty
Balance Sheet
May 31, 2018

Assets

Cash	$123,200
Supplies..	12,800
Land	H
Total assets	$ I

Liabilities

Accounts payable	$ 48,000

Stockholders' Equity

Common stock...	$ J	
Retained earnings..	K	
Total stockholders' equity...............................		L
Total liabilities and stockholders' equity...............		$ M

Atlas Realty
Statement of Cash Flows
For the Month Ended May 31, 2018

Cash flows from operating activities:		
Cash received from customers.....................................	$ N	
Cash payments for expenses and payments to creditors............	(252,800)	
Net cash flows from operating activities		$ O
Cash flows from investing activities:		
Cash payments for acquisition of land		(120,000)
Cash flows from financing activities:		
Cash received from issuing common stock	$160,000	
Cash dividends	(64,000)	
Net cash flows from financing activities...........................		P
Net increase (decrease) in cash and May 31, 2018, cash balance.........		$ Q

Instructions

By analyzing the interrelationships among the four financial statements, determine the proper amounts for A through Q.

Continuing Problem

✔ 2. Net income: $1,340

Peyton Smith enjoys listening to all types of music and owns countless CDs. Over the years, Peyton has gained a local reputation for knowledge of music from classical to rap and the ability to put together sets of recordings that appeal to all ages.

During the last several months, Peyton served as a guest disc jockey on a local radio station. In addition, Peyton has entertained at several friends' parties as the host deejay.

On June 1, 2018, Peyton established a corporation known as PS Music. Using an extensive collection of music MP3 files, Peyton will serve as a disc jockey on a fee basis for weddings, college parties, and other events. During June, Peyton entered into the following transactions:

June 1. Deposited $4,000 in a checking account in the name of PS Music in exchange for common stock.
2. Received $3,500 from a local radio station for serving as the guest disc jockey for June.
2. Agreed to share office space with a local real estate agency, Pinnacle Realty. PS Music will pay one-fourth of the rent. In addition, PS Music agreed to pay a portion of the wages of the receptionist and to pay one-fourth of the utilities. Paid $800 for the rent of the office.
4. Purchased supplies from City Office Supply Co. for $350. Agreed to pay $100 within 10 days and the remainder by July 5, 2018.
6. Paid $500 to a local radio station to advertise the services of PS Music twice daily for two weeks.
8. Paid $675 to a local electronics store for renting digital recording equipment.
12. Paid $350 (music expense) to Cool Music for the use of its current music demos to make various music sets.
13. Paid City Office Supply Co. $100 on account.
16. Received $300 from a dentist for providing two music sets for the dentist to play for her patients.
22. Served as disc jockey for a wedding party. The father of the bride agreed to pay $1,000 in July.
25. Received $500 for serving as the disc jockey for a cancer charity ball hosted by the local hospital.
29. Paid $240 (music expense) to Galaxy Music for the use of its library of music demos.
30. Received $900 for serving as PS disc jockey for a local club's monthly dance.
30. Paid Pinnacle Realty $400 for PS Music's share of the receptionist's wages for June.
30. Paid Pinnacle Realty $300 for PS Music's share of the utilities for June.
30. Determined that the cost of supplies on hand is $170. Therefore, the cost of supplies used during the month was $180.
30. Paid for miscellaneous expenses, $415.
30. Paid $1,000 royalties (music expense) to National Music Clearing for use of various artists' music during the month.
30. Paid dividends, $500.

Instructions

1. Indicate the effect of each transaction and the balances after each transaction, using the following tabular headings:

Assets	=	Liabilities +						Stockholders' Equity							
										Office	Equipment					
		Accts.	Accounts	Common			Fees	Music	Rent	Rent	Advertising	Wages	Utilities	Supplies	Misc.
Cash +	Rec. +	Supplies =	Payable +	Stock	– Dividends +	Earned –	Exp. –	Exp. –	Exp. –	Exp. –	Exp. –	Exp. –	Exp. –	Exp.

2. Prepare an income statement for PS Music for the month ended June 30, 2018.
3. Prepare a retained earnings statement for PS Music for the month ended June 30, 2018.
4. Prepare a balance sheet for PS Music as of June 30, 2018.

Analysis for Decision Making

REAL WORLD

ADM-1   Continuing Company Analysis—Amazon and Best Buy: Ratio of liabilities to stockholders' equity

Amazon.com, Inc. is one of the largest Internet retailers in the world. We will use Amazon as a continuing company exercise to reinforce the various tools and techniques for analyzing financial statements. We will begin with the ratio of liabilities to stockholders' equity.

Ratios can be used to compare companies in the same industry. For Amazon, there are a number of competitors that sell media, electronic, and other merchandise. Best Buy, Inc. is one such company. The following total liabilities and stockholders' equity information (in millions) is provided for Amazon and Best Buy for the end of a recent year:

	Amazon	Best Buy
Total liabilities	$43,764	$10,024
Total stockholders' equity	10,741	3,989

A.   Compute the ratio of liabilities to stockholders' equity for each company. (Round to two decimal places.)

B.   ━━━━▶ What conclusions regarding the margin of protection to creditors can you draw for these two companies?

SHOW ME HOW

REAL WORLD

ADM-2   Home Depot: Ratio of liabilities to stockholders' equity

The Home Depot, Inc., is the world's largest home improvement retailer and one of the largest retailers in the United States based on sales volume. Home Depot operates over 2,200 stores that sell a wide assortment of building, home improvement, and lawn and garden items.

Home Depot recently reported the following end-of-year balance sheet data (in millions):

	Year 3	Year 2	Year 1
Total assets	$40,518	$41,804	$40,518
Total stockholders' equity	12,522	17,777	17,898

A.   Determine the total liabilities at the end of Years 1, 2, and 3.

B.   Compute the ratio of liabilities to stockholders' equity for all three years. (Round to two decimal places.)

C.   ━━━━▶ What conclusions regarding the margin of protection to creditors can you draw from the trend in this ratio for the three years?

REAL WORLD

ADM-3   Lowe's: Ratio of liabilities to stockholders' equity

Lowe's Companies, Inc., a major competitor to The Home Depot in the home improvement retail business, operates over 1,800 stores. Lowe's recently reported the following end-of-year balance sheet data (in millions):

	Year 3	Year 2	Year 1
Total assets	$32,732	$32,666	$33,559
Total liabilities	20,879	18,809	17,026

A.   Determine the total stockholders' equity at the end of Years 1, 2, and 3.

B.   Compute the ratio of liabilities to stockholders' equity for all three years. (Round to two decimal places.)

C.   ━━━━▶ What conclusions regarding the margin of protection to creditors can you draw from the trend in this ratio for the three years?

D.   ━━━━▶ Using the balance sheet data for Home Depot in ADM-2, how does Lowe's ratio of liabilities to stockholders' equity compare to that of Home Depot?

REAL WORLD

ADM-4   Papa Johns and Yum! Brands: Ratio of liabilities to stockholders' equity

The following total liabilities and stockholders' equity information (in millions) is provided for Papa John's International, Inc. and Yum! Brands, Inc. at the end of a recent year:

	Papa John's	Yum! Brands
Total liabilities	$405	$6,732
Total stockholders' equity	99	1,604

Yum! Brands is a much larger company than is Papa John's, however both companies compete internationally in the fast food business. Papa John's is primarily in the carry-out and delivery pizza business, while Yum! Brands is in the quick-service restaurant business with its Pizza Hut, Taco Bell, and KFC brands.

A. Compute the ratio of liabilities to stockholders' equity for each company. (Round to one decimal place.)

B. ━━━► What conclusions regarding the margin of protection to creditors can you draw for these two companies?

C. Which company is more risky to creditors?

Take It Further

ETHICS

TIF 1-1   Ethics in Action

Marco Brolo is one of three partners who own and operate Silkroad Partners, a global import–export business. Marco is the partner in charge of recording partnership transactions in the accounts. On his way to work one day, Marco's car broke down. At the repair shop, Marco learned that his car's engine had significant damage, and it will cost over $2,000 to repair the damage. He does not have enough money in his bank account to cover the cost of the repair, and his credit cards are at their limit. This car is the only form of transportation that Marco has to get to and from work every day. He does not use his car for any business travel.

After considering his options, Marco decides to take $2,000 from the partnership for the repair, and record it as an expense of the partnership. He believes that this is appropriate since he needs his car to get to work every day.

1. ━━━► Is Marco behaving ethically? Why?
2. ━━━► Who is affected by Marco's decision?
3. ━━━► What other alternatives might Marco consider?

REAL WORLD

TIF 1-2   Team Activity

In teams, select a public company that interests you. Obtain the company's most recent annual report on Form 10-K. The Form 10-K is a company's annually required filing with the Securities and Exchange Commission (SEC). It includes the company's financial statements and accompanying notes. The Form 10-K can be obtained either (A) from the investor relations section of the company's Web site or (B) by using the company search feature of the SEC's EDGAR database service found at www.sec.gov/edgar/searchedgar/companysearch.html.

Based on the information in the company's most recent annual report, answer the following questions:

1. What is the official name of the company?
2. Where are the company's principal offices located?
3. Who is the company's chief executive officer?
4. Is the company primarily a service, merchandising, or manufacturing business?
5. How does the company describe its business?
6. Which financial statements are included in the annual report?

TIF 1-3   Communication

There are two common causes of business and accounting fraud:

■ a failure of individual character, and
■ a culture of greed or ethical indifference within an organization.

━━━► Write a brief memo describing how these two factors could lead to accounting fraud.

2 Analyzing Transactions

Chapter 1

Transactions

Accounting System

Accounting Equation

Assets = Liabilities + Equity

Chapter 2

Account	
Debits	Credits

Rules of Debit and Credit

Balance Sheet Accounts

ASSETS Asset Accounts		=	LIABILITIES Liability Accounts		+	STOCKHOLDERS' EQUITY			

ASSETS
Asset Accounts

Debit for increases (+)	Credit for decreases (−)
Balance	

LIABILITIES
Liability Accounts

Debit for decreases (−)	Credit for increases (+)
	Balance

STOCKHOLDERS' EQUITY

Common Stock

Debit for decreases (−)	Credit for increases (+)
	Balance

Retained Earnings

Debit for decreases (−)	Credit for increases (+)
	Balance

Dividends

Debit for increases (+)	Credit for decreases (−)
Balance	

Income Statement Accounts

Revenue Accounts

Debit for decreases (−)	Credit for increases (+)
	Balance

− Expense Accounts

Debit for increases (+)	Credit for decreases (−)
Balance	

Unadjusted Trial Balance
Total Debit Balances = Total Credit Balances

Apple Inc.™

Every day it seems like we get an incredible amount of incoming e-mail messages—from friends, relatives, subscribed e-mail lists, and even spammers! But how do you organize all of these messages? You might create folders to sort messages by sender, topic, or project. Perhaps you use keyword search utilities. You might even use filters or rules to automatically delete spam or send messages from your best friend to a special folder. In any case, you are organizing information so that it is simple to retrieve and allows you to understand, respond, or refer to the messages.

In the same way that you organize your e-mail, companies develop an organized method for processing, recording, and summarizing financial transactions. For example, **Apple Inc.** has a huge volume of financial transactions, resulting from sales of its innovative computers, digital media (iTunes),

iPods, iPhones, and iPads. When Apple sells an iPad, a customer has the option of paying with a credit card, a debit or check card, an Apple gift card, a financing arrangement, or cash. In order to analyze only the information related to Apple's cash transactions, the company must record or summarize all these similar sales using a single category or "cash" account. Similarly, Apple will record credit card payments for iPads and sales from financing arrangements in different accounts (records).

While Chapter 1 used the accounting equation (Assets = Liabilities + Equity) to analyze and record financial transactions, this chapter presents more practical and efficient recording methods. In addition, this chapter discusses possible accounting errors that may occur, along with methods to detect and correct them.

What's Covered

Analyzing Transactions

Elements of Accounting Systems	Analyzing and Recording Transactions	Preparing a Trial Balance
■ Accounts (Obj. 1)	■ Double-Entry Accounting System (Obj. 2)	■ Steps in Preparation (Obj. 4)
■ Journal (Obj. 2)	■ Journalizing (Obj. 2, 3)	■ Interpretation (Obj. 4)
■ Ledger (Obj. 2)	■ Posting (Obj. 3)	■ Types of Errors (Obj. 4)

Learning Objectives

Obj. 1 Describe the characteristics of an account and a chart of accounts.

Obj. 2 Describe and illustrate journalizing transactions using the double-entry accounting system.

Obj. 3 Describe and illustrate the journalizing and posting of transactions to accounts.

Obj. 4 Prepare an unadjusted trial balance and explain how it can be used to discover errors.

Analysis for Decision Making

Describe and illustrate the use of horizontal analysis in evaluating a company's performance and financial condition.

Objective 1
Describe the characteristics of an account and a chart of accounts.

Using Accounts to Record Transactions

In Chapter 1, the November transactions for **NetSolutions** were recorded using the accounting equation format shown in Exhibit 1. However, this format is not efficient or practical for companies that have to record thousands or millions of transactions daily. As a result, accounting systems are designed to show the increases and decreases in each accounting equation element as a separate record. This record is called an **account**.

To illustrate, the Cash column of Exhibit 1 records the increases and decreases in cash. Likewise, the other columns in Exhibit 1 record the increases and decreases in the other accounting equation elements. Each of these columns can be organized into a separate account.

Exhibit 1 NetSolutions' November Transactions

	Assets			=	Liabilities +			Stockholders' Equity						
					Accounts	**Common**		**Fees**	**Wages**	**Rent**	**Supplies**	**Utilities**	**Misc.**
	Cash	**+ Supp. +**	**Land**	**=**	**Payable**	**+ Stock**	**– Dividends +**	**Earned –**	**Exp. –**	**Exp. –**	**Exp. –**	**Exp. –**	**Exp.**
A.	+25,000					+25,000							
B.	–20,000		+20,000										
Bal.	5,000		20,000			25,000							
C.		+1,350			+1,350								
Bal.	5,000	1,350	20,000		1,350	25,000							
D.	+7,500							+7,500					
Bal.	12,500	1,350	20,000		1,350	25,000		7,500					
E.	–3,650								–2,125	–800		–450	–275
Bal.	8,850	1,350	20,000		1,350	25,000		7,500	–2,125	–800		–450	–275
F.	–950				–950								
Bal.	7,900	1,350	20,000		400	25,000		7,500	–2,125	–800		–450	–275
G.		–800									–800		
Bal.	7,900	550	20,000		400	25,000		7,500	–2,125	–800	–800	–450	–275
H.	–2,000						–2,000						
Bal.	5,900	550	20,000		400	25,000	–2,000	7,500	–2,125	–800	–800	–450	–275

An account, in its simplest form, has three parts.

■ A title, which is the name of the accounting equation element recorded in the account
■ A space for recording increases in the amount of the element
■ A space for recording decreases in the amount of the element

The account form that follows is called a **T account** because it resembles the letter T. The left side of the account is called the *debit* side, and the right side is called the *credit* side.[1]

Title

Left side	Right side
debit	*credit*

The amounts shown in the Cash column of Exhibit 1 would be recorded in a cash account as follows:

note:
Amounts entered on the left side of an account are debits, and amounts entered on the right side of an account are credits.

Cash

	(A)	25,000	(B)	20,000
Debit	(D)	7,500	(E)	3,650
Side of			(F)	950
Account			(H)	2,000
	Balance	5,900		

Balance of Account ⟶

Recording transactions in accounts must follow certain rules. For example, increases in assets are recorded on the **debit** (left side) of an account. Likewise, decreases in assets are recorded on the **credit** (right side) of an account. The excess of the debits of an asset account over its credits is the **balance of the account**.

To illustrate, the receipt (increase in Cash) of $25,000 in transaction (A) is entered on the debit (left) side of the cash account. The letter or date of the transaction is also entered into the account. That way, if any questions later arise related to the entry, the entry can be traced back to the underlying transaction data. In contrast, the payment (decrease in Cash) of $20,000 to purchase land in transaction (B) is entered on the credit (right) side of the account.

The balance of the cash account of $5,900 is the excess of the debits over the credits, computed as follows:

Debits ($25,000 + $7,500)	$32,500
Less credits ($20,000 + $3,650 + $950 + $2,000)	26,600
Balance of Cash as of November 30, 2017	$ 5,900

The balance of the cash account is inserted in the account, in the Debit column. In this way, the balance is identified as a debit balance.[2] This balance represents NetSolutions' cash on hand as of November 30, 2017. This balance of $5,900 is reported on the November 30, 2017, balance sheet for **NetSolutions** as shown in Exhibit 8 of Chapter 1.

In a recent balance sheet, **Apple Inc.** reported $13.8 billion of cash.   *Link to Apple*

In an actual accounting system, a more formal account form replaces the T account. Later in this chapter, a four-column account is illustrated. The T account, however, is a simple way to illustrate the effects of transactions on accounts and financial statements. For this reason, T accounts are often used in business to explain transactions.

Each of the columns in Exhibit 1 can be converted into an account form in a similar manner as was done for the Cash column of Exhibit 1. However, as mentioned earlier, recording increases and decreases in accounts must follow certain rules. These rules are discussed after the chart of accounts is described.

Chart of Accounts

A group of accounts for a business entity is called a **ledger**. A list of the accounts in the ledger is called a **chart of accounts**. The accounts are normally listed in the order in which they appear in the financial statements. The balance sheet accounts are listed first, in the order of

---

[1] The terms *debit* and *credit* are derived from the Latin *debere* and *credere*.

[2] The totals of the debit and credit columns may be shown separately in an account. When this is done, these amounts should be identified in some way so that they are not mistaken for entries or the ending balance of the account.

assets, liabilities, and stockholders' equity. The income statement accounts are then listed in the order of revenues and expenses.

Assets Assets are resources owned by the business entity. These resources can be physical items, such as cash and supplies, or intangibles that have value. Examples of intangible assets include patent rights, copyrights, and trademarks. Assets also include accounts receivable, prepaid expenses (such as insurance), buildings, equipment, and land.

Liabilities Liabilities are debts owed to outsiders (creditors). Liabilities are often identified on the balance sheet by titles that include *payable*. Examples of liabilities include accounts payable, notes payable, and wages payable. Cash received before services are delivered creates a liability to perform the services. These future service commitments are called *unearned revenues*. Examples of *unearned revenues* include magazine subscriptions received by a publisher and tuition received at the beginning of a term by a college.

Stockholders' equity Stockholders' equity is the stockholders' right to the assets of the business. Stockholders' equity is represented by the balance of the **common stock** and **retained earnings** accounts. A **dividends** account represents distributions of earnings to stockholders.

Revenues Revenues are increases in assets and stockholders' equity as a result of selling services or products to customers. Examples of revenues include fees earned, fares earned, commissions revenue, and rent revenue.

Expenses Expenses result from using up assets or consuming services in the process of generating revenues. Examples of expenses include wages expense, rent expense, utilities expense, supplies expense, and miscellaneous expense.

Illustration of Chart of Accounts A chart of accounts should meet the needs of a company's managers and other users of its financial statements. The accounts within the chart of accounts are numbered for use as references. A numbering system is normally used, so that new accounts can be added without affecting other account numbers.

Exhibit 2 is **NetSolutions**' chart of accounts that is used in this chapter. Additional accounts will be introduced in later chapters. In Exhibit 2, each account number has two digits. The first digit indicates the major account group of the ledger in which the account is located. Accounts beginning with 1 represent assets; 2, liabilities; 3, stockholders' equity; 4, revenue; and 5, expenses. The second digit indicates the location of the account within its group.

Exhibit 2 Chart of Accounts for NetSolutions		

Balance Sheet Accounts		**Income Statement Accounts**	
1. Assets		**4. Revenue**	
11	Cash	41	Fees Earned
12	Accounts Receivable	**5. Expenses**	
14	Supplies	51	Wages Expense
15	Prepaid Insurance	52	Supplies Expense
17	Land	53	Rent Expense
18	Office Equipment	54	Utilities Expense
2. Liabilities		59	Miscellaneous Expense
21	Accounts Payable		
23	Unearned Rent		
3. Stockholders' Equity			
31	Common Stock		
32	Retained Earnings		
33	Dividends		

Each of the columns in Exhibit 1 has been assigned an account number in the chart of accounts shown in Exhibit 2. In addition, Accounts Receivable, Prepaid Insurance, Office Equipment, and Unearned Rent have been added. These accounts will be used in recording NetSolutions' December transactions.

Why It Matters

The Hijacking Receivable

A company's chart of accounts should reflect the basic nature of its operations. Occasionally, however, transactions take place that give rise to unusual accounts. The following is a story of one such account.

Before strict airport security was implemented across the United States, several airlines experienced hijacking incidents. One such incident occurred when a Southern Airways jet en route from Memphis to Miami was hijacked during a stopover in Birmingham, Alabama. The three hijackers boarded the plane in Birmingham armed with handguns and hand grenades. At gunpoint, the hijackers took the plane, the plane's crew, and the passengers to nine American cities, Toronto, and eventually to Havana, Cuba.

During the long flight, the hijackers demanded a ransom of $10 million. Southern Airways, however, was only able to come up with $2 million. Eventually, the pilot talked the hijackers into settling for the $2 million when the plane landed in Chattanooga for refueling.

Upon landing in Havana, the Cuban authorities arrested the hijackers and, after a brief delay, sent the plane, passengers, and crew back to the United States. The hijackers and the $2 million stayed in Cuba.

How did Southern Airways account for and report the hijacking payment in its subsequent financial statements? As you might have analyzed, the initial entry credited Cash for $2 million. The debit was to an account entitled "Hijacking Payment." This account was reported as a type of receivable under "other assets" on Southern Airways' balance sheet. The company maintained that it would be able to collect the cash from the Cuban government and that, therefore, a receivable existed. In fact, Southern Airways was later repaid $2 million by the Cuban government, which was, at that time, attempting to improve relations with the United States.

Double-Entry Accounting System

Objective 2
Describe and illustrate journalizing transactions using the double-entry accounting system.

All businesses use what is called the **double-entry accounting system**. This system is based on the accounting equation and requires:

- Every business transaction to be recorded in at least two accounts.
- The total debits recorded for each transaction to be equal to the total credits recorded.

The double-entry accounting system also has specific **rules of debit and credit** for recording transactions in the accounts.

Apple records transactions using generally accepted accounting principles and double-entry accounting.   *Link to Apple*

Balance Sheet Accounts

The debit and credit rules for balance sheet accounts are as follows:

Balance Sheet Accounts

ASSETS Asset Accounts		=	LIABILITIES Liability Accounts		+	STOCKHOLDERS' EQUITY Stockholders' Equity Accounts	
Debit for increases (+)	Credit for decreases (−)		Debit for decreases (−)	Credit for increases (+)		Debit for decreases (−)	Credit for increases (+)

Income Statement Accounts

The debit and credit rules for income statement accounts are based on their relationship with stockholders' equity. As shown for balance sheet accounts, stockholders' equity accounts are increased by credits. Because revenues increase stockholders' equity, revenue accounts are increased by credits and decreased by debits. Because stockholders' equity accounts are decreased by debits, expense accounts are increased by debits and decreased by credits. Thus, the rules of debit and credit for revenue and expense accounts are as follows:

Income Statement Accounts

Revenue Accounts		Expense Accounts	
Debit for decreases (−)	Credit for increases (+)	Debit for increases (+)	Credit for decreases (−)

Retained Earnings Statement Accounts (Dividends)

The debit and credit rules for recording dividends are based on the effect of dividends on stockholders' equity (retained earnings). Since dividends decrease stockholders' equity (retained earnings), the dividends account is increased by debits. Likewise, the dividends account is decreased by credits. Thus, the rules of debit and credit for the dividends account are as follows:

Dividends Account	
Debit for increases (+)	Credit for decreases (–)

Normal Balances

The sum of the increases in an account is usually equal to or greater than the sum of the decreases in the account. Thus, the **normal balance of an account** is either a debit or credit depending on whether increases in the account are recorded as debits or credits. For example, because asset accounts are increased with debits, asset accounts normally have debit balances. Likewise, liability accounts normally have credit balances.

The rules of debit and credit and the normal balances of the various types of accounts are summarized in Exhibit 3. Debits and credits are sometimes abbreviated as Dr. for debit and Cr. for credit.

Exhibit 3   Rules of Debit and Credit, Normal Balances of Accounts

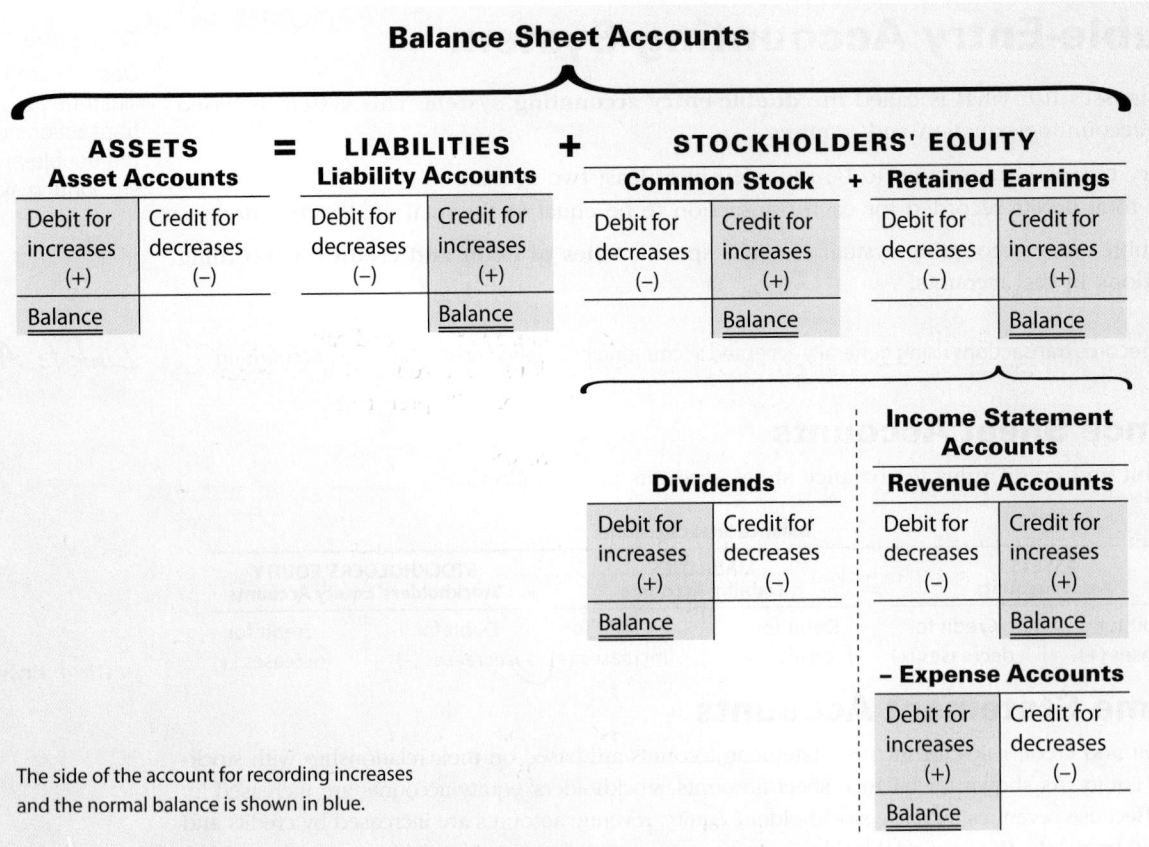

The side of the account for recording increases and the normal balance is shown in blue.

When an account normally having a debit balance has a credit balance, or vice versa, an error may have occurred or an unusual situation may exist. For example, a credit balance in the office equipment account could result only from an error. This is because a business cannot have more decreases than increases of office equipment. On the other hand, a debit balance in an accounts payable account could result from an overpayment.

Why It Matters

Debits and Credits at the Bank

If you make a deposit at the bank, you are said to *credit* your account. Likewise, when you make a withdrawal, you are said to *debit* your account. At first, this may seem opposite to the debit and credit normal balance rules. Additions to cash are debits, not credits. However, while the cash in your account is an asset to you, it is a liability to the bank. Thus, when the bank credits your account for a deposit, it is increasing its liability account to you. Likewise, when the bank debits your account for a withdrawal, it is decreasing its liability account to you. Thus, the debit and credit normal balance rules are being followed from the bank's perspective.

Check Up Corner 2-1 | **Balance Sheet Accounts**

David Simmons, M.D., recently organized Simmons Urgent Care Inc. as a walk-in clinic. The clinic has purchased medical supplies and office equipment on account. In addition, David has invested cash in the business in exchange for common stock.

Identify the balance sheet accounts that Simmons Urgent Care will use to record these transactions, indicating whether each is an asset, liability, or stockholders' equity account and whether the normal balance is a debit or a credit.

Solution:

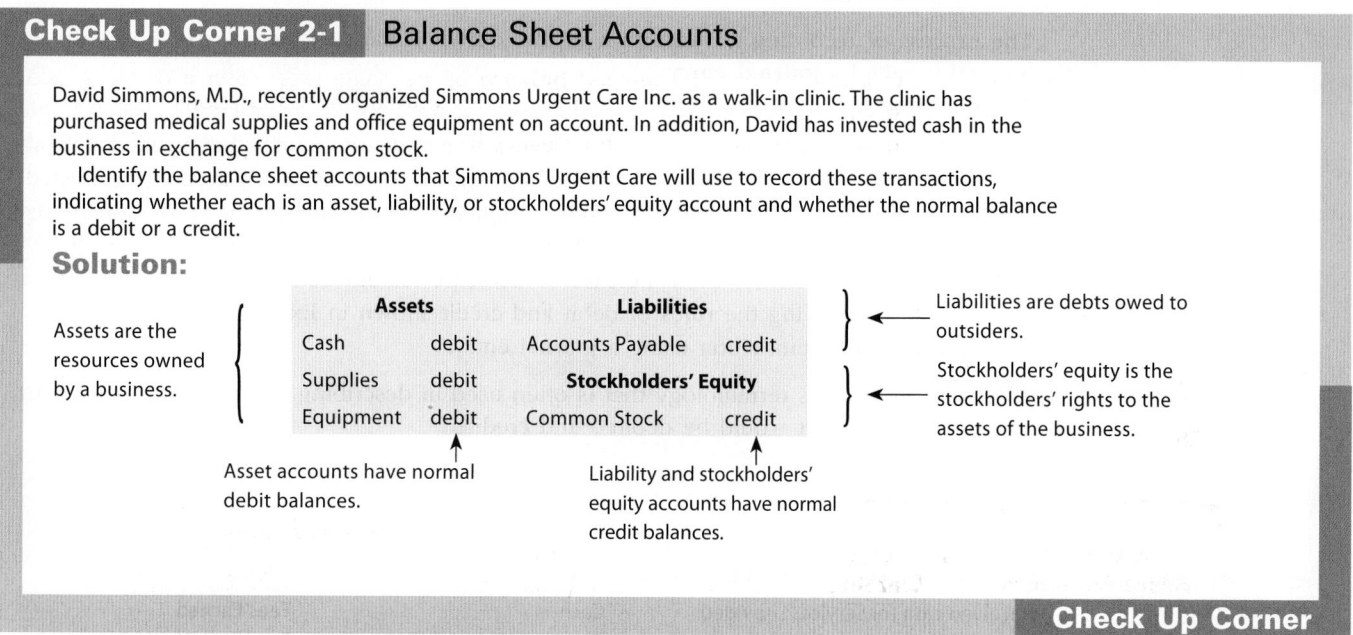

Assets are the resources owned by a business.

Assets		**Liabilities**	
Cash	debit	Accounts Payable	credit
Supplies	debit	**Stockholders' Equity**	
Equipment	debit	Common Stock	credit

Asset accounts have normal debit balances.

Liability and stockholders' equity accounts have normal credit balances.

Liabilities are debts owed to outsiders.

Stockholders' equity is the stockholders' rights to the assets of the business.

Check Up Corner

Journalizing

Using the rules of debit and credit, transactions are initially entered in a record called a **journal**. In this way, the journal serves as a record of when transactions occurred and were recorded. To illustrate, the November 2017 transactions of **NetSolutions** from Chapter 1 are used.

Nov. 1	*Chris Clark deposited $25,000 in a bank account in the name of NetSolutions in exchange for common stock.*	**Transaction A**

This transaction increases an asset account and increases an stockholders' equity account. It is recorded in the journal as an increase (debit) to Cash and an increase (credit) to Common Stock.

Analysis

Journal Entry

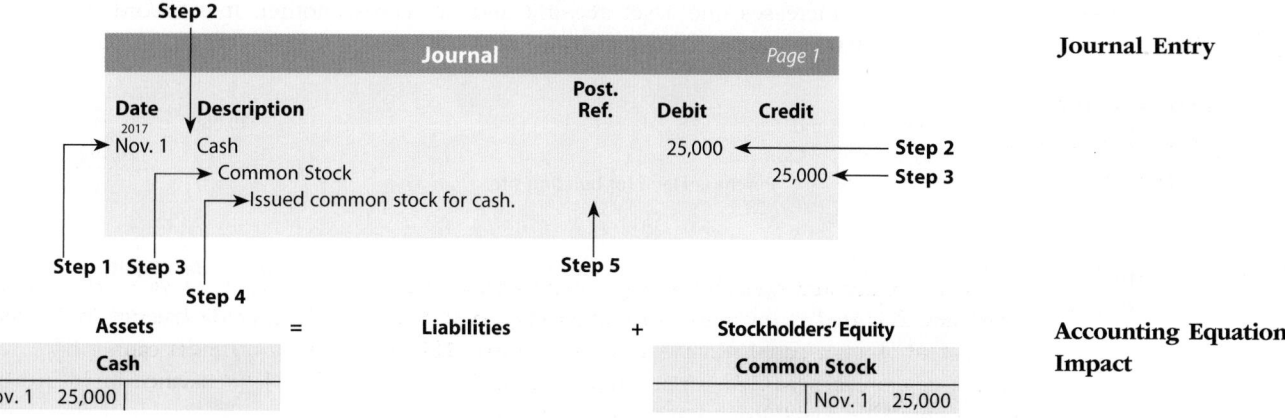

Accounting Equation Impact

The transaction is recorded in the journal using the following steps:

- Step 1. The date of the transaction is entered in the Date column.
- Step 2. The title of the account to be debited is recorded in the left-hand margin under the Description column, and the amount to be debited is entered in the Debit column.
- Step 3. The title of the account to be credited is listed below and to the right of the debited account title, and the amount to be credited is entered in the Credit column.
- Step 4. A brief description may be entered below the credited account.
- Step 5. The Post. Ref. (Posting Reference) column is left blank when the journal entry is initially recorded. This column is used later in this chapter when the journal entry amounts are transferred to the accounts in the ledger.

The process of recording a transaction in the journal is called **journalizing**. The entry in the journal is called a **journal entry**.

The following is a useful method for analyzing and journalizing transactions:

- Step 1. Carefully read the description of the transaction to determine whether an asset, a liability, a stockholders' equity, a revenue, an expense, or a dividends account is affected.
- Step 2. For each account affected by the transaction, determine whether the account increases or decreases.
- Step 3. Determine whether each increase or decrease should be recorded as a debit or a credit, following the rules of debit and credit shown in Exhibit 3.
- Step 4. Record the transaction using a journal entry.

Exhibit 4 summarizes terminology that is often used in describing a transaction along with the related accounts that would be debited and credited.

Exhibit 4
Transaction Terminology and Related Journal Entry Accounts

Common Transaction Terminology	Journal Entry Account	
	Debit	Credit
Received cash for services provided	Cash	Fees Earned
Services provided on account	Accounts Receivable	Fees Earned
Received cash on account	Cash	Accounts Receivable
Purchased on account	Asset account	Accounts Payable
Paid on account	Accounts Payable	Cash
Paid cash	Asset or expense account	Cash
Issued common stock	Cash and/or other assets	Common Stock
Paid dividends	Dividends	Cash

The remaining transactions of **NetSolutions** for November are analyzed and journalized next.

Transaction B   *Nov. 5   NetSolutions paid $20,000 for the purchase of land as a future building site.*

Analysis   This transaction increases one asset account and decreases another. It is recorded in the journal as a $20,000 increase (debit) to Land and a $20,000 decrease (credit) to Cash.

Journal Entry

Nov. 5	Land	20,000	
	Cash		20,000
	Purchased land for building site.		

Accounting Equation Impact

Assets = Liabilities + Stockholders' Equity

Land	
Nov. 5 20,000	

Cash	
	Nov. 5 20,000

Nov. 10   NetSolutions purchased supplies on account for $1,350.   **Transaction C**

This transaction increases an asset account and increases a liability account. It is recorded in the journal as a $1,350 increase (debit) to Supplies and a $1,350 increase (credit) to Accounts Payable.   **Analysis**

Journal Entry

Nov. 10	Supplies	1,350	
	Accounts Payable		1,350
	Purchased supplies on account.		

Accounting Equation Impact

Assets	=	Liabilities	+	Stockholders' Equity
Supplies		**Accounts Payable**		
Nov. 10 1,350		Nov. 10 1,350		

Nov. 18   NetSolutions received cash of $7,500 from customers for services provided.   **Transaction D**

This transaction increases an asset account and increases a revenue account. It is recorded in the journal as a $7,500 increase (debit) to Cash and a $7,500 increase (credit) to Fees Earned.   **Analysis**

Journal Entry

Nov. 18	Cash	7,500	
	Fees Earned		7,500
	Received fees from customers.		

Accounting Equation Impact

Assets	=	Liabilities	+	Stockholders' Equity (Revenue)
Cash				**Fees Earned**
Nov. 18 7,500				Nov. 18 7,500

Nov. 30   NetSolutions incurred the following expenses: wages, $2,125; rent, $800;   **Transaction E**
utilities, $450; and miscellaneous, $275.

This transaction increases various expense accounts and decreases an asset (Cash) account. You should note that regardless of the number of accounts, *the sum of the debits is always equal to the sum of the credits in a journal entry*. It is recorded in the journal with increases (debits) to the expense accounts (Wages Expense, $2,125; Rent Expense, $800; Utilities Expense, $450; and Miscellaneous Expense, $275) and a decrease (credit) to Cash, $3,650.   **Analysis**

Journal Entry

Nov. 30	Wages Expense	2,125	
	Rent Expense	800	
	Utilities Expense	450	
	Miscellaneous Expense	275	
	Cash		3,650
	Paid expenses.		

Accounting Equation Impact

Assets	=	Liabilities	+	Stockholders' Equity (Expense)
Cash				**Wages Expense**
	Nov. 30 3,650			Nov. 30 2,125
				Rent Expense
				Nov. 30 800
				Utilities Expense
				Nov. 30 450
				Miscellaneous Expense
				Nov. 30 275

Transaction F   *Nov. 30 NetSolutions paid creditors on account, $950.*

Analysis   This transaction decreases a liability account and decreases an asset account. It is recorded in the journal as a $950 decrease (debit) to Accounts Payable and a $950 decrease (credit) to Cash.

Journal Entry

Nov. 30	Accounts Payable	950	
	Cash		950
	Paid creditors on account.		

Accounting Equation Impact

Assets	=	Liabilities	+	Stockholders' Equity
Cash		**Accounts Payable**		
Nov. 30	950	Nov. 30	950	

Transaction G   *Nov. 30   NetSolutions determined that the cost of supplies on hand at November 30 was $550.*

Analysis   NetSolutions purchased $1,350 of supplies on November 10. Thus, $800 ($1,350 – $550) of supplies must have been used during November. This transaction is recorded in the journal as an $800 increase (debit) to Supplies Expense and an $800 decrease (credit) to Supplies.

Journal Entry

Nov. 30	Supplies Expense	800	
	Supplies		800
	Supplies used during November.		

Accounting Equation Impact

Assets	=	Liabilities	+	Stockholders' Equity (Expense)
Supplies				**Supplies Expense**
	Nov. 30 800			Nov. 30 800

Transaction H   *Nov. 30 Paid dividends, $2,000.*

Analysis   This transaction decreases assets and stockholders' equity. This transaction is recorded in the journal as a $2,000 increase (debit) to Dividends and a $2,000 decrease (credit) to Cash.

Journal Entry

Journal					Page 2
Date	**Description**		**Post. Ref.**	**Debit**	**Credit**
2017					
Nov. 30	Dividends			2,000	
	Cash				2,000
	Paid dividends.				

Accounting Equation Impact

Assets	=	Liabilities	+	Stockholders' Equity (Dividends)
Cash				**Dividends**
	Nov. 30 2,000			Nov. 30 2,000

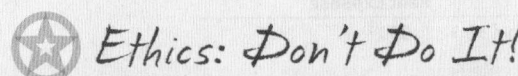 *Ethics: Don't Do It!*

Will Journalizing Prevent Fraud?

While journalizing transactions reduces the possibility of fraud, it by no means eliminates it. For example, embezzlement can be hidden within the double-entry bookkeeping system by creating fictitious suppliers to whom checks are issued.

Check Up Corner 2-2 | Journal Entries

During the first month of operations, Simmons Urgent Care Inc. completed the following transactions:

Jan. 1 David Simmons deposited $30,000 in a bank account in the name of Simmons Urgent Care Inc. in exchange for common stock.

2 Purchased medical supplies on account, $6,000.

6 Paid cash to creditors on account, $3,200.

7 Purchased office equipment on account, $62,500

Prepare the journal entries to record these transactions, and illustrate their impact on the accounting equation.

Solution:

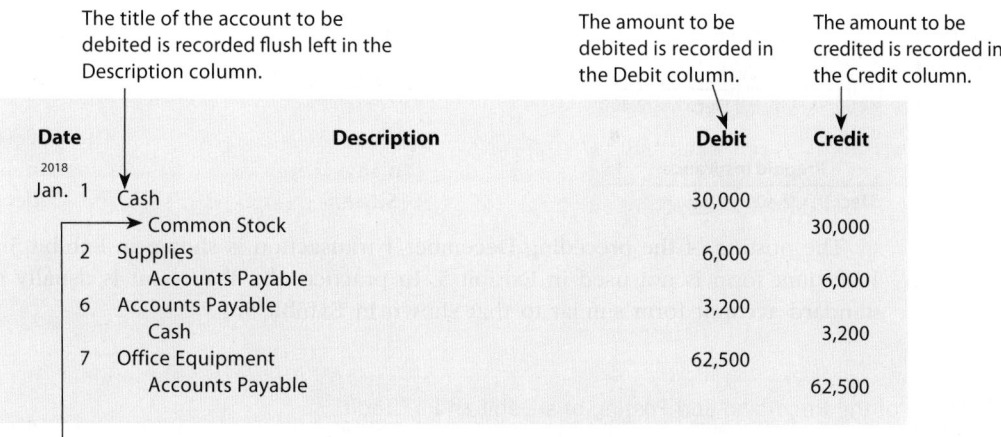

The title of the account to be debited is recorded flush left in the Description column.

The amount to be debited is recorded in the Debit column.

The amount to be credited is recorded in the Credit column.

The title of the account to be credited is recorded below the debit in the Description column and indented slightly.

Increases in asset accounts are recorded on the debit (left) side of the account.

Increases in liability and stockholders' equity accounts are recorded on the credit (right) side of the account.

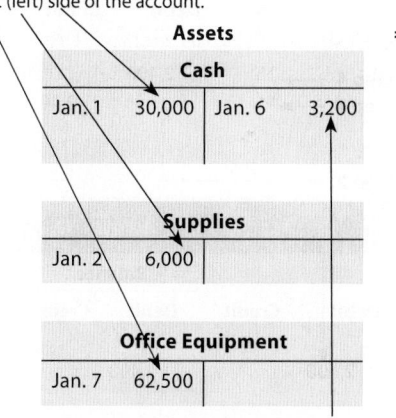
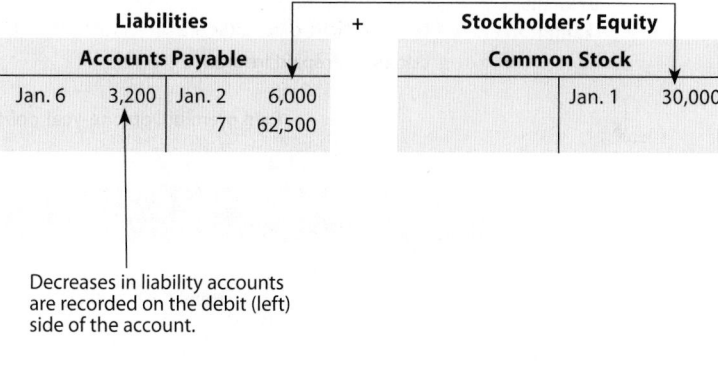

Decreases in liability accounts are recorded on the debit (left) side of the account.

Decreases in asset accounts are recorded on the credit (right) side of the account.

Posting Journal Entries to Accounts

Objective 3
Describe and illustrate the journalizing and posting of transactions to accounts.

As illustrated, a transaction is first recorded in a journal. Periodically, the journal entries are transferred to the accounts in the ledger. The process of transferring the debits and credits from the journal entries to the accounts is called **posting**.

The December 2017 transactions of **NetSolutions** are used to illustrate posting from the journal to the ledger. By using the December transactions, an additional review of analyzing and journalizing transactions is provided.

Transaction   *Dec. 1   NetSolutions paid a premium of $2,400 for an insurance policy for liability, theft, and fire. The policy covers a one-year period.*

Analysis   Advance payments of expenses, such as for insurance premiums, are called prepaid expenses. Prepaid expenses are assets. For NetSolutions, the asset purchased is insurance protection for 12 months. This transaction is recorded as a $2,400 increase (debit) to Prepaid Insurance and a $2,400 decrease (credit) to Cash.

Journal Entry

Dec.	1	Prepaid Insurance	15	2,400	
		Cash	11		2,400
		Paid premium on one-year policy.			

Accounting Equation Impact

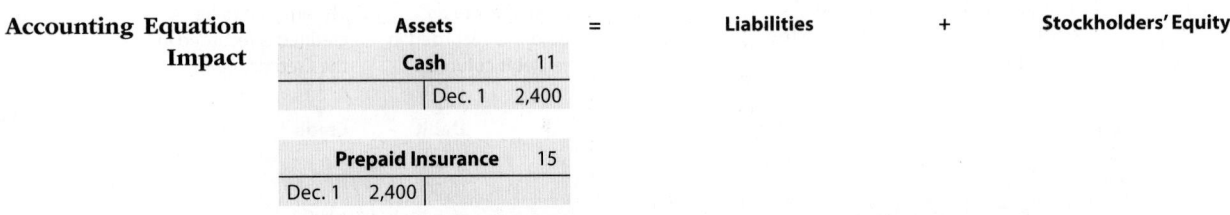

Assets		=	**Liabilities**	+	**Stockholders' Equity**

Cash	11
Dec. 1	2,400

Prepaid Insurance	15
Dec. 1	2,400	

The posting of the preceding December 1 transaction is shown in Exhibit 5. Notice that the T account form is not used in Exhibit 5. In practice, the T account is usually replaced with a standard account form similar to that shown in Exhibit 5.

Exhibit 5   Diagram of the Recording and Posting of a Debit and a Credit

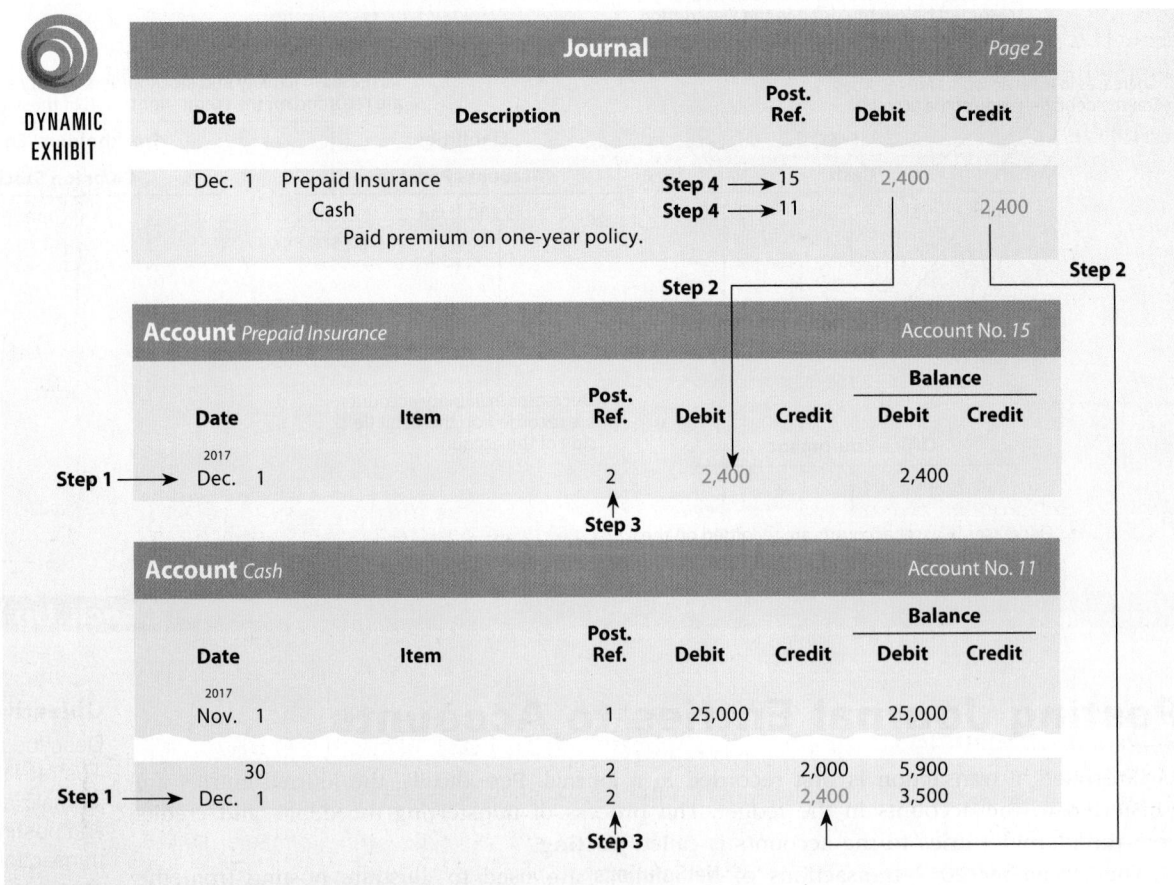

The debits and credits for each journal entry are posted to the accounts in the order in which they occur in the journal. To illustrate, the debit portion of the December 1 journal entry is posted to the prepaid account in Exhibit 5 using the following four steps:

■ Step 1. The date (Dec. 1) of the journal entry is entered in the Date column of Prepaid Insurance.
■ Step 2. The amount (2,400) is entered into the Debit column of Prepaid Insurance.
■ Step 3. The journal page number (2) is entered in the Posting Reference (Post. Ref.) column of Prepaid Insurance.
■ Step 4. The account number (15) is entered in the Posting Reference (Post. Ref.) column in the journal.

As shown in Exhibit 5, the credit portion of the December 1 journal entry is posted to the cash account in a similar manner.

The remaining December transactions for **NetSolutions** are analyzed and journalized in the following paragraphs. These transactions are posted to the ledger later in this chapter (see Exhibit 6). To simplify, some of the December transactions are stated in summary form. For example, cash received for services is normally recorded on a daily basis. However, only summary totals are recorded at the middle and end of the month for NetSolutions.

Dec. 1 NetSolutions paid rent for December, $800. The company from which NetSolutions is renting its office space now requires the payment of rent on the first of each month, rather than at the end of the month.	**Transaction**

The advance payment of rent is an asset, much like the advance payment of the insurance premium in the preceding transaction. However, unlike the insurance premium, this prepaid rent will expire in one month. When an asset is purchased with the expectation that it will be used up in a short period of time, such as a month, it is normal to debit an expense account initially. This avoids having to transfer the balance from an asset account (Prepaid Rent) to an expense account (Rent Expense) at the end of the month. Thus, this transaction is recorded as an $800 increase (debit) to Rent Expense and an $800 decrease (credit) to Cash. — **Analysis**

Dec. 1	Rent Expense	53	800	
	Cash	11		800
	Paid rent for December.			

— **Journal Entry**

Assets	=	Liabilities	+	Stockholders' Equity (Expense)
Cash 11				**Rent Expense** 53
Dec. 1 800				Dec. 1 800

— **Accounting Equation Impact**

Dec. 1 NetSolutions received an offer from a local retailer to rent the land purchased on November 5. The retailer plans to use the land as a parking lot for its employees and customers. NetSolutions agreed to rent the land to the retailer for three months, with the rent payable in advance. NetSolutions received $360 for three months' rent beginning December 1.	**Transaction**

By agreeing to rent the land and accepting the $360, NetSolutions has incurred an obligation (liability) to the retailer. This obligation is to make the land available for use for three months and not to interfere with its use. The liability created by receiving the cash in advance of providing the service is called **unearned revenue**. As time passes, the unearned rent liability will decrease and will become revenue. Thus, this transaction is recorded as a $360 increase (debit) to Cash and a $360 increase (credit) to Unearned Rent. — **Analysis**

Journal Entry

Dec. 1	Cash		11	360
	Unearned Rent		23		360
	Received advance payment for three			
	months' rent on land.			

Accounting Equation Impact

Assets	=	Liabilities	+	Stockholders' Equity
Cash 11		**Unearned Rent** 23		
Dec. 1 360		Dec. 1 360		

Link to Apple   In a recent balance sheet, Apple reported over $11 billion in unearned revenue, sometimes called deferred revenue.

Transaction   *Dec. 4   NetSolutions purchased office equipment on account from Executive Supply Co. for $1,800.*

Analysis   The asset (Office Equipment) and liability accounts (Accounts Payable) increase. This transaction is recorded as an $1,800 increase (debit) to Office Equipment and an $1,800 increase (credit) to Accounts Payable.

Journal Entry

Dec. 4	Office Equipment		18	1,800
	Accounts Payable		21		1,800
	Purchased office equipment on account.			

Accounting Equation Impact

Assets	=	Liabilities	+	Stockholders' Equity
Office Equipment 18		**Accounts Payable** 21		
Dec. 4 1,800		Dec. 4 1,800		

Link to Apple   In a recent balance sheet, Apple reported equipment, buildings, and land of over $34 billion.

Transaction   *Dec. 6   NetSolutions paid $180 for a newspaper advertisement.*

Analysis   An expense increases, and an asset (Cash) decreases. Expense items that are expected to be minor in amount are normally included as part of the miscellaneous expense. This transaction is recorded as a $180 increase (debit) to Miscellaneous Expense and a $180 decrease (credit) to Cash.

Journal Entry

Dec. 6	Miscellaneous Expense		59	180
	Cash		11		180
	Paid for newspaper advertisement.			

Accounting Equation Impact

Assets	=	Liabilities	+	Stockholders' Equity (Expense)
Cash 11				**Miscellaneous Exp.** 59
Dec. 6 180				Dec. 6 180

Link to Apple   In a recent year, Apple incurred advertising expense of $1.2 billion. Apple reports advertising expense as part of Selling, General, and Administrative expenses.

Why It Matters
Computerized Accounting Systems

Computerized accounting systems like QuickBooks and PeachTree are widely used by even the smallest companies. These systems simplify the journalizing process and eliminate the need for manual posting. For example, in a computerized accounting system, when a customer payment is processed, the date, customer name, and payment amount are entered in the "Receive Payment" window. The entered data are automatically journalized and posted to the ledger accounts. In this way, posting is seamless and instant.

Dec. 11   NetSolutions paid creditors $400.   **Transaction**

A liability (Accounts Payable) and an asset (Cash) decrease. This transaction is recorded as   **Analysis**
a $400 decrease (debit) to Accounts Payable and a $400 decrease (credit) to Cash.

Journal Entry

Dec. 11	Accounts Payable	21	400	
	Cash	11		400
	Paid creditors on account.			

Accounting Equation Impact

Assets	=	Liabilities	+	Stockholders' Equity
Cash 11		**Accounts Payable** 21		
Dec. 11 400		Dec. 11 400		

Dec. 13   NetSolutions paid a receptionist and a part-time assistant $950 for two weeks' wages.   **Transaction**

This transaction is similar to the December 6 transaction, where an expense account is   **Analysis**
increased and Cash is decreased. This transaction is recorded as a $950 increase (debit) to
Wages Expense and a $950 decrease (credit) to Cash.

Journal Entry

	Journal			Page 3
Date	**Description**	**Post. Ref.**	**Debit**	**Credit**
2017				
Dec. 13	Wages Expense	51	950	
	Cash	11		950
	Paid two weeks' wages.			

Accounting Equation Impact

Assets	=	Liabilities	+	Stockholders' Equity (Expense)
Cash 11				**Wages Expense** 51
Dec. 13 950				Dec. 13 950

Dec. 16   NetSolutions received $3,100 from fees earned for the first half of December.   **Transaction**

An asset account (Cash) and a revenue account (Fees Earned) increase. This transaction is   **Analysis**
recorded as a $3,100 increase (debit) to Cash and a $3,100 increase (credit) to Fees Earned.

Journal Entry

Dec. 16	Cash	11	3,100	
	Fees Earned	41		3,100
	Received fees from customers.			

Accounting Equation Impact

Assets	=	Liabilities	+	Stockholders' Equity (Revenue)
Cash 11				**Fees Earned** 41
Dec. 16 3,100				Dec. 16 3,100

Dec. 16   Fees earned on account totaled $1,750 for the first half of December.   **Transaction**

When a business agrees that a customer may pay for services provided at a later date, an   **Analysis**
account receivable is created. An account receivable is a claim against the customer. An account
receivable is an asset, and the revenue is earned even though no cash has been received. Thus,
this transaction is recorded as a $1,750 increase (debit) to Accounts Receivable and a $1,750
increase (credit) to Fees Earned.

Journal Entry

Dec. 16	Accounts Receivable	12	1,750	
	Fees Earned	41		1,750
	Fees earned on account.			

Accounting Equation Impact

Assets	=	Liabilities	+	Stockholders' Equity (Revenue)
Accounts Receivable 12				**Fees Earned 41**
Dec. 16 1,750				Dec. 16 1,750

Transaction *Dec. 20 NetSolutions paid $900 to Executive Supply Co. on the $1,800 debt owed from the December 4 transaction.*

Analysis This is similar to the transaction of December 11. This transaction is recorded as a $900 decrease (debit) to Accounts Payable and a $900 decrease (credit) to Cash.

Journal Entry

Dec. 20	Accounts Payable	21	900	
	Cash	11		900
	Paid creditors on account.			

Accounting Equation Impact

Assets	=	Liabilities	+	Stockholders' Equity
Cash 11		**Accounts Payable 21**		
Dec. 20 900		Dec. 20 900		

Link to Apple   On a recent balance sheet, **Apple** reported $30.2 billion in accounts payable.

Transaction *Dec. 21 NetSolutions received $650 from customers in payment of their accounts.*

Analysis When customers pay amounts owed for services they have previously received, one asset increases and another asset decreases. This transaction is recorded as a $650 increase (debit) to Cash and a $650 decrease (credit) to Accounts Receivable.

Journal Entry

Dec. 21	Cash	11	650	
	Accounts Receivable	12		650
	Received cash from customers on account.			

Accounting Equation Impact

Assets	=	Liabilities	+	Stockholders' Equity
Cash 11				
Dec. 21 650				

Accounts Receivable   12
Dec. 21   650

Transaction *Dec. 23 NetSolutions paid $1,450 for supplies.*

Analysis One asset account (Supplies) increases, and another asset account (Cash) decreases. This transaction is recorded as a $1,450 increase (debit) to Supplies and a $1,450 decrease (credit) to Cash.

Journal Entry

Dec. 23	Supplies	14	1,450	
	Cash	11		1,450
	Purchased supplies.			

Assets			=	Liabilities	+	Stockholders' Equity	Accounting Equation Impact

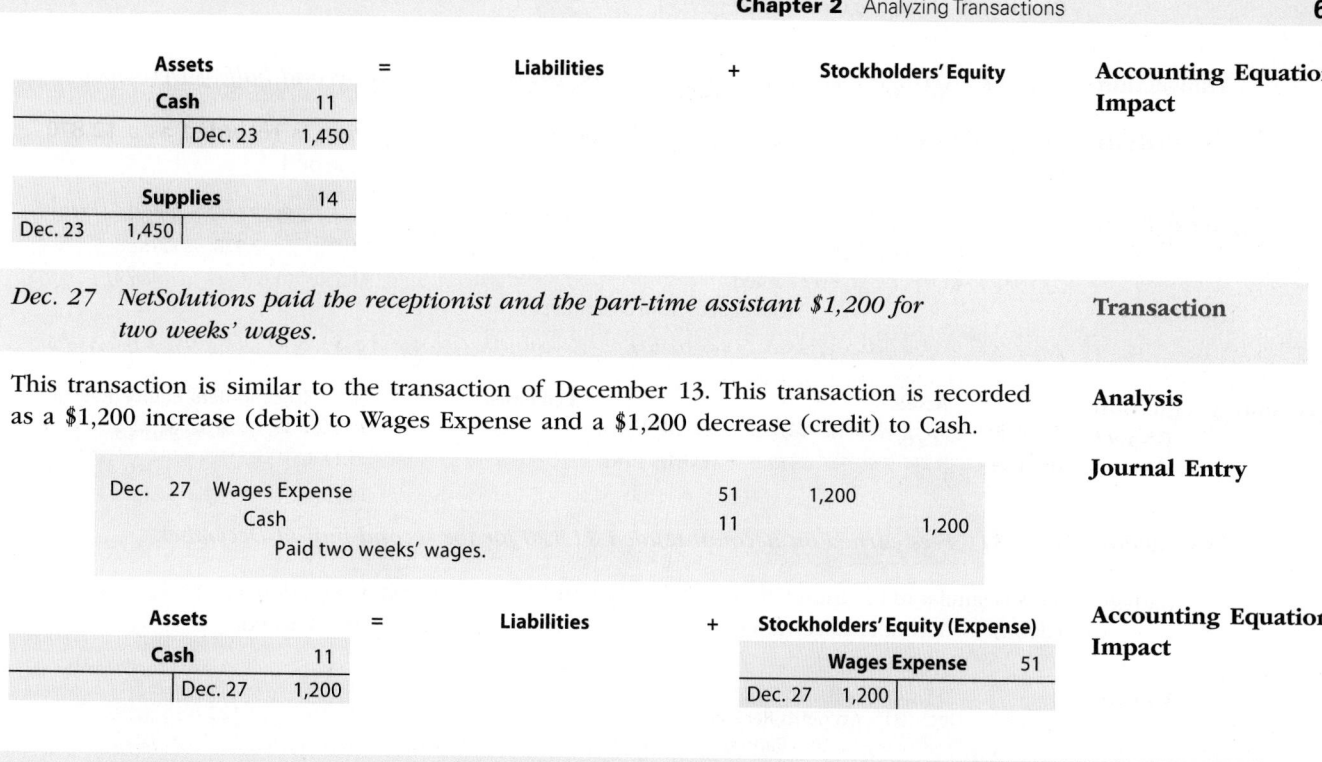

Cash 11
Dec. 23 1,450

Supplies 14
Dec. 23 1,450

Dec. 27 NetSolutions paid the receptionist and the part-time assistant $1,200 for two weeks' wages.   *Transaction*

This transaction is similar to the transaction of December 13. This transaction is recorded as a $1,200 increase (debit) to Wages Expense and a $1,200 decrease (credit) to Cash.   *Analysis*

Journal Entry

Dec. 27 Wages Expense   51   1,200
           Cash   11   1,200
              Paid two weeks' wages.

Accounting Equation Impact

Assets   = **Liabilities**   + **Stockholders' Equity (Expense)**

Cash 11   **Wages Expense** 51
Dec. 27 1,200   Dec. 27 1,200

Dec. 31 NetSolutions paid its $310 telephone bill for the month.   *Transaction*

This is similar to the transaction of December 6. This transaction is recorded as a $310 increase (debit) to Utilities Expense and a $310 decrease (credit) to Cash.   *Analysis*

Journal Entry

Dec. 31 Utilities Expense   54   310
           Cash   11   310
              Paid telephone bill.

Accounting Equation Impact

Assets   = **Liabilities**   + **Stockholders' Equity (Expense)**

Cash 11   **Utilities Expense** 54
Dec. 31 310   Dec. 31 310

Dec. 31 NetSolutions paid its $225 electric bill for the month.   *Transaction*

This is similar to the preceding transaction. This transaction is recorded as a $225 increase (debit) to Utilities Expense and a $225 decrease (credit) to Cash.   *Analysis*

Journal Entry

Journal					Page 4
Date	Description	Post. Ref.	Debit	Credit	
2017					
Dec. 31	Utilities Expense	54	225		
	Cash	11		225	
	Paid electric bill.				

Accounting Equation Impact

Assets   = **Liabilities**   + **Stockholders' Equity (Expense)**

Cash 11   **Utilities Expense** 54
Dec. 31 225   Dec. 31 225

Transaction	*Dec. 31 NetSolutions received $2,870 from fees earned for the second half of December.*

Analysis	This is similar to the transaction of December 16. This transaction is recorded as a $2,870 increase (debit) to Cash and a $2,870 increase (credit) to Fees Earned.

Journal Entry

Dec.	31	Cash	11	2,870	
		Fees Earned	41		2,870
		Received fees from customers.			

Accounting Equation Impact

Assets		=	Liabilities	+	Stockholders' Equity (Revenue)	
Cash	11				**Fees Earned**	41
Dec. 31 2,870					Dec. 31 2,870	

Transaction	*Dec. 31 Fees earned on account totaled $1,120 for the second half of December.*

Analysis	This is similar to the transaction of December 16. This transaction is recorded as a $1,120 increase (debit) to Accounts Receivable and a $1,120 increase (credit) to Fees Earned.

Journal Entry

Dec.	31	Accounts Receivable	12	1,120	
		Fees Earned	41		1,120
		Fees earned on account.			

Accounting Equation Impact

Assets		=	Liabilities	+	Stockholders' Equity (Revenue)	
Accounts Receivable	12				**Fees Earned**	41
Dec. 31 1,120					Dec. 31 1,120	

Link to Apple	On a recent balance sheet, **Apple** reported $17.5 billion in accounts receivable.

Transaction	*Dec. 31 Paid dividends, $2,000.*

Analysis	This transaction decreases stockholders' equity and assets. This transaction is recorded as a $2,000 increase (debit) to Dividends and a $2,000 decrease (credit) to Cash.

Journal Entry

Dec.	31	Dividends	33	2,000	
		Cash	11		2,000
		Paid dividends.			

Accounting Equation Impact

Assets		=	Liabilities	+	Stockholders' Equity (Dividends)	
Cash	11				**Dividends**	33
	Dec. 31 2,000				Dec. 31 2,000	

Link to Apple	In a recent year, **Apple** paid $11 billion in dividends.

Exhibit 6 shows the ledger for **NetSolutions** after the transactions for both November and December have been posted.

Exhibit 6 General Ledger for NetSolutions

Ledger

Account Cash — Account No. 11

Date	Item	Post. Ref.	Debit	Credit	Balance Debit	Credit
2017						
Nov. 1		1	25,000		25,000	
5		1		20,000	5,000	
18		1	7,500		12,500	
30		1		3,650	8,850	
30		1		950	7,900	
30		2		2,000	5,900	
Dec. 1		2		2,400	3,500	
1		2		800	2,700	
1		2	360		3,060	
6		2		180	2,880	
11		2		400	2,480	
13		3		950	1,530	
16		3	3,100		4,630	
20		3		900	3,730	
21		3	650		4,380	
23		3		1,450	2,930	
27		3		1,200	1,730	
31		3		310	1,420	
31		4		225	1,195	
31		4	2,870		4,065	
31		4		2,000	2,065	

Account Accounts Receivable — Account No. 12

Date	Item	Post. Ref.	Debit	Credit	Balance Debit	Credit
2017						
Dec. 16		3	1,750		1,750	
21		3		650	1,100	
31		4	1,120		2,220	

Account Supplies — Account No. 14

Date	Item	Post. Ref.	Debit	Credit	Balance Debit	Credit
2017						
Nov. 10		1	1,350		1,350	
30		1		800	550	
Dec. 23		3	1,450		2,000	

Account Prepaid Insurance — Account No. 15

Date	Item	Post. Ref.	Debit	Credit	Balance Debit	Credit
2017						
Dec. 1		2	2,400		2,400	

Account Land — Account No. 17

Date	Item	Post. Ref.	Debit	Credit	Balance Debit	Credit
2017						
Nov. 5		1	20,000		20,000	

Account Office Equipment — Account No. 18

Date	Item	Post. Ref.	Debit	Credit	Balance Debit	Credit
2017						
Dec. 4		2	1,800		1,800	

Account Accounts Payable — Account No. 21

Date	Item	Post. Ref.	Debit	Credit	Balance Debit	Credit
2017						
Nov. 10		1		1,350		1,350
30		1	950			400
Dec. 4		2		1,800		2,200
11		2	400			1,800
20		3	900			900

Account Unearned Rent — Account No. 23

Date	Item	Post. Ref.	Debit	Credit	Balance Debit	Credit
2017						
Dec. 1		2		360		360

Account Common Stock — Account No. 31

Date	Item	Post. Ref.	Debit	Credit	Balance Debit	Credit
2017						
Nov. 1		1		25,000		25,000

Account Dividends — Account No. 33

Date	Item	Post. Ref.	Debit	Credit	Balance Debit	Credit
2017						
Nov. 30		2	2,000		2,000	
Dec. 31		4	2,000		4,000	

(Continued)

Exhibit 6 General Ledger for NetSolutions *(Concluded)*

Account *Fees Earned* — Account No. *41*

Date	Item	Post. Ref.	Debit	Credit	Balance Debit	Balance Credit
2017						
Nov. 18		1		7,500		7,500
Dec. 16		3		3,100		10,600
16		3		1,750		12,350
31		4		2,870		15,220
31		4		1,120		16,340

Account *Wages Expense* — Account No. *51*

Date	Item	Post. Ref.	Debit	Credit	Balance Debit	Balance Credit
2017						
Nov. 30		1	2,125		2,125	
Dec. 13		3	950		3,075	
27		3	1,200		4,275	

Account *Supplies Expense* — Account No. *52*

Date	Item	Post. Ref.	Debit	Credit	Balance Debit	Balance Credit
2017						
Nov. 30		1	800		800	

Account *Rent Expense* — Account No. *53*

Date	Item	Post. Ref.	Debit	Credit	Balance Debit	Balance Credit
2017						
Nov. 30		1	800		800	
Dec. 1		2	800		1,600	

Account *Utilities Expense* — Account No. *54*

Date	Item	Post. Ref.	Debit	Credit	Balance Debit	Balance Credit
2017						
Nov. 30		1	450		450	
Dec. 31		3	310		760	
31		4	225		985	

Account *Miscellaneous Expense* — Account No. *59*

Date	Item	Post. Ref.	Debit	Credit	Balance Debit	Balance Credit
2017						
Nov. 30		1	275		275	
Dec. 6		2	180		455	

Trial Balance

Objective 4

Prepare an unadjusted trial balance and explain how it can be used to discover errors.

Errors may occur in posting debits and credits from the journal to the ledger. One way to detect such errors is by preparing a **trial balance**. Double-entry accounting requires that debits must always equal credits. The trial balance verifies this equality. The steps in preparing a trial balance are as follows:

- Step 1. List the name of the company, the title of the trial balance, and the date the trial balance is prepared.
- Step 2. List the accounts from the ledger, and enter their debit or credit balance in the Debit or Credit column of the trial balance.
- Step 3. Total the Debit and Credit columns of the trial balance.
- Step 4. Verify that the total of the Debit column equals the total of the Credit column.

The trial balance for **NetSolutions** as of December 31, 2017, is shown in Exhibit 7. The account balances in Exhibit 7 are taken from the ledger shown in Exhibit 6. Before a trial balance is prepared, each account balance in the ledger must be determined. When the standard account form is used as in Exhibit 6, the balance of each account appears in the Balance column on the same line as the last posting to the account.

The trial balance shown in Exhibit 7 is titled an **unadjusted trial balance**. This is to distinguish it from other trial balances that will be prepared in later chapters. These other trial balances include an adjusted trial balance and a post-closing trial balance.[3]

[3] The adjusted trial balance will be discussed in Chapter 3 and the post-closing trial balance in Chapter 4.

Exhibit 7 Trial Balance

Step 1

NetSolutions
Unadjusted Trial Balance
December 31, 2017

Step 2

	Account No.	Debit Balances	Credit Balances
Cash	11	2,065	
Accounts Receivable	12	2,220	
Supplies	14	2,000	
Prepaid Insurance	15	2,400	
Land	17	20,000	
Office Equipment	18	1,800	
Accounts Payable	21		900
Unearned Rent	23		360
Common Stock	31		25,000
Dividends	33	4,000	
Fees Earned	41		16,340
Wages Expense	51	4,275	
Supplies Expense	52	800	
Rent Expense	53	1,600	
Utilities Expense	54	985	
Miscellaneous Expense	59	455	
		42,600	42,600

Steps 3–4

Errors Affecting the Trial Balance

If the trial balance totals are not equal, an error has occurred. In this case, the error must be found and corrected. A method useful in discovering errors is as follows:

1. If the difference between the Debit and Credit column totals is 10, 100, or 1,000, an error in addition may have occurred. In this case, re-add the trial balance column totals. If the error still exists, recompute the account balances.

2. If the difference between the Debit and Credit column totals can be evenly divisible by 2, the error may be due to the entering of a debit balance as a credit balance, or vice versa. In this case, review the trial balance for account balances of one-half the difference that may have been entered in the wrong column. For example, if the Debit column total is $20,640 and the Credit column total is $20,236, the difference of $404 ($20,640 − $20,236) may be due to a credit account balance of $202 that was entered as a debit account balance.

3. If the difference between the Debit and Credit column totals is evenly divisible by 9, trace the account balances back to the ledger to see if an account balance was incorrectly copied from the ledger. Two common types of copying errors are transpositions and slides. A **transposition** occurs when the order of the digits is copied incorrectly, such as writing $542 as $452 or $524. In a **slide**, the entire number is copied incorrectly one or more spaces to the right or the left, such as writing $542.00 as $54.20 or $5,420.00. In both cases, the resulting error will be evenly divisible by 9.

4. If the difference between the Debit and Credit column totals is not evenly divisible by 2 or 9, review the ledger to see if an account balance in the amount of the error has been omitted from the trial balance. If the error is not discovered, review the journal postings to see if a posting of a debit or credit may have been omitted.

5. If an error is not discovered by the preceding steps, the accounting process must be retraced, beginning with the last journal entry.

The trial balance does not provide complete proof of the accuracy of the ledger. It indicates only that the debits and the credits are equal. This proof is of value, however, because errors often affect the equality of debits and credits.

Errors Not Affecting the Trial Balance

An error may occur that does not cause the trial balance totals to be unequal. Such an error may be discovered when preparing the trial balance or may be indicated by an unusual account balance. For example, a credit balance in the supplies account indicates an error has occurred. This is because a business cannot have "negative" supplies. When such errors are discovered, they should be corrected. If the error has already been journalized and posted to the ledger, a **correcting journal entry** is normally prepared.

To illustrate, assume that on May 5 a $12,500 purchase of office equipment on account was incorrectly journalized and posted as a debit to Supplies and a credit to Accounts Payable for $12,500. This posting of the incorrect entry is shown in the following T accounts:

Incorrect:

Supplies	14		Accounts Payable	21
12,500				12,500

Before making a correcting journal entry, it is best to determine the debit(s) and credit(s) that should have been recorded. These are shown in the following T accounts:

Correct:

Office Equipment	18		Accounts Payable	21
12,500				12,500

Comparing the two sets of T accounts shows that the incorrect debit to Supplies may be corrected by debiting Office Equipment for $12,500 and crediting Supplies for $12,500. The following correcting entry is then journalized and posted:

Entry to Correct Error:

May	31	Office Equipment	18	12,500	
		Supplies	14		12,500
		To correct erroneous debit			
		to Supplies on May 5. See invoice			
		from Bell Office Equipment Co.			

Check Up Corner 2-3 Trial Balance

The accounts in the ledger of Simmons Urgent Care Inc. as of December 31 2018, are listed in alphabetical order as follows. All accounts have normal balances.

Accounts Payable	$ 7,200	Miscellaneous Expense	$ 2,200
Accounts Receivable	22,000	Retained Earnings	36,300
Cash	21,000	Supplies	7,800
Common Stock	30,000	Supplies Expense	22,000
Dividends	15,000	Rent Expense	12,000
Fees Earned	250,000	Utilities Expense	4,000
Office Equipment	62,500	Wages Expense	155,000

Prepare an unadjusted trial balance, listing the accounts in their normal order.

Solution:

Balances from accounts with a normal debit balance are shown in the left column.

Balances from accounts with a normal credit balance are shown in the right column.

Accounts from the general ledger are presented in the order in which they appear in the ledger.

Simmons Urgent Care Inc. Unadjusted Trial Balance December 31, 2018	Debit Balances	Credit Balances
Cash	21,000	
Accounts Receivable...	22,000	
Supplies..	7,800	
Office Equipment	62,500	
Accounts Payable		7,200
Common Stock...		30,000
Retained Earnings...		36,300
Dividends	15,000	
Fees Earned...		250,000
Wages Expense	155,000	
Supplies Expense..	22,000	
Rent Expense	12,000	
Utilities Expense	4,000	
Miscellaneous Expense	2,200	
	323,500	323,500

The trial balance verifies that the total debits equal total credits. If total debits do not equal total credits, an error has occurred.

Check Up Corner

Analysis for Decision Making

Horizontal Analysis

A single item in a financial statement, such as net income, is often useful in interpreting the financial performance of a company. However, a comparison with prior periods often makes the financial information even more useful. For example, comparing net income of the current period with the net income of the prior period will indicate whether the company's operating performance has improved.

In **horizontal analysis**, the amount of each item on a current financial statement is compared with the same item on an earlier statement. The increase or decrease in the *amount* of the item is computed together with the *percent* of increase or decrease. When two statements are being compared, the earlier statement is used as the base for computing the amount and the percent of change.

Objective

Describe and illustrate the use of horizontal analysis in evaluating a company's performance and financial condition.

To illustrate, the horizontal analysis of two income statements for J. Holmes, Attorney-at-Law follows:

J. Holmes, Attorney-at-Law
Income Statements
For the Years Ended December 31

	Year 2	Year 1	Increase (Decrease)	Percent
Fees earned	$187,500	$150,000	$37,500	25.0%*
Operating expenses:				
Wages expense	$ 60,000	$ 45,000	$15,000	33.3%
Rent expense	15,000	12,000	3,000	25.0%
Utilities expense	12,500	9,000	3,500	38.9%
Supplies expense	2,700	3,000	(300)	(10.0)%
Miscellaneous expense	2,300	1,800	500	27.8%
Total operating expenses	$ 92,500	$ 70,800	$21,700	30.6%
Net income	$ 95,000	$ 79,200	$15,800	19.9%

*$37,500 ÷ $150,000

The horizontal analysis for J. Holmes, Attorney-at-Law, indicates both favorable and unfavorable trends. The increase in fees earned is a favorable trend, as is the decrease in supplies expense. Unfavorable trends include the increase in wages expense, utilities expense, and miscellaneous expense. These expenses increased the same as or faster than the increase in revenues, with total operating expenses increasing by 30.6%. Overall, net income increased by $15,800, or 19.9%, a favorable trend.

The significance of the various increases and decreases in the revenue and expense items should be investigated to see if operations could be further improved. For example, the increase in utilities expense of 38.9% was the result of renting additional office space for use by a part-time law student in performing paralegal services. This explains the increase in rent expense of 25.0% and the increase in wages expense of 33.3%. The increase in revenues of 25.0% reflects the fees generated by the new paralegal.

The preceding example illustrates how horizontal analysis can be useful in interpreting and analyzing the income statement. Horizontal analyses can also be performed for the balance sheet, the retained earnings statement, and the statement of cash flows.

To illustrate, horizontal analysis for two recent years of **Apple Inc.**'s statements of cash flows follows:

Apple Inc.
Statements of Cash Flows
(in millions)

	Year 2	Year1	Increase (Decrease)	Percent
Cash flows from operating activities	$ 59,713	$ 53,666	$ 6,047	11.3%
Cash flows used for investing activities	(22,579)	(33,774)	11,195	33.1%
Cash flows used for financing activities	(37,549)	(16,379)	(21,170)	(129.3)%
Net increase (decrease) in cash	$ (415)	$ 3,513	$ (3,928)	(111.8)%
Beginning of the year cash balance	14,259	10,746	3,513	32.7%
End of the year cash balance	$ 13,844	$ 14,259	$ (415)	(2.9)%

The horizontal analysis of the cash flows for Apple indicates an increase of cash flows from operating activities of 11.3%, which is a favorable change. Apple decreased the amount of cash used for investing activities, which increased cash by 33.1% from the prior year. In addition, Apple increased the amount of cash used for financing activities, which decreased cash by 129.3% from the prior year. These changes in cash from investing and financing activities are neither favorable nor unfavorable, but reflect management's financing and investing decisions. Overall, Apple decreased cash by $415 million in Year 2, compared to increasing cash by $3,513 million in Year 1.

Make a Decision | Horizontal Analysis

Vera Bradley, Inc. is a leading designer, producer, and retailer of fashion handbags, accessories, and travel items for women. Income statements for two recent years for Vera Bradley are as follows:

Vera Bradley, Inc.
Income Statements
(in thousands)

	Year 2	Year 1
Revenues....................................	$536,021	$541,148
Cost of sales	240,589	232,867
Gross profit.................................	$295,432	$308,281
Selling, general, and administrative expenses ..	205,957	204,412
Other income...............................	4,776	6,277
Operating income	$ 94,251	$110,146
Interest expense............................	382	679
Income before income taxes.................	$ 93,869	$109,467
Income tax expense........................	35,057	40,597
Net income................................	$ 58,812	$ 68,870

A. Prepare a horizontal analysis of the two income statements.

B. Assume you were a shareholder of Vera Bradley. Would you be inclined to view Vera Bradley's change in net income favorably or unfavorably?

C. Using the income statement information, why did the net income change during the two years?

Solution:

A.

	Year 2	Year 1	Increase (Decrease)	Percent
Revenues.....................................	$536,021	$541,148	$ (5,127)	(0.9)%
Cost of sales.................................	240,589	232,867	7,722	3.3%
Gross profit.................................	$295,432	$308,281	$(12,849)	(4.2)%
Selling, general, and administrative expenses	205,957	204,412	1,545	0.8%
Other income................................	4,776	6,277	(1,501)	(23.9)%
Operating income	$ 94,251	$110,146	$(15,895)	(14.4)%
Interest expense..............................	382	679	(297)	(43.7)%
Income before income taxes....................	$ 93,869	$109,467	$(15,598)	(14.2)%
Income tax expense...........................	35,057	40,597	(5,540)	(13.6)%
Net income...................................	$ 58,812	$ 68,870	$(10,058)	(14.6)%

B. The net income decreased between the two years by $10,058,000. This represented a 14.6% decrease between the two years [($10,058)÷$68,870]. Thus, as a shareholder, you would view this decrease in net income between the two years as unfavorable.

C. The net income decreased between the two years for a number of reasons. The revenues decreased by 0.9%, while the cost of sales increased by 3.3%. The increase in the cost of sales suggests that the price for purchased goods increased over the two years, and the company was not able to pass along the increases to customers. These factors combined to decrease gross profit by 4.2%. In addition, selling, general, and administrative expenses increased by 0.8%, while other income decreased by 23.9%. Together, all these changes caused operating income to decrease by 14.4%, which is close to the percentage decrease in net income.

Make a Decision

Let's Review

Chapter Summary

1. The simplest form of an account, a T account, has three parts: (1) a title, which is the name of the item recorded in the account; (2) a left side, called the debit side; and (3) a right side, called the credit side. Periodically, the debits in an account are added, the credits in the account are added, and the balance of the account is determined. The system of accounts that make up a ledger is called a chart of accounts.

2. Transactions are initially entered in a record called a journal. The rules of debit and credit for recording increases or decreases in accounts are shown in Exhibit 3. Each transaction is recorded so that the sum of the debits is always equal to the sum of the credits. The normal balance of an account is indicated by the side of the account (debit or credit) that receives the increases.

3. Transactions are journalized and posted to the ledger using the rules of debit and credit. The debits and credits for each journal entry are posted to the accounts in the order in which they occur in the journal.

4. A trial balance is prepared by listing the accounts from the ledger and their balances. The totals of the Debit column and Credit column of the trial balance must be equal. If the two totals are not equal, an error has occurred. Errors may occur even though the trial balance totals are equal. Such errors may require a correcting journal entry.

Key Terms

account (54)	double-entry accounting system (57)	retained earnings (56)
account receivable (67)	expenses (56)	revenues (56)
assets (56)	horizontal analysis (75)	rules of debit and credit (57)
balance of the account (55)	journal (59)	slide (73)
chart of accounts (55)	journal entry (60)	stockholders' equity (56)
common stock (56)	journalizing (60)	T account (55)
correcting journal entry (74)	ledger (55)	transposition (73)
credit (55)	liabilities (56)	trial balance (72)
debit (55)	normal balance of an account (58)	unadjusted trial balance (72)
dividends (56)	posting (63)	unearned revenue (65)

Practice

Multiple-Choice Questions

1. A debit may signify a(n):
   A. increase in an asset account.
   B. decrease in an asset account.
   C. increase in a liability account.
   D. increase in the stockholders' equity (common stock) account.

2. The type of account with a normal credit balance is:
   A. an asset.
   B. stockholders' equity (dividend).
   C. a revenue.
   D. an expense.

3. A debit balance in which of the following accounts would indicate a likely error?
   A. Accounts Receivable
   B. Cash
   C. Fees Earned
   D. Miscellaneous Expense

4. The receipt of cash from customers in payment of their accounts would be recorded by:
   A. a debit to Cash and a credit to Accounts Receivable.
   B. a debit to Accounts Receivable and a credit to Cash.
   C. a debit to Cash and a credit to Accounts Payable.
   D. a debit to Accounts Payable and a credit to Cash.

5. The form listing the titles and balances of the accounts in the ledger on a given date is the:
   A. income statement.
   B. balance sheet.
   C. retained earnings statement.
   D. trial balance.

Answers provided after Problem. Need more practice? Find additional multiple-choice questions, exercises, and problems in CengageNOWv2.

Exercises

SHOW ME HOW

1. Rules of debit and credit and normal balances
Obj. 2

State for each account whether it is likely to have (A) debit entries only, (B) credit entries only, or (C) both debit and credit entries. Also, indicate its normal balance.

1. Accounts Receivable
2. Commissions Earned
3. Notes Payable
4. Common Stock
5. Rent Revenue
6. Wages Expense

SHOW ME HOW

2. Journal entry for asset purchase
Obj. 2

Prepare a journal entry for the purchase of office equipment on October 27 for $32,750, paying $6,550 cash and the remainder on account.

SHOW ME HOW

3. Journal entry for fees earned
Obj. 3

Prepare a journal entry on March 16 for fees earned on account, $9,450.

SHOW ME HOW

4. Journal entry for dividends
Obj. 3

Prepare a journal entry on December 23 for dividends paid of $20,000.

SHOW ME HOW

5. Missing amount from an account
Obj. 3

On July 1, the cash account balance was $37,450. During July, cash payments totaled $115,860 and the July 31 balance was $29,600. Determine the cash receipts during July.

SHOW ME HOW

6. Trial balance errors
Obj. 4

For each of the following errors, considered individually, indicate whether the error would cause the trial balance totals to be unequal. If the error would cause the trial balance totals to be unequal, indicate whether the debit or credit total is higher and by how much.

A. The payment of an insurance premium of $5,400 for a three-year policy was debited to Prepaid Insurance for $5,400 and credited to Cash for $4,500.

B. A payment of $270 on account was debited to Accounts Payable for $720 and credited to Cash for $720.

C. A purchase of supplies on account for $1,600 was debited to Supplies for $1,600 and debited to Accounts Payable for $1,600.

SHOW ME HOW

7. Correcting entries
Obj.4

The following errors took place in journalizing and posting transactions:

A. Rent expense of $4,650 paid for the current month was recorded as a debit to Miscellaneous Expense and a credit to Rent Expense.

B. The payment of $3,700 from a customer on account was recorded as a debit to Cash and a credit to Accounts Payable.

Journalize the entries to correct the errors. Omit explanations.

Answers provided after Problem. Need more practice? Find additional multiple-choice questions, exercises, and problems in CengageNOWv2.

Problem

J.F. Outz, M.D., organized Hearts Inc. three years ago to practice cardiology. During April 2017, Hearts Inc. completed the following transactions:

Apr. 1. Paid office rent for April, $800.

3. Purchased equipment on account, $2,100.

5. Received cash on account from patients, $3,150.

8. Purchased X-ray film and other supplies on account, $245.

9. One of the items of equipment purchased on April 3 was defective. It was returned with the permission of the supplier, who agreed to reduce the account for the amount charged for the item, $325.

12. Paid cash to creditors on account, $1,250.

17. Paid cash for renewal of a six-month property insurance policy, $370.

20. Discovered that the balances of the cash account and the accounts payable account as of April 1 were overstated by $200. A payment of that amount to a creditor in March had not been recorded. Journalize the $200 payment as of April 20.

24. Paid cash for laboratory analysis, $545.

27. Paid dividends, $1,250.

30. Recorded the cash received in payment of services (on a cash basis) to patients during April, $1,720.

30. Paid salaries of receptionist and nurses, $1,725.

30. Paid various utility expenses, $360.

30. Recorded fees charged to patients on account for services performed in April, $5,145.

30. Paid miscellaneous expenses, $132.

Hearts Inc.'s account titles, numbers, and balances as of April 1 (all normal balances) are listed as follows: Cash, 11, $4,123; Accounts Receivable, 12, $6,725; Supplies, 13, $290; Prepaid Insurance, 14, $465; Equipment, 18, $19,745; Accounts Payable, 22, $765; Common Stock, 31, $10,000; Retained Earnings, 32, $20,583; Dividends, 33, $0; Professional Fees, 41, $0; Salary Expense, 51, $0; Rent Expense, 53, $0; Laboratory Expense, 55, $0; Utilities Expense, 56, $0; Miscellaneous Expense, 59, $0.

Instructions

1. Open a ledger of standard four-column accounts for Hearts Inc. as of April 1. Enter the balances in the appropriate balance columns and place a check mark (✓) in the Posting Reference column. (*Hint:* Verify the equality of the debit and credit balances in the ledger before proceeding with the next instruction.)

2. Journalize each transaction in a two-column journal.

3. Post the journal to the ledger, extending the month-end balances to the appropriate balance columns after each posting.

4. Prepare an unadjusted trial balance as of April 30.

Need more practice? Find additional multiple-choice questions, exercises, and problems in CengageNOWv2.

Answers

Multiple-Choice Questions

1. **A** A debit may signify an increase in an asset account (answer A) or a decrease in a liability or stockholders' equity (common stock) account. A credit may signify a decrease in an asset account (answer B) or an increase in a liability or stockholders' equity (common stock) account (answers C and D).

2. **C** Liability, stockholders' equity (common stock), and revenue (answer C) accounts have normal credit balances. Asset (answer A), stockholders' equity (dividend) (answer B), and expense (answer D) accounts have normal debit balances.

3. **C** Accounts Receivable (answer A), Cash (answer B), and Miscellaneous Expense (answer D) would all normally have debit balances. Fees Earned should normally have a credit balance. Hence, a debit balance in Fees Earned (answer C) would indicate a likely error in the recording process.

4. **A** The receipt of cash from customers on account debits (increases) the asset Cash and credits (decreases) the asset Accounts Receivable, as indicated by answer A. Answer B has the debit and credit reversed, and answers C and D involve transactions with creditors (accounts payable) and not customers (accounts receivable).

5. **D** The trial balance (answer D) is a listing of the balances and the titles of the accounts in the ledger on a given date, so that the equality of the debits and credits in the ledger can be verified. The income statement (answer A) is a summary of revenue and expenses for a period of time. The balance sheet (answer B) is a presentation of the assets, liabilities, and stockholders' equity on a given date. The retained earnings statement (answer C) is a summary of the changes in retained earnings for a period of time.

Exercises

1.

    1. Debit and credit entries, normal debit balance
    2. Credit entries only, normal credit balance
    3. Debit and credit entries, normal credit balance
    4. Credit entries only, normal credit balance
    5. Credit entries only, normal credit balance
    6. Debit entries only, normal debit balance

2.

Oct. 27	Office Equipment	32,750	
	Cash		6,550
	Accounts Payable		26,200

3.

Mar. 16	Accounts Receivable	9,450	
	Fees Earned		9,450

4.

Dec. 23	Dividends	20,000	
	Cash		20,000

5. Using the following T account, solve for the amount of cash receipts (indicated by ? below).

Cash			
July 1 Bal.	37,450	115,860	Cash payments
Cash receipts	?		
July 31 Bal.	29,600		

$29,600 = $37,450 + Cash receipts − $115,860
Cash receipts = $29,600 + $115,860 − $37,450 = $108,010

6.

    A. The totals are unequal. The debit total is higher by $900 ($5,400 − $4,500).
    B. The totals are equal because both the debit and credit entries were journalized and posted for $720.
    C. The totals are unequal. The debit total is higher by $3,200 ($1,600 + $1,600).

7.

A.

Rent Expense	4,650	
Miscellaneous Expense		4,650

Rent Expense	4,650	
Cash		4,650

Note: The first entry in (A) reverses the incorrect entry, and the second entry records the correct entry. These two entries could also be combined into one entry as shown below; however, preparing two entries would make it easier for someone to understand later what happened and why the entries were necessary.

Rent Expense	9,300	
Miscellaneous Expense		4,650
Cash		4,650

B.

Accounts Payable	3,700	
Accounts Receivable		3,700

Need more help? Watch step-by-step videos of how to compute answers to these Exercises in CengageNOWv2.

Problem

1., 2., and 3.

Journal				Page 27
Date	**Description**	**Post. Ref.**	**Debit**	**Credit**
2017				
Apr. 1	Rent Expense	53	800	
	Cash	11		800
	Paid office rent for April.			
3	Equipment	18	2,100	
	Accounts Payable	22		2,100
	Purchased equipment			
	on account.			
5	Cash	11	3,150	
	Accounts Receivable	12		3,150
	Received cash on			
	account.			
8	Supplies	13	245	
	Accounts Payable	22		245
	Purchased supplies.			
9	Accounts Payable	22	325	
	Equipment	18		325
	Returned defective			
	equipment.			
12	Accounts Payable	22	1,250	
	Cash	11		1,250
	Paid creditors on			
	account.			
17	Prepaid Insurance	14	370	
	Cash	11		370
	Renewed six-month			
	property policy.			
20	Accounts Payable	22	200	
	Cash	11		200
	Recorded March			
	payment to creditor.			

Journal				Page 28
Date	**Description**	**Post. Ref.**	**Debit**	**Credit**
2017				
Apr. 24	Laboratory Expense	55	545	
	Cash	11		545
	Paid for laboratory			
	analysis.			
27	Dividends	33	1,250	
	Cash	11		1,250
	Paid dividends.			
30	Cash	11	1,720	
	Professional Fees	41		1,720
	Received fees from			
	patients.			
30	Salary Expense	51	1,725	
	Cash	11		1,725
	Paid salaries.			
30	Utilities Expense	56	360	
	Cash	11		360
	Paid utilities.			
30	Accounts Receivable	12	5,145	
	Professional Fees	41		5,145
	Recorded fees earned			
	on account.			
30	Miscellaneous Expense	59	132	
	Cash	11		132
	Paid expenses.			

Account *Cash*   Account No. *11*

Date	Item	Post. Ref.	Debit	Credit	Balance Debit	Balance Credit
2017						
Apr. 1	Balance	✓			4,123	
1		27		800	3,323	
5		27	3,150		6,473	
12		27		1,250	5,223	
17		27		370	4,853	
20		27		200	4,653	
24		28		545	4,108	
27		28		1,250	2,858	
30		28	1,720		4,578	
30		28		1,725	2,853	
30		28		360	2,493	
30		28		132	2,361	

Account *Accounts Receivable*   Account No. *12*

Date	Item	Post. Ref.	Debit	Credit	Balance Debit	Balance Credit
2017						
Apr. 1	Balance	✓			6,725	
5		27		3,150	3,575	
30		28	5,145		8,720	

Account *Supplies*   Account No. *13*

Date	Item	Post. Ref.	Debit	Credit	Balance Debit	Balance Credit
2017						
Apr. 1	Balance	✓			290	
8		27	245		535	

Account *Prepaid Insurance*   Account No. *14*

Date	Item	Post. Ref.	Debit	Credit	Balance Debit	Balance Credit
2017						
Apr. 1	Balance	✓			465	
17		27	370		835	

Account *Equipment*   Account No. *18*

Date	Item	Post. Ref.	Debit	Credit	Balance Debit	Balance Credit
2017						
Apr. 1	Balance	✓			19,745	
3		27	2,100		21,845	
9		27		325	21,520	

Account *Accounts Payable*   Account No. *22*

Date	Item	Post. Ref.	Debit	Credit	Balance Debit	Balance Credit
2017						
Apr. 1	Balance	✓				765
3		27		2,100		2,865
8		27		245		3,110
9		27	325			2,785
12		27	1,250			1,535
20		27	200			1,335

Account *Common Stock*   Account No. *31*

Date	Item	Post. Ref.	Debit	Credit	Balance Debit	Balance Credit
2017						
Apr. 1	Balance	✓				10,000

Account *Retained Earnings*   Account No. *32*

Date	Item	Post. Ref.	Debit	Credit	Balance Debit	Balance Credit
2017						
Apr. 1	Balance	✓				20,583

Account *Dividends*   Account No. *33*

Date	Item	Post. Ref.	Debit	Credit	Balance Debit	Balance Credit
2017						
Apr. 27		28	1,250		1,250	

Account *Professional Fees*   Account No. *41*

Date	Item	Post. Ref.	Debit	Credit	Balance Debit	Balance Credit
2017						
Apr. 30		28		1,720		1,720
30		28		5,145		6,865

Account *Salary Expense*   Account No. *51*

Date	Item	Post. Ref.	Debit	Credit	Balance Debit	Balance Credit
2017						
Apr. 30		28	1,725		1,725	

(Continued)

Account Rent Expense						Account No. 53

Date	Item	Post. Ref.	Debit	Credit	Balance Debit	Balance Credit
2017 Apr. 1		27	800		800	

Account Utilities Expense						Account No. 56

Date	Item	Post. Ref.	Debit	Credit	Balance Debit	Balance Credit
2017 Apr. 30		28	360		360	

Account Laboratory Expense						Account No. 55

Date	Item	Post. Ref.	Debit	Credit	Balance Debit	Balance Credit
2017 Apr. 24		28	545		545	

Account Miscellaneous Expense						Account No. 59

Date	Item	Post. Ref.	Debit	Credit	Balance Debit	Balance Credit
2017 Apr. 30		28	132		132	

4.

J. F. Outz, M.D.
Unadjusted Trial Balance
April 30, 2017

	Account No.	Debit Balances	Credit Balances
Cash	11	2,361	
Accounts Receivable	12	8,720	
Supplies	13	535	
Prepaid Insurance	14	835	
Equipment	18	21,520	
Accounts Payable	22		1,335
Common Stock	31		10,000
Retained Earnings	32		20,583
Dividends	33	1,250	
Professional Fees	41		6,865
Salary Expense	51	1,725	
Rent Expense	53	800	
Laboratory Expense	55	545	
Utilities Expense	56	360	
Miscellaneous Expense	59	132	
		38,783	38,783

Discussion Questions

1. What is the difference between an account and a ledger?

2. Do the terms *debit* and *credit* signify increase or decrease or can they signify either? Explain.

3. McIntyre Company adheres to a policy of depositing all cash receipts in a bank account and making all payments by check. The cash account as of December 31 has a credit balance of $1,850, and there is no undeposited cash on hand. (A) Assuming no errors occurred during journalizing or posting, what caused this unusual balance? (B) Is the $1,850 credit balance in the cash account an asset, a liability, stockholders' equity, a revenue, or an expense?

4. eCatalog Services Company performed services in October for a specific customer, for a fee of $7,890. Payment was received the following November. (A) Was the revenue earned in October or November? (B) What accounts should be debited and credited in (1) October and (2) November?

5. If the two totals of a trial balance are equal, does it mean that there are no errors in the accounting records? Explain.

6. Assume that a trial balance is prepared with an account balance of $8,900 listed as $9,800 and an account balance of $1,000 listed as $100. Identify the transposition and the slide.

7. Assume that when a purchase of supplies of $2,650 for cash was recorded, both the debit and the credit were journalized and posted as $2,560. (A) Would this error cause the trial balance to be out of balance? (B) Would the trial balance be out of balance if the $2,650 entry had been journalized correctly but the credit to Cash had been posted as $2,560?

8. Assume that Muscular Consulting erroneously recorded the payment of $7,500 of dividends as a debit to Salary Expense. (A) How would this error affect the equality of the trial balance? (B) How would this error affect the income statement, retained earnings statement, and balance sheet?

9. Assume that Sunshine Realty Co. borrowed $300,000 from Columbia First Bank and Trust. In recording the transaction, Sunshine erroneously recorded the receipt as a debit to Cash, $300,000, and a credit to Fees Earned, $300,000. (A) How would this error affect the equality of the trial balance? (B) How would this error affect the income statement, retained earnings statement, and balance sheet?

10. Checking accounts are one of the most common forms of deposits for banks. Assume that Surety Storage has a checking account at Ada Savings Bank. What type of account (asset, liability, stockholders' equity, revenue, expense, dividends) does the account balance of $11,375 represent from the viewpoint of (A) Surety Storage and (B) Ada Savings Bank?

Basic Exercises

SHOW ME HOW

BE 2-1 Rules of debit and credit and normal balances   Obj. 2

State for each account whether it is likely to have (A) debit entries only, (B) credit entries only, or (C) both debit and credit entries. Also, indicate its normal balance.

1. Accounts Payable
2. Cash
3. Dividends
4. Miscellaneous Expense
5. Insurance Expense
6. Fees Earned

SHOW ME HOW

BE 2-2 Journal entry for asset purchase   Obj. 2

Prepare a journal entry for the purchase of office supplies on March 9 for $1,775, paying $275 cash and the remainder on account.

SHOW ME HOW

BE 2-3 Journal entry for fees earned   Obj. 3

Prepare a journal entry on August 13 for cash received for services rendered, $9,000.

SHOW ME HOW

BE 2-4 Journal entry for dividends   Obj. 3

Prepare a journal entry on June 30 for dividends of $11,500.

SHOW ME HOW

BE 2-5 Missing amount from an account   Obj. 3

On August 1, the supplies account balance was $1,025. During August, supplies of $3,110 were purchased, and $1,324 of supplies were on hand as of August 31. Determine supplies expense for August.

SHOW ME HOW

BE 2-6 Trial balance errors   Obj. 4

For each of the following errors, considered individually, indicate whether the error would cause the trial balance totals to be unequal. If the error would cause the trial balance totals to be unequal, indicate whether the debit or credit total is higher and by how much.

A. The payment of cash for the purchase of office equipment of $12,900 was debited to Land for $12,900 and credited to Cash for $12,900.

B. The payment of $1,840 on account was debited to Accounts Payable for $184 and credited to Cash for $1,840.

C. The receipt of cash on account of $3,800 was recorded as a debit to Cash for $8,300 and a credit to Accounts Receivable for $3,800.

SHOW ME HOW

BE 2-7 Correcting entries   Obj. 4

The following errors took place in journalizing and posting transactions:

A. The receipt of $8,400 for services rendered was recorded as a debit to Accounts Receivable and a credit to Fees Earned.

B. The purchase of supplies of $2,500 on account was recorded as a debit to Office Equipment and a credit to Supplies.

Journalize the entries to correct the errors. Omit explanations.

Exercises

REAL WORLD

EX 2-1 Chart of accounts   Obj. 1

The following accounts appeared in recent financial statements of **Delta Air Lines**:

Accounts Payable	Flight Equipment
Advanced Payments for Equipment	Frequent Flyer (Obligations)
Air Traffic Liability	Fuel Inventory
Aircraft Fuel (Expense)	Landing Fees (Expense)
Aircraft Maintenance (Expense)	Parts and Supplies Inventories
Aircraft Rent (Expense)	Passenger Commissions (Expense)
Cargo Revenue	Passenger Revenue
Cash	Prepaid Expenses
Contract Carrier Arrangements (Expense)	Taxes Payable

Identify each account as either a balance sheet account or an income statement account. For each balance sheet account, identify it as an asset, a liability, or stockholders' equity. For each income statement account, identify it as a revenue or an expense.

EX 2-2 Chart of accounts   Obj. 1

Innerscape Interiors is owned and operated by Jackie Vargo, an interior decorator. In the ledger of Innerscape Interiors, the first digit of the account number indicates its major account classification (1—assets, 2—liabilities, 3—stockholders' equity, 4—revenues, 5—expenses). The second digit of the account number indicates the specific account within each of the preceding major account classifications.

Match each account number with its most likely account in the list that follows. The account numbers are 11, 12, 13, 21, 31, 32, 33, 41, 51, 52, and 53.

Accounts Payable	Land
Accounts Receivable	Miscellaneous Expense
Cash	Retained Earnings
Common Stock	Supplies Expense
Dividends	Wages Expense
Fees Earned	

EX 2-3 Chart of accounts

Obj. 1

LeadCo School is a newly organized business that teaches people how to inspire and influence others. The list of accounts to be opened in the general ledger is as follows:

Accounts Payable	Prepaid Insurance
Accounts Receivable	Rent Expense
Cash	Retained Earnings
Common Stock	Supplies
Dividends	Supplies Expense
Equipment	Unearned Rent
Fees Earned	Wages Expense
Miscellaneous Expense	

List the accounts in the order in which they should appear in the ledger of LeadCo School and assign account numbers. Each account number is to have two digits: the first digit is to indicate the major classification (1 for assets, etc.), and the second digit is to identify the specific account within each major classification (11 for Cash, etc.).

EX 2-4 Rules of debit and credit

Obj. 1, 2

The following table summarizes the rules of debit and credit. For each of the items A through L, indicate whether the proper answer is a debit or a credit.

	Increase	Decrease	Normal Balance
Balance sheet accounts:			
Asset	A	B	Debit
Liability	C	Debit	D
Stockholders' equity:			
Common Stock	Credit	E	F
Retained Earnings	G	H	Credit
Dividends	Debit	Credit	I
Income statement accounts:			
Revenue	J	K	Credit
Expense	L	Credit	Debit

EX 2-5 Normal entries for accounts

Obj. 2

During the month, Gates Labs Co. has a substantial number of transactions affecting each of the following accounts. State for each account whether it is likely to have (A) debit entries only, (B) credit entries only, or (C) both debit and credit entries.

1. Accounts Payable
2. Accounts Receivable
3. Cash
4. Fees Earned
5. Insurance Expense
6. Dividends
7. Utilities Expense

EX 2-6 Normal balances of accounts

Obj. 1, 2

Identify each of the following accounts of Kaiser Services Co. as asset, liability, stockholders' equity, revenue, or expense, and state in each case whether the normal balance is a debit or a credit:

A. Accounts Payable
B. Accounts Receivable
C. Cash
D. Common Stock
E. Dividends
F. Fees Earned
G. Office Equipment
H. Rent Expense
I. Supplies
J. Wages Expense

EX 2-7 Transactions   Obj. 2

Zenith Consulting Co. has the following accounts in its ledger: Cash, Accounts Receivable, Supplies, Office Equipment, Accounts Payable, Common Stock, Retained Earnings, Dividends, Fees Earned, Rent Expense, Advertising Expense, Utilities Expense, Miscellaneous Expense.

Journalize the following selected transactions for March 2018 in a two-column journal. Journal entry explanations may be omitted.

Mar. 1. Paid rent for the month, $4,000.
     3. Paid advertising expense, $1,350.
     5. Paid cash for supplies, $1,800.
     6. Purchased office equipment on account, $11,500.
    10. Received cash from customers on account, $8,600.
    15. Paid creditor on account, $3,180.
    27. Paid cash for miscellaneous expenses, $700.
    30. Paid telephone bill for the month, $550.
    31. Fees earned and billed to customers for the month, $37,200.
    31. Paid electricity bill for the month, $830.
    31. Paid dividends, $2,000.

EX 2-8 Journalizing and posting   Obj. 2, 3

On October 3, 2018, Regal Company purchased $3,600 of supplies on account. In Regal's chart of accounts, the supplies account is No. 15, and the accounts payable account is No. 21.

A. Journalize the October 3, 2018, transaction on page 91 of Regal Company's two-column journal. Include an explanation of the entry.

B. Prepare a four-column account for Supplies. Enter a debit balance of $770 as of October 1, 2018. Place a check mark (✓) in the Posting Reference column.

C. Prepare a four-column account for Accounts Payable. Enter a credit balance of $26,200 as of October 1, 2018. Place a check mark (✓) in the Posting Reference column.

D. Post the October 3, 2018, transaction to the accounts.

E. ▬▬▬▶ Do the rules of debit and credit apply to all companies?

EX 2-9 Transactions and T accounts   Obj. 2, 3

The following selected transactions were completed during March of the current year:

1. Billed customers for fees earned, $54,100.
2. Purchased supplies on account, $1,250.
3. Received cash from customers on account, $43,800.
4. Paid creditors on account, $600.

A. Journalize these transactions in a two-column journal, using the appropriate number to identify the transactions. Journal entry explanations may be omitted.

B. Post the entries prepared in (A) to the following T accounts: Cash, Supplies, Accounts Receivable, Accounts Payable, Fees Earned. To the left of each amount posted in the accounts, place the appropriate number to identify the transaction.

C. ▬▬▬▶ Assume that the unadjusted trial balance on March 31 shows a credit balance for Accounts Receivable. Does this credit balance mean an error has occurred?

EX 2-10 Cash account balance   Obj. 1, 2, 3

During the month, Warwick Co. received $515,000 in cash and paid out $375,000 in cash.

A. ▬▬▬▶ Does this information indicate that Warwick Co. had net income of $140,000 during the month? Explain.

B. If the balance of the cash account is $200,000 at the end of the month, what was the cash balance at the beginning of the month?

EX 2-11 Account balances

Obj. 1, 2, 3

SHOW ME HOW

A. During February, $186,500 was paid to creditors on account, and purchases on account were $201,400. Assuming the February 28 balance of Accounts Payable was $59,900, determine the account balance on February 1.

B. On October 1, the accounts receivable account balance was $115,800. During October, $449,600 was collected from customers on account. Assuming the October 31 balance was $130,770, determine the fees billed to customers on account during October.

C. On April 1, the cash account balance was $46,220. During April, cash receipts totaled $248,600 and the April 30 balance was $56,770. Determine the cash payments made during April.

EX 2-12 Retained earnings account balance

Obj. 1, 2

SHOW ME HOW

As of January 1, Retained Earnings had a credit balance of $314,000. During the year, dividends totaled $10,000, and the business incurred a net loss of $320,000.

A. Compute the balance of Retained Earnings as of the end of the year.

B. ━━━▶ Assuming that there have been no recording errors, will the balance sheet prepared at December 31 balance? Explain.

EX 2-13 Identifying transactions

Obj. 1, 2

SHOW ME HOW

Napa Tours Co. is a travel agency. The nine transactions recorded by Napa Tours during April 2018, its first month of operations, are indicated in the following T accounts:

	Cash				Equipment			Dividends	
(1)	50,000	(2)	3,400	(3)	15,000		(9)	1,000	
(7)	8,700	(3)	5,000						
		(4)	4,850						
		(6)	2,500						
		(9)	1,000						

	Accounts Receivable				Accounts Payable			Service Revenue	
(5)	18,200	(7)	8,700	(6)	2,500	(3)	10,000	(5)	18,200

	Supplies				Common Stock			Operating Expenses	
(2)	3,400	(8)	1,100			(1)	50,000	(4)	4,850
								(8)	1,100

Indicate for each debit and each credit: (A) whether an asset, liability, stockholders' equity, dividend, revenue, or expense account was affected and (B) whether the account was increased (+) or decreased (−). Present your answers in the following form, with transaction (1) given as an example:

	Account Debited		Account Credited	
Transaction	Type	Effect	Type	Effect
(1)	asset	+	stockholders' equity	+

EX 2-14 Journal entries

Obj. 1, 2

SHOW ME HOW

Based upon the T accounts in Exercise 2-13, prepare the nine journal entries from which the postings were made. Journal entry explanations may be omitted.

EX 2-15 Trial balance

Obj. 4

Based upon the data presented in Exercise 2-13, (A) prepare an unadjusted trial balance, listing the accounts in their proper order. (B) Based upon the unadjusted trial balance, determine the net income or net loss.

SHOW ME HOW   EXCEL TEMPLATE

EX 2-16 Trial balance

✔ Total of Credit column:
$3,260,000

SHOW ME HOW

Obj. 4

The accounts in the ledger of Atlantic Furniture Company as of July 2018 are listed in alphabetical order as follows. All accounts have normal balances. The balance of the cash account has been intentionally omitted.

Accounts Payable	$ 92,400	Notes Payable	$ 25,000
Accounts Receivable	483,600	Prepaid Insurance	21,600
Cash	?	Rent Expense	140,000
Common Stock	75,000	Retained Earnings	311,600
Dividends	24,000	Supplies	3,975
Fees Earned	2,750,000	Supplies Expense	11,200
Insurance Expense	9,000	Unearned Rent	6,000
Land	50,000	Utilities Expense	49,100
Miscellaneous Expense	10,200	Wages Expense	2,250,000

Prepare an unadjusted trial balance, listing the accounts in their normal order and inserting the missing figure for cash.

EX 2-17 Effect of errors on trial balance

Obj. 4

Indicate which of the following errors, each considered individually, would cause the trial balance totals to be unequal:

A. A fee of $21,000 earned and due from a client was not debited to Accounts Receivable or credited to a revenue account, because the cash had not been received.

B. A receipt of $11,300 from an account receivable was journalized and posted as a debit of $11,300 to Cash and a credit of $11,300 to Fees Earned.

C. A payment of $4,950 to a creditor was posted as a debit of $4,950 to Accounts Payable and a debit of $4,950 to Cash.

D. A payment of $5,000 for equipment purchased was posted as a debit of $500 to Equipment and a credit of $500 to Cash.

E. Payment of cash dividends of $19,000 was journalized and posted as a debit of $1,900 to Salary Expense and a credit of $19,000 to Cash.

Indicate which of the preceding errors would require a correcting entry.

EX 2-18 Errors in trial balance

✔ Total of Credit column:
$525,000

Obj. 4

The following preliminary unadjusted trial balance of Ranger Co., a sports ticket agency, does not balance:

Ranger Co.
Unadjusted Trial Balance
August 31, 2018

	Debit Balances	Credit Balances
Cash	77,600	
Accounts Receivable....................................	37,750	
Prepaid Insurance		12,000
Equipment..	19,000	
Accounts Payable		29,100
Unearned Rent..		10,800
Common Stock..	40,000	
Retained Earnings......................................	70,000	
Dividends	13,000	
Service Revenue		385,000
Wages Expense		213,000
Advertising Expense....................................	16,350	
Miscellaneous Expense		18,400
	273,700	668,300

When the ledger and other records are reviewed, you discover the following: (1) the debits and credits in the cash account total $77,600 and $62,100, respectively; (2) a billing of $9,000 to a customer on account was not posted to the accounts receivable account; (3) a payment of $4,500 made to a creditor on account was not posted to the accounts payable account;

(4) the balance of the unearned rent account is $5,400; (5) the correct balance of the equipment account is $190,000; and (6) each account has a normal balance.

Prepare a corrected unadjusted trial balance.

EX 2-19 Effect of errors on trial balance

Obj. 4

The following errors occurred in posting from a two-column journal:

1. A credit of $6,000 to Accounts Payable was not posted.
2. An entry debiting Accounts Receivable and crediting Fees Earned for $5,300 was not posted.
3. A debit of $2,700 to Accounts Payable was posted as a credit.
4. A debit of $480 to Supplies was posted twice.
5. A debit of $3,600 to Cash was posted to Miscellaneous Expense.
6. A credit of $780 to Cash was posted as $870.
7. A debit of $12,620 to Wages Expense was posted as $12,260.

Considering each case individually (i.e., assuming that no other errors had occurred), indicate: (A) by "yes" or "no" whether the trial balance would be out of balance; (B) if answer to (A) is "yes," the amount by which the trial balance totals would differ; and (C) whether the Debit or Credit column of the trial balance would have the larger total. Answers should be presented in the following form, with error (1) given as an example:

	(A)	(B)	(C)
Error	Out of Balance	Difference	Larger Total
1.	yes	$6,000	debit

EX 2-20 Errors in trial balance

Obj. 4

✔ Total of Credit column: $1,450,000

SHOW ME HOW

Identify the errors in the following trial balance. All accounts have normal balances.

Ensemble Co.
Unadjusted Trial Balance
For the Year Ending December 31, 2018

	Debit Balances	Credit Balances
Cash	42,900	
Accounts Receivable...		123,500
Prepaid Insurance	27,000	
Equipment...	300,000	
Accounts Payable	52,000	
Salaries Payable...		4,800
Common Stock		40,000
Retained Earnings		137,200
Dividends		5,000
Service Revenue		1,216,000
Salary Expense...	660,000	
Advertising Expense...		275,000
Miscellaneous Expense	16,600	
	1,801,500	1,801,500

EX 2-21 Entries to correct errors

Obj. 4

SHOW ME HOW

The following errors took place in journalizing and posting transactions:

A. Insurance of $18,000 paid for the current year was recorded as a debit to Insurance Expense and a credit to Prepaid Insurance.
B. Dividends of $10,000 were recorded as a debit to Wages Expense and a credit to Cash.

Journalize the entries to correct the errors. Omit explanations.

EX 2-22 Entries to correct errors

Obj. 4

SHOW ME HOW

The following errors took place in journalizing and posting transactions:

A. Cash of $8,800 received on account was recorded as a debit to Fees Earned and a credit to Cash.
B. A $1,760 purchase of supplies for cash was recorded as a debit to Supplies Expense and a credit to Accounts Payable.

Journalize the entries to correct the errors. Omit explanations.

Problems: Series A

PR 2-1A   Entries into T accounts and trial balance

Obj. 1, 2, 3, 4

✔ 3. Total of Debit column: $100,525

Marjorie Knaus, an architect, organized Knaus Architects on January 1, 2018. During the month, Knaus Architects completed the following transactions:

A.   Issued common stock to Marjorie Knaus in exchange for $30,000.
B.   Paid January rent for office and workroom, $2,500.
C.   Purchased used automobile for $28,500, paying $6,000 cash and giving a note payable for the remainder.
D.   Purchased office and computer equipment on account, $8,000.
E.   Paid cash for supplies, $2,100.
F.   Paid cash for annual insurance policies, $3,600.
G.   Received cash from client for plans delivered, $9,000.
H.   Paid cash for miscellaneous expenses, $2,600.
I.   Paid cash to creditors on account, $4,000.
J.   Paid installment due on note payable, $1,875.
K.   Received invoice for blueprint service, due in February, $5,500.
L.   Recorded fees earned on plans delivered, payment to be received in February, $31,400.
M.   Paid salary of assistants, $6,000.
N.   Paid gas, oil, and repairs on automobile for January, $1,300.

Instructions

1.   Record these transactions directly in the following T accounts, without journalizing: Cash, Accounts Receivable, Supplies, Prepaid Insurance, Automobiles, Equipment, Notes Payable, Accounts Payable, Common Stock, Professional Fees, Salary Expense, Blueprint Expense, Rent Expense, Automobile Expense, Miscellaneous Expense. To the left of the amount entered in the accounts, place the appropriate letter to identify the transaction.

2.   Determine account balances of the T accounts. Accounts containing a single entry only (such as Prepaid Insurance) do not need a balance.

3.   Prepare an unadjusted trial balance for Knaus Architects as of January 31, 2018.

4.   Determine the net income or net loss for January.

PR 2-2A   Journal entries and trial balance

Obj. 1, 2, 3, 4

✔ 4. C. $6,770

On October 1, 2018, Jay Crowley established Affordable Realty, which completed the following transactions during the month:

A.   Jay Crowley transferred cash from a personal bank account to an account to be used for the business in exchange for common stock, $40,000.
B.   Paid rent on office and equipment for the month, $4,800.
C.   Purchased supplies on account, $2,150.
D.   Paid creditor on account, $1,100.
E.   Earned sales commissions, receiving cash, $18,750.
F.   Paid automobile expenses (including rental charge) for month, $1,580, and miscellaneous expenses, $800.
G.   Paid office salaries, $3,500.
H.   Determined that the cost of supplies used was $1,300.
I.   Paid dividends, $1,500.

SHOW ME HOW   EXCEL TEMPLATE

GENERAL LEDGER

Instructions

1.   Journalize entries for transactions (A) through (I), using the following account titles: Cash, Supplies, Accounts Payable, Common Stock, Dividends, Sales Commissions, Rent Expense, Office Salaries Expense, Automobile Expense, Supplies Expense, Miscellaneous Expense. Explanations may be omitted.

2. Prepare T accounts, using the account titles in (1). Post the journal entries to these accounts, placing the appropriate letter to the left of each amount to identify the transactions. Determine the account balances after all posting is complete. Accounts containing only a single entry do not need a balance.

3. Prepare an unadjusted trial balance as of October 31, 2018.

4. Determine the following:

   A. Amount of total revenue recorded in the ledger.

   B. Amount of total expenses recorded in the ledger.

   C. Amount of net income for October.

5. Determine the increase or decrease in retained earnings for October.

PR 2-3A Journal entries and trial balance

Obj. 1, 2, 3, 4

SHOW ME HOW

EXCEL TEMPLATE

GENERAL LEDGER

✔ 3. Total of Credit column: $111,450

On November 1, 2018, Kris Lehman established an interior decorating business, Modern Designs. During the month, Kris completed the following transactions related to the business:

Nov. 1. Kris transferred cash from a personal bank account to an account to be used for the business in exchange for common stock, $36,000.

1. Paid rent for period of November 1 to end of month, $4,000.

6. Purchased office equipment on account, $16,000.

8. Purchased a truck for $43,000 paying $4,300 cash and giving a note payable for the remainder.

10. Purchased supplies for cash, $1,860.

12. Received cash for job completed, $8,000.

15. Paid annual premiums on property and casualty insurance, $2,400.

23. Recorded jobs completed on account and sent invoices to customers, $15,500.

24. Received an invoice for truck expenses, to be paid in November, $1,250.

Enter the following transactions on Page 2 of the two-column journal:

29. Paid utilities expense, $3,660.

29. Paid miscellaneous expenses, $1,700.

30. Received cash from customers on account, $10,500.

30. Paid wages of employees, $4,750.

30. Paid creditor a portion of the amount owed for equipment purchased on November 6, $4,000.

30. Paid dividends, $1,600.

Instructions

1. Journalize each transaction in a two-column journal beginning on Page 1, referring to the following chart of accounts in selecting the accounts to be debited and credited. (Do not insert the account numbers in the journal at this time.) Explanations may be omitted.

11 Cash	31 Common Stock
12 Accounts Receivable	33 Dividends
13 Supplies	41 Fees Earned
14 Prepaid Insurance	51 Wages Expense
16 Equipment	53 Rent Expense
18 Truck	54 Utilities Expense
21 Notes Payable	55 Truck Expense
22 Accounts Payable	59 Miscellaneous Expense

2. Post the journal to a ledger of four-column accounts, inserting appropriate posting references as each item is posted. Extend the balances to the appropriate balance columns after each transaction is posted.

3. Prepare an unadjusted trial balance for Modern Designs as of November 30, 2018.

4. Determine the excess of revenues over expenses for November.

5. ➤ Can you think of any reason why the amount determined in (4) might not be the net income for November?

PR 2-4A   Journal entries and trial balance   Obj. 1, 2, 3, 4

✔ **4. Total of Debit column:** **$532,525**

GENERAL LEDGER

Elite Realty acts as an agent in buying, selling, renting, and managing real estate. The unadjusted trial balance on March 31, 2018, follows:

Elite Realty
Unadjusted Trial Balance
March 31, 2018

	Account No.	Debit Balances	Credit Balances
Cash	11	26,300	
Accounts Receivable.....................................	12	61,500	
Prepaid Insurance	13	3,000	
Office Supplies..	14	1,800	
Land	16	—	
Accounts Payable	21		14,000
Unearned Rent..	22		—
Notes Payable...	23		—
Common Stock...	31		10,000
Retained Earnings.......................................	32		36,000
Dividends	33	2,000	
Fees Earned...	41		240,000
Salary and Commission Expense.........................	51	148,200	
Rent Expense	52	30,000	
Advertising Expense.....................................	53	17,800	
Automobile Expense	54	5,500	
Miscellaneous Expense	59	3,900	
		300,000	300,000

The following business transactions were completed by Elite Realty during April 2018:

Apr. 1.   Paid rent on office for month, $6,500.

     2.   Purchased office supplies on account, $2,300.

     5.   Paid insurance premiums, $6,000.

     10.   Received cash from clients on account, $52,300.

     15.   Purchased land for a future building site for $200,000, paying $30,000 in cash and giving a note payable for the remainder.

     17.   Paid creditors on account, $6,450.

     20.   Returned a portion of the office supplies purchased on April 2, receiving full credit for their cost, $325.

     23.   Paid advertising expense, $4,300.

Enter the following transactions on Page 19 of the two-column journal:

     27.   Discovered an error in computing a commission; received cash from the salesperson for the overpayment, $2,500.

     28.   Paid automobile expense (including rental charges for an automobile), $1,500.

     29.   Paid miscellaneous expenses, $1,400.

     30.   Recorded revenue earned and billed to clients during the month, $57,000.

     30.   Paid salaries and commissions for the month, $11,900.

     30.   Paid dividends, $4,000.

     30.   Rented land purchased on April 15 to local merchants association for use as a parking lot in May and June, during a street rebuilding program; received advance payment of $10,000.

Instructions

1. Record the April 1, 2018, balance of each account in the appropriate balance column of a four-column account, write *Balance* in the item section, and place a check mark (✓) in the Posting Reference column.

2. Journalize the transactions for April in a two-column journal beginning on Page 18. Journal entry explanations may be omitted.

3. Post to the ledger, extending the account balance to the appropriate balance column after each posting.

4. Prepare an unadjusted trial balance of the ledger as of April 30, 2018.

5. Assume that the April 30 transaction for salaries and commissions should have been $19,100. (A) Why did the unadjusted trial balance in (4) balance? (B) Journalize the correcting entry. (C) Is this error a transposition or slide?

PR 2-5A   Corrected trial balance

Obj. 4

✔ 1. Total of Debit column: $650,000

The Lexington Group has the following unadjusted trial balance as of May 31, 2018:

The Lexington Group
Unadjusted Trial Balance
May 31, 2018

	Debit Balances	Credit Balances
Cash	20,350	
Accounts Receivable	37,000	
Supplies	1,100	
Prepaid Insurance	200	
Equipment	171,175	
Notes Payable		36,000
Accounts Payable		26,000
Common Stock		50,000
Retained Earnings		94,150
Dividends	15,000	
Fees Earned		429,850
Wages Expense	270,000	
Rent Expense	63,000	
Advertising Expense	25,200	
Miscellaneous Expense	5,100	
	608,125	636,000

The debit and credit totals are not equal as a result of the following errors:

A. The cash entered on the trial balance was overstated by $7,000.
B. A cash receipt of $8,200 was posted as a debit to Cash of $2,800.
C. A debit of $16,500 to Accounts Receivable was not posted.
D. A return of $125 of defective supplies was erroneously posted as a $1,250 credit to Supplies.
E. An insurance policy acquired at a cost of $3,600 was posted as a credit to Prepaid Insurance.
F. The balance of Notes Payable was understated by $9,000.
G. A credit of $10,000 in Accounts Payable was overlooked when determining the balance of the account.
H. A debit of $5,000 for dividends was posted as a credit to Retained Earnings.
I. The balance of $60,300 in Rent Expense was entered as $63,000 in the trial balance.
J. Gas, Electricity, and Water Expense, with a balance of $16,350, was omitted from the trial balance.

Instructions

1. Prepare a corrected unadjusted trial balance as of May 31, 2018.

2. ▬▬▶ Does the fact that the unadjusted trial balance in (1) is balanced mean that there are no errors in the accounts? Explain.

Problems: Series B

PR 2-1B   Entries into T accounts and trial balance

Obj. 1, 2, 3, 4

✔ 3. Total of Debit column: $69,550

Ken Jones, an architect, organized Jones Architects on April 1, 2018. During the month, Jones Architects completed the following transactions:

A. Transferred cash from a personal bank account to an account to be used for the business in exchange for common stock, $18,000.
B. Purchased used automobile for $19,500, paying $2,500 cash and giving a note payable for the remainder.
C. Paid April rent for office and workroom, $3,150.
D. Paid cash for supplies, $1,450.
E. Purchased office and computer equipment on account, $6,500.
F. Paid cash for annual insurance policies on automobile and equipment, $2,400.
G. Received cash from a client for plans delivered, $12,000.
H. Paid cash to creditors on account, $1,800.
I. Paid cash for miscellaneous expenses, $375.

(Continued)

J. Received invoice for blueprint service, due in May, $2,500.

K. Recorded fees earned on plans delivered, payment to be received in May, $15,650.

L. Paid salary of assistant, $2,800.

M. Paid cash for miscellaneous expenses, $200.

N. Paid installment due on note payable, $300.

O. Paid gas, oil, and repairs on automobile for April, $550.

Instructions

1. Record these transactions directly in the following T accounts, without journalizing: Cash, Accounts Receivable, Supplies, Prepaid Insurance, Automobiles, Equipment, Notes Payable, Accounts Payable, Common Stock, Professional Fees, Rent Expense, Salary Expense, Blueprint Expense, Automobile Expense, Miscellaneous Expense. To the left of each amount entered in the accounts, place the appropriate letter to identify the transaction.

2. Determine account balances of the T accounts. Accounts containing a single entry only (such as Prepaid Insurance) do not need a balance.

3. Prepare an unadjusted trial balance for Jones Architects as of April 30, 2018.

4. Determine the net income or net loss for April.

PR 2-2B   Journal entries and trial balance   Obj. 1, 2, 3, 4

✔ 4. C. $4,550

On August 1, 2018, Rafael Masey established Planet Realty, which completed the following transactions during the month:

SHOW ME HOW   EXCEL TEMPLATE

GENERAL LEDGER

A. Rafael Masey transferred cash from a personal bank account to an account to be used for the business in exchange for common stock, $17,500.

B. Purchased supplies on account, $2,300.

C. Earned sales commissions, receiving cash, $13,300.

D. Paid rent on office and equipment for the month, $3,000.

E. Paid creditor on account, $1,150.

F. Paid dividends, $1,800.

G. Paid automobile expenses (including rental charge) for month, $1,500, and miscellaneous expenses, $400.

H. Paid office salaries, $2,800.

I. Determined that the cost of supplies used was $1,050.

Instructions

1. Journalize entries for transactions (A) through (I), using the following account titles: Cash, Supplies, Accounts Payable, Common Stock, Dividends, Sales Commissions, Rent Expense, Office Salaries Expense, Automobile Expense, Supplies Expense, Miscellaneous Expense. Journal entry explanations may be omitted.

2. Prepare T accounts, using the account titles in (1). Post the journal entries to these accounts, placing the appropriate letter to the left of each amount to identify the transactions. Determine the account balances, after all posting is complete. Accounts containing only a single entry do not need a balance.

3. Prepare an unadjusted trial balance as of August 31, 2018.

4. Determine the following:

    A. Amount of total revenue recorded in the ledger.

    B. Amount of total expenses recorded in the ledger.

    C. Amount of net income for August.

5. Determine the increase or decrease in retained earnings for August.

PR 2-3B   Journal entries and trial balance   Obj. 1, 2, 3, 4

✔ 3. Total of Credit column:
$70,300

On October 1, 2018, Jay Pryor established an interior decorating business, Pioneer Designs. During the month, Jay completed the following transactions related to the business:

SHOW ME HOW   EXCEL TEMPLATE

GENERAL LEDGER

Oct. 1. Jay transferred cash from a personal bank account to an account to be used for the business in exchange for common stock, $18,000.

4. Paid rent for period of October 4 to end of month, $3,000.

10. Purchased a used truck for $23,750, paying $3,750 cash and giving a note payable for the remainder.

13. Purchased equipment on account, $10,500.

14. Purchased supplies for cash, $2,100.

Oct. 15. Paid annual premiums on property and casualty insurance, $3,600.

15. Received cash for job completed, $8,950.

Enter the following transactions on Page 2 of the two-column journal:

21. Paid creditor a portion of the amount owed for equipment purchased on October 13, $2,000.

24. Recorded jobs completed on account and sent invoices to customers, $14,150.

26. Received an invoice for truck expenses, to be paid in November, $700.

27. Paid utilities expense, $2,240.

27. Paid miscellaneous expenses, $1,100.

29. Received cash from customers on account, $7,600.

30. Paid wages of employees, $4,800.

31. Paid dividends, $3,500.

Instructions

1. Journalize each transaction in a two-column journal beginning on Page 1, referring to the following chart of accounts in selecting the accounts to be debited and credited. (Do not insert the account numbers in the journal at this time.) Journal entry explanations may be omitted.

11 Cash	31 Common Stock
12 Accounts Receivable	33 Dividends
13 Supplies	41 Fees Earned
14 Prepaid Insurance	51 Wages Expense
16 Equipment	53 Rent Expense
18 Truck	54 Utilities Expense
21 Notes Payable	55 Truck Expense
22 Accounts Payable	59 Miscellaneous Expense

2. Post the journal to a ledger of four-column accounts, inserting appropriate posting references as each item is posted. Extend the balances to the appropriate balance columns after each transaction is posted.

3. Prepare an unadjusted trial balance for Pioneer Designs as of October 31, 2018.

4. Determine the excess of revenues over expenses for October.

5. ➡ Can you think of any reason why the amount determined in (4) might not be the net income for October?

PR 2-4B Journal entries and trial balance

Obj. 1, 2, 3, 4

✔ 4. Total of Debit column: $945,000

GENERAL LEDGER

Valley Realty acts as an agent in buying, selling, renting, and managing real estate. The unadjusted trial balance on July 31, 2018, follows:

Valley Realty
Unadjusted Trial Balance
July 31, 2018

	Account No.	Debit Balances	Credit Balances
Cash	11	52,500	
Accounts Receivable.............................	12	100,100	
Prepaid Insurance	13	12,600	
Office Supplies....................................	14	2,800	
Land	16	—	
Accounts Payable	21		21,000
Unearned Rent....................................	22		—
Notes Payable.....................................	23		—
Common Stock....................................	31		17,500
Retained Earnings................................	32		70,000
Dividends	33	44,800	
Fees Earned..	41		591,500
Salary and Commission Expense..............	51	385,000	
Rent Expense	52	49,000	
Advertising Expense..............................	53	32,200	
Automobile Expense	54	15,750	
Miscellaneous Expense	59	5,250	
		700,000	700,000

(Continued)

The following business transactions were completed by Valley Realty during August 2018:

Aug. 1.	Purchased office supplies on account, $3,150.
2.	Paid rent on office for month, $7,200.
3.	Received cash from clients on account, $83,900.
5.	Paid insurance premiums, $12,000.
9.	Returned a portion of the office supplies purchased on August 1, receiving full credit for their cost, $400.
17.	Paid advertising expense, $8,000.
23.	Paid creditors on account, $13,750.

Enter the following transactions on Page 19 of the two-column journal:

29.	Paid miscellaneous expenses, $1,700.
30.	Paid automobile expense (including rental charges for an automobile), $2,500.
31.	Discovered an error in computing a commission during July; received cash from the salesperson for the overpayment, $2,000.
31.	Paid salaries and commissions for the month, $53,000.
31.	Recorded revenue earned and billed to clients during the month, $183,500.
31.	Purchased land for a future building site for $75,000, paying $7,500 in cash and giving a note payable for the remainder.
31.	Paid dividends, $1,000.
31.	Rented land purchased on August 31 to a local university for use as a parking lot during football season (September, October, and November); received advance payment of $5,000.

Instructions

1. Record the August 1 balance of each account in the appropriate balance column of a four-column account, write *Balance* in the item section, and place a check mark (✓) in the Posting Reference column.

2. Journalize the transactions for August in a two-column journal beginning on Page 18. Journal entry explanations may be omitted.

3. Post to the ledger, extending the account balance to the appropriate balance column after each posting.

4. Prepare an unadjusted trial balance of the ledger as of August 31, 2018.

5. Assume that the August 31 transaction for dividends should have been $10,000. (A) Why did the unadjusted trial balance in (4) balance? (B) Journalize the correcting entry. (C) Is this error a transposition or slide?

PR 2-5B   Corrected trial balance   **Obj. 4**

✔ 1. Total of Debit column:
$712,500

Tech Support Services has the following unadjusted trial balance as of January 31, 2018:

Tech Support Services
Unadjusted Trial Balance
January 31, 2018

	Debit Balances	Credit Balances
Cash	25,550	
Accounts Receivable..	44,050	
Supplies	6,660	
Prepaid Insurance	3,600	
Equipment...	162,000	
Notes Payable...		75,000
Accounts Payable		13,200
Common Stock...		18,000
Retained Earnings...		83,850
Dividends	33,000	
Fees Earned...		534,000
Wages Expense	306,000	
Rent Expense	62,550	
Advertising Expense...	23,850	
Gas, Electricity, and Water Expense	17,000	
	684,260	724,050

The debit and credit totals are not equal as a result of the following errors:

A. The cash entered on the trial balance was overstated by $8,000.
B. A cash receipt of $4,100 was posted as a debit to Cash of $1,400.
C. A debit of $12,350 to Accounts Receivable was not posted.
D. A return of $235 of defective supplies was erroneously posted as a $325 credit to Supplies.
E. An insurance policy acquired at a cost of $3,000 was posted as a credit to Prepaid Insurance.
F. The balance of Notes Payable was overstated by $21,000.
G. A credit of $3,450 in Accounts Payable was overlooked when the balance of the account was determined.
H. A debit of $6,000 for dividends was posted as a debit to Retained Earnings.
I. The balance of $28,350 in Advertising Expense was entered as $23,850 in the trial balance.
J. Miscellaneous Expense, with a balance of $4,600, was omitted from the trial balance.

Instructions

1. Prepare a corrected unadjusted trial balance as of January 31, 2018.

2. ➤ Does the fact that the unadjusted trial balance in (1) is balanced mean that there are no errors in the accounts? Explain.

Continuing Problem

✔ **4. Total of Debit column:**
$40,750

GENERAL LEDGER

The transactions completed by PS Music during June 2018 were described at the end of Chapter 1. The following transactions were completed during July, the second month of the business's operations:

July 1. Peyton Smith made an additional investment in PS Music in exchange for common stock by depositing $5,000 in PS Music's checking account.

1. Instead of continuing to share office space with a local real estate agency, Peyton decided to rent office space near a local music store. Paid rent for July, $1,750.

1. Paid a premium of $2,700 for a comprehensive insurance policy covering liability, theft, and fire. The policy covers a one-year period.

2. Received $1,000 on account.

3. On behalf of PS Music, Peyton signed a contract with a local radio station, KXMD, to provide guest spots for the next three months. The contract requires PS Music to provide a guest disc jockey for 80 hours per month for a monthly fee of $3,600. Any additional hours beyond 80 will be billed to KXMD at $40 per hour. In accordance with the contract, Peyton received $7,200 from KXMD as an advance payment for the first two months.

3. Paid $250 on account.

4. Paid an attorney $900 for reviewing the July 3 contract with KXMD. (Record as Miscellaneous Expense.)

5. Purchased office equipment on account from Office Mart, $7,500.

8. Paid for a newspaper advertisement, $200.

11. Received $1,000 for serving as a disc jockey for a party.

13. Paid $700 to a local audio electronics store for rental of digital recording equipment.

14. Paid wages of $1,200 to receptionist and part-time assistant.

Enter the following transactions on Page 2 of the two-column journal:

16. Received $2,000 for serving as a disc jockey for a wedding reception.

18. Purchased supplies on account, $850.

21. Paid $620 to Upload Music for use of its current music demos in making various music sets.

22. Paid $800 to a local radio station to advertise the services of PS Music twice daily for the remainder of July.

23. Served as disc jockey for a party for $2,500. Received $750, with the remainder due August 4, 2018.

27. Paid electric bill, $915.

28. Paid wages of $1,200 to receptionist and part-time assistant.

29. Paid miscellaneous expenses, $540.

30. Served as a disc jockey for a charity ball for $1,500. Received $500, with the remainder due on August 9, 2018.

31. Received $3,000 for serving as a disc jockey for a party.

(Continued)

July 31. Paid $1,400 royalties (music expense) to National Music Clearing for use of various artists' music during July.

31. Paid dividends, $1,250.

PS Music's chart of accounts and the balance of accounts as of July 1, 2018 (all normal balances), are as follows:

11	Cash	$3,920	41	Fees Earned	$6,200
12	Accounts Receivable	1,000	50	Wages Expense	400
14	Supplies	170	51	Office Rent Expense	800
15	Prepaid Insurance	—	52	Equipment Rent Expense	675
17	Office Equipment	—	53	Utilities Expense	300
21	Accounts Payable	250	54	Music Expense	1,590
23	Unearned Revenue	—	55	Advertising Expense	500
31	Common Stock	4,000	56	Supplies Expense	180
33	Dividends	500	59	Miscellaneous Expense	415

Instructions

1. Enter the July 1, 2018, account balances in the appropriate balance column of a four-column account. Write *Balance* in the Item column, and place a check mark (✓) in the Posting Reference column. (*Hint:* Verify the equality of the debit and credit balances in the ledger before proceeding with the next instruction.)

2. Analyze and journalize each transaction in a two-column journal beginning on Page 1, omitting journal entry explanations.

3. Post the journal to the ledger, extending the account balance to the appropriate balance column after each posting.

4. Prepare an unadjusted trial balance as of July 31, 2018.

Analysis for Decision Making

REAL WORLD

ADM-1 Continuing Company Analysis—Amazon: Horizontal analysis

Amazon.com, Inc. is the largest Internet retailer in the United States. Amazon's income statements through income from operations for two recent years follow:

Amazon.com, Inc.
Operating Income Statements
For the Years Ended December 31
(in millions)

	Year 2	Year 1
Product sales	$70,080	$60,903
Service sales	18,908	13,549
Total sales	$88,988	$74,452
Cost of sales	$62,752	$54,181
Fulfillment	10,766	8,585
Marketing	4,332	3,133
Technology and content	9,275	6,565
General and administrative	1,552	1,129
Other operating expense (income), net	133	114
Total operating expenses	$88,810	$73,707
Income from operations	$ 178	$ 745

A. Prepare a horizontal analysis of the operating income statements. (Round percentages to one decimal place.)

B. ➡ Interpret the results of the horizontal analysis.

ADM-2 Chipotle: Horizontal analysis

Chipotle Mexican Grill, Inc. is a quick-service restaurant providing a focused menu of burritos, tacos, and salads. Chipotle's balance sheets for the end of two recent years are as follows:

Chipotle Mexican Grill, Inc.
Balance Sheets
December 31
(in thousands)

	Year 2	Year 1
Assets		
Current assets		
Cash...	$ 419,465	$ 323,203
Accounts receivable, net..........................	34,839	24,016
Inventory	15,332	13,044
Other current assets..............................	70,251	51,073
Investments.....................................	338,592	254,971
Total current assets	$ 878,479	$ 666,307
Property, plant, and equipment	1,106,984	963,238
Long-term investments.............................	496,106	313,863
Other assets.....................................	64,716	65,872
Total assets	$2,546,285	$2,009,280
Liabilities and Stockholders' Equity		
Current liabilities		
Accounts payable................................	$ 69,613	$ 59,022
Other current liabilities...........................	176,097	140,206
Total current liabilities.........................	$ 245,710	$ 199,228
Long-term liabilities.............................	288,206	271,764
Total liabilities.....................................	$ 533,916	$ 470,992
Stockholders' Equity		
Common stock	$ 354	$ 352
Additional paid-in capital	1,038,932	919,840
Retained earnings.................................	1,722,271	1,276,897
Treasury stock	(748,759)	(660,421)
Other adjustments.................................	(429)	1,620
Total stockholders' equity..........................	$2,012,369	$1,538,288
Total liabilities and stockholders' equity	$2,546,285	$2,009,280

A. Prepare a horizontal analysis of the two balance sheets. (Round percentages to one decimal place.)

B. ━━━▶ Interpret the horizontal analysis with respect to the change in total assets, total liabilities, and total stockholders' equity. (Treasury stock will be discussed in a later chapter and may be omitted from your analysis.)

ADM-3 Target: Horizontal analysis

The following data (in millions) are taken from the financial statements of **Target Corporation**, the owner of Target stores:

	Year 2	Year 1
Revenue	$72,618	$71,279
Operating expenses	67,857	66,320
Operating income	$ 4,761	$ 4,959

(Continued)

A. For Target, determine the amount of change in millions and the percent of change (rounded to one decimal place) from Year 1 to Year 2 for:

1. Revenue
2. Operating expenses
3. Operating income

B. ━━━━▶ What conclusions can you draw from your analysis of the revenue and total operating expenses?

REAL WORLD

ADM-4   Walmart: Horizontal analysis

The following data (in millions) are taken from the financial statements of **Walmart Stores, Inc.**:

	Year 2	Year 1
Revenue	$485,651	$476,294
Operating expenses	458,504	449,422
Operating income	$ 27,147	$ 26,872

A. For Walmart, determine the amount of change in millions and the percent of change (rounded to one decimal place) from Year 1 to Year 2 for:

1. Revenue
2. Operating expenses
3. Operating income

B. ━━━━▶ Comment on the results of your horizontal analysis in requirement (A).

C. ━━━━▶ Based on ADM-3, compare and comment on the two-year change in operating results between Target and Walmart.

Take It Further

ETHICS

TIF 2-1   Ethics in Action

Buddy Dupree is the accounting manager for On-Time Geeks, a tech support company for individuals and small businesses. As part of his job, Buddy is responsible for preparing the company's trial balance. His supervisor placed a "hard deadline" of Friday at 5 PM for the completion of the trial balance. Unfortunately, Buddy was unable to get the trial balance to balance by the due date. The credit side of the trial balance exceeded the debit side by $3,000. To make the deadline, Buddy decided to add a $3,000 debit to the vehicles account balance. He selected the vehicles account because it will not be significantly affected by the additional $3,000.

1. ➤ Is Buddy behaving ethically? Why?
2. ➤ Who is affected by Buddy's decision?
3. ➤ How should Buddy have handled this situation?

REAL WORLD

TIF 2-2   Team Activity

In teams, select a public company that interests you. Obtain the company's most recent annual report on Form 10-K. The Form 10-K is a company's annually required filing with the Securities and Exchange Commission (SEC). It includes the company's financial statements and accompanying notes. The Form 10-K can be obtained either (A) from the investor relations section of the company's Web site or (B) by using the company search feature of the SEC's EDGAR database service found at www.sec.gov/edgar/searchedgar/companysearch.html.

Based on the information in the company's most recent annual report, answer the following questions:

1. What amount of total assets does the company report on its balance sheet?
2. What amount of total liabilities does the company report on its balance sheet?
3. Using the accounting equation, determine the company's stockholders' equity. Compare this amount to the amount of stockholders' equity reported on the company's balance sheet.
4. How many years of information are reported on the company's income statement?
5. How many years of information are reported on the company's balance sheet?
6. ➤ What is the difference between the information reported on the income statement and the information reported on the balance sheet?

TIF 2-3   Communication and Decision Making

The complexity of the current business and regulatory environment has increased the demand for individuals in all fields of business who have the ability to analyze business transactions and interpret their effects on the financial statements. Search the Internet or your local newspaper for job opportunities in business. One possible Web site is www.careerbuilder.com.

➤ Select a job opportunity to explore further. Write a brief memo to your instructor describing how the ability to analyze business transactions and interpret their effects on the financial statements would be needed for the job opportunity you have selected.

Chapter 1

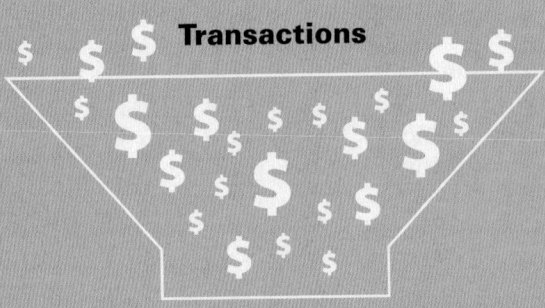

Transactions

Accounting System

Accounting Equation

Assets = Liabilities + Equity

Chapter 2

Account	
Debits	Credits

Rules of Debit and Credit

Balance Sheet Accounts

ASSETS = **LIABILITIES** + **STOCKHOLDERS' EQUITY**

Asset Accounts

Debit for increases (+)	Credit for decreases (−)
Balance	

Liability Accounts

Debit for decreases (−)	Credit for increases (+)
	Balance

Common Stock

Debit for decreases (−)	Credit for increases (+)
	Balance

+ **Retained Earnings**

Debit for decreases (−)	Credit for increases (+)
	Balance

Income Statement Accounts

Dividends

Debit for increases (+)	Credit for decreases (−)
Balance	

Revenue Accounts

Debit for decreases (−)	Credit for increases (+)
	Balance

– Expense Accounts

Debit for increases (+)	Credit for decreases (−)
Balance	

Unadjusted Trial Balance

Total Debit Balances = Total Credit Balances

The Adjusting Process

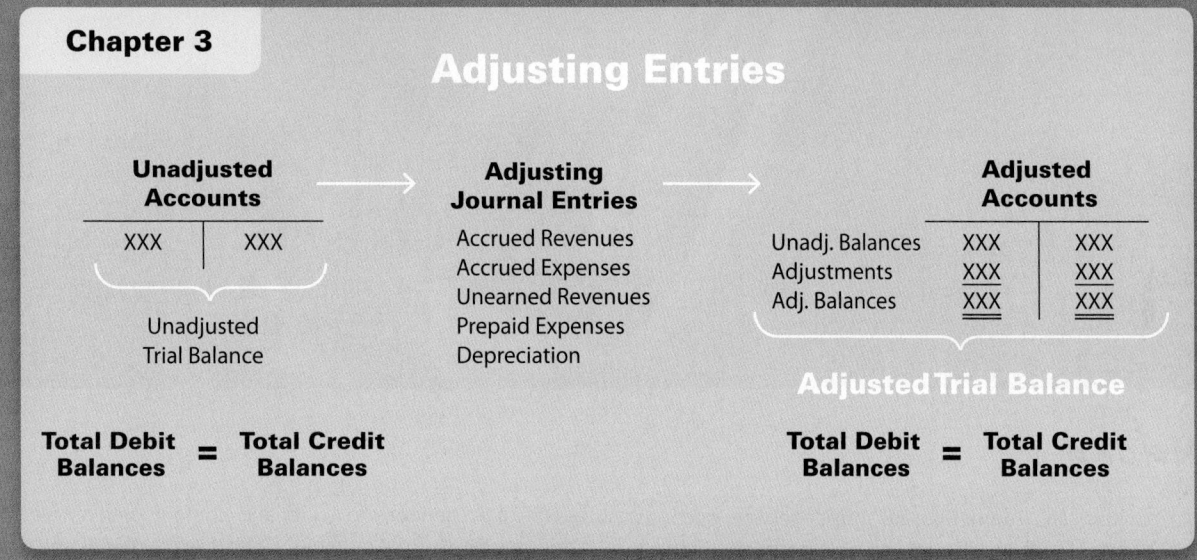

Pandora

Do you use an Internet-based music service such as **Pandora**? Using playlist-generating algorithms, Pandora predicts a listener's music preferences based on his or her initial music selections. Pandora selects music it thinks the listener will enjoy, including music of new artists that match the listener's preferences. Recently, Pandora developed similar comedy-generating algorithms that match a listener's preferences for comedy with more than 1,000 comedians.

Most of Pandora's services are offered free to listeners with only 12.5% of its revenues generated from subscription services. So, where do most of Pandora's revenues come from?

Pandora generates more than 85% of its revenues from selling advertising banners that surround the video displays on its tuner. By analyzing its listener interactions, Pandora identifies listener age, gender, zip code, and content preferences. These attributes can then be matched with advertiser needs and desires.

When should Pandora record revenue from its advertisers and subscribers? Revenue should be recorded when earned. Advertising revenue is earned as ads are displayed, while subscriber revenue is earned when the service has been delivered to the listener. As a result, companies like Pandora must update their accounting records for such items as unearned advertising and subscription revenue before preparing financial statements.

This chapter describes and illustrates the process by which companies update their accounting records before preparing financial statements. This discussion includes the adjustments to update revenue and expense accounts at the end of the accounting period.

What's Covered

The Adjusting Process

Nature of Adjusting Process	Adjusting Entries for Accruals	Adjusting Entries for Deferrals	Adjusting Entries for Depreciation	Concluding the Adjusting Process
■ Accrual v. Cash Basis (Obj. 1) ■ Revenue and Expense Recognition (Obj. 1) ■ Accruals (Obj. 1) ■ Deferrals (Obj. 1)	■ Accrued Revenues (Obj. 2) ■ Accrued Expenses (Obj. 2)	■ Unearned Revenue (Obj. 3) ■ Prepaid Expenses (Obj. 3)	■ Fixed Assets (Obj. 4) ■ Accumulated Depreciation (Obj. 4) ■ Book Value (Obj. 4)	■ Summary (Obj. 5) ■ Adjusted Trial Balance (Obj. 6)

Learning Objectives

Obj. 1 Describe the nature of the adjusting process.

Obj. 2 Prepare adjusting entries for accruals.

Obj. 3 Prepare adjusting entries for deferrals.

Obj. 4 Prepare adjusting entries for depreciation.

Obj. 5 Summarize the adjusting process.

Obj. 6 Prepare an adjusted trial balance.

Analysis for Decision Making

Describe and Illustrate the use of vertical analysis in evaluating a company's performance and financial condition.

Nature of the Adjusting Process

Objective 1
Describe the nature of the adjusting process.

In Chapter 2, the November and December transactions for **NetSolutions** were recorded using the double-entry accounting system. After the transactions were recorded, an unadjusted trial balance was prepared on December 31 verifying that the total debit balances equal the total credit balances. Before financial statements can be prepared, however, some accounts in the unadjusted trial balance must be adjusted. These adjustments are necessary because the transactions for NetSolutions were recorded using the accrual basis of accounting.

Accrual and Cash Basis of Accounting

Under the **accrual basis of accounting**, revenues are reported on the income statement in the period in which a service has been performed or a product has been delivered. Cash may or may not be received from customers during this period. For example, a cleaning company will record revenue after it cleans an office building, even if it is not paid for several weeks. The accrual basis of accounting also requires expenses to be recorded when they are incurred, not necessarily when cash is paid.

Pandora uses the accrual basis of accounting in preparing its financial statements.

Link to Pandora

Although generally accepted accounting principles (GAAP) require the accrual basis of accounting, most individuals and some businesses use the cash basis of accounting. Under the **cash basis of accounting**, revenues and expenses are reported on the income statement in the period in which cash is received or paid. For example, fees are recorded when cash is received from clients; likewise, wages are recorded when cash is paid to employees. The net income (or net loss) is the difference between the cash receipts (revenues) and the cash payments (expenses).

Small service businesses may use the cash basis because they have few receivables and payables. For example, attorneys, physicians, and real estate agents may use the cash basis. For them, the cash basis provides financial statements similar to those of the accrual basis. For most large businesses, however, the cash basis will not provide accurate financial statements for user needs. For this reason, the accrual basis is required by GAAP and is used in this text.

Revenue and Expense Recognition

To be useful for decision making, financial statements must be provided on a periodic basis. As a result, the economic life of a business is divided into time periods such as a month, quarter of a year, or full year. Under accrual accounting, the net income of a period is reported using revenue and expense recognition principles.

Under the **revenue recognition principle**, revenues are recorded when services have been performed or products have been delivered to customers. Revenue is normally measured as the assets received, such as cash or accounts receivable.[1] The process of recognizing revenues is called **revenue recognition**.[2]

Link to Pandora   Subscription revenues from **Pandora**'s customers are recorded equally over the subscription periods. For example, a yearly subscription would be recorded equally over 12 months.

Under the **expense recognition principle**, the expenses incurred in generating revenue must be reported in the same period as the related revenue. This is also called the **matching principle**. By matching revenues and expenses, net income or loss for the period is properly reported on the income statement. Adjusting entries are required to properly match revenues and expenses.

Link to Pandora   **Pandora** computes royalty expense paid to an artist for a song that is streamed to listeners based upon the number of times it is played/streamed.

The Adjusting Process

At the end of an accounting period, an unadjusted trial balance is prepared to verify that the total debit balances equal the total credit balances. Many of these account balances are reported in the financial statements without change. For example, the balances of the cash and land accounts are normally the amounts reported on the balance sheet.

Some accounts on the unadjusted trial balance, however, require adjustments for the following reasons:

- Some expenses are not recorded daily. For example, the daily use of supplies would require many entries with small amounts. Also, the amount of supplies on hand on a day-to-day basis is normally not needed.
- Some revenues and expenses are incurred as time passes rather than as separate transactions. For example, rent received in advance (unearned rent) expires and becomes revenue with the passage of time. Likewise, prepaid insurance expires and becomes an expense with the passage of time.
- Some revenues and expenses may be unrecorded at the end of the accounting period. For example, a company may have provided services to customers that it has not billed or recorded at the end of the accounting period. Likewise, a company may not pay its employees until the next accounting period even though the employees have earned their wages in the current period.

---

[1] As will be illustrated later in this chapter, revenues may also be measured as a decrease in a liability such as unearned revenue.
[2] FASB Accounting Standards Update, Revenue from Contracts with Customers (Topic 606), Financial Accounting Standards Board, May 2014, Norwalk, CT.

The analysis and updating of accounts at the end of the period before the financial statements are prepared is called the **adjusting process**. The journal entries that bring the accounts up to date at the end of the accounting period are called **adjusting entries**. All adjusting entries affect at least one income statement account and one balance sheet account. Thus, an adjusting entry will always involve a revenue or an expense account *and* an asset or a liability account.

Types of Accounts Requiring Adjustment

The two general classifications of accounts requiring adjustment are as follows:

- Accruals
- Deferrals

Accruals An **accrual** occurs when revenue has been earned or an expense has been incurred but has not been recorded. If the accrual is for revenue, the adjusting entry debits an asset (Accounts Receivable) and credits a revenue account. If the accrual is for an expense, the adjusting entry debits an expense account and credits a related liability account such as Accounts Payable or Wages Payable. Exhibit 1 summarizes the accounting for accruals.

Exhibit 1 Accruals

ACCRUED REVENUE		
Adjustment Data	**Journal Entry**	**Adjusting Entry**
Revenue has been earned.	No entry has been made.	Accounts Receivable XXX
		Revenue XXX
ACCRUED EXPENSE		
Adjustment Data	**Journal Entry**	**Adjusting Entry**
Expense has been incurred.	No entry has been made.	Expense XXX
		Accounts (Wages) Payable XXX

Deferrals A **deferral** occurs when cash related to a future revenue or expense has been initially recorded as a liability or an asset. If the cash received is related to future revenue, it is initially recorded as a liability called **unearned revenue**. The adjusting entry in the period when the revenue is earned debits an unearned revenue account and credits a revenue account. If the cash paid is related to a future expense, it is initially recorded as an asset called **prepaid expense**. The adjusting entry in the period when the expense is incurred debits an expense account and credits a prepaid expense (asset) account. Exhibit 2 summarizes the accounting for deferrals.

Exhibit 2 Deferrals

UNEARNED REVENUE			
Initial Recording		**End-of-Period**	
Transaction	**Journal Entry**	**Adjustment Data**	**Adjusting Entry**
Cash has been received for revenue that will be earned in a future period.	Cash XXX Unearned Revenue XXX	Revenue has been earned.	Unearned Revenue XXX Revenue XXX
PREPAID EXPENSE			
Initial Recording		**End-of-Period**	
Transaction	**Journal Entry**	**Adjustment Data**	**Adjusting Entry**
Cash has been paid for a future expense.	Prepaid Expense XXX Cash XXX	Prepaid expense has been used to generate revenue.	Expense XXX Prepaid Expense XXX

Adjusting Entries for Accruals

To illustrate adjusting entries, the December 31, 2017, unadjusted trial balance of **NetSolutions**, shown in Exhibit 3, is used. An expanded chart of accounts for NetSolutions is shown in Exhibit 4. The additional accounts used in this chapter are highlighted. The rules of debit and credit shown in Exhibit 3 of Chapter 2 are used to record the adjusting entries.

Exhibit 3
Unadjusted Trial Balance for NetSolutions

NetSolutions Unadjusted Trial Balance December 31, 2017			
	Account No.	Debit Balances	Credit Balances
Cash	11	2,065	
Accounts Receivable......................................	12	2,220	
Supplies	14	2,000	
Prepaid Insurance	15	2,400	
Land	17	20,000	
Office Equipment	18	1,800	
Accounts Payable	21		900
Unearned Rent	23		360
Common Stock	31		25,000
Dividends	33	4,000	
Fees Earned	41		16,340
Wages Expense	51	4,275	
Supplies Expense	52	800	
Rent Expense	53	1,600	
Utilities Expense	54	985	
Miscellaneous Expense	59	455	
		42,600	42,600

Exhibit 4
Expanded Chart of Accounts for NetSolutions

Balance Sheet Accounts	Income Statement Accounts
1. Assets	**4. Revenue**
11 Cash	41 Fees Earned
12 Accounts Receivable	42 Rent Revenue
14 Supplies	**5. Expenses**
15 Prepaid Insurance	51 Wages Expense
17 Land	52 Supplies Expense
18 Office Equipment	53 Rent Expense
19 Accumulated Depreciation—Office Equipment	54 Utilities Expense
2. Liabilities	55 Insurance Expense
21 Accounts Payable	56 Depreciation Expense
22 Wages Payable	59 Miscellaneous Expense
23 Unearned Rent	
3. Stockholders' Equity	
31 Common Stock	
32 Retained Earnings	
33 Dividends	

Accrued Revenues

During an accounting period, some revenues are recorded only when cash is received. Thus, at the end of an accounting period, there may be revenue that has been earned *but has not been recorded*. In such cases, the revenue is recorded by increasing (debiting) an asset account and increasing (crediting) a revenue account.

To illustrate, assume that **NetSolutions** signed an agreement with Dankner Co. on December 15. The agreement provides that NetSolutions will answer computer questions and render assistance to Dankner Co.'s employees. The services will be billed to Dankner Co. on the fifteenth of each month at a rate of $20 per hour. As of December 31, NetSolutions had provided 25 hours of assistance to Dankner Co. The revenue of $500 (25 hours × $20) will be billed on January 15. However, NetSolutions earned the revenue in December.

The claim against the customer for payment of the $500 is an account receivable (*an asset*). Thus, the accounts receivable account is increased (debited) by $500, and the fees earned account is increased (credited) by $500. The adjusting journal entry and T accounts are as follows:

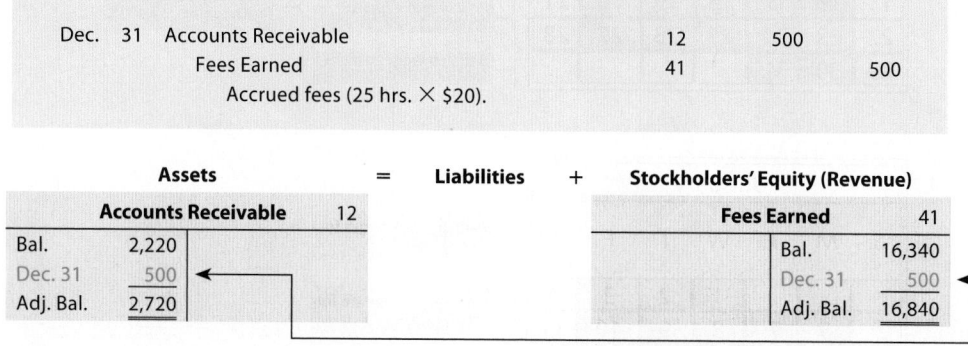

Adjusting Journal Entry

Accounting Equation Impact

If the adjustment for the accrued revenue ($500) is not recorded, Fees Earned and the net income will be understated by $500 on the income statement. On the balance sheet, assets (Accounts Receivable) and stockholders' equity (Retained Earnings) will be understated by $500. The effects of omitting this adjusting entry are as follows:

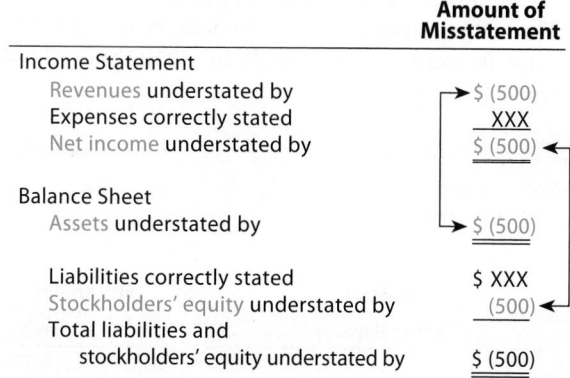

Pandora's accrued revenues from advertising are recorded in its accounts receivable at the end of the year.

Link to Pandora

Accrued Expenses

Some types of services used in earning revenues are paid for *after* the service has been performed. For example, wages expense is used hour by hour but is paid only daily, weekly, biweekly, or monthly. At the end of the accounting period, the amount of such *accrued* but unpaid items is an expense and a liability.

For example, if the last day of the employees' pay period is not the last day of the accounting period, an accrued expense (wages expense) and the related liability (wages payable) must be recorded by an adjusting entry. This adjusting entry is necessary so that expenses are properly matched to the period in which they were incurred in earning revenue.

To illustrate, **NetSolutions** pays its employees biweekly. During December, NetSolutions paid wages of $950 on December 13 and $1,200 on December 27. These payments covered pay periods ending on those days as shown in Exhibit 5.

Exhibit 5
Accrued Wages

DYNAMIC
EXHIBIT

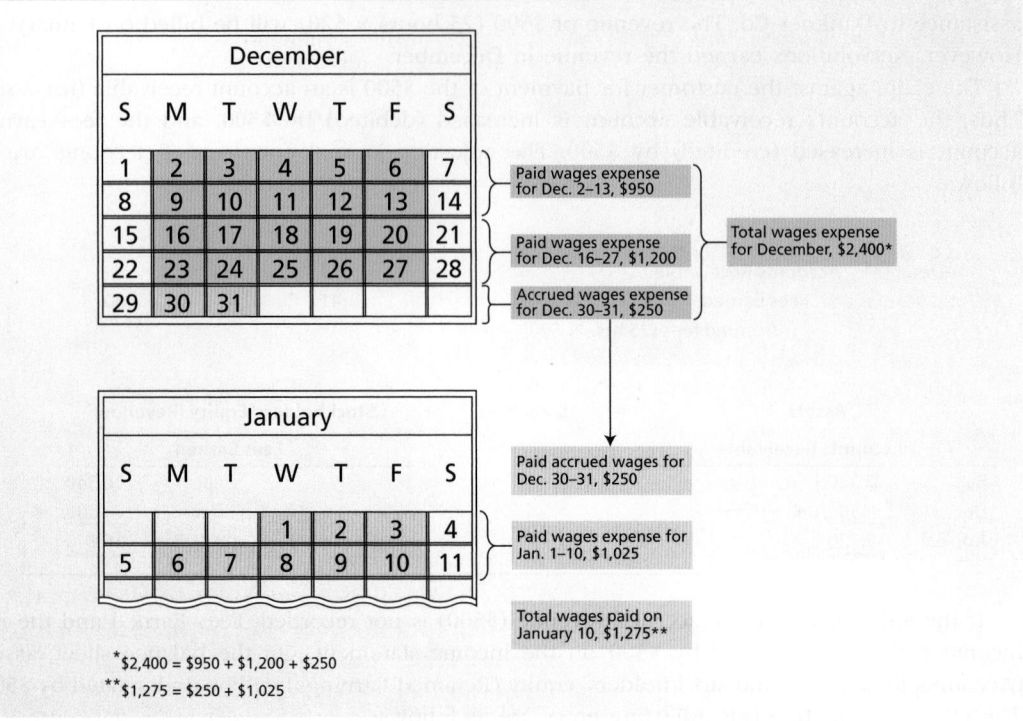

As of December 31, NetSolutions owes $250 of wages to employees for Monday and Tuesday, December 30 and 31. Thus, the wages expense account is increased (debited) by $250, and the wages payable account is increased (credited) by $250. The adjusting journal entry and T accounts are as follows:

Adjusting
Journal Entry

Dec.	31	Wages Expense		51	250	
		Wages Payable		22		250
		Accrued wages.				

Accounting Equation
Impact

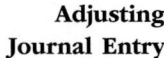

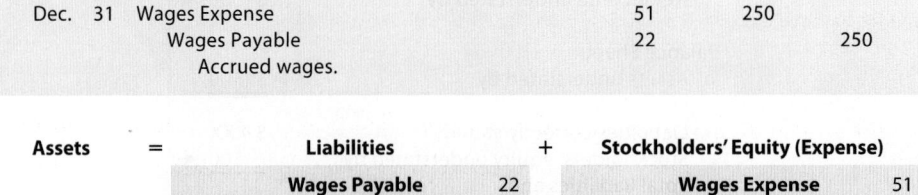

After the adjusting entry is recorded and posted, the debit balance of the wages expense account is $4,525. This balance of $4,525 is the wages expense for two months, November and December. The credit balance of $250 in Wages Payable is the liability for wages owed on December 31.

As shown in Exhibit 5, NetSolutions paid wages of $1,275 on January 10. This payment includes the $250 of accrued wages recorded on December 31. Thus, on January 10, the wages payable account is decreased (debited) by $250. Also, the wages expense account is increased (debited) by $1,025 ($1,275 – $250), which is the wages expense for January 1–10. Finally, the cash account is decreased (credited) by $1,275. The journal entry for the payment of wages on January 10 follows:[3]

Jan.	10	Wages Expense		51	1,025	
		Wages Payable		22	250	
		Cash		11		1,275

[3] To simplify the subsequent recording of the following period's transactions, some accountants use what is known as reversing entries for certain types of adjustments. Reversing entries are discussed and illustrated in an appendix to Chapter 4.

If the adjustment for wages ($250) is not recorded, Wages Expense will be understated by $250, and the net income will be overstated by $250 on the income statement. On the balance sheet, liabilities (Wages Payable) will be understated by $250, and stockholders' equity (Retained Earnings) will be overstated by $250. The effects of omitting this adjusting entry are as follows:

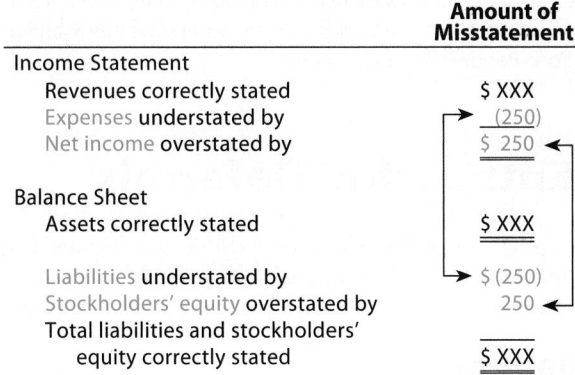

	Amount of Misstatement
Income Statement	
Revenues correctly stated	$ XXX
Expenses understated by	(250)
Net income overstated by	$ 250
Balance Sheet	
Assets correctly stated	$ XXX
Liabilities understated by	$ (250)
Stockholders' equity overstated by	250
Total liabilities and stockholders' equity correctly stated	$ XXX

In a recent balance sheet, **Pandora** reported accrued royalties payable of $66 million, which it pays to owners of the music it plays.   *Link to Pandora*

Check Up Corner 3-1   Adjusting Entries for Accruals

On December 31, the following data were accumulated for preparing the adjusting entries for the Atlanta Rhythm Company:

- At the end of the year, $13,680 of fees have been earned, but have not been billed to clients.
- Wages of $12,500 are paid on Friday for a five-day work week. The accounting period ends on Thursday, December 31.

Journalize the adjusting entries necessary on December 31, the end of the accounting period.

Solution:

An accrual occurs when revenue has been earned or an expense has been incurred, but has not been recorded.

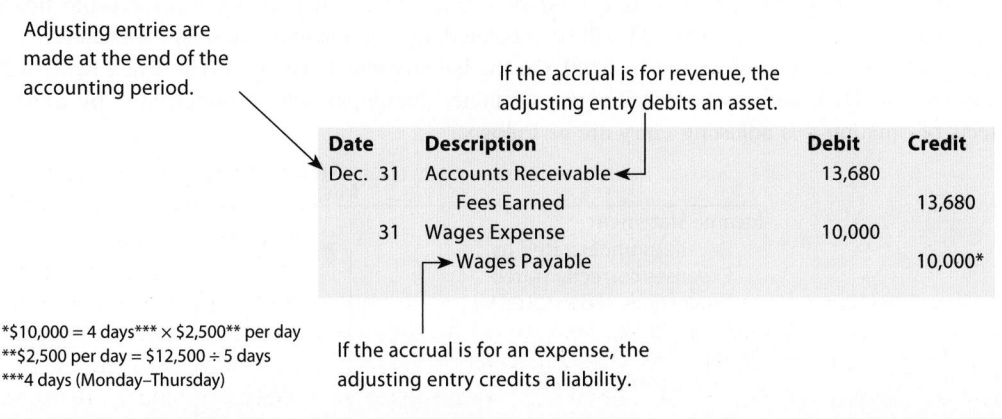

Adjusting entries are made at the end of the accounting period.

If the accrual is for revenue, the adjusting entry debits an asset.

Date	Description	Debit	Credit
Dec. 31	Accounts Receivable	13,680	
	Fees Earned		13,680
31	Wages Expense	10,000	
	Wages Payable		10,000*

If the accrual is for an expense, the adjusting entry credits a liability.

*$10,000 = 4 days*** × $2,500** per day
**$2,500 per day = $12,500 ÷ 5 days
***4 days (Monday–Thursday)

Check Up Corner

Why It Matters

Earning Revenues from Season Tickets

Madison Square Garden Company (MSG) owns the New York Knicks basketball team and the New York Rangers

hockey team. The company sells season tickets prior to the season. The amounts received for season tickets are recognized as unearned revenue, a current liability. MSG recognizes revenue and reduces unearned revenue as the games are played through the season.

Objective 3
Prepare adjusting entries for deferrals.

Adjusting Entries for Deferrals

The unadjusted trial balance for **NetSolutions** in Exhibit 3 indicates Unearned Rent of $360. In addition, Exhibit 3 indicates that NetSolutions has prepaid assets consisting of Supplies of $2,000 and Prepaid Insurance of $2,400. Each of these deferrals requires an adjusting entry.

Unearned Revenues

The December 31 unadjusted trial balance of **NetSolutions** indicates a balance in the unearned rent account of $360. This balance represents the receipt of three months' rent on December 1 for December, January, and February. At the end of December, one month's rent has been earned. Thus, the unearned rent account is decreased (debited) by $120, and the rent revenue account is increased (credited) by $120. The $120 represents the rental revenue for one month ($360 ÷ 3). The adjusting journal entry and T accounts are as follows:

Adjusting Journal Entry

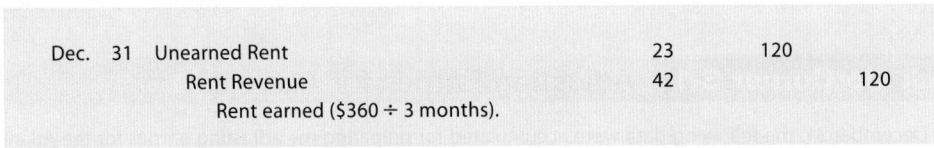

Dec. 31	Unearned Rent	23	120	
	Rent Revenue	42		120
	Rent earned ($360 ÷ 3 months).			

Accounting Equation Impact

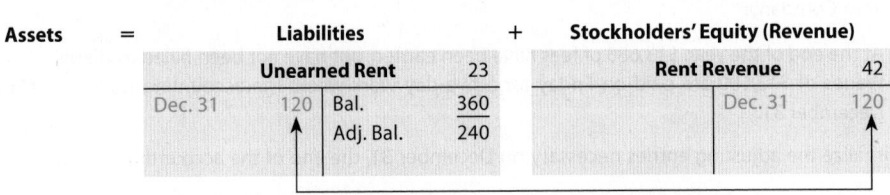

Assets = **Liabilities** + **Stockholders' Equity (Revenue)**

Unearned Rent		23
Dec. 31	120	Bal.	360
		Adj. Bal.	240

Rent Revenue		42
	Dec. 31	120

After the adjusting entry is recorded and posted, the unearned rent account has a credit balance of $240. This balance is a liability that will become revenue in a future period. Rent Revenue has a balance of $120, which is revenue of the current period.[4]

If the preceding adjustment of unearned rent and rent revenue is not recorded, the financial statements prepared on December 31 will be misstated. On the income statement, Rent Revenue and the net income will be understated by $120. On the balance sheet, liabilities (Unearned Rent) will be overstated by $120, and stockholders' equity (Retained Earnings) will be understated by $120. The effects of omitting this adjusting entry are as follows:

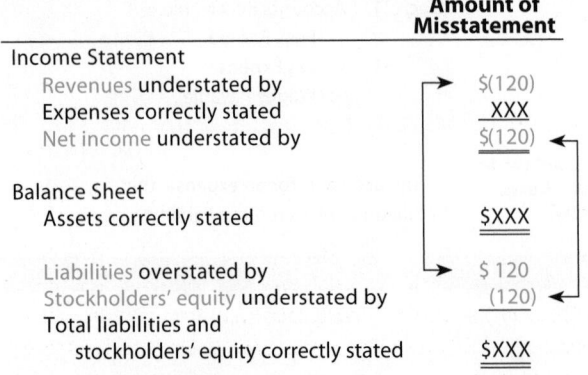

	Amount of Misstatement
Income Statement	
Revenues understated by	$(120)
Expenses correctly stated	XXX
Net income understated by	$(120)
Balance Sheet	
Assets correctly stated	$XXX
Liabilities overstated by	$ 120
Stockholders' equity understated by	(120)
Total liabilities and	
stockholders' equity correctly stated	$XXX

[4] An alternative treatment of recording revenues received in advance of their being earned is discussed in an appendix that can be downloaded from the book's companion Web site (www.cengagebrain.com).

In a recent balance sheet, **Pandora** reported deferred revenue of $43 million.

Link to Pandora

Prepaid Expenses

The December 31, 2017, unadjusted trial balance of **NetSolutions** indicates a balance in the supplies account of $2,000. In addition, the prepaid insurance account has a balance of $2,400. Each of these accounts requires an adjusting entry.

Supplies The balance in NetSolutions' supplies account on December 31 is $2,000. Some of these supplies (CDs, paper, envelopes, etc.) were used during December, and some are still on hand (not used). If either amount is known, the other can be determined. It is normally easier to determine the cost of the supplies on hand at the end of the month than to record daily supplies used.

Assuming that on December 31 the amount of supplies on hand is $760, the amount to be transferred from the asset account to the expense account is $1,240, computed as follows:

Supplies available during December (balance of account)	$2,000
Supplies on hand, December 31	760
Supplies used (amount of adjustment)	$1,240

At the end of December, the supplies expense account is increased (debited) for $1,240, and the supplies account is decreased (credited) for $1,240 to record the supplies used during December. The adjusting journal entry and T accounts for Supplies and Supplies Expense are as follows:

Adjusting Journal Entry

	Journal			Page 5	
Date	**Description**	**Post. Ref.**	**Debit**	**Credit**	
2017					
Dec. 31	Supplies Expense	52	1,240		
	Supplies	14		1,240	
	Supplies used ($2,000 – $760).				

Accounting Equation Impact

Assets	=	**Liabilities**	+	**Stockholders' Equity (Expense)**

	Supplies	14			**Supplies Expense**	52
Bal.	2,000	Dec. 31 1,240		Bal.	800	
Adj. Bal.	760			Dec. 31	1,240	
				Adj. Bal.	2,040	

The adjusting entry is highlighted in the T accounts to separate it from other transactions. After the adjusting entry is recorded and posted, the supplies account has a debit balance of $760. This balance is an asset that will become an expense in a future period.

Why It Matters

Sports Signing Bonus

The **National Football League** (NFL), **National Basketball Association** (NBA), and **National Hockey League** (NHL) all have team salary caps that are used to create parity in the sport league. The salary cap limits the total salaries that a team can pay each year. Teams use signing bonuses as a way to reduce the impact of salaries on the salary cap. Under cap rules, the bonus is spread over the length of the player's contract. For example, if a player receives a $6 million bonus for a six-year contract, the player will receive the complete $6 million upon signing the contract, but only $1 million will be applied to the salary cap for each year of the contract. This is similar to how GAAP also accounts for the bonus. The bonus is treated as a prepaid salary expense that is amortized over the life of the contract. If a player is released prior to the end of the contract, any remaining unamortized balance is expensed immediately.

Prepaid Insurance The debit balance of $2,400 in **NetSolutions**' prepaid insurance account represents a December 1 prepayment of insurance for 12 months. At the end of December, the insurance expense account is increased (debited), and the prepaid insurance account is decreased (credited) by $200, the insurance for one month. The adjusting journal entry and T accounts for Prepaid Insurance and Insurance Expense are as follows:

Adjusting Journal Entry

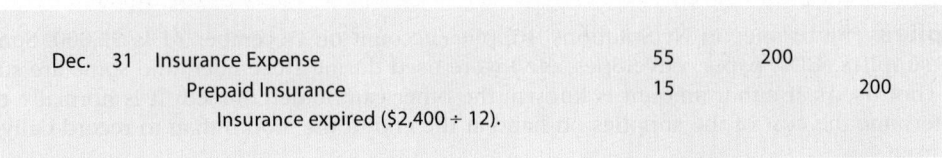

Dec. 31	Insurance Expense	55	200	
	Prepaid Insurance	15		200
	Insurance expired ($2,400 ÷ 12).			

Accounting Equation Impact

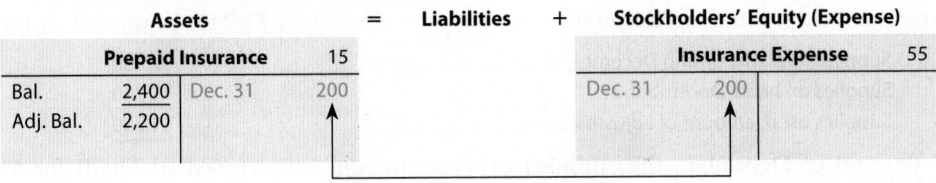

Assets	=	Liabilities	+	Stockholders' Equity (Expense)
Prepaid Insurance 15				**Insurance Expense** 55

		Dec. 31	200		Dec. 31	200
Bal.	2,400					
Adj. Bal.	2,200					

After the adjusting entry is recorded and posted, the prepaid insurance account has a debit balance of $2,200. This balance is an asset that will become an expense in future periods. The insurance expense account has a debit balance of $200, which is an expense of the current period.

If the preceding adjustments for supplies ($1,240) and insurance ($200) are not recorded, the financial statements prepared as of December 31 will be misstated. On the income statement, Supplies Expense and Insurance Expense will be understated by a total of $1,440 ($1,240 + $200), and net income will be overstated by $1,440. On the balance sheet, Supplies and Prepaid Insurance will be overstated by a total of $1,440. Because net income increases retained earnings, stockholders' equity will also be overstated by $1,440 on the balance sheet. The effects of omitting these adjusting entries on the income statement and balance sheet are as follows:

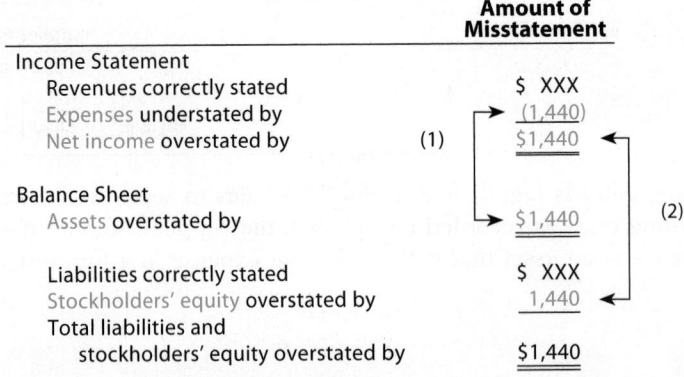

		Amount of Misstatement
Income Statement		
Revenues correctly stated		$ XXX
Expenses understated by		(1,440)
Net income overstated by	(1)	$1,440
Balance Sheet		
Assets overstated by		$1,440 (2)
Liabilities correctly stated		$ XXX
Stockholders' equity overstated by		1,440
Total liabilities and		
stockholders' equity overstated by		$1,440

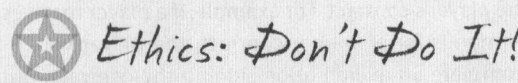 *Ethics: Don't Do It!*

Free Issue

Office supplies are often available to employees on a "free issue" basis. This means that employees do not have to "sign" for the release of office supplies but merely obtain the necessary supplies from a local storage area as needed. Just because supplies are easily available, however, doesn't mean they can be taken for personal use. There are many instances where employees have been terminated for taking supplies home for personal use.

Arrow (1) indicates the effect of the understated expenses on assets. Arrow (2) indicates the effect of the overstated net income on stockholders' equity.

Payments for prepaid expenses are sometimes made at the beginning of the period in which they will be *entirely used or consumed*. To illustrate, the following December 1 transaction of NetSolutions is used:

> *Dec. 1   NetSolutions paid rent of $800 for the month.*

On December 1, the rent payment of $800 represents Prepaid Rent. However, the Prepaid Rent expires daily, and at the end of December there will be no asset left. In such cases, the payment of $800 is recorded as Rent Expense rather than as Prepaid Rent. In this way, no adjusting entry is needed at the end of the period.[5]

Check Up Corner 3-2   Adjusting Entries for Deferrals

For the Atlanta Rhythm Company, selected account balances before adjustment at December 31, the end of the current year, are as follows:

	Debit Balances	Credit Balances
Supplies	$ 2,700	
Prepaid Insurance	12,000	
Unearned Fees		$44,900

Additional data needed to determine year-end adjustments are as follows:

- Supplies on hand at December 31, $1,100.
- Insurance premiums expired during the year, $10,000.
- The balance in the Unearned Fees account on December 31, after adjusting entries, is $15,600.

Journalize the adjusting entries necessary on December 31.

Solution:

A deferral occurs when cash has been received for a future revenue, or cash has been paid for a future expense.

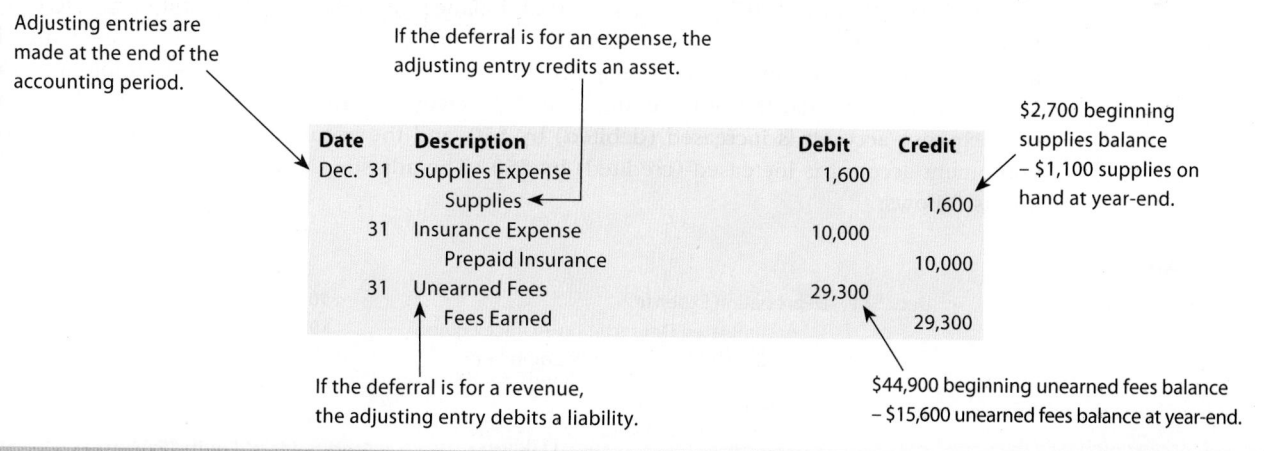

Adjusting entries are made at the end of the accounting period.

If the deferral is for an expense, the adjusting entry credits an asset.

$2,700 beginning supplies balance − $1,100 supplies on hand at year-end.

Date	Description	Debit	Credit
Dec. 31	Supplies Expense	1,600	
	Supplies		1,600
31	Insurance Expense	10,000	
	Prepaid Insurance		10,000
31	Unearned Fees	29,300	
	Fees Earned		29,300

If the deferral is for a revenue, the adjusting entry debits a liability.

$44,900 beginning unearned fees balance − $15,600 unearned fees balance at year-end.

Check Up Corner

---

[5] An alternative treatment of recording the cost of supplies, rent, and other prepayments of expenses is discussed in an appendix that can be downloaded from the book's companion Web site (www.cengagebrain.com).

Objective 4

Prepare adjusting
entries for
depreciation.

Adjusting Entries for Depreciation

Fixed assets, or **plant assets**, are physical resources that are owned and used by a business and are permanent or have a long life. Examples of fixed assets include land, buildings, and equipment. In a sense, fixed assets are a type of *long-term* prepaid expense. However, because of their unique nature and long life, they are discussed separately from other prepaid expenses.

Fixed assets, such as office equipment, are used to generate revenue much like supplies are used to generate revenue. Unlike supplies, however, there is no visible reduction in the quantity of the equipment. Instead, as time passes, the equipment loses its ability to provide useful services. This decrease in usefulness is called **depreciation**.

All fixed assets, except land, lose their usefulness and, thus, are said to **depreciate**. As a fixed asset depreciates, a portion of its cost should be recorded as an expense. This periodic expense is called **depreciation expense**.

The adjusting entry to record depreciation expense is similar to the adjusting entry for supplies used. The depreciation expense account is increased (debited) for the amount of depreciation. However, the fixed asset account is not decreased (credited). This is because both the original cost of a fixed asset and the depreciation recorded since its purchase are reported on the balance sheet. Instead, an account entitled **Accumulated Depreciation** is increased (credited).

Accumulated depreciation accounts are called **contra accounts**, or **contra asset accounts**. This is because accumulated depreciation accounts are deducted from their related fixed asset accounts on the balance sheet. The normal balance of a contra account is opposite to the account from which it is deducted. Because the normal balance of a fixed asset account is a debit, the normal balance of an accumulated depreciation account is a credit.

The normal titles for fixed asset accounts and their related contra asset accounts are as follows:

Fixed Asset Account	Contra Asset Account
Land	None—Land is not depreciated.
Buildings	Accumulated Depreciation—Buildings
Store Equipment	Accumulated Depreciation—Store Equipment
Office Equipment	Accumulated Depreciation—Office Equipment

The December 31, 2017, unadjusted trial balance of **NetSolutions** (Exhibit 5) indicates that NetSolutions owns two fixed assets: land and office equipment. Land does not depreciate; however, an adjusting entry is recorded for the depreciation of the office equipment for December. Assume that the office equipment depreciates $50 during December. The depreciation expense account is increased (debited) by $50, and the accumulated depreciation—office equipment account is increased (credited) by $50.[6] The adjusting journal entry and T accounts are as follows:

**Adjusting
Journal Entry**

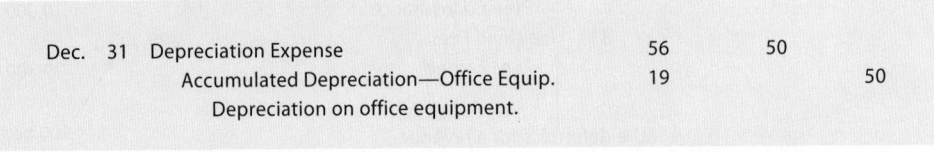

Dec.	31	Depreciation Expense	56	50
		Accumulated Depreciation—Office Equip.	19	50
		Depreciation on office equipment.		

**Accounting Equation
Impact**

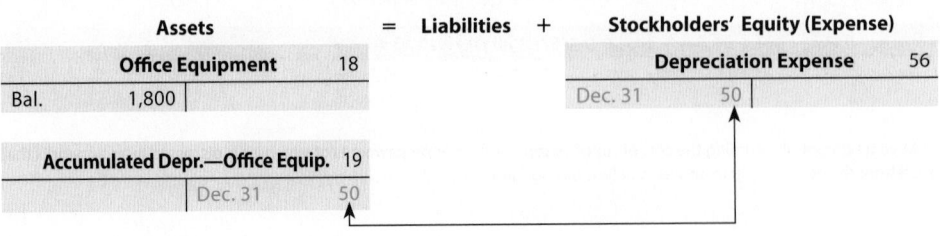

Assets	= Liabilities +	Stockholders' Equity (Expense)
Office Equipment 18		**Depreciation Expense** 56
Bal. 1,800		Dec. 31 50
Accumulated Depr.—Office Equip. 19		
Dec. 31 50		

---

[6] Methods of computing depreciation expense are described and illustrated in Chapter 9.

After the adjusting journal entry is recorded and posted, the office equipment account still has a debit balance of $1,800. This is the original cost of the office equipment that was purchased on December 4. The accumulated depreciation—office equipment account has a credit balance of $50. The difference between these two balances is the cost of the office equipment that has not yet been depreciated. This amount, called the **book value of the asset** (or **net book value**), is computed as follows:

Book Value of Asset = Cost of Asset – Accumulated Depreciation of Asset

Book Value of Office Equipment = Cost of Office Equipment – Accumulated Depr. of Office Equipment
= $1,800 – $50
= $1,750

The office equipment and its related accumulated depreciation are reported on the December 31, 2017, balance sheet as follows:

| Office equipment | $1,800 | |
| Accumulated depreciation | (50) | $1,750 |

In a recent balance sheet, Pandora reported property, plant, and equipment of $57 million, accumulated depreciation of $22 million, and a net book value of $35 million.

Link to Pandora

The market value of a fixed asset usually differs from its book value. This is because depreciation is an *allocation* method, not a *valuation* method. That is, depreciation allocates the cost of a fixed asset to expense over its estimated life. Depreciation does not measure changes in market values, which vary from year to year. Thus, on December 31, 2017, the market value of NetSolutions' office equipment could be more or less than $1,750.

If the adjustment for depreciation ($50) is not recorded, Depreciation Expense on the income statement will be understated by $50, and the net income will be overstated by $50. On the balance sheet, assets (the book value of Office Equipment) and stockholders' equity (Retained Earnings) will be overstated by $50. The effects of omitting the adjustment for depreciation are as follows:

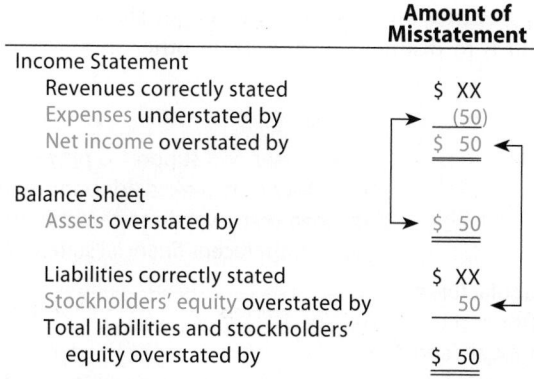

	Amount of Misstatement
Income Statement	
Revenues correctly stated	$ XX
Expenses understated by	(50)
Net income overstated by	$ 50
Balance Sheet	
Assets overstated by	$ 50
Liabilities correctly stated	$ XX
Stockholders' equity overstated by	50
Total liabilities and stockholders' equity overstated by	$ 50

Check Up Corner 3-3   Depreciation

For the Atlanta Rhythm Company, selected account balances before adjustment at December 31, the end of the current year, are as follows:

	Debit Balances	Credit Balances
Equipment	$40,000	
Accumulated Depreciation—Equipment		$12,000

Depreciation on equipment during the year is $4,000.

A. Journalize the adjusting entry necessary for depreciation on December 31.
B. Compute the book value of the equipment that will be reported on the balance sheet.

Solution:

A. Adjusting entries are made at the end of the accounting period.

The debit to Depreciation Expense reflects the portion of the asset's cost that is used during the period.

The credit to Accumulated Depreciation—Equipment increases the account balance, which is reported on the balance sheet.

Date	Description	Debit	Credit
Dec. 31	Depreciation Expense	4,000	
	Accumulated Depreciation—Equipment		4,000

B. Book Value of Equipment = Cost of Equipment − Accumulated Depreciation of Equipment
$24,000 = $40,000 (cost) − $12,000 (beginning balance in accumulated depreciation)
− $4,000 (current year depreciation)

Check Up Corner

Objective 5
Summarize the adjusting process.

Summary of Adjusting Process

A summary of the basic types of adjusting entries is shown in Exhibit 6. The adjusting entries for **NetSolutions** are shown in Exhibit 7. The adjusting entries are dated as of the last day of the period. However, because collecting the adjustment data requires time, the entries are usually recorded at a later date. An explanation is normally included with each adjusting entry.

NetSolutions' adjusting entries are posted to the ledger shown in Exhibit 8. The adjustments are highlighted in Exhibit 8 to distinguish them from other transactions.

Why It Matters

Microsoft's Deferred Revenues

Microsoft Corporation develops, manufactures, licenses, and supports a wide range of computer software products, including Windows® operating systems, Word®, Excel®, and the Xbox® gaming system. When Microsoft sells its products, it incurs an obligation to support its software with technical support and periodic updates. As a result, not all the revenue is earned on the date of sale; some of the revenue on the date of sale is unearned. The portion of revenue related to support services, such as updates and technical support, is earned as time passes and support is provided to customers. Thus, each year Microsoft makes adjusting entries transferring some of its unearned revenue to revenue. The following excerpts were taken from recent financial statements of Microsoft:

	Year 2	Year 1
Unearned revenue (in millions)	$25,158	$22,348

The Year 2 balance is equal to 28% of Year 2 revenues, indicating the significant impact of unearned revenue to Microsoft's operating results. During Year 3, Microsoft expects to recognize $23,150 of revenue from the $25,158 of unearned revenue. At the same time, Microsoft will record additional unearned revenue from Year 3 sales.

Exhibit 6 Summary of Adjustments

ACCRUED REVENUES				
Examples	**Reason for Adjustment**	**Adjusting Entry**	**Examples from NetSolutions**	**Financial Statement Impact if Adjusting Entry Is Omitted**
Services performed but not billed, interest to be received	Services have been provided to the customer, but have not been billed or recorded. Interest has been earned, but has not been received or recorded.	Asset Dr. Revenue Cr.	Accounts Receivable 500 Fees Earned 500	Income Statement: Revenues Understated Expenses No effect Net income Understated Balance Sheet: Assets Understated Liabilities No effect Stockholders' equity Understated (Retained earnings)
ACCRUED EXPENSES				
Wages or salaries incurred but not paid, interest incurred but not paid	Expenses have been incurred, but have not been paid or recorded.	Expense Dr. Liability Cr.	Wages Expense 250 Wages Payable 250	Income Statement: Revenues No effect Expenses Understated Net income Overstated Balance Sheet: Assets No effect Liabilities Understated Stockholders' equity Overstated (Retained earnings)
UNEARNED REVENUES				
Unearned rent, magazine subscriptions received in advance, fees received in advance of services	Cash received before the services have been provided is recorded as a liability. Some services have been provided to the customer before the end of the accounting period.	Liability Dr. Revenue Cr.	Unearned Rent 120 Rent Revenue 120	Income Statement: Revenues Understated Expenses No effect Net income Understated Balance Sheet: Assets No effect Liabilities Overstated Stockholders' equity Understated (Retained earnings)
PREPAID EXPENSES				
Supplies, prepaid insurance	Prepaid expenses (assets) have been used or consumed in the business operations.	Expense Dr. Asset Cr.	Supplies Expense 1,240 Supplies 1,240 Insurance Expense 200 Prepaid Insurance 200	Income Statement: Revenues No effect Expenses Understated Net income Overstated Balance Sheet: Assets Overstated Liabilities No effect Stockholders' equity Overstated (Retained earnings)
DEPRECIATION				
Depreciation of equipment and buildings	Fixed assets depreciate as they are used or consumed in the business operations.	Expense Dr. Contra Asset Cr.	Depreciation Expense 50 Accum. Depreciation— Office Equipment 50	Income Statement: Revenues No effect Expenses Understated Net income Overstated Balance Sheet: Assets Overstated Liabilities No effect Stockholders' equity Overstated (Retained earnings)

Exhibit 7

Adjusting Entries—
NetSolutions

		Journal			Page 5
Date		**Description**	**Post. Ref.**	**Debit**	**Credit**
		Adjusting Entries			
2017					
Dec. 31		Supplies Expense	52	1,240	
		Supplies	14		1,240
		Supplies used ($2,000 – $760).			
	31	Insurance Expense	55	200	
		Prepaid Insurance	15		200
		Insurance expired ($2,400 ÷ 12 months).			
	31	Unearned Rent	23	120	
		Rent Revenue	42		120
		Rent earned ($360 ÷ 3 months).			
	31	Accounts Receivable	12	500	
		Fees Earned	41		500
		Accrued fees (25 hrs. × $20).			
	31	Wages Expense	51	250	
		Wages Payable	22		250
		Accrued wages.			
	31	Depreciation Expense	56	50	
		Accum. Depreciation—Office Equipment	19		50
		Depreciation on office equipment.			

Exhibit 8 Ledger with Adjusting Entries—NetSolutions

Account Cash — Account No. 11

Date	Item	Post. Ref.	Debit	Credit	Balance Debit	Balance Credit
2017						
Nov. 1		1	25,000		25,000	
5		1		20,000	5,000	
18		1	7,500		12,500	
30		1		3,650	8,850	
30		1		950	7,900	
30		2		2,000	5,900	
Dec. 1		2		2,400	3,500	
1		2		800	2,700	
1		2	360		3,060	
6		2		180	2,880	
11		2		400	2,480	
13		3		950	1,530	
16		3	3,100		4,630	
20		3		900	3,730	
21		3	650		4,380	
23		3		1,450	2,930	
27		3		1,200	1,730	
31		3		310	1,420	
31		4		225	1,195	
31		4	2,870		4,065	
31		4		2,000	2,065	

Account Accounts Receivable — Account No. 12

Date	Item	Post. Ref.	Debit	Credit	Balance Debit	Balance Credit
2017						
Dec. 16		3	1,750		1,750	
21		3		650	1,100	
31		4	1,120		2,220	
31	Adjusting	5	500		2,720	

Account Supplies — Account No. 14

Date	Item	Post. Ref.	Debit	Credit	Balance Debit	Balance Credit
2017						
Nov. 10		1	1,350		1,350	
30		1		800	550	
Dec. 23		3	1,450		2,000	
31	Adjusting	5		1,240	760	

Exhibit 8 Ledger with Adjusting Entries—NetSolutions *(Continued)*

Account *Prepaid Insurance* Account No. *15*

Date	Item	Post. Ref.	Debit	Credit	Balance Debit	Balance Credit
2017						
Dec. 1		2	2,400		2,400	
31	Adjusting	5		200	2,200	

Account *Land* Account No. *17*

Date	Item	Post. Ref.	Debit	Credit	Balance Debit	Balance Credit
2017						
Nov. 5		1	20,000		20,000	

Account *Office Equipment* Account No. *18*

Date	Item	Post. Ref.	Debit	Credit	Balance Debit	Balance Credit
2017						
Dec. 4		2	1,800		1,800	

Account *Accum. Depr.—Office Equip.* Account No. *19*

Date	Item	Post. Ref.	Debit	Credit	Balance Debit	Balance Credit
2017						
Dec. 31	Adjusting	5		50		50

Account *Accounts Payable* Account No. *21*

Date	Item	Post. Ref.	Debit	Credit	Balance Debit	Balance Credit
2017						
Nov. 10		1		1,350		1,350
30		1	950			400
Dec. 4		2		1,800		2,200
11		2	400			1,800
20		3	900			900

Account *Wages Payable* Account No. *22*

Date	Item	Post. Ref.	Debit	Credit	Balance Debit	Balance Credit
2017						
Dec. 31	Adjusting	5		250		250

Account *Unearned Rent* Account No. *23*

Date	Item	Post. Ref.	Debit	Credit	Balance Debit	Balance Credit
2017						
Dec. 1		2		360		360
31	Adjusting	5	120			240

Account *Common Stock* Account No. *31*

Date	Item	Post. Ref.	Debit	Credit	Balance Debit	Balance Credit
2017						
Nov. 1		1		25,000		25,000

Account *Dividends* Account No. *33*

Date	Item	Post. Ref.	Debit	Credit	Balance Debit	Balance Credit
2017						
Nov. 30		2	2,000		2,000	
Dec. 31		4	2,000		4,000	

Account *Fees Earned* Account No. *41*

Date	Item	Post. Ref.	Debit	Credit	Balance Debit	Balance Credit
2017						
Nov. 18		1		7,500		7,500
Dec. 16		3		3,100		10,600
16		3		1,750		12,350
31		4		2,870		15,220
31		4		1,120		16,340
31	Adjusting	5		500		16,840

Account *Rent Revenue* Account No. *42*

Date	Item	Post. Ref.	Debit	Credit	Balance Debit	Balance Credit
2017						
Dec. 31	Adjusting	5		120		120

Account *Wages Expense* Account No. *51*

Date	Item	Post. Ref.	Debit	Credit	Balance Debit	Balance Credit
2017						
Nov. 30		1	2,125		2,125	
Dec. 13		3	950		3,075	
27		3	1,200		4,275	
31	Adjusting	5	250		4,525	

(Continued)

Exhibit 8   Ledger with Adjusting Entries—NetSolutions (*Concluded*)

Account *Supplies Expense*   Account No. 52

Date	Item	Post. Ref.	Debit	Credit	Balance Debit	Balance Credit
2017						
Nov. 30		1	800		800	
Dec. 31	Adjusting	5	1,240		2,040	

Account *Rent Expense*   Account No. 53

Date	Item	Post. Ref.	Debit	Credit	Balance Debit	Balance Credit
2017						
Nov. 30		1	800		800	
Dec. 1		2	800		1,600	

Account *Utilities Expense*   Account No. 54

Date	Item	Post. Ref.	Debit	Credit	Balance Debit	Balance Credit
2017						
Nov. 30		1	450		450	
Dec. 31		3	310		760	
31		4	225		985	

Account *Insurance Expense*   Account No. 55

Date	Item	Post. Ref.	Debit	Credit	Balance Debit	Balance Credit
2017						
Dec. 31	Adjusting	5	200		200	

Account *Depreciation Expense*   Account No. 56

Date	Item	Post. Ref.	Debit	Credit	Balance Debit	Balance Credit
2017						
Dec. 31	Adjusting	5	50		50	

Account *Miscellaneous Expense*   Account No. 59

Date	Item	Post. Ref.	Debit	Credit	Balance Debit	Balance Credit
2017						
Nov. 30		1	275		275	
Dec. 6		2	180		455	

Objective 6

Prepare an adjusted trial balance.

Adjusted Trial Balance

After the adjusting entries are posted, an **adjusted trial balance** is prepared. The adjusted trial balance verifies the equality of the total debit and credit balances before the financial statements are prepared. If the adjusted trial balance does not balance, an error has occurred. However, as discussed in Chapter 2, errors may occur even though the adjusted trial balance totals agree. For example, if an adjusting entry were omitted, the adjusted trial balance totals would still agree.

Exhibit 9 shows the adjusted trial balance for **NetSolutions** as of December 31, 2017. Chapter 4 discusses how financial statements, including a classified balance sheet, are prepared from an adjusted trial balance.

NetSolutions Adjusted Trial Balance December 31, 2017	Account No.	Debit Balances	Credit Balances
Cash	11	2,065	
Accounts Receivable...	12	2,720	
Supplies..	14	760	
Prepaid Insurance	15	2,200	
Land	17	20,000	
Office Equipment	18	1,800	
Accumulated Depreciation—Office Equipment..................	19		50
Accounts Payable...	21		900
Wages Payable...	22		250
Unearned Rent...	23		240
Common Stock	31		25,000
Dividends	33	4,000	
Fees Earned..	41		16,840
Rent Revenue	42		120
Wages Expense	51	4,525	
Supplies Expense...	52	2,040	
Rent Expense	53	1,600	
Utilities Expense	54	985	
Insurance Expense	55	200	
Depreciation Expense	56	50	
Miscellaneous Expense	59	455	
		43,400	43,400

Exhibit 9

Adjusted Trial Balance

Analysis for Decision Making

Vertical Analysis

Comparing each item on a financial statement with a total amount from the same statement is useful in analyzing relationships within the financial statement. **Vertical analysis** is the term used to describe such comparisons.

In vertical analysis of a balance sheet, each asset item is stated as a percent of the total assets. Each liability and stockholders' equity item is stated as a percent of total liabilities and stockholders' equity. In vertical analysis of an income statement, each item is stated as a percent of revenues or fees earned.

Vertical analysis is also useful for analyzing changes in financial statements over time. To illustrate, a vertical analysis of two years of income statements for J. Holmes, Attorney-at-Law, follows:

Objective

Describe and illustrate the use of vertical analysis in evaluating a company's performance and financial condition.

J. Holmes, Attorney-at-Law
Income Statements
For the Years Ended December 31

	Year 2		Year 1	
	Amount	Percent*	Amount	Percent*
Fees earned....................................	$187,500	100.0%	$150,000	100.0%
Operating expenses:				
Wages expense	$ 60,000	32.0%	$ 45,000	30.0%
Rent expense.............................	15,000	8.0%	12,000	8.0%
Utilities expense	12,500	6.7%	9,000	6.0%
Supplies expense	2,700	1.4%	3,000	2.0%
Miscellaneous expense.................	2,300	1.2%	1,800	1.2%
Total operating expenses...........	$ 92,500	49.3%	$ 70,800	47.2%
Net income.................................	$ 95,000	50.7%	$ 79,200	52.8%

*Rounded to one decimal place

The preceding vertical analysis indicates both favorable and unfavorable trends affecting the income statement of J. Holmes, Attorney-at-Law. The increase in wages expense of 2% (32.0% − 30.0%) is an unfavorable trend, as is the increase in utilities expense of 0.7% (6.7% − 6.0%). A favorable trend is the decrease in supplies expense of 0.6% (2.0% − 1.4%). Rent expense and miscellaneous expense as a percent of fees earned were constant. The net result of these trends is that net income decreased as a percent of fees earned from 52.8% to 50.7%.

The analysis of the various percentages shown for J. Holmes, Attorney-at-Law, can be enhanced by comparisons with industry averages. Such averages are published by trade associations and financial information services. Any major differences between industry averages should be investigated.

Vertical analysis of operating income taken from two recent years of income statements for **Pandora Media, Inc.** follows:

Pandora Media, Inc.
Operating Income Statements
For the Years Ended January 31
(in thousands)

	Year 2		Year 1	
	Amount	**Percent***	**Amount**	**Percent***
Revenues:				
Advertising...............................	$732,338	79.5%	$489,340	81.5%
Subscription	188,464	20.5%	110,893	18.5%
Total revenues........................	$920,802	100.0%	$600,233	100.0%
Expenses:				
Cost of revenues........................	$508,004	55.2%	$357,083	59.5%
Sales and marketing	277,330	30.1%	169,005	28.2%
General and administrative............	112,443	12.2%	69,300	11.5%
Product development	53,153	5.8%	31,294	5.2%
Total expenses	$950,930	103.3%	$626,682	104.4%
Operating income (loss)...................	$ (30,128)	(3.3)%	$ (26,449)	(4.4)%

*Rounded to one decimal place

The preceding illustration shows the usefulness of vertical analysis. Since Year 2 revenues are almost 50% larger than those of Year 1, it is difficult to compare operating results using only dollar amounts. Vertical analysis, however, provides a relative comparison. The analysis reveals that the operating loss decreased from 4.4% to 3.3% as a percent of total revenues. This improvement was the result of the net change in expenses as a percent of revenue. The cost of revenues decreased from 59.5% to 55.2% of revenues, while sales and marketing, general and administrative, and product development expenses all increased as a percent of sales. The percentage increase in these latter expenses was less than the percentage decrease in the cost of revenues. Thus, total expenses decreased from 104.4% to 103.3% as a percent of revenues.

Make a Decision   Vertical Analysis

World Wrestling Entertainment, Inc. is a sports media and entertainment company primarily focused on professional wrestling. Operating income statements for two recent years follow:

World Wrestling Entertainment, Inc.
Operating Income Statements
For the Years Ended December 31
(in thousands)

	Year 2	Year 1
Revenues	$542,620	$507,970
Expenses:		
Cost of revenues...	$377,615	$323,028
Selling, general, and administrative expenses	180,457	154,582
Depreciation expense	26,705	24,469
Total expenses..	$584,777	$502,079
Operating income (loss).....................................	$ (42,157)	$ 5,891

A. Prepare a vertical analysis of the operating income statements for both years.

B. Using the vertical analysis, explain why there is a loss in Year 2.

Solution:
A.

World Wrestling Entertainment, Inc.
Operating Income Statements
For the Years Ended December 31
(in thousands)

	Year 2		Year 1	
	Amount	Percent*	Amount	Percent*
Revenues	$542,620	100%	$507,970	100%
Expenses:				
Cost of revenues...........................	$377,615	70%	$323,028	64%
Selling, general, and administrative				
expenses..................................	180,457	33%	154,582	30%
Depreciation expense....................	26,705	5%	24,469	5%
Total expenses	$584,777	108%	$502,079	99%
Operating income (loss)...................	$ (42,157)	(8)%	$ 5,891	1%

B. The vertical analysis shows the expenses and operating income as a percent of total revenues for each year. The total expenses for the company have increased as a percent of revenues from Year 1 to Year 2, or from 99% to 108% of total revenues. The cost of revenues increased from 64% to 70%, while the selling, general, and administrative expenses increased from 30% to 33% of total revenues. These two expense categories caused a 9% decrease in the operating income as a percent of revenues, or from 1% to –8% between the two years. Management should investigate why these expenses increased faster than revenues.

Make a Decision

Let's Review

Chapter Summary

1. The accrual basis of accounting requires that revenues are reported in the period in which they are earned and expenses are matched with the revenues they generate. The updating of accounts at the end of the accounting period is called the adjusting process. Each adjusting entry affects an income statement and balance sheet account. The two general classifications for accounts requiring adjustment are accruals and deferrals. Accruals include accrued revenues and accrued expenses. Deferrals include unearned revenues and prepaid expenses.

2. Adjusting entries for accruals include accrued revenues and expenses. The adjusting entry for an accrued revenue debits Accounts Receivable and credits a revenue account such as Fees Earned. The adjusting entry for an accrued expense debits an expense account such as Wages Expense and credits a liability account such as Wages Payable.

3. Adjusting entries for deferrals include unearned revenues and prepaid expenses. The adjusting entry for an unearned revenue debits an unearned revenue account such as Unearned Rent and credits a revenue account such as Rent Revenue. The adjusting entry for an accrued expense debits an expense account such as Wages Expense and credits a liability account such as Wages Payable.

4. The adjusting entry for depreciation of a fixed asset debits Depreciation Expense and credits a contra asset account, Accumulated Depreciation. The book value of a fixed asset equals its cost less its accumulated depreciation. Land is a fixed asset that does not depreciate.

5. A summary of adjustments, including the type of adjustment, reason for the adjustment, the adjusting entry, and the effect of omitting an adjustment on the financial statements, is shown in Exhibit 6.

6. After all of the adjusting entries have been posted, the equality of the total debit balances and the total credit balances is verified by an adjusted trial balance.

Key Terms

accrual (109)
accrual basis of accounting (107)
Accumulated Depreciation (118)
adjusted trial balance (124)
adjusting entries (109)
adjusting process (109)
book value of the asset
    (or net book value) (119)

cash basis of accounting (107)
contra accounts (or contra
    asset accounts) (118)
deferral (109)
depreciate (118)
depreciation (118)
depreciation expense (118)
expense recognition principle (108)

fixed assets (or plant assets) (118)
matching principle (108)
prepaid expense (109)
revenue recognition (108)
revenue recognition principle (108)
unearned revenue (109)
vertical analysis (125)

Practice

Multiple-Choice Questions

1. Which of the following items represents a deferral?
   A. Prepaid insurance
   B. Wages payable
   C. Fees earned
   D. Accumulated depreciation

2. The balance in the unearned rent account for Jones Co. as of December 31 is $1,200. If Jones Co. failed to record the adjusting entry for $600 of rent earned during December, the effect on the balance sheet and income statement for December would be:
   A. assets understated $600; net income overstated $600.
   B. liabilities understated $600; net income understated $600.
   C. liabilities overstated $600; net income understated $600.
   D. liabilities overstated $600; net income overstated $600.

3. If the supplies account, before adjustment on May 31, indicated a balance of $2,250, and supplies on hand at May 31 totaled $950, the adjusting entry would be:
   A. debit Supplies, $950; credit Supplies Expense, $950.
   B. debit Supplies, $1,300; credit Supplies Expense, $1,300.
   C. debit Supplies Expense, $950; credit Supplies, $950.
   D. debit Supplies Expense, $1,300; credit Supplies, $1,300.

4. If the estimated amount of depreciation on equipment for a period is $2,000, the adjusting entry to record depreciation would be:
   A. debit Depreciation Expense, $2,000; credit Equipment, $2,000.
   B. debit Equipment, $2,000; credit Depreciation Expense, $2,000.
   C. debit Depreciation Expense, $2,000; credit Accumulated Depreciation, $2,000.
   D. debit Accumulated Depreciation, $2,000; credit Depreciation Expense, $2,000.

5. If the equipment account has a balance of $22,500 and its accumulated depreciation account has a balance of $14,000, the book value of the equipment is:
   A. $36,500.
   B. $22,500.
   C. $14,000.
   D. $8,500.

6. If the adjusting entry for accrued wages of $7,500 was omitted, the adjusted trial balance totals would be:
   A. Unequal, the debit total would exceed the credit total by $7,500.
   B. Unequal, the debit total would exceed the credit total by $15,000.
   C. Unequal, the credit total would exceed the credit total by $7,500.
   D. Equal, assuming no other errors or omissions.

Answers provided after Problem. Need more practice? Find additional multiple-choice questions, exercises, and problems in CengageNOWv2.

Exercises

SHOW ME HOW

1. Accounts requiring adjustment
Obj. 1, 2, 3

Indicate with a Yes or No whether or not each of the following accounts normally requires an adjusting entry:

A. Accumulated Depreciation
B. Dividends
C. Land
D. Salaries Payable
E. Supplies
F. Unearned Rent

SHOW ME HOW

2. Type of adjustment
Obj. 1, 2, 3

Classify the following items as (1) prepaid expense, (2) unearned revenue, (3) accrued revenue, or (4) accrued expense:

A. Cash received for services not yet rendered

B. Insurance paid for the next year

C. Rent revenue earned but not received

D. Salaries owed but not yet paid

SHOW ME HOW

3. Adjustment for accrued revenues
Obj. 2

At the end of the current year, $23,570 of fees have been earned but have not been billed to clients. Journalize the adjusting entry to record the accrued fees.

SHOW ME HOW

4. Adjustment for accrued expense
Obj. 2

We-Sell Realty Co. pays weekly salaries of $11,800 on Friday for a five-day workweek ending on that day. Journalize the necessary adjusting entry at the end of the accounting period, assuming that the period ends on Wednesday.

SHOW ME HOW

5. Adjustment for unearned revenue
Obj. 3

The balance in the unearned fees account, before adjustment at the end of the year, is $272,500. Journalize the adjusting entry required, assuming the amount of unearned fees at the end of the year is $189,750.

SHOW ME HOW

6. Adjustment for prepaid expense
Obj. 3

The supplies account had a beginning balance of $3,375 and was debited for $6,450 for supplies purchased during the year. Journalize the adjusting entry required at the end of the year, assuming the amount of supplies on hand is $2,980.

SHOW ME HOW

7. Adjustment for depreciation
Obj. 4

The estimated amount of depreciation on equipment for the current year is $6,880. Journalize the adjusting entry to record the depreciation.

SHOW ME HOW

8. Effect of omitting adjustments
Obj. 5

For the year ending August 31, Mammalia Medical Co. mistakenly omitted adjusting entries for (1) depreciation of $5,800, (2) fees earned that were not billed of $44,500, and (3) accrued wages of $7,300. Indicate the combined effect of the errors on (A) revenues, (B) expenses, and (C) net income for the year ended August 31.

SHOW ME HOW

9. Effect of errors on adjusted trial balance
Obj. 6

For each of the following errors, considered individually, indicate whether the error would cause the adjusted trial balance totals to be unequal. If the error would cause the adjusted trial balance totals to be unequal, indicate whether the debit or credit total is higher and by how much.

A. The adjustment of $9,800 for accrued fees earned was journalized as a debit to Accounts Receivable for $9,800 and a credit to Fees Earned for $8,900.

B. The adjustment of depreciation of $3,600 was omitted from the end-of-period adjusting entries.

Answers provided after Problem. Need more practice? Find additional multiple-choice questions, exercises, and problems in CengageNOWv2.

Problem

Three years ago, T. Roderick organized Harbor Realty. At July 31, 2018, the end of the current year, the unadjusted trial balance of Harbor Realty follows:

Harbor Realty Unadjusted Trial Balance July 31, 2018		
	Debit Balances	Credit Balances
Cash	3,425	
Accounts Receivable..	7,000	
Supplies...	1,270	
Prepaid Insurance	620	
Office Equipment	51,650	
Accumulated Depreciation—Office Equipment..................		9,700
Accounts Payable		925
Wages Payable...		0
Unearned Fees...		1,250
Common Stock		5,000
Retained Earnings		24,000
Dividends	5,200	
Fees Earned...		59,125
Wages Expense	22,415	
Depreciation Expense	0	
Rent Expense	4,200	
Utilities Expense	2,715	
Supplies Expense...	0	
Insurance Expense	0	
Miscellaneous Expense	1,505	
	100,000	100,000

The data needed to determine year-end adjustments follow:
- Supplies on hand at July 31, 2018, $380.
- Insurance premiums expired during the year, $315.
- Depreciation of equipment during the year, $4,950.
- Wages accrued but not paid at July 31, 2018, $440.
- Accrued fees earned but not recorded at July 31, 2018, $1,000.
- Unearned fees on July 31, 2018, $750.

Instructions

1. Prepare the necessary adjusting journal entries on July 31. Include journal entry explanations.

2. Determine the balance of the accounts affected by the adjusting entries, and prepare an adjusted trial balance.

Need more practice? Find additional multiple-choice questions, exercises, and problems in CengageNOWv2.

Answers

Multiple-Choice Questions

1. **A** A deferral is the delay in recording an expense already paid, such as prepaid insurance (answer A). Wages payable (answer B) is considered an accrued expense or accrued liability. Fees earned (answer C) is a revenue item. Accumulated depreciation (answer D) is a contra item to a fixed asset.

2. **C** The failure to record the adjusting entry debiting Unearned Rent, $600, and crediting Rent Revenue, $600, would have the effect of overstating liabilities by $600 and understating net income by $600 (answer C).

3. **D** The balance in the supplies account, before adjustment, represents the amount of supplies available. From this amount ($2,250) is subtracted the amount of supplies on hand ($950) to determine the supplies used ($1,300). Since increases in expense accounts are recorded by debits and decreases in asset accounts are recorded by credits, answer D is the correct entry.

4. **C** Since increases in expense accounts (such as depreciation expense) are recorded by debits and it is customary to record the decreases in usefulness of fixed assets as credits to accumulated depreciation accounts, answer C is the correct entry.

5. **D** The book value of a fixed asset is the difference between the balance in the asset account and the balance in the related accumulated depreciation account, or $22,500 – $14,000, as indicated by answer D ($8,500).

6. **D** Assuming no other errors or omission, the adjusted trial balance totals would be equal even though the adjusting entry for accrued wages was omitted. This illustrates that equal debit and credit totals on a trial balance don't necessarily mean that errors don't exist in the accounts.

Exercises

1.

A. Yes	C. No	E. Yes
B. No	D. Yes	F. Yes

2.

A. Unearned revenue	C. Accrued revenue
B. Prepaid expense	D. Accrued expense

3.

Dec. 31	Accounts Receivable	23,570	
	Fees Earned		23,570
	Accrued fees.		

4.

Dec. 31	Salaries Expense	7,080	
	Salaries Payable		7,080
	Accrued salaries [($11,800 ÷ 5 days) × 3 days].		

5.

Dec. 31	Unearned Fees	82,750	
	Fees Earned		82,750
	Fees earned ($272,500 – $189,750).		

6.

			Debit	Credit
Dec. 31	Supplies Expense		6,845	
	Supplies			6,845
	Supplies used ($3,375 + $6,450 − $2,980).			

7.

			Debit	Credit
Dec. 31	Depreciation Expense		6,880	
	Accumulated Depreciation–Equipment			6,880
	Depreciattion on equipment.			

8.

A. Revenues were understated by $44,500.
B. Expenses were understated by $13,100 ($5,800 + $7,300).
C. Net income was understated by $31,400 ($44,500 − $13,100).

9.

A. The totals are unequal. The debit total is higher by $900 ($9,800 − $8,900).
B. The totals are equal because the adjusting entry was omitted.

Need more help? Watch step-by-step videos of how to compute answers to these Exercises in CengageNOWv2.

Problem

1.

Journal					
Date		**Description**	**Post. Ref.**	**Debit**	**Credit**
2018 July	31	Supplies Expense		890	
		Supplies			890
		Supplies used ($1,270 − $380).			
	31	Insurance Expense		315	
		Prepaid Insurance			315
		Insurance expired.			
	31	Depreciation Expense		4,950	
		Accumulated Depreciation—Office Equipment			4,950
		Depreciation expense.			
	31	Wages Expense		440	
		Wages Payable			440
		Accrued wages.			
	31	Accounts Receivable		1,000	
		Fees Earned			1,000
		Accrued fees.			
	31	Unearned Fees		500	
		Fees Earned			500
		Fees earned ($1,250 − $750).			

2.

Harbor Realty
Adjusted Trial Balance
July 31, 2018

	Debit Balances	Credit Balances
Cash	3,425	
Accounts Receivable	8,000	
Supplies	380	
Prepaid Insurance	305	
Office Equipment	51,650	
Accumulated Depreciation—Office Equipment		14,650
Accounts Payable		925
Wages Payable		440
Unearned Fees		750
Common Stock		5,000
Retained Earnings		24,000
Dividends	5,200	
Fees Earned		60,625
Wages Expense	22,855	
Depreciation Expense	4,950	
Rent Expense	4,200	
Utilities Expense	2,715	
Supplies Expense	890	
Insurance Expense	315	
Miscellaneous Expense	1,505	
	106,390	106,390

Discussion Questions

1. How are revenues and expenses reported on the income statement under (A) the cash basis of accounting and (B) the accrual basis of accounting?

2. Is the matching concept related to (A) the cash basis of accounting or (B) the accrual basis of accounting?

3. Why are adjusting entries needed at the end of an accounting period?

4. What is the difference between *adjusting entries* and *correcting entries*?

5. Identify the four different categories of adjusting entries frequently required at the end of an accounting period.

6. If the effect of the debit portion of an adjusting entry is to increase the balance of an asset account, which of the following statements describes the effect of the credit portion of the entry?

   A. Increases the balance of a revenue account.

   B. Increases the balance of an expense account.

   C. Increases the balance of a liability account.

7. If the effect of the credit portion of an adjusting entry is to increase the balance of a liability account, which of the following statements describes the effect of the debit portion of the entry?

   A. Increases the balance of a revenue account.

   B. Increases the balance of an expense account.

   C. Increases the balance of an asset account.

8. Does every adjusting entry have an effect on determining the amount of net income for a period? Explain.

9. On November 1 of the current year, a business paid the November rent on the building that it occupies. (A) Do the rights acquired at November 1 represent an asset or an expense? (B) What is the justification for debiting Rent Expense at the time of payment?

10. (A) Explain the purpose of the two accounts: Depreciation Expense and Accumulated Depreciation. (B) What is the normal balance of each account? (C) Is it customary for the balances of the two accounts to be equal in amount? (D) In what financial statements, if any, will each account appear?

Basic Exercises

SHOW ME HOW

BE 3-1 Accounts requiring adjustment   Obj. 1, 2, 3

Indicate with a Yes or No whether or not each of the following accounts normally requires an adjusting entry:

A. Building   C. Wages Expense   E. Common Stock

B. Cash   D. Miscellaneous Expense   F. Prepaid Insurance

SHOW ME HOW

BE 3-2 Type of adjustment   Obj. 1, 2, 3

Classify the following items as (1) prepaid expense, (2) unearned revenue, (3) accrued revenue, or (4) accrued expense:

A. Cash received for use of land next month   C. Rent expense owed but not yet paid

B. Fees earned but not received   D. Supplies on hand

SHOW ME HOW

BE 3-3 Adjustment for accrued revenues   Obj. 2

At the end of the current year, $17,555 of fees have been earned but have not been billed to clients. Journalize the adjusting entry to record the accrued fees.

SHOW ME HOW

BE 3-4 Adjustment for accrued expense   Obj. 2

Prospect Realty Co. pays weekly salaries of $27,600 on Monday for a six-day workweek ending the preceding Saturday. Journalize the necessary adjusting entry at the end of the accounting period, assuming that the period ends on Friday.

SHOW ME HOW

BE 3-5 Adjustment for unearned revenue   Obj. 3

On June 1, 2018, Herbal Co. received $18,900 for the rent of land for 12 months. Journalize the adjusting entry required for unearned rent on December 31, 2018.

SHOW ME HOW

BE 3-6 Adjustment for prepaid expense   Obj. 3

The prepaid insurance account had a beginning balance of $4,500 and was debited for $16,600 of premiums paid during the year. Journalize the adjusting entry required at the end of the year, assuming the amount of unexpired insurance related to future periods is $5,600.

SHOW ME HOW

BE 3-7 Adjustment for depreciation   Obj. 4

The estimated amount of depreciation on equipment for the current year is $7,700. Journalize the adjusting entry to record the depreciation.

SHOW ME HOW

BE 3-8 Effect of omitting adjustments   Obj. 5

For the year ending April 30, Urology Medical Services Co. mistakenly omitted adjusting entries for (1) $1,400 of supplies that were used, (2) unearned revenue of $6,600 that was earned, and (3) insurance of $9,000 that expired. Indicate the combined effect of the errors on (A) revenues, (B) expenses, and (C) net income for the year ended April 30.

SHOW ME HOW

BE 3-9 Effect of errors on adjusted trial balance   Obj. 6

For each of the following errors, considered individually, indicate whether the error would cause the adjusted trial balance totals to be unequal. If the error would cause the adjusted trial balance totals to be unequal, indicate whether the debit or credit total is higher and by how much.

A. The adjustment for accrued wages of $5,200 was journalized as a debit to Wages Expense for $5,200 and a credit to Accounts Payable for $5,200.

B. The entry for $1,125 of supplies used during the period was journalized as a debit to Supplies Expense of $1,125 and a credit to Supplies of $1,152.

Exercises

EX 3-1 Classifying types of adjustments

Obj. 1, 2, 3

Classify the following items as (A) prepaid expense, (B) unearned revenue, (C) accrued revenue, or (D) accrued expense:

1. A two-year premium paid on a fire insurance policy.
2. Fees earned but not yet received.
3. Fees received but not yet earned.
4. Salary owed but not yet paid.
5. Subscriptions received in advance by a magazine publisher.
6. Supplies on hand.
7. Taxes owed but payable in the following period.
8. Utilities owed but not yet paid.

EX 3-2 Classifying adjusting entries

Obj. 1, 2, 3

The following accounts were taken from the unadjusted trial balance of Orion Co., a congressional lobbying firm. Indicate whether or not each account would normally require an adjusting entry. If the account normally requires an adjusting entry, use the following notation to indicate the type of adjustment:

AE—Accrued Expense
AR—Accrued Revenue
PE—Prepaid Expense
UR—Unearned Revenue

To illustrate, the answer for the first account follows:

Account	Answer
Accounts Receivable	Normally requires adjustment (AR).
Cash	
Common Stock	
Interest Expense	
Interest Receivable	
Land	
Office Equipment	
Prepaid Rent	
Supplies	
Unearned Fees	
Wages Expense	

SHOW ME HOW

EX 3-3 Adjusting entry for accrued fees

Obj. 2

At the end of the current year, $59,500 of fees have been earned but have not been billed to clients.

A. Journalize the adjusting entry to record the accrued fees.

B. ━━━➤ If the cash basis rather than the accrual basis had been used, would an adjusting entry have been necessary? Explain.

EX 3-4   Effect of omitting adjusting entry
Obj. 2, 5

The adjusting entry for accrued fees was omitted at October 31, the end of the current year. Indicate which items will be in error, because of the omission, on (A) the income statement for the current year and (B) the balance sheet as of October 31. Also indicate whether the items in error will be overstated or understated.

EX 3-5   Adjusting entries for accrued salaries
Obj. 2

✔ A. Amount of entry: $10,350

SHOW ME HOW

Garcia Realty Co. pays weekly salaries of $17,250 on Friday for a five-day workweek ending on that day. Journalize the necessary adjusting entry at the end of the accounting period, assuming that the period ends (A) on Wednesday and (B) on Thursday.

EX 3-6   Determining wages paid
Obj. 2

The wages payable and wages expense accounts at May 31, after adjusting entries have been posted at the end of the first month of operations, are shown in the following T accounts:

Wages Payable		Wages Expense	
Bal.	7,175	Bal. 73,250	

Determine the amount of wages paid during the month.

EX 3-7   Effect of omitting adjusting entry
Obj. 2, 5

Accrued salaries owed to employees for October 30 and 31 are not considered in preparing the financial statements for the year ended October 31. Indicate which items will be erroneously stated, because of the error, on (A) the income statement for the year and (B) the balance sheet as of October 31. Also indicate whether the items in error will be overstated or understated.

EX 3-8   Effect of omitting adjusting entry
Obj. 2, 5

When preparing the financial statements for the year ended October 31, accrued salaries owed to employees for October 30 and 31 were overlooked. The accrued salaries were included in the first salary payment in November. Indicate which items will be erroneously stated, because of failure to correct the initial error, on (A) the income statement for the month of November and (B) the balance sheet as of November 30.

EX 3-9   Adjusting entries for unearned fees
Obj. 3

SHOW ME HOW

The balance in the unearned fees account, before adjustment at the end of the year, is $18,000. Journalize the adjusting entry required if the amount of unearned fees at the end of the year is $3,600.

EX 3-10   Effect of omitting adjusting entry
Obj. 3, 5

At the end of July, the first month of the business year, the usual adjusting entry transferring rent earned to a revenue account from the unearned rent account was omitted. Indicate which items will be incorrectly stated, because of the error, on (A) the income statement for July and (B) the balance sheet as of July 31. Also indicate whether the items in error will be overstated or understated.

EX 3-11   Adjusting entry for supplies
Obj. 3

SHOW ME HOW

The balance in the supplies account, before adjustment at the end of the year, is $4,850. Journalize the adjusting entry required if the amount of supplies on hand at the end of the year is $880.

SHOW ME HOW

EX 3-12 Determining supplies purchased

Obj. 3

The supplies and supplies expense accounts at December 31, after adjusting entries have been posted at the end of the first year of operations, are shown in the following T accounts:

Supplies		Supplies Expense	
Bal. 2,550		Bal. 7,120	

Determine the amount of supplies purchased during the year.

EX 3-13 Effect of omitting adjusting entry

Obj. 3, 5

At March 31, the end of the first month of operations, the usual adjusting entry transferring prepaid insurance expired to an expense account is omitted. Which items will be incorrectly stated, because of the error, on (A) the income statement for March and (B) the balance sheet as of March 31? Also indicate whether the items in error will be overstated or understated.

SHOW ME HOW

EX 3-14 Adjusting entries for prepaid insurance

Obj. 3

The balance in the prepaid insurance account, before adjustment at the end of the year, is $27,000. Journalize the adjusting entry required under each of the following *alternatives* for determining the amount of the adjustment: (A) the amount of insurance expired during the year is $20,250; (B) the amount of unexpired insurance applicable to future periods is $6,750.

SHOW ME HOW

EX 3-15 Adjusting entries for prepaid insurance

Obj. 3

The prepaid insurance account had a balance of $3,000 at the beginning of the year. The account was debited for $32,500 for premiums on policies purchased during the year. Journalize the adjusting entry required under each of the following *alternatives* for determining the amount of the adjustment: (A) the amount of unexpired insurance applicable to future periods is $4,800; (B) the amount of insurance expired during the year is $30,700.

SHOW ME HOW

EX 3-16 Adjusting entries for unearned and accrued fees

Obj. 2, 3

The balance in the unearned fees account, before adjustment at the end of the year, is $97,770. Of these fees, $39,750 have been earned. In addition, $24,650 of fees have been earned but have not been billed. Journalize the adjusting entries (A) to adjust the unearned fees account and (B) to record the accrued fees.

EX 3-17 Adjusting entries for prepaid and accrued taxes

Obj. 2, 3

✔ B. $57,320

SHOW ME HOW

A-Z Construction Company was organized on May 1 of the current year. On May 2, A-Z Construction prepaid $18,480 to the city for taxes (license fees) for the *next* 12 months and debited the prepaid taxes account. A-Z Construction is also required to pay in January an annual tax (on property) for the *previous* calendar year. The estimated amount of the property tax for the current year (May 1 to December 31) is $45,000.

A. Journalize the two adjusting entries required to bring the accounts affected by the two taxes up to date as of December 31, the end of the current year.

B. What is the amount of tax expense for the current year?

SHOW ME HOW

EX 3-18 Adjustment for depreciation

Obj. 4

The estimated amount of depreciation on equipment for the current year is $8,200. Journalize the adjusting entry to record the depreciation.

SHOW ME HOW

EX 3-19 Determining fixed asset's book value

Obj. 4

The balance in the equipment account is $3,150,000, and the balance in the accumulated depreciation—equipment account is $2,075,000.

A. What is the book value of the equipment?

B. ━━━▶ Does the balance in the accumulated depreciation account mean that the equipment's loss of value is $2,075,000? Explain.

REAL WORLD

EX 3-20 Book value of fixed assets

Obj. 4

In a recent balance sheet, **Microsoft Corporation** reported *Property, Plant, and Equipment* of $27,804 million and *Accumulated Depreciation* of $14,793 million.

A. What was the book value of the fixed assets?

B. ━━━▶ Would the book value of Microsoft's fixed assets normally approximate their fair market values?

REAL WORLD

EX 3-21 Effects of errors on financial statements

Obj. 2, 5

For a recent period, the balance sheet for **Costco Wholesale Corporation** reported accrued expenses of $3,446 million. For the same period, Costco reported income before income taxes of $3,197 million. Assume that the adjusting entry for $3,446 million of accrued expenses was not recorded at the end of the current period. What would have been the income (loss) before income taxes?

REAL WORLD

EX 3-22 Effects of errors on financial statements

Obj. 2, 5

For a recent year, the balance sheet for **The Campbell Soup Company** includes accrued expenses of $553 million. The income before taxes for Campbell for the year was $1,073 million.

A. Assume the adjusting entry for $553 million of accrued expenses was not recorded at the end of the year. By how much would income before taxes have been misstated?

B. What is the percentage of the misstatement in (A) to the reported income of $1,073 million? (Round to one decimal place.)

EX 3-23 Effects of errors on financial statements

Obj. 2, 3, 5

✔ 1. A. Revenue understated, $34,900

The accountant for Healthy Life Company, a medical services consulting firm, mistakenly omitted adjusting entries for (A) unearned revenue earned during the year ($34,900) and (B) accrued wages ($12,770). Indicate the effect of each error, considered individually, on the income statement for the current year ended July 31. Also indicate the effect of each error on the July 31 balance sheet. Set up a table similar to the following, and record your answers by inserting the dollar amount in the appropriate spaces. Insert a zero if the error does not affect the item.

	Error (A)		Error (B)	
	Over-stated	Under-stated	Over-stated	Under-stated
1. Revenue for the year would be	$ _____	$ _____	$ _____	$ _____
2. Expenses for the year would be	$ _____	$ _____	$ _____	$ _____
3. Net income for the year would be	$ _____	$ _____	$ _____	$ _____
4. Assets at July 31 would be	$ _____	$ _____	$ _____	$ _____
5. Liabilities at July 31 would be	$ _____	$ _____	$ _____	$ _____
6. Stockholders' equity at July 31 would be	$ _____	$ _____	$ _____	$ _____

EX 3-24   Effects of errors on financial statements   Obj. 2, 3, 5

If the net income for the current year had been $196,400 in Exercise 3-23, what would have been the correct net income if the proper adjusting entries had been made?

SHOW ME HOW

EX 3-25   Adjusting entries for depreciation; effect of error   Obj. 4, 5

On December 31, a business estimates depreciation on equipment used during the first year of operations to be $13,900.

A. Journalize the adjusting entry required as of December 31.

B. If the adjusting entry in (A) were omitted, which items would be erroneously stated on (1) the income statement for the year and (2) the balance sheet as of December 31?

SHOW ME HOW

EX 3-26   Adjusting entries from trial balances   Obj. 6

The unadjusted and adjusted trial balances for American Leaf Company on October 31, 2018, follow:

American Leaf Company
Trial Balances
October 31, 2018

	Unadjusted		Adjusted	
	Debit Balances	Credit Balances	Debit Balances	Credit Balances
Cash	16		16	
Accounts Receivable............................	38		44	
Supplies......................................	12		10	
Prepaid Insurance	20		8	
Land	26		26	
Equipment.....................................	40		40	
Accumulated Depreciation—Equipment		8		12
Accounts Payable		26		26
Wages Payable.................................		0		2
Common Stock.................................		20		20
Retained Earnings		72		72
Dividends	8		8	
Fees Earned....................................		74		80
Wages Expense	24		26	
Rent Expense	8		8	
Insurance Expense	0		12	
Utilities Expense	4		4	
Depreciation Expense	0		4	
Supplies Expense..............................	0		2	
Miscellaneous Expense	4		4	
	200	200	212	212

Journalize the five entries that adjusted the accounts at October 31, 2018. None of the accounts were affected by more than one adjusting entry.

EX 3-27   Adjusting entries from trial balances   Obj. 6

✔ Corrected trial balance totals, $369,000

The accountant for Eva's Laundry prepared the following unadjusted and adjusted trial balances. Assume that all balances in the unadjusted trial balance and the amounts of the adjustments are correct. Identify the errors in the accountant's adjusting entries, assuming that none of the accounts were affected by more than one adjusting entry.

Eva's Laundry
Trial Balances
May 31, 2018

	Unadjusted		Adjusted	
	Debit Balances	Credit Balances	Debit Balances	Credit Balances
Cash	7,500		7,500	
Accounts Receivable............................	18,250		23,250	
Laundry Supplies................................	3,750		6,750	
Prepaid Insurance*	5,200		1,600	
Laundry Equipment	190,000		177,000	
Accumulated Depreciation—Laundry Equipment....		48,000		48,000
Accounts Payable		9,600		9,600
Wages Payable...................................				1,000
Common Stock		35,000		35,000
Retained Earnings...............................		75,300		75,300
Dividends	28,775		28,775	
Laundry Revenue................................		182,100		182,100
Wages Expense	49,200		49,200	
Rent Expense	25,575		25,575	
Utilities Expense	18,500		18,500	
Depreciation Expense			13,000	
Laundry Supplies Expense			3,000	
Insurance Expense			600	
Miscellaneous Expense	3,250		3,250	
	350,000	350,000	358,000	351,000

* $3,600 of insurance expired during the year.

Problems: Series A

PR 3-1A   Adjusting entries
Obj. 2, 3, 4

On March 31, the following data were accumulated to assist the accountant in preparing the adjusting entries for Potomac Realty:

- The supplies account balance on March 31 is $5,620. The supplies on hand on March 31 are $1,290.
- The unearned rent account balance on March 31 is $5,000 representing the receipt of an advance payment on March 1 of four months' rent from tenants.
- Wages accrued but not paid at March 31 are $2,290.
- Fees accrued but unbilled at March 31 are $16,825.
- Depreciation of office equipment is $4,600.

Instructions

1. Journalize the adjusting entries required at March 31.

2. ➡ Briefly explain the difference between adjusting entries and entries that would be made to correct errors.

PR 3-2A   Adjusting entries
Obj. 2, 3, 4, 5

Selected account balances before adjustment for Atlantic Coast Realty at July 31, the end of the current year, are as follows:

(Continued)

	Debits	Credits
Accounts Receivable	$ 75,000	
Equipment	345,700	
Accumulated Depreciation—Equipment		$112,500
Prepaid Rent	9,000	
Supplies	3,350	
Wages Payable		—
Unearned Fees		12,000
Fees Earned		660,000
Wages Expense	325,000	
Rent Expense	—	
Depreciation Expense	—	
Supplies Expense	—	

Data needed for year-end adjustments are as follows:

- Unbilled fees at July 31, $11,150.
- Supplies on hand at July 31, $900.
- Rent expired, $6,000.
- Depreciation of equipment during year, $8,950.
- Unearned fees at July 31, $2,000.
- Wages accrued but not paid at July 31, $4,840.

Instructions

1. Journalize the six adjusting entries required at July 31, based on the data presented.

2. What would be the effect on the income statement if the adjustments for unbilled fees and accrued wages were omitted at the end of the year?

3. What would be the effect on the balance sheet if the adjustments for unbilled fees and accrued wages were omitted at the end of the year?

4. What would be the effect on the "Net increase or decrease in cash" on the statement of cash flows if the adjustments for unbilled fees and accrued wages were omitted at the end of the year?

GENERAL LEDGER

PR 3-3A   Adjusting entries

Obj. 2, 3, 4, 5

Reliable Repairs & Service, an electronics repair store, prepared the following unadjusted trial balance at the end of its first year of operations:

Reliable Repairs & Service
Unadjusted Trial Balance
April 30, 2018

	Debit Balances	Credit Balances
Cash	10,350	
Accounts Receivable	67,500	
Supplies	16,200	
Equipment	116,100	
Accounts Payable		15,750
Unearned Fees		18,000
Common Stock		10,000
Retained Earnings		111,500
Dividends	13,500	
Fees Earned		294,750
Wages Expense	94,500	
Rent Expense	72,000	
Utilities Expense	51,750	
Miscellaneous Expense	8,100	
	450,000	450,000

For preparing the adjusting entries, the following data were assembled:

- Fees earned but unbilled on April 30 were $9,850.
- Supplies on hand on April 30 were $4,660.

- Depreciation of equipment was estimated to be $6,470 for the year.
- The balance in unearned fees represented the April 1 receipt in advance for services to be provided. During April, $15,000 of the services were provided.
- Unpaid wages accrued on April 30 were $5,200.

Instructions

1. Journalize the adjusting entries necessary on April 30, 2018.

2. Determine the revenues, expenses, and net income of Reliable Repairs & Service before the adjusting entries.

3. Determine the revenues, expense, and net income of Reliable Repairs & Service after the adjusting entries.

4. Determine the effect of the adjusting entries on Retained Earnings.

GENERAL LEDGER

PR 3-4A   Adjusting entries

Obj. 2, 3, 4, 5, 6

Good Note Company specializes in the repair of music equipment and is owned and operated by Robin Stahl. On November 30, 2018, the end of the current year, the accountant for Good Note prepared the following trial balances:

Good Note Company
Trial Balances
November 30, 2018

	Unadjusted		Adjusted	
	Debit Balances	Credit Balances	Debit Balances	Credit Balances
Cash	38,250		38,250	
Accounts Receivable	89,500		89,500	
Supplies	11,250		2,400	
Prepaid Insurance	14,250		3,850	
Equipment	290,450		290,450	
Accumulated Depreciation—Equipment		94,500		106,100
Automobiles	129,500		129,500	
Accumulated Depreciation—Automobiles		54,750		62,050
Accounts Payable		24,930		26,130
Salaries Payable		—		8,100
Unearned Service Fees		18,000		9,000
Common Stock		100,000		100,000
Retained Earnings		224,020		224,020
Dividends	75,000		75,000	
Service Fees Earned		733,800		742,800
Salary Expense	516,900		525,000	
Rent Expense	54,000		54,000	
Supplies Expense	—		8,850	
Depreciation Expense—Equipment	—		11,600	
Depreciation Expense—Automobiles	—		7,300	
Utilities Expense	12,900		14,100	
Taxes Expense	8,175		8,175	
Insurance Expense	—		10,400	
Miscellaneous Expense	9,825		9,825	
	1,250,000	1,250,000	1,278,200	1,278,200

Instructions

Journalize the seven entries that adjusted the accounts at November 30. None of the accounts were affected by more than one adjusting entry.

PR 3-5A   Adjusting entries and adjusted trial balances

Obj. 2, 3, 4, 5, 6

✔ 2. Total of Debit column: $776,180

Rowland Company is a small editorial services company owned and operated by Marlene Rowland. On August 31, 2018, the end of the current year, Rowland Company's accounting clerk prepared the following unadjusted trial balance:

EXCEL TEMPLATE

GENERAL LEDGER

(Continued)

Rowland Company
Unadjusted Trial Balance
August 31, 2018

	Debit Balances	Credit Balances
Cash	7,500	
Accounts Receivable	38,400	
Prepaid Insurance	7,200	
Supplies	1,980	
Land	112,500	
Building	150,250	
Accumulated Depreciation—Building		87,550
Equipment	135,300	
Accumulated Depreciation—Equipment		97,950
Accounts Payable		12,150
Unearned Rent		6,750
Common Stock		75,000
Retained Earnings		146,000
Dividends	15,000	
Fees Earned		324,600
Salaries and Wages Expense	193,370	
Utilities Expense	42,375	
Advertising Expense	22,800	
Repairs Expense	17,250	
Miscellaneous Expense	6,075	
	750,000	750,000

The data needed to determine year-end adjustments are as follows:

- Unexpired insurance at August 31, $6,000.
- Supplies on hand at August 31, $480.
- Depreciation of building for the year, $7,500.
- Depreciation of equipment for the year, $4,150.
- Rent unearned at August 31, $1,550.
- Accrued salaries and wages at August 31, $3,200.
- Fees earned but unbilled on August 31, $11,330.

Instructions

1. Journalize the adjusting entries using the following additional accounts: Salaries and Wages Payable; Rent Revenue; Insurance Expense; Depreciation Expense—Building; Depreciation Expense—Equipment; and Supplies Expense.

2. Determine the balances of the accounts affected by the adjusting entries, and prepare an adjusted trial balance.

PR 3-6A Adjusting entries and errors

Obj. 2, 3, 4, 5

✔ 2. Corrected net income: $137,750

At the end of April, the first month of operations, the following selected data were taken from the financial statements of Shelby Crawford, an attorney:

EXCEL TEMPLATE

Net income for April	$120,000
Total assets at April 30	750,000
Total liabilities at April 30	300,000
Total stockholders' equity at April 30	450,000

In preparing the financial statements, adjustments for the following data were overlooked:

- Supplies used during April, $2,750.
- Unbilled fees earned at April 30, $23,700.
- Depreciation of equipment for April, $1,800.
- Accrued wages at April 30, $1,400.

Instructions

1. Journalize the entries to record the omitted adjustments.

2. Determine the correct amount of net income for April and the total assets, liabilities, and stockholders' equity at April 30. In addition to indicating the corrected amounts, indicate the effect of each omitted adjustment by setting up and completing a columnar table similar to the following. The adjustment for supplies used is presented as an example.

	Net Income	Total Assets	=	Total Liabilities	+ Total Stockholders' Equity
Reported amounts	$120,000	$750,000		$300,000	$450,000
Corrections:					
Supplies used	–2,750	–2,750		0	–2,750
Unbilled fees earned	_____	_____		_____	_____
Equipment depreciation	_____	_____		_____	_____
Accrued wages	_____	_____		_____	_____
Corrected amounts	_____	_____		_____	_____

Problems: Series B

SHOW ME HOW   EXCEL TEMPLATE

PR 3-1B Adjusting entries   Obj. 2, 3, 4

On May 31, the following data were accumulated to assist the accountant in preparing the adjusting entries for Oceanside Realty:

- Fees accrued but unbilled at May 31 are $19,750.
- The supplies account balance on May 31 is $12,300. The supplies on hand at May 31 are $4,150.
- Wages accrued but not paid at May 31 are $2,700.
- The unearned rent account balance at May 31 is $9,000, representing the receipt of an advance payment on May 1 of three months' rent from tenants.
- Depreciation of office equipment is $3,200.

Instructions

1. Journalize the adjusting entries required at May 31.

2. ══════► Briefly explain the difference between adjusting entries and entries that would be made to correct errors.

SHOW ME HOW

PR 3-2B Adjusting entries   Obj. 2, 3, 4, 5

Selected account balances before adjustment for Intuit Realty at November 30, the end of the current year, follow:

	Debits	Credits
Accounts Receivable	$ 75,000	
Equipment	250,000	
Accumulated Depreciation—Equipment		$ 12,000
Prepaid Rent	12,000	
Supplies	3,170	
Wages Payable		—
Unearned Fees		10,000
Fees Earned		400,000
Wages Expense	140,000	
Rent Expense	—	
Depreciation Expense	—	
Supplies Expense	—	

Data needed for year-end adjustments are as follows:

- Supplies on hand at November 30, $550.
- Depreciation of equipment during year, $1,675.
- Rent expired during year, $8,500.

- Wages accrued but not paid at November 30, $2,000.
- Unearned fees at November 30, $4,000.
- Unbilled fees at November 30, $5,380.

(Continued)

Instructions

1. Journalize the six adjusting entries required at November 30, based on the data presented.

2. What would be the effect on the income statement if the adjustments for equipment depreciation and unearned fees were omitted at the end of the year?

3. What would be the effect on the balance sheet if the adjustments for equipment depreciation and unearned fees were omitted at the end of the year?

4. What would be the effect on the "Net increase or decrease in cash" on the statement of cash flows if the adjustments for equipment depreciation and unearned fees were omitted at the end of the year?

GENERAL LEDGER

PR 3-3B   Adjusting entries

Obj. 2, 3, 4, 5

Crazy Mountain Outfitters Co., an outfitter store for fishing treks, prepared the following unadjusted trial balance at the end of its first year of operations:

Crazy Mountain Outfitters Co.
Unadjusted Trial Balance
April 30, 2018

	Debit Balances	Credit Balances
Cash	11,400	
Accounts Receivable.....................................	72,600	
Supplies	7,200	
Equipment...	112,000	
Accounts Payable		12,200
Unearned Fees		19,200
Common Stock		20,000
Retained Earnings		117,800
Dividends	10,000	
Fees Earned..		305,800
Wages Expense	157,800	
Rent Expense	55,000	
Utilities Expense	42,000	
Miscellaneous Expense	7,000	
	475,000	475,000

For preparing the adjusting entries, the following data were assembled:

- Supplies on hand on April 30 were $1,380.
- Fees earned but unbilled on April 30 were $3,900.
- Depreciation of equipment was estimated to be $3,000 for the year.
- Unpaid wages accrued on April 30 were $2,475.
- The balance in unearned fees represented the April 1 receipt in advance for services to be provided. Only $14,140 of the services was provided between April 1 and April 30.

Instructions

1. Journalize the adjusting entries necessary on April 30, 2018.

2. Determine the revenues, expenses, and net income of Crazy Mountain Outfitters Co. before the adjusting entries.

3. Determine the revenues, expense, and net income of Crazy Mountain Outfitters Co. after the adjusting entries.

4. Determine the effect of the adjusting entries on Retained Earnings.

GENERAL LEDGER

PR 3-4B   Adjusting entries

Obj. 2, 3, 4, 5, 6

The Signage Company specializes in the maintenance and repair of signs, such as billboards. On March 31, 2018, the accountant for The Signage Company prepared the trial balances shown at the top of the following page.

Instructions

Journalize the seven entries that adjusted the accounts at March 31. None of the accounts were affected by more than one adjusting entry.

The Signage Company
Trial Balances
March 31, 2018

	Unadjusted		Adjusted	
	Debit Balances	Credit Balances	Debit Balances	Credit Balances
Cash	4,750		4,750	
Accounts Receivable	17,400		17,400	
Supplies	6,200		2,175	
Prepaid Insurance	9,000		1,150	
Land	100,000		100,000	
Buildings	170,000		170,000	
Accumulated Depreciation—Buildings		51,500		61,000
Trucks	75,000		75,000	
Accumulated Depreciation—Trucks		12,000		17,000
Accounts Payable		6,920		8,750
Salaries Payable		—		1,400
Unearned Service Fees		10,500		3,850
Common Stock		50,000		50,000
Retained Earnings		206,400		206,400
Dividends	7,500		7,500	
Service Fees Earned		162,680		169,330
Salary Expense	80,000		81,400	
Depreciation Expense—Trucks	—		5,000	
Rent Expense	11,900		11,900	
Supplies Expense	—		4,025	
Utilities Expense	6,200		8,030	
Depreciation Expense—Buildings	—		9,500	
Taxes Expense	2,900		2,900	
Insurance Expense	—		7,850	
Miscellaneous Expense	9,150		9,150	
	500,000	500,000	517,730	517,730

PR 3-5B Adjusting entries and adjusted trial balances   Obj. 2, 3, 4, 5, 6

✔ 2. Total of Debit column: $420,300

EXCEL TEMPLATE   GENERAL LEDGER

Reece Financial Services Co., which specializes in appliance repair services, is owned and operated by Joni Reece. Reece Financial Services' accounting clerk prepared the following unadjusted trial balance at July 31, 2018:

Reece Financial Services Co.
Unadjusted Trial Balance
July 31, 2018

	Debit Balances	Credit Balances
Cash	10,200	
Accounts Receivable	34,750	
Prepaid Insurance	6,000	
Supplies	1,725	
Land	50,000	
Building	155,750	
Accumulated Depreciation—Building		62,850
Equipment	45,000	
Accumulated Depreciation—Equipment		17,650
Accounts Payable		3,750
Unearned Rent		3,600
Common Stock		60,000
Retained Earnings		93,550
Dividends	8,000	
Fees Earned		158,600
Salaries and Wages Expense	56,850	
Utilities Expense	14,100	
Advertising Expense	7,500	
Repairs Expense	6,100	
Miscellaneous Expense	4,025	
	400,000	400,000

(Continued)

The data needed to determine year-end adjustments are as follows:

- Depreciation of building for the year, $6,400.
- Depreciation of equipment for the year, $2,800.
- Accrued salaries and wages at July 31, $900.
- Unexpired insurance at July 31, $1,500.
- Fees earned but unbilled on July 31, $10,200.
- Supplies on hand at July 31, $615.
- Rent unearned at July 31, $300.

Instructions

1. Journalize the adjusting entries using the following additional accounts: Salaries and Wages Payable; Rent Revenue; Insurance Expense; Depreciation Expense—Building; Depreciation Expense—Equipment; and Supplies Expense.

2. Determine the balances of the accounts affected by the adjusting entries, and prepare an adjusted trial balance.

PR 3-6B   Adjusting entries and errors   Obj. 2, 3, 4, 5

✔ 2. Corrected net
income: $128,700

EXCEL TEMPLATE

At the end of August, the first month of operations, the following selected data were taken from the financial statements of Tucker Jacobs, an attorney:

Net income for August	$112,500
Total assets at August 31	650,000
Total liabilities at August 31	225,000
Total stockholders' equity at August 31	425,000

In preparing the financial statements, adjustments for the following data were overlooked:

- Unbilled fees earned at August 31, $31,900.
- Depreciation of equipment for August, $7,500.
- Accrued wages at August 31, $5,200.
- Supplies used during August, $3,000.

Instructions

1. Journalize the entries to record the omitted adjustments.

2. Determine the correct amount of net income for August and the total assets, liabilities, and stockholders' equity at August 31. In addition to indicating the corrected amounts, indicate the effect of each omitted adjustment by setting up and completing a columnar table similar to the following. The first adjustment is presented as an example.

	Net Income	Total Assets	=	Total Liabilities	+	Total Stockholders' Equity
Reported amounts	$112,500	$650,000		$225,000		$425,000
Corrections:						
Unbilled fees earned	+31,900	+31,900		0		+31,900
Equipment depreciation	_____	_____		_____		_____
Accrued wages	_____	_____		_____		_____
Supplies used	_____	_____		_____		_____
Corrected amounts						

Continuing Problem

GENERAL LEDGER

The unadjusted trial balance that you prepared for PS Music at the end of Chapter 2 should appear as follows:

PS Music
Unadjusted Trial Balance
July 31, 2018

	Account No.	Debit Balances	Credit Balances
Cash	11	9,945	
Accounts Receivable.	12	2,750	
Supplies	14	1,020	
Prepaid Insurance	15	2,700	
Office Equipment	17	7,500	
Accounts Payable	21		8,350
Unearned Revenue.	23		7,200
Common Stock	31		9,000
Dividends	33	1,750	
Fees Earned.	41		16,200
Wages Expense	50	2,800	
Office Rent Expense	51	2,550	
Equipment Rent Expense	52	1,375	
Utilities Expense	53	1,215	
Music Expense	54	3,610	
Advertising Expense.	55	1,500	
Supplies Expense.	56	180	
Miscellaneous Expense	59	1,855	
		40,750	40,750

The data needed to determine adjustments are as follows:

- During July, PS Music provided guest disc jockeys for KXMD for a total of 115 hours. For information on the amount of the accrued revenue to be billed to KXMD, see the contract described in the July 3 transaction at the end of Chapter 2.
- Supplies on hand at July 31, $275.
- The balance of the prepaid insurance account relates to the July 1 transaction at the end of Chapter 2.
- Depreciation of the office equipment is $50.
- The balance of the unearned revenue account relates to the contract between PS Music and KXMD, described in the July 3 transaction at the end of Chapter 2.
- Accrued wages as of July 31 were $140.

Instructions

1. Prepare adjusting journal entries. You will need the following additional accounts:

   18 Accumulated Depreciation—Office Equipment
   22 Wages Payable
   57 Insurance Expense
   58 Depreciation Expense

2. Post the adjusting entries, inserting balances in the accounts affected.

3. Prepare an adjusted trial balance.

Analysis for Decision Making

ADM-1   Continuing Company Analysis—Amazon: Vertical analysis

Amazon.com, Inc. is the largest Internet retailer in the United States. Amazon's income statements through income from operations for two recent years are as follows (in millions):

Amazon.com, Inc.
Operating Income Statements
For the Years Ended December 31
(in millions)

	Year 2	Year 1
Product sales..	$70,080	$60,903
Service sales...	18,908	13,549
Total sales..	$88,988	$74,452
Cost of sales...	$62,752	$54,181
Fulfillment..	10,766	8,585
Marketing	4,332	3,133
Technology and content..	9,275	6,565
General and administrative	1,552	1,129
Other operating expense (income), net	133	114
Total operating expenses...	$88,810	$73,707
Income from operations...	$ 178	$ 745

A.   Prepare a vertical analysis of the two operating income statements. (Round percentages to one decimal place.)

B.   ▬▬▬▶   Use the vertical analysis to explain the decrease in income from operations.

ADM-2   Chipotle: Vertical analysis

Chipotle Mexican Grill, Inc. is a quick-service restaurant providing a focused menu of burritos, tacos, and salads. Chipotle's balance sheets for the end of two recent years are as follows (in thousands):

Chipotle Mexican Grill, Inc.
Balance Sheets
December 31
(in thousands)

	Year 2	Year 1
Assets		
Current assets		
Cash	$ 419,465	$ 323,203
Accounts receivable, net	34,839	24,016
Inventory..	15,332	13,044
Other current assets..	70,251	51,073
Investments..	338,592	254,971
Total current assets	$ 878,479	$ 666,307
Property, plant, and equipment..................................	1,106,984	963,238
Long-term investments...	496,106	313,863
Other assets..	64,716	65,872
Total assets..	$2,546,285	$2,009,280

Liabilities and Stockholders' Equity

Current liabilities

Accounts payable...	$ 69,613	$ 59,022
Other current liabilities.....................................	176,097	140,206
Total current liabilities.................................	$ 245,710	$ 199,228
Long-term liabilities..	288,206	271,764
Total liabilities.......................................	$ 533,916	$ 470,992

Stockholders' Equity

Common stock	$ 354	$ 352
Additional paid-in capital	1,038,932	919,840
Retained earnings	1,722,271	1,276,897
Treasury stock	(748,759)	(660,421)
Other adjustments...	(429)	1,620
Total stockholders' equity............................	$2,012,369	$1,538,288
Total liabilities and stockholders' equity...........	$2,546,285	$2,009,280

A. Prepare a vertical analysis of the two balance sheets. (Round percentages to one decimal place.)

B. ━━➤ Interpret the vertical analysis with respect to the change in the percent of asset, liability, and stockholders' equity components to total assets. (Treasury stock will be discussed in a later chapter and may be omitted from your analysis.)

REAL WORLD

ADM-3 Nike: Vertical analysis

The following data are taken from recent financial statement of Nike, Inc. (in millions):

	Year 2	Year 1
Sales (revenues)	$27,799	$25,313
Net income	2,693	2,472

A. Determine the amount of change (in millions) and percent of change in net income from Year 1 to Year 2. (Round to one decimal place.)

B. Determine the percentage relationship between net income and sales for Year 2 and Year 1. (Round to one decimal place.)

C. ━━➤ What conclusions can you draw from your analyses?

REAL WORLD

ADM-4 AT&T and Verizon: Vertical analysis

The following income statement data for AT&T Inc. and Verizon Communications Inc. were taken from their recent annual reports (in millions):

	AT&T	Verizon
Revenues	$132,447	$127,079
Cost of services (expense)	(60,611)	(49,931)
Selling and marketing expense	(39,697)	(41,016)
Depreciation and other expenses	(20,393)	(16,533)
Operating income	$ 11,746	$ 19,599

A. Prepare a vertical analysis of the income statement for AT&T. (Round to one decimal place.)

B. Prepare a vertical analysis of the income statement for Verizon. (Round to one decimal place.)

C. ━━➤ Based on Requirements A and B, how does AT&T compare to Verizon?

Take It Further

ETHICS

TIF 3-1 Ethics in Action

Chris P. Bacon is the chief accountant for CV Industries, a large manufacturing company. In addition to its normal business activities, the company has excess warehouse space that it rents out to local businesses. Because the typical renter is a small business, CV Industries requires renters to make lease payments for the entire rental period on the day the lease is signed. As a result, CV Industries typically reports a large unearned rent balance on its balance sheet.

After making adjusting entries for the current year, Chris prepares the adjusted trial balance and notices that the company's earnings will decline significantly. He presents the adjusted trial balance to the company's CFO, Antonio Beldin, who is concerned about the earnings decline. Mr. Beldin notices the large unearned rent balance and proposes making an additional end-of-period adjusting entry to recognize the entire unearned rent balance as revenue in the current period. Chris protests, reminding Mr. Beldin that the adjusting entry for unearned rent has already been made. Mr. Beldin assures Chris that his proposal is acceptable, reminding Chris that "because we have already received the cash, we have the right to recognize the revenue in the current period." He instructs Chris to make the additional adjusting journal entry. Chris is hesitant to follow these instructions, but he is sensitive to the company's emphasis on earnings growth and makes the adjusting entry as instructed.

1. ▬▬▶ Is Chris behaving ethically? Why?
2. ▬▬▶ Who is affected by Chris's decision?

REAL WORLD

TIF 3-2 Team Activity

In teams, select a public company that interests you. Obtain the company's most recent annual report on Form 10-K. The Form 10-K is a company's annually required filing with the Securities and Exchange Commission (SEC). It includes the company's financial statements and accompanying notes. The Form 10-K can be obtained either (A) from the investor relations section of the company's Web site or (B) by using the company search feature of the SEC's EDGAR database service found at www.sec.gov/edgar/searchedgar/companysearch.html.

1. Based on the information in the company's most recent annual report, answer the following questions:
   A. In what industry does the company operate?
   B. How many years of information are reported on the company's income statement?
   C. How much net income does the company report on its income statement for each year presented?
   D. How much revenue does the company report on its income statement for each year presented?
   E. Within the notes to the financial statements, find the note on significant accounting policies. Based on the information in this note, when does the company recognize revenue?
2. ▬▬▶ Based solely on the company's net income, has the company's performance improved, remained constant, or deteriorated over the periods presented? Briefly explain your answer.

REAL WORLD

TIF 3-3 Communication

Delta Air Lines is a major passenger airline headquartered in the United States. Most Delta passengers purchase their tickets several weeks prior to taking the trip and use a credit card such as VISA or American Express to pay for their ticket. The credit card company pays the airline at the time the flight is booked, several weeks prior to the flight.

▬▬▶ Write a brief memo to your instructor explaining when Delta should recognize revenue from ticket sales.

Chapter 1

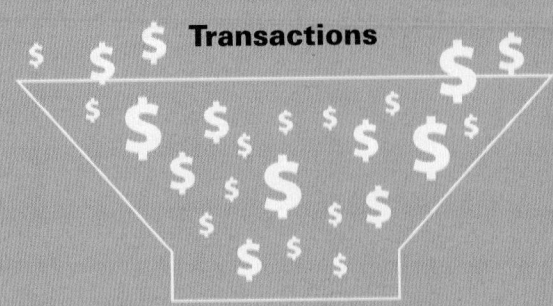

Transactions

Accounting System

Accounting Equation

Assets = Liabilities + Equity

Chapter 2

Account	
Debits	Credits

Rules of Debit and Credit

Balance Sheet Accounts

ASSETS = **LIABILITIES** + **STOCKHOLDERS' EQUITY**

ASSETS
Asset Accounts

Debit for increases (+)	Credit for decreases (−)
Balance	

LIABILITIES
Liability Accounts

Debit for decreases (−)	Credit for increases (+)
	Balance

STOCKHOLDERS' EQUITY

Common Stock

Debit for decreases (−)	Credit for increases (+)
	Balance

Retained Earnings

Debit for decreases (−)	Credit for increases (+)
	Balance

Dividends

Debit for increases (+)	Credit for decreases (−)
Balance	

Income Statement Accounts

Revenue Accounts

Debit for decreases (−)	Credit for increases (+)
	Balance

− Expense Accounts

Debit for increases (+)	Credit for decreases (−)
Balance	

Unadjusted Trial Balance

Total Debit Balances = Total Credit Balances

4 Completing the Accounting Cycle

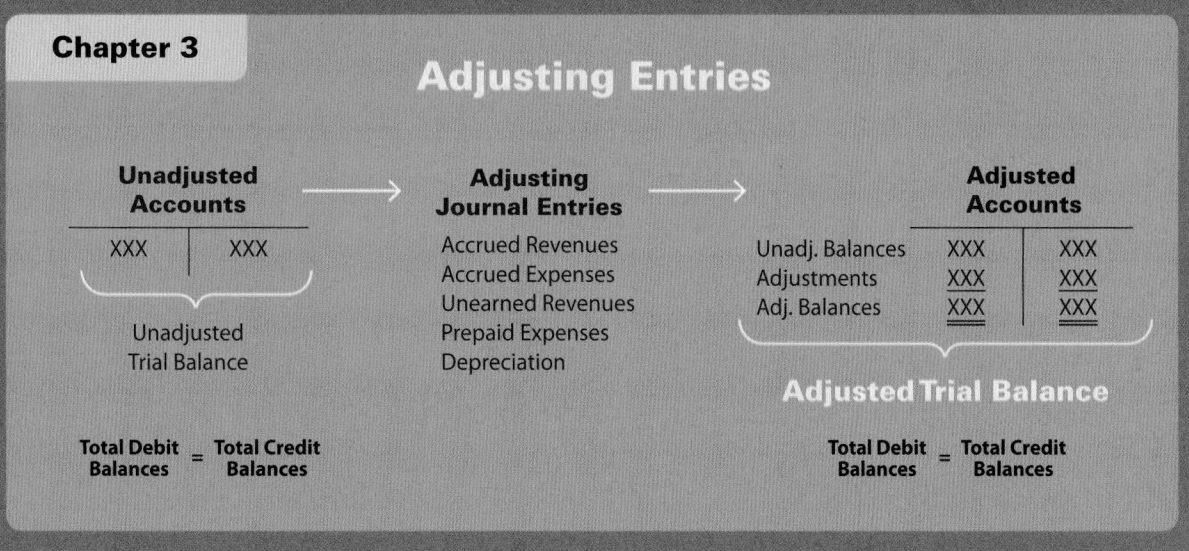

Chapter 3

Adjusting Entries

Unadjusted Accounts

| XXX | XXX |

Unadjusted Trial Balance

Adjusting Journal Entries

Accrued Revenues
Accrued Expenses
Unearned Revenues
Prepaid Expenses
Depreciation

Adjusted Accounts

Unadj. Balances	XXX	XXX
Adjustments	XXX	XXX
Adj. Balances	XXX	XXX

Adjusted Trial Balance

Total Debit Balances = Total Credit Balances

Total Debit Balances = Total Credit Balances

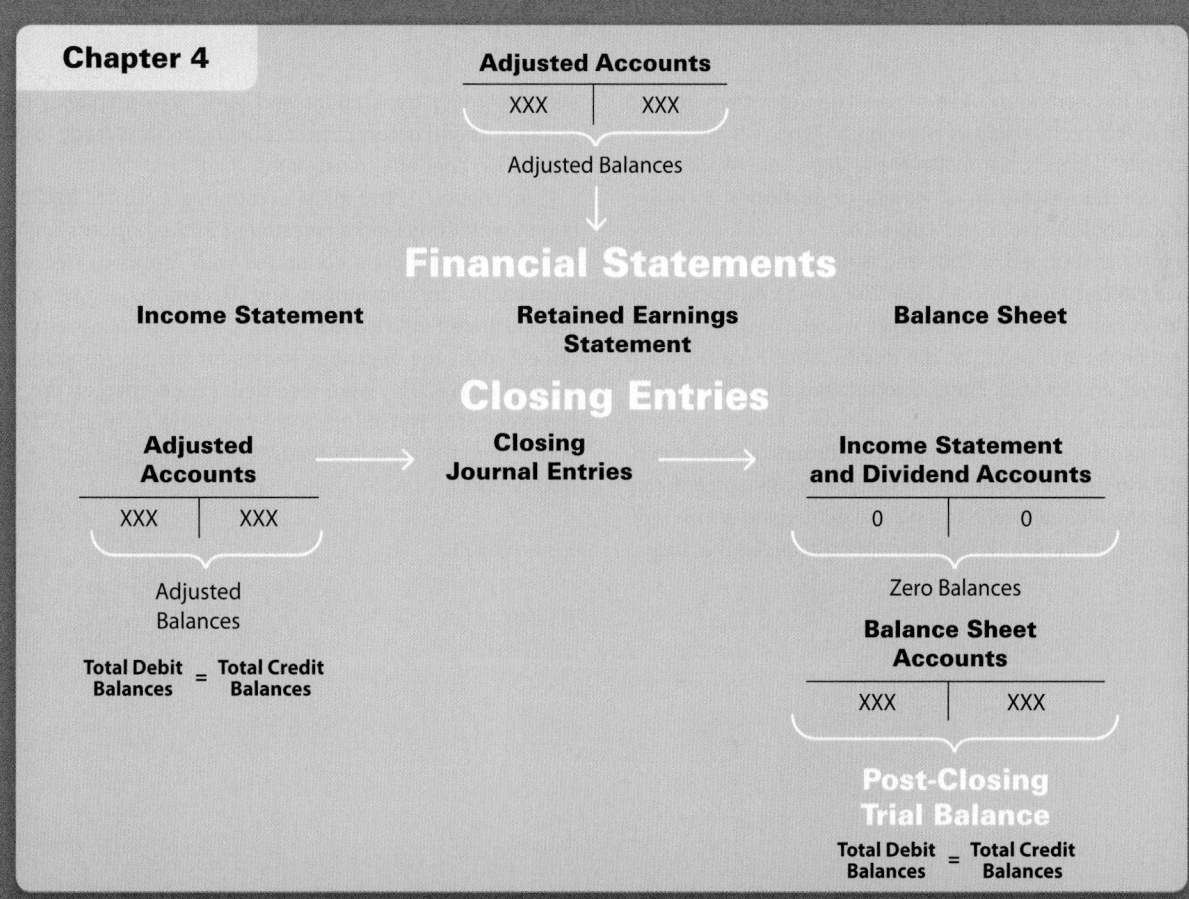

Chapter 4

Adjusted Accounts

| XXX | XXX |

Adjusted Balances

Financial Statements

| **Income Statement** | **Retained Earnings Statement** | **Balance Sheet** |

Closing Entries

Adjusted Accounts

| XXX | XXX |

Adjusted Balances

Total Debit Balances = Total Credit Balances

Closing Journal Entries

Income Statement and Dividend Accounts

| 0 | 0 |

Zero Balances

Balance Sheet Accounts

| XXX | XXX |

Post-Closing Trial Balance

Total Debit Balances = Total Credit Balances

Zynga

Zynga is a leading provider of social games with more than 240 million active players per month. Zynga's games, such as CastleVille Legends, FarmVille, Mafia Wars, and Words With Friends, can be played on a variety of platforms including Facebook, Google Android, and Apple IOS.

Zynga was founded in 2007 and is named after CEO (Chief Executive Officer) Mark Pincus's dog. Zinga is an American Bulldog who is known for her human-like qualities, which include sitting on chairs and eating at the dinner table. Because she is playful, loyal, and lovable, Zinga is considered the guiding spirit of the company.

In developing its games, Zynga goes through a game development cycle that starts with the initial gaming concept, program development, and ends with testing and debugging errors. Businesses also go through a cycle of accounting activities that begins with recording transactions and ends with preparing financial statements and getting the accounting records ready for recording the next period's transactions.

In Chapter 1, the initial accounting cycle for **NetSolutions** began with Chris Clark's investment in the business on November 1, 2017. The cycle continued with recording NetSolutions' transactions for November and December, as we discussed and illustrated in Chapters 1 and 2. In Chapter 3, the cycle continued when the adjusting entries for the two months ending December 31, 2017, were recorded. In this chapter, the cycle is completed for NetSolutions by preparing financial statements and getting the accounts ready for recording transactions of the next period.

Source: Zynga.com

What's Covered

Completing the Accounting Cycle

Preparing Classified Financial Statements	**Closing the Accounts**	**The Accounting Cycle**	**Reporting Using a Fiscal Year**
■ Flow of Accounting Information (Obj. 1)	■ Closing Entries (Obj. 3)	■ Summary (Obj. 4)	■ Calendar Year (Obj. 6)
■ Income Statement (Obj. 2)	■ Post-Closing Trial Balance (Obj. 3)	■ Illustration (Obj. 5)	■ Natural Business Year (Obj. 6)
■ Retained Earnings Statement (Obj. 2)			
■ Balance Sheet (Obj. 2)			

Learning Objectives

Obj. 1 Describe the flow of accounting information from the unadjusted trial balance into the adjusted trial balance and financial statements.

Obj. 2 Prepare financial statements from adjusted account balances.

Obj. 3 Prepare closing entries.

Obj. 4 Describe the accounting cycle.

Obj. 5 Illustrate the accounting cycle for one period.

Obj. 6 Explain what is meant by the fiscal year and the natural business year.

Analysis for Decision Making

Describe and illustrate the use of working capital and the current ratio in evaluating a company's financial condition.

Flow of Accounting Information

Objective 1
Describe the flow of accounting information from the unadjusted trial balance into the adjusted trial balance and financial statements.

The process of adjusting the accounts and preparing financial statements is one of the most important in accounting. Using the **NetSolutions** illustration from Chapters 1–3 and an end-of-period spreadsheet, the flow of accounting data in adjusting accounts and preparing financial statements are summarized in Exhibit 1.

The end-of-period spreadsheet in Exhibit 1 begins with the unadjusted trial balance. The unadjusted trial balance verifies that the total of the debit balances equals the total of the credit balances. If the trial balance totals are unequal, an error has occurred. Any errors must be found and corrected before the end-of-period process can continue.

The adjustments for NetSolutions from Chapter 3 are shown in the Adjustments columns of the spreadsheet. Cross-referencing (by letters) the debit and credit of each adjustment is useful in reviewing the effect of the adjustments on the unadjusted account balances. The adjustments are normally entered in the order in which the data are assembled. If the titles of the accounts to be adjusted do not appear in the unadjusted trial balance, the accounts are inserted in their proper order in the Account Title column. The total of the Adjustments columns verifies that the total debits equal the total credits for the adjusting entries. The total of the Debit column must equal the total of the Credit column.

The adjustments in the spreadsheet are added to or subtracted from the amounts in the Unadjusted Trial Balance columns to arrive at the amounts inserted in the Adjusted Trial Balance columns. In this way, the Adjusted Trial Balance columns of the spreadsheet illustrate the effect of the adjusting entries on the unadjusted accounts. The totals of the Adjusted Trial Balance columns verify that the totals of the debit and credit balances are equal after adjustment.

Exhibit 1 End-of-Period Spreadsheet and Flow of Accounting Data—NetSolutions

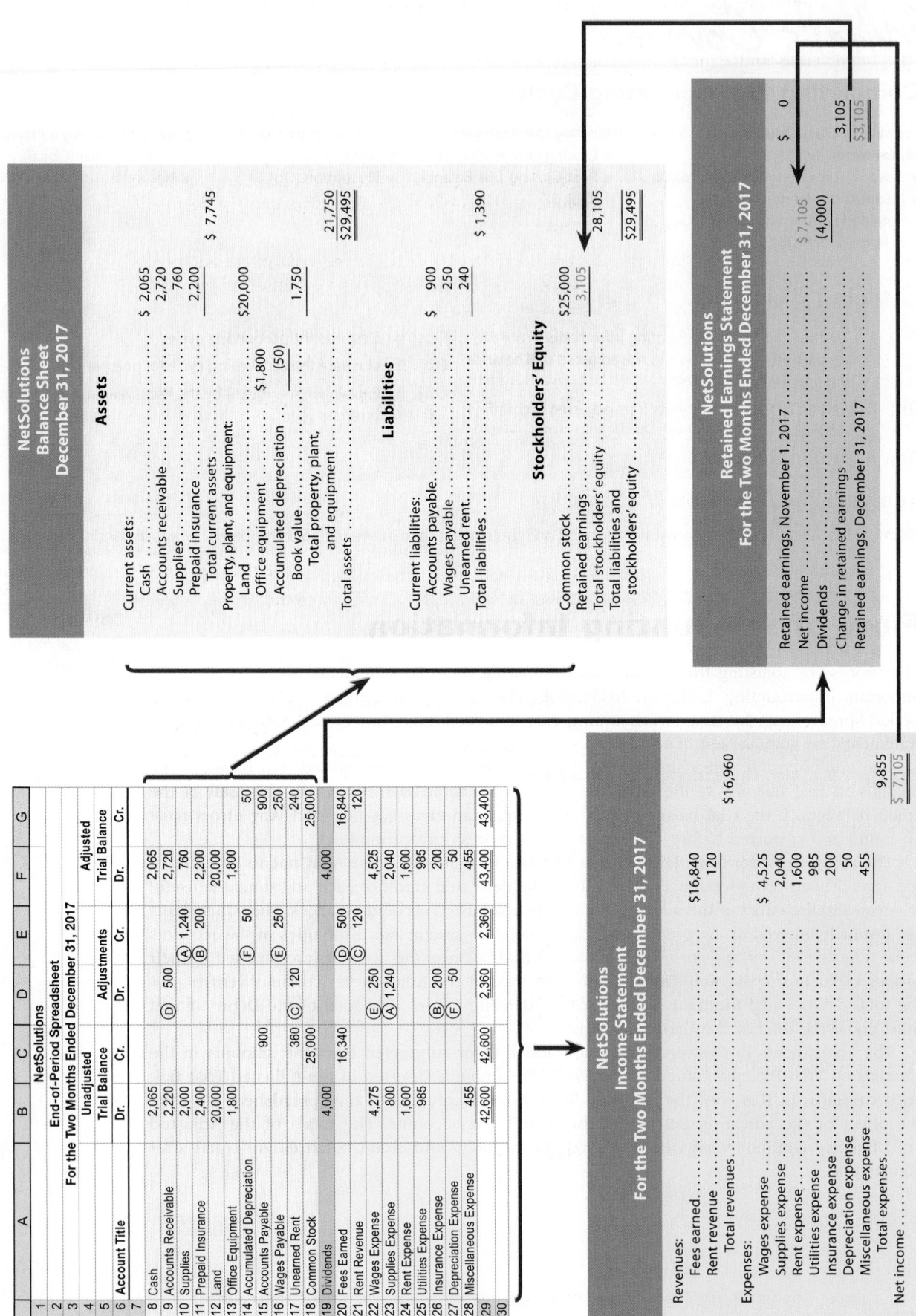

Exhibit 1 illustrates the flow of accounts from the adjusted trial balance into the financial statements as follows:

1. The revenue and expense accounts (spreadsheet lines 20–28) flow into the income statement.

2. The dividends account (spreadsheet line 19) flows into the retained earnings statement. The net income of $7,105 also flows into the retained earnings statement from the income statement.

3. The asset, liability, and common stock accounts (spreadsheet lines 8–18) flow into the balance sheet. The end-of-the-period retained earnings of $3,105 also flows into the balance sheet from the retained earnings statement.

To summarize, Exhibit 1 illustrates the process by which accounts are adjusted. In addition, Exhibit 1 illustrates how the adjusted accounts flow into the financial statements. The financial statements for NetSolutions can be prepared directly from Exhibit 1.

The spreadsheet in Exhibit 1 is not required. However, many accountants prepare such a spreadsheet, sometimes called a *work sheet*, as part of the normal end-of-period process. The primary advantage in doing so is that it allows managers and accountants to see the effect of adjustments on the financial statements. This is especially useful for adjustments that depend upon estimates. Such estimates and their effect on the financial statements are discussed in later chapters.[1]

Financial Statements

Objective 2
Prepare financial statements from adjusted account balances.

Using the adjusted trial balance shown in Exhibit 1, the financial statements for **NetSolutions** can be prepared. The income statement, the retained earnings statement, and the balance sheet are shown in Exhibit 2.

Income Statement

The income statement is prepared directly from the Adjusted Trial Balance columns of the Exhibit 1 spreadsheet, beginning with fees earned of $16,840. The expenses in the income statement in Exhibit 2 are listed in order of size, beginning with the larger items. Miscellaneous expense is the last item, regardless of its amount.

In a recent income statement, **Zynga** reported a net loss from operations of $226 million.

Link to Zynga

Retained Earnings Statement

The first item normally presented on the retained earnings statement is the balance of the retained earnings account at the beginning of the period. Since **NetSolutions** began operations on November 1, this balance is zero in Exhibit 2. Then, the retained earnings statement shows the net income for the two months ended December 31, 2017. The amount of dividends is deducted from the net income to arrive at the retained earnings as of December 31, 2017.

Zynga has never declared or paid a cash dividend since its inception.

Link to Zynga

---

[1] Appendix 1 to this chapter describes and illustrates how to prepare an end-of-period spreadsheet that includes financial statement columns.

Exhibit 2
Financial
Statements—
NetSolutions

DYNAMIC
EXHIBIT

NetSolutions
Income Statement
For the Two Months Ended December 31, 2017

Revenues:		
Fees earned...		$16,840
Rent revenue...		120
Total revenues		$16,960
Expenses:		
Wages expense..	$ 4,525	
Supplies expense..	2,040	
Rent expense	1,600	
Utilities expense..	985	
Insurance expense..	200	
Depreciation expense..	50	
Miscellaneous expense	455	
Total expenses		9,855
Net income		$ 7,105

NetSolutions
Retained Earnings Statement
For the Two Months Ended December 31, 2017

Retained earnings, November 1, 2017......................................		$ 0
Net income	$ 7,105	
Dividends	(4,000)	
Change in retained earnings		3,105
Retained earnings, December 31, 2017....................................		$3,105

NetSolutions
Balance Sheet
December 31, 2017

Assets

Current assets:			
Cash..		$ 2,065	
Accounts receivable		2,720	
Supplies		760	
Prepaid insurance		2,200	
Total current assets			$ 7,745
Property, plant, and equipment:			
Land..		$20,000	
Office equipment...	$1,800		
Accumulated depreciation....................................	(50)		
Book value...		1,750	
Total property, plant, and equipment			21,750
Total assets...			$29,495

Liabilities

Current liabilities:		
Accounts payable...	$ 900	
Wages payable	250	
Unearned rent...	240	
Total liabilities...		$ 1,390

Stockholders' Equity

Common stock	$25,000	
Retained earnings...	3,105	
Total stockholders' equity....................................		28,105
Total liabilities and stockholders' equity......................		$29,495

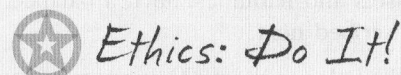 Ethics: Do It!

CEO's Health?

How much and what information to disclose in financial statements and to investors presents a common ethical dilemma for managers and accountants. For example, Steve Jobs, co-founder and CEO of **Apple Inc.**, had been diagnosed and treated for pancreatic cancer. Apple Inc. had insisted that the status of Steve Jobs's health was a "private" matter and did not have to be disclosed to investors. Apple maintained this position even though Jobs was a driving force behind Apple's innovation and financial success.

Steve Jobs's health deteriorated significantly, however, and that disclosure was eventually provided. On October 5, 2011, Steve Jobs died at the age of 56.

For the following period, the beginning balance of retained earnings for NetSolutions is the ending balance that was reported for the previous period. For example, assume that during 2018, NetSolutions earned net income of $149,695 and paid dividends of $24,000. The retained earnings statement for the year ending December 31, 2018, for NetSolutions is as follows:

NetSolutions
Retained Earnings Statement
For the Year Ended December 31, 2018

Retained earnings, January 1, 2018		$ 3,105
Net income	$149,695	
Dividends	(24,000)	
Change in retained earnings		125,695
Retained earnings, December 31, 2018		$128,800

For NetSolutions, the amount of dividends was less than the net income. If the dividends had exceeded the net income, the order of the net income and the dividends would have been reversed. The difference between the two items would then be deducted from the beginning Retained Earnings balance. Other factors, such as a net loss, may also require some change in the form of the retained earnings statement, as shown in the following example:

Retained earnings, January 1, 20—		$45,000
Net loss	$(5,600)	
Dividends	(9,500)	
Change in retained earnings		(15,100)
Retained earnings, December 31, 20—		$29,900

In recent financial statements, **Zynga** reported a net loss of $226 million and an accumulated deficit in retained earnings of $1.2 billion.

Link to Zynga

Balance Sheet

The balance sheet is prepared directly from the Adjusted Trial Balance columns of the Exhibit 1 spreadsheet, beginning with Cash of $2,065. The asset and liability amounts are taken from the spreadsheet. The retained earnings amount, however, is taken from the retained earnings statement, as illustrated in Exhibit 2.

The balance sheet in Exhibit 2 shows subsections for assets and liabilities. Such a balance sheet is a *classified balance sheet*. These subsections are described next.

note:
Two common classes of assets are current assets and property, plant, and equipment.

Assets Assets are commonly divided into two sections on the balance sheet: (1) current assets and (2) property, plant, and equipment.

Current Assets Cash and other assets that are expected to be converted to cash or sold or used up usually within one year or less, through the normal operations of the business, are called **current assets**. In addition to cash, the current assets may include notes receivable, accounts receivable, supplies, and other prepaid expenses.

  Notes receivable are amounts that customers owe. They are written promises to pay the amount of the note and interest. Accounts receivable are also amounts customers owe, but they are less formal than notes. Accounts receivable normally result from providing services or selling merchandise on account. Notes receivable and accounts receivable are current assets because they are usually converted to cash within one year or less.

Property, Plant, and Equipment The **property, plant, and equipment** section may also be described as **fixed assets** or **plant assets**. These assets include equipment, machinery, buildings, and land. With the exception of land, as discussed in Chapter 3, fixed assets depreciate over a period of time. The original cost, accumulated depreciation, and book value of each major type of fixed asset are normally reported on the balance sheet or in the notes to the financial statements.

Link to Zynga   In a recent balance sheet, Zynga reported current assets of $1.1 billion; property, plant, and equipment and other assets of $1.2 billion; and total assets of $2.3 billion.

note:
Two common classes of liabilities are current liabilities and long-term liabilities.

Liabilities Liabilities are the amounts the business owes to creditors. Liabilities are commonly divided into two sections on the balance sheet: (1) current liabilities and (2) long-term liabilities.

Current Liabilities Liabilities that will be due within a short time (usually one year or less) and that are to be paid out of current assets are called **current liabilities**. The most common liabilities in this group are notes payable and accounts payable. Other current liabilities may include wages payable, interest payable, taxes payable, and unearned fees.

Long-Term Liabilities Liabilities that will not be due for a long time (usually more than one year) are called **long-term liabilities**. If NetSolutions had long-term liabilities, they would be reported below the current liabilities. As long-term liabilities come due and are to be paid within one year, they are reported as current liabilities. If they are to be renewed rather than paid, they would continue to be reported as long term. When an asset is pledged as security for a liability, the obligation may be called a *mortgage note payable* or a *mortgage payable*.

Link to Zynga   In a recent balance sheet, Zynga reported current liabilities of $369 million, long-term and other liabilities of $84 million, and total liabilities of $453 million.

Stockholders' Equity The stockholders' right to the assets of the business is presented on the balance sheet below the liabilities section. The stockholders' equity of NetSolutions consists of common stock and retained earnings. The stockholders' equity is added to the total liabilities, and this total must be equal to the total assets.

Link to Zynga   In a recent balance sheet, Zynga reported common stock of $3.1 billion, a retained earnings deficit of $1.2 billion, and total stockholders' equity of $1.9 billion.

Check Up Corner 4-1 Financial Statements from Adjusted Trial Balance

The following account balances were taken from the adjusted trial balance for Laser Corrective Vision Company, a health care company, for the fiscal year ended December 31, 2018:

Depreciation Expense	$ 25,000	Rent Expense	$ 20,000
Dividends	6,000	Salaries Expense	165,000
Fees Earned	312,000	Supplies Expense	18,500
Insurance Expense	6,000	Utilities Expense	12,000
Miscellaneous Expense	5,500		

On January 1, 2018, Retained Earnings had a balance of $100,000.

Prepare an income statement and retained earnings statement for Laser Corrective Vision.

Solution:

The income statement is prepared directly from the adjusted trial balance.

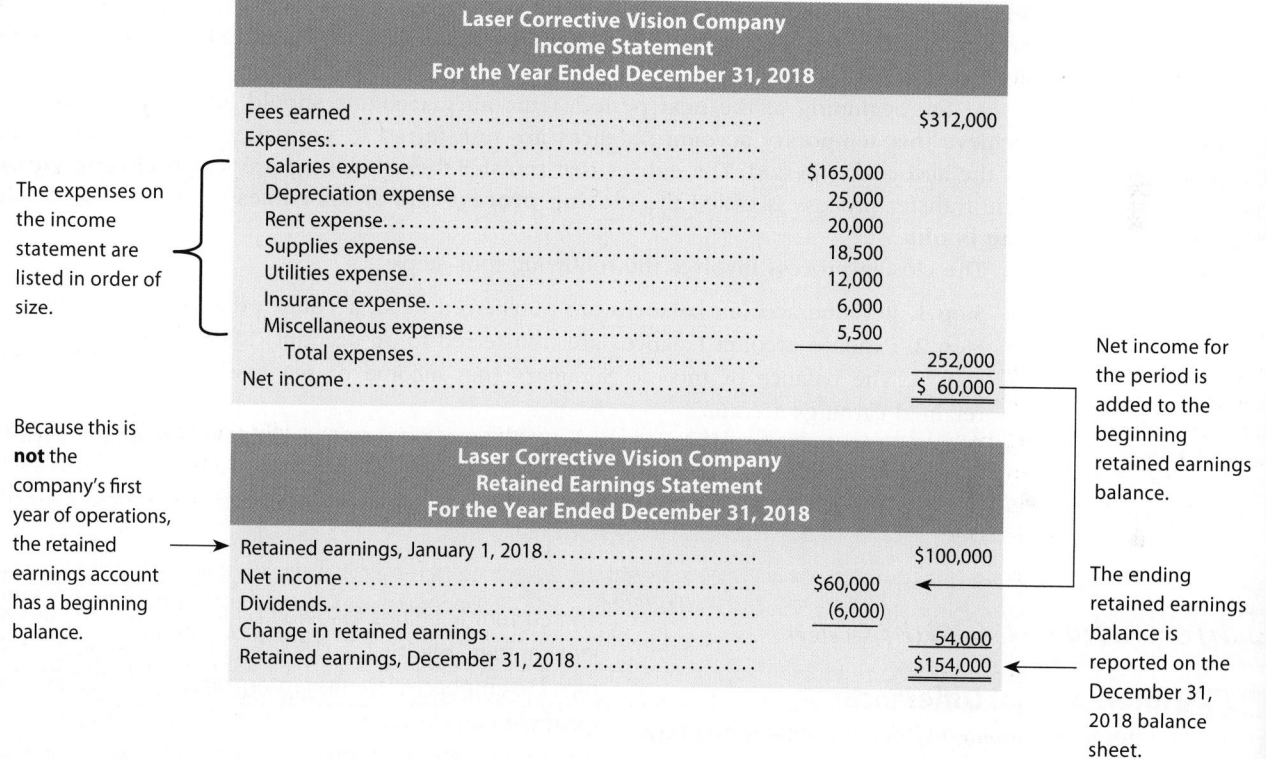

The expenses on the income statement are listed in order of size.

Because this is **not** the company's first year of operations, the retained earnings account has a beginning balance.

Laser Corrective Vision Company
Income Statement
For the Year Ended December 31, 2018

Fees earned		$312,000
Expenses:		
Salaries expense	$165,000	
Depreciation expense	25,000	
Rent expense	20,000	
Supplies expense	18,500	
Utilities expense	12,000	
Insurance expense	6,000	
Miscellaneous expense	5,500	
Total expenses		252,000
Net income		$ 60,000

Laser Corrective Vision Company
Retained Earnings Statement
For the Year Ended December 31, 2018

Retained earnings, January 1, 2018		$100,000
Net income	$60,000	
Dividends	(6,000)	
Change in retained earnings		54,000
Retained earnings, December 31, 2018		$154,000

Net income for the period is added to the beginning retained earnings balance.

The ending retained earnings balance is reported on the December 31, 2018 balance sheet.

Check Up Corner

Objective 3
Prepare closing entries.

Closing Entries

As discussed in Chapter 3, the adjusting entries are recorded in the journal at the end of the accounting period. For **NetSolutions**, the adjusting entries are shown in Exhibit 7 of Chapter 3.

After the adjusting entries are posted to NetSolutions' ledger, shown in Exhibit 6 of this chapter, the ledger agrees with the data reported on the financial statements.

The balances of the accounts reported on the balance sheet are carried forward from year to year. Because they are relatively permanent, these accounts are called **permanent accounts** or **real accounts**. For example, Cash, Accounts Receivable, Equipment, Accumulated Depreciation, Accounts Payable, Common Stock, and Retained Earnings are permanent accounts.

The balances of the accounts reported on the income statement are not carried forward from year to year. Also, the balance of the dividends account, which is reported on the retained earnings statement, is not carried forward. Because these accounts report amounts for only one period, they are called **temporary accounts** or **nominal accounts**. Temporary accounts are not carried forward because they relate only to one period. For example, the Fees Earned of $16,840 and Wages Expense of $4,525 for NetSolutions shown in Exhibit 2 are for the two months ending December 31, 2017, and should not be carried forward to 2018.

note:

Closing entries transfer the balances of temporary accounts to the retained earnings account.

At the beginning of the next period, temporary accounts should have zero balances. To achieve this, temporary account balances are transferred to permanent accounts at the end of the accounting period. The entries that transfer these balances are called **closing entries**. The transfer process is called the **closing process** and is sometimes referred to as **closing the books**.

The closing process involves the following four steps:

- Step 1. Revenue account balances are transferred to an account called Income Summary.
- Step 2. Expense account balances are transferred to an account called Income Summary.
- Step 3. The balance of Income Summary (net income or net loss) is transferred to the retained earnings account.
- Step 4. The balance of the dividends account is transferred to the retained earnings account.

International Connection

IFRS **International Differences**

Financial statements prepared under accounting practices in other countries often differ from those prepared under generally accepted accounting principles in the United States. This is to be expected because cultures and market structures differ from country to country.

To illustrate, BMW Group prepares its financial statements under International Financial Reporting Standards as adopted by the European Union. In doing so, BMW's balance sheet reports fixed assets first, followed by current assets. It also reports stockholders' equity before the liabilities. In contrast, balance sheets prepared under U.S. accounting principles report current assets followed by fixed assets and current liabilities followed by long-term liabilities and stockholders' equity. The U.S. form of balance sheet is organized to emphasize creditor interpretation and analysis. For example, current assets and current liabilities are presented first to facilitate their interpretation and analysis by creditors. Likewise, to emphasize their importance, liabilities are reported before stockholders' equity.*

Regardless of these differences, the basic principles underlying the accounting equation and the double-entry accounting system are the same in Germany and the United States. Even though differences in recording and reporting exist, the accounting equation holds true: The total assets still equal the total liabilities and stockholders' equity.

*Examples of U.S. and IFRS financial statement reporting differences are further discussed and illustrated in Appendix C.

Exhibit 3 diagrams the closing process.

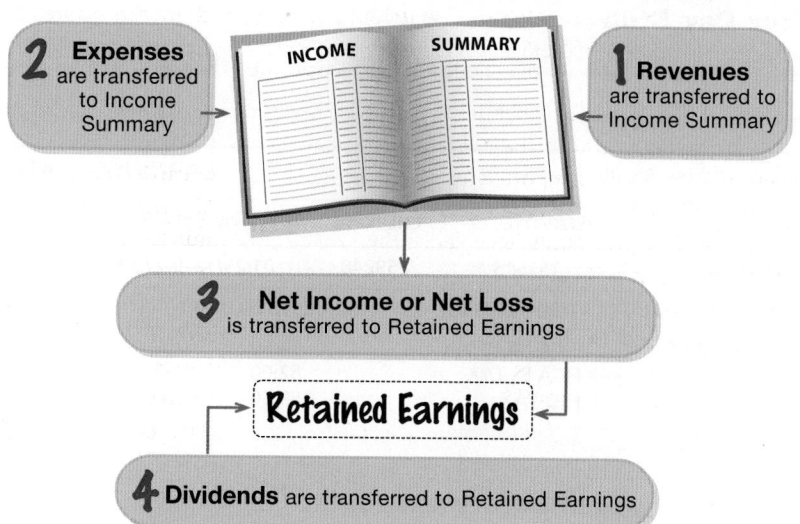

Exhibit 3
The Closing Process

Income Summary is a temporary account that is only used during the closing process. At the beginning of the closing process, Income Summary has no balance. During the closing process, Income Summary will be debited and credited for various amounts. At the end of the closing process, Income Summary will again have no balance. Because Income Summary has the effect of clearing the revenue and expense accounts of their balances, it is sometimes called a **clearing account**. Other titles used for this account include Revenue and Expense Summary, Profit and Loss Summary, and Income and Expense Summary.

note:

The income summary account does not appear on the financial statements.

The four closing entries required in the closing process are as follows:

1. Debit each revenue account for its balance and credit Income Summary for the total revenue.
2. Credit each expense account for its balance and debit Income Summary for the total expenses.
3. Debit Income Summary for its balance (net income) and credit the retained earnings account.
4. Debit the retained earnings account for the balance of the dividends account and credit the dividends account.

In the case of a net loss, Income Summary will have a debit balance after the first two closing entries. In this case, credit Income Summary for the amount of its balance and debit the retained earnings account for the amount of the net loss.

Closing entries are recorded in the journal and are dated as of the last day of the accounting period. In the journal, closing entries are recorded immediately following the adjusting entries. The caption, *Closing Entries*, is often inserted above the closing entries to separate them from the adjusting entries.

It is possible to close the temporary revenue and expense accounts without using a clearing account such as Income Summary. In this case, the balances of the revenue and expense accounts are closed directly to the retained earnings account.

Why It Matters

Temporary Accounts on Your Pay Stub

At the end of every pay period, employees receive a paycheck (or direct deposit) and a pay stub. The pay stub might look something like this:

Sample Company Name, Sample Company Address, 95220					**EARNINGS STATEMENT**	
EMPLOYEE NAME	**SOCIAL SEC. ID**		**EMPLOYEE ID**	**CHECK No.**	**PAY PERIOD**	**PAY DATE**
James Robert	XXX-XX-6666		151515	259248	01/23/18–01/29/18	01/31/18

INCOME	RATE	HOURS	CURRENT TOTAL	DEDUCTIONS	CURRENT TOTAL	YEAR-TO-DATE
GROSS WAGES			1,000.00	FICA MED TAX	14.50	72.50
				FICA SS TAX	62.00	310.00
				FED TAX	159.50	797.50

Temporary Accounts

YTD GROSS	YTD DEDUCTIONS	YTD NET PAY	TOTAL	DEDUCTIONS	NET PAY
5,000.00	1,180.00	3,820.00	1,000.00	236.00	764.00

Each of the year-to-date accounts shown on the pay stub are temporary accounts. Each account describes the increases and decreases in the net cash received for the employee's work over the year. Increases are the gross pay, while decreases are deductions, such as Medicare taxes, social security taxes, and federal withholding taxes (FICA MED TAX, FICA SS TAX, and FED TAX in the illustration). These amounts are accumulated so that year-to-date summaries are provided as the year progresses. This is similar to income statement accounts that accumulate revenues and expenses over the period. At the end of the year, all of the year-to-date accounts are reset to zero to prepare for the next year's accumulation. This is similar to closing income statement accounts, which are also set to zero at the beginning of the new period.

Journalizing and Posting Closing Entries

A flowchart of the four closing entries for **NetSolutions** is shown in Exhibit 4. The balances in the accounts are those shown in the Adjusted Trial Balance columns of the end-of-period spreadsheet shown in Exhibit 1.

The closing entries for **NetSolutions** are shown in Exhibit 5. The account titles and balances for these entries may be obtained from the end-of-period spreadsheet, the adjusted trial balance, the income statement, the retained earnings statement, or the ledger.

The closing entries are posted to NetSolutions' ledger as shown in Exhibit 6. Income Summary has been added to NetSolutions' ledger in Exhibit 6 as account number 34. After the closing entries are posted, NetSolutions' ledger has the following characteristics:

- The balance of Retained Earnings of $3,105 agrees with the amount reported on the retained earnings statement and the balance sheet.
- The revenue, expense, and dividends accounts will have zero balances.

Exhibit 4 Flowchart of Closing Entries for NetSolutions

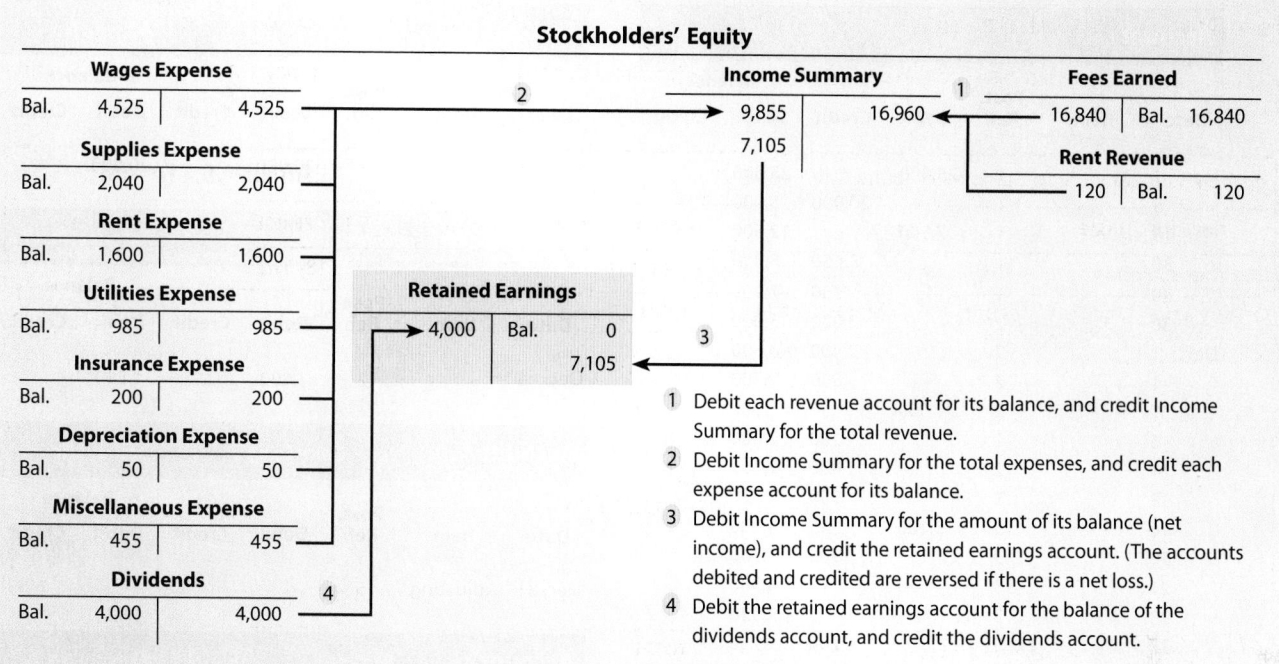

Stockholders' Equity

1 Debit each revenue account for its balance, and credit Income Summary for the total revenue.

2 Debit Income Summary for the total expenses, and credit each expense account for its balance.

3 Debit Income Summary for the amount of its balance (net income), and credit the retained earnings account. (The accounts debited and credited are reversed if there is a net loss.)

4 Debit the retained earnings account for the balance of the dividends account, and credit the dividends account.

Exhibit 5

Closing Entries, NetSolutions

Date		Description	Post. Ref.	Debit	Credit
		Journal Page 6			
		Closing Entries			
2017 Dec.	31	Fees Earned	41	16,840	
		Rent Revenue	42	120	
		Income Summary	34		16,960
	31	Income Summary	34	9,855	
		Wages Expense	51		4,525
		Supplies Expense	52		2,040
		Rent Expense	53		1,600
		Utilities Expense	54		985
		Insurance Expense	55		200
		Depreciation Expense	56		50
		Miscellaneous Expense	59		455
	31	Income Summary	34	7,105	
		Retained Earnings	32		7,105
	31	Retained Earnings	32	4,000	
		Dividends	33		4,000

As shown in Exhibit 6, the closing entries are normally identified in the ledger as "Closing." In addition, a line is often inserted in both balance columns after a closing entry is posted. This separates next period's revenue, expense, and dividend transactions from those of the current period. Next period's transactions will be posted directly below the closing entry.

Exhibit 6 Ledger with Closing Entries—NetSolutions

Account *Cash*   Account No. *11*

Date	Item	Post. Ref.	Debit	Credit	Balance Debit	Balance Credit
2017						
Nov. 1		1	25,000		25,000	
5		1		20,000	5,000	
18		1	7,500		12,500	
30		1		3,650	8,850	
30		1		950	7,900	
30		2		2,000	5,900	
Dec. 1		2		2,400	3,500	
1		2		800	2,700	
1		2	360		3,060	
6		2		180	2,880	
11		2		400	2,480	
13		3		950	1,530	
16		3	3,100		4,630	
20		3		900	3,730	
21		3	650		4,380	
23		3		1,450	2,930	
27		3		1,200	1,730	
31		3		310	1,420	
31		4		225	1,195	
31		4	2,870		4,065	
31		4		2,000	2,065	

Account *Accounts Receivable*   Account No. *12*

Date	Item	Post. Ref.	Debit	Credit	Balance Debit	Balance Credit
2017						
Dec. 16		3	1,750		1,750	
21		3		650	1,100	
31		4	1,120		2,220	
31	Adjusting	5	500		2,720	

Account *Supplies*   Account No. *14*

Date	Item	Post. Ref.	Debit	Credit	Balance Debit	Balance Credit
2017						
Nov. 10		1	1,350		1,350	
30		1		800	550	
Dec. 23		3	1,450		2,000	
31	Adjusting	5		1,240	760	

Account *Prepaid Insurance*   Account No. *15*

Date	Item	Post. Ref.	Debit	Credit	Balance Debit	Balance Credit
2017						
Dec. 1		2	2,400		2,400	
31	Adjusting	5		200	2,200	

Account *Land*   Account No. *17*

Date	Item	Post. Ref.	Debit	Credit	Balance Debit	Balance Credit
2017						
Nov. 5		1	20,000		20,000	

Account *Office Equipment*   Account No. *18*

Date	Item	Post. Ref.	Debit	Credit	Balance Debit	Balance Credit
2017						
Dec. 4		2	1,800		1,800	

Account *Accum. Depr.—Office Equip.*   Account No. *19*

Date	Item	Post. Ref.	Debit	Credit	Balance Debit	Balance Credit
2017						
Dec. 31	Adjusting	5		50		50

Account *Accounts Payable*   Account No. *21*

Date	Item	Post. Ref.	Debit	Credit	Balance Debit	Balance Credit
2017						
Nov. 10		1		1,350		1,350
30		1	950			400
Dec. 4		2		1,800		2,200
11		2	400			1,800
20		3	900			900

Account *Wages Payable*   Account No. *22*

Date	Item	Post. Ref.	Debit	Credit	Balance Debit	Balance Credit
2017						
Dec. 31	Adjusting	5		250		250

Account *Unearned Rent*   Account No. *23*

Date	Item	Post. Ref.	Debit	Credit	Balance Debit	Balance Credit
2017						
Dec. 1		2		360		360
31	Adjusting	5	120			240

Account *Common Stock*   Account No. *31*

Date	Item	Post. Ref.	Debit	Credit	Balance Debit	Balance Credit
2017						
Nov. 1				25,000		25,000

Exhibit 6 Ledger, NetSolutions (*Concluded*)

Account *Retained Earnings*   Account No. *32*

Date	Item	Post. Ref.	Debit	Credit	Balance Debit	Balance Credit
2017						
Nov. 1						0
Dec. 31	Closing	6		7,105		7,105
31	Closing	6	4,000			3,105

Account *Dividends*   Account No. *33*

Date	Item	Post. Ref.	Debit	Credit	Balance Debit	Balance Credit
2017						
Nov. 30		2	2,000		2,000	
Dec. 31		4	2,000		4,000	
31	Closing	6		4,000	—	—

Account *Income Summary*   Account No. *34*

Date	Item	Post. Ref.	Debit	Credit	Balance Debit	Balance Credit
2017						
Dec. 31	Closing	6		16,960		16,960
31	Closing	6	9,855			7,105
31	Closing	6	7,105		—	—

Account *Fees Earned*   Account No. *41*

Date	Item	Post. Ref.	Debit	Credit	Balance Debit	Balance Credit
2017						
Nov. 18		1		7,500		7,500
Dec. 16		3		3,100		10,600
16		3		1,750		12,350
31		4		2,870		15,220
31		4		1,120		16,340
31	Adjusting	5		500		16,840
31	Closing	6	16,840		—	—

Account *Rent Revenue*   Account No. *42*

Date	Item	Post. Ref.	Debit	Credit	Balance Debit	Balance Credit
2017						
Dec. 31	Adjusting	5		120		120
31	Closing	6	120		—	—

Account *Wages Expense*   Account No. *51*

Date	Item	Post. Ref.	Debit	Credit	Balance Debit	Balance Credit
2017						
Nov. 30		1	2,125		2,125	
Dec. 13		3	950		3,075	
27		3	1,200		4,275	
31	Adjusting	5	250		4,525	
31	Closing	6		4,525	—	—

Account *Supplies Expense*   Account No. *52*

Date	Item	Post. Ref.	Debit	Credit	Balance Debit	Balance Credit
2017						
Nov. 30		1	800		800	
Dec. 31	Adjusting	5	1,240		2,040	
31	Closing	6		2,040	—	—

Account *Rent Expense*   Account No. *53*

Date	Item	Post. Ref.	Debit	Credit	Balance Debit	Balance Credit
2017						
Nov. 30		1	800		800	
Dec. 1		2	800		1,600	
31	Closing	6		1,600	—	—

Account *Utilities Expense*   Account No. *54*

Date	Item	Post. Ref.	Debit	Credit	Balance Debit	Balance Credit
2017						
Nov. 30		1	450		450	
Dec. 31		3	310		760	
31		4	225		985	
31	Closing	6		985	—	—

Account *Insurance Expense*   Account No. *55*

Date	Item	Post. Ref.	Debit	Credit	Balance Debit	Balance Credit
2017						
Dec. 31	Adjusting	5	200		200	
31	Closing	6		200	—	—

Account *Depreciation Expense*   Account No. *56*

Date	Item	Post. Ref.	Debit	Credit	Balance Debit	Balance Credit
2017						
Dec. 31	Adjusting	5	50		50	
31	Closing	6		50	—	—

Account *Miscellaneous Expense*   Account No. *59*

Date	Item	Post. Ref.	Debit	Credit	Balance Debit	Balance Credit
2017						
Nov. 30		1	275		275	
Dec. 6		2	180		455	
31	Closing	6		455	—	—

Check Up Corner 4-2 Closing Entries

After the accounts have been adjusted at December 31, the end of the fiscal year, the following balances are taken from the ledger of Socizo Services Co.:

Retained Earnings	$615,850
Dividends	25,000
Fees Earned	380,450
Wages Expense	250,000
Rent Expense	65,000
Supplies Expense	18,250
Miscellaneous Expense	6,200

Journalize the entries required to close the accounts.

Solution:

Debit the revenue account for its balance.

Credit Income Summary for total revenue.

Closing Entries

Dec. 31	Fees Earned	380,450	
	Income Summary		380,450
31	Income Summary	339,450	
	Wages Expense		250,000
	Rent Expense		65,000
	Supplies Expense		18,250
	Miscellaneous Expense		6,200
31	Income Summary	41,000	
	Retained Earnings		41,000
31	Retained Earnings	25,000	
	Dividends		25,000

Debit Income Summary for total expenses.

Credit each expense account for its balance.

The income summary account is debited and the retained earnings account is credited when earnings are positive.

The balance in Dividends is debited to Retained Earnings.

At the completion of the closing process, the revenue, expense, dividends, and income summary accounts have a zero balance.

Check Up Corner

Post-Closing Trial Balance

A post-closing trial balance is prepared after the closing entries have been posted. The purpose of the post-closing (after closing) trial balance is to verify that the ledger is in balance at the beginning of the next period. The accounts and amounts should agree exactly with the accounts and amounts listed on the balance sheet at the end of the period. The post-closing trial balance for **NetSolutions** is shown in Exhibit 7.

NetSolutions Post-Closing Trial Balance December 31, 2017	Account No.	Debit Balances	Credit Balances
Cash	11	2,065	
Accounts Receivable	12	2,720	
Supplies	14	760	
Prepaid Insurance	15	2,200	
Land	17	20,000	
Office Equipment	18	1,800	
Accumulated Depreciation—Office Equipment	19		50
Accounts Payable	21		900
Wages Payable	22		250
Unearned Rent	23		240
Common Stock	31		25,000
Retained Earnings	32		3,105
		29,545	29,545

Exhibit 7
Post-Closing
Trial Balance,
NetSolutions

Accounting Cycle

The accounting process that begins with analyzing and journalizing transactions and ends with the post-closing trial balance is called the **accounting cycle**. The steps in the accounting cycle are as follows:

- Step 1. Transactions are analyzed and recorded in the journal.
- Step 2. Transactions are posted to the ledger.
- Step 3. An unadjusted trial balance is prepared.
- Step 4. Adjustment data are assembled and analyzed.
- Step 5. An optional end-of-period spreadsheet is prepared.
- Step 6. Adjusting entries are journalized and posted to the ledger.
- Step 7. An adjusted trial balance is prepared.
- Step 8. Financial statements are prepared.
- Step 9. Closing entries are journalized and posted to the ledger.
- Step 10. A post-closing trial balance is prepared.[2]

Exhibit 8 illustrates the accounting cycle in graphic form. It also illustrates how the accounting cycle begins with transactions that flow through the accounting system into the financial statements.

Objective 4
Describe the
accounting cycle.

Illustration of the Accounting Cycle

In this section, the complete accounting cycle for one period is illustrated. Assume that for several years Kelly Pitney has operated a part-time consulting business from her home. As of April 1, 2018, Kelly decided to move to rented quarters and to operate the business on a full-time basis. The business will be known as Kelly Consulting. During April, Kelly Consulting entered into the following transactions:

Apr. 1. The following assets were received from Kelly Pitney in exchange for common stock: cash, $13,100; accounts receivable, $3,000; supplies, $1,400; and office equipment, $12,500. There were no liabilities received.

1. Paid three months' rent on a lease rental contract, $4,800.

Objective 5
Illustrate the
accounting cycle for
one period.

[2] Some accountants include the journalizing and posting of "reversing entries" as the last step in the accounting cycle. Because reversing entries are not required, they are described and illustrated in Appendix 2 to this chapter.

Exhibit 8

Accounting Cycle

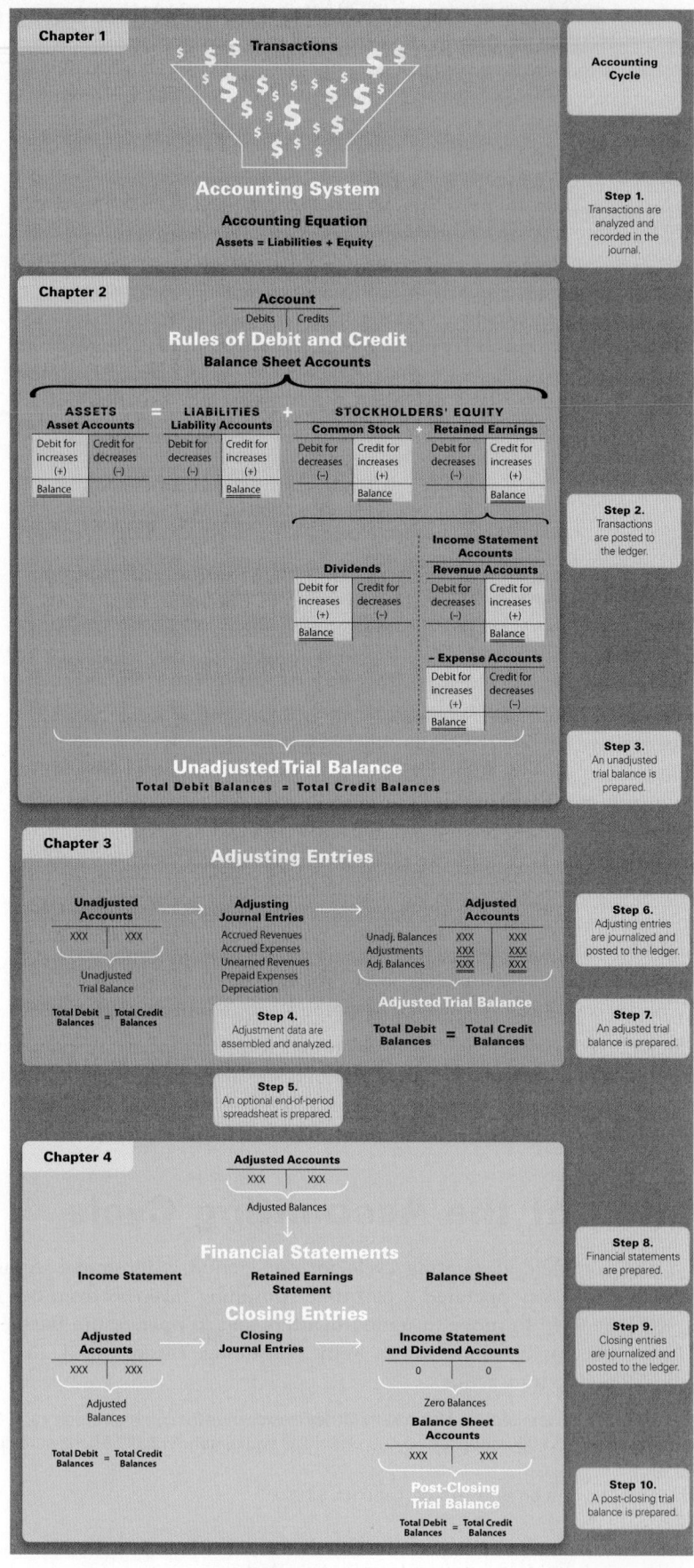

Apr. 2. Paid the premiums on property and casualty insurance policies, $1,800.

4. Received cash from clients as an advance payment for services to be provided and recorded it as unearned fees, $5,000.

5. Purchased additional office equipment on account from Office Station Co., $2,000.

6. Received cash from clients on account, $1,800.

10. Paid cash for a newspaper advertisement, $120.

12. Paid Office Station Co. for part of the debt incurred on April 5, $1,200.

12. Recorded services provided on account for the period April 1–12, $4,200.

14. Paid part-time receptionist for two weeks' salary, $750.

17. Recorded cash from cash clients for fees earned during the period April 1–16, $6,250.

18. Paid cash for supplies, $800.

20. Recorded services provided on account for the period April 13–20, $2,100.

24. Recorded cash from cash clients for fees earned for the period April 17–24, $3,850.

26. Received cash from clients on account, $5,600.

27. Paid part-time receptionist for two weeks' salary, $750.

29. Paid telephone bill for April, $130.

30. Paid electricity bill for April, $200.

30. Recorded cash from cash clients for fees earned for the period April 25–30, $3,050.

30. Recorded services provided on account for the remainder of April, $1,500.

30. Paid dividends, $6,000.

Step 1. Analyzing and Recording Transactions in the Journal

The first step in the accounting cycle is to analyze and record transactions in the journal using the double-entry accounting system. As illustrated in Chapter 2, transactions are analyzed and journalized using the following steps:

- Step 1. Carefully read the description of the transaction to determine whether an asset, liability, common stock, retained earnings, dividends, revenue, or expense account is affected.
- Step 2. For each account affected by the transaction, determine whether the account increases or decreases.
- Step 3. Determine whether each increase or decrease should be recorded as a debit or a credit, following the rules of debit and credit shown in Exhibit 3 of Chapter 2.
- Step 4. Record the transaction using a journal entry.

The company's chart of accounts is useful in determining which accounts are affected by the transaction. The chart of accounts for Kelly Consulting is shown in Exhibit 9.

11 Cash	32 Retained Earnings
12 Accounts Receivable	33 Dividends
14 Supplies	34 Income Summary
15 Prepaid Rent	41 Fees Earned
16 Prepaid Insurance	51 Salary Expense
18 Office Equipment	52 Rent Expense
19 Accumulated Depreciation	53 Supplies Expense
21 Accounts Payable	54 Depreciation Expense
22 Salaries Payable	55 Insurance Expense
23 Unearned Fees	59 Miscellaneous Expense
31 Common Stock	

Exhibit 9

Chart of Accounts for Kelly Consulting

After analyzing each of Kelly Consulting's transactions for April, the journal entries are recorded as shown in Exhibit 10.

Exhibit 10

Journal Entries
for April, Kelly
Consulting

		Journal			Page 1
Date		Description	Post. Ref.	Debit	Credit
2018					
Apr.	1	Cash	11	13,100	
		Accounts Receivable	12	3,000	
		Supplies	14	1,400	
		Office Equipment	18	12,500	
		Common Stock	31		30,000
	1	Prepaid Rent	15	4,800	
		Cash	11		4,800
	2	Prepaid Insurance	16	1,800	
		Cash	11		1,800
	4	Cash	11	5,000	
		Unearned Fees	23		5,000
	5	Office Equipment	18	2,000	
		Accounts Payable	21		2,000
	6	Cash	11	1,800	
		Accounts Receivable	12		1,800
	10	Miscellaneous Expense	59	120	
		Cash	11		120
	12	Accounts Payable	21	1,200	
		Cash	11		1,200
	12	Accounts Receivable	12	4,200	
		Fees Earned	41		4,200
	14	Salary Expense	51	750	
		Cash	11		750

		Journal			Page 2
Date		Description	Post. Ref.	Debit	Credit
2018					
Apr.	17	Cash	11	6,250	
		Fees Earned	41		6,250
	18	Supplies	14	800	
		Cash	11		800
	20	Accounts Receivable	12	2,100	
		Fees Earned	41		2,100
	24	Cash	11	3,850	
		Fees Earned	41		3,850
	26	Cash	11	5,600	
		Accounts Receivable	12		5,600
	27	Salary Expense	51	750	
		Cash	11		750
	29	Miscellaneous Expense	59	130	
		Cash	11		130

	Journal				Page 2
Date	**Description**	**Post. Ref.**	**Debit**	**Credit**	
30	Miscellaneous Expense	59	200		
	Cash	11		200	
30	Cash	11	3,050		
	Fees Earned	41		3,050	
30	Accounts Receivable	12	1,500		
	Fees Earned	41		1,500	
30	Dividends	33	6,000		
	Cash	11		6,000	

Exhibit 10

Journal Entries for April, Kelly Consulting (*Concluded*)

Step 2. Posting Transactions to the Ledger

Periodically, the transactions recorded in the journal are posted to the accounts in the ledger. The debits and credits for each journal entry are posted to the accounts in the order in which they occur in the journal. As illustrated in Chapters 2 and 3, journal entries are posted to the accounts using the following four steps:

- Step 1. The date is entered in the Date column of the account.
- Step 2. The amount is entered into the Debit or Credit column of the account.
- Step 3. The journal page number is entered in the Posting Reference column.
- Step 4. The account number is entered in the Posting Reference (Post. Ref.) column in the journal.

The journal entries for Kelly Consulting have been posted to the ledger shown in Exhibit 18.

Step 3. Preparing an Unadjusted Trial Balance

An unadjusted trial balance is prepared to determine whether any errors have been made in posting the debits and credits to the ledger. The unadjusted trial balance shown in Exhibit 11 does not provide complete proof of the accuracy of the ledger. It indicates only that the debits and the credits are equal. This proof is of value, however, because errors often affect the equality of debits and credits. If the two totals of a trial balance are not equal, an error has occurred that must be discovered and corrected.

The unadjusted account balances shown in Exhibit 11 were taken from Kelly Consulting's ledger shown in Exhibit 18, before any adjusting entries were recorded.

Step 4. Assembling and Analyzing Adjustment Data

Before the financial statements can be prepared, the accounts must be updated. The four types of accounts that normally require adjustment include prepaid expenses, unearned revenue, accrued revenue, and accrued expenses. In addition, depreciation expense must be recorded for fixed assets other than land. The following data have been assembled on April 30, 2018, for analysis of possible adjustments for Kelly Consulting:

A. Insurance expired during April is $300.
B. Supplies on hand on April 30 are $1,350.
C. Depreciation of office equipment for April is $330.
D. Accrued receptionist salary on April 30 is $120.
E. Rent expired during April is $1,600.
F. Unearned fees on April 30 are $2,500.

Kelly Consulting
Unadjusted Trial Balance
April 30, 2018

	Account No.	Debit Balances	Credit Balances
Cash	11	22,100	
Accounts Receivable	12	3,400	
Supplies	14	2,200	
Prepaid Rent	15	4,800	
Prepaid Insurance	16	1,800	
Office Equipment	18	14,500	
Accumulated Depreciation	19		0
Accounts Payable	21		800
Salaries Payable	22		0
Unearned Fees	23		5,000
Common Stock	31		30,000
Dividends	33	6,000	
Fees Earned	41		20,950
Salary Expense	51	1,500	
Rent Expense	52	0	
Supplies Expense	53	0	
Depreciation Expense	54	0	
Insurance Expense	55	0	
Miscellaneous Expense	59	450	
		56,750	56,750

Step 5. Preparing an Optional End-of-Period Spreadsheet

Although an end-of-period spreadsheet is not required, it is useful in showing the flow of accounting information from the unadjusted trial balance to the adjusted trial balance. In addition, an end-of-period spreadsheet is useful in analyzing the impact of proposed adjustments on the financial statements. The end-of-period spreadsheet for Kelly Consulting is shown in Exhibit 12.

	A	B	C	D	E	F	G
1	Kelly Consulting						
2	End-of-Period Spreadsheet						
3	For the Month Ended April 30, 2018						
4		Unadjusted				Adjusted	
5		Trial Balance		Adjustments		Trial Balance	
6	Account Title	Dr.	Cr.	Dr.	Cr.	Dr.	Cr.
7							
8	Cash	22,100				22,100	
9	Accounts Receivable	3,400				3,400	
10	Supplies	2,200			(B) 850	1,350	
11	Prepaid Rent	4,800			(E) 1,600	3,200	
12	Prepaid Insurance	1,800			(A) 300	1,500	
13	Office Equipment	14,500				14,500	
14	Accum. Depreciation				(C) 330		330
15	Accounts Payable		800				800
16	Salaries Payable				(D) 120		120
17	Unearned Fees		5,000	(F) 2,500			2,500
18	Common Stock		30,000				30,000
19	Dividends	6,000				6,000	
20	Fees Earned		20,950		(F) 2,500		23,450
21	Salary Expense	1,500		(D) 120		1,620	
22	Rent Expense			(E) 1,600		1,600	
23	Supplies Expense			(B) 850		850	
24	Depreciation Expense			(C) 330		330	
25	Insurance Expense			(A) 300		300	
26	Miscellaneous Expense	450				450	
27		56,750	56,750	5,700	5,700	57,200	57,200
28							

Step 6. Journalizing and Posting Adjusting Entries

Based on the adjustment data shown in Step 4, adjusting entries for Kelly Consulting are prepared as shown in Exhibit 13. Each adjusting entry affects at least one income statement account and one balance sheet account. Explanations for each adjustment including any computations are normally included with each adjusting entry.

Each of the adjusting entries shown in Exhibit 13 is posted to Kelly Consulting's ledger shown in Exhibit 18. The adjusting entries are identified in the ledger as "Adjusting."

Journal				Page 3
Date	**Description**	**Post. Ref.**	**Debit**	**Credit**
	Adjusting Entries			
2018 Apr. 30	Insurance Expense	55	300	
	Prepaid Insurance	16		300
	Expired insurance.			
30	Supplies Expense	53	850	
	Supplies	14		850
	Supplies used ($2,200 – $1,350).			
30	Depreciation Expense	54	330	
	Accumulated Depreciation	19		330
	Depreciation of office equipment.			
30	Salary Expense	51	120	
	Salaries Payable	22		120
	Accrued salary.			
30	Rent Expense	52	1,600	
	Prepaid Rent	15		1,600
	Rent expired during April.			
30	Unearned Fees	23	2,500	
	Fees Earned	41		2,500
	Fees earned ($5,000 – $2,500).			

Exhibit 13

Adjusting Entries, Kelly Consulting

Step 7. Preparing an Adjusted Trial Balance

After the adjustments have been journalized and posted, an adjusted trial balance is prepared to verify the equality of the total of the debit and credit balances. This is the last step before preparing the financial statements. If the adjusted trial balance does not balance, an error has occurred and must be found and corrected. The adjusted trial balance for Kelly Consulting as of April 30, 2018, is shown in Exhibit 14.

Step 8. Preparing the Financial Statements

The most important outcome of the accounting cycle is the financial statements. The income statement is prepared first, followed by the retained earnings statement and then the balance sheet. The statements can be prepared directly from the adjusted trial balance, the end-of-period spreadsheet, or the ledger. The net income or net loss shown on the income statement is reported on the retained earnings statement along with any dividends. The ending retained earnings is reported on the balance sheet with common stock as part of stockholders' equity. Stockholders' equity is then added with total liabilities to equal total assets.

Exhibit 14
Adjusted Trial Balance, Kelly Consulting

Kelly Consulting Adjusted Trial Balance April 30, 2018			
	Account No.	Debit Balances	Credit Balances
Cash	11	22,100	
Accounts Receivable	12	3,400	
Supplies	14	1,350	
Prepaid Rent	15	3,200	
Prepaid Insurance	16	1,500	
Office Equipment	18	14,500	
Accumulated Depreciation	19		330
Accounts Payable	21		800
Salaries Payable	22		120
Unearned Fees	23		2,500
Common Stock	31		30,000
Dividends	33	6,000	
Fees Earned	41		23,450
Salary Expense	51	1,620	
Rent Expense	52	1,600	
Supplies Expense	53	850	
Depreciation Expense	54	330	
Insurance Expense	55	300	
Miscellaneous Expense	59	450	
		57,200	57,200

The financial statements for Kelly Consulting are shown in Exhibit 15. Kelly Consulting earned net income of $18,300 for April. As of April 30, 2018, Kelly Consulting has total assets of $45,720, total liabilities of $3,420, and total stockholders' equity of $42,300.

Exhibit 15
Financial Statements, Kelly Consulting

Kelly Consulting Income Statement For the Month Ended April 30, 2018		
Fees earned		$23,450
Expenses:		
Salary expense	$1,620	
Rent expense	1,600	
Supplies expense	850	
Depreciation expense	330	
Insurance expense	300	
Miscellaneous expense	450	
Total expenses		5,150
Net income		$18,300

Kelly Consulting Retained Earnings Statement For the Month Ended April 30, 2018		
Retained earnings, April 1, 2018		$ 0
Net income	$ 18,300	
Dividends	(6,000)	
Change in retained earnings		12,300
Retained earnings, April 30, 2018		$12,300

(Continued)

Kelly Consulting Balance Sheet April 30, 2018			
Assets			
Current assets:			
Cash.........		$22,100	
Accounts receivable		3,400	
Supplies		1,350	
Prepaid rent...		3,200	
Prepaid insurance		1,500	
Total current assets...			$31,550
Property, plant, and equipment:			
Office equipment...		$14,500	
Accumulated depreciation		(330)	
Total property, plant, and equipment			14,170
Total assets...			$45,720
Liabilities			
Current liabilities:			
Accounts payable...		$ 800	
Salaries payable		120	
Unearned fees..		2,500	
Total liabilities...			$ 3,420
Stockholders' Equity			
Common stock		$30,000	
Retained earnings		12,300	
Total stockholders' equity			42,300
Total liabilities and stockholders' equity			$45,720

Exhibit 15

Financial Statements, Kelly Consulting (*Concluded*)

Step 9. Journalizing and Posting Closing Entries

As described earlier in this chapter, four closing entries are required at the end of an accounting period. These four closing entries are as follows:

1. Debit each revenue account for its balance, and credit Income Summary for the total revenue.
2. Credit each expense account for its balance, and debit Income Summary for the total expenses.
3. Debit Income Summary for its balance, and credit the retained earnings account.
4. Debit the retained earnings account for the balance of the dividends account, and credit the dividends account.

The four closing entries for Kelly Consulting are shown in Exhibit 16. The closing entries are posted to Kelly Consulting's ledger as shown in Exhibit 18. After the closing entries are posted, Kelly Consulting's ledger has the following characteristics:

■ The balance of Retained Earnings of $12,300 agrees with the amount reported on the retained earnings statement and the balance sheet.
■ The revenue, expense, and dividends accounts will have zero balances.

The closing entries are normally identified in the ledger as "Closing." In addition, a line is often inserted in both balance columns after a closing entry is posted. This separates next period's revenue, expense, and dividend transactions from those of the current period.

Exhibit 16

Closing Entries,
Kelly Consulting

			Journal			Page 4
Date			**Description**	**Post. Ref.**	**Debit**	**Credit**
			Closing Entries			
2018 Apr.	30	Fees Earned		41	23,450	
			Income Summary	34		23,450
	30	Income Summary		34	5,150	
			Salary Expense	51		1,620
			Rent Expense	52		1,600
			Supplies Expense	53		850
			Depreciation Expense	54		330
			Insurance Expense	55		300
			Miscellaneous Expense	59		450
	30	Income Summary		34	18,300	
			Retained Earnings	32		18,300
	30	Retained Earnings		32	6,000	
			Dividends	33		6,000

Step 10. Preparing a Post-Closing Trial Balance

A post-closing trial balance is prepared after the closing entries have been posted. The purpose of the post-closing trial balance is to verify that the ledger is in balance at the beginning of the next period. The accounts and amounts in the post-closing trial balance should agree exactly with the accounts and amounts listed on the balance sheet at the end of the period.

The post-closing trial balance for Kelly Consulting is shown in Exhibit 17. The balances shown in the post-closing trial balance are taken from the ending balances in the ledger shown in Exhibit 18. These balances agree with the amounts shown on Kelly Consulting's balance sheet in Exhibit 15.

Exhibit 17

Post-Closing
Trial Balance, Kelly
Consulting

Kelly Consulting Post-Closing Trial Balance April 30, 2018			
	Account No.	**Debit Balances**	**Credit Balances**
Cash..	11	22,100	
Accounts Receivable...................................	12	3,400	
Supplies	14	1,350	
Prepaid Rent	15	3,200	
Prepaid Insurance......................................	16	1,500	
Office Equipment.......................................	18	14,500	
Accumulated Depreciation	19		330
Accounts Payable.......................................	21		800
Salaries Payable	22		120
Unearned Fees	23		2,500
Common Stock...	31		30,000
Retained Earnings	32		12,300
		46,050	46,050

Exhibit 18 Ledger, Kelly Consulting

Account *Cash* Account No. 11

Date	Item	Post. Ref.	Debit	Credit	Balance Debit	Balance Credit
2018						
Apr. 1		1	13,100		13,100	
1		1		4,800	8,300	
2		1		1,800	6,500	
4		1	5,000		11,500	
6		1	1,800		13,300	
10		1		120	13,180	
12		1		1,200	11,980	
14		1		750	11,230	
17		2	6,250		17,480	
18		2		800	16,680	
24		2	3,850		20,530	
26		2	5,600		26,130	
27		2		750	25,380	
29		2		130	25,250	
30		2		200	25,050	
30		2	3,050		28,100	
30		2		6,000	22,100	

Account *Accounts Receivable* Account No. 12

Date	Item	Post. Ref.	Debit	Credit	Balance Debit	Balance Credit
2018						
Apr. 1		1	3,000		3,000	
6		1		1,800	1,200	
12		1	4,200		5,400	
20		2	2,100		7,500	
26		2		5,600	1,900	
30		2	1,500		3,400	

Account *Supplies* Account No. 14

Date	Item	Post. Ref.	Debit	Credit	Balance Debit	Balance Credit
2018						
Apr. 1		1	1,400		1,400	
18		2	800		2,200	
30	Adjusting	3		850	1,350	

Account *Prepaid Rent* Account No. 15

Date	Item	Post. Ref.	Debit	Credit	Balance Debit	Balance Credit
2018						
Apr. 1		1	4,800		4,800	
30	Adjusting	3		1,600	3,200	

Account *Prepaid Insurance* Account No. 16

Date	Item	Post. Ref.	Debit	Credit	Balance Debit	Balance Credit
2018						
Apr. 2		1	1,800		1,800	
30	Adjusting	3		300	1,500	

Account *Office Equipment* Account No. 18

Date	Item	Post. Ref.	Debit	Credit	Balance Debit	Balance Credit
2018						
Apr. 1		1	12,500		12,500	
5		1	2,000		14,500	

Account *Accumulated Depreciation* Account No. 19

Date	Item	Post. Ref.	Debit	Credit	Balance Debit	Balance Credit
2018						
Apr. 30	Adjusting	3		330		330

Account *Accounts Payable* Account No. 21

Date	Item	Post. Ref.	Debit	Credit	Balance Debit	Balance Credit
2018						
Apr. 5		1		2,000		2,000
12		1	1,200			800

Account *Salaries Payable* Account No. 22

Date	Item	Post. Ref.	Debit	Credit	Balance Debit	Balance Credit
2018						
Apr. 30	Adjusting	3		120		120

Account *Unearned Fees* Account No. 23

Date	Item	Post. Ref.	Debit	Credit	Balance Debit	Balance Credit
2018						
Apr. 4		1		5,000		5,000
30	Adjusting	3	2,500			2,500

Account *Common Stock* Account No. 31

Date	Item	Post. Ref.	Debit	Credit	Balance Debit	Balance Credit
2018						
Apr. 1		1		30,000		30,000

Account *Retained Earnings* Account No. 32

Date	Item	Post. Ref.	Debit	Credit	Balance Debit	Balance Credit
2018						
Apr. 1		1				0
30	Closing	4		18,300		18,300
30	Closing	4	6,000			12,300

(Continued)

Exhibit 18 Ledger, Kelly Consulting (*Concluded*)

Account *Dividends* — Account No. 33

Date	Item	Post. Ref.	Debit	Credit	Balance Debit	Balance Credit
2018 Apr. 30		2	6,000		6,000	
30	Closing	4		6,000	—	—

Account *Income Summary* — Account No. 34

Date	Item	Post. Ref.	Debit	Credit	Balance Debit	Balance Credit
2018 Apr. 30	Closing	4		23,450		23,450
30	Closing	4	5,150			18,300
30	Closing	4	18,300		—	—

Account *Fees Earned* — Account No. 41

Date	Item	Post. Ref.	Debit	Credit	Balance Debit	Balance Credit
2018 Apr. 12		1		4,200		4,200
17		2		6,250		10,450
20		2		2,100		12,550
24		2		3,850		16,400
30		2		3,050		19,450
30		2		1,500		20,950
30	Adjusting	3		2,500		23,450
30	Closing	4	23,450		—	—

Account *Salary Expense* — Account No. 51

Date	Item	Post. Ref.	Debit	Credit	Balance Debit	Balance Credit
2018 Apr. 14		1	750		750	
27		2	750		1,500	
30	Adjusting	3	120		1,620	
30	Closing	4		1,620	—	—

Account *Rent Expense* — Account No. 52

Date	Item	Post. Ref.	Debit	Credit	Balance Debit	Balance Credit
2018 Apr. 30	Adjusting	3	1,600		1,600	
30	Closing	4		1,600	—	—

Account *Supplies Expense* — Account No. 53

Date	Item	Post. Ref.	Debit	Credit	Balance Debit	Balance Credit
2018 Apr. 30	Adjusting	3	850		850	
30	Closing	4		850	—	—

Account *Depreciation Expense* — Account No. 54

Date	Item	Post. Ref.	Debit	Credit	Balance Debit	Balance Credit
2018 Apr. 30	Adjusting	3	330		330	
30	Closing	4		330	—	—

Account *Insurance Expense* — Account No. 55

Date	Item	Post. Ref.	Debit	Credit	Balance Debit	Balance Credit
2018 Apr. 30	Adjusting	3	300		300	
30	Closing	4		300	—	—

Account *Miscellaneous Expense* — Account No. 59

Date	Item	Post. Ref.	Debit	Credit	Balance Debit	Balance Credit
2018 Apr. 10		1	120		120	
29		2	130		250	
30		2	200		450	
30	Closing	4		450	—	—

Objective 6

Explain what is meant by the fiscal year and the natural business year.

Fiscal Year

The annual accounting period adopted by a business is known as its **fiscal year**. Fiscal years begin with the first day of the month selected and end on the last day of the following twelfth month. The period most commonly used is the calendar year. Other periods are not unusual, especially for businesses organized as corporations. For example, a corporation may adopt a fiscal year that ends when business activities have reached the lowest point in its annual operating cycle. Such a fiscal year is called the **natural business year**. At the low point in its operating cycle, a business has more time to analyze the results of operations and to prepare financial statements.

Because companies with fiscal years often have highly seasonal operations, investors and others should be careful in interpreting partial-year reports for such companies. That is, you should expect the results of operations for these companies to vary significantly throughout the fiscal year.

Zynga uses an accounting period ending December 31.

Link to Zynga

The financial history of a business may be shown by a series of balance sheets and income statements for several fiscal years. If the life of a business is expressed by a line moving from left to right, the series of balance sheets and income statements may be graphed as shown in Exhibit 19.

Exhibit 19 Financial History of a Business

Income Statement 2016 | Income Statement 2017 | Income Statement 2018

2016 | 2016 | 2017 | 2018

Jan. 1 | 2016 | Dec. 31 | 2017 | Dec. 31 | 2018 | Dec. 31

Balance Sheet 2016 | Balance Sheet 2017 | Balance Sheet 2018

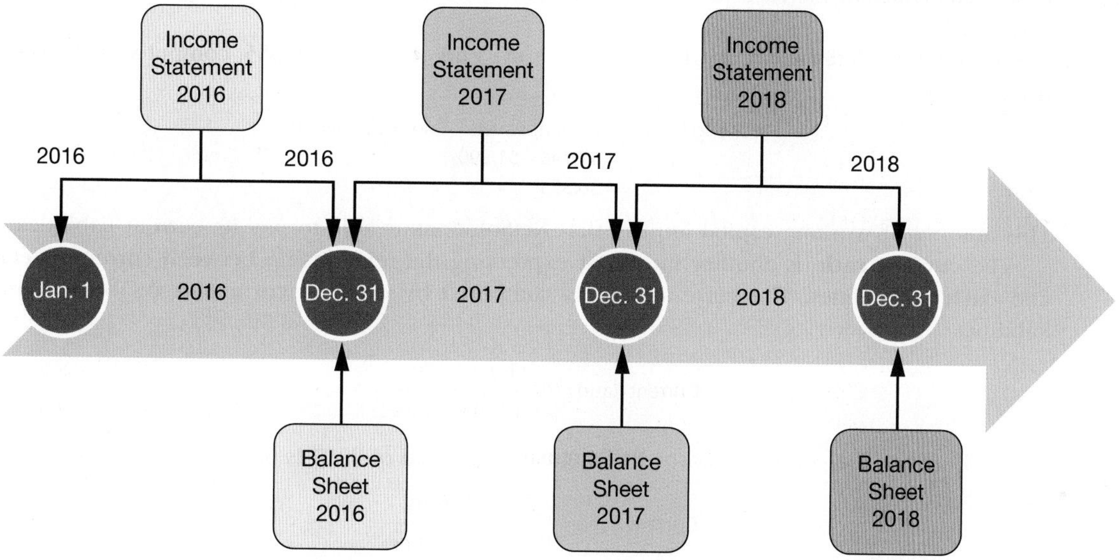

Why It Matters

Choosing a Fiscal Year

CVS Caremark Corporation (CVS) operates more than 7,000 pharmacies throughout the United States and fills more than one billion prescriptions annually. CVS recently chose December 31 as its fiscal year-end and described its decision as follows:

… our Board of Directors approved a change in our fiscal year-end … to December 31 of each year to better reflect our position in the health care … industry.

In contrast, most large retailers such as Walmart and Target use fiscal years ending January 31 so that all of the Christmas sales and returns can be properly captured before closing the income statement accounts. Thus, January 31 is the end of the natural business year for most retailers.

Analysis for Decision Making

Objective

Describe and illustrate the use of working capital and the current ratio in evaluating a company's financial condition.

Working Capital and Current Ratio

The ability to convert assets into cash is called **liquidity**, while the ability of a business to pay its debts is called **solvency**. Two financial measures for evaluating a business's short-term liquidity and solvency are *working capital* and the *current ratio*.

Working capital is the excess of the current assets of a business over its current liabilities:

$$\text{Working Capital} = \text{Current Assets} - \text{Current Liabilities}$$

Current assets are more liquid than long-term assets, because they can be more readily turned into cash to meet short-term obligations. Thus, an increase in a company's current assets increases or improves its liquidity because these assets are available for uses other than paying current liabilities.

A positive working capital implies that the business is able to pay its current liabilities and is solvent. Thus, an increase in working capital increases or improves a company's short-term solvency.

To illustrate, **NetSolutions**' working capital at the end of 2017 is $6,355, computed as follows from Exhibit 1:

$$\text{Working Capital} = \text{Current Assets} - \text{Current Liabilities}$$
$$= \$7,745 - \$1,390$$
$$= \$6,355$$

This amount of working capital implies that NetSolutions is able to pay its current liabilities.

The **current ratio** is another means of expressing the relationship between current assets and current liabilities. The current ratio is computed by dividing current assets by current liabilities:

$$\text{Current Ratio} = \frac{\text{Current Assets}}{\text{Current Liabilities}}$$

To illustrate, the current ratio for **NetSolutions** at the end of 2017 is 5.6, computed as follows:

$$\text{Current Ratio} = \frac{\text{Current Assets}}{\text{Current Liabilities}}$$
$$= \frac{\$7,745}{\$1,390}$$
$$= 5.6 \text{ (Rounded)}$$

The current ratio is more useful than working capital in making comparisons across companies or with industry averages. To illustrate, the following data (in millions) were taken from recent financial statements of **Electronic Arts Inc.**, **Take-Two Interactive Software, Inc.**, and **Zynga, Inc.**:

	Electronic Arts		Take-Two		Zynga	
	Year 2	Year 1	Year 2	Year 1	Year 2	Year 1
Current assets	$3,138	$2,325	$1,399	$866	$1,083	$1,242
Current liabilities	2,390	1,917	475	337	369	277
Working capital	$ 748	$ 408	$ 924	$529	$ 714	$ 965
Current ratio*	1.3	1.2	2.9	2.6	2.9	4.5

* Current Assets ÷ Current Liabilities, rounded to one decimal place.

Electronic Arts' current assets are more than 2.2 times ($3,138 compared to $1,399) those of Take-Two and nearly 2.9 times ($3,138 compared to $1,083) those of Zynga. Such size differences make meaningful comparisons difficult across companies. For this reason, the current ratio is computed.

Although Electronic Arts has larger current asset and current liability balances, the current ratios of Take-Two and Zynga are more than twice as large as the current ratio of Electronic Arts at the end of Year 2 (2.9 for Take-Two and Zynga and 1.3 for Electronic Arts). Overall, the short-term liquidity positions of Take-Two and Zynga appear to be stronger than Electronic Arts' liquidity position. In addition, the two-year comparison shows that the current ratio has decreased significantly for Zynga (4.5 to 2.9) and increased slightly for Take-Two (2.6 to 2.9) and Electronic Arts (1.2 to 1.3).

Make a Decision   Working Capital and Current Ratio

The Finish Line, Inc. and **Foot Locker, Inc.** are two retail athletic footwear chains. The current assets and current liabilities from two recent balance sheet dates follow (in millions):

	Foot Locker		The Finish Line	
	Year 2	**Year 1**	**Year 2**	**Year 1**
Current assets	$2,456	$2,350	$567	$492
Current liabilities	696	626	194	134

A. Compute the working capital for each company at the end of each year.

B. Compute the current ratio for each company at the end of each year.

C. If you were a supplier to these two companies, which company provides the greater protection for trade payments (accounts payable)?

D. Did liquidity improve or decline for the two companies between the two years?

Solution:

A. and B.

	Foot Locker		The Finish Line	
	Year 2	**Year 1**	**Year 2**	**Year 1**
Current assets	$2,456	$2,350	$567	$492
Current liabilities	696	626	194	134
A. Working capital	$1,760	$1,724	$373	$358
B. Current ratio*	3.5	3.8	2.9	3.7

*Current Assets ÷ Current Liabilities, rounded to one decimal place.

C. For both years, it appears that Foot Locker has the greater relative liquidity, as measured by the current ratio (3.5 and 3.8 compared to The Finish Line's 2.9 and 3.7). However, both companies have current ratios near or above 3.0, which would be adequate under most conditions. Thus, while Foot Locker provides greater protection for satisfying trade payments, both companies appear to have sufficient liquidity to meet short-term obligations to suppliers.

D. Both companies have shown some decrease in their current ratios, indicating some modest decline in their respective short-term liquidity. Foot Locker's current ratio decreased from 3.8 to 3.5, or nearly 8% [(3.5 − 3.8) ÷ 3.8]. The Finish Line's current ratio decreased from 3.7 to 2.9, or nearly 22% [(2.9 − 3.7) ÷ 3.7]. Neither of these results is cause for concern. Normal business conditions will cause the current ratio to change from year to year.

Make a Decision

Appendix 1 End-of-Period Spreadsheet

Accountants often use spreadsheets for analyzing and summarizing data. Such spreadsheets are not a formal part of the accounting records. This is in contrast to the chart of accounts, the journal, and the ledger, which are essential parts of an accounting system. Spreadsheets are usually prepared by using a computer program such as Microsoft's Excel.®

Exhibit 1 is an end-of-period spreadsheet used to summarize adjusting entries and their effects on the accounts. As illustrated in the chapter, the financial statements for **NetSolutions** can be prepared directly from the spreadsheet's Adjusted Trial Balance columns.

Some accountants prefer to expand the end-of-period spreadsheet shown in Exhibit 1 to include financial statement columns. Exhibits 20 through 24 illustrate the step-by-step process of how to prepare this spreadsheet. As a basis for illustration, NetSolutions is used.

Step 1. Enter the Title

The spreadsheet is started by entering the following data:

1. Name of the business: *NetSolutions*
2. Type of spreadsheet: *End-of-Period Spreadsheet*
3. The period of time: *For the Two Months Ended December 31, 2017*

Exhibit 20 shows the preceding data entered for NetSolutions.

Step 2. Enter the Unadjusted Trial Balance

Enter the unadjusted trial balance on the spreadsheet. The spreadsheet in Exhibit 20 shows the unadjusted trial balance for NetSolutions at December 31, 2017.

Exhibit 20   Spreadsheet with Unadjusted Trial Balance Entered

	A	B	C	D	E	F	G	H	I	J	K
1					NetSolutions						
2					End-of-Period Spreadsheet						
3					For the Two Months Ended December 31, 2017						
4		Unadjusted				Adjusted					
5		Trial Balance		Adjustments		Trial Balance		Income Statement		Balance Sheet	
6	**Account Title**	Dr.	Cr.	Dr.	Cr.	Dr.	Cr.	Dr.	Cr.	Dr.	Cr.
7											
8	Cash	2,065									
9	Accounts Receivable	2,220									
10	Supplies	2,000									
11	Prepaid Insurance	2,400									
12	Land	20,000									
13	Office Equipment	1,800									
14	Accumulated Depreciation										
15	Accounts Payable		900								
16	Wages Payable										
17	Unearned Rent		360								
18	Common Stock		25,000								
19	Dividends	4,000									
20	Fees Earned		16,340								
21	Rent Revenue										
22	Wages Expense	4,275									
23	Supplies Expense	800									
24	Rent Expense	1,600									
25	Utilities Expense	985									
26	Insurance Expense										
27	Depreciation Expense										
28	Miscellaneous Expense	455									
29		42,600	42,600								
30											

The spreadsheet is used for summarizing the effects of adjusting entries. It also aids in preparing financial statements.

Step 3. Enter the Adjustments

The adjustments for NetSolutions from Chapter 3 are entered in the Adjustments columns, as shown in Exhibit 21. Cross-referencing (by letters) the debit and credit of each adjustment is useful in reviewing the spreadsheet. It is also helpful for identifying the adjusting entries that need to be recorded in the journal. This cross-referencing process is sometimes referred to as *keying* the adjustments.

Exhibit 21 Spreadsheet with Unadjusted Trial Balance and Adjustments

	A	B	C	D	E	F	G	H	I	J	K
1				NetSolutions							
2				End-of-Period Spreadsheet							
3				For the Two Months Ended December 31, 2017							
4		Unadjusted				Adjusted					
5		Trial Balance		Adjustments		Trial Balance		Income Statement		Balance Sheet	
6	Account Title	Dr.	Cr.	Dr.	Cr.	Dr.	Cr.	Dr.	Cr.	Dr.	Cr.
7											
8	Cash	2,065									
9	Accounts Receivable	2,220		(D) 500							
10	Supplies	2,000			(A) 1,240						
11	Prepaid Insurance	2,400			(B) 200						
12	Land	20,000									
13	Office Equipment	1,800									
14	Accumulated Depreciation				(F) 50						
15	Accounts Payable		900								
16	Wages Payable				(E) 250						
17	Unearned Rent		360	(C) 120							
18	Common Stock		25,000								
19	Dividends	4,000									
20	Fees Earned		16,340		(D) 500						
21	Rent Revenue				(C) 120						
22	Wages Expense	4,275		(E) 250							
23	Supplies Expense	800		(A) 1,240							
24	Rent Expense	1,600									
25	Utilities Expense	985									
26	Insurance Expense			(B) 200							
27	Depreciation Expense			(F) 50							
28	Miscellaneous Expense	455									
29		42,600	42,600	2,360	2,360						
30											

> The adjustments on the spreadsheet are used in preparing the adjusting journal entries.

The adjustments are normally entered in the order in which the data are assembled. If the titles of the accounts to be adjusted do not appear in the unadjusted trial balance, the accounts are inserted in their proper order in the Account Title column.

The adjusting entries for NetSolutions are entered in the Adjustments columns as follows:

(A) **Supplies.** The supplies account has a debit balance of $2,000. The cost of the supplies on hand at the end of the period is $760. The supplies expense for December is the difference between the two amounts, or $1,240 ($2,000 – $760). The adjustment is entered as (1) $1,240 in the Adjustments Debit column on the same line as Supplies Expense and (2) $1,240 in the Adjustments Credit column on the same line as Supplies.

(B) **Prepaid Insurance.** The prepaid insurance account has a debit balance of $2,400. This balance represents the prepayment of insurance for 12 months beginning December 1. Thus, the insurance expense for December is $200 ($2,400 ÷ 12). The adjustment is entered as (1) $200 in the Adjustments Debit column on the same line as Insurance Expense and (2) $200 in the Adjustments Credit column on the same line as Prepaid Insurance.

(C) **Unearned Rent.** The unearned rent account has a credit balance of $360. This balance represents the receipt of three months' rent, beginning with December. Thus, the rent revenue for December is $120 ($360 ÷ 3). The adjustment is entered as (1) $120 in the Adjustments Debit column on the same line as Unearned Rent and (2) $120 in the Adjustments Credit column on the same line as Rent Revenue.

(D) **Accrued Fees.** Fees accrued at the end of December but not recorded total $500. This amount is an increase in an asset and an increase in revenue. The adjustment is entered as (1) $500 in the Adjustments Debit column on the same line as Accounts Receivable and (2) $500 in the Adjustments Credit column on the same line as Fees Earned.

(E) **Wages.** Wages accrued but not paid at the end of December total $250. This amount is an increase in expenses and an increase in liabilities. The adjustment is entered as (1) $250 in the Adjustments Debit column on the same line as Wages Expense and (2) $250 in the Adjustments Credit column on the same line as Wages Payable.

(F) **Depreciation.** Depreciation of the office equipment is $50 for December. The adjustment is entered as (1) $50 in the Adjustments Debit column on the same line as Depreciation Expense and (2) $50 in the Adjustments Credit column on the same line as Accumulated Depreciation.

After the adjustments have been entered, the Adjustments columns are totaled to verify the equality of the debits and credits. The total of the Debit column must equal the total of the Credit column.

Step 4. Enter the Adjusted Trial Balance

The adjusted trial balance is entered by combining the adjustments with the unadjusted balances for each account. The adjusted amounts are then extended to the Adjusted Trial Balance columns, as shown in Exhibit 22.

To illustrate, the cash amount of $2,065 is extended to the Adjusted Trial Balance Debit column since no adjustments affected Cash. Accounts Receivable has an initial balance of $2,220 and a debit adjustment of $500. Thus, $2,720 ($2,220 + $500) is entered in the Adjusted Trial Balance

Exhibit 22 Spreadsheet with Unadjusted Trial Balance, Adjustments, and Adjusted Trial Balance Entered

	A	B	C	D	E	F	G	H	I	J	K
1					NetSolutions						
2					End-of-Period Spreadsheet						
3					For the Two Months Ended December 31, 2017						
4		Unadjusted				Adjusted					
5		Trial Balance		Adjustments		Trial Balance		Income Statement		Balance Sheet	
6	Account Title	Dr.	Cr.	Dr.	Cr.	Dr.	Cr.	Dr.	Cr.	Dr.	Cr.
7											
8	Cash	2,065				2,065					
9	Accounts Receivable	2,220		(D) 500		2,720					
10	Supplies	2,000			(A) 1,240	760					
11	Prepaid Insurance	2,400			(B) 200	2,200					
12	Land	20,000				20,000					
13	Office Equipment	1,800				1,800					
14	Accumulated Depreciation				(F) 50		50				
15	Accounts Payable		900				900				
16	Wages Payable				(E) 250		250				
17	Unearned Rent		360	(C) 120			240				
18	Common Stock		25,000				25,000				
19	Dividends	4,000				4,000					
20	Fees Earned		16,340		(D) 500		16,840				
21	Rent Revenue				(C) 120		120				
22	Wages Expense	4,275		(E) 250		4,525					
23	Supplies Expense	800		(A) 1,240		2,040					
24	Rent Expense	1,600				1,600					
25	Utilities Expense	985				985					
26	Insurance Expense			(B) 200		200					
27	Depreciation Expense			(F) 50		50					
28	Miscellaneous Expense	455				455					
29		42,600	42,600	2,360	2,360	43,400	43,400				
30											

The adjusted trial balance amounts are determined by adding the adjustments to or subtracting the adjustments from the trial balance amounts. For example, the Wages Expense debit of $4,525 is the trial balance amount of $4,275 plus the $250 adjustment debit.

Debit column for Accounts Receivable. The same process continues until all account balances are extended to the Adjusted Trial Balance columns.

After the accounts and adjustments have been extended, the Adjusted Trial Balance columns are totaled to verify the equality of debits and credits. The total of the Debit column must equal the total of the Credit column.

Step 5. Extend the Accounts to the Income Statement and Balance Sheet Columns

The adjusted trial balance amounts are extended to the Income Statement and Balance Sheet columns. The amounts for revenues and expenses are extended to the Income Statement columns. The amounts for assets, liabilities, and stockholders' equity (Common Stock, Retained Earnings, Dividends) are extended to the Balance Sheet columns.[3]

The first account listed in the Adjusted Trial Balance columns is Cash with a debit balance of $2,065. Cash is an asset, is listed on the balance sheet, and has a debit balance. Therefore, $2,065 is extended to the Balance Sheet Debit column. Accounts Receivable and the other balance sheet accounts are extended in the same manner. Fees Earned is the first account extended to the Income Statement columns. Its balance of $16,840 is extended to the Income Statement Credit column. The same process continues until all account balances have been extended to the proper columns, as shown in Exhibit 23.

Exhibit 23 Spreadsheet with Amounts Extended to Income Statement and Balance Sheet Columns

	A	B	C	D	E	F	G	H	I	J	K
1				NetSolutions							
2				End-of-Period Spreadsheet							
3				For the Two Months Ended December 31, 2017							
4		Unadjusted				Adjusted					
5		Trial Balance		Adjustments		Trial Balance		Income Statement		Balance Sheet	
6	Account Title	Dr.	Cr.	Dr.	Cr.	Dr.	Cr.	Dr.	Cr.	Dr.	Cr.
7											
8	Cash	2,065				2,065				2,065	
9	Accounts Receivable	2,220		(D) 500		2,720				2,720	
10	Supplies	2,000			(A) 1,240	760				760	
11	Prepaid Insurance	2,400			(B) 200	2,200				2,200	
12	Land	20,000				20,000				20,000	
13	Office Equipment	1,800				1,800				1,800	
14	Accumulated Depreciation				(F) 50		50				50
15	Accounts Payable		900				900				900
16	Wages Payable				(E) 250		250				250
17	Unearned Rent		360	(C) 120			240				240
18	Common Stock		25,000				25,000				25,000
19	Dividends	4,000				4,000				4,000	
20	Fees Earned		16,340		(D) 500		16,840		16,840		
21	Rent Revenue				(C) 120		120		120		
22	Wages Expense	4,275		(E) 250		4,525		4,525			
23	Supplies Expense	800		(A) 1,240		2,040		2,040			
24	Rent Expense	1,600				1,600		1,600			
25	Utilities Expense	985				985		985			
26	Insurance Expense			(B) 200		200		200			
27	Depreciation Expense			(F) 50		50		50			
28	Miscellaneous Expense	455				455		455			
29		42,600	42,600	2,360	2,360	43,400	43,400				
30											

The revenue and expense amounts are extended to (entered in) the Income Statement columns.

The asset, liability, common stock, and dividends amounts are extended to (entered in) the Balance Sheet columns.

[3] The balance of the dividends account is extended to the Balance Sheet columns because the spreadsheet does not have separate Retained Earnings Statement columns.

Step 6. Total the Income Statement and Balance Sheet Columns, Compute the Net Income or Net Loss, and Complete the Spreadsheet

After the account balances are extended to the Income Statement and Balance Sheet columns, each of the columns is totaled. The difference between the two Income Statement column totals is the amount of the net income or the net loss for the period. This difference (net income or net loss) will also be the difference between the two Balance Sheet column totals.

If the Income Statement Credit column total (total revenue) is greater than the Income Statement Debit column total (total expenses), the difference is the net income. If the Income Statement Debit column total is greater than the Income Statement Credit column total, the difference is a net loss.

As shown in Exhibit 24, the total of the Income Statement Credit column is $16,960, and the total of the Income Statement Debit column is $9,855. Thus, the net income for NetSolutions is $7,105, computed as follows:

Total of Income Statement Credit column (revenues)	$16,960
Total of Income Statement Debit column (expenses)	9,855
Net income (excess of revenues over expenses)	$ 7,105

Exhibit 24 Completed Spreadsheet with Net Income Shown

	A	B	C	D	E	F	G	H	I	J	K
1					NetSolutions						
2					End-of-Period Spreadsheet						
3					For the Two Months Ended December 31, 2017						
4		Unadjusted				Adjusted					
5		Trial Balance		Adjustments		Trial Balance		Income Statement		Balance Sheet	
6	Account Title	Dr.	Cr.	Dr.	Cr.	Dr.	Cr.	Dr.	Cr.	Dr.	Cr.
7											
8	Cash	2,065				2,065				2,065	
9	Accounts Receivable	2,220		(D) 500		2,720				2,720	
10	Supplies	2,000			(A) 1,240	760				760	
11	Prepaid Insurance	2,400			(B) 200	2,200				2,200	
12	Land	20,000				20,000				20,000	
13	Office Equipment	1,800				1,800				1,800	
14	Accumulated Depreciation				(F) 50		50				50
15	Accounts Payable		900				900				900
16	Wages Payable				(E) 250		250				250
17	Unearned Rent		360	(C) 120			240				240
18	Common Stock		25,000				25,000				25,000
19	Dividends	4,000				4,000				4,000	
20	Fees Earned		16,340		(D) 500		16,840		16,840		
21	Rent Revenue				(C) 120		120		120		
22	Wages Expense	4,275		(E) 250		4,525		4,525			
23	Supplies Expense	800		(A) 1,240		2,040		2,040			
24	Rent Expense	1,600				1,600		1,600			
25	Utilities Expense	985				985		985			
26	Insurance Expense			(B) 200		200		200			
27	Depreciation Expense			(F) 50		50		50			
28	Miscellaneous Expense	455				455		455			
29		42,600	42,600	2,360	2,360	43,400	43,400	9,855	16,960	33,545	26,440
30	Net income							7,105			7,105
31								16,960	16,960	33,545	33,545
32											

The difference between the Income Statement column totals is the net income (or net loss) for the period. The difference between the Balance Sheet column totals is also the net income (or net loss) for the period.

The amount of the net income, $7,105, is entered in the Income Statement Debit column and the Balance Sheet Credit column. *Net income* is also entered in the Account Title column. Entering the net income of $7,105 in the Balance Sheet Credit column has the effect of transferring the net balance of the revenue and expense accounts to the retained earnings account.

If there was a net loss instead of net income, the amount of the net loss would be entered in the Income Statement Credit column and the Balance Sheet Debit column. *Net loss* would also be entered in the Account Title column.

After the net income or net loss is entered on the spreadsheet, the Income Statement and Balance Sheet columns are totaled. The totals of the two Income Statement columns must now be equal. The totals of the two Balance Sheet columns must also be equal.

Preparing the Financial Statements from the Spreadsheet

The spreadsheet can be used to prepare the income statement, the retained earnings statement, and the balance sheet shown in Exhibit 2. The income statement is normally prepared directly from the spreadsheet. The expenses are listed in the income statement in Exhibit 2 in order of size, beginning with the larger items. Miscellaneous expense is the last item, regardless of its amount.

The first item normally presented on the retained earnings statement is the balance of the retained earnings account at the beginning of the period. This amount along with the net income (or net loss) and the dividends amount shown in the spreadsheet are used to determine the ending retained earnings account balance.

The balance sheet can be prepared directly from the spreadsheet columns except for the ending balance of retained earnings. The ending balance of retained earnings is taken from the retained earnings statement.

When a spreadsheet is used, the adjusting and closing entries are normally not journalized or posted until after the spreadsheet and financial statements have been prepared. The data for the adjusting entries are taken from the Adjustments columns of the spreadsheet. The data for the first two closing entries are taken from the Income Statement columns of the spreadsheet. The amount for the third closing entry is the net income or net loss appearing at the bottom of the spreadsheet. The amount for the fourth closing entry is the dividends account balance that appears in the Balance Sheet Debit column of the spreadsheet.

Appendix 2 Reversing Entries

Some adjusting entries recorded at the end of an accounting period affect how transactions are recorded in the next period. For this reason, some companies add another step to the accounting cycle. This additional step records journal entries on the first day of the next period that are the exact *opposite* of the related adjusting entry from the last day of the prior period. These journal entries are called **reversing entries**.

To illustrate, the **NetSolutions** data for accrued wages from Chapter 3 is used. This data is summarized in Exhibit 25.

Exhibit 25
Accrued Wages

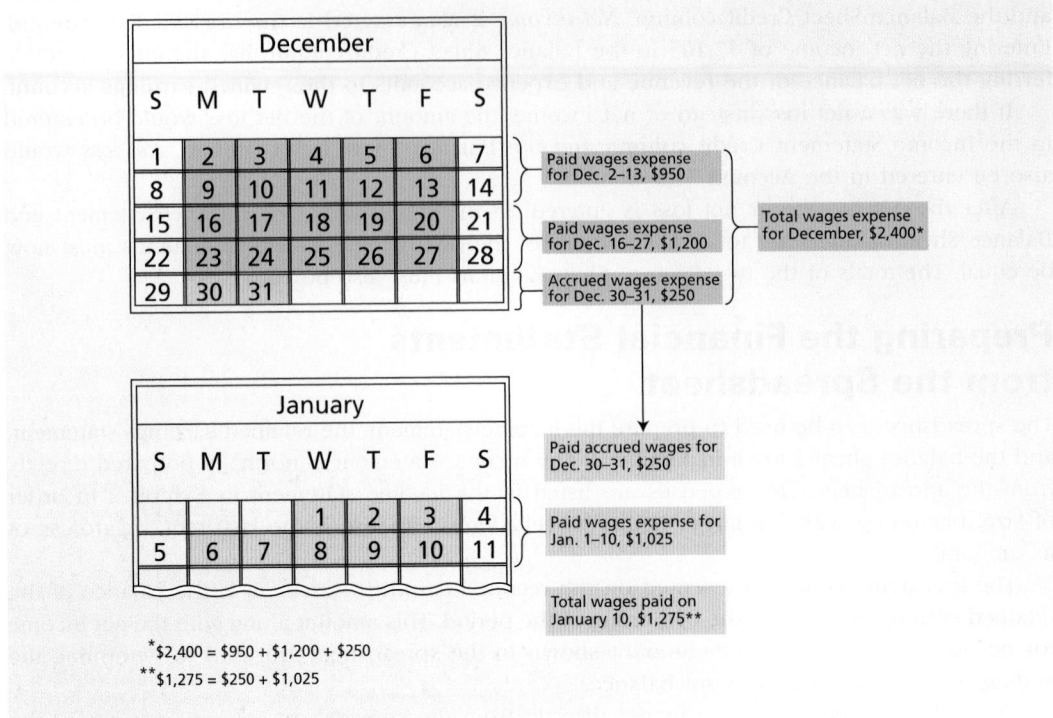

Based upon Exhibit 25, accrued wages for December 30 and 31 of $250 were recorded with the following adjusting entry:

2017				
Dec.	31	Wages Expense	51	250
		Wages Payable	22	250

Exhibit 26 shows Wages Payable and Wages Expense after the adjusting entry has been recorded and posted. Wages Payable has a credit balance of $250 and Wages Expense has a debit balance of $4,525.

Exhibit 26
Wages Expense and Wages Payable

After Adjustment

Account Wages Payable   Account No. 22

		Post.			Balance	
Date	Item	Ref.	Debit	Credit	Debit	Credit
2017						
Dec. 31	Adjusting	5		250		250

Account Wages Expense   Account No. 51

		Post.			Balance	
Date	Item	Ref.	Debit	Credit	Debit	Credit
2017						
Nov. 30		1	2,125		2,125	
Dec. 13		3	950		3,075	
24		3	1,200		4,275	
31	Adjusting	5	250		4,525	

After the closing entries are recorded, Wages Expense has a zero balance. Since Wages Payable is a liability account, it is not closed. Thus, Wages Payable has a credit balance of $250 as of January 1, 2018.

On January 10, 2018, NetSolutions pays wages of $1,275. The *normal* entry for paying wages is as follows:

Jan.	10	Wages Expense	51	1,275	
		Cash	11		1,275

However, the preceding entry is incorrect. Specifically, Wages Payable should have been debited for $250, and the wages for January 1–10 are $1,025 ($1,275 – $250), not $1,275. The correct entry to record the January 10 payroll is as follows:

Jan.	10	Wages Payable	22	250	
		Wages Expense	51	1,025	
		Cash	11		1,275

Because the correct entry is not the same as the normal journal entry, there is a chance that Wages Payable will be overlooked and an error made. To avoid this and to simplify the recording of next period's transactions, many companies use reversing entries.

A reversing entry is the opposite of the adjusting entry to which it relates. For example, the reversing entry for the accrued payroll for NetSolutions is as follows:

Jan.	1	Wages Payable	22	250	
		Wages Expense	51		250
		Reversing entry.			

Reversing entries are recorded on the first day of the subsequent accounting period. Exhibit 27 shows the wages payable and wages expense accounts after the reversing entry has been recorded and posted.

After Reversing Entry

Account Wages Payable — Account No. 22

Date	Item	Post. Ref.	Debit	Credit	Balance Debit	Balance Credit
2017						
Dec. 31	Adjusting	5		250		250
2018						
Jan. 1	Reversing	7	250		—	—

Account Wages Expense — Account No. 51

Date	Item	Post. Ref.	Debit	Credit	Balance Debit	Balance Credit
2017						
Nov. 30		1	2,125		2,125	
Dec. 13		3	950		3,075	
27		3	1,200		4,275	
31	Adjusting	5	250		4,525	
31	Closing	6		4,525	—	—
2017						
Jan. 1	Reversing	7		250		250

Exhibit 27
Wages Expense and Wages Payable

Exhibit 27 indicates that on January 1, Wages Payable has a zero balance and Wages Expense has a credit balance of $250. The Wages Expense credit balance of $250 is only temporary. Wages Expense will have a debit balance as soon as the first payroll is paid on January 10.

To illustrate, the January 10 payroll of $1,275 would be recorded in the normal manner as follows:

| Jan. | 10 | Wages Expense | 51 | 1,275 | |
| | | Cash | 11 | | 1,275 |

After the preceding entry is posted, Wages Expense will have a debit balance of $1,025 ($1,275 – $250), which is the correct wages expense for January 1–10.

The use of reversing entries is optional. However, in computerized accounting systems, routine transactions are processed in standard manner. In such cases, reversing entries are useful in avoiding errors and simplifying the recording of the subsequent period's transactions.

Let's Review

Chapter Summary

1. Exhibit 1 illustrates the end-of-period process by which accounts are adjusted and how the adjusted accounts flow into the financial statements.

2. Using the end-of-period spreadsheet shown in Exhibit 1, the income statement, retained earnings statement, and balance sheet can be prepared. A classified balance sheet has sections for current assets; property, plant, and equipment; current liabilities; long-term liabilities; and stockholders' equity.

3. Four entries are required in closing the temporary accounts. The first entry closes the revenue accounts to Income Summary. The second entry closes the expense accounts to Income Summary. The third entry closes the balance of Income Summary (net income or net loss) to the retained earnings account. The fourth entry closes the dividends account to the retained earnings account. After the closing entries have been posted to the ledger, the balance in the retained earnings account agrees with the amount reported on the retained earnings statement and balance sheet. In addition, the revenue, expense, and dividends accounts will have zero balances.

4. The 10 basic steps of the accounting cycle are as follows:
   1. Transactions are analyzed and recorded in the journal.
   2. Transactions are posted to the ledger.
   3. An unadjusted trial balance is prepared.
   4. Adjustment data are assembled and analyzed.
   5. An optional end-of-period spreadsheet is prepared.
   6. Adjusting entries are journalized and posted to the ledger.
   7. An adjusted trial balance is prepared.
   8. Financial statements are prepared.
   9. Closing entries are journalized and posted to the ledger.
   10. A post-closing trial balance is prepared.

5. The complete accounting cycle for Kelly Consulting for the month of April is described and illustrated in this chapter.

6. The annual accounting period adopted by a business is its fiscal year. A company's fiscal year that ends when business activities have reached the lowest point in its annual operating cycle is called the natural business year.

Key Terms

accounting cycle (171)	current ratio (184)	notes receivable (162)
clearing account (165)	fiscal year (182)	permanent (real) accounts (164)
closing entries (164)	fixed (plant) assets (162)	property, plant, and equipment (162)
closing process (164)	Income Summary (165)	reversing entries (191)
closing the books (164)	liquidity (184)	solvency (184)
current assets (162)	long-term liabilities (162)	temporary (nominal) accounts (164)
current liabilities (162)	natural business year (182)	working capital (184)

Practice

Multiple-Choice Questions

1. Which of the following accounts in the Adjusted Trial Balance columns of the end-of-period spreadsheet (work sheet) would be reported on the retained earnings statement?
   A. Utilities Expense
   B. Rent Revenue
   C. Dividends
   D. Miscellaneous Expense

2. Which of the following accounts would be classified as a current asset on the balance sheet?
   A. Office Equipment
   B. Land
   C. Accumulated Depreciation
   D. Accounts Receivable

3. Which of the following entries closes the dividends account at the end of the period?
   A. Debit the dividends account, credit the income summary account.
   B. Debit the retained earnings account, credit the dividends account.
   C. Debit the income summary account, credit the dividends account.
   D. Debit the dividends account, credit the retained earnings account.

4. Which of the following accounts would not be closed to the income summary account at the end of a period?
   A. Fees Earned
   B. Wages Expense
   C. Rent Expense
   D. Accumulated Depreciation

5. Which of the following accounts would not be included in a post-closing trial balance?
   A. Cash
   B. Fees Earned
   C. Accumulated Depreciation
   D. Retained Earnings

Answers provided after Problem. Need more practice? Find additional multiple-choice questions, exercises, and problems in CengageNOWv2.

Exercises

SHOW ME HOW

---

1. Flow of accounts into financial statements   Obj. 1

The balances for the accounts that follow appear in the Adjusted Trial Balance columns of the end-of-period spreadsheet. Indicate whether each account would flow into the income statement, retained earnings statement, or balance sheet.

1. Accounts Receivable
2. Depreciation Expense—Equipment
3. Retained Earnings
4. Office Equipment
5. Rent Revenue
6. Supplies Expense
7. Unearned Revenue
8. Wages Payable

SHOW ME HOW

2. Retained earnings statement

Obj. 2

Marcie Davies owns and operates Gemini Advertising Services. On January 1, 2018, Retained Earnings had a balance of $618,500. During the year, Marcie invested an additional $40,000 in exchange for common stock, and $15,000 of dividends were paid. For the year ended December 31, 2018, Gemini Advertising reported a net income of $92,330. Prepare a retained earnings statement for the year ended December 31, 2018.

SHOW ME HOW

3. Classified balance sheet

Obj. 2

The following accounts appear in an adjusted trial balance of San Jose Consulting. Indicate whether each account would be reported in the (A) current asset; (B) property, plant, and equipment; (C) current liability; (D) long-term liability; or (E) stockholders' equity section of the December 31, 2018, balance sheet of San Jose Consulting.

1. Building
2. Common Stock
3. Notes Payable (due in five years)
4. Prepaid Rent
5. Salaries Payable
6. Supplies
7. Taxes Payable
8. Unearned Service Fees

SHOW ME HOW

4. Closing entries

Obj. 3

After the accounts have been adjusted at October 31, the end of the fiscal year, the following balances were taken from the ledger of Smart Delivery Services Co.:

Retained Earnings	$3,550,000
Dividends	40,000
Fees Earned	1,145,000
Wages Expense	740,000
Rent Expense	65,000
Supplies Expense	14,750
Miscellaneous Expense	8,800

Journalize the four entries required to close the accounts.

SHOW ME HOW

5. Accounting cycle

Obj. 4

From the following list of steps in the accounting cycle, identify what two steps are missing:

A. Transactions are analyzed and recorded in the journal.

B. An unadjusted trial balance is prepared.

C. Adjustment data are assembled and analyzed.

D. An optional end-of-period spreadsheet is prepared.

E. Adjusting entries are journalized and posted to the ledger.

F. An adjusted trial balance is prepared.

G. Closing entries are journalized and posted to the ledger.

H. A post-closing trial balance is prepared.

Answers provided after Problem. Need more practice? Find additional multiple-choice questions, exercises, and problems in CengageNOWv2.

Problem

Three years ago, T. Roderick organized Harbor Realty. At July 31, 2018, the end of the fiscal year, the following end-of-period spreadsheet was prepared:

	A	B	C	D	E	F	G
1		Harbor Realty					
2		End-of-Period Spreadsheet					
3		For the Year Ended July 31, 2018					
4		Unadjusted				Adjusted	
5		Trial Balance		Adjustments		Trial Balance	
6	**Account Title**	Dr.	Cr.	Dr.	Cr.	Dr.	Cr.
7							
8	Cash	3,425				3,425	
9	Accounts Receivable	7,000		1,000		8,000	
10	Supplies	1,270			890	380	
11	Prepaid Insurance	620			315	305	
12	Office Equipment	51,650				51,650	
13	Accumulated Depreciation		9,700		4,950		14,650
14	Accounts Payable		925				925
15	Unearned Fees		1,250	500			750
16	Wages Payable				440		440
17	Common Stock		5,000				5,000
18	Retained Earnings		24,000				24,000
19	Dividends	5,200				5,200	
20	Fees Earned		59,125		1,000		60,625
21					500		
22	Wages Expense	22,415		440		22,855	
23	Depreciation Expense			4,950		4,950	
24	Rent Expense	4,200				4,200	
25	Utilities Expense	2,715				2,715	
26	Supplies Expense			890		890	
27	Insurance Expense			315		315	
28	Miscellaneous Expense	1,505				1,505	
29		100,000	100,000	8,095	8,095	106,390	106,390
30							

Instructions

1. Prepare an income statement, a retained earnings statement, and a balance sheet.
2. On the basis of the data in the end-of-period spreadsheet, journalize the closing entries.

Need more practice? Find additional multiple-choice questions, exercises, and problems in CengageNOWv2.

Answers

Multiple-Choice Questions

1. **C** Dividends (answer C) would be reported on the retained earnings statement. Utilities Expense (answer A), Rent Revenue (answer B), and Miscellaneous Expense (answer D) would all be reported on the income statement.

2. **D** Cash or other assets that are expected to be converted to cash or sold or used up within one year or less through the normal operations of the business are classified as current assets on the balance sheet. Accounts Receivable (answer D) is a current asset, since it will normally be converted to cash within one year. Office Equipment (answer A), Land (answer B), and Accumulated Depreciation (answer C) are all reported in the property, plant, and equipment section of the balance sheet.

3. **B** The entry to close the dividends account is to debit the retained earnings account and credit the dividends account (answer B).

4. **D** Since all revenue and expense accounts are closed at the end of the period, Fees Earned (answer A), Wages Expense (answer B), and Rent Expense (answer C) would all be closed to Income Summary. Accumulated Depreciation (answer D) is a contra asset account that is not closed.

5. **B** Since the post-closing trial balance includes only balance sheet accounts (all of the revenue, expense, and dividend accounts are closed), Cash (answer A), Accumulated Depreciation (answer C), and Retained Earnings (answer D) would appear on the post-closing trial balance. Fees Earned (answer B) is a temporary account that is closed prior to preparing the post-closing trial balance.

Exercises

1.

1. Balance sheet	5. Income statement
2. Income statement	6. Income statement
3. Retained earnings statement	7. Balance sheet
4. Balance sheet	8. Balance sheet

2.

Gemini Advertising Services Retained Earnings Statement For the Year Ended December 31, 2018		
Retained earnings, January 1, 2018		$618,500
Net income	$ 92,330	
Dividends	(15,000)	
Change in retained earnings..		77,330
Retained earnings, December 31, 2018.......................................		$695,830

3.

1. Property, plant, and equipment	5. Current liability
2. Stockholders' equity	6. Current asset
3. Long-term liability	7. Current liability
4. Current asset	8. Current liability

4.

Journal		
Closing Entries		
Oct. 31 Fees Earned	1,145,000	
Income Summary		1,145,000
31 Income Summary	828,550	
Wages Expense		740,000
Rent Expense		65,000
Supplies Expense		14,750
Miscellaneous Expense		8,800
31 Income Summary	316,450	
Retained Earnings		316,450
31 Retained Earnings	40,000	
Dividends		40,000

5. The following two steps are missing: (1) posting the transactions to the ledger and (2) the preparation of the financial statements. Transactions should be posted to the ledger after step (A). The financial statements should be prepared after step (F).

Need more help? Watch step-by-step videos of how to compute answers to these Exercises in CengageNOWv2.

Problem

1.

Harbor Realty
Income Statement
For the Year Ended July 31, 2018

Fees earned..		$60,625
Expenses:		
Wages expense	$22,855	
Depreciation expense	4,950	
Rent expense...	4,200	
Utilities expense	2,715	
Supplies expense	890	
Insurance expense	315	
Miscellaneous expense	1,505	
Total expenses..		37,430
Net income		$23,195

Harbor Realty
Retained Earnings Statement
For the Year Ended July 31, 2018

Retained earnings, August 1, 2017..		$24,000
Net income	$23,195	
Dividends	(5,200)	
Change in retained earnings		17,995
Retained earnings, July 31, 2018...		$41,995

Harbor Realty
Balance Sheet
July 31, 2018

Assets		
Current assets:		
Cash...	$ 3,425	
Accounts receivable	8,000	
Supplies	380	
Prepaid insurance	305	
Total current assets		$12,110
Property, plant, and equipment:		
Office equipment..	$51,650	
Accumulated depreciation...	(14,650)	
Total property, plant, and equipment		37,000
Total assets..		$49,110

Liabilities		
Current liabilities:		
Accounts payable..	$ 925	
Unearned fees	750	
Wages payable	440	
Total liabilities..		$ 2,115

Stockholders' Equity		
Common stock	$ 5,000	
Retained earnings	41,995	
Total stockholders' equity		46,995
Total liabilities and stockholders' equity		$49,110

2.

Journal					
Date		**Description**	**Post. Ref.**	**Debit**	**Credit**
		Closing Entries			
2018					
July	31	Fees Earned		60,625	
		Income Summary			60,625
	31	Income Summary		37,430	
		Wages Expense			22,855
		Depreciation Expense			4,950
		Rent Expense			4,200
		Utilities Expense			2,715
		Supplies Expense			890
		Insurance Expense			315
		Miscellaneous Expense			1,505
	31	Income Summary		23,195	
		Retained Earnings			23,195
	31	Retained Earnings		5,200	
		Dividends			5,200

Discussion Questions

1. Why do some accountants prepare an end-of-period spreadsheet?

2. Describe the nature of the assets that compose the following sections of a balance sheet: (A) current assets, (B) property, plant, and equipment.

3. What is the difference between a current liability and a long-term liability?

4. What types of accounts are referred to as temporary accounts?

5. Why are closing entries required at the end of an accounting period?

6. What is the difference between adjusting entries and closing entries?

7. What is the purpose of the post-closing trial balance?

8. (A) What is the most important output of the accounting cycle? (B) Do all companies have an accounting cycle? Explain.

9. What is the natural business year?

10. Recent fiscal years for several well-known companies are as follows:

Company	Fiscal Year Ending
J. C. Penney Company, Inc.	January 27
L Brands, Inc.	January 27
Sears Holdings Corporation	January 27
Target Corporation	January 27
The Home Depot, Inc.	January 28
Tiffany & Co.	January 30

What general characteristic shared by these companies explains why they do not have fiscal years ending December 31?

Basic Exercises

SHOW ME HOW

BE 4-1 Flow of accounts into financial statements
Obj. 1

The balances for the accounts that follow appear in the Adjusted Trial Balance columns of the end-of-period spreadsheet. Indicate whether each account would flow into the income statement, retained earnings statement, or balance sheet.

1. Accumulated Depreciation—Building
2. Cash
3. Fees Earned
4. Insurance Expense

5. Prepaid Rent
6. Supplies
7. Dividends
8. Wages Expense

SHOW ME HOW

BE 4-2 Retained earnings statement
Obj. 2

Blake Knudson owns and operates Grab Bag Delivery Services. On January 1, 2018, Retained Earnings had a balance of $918,000. During the year, no additional common stock was issued, and $15,000 of dividends were paid. For the year ended December 31, 2018, Grab Bag Delivery reported a net loss of $43,500. Prepare a retained earnings statement for the year ended December 31, 2018.

SHOW ME HOW

BE 4-3 Classified balance sheet
Obj. 2

The following accounts appear in an adjusted trial balance of Kangaroo Consulting. Indicate whether each account would be reported in the (A) current asset; (B) property, plant, and equipment; (C) current liability; (D) long-term liability; or (E) stockholders' equity section of the December 31, 2018, balance sheet of Kangaroo Consulting.

1. Accounts Payable
2. Accounts Receivable
3. Accumulated Depreciation—Building
4. Cash

5. Common Stock
6. Note Payable (due in ten years)
7. Supplies
8. Wages Payable

SHOW ME HOW

BE 4-4 Closing entries
Obj. 3

After the accounts have been adjusted at April 30, the end of the fiscal year, the following balances were taken from the ledger of Nuclear Landscaping Co.:

Retained Earnings	$643,600
Dividends	10,500
Fees Earned	356,500
Wages Expense	283,100
Rent Expense	56,000
Supplies Expense	11,500
Miscellaneous Expense	13,000

Journalize the four entries required to close the accounts.

SHOW ME HOW

BE 4-5 Accounting cycle
Obj. 4

From the following list of steps in the accounting cycle, identify what two steps are missing:

A. Transactions are analyzed and recorded in the journal.
B. Transactions are posted to the ledger.
C. An unadjusted trial balance is prepared.
D. An optional end-of-period spreadsheet is prepared.
E. Adjusting entries are journalized and posted to the ledger.
F. An adjusted trial balance is prepared.
G. Financial statements are prepared.
H. A post-closing trial balance is prepared.

Exercises

EX 4-1   Flow of accounts into financial statements   Obj. 1, 2

The balances for the accounts that follow appear in the Adjusted Trial Balance columns of the end-of-period spreadsheet. Indicate whether each account would flow into the income statement, retained earnings statement, or balance sheet.

1. Accounts Payable	6. Supplies
2. Accounts Receivable	7. Unearned Rent
3. Cash	8. Utilities Expense
4. Dividends	9. Wages Expense
5. Fees Earned	10. Wages Payable

EX 4-2   Classifying accounts   Obj. 1, 2

Balances for each of the following accounts appear in an adjusted trial balance. Identify each as (A) asset, (B) liability, (C) revenue, or (D) expense.

1. Accounts Receivable	7. Rent Revenue
2. Equipment	8. Salary Expense
3. Fees Earned	9. Salary Payable
4. Insurance Expense	10. Supplies
5. Prepaid Advertising	11. Supplies Expense
6. Prepaid Rent	12. Unearned Rent

SHOW ME HOW

EX 4-3   Financial statements from the end-of-period spreadsheet   Obj. 1, 2

Taser Consulting is a consulting firm owned and operated by Annamarie Phipps. The following end-of-period spreadsheet was prepared for the year ended October 31, 2018:

	A	B	C	D	E	F	G
1		Taser Consulting					
2		End-of-Period Spreadsheet					
3		For the Year Ended October 31, 2018					
4		Unadjusted				Adjusted	
5		Trial Balance		Adjustments		Trial Balance	
6	Account Title	Dr.	Cr.	Dr.	Cr.	Dr.	Cr.
7							
8	Cash	45,000				45,000	
9	Accounts Receivable	119,200				119,200	
10	Supplies	11,900			7,500	4,400	
11	Office Equipment	400,000				400,000	
12	Accumulated Depreciation		56,000		6,000		62,000
13	Accounts Payable		20,500				20,500
14	Salaries Payable				9,000		9,000
15	Common Stock		75,000				75,000
16	Retained Earnings		180,700				180,700
17	Dividends	25,000				25,000	
18	Fees Earned		800,000				800,000
19	Salary Expense	520,000		9,000		529,000	
20	Supplies Expense			7,500		7,500	
21	Depreciation Expense			6,000		6,000	
22	Miscellaneous Expense	11,100				11,100	
23		1,132,200	1,132,200	22,500	22,500	1,147,200	1,147,200
24							

Based on the preceding spreadsheet, prepare an income statement, retained earnings statement, and balance sheet for Taser Consulting.

EX 4-4 Financial statements from the end-of-period spreadsheet

Obj. 1, 2

Triton Consulting is a consulting firm owned and operated by Jayson Neese. The following end-of-period spreadsheet was prepared for the year ended April 30, 2018:

	A	B	C	D	E	F	G
1		Triton Consulting					
2		End-of-Period Spreadsheet					
3		For the Year Ended April 30, 2018					
4		Unadjusted				Adjusted	
5		Trial Balance		Adjustments		Trial Balance	
6	Account Title	Dr.	Cr.	Dr.	Cr.	Dr.	Cr.
7							
8	Cash	21,500				21,500	
9	Accounts Receivable	51,150				51,150	
10	Supplies	2,400			1,650	750	
11	Office Equipment	32,000				32,000	
12	Accumulated Depreciation		4,500		900		5,400
13	Accounts Payable		3,350				3,350
14	Salaries Payable				2,000		2,000
15	Common Stock		20,000				20,000
16	Retained Earnings		52,200				52,200
17	Dividends	10,000				10,000	
18	Fees Earned		279,000				279,000
19	Salary Expense	240,000		2,000		242,000	
20	Supplies Expense			1,650		1,650	
21	Depreciation Expense			900		900	
22	Miscellaneous Expense	2,000				2,000	
23		359,050	359,050	4,550	4,550	361,950	361,950
24							

Based on the preceding spreadsheet, prepare an income statement, retained earnings statement, and balance sheet for Triton Consulting.

EX 4-5 Income statement

Obj. 2

✔ Net income, $186,750

The following account balances were taken from the adjusted trial balance for Urgent Messenger Service, a delivery service firm, for the fiscal year ended November 30, 2018:

Depreciation Expense	$ 10,650	Rent Expense	$ 75,000
Fees Earned	724,500	Salaries Expense	393,100
Insurance Expense	5,000	Supplies Expense	6,150
Miscellaneous Expense	6,650	Utilities Expense	41,200

Prepare an income statement.

EX 4-6 Income statement; net loss

Obj. 2

✔ Net loss, $(49,250)

The following revenue and expense account balances were taken from the ledger of Acorn Health Services Co. after the accounts had been adjusted on January 31, 2018, the end of the fiscal year:

Depreciation Expense	$10,000	Service Revenue	$634,900
Insurance Expense	9,000	Supplies Expense	4,100
Miscellaneous Expense	8,150	Utilities Expense	44,700
Rent Expense	60,000	Wages Expense	548,200

Prepare an income statement.

EX 4-7 Income statement

Obj. 2

FedEx Corporation had the following revenue and expense account balances (in millions) for a recent year ending May 31:

Depreciation Expense	$2,587	Purchased Transportation	$ 8,011
Fuel Expense	4,557	Rentals and Landing Fees	2,622
Maintenance and Repairs Expense	1,862	Revenues	45,567
Other Expense (Income) Net	6,084	Salaries and Employee Benefits	16,555
Provision for Income Taxes	1,192		

A. Prepare an income statement.

B. ━━━━▶ Compare your income statement with the income statement that is available at FedEx's Web site (http://investors.fedex.com). Under Annual Report, select Download PDF. What similarities and differences do you see?

EX 4-8 Retained earnings statement

Obj. 2

Climate Control Systems Co. offers its services to residents in the Spokane area. Selected accounts from the ledger of Climate Control Systems for the fiscal year ended December 31, 2018, are as follows:

Retained Earnings					Dividends			
Dec. 31	160,000	Jan. 1 (2018)	4,150,800	Mar. 31	40,000	Dec. 31	160,000
		Dec. 31	700,000	June 30	40,000		
				Sept. 30	40,000		
				Dec. 31	40,000		

Income Summary			
Dec. 31	4,530,000	Dec. 31	5,230,000
31	700,000		

Prepare a retained earnings statement for the year.

EX 4-9 Retained earnings statement; net loss

Obj. 2

Selected accounts from the ledger of Restoration Arts for the fiscal year ended April 30, 2018, are as follows:

Retained Earnings					Dividends			
Apr. 30	31,200	May 1 (2017)	475,500	Sept. 30	1,250	Apr. 30	5,000
30	5,000			Dec. 31	1,250		
				March 31	1,250		
				June 30	1,250		

Income Summary			
Apr. 30	197,000	Apr. 30	165,800
		30	31,200

Prepare a retained earnings statement for the year.

EX 4-10 Classifying assets

Obj. 2

Identify each of the following as (A) a current asset or (B) property, plant, and equipment:

1. Accounts Receivable
2. Building
3. Cash

4. Equipment
5. Prepaid Insurance
6. Supplies

EX 4-11   Balance sheet classification   Obj. 2

At the balance sheet date, a business owes a mortgage note payable of $375,000, the terms of which provide for monthly payments of $1,250.

➤ Explain how the liability should be classified on the balance sheet.

EX 4-12   Balance sheet   Obj. 2

✔ Total assets: $800,000

SHOW ME HOW

Dynamic Weight Loss Co. offers personal weight reduction consulting services to individuals. After all the accounts have been closed on June 30, 2018, the end of the fiscal year, the balances of selected accounts from the ledger of Dynamic Weight Loss are as follows:

Accounts Payable	$ 51,200	Prepaid Insurance	$ 8,400
Accounts Receivable	187,500	Prepaid Rent	6,000
Accumulated Depreciation—Equipment	186,000	Retained Earnings	620,300
Cash	?	Salaries Payable	7,500
Common Stock	100,000	Supplies	11,200
Equipment	325,900	Unearned Fees	21,000
Land	375,000		

Prepare a classified balance sheet that includes the correct balance for Cash.

EX 4-13   Balance sheet   Obj. 2

✔ Corrected balance sheet, total assets: $625,000

List the errors you find in the following balance sheet. Prepare a corrected balance sheet.

Labyrinth Services Co.
Balance Sheet
For the Year Ended August 31, 2018

Assets

Current assets:

Cash..	$ 18,500	
Accounts payable..	31,300	
Supplies	6,500	
Prepaid insurance	16,600	
Land...	225,000	
Total current assets		$297,900

Property, plant, and equipment:

Building...	$400,000	
Equipment	97,000	
Total property, plant, and equipment..............		635,400
Total assets		$933,300

Liabilities

Current liabilities:

Accounts receivable......................................	$ 41,400	
Accumulated depreciation—building...............	155,000	
Accumulated depreciation—equipment	25,000	
Net income..	118,200	
Total liabilities		$339,600

Stockholders' Equity

Wages payable	$ 6,500	
Common stock..	75,000	
Retained earnings...	512,200	
Total stockholders' equity..................................		593,700
Total liabilities and stockholders' equity..............		$933,300

EX 4-14 Identifying accounts to be closed

Obj. 3

From the list that follows, identify the accounts that should be closed to Income Summary at the end of the fiscal year:

A. Accounts Payable

B. Accumulated Depreciation—Equipment

C. Depreciation Expense—Equipment

D. Equipment

E. Common Stock

F. Dividends

G. Fees Earned

H. Land

I. Supplies

J. Supplies Expense

K. Wages Expense

L. Wages Payable

EX 4-15 Closing entries

Obj. 3

Prior to its closing, Income Summary had total debits of $1,190,500 and total credits of $1,476,300.

➤ Briefly explain the purpose served by the income summary account and the nature of the entries that resulted in the $1,190,500 and the $1,476,300.

SHOW ME HOW

EX 4-16 Closing entries with net income

Obj. 3

After all revenue and expense accounts have been closed at the end of the fiscal year, Income Summary has a debit of $2,450,000 and a credit of $3,000,000. At the same date, Retained Earnings has a credit balance of $8,222,600 and Dividends has a balance of $125,000.

(A) Journalize the entries required to complete the closing of the accounts.

(B) Determine the amount of Retained Earnings at the end of the period.

SHOW ME HOW

EX 4-17 Closing entries with net loss

Obj. 3

Rainbow Services Co. offers its services to individuals desiring to improve their personal images. After the accounts have been adjusted at August 31, the end of the fiscal year, the following balances were taken from the ledger of Rainbow Services:

Retained Earnings	$2,650,000	Rent Expense	$185,000
Dividends	10,000	Supplies Expense	26,200
Fees Earned	1,050,000	Miscellaneous Expense	28,600
Wages Expense	886,000		

Journalize the four entries required to close the accounts.

EX 4-18 Identifying permanent accounts

Obj. 3

Which of the following accounts will usually appear in the post-closing trial balance?

A. Accounts Payable

B. Accumulated Depreciation

C. Cash

D. Common Stock

E. Dividends

F. Depreciation Expense

G. Fees Earned

H. Office Equipment

I. Salaries Expense

J. Salaries Payable

K. Supplies

EX 4-19 Post-closing trial balance

✔ Correct column totals, $526,250

Obj. 3

An accountant prepared the following post-closing trial balance:

SHOW ME HOW

Security Services Co.
Post-Closing Trial Balance
July 31, 2018

	Debit Balances	Credit Balances
Cash	41,100	
Accounts Receivable	317,400	
Supplies		5,000
Equipment		162,750
Accumulated Depreciation—Equipment...........................	73,300	
Accounts Payable	82,500	
Salaries Payable		5,500
Unearned Rent	12,000	
Common Stock	65,000	
Retained Earnings	287,950	
	879,250	173,250

Prepare a corrected post-closing trial balance. Assume that all accounts have normal balances and that the amounts shown are correct.

EX 4-20 Steps in the accounting cycle

Obj. 4

Rearrange the following steps in the accounting cycle in proper sequence:

A. A post-closing trial balance is prepared.

B. Adjustment data are asssembled and analyzed.

C. Adjusting entries are journalized and posted to the ledger.

D. An adjusted trial balance is prepared.

E. An optional end-of-period spreadsheet is prepared.

F. An unadjusted trial balance is prepared.

G. Closing entries are journalized and posted to the ledger.

H. Financial statements are prepared.

I. Transactions are analyzed and recorded in the journal.

J. Transactions are posted to the ledger.

Appendix 1

EX 4-21 Completing an end-of-period spreadsheet

List (A) through (J) in the order they would be performed in preparing and completing an end-of-period spreadsheet.

A. Add the Debit and Credit columns of the Unadjusted Trial Balance columns of the spreadsheet to verify that the totals are equal.

B. Add the Debit and Credit columns of the Balance Sheet and Income Statement columns of the spreadsheet to verify that the totals are equal.

C. Add or deduct adjusting entry data to trial balance amounts, and extend amounts to the Adjusted Trial Balance columns.

D. Add the Debit and Credit columns of the Adjustments columns of the spreadsheet to verify that the totals are equal.

(Continued)

E. Add the Debit and Credit columns of the Balance Sheet and Income Statement columns of the spreadsheet to determine the amount of net income or net loss for the period.

F. Add the Debit and Credit columns of the Adjusted Trial Balance columns of the spreadsheet to verify that the totals are equal.

G. Enter the adjusting entries into the spreadsheet, based on the adjustment data.

H. Enter the amount of net income or net loss for the period in the proper Income Statement column and Balance Sheet column.

I. Enter the unadjusted account balances from the general ledger into the Unadjusted Trial Balance columns of the spreadsheet.

J. Extend the adjusted trial balance amounts to the Income Statement columns and the Balance Sheet columns.

Appendix 1

EX 4-22   Adjustment data on an end-of-period spreadsheet

✔ Total debits of Adjustments column: $31

EXCEL TEMPLATE

Alert Security Services Co. offers security services to business clients. The trial balance for Alert Security Services has been prepared on the following end-of-period spreadsheet for the year ended October 31, 2018:

Alert Security Services Co.
End-of-Period Spreadsheet
For the Year Ended October 31, 2018

Account Title	Unadjusted Trial Balance Dr.	Cr.	Adjustments Dr.	Cr.	Adjusted Trial Balance Dr.	Cr.
Cash	12					
Accounts Receivable	90					
Supplies	8					
Prepaid Insurance	12					
Land	190					
Equipment	50					
Accum. Depr.—Equipment		4				
Accounts Payable		36				
Wages Payable		0				
Common Stock		50				
Retained Earnings		210				
Dividends	8					
Fees Earned		200				
Wages Expense	110					
Rent Expense	12					
Insurance Expense	0					
Utilities Expense	6					
Supplies Expense	0					
Depreciation Expense—Equip.	0					
Miscellaneous Expense	2					
	500	500				

The data for year-end adjustments are as follows:

A. Fees earned, but not yet billed, $13.

B. Supplies on hand, $4.

C. Insurance premiums expired, $10.

D. Depreciation expense, $3.

E. Wages accrued, but not paid, $1.

Enter the adjustment data, and place the balances in the Adjusted Trial Balance columns.

Appendix 1

EX 4-23   Completing an end-of-period spreadsheet

✔ Net income: $65

EXCEL TEMPLATE

Alert Security Services Co. offers security services to business clients. Complete the following end-of-period spreadsheet for Alert Security Services Co.:

Alert Security Services Co.
End-of-Period Spreadsheet
For the Year Ended October 31, 2018

Account Title	Adjusted Trial Balance		Income Statement		Balance Sheet	
	Dr.	Cr.	Dr.	Cr.	Dr.	Cr.
Cash	12					
Accounts Receivable	103					
Supplies	4					
Prepaid Insurance	2					
Land	190					
Equipment	50					
Accum. Depr.—Equipment		7				
Accounts Payable		36				
Wages Payable		1				
Common Stock		50				
Retained Earnings		210				
Dividends	8					
Fees Earned		213				
Wages Expense	111					
Rent Expense	12					
Insurance Expense	10					
Utilities Expense	6					
Supplies Expense	4					
Depreciation Expense—Equip.	3					
Miscellaneous Expense	2					
	517	517				
Net income (loss)						

✔ Retained earnings, October 31, 2018: $267

EXCEL TEMPLATE

Appendix 1

EX 4-24   Financial statements from an end-of-period spreadsheet

Based on the data in Exercise 4-23, prepare an income statement, retained earnings statement, and balance sheet for Alert Security Services Co.

Appendix 1

EX 4-25   Adjusting entries from an end-of-period spreadsheet

Based on the data in Exercise 4-22, prepare the adjusting entries for Alert Security Services Co.

Appendix 1

EX 4-26   Closing entries from an end-of-period spreadsheet

Based on the data in Exercise 4-23, prepare the closing entries for Alert Security Services Co.

Appendix 2

EX 4-27   Reversing entry

The following adjusting entry for accrued wages was recorded on December 31:

| Dec. 31 | Wages Expense | 5,500 | |
| | Wages Payable | | 5,500 |

(Continued)

A. Journalize the reversing entry that would be made on January 1 of the next period.

B. Assume that the first paid period of the following year ends on January 6 and that wages of $61,375 were paid. Journalize the entry to record the payment of the January 6 wages.

C. Journalize the entry to record the payment of the January 6 wages assuming that a reversing entry was not made on January 1.

D. What is wages expense for the period January 1–6?

___

Appendix 2

EX 4-28   Adjusting and reversing entries

On the basis of the following data, (A) journalize the adjusting entries at December 31, the end of the current fiscal year, and (B) journalize the reversing entries on January 1, the first day of the following year:

1. Sales salaries are uniformly $11,750 for a five-day workweek, ending on Friday. The last payday of the year was Friday, December 26.
2. Accrued fees earned but not recorded at December 31, $51,300.

___

Appendix 2

EX 4-29   Adjusting and reversing entries

On the basis of the following data, (A) journalize the adjusting entries at June 30, the end of the current fiscal year, and (B) journalize the reversing entries on July 1, the first day of the following year:

1. Wages are uniformly $66,000 for a five-day workweek, ending on Friday. The last payday of the year was Thursday, June 27.
2. Accrued fees earned but not recorded at June 30, $25,000.

___

Appendix 2

EX 4-30   Entries posted to wages expense account

Portions of the wages expense account of a business follow:

					Balance	
Account Wages Expense					Account No. 53	
Date	Item	Post. Ref.	Dr.	Cr.	Dr.	Cr.
2017						
Dec. 26	(1)	125	15,400		800,000	
31	(2)	126	9,250		809,250	
31	(3)	127		809,250	—	—
2018						
Jan. 1	(4)	128		9,250		9,250
2	(5)	129	14,800		5,550	

A. Indicate the nature of the entry (payment, adjusting, closing, reversing) from which each numbered posting was made.

B. Journalize the complete entry from which each numbered posting was made.

Appendix 2

EX 4-31 Entries posted to wages expense account

Portions of the salaries expense account of a business follow:

Account Salaries Expense						Account No. 62
		Post.			**Balance**	
Date	**Item**	**Ref.**	**Dr.**	**Cr.**	**Dr.**	**Cr.**
2017						
Dec. 27	(1)	29	22,000		1,200,000	
31	(2)	30	13,200		1,213,200	
31	(3)	31		1,213,200	—	—
2018						
Jan. 1	(4)	32		13,200		13,200
2	(5)	33	24,000		10,800	

A. Indicate the nature of the entry (payment, adjusting, closing, reversing) from which each numbered posting was made.

B. Journalize the complete entry from which each numbered posting was made.

Problems: Series A

PR 4-1A Financial statements and closing entries   Obj. 1, 2, 3

✔ 3. Total assets: $354,500

SHOW ME HOW

EXCEL TEMPLATE

GENERAL LEDGER

Lamp Light Company maintains and repairs warning lights, such as those found on radio towers and lighthouses. Lamp Light prepared the following end-of-period spreadsheet at December 31, 2018, the end of the fiscal year:

	A	B	C	D	E	F	G
1		Lamp Light Company					
2		End-of-Period Spreadsheet					
3		For the Year Ended December 31, 2018					
4		Unadjusted				Adjusted	
5		Trial Balance		Adjustments		Trial Balance	
6	**Account Title**	Dr.	Cr.	Dr.	Cr.	Dr.	Cr.
7							
8	Cash	10,800				10,800	
9	Accounts Receivable	38,900		11,300		50,200	
10	Prepaid Insurance	4,200			3,000	1,200	
11	Supplies	2,730			2,250	480	
12	Land	98,000				98,000	
13	Building	400,000				400,000	
14	Accum. Depr.—Building		205,300		10,100		215,400
15	Equipment	101,000				101,000	
16	Accum. Depr.—Equipment		85,100		6,680		91,780
17	Accounts Payable		15,700				15,700
18	Salaries & Wages Payable				4,900		4,900
19	Unearned Rent		2,100	1,300			800
20	Common Stock		75,000				75,000
21	Retained Earnings		128,100				128,100
22	Dividends	10,000				10,000	
23	Fees Earned		363,700		11,300		375,000
24	Rent Revenue				1,300		1,300
25	Salaries & Wages Expense	163,100		4,900		168,000	
26	Advertising Expense	21,700				21,700	
27	Utilities Expense	11,400				11,400	
28	Depr. Exp.—Building			10,100		10,100	
29	Repairs Expense	8,850				8,850	
30	Depr. Exp.—Equipment			6,680		6,680	
31	Insurance Expense			3,000		3,000	
32	Supplies Expense			2,250		2,250	
33	Misc. Expense	4,320				4,320	
34		875,000	875,000	39,530	39,530	907,980	907,980
35							

(Continued)

Instructions

1. Prepare an income statement for the year ended December 31.

2. Prepare a retained earnings statement for the year ended December 31.

3. Prepare a balance sheet as of December 31.

4. Based upon the end-of-period spreadsheet, journalize the closing entries.

5. Prepare a post-closing trial balance.

PR 4-2A Financial statements and closing entries

Obj. 2, 3

✔ 1. Retained earnings, November 30: $185,800

Foxy Investigative Services is an investigative services firm that is owned and operated by Shirley Vickers. On November 30, 2018, the end of the fiscal year, the accountant for Foxy Investigative Services prepared an end-of-period spreadsheet, a part of which follows:

	A	F	G
1	Foxy Investigative Services		
2	End-of-Period Spreadsheet		
3	For the Year Ended November 30, 2018		
4		Adjusted	
5		Trial Balance	
6	Account Title	Dr.	Cr.
7			
8	Cash	27,500	
9	Accounts Receivable	71,800	
10	Supplies	3,550	
11	Prepaid Insurance	750	
12	Building	330,500	
13	Accumulated Depreciation—Building		184,100
14	Accounts Payable		16,100
15	Salaries Payable		6,600
16	Unearned Rent		1,500
17	Common Stock		40,000
18	Retained Earnings		70,300
19	Dividends	30,000	
20	Service Fees		675,500
21	Rent Revenue		9,000
22	Salaries Expense	435,000	
23	Rent Expense	55,000	
24	Supplies Expense	11,850	
25	Depreciation Expense—Building	10,000	
26	Utilities Expense	8,800	
27	Repairs Expense	4,250	
28	Insurance Expense	3,000	
29	Miscellaneous Expense	11,100	
30		1,003,100	1,003,100

Instructions

1. Prepare an income statement, a retained earnings statement, and a balance sheet.

2. Journalize the entries that were required to close the accounts at November 30.

3. If Retained Earnings had instead decreased $46,000 after the closing entries were posted, and the dividends remained the same, what would have been the amount of net income or net loss?

PR 4-3A T accounts, adjusting entries, financial statements, and closing entries; optional end-of-period spreadsheet

Obj. 2, 3

✔ 5. Net income: $10,700

EXCEL TEMPLATE   GENERAL LEDGER

The unadjusted trial balance of Epicenter Laundry at June 30, 2018, the end of the fiscal year, follows:

Epicenter Laundry
Unadjusted Trial Balance
June 30, 2018

	Debit Balances	Credit Balances
Cash	11,000	
Laundry Supplies	21,500	
Prepaid Insurance.	9,600	
Laundry Equipment.	232,600	
Accumulated Depreciation		125,400
Accounts Payable.		11,800
Common Stock		40,000
Retained Earnings		65,600
Dividends	10,000	
Laundry Revenue		232,200
Wages Expense.	125,200	
Rent Expense.	40,000	
Utilities Expense.	19,700	
Miscellaneous Expense.	5,400	
	475,000	475,000

The data needed to determine year-end adjustments are as follows:

(A) Laundry supplies on hand at June 30 are $3,600.

(B) Insurance premiums expired during the year are $5,700.

(C) Depreciation of laundry equipment during the year is $6,500.

(D) Wages accrued but not paid at June 30 are $1,100.

Instructions

1. For each account listed in the unadjusted trial balance, enter the balance in a T account. Identify the balance as "June 30 Bal." In addition, add T accounts for Wages Payable, Depreciation Expense, Laundry Supplies Expense, Insurance Expense, and Income Summary.

2. *(Optional)* Enter the unadjusted trial balance on an end-of-period spreadsheet and complete the spreadsheet. Add the accounts listed in part (1) as needed.

3. Journalize and post the adjusting entries. Identify the adjustments by "Adj." and the new balances as "Adj. Bal."

4. Prepare an adjusted trial balance.

5. Prepare an income statement, a retained earnings statement, and a balance sheet.

6. Journalize and post the closing entries. Identify the closing entries by "Clos."

7. Prepare a post-closing trial balance.

PR 4-4A   Ledger accounts, adjusting entries, financial statements, and closing entries; optional spreadsheet   Obj. 2, 3

✔ 5. Net income:
$51,150

EXCEL TEMPLATE   GENERAL LEDGER

The unadjusted trial balance of Lakota Freight Co. at March 31, 2018, the end of the year, follows:

Lakota Freight Co.
Unadjusted Trial Balance
March 31, 2018

	Account No.	Debit Balances	Credit Balances
Cash	11	12,000	
Supplies	13	30,000	
Prepaid Insurance.	14	3,600	
Equipment	16	110,000	
Accumulated Depreciation—Equipment.	17		25,000
Trucks.	18	60,000	
Accumulated Depreciation—Trucks	19		15,000
Accounts Payable	21		4,000
Common Stock	31		26,000
Retained Earnings	32		70,000
Dividends	33	15,000	
Service Revenue	41		160,000
Wages Expense	51	45,000	
Rent Expense.	53	10,600	
Truck Expense	54	9,000	
Miscellaneous Expense.	59	4,800	
		300,000	300,000

The data needed to determine year-end adjustments are as follows:

(A) Supplies on hand at March 31 are $7,500.

(B) Insurance premiums expired during year are $1,800.

(C) Depreciation of equipment during year is $8,350.

(D) Depreciation of trucks during year is $6,200.

(E) Wages accrued but not paid at March 31 are $600.

Instructions

1. For each account listed in the trial balance, enter the balance in the appropriate Balance column of a four-column account and place a check mark (✓) in the Posting Reference column.

2. *(Optional)* Enter the unadjusted trial balance on an end-of-period spreadsheet and complete the spreadsheet. Add the accounts listed in part (3) as needed.

3. Journalize and post the adjusting entries, inserting balances in the accounts affected. Record the adjusting entries on Page 26 of the journal. The following additional accounts from Lakota Freight Co.'s chart of accounts should be used: Wages Payable, 22; Supplies Expense, 52; Depreciation Expense—Equipment, 55; Depreciation Expense—Trucks, 56; Insurance Expense, 57.

4. Prepare an adjusted trial balance.

5. Prepare an income statement, a retained earnings statement, and a balance sheet.

6. Journalize and post the closing entries. Record the closing entries on Page 27 of the journal. (Income Summary is account #34 in the chart of accounts.) Indicate closed accounts by inserting a line in both Balance columns opposite the closing entry.

7. Prepare a post-closing trial balance.

PR 4-5A Complete accounting cycle Obj. 4, 5

✔ 8. Net income: $33,475

EXCEL TEMPLATE

For the past several years, Steffy Lopez has operated a part-time consulting business from his home. As of July 1, 2018, Steffy decided to move to rented quarters and to operate the business, which was to be known as Diamond Consulting, on a full-time basis. Diamond entered into the following transactions during July:

July 1. The following assets were received from Steffy Lopez in exchange for common stock: cash, $13,500; accounts receivable, $20,800; supplies, $3,200; and office equipment, $7,500. There were no liabilities received.

  1. Paid two months' rent on a lease rental contract, $4,800.

  2. Paid the premiums on property and casualty insurance policies, $4,500.

  4. Received cash from clients as an advance payment for services to be provided, and recorded it as unearned fees, $5,500.

  5. Purchased additional office equipment on account from Office Station Co., $6,500.

  6. Received cash from clients on account, $15,300.

  10. Paid cash for a newspaper advertisement, $400.

  12. Paid Office Station Co. for part of the debt incurred on July 5, $5,200.

  12. Recorded services provided on account for the period July 1–12, $13,300.

  14. Paid receptionist for two weeks' salary, $1,750.

Record the following transactions on Page 2 of the journal:

  17. Recorded cash from cash clients for fees earned during the period July 1–17, $9,450.

  18. Paid cash for supplies, $600.

  20. Recorded services provided on account for the period July 13–20, $6,650.

  24. Recorded cash from cash clients for fees earned for the period July 17–24, $4,000.

  26. Received cash from clients on account, $12,000.

  27. Paid receptionist for two weeks' salary, $1,750.

  29. Paid telephone bill for July, $325.

  31. Paid electricity bill for July, $675.

  31. Recorded cash from cash clients for fees earned for the period July 25–31, $5,200.

  31. Recorded services provided on account for the remainder of July, $3,000.

  31. Paid dividends, $12,500.

Instructions

1. Journalize each transaction in a two-column journal starting on Page 1, referring to the following chart of accounts in selecting the accounts to be debited and credited. (Do not insert the account numbers in the journal at this time.)

11	Cash	31	Common Stock
12	Accounts Receivable	32	Retained Earnings
14	Supplies	33	Dividends
15	Prepaid Rent	41	Fees Earned
16	Prepaid Insurance	51	Salary Expense
18	Office Equipment	52	Rent Expense
19	Accumulated Depreciation	53	Supplies Expense
21	Accounts Payable	54	Depreciation Expense
22	Salaries Payable	55	Insurance Expense
23	Unearned Fees	59	Miscellaneous Expense

2. Post the journal to a ledger of four-column accounts.

3. Prepare an unadjusted trial balance.

(Continued)

4. At the end of July, the following adjustment data were assembled. Analyze and use these data to complete parts (5) and (6).

   (A) Insurance expired during July is $375.
   (B) Supplies on hand on July 31 are $1,525.
   (C) Depreciation of office equipment for July is $750.
   (D) Accrued receptionist salary on July 31 is $175.
   (E) Rent expired during July is $2,400.
   (F) Unearned fees on July 31 are $2,750.

5. *(Optional)* Enter the unadjusted trial balance on an end-of-period spreadsheet and complete the spreadsheet.

6. Journalize and post the adjusting entries. Record the adjusting entries on Page 3 of the journal.

7. Prepare an adjusted trial balance.

8. Prepare an income statement, a retained earnings statement, and a balance sheet.

9. Prepare and post the closing entries. (Income Summary is account #34 in the chart of accounts.) Record the closing entries on Page 4 of the journal. Indicate closed accounts by inserting a line in both the Balance columns opposite the closing entry.

10. Prepare a post-closing trial balance.

Problems: Series B

PR 4-1B Financial statements and closing entries

Obj. 1, 2, 3

✔ 3. Total assets: $342,425

Last Chance Company offers legal consulting advice to prison inmates. Last Chance prepared the end-of-period spreadsheet that follows at June 30, 2018, the end of the fiscal year.

SHOW ME HOW

EXCEL TEMPLATE

GENERAL LEDGER

	A	B	C	D	E	F	G
1		Last Chance Company					
2		End-of-Period Spreadsheet					
3		For the Year Ended June 30, 2018					
4		Unadjusted				Adjusted	
5		Trial Balance		Adjustments		Trial Balance	
6	Account Title	Dr.	Cr.	Dr.	Cr.	Dr.	Cr.
7							
8	Cash	5,100				5,100	
9	Accounts Receivable	22,750		3,750		26,500	
10	Prepaid Insurance	3,600			1,300	2,300	
11	Supplies	2,025			1,500	525	
12	Land	80,000				80,000	
13	Building	340,000				340,000	
14	Accum. Depr.—Building		190,000		3,000		193,000
15	Equipment	140,000				140,000	
16	Accum. Depr.—Equipment		54,450		4,550		59,000
17	Accounts Payable		9,750				9,750
18	Salaries & Wages Payable				1,900		1,900
19	Unearned Rent		4,500	3,000			1,500
20	Common Stock		90,000				90,000
21	Retained Earnings		271,300				271,300
22	Dividends	20,000				20,000	
23	Fees Earned		280,000		3,750		283,750
24	Rent Revenue				3,000		3,000
25	Salaries & Wages Expense	145,100		1,900		147,000	
26	Advertising Expense	86,800				86,800	
27	Utilities Expense	30,000				30,000	
28	Travel Expense	18,750				18,750	
29	Depr. Exp.—Equipment			4,550		4,550	
30	Depr. Exp.—Building			3,000		3,000	
31	Supplies Expense			1,500		1,500	
32	Insurance Expense			1,300		1,300	
33	Misc. Expense	5,875				5,875	
34		900,000	900,000	19,000	19,000	913,200	913,200
35							

Instructions

1. Prepare an income statement for the year ended June 30.

2. Prepare a retained earnings statement for the year ended June 30.

3. Prepare a balance sheet as of June 30.

4. On the basis of the end-of-period spreadsheet, journalize the closing entries.

5. Prepare a post-closing trial balance.

PR 4-2B Financial statements and closing entries   Obj. 2, 3

✔ 1. Retained earnings, October 31: $288,000

The Gorman Group is a financial planning services firm owned and operated by Nicole Gorman. As of October 31, 2018, the end of the fiscal year, the accountant for The Gorman Group prepared an end-of-period spreadsheet, part of which follows:

	A	F	G
1	The Gorman Group		
2	End-of-Period Spreadsheet		
3	For the Year Ended October 31, 2018		
4		Adjusted	
5		Trial Balance	
6	Account Title	Dr.	Cr.
7			
8	Cash	11,000	
9	Accounts Receivable	28,150	
10	Supplies	6,350	
11	Prepaid Insurance	9,500	
12	Land	75,000	
13	Buildings	250,000	
14	Accumulated Depreciation—Buildings		117,200
15	Equipment	240,000	
16	Accumulated Depreciation—Equipment		151,700
17	Accounts Payable		33,300
18	Salaries Payable		3,300
19	Unearned Rent		1,500
20	Common Stock		25,000
21	Retained Earnings		195,000
22	Dividends	20,000	
23	Service Fees		468,000
24	Rent Revenue		5,000
25	Salaries Expense	291,000	
26	Depreciation Expense—Equipment	17,500	
27	Rent Expense	15,500	
28	Supplies Expense	9,000	
29	Utilities Expense	8,500	
30	Depreciation Expense—Buildings	6,600	
31	Repairs Expense	3,450	
32	Insurance Expense	3,000	
33	Miscellaneous Expense	5,450	
34		1,000,000	1,000,000

Instructions

1. Prepare an income statement, a retained earnings statement, and a balance sheet.

2. Journalize the entries that were required to close the accounts at October 31.

3. If the balance of Retained Earnings had instead increased $115,000 after the closing entries were posted, and the dividends remained the same, what would have been the amount of net income or net loss?

PR 4-3B T accounts, adjusting entries, financial statements, and closing entries; optional end-of-period spreadsheet

Obj. 2, 3

✔ 5. Net income: $27,350

The unadjusted trial balance of La Mesa Laundry at August 31, 2018, the end of the fiscal year, follows:

EXCEL TEMPLATE

GENERAL LEDGER

La Mesa Laundry
Unadjusted Trial Balance
August 31, 2018

	Debit Balances	Credit Balances
Cash	3,800	
Laundry Supplies	9,000	
Prepaid Insurance..	6,000	
Laundry Equipment...	180,800	
Accumulated Depreciation		49,200
Accounts Payable..		7,800
Common Stock		15,000
Retained Earnings		80,000
Dividends	2,400	
Laundry Revenue..		248,000
Wages Expense...	135,800	
Rent Expense...	43,200	
Utilities Expense..	16,000	
Miscellaneous Expense.......................................	3,000	
	400,000	400,000

The data needed to determine year-end adjustments are as follows:

(A) Wages accrued but not paid at August 31 are $2,200.
(B) Depreciation of equipment during the year is $8,150.
(C) Laundry supplies on hand at August 31 are $2,000.
(D) Insurance premiums expired during the year are $5,300.

Instructions

1. For each account listed in the unadjusted trial balance, enter the balance in a T account. Identify the balance as "Aug. 31 Bal." In addition, add T accounts for Wages Payable, Depreciation Expense, Laundry Supplies Expense, Insurance Expense, and Income Summary.

2. *(Optional)* Enter the unadjusted trial balance on an end-of-period spreadsheet and complete the spreadsheet. Add the accounts listed in part (1) as needed.

3. Journalize and post the adjusting entries. Identify the adjustments by "Adj." and the new balances as "Adj. Bal."

4. Prepare an adjusted trial balance.

5. Prepare an income statement, a retained earnings statement, and a balance sheet.

6. Journalize and post the closing entries. Identify the closing entries by "Clos."

7. Prepare a post-closing trial balance.

PR 4-4B   Ledger accounts, adjusting entries, financial statements, and closing entries; optional end-of-period spreadsheet

Obj. 2, 3

✔ 5. Net income:
$46,150

EXCEL TEMPLATE   GENERAL LEDGER

The unadjusted trial balance of Recessive Interiors at January 31, 2018, the end of the year, follows:

Recessive Interiors
Unadjusted Trial Balance
January 31, 2018

	Account No.	Debit Balances	Credit Balances
Cash	11	13,100	
Supplies	13	8,000	
Prepaid Insurance	14	7,500	
Equipment	16	113,000	
Accumulated Depreciation—Equipment	17		12,000
Trucks	18	90,000	
Accumulated Depreciation—Trucks	19		27,100
Accounts Payable	21		4,500
Common Stock	31		30,000
Retained Earnings	32		96,400
Dividends	33	3,000	
Service Revenue	41		155,000
Wages Expense	51	72,000	
Rent Expense	52	7,600	
Truck Expense	53	5,350	
Miscellaneous Expense	59	5,450	
		325,000	325,000

The data needed to determine year-end adjustments are as follows:

(A) Supplies on hand at January 31 are $2,850.

(B) Insurance premiums expired during the year are $3,150.

(C) Depreciation of equipment during the year is $5,250.

(D) Depreciation of trucks during the year is $4,000.

(E) Wages accrued but not paid at January 31 are $900.

Instructions

1. For each account listed in the unadjusted trial balance, enter the balance in the appropriate Balance column of a four-column account and place a check mark (✓) in the Posting Reference column.

2. *(Optional)* Enter the unadjusted trial balance on an end-of-period spreadsheet and complete the spreadsheet. Add the accounts listed in part (3) as needed.

3. Journalize and post the adjusting entries, inserting balances in the accounts affected. Record the adjusting entries on Page 26 of the journal. The following additional accounts from Recessive Interiors' chart of accounts should be used: Wages Payable, 22; Depreciation Expense—Equipment, 54; Supplies Expense, 55; Depreciation Expense—Trucks, 56; Insurance Expense, 57.

4. Prepare an adjusted trial balance.

5. Prepare an income statement, a retained earnings statement, and a balance sheet.

6. Journalize and post the closing entries. Record the closing entries on Page 27 of the journal. (Income Summary is account #34 in the chart of accounts.) Indicate closed accounts by inserting a line in both Balance columns opposite the closing entry.

7. Prepare a post-closing trial balance.

PR 4-5B   Complete accounting cycle

Obj. 4, 5

✔ 8. Net income:
$53,775

EXCEL TEMPLATE

For the past several years, Jeff Horton has operated a part-time consulting business from his home. As of April 1, 2018, Jeff decided to move to rented quarters and to operate the business, which was to be known as Rosebud Consulting, on a full-time basis. Rosebud entered into the following transactions during April:

Apr. 1.   The following assets were received from Jeff Horton in exchange for common stock: cash, $20,000; accounts receivable, $14,700; supplies, $3,300; and office equipment, $12,000. There were no liabilities received.

   1.   Paid three months' rent on a lease rental contract, $6,000.

   2.   Paid the premiums on property and casualty insurance policies, $4,200.

   4.   Received cash from clients as an advance payment for services to be provided and recorded it as unearned fees, $9,400.

   5.   Purchased additional office equipment on account from Smith Office Supply Co., $8,000.

   6.   Received cash from clients on account, $11,700.

   10.   Paid cash for a newspaper advertisement, $350.

   12.   Paid Smith Office Supply Co. for part of the debt incurred on April 5, $6,400.

   12.   Recorded services provided on account for the period April 1–12, $21,900.

   14.   Paid receptionist for two weeks' salary, $1,650.

Record the following transactions on Page 2 of the journal:

   17.   Recorded cash from cash clients for fees earned during the period April 1–16, $6,600.

   18.   Paid cash for supplies, $725.

   20.   Recorded services provided on account for the period April 13–20, $16,800.

   24.   Recorded cash from cash clients for fees earned for the period April 17–24, $4,450.

   26.   Received cash from clients on account, $26,500.

   27.   Paid receptionist for two weeks' salary, $1,650.

   29.   Paid telephone bill for April, $540.

   30.   Paid electricity bill for April, $760.

   30.   Recorded cash from cash clients for fees earned for the period April 25–30, $5,160.

   30.   Recorded services provided on account for the remainder of April, $2,590.

   30.   Paid dividends, $18,000.

Instructions

1. Journalize each transaction in a two-column journal starting on Page 1, referring to the following chart of accounts in selecting the accounts to be debited and credited. (Do not insert the account numbers in the journal at this time.)

11	Cash	31	Common Stock
12	Accounts Receivable	32	Retained Earnings
14	Supplies	33	Dividends
15	Prepaid Rent	41	Fees Earned
16	Prepaid Insurance	51	Salary Expense
18	Office Equipment	52	Supplies Expense
19	Accumulated Depreciation	53	Rent Expense
21	Accounts Payable	54	Depreciation Expense
22	Salaries Payable	55	Insurance Expense
23	Unearned Fees	59	Miscellaneous Expense

2. Post the journal to a ledger of four-column accounts.

3. Prepare an unadjusted trial balance.

4. At the end of April, the following adjustment data were assembled. Analyze and use these data to complete parts (5) and (6).

   (A)   Insurance expired during April is $350.

   (B)   Supplies on hand on April 30 are $1,225.

   (C)   Depreciation of office equipment for April is $400.

   (D)   Accrued receptionist salary on April 30 is $275.

   (E)   Rent expired during April is $2,000.

   (F)   Unearned fees on April 30 are $2,350.

5. *(Optional)* Enter the unadjusted trial balance on an end-of-period spreadsheet and complete the spreadsheet.

6. Journalize and post the adjusting entries. Record the adjusting entries on Page 3 of the journal.

7. Prepare an adjusted trial balance.

8. Prepare an income statement, a retained earnings statement, and a balance sheet.

9. Prepare and post the closing entries. Record the closing entries on Page 4 of the journal. (Income Summary is account #34 in the chart of accounts.) Indicate closed accounts by inserting a line in both the Balance columns opposite the closing entry.

10. Prepare a post-closing trial balance.

Continuing Problem

✔ **2. Net income: $4,955**

The unadjusted trial balance of PS Music as of July 31, 2018, along with the adjustment data for the two months ended July 31, 2018, are shown in Chapter 3. Based upon the adjustment data, the following adjusted trial balance was prepared:

PS Music
Adjusted Trial Balance
July 31, 2018

	Account No.	Debit Balances	Credit Balances
Cash	11	9,945	
Accounts Receivable................................	12	4,150	
Supplies...	14	275	
Prepaid Insurance	15	2,475	
Office Equipment	17	7,500	
Accumulated Depreciation—Office Equipment..........	18		50
Accounts Payable	21		8,350
Wages Payable.....................................	22		140
Unearned Revenue.................................	23		3,600
Common Stock	31		9,000
Dividends	33	1,750	
Fees Earned.......................................	41		21,200
Music Expense	54	3,610	
Wages Expense	50	2,940	
Office Rent Expense	51	2,550	
Advertising Expense................................	55	1,500	
Equipment Rent Expense	52	1,375	
Utilities Expense	53	1,215	
Supplies Expense...................................	56	925	
Insurance Expense	57	225	
Depreciation Expense	58	50	
Miscellaneous Expense	59	1,855	
		42,340	42,340

Instructions

1. *(Optional)* Using the data from Chapter 3, prepare an end-of-period spreadsheet.

2. Prepare an income statement, a retained earnings statement, and a balance sheet.

3. Journalize and post the closing entries. The retained earnings account is #33 and the income summary account is #34 in the ledger of PS Music. Indicate closed accounts by inserting a line in both Balance columns opposite the closing entry.

4. Prepare a post-closing trial balance.

Comprehensive Problem 1

✔ 8. Net income,
   $33,425

EXCEL TEMPLATE

Kelly Pitney began her consulting business, Kelly Consulting, on April 1, 2018. The accounting cycle for Kelly Consulting for April, including financial statements, was illustrated in this chapter. During May, Kelly Consulting entered into the following transactions:

May 3. Received cash from clients as an advance payment for services to be provided and recorded it as unearned fees, $4,500.

5. Received cash from clients on account, $2,450.

9. Paid cash for a newspaper advertisement, $225.

13. Paid Office Station Co. for part of the debt incurred on April 5, $640.

15. Recorded services provided on account for the period May 1–15, $9,180.

16. Paid part-time receptionist for two weeks' salary including the amount owed on April 30, $750.

17. Recorded cash from cash clients for fees earned during the period May 1–16, $8,360.

Record the following transactions on Page 6 of the journal:

20. Purchased supplies on account, $735.

21. Recorded services provided on account for the period May 16–20, $4,820.

25. Recorded cash from cash clients for fees earned for the period May 17–23, $7,900.

27. Received cash from clients on account, $9,520.

28. Paid part-time receptionist for two weeks' salary, $750.

30. Paid telephone bill for May, $260.

31. Paid electricity bill for May, $810.

31. Recorded cash from cash clients for fees earned for the period May 26–31, $3,300.

31. Recorded services provided on account for the remainder of May, $2,650.

31. Paid dividends, $10,500.

Instructions

1. The chart of accounts for Kelly Consulting is shown in Exhibit 9, and the post-closing trial balance as of April 30, 2018, is shown in Exhibit 17. For each account in the post-closing trial balance, enter the balance in the appropriate Balance column of a four-column account. Date the balances May 1, 2018, and place a check mark (✓) in the Posting Reference column. Journalize each of the May transactions in a two-column journal starting on Page 5 of the journal and using Kelly Consulting's chart of accounts. (Do not insert the account numbers in the journal at this time.)

2. Post the journal to a ledger of four-column accounts.

3. Prepare an unadjusted trial balance.

4. At the end of May, the following adjustment data were assembled. Analyze and use these data to complete parts (5) and (6).

   (A) Insurance expired during May is $275.

   (B) Supplies on hand on May 31 are $715.

   (C) Depreciation of office equipment for May is $330.

   (D) Accrued receptionist salary on May 31 is $325.

   (E) Rent expired during May is $1,600.

   (F) Unearned fees on May 31 are $3,210.

5. *(Optional)* Enter the unadjusted trial balance on an end-of-period spreadsheet and complete the spreadsheet.

6. Journalize and post the adjusting entries. Record the adjusting entries on Page 7 of the journal.

7. Prepare an adjusted trial balance.

8. Prepare an income statement, a retained earnings statement, and a balance sheet.

9. Prepare and post the closing entries. Record the closing entries on Page 8 of the journal. (Income Summary is account #34 in the chart of accounts.) Indicate closed accounts by inserting a line in both the Balance columns opposite the closing entry.

10. Prepare a post-closing trial balance.

Analysis for Decision Making

REAL WORLD

ADM-1 Continuing Company Analysis—Amazon: Working capital and current ratio

Amazon.com, Inc. is the largest Internet retailer in the United States. Best Buy, Inc. is a leading retailer of technology and media products in the United States. Amazon and Best Buy compete in similar markets; however, Best Buy sells through both traditional retail stores and the Internet, while Amazon sells only through the Internet. The current assets and current liabilities from recent balance sheets for both companies are provided as follows (in millions):

	Amazon	Best Buy
Current assets	$31,327	$10,485
Current liabilities	28,089	7,436

A. Compute the working capital for each company.
B. Which company has the largest working capital?
C. ➤ Is working capital a good measure of relative liquidity in comparing the two companies? Explain.
D. Compute the current ratio for both companies. (Round to one decimal place.)
E. Which company has the larger relative liquidity based on the current ratio?

SHOW ME HOW

REAL WORLD

ADM-2 Under Armour: Current ratio

The following year-end data were taken from recent balance sheets of Under Armour, Inc. (in millions):

	December 31	
	Year 2	Year 1
Current assets	$1,129	$903
Current liabilities	427	252

A. Compute the working capital and the current ratio as of December 31, Year 2 and Year 1. (Round to one decimal place.)
B. ➤ What conclusions concerning the company's ability to meet its short-term obligations can you draw from part (A)?

REAL WORLD

ADM-3 Sears: Current ratio

Sears Holdings Corporation is one of the largest mall-based retailers in the United States. The following year-end data were taken from a recent Sears balance sheet (in millions):

	December 31	
	Year 2	Year 1
Current assets	$5,863	$8,959
Current liabilities	6,076	8,185

A. Compute the working capital and the current ratio as of December 31, Year 1 and Year 2. (Round to two decimal places.)
B. ➤ What conclusions concerning the company's ability to meet its short-term obligations can you draw from part (A)?

REAL WORLD

ADM-4 Google and Microsoft: Current ratio

Google, Inc. and Microsoft Corporation design and distribute consumer and enterprise software, including overlaps in search, business productivity, and mobile operating systems. Google's primary source of revenue is from advertising, while Microsoft's is from software subscription and support fees. The following year-end data (in millions) were taken from recent balance sheets for both companies:

	Microsoft		Google	
	Year 2	Year 1	Year 2	Year 1
Current assets	$114,246	$101,466	$72,886	$80,685
Current liabilities	45,625	37,417	15,908	16,805

A. Compute the working capital for each company for both years.

B. Which company has the larger working capital at the end of Year 2?

C. ━━━━━▶ Is working capital a good measure of relative liquidity in comparing the two companies? Explain.

D. Compute the current ratio for both companies. (Round to one decimal place.)

E. Which company has the larger relative liquidity based on the current ratio?

F. ━━━━━▶ Based on your analysis, comment on the short-term debt-paying ability of these two companies.

Take It Further

ETHICS

TIF 4-1 Ethics in Action

New Wave Images is a graphics design firm that prepares its financial statements using a calendar year. Manny Kinn, the company treasurer and vice president of finance, has prepared a classified balance sheet as of December 31. In January, this balance sheet will be submitted along with an application for a loan from First Peoples Community Bank. An excerpt from the balance sheet follows:

Cash	$ 25,000
Accounts receivable	85,000
......	
Total assets	$250,000

The accounts receivable balance includes a $56,000 loan to Tom Morrow, the company president. Tom borrowed the money from New Wave 18 months earlier for a down payment on a new home. Tom has orally assured Manny that he will pay off the loan within the next year. Because Tom is the company president, Manny treats the amount due as a trade account receivable. In addition, Manny knows that the bank will consider a large balance in trade accounts receivable more favorably than a large personal loan to a single individual. Manny reported the $56,000 in the same manner on the preceding year's balance sheet.

1. ━━━━▶ Is Manny behaving ethically by reporting the loan to Tom as a trade account receivable? Why?

2. ━━━━▶ Who will be affected by Manny's decision?

TIF 4-2 Team Activity

In teams, select two public companies of different industries that interest you. Obtain each company's most recent annual report on Form 10-K. The Form 10-K is a company's annually required filing with the Securities and Exchange Commission (SEC). It includes the company's financial statements and accompanying notes. The Form 10-K can be obtained either (A) from the investor relations section of the company's Web site or (B) by using the company search feature of the SEC's EDGAR database service found at www.sec.gov/edgar/searchedgar/companysearch.html.

Find the balance sheet for each of the two companies you have selected. Compare the balance sheets of the two companies as follows:

1. What is each company's fiscal year?
2. Which balance sheet accounts do the two companies have in common?
3. ➤ Which balance sheet accounts stand out as different between the two companies? Why do these differences exist?

TIF 4-3 Communication

Your friend, Daniel Nat, recently began work as the lead accountant for the Asheville Company. Dan prepared the following balance sheet for December 31, 2018:

Asheville Company Balance Sheet For the Year Ended December 31, 2018	
Assets	
Land..	$100,000
Accounts payable..	10,000
Accounts receivable...	12,500
Cash...	10,000
Common stock...	115,000
Total assets..	$247,500
Liabilities	
Equipment	$125,000
Retained earnings...	120,000
Wages payable..	2,500
Total liabilities	$247,500

➤ White a brief memo to Daniel explaining the errors in the Asheville Company balance sheet and the correct presentation for the balance sheet.

Chapter 5

Accounting for Merchandising Businesses

Chapters 1–4
Accounting Cycle

Income Statement	Retained Earnings Statement	Balance Sheet	Statement of Cash Flows

Chapter 5 Accounting for Merchandising Businesses

Chapter 12 *Corporations*

Chapter 13 *Cash Flows*

Assets	=	Liabilities	+	Stockholders' Equity

Chapter 7 *Cash*
Chapter 6 *Inventories*
Chapter 8 *Receivables*
Chapter 9 *Fixed and Intangible Assets*

Chapter 10 *Current Liabilities*
Chapter 11 *Bonds Payable*

Chapter 12 *Common Stock*

Chapter 14
Financial Statement Analysis

Statement of Retained Earnings

Retained earnings, Jan. 1		$XXX
Net income	$ XXX	
Dividends	(XXX)	

Statement of Cash Flows

Cash flows from (used in) operating activities	$XXX
Cash flows from (used in) investing activities	XXX
Cash flows from (used in) financing activities	XXX
	$XXX
	XXX
	$XXX

Income Statement

Sales		$XXX
Cost of goods sold		XXX
Gross profit		$XXX
Operating expenses:		
Advertising expense	$XXX	
Depreciation expense	XXX	
Amortization expense	XXX	
Depletion expense	XXX	
...	XXX	
...	XXX	
Total operating expenses		XXX
Income from operations		$XXX
Other revenue and expense		XXX
Net income		$XXX

Balance Sheet

Current assets:		
Cash	$XXX	
Accounts receivable	XXX	
Inventory	XXX	
Total current assets		$XXX
Property, plant and equipment	$XXX	
Intangible assets	XXX	
Total long-term assets		XXX
Total assets		$XXX
Liabilities:		
Current liabilities	$XXX	
Long-term liabilities	XXX	
Total liabilities		$XXX
Stockholders' equity		XXX
Total liabilities and stockholders' equity		$XXX

226

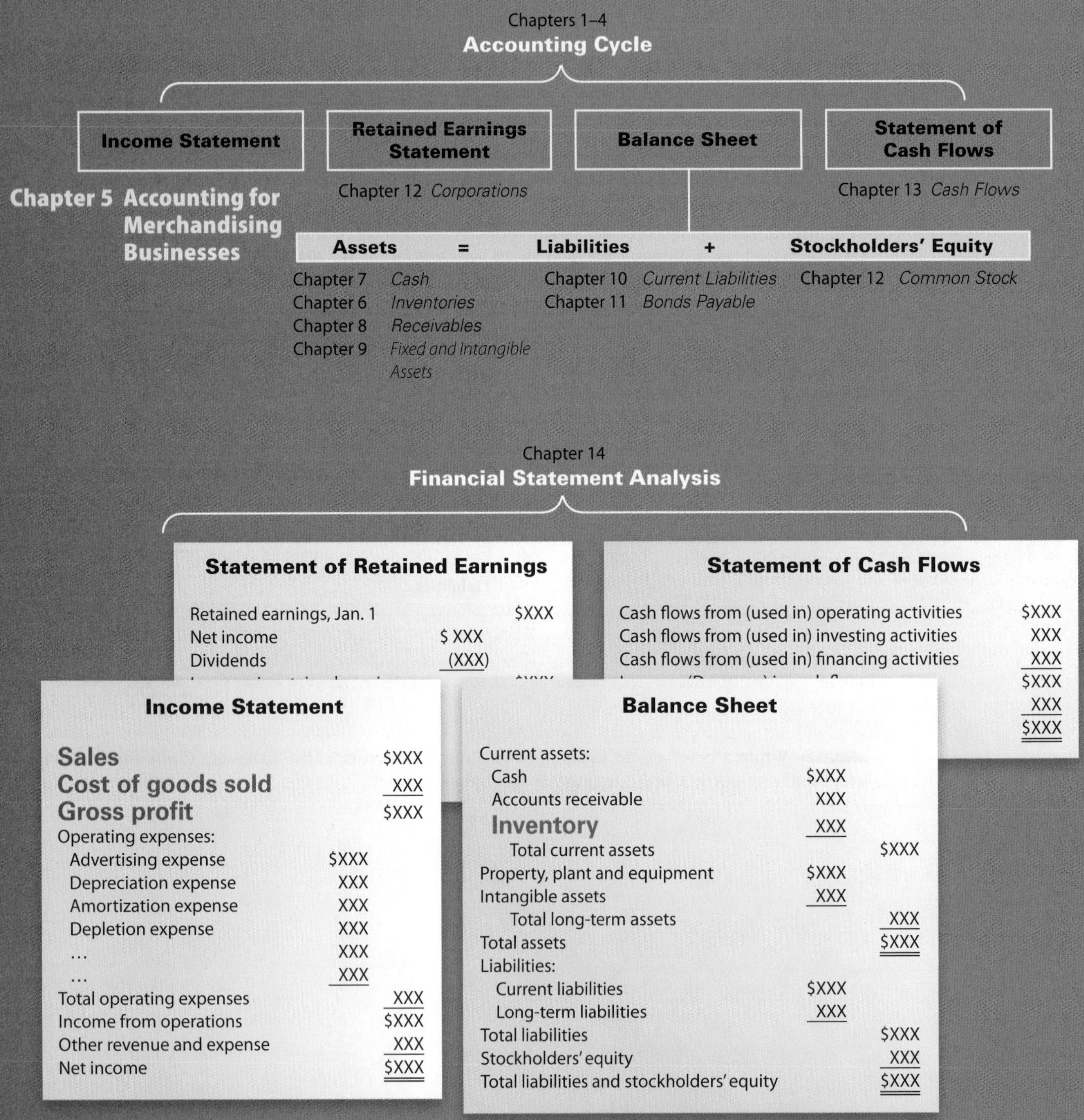

Dollar Tree, Inc.

When you are low on cash but need to pick up party supplies, housewares, or other consumer items, where do you go? Many shoppers are turning to **Dollar Tree, Inc.**, the nation's largest single price point dollar retailer with more than 5,000 stores in 48 states. For the fixed price of $1 on merchandise in its stores, Dollar Tree has worked hard providing "new treasures" every week for the entire family.

Despite the fact that items cost only $1, the accounting for a merchandiser, like Dollar Tree, is more complex than for a service company. This is because a service company sells only services and has no inventory. With Dollar Tree's locations and merchandise, the company must design its accounting system to not only record the receipt of goods for resale, but also to keep track of what merchandise is available for sale as well as where the merchandise is located. In addition, Dollar Tree must record the sales and costs of the goods sold for each of its stores. Finally, Dollar Tree must record such data as delivery costs, merchandise discounts, and merchandise returns.

This chapter focuses on the accounting principles and concepts for a merchandising business. In doing so, the basic differences between merchandiser and service company activities are highlighted. The financial statements of a merchandising business and accounting for merchandise transactions are also described and illustrated.

What's Covered

Accounting for Merchandising Businesses

Nature of Merchandising Businesses	Purchase Transactions	Sales Transactions	Merchandising Financial Statements
■ Operating Cycle (Obj. 1) ■ Income Statement (Obj. 1) ■ Subsidiary Ledgers (Obj. 2) ■ Inventory Systems (Obj. 2)	■ Purchase Discounts (Obj. 2) ■ Purchase Returns and Allowances (Obj. 2) ■ Freight (Obj. 2) ■ Buyer/Seller Transactions (Obj. 2)	■ Customer Discounts (Obj. 2) ■ Customer Returns and Allowances (Obj. 2) ■ Freight (Obj. 2) ■ Buyer/Seller Transactions (Obj. 2)	■ Single-Step Income Statement (Obj. 3) ■ Multiple-Step Income Statement (Obj. 3) ■ Retained Earnings Statement (Obj. 3) ■ Balance Sheet (Obj. 3) ■ Adjusting Entries (Obj. 4) ■ Closing Entries (Obj. 4)

Learning Objectives

Obj. 1   Distinguish between the activities and financial statements of service and merchandising businesses.

Obj. 2   Describe and illustrate the accounting for merchandise transactions.

Obj. 3   Describe and illustrate the financial statements of a merchandising business.

Obj. 4   Describe the adjusting and closing process for a merchandising business.

Analysis for Decision Making

Describe and illustrate the use of the asset turnover ratio in evaluating a company's operating performance.

Objective 1

Distinguish between the activities and financial statements of service and merchandising businesses.

Nature of Merchandising Businesses

The activities of a service business differ from those of a merchandising business. These differences are reflected in the operating cycles of a service and merchandising business as well as in their financial statements.

Operating Cycle

The **operating cycle** is the process by which a company spends cash, generates revenues, and receives cash either at the time the revenues are generated or later by collecting an accounts receivable. The operating cycle of a service and merchandising business differs in that a merchandising business must purchase merchandise for sale to customers. The operating cycle for a merchandise business is shown in Exhibit 1.

Exhibit 1

The Operating Cycle for a Merchandising Business

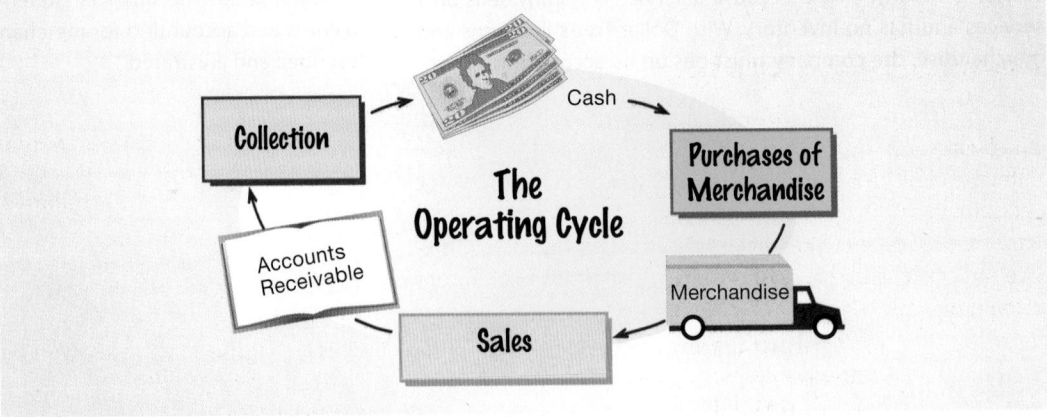

The time in days to complete an operating cycle differs significantly among merchandise businesses. Grocery stores normally have short operating cycles because of the nature of their merchandise. For example, many grocery items, such as milk, must be sold within their expiration dates of a week or two. In contrast, jewelry stores often carry expensive items that are displayed months before being sold to customers.

Financial Statements

The differences between service and merchandising businesses are also reflected in their financial statements. For example, these differences are illustrated in the following condensed income statements:

Service Business		Merchandising Business	
Fees earned	$ XXX	Sales	$ XXX
Operating expenses	(XXX)	Cost of goods sold	(XXX)
Operating income	$ XXX	Gross profit	$ XXX
		Operating expenses	(XXX)
		Operating income	$ XXX

The revenue activities of a service business involve providing services to customers. On the income statement for a service business, the revenues from services are reported as *fees earned.* The operating expenses incurred in providing the services are subtracted from the fees earned to arrive at *operating income.*

In contrast, the revenue activities of a merchandising business involve the buying and selling of merchandise. A merchandising business first purchases merchandise to sell to its customers. When this merchandise is sold, the revenue is reported as **sales**, and its cost is recognized as an expense. This expense is called the **cost of goods sold** or *cost of merchandise sold.* The cost of goods sold is subtracted from sales to arrive at gross profit. This amount is called **gross profit** because it is the profit *before* deducting operating expenses. The operating expenses are subtracted from gross profit to arrive at operating income.

Merchandise on hand (not sold) at the end of an accounting period is called **inventory** or *merchandise inventory.* Inventory is reported as a current asset on the balance sheet.

In a recent income statement, **Dollar Tree** reported the following (in billions):

Sales	$ 8.6
Cost of goods sold	(5.6)
Gross profit	$ 3.0
Operating expenses	(2.0)
Operating income	$ 1.0

On its balance sheet, it reported inventory of $1.0 billion.

Link to Dollar Tree

Why It Matters

Comcast Versus Lowe's

Comcast Corporation is a service business that offers cable communications, broadcast television (NBC television), filmed entertainment (Universal Pictures), and theme parks (Universal Parks) to its customers. **Lowe's Companies** is a large home improvement retailer. The differences in the operations of a service and merchandising business are illustrated in their recent income statements, as follows.

Comcast Corporation
Condensed Income Statement
(in millions)

Revenue	$ 68,775
Programming and production expenses	(20,912)
Selling and administrative expenses	(24,940)
Depreciation and amortization expenses	(8,019)
Operating income	$ 14,904

Lowe's Companies
Condensed Income Statement
(in millions)

Sales	$ 56,223
Cost of goods sold	(36,665)
Gross profit	$ 19,558
Selling, general, and administrative expenses	(13,281)
Depreciation expense	(1,485)
Operating income	$ 4,792

As a merchandising company, Lowe's subtracts cost of goods sold from sales to disclose gross profit. As a service company, Comcast does not show cost of goods sold, nor a gross profit line. Rather, service expenses are subtracted from revenue straight to operating income.

Objective 2

Describe and illustrate the accounting for merchandise transactions.

Merchandising Transactions

This section illustrates merchandise transactions for **NetSolutions** after it becomes a retailer of computer hardware and software. During 2017, Chris Clark implemented the second phase of NetSolutions' business plan. In doing so, Chris notified clients that beginning July 1, 2018, NetSolutions would no longer offer consulting services. Instead, it would become a retailer.

NetSolutions' business strategy is to offer personalized service to individuals and small businesses that are upgrading or purchasing new computer systems. NetSolutions' personal service includes a no-obligation, on-site assessment of the customer's computer needs. By providing personalized service and follow-up, Chris feels that NetSolutions can compete effectively against such retailers as **Best Buy**, **Office Max**, **Office Depot**, and **Dell**.

Merchandise transactions are recorded in the accounts, using the rules of debit and credit that are described and illustrated in Chapter 2. However, the accounting system for merchandise businesses is often modified to more efficiently record transactions. For example, an accounting system should be designed to provide information on the amounts due from various customers (accounts receivable) and amounts owed to various creditors (accounts payable). A separate account for each customer and creditor could be added to the ledger. However, as the number of customers and creditors increased, the ledger would become large and awkward to use.

A large number of individual accounts with a common characteristic can be grouped together in a separate ledger, called a **subsidiary ledger**. The primary ledger, which contains all of the balance sheet and income statement accounts, is then called the **general ledger**. Each subsidiary ledger is represented in the general ledger by a summarizing account, called a **controlling account**. The sum of the balances of the accounts in the subsidiary ledger must equal the balance of the related controlling account. Thus, a subsidiary ledger is a secondary ledger that supports a controlling account in the general ledger.

Common subsidiary ledgers are:

- The **accounts receivable subsidiary ledger**, or *customers ledger*, lists the individual customer accounts in alphabetical order. The controlling account in the general ledger is Accounts Receivable.
- The **accounts payable subsidiary ledger**, or *creditors ledger*, lists individual creditor accounts in alphabetical order. The controlling account in the general ledger is Accounts Payable.
- The **inventory subsidiary ledger**, or *inventory ledger*, lists individual inventory by item (bar code) number. The controlling account in the general ledger is Inventory. An inventory subsidiary ledger is used in a perpetual inventory system.

Most merchandising companies also use computerized accounting systems that record similar transactions in separate journals, which generate purchase, sales, and inventory reports. These separate journals are called **special journals**. However, for simplicity, the journal entries in this chapter will be illustrated using a two-column general journal.[1]

Purchases Transactions

There are two systems for accounting for merchandise transactions: perpetual and periodic. In a **perpetual inventory system**, each purchase and sale of merchandise is recorded in the inventory account and related subsidiary ledger. In this way, the amount of merchandise available for sale and the amount sold are continuously (perpetually) updated in the inventory records. In a **periodic inventory system**, the inventory does not show the amount of merchandise available for sale and the amount sold. Instead, a listing of inventory on hand, called a **physical inventory**, is prepared at the end of the accounting period. This physical inventory is used to determine the cost of inventory on hand at the end of the period and the cost of goods sold during the period.

Most merchandise companies use computerized perpetual inventory systems. Such systems use bar codes or radio frequency identification codes embedded in a product. An optical scanner or radio frequency identification device is then used to read the product codes and track inventory on hand and sold.

---

[1] Subsidiary ledgers and special journals are further described and illustrated in an online appendix at www.cengagebrain.com.

Because computerized perpetual inventory systems are widely used, this chapter illustrates merchandise transactions using a perpetual inventory system. The periodic system is described and illustrated in an appendix at the end of this chapter.

Dollar Tree uses point-of-sale computerized software to plan purchases and track inventory. This system automatically reorders key items based on sales and inventory levels.

Link to Dollar Tree

Under the perpetual inventory system, cash purchases of merchandise are recorded as follows:

2019				
Jan.	3	Inventory	2,510	
		Cash		2,510
		Purchased inventory from Bowen Co.		

A = L + E
+ −

Purchases of inventory on account are recorded as follows:

Jan.	4	Inventory	9,250	
		Accounts Payable—Thomas Corporation		9,250
		Purchased inventory on account.		

A = L + E
+   +

The terms of purchases on account are normally indicated on the **invoice** or bill that the seller sends the buyer. An example of an invoice sent to **NetSolutions** by Alpha Technologies is shown in Exhibit 2.

Alpha Technologies		**Invoice**
1000 Matrix Blvd.		**106-8**
San Jose, CA 95116-1000		
		Made in U.S.A.

SOLD TO	**CUSTOMER**	**ORDER**
NetSolutions	**ORDER NO.**	**DATE**
5101 Washington Ave.	412	Jan. 3, 2019
Cincinnati, OH 45227-5101		

DATE SHIPPED	**HOW SHIPPED AND ROUTE**	**TERMS**	**INVOICE DATE**
Jan. 5, 2019	US Express Trucking Co.	2/10, n/30	Jan. 5, 2019

FROM	**F.O.B.**
San Jose	Cincinnati

QUANTITY	**DESCRIPTION**	**UNIT PRICE**	**AMOUNT**
20	HC9 Printer/Fax/Copiers	150.00	3,000.00

Exhibit 2
Invoice

The terms for when payments for merchandise are to be made are called the **credit terms**. If payment is required on delivery, the terms are cash or net cash. Otherwise, the buyer is allowed an amount of time, known as the **credit period**, in which to pay. The credit period usually begins with the date of the sale as shown on the invoice.

If payment is due within a stated number of days after the invoice date, such as 30 days, the terms are net 30 days. These terms may be written as *n/30*.[2] If payment is due by the end of the month in which the sale was made, the terms are written as *n/eom*.

Why It Matters

Apple's Credit Terms

Working capital efficiency is influenced by the relationship between the suppliers' and customers' credit terms. If the suppliers' credit terms are longer than the customers'

credit terms, then the company is able to use suppliers to finance the operating cycle. For example, **Apple** is able to collect on sales within an average of approximately 30 days. However, Apple uses an average of 85 days to pay its suppliers. Thus, Apple collects faster than it pays, allowing Apple to use the suppliers' money as an interest-free loan for the 55-day (85 days – 30 days) difference.

Purchases Discounts To encourage the buyer to pay before the end of the credit period, the seller may offer a discount. For example, a seller may offer a 2% discount if the buyer pays within 10 days of the invoice date. If the buyer does not take the discount, the total invoice amount is due within 30 days. These terms are expressed as 2/10, n/30 and are read as "2% discount if paid within 10 days, net amount due within 30 days." The credit terms of 2/10, n/30 are summarized in Exhibit 3, using the invoice in Exhibit 2.

Exhibit 3 Credit Terms

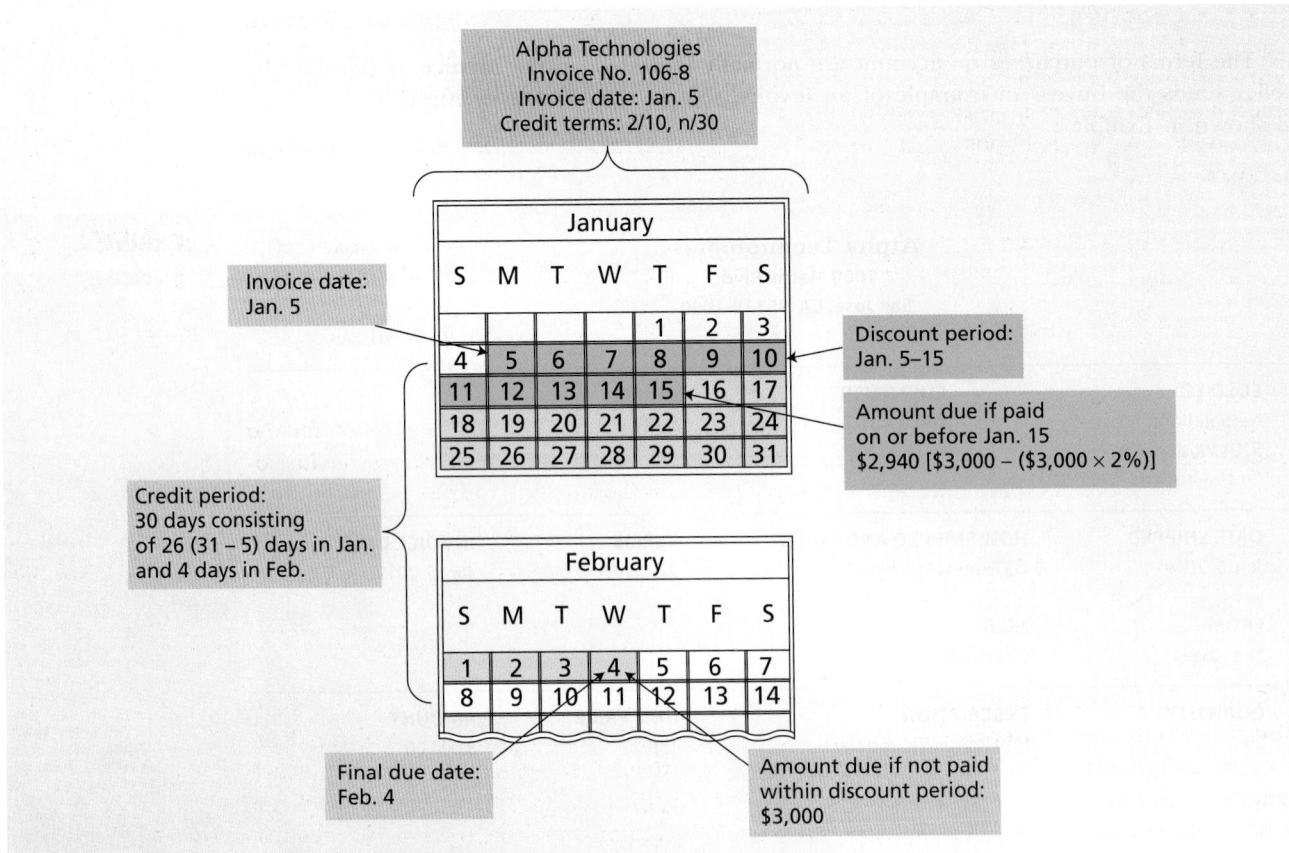

[2] The word *net* as used here does not have the usual meaning of a number after deductions have been subtracted, as in *net income*.

Discounts taken by the buyer for early payment of an invoice are called **purchases discounts**. Purchases discounts taken by a buyer reduce the cost of the merchandise purchased. Even if the buyer has to borrow to pay within a discount period, it is normally to the buyer's advantage to do so. For this reason, accounting systems are normally designed so that all available discounts are taken.

To illustrate, the invoice shown in Exhibit 2 is used. The last day of the discount period is January 15 (invoice date of January 5 plus 10 days). Assume that in order to pay the invoice on January 15, **NetSolutions** borrows $2,940, which is $3,000 less the discount of $60 ($3,000 × 2%). If an annual interest rate of 6% and a 360-day year is also assumed, the interest on the loan of $2,940 for the remaining 20 days of the credit period is $9.80 ($2,940 × 6% × 20 ÷ 360).[3]

The net savings to NetSolutions of taking the discount is $50.20, computed as follows:

Discount of 2% on $3,000	$60.00
Interest for 20 days at a rate of 6% on $2,940	9.80
Savings from taking the discount	$50.20

The savings can also be seen by comparing the interest rate on the money *saved* by taking the discount and the interest rate on the money *borrowed* to take the discount. The interest rate on the money saved in the prior example is estimated by converting 2% for 20 days to a yearly rate, as follows:

$$2\% \times \frac{360 \text{ days}}{20 \text{ days}} = 2\% \times 18 = 36\%$$

NetSolutions borrowed $2,940 at 6% to take the discount. If NetSolutions does not take the discount, it *pays* an estimated interest rate of 36% for using the $2,940 for the remaining 20 days of the credit period. Thus, buyers should normally take all available purchase discounts.

Since buyers normally take all purchases discounts, Inventory is debited for the net purchase price under the perpetual inventory system. That is, the buyer debits Inventory for the amount of the invoice less the discount.

To illustrate, NetSolutions would record the Alpha Technologies invoice and its payment as follows:

Jan.	5	Inventory	2,940		A = L + E	
		Accounts Payable—Alpha Technologies		2,940	+ +	
	15	Accounts Payable—Alpha Technologies	2,940		A = L + E	
		Cash		2,940	– –	

If NetSolutions did not pay within the discount period, inventory would be debited for the amount of the missed discount. For example, assuming that NetSoltuions paid Alpha Technologies on February 4, the payment would be recorded as follows:

Feb.	4	Accounts Payable—Alpha Technologies	2,940		A = L + E	
		Inventory	60		+– –	
		Cash		3,000		

Purchases Returns and Allowances A buyer may request an allowance for merchandise that is returned (purchases return) or a price allowance (purchases allowance) for damaged or defective merchandise. From a buyer's perspective, such returns and allowances are called **purchases returns and allowances**. In both cases, the buyer normally sends the seller a debit memorandum to notify the seller of reasons for the return (purchase return) or to request a price reduction (purchase allowance).

A **debit memorandum**, often called a **debit memo**, is shown in Exhibit 4. A debit memo informs the seller of the amount the buyer proposes to *debit* to the account payable due the seller. It also states the reasons for the return or the request for the price allowance.

---

[3] To simplify computations and rounding, we use a 360-day year rather than a 365-year.

Exhibit 4

Debit Memo

NetSolutions   No. 18

5101 Washington Ave.

Cincinnati, OH 45227-5101

DEBIT MEMO

TO	DATE
Maxim Systems	March 7, 2019
7519 East Wilson Ave.	
Seattle, WA 98101-7519	

WE DEBITED YOUR ACCOUNT AS FOLLOWS

10	Server Network Interface Cards, your invoice No. 7291,	@90.00	900.00
	are being returned via parcel post. Our order specified No. 825X.		

The buyer may use the debit memo as the basis for recording the return or allowance or wait for approval from the seller (creditor). In either case, the buyer debits Accounts Payable and credits Inventory.

To illustrate, **NetSolutions** records the return of the inventory indicated in the debit memo in Exhibit 4 as follows:

A = L + E

− −

Mar. 7	Accounts Payable—Maxim Systems	900	
	Inventory		900
	Debit Memo No. 18.		

Before paying an invoice, a buyer may return inventory or be granted a price allowance for an invoice with a purchase discount. In this case, the amount of the return is recorded at its invoice amount less the discount.

To illustrate, assume the following data concerning a purchase of inventory by NetSolutions on May 2:

May 2. Purchased $5,000 of inventory on account from Delta Data Link, terms 2/10, n/30.

   4. Returned $1,000 of the inventory purchased on May 2.

   12. Paid for the purchase of May 2 less the return and discount.

NetSolutions would record these transactions as follows:

A = L + E

+ +

May	2	Inventory	4,900	
		Accounts Payable—Delta Data Link		4,900
		Purchased inventory.		
		[$5,000 − ($5,000 × 2%)]		

A = L + E

− −

	4	Accounts Payable—Delta Data Link	980	
		Inventory		980
		Returned portion of merchandise purchased.		
		[$1,000 − ($1,000 × 2%)]		

A = L + E

− −

	12	Accounts Payable—Delta Data Link	3,920	
		Cash		3,920
		($4,900 − $980)		

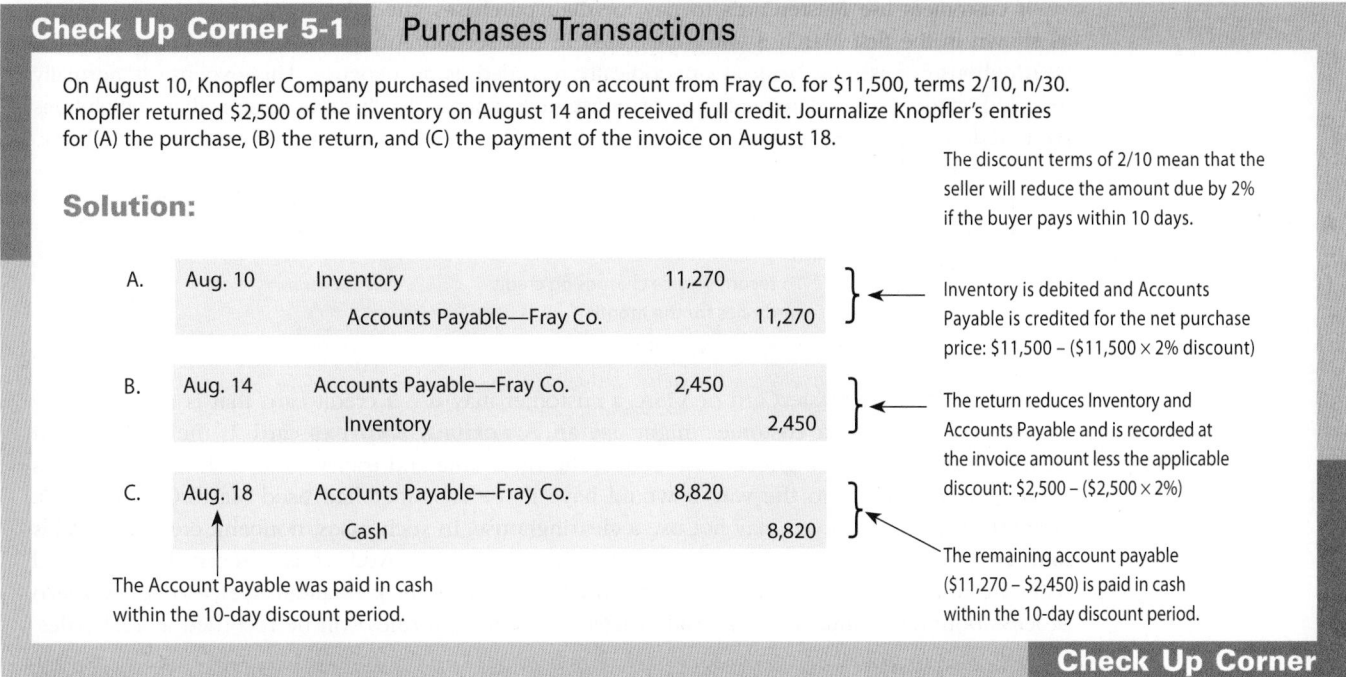

Sales Transactions

Revenue from merchandise sales is usually recorded as *Sales*. Sometimes a business may use the title *Sales of Merchandise*.

Cash Sales A business may sell merchandise for cash. Cash sales are normally entered on a cash register and recorded in the accounts. To illustrate, assume that on March 3, **NetSolutions** sells merchandise for $1,800. These cash sales are recorded as follows:

2019				
Mar.	3	Cash	1,800	
		Sales		1,800
		To record cash sales.		

A = L + E
+   + Rev

Using the perpetual inventory system, the cost of goods sold and the decrease in inventory are also recorded. In this way, the inventory account indicates the amount of inventory on hand (not sold).

To illustrate, assume that the cost of goods sold on March 3 is $1,200. The entry to record the cost of goods sold and the decrease in the inventory is as follows:

Mar.	3	Cost of Goods Sold	1,200	
		Inventory		1,200
		To record the cost of goods sold.		

A = L + E
−   − Exp

Sales may be made to customers using credit cards such as **MasterCard** or **VISA**. Such sales are recorded as cash sales. This is because these sales are normally processed by a clearinghouse that contacts the bank that issued the card. The issuing bank then electronically transfers cash directly to the retailer's bank account.[4] Thus, the retailer normally receives cash within a few days of making the credit card sale.

Dollar Tree normally receives cash from credit card sales within three business days, and thus records credit card sales as cash sales.

Link to Dollar Tree

[4] CyberSource is one of the major credit card clearinghouses. For a more detailed description of how credit card sales are processed, see the following CyberSource Web page: www.cybersource.com, click on Products, and under Payment Processing, click on Payment Cards, and then on How It Works.

If customers use MasterCards to pay for their purchases, the sales would be recorded exactly as shown in the first March 3 entry illustrated in this section. Any processing fees charged by the clearinghouse or issuing bank are periodically recorded as an expense. This expense is normally reported on the income statement as an administrative expense. To illustrate, assume that NetSolutions paid credit card processing fees of $4,150 on March 31. These fees would be recorded as follows:

```
A  =  L  +  E
-           -  Exp
```

Mar.	31	Credit Card Expense	4,150	
		Cash		4,150
		To record service charges on credit card sales for the month.		

Instead of using MasterCard or VISA, a customer may use a credit card that is not issued by a bank. For example, a customer might use an **American Express** card. If the seller uses a clearinghouse, the clearinghouse will collect the receivable and transfer the cash to the retailer's bank account, similar to the way it would have if the customer had used MasterCard or VISA. Large businesses, however, may not use a clearinghouse. In such cases, nonbank credit card sales must first be reported to the card company before cash is received. Thus, a receivable is created with the nonbank credit card company. However, because most retailers use clearinghouses to process both bank and nonbank credit cards, all credit card sales will be recorded as cash sales.

Link to Dollar Tree

Dollar Tree only accepts cash, checks, credit cards, and debit cards from its customers.

Sales on Account A business may sell merchandise on account. The seller records such sales as a debit to Accounts Receivable and a credit to Sales. An example of an entry for a **NetSolutions** sale on account of $18,000 follows. The cost of goods sold was $10,800.

```
A  =  L  +  E
+           +  Rev
```

Mar.	10	Accounts Receivable—Digital Technologies	18,000	
		Sales		18,000
		Invoice No. 7172.		

```
A  =  L  +  E
-           -  Exp
```

	10	Cost of Goods Sold	10,800	
		Inventory		10,800
		Cost of merch. sold on Invoice No. 7172.		

Link to Dollar Tree

Because **Dollar Tree** does not sell merchandise to customers on account, but only accepts cash, checks, credit cards, and debit cards, it did not report any accounts receivable on a recent balance sheet.

Customer Discounts A seller may grant customers a variety of discounts, called **customer discounts**, as incentives to encourage customers to act in a way benefiting the seller. For example, a seller may offer customer discounts to encourage customers to purchase in volume or order early.

A common discount, called a **sales discount**, encourages customers to pay their invoice early. For example, a seller may offer credit terms of 2/10, n/30, which provides a 2% sales discount if the invoice is paid within 10 days. If not paid within 10 days, the total invoice amount is due within 30 days.[5]

To illustrate the accounting for sales discounts, assume that **NetSolutions** sold $18,000 of merchandise to Digital Technologies on March 10 with credit terms 2/10, n/30. The March 10 sale would be recorded as follows:[6]

```
A  =  L  +  E
+           +  Rev
```

Mar.	10	Accounts Receivable—Digital Technologies	17,640	
		Sales [$18,000 - ($18,000 × 2%)]		17,640

[5] From the buyer's perspective, a sales discount is referred to as a purchases discount, which was discussed earlier in this chapter.
[6] The accounting for customer discounts other than sales discounts is discussed in advanced accounting courses.

The sale to Digital Technologies is recorded by NetSolutions as $17,640, which is the invoice amount of $18,000 less the sales discount of $360 ($18,000 × 2%).[7]

The payment by Digital Technologies on March 19 is recorded as follows:

Mar.	19	Cash	17,640	
		Accounts Receivable—Digital Technologies		17,640

A = L + E
+ –

If Digital Technologies did not pay within the discount period, NetSolutions would receive $18,000 and Sales would be credited for the amount of the discount. For example, assuming that Digital Technologies paid NetSolutions on April 9, the payment would be recorded by NetSolutions as follows:

Apr.	9	Cash	18,000	
		Accounts Receivable—Digital Technologies		17,640
		Sales		360

A = L + E
+ – + Rev

Cash Refunds and Allowances

A buyer may receive merchandise that is defective, damaged during shipment, or does not meet the buyer's expectations. In these cases, the seller may pay the buyer a **cash refund** or grant a **customer allowance** that reduces the accounts receivable owed on the original selling price.

If the buyer is paid a refund, the seller debits Customer Refunds Payable and credits Cash. For example, assume that on March 4 **NetSolutions** pays Blake & Sons a refund of $900 for merchandise that was damaged in shipment. Blake & Sons has agreed to keep the merchandise and make any necessary repairs. Netsolutions would record the payment of the refund as follows:

Mar.	4	Customer Refunds Payable	900	
		Cash		900

A = L + E
– –

Customer refunds payable is a liability account for estimated refunds and allowances that will be paid or granted customers in the future. It is recorded at the end of the accounting period as part of the adjusting process. The adjusting entry for customer refunds payable is illustrated later in this chapter.

In some cases, a customer who is due a refund has an outstanding account receivable balance. Instead of paying a cash refund, the seller may grant the customer an allowance against the customer's account receivable. When this is done, the seller sends the buyer a **credit memorandum**, or **credit memo**, indicating its intent to credit the customer's account receivable.

To illustrate, assume that instead of paying a cash refund to Blake & Sons, NetSolutions granted Blake & Sons a customer allowance of $900. NetSolutions notifies Blake & Sons of the allowance by issuing the credit memo shown in Exhibit 5.

NetSolutions
5101 Washington Ave.
Cincinnati, OH 45227-5101

Exhibit 5
Credit Memo

CREDIT MEMO

TO	**DATE**
Blake & Sons	March 4, 2019
7608 Melton Avenue	
Los Angeles, CA 90025-3942	

THE CUSTOMER ACCOUNT IS CREDITED

Allowance for merchandise damaged in shipment	900

[7] This is consistent with *Revenue from Contracts with Customers, Topic 606, FASB Accounting Standards Update,* Financial Accounting Standards Board, Norwalk, CT, May 2014.

The credit memo indicates that NetSolutions intends to reduce Blake & Sons' accounts receivable for $900 due to merchandise damaged in shipment. NetSolutions would record the granting of the customer allowance as follows:

A = L + E		
– –		

	Mar.	4	Customer Refunds Payable	900	
			Accounts Receivable—Blake & Sons		900

Link to Dollar Tree

Dollar Tree does not offer refunds and all sales are final.

Customer Returns In the preceding example, Blake & Sons did not return merchandise. When customers return merchandise for a cash refund or allowance, an additional entry must be made. This additional entry debits Inventory and credits Estimated Returns Inventory for the seller's original cost of the returned merchandise.

To illustrate, assume that on January 15 Bormann Enterprises returned merchandise with a selling price of $3,000 for a cash refund. The merchandise originally cost **NetSolutions** $2,100. NetSolutions would record the cash refund and the return with the following two entries:

A = L + E		
– –		

	Jan.	15	Customer Refunds Payable	3,000	
			Cash		3,000

A = L + E		
+ –		

		15	Inventory	2,100	
			Estimated Returns Inventory		2,100

The first entry records the cash refund payment of $3,000. The second entry records the receipt of the $2,100 of returned merchandise by debiting Inventory and crediting Estimated Returns Inventory.[8]

Estimated returns inventory is a current asset that is reported on the balance sheet after Inventory. It represents an estimate of merchandise that will be returned by customers. It is recorded at the end of the accounting period as part of the adjusting process. The adjusting entry for estimated returns inventory is illustrated later in this chapter.

If Bormann Enterprises had an outstanding accounts receivable balance on January 15, NetSolutions could have issued a $3,000 credit memo to Bormann Enterprises. In this case, NetSolutions would have credited Accounts Receivable—Bormann Enterprises instead of Cash.

The journal entries to record customer refunds, allowances, and returns are summarized in Exhibit 6.

Exhibit 6   Journal Entries to Record Customer Refunds, Allowances, and Returns

	Cash Refund Paid		Credit Memorandum Issued	
Customer does not return merchandise	Customer Refunds Payable XXX		Customer Refunds Payable XXX	
	Cash	XXX	Accounts Receivable..........	XXX
Customer returns merchandise	Customer Refunds Payable XXX		Customer Refunds Payable XXX	
	Cash	XXX	Accounts Receivable..........	XXX
	Inventory..................... XXX		Inventory..................... XXX	
	Estimated Returns Inventory ...	XXX	Estimated Returns Inventory ...	XXX

Link to Dollar Tree

Although all sales are final, **Dollar Tree** will "exchange" any unopened item with the original receipt.

[8] Because of wear, tear, and damage, companies may segregate returned items from normal inventory by using a separate returns inventory account.

 *Ethics: Don't Do It!*

The Case of the Fraudulent Price Tags

One of the challenges for a retailer is policing its sales return policy. There are many ways in which customers can unethically or illegally abuse such policies. In one case, a couple was accused of attaching **Marshalls**' store price tags to cheaper merchandise bought or obtained elsewhere. The couple then returned the cheaper goods and received the substantially higher refund amount. Company security officials discovered the fraud and had the couple arrested after they had allegedly bilked the company for more than $1 million.

Check Up Corner 5-2 | **Sales Transactions**

On December 30, Burrows Inc. sold $12,000 of merchandise to Wall Company on account, with terms 2/10, n/30. The merchandise originally cost Burrows $8,000. On January 3, Wall determines that a portion of the merchandise received does not operate properly, and Burrows issues a credit memo for the returned items. The selling price of the returned merchandise is $3,000. It originally cost Burrows $2,000. Journalize the entries by Burrows to record (A) the December 30 sale, (B) the January 3 return, and (C) the receipt of the amount due from Wall on January 6.

Solution:

A. Dec. 30   Accounts Receivable—Wall Company   11,760
            Sales   11,760*

The sale is recorded at the invoice amount ($12,000) less the 2% discount ($240).

B. Jan. 3   Customer Refunds Payable   2,940
            Accounts Receivable—Wall Company   2,940

The customer refund is recorded at the invoice amount ($3,000) less the 2% discount ($60).

          Inventory   2,000
            Estimated Returns Inventory   2,000

When goods are returned, Estimated Returns Inventory is credited and Inventory is debited for the original cost of the inventory.

Instead of paying a cash refund, the seller grants the customer an allowance against its account receivable.

Customer Refunds Payable is a liability account for estimated refunds.

The account receivable was paid in cash within the 10-day discount period.

C. Jan. 6   Cash   8,820
            Accounts Receivable—Wall Company   8,820**

The remaining account receivable ($11,760 – $2,940) is paid in cash within the discount period.

Check Up Corner

Freight

Purchases and sales of merchandise often involve freight. The terms of a sale indicate when ownership (title and control) of the merchandise passes from the seller to the buyer. This point determines whether the buyer or the seller pays the freight costs.[9]

The ownership of the merchandise may pass to the buyer when the seller delivers the merchandise to the freight carrier. In this case, the terms are said to be **FOB (free on board) shipping point**. This term means that the buyer pays the freight costs from the shipping point to the final destination. Such costs are part of the buyer's total cost of purchasing inventory and are added to the cost of the inventory by debiting Inventory.

note:
The buyer bears the freight costs if the shipping terms are FOB shipping point.

---

[9] The passage of title also determines whether the buyer or seller must pay other costs, such as the cost of insurance, while the merchandise is in transit.

To illustrate, assume that on June 10, **NetSolutions** purchased merchandise as follows:

June 10. Purchased merchandise from Magna Data, $900, terms FOB shipping point.
   10. Paid freight of $50 on June 10 purchase from Magna Data.

NetSolutions would record these two transactions as follows:

A = L + E
+   +

A = L + E
+ –

	June	10	Inventory	900	
			Accounts Payable—Magna Data		900
			Purchased merchandise, terms FOB		
			shipping point.		
		10	Inventory	50	
			Cash		50
			Paid shipping cost on merchandise		
			purchased.		

note:

The seller bears the freight costs if the shipping terms are FOB destination.

The ownership of the merchandise may pass to the buyer when the buyer receives the merchandise. In this case, the terms are said to be **FOB (free on board) destination**. This term means that the seller pays the freight costs from the shipping point to the buyer's final destination. When the seller pays the delivery charges, the seller debits Delivery Expense or Freight Out. Delivery Expense is reported on the seller's income statement as a selling expense.

To illustrate, assume that **NetSolutions** sells merchandise as follows:

June 15. Sold merchandise to Kranz Company on account, $700, terms FOB destination. The cost of the goods sold is $480.
   15. NetSolutions pays freight of $40 on the sale of June 15.

NetSolutions records the sale, the cost of the sale, and the freight cost as follows:

A = L + E
+   + Rev

A = L + E
–   – Exp

A = L + E
–   – Exp

	June	15	Accounts Receivable—Kranz Company	700	
			Sales		700
			Sold merchandise, terms FOB destination.		
		15	Cost of Goods Sold	480	
			Inventory		480
			Recorded cost of goods sold to		
			Kranz Company.		
		15	Delivery Expense	40	
			Cash		40
			Paid shipping cost on merchandise sold.		

The seller may prepay the freight, even though the terms are FOB shipping point. The seller will then add the freight to the invoice. The buyer debits Inventory for the total amount of the invoice, including the freight. Any discount terms would not apply to the prepaid freight.

To illustrate, assume that **NetSolutions** sells merchandise as follows:

June 20. Sold merchandise to Planter Company on account, $800, terms FOB shipping point. NetSolutions paid freight of $45, which was added to the invoice. The cost of the goods sold is $360.

NetSolutions records the sale, the cost of the sale, and the freight as follows:

June	20	Accounts Receivable—Planter Company		800	
		Sales			800
		Sold merchandise, terms FOB shipping point.			
	20	Cost of Goods Sold		360	
		Inventory			360
		Recorded cost of goods sold to Planter Company.			
	20	Accounts Receivable—Planter Company		45	
		Cash			45
		Prepaid shipping cost on merchandise sold.			

A = L + E
+   + Rev

A = L + E
−   − Exp

A = L + E
+ −

Shipping terms, the passage of title (control), and whether the buyer or seller is to pay the freight costs are summarized in Exhibit 7.

Exhibit 7 Freight Terms

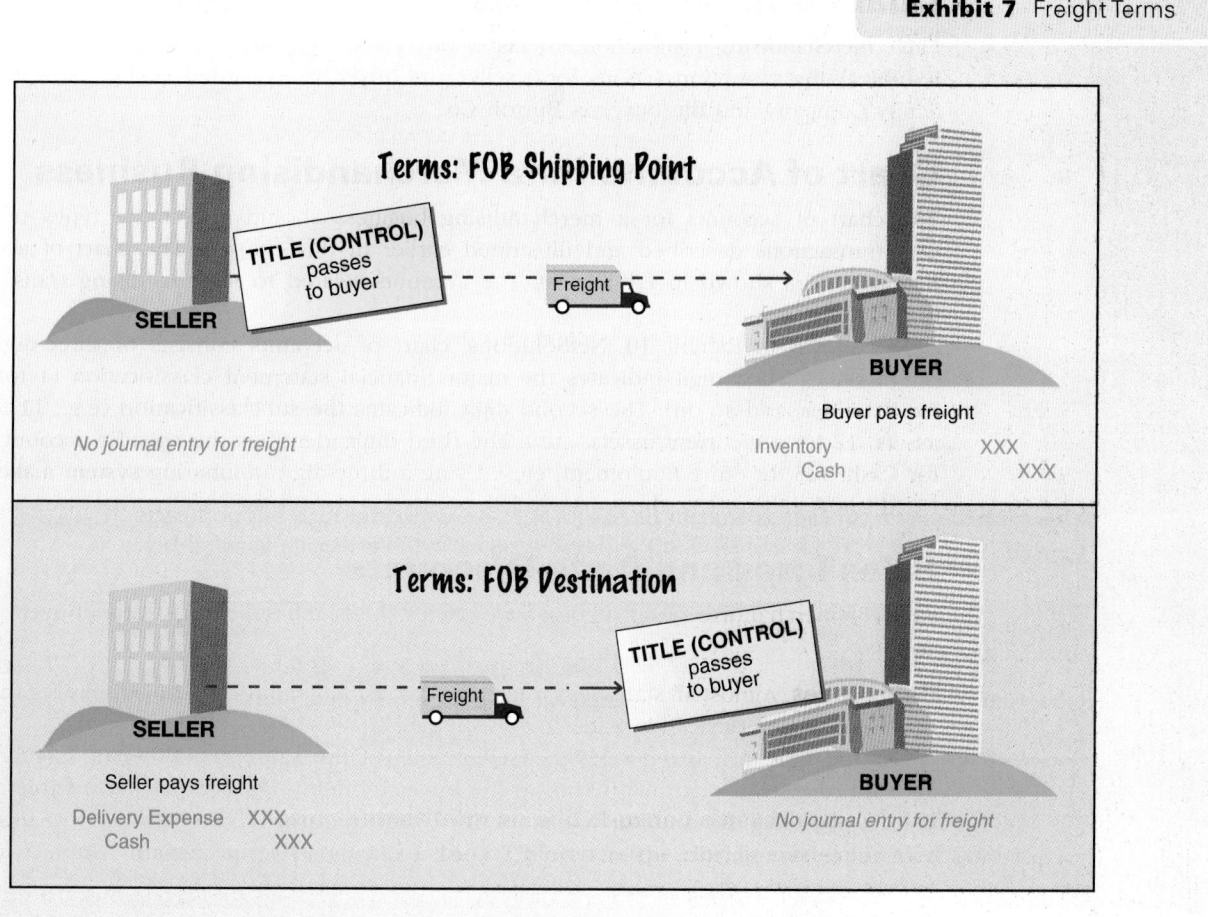

Summary: Recording Inventory Transactions

Recording inventory transactions under the perpetual inventory system has been described and illustrated in the preceding sections. These transactions involved purchases, purchases returns and allowances, freight, cost of goods sold (from sales), and customer returns. Exhibit 8 summarizes how these transactions are recorded in T account form.

Exhibit 8
Recording Inventory
Transactions

Inventory			
Purchases (net of discounts)	XXX	Purchases returns and allowances (net of discounts)	XXX
Freight for merchandise purchased FOB shipping point	XXX	Cost of goods sold	XXX
Customer returns	XXX		

Estimated Returns Inventory			
Adjusting entry for estimated customer returns	XXX	Customer returns	XXX

Cost of Goods Sold			
Cost of goods sold	XXX	Adjusting entry for estimated customer returns	XXX

Dual Nature of Merchandise Transactions

Each merchandising transaction affects a buyer and a seller. In the illustration shown in Exhibit 9, the same transactions for a seller and buyer are recorded. In Exhibit 9, the seller is Scully Company and the buyer is Burton Co.

Chart of Accounts for a Merchandising Business

The chart of accounts for a merchandising business should reflect the types of merchandise transactions described and illustrated earlier in this chapter. The chart of accounts for **NetSolutions** is shown in Exhibit 10. The accounts related to merchandising transactions are highlighted.

As shown in Exhibit 10, NetSolutions' chart of accounts consists of three-digit account numbers. The first digit indicates the major financial statement classification (1 for assets, 2 for liabilities, and so on). The second digit indicates the subclassification (e.g., 11 for current assets, 12 for noncurrent assets, etc.). The third digit identifies the specific account (e.g., 110 for Cash, 123 for Store Equipment, etc.). Using a three-digit numbering system makes it easier to add new accounts as they are needed.

Sales Taxes and Trade Discounts

Sales of merchandise often involve sales taxes. Also, the seller may offer buyers trade discounts.

Sales Taxes Almost all states levy a tax on sales of merchandise.[10] The liability for the sales tax is incurred when the sale is made.

At the time of a cash sale, the seller collects the sales tax. When a sale is made on account, the seller charges the tax to the buyer by debiting Accounts Receivable. The seller credits the sales account for the amount of the sale and credits the tax to Sales Tax Payable. For example, the seller would record a sale of $100 on account, subject to a tax of 6%, as follows:

A = L + E
+   +   + Rev

Aug.	12	Accounts Receivable—Lemon Co.	106	
		Sales		100
		Sales Tax Payable		6
		Invoice No. 339.		

[10] Businesses that purchase merchandise for resale to others are normally exempt from paying sales taxes on their purchases. Only final buyers of merchandise normally pay sales taxes.

Exhibit 9 Illustration of Inventory Transactions for Seller and Buyer

Transaction	Scully Company (Seller)		Burton Co. (Buyer)	

July 1. Scully Company sold merchandise on account to Burton Co., $7,500, terms FOB shipping point, n/45. The cost of the goods sold was $4,500.	Accounts Receivable—Burton Co. ... 7,500
	    Sales............................
	
	Cost of Goods Sold 4,500
	    Inventory ....
	
		7,500
		
		4,500
			Inventory 7,500
			    Accounts Payable—Scully Co. ..
				7,500

July 2. Burton Co. paid freight of $150 on July 1 purchase from Scully Company.	No journal entry.		Inventory .... 150 Cash...........................	150

July 5. Scully Company sold merchandise on account to Burton Co., $5,000, terms FOB destination, n/30. The cost of the goods sold was $3,500.	Accounts Receivable—Burton Co. ... 5,000
	    Sales............................
	
	Cost of Goods Sold 3,500
	    Inventory ....
	
		5,000
		
		3,500
			Inventory 5,000
			    Accounts Payable—Scully Co. ..
				5,000

July 7. Scully Company paid freight of $250 for delivery of merchandise sold to Burton Co. on July 5.	Delivery Expense .... 250 Cash...........................	250	No journal entry.	

July 15. Scully Company received payment from Burton Co. for purchase of July 5.	Cash 5,000
	    Accounts Receivable—Burton Co.
		5,000	Accounts Payable—Scully Co. 5,000
			    Cash...........................
				5,000

July 18. Scully Company sold merchandise on account to Burton Co., $12,000, terms FOB shipping point, 2/10, n/eom. Scully Company prepaid freight of $500, which was added to the invoice. The cost of the goods sold was $7,200.	Accounts Receivable—Burton Co. ... 11,760
	    Sales............................
	
	Accounts Receivable—Burton Co. ... 500
	    Cash...........................
	
	Cost of Goods Sold 7,200
	    Inventory ....
	
		11,760
		
		500
		
		7,200
			Inventory 12,260
			    Accounts Payable—Scully Co. ..
				12,260

July 22. Scully Company paid Burton Company a refund of $750 for merchandise damaged in the July 5 purchase. Burton kept the merchandise.	Customer Refunds Payable 750
	    Cash...........................
		750	Cash 750
			    Inventory ....
				750

July 28. Scully Company received payment from Burton Co. for purchase of July 18.	Cash 12,260
	    Accounts Receivable—Burton Co. .
		12,260	Accounts Payable—Scully Co. 12,260
			    Cash...........................
				12,260

July 31. Scully Company granted a customer allowance (credit memo) to Burton Co. for $2,500 for merchandise returned from July 1 purchase. The cost of the merchandise returned was $1,500.	Customer Refunds Payable 2,500
	    Accounts Receivable—Burton Co. .
	
	Inventory 1,500
	    Estimated Returns Inventory....
	
		2,500
		
		1,500
			Accounts Payable—Scully Co. 2,500
			    Inventory......................
				2,500

Exhibit 10	Balance Sheet Accounts	Income Statement Accounts

Exhibit 10
Chart of Accounts for NetSolutions, a Merchandising Business

Balance Sheet Accounts

100 Assets
- 110 Cash
- 112 Accounts Receivable
- 115 Inventory
- 116 Estimated Returns Inventory
- 117 Office Supplies
- 118 Prepaid Insurance
- 120 Land
- 123 Store Equipment
- 124 Accumulated Depreciation— Store Equipment
- 125 Office Equipment
- 126 Accumulated Depreciation— Office Equipment

200 Liabilities
- 210 Accounts Payable
- 211 Salaries Payable
- 212 Unearned Rent
- 213 Customer Refunds Payable
- 215 Notes Payable

300 Stockholders' Equity
- 310 Common Stock
- 311 Retained Earnings

Income Statement Accounts

- 312 Dividends
- 313 Income Summary

400 Revenues
- 410 Sales

500 Costs and Expenses
- 510 Cost of Goods Sold
- 520 Sales Salaries Expense
- 521 Advertising Expense
- 522 Depreciation Expense— Store Equipment
- 523 Delivery Expense
- 529 Miscellaneous Selling Expense
- 530 Office Salaries Expense
- 531 Rent Expense
- 532 Depreciation Expense— Office Equipment
- 533 Insurance Expense
- 534 Office Supplies Expense
- 539 Misc. Administrative Expense

600 Other Income
- 610 Rent Revenue

700 Other Expense
- 710 Interest Expense

On a regular basis, the seller pays to the taxing authority (state) the amount of the sales tax collected. The seller records such a payment as follows:

A = L + E				
– –	Sept. 15	Sales Tax Payable	2,900	
		Cash		2,900
		Payment for sales taxes collected during August.		

Why It Matters

E-commerce Shopping Carts

When you shop on an e-commerce site, you will often select items that fill out a shopping cart form that identifies the items to be purchased and their prices. This illustration is from **Apple**'s shopping cart. The shopping cart has a set of Apple EarPods at a price of $29. When checking out, the e-commerce site will automatically record the sales transaction for this purchase at a sales price of $29, plus appropriate sales tax and shipping. In addition, completing the checkout will record the reduction of EarPod inventory by one unit and record the appropriate cost of goods sold. Thus, all the merchandising transactions are generated from the shopping cart check-out process.

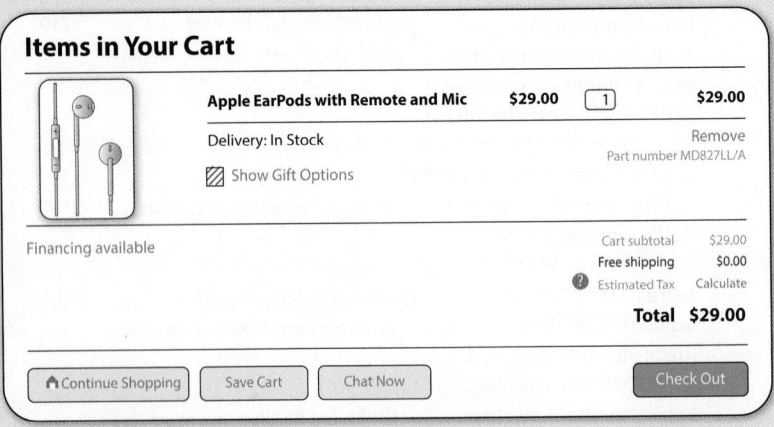

Items in Your Cart

	Apple EarPods with Remote and Mic	$29.00	1	$29.00
	Delivery: In Stock			Remove
	Show Gift Options			Part number MD827LL/A

Financing available

Cart subtotal $29.00
Free shipping $0.00
? Estimated Tax Calculate

Total $29.00

Continue Shopping | Save Cart | Chat Now | Check Out

Source: Apple®

Trade Discounts Wholesalers are companies that sell merchandise to other businesses rather than to the public. Many wholesalers publish or upload sales catalogs online. However, wholesalers often offer special discounts to government agencies or businesses that order large quantities. Such discounts are called **trade discounts**.

Sellers and buyers do not normally record the list prices of merchandise and trade discounts in their accounts. For example, assume that an item has a list price of $1,000 and a 40% trade discount. The seller records the sale of the item at $600 [$1,000 less the trade discount of $400 ($1,000 × 40%)]. Likewise, the buyer records the purchase at $600.

Financial Statements for a Merchandising Business

Objective 3
Describe and illustrate the financial statements of a merchandising business.

Although merchandising transactions affect the balance sheet in reporting inventory, they primarily affect the income statement. An income statement for a merchandising business is normally prepared using either a *multiple-step* or *single-step* format.

Multiple-Step Income Statement

The 2019 income statement for NetSolutions is shown in Exhibit 11.[11] This form of income statement, called a **multiple-step income statement**, contains several sections, subsections, and subtotals.

NetSolutions Income Statement For the Year Ended December 31, 2019			
Sales			$708,255
Cost of goods sold			520,305
Gross profit			$187,950
Operating expenses:			
Selling expenses:			
Sales salaries expense	$53,430		
Advertising expense	10,860		
Depreciation expense—store equipment	3,100		
Delivery expense	2,800		
Miscellaneous selling expense	630		
Total selling expenses		$70,820	
Administrative expenses:			
Office salaries expense	$21,020		
Rent expense	8,100		
Depreciation expense—office equipment	2,490		
Insurance expense	1,910		
Office supplies expense	610		
Miscellaneous administrative expense	760		
Total administrative expenses		34,890	
Total operating expenses			105,710
Income from operations			$ 82,240
Other revenue and expense:			
Rent revenue		$ 600	
Interest expense		(2,440)	(1,840)
Net income			$ 80,400

Exhibit 11
Multiple-Step Income Statement

[11] The NetSolutions income statement for 2019 is used because it allows a better illustration of the computation of the cost of goods sold in the appendix to this chapter.

Sales The total amount of sales to customers for cash and on account is reported in this section. NetSolutions reported sales of $708,255 for the year ended December 31, 2019.

Cost of Goods Sold As shown in Exhibit 11, NetSolutions reported cost of goods sold of $520,305 during 2019. This amount is the cost of goods sold to customers. Cost of goods sold may also be reported as *cost of merchandise sold* or *cost of sales*.

Gross Profit The excess of sales over cost of goods sold is gross profit. As shown in Exhibit 11, NetSolutions reported gross profit of $187,950 in 2019.

Income from Operations Income from operations, sometimes called **operating income**, is determined by subtracting operating expenses from gross profit. Operating expenses are normally classified as either selling expenses or administrative expenses.

 Selling expenses are incurred directly in the selling of merchandise. Examples of selling expenses include sales salaries, store supplies used, depreciation of store equipment, delivery expense, and advertising.

 Administrative expenses, sometimes called **general expenses**, are incurred in the administration or general operations of the business. Examples of administrative expenses include office salaries, depreciation of office equipment, and office supplies used.

 Each selling and administrative expense may be reported separately as shown in Exhibit 11. However, many companies report selling, administrative, and operating expenses as single line items, as follows for NetSolutions:

IFRS

See Appendix C for more information.

Gross profit		$187,950
Operating expenses:		
Selling expenses	$70,820	
Administrative expenses	34,890	
Total operating expenses		105,710
Income from operations		$ 82,240

Other Revenue and Expense Other income and expense items are not related to the primary operations of the business. **Other revenue** is revenue from sources other than the primary operating activity of a business. Examples of other income include income from interest, rent, and gains resulting from the sale of fixed assets. **Other expense** is an expense that cannot be traced directly to the normal operations of the business. Examples of other expenses include interest expense and losses from disposing of fixed assets.

 Other income and other expense are offset against each other on the income statement. If the total of other income exceeds the total of other expense, the difference is added to income from operations to determine net income. If the reverse is true, the difference is subtracted from income from operations. The other income and expense items of NetSolutions are reported as follows and in Exhibit 11:

Income from operations		$82,240
Other revenue and expense:		
Rent revenue	$ 600	
Interest expense	(2,440)	(1,840)
Net income		$80,400

Link to Dollar Tree

Dollar Tree reports its income using the multiple-step income statement format.

Check Up Corner 5-3   Multiple-Step Income Statement

The following account balances were taken from the adjusted trial balance for Laser-Tek Company for the fiscal year ended December 31, 2018:

Advertising Expense	$ 32,500	Miscellaneous Selling Expense	$ 4,320
Cost of Goods Sold	512,400	Office Salaries Expense	82,400
Depreciation Expense—Office Equipment	20,000	Office Supplies Expense	1,650
Interest Revenue	1,425	Sales	912,500
Miscellaneous Administrative Expense	1,200	Sales Salaries Expense	160,000

Prepare a multiple-step income statement for Laser-Tek Company.

Solution:

Laser-Tek Company
Income Statement
For the Year Ended December 31, 2018

Sales			$912,500
Cost of goods sold			512,400
Gross profit.			$400,100
Operating expenses:			
Selling expenses:			
Sales salaries expense.	$160,000		
Advertising expense	32,500		
Miscellaneous selling expense	4,320		
Total selling expenses.		$196,820	
Administrative expenses:			
Office salaries expense	$ 82,400		
Depreciation expense—office equipment . . .	20,000		
Office supplies expense	1,650		
Miscellaneous administrative expense.	1,200		
Total administrative expenses		105,250	
Total operating expenses			302,070
Income from operations.			$ 98,030
Other revenue and expense:			
Interest revenue			1,425
Net income.			$ 99,455

Gross profit is the excess of sales over the cost of goods sold.

Income from operations is computed by subtracting operating expenses from gross profit.

Other income and expense items are not related to the company's primary business.

Check Up Corner

Single-Step Income Statement

An alternate form of income statement is the **single-step income statement.** As shown in Exhibit 12, the income statement for **NetSolutions** deducts the total of all expenses *in one step* from the total of all revenues.

The single-step form emphasizes total revenues and total expenses in determining net income. A criticism of the single-step form is that gross profit and income from operations are not reported.

Exhibit 12
Single-Step Income
Statement

NetSolutions Income Statement For the Year Ended December 31, 2019		
Revenues:		
Sales		$708,255
Rent revenue		600
Total revenues		$708,855
Expenses:		
Cost of goods sold...	$520,305	
Selling expenses	70,820	
Administrative expenses	34,890	
Interest expense..	2,440	
Total expenses		628,455
Net income		$ 80,400

Retained Earnings Statement

The retained earnings statement for **NetSolutions** is shown in Exhibit 13. This statement is prepared in the same manner as for a service business.

Exhibit 13
Retained Earnings
Statement for
Merchandising
Business

NetSolutions Retained Earnings Statement For the Year Ended December 31, 2019		
Retained earnings, January 1, 2019		$128,800
Net income	$ 80,400	
Dividends	(18,000)	
Change in retained earnings		62,400
Retained earnings, December 31, 2019.............................		$191,200

Balance Sheet

The balance sheet for **NetSolutions** is shown in Exhibit 14. In Exhibit 14, inventory is reported as a current asset and the current portion of the note payable of $5,000 is reported as a current liability.

Link to Dollar Tree

In a recent balance sheet, **Dollar Tree** reported inventory as a current asset and the current portion of long-term debt as a current liability.

Objective 4

Describe the adjusting and closing process for a merchandising business.

The Adjusting and Closing Process

Thus far, the recording of transactions, chart of accounts, and financial statements for a merchandising business (NetSolutions) have been described and illustrated. In the remainder of this chapter, the adjusting and closing process for a merchandising business will be described. In this discussion, the focus will be on the elements of the accounting cycle that differ from those of a service business.

Exhibit 14
Balance Sheet for Merchandising Business

NetSolutions
Balance Sheet
December 31, 2019

Assets

Current assets:

Cash..		$ 52,650	
Accounts receivable		91,080	
Inventory..		62,150	
Estimated returns inventory.....................		5,300	
Office supplies		480	
Prepaid insurance		2,650	
Total current assets..........................			$214,310

Property, plant, and equipment:

Land		$ 20,000	
Store equipment	$27,100		
Accumulated depreciation	(5,700)		
Book value......................................		21,400	
Office equipment................................	$15,570		
Accumulated depreciation	(4,720)		
Book value		10,850	
Total property, plant, and equipment.......			52,250
Total assets			$266,560

Liabilities

Current liabilities:

Accounts payable	$ 14,466	
Customer refunds payable	7,954	
Note payable (current portion)	5,000	
Salaries payable................................	1,140	
Unearned rent	1,800	
Total current liabilities........................		$ 30,360

Long-term liabilities:

Note payable (final payment due in ten years)		20,000
Total liabilities		$ 50,360

Stockholders' Equity

Common stock	$ 25,000	
Retained earnings...................................	191,200	
Total stockholders' equity............................		216,200
Total liabilities and stockholders' equity..............		$266,560

Adjusting Entries for Customer Returns and Allowances

Sellers are required to estimate returns and allowances at the end of an accounting period and prepare two adjusting entries:

1. The first adjusting entry reduces the sales account and creates a customer refund liability account.
2. The second adjusting entry creates an estimated returns inventory account for merchandise that is expected to be returned and reduces cost of goods sold.

To illustrate, assume the following for **NetSolutions** on December 31, 2019, before any adjustments:

Estimated cost of merchandise returned for 2019 sales	$5,000
Estimated percent of refunds of 2019 sales	1%

	Unadjusted Balances December 31, 2019	
	Debit	**Credit**
Sales	$715,409	
Cost of goods sold		$523,505
Estimated returns inventory	300	
Customer refunds payable		800

On December 31, 2019, NetSolutions makes the following two adjusting entries:[12]

A = L + E
+   − Rev

A = L + E
+   − Exp

Dec.	31	Sales (1% × $715,409)	7,154	
		Customer Refunds Payable		7,154
	31	Estimated Returns Inventory	5,000	
		Cost of Goods Sold		5,000

The first adjusting entry reduces 2019 sales by the amount of estimated refunds that may occur in 2020. Since 1% of sales are expected to be refunded, Sales is debited for $7,154 (1% × $715,409). In addition, a liability is recorded for $7,154 by crediting Customer Refunds Payable for the estimated customer refunds in 2020.

The second adjusting entry debits the asset Estimated Returns Inventory and reduces Cost of Goods Sold for the cost of merchandise that is expected to be returned in 2020 of $5,000. Estimated Returns Inventory is debited rather than the Inventory because the type of merchandise returned will not be known until the returns actually occur.

After the adjusting entries are posted to the ledger, Estimated Returns Inventory will have an adjusted balance of $5,300 ($300 + $5,000) and Customer Refunds Payable will have a balance of $7,954 ($800 + $7,154). Estimated returns inventory of $5,300 is reported on the balance sheet in Exhibit 14 as a current asset following Inventory. Customer refunds payable of $7,954 is reported in Exhibit 14 as a current liability following accounts payable. In addition, the adjusting entries ensure that the current period sales are matched with the related cost of goods sold on the income statement.

Adjusting Entry for Inventory Shrinkage

Under the perpetual inventory system, the inventory account is continually updated for purchase and sales transactions. As a result, the balance of the inventory account is the amount of merchandise available for sale at that point in time. However, retailers normally experience some loss of inventory due to shoplifting, employee theft, or errors. Thus, the physical inventory on hand at the end of the accounting period is usually less than the balance of Inventory. This difference is called **inventory shrinkage** or **inventory shortage**.

To illustrate, **NetSolutions**' inventory records indicate the following on December 31, 2019:

Account balance of Inventory	$63,950
Physical inventory on hand	62,150
Inventory shrinkage	$ 1,800

At the end of the accounting period, inventory shrinkage is recorded by the following adjusting entry:

A = L + E
−   − Exp

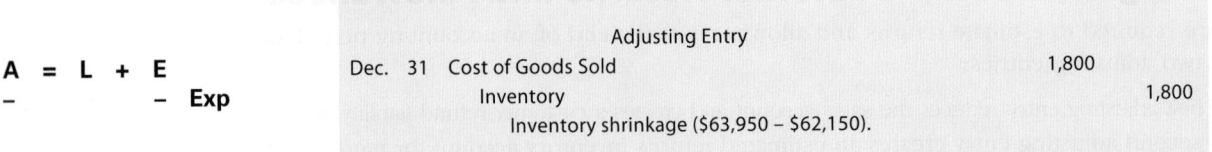

		Adjusting Entry		
Dec.	31	Cost of Goods Sold	1,800	
		Inventory		1,800
		Inventory shrinkage ($63,950 − $62,150).		

After the preceding entry is recorded, the balance of Inventory agrees with the physical inventory on hand at the end of the period. Since inventory shrinkage cannot be totally eliminated, it is considered a normal cost of operations. If, however, the amount of the shrinkage is unusually large, it may be disclosed separately on the income statement. In such cases, the shrinkage may be recorded in a separate account, such as Loss from Inventory Shrinkage.

---

[12] The accounting illustrated is based upon *Revenue from Contracts with Customers, Topic 606, FASB Accounting Standards Update*, Financial Accounting Standards Board, Norwalk, CT, May 2014.

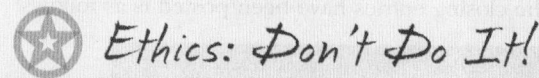 *Ethics: Don't Do It!*

The Cost of Employee Theft

One survey reported that the 24 largest U.S. retail store chains have lost more than $6 billion to shoplifting and employee theft. The stores apprehended over 1 million shoplifters and dishonest employees and recovered more than $161

million from these thieves. Approximately 1 out of every 36 employees was apprehended for theft from his or her employer. Each dishonest employee stole approximately 6 times the amount stolen by shoplifters ($665.77 versus $113.30).

Source: Jack L. Hayes International, 24th Annual Retail Theft Survey, 2012.

Closing Entries

The closing entries for a merchandising business are similar to those for a service business. The four closing entries for a merchandising business are as follows:

1. Debit each temporary account with a credit balance, such as Sales, for its balance and credit Income Summary.
2. Credit each temporary account with a debit balance, such as the various expenses, and debit Income Summary. Since Cost of Goods Sold is a temporary account with a debit balance, it is credited for its balance.
3. Debit Income Summary for the amount of its balance (net income) and credit the retained earnings account. The accounts debited and credited are reversed if there is a net loss.
4. Debit the retained earnings account for the balance of the dividends account and credit the dividends account.

The four closing entries for **NetSolutions** follow:

					Journal		Page 29
Date			**Item**		**Post. Ref.**	**Debit**	**Credit**
2019			Closing Entries				
Dec.	31	Sales			410	708,255	
		Rent Revenue			610	600	
		Income Summary			313		708,855
	31	Income Summary			313	628,455	
		Cost of Goods Sold			510		520,305
		Sales Salaries Expense			520		53,430
		Advertising Expense			521		10,860
		Depr. Expense—Store Equipment			522		3,100
		Delivery Expense			523		2,800
		Miscellaneous Selling Expense			529		630
		Office Salaries Expense			530		21,020
		Rent Expense			531		8,100
		Depr. Expense—Office Equipment			532		2,490
		Insurance Expense			533		1,910
		Office Supplies Expense			534		610
		Misc. Administrative Expense			539		760
		Interest Expense			710		2,440
	31	Income Summary			313	80,400	
		Retained Earnings			311		80,400
	31	Retained Earnings			311	18,000	
		Dividends			312		18,000

NetSolutions' income summary account after the closing entries have been posted is as follows:

Account Income Summary						Account No. 313
		Post.			**Balance**	
Date	Item	Ref.	Debit	Credit	Debit	Credit
2019						
Dec. 31	Revenues	29		708,855		708,855
31	Expenses	29	628,455			80,400
31	Net income	29	80,400		—	—

After the closing entries are posted to the accounts, a post-closing trial balance is prepared. The only accounts that should appear on the post-closing trial balance are the asset, contra asset, liability, and stockholders' equity accounts with balances. These are the same accounts that appear on the end-of-period balance sheet. If the two totals of the trial balance columns are not equal, an error has occurred that must be found and corrected.

Analysis for Decision Making

Objective

Describe and illustrate the use of the asset turnover ratio in evaluating a company's operating performance.

Asset Turnover Ratio

The **asset turnover ratio** measures how effectively a business is using its assets to generate sales. A high ratio indicates an effective use of assets.

The asset turnover ratio is computed as follows:

$$\text{Asset Turnover Ratio} = \frac{\text{Sales}}{\text{Average Total Assets}}$$

The denominator is the average of the total assets at the beginning and end of the year. To illustrate the use of this ratio, the following data (in millions) were taken from recent annual reports of **Dollar Tree, Inc.**:

	Year 2	Year 1
Total sales	$7,840	$7,394
Total assets:		
Beginning of year	2,752	2,329
End of year	2,772	2,752

The asset turnover ratio for each year is as follows:

	Year 2	Year 1
Asset turnover ratio*	2.84	2.91
	$7,840 ÷ [($2,752 + $2,772) ÷ 2]	$7,394 ÷ [($2,329 + $2,752) ÷ 2]

*Rounded to two decimal places.

Dollar Tree's asset turnover ratio decreased from 2.91 in Year 1 to 2.84 in Year 2. Thus, Dollar Tree had an insignificant decline in the use of its assets to generate sales in Year 2.

Using the asset turnover ratio for comparisons to competitors and with industry averages could also be beneficial in interpreting Dollar Tree's use of its assets. For example, the following data (in millions) were taken from a recent annual report of **Dollar General Corporation**, one of Dollar Tree's competitors:

	Year 2
Total sales	$18,910
Total assets:	
Beginning of year	10,867
End of year	11,224

Dollar General's asset turnover ratio for Year 2 is as follows:

	Year 2
Asset turnover ratio*	1.71

$$\$18,910 \div [(\$10,867 + \$11,224) \div 2]$$

*Rounded to two decimal places.

Comparing Dollar General's Year 2 ratio of 1.71 to Dollar Tree's Year 2 ratio of 2.84 implies that Dollar Tree is using its assets more efficiently than is Dollar General.

Make a Decision — Asset Turnover Ratio

CSX Corporation and **Union Pacific Corporation** are major railroads, operating primarily in the eastern and western portion of the United States, respectively. **YRC Worldwide Inc.** (Yellow Freight) is one of the largest trucking companies in the United States. The sales and total assets for a recent year for each company are as follows:

	CSX	Union Pacific	YRC Worldwide
Total sales	$12,669	$23,988	$5,069
Total assets:			
Beginning of year	31,782	49,731	2,065
End of year	33,053	52,716	1,985

A. Compute the asset turnover ratio for each company. (Round to two decimal places.)
B. Which railroad is more efficient in generating revenues from its assets?
C. How does YRC's asset turnover ratio compare to the two railroads? Why?

Solution:
A.

	CSX	Union Pacific	YRC Worldwide
Asset turnover ratio	0.39	0.47	2.50
	$12,669 ÷ [($31,782 + $33,053) ÷ 2]	$23,988 ÷ [($49,731 + $52,716) ÷ 2]	$5,069 ÷ [($2,065 + $1,985) ÷ 2]

B. Union Pacific's asset turnover ratio is 0.47, while CSX's is 0.39. Thus, Union Pacific is more efficient in using its assets in generating revenue. For every dollar of assets, Union Pacific generates 47 cents of revenue.
C. YRC's asset turnover ratio is over five times larger than that of the railroads. Clearly, YRC is much more efficient in generating revenues from its total assets than are the railroads. Railroads are very capital intensive, which means that their operations require a large asset base. Railroads require track, engines, railcars, computers, and switching yards to maintain the rail system. A trucking company is much less capital intensive. A trucking company requires an investment in trucks, computers, and terminals. Trucks run on highways that are an asset of the government, whereas the railroads must own their own rails.

Make a Decision

Appendix The Periodic Inventory System

Throughout this chapter, the perpetual inventory system was used to record purchases and sales of merchandise. Not all merchandise businesses, however, use the perpetual inventory system. For example, small merchandise businesses, such as a local hardware store, may use a manual accounting system. A manual perpetual inventory system is time consuming and costly to maintain. In this case, the periodic inventory system may be used.

Under the periodic inventory system, purchases are normally recorded at their invoice amount as a debit to Purchases. If the invoice is paid within the discount period, the discount is recorded as a credit in a separate account called Purchases Discounts. Likewise, purchases returns are recorded as a credit in a separate account called Purchases Returns and Allowances.

Chart of Accounts Under the Periodic Inventory System

The chart of accounts for **NetSolutions** under a periodic inventory system is shown in Exhibit 15. The accounts used to record transactions under the periodic inventory system are highlighted in Exhibit 15.

Exhibit 15

Chart of Accounts Under the Periodic Inventory System

Balance Sheet Accounts		Income Statement Accounts	
100	Assets	400	Revenues
110	Cash	410	Sales
111	Notes Receivable	500	Costs and Expenses
112	Accounts Receivable	510	Purchases
115	Inventory	511	Purchases Returns and Allowances
116	Estimated Returns Inventory		
117	Office Supplies	512	Purchases Discounts
118	Prepaid Insurance	513	Freight In
120	Land	520	Sales Salaries Expense
123	Store Equipment	521	Advertising Expense
124	Accumulated Depreciation— Store Equipment	522	Depreciation Expense— Store Equipment
125	Office Equipment	523	Delivery Expense
126	Accumulated Depreciation— Office Equipment	529	Miscellaneous Selling Expense
		530	Office Salaries Expense
200	Liabilities	531	Rent Expense
210	Accounts Payable	532	Depreciation Expense— Office Equipment
211	Salaries Payable		
212	Unearned Rent	533	Insurance Expense
213	Customer Refunds Payable	534	Office Supplies Expense
215	Notes Payable	539	Misc. Administrative Expense
300	Stockholders' Equity	600	Other Revenue
310	Common Stock	610	Rent Revenue
311	Retained Earnings		
312	Dividends	700	Other Expense
313	Income Summary	710	Interest Expense

Recording Merchandise Transactions Under the Periodic Inventory System

Using the periodic inventory system, purchases of inventory are not recorded in the inventory account. Instead, purchases, purchases discounts, and purchases returns and allowances accounts are used. In addition, the sales of merchandise are not recorded in the inventory account. Thus, there is no detailed record of the amount of inventory on hand at any given time. At the end of the period, a physical count of inventory on hand is taken. This physical count is used to determine the cost of goods sold as will be illustrated later.

The use of purchases, purchases discounts, purchases returns and allowances, and freight in accounts are described in this section.

Purchases Purchases of inventory are recorded in a purchases account rather than in the inventory account. Purchases is debited for the invoice amount of a purchase.

Purchases Discounts Purchases discounts are normally recorded in a separate purchases discounts account. The balance of the purchases discounts account is reported as a deduction from Purchases for the period. Thus, Purchases Discounts is a contra (or offsetting) account to Purchases.

Purchases Returns and Allowances Purchases returns and allowances are recorded in a similar manner as purchases discounts. A separate purchases returns and allowances account is used to record returns and allowances. Purchases returns and allowances are reported as a deduction from Purchases for the period. Thus, Purchases Returns and Allowances is a contra (or offsetting) account to Purchases.

Freight In When merchandise is purchased FOB shipping point, the buyer pays for the freight. Under the periodic inventory system, freight paid when purchasing merchandise FOB shipping point is debited to Freight In, Transportation In, or a similar account.

The preceding periodic inventory accounts and their effect on the cost of merchandise purchased are summarized as follows:

Account	Entry to Increase	Normal Balance	Effect on Cost of Merchandise Purchased
Purchases	Debit	Debit	Increases
Purchases Discounts	Credit	Credit	Decreases
Purchases Returns and Allowances	Credit	Credit	Decreases
Freight In	Debit	Debit	Increases

Exhibit 16 illustrates the recording of merchandise transactions using the periodic system.

Transaction	Periodic Inventory System	
June 5. Purchased $30,000 of merchandise on account, terms 2/10, n/30.	Purchases . . . . 30,000 Accounts Payable	30,000

June 8. Returned merchandise purchased on account on June 5, $500.	Accounts Payable 500
	    Purchases Returns and
	      Allowances . . . .
		500

June 15. Paid for purchase of June 5, less return of $500 and discount of $590 [($30,000 – $500) × 2%].	Accounts Payable 29,500
	    Cash . . . .
	    Purchases Discounts . . . .
		28,910
		590

June 18. Sold merchandise on account, $12,500, 1/10, n/30. The cost of the goods sold was $9,000.	Accounts Receivable 12,375
	    Sales . . . .
	    [$12,500 – ($12,500 × 1%)]
		12,375

June 22. Purchased merchandise, $15,000, terms FOB shipping point, 2/15, n/30, with prepaid freight of $750 added to the invoice.	Purchases . . . . 15,000 Freight In. . . . . 750 Accounts Payable	15,750
June 28. Received payment on account from June 18 sale	Cash . . . . 12,375 Accounts Receivable	12,375
June 29. Received $19,600 from cash sales. The cost of the goods sold was $13,800.	Cash . . . . 19,600 Sales	19,600

Exhibit 16

Transactions Using the Periodic Inventory System

Adjusting Process Under the Periodic Inventory System

The adjusting process is the same under the periodic and perpetual inventory systems except for the inventory shrinkage adjustment and customer refunds and allowances. The ending inventory is determined by a physical count under both systems.

Under the perpetual inventory system, the ending inventory physical count is compared to the balance of Inventory. The difference is the amount of inventory shrinkage. The inventory shrinkage is then recorded as a debit to Cost of Goods Sold and a credit to Inventory.

Under the periodic inventory system, the inventory account is not kept up to date for purchases and sales. As a result, the inventory shrinkage cannot be directly determined. Instead, any inventory shrinkage is included indirectly in the computation of the cost of goods sold as shown in Exhibit 17. This is a major disadvantage of the periodic inventory system. That is, inventory shrinkage is not separately determined.

Like the perpetual inventory system, the periodic system records the same adjusting entry debiting Sales and crediting Customer Refunds Payable for estimated customer refunds and allowances of $7,154. No entry, however, is made for estimated returns inventory. Instead, cost of goods sold is reduced by the cost of the estimated returns inventory for the current year. The estimated cost of the returns for **NetSolutions**' 2019 sales is $5,000. This amount is subtracted from the cost of goods sold before estimated returns of $525,305 to yield cost of goods sold of $520,305 shown in Exhibit 17.

Exhibit 17 Determining Cost of Goods Sold Using the Periodic System			
Inventory, January 1, 2019..............................			$ 59,700
Cost of merchandise purchased:			
Purchases		$521,980	
Purchases returns and allowances		(9,100)	
Purchases discounts................................		(2,525)	
Net purchases......................................		$510,355	
Freight in..		17,400	
Total cost of merchandise purchased.............			527,755
Inventory available for sale			$587,455
Inventory, December 31, 2019...........................			62,150
Cost of goods sold before estimated returns			$ 525,305
Increase in estimated returns inventory			(5,000)
Cost of goods sold			$520,305

Financial Statements Under the Periodic Inventory System

The financial statements are similar under the perpetual and periodic inventory systems. When the multiple-step format of income statement is used, the cost of goods sold may be reported as shown in Exhibit 17.

Closing Entries Under the Periodic Inventory System

The closing entries differ in the periodic inventory system in that there is no cost of goods sold account to close to Income Summary. Instead, the purchases, purchases discounts, purchases returns and allowances, and freight in accounts are closed to Income Summary. In addition, the inventory account is adjusted to the end-of-period physical inventory count during the closing process. The estimated returns inventory account is also adjusted for the estimated returns from the current period's sales.

The four closing entries under the periodic inventory system are as follows:

1. Debit each temporary account with a credit balance, such as Sales, for its balance and credit Income Summary. Since Purchases Discounts and Purchases Returns and Allowances are temporary accounts with credit balances, they are debited for their balances. In addition, debit the estimated returns inventory account for the cost of the future estimated returns of

the current period's sales. Finally, Inventory is debited for its end-of-period balance based on the end-of-period physical inventory.

2. Credit each temporary account with a debit balance, such as the various expenses, and debit Income Summary. Since Freight In is a temporary account with a debit balance, it is credited for its balance. In addition, Inventory is credited for its balance as of the beginning of the period.

3. Debit Income Summary for the amount of its balance (net income) and credit the retained earnings account. The accounts debited and credited are reversed if there is a net loss.

4. Debit the retained earnings account for the balance of the dividends account and credit the dividends account.

The four closing entries for **NetSolutions** under the periodic inventory system are shown in Exhibit 18.

		Journal				**Exhibit 18**
Date		**Item**	**Post. Ref.**	**Debit**	**Credit**	Closing Entries for Periodic
2019		Closing Entries				Inventory System
Dec. 31		Inventory	115	62,150		
		Estimated Returns Inventory	116	5,000		
		Sales	410	708,255		
		Purchases Returns and Allowances	511	9,100		
		Purchases Discounts	512	2,525		
		Rent Revenue	610	600		
		Income Summary	313		787,630	
31		Income Summary	313	707,230		
		Inventory	115		59,700	
		Purchases	510		521,980	
		Freight In	513		17,400	
		Sales Salaries Expense	520		53,430	
		Advertising Expense	521		10,860	
		Depreciation Expense—Store Equipment	522		3,100	
		Delivery Expense	523		2,800	
		Miscellaneous Selling Expense	529		630	
		Office Salaries Expense	530		21,020	
		Rent Expense	531		8,100	
		Depreciation Expense—Office Equipment	532		2,490	
		Insurance Expense	533		1,910	
		Office Supplies Expense	534		610	
		Miscellaneous Administrative Expense	539		760	
		Interest Expense	710		2,440	
31		Income Summary	313	80,400		
		Retained Earnings	311		80,400	
31		Retained Earnings	311	18,000		
		Dividends	312		18,000	

In the first closing entry, Inventory is debited for $62,150. This is the ending physical inventory count on December 31, 2019. In addition, the cost of the estimated merchandise returns from 2019 sales is debited to Estimated Returns Inventory for $5,000.

In the second closing entry, Inventory is credited for its January 1, 2019, balance of $59,700. In this way, the closing entries reflect the effects of the beginning and ending Inventory in determining the cost of goods sold, as shown in Exhibit 17. After the closing entries are posted, Inventory will have a balance of $62,150 and Estimated Returns Inventory will have a balance of $5,300, which are the amounts reported on the December 31, 2019, balance sheet.

In Exhibit 18, the periodic inventory accounts are highlighted. Under the perpetual inventory system, the highlighted periodic inventory accounts are replaced by the cost of goods sold account.

Let's Review

Chapter Summary

1. Merchandising businesses purchase merchandise for selling to customers. On a merchandising business's income statement, revenue from selling merchandise is reported as sales. The cost of the goods sold is subtracted from sales to arrive at gross profit. The operating expenses are subtracted from gross profit to arrive at net income. Inventory, which is merchandise not sold, is reported as a current asset on the balance sheet.

2. Purchases of merchandise for cash or on account are recorded as Inventory. Discounts for early payment of purchases on account are purchases discounts. Purchases of inventory subject to purchases discounts are recorded net of the discount. Price adjustments or returned merchandise are purchases returns. Price adjustments or returned merchandise are recorded net of any purchase discount.

   Sales of merchandise for cash or on account are recorded as sales. The cost of goods sold and the reduction in Inventory are also recorded at the time of sale.

   A seller may grant customers a variety of discounts, called customer discounts. A sales discount encourages customers to pay their invoices early. Sales subject to a sales discount are recorded net of the discount.

   A seller may pay a customer a refund or grant a price allowance for returned or damaged merchandise, called customer returns and allowances. When merchandise is returned for a refund, Customer Refunds Payable is debited and Cash is credited for the amount of the refund. The returned merchandise is recorded as a debit to Inventory and credit to Estimated Returns Inventory. When a customer doesn't return merchandise but is granted an allowance, Customer Refunds Payable is debited and either Cash, if the customer has already paid for the merchandise, or Account Receivable is credited.

   When merchandise is shipped FOB shipping point, the buyer pays the freight and debits Inventory. When merchandise is shipped FOB destination, the seller pays the freight and debits Delivery Expense or Freight Out. Merchandise transactions can be summarized in T account form as shown in Exhibit 8. Each merchandising transaction affects a buyer and a seller. The chart of accounts for a merchandising business (NetSolutions) is shown in Exhibit 10. The liability for sales tax is incurred when the sale is made and is recorded by the seller as a credit to the sales tax payable account. Trade discounts are discounts off the list price of merchandise.

3. The multiple-step income statement of a merchandiser reports sales. The cost of the goods sold is subtracted from sales to determine the gross profit. Operating income is determined by subtracting selling and administrative expenses from gross profit. Net income is determined by adding or subtracting the net of other income and expense. The income statement may also be reported in a single-step form. The retained earnings statement is similar to that for a service business. The balance sheet reports inventory at the end of the period as a current asset.

4. At the end of the accounting period, a seller must record two adjusting entries for expected returns and allowances. The first adjusting entry debits Sales and credits Customer Refunds Payable. The second entry debits Estimated Returns Inventory and credits Cost of Goods Sold.

   The normal adjusting entry for inventory shrinkage is to debit Cost of Goods Sold and credit Inventory. The closing entries for a merchandising business are similar to those for a service business except that the cost of goods sold is also closed to Income Summary.

Key Terms

accounts payable subsidiary ledger (230)

accounts receivable subsidiary ledger (216)

administrative expenses (general expenses) (246)

asset turnover ratio (252)

cash refund (237)

controlling account (230)

cost of goods sold (229)

credit memorandum (credit memo) (237)

credit period (231)

credit terms (231)

customer allowance (237)

customer discounts (236)

customer refunds payable (237)

debit memorandum (debit memo) (233)

estimated returns inventory (238)

FOB (free on board) destination (240)

FOB (free on board) shipping point (239)

general ledger (230)

gross profit (229)

income from operations (operating income) (246)

inventory (229)

inventory shrinkage (inventory shortage) (250)

inventory subsidiary ledger (230)

invoice (231)

multiple-step income statement (245)

operating cycle (228)

operating income (246)

other expense (246)

other revenue (246)

periodic inventory system (230)

perpetual inventory system (230)

physical inventory (230)

purchases discounts (233)

purchases returns and allowances (233)

sales (229)

sales discount (236)

selling expenses (246)

single-step income statement (247)

special journals (230)

subsidiary ledger (230)

trade discounts (245)

Practice

Multiple-Choice Questions

1. If merchandise purchased on account is returned, the buyer may inform the seller of the details by issuing a(n):
   A. debit memo.
   B. credit memo.
   C. invoice.
   D. bill.

2. If merchandise is sold on account to a customer for $1,000, terms FOB shipping point, 1/10, n/30, and the seller prepays $50 in freight, the amount of the discount for early payment would be:
   A. $0.
   B. $5.00.
   C. $10.00.
   D. $10.50.

3. The income statement in which the total of all expenses is deducted from the total of all revenues is termed the:
   A. multiple-step form.
   B. single-step form.
   C. account form.
   D. report form.

4. On a multiple-step income statement, the excess of net sales over the cost of goods sold is called:
   A. operating income.
   B. income from operations.
   C. gross profit.
   D. net income.

5. Which of the following expenses would normally be classified as other expense on a multiple-step income statement?
   A. Depreciation expense—office equipment
   B. Sales salaries expense
   C. Insurance expense
   D. Interest expense

Answers provided after Problem. Need more practice? Find additional multiple-choice questions, exercises, and problems in CengageNOWv2.

Exercises

SHOW ME HOW

1. Gross profit   Obj. 1

During the current year, merchandise is sold for $615,000 cash and $4,110,000 on account. The cost of the goods sold is $2,835,000. What is the amount of the gross profit?

SHOW ME HOW

2. Purchases transactions   Obj. 2

Halibut Company purchased merchandise on account from a supplier for $18,600, terms 2/10, n/30. Halibut returned $5,000 of the merchandise and received full credit.

A. If Halibut Company pays the invoice within the discount period, what is the amount of cash required for the payment?

B. What account is credited by Halibut Company to record the return?

SHOW ME HOW

3. Sales transactions   Obj. 2

Journalize the following merchandise transactions:

A. Sold merchandise on account, $72,500 with terms 2/10, n/30. The cost of the goods sold was $43,500.
B. Received payment less the discount.
C. Refunded $1,000 to customer for defective merchandise that was not returned.

SHOW ME HOW

4. Freight terms   Obj. 2

Determine the amount to be paid in full settlement of each of two invoices, (A) and (B), assuming that credit for returns and allowances was received prior to payment and that all invoices were paid within the discount period.

	Merchandise	Freight Paid by Seller	Freight Terms	Returns and Allowances
A.	$ 90,000	$1,000	FOB shipping point, 1/10, n/30	$15,000
B.	110,000	1,575	FOB destination, 2/10, n/30	8,500

SHOW ME HOW

5. Transactions for buyer and seller   Obj. 2

Sather Co. sold merchandise to Boone Co. on account, $31,800, terms 2/15, n/30. The cost of the goods sold is $19,000. Journalize the entries for Sather Co. and Boone Co. for the sale, purchase, and payment of amount due.

SHOW ME HOW

6. Adjusting entries   Obj. 4

Castle Furnishings Company uses a perpetual inventory system. Journalize the November 30 adjusting entries based upon the following:

A. Sales returns of $40,000 and merchandise returns of $15,000 are estimated for the current year's sales.
B. The inventory account has a balance of $675,400, while physical inventory indicates that $663,800 of merchandise is on hand. Assume any shrinkage is a normal amount.

Answers provided after Problem. Need more practice? Find additional multiple-choice questions, exercises, and problems in CengageNOWv2.

Problem

The following transactions were completed by Montrose Company during May of the current year. Montrose uses a perpetual inventory system.

May 3. Purchased merchandise on account from Floyd Co., $4,000, terms FOB shipping point, 2/10, n/30, with prepaid freight of $120 added to the invoice.

5. Purchased merchandise on account from Kramer Co., $8,500, terms FOB destination, 1/10, n/30.

6. Sold merchandise on account to C. F. Howell Co., list price $4,000, trade discount 30%, terms 2/10, n/30. The cost of the goods sold was $1,125.

8. Purchased office supplies for cash, $150.

May 10. Returned merchandise purchased on May 5 from Kramer Co., $1,300.

13. Paid Floyd Co. on account for purchase of May 3.

14. Purchased merchandise for cash, $10,500.

15. Paid Kramer Co. on account for purchase of May 5, less return of May 10.

16. Received cash on account from sale of May 6 to C. F. Howell Co.

19. Sold merchandise on MasterCard credit cards, $2,450. The cost of the goods sold was $980.

22. Sold merchandise for cash to Comer Co., $3,480. The cost of the goods sold was $1,400.

24. Sold merchandise on account to Smith Co., $4,350. The cost of the goods sold was $1,750.

25. Refunded Comer Co. $1,480 for returned merchandise from sale on May 22. The cost of the returned merchandise was $600.

31. Paid a service processing fee of $140 for MasterCard sales.

Instructions

1. Journalize the preceding transactions.

2. Journalize the adjusting entries for estimated customer refunds and returns. Assume that sales of $3,000 are estimated to be refunded and inventory costing $1,800 is estimated to be returned.

3. Journalize the adjusting entry for inventory shrinkage, $3,750.

Need more practice? Find additional multiple-choice questions, exercises, and problems in CengageNOWv2.

Answers

Multiple-Choice Questions

1. **A** A debit memo (answer A), issued by the buyer, indicates the amount the buyer proposes to debit to the accounts payable account. A credit memo (answer B), issued by the seller, indicates the amount the seller proposes to credit to the accounts receivable account. An invoice (answer C) or a bill (answer D), issued by the seller, indicates the amount and terms of the sale.

2. **C** The amount of discount for early payment is $10 (answer C), or 1% of $1,000. Although the $50 of freight paid by the seller is debited to the customer's account, the customer is not entitled to a discount on that amount.

3. **B** The single-step form of income statement (answer B) is so named because the total of all expenses is deducted in one step from the total of all revenues. The multiple-step form (answer A) includes numerous sections and subsections with several subtotals. The account form (answer C) and the report form (answer D) are two common forms of the balance sheet.

4. **C** Gross profit (answer C) is the excess of net sales over the cost of goods sold. Operating income (answer A) or income from operations (answer B) is the excess of gross profit over operating expenses. Net income (answer D) is the final figure on the income statement after all revenues and expenses have been reported.

5. **D** Expenses such as interest expense (answer D) that cannot be associated directly with operations are identified as other expense or nonoperating expense. Depreciation expense— office equipment (answer A) is an administrative expense. Sales salaries expense (answer B) is a selling expense. Insurance expense (answer C) is a mixed expense with elements of both selling expense and administrative expense. For small businesses, insurance expense is usually reported as an administrative expense.

Exercises

1. $1,890,000 ($615,000 + $4,110,000 − $2,835,000)

2.

   A. $13,328. Purchase of $18,228 [$18,600 − ($18,600 × 2%)] less the return of $4,900 [$5,000 − ($5,000 × 2%)]

   B. Inventory

3.

   A.

Accounts Receivable	71,050	
Sales		71,050
[$72,500 − ($72,500 × 2%)]		
Cost of Good Sold	43,500	
Inventory		43,500

   B.

Cash	71,050	
Accounts Receivable		71,050

   C.

Customer Refunds Payable	1,000	
Cash		1,000

4.

   A. $75,250. Purchase of $89,100 [$90,000 ($90,000 × 1%)] less return of $14,850 [$15,000 − ($15,000 × 1%)] plus $1,000 of shipping.

   B. $99,470. Purchase of $107,800 [$110,000 − ($110,000 × 2%)] less return of $8,330 [$8,500 − ($8,500 × 2%)].

5.

Sather Co. journal entries:

Accounts Receivable—Boone Co.	31,164	
Sales		31,164
[$31,800 − ($31,800 × 2%)]		
Cost of Goods Sold	19,000	
Inventory		19,000
Cash	31,164	
Accounts Receivable—Boone Co.		31,164

Boone Co. journal entries:

Inventory [$31,800 − ($31,800 × 2%)]	31,164	
Accounts Payable—Sather Co.		31,164
Accounts Payable—Sather Co.	31,164	
Cash		31,164

6.

   A.

Sales	40,000	
Customer Refunds Payable		40,000
Estimated Returns Inventory	15,000	
Cost of Goods Sold		15,000

   B.

Nov.	30	Cost of Goods Sold	11,600	
		Inventory		11,600
		($675,400 − $663,800)		

Need more help? Watch step-by-step videos of how to compute answers to these Exercises in CengageNOWv2.

Problem

1.	May 3	Inventory [$4,000 − ($4,000 × 2%)] + $120		4,040	
		Accounts Payable—Floyd Co.			4,040
	5	Inventory [$8,500 − ($8,500 × 1%)]		8,415	
		Accounts Payable—Kramer Co.			8,415
	6	Accounts Receivable—C. F. Howell Co.		2,744	
		Sales			2,744
		[$4,000 − (30% × $4,000)] = $2,800			
		[$2,800 − ($2,800 × 2%)] = $2,744			
	6	Cost of Goods Sold		1,125	
		Inventory			1,125
	8	Office Supplies		150	
		Cash			150
	10	Accounts Payable—Kramer Co. [$1,300 − ($1,300 × 1%)]		1,287	
		Inventory			1,287
	13	Accounts Payable—Floyd Co.		4,040	
		Cash			4,040
	14	Inventory		10,500	
		Cash			10,500
	15	Accounts Payable—Kramer Co. ($8,415 − $1,287)		7,128	
		Cash			7,128
	16	Cash		2,744	
		Accounts Receivable—C. F. Howell Co.			2,744
	19	Cash		2,450	
		Sales			2,450
	19	Cost of Goods Sold		980	
		Inventory			980
	22	Cash		3,480	
		Sales			3,480
	22	Cost of Goods Sold		1,400	
		Inventory			1,400
	24	Accounts Receivable—Smith Co.		4,350	
		Sales			4,350
	24	Cost of Goods Sold		1,750	
		Inventory			1,750
	25	Customer Refunds Payable		1,480	
		Cash			1,480
	25	Inventory		600	
		Estimated Returns Inventory			600
	31	Credit Card Expense		140	
		Cash			140
2.	May 31	Sales		3,000	
		Customer Refunds Payable			3,000
	31	Estimated Returns Inventory		1,800	
		Cost of Goods Sold			1,800
3.	May 31	Cost of Goods Sold		3,750	
		Inventory			3,750

Discussion Questions

1. What distinguishes a merchandising business from a service business?

2. Can a business earn a gross profit but incur a net loss? Explain.

3. The credit period during which the buyer of merchandise is allowed to pay usually begins with what date?

4. What is the meaning of (A) 1/15, n/60; (B) n/30; (c) n/eom?

5. How are sales to customers using MasterCard and VISA recorded?

6. What is the nature of (A) a credit memo issued by the seller of merchandise, (B) a debit memo issued by the buyer of merchandise?

7. Who is responsible for freight when the terms of sale are (A) FOB shipping point, (B) FOB destination?

8. Name three accounts that would normally appear in the chart of accounts of a merchandising business but would not appear in the chart of accounts of a service business.

9. Audio Outfitter Inc., which uses a perpetual inventory system, experienced a normal inventory shrinkage of $13,675. What accounts would be debited and credited to record the adjustment for the inventory shrinkage at the end of the accounting period?

10. Assume that Audio Outfitter Inc. in Discussion Question 9 experienced an abnormal inventory shrinkage of $98,600. Audio Outfitter has decided to record the abnormal inventory shrinkage so that it would be separately disclosed on the income statement. What account would be debited for the abnormal inventory shrinkage?

Basic Exercises

SHOW ME HOW

BE 5-1   Gross profit   **Obj. 1**

During the current year, merchandise is sold for $18,300 cash and $295,700 on account. The cost of the goods sold is $188,000. What is the amount of the gross profit?

SHOW ME HOW

BE 5-2   Purchases transactions   **Obj. 2**

Hoffman Company purchased merchandise on account from a supplier for $65,000, terms 1/10, n/30. Hoffman returned $7,500 of the merchandise and received full credit.

A.   If Hoffman Company pays the invoice within the discount period, what is the amount of cash required for the payment?

B.   What account is debited by Hoffman Company to record the return?

SHOW ME HOW

BE 5-3   Sales transactions   **Obj. 2**

Journalize the following merchandise transactions:

A.   Sold merchandise on account, $92,500 with terms 1/10, n/30. The cost of the goods sold was $55,500.

B.   Received payment less the discount.

C.   Refunded $750 to customer for defective merchandise that was not returned.

SHOW ME HOW

BE 5-4   Freight terms   **Obj. 2**

Determine the amount to be paid in full settlement of each of two invoices, (A) and (B), assuming that credit for returns and allowances was received prior to payment and that all invoices were paid within the discount period.

	Merchandise	Freight Paid by Seller	Freight Terms	Returns and Allowances
A.	$36,000	$800	FOB destination, 1/10, n/30	$4,000
B.	44,900	375	FOB shipping point, 2/10, n/30	2,400

SHOW ME HOW

BE 5-5 Transactions for buyer and seller　　　　　　　　　　　　　　　Obj. 2

Shore Co. sold merchandise to Blue Star Co. on account, $112,000, terms FOB shipping point, 2/10, n/30. The cost of the goods sold is $67,200. Shore paid freight of $1,800. Journalize the entries for Shore and Blue Star for the sale, purchase, and payment of amount due.

SHOW ME HOW

BE 5-6 Adjusting entries　　　　　　　　　　　　　　　　　　　　　　Obj. 4

Hahn Flooring Company uses a perpetual inventory system. Journalize the December 31 adjusting entries based upon the following:

A.　Sales returns of $125,000 and merchandise returns of $80,000 are estimated for the current year's sales.

B.　The inventory account has a balance of $1,333,150, while physical inventory indicates that $1,309,900 of merchandise is on hand. Assume any shrinkage is a normal amount.

Exercises

SHOW ME HOW

EX 5-1 Determining gross profit　　　　　　　　　　　　　　　　　　　Obj. 1

During the current year, merchandise is sold for $11,750,000. The cost of the goods sold is $7,050,000.

A.　What is the amount of the gross profit?

B.　Compute the gross profit percentage (gross profit divided by sales).

C.　━━━▶ Will the income statement always report a net income? Explain.

SHOW ME HOW　
REAL WORLD

EX 5-2 Determining cost of goods sold　　　　　　　　　　　　　　　　Obj. 1

For a recent year, **Best Buy** reported sales of $42,410 million. Its gross profit was $9,690 million. What was the amount of Best Buy's cost of goods sold?

SHOW ME HOW

EX 5-3 Purchase-related transactions　　　　　　　　　　　　　　　　Obj. 2

The Stationery Company purchased merchandise on account from a supplier for $28,900, terms 1/10, n/30. The Stationery Company returned $6,100 of the merchandise and received full credit.

A.　What is the amount of cash required for the payment?

B.　Under a perpetual inventory system, what account is credited by The Stationery Company to record the return?

EX 5-4 Purchase-related transactions　　　　　　　　　　　　　　　　Obj. 2

A retailer is considering the purchase of 250 units of a specific item from either of two suppliers. Their offers are as follows:

Supplier One: $400 a unit, total of $100,000, 1/10, n/30, no charge for freight.

Supplier Two: $399 a unit, total of $99,750, 2/10, n/30, plus freight of $975.

Which of the two offers, Supplier One or Supplier Two, yields the lower price?

EX 5-5 Purchase-related transactions　　　　　　　　　　　　　　　　Obj. 2

━━━▶ The debits and credits from four related transactions, A through D, are presented in the following T accounts. Describe each transaction.

Cash		
	B	300
	D	16,660

Accounts Payable				
C	3,920	A	20,580
D	16,660		

Inventory			
A	20,580	C	3,920
B	300		

SHOW ME HOW

EX 5-6   Purchase-related transactions   Obj. 2

Warwick's Co., a women's clothing store, purchased $75,000 of merchandise from a supplier on account, terms FOB destination, 2/10, n/30. Warwick's returned $9,000 of the merchandise, receiving a credit memo. Journalize Warwick's entries to record (A) the purchase, (B) the merchandise return, and (C) the payment within the discount period of ten days, and (D) payment beyond the discount period of ten days.

SHOW ME HOW

EX 5-7   Purchase-related transactions   Obj. 2

Journalize entries for the following related transactions of Lilly Heating & Air Company:

A. Purchased $36,000 of merchandise from Schell Co. on account, terms 1/10, n/30.
B. Paid the amount owed on the invoice within the discount period.
C. Discovered that $9,000 of the merchandise purchased in (A) was defective and returned items, receiving credit.
D. Purchased $5,000 of merchandise from Schell Co. on account, terms n/30.
E. Received a refund from Schell Co. for return in (C) less the purchase in (D).

EX 5-8   Sales-related transactions, including the use of credit cards   Obj. 2

Journalize the entries for the following transactions:

A. Sold merchandise for cash, $25,000. The cost of the goods sold was $17,500.
B. Sold merchandise on account, $98,000. The cost of the goods sold was $58,800.
C. Sold merchandise to customers who used MasterCard and VISA, $475,000. The cost of the goods sold was $280,000.
D. Sold merchandise to customers who used American Express, $63,000. The cost of the goods sold was $39,000.
E. Received an invoice from National Clearing House Credit Co. for $13,450 representing a service fee paid for processing MasterCard, VISA, and American Express sales.

EX 5-9   Customer refund   Obj. 2

Senger Company sold merchandise of $15,500, terms 2/10, n/30, to Burris Inc. on April 23. Burris paid Senger for the merchandise on May 2. On May 12, Senger paid Burris $650 for costs incurred by Burris to repair defective merchandise. (A) Journalize the entry by Senger Company to record the customer refund to Burris Inc. (B) Assume that instead of paying Burris cash, Senger issued a credit memo to Burris to be used against Burris's outstanding account receivable balance. Journalize the entry by Senger Company to record the issuance of the credit memo.

EX 5-10   Customer return and refund   Obj. 2

On December 28, Silverman Enterprises sold $18,500 of merchandise to Beasley Co. with terms 2/10, n/30. The cost of the goods sold was $11,200. On December 31, Silverman prepared its adjusting entries, yearly financial statements, and closing entries. On January 3, Silverman issued Beasley a credit memo for returned merchandise. The returned merchandise originally cost Silverman $2,350 and was billed (invoiced) for $4,000 with terms 2/10, n/30. (A) Journalize the entries by Silverman Enterprises to record the December 28 sale. Beasley paid the balance due on January 7. (B) Journalize the entries by Silverman Enterprises to record the merchandise returned January 3. (C) Journalize the entry to record the receipt of the amount due by Beasley Co. on January 7.

SHOW ME HOW

EX 5-11   Sales-related transactions   Obj. 2

After the amount due on a sale of $28,000, terms 2/10, n/eom, is received from a customer within the discount period, the seller consents to the return of the entire shipment for a cash refund. The cost of the merchandise returned is $16,800. (A) What is the amount of the refund owed to the customer? (B) Journalize the entries made by the seller to record the return and the refund.

EX 5-12 Sales-related transactions

Obj. 2

The debits and credits for five related transactions, A through E, are presented in the following T accounts. Describe each transaction.

Cash				Sales		
E	39,200				A	41,160

Accounts Receivable				Cost of Goods Sold		
A	41,160	C	1,960	B	25,200	
		E	39,200			

Inventory			
D	1,200	B	25,200

Estimated Returns Inventory		
	D	1,200

Customer Refunds Payable		
C	1,960	

EX 5-13 Sales-related transactions

Obj. 2

Sayers Co. sold merchandise on account to a customer for $80,000 terms 2/10, n/30. The cost of the goods sold was $58,000. Journalize Sayers' entries to record (A) the sale, (B) the receipt of payment within the discount period, and (C) the receipt of payment beyond the discount period of ten days.

✔ A. $30,400

EX 5-14 Determining amounts to be paid on invoices

Obj. 2

Determine the amount to be paid in full settlement of each of the following invoices, assuming that credit for returns and allowances was received prior to payment and that all invoices were paid within the discount period:

	Merchandise	Freight Paid by Seller		Customer Returns and Allowances
A.	$32,000	—	FOB destination, n/30	$1,600
B.	12,800	$300	FOB shipping point, 2/10, n/30	2,500
C.	21,000	—	FOB shipping point, 1/10, n/30	4,000
D.	9,000	175	FOB shipping point, 2/10, n/30	1,000
E.	77,400	—	FOB destination, 1/10, n/30	—

EX 5-15 Sales-related transactions

Obj. 2

Showcase Co., a furniture wholesaler, sells merchandise to Balboa Co. on account, $254,500, terms n/30. The cost of the goods sold is $152,700. Showcase issues a credit memo for $30,000 for merchandise returned prior to Balboa paying the original invoice. The cost of the merchandise returned is $17,500. Journalize Showcase Co.'s entries for (A) the sale, including the cost of the goods sold, (B) the credit memo, including the cost of the returned merchandise, and (C) the receipt of the check for the amount due from Balboa Co.

EX 5-16 Purchase-related transactions

Obj. 2

Based on the data presented in Exercise 5-15, journalize Balboa Co.'s entries for (A) the purchase, (B) the return of the merchandise for credit, and (C) the payment of the invoice.

EX 5-17 Chart of accounts

Obj. 2

Monet Paints Co. is a newly organized business with a list of accounts arranged in alphabetical order, as follows:

Accounts Payable	Inventory
Accounts Receivable	Land
Accumulated Depreciation—Office Equipment	Miscellaneous Administrative Expense
Accumulated Depreciation—Store Equipment	Miscellaneous Selling Expense
Advertising Expense	Notes Payable
Cash	Office Equipment
Common Stock	Office Salaries Expense
Cost of Goods Sold	Office Supplies
Customer Refunds Payable	Office Supplies Expense
Delivery Expense	Prepaid Insurance
Depreciation Expense—Office Equipment	Rent Expense
Depreciation Expense—Store Equipment	Retained Earnings
Dividends	Salaries Payable
Estimated Returns Inventory	Sales
Income Summary	Sales Salaries Expense
Insurance Expense	Store Equipment
Interest Expense	Store Supplies
Interest Revenue	Store Supplies Expense

Construct a chart of accounts, assigning account numbers and arranging the accounts in balance sheet and income statement order, as illustrated in Exhibit 10. Each account number is three digits: the first digit is to indicate the major classification (1 for assets, and so on); the second digit is to indicate the subclassification (11 for current assets, and so on); and the third digit is to identify the specific account (110 for Cash, 112 for Accounts Receivable, 114 for Inventory, 115 for Estimated Returns Inventory, and so on).

EX 5-18 Sales tax

Obj. 2

✔C. $38,880

SHOW ME HOW

A sale of merchandise on account for $36,000 is subject to an 8% sales tax. (A) Should the sales tax be recorded at the time of sale or when payment is received? (B) What is the amount credited to sales? (C) What is the amount debited to Accounts Receivable? (D) What is the account to which the $2,880 ($36,000 × 8%) is credited?

EX 5-19 Sales tax transactions

Obj. 2

SHOW ME HOW

Journalize the entries to record the following selected transactions:

A. Sold $640,000 of merchandise on account, subject to a sales tax of 7%. The cost of the goods sold was $385,000.
B. Paid $61,750 to the state sales tax department for taxes collected.

EX 5-20 Normal balances of merchandise accounts

Obj. 2

What is the normal balance of the following accounts: (A) Cost of Goods Sold, (B) Customer Refunds Payable, (C) Delivery Expense, (D) Estimated Returns Inventory, (E) Inventory, (F) Sales, (G) Sales Tax Payable.

EX 5-21 Income statement and accounts for merchandiser

Obj. 3

SHOW ME HOW

For the fiscal year, sales were $46,680,000 and the cost of goods sold was $28,000,000.

A. What was the amount of gross profit?
B. If total operating expenses were $5,000,000 could you determine net income?
C. Is Customer Refunds Payable an asset, liability, or stockholders' equity account and what is its normal balance?
D. Is Estimated Returns Inventory an asset, liability, or stockholders' equity account and what is its normal balance?

EX 5-22 Income statement for merchandiser

Obj. 3

The following expenses were incurred by a merchandising business during the year. In which expense section of the income statement should each be reported: (A) selling, (B) administrative, or (C) other?

1. Advertising expense
2. Depreciation expense on store equipment
3. Insurance expense on office equipment
4. Interest expense on notes payable
5. Rent expense on office building
6. Salaries of office personnel
7. Salary of sales manager
8. Sales supplies used

SHOW ME HOW

EX 5-23 Determining amounts for items omitted from income statement

Obj. 3

One item is omitted in each of the following four lists of income statement data. Determine the amounts of the missing items, identifying them by letter.

	Chase Company	Jessup Inc.	Osterman Company	Snyder Co.
Sales	$735,000	B	$8,220,000	D
Cost of goods sold	A	$157,850	C	44,500
Gross profit	110,000	42,150	2,300,000	15,500

✔ A. Net income:
$1,720,000

SHOW ME HOW

EXCEL TEMPLATE

EX 5-24 Multiple-step income statement

Obj. 3

On March 31, 2018, the balances of the accounts appearing in the ledger of Royal Furnishings Company, a furniture wholesaler, are as follows:

Accounts Receivable	$ 170,000	Inventory	$ 980,000
Accumulated Depreciation—Building	750,000	Notes Payable	250,000
Administrative Expenses	435,000	Office Supplies	20,000
Building	3,500,000	Retained Earnings	1,987,000
Cash	80,000	Salaries Payable	8,000
Common Stock	300,000	Sales	8,245,000
Cost of Goods Sold	5,500,000	Selling Expenses	575,000
Dividends	175,000	Store Supplies	90,000
Interest Expense	15,000		

A. Prepare a multiple-step income statement for the year ended March 31, 2018.

B. ➡ Compare the major advantages and disadvantages of the multiple-step and single-step forms of income statements.

EX 5-25 Multiple-step income statement

Obj. 3

The following income statement for Curbstone Company was prepared for the year ended August 31, 2018:

Curbstone Company
Income Statement
For the Year Ended August 31, 2018

Sales		$8,595,000
Cost of goods sold		6,110,000
Income from operations		$2,485,000
Expenses:		
Selling expenses	$800,000	
Administrative expenses	575,000	
Delivery expense	425,000	
Total expenses		1,800,000
		$ 685,000
Other expense:		
Interest revenue		45,000
Gross profit		$ 640,000

A. Identify the errors in the income statement.

B. Prepare a corrected income statement.

EX 5-26 Single-step income statement   Obj. 3

Summary operating data for Custom Wire & Tubing Company during the year ended April 30, 2018, are as follows: cost of goods sold, $6,100,000; administrative expenses, $740,000; interest expense, $25,000; rent revenue, $60,000; sales, $9,332,500; and selling expenses, $1,250,000. Prepare a single-step income statement.

EX 5-27 Adjusting entry for customer refunds, allowances, and returns   Obj. 4

Scott Company had sales of $12,350,000 and related cost of goods sold of $7,500,000. Scott provides customers a refund for any returned or damaged merchandise. At the end of the year, Scott estimates that customers will request refunds for 0.8% of sales and estimates that merchandise costing $48,000 will be returned. Journalize the adjusting entries on December 31 to record the expected customer returns.

EX 5-28 Adjusting entry for customer refunds, allowances, and returns   Obj. 4

Statz Company had sales of $1,800,000 and related cost of goods sold of $1,150,000 for its first year of operations ending December 31. Statz provides customers a refund for any returned or damaged merchandise. At the end of the year, Statz estimates that customers will request refunds for 1.5% of sales and estimates that merchandise costing $16,000 will be returned. Assume that on February 3 of the following year, Buck Co. returned merchandise with a selling price of $5,000 for a cash refund. The returned merchandise originally cost Statz $3,100. (A) Journalize the adjusting entries on December 31 to record the expected customer returns. (B) Journalize the entries to record the returned merchandise and cash refund to Buck Co. on February 3.

EX 5-29 Adjusting entry for inventory shrinkage   Obj. 4

Omega Tire Co.'s perpetual inventory records indicate that $3,145,000 of merchandise should be on hand on August 31. The physical inventory indicates that $3,113,500 of merchandise is actually on hand. Journalize the adjusting entry for the inventory shrinkage for Omega Tire Co. for the fiscal year ended August 31.

EX 5-30 Closing the accounts of a merchandiser   Obj. 4

From the following list, identify the accounts that should be closed to Income Summary at the end of the fiscal year under a perpetual inventory system: (A) Accounts Payable, (B) Advertising Expense, (C) Cost of Goods Sold, (D) Dividends, (E) Inventory, (F) Sales, (G) Supplies, (H) Supplies Expense, (I) Wages Payable.

EX 5-31 Closing entries; net income   Obj. 4

Based on the data presented in Exercise 5-24, journalize the closing entries.

EX 5-32 Closing entries   Obj. 4

On July 31, the close of the fiscal year, the balances of the accounts appearing in the ledger of Serbian Interiors Company, a furniture wholesaler, are as follows:

Accumulated Depr.—Building	$365,000	Inventory	$ 115,000
Administrative Expenses	440,000	Notes Payable	100,000
Building	810,000	Retained Earnings	455,000
Cash	78,000	Sales	1,437,000
Common Stock	75,000	Sales Tax Payable	4,500
Cost of Goods Sold	775,000	Selling Expenses	160,000
Dividends	15,000	Store Supplies	16,000
Interest Expense	6,000	Store Supplies Expense	21,500

Prepare the July 31 closing entries for Serbian Interiors Company.

Appendix

EX 5-33 Rules of debit and credit for periodic inventory accounts

Complete the following table by indicating for A through G whether the proper answer is debit or credit:

Account	Increase	Decrease	Normal Balance
Purchases	debit	A	B
Purchases Discounts	credit	C	credit
Purchases Returns and Allowances	D	E	F
Freight In	debit	G	debit

Appendix

EX 5-34 Journal entries using the periodic inventory system

The following selected transactions were completed by Air Systems Company during January of the current year. Air Systems uses the periodic inventory system.

Jan. 2. Purchased $18,200 of merchandise on account, FOB shipping point, terms 2/15, n/30.
  5. Paid freight of $190 on the January 2 purchase.
  6. Returned $2,750 of the merchandise purchased on January 2.
  13. Sold merchandise on account, $37,300, FOB destination, 1/10, n/30. The cost of goods sold was $22,400.
  15. Paid freight of $215 for the merchandise sold on January 13.
  17. Paid for the purchase of January 2 less the return and discount.
  23. Received payment on account for the sale of January 13 less the discount.

Journalize the entries to record the transactions of Air Systems Company.

Appendix

EX 5-35 Identify items missing in determining cost of goods sold

For (A) through (E), identify the items designated by X and Y.

A. Purchases – (X + Y) = Net purchases
B. Net purchases + X = Cost of inventory purchased
C. Inventory (beginning) + Cost of inventory purchased = X
D. Inventory available for sale – X = Cost of inventory before estimated returns
E. Cost of goods sold before estimated returns – X = Cost of goods sold

Appendix

EX 5-36 Cost of goods sold and related items

✔ A. Cost of goods sold, $3,540,000

The following data were extracted from the accounting records of Harkins Company for the year ended April 30, 2018:

Estimated returns of current year sales	$ 11,600
Inventory, May 1, 2017	380,000
Inventory, April 30, 2018	415,000
Purchases	3,800,000
Purchases returns and allowances	150,000
Purchases discounts	80,000
Sales	5,850,000
Freight in	16,600

A. Prepare the cost of goods sold section of the income statement for the year ended April 30, 2018, using the periodic inventory system.

B. Determine the gross profit to be reported on the income statement for the year ended April 30, 2018.

C. ➤ Would gross profit be different if the perpetual inventory system was used instead of the periodic inventory system?

Appendix

EX 5-37 Cost of goods sold

Based on the following data, determine the cost of goods sold for November:

Estimated returns of November sales	$ 14,500
Inventory, November 1	28,000
Inventory, November 30	31,500
Purchases	475,000
Purchases returns and allowances	15,000
Purchases discounts	9,000
Freight in	7,000

Appendix

EX 5-38 Cost of goods sold

Based on the following data, determine the cost of goods sold for July:

Estimated returns of July sales	$ 34,900
Inventory, July 1	190,850
Inventory, July 31	160,450
Purchases	1,126,000
Purchases returns and allowances	46,000
Purchases discounts	23,000
Freight in	17,500

Appendix

EX 5-39 Cost of goods sold

✔ Correct cost of goods sold, $990,000

Identify the errors in the following schedule of the cost of goods sold for the year ended May 31, 2018:

Cost of goods sold:		
Inventory, May 31, 2018		$ 105,000
Cost of merchandise purchased:		
Purchases	$1,110,000	
Purchases returns and allowances	55,000	
Purchases discounts.....................................	30,000	
Freight in..	(22,000)	
Total cost of merchandise purchased..................		1,173,000
Inventory available for sale		$1,278,000
Less inventory, June 1, 2017		91,300
Cost of goods sold before estimated returns		$1,186,700
Estimated returns of this year's sales		43,300
Cost of goods sold		$1,230,000

Appendix

EX 5-40 Closing entries using periodic inventory system

United Rug Company is a small rug retailer owned and operated by Pat Kirwan. After the accounts have been adjusted on December 31, the following selected account balances were taken from the ledger:

Advertising Expense...	$ 36,000
Depreciation Expense	13,000
Dividends	65,000
Freight In..	17,000
Inventory, December 1...	375,000
Inventory, December 31	460,000
Miscellaneous Expense	9,000
Purchases..	1,760,000
Purchases Discounts...	35,000
Purchases Returns and Allowances	45,000
Salaries Expense	375,000
Sales	2,220,000

The estimated cost of merchandise returns from December sales is $20,000. Journalize the closing entries.

Problems: Series A

GENERAL LEDGER

PR 5-1A Purchase-related transactions using perpetual inventory system   Obj. 2

The following selected transactions were completed by Capers Company during October of the current year:

Oct. 1. Purchased merchandise from UK Imports Co., $14,448, terms FOB destination, n/30.
   3. Purchased merchandise from Hoagie Co., $9,950, terms FOB shipping point, 2/10, n/eom. Prepaid freight of $220 was added to the invoice.
   4. Purchased merchandise from Taco Co., $13,650, terms FOB destination, 2/10, n/30.
   6. Issued debit memo to Taco Co. for $4,550 of merchandise returned from purchase on October 4.
  13. Paid Hoagie Co. for invoice of October 3.
  14. Paid Taco Co. for invoice of October 4, less debit memo of October 6.
  19. Purchased merchandise from Veggie Co., $27,300, terms FOB shipping point, n/eom.
  19. Paid freight of $400 on October 19 purchase from Veggie Co.
  20. Purchased merchandise from Caesar Salad Co., $22,000, terms FOB destination, 1/10, n/30.
  30. Paid Caesar Salad Co. for invoice of October 20.
  31. Paid UK Imports Co. for invoice of October 1.
  31. Paid Veggie Co. for invoice of October 19.

Instructions

Journalize the entries to record the transactions of Capers Company for October.

SHOW ME HOW

EXCEL TEMPLATE

GENERAL LEDGER

PR 5-2A Sales-related transactions using perpetual inventory system   Obj. 2

The following selected transactions were completed by Amsterdam Supply Co., which sells office supplies primarily to wholesalers and occasionally to retail customers:

Mar. 2. Sold merchandise on account to Equinox Co., $18,900, terms FOB destination, 1/10, n/30. The cost of the goods sold was $13,300.
   3. Sold merchandise for $11,350 plus 6% sales tax to retail cash customers. The cost of the goods sold was $7,000.
   4. Sold merchandise on account to Empire Co., $55,400, terms FOB shipping point, n/eom. The cost of the goods sold was $33,200.
   5. Sold merchandise for $30,000 plus 6% sales tax to retail customers who used MasterCard. The cost of the goods sold was $19,400.
  12. Received check for amount due from Equinox Co. for sale on March 2.
  14. Sold merchandise to customers who used American Express cards, $13,700. The cost of the goods sold was $8,350.
  16. Sold merchandise on account to Targhee Co., $27,500, terms FOB shipping point, 1/10, n/30. The cost of the goods sold was $16,000.
  18. Issued credit memo for $4,800 to Targhee Co. for merchandise returned from sale on March 16. The cost of the merchandise returned was $2,900.
  19. Sold merchandise on account to Vista Co., $8,250, terms FOB shipping point, 2/10, n/30. Added $75 to the invoice for prepaid freight. The cost of the goods sold was $5,000.
  26. Received check for amount due from Targhee Co. for sale on March 16 less credit memo of March 18.
  28. Received check for amount due from Vista Co. for sale of March 19.
  31. Received check for amount due from Empire Co. for sale of March 4.
  31. Paid Fleetwood Delivery Service $5,600 for merchandise delivered during March to customers under shipping terms of FOB destination.
Apr. 3. Paid City Bank $940 for service fees for handling MasterCard and American Express sales during March.
  15. Paid $6,544 to state sales tax division for taxes owed on sales.

Instructions

Journalize the entries to record the transactions of Amsterdam Supply Co.

SHOW ME HOW   GENERAL LEDGER

PR 5-3A   Sales-related and purchase-related transactions using perpetual inventory system

Obj. 2

The following were selected from among the transactions completed by Babcock Company during November of the current year:

Nov. 3. Purchased merchandise on account from Moonlight Co., list price $85,000, trade discount 25%, terms FOB destination, 2/10, n/30.

4. Sold merchandise for cash, $37,680. The cost of the goods sold was $22,600.

5. Purchased merchandise on account from Papoose Creek Co., $47,500, terms FOB shipping point, 2/10, n/30, with prepaid freight of $810 added to the invoice.

6. Returned $13,500 ($18,000 list price less trade discount of 25%) of merchandise purchased on November 3 from Moonlight Co.

8. Sold merchandise on account to Quinn Co., $15,600 with terms n/15. The cost of the goods sold was $9,400.

13. Paid Moonlight Co. on account for purchase of November 3, less return of November 6.

14. Sold merchandise on VISA, $236,000. The cost of the goods sold was $140,000.

15. Paid Papoose Creek Co. on account for purchase of November 5.

23. Received cash on account from sale of November 8 to Quinn Co.

24. Sold merchandise on account to Rabel Co., $56,900, terms 1/10, n/30. The cost of the goods sold was $34,000.

28. Paid VISA service fee of $3,540.

30. Paid Quinn Co. a cash refund of $6,000 for returned merchandise from sale of November 8. The cost of the returned merchandise was $3,300.

Instructions

Journalize the transactions.

PR 5-4A   Sales-related and purchase-related transactions for seller and buyer using perpetual inventory system

Obj. 2

The following selected transactions were completed during August between Summit Company and Beartooth Co.:

Aug. 1. Summit Company sold merchandise on account to Beartooth Co., $48,000, terms FOB destination, 2/15, n/eom. The cost of the goods sold was $28,800.

2. Summit Company paid freight of $1,150 for delivery of merchandise sold to Beartooth Co. on August 1.

5. Summit Company sold merchandise on account to Beartooth Co., $66,000, terms FOB shipping point, n/eom. The cost of the goods sold was $40,000.

9. Beartooth Co. paid freight of $2,300 on August 5 purchase from Summit Company.

15. Summit Company sold merchandise on account to Beartooth Co., $58,700, terms FOB shipping point, 1/10, n/30. Summit paid freight of $1,675, which was added to the invoice. The cost of the goods sold was $35,000.

16. Beartooth Co. paid Summit Company for purchase of August 1.

25. Beartooth Co. paid Summit Company on account for purchase of August 15.

31. Beartooth Co. paid Summit Company on account for purchase of August 5.

Instructions

Journalize the August transactions for (1) Summit Company and (2) Beartooth Co.

PR 5-5A   Multiple-step income statement and balance sheet

Obj. 3

✔ 1. Net income
$943,400

EXCEL TEMPLATE   GENERAL LEDGER

The following selected accounts and their current balances appear in the ledger of Clairemont Co. for the fiscal year ended May 31, 2018:

Cash	$ 240,000	Retained Earnings	$ 2,949,100
Accounts Receivable	966,000	Dividends	100,000
Inventory	1,690,000	Sales	11,343,000
Estimated Returns Inventory	22,500	Cost of Goods Sold	7,850,000
Office Supplies	13,500	Sales Salaries Expense	916,000
Prepaid Insurance	8,000	Advertising Expense	550,000
Office Equipment	830,000	Depreciation Expense—	
Accumulated Depreciation—		Store Equipment	140,000
Office Equipment	550,000	Miscellaneous Selling Expense	38,000
Store Equipment	3,600,000	Office Salaries Expense	650,000
Accumulated Depreciation—		Rent Expense	94,000
Store Equipment	1,820,000	Depreciation Expense—	
Accounts Payable	326,000	Office Equipment	50,000
Customer Refunds Payable	40,000	Insurance Expense	48,000
Salaries Payable	41,500	Office Supplies Expense	28,100
Note Payable		Miscellaneous Administrative Exp.	14,500
(final payment due 2024)	300,000	Interest Expense	21,000
Common Stock	500,000		

Instructions

1. Prepare a multiple-step income statement.

2. Prepare a retained earnings statement.

3. Prepare a balance sheet, assuming that the current portion of the note payable is $50,000.

4. ➤ Briefly explain how multiple-step and single-step income statements differ.

PR 5-6A   Single-step income statement and balance sheet

Obj. 3, 4

✔ 3. Total assets:
$5,000,000

EXCEL TEMPLATE

Selected accounts and related amounts for Clairemont Co. for the fiscal year ended May 31, 2018, are presented in Problem 5-5A.

Instructions

1. Prepare a single-step income statement in the format shown in Exhibit 12.

2. Prepare a retained earnings statement.

3. Prepare balance sheet, assuming that the current portion of the note payable is $50,000.

4. Prepare closing entries as of May 31, 2018.

Appendix

PR 5-7A   Purchase-related transactions using periodic inventory system

Selected transactions for Capers Company during October of the current year are listed in Problem 5-1A.

Instructions

Journalize the entries to record the transactions of Capers Company for October using the periodic inventory system.

Appendix

PR 5-8A   Sales-related and purchase-related transactions using periodic inventory system

Selected transactions for Babcock Company during November of the current year are listed in Problem 5-3A.

Instructions

Journalize the entries to record the transactions of Babcock Company for November using the periodic inventory system.

Appendix

PR 5-9A   Sales-related and purchase-related transactions for buyer and seller using periodic inventory system

Selected transactions during August between Summit Company and Beartooth Co. are listed in Problem 5-4A.

Instructions

Journalize the entries to record the transactions for (1) Summit Company and (2) Beartooth Co., assuming that both companies use the periodic inventory system.

Appendix

PR 5-10A   Periodic inventory accounts, multiple-step income statement, closing entries

✔ 2. Net income, $185,000

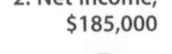

EXCEL TEMPLATE

On December 31, 2018, the balances of the accounts appearing in the ledger of Wyman Company are as follows:

Cash	$ 13,500	Dividends	$ 25,000
Accounts Receivable	72,000	Sales	3,280,000
Inventory, January 1, 2018	257,000	Purchases	2,650,000
Estimated Returns Inventory,		Purchases Returns and Allowances	93,000
January 1, 2018	35,000	Purchases Discounts	37,000
Office Supplies	3,000	Freight In	48,000
Prepaid Insurance	4,500	Sales Salaries Expense	300,000
Land	150,000	Advertising Expense	45,000
Store Equipment	270,000	Delivery Expense	9,000
Accumulated Depreciation—		Depreciation Expense—	
Store Equipment	55,900	Store Equipment	6,000
Office Equipment	78,500	Miscellaneous Selling Expense	12,000
Accumulated Depreciation—		Office Salaries Expense	175,000
Office Equipment	16,000	Rent Expense	28,000
Accounts Payable	77,800	Insurance Expense	3,000
Salaries Payable	3,000	Office Supplies Expense	2,000
Customer Refunds Payable	50,000	Depreciation Expense—	
Unearned Rent	8,300	Office Equipment	1,500
Notes Payable	50,000	Miscellaneous Administrative Expense	3,500
Common Stock	150,000	Rent Revenue	7,000
Retained Earnings	365,600	Interest Expense	2,000

Instructions

1. ➤ Does Wyman Company use a periodic or perpetual inventory system? Explain.

2. Prepare a multiple-step income statement for Wyman Company for the year ended December 31, 2018. The inventory as of December 31, 2018, was $305,000. The estimated cost of customer returns inventory for December 31, 2018, is estimated to increase to $40,000.

3. Prepare the closing entries for Wyman Company as of December 31, 2018.

4. What would be the net income if the perpetual inventory system had been used?

Problems: Series B

GENERAL LEDGER

PR 5-1B   Purchase-related transactions using perpetual inventory system   Obj. 2

The following selected transactions were completed by Niles Co. during March of the current year:

Mar. 1. Purchased merchandise from Haas Co., $43,250, terms FOB shipping point, 2/10, n/eom. Prepaid freight of $650 was added to the invoice.

 5. Purchased merchandise from Whitman Co., $19,175, terms FOB destination, n/30.

 10. Paid Haas Co. for invoice of March 1.

Mar. 13. Purchased merchandise from Jost Co., $15,550, terms FOB destination, 2/10, n/30.

14. Issued debit memo to Jost Co. for $3,750 of merchandise returned from purchase on March 13.

18. Purchased merchandise from Fairhurst Company, $13,560, terms FOB shipping point, n/eom.

18. Paid freight of $140 on March 18 purchase from Fairhurst Company.

19. Purchased merchandise from Bickle Co., $6,500, terms FOB destination, 2/10, n/30.

23. Paid Jost Co. for invoice of March 13, less debit memo of March 14.

29. Paid Bickle Co. for invoice of March 19.

31. Paid Fairhurst Company for invoice of March 18.

31. Paid Whitman Co. for invoice of March 5.

Instructions

Journalize the entries to record the transactions of Niles Co. for March.

SHOW ME HOW   EXCEL TEMPLATE

GENERAL LEDGER

PR 5-2B Sales-related transactions using perpetual inventory system   Obj. 2

The following selected transactions were completed by Green Lawn Supplies Co., which sells irrigation supplies primarily to wholesalers and occasionally to retail customers:

July 1. Sold merchandise on account to Landscapes Co., $33,450, terms FOB shipping point, n/eom. The cost of the goods sold was $20,000.

2. Sold merchandise for $86,000 plus 8% sales tax to retail cash customers. The cost of the goods sold was $51,600.

5. Sold merchandise on account to Peacock Company, $17,500, terms FOB destination, 1/10, n/30. The cost of the goods sold was $10,000.

8. Sold merchandise for $112,000 plus 8% sales tax to retail customers who used VISA cards. The cost of the goods sold was $67,200.

13. Sold merchandise to customers who used MasterCard cards, $96,000. The cost of the goods sold was $57,600.

14. Sold merchandise on account to Loeb Co., $16,000, terms FOB shipping point, 1/10, n/30. The cost of the goods sold was $9,000.

15. Received check for amount due from Peacock Company for sale on July 5.

16. Issued credit memo for $3,000 to Loeb Co. for merchandise returned from the sale on July 14. The cost of the merchandise returned was $1,800.

18. Sold merchandise on account to Jennings Company, $11,350, terms FOB shipping point, 2/10, n/30. Paid $475 for freight and added it to the invoice. The cost of the goods sold was $6,800.

24. Received check for amount due from Loeb Co. for sale on July 14 less credit memo of July 16.

28. Received check for amount due from Jennings Company for sale of July 18.

31. Paid Black Lab Delivery Service $8,550 for merchandise delivered during July to customers under shipping terms of FOB destination.

31. Received check for amount due from Landscapes Co. for sale of July 1.

Aug. 3. Paid Hays Federal Bank $3,770 for service fees for handling MasterCard and VISA sales during July.

10. Paid $41,260 to state sales tax division for taxes owed on sales.

Instructions

Journalize the entries to record the transactions of Green Lawn Supplies Co.

SHOW ME HOW   GENERAL LEDGER

PR 5-3B Sales-related and purchase-related transactions using perpetual   Obj. 2
inventory system

The following were selected from among the transactions completed by Essex Company during July of the current year:

July 3. Purchased merchandise on account from Hamling Co., list price $72,000, trade discount 15%, terms FOB shipping point, 2/10, n/30, with prepaid freight of $1,450 added to the invoice.

5. Purchased merchandise on account from Kester Co., $33,450, terms FOB destination, 2/10, n/30.

6. Sold merchandise on account to Parsley Co., $36,000, terms n/15. The cost of the goods sold was $25,000.

7. Returned $6,850 of merchandise purchased on July 5 from Kester Co.

13. Paid Hamling Co. on account for purchase of July 3.

15. Paid Kester Co. on account for purchase of July 5, less return of July 7.

(Continued)

July 21. Received cash on account from sale of July 6 to Parsley Co.

21. Sold merchandise on MasterCard, $108,000. The cost of the goods sold was $64,800.

22. Sold merchandise on account to Tabor Co., $16,650, terms 2/10, n/30. The cost of the goods sold was $10,000.

23. Sold merchandise for cash, $91,200. The cost of the goods sold was $55,000.

28. Paid Parsley Co. a cash refund of $7,150 for returned merchandise from sale of July 6. The cost of the returned merchandise was $4,250.

31. Paid MasterCard service fee of $1,650.

Instructions
Journalize the transactions.

PR 5-4B   Sales-related and purchase-related transactions for seller and buyer using perpetual inventory system   Obj. 2

The following selected transactions were completed during April between Swan Company and Bird Company:

Apr. 2. Swan Company sold merchandise on account to Bird Company, $32,000, terms FOB shipping point, 2/10, n/30. Swan paid freight of $330, which was added to the invoice. The cost of the goods sold was $19,200.

8. Swan Company sold merchandise on account to Bird Company, $49,500, terms FOB destination, 1/15, n/eom. The cost of the goods sold was $29,700.

8. Swan Company paid freight of $710 for delivery of merchandise sold to Bird Company on April 8.

12. Bird Company paid Swan Company for purchase of April 2.

23. Bird Company paid Swan Company for purchase of April 8.

24. Swan Company sold merchandise on account to Bird Company, $67,350, terms FOB shipping point, n/eom. The cost of the goods sold was $40,400.

26. Bird Company paid freight of $875 on April 24 purchase from Swan Company.

30. Bird Company paid Swan Company on account for purchase of April 24.

Instructions
Journalize the April transactions for (1) Swan Company and (2) Bird Company.

PR 5-5B   Multiple-step income statement and balance sheet   Obj. 3

✔ 1. Net income:
$1,340,000

The following selected accounts and their current balances appear in the ledger of Kanpur Co. for the fiscal year ended June 30, 2018:

EXCEL TEMPLATE   GENERAL LEDGER

Cash	$ 92,000	Retained Earnings		$ 381,000
Accounts Receivable	450,000	Dividends		300,000
Inventory	370,000	Sales		8,925,000
Estimated Returns Inventory	5,000	Cost of Goods Sold		5,620,000
Office Supplies	10,000	Sales Salaries Expense		850,000
Prepaid Insurance	12,000	Advertising Expense		420,000
Office Equipment	220,000	Depreciation Expense—		
Accumulated Depreciation—		Store Equipment		33,000
Office Equipment	58,000	Miscellaneous Selling Expense		18,000
Store Equipment	650,000	Office Salaries Expense		540,000
Accumulated Depreciation—		Rent Expense		48,000
Store Equipment	87,500	Insurance Expense		24,000
Accounts Payable	38,500	Depreciation Expense—		
Customers Refunds Payable	10,000	Office Equipment		10,000
Salaries Payable	4,000	Office Supplies Expense		4,000
Note Payable		Miscellaneous Administrative		
(final payment due 2034)	140,000	Exp.		6,000
Common Stock	50,000	Interest Expense		12,000

Instructions

1. Prepare a multiple-step income statement.

2. Prepare a retained earnings statement.

3. Prepare a balance sheet, assuming that the current portion of the note payable is $7,000.

4. ➡ Briefly explain how multiple-step and single-step income statements differ.

PR 5-6B   Single-step income statement and balance sheet   **Obj. 3, 4**

✔ 3. Total assets: $1,663,500

Selected accounts and related amounts for Kanpur Co. for the fiscal year ended June 30, 2018, are presented in Problem 5-5B.

EXCEL TEMPLATE

Instructions

1. Prepare a single-step income statement in the format shown in Exhibit 12.

2. Prepare a retained earnings statement.

3. Prepare a balance sheet, assuming that the current portion of the note payable is $7,000.

4. Prepare closing entries as of June 30, 2018.

Appendix

PR 5-7B   Purchase-related transactions using periodic inventory system

Selected transactions for Niles Co. during March of the current year are listed in Problem 5-1B.

Instructions

Journalize the entries to record the transactions of Niles Co. for March using the periodic inventory system.

Appendix

PR 5-8B   Sales-related and purchase-related transactions using periodic inventory system

Selected transactions for Essex Company during July of the current year are listed in Problem 5-3B.

Instructions

Journalize the entries to record the transactions of Essex Company for July using the periodic inventory system.

Appendix

PR 5-9B   Sales-related and purchase-related transactions for buyer and seller using periodic inventory system

Selected transactions during April between Swan Company and Bird Company are listed in Problem 5-4B.

Instructions

Journalize the entries to record the transactions for (1) Swan Company and (2) Bird Company assuming that both companies use the periodic inventory system.

Appendix

PR 5-10B   Periodic inventory accounts, multiple-step income statement, closing entries

✔ 2. Net income,
$1,208,000

EXCEL TEMPLATE

On June 30, 2018, the balances of the accounts appearing in the ledger of Simkins Company are as follows:

Cash	$ 125,000	Dividends	$ 275,000
Accounts Receivable	340,000	Sales	6,590,000
Inventory, July 1, 2017	415,000	Purchases	4,100,000
Estimated Returns Inventory,		Purchases Returns and Allowances	32,000
July 1, 2017	25,000	Purchases Discounts	13,000
Office Supplies	9,000	Freight In	45,000
Prepaid Insurance	18,000	Sales Salaries Expense	580,000
Land	300,000	Advertising Expense	315,000
Store Equipment	550,000	Delivery Expense	18,000
Accumulated Depreciation—		Depreciation Expense—	
Store Equipment	190,000	Store Equipment	12,000
Office Equipment	250,000	Miscellaneous Selling Expense	28,000
Accumulated Depreciation—		Office Salaries Expense	375,000
Office Equipment	110,000	Rent Expense	43,000
Accounts Payable	85,000	Insurance Expense	17,000
Customer Refunds Payable	30,000	Office Supplies Expense	5,000
Salaries Payable	9,000	Depreciation Expense—	
Unearned Rent	6,000	Office Equipment	4,000
Notes Payable	50,000	Miscellaneous Administrative Expense	16,000
Common Stock	300,000	Rent Revenue	32,500
Retained Earnings	520,000	Interest Expense	2,500

Instructions

1. ▬▬▬▬▶ Does Simkins Company use a periodic or perpetual inventory system? Explain.

2. Prepare a multiple-step income statement for Simkins Company for the year ended June 30, 2018. The inventory as of June 30, 2018, was $508,000. The estimated cost of customer returns inventory for June 30, 2018 is estimated to increase to $33,000.

3. Prepare the closing entries for Simkins Company as of June 30, 2018.

4. What would be the net income if the perpetual inventory system had been used?

Comprehensive Problem 2

✔ 8. Net income:
$741,855

Palisade Creek Co. is a merchandising business that uses the perpetual inventory system. The account balances for Palisade Creek as of May 1, 2018 (unless otherwise indicated), are as follows:

110	Cash	$ 83,600	312	Dividends	$ 135,000
112	Accounts Receivable	233,900	313	Income Summary	—
115	Inventory	624,400	410	Sales	5,069,000
116	Estimated Returns Inventory	28,000	510	Cost of Goods Sold	2,823,000
117	Prepaid Insurance	16,800	520	Sales Salaries Expense	664,800
118	Store Supplies	11,400	521	Advertising Expense	281,000
123	Store Equipment	569,500	522	Depreciation Expense	—
124	Accumulated Depreciation—		523	Store Supplies Expense	—
	Store Equipment	56,700	529	Miscellaneous Selling Expense	12,600
210	Accounts Payable	96,600	530	Office Salaries Expense	382,100
211	Salaries Payable	—	531	Rent Expense	83,700
212	Customers Refunds Payable	50,000	532	Insurance Expense	—
310	Common Stock	100,000	539	Miscellaneous Administrative	
311	Retained Earnings	585,300		Expense	7,800

During May, the last month of the fiscal year, the following transactions were completed:

May 1. Paid rent for May, $5,000.

    3. Purchased merchandise on account from Martin Co., terms 2/10, n/30, FOB shipping point, $36,000.

May 4. Paid freight on purchase of May 3, $600.

6. Sold merchandise on account to Korman Co., terms 2/10, n/30, FOB shipping point, $68,500. The cost of the goods sold was $41,000.

7. Received $22,300 cash from Halstad Co. on account.

10. Sold merchandise for cash, $54,000. The cost of the goods sold was $32,000.

13. Paid for merchandise purchased on May 3.

15. Paid advertising expense for last half of May, $11,000.

16. Received cash from sale of May 6.

19. Purchased merchandise for cash, $18,700.

19. Paid $33,450 to Buttons Co. on account.

20. Paid Korman Co. a cash refund of $13,230 for returned merchandise from sale of May 6. The invoice amount of the returned merchandise was $13,500 and the cost of the returned merchandise was $8,000.

Record the following transactions on Page 21 of the journal:

May 20. Sold merchandise on account to Crescent Co., terms 1/10, n/30, FOB shipping point, $110,000. The cost of the goods sold was $70,000.

21. For the convenience of Crescent Co., paid freight on sale of May 20, $2,300.

21. Received $42,900 cash from Gee Co. on account.

21. Purchased merchandise on account from Osterman Co., terms 1/10, n/30, FOB destination, $88,000.

24. Returned of damaged merchandise purchased on May 21, receiving a credit memo from the seller for $5,000.

26. Refunded cash on sales made for cash, $7,500. The cost of the merchandise returned was $4,800.

28. Paid sales salaries of $56,000 and office salaries of $29,000.

29. Purchased store supplies for cash, $2,400.

30. Sold merchandise on account to Turner Co., terms 2/10, n/30, FOB shipping point, $78,750. The cost of the goods sold was $47,000.

30. Received cash from sale of May 20 plus freight paid on May 21.

31. Paid for purchase of May 21, less return of May 24.

Instructions

1. Enter the balances of each of the accounts in the appropriate balance column of a four-column account. Write *Balance* in the item section, and place a check mark (⊘) in the Posting Reference column. Journalize the transactions for July, starting on Page 20 of the journal.

2. Post the journal to the general ledger, extending the month-end balances to the appropriate balance columns after all posting is completed. In this problem, you are not required to update or post to the accounts receivable and accounts payable subsidiary ledgers.

3. Prepare an unadjusted trial balance.

4. At the end of May, the following adjustment data were assembled. Analyze and use these data to complete (5) and (6).

A.	Inventory on May 31	$570,000
B.	Insurance expired during the year	12,000
C.	Store supplies on hand on May 31	4,000
D.	Depreciation for the current year	14,000
E.	Accrued salaries on May 31:	

Sales salaries	$7,000	
Office salaries	6,600	13,600

F. The adjustment for customer returns and allowances is $60,000 for sales and $35,000 for cost of goods sold.

5. *(Optional)* Enter the unadjusted trial balance on a 10-column end-of-period spreadsheet (work sheet), and complete the spreadsheet.

6. Journalize and post the adjusting entries. Record the adjusting entries on Page 22 of the journal.

7. Prepare an adjusted trial balance.

8. Prepare an income statement, a retained earnings statement, and a balance sheet.

9. Prepare and post the closing entries. Record the closing entries on Page 23 of the journal. Indicate closed accounts by inserting a line in both the Balance columns opposite the closing entry. Insert the new balance in the retained earnings account.

10. Prepare a post-closing trial balance.

Analysis for Decision Making

REAL WORLD

ADM-1 Continuing Company Analysis—Amazon: Asset turnover ratio

Amazon.com, Inc. is one of the largest Internet retailers in the world. Netflix, Inc. provides digital streaming and DVD rentals in the United States. Amazon and Netflix compete in streaming and digital services, however Amazon also sells many other products through the Internet. The sales and total assets (in millions) from recent financial statements were reported as follows for both companies:

	Amazon	Netflix
Total revenues (sales)	$88,988	$5,505
Total assets:		
Beginning of year	40,159	5,413
End of year	54,505	7,057

A. Based on your knowledge of each company, identify three major assets used by each company in generating revenue.

B. Compute the asset turnover ratio for each company. (Round to two decimal places).

C. Which company generates sales from total assets more efficiently?

SHOW ME HOW

REAL WORLD

ADM-2 Home Depot: Asset turnover ratio

The Home Depot reported the following data (in millions) in its recent financial statements:

	Year 2	Year 1
Total sales	$83,176	$78,812
Total assets:		
Beginning of year	40,518	41,084
End of year	39,946	40,518

A. Determine the asset turnover ratio for Home Depot for Year 2 and Year 1. (Round to two decimal places).

B. ▬▬▬ What conclusions can be drawn from these ratios concerning the trend in the ability of Home Depot to effectively use its assets to generate sales?

REAL WORLD

ADM-3 Kroger: Asset turnover ratio

The Kroger Company, a national supermarket chain, reported the following data (in millions) in its financial statements for a recent year:

Total sales	$108,465
Total assets:	
Beginning of year	29,281
End of year	30,556

A. Compute the asset turnover ratio. (Round to two decimal places.)

B. ▬▬▬ Tiffany & Co. is a large North American retailer of jewelry. Tiffany's asset turnover ratio is 0.92. Why would Tiffany's asset turnover ratio be lower than that of Kroger?

REAL WORLD

ADM-4 J. C. Penney: Asset turnover ratio

J. C. Penney Company, Inc. is a large general merchandise retailer in the United States. The following data were obtained from its financial statements for four recent years:

	Year 4	Year 3	Year 2	Year 1
Total sales	$12,257	$11,859	$12,985	$17,260
Total assets:				
Beginning of year	11,801	9,781	11,424	13,068
End of year	10,404	11,801	9,781	11,424

A. Compute the asset turnover ratio for each year. (Round to two decimal places).

B. Plot the asset turnover ratio on a line chart with the year on the horizontal axis.

C. ▬▬▬ Interpret the trend in this ratio over the four years.

Take It Further

ETHICS

TIF 5-1 Ethics in Action

Margie Johnson is a staff accountant at ToolEx Company, a manufacturer of tools and equipment. The company is under pressure from investors to increase earnings, and the president of the company expects the accounting department to "make this happen." Margie's boss, who has been a mentor to her, is concerned that if earnings do not increase, he will be terminated.

Shortly after the end of the fiscal year, the company performs a physical count of the inventory. When Margie compares the physical count to the balance in the inventory account, she finds a significant amount of inventory shrinkage. The amount is so large that it will result in a significant drop in earnings this period. Margie's boss asks her not to make the adjusting entry for shrinkage this period. He assures her that they will get "caught up" on shrinkage in the next period, after the pressure is off to reach this period's earnings goal. Margie's boss asks her to do this as a personal favor to him.

What should Margie do in this situation? Why?

REAL WORLD

TIF 5-2 Team Activity

In teams, select a public company that interests you. Obtain the company's most recent annual report on Form 10-K. The Form 10-K is a company's annually required filing with the Securities and Exchange Commission (SEC). It includes the company's financial statements and accompanying notes. The Form 10-K can be obtained either (A) from the investor relations section of the company's Web site or (B) by using the company search feature of the SEC's EDGAR database service found at www.sec.gov/edgar/searchedgar/companysearch.html.

1. Based on the information in the company's most recent annual report, determine each of the following for all the years presented:
   A. Gross profit
   B. Gross profit rate (Gross profit ÷ Sales)
   C. Income from operations
   D. Percentage change in income from operations
   E. Net income
   F. Percentage change in net income
2. Based solely on your responses to item 1, has the company's performance improved, remained constant, or deteriorated over the periods presented? Briefly explain your answer.

TIF 5-3 Communication

Suzi Nomro operates Watercraft Supply Company, an online boat parts distributorship that is in its third year of operation. The following income statement was prepared for the year ended October 31, 2018.

Watercraft Supply Company Income Statement For the Year Ended October 31, 2018		
Revenues:		
Sales		$1,350,000
Interest		15,000
Total revenues		$1,365,000
Expenses:		
Cost of goods sold	$810,000	
Selling expenses	140,000	
Administrative expenses	90,000	
Interest expense	4,000	
Total expenses		1,044,000
Net income		$ 321,000

(Continued)

Suzi is considering a proposal to increase net income by offering sales discounts of 2/15, n/30 and by shipping all merchandise FOB shipping point. Currently, no sales discounts are allowed and merchandise is shipped FOB destination. It is estimated that the new terms will increase sales by 10%. The ratio of the cost of goods sold to sales is expected to be 60%. All selling and administrative expenses are expected to remain unchanged, except for store supplies and miscellaneous selling expenses, which are expected to increase proportionately with increased sales. The amounts of these items for the year ended October 31, 2018, were as follows:

Store supplies expense	$12,000
Miscellaneous selling expenses	6,000

The interest revenue and expense items will remain unchanged. The shipment of all merchandise FOB shipping point will eliminate all delivery expenses, which for the year ended October 31, 2018, were $12,000.

Write a brief memo to Suzi discussing the potential benefits and limitations of this proposal. Include a determination of the net income that Watercraft Supply could generate next year, under the new proposal, assuming that all sales are collected within the discount period.

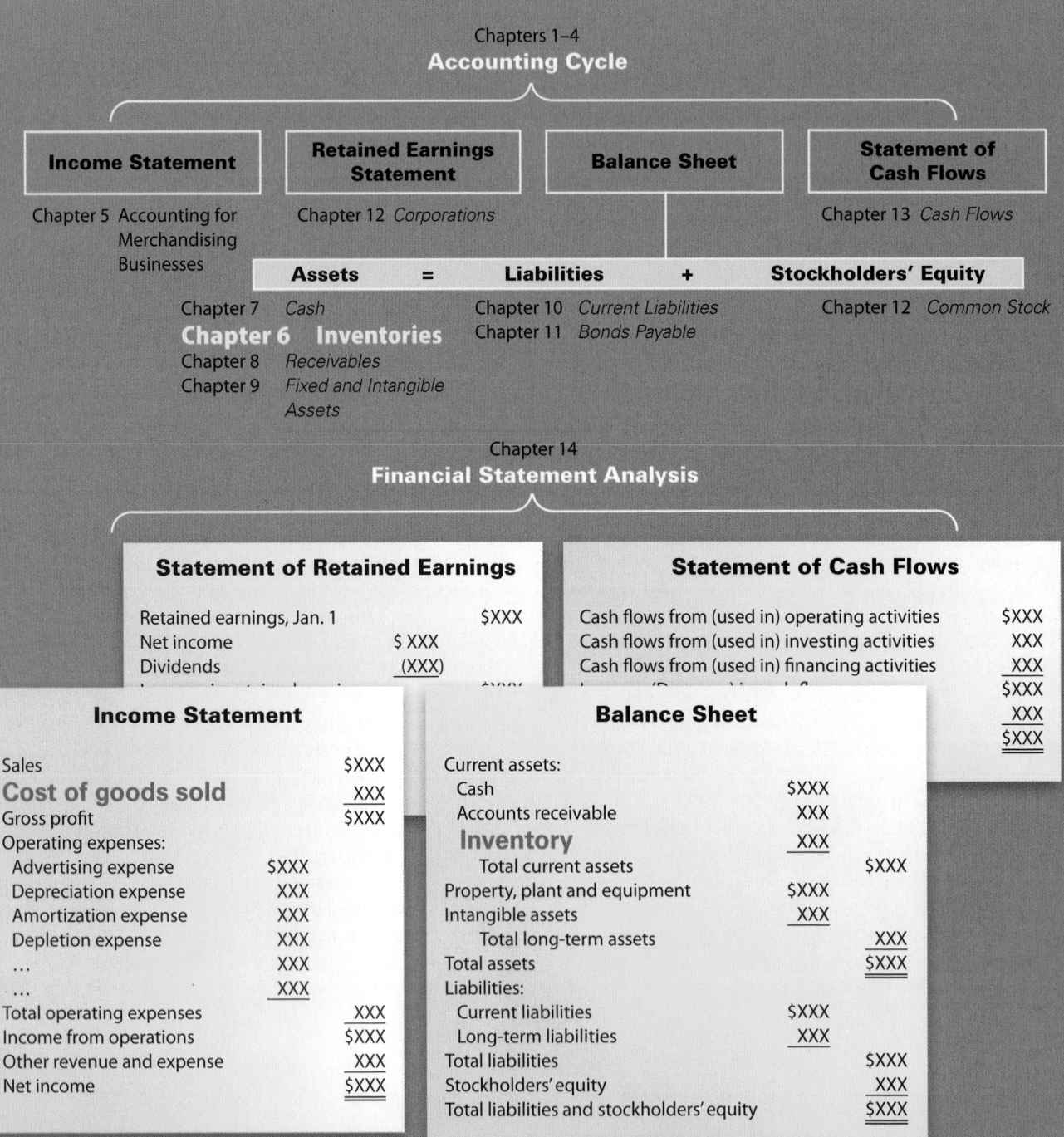

Chapter **6** Inventories

Chapters 1–4
Accounting Cycle

Income Statement	**Retained Earnings Statement**	**Balance Sheet**	**Statement of Cash Flows**

Chapter 5 Accounting for Merchandising Businesses

Chapter 12 *Corporations*

Chapter 13 *Cash Flows*

Assets	**=**	**Liabilities**	**+**	**Stockholders' Equity**

Chapter 7 *Cash*

Chapter 6 Inventories
Chapter 8 *Receivables*
Chapter 9 *Fixed and Intangible Assets*

Chapter 10 *Current Liabilities*
Chapter 11 *Bonds Payable*

Chapter 12 *Common Stock*

Chapter 14
Financial Statement Analysis

Statement of Retained Earnings

Retained earnings, Jan. 1		$XXX
Net income	$ XXX	
Dividends	(XXX)	

Statement of Cash Flows

Cash flows from (used in) operating activities	$XXX
Cash flows from (used in) investing activities	XXX
Cash flows from (used in) financing activities	XXX
	$XXX
	XXX
	$XXX

Income Statement

Sales		$XXX
Cost of goods sold		XXX
Gross profit		$XXX
Operating expenses:		
Advertising expense	$XXX	
Depreciation expense	XXX	
Amortization expense	XXX	
Depletion expense	XXX	
…	XXX	
…	XXX	
Total operating expenses		XXX
Income from operations		$XXX
Other revenue and expense		XXX
Net income		$XXX

Balance Sheet

Current assets:		
Cash	$XXX	
Accounts receivable	XXX	
Inventory	XXX	
Total current assets		$XXX
Property, plant and equipment	$XXX	
Intangible assets	XXX	
Total long-term assets		XXX
Total assets		$XXX
Liabilities:		
Current liabilities	$XXX	
Long-term liabilities	XXX	
Total liabilities		$XXX
Stockholders' equity		XXX
Total liabilities and stockholders' equity		$XXX

Best Buy

Assume that in September you purchased a Sony HDTV from **Best Buy**. At the same time, you purchased a Denon surround sound system for $599.99. You liked your surround sound so well that in November you purchased an identical Denon system on sale for $549.99 for your bedroom TV. Over the holidays, you moved to a new apartment and in the process of unpacking discovered that one of the Denon surround sound systems was missing. Luckily, your renters or homeowners insurance policy will cover the theft; but the insurance company needs to know the cost of the system that was stolen.

The Denon systems were identical. However, to respond to the insurance company, you will need to identify which system was stolen. Was it the first system, which cost $599.99, or was it the second system, which cost $549.99? Whichever assumption you make may determine the amount that you receive from the insurance company.

Merchandising businesses such as Best Buy make similar assumptions when identical merchandise is purchased at different costs. For example, Best Buy may have purchased thousands of Denon surround sound systems over the past year at different costs. At the end of a period, some of the Denon systems will still be in inventory, and some will have been sold. But which costs relate to the sold systems, and which costs relate to the Denon systems still in inventory? Best Buy's assumption about inventory costs can involve large dollar amounts and, thus, can have a significant impact on the financial statements. For example, Best Buy reported $5,174 million of inventory and net income of $1,233 million for a recent year.

This chapter discusses such issues as how to determine the cost of merchandise in inventory and the cost of goods sold. However, this chapter begins by discussing the importance of control over inventory.

What's Covered

Inventories

Nature of Inventory	**Perpetual Inventory System**	**Periodic Inventory System**	**Valuing Inventory**
■ Safeguarding Inventory (Obj. 1) ■ Cost Flow Overview (Obj. 2)	■ First-In, First-Out Method (Obj. 3) ■ Last-In, First-Out Method (Obj. 3) ■ Weighted Average Cost Method (Obj. 3)	■ First-In, First-Out Method (Obj. 4) ■ Last-In, First-Out Method (Obj. 4) ■ Weighted Average Cost Method (Obj. 4)	■ Comparing FIFO, LIFO, and Weighted-Average Methods (Obj. 5) ■ Lower of Cost or Market (Obj. 6) ■ Balance Sheet (Obj. 6) ■ Effect of Errors (Obj. 6)

Learning Objectives

Obj. 1 Describe the importance of control over inventory.

Obj. 2 Describe three inventory cost flow assumptions and how they impact the income statement and balance sheet.

Obj. 3 Determine the cost of inventory under the perpetual inventory system, using the FIFO, LIFO, and weighted average cost methods.

Obj. 4 Determine the cost of inventory under the periodic inventory system, using the FIFO, LIFO, and weighted average cost methods.

Obj. 5 Compare and contrast the use of the three inventory costing methods.

Obj. 6 Describe and illustrate the reporting of inventory in the financial statements.

Analysis for Decision Making

Describe and illustrate the inventory turnover and the number of days' sales in inventory in analyzing the efficiency and effectiveness of inventory management.

Objective 1

Describe the importance of control over inventory.

Control of Inventory

Two primary objectives of control over inventory are as follows:[1]

■ Safeguarding the inventory from damage or theft.
■ Reporting inventory in the financial statements.

Safeguarding Inventory

Controls for safeguarding inventory begin as soon as the inventory is ordered. The following documents are often used for inventory control:

■ Purchase order
■ Receiving report
■ Vendor's invoice

The **purchase order** authorizes the purchase of the inventory from an approved vendor. As soon as the inventory is received, a receiving report is completed. The **receiving report** establishes an initial record of the receipt of the inventory. To make sure the inventory received is what was ordered, the receiving report is compared with the purchase order. The price, quantity, and description of the item on the purchase order and receiving report are then compared to the vendor's invoice. If the receiving report, purchase order, and vendor's invoice agree, the inventory is recorded in the accounting records. If any differences exist, they should be investigated and reconciled.

Recording inventory using a perpetual inventory system is also an effective means of control. The amount of inventory is always available in the **subsidiary inventory ledger**. This helps keep inventory quantities at proper levels. For example, comparing inventory quantities with maximum and minimum levels allows for the timely reordering of inventory and prevents ordering excess inventory.

---

[1] Additional controls used by businesses are described and illustrated in Chapter 7, "Internal Control and Cash."

Finally, controls for safeguarding inventory should include security measures to prevent damage and customer or employee theft. Some examples of security measures include the following:

- Storing inventory in areas that are restricted to only authorized employees
- Locking high-priced inventory in cabinets
- Using two-way mirrors, cameras, security tags, and guards

Best Buy uses scanners to screen customers as they leave the store for merchandise that has not been purchased. In addition, Best Buy stations greeters at the store's entrance to keep customers from bringing in bags that can be used to shoplift merchandise.

Link to Best Buy

Reporting Inventory

A **physical inventory** or *count of inventory* should be taken near year-end to make sure that the quantity of inventory reported in the financial statements is accurate. After the quantity of inventory on hand is determined, the cost of the inventory is assigned for reporting in the financial statements. Most companies assign costs to inventory using one of three inventory cost flow assumptions. If a physical count is not possible or inventory records are not available, the inventory cost may be estimated as described in the appendix at the end of this chapter.

Best Buy conducts ongoing physical counts of inventory throughout the year as a basis for monitoring and predicting loss adjustments for theft.

Link to Best Buy

Inventory Cost Flow Assumptions

Objective 2
Describe three inventory cost flow assumptions and how they impact the income statement and balance sheet.

An accounting issue arises when identical units of merchandise are acquired at different unit costs during a period. In such cases, when an item is sold, it is necessary to determine its cost using a cost flow assumption and related inventory costing method. Three common cost flow assumptions and related inventory costing methods are shown in Exhibit 1.

Exhibit 1   Cost Flow Assumptions

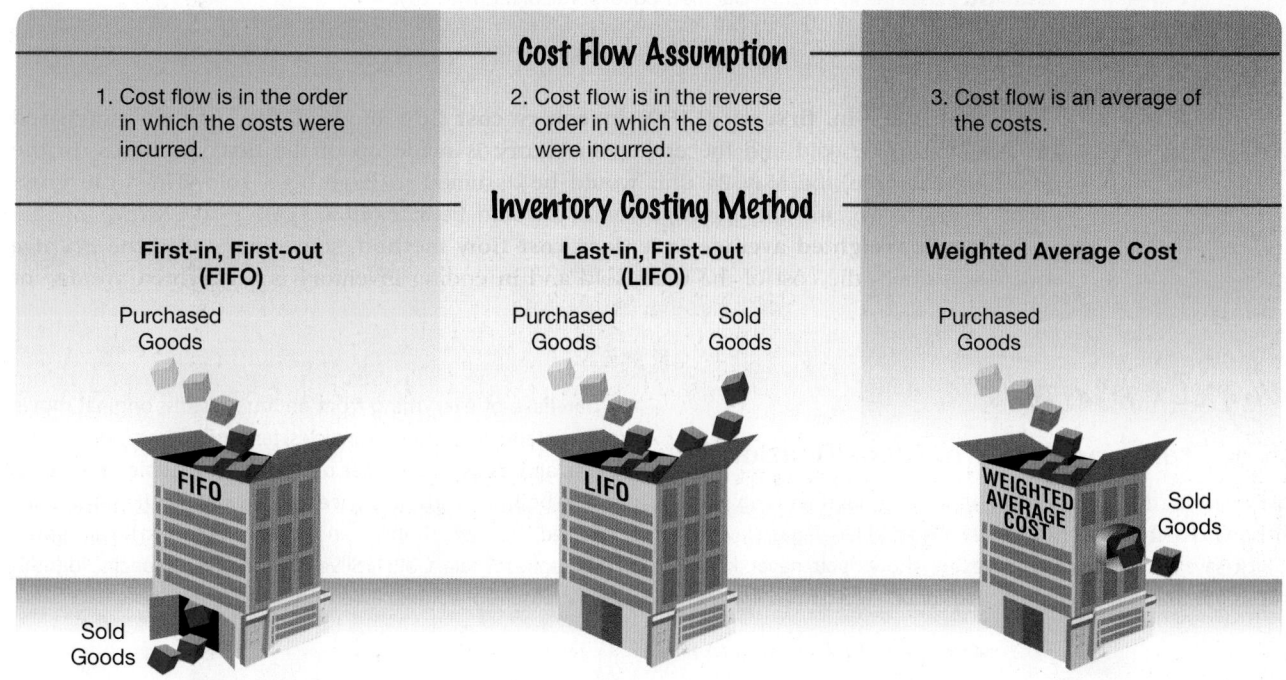

To illustrate, assume that three identical units of merchandise are purchased during May, as follows:

			Units	Cost
May	10	Purchase	1	$ 9
	18	Purchase	1	13
	24	Purchase	1	14
	Total		3	$36

Average cost per unit: $12 ($36 ÷ 3 units)

Assume that one unit is sold on May 30 for $20. Depending upon which unit was sold, the gross profit varies from $11 to $6, computed as follows:

	May 10 Unit Sold	May 18 Unit Sold	May 24 Unit Sold
Sales	$20	$20	$20
Cost of goods sold	9	13	14
Gross profit	$11	$ 7	$ 6
Ending inventory	$27	$23	$22
	($13 + $14)	($9 + $14)	($9 + $13)

Under the **specific identification inventory cost flow method**, the unit sold is identified with a specific purchase. The ending inventory is made up of the remaining units on hand. Thus, the gross profit, cost of goods sold, and ending inventory can vary as illustrated. For example, if the May 18 unit was sold, the cost of goods sold is $13, the gross profit is $7, and the ending inventory is $23.

The specific identification method is not practical unless each inventory unit can be separately identified. For example, an automobile dealer may use the specific identification method because each automobile has a unique serial number. However, most businesses cannot identify each inventory unit separately. In such cases, one of the following three inventory cost flow methods is used.

Under the **first-in, first-out (FIFO) inventory cost flow method**, the first units purchased are assumed to be sold and the ending inventory is made up of the most recent purchases. In the preceding example, the May 10 unit would be assumed to have been sold. Thus, the gross profit would be $11, and the ending inventory would be $27 ($13 + $14).

Link to Best Buy

Best Buy uses the first-in, first-out method for some of its inventory.

Under the **last-in, first-out (LIFO) inventory cost flow method**, the last units purchased are assumed to be sold and the ending inventory is made up of the first purchases. In the preceding example, the May 24 unit would be assumed to have been sold. Thus, the gross profit would be $6, and the ending inventory would be $22 ($9 + $13).

Under the **weighted average inventory cost flow method**, sometimes called the *average cost flow method*, the cost of the units sold and in ending inventory is a weighted average of

Why It Matters

Pawn Stars and Specific Identification

Pawn Stars is the History Channel's TV series featuring Rick Harrison's **Gold & Silver Pawn Shop** of Las Vegas, Nevada. As Rick says in the opening of every show, "you never know what is gonna come through that door." The show features the purchase of everything from antique pistols, original movie props, vintage cars and motorcycles, famous autographed memorabilia, and many other types of unusual collectibles. Each item needs to be appraised and a price negotiated with the seller. Once purchased, the pawn shop has an item of inventory to be presented to the public for sale. Gold & Silver Pawn uses the specific identification method for valuing inventory.

the purchase costs. The purchase costs are weighted by the quantities purchased at each cost, thus the term *weighted average*. In the preceding example, the cost of the unit sold would be $12 ($36 ÷ 3 units), the gross profit would be $8 ($20 – $12), and the ending inventory would be $24 ($12 × 2 units). In this example, the purchase costs are weighted equally, since the same quantity (one) was purchased at each cost.

Best Buy also uses the weighted average cost method for some of its inventory.

Link to Best Buy

The three inventory cost flow methods, FIFO, LIFO, and weighted average, are shown in Exhibit 2.

Exhibit 2 Inventory Costing Methods

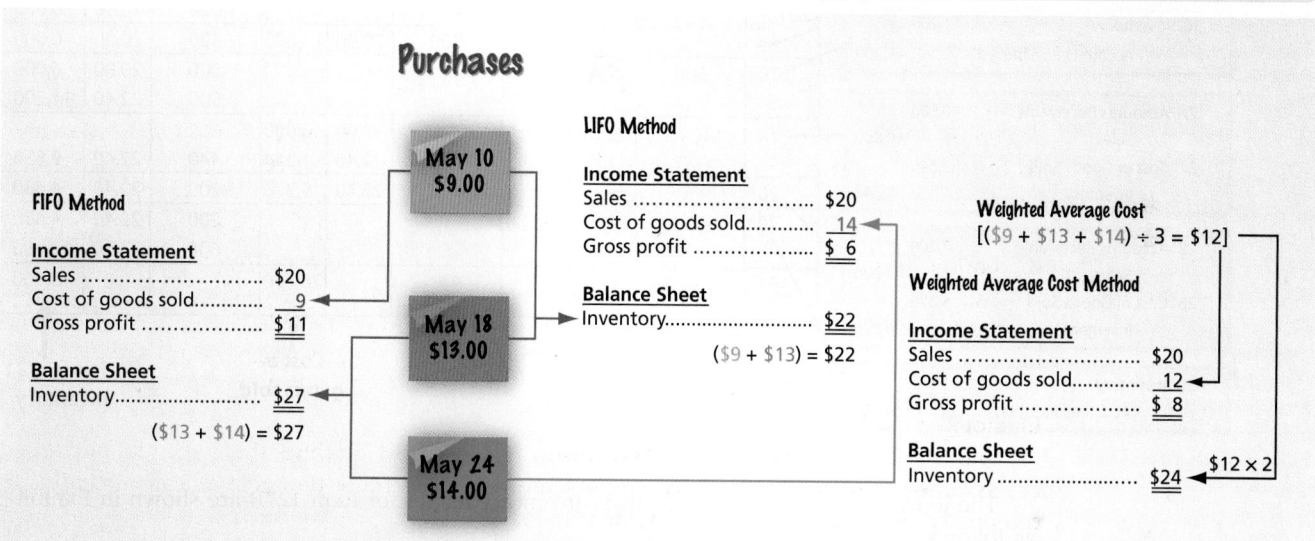

Inventory Costing Methods Under a Perpetual Inventory System

Objective 3
Determine the cost of inventory under the perpetual inventory system, using the FIFO, LIFO, and weighted average cost methods.

As illustrated in the prior section, when identical units of an item are purchased at different unit costs, an inventory cost flow method must be used. This is true regardless of whether the perpetual or periodic inventory system is used.

In this section, the FIFO, LIFO, and weighted average cost methods are illustrated under a perpetual inventory system. For purposes of illustration, the following data for **Item 127B** are used:

	Item 127B	**Units**	**Cost**
Jan. 1	Inventory	1,000	$20.00
4	Sale at $30 per unit	700	
10	Purchase	500	22.40
22	Sale at $30 per unit	360	
28	Sale at $30 per unit	240	
30	Purchase	600	23.30

First-In, First-Out Method

When the FIFO method is used, costs are included in the cost of goods sold in the order in which they were purchased. This is often the same as the physical flow of the goods.

Thus, the FIFO method often provides results that are about the same as those that would have been obtained using the specific identification method. For example, grocery stores shelve milk and other perishable products by expiration dates. Products with early expiration dates are stocked in front. In this way, the oldest products (earliest purchases) are sold first.

DYNAMIC EXHIBIT

To illustrate, Exhibit 3 shows the use of FIFO under a perpetual inventory system for **Item 127B.**

Exhibit 3   Entries and Perpetual Inventory Account (FIFO)

Jan. 4	Accounts Receivable	21,000	
	Sales		21,000
4	Cost of Goods Sold	14,000	
	Inventory		14,000

10	Inventory	11,200	
	Accounts Payable		11,200

22	Accounts Receivable	10,800	
	Sales		10,800
22	Cost of Goods Sold	7,344	
	Inventory		7,344

28	Accounts Receivable	7,200	
	Sales		7,200
28	Cost of Goods Sold	5,376	
	Inventory		5,376

30	Inventory	13,980	
	Accounts Payable		13,980

Item 127B

	Purchases			Cost of Goods Sold			Inventory		
Date	Quantity	Unit Cost	Total Cost	Quantity	Unit Cost	Total Cost	Quantity	Unit Cost	Total Cost
Jan. 1							1,000	20.00	20,000
4				700	20.00	14,000	300	20.00	6,000
10	500	22.40	11,200				300	20.00	6,000
							500	22.40	11,200
22				300	20.00	6,000			
				60	22.40	1,344	440	22.40	9,856
28				240	22.40	5,376	200	22.40	4,480
30	600	23.30	13,980				200	22.40	4,480
							600	23.30	13,980
31	Balances					26,720			18,460

Cost of goods sold

January 31 inventory

The journal entries and the subsidiary inventory ledger for Item 127B are shown in Exhibit 3 as follows:

1. The beginning balance on January 1 is $20,000 (1,000 units at a unit cost of $20.00).
2. On January 4, 700 units were sold at a price of $30 each for sales of $21,000 (700 units at a selling price of $30 per unit). The cost of goods sold is $14,000 (700 units at a unit cost of $20). After the sale, there remains $6,000 of inventory (300 units at a unit cost of $20).
3. On January 10, $11,200 is purchased (500 units at a unit cost of $22.40). After the purchase, the inventory is reported on two lines, $6,000 (300 units at a unit cost of $20.00) from the beginning inventory and $11,200 (500 units at a unit cost of $22.40) from the January 10 purchase.
4. On January 22, 360 units are sold at a price of $30 each for sales of $10,800 (360 units at a selling price of $30 per unit). Using FIFO, the cost of goods sold of $7,344 consists of $6,000 (300 units at a unit cost of $20.00) from the beginning inventory plus $1,344 (60 units at a unit cost of $22.40) from the January 10 purchase. After the sale, there remains $9,856 of inventory (440 units at a unit cost of $22.40) from the January 10 purchase.
5. The January 28 sale and January 30 purchase are recorded in a similar manner.
6. The ending balance on January 31 is $18,460. This balance is made up of two layers of inventory as follows:

	Date of Purchase	Quantity	Unit Cost	Total Cost
Layer 1:	Jan. 10	200	$22.40	$ 4,480
Layer 2:	Jan. 30	600	23.30	13,980
Total		800		$18,460

Last-In, First-Out Method

When the LIFO method is used, the cost of the units sold is the cost of the most recent purchases. The LIFO method was originally used in those rare cases where the units sold were taken from the most recently purchased units. However, for tax purposes, LIFO is now widely used even when it does not represent the physical flow of units. The tax impact of LIFO is discussed later in this chapter.

DYNAMIC EXHIBIT

To illustrate, Exhibit 4 shows the use of LIFO under a perpetual inventory system for Item 127B.

Exhibit 4 Entries and Perpetual Inventory Account (LIFO)

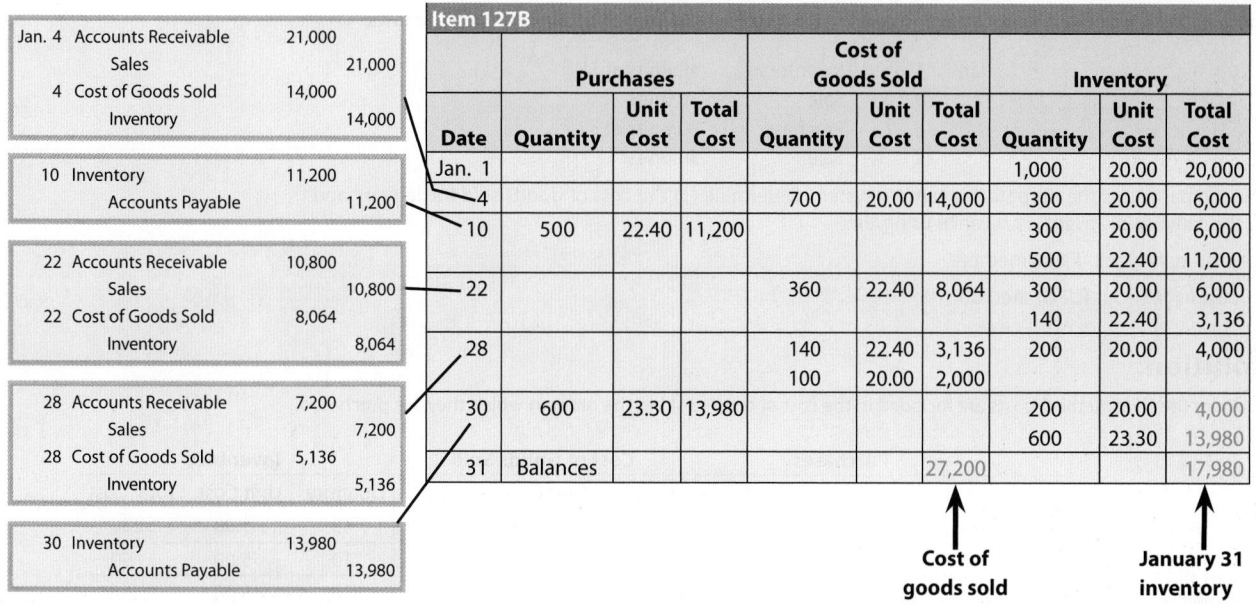

Accounts	Debit	Credit
Jan. 4 Accounts Receivable	21,000	
Sales		21,000
4 Cost of Goods Sold	14,000	
Inventory		14,000
10 Inventory	11,200	
Accounts Payable		11,200
22 Accounts Receivable	10,800	
Sales		10,800
22 Cost of Goods Sold	8,064	
Inventory		8,064
28 Accounts Receivable	7,200	
Sales		7,200
28 Cost of Goods Sold	5,136	
Inventory		5,136
30 Inventory	13,980	
Accounts Payable		13,980

Item 127B

	Purchases			Cost of Goods Sold			Inventory		
Date	Quantity	Unit Cost	Total Cost	Quantity	Unit Cost	Total Cost	Quantity	Unit Cost	Total Cost
Jan. 1							1,000	20.00	20,000
4				700	20.00	14,000	300	20.00	6,000
10	500	22.40	11,200				300	20.00	6,000
							500	22.40	11,200
22				360	22.40	8,064	300	20.00	6,000
							140	22.40	3,136
28				140	22.40	3,136	200	20.00	4,000
				100	20.00	2,000			
30	600	23.30	13,980				200	20.00	4,000
							600	23.30	13,980
31	Balances					27,200			17,980

Cost of goods sold ↑

January 31 inventory ↑

The journal entries and the subsidiary inventory ledger for Item 127B are shown in Exhibit 4 as follows:

1. The beginning balance on January 1 is $20,000 (1,000 units at a unit of cost of $20.00).

2. On January 4, 700 units were sold at a price of $30 each for sales of $21,000 (700 units at a selling price of $30 per unit). The cost of goods sold is $14,000 (700 units at a unit cost of $20). After the sale, there remains $6,000 of inventory (300 units at a unit cost of $20).

3. On January 10, $11,200 is purchased (500 units at a unit cost of $22.40). After the purchase, the inventory is reported on two lines, $6,000 (300 units at a unit cost of $20.00) from the beginning inventory and $11,200 (500 units at a unit cost of $22.40) from the January 10 purchase.

IFRS
See Appendix C for more information.

4. On January 22, 360 units are sold at a price of $30 each for sales of $10,800 (360 units at a selling price of $30 per unit). Using LIFO, the cost of goods sold is $8,064 (360 units at unit cost of $22.40) from the January 10 purchase. After the sale, there remains $9,136 of inventory consisting of $6,000 (300 units at a unit cost of $20.00) from the beginning inventory and $3,136 (140 units at a unit cost of $22.40) from the January 10 purchase.

5. The January 28 sale and January 30 purchase are recorded in a similar manner.

6. The ending balance on January 31 is $17,980. This balance is made up of two layers of inventory as follows:

	Date of Purchase	Quantity	Unit Cost	Total Cost
Layer 1:	Beg. inv. (Jan. 1)	200	$20.00	$ 4,000
Layer 2:	Jan. 30	600	23.30	13,980
Total		800		$17,980

When the LIFO method is used, the subsidiary inventory ledger is sometimes maintained in units only. The units are converted to dollars when the financial statements are prepared at the end of the period.

Check Up Corner 6-1 Perpetual Inventory

The beginning inventory, purchases, and sales of Item QX3 for the month of January are as follows:

Jan.	1	Inventory	40 units at $5
	9	Sale	30 units
	18	Purchase	70 units at $7
	22	Sale	36 units

The company uses the perpetual inventory system. Determine (1) the cost of goods sold for January and (2) the January 31 inventory balance using the:

A. first-in, first-out (FIFO) method.

B. last-in, first-out (LIFO) method.

Solution:

A. Under the FIFO method, costs are included in the cost of goods sold in the order in which they are purchased.

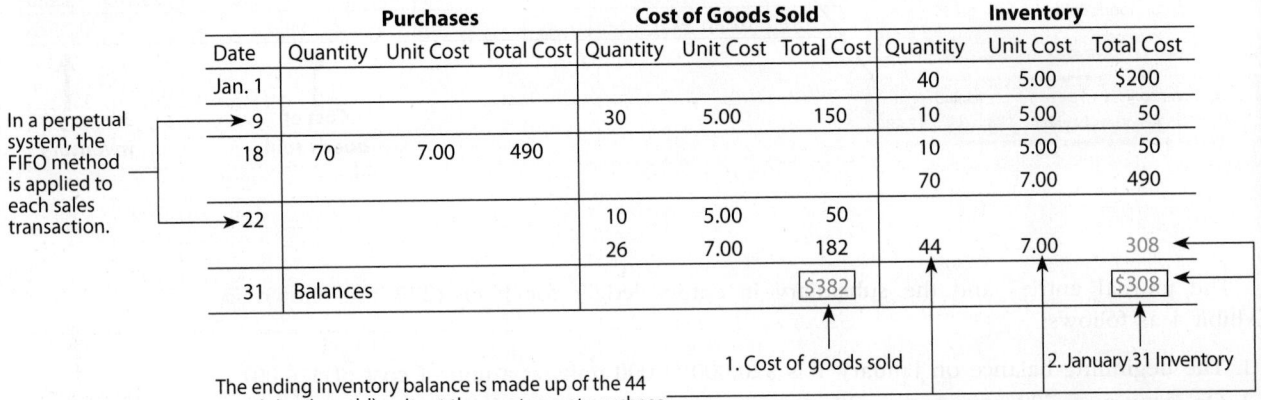

In a perpetual system, the FIFO method is applied to each sales transaction.

Date	Purchases Quantity	Unit Cost	Total Cost	Cost of Goods Sold Quantity	Unit Cost	Total Cost	Inventory Quantity	Unit Cost	Total Cost
Jan. 1							40	5.00	$200
9				30	5.00	150	10	5.00	50
18	70	7.00	490				10	5.00	50
							70	7.00	490
22				10	5.00	50			
				26	7.00	182	44	7.00	308
31	Balances					$382			$308

1. Cost of goods sold

2. January 31 Inventory

The ending inventory balance is made up of the 44 remaining (unsold) units at the most recent purchase price ($7 per unit).

B. Under the LIFO method, the costs of the most recent purchases are included in the cost of goods sold.

The ending inventory balance is made up of two layers: 10 units at the beginning inventory unit cost ($5 per unit), and 34 units at the Jan. 18 purchase price ($7 per unit).

In a perpetual system, the LIFO method is applied to each sales transaction.

Date	Purchases Quantity	Unit Cost	Total Cost	Cost of Goods Sold Quantity	Unit Cost	Total Cost	Inventory Quantity	Unit Cost	Total Cost
Jan. 1							40	5.00	$200
9				30	5.00	150	10	5.00	50
18	70	7.00	490				10	5.00	50
							70	7.00	490
22				36	7.00	252	10	5.00	50
							34	7.00	238
31	Balances					$402			$288

1. Cost of goods sold

2. January 31 Inventory

Check Up Corner

Weighted Average Cost Method

When the weighted average cost method is used in a perpetual inventory system, a weighted average unit cost for each item is computed each time a purchase is made. This unit cost is used to determine the cost of each sale until another purchase is made and a new average is computed. This technique is called a *moving average*.

To illustrate, Exhibit 5 shows the use of weighted average under a perpetual inventory system for **Item 127B**.

DYNAMIC EXHIBIT

Exhibit 5   Entries and Perpetual Inventory Account (Weighted Average)

Jan. 4	Accounts Receivable	21,000	
	Sales		21,000
4	Cost of Goods Sold	14,000	
	Inventory		14,000
10	Inventory	11,200	
	Accounts Payable		11,200
22	Accounts Receivable	10,800	
	Sales		10,800
22	Cost of Goods Sold	7,740	
	Inventory		7,740
28	Accounts Receivable	7,200	
	Sales		7,200
28	Cost of Goods Sold	5,160	
	Inventory		5,160
30	Inventory	13,980	
	Accounts Payable		13,980

Item 127B

| | | Purchases | | | Cost of Goods Sold | | | Inventory | | |
| | | | Unit | Total | | Unit | Total | | Unit | Total |
Date	Quantity	Cost	Cost	Quantity	Cost	Cost	Quantity	Cost	Cost
Jan. 1							1,000	20.00	20,000
4				700	20.00	14,000	300	20.00	6,000
10	500	22.40	11,200				800	21.50	17,200
22				360	21.50	7,740	440	21.50	9,460
28				240	21.50	5,160	200	21.50	4,300
30	600	23.30	13,980				800	22.85	18,280
31	Balances					26,900	800	22.85	18,280

↑ Cost of goods sold   ↑ January 31 inventory

The journal entries and the subsidiary inventory ledger for Item 127B are shown in Exhibit 5 as follows:

1. The beginning balance on January 1 is $20,000 (1,000 units at a unit cost of $20.00).

2. On January 4, 700 units were sold at a price of $30 each for sales of $21,000 (700 units at a selling price of $30 per unit). The cost of goods sold is $14,000 (700 units at a unit cost of $20). After the sale, there remains $6,000 of inventory (300 units at a unit cost of $20).

3. On January 10, $11,200 is purchased (500 units at a unit cost of $22.40). After the purchase, the weighted average unit cost of $21.50 is determined by dividing the total cost of the inventory on hand of $17,200 ($6,000 + $11,200) by the total quantity of inventory on hand of 800 (300 + 500) units. Thus, after the purchase, the inventory consists of 800 units at $21.50 per unit for a total cost of $17,200.

4. On January 22, 360 units are sold at a price of $30 each for sales of $10,800 (360 units at a selling price of $30 per unit). Using weighted average, the cost of goods sold is $7,740 (360 units × $21.50 per unit). After the sale, there remains $9,460 of inventory (440 units × $21.50 per unit).

5. The January 28 sale and January 30 purchase are recorded in a similar manner.

6. The ending balance on January 31 is $18,280 (800 units × $22.85 per unit).

Why It Matters

Computerized Perpetual Inventory Systems

Your purchases are scanned when you go through the checkout line at Best Buy. The scanned data is used to identify the price and adjust the inventory levels. Computerized perpetual inventory systems are used like this when there are many inventory transactions and a manual system is simply not feasible.

Computerized perpetual inventory systems are useful to managers in controlling and managing inventory. For example, if Best Buy has fast-selling items, they can be reordered before the stock runs out. Sales patterns can also be analyzed to determine when to mark down merchandise or when to restock seasonal merchandise. Finally, computerized inventory data can be used to evaluate the effectiveness of advertising campaigns and promotions.

Objective 4
Determine the cost of inventory under the periodic inventory system, using the FIFO, LIFO, and weighted average cost methods.

Inventory Costing Methods Under a Periodic Inventory System

When the periodic inventory system is used, only revenue is recorded each time a sale is made. No entry is made at the time of the sale to record the cost of the goods sold. At the end of the accounting period, a physical inventory is taken to determine the cost of the inventory and the cost of the goods sold.[2]

Like the perpetual inventory system, a cost flow assumption must be made when identical units are acquired at different unit costs during a period. In such cases, the FIFO, LIFO, or weighted average cost method is used.

First-In, First-Out Method

To illustrate the use of the FIFO method in a periodic inventory system, we use the same data for **Item 127B** as in the perpetual inventory example. The beginning inventory and purchases of Item 127B in January are as follows:

Jan. 1	Inventory	1,000 units at	$20.00	$20,000
10	Purchase	500 units at	22.40	11,200
30	Purchase	600 units at	23.30	13,980
	Available for sale during month	2,100		$45,180

The physical count on January 31 shows that 800 units are on hand. Using the FIFO method, the cost of the goods on hand at the end of the period is made up of the most recent costs. The cost of the 800 units in the ending inventory on January 31 is determined as follows:

Most recent costs, January 30 purchase	600 units at	$23.30	$13,980
Next most recent costs, January 10 purchase	200 units at	22.40	4,480
Inventory, January 31	800 units		$18,460

Deducting the cost of the January 31 inventory of $18,460 from the cost of goods available for sale of $45,180 yields the cost of goods sold of $26,720, computed as follows:

Beginning inventory, January 1	$20,000
Purchases ($11,200 + $13,980)	25,180
Cost of goods available for sale in January	$45,180
Ending inventory, January 31	18,460
Cost of goods sold	$26,720

---

[2] Determining the cost of goods sold using the periodic system was illustrated in the appendix to Chapter 5.

The $18,460 cost of the ending inventory on January 31 is made up of the most recent costs. The $26,720 cost of goods sold is made up of the beginning inventory and the earliest costs. Exhibit 6 shows the relationship of the cost of goods sold for January and the ending inventory on January 31.

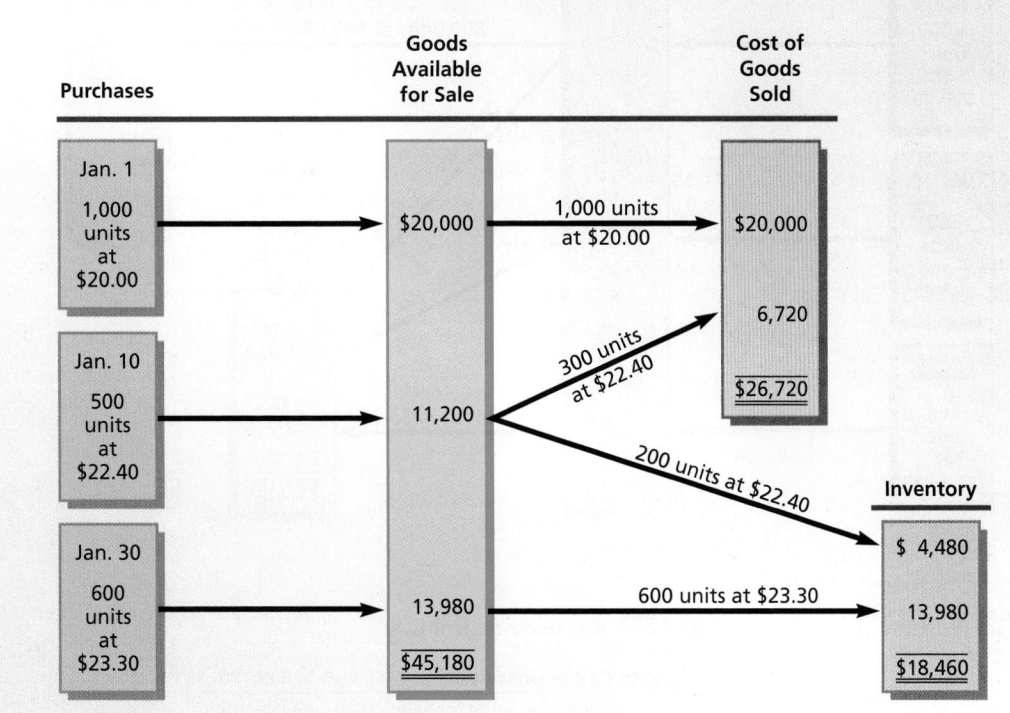

Exhibit 6
First-In, First-Out
Flow of Costs

Last-In, First-Out Method

When the LIFO method is used, the cost of goods on hand at the end of the period is made up of the earliest costs. Based on the same data for **Item 127B** as in the FIFO example, the cost of the 800 units in ending inventory on January 31 is $16,000, which consists of 800 units from the beginning inventory at a cost of $20.00 per unit.

IFRS
See Appendix C for more information.

Deducting the cost of the January 31 inventory of $16,000 from the cost of goods available for sale of $45,180 yields the cost of goods sold of $29,180, computed as follows:

Beginning inventory, January 1	$20,000
Purchases ($11,200 + $13,980)	25,180
Cost of goods available for sale in January	$45,180
Ending inventory, January 31	16,000
Cost of goods sold	$29,180

The $16,000 cost of the ending inventory on January 31 is made up of the earliest costs. The $29,180 cost of goods sold is made up of the most recent costs. Exhibit 7 shows the relationship of the cost of goods sold for January and the ending inventory on January 31.

Weighted Average Cost Method

The weighted average cost method uses the weighted average unit cost for determining the cost of goods sold and the ending inventory. If purchases are relatively uniform during a period, the weighted average cost method provides results that are similar to the physical flow of goods.

The weighted average unit cost is determined as follows:

$$\text{Weighted Average Unit Cost} = \frac{\text{Total Cost of Units Available for Sale}}{\text{Units Available for Sale}}$$

Exhibit 7

Last-In, First-Out
Flow of Costs

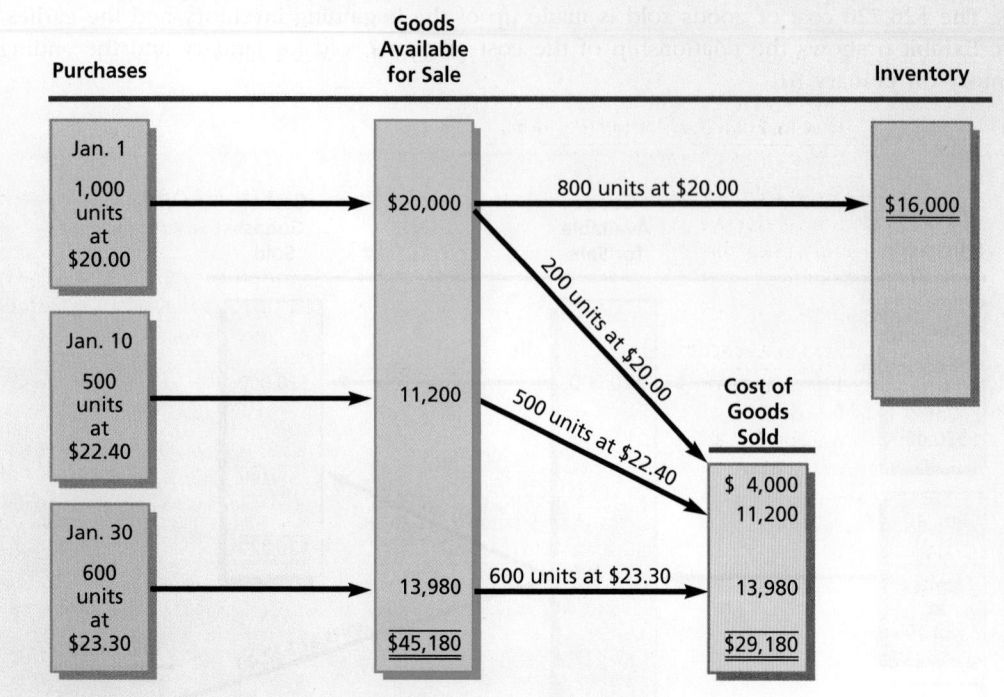

To illustrate, the data for **Item 127B** are used as follows:

$$\text{Weighted Average Unit Cost} = \frac{\text{Total Cost of Units Available for Sale}}{\text{Units Available for Sale}} = \frac{\$45,180}{2,100 \text{ units}}$$

$$= \$21.51 \text{ per unit (Rounded)}$$

The cost of the January 31 ending inventory is as follows:

Inventory, January 31: $17,208 (800 units × $21.51)

Deducting the cost of the January 31 inventory of $17,208 from the cost of goods available for sale of $45,180 yields the cost of goods sold of $27,972, computed as follows:

Beginning inventory, January 1	$20,000
Purchases ($11,200 + $13,980)	25,180
Cost of goods available for sale in January	$45,180
Ending inventory, January 31	17,208
Cost of goods sold	$27,972

Check Up Corner 6-2　Periodic Inventory

The beginning inventory, purchases, and sales of Item PEAR4 for a recent year are as follows:

Jan. 1	Inventory	6 units at $50	$ 300
Mar. 20	Purchase	14 units at $55	770
Oct. 30	Purchase	20 units at $62	1,240
	Available for sale	40 units	$2,310

There are 16 units of the item in the physical inventory at December 31, the end of the fiscal year. The company uses the periodic inventory system. Determine (1) the December 31 inventory balance and (2) the cost of goods sold for the year, using the:

A. first-in, first-out (FIFO) method.

B. last-in, first-out (LIFO) method.

Solution:

Under the periodic system, the LIFO and FIFO methods are applied at the end of the accounting period.

A.

First-In, First-Out Method (Periodic)	
Beginning inventory, January 1 (6 units × $50)	$ 300
Purchases ($770 + $1,240)	2,010
Cost of goods available for sale	$2,310
1. Ending inventory, December 31 (16 units × $62)	992
2. Cost of goods sold	$1,318

Under FIFO, the cost of the ending inventory is made up of the most recent costs.

Deducting the cost of ending inventory under FIFO from the cost of goods available for sale yields the cost of goods sold.

B.

Last-In, Last-Out Method (Periodic)	
Beginning inventory, January 1 (6 units × $50)	$ 300
Purchases ($770 + $1,240)	2,010
Cost of goods available for sale	$2,310
1. Ending inventory, December 31:	
[(6 units × $50) + (10 units × $55)] = $300 + $550	850
2. Cost of goods sold	$1,460

Under LIFO, the cost of the ending inventory is made up of the earliest costs.

Deducting the cost of ending inventory under LIFO from the cost of goods available for sale yields the cost of goods sold.

Check Up Corner

Comparing Inventory Costing Methods

Objective 5
Compare and contrast the use of the three inventory costing methods.

A different cost flow is assumed for the FIFO, LIFO, and weighted average inventory cost flow methods. As a result, the three methods normally yield different amounts for the following:

- Cost of goods sold
- Gross profit
- Net income
- Ending inventory

Using the perpetual inventory system illustration with sales of $39,000 (1,300 units × $30), the following differences are apparent:[3]

IFRS

See Appendix C for more information.

Partial Income Statements			
	First-In, First-Out	Weighted Average Cost	Last-In, First-Out
Sales	$39,000	$39,000	$39,000
Cost of goods sold:	26,720	26,900	27,200
Gross profit	$12,280	$12,100	$11,800
Inventory, Jan. 31	$18,460	$18,280	$17,980

The preceding differences show the effect of increasing costs (prices). If costs (prices) remain the same, all three methods would yield the same results. However, costs (prices) normally do change. The effects of changing costs (prices) on the FIFO and LIFO methods are summarized in Exhibit 8. The weighted average cost method will always yield results between those of FIFO and LIFO.

---

[3] Similar results would also occur when comparing inventory costing methods under a periodic inventory system.

Exhibit 8

Effects of
Changing Costs
(Prices): FIFO
and LIFO Cost
Methods

	+ Increasing Costs (Prices)		− Decreasing Costs (Prices)	
	↑ Highest Amount	↓ Lowest Amount	↑ Highest Amount	↓ Lowest Amount
Cost of goods sold	LIFO	FIFO	FIFO	LIFO
Gross profit	FIFO	LIFO	LIFO	FIFO
Net income	FIFO	LIFO	LIFO	FIFO
Ending inventory	FIFO	LIFO	LIFO	FIFO

FIFO reports higher gross profit and net income than the LIFO method when costs (prices) are increasing, as shown in Exhibit 8. However, in periods of rapidly rising costs, the inventory that is sold must be replaced at increasingly higher costs. In such cases, the larger FIFO gross profit and net income are sometimes called *inventory profits* or *illusory profits*.

During a period of increasing costs, LIFO matches more recent costs against sales on the income statement. Thus, it can be argued that the LIFO method more nearly matches current costs with current revenues. LIFO also offers an income tax savings during periods of increasing costs. This is because LIFO reports the lowest amount of gross profit and, thus, taxable net income.[4] However, under LIFO, the ending inventory on the balance sheet may be quite different from its current replacement cost. In such cases, the financial statements normally include a note that estimates what the inventory would have been if FIFO had been used.

The weighted average cost method is, in a sense, a compromise between FIFO and LIFO. The effect of cost (price) trends is averaged in determining the cost of goods sold and the ending inventory.

Objective 6

Describe and illustrate the reporting of inventory in the financial statements.

Reporting Inventory in the Financial Statements

Cost is the primary basis for valuing and reporting inventories in the financial statements. However, inventory may be valued at other than cost in the following cases:

- The cost of replacing items in inventory is below the recorded cost.
- The inventory cannot be sold at normal prices due to imperfections, style changes, spoilage, damage, obsolescence, or other causes.

Valuation at Lower of Cost or Market

IFRS

See Appendix C for more information.

If the market is lower than the purchase cost, the **lower-of-cost-or-market (LCM) method** is used to value the inventory. *Market,* as used in *lower of cost or market*, is the **net realizable value** of the inventory.[5] Net realizable value is determined as follows:

Net Realizable Value = Estimated Selling Price − Direct Costs of Disposal

 Ethics: Don't Do It!

Where's the Bonus?

Managers are often given bonuses based on reported earnings numbers. This can create a conflict. For example,

LIFO can improve the value of the company through lower taxes. However, using LIFO also lowers management bonuses that are based on reported income. Thus, a manager might use FIFO to maximize his or her bonus even though LIFO is better for the company.

---

[4] A proposal currently exists to not allow the use of LIFO for tax purposes.

[5] Accounting Standards Update, *Inventory (Topic 330): Simplifying the Measurement of Inventory*, July 2015, FASB.

Direct costs of disposal include selling expenses such as special advertising or sales commissions.

To illustrate, assume the following data about an item of damaged inventory:

Original cost	$1,000
Estimated selling price	800
Estimated selling expenses	150

In applying LCM, the market value of the inventory is $650, computed as follows:

Market Value (Net Realizable Value) = $800 − $150 = $650

Thus, the inventory would be valued at $650, which is the lower of its cost of $1,000 and its market value of $650.

The lower-of-cost-or-market method can be applied in one of three ways. The cost, market price, and any declines could be determined for the following:

- Each item in the inventory
- Each major class or category of inventory
- Total inventory as a whole

The amount of any price decline is included in the cost of goods sold. This, in turn, reduces gross profit and net income in the period in which the price declines occur. This matching of price declines to the period in which they occur is the primary advantage of using the lower-of-cost-or-market method.

Best Buy values its inventory at lower of cost or market based upon cost and the amount it expects to realize from the sale.

Link to Best Buy

To illustrate, assume the following data for 400 identical units of Item A in inventory on December 31:

Cost per unit	$10.25
Market value (net realizable value) per unit	9.50

Since the market value of Item A is $9.50 per unit, $9.50 is used under the lower-of-cost-or-market method.

Exhibit 9 illustrates applying the lower-of-cost-or-market method to each inventory item (Echo, Foxtrot, Sierra, Tango). As applied on an item-by-item basis, the total lower-of-cost-or-market is $15,070, which is a market decline of $450 ($15,520 − $15,070). This market decline of $450 is included in the cost of goods sold.

	A	B	C	D	E	F	G
1				Market Value			
2		Inventory	Cost per	per Unit			
3	Item	Quantity	Unit	(Net Realizable Value)	Cost	Market	LCM
4	Echo	400	$10.25	$ 9.50	$ 4,100	$ 3,800	$ 3,800
5	Foxtrot	120	22.50	24.10	2,700	2,892	2,700
6	Sierra	600	8.00	7.75	4,800	4,650	4,650
7	Tango	280	14.00	14.75	3,920	4,130	3,920
8	Total				$15,520	$15,472	$15,070
9							

Exhibit 9

Determining Inventory at Lower of Cost or Market (LCM)

The excess of cost over the amount **Best Buy** expects to receive from the sale of an item is called a markdown.

Link to Best Buy

In Exhibit 9, Items Echo, Foxtrot, Sierra, and Tango could be viewed as a class of inventory items. If the lower-of-cost-or-market method is applied to the class, the inventory would be valued at $15,472, which is a market decline of $48 ($15,520 − $15,472). Likewise, if Items Echo, Foxtrot, Sierra, and Tango make up the total inventory, the lower-of-cost-or-market method as applied to the total inventory would be the same amount, $15,472.

Check Up Corner 6-3 Lower of Cost or Market

JJ's Electronics Company has three products in inventory (PCs, tablets, and smartphones). Each product's quantity, cost per unit, and market value per unit are as follows:

Item	Inventory Quantity	Cost per Unit	Market Value per Unit (Net Realizable Value)
PC	10	$175	$168
Tablet	12	132	150
Smartphone	8	199	187

Apply the lower-of-cost-or-market method to each inventory item in a form similar to Exhibit 9.

Solution:

The cost of each item is determined by multiplying the inventory quantity by the cost per unit.

The market value of each item is determined by multiplying the inventory quantity by the market value per unit.

	A	B	C	D	E	F	G
1				Market Value			
2		Inventory	Cost per	per Unit			
3	Item	Quantity	Unit	(Net Realizable Value)	Cost	Market	LCM
4	PC	10	$175	$168	$1,750	$1,680	$1,680
5	Tablet	12	132	150	1,584	1,800	1,584
6	Smartphone	8	199	187	1,592	1,496	1,496
7	Total				$4,926	$4,976	$4,760
8							

When applying the LCM method to each inventory item, the lower of the cost or market is selected.

The total inventory value is the sum of the lower of the cost or market value for each item in inventory.

Check Up Corner

Inventory on the Balance Sheet

IFRS
See Appendix C for more information.

Inventory is usually reported in the current assets section of the balance sheet. In addition to this amount, the following are reported:

- The method of determining the cost of the inventory (FIFO, LIFO, or weighted average)
- The method of valuing the inventory (cost or the lower of cost or market)

Why It Matters

Good Samaritan

A corporation may decide that the best way to dispose of unwanted inventory is to give it to charity. Under the Internal Revenue Code, a corporation may take an "enhanced" deduction for charitable contributions of select inventory, such as food, clothing, and medical supplies, used for the ill, the needy, or infants. Thus, for example, disaster relief contributions would be subject to the "enhanced" deduction. The enhanced deduction is for amounts up to half the planned profit on the item, but not greater than twice what the company paid for it. There are Web sites that can help place unwanted items to charitable uses, such as www.wastetocharity.org.

The financial statement reporting for the topics covered in Chapters 6–12 are illustrated using excerpts from the financial statements of **Mornin' Joe**. Mornin' Joe is a fictitious company that offers drip and espresso coffee in a coffeehouse setting. The complete financial statements of Mornin' Joe are illustrated at the end of Chapter 14.

The balance sheet presentation for inventory for Mornin' Joe within the current asset section is as follows:

Mornin' Joe

Mornin' Joe Balance Sheet December 31, 20Y6		
Assets		
Current assets:		
Cash and cash equivalents...		$235,000
Trading investments (at cost)...	$420,000	
Valuation allowance for trading investments........................	45,000	
Trading investments (at fair value)................................		465,000
Accounts receivable	$305,000	
Allowance for doubtful accounts....................................	(12,300)	
Accounts receivable, net..		292,700
Inventory—at lower of cost (first-in, first-out method) or net realizable value..................................		120,000

It is not unusual for a large business to use different costing methods for segments of its inventories. Also, a business may change its inventory costing method. In such cases, the effect of the change and the reason for the change are disclosed in the notes to the financial statements.

Best Buy uses the weighted average cost and first-in, first-out methods for recording inventory.

Link to Best Buy

Effect of Inventory Errors on the Financial Statements

Any errors in inventory will affect the balance sheet and income statement. Some reasons that inventory errors may occur include the following:

- Physical inventory on hand was miscounted.
- Costs were incorrectly assigned to inventory. For example, the FIFO, LIFO, or weighted average cost method was incorrectly applied.
- Inventory in transit was incorrectly included or excluded from inventory.
- Consigned inventory was incorrectly included or excluded from inventory.

Inventory errors often arise from merchandise that is in transit at year-end. As discussed in Chapter 5, shipping terms determine when the title to merchandise passes. When goods are purchased or sold *FOB shipping point*, title passes to the buyer when the goods are shipped. When the terms are *FOB destination*, title passes to the buyer when the goods are received.

To illustrate, assume that SysExpress ordered the following merchandise from American Products:

Date ordered:	December 27, 20Y6
Amount:	$10,000
Terms:	FOB shipping point, 2/10, n/30
Date shipped by seller:	December 30, 20Y6
Date delivered:	January 3, 20Y7

When SysExpress counts its physical inventory on December 31, 20Y6, the merchandise is still in transit. In such cases, it would be easy for SysExpress to not include the $10,000 of merchandise in its December 31 physical inventory. However, since the merchandise was purchased *FOB shipping point*, SysExpress owns the merchandise. Thus, it should be included in the December 31 inventory, even though it is not on hand. Likewise, any merchandise *sold* by

SysExpress *FOB destination* is still SysExpress's inventory, even if it is in transit to the buyer on December 31.

Inventory errors often arise from **consigned inventory**. Manufacturers sometimes ship merchandise to retailers who act as the manufacturer's selling agent. The manufacturer, called the **consignor**, retains title until the goods are sold. Such merchandise is said to be shipped *on consignment* to the retailer, called the **consignee**. Any unsold merchandise at year-end is a part of the manufacturer's (consignor's) inventory, even though the merchandise is in the hands of the retailer (consignee). At year-end, it would be easy for the retailer (consignee) to incorrectly include the consigned merchandise in its physical inventory. Likewise, the manufacturer (consignor) should include consigned inventory in its physical inventory, even though the inventory is not on hand.

Income Statement Effects   Inventory errors will misstate the income statement amounts for cost of goods sold, gross profit, and net income. The effects of inventory errors on the current period's income statement are summarized in Exhibit 10.

Exhibit 10

Effect of Inventory Errors on Current Period's Income Statement

	Income Statement Effect		
Inventory Error	**Cost of Goods Sold**	**Gross Profit**	**Net Income**
Beginning inventory is:			
↓ Understated	↓ Understated	↑ Overstated	↑ Overstated
↑ Overstated	↑ Overstated	↓ Understated	↓ Understated
Ending inventory is:			
↓ Understated	↑ Overstated	↓ Understated	↓ Understated
↑ Overstated	↓ Understated	↑ Overstated	↑ Overstated

To illustrate, the income statements of SysExpress shown in Exhibit 11 are used.[6] On December 31, 20Y6, assume that SysExpress incorrectly records its physical inventory as $50,000 instead of the correct amount of $60,000. Thus, the December 31, 20Y6, inventory is understated by $10,000 ($60,000 – $50,000). As a result, the cost of goods sold is overstated by $10,000. The gross profit and the net income for the year will also be understated by $10,000.

The December 31, 20Y6, inventory becomes the January 1, 20Y7, inventory. Thus, the beginning inventory for 20Y7 is understated by $10,000. As a result, the cost of goods sold is understated by $10,000 for 20Y7. The gross profit and net income for 20Y7 will be overstated by $10,000.

As shown in Exhibit 11, because the ending inventory of one period is the beginning inventory of the next period, the effects of inventory errors carry forward to the next period. Specifically, if uncorrected, the effects of inventory errors reverse themselves in the next period. In Exhibit 11, the combined net income for the two years of $525,000 is correct, even though the 20Y6 and 20Y7 income statements were incorrect.

Balance Sheet Effects   Inventory errors misstate the inventory, current assets, total assets, and stockholders' equity on the balance sheet. The effects of inventory errors on the current period's balance sheet are summarized in Exhibit 12.

For the SysExpress illustration shown in Exhibit 11, the December 31, 20Y6, ending inventory was understated by $10,000. As a result, the inventory, current assets, and total assets would be understated by $10,000 on the December 31, 20Y6, balance sheet. Because the ending physical inventory is understated, the cost of goods sold for 20Y6 will be overstated by $10,000. Thus, the gross profit and the net income for 20Y6 are understated by $10,000. Because the net income is closed to Retained Earnings at the end of the period, the stockholders' equity on the December 31, 20Y6, balance sheet is also understated by $10,000.

---

[6] The effect of inventory errors will be illustrated using the periodic system. This is because it is easier to see the impact of inventory errors on the income statement using the periodic system. The effect of inventory errors would be the same under the perpetual inventory system.

Exhibit 11 Effects of Inventory Errors on Two Years' Income Statements

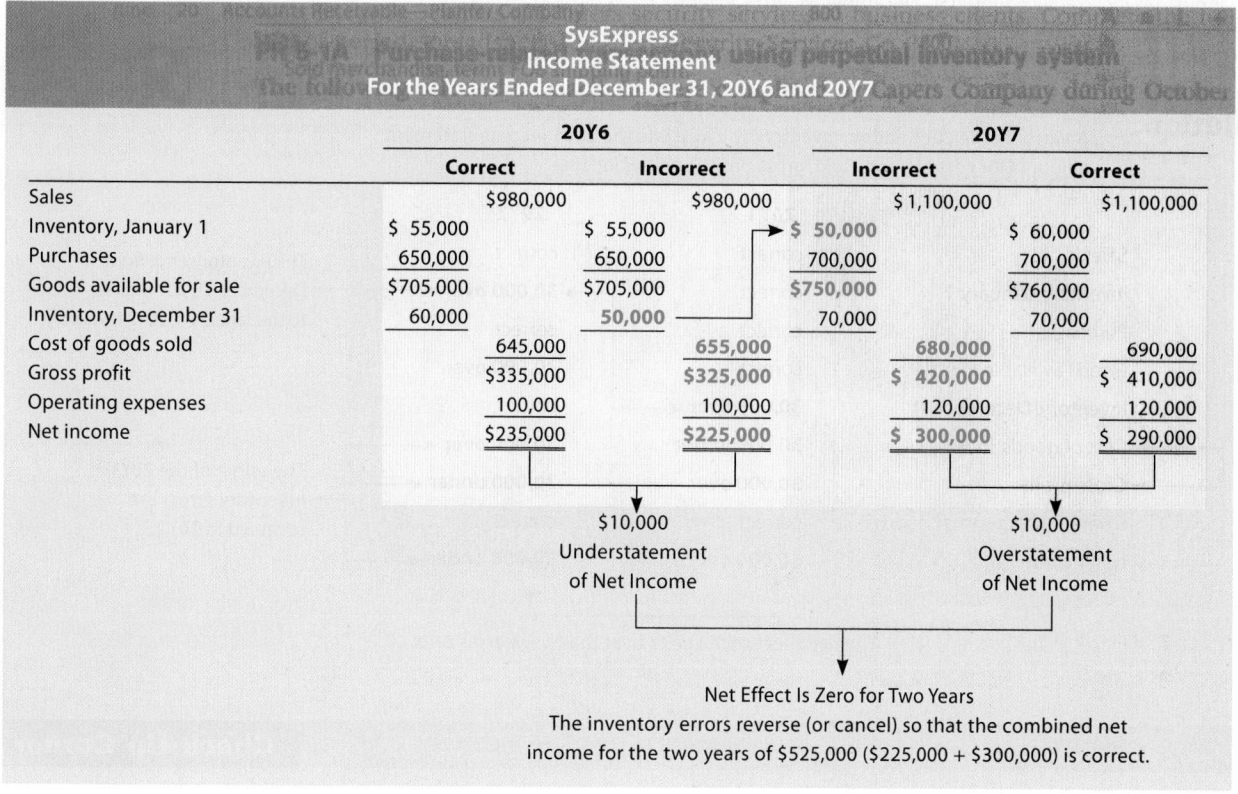

SysExpress
Income Statement
For the Years Ended December 31, 20Y6 and 20Y7

	20Y6		20Y7	
	Correct	Incorrect	Incorrect	Correct
Sales	$980,000	$980,000	$1,100,000	$1,100,000
Inventory, January 1	$ 55,000	$ 55,000	$ 50,000	$ 60,000
Purchases	650,000	650,000	700,000	700,000
Goods available for sale	$705,000	$705,000	$750,000	$760,000
Inventory, December 31	60,000	50,000	70,000	70,000
Cost of goods sold	645,000	655,000	680,000	690,000
Gross profit	$335,000	$325,000	$ 420,000	$ 410,000
Operating expenses	100,000	100,000	120,000	120,000
Net income	$235,000	$225,000	$ 300,000	$ 290,000

$10,000
Understatement
of Net Income

$10,000
Overstatement
of Net Income

Net Effect Is Zero for Two Years
The inventory errors reverse (or cancel) so that the combined net
income for the two years of $525,000 ($225,000 + $300,000) is correct.

Inventory errors reverse themselves within two years. As a result, the balance sheet will be correct as of December 31, 20Y7. Using the SysExpress illustration from Exhibit 11, these effects are summarized as follows:

	Amount of Misstatement	
Balance Sheet:	**December 31, 20Y6**	**December 31, 20Y7**
Inventory overstated (understated)	$(10,000)	Correct
Current assets overstated (understated)	(10,000)	Correct
Total assets overstated (understated)	(10,000)	Correct
Stockholders' equity overstated (understated)	(10,000)	Correct
Income Statement:	**20Y6**	**20Y7**
Cost of goods sold overstated (understated)	$ 10,000	$(10,000)
Gross profit overstated (understated)	(10,000)	10,000
Net income overstated (understated)	(10,000)	10,000

Balance Sheet Effect				
Ending Inventory Error	Inventory	Current Assets	Total Assets	Stockholders' Equity (Retained Earnings)
↓ Understated	↓ Understated	↓ Understated	↓ Understated	↓ Understated
↑ Overstated	↑ Overstated	↑ Overstated	↑ Overstated	↑ Overstated

Exhibit 12

Effect of Inventory Errors on Current Period's Balance Sheet

Check Up Corner 6-4 | Effects of Inventory Errors

Zulu Industries incorrectly counted its December 31, 20Y1 inventory at $250,000 instead of the correct amount of $220,000. Indicate the effect of the misstatement on Zulu's income statement for the current year (20Y1) and the following year (20Y2). What is the net effect of the error for the two years?

Solution:

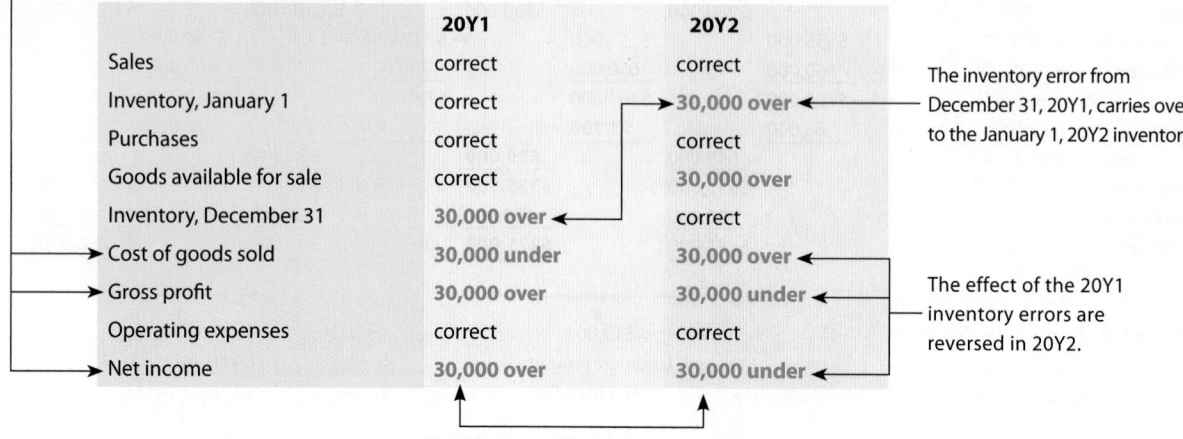

An error in the 20Y1 ending inventory will misstate the 20Y1 income statement amounts for cost of goods sold, gross profit, and net income.

	20Y1	20Y2	
Sales	correct	correct	
Inventory, January 1	correct	30,000 over	The inventory error from December 31, 20Y1, carries over to the January 1, 20Y2 inventory.
Purchases	correct	correct	
Goods available for sale	correct	30,000 over	
Inventory, December 31	30,000 over	correct	
Cost of goods sold	30,000 under	30,000 over	
Gross profit	30,000 over	30,000 under	The effect of the 20Y1 inventory errors are reversed in 20Y2.
Operating expenses	correct	correct	
Net income	30,000 over	30,000 under	

The net effect of the error over the two years is zero.

Check Up Corner

Analysis for Decision Making

Objective

Describe and illustrate the inventory turnover and the number of days' sales in inventory in analyzing the efficiency and effectiveness of inventory management.

Inventory Turnover and Number of Days' Sales in Inventory

A merchandising business should keep enough inventory on hand to meet its customers' needs. A failure to do so may result in lost sales. However, too much inventory ties up funds that could be used to improve operations. Also, excess inventory increases expenses such as storage and property taxes. Finally, excess inventory increases the risk of losses due to price decreases, damage, or changes in customer tastes.

Two measures to analyze inventory management are:

- inventory turnover and
- number of days' sales in inventory.

Inventory turnover measures the relationship between the cost of goods sold and the amount of inventory carried during the period. It measures the number of times inventory is turned into sold goods during the year. It is computed as follows:

$$\text{Inventory Turnover} = \frac{\text{Cost of Goods Sold}}{\text{Average Inventory}}$$

To illustrate, inventory turnover for **Best Buy** is computed from the following data (in millions) from two recent annual reports:

	Year 2	Year 1
Cost of goods sold	$31,292	$31,212
Inventories:		
Beginning of year	5,376	6,781
End of year	5,174	5,376
Average inventory:*		
($5,376 + $5,174) ÷ 2	5,275.0	
($6,781 + $5,376) ÷ 2		6,078.5
Inventory turnover:*		
$31,292 ÷ $5,275.0	5.9	
$31,212 ÷ $6,078.5		5.1

* Rounded to one decimal place.

Generally, the larger the inventory turnover, the more efficient and effective the company is in managing inventory. In the preceding example, inventory turnover increased slightly from 5.1 to 5.9 during Year 2, and thus Best Buy's inventory management improved during Year 2.

The **number of days' sales in inventory** measures the length of time it takes to acquire, sell, and replace the inventory. It is computed as follows:[7]

$$\text{Number of Days' Sales in Inventory} = \frac{\text{Average Inventory}}{\text{Average Daily Cost of Goods Sold}}$$

The average daily cost of goods sold is determined by dividing the cost of goods sold by 365.[8] Based upon the preceding data, the number of days' sales in inventory for **Best Buy** is computed as follows:

	Year 2	Year 1
Cost of goods sold	$31,292	$31,212
Average daily cost of goods sold:*		
$31,292 ÷ 365 days	85.7	
$31,212 ÷ 365 days		85.5
Average inventory:*		
($5,376 + $5,174) ÷ 2	5,275.0	
($6,781 + $5,376) ÷ 2		6,078.5
Number of days' sales in inventory:*		
$5,275.0 ÷ $85.7	61.6 days	
$6,078.5 ÷ $85.5		71.1 days

* Rounded to one decimal place.

Generally, the lower the number of days' sales in inventory, the more efficient and effective the company is in managing inventory. The number of days' sales in inventory decreased from 71.1 to 61.6 days, and thus Best Buy's inventory management improved. This is consistent with the increase in inventory turnover during the year.

As with most financial ratios, differences exist among industries. To illustrate, **Whole Foods Market, Inc.** is a leading retailer of organic and natural foods in the United States. Because food is perishable, it will sell more rapidly than Best Buy's consumer electronics. Thus, Whole Foods' inventory management should be significantly more efficient than Best Buy's. For a recent year, this is confirmed as follows:

	Best Buy	Whole Foods
Inventory turnover	5.9	21.2
Number of days' sales in inventory	61.5 days	17.2 days

[7] Number of days' sales in inventory may also be computed as 365 days divided by the inventory turnover.

[8] We use 365 days for all computations involving real world companies and data. We do this to highlight differences among companies and because computations using real world data normally require rounding.

Make a Decision   Inventory Turnover and Number of Days' Sales in Inventory

Darden Restaurants, Inc. is the largest full-service restaurant company in the world. It operates over 2,200 restaurants under a variety of brand names, including Olive Garden, Bahama Breeze, and LongHorn Steakhouse. **Panera Bread Company** operates over 1,800 bakery-café locations across North America. It is one of the largest food service companies in the United States. The cost of food, beverage, and packaging and the beginning and ending inventory balances from recent annual reports for Darden and Panera are as follows (in millions):

	Darden	Panera
Cost of goods sold (food, beverage, and packaging)	$1,892	$670
Inventories:		
Beginning of year	357	22
End of year	197	23

A. Compute the inventory turnover for both companies. (Round calculations to one decimal place.)

B. Compute the number of days' sales in inventory for both companies. (Round calculations to one decimal place.)

C. Which company is more efficient in managing inventory?

D. What might explain the difference in the inventory management efficiency of the two companies?

Solution:

A.

$$\text{Inventory Turnover} = \frac{\text{Cost of Goods Sold (Food, Beverage, and Packaging)}}{\text{Average Inventory}}$$

Darden: $\dfrac{\$1,892}{(\$357 + \$197) \div 2} = \dfrac{\$1,892}{\$277} = 6.8$

Panera: $\dfrac{\$670}{(\$22 + \$23) \div 2} = \dfrac{\$670}{\$22.5} = 29.8$

B.

$$\text{Number of Days' Sales in Inventory} = \frac{\text{Average Inventory}}{\text{Average Daily Cost of Goods Sold (Food, Beverage, and Packaging)}}$$

Darden: $\dfrac{(\$357 + \$197) \div 2}{\$1,892 \div 365} = \dfrac{\$277}{\$5.2} = 53.3 \text{ days}$

Panera: $\dfrac{(\$22 + \$23) \div 2}{\$670 \div 365} = \dfrac{\$22.5}{\$1.8} = 12.5 \text{ days}$

C. Panera appears to manage its food, beverage, and packaging inventories more efficiently. Panera has an inventory turnover of 29.8 and number of days' sales in inventory of 12.5 days. This compares to Darden's inventory turnover of 6.8 and number of days' sales in inventory of 53.3 days.

D. One major explanation for the difference in inventory management efficiency may relate to the types of food the restaurants serve. Darden's restaurants offer food that can be stored, refrigerated, or frozen. Thus, Darden's food turnover can be slower. However, Panera offers bread products that must be sold fresh. Thus, Panera must manage its inventory more carefully.

Make a Decision

Appendix Estimating Inventory Cost

A business may need to estimate the amount of inventory for the following reasons:

- Perpetual inventory records are not maintained.
- A disaster such as a fire or flood has destroyed the inventory records and the inventory.
- Monthly or quarterly financial statements are needed, but a physical inventory is taken only once a year.

This appendix describes and illustrates two widely used methods of estimating inventory cost.

Retail Method of Inventory Costing

The **retail inventory method** of estimating inventory cost requires costs and retail prices to be maintained for the merchandise available for sale. A ratio of cost to retail price is then used to convert ending inventory at retail to estimate the ending inventory cost.

The retail inventory method is applied as follows:

- Step 1. Determine the total merchandise available for sale at cost and retail.
- Step 2. Determine the ratio of the cost to retail of the merchandise available for sale.
- Step 3. Determine the ending inventory at retail by deducting the sales from the merchandise available for sale at retail.
- Step 4. Estimate the ending inventory cost by multiplying the ending inventory at retail by the cost to retail ratio.

Exhibit 13 illustrates the retail inventory method.

	A	B	C
1		Cost	Retail
2	Inventory, January 1	$19,400	$ 36,000
3	Purchases in January (net)	42,600	64,000
Step 1 → 4	Merchandise available for sale	$62,000	$100,000
Step 2 → 5	Ratio of cost to retail price: $\dfrac{\$62,000}{\$100,000} = 62\%$		
6	Sales for January		70,000
Step 3 → 7	Inventory, January 31, at retail		$ 30,000
Step 4 → 8	Inventory, January 31, at estimated cost		
9	($30,000 × 62%)		$ 18,600
10			

Exhibit 13
Determining Inventory by the Retail Method

When estimating the cost to retail ratio, the mix of items in the ending inventory is assumed to be the same as the merchandise available for sale. If the ending inventory is made up of different classes of merchandise, cost to retail ratios may be developed for each class of inventory.

An advantage of the retail method is that it provides inventory figures for preparing monthly statements. Department stores and similar retailers often determine gross profit and operating income each month but may take a physical inventory only once or twice a year. Thus, the retail method allows management to monitor operations more closely.

The retail method may also be used as an aid in taking a physical inventory. In this case, the items are counted and recorded at their retail (selling) prices instead of their costs. The physical inventory at retail is then converted to cost by using the cost to retail ratio.

Gross Profit Method of Inventory Costing

The **gross profit method** uses the estimated gross profit for the period to estimate the inventory at the end of the period. The gross profit is estimated from the preceding year, adjusted for any current-period changes in the cost and sales prices.

The gross profit method is applied as follows:

- Step 1. Determine the merchandise available for sale at cost.
- Step 2. Determine the estimated gross profit by multiplying the sales by the gross profit percentage, assumed to be 30% in this illustration.
- Step 3. Determine the estimated cost of goods sold by deducting the estimated gross profit from the sales.
- Step 4. Estimate the ending inventory cost by deducting the estimated cost of goods sold from the merchandise available for sale.

Exhibit 14 illustrates the gross profit method.

Exhibit 14

Estimating Inventory by Gross Profit Method

	A	B	C
1			Cost
2	Inventory, January 1		$ 57,000
3	Purchases in January (net)		180,000
Step 1 → 4	Merchandise available for sale		$237,000
5	Sales for January	$250,000	
Step 2 → 6	Estimated gross profit ($250,000 × 30%)	75,000	
Step 3 → 7	Estimated cost of goods sold		175,000
Step 4 → 8	Estimated inventory, January 31		$ 62,000
9			

The gross profit method is useful for estimating inventories for monthly or quarterly financial statements. It is also useful in estimating the cost of inventory destroyed by fire or other disasters.

Let's Review

Chapter Summary

1. Two objectives of inventory control are safeguarding the inventory and properly reporting it in the financial statements. The perpetual inventory system and physical count enhance control over inventory.

2. The three common inventory cost flow assumptions used in business are the (1) first-in, first-out method (FIFO); (2) last-in, first-out method (LIFO); and (3) weighted average cost method. The cost flow assumption affects the income statement and balance sheet.

3. In a perpetual inventory system, the number of units and the cost of each type of merchandise are recorded in a subsidiary inventory ledger, with a separate account for each type of merchandise.

4. In a periodic inventory system, a physical inventory is taken to determine the cost of the inventory and the cost of goods sold.

5. The three inventory costing methods will normally yield different amounts for (1) the ending inventory, (2) the cost of goods sold for the period, and (3) the gross profit (and net income) for the period.

6. The lower-of-cost-or-market (LCM) method is used to value inventory. The market value is the net realizable value of the merchandise. Inventory is usually presented in the current assets section of the balance sheet, following receivables. The methods of determining the cost and valuing the inventory are reported. Errors in reporting inventory will affect the balance sheet and income statement.

Key Terms

consigned inventory (304)
consignee (304)
consignor (304)
first-in, first-out (FIFO)
    inventory cost flow
    method (290)
gross profit method (309)
inventory turnover (306)

last-in, first-out (LIFO) inventory
    cost flow method (290)
lower-of-cost-or-market
    (LCM) method (300)
net realizable value (300)
number of days' sales in
    inventory (307)
physical inventory (289)

purchase order (288)
receiving report (288)
retail inventory method (309)
specific identification inventory
    cost flow method (290)
subsidiary inventory ledger (288)
weighted average inventory
    cost flow method (290)

Practice

Multiple-Choice Questions

1. The inventory costing method that is based on the assumption that costs should be charged against revenue in the order in which they were incurred is:
   A. FIFO.
   B. LIFO.
   C. weighted average cost.
   D. perpetual inventory.

2. The following units of a particular item were purchased and sold during the period:

Beginning inventory	40 units at $20
First purchase	50 units at $21
Second purchase	50 units at $22
First sale	110 units
Third purchase	50 units at $23
Second sale	45 units

   What is the cost of the 35 units on hand at the end of the period as determined under the perpetual inventory system by the LIFO costing method?
   A. $715
   B. $705
   C. $700
   D. $805

3. The following units of a particular item were available for sale during the period:

Beginning inventory	40 units at $20
First purchase	50 units at $21
Second purchase	50 units at $22
Third purchase	50 units at $23

   What is the unit cost of the 35 units on hand at the end of the period as determined under the periodic inventory system by the FIFO costing method?
   A. $20
   B. $21
   C. $22
   D. $23

4. If inventory is being valued at cost and the price level is steadily rising, the method of costing that will yield the highest net income is:
   A. LIFO.
   B. FIFO.
   C. average.
   D. periodic.

5. If the inventory at the end of the year is understated by $7,500, the error will cause an:
   A. understatement of cost of goods sold for the year by $7,500.
   B. overstatement of gross profit for the year by $7,500.
   C. overstatement of beginning inventory for the following year by $7,500.
   D. understatement of net income for the year by $7,500.

Answers provided after Problem. Need more practice? Find additional multiple-choice questions, exercises, and problems in CengageNOWv2.

Exercises

SHOW ME HOW

1. Cost flow methods

Obj. 2

The following three identical units of Item BZ1810 are purchased during November:

	Item BZ1810	Units	Cost
Nov. 2	Purchase	1	$ 55
14	Purchase	1	57
28	Purchase	1	62
	Total	3	$174
	Average cost per unit		$ 58 ($174 ÷ 3 units)

Assume that one unit is sold on November 30 for $90.

Determine the gross profit for November and ending inventory on November 30 using the (A) first-in, first-out (FIFO); (B) last-in, first-out (LIFO); and (C) weighted average cost methods.

SHOW ME HOW

2. Perpetual inventory using FIFO

Obj. 3

Beginning inventory, purchases, and sales for Item ProX2 are as follows:

Jan. 1	Inventory	60 units at $100
9	Sale	35 units
13	Purchase	50 units at $110
25	Sale	48 units

Assuming a perpetual inventory system and using the first-in, first-out (FIFO) method, determine (A) the cost of goods sold on January 25 and (B) the inventory on January 31.

SHOW ME HOW

3. Perpetual inventory using LIFO

Obj. 3

Beginning inventory, purchases, and sales for Item Zebra 9x are as follows:

April 1	Inventory	420 units at $8
10	Sale	300 units
18	Purchase	280 units at $9
27	Sale	250 units

Assuming a perpetual inventory system and using the last-in, first-out (LIFO) method, determine (A) the cost of goods sold on April 27 and (B) the inventory on April 30.

SHOW ME HOW

4. Perpetual inventory using weighted average

Obj. 3

Beginning inventory, purchases, and sales for 30xT are as follows:

May 1	Inventory	50 units at $80
12	Sale	35 units
23	Purchase	60 units at $90
26	Sale	55 units

Assuming a perpetual inventory system and using the weighted average method, determine the (A) weighted average unit cost after the May 23 purchase, (B) cost of goods sold on May 26, and (C) inventory on May 31.

SHOW ME HOW

5. Periodic inventory using FIFO, LIFO, and weighted average cost methods

Obj. 4

The units of an item available for sale during the year were as follows:

Jan. 1	Inventory	12 units at $5,400	$ 64,800
Aug. 7	Purchase	18 units at $6,000	108,000
Dec. 11	Purchase	15 units at $6,480	97,200
	Available for sale	45 units	$270,000

There are 14 units of the item in the physical inventory at December 31. The periodic inventory system is used. Determine the inventory cost using the (A) first-in, first-out (FIFO) method; (B) last-in, first-out (LIFO) method; and (C) weighted average cost method.

SHOW ME HOW

6. Lower-of-cost-or-market method

Obj. 6

On the basis of the following data, determine the value of the inventory at the lower of cost or market. Apply lower of cost or market to each inventory item, as shown in Exhibit 9.

Item	Inventory Quantity	Cost per Unit	Market Value per Unit (Net Realizable Value)
Raven 10	1,200	$115	$112
Dove 23	6,500	17	22

SHOW ME HOW

7. Effect of inventory errors

Obj. 6

During the taking of its physical inventory on August 31, 20Y4, Kate Interiors Company incorrectly counted its inventory as $366,900 instead of the correct amount of $378,500. Indicate the effect of the misstatement on Kate Interiors' August 31, 20Y4, balance sheet and income statement for the year ended August 31, 20Y4.

Answers provided after Problem. Need more practice? Find additional multiple-choice questions, exercises, and problems in CengageNOWv2.

Problem

Stewart Co.'s beginning inventory and purchases during the year ended December 31, 20Y2, were as follows:

		Unit	Unit Cost	Total Cost
January 1	Inventory	1,000	$50.00	$ 50,000
March 10	Purchase	3,000	52.00	156,000
June 25	Sold 1,600 units			
August 30	Purchase	2,600	55.00	143,000
October 5	Sold 4,000 units			
November 26	Purchase	1,000	57.68	57,680
December 31	Sold 800 units			
Total		7,600		$406,680

Instructions

1. Determine the cost of inventory on December 31, 20Y2, using the perpetual inventory system and each of the following inventory costing methods:
   A. first-in, first-out
   B. last-in, first-out
   C. weighted average (round weighted average cost per unit to two decimal places)
2. Determine the cost of inventory on December 31, 20Y2, using the periodic inventory system and each of the following inventory costing methods:
   A. first-in, first-out
   B. last-in, first-out
   C. weighted average cost (round weighted average cost per unit to two decimal places)
3. (*Appendix*) Assume that during the fiscal year ended December 31, 20Y2, sales were $530,000 and the estimated gross profit rate was 36%. Estimate the ending inventory at December 31, 20Y2, using the gross profit method.

Need more practice? Find additional multiple-choice questions, exercises, and problems in CengageNOWv2.

Answers

Multiple-Choice Questions

1. **A** The FIFO method (answer A) is based on the assumption that costs are charged against revenue in the order in which they were incurred. The LIFO method (answer B) charges the most recent costs incurred against revenue, and the weighted average cost method (answer C) charges a weighted average of unit costs of items sold against revenue. The perpetual inventory system (answer D) is a system and not a method of costing.

2. **A** The LIFO method of costing is based on the assumption that costs should be charged against revenue in the reverse order in which costs were incurred. Thus, the oldest costs are assigned to ending inventory. Thirty of the 35 units would be assigned a unit cost of $20

(since 10 of the beginning inventory units were sold on the first sale), and the remaining 5 units would be assigned a cost of $23, for a total of $715 (answer A).

3. **D** The FIFO method of costing is based on the assumption that costs should be charged against revenue in the order in which they were incurred (first-in, first-out). Thus, the most recent costs are assigned to inventory. The 35 units would be assigned a unit cost of $23 (answer D).

4. **B** When the price level is steadily rising, the earlier unit costs are lower than recent unit costs. Under the FIFO method (answer B), these earlier costs are matched against revenue to yield the highest possible net income. The periodic inventory system (answer D) is a system and not a method of costing.

5. **D** The understatement of inventory by $7,500 at the end of the year will cause the cost of goods sold for the year to be overstated by $7,500, the gross profit for the year to be understated by $7,500, next year's beginning inventory to be understated by $7,500, and the net income for the year to be understated by $7,500 (answer D).

Exercises

1.

	Gross Profit November	Ending Inventory November 30
A. First-in, first-out (FIFO)	$35 ($90 – $55)	$119 ($57 + $62)
B. Last-in, first-out (LIFO)	$28 ($90 – $62)	$112 ($55 + $57)
C. Weighted average cost	$32 ($90 – $58)	$116 ($58 × 2)

2.

A. Cost of goods sold (January 25):

25 units @ $100	$2,500
23 units @ $110	2,530
48	$5,030

B. Inventory, January 31: $2,970 = 27 units × $110

3.

A. Cost of goods sold (April 27): $2,250 = 250 units × $9
B. Inventory, April 30:

120 units @ $8	$ 960
30 units @ $ 9	270
150	$1,230

4.

A. Weighted average unit cost: $88
Inventory total cost after purchase on May 23:

15 units @ $80	$1,200
60 units @ $90	5,400
75	$6,600

Weighted average unit cost = $88 ($6,600 ÷ 75 units)
B. Cost of goods sold (May 26): $4,840 (55 units × $88)
C. Inventory, May 31: $1,760 = 20 units × $88

5.

A. First-in, first-out (FIFO) method: $90,720 = 14 units × $6,480
B. Last-in, first-out (LIFO) method: $76,800 = [(12 units × $5,400) + (2 units × $6,000)]
C. Weighted average cost method: $84,000 (14 units × $6,000),
where average cost = $6,000 = $270,000 ÷ 45 units

6.

Commodity	Inventory Quantity	Cost per unit	Market Value per Unit (Net Realizable Value)	Total Cost	Total Market	Total LCM
Raven 10	1,200	$115	$112	$138,000	$134,400	$134,400
Dove 23	6,500	17	22	110,500	143,000	110,500
Total				$248,500	$277,400	$244,900

7.

	Amount of Misstatement Overstatement (Understatement)
Balance Sheet:	
Inventory understated*	$(11,600)
Current assets understated	(11,600)
Total assets understated	(11,600)
Stockholders' equity understated	(11,600)
Income Statement:	
Cost of goods sold overstated	$ 11,600
Gross profit understated	(11,600)
Net income understated	(11,600)

* $378,500 – $366,900 = $11,600

Need more help? Watch step-by-step videos of how to compute answers to these Exercises in CengageNOWv2.

Problem

1.
   A. First-in, first-out method: $68,680 ($11,000 + $57,680)
   B. Last-in, first-out method: $61,536 ($50,000 + $11,536)
   C. Weighted average cost method: $66,600 (1,200 units × $55.50)
      The subsidiary ledgers shown below and on the next page support the preceding perpetual inventory amounts.

2. A. First-in, first-out method:

1,000 units at $57.68	$57,680
200 units at $55.00	11,000
1,200 units	$68,680

   B. Last-in, first-out method:

1,000 units at $50.00	$50,000
200 units at $52.00	10,400
1,200 units	$60,400

   C. Weighted average cost method:

Weighted average cost per unit: $406,680 ÷ 7,600 units = $53.51 (Rounded)
Inventory, December 31, 20Y2: 1,200 units × $53.51 = $64,212

1. A. First-in, first-out method: $68,680 ($11,000 + $57,680)

Date	Purchases			Cost of Goods Sold			Inventory		
	Quantity	Unit Cost	Total Cost	Quantity	Unit Cost	Total Cost	Quantity	Unit Cost	Total Cost
20Y2									
Jan. 1							1,000	50.00	50,000
Mar. 10	3,000	52.00	156,000				1,000	50.00	50,000
							3,000	52.00	156,000
June 25				1,000	50.00	50,000	2,400	52.00	124,800
				600	52.00	31,200			
Aug. 30	2,600	55.00	143,000				2,400	52.00	124,800
							2,600	55.00	143,000
Oct. 5				2,400	52.00	124,800	1,000	55.00	55,000
				1,600	55.00	88,000			
Nov. 26	1,000	57.68	57,680				1,000	55.00	55,000
							1,000	57.68	57,680
Dec. 31				800	55.00	44,000	200	55.00	11,000
							1,000	57.68	57,680
31	Balances					338,000			68,680

(Continued)

B. Last-in, first-out method: $61,536 ($50,000 + $11,536)

Date	Purchases Quantity	Purchases Unit Cost	Purchases Total Cost	Cost of Goods Sold Quantity	Cost of Goods Sold Unit Cost	Cost of Goods Sold Total Cost	Inventory Quantity	Inventory Unit Cost	Inventory Total Cost
20Y2 Jan. 1							1,000	50.00	50,000
Mar. 10	3,000	52.00	156,000				1,000	50.00	50,000
							3,000	52.00	156,000
June 25				1,600	52.00	83,200	1,000	50.00	50,000
							1,400	52.00	72,800
Aug. 30	2,600	55.00	143,000				1,000	50.00	50,000
							1,400	52.00	72,800
							2,600	55.00	143,000
Oct. 5				2,600	55.00	143,000	1,000	50.00	50,000
				1,400	52.00	72,800			
Nov. 26	1,000	57.68	57,680				1,000	50.00	50,000
							1,000	57.68	57,680
Dec. 31				800	57.68	46,144	1,000	50.00	50,000
							200	57.68	11,536
31	Balances					345,144			61,536

C. Weighted average cost method: $66,600 (1,200 units × $55.50)

Date	Purchases Quantity	Purchases Unit Cost	Purchases Total Cost	Cost of Goods Sold Quantity	Cost of Goods Sold Unit Cost	Cost of Goods Sold Total Cost	Inventory Quantity	Inventory Unit Cost	Inventory Total Cost
20Y2 Jan. 1							1,000	50.00	50,000
Mar. 10	3,000	52.00	156,000				4,000	51.50	206,000
June 25				1,600	51.50	82,400	2,400	51.50	123,600
Aug. 30	2,600	55.00	143,000				5,000	53.32	266,600
Oct. 5				4,000	53.32	213,280	1,000	53.32	53,320
Nov. 26	1,000	57.68	57,680				2,000	55.50	111,000
Dec. 31				800	55.50	44,400	1,200	55.50	66,600
31	Balances					340,080	1,200	55.50	66,600

3. (*Appendix*)

	Cost
Inventory, January 1, 20Y2	$ 50,000
Purchases (net)	356,680
Merchandise available for sale	$406,680
Sales $530,000	
Estimated gross profit ($530,000 × 36%) 190,800	
Estimated cost of goods sold	339,200
Estimated inventory, December 31, 20Y2	$ 67,480

Discussion Questions

1. Before inventory purchases are recorded, the receiving report should be reconciled to what documents?

2. Why is it important to periodically take a physical inventory when using a perpetual inventory system?

3. Do the terms *FIFO, LIFO,* and *weighted average* refer to techniques used in determining quantities of the various classes of inventory on hand? Explain.

4. If inventory is being valued at cost and the price level is decreasing, which of the three methods of costing—FIFO, LIFO, or weighted average cost—will yield (A) the highest inventory cost, (B) the lowest inventory cost, (C) the highest gross profit, and (D) the lowest gross profit?

5. Which of the three methods of inventory costing—FIFO, LIFO, or weighted average cost—will in general

yield an inventory cost most nearly approximating current replacement cost?

6. If inventory is being valued at cost and the price level is steadily rising, which of the three methods of costing—FIFO, LIFO, or weighted average cost—will yield the lowest annual income tax expense? Explain.

7. Using the following data, how should the inventory be valued under lower of cost or market?

Original cost	$1,350
Estimated selling price	1,475
Selling expenses	180

8. The inventory at the end of the year was understated by $14,750. (A) Did the error cause an overstatement or an understatement of the gross profit for the year? (B) Which items on the balance sheet at the end of the year were overstated or understated as a result of the error?

9. Hutch Co. sold merchandise to Bibbins Company on May 31, FOB shipping point. If the merchandise is in transit on May 31, the end of the fiscal year, which company would report it in its financial statements? Explain.

10. A manufacturer shipped merchandise to a retailer on a consignment basis. If the merchandise is unsold at the end of the period, in whose inventory should the merchandise be included?

Basic Exercises

SHOW ME HOW

BE 6-1 Cost flow methods   Obj. 2

The following three identical units of Item P401C are purchased during April:

Item Beta		Units	Cost
April	2 Purchase	1	$100
	15 Purchase	1	120
	20 Purchase	1	140
	Total	3	$360
	Average cost per unit		$120 ($360 ÷ 3 units)

Assume that one unit is sold on April 27 for $300.

Determine the gross profit for April and ending inventory on April 30 using the (A) first-in, first-out (FIFO); (B) last-in, first-out (LIFO); and (C) weighted average cost methods.

SHOW ME HOW

BE 6-2 Perpetual inventory using FIFO   Obj. 3

Beginning inventory, purchases, and sales for Item Zeta9 are as follows:

Oct.	1	Inventory	175 units at $30
	7	Sale	155 units
	15	Purchase	200 units at $33
	24	Sale	140 units

Assuming a perpetual inventory system and using the first-in, first-out (FIFO) method, determine (A) the cost of goods sold on October 24 and (B) the inventory on October 31.

SHOW ME HOW

BE 6-3 Perpetual inventory using LIFO   Obj. 3

Beginning inventory, purchases, and sales for Item 88-HX are as follows:

July	1	Inventory	90 units at $54
	8	Sale	75 units
	15	Purchase	125 units at $60
	27	Sale	80 units

Assuming a perpetual inventory system and using the last-in, first-out (LIFO) method, determine (A) the cost of goods sold on July 27 and (B) the inventory on July 31.

BE 6-4   Perpetual inventory using weighted average   **Obj. 3**

Beginning inventory, purchases, and sales for WCS12 are as follows:

Oct.	1	Inventory	300 units at $8
	13	Sale	175 units
	22	Purchase	375 units at $10
	29	Sale	280 units

Assuming a perpetual inventory system and using the weighted average method, determine (A) the weighted average unit cost after the October 22 purchase, (B) the cost of goods sold on October 29, and (C) the inventory on October 31.

BE 6-5   Periodic inventory using FIFO, LIFO, and weighted average cost methods   **Obj. 4**

The units of an item available for sale during the year were as follows:

Jan.	1	Inventory	20 units at $360	$ 7,200
Aug.	13	Purchase	260 units at $342	88,920
Nov.	30	Purchase	40 units at $357	14,280
		Available for sale	320 units	$110,400

There are 57 units of the item in the physical inventory at December 31. The periodic inventory system is used. Determine the inventory cost using the (A) first-in, first-out (FIFO) method; (B) last-in, first-out (LIFO) method; and (C) weighted average cost method.

BE 6-6   Lower-of-cost-or-market method   **Obj. 6**

On the basis of the following data, determine the value of the inventory at the lower of cost or market. Apply lower of cost or market to each inventory item, as shown in Exhibit 9.

Item	Inventory Quantity	Cost per Unit	Market Value per Unit (Net Realizable Value)
JFW1	6,330	$10	$11
SAW9	1,140	36	34

BE 6-7   Effect of inventory errors   **Obj. 6**

During the taking of its physical inventory on December 31, 20Y3, Waterjet Bath Company incorrectly counted its inventory as $728,660 instead of the correct amount of $719,880. Indicate the effect of the misstatement on Waterjet Bath's December 31, 20Y3, balance sheet and income statement for the year ended December 31, 20Y3.

Exercises

EX 6-1   Control of inventories   **Obj. 1**

Triple Creek Hardware Store currently uses a periodic inventory system. Kevin Carlton, the owner and sole stockholder, is considering the purchase of a computer system that would make it feasible to switch to a perpetual inventory system.

Kevin is unhappy with the periodic inventory system because it does not provide timely information on inventory levels. Kevin has noticed on several occasions that the store runs out of good-selling items, while too many poor-selling items are on hand.

Kevin is also concerned about lost sales while a physical inventory is being taken. Triple Creek currently takes a physical inventory twice a year. To minimize distractions, the store is closed on the day inventory is taken. Kevin believes that closing the store is the only way to get an accurate inventory count.

➡ Will switching to a perpetual inventory system strengthen Triple Creek Hardware's control over inventory items? Will switching to a perpetual inventory system eliminate the need for a physical inventory count? Explain.

EX 6-2 Control of inventories

Obj. 1

Hardcase Luggage Shop is a small retail establishment located in a large shopping mall. This shop has implemented the following procedures regarding inventory items:

A. Because the shop carries mostly high-quality, designer luggage, all inventory items are tagged with a control device that activates an alarm if a tagged item is removed from the store.

B. Because the display area of the store is limited, only a sample of each piece of luggage is kept on the selling floor. Whenever a customer selects a piece of luggage, the salesclerk gets the appropriate piece from the store's stockroom. Because all salesclerks need access to the stockroom, it is not locked. The stockroom is adjacent to the break room used by all mall employees.

C. Whenever Hardcase receives a shipment of new inventory, the items are taken directly to the stockroom. Hardcase's accountant uses the vendor's invoice to record the amount of inventory received.

State whether each of these procedures is appropriate or inappropriate. If it is inappropriate, state why.

✔ Inventory balance, November 30, $7,480

SHOW ME HOW

EX 6-3 Perpetual inventory using FIFO

Obj. 2, 3

Beginning inventory, purchases, and sales data for DVD players are as follows:

November	1	Inventory	120 units at $39
	10	Sale	90 units
	15	Purchase	140 units at $40
	20	Sale	110 units
	24	Sale	45 units
	30	Purchase	160 units at $43

The business maintains a perpetual inventory system, costing by the first-in, first-out method.

A. Determine the cost of goods sold for each sale and the inventory balance after each sale, presenting the data in the form illustrated in Exhibit 3.

B. Based upon the preceding data, would you expect the inventory to be higher or lower using the last-in, first-out method?

✔ Inventory balance, November 30, $7,465

SHOW ME HOW   EXCEL TEMPLATE

EX 6-4 Perpetual inventory using LIFO

Obj. 2, 3

Assume that the business in Exercise 6-3 maintains a perpetual inventory system, costing by the last-in, first-out method. Determine the cost of goods sold for each sale and the inventory balance after each sale, presenting the data in the form illustrated in Exhibit 4.

✔ Inventory balance, December 31, $8,064

SHOW ME HOW   EXCEL TEMPLATE

EX 6-5 Perpetual inventory using LIFO

Obj. 2, 3

Beginning inventory, purchases, and sales data for prepaid cell phones for December are as follows:

Inventory		Purchases		Sales	
Dec. 1	310 units at $88	Dec. 10	144 units at $90	Dec. 12	240 units
		20	240 units at $96	14	166 units
				31	200 units

A. Assuming that the perpetual inventory system is used, costing by the LIFO method, determine the cost of goods sold for each sale and the inventory balance after each sale, presenting the data in the form illustrated in Exhibit 4.

B. Based upon the preceding data, would you expect the inventory to be higher or lower using the first-in, first-out method?

✔ Inventory balance, December 31, $8,448

SHOW ME HOW   EXCEL TEMPLATE

EX 6-6 Perpetual inventory using FIFO

Obj. 2, 3

Assume that the business in Exercise 6-5 maintains a perpetual inventory system, costing by the first-in, first-out method. Determine the cost of goods sold for each sale and the inventory balance after each sale, presenting the data in the form illustrated in Exhibit 3.

EX 6-7 FIFO and LIFO costs under perpetual inventory system

Obj. 2, 3

✔ B. $1,760,000

SHOW ME HOW

The following units of an item were available for sale during the year:

Beginning inventory	7,200 units at $160
Sale	4,800 units at $300
First purchase	16,000 units at $168
Sale	12,000 units at $300
Second purchase	15,000 units at $176
Sale	11,000 units at $300

The firm uses the perpetual inventory system, and there are 10,400 units of the item on hand at the end of the year. What is the total cost of the ending inventory according to (A) FIFO and (B) LIFO?

EX 6-8 Weighted average cost flow method under perpetual inventory system

Obj. 3

✔ Total Cost of goods sold, $1,758,750

SHOW ME HOW

The following units of a particular item were available for sale during the calendar year:

Jan.	1	Inventory	10,000 units at $75.00
Mar.	18	Sale	8,000 units
May	2	Purchase	18,000 units at $77.50
Aug.	9	Sale	15,000 units
Oct.	20	Purchase	7,000 units at $80.25

The firm uses the weighted average cost method with a perpetual inventory system. Determine the cost of goods sold for each sale and the inventory balance after each sale. Present the data in the form illustrated in Exhibit 5.

EX 6-9 Weighted average cost flow method under perpetual inventory system

Obj. 3

✔ Total Cost of goods sold, $154,400

The following units of a particular item were available for sale during the calendar year:

Jan.	1	Inventory	4,000 units at $20
Apr.	19	Sale	2,500 units
June	30	Purchase	6,000 units at $24
Sept.	2	Sale	4,500 units
Nov.	15	Purchase	1,000 units at $25

The firm uses the weighted average cost method with a perpetual inventory system. Determine the cost of goods sold for each sale and the inventory balance after each sale. Present the data in the form illustrated in Exhibit 5.

EX 6-10 Perpetual inventory using FIFO

Obj. 3

✔ Total Cost of goods sold, $152,000

Assume that the business in Exercise 6-9 maintains a perpetual inventory system. Determine the cost of goods sold for each sale and the inventory balance after each sale, assuming the first-in, first-out method. Present the data in the form illustrated in Exhibit 3.

EX 6-11 Perpetual inventory using LIFO

Obj. 3

✔ Total Cost of goods sold, $158,000

Assume that the business in Exercise 6-9 maintains a perpetual inventory system. Determine the cost of goods sold for each sale and the inventory balance after each sale, assuming the last-in, first-out method. Present the data in the form illustrated in Exhibit 4.

EX 6-12 Periodic inventory by three methods

Obj. 2, 4

✔ B. $16,600

SHOW ME HOW

The units of an item available for sale during the year were as follows:

Jan.	1	Inventory	1,000 units at $15
Feb.	17	Purchase	1,375 units at $16
July	21	Purchase	1,500 units at $17
Nov.	23	Purchase	1,125 units at $18

There are 1,100 units of the item in the physical inventory at December 31. The periodic inventory system is used. Determine the inventory cost by the (A) first-in, first-out method, (B) last-in, first-out method, and (C) weighted average cost method.

EX 6-13 Periodic inventory by three methods; cost of goods sold

Obj. 2, 4

✔ A. Inventory, $24,912

SHOW ME HOW

The units of an item available for sale during the year were as follows:

Jan.	1	Inventory	180 units at $108
Mar.	10	Purchase	224 units at $110
Aug.	30	Purchase	200 units at $116
Dec.	12	Purchase	196 units at $120

There are 208 units of the item in the physical inventory at December 31. The periodic inventory system is used. Determine the ending inventory cost and the cost of goods sold by three methods, presenting your answers in the following form:

Inventory Method	Ending Inventory	Cost of Goods Sold
A. First-in, first-out	$	$
B. Last-in, first-out		
C. Weighted average cost		

EX 6-14 Comparing inventory methods

Obj. 5

Assume that a firm separately determined inventory under FIFO and LIFO and then compared the results.

A. In each space that follows, place the correct sign [less than (<), greater than (>), or equal (=)] for each comparison, assuming periods of rising prices.

1. FIFO inventory	_____	LIFO inventory
2. FIFO cost of goods sold	_____	LIFO cost of goods sold
3. FIFO net income	_____	LIFO net income
4. FIFO income taxes	_____	LIFO income taxes

B. ➤ Why would management prefer to use LIFO over FIFO in periods of rising prices?

SHOW ME HOW

EXCEL TEMPLATE

EX 6-15 Lower-of-cost-or-market inventory

Obj. 6

On the basis of the following data, determine the value of the inventory at the lower of cost or market. Assemble the data in the form illustrated in Exhibit 9.

Product	Inventory Quantity	Cost per Unit	Market Value per Unit (Net Realizable Value)
Model A	300	$140	$125
Model B	500	90	112
Model C	150	60	59
Model D	800	120	115
Model E	400	140	145

EX 6-16 Inventory on the balance sheet

Obj. 6

Based on the data in Exercise 6-15 and assuming that cost was determined by the FIFO method, show how the inventory would appear on the balance sheet.

EX 6-17 Effect of errors in physical inventory

Obj. 6

Madison River Supply Co. sells canoes, kayaks, whitewater rafts, and other boating supplies. During the taking of its physical inventory on December 31, 20Y8, Madison incorrectly counted its inventory as $545,000 instead of the correct amount of $555,400.

(Continued)

A. State the effects of the error on the December 31, 20Y8, balance sheet of Madison River Supply.

B. State the effects of the error on the income statement of Madison River Supply for the year ended December 31, 20Y8.

C. If uncorrected, what would be the effects of the error on the 20Y9 income statement?

D. If uncorrected, what would be the effects of the error on the December 31, 20Y9, balance sheet?

EX 6-18   Effect of errors in physical inventory   Obj. 6

Fonda Motorcycle Shop sells motorcycles, ATVs, and other related supplies and accessories. During the taking of its physical inventory on December 31, 20Y1, Fonda incorrectly counted its inventory as $337,500 instead of the correct amount of $328,850.

A. State the effects of the error on the December 31, 20Y1, balance sheet of Fonda Motorcycle Shop.

B. State the effects of the error on the income statement of Fonda Motorcycle Shop for the year ended December 31, 20Y1.

C. If uncorrected, what would be the effects of the error on the 20Y2 income statement?

D. If uncorrected, what would be the effects of the error on the December 31, 20Y2, balance sheet?

EX 6-19   Error in inventory   Obj. 6

During 20Y5, the accountant discovered that the physical inventory at the end of 20Y4 had been understated by $42,750. Instead of correcting the error, however, the accountant assumed that the error would balance out (correct itself) in 20Y5.

➤ Are there any flaws in the accountant's assumption? Explain.

Appendix
EX 6-20   Retail method

A business using the retail method of inventory costing determines that inventory at retail is $1,235,000. If the ratio of cost to retail price is 54%, what is the amount of inventory to be reported on the financial statements?

Appendix
EX 6-21   Retail method

A business using the retail method of inventory costing determines that inventory at retail is $396,400. If the ratio of cost to retail price is 61%, what is the amount of inventory to be reported on the financial statements?

Appendix
EX 6-22   Retail method

A business using the retail method of inventory costing determines that inventory at retail is $775,000. If the ratio of cost to retail price is 66%, what is the amount of inventory to be reported on the financial statements?

Appendix
EX 6-23   Retail method

EXCEL TEMPLATE

On the basis of the following data, estimate the cost of the inventory at June 30 by the retail method:

		Cost	Retail
June 1	Inventory	$ 165,000	$ 275,000
June 1–30	Purchases (net)	2,361,500	3,800,000
June 1–30	Sales		3,550,000

Appendix
EX 6-24   Gross profit method

✔ A. Inventory
destroyed: $414,000

The inventory was destroyed by fire on December 31. The following data were obtained from the accounting records:

Jan. 1	Inventory	$ 350,000
Jan. 1–Dec. 31	Purchases (net)	2,950,000
	Sales	4,440,000
	Estimated gross profit rate	35%

A. Estimate the cost of the inventory destroyed.

B. ➤ Briefly describe the situations in which the gross profit method is useful.

Appendix
EX 6-25   Gross profit method

Based on the following data, estimate the cost of the ending inventory:

Sales	$9,250,000
Estimated gross profit rate	36%
Beginning inventory	$ 180,000
Purchases (net)	5,945,000
Merchandise available for sale	$6,125,000

Appendix
EX 6-26   Gross profit method

Based on the following data, estimate the cost of the ending inventory:

Sales	$1,450,000
Estimated gross profit rate	42%
Beginning inventory	$ 100,000
Purchases (net)	860,000
Merchandise available for sale	$ 960,000

Problems: Series A

PR 6-1A   FIFO perpetual inventory

Obj. 2, 3

✔ 3. $8,983,125

SHOW ME HOW   EXCEL TEMPLATE

The beginning inventory at Midnight Supplies and data on purchases and sales for a three-month period ending March 31 are as follows:

Date		Transaction	Number of Units	Per Unit	Total
Jan.	1	Inventory	7,500	$ 75.00	$ 562,500
	10	Purchase	22,500	85.00	1,912,500
	28	Sale	11,250	150.00	1,687,500
	30	Sale	3,750	150.00	562,500
Feb.	5	Sale	1,500	150.00	225,000
	10	Purchase	54,000	87.50	4,725,000
	16	Sale	27,000	160.00	4,320,000
	28	Sale	25,500	160.00	4,080,000
Mar.	5	Purchase	45,000	89.50	4,027,500
	14	Sale	30,000	160.00	4,800,000
	25	Purchase	7,500	90.00	675,000
	30	Sale	26,250	160.00	4,200,000

(Continued)

Instructions

1. Record the inventory, purchases, and cost of goods sold data in a perpetual inventory record similar to the one illustrated in Exhibit 3, using the first-in, first-out method.

2. Determine the total sales and the total cost of goods sold for the period. Journalize the entries in the sales and cost of goods sold accounts. Assume that all sales were on account.

3. Determine the gross profit from sales for the period.

4. Determine the ending inventory cost as of March 31.

5. Based upon the preceding data, would you expect the ending inventory using the last-in, first-out method to be higher or lower?

PR 6-2A   LIFO perpetual inventory   Obj. 2, 3

✔ 2. Gross profit, $5,773,125

SHOW ME HOW   EXCEL TEMPLATE

The beginning inventory at Midnight Supplies and data on purchases and sales for a three-month period are shown in Problem 6-1A.

Instructions

1. Record the inventory, purchases, and cost of goods sold data in a perpetual inventory record similar to the one illustrated in Exhibit 4, using the last-in, first-out method.

2. Determine the total sales, the total cost of goods sold, and the gross profit from sales for the period.

3. Determine the ending inventory cost as of March 31.

PR 6-3A   Weighted average cost method with perpetual inventory   Obj. 2, 3

✔ 2. Gross profit, $5,893,125

The beginning inventory for Midnight Supplies and data on purchases and sales for a three-month period are shown in Problem 6-1A.

Instructions

1. Record the inventory, purchases, and cost of goods sold data in a perpetual inventory record similar to the one illustrated in Exhibit 5, using the weighted average cost method.

2. Determine the total sales, the total cost of goods sold, and the gross profit from sales for the period.

3. Determine the ending inventory cost as of March 31.

PR 6-4A   Periodic inventory by three methods   Obj. 2, 3

✔ 2. Inventory, $881,250

The beginning inventory for Midnight Supplies and data on purchases and sales for a three-month period are shown in Problem 6-1A.

Instructions

1. Determine the inventory on March 31 and the cost of goods sold for the three-month period, using the first-in, first-out method and the periodic inventory system.

2. Determine the inventory on March 31 and the cost of goods sold for the three-month period, using the last-in, first-out method and the periodic inventory system.

3. Determine the inventory on March 31 and the cost of goods sold for the three-month period, using the weighted average cost method and the periodic inventory system. (Round the weighted average unit cost to the nearest cent.)

4. Compare the gross profit and the March 31 inventories, using the following column headings:

	FIFO	LIFO	Weighted Average
Sales			
Cost of goods sold			
Gross profit			
Inventory, March 31			

PR 6-5A Periodic inventory by three methods

Obj. 2, 4

✔ 1. $10,700

SHOW ME HOW   EXCEL TEMPLATE

Dymac Appliances uses the periodic inventory system. Details regarding the inventory of appliances at January 1, purchases invoices during the next 12 months, and the inventory count at December 31 are summarized as follows:

Model	Inventory, January 1	Purchases Invoices			Inventory Count, December 31
		1st	2nd	3rd	
A10	—	4 at $ 64	4 at $ 70	4 at $ 76	6
B15	8 at $176	4 at 158	3 at 170	6 at 184	8
E60	3 at 75	3 at 65	15 at 68	9 at 70	5
G83	7 at 242	6 at 250	5 at 260	10 at 259	9
J34	12 at 240	10 at 246	16 at 267	16 at 270	15
M90	2 at 108	2 at 110	3 at 128	3 at 130	5
Q70	5 at 160	4 at 170	4 at 175	7 at 180	8

Instructions

1. Determine the cost of the inventory on December 31 by the first-in, first-out method. Present data in columnar form, using the following headings:

Model	Quantity	Unit Cost	Total Cost

If the inventory of a particular model comprises one entire purchase plus a portion of another purchase acquired at a different unit cost, use a separate line for each purchase.

2. Determine the cost of the inventory on December 31 by the last-in, first-out method, following the procedures indicated in (1).

3. Determine the cost of the inventory on December 31 by the weighted average cost method, using the columnar headings indicated in (1).

4. ━━━━▶ Discuss which method (FIFO or LIFO) would be preferred for income tax purposes in periods of (A) rising prices and (B) declining prices.

PR 6-6A Lower-of-cost-or-market inventory

Obj. 6

✔ Total LCM, $39,873

Data on the physical inventory of Ashwood Products Company as of December 31 follows:

Description	Inventory Quantity	Market Value per Unit (Net Realizable Value)
B12	38	$ 57
E41	18	180
G19	33	126
L88	18	550
N94	400	7
P24	90	18
R66	8	250
T33	140	20
Z16	15	752

Quantity and cost data from the last purchases invoice of the year and the next-to-the-last purchases invoice are summarized as follows:

Description	Last Purchases Invoice		Next-to-the-Last Purchases Invoice	
	Quantity Purchased	Unit Cost	Quantity Purchased	Unit Cost
B12	30	$ 60	30	$ 59
E41	35	178	20	180
G19	20	128	25	129
L88	10	563	10	560
N94	500	8	500	7
P24	80	22	50	21
R66	5	248	4	260
T33	100	21	100	19
Z16	10	750	9	745

(Continued)

Instructions

Determine the inventory at cost and also at the lower of cost or market, using the first-in, first-out method. Record the appropriate unit costs on the inventory sheet, and complete the pricing of the inventory. When there are two different unit costs applicable to an item, proceed as follows:

1. Draw a line through the quantity, and insert the quantity and unit cost of the last purchase.

2. On the following line, insert the quantity and unit cost of the next-to-the-last purchase.

3. Total the cost and market columns and insert the lower of the two totals in the LCM column. The first item on the inventory sheet has been completed as an example.

Inventory Sheet

December 31

Description	Inventory Quantity	Cost per Unit	Market Value per Unit (Net Realizable Value)	Cost	Market	LCM
B12	38 30	$60	$57	$1,800	$1,710	
	8	59	57	472	456	
				$2,272	$2,166	$2,166

Appendix
PR 6-7A Retail method; gross profit method

✔ 1. $306,900

Selected data on inventory, purchases, and sales for Celebrity Tan Co. and Ranchworks Co. are as follows:

	Cost	Retail
Celebrity Tan Co.		
Inventory, August 1	$ 300,000	$ 575,000
Transactions during August:		
Purchases (net)	2,021,900	3,170,000
Sales		3,250,000
Ranchworks Co.		
Inventory, March 1	$ 880,000	
Transactions during March through November:		
Purchases (net)	9,500,000	
Sales	15,800,000	
Estimated gross profit rate	38%	

Instructions

1. Determine the estimated cost of the inventory of Celebrity Tan Co. on August 31 by the retail method, presenting details of the computations.

2. A. Estimate the cost of the inventory of Ranchworks Co. on November 30 by the gross profit method, presenting details of the computations.

   B. Assume that Ranchworks Co. took a physical inventory on November 30 and discovered that $369,750 of inventory was on hand. What was the estimated loss of inventory due to theft or damage during March through November?

Problems: Series B

PR 6-1B FIFO perpetual inventory
Obj. 2, 3

✔ 3. $214,474

SHOW ME HOW   EXCEL TEMPLATE

The beginning inventory at Dunne Co. and data on purchases and sales for a three-month period ending June 30 are as follows:

Date		Transaction	Number of Units	Per Unit	Total
Apr.	3	Inventory	25	$1,200	$ 30,000
	8	Purchase	75	1,240	93,000
	11	Sale	40	2,000	80,000
	30	Sale	30	2,000	60,000
May	8	Purchase	60	1,260	75,600
	10	Sale	50	2,000	100,000
	19	Sale	20	2,000	40,000
	28	Purchase	80	1,260	100,800
June	5	Sale	40	2,250	90,000
	16	Sale	25	2,250	56,250
	21	Purchase	35	1,264	44,240
	28	Sale	44	2,250	99,000

Instructions

1. Record the inventory, purchases, and cost of goods sold data in a perpetual inventory record similar to the one illustrated in Exhibit 3, using the first-in, first-out method.

2. Determine the total sales and the total cost of goods sold for the period. Journalize the entries in the sales and cost of goods sold accounts. Assume that all sales were on account.

3. Determine the gross profit from sales for the period.

4. Determine the ending inventory cost on June 30.

5. Based upon the preceding data, would you expect the ending inventory using the last-in, first-out method to be higher or lower?

PR 6-2B LIFO perpetual inventory
Obj. 2, 3

✔ 2. Gross profit, $213,170

SHOW ME HOW   EXCEL TEMPLATE

The beginning inventory for Dunne Co. and data on purchases and sales for a three-month period are shown in Problem 6-1B.

Instructions

1. Record the inventory, purchases, and cost of goods sold data in a perpetual inventory record similar to the one illustrated in Exhibit 4, using the last-in, first-out method.

2. Determine the total sales, the total cost of goods sold, and the gross profit from sales for the period.

3. Determine the ending inventory cost on June 30.

PR 6-3B Weighted average cost method with perpetual inventory
Obj. 2, 3

✔ 2. Gross profit, $214,396

The beginning inventory for Dunne Co. and data on purchases and sales for a three-month period are shown in Problem 6-1B.

Instructions

1. Record the inventory, purchases, and cost of goods sold data in a perpetual inventory record similar to the one illustrated in Exhibit 5, using the weighted average cost method.

2. Determine the total sales, the total cost of goods sold, and the gross profit from sales for the period.

3. Determine the ending inventory cost on June 30.

PR 6-4B   Periodic inventory by three methods

Obj. 2, 3

✔ 2. Inventory, $31,240

The beginning inventory for Dunne Co. and data on purchases and sales for a three-month period are shown in Problem 6-1B.

Instructions

1. Determine the inventory on June 30 and the cost of goods sold for the three-month period, using the first-in, first-out method and the periodic inventory system.

2. Determine the inventory on June 30 and the cost of goods sold for the three-month period, using the last-in, first-out method and the periodic inventory system.

3. Determine the inventory on June 30 and the cost of goods sold for the three-month period, using the weighted average cost method and the periodic inventory system. (Round the weighted average unit cost to the dollar.)

4. Compare the gross profit and June 30 inventories using the following column headings:

	FIFO	LIFO	Weighted Average
Sales			
Cost of goods sold			
Gross profit			
Inventory, June 30			

PR 6-5B   Periodic inventory by three methods

Obj. 2, 4

✔ 1. $18,545

Pappa's Appliances uses the periodic inventory system. Details regarding the inventory of appliances at January 1, purchases invoices during the year, and the inventory count at December 31 are summarized as follows:

SHOW ME HOW   EXCEL TEMPLATE

Model	Inventory, January 1	Purchases Invoices 1st	2nd	3rd	Inventory Count, December 31
C55	3 at $1,040	3 at $1,054	3 at $1,060	3 at $1,070	4
D11	9 at 639	7 at 645	6 at 666	6 at 675	11
F32	5 at 240	3 at 260	1 at 260	1 at 280	2
H29	6 at 305	3 at 310	3 at 316	4 at 317	4
K47	6 at 520	8 at 531	4 at 549	6 at 542	8
S33	—	4 at 222	4 at 232	—	2
X74	4 at 35	6 at 36	8 at 37	7 at 39	7

Instructions

1. Determine the cost of the inventory on December 31 by the first-in, first-out method. Present data in columnar form, using the following headings:

Model	Quantity	Unit Cost	Total Cost

If the inventory of a particular model comprises one entire purchase plus a portion of another purchase acquired at a different unit cost, use a separate line for each purchase.

2. Determine the cost of the inventory on December 31 by the last-in, first-out method, following the procedures indicated in (1).

3. Determine the cost of the inventory on December 31 by the weighted average cost method, using the columnar headings indicated in (1).

4. ➡ Discuss which method (FIFO or LIFO) would be preferred for income tax purposes in periods of (A) rising prices and (B) declining prices.

PR 6-6B Lower-of-cost-or-market inventory

Obj. 6

✔ Total LCM, $41,873

Data on the physical inventory of Katus Products Co. as of December 31 follows:

Description	Inventory Quantity	Market Value per Unit (Net Realizable Value)
A54	37	$ 56
C77	24	178
F66	30	132
H83	21	545
K12	375	5
Q58	90	18
S36	8	235
V97	140	20
Y88	17	744

Quantity and cost data from the last purchases invoice of the year and the next-to-the-last purchases invoice are summarized as follows:

Description	Last Purchases Invoice		Next-to-the-Last Purchases Invoice	
	Quantity Purchased	Unit Cost	Quantity Purchased	Unit Cost
A54	30	$ 60	40	$ 58
C77	25	174	15	180
F66	20	130	15	128
H83	6	547	15	540
K12	500	6	500	7
Q58	75	25	80	26
S36	5	256	4	260
V97	100	17	115	16
Y88	10	750	8	740

Instructions

Determine the inventory at cost and also at the lower of cost or market, using the first-in, first-out method. Record the appropriate unit costs on the inventory sheet, and complete the pricing of the inventory. When there are two different unit costs applicable to an item, proceed as follows:

1. Draw a line through the quantity, and insert the quantity and unit cost of the last purchase.

2. On the following line, insert the quantity and unit cost of the next-to-the-last purchase.

3. Total the cost and market columns and insert the lower of the two totals in the LCM column. The first item on the inventory sheet has been completed as an example.

Inventory Sheet

December 31

Description	Unit Inventory Quantity	Cost per Unit	Market Value per Unit (Net Realizable Value)	Total		
				Cost	Market	LCM
A54	37̶ 30	$60	$56	$1,800	$1,680	
	7	58	56	406	392	
				$2,206	$2,072	$2,072

Appendix
PR 6-7B   Retail method; gross profit method

✔ 1. $630,000   Selected data on inventory, purchases, and sales for Jaffe Co. and Coronado Co. are as follows:

	Cost	Retail
Jaffe Co.		
Inventory, February 1	$ 400,000	$ 615,000
Transactions during February:		
Purchases (net)	4,055,000	5,325,000
Sales		5,100,000
Coronado Co.		
Inventory, May 1	$ 400,000	
Transactions during May thru October:		
Purchases (net)	3,150,000	
Sales	4,750,000	
Estimated gross profit rate	35%	

Instructions

1. Determine the estimated cost of the inventory of Jaffe Co. on February 28 by the retail method, presenting details of the computations.

2. A. Estimate the cost of the inventory of Coronado Co. on October 31 by the gross profit method, presenting details of the computations.

   B. Assume that Coronado Co. took a physical inventory on October 31 and discovered that $366,500 of inventory was on hand. What was the estimated loss of inventory due to theft or damage during May through October?

Analysis for Decision Making

REAL WORLD

ADM-1   Continuing Company Analysis—Amazon: Inventory turnover and number of days' sales in inventory

Amazon.com, Inc. is one of the largest Internet retailers in the world. **Target Corporation** is one of the largest value-priced general merchandisers operating in the United States. Target sells through nearly 1,800 brick-and-mortar stores and through the Internet. Amazon and Target compete for customers across a wide variety of products, including media, general merchandise, apparel, and consumer electronics. Cost of goods sold and inventory information from a recent annual report are provided for both companies as follows (in millions):

	Amazon	Target
Cost of goods sold	$62,752	$51,160
Inventories:		
Beginning of year	7,411	7,903
End of year	8,299	8,766

A. Compute the inventory turnover for both companies. (Round all calculations to one decimal place.)

B. Compute the number of days' sales in inventory for both companies. (Use 365 days and round all calculations to one decimal place.)

C. Which company has the better inventory efficiency?

D. What might explain the difference in inventory efficiency between the two companies?

ADM-2   Costco, Walmart, Nordstrom: Inventory turnover and number of days' sales in inventory

The general merchandise retail industry has a number of segments represented by the following companies:

Company Name	Merchandise Concept
Costco Wholesale Corporation	Membership warehouse
Walmart Stores, Inc.	Discount general merchandise
Nordstrom, Inc.	Fashion department store

For a recent year, the following cost of goods sold and beginning and ending inventories are provided from corporate annual reports (in millions) for these three companies:

	Costco	Walmart	Nordstrom
Cost of goods sold	$98,458	$365,086	$8,406
Inventories:			
Beginning of year	7,894	44,858	1,531
End of year	8,456	45,141	1,733

A. Determine the inventory turnover ratio for all three companies. (Round all calculations to one decimal place.)

B. Determine the number of days' sales in inventory for all three companies. (Use 365 days and round all calculations to one decimal place.)

C. Interpret these results based on each company's merchandising concept.

ADM-3   Monster Beverage and Brown-Forman: Inventory turnover and number of days' sales in inventory

Monster Beverage Corporation develops, markets, and sells energy and other alternative beverage brands. Brown-Forman Corporation manufactures and sells a wide variety of spirit and wine beverages, such as Jack Daniel's®. The cost of goods sold and inventory were obtained from a recent annual report for both companies as follows (in millions):

	Monster Beverage	Brown-Forman
Cost of goods sold	$1,125	$928
Inventories:		
Beginning of year	222	882
End of year	175	827

A. Determine the inventory turnover for both companies. (Round all calculations to one decimal place.)

B. Determine the number of days' sales in inventory for both companies. (Use 365 days and round all calculations to one decimal place.)

C. Interpret the difference in inventory efficiency based on the companies' respective product types.

ADM-4   Hewlett-Packard and Apple: Inventory turnover and number of days' sales in inventory

Hewlett-Packard Company (HP) and Apple Inc. are both developers and marketers of computer equipment and peripherals. However, the two companies follow different manufacturing strategies. HP maintains a significant portion of its own manufacturing capabilities,

(Continued)

while Apple outsources manufacturing to other companies. The following financial statement information is provided for both companies for a recent year (in millions):

	HP	Apple
Cost of goods sold	$73,726	$112,258
Inventories:		
Beginning of year	6,046	1,764
End of year	6,415	2,111

A. Determine the inventory turnover for each company. (Round all calculations to one decimal place.)

B. Determine the number of days' sales in inventory for each company. (Use 365 days and round all calculations to one decimal place.)

C. ━━━▶ Interpret the difference between the ratios for the two companies.

Take It Further

ETHICS

TIF 6-1   Ethics in Action

Sizemo Elektroniks sells semiconductors that are used in games and small toys. The company has been extremely successful in recent years, recording an increase in earnings each of the past six quarters. At the end of the current quarter, Jay Shulz, the company's staff accountant, calculated the ending inventory for the semiconductors and was surprised to find that the quantity of the Hayden X537 model had not changed during the quarter. Jay confirmed his calculation with the inventory control manager, who indicated that sales of the Hayden 537X had stopped when the Hayden 637X semiconductor was released early in the quarter. Jay researched the issue further and found that the Hayden 637X semiconductor has the same applications as the Hayden 537X, but has more computing power and a lower cost than the 537X. Jay emailed this information to Tina Vereen, the chief financial officer, and recommended that the company apply the lower-of-cost-or-market method to the Hayden 537X semiconductors in inventory. Later that day, Tina emailed Jay back instructing him not to apply the lower-of-cost-or-market method to the 537X inventory because "the company is under considerable pressure to maintain its track record of earnings growth, and a lower-of-cost-or-market adjustment would result in a significant decline in earnings this quarter." Reluctantly, Jay followed Tina's instructions.

Evaluate the decision not to apply the lower-of-cost-or-market method in the current quarter.

1. ━━━▶ Who benefits from this decision?

2. ━━━▶ Who is harmed by this decision?

3. ━━━▶ Are Jay and Tina acting in an ethical manner? Explain.

REAL WORLD

TIF 6-2   Team Activity

In teams, select a public company that interests you and is a business that requires inventory. Obtain the company's most recent annual report on Form 10-K. The Form 10-K is a company's annually required filing with the Securities and Exchange Commission (SEC). It includes the company's financial statements and accompanying notes. The Form 10-K can be obtained either (A) from the investor relations section of the company's Web site or (B) by using the company search feature of the SEC's EDGAR database service found at www.sec.gov/edgar/searchedgar/companysearch.html.

1. Based on the information in the company's most recent annual report, answer the following questions:

    A. What types of items are included in the company's inventory?

    B. What inventory costing method or methods does the company use to determine the inventory amount reported on its balance sheet?

    C. How much inventory does the company have at the end of the most recent year?

D. What percentage of total current assets is inventory during the three years presented? Has this percentage increased, decreased, or remained the same during this period?

E. How much cost of goods sold does the company report for the most recent year?

2. ➤ Using the information presented in the company's annual report, calculate the company's inventory turnover for the current and previous years. Based on this information, has the company's performance improved? Briefly explain your answer.

TIF 6-3 Communication

Golden Eagle Company began operations on April 1 by selling a single product. Data on purchases and sales for the year are as follows:

Purchases:

Date	Units Purchased	Unit Cost	Total Cost
April 6	31,000	$36.60	$1,134,600
May 18	33,000	39.00	1,287,000
June 6	40,000	39.60	1,584,000
July 10	40,000	42.00	1,680,000
August 10	27,200	42.75	1,162,800
October 25	12,800	43.50	556,800
November 4	8,000	44.85	358,800
December 10	8,000	48.00	384,000
	200,000		$8,148,000

Sales:

April	16,000 units
May	16,000
June	20,000
July	24,000
August	28,000
September	28,000
October	18,000
November	10,000
December	8,000
Total units	168,000
Total sales	$10,000,000

The president of the company, Connie Kilmer, has asked for your advice on which inventory cost flow method should be used for the 32,000-unit physical inventory that was taken on December 31. The company plans to expand its product line in the future and uses the periodic inventory system.

➤ Write a brief memo to Ms. Kilmer comparing and contrasting the LIFO and FIFO inventory cost flow methods and their potential impacts on the company's financial statements.

7 Internal Control and Cash

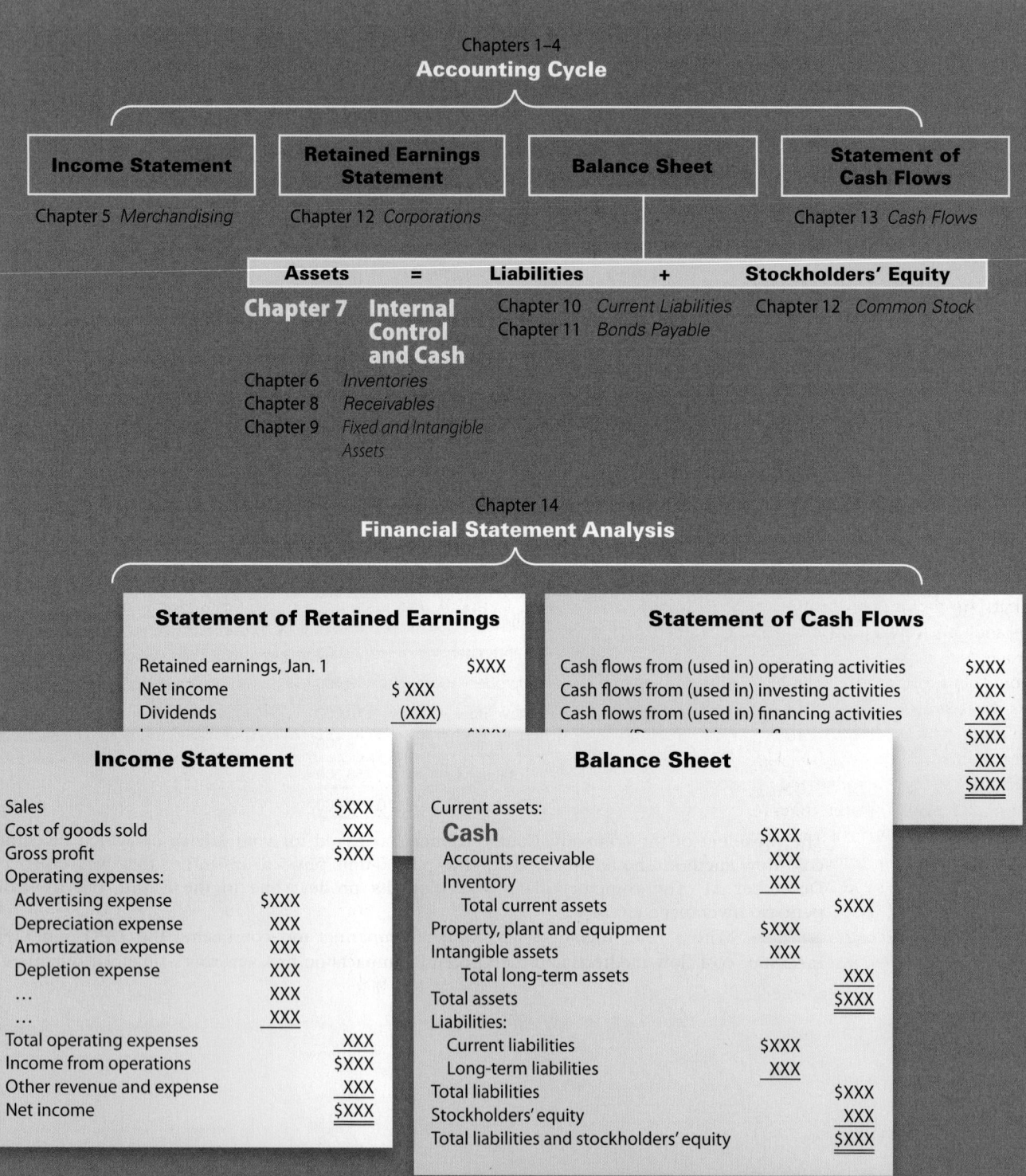

Chapters 1–4
Accounting Cycle

Income Statement	Retained Earnings Statement	Balance Sheet	Statement of Cash Flows

Chapter 5 *Merchandising*   Chapter 12 *Corporations*   Chapter 13 *Cash Flows*

Assets	=	Liabilities	+	Stockholders' Equity

Chapter 7 Internal Control and Cash

Chapter 6 *Inventories*
Chapter 8 *Receivables*
Chapter 9 *Fixed and Intangible Assets*

Chapter 10 *Current Liabilities*
Chapter 11 *Bonds Payable*

Chapter 12 *Common Stock*

Chapter 14
Financial Statement Analysis

Statement of Retained Earnings

Retained earnings, Jan. 1		$XXX
Net income	$ XXX	
Dividends	(XXX)	

Statement of Cash Flows

Cash flows from (used in) operating activities	$XXX
Cash flows from (used in) investing activities	XXX
Cash flows from (used in) financing activities	XXX
	$XXX
	XXX
	$XXX

Income Statement

Sales		$XXX
Cost of goods sold		XXX
Gross profit		$XXX
Operating expenses:		
Advertising expense	$XXX	
Depreciation expense	XXX	
Amortization expense	XXX	
Depletion expense	XXX	
…	XXX	
…	XXX	
Total operating expenses		XXX
Income from operations		$XXX
Other revenue and expense		XXX
Net income		$XXX

Balance Sheet

Current assets:		
Cash	$XXX	
Accounts receivable	XXX	
Inventory	XXX	
Total current assets		$XXX
Property, plant and equipment	$XXX	
Intangible assets	XXX	
Total long-term assets		XXX
Total assets		$XXX
Liabilities:		
Current liabilities	$XXX	
Long-term liabilities	XXX	
Total liabilities		$XXX
Stockholders' equity		XXX
Total liabilities and stockholders' equity		$XXX

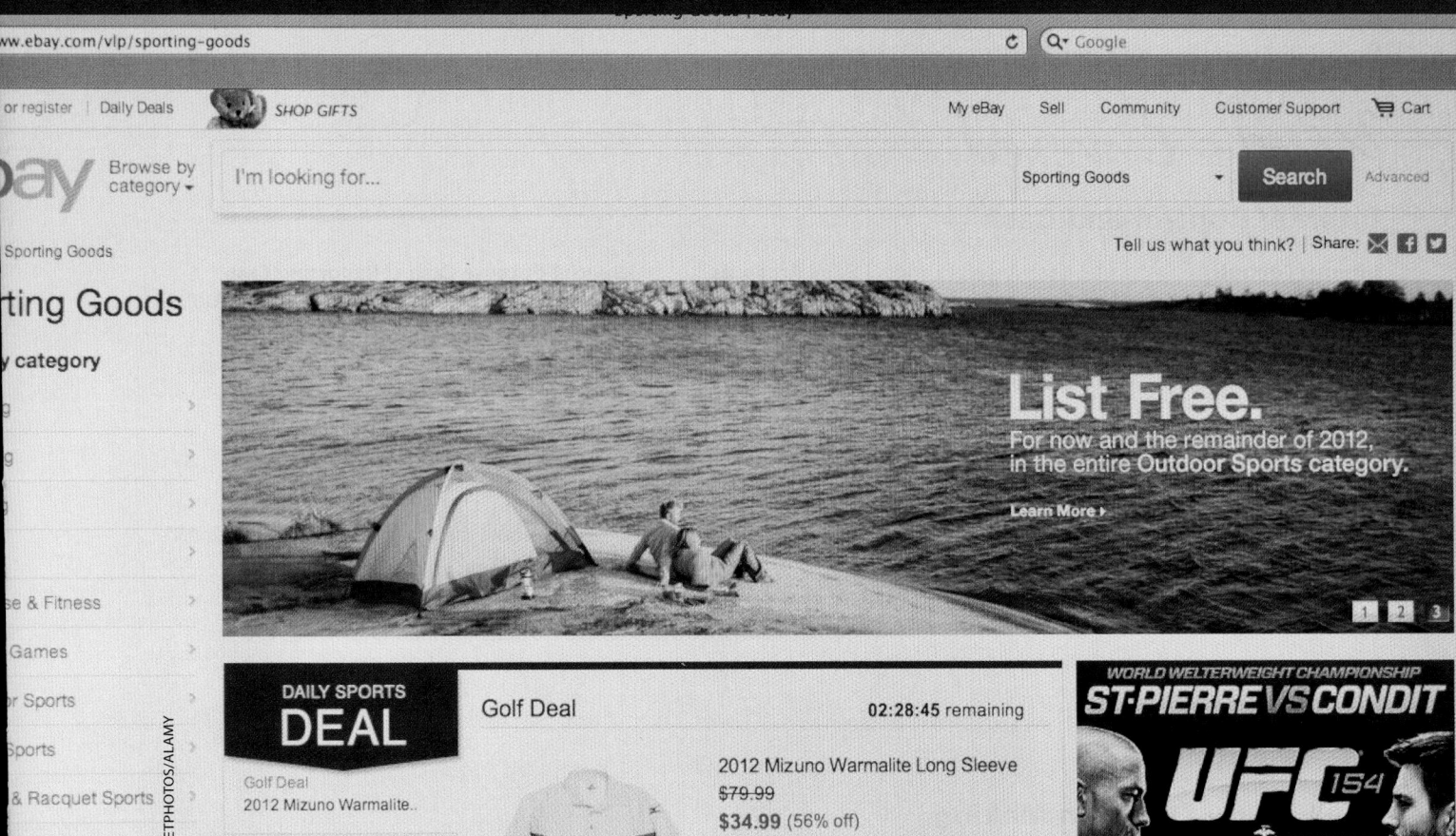

eBay Inc.

Controls are a part of your everyday life. At one extreme, laws are used to limit your behavior. For example, speed limits are designed to control your driving for traffic safety. In addition, you may also use many nonlegal controls. For example, you can keep credit card receipts in order to compare your transactions to the monthly credit card statement. Comparing receipts to the monthly statement is a control designed to catch mistakes made by the credit card company. In addition, banks give you a personal identification number (PIN) as a control against unauthorized access to your cash if you lose your automated teller machine (ATM) card. Dairies use freshness dating on their milk containers as a control to prevent the purchase or sale of soured milk. As you can see, you use and encounter controls every day.

Just as there are many examples of controls throughout society, businesses must also implement controls to help guide the behavior of their managers, employees, and customers. For example, **eBay Inc.** maintains an Internet-based marketplace for the sale of goods and services. Using eBay's online platform, buyers and sellers can browse, buy, and sell a wide variety of items including antiques and used cars. However, in order to maintain the integrity and trust of its buyers and sellers, eBay must have controls to ensure that buyers pay for their items and sellers don't misrepresent their items or fail to deliver sales. One such control eBay uses is a feedback forum that establishes buyer and seller reputations. A prospective buyer or seller can view the member's reputation and feedback comments before completing a transaction. Dishonest or unfair trading can lead to a negative reputation and even suspension or cancellation of the member's ability to trade on eBay.

This chapter discusses controls that can be included in accounting systems to provide reasonable assurance that the financial statements are reliable. Controls to discover and prevent errors to a bank account are also discussed. This chapter begins by discussing the Sarbanes-Oxley Act and its impact on controls and financial reporting.

What's Covered

Internal Control and Cash

Internal Controls	**Cash Receipts and Payments**	**Bank Accounts**	**Special-Purpose Cash Funds**	**Reporting Cash**
■ Sarbanes-Oxley Act (Obj. 1) ■ Elements (Obj. 2) ■ Limitations (Obj. 2)	■ Control of Cash Receipts (Obj. 3) ■ Control of Cash Payments (Obj. 3)	■ Bank Statement (Obj. 4) ■ Bank Reconciliation (Obj. 5)	■ Petty Cash (Obj. 6)	■ Balance Sheet (Obj. 7)

Learning Objectives

Obj. 1   Describe the Sarbanes-Oxley Act and its impact on internal controls and financial reporting.

Obj. 2   Describe and illustrate the objectives and elements of internal control.

Obj. 3   Describe and illustrate the application of internal controls to cash.

Obj. 4   Describe the nature of a bank account and its use in controlling cash.

Obj. 5   Describe and illustrate the use of a bank reconciliation in controlling cash.

Obj. 6   Describe the accounting for special-purpose cash funds.

Obj. 7   Describe and illustrate the reporting of cash and cash equivalents in the financial statements.

Analysis for Decision Making

Describe and illustrate the use of days' cash on hand to assess a company's ability to meet its cash commitments.

Objective 1

Describe the Sarbanes-Oxley Act and its impact on internal controls and financial reporting.

Sarbanes-Oxley Act

During recent financial scandals, stockholders, creditors, and other investors lost billions of dollars.[1] As a result, the U.S. Congress passed the **Sarbanes-Oxley Act**. This act is one of the most important laws affecting U.S. companies in recent history. The purpose of Sarbanes-Oxley is to maintain public confidence and trust in the financial reporting of companies.

Sarbanes-Oxley applies only to companies whose stock is traded on public exchanges, referred to as *publicly held companies*. However, Sarbanes-Oxley highlighted the importance of assessing the financial controls and reporting of all companies. As a result, companies of all sizes have been influenced by Sarbanes-Oxley.

Sarbanes-Oxley emphasizes the importance of effective internal control.[2] **Internal control** is defined as the procedures and processes used by a company to:

■ Safeguard its assets.
■ Process information accurately.
■ Ensure compliance with laws and regulations.

Sarbanes-Oxley requires companies to maintain effective internal controls over the recording of transactions and the preparing of financial statements. Such controls are important because they deter fraud and prevent misleading financial statements as shown in Exhibit 1.

---

[1] Exhibit 2 in Chapter 1 briefly summarizes these scandals.
[2] Sarbanes-Oxley also has important implications for corporate governance and the regulation of the public accounting profession. This chapter, however, focuses on the internal control implications of Sarbanes-Oxley.

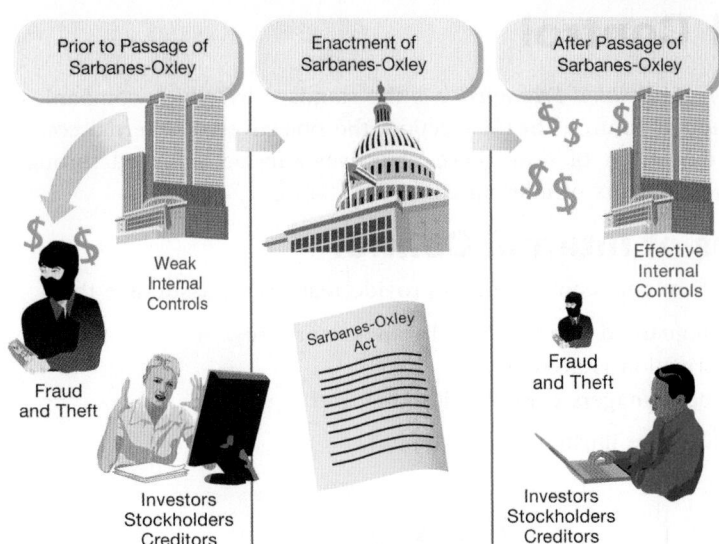

Exhibit 1
Effect of Sarbanes-Oxley

Sarbanes-Oxley also requires companies and their independent accountants to report on the effectiveness of the company's internal controls.[3] These reports are required to be filed with the company's annual 10-K report with the Securities and Exchange Commission. Companies are also encouraged to include these reports in their annual reports to stockholders. An example of such a report by the management of **eBay** is shown in Exhibit 2.

Management's Annual Report on Internal Control Over Financial Reporting

Our management is responsible for establishing and maintaining adequate internal control over financial reporting. Our management, including our principal executive officer and principal financial officer, conducted an evaluation of the effectiveness of our internal control over financial reporting based on the framework in Internal Control— Integrated Framework (2013) issued by the Committee of Sponsoring Organizations of the Treadway Commission. Based on its evaluation under the framework in Internal Control—Integrated Framework, our management concluded that our internal control over financial reporting was effective as of December 31, ...

Source: eBay, Form 10-K for the Fiscal Year Ended December 31, 2014.

Exhibit 2
eBay's Report of Compliance with Sarbanes-Oxley

Exhibit 2 is taken from the annual (10-K) report of **eBay**.

Link to eBay

Exhibit 2 indicates that the evaluation of internal controls is based on *Internal Control— Integrated Framework*, which was issued by the Committee of Sponsoring Organizations (COSO) of the Treadway Commission. This framework is the standard by which companies design, analyze, and evaluate internal controls. For this reason, this framework is used as the basis for discussing internal controls.[4]

---

[3] These reporting requirements are required under Section 404 of the act. As a result, these requirements and reports are often referred to as 404 requirements and 404 reports.

[4] Additional information on *Internal Control—Integrated Framework* can be found on COSO's Web site at www.coso.org.

Objective 2

Describe and illustrate the objectives and elements of internal control.

Internal Control

Internal Control—Integrated Framework is the standard by which companies design, analyze, and evaluate internal control.[5] In this section, the objectives of internal control are described, followed by a discussion of how these objectives can be achieved through the *Integrated Framework's* five elements of internal control.

Objectives of Internal Control

The objectives of internal control are to provide reasonable assurance that:

- Assets are safeguarded and used for business purposes.
- Business information is accurate.
- Employees and managers comply with laws and regulations.

These objectives are illustrated in Exhibit 3.

Exhibit 3

Objectives of Internal Control

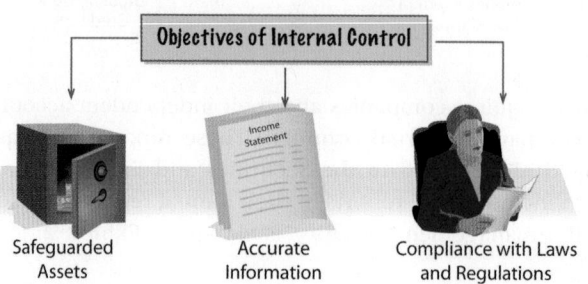

Safeguarded Assets

Accurate Information

Compliance with Laws and Regulations

Internal control can safeguard assets by preventing theft, fraud, misuse, or misplacement. A serious concern of internal control is preventing employee fraud. **Employee fraud** is the intentional act of deceiving an employer for personal gain. Such fraud may range from minor overstating of a travel expense report to stealing millions of dollars. Employees stealing from a business often adjust the accounting records in order to hide their fraud. Thus, employee fraud usually affects the accuracy of business information.

Accurate information is necessary to successfully operate a business. Businesses must also comply with laws, regulations, and financial reporting standards. Examples of such standards include environmental regulations, safety regulations, and generally accepted accounting principles (GAAP).

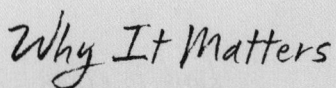

Employee Fraud

The Association of Fraud Examiners estimates that 5% of annual revenues worldwide or more than $3.7 trillion is lost to employee fraud. A common *cash receipts* employee fraud can occur when employees accept cash payments from customers, do not record the sale, and then pocket the cash. A common *cash payments* employee fraud can occur when employees bill their employer for false services or personal items.

Source: *2014 Report to the Nation on Occupational Fraud and Abuse,* Association of Fraud Examiners.

Elements of Internal Control

The three internal control objectives can be achieved by applying the five **elements of internal control** set forth by the *Integrated Framework.*[6] These elements are as follows:

- Control environment
- Risk assessment
- Control procedures

[5] *Internal Control—Integrated Framework* by the Committee of Sponsoring Organizations of the Treadway Commission, 2013.
[6] Ibid., pp. 12–14.

- Monitoring
- Information and communication

The elements of internal control are illustrated in Exhibit 4.

Exhibit 4
Elements of
Internal Control

In Exhibit 4, the elements of internal control form an umbrella over the business to protect it from control threats. The control environment is the size of the umbrella. Risk assessment, control procedures, and monitoring are the fabric of the umbrella, which keep it from leaking. Information and communication connect the umbrella to management and the business.

As technology changes, **eBay** must continually monitor and strengthen its controls over its e-commerce transactions.

Link to eBay

Control Environment

The **control environment** is the overall attitude of management and employees about the importance of controls. Three factors influencing a company's control environment include the following, as shown in Exhibit 5:

- Management's philosophy and operating style
- The company's organizational structure
- The company's personnel policies

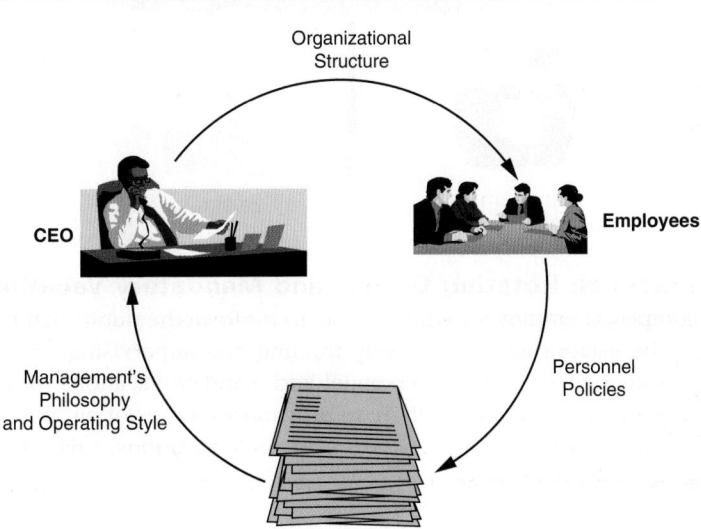

Exhibit 5
Control
Environment

Management's philosophy and operating style relates to whether management emphasizes the importance of internal controls. An emphasis on controls and adherence to control policies creates an effective control environment. In contrast, overemphasizing operating goals and tolerating deviations from control policies creates an ineffective control environment.

The business's organizational structure is the framework for planning and controlling operations. For example, a retail store chain might organize each of its stores as separate business units. Each store manager has full authority over pricing and other operating activities. In such a structure, each store manager has the responsibility for establishing an effective control environment.

The business's personnel policies involve the hiring, training, evaluation, compensation, and promotion of employees. In addition, job descriptions, employee codes of ethics, and conflict-of-interest policies are part of the personnel policies. Such policies can enhance the internal control environment if they provide reasonable assurance that only competent, honest employees are hired and retained.

Risk Assessment

All businesses face risks such as changes in customer requirements, competitive threats, regulatory changes, and changes in economic factors. Management should identify such risks, analyze their significance, assess their likelihood of occurring, and take any necessary actions to minimize them.

Control Procedures

Control procedures provide reasonable assurance that business goals will be achieved, including the prevention of fraud. Control procedures, which constitute one of the most important elements of internal control, include the following as shown in Exhibit 6:

- Competent personnel, rotating duties, and mandatory vacations
- Separating responsibilities for related operations
- Separating operations, custody of assets, and accounting
- Proofs and security measures

Exhibit 6

Internal Control Procedures

Competent Personnel, Rotating Duties, and Mandatory Vacations A successful company needs competent employees who are able to perform the duties that they are assigned. Procedures should be established for properly training and supervising employees. It is also advisable to rotate duties of accounting personnel and mandate vacations for all employees. In this way, employees are encouraged to adhere to procedures. Cases of employee fraud are often discovered when a long-term employee, who never took vacations, missed work because of an illness or another unavoidable reason.

Separating Responsibilities for Related Operations The responsibility for related operations should be divided among two or more people. This decreases the possibility of errors and fraud. For example, if the same person orders supplies, verifies the receipt of the supplies, and pays the supplier, the following abuses may occur:

- Orders may be placed on the basis of friendship with a supplier, rather than on price, quality, and other objective factors.
- The quantity and quality of supplies received may not be verified; thus, the company may pay for supplies not received or that are of poor quality.
- Supplies may be stolen by the employee.
- The validity and accuracy of invoices may not be verified; hence, the company may pay false or inaccurate invoices.

For the preceding reasons, the responsibilities for purchasing, receiving, and paying for supplies should be divided among three persons or departments.

Separating Operations, Custody of Assets, and Accounting The responsibilities for operations, custody of assets, and accounting should be separated. In this way, the accounting records serve as an independent check on the operating managers and the employees who have custody of assets.

To illustrate, employees who handle cash receipts should not record cash receipts in the accounting records. To do so would allow employees to borrow or steal cash and hide the theft in the accounting records. Likewise, operating managers should not also record the results of operations. To do so would allow the managers to distort the accounting reports to show favorable results, which might allow them to receive larger bonuses.

Proofs and Security Measures Proofs and security measures are used to safeguard assets and ensure reliable accounting data. Proofs involve procedures such as authorization, approval, and reconciliation. For example, an employee planning to travel on company business may be required to complete a "travel request" form for a manager's authorization and approval.

Documents used for authorization and approval should be prenumbered, accounted for, and safeguarded. Prenumbering of documents helps prevent transactions from being recorded more than once or not at all. In addition, accounting for and safeguarding prenumbered documents helps prevent fraudulent transactions from being recorded. For example, blank checks are prenumbered and safeguarded. Once a payment has been properly authorized and approved, the checks are filled out and issued.

Reconciliations are also an important control. Later in this chapter, the use of bank reconciliations as an aid in controlling cash is described and illustrated.

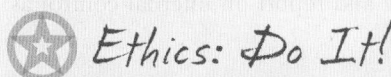 Ethics: Do It!

Tips on Preventing Employee Fraud in Small Companies

- Do not have the same employee write company checks and keep the books. Look for payments to vendors you don't know or payments to vendors whose names appear to be misspelled.
- If your business has a computer system, restrict access to accounting files as much as possible. Also, keep a backup copy of your accounting files and store it at an off-site location.
- Be wary of anybody working in finance who declines to take vacations. They may be afraid that a replacement will uncover fraud.

- Require and monitor supporting documentation (such as vendor invoices) before signing checks.
- Track the number of credit card bills you sign monthly.
- Limit and monitor access to important documents and supplies, such as blank checks and signature stamps.
- Check W-2 forms against your payroll annually to make sure you're not carrying any fictitious employees.
- Rely on yourself, not on your accountant, to spot fraud.

Source: Steve Kaufman, "Embezzlement Common at Small Companies," Knight-Ridder Newspapers, reported in *Athens Daily News/Athens Banner-Herald,* March 10, 1996, p. 4D.

Security measures involve measures to safeguard assets. For example, cash on hand should be kept in a cash register or safe. Inventory not on display should be stored in a locked storeroom or warehouse. Accounting records such as the accounts receivable subsidiary ledger should also be safeguarded to prevent their loss. For example, electronically maintained accounting records should be safeguarded with access codes and backed up so that any lost or damaged files could be recovered if necessary.

Monitoring

Monitoring the internal control system is used to locate weaknesses and improve controls. Monitoring often includes observing employee behavior and the accounting system for indicators of control problems. Some such indicators are shown in Exhibit 7.[7]

Exhibit 7 Warning Signs of Internal Control Problems

Warning signs with regard to people	**Warning signs from the accounting system**
• Abrupt change in lifestyle (without winning the lottery). • Close social relationships with suppliers. • Refusing to take a vacation. • Frequent borrowing from other employees. • Excessive use of alcohol or drugs.	• Missing documents or gaps in transaction numbers (could mean documents are being used for fraudulent transactions). • An unusual increase in customer refunds (refunds may be phony). • Differences between daily cash receipts and bank deposits (could mean receipts are being pocketed before being deposited). • Sudden increase in slow payments (employee may be pocketing the payments). • Backlog in recording transactions (possibly an attempt to delay detection of fraud).

Evaluations of controls are often performed when there are major changes in strategy, senior management, business structure, or operations. Internal auditors, who are independent of operations, usually perform such evaluations. Internal auditors are also responsible for day-to-day monitoring of controls. External auditors also evaluate and report on internal control as part of their annual financial statement audit.

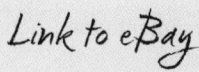 *Link to eBay* **eBay** reduces fraudulent activities by restricting or suspending buyers and sellers with questionable transaction histories.

Information and Communication

Information and communication is an essential element of internal control. Information about the control environment, risk assessment, control procedures, and monitoring is used by management for guiding operations and ensuring compliance with reporting, legal, and regulatory requirements. Management also uses external information to assess events and conditions that impact decision making and external reporting. For example, management uses pronouncements of the Financial Accounting Standards Board (FASB) to assess the impact of changes in reporting standards on the financial statements.

---

[7] Edwin C. Bliss, "Employee Theft," *Boardroom Reports*, July 15, 1994, pp. 5–6.

Check Up Corner 7-1 | Internal Controls

Identify the control procedure violated in each of the following scenarios:

A. Todd Leone is the accounting clerk for Home Chic, a small boutique retail store that is owned and operated by Al Dente. Al does not care much for the accounting side of the business and allows Todd to make all payments to the company's suppliers. Todd pays all invoices that Home Chic receives. Al does not review the payments Todd makes.

B. Jose Muldoon's Mobile Foods is a food truck with two trusted employees. One employee stocks the food truck each day, prepares the orders, and cleans up the kitchen at the end of the day. The other employee takes orders, collects payment from customers, counts the cash at the end of the day, records the cash receipts, and deposits the cash in the night depository slot at the bank.

C. Tad is the treasurer and chief financial officer of a local bank in Wisteria, California. Tad was born and raised in the community and has never had a desire to travel. As a result, he has not taken a vacation or a day off of work in over 6 years.

Solution:

A. Separating operations, custody of assets, and accounting. The responsibility for maintaining the accounting records, operations, and custody of assets should be separated. This is a violation of this control procedure because the payments do not require approval by an independent party.

B. Separating operations, custody of assets, and accounting. The responsibility for maintaining the accounting records, operations, and custody of assets should be separated. This is a violation of this control procedure because the same employee collects the cash (operations and custody of assets), records the cash receipts (accounting records), and deposits the cash (custody of assets).

C. Competent personnel, rotating duties, and mandatory vacations. Procedures should be established to rotate duties of accounting personnel and mandate vacations for all employees. This is a violation of this control procedure.

Check Up Corner

Limitations of Internal Control

Internal control systems can provide only reasonable assurance for safeguarding assets, processing accurate information, and compliance with laws and regulations. In other words, internal controls are not a guarantee. This is due to the following factors:

- The human element of controls
- Cost-benefit considerations

The *human element* recognizes that controls are applied and used by humans. As a result, human errors can occur because of fatigue, carelessness, confusion, or misjudgment. For example, an employee may unintentionally shortchange a customer or miscount the amount of inventory received from a supplier. In addition, two or more employees may collude together to defeat or circumvent internal controls. This latter case often involves fraud and the theft of assets. For example, the cashier and the accounts receivable clerk might collude to steal customer payments on account.

Cost-benefit considerations recognize that the cost of internal controls should not exceed their benefits. For example, retail stores could eliminate shoplifting by searching all customers before they leave the store. However, such a control procedure would upset customers and result in lost sales. Instead, retailers use cameras or signs saying, "*We prosecute all shoplifters.*"

The auditor's report for **eBay** includes the statement: . . . internal control over financial reporting is a process designed to provide reasonable assurance regarding the reliability of financial reporting . . .

Link to eBay

Objective 3

Describe and illustrate the application of internal controls to cash.

Cash Controls over Receipts and Payments

Cash includes coins, currency (paper money), checks, and money orders. Money on deposit with a bank or other financial institution that is available for withdrawal is also considered cash. Normally, you can think of cash as anything that a bank would accept for deposit in your account. For example, a check made payable to you could normally be deposited in a bank and, thus, is considered cash.

Businesses usually have several bank accounts. For example, a business might have one bank account for general cash payments and another for payroll. A separate ledger account is normally used for each bank account. For example, a bank account at City Bank could be identified in the ledger as *Cash in Bank—City Bank*. To simplify, this chapter assumes that a company has only *one* bank account, which is identified in the ledger as *Cash*.

Cash is the asset most likely to be stolen or used improperly in a business. For this reason, businesses must carefully control cash and cash transactions.

Control of Cash Receipts

To protect cash from theft and misuse, a business must control cash from the time it is received until it is deposited in a bank. Businesses normally receive cash from two main sources.

- Customers purchasing products or services
- Customers making payments on account

Cash Received from Cash Sales An important control to protect cash received in over-the-counter sales is a cash register. The use of a cash register to control cash is shown in Exhibit 8.

Exhibit 8

Cash Register as a Control

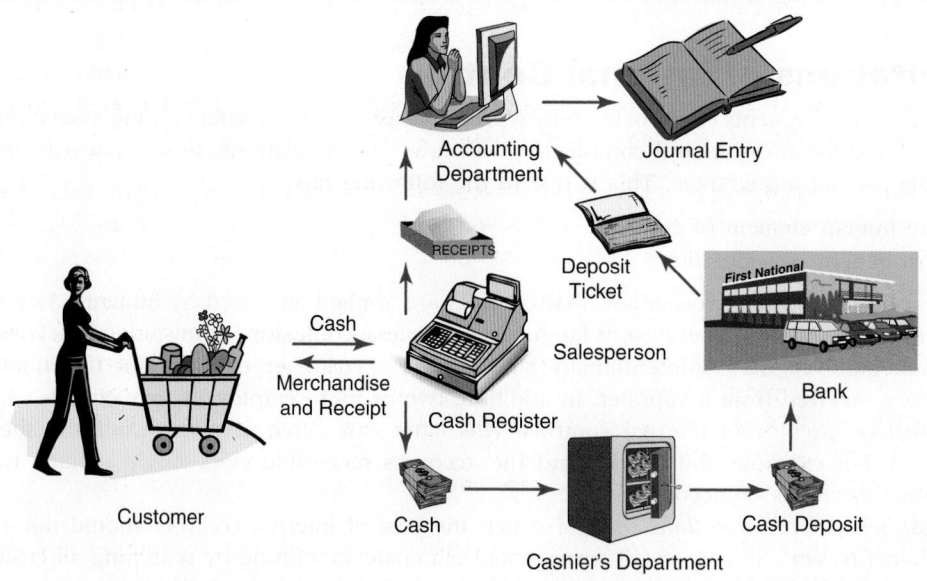

A cash register controls cash as follows:

1. At the beginning of every work shift, each cash register clerk is given a cash drawer containing a predetermined amount of cash. This amount is used for making change for customers and is sometimes called a *change fund*.
2. When a salesperson enters the amount of a sale, the cash register displays the amount to the customer. This allows the customer to verify that the clerk has charged the correct amount. The customer also receives a cash receipt.
3. At the end of the shift, the clerk and the supervisor count the cash in the clerk's cash drawer. The amount of cash in each drawer should equal the beginning amount of cash plus the cash sales for the day.

4. The supervisor takes the cash to the Cashier's Department where it is placed in a safe.

5. The supervisor forwards the clerk's cash register receipts to the Accounting Department.

6. The cashier prepares a bank deposit ticket.

7. The cashier deposits the cash in the bank, or the cash is picked up by an armored car service, such as Wells Fargo.

8. The Accounting Department summarizes the cash receipts and records the day's cash sales.

9. When cash is deposited in the bank, the bank normally stamps a duplicate copy of the deposit ticket with the amount received. This bank receipt is returned to the Accounting Department, where it is compared to the total amount that should have been deposited. This control helps ensure that all the cash is deposited and that no cash is lost or stolen on the way to the bank. Any shortages are thus promptly detected.

Salespersons may make errors in making change for customers or in ringing up cash sales. As a result, the amount of cash on hand may differ from the amount of cash sales. Such differences are recorded in a **cash short and over account**.

To illustrate, assume the following cash register data for May 3:

Cash register total for cash sales	$35,690
Cash receipts from cash sales	35,668

The cash sales, receipts, and shortage of $22 ($35,690 – $35,668) would be journalized as follows:

May 3	Cash	35,668	
	Cash Short and Over	22	
	Sales		35,690

A = L + E
\+ + Rev
  – Exp

If there had been cash over, Cash Short and Over would have been credited for the overage. At the end of the accounting period, a debit balance in Cash Short and Over is included in miscellaneous expense on the income statement. A credit balance is included in the Other Revenue section. If a salesperson consistently has large cash short and over amounts, the supervisor may require the clerk to take additional training.

Cash Received in the Mail Cash is received in the mail when customers pay their bills. This cash is usually in the form of checks and money orders. Most companies design their invoices so that customers return a portion of the invoice, called a *remittance advice*, with their payment. Remittance advices may be used to control cash received in the mail as follows:

1. An employee opens the incoming mail and compares the amount of cash received with the amount shown on the remittance advice. If a customer does not return a remittance advice, the employee prepares one. The remittance advice serves as a record of the cash initially received. It also helps ensure that the posting to the customer's account is for the amount of cash received.

2. The employee opening the mail stamps checks and money orders "For Deposit Only" in the bank account of the business.

3. The remittance advices and their summary totals are delivered to the Accounting Department.

4. All cash and money orders are delivered to the Cashier's Department.

5. The cashier prepares a bank deposit ticket.

6. The cashier deposits the cash in the bank, or the cash is picked up by an armored car service, such as Wells Fargo.

7. An accounting clerk records the cash received and posts the amounts to the customer accounts.

8. When cash is deposited in the bank, the bank normally stamps a duplicate copy of the deposit ticket with the amount received. This bank receipt is returned to the Accounting Department, where it is compared to the total amount that should have been deposited. This control helps ensure that all cash is deposited and that no cash is lost or stolen on the way to the bank. Any shortages are thus promptly detected.

Separating the duties of the Cashier's Department, which handles cash, and the Accounting Department, which records cash, is a control. If Accounting Department employees both handle and record cash, an employee could steal cash and change the accounting records to hide the theft.

Cash Received by EFT Cash may also be received from customers through **electronic funds transfer (EFT)**. For example, customers may authorize automatic electronic transfers from their checking accounts to pay monthly bills for such items as cell phone, Internet, and electric services. In such cases, the company sends the customer's bank a signed form from the customer authorizing the monthly electronic transfers. Each month, the company notifies the customer's bank of the amount of the transfer and the date the transfer should take place. On the due date, the company records the electronic transfer as a receipt of cash to its bank account and posts the amount paid to the customer's account.

Companies encourage customers to use EFT for the following reasons:

- EFTs cost less than receiving cash payments through the mail.
- EFTs enhance internal controls over cash, since the cash is received directly by the bank without any employees handling cash.
- EFTs reduce late payments from customers and speed up the processing of cash receipts.

Link to eBay   In a recent year, eBay generated over $5 billion in cash from operations.

Control of Cash Payments

The control of cash payments should provide reasonable assurance that:

- Payments are made for only authorized transactions.
- Cash is used effectively and efficiently. For example, controls should ensure that all available purchase discounts are taken.

In a small business, an owner/manager may authorize payments based on personal knowledge. In a large business, however, purchasing goods, inspecting the goods received, and verifying the invoices are usually performed by different employees. These duties must be coordinated to ensure that proper payments are made to creditors. One system used for this purpose is the voucher system.

Voucher System A **voucher system** is a set of procedures for authorizing and recording liabilities and cash payments. A **voucher** is any document that serves as proof of authority to pay cash or issue an electronic funds transfer. An invoice that has been approved for payment could be considered a voucher. In many businesses, however, a voucher is a special form used to record data about a liability and the details of its payment.

In a manual system, a voucher is normally prepared after all necessary supporting documents have been received. For the purchase of goods, a voucher is supported by the supplier's invoice, a purchase order, and a receiving report. After a voucher is prepared, it is submitted for approval. Once approved, the voucher is recorded in the accounts and filed by due date. Upon payment, the voucher is recorded in the same manner as the payment of an account payable.

In a computerized system, data from the supporting documents (such as purchase orders, receiving reports, and suppliers' invoices) are entered directly into computer files. At the due date, the checks are automatically generated and mailed to creditors. At that time, the voucher is electronically transferred to a paid voucher file.

Cash Paid by EFT Cash can also be paid by electronic funds transfer (EFT) systems. For example, you can withdraw cash from your bank account using an ATM machine. Your withdrawal is a type of EFT transfer.

Companies also use EFT transfers. For example, many companies pay their employees via EFT. Under such a system, employees authorize the deposit of their payroll checks directly into their checking accounts. Each pay period, the company transfers the employees' net pay to their checking accounts through the use of EFT. Many companies also use EFT systems to pay their suppliers and other vendors.

Why It Matters
Mobile Payments

A rapidly emerging method of payments using EFT are mobile payments, such as those made with Apple Pay™. With mobile payments, our phones become our wallets and our cash is electronic, transferred digitally from our bank accounts or credit cards.

Security is enhanced with fingerprint login to the smartphone. In this way, only the phone's owner can open the "wallet." Many of the internal control features required for managing cash payments are eliminated by this technology, much like EFT transactions. Moreover, even credit card slips are replaced by electronic authorizations and transactions. Internal controls are still required to verify that prices are accurate and goods are properly delivered for authenticated purchases.

Link to eBay

eBay purchased PayPal, which was developed to enable individuals and businesses to safely send and receive payments online. Because of new online payment systems such as Apple Pay, eBay discontinued its PayPal operations in 2015 and established PayPal as a separate, publicly held company.

Bank Accounts

Objective 4

Describe the nature of a bank account and its use in controlling cash.

A major reason that companies use bank accounts is for internal control. Some of the control advantages of using bank accounts are as follows:

- Bank accounts reduce the amount of cash on hand.
- Bank accounts provide an independent recording of cash transactions. Reconciling the balance of the cash account in the company's records with the cash balance according to the bank is an important control.
- Use of bank accounts facilitates the transfer of funds using EFT systems.

Bank Statement

Banks maintain a record of all checking account transactions. A summary of all transactions, called a **bank statement**, is mailed, usually each month, to the company (depositor) or made available online. The bank statement shows the beginning balance, additions, deductions, and the ending balance. A typical bank statement is shown in Exhibit 9 for **Power Networking**.

Checks or copies of the checks listed in the order that they were paid by the bank may accompany the bank statement. If paid checks are returned, they are stamped "Paid," together with the date of payment. Many banks no longer return checks or check copies. Instead, the check payment information is available online.

The company's checking account balance *in the bank records* is a liability. Thus, in the bank's records, the company's account has a credit balance. Because the bank statement is prepared from the bank's point of view, a credit memo entry on the bank statement indicates an increase (a credit) to the company's account. Likewise, a debit memo entry on the bank statement indicates a decrease (a debit) in the company's account. This relationship is shown in Exhibit 10.

Exhibit 9

Bank Statement

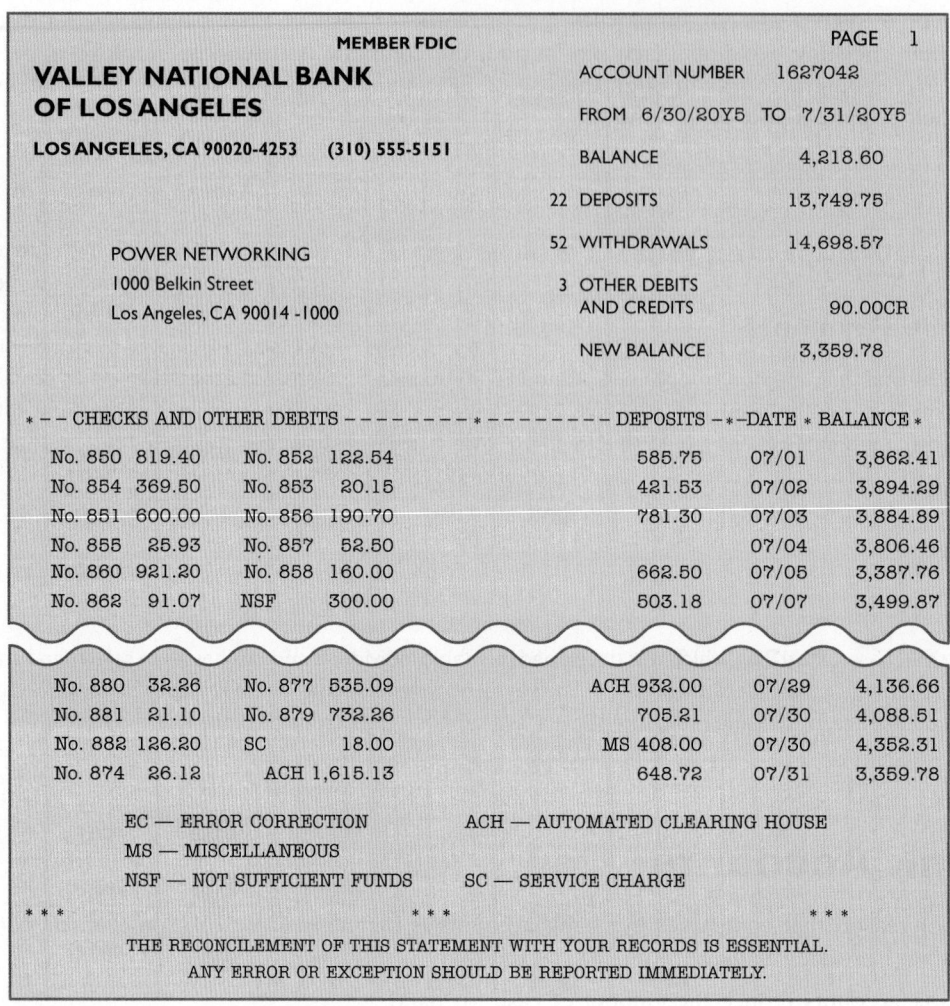

MEMBER FDIC

PAGE 1

**VALLEY NATIONAL BANK
OF LOS ANGELES**

LOS ANGELES, CA 90020-4253 **(310) 555-5151**

ACCOUNT NUMBER 1627042

FROM 6/30/20Y5 TO 7/31/20Y5

BALANCE 4,218.60

22 DEPOSITS 13,749.75

52 WITHDRAWALS 14,698.57

3 OTHER DEBITS
AND CREDITS 90.00CR

NEW BALANCE 3,359.78

POWER NETWORKING
1000 Belkin Street
Los Angeles, CA 90014-1000

--CHECKS AND OTHER DEBITS---------------- DEPOSITS -*-DATE * BALANCE *

No. 850	819.40	No. 852	122.54	585.75	07/01	3,862.41
No. 854	369.50	No. 853	20.15	421.53	07/02	3,894.29
No. 851	600.00	No. 856	190.70	781.30	07/03	3,884.89
No. 855	25.93	No. 857	52.50		07/04	3,806.46
No. 860	921.20	No. 858	160.00	662.50	07/05	3,387.76
No. 862	91.07	NSF	300.00	503.18	07/07	3,499.87

No. 880	32.26	No. 877	535.09	ACH 932.00	07/29	4,136.66
No. 881	21.10	No. 879	732.26	705.21	07/30	4,088.51
No. 882	126.20	SC	18.00	MS 408.00	07/30	4,352.31
No. 874	26.12	ACH	1,615.13	648.72	07/31	3,359.78

EC — ERROR CORRECTION   ACH — AUTOMATED CLEARING HOUSE

MS — MISCELLANEOUS

NSF — NOT SUFFICIENT FUNDS   SC — SERVICE CHARGE

* * *   * * *   * * *

THE RECONCILEMENT OF THIS STATEMENT WITH YOUR RECORDS IS ESSENTIAL.
ANY ERROR OR EXCEPTION SHOULD BE REPORTED IMMEDIATELY.

Exhibit 10 Checking Account: Company and Bank Perspectives

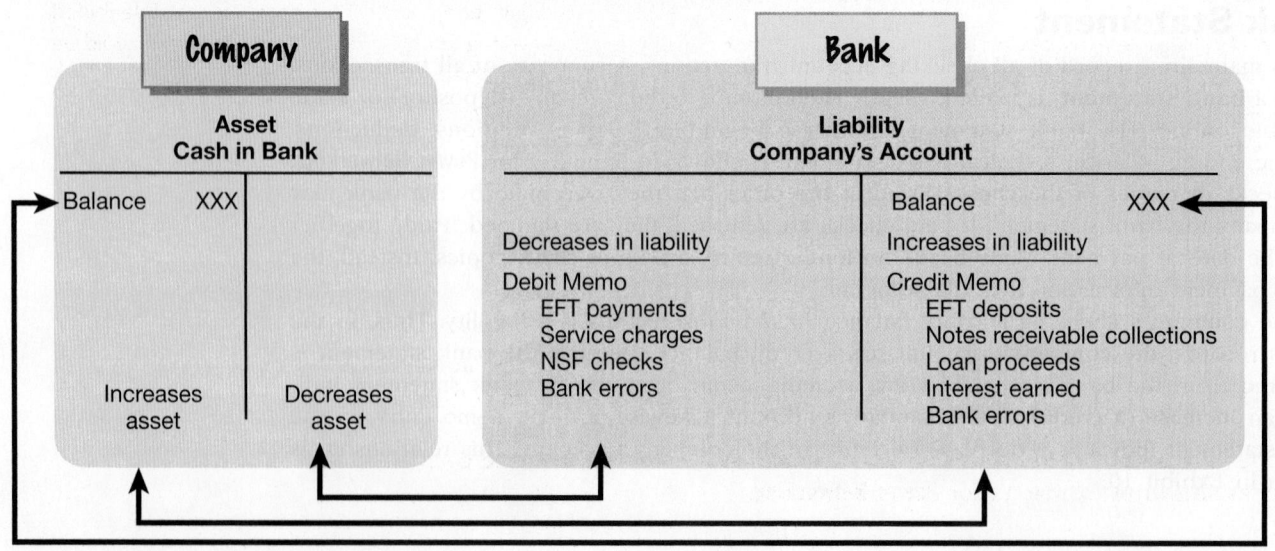

A bank makes credit entries (issues credit memos) for the following:

- Deposits made by electronic funds transfer (EFT)
- Collections of notes receivable for the company
- Proceeds for a loan made to the company by the bank
- Interest earned on the company's account
- Correction (if any) of bank errors

A bank makes debit entries (issues debit memos) for the following:

- Payments made by electronic funds transfer (EFT)
- Service charges
- Customer checks returned for not sufficient funds
- Correction (if any) of bank errors

Customers' checks returned for not sufficient funds, called *NSF checks*, are customer checks that were initially deposited but were not paid by the customer's bank. Because the company's bank credited the customer's check to the company's account when it was deposited, the bank debits the company's account (issues a debit memo) when the check is returned without payment.

The reason for a credit or debit memo entry is indicated on the bank statement. Exhibit 9 identifies the following types of credit and debit memo entries:

- EC: Error correction to correct bank error
- NSF: Not sufficient funds check
- SC: Service charge
- ACH: Automated clearing house entry for electronic funds transfer
- MS: Miscellaneous item such as collection of a note receivable on behalf of the company or receipt of a loan by the company from the bank

The preceding list includes the notation "ACH" for electronic funds transfers. ACH is a network for clearing electronic funds transfers among individuals, companies, and banks.[8] Because electronic funds transfers may be either deposits or payments, ACH entries may indicate either a debit or credit entry to the company's account. Likewise, entries to correct bank errors and miscellaneous items may indicate a debit or credit entry to the company's account.

Why It Matters

Bank Error in Your Favor (or Maybe Not)

A New Zealand couple expected a $100,000 deposit into their checking account, but discovered the bank accidentally deposited $10,000,000. The couple immediately transferred the $10,000,000 to another account and left the country, hoping to cash in on this supposed windfall. Not surprisingly, they were found, arrested, and prosecuted for fraud. So, if you find a bank error in your favor, it really isn't like getting a Monopoly card. You cannot keep the cash, but must return it to the bank. Banks typically have a long time to correct such errors, and if it can be reasonably determined that you knew of the error, but failed to report it, you could be prosecuted for bank fraud.

Source: Nickel, "Bank Error in Your Favor?," *Forbes.com*, May 2012 (www.forbes.com/sites/moneybuilder/2012/05/24/bank-error-in-your-favor/).

Using the Bank Statement as a Control over Cash

The bank statement is a primary control that a company uses over cash. A company uses the bank's statement by comparing the company's record of cash transactions to those recorded by the bank.

The cash balance shown by a bank statement is usually different from the company's cash balance, as shown in Exhibit 11 for **Power Networking**.

---

[8] For further information on ACH, go to www.nacha.org/. Click on "NACHA and the ACH Network" and then click on "ACH Network: How It Works."

Exhibit 11

Power Networking's Bank Statement and Records

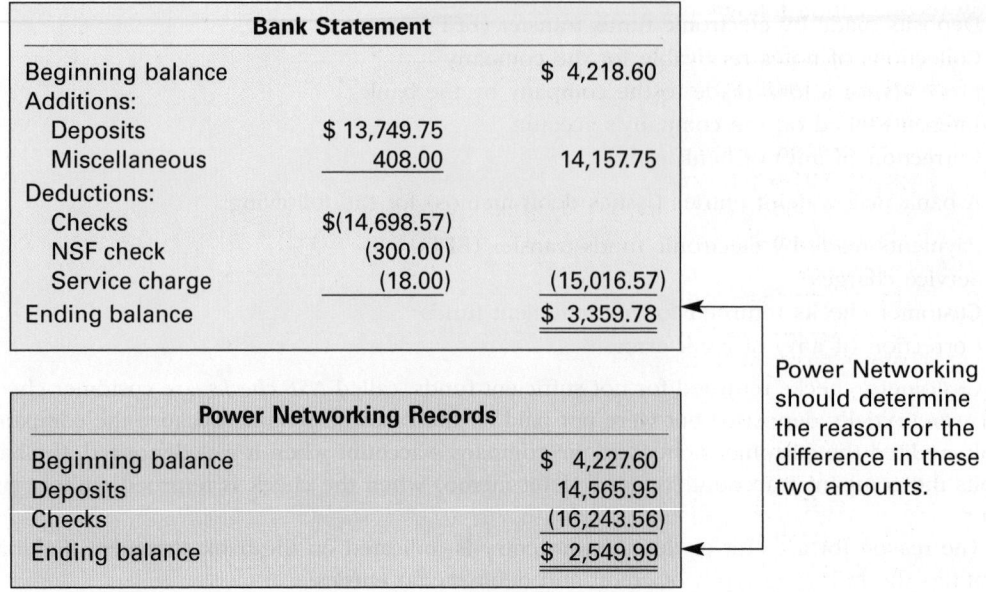

Bank Statement		
Beginning balance		$ 4,218.60
Additions:		
Deposits	$ 13,749.75	
Miscellaneous	408.00	14,157.75
Deductions:		
Checks	$(14,698.57)	
NSF check	(300.00)	
Service charge	(18.00)	(15,016.57)
Ending balance		$ 3,359.78

Power Networking Records	
Beginning balance	$ 4,227.60
Deposits	14,565.95
Checks	(16,243.56)
Ending balance	$ 2,549.99

Power Networking should determine the reason for the difference in these two amounts.

Differences between the company balance and bank balance may arise because of a delay by either the company or bank in recording transactions. For example, there is normally a time lag of one or more days between the date a check is written and the date that it is paid by the bank. Likewise, there is normally a time lag between when the company mails a deposit to the bank (or uses the night depository) and when the bank receives and records the deposit.

Differences may also arise because the bank has debited or credited the company's account for transactions that the company will not know about until the bank statement is received. Finally, differences may arise from errors made by either the company or the bank. For example, the company may incorrectly post to Cash a check written for $4,500 as $450. Likewise, a bank may incorrectly record the amount of a check.

Objective 5

Describe and illustrate the use of a bank reconciliation in controlling cash.

Bank Reconciliation

A **bank reconciliation** is an analysis of the items and amounts creating the difference between the cash balance reported in the bank statement and the balance of the cash account in the ledger. The adjusted cash balance determined in the bank reconciliation is reported on the balance sheet.

A bank reconciliation is usually divided into two sections as follows:

1. The *bank section* begins with the cash balance according to the bank statement and ends with the *adjusted balance*.

2. The *company section* begins with the cash balance according to the company's records and ends with the *adjusted balance*.

The *adjusted balance* from bank and company sections must be equal. The format of the bank reconciliation follows:

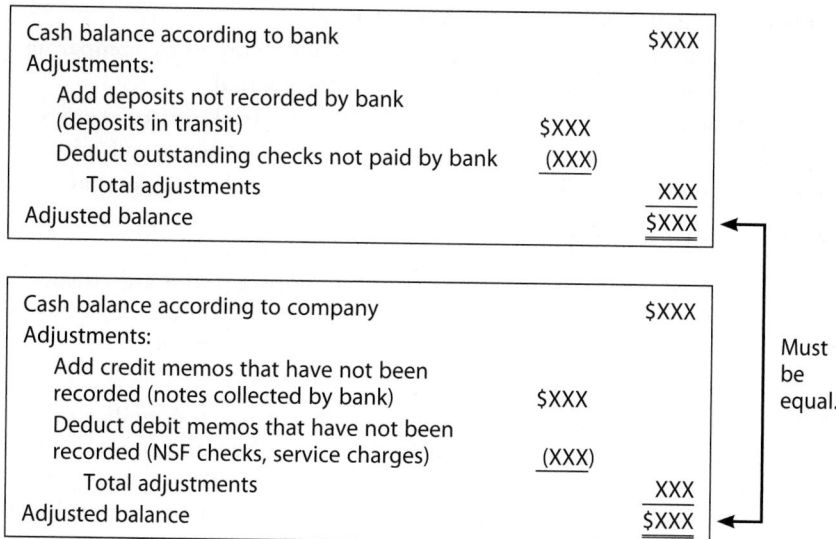

Cash balance according to bank			$XXX
Adjustments:			
Add deposits not recorded by bank (deposits in transit)		$XXX	
Deduct outstanding checks not paid by bank		(XXX)	
Total adjustments			XXX
Adjusted balance			$XXX

Cash balance according to company			$XXX
Adjustments:			
Add credit memos that have not been recorded (notes collected by bank)		$XXX	
Deduct debit memos that have not been recorded (NSF checks, service charges)		(XXX)	
Total adjustments			XXX
Adjusted balance			$XXX

Must be equal.

A bank reconciliation is prepared using steps illustrated in Exhibit 12.

Exhibit 12

How to Prepare a Bank Reconcilation

Bank Section of Reconciliation

- Step 1.   Enter the *Cash balance according to bank* from the ending cash balance according to the bank statement.

- Step 2.   *Add deposits not recorded by the bank.*
  Identify deposits not recorded by the bank by comparing each deposit listed on the bank statement with unrecorded deposits appearing in the preceding period's reconciliation and with the current period's deposits.
  Examples: Deposits in transit at the end of the period.

- Step 3.   *Deduct outstanding checks that have not been paid by the bank.*
  Identify outstanding checks by comparing paid checks with outstanding checks appearing on the preceding period's reconciliation and with recorded checks.
  Examples: Outstanding checks at the end of the period.

- Step 4.   Determine the *Adjusted balance* by totaling the adjustments and adding (subtracting) the total to (from) the cash balance according to bank.

Company Section of Reconciliation

- Step 5.   Enter the *Cash balance according to company* from the ending cash balance in the ledger.

- Step 6.   *Add credit memos that have not been recorded.*
  Identify the bank credit memos that have not been recorded by comparing the bank statement credit memos to entries in the journal.
  Examples: A note receivable and interest that the bank has collected for the company.

(Continued)

Exhibit 12

How to Prepare a
Bank Reconcilation
(Concluded)

- Step 7.   *Deduct debit memos that have not been recorded.*
  Identify the bank debit memos that have not been recorded by comparing the bank statement debit memos to entries in the journal.
  Examples: Customers' not sufficient funds (NSF) checks; bank service charges.
- Step 8.   Determine the *Adjusted balance* by totaling the adjustments and adding (subtracting) the total to (from) the cash balance according to company.

Verify That Adjusted Balances Are Equal

- Step 9.   Verify that the adjusted balances determined in Steps 4 and 8 are equal.

The adjusted balances in the bank and company sections of the reconciliation must be equal. If the balances are not equal, an item has been overlooked and must be found.

Sometimes, the adjusted balances are not equal because either the company or the bank has made an error. In such cases, the error is often discovered by comparing the amount of each item (deposit and check) on the bank statement with that in the company's records.

Any bank or company errors discovered should be added to or deducted from the bank or company section of the reconciliation, depending on the nature of the error. For example, assume that the bank incorrectly recorded a company check for $50 as $500. This bank error of $450 ($500 – $50) would be added to the bank balance in the bank section of the reconciliation. In addition, the bank would be notified of the error so that it could be corrected. On the other hand, assume that the company recorded a deposit of $1,200 as $2,100. This company error of $900 ($2,100 – $1,200) would be deducted from the cash balance in the company section of the bank reconciliation. The company would correct the error using a journal entry.

To illustrate, the bank statement for **Power Networking** in Exhibit 9 is used. This bank statement shows a balance of $3,359.78 as of July 31. The cash balance in Power Networking's ledger on the same date is $2,549.99. Using the preceding steps, the following reconciling items were identified:

- Step 2.   Deposit of July 31, not recorded on bank statement: $816.20
- Step 3.   Outstanding checks:

Check No. 812	$1,061.00
Check No. 878	435.39
Check No. 883	48.60
Total	$1,544.99

- Step 6.   Note receivable of $400 plus interest of $8 collected by bank not recorded in the journal as indicated by a credit memo of $408.
- Step 7.   Check from customer (Thomas Ivey) for $300 returned by bank because of insufficient funds (NSF) as indicated by a debit memo of $300.00.
  Bank service charges of $18, not recorded in the journal as indicated by a debit memo of $18.00.

In addition, an error of $9 was discovered. This error occurred when Check No. 879 for $732.26 to Taylor Co., on account, was recorded in the company's journal as $723.26.

The bank reconciliation, based on the Exhibit 9 bank statement and the preceding reconciling items, is shown in Exhibit 13 for **Power Networking**.

Exhibit 13 Bank Reconciliation for Power Networking

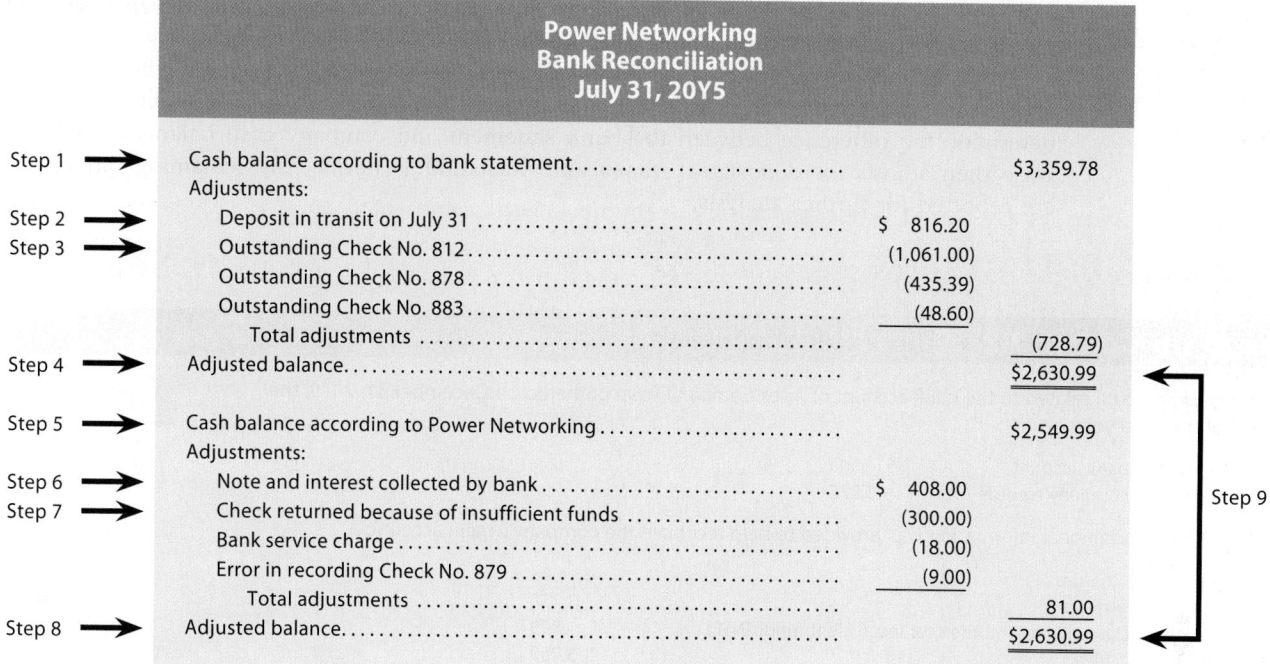

Power Networking		
Bank Reconciliation		
July 31, 20Y5		

Step 1 → Cash balance according to bank statement............................ $3,359.78
Adjustments:
Step 2 →   Deposit in transit on July 31 .... $ 816.20
Step 3 →   Outstanding Check No. 812...................................... (1,061.00)
   Outstanding Check No. 878...................................... (435.39)
   Outstanding Check No. 883...................................... (48.60)
      Total adjustments .... (728.79)
Step 4 → Adjusted balance... $2,630.99

Step 5 → Cash balance according to Power Networking......................... $2,549.99
Adjustments:
Step 6 →   Note and interest collected by bank............................... $ 408.00
Step 7 →   Check returned because of insufficient funds .... (300.00)
   Bank service charge... (18.00)
   Error in recording Check No. 879 .... (9.00)
      Total adjustments 81.00
Step 8 → Adjusted balance... $2,630.99

Step 9

The company's records do not need to be updated for any items in the *bank section* of the reconciliation. This section begins with the cash balance according to the bank statement. However, the bank should be notified of any errors that need to be corrected.

The company's records do need to be updated for any items in the *company section* of the bank reconciliation. The company's records are updated using journal entries. For example, journal entries should be made for any unrecorded bank memos and any company errors.

The journal entries for **Power Networking**, based on the bank reconciliation shown in Exhibit 13, are as follows:

July 31	Cash	408	
	Notes Receivable		400
	Interest Revenue		8
31	Accounts Receivable—Thomas Ivey	300	
	Miscellaneous Expense	18	
	Accounts Payable—Taylor Co.	9	
	Cash		327

A = L + E
\+ –   + Rev

A = L + E
\+ – – – Exp

After the preceding journal entries are recorded and posted, the cash account will have a debit balance of $2,630.99. This cash balance agrees with the adjusted balance shown on the bank reconciliation. This is the amount of cash on July 31 and is the amount that is reported on Power Networking's July 31 balance sheet.

Businesses may reconcile their bank accounts in a slightly different format from that shown in Exhibit 13. Regardless, the objective is to control cash by reconciling the company's records with the bank statement. In doing so, any errors or misuse of cash may be detected.

To enhance internal control, the bank reconciliation should be prepared by an employee who does not take part in or record cash transactions. Otherwise, mistakes may occur, and it is more likely that cash will be stolen or misapplied. For example, an employee who handles cash and also reconciles the bank statement could steal a cash deposit, omit the deposit from the accounts, and omit it from the reconciliation.

Bank reconciliations are also an important part of computerized systems where deposits and checks are stored in electronic files and records. Some systems use computer software to determine the difference between the bank statement and company cash balances. The software then adjusts for deposits in transit and outstanding checks. Any remaining differences are reported for further analysis.

Check Up Corner 7-2   Bank Reconciliation

The following data related to the bank account of Apex Company were gathered on December 31, 20Y9, the end of the fiscal year:

Balance per bank account	$14,500
Balance per company records	13,875

The following additional information was provided to help reconcile the company's bank account:

Bank service charges	$ 75
Deposit in transit	3,750
Check from Dave Hilman returned for insufficient funds (NSF)	800
Outstanding checks	5,250

Prepare a bank reconciliation for Apex Company on December 31, 20Y9.

Solution:

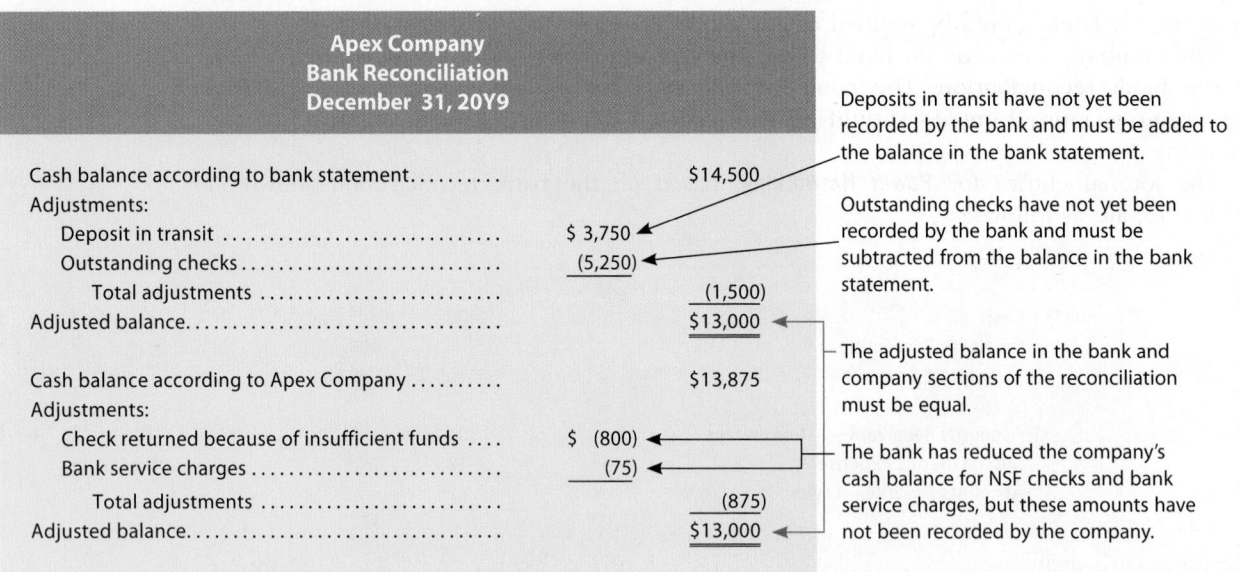

Apex Company
Bank Reconciliation
December 31, 20Y9

Cash balance according to bank statement..........		$14,500
Adjustments:		
Deposit in transit	$ 3,750	
Outstanding checks...........................	(5,250)	
Total adjustments		(1,500)
Adjusted balance.................................		$13,000
Cash balance according to Apex Company		$13,875
Adjustments:		
Check returned because of insufficient funds	$ (800)	
Bank service charges	(75)	
Total adjustments		(875)
Adjusted balance.................................		$13,000

Deposits in transit have not yet been recorded by the bank and must be added to the balance in the bank statement.

Outstanding checks have not yet been recorded by the bank and must be subtracted from the balance in the bank statement.

The adjusted balance in the bank and company sections of the reconciliation must be equal.

The bank has reduced the company's cash balance for NSF checks and bank service charges, but these amounts have not been recorded by the company.

Check Up Corner

Special-Purpose Cash Funds

A company often has to pay small amounts for such items as postage, office supplies, or minor repairs. Although small, such payments may occur often enough to total a significant amount. Thus, it is desirable to control such payments. However, writing a check for each small payment is not practical. Instead, a special cash fund, called a **petty cash fund**, is used.

A petty cash fund is established by estimating the amount of payments needed from the fund during a period, such as a week or a month. A check is then written and cashed for this amount. The money obtained from cashing the check is then given to an employee, called the *petty cash custodian*. The petty cash custodian disburses monies from the fund as needed. For control purposes, the company may place restrictions on the maximum amount and the types of payments that can be made from the fund. Each time money is paid from petty cash, the custodian records the details on a petty cash receipts form.

The petty cash fund is normally replenished at periodic intervals, when it is depleted, or when it reaches a minimum amount. When a petty cash fund is replenished, the accounts debited are determined by summarizing the petty cash receipts. A check is then written for this amount, payable to Petty Cash.

To illustrate, assume that a petty cash fund of $500 is established on August 1. The entry to journalize this transaction is as follows:

Aug. 1 Petty Cash	500	
Cash		500

$A = L + E$
$+ -$

The only time Petty Cash is debited is when the fund is initially established, as shown in the preceding entry, or when the fund is being increased. The only time Petty Cash is credited is when the fund is being decreased or eliminated.

At the end of August, the petty cash receipts indicate expenditures for the following items:

Office supplies	$380
Postage (debit Office Supplies)	22
Store supplies	35
Miscellaneous administrative expense	30
Total	$467

The entry to replenish the petty cash fund on August 31 is as follows:

Aug. 31 Office Supplies	402	
Store Supplies	35	
Miscellaneous Administrative Expense	30	
Cash		467

$A = L + E$
$+ -$ $- Exp$

Petty Cash is not debited when the fund is replenished. Instead, the accounts affected by the petty cash disbursements are debited, as shown in the preceding entry. Replenishing the petty cash fund restores the fund to its original amount of $500.

Companies often use other cash funds for special needs, such as payroll or travel expenses. Such funds are called **special-purpose funds**. For example, each salesperson might be given $1,000 for travel-related expenses. Periodically, each salesperson submits an expense report, and the fund is replenished. Special-purpose funds are established and controlled in a manner similar to that of the petty cash fund.

Financial Statement Reporting of Cash

Cash is normally listed as the first asset in the current assets section of the balance sheet. Most companies present only a single cash amount on the balance sheet by combining all their bank and cash fund accounts.

A company may temporarily have excess cash. In such cases, the company normally invests in highly liquid investments in order to earn interest. These investments are called **cash equivalents**.[9] Examples of cash equivalents include U.S. Treasury bills, notes issued by major corporations (referred to as *commercial paper*), and money market funds. In such cases, companies usually report *Cash and cash equivalents* as one amount on the balance sheet.

Link to eBay   On a recent balance sheet, **eBay** reported over $6 billion in cash and cash equivalents.

The balance sheet presentation for cash for **Mornin' Joe** follows:

Mornin' Joe

Mornin' Joe Balance Sheet December 31, 20Y6

Assets	
Current assets:	
Cash and cash equivalents	$235,000

Banks may require that companies maintain minimum cash balances in their bank accounts. Such a balance is called a **compensating balance**. This is often required by the bank as part of a loan agreement or line of credit. A *line of credit* is a preapproved amount the bank is willing to lend to a customer upon request. Compensating balance requirements are normally disclosed in notes to the financial statements.

Why It Matters

Managing Apple's Cash

Apple Inc. has investments and cash that total over $155 billion. This represents over 65% of Apple's total assets, and thus requires significant management attention. How does Apple manage these assets? Apple owns **Braeburn Capital**, a Nevada-based asset management company. Braeburn was established in 2006 for one purpose: to manage Apple's cash and investments. Braeburn operates under a veil of secrecy, and little is known about the firm. It is simply described as "Braeburn Capital Inc. is the asset management arm of Apple Inc. The firm invests in the public equity markets." Apple's financial statement footnotes provide some detail describing its holdings. More than $13 billion is incuded as cash or cash equivalents, such as money market funds. The remainder is divided between short- and long-term investments.

Source: Apple Inc. annual report, Form 10-K, For the Year Ended September 27, 2014.

---

[9] To be classified as a cash equivalent, according to FASB *Accounting Standards Codification*, Section 305.10, the investment is expected to be converted to cash within three months.

Analysis for Decision Making

Days' Cash on Hand

Objective

Describe and illustrate the use of days' cash on hand to assess a company's ability to meet its cash commitments.

Days' cash on hand measures how long a company could survive if its sources of revenue were to decline significantly. A higher number of days implies a higher liquidity and is thus viewed favorably by creditors. However, a number of days' cash on hand that is too high may indicate that the company has not invested cash back into the business or returned profits back to the owners. Days' cash on hand greater than 50 days would be considered adequate for businesses.

Days' cash on hand is calculated as follows:

$$\text{Days' Cash on Hand} = \frac{\text{Cash and Short-Term Investments}}{\text{Daily Cash Operating Expenses}}$$

The cash and short-term investments are taken from the year-end balance sheet and represent the most liquid assets. The daily cash operating expenses are computed from income statement information, as follows:

$$\text{Daily Cash Operating Expenses} = (\text{Operating Expenses} - \text{Depreciation Expense}) \div 365 \text{ days}$$

Depreciation expense is subtracted from the operating expenses because it is a noncash expense. The net amount is divided by 365 days in order to convert the annual cash operating expense amount into a daily amount.

Days' cash on hand is the number of days the daily cash operating expenses can be supported by cash and near-cash balances. It is a popular measure used by nonprofits whose revenues are based on contributions. It reveals how long the nonprofit could survive if contributions dropped significantly. It is also used by start-up companies to measure how long cash is available to support operations until revenues begin to be earned. The measure can be used to estimate how long a business could survive a catastrophic event, such as a software virus for an Internet company or a national health emergency for an airline.

To illustrate, the following information is provided from three recent annual financial statements for **eBay** (in millions):

	Year 3	Year 2	Year 1
Cash (end of year)	$6,328	$4,494	$6,817
Short-term investments (end of year)	3,770	4,531	2,591
Operating expenses	8,656	7,640	6,968
Depreciation expense	1,490	1,400	1,200

The days' cash on hand for all three years is computed as:

	Year 3	Year 2	Year 1
Cash and short-term investments:			
$6,328 + $3,770	$10,098		
$4,494 + $4,531		$9,025	
$6,817 + $2,591			$9,408
Daily cash operating expenses:*			
($8,656 − $1,490) ÷ 365 days	$ 19.6		
($7,640 − $1,400) ÷ 365 days		$ 17.1	
($6,968 − $1,200) ÷ 365 days			$ 15.8
Days' cash on hand:*			
$10,098 ÷ $19.6	515.2		
$9,025 ÷ $17.1		527.8	
$9,408 ÷ $15.8			595.4

*Rounded to one decimal place

As can be seen, eBay's days' cash on hand declined from 595.4 days in Year 1 to 515.2 days in Year 3. However, the days' cash on hand exceeds 500 days for all three years. Thus, the three-year decline is not a concern. This high number of days suggests that a catastrophic event would not threaten eBay's survival. eBay appears to have sufficient liquidity to support operations and business growth.

Make a Decision   Days' Cash on Hand

J. C. Penney Company, Inc. and **Macy's, Inc.** are large department store chains in the United States. Information from recent annual reports for both companies is as follows (in millions):

	J. C. Penney	Macy's
Cash (end of year)	$ 119	$2,246
Short-term investments (end of year)	1,199	—
Operating expenses	4,569	8,355
Depreciation expense	631	1,036

A. Determine the days' cash on hand for each company. (Round to one decimal place.)

B. Which company has the better liquidity position?

Solution:

A.

$$\text{Days' Cash on Hand} = \frac{\text{Cash and Short-Term Investments}}{(\text{Operating Expenses} - \text{Depreciation Expense}) \div 365 \text{ days}}$$

$$\text{J. C. Penney:} \quad \frac{\$119 + \$1,199}{(\$4,569 - \$631) \div 365 \text{ days}} = 122.0 \text{ days}$$

$$\text{Macy's:} \quad \frac{\$2,246}{(\$8,355 - \$1,036) \div 365 \text{ days}} = 111.7 \text{ days}$$

B. J. C. Penney has days' cash on hand of 122.0 days, which is 10.3 days better than Macy's 111.7 days. However, both companies have sufficient cash to meet operating needs.

Make a Decision

Let's Review

Chapter Summary

1. Sarbanes-Oxley requires companies to maintain strong and effective internal controls and to report on the effectiveness of the internal controls.

2. The objectives of internal control are to provide reasonable assurance that (1) assets are safeguarded and used for business purposes, (2) business information is accurate, and (3) the company is complying with laws and regulations. The elements of internal control are the control environment, risk assessment, control procedures, monitoring, and information and communication.

3. A cash register is a control for protecting cash received in over-the-counter sales. A remittance advice is a control for cash received through the mail. Separating the duties of handling cash and recording cash is also a control. A voucher system is a control system for cash payments. Many companies use electronic funds transfers for cash receipts and cash payments.

4. Bank accounts control cash by reducing the amount of cash on hand and facilitating the transfer of cash between businesses and locations. In addition, the bank statement allows a business to reconcile the cash transactions recorded in the accounting records to those recorded by the bank.

5. A bank reconciliation is prepared using the nine steps as summarized in Exhibit 12. The items in the company section of a bank reconciliation must be journalized on the company's records.

6. Special-purpose cash funds, such as a petty cash fund or a travel fund, are used by businesses to meet specific needs. Each fund is established by cashing a check for the amount of cash needed. At periodic intervals, the fund is replenished and the disbursements recorded.

7. Cash is listed as the first asset in the current assets section of the balance sheet. Companies that have invested excess cash in highly liquid investments usually report *Cash and cash equivalents* on the balance sheet.

Key Terms

bank reconciliation (350)
bank statement (347)
cash (344)
cash equivalents (356)
cash short and over account (345)
compensating balance (356)

control environment (339)
days' cash on hand (357)
electronic funds transfer (EFT) (346)
elements of internal control (338)
employee fraud (338)
internal control (336)

petty cash fund (355)
Sarbanes-Oxley Act (336)
special-purpose funds (355)
voucher (346)
voucher system (346)

Practice

Multiple-Choice Questions

1. Which of the following is *not* an element of internal control?
   A. Control environment
   B. Monitoring
   C. Compliance with laws and regulations
   D. Control procedures

2. The bank erroneously charged Tropical Services' account for $450.50 for a check that was correctly written and recorded by Tropical Services as $540.50. To reconcile the bank account of Tropical Services at the end of the month, you would:

A. add $90 to the cash balance according to the bank statement.

B. add $90 to the cash balance according to Tropical Services' records.

C. deduct $90 from the cash balance according to the bank statement.

D. deduct $90 from the cash balance according to Tropical Services' records.

3. In preparing a bank reconciliation, the amount of checks outstanding would be:

A. added to the cash balance according to the bank statement.

B. deducted from the cash balance according to the bank statement.

C. added to the cash balance according to the company's records.

D. deducted from the cash balance according to the company's records.

4. Journal entries based on the bank reconciliation are required for:

A. additions to the cash balance according to the company's records.

B. deductions from the cash balance according to the company's records.

C. both A and B.

D. neither A nor B.

5. A petty cash fund is:

A. used to pay relatively small amounts.

B. established by estimating the amount of cash needed for disbursements of relatively small amounts during a specified period.

C. reimbursed when the amount of money in the fund is reduced to a predetermined minimum amount.

D. all of the above.

Answers provided after Problem. Need more practice? Find additional multiple-choice questions, exercises, and problems in CengageNOWv2.

Exercises

SHOW ME HOW

1. Internal control elements   Obj. 2

Identify each of the following as relating to (A) the control environment, (B) control procedures, or (C) information and communication:

1. Organizational structure
2. Report of company's conformity with environmental laws and regulations
3. Proofs and security measures

SHOW ME HOW

2. Items on company's bank statement   Obj. 4

The following items may appear on a bank statement:

1. Bank correction of an error from recording a $6,200 deposit as $2,600
2. EFT payment
3. Note collected for company
4. Service charge

Using the following format, indicate whether each item would appear as a debit or credit memo on the bank statement and whether the item would increase or decrease the balance of the company's account:

Item No.	Appears on the Bank Statement as a Debit or Credit Memo	Increases or Decreases the Balance of the Company's Bank Account

SHOW ME HOW

3. Bank reconciliation   Obj. 5

The following data were gathered to use in reconciling the bank account of Eves Company:

Balance per bank	$9,350
Balance per company records	8,510
Bank service charges	35
Deposit in transit	2,350
NSF check	1,875
Outstanding checks	5,100

A. What is the adjusted balance on the bank reconciliation?

B. Journalize any necessary entries for Eves Company based on the bank reconciliation.

SHOW ME HOW

4. Petty cash fund   Obj. 6

Prepare journal entries for each of the following:

A. Issued a check to establish a petty cash fund of $750.

B. The amount of cash in the petty cash fund is $115. Issued a check to replenish the fund, based on the following summary of petty cash receipts: repair expense, $515 and miscellaneous selling expense, $88. Record any missing funds in the cash short and over account.

Answers provided after Problem. Need more practice? Find additional multiple-choice questions, exercises, and problems in CengageNOWv2.

Problem

The bank statement for Urethane Company for June 30, 20Y2, indicates a balance of $9,293.11. All cash receipts are deposited each evening in a night depository, after banking hours. The accounting records indicate the following summary data for cash receipts and payments for June:

Cash balance as of June 1	$ 3,943.50
Total cash receipts for June	28,971.60
Total amount of checks issued in June	28,388.85

Comparing the bank statement and the accompanying canceled checks and memos with the records reveals the following reconciling items:

A. The bank had collected for Urethane Company $1,030 on a note left for collection. The face amount of the note was $1,000.

B. A deposit of $1,852.21, representing receipts of June 30, had been made too late to appear on the bank statement.

C. Checks outstanding totaled $5,265.27.

D. A check drawn for $139 had been incorrectly charged by the bank as $157.

E. A check for $370 returned with the statement had been recorded in the company's records as $730. The check was for the payment of an obligation to Avery Equipment Company for the purchase of office supplies on account.

F. Bank service charges for June amounted to $18.20.

Instructions

1. Prepare a bank reconciliation for June.

2. Journalize the entries that should be made by Urethane Company.

Need more practice? Find additional multiple-choice questions, exercises, and problems in CengageNOWv2.

Answers

Multiple-Choice Questions

1. **C** Compliance with laws and regulations (answer C) is an objective, not an element, of internal control. The control environment (answer A), monitoring (answer B), control procedures (answer D), risk assessment, and information and communication are the five elements of internal control.

2. **C** The error was made by the bank, so the cash balance according to the bank statement needs to be adjusted. Since the bank deducted $90 ($540.50 – $450.50) too little, the error of $90 should be deducted from the cash balance according to the bank statement (answer C).

3. **B** On any specific date, the cash account in a company's ledger may not agree with the account in the bank's ledger because of delays and/or errors by either party in recording transactions. The purpose of a bank reconciliation is to determine the reasons for any differences between the two account balances. All errors should then be corrected by the company or the bank, as appropriate. In arriving at the adjusted cash balance according to the bank statement, outstanding checks must be deducted (answer B) to adjust for checks that have been written by the company but that have not yet been presented to the bank for payment.

4. **C** All reconciling items that are added to and deducted from the cash balance according to the company's records on the bank reconciliation (answer C) require that journal entries be made by the company to correct errors made in recording transactions or to bring the cash account up to date for delays in recording transactions.

5. **D** To avoid the delay, annoyance, and expense that is associated with paying all obligations by check, relatively small amounts (answer A) are paid from a petty cash fund. The fund is established by estimating the amount of cash needed to pay these small amounts during a specified period (answer B), and it is then reimbursed when the amount of money in the fund is reduced to a predetermined minimum amount (answer C).

Exercises

1.

   1. (A) the control environment
   2. (C) information and communication
   3. (B) control procedures

2.

Item No.	Appears on the Bank Statement as a Debit or Credit Memo	Increases or Decreases the Balance of the Company's Bank Account
1	credit memo	increases
2	debit memo	decreases
3	credit memo	increases
4	debit memo	decreases

3.

  A. $6,600 as shown below.
    Bank section of reconciliation: $9,350 + $2,350 – $5,100 = $6,600
    Company section of reconciliation: $8,510 – $35 – $1,875 = $6,600

  B.

Accounts Receivable	1,875	
Miscellaneous Expense	35	
Cash		1,910

4.

A.

Petty Cash	750	
Cash		750

B.

Repairs Expense	515	
Miscellaneous Selling Expense	88	
Cash Short and Over	32	
Cash		635

Need more help? Watch step-by-step videos of how to compute answers to these Exercises in CengageNOWv2.

Problem

1.

Urethane Company Bank Reconciliation June 30, 20Y2		
Cash balance according to bank statement		$ 9,293.11
Adjustments:		
Deposit of June 30 not recorded by bank.............................	$ 1,852.21	
Bank error in charging check as $157 instead of $139	18.00	
Outstanding checks	(5,265.27)	
Total adjustments		(3,395.06)
Adjusted balance		$ 5,898.05
Cash balance according to company's records		$ 4,526.25*
Adjustments:		
Proceeds of note collected by bank, including $30 interest	$ 1,030.00	
Error in recording check...	360.00	
Bank service charges...	(18.20)	
Total adjustments		1,371.80
Adjusted balance		$ 5,898.05
*$3,943.50 + $28,971.60 – $28,388.85		

2.

June	30	Cash	1,390.00	
		Notes Receivable		1,000.00
		Interest Revenue		30.00
		Accounts Payable—Avery Equipment Company		360.00
	30	Miscellaneous Administrative Expense	18.20	
		Cash		18.20

Discussion Questions

1. (A) Name and describe the five elements of internal control. (B) Is any one element of internal control more important than another?

2. Why should the employee who handles cash receipts not have the responsibility for maintaining the accounts receivable records? Explain.

3. The ticket seller at a movie theater doubles as a ticket taker for a few minutes each day while the ticket taker is on a break. Which control procedure of a business's system of internal control is violated in this situation?

4. Why should the responsibility for maintaining the accounting records be separated from the responsibility for operations? Explain.

5. Assume that Brooke Miles, accounts payable clerk for West Coast Design Inc., stole $48,350 by paying fictitious invoices for goods that were never received. The clerk set up accounts in the names of the fictitious companies and cashed the checks at a local bank. Describe a control procedure that would have prevented or detected the fraud.

6. Before a voucher for the purchase of merchandise is approved for payment, supporting documents should be compared to verify the accuracy of the liability. Give an example of supporting documents for the purchase of merchandise.

7. The balance of Cash is likely to differ from the bank statement balance. What two factors are likely to be responsible for the difference?

8. What is the purpose of preparing a bank reconciliation?

9. Knott Inc. has a petty cash fund of $750. (A) Since the petty cash fund is only $750, should Knott implement controls over petty cash? (B) What controls, if any, could be used for the petty cash fund?

10. (A) How are cash equivalents reported in the financial statements? (B) What are some examples of cash equivalents?

Basic Exercises

SHOW ME HOW

BE 7-1 Internal control elements   Obj. 2

Identify each of the following as relating to (A) the control environment, (B) control procedures, or (C) monitoring:

1. Hiring of external auditors to review the adequacy of controls
2. Personnel policies
3. Safeguarding inventory in a locked warehouse

SHOW ME HOW

BE 7-2 Items on company's bank statement   Obj. 4

The following items may appear on a bank statement:

1. Bank correction of an error from posting another customer's check (disbursement) to the company's account
2. EFT deposit
3. Loan proceeds
4. NSF check

Using the following format, indicate whether each item would appear as a debit or credit memo on the bank statement and whether the item would increase or decrease the balance of the company's account:

Item No.	Appears on the Bank Statement as a Debit or Credit Memo	Increases or Decreases the Balance of the Company's Bank Account

SHOW ME HOW

BE 7-3 Bank reconciliation

Obj. 5

The following data were gathered to use in reconciling the bank account of Reddan Company:

Balance per bank	$18,250
Balance per company records	12,045
Bank service charges	30
Deposit in transit	3,500
Note collected by bank with $160 interest	4,160
Outstanding checks	5,575

A. What is the adjusted balance on the bank reconciliation?

B. Journalize any necessary entries for Reddan Company based on the bank reconciliation.

SHOW ME HOW

BE 7-4 Petty cash fund

Obj. 6

Prepare journal entries for each of the following:

A. Issued a check to establish a petty cash fund of $600.

B. The amount of cash in the petty cash fund is $130. Issued a check to replenish the fund, based on the following summary of petty cash receipts: store supplies, $410, and miscellaneous selling expense, $50. Record any missing funds in the cash short and over account.

Exercises

Internet Project

EX 7-1 Sarbanes-Oxley internal control report

Obj. 1

Using Wikipedia (www.wikipedia.com), look up the entry for Sarbanes-Oxley Act. Look over the table of contents and find the section that describes Section 404.

 What does Section 404 require of management's internal control report?

EX 7-2 Internal controls

Obj. 2, 3

Faith Cassen has recently been hired as the manager of Gibraltar Coffee Shop. Gibraltar Coffee Shop is a national chain of franchised coffee shops. During her first month as store manager, Faith encountered the following internal control situations:

A. Faith caught an employee putting a case of 1,000 single-serving tea bags in his car. Not wanting to create a scene, Faith smiled and said, "I don't think you're putting those tea bags on the right shelf. Don't they belong inside the coffee shop?" The employee returned the tea bags to the stockroom.

B. Gibraltar Coffee Shop has one cash register. Prior to Faith's joining the coffee shop, each employee working on a shift would take a customer order, accept payment, and then prepare the order. Faith made one employee on each shift responsible for taking orders and accepting the customer's payment. Other employees prepare the orders.

C. Because only one employee uses the cash register, that employee is responsible for counting the cash at the end of the shift and verifying that the cash in the drawer matches the amount of cash sales recorded by the cash register. Faith expects each cashier to balance the drawer to the penny *every* time—no exceptions.

State whether you agree or disagree with Faith's method of handling each situation and explain your answer.

EX 7-3 Internal controls

Obj. 2, 3

Ramona's Clothing is a retail store specializing in women's clothing. The store has established a liberal return policy for the holiday season in order to encourage gift purchases. Any item purchased during November and December may be returned through January 31, with a receipt, for cash or exchange. If the customer does not have a receipt, cash will still be refunded for any item under $75. If the item is more than $75, a check is mailed to the customer.

Whenever an item is returned, a store clerk completes a return slip, which the customer signs. The return slip is placed in a special box. The store manager visits the return counter

(Continued)

approximately once every two hours to authorize the return slips. Clerks are instructed to place the returned merchandise on the proper rack on the selling floor as soon as possible.

This year, returns at Ramona's have reached an all-time high. There are a large number of returns under $75 without receipts.

A. ━━━▶How can sales clerks employed at Ramona's Clothing use the store's return policy to steal money from the cash register?

B. ━━━▶What internal control weaknesses do you see in the return policy that make cash thefts easier?

C. ━━━▶Would issuing a store credit in place of a cash refund for all merchandise returned without a receipt reduce the possibility of theft? List some advantages and disadvantages of issuing a store credit in place of a cash refund.

D. ━━━▶Assume that Ramona's Clothing is committed to the current policy of issuing cash refunds without a receipt. What changes could be made in the store's procedures regarding customer refunds in order to improve internal control?

EX 7-4 Internal controls for bank lending
Obj. 2, 3

Pacific Bank provides loans to businesses in the community through its Commercial Lending Department. Small loans (less than $100,000) may be approved by an individual loan officer, while larger loans (greater than $100,000) must be approved by a board of loan officers. Once a loan is approved, the funds are made available to the loan applicant under agreed-upon terms. Pacific Bank has instituted a policy whereby its president has the individual authority to approve loans up to $5,000,000. The president believes that this policy will allow flexibility to approve loans to valued clients much quicker than under the previous policy.

━━━▶As an internal auditor of Pacific Bank, how would you respond to this change in policy?

REAL WORLD

EX 7-5 Internal controls
Obj. 2, 3

One of the largest losses in history from unauthorized securities trading involved a securities trader for the French bank, **Societe Generale**. The trader was able to circumvent internal controls and create more than $7 billion in trading losses in six months. The trader apparently escaped detection by using knowledge of the bank's internal control systems learned from a previous back-office monitoring job. Much of this monitoring involved the use of software to monitor trades. In addition, traders were usually kept to tight trading limits. Apparently, these controls failed in this case.

━━━▶ What general weaknesses in Societe Generale's internal controls contributed to the occurrence and size of the losses?

REAL WORLD

EX 7-6 Internal controls
Obj. 2, 3

An employee of **JHT Holdings, Inc.**, a trucking company, was responsible for resolving roadway accident claims under $25,000. The employee created fake accident claims and wrote settlement checks of between $5,000 and $25,000 to friends or acquaintances acting as phony "victims." One friend recruited subordinates at his place of work to cash some of the checks. Beyond this, the JHT employee also recruited lawyers, whom he paid to represent both the trucking company and the fake victims in the bogus accident settlements. When the lawyers cashed the checks, they allegedly split the money with the corrupt JHT employee. This fraud went undetected for two years.

━━━▶ Why would it take so long to discover such a fraud?

EX 7-7 Internal controls
Obj. 2, 3

All-Around Sound Co. discovered a fraud whereby one of its front office administrative employees used company funds to purchase goods, such as computers, digital cameras, and other electronic items for her own use. The fraud was discovered when employees noticed an increase in delivery frequency from vendors and the use of unusual vendors. After some investigation, it was discovered that the employee would alter the description or change the quantity on an invoice in order to explain the cost on the bill.

━━━▶ What general internal control weaknesses contributed to this fraud?

REAL WORLD

EX 7-8 Financial statement fraud
Obj. 2, 3

A former chairman, CFO, and controller of **Donnkenny, Inc.**, an apparel company that makes sportswear for Pierre Cardin and Victoria Jones, pleaded guilty to financial statement fraud. These managers used false journal entries to record fictitious sales, hid inventory in public warehouses so that it could be recorded as "sold," and required sales orders to be backdated so that the sale could be moved back to an earlier period. The combined effect of these actions caused $25 million out of $40 million in quarterly sales to be phony.

A. ➤ Why might control procedures listed in this chapter be insufficient in stopping this type of fraud?

B. ➤ How could this type of fraud be stopped?

EX 7-9 Internal control of cash receipts
Obj. 2, 3

The procedures used for over-the-counter receipts are as follows. At the close of each day's business, the sales clerks count the cash in their respective cash drawers, after which they determine the amount recorded by the cash register and prepare the memo cash form, noting any discrepancies. An employee from the cashier's office counts the cash, compares the total with the memo, and takes the cash to the cashier's office.

A. ➤ Indicate the weak link in internal control.

B. ➤ How can the weakness be corrected?

EX 7-10 Internal control of cash receipts
Obj. 2, 3

Sergio Flores works at the drive-through window of Big & Bad Burgers. Occasionally, when a drive-through customer orders, Sergio fills the order and pockets the customer's money. He does not ring up the order on the cash register.

➤ Identify the internal control weaknesses that exist at Big & Bad Burgers, and discuss what can be done to prevent this theft.

EX 7-11 Internal control of cash receipts
Obj. 2, 3

The mailroom employees send all remittances and remittance advices to the cashier. The cashier deposits the cash in the bank and forwards the remittance advices and duplicate deposit slips to the Accounting Department.

A. ➤ Indicate the weak link in internal control in the handling of cash receipts.

B. ➤ How can the weakness be corrected?

SHOW ME HOW

EX 7-12 Entry for cash sales; cash short
Obj. 3

The actual cash received from cash sales was $61,355, and the amount indicated by the cash register total was $61,380. Journalize the entry to record the cash receipts and cash sales.

SHOW ME HOW

EX 7-13 Entry for cash sales; cash over
Obj. 3

The actual cash received from cash sales was $295,455, and the amount indicated by the cash register total was $295,340. Journalize the entry to record the cash receipts and cash sales.

EX 7-14 Internal control of cash payments
Obj. 3

Abbe Co. is a small merchandising company with a manual accounting system. An investigation revealed that in spite of a sufficient bank balance, a significant amount of available cash discounts had been lost because of failure to make timely payments. In addition, it was discovered that the invoices for several purchases had been paid twice.

➤ Outline procedures for the payment of vendors' invoices so that the possibilities of losing available cash discounts and of paying an invoice a second time will be minimized.

EX 7-15 Internal control of cash payments

Obj. 2, 3

Paragon Tech Company, a communications equipment manufacturer, recently fell victim to a fraud scheme developed by one of its employees. To understand the scheme, it is necessary to review Paragon's procedures for the purchase of services.

The purchasing agent is responsible for ordering services (such as repairs to a photocopy machine or office cleaning) after receiving a service requisition from an authorized manager. However, because no tangible goods are delivered, a receiving report is not prepared. When the Accounting Department receives an invoice billing Paragon Tech for a service call, the accounts payable clerk calls the manager who requested the service in order to verify that it was performed.

The fraud scheme involves Mae Jansma, the manager of plant and facilities. Mae arranged for her uncle's company, Radiate Systems, to be placed on Paragon's approved vendor list. Mae did not disclose the family relationship.

On several occasions, Mae would submit a requisition for services to be provided by Radiate. However, the service requested was really not needed, and it was never performed. Radiate would bill Paragon for the service and then split the cash payment with Mae.

Explain what changes should be made to Paragon Tech Company's procedures for ordering and paying for services in order to prevent such occurrences in the future.

EX 7-16 Bank reconciliation

Obj. 5

Identify each of the following reconciling items as: (A) an addition to the cash balance according to the bank statement, (B) a deduction from the cash balance according to the bank statement, (C) an addition to the cash balance according to the company's records, or (D) a deduction from the cash balance according to the company's records. (None of the transactions reported by bank debit and credit memos have been recorded by the company.)

1. Bank service charges, $75.
2. Check of a customer returned by bank to company because of insufficient funds, $880.
3. Check for $275 incorrectly recorded by the company as $725.
4. Check for $100 incorrectly charged by bank as $1,000.
5. Deposit in transit, $5,550.
6. Outstanding checks, $10,350.
7. Note collected by bank, $12,720.

EX 7-17 Entries based on bank reconciliation

Obj. 5

Which of the reconciling items listed in Exercise 7-16 require an entry in the company's accounts?

EX 7-18 Bank reconciliation

Obj. 5

✔ Adjusted balance: $21,725

SHOW ME HOW

The following data were accumulated for use in reconciling the bank account of Creative Design Co. for August 20Y6:

1. Cash balance according to the company's records at August 31, $20,870.
2. Cash balance according to the bank statement at August 31, $37,600.
3. Checks outstanding, $23,375.
4. Deposit in transit not recorded by bank, $7,500.
5. A check for $100 in payment of an account was erroneously recorded in the check register as $1,000.
6. Bank debit memo for service charges, $45.

A. Prepare a bank reconciliation, using the format shown in Exhibit 13.

B. If the balance sheet were prepared for Creative Design Co. on August 31 what amount should be reported for cash?

C. Must a bank reconciliation always balance (reconcile)?

SHOW ME HOW

EX 7-19 Entries for bank reconciliation

Obj. 5

Using the data presented in Exercise 7-18, journalize the entry or entries that should be made by the company.

SHOW ME HOW

EX 7-20 Entries for note collected by bank

Obj. 5

Accompanying a bank statement for Borden Company is a credit memo for $21,200 representing the principal ($20,000) and interest ($1,200) on a note that had been collected by the bank. The company had been notified by the bank at the time of the collection but had made no entries. Journalize the entry that should be made by the company to bring the accounting records up to date.

SHOW ME HOW

EX 7-21 Bank reconciliation

Obj. 5

An accounting clerk for Chesner Co. prepared the following bank reconciliation:

Chesner Co.
Bank Reconciliation
July 31, 20Y4

Cash balance according to company's records		$11,100
Adjustments:		
Outstanding checks	$ 3,585	
Error by Chesner Co. in recording Check		
No. 1056 as $950 instead of $590	360	
Note for $12,000 collected by bank, including interest	12,480	
Deposit in transit on July 31	(7,200)	
Bank service charges	(25)	
Total adjustments		9,200
Cash balance according to bank statement		$20,300

A. From the data in this bank reconciliation, prepare a new bank reconciliation for Chesner Co., using the format shown in the Let's Review section.

B. If a balance sheet were prepared for Chesner Co. on July 31, 20Y4, what amount should be reported for cash?

EX 7-22 Bank reconciliation

Obj. 5

✔ Corrected adjusted balance: $19,780

The following bank reconciliation was prepared as of June 30, 20Y7:

Poway Co.
Bank Reconciliation
For the Month Ended June 30, 20Y7

Cash balance according to bank statement		$16,185
Adjustments:		
Outstanding Check No. 1067	$ 575	
Outstanding Check No. 1106	470	
Outstanding Check No. 1110	1,050	
Outstanding Check No. 1113	910	
Deposit of June 30 not recorded by bank	(6,600)	
Total adjustments		(3,595)
Adjusted balance		$12,590
Cash balance according to company's records		$ 8,985
Adjustments:		
Proceeds of note collected by bank: Face value	$ 6,000	
Proceeds of note collected by bank: Interest	300	
Service charges	15	
Check returned because of insufficient funds	(890)	
Error in recording June 17 deposit of $7,150 as $1,750	(5,400)	
Total adjustments		25
Adjusted balance		$ 9,010

A. Identify the errors in the bank reconciliation.

B. Prepare a corrected bank reconciliation.

SHOW ME HOW

EX 7-23 Using bank reconciliation to determine cash receipts stolen   Obj. 2, 3, 5

Alaska Impressions Co. records all cash receipts on the basis of its cash register tapes. Alaska Impressions discovered during October 20Y3 that one of its sales clerks had stolen an undetermined amount of cash receipts by taking the daily deposits to the bank. The following data have been gathered for October:

Cash in bank according to the general ledger	$11,680
Cash according to the October 31, 20Y3, bank statement	13,275
Outstanding checks as of October 31, 20Y3	3,670
Bank service charge for October	40
Note receivable, including interest collected by bank in October	2,100

No deposits were in transit on October 31.

A. Determine the amount of cash receipts stolen by the sales clerk.

B. ➤ What accounting controls would have prevented or detected this theft?

SHOW ME HOW

EX 7-24 Petty cash fund entries   Obj. 6

Journalize the entries to record the following:

A. Check No. 12-375 is issued to establish a petty cash fund of $750.

B. The amount of cash in the petty cash fund is now $80. Check No. 12-476 is issued to replenish the fund, based on the following summary of petty cash receipts: office supplies, $288; miscellaneous selling expense, $226; miscellaneous administrative expense, $123. (Because the amount of the check to replenish the fund plus the balance in the fund do not equal $750, record the discrepancy in the cash short and over account.)

Problems: Series A

PR 7-1A Evaluating internal control of cash   Obj. 2, 3

The following procedures were recently installed by Raspberry Creek Company:

A. After necessary approvals have been obtained for the payment of a voucher, the treasurer signs and mails the check. The treasurer then stamps the voucher and supporting documentation as paid and returns the voucher and supporting documentation to the accounts payable clerk for filing.

B. The accounts payable clerk prepares a voucher for each disbursement. The voucher along with the supporting documentation is forwarded to the treasurer's office for approval.

C. Along with petty cash expense receipts for postage, office supplies, etc., several postdated employee checks are in the petty cash fund.

D. At the end of the day, cash register clerks are required to use their own funds to make up any cash shortages in their registers.

E. At the end of each day, all cash receipts are placed in the bank's night depository.

F. At the end of each day, an accounting clerk compares the duplicate copy of the daily cash deposit slip with the deposit receipt obtained from the bank.

G. All mail is opened by the mail clerk, who forwards all cash remittances to the cashier. The cashier prepares a listing of the cash receipts and forwards a copy of the list to the accounts receivable clerk for recording in the accounts.

H. The bank reconciliation is prepared by the cashier, who works under the supervision of the treasurer.

Instructions

➤ Indicate whether each of the procedures of internal control over cash represents (1) a strength or (2) a weakness. For each weakness, indicate why it exists.

SHOW ME HOW   EXCEL TEMPLATE

PR 7-2A Transactions for petty cash, cash short and over

Obj. 3, 6

Wyoming Restoration Company completed the following selected transactions during July 20Y1:

July 1. Established a petty cash fund of $1,100.

12. The cash sales for the day, according to the cash register records, totaled $8,192. The actual cash received from cash sales was $8,220.

31. Petty cash on hand was $47. Replenished the petty cash fund for the following disbursements, each evidenced by a petty cash receipt:

July 3. Store supplies, $580.

7. Express charges on merchandise sold, $90 (Delivery Expense).

9. Office supplies, $30.

13. Office supplies, $35.

19. Postage stamps, $50 (Office Supplies).

21. Repair to office file cabinet lock, $60 (Miscellaneous Administrative Expense).

22. Postage due on special delivery letter, $28 (Miscellaneous Administrative Expense).

24. Express charges on merchandise sold, $135 (Delivery Expense).

30. Office supplies, $25.

31. The cash sales for the day, according to the cash register records, totaled $10,241. The actual cash received from cash sales was $10,232.

31. Decreased the petty cash fund by $150.

Instructions
Journalize the transactions.

PR 7-3A Bank reconciliation and entries

Obj. 5

✔ 1. Adjusted balance: $175,960

SHOW ME HOW   EXCEL TEMPLATE

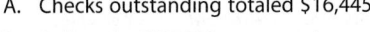

GENERAL LEDGER

The cash account for Pala Medical Co. at June 30, 20Y1, indicated a balance of $146,035. The bank statement indicated a balance of $181,965 on June 30, 20Y1. Comparing the bank statement and the accompanying canceled checks and memos with the records revealed the following reconciling items:

A. Checks outstanding totaled $16,445.

B. A deposit of $9,900, representing receipts of June 30, had been made too late to appear on the bank statement.

C. The bank collected $31,800 on a $30,000 note, including interest of $1,800.

D. A check for $2,000 returned with the statement had been incorrectly recorded by Pala Medical Co. as $200. The check was for the payment of an obligation to Skyline Supply Co. for a purchase on account.

E. A check drawn for $170 had been erroneously charged by the bank as $710.

F. Bank service charges for June amounted to $75.

Instructions

1. Prepare a bank reconciliation.

2. Journalize the necessary entries.

3. If a balance sheet were prepared for Pala Medical Co. on June 30, 20Y1, what amount should be reported as cash?

PR 7-4A Bank reconciliation and entries

Obj. 5

✔ 1. Adjusted balance: $4,830

SHOW ME HOW   EXCEL TEMPLATE

GENERAL LEDGER

The cash account for Coastal Bike Co. at October 1, 20Y9, indicated a balance of $5,140. During October, the total cash deposited was $39,175, and checks written totaled $40,520. The bank statement indicated a balance of $8,980 on October 31, 20Y9. Comparing the bank statement, the canceled checks, and the accompanying memos with the records revealed the following reconciling items:

A. Checks outstanding totaled $5,560.

B. A deposit of $1,050 representing receipts of October 31 had been made too late to appear on the bank statement.

C. The bank had collected for Coastal Bike Co. $2,120 on a note left for collection. The face of the note was $2,000.

D. A check for $370 returned with the statement had been incorrectly charged by the bank as $730.

(Continued)

E. A check for $310 returned with the statement had been recorded by Coastal Bike Co. as $130. The check was for the payment of an obligation to Rack Pro Co. on account.

F. Bank service charges for October amounted to $25.

G. A check for $880 from Bay View Condos was returned by the bank due to insufficient funds.

Instructions

1. Prepare a bank reconciliation as of October 31, 20Y9.

2. Journalize the necessary entries.

3. If a balance sheet were prepared for Coastal Bike Co. on October 31, 20Y9, what amount should be reported as cash?

PR 7-5A Bank reconciliation and entries   Obj. 5

✔ 1. Adjusted balance: $13,216

EXCEL TEMPLATE   GENERAL LEDGER

Beeler Furniture Company deposits all cash receipts each Wednesday and Friday in a night depository, after banking hours. The data required to reconcile the bank statement as of June 30, 20Y2, have been taken from various documents and records and are reproduced as follows. The sources of the data are printed in capital letters. All checks were written for payments on account.

CASH ACCOUNT:

Balance as of June 1	$9,317.40
CASH RECEIPTS FOR MONTH OF JUNE	9,223.76

DUPLICATE DEPOSIT TICKETS:

Date and amount of each deposit in June:

Date	Amount	Date	Amount	Date	Amount
June 1	$1,080.50	June 10	$ 996.61	June 22	$ 897.34
3	854.17	15	882.95	24	947.21
8	840.50	17	1,606.74	30	1,117.74

CHECKS WRITTEN:

Number and amount of each check issued in June:

Check No.	Amount	Check No.	Amount	Check No.	Amount
740	$237.50	747	Void	754	$ 449.75
741	495.15	748	$450.90	755	272.75
742	501.90	749	640.13	756	113.95
743	761.30	750	276.77	757	407.95
744	506.88	751	299.37	758	259.60
745	117.25	752	537.01	759	901.50
746	298.66	753	380.95	760	486.39
Total amount of checks issued in June					$8,395.66

BANK RECONCILIATION FOR PRECEDING MONTH:

Beeler Furniture Company
Bank Reconciliation
May 31, 20Y2

Cash balance according to bank statement.........................		$9,447.20
Adjustments:		
Deposit of May 31 not recorded by bank.........................	$ 690.25	
Outstanding Check No. 731	(162.15)	
Outstanding Check No. 736	(345.95)	
Outstanding Check No. 738	(251.40)	
Outstanding Check No. 739	(60.55)	
Total adjustments		(129.80)
Adjusted balance...		$9,317.40
Cash balance according to company's records		$9,352.50
Adjustments:		
Bank service charges		(35.10)
Adjusted balance...		$9,317.40

JUNE BANK STATEMENT:

```
        A          MEMBER FDIC                              PAGE    1
        N B    AMERICAN NATIONAL BANK        ACCOUNT NUMBER
                  OF CHICAGO                 FROM 6/01/20Y2   TO 6/30/20Y2
     CHICAGO, IL 60603   (312) 441-1239      BALANCE             9,447.20

                                           9 DEPOSITS            8,691.77

                                          20 WITHDRAWALS         7,599.26

        BEELER FURNITURE COMPANY           4 OTHER DEBITS
                                             AND CREDITS         3,085.00CR

                                             NEW BALANCE        13,624.71
```

```
* - - - CHECKS AND OTHER DEBITS - - - * - - DEPOSITS - - * - DATE - * - - BALANCE- - *
   No. 731   162.15   No. 736   345.95       690.25    6/01      9,629.35
   No. 739    60.55   No. 740   237.50     1,080.50    6/02     10,411.80
   No. 741   495.15   No. 742   501.90       854.17    6/04     10,268.92
   No. 743   671.30   No. 744   506.88       840.50    6/09      9,931.24
   No. 745   117.25   No. 746   298.66   MS 3,500.00   6/09     13,015.33
   No. 748   450.90   No. 749   640.13   MS   210.00   6/09     12,134.30
   No. 750   276.77   No. 751   299.37       896.61    6/11     12,454.77
   No. 752   537.01   No. 753   380.95       882.95    6/16     12,419.76
   No. 754   449.75   No. 755   272.75     1,606.74    6/18     13,304.00
   No. 757   407.95   No. 760   486.39       897.34    6/23     13,307.00
                                             942.71    6/25     14,249.71
                                  NSF 550.00           6/28     13,699.71
                                  SC   75.00           6/30     13,624.71
```

```
        EC — ERROR CORRECTION              OD — OVERDRAFT
        MS — MISCELLANEOUS                 PS — PAYMENT STOPPED
        NSF — NOT SUFFICIENT FUNDS         SC — SERVICE CHARGE
 * * *                          * * *                              * * *
        THE RECONCILEMENT OF THIS STATEMENT WITH YOUR RECORDS IS ESSENTIAL.
           ANY ERROR OR EXCEPTION SHOULD BE REPORTED IMMEDIATELY.
```

Instructions

1. Prepare a bank reconciliation as of June 30, 20Y2. If errors in recording deposits or checks are discovered, assume that the errors were made by the company. Assume that all deposits are from cash sales. All checks are written to satisfy accounts payable.

2. Journalize the necessary entries.

3. What is the amount of cash that should appear on the balance sheet as of June 30, 20Y2?

4. ━━━━► Assume that a canceled check for $390 has been incorrectly recorded by the bank as $930. Briefly explain how the error would be included in a bank reconciliation and how it should be corrected.

Problems: Series B

PR 7-1B   Evaluating internal control of cash   Obj. 2, 3

The following procedures were recently installed by The China Shop:

A. All sales are rung up on the cash register, and a receipt is given to the customer. All sales are recorded on a record locked inside the cash register.

B. Each cashier is assigned a separate cash register drawer to which no other cashier has access.

C. At the end of a shift, each cashier counts the cash in his or her cash register, unlocks the cash register record, and compares the amount of cash with the amount on the record to determine cash shortages and overages.

D. Checks received through the mail are given daily to the accounts receivable clerk for recording collections on account and for depositing in the bank.

E. Vouchers and all supporting documents are perforated with a PAID designation after being paid by the treasurer.

F. Disbursements are made from the petty cash fund only after a petty cash receipt has been completed and signed by the payee.

G. The bank reconciliation is prepared by the cashier.

Instructions

Indicate whether each of the procedures of internal control over cash represents (1) a strength or (2) a weakness. For each weakness, indicate why it exists.

SHOW ME HOW   EXCEL TEMPLATE

PR 7-2B   Transactions for petty cash, cash short and over   Obj. 3, 6

Cedar Springs Company completed the following selected transactions during June 20Y3:

June 1. Established a petty cash fund of $1,000.

   12. The cash sales for the day, according to the cash register records, totaled $9,440. The actual cash received from cash sales was $9,506.

   30. Petty cash on hand was $46. Replenished the petty cash fund for the following disbursements, each evidenced by a petty cash receipt:

   June   2. Store supplies, $375.

   10. Express charges on merchandise purchased, $105 (Inventory).

   14. Office supplies, $85.

   15. Office supplies, $90.

   18. Postage stamps, $33 (Office Supplies).

   20. Repair to fax, $100 (Miscellaneous Administrative Expense).

   21. Repair to office door lock, $25 (Miscellaneous Administrative Expense).

   22. Postage due on special delivery letter, $9 (Miscellaneous Administrative Expense).

   28. Express charges on merchandise purchased, $110 (Inventory).

   30. The cash sales for the day, according to the cash register records, totaled $13,390. The actual cash received from cash sales was $13,350.

   30. Increased the petty cash fund by $200.

Instructions

Journalize the transactions.

✔ 1. Adjusted balance: $24,305

SHOW ME HOW   EXCEL TEMPLATE

GENERAL LEDGER

PR 7-3B   Bank reconciliation and entries   Obj. 5

The cash account for Stone Systems at July 31, 20Y5, indicated a balance of $17,750. The bank statement indicated a balance of $33,650 on July 31, 20Y5. Comparing the bank statement and the accompanying canceled checks and memos with the records reveals the following reconciling items:

A. Checks outstanding totaled $17,865.

B. A deposit of $9,150, representing receipts of July 31, had been made too late to appear on the bank statement.

C. The bank had collected $6,095 on a note left for collection. The face of the note was $5,750.

D. A check for $390 returned with the statement had been incorrectly recorded by Stone Systems as $930. The check was for the payment of an obligation to Holland Co. for the purchase of office supplies on account.

E. A check drawn for $1,810 had been incorrectly charged by the bank as $1,180.

F. Bank service charges for July amounted to $80.

Instructions

1. Prepare a bank reconciliation.

2. Journalize the necessary entries.

3. If a balance sheet were prepared for Stone Systems on July 31, 20Y5, what amount should be reported as cash?

PR 7-4B **Bank reconciliation and entries** **Obj. 5**

✔ 1. Adjusted balance: $78,535

SHOW ME HOW

EXCEL TEMPLATE

GENERAL LEDGER

The cash account for Collegiate Sports Co. on November 1, 20Y9, indicated a balance of $81,145. During November, the total cash deposited was $293,150, and checks written totaled $307,360. The bank statement indicated a balance of $112,675 on November 30, 20Y9. Comparing the bank statement, the canceled checks, and the accompanying memos with the records revealed the following reconciling items:

A. Checks outstanding totaled $41,840.

B. A deposit of $12,200, representing receipts of November 30, had been made too late to appear on the bank statement.

C. A check for $7,250 had been incorrectly charged by the bank as $2,750.

D. A check for $760 returned with the statement had been recorded by Collegiate Sports Co. as $7,600. The check was for the payment of an obligation to Ramirez Co. on account.

E. The bank had collected for Collegiate Sports Co. $7,385 on a note left for collection. The face of the note was $7,000.

F. Bank service charges for November amounted to $125.

G. A check for $2,500 from Hallen Academy was returned by the bank because of insufficient funds.

Instructions

1. Prepare a bank reconciliation as of November 30, 20Y9.

2. Journalize the necessary entries.

3. If a balance sheet were prepared for Collegiate Sports Co. on November 30, 20Y9, what amount should be reported as cash?

PR 7-5B **Bank reconciliation and entries** **Obj. 5**

✔ 1. Adjusted balance: $11,494

EXCEL TEMPLATE

GENERAL LEDGER

Sunshine Interiors deposits all cash receipts each Wednesday and Friday in a night depository, after banking hours. The data required to reconcile the bank statement as of July 31, 20Y0, have been taken from various documents and records and are reproduced as follows. The sources of the data are printed in capital letters. All checks were written for payments on account.

CASH ACCOUNT:

Balance as of July 1	$9,578.00
CASH RECEIPTS FOR MONTH OF JULY	6,465.42

DUPLICATE DEPOSIT TICKETS:

Date and amount of each deposit in July:

Date	Amount	Date	Amount	Date	Amount
July 2	$569.50	July 12	$580.70	July 23	$ 713.45
5	701.80	16	600.10	26	601.50
9	819.24	19	701.26	31	1,177.87

CHECKS WRITTEN:

Number and amount of each check issued in July:

Check No.	Amount	Check No.	Amount	Check No.	Amount
614	$243.50	621	$309.50	628	$ 837.70
615	350.10	622	Void	629	329.90
616	279.90	623	Void	630	882.80
617	395.50	624	707.01	631	1,081.56
618	435.40	625	158.63	632	325.40
619	320.10	626	550.03	633	310.08
620	238.87	627	381.73	634	241.71
Total amount of checks issued in July					$8,379.42

(Continued)

BANK RECONCILIATION FOR PRECEDING MONTH:

Sunshine Interiors
Bank Reconciliation
June 30, 20Y0

Cash balance according to bank statement............................		$9,422.80
Adjustments:		
Deposit of June 30 not recorded by bank	$ 780.80	
Outstanding Check No. 580	(310.10)	
Outstanding Check No. 602	(85.50)	
Outstanding Check No. 612	(92.50)	
Outstanding Check No. 613	(137.50)	
Total adjustments		155.20
Adjusted balance..		$9,578.00
Cash balance according to company's records		$9,605.70
Adjustments:		
Bank service charges		(27.70)
Adjusted balance..		$9,578.00

JULY BANK STATEMENT:

```
                                   MEMBER FDIC                          PAGE    1

A   AMERICAN NATIONAL BANK              ACCOUNT NUMBER
NB      OF DETROIT
                                        FROM  7/01/20Y0   TO  7/31/20Y0
DETROIT, MI 48201-2500   (313) 933-8547
                                        BALANCE              9,422.80

                                     9  DEPOSITS             6,086.35

                                    20  WITHDRAWALS          7,656.74

        SUNSHINE INTERIORS
                                     4  OTHER DEBITS
                                        AND CREDITS          3,749.00CR

                                        NEW BALANCE         11,601.41

* – – – – – CHECKS AND OTHER DEBITS – – – – – * – DEPOSITS – * – DATE – * – BALANCE– *

No. 580  310.10   No. 612    92.50            780.80      07/01     9,801.00
No. 602   85.50   No. 614   243.50            569.50      07/03    10,041.50
No. 615  350.10   No. 616   279.90            701.80      07/06    10,113.30
No. 617  395.50   No. 618   435.40            819.24      07/11    10,101.64
No. 619  320.10   No. 620   238.87            580.70      07/13    10,123.37
No. 621  309.50   No. 624   707.01    MS 4,000.00         07/14    13,106.86
No. 625  158.63   No. 626   550.03    MS   160.00         07/14    12,558.20
No. 627  318.73   No. 629   329.90            600.10      07/17    12,509.67
No. 630  882.80   No. 631 1,081.56  NSF 375.00            07/20    10,170.31
No. 632  325.40   No. 634   241.71            701.26      07/21    10,304.46
                                              731.45      07/24    11,035.91
                                              601.50      07/28    11,637.41
                          SC     36.00                    07/31    11,601.41

        EC — ERROR CORRECTION            OD — OVERDRAFT
        MS — MISCELLANEOUS               PS — PAYMENT STOPPED
        NSF — NOT SUFFICIENT FUNDS       SC — SERVICE CHARGE

 * * *                          * * *                         * * *
        THE RECONCILEMENT OF THIS STATEMENT WITH YOUR RECORDS IS ESSENTIAL.
          ANY ERROR OR EXCEPTION SHOULD BE REPORTED IMMEDIATELY.
```

Instructions

1. Prepare a bank reconciliation as of July 31, 20Y0. If errors in recording deposits or checks are discovered, assume that the errors were made by the company. Assume that all deposits are from cash sales. All checks are written to satisfy accounts payable.

2. Journalize the necessary entries.

3. What is the amount of cash that should appear on the balance sheet as of July 31, 20Y0?

4. ➤ Assume that a canceled check for $180 has been incorrectly recorded by the bank as $1,800. Briefly explain how the error would be included in a bank reconciliation and how it should be corrected.

Analysis for Decision Making

REAL WORLD

ADM-1 Continuing Company Analysis—Amazon: Days' cash on hand

Amazon.com, Inc. is one of the largest Internet retailers in the world. Netflix, Inc. provides digital streaming and DVD rentals in the United States. Amazon and Netflix compete in streaming and digital services; however, Amazon also sells many other products online. The cash, temporary investments, operating expenses, and depreciation expense from recent financial statements were reported as follows for both companies (in millions):

	Amazon	Netflix
Balance sheet, end of year:		
Cash	$14,557	$1,114
Temporary investments	—	495
Income statement:		
Operating expenses	88,810	5,102
Depreciation expense	4,746	2,781

A. Determine the days' cash on hand for Amazon and Netflix. (Round all calculations to one decimal place.)

B. ➤ Interpret the results.

REAL WORLD

ADM-2 Apache: Days' cash on hand

Apache Corporation is an independent energy company that explores, develops, and produces oil and gas products. Apache operates worldwide, including in the United States, Canada, and the North Sea. The profitability of the oil and gas business is highly influenced by the price of crude oil and natural gas, and by the success in finding oil and gas. Selected financial information for Apache for three recent years follows (in millions):

	Year 3	Year 2	Year 1
Balance sheet, end of year:			
Cash	$ 769	$ 1,906	$ 160
Income statement:			
Operating expenses	16,575	11,156	11,724
Depreciation expense	10,158	6,289	6,881

A. Determine the days' cash on hand for each year. (Round all calculations to one decimal place.)

B. ➤ Interpret the results.

C. ➤ What are some ways a company can respond to a liquidity squeeze?

REAL WORLD

ADM-3   Krispy Kreme and Dunkin': Days' cash on hand

Krispy Kreme Doughnuts, Inc. is a leading retailer and wholesaler of doughnuts. Krispy Kreme owns or franchises 1,000 stores where the "hot" light tells you if doughnuts are cooking. **Dunkin' Brands Group, Inc.** is a leading franchisor of doughnut (Dunkin' Donuts) and ice cream (Baskin-Robbins) shops with more than 19,000 stores worldwide. Selected financial statement information for a recent year for both companies follows (in thousands):

	Krispy Kreme	Dunkin' Brands
Operating expenses	$442,097	$432,535
Depreciation expense	12,840	19,779
Cash (end of year balance)	50,971	208,080

A. Determine the days' cash on hand for each company. (Round all calculations to one decimal place.)

B. Which company appears to have the stronger cash liquidity position?

REAL WORLD

ADM-4   Nike, lululemon, and Under Armour: Days' cash on hand

Three companies that compete in the athletic and activewear market segment are **Nike, Inc.**, **lululemon athletica inc.**, and **Under Armour, Inc.** Nike is the largest designer and seller of athletic footwear and apparel in the world. Lululemon designs and sells technical athletic apparel featuring yoga, fitness, and dance-inspired wear. Under Armour designs and sells athletic apparel featuring high-performance fabrics for men and women around the world. Selected financial information for a recent year follows (in millions):

	Nike	lululemon	Under Armour
Balance sheet:			
Cash	$ 2,220	$ 664	$ 593
Temporary investments	2,922		
Income statement:			
Operating expenses	8,766	538	1,158
Depreciation expense	518	58	72
Total revenues	27,799	1,797	3,084

A. ➤ How does the size of these companies, as represented by total revenues, compare to each other?

B. Compute the days' cash on hand for all three companies. (Round all calculations to one decimal place.)

C. ➤ Comment on the cash sufficiency for these three companies.

D. Which company appears to have the greatest cash liquidity?

E. ➤ Why is a ratio used to compare cash sufficiency across the three companies rather than just the companies' cash balances?

Take It Further

ETHICS

TIF 7-1   Ethics in Action

Tehra Dactyl is an accountant for Skeds, Inc., a footwear and apparel company. The company's revenue and net income have increased by more than 100% over the past three years. During the same period, Tehra and her colleagues in the accounting department have not received a raise or salary increase. Frustrated by not receiving a raise while the company has thrived, Tehra has begun submitting expense reimbursements for personal purchases. Tehra has a good relationship with her supervisor, and he simply "signs off" on Tehra's expense reimbursements. Tehra suspects that he knows that she is submitting personal expenses for reimbursement and is "looking the other way" because Tehra has not received a raise in the past three years.

> Are Tehra and her supervisor acting in an ethical manner? Why?

REAL WORLD

TIF 7-2   Team Activity

In teams, select a public company that interests you. Obtain the company's most recent annual report on Form 10-K. The Form 10-K is a company's annually required filing with the Securities and Exchange Commission (SEC). It includes the company's financial statements and accompanying notes. The Form 10-K can be obtained either (A) from the investor relations section of the company's Web site or (B) by using the company search feature of the SEC's EDGAR database service found at www.sec.gov/edgar/searchedgar/companysearch.html.

1. Based on the information in the company's most recent annual report, answer the following questions:
   A. How much cash does the company have at the end of the most recent year?
   B. What percentage of total current assets is cash during the most recent two years presented? Has this percentage increased, decreased, or remained the same during this period?
2. Review Management's Annual Report on Internal Control Over Financial Reporting. Based on this information, answer the following questions:
   A. Who has responsibility for establishing and maintaining adequate internal controls over a company's financial reporting?
   B. How is "internal control over financial reporting" defined in this report?
   C. What level of assurance is provided that fraud will be detected?

TIF 7-3   Communication

Wholesome and Happy Foods is a farm-to-family grocery store located in the Pacific Northwest. The company recently installed four self-checkout lanes that allow customers to scan their own groceries and pay for their purchases using an automated checkout kiosk. The kiosks are monitored by a single attendant. In recent weeks, management has become concerned that some customers are not scanning all of the items that they bring through the self-checkout lanes.

> Write a brief memo to your instructor suggesting features and capabilities for the kiosks that would serve as control procedures, ensuring that all items brought through the self-checkout lanes are properly scanned and purchased.

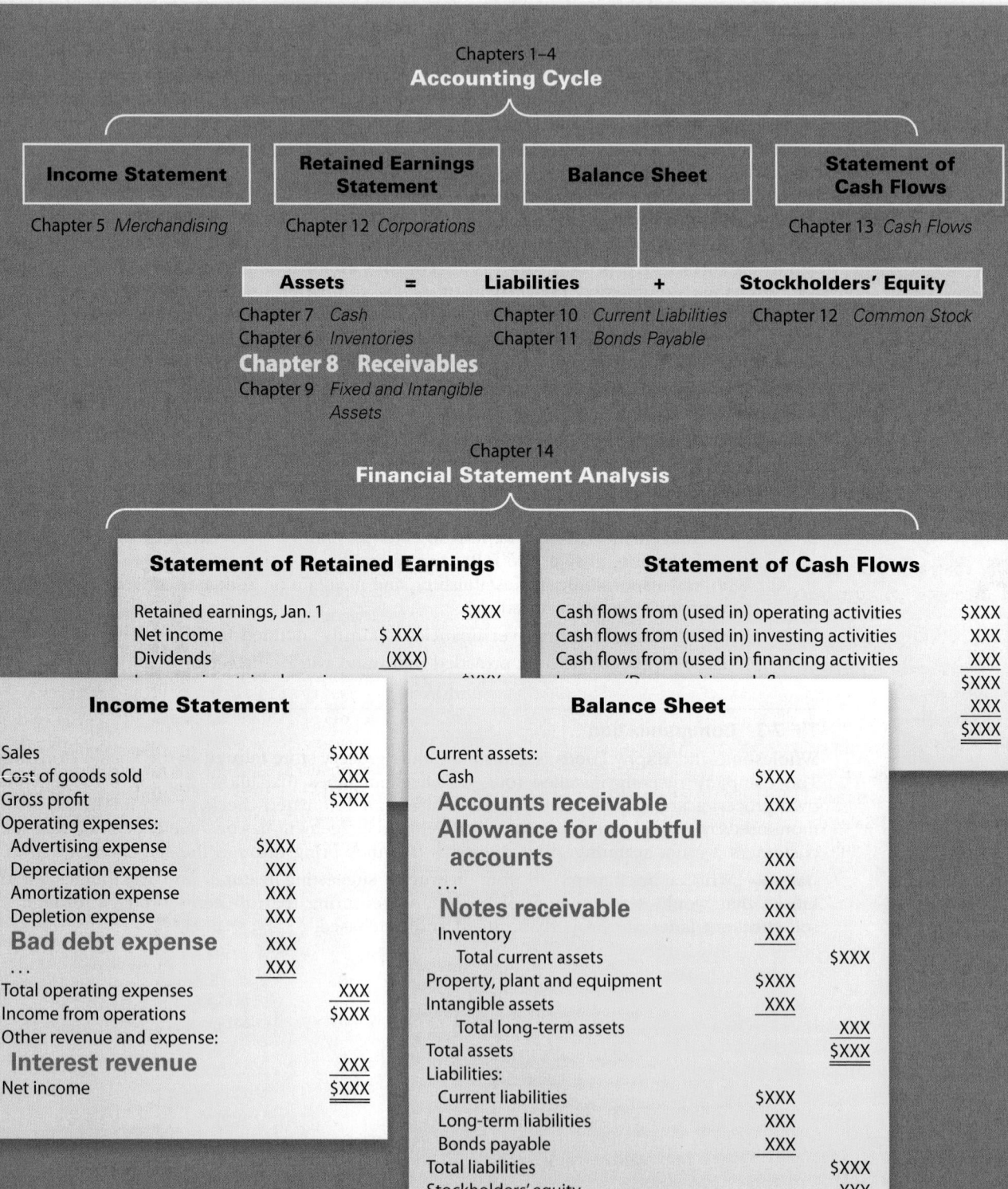

Keurig Green Mountain, Inc.*

A company generates revenues by providing goods or services to customers. For example, **Keurig Green Mountain, Inc.**, sells brewing systems and related beverage packets to supermarkets, department stores, convenience stores, and club stores. Keurig also sells directly to consumers through its Web site at www.keurig.com.

If you were to purchase a brewing system at Keurig.com, you would use a credit card to complete the purchase. In this case, Keurig would record the transaction as a cash sale. However, Keurig allows its business customers to purchase its products "on account." Sales on account create accounts receivable with credit terms requiring payment within the credit period.

Unlike cash sales, not all credit sales will generate cash. That is, some customers will not pay their account receivable and the company will have to record a bad debt expense. Companies like Keurig try to reduce uncollectible accounts by reviewing customer credit rating and payment history prior to a sale. Even with such procedures, however, companies will experience bad debts.

This chapter describes common classifications of receivables, including notes receivable. In addition, methods of accounting for and estimating uncollectible accounts are described and illustrated. Finally, the reporting of receivables, the allowance for uncollectible accounts, and bad debt expense in the financial statements is described and illustrated.

*Keurig Green Mountain was sold to private equity firm JAB Holding Co. in December 2015.

What's Covered

Learning Objectives

Obj. 1 Describe the common classes of receivables.

Obj. 2 Describe the accounting for uncollectible receivables.

Obj. 3 Describe the direct write-off method of accounting for uncollectible receivables.

Obj. 4 Describe the allowance method of accounting for uncollectible receivables.

Obj. 5 Compare the direct write-off and allowance methods of accounting for uncollectible accounts.

Obj. 6 Describe the accounting for notes receivable.

Obj. 7 Describe the reporting of receivables on the balance sheet.

Analysis for Decision Making

Describe and illustrate the use of accounts receivable turnover and number of days' sales in receivables to evaluate a company's efficiency in collecting its receivables.

Objective 1
Describe the common classes of receivables.

Classification of Receivables

The receivables that result from sales on account are normally accounts receivable or notes receivable. The term **receivables** includes all money claims against other entities, including people, companies, and other organizations. Receivables are usually a significant portion of the total current assets.

Accounts Receivable

The most common transaction creating a receivable is selling merchandise or services on account (on credit). The receivable is recorded as a debit to Accounts Receivable. Such **accounts receivable** are normally collected within a short period, such as 30 or 60 days. They are classified on the balance sheet as a current asset.

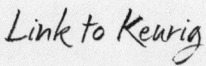 *Link to Keurig*   In a recent annual report, **Keurig** reported an account receivable from **Costco** of over $100 million.

Notes Receivable

Notes receivable are amounts that customers owe for which a formal, written instrument of credit has been issued. If notes receivable are expected to be collected within a year, they are classified on the balance sheet as a current asset.

Notes are often used for credit periods of more than 60 days. For example, an automobile dealer may require a down payment at the time of sale and accept a note or a series of notes for the remainder. Such notes usually provide for monthly payments.

Notes may also be used to settle a customer's account receivable. Notes and accounts receivable that result from sales transactions are sometimes called *trade receivables*. In this chapter, all notes and accounts receivable are from sales transactions.

Other Receivables

Other receivables include interest receivable, taxes receivable, and receivables from officers or employees. Other receivables are normally reported separately on the balance sheet. If they are expected to be collected within one year, they are classified as current assets. If collection is expected beyond one year, they are classified as noncurrent assets and reported under the caption *Investments*.

Uncollectible Receivables

Objective 2
Describe the accounting for uncollectible receivables.

In prior chapters, the accounting for sales of merchandise or services on account (on credit) was described and illustrated. A major issue that has not yet been discussed is that some customers will not pay their accounts. That is, some accounts receivable will be uncollectible.

Companies may shift the risk of uncollectible receivables to other companies. For example, some retailers do not accept sales on account but will only accept cash or credit cards. Such policies shift the risk to the credit card companies.

Companies may also sell their receivables. This is often the case when a company issues its own credit card. For example, **Macy's** and **JCPenney** issue their own credit cards. Selling receivables is called *factoring* the receivables. The buyer of the receivables is called a *factor*. An advantage of factoring is that the company selling its receivables immediately receives cash for operating and other needs. Also, depending on the factoring agreement, some of the risk of uncollectible accounts is shifted to the factor.

Regardless of how careful a company is in granting credit, some credit sales will be uncollectible. The operating expense recorded from uncollectible receivables is called **bad debt expense**, *uncollectible accounts expense*, or *doubtful accounts expense*.

There is no general rule for when an account becomes uncollectible. Some indications that an account may be uncollectible include the following:

- The receivable is past due.
- The customer does not respond to the company's attempts to collect.
- The customer files for bankruptcy.
- The customer closes its business.
- The company cannot locate the customer.

If a customer doesn't pay, a company may turn the account over to a collection agency. After the collection agency attempts to collect payment, any remaining balance in the account is considered worthless.

The two methods of accounting for uncollectible receivables are as follows:

- The **direct write-off method** records bad debt expense only when an account is determined to be worthless.
- The **allowance method** records bad debt expense by estimating uncollectible accounts at the end of the accounting period.

Keurig uses the allowance method and estimates uncollectible accounts based upon historical experience and specific customer risk, such as a customer who is experiencing financial difficulties.

Link to Keurig

Why It Matters

Warning Signs

A business must manage the risk of extending credit. The following early warning signs can be used to signal the need to moderate future sales and accelerate collection efforts:

- You're only receiving partial payments.
- The customer's ordering pattern has declined dramatically, or the customer has stopped buying from you.
- The customer requests frequent changes in the payment schedule.
- You are repeatedly told that late payments are in the mail.
- The customer refuses to make payment, claiming dissatisfaction with the product.
- You can't reach your customer, or the customer refuses to acknowledge you.

Source: BMO Harris Bank Web site, Small Business Learning Center, Managing Your Trade Credit, 2015, https://www.bmoharris.com/us/small-business/learning-center/101/trade-credit

The direct write-off method is often used by small companies and companies with few receivables.[1] Generally accepted accounting principles (GAAP), however, require companies with a large amount of receivables to use the allowance method. As a result, most well-known companies such as **General Electric**, **Pepsi**, **Intel**, and **FedEx** use the allowance method.

Direct Write-Off Method for Uncollectible Accounts

Objective 3

Describe the direct write-off method of accounting for uncollectible receivables.

Under the direct write-off method, Bad Debt Expense is not recorded until the customer's account is determined to be worthless. At that time, the customer's account receivable is written off.

To illustrate, assume that a $4,200 account receivable from D. L. Ross has been determined to be uncollectible. The entry to write off the account is as follows:

A = L + E
−   − Exp

| May 10 | Bad Debt Expense | 4,200 | |
| | Accounts Receivable—D. L. Ross | | 4,200 |

An account receivable that has been written off may be collected later. In such cases, the account is reinstated by an entry that reverses the write-off entry. The cash received in payment is then recorded as a receipt on account.

To illustrate, assume that the D. L. Ross account of $4,200 written off on May 10 is later collected on November 21. The reinstatement and receipt of cash is journalized as follows:

A = L + E
+   + Exp

A = L + E
+ −

Nov. 21	Accounts Receivable—D. L. Ross	4,200	
	Bad Debt Expense		4,200
21	Cash	4,200	
	Accounts Receivable—D. L. Ross		4,200

The direct write-off method is used by businesses that sell most of their goods or services for cash or through the acceptance of **MasterCard** or **VISA**, which are recorded as cash sales. In such cases, receivables are a small part of the current assets and any bad debt expense is small. Examples of such businesses are a restaurant, a convenience store, and a small retail store.

Allowance Method for Uncollectible Accounts

Objective 4

Describe the allowance method of accounting for uncollectible receivables.

The allowance method estimates the uncollectible accounts receivable at the end of the accounting period. Based on this estimate, Bad Debt Expense is recorded by an adjusting entry.

To illustrate, assume that **ExTone Company** began operations August 1. As of the end of its accounting period on December 31, ExTone has an accounts receivable balance of $200,000.

Why It Matters

Failure to Collect

When customers fail to pay their accounts, a business has the option of seeking payment through a variety of means. The easiest recourse is to simply inquire about the cause of non-payment and adjust terms to maximize the potential for collection. For large amounts, the cost and time of legal remedies can be appropriate. However, for smaller amounts, most businesses wish to minimize the time, effort, and cost of collecting amounts past due. Thus, after exhausting their internal efforts to collect, it is typical to use the services of a collection agency to collect overdue accounts. Such services must abide by a number of consumer protection laws in collecting overdue accounts. The final amount collected will often be less than the full amount due, of which the collection agency will often keep 25–45% as a contingency fee. Thus, the collection agency is often the last resort before a final write-off.

---

[1] The direct write-off method is also required for federal income tax purposes.

This balance includes some past due accounts. Based on industry averages, ExTone estimates that $30,000 of the December 31 accounts receivable will be uncollectible. However, on December 31, ExTone doesn't know which customer accounts will be uncollectible. Thus, specific customer accounts cannot be decreased or credited. Instead, a contra asset account, **Allowance for Doubtful Accounts**, is credited for the estimated bad debts.

Using the $30,000 estimate, the following adjusting entry is made on December 31:

Dec. 31	Bad Debt Expense	30,000	
	Allowance for Doubtful Accounts		30,000
	Uncollectible accounts estimate.		

A = L + E
−   − Exp

The preceding adjusting entry affects the income statement and balance sheet. On the income statement, the $30,000 of Bad Debt Expense will be matched against the related revenues of the period. On the balance sheet, the value of the receivables is reduced to the amount that is expected to be collected or realized. This amount, $170,000 ($200,000 − $30,000), is called the **net realizable value** of the receivables.

After the preceding adjusting entry is recorded, Accounts Receivable still has a debit balance of $200,000. This balance is the total amount owed by customers on account on December 31 as supported by the accounts receivable subsidiary ledger. The accounts receivable contra account, Allowance for Doubtful Accounts, has a credit balance of $30,000.

Note:
The adjusting entry reduces receivables to their net realizable value and matches the uncollectible expense with revenues.

Write-Offs to the Allowance Account

When a customer's account is identified as uncollectible, it is written off against the allowance account. This requires the company to remove the specific accounts receivable and an equal amount from the allowance account.

To illustrate, on January 21 of the following year, John Parker's account of $6,000 with **ExTone Company** is written off as follows:

Jan. 21	Allowance for Doubtful Accounts	6,000	
	Accounts Receivable—John Parker		6,000

A = L + E
+ −

At the end of a period, Allowance for Doubtful Accounts will normally have a balance. This is because Allowance for Doubtful Accounts is based on an estimate. As a result, the total write-offs to the allowance account during the period will rarely equal the balance of the account at the beginning of the period. The allowance account will have a credit balance at the end of the period if the write-offs during the period are less than the beginning balance. It will have a debit balance if the write-offs exceed the beginning balance.

Ethics: Don't Do It!

Collecting Past Due Accounts

Companies should make reasonable attempts (steps) to collect past due accounts, as we discussed in the previous Why It Matters. Many companies first send a collection reminder as a first step. As a second step, a company may send a collection letter which offers options such as a willingness to negotiate a schedule for future payments. The next step is normally to turn the past due amount over to a collection agency or to file action in court. However, in no case should a company employee harass or misrepresent themselves as an attorney, collection agent, or agent of the court to the customer.

Exhibit 1
The Allowance
Method

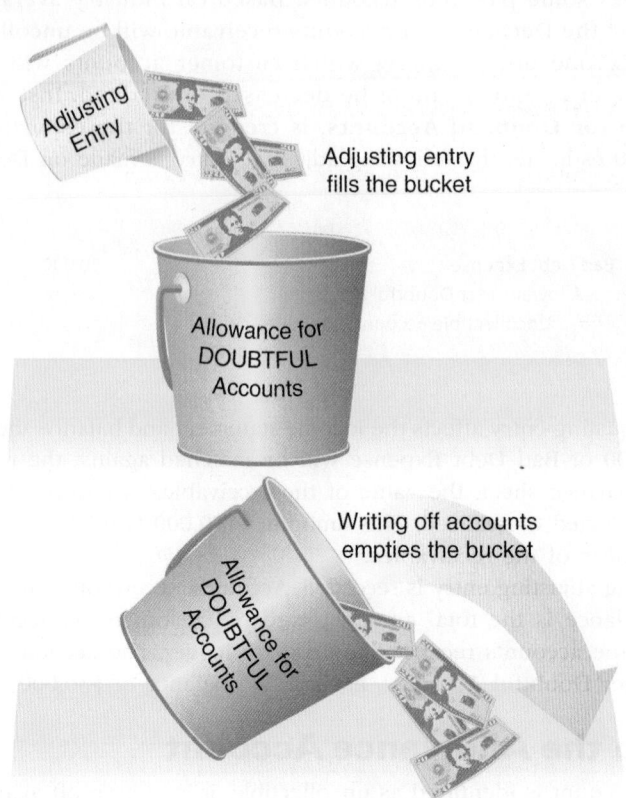

Exhibit 1 illustrates the allowance method where the adjusting entry increases the Allowance for Doubtful Accounts (fills the bucket) while writing off accounts decreases the Allowance for Doubtful Accounts (empties the bucket).

To illustrate, assume that during the second year of operations, **ExTone Company** writes off $26,750 of uncollectible accounts, including the $6,000 account of John Parker recorded on January 21. Allowance for Doubtful Accounts will have a credit balance of $3,250 ($30,000 − $26,750), computed as follows:

Allowance for Doubtful Accounts

			Jan. 1	Balance	30,000
Jan. 21	6,000				
Total accounts	Feb. 2	3,900			
written off $26,750	⋮	⋮			
			Dec. 31	Unadjusted balance	3,250

If ExTone had written off $32,100 in accounts receivable during the second year, Allowance for Doubtful Accounts would have a debit balance of $2,100, computed as follows:

Allowance for Doubtful Accounts

			Jan. 1	Balance	30,000
	Jan. 21	6,000			
Total accounts	Feb. 2	3,900			
written off $32,100	⋮	⋮			
Dec. 31	Unadjusted balance	2,100			

The allowance account balances (credit balance of $3,250 and debit balance of $2,100) in the preceding illustrations are *before* the end-of-period adjusting entry. After the end-of-period adjusting entry is recorded, Allowance for Doubtful Accounts should always have a credit balance.

An account receivable that has been written off against the allowance account may be collected later. Like the direct write-off method, the account is reinstated by an entry that reverses the write-off entry. The cash received in payment is then recorded as a receipt on account.

Why It Matters

Allowance Percentages Across Companies

The percent of the allowance for doubtful accounts to total accounts receivable will vary across companies and industries. For example, the following percentages were computed from recent annual reports:

Company	Industry	Percent of Allowance for Doubtful Accounts to Total Accounts Receivable
Coca-Cola	Beverages	7.1%
DuPont	Chemicals	3.8%
HCA	Health services	46.8%
Nike	Apparel	2.2%
Union Pacific	Transportation services	0.3%
Wynn Resorts	Casino gaming	23.9%

Coca-Cola had an unusual increase in its estimated bad debts stemming from collection issues regarding its Venezuelan bottling partner. HCA's higher percentage is due in part because of charity care and collection challenges with deductibles and copays. Wynn Resorts' high percentage is typical for casinos, representing the challenges in collecting gambling debts.

To illustrate, assume that Nancy Smith's account of $5,000, which was written off on April 2, is collected later on June 10. **ExTone Company** journalizes the reinstatement and the collection as follows:

June	10	Accounts Receivable—Nancy Smith	5,000	
		Allowance for Doubtful Accounts		5,000
	10	Cash	5,000	
		Accounts Receivable—Nancy Smith		5,000

A = L + E
+ −

A = L + E
+ −

Estimating Uncollectibles

The allowance method requires an estimate of uncollectible accounts at the end of the period. This estimate is normally based on past experience, industry averages, and forecasts of the future.

The two methods used to estimate uncollectible accounts are as follows:

- Percent of sales method.
- Analysis of receivables method.

Percent of Sales Method Since accounts receivable are created by credit sales, uncollectible accounts can be estimated as a percent of credit sales. If the portion of credit sales to sales is relatively constant, the percent may be applied to total sales.

To illustrate, assume the following data for **ExTone Company** on December 31, before any adjustments:

Balance of Accounts Receivable	$ 240,000
Balance of Allowance for Doubtful Accounts	3,250 (Cr.)
Total credit sales	3,000,000
Bad debt as a percent of credit sales	¾%

Bad Debt Expense of $22,500 is estimated as follows:

Bad Debt Expense = Credit Sales × Bad Debt as a Percent of Credit Sales

Bad Debt Expense = $3,000,000 × ¾% = $22,500

The adjusting entry for uncollectible accounts on December 31 is as follows:

A = L + E
− − Exp

Dec.	31	Bad Debt Expense	22,500	
		Allowance for Doubtful Accounts		22,500
		Uncollectible accounts estimate		
		($3,000,000 × ¾% = $22,500).		

After the adjusting entry is posted to the ledger, Bad Debt Expense will have an adjusted balance of $22,500. Allowance for Doubtful Accounts will have an adjusted balance of $25,750 ($3,250 + $22,500). Both T accounts follow:

Bad Debt Expense

Dec. 31	Adjusting entry	22,500 ◄
Dec. 31	Adjusted balance	22,500

Allowance for Doubtful Accounts

			Jan. 1	Balance	30,000
Total accounts written off $26,750	Jan. 21 6,000				
	Feb. 2 3,900				
	⋮	⋮	Dec. 31	Unadjusted balance	3,250
			Dec. 31	Adjusting entry	22,500 ◄
			Dec. 31	Adjusted balance	25,750

Under the percent of sales method, the amount of the adjusting entry is the amount estimated for Bad Debt Expense. This estimate is credited to whatever the unadjusted balance is for Allowance for Doubtful Accounts.

To illustrate, assume that in the preceding example the unadjusted balance of Allowance for Doubtful Accounts on December 31 had been a $2,100 debit balance instead of a $3,250 credit balance. The adjustment would still have been $22,500. However, the December 31 ending adjusted balance of Allowance for Doubtful Accounts would have been $20,400 ($22,500 − $2,100).

Note:

The estimate based on sales is added to any balance in Allowance for Doubtful Accounts.

Check Up Corner 8-1   Percent of Sales Method

At the end of the current year, ARS Industries has the following account balances before making an adjusting entry for uncollectible accounts:

Accounts Receivable	$800,000 debit
Allowance for Doubtful Accounts	7,500 credit

The company recorded $3,500,000 of credit sales during the year. The company uses the percent of sales method and estimates that ½ of 1% of credit sales for the year will be uncollectible.

A. Determine the bad debt expense for the period, and journalize the adjusting entry.

B. Determine the adjusted balances of Allowance for Doubtful Accounts and Accounts Receivable.

C. Determine the net realizable value of accounts receivable at the end of the period.

Solution:

A. Bad Debt Expense = Credit Sales × Bad Debt as a Percent of Credit Sales
$17,500 = $3,500,000 × 0.5%

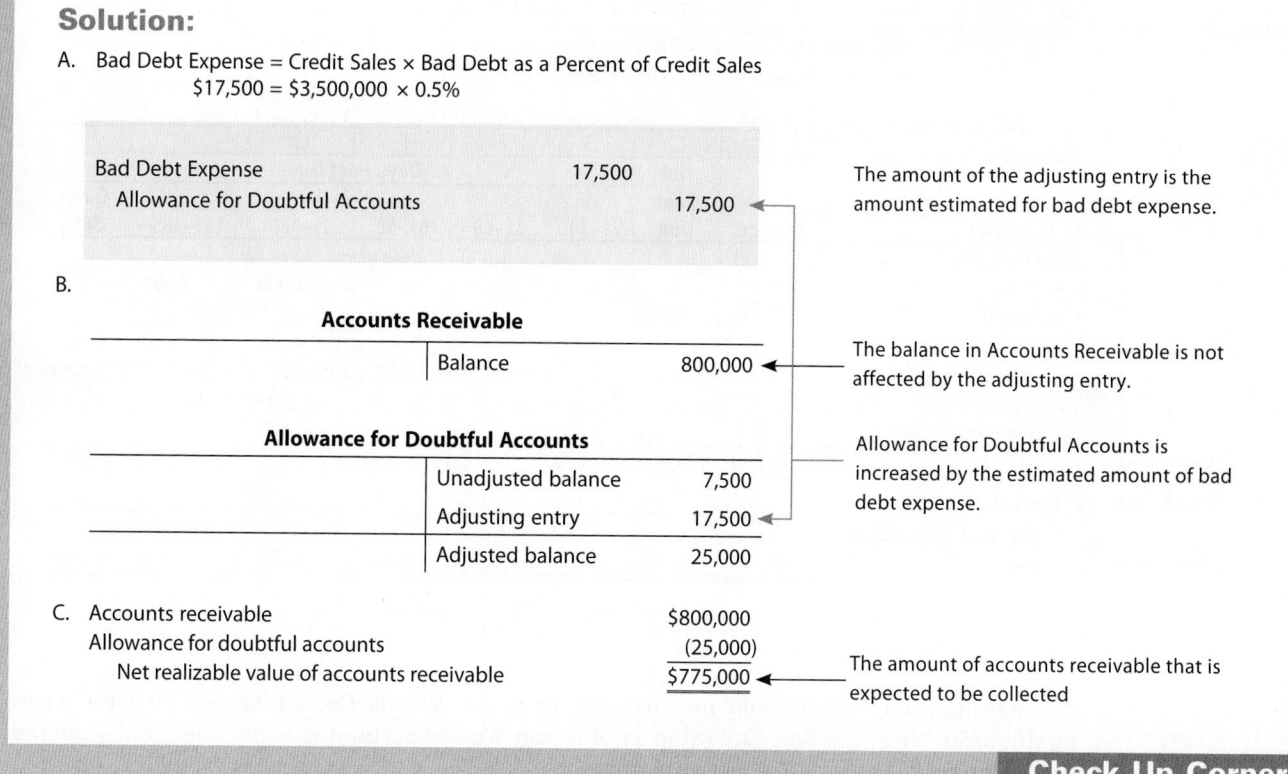

| Bad Debt Expense | 17,500 | |
| Allowance for Doubtful Accounts | | 17,500 |

The amount of the adjusting entry is the amount estimated for bad debt expense.

B.

Accounts Receivable

| Balance | 800,000 |

The balance in Accounts Receivable is not affected by the adjusting entry.

Allowance for Doubtful Accounts

Unadjusted balance	7,500
Adjusting entry	17,500
Adjusted balance	25,000

Allowance for Doubtful Accounts is increased by the estimated amount of bad debt expense.

C.
Accounts receivable	$800,000
Allowance for doubtful accounts	(25,000)
Net realizable value of accounts receivable	$775,000

The amount of accounts receivable that is expected to be collected

Check Up Corner

Analysis of Receivables Method The analysis of receivables method is based on the assumption that the longer an account receivable is outstanding, the less likely that it will be collected. The analysis of receivables method is applied as follows:

- Step 1. The due date of each account receivable is determined.
- Step 2. The number of days each account is past due is determined. This is the number of days between the due date of the account and the date of the analysis.
- Step 3. Each account is placed in an aged class according to its days past due. Typical aged classes include the following:

Days Past Due
Not past due
1–30
31–60
61–90
91–180
181–365
Over 365

- Step 4. The totals for each aged class are determined.
- Step 5. The total for each aged class is multiplied by an estimated percentage of uncollectible accounts for that class.
- Step 6. The estimated total of uncollectible accounts is determined as the sum of the uncollectible accounts for each aged class.

The preceding steps are summarized in an aging schedule, and this overall process is called **aging the receivables**.

To illustrate, assume that **ExTone Company** uses the analysis of receivables method instead of the percent of sales method. ExTone prepared an aging schedule for its accounts receivable of $240,000 as of December 31 as shown in Exhibit 2.

Exhibit 2   Aging of Receivables Schedule, December 31

DYNAMIC EXHIBIT

Steps 1–3

	A	B	C	D	E	F	G	H	I
1			Not			Days Past Due			
2			Past						Over
3	Customer	Balance	Due	1–30	31–60	61–90	91–180	181–365	365
4	Ashby & Co.	1,500			1,500				
5	B. T. Barr	6,100					3,500	2,600	
6	Brock Co.	4,700	4,700						
7									
21									
22	Saxon Woods Co.	600					600		
23	Total	240,000	125,000	64,000	13,100	8,900	5,000	10,000	14,000
24	Percent uncollectible		2%	5%	10%	20%	30%	50%	80%
25	Estimate of uncollectible accounts	26,490	2,500	3,200	1,310	1,780	1,500	5,000	11,200

Step 4 → 23
Step 5 → 24
Step 6 → 25

Assume that ExTone sold merchandise to Saxon Woods Co. on August 29 with terms 2/10, n/30. Thus, the due date (Step 1) of Saxon Woods' account is September 28, computed as follows:

Credit terms, net	30 days
Less: Aug. 30 and Aug. 31	(2) days
Days in September	28 days

As of December 31, Saxon Woods' account is 94 days past due (Step 2), computed as follows:

Number of days past due in September	2 days (30 – 28)
Number of days past due in October	31 days
Number of days past due in November	30 days
Number of days past due in December	31 days
Total number of days past due	94 days

Exhibit 2 shows that the $600 account receivable for Saxon Woods Co. was placed in the 91–180 days past due class (Step 3).

The total for each of the aged classes is determined (Step 4). Exhibit 2 shows that $125,000 of the accounts receivable are not past due, while $64,000 are 1–30 days past due. ExTone applies a different estimated percentage of uncollectible accounts to the totals of each of the aged classes (Step 5). As shown in Exhibit 2, the percent is 2% for accounts not past due, while the percent is 80% for accounts over 365 days past due.

The sum of the estimated uncollectible accounts for each aged class (Step 6) is the estimated uncollectible accounts on December 31. This is the desired adjusted balance for Allowance for Doubtful Accounts. For ExTone, this amount is $26,490, as shown in Exhibit 2.

Comparing the estimate of $26,490 with the unadjusted balance of the allowance account determines the amount of the adjustment for Bad Debt Expense. For ExTone, the unadjusted balance of the allowance account is a credit balance of $3,250. The amount to be added to this balance is therefore $23,240 ($26,490 – $3,250). The adjusting entry is as follows:

Note:

The estimate based on receivables is compared to the balance in the allowance account to determine the amount of the adjusting entry.

A = L + E
–   – Exp

Dec. 31	Bad Debt Expense	23,240	
	Allowance for Doubtful Accounts		23,240
	Uncollectible accounts estimate		
	($26,490 – $3,250).		

After the preceding adjusting entry is posted to the ledger, Bad Debt Expense will have an adjusted balance of $23,240. Allowance for Doubtful Accounts will have an adjusted balance of $26,490, and the net realizable value of the receivables is $213,510 ($240,000 − $26,490). Both T accounts follow:

Bad Debt Expense

Dec. 31	Adjusting entry	23,240
Dec. 31	Adjusted balance	23,240

Allowance for Doubtful Accounts

		Dec. 31	Unadjusted balance	3,250
		Dec. 31	Adjusting entry	23,240
		Dec. 31	Adjusted balance	26,490

Under the analysis of receivables method, the amount of the adjusting entry is the amount that will yield an adjusted balance for Allowance for Doubtful Accounts equal to that estimated by the aging schedule.

To illustrate, if the unadjusted balance of the allowance account had been a debit balance of $2,100, the amount of the adjustment would have been $28,590 ($26,490 + $2,100). In this case, Bad Debt Expense would have an adjusted balance of $28,590. However, the adjusted balance of Allowance for Doubtful Accounts would still have been $26,490. After the adjusting entry is posted, both T accounts follow:

Bad Debt Expense

Dec. 31	Adjusting entry	28,590
Dec. 31	Adjusted balance	28,590

Allowance for Doubtful Accounts

Dec. 31	Unadjusted balance	2,100	
		Dec. 31	Adjusting entry	28,590
		Dec. 31	Adjusted balance	26,490

Check Up Corner 8-2 Analysis of Receivables Method

At the end of the current year, ARS Industries has the following account balances before making an adjusting entry for uncollectible accounts:

Accounts Receivable	$800,000 debit
Allowance for Doubtful Accounts	7,500 credit

The company recorded $3,500,000 of credit sales during the year. An aging of the company's accounts receivable on December 31 and a historical analysis of the percentage of uncollectible accounts in each age class follow:

Age Class	Balance	Percent Uncollectible
Not past due	$658,000	1%
1–30 days	69,000	6
31–90 days	47,000	14
Over 90 days	26,000	20
	$800,000	

The company estimates the allowance for doubtful accounts based on the analysis of receivables method.

A. Determine the bad debt expense for the period, and journalize the adjusting entry.

B. Determine the adjusted balances of Allowance for Doubtful Accounts and Accounts Receivable.

C. Determine the net realizable value of accounts receivable at the end of the period.

Solution:

A.

Bad Debt Expense ($22,500 – $7,500)	15,000	
Allowance for Doubtful Accounts		15,000

Age Class	Balance	Percent Uncollectible	Estimate of Uncollectible Accounts
Not past due	$658,000	1%	$ 6,580
1–30 days	69,000	6	4,140
31–90 days	47,000	14	6,580
Over 90 days	26,000	20	5,200
	$800,000		$22,500

The adjusting entry to record Bad Debt Expense ($15,000) is the amount necessary to adjust the beginning balance ($7,500) to the desired ending balance ($22,500) in Allowance for Doubtful Accounts (calculated in the aging of accounts).

B.

Allowance for Doubtful Accounts

	Unadjusted balance	7,500
	Adjusting entry	15,000
	Adjusted balance	22,500

The ending balance in Allowance for Doubtful Accounts is the amount estimated in the aging of accounts.

Accounts Receivable

	Balance	800,000

The balance in Accounts Receivable is not affected by the adjusting entry.

C.
Accounts receivable	$800,000
Allowance for doubtful accounts	(22,500)
Net realizable value of accounts receivable	$777,500

The amount of accounts receivable that is expected to be collected

Check Up Corner

Comparing Estimation Methods Both the percent of sales and analysis of receivables methods estimate uncollectible accounts. However, each method has a slightly different focus and financial statement emphasis.

Under the percent of sales method, Bad Debt Expense is the focus of the estimation process. The percent of sales method places more emphasis on matching revenues and expenses and, thus, emphasizes the income statement. That is, the amount of the adjusting entry is based on the estimate of Bad Debt Expense for the period. Allowance for Doubtful Accounts is then credited for this amount.

Under the analysis of receivables method, Allowance for Doubtful Accounts is the focus of the estimation process. The analysis of receivables method places more emphasis on the net realizable value of the receivables and, thus, emphasizes the balance sheet. That is, the amount of the adjusting entry is the amount that will yield an adjusted balance for Allowance for Doubtful Accounts equal to that estimated by the aging schedule. Bad Debt Expense is then debited for this amount.

Exhibit 3 summarizes these differences between the percent of sales and the analysis of receivables methods. Exhibit 3 also shows the results of the ExTone Company illustration for the percent of sales and analysis of receivables methods. The amounts shown in Exhibit 3 assume

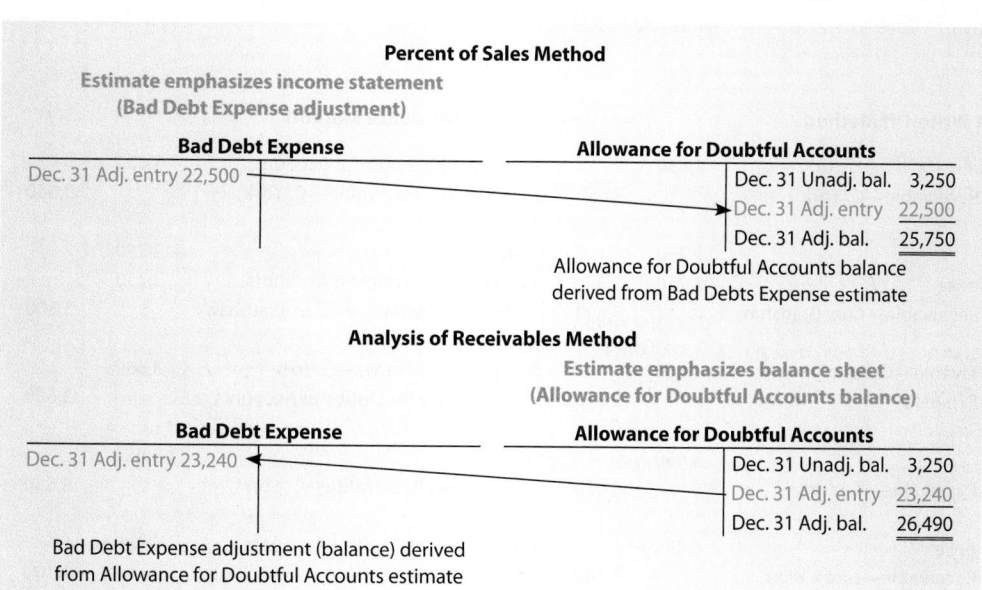

Exhibit 3
Difference
Between
Estimation
Methods

an unadjusted credit balance of $3,250 for Allowance for Doubtful Accounts. While the methods normally yield different amounts for any one period, over several periods the amounts should be similar.

Comparing Direct Write-Off and Allowance Methods

Objective 5
Compare the direct write-off and allowance methods of accounting for uncollectible accounts.

Journal entries for the direct write-off and allowance methods are illustrated and compared in this section. As a basis for illustration, the following transactions, taken from the records of Hobbs Company for the year ending December 31, are used:

Mar. 1. Wrote off account of C. York, $3,650.

Apr. 12. Received $2,250 as partial payment on the $5,500 account of Cary Bradshaw. Wrote off the remaining balance as uncollectible.

June 22. Received the $3,650 from C. York, which had been written off on March 1. Reinstated the account and recorded the cash receipt.

Sept. 7. Wrote off the following accounts as uncollectible (record as one journal entry):

Jason Bigg	$1,100
Steve Bradey	2,220
Samantha Neeley	775
Stanford Noonan	1,360
Aiden Wyman	990

Dec. 31. Hobbs Company uses the percent of credit sales method of estimating uncollectible expenses. Based on past history and industry averages, 1.25% of credit sales are expected to be uncollectible. Hobbs recorded $3,400,000 of credit sales during the year.

Exhibit 4 illustrates the journal entries for Hobbs using the direct write-off and allowance methods. Using the direct write-off method, there is no adjusting entry on December 31 for uncollectible accounts. In contrast, the allowance method records an adjusting entry for estimated uncollectible accounts of $42,500.

Exhibit 4 Comparing Direct Write-Off and Allowance Methods

		Direct Write-Off Method			Allowance Method		
Mar.	1	Bad Debt Expense	3,650		Allowance for Doubtful Accounts	3,650	
		Accounts Receivable—C. York		3,650	Accounts Receivable—C. York		3,650
Apr.	12	Cash	2,250		Cash	2,250	
		Bad Debt Expense	3,250		Allowance for Doubtful Accounts	3,250	
		Accounts Receivable—Cary Bradshaw		5,500	Accounts Receivable—Cary Bradshaw		5,500
June	22	Accounts Receivable—C. York	3,650		Accounts Receivable—C. York	3,650	
		Bad Debt Expense		3,650	Allowance for Doubtful Accounts		3,650
	22	Cash	3,650		Cash	3,650	
		Accounts Receivable—C. York		3,650	Accounts Receivable—C. York		3,650
Sept.	7	Bad Debt Expense	6,445		Allowance for Doubtful Accounts	6,445	
		Accounts Receivable—Jason Bigg		1,100	Accounts Receivable—Jason Bigg		1,100
		Accounts Receivable—Steve Bradey		2,220	Accounts Receivable—Steve Bradey		2,220
		Accounts Receivable—Samantha Neeley		775	Accounts Receivable—Samantha Neeley		775
		Accounts Receivable—Stanford Noonan		1,360	Accounts Receivable—Stanford Noonan		1,360
		Accounts Receivable—Aiden Wyman		990	Accounts Receivable—Aiden Wyman		990
Dec.	31	No Entry			Bad Debt Expense	42,500	
					Allowance for Doubtful Accounts		42,500
					Uncollectible accounts estimate ($3,400,000 × 0.0125 = $42,500).		

The primary differences between the direct write-off and allowance methods are summarized in Exhibit 5.

Exhibit 5
Direct Write-Off and Allowance Methods

	Direct Write-Off Method	Allowance Method
Bad debt expense is recorded	When the specific customer accounts are determined to be uncollectible.	Using estimate based on (1) a percent of sales or (2) an analysis of receivables.
Allowance account	No allowance account is used.	The allowance account is used.
Primary users	Small companies and companies with few receivables.	Large companies and those with a large amount of receivables.

Objective 6
Describe the accounting for notes receivable.

Notes Receivable

A note has some advantages over an account receivable. By signing a note, the debtor recognizes the debt and agrees to pay it according to its terms. Thus, a note is a stronger legal claim.

Characteristics of Notes Receivable

A promissory note is a written promise to pay the face amount, usually with interest, on demand or at a date in the future.[2] Characteristics of a promissory note are as follows:

1. The *maker* is the party making the promise to pay.
2. The *payee* is the party to whom the note is payable.

[2] You may see references to non-interest-bearing notes. Such notes are not widely used and carry an assumed or implicit interest rate.

3. The *face amount* is the amount for which the note is written on its face.

4. The *issuance date* is the date a note is issued.

5. The *due date* or *maturity date* is the date the note is to be paid.

6. The *term* of a note is the amount of time between the issuance and due dates.

7. The *interest rate* is that rate of interest that must be paid on the face amount for the term of the note.

Exhibit 6 illustrates a promissory note.

Exhibit 6 Promissory Note

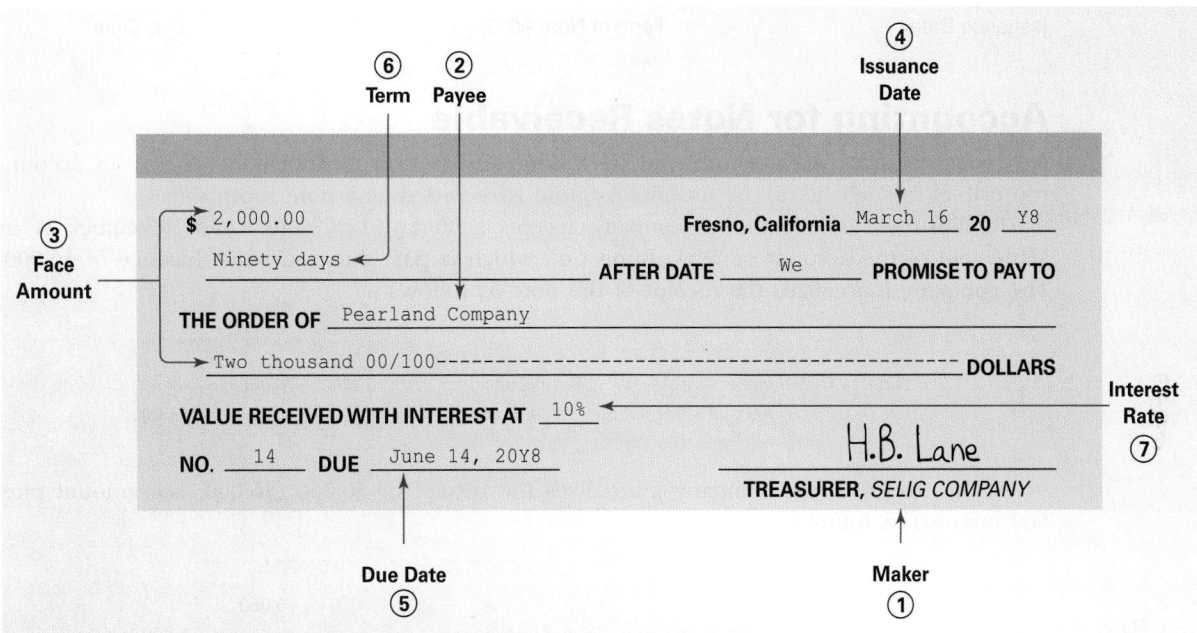

The maker of the note is Selig Company, and the payee is Pearland Company. The face value of the note is $2,000, the interest rate is 10%, and the issuance date is March 16, 20Y8. The term of the note is 90 days, which results in a due date of June 14, 20Y8, computed as follows and shown in Exhibit 7:

Days in March	31 days
Minus issuance date of note	16
Days remaining in March	15 days
Add days in April	30
Add days in May	31
Add days in June (due date of June 14)	14
Term of note	90 days

The interest on a note is computed as follows:

$$\text{Interest} = \text{Face Amount} \times \text{Interest Rate} \times (\text{Term} \div 360 \text{ days})$$

The interest rate is stated on an annual (yearly) basis, while the term is expressed as days. Thus, the interest on the note in Exhibit 6 is computed as follows:

$$\text{Interest} = \$2,000 \times 10\% \times (90 \div 360) = \$50$$

To simplify, 360 days per year will be used. In practice, companies such as banks and mortgage companies use the exact number of days in a year, 365.

The **maturity value** is the amount that must be paid at the due date of the note, which is the sum of the face amount and the interest. The maturity value of the note in Exhibit 6 is $2,050 ($2,000 + $50).

Exhibit 7
Determining Due
Date of Promissory
Note

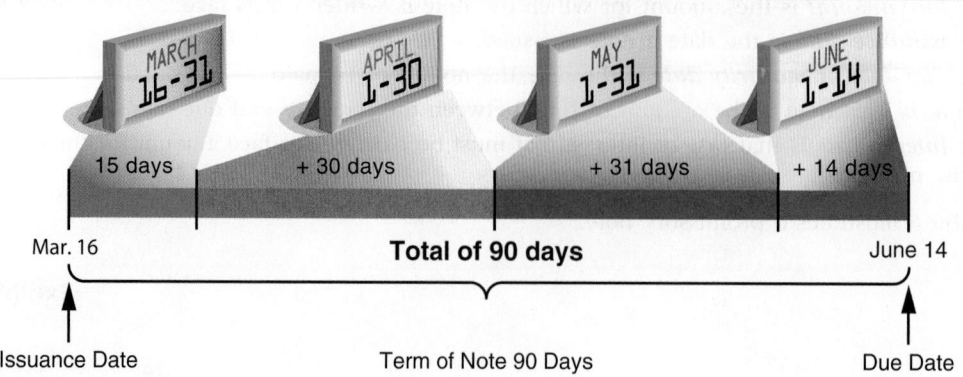

| 15 days | + 30 days | + 31 days | + 14 days |

Mar. 16   **Total of 90 days**   June 14

↑   ↑
Issuance Date   Term of Note 90 Days   Due Date

Accounting for Notes Receivable

A promissory note may be received by a company from a customer to replace an account receivable. In such cases, the promissory note is recorded as a note receivable.[3]

To illustrate, assume that a company accepts a 30-day, 12% note dated November 21 in settlement of the account of W. A. Bunn Co., which is past due and has a balance of $6,000. The company journalizes the receipt of the note as follows:

A = L + E
+ –

Nov.	21	Notes Receivable—W. A. Bunn Co.	6,000	
		Accounts Receivable—W. A. Bunn Co.		6,000

At the due date, the company journalizes the receipt of $6,060 ($6,000 face amount plus $60 interest) as follows:

A = L + E
+ –   + Rev

Dec.	21	Cash	6,060	
		Notes Receivable—W. A. Bunn Co.		6,000
		Interest Revenue		60
		[$6,060 = $6,000 + ($6,000 × 12% × 30 ÷ 360)].		

If the maker of a note fails to pay the note on the due date, the note is a **dishonored note receivable**. A company that holds a dishonored note transfers the face amount of the note plus any interest due back to an accounts receivable account. For example, assume that the $6,000, 30-day, 12% note received from W. A. Bunn Co. and recorded on November 21 is dishonored. The company holding the note transfers the note and interest back to the customer's account as follows:

A = L + E
+ –   + Rev

Dec.	21	Accounts Receivable—W. A. Bunn Co.	6,060	
		Notes Receivable—W. A. Bunn Co.		6,000
		Interest Revenue		60

The company has earned the interest of $60, even though the note is dishonored. If the account receivable is uncollectible, the company will write off $6,060 against Allowance for Doubtful Accounts.

A company receiving a note should record an adjusting entry for any accrued interest at the end of the period. For example, assume that Crawford Company issues a $4,000, 90-day, 12% note dated December 1, 20Y3, to settle its account receivable. If the accounting

---

[3] The accounting for notes payable is described and illustrated in Chapter 10.

period ends on December 31, the company receiving the note would journalize the following entries:

20Y3					
Dec.	1	Notes Receivable—Crawford Company	4,000		
		Accounts Receivable—Crawford Company		4,000	

A = L + E
+ −

	31	Interest Receivable	40		
		Interest Revenue		40	
		Accrued interest			
		($4,000 × 12% × 30 ÷ 360).			

A = L + E
+   + Rev

20Y4					
Mar.	1	Cash	4,120		
		Notes Receivable—Crawford Company		4,000	
		Interest Receivable		40	
		Interest Revenue		80	
		Total interest of $120			
		($4,000 × 12% × 90 ÷ 360).			

A = L + E
+ −   + Rev

The interest revenue account is closed at the end of each accounting period. The amount of interest revenue is normally reported in the Other revenue and expense section of the income statement.

Check Up Corner 8-3   Notes Receivable

Icebreaker Company receives a 120-day, 6% note for $40,000, dated May 14, in settlement of an account that is past due. The balance in the account is $40,000.

A. Determine the due date of the note.

B. Determine the maturity value of the note.

C. Prepare the journal entries to record the (1) receipt of the note and (2) collection at maturity.

Solution:

A. The due date of the note is September 11, determined as follows:

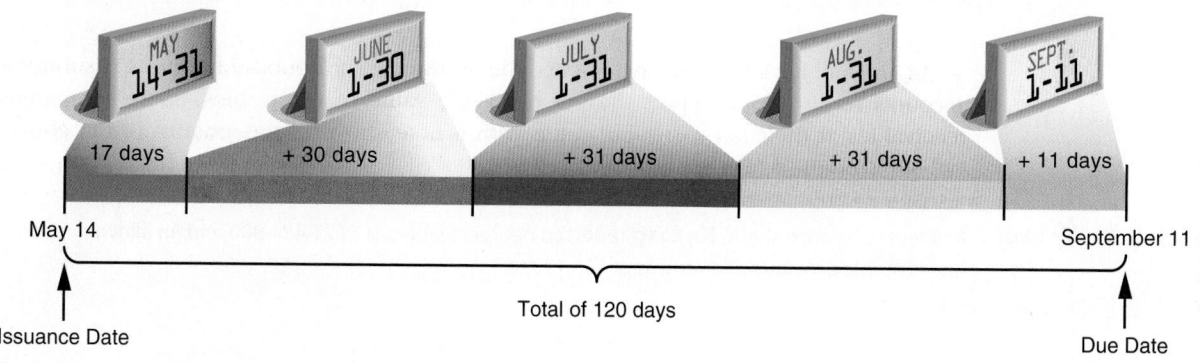

B. The maturity value of the note is the sum of the face amount and interest. The interest is computed as follows:

Interest = Face Amount × Interest Rate × (Term ÷ 360 days)

      = $40,000   × 6%   × 120 ÷ 360

      = $800

Face amount	$40,000
Interest	800
Maturity value of the note	$40,800

The maturity value is the amount that must be collected at the due date of the note.

C.   The journal entries to record the (1) receipt of the note and (2) collection at maturity are as follows:

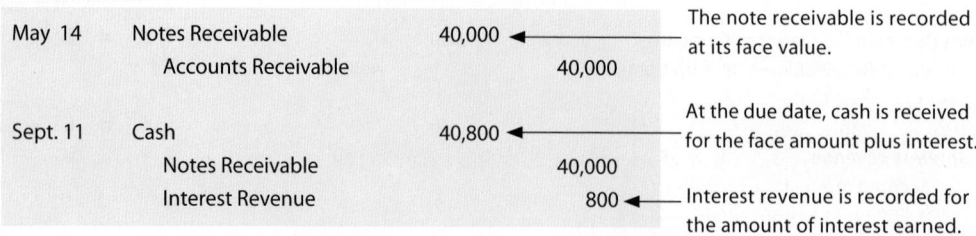

May 14	Notes Receivable	40,000		The note receivable is recorded at its face value.
	Accounts Receivable		40,000	
Sept. 11	Cash	40,800		At the due date, cash is received for the face amount plus interest.
	Notes Receivable		40,000	
	Interest Revenue		800	Interest revenue is recorded for the amount of interest earned.

Check Up Corner

Objective 7
Describe the reporting of receivables on the balance sheet.

Reporting Receivables on the Balance Sheet

All receivables that are expected to be realized in cash within a year are reported in the current assets section of the balance sheet. Current assets are normally reported in the order of their liquidity, beginning with cash and cash equivalents.

The balance sheet presentation for receivables for **Mornin' Joe** follows:

Mornin' Joe

Mornin' Joe
Balance Sheet
December 31, 20Y6

Assets

Current assets:		
Cash and cash equivalents....................................		$235,000
Accounts receivable	$305,000	
Allowance for doubtful accounts.............................	(12,300)	
Accounts receivable, net.		292,700

In Mornin' Joe's financial statements, the allowance for doubtful accounts is subtracted from accounts receivable to report the net realizable value of receivables. Some companies report receivables at their net realizable value with a note showing the amount of the allowance.

Link to Keurig   In a recent balance sheet, **Keurig** reported net receivables of $621,451,000 and an allowance for uncollectible accounts and returns of $66,120,000.

Other disclosures, such as unusual credit risks within the receivables, are reported in the financial statement notes. For example, if the majority of the receivables are due from one customer or are due from customers located in one area of the country or one industry, these facts are disclosed.[4]

Link to Keurig   **Keurig** uses **M. Block & Sons** to process its sales to department stores, supermarkets, and other retailers in the United States. As a result, Keurig reported a significant credit risk related to its account receivable from M Block.

[4] *FASB Accounting Standards Codification*, Section 210-10-50.

Analysis for Decision Making

Accounts Receivable Turnover and Number of Days' Sales in Receivables

Objective

Describe and illustrate the use of accounts receivable turnover and number of days' sales in receivables to evaluate a company's efficiency in collecting its receivables.

Two financial measures that are useful in evaluating efficiency in collecting receivables are the following:

- accounts receivable turnover
- number of days' sales in receivables

The **accounts receivable turnover** measures how frequently during the year the accounts receivable are being converted to cash. For example, with credit terms of n/30, the accounts receivable should turn over about 12 times per year.

The accounts receivable turnover is computed as follows:[5]

$$\text{Accounts Receivable Turnover} = \frac{\text{Sales}}{\text{Average Accounts Receivable}}$$

The average accounts receivable can be determined by adding the beginning and ending accounts receivable balances and dividing by two. For example, consider the following financial data (in millions) for **Keurig Green Mountain, Inc.**:

	Year 2	Year 1
Sales	$4,708	$4,358
Accounts receivable:		
Beginning of year	468	364
End of year	621	468

The accounts receivable turnover for Years 1 and 2 can be computed as follows (rounding to one decimal place):

$$\text{Accounts Receivable Turnover, Year 1} = \frac{\$4,358}{(\$364 + \$468) \div 2}$$

$$= \frac{\$4,358}{\$416} = 10.5$$

$$\text{Accounts Receivable Turnover, Year 2} = \frac{\$4,708}{(\$468 + \$621) \div 2}$$

$$= \frac{\$4,708}{\$544.5} = 8.6$$

The accounts receivable turnover has declined in Year 2. This suggests that Keurig is allowing customers to take longer to pay their accounts.

The **number of days' sales in receivables** is an estimate of the length of time the accounts receivable have been outstanding. With credit terms of n/30, the number of days' sales in receivables should be about 30 days. It is computed as follows:[6]

$$\text{Number of Days' Sales in Receivables} = \frac{\text{Average Accounts Receivable}}{\text{Average Daily Sales}}$$

[5] If known, credit sales can be used in the numerator. However, because credit sales are not normally disclosed to external users, most analysts use sales in the numerator.
[6] The number of days' sales in receivables can also be computed as (365 days ÷ Accounts Receivable Turnover).

Average daily sales are determined by dividing sales by 365 days.[7] For example, using the preceding data for Keurig, the number of days' sales in receivables for Years 1 and 2 is computed as follows (rounding all calculations to one decimal place):

$$\text{Number of Days' Sales in Receivables, Year 1} = \frac{\$416}{\$4{,}358 \div 365}$$

$$= \frac{\$416}{\$11.9} = 35.0$$

$$\text{Number of Days' Sales in Receivables, Year 2} = \frac{\$544.5}{\$4{,}708 \div 365}$$

$$= \frac{\$544.5}{\$12.9} = 42.2$$

The number of days' sales in receivables confirms that Keurig's efficiency in collecting accounts receivable declined from Year 1 to Year 2. Lengthening the credit terms or selling in markets where longer credit terms are standard could cause this decline. The efficiency in collecting accounts receivable has declined when the accounts receivable turnover decreases or the number of days' sales in receivables increases.

The efficiency in collecting accounts receivable can be compared across companies in similar industries. For example, the accounts receivable turnover and number of days' sales in receivables for Keurig can be compared to a competitor, such as **Starbucks**, as shown in Exhibit 8.

Exhibit 8

Accounts Receivable Turnover and Number of Days' Sales in Receivables for Keurig and Starbucks

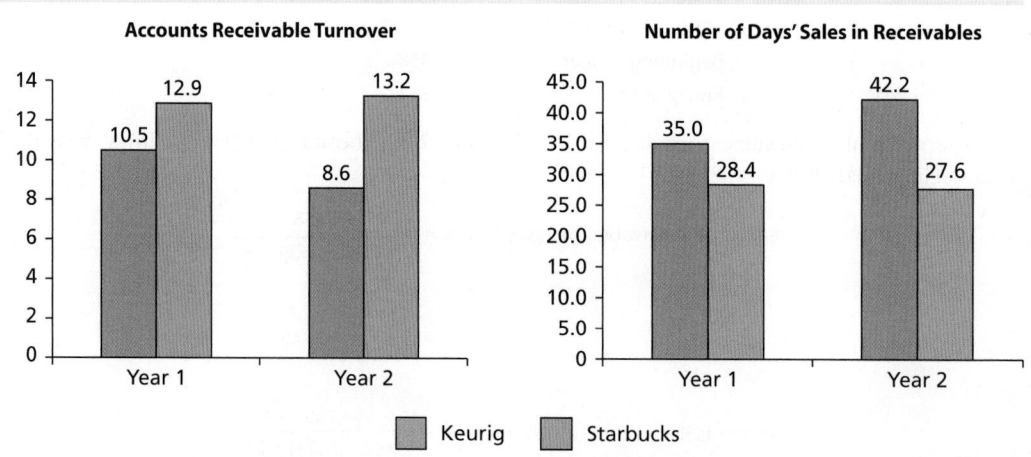

In this analysis, Starbucks is more efficient in collecting accounts receivable than is Keurig. This is likely because Starbucks, unlike Keurig, sells a portion of its coffee in its own retail stores. Such sales are mostly for cash, thus causing these ratios to favor Starbucks.

---

[7] We use 365 days for all computations involving real world companies and data. We do this to highlight differences among companies and because computations using real world data normally require rounding.

Make a Decision | Accounts Receivable Turnover and Number of Days' Sales in Receivables

DIRECTV and **DISH Network Corporation** provide satellite-based entertainment services to retail and commercial customers. Services are billed and collected on a monthly basis. Sales and accounts receivable information for both companies for a recent period follow:

	DIRECTV	DISH Network
Sales	$33,260	$14,643
Accounts receivable:		
Beginning of the year	2,547	958
End of the year	2,800	951

A. Determine the accounts receivable turnover and number of days' sales in receivables for each company. Round all calculations to one decimal place.

B. Based on these ratios, which satellite company appears to be more efficient in collecting accounts receivable?

Solution:

A.

	DIRECTV	DISH Network
Average accounts receivable:		
($2,547 + $2,800) ÷ 2	$2,673.5	
($958 + $951) ÷ 2		$954.5
Accounts receivable turnover:		
$33,260 ÷ $2,673.5	12.4	
$14,643 ÷ $954.5		15.3
Number of days' sales in receivables:		
$2,673.5 ÷ ($33,260 ÷ 365)	29.3	
$954.5 ÷ ($14,643 ÷ 365)		23.8

B. DISH Network has an accounts receivable turnover of 15.3, compared to DIRECTV's 12.4. The larger number suggests that DISH Network is able to convert accounts receivable into cash more frequently than DIRECTV. The number of days' sales in receivables ratio confirms this result. DISH Network averages 23.8 days, while DIRECTV averages 29.3 days, to convert receivables into cash. Thus, DISH Network appears more efficient in collecting accounts receivable.

Make a Decision

Let's Review

Chapter Summary

1. *Receivables* include all money claims against other entities. Receivables are normally classified as accounts receivable, notes receivable, or other receivables.

2. The operating expense recorded from uncollectible receivables is called *bad debt expense*. The two methods of accounting for uncollectible receivables are the direct write-off method and the allowance method.

3. Under the direct write-off method, the entry to write off an account debits Bad Debt Expense and credits Accounts Receivable. Neither an allowance account nor an adjusting entry is needed at the end of the period.

4. Under the allowance method, an adjusting entry is made for uncollectible accounts. When an account is determined to be uncollectible, it is written off against the allowance account. The allowance account is a contra asset account that normally has a credit balance after the adjusting entry has been posted. The estimate of uncollectibles may be based on a percent of sales or an analysis of receivables. Exhibit 3 compares and contrasts these two methods.

5. Exhibit 4 illustrates the differences between the direct write-off and allowance methods of accounting for uncollectible accounts.

6. A note received to settle an account receivable is journalized as a debit to Notes Receivable and a credit to Accounts Receivable. When a note is paid at maturity, Cash is debited, Notes Receivable is credited, and Interest Revenue is credited. If the maker of a note fails to pay, the dishonored note is journalized by debiting an account receivable for the amount due from the maker of the note.

7. All receivables that are expected to be realized in cash within a year are reported in the current assets section of the balance sheet. In addition to the allowance for doubtful accounts, additional receivable disclosures include the market (fair) value and unusual credit risks.

Key Terms

accounts receivable (382)
accounts receivable turnover (399)
aging the receivables (389)
Allowance for Doubtful
   Accounts (385)

allowance method (383)
bad debt expense (383)
direct write-off method (383)
dishonored note receivable (396)
maturity value (395)

net realizable value (385)
notes receivable (382)
number of days' sales in
   receivables (399)
receivables (382)

Practice

Multiple-Choice Questions

1. At the end of the fiscal year, before the accounts are adjusted, Accounts Receivable has a balance of $200,000 and Allowance for Doubtful Accounts has a credit balance of $2,500. If the estimate of uncollectible accounts determined by aging the receivables is $8,500, the amount of bad debt expense is:
   A. $2,500
   B. $6,000
   C. $8,500
   D. $11,000

2. At the end of the fiscal year, Accounts Receivable has a balance of $100,000 and Allowance for Doubtful Accounts has a balance of $7,000. The expected net realizable value of the accounts receivable is:
   A. $7,000
   B. $93,000
   C. $100,000
   D. $107,000

3. What is the maturity value of a 90-day, 12% note for $10,000?
   A. $8,800
   B. $10,000
   C. $10,300
   D. $11,200

4. What is the due date of a $12,000, 90-day, 8% note receivable dated August 5?
   A. October 31
   B. November 2
   C. November 3
   D. November 4

5. When a note receivable is dishonored, Accounts Receivable is debited for what amount?
   - A. The face value of the note
   - B. The maturity value of the note
   - C. The maturity value of the note less accrued interest
   - D. The maturity value of the note plus accrued interest

Answers provided after Problem. Need more practice? Find additional multiple-choice questions, exercises, and problems in CengageNOWv2.

Exercises

SHOW ME HOW

1. Direct write-off method   Obj. 3

Journalize the following transactions, using the direct write-off method of accounting for uncollectible receivables:

June 2. Received $1,200 from Melissa Crone and wrote off the remainder owed of $4,000 as uncollectible.

Oct. 9. Reinstated the account of Melissa Crone and received $4,000 cash in full payment.

SHOW ME HOW

2. Allowance method   Obj. 4

Journalize the following transactions, using the allowance method of accounting for uncollectible receivables:

June 2. Received $1,200 from Melissa Crone and wrote off the remainder owed of $4,000 as uncollectible.

Oct. 9. Reinstated the account of Melissa Crone and received $4,000 cash in full payment.

SHOW ME HOW

3. Percent of sales method   Obj. 4

At the end of the current year, Accounts Receivable has a balance of $1,975,000; Allowance for Doubtful Accounts has a credit balance of $19,670; and sales for the year total $28,550,000. Bad debt expense is estimated at ¾ of 1% of sales.

Determine (A) the amount of the adjusting entry for uncollectible accounts; (B) the adjusted balances of Accounts Receivable, Allowance for Doubtful Accounts, and Bad Debt Expense; and (C) the net realizable value of accounts receivable.

SHOW ME HOW

4. Analysis of receivables method   Obj. 4

At the end of the current year, Accounts Receivable has a balance of $1,975,000; Allowance for Doubtful Accounts has a credit balance of $19,670; and sales for the year total $28,550,000. Using the aging method, the balance of Allowance for Doubtful Accounts is estimated as $225,000.

Determine (A) the amount of the adjusting entry for uncollectible accounts; (B) the adjusted balances of Accounts Receivable, Allowance for Doubtful Accounts, and Bad Debt Expense; and (C) the net realizable value of accounts receivable.

SHOW ME HOW

5. Note receivable   Obj. 6

Guzman Company received a 60-day, 5% note for $54,000 dated July 12 from a customer on account.

A. Determine the due date of the note.

B. Determine the maturity value of the note.

C. Journalize the entry to record the receipt of the payment of the note at maturity.

Answers provided after Problem. Need more practice? Find additional multiple-choice questions, exercises, and problems in CengageNOWv2.

Problem

Ditzler Company, a construction supply company, uses the allowance method of accounting for uncollectible accounts receivable. Selected transactions completed by Ditzler are as follows:

Feb. 1. Sold merchandise on account to Ames Co., $8,000. The cost of the goods sold was $4,500.

Mar. 15. Accepted a 60-day, 12% note for $8,000 from Ames Co. on account.

Apr. 9. Wrote off a $2,500 account from Dorset Co. as uncollectible.

21. Loaned $7,500 cash to Jill Klein, receiving a 90-day, 14% note.

May 14. Received the interest due from Ames Co. and a new 90-day, 14% note as a renewal of the loan. (Record both the debit and the credit to the notes receivable account.)

June 13. Reinstated the account of Dorset Co., written off on April 9, and received $2,500 in full payment.

July 20. Jill Klein dishonored her note.

Aug. 12. Received from Ames Co. the amount due on its note of May 14.

19. Received from Jill Klein the amount owed on the dishonored note, plus interest for 30 days at 15%, computed on the maturity value of the note. Round to the nearest cent.

Dec. 16. Accepted a 60-day, 12% note for $12,000 from Global Company on account.

31. It is estimated that 3% of the credit sales of $1,375,000 for the year ended December 31 will be uncollectible.

Instructions

1. Journalize the transactions.

2. Journalize the adjusting entry to record the accrued interest on December 31 on the Global Company note.

Need more practice? Find additional multiple-choice questions, exercises, and problems in CengageNOWv2.

Answers

Multiple-Choice Questions

1. **B** The estimate of uncollectible accounts, $8,500 (answer C), is the amount of the desired balance of Allowance for Doubtful Accounts after adjustment. The amount of the current provision to be made for uncollectible accounts expense is thus $6,000 (answer B), which is the amount that must be added to the Allowance for Doubtful Accounts credit balance of $2,500 (answer A) so that the account will have the desired balance of $8,500.

2. **B** The amount expected to be realized from accounts receivable is the balance of Accounts Receivable, $100,000, less the balance of Allowance for Doubtful Accounts, $7,000, or $93,000 (answer B).

3. **C** Maturity value is the amount that is due at the maturity or due date. The maturity value of $10,300 (answer C) is determined as follows:

Face amount of note	$10,000
Plus interest ($10,000 × 0.12 × 90 ÷ 360)	300
Maturity value of note	$10,300

4. **C** November 3 is the due date of a $12,000, 90-day, 8% note receivable dated August 5 [26 days in August (31 days − 5 days) + 30 days in September + 31 days in October + 3 days in November].

5. **B** If a note is dishonored, Accounts Receivable is debited for the maturity value of the note (answer B). The maturity value of the note is its face value (answer A) plus the accrued interest. The maturity value of the note less accrued interest (answer C) is equal to the face value of the note. The maturity value of the note plus accrued interest (answer D) is incorrect, since the interest would be added twice.

Exercises

1.

June 2	Cash	1,200	
	Bad Debt Expense	4,000	
	Accounts Receivable—Melissa Crone		5,200
Oct. 9	Accounts Receivable—Melissa Crone	4,000	
	Bad Debt Expense		4,000
9	Cash	4,000	
	Accounts Receivable—Melissa Crone		4,000

2.

June 2	Cash	1,200	
	Allowance for Doubtful Accounts	4,000	
	Accounts Receivable—Melissa Crone		5,200
Oct. 9	Accounts Receivable—Melissa Crone	4,000	
	Allowance for Doubtful Accounts		4,000
9	Cash	4,000	
	Accounts Receivable—Melissa Crone		4,000

3.
   A. $214,125 [$28,550,000 × (3 ÷ 4 × 1%)]$
   B.

	Adjusted Balances
Accounts Receivable	$1,975,000
Allowance for Doubtful Accounts ($19,670 + $214,125)	233,795
Bad Debt Expense	214,125

   C. Net realizable value ($1,975,000 − $233,795) = $1,741,205

4.
   A. $205,330 ($225,000 − $19,670)$
   B.

	Adjusted Balances
Accounts Receivable	$1,975,000
Allowance for Doubtful Accounts	225,000
Bad Debt Expense	205,330

   C. Net realizable value ($1,975,000 − $225,000) = $1,750,000

5.
   A. The due date for the note is September 10, determined as follows:

July	19 days (31 − 12)
August	31
September	10
Total	60 days

   B. $54,450 [$54,000 + ($54,000 × 5% × 60 ÷ 360)]$

(Continued)

C.

Sept.	10	Cash	54,450	
		Notes Receivable		54,000
		Interest Revenue		450

Need more help? Watch step-by-step videos of how to compute answers to these Exercises in CengageNOWv2.

Problem

1.

Feb.	1	Accounts Receivable—Ames Co.	8,000.00	
		Sales		8,000.00
	1	Cost of Goods Sold	4,500.00	
		Inventory		4,500.00
Mar.	15	Notes Receivable—Ames Co.	8,000.00	
		Accounts Receivable—Ames Co.		8,000.00
Apr.	9	Allowance for Doubtful Accounts	2,500.00	
		Accounts Receivable—Dorset Co.		2,500.00
	21	Notes Receivable—Jill Klein	7,500.00	
		Cash		7,500.00
May	14	Notes Receivable—Ames Co.	8,000.00	
		Cash	160.00	
		Notes Receivable—Ames Co.		8,000.00
		Interest Revenue		160.00
		($8,000 × 12% × 60 ÷ 360)		
June	13	Accounts Receivable—Dorset Co.	2,500.00	
		Allowance for Doubtful Accounts		2,500.00
	13	Cash	2,500.00	
		Accounts Receivable—Dorset Co.		2,500.00
July	20	Accounts Receivable—Jill Klein	7,762.50	
		Notes Receivable—Jill Klein		7,500.00
		Interest Revenue		262.50
		[$7,500 + ($7,500 × 14% × 90 ÷ 360)]		
Aug.	12	Cash	8,280.00	
		Notes Receivable—Ames Co.		8,000.00
		Interest Revenue		280.00
		[$8,000 + ($8,000 × 14% × 90 ÷ 360)]		
	19	Cash	7,859.53	
		Accounts Receivable—Jill Klein		7,762.50
		Interest Revenue		97.03
		($7,762.50 × 15% × 30 ÷ 360).		
Dec.	16	Notes Receivable—Global Company	12,000.00	
		Accounts Receivable—Global Company		12,000.00
	31	Bad Debt Expense	41,250.00	
		Allowance for Doubtful Accounts		41,250.00
		Uncollectible accounts estimate		
		($1,375,000 × 3%).		

2.

Dec.	31	Interest Receivable	60.00	
		Interest Revenue		60.00
		Accrued interest		
		($12,000 × 12% × 15 ÷ 360).		

Discussion Questions

1. What are the three classifications of receivables?

2. Dan's Hardware is a small hardware store in the rural township of Twin Bridges. It rarely extends credit to its customers in the form of an account receivable. The few customers who are allowed to carry accounts receivable are long-time residents of Twin Bridges with a history of doing business at Dan's Hardware. What method of accounting for uncollectible receivables should Dan's Hardware use? Why?

3. What kind of an account (asset, liability, etc.) is Allowance for Doubtful Accounts, and is its normal balance a debit or a credit?

4. After the accounts are adjusted and closed at the end of the fiscal year, Accounts Receivable has a balance of $673,400, and Allowance for Doubtful Accounts has a balance of $11,900. Describe how the accounts receivable and the allowance for doubtful accounts are reported on the balance sheet.

5. A firm has consistently adjusted its allowance account at the end of the fiscal year by adding a fixed percent of the period's sales on account. After seven years, the balance in Allowance for Doubtful Accounts has become very large in relationship to the balance in Accounts Receivable. Give two possible explanations.

6. Which of the two methods of estimating uncollectibles provides for the most accurate estimate of the current net realizable value of the receivables?

7. Neptune Company issued a note receivable to Sailfish Company. (A) Who is the payee? (B) What is the title of the account used by Sailfish Company in recording the note?

8. If a note provides for payment of principal of $85,000 and interest at the rate of 6%, will the interest amount to $5,100? Explain.

9. The maker of a $240,000, 6%, 90-day note receivable failed to pay the note on the due date of November 30. What accounts should be debited and credited by the payee to record the dishonored note receivable?

10. The note receivable dishonored in Discussion Question 9 is paid on December 30 by the maker, plus interest for 30 days at 9%. What entry should be made to record the receipt of the payment?

Basic Exercises

SHOW ME HOW

BE 8-1 Direct write-off method Obj. 3

Journalize the following transactions, using the direct write-off method of accounting for uncollectible receivables:

Mar. 17 Received $275 from Shawn McNeely and wrote off the remainder owed of $1,000 as uncollectible.

July 29 Reinstated the account of Shawn McNeely and received $1,000 cash in full payment.

SHOW ME HOW

BE 8-2 Allowance method Obj. 4

Journalize the following transactions, using the allowance method of accounting for uncollectible receivables:

Mar. 17 Received $275 from Shawn McNeely and wrote off the remainder owed of $1,000 as uncollectible.

July 29 Reinstated the account of Shawn McNeely and received $1,000 cash in full payment.

SHOW ME HOW

BE 8-3   Percent of sales method   Obj. 4

At the end of the current year, Accounts Receivable has a balance of $2,150,000; Allowance for Doubtful Accounts has a debit balance of $10,500; and sales for the year total $51,850,000. Bad debt expense is estimated at ¼ of 1% of sales.

Determine (A) the amount of the adjusting entry for uncollectible accounts; (B) the adjusted balances of Accounts Receivable, Allowance for Doubtful Accounts, and Bad Debt Expense; and (C) the net realizable value of accounts receivable.

SHOW ME HOW

BE 8-4   Analysis of receivables method   Obj. 4

At the end of the current year, Accounts Receivable has a balance of $2,150,000; Allowance for Doubtful Accounts has a debit balance of $10,500; and sales for the year total $51,850,000. Using the aging method, the balance of Allowance for Doubtful Accounts is estimated as $110,000.

Determine (A) the amount of the adjusting entry for uncollectible accounts; (B) the adjusted balances of Accounts Receivable, Allowance for Doubtful Accounts, and Bad Debt Expense; and (C) the net realizable value of accounts receivable.

SHOW ME HOW

BE 8-5   Note receivable   Obj. 6

Prefix Supply Company received a 120-day, 8% note for $450,000, dated April 9 from a customer on account.

A. Determine the due date of the note.

B. Determine the maturity value of the note.

C. Journalize the entry to record the receipt of the payment of the note at maturity.

Exercises

REAL WORLD

EX 8-1   Classifications of receivables   Obj. 1

The Boeing Company is one of the world's major aerospace firms with operations involving commercial aircraft, military aircraft, missiles, satellite systems, and information and battle management systems. As of a recent year, Boeing had $4,281 million of receivables involving U.S. government contracts and $1,749 million of receivables involving commercial aircraft customers, such as **Delta Air Lines** and **United Airlines**.

➤Should Boeing report these receivables separately in the financial statements or combine them into one overall accounts receivable amount? Explain.

EX 8-2   Nature of uncollectible accounts   Obj. 2

✔ A. 15.9%

SHOW ME HOW   REAL WORLD

MGM Resorts International owns and operates hotels and casinos including the MGM Grand and the Bellagio in Las Vegas, Nevada. As of a recent year, MGM reported accounts receivable of $562,947,000 and allowance for doubtful accounts of $89,602,000. **Johnson & Johnson** manufactures and sells a wide range of healthcare products including Band-Aids and Tylenol. As of a recent year, J&J reported accounts receivable of $11,260,000,000 and allowance for doubtful accounts of $275,000,000.

A. Compute the percentage of the allowance for doubtful accounts to the accounts receivable for MGM. (Round to one decimal place.)

B. Compute the percentage of the allowance for doubtful accounts to the accounts receivable for J&J. (Round to one decimal place.)

C. ➤Discuss possible reasons for the difference in the two ratios computed in (A) and (B).

SHOW ME HOW

EX 8-3 Entries for uncollectible accounts, using direct write-off method Obj. 3

Journalize the following transactions in the accounts of Canyon River Medical Co., a medical equipment company that uses the direct write-off method of accounting for uncollectible receivables:

Jan. 19 Sold merchandise on account to Dr. Kyle Norby, $6,400. The cost of goods sold was $3,000.

June 2 Received $500 from Dr. Kyle Norby and wrote off the remainder owed on the sale of January 19 as uncollectible.

Oct. 23 Reinstated the account of Dr. Kyle Norby that had been written off on June 2 and received $5,900 cash in full payment.

SHOW ME HOW

EX 8-4 Entries for uncollectible receivables, using allowance method Obj. 4

Journalize the following transactions in the accounts of Zippy Interiors Company, a restaurant supply company that uses the allowance method of accounting for uncollectible receivables:

May 24 Sold merchandise on account to Old Town Cafe $18,450. The cost of goods sold was $11,000.

Sept. 30 Received $6,000 from Old Town Cafe and wrote off the remainder owed on the sale of May 24 as uncollectible.

Dec. 7 Reinstated the account of Old Town Cafe that had been written off on September 30 and received $12,450 cash in full payment.

EX 8-5 Entries to write off accounts receivable Obj. 3, 4

Creative Solutions Company, a computer consulting firm, has decided to write off the $11,750 balance of an account owed by a customer, Wil Treadwell. Journalize the entry to record the write-off, assuming that (A) the direct write-off method is used and (B) the allowance method is used.

EX 8-6 Providing for doubtful accounts Obj. 4

✔ A. $205,500

✔ B. $197,500

SHOW ME HOW

At the end of the current year, the accounts receivable account has a debit balance of $2,950,000 and sales for the year total $27,400,000. Determine the amount of the adjusting entry to provide for doubtful accounts under each of the following assumptions:

A. The allowance account before adjustment has a debit balance of $9,500. Bad debt expense is estimated at ¾ of 1% of sales.

B. The allowance account before adjustment has a debit balance of $9,500. An aging of the accounts in the customer ledger indicates estimated doubtful accounts of $188,000.

C. The allowance account before adjustment has a credit balance of $31,400. Bad debt expense is estimated at ½ of 1% of sales.

D. The allowance account before adjustment has a credit balance of $31,400. An aging of the accounts in the customer ledger indicates estimated doubtful accounts of $175,000.

EX 8-7 Number of days past due Obj. 4

✔ Avalanche Auto, 84 days

Toot Auto Supply distributes new and used automobile parts to local dealers throughout the Midwest. Toot's credit terms are n/30. As of the end of business on October 31, the following accounts receivable were past due:

Account	Due Date	Amount
Avalanche Auto	August 8	$12,000
Bales Auto	October 11	2,400
Derby Auto Repair	June 23	3,900
Lucky's Auto Repair	September 2	6,600
Pit Stop Auto	September 19	1,100
Reliable Auto Repair	July 15	9,750
Trident Auto	August 24	1,800
Valley Repair & Tow	May 17	4,000

Determine the number of days each account is past due as of October 31.

SHOW ME HOW   EXCEL TEMPLATE

EX 8-8 Aging of receivables schedule

Obj. 4

The accounts receivable clerk for Evers Industries prepared the following partially completed aging of receivables schedule as of the end of business on July 31:

	A	B	C	D	E	F	G
1			Not	Days Past Due			
2			Past				Over
3	Customer	Balance	Due	1–30	31–60	61–90	90
4	Acme Industries Inc.	3,000	3,000				
5	Alliance Company	4,500		4,500			
21	Zollinger Company	5,000			5,000		
22	Subtotals	1,050,000	600,000	220,000	115,000	85,000	30,000

The following accounts were unintentionally omitted from the aging schedule and not included in the preceding subtotals:

Customer	Balance	Due Date
Boyd Industries	$36,000	April 7
Hodges Company	11,500	May 29
Kent Creek Inc.	6,600	June 8
Lockwood Company	7,400	August 10
Van Epps Company	13,000	July 2

A. Determine the number of days past due for each of the preceding accounts as of July 31.

B. Complete the aging of receivables schedule by adding the omitted accounts to the bottom of the schedule and updating the totals.

EX 8-9 Estimating allowance for doubtful accounts

Obj. 4

✔ Allowance for
doubtful accounts,
$106,106

SHOW ME HOW   EXCEL TEMPLATE

Evers Industries has a past history of uncollectible accounts, as follows. Estimate the allowance for doubtful accounts, based on the aging of receivables schedule you completed in Exercise 8-8.

Age Class	Percent Uncollectible
Not past due	1%
1–30 days past due	3
31–60 days past due	12
61–90 days past due	30
Over 90 days past due	75

EX 8-10 Adjustment for uncollectible accounts

Obj. 4

SHOW ME HOW

Using data in Exercise 8-9, assume that the allowance for doubtful accounts for Evers Industries has a credit balance of $8,240 before adjustment on July 31. Journalize the adjusting entry for uncollectible accounts as of July 31.

EX 8-11 Estimating doubtful accounts

Obj. 4

SHOW ME HOW

Outlaw Bike Co. is a wholesaler of motorcycle supplies. An aging of the company's accounts receivable on December 31 and a historical analysis of the percentage of uncollectible accounts in each age category are as follows:

Age Class	Balance	Percent Uncollectible
Not past due	$ 892,000	¾%
1–30 days past due	285,000	1
31–60 days past due	101,000	8
61–90 days past due	63,000	16
91–180 days past due	43,100	50
Over 180 days past due	17,700	80
	$1,401,800	

Estimate what the proper balance of the allowance for doubtful accounts should be as of December 31.

SHOW ME HOW

EX 8-12   Entry for uncollectible accounts   **Obj. 4**

Using the data in Exercise 8-11, assume that the allowance for doubtful accounts for Outlaw Bike Co. had a debit balance of $5,140 as of December 31.

Journalize the adjusting entry for uncollectible accounts as of December 31.

EX 8-13   Entries for bad debt expense under the direct write-off and allowance   **Obj. 5**
methods

✔ C. $8,225 higher

The following selected transactions were taken from the records of Shipway Company for the first year of its operations ending December 31:

SHOW ME HOW

Apr. 13. Wrote off account of Dean Sheppard, $8,450.

May 15. Received $500 as partial payment on the $7,100 account of Dan Pyle. Wrote off the remaining balance as uncollectible.

July 27. Received $8,450 from Dean Sheppard, whose account had been written off on April 13. Reinstated the account and recorded the cash receipt.

Dec. 31. Wrote off the following accounts as uncollectible (record as one journal entry):

Paul Chapman	$2,225
Duane DeRosa	3,550
Teresa Galloway	4,770
Ernie Klatt	1,275
Marty Richey	1,690

31. If necessary, record the year-end adjusting entry for uncollectible accounts.

A. Journalize the transactions under the direct write-off method.

B. Journalize the transactions under the allowance method. Shipway Company uses the percent of credit sales method of estimating uncollectible accounts expense. Based on past history and industry averages, ¾% of credit sales are expected to be uncollectible. Shipway recorded $3,778,000 of credit sales during the year.

C. How much higher (lower) would Shipway Company's net income have been under the direct write-off method than under the allowance method?

EX 8-14   Entries for bad debt expense under the direct write-off and allowance   **Obj. 5**
methods

✔ C. $11,090 higher

The following selected transactions were taken from the records of Rustic Tables Company for the year ending December 31:

SHOW ME HOW   EXCEL TEMPLATE

June 8. Wrote off account of Kathy Quantel, $8,440.

Aug. 14. Received $3,000 as partial payment on the $12,500 account of Rosalie Oakes. Wrote off the remaining balance as uncollectible.

Oct. 16. Received the $8,440 from Kathy Quantel, whose account had been written off on June 8. Reinstated the account and recorded the cash receipt.

Dec. 31. Wrote off the following accounts as uncollectible (record as one journal entry):

Wade Dolan	$4,600
Greg Gagne	3,600
Amber Kisko	7,150
Shannon Poole	2,975
Niki Spence	6,630

31. If necessary, record the year-end adjusting entry for uncollectible accounts.

(Continued)

A. Journalize the transactions under the direct write-off method.

B. Journalize the transactions under the allowance method, assuming that the allowance account had a beginning balance of $36,000 at the beginning of the year and the company uses the analysis of receivables method. Rustic Tables Company prepared the following aging schedule for its accounts receivable:

Aging Class (Number of Days Past Due)	Receivables Balance on December 31	Estimated Percent of Uncollectible Accounts
0–30 days	$320,000	1%
31–60 days	110,000	3
61–90 days	24,000	10
91–120 days	18,000	33
More than 120 days	43,000	75
Total receivables	$515,000	

C. How much higher (lower) would Rustic Tables' net income have been under the direct write-off method than under the allowance method?

EX 8-15   Effect of doubtful accounts on net income   Obj. 5

During its first year of operations, Mack's Plumbing Supply Co. had sales of $3,250,000, wrote off $27,800 of accounts as uncollectible using the direct write-off method, and reported net income of $487,500. Determine what the net income would have been if the allowance method had been used and the company estimated that 1% of sales would be uncollectible.

EX 8-16   Effect of doubtful accounts on net income   Obj. 5

✔ B. $11,700 credit balance

Using the data in Exercise 8-15, assume that during the second year of operations Mack's Plumbing Supply Co. had sales of $4,100,000, wrote off $34,000 of accounts as uncollectible using the direct write-off method, and reported net income of $600,000.

A. Determine what net income would have been in the second year if the allowance method (using 1% of sales) had been used in both the first and second years.

B. Determine what the balance of the allowance for doubtful accounts would have been at the end of the second year if the allowance method had been used in both the first and second years.

EX 8-17   Entries for bad debt expense under the direct write-off and allowance   Obj. 5
methods

✔ C. 9,375 higher

Casebolt Company wrote off the following accounts receivable as uncollectible for the first year of its operations ending December 31:

SHOW ME HOW

Customer	Amount
Shawn Brooke	$ 4,650
Eve Denton	5,180
Art Malloy	11,050
Cassie Yost	9,120
Total	$30,000

A. Journalize the write-offs under the direct write-off method.

B. Journalize the write-offs under the allowance method. Also, journalize the adjusting entry for uncollectible accounts. The company recorded $5,250,000 of credit sales during the year. Based on past history and industry averages, ¾% of credit sales are expected to be uncollectible.

C. How much higher (lower) would Casebolt Company's net income have been under the direct write-off method than under the allowance method?

EX 8-18 Entries for bad debt expense under the direct write-off and allowance methods   Obj. 5

Seaforth International wrote off the following accounts receivable as uncollectible for the year ending December 31:

Customer	Amount
Kim Abel	$ 21,550
Lee Drake	33,925
Jenny Green	27,565
Mike Lamb	19,460
Total	$102,500

The company prepared the following aging schedule for its accounts receivable on December 31:

Aging Class (Number of Days Past Due)	Receivables Balance on December 31	Estimated Percent of Uncollectible Accounts
0–30 days	$ 715,000	1%
31–60 days	310,000	2
61–90 days	102,000	15
91–120 days	76,000	30
More than 120 days	97,000	60
Total receivables	$1,300,000	

A. Journalize the write-offs under the direct write-off method.

B. Journalize the write-offs and the year-end adjusting entry under the allowance method, assuming that the allowance account had a beginning balance of $95,000 and the company uses the analysis of receivables method.

C. How much higher (lower) would Seaforth International's net income have been under the allowance method than under the direct write-off method?

EX 8-19 Determine due date and interest on notes   Obj. 6

✔ A. May 2, $1,600

Determine the due date and the amount of interest due at maturity on the following notes:

	Date of Note	Face Amount	Interest Rate	Term of Note
A.	January 3*	$80,000	6%	120 days
B.	February 20*	27,000	4	30 days
C.	May 24	62,500	8	45 days
D.	August 30	30,000	5	90 days
E.	October 4	40,000	7	90 days

* Assume a leap year in which February has 29 days.

 SHOW ME HOW   EXCEL TEMPLATE

EX 8-20 Entries for notes receivable   Obj. 6

✔ B. $61,000

Valley Designs issued a 120-day, 5% note for $60,000 dated April 15 to Bork Furniture Company on account.

A. Determine the due date of the note.

B. Determine the maturity value of the note.

C. Journalize the entries to record the following: (1) receipt of the note by Bork Furniture and (2) receipt of payment of the note at maturity.

 SHOW ME HOW

EX 8-21   Entries for notes receivable

Obj. 6

The series of five transactions, A through E, recorded in the following T accounts were related to a sale to a customer on account and the receipt of the amount owed. Briefly describe each transaction.

	Cash				Notes Receivable	
E	76,500			C	75,000	D	75,000

	Accounts Receivable				Cost of Goods Sold	
A	75,000	C	75,000	B	45,000	
D	75,400	E	75,400			

	Inventory				Interest Revenue	
		B	45,000		D	400
					E	1,100

	Sales	
		A	75,000

EX 8-22   Entries for notes receivable, including year-end entries

Obj. 6

The following selected transactions were completed by Interlocking Devices Co., a supplier of zippers for clothing:

20Y7

Dec.   7. Received from Unitarian Clothing & Bags Co., on account, a $75,000, 60-day, 3% note dated December 7.

31. Recorded an adjusting entry for accrued interest on the note of December 7.

31. Recorded the closing entry for interest revenue.

20Y8

Feb.   5. Received payment of note and interest from Unitarian Clothing & Bags Co.

Journalize the entries to record the transactions.

EX 8-23   Entries for receipt and dishonor of note receivable

Obj. 6

Journalize the following transactions of Trapper Jon's Productions:

June 23. Received a $48,000, 90-day, 8% note dated June 23 from Radon Express Co. on account.

Sept. 21. The note is dishonored by Radon Express Co.

Oct. 21. Received the amount due on the dishonored note plus interest for 30 days at 10% on the total amount charged to Radon Express Co. on September 21.

EX 8-24   Entries for receipt and dishonor of notes receivable

Obj. 4, 6

Journalize the following transactions in the accounts of Missouri Gaming Co., which operates a riverboat casino:

Mar. 29 Received a $30,000, 60-day, 5% note dated March 29 from Karie Platt on account.

Apr. 30. Received a $24,000 60-day, 8% note dated April 30 from Jon Kelly on account.

May 28. The note dated March 29 from Karie Platt is dishonored, and the customer's account is charged for the note, including interest.

June 29. The note dated April 30 from Jon Kelly is dishonored, and the customer's account is charged for the note, including interest.

Aug. 26. Cash is received for the amount due on the dishonored note dated March 29 plus interest for 90 days at 8% on the total amount debited to Karie Platt on May 28.

Oct. 22. Wrote off against the allowance account the amount charged to Jon Kelly on June 29 for the dishonored note dated April 30.

SHOW ME HOW

EX 8-25 Receivables on the balance sheet

Obj. 7

List any errors you can find in the following partial balance sheet:

Napa Vino Company
Balance Sheet
December 31, 20Y6

Assets		
Current assets:		
Cash		$ 78,500
Notes receivable	$ 300,000	
Interest receivable	(4,500)	
Notes receivable, net		295,500
Accounts receivable	$1,200,000	
Allowance for doubtful accounts	11,500	
Accounts receivable, net		1,211,500

Problems: Series A

PR 8-1A Allowance method entries

Obj. 4

✔ 3. $1,749,300

SHOW ME HOW   GENERAL LEDGER

The following transactions were completed by Irvine Company during the current fiscal year ended December 31:

Feb. 8. Received 40% of the $18,000 balance owed by DeCoy Co., a bankrupt business, and wrote off the remainder as uncollectible.

May 27. Reinstated the account of Seth Nelsen, which had been written off in the preceding year as uncollectible. Journalized the receipt of $7,350 cash in full payment of Seth's account.

Aug. 13. Wrote off the $6,400 balance owed by Kat Tracks Co., which has no assets.

Oct. 31. Reinstated the account of Crawford Co., which had been written off in the preceding year as uncollectible. Journalized the receipt of $3,880 cash in full payment of the account.

Dec. 31. Wrote off the following accounts as uncollectible (compound entry): Newbauer Co., $7,190; Bonneville Co., $5,500; Crow Distributors, $9,400; Fiber Optics, $1,110.

31. Based on an analysis of the $1,785,000 of accounts receivable, it was estimated that $35,700 will be uncollectible. Journalized the adjusting entry.

Instructions

1. Record the January 1 credit balance of $26,000 in a T account for Allowance for Doubtful Accounts.

2. Journalize the transactions. Post each entry that affects the following selected T accounts and determine the new balances:

    Allowance for Doubtful Accounts
    Bad Debt Expense

3. Determine the expected net realizable value of the accounts receivable as of December 31.

4. Assuming that instead of basing the provision for uncollectible accounts on an analysis of receivables, the adjusting entry on December 31 had been based on an estimated expense of ¼ of 1% of the sales of $18,200,000 for the year, determine the following:

    A. Bad debt expense for the year.

    B. Balance in the allowance account after the adjustment of December 31.

    C. Expected net realizable value of the accounts receivable as of December 31.

EXCEL TEMPLATE

PR 8-2A Aging of receivables; estimating allowance for doubtful accounts   Obj. 4

✔ 3. $121,000

Trophy Fish Company supplies flies and fishing gear to sporting goods stores and outfitters throughout the western United States. The accounts receivable clerk for Trophy Fish prepared the following partially completed aging of receivables schedule as of the end of business on December 31, 20Y4:

	A	B	C	D	E	F	G	H
1			Not		Days Past Due			
2			Past					
3	Customer	Balance	Due	1–30	31–60	61–90	91–120	Over 120
4	AAA Outfitters	20,000	20,000					
5	Brown Trout Fly Shop	7,500			7,500			
30	Zigs Fish Adventures	4,000		4,000				
31	Subtotals	1,300,000	750,000	290,000	120,000	40,000	20,000	80,000

The following accounts were unintentionally omitted from the aging schedule. Assume all due dates are for the current year except for Wolfe Sports, which is due in the next year.

Customer	Due Date	Balance
Adams Sports & Flies	May 22	$5,000
Blue Dun Flies	Oct. 10	4,900
Cicada Fish Co.	Sept. 29	8,400
Deschutes Sports	Oct. 20	7,000
Green River Sports	Nov. 7	3,500
Smith River Co.	Nov. 28	2,400
Western Trout Company	Dec. 7	6,800
Wolfe Sports	Jan. 20	4,400

Trophy Fish has a past history of uncollectible accounts by age category, as follows:

Age Class	Percent Uncollectible
Not past due	1%
1–30 days past due	2
31–60 days past due	10
61–90 days past due	30
91–120 days past due	40
Over 120 days past due	80

Instructions

1. Determine the number of days past due for each of the preceding accounts.

2. Complete the aging of receivables schedule by adding the omitted accounts to the bottom of the schedule and updating the totals.

3. Estimate the allowance for doubtful accounts, based on the aging of receivables schedule.

4. Assume that the allowance for doubtful accounts for Trophy Fish Company has a debit balance of $3,600 before adjustment on December 31. Journalize the adjusting entry for uncollectible accounts.

5. ➤ Assume that the adjusting entry in (4) was inadvertently omitted, how would the omission affect the balance sheet and income statement?

PR 8-3A Compare two methods of accounting for uncollectible receivables   Obj. 3, 4, 5

✔ 1. Year 4: Balance of allowance account, end of year, $15,050

Call Systems Company, a telephone service and supply company, has just completed its fourth year of operations. The direct write-off method of recording bad debt expense has been used during the entire period. Because of substantial increases in sales volume and the amount of uncollectible accounts, the company is considering changing to the allowance method. Information is requested as to the effect that an annual provision of 1% of sales would have had on the amount of bad debt expense reported for each of the past four years. It is also considered desirable to know what the balance of Allowance for Doubtful Accounts would have been at the end of each year. The following data have been obtained from the accounts:

Year	Sales	Uncollectible Accounts Written Off	1	2	3	4
			Year of Origin of Accounts Receivable Written Off as Uncollectible			
1	$ 900,000	$ 4,500	$4,500			
2	1,250,000	9,600	3,000	$6,600		
3	1,500,000	12,800	1,000	3,700	$8,100	
4	2,200,000	16,550		1,500	4,300	$10,750

Instructions

1. Assemble the desired data, using the following column headings:

Year	Bad Debt Expense		Increase (Decrease) in Amount of Expense	Balance of Allowance Account, End of Year
	Expense Actually Reported	Expense Based on Estimate		

2. ➤ Experience during the first four years of operations indicated that the receivables were either collected within two years or had to be written off as uncollectible. Does the estimate of 1% of sales appear to be reasonably close to the actual experience with uncollectible accounts originating during the first two years? Explain.

PR 8-4A Details of notes receivable and related entries
Obj. 6

✔ 1. Note 2: Due date, May 22; Interest due at maturity, $300

SHOW ME HOW

Water Closet Co. wholesales bathroom fixtures. During the current year ending December 31, Water Closet received the following notes:

	Date	Face Amount	Term	Interest Rate
1.	Mar. 6	$75,000	60 days	4%
2.	Apr. 7	40,000	45 days	6
3.	Aug. 12	36,000	120 days	5
4.	Oct. 22	27,000	30 days	8
5.	Nov. 19	48,000	90 days	3
6.	Dec. 15	72,000	45 days	5

Instructions

1. Determine for each note (A) the due date and (B) the amount of interest due at maturity, identifying each note by number.

2. Journalize the entry to record the dishonor of Note (3) on its due date.

3. Journalize the adjusting entry to record the accrued interest on Notes (5) and (6) on December 31.

4. Journalize the entries to record the receipt of the amounts due on Notes (5) and (6) in January and February.

PR 8-5A Notes receivable entries
Obj. 6

The following data relate to notes receivable and interest for CGH Cable Co., a cable manufacturer and supplier. (All notes are dated as of the day they are received.)

Apr. 10. Received a $144,000, 5%, 60-day note on account.

May 15. Received a $270,000, 7%, 120-day note on account.

June 9. Received $145,200 on note of April 10.

Aug. 22. Received a $150,000, 4%, 45-day note on account.

Sept. 12. Received $276,300 on note of May 15.

30. Received a $210,000, 8%, 60-day note on account.

Oct. 6. Received $150,750 on note of August 22.

18. Received a 120,000, 5%, 60-day note on account.

Nov. 29. Received $212,800 on note of September 30.

Dec. 17. Received $121,000 on note of October 18.

Instructions

Journalize the entries to record the transactions.

GENERAL LEDGER

PR 8-6A   Sales and notes receivable transactions   Obj. 6

The following were selected from among the transactions completed by Caldemeyer Co. during the current year. Caldemeyer sells and installs home and business security systems.

Jan.   3.   Loaned $18,000 cash to Trina Gelhaus, receiving a 90-day, 8% note.

Feb.   10.   Sold merchandise on account to Bradford & Co., $24,000. The cost of goods sold was $14,400.

     13.   Sold merchandise on account to Dry Creek Co., $60,000. The cost of goods sold was $54,000.

Mar.   12.   Accepted a 60-day, 7% note for $24,000 from Bradford & Co. on account.

     14.   Accepted a 60-day, 9% note for $60,000 from Dry Creek Co. on account.

Apr.   3.   Received the interest due from Trina Gelhaus and a new 120-day, 9% note as a renewal of the loan of January 3. (Record both the debit and the credit to the notes receivable account.)

May   11.   Received from Bradford & Co. the amount due on the note of March 12.

     13.   Dry Creek Co. dishonored its note dated March 14.

July   12.   Received from Dry Creek Co. the amount owed on the dishonored note, plus interest for 60 days at 12% computed on the maturity value of the note.

Aug.   1.   Received from Trina Gelhaus the amount due on her note of April 3.

Oct.   5.   Sold merchandise on account, terms 2/10, n/30, to Halloran Co., $13,500. Record the sale net of the 2% discount. The cost of goods sold was $8,100.

     15.   Received from Halloran Co. the amount of the invoice of October 5, less 2% discount.

Instructions

Journalize the entries to record the transactions.

Problems: Series B

PR 8-1B   Allowance method entries   Obj. 4

✔ 3. $2,290,000

SHOW ME HOW   GENERAL LEDGER

The following transactions were completed by Wild Trout Gallery during the current fiscal year ended December 31:

Jan.   19.   Reinstated the account of Arlene Gurley, which had been written off in the preceding year as uncollectible. Journalized the receipt of $2,660 cash in full payment of Arlene's account.

Apr.   3.   Wrote off the $12,750 balance owed by Premier GS Co., which is bankrupt.

July   16.   Received 25% of the $22,000 balance owed by Hayden Co., a bankrupt business, and wrote off the remainder as uncollectible.

Nov.   23.   Reinstated the account of Harry Carr, which had been written off two years earlier as uncollectible. Recorded the receipt of $4,000 cash in full payment.

Dec.   31.   Wrote off the following accounts as uncollectible (compound entry): Cavey Co., $3,300; Fogle Co., $8,100; Lake Furniture, $11,400; Melinda Shryer, $1,200.

     31.   Based on an analysis of the $2,350,000 of accounts receivable, it was estimated that $60,000 will be uncollectible. Journalized the adjusting entry.

Instructions

1. Record the January 1 credit balance of $50,000 in a T account for Allowance for Doubtful Accounts.

2. Journalize the transactions. Post each entry that affects the following selected T accounts and determine the new balances:

          Allowance for Doubtful Accounts
          Bad Debt Expense

3. Determine the expected net realizable value of the accounts receivable as of December 31.

4. Assuming that instead of basing the provision for uncollectible accounts on an analysis of receivables, the adjusting entry on December 31 had been based on an estimated expense of ½ of 1% of the sales of $15,800,000 for the year, determine the following:

A. Bad debt expense for the year.

B. Balance in the allowance account after the adjustment of December 31.

C. Expected net realizable value of the accounts receivable as of December 31.

PR 8-2B Aging of receivables; estimating allowance for doubtful accounts **Obj. 4**

✔ 3. $123,235

EXCEL TEMPLATE

Wig Creations Company supplies wigs and hair care products to beauty salons throughout Texas and the Southwest. The accounts receivable clerk for Wig Creations prepared the following partially completed aging of receivables schedule as of the end of business on December 31, 20Y7:

	A	B	C	D	E	F	G	H
1			Not			Days Past Due		
2			Past					
3	Customer	Balance	Due	1–30	31–60	61–90	91–120	Over 120
4	ABC Beauty	15,000	15,000					
5	Angel Wigs	8,000			8,000			
30	Zodiac Beauty	3,000		3,000				
31	Subtotals	875,000	415,000	210,000	112,000	55,000	18,000	65,000

The following accounts were unintentionally omitted from the aging schedule. Assume all due dates are for the current year except for Visions Hair & Nail, which is due in the next year.

Customer	Due Date	Balance
Arcade Beauty	Aug. 17	$10,000
Creative Images	Oct. 30	8,500
Excel Hair Products	July 3	7,500
First Class Hair Care	Sept. 8	6,600
Golden Images	Nov. 23	3,600
Oh That Hair	Nov. 29	1,400
One Stop Hair Designs	Dec. 7	4,000
Visions Hair & Nail	Jan. 11	9,000

Wig Creations has a past history of uncollectible accounts by age category, as follows:

Age Class	Percent Uncollectible
Not past due	1%
1–30 days past due	4
31–60 days past due	16
61–90 days past due	25
91–120 days past due	40
Over 120 days past due	80

Instructions

1. Determine the number of days past due for each of the preceding accounts.

2. Complete the aging of receivables schedule by adding the omitted accounts to the bottom of the schedule and updating the totals.

3. Estimate the allowance for doubtful accounts, based on the aging of receivables schedule.

4. Assume that the allowance for doubtful accounts for Wig Creations has a credit balance of $7,375 before adjustment on December 31. Journalize the adjustment for uncollectible accounts.

5. ▬▬▶ Assume that the adjusting entry in (4) was inadvertently omitted, how would the omission affect the balance sheet and income statement?

PR 8-3B Compare two methods of accounting for uncollectible receivables **Obj. 3, 4, 5**

✔ 1. Year 4: Balance of allowance account, end of year, $32,550

Digital Depot Company, which operates a chain of 40 electronics supply stores, has just completed its fourth year of operations. The direct write-off method of recording bad debt expense has been used during the entire period. Because of substantial increases in sales volume and

(Continued)

the amount of uncollectible accounts, the firm is considering changing to the allowance method. Information is requested as to the effect that an annual provision of ¼% of sales would have had on the amount of bad debt expense reported for each of the past four years. It is also considered desirable to know what the balance of Allowance for Doubtful Accounts would have been at the end of each year. The following data have been obtained from the accounts:

| | | | Year of Origin of Accounts Receivable Written Off as Uncollectible | | | |
Year	Sales	Uncollectible Accounts Written Off	1	2	3	4
1	$12,500,000	$18,000	$18,000			
2	14,800,000	30,200	9,000	$21,200		
3	18,000,000	39,900	3,600	9,300	$27,000	
4	24,000,000	52,600		5,100	12,500	$35,000

Instructions

1. Assemble the desired data, using the following column headings:

| | Bad Debt Expense | | | |
Year	Expense Actually Reported	Expense Based on Estimate	Increase (Decrease) in Amount of Expense	Balance of Allowance Account, End of Year

2. ▬▬▬▶ Experience during the first four years of operations indicated that the receivables were either collected within two years or had to be written off as uncollectible. Does the estimate of ¼% of sales appear to be reasonably close to the actual experience with uncollectible accounts originating during the first two years? Explain.

PR 8-4B Details of notes receivable and related entries Obj. 6

✔ 1. Note 1: Due date, Feb. 13; Interest due at maturity, $110

SHOW ME HOW

Gen-X Ads Co. produces advertising videos. During the current year ending December 31, Gen-X Ads received the following notes:

	Date	Face Amount	Term	Interest Rate
1.	Jan. 14	$33,000	30 days	4%
2.	Mar. 9	60,000	45 days	7
3.	July 12	48,000	90 days	5
4.	Aug. 23	16,000	75 days	6
5.	Nov. 15	36,000	60 days	8
6.	Dec. 10	24,000	60 days	6

Instructions

1. Determine for each note (A) the due date and (B) the amount of interest due at maturity, identifying each note by number.

2. Journalize the entry to record the dishonor of Note (3) on its due date.

3. Journalize the adjusting entry to record the accrued interest on Notes (5) and (6) on December 31.

4. Journalize the entries to record the receipt of the amounts due on Notes (5) and (6) in January and February.

PR 8-5B Notes receivable entries Obj. 6

The following data relate to notes receivable and interest for Owens Co., a financial services company. (All notes are dated as of the day they are received.)

Mar.   8. Received a $33,000, 5%, 60-day note on account.

    31. Received an $80,000, 7%, 90-day note on account.

May   7. Received $33,275 on note of March 8.

    16. Received a $72,000, 7%, 90-day note on account.

June 11. Received a $36,000, 6%, 45-day note on account.

    29. Received $81,400 on note of March 31.

July 26. Received $36,270 on note of June 11.

Aug. 4. Received a $48,000, 9%, 120-day note on account.

    14. Received $73,260 on note of May 16.

Dec. 2. Received $49,440 on note of August 4.

Instructions

Journalize the entries to record the transactions.

GENERAL LEDGER

PR 8-6B   Sales and notes receivable transactions

Obj. 6

The following were selected from among the transactions completed during the current year by Danix Co., an appliance wholesale company:

Jan. 21. Sold merchandise on account to Black Tie Co., $28,000. The cost of goods sold was $16,800.

Mar. 18. Accepted a 60-day, 6% note for $28,000 from Black Tie Co. on account.

May 17. Received from Black Tie Co. the amount due on the note of March 18.

June 15. Sold merchandise on account, terms 1/10, n/30, to Pioneer Co. for $17,700. Record the sale net of the discount. The cost of goods sold was $10,600.

    21. Loaned $18,000 cash to JR Stutts, receiving a 30-day, 8% note.

    25. Received from Pioneer Co. the amount due on the invoice of June 15, less 1% discount.

July 21. Received the interest due from JR Stutts and a new 60-day, 9% note as a renewal of the loan of June 21. (Record both the debit and the credit to the notes receivable account.)

Sept. 19. Received from JR Stutts the amount due on her note of July 21.

    22. Sold merchandise on account to Wycoff Co., $20,000. The cost of goods sold was $12,000.

Oct. 14. Accepted a 30-day, 6% note for $20,000 from Wycoff Co. on account.

Nov. 13. Wycoff Co. dishonored the note dated October 14.

Dec. 28. Received from Wycoff Co. the amount owed on the dishonored note, plus interest for 45 days at 8% computed on the maturity value of the note.

Instructions

Journalize the entries to record the transactions.

Analysis for Decision Making

REAL WORLD

ADM-1   Continuing Company Analysis—Amazon: Accounts receivable turnover and number of days' sales in receivables

Amazon.com, Inc. is one of the largest Internet retailers in the world. **Best Buy, Inc.** is a leading retailer of consumer electronics and media products in the United States. Amazon and Best Buy compete in similar markets; however, Best Buy sells through both traditional retail stores and the Internet, while Amazon sells only through the Internet. Sales and accounts receivable information for both companies for a recent period follows (in millions):

	Amazon	Best Buy
Sales	$88,988	$40,339
Accounts receivable:		
Beginning of year	4,767	1,308
End of year	5,612	1,280

(Continued)

A. Determine the accounts receivable turnover for each company. (Round all calculations to one decimal place.)

B. Determine the number of days' sales in receivables for each company. (Round all calculations to one decimal place.)

C. ▬▬▬▶ Evaluate the relative efficiency in collecting accounts receivables between the two companies.

D. ▬▬▬▶ What might explain this difference?

SHOW ME HOW   REAL WORLD

ADM-2   Ralph Lauren: Accounts receivable turnover and number of days' sales in receivables

Ralph Lauren Corporation designs, markets, and distributes a variety of apparel, home décor, accessory, and fragrance products. The company's products include such brands as Ralph Lauren, Polo by Ralph Lauren, and Chaps. For two recent years, the company reported the following (in millions):

	Year 2	Year 1
Sales	$7,620	$7,450
Accounts receivable (end of year)	655	588

The accounts receivable at the beginning of Year 1 was $458 million.

A. Compute the accounts receivable turnover for Year 1 and Year 2. (Round to one decimal place.)

B. Compute the number of days' sales in receivables for Year 1 and Year 2. (Use 365 days and round all calculations to one decimal place.)

C. ▬▬▬▶ What conclusions can be drawn from these analyses regarding Ralph Lauren's efficiency in collecting receivables?

REAL WORLD

ADM-3   L Brands: Accounts receivable turnover and number of days' sales in receivables

L Brands, Inc. sells women's clothing and personal health care products through specialty retail stores including Victoria's Secret and Bath & Body Works stores. L Brands reported the following (in millions) for two recent years:

	Year 2	Year 1
Sales	$11,454	$10,773
Accounts receivable:		
Beginning of year	244	203
End of year	252	244

A. Determine the accounts receivable turnover for Year 1 and Year 2. (Round all calculations to one decimal place.)

B. Compute the number of days' sales in receivables for Year 1 and Year 2. (Use 365 days and round all calculations to one decimal place.)

C. ▬▬▬▶ What conclusions can be drawn from these analyses regarding L Brands' efficiency in collecting receivables?

REAL WORLD

ADM-4   Ralph Lauren and L Brands: Average accounts receivable turnover

Use the data in ADM-2 and ADM-3 to analyze the accounts receivable turnover ratios of **Ralph Lauren Corporation** and **L Brands, Inc.**

A. Compute the accounts receivable turnover ratios for Ralph Lauren and L Brands for the years shown in ADM-2 and ADM-3. Average the accounts receivable turnover ratio for the two years. Round all calculations to one decimal place.

B. Does L Brands or Ralph Lauren have the higher average accounts receivable turnover ratio?

C. ▬▬▬▶ What might explain the difference in the average accounts receivable turnover ratios between the two companies?

Take It Further

ETHICS

TIF 8-1 Ethics In Action

Bud Lighting Co. is a retailer of commercial and residential lighting products. Gowen Geter, the company's chief accountant, is in the process of making year-end adjusting entries for uncollectible accounts receivable. In recent years, the company has experienced an increase in accounts that have become uncollectible. As a result, Gowen believes that the company should increase the percentage used for estimating doubtful accounts from 2% to 4% of credit sales. This change will significantly increase bad debt expense, resulting in a drop in earnings for the first time in company history. The company president, Tim Burr, is under considerable pressure to meet earnings goals. He suggests that this is "not the right time" to change the estimate. He instructs Gowen to keep the estimate at 2%. Gowen is confident that 2% is too low, but he follows Tim's instructions.

⟹ Evaluate the decision to use the lower percentage to improve earnings. Are Tim and Gowen acting in an ethical manner?

REAL WORLD

TIF 8-2 Team Activity

In teams, select a public company that interests you and is a business that has accounts receivable. Obtain the company's most recent annual report on Form 10-K. The Form 10-K is a company's annually required filing with the Securities and Exchange Commission (SEC). It includes the company's financial statements and accompanying notes. The Form 10-K can be obtained either (A) from the investor relations section of the company's Web site or (B) by using the company search feature of the SEC's EDGAR database service found at www.sec.gov/edgar/searchedgar/companysearch.html.

1. Based on the information in the company's most recent annual report, answer the following questions:
   A. What amount of accounts receivable did the company report at the end of the most recent year?
   B. What is the balance in the company's Allowance for Uncollectible Accounts at the end of the most recent year?
   C. What percentage of total current assets is accounts receivable at the end of each of the two years presented? Has this percentage increased, decreased, or remained the same during this period?
   D. How much bad debt expense did the company report for the most recent year?

2. ⟹ Using the information presented in the company's annual report, calculate the company's accounts receivable turnover for the current and previous years. Based on this information, has the company's management of accounts receivable improved? Briefly explain your answer.

TIF 8-3 Communication

On January 1, Xtreme Co. began offering credit with terms of n/30. Uncollectible accounts are estimated to be 1% of credit sales, which is the average for the industry. The CEO, Todd Hurley, has no background in accounting and is struggling to understand the allowance method.

⟹ Write a brief memo to Todd explaining the allowance method and how this information is reported in the financial statements.

Long-Term Assets: Fixed and Intangible

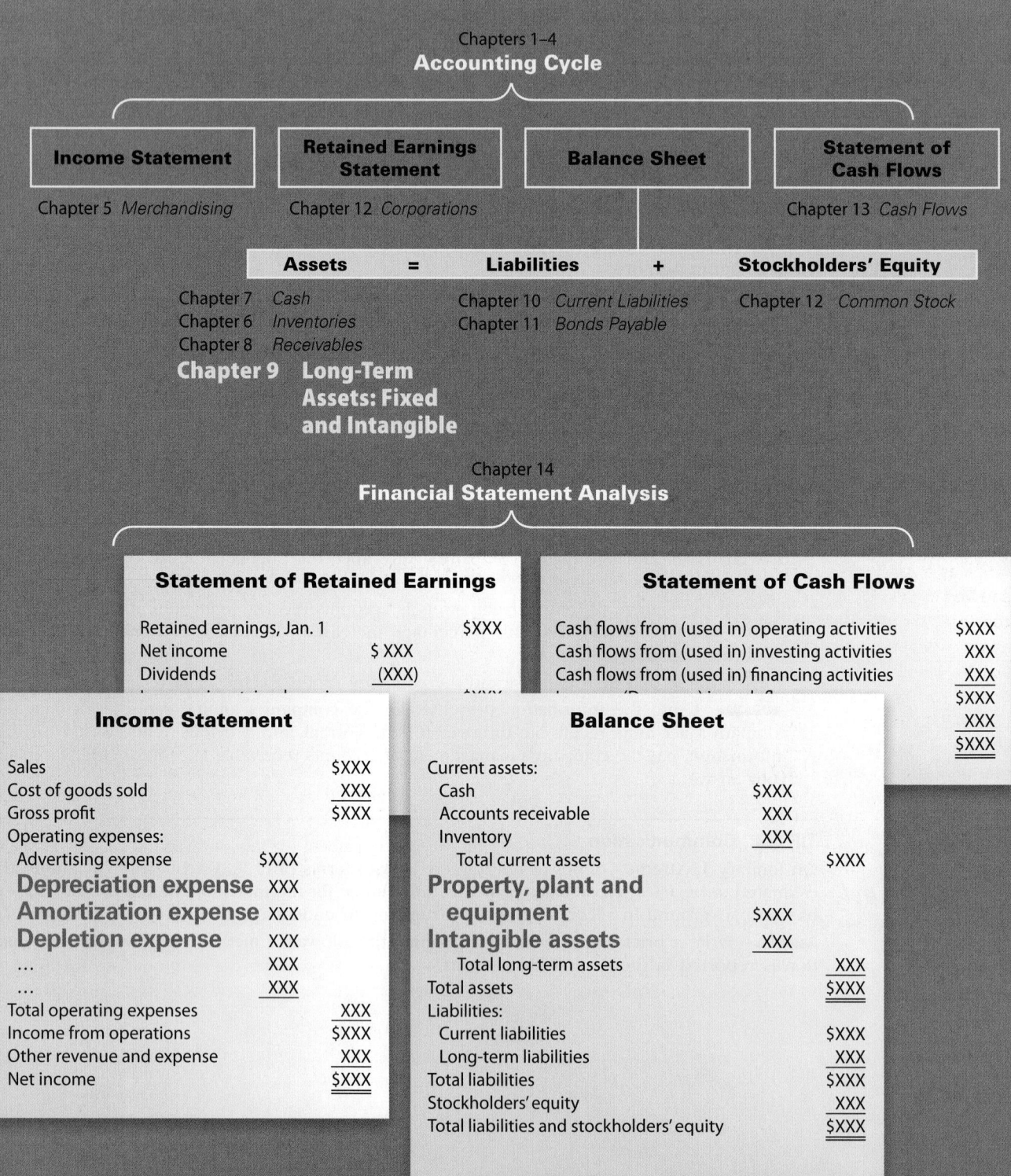

Chapters 1–4
Accounting Cycle

| Income Statement | Retained Earnings Statement | Balance Sheet | Statement of Cash Flows |

Chapter 5 *Merchandising*   Chapter 12 *Corporations*   Chapter 13 *Cash Flows*

| Assets | = | Liabilities | + | Stockholders' Equity |

Chapter 7 *Cash*   Chapter 10 *Current Liabilities*   Chapter 12 *Common Stock*
Chapter 6 *Inventories*   Chapter 11 *Bonds Payable*
Chapter 8 *Receivables*
Chapter 9 Long-Term Assets: Fixed and Intangible

Chapter 14
Financial Statement Analysis

Statement of Retained Earnings

Retained earnings, Jan. 1	$XXX
Net income	$ XXX
Dividends	(XXX)

Statement of Cash Flows

Cash flows from (used in) operating activities	$XXX
Cash flows from (used in) investing activities	XXX
Cash flows from (used in) financing activities	XXX
	$XXX
	XXX
	$XXX

Income Statement

Sales		$XXX
Cost of goods sold		XXX
Gross profit		$XXX
Operating expenses:		
Advertising expense	$XXX	
Depreciation expense	XXX	
Amortization expense	XXX	
Depletion expense	XXX	
…	XXX	
…	XXX	
Total operating expenses		XXX
Income from operations		$XXX
Other revenue and expense		XXX
Net income		$XXX

Balance Sheet

Current assets:		
Cash	$XXX	
Accounts receivable	XXX	
Inventory	XXX	
Total current assets		$XXX
Property, plant and equipment	$XXX	
Intangible assets	XXX	
Total long-term assets		XXX
Total assets		$XXX
Liabilities:		
Current liabilities		$XXX
Long-term liabilities		XXX
Total liabilities		$XXX
Stockholders' equity		XXX
Total liabilities and stockholders' equity		$XXX

McDonald's

McDonald's began in 1940 in San Bernardino, California, as a Bar-B-Q restaurant operated by two brothers, Dick and Mac McDonald. In 1954, Ray Kroc visited the restaurant and convinced the McDonald brothers to let him franchise its operations nationwide. Ray Kroc opened his first McDonald's in Des Plaines, Illinois, in 1955, with its distinguishing, newly designed Golden Arches. Today, McDonald's operates in more than 100 countries, has more than 30,000 restaurants, employs more than 400,000 people, has sold billions of hamburgers, and generates yearly revenues in excess of $27 billion.

Would you like to own and operate a McDonald's restaurant? McDonald's grants 20-year franchises to individuals who want to become owner/operators of a restaurant. Individuals may purchase either an existing or a new restaurant. When opening a new restaurant, the owner must invest in the store equipment, signs, seating, and décor. The company normally owns the land and the building. McDonald's also provides training for its owner/operators. In return, the company is paid a monthly service charge, which is either a fixed amount or a percent of sales. The total cost of opening a new restaurant may exceed several million dollars.

Obviously, the decision to open a McDonald's restaurant is a major commitment with long-lasting implications. This chapter discusses the accounting for investments in long-term, fixed assets such as a new restaurant. This accounting addresses such issues as how much of the investment should be recorded as an asset, how much should be written off as an expense each year, and how the disposal of a fixed asset should be recorded. Finally, accounting for natural resources, such as mineral deposits, and intangible assets, such as patents and copyrights, are discussed.

Source: www.aboutmcdonalds.com

What's Covered

Long-Term Assets: Fixed and Intangible

Fixed Assets
- Cost (Obj. 1)
- Depreciation (Obj. 2)
- Repairs and Improvements (Obj. 2)
- Disposal (Obj. 3)

Natural Resources
- Cost (Obj. 4)
- Depletion (Obj. 4)

Intangible Assets
- Patents, Copyrights, Trademarks, and Goodwill (Obj. 5)
- Amortization and Impairment (Obj. 5)

Reporting Long-Term Assets
- Income Statement (Obj. 6)
- Balance Sheet (Obj. 6)

Learning Objectives

Obj. 1 Define, classify, and account for the cost of fixed assets.

Obj. 2 Compute depreciation using the following methods: straight-line, units-of-activity, and double-declining-balance.

Obj. 3 Journalize the disposal of fixed assets.

Obj. 4 Describe the accounting for natural resources, including the journal entry for depletion.

Obj. 5 Describe the accounting for intangible assets, such as patents, copyrights, and goodwill.

Obj. 6 Describe how depreciation expense is reported on an income statement and prepare a balance sheet that includes fixed assets and intangible assets.

Analysis for Decision Making

Describe and illustrate the fixed asset turnover ratio to assess the efficiency of a company's use of its fixed assets.

Objective 1
Define, classify, and account for the cost of fixed assets.

Nature of Fixed Assets

Fixed assets are long-term or relatively permanent assets such as equipment, machinery, buildings, and land. Other descriptive titles for fixed assets are *plant assets* or *property, plant, and equipment*. Fixed assets have the following characteristics:

- They exist physically and, thus, are *tangible* assets.
- They are owned and used by the company in its normal operations.
- They are not offered for sale as part of normal operations.

Fixed assets are critical to the success of many businesses. For example, computers and Internet servers are critical fixed assets for a business that provides online retail or technology services.

IFRS
See Appendix C for more information.

Classifying Costs

A cost that has been incurred may be classified as a fixed asset, an investment, or an expense. Exhibit 1 shows how to determine the proper classification of a cost and how it should be recorded.

Exhibit 1
Classifying Costs

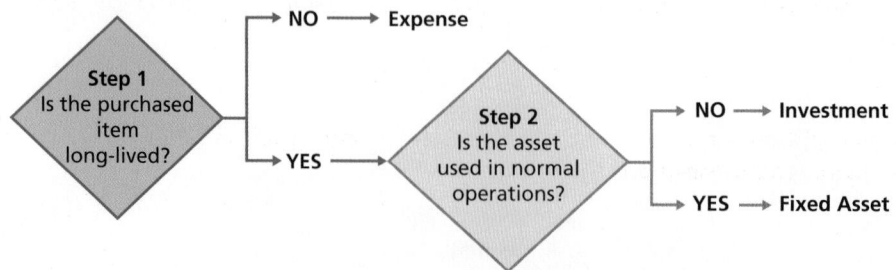

Why It Matters

Fixed Assets

Fixed assets often represent a significant portion of a company's total assets. The table that follows shows the fixed assets as a percent of total assets for some select companies across a variety of industries.

As can be seen, the type of industry will impact the proportion of fixed assets to total assets. Retail has the highest percent of fixed assets to total assets, while social media and software are on the lower end of the scale. High-tech service companies often use fewer fixed assets to deliver their services than will companies that use stores, equipment, planes, cell towers, or theme parks.

Company	Industry	Percent of Fixed Assets to Total Assets
McDonald's Corporation	Food Retail	72%
Target Corporation	Merchandise Retail	63%
Alcoa Inc.	Heavy Industry	44%
Delta Air Lines, Inc.	Transportation	41%
Verizon Communications Inc.	Communications	39%
The Walt Disney Company	Entertainment	28%
Facebook, Inc.	Social Media	10%
Microsoft Corporation	Software	8%

Fixed assets have important properties that require management attention:

- Fixed assets require a long-term commitment. Mistakes in acquiring fixed assets can be very costly and difficult to reverse, thus managers must take special care in acquiring fixed assets.
- Fixed assets wear out over time and need to be replaced. Managers must monitor fixed assets and know when to replace fixed assets due to wear and tear or obsolescence.

- Fixed assets need to be maintained during use. Managers need to develop maintenance programs to keep the investment in fixed assets productive.
- Fixed assets often require significant acquisition funds. Managers need to acquire funding internally or by other sources to finance the purchase of fixed assets.

As shown in Exhibit 1, classifying a cost involves the following steps:

- Step 1.   Is the purchased item long-lived?

   If *yes*, the item is recorded as an asset on the balance sheet, either as a fixed asset or an investment. Proceed to Step 2.

   If *no*, the item is classified and recorded as an *expense*.

- Step 2.   Is the asset used in normal operations?

   If *yes*, the asset is classified and recorded as a *fixed asset*.

   If *no*, the asset is classified and recorded as an *investment*.

Items that are classified and recorded as fixed assets include land, buildings, or equipment. Such assets normally last more than a year and are used in the normal operations of the business. However, standby equipment for use during peak periods or when other equipment breaks down is still classified as a fixed asset, even though it is not used very often. In contrast, fixed assets that have been abandoned or are no longer used in operations are not classified as fixed assets.

In a recent financial statement, McDonald's reported total property, plant, and equipment of over $40 billion, which consists of land, buildings, and equipment.

Link to McDonald's

Although fixed assets may be sold, they should not be offered for sale as part of normal operations. For example, cars and trucks offered for sale by an automotive dealership are not fixed assets of the dealership. On the other hand, a tow truck used in the normal operations of the dealership is a fixed asset of the dealership.

Investments are long-lived assets that are not used in the normal operations and are held for future resale. Such assets are reported on the balance sheet in a section entitled *Investments*. For example, undeveloped land acquired for future resale would be classified and reported as an investment, not land.

The Cost of Fixed Assets

In addition to purchase price, the costs of acquiring fixed assets include all amounts spent getting the asset in place and ready for use. For example, freight costs and the costs of installing equipment are part of the asset's total cost.

Exhibit 2 summarizes some of the common costs of acquiring fixed assets. These costs are recorded by debiting the related fixed asset account, such as Land,[1] Building, Land Improvements, or Machinery and Equipment.

Exhibit 2 Costs of Acquiring Fixed Assets

Building

- Architects' fees
- Engineers' fees
- Insurance costs incurred during construction
- Interest on money borrowed to finance construction
- Sales taxes
- Repairs (purchase of existing building)
- Reconditioning (purchase of existing building)
- Modifying for use
- Permits from government agencies

Machinery & Equipment

- Sales taxes
- Freight
- Installation
- Repairs (purchase of used equipment)
- Reconditioning (purchase of used equipment)
- Insurance while in transit
- Assembly
- Modifying for use
- Testing for use
- Permits from government agencies

Land

- Purchase price
- Sales taxes
- Permits from government agencies
- Broker's commissions
- Title fees
- Surveying fees
- Delinquent real estate taxes
- Removing unwanted building less any salvage
- Grading and leveling

Land Improvements

- Trees and shrubs
- Fences
- Outdoor lighting
- Paved parking areas or walkways

Only costs necessary for preparing the fixed asset for use are included as a cost of the asset. Unnecessary costs that do not increase the asset's usefulness are recorded as an expense. For example, the following costs are included as an expense:

- Vandalism
- Mistakes in installation

---

[1] As discussed here, land is assumed to be used only as a location or site and not for its mineral deposits or other natural resources.

- Uninsured theft
- Damage during unpacking and installing
- Fines for not obtaining proper permits from governmental agencies

To illustrate, assume Kimble Inc. purchased equipment for $12,000. Freight costs of $600 were incurred to transport the equipment to the installation site. On site, installation costs of $1,500 were incurred, including $500 due to an error in installation. The journal entry to record the equipment is as follows:

Equipment ($12,000 + $600 + $1,500 − $500)	13,600	
Cash		13,600

A = L + E
+ −

The cost of the error in installing the equipment of $500 is not included in the cost of the equipment, but instead is recorded as an expense.

A company may incur costs associated with constructing a fixed asset such as a new building. The direct costs incurred in the construction, such as labor and materials, should be capitalized as a debit to an account entitled *Construction in Progress*. When the construction is complete, the costs are reclassified by crediting Construction in Progress and debiting the proper fixed asset account such as Building.

Leasing Fixed Assets

A *lease* is a contract for the use of an asset for a period of time. Leases are often used in business. For example, automobiles, computers, medical equipment, buildings, and airplanes are often leased.

The two parties to a lease contract are as follows:

- The *lessor* is the party who owns the asset.
- The *lessee* is the party to whom the rights to use the asset are granted by the lessor.

Under a lease contract, the lessee pays rent on a periodic basis for the lease term. An advantage of leasing an asset is that the lessee has access to an asset without having to spend funds or obtain financing to buy the asset. In addition, expenses such as maintenance and repair costs may be the responsibility of the lessor. Finally, the risk of incurring additional cost because the asset becomes obsolete before the end of its useful life can be mitigated by leasing an asset.

McDonald's recently reported that it is the lessee in over 14,000 locations. The leases are normally for 20 years with an option to renew.

Link to McDonald's

The Financial Accounting Standards Board (FASB) and the International Accounting Standards Board (IASB) recently completed a project to merge U.S. and international standards on leasing.[2] The new FASB standard distinguishes between finance leases and operating leases. Under a finance lease, the lessee records an asset and liability similar to having purchased the asset. Under an operating lease, the lessee records prepaid rent (and, if necessary, a liability for future lease payments) and records rent expense as the asset is used.

For purposes of this text, we assume that all leases are operating leases that do not extend beyond one year. Thus, lease payments are recorded by debiting Rent Expense and crediting Cash. In some cases, like those illustrated in earlier chapters, Prepaid Rent is initially recorded with an adjusting entry at the end of the period to record Rent Expense.

Regardless of the type of lease, lease terms should be disclosed in the notes to the financial statements. These disclosures would include such items as the length of the lease, termination rights, and renewal options.

IFRS
See Appendix C for more information.

---

[2] Accounting Standards Update, *Leases (Topic 842)*, February, 2016, FASB (Norwalk, CT).

Objective 2
Compute depreciation using the following methods: straight-line, units-of-activity, and double-declining-balance.

Accounting for Depreciation

Over time, fixed assets, with the exception of land, lose their ability to provide services. Thus, the costs of fixed assets such as equipment and buildings should be recorded as an expense over their useful lives. Recording the cost of fixed assets as an expense is called **depreciation**. Because land has an unlimited life, it is not depreciated.

Depreciation can be caused by physical or functional factors.

- *Physical depreciation* factors include wear and tear during use or from exposure to weather.
- *Functional depreciation* factors include obsolescence and changes in customer needs that cause the asset to no longer provide services for which it was intended. For example, equipment may become obsolete due to changing technology.

Two common misunderstandings that exist about depreciation as used in accounting include:

- Depreciation does not measure a decline in the market value of a fixed asset. Instead, depreciation is an allocation of a fixed asset's cost to expense over the asset's useful life. Thus, the **book value** of a fixed asset (cost less accumulated depreciation) usually does not agree with the asset's market value. This is justified in accounting because a fixed asset is for use in a company's operations rather than for resale.
- Depreciation does not provide cash to replace fixed assets as they wear out. This misunderstanding may occur because depreciation, unlike most expenses, does not require an outlay of cash when it is recorded.

Factors in Computing Depreciation Expense

The three factors that determine the depreciation expense for a fixed asset are as follows:

- The asset's initial cost
- The asset's expected useful life
- The asset's estimated residual value

The **initial cost** of a fixed asset is the purchase price of the asset plus all costs to obtain and ready it for use. This initial cost is determined using the concepts discussed and illustrated earlier in this chapter.

The **expected useful life** of a fixed asset is the estimated length of time the asset will be used in normal operations. It is estimated at the time the asset is placed into service. Estimates of expected useful lives are available from industry trade associations. The Internal Revenue Service also publishes guidelines for useful lives, which may be helpful for financial reporting purposes. However, it is not uncommon for different companies to use a different useful life for similar assets.

McDonald's uses a useful life of up to 40 years for its buildings and from 3–5 years for its equipment.

The **residual value** of a fixed asset is the estimated value of the asset at the end of its useful life. It is estimated at the time the asset is placed into service. Residual value is sometimes referred to as *scrap value, salvage value,* or *trade-in value.*

The difference between a fixed asset's initial cost and its residual value is called the asset's **depreciable cost**. This is the asset's cost that is allocated over its useful life as depreciation expense. If a fixed asset has no residual value, then its entire cost should be allocated to depreciation.

To illustrate depreciation methods, assume **Exeter Company** purchased a new forklift on January 1 as follows:

Initial cost	$24,000
Expected useful life	5 years
Estimated residual value	$2,000

Exhibit 3 shows the relationship between depreciation expense and the forklift's initial cost, expected useful life, and estimated residual value.

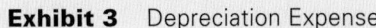

Exhibit 3   Depreciation Expense

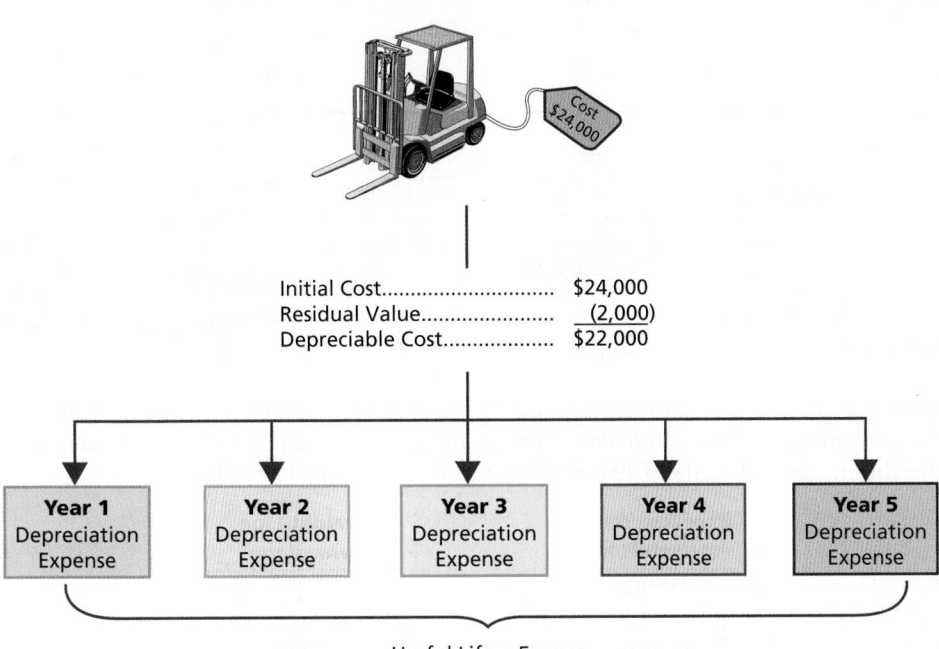

The three depreciation methods used most often are as follows:[3]

- Straight-line depreciation
- Units-of-activity depreciation
- Double-declining-balance depreciation

It is not necessary for a company to use only one method of computing depreciation for all of its fixed assets. For example, a company may use one method for depreciating equipment and another method for depreciating buildings.

Straight-Line Method

The **straight-line method** provides for the same amount of depreciation expense for each year of the asset's useful life. The annual straight-line depreciation for **Exeter**'s forklift is $4,400, computed as follows:

$$\text{Annual Depreciation} = \frac{\text{Cost} - \text{Residual Value}}{\text{Useful Life}} = \frac{\$24,000 - \$2,000}{5 \text{ Years}} = \$4,400$$

The straight-line method reports the same amount of depreciation expense each year, as illustrated in Exhibit 4.

[3] Another method not often used today, called the *sum-of-the-years-digits method*, is described and illustrated in an online appendix located at www.cengagebrain.com.

Exhibit 4 Straight-Line Method

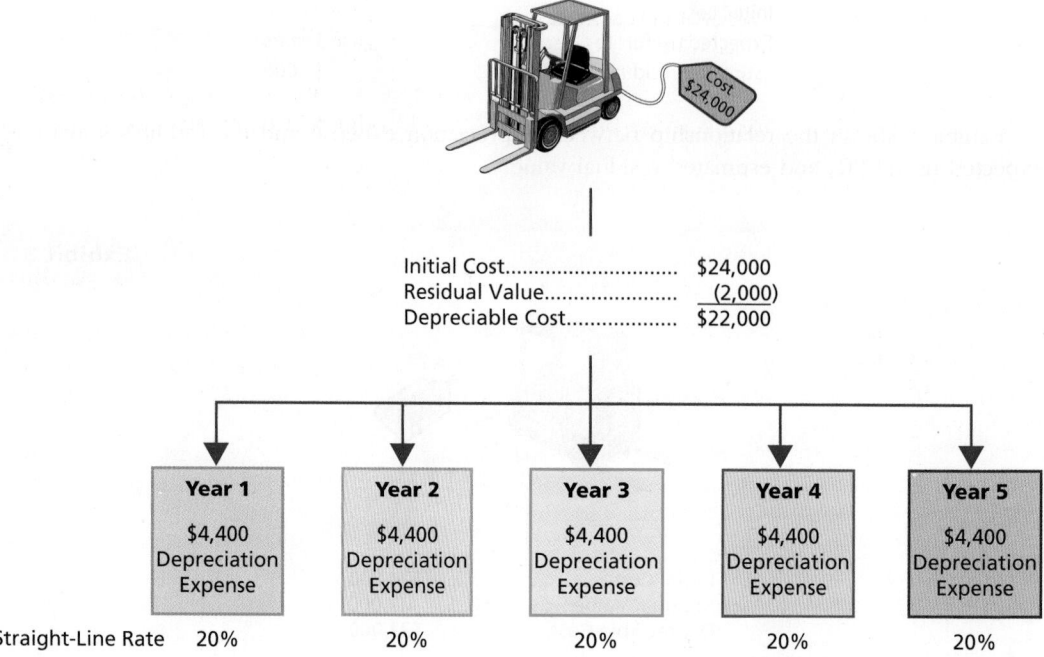

Computing straight-line depreciation may be simplified by converting the annual depreciation to a percentage of depreciable cost.[4] The straight-line percentage is determined by dividing 100% by the number of years of expected useful life, computed as follows:

Expected Years of Useful Life	Straight-Line Percentage
5 years	20% (100% ÷ 5)
8 years	12.5% (100% ÷ 8)
10 years	10% (100% ÷ 10)
20 years	5% (100% ÷ 20)
25 years	4% (100% ÷ 25)

For the preceding equipment, the annual depreciation of $4,400 can be computed by multiplying the depreciable cost of $22,000 by 20% (100% ÷ 5).

Depreciation of the forklift for the first year using the straight-line method is recorded as follows:

A = L + E
− − Exp

Dec. 31	Depreciation Expense—Forklift	4,400	
	Accumulated Depreciation—Forklift		4,400

Accumulated depreciation accounts are called *contra accounts*, or *contra asset accounts*. This is because accumulated depreciation accounts are deducted from their related fixed asset accounts on the balance sheet. The difference between the fixed asset account and its related accumulated depreciation account is called the asset's **book value** or *net book value of the asset*.

---

[4] The depreciation rate may also be expressed as a fraction. For example, the annual straight-line rate for an asset with a three-year useful life is 1/3.

The book value of the forklift at the end of the first year is $19,600. It would be reported on the balance sheet as follows:

Equipment	$24,000
Accumulated depreciation	(4,400)
Book value	$19,600

As shown in Exhibit 5, as depreciation expense is recorded each year, Accumulated Depreciation—Forklift will increase and the book value of the forklift will decrease.

Exhibit 5 Straight-Line Method: Depreciation Expense and Book Value

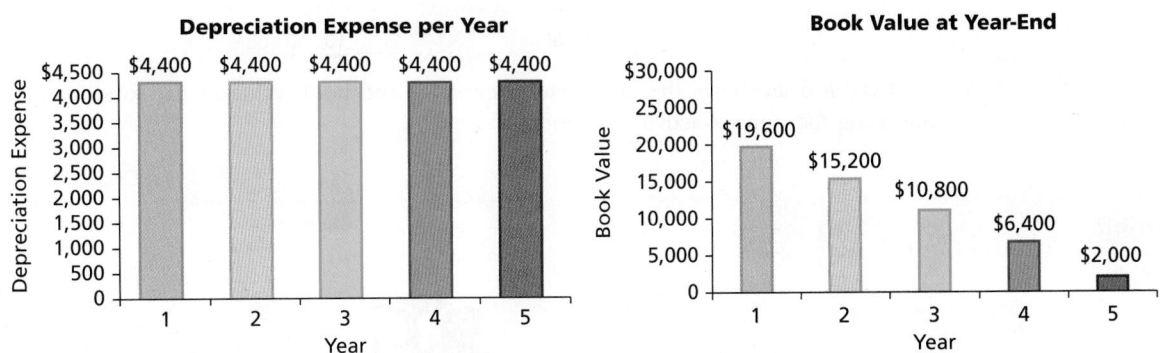

The straight-line method is simple to use. When an asset's revenues are about the same from period to period, straight-line depreciation provides a good matching of depreciation expense with the asset's revenues.

Units-of-Activity Method

The **units-of-activity method** provides the same amount of depreciation expense for each unit of activity of the asset. Depending on the asset, the units of activity can be expressed in terms of hours, miles driven, or quantity produced. For example, the unit of activity for a truck is normally expressed in miles driven. For manufacturing assets, the units of activity are often expressed as units of product. In this case, the units-of-activity method may be called the *units-of-production method* or *units-of-output method*.

The units-of-activity method is applied in the following two steps:

- Step 1. Determine the depreciation per unit as follows:

$$\text{Depreciation per Unit} = \frac{\text{Cost} - \text{Residual Value}}{\text{Total Estimated Units of Activity}}$$

- Step 2. Compute the depreciation expense as follows:

$$\text{Depreciation Expense} = \text{Depreciation per Unit} \times \text{Units of Activity for Period}$$

To illustrate, assume that Exeter's forklift is estimated to have a useful life of 10,000 operating hours over the life of the asset. During the first year, the forklift was operated 2,100 hours. The units-of-activity depreciation for the year is $4,620, computed as follows:

- Step 1. Determine the depreciation per hour as follows:

$$\text{Depreciation per Hour} = \frac{\text{Cost} - \text{Residual Value}}{\text{Total Estimated Units of Activity}} = \frac{\$24,000 - \$2,000}{10,000 \text{ Hours}} = \$2.20 \text{ per Hour}$$

- Step 2. Compute the depreciation expense as follows:

$$\text{Depreciation Expense} = \text{Depreciation per Unit} \times \text{Units of Activity for Period}$$
$$= \$2.20 \text{ per Hour} \times 2,100 \text{ Hours} = \$4,620$$

Depreciation for the first year using the units-of-activity method is recorded as follows:

A = L + E
−   − Exp

| Dec. 31 | Depreciation Expense—Forklift | 4,620 | |
| | Accumulated Depreciation—Forklift | | 4,620 |

Assume that during its five-year life, the forklift was used as follows:

Year 1	2,100 hours
Year 2	1,500
Year 3	2,600
Year 4	1,800
Year 5	2,000
Total	10,000 hours

Exhibit 6 illustrates the depreciation expense and book value of the forklift over its five-year life using the units-of-activity method.

Exhibit 6 Units-of-Activity Method

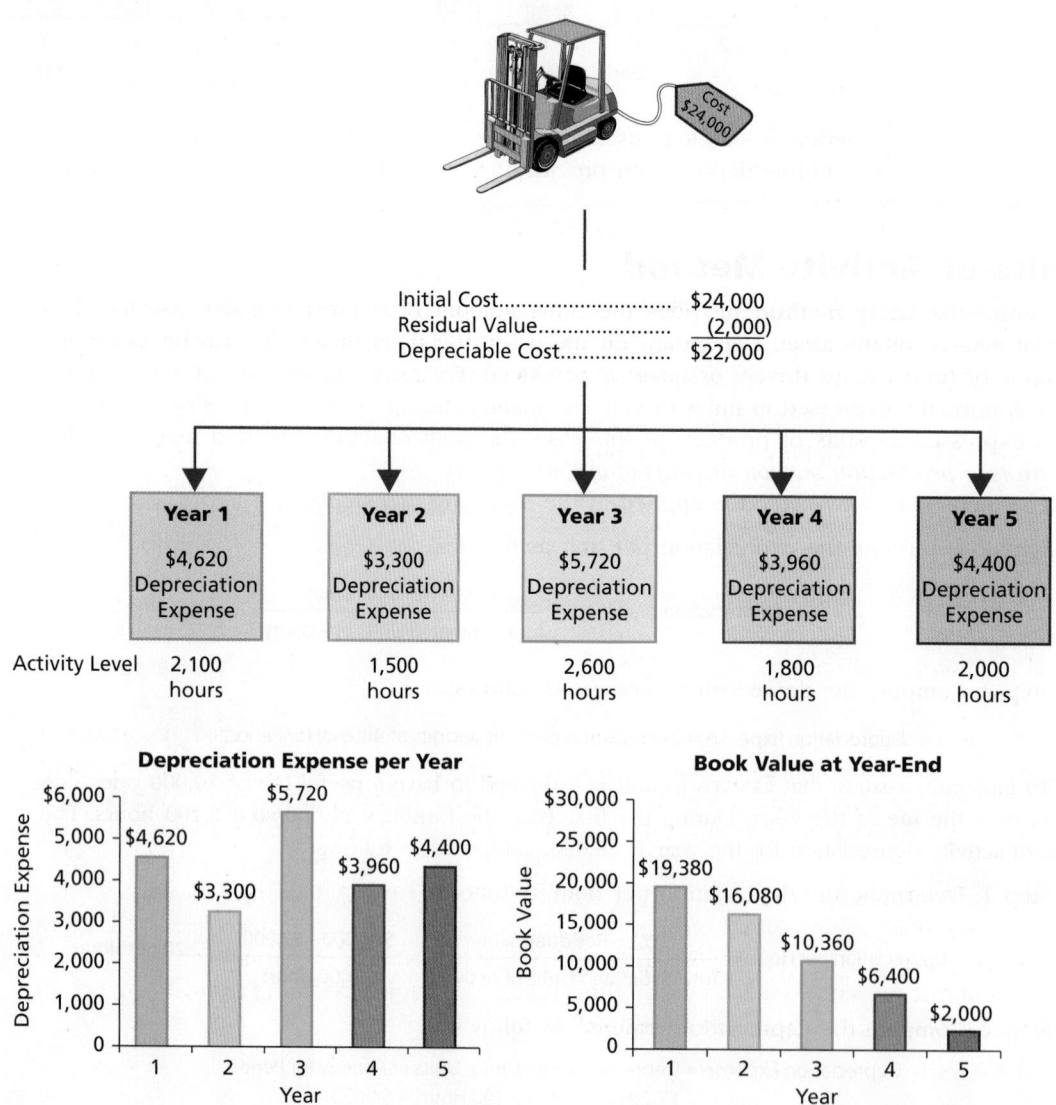

As shown in Exhibit 6, depreciation expense and book value varies each year depending on the hours the forklift is operated.

The units-of-activity method is often used when a fixed asset's use varies from year to year. In such cases, the units-of-activity method matches depreciation expense with the asset's revenues.

Double-Declining-Balance Method

The **double-declining-balance method** provides for a declining periodic expense over the expected useful life of the asset. The double-declining-balance method is applied in the following three steps:

- Step 1. Determine the straight-line percentage, using the expected useful life.
- Step 2. Determine the double-declining-balance rate by multiplying the straight-line rate (from Step 1) by 2.
- Step 3. Compute the depreciation expense by multiplying the double-declining-balance rate (from Step 2) times the book value of the asset.

To illustrate, the purchase of **Exeter**'s forklift is used to compute double-declining-balance depreciation. For the first year, the depreciation is $9,600, computed as follows:

- Step 1. Straight-line percentage = 20% (100% ÷ 5)
- Step 2. Double-declining-balance rate = 40% (20% × 2)
- Step 3. Depreciation expense = $9,600 ($24,000 × 40%)

Depreciation of the forklift for the first year using the double-declining-balance method is recorded as follows:

Dec. 31	Depreciation Expense—Forklift	9,600	
	Accumulated Depreciation—Forklift		9,600

A = L + E
–   – Exp

For the first year, the book value of the equipment is its initial cost of $24,000. After the first year, the book value declines, and thus, the depreciation also declines. The double-declining-balance depreciation for the full five-year life of the forklift is as follows:

Year	Cost	Acc. Dep. at Beginning of Year	Book Value at Beginning of Year	Double-Declining-Balance Rate		Depreciation for Year	Book Value at End of Year
1	$24,000		$24,000.00	×	40%	$9,600.00	$14,400.00
2	24,000	$ 9,600.00	14,400.00	×	40%	5,760.00	8,640.00
3	24,000	15,360.00	8,640.00	×	40%	3,456.00	5,184.00
4	24,000	18,816.00	5,184.00	×	40%	2,073.60	3,110.40
5	24,000	20,889.60	3,110.40		—	1,110.40	2,000.00

When the double-declining-balance method is used, the estimated residual value is *not* considered. However, the asset should not be depreciated below its estimated residual value. In the preceding example, the estimated residual value was $2,000. Therefore, the depreciation for the fifth year is $1,110.40 ($3,110.40 − $2,000.00) instead of $1,244.16 (40% × $3,110.40).

Exhibit 7 illustrates the depreciation expense and book value of the forklift over its five-year life using the double-declining-balance method. As shown in Exhibit 7, the double-declining-balance method has higher depreciation in the first year of the asset's life, followed by declining depreciation amounts. For this reason, the double-declining-balance method is called an **accelerated depreciation method**.

Exhibit 7   Double-Declining-Balance Method

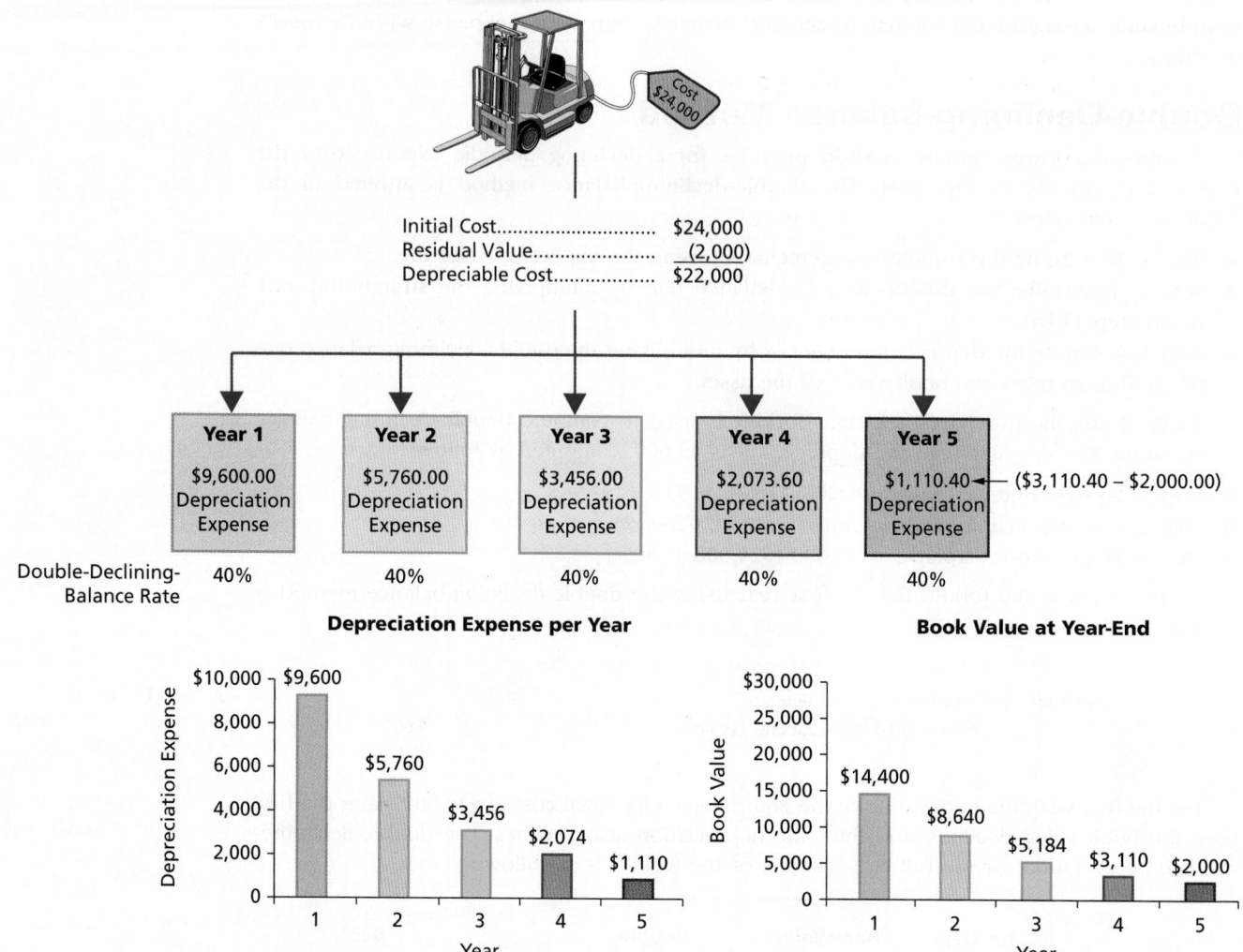

Revenues generated by an asset are often greater in the early years of its use than in later years. In such cases, the double-declining-balance method provides a good matching of depreciation expense with the asset's revenues.

Comparing Depreciation Methods

The three depreciation methods are summarized in Exhibit 8. All three methods allocate a portion of the total cost of an asset to an accounting period, while never depreciating an asset below its residual value.

Exhibit 8

Summary of Depreciation Methods

Method	Useful Life	Depreciable Cost	Depreciation Rate	Depreciation Expense
Straight-line	Years	Cost less residual value	Straight-line rate*	Constant
Units-of-activity	Units of activity	Cost less residual value	$\dfrac{\text{Cost} - \text{Residual value}}{\text{Total units of activity}}$	Variable
Double-declining-balance	Years	Declining book value, but not below residual value	Straight-line rate* × 2	Declining

*Straight-line rate = (100% ÷ Useful life)

The straight-line method provides for the same periodic amounts of depreciation expense over the life of the asset. The units-of-activity method provides for periodic amounts of depreciation expense that vary, depending on the amount the asset is used. The double-declining-balance method provides for a higher depreciation amount in the first year of the asset's use, followed by declining amounts.

Exhibit 9 illustrates depreciation expense for each depreciation method over the five-year life of the forklift.

| | Depreciation Expense | | |
| | Straight-Line | Units-of-Activity | Double-Declining-Balance |
Year	Method	Method	Method
1	$ 4,400*	$ 4,620 ($2.20 × 2,100 hrs.)	$ 9,600.00 ($24,000 × 40%)
2	4,400	3,300 ($2.20 × 1,500 hrs.)	5,760.00 ($14,400 × 40%)
3	4,400	5,720 ($2.20 × 2,600 hrs.)	3,456.00 ($8,640 × 40%)
4	4,400	3,960 ($2.20 × 1,800 hrs.)	2,073.60 ($5,184 × 40%)
5	4,400	4,400 ($2.20 × 2,000 hrs.)	1,110.40**
Total	$22,000	$22,000	$22,000.00

Exhibit 9
Comparing Depreciation Methods

DYNAMIC EXHIBIT

*$4,400 = ($24,000 – $2,000) ÷ 5 years

**$3,110.40 – $2,000.00 because the equipment cannot be depreciated below its residual value of $2,000.

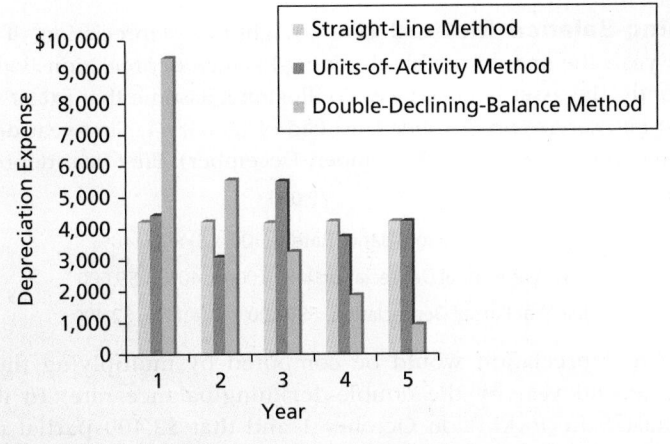

Partial-Year Depreciation

A fixed asset may be purchased and placed in service other than the first month of an accounting period. In such cases, depreciation is prorated based on the month the asset is placed in service. For example, assume an asset is placed in service on March 1. For an accounting period ending December 31, depreciation would be computed (prorated) for 10 months (March 1 to December 31).

Why It Matters

Tax Return Depreciation

The Internal Revenue Code uses the Modified Cost Recovery System (MACRS) to compute depreciation for tax purposes. Depreciation under MACRS is similar to that computed under the double-declining-balance method. MACRS is beneficial for tax purposes since depreciation is accelerated, thus creating faster tax deductions. Thus, most companies use straight-line depreciation for their financial statements and MACRS for their tax accounting. This is a major reason for accounting and tax income to differ.

Assets may also be placed in service other than the first day of a month. In such cases, assets placed in service during the first half of a month are normally treated as having been purchased on the first day of *that* month. Likewise, asset purchases during the second half of a month are treated as having been purchased on the first day of the *next* month.

Straight-Line Method Under the straight-line method, depreciation is prorated based on the number of months the asset is in service. To illustrate, assume that **Exeter Company** purchased the forklift on October 1 instead of January 1. The first-year depreciation would be based upon three months (October, November, December). First-year depreciation would be $1,100, computed as follows:

$$\text{Annual Depreciation} = (\$24,000 - \$2,000) \div 5 \text{ years} = \$4,400$$
$$\text{First-Year Depreciation} = \$4,400 \times (3 \div 12) = \$1,100$$

Units-of-Activity Method The units-of-activity method computes depreciation expense using an activity rate and the activity level for the period. To illustrate, assume that **Exeter** purchased the forklift on October 1 instead of January 1. Assume that during October 1 to December 31, the forklift was used for 400 hours. First-year depreciation would be $880, computed as follows:

$$\text{Depreciation per Hour} = (\$24,000 - \$2,000) \div 10,000 \text{ Hours} = \$2.20 \text{ per Hour}$$
$$\text{First-Year Depreciation} = \$2.20 \text{ per Hour} \times 400 \text{ Hours} = \$880$$

Double-Declining-Balance Method Like straight-line depreciation, if an asset is used for only part of a year, the annual double-declining-balance depreciation is prorated based on the number of months the asset is in service. To illustrate, assume that **Exeter**'s forklift was purchased and placed into service on October 1 instead of January 1. First-year depreciation would be based upon three months (October, November, December). First-year depreciation would be $2,400, computed as follows:

$$\text{Double-Declining-Balance Rate} = (100 \div 5) \times 2 = 40\%$$
$$\text{First-Year Annual Depreciation} = \$24,000 \times 40\% = \$9,600$$
$$\text{First-Year Partial Depreciation} = \$9,600 \times (3 \div 12) = \$2,400$$

The second-year depreciation would be computed by multiplying the book value on January 1 of the second year by the double-declining-balance rate. To illustrate, assume that Exeter purchased the forklift on October 1 and that $2,400 partial depreciation was recorded on December 31. The book value on January 1 of the second year is $21,600 ($24,000 − $2,400). The second-year depreciation would then be $8,640, computed as follows:

$$\text{Second-Year Annual Depreciation} = \$21,600 \times 40\% = \$8,640$$

Revising Depreciation Estimates

Estimates of residual values and useful lives of fixed assets may change due to abnormal wear and tear or obsolescence. When new estimates are made by management, they are used to determine the depreciation expense in future periods. The depreciation expense recorded in earlier years is not affected.[5]

To illustrate, assume the following data for a machine that was purchased on January 1:

Initial machine cost	$140,000
Expected useful life	5 years
Estimated residual value	$10,000
Annual depreciation using the straight-line method	
[($140,000 − $10,000) ÷ 5 years]	$26,000

---

[5] *FASB Accounting Standards Codification*, Section 250-10-05.

At the end of the second year, the machine's book value (undepreciated cost) is $88,000, computed as follows:

Initial machine cost	$140,000
Accumulated depreciation ($26,000 per year × 2 years)	(52,000)
Book value (undepreciated cost), end of second year	$ 88,000

At the beginning of the third year, the company estimates that the machine's remaining useful life is eight years (instead of three) and that its residual value is $8,000 (instead of $10,000). The depreciation expense for each of the remaining eight years is $10,000, computed as follows:

$$\text{Revised Depreciation Expense} = \frac{\text{Book Value} - \text{Revised Residual Value}}{\text{Revised Remaining Useful Life}} = \frac{\$88,000 - \$8,000}{8\,\text{Years}} = \$10,000$$

Exhibit 10 shows the book value of the asset over its original and revised lives. After the depreciation is revised at the end of the second year, book value declines at a slower rate. At the end of the tenth year, the book value reaches the revised residual value of $8,000.

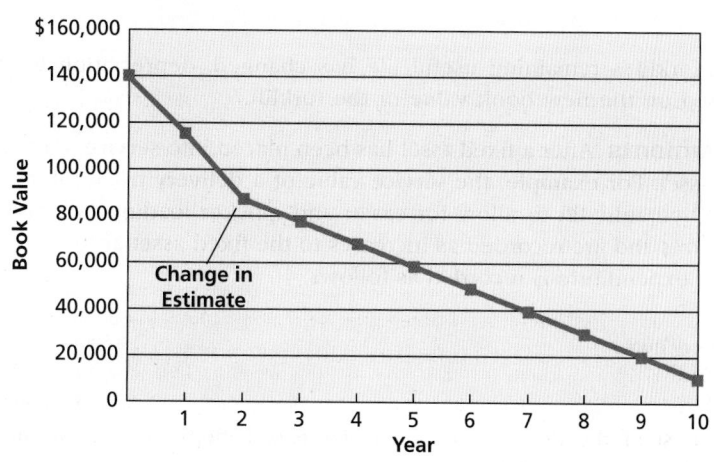

Exhibit 10
Book Value of Asset with Change in Estimate

Repair and Improvements

Once a fixed asset has been acquired and placed into service, costs may be incurred for ordinary maintenance and repairs. In addition, costs may be incurred for improving an asset or for extraordinary repairs that extend the asset's useful life. Costs that benefit only the current period are called **revenue expenditures**. Costs that improve the asset or extend its useful life are **capital expenditures**.

IFRS

See Appendix C for more information.

Ordinary Maintenance and Repairs Costs related to the ordinary maintenance and repairs of a fixed asset are recorded as an expense of the current period. Such expenditures are *revenue expenditures* and are recorded as increases to Repairs and Maintenance Expense. For example, $300 paid for a tune-up of a delivery truck is recorded as follows:

Repairs and Maintenance Expense	300	
Cash		300

A = L + E
−   − Exp

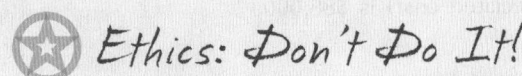 Ethics: Don't Do It!

Capital Crime

One of the largest accounting frauds in history involved the improper accounting for maintenance expenditures. WorldCom, the second largest telecommunications company in the United States at the time, improperly treated maintenance expenditures on its telecommunications network as capital expenditures. As a result, the company had to restate its prior years' earnings downward by nearly $4 billion to correct this error. The company declared bankruptcy within months of disclosing the error, and the CEO was sentenced to 25 years in prison.

Extraordinary Repairs After a fixed asset has been placed into service, costs may be incurred to extend the asset's useful life. For example, the engine of a forklift that is near the end of its useful life may be overhauled at a cost of $4,500, extending its useful life by eight years. Such costs are *capital expenditures* and are recorded as a decrease in an accumulated depreciation account. In the case of the forklift, the expenditure is recorded as follows:

A = L + E
+ –

Accumulated Depreciation—Forklift	4,500	
Cash		4,500

Because the forklift's remaining useful life has changed, depreciation for the forklift will also change based on the new book value of the forklift.

Asset Improvements After a fixed asset has been placed into service, costs may be incurred to improve the asset. For example, the service value of a delivery truck might be improved by adding a $5,500 hydraulic lift to allow for easier and quicker loading of cargo. Such costs are *capital expenditures* and are recorded as increases to the fixed asset account. In the case of the hydraulic lift, the expenditure is recorded as follows:

A = L + E
+ –

Delivery Truck	5,500	
Cash		5,500

Because the cost of the delivery truck has increased, depreciation for the truck will also change over its remaining useful life.

The accounting for revenue and capital expenditures is summarized in Exhibit 11.

Exhibit 11
Revenue
and Capital
Expenditures

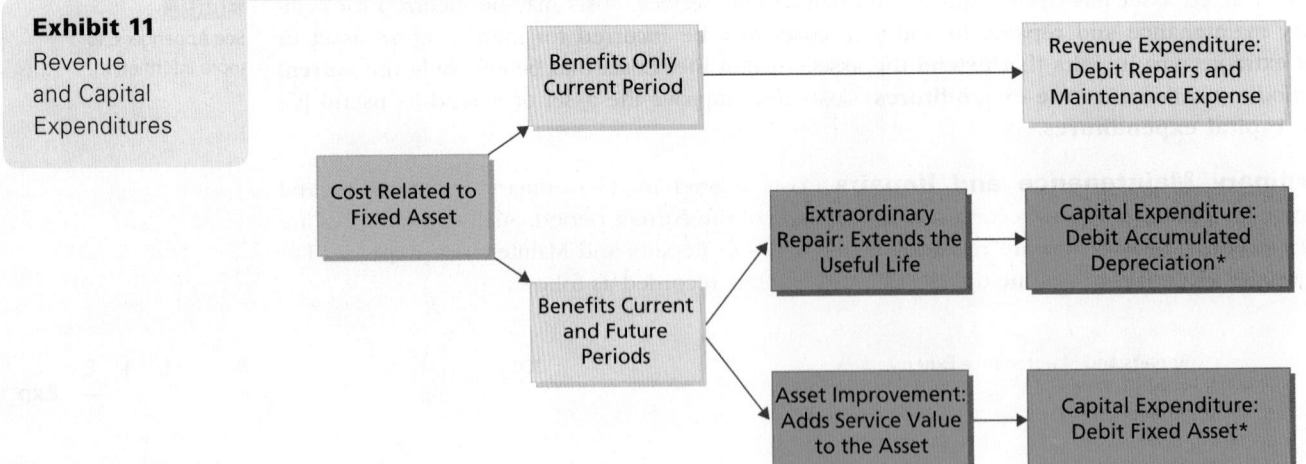

* Revise depreciation.

Disposal of Fixed Assets

Fixed assets that are no longer useful may be discarded or sold.[6] In such cases, the fixed asset is removed from the accounts. Just because a fixed asset is fully depreciated, however, does not mean that it should be removed from the accounts.

If a fixed asset is still being used, its cost and accumulated depreciation should remain in the ledger even if the asset is fully depreciated. If the asset was removed from the ledger, the accounts would contain no evidence of their continued existence. In addition, cost and accumulated depreciation data on such assets are often needed for property tax and income tax reports.

Discarding Fixed Assets

If a fixed asset is no longer used and has no residual value, it is discarded. For example, assume that a fixed asset is fully depreciated, has no residual value, and is discarded. The discarded asset and its accumulated depreciation are removed from the accounts and ledger.

To illustrate, assume that equipment acquired at a cost of $25,000 is fully depreciated. On February 14, the equipment is discarded. The entry to record the discard is as follows:

Feb. 14	Accumulated Depreciation—Equipment	25,000	
	Equipment		25,000
	To write off equipment discarded.		

$$A = L + E$$
$$+ -$$

If an asset has not been fully depreciated, depreciation should be recorded before removing the asset from the accounting records. To illustrate, assume that equipment costing $6,000 with no estimated residual value is depreciated at a straight-line rate of 10%. The accumulated depreciation balance, after adjusting entries, is $4,650 on December 31. On March 24 of the following year, the asset is removed from service and discarded. The entry to record the depreciation for the three months before the asset is discarded is as follows:

Mar. 24	Depreciation Expense—Equipment	150	
	Accumulated Depreciation—Equipment		150
	To record current depreciation on equipment discarded ($600 × 3/12).		

$$A = L + E$$
$$- \qquad - Exp$$

The discarding of the equipment is then recorded as follows:

Mar. 24	Accumulated Depreciation—Equipment	4,800	
	Loss on Disposal of Equipment	1,200	
	Equipment		6,000
	To write off equipment discarded.		

$$A = L + E$$
$$+ - \qquad - Loss$$

The loss of $1,200 is recorded because the balance of the accumulated depreciation account ($4,800) is less than the balance in the equipment account ($6,000). Losses on the discarding of fixed assets are reported on the income statement.

---

[6] The accounting for the exchange of fixed assets is described and illustrated in the appendix at the end of this chapter.

Selling Fixed Assets

The entry to record the sale of a fixed asset is similar to the entry for discarding an asset. The only difference is that the receipt of cash is also recorded. If the selling price is more than the book value of the asset, a gain is recorded. If the selling price is less than the book value, a loss is recorded.

To illustrate, assume that equipment is purchased at a cost of $10,000 with no estimated residual value and is depreciated at a straight-line rate of 10%. The equipment is sold for cash on October 12 of the eighth year of its use. The balance of the accumulated depreciation account as of the preceding December 31 is $7,000. The entry to update the depreciation for the nine months of the current year is as follows:

A = L + E
−   − Exp

Oct. 12	Depreciation Expense—Equipment		750	
	Accumulated Depreciation—Equipment			750
	To record current depreciation on			
	equipment sold ($10,000 × $^{9}/_{12}$ × 10%).			

After the current depreciation is recorded, the book value of the asset is $2,250 ($10,000 − $7,750). The entries to record the sale, assuming three different selling prices, are as follows:

Sold at book value, for $2,250. No gain or loss.

A = L + E
+ −

Oct. 12	Cash		2,250	
	Accumulated Depreciation—Equipment		7,750	
	Equipment			10,000

Sold below book value, for $1,000. Loss of $1,250.

A = L + E
+ −   − Loss

Oct. 12	Cash		1,000	
	Accumulated Depreciation—Equipment		7,750	
	Loss on Sale of Equipment		1,250	
	Equipment			10,000

Sold above book value, for $2,800. Gain of $550.

A = L + E
+ −   + Gain

Oct. 12	Cash		2,800	
	Accumulated Depreciation—Equipment		7,750	
	Equipment			10,000
	Gain on Sale of Equipment			550

Why It Matters

Downsizing

Management may decide to sell a fixed asset when it is perceived to no longer meet business objectives. This can happen when the strategy of the business changes or the business is downsizing operations. For example, Ruby Tuesday, a national restaurant chain, sold stores and equipment at a book value of $14 million for cash proceeds of $15.4 million, resulting in a $1.4 million gain. These fixed assets were sold in order to focus on more profitable restaurants.

Check Up Corner 9-1 Fixed Assets

On the first day of the year, Firefall Company acquired equipment for use in operations at a cost of $340,000. The equipment was expected to have a useful life of four years or 1,000 hours, and a residual value of $20,000. The equipment was used for 280 hours during the first year, 260 hours during the second year, 240 hours during the third year, and 220 hours during the fourth year.

A. Determine the annual depreciation expense in each year and the book value of the equipment at the end of each year under the:
   1. straight-line method
   2. units-of-activity method
   3. double-declining-balance method

B. Assuming the equipment was sold for $95,000 on the first day of the fourth year of operations, journalize the entry to record the sale if the equipment was depreciated under the:
   1. straight-line method
   2. units-of-activity method
   3. double-declining-balance method

Solution:

A. 1. Straight-Line Method:

$$\frac{\text{Annual}}{\text{Depreciation Expense}} = \frac{\text{Cost} - \text{Residual Value}}{\text{Useful Life}} = \frac{\$340,000 - \$20,000}{4 \text{ Years}} = \$80,000$$

The straight-line percentage is computed as follows:

$$\text{Straight-Line Percentage} = \frac{100\%}{4 \text{ Years}} = 25\%$$

Annual depreciation expense and end-of-year book value are computed as follows:

| | Calculation of Depreciation | | | | | End of Year | |
Year	Straight-Line Percentage	×	Depreciable Cost	=	Annual Depreciation Expense	Accumulated Depreciation	Book Value
1	25%	×	$320,000	=	$80,000	$ 80,000	$260,000
2	25%	×	320,000	=	80,000	160,000	180,000
3	25%	×	320,000	=	80,000	240,000	100,000
4	25%	×	320,000	=	80,000	320,000	20,000

Book Value = Asset Cost ($340,000) − Accumulated Depreciation

Ending Book Value = Residual Value

2. Units-of-Activity Method:

$$\frac{\text{Depreciation per}}{\text{Hour of Use}} = \frac{\text{Cost} - \text{Residual Value}}{\text{Total Number of Hours}} = \frac{\$340,000 - \$20,000}{1,000 \text{ Hours}} = \$320 \text{ per Hour}$$

Annual depreciation expense and end-of-year book value are computed as follows:

| | Calculation of Depreciation | | | | | End of Year | |
Year	Depreciation per Hour of Use	×	Total Hours of Activity Used	=	Annual Depreciation Expense	Accumulated Depreciation	Book Value
1	$320	×	280	=	$89,600	$ 89,600	$250,400
2	320	×	260	=	83,200	172,800	167,200
3	320	×	240	=	76,800	249,600	90,400
4	320	×	220	=	70,400	320,000	20,000

Book Value = Asset Cost ($340,000) − Accumulated Depreciation

Ending Book Value = Residual Value

3. Double-Declining-Balance Method:

$$\text{Straight-Line Percentage} = \frac{100\%}{4 \text{ Years}} = 25\%$$

$$\text{Double-Declining-Balance Rate} = 2 \times 25\% = 50\%$$

Annual depreciation expense and end-of-year book value are computed as follows:

Year	Book Value at Beginning of Year	×	Double-Declining-Balance Rate	=	Annual Depreciation Expense	Accumulated Depreciation	Book Value
1	$340,000	×	50%	=	$170,000	$170,000	$170,000
2	170,000	×	50%	=	85,000	255,000	85,000
3	85,000	×	50%	=	42,500	297,500	42,500
4	42,500		not applicable		22,500	320,000	20,000

Book Value =
Asset Cost ($340,000) −
Accumulated Depreciation

Ending Book Value =
Residual Value

Final Year Depreciation Expense = Book Value at Beginning of
Final Year − Residual Value
= $42,500 − $20,000

B. 1. Straight-Line Method:

Cash	95,000	
Accumulated Depreciation—Equipment	240,000	
Loss on Sale of Equipment	5,000	
Equipment		340,000

2. Units-of-Activity Method:

Cash	95,000	
Accumulated Depreciation—Equipment	249,600	
Equipment		340,000
Gain on Sale of Equipment		4,600

Accumulated Depreciation
at the End of Year 3

3. Double-Declining-Balance Method:

Cash	95,000	
Accumulated Depreciation—Equipment	297,500	
Equipment		340,000
Gain on Sale of Equipment		52,500

Check Up Corner

Natural Resources

Objective 4
Describe the accounting for natural resources, including the journal entry for depletion.

Some businesses own natural resources such as timber, minerals, or oil. The characteristics of natural resources are as follows:

- **Naturally Occurring:** An asset that is created through natural growth or naturally through the passage of time. For example, timber is a natural resource that naturally grows over time.
- **Removed for Sale:** The asset is consumed by removing it from its land source. For example, timber is removed for use when it is harvested, and minerals are removed when they are mined.
- **Removed and Sold over More Than One Year:** The natural resource is removed and sold over a period of more than one year.

Natural resources are classified as a type of fixed asset. The cost of a natural resource includes the cost of obtaining and preparing it for use. For example, legal fees incurred in purchasing a natural resource are included as part of its cost.

As natural resources are harvested or mined and then sold, a portion of their cost is debited to an expense account called **depletion expense**.

Depletion is determined as follows:[7]

- Step 1. Determine the depletion rate as follows:

$$\text{Depletion Rate} = \frac{\text{Cost of Resource}}{\text{Estimated Total Units of Resource}}$$

- Step 2. Multiply the depletion rate by the quantity removed from the resource during the period.

$$\text{Depletion Expense} = \text{Depletion Rate} \times \text{Quantity Removed}$$

To illustrate, assume that Karst Company purchased mining rights as follows:

Cost of mineral deposit	$400,000
Estimated total units of resource	1,000,000 tons
Tons mined during year	90,000 tons

The depletion expense of $36,000 for the year is computed as follows:

$$\text{Step 1. Depletion Rate} = \frac{\text{Cost of Resource}}{\text{Estimated Total Units of Resource}} = \frac{\$400,000}{1,000,000 \text{ Tons}} = \$0.40 \text{ per Ton}$$

Step 2. Depletion Expense = $0.40 per Ton × 90,000 Tons = $36,000

The adjusting entry to record the depletion is as follows:

Dec. 31	Depletion Expense		36,000	
	Accumulated Depletion			36,000
	Depletion of mineral deposit.			

A = L + E
–   – Exp

Like the accumulated depreciation account, Accumulated Depletion is a contra asset account. It is reported on the balance sheet as a deduction from the cost of the mineral deposit.

---

[7] We assume that there is no significant residual value after all the natural resource is removed.

Check Up Corner 9-2   Natural Resources

Caldwell Mining Co. acquired mineral rights for $126,000,000. The mineral deposit is estimated at 42,000,000 tons. During the current year, 3,800,000 tons were mined and sold.

A. What is the depletion rate per ton?
B. Determine the amount of depletion expense for the current year.
C. Journalize the adjusting entry to recognize depletion expense at the end of the year.

Solution:

A. Depletion Rate $= \dfrac{\text{Cost of Resource}}{\text{Estimated Total Units of Resource}} = \dfrac{\$126,000,000}{42,000,000 \text{ Tons}} = \$3.00 \text{ per Ton}$

B. Depletion Expense = Depletion Rate × Quantity Removed
= $3.00 per Ton × 3,800,000 Tons
= $11,400,000

C.

Depletion Expense	11,400,000	
Accumulated Depletion		11,400,000

Check Up Corner

Objective 5
Describe the accounting for intangible assets, such as patents, copyrights, and goodwill.

IFRS
See Appendix C for more information.

Intangible Assets

Long-term assets that are used in the operations of the business, but do not exist physically, are called intangible assets. **Intangible assets** may be acquired through innovative, creative activities or from purchasing the rights from another company. Examples of intangible assets include patents, copyrights, trademarks, and goodwill.

The accounting for intangible assets is similar to that for fixed assets. The major issues are:

- Determining the initial cost.
- Determining the **amortization**, which is the amount of cost to transfer to expense.

Amortization results from the passage of time or a decline in the usefulness of the intangible asset.

Patents

Manufacturers may acquire exclusive rights to produce and sell goods with one or more unique features. Such rights are granted by **patents**, which the federal government issues to inventors. These rights continue in effect for 20 years. A business may purchase patent rights from others, or it may obtain patents developed by its own research and development.

Why It Matters

Facebook Value

The market value of Facebook can be determined by multiplying the common stock outstanding by the market price per share. The market value of Facebook at the end of a recent year was $160 billion. The book value of stockholder's equity (net assets) of Facebook on the same date was $15.5 billion. The difference of $144.5 billion is the unrecognized intangible assets of Facebook. Intangible assets that are recognized for accounting purposes are only those that are supported by a business transaction. For Facebook, these include acquired goodwill, patents, technology, and trade name, which total only $1.7 billion. Technology companies, such as Facebook, will typically have large unrecognized intangible value beyond that recorded for accounting purposes.

The initial cost of a purchased patent, including any legal fees, is debited to an asset account. This cost is written off, or amortized, over the years of the patent's expected useful life. The expected useful life of a patent may be less than its legal life. For example, a patent may become worthless due to changing technology or consumer tastes.

Patent amortization is normally computed using the straight-line method. The amortization is recorded by debiting an amortization expense account and crediting the patents account. A separate contra asset account is usually *not* used for intangible assets.

To illustrate, assume that at the beginning of its fiscal year, a company acquires patent rights for $100,000. Although the patent will not expire for 14 years, its remaining useful life is estimated as five years. The adjusting entry to amortize the patent at the end of the year is as follows:

Dec. 31	Amortization Expense—Patents		20,000	
	Patents			20,000
	Patent amortization ($100,000 ÷ 5).			

$$A = L + E$$
$$- \qquad\qquad - \text{Exp}$$

Some companies develop their own patents through research and development. In such cases, any *research and development costs* are usually recorded as current operating expenses in the period in which they are incurred. This accounting for research and development costs is justified on the basis that any future benefits from current research and development are highly uncertain.

Copyrights and Trademarks

The exclusive right to publish and sell a literary, artistic, or musical composition is granted by a **copyright**. Copyrights are issued by the federal government and extend for 70 years beyond the author's death. The costs of a copyright include all costs of creating the work plus any other costs of obtaining the copyright. A copyright that is purchased is recorded at the price paid for it. Copyrights are amortized over their estimated useful lives.

A **trademark** is a name, term, or symbol used to identify a business and its products. Under federal law, businesses can protect their trademarks by registering them for 10 years and renewing the registration for 10-year periods. Like a copyright, the legal costs of registering a trademark are recorded as an asset. Most businesses identify their registered trademarks with ® in their advertisements and on their products.

If a trademark is purchased from another business, its cost is recorded as an asset. In such cases, the cost of the trademark is considered to have an indefinite useful life. Thus, trademarks are not amortized. Instead, trademarks are reviewed periodically for impaired value. When a trademark is impaired, the trademark should be written down and a loss recognized.

McDonald's Corporation owns trademarks on "McDonald's" and the Golden Arches logo.

Link to McDonald's

Goodwill

Goodwill refers to an intangible asset of a business that is created from such favorable factors as location, product quality, reputation, and managerial skill. Goodwill allows a business to earn a greater rate of return than normal.

Generally accepted accounting principles (GAAP) allow goodwill to be recorded only if it is objectively determined by a transaction. An example of such a transaction is the purchase of a business at a price in excess of the fair value of its net assets (assets less liabilities). The excess is recorded as goodwill and reported as an intangible asset.

Link to McDonald's

On a recent balance sheet, **McDonald's** reported goodwill of $2.9 billion. Most of McDonald's goodwill arises when it purchases existing restaurants from franchisees.

Unlike patents and copyrights, goodwill is not amortized. However, a loss should be recorded if the future prospects of the purchased firm become impaired. This loss would normally be disclosed in the Other Expense section of the income statement.

To illustrate, assume that on December 31 FaceCard Company has determined that $250,000 of the goodwill created from the purchase of Electronic Systems is impaired. The entry to record the impairment is as follows:

A = L + E
–   – **Loss**

Dec. 31	Loss from Impaired Goodwill	250,000	
	Goodwill		250,000
	Impaired goodwill.		

Link to McDonald's

McDonald's compares fair value to book (carrying) value to determine whether goodwill is impaired. In a recent annual report, McDonald's reported that it did not have any goodwill at risk of impairment.

Exhibit 12 shows common intangible asset disclosures for 500 large firms. Goodwill is the most often reported intangible asset. This is because goodwill arises from merger transactions, which are common.

Exhibit 12

Frequency of Intangible Asset Disclosures for 500 Firms

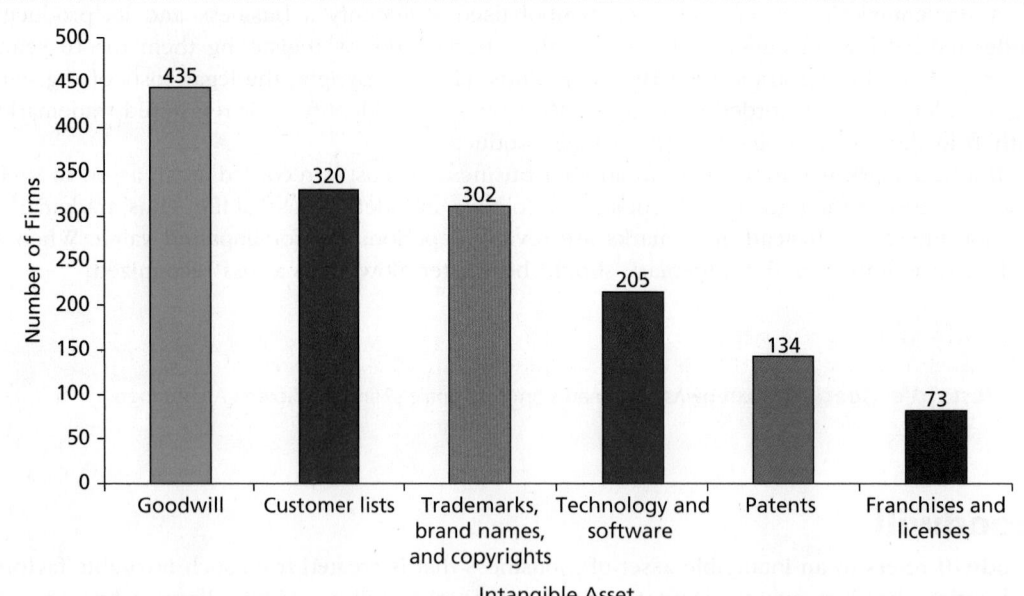

Note: Some firms have multiple disclosures.
Source: *Accounting Trends & Techniques,* 66th ed., American Institute of Certified Public Accountants, New York, 2012.

Exhibit 13 summarizes the characteristics of intangible assets.

Exhibit 13
Comparison of Intangible Assets

Intangible Asset	Description	Amortization Period	Periodic Expense
Patent	Exclusive right to benefit from an innovation	Estimated useful life not to exceed legal life	Amortization expense
Copyright	Exclusive right to benefit from a literary, artistic, or musical composition	Estimated useful life not to exceed legal life	Amortization expense
Trademark	Exclusive use of a name, term, or symbol	None	Impairment loss if fair value less than carrying value (impaired)
Goodwill	Excess of purchase price of a business over the fair value of its net assets (assets − liabilities)	None	Impairment loss if fair value less than carrying value (impaired)

International Connection

IFRS International Financial Reporting Standards (IFRS)

IFRS allow certain research and development (R&D) costs to be recorded as assets when incurred. Typically, R&D costs are classified as either research costs or development costs. If certain criteria are met, research costs can be recorded as an expense, while development costs can be recorded as an asset. This criterion includes such considerations as the company's intent to use or to sell the intangible asset. For example, Nokia Corporation (Finland) reported capitalized development costs of €40 million in a recent statement of financial position (balance sheet), where € represents the euro, the common currency of the European Economic Union.*

*Differences between U.S. GAAP and IFRS are further discussed and illustrated in Appendix C.

Check Up Corner 9-3 Intangible Assets

Hollis Company acquired patents for $125,000 on July 1 of the current year. The technology supported by these patents was expected to have a 10-year life. In addition, goodwill from acquiring Logan Company in a prior year was impaired by $30,000 due to new competitive technologies.

A. Journalize the acquisition of the patent on July 1.
B. Journalize the adjusting entry for the amortization of the patent on December 31.
C. Journalize the adjusting entry for the impairment of goodwill on December 31.

Solution:

A.

July 1	Patents		125,000	
	Cash			125,000

B.

Dec. 31	Amortization Expense—Patents		6,250	
	Patents [($125,000 ÷ 10 years) × 1/2]			6,250

C.

Dec. 31	Loss from Impaired Goodwill		30,000	
	Goodwill			30,000

Check Up Corner

Objective 6

Describe how depreciation expense is reported on an income statement and prepare a balance sheet that includes fixed assets and intangible assets.

Financial Reporting for Long-Term Assets: Fixed and Intangible

On the income statement, depreciation and amortization expense should be reported separately or disclosed in a note. A description of the methods used in computing depreciation should also be reported.

On the balance sheet, each class of fixed assets should be disclosed on the face of the statement or in the notes. The related accumulated depreciation should also be disclosed, either by class or in total. The fixed assets may be shown at their *book value* (cost less accumulated depreciation), which can also be described as their *net* amount.

If there are many classes of fixed assets, a single amount may be presented on the balance sheet, supported by a note with a separate listing. Fixed assets may be reported under the more descriptive caption of property, plant, and equipment.

Intangible assets are usually reported on the balance sheet in a separate section following fixed assets. The balance of each class of intangible assets should be disclosed net of any amortization.

The balance sheet presentation for **Mornin' Joe**'s fixed and intangible assets follows:

Mornin' Joe

Mornin' Joe
Balance Sheet
December 31, 20Y6

Property, plant, and equipment:			
Land			$1,850,000
Buildings		$2,650,000	
Accumulated depreciation		(420,000)	
Buildings, book value			2,230,000
Office equipment		$ 350,000	
Accumulated depreciation		(102,000)	
Office equipment, book value			248,000
Total property, plant, and equipment, book value			$4,328,000
Intangible assets:			
Patents			140,000

The cost and related accumulated depletion of mineral rights are normally shown as part of the fixed assets section of the balance sheet. The mineral rights may be shown net of depletion on the face of the balance sheet. In such cases, a supporting note discloses the accumulated depletion.

Analysis for Decision Making

Objective

Describe and illustrate the fixed asset turnover ratio to assess the efficiency of a company's use of its fixed assets.

Fixed Asset Turnover Ratio

The **fixed asset turnover ratio** measures the number of sales dollars earned per dollar of fixed assets. The higher the ratio, the more efficiently a company is using its fixed assets in generating sales. The ratio is computed as follows:

$$\text{Fixed Asset Turnover Ratio} = \frac{\text{Sales}}{\text{Average Book Value of Fixed Assets}}$$

To illustrate, the following data (in millions) were taken from a recent financial statement of **McDonald's Corporation**:

Sales	$28,106
Fixed assets (net):	
Beginning of year	24,677
End of year	25,747

McDonald's fixed asset turnover ratio for the year is computed as follows (rounded to one decimal place):

$$\text{Fixed Asset Turnover Ratio} = \frac{\text{Sales}}{\text{Average Book Value of Fixed Assets}}$$

$$= \frac{\$28,106}{(\$24,677 + \$25,747) \div 2}$$

$$= 1.1$$

Is 1.1 efficient? To answer this question, McDonald's fixed asset turnover ratio can be compared to other quick-service restaurant companies, as shown in Exhibit 14. **Yum! Brands** operates **KFC**, **Pizza Hut**, and **Taco Bell** quick-service restaurants. The other restaurants are likely familiar by name.

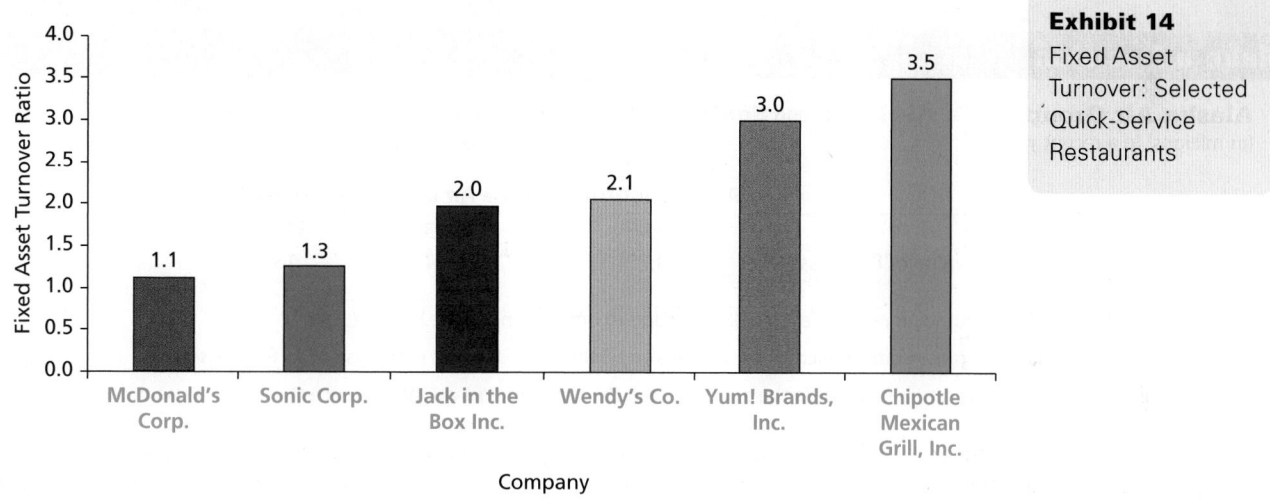

Exhibit 14
Fixed Asset Turnover: Selected Quick-Service Restaurants

Differences in the fixed asset turnover between these companies can be due to a number of factors, including differences in both the average fixed asset book value and sales per restaurant. Explaining McDonald's low fixed asset turnover ratio relative to the other restaurants would require a deeper analysis into these variables.

Comparing companies within industries is useful because the fixed asset turnover ratio should be comparable within an industry. The fixed asset turnover ratio will vary across industries because of differences in how industries use fixed assets. For example, the fixed asset turnover ratio for selected companies in different industries is shown in Exhibit 15.

Exhibit 15

Fixed Asset Turnover Ratio: Various Industries

Company (Industry)	Fixed Asset Turnover Ratio
Disney (entertainment)	2.0
ExxonMobil (petrochemical)	1.7
Google (Internet)	4.2
Macy's (retail)	3.5
ManpowerGroup (temporary employment)	115.4
McDonald's (quick-service restaurant)	1.1
Union Pacific (railroad)	0.5

The smaller fixed asset turnover ratios are associated with industries that require large fixed asset investments to generate revenues. The larger fixed asset turnover ratios are associated with industries that require smaller fixed asset investments to generate revenues. Thus, for example, the difference in the fixed asset turnover ratio between Union Pacific and ManpowerGroup is due to the difference in the way fixed assets are used in their respective industries. Railroads require extensive investments in track, engines, and railcars while temporary employment agencies require few investments in fixed assets.

Make a Decision | **Fixed Asset Turnover Ratio**

Alaska Air Group, Delta Air Lines, and Southwest Airlines reported the following financial information (in millions) in a recent year:

	Alaska Air Group	Delta Air Lines	Southwest Airlines
Sales	$4,964	$37,773	$17,699
Average book value of fixed assets	3,751	21,284	13,078

A. Determine the fixed asset turnover ratio for each airline. (Round to one decimal place.)

B. Based on the fixed asset turnover ratio, which airline appears to be the most efficient in the use of its fixed assets?

C. The most important fixed asset to an airline is the aircraft. Given this, what factors might influence the efficient use of fixed assets for an airline?

Solution:

A. Fixed Asset Turnover Ratio = $\dfrac{\text{Sales}}{\text{Average Book Value of Fixed Assets}}$

Alaska Air Group: $\dfrac{\$4,964}{\$3,751} = 1.3$

Delta Air Lines: $\dfrac{\$37,773}{\$21,284} = 1.8$

Southwest Airlines: $\dfrac{\$17,699}{\$13,078} = 1.3$

B. Delta Air Lines has the largest fixed asset turnover ratio and, thus, is more efficient in using fixed assets than the other two airlines. Delta's sales are $1.77 for every dollar of fixed assets, which is approximately 30% better than the other two airlines.

C. The efficient use of aircraft can yield a higher fixed asset turnover ratio. An airline can increase aircraft efficiency by maximizing the number of seats sold on a flight. This is called the load factor. The higher the load factor, the more efficient is the aircraft's use in generating revenues. High load factors are often obtained by matching aircraft size and capacity with the demand for seats. Other than filling seats, airlines can maximize aircraft efficiency by minimizing the ground time between flights. This can be accomplished with improved scheduling, maintenance, and operating procedures.

Make a Decision

Appendix Exchanging Similar Fixed Assets

Old equipment is often traded in for new equipment having a similar use. In such cases, the seller allows the buyer an amount for the old equipment traded in. This amount, called the **trade-in allowance**, may be either greater or less than the book value of the old equipment. The remaining balance—the amount owed—is either paid in cash or recorded as a liability. It is normally called **boot**, which is its tax name.

Accounting for the exchange of similar assets depends on whether the transaction has *commercial substance*.[8] An exchange has commercial substance if future cash flows change as a result of the exchange. If an exchange of similar assets has commercial substance, a gain or loss is recognized. In such cases, the exchange is accounted for similar to that of a sale of a fixed asset. The gain or loss is determined as the difference between the fair market value (trade-in allowance) of the asset given up (exchanged) and its book value. Alternatively, the gain or loss can be determined as the difference between the fair market value of the new asset received and the assets given up in the exchange (cash and book value of the old asset).

Gain on Exchange

To illustrate a gain on an exchange of similar assets, assume the following:

Similar equipment acquired (new):

Price (fair market value) of new equipment	$ 5,000
Trade-in allowance on old equipment	(1,100)
Cash paid at June 19, date of exchange	$ 3,900

Equipment traded in (old):

Cost of old equipment	$ 4,000
Accumulated depreciation at date of exchange	(3,200)
Book value at June 19, date of exchange	$ 800

The entry to record this exchange and payment of cash is as follows:

June 19	Accumulated Depreciation—Equipment	3,200	
	Equipment (new equipment)	5,000	
	Equipment (old equipment)		4,000
	Cash		3,900
	Gain on Exchange of Equipment		300

A = L + E
+ −   + Gain

The gain on the exchange, $300, is the difference between the fair market value (trade-in allowance) of the asset given up (exchanged) of $1,100 and its book value of $800, computed as follows:

Fair market value (trade-in allowance) of old equipment	$1,100
Book value of old equipment	(800)
Gain on exchange of assets	$ 300

The gain on the exchange, $300, can also be determined as the difference between the fair market value of the new asset of $5,000 and the book value of the old asset traded in of $800 plus the cash paid of $3,900, computed as follows:

Price (fair market value) of new equipment		$ 5,000
Assets given up in exchange:		
Book value of old equipment ($4,000 – $3,200)	$ 800	
Cash paid on the exchange	3,900	(4,700)
Gain on exchange of assets		$ 300

[8] *FASB Accounting Standards Codification*, Section 360-10-30.

Loss on Exchange

To illustrate a loss on an exchange of similar assets, assume that instead of a trade-in allowance of $1,100, a trade-in allowance of only $675 was allowed in the preceding example. In this case, the cash paid on the exchange is $4,325, computed as follows:

Price (fair market value) of new equipment	$5,000
Trade-in allowance of old equipment	(675)
Cash paid at June 19, date of exchange	$4,325

The entry to record this exchange and payment of cash is as follows:

A = L + E
+ –   – Loss

June 19	Accumulated Depreciation—Equipment	3,200	
	Equipment (new equipment)	5,000	
	Loss on Exchange of Equipment	125	
	Equipment (old equipment)		4,000
	Cash		4,325

The loss on the exchange, $125, is the difference between the fair market value (trade-in allowance) of the asset given up (exchanged) of $675 and its book value of $800, computed as follows:

Fair market value (trade-in allowance) of old equipment	$ 675
Book value of old equipment	(800)
Loss on exchange of assets	$(125)

The loss on the exchange, $125, can also be determined as the difference between the fair market value of the new asset of $5,000 and the book value of the old asset traded in of $800 plus the cash paid of $4,325, computed as follows:

Price (fair market value) of new equipment		$ 5,000
Assets given up in exchange:		
Book value of old equipment ($4,000 – $3,200)	$ 800	
Cash paid on the exchange	4,325	(5,125)
Loss on exchange of assets		$ (125)

In those cases where an asset exchange *lacks commercial substance*, no gain is recognized on the exchange. Instead, the cost of the new asset is adjusted for any gain. For example, in the first illustration, the gain of $300 would be subtracted from the purchase price of $5,000 and the new asset would be recorded at $4,700. Accounting for the exchange of assets that lack commercial substance is discussed in more advanced accounting texts.[9]

---

[9] The exchange of similar assets also involves complex tax issues which are discussed in advanced accounting courses.

Let's Review

Chapter Summary

1. Fixed assets are long-term tangible assets used in the normal operations of the business such as equipment, buildings, and land. The initial cost of a fixed asset includes all amounts spent to get the asset in place and ready for use.

2. All fixed assets except land should be depreciated over time. Three factors are considered in determining depreciation: (1) the fixed asset's initial cost, (2) the useful life of the asset, and (3) the residual value of the asset. Depreciation may be determined using the straight-line, units-of-activity, and double-declining-balance methods. Depreciation may be revised into the future for changes in an asset's useful life or residual value. Revenue expenditures include ordinary repairs and maintenance. Capital expenditures include asset improvements and extraordinary repairs.

3. When discarding a fixed asset, any depreciation for the current period is recorded, and the book value of the asset is then removed from the accounts. When a fixed asset is sold, the book value is removed, and the cash or other asset received is recorded. If the selling price is more than the book value of the asset, the transaction results in a gain. If the selling price is less than the book value, there is a loss.

4. The amount of periodic depletion is computed by multiplying the quantity of minerals extracted during the period by a depletion rate. The depletion rate is computed by dividing the cost of the mineral deposit by its estimated total units of resource. The entry to record depletion debits a depletion expense account and credits an accumulated depletion account.

5. Long-term assets such as patents, copyrights, trademarks, and goodwill are intangible assets. The cost of patents and copyrights should be amortized over the years of the asset's expected usefulness by debiting an expense account and crediting the intangible asset account. Trademarks and goodwill are not amortized but are written down only upon impairment.

6. The amount of depreciation expense and the depreciation methods used should be disclosed in the financial statements. Each major class of fixed assets should be disclosed, along with the related accumulated depreciation. Intangible assets are usually presented in a separate section following fixed assets. Each major class of intangible assets should be disclosed net of the amortization recorded to date.

Key Terms

accelerated depreciation method (435)
amortization (446)
book value (430)
boot (453)
capital expenditures (439)
copyright (447)
depletion expense (445)
depreciable cost (430)

depreciation (430)
double-declining-balance method (435)
expected useful life (430)
fixed asset turnover ratio (450)
fixed assets (426)
goodwill (447)
initial cost (430)
intangible assets (446)

patents (446)
residual value (430)
revenue expenditures (439)
straight-line method (431)
trade-in allowance (453)
trademark (447)
units-of-activity method (433)

Practice

Multiple-Choice Questions

1. Which of the following expenditures incurred in connection with acquiring machinery is a proper charge to the asset account?
   A. Freight
   B. Installation costs
   C. Both A and B
   D. Neither A nor B

2. What is the amount of depreciation, using the double-declining-balance method for the second year of use for equipment costing $9,000, with an estimated residual value of $600 and an estimated life of three years?
   A. $6,000
   B. $3,000
   C. $2,000
   D. $400

3. An example of an accelerated depreciation method is:
   A. straight-line.
   B. double-declining-balance.
   C. units-of-activity.
   D. depletion.

4. Equipment purchased on January 3 for $80,000 was depreciated using the straight-line method based upon a five-year life and $7,500 residual value. The equipment was sold three years later on December 31 for $40,000. What is the gain on the sale of the equipment?
   A. $3,500
   B. $14,500
   C. $36,500
   D. $43,500

5. Which of the following is an example of an intangible asset?
   A. Patents
   B. Goodwill
   C. Copyrights
   D. All of these

Answers provided after Problem. Need more practice? Find additional multiple-choice questions, exercises, and problems in CengageNOWv2.

Exercises

SHOW ME HOW

1. Straight-line depreciation   Obj. 2

Equipment acquired at the beginning of the year at a cost of $340,000 has an estimated residual value of $45,000 and an estimated useful life of 10 years. Determine (A) the depreciable cost, (B) the straight-line rate, and (C) the annual straight-line depreciation.

SHOW ME HOW

2. Units-of-activity depreciation   Obj. 2

A tractor acquired at a cost of $420,000 has an estimated residual value of $30,000, has an estimated useful life of 25,000 hours, and was operated 1,850 hours during the year. Determine (A) the depreciable cost, (B) the depreciation rate, and (C) the units-of-activity depreciation for the year.

SHOW ME HOW

3. Double-declining-balance depreciation   Obj. 2

Equipment acquired at the beginning of the year at a cost of $175,000 has an estimated residual value of $12,000 and an estimated useful life of 10 years. Determine (A) the double-declining-balance rate and (B) the double-declining-balance depreciation for the first year.

SHOW ME HOW

4. Revision of depreciation
Obj. 2

A truck with a cost of $82,000 has an estimated residual value of $16,000, an estimated useful life of 12 years, and is depreciated by the straight-line method. (A) Determine the amount of the annual depreciation. (B) Determine the book value at the end of the seventh year of use. (C) Assuming that at the start of the eighth year the remaining life is estimated to be six years and the residual value is estimated to be $12,000, determine the depreciation expense for each of the remaining six years.

SHOW ME HOW

5. Capital and revenue expenditures
Obj. 2

On August 7, Green River Inflatables Co. paid $1,675 to install a hydraulic lift and $40 for an air filter for one of its delivery trucks. Journalize the entries for the new lift and air filter expenditures.

SHOW ME HOW

6. Sale of equipment
Obj. 3

Equipment was acquired at the beginning of the year at a cost of $465,000. The equipment was depreciated using the straight-line method based on an estimated useful life of 15 years and an estimated residual value of $45,000.

A. What was the depreciation for the first year?

B. Assuming the equipment was sold at the end of the eighth year for $235,000, determine the gain or loss on the sale of the equipment.

C. Journalize the entry to record the sale.

SHOW ME HOW

7. Depletion
Obj. 4

Caldwell Mining Co. acquired mineral rights for $127,500,000. The mineral deposit is estimated at 425,000,000 tons. During the current year, 42,000,000 tons were mined and sold.

A. Determine the depletion rate.

B. Determine the amount of depletion expense for the current year.

C. Journalize the adjusting entry on December 31 to recognize the depletion expense.

SHOW ME HOW

8. Impaired goodwill and amortization of patent
Obj. 5

On December 31, it was estimated that goodwill of $4,000,000 was impaired. In addition, a patent with an estimated useful economic life of 15 years was acquired for $900,000 on August 1.

A. Journalize the adjusting entry on December 31 for the impaired goodwill.

B. Journalize the adjusting entry on December 31 for the amortization of the patent rights.

Answers provided after Problem. Need more practice? Find additional multiple-choice questions, exercises, and problems in CengageNOWv2.

Problem

McCollum Company, a furniture wholesaler, acquired new equipment at a cost of $150,000 at the beginning of the fiscal year. The equipment has an estimated life of five years and an estimated residual value of $12,000. Ellen McCollum, the president, has requested information regarding alternative depreciation methods.

Instructions

1. Determine the annual depreciation for each of the five years of estimated useful life of the equipment, the accumulated depreciation at the end of each year, and the book value of the equipment at the end of each year by (A) the straight-line method and (B) the double-declining-balance method.
2. Assume that the equipment was depreciated under the double-declining-balance method. In the first week of the fifth year, the equipment was sold for $10,000. Journalize the entry to record the sale.

Need more practice? Find additional multiple-choice questions, exercises, and problems in CengageNOWv2.

Answers

Multiple-Choice Questions

1. **C** All amounts spent to get a fixed asset (such as machinery) in place and ready for use are proper charges to the asset account. In the case of machinery acquired, the freight (answer A) and the installation costs (answer B) are both (answer C) proper charges to the machinery account.

2. **C** The periodic charge for depreciation under the double-declining-balance method for the second year is determined as follows:

   Step 1: Determine the straight-line percentage, using the expected useful life.

   $$\text{Straight-line percentage} = 100\% \div 3 \text{ years}$$
   $$= 33.333\%$$

   Step 2: Determine the double-declining-balance rate by multiplying the straight-line rate from Step 1 by 2.

   $$\text{Double-declining-balance rate} = 33.333\% \times 2$$
   $$= 66.666\%$$

   Step 3: Compute the depreciation expense by multiplying the double-declining-balance rate from Step 2 times the book value of the asset.

   $$\text{First-Year Depreciation} = 66.666\% \times \$9,000$$
   $$= \$6,000 \qquad \text{(answer A)}$$

   $$\text{Book Value at End of Year 1} = \$9,000 - \$6,000$$
   $$= \$3,000$$

   $$\text{Second-Year Depreciation} = \$3,000 \times 66.666\%$$
   $$= \$2,000 \qquad \text{(answer C)}$$

   $$\text{Third-Year Depreciation} = (\$3,000 - \$2,000) \times 66.666\%$$
   $$= \$667$$

   The equipment cannot be depreciated below its residual value of $600; thus, the third-year depreciation is $400 ($1,000 – $600) (answer D).

3. **B** A depreciation method that provides for a higher depreciation amount in the first year of the use of an asset and a gradually declining periodic amount thereafter is called an accelerated depreciation method. The double-declining-balance method (answer B) is an example of such a method.

4. **A** A gain of $3,500 is recognized on the sale of the equipment, computed as follows:

Annual depreciation [($80,000 – $7,500) ÷ 5 years]	$14,500 (answer B)
Cost of equipment	$80,000
Accumulated depreciation on December 31 ($14,500 × 3)	43,500 (answer D)
Book value of equipment on December 31	$36,500 (answer C)
Selling price	$40,000
Book value of equipment on December 31	36,500
Gain on sale of equipment	$ 3,500

5. **D** Long-lived assets that are useful in operations, not held for sale, and without physical qualities are called intangible assets. Patents, goodwill, and copyrights are examples of intangible assets (answer D).

Exercises

1.

A. $295,000 ($340,000 − $45,000)

B. 10.0% = (1 ÷ 10)

C. $29,500 ($295,000 × 10.0%), or ($295,000 ÷ 10 years)

2.

A. $390,000 ($420,000 − $30,000)

B. $15.60 per hour ($390,000 ÷ 25,000 hours)

C. $28,860 (1,850 hours × $15.60)

3.

A. 20.0% = [(1 ÷ 10) × 2]

B. $35,000 ($175,000 × 20.0%)

4.

A. $5,500 [($82,000 − $16,000) ÷ 12]

B. $43,500 [$82,000 − ($5,500 × 7)]

C. $5,250 [($43,500 − $12,000) ÷ 6]

5.

Aug. 7	Delivery Truck	1,675	
	Cash		1,675
7	Repairs and Maintenance Expense	40	
	Cash		40

6.

A. $28,000 [($465,000 − $45,000) ÷ 15]

B. $6,000 loss {$235,000 − [$465,000 − ($28,000 × 8)]}

C.

Cash	235,000	
Accumulated Depreciation—Equipment	224,000	
Loss on Sale of Equipment	6,000	
Equipment		465,000

7.

A. $0.30 per ton = $127,500,000 ÷ 425,000,000 tons

B. $12,600,000 = 42,000,000 tons × $0.30 per ton

C.

Dec. 31	Depletion Expense	12,600,000	
	Accumulated Depletion		12,600,000
	Depletion of mineral deposit.		

8.

A.

Dec. 31	Loss from Impaired Goodwill	4,000,000	
	Goodwill		4,000,000
	Impaired goodwill.		

B.

Dec. 31	Amortization Expense—Patents	25,000	
	Patents		25,000
	Amortized patent rights		
	[($900,000 ÷ 15) × 5/12].		

Need more help? Watch step-by-step videos of how to compute answers to these Exercises in CengageNOWv2.

Problem

1.

	Year	Depreciation Expense	Accumulated Depreciation, End of Year	Book Value, End of Year
A.	1	$27,600*	$ 27,600	$122,400
	2	27,600	55,200	94,800
	3	27,600	82,800	67,200
	4	27,600	110,400	39,600
	5	27,600	138,000	12,000

*$27,600 = ($150,000 − $12,000) ÷ 5

	Year	Depreciation Expense	Accumulated Depreciation, End of Year	Book Value, End of Year
B.	1	$60,000**	$ 60,000	$90,000
	2	36,000	96,000	54,000
	3	21,600	117,600	32,400
	4	12,960	130,560	19,440
	5	7,440***	138,000	12,000

**$60,000 = $150,000 × 40%

***The asset is not depreciated below the estimated residual value of $12,000.
$7,440 = $150,000 − $130,560 − $12,000

2.

Cash	10,000	
Accumulated Depreciation—Equipment	130,560	
Loss on Sale of Equipment	9,440	
Equipment		150,000

Discussion Questions

1. O'Neil Office Supplies has a fleet of automobiles and trucks for use by salespersons and for delivery of office supplies and equipment. Collins Auto Sales Co. has automobiles and trucks for sale. Under what caption would the automobiles and trucks be reported in the balance sheet of (A) O'Neil Office Supplies and (B) Collins Auto Sales Co.?

2. Bullwinkle Co. acquired an adjacent vacant lot with the hope of selling it in the future at a gain. The lot is not intended to be used in Bullwinkle business operations. Where should such real estate be listed on the balance sheet?

3. Alpine Company solicited bids from several contractors to construct an addition to its office building. The lowest bid received was for $1,200,000. Alpine decided to construct the addition itself at a cost of $1,100,000. What amount should be recorded in the building account?

4. Distinguish between the accounting for capital expenditures and revenue expenditures.

5. Immediately after a used truck is acquired, a new motor is installed at a total cost of $3,850. Is this a capital expenditure or a revenue expenditure?

6. Keyser Company purchased a machine that has a manufacturer's suggested life of 20 years. The company plans to use the machine on a special project that will last 12 years. At the completion of the project, the machine will be sold. Over how many years should the machine be depreciated?

7. Is it necessary for a business to use the same method of computing depreciation (A) for all classes of its depreciable assets and (B) for financial statement purposes and in determining income taxes?

8. A. Under what conditions is the use of an accelerated depreciation method most appropriate?
   B. Why is an accelerated depreciation method often used for income tax purposes?

9. For some of the fixed assets of a business, the balance in Accumulated Depreciation is exactly equal to the cost of the asset. (A) Is it permissible to record additional depreciation on the assets if they are still useful to the business? Explain. (B) When should an entry be made to remove the cost and the accumulated depreciation from the accounts?

10. A. Over what period of time should the cost of a patent acquired by purchase be amortized?
    B. In general, what is the required accounting treatment for research and development costs?
    C. How should goodwill be amortized?

Basic Exercises

SHOW ME HOW

BE 9-1   Straight-line depreciation   Obj. 2

A building acquired at the beginning of the year at a cost of $1,450,000 has an estimated residual value of $300,000 and an estimated useful life of 10 years. Determine (A) the depreciable cost, (B) the straight-line rate, and (C) the annual straight-line depreciation.

SHOW ME HOW

BE 9-2   Units-of-activity depreciation   Obj. 2

A truck acquired at a cost of $69,000 has an estimated residual value of $12,000, has an estimated useful life of 300,000 miles, and was driven 77,000 miles during the year. Determine (A) the depreciable cost, (B) the depreciation rate, and (C) the units-of-activity depreciation for the year.

SHOW ME HOW

BE 9-3   Double-declining-balance depreciation   Obj. 2

A building acquired at the beginning of the year at a cost of $1,375,000 has an estimated residual value of $250,000 and an estimated useful life of 40 years. Determine (A) the double-declining-balance rate and (B) the double-declining-balance depreciation for the first year.

SHOW ME HOW

BE 9-4   Revision of depreciation   Obj. 2

Equipment with a cost of $180,000 has an estimated residual value of $14,400, has an estimated useful life of 16 years, and is depreciated by the straight-line method. (A) Determine the amount of the annual depreciation. (B) Determine the book value at the end of the tenth year of use. (C) Assuming that at the start of the eleventh year the remaining life is estimated to be eight years and the residual value is estimated to be $10,500, determine the depreciation expense for each of the remaining eight years.

SHOW ME HOW

BE 9-5   Capital and revenue expenditures   Obj. 2

On February 14, Garcia Associates Co. paid $2,300 to repair the transmission on one of its delivery vans. In addition, Garcia paid $450 to install a GPS system in its van. Journalize the entries for the transmission and GPS system expenditures.

SHOW ME HOW

BE 9-6   Sale of equipment   Obj. 3

Equipment was acquired at the beginning of the year at a cost of $600,000. The equipment was depreciated using the double-declining-balance method based on an estimated useful life of 16 years and an estimated residual value of $60,000.

A. What was the depreciation for the first year?

B. Assuming the equipment was sold at the end of the second year for $480,000, determine the gain or loss on the sale of the equipment.

C. Journalize the entry on Dec. 31 to record the sale.

SHOW ME HOW

BE 9-7   Depletion   Obj. 4

Glacier Mining Co. acquired mineral rights for $494,000,000. The mineral deposit is estimated at 475,000,000 tons. During the current year, 31,500,000 tons were mined and sold.

A. Determine the depletion rate.

B. Determine the amount of depletion expense for the current year.

C. Journalize the adjusting entry on December 31 to recognize the depletion expense.

SHOW ME HOW

BE 9-8   Impaired goodwill and amortization of patent   Obj. 5

On December 31, it was estimated that goodwill of $6,000,000 was impaired. In addition, a patent with an estimated useful economic life of 12 years was acquired for $1,500,000 on April 1.

A. Journalize the adjusting entry on December 31 for the impaired goodwill.

B. Journalize the adjusting entry on December 31 for the amortization of the patent rights.

Exercises

EX 9-1   Costs of acquiring fixed assets
Obj. 1

Melinda Stoffers owns and operates ABC Print Co. During February, ABC incurred the following costs in acquiring two printing presses. One printing press was new, and the other was purchased from a business that recently filed for bankruptcy.

Costs related to new printing press:

1. Fee paid to factory representative for installation
2. Freight
3. Insurance while in transit
4. New parts to replace those damaged in unloading
5. Sales tax on purchase price
6. Special foundation

Costs related to used printing press:

7. Fees paid to attorney to review purchase agreement
8. Freight
9. Installation
10. Repair of damage incurred in reconditioning the press
11. Replacement of worn-out parts
12. Vandalism repairs during installation

A. Indicate which costs incurred in acquiring the new printing press should be debited to the asset account.

B. Indicate which costs incurred in acquiring the used printing press should be debited to the asset account.

EX 9-2   Determining cost of land
Obj. 1, 2

Bridger Ski Co. has developed a tract of land into a ski resort. The company has cut the trees, cleared and graded the land and hills, and constructed ski lifts.
━━━━▶ (A) Should the tree cutting, land clearing, and grading costs of constructing the ski slopes be debited to the land account? (B) If such costs are debited to Land, should they be depreciated? Explain.

EX 9-3   Determining cost of land
Obj. 1

SHOW ME HOW

On-Time Delivery Company acquired an adjacent lot to construct a new warehouse, paying $90,000 and giving a short-term note for $50,000. Legal fees paid were $1,750, delinquent taxes assumed were $25,000, and fees paid to remove an old building from the land were $9,000. Materials salvaged from the demolition of the building were sold for $1,000. A contractor was paid $415,000 to construct a new warehouse. Determine the cost of the land to be reported on the balance sheet.

EX 9-4   Nature of depreciation
Obj. 2

Tri-City Ironworks Co. reported $44,500,000 for equipment and $29,800,000 for accumulated depreciation—equipment on its balance sheet.
━━━━▶ Does this mean (A) that the replacement cost of the equipment is $44,500,000 and (B) that $29,800,000 is set aside in a special fund for the replacement of the equipment? Explain.

EX 9-5   Straight-line depreciation rates
Obj. 2

✔ C. 10%

Convert each of the following estimates of useful life to a straight-line depreciation rate, stated as a percentage: (A) 4 years, (B) 8 years, (C) 10 years, (D) 16 years, (E) 25 years, (F) 40 years, (G) 50 years.

SHOW ME HOW

EX 9-6 Straight-line depreciation
Obj. 2

A refrigerator used by a wholesale warehouse has a cost of $64,000, an estimated residual value of $5,200, and an estimated useful life of 12 years. What is the amount of the annual depreciation computed by the straight-line method?

SHOW ME HOW

EX 9-7 Depreciation by units-of-activity method
Obj. 2

A diesel-powered tractor with a cost of $90,000 and estimated residual value of $15,000 is expected to have a useful operating life of 30,000 hours. During April, the tractor was operated 120 hours. Determine the depreciation for the month.

✔ A. Truck #1, credit
to Accumulated
Depreciation, $5,460

SHOW ME HOW

EX 9-8 Depreciation by units-of-activity method
Obj. 2

Prior to adjustment at the end of the year, the balance in Trucks is $296,900 and the balance in Accumulated Depreciation—Trucks is $99,740. Details of the subsidiary ledger are as follows:

Truck No.	Cost	Estimated Residual Value	Estimated Useful Life	Accumulated Depreciation at Beginning of Year	Miles Operated During Year
1	$80,000	$15,000	250,000 miles	—	21,000 miles
2	54,000	6,000	300,000	$14,400	33,500
3	72,900	10,900	200,000	60,140	8,000
4	90,000	22,800	240,000	25,200	22,500

A. Determine the depreciation rates per mile and the amount to be credited to the accumulated depreciation section of each of the subsidiary accounts for the miles operated during the current year.

B. Journalize the entry on Dec. 31 to record depreciation for the year.

✔ A. $8,500

SHOW ME HOW

EX 9-9 Depreciation by two methods
Obj. 2

A Kubota tractor acquired on January 8 at a cost of $85,000 has an estimated useful life of 10 years. Assuming that it will have no residual value, determine the depreciation for each of the first two years (A) by the straight-line method and (B) by the double-declining-balance method.

✔ A. $3,250

SHOW ME HOW

EX 9-10 Depreciation by two methods
Obj. 2

A storage tank acquired at the beginning of the fiscal year at a cost of $75,000 has an estimated residual value of $10,000 and an estimated useful life of 20 years. Determine the following: (A) the amount of annual depreciation by the straight-line method and (B) the amount of depreciation for the first and second years computed by the double-declining-balance method.

✔ A. First year, $6,200

SHOW ME HOW

EX 9-11 Partial-year depreciation
Obj. 2

Equipment acquired at a cost of $105,000 has an estimated residual value of $12,000 and an estimated useful life of 10 years. It was placed into service on May 1 of the current fiscal year, which ends on December 31. Determine the depreciation for the current fiscal year and for the following fiscal year by (A) the straight-line method and (B) the double-declining-balance method.

✔ A. $23,750

SHOW ME HOW

EX 9-12 Revision of depreciation
Obj. 2

A building with a cost of $1,200,000 has an estimated residual value of $250,000, has an estimated useful life of 40 years, and is depreciated by the straight-line method. (A) What is the amount of the annual depreciation? (B) What is the book value at the end of the twenty-eighth year of use? (C) If at the start of the twenty-ninth year it is estimated that the remaining life is 10 years and that the residual value is $180,000, what is the depreciation expense for each of the remaining 10 years?

EX 9-13 Capital and revenue expenditures

Obj. 1

Warner Freight Lines Co. incurred the following costs related to trucks and vans used in operating its delivery service:

1. Changed the oil and greased the joints of all the trucks and vans.
2. Changed the radiator fluid on a truck that had been in service for the past four years.
3. Installed a hydraulic lift to a van.
4. Installed security systems on four of the newer trucks.
5. Overhauled the engine on one of the trucks purchased three years ago.
6. Rebuilt the transmission on one of the vans that had been driven 40,000 miles. The van was no longer under warranty.
7. Removed a two-way radio from one of the trucks and installed a new radio with a greater range of communication.
8. Repaired a flat tire on one of the vans.
9. Replaced a truck's suspension system with a new suspension system that allows for the delivery of heavier loads.
10. Tinted the back and side windows of one of the vans to discourage theft of contents.

Classify each of the costs as a capital expenditure or a revenue expenditure.

EX 9-14 Capital and revenue expenditures

Obj. 1

Jackie Fox owns and operates Platinum Transport Co. During the past year, Jackie incurred the following costs related to an 18-wheel truck:

1. Changed engine oil.
2. Installed a television in the sleeping compartment of the truck.
3. Installed a wind deflector on top of the cab to increase fuel mileage.
4. Modified the factory-installed turbo charger with a special-order kit designed to add 50 more horsepower to the engine performance.
5. Replaced a headlight that had burned out.
6. Replaced a shock absorber that had worn out.
7. Replaced fog and cab light bulbs.
8. Replaced the hydraulic brake system that had begun to fail during his latest trip through the Rocky Mountains.
9. Removed the old radio and replaced it with a new communications module.
10. Replaced the old radar detector with a newer model that is fastened to the truck with a locking device that prevents its removal.

Classify each of the costs as a capital expenditure or a revenue expenditure.

SHOW ME HOW

EX 9-15 Capital and revenue expenditures

Obj. 1, 2

Quality Move Company made the following expenditures on one of its delivery trucks:

Mar. 20. Replaced the transmission at a cost of $1,890.
June 11. Paid $1,350 for installation of a hydraulic lift.
Nov. 30. Paid $55 to change the oil and air filter.

Prepare journal entries for each expenditure.

EX 9-16 Capital expenditure and depreciation

Obj. 1, 2

✔ B. Depreciation Expense, $800

Willow Creek Company purchased and installed carpet in its new general offices on April 30 for a total cost of $18,000. The carpet is estimated to have a 15-year useful life and no residual value.

A. Prepare the journal entry necessary for recording the purchase of the new carpet.

B. Record the December 31 adjusting entry for the partial-year depreciation expense for the carpet, assuming that Willow Creek uses the straight-line method.

SHOW ME HOW

EX 9-17 Entries for sale of fixed asset

Obj. 3

Equipment acquired on January 8 at a cost of $168,000 has an estimated useful life of 18 years, has an estimated residual value of $15,000, and is depreciated by the straight-line method.

A. What was the book value of the equipment at December 31 the end of the fourth year?

B. Assuming that the equipment was sold on April 1 of the fifth year for $125,000, journalize the entries to record (1) depreciation for the three months until the sale date, and (2) the sale of the equipment.

EX 9-18 Disposal of fixed asset

Obj. 3

✔ B. $322,500

SHOW ME HOW

Equipment acquired on January 6 at a cost of $375,000 has an estimated useful life of 20 years and an estimated residual value of $25,000.

A. What was the annual amount of depreciation for the Years 1–3 using the straight-line method of depreciation?

B. What was the book value of the equipment on January 1 of Year 4?

C. Assuming that the equipment was sold on January 3 of Year 4 for $300,000, journalize the entry to record the sale.

D. Assuming that the equipment had been sold on January 3 of Year 4 for $325,000 instead of $300,000, journalize the entry to record the sale.

EX 9-19 Depletion entries

Obj. 4

✔ A. $9,000,000

SHOW ME HOW

Alaska Mining Co. acquired mineral rights for $67,500,000. The mineral deposit is estimated at 30,000,000 tons. During the current year, 4,000,000 tons were mined and sold.

A. Determine the amount of depletion expense for the current year.

B. Journalize the adjusting entry on December 31 to recognize the depletion expense.

EX 9-20 Amortization entries

Obj. 5

✔ A. $357,600

SHOW ME HOW

Kleen Company acquired patent rights on January 10 of Year 1 for $2,800,000. The patent has a useful life equal to its legal life of eight years. On January 7 of Year 4, Kleen successfully defended the patent in a lawsuit at a cost of $38,000.

A. Determine the patent amortization expense for Year 4 ended December 31.

B. Journalize the adjusting entry on December 31 of Year 4 to recognize the amortization.

REAL WORLD

EX 9-21 Book value of fixed assets

Obj. 6

Apple Inc. designs, manufactures, and markets personal computers and related software. Apple also manufactures and distributes music players (iPod) and mobile phones (iPhone) along with related accessories and services, including online distribution of third-party music, videos, and applications. The following information was taken from a recent annual report of Apple:

Property, Plant, and Equipment (in millions):

	Current Year	Preceding Year
Land and buildings	$ 4,863	$ 3,309
Machinery, equipment, and internal-use software	29,639	21,242
Other fixed assets	4,513	3,968
Accumulated depreciation and amortization	(18,391)	(11,922)

A. Compute the book value of the fixed assets for the current year and the preceding year and explain the differences, if any.

B. ➡ Would you normally expect Apple's book value of fixed assets to increase or decrease during the year? Why?

EX 9-22 Balance sheet presentation

Obj. 6

List the errors you find in the following partial balance sheet:

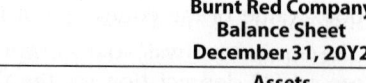

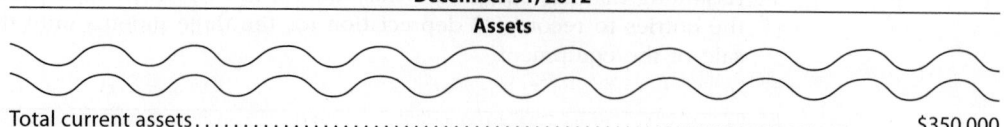

Burnt Red Company
Balance Sheet
December 31, 20Y2

Assets

Total current assets... $350,000

Property, plant, and equipment:	Replacement Cost	Accumulated Depreciation	Book Value
Land.....................................	$ 250,000	$ 50,000	$200,000
Buildings................................	450,000	160,000	290,000
Factory equipment	375,000	140,000	235,000
Office equipment.........................	125,000	60,000	65,000
Patents	90,000	—	90,000
Goodwill.................................	60,000	10,000	50,000
Total property, plant, and equipment........	$1,350,000	$420,000	$930,000

Appendix

EX 9-23 Asset traded for similar asset

✔ A. $185,000

A printing press priced at a fair market value of $275,000 is acquired in a transaction that has commercial substance by trading in a similar press and paying cash for the difference between the trade-in allowance and the price of the new press.

A. Assuming that the trade-in allowance is $90,000, what is the amount of cash given?

B. Assuming that the book value of the press traded in is $68,000, what is the gain or loss on the exchange?

Appendix

EX 9-24 Asset traded for similar asset

✔ B. $18,500 loss

Assume the same facts as in Exercise 9-23, except that the book value of the press traded in is $108,500. (A) What is the amount of cash given? (B) What is the gain or loss on the exchange?

Appendix

EX 9-25 Entries for trade of fixed asset

On July 1, Twin Pines Co., a water distiller, acquired new bottling equipment with a list price (fair market value) of $220,000. Twin Pines received a trade-in allowance (fair market value) of $45,000 on the old equipment of a similar type and paid cash of $175,000. The following information about the old equipment is obtained from the account in the equipment ledger: cost, $180,000; accumulated depreciation on December 31, the end of the preceding fiscal year, $120,000; annual depreciation, $12,000. Assuming the exchange has commercial substance, journalize the entries to record (A) the current depreciation of the old equipment to the date of trade-in and (B) the exchange transaction on July 1.

Appendix

EX 9-26 Entries for trade of fixed asset

On October 1, Bentley Delivery Services acquired a new truck with a list price (fair market value) of $75,000. Bentley Delivery received a trade-in allowance (fair market value) of $24,000 on an old truck of similar type and paid cash of $51,000. The following information about the old truck is obtained from the account in the equipment ledger: cost, $56,000; accumulated depreciation on December 31, the end of the preceding fiscal year, $35,000; annual depreciation, $7,000. Assuming the exchange has commercial substance, journalize the entries to record (A) the current depreciation of the old truck to the date of trade-in and (B) the transaction on October 1.

Problems: Series A

PR 9-1A Allocating payments and receipts to fixed asset accounts Obj. 1

✔ Land, $400,000

The following payments and receipts are related to land, land improvements, and buildings acquired for use in a wholesale ceramic business. The receipts are identified by an asterisk.

A. Fee paid to attorney for title search	$ 2,500
B. Cost of real estate acquired as a plant site: Land	285,000
Building (to be demolished)	55,000
C. Delinquent real estate taxes on property, assumed by purchaser	15,500
D. Cost of razing and removing building acquired in B	5,000
E. Proceeds from sale of salvage materials from old building	4,000*
F. Special assessment paid to city for extension of water main to the property	29,000
G. Architect's and engineer's fees for plans and supervision	60,000
H. Premium on one-year insurance policy during construction	6,000
I. Cost of filling and grading land	12,000
J. Money borrowed to pay building contractor	900,000*
K. Cost of repairing windstorm damage during construction	5,500
L. Cost of paving parking lot to be used by customers	32,000
M. Cost of trees and shrubbery planted	11,000
N. Cost of floodlights installed on parking lot	2,000
O. Cost of repairing vandalism damage during construction	2,500
P. Proceeds from insurance company for windstorm and vandalism damage	7,500*
Q. Payment to building contractor for new building	800,000
R. Interest incurred on building loan during construction	34,500
S. Refund of premium on insurance policy (H) canceled after 11 months	500*

Instructions

1. Assign each payment and receipt to Land (unlimited life), Land Improvements (limited life), Building, or Other Accounts. Indicate receipts by an asterisk. Identify each item by letter and list the amounts in columnar form, as follows:

Item	Land	Land Improvements	Building	Other Accounts

2. Determine the amount debited to Land, Land Improvements, and Building.

3. ━━━▶ The costs assigned to the land, which is used as a plant site, will not be depreciated, while the costs assigned to land improvements will be depreciated. Explain this seemingly contradictory application of the concept of depreciation.

4. What would be the effect on the income statement and balance sheet if the cost of filling and grading land of $12,000 [payment (I)] was incorrectly classified as Land Improvements rather than Land? Assume Land Improvements are depreciated over a 20-year life using the double-declining-balance method.

PR 9-2A Comparing three depreciation methods Obj. 2

✔ 1. a. Year 1: straight-line depreciation, $22,500

SHOW ME HOW

EXCEL TEMPLATE

Dexter Industries purchased packaging equipment on January 8 for $72,000. The equipment was expected to have a useful life of three years, or 18,000 operating hours, and a residual value of $4,500. The equipment was used for 7,600 hours during Year 1, 6,000 hours in Year 2, and 4,400 hours in Year 3.

Instructions

1. Determine the amount of depreciation expense for the three years ending December 31, by (A) the straight-line method, (B) the units-of-activity method, and (C) the double-declining-balance method. Also determine the total depreciation expense for the three years by each

(Continued)

method. The following columnar headings are suggested for recording the depreciation expense amounts:

	Depreciation Expense		
Year	Straight-Line Method	Units-of-Activity Method	Double-Declining-Balance Method

2. What method yields the highest depreciation expense for Year 1?

3. What method yields the most depreciation over the three-year life of the equipment?

PR 9-3A Depreciation by three methods; partial years   Obj. 2

✔ A. Year 1: $65,250

EXCEL TEMPLATE

Perdue Company purchased equipment on April 1 for $270,000. The equipment was expected to have a useful life of three years or 18,000 operating hours, and a residual value of $9,000. The equipment was used for 7,500 hours during Year 1, 5,500 hours in Year 2, 4,000 hours in Year 3, and 1,000 hours in Year 4.

Instructions

Determine the amount of depreciation expense for the years ended December 31, Year 1, Year 2, Year 3, and Year 4, by (A) the straight-line method, (B) the units-of-activity method, and (C) the double-declining-balance method.

PR 9-4A Depreciation by two methods; sale of fixed asset   Obj. 2, 3

✔ 1. B. Year 1: $320,000 depreciation expense

EXCEL TEMPLATE   GENERAL LEDGER

New lithographic equipment, acquired at a cost of $800,000 on March 1 at the beginning of a fiscal year, has an estimated useful life of five years and an estimated residual value of $90,000. The manager requested information regarding the effect of alternative methods on the amount of depreciation expense each year.

In the first week of the fifth year, on March 4, the equipment was sold for $135,000.

Instructions

1. Determine the annual depreciation expense for each of the estimated five years of use, the accumulated depreciation at the end of each year, and the book value of the equipment at the end of each year by (A) the straight-line method and (B) the double-declining-balance method. The following columnar headings are suggested for each schedule:

Year	Depreciation Expense	Accumulated Depreciation, End of Year	Book Value, End of Year

2. Journalize the entry to record the sale assuming the manager chose the double-declining-balance method.

3. Journalize the entry to record the sale in (2), assuming that the equipment was sold for $88,750 instead of $135,000.

GENERAL LEDGER

PR 9-5A Transactions for fixed assets, including sale   Obj. 1, 2, 3

The following transactions and adjusting entries were completed by Legacy Furniture Co. during a three-year period. All are related to the use of delivery equipment. The double-declining-balance method of depreciation is used.

Year 1

Jan. 4. Purchased a used delivery truck for $28,000, paying cash.

Nov. 2. Paid garage $675 for miscellaneous repairs to the truck.

Dec. 31. Recorded depreciation on the truck for the year. The estimated useful life of the truck is four years, with a residual value of $5,000 for the truck.

Year 2

Jan. 6. Purchased a new truck for $48,000, paying cash.

Apr. 1. Sold the used truck for $15,000. (Record depreciation to date in Year 2 for the truck.)

June 11. Paid garage $450 for miscellaneous repairs to the truck.

Dec. 31. Record depreciation for the new truck. It has an estimated residual value of $9,000 and an estimated life of five years.

Year 3

July 1. Purchased a new truck for $54,000, paying cash.

Oct. 2. Sold the truck purchased January 6, Year 2, for $16,750. (Record depreciation to date for Year 3 for the truck.)

Dec. 31. Recorded depreciation on the remaining truck. It has an estimated residual value of $12,000 and an estimated useful life of eight years.

Instructions

Journalize the transactions and the adjusting entries.

PR 9-6A Amortization and depletion entries Obj. 4, 5

✔ 1. A. $352,000 Data related to the acquisition of timber rights and intangible assets during the current year ended December 31 are as follows:

A. Timber rights on a tract of land were purchased for $1,600,000 on February 22. The stand of timber is estimated at 5,000,000 board feet. During the current year, 1,100,000 board feet of timber were cut and sold.

B. On December 31, the company determined that $3,750,000 of goodwill was impaired.

C. Governmental and legal costs of $6,600,000 were incurred on April 3 in obtaining a patent with an estimated economic life of 12 years. Amortization is to be for three-fourths of a year.

Instructions

1. Determine the amount of the amortization, depletion, or impairment for the current year for each of the foregoing items.

2. Journalize the adjusting entries required to record the amortization, depletion, or impairment for each item.

Problems: Series B

PR 9-1B Allocating payments and receipts to fixed asset accounts Obj. 1

✔ Land, $860,000 The following payments and receipts are related to land, land improvements, and buildings acquired for use in a wholesale apparel business. The receipts are identified by an asterisk.

A.	Fee paid to attorney for title search	$ 3,600
B.	Cost of real estate acquired as a plant site: Land	720,000
	Building (to be demolished)	60,000
C.	Finder's fee paid to real estate agency	23,400
D.	Delinquent real estate taxes on property, assumed by purchaser	15,000
E.	Architect's and engineer's fees for plans for new building	75,000
F.	Cost of removing building purchased with land in (B)	10,000
G.	Proceeds from sale of salvage materials from old building	3,400*
H.	Cost of filling and grading land	18,000
I.	Premium on one-year insurance policy during construction	8,400
J.	Money borrowed to pay building contractor	800,000*
K.	Special assessment paid to city for extension of water main to the property	13,400
L.	Cost of repairing windstorm damage during construction	3,000
M.	Cost of repairing vandalism damage during construction	2,000
N.	Cost of trees and shrubbery planted	14,000
O.	Cost of paving parking lot to be used by customers	21,600
P.	Interest incurred on building loan during construction	40,000
Q.	Proceeds from insurance company for windstorm and vandalism damage	4,500*
R.	Payment to building contractor for new building	800,000
S.	Refund of premium on insurance policy (I) canceled after 10 months	1,400*

(Continued)

Instructions

1. Assign each payment and receipt to Land (unlimited life), Land Improvements (limited life), Building, or Other Accounts. Indicate receipts by an asterisk. Identify each item by letter and list the amounts in columnar form, as follows:

Item	Land	Land Improvements	Building	Other Accounts

2. Determine the amount debited to Land, Land Improvements, and Building.

3. ➤ The costs assigned to the land, which is used as a plant site, will not be depreciated, while the costs assigned to land improvements will be depreciated. Explain this seemingly contradictory application of the concept of depreciation.

4. What would be the effect on the income statement and balance sheet if the cost of paving the parking lot of $21,600 [payment (O)] was incorrectly classified as Land rather than Land Improvements? Assume Land Improvements are depreciated over a 10-year life using the double-declining-balance method.

PR 9-2B Comparing three depreciation methods   Obj. 2

✔ 1. A. Year 1: straight-
line depreciation,
$71,250

SHOW ME HOW

EXCEL TEMPLATE

Waylander Coatings Company purchased waterproofing equipment on January 6 for $320,000. The equipment was expected to have a useful life of four years, or 20,000 operating hours, and a residual value of $35,000. The equipment was used for 7,200 hours during Year 1, 6,400 hours in Year 2, 4,400 hours in Year 3, and 2,000 hours in Year 4.

Instructions

1. Determine the amount of depreciation expense for the years ended December 31, Year 1, Year 2, Year 3, and Year 4, by (A) the straight-line method, (B) the units-of-activity method, and (C) the double-declining-balance method. Also determine the total depreciation expense for the four years by each method. The following columnar headings are suggested for recording the depreciation expense amounts:

	Depreciation Expense		
Year	Straight-Line Method	Units-of-Activity Method	Double-Declining-Balance Method

2. What method yields the highest depreciation expense for Year 1?

3. What method yields the most depreciation over the four-year life of the equipment?

PR 9-3B Depreciation by three methods; partial years   Obj. 2

✔ A. Year 1, $8,400

EXCEL TEMPLATE

Layton Company purchased tool sharpening equipment on October 1 for $108,000. The equipment was expected to have a useful life of three years or 12,000 operating hours, and a residual value of $7,200. The equipment was used for 1,350 hours during Year 1, 4,200 hours in Year 2, 3,650 hours in Year 3, and 2,800 hours in Year 4.

Instructions

Determine the amount of depreciation expense for the years ended December 31, Year 1, Year 2, Year 3, and Year 4, by (A) the straight-line method, (B) the units-of-activity method, and (C) the double-declining-balance method.

PR 9-4B Depreciation by two methods; sale of fixed asset   Obj. 2, 3

✔ 1. B. Year 1, $55,000
depreciation expense

EXCEL TEMPLATE

GENERAL LEDGER

New tire retreading equipment, acquired at a cost of $110,000 on September 1 at the beginning of a fiscal year, has an estimated useful life of four years and an estimated residual value of $7,500. The manager requested information regarding the effect of alternative methods on the amount of depreciation expense each year. On the basis of the data presented to the manager, the double-declining-balance method was selected.

In the first week of the fourth year, on September 6, the equipment was sold for $18,000.

Instructions

1. Determine the annual depreciation expense for each of the estimated four years of use, the accumulated depreciation at the end of each year, and the book value of the equipment at the end of each year by (A) the straight-line method and (B) the double-declining-balance method. The following columnar headings are suggested for each schedule:

Year	Depreciation Expense	Accumulated Depreciation, End of Year	Book Value, End of Year

2. Journalize the entry to record the sale.

3. Journalize the entry to record the sale, assuming that the equipment sold for $10,500 instead of $18,000.

GENERAL LEDGER

PR 9-5B Transactions for fixed assets, including sale   Obj. 1, 2, 3

The following transactions and adjusting entries were completed by Robinson Furniture Co. during a three-year period. All are related to the use of delivery equipment. The double-declining-balance method of depreciation is used.

Year 1

Jan. 8. Purchased a used delivery truck for $24,000, paying cash.

Mar. 7. Paid garage $900 for changing the oil, replacing the oil filter, and tuning the engine on the delivery truck.

Dec. 31. Recorded depreciation on the truck for the fiscal year. The estimated useful life of the truck is four years, with a residual value of $4,000 for the truck.

Year 2

Jan. 9. Purchased a new truck for $50,000, paying cash.

Feb. 28. Paid garage $250 to tune the engine and make other minor repairs on the used truck.

Apr. 30. Sold the used truck for $9,500. (Record depreciation to date in Year 2 for the truck.)

Dec. 31. Record depreciation for the new truck. It has an estimated residual value of $12,000 and an estimated life of eight years.

Year 3

Sept. 1. Purchased a new truck for $58,500, paying cash.

       4. Sold the truck purchased January 9, Year 2, for $36,000. (Record depreciation to date for Year 3 for the truck.)

Dec. 31. Recorded depreciation on the remaining truck. It has an estimated residual value of $16,000 and an estimated useful life of 10 years.

Instructions

Journalize the transactions and the adjusting entries.

PR 9-6B Amortization and depletion entries   Obj. 4, 5

✔ B. $150,000   Data related to the acquisition of timber rights and intangible assets during the current year ended December 31 are as follows:

A. On December 31, the company determined that $3,400,000 of goodwill was impaired.

B. Governmental and legal costs of $4,800,000 were incurred on September 30 in obtaining a patent with an estimated economic life of eight years. Amortization is to be for one-fourth of a year.

C. Timber rights on a tract of land were purchased for $2,975,000 on February 4. The stand of timber is estimated at 12,500,000 board feet. During the current year, 4,150,000 board feet of timber were cut and sold.

Instructions

1. Determine the amount of the amortization, depletion, or impairment for the current year for each of the foregoing items.

2. Journalize the adjusting entries to record the amortization, depletion, or impairment for each item.

Analysis for Decision Making

REAL WORLD

ADM-1 Continuing Company Analysis—Amazon: Fixed asset turnover ratio

Amazon.com, Inc. is the world's leading Internet retailer of merchandise and media. Amazon also designs and sells electronic products, such as e-readers. **Netflix, Inc.** is the world's leading Internet television network. Both companies compete in the digital media and streaming space. However, Netflix is more narrowly focused in the digital streaming business than is Amazon. Sales and average book value of fixed assets information (in millions) are provided for Amazon and Netflix for a recent year as follows:

	Amazon	Netflix
Sales	$88,988	$5,505
Average book value of fixed assets	13,958	142

A. Compute the fixed asset turnover ratio for each company. (Round to one decimal place.)

B. Which company is more efficient in generating sales from fixed assets?

C. ➤ Interpret your results.

REAL WORLD

ADM-2 Verizon: Fixed asset turnover ratio

Verizon Communications Inc. is a major telecommunications company in the United States. Two recent balance sheets for Verizon disclosed the following information regarding fixed assets:

	End of Year (in millions)	Beginning of Year (in millions)
Property, plant, and equipment	$220,865	$ 209,575
Accumulated depreciation	(131,909)	(120,933)
Property, plant, and equipment (net)	$ 88,956	$ 88,642

Verizon's revenue for the year was $120,550 million. Assume the fixed asset turnover ratio for the telecommunications industry averages approximately 1.1.

A. Determine Verizon's fixed asset turnover ratio. (Round to one decimal place.)

B. ➤ Interpret this ratio with respect to the industry average.

REAL WORLD

ADM-3 FedEx and UPS: Fixed asset turnover ratio

FedEx Corporation and **United Parcel Service, Inc.** compete in the package delivery business. The major fixed assets for each business include aircraft, sorting and handling facilities, delivery vehicles, and information technology. The sales and average book value of fixed assets reported on recent financial statements for each company were as follows:

	FedEx	UPS
Sales (in millions)	$45,567	$55,438
Average book value of fixed assets (in millions)	19,017	17,927

A. Compute the fixed asset turnover ratio for each company. (Round to one decimal place.)

B. Which company appears more efficient in using fixed assets?

C. ➤ Interpret the meaning of the ratio for the more efficient company.

REAL WORLD

ADM-4 Comcast, Google, and Walmart: Fixed asset turnover ratio

The following table shows the sales and average book value of fixed assets for three different companies from three different industries for a recent year:

Company (Industry)	Sales (in millions)	Average Book Value of Fixed Assets (in millions)
Comcast Corporation (communications)	$ 64,657	$ 28,536
Google Inc. (Internet)	59,825	14,189
Walmart Stores, Inc. (retail)	474,259	117,294

A. For each company, determine the fixed asset turnover ratio. (Round to one decimal place.)

B. ▬▬▬► Explain Comcast's fixed asset turnover ratio relative to the other two companies.

Take It Further

ETHICS

TIF 9-1 Ethics in Action

Hard Bodies Co. is a fitness chain that has just completed its second year of operations. At the beginning of its first fiscal year, the company purchased fitness equipment at a cost of $600,000 and estimated that the equipment would have a useful life of five years and no residual value. The company uses the straight-line depreciation method. The company reported net income for the first two years of operations as follows:

Year	Net Income (Loss)
1	$50,000
2	(2,000)

Mike Gambit, the company's chief financial officer (CFO), has recently run financial models to predict future net income, and he expects net losses to continue at $(2,000) per year for the next three years. James Steed, the president of Hard Bodies, is concerned about these predictions, as he is under pressure from the company's owner to return the company to Year 1 net income levels. If the company does not meet these goals, both he and Mike will likely be fired. Mike suggests that the company change the estimated useful life of the fitness equipment to 10 years and increase the equipment's estimated residual value to $50,000. This will reduce depreciation expense and increase net income.

1. ▬▬▬► Evaluate the decision to change the equipment's estimated useful life and estimated residual value to improve earnings. How does this change impact the usefulness of the company's net income for external decision makers?

2. ▬▬▬► If Mike and James make the change, are they acting in an ethical manner? Explain.

REAL WORLD

TIF 9-2 Team Activity

In teams, select a public company that interests you. Obtain the company's most recent annual report on Form 10-K. The Form 10-K is a company's annually required filing with the Securities and Exchange Commission (SEC). It includes the company's financial statements and accompanying notes. The Form 10-K can be obtained either (A) from the investor relations section of the company's Web site or (B) by using the company search feature of the SEC's EDGAR database service found at www.sec.gov/edgar/searchedgar/companysearch.html.

1. Based on the information in the company's most recent annual report, answer the following questions:

   A. What depreciation methods does the company use to compute depreciation expense?

   B. How much depreciation expense does the company report on its income statement?

   C. What is the initial cost of the company's fixed assets?

(Continued)

D. What is the book value of the company's fixed assets?

E. What types of intangible assets, if any, does the company report on its balance sheet?

2. ➤ Does the book value of the company's fixed assets reflect their current market value? Explain your answer.

TIF 9-3   Communication

Godwin Co. owns three delivery trucks. Details for each truck at the end of the most recent year follow:

	Age	Expected Useful Life	Initial Cost	Accumulated Depreciation
Truck 1	3	6	$22,500	$11,250
Truck 2	5	6	26,250	21,875
Truck 3	2	6	28,500	9,500

- At the beginning of the year, a hydraulic lift is added to Truck 1 at a cost of $4,500. The addition of the hydraulic lift will allow the company to deliver much larger objects than could previously be delivered.
- At the beginning of the year, the engine of Truck 2 is overhauled at a cost of $5,000. The engine overhaul will extend the truck's useful life by three years.

➤ Write a short memo to Godwin's chief financial officer explaining the financial statement effects of the expenditures associated with Trucks 1 and 2.

Chapter 10

Liabilities: Current, Installment Notes, Contingencies

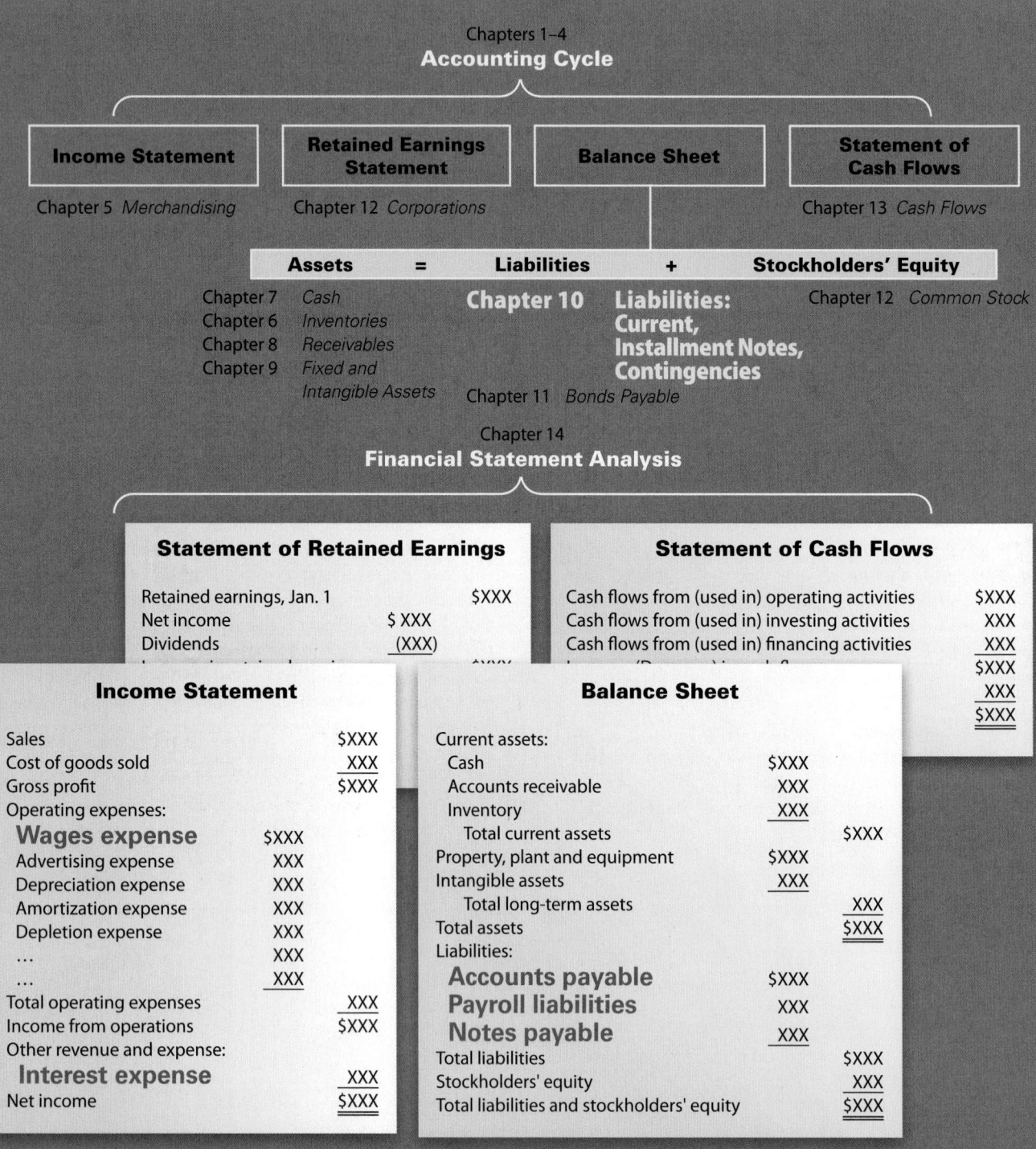

Chapters 1–4
Accounting Cycle

Income Statement	Retained Earnings Statement	Balance Sheet	Statement of Cash Flows

Chapter 5 *Merchandising* Chapter 12 *Corporations* Chapter 13 *Cash Flows*

Assets = Liabilities + Stockholders' Equity

Chapter 7 *Cash*
Chapter 6 *Inventories*
Chapter 8 *Receivables*
Chapter 9 *Fixed and Intangible Assets*

Chapter 10 Liabilities: Current, Installment Notes, Contingencies

Chapter 11 *Bonds Payable*

Chapter 12 *Common Stock*

Chapter 14
Financial Statement Analysis

Statement of Retained Earnings

Retained earnings, Jan. 1	$XXX
Net income	$ XXX
Dividends	(XXX)

Statement of Cash Flows

Cash flows from (used in) operating activities	$XXX
Cash flows from (used in) investing activities	XXX
Cash flows from (used in) financing activities	XXX
	$XXX
	XXX
	$XXX

Income Statement

Sales	$XXX
Cost of goods sold	XXX
Gross profit	$XXX
Operating expenses:	
Wages expense	$XXX
Advertising expense	XXX
Depreciation expense	XXX
Amortization expense	XXX
Depletion expense	XXX
…	XXX
…	XXX
Total operating expenses	XXX
Income from operations	$XXX
Other revenue and expense:	
Interest expense	XXX
Net income	$XXX

Balance Sheet

Current assets:		
Cash	$XXX	
Accounts receivable	XXX	
Inventory	XXX	
Total current assets		$XXX
Property, plant and equipment	$XXX	
Intangible assets	XXX	
Total long-term assets		XXX
Total assets		$XXX
Liabilities:		
Accounts payable	$XXX	
Payroll liabilities	XXX	
Notes payable	XXX	
Total liabilities		$XXX
Stockholders' equity		XXX
Total liabilities and stockholders' equity		$XXX

476

Starbucks

Buying goods on credit is essential for businesses to run efficiently. The use of credit makes transactions more convenient and improves buying power. For *individuals*, the most common form of short-term credit is a credit card. Credit cards allow individuals to purchase items before they are paid for, while removing the need for individuals to carry large amounts of cash. They also provide documentation of purchases through a monthly credit card statement.

Short-term credit is also used by *businesses* to make purchasing items more convenient. It also gives the business control over the payment for goods and services. When **Starbucks** opened its first coffee shop in 1971, it relied on short-term trade credit, or accounts payable, to purchase ingredients for its coffee shop in Seattle's historic Pike Place Market. Today, Starbucks still relies on accounts payable and short-term trade credit, which also gives it control over cash payments by separating the purchase function from the payment function. Thus, the employee responsible for purchasing the ingredients is separated from the employee responsible for paying for the purchase. This separation of duties can help prevent unauthorized purchases or payments.

In addition to accounts payable, Starbucks has liabilities related to payroll, notes, and contingencies. This chapter describes and illustrates the accounting for each of these liabilities.

What's Covered

Liabilities: Current, Installment Notes, Contingencies

Current Liabilities	**Installment Notes**	**Contingent Liabilities**	**Reporting Liabilities**
■ Accounts Payable and Accruals (Obj. 1)	■ Issuance (Obj. 4)	■ Probable Estimable (Obj. 5)	■ Balance Sheet (Obj. 6)
■ Notes Payable (Obj. 1)	■ Periodic Payments (Obj. 4)	■ Probable Not Estimable (Obj. 5)	
■ Current Portion of Long-Term Debt (Obj. 1)		■ Reasonably Possible (Obj. 5)	
■ Payroll (Obj. 2)		■ Remote (Obj. 5)	
■ Fringe Benefits (Obj. 3)			

Learning Objectives

Obj. 1 Describe and illustrate current liabilities, including those related to accounts payable, accruals, notes payable, and the current portion of long-term debt.

Obj. 2 Describe and illustrate the accounting for payroll liabilities.

Obj. 3 Describe and illustrate the accounting for employee fringe benefits, including vacation pay and pensions.

Obj. 4 Describe and illustrate the accounting for installment notes.

Obj. 5 Describe and illustrate the accounting for contingent liabilities, including product warranties.

Obj. 6 Describe the reporting of liabilities on the balance sheet.

Analysis for Decision Making

Describe and illustrate the use of the quick ratio in analyzing a company's ability to pay its current liabilities.

Objective 1

Describe and illustrate current liabilities, including those related to accounts payable, accruals, notes payable, and the current portion of long-term debt.

Current Liabilities

When a company or a bank advances *credit*, it is making a loan. The company or bank is called a *creditor* (or *lender*). The individuals or companies receiving the loan are called *debtors* (or *borrowers*).

Debt is recorded as a liability by the debtor. *Long-term liabilities* are debts due beyond one year. Thus, a 30-year mortgage used to purchase property is a long-term liability. *Current liabilities* are debts that will be paid out of current assets and are due within one year.

Types of current liabilities discussed in this section include the following:

■ Accounts payable and accruals
■ Short-term notes payable
■ Current portion of long-term debt

Accounts Payable and Accruals

Accounts payable transactions have been described and illustrated in earlier chapters. These transactions involve a variety of purchases on account, including the purchase of merchandise and supplies.

Accruals have also been described and illustrated in earlier chapters. Accrued liabilities reflect an obligation to pay current assets in the future. Accrued liabilities are normally recorded at the end of an accounting period as part of the adjustment process. For example, wages due employees at the end of the period are recorded as an expense (Wages Expense) and an accrued liability (Wages Payable).

For most companies, accounts payable and accrued liabilities are the largest portion of current liabilities.

Link to Starbucks

On a recent balance sheet, **Starbucks** reported $533.7 million of accounts payable and $1,524.4 million of accrued liabilities, which make up over two-thirds of its current liabilities.

Short-Term Notes Payable

Notes may be issued to purchase merchandise or other assets. Notes may also be issued to creditors to satisfy an account payable created earlier.[1]

To illustrate, assume that Nature's Sunshine Company issued a 90-day, 12% note for $1,000, dated August 1, to Murray Co. for a $1,000 overdue account. The entry to record the issuance of the note is as follows:

Aug. 1	Accounts Payable—Murray Co.	1,000	
	Notes Payable		1,000
	Issued a 90-day, 12% note on account.		

$$A = L + E$$
$$+ -$$

When the note matures, the entry to record the payment of $1,000 plus $30 interest ($1,000 × 12% × 90 ÷ 360[2]) is as follows:

Oct. 30	Notes Payable	1,000	
	Interest Expense	30	
	Cash		1,030
	Paid principal and interest due on note.		

$$A = L + E$$
$$- \quad - \quad - Exp$$

The interest expense is reported in the Other Expense section of the income statement for the year ended December 31. The interest expense account is closed at December 31.

Each note transaction affects a debtor (borrower) and creditor (lender). Exhibit 1 shows how the same transactions are recorded by the debtor and creditor. In Exhibit 1, the debtor (borrower) is Bowden Co., and the creditor (lender) is Coker Co.

Exhibit 1 Note Transactions: Borrower and Creditor

	Bowden Co. (Borrower)			Coker Co. (Creditor)		
May 1. Bowden Co. purchased merchandise on account from Coker Co., $10,000, 2/10, n/30. The merchandise cost Coker Co. $7,500.	Inventory	10,000		Accounts Receivable	10,000	
	Accounts Payable		10,000	Sales		10,000
				Cost of Goods Sold	7,500	
				Merchandise Inventory		7,500
May 31. Bowden Co. issued a 60-day, 12% note for $10,000 to Coker Co. on account.	Accounts Payable	10,000		Notes Receivable	10,000	
	Notes Payable		10,000	Accounts Receivable		10,000
July 30. Bowden Co. paid Coker Co. the amount due on the note of May 31. Interest: $10,000 × 12% × 60 ÷ 360.	Notes Payable	10,000		Cash	10,200	
	Interest Expense	200		Interest Revenue		200
	Cash		10,200	Notes Receivable		10,000

A company may also borrow from a bank by issuing a note. To illustrate, assume that on September 19, Iceburg Company borrowed cash from First National Bank by issuing a $4,000, 90-day, 15% note to the bank. The entry to record the issuance of the note and the cash proceeds is as follows:

Sept. 19	Cash	4,000	
	Notes Payable		4,000
	Issued a 90-day, 15% note		
	to First National Bank.		

$$A = L + E$$
$$+ \quad +$$

[1] The accounting for notes received to satisfy an account receivable was described and illustrated in Chapter 8, *Receivables*.
[2] To simplify computations and rounding, 360 days per year are used. In practice, companies use 365 days.

On the due date of the note (December 18), Iceburg Company owes First National Bank $4,000 plus interest of $150 ($4,000 × 15% × 90 ÷ 360). The entry to record the payment of the note is as follows:

A = L + E
–   –   – **Exp**

Dec. 18	Notes Payable	4,000	
	Interest Expense	150	
	Cash		4,150
	Paid principal and interest due on note.		

In some cases, a *discounted note* may be issued rather than an interest-bearing note. A discounted note has the following characteristics:

- The interest rate on the note is called the *discount rate*.
- The amount of interest on the note, called the *discount*, is computed by multiplying the discount rate times the face amount of the note.
- The debtor (borrower) receives the face amount of the note less the discount, called the *proceeds*.
- The debtor must repay the face amount of the note on the due date.

To illustrate, assume that on August 10, Cary Company issues a $20,000, 90-day discounted note to Western National Bank. The discount rate is 15%, and the amount of the discount is $750 ($20,000 × 15% × 90 ÷ 360). Thus, the proceeds received by Cary are $19,250. The entry by Cary is as follows:

A = L + E
+   +   – **Exp**

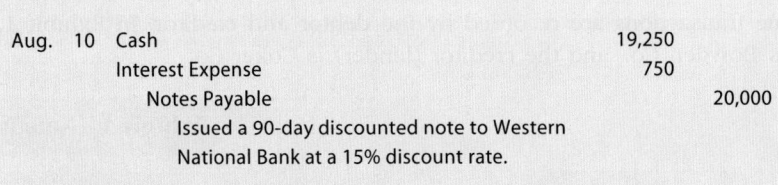

Aug. 10	Cash	19,250	
	Interest Expense	750	
	Notes Payable		20,000
	Issued a 90-day discounted note to Western		
	National Bank at a 15% discount rate.		

The entry when Cary pays the discounted note on November 8 is as follows:[3]

A = L + E
–   –

Nov. 8	Notes Payable	20,000	
	Cash		20,000
	Paid note due.		

Current Portion of Long-Term Debt

The current portions of long-term debt, such as the current portion of installment notes, are reported on the balance sheet as a current liability. An **installment note** is a debt that requires the borrower to make equal periodic payments to the lender for the term of the note. Installment notes are often used to purchase property, plant, and equipment. The accounting for installment notes is described and illustrated later in this chapter.

Check Up Corner 10-1 Short-Term Notes Payable

On October 3, Bering Industries Inc. is considering two alternatives for a short-term loan from Community Bank: (1) issue a $60,000, 60-day, 5% note or (2) issue a $60,000, 60-day note that the bank discounts at 5%.
A. Journalize the entries to record the issuance and repayment of the note, assuming the company selects the $60,000, 60-day, 5% note.
B. Journalize the entries to record the issuance and repayment of the note, assuming the company selects the $60,000, 60-day note that the bank discounts at 5%.

[3] If the accounting period ends before a discounted note is paid, an adjusting entry should record the prepaid (deferred) interest that is not yet an expense. This deferred interest would be deducted from Notes Payable in the current liabilities section of the balance sheet.

Solution:

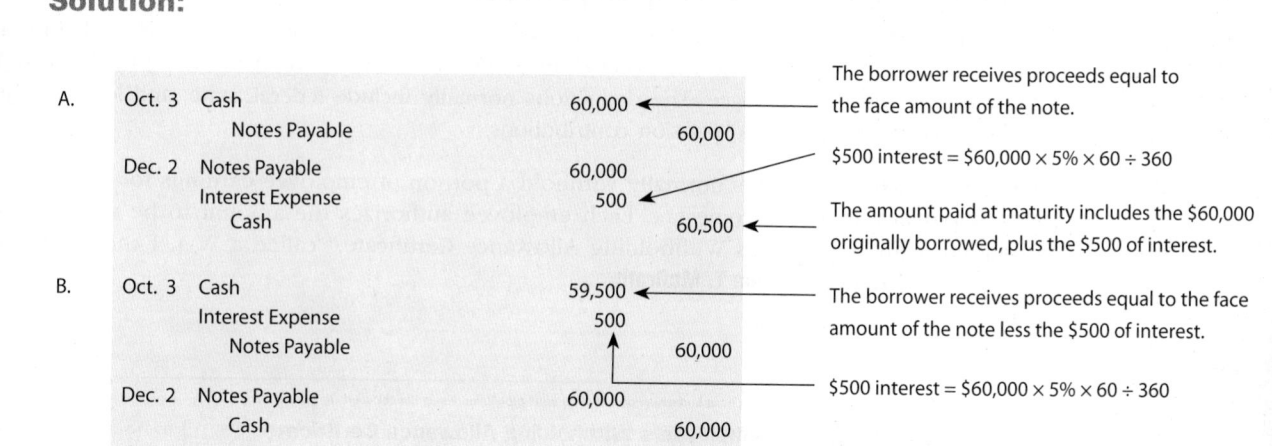

The borrower receives proceeds equal to the face amount of the note.

A. Oct. 3 Cash 60,000
Notes Payable 60,000

Dec. 2 Notes Payable 60,000
Interest Expense 500
Cash 60,500

$500 interest = $60,000 × 5% × 60 ÷ 360

The amount paid at maturity includes the $60,000 originally borrowed, plus the $500 of interest.

B. Oct. 3 Cash 59,500
Interest Expense 500
Notes Payable 60,000

Dec. 2 Notes Payable 60,000
Cash 60,000

The borrower receives proceeds equal to the face amount of the note less the $500 of interest.

$500 interest = $60,000 × 5% × 60 ÷ 360

The amount repaid equals the $60,000 face amount.

Check Up Corner

Payroll Liabilities

Objective 2
Describe and illustrate the accounting for payroll liabilities.

In accounting, **payroll** refers to the amount paid to employees for services they provided during the period. A company's payroll is important for the following reasons:

- Payroll and related payroll taxes significantly affect the net income of most companies.
- Payroll is subject to federal and state regulations.
- Good employee morale requires payroll to be paid timely and accurately.

Liability for Employee Earnings

Salary usually refers to payment for managerial and administrative services. Salary is normally expressed in terms of a month or a year. *Wages* usually refers to payment for employee manual labor. The rate of wages is normally stated on an hourly or a weekly basis. The salary or wage of an employee may be increased by bonuses, commissions, profit sharing, or cost-of-living adjustments.

Companies engaged in interstate commerce must follow the Fair Labor Standards Act. This act, sometimes called the Federal Wage and Hour Law, requires employers to pay a minimum rate of 1½ times the regular rate for all hours worked in excess of 40 hours per week. Exemptions are provided for executive, administrative, and some supervisory positions. Increased rates for working overtime, nights, or holidays are common, even when not required by law. These rates may be as much as twice the regular rate.

To illustrate computing an employee's earnings, assume that **John T. McGrath** is a salesperson employed by **McDermott Supply Co.** McGrath's regular rate is $34 per hour, and any hours worked in excess of 40 hours per week are paid at 1½ times the regular rate. McGrath worked 42 hours for the week ended December 27. His earnings of $1,462 for the week are computed as follows:

Earnings at regular rate (40 hrs. × $34)	$1,360
Earnings at overtime rate [2 hrs. × ($34 × 1½)]	102
Total earnings	$1,462

Deductions from Employee Earnings

The total earnings of an employee for a payroll period, including any overtime pay, are called **gross pay**. From this amount is subtracted one or more *deductions* to arrive at the **net pay**. Net pay is the amount paid the employee. The deductions normally include federal, state, and local income taxes, medical insurance, and pension contributions.

Income Taxes Employers normally withhold a portion of employee earnings for payment of the employees' federal income tax. Each employee authorizes the amount to be withheld by completing an "Employee's Withholding Allowance Certificate," called a W-4. Exhibit 2 is the W-4 form submitted by **John T. McGrath**.

Exhibit 2

Employee's Withholding Allowance Certificate (W-4 Form)

```
-------------------- Separate here and give Form W-4 to your employer. Keep the top part for your records. --------------------

Form  W-4        Employee's Withholding Allowance Certificate              OMB No. 1545-0074
Department of the Treasury   ▶ Whether you are entitled to claim a certain number of allowances or exemption from withholding is       20--
Internal Revenue Service       subject to review by the IRS. Your employer may be required to send a copy of this form to the IRS.
1   Your first name and middle initial      Last name                      2  Your social security number
    John T.                                 McGrath                            381  48  9120
    Home address (number and street or rural route)      3 [X] Single  [ ] Married  [ ] Married, but withhold at higher Single rate.
    1830 4th Street                                      Note. If married, but legally separated, or spouse is a nonresident alien, check the "Single" box.
    City or town, state, and ZIP code                    4  If your last name differs from that shown on your social security card,
    Clinton, Iowa 52732-6142                                check here. You must call 1-800-772-1213 for a replacement card. ▶ [ ]
5   Total number of allowances you are claiming (from line H above or from the applicable worksheet on page 2)   5 | 1
6   Additional amount, if any, you want withheld from each paycheck  . . . . . . . . . . . . . .                 6 | $
7   I claim exemption from withholding for 20--, and I certify that I meet both of the following conditions for exemption.
    • Last year I had a right to a refund of all federal income tax withheld because I had no tax liability, and
    • This year I expect a refund of all federal income tax withheld because I expect to have no tax liability.
    If you meet both conditions, write "Exempt" here . . . . . . . . . . . . . ▶ | 7
Under penalties of perjury, I declare that I have examined this certificate and, to the best of my knowledge and belief, it is true, correct, and complete.
Employee's signature
(This form is not valid unless you sign it.) ▶  John T. McGrath        Date ▶  June 2, 20--
8   Employer's name and address (Employer: Complete lines 8 and 10 only if sending to the IRS.)  9 Office code (optional)  10 Employer identification number (EIN)

For Privacy Act and Paperwork Reduction Act Notice, see page 2.      Cat. No. 10220Q              Form W-4 (20--)
```

On the W-4, an employee indicates marital status and the number of withholding allowances. A single employee may claim one withholding allowance. A married employee may claim an additional allowance for a spouse. An employee may also claim an allowance for each dependent other than a spouse. Each allowance reduces the federal income tax withheld from the employee's pay. Exhibit 2 indicates that McGrath is single and, thus, claimed one withholding allowance.

The federal income tax withheld depends on each employee's gross pay and W-4 allowance. Withholding tables issued by the Internal Revenue Service (IRS) are used to determine amounts to withhold.

FICA Tax Employers are required by the Federal Insurance Contributions Act (FICA) to withhold a portion of the earnings of each employee. The **FICA tax** withheld contributes to the following two federal programs:

- *Social security*, which provides payments for retirees, survivors, and disability insurance.
- *Medicare*, which provides health insurance for senior citizens.

The amount withheld from each employee is based on the employee's earnings *paid* in the *calendar* year. The withholding tax rates and maximum earnings subject to tax are often revised by Congress.[4] To simplify, this chapter assumes the following rates and earnings subject to tax:

- Social security: 6% on all earnings
- Medicare: 1.5% on all earnings

[4] For 2015, the social security tax rate was 6.2% and the Medicare tax rate was 1.45%. Earnings subject to the social security tax are limited to an annual threshold amount. To simplify, we assume all earnings are subject to social security taxes.

To illustrate, assume that John T. McGrath's earnings for the week ending December 27 are $1,462 and the total FICA tax to be withheld is $109.65, computed as follows:

Earnings subject to 6% social security tax	$1,462	
Social security tax rate	× 6%	
Social security tax		$ 87.72
Earnings subject to 1.5% Medicare tax	$1,462	
Medicare tax rate	× 1.5%	
Medicare tax		21.93
Total FICA tax		$109.65

Other Deductions Employees may choose to have additional amounts deducted from their gross pay. For example, an employee may authorize deductions for retirement savings, charitable contributions, or life insurance. A union contract may also require the deduction of union dues.

Computing Employee Net Pay

Gross earnings less payroll deductions equals *net pay*, sometimes called *take-home pay*. Assume that John T. McGrath authorized weekly deductions of $20 for retirement savings and $5 for a United Fund contribution. Assuming that $257.95 of federal income tax is withheld, McGrath's net pay for the week ended December 27 is $1,069.40, computed as follows:

Gross earnings for the week		$1,462.00
Deductions:		
Social security tax	$ 87.72	
Medicare tax	21.93	
Federal income tax	257.95	
Retirement savings	20.00	
United Fund	5.00	
Total deductions		392.60
Net pay		$1,069.40

Employer's Payroll Taxes

Employers are subject to the following payroll taxes for amounts paid their employees:

- *FICA Tax:* Employers must match the employee's FICA tax contribution.
- *Federal Unemployment Compensation Tax (FUTA):* This employer tax provides for temporary payments to those who become unemployed. The tax collected by the federal government is allocated among the states for use in state programs rather than paid directly to employees. Congress often revises the FUTA tax rate and maximum earnings subject to tax.

Why It Matters

The Most You Will Ever Pay

In 1936, the Social Security Board described how the tax was expected to affect a worker's pay, as follows:

The taxes called for in this law will be paid both by your employer and by you. For the next 3 years, you will pay maybe 15 cents a week, maybe 25 cents a week, maybe 30 cents or more, according to what you earn. That is to say, during the next 3 years, beginning January 1, 1937, you will pay 1 cent for every dollar you earn, and at the same time, your employer will pay 1 cent for every dollar you earn, up to $3,000 a year....

...Beginning in 1940 you will pay, and your employer will pay, 1½ cents for each dollar you earn, up to $3,000 a year...and then beginning

in 1943, you will pay 2 cents, and so will your employer, for every dollar you earn for the next three years. After that, you and your employer will each pay half a cent more for 3 years, and finally, beginning in 1949, ... you and your employer will each pay 3 cents on each dollar you earn, up to $3,000 a year. That is the most you will ever pay.

The rate on January 1, 2015, was 7.65 cents per dollar earned (7.65%). The social security portion was 6.20% on the first $118,500 of earnings. The Medicare portion was 1.45% on all earnings. In addition, there is an additional Medicare tax of 0.9% on wages in excess of $200,000 for the calendar year.

Source: Arthur Lodge, "That Is the Most You Will Ever Pay," *Journal of Accountancy,* October 1985, p. 44.

■ *State Unemployment Compensation Tax (SUTA):* This employer tax also provides temporary payments to those who become unemployed. The FUTA and SUTA programs are closely coordinated, with the states distributing the unemployment checks.[5] SUTA tax rates and earnings subject to tax vary by state.[6]

The preceding employer taxes are an operating expense of the company. Exhibit 3 summarizes the responsibility for employee and employer payroll taxes.

Exhibit 3
Responsibility for Tax Payments

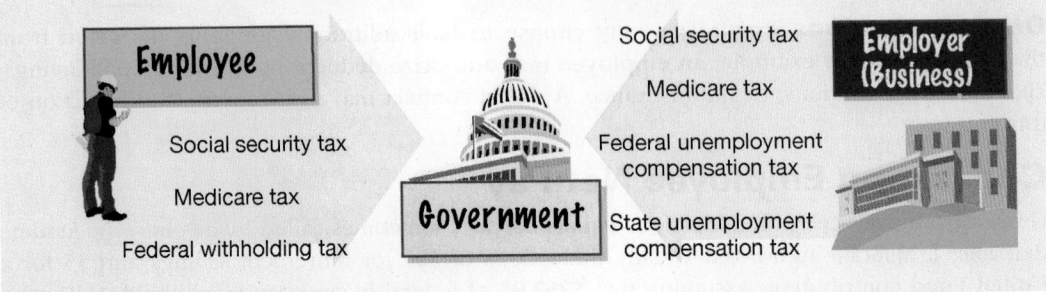

Recording Payroll

The payroll liabilities are normally recorded at the end of each payroll period. To illustrate, the following data for **McDermott Supply** for its payroll period ending March 21 is used.

Payroll:	
Sales salaries	$20,000
Office salaries	5,000
Total payroll	$25,000
Salaries subject to payroll taxes:	
Social security and Medicare	$25,000
State and federal unemployment tax	10,000
Payroll tax rates:	
Social security tax	6.0%
Medicare tax	1.5
State unemployment compensation tax	5.4
Federal unemployment compensation tax	0.8
Employee deductions:	
Federal income tax withholdings	$2,100
State income tax withholdings	550
Retirement contributions	1,200
Charitable contributions	250

The journal entry to record the March 21 payroll is as follows:

A = L + E
   +   – Exp

Mar. 21	Sales Salaries Expense	20,000	
	Office Salaries Expense	5,000	
	Social Security Tax Payable ($25,000 × 6%)		1,500
	Medicare Tax Payable ($25,000 × 1.5%)		375
	Employees Federal Income Tax Payable		2,100
	Employees State Income Tax Payable		550
	Retirement Contributions Payable		1,200
	Charitable Contributions Payable		250
	Salaries Payable		19,025

[5] This rate may be reduced to 0.8% for credits for state unemployment compensation tax.
[6] For 2015, the maximum state rate credited against the federal unemployment rate was 5.4% of the first $7,000 of each employee's earnings during a calendar year.

Employers must match the employees' social security and Medicare taxes. In addition, an employer must pay state and federal unemployment compensation taxes. The employer's payroll taxes of $2,495 for the March 21 payroll are as follows:

Social security tax ($25,000 × 6%)	$1,500
Medicare tax ($25,000 × 1.5%)	375
State unemployment tax ($10,000 × 5.4%)	540
Federal unemployment tax ($10,000 × 0.8%)	80
Total payroll taxes	$2,495

The journal entry to record the payroll tax expense is as follows:

Mar. 21	Payroll Tax Expense	2,495	
	Social Security Tax Payable		1,500
	Medicare Tax Payable		375
	State Unemployment Tax Payable		540
	Federal Unemployment Tax Payable		80

A = L + E
  + − Exp

When the preceding liabilities are paid, a journal entry is recorded debiting the liability accounts and crediting Cash.

Check Up Corner 10-2 Payroll Entries

Wildcat Company had gross wages of $180,000 for the week ended March 20. All $180,000 of wages are subject to social security and Medicare taxes, while $30,000 of wages are subject to federal and state unemployment taxes. Tax rates are as follows:

Social security tax	6.0%
Medicare tax	1.5
State unemployment compensation tax	5.4
Federal unemployment compensation tax	0.8

The total amount withheld from employee wages for federal taxes was $38,500.

A. Journalize the entry to record the payroll for the week of March 20.

B. Journalize the entry to record the employer's payroll tax expense incurred for the week of March 20.

Solution:

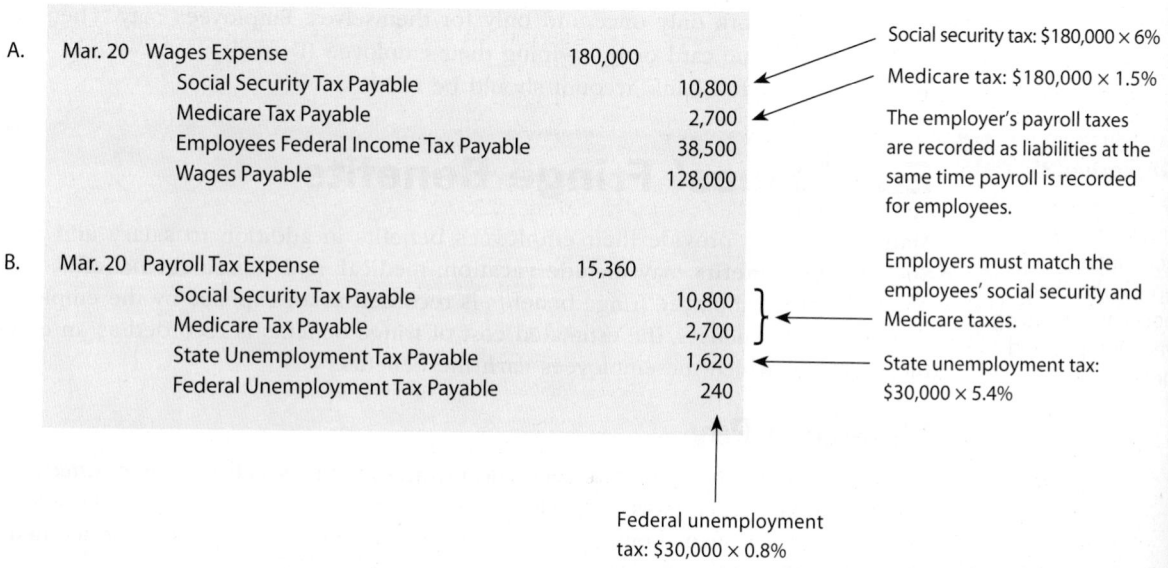

A.	Mar. 20	Wages Expense	180,000	
		Social Security Tax Payable		10,800
		Medicare Tax Payable		2,700
		Employees Federal Income Tax Payable		38,500
		Wages Payable		128,000
B.	Mar. 20	Payroll Tax Expense	15,360	
		Social Security Tax Payable		10,800
		Medicare Tax Payable		2,700
		State Unemployment Tax Payable		1,620
		Federal Unemployment Tax Payable		240

Social security tax: $180,000 × 6%

Medicare tax: $180,000 × 1.5%

The employer's payroll taxes are recorded as liabilities at the same time payroll is recorded for employees.

Employers must match the employees' social security and Medicare taxes.

State unemployment tax: $30,000 × 5.4%

Federal unemployment tax: $30,000 × 0.8%

Check Up Corner

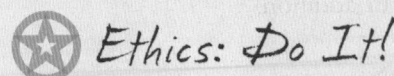 *Ethics: Do It!*

$8 Million for 18 Minutes of Work

Computer system controls can be very important in issuing payroll checks. In one case, a Detroit schoolteacher was paid $4,015,625 after deducting $3,884,375 in payroll deductions for 18 minutes of overtime work. The error was caused by a computer glitch when the teacher's employee identification number was substituted incorrectly in the "hourly wage" field and wasn't caught by the payroll software. After six days, the error was discovered, and the money was returned. "One of the things that came with (the software) is a fail-safe that prevents that. It doesn't work," a financial officer said. The district has since installed a program to flag any paycheck exceeding $10,000.

Source: Associated Press, September 27, 2002.

Paying Payroll

Companies pay employees either by electronic funds transfer or by issuing *payroll checks*. With electronic funds transfers, the employee's net pay is electronically deposited into their bank account each period. The employees receive a payroll statement summarizing how the net pay was computed.

Most companies use a special payroll bank account for payroll. In such cases, payroll is processed as follows:

1. The total net pay for the period is determined.
2. The company authorizes an electronic funds transfer (EFT) from its regular bank account to the special payroll bank account for the total net pay.
3. Individual EFTs or payroll checks are disbursed from the payroll account.

An advantage of using a separate payroll bank account is that reconciling the bank statements is simplified.

Internal Controls for Payroll

The controls described in Chapter 7 also apply to payrolls. Some examples of payroll controls include the following:

- The hiring and firing of employees should be properly authorized and approved in writing.
- All changes in pay rates should be properly authorized and approved in writing.
- Employees should be observed when arriving for work to verify that employees are "checking in" for work only once and only for themselves. Employees may "check in" for work by using a time card or by swiping their employee ID card.
- A special payroll bank account should be used.

Objective 3

Describe and illustrate the accounting for employee fringe benefits, including vacation pay and pensions.

Employees' Fringe Benefits

Many companies provide their employees benefits in addition to salary and wages earned. Such **fringe benefits** may include vacation, medical, and retirement benefits.

The cost of employee fringe benefits is recorded as an expense by the employer. To match revenues and expenses, the estimated cost of fringe benefits is recorded as an expense during the period in which the employees earn the benefits.

Vacation Pay

Most employers provide employees vacations, sometimes called *compensated absences*. The liability to pay for employee vacations could be accrued as a liability at the end of each pay period. However, many companies wait and record an adjusting entry for accrued vacation at the end of the year.

To illustrate, assume that employees earn one day of vacation for each month worked. The estimated vacation pay for the year ending December 31 is $325,000. The adjusting entry for the accrued vacation is as follows:

Dec. 31	Vacation Pay Expense	325,000	
	Vacation Pay Payable		325,000
	Accrued vacation pay for the year.		

A = L + E
+   – Exp

Employees may be required to take all their vacation time within one year. In such cases, any accrued vacation pay will be paid within one year. Thus, the vacation pay payable is reported as a current liability on the balance sheet. If employees are allowed to accumulate their vacation pay, the estimated vacation pay payable that will *not* be taken within a year is reported as a long-term liability.

When employees take vacations, the liability for vacation pay is decreased by debiting Vacation Pay Payable. Salaries or Wages Payable and the other related payroll accounts for taxes and withholdings are credited.

Pensions

A **pension** is a cash payment to retired employees. Pension rights are accrued by employees as they work, based on the employer's pension plan. Two basic types of pension plans are defined contribution and defined benefit plans.[7]

Defined Contribution Plans In a **defined contribution plan**, the company invests contributions on behalf of the employee during the employee's working years. Normally, the employee and employer contribute to the plan. The employee's pension depends on the total contributions and the investment returns earned on those contributions.

One of the more popular defined contribution plans is the 401k plan. Under this plan, employees contribute a portion of their gross pay to investments, such as mutual funds. A 401k plan offers employees two advantages.

- The employee contribution is deducted before taxes.
- The contributions and related earnings are not taxed until withdrawn at retirement.

In most cases, the employer matches some portion of the employee's contribution. The employer's cost is debited to *Pension Expense*. To illustrate, assume that Heaven Scent Perfumes Company contributes 10% of employee monthly salaries to an employee 401k plan. Assuming $500,000 of monthly salaries, the journal entry to record the monthly contribution is as follows:

Dec. 31	Pension Expense	50,000	
	Cash		50,000
	Contributed 10% of monthly salaries		
	to pension plan.		

A = L + E
–   – Exp

Defined Benefit Plans In a **defined benefit plan**, the company pays the employee a fixed annual pension based on a formula. The formula is normally based on such factors as the employee's years of service, age, and past salary.

In a defined benefit plan, the employer is obligated to pay for (fund) the employee's future pension benefits. As a result, many companies are replacing their defined benefit plans with defined contribution plans.

The pension cost of a defined benefit plan is debited to *Pension Expense*. Cash is credited for the amount contributed (funded) by the employer. Any unfunded amount is credited to *Unfunded Pension Liability*.

---

[7] The accounting for pensions is complex due to the uncertainties of estimating future pension liabilities. These estimates depend on such factors as employee life expectancies, employee turnover, expected employee compensation levels, and investment income on pension contributions. Additional accounting and disclosures related to pensions are covered in advanced accounting courses.

To illustrate, assume that the defined benefit plan of Hinkle Co. requires an annual pension cost of $80,000. This annual contribution is based on estimates of Hinkle's future pension liabilities. On December 31, Hinkle pays $60,000 to the pension fund. The entry to record the payment and the unfunded liability is as follows:

A = L + E
–   +   – Exp

Dec. 31	Pension Expense	80,000	
	Cash		60,000
	Unfunded Pension Liability		20,000
	Annual pension cost and contribution.		

If the unfunded pension liability is to be paid within one year, it is reported as a current liability on the balance sheet. Any portion of the unfunded pension liability that will be paid beyond one year is a long-term liability.

Why It Matters

State Pension Obligations

Each state has a pension plan for its employees. The plan is determined by the state legislature through the normal political process. The funding of each state's plan relative to the outstanding obligation differs across the states, again according to political decisions regarding the funding level.

Some states are well funded, while others face significant pension shortfalls. Only 13 out of 50 states have pension assets greater than 80% of their pension obligations, which is considered a healthy funding ratio. The U.S. Census Bureau provides an annual survey on the status of state pension plans. According to a recent survey, the top and bottom five states by the percent of pension obligations funded are as follows:

Rank	State	Percent of Pension Funded	Pension Contributions as a Percent of State Payroll	Pension Liability per State Resident
1	Wisconsin	102%	12.6%	$ 0
2	North Carolina	95	12.7	407
3	New York	93	15.7	877
4	South Dakota	93	13.3	730
5	Tennessee	89	15.1	693
46	New Jersey	55	16.4	6,447
47	Alaska	53	31.6	11,028
48	Kentucky	50	21.6	5,907
49	Connecticut	49	25.7	7,027
50	Illinois	47	31.9	7,636

As can be seen, the states with the most severe underfunding are also the states making the largest contributions to their pension plans as a percent of the state's governmental payroll. This is likely an attempt to "catch up" to their obligations, but is coming at a high cost to the state's taxpayers.

Postretirement Benefits Other than Pensions

Employees may earn rights to other postretirement benefits from their employer. Such benefits may include dental care, eye care, medical care, life insurance, tuition assistance, tax services, and legal services.

The accounting for other postretirement benefits is similar to that of defined benefit pension plans. The estimate of the annual benefits expense is recorded by debiting *Postretirement Benefits Expense*. If the benefits are fully funded, Cash is credited for the same amount. If the benefits are not fully funded, a postretirement benefits plan liability account is also credited.

The financial statements should disclose the nature of the postretirement benefits liabilities. These disclosures are usually included as notes to the financial statements. Additional accounting and disclosures for postretirement benefits are covered in advanced accounting courses.

Installment Notes

Objective 4

Describe and illustrate the accounting for installment notes.

An **installment note** is a debt that requires the borrower to make equal periodic payments to the lender for the term of the note. Each note payment includes the following:

- Payment of a portion of the amount initially borrowed, called the *principal*
- Payment of interest on the outstanding balance

At the end of the note's term, the principal will have been repaid in full.

Installment notes are often used to purchase specific assets such as equipment, and are often secured by the purchased asset. If the borrower fails to pay the note, the lender has the right to take possession of the pledged asset and sell it to pay off the debt. Installment notes that are secured by purchased assets are sometimes called *mortgage notes*.

Issuance

When an installment note is issued, an entry is recorded debiting Cash and crediting Notes Payable. To illustrate, assume that on January 1 of Year 1 Lewis Company issues the following installment note to City National Bank:

Principal amount of note	$24,000
Interest rate	6%
Term of note	5 years
Annual payments	$5,698[8]

The entry to record the issuance of the note is as follows:

Year 1			
Jan. 1	Cash	24,000	
	Notes Payable		24,000
	Issued installment note for cash.		

$$A = L + E$$
$$+ \quad +$$

Periodic Payments

The preceding note payable requires Lewis Company to repay the principal and interest in equal payments of $5,698 beginning December 31 of Year 1 for each of the next five years. Each installment note payment includes an interest and principal component.

The interest portion of an installment note payment is computed by multiplying the interest rate by the carrying amount (book value) of the note at the beginning of the period. The principal portion of the payment is then computed as the difference between the total installment note payment (cash paid) and the interest component. These computations are illustrated in Exhibit 4 (rounded to the nearest dollar).

[8] The annual payment is computed using present value concepts that are discussed in advanced accounting courses.

Exhibit 4 Allocation of Periodic Payments

For the Year Ending December 31	A January 1 Carrying Amount	B Note Payment (cash paid)	C Interest Expense (6% of January 1 Note Carrying Amount)	D Decrease in Notes Payable (B – C)	E December 31 Carrying Amount (A – D)
Year 1	$24,000	$ 5,698	$ 1,440 (6% of $24,000)	$ 4,258	$19,742
Year 2	19,742	5,698	1,185 (6% of $19,742)	4,513	15,229
Year 3	15,229	5,698	914 (6% of $15,229)	4,784	10,445
Year 4	10,445	5,698	627 (6% of $10,445)	5,071	5,374
Year 5	5,374	5,698	324* (6% of $5,374)	5,374	0
		$28,490	$4,490	$24,000	

*Rounded ($5,698 – $5,374).

1. The January 1 carrying value (Column A) for Year 1 equals the amount borrowed from the bank. The January 1 balance in the following years equals the December 31 balance from the prior year.

2. The note payment (Column B) remains constant at $5,698, the annual cash payment required by the bank.

3. The interest expense (Column C) is computed at 6% of the installment note carrying amount at the beginning of each year. As a result, the interest expense decreases each year.

4. Notes payable decreases each year by the amount of the principal repayment (Column D). The principal repayment is computed by subtracting the interest expense (Column C) from the total payment (Column B). The principal repayment (Column D) increases each year as the interest expense decreases (Column C).

5. The carrying amount on December 31 (Column E) of the note decreases from $24,000, the initial amount borrowed, to $0 at the end of Year 5.

The entry to record the first payment on December 31 of Year 1 is as follows:

A = L + E
–   –   – Exp

Year 1			
Dec. 31	Interest Expense	1,440	
	Notes Payable	4,258	
	Cash		5,698
	Paid principal and interest on installment note.		

The entry to record the second payment on December 31 of Year 2 is as follows:

A = L + E
–   –   – Exp

Year 2			
Dec. 31	Interest Expense	1,185	
	Notes Payable	4,513	
	Cash		5,698
	Paid principal and interest on installment note.		

As the preceding entries show, the cash payment of $5,698 is the same in each year. The interest and principal repayment, however, change each year. This is because the carrying amount (book value) of the note decreases each year as principal is repaid, which decreases the interest component the next period.

The entry to record the final payment on December 31 of Year 5 is as follows:

A = L + E
–   –   – Exp

Year 5			
Dec. 31	Interest Expense	324	
	Notes Payable	5,374	
	Cash		5,698
	Paid principal and interest on installment note.		

After the final payment, the carrying amount on the note is zero, indicating that the note has been paid in full. Any assets that secure the note would then be released by the bank.

Why It Matters

Installment Credit

The type of loan most often obtained by a consumer for large purchases such as an automobile or a home is the installment loan. The installment payments consist of both principal and interest. The interest portion starts large at the beginning of the installment period and gets smaller toward the end of an installment period. For example, the payment for a 30-year, $150,000 mortgage at 5% interest would be $805. At the beginning of the 30-year period, 76% or $610 would go toward interest, with the remainder going toward principal reduction. At the end of the 30-year period, nearly all of the $805 payment would go toward principal reduction. The reason for this pattern is because the principal balance is large at the beginning of the installment period, and gradually reduces as payments are made. Thus, the amount of interest paid per period is trending with the declining loan balance.

Check Up Corner 10-3 — Installment Notes

On January 1, the first day of the fiscal year, Anchor Company issues a $30,000, 10%, five-year installment note that has annual payments of $7,914.

A. Journalize the annual note payment at the end of Year 1 and Year 2.

B. Determine the carrying amount of the note at the end of Year 1 and Year 2.

Solution:

For the Year Ending December 31	January 1 Carrying Amount	Note Payment	Interest Expense	Decrease in Notes Payable	December 31 Carrying Amount
Year 1	$30,000	$7,914	$3,000 (10% × $30,000)	$4,914	$25,086
Year 2	25,086	7,914	2,509 (10% × $25,086)	5,405	19,681

A.

Year 1					Payment of interest on the original $30,000 balance
Dec. 31	Interest Expense		3,000		
	Notes Payable		4,914		Payment of a portion of the amount initially borrowed
	Cash			7,914	

Year 2					Payment of interest on the Dec. 31, Year 1 balance
Dec. 31	Interest Expense		2,509		
	Notes Payable		5,405		Payment of a portion of the amount initially borrowed
	Cash			7,914	

B.
December 31, Year 1	$25,086	The remaining balance on the installment note at the end of each year (see table)
December 31, Year 2	19,681	

Check Up Corner

Objective 5

Describe and illustrate the accounting for contingent liabilities, including product warranties.

Contingent Liabilities

Some liabilities may arise from past transactions only if certain events occur in the future. These *potential* liabilities are called **contingent liabilities**.

The accounting for contingent liabilities depends on the following two factors:

- *Likelihood of occurring*
- *Measurement*

The likelihood of occurring is classified as *probable, reasonably possible,* or *remote.* The ability to measure the potential liability is classified as *estimable* or *not estimable.*

Probable and Estimable

If a contingent liability is *probable* and the amount of the liability can be *reasonably estimated,* it is recorded and disclosed. The liability is recorded by debiting an expense and crediting a liability.

To illustrate, assume that during June a company sold a product for $60,000 that includes a 36-month warranty for repairs.[9] The average cost of repairs over the warranty period is estimated at 5% of the sales price. The entry to record the estimated product warranty expense for June is as follows:

A = L + E
　　+　 – Exp

June 30	Product Warranty Expense	3,000	
	Product Warranty Payable		3,000
	Warranty expense for June (5% × $60,000).		

The preceding entry records warranty expense in the same period in which the sale is recorded. In this way, warranty expense is matched with the related revenue (sales).

If the product is repaired under warranty, the repair costs are recorded by debiting *Product Warranty Payable* and crediting *Cash, Supplies, Wages Payable,* or other appropriate accounts. Thus, if a $200 part is replaced under warranty on August 16, the entry is as follows:

A = L + E
–　　 –

Aug. 16	Product Warranty Payable	200	
	Supplies		200
	Replaced defective part under warranty.		

Link to Starbucks

In 2011, **Starbucks** terminated a contract with **Kraft Foods** that allowed Kraft to sell bagged Starbucks coffee in grocery stores. The early termination resulted in litigation between Kraft and Starbucks. After an arbitrator found in Kraft's favor, Starbucks recorded a liability for $2.8 billion.

Probable and Not Estimable

A contingent liability may be probable, but cannot be estimated. In this case, the contingent liability is disclosed in the notes to the financial statements. For example, a company may have accidentally polluted a local river by dumping waste products. At the end of the period, the cost of the cleanup and any fines may not be able to be estimated.

---

[9] This discussion is limited to a discussion of assurance type warranties. A more detailed discussion of the types of warranties and their accounting is covered in intermediate and advanced accounting texts.

Reasonably Possible

A contingent liability may be only possible. For example, a company may have lost a lawsuit for infringing on another company's patent rights. However, the verdict is under appeal and the company's lawyers feel that the verdict will be reversed or significantly reduced. In this case, the contingent liability is disclosed in the notes to the financial statements.

Remote

A contingent liability may be remote. For example, a ski resort may be sued for injuries incurred by skiers. In most cases, the courts have found that a skier accepts the risk of injury when participating in the activity. Thus, unless the ski resort is grossly negligent, the resort will not incur a liability for ski injuries. In such cases, no disclosure needs to be made in the notes to the financial statements. The accounting treatment of contingent liabilities is summarized in Exhibit 5.

Exhibit 5 Accounting Treatment of Contingent Liabilities

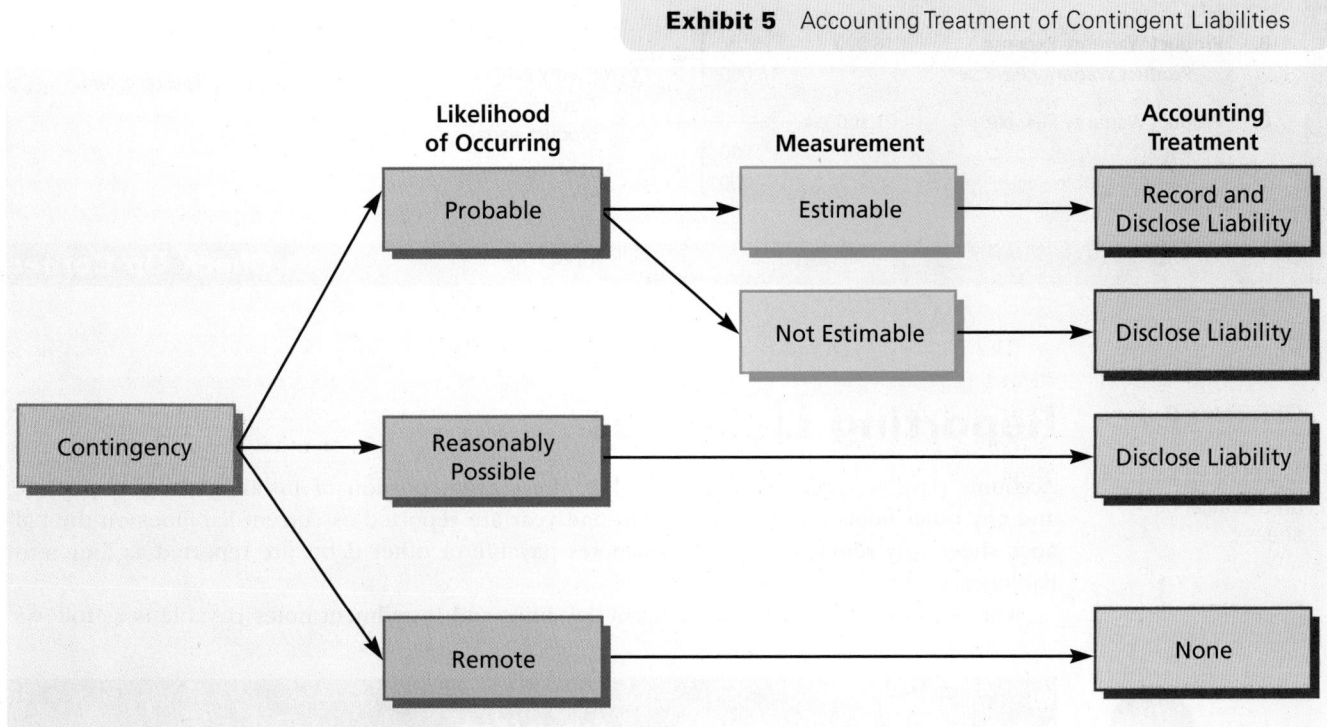

Common examples of contingent liabilities disclosed in notes to the financial statements are litigation, environmental matters, guarantees, and contingencies from the sale of receivables.

Professional judgment is necessary in distinguishing between classes of contingent liabilities. This is especially the case when distinguishing between probable and reasonably possible contingent liabilities.

In a recent annual report, **Starbucks** reported that in its normal course of business, it is party to a variety of legal actions. However, the management of Starbucks believes none of these actions will have a material effect on its financial statements.

Link to Starbucks

Check Up Corner 10-4 Contingent Liabilities

Scooter General Inc. is in its first year of manufacturing and selling high-end scooters. The company warrants its products for one year and estimates product warranty costs at 2% of sales. During January, a customer sued the company for false advertising. The company's legal counsel has been in negotiations with the customer's attorney and believes that it is probable the company will reach an out-of-court settlement for $85,000 in the coming weeks. The lawsuit will not impact the company's warranty cost estimate.

A. Should the company journalize the contingent liability associated with the lawsuit?

B. Journalize the adjusting entry required at the end of January to record the estimated product warranty costs. Sales were $800,000 during January.

C. In February, the company made warranty repairs requiring $900 of replacement parts and $400 of labor costs. Journalize the entry to record the warranty work provided in February.

Solution:

A. Yes. The amount should be recognized as a contingent liability. Legal counsel believes an out-of-court settlement is probable, and the amount of the settlement can be reasonably estimated.

B.
Product Warranty Expense	16,000	
Product Warranty Payable		16,000

$800,000 × 2% product warranty estimate

Product warranty expense is recorded in the same period in which the sale is recorded.

C.
Product Warranty Payable	1,300	
Parts		900
Wages Payable		400

Actual repair costs reduce the product warranty liability.

Actual repair costs

Check Up Corner

Objective 6

Describe the reporting of liabilities on the balance sheet.

Reporting Liabilities

Accounts payable, accruals, notes payable, the current portion of installment notes payable, and any other debts that are due within one year are reported as current liabilities on the balance sheet. Any remaining installment notes payable or other debts are reported as long-term liabilities.

The reporting of **Mornin' Joe's** current liabilities and installment notes payable is as follows:

Mornin' Joe

Mornin' Joe **Balance Sheet** **December 31, 20Y6**		

Current liabilities:		
Accounts payable.....................................	$133,000	
Notes payable (current portion).......................	200,000	
Salaries and wages payable...........................	42,000	
Payroll taxes payable.................................	16,400	
Interest payable	40,000	
Total current liabilities		$ 431,400
Long-term liabilities:		
Notes payable..		1,400,000

Analysis for Decision Making

Quick Ratio

Objective

Describe and illustrate the use of the quick ratio in analyzing a company's ability to pay its current liabilities.

Current position analysis helps creditors evaluate a company's ability to pay its current liabilities. This analysis is based on the following three measures:

- Working capital
- Current ratio
- Quick ratio

Working capital and the current ratio were discussed in Chapter 4 and are computed as follows:

$$\text{Working Capital} = \text{Current Assets} - \text{Current Liabilities}$$

$$\text{Current Ratio} = \frac{\text{Current Assets}}{\text{Current Liabilities}}$$

While these two measures can be used to weigh a company's ability to pay its current liabilities, they do not show the company's ability to pay these liabilities within a short period of time. This is because some current assets, such as inventory, cannot be converted into cash as quickly as other current assets, such as cash and accounts receivable.

The **quick ratio** overcomes this limitation by measuring the "instant" debt-paying ability of a company and is computed as follows:

$$\text{Quick Ratio} = \frac{\text{Quick Assets}}{\text{Current Liabilities}}$$

Quick assets are cash and other current assets that can be easily converted to cash, such as temporary investments and accounts receivable. Temporary investments include securities that can be easily sold and turned into cash. The other current assets are not included as part of quick assets because they often include prepaid expenses or other deferred assets that are not easily converted to cash. To illustrate, consider the following data for TechSolutions, Inc., at the end of a recent year:

Current assets:	
Cash	$2,020
Temporary investments	3,400
Accounts receivable	1,600
Inventory	2,000
Other current assets	160
Total current assets	$9,180
Current liabilities:	
Accounts payable	$3,000
Other current liabilities	2,400
Total current liabilities	$5,400
Working capital (current assets – current liabilities)	$3,780
Current ratio (current assets ÷ current liabilities)	1.7

The quick ratio for TechSolutions, Inc., is computed as follows:

$$\text{Quick Ratio} = \frac{\$2,020 + \$3,400 + \$1,600}{\$5,400} = 1.3$$

The quick ratio of 1.3 indicates that the company has more than enough quick assets to pay its current liabilities in a short period of time. A quick ratio below 1.0 would indicate that the company does not have enough quick assets to cover its current liabilities.

Like the current ratio, the quick ratio is particularly useful in making comparisons across companies. To illustrate, the following selected balance sheet data (excluding ratios) were taken from recent financial statements of **Panera Bread Company** and **Starbucks Corporation** (in thousands):

	Panera	Starbucks
Current assets:		
Cash and cash equivalents	$196,493	$1,708,400
Temporary investments	—	135,400
Accounts receivable	106,653	631,000
Inventory	22,811	1,090,900
Other current assets	80,209	603,000
Total current assets	$406,166	$4,168,700
Current liabilities:		
Accounts payable	$ 19,511	$ 533,700
Other current liabilities	333,201	2,505,000
Total current liabilities	$352,712	$3,038,700
Working capital (current assets – current liabilities)	$53,454	$1,130,000
Current ratio (current assets ÷ current liabilities)	1.2	1.4
Quick ratio (quick assets ÷ current liabilities)*	0.9	0.8

*The quick ratio for each company is computed as follows:
Panera: ($196,493 + $106,653) ÷ $352,712 = 0.9
Starbucks: ($1,708,400 + $135,400 + $631,000) ÷ $3,038,700 = 0.8

Starbucks is larger than Panera and has more than 20 times the amount of working capital. Such size differences make working capital comparisons between companies difficult. In contrast, current and quick ratios provide more meaningful comparisons across companies. In this example, Starbucks has a slightly higher current ratio than Panera. However, Starbucks' quick ratio (0.8) is weaker than Panera's quick ratio (0.9). This is mostly due to the larger relative inventory held by Starbucks. Both companies have quick ratios below 1.0, indicating that quick assets do not fully cover current liabilities. This is not a concern, because inventory turns into cash quickly for these two food companies.

Make a Decision   Quick Ratio

Abercrombie & Fitch Co. (A&F) and **The Gap, Inc.** are two U.S. apparel retailers. The current assets and current liabilities for each company from recent balance sheets are as follows (in thousands):

	A&F	The Gap
Current assets:		
Cash	$ 520,708	$1,515,000
Accounts receivable	52,910	—
Inventories	460,794	1,889,000
Other current assets	130,560	913,000
Total current assets	$1,164,972	$4,317,000
Current liabilities:		
Accounts payable	$ 141,685	$1,173,000
Other current liabilities	344,271	1,061,000
Total current liabilities	$ 485,956	$2,234,000

A. Compute the quick ratio for each company. (Round to one decimal place.)

B. Based on the quick ratio, which company appears to have the greater short-term liquidity? Why?

Solution:

A.

$$\text{Quick Ratio} = \frac{\text{Quick Assets}}{\text{Current Liabilities}}$$

A&F: $\dfrac{\$520,708 + \$52,910}{\$485,956} = 1.2$

The Gap: $\dfrac{\$1,515,000}{\$2,234,000} = 0.7$

B. Using the quick ratio, A&F's short-term liquidity is stronger than The Gap's. A&F's quick ratio of 1.2 is significantly larger than The Gap's 0.7. Part of this difference is because A&F's cash is a much larger portion of its total current assets ($520,708 ÷ $1,164,972 = 45%) than are The Gap's ($1,515,000 ÷ $4,317,000 = 35%). In contrast, The Gap's inventory is a larger percent of its current assets ($1,889,000 ÷ $4,317,000 = 44%) than are A&F's ($460,794 ÷ $1,164,972 = 40%). Thus, A&F's stronger quick ratio appears to be the result of a stronger relative cash position and a more efficient inventory position. Note that The Gap has no receivables listed. Most of The Gap's customers pay by credit card or cash. Thus, no receivables are recorded on sales. A&F is similar but appears to have some trade credit relationships, producing some receivables.

Make a Decision

Let's Review

Chapter Summary

1. Current liabilities are obligations that are to be paid out of current assets and are due within a short time, usually within one year. The primary types of current liabilities are accounts payable, accruals, notes payable, and the current portion of long-term debt.

2. Payroll liabilities include those for employee earnings and employer's payroll taxes. An employer's liability for employee earnings is determined from employee total earnings, including overtime pay. From this amount, employee deductions are subtracted to arrive at the net pay to be paid to each employee. Employers also incur liabilities for payroll taxes, such as social security tax, Medicare tax, federal unemployment compensation tax, and state unemployment compensation tax.

3. Fringe benefits are expenses of the period in which the employees earn the benefits. Fringe benefits are recorded by debiting an expense account and crediting a liability account.

4. An installment note requires the borrower to make equal periodic payments to the lender for the term of the note. Each payment consists of principal and interest. The journal entry for the payment debits Interest Expense and Notes Payable and credits Cash for the amount of the payment. After the final payment, the carrying amount on the note is zero.

5. A contingent liability is a potential obligation that results from a past transaction but depends on a future event. The accounting for contingent liabilities is summarized in Exhibit 5.

6. Accounts payable, accruals, notes payable, the current portion of installment notes payable, and any other debts that are due within one year are reported as current liabilities on the balance sheet. Any remaining installment notes payable or other debts are reported as long-term liabilities.

Key Terms

contingent liabilities (492)
defined benefit plan (487)
defined contribution plan (487)
FICA tax (482)

fringe benefits (486)
gross pay (482)
installment note (480)
net pay (482)

payroll (481)
pension (487)
quick assets (495)
quick ratio (495)

Practice

Multiple-Choice Questions

1. A business issued a $5,000, 60-day, 12% note to the bank. The amount due at maturity is:
   A. $4,900
   B. $5,000
   C. $5,100
   D. $5,600

2. A business issued a $5,000, 60-day note to a supplier, which discounted the note at 12%. The proceeds are:
   A. $4,400
   B. $4,900
   C. $5,000
   D. $5,100

3. Which of the following taxes are employers usually not required to withhold from employees?
   A. Federal income tax
   B. Federal unemployment compensation tax
   C. Medicare tax
   D. State and local income tax

4. An employee's rate of pay is $36 per hour, with time and a half for all hours worked in excess of 40 during a week. The employee worked 45 hours during the week. The amount of the employee's gross pay for the week is:
   A. $1,440
   B. $1,620
   C. $1,710
   D. $1,800

5. Which of the following is the journal entry to record a periodic payment on an installment note?
   A. Debit Notes Payable; credit Cash
   B. Debit Interest Expense; credit Cash
   C. Debit Interest Expense; debit Notes Payable; credit Cash
   D. Debit Interest Expense; credit Notes Payable; credit Cash

Answers provided after Problem. Need more practice? Find additional multiple-choice questions, exercises, and problems in CengageNOWv2.

Exercises

SHOW ME HOW

1. Proceeds from notes payable   Obj. 1

On October 12, Belleville Co. borrowed cash from Texas Bank by issuing a 30-day note with a face amount of $70,000.
A. Determine the proceeds of the note, assuming the note carries an interest rate of 6%.
B. Determine the proceeds of the note, assuming the note is discounted at 6%.

SHOW ME HOW

2. Employee net pay   Obj. 2

Lily Flower's weekly gross earnings for the week ended October 20 were $2,500, and her federal income tax withholding was $517.24. Assuming the social security rate is 6% and Medicare is 1.5% of all earnings, what is Flower's net pay?

SHOW ME HOW

3. Journalize period payroll

Obj. 2

The payroll register of Konrath Co. indicates $13,200 of social security withheld and $3,300 of Medicare tax withheld on total salaries of $220,000 for the period. Federal withholding for the period totaled $43,560.

Journalize the entry to record the period's payroll.

SHOW ME HOW

4. Journalize payroll tax

Obj. 2

The payroll register of Konrath Co. indicates $13,200 of social security withheld and $3,300 of Medicare tax withheld on total salaries of $220,000 for the period. Earnings of $35,000 are subject to state and federal unemployment compensation taxes at the federal rate of 0.8% and the state rate of 5.4%.

Journalize the entry to record the payroll tax expense for the period.

SHOW ME HOW

5. Vacation pay and pension benefits

Obj. 3

Fukushima Company provides its employees with vacation benefits and a defined contribution pension plan. Employees earned vacation pay of $19,500 for the period. The pension plan requires a contribution to the plan administrator equal to 6% of employee salaries. Salaries were $260,000 during the period, and the full amount due was contributed to the pension plan administrator.

Journalize the entry to record the (A) vacation pay and (B) pension benefit.

SHOW ME HOW

6. Journalizing installment notes

Obj. 4

On the first day of the fiscal year, a company issues $65,000, 6%, five-year installment notes that have annual payments of $15,431. The first note payment consists of $3,900 of interest and $11,531 of principal repayment.

A. Journalize the entry to record the issuance of the installment notes.

B. Journalize the first annual note payment.

SHOW ME HOW

7. Estimated warranty liability

Obj. 5

Chloe Co. sold $300,000 of equipment during January under a one-year warranty. The cost to repair defects under the warranty is estimated at 5% of the sales price. On June 20, a customer required a $90 part replacement plus $42 of labor under the warranty.

Journalize the entry to record (A) the estimated warranty expense on January 31 for January sales, and (B) the June 20 warranty work.

Answers provided after Problem. Need more practice? Find additional multiple-choice questions, exercises, and problems in CengageNOWv2.

Problem

Selected transactions of Taylor Company, completed during the fiscal year ended December 31, are as follows:

Mar. 1. Purchased merchandise on account from Kelvin Co., $20,000.

Apr. 10. Issued a 60-day, 12% note for $20,000 to Kelvin Co. on account.

June 9. Paid Kelvin Co. the amount owed on the note of April 10.

Aug. 1. Issued a $50,000, 90-day note to Harold Co. in exchange for a building. Harold Co. discounted the note at 15%.

Oct. 30. Paid Harold Co. the amount due on the note of August 1.

(Continued)

Dec. 27. Journalized the entry to record the biweekly payroll. A summary of the payroll record follows:

Salary distribution:

Sales	$63,400	
Officers	36,600	
Office	10,000	$110,000

Deductions:

Social security tax	$ 6,600	
Medicare tax	1,650	
Federal income tax withheld	17,600	
State income tax withheld	4,950	
Savings bond deductions	850	
Medical insurance deductions	1,120	32,770
Net amount		$ 77,230

27. Journalized the entry to record payroll taxes for social security and Medicare from the biweekly payroll.

30. Issued a check in payment of liabilities for employees' federal income tax of $17,600, social security tax of $13,200, and Medicare tax of $3,300.

31. Issued a check for $9,500 to the pension fund trustee to fully fund the pension cost for December.

31. Journalized an entry to record the employees' accrued vacation pay, $36,100.

31. Journalized an entry to record the estimated accrued product warranty liability, $37,240.

Instructions

Journalize the preceding transactions.

Need more practice? Find additional multiple-choice questions, exercises, and problems in CengageNOWv2.

Answers

Multiple-Choice Questions

1. **C** The maturity value is $5,100, determined as follows:

Face amount of note	$5,000
Interest ($5,000 × 12% × 60 ÷ 360)	100
Maturity value	$5,100

2. **B** The net amount available to a borrower from discounting a note payable is called the proceeds. The proceeds of $4,900 (answer B) is determined as follows:

Face amount of note	$5,000
Discount ($5,000 × 12% × 60 ÷ 360)	(100)
Proceeds	$4,900

3. **B** Employers are usually required to withhold a portion of their employees' earnings for payment of federal income taxes (answer A), Medicare tax (answer C), and state and local income taxes (answer D). Generally, federal unemployment compensation taxes (answer B) are levied against the employer only and thus are not deducted from employee earnings.

4. **C** The amount of gross pay of $1,710 (answer C) is determined as follows:

$1,710 = (40 hours × $36) + [(45 hrs. − 40 hrs.) × ($36 × 1.5)]
$1,710 = $1,440 + (5 hrs. × $54) = $1,440 + $270

5. **C** The journal entry to record a periodic payment on an installment note debits Interest Expense, debits Notes Payable, and credits Cash (answer C).

Exercises

1.

A. $70,000

B. $69,650 [$70,000 − ($70,000 × 30 ÷ 360 × 6%)]

2.

Total wage payment		$2,500.00
Deductions:		
Federal income tax	$(517.24)	
Social security tax ($2,500 × 6%)	(150.00)	
Medicare tax ($2,500 × 1.5%)	(37.50)	
Total deductions		(704.74)
Net pay		$1,795.26

3.

Salaries Expense	220,000	
Social Security Tax Payable		13,200
Medicare Tax Payable		3,300
Employees Federal Income Tax Payable		43,560
Salaries Payable		159,940

4.

Payroll Tax Expense	18,670	
Social Security Tax Payable		13,200
Medicare Tax Payable		3,300
State Unemployment Tax Payable*		1,890
Federal Unemployment Tax Payable**		280

*$35,000 × 5.4%
**$35,000 × 0.8%

5. A.

Vacation Pay Expense	19,500	
Vacation Pay Payable		19,500
Vacation pay accrued for the period.		

B.

Pension Expense	15,600	
Cash		15,600
To record pension contribution		
(6% × $260,000).		

6. A.

Cash	65,000	
Notes Payable		65,000
Issued installment notes for cash.		

B.

Interest Expense	3,900	
Notes Payable	11,531	
Cash		15,431
Paid principal and interest on installment notes.		

7. A.

Jan. 31 Product Warranty Expense	15,000	
Product Warranty Payable		15,000
To record warranty expense for		
February (5% × $300,000).		

B.

June 20 Product Warranty Payable	132	
Supplies		90
Wages Payable		42

Need more help? Watch step-by-step videos of how to compute answers to these Exercises in CengageNOWv2.

Problem

Mar.	1	Merchandise Inventory	20,000	
		Accounts Payable—Kelvin Co.		20,000
Apr.	10	Accounts Payable—Kelvin Co.	20,000	
		Notes Payable		20,000
June	9	Notes Payable	20,000	
		Interest Expense	400	
		Cash		20,400
		($20,000 × 12% × 60/360)		
Aug.	1	Building	48,125	
		Interest Expense	1,875	
		Notes Payable		50,000
		($50,000 × 15% × 90/360)		
Oct.	30	Notes Payable	50,000	
		Cash		50,000
Dec.	27	Sales Salaries Expense	63,400	
		Officers Salaries Expense	36,600	
		Office Salaries Expense	10,000	
		Social Security Tax Payable		6,600
		Medicare Tax Payable		1,650
		Employees Federal Income Tax Payable		17,600
		Employees State Income Tax Payable		4,950
		Bond Deductions Payable		850
		Medical Insurance Payable		1,120
		Salaries Payable		77,230
	27	Payroll Tax Expense	8,250	
		Social Security Tax Payable		6,600
		Medicare Tax Payable		1,650
	30	Employees Federal Income Tax Payable	17,600	
		Social Security Tax Payable	13,200	
		Medicare Tax Payable	3,300	
		Cash		34,100
	31	Pension Expense	9,500	
		Cash		9,500
		Fund pension cost.		
	31	Vacation Pay Expense	36,100	
		Vacation Pay Payable		36,100
		Accrue vacation pay.		
	31	Product Warranty Expense	37,240	
		Product Warranty Payable		37,240
		Accrue warranty expense.		

Discussion Questions

1. Does a discounted note payable provide credit without interest? Discuss.

2. Employees are subject to taxes withheld from their paychecks.

   A. List the federal taxes withheld from most employee paychecks.

   B. Give the title of the accounts credited by amounts withheld.

3. Why are deductions from employees' earnings classified as liabilities for the employer?

4. For each of the following payroll-related taxes, indicate whether they generally apply to (A) employees only, (B) employers only, or (C) both employees and employers:

   1. Federal income tax
   2. Medicare tax
   3. Social security tax
   4. Federal unemployment compensation tax
   5. State unemployment compensation tax

5. What are the principal reasons for using a special payroll bank account?

6. To match revenues and expenses properly, should the expense for employee vacation pay be recorded in the period during which the vacation privilege is earned or during the period in which the vacation is taken? Discuss.

7. Explain how a defined contribution pension plan works.

8. Installment notes require equal periodic payments.

   A. What is included in each periodic payment?

   B. Does the periodic interest expense on an installment note increase or decrease over the life of the note?

9. When should the liability associated with a product warranty be recorded? Discuss.

10.  **General Motors Corporation** reported $2.6 billion of product warranties in the current liabilities section of a recent balance sheet. How would costs of repairing a defective product be recorded?

   REAL WORLD

Basic Exercises

SHOW ME HOW

BE 10-1 Proceeds from notes payable   Obj. 1

On January 26, Nyree Co. borrowed cash from Conrad Bank by issuing a 45-day note with a face amount of $150,000.

A. Determine the proceeds of the note, assuming the note carries an interest rate of 10%.

B. Determine the proceeds of the note, assuming the note is discounted at 10%.

SHOW ME HOW

BE 10-2 Employee net pay   Obj. 2

Lindsey Vater's weekly gross earnings for the week ended March 9 were $1,000, and her federal income tax withholding was $161.20. Assuming the social security tax rate is 6% and Medicare tax is 1.5% of all earnings, what is Lindsey's net pay?

SHOW ME HOW

BE 10-3 Journalize period payroll   Obj. 2

The payroll register of Heritage Co. indicates $3,900 of social security withheld and $975 of Medicare tax withheld on total salaries of $65,000 for the period. Federal withholding for the period totaled $14,250. Retirement savings withheld from employee paychecks were $2,600 for the period.

   Journalize the entry to record the period's payroll.

SHOW ME HOW

BE 10-4 Journalize payroll tax   Obj. 2

The payroll register of Heritage Co. indicates $3,900 of social security withheld and $975 of Medicare tax withheld on total salaries of $65,000 for the period. Earnings of $10,000 are subject to state and federal unemployment compensation taxes at the federal rate of 0.8% and the state rate of 5.4%.

   Journalize the entry to record the payroll tax expense for the period.

SHOW ME HOW

BE 10-5   Vacation pay and pension benefits   **Obj. 3**

Regling Company provides its employees vacation benefits and a defined benefit pension plan. Employees earned vacation pay of $35,000 for the period. The pension formula calculated a pension cost of $201,250. Only $175,000 was contributed to the pension plan administrator.

Journalize the entry to record the (A) vacation pay and (B) pension benefit.

SHOW ME HOW

BE 10-6   Journalizing installment notes   **Obj. 4**

On the first day of the fiscal year, a company issues $45,000, 8%, six-year installment notes that have annual payments of $9,734. The first note payment consists of $3,600 of interest and $6,134 of principal repayment.

A. Journalize the entry to record the issuance of the installment notes.

B. Journalize the first annual note payment.

SHOW ME HOW

BE 10-7   Estimated warranty liability   **Obj. 5**

Quantas Industries sold $325,000 of consumer electronics during July under a nine-month warranty. The cost to repair defects under the warranty is estimated at 4.5% of the sales price. On November 11, a customer was given $220 cash under terms of the warranty.

Journalize the entry to record (A) the estimated warranty expense on July 31 for July sales, and (B) the November 11 cash payment.

Exercises

✔ Total current
liabilities, $1,929,750

SHOW ME HOW

EX 10-1   Current liabilities   **Obj. 1**

Bon Nebo Co. sold 25,000 annual subscriptions of *Bjorn* for $85 during December 20Y5. These new subscribers will receive monthly issues, beginning in January 20Y6. In addition, the business had taxable income of $840,000 during the first calendar quarter of 20Y6. The federal tax rate is 40%. A quarterly tax payment will be made on April 12, 20Y6.

Prepare the current liabilities section of the balance sheet for Bon Nebo Co. on March 31, 20Y6.

SHOW ME HOW

EX 10-2   Entries for notes payable   **Obj. 1**

Bennett Enterprises issues a $400,000, 90-day, 5% note to Spectrum Industries for merchandise inventory.

A. Journalize Bennett Enterprises' entries to record:

1. the issuance of the note.

2. the payment of the note at maturity.

B. Journalize Spectrum Industries' entries to record:

1. the receipt of the note.

2. the receipt of the payment of the note at maturity.

SHOW ME HOW

EX 10-3   Evaluating alternative notes   **Obj. 1**

A borrower has two alternatives for a loan: (1) issue a $150,000, 45-day, 4% note or (2) issue a $150,000, 45-day note that the creditor discounts at 4%.

A. Calculate the amount of the interest expense for each option.

B. Determine the proceeds received by the borrower in each situation.

C. ━━━━▶ Which alternative is more favorable to the borrower? Explain.

SHOW ME HOW

EX 10-4 Entries for notes payable
Obj. 1

A business issued a 120-day, 5% note for $90,000 to a creditor on account. Journalize the entries to record (A) the issuance of the note and (B) the payment of the note at maturity, including interest.

SHOW ME HOW

EX 10-5 Entries for discounted note payable
Obj. 1

A business issued a 60-day note for $75,000 to a creditor on account. The note was discounted at 7%. Journalize the entries to record (A) the issuance of the note and (B) the payment of the note at maturity.

SHOW ME HOW

EX 10-6 Fixed asset purchases with note
Obj. 1

On June 30, Collins Management Company purchased land for $400,000 and a building for $560,000, paying $360,000 cash and issuing a 5% note for the balance, secured by a mortgage on the property. The terms of the note provide for 20 semiannual payments of $30,000 on the principal plus the interest accrued from the date of the preceding payment. Journalize the entry to record (A) the transaction on June 30, (B) the payment of the first installment on December 31, and (C) the payment of the second installment the following June 30.

REAL WORLD

EX 10-7 Current portion of long-term debt
Obj. 1

PepsiCo, Inc., reported the following information about its long-term debt in the notes to a recent financial statement (in millions):

Long-term debt is composed of the following:

	December 31	
	Current Year	**Prior Year**
Total long term-debt	$27,917	$26,557
Current portion	(4,096)	(2,224)
Long-term debt	$23,821	$24,333

A. How much of the long-term debt was disclosed as a current liability on the current year's December 31 balance sheet?

B. How much did the total current liabilities change between the preceding year and the current year as a result of the current portion of long-term debt?

C. If PepsiCo did not issue additional long-term debt next year, what would be the total long-term debt on December 31 of the upcoming year?

✔ B. Net pay, $1,896.55

EX 10-8 Calculate payroll
Obj. 2

An employee earns $44 per hour and 1.5 times that rate for all hours in excess of 40 hours per week. If the employee worked 51 hours during the week, determine the employee's (A) gross pay and (B) net pay for the week. Assume that the social security tax rate is 6.0%, the Medicare tax rate is 1.5%, and the employee's federal income tax withheld is $403.

SHOW ME HOW

✔ Consultant net pay, $2,775.00

EX 10-9 Calculate payroll
Obj. 2

K. Mello Company has three employees—a consultant, a computer programmer, and an administrator. The following payroll information is available for each employee:

	Consultant	Computer Programmer	Administrator
Regular earnings rate	$4,000 per week	$30 per hour	$40 per hour
Overtime earnings rate	Not applicable	2 times hourly rate	1.5 times hourly rate
Federal income tax withheld	$925.00	$248.00	$505.00

For hourly employees, overtime is paid for hours worked in excess of 40 hours per week.

SHOW ME HOW

(Continued)

For the current pay period, the computer programmer worked 44 hours and the administrator worked 48 hours. Assume that the social security tax rate was 6.0%, the Medicare tax rate was 1.5%.

Determine the gross pay and the net pay for each of the three employees for the current pay period.

EX 10-10   Summary payroll data   Obj. 2

✔ A. (3) Total
earnings, $540,000

EXCEL TEMPLATE

In the following summary of data for a payroll period, some amounts have been intentionally omitted:

Earnings:		
1.	At regular rate	?
2.	At overtime rate	$ 80,000
3.	Total earnings	?
Deductions:		
4.	Social security tax	32,400
5.	Medicare tax	8,100
6.	Income tax withheld	135,000
7.	Medical insurance	18,900
8.	Union dues	?
9.	Total deductions	201,150
10.	Net amount paid	$338,850
Accounts debited:		
11.	Factory Wages	285,000
12.	Sales Salaries	?
13.	Office Salaries	120,000

A. Calculate the amounts omitted in lines (1), (3), (8), and (12).

B. Journalize the entry to record the payroll accrual.

C. Journalize the entry to record the payment of the payroll.

EX 10-11   Payroll tax entries   Obj. 2

✔ A. $11,790

SHOW ME HOW

EXCEL TEMPLATE

According to a summary of the payroll of Mountain Streaming Co., $120,000 was subject to the 6.0% social security tax and the 1.5% Medicare tax. Also, $45,000 was subject to state and federal unemployment taxes.

A. Calculate the employer's payroll taxes, using the following rates: state unemployment, 5.4%; federal unemployment, 0.8%.

B. Journalize the entry to record the accrual of payroll taxes.

EX 10-12   Payroll entries   Obj. 2

SHOW ME HOW

The payroll register for D. Salah Company for the week ended May 18 indicated the following:

Salaries	$660,000
Federal income tax withheld	180,000

The salaries were all subject to the 6.0% social security tax and the 1.5% Medicare tax. In addition, state and federal unemployment taxes were calculated at the rate of 5.4% and 0.8%, respectively, on $50,000 of salaries.

A. Journalize the entry to record the payroll for the week of May 18.

B. Journalize the entry to record the payroll tax expense incurred for the week of May 18.

SHOW ME HOW

EX 10-13 Payroll entries

Obj. 2

Widmer Company had gross wages of $240,000 during the week ended June 17. The amount of wages subject to social security tax was $240,000, while the amount of wages subject to federal and state unemployment taxes was $35,000. Tax rates are as follows:

Social security	6.0%
Medicare	1.5%
State unemployment	5.4%
Federal unemployment	0.8%

The total amount withheld from employee wages for federal taxes was $48,000.

A. Journalize the entry to record the payroll for the week of June 17.

B. Journalize the entry to record the payroll tax expense incurred for the week of June 17.

EX 10-14 Payroll internal control procedures

Obj. 2

Big Howie's Hot Dog Stand is a fast-food restaurant specializing in hot dogs and hamburgers. The store employs 8 full-time and 12 part-time workers. The store's weekly payroll averages $5,600 for all 20 workers.

Big Howie's uses a personal computer to assist in preparing paychecks. Each week, the store's accountant collects employee time cards and enters the hours worked into the payroll program. The payroll program calculates each employee's pay and prints a paycheck. The accountant uses a check-signing machine to sign the paychecks. Next, the restaurant's owner/manager authorizes the transfer of funds from the restaurant's regular bank account to the payroll account.

For the week of May 12, the accountant accidentally recorded 100 hours worked instead of 40 hours for one of the full-time employees.

Does Big Howie's Hot Dog Stand have internal controls in place to catch this error? If so, how will this error be detected?

EX 10-15 Internal control procedures

Obj. 2

Dave's Scooters is a small manufacturer of specialty scooters. The company employs 14 production workers and four administrative persons. The following procedures are used to process the company's weekly payroll:

A. Whenever an employee receives a pay raise, the supervisor must fill out a wage adjustment form, which is signed by the company president. This form is used to change the employee's wage rate in the payroll system.

B. All employees are required to record their hours worked by clocking in and out on a time clock. Employees must clock out for lunch break. Due to congestion around the time clock area at lunch time, management has not objected to having one employee clock their entire department in and out.

C. Whenever a salaried employee is terminated, Personnel authorizes Payroll to remove the employee from the payroll system. However, this procedure is not required when an hourly worker is fired. Hourly employees only receive a paycheck if their time cards show hours worked. The computer automatically drops an employee from the payroll system when that employee has six consecutive weeks with no hours worked.

D. Paychecks are signed by using a check-signing machine. This machine is located in the main office so that it can be easily accessed by anyone needing a check signed.

E. Dave's Scooters maintains a separate checking account for payroll checks. Each week, the total net pay for all employees is transferred from the company's regular bank account to the payroll account.

State whether each of the procedures is appropriate or inappropriate, after considering the principles of internal control. If a procedure is inappropriate, describe the appropriate procedure.

EX 10-16   Accrued vacation pay   Obj. 3

A business provides its employees with varying amounts of vacation per year, depending on the length of employment. The estimated amount of the current year's vacation pay is $42,000.

A. Journalize the adjusting entry required on January 31, the end of the first month of the current year, to record the accrued vacation pay.

B. ▬▬▶ How is the vacation pay reported on the company's balance sheet? When is this amount removed from the company's balance sheet?

EX 10-17   Pension plan entries   Obj. 3

Yuri Co. operates a chain of gift shops. The company maintains a defined contribution pension plan for its employees. The plan requires quarterly installments to be paid to the funding agent, Whims Funds, by the fifteenth of the month following the end of each quarter. Assume that the pension cost is $365,000 for the quarter ended December 31.

A. Journalize the entries to record the accrued pension liability on December 31 and the payment to the funding agent on January 15.

B. ▬▬▶ How does a defined contribution plan differ from a defined benefit plan?

EX 10-18   Defined benefit pension plan terms   Obj. 3

In a recent year's financial statements, **Procter & Gamble** showed an unfunded pension liability of $5,955 million and a periodic pension cost of $432 million.

▬▬▶ Explain the meaning of the $5,955 million unfunded pension liability and the $432 million periodic pension cost.

EX 10-19   Entries for installment note transactions   Obj. 4

On the first day of the fiscal year, Shiller Company borrowed $85,000 by giving a seven–year, 7% installment note to Soros Bank. The note requires annual payments of $15,772, with the first payment occurring on the last day of the fiscal year. The first payment consists of interest of $5,950 and principal repayment of $9,822.

A. Journalize the entries to record the following:

1. Issued the installment note for cash on the first day of the fiscal year.

2. Paid the first annual payment on the note.

B. ▬▬▶ Explain how the notes payable would be reported on the balance sheet at the end of the first year.

EX 10-20   Entries for installment note transactions   Obj. 4

On January 1 of 20Y2, Hebron Company issued a $175,000, five-year, 8% installment note to Ventsam Bank. The note requires annual payments of $43,830, beginning on December 31 of 20Y2. Journalize the entries to record the following:

20Y2

Jan.   1. Issued the note for cash at its face amount.

Dec. 31. Paid the annual payment on the note, which consisted of interest of $14,000 and principal of $29,830.

20Y5

Dec. 31. Paid the annual payment on the note, included $6,253 of interest. The remainder of the payment reduced the principal balance on the note.

SHOW ME HOW

EXCEL TEMPLATE

EX 10-21 Entries for installment note transactions

Obj. 4

On January 1 of Year 1, Bryson Company obtained a $147,750, four-year, 7% installment note from Campbell Bank. The note requires annual payments of $43,620, beginning on December 31 of Year 1.

A. Prepare a table for this installment note, similar to the one presented in Exhibit 4. Round to the nearest dollar.

B. Journalize the entries for the issuance of the note and the four annual note payments.

C. ➤ Describe how the annual note payment would be reported on the Year 1 income statement.

SHOW ME HOW

EX 10-22 Accrued product warranty

Obj. 5

Fosters Manufacturing Co. warrants its products for one year. The estimated product warranty is 3% of sales. Assume that sales were $1,100,000 for January. On February 7, a customer received warranty repairs requiring $175 of parts and $80 of labor.

A. Journalize the adjusting entry required at January 31, the end of the first month of the current fiscal year, to record the accrued product warranty.

B. Journalize the entry to record the warranty work provided in February.

REAL WORLD

EX 10-23 Accrued product warranty

Obj. 5

General Motors Company (GM) disclosed estimated product warranty payable for comparative years as follows:

	(in millions)	
	Current Year	Prior Year
Current estimated product warranty payable	$3,582	$2,721
Noncurrent estimated product warranty payable	6,064	4,880
Total	$9,646	$7,601

Assume that GM's sales were $155,929 million in the current year and that the total paid on warranty claims during the current year was $4,326 million.

A. ➤ Why are short- and long-term estimated warranty liabilities separately disclosed?

B. Provide the journal entry for the current year product warranty expense.

C. What two conditions must be met in order for a product warranty liability to be reported in the financial statements?

EX 10-24 Contingent liabilities

Obj. 6

Several months ago, Ayers Industries Inc. experienced a hazardous materials spill at one of its plants. As a result, the Environmental Protection Agency (EPA) fined the company $240,000. The company is contesting the fine. In addition, an employee is seeking $220,000 in damages related to the spill. Lastly, a homeowner has sued the company for $310,000. The homeowner lives 35 miles from the plant but believes that the incident has reduced the home's resale value by $310,000.

Ayers' legal counsel believes that it is probable that the EPA fine will stand. In addition, counsel indicates that an out-of-court settlement of $125,000 has recently been reached with the employee. The final papers will be signed next week. Counsel believes that the homeowner's case is much weaker and will be decided in favor of Ayers. Other litigation related to the spill is possible, but the damage amounts are uncertain.

A. Journalize the contingent liabilities associated with the hazardous materials spill. Use the account "Damage Awards and Fines" to recognize the expense for the period.

B. ➤ Prepare a note disclosure relating to this incident.

Problems: Series A

PR 10-1A Liability transactions
Obj. 1, 5

The following items were selected from among the transactions completed by Sherwood Co. during the current year:

Mar. 1. Purchased merchandise on account from Kirkwood Co., $175,000, terms n/30.

  31. Issued a 30-day, 6% note for $175,000 to Kirkwood Co., on account.

Apr. 30. Paid Kirkwood Co. the amount owed on the note of March 31.

June 1. Borrowed $400,000 from Triple Creek Bank, issuing a 45-day, 5% note.

July 1. Purchased tools by issuing a $45,000, 60-day note to Poulin Co., which discounted the note at the rate of 7%.

  16. Paid Triple Creek Bank the interest due on the note of June 1 and renewed the loan by issuing a new 30-day, 6% note for $400,000. (Journalize both the debit and credit to the notes payable account.)

Aug. 15. Paid Triple Creek Bank the amount due on the note of July 16.

  30. Paid Poulin Co. the amount due on the note of July 1.

Dec. 1. Purchased equipment from Greenwood Co. for $260,000, paying $40,000 cash and issuing a series of ten 9% notes for $22,000 each, coming due at 30-day intervals.

  22. Settled a product liability lawsuit with a customer for $50,000, payable in January. Accrued the loss in a litigation claims payable account.

  31. Paid the amount due to Greenwood Co. on the first note in the series issued on December 1.

Instructions

1. Journalize the transactions.

2. Journalize the adjusting entry for each of the following accrued expenses at the end of the current year:

 A. Product warranty cost, $80,000.

 B. Interest on the nine remaining notes owed to Greenwood Co.

PR 10-2A Entries for payroll and payroll taxes
Obj. 2

✔ 1. (B) Dr. Payroll Tax Expense, $61,476

GENERAL LEDGER

The following information about the payroll for the week ended December 30 was obtained from the records of Boltz Co.:

Salaries:		Deductions:	
Sales salaries	$540,000	Income tax withheld	$160,000
Warehouse salaries	155,000	U.S. savings bonds	10,500
Office salaries	85,000	Group insurance	9,000
	$780,000		

Tax rates assumed:

  Social security, 6%   State unemployment (employer only), 5.4%

  Medicare, 1.5%   Federal unemployment (employer only), 0.8%

Instructions

1. Assuming that the payroll for the last week of the year is to be paid on December 31, journalize the following entries:

 A. December 30, to record the payroll.

 B. December 30, to record the employer's payroll taxes on the payroll to be paid on December 31. Of the total payroll for the last week of the year, $48,000 is subject to unemployment compensation taxes.

2. Assuming that the payroll for the last week of the year is to be paid on January 5 of the following fiscal year, journalize the following entries:

 A. December 30, to record the payroll.

 B. January 5, to record the employer's payroll taxes on the payroll to be paid on January 5. Since it is a new fiscal year, all $780,000 in salaries is subject to unemployment compensation taxes.

PR 10-3A Wage and tax statement data on employer FICA tax

Obj. 2

✔ 2. (E) $28,574.96

EXCEL TEMPLATE

Ehrlich Co. began business on January 2. Salaries were paid to employees on the last day of each month, and social security tax, Medicare tax, and federal income tax were withheld in the required amounts. An employee who is hired in the middle of the month receives half the monthly salary for that month. All required payroll tax reports were filed, and the correct amount of payroll taxes was remitted by the company for the calendar year. Early in the following year, before the Wage and Tax Statements (Form W-2) could be prepared for distribution to employees and for filing with the Social Security Administration, the employees' earnings records were inadvertently destroyed.

None of the employees resigned or were discharged during the year, and there were no changes in salary rates. The social security tax was withheld at the rate of 6.0% and Medicare tax at the rate of 1.5% on salary. Data on dates of employment, salary rates, and employees' income taxes withheld, which are summarized as follows, were obtained from personnel records and payroll records:

Employee	Date First Employed	Monthly Salary	Monthly Income Tax Withheld
Arnett	Nov. 16	$ 5,500	$ 944
Cruz	Jan. 2	4,800	833
Edwards	Oct. 1	8,000	1,592
Harvin	Dec. 1	6,000	1,070
Nicks	Feb. 1	10,000	2,350
Shiancoe	Mar. 1	11,600	2,600
Ward	Nov. 16	5,220	876

Instructions

1. Compute the amounts to be reported for the year on each employee's Wage and Tax Statement (Form W-2), arranging the data as follows (round to the nearest cent):

Employee	Gross Earnings	Federal Income Tax Withheld	Social Security Tax Withheld	Medicare Tax Withheld

2. Compute the following employer payroll taxes for the year: (A) social security, (B) Medicare, (C) state unemployment compensation at 5.4% on the first $10,000 of each employee's earnings, (D) federal unemployment compensation at 0.8% on the first $10,000 of each employee's earnings, (E) total.

PR 10-4A Payroll summary

Obj. 2

✔ 1. Total net pay $15,424.12

EXCEL TEMPLATE

The following data for Throwback Industries Inc. relate to the payroll for the week ended December 9.

Employee	Hours Worked	Hourly Rate	Weekly Salary	Federal Income Tax	U.S. Savings Bonds
Aaron	46	$68.00		$750.20	$100
Cobb	41	62.00		537.68	110
Clemente	48	70.00		832.64	120
DiMaggio	35	56.00		366.04	0
Griffey, Jr.	45	62.00		641.84	130
Mantle			$1,800	342.45	120
Robinson	36	54.00		382.56	130
Williams			2,000	398.24	125
Vaughn	42	62.00		584.72	50

Employees Mantle and Williams are office staff, and all of the other employees are sales personnel. All sales personnel are paid 1½ times the regular rate for all hours in excess of 40 hours per week. The social security tax rate is 6.0%, and Medicare tax is 1.5% of each employee's annual earnings. The next payroll check to be used is No. 901.

(Continued)

Instructions

1. Prepare a payroll summary for Throwback Industries Inc. for the week ended December 9. Use the following columns: Employee, Total Hours, Regular Earnings, Overtime Earnings, Total Earnings, Social Security Tax, Medicare Tax, Federal Income Tax, U.S. Savings Bonds, Total Deductions, Net Pay, Ck. No., Sales Salaries Expense, and Office Salaries Expense.

2. Journalize the entry to record the payroll for the week.

GENERAL LEDGER

PR 10-5A   Payroll accounts and year-end entries   Obj. 2, 3

The following accounts, with the balances indicated, appear in the ledger of Garcon Co. on December 1 of the current year:

211	Salaries Payable	—	218	Bond Deductions Payable	$ 3,400
212	Social Security Tax Payable	$ 9,273	219	Medical Insurance Payable	27,000
213	Medicare Tax Payable	2,318	411	Operations Salaries Expense	950,000
214	Employees Federal Income Tax Payable	15,455	511	Officers Salaries Expense	600,000
215	Employees State Income Tax Payable	13,909	512	Office Salaries Expense	150,000
216	State Unemployment Tax Payable	1,400	519	Payroll Tax Expense	137,951
217	Federal Unemployment Tax Payable	500			

The following transactions relating to payroll, payroll deductions, and payroll taxes occurred during December:

Dec. 2. Issued Check No. 410 for $3,400 to Jay Bank to purchase U.S. savings bonds for employees.

2. Issued Check No. 411 to Jay Bank for $27,046 in payment of $9,273 of social security tax, $2,318 of Medicare tax, and $15,455 of employees' federal income tax due.

13. Journalized the entry to record the biweekly payroll. A summary of the payroll record follows:

Salary distribution:		
Operations	$43,200	
Officers	27,200	
Office	6,800	$77,200
Deductions:		
Social security tax	$ 4,632	
Medicare tax	1,158	
Federal income tax withheld	15,440	
State income tax withheld	3,474	
Savings bond deductions	1,700	
Medical insurance deductions	4,500	30,904
Net amount		$46,296

13. Issued Check No. 420 in payment of the net amount of the biweekly payroll.

13. Journalized the entry to record payroll taxes on employees' earnings of December 13: social security tax, $4,632; Medicare tax, $1,158; state unemployment tax, $350; federal unemployment tax, $125.

16. Issued Check No. 424 to Jay Bank for $27,020, in payment of $9,264 of social security tax, $2,316 of Medicare tax, and $15,440 of employees' federal income tax due.

19. Issued Check No. 429 to Sims-Walker Insurance Company for $31,500 in payment of the semiannual premium on the group medical insurance policy.

27. Journalized the entry to record the biweekly payroll. A summary of the payroll record follows:

Salary distribution:		
Operations	$42,800	
Officers	28,000	
Office	7,000	$77,800
Deductions:		
Social security tax	$ 4,668	
Medicare tax	1,167	
Federal income tax withheld	15,404	
State income tax withheld	3,501	
Savings bond deductions	1,700	26,440
Net amount		$51,360

Dec. 27. Issued Check No. 541 in payment of the net amount of the biweekly payroll.

27. Journalized the entry to record payroll taxes on employees' earnings of December 27: social security tax, $4,668; Medicare tax, $1,167; state unemployment tax, $225; federal unemployment tax, $75.

27. Issued Check No. 543 for $20,884 to State Department of Revenue in payment of employees' state income tax due on December 31.

31. Issued Check No. 545 to Jay Bank for $3,400 to purchase U.S. savings bonds for employees.

31. Paid $45,000 to the employee pension plan. The annual pension cost is $60,000. (Record both the payment and unfunded pension liability.)

Instructions

1. Journalize the transactions.

2. Journalize the following adjusting entries on December 31:

   A. Salaries accrued: operations salaries, $8,560; officers salaries, $5,600; office salaries, $1,400. The payroll taxes are immaterial and are not accrued.

   B. Vacation pay, $15,000.

Problems: Series B

SHOW ME HOW   GENERAL LEDGER

PR 10-1B Liability transactions   Obj. 1, 5

The following items were selected from among the transactions completed by Aston Martin Inc. during the current year:

Apr. 15. Borrowed $225,000 from Audi Company, issuing a 30-day, 6% note for that amount.

May   1. Purchased equipment by issuing a $320,000, 180-day note to Spyder Manufacturing Co., which discounted the note at the rate of 6%.

15. Paid Audi Company the interest due on the note of April 15 and renewed the loan by issuing a new 60-day, 8% note for $225,000. (Record both the debit and credit to the notes payable account.)

July 14. Paid Audi Company the amount due on the note of May 15.

Aug. 16. Purchased merchandise on account from Exige Co., $90,000, terms, n/30.

Sept. 15. Issued a 45-day, 6% note for $90,000 to Exige Co., on account.

Oct. 28. Paid Spyder Manufacturing Co. the amount due on the note of May 1.

30. Paid Exige Co. the amount owed on the note of September 15.

Nov. 16. Purchased store equipment from Gallardo Co. for $450,000, paying $50,000 and issuing a series of twenty 9% notes for $20,000 each, coming due at 30-day intervals.

Dec. 16. Paid the amount due Gallardo Co. on the first note in the series issued on November 16.

28. Settled a personal injury lawsuit with a customer for $87,500, to be paid in January. Aston Martin Inc. accrued the loss in a litigation claims payable account.

Instructions

1. Journalize the transactions.

2. Journalize the adjusting entry for each of the following accrued expenses at the end of the current year:

   A. Product warranty cost, $26,800.

   B. Interest on the 19 remaining notes owed to Gallardo Co.

PR 10-2B   Entries for payroll and payroll taxes

Obj. 2

✔ 1. (B) Dr. Payroll
Tax Expense,
$90,735

GENERAL LEDGER

The following information about the payroll for the week ended December 30 was obtained from the records of Saine Co.:

Salaries:			Deductions:	
Sales salaries	$ 625,000		Income tax withheld	$232,260
Warehouse salaries	240,000		U.S. savings bonds	35,500
Office salaries	320,000		Group insurance	53,325
	$1,185,000			

Tax rates assumed:

Social security, 6%

Medicare, 1.5%

State unemployment (employer only), 5.4%

Federal unemployment (employer only), 0.8%

Instructions

1. Assuming that the payroll for the last week of the year is to be paid on December 31, journalize the following entries:

   A. December 30, to record the payroll.

   B. December 30, to record the employer's payroll taxes on the payroll to be paid on December 31. Of the total payroll for the last week of the year, $30,000 is subject to unemployment compensation taxes.

2. Assuming that the payroll for the last week of the year is to be paid on January 4 of the following fiscal year, journalize the following entries:

   A. December 30, to record the payroll.

   B. January 4, to record the employer's payroll taxes on the payroll to be paid on January 4. Because it is a new fiscal year, all $1,185,000 in salaries is subject to unemployment compensation taxes.

PR 10-3B   Wage and tax statement data and employer FICA tax

Obj. 2

✔ 2. (E) $25,136.13

EXCEL TEMPLATE

Jocame Inc. began business on January 2. Salaries were paid to employees on the last day of each month, and social security tax, Medicare tax, and federal income tax were withheld in the required amounts. An employee who is hired in the middle of the month receives half the monthly salary for that month. All required payroll tax reports were filed, and the correct amount of payroll taxes was remitted by the company for the calendar year. Early in the following year, before the Wage and Tax Statements (Form W-2) could be prepared for distribution to employees and for filing with the Social Security Administration, the employees' earnings records were inadvertently destroyed.

None of the employees resigned or were discharged during the year, and there were no changes in salary rates. The social security tax was withheld at the rate of 6.0% and Medicare tax at the rate of 1.5% on salary. Data on dates of employment, salary rates, and employees' income taxes withheld, which are summarized as follows, were obtained from personnel records and payroll records:

Employee	Date First Employed	Monthly Salary	Monthly Income Tax Withheld
Addai	July 16	$ 8,160	$1,704
Kasay	June 1	3,600	533
McGahee	Feb. 16	6,420	1,238
Moss	Jan. 1	4,600	783
Stewart	Dec. 1	4,500	758
Tolbert	Nov. 16	3,250	446
Wells	May 1	10,500	2,359

Instructions

1. Compute the amounts to be reported for the year on each employee's Wage and Tax Statement (Form W-2), arranging the data as follows (round to the nearest cent):

Employee	Gross Earnings	Federal Income Tax Withheld	Social Security Tax Withheld	Medicare Tax Withheld

2. Compute the following employer payroll taxes for the year: (A) social security, (B) Medicare, (C) state unemployment compensation at 5.4% on the first $10,000 of each employee's earnings, (D) federal unemployment compensation at 0.8% on the first $10,000 of each employee's earnings, (E) total.

PR 10-4B   Payroll summary   Obj. 2

✔ 1. Total net pay,
   $16,592.58

EXCEL TEMPLATE

The following data for Flexco Inc. relate to the payroll for the week ended December 9:

Employee	Hours Worked	Hourly Rate	Weekly Salary	Federal Income Tax	U.S. Savings Bonds
Carlton	52	$50.00		$667.00	$ 60
Grove			$4,000	860.00	100
Johnson	36	52.00		355.68	0
Koufax	45	58.00		578.55	44
Maddux	37	45.00		349.65	62
Seaver			3,200	768.00	120
Spahn	46	52.00		382.20	0
Winn	48	50.00		572.00	75
Young	43	54.00		480.60	80

Employees Grove and Seaver are office staff, and all of the other employees are sales personnel. All sales personnel are paid 1½ times the regular rate for all hours in excess of 40 hours per week. The social security tax rate is 6.0% of each employee's annual earnings, and Medicare tax is 1.5% of each employee's annual earnings. The next payroll check to be used is No. 328.

Instructions

1. Prepare a payroll summary for Flexco Inc. for the week ended December 9. Use the following columns: Employee, Total Hours, Regular Earnings, Overtime Earnings, Total Earnings, Social Security Tax, Medicare Tax, Federal Income Tax, U.S. Savings Bonds, Total Deductions, Net Pay, Ck. No., Sales Salaries Expense, and Office Salaries Expense. (Round to the nearest cent.)

2. Journalize the entry to record the payroll for the week.

PR 10-5B   Payroll accounts and year-end entries   Obj. 2, 3

GENERAL LEDGER

The following accounts, with the balances indicated, appear in the ledger of Codigo Co. on December 1 of the current year:

101	Salaries Payable	—	108	Bond Deductions Payable	$ 2,300
102	Social Security Tax Payable	$2,913	109	Medical Insurance Payable	2,520
103	Medicare Tax Payable	728	201	Sales Salaries Expense	700,000
104	Employees Federal Income Tax Payable	4,490	301	Officers Salaries Expense	340,000
105	Employees State Income Tax Payable	4,078	401	Office Salaries Expense	125,000
106	State Unemployment Tax Payable	1,260	408	Payroll Tax Expense	59,491
107	Federal Unemployment Tax Payable	360			

The following transactions relating to payroll, payroll deductions, and payroll taxes occurred during December:

Dec. 1. Issued Check No. 815 to Aberderas Insurance Company for $2,520, in payment of the semiannual premium on the group medical insurance policy.

1. Issued Check No. 816 to Alvarez Bank for $8,131, in payment for $2,913 of social security tax, $728 of Medicare tax, and $4,490 of employees' federal income tax due.

2. Issued Check No. 817 for $2,300 to Alvarez Bank to purchase U.S. savings bonds for employees.

(Continued)

Dec. 12. Journalized the entry to record the biweekly payroll. A summary of the payroll record follows:

Salary distribution:		
Sales	$14,500	
Officers	7,100	
Office	2,600	$24,200
Deductions:		
Social security tax	$ 1,452	
Medicare tax	363	
Federal income tax withheld	4,308	
State income tax withheld	1,089	
Savings bond deductions	1,150	
Medical insurance deductions	420	8,782
Net amount		$15,418

12. Issued Check No. 822 in payment of the net amount of the biweekly payroll.

12. Journalized the entry to record payroll taxes on employees' earnings of December 12: social security tax, $1,452; Medicare tax, $363; state unemployment tax, $315; federal unemployment tax, $90.

15. Issued Check No. 830 to Alvarez Bank for $7,938, in payment of $2,904 of social security tax, $726 of Medicare tax, and $4,308 of employees' federal income tax due.

26. Journalized the entry to record the biweekly payroll. A summary of the payroll record follows:

Salary distribution:		
Sales	$14,250	
Officers	7,250	
Office	2,750	$24,250
Deductions:		
Social security tax	$ 1,455	
Medicare tax	364	
Federal income tax withheld	4,317	
State income tax withheld	1,091	
Savings bond deductions	1,150	8,377
Net amount		$15,873

26. Issued Check No. 840 for the net amount of the biweekly payroll.

26. Journalized the entry to record payroll taxes on employees' earnings of December 26: social security tax, $1,455; Medicare tax, $364; state unemployment tax, $150; federal unemployment tax, $40.

30. Issued Check No. 851 for $6,258 to State Department of Revenue, in payment of employees' state income tax due on December 31.

30. Issued Check No. 852 to Alvarez Bank for $2,300 to purchase U.S. savings bonds for employees.

31. Paid $55,400 to the employee pension plan. The annual pension cost is $65,500. (Record both the payment and the unfunded pension liability.)

Instructions

1. Journalize the transactions.

2. Journalize the following adjusting entries on December 31:

   A. Salaries accrued: sales salaries, $4,275; officers salaries, $2,175; office salaries, $825. The payroll taxes are immaterial and are not accrued.

   B. Vacation pay, $13,350.

Comprehensive Problem 3

✔ **5. Total assets, $3,569,300**

GENERAL LEDGER

Selected transactions completed by Kornett Company during its first fiscal year ended December 31, 20Y5, were as follows:

Jan. 3. Issued a check to establish a petty cash fund of $4,500.

Feb. 26. Replenished the petty cash fund, based on the following summary of petty cash receipts: office supplies, $1,680; miscellaneous selling expense, $570; miscellaneous administrative expense, $880.

Apr. 14. Purchased $31,300 of merchandise on account, terms 1/10, n/30. The perpetual inventory system is used to account for inventory.

May 13. Paid the invoice of April 14 after the discount period had passed.

17. Received cash from daily cash sales for $21,200. The amount indicated by the cash register was $21,240.

June 2. Received a 60-day, 8% note for $180,000 on the Ryanair account.

Aug. 1. Received amount owed on June 2 note, plus interest at the maturity date.

24. Received $7,600 on the Finley account and wrote off the remainder owed on a $9,000 accounts receivable balance. (The allowance method is used in accounting for uncollectible receivables.)

Sept. 15. Reinstated the Finley account written off on August 24 and received $1,400 cash in full payment.

15. Purchased land by issuing a $670,000, 90-day note to Zahorik Co., which discounted it at 9%.

Oct. 17. Sold office equipment in exchange for $135,000 cash plus receipt of a $100,000, 90-day, 9% note. The equipment had a cost of $320,000 and accumulated depreciation of $64,000 as of October 17.

Nov. 30. Journalized the monthly payroll for November, based on the following data:

Salaries		Deductions	
Sales salaries	$135,000	Income tax withheld	$39,266
Office salaries	77,250	Social security tax withheld	12,735
	$212,250	Medicare tax withheld	3,184

Unemployment tax rates:	
State unemployment	5.4%
Federal unemployment	0.8%
Amount subject to unemployment taxes:	
State unemployment	$5,000
Federal unemployment	5,000

30. Journalized the employer's payroll taxes on the payroll.

Dec. 14. Journalized the payment of the September 15 note at maturity.

31. The pension cost for the year was $190,400, of which $139,700 was paid to the pension plan trustee.

Instructions

1. Journalize the selected transactions.

2. Based on the following data, prepare a bank reconciliation for December of the current year:

- Balance according to the bank statement at December 31, $283,000.
- Balance according to the ledger at December 31, $245,410.
- Checks outstanding at December 31, $68,540.
- Deposit in transit, not recorded by bank, $29,500.
- Bank debit memo for service charges, $750.
- A check for $12,700 in payment of an invoice was incorrectly recorded in the accounts as $12,000.

3. Based on the bank reconciliation prepared in (2), journalize the entry or entries to be made by Kornett Company. Use the Miscellaneous Administrative Expense account to record bank service charges.

4. Based on the following selected data, journalize the adjusting entries as of December 31 of the current year:

A. Estimated uncollectible accounts at December 31, $16,000, based on an aging of accounts receivable. The balance of Allowance for Doubtful Accounts at December 31 was $2,000 (debit).

B. The physical inventory on December 31 indicated an inventory shrinkage of $3,300.

C. Prepaid insurance expired during the year, $22,820.

D. Office supplies used during the year, $3,920.

E. Depreciation is computed as follows:

Asset	Cost	Residual Value	Acquisition Date	Useful Life in Years	Depreciation Method Used
Buildings	$900,000	$ 0	January 2	50	Double-declining-balance
Office Equip.	246,000	26,000	January 3	5	Straight-line
Store Equip.	112,000	12,000	July 1	10	Straight-line

F. A patent costing $48,000 when acquired on January 2 has a remaining legal life of 10 years and is expected to have value for 8 years.

(Continued)

G. The cost of mineral rights was $546,000. Of the estimated deposit of 910,000 tons of ore, 50,000 tons were mined and sold during the year.

H. Vacation pay expense for December, $10,500.

I. A product warranty was granted beginning December 1 and covering a one-year period. The estimated cost is 4% of sales, which totaled $1,900,000 in December.

J. Interest was accrued on the note receivable received on October 17.

5. Based on the following information and the post-closing trial balance that follows, prepare a balance sheet in report form at December 31 of the current year:

The merchandise inventory is stated at cost by the LIFO method.
The product warranty payable is a current liability.

Vacation pay payable:
Current liability	$7,140
Long-term liability	3,360

The unfunded pension liability is a long-term liability.

Notes payable:
Current liability	$ 70,000
Long-term liability	630,000

Kornett Company
Post-Closing Trial Balance
December 31, 20Y5

	Debit Balances	Credit Balances
Petty Cash	4,500	
Cash	243,960	
Notes Receivable	100,000	
Accounts Receivable	470,000	
Allowance for Doubtful Accounts		16,000
Inventory	320,000	
Interest Receivable	1,875	
Prepaid Insurance	45,640	
Office Supplies	13,400	
Land	654,925	
Buildings	900,000	
Accumulated Depreciation—Buildings		36,000
Office Equipment	246,000	
Accumulated Depreciation—Office Equipment		44,000
Store Equipment	112,000	
Accumulated Depreciation—Store Equipment		5,000
Mineral Rights	546,000	
Accumulated Depletion		30,000
Patents	42,000	
Social Security Tax Payable		25,470
Medicare Tax Payable		4,710
Employees Federal Income Tax Payable		40,000
State Unemployment Tax Payable		270
Federal Unemployment Tax Payable		40
Salaries Payable		157,000
Accounts Payable		131,600
Interest Payable		28,000
Product Warranty Payable		76,000
Vacation Pay Payable		10,500
Unfunded Pension Liability		50,700
Notes Payable		700,000
Common Stock		500,000
Retained Earnings		1,845,010
	3,700,300	3,700,300

Analysis for Decision Making

REAL WORLD

ADM-1 Continuing Company Analysis—Amazon: Short-term liquidity analysis

Amazon.com, Inc. is one of the largest Internet retailers in the world. Best Buy, Inc. is a leading retailer of consumer electronics and media products in the United States. Amazon and Best Buy compete in similar markets; however, Best Buy sells through both traditional retail stores and the Internet, while Amazon sells only through the Internet. Current asset and current liability information from recent financial statements are as follows (in millions):

	Amazon	Best Buy
Current assets:		
Cash	$14,557	$ 2,432
Short-term investments	2,859	1,456
Accounts receivable	5,612	1,280
Inventories	8,299	5,174
Other current assets	—	1,387
Total current assets	$31,327	$11,729
Current liabilities:		
Accounts payable	$16,459	$ 5,122
Other current liabilities	11,630	2,314
Total current liabilities	$28,089	$ 7,436

A. Compute working capital for each company
B. Compute the current ratio for each company. (Round to one decimal place.)
C. Compute the quick ratio for each company. (Round to one decimal place.)
D. ▬▬▬▶ Can the working capital be usefully compared between the two companies? Explain.
E. Which company has the greater debt-paying ability according to the current ratio?
F. Which company has the greater short-term debt-paying ability according to the quick ratio?
G. ▬▬▬▶ Why are the results different between (E) and (F)? (*Hint:* Perform a vertical analysis of the current assets.)

REAL WORLD

ADM-2 Hershey: Short-term liquidity analysis

The Hershey Company is the largest producer of chocolate in North America under the Hershey's and Reese's brand names. The following balance sheet information is provided at the end of three recent years (in thousands):

	December 31,		
	Year 3	Year 2	Year 1
Current assets:			
Cash	$ 374,854	$1,118,508	$ 728,272
Short-term investments	97,131	—	—
Accounts receivable	596,940	477,912	461,383
Inventories	801,036	659,541	633,262
Other current assets	377,086	231,373	290,568
Total current assets	$2,247,047	$2,487,334	$2,113,485
Current liabilities:			
Accounts payable	$ 482,017	$ 461,514	$ 441,977
Other current liabilities	1,453,630	946,508	1,029,133
Total current liabilities	$1,935,647	$1,408,022	$1,471,110

A. Compute the working capital for the three years.
B. Compute the current ratio for the three years. (Round to one decimal place.)
C. Compute the quick ratio for the three years. (Round to one decimal place.)
D. ▬▬▬▶ Interpret the short-term liquidity for the three years from (C).
E. ▬▬▬▶ Are the other two measures in (A) and (B) consistent with your analysis in (D)?

ADM-3   Neiman Marcus and Kohl's: Short-term liquidity analysis

Neiman Marcus Group is one of the largest luxury fashion retailers in the world. **Kohl's Corporation** sells moderately priced private and national branded products through more than 1,100 department stores located throughout the United States. The current assets and current liabilities at the end of a recent year for both companies are as follows (in millions):

	Neiman Marcus	Kohl's
Current assets:		
Cash	$ 197	$1,407
Inventories	1,069	3,814
Other current assets	144	477
Total current assets	$1,410	$5,698
Current liabilities:		
Accounts payable	$ 375	$1,511
Other current liabilities	482	1,348
Total current liabilities	$ 857	$2,859

A. ━━━━▶ Would an analysis of working capital between the two companies be meaningful? Explain.

B. Compute the quick ratio for both companies. (Round to the nearest decimal.)

C. ━━━━▶ Interpret your results.

ADM-4   Cabela's and Dick's Sporting Goods: Short-term liquidity analysis

Cabela's Incorporated is a leading specialty retailer of outdoor sports merchandise. **Dick's Sporting Goods, Inc.** is a leading full-line retailer of sporting equipment and apparel. The current assets and current liabilities of both companies are provided as follows from recent financial statements (in millions):

	Cabela's	Dick's
Current assets:		
Cash	$ 478	$ 345
Accounts receivable	62	35
Credit card loans	4,422	—
Inventories	760	1,096
Other current assets	216	120
Total current assets	$5,938	$1,596
Current liabilities:		
Accounts payable	$ 336	$ 508
Gift cards	340	—
Other current liabilities	1,445	493
Total current liabilities	$2,121	$1,001

Cabela's has a branded credit card that is the basis for its financial services business. "Credit card loans" in Cabela's current assets represent the amounts due from Cabela's CLUB® Visa credit card customers. The credit card loans represent 1,817,012 active accounts with an average balance of $2,167. The credit card holders have a median FICO score of 795, which denotes highly creditworthy customers. Cabela's other current liabilities include, among other items, short-term funding to support credit card purchases from its CLUB members.

A. What do the "gift cards" listed under Cabela's current liabilities represent?

B. ━━━━▶ Should the "credit card loans" be considered part of quick assets for Cabela's computation of the quick ratio? Explain.

C. Compute the current ratio for Cabela's and Dick's Sporting Goods. (Round to one decimal place.)

D. Compute the quick ratio for Cabela's and Dick's Sporting Goods. (Round to one decimal place.)

E. ━━━━▶ Compare the two companies using the computations in (C) and (D).

Take It Further

ETHICS

TIF 10-1 Ethics in Action

Tonya Latirno is a staff accountant for Cannally and Kennedy, a local CPA firm. For the past 10 years, the firm has given employees a year-end bonus equal to two weeks' salary. On November 15, the firm's management team announced that there would be no annual bonus this year. Because of the firm's long history of giving a year-end bonus, Tonya and her co-workers had come to expect the bonus and felt that Cannally and Kennedy had breached an implicit agreement by discontinuing the bonus. As a result, Tonya decided that she would make up for the lost bonus by working an extra six hours of overtime per week for the rest of the year. Cannally and Kennedy's policy is to pay overtime at 150% of straight time.

Tonya's supervisor was surprised to see overtime being reported, because there is generally very little additional or unusual client service demands at the end of the calendar year. However, the overtime was not questioned, because employees are on the "honor system" in reporting their work hours.

1. ▰▰▰➤ Is Cannally and Kennedy acting in an ethical manner by eliminating the bonus? Explain your answer.
2. ▰▰▰➤ Is Tonya behaving ethically by making up the bonus with unnecessary overtime? Why?

REAL WORLD

TIF 10-2 Team Activity

In teams, select a public company that interests you. Obtain the company's most recent annual report on Form 10-K. The Form 10-K is a company's annually required filing with the Securities and Exchange Commission (SEC). It includes the company's financial statements and accompanying notes. The Form 10-K can be obtained either (A) from the investor relations section of the company's Web site or (B) by using the company search feature of the SEC's EDGAR database service found at www.sec.gov/edgar/searchedgar/companysearch.html.

Based on the information in the company's annual report answer the following questions:

1. What amount of current liabilities does the company report on its balance sheet at the end of the most recent year? What types of current liabilities does the company report?
2. Have current liabilities increased or decreased from the prior year? By what amount?
3. Does the company disclose any contingent liabilities in the notes to the financial statements? If so, briefly describe the nature of these contingent liabilities.
4. How much of the company's long-term debt will come due in the coming year?

TIF 10-3 Communication

WBM Motorworks is a manufacturer of high-end touring and off-road motorcycles. On November 30, the company was sued by a customer who was injured when the front shock absorber on the WBM Series 3 motorcycle cracked during use. The company conducted a preliminary investigation into the matter during December and found evidence of a manufacturing defect in the shock absorber. While it is uncertain whether the manufacturing defect is the source of the product failure, the company has voluntarily recalled the front shock absorbers on the Series 3 motorcycles. The company is uncertain how the lawsuit will be resolved. Similar lawsuits against other manufacturers have been settled for approximately $2,000,000.

▰▰▰➤ Write a brief memo to the president of WBM Motorworks, U. D. Mach III, discussing how the lawsuit might be reported in the financial statements.

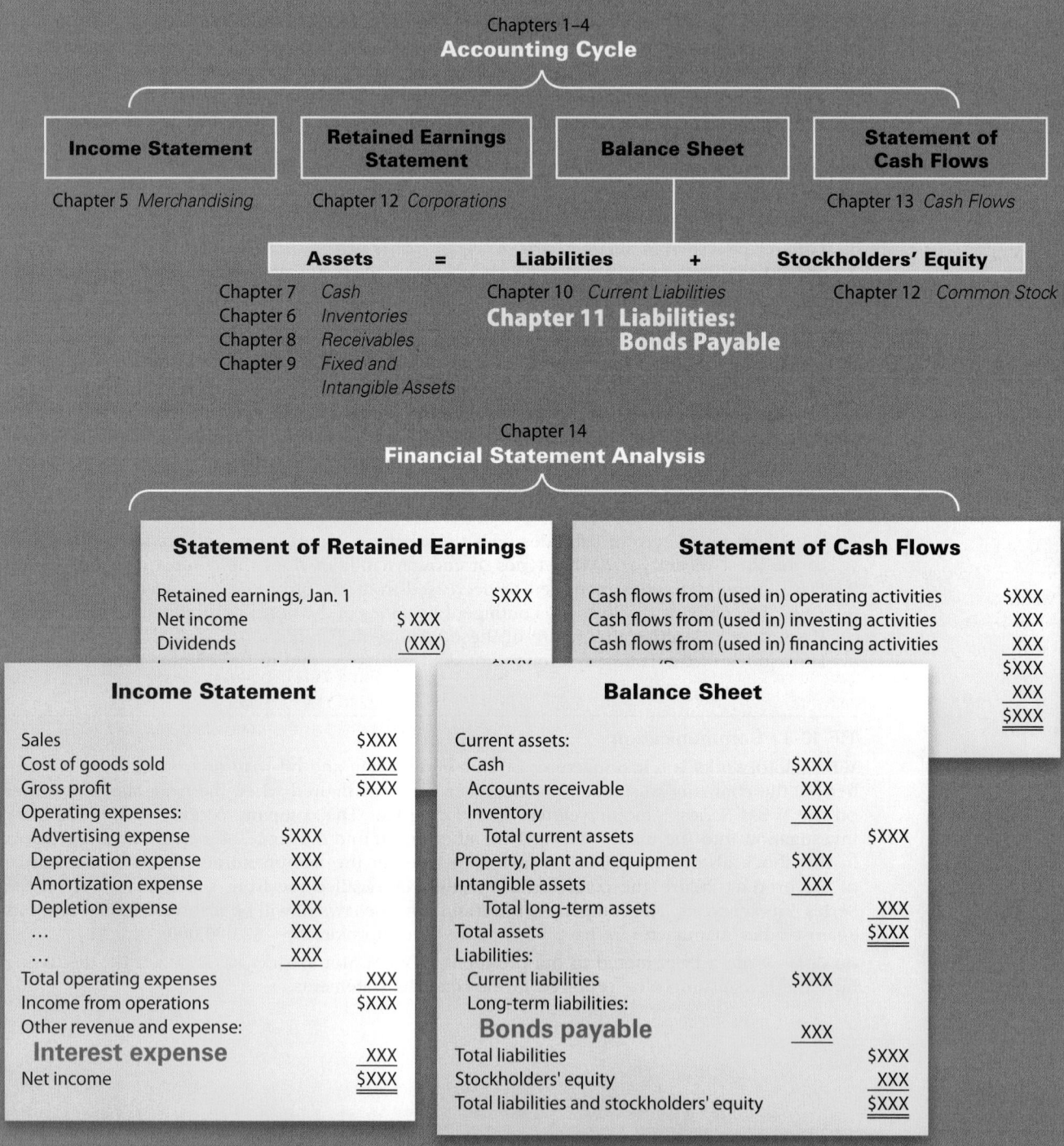

Chapters 1–4
Accounting Cycle

| Income Statement | Retained Earnings Statement | Balance Sheet | Statement of Cash Flows |

Chapter 5 *Merchandising*   Chapter 12 *Corporations*   Chapter 13 *Cash Flows*

| Assets | = | Liabilities | + | Stockholders' Equity |

Chapter 7   *Cash*   Chapter 10 *Current Liabilities*   Chapter 12 *Common Stock*
Chapter 6   *Inventories*   **Chapter 11 Liabilities:**
Chapter 8   *Receivables*   **Bonds Payable**
Chapter 9   *Fixed and*
                Intangible Assets

Chapter 14
Financial Statement Analysis

Statement of Retained Earnings

Retained earnings, Jan. 1		$XXX
Net income	$ XXX	
Dividends	(XXX)	

Statement of Cash Flows

Cash flows from (used in) operating activities	$XXX
Cash flows from (used in) investing activities	XXX
Cash flows from (used in) financing activities	XXX
	$XXX
	XXX
	$XXX

Income Statement

Sales		$XXX
Cost of goods sold		XXX
Gross profit		$XXX
Operating expenses:		
Advertising expense	$XXX	
Depreciation expense	XXX	
Amortization expense	XXX	
Depletion expense	XXX	
...	XXX	
...	XXX	
Total operating expenses		XXX
Income from operations		$XXX
Other revenue and expense:		
Interest expense		XXX
Net income		$XXX

Balance Sheet

Current assets:		
Cash	$XXX	
Accounts receivable	XXX	
Inventory	XXX	
Total current assets		$XXX
Property, plant and equipment	$XXX	
Intangible assets	XXX	
Total long-term assets		XXX
Total assets		$XXX
Liabilities:		
Current liabilities	$XXX	
Long-term liabilities:		
Bonds payable	XXX	
Total liabilities		$XXX
Stockholders' equity		XXX
Total liabilities and stockholders' equity		$XXX

PepsiCo, Inc.

PepsiCo, Inc. is best known for its beverages, which include Pepsi, Diet Pepsi, Gatorade, Mountain Dew, Diet Mountain Dew, Tropicana fruit juices, and Aquafina water.* However, PepsiCo also produces a variety of foods, which include Lay's potato chips, Fritos corn chips, Doritos, Cheetos, Quaker oatmeal, Aunt Jemima mixes and syrups, and Cap'n Crunch cereal. PepsiCo produces, distributes, and sells its products in over 200 countries.

* The brands listed here are trademarked by PepsiCo.

PepsiCo uses a variety of methods to finance its operations, including long-term debt and stock. A recent balance sheet revealed that over 75% of its total assets are financed with liabilities, and 66% of these liabilities are long-term. Included in PepsiCo's long-term liabilities are a variety of notes and bonds. For example, PepsiCo has $13,640 million of bonds maturing throughout 2020–2044 with interest rates of 3.9% and 4.0%. In this chapter, we will discuss the accounting and reporting of bonds payable.

What's Covered

Learning Objectives

Obj. 1   Describe the characteristics and terminology of bonds payable.

Obj. 2   Describe and illustrate the accounting for bonds payable.

Obj. 3   Describe and illustrate the reporting of bonds payable.

Analysis for Decision Making

Describe and illustrate how the times interest earned ratio is used to evaluate a company's financial condition.

Objective 1

Describe the characteristics and terminology of bonds payable.

Nature of Bonds Payable

A **bond** is a form of interest-bearing note. Like a note, a bond requires periodic interest payments, with the face amount to be repaid at the maturity date. For example, a 12% bond requires the company issuing the bond to pay 12% interest on the face amount of the bonds every year. As creditors of the corporation, bondholder claims on the corporation's assets rank ahead of stockholders.

Corporate bonds normally differ in face amount, interest rates, interest payment dates, and maturity dates. Bonds also differ in other ways such as whether corporate assets are pledged in support of the bonds.

Bond Characteristics and Terminology

A bond issue is normally divided into a number of individual bonds. The face amount of each bond is called the *principal*. This is the amount that must be repaid on the dates the bonds mature. The principal is usually $1,000, or a multiple of $1,000. The interest on bonds may be payable annually, semiannually, or quarterly. Most bonds pay interest semiannually.

The underlying contract between the company issuing bonds and the bondholders is called a **bond indenture**. This contract can be written in different ways, depending on the financing needs of the company. The two most common types of bonds are term bonds and serial bonds. When all bonds of an issue mature at the same time, they are called *term bonds*. If the bonds mature over several dates, they are called *serial bonds*. For example, one-tenth of an issue of $1,000,000 bonds, or $100,000, may mature 16 years from the issue date, another $100,000 in the 17th year, and so on.

There are also a variety of more complicated bond structures. For example, *convertible bonds* may be exchanged for shares of common stock, and *callable bonds* may be redeemed by the corporation prior to maturity. These bonds are discussed in intermediate and advanced accounting texts.

Proceeds from Issuing Bonds

When a corporation issues bonds, the proceeds received for the bonds depend on:

■ The face amount of the bonds, which is the amount due at the maturity date.

■ The interest rate on the bonds.

■ The market rate of interest for similar bonds.

The face amount and the interest rate on the bonds are identified in the bond indenture. The interest rate to be paid on the face amount of the bond is called the **contract rate** or *coupon rate*.

The **market rate of interest**, sometimes called the **effective rate of interest**, is the rate determined from sales and purchases of similar bonds. The market rate of interest is affected by a variety of factors, including investors' expectations of current and future economic conditions.

By comparing the market and contract rates of interest, it can be determined whether the bonds will sell for more than, less than, or at their face amount, as shown in Exhibit 1.

Exhibit 1   Issuing Bonds at a Discount, at Face Amount, and at a Premium

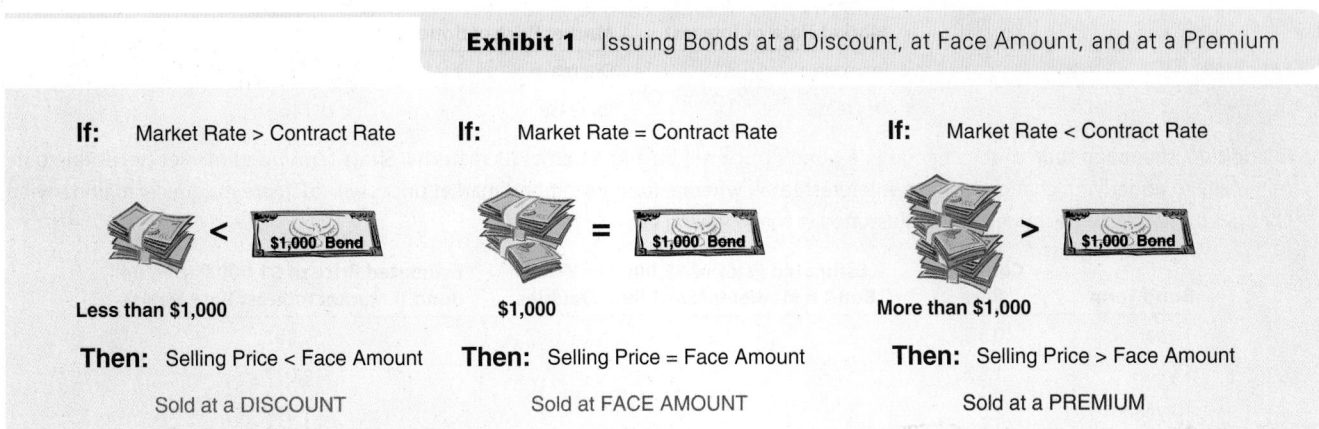

If the market rate equals the contract rate, bonds will sell at the **face amount**. If the market rate is greater than the contract rate, the bonds will sell for less than their face value. The face amount of the bonds less the selling price is called a **discount**. A bond sells at a discount because buyers are not willing to pay the full face amount for bonds with a contract rate that is lower than the market rate.

PepsiCo's 2.75% bonds maturing in 2023 were recently selling for less than their face value.   *Link to PepsiCo*

If the market rate is less than the contract rate, the bonds will sell for more than their face value. The selling price of the bonds less the face amount is called a **premium**. A bond sells at a premium because buyers are willing to pay more than the face amount for bonds with a contract rate that is higher than the market rate.

PepsiCo's 4.25% bonds maturing in 2044 were recently selling for more than their face value.   *Link to PepsiCo*

The price of a bond is quoted as a percentage of the bond's face value. For example, a $1,000 bond quoted at 98 could be purchased or sold for $980 ($1,000 × 0.98). Likewise, bonds quoted at 109 could be purchased or sold for $1,090 ($1,000 × 1.09).

PepsiCo's 4.5% bonds maturing in 2023 were selling for over 111% of their face value.   *Link to PepsiCo*

Why It Matters

Investor Bond Price Risk

Corporate bonds are purchased as investments by individuals and institutions, such as pension funds. Bonds issued by financially strong issuers provide the investor a contracted stream of interest payments and return of principal. Thus, high-quality bond investments are considered less risky than equity investments. However, this does not mean the investor has no price risk. Bond prices move opposite to changes in market interest rates, as follows:

Market Rate of Interest	Market Price of Bonds
Increase	Decrease
Decrease	Increase

In addition, the magnitude of the change in a bond's price will be a function of its maturity. Short-term bond market prices fluctuate minimally to underlying changes in market interest rates, whereas long-term bond market prices will fluctuate maximally to underlying changes in market interest rates. This is illustrated in the following table:

Bond Term	Contract Rate	Estimated Price of $1,000 Par Value Bond if Market Interest Rate Doubles	Estimated Price of $1,000 Par Value Bond if Market Interest Rate Halves
1 year	0.5%	$995	$1,002
5 years	1.5%	931	1,037
10 years	2.0%	836	1,095
30 years	3.0%	585	1,361

This table shows that the price of the bond is much more variable, and hence riskier, to changes in the market interest rate as the term of the bond gets longer. This relationship is one of the reasons long-term bonds often have higher coupon rates than do shorter-term bonds. The bond's term must be considered in managing the risk versus return of a bond investment.

Check Up Corner 11-1   Nature of Bonds Payable

Match the bond terminology in the left column to the correct definition from the right column.

Bond Terminology	Definitions
1. Contract rate of interest	A. The amount due at the maturity date
2. Discount	B. The interest rate to be paid on the face amount of the bond
3. Face amount	C. The interest rate determined from sales and purchases of similar bonds
4. Market rate of interest	D. When bonds sell for less than their face value
5. Premium	E. When bonds sell for more than their face value

Solution:

1. B
2. D
3. A
4. C
5. E

Check Up Corner

Accounting for Bonds Payable

Objective 2

Describe and illustrate the accounting for bonds payable.

Bonds may be issued at their face amount, a discount, or a premium. When bonds are issued at less or more than their face amount, the discount or premium must be amortized over the life of the bonds. At the maturity date, the face amount must be repaid. In some situations, a corporation may redeem bonds before their maturity date by repurchasing them from investors.

Bonds Issued at Face Amount

If the market rate of interest is equal to the contract rate of interest, the bonds will sell for their face amount or at a price of 100. To illustrate, assume that on January 1, Year 1, Eastern Montana Communications Inc. issued the following bonds:

Face amount	$100,000
Contract rate of interest	12%
Interest paid semiannually on June 30 and December 31.	
Term of bonds	5 years
Market rate of interest	12%

Since the contract rate of interest and the market rate of interest are the same, the bonds will sell at their face amount. The entry to record the issuance of the bonds is as follows:

Year 1			
Jan. 1	Cash	100,000	
	Bonds Payable		100,000
	Issued $100,000 bonds payable at face amount.		

A = L + E
+   +

Every six months (on June 30 and December 31) after the bonds are issued, interest of $6,000 ($100,000 × 12% × ½ year) is paid. The first interest payment on June 30, Year 1, is recorded as follows:

Year 1			
June 30	Interest Expense	6,000	
	Cash		6,000
	Paid six months' interest on bonds.		

A = L + E
–   – Exp

At the maturity date, the payment of the principal of $100,000 is recorded as follows:

Year 5			
Dec. 31	Bonds Payable	100,000	
	Cash		100,000
	Paid bond principal at maturity date.		

A = L + E
–   –

Bonds Issued at a Discount

If the market rate of interest is greater than the contract rate of interest, the bonds will sell for less than their face amount. This is because investors are not willing to pay the full face amount for bonds that pay a lower contract rate of interest than the rate they could earn on similar bonds (market rate). The difference between the face amount and the selling price of the bonds is the bond discount.[1]

note:

Bonds will sell at a discount when the market rate of interest is higher than the contract rate.

To illustrate, assume that on January 1, Year 1, Western Wyoming Distribution Inc. issued the following bonds:

Face amount	$100,000
Contract rate of interest	12%
Interest paid semiannually on June 30 and December 31.	
Term of bonds	5 years
Market rate of interest	13%

[1] The price that investors are willing to pay for the bonds depends on present value concepts. Present value concepts, including the computation of bond prices, are described and illustrated in Appendix 1 at the end of this chapter.

Because the contract rate of interest is less than the market rate of interest, the bonds will sell at less than their face amount. Assuming the bonds sell for $96,406, the entry to record the issuance of the bonds is as follows:

A = L + E
+   +

Year 1			
Jan. 1	Cash	96,406	
	Discount on Bonds Payable	3,594	
	Bonds Payable		100,000
	Issued $100,000 bonds at discount.		

The $96,406 is the amount investors are willing to pay for bonds that have a lower contract rate of interest (12%) than the market rate (13%). The discount is the market's way of adjusting the contract rate of interest to the higher market rate of interest.

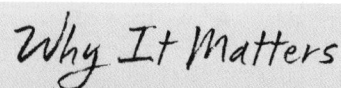

Link to PepsiCo

PepsiCo's 3.6% bonds maturing in 2042 were selling for less than 94% of their face value, which implies that the market rate of interest for equivalent bonds is more than 3.6%.

The account, Discount on Bonds Payable, is a contra account to Bonds Payable and has a normal debit balance. It is subtracted from Bonds Payable to determine the carrying amount (or book value) of the bonds payable. The **carrying amount** of bonds payable is the face amount of the bonds less any unamortized discount or plus any unamortized premium. Thus, after the preceding entry, the carrying amount of the bonds payable is $96,406 ($100,000 − $3,594).

Amortizing a Bond Discount

Every period, a portion of the bond discount must be reduced and added to interest expense to reflect the passage of time. This process, called **amortization**, increases the contract rate of interest on a bond to the market rate of interest that existed on the date the bonds were issued. The entry to amortize a bond discount is as follows:

Interest Expense	XXX	
Discount on Bonds Payable		XXX

Why It Matters

U.S. Government Debt

Like many corporations, the U.S. government issues debt to finance its operations. Currently, debt provides approximately 15% of the total annual funding needs of the U.S. government. The remainder comes from taxes. The debt is issued by the U.S. Treasury Department in the form of U.S. Treasury bills, notes, and bonds. An individual investor can purchase these as an investment through the TreasuryDirect® Web site or through a broker. Treasury securities have the following characteristics:

	Issued at	Interest Paid	Term
U.S. Treasury bills	Discount	None	1 year or less
U.S. Treasury notes	Face value	Semiannual	1 to 10 years
U.S. Treasury bonds	Face value	Semiannual	30 years

Recently, 10-year notes had a contract rate of 2.26%. The contract interest rate for government securities will normally be lowest for Treasury bills and largest for Treasury bonds. A plot of contract interest rates by the term of the debt is called the "yield curve."

The preceding entry may be made annually as an adjusting entry, or it may be combined with the semiannual interest payment. In the latter case, the entry would be as follows:

Interest Expense	XXX	
Discount on Bonds Payable		XXX
Cash (amount of semiannual interest)		XXX

The two methods of computing the amortization of a bond discount are:

- *Straight-line method*
- *Effective interest rate method,* sometimes called the *interest method*

The **effective interest rate method** is required by generally accepted accounting principles. However, the straight-line method may be used if the results do not differ significantly from the interest method. The straight-line method is used in this chapter. The effective interest rate method is described and illustrated in Appendix 2 at the end of this chapter.

The **straight-line method of amortization** provides equal amounts of discount (or premium) to be written off to interest expense each period. To illustrate, amortization of the Western Wyoming Distribution bond discount of $3,594 is computed as follows:

Discount on bonds payable	$3,594
Term of bonds	5 years
Semiannual amortization	$359.40 ($3,594 ÷ 10 periods)

The combined entry to record the first interest payment and the amortization of the discount is as follows:

Year 1			
June 30	Interest Expense	6,359.40	
	Discount on Bonds Payable		359.40
	Cash		6,000.00
	Paid semiannual interest and amortized ¹/₁₀ of bond discount.		

A = L + E
− + − Exp

The preceding entry is made on each interest payment date. Thus, the amount of the semiannual interest expense on the bonds ($6,359.40) remains the same over the life of the bonds.

The effect of the discount amortization is to increase the interest expense from $6,000.00 to $6,359.40 on every semiannual interest payment date. In effect, this increases the contract rate of interest from 12% to a rate of interest that approximates the market rate of 13%. In addition, as the discount is amortized, the carrying amount of the bonds increases until it equals the face amount of the bonds on the maturity date.

Check Up Corner 11-2 Bonds Issued at a Discount

On January 1, the first day of the fiscal year, Nickson Company issues a $1,000,000, 6%, five-year bond, receiving cash of $936,420. The bond pays interest semiannually on June 30 and December 31, and is amortized semiannually using the straight-line method.

A. Journalize the issuance of the bond on January 1.
B. Journalize the semiannual interest payments on June 30 and December 31 of the first year. The bond discount amortization is combined with the semiannual interest payment.
C. Determine the carrying amount of the bond at the end of the first year.

Solution:

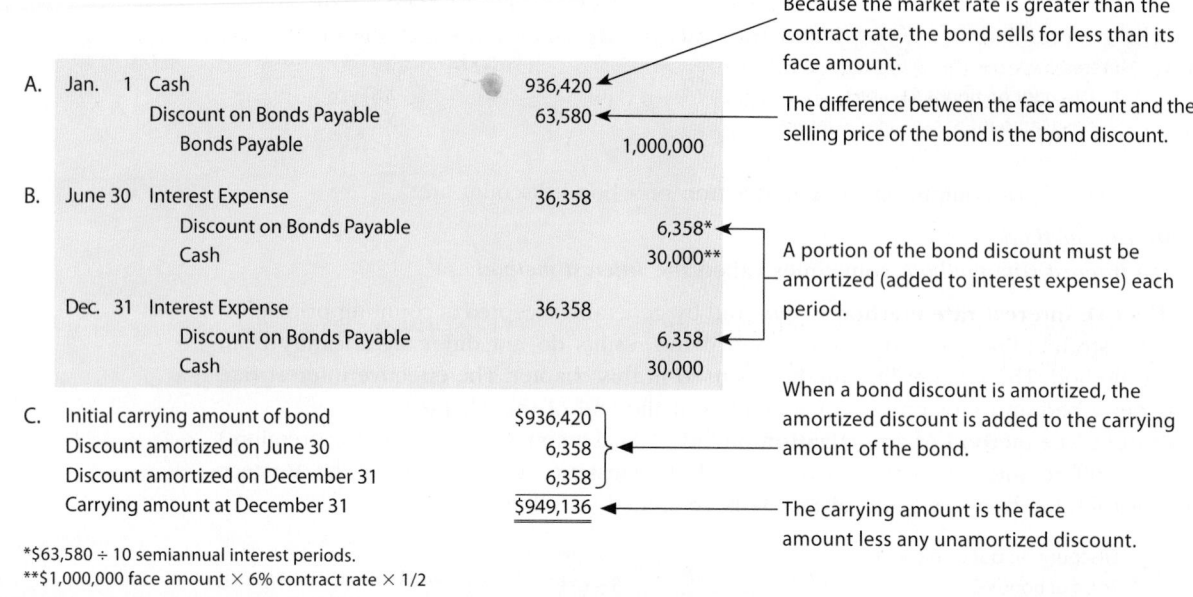

A.	Jan. 1	Cash	936,420
		Discount on Bonds Payable	63,580
		Bonds Payable	1,000,000

Because the market rate is greater than the contract rate, the bond sells for less than its face amount.

The difference between the face amount and the selling price of the bond is the bond discount.

B.	June 30	Interest Expense	36,358
		Discount on Bonds Payable	6,358*
		Cash	30,000**
	Dec. 31	Interest Expense	36,358
		Discount on Bonds Payable	6,358
		Cash	30,000

A portion of the bond discount must be amortized (added to interest expense) each period.

C.	Initial carrying amount of bond	$936,420
	Discount amortized on June 30	6,358
	Discount amortized on December 31	6,358
	Carrying amount at December 31	$949,136

When a bond discount is amortized, the amortized discount is added to the carrying amount of the bond.

The carrying amount is the face amount less any unamortized discount.

*$63,580 ÷ 10 semiannual interest periods.
**$1,000,000 face amount × 6% contract rate × 1/2

Check Up Corner

Bonds Issued at a Premium

If the market rate of interest is less than the contract rate of interest, the bonds will sell for more than their face amount. This is because investors are willing to pay more for bonds that pay a higher contract rate of interest than the rate they could earn on similar bonds (market rate).

To illustrate, assume that on January 1, Year 1, Northern Idaho Transportation Inc. issued the following bonds:

Face amount	$100,000
Contract rate of interest	12%
Interest paid semiannually on June 30 and December 31.	
Term of bonds	5 years
Market rate of interest	11%

Because the contract rate of interest is more than the market rate of interest, the bonds will sell for more than their face amount. Assuming the bonds sell for $103,769, the entry to record the issuance of the bonds is as follows:

A = L + E
+   +

Year 1				
Jan. 1	Cash		103,769	
	Bonds Payable			100,000
	Premium on Bonds Payable			3,769
	Issued $100,000 bonds at a premium.			

The $3,769 premium is the extra amount investors are willing to pay for bonds that have a higher contract rate of interest (12%) than the market rate (11%). The premium is the market's way of adjusting the contract rate of interest to the lower market rate of interest.

Link to PepsiCo PepsiCo's 3.6% bonds maturing in 2042 were selling for less than 94% of their face value, which implies that the market rate of interest for equivalent bonds is more than 3.6%.

The account, Premium on Bonds Payable, has a normal credit balance. It is added to Bonds Payable to determine the carrying amount (or book value) of the bonds payable. Thus, after the preceding entry, the carrying amount of the bonds payable is $103,769 ($100,000 + $3,769).

Amortizing a Bond Premium

Like bond discounts, a bond premium must be amortized over the life of the bond. The amortization of a bond premium decreases the contract rate of interest on a bond to the market rate of interest that existed on the date the bonds were issued. The amortization can be computed using either the straight-line or the effective interest rate method. The entry to amortize a bond premium is as follows:

Premium on Bonds Payable	XXX	
Interest Expense		XXX

The preceding entry may be made annually as an adjusting entry, or it may be combined with the semiannual interest payment. In the latter case, it would be:

Interest Expense	XXX	
Premium on Bonds Payable	XXX	
Cash (amount of semiannual interest)		XXX

To illustrate, amortization of the preceding premium of $3,769 is computed as follows using the straight-line method:

Premium on bonds payable..................	$3,769
Term of bonds..............................	5 years
Semiannual amortization	$376.90 ($3,769 ÷ 10 periods)

The combined entry to record the first interest payment and the amortization of the premium is as follows:

Year 1			
June 30	Interest Expense	5,623.10	
	Premium on Bonds Payable	376.90	
	Cash		6,000.00
	Paid semiannual interest and amortized ¹/₁₀ of bond premium.		

$$A = L + E$$
$$- \quad - \quad - \text{ Exp}$$

The preceding entry is made on each interest payment date. Thus, the amount of the semiannual interest expense ($5,623.10) on the bonds remains the same over the life of the bonds.

The effect of the premium amortization is to decrease the interest expense from $6,000.00 to $5,623.10. In effect, this decreases the rate of interest from 12% to a rate of interest that approximates the market rate of 11%. In addition, as the premium is amortized, the carrying amount of the bonds decreases until it equals the face amount of bonds on the maturity date.

Why It Matters

Bond Ratings

When purchasing bonds, investors are very interested in the likelihood that the bond issuer will not be able to repay bond principal and associated interest. This is termed the *likelihood of default*. To help them assess the likelihood of default, independent rating agencies review and grade the financial condition of companies that issue bonds. For example, the

Standard & Poor's rating agency rates bonds on a scale from D (lowest) to AAA (highest). Bonds with a rating of BBB– or higher are called *investment grade* (or *IG*) bonds because they are issued by companies who are unlikely to default. Bonds issued by companies in weaker financial condition receive ratings below BBB–, reflecting the higher potential for default. These lesser-quality bonds are referred to as *noninvestment grade* or *high-yield* (or *HY*) bonds. Noninvestment grade bonds have a higher yield to compensate investors for their higher risk of default.

Check Up Corner 11-3   Bonds Issued at a Premium

On January 1, the first day of the fiscal year, Johnson Company issues a $2,000,000, 8%, five-year bond, receiving cash of $2,170,600. The bond pays interest semiannually on June 30 and December 31 and is amortized semiannually using the straight-line method.

A.   Journalize the issuance of the bond on January 1.

B.   Journalize the semiannual interest payments on June 30 and December 31 of the first year. The bond premium amortization is combined with the semiannual interest payment.

C.   Determine the carrying amount of the bond at the end of the first year.

Solution:

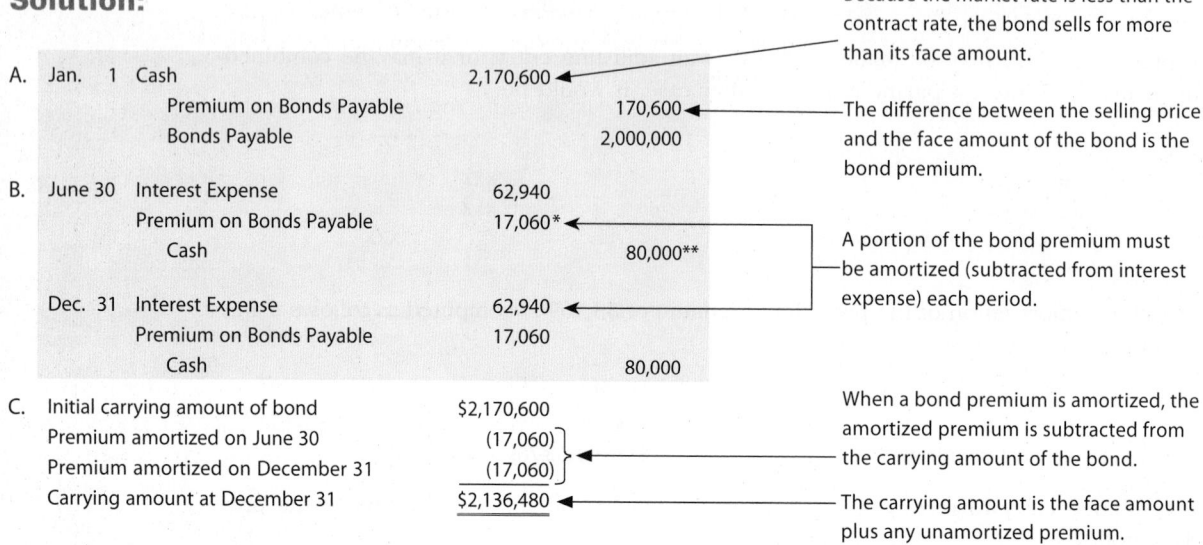

Because the market rate is less than the contract rate, the bond sells for more than its face amount.

A.	Jan.	1	Cash	2,170,600	
			Premium on Bonds Payable		170,600
			Bonds Payable		2,000,000

The difference between the selling price and the face amount of the bond is the bond premium.

B.	June 30	Interest Expense	62,940	
		Premium on Bonds Payable	17,060*	
		Cash		80,000**

A portion of the bond premium must be amortized (subtracted from interest expense) each period.

	Dec. 31	Interest Expense	62,940	
		Premium on Bonds Payable	17,060	
		Cash		80,000

C.	Initial carrying amount of bond	$2,170,600
	Premium amortized on June 30	(17,060)
	Premium amortized on December 31	(17,060)
	Carrying amount at December 31	$2,136,480

When a bond premium is amortized, the amortized premium is subtracted from the carrying amount of the bond.

The carrying amount is the face amount plus any unamortized premium.

*$170,600 ÷ 10 semiannual interest periods
**$2,000,000 face amount × 8% contract rate × 1/2

Check Up Corner

Bond Redemption

A corporation may redeem or call bonds before they mature. This is often done when the market rate of interest declines below the contract rate of interest. In such cases, the corporation may issue new bonds at a lower interest rate and use the proceeds to redeem the original bond issue.

Callable bonds can be redeemed by the issuing corporation within the period of time and at the price stated in the bond indenture. Normally, the call price is above the face value. A corporation may also redeem its bonds by purchasing them on the open market.[2]

A corporation usually redeems its bonds at a price different from the carrying amount (or book value) of the bonds. A gain or loss may be realized on a bond redemption as follows:

- A *gain* is recorded if the price paid for redemption is below the bond carrying amount.
- A *loss* is recorded if the price paid for the redemption is above the carrying amount.

Gains and losses on the redemption of bonds are reported in the *Other income (loss)* section of the income statement.

To illustrate, assume that on June 30, a corporation has the following bond issue:

| Face amount of bonds | $100,000 |
| Premium on bonds payable | 4,000 |

[2] Some bond indentures require the corporation issuing the bonds to transfer cash to a special cash fund, called a *sinking fund,* over the life of the bond. Such funds help assure investors that there will be adequate cash to pay the bonds at their maturity date.

On June 30 the corporation redeemed one-fourth ($25,000) of these bonds in the market for $24,000. The entry to record the redemption is as follows:

June 30	Bonds Payable	25,000	
	Premium on Bonds Payable	1,000	
	Cash		24,000
	Gain on Redemption of Bonds		2,000
	Redeemed $25,000 bonds for $24,000.		

A = L + E
− − + Gain

In the preceding entry, only the portion of the premium related to the redeemed bonds ($4,000 × 25% = $1,000) is written off. The difference between the carrying amount of the bonds redeemed, $26,000 ($25,000 + $1,000), and the redemption price, $24,000, is recorded as a gain.

Assume that the corporation calls the remaining $75,000 of outstanding bonds, which are held by a private investor, for $79,500 on July 1. The entry to record the redemption is as follows:

July 1	Bonds Payable	75,000	
	Premium on Bonds Payable	3,000	
	Loss on Redemption of Bonds	1,500	
	Cash		79,500
	Redeemed $75,000 bonds for $79,500.		

A = L + E
− − − Loss

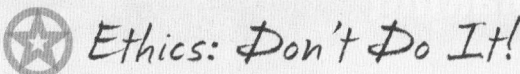

Ethics: Don't Do It!

The Ratings Game

In February 2013, the United States Justice Department filed a lawsuit against **Standard & Poor's** for inflating its ratings on high-risk bond issuances between 2004 and 2007. During this time period, Standard & Poor's gave its highest rating (AAA) to debt securities that were, in fact, highly risky. During the financial crisis of 2008, most of these bonds experienced significant drops in value, leaving investors with huge losses. The Justice Department lawsuit alleged that Standard & Poor's was aware of the high risks associated with these bonds but inflated its ratings because of the large fee it received for providing a rating on these bonds. In 2015, Standard & Poor's settled this and related lawsuits for $1.5 billion.

Source: "U.S. vs. S&P: The Rating Game," *The Chicago Tribune*, February 6, 2013. "S&P reaches $1.5 billion deal with U.S., states over crisis-era ratings," Reuters, Business News, February 3, 2015.

Reporting Bonds Payable

Objective 3

Describe and illustrate the reporting of bonds payable.

Bonds payable are reported as liabilities on the balance sheet. As illustrated in Chapter 10 with notes payable, any portion of the bonds that is due within one year is reported as a current liability. Any remaining bonds are reported as a long-term liability. In this case, no portion of the bonds payable are due currently.

Any unamortized premium is reported as an addition to the face amount of the bonds. Any unamortized discount is reported as a deduction from the face amount of the bonds. A description of the bonds and notes should also be reported either on the face of the financial statements or in the accompanying notes.

The reporting of bonds payable for **Mornin' Joe** follows:

Mornin' Joe

Mornin' Joe **Balance Sheet** **December 31, 20Y6**		
Current liabilities:		
Accounts payable..	$133,000	
Notes payable (current portion)................................	200,000	
Salaries and wages payable.....................................	42,000	
Payroll taxes payable...	16,400	
Interest payable	40,000	
Total current liabilities		$ 431,400
Long-term liabilities:		
Bonds payable, 8%, due in 10 years	$500,000	
Less unamortized discount	16,000	$ 484,000
Notes payable		1,400,000
Total long-term liabilities......................................		$1,884,000
Total liabilities		$2,315,400

Analysis for Decision Making

Objective

Describe and illustrate how the times interest earned ratio is used to evaluate a company's financial condition.

Times Interest Earned

As we have discussed, the assets of a company are subject to (1) the claims of creditors and (2) the rights of owners. As creditors, bondholders are primarily concerned with the company's ability to make its periodic interest payments and repay the face amount of the bonds at maturity.

Analysts assess the risk that bondholders will not receive their interest payments by computing the **times interest earned** ratio during the year as follows:

$$\text{Times Interest Earned} = \frac{\text{Income Before Income Tax} + \text{Interest Expense}}{\text{Interest Expense}}$$

This ratio computes the number of times interest payments could be paid out of current-period earnings. Because interest payments reduce income tax expense, the ratio is computed using income before tax. High values of this ratio are considered favorable. In contrast, low values are considered unfavorable. Values of this ratio less than 1.0 suggest that the firm is unable to cover interest payments from current-period income before tax. Such a situation could eventually lead to loan defaults.

To illustrate, the following data were taken from recent annual reports of four companies in the soft drink beverage industry—**PepsiCo, Inc.**, **The Coca-Cola Company**, **Dr Pepper Snapple Group, Inc.**, and **Monster Beverage Corporation** (in thousands):

	PepsiCo	Coca-Cola	Dr Pepper Snapple	Monster
Interest expense	$ 909,000	$ 483,000	$ 109,000	$ 1,676
Income before income tax expense	8,757,000	9,325,000	1,073,000	745,788

The times interest earned is computed as follows for all four companies:

	PepsiCo	Coca-Cola	Dr Pepper Snapple	Monster
Interest expense	$ 909,000	$ 483,000	$ 109,000	$ 1,676
Income before income tax expense	8,757,000	9,325,000	1,073,000	745,788
Income before income tax expense + Interest expense	$9,666,000	$9,808,000	$1,182,000	$747,464
Times interest earned	10.6	20.3	10.8	446.0
	($9,666,000 ÷ $909,000)	($9,808,000 ÷ $483,000)	($1,182,000 ÷ $109,000)	($747,464 ÷ $1,676)

Monster is much smaller than the other three beverage companies. However, it has a times interest earned ratio of 446, which is much greater than the other three companies. This is because Monster has no long-term debt and only a small amount of short-term bank loans. Among the other three beverage companies, Coca-Cola has twice the interest coverage of PepsiCo and Dr Pepper Snapple. Since all of the ratios are in excess of 10, all of the companies generate enough income before tax to pay (cover) their interest payments. As a result, bondholders of these companies have extremely good protection in the event of an earnings decline.

Make a Decision   Times Interest Earned

The Clorox Company and **The Procter & Gamble Company** (P&G) produce and sell packaged consumer products around the world. Income and interest expense information from financial statements for a recent year follows (in millions):

	Clorox	P&G
Interest expense	$122	$ 709
Income before income tax expense	853	14,885

A. Compute the times interest earned for each company. (Round to one decimal place.)

B. If you were a lender to these two companies, which one appears to have the greater coverage of interest expense and thus the greater protection for your loan interest?

Solution:

A.

	Clorox	P&G
Interest expense	$122	$ 709
Income before income tax expense	853	14,885
Income before income tax expense + Interest expense	$975	$15,594
Times interest earned	8.0	22.0
	($975 ÷ $122)	($15,594 ÷ $709)

B. P&G has a times interest earned ratio of 22, which is 2.75 times greater than Clorox's ratio of 8 (22 ÷ 8). This is because the relative size of P&G's long-term debt to total assets is 14%, which is much smaller than Clorox's 50%. While P&G's coverage ratio demonstrates greater protection for creditors, Clorox's ratio of 8 is considered more than sufficient and, thus, not a cause for concern. Thus, as a lender, you would have greater interest protection from P&G, but both companies have adequate interest coverage.

Make a Decision

Appendix 1 Present Value Concepts and Pricing Bonds Payable

When a corporation issues bonds, the price that investors are willing to pay for the bonds depends on the following:

- The face amount of the bonds, which is the amount due at the maturity date.
- The periodic interest to be paid on the bonds.
- The market rate of interest.

An investor determines how much to pay for the bonds by computing the present value of the bond's future cash receipts, using the market rate of interest. A bond's future cash receipts include its face value at maturity and the periodic interest payments.

Present Value Concepts

The concept of present value is based on the time value of money. The *time value of money concept* recognizes that cash received today is worth more than the same amount of cash to be received in the future.

To illustrate, what would you rather have: $1,000 today or $1,000 one year from now? You would rather have the $1,000 today because it could be invested to earn interest. For example, if the $1,000 could be invested to earn 10% per year, the $1,000 will accumulate to $1,100 ($1,000 plus $100 interest) in one year. In this sense, you can think of the $1,000 in hand today as the **present value** of $1,100 to be received a year from today. This present value is illustrated in Exhibit 2.

Exhibit 2

Present Value and Future Value

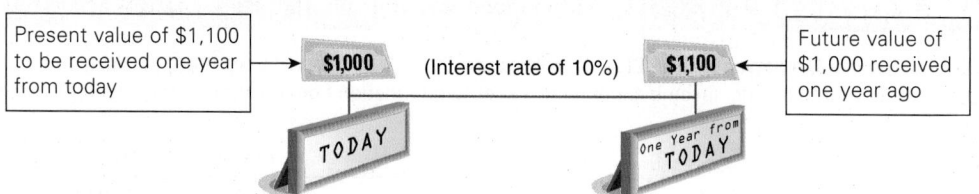

A related concept to present value is **future value**. To illustrate, using the preceding example illustrated in Exhibit 2, the $1,100 to be received one year from today is the *future value* of $1,000 today, assuming an interest rate of 10%.

Present Value of an Amount To illustrate the present value of an amount, assume that $1,000 is to be received in one year. If the market rate of interest is 10%, the present value of the $1,000 is $909.09 ($1,000 ÷ 1.10). This present value is illustrated in Exhibit 3.

Exhibit 3

Present Value of an Amount to Be Received in One Year

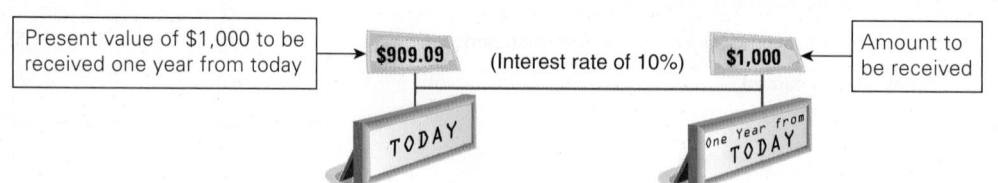

If the $1,000 is to be received in two years, with interest of 10% compounded at the end of the first year, the present value is $826.45 ($909.09 ÷ 1.10).[3] This present value is illustrated in Exhibit 4.

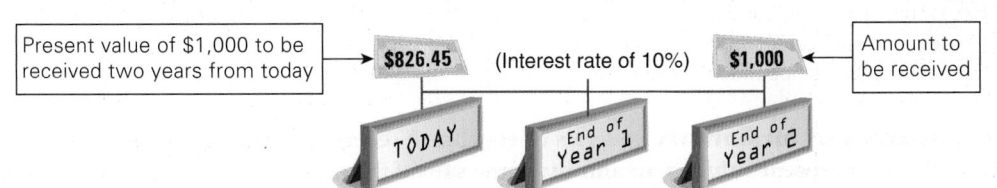

Exhibit 4

Present Value of an Amount to Be Received in Two Years

The present value of an amount to be received in the future can be determined by a series of divisions as illustrated in Exhibits 2, 3, and 4. In practice, however, it is easier to use a table of present values.

The *present value of $1* table is used to find the present value factor for $1 to be received after a number of periods in the future. The amount to be received is then multiplied by this factor to determine its present value.

To illustrate, Exhibit 5 is a partial table of the present value of $1.[4] Exhibit 5 indicates that the present value of $1 to be received in two years with a market rate of interest of 10% a year is 0.82645. Multiplying $1,000 to be received in two years by 0.82645 yields $826.45 ($1,000 × 0.82645). This amount is the same amount computed earlier. In Exhibit 5, the Periods column represents the number of compounding periods, and the percentage columns represent the compound interest rate per period. Thus, the present value factor from Exhibit 5 for 12% for five years is 0.56743. If the interest is compounded semiannually, the interest rate is 6% (12% ÷ 2), and the number of periods is 10 (5 years × 2 times per year). Thus, the present value factor from Exhibit 5 for 6% and 10 periods is 0.55839.

Exhibit 5   Present Value of $1 at Compound Interest

Periods	4%	4½%	5%	5½%	6%	6½%	7%	10%	11%	12%	13%
1	0.96154	0.956940	0.95238	0.94787	0.94340	0.93897	0.93458	0.90909	0.90090	0.89286	0.88496
2	0.92456	0.915730	0.90703	0.89845	0.89000	0.88166	0.87344	0.82645	0.81162	0.79719	0.78315
3	0.88900	0.876300	0.86384	0.85161	0.83962	0.82785	0.81630	0.75131	0.73119	0.71178	0.69305
4	0.85480	0.838560	0.82270	0.80722	0.79209	0.77732	0.76290	0.68301	0.65873	0.63552	0.61332
5	0.82193	0.802450	0.78353	0.76513	0.74726	0.72988	0.71299	0.62092	0.59345	0.56743	0.54276
6	0.79031	0.767900	0.74622	0.72525	0.70496	0.68533	0.66634	0.56447	0.53464	0.50663	0.48032
7	0.75992	0.734830	0.71068	0.68744	0.66506	0.64351	0.62275	0.51316	0.48166	0.45235	0.42506
8	0.73069	0.703190	0.67684	0.65160	0.62741	0.60423	0.58201	0.46651	0.43393	0.40388	0.37616
9	0.70259	0.672900	0.64461	0.61763	0.59190	0.56735	0.54393	0.42410	0.39092	0.36061	0.33288
10	0.67556	0.643930	0.61391	0.58543	0.55839	0.53273	0.50835	0.38554	0.35218	0.32197	0.29459

[3] Note that the future value of $826.45 in two years, at an interest rate of 10% compounded annually, is $1,000.

[4] To simplify the illustrations and homework assignments, the tables presented in this chapter are limited to 10 periods for a small number of interest rates, and the amounts are carried to only five decimal places. Computer programs and business function calculators can be used to determine present values for any number of interest rates, decimal places, or periods. More complete interest tables are presented in Appendix A of the text.

Some additional examples using Exhibit 5 follow:

	Number of Periods	Interest Rate	Present Value of $1 Factor from Exhibit 5
10% for *two* years compounded *annually*	2	10%	0.82645
10% for *two* years compounded *semiannually*	4	5%	0.82270
10% for *three* years compounded *semiannually*	6	5%	0.74622
12% for *five* years compounded *semiannually*	10	6%	0.55839

Present Value of an Annuity A series of equal cash receipts spaced equally in time is called an **annuity**. The **present value of an annuity** is the sum of the present values of each cash receipt. To illustrate, assume that $100 is to be received annually for two years and that the market rate of interest is 10%. Using Exhibit 5, the present value of the receipt of the two amounts of $100 is $173.55, as shown in Exhibit 6.

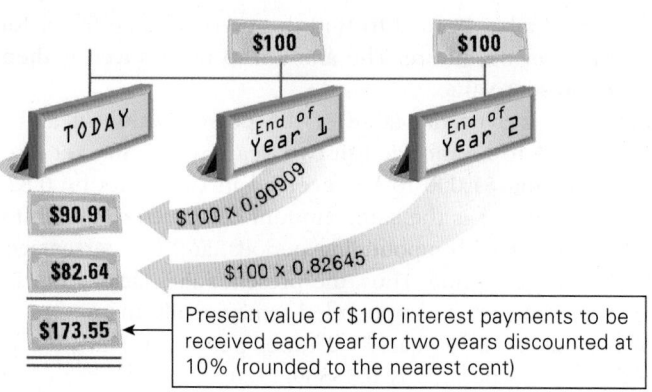

Instead of using present value of $1 tables to determine the present value of each cash flow separately, such as in Exhibit 5, the present value of an annuity can be computed in a single step. Using a value from the *present value of an annuity of $1* table in Exhibit 7, the present value of the entire annuity can be calculated by multiplying the equal cash payment times the appropriate present value of an annuity of $1.

Exhibit 7   Present Value of an Annuity of $1 at Compound Interest

Periods	4%	4½%	5%	5½%	6%	6½%	7%	10%	11%	12%	13%
1	0.96154	0.95694	0.95238	0.94787	0.94340	0.93897	0.93458	0.90909	0.90090	0.89286	0.88496
2	1.88609	1.87267	1.85941	1.84632	1.83339	1.82063	1.80802	1.73554	1.71252	1.69005	1.66810
3	2.77509	2.74896	2.72325	2.69793	2.67301	2.64848	2.62432	2.48685	2.44371	2.40183	2.36115
4	3.62990	3.58753	3.54595	3.50515	3.46511	3.42580	3.38721	3.16987	3.10245	3.03735	2.97447
5	4.45182	4.38998	4.32948	4.27028	4.21236	4.15568	4.10020	3.79079	3.69590	3.60478	3.51723
6	5.24214	5.15787	5.07569	4.99553	4.91732	4.84101	4.76654	4.35526	4.23054	4.11141	3.99755
7	6.00205	5.89270	5.78637	5.68297	5.58238	5.48452	5.38929	4.86842	4.71220	4.56376	4.42261
8	6.73274	6.59589	6.46321	6.33457	6.20979	6.08875	5.97130	5.33493	5.14612	4.96764	4.79677
9	7.43533	7.26879	7.10782	6.95220	6.80169	6.65610	6.51523	5.75902	5.53705	5.32825	5.13166
10	8.11090	7.91272	7.72173	7.53763	7.36009	7.18883	7.02358	6.14457	5.88923	5.65022	5.42624

To illustrate, the present value of $100 to be received at the end of each of the next two years at 10% compound interest per period is $173.55 ($100 × 1.73554). This amount is the same amount computed previously using the present value of $1.

Pricing Bonds

The selling price of a bond is the sum of the present values of:

■ The face amount of the bonds due at the maturity date
■ The periodic interest to be paid on the bonds

The market rate of interest is used to compute the present value of both the face amount and the periodic interest.

To illustrate the pricing of bonds, assume that Southern Utah Communications Inc. issued the following bond on January 1:

Face amount	$100,000
Contract rate of interest	12%
Interest paid semiannually on June 30 and December 31.	
Term of bonds	5 years

Market Rate of Interest of 12% Assuming a market rate of interest of 12%, the bonds would sell for their face amount. As shown by the following present value computations, the bonds would sell for $100,000:

Present value of face amount of $100,000 due in five years, at 12% compounded semiannually: $100,000 × 0.55839 (present value of $1 for 10 periods at 6% from Exhibit 5).................................	$ 55,839
Present value of 10 semiannual interest payments of $6,000, at 12% compounded semiannually: $6,000 × 7.36009 (present value of an annuity of $1 for 10 periods at 6% from Exhibit 7)	44,161
Total present value of bonds...	$100,000

Market Rate of Interest of 13% Assuming a market rate of interest of 13%, the bonds would sell at a discount. As shown by the following present value computations, the bonds would sell for $96,406:[5]

Present value of face amount of $100,000 due in five years, at 13% compounded semiannually: $100,000 × 0.53273 (present value of $1 for 10 periods at 6½% from Exhibit 5)...............................	$53,273
Present value of 10 semiannual interest payments of $6,000, at 13% compounded semiannually: $6,000 × 7.18883 (present value of an annuity of $1 for 10 periods at 6½% from Exhibit 7)	43,133
Total present value of bonds...	$96,406

Market Rate of Interest of 11% Assuming a market rate of interest of 11%, the bonds would sell at a premium. As shown by the following present value computations, the bonds would sell for $103,769:

Present value of face amount of $100,000 due in five years, at 11% compounded semiannually: $100,000 × 0.58543 (present value of $1 for 10 periods at 5½% from Exhibit 5)...............................	$ 58,543
Present value of 10 semiannual interest payments of $6,000, at 11% compounded semiannually: $6,000 × 7.53763 (present value of an annuity of $1 for 10 periods at 5½% from Exhibit 7)	45,226
Total present value of bonds...	$103,769

As shown, the selling price of the bond varies with the present value of the bond's face amount at maturity, the interest payments, and the market rate of interest.

[5] Some corporations issue bonds called *zero-coupon bonds* that provide for only the payment of the face amount at maturity. Such bonds sell for large discounts. in this example, such a bond would sell for $53,273, which is the present value of the face amount.

Appendix 2 Effective Interest Rate Method of Amortization

The **effective interest rate method** of amortization provides for a constant *rate* of interest over the life of the bonds. As the discount or premium is amortized, the carrying amount of the bonds changes. As a result, interest expense also changes each period. This is in contrast to the straight-line method, which provides for a constant *amount* of interest expense each period.

The interest rate used in the effective interest rate method of amortization, sometimes called the *interest method*, is the market rate on the date the bonds are issued. The carrying amount of the bonds is multiplied by this interest rate to determine the interest expense for the period. The difference between the interest expense and the interest payment is the amount of discount or premium to be amortized for the period.

Amortization of Discount by the Interest Method

To illustrate, the following data taken from the chapter illustration of issuing bonds at a discount are used:

Face value of 12%, five-year bonds, interest compounded semiannually...................	$100,000
Present value of bonds at effective (market) rate of interest of 13%	96,406
Discount on bonds payable..	$ 3,594

Exhibit 8 illustrates the interest method for the preceding bonds. Exhibit 8 begins with six columns. The first column is not lettered. The remaining columns are lettered A through E. The exhibit was then prepared as follows:

- Step 1. List the interest payments dates in the first column, which for the preceding bond are 10 interest payment dates (semiannual interest over five years). Also, list on the first line the initial amount of discount in Column D and the initial carrying amount (selling price) of the bonds in Column E.
- Step 2. List in Column A the semiannual interest payments, which for the preceding bond are $6,000 ($100,000 × 6%).
- Step 3. Compute the interest expense in Column B by multiplying the bond carrying amount at the beginning of each period times 6½%, which is the semiannual effective interest (market) rate (13% ÷ 2).

Exhibit 8 Amortization of Discount on Bonds Payable

Interest Payment Date	A Interest Paid (6% of Face Amount)	B Interest Expense (6½% of Bond Carrying Amount)	C Discount Amortization (B – A)	D Unamortized Discount (D – C)	E Bond Carrying Amount ($100,000 – D)
				$3,594	$ 96,406
June 30, Year 1	$6,000	$6,266 (6½% of $96,406)	$266	3,328	96,672
Dec. 31, Year 1	6,000	6,284 (6½% of $96,672)	284	3,044	96,956
June 30, Year 2	6,000	6,302 (6½% of $96,956)	302	2,742	97,258
Dec. 31, Year 2	6,000	6,322 (6½% of $97,258)	322	2,420	97,580
June 30, Year 3	6,000	6,343 (6½% of $97,580)	343	2,077	97,923
Dec. 31, Year 3	6,000	6,365 (6½% of $97,923)	365	1,712	98,288
June 30, Year 4	6,000	6,389 (6½% of $98,288)	389	1,323	98,677
Dec. 31, Year 4	6,000	6,414 (6½% of $98,677)	414	909	99,091
June 30, Year 5	6,000	6,441 (6½% of $99,091)	441	468	99,532
Dec. 31, Year 5	6,000	6,470 (6½% of $99,532)	468*	—	100,000

*Cannot exceed unamortized discount.

- Step 4. In Column C, compute the discount to be amortized each period by subtracting the interest payment in Column A ($6,000) from the interest expense for the period shown in Column B.
- Step 5. Compute the remaining unamortized discount by subtracting the amortized discount in Column C for the period from the unamortized discount at the beginning of the period in Column D.
- Step 6. Compute the bond carrying amount at the end of the period by subtracting the unamortized discount at the end of the period in Column D from the face amount of the bonds ($100,000).

Steps 3–6 are repeated for each interest payment.

As shown in Exhibit 8, the interest expense increases each period as the carrying amount of the bond increases. Also, the unamortized discount decreases each period to zero at the maturity date. Finally, the carrying amount of the bonds increases from $96,406 to $100,000 (the face amount) at maturity.

The entry to record the first interest payment on June 30, Year 1, and the related discount amortization is as follows:

Year 1				
June 30	Interest Expense	6,266		
	Discount on Bonds Payable		266	
	Cash		6,000	
	Paid semiannual interest and amortized bond discount for ½ year.			

$$A = L + E$$
$$- \quad + \quad - \text{Exp}$$

If the amortization is recorded only at the end of the year, the amount of the discount amortized on December 31, Year 1, would be $550. This is the sum of the first two semiannual amortization amounts ($266 and $284) from Exhibit 8.

Amortization of Premium by the Interest Method

To illustrate, the following data taken from the chapter illustration of issuing bonds at a premium are used:

Present value of bonds at effective (market) rate of interest of 11%.........................	$103,769
Face value of 12%, five-year bonds, interest compounded semiannually.....................	100,000
Premium on bonds payable...	$ 3,769

Exhibit 9 illustrates the interest method for the preceding bonds. Exhibit 9 begins with six columns. The first column is not lettered. The remaining columns are lettered A through E. The exhibit was then prepared as follows:

- Step 1. List the number of interest payments in the first column, which for the preceding bond are 10 interest payments (semiannual interest over five years). Also, list on the first line the initial amount of premium in Column D and the initial carrying amount of the bonds in Column E.
- Step 2. List in Column A the semiannual interest payments, which for the preceding bond are $6,000 ($100,000 × 6%).
- Step 3. Compute the interest expense in Column B by multiplying the bond carrying amount at the beginning of each period times 5½%, which is the semiannual effective interest (market) rate (11% ÷ 2).
- Step 4. In Column C, compute the premium to be amortized each period by subtracting the interest expense for the period shown in Column B from the interest payment in Column A ($6,000).
- Step 5. Compute the remaining unamortized premium by subtracting the amortized premium in Column C for the period from the unamortized premium at the beginning of the period in Column D.

Exhibit 9   Amortization of Premium on Bonds Payable

Interest Payment Date	A Interest Paid (6% of Face Amount)	B Interest Expense (5½% of Bond Carrying Amount)	C Premium Amortization (A – B)	D Unamortized Premium (D – C)	E Bond Carrying Amount ($100,000 + D)
				$3,769	$103,769
June 30, Year 1	$6,000	$5,707 (5½% of $103,769)	$293	3,476	103,476
Dec. 31, Year 1	6,000	5,691 (5½% of $103,476)	309	3,167	103,167
June 30, Year 2	6,000	5,674 (5½% of $103,167)	326	2,841	102,841
Dec. 31, Year 2	6,000	5,656 (5½% of $102,841)	344	2,497	102,497
June 30, Year 3	6,000	5,637 (5½% of $102,497)	363	2,134	102,134
Dec. 31, Year 3	6,000	5,617 (5½% of $102,134)	383	1,751	101,751
June 30, Year 4	6,000	5,596 (5½% of $101,751)	404	1,347	101,347
Dec. 31, Year 4	6,000	5,574 (5½% of $101,347)	426	921	100,921
June 30, Year 5	6,000	5,551 (5½% of $100,921)	449	472	100,472
Dec. 31, Year 5	6,000	5,526 (5½% of $100,472)	472*	—	100,000

*Cannot exceed unamortized premium.

- Step 6. Compute the bond carrying amount at the end of the period by adding the unamortized premium at the end of the period in Column D to the face amount of the bonds ($100,000).

Steps 3–6 are repeated for each interest payment.

As shown in Exhibit 9, the interest expense decreases each period as the carrying amount of the bond decreases. Also, the unamortized premium decreases each period to zero at the maturity date. Finally, the carrying amount of the bonds decreases from $103,769 to $100,000 (the face amount) at maturity.

The entry to record the first interest payment on June 30, Year 1, and the related premium amortization is as follows:

A = L + E
–   –   – Exp

Year 1				
June 30	Interest Expense		5,707	
	Premium on Bonds Payable		293	
	Cash			6,000
	Paid semiannual interest and amortized bond premium for ½ year.			

If the amortization is recorded only at the end of the year, the amount of the premium amortized on December 31, Year 1, would be $602. This is the sum of the first two semiannual amortization amounts ($293 and $309) from Exhibit 9.

Let's Review

Chapter Summary

1. The face amount of a bond is called the principal, and the underlying contract is called a bond indenture. When all the bonds of an issue mature at the same time, they are called term bonds. If the bonds mature over several dates, they are called serial bonds. Convertible bonds may be exchanged with common stock, while callable bonds may be redeemed prior to maturity.

   When a corporation issues bonds, the price that buyers are willing to pay for the bonds depends on (1) the face amount of the bonds, (2) the contract rate of interest to be paid on the bonds, and (3) the market rate of interest. If the contract rate of interest equals the market rate of interest, the bonds will sell at their face amount. If the contract rate of interest is less than the market rate of interest, the bonds will sell at a discount. If the contract rate of interest is more than the market rate of interest, the bonds will sell at a premium.

2. The journal entry for issuing bonds payable debits Cash and credits Bonds Payable. Any difference between the face amount of the bonds and the selling price is debited to Discount on Bonds Payable or credited to Premium on Bonds Payable when the bonds are issued. Any discount or premium on bonds payable is amortized to interest expense over the life of the bonds. At the maturity date, the entry to record the repayment of the face value of a bond is a debit to Bonds Payable and a credit to Cash.

   When a corporation redeems bonds before they mature, Bonds Payable is debited for the face amount of the bonds, Premium (Discount) on Bonds Payable is debited (credited) for its unamortized balance, Cash is credited, and any gain or loss on the redemption is recorded.

3. Bonds payable are usually reported as long-term liabilities. If the bonds are due within one year of the balance sheet date, they are reported as current liabilities. A discount on bonds is reported as a deduction from the related bonds payable. A premium on bonds is reported as an addition to the related bonds payable.

Key Terms

amortization (528)	discount (525)	premium (525)
annuity (538)	effective interest rate method (529, 540)	present value (536)
bond (524)	effective rate of interest (525)	present value of annuity (538)
bond indenture (524)	face amount (525)	straight-line method of
carrying amount (528)	future value (536)	amortization (529)
contract rate (525)	market rate of interest (525)	times interest earned (534)

Practice

Multiple-Choice Questions

1. The proceeds received from issuing bonds depends on which of the following?
   A. Coupon rate of interest   C. Principal
   B. Market rate of interest   D. All of these

2. If a corporation plans to issue $1,000,000 of 5% bonds at a time when the market rate for similar bonds is 4%, the bonds can be expected to sell at:
   A. their face amount.   C. a discount.
   B. a premium.   D. a premium or discount.

3. If the bonds payable account has a balance of $900,000 and the discount on bonds payable account has a balance of $72,000, what is the carrying amount of the bonds?
   A. $828,000   C. $972,000
   B. $900,000   D. $580,000

4. Which of the following is the entry to amortize a discount on bonds?
   A. Debit Discount on Bonds Payable;   C. Debit Interest Expense; credit Discount
      credit Interest Expense   on Bonds Payable
   B. Debit Bonds Payable; credit   D. Debit Premium on Bonds Payable; credit
      Discount on Bonds Payable   Interest Expense

5. The balance in the discount on bonds payable account would usually be reported on the balance sheet in the:
   A. Current assets section.   C. Long-term liabilities section.
   B. Current liabilities section.   D. Investments section.

Answers provided after Problem. Need more practice? Find additional multiple-choice questions, exercises, and problems in CengageNOWv2.

Exercises

SHOW ME HOW

1. Issuing bonds at face amount   Obj. 2

On January 1, the first day of the fiscal year, a company issues a $500,000, 5%, 10-year bond that pays semiannual interest of $12,500 ($500,000 × 5% × ½ year), receiving cash of $500,000. Journalize the entries to record (A) the issuance of the bonds, (B) the first interest payment on June 30, and (C) the payment of the principal on the maturity date.

SHOW ME HOW

2. Issuing bonds at a discount   Obj. 2

On the first day of the fiscal year, a company issues a $1,200,000, 9%, five-year bond that pays semiannual interest of $54,000 ($1,200,000 × 9% × ½), receiving cash of $1,153,670. Journalize the bond issuance.

SHOW ME HOW

3. Discount amortization   Obj. 2

Using the bond from Exercise 2, journalize the first interest payment and the amortization of the related bond discount. (Round to the nearest dollar.)

SHOW ME HOW

4. Issuing bonds at a premium   Obj. 2

On the first day of the fiscal year, a company issues a $2,000,000, 8%, five-year bond that pays semiannual interest of $80,000 ($2,000,000 × 8% × ½), receiving cash of $2,170,604. Journalize the bond issuance.

SHOW ME HOW

5. Premium amortization   Obj. 2

Using the bond from Exercise 4, journalize the first interest payment and the amortization of the related bond premium. (Round to the nearest dollar.)

SHOW ME HOW

6. Redemption of bonds payable   Obj. 2

A $1,500,000 bond issue on which there is an unamortized discount of $70,100 is redeemed for $1,455,000. Journalize the redemption of the bonds.

Answers provided after Problem. Need more practice? Find additional multiple-choice questions, exercises, and problems in CengageNOWv2.

Problem

The fiscal year of Russell Inc., a manufacturer of acoustical supplies, ends December 31. Selected transactions for the period Year 1 through Year 6 involving bonds payable issued by Russell Inc. are as follows:

Year 1

June 30.   Issued $2,000,000 of 25-year, 7% callable bonds dated June 30, Year 1, for cash of $1,920,000. Interest is payable semiannually on June 30 and December 31.

Dec. 31.   Paid the semiannual interest on the bonds.

       31.   Closed the interest expense account.

Year 2

June 30.   Paid the semiannual interest on the bonds.

Dec. 31.   Paid the semiannual interest on the bonds.

       31.   Closed the interest expense account.

Year 6

June 30.   Recorded the redemption of the bonds, which were called at 101.5. The balance in the bond discount account is $57,600 after the payment of interest and amortization of discount have been recorded. (Record the redemption only.)

Instructions

1. Journalize entries to record the preceding transactions.

2. Determine the amount of interest expense for Year 1 and Year 2.

3. Determine the carrying amount of the bonds as of December 31, Year 2.

Need more practice? Find additional multiple-choice questions, exercises, and problems in CengageNOWv2.

Answers

Multiple-Choice Questions

1. **D** The proceeds received from issuing bonds depends upon the coupon rate of interest (answer A), the market rate of interest (answer B), and the principal (answer C).

2. **B** Since the contract rate on the bonds is higher than the prevailing market rate, a rational investor would be willing to pay more than the face amount, or a premium (answer B), for the bonds. If the contract rate and the market rate were equal, the bonds could be expected to sell at their face amount (answer A). Likewise, if the market rate is higher than the contract rate, the bonds would sell at a discount (answer C).

3. **A** The bond carrying amount is the face amount plus any unamortized premium or less any unamortized discount. For this question, the carrying amount is $900,000 less $72,000, or $828,000 (answer A).

4. **C** The entry to amortize a discount on bonds payable debits Interest Expense and credits Discount on Bonds Payable (answer C). The entry to amortize a premium on bonds payable debits Premium on Bonds Payable and credits Interest Expense (answer D).

5. **C** The balance of Discount on Bonds Payable is usually reported as a deduction from Bonds Payable in the Long-term liabilities section (answer C) of the balance sheet. Likewise, a balance in Premium on Bonds Payable would be reported as an addition to Bonds Payable in the Long-term liabilities section of the balance sheet.

Exercises

1.

   A.

Cash	500,000	
Bonds Payable		500,000

   B.

Interest Expense	12,500	
Cash		12,500

   C.

Bonds Payable	500,000	
Cash		500,000

2.

Cash	1,153,670	
Discount on Bonds Payable	46,330	
Bonds Payable		1,200,000

3.

Interest Expense	58,633	
Discount on Bonds Payable		4,633
Cash		54,000

   Discount on Bonds Payable = $46,330 ÷ 10 semiannual payments

4.

Cash	2,170,604	
Premium on Bonds Payable		170,604
Bonds Payable		2,000,000

5.

Interest Expense	62,940	
Premium on Bonds Payable	17,060	
Cash		80,000

   Premium on Bonds Payable = $170,604 ÷ 10 semiannual payments

6.

Bonds Payable	1,500,000	
Loss on Redemption of Bonds	25,100	
Discount on Bonds Payable		70,100
Cash		1,455,000

Need more help? Watch step-by-step videos of how to compute answers to these Exercises in CengageNOWv2.

Problem

1.

Year 1				
June 30	Cash		1,920,000	
	Discount on Bonds Payable		80,000	
	Bonds Payable			2,000,000
Dec. 31	Interest Expense		71,600	
	Discount on Bonds Payable			1,600
	Cash			70,000
31	Income Summary		71,600	
	Interest Expense			71,600
Year 2				
June 30	Interest Expense		71,600	
	Discount on Bonds Payable			1,600
	Cash			70,000
Dec. 31	Interest Expense		71,600	
	Discount on Bonds Payable			1,600
	Cash			70,000
31	Income Summary		143,200	
	Interest Expense			143,200
Year 6				
June 30	Bonds Payable		2,000,000	
	Loss on Redemption of Bonds Payable		87,600	
	Discount on Bonds Payable			57,600
	Cash			2,030,000

2. Year 1: $71,600 = $70,000 + $1,600
   Year 2: $143,200 = $71,600 + $71,600

3.

Initial carrying amount of bonds	$1,920,000
Discount amortized on December 31, Year 1	1,600
Discount amortized on December 31, Year 2	3,200
Carrying amount of bonds, December 31, Year 2	$1,924,800

Discussion Questions

1. Describe the two distinct obligations incurred by a corporation when issuing bonds.

2. Explain the meaning of each of the following terms as they relate to a bond issue: (A) convertible, and (B) callable.

3. If you asked your broker to purchase for you a 12% bond when the market interest rate for such bonds was 11%, would you expect to pay more or less than the face amount for the bond? Explain.

4. A corporation issues $26,000,000 of 9% bonds to yield interest at the rate of 7%. (A) Was the amount of cash received from the sale of the bonds greater or less than $26,000,000? (B) Identify the following amounts as they relate to the bond issue: (1) face amount, (2) market or effective rate of interest, (3) contract rate of interest, and (4) maturity amount.

5. If bonds issued by a corporation are sold at a discount, is the market rate of interest greater or less than the contract rate?

6. The following data relate to a $2,000,000, 8% bond issued for a selected semiannual interest period:

Bond carrying amount at beginning of period	$2,125,000
Interest paid during period	160,000
Interest expense allocable to the period	148,750

(A) Were the bonds issued at a discount or at a premium? (B) What is the unamortized amount of the discount or premium account at the beginning of the period? (C) What account was debited to amortize the discount or premium?

7. Bonds Payable has a balance of $5,000,000 and Discount on Bonds Payable has a balance of $150,000. If the issuing corporation redeems the bonds at 98, is there a gain or loss on the bond redemption?

8. Fleeson Company needs additional funds to purchase equipment for a new production facility and is considering either issuing bonds payable or borrowing the money from a local bank in the form of an installment note. How does an installment note differ from a bond payable?

9. In what section of the balance sheet would a bond payable be reported if (A) it is payable within one year and (B) it is payable beyond one year?

Basic Exercises

SHOW ME HOW

BE 11-1 Issuing bonds at face amount
Obj. 2

On January 1, the first day of the fiscal year, Designer Fabric Inc. issues a $5,000,000, 6%, 10-year bond that pays semiannual interest of $150,000 ($5,000,000 × 6% × ½ year), receiving cash of $5,000,000. Journalize the entries to record (A) the issuance of the bonds, (B) the first interest payment on June 30, and (C) the payment of the principal on the maturity date.

SHOW ME HOW

BE 11-2 Issuing bonds at a discount
Obj. 2

On the first day of the fiscal year, a company issues a $2,500,000, 4%, five-year bond that pays semiannual interest of $50,000 ($2,500,000 × 4% × ½), receiving cash of $2,400,000. Journalize the bond issuance.

SHOW ME HOW

BE 11-3 Discount amortization
Obj. 2

Using the bond from Basic Exercise 11-2, journalize the first interest payment and the amortization of the related bond discount.

SHOW ME HOW

BE 11-4 Issuing bonds at a premium
Obj. 2

On the first day of the fiscal year, a company issues an $7,500,000, 8%, five-year bond that pays semiannual interest of $300,000 ($7,500,000 × 8% × ½), receiving cash of $7,740,000. Journalize the bond issuance.

SHOW ME HOW

BE 11-5 Premium amortization

Obj. 2

Using the bond from Basic Exercise 11-4, journalize the first interest payment and the amortization of the related bond premium.

SHOW ME HOW

BE 11-6 Redemption of bonds payable

Obj. 2

A $500,000 bond issue on which there is an unamortized premium of $67,000 is redeemed for $490,000. Journalize the redemption of the bonds.

Exercises

REAL WORLD

EX 11-1 Bond price

Obj. 1

United States Steel Corporation's 7.5% bonds due in 2022 were reported as selling for 104.5. ━━━▶ Were the bonds selling at a premium or at a discount? Why is United States Steel able to sell its bonds at this price?

SHOW ME HOW

EX 11-2 Entries for issuing bonds

Obj. 2

Thomson Co. produces and distributes semiconductors for use by computer manufacturers. Thomson issued $900,000 of 10-year, 7% bonds on May 1 of the current year at face value, with interest payable on May 1 and November 1. The fiscal year of the company is the calendar year. Journalize the entries to record the following selected transactions for the current year:

May   1. Issued the bonds for cash at their face amount.
Nov. 1. Paid the interest on the bonds.
Dec. 31. Recorded accrued interest for two months.

EX 11-3 Entries for issuing bonds and amortizing discount by straight-line method Obj. 2

✔ B. $781,118

SHOW ME HOW

On the first day of its fiscal year, Chin Company issued $10,000,000 of five-year, 7% bonds to finance its operations of producing and selling home improvement products. Interest is payable semiannually. The bonds were issued at a market (effective) interest rate of 8%, resulting in Chin receiving cash of $9,594,415.

A. Journalize the entries to record the following:

1. Issuance of the bonds.

2. First semiannual interest payment. The bond discount is combined with the semiannual interest payment. (Round to the nearest dollar.)

3. Second semiannual interest payment. The bond discount is combined with the semiannual interest payment. (Round to the nearest dollar.)

B. Determine the amount of the bond interest expense for the first year.

C. ━━━▶ Explain why the company was able to issue the bonds for only $9,594,415 rather than for the face amount of $10,000,000.

SHOW ME HOW

EX 11-4 Entries for issuing bonds and amortizing premium by straight-line method Obj. 2

Smiley Corporation wholesales repair products to equipment manufacturers. On April 1, Year 1, Smiley issued $20,000,000 of five-year, 9% bonds at a market (effective) interest rate of 8%, receiving cash of $20,811,010. Interest is payable semiannually on April 1 and October 1. Journalize the entries to record the following:

A. Issuance of bonds on April 1, Year 1.

B. First interest payment on October 1, Year 1, and amortization of bond premium for six months, using the straight-line method.

C. ━━━▶ Explain why the company was able to issue the bonds for $20,811,010 rather than for the face amount of $20,000,000.

EX 11-5   Entries for issuing and calling bonds; loss   Obj. 2

Hoover Corp., a wholesaler of music equipment, issued $30,000,000 of 20-year, 8% callable bonds on March 1, Year 1, at their face amount, with interest payable on March 1 and September 1. The fiscal year of the company is the calendar year. Journalize the entries to record the following selected transactions:

Year 1

Mar. 1.   Issued the bonds for cash at their face amount.

Sept. 1.   Paid the interest on the bonds.

Year 3

Sept. 1.   Called the bond issue at 101.5, the rate provided in the bond indenture. (Omit entry for payment of interest.)

EX 11-6   Entries for issuing and calling bonds; gain   Obj. 2

Mia Breen Corp. produces and sells wind-energy-driven engines. To finance its operations, Mia Breen issued $18,000,000 of 20-year, 4% callable bonds on May 1, Year 1, at their face amount, with interest payable on May 1 and November 1. The fiscal year of the company is the calendar year. Journalize the entries to record the following selected transactions:

Year 1

May 1.   Issued the bonds for cash at their face amount.

Nov. 1.   Paid the interest on the bonds.

Year 5

Nov. 1.   Called the bond issue at 99, the rate provided in the bond indenture. (Omit entry for payment of interest.)

EX 11-7   Reporting bonds   Obj. 3

At the beginning of the current year, two bond issues (Simmons Industries 7%, 20-year bonds and Hunter Corporation 8%, 10-year bonds) were outstanding. During the year, the Simmons Industries bonds were redeemed and a significant loss on the redemption of bonds was reported on the income statement. At the end of the year, the Hunter bonds were reported as a noncurrent liability. The maturity date on the Hunter bonds was early in the following year.

➤ Identify the flaws in the reporting practices related to the two bond issues.

Appendix 1

EX 11-8   Present value of amounts due

Assume that you are going to receive $50,000 in 10 years. The current market rate of interest is 4%.

A. Using the present value of $1 table in Exhibit 5, determine the present value of this amount compounded annually.

B. ➤ Why is the present value less than the $50,000 to be received in the future?

Appendix 1

EX 11-9   Present value of an annuity

Determine the present value of $200,000 to be received at the end of each of four years, using an interest rate of 7%, compounded annually, as follows:

A. By successive computations, using the present value of $1 table in Exhibit 5.

B. By using the present value of an annuity of $1 table in Exhibit 7.

C. ➤ Why is the present value of the four $200,000 cash receipts less than the $800,000 to be received in the future?

Appendix 1

EX 11-10 Present value of an annuity

On January 1 you win $50,000,000 in the state lottery. The $50,000,000 prize will be paid in equal installments of $6,250,000 over eight years. The payments will be made on December 31 of each year, beginning on December 31 of this year. If the current interest rate is 5%, determine the present value of your winnings. Use the present value tables in Appendix A.

Appendix 1

EX 11-11 Present value of an annuity

Assume the same data as in Exercise 11-10, except that the current interest rate is 12%.

➤ Will the present value of your winnings using an interest rate of 12% be more than the present value of your winnings using an interest rate of 5%? Why or why not?

Appendix 1

EX 11-12 Present value of bonds payable; discount

Pinder Co. produces and sells high-quality video equipment. To finance its operations, Pinder issued $25,000,000 of five-year, 7% bonds, with interest payable semiannually, at a market (effective) interest rate of 9%. Determine the present value of the bonds payable, using the present value tables in Exhibits 5 and 7. (Round to the nearest dollar.)

Appendix 1

EX 11-13 Present value of bonds payable; premium

Moss Co. issued $42,000,000 of five-year, 11% bonds, with interest payable semiannually, at a market (effective) interest rate of 9%. Determine the present value of the bonds payable using the present value tables in Exhibits 5 and 7. (Round to the nearest dollar.)

Appendix 2

EX 11-14 Amortize discount by interest method

✔ B. $3,923,959

On the first day of its fiscal year, Ebert Company issued $50,000,000 of 10-year, 7% bonds to finance its operations. Interest is payable semiannually. The bonds were issued at a market (effective) interest rate of 9%, resulting in Ebert receiving cash of $43,495,895. The company uses the interest method.

A. Journalize the entries to record the following:

1. Sale of the bonds.

2. First semiannual interest payment, including amortization of discount. (Round to the nearest dollar.)

3. Second semiannual interest payment, including amortization of discount. (Round to the nearest dollar.)

B. Compute the amount of the bond interest expense for the first year.

C. ➤ Explain why the company was able to issue the bonds for only $43,495,895 rather than for the face amount of $50,000,000.

Appendix 2

EX 11-15 Amortize premium by interest method

✔ B. $1,662,619

Shunda Corporation wholesales parts to appliance manufacturers. On January 1, Shunda issued $22,000,000 of five-year, 9% bonds at a market (effective) interest rate of 7%, receiving cash of $23,829,684. Interest is payable semiannually. Shunda's fiscal year begins on January 1. The company uses the interest method.

A. Journalize the entries to record the following:

1. Sale of the bonds.

2. First semiannual interest payment, including amortization of premium. (Round to the nearest dollar.)

(Continued)

3. Second semiannual interest payment, including amortization of premium. (Round to the nearest dollar.)

B. Determine the bond interest expense for the first year.

C. ━━━━▶Explain why the company was able to issue the bonds for $23,829,684 rather than for the face amount of $22,000,000.

Appendix 1 and Appendix 2

EX 11-16 Compute bond proceeds, amortizing premium by interest method, and interest expense

✔ A. $37,702,483
✔ C. $225,620

Ware Co. produces and sells motorcycle parts. On the first day of its fiscal year, Ware issued $35,000,000 of five-year, 12% bonds at a market (effective) interest rate of 10%, with interest payable semiannually. Compute the following, presenting figures used in your computations:

A. The amount of cash proceeds from the sale of the bonds. Use the tables of present values in Exhibits 5 and 7. (Round to the nearest dollar.)

B. The amount of premium to be amortized for the first semiannual interest payment period, using the interest method. (Round to the nearest dollar.)

C. The amount of premium to be amortized for the second semiannual interest payment period, using the interest method. (Round to the nearest dollar.)

D. The amount of the bond interest expense for the first year.

Appendix 1 and Appendix 2

EX 11-17 Compute bond proceeds, amortizing discount by interest method, and interest expense

✔ A. $71,167,524
✔ B. $670,051

Boyd Co. produces and sells aviation equipment. On the first day of its fiscal year, Boyd issued $80,000,000 of five-year, 9% bonds at a market (effective) interest rate of 12%, with interest payable semiannually. Compute the following, presenting figures used in your computations:

A. The amount of cash proceeds from the sale of the bonds. Use the tables of present values in Exhibits 5 and 7. (Round to the nearest dollar.)

B. The amount of discount to be amortized for the first semiannual interest payment period, using the interest method. (Round to the nearest dollar.)

C. The amount of discount to be amortized for the second semiannual interest payment period, using the interest method. (Round to the nearest dollar.)

D. The amount of the bond interest expense for the first year.

Problems: Series A

PR 11-1A Bond discount, entries for bonds payable transactions Obj. 2

✔ 3. $1,535,897

SHOW ME HOW   GENERAL LEDGER

On July 1, Year 1, Danzer Industries Inc. issued $40,000,000 of 10-year, 7% bonds at a market (effective) interest rate of 8%, receiving cash of $37,282,062. Interest on the bonds is payable semiannually on December 31 and June 30. The fiscal year of the company is the calendar year.

Instructions

1. Journalize the entry to record the amount of cash proceeds from the issuance of the bonds on July 1, Year 1.

2. Journalize the entries to record the following:

A. The first semiannual interest payment on December 31, Year 1, and the amortization of the bond discount, using the straight-line method. (Round to the nearest dollar.)

B. The interest payment on June 30, Year 2, and the amortization of the bond discount, using the straight-line method. (Round to the nearest dollar.)

3. Determine the total interest expense for Year 1.

4. Will the bond proceeds always be less than the face amount of the bonds when the contract rate is less than the market rate of interest?

5. *(Appendix 1)* Compute the price of $37,282,062 received for the bonds by using the present value tables in Appendix A at the end of the text. (Round to the nearest dollar.)

PR 11-2A   Bond premium, entries for bonds payable transactions   Obj. 2

✔ 3. $1,168,704

GENERAL LEDGER

Campbell Inc. produces and sells outdoor equipment. On July 1, Year 1, Campbell issued $25,000,000 of 10-year, 10% bonds at a market (effective) interest rate of 9%, receiving cash of $26,625,925. Interest on the bonds is payable semiannually on December 31 and June 30. The fiscal year of the company is the calendar year.

Instructions

1. Journalize the entry to record the amount of cash proceeds from the issuance of the bonds on July 1, Year 1.

2. Journalize the entries to record the following:

   A. The first semiannual interest payment on December 31, Year 1, and the amortization of the bond premium, using the straight-line method. (Round to the nearest dollar.)

   B. The interest payment on June 30, Year 2, and the amortization of the bond premium, using the straight-line method. (Round to the nearest dollar.)

3. Determine the total interest expense for Year 1.

4. Will the bond proceeds always be greater than the face amount of the bonds when the contract rate is greater than the market rate of interest?

5. *(Appendix 1)* Compute the price of $26,625,925 received for the bonds by using the present value tables in Appendix A at the end of the text. (Round to the nearest dollar.)

PR 11-3A   Entries for bonds payable, including bond redemption   Obj. 2

✔ 3. $64,317,346

SHOW ME HOW

EXCEL TEMPLATE

GENERAL LEDGER

The following transactions were completed by Winklevoss Inc., whose fiscal year is the calendar year:

Year 1

July   1. Issued $74,000,000 of 20-year, 11% callable bonds dated July 1, Year 1, at a market (effective) rate of 13%, receiving cash of $63,532,267. Interest is payable semiannually on December 31 and June 30.

Dec. 31. Paid the semiannual interest on the bonds. The bond discount amortization of $261,693 is combined with the semiannual interest payment.

        31. Closed the interest expense account.

Year 2

June 30. Paid the semiannual interest on the bonds. The bond discount amortization of $261,693 is combined with the semiannual interest payment.

Dec. 31. Paid the semiannual interest on the bonds. The bond discount amortization of $261,693 is combined with the semiannual interest payment.

        31. Closed the interest expense account.

Year 3

June 30. Recorded the redemption of the bonds, which were called at 98. The balance in the bond discount account is $9,420,961 after payment of interest and amortization of discount have been recorded. (Record the redemption only.)

Instructions

1. Journalize the entries to record the transactions. (Round all amounts to the nearest dollar.)

2. Indicate the amount of the interest expense in (A) Year 1 and (B) Year 2.

3. Determine the carrying amount of the bonds as of December 31, Year 2.

Appendix 1 and Appendix 2

PR 11-4A   Bond discount, entries for bonds payable transactions, interest method of amortizing bond discount

✔ 3. $1,491,277

On July 1, Year 1, Danzer Industries Inc. issued $40,000,000 of 10-year, 7% bonds at a market (effective) interest rate of 8%, receiving cash of $37,282,062. Interest on the bonds is payable semiannually on December 31 and June 30. The fiscal year of the company is the calendar year.

Instructions

1. Journalize the entry to record the amount of cash proceeds from the issuance of the bonds.

2. Journalize the entries to record the following:

   A. The first semiannual interest payment on December 31, Year 1, and the amortization of the bond discount, using the interest method. (Round to the nearest dollar.)

   B. The interest payment on June 30, Year 2, and the amortization of the bond discount, using the interest method. (Round to the nearest dollar.)

3. Determine the total interest expense for Year 1.

Appendix 1 and Appendix 2

PR 11-5A   Bond premium, entries for bonds payable transactions, interest method of amortizing bond premium

✔ 3. $1,198,167

Campbell, Inc. produces and sells outdoor equipment. On July 1, Year 1. Campbell issued $25,000,000 of 10-year, 10% bonds at a market (effective) interest rate of 9%, receiving cash of $26,625,925. Interest on the bonds is payable semiannually on December 31 and June 30. The fiscal year of the company is the calendar year.

Instructions

1. Journalize the entry to record the amount of cash proceeds from the issuance of the bonds.

2. Journalize the entries to record the following:

   A. The first semiannual interest payment on December 31, Year 1, and the amortization of the bond premium, using the interest method. (Round to the nearest dollar.)

   B. The interest payment on June 30, Year 2, and the amortization of the bond premium, using the interest method. (Round to the nearest dollar.)

3. Determine the total interest expense for Year 1.

Problems: Series B

PR 11-1B   Bond discount, entries for bonds payable transactions   Obj. 2

✔ 3. $2,392,269

SHOW ME HOW   GENERAL LEDGER

On July 1, Year 1, Livingston Corporation, a wholesaler of manufacturing equipment, issued $46,000,000 of 20-year, 10% bonds at a market (effective) interest rate of 11%, receiving cash of $42,309,236. Interest on the bonds is payable semiannually on December 31 and June 30. The fiscal year of the company is the calendar year.

Instructions

1. Journalize the entry to record the amount of cash proceeds from the issuance of the bonds on July 1, Year 1.

2. Journalize the entries to record the following:

   A. The first semiannual interest payment on December 31, Year 1, and the amortization of the bond discount, using the straight-line method. (Round to the nearest dollar.)

   B. The interest payment on June 30, Year 2, and the amortization of the bond discount, using the straight-line method. (Round to the nearest dollar.)

3. Determine the total interest expense for Year 1.

4. Will the bond proceeds always be less than the face amount of the bonds when the contract rate is less than the market rate of interest?

5. *(Appendix 1)* Compute the price of $42,309,236 received for the bonds by using the present value tables in Appendix A at the end of the text. (Round to the nearest dollar.)

PR 11-2B   Bond premium, entries for bonds payable transactions   Obj. 2

✔ 3. $3,494,977

GENERAL LEDGER

Rodgers Corporation produces and sells football equipment. On July 1, Year 1, Rodgers issued $65,000,000 of 10-year, 12% bonds at a market (effective) interest rate of 10%, receiving cash of $73,100,469. Interest on the bonds is payable semiannually on December 31 and June 30. The fiscal year of the company is the calendar year.

Instructions

1. Journalize the entry to record the amount of cash proceeds from the issuance of the bonds on July 1, Year 1.

2. Journalize the entries to record the following:

   A. The first semiannual interest payment on December 31, Year 1, and the amortization of the bond premium, using the straight-line method. (Round to the nearest dollar.)

   B. The interest payment on June 30, Year 2, and the amortization of the bond premium, using the straight-line method. (Round to the nearest dollar.)

3. Determine the total interest expense for Year 1.

4. Will the bond proceeds always be greater than the face amount of the bonds when the contract rate is greater than the market rate of interest?

5. *(Appendix 1)* Compute the price of $73,100,469 received for the bonds by using the present value tables in Appendix A at the end of the text. (Round to the nearest dollar.)

PR 11-3B   Entries for bonds payable, including bond redemption   Obj. 2

✔ 3. $61,644,484

SHOW ME HOW

EXCEL TEMPLATE

GENERAL LEDGER

The following transactions were completed by Montague Inc., whose fiscal year is the calendar year:

Year 1

July   1.   Issued $55,000,000 of 10-year, 9% callable bonds dated July 1, Year 1, at a market (effective) rate of 7%, receiving cash of $62,817,040. Interest is payable semiannually on December 31 and June 30.

Dec.   31.   Paid the semiannual interest on the bonds. The bond discount amortization of $390,852 is combined with the semiannual interest payment.

        31.   Closed the interest expense account.

Year 2

June   30.   Paid the semiannual interest on the bonds. The bond discount amortization of $390,852 is combined with the semiannual interest payment.

Dec.   31.   Paid the semiannual interest on the bonds. The bond discount amortization of $390,852 is combined with the semiannual interest payment.

        31.   Closed the interest expense account.

Year 3

June   30.   Recorded the redemption of the bonds, which were called at 103. The balance in the bond premium account is $6,253,632 after payment of interest and amortization of premium have been recorded. (Record the redemption only.)

Instructions

1. Journalize the entries to record the foregoing transactions.

2. Indicate the amount of the interest expense in (A) Year 1 and (B) Year 2.

3. Determine the carrying amount of the bonds as of December 31, Year 2.

Appendix 1 and Appendix 2

PR 11-4B   Bond discount, entries for bonds payable transactions, interest method of amortizing bond discount

✔ 3. $2,327,008

On July 1, Year 1, Livingston Corporation, a wholesaler of manufacturing equipment, issued $46,000,000 of 20-year, 10% bonds at a market (effective) interest rate of 11%, receiving cash of $42,309,236. Interest on the bonds is payable semiannually on December 31 and June 30. The fiscal year of the company is the calendar year.

Instructions

1. Journalize the entry to record the amount of cash proceeds from the issuance of the bonds.

2. Journalize the entries to record the following:

   A. The first semiannual interest payment on December 31, Year 1, and the amortization of the bond discount, using the interest method. (Round to the nearest dollar.)

   B. The interest payment on June 30, Year 2, and the amortization of the bond discount, using the interest method. (Round to the nearest dollar.)

3. Determine the total interest expense for Year 1.

Appendix 1 and Appendix 2

PR 11-5B   Bond premium, entries for bonds payable transactions, interest method of amortizing bond premium

✔ 3. $3,655,023

Rodgers Corporation produces and sells football equipment. On July 1, Year 1, Rodgers issued $65,000,000 of 10-year, 12% bonds at a market (effective) interest rate of 10%, receiving cash of $73,100,469. Interest on the bonds is payable semiannually on December 31 and June 30. The fiscal year of the company is the calendar year.

Instructions

1. Journalize the entry to record the amount of cash proceeds from the issuance of the bonds.

2. Journalize the entries to record the following:

   A. The first semiannual interest payment on December 31, Year 1, and the amortization of the bond premium, using the interest method. (Round to the nearest dollar.)

   B. The interest payment on June 30, Year 2, and the amortization of the bond premium, using the interest method. (Round to the nearest dollar.)

3. Determine the total interest expense for Year 1.

Analysis for Decision Making

REAL WORLD

ADM-1 Continuing Company Analysis—Amazon: Times interest earned

Amazon.com, Inc. is one of the largest Internet retailers in the world. **Walmart Stores, Inc.** is the largest retailer in the United States. Amazon and Walmart compete in similar markets; however, Walmart sells through both traditional retail stores and the Internet, while Amazon sells only through the Internet. Interest expense and income before income tax expense from the financial statements of both companies for two recent years follow (in millions):

	Amazon		Walmart	
	Year 2	Year 1	Year 2	Year 1
Interest expense	$ 210	$141	$ 2,461	$ 2,335
Income (loss) before income tax expense	(111)	274	24,799	24,656

A. Compute the times interest earned ratio for both companies for the two years. (Round to one decimal place.)
B. ➤ Interpret Amazon's interest coverage from Year 1 to Year 2.
C. Does a times interest earned ratio less than 1.0 mean that creditors will not get paid interest?
D. ➤ Interpret Walmart's interest coverage from Year 1 to Year 2.
E. Which company appears to have the greater protection for creditors?

REAL WORLD

ADM-2 Arch Coal: Times interest earned

Arch Coal, Inc. is a major coal mining company in the United States. Condensed income statement information for three recent years follows (in millions):

	Year 3	Year 2	Year 1
Revenues	$2,937	$ 3,014	$ 3,768
Costs and expenses	3,087	3,677	4,525
Loss from operations	$ (150)	$ (663)	$ (757)
Interest expense (net)	383	375	312
Loss before income taxes	$ (533)	$(1,038)	$(1,069)

A. Compute the times interest earned ratio for the three years. (Round to one decimal place.)
B. ➤ How would you interpret a negative ratio?
C. Is the trend improving or deteriorating?

REAL WORLD

ADM-3 Aeropostale: Times interest earned

Aeropostale, Inc. is a specialty fashion retailer targeting young adults. The income before income tax expense and interest expense for four recent years follow (in millions):

	Year 4	Year 3	Year 2	Year 1
Income (loss) before income tax expense	$(132.1)	$(135.6)	$91.7	$129.1
Interest expense	8.8	0.9	0.5	0.4

A. Compute the time interest earned ratio for each year. (Round to one decimal place.)
B. Plot the four points on a graph with the year numbers on the horizontal axis, beginning with Year 1.
C. ➤ Interpret the trend in the ratio from your graph.
D. ➤ What happened to interest expense in Year 4? What might be the cause?

REAL WORLD

ADM-4   Hilton and Marriott: Times interest earned

Hilton Worldwide Holdings, Inc. and Marriott International, Inc. are two of the largest hotel operators in the world. Selected financial information from recent income statements for both companies follows (in millions):

	Hilton	Marriott
Operating income	$1,673	$1,159
Interest expense	618	115
Other expense items	92	44
Income before income taxes	$1,147	$1,088
Income tax expense	465	335
Net income	$ 682	$ 753

A. Compute the times interest earned ratio for each company. (Round to one decimal place.)
B. ➤ Which company appears to better protect creditor interest? Why?

Take It Further

ETHICS

TIF 11-1   Ethics in Action

CEG Capital Inc. is a large holding company that uses long-term debt extensively to fund its operations. At December 31, the company reported total assets of $100 million, total debt of $55 million, and total equity of $45 million. In January, the company issued $11 billion in long-term bonds to investors at par value. This was the largest debt issuance in the company's history, and it significantly increased the company's ratio of total debt to total equity. Five days after the debt issuance, CEG filed legal documents to prepare for an additional $50 billion long-term bond issue. As a result of this filing, the price of the $11 billion in bonds that the company issued earlier in the week dropped to 94 because of the increased risk associated with the company's debt. The investors in the original $11 billion bond issuance were not informed of the company's plans to issue additional debt so quickly after the initial bond issue.

➤ Did CEG Capital act unethically by not disclosing to initial bond investors its immediate plans to issue an additional $50 billion debt offering?

REAL WORLD

TIF 11-2   Team Activity

In teams, select a public company that interests you. Obtain the company's most recent annual report on Form 10-K. The Form 10-K is a company's annually required filing with the Securities and Exchange Commission (SEC). It includes the company's financial statements and accompanying notes. The Form 10-K can be obtained either (A) from the investor relations section of the company's Web site or (B) by using the company search feature of the SEC's EDGAR database service found at www.sec.gov/edgar/searchedgar/companysearch.html.

1. Based on the information in the company's most recent annual report, answer the following questions:
   A. How much long-term debt does the company report at the end of the most recent year presented?
   B. Does the company have any bonds outstanding at the end of the most recent year? If so, read the supporting notes to the financial statements and determine:
      (1)   The contract rate of interest on the bond issue(s).
      (2)   The discount or premium on the bond issue(s).
      (3)   The due date of the bond issue(s).
      (4)   The total amount of any bonds that will mature within one year of the balance sheet date.
2. ➤ Based on your answers to the questions in requirement 1, evaluate the company's debt position.

TIF 11-3 Communication

Nordbock Inc. reports the following outstanding bond issue on its December 31, 20Y1, balance sheet:

$1,000,000, 7%, 10-year bonds that pay interest semiannually.

The bonds have been outstanding for five years and were originally issued at face amount. The company is considering redeeming these bonds on January 1, 20Y2, at 103 and issuing new $1,000,000, 5%, five-year bonds at their face amount. These bonds would pay interest semiannually on June 30 and December 31.

Write a brief memo to Liz Nolan, the chief financial officer, discussing the costs of redeeming the existing bonds, the proceeds from issuing the new bonds, and whether this is a good financial decision.

12

Corporations: Organization, Stock Transactions, and Dividends

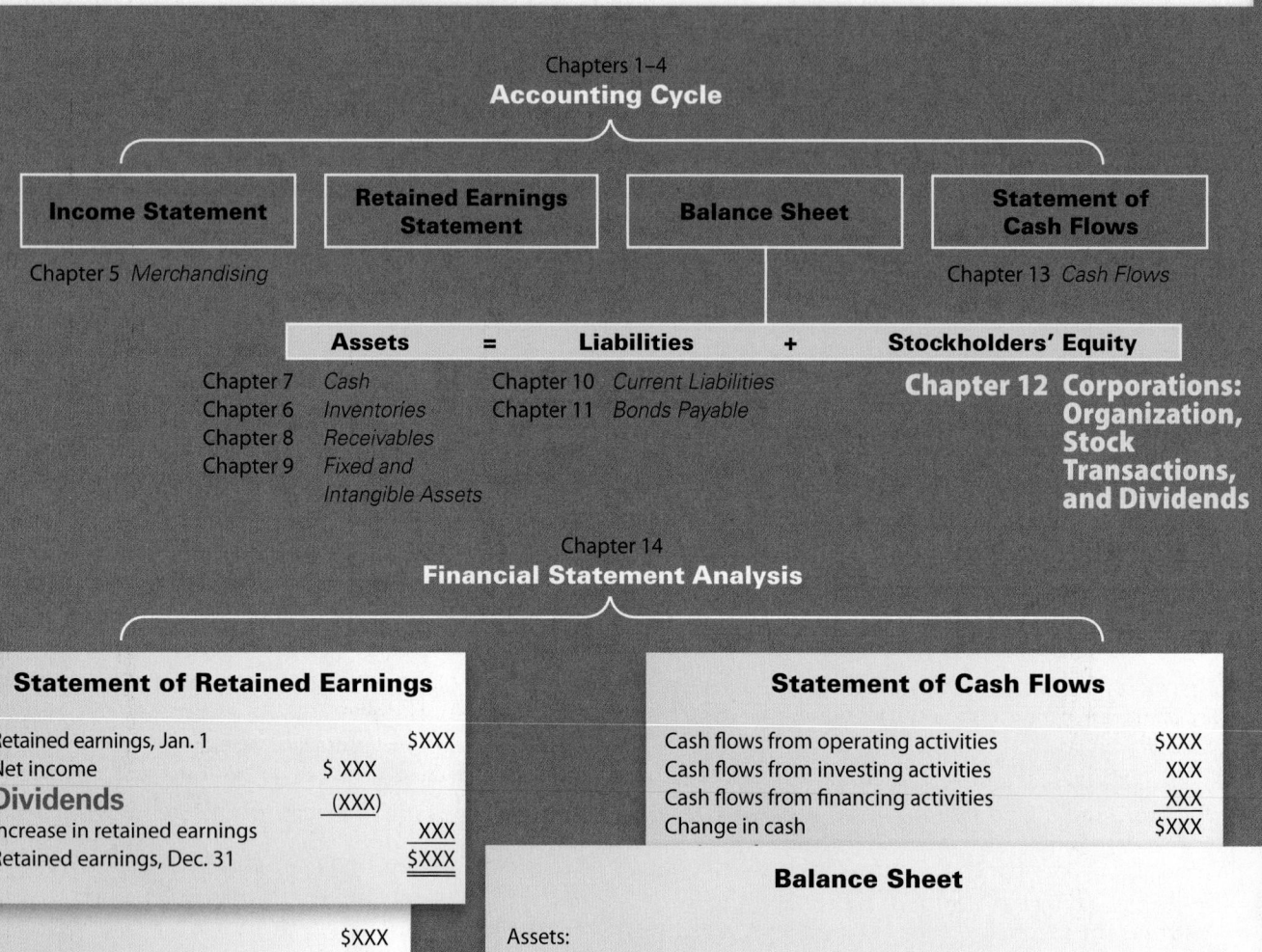

Chapters 1–4
Accounting Cycle

Income Statement	Retained Earnings Statement	Balance Sheet	Statement of Cash Flows

Chapter 5 *Merchandising*   Chapter 13 *Cash Flows*

Assets	=	Liabilities	+	Stockholders' Equity

Chapter 7 *Cash*   Chapter 10 *Current Liabilities*   **Chapter 12 Corporations:**
Chapter 6 *Inventories*   Chapter 11 *Bonds Payable*   **Organization,**
Chapter 8 *Receivables*   **Stock**
Chapter 9 *Fixed and*   **Transactions,**
         Intangible Assets   **and Dividends**

Chapter 14
Financial Statement Analysis

Statement of Retained Earnings

Retained earnings, Jan. 1		$XXX
Net income	$ XXX	
Dividends	(XXX)	
Increase in retained earnings		XXX
Retained earnings, Dec. 31		$XXX

Statement of Cash Flows

Cash flows from operating activities	$XXX
Cash flows from investing activities	XXX
Cash flows from financing activities	XXX
Change in cash	$XXX

Balance Sheet

Assets:		
Current assets		$XXX
Property, plant, and equipment		XXX
Intangible assets		XXX
Total assets		$XXX
Liabilities:		
Current liabilities	$ XXX	
Long-term liabilities	XXX	
Total liabilities		$XXX
Stockholders' equity:		
Retained earnings	$ XXX	
Common stock	XXX	
Preferred stock	XXX	
Paid-in capital in excess of par	XXX	
Treasury stock	(XXX)	
Paid-in capital from sale of treasury stock	XXX	
Total stockholders' equity		XXX
Total liabilities and stockholders' equity		$XXX

Sales		$XXX
Cost of goods sold		XXX
Gross profit		$XXX
Operating expenses:		
Advertising expense	$XXX	
Depreciation expense	XXX	
Amortization expense	XXX	
Depletion expense	XXX	
…	XXX	
…	XXX	
Total operating expenses		XXX
Income from operations		$XXX
Other revenue and expense		XXX
Net income		$XXX

Alphabet (Google), Inc.*

If you purchase a share of stock from **Google**, you own a small interest in the company. You may request a Google stock certificate as an indication of your ownership.

Google is one of the most visible companies on the Internet. Many of us cannot visit the Web without using Google to power a search or to retrieve our e-mail using Google's Gmail. Yet Google's Internet tools are free to online browsers. Google generates most of its revenue through online advertising.

Purchasing a share of stock from Google may be a great gift idea for the "hard-to-shop-for person." However, a stock certificate represents more than just a picture that you can frame. In fact, the stock certificate is a document that reflects legal ownership of the future financial prospects of Google. In addition, as a shareholder, it represents your claim against the assets and earnings of the corporation.

If you are purchasing Google stock as an investment, you should analyze Google's financial statements and management's plans for the future. For example, Google first offered its stock to the public on August 19, 2004, for $100 per share. Google's stock has sold for more than $1,000 per share, even though it pays no dividends. In addition, Google recently expanded into developing and offering free software platforms for mobile devices such as cell phones. For example, your cell phone may use Google's Android™ operating system. So, should you purchase Google stock?

This chapter describes and illustrates the nature of corporations, including the accounting for stock and dividends. This discussion will aid you in making decisions such as whether or not to buy stock in a company.

* In August 2015, Google, Inc. announced that it was reorganizing and changing the name of its company from Google to Alphabet. Alphabet will be the parent company for a number of different brands, including Google, Android, and YouTube. Since Google is the more commonly used name, we use Google throughout this chapter.

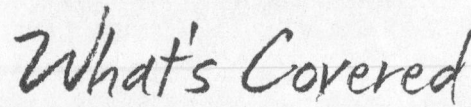

What's Covered

Corporations: Organization, Stock Transactions, and Dividends

Corporations	**Classes of Stock**	**Dividends and Stock Splits**	**Treasury Stock**	**Reporting Stockholders' Equity**
■ Characteristics (Obj. 1)	■ Common Stock (Obj. 2)	■ Cash Dividends (Obj. 3)	■ Purchasing (Obj. 5)	■ Common Stock (Obj. 6)
■ Forming a Corporation (Obj. 1)	■ Preferred Stock (Obj. 2)	■ Stock Dividends (Obj. 3)	■ Selling (Obj. 5)	■ Preferred Stock (Obj. 6)
	■ Paid-In Capital (Obj. 2)	■ Stock Splits (Obj. 4)		■ Paid-In Capital (Obj. 6)
				■ Retained Earnings (Obj. 6)

Learning Objectives

Obj. 1 Describe the nature of the corporate form of organization.

Obj. 2 Describe and illustrate the characteristics of stock, classes of stock, and entries for issuing stock.

Obj. 3 Describe and illustrate the accounting for cash dividends and stock dividends.

Obj. 4 Describe the effect of stock splits on stockholders' equity.

Obj. 5 Describe and illustrate the accounting for treasury stock transactions.

Obj. 6 Describe and illustrate the reporting of stockholders' equity.

Analysis for Decision Making

Describe and illustrate the use of earnings per share in evaluating a company's profitability.

Objective 1
Describe the nature of the corporate form of organization.

Nature of a Corporation

Most large businesses are organized as corporations. As a result, corporations generate more than 90% of the total business dollars in the United States. In contrast, most small businesses are organized as proprietorships, partnerships, or limited liability companies.

Characteristics of a Corporation

A *corporation* is a legal entity, distinct and separate from the individuals who create and operate it. As a legal entity, a corporation may acquire, own, and dispose of property in its own name. It may also incur liabilities and enter into contracts. Most importantly, it can sell shares of ownership, called **stock**. This characteristic gives corporations the ability to raise large amounts of capital.

The **stockholders** or *shareholders* who own the stock own the corporation. They can buy and sell stock without affecting the corporation's operations or continued existence. Corporations whose shares of stock are traded in public markets are called *public corporations*. Corporations whose shares are not traded publicly are usually owned by a small group of investors and are called *nonpublic* or *private corporations*.

The stockholders of a corporation have *limited liability*. This means that creditors usually may not go beyond the assets of the corporation to satisfy their claims. Thus, the financial loss that a stockholder may suffer is limited to the amount invested.

The stockholders control a corporation by electing a *board of directors*. This board meets periodically to establish corporate policies. It also selects the chief executive officer (CEO) and other major officers to manage the corporation's day-to-day affairs. Exhibit 1 shows the organizational structure of a corporation.

note:

Corporations have a separate legal existence, transferable units of ownership, and limited stockholder liability.

As a separate entity, a corporation is subject to taxes. For example, corporations must pay federal income taxes on their income.[1] Thus, corporate income that is distributed to stockholders in the form of *dividends* has already been taxed. In turn, stockholders must pay income taxes on the dividends they receive. This *double taxation* of corporate earnings is a major disadvantage of the corporate form. The advantages and disadvantages of the corporate form are listed in Exhibit 2.

[1] A majority of states also require corporations to pay income taxes.

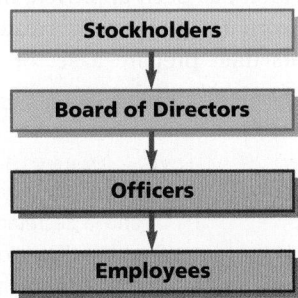

Exhibit 1

Organizational Structure of a Corporation

Exhibit 2 Advantages and Disadvantages of the Corporate Form

Advantages	Explanation
Separate legal existence	A corporation exists separately from its owners.
Continuous life	A corporation's life is separate from its owners; therefore, it exists indefinitely.
Raising large amounts of capital	The corporate form is suited for raising large amounts of money from shareholders.
Ownership rights are easily transferable	A corporation sells shares of ownership, called *stock*. The stockholders of a public company can transfer their shares of stock to other stockholders through stock markets, such as the New York Stock Exchange.
Limited liability	A corporation's creditors usually may not go beyond the assets of the corporation to satisfy their claims. Thus, the financial loss that a stockholder may suffer is limited to the amount invested.

Disadvantages	Explanation
Owner is separate from management	Stockholders control management through a board of directors. The board of directors should represent shareholder interests; however, the board is often more closely tied to management than to shareholders. As a result, the board of directors and management may not always behave in the best interests of stockholders.
Double taxation of dividends	As a separate legal entity, a corporation is subject to taxation. Thus, net income distributed as dividends will be taxed once at the corporation level, and then again at the individual level.
Regulatory costs	Corporations must satisfy many requirements, such as those required by the Sarbanes-Oxley Act.

Forming a Corporation

The first step in forming a corporation is to file an *application of incorporation* with the state. State incorporation laws differ, and corporations often organize in those states with the more favorable laws. For this reason, more than half of the largest companies are incorporated in Delaware. Exhibit 3 lists some corporations, their states of incorporation, and the location of their headquarters.

Corporation	State of Incorporation	Headquarters
Caterpillar	Delaware	Peoria, IL
Delta Air Lines	Delaware	Atlanta, GA
The Dow Chemical Company	Delaware	Midland, MI
Google Inc.	Delaware	Mountain View, CA
General Electric Company	New York	Fairfield, CT
The Home Depot	Delaware	Atlanta, GA
Kellogg Company	Delaware	Battle Creek, MI
Reynolds American	Delaware	Winston-Salem, NC
Starbucks Corporation	Washington	Seattle, WA
3M Company	Delaware	St. Paul, MN
Walt Disney Company	Delaware	Burbank, CA
Whirlpool Corporation	Delaware	Benton Harbor, MI

Exhibit 3

Examples of Corporations and Their States of Incorporation

After the application of incorporation has been approved, the state grants a *charter* or *articles of incorporation*. The articles of incorporation formally create the corporation.[2] The corporate management and board of directors then prepare a set of *bylaws*, which are the rules and procedures for conducting the corporation's affairs.

Link to Google

Some excepts from **Google**'s bylaws follow:

ARTICLE I—CORPORATE OFFICES

1.1 REGISTERED OFFICE.
The registered office of Google Inc. shall be fixed in the corporation's certificate of incorporation. ...

1.2 OTHER OFFICES.
The corporation's Board of Directors (the "Board") may at any time establish other offices at any place or places where the corporation is qualified to do business.

ARTICLE II—MEETINGS OF STOCKHOLDERS

2.2 ANNUAL MEETING.
The annual meeting of stockholders shall be held each year on a date and at a time designated by the Board. At the annual meeting, directors shall be elected and any other proper business may be transacted.

2.4 NOTICE OF STOCKHOLDERS' MEETINGS.
All notices of meetings of stockholders shall be sent ... not less than ten (10) nor more than sixty (60) days before the date of the meeting to each stockholder entitled to vote at such meeting.... The notice shall specify the place, if any, date and hour of the meeting, the means of remote communication, if any, by which stockholders and proxy holders may be deemed to be present in person and vote at such meeting. ...

2.8 ADMINISTRATION OF THE MEETING.
Meetings of stockholders shall be presided over by the chairman of the Board. ...

ARTICLE V—OFFICERS

5.1 OFFICERS.
The officers of the corporation shall be a chief executive officer, one or more presidents (at the discretion of the Board), a chairman of the Board and a secretary. The corporation may also have, at the discretion of the Board, a vice chairman of the Board, a chief financial officer, a treasurer, one or more vice presidents, one or more assistant vice presidents, one or more assistant treasurers, one or more assistant secretaries, and any such other officers as may be appointed in accordance with the provisions of these bylaws.

5.6 CHAIRMAN OF THE BOARD.
The chairman of the Board shall be a member of the Board and, if present, preside at meetings of the Board. ...

5.7 CHIEF EXECUTIVE OFFICER.
Subject to the control of the Board, ... the chief executive officer shall, together with the president or presidents of the corporation, have general supervision, direction, and control of the business and affairs of the corporation. ... The chief executive officer shall ... preside at all meetings of the stockholders.

5.11 CHIEF FINANCIAL OFFICER.
The chief financial officer shall keep and maintain ... adequate and correct books and records of accounts of the properties and business transactions of the corporation, including accounts of its assets, liabilities, receipts, disbursements, gains, losses, capital, retained earnings and shares. ...

5.12 TREASURER.
The treasurer shall deposit all moneys and other valuables in the name and to the credit of the corporation. ...

Source: http://investor.google.com/corporate/bylaws.html

Costs may be incurred in organizing a corporation. These costs include legal fees, taxes, state incorporation fees, license fees, and promotional costs. Such costs are debited to an expense account entitled *Organizational Expenses*.

To illustrate, a corporation's organizing costs of $8,500 on January 5 are recorded as follows:

A = L + E
–   – Exp

Jan. 5	Organizational Expenses	8,500	
	Cash		8,500
	Paid costs of organizing the corporation.		

[2] The articles of incorporation may also restrict a corporation's activities in certain areas, such as owning certain types of real estate, conducting certain types of business activities, or purchasing its own stock.

Why It Matters

Red Tape and Starting a Business

The ease of starting a business varies around the world depending upon the number of regulatory procedures, time, cost, and minimum capital requirements imposed by governments. Countries that maintain minimum barriers to starting a business allow for creativity to be more easily expressed in the marketplace by entrepreneurs. The World Bank Group provides an annual survey of the ease of starting a business by country. Some of their recent selected findings are as follows:

Country	Ease of Starting a Business World Rank
Singapore	1
New Zealand	2
United States	7
United Kingdom	8
Germany	14
Canada	16
Japan	29

Country	Ease of Starting a Business World Rank
Mexico	39
Russia	62
China	90
India	142
Haiti	180
Libya	188

Source: Doing Business 2015, World Bank Group.

Paid-In Capital from Stock

Objective 2

Describe and illustrate the characteristics of stock, classes of stock, and entries for issuing stock.

The two main sources of stockholders' equity are paid-in capital (or contributed capital) and retained earnings. The main source of paid-in capital is from issuing stock.

Characteristics of Stock

The number of shares of stock that a corporation is *authorized* to issue is stated in its charter. The term *issued* refers to the shares issued to the stockholders. A corporation may reacquire some of the stock that it has issued. The stock remaining in the hands of stockholders is then called **outstanding stock**. The relationship between authorized, issued, and outstanding stock is shown in Exhibit 4.

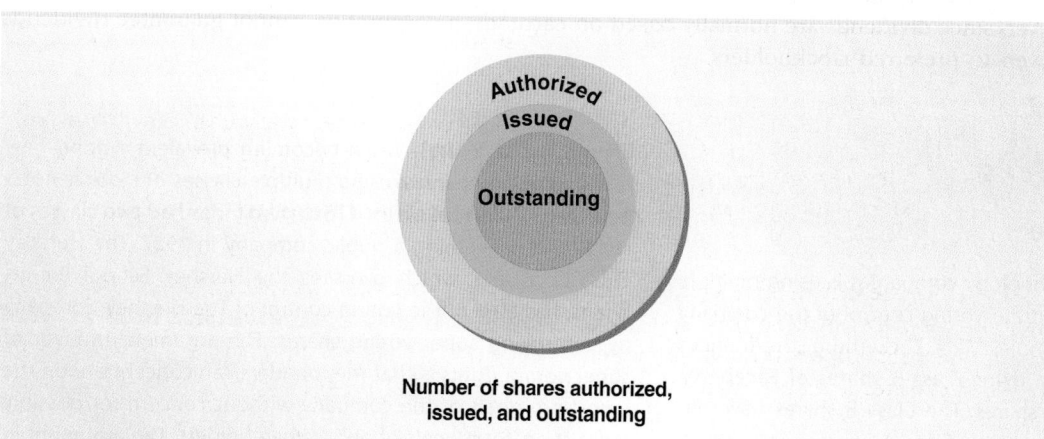

Number of shares authorized, issued, and outstanding

Exhibit 4

Authorized, Issued, and Outstanding Stock

Upon request, corporations may issue stock certificates to stockholders to document their ownership. Printed on a stock certificate is the name of the company, the name of the stockholder, and the number of shares owned. The stock certificate may also indicate a dollar amount assigned to each share of stock, called **par value**. Stock may be issued without par, in which case it is called *no-par stock*. In some states, the board of directors of a corporation is required to assign a *stated value* to no-par stock.

Link to Google   The par value of Google's stock is $0.001 per share.

Corporations have limited liability, and thus, creditors have no claim against stockholders' personal assets. To protect creditors, however, some states require corporations to maintain a minimum amount of paid-in capital. This minimum amount, called *legal capital,* usually includes the par or stated value of the shares issued.

The major rights that accompany ownership of a share of stock are as follows:

- The right to vote in matters concerning the corporation.
- The right to share in distributions of earnings.
- The right to share in assets upon liquidation.

These stock rights normally vary with the class of stock.

Link to Google   Google has three classes of common stock outstanding. Class A has one vote per share; Class B has ten votes per share; and Class C has no voting rights. The current executive chairman and the two original founders control over 60% of the voting power through their ownership of Class B stock.

Types of Stock

note:
The two primary classes of paid-in capital are common stock and preferred stock.

When only one class of stock is issued, it is called **common stock**. Each share of common stock has equal rights.

A corporation may also issue one or more classes of stock with various preference rights such as a preference to dividends. Such a stock is called a **preferred stock**. The dividend rights of preferred stock are stated either as dollars per share or as a percent of par. For example, a $50 par value preferred stock with a $4 per share dividend may be described as either:[3]

preferred $4 stock, $50 par

or

preferred 8% stock, $50 par

As shown in Exhibit 5, preferred stockholders have first rights (preference) to any dividends, and thus, they have a greater chance of receiving dividends than common stockholders. However, since dividends are normally based on earnings, a corporation cannot guarantee dividends even to preferred stockholders.

Why It Matters

You Have No Vote

An emerging trend in technology companies is using multiple classes of stock to concentrate voting control of the company to the founders. For example, Mark Zuckerburg, the founder and CEO of Facebook, owns Class B shares of Facebook. The public owns Class A shares. The Class B shares have ten votes for every one vote in the Class A shares. As a result, Zuckerburg owns 18% of the stock, but 57% of the voting rights of Facebook. Other companies using multiple classes of stock in this way include Google, Groupon, LinkedIn, Zynga, and Yelp!. While becoming prevalent among new technology companies, using multiple classes of stock is not a new idea. The Hershey Company has had two classes of stock since becoming a public company in 1927. The Hershey Trust Company, which oversees the Hershey School for orphans, has 80% of the voting control of The Hershey Company by controlling super voting shares. The argument in favor of super voting rights is that the founders can concentrate on the long-term goals of the company without concern for possibly more short-term goals of public shareholders. The argument in opposition is that concentrating control among the founders can eliminate or reduce the public shareholders' ability to hold management accountable.

[3] In some cases, preferred stock may receive additional dividends if certain conditions are met. Such stock, called *participating preferred stock,* is not often issued.

Exhibit 5

Dividend
Preferences

Google has 100,000,000 shares of authorized preferred stock with a par of $0.001, which are convertible to common stock. However, there are no shares of preferred stock issued or outstanding.

Link to Google

The payment of dividends is authorized by the corporation's board of directors. When authorized, the directors are said to have *declared* a dividend.

Cumulative preferred stock has a right to receive regular dividends that were not declared (paid) in prior years. Noncumulative preferred stock does not have this right.

Cumulative preferred stock dividends that have not been paid in prior years are said to be **in arrears**. Any preferred dividends in arrears must be paid before any common stock dividends are paid. In addition, any dividends in arrears are normally disclosed in notes to the financial statements.

To illustrate, assume that a corporation has issued the following preferred and common stock:

> 1,000 shares of cumulative preferred $4 stock, $50 par
> 4,000 shares of common stock, $15 par

The corporation was organized on January 1 of Year 1 and paid no dividends in Year 1 and Year 2. In Year 3, the corporation paid $22,000 in dividends, of which $12,000 was paid to preferred stockholders and $10,000 was paid to common stockholders, computed as shown in Exhibit 6.

Total dividends paid		$ 22,000
Preferred stockholders:		
Year 1 dividends in arrears (1,000 shares × $4).........................	$4,000	
Year 2 dividends in arrears (1,000 shares × $4).........................	4,000	
Year 3 dividend (1,000 shares × $4)	4,000	
Total preferred dividends paid		(12,000)
Dividends available to common stockholders		$ 10,000

Exhibit 6

Preferred Dividends
in Arrears

As a result, preferred stockholders received $12.00 per share ($12,000 ÷ 1,000 shares) in dividends, while common stockholders received $2.50 per share ($10,000 ÷ 4,000 shares).

In addition to dividend preference, preferred stock may be given preferences to assets if the corporation goes out of business and is liquidated. However, claims of creditors must be satisfied first. Preferred stockholders are next in line to receive any remaining assets, followed by the common stockholders.

Why It Matters

Buying and Selling Stock

A company will issue stock as part of an IPO, or initial public offering. This event creates the accounting entries for issuing stock. Once the stock is issued, it will trade publicly between buyers and sellers of the stock. These transactions are not recorded on the company's books, unless the company is repurchasing its own stock. Public trading of stock occurs on the New York Stock Exchange (NYSE) and NASDAQ markets. For example, General Electric trades on the NYSE and Facebook trades on the NASDAQ.

Issuing Stock

A separate account is used for recording the amount of each class of stock issued to investors in a corporation. For example, assume that a corporation is authorized to issue 10,000 shares of $100 par preferred stock and 100,000 shares of $20 par common stock. The corporation issued 5,000 shares of preferred stock and 50,000 shares of common stock at par for cash. The corporation's entry to record the stock issue is as follows:[4]

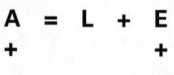

Cash	1,500,000	
Preferred Stock		500,000
Common Stock		1,000,000
Issued preferred stock and common stock at par for cash.		

Stock is often issued by a corporation at a price other than its par. The price at which stock is sold depends on a variety of factors, such as the following:

- The financial condition, earnings record, and dividend record of the corporation.
- Investor expectations of the corporation's potential earning power.
- General business and economic conditions and expectations.

If stock is issued (sold) for a price that is more than its par, the stock has been sold at a **premium**. For example, if common stock with a par of $50 is sold for $60 per share, the stock has sold at a premium of $10.

If stock is issued (sold) for a price that is less than its par, the stock has been sold at a **discount**. For example, if common stock with a par of $50 is sold for $45 per share, the stock has sold at a discount of $5. Many states do not permit stock to be sold at a discount. In other states, stock may be sold at a discount in only unusual cases. Because stock is rarely sold at a discount, it is not illustrated.

In order to distribute dividends, financial statements, and other reports, a corporation must keep track of its stockholders. Large public corporations normally use a financial institution, such as a bank, for this purpose.[5] In such cases, the financial institution is referred to as a *transfer agent* or *registrar*.

Premium on Stock

When stock is issued at a premium, Cash is debited for the amount received. Common Stock or Preferred Stock is credited for the par amount. The excess of the amount paid over par is part of the paid-in capital. An account entitled *Paid-In Capital in Excess of Par* is credited for this amount.

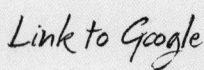 **Google** recently reported paid-in capital of almost $26 billion.

To illustrate, assume that Caldwell Company issues 2,000 shares of $50 par preferred stock for cash at $55. The entry to record this transaction is as follows:

Cash	110,000	
Preferred Stock		100,000
Paid-In Capital in Excess of Par—Preferred Stock		10,000
Issued $50 par preferred stock at $55.		

[4] The accounting for investments in stocks from the point of view of the investor is discussed in Appendix D.

[5] Small corporations may use a subsidiary ledger, called a *stockholders ledger.* in this case, the stock accounts (Preferred Stock and Common Stock) are controlling accounts for the subsidiary ledger.

When stock is issued in exchange for assets other than cash, such as land, buildings, and equipment, the assets acquired are recorded at their fair market value. If this value cannot be determined, the fair market price of the stock issued is used.

To illustrate, assume that a corporation acquired land with a fair market value that cannot be determined. In exchange, the corporation issued 10,000 shares of its $10 par common stock. If the stock has a market price of $12 per share, the transaction is recorded as follows:

Land	120,000		A = L + E	
Common Stock		100,000	+	+
Paid-In Capital in Excess of Par		20,000		
Issued $10 par common stock, valued				
at $12 per share, for land.				

No-Par Stock

In most states, no-par preferred and common stock may be issued. When no-par stock is issued, Cash is debited and Common Stock is credited for the proceeds. As no-par stock is issued over time, this entry is the same even if the issuing price varies.

To illustrate, assume that on January 9, a corporation issues 10,000 shares of no-par common stock at $40 a share. On June 27, the corporation issues an additional 1,000 shares at $36. The entries to record these issuances of the no-par stock are as follows:

Jan. 9	Cash	400,000		A = L + E	
	Common Stock		400,000	+	+
	Issued 10,000 shares of no-par				
	common stock at $40.				
June 27	Cash	36,000		A = L + E	
	Common Stock		36,000	+	+
	Issued 1,000 shares of no-par				
	common stock at $36.				

In some states, no-par stock may be assigned a *stated value per share.* The stated value is recorded like a par value. Any excess of the proceeds over the stated value is credited to *Paid-In Capital in Excess of Stated Value.*

To illustrate, assume that in the preceding example the no-par common stock is assigned a stated value of $25. The issuance of the stock on January 9 and June 27 is recorded as follows:

Jan. 9	Cash	400,000		A = L + E	
	Common Stock		250,000	+	+
	Paid-In Capital in Excess of Stated Value		150,000		
	Issued 10,000 shares of no-par common stock				
	at $40; stated value, $25.				
June 27	Cash	36,000		A = L + E	
	Common Stock		25,000	+	+
	Paid-In Capital in Excess of Stated Value		11,000		
	Issued 1,000 shares of no-par common stock				
	at $36; stated value, $25.				

Check Up Corner 12-1 Classes of Stock

On January 1, 20Y1, DeFrance Corporation issued for cash 40,000 shares of $10 par common stock at $24. On March 30, 20Y1, DeFrance issued 6,000 shares of cumulative preferred 3% stock of $100 par at $142. The following amounts were distributed as dividends on December 31 of each year:

20Y1	$ 6,000
20Y2	46,000
20Y3	80,000

A. Journalize the entries to record the January 1 and March 30, 20Y1 transactions.
B. Determine the dividends per share for preferred and common stock for 20Y1, 20Y2, and 20Y3.

Solution:

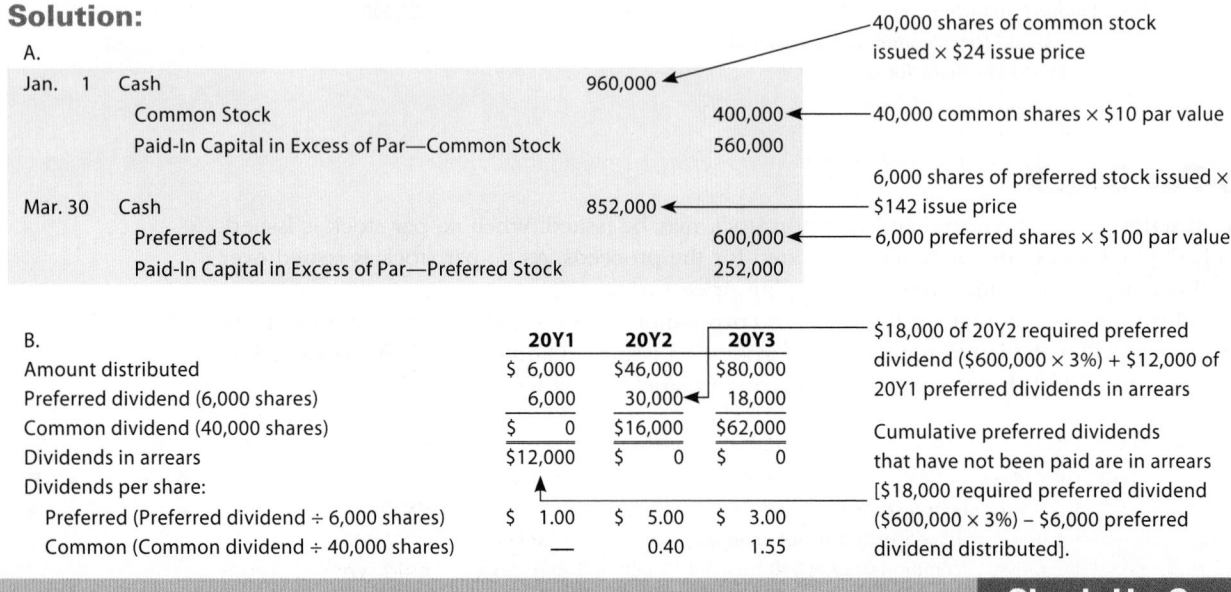

A.

Jan. 1	Cash	960,000	
	Common Stock		400,000
	Paid-In Capital in Excess of Par—Common Stock		560,000
Mar. 30	Cash	852,000	
	Preferred Stock		600,000
	Paid-In Capital in Excess of Par—Preferred Stock		252,000

40,000 shares of common stock issued × $24 issue price

40,000 common shares × $10 par value

6,000 shares of preferred stock issued × $142 issue price

6,000 preferred shares × $100 par value

B.

	20Y1	20Y2	20Y3
Amount distributed	$ 6,000	$46,000	$80,000
Preferred dividend (6,000 shares)	6,000	30,000	18,000
Common dividend (40,000 shares)	$ 0	$16,000	$62,000
Dividends in arrears	$12,000	$ 0	$ 0
Dividends per share:			
Preferred (Preferred dividend ÷ 6,000 shares)	$ 1.00	$ 5.00	$ 3.00
Common (Common dividend ÷ 40,000 shares)	—	0.40	1.55

$18,000 of 20Y2 required preferred dividend ($600,000 × 3%) + $12,000 of 20Y1 preferred dividends in arrears

Cumulative preferred dividends that have not been paid are in arrears [$18,000 required preferred dividend ($600,000 × 3%) – $6,000 preferred dividend distributed].

Check Up Corner

 Ethics: Don't Do It!

The Professor Who Knew Too Much

A major Midwestern university released a quarterly "American Customer Satisfaction Index" based on its research of customers of popular U.S. products and services. Before the release of the index to the public, the professor in charge of the research bought and sold stocks of some of the companies in the report. The professor was quoted as saying that he thought it was important to test his theories of customer satisfaction with "real" [his own] money.

Is this proper or ethical? Apparently, the dean of the Business School didn't think so. In a statement to the press, the dean stated: "I have instructed anyone affiliated with the (index) not to make personal use of information gathered in the course of producing the quarterly index, prior to the index's release to the general public, and they [the researchers] have agreed."

Sources: Jon E. Hilsenrath and Dan Morse, "Researcher Uses Index to Buy, Short Stocks," *The Wall Street Journal*, February 18, 2003; and Jon E. Hilsenrath, "Satisfaction Theory: Mixed Results," *The Wall Street Journal*, February 19, 2003.

Accounting for Dividends

Objective 3
Describe and illustrate the accounting for cash dividends and stock dividends.

When a board of directors declares a cash dividend, it authorizes the distribution of cash to stockholders. When a board of directors declares a stock dividend, it authorizes the distribution of its stock. In both cases, declaring a dividend reduces the retained earnings of the corporation.[6]

Google has never paid a cash dividend and has no intention of doing so in the foreseeable future.

Link to Google

Cash Dividends

A cash distribution of earnings by a corporation to its shareholders is a **cash dividend**. Although dividends may be paid in other assets, cash dividends are the most common.

Three conditions for a cash dividend are as follows:

- Sufficient retained earnings
- Sufficient cash
- Formal action by the board of directors

There must be a sufficient (large enough) balance in Retained Earnings to declare a cash dividend. That is, the balance of Retained Earnings must be large enough so that the dividend does not create a debit balance in the retained earnings account. However, a large Retained Earnings balance does not mean that there is cash available to pay dividends. This is because the balances of Cash and Retained Earnings are often unrelated.

Even if there are sufficient retained earnings and cash, a corporation's board of directors is not required to pay dividends. Nevertheless, many corporations pay quarterly cash dividends to make their stock more attractive to investors. *Special* or *extra dividends* may also be paid when a corporation experiences higher than normal profits.

Three dates included in a dividend announcement are as follows:

1. Date of declaration
2. Date of record
3. Date of payment

The *date of declaration* is the date the board of directors formally authorizes the payment of the dividend. On this date, the corporation incurs the liability to pay the amount of the dividend.

The *date of record* is the date the corporation uses to determine which stockholders will receive the dividend. During the period of time between the date of declaration and the date of record, the stock price is quoted as selling *with-dividends*. This means that any investors purchasing the stock before the date of record will receive the dividend.

The *date of payment* is the date the corporation will pay the dividend to the stockholders who owned the stock on the date of record. During the period of time between the record date and the payment date, the stock price is quoted as selling *ex-dividends*. This means that since the date of record has passed, any new investors will not receive the dividend.

To illustrate, assume that on October 1, Hiber Corporation declares the following cash dividends with a date of record of November 10 and a date of payment of December 2:

	Dividend per Share	Total Dividends
Preferred stock, $100 par, 5,000 shares outstanding	$2.50	$12,500
Common stock, $10 par, 100,000 shares outstanding	$0.30	30,000
Total		$42,500

[6] In rare cases, when a corporation is reducing its operations or going out of business, a dividend may be a distribution of paid-in capital. Such a dividend is called a *liquidating dividend*.

Declaration Date

On October 1, the declaration date, Hiber Corporation records the following entry:

A = L + E
 +   − Div

Oct. 1	Cash Dividends	42,500	
	Cash Dividends Payable		42,500
	Declared cash dividends.		

Date of Record

On November 10, the date of record, no entry is necessary. This date merely determines which stockholders will receive the dividends.

Date of Payment

On December 2, the date of payment, Hiber Corporation records the payment of the dividends as follows:

A = L + E
 −   −

Dec. 2	Cash Dividends Payable	42,500	
	Cash		42,500
	Paid cash dividends.		

At the end of the accounting period, the balance in Cash Dividends will be transferred to Retained Earnings as part of the closing process. This closing entry debits Retained Earnings and credits Cash Dividends for the balance of the cash dividends account. If the cash dividends have not been paid by the end of the period, Cash Dividends Payable will be reported on the balance sheet as a current liability.

Stock Dividends

A **stock dividend** is a distribution of shares of stock to stockholders. Stock dividends are normally declared only on common stock and issued to common stockholders.

A stock dividend affects only stockholders' equity. Specifically, the amount of the stock dividend is transferred from Retained Earnings to Paid-In Capital. The amount transferred is normally the fair value (market price) of the shares issued in the stock dividend.[7]

To illustrate, assume that the stockholders' equity accounts of Hendrix Corporation as of December 15 are as follows:

Common Stock, $20 par (2,000,000 shares issued)	$40,000,000
Paid-In Capital in Excess of Par—Common Stock	9,000,000
Retained Earnings	26,600,000

On December 15, Hendrix Corporation declares a stock dividend of 5% or 100,000 shares (2,000,000 shares × 5%) to be issued on January 10 to stockholders of record on December 31. The market price of the stock on December 15 (the date of declaration) is $31 per share.

The entry to record the stock dividend is as follows:

A = L + E
      + −

Dec. 15	Stock Dividends	3,100,000	
	Stock Dividends Distributable		2,000,000
	Paid-In Capital in Excess of Par—Common Stock		1,100,000
	Declared 5% (100,000 shares) stock		
	dividend on $20 par common stock		
	with a market price of $31 per share.		

After the preceding entry is recorded, Stock Dividends will have a debit balance of $3,100,000. Like cash dividends, the stock dividends account is closed to Retained Earnings at the end of the accounting period. This closing entry debits Retained Earnings and credits Stock Dividends.

---

[7] The use of fair market value is justified as long as the number of shares issued for the stock dividend is small (less than 25% of the shares outstanding).

At the end of the period, the *stock dividends distributable* and *paid-in capital in excess of par—common stock* accounts are reported in the Paid-In Capital section of the balance sheet. Thus, the effect of the preceding stock dividend is to transfer $3,100,000 of retained earnings to paid-in capital.

On January 10, the stock dividend is distributed to stockholders by issuing 100,000 shares of common stock. The issuance of the stock is recorded by the following entry:

Jan. 10	Stock Dividends Distributable	2,000,000	
	Common Stock		2,000,000
	Issued stock as stock dividend.		

A = L + E
+ −

A stock dividend does not change the assets, liabilities, or total stockholders' equity of a corporation. Likewise, a stock dividend does not change an individual stockholder's proportionate interest (equity) in the corporation.

To illustrate, assume a stockholder owns 1,000 of a corporation's 10,000 shares outstanding. If the corporation declares a 6% stock dividend, the stockholder's proportionate interest will not change, computed as follows:

	Before Stock Dividend	After Stock Dividend
Total shares issued	10,000	10,600 [10,000 + (10,000 × 6%)]
Number of shares owned	1,000	1,060 [1,000 + (1,000 × 6%)]
Proportionate ownership	10% (1,000 ÷ 10,000)	10% (1,060 ÷ 10,600)

Check Up Corner 12-2 Dividends

Borzilova Company has 150,000 shares of $20 par common stock outstanding on January 1. During the year, the company had the following dividend transactions:

A. On April 7, the company declared a cash dividend of $0.06 per share on common stock to shareholders of record on April 28. The cash dividend is paid on March 10.

B. On August 30, the company declared a 2% stock dividend to stockholders of record on October 20. The stock certificates for the stock dividend are distributed on October 31.

The market price of the company's stock was $60 on August 30, $64 on October 20, and $67 on October 31. Journalize the entries required on each date.

Solution:

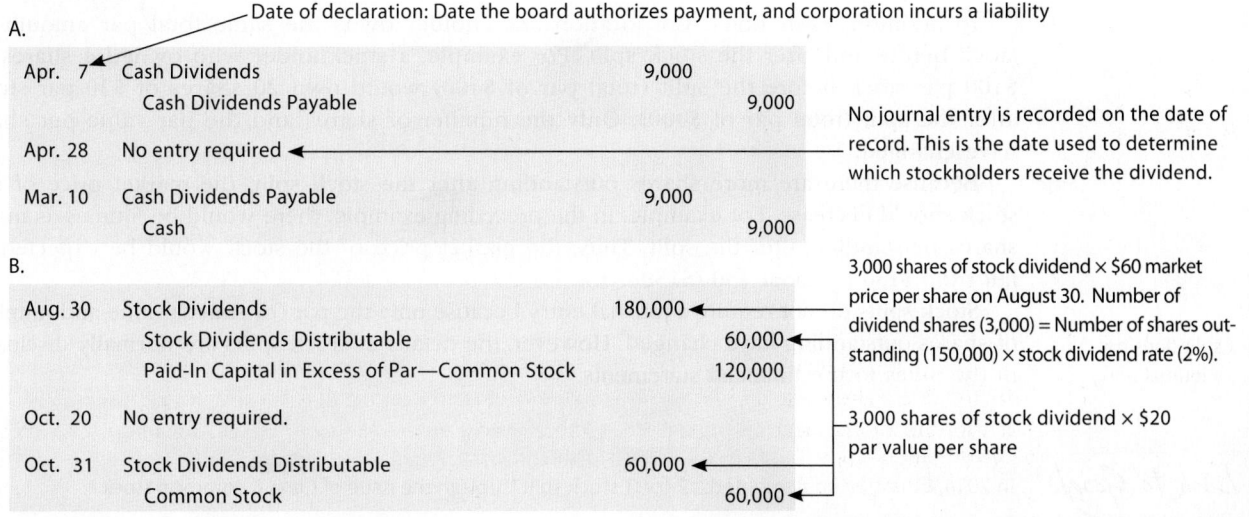

A. Date of declaration: Date the board authorizes payment, and corporation incurs a liability

Apr. 7	Cash Dividends	9,000	
	Cash Dividends Payable		9,000
Apr. 28	No entry required		
Mar. 10	Cash Dividends Payable	9,000	
	Cash		9,000

No journal entry is recorded on the date of record. This is the date used to determine which stockholders receive the dividend.

B.

Aug. 30	Stock Dividends	180,000	
	Stock Dividends Distributable		60,000
	Paid-In Capital in Excess of Par—Common Stock		120,000
Oct. 20	No entry required.		
Oct. 31	Stock Dividends Distributable	60,000	
	Common Stock		60,000

3,000 shares of stock dividend × $60 market price per share on August 30. Number of dividend shares (3,000) = Number of shares outstanding (150,000) × stock dividend rate (2%).

3,000 shares of stock dividend × $20 par value per share

Check Up Corner

Objective 4

Describe the effect
of stock splits on
stockholders' equity.

Stock Splits

A **stock split** is a process by which a corporation reduces the par or stated value of its common stock and issues a proportionate number of additional shares. A stock split applies to all common shares including the unissued and issued shares.

A major objective of a stock split is to reduce the market price per share of the stock. This attracts more investors and broadens the types and numbers of stockholders.

To illustrate, assume that Rojek Corporation has 10,000 shares of $100 par common stock outstanding with a current market price of $150 per share. The board of directors declares the following stock split:

1. Each common shareholder will receive 5 shares for each share held. This is called a 5-for-1 stock split. As a result, 50,000 shares (10,000 shares × 5) will be outstanding.
2. The par of each share of common stock will be reduced to $20 ($100 ÷ 5).

The par value of the common stock outstanding is $1,000,000 both before and after the stock split as shown in Exhibit 7 and computed as follows:

	Before Split	After Split
Number of shares	10,000	50,000
Par value per share	× $100	× $20
Total	$1,000,000	$1,000,000

Exhibit 7

Stock Split:
Before and After

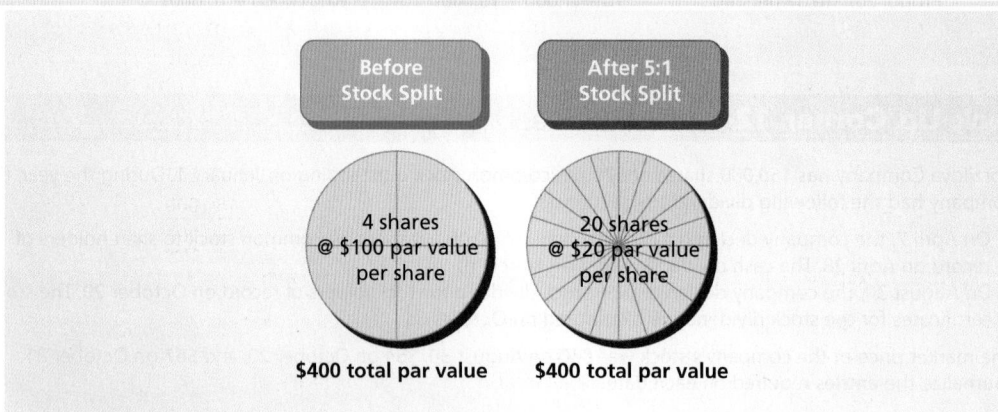

In addition, each Rojek Corporation shareholder owns the same total par amount of stock before and after the stock split. For example, a stockholder who owned 4 shares of $100 par stock before the split (total par of $400) would own 20 shares of $20 par stock after the split (total par of $400). Only the number of shares and the par value per share have changed.

Because there are more shares outstanding after the stock split, the market price of the stock should decrease. For example, in the preceding example, there would be 5 times as many shares outstanding after the split. Thus, the market price of the stock would be expected to fall from $150 to about $30 ($150 ÷ 5).

note:

A stock split does not
require a journal entry.

Stock splits do not require a journal entry because only the par (or stated) value and number of shares outstanding have changed. However, the details of stock splits are normally disclosed in the notes to the financial statements.

Link to Google   In 2014, **Google** implemented a 2-for-1 stock split through the issue of Class C common stock.

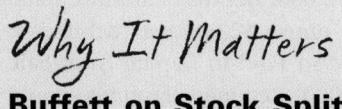

Buffett on Stock Splits

Warren E. Buffett, chief executive officer of Berkshire Hathaway Inc., opposes stock splits on the basis that they add no value to the company. Since its inception, Berkshire Hathaway has never declared a stock split on its primary (Class A) common stock. As a result, Berkshire Hathaway's Class A common stock sells well above $200,000 per share, which is the most expensive stock on the New York Stock Exchange. Such a high price doesn't bother Buffet because he believes that high stock prices attract more sophisticated and long-term investors and discourage stock speculators and short-term investors.

In contrast, Microsoft Corporation has split its stock nine times since it went public in 1986. As a result, one share of Microsoft purchased in 1986 is equivalent to 288 shares today, which would be worth more than $12,000.

Treasury Stock Transactions

Objective 5

Describe and illustrate the accounting for treasury stock transactions.

Treasury stock is stock that a corporation has issued and then reacquired. A corporation may reacquire (purchase) its own stock for a variety of reasons, including the following:

- To provide shares for resale to employees
- To reissue as bonuses to employees, or
- To support the market price of the stock

The *cost method* is normally used for recording the purchase and resale of treasury stock.[8] Using the cost method, *Treasury Stock* is debited for the cost (purchase price) of the stock. When the stock is resold, Treasury Stock is credited for its cost. Any difference between the cost and the selling price is debited or credited to *Paid-In Capital from Sale of Treasury Stock.*

To illustrate, assume that a corporation has the following paid-in capital on January 1:

Common stock, $25 par (20,000 shares authorized and issued)	$500,000
Excess of issue price over par	150,000
	$650,000

The corporation entered into the following treasury stock transactions:

Feb. 13. Purchased 1,000 shares of its common stock at $45 per share.
Apr. 29. Sold 600 shares of the treasury stock for $60.
Oct. 4. Sold the remaining 400 shares of treasury stock for $40 per share.

The journal entries to record the preceding transactions are shown in Exhibit 8.

Exhibit 8

Treasury Stock Transactions

DYNAMIC EXHIBIT

Feb. 13	Treasury Stock	45,000		A = L + E
	Cash		45,000	– –
	Purchased 1,000 shares of treasury stock at $45.			

Apr. 29	Cash	36,000		A = L + E
	Treasury Stock		27,000	+ +
	Paid-In Capital from Sale of Treasury Stock		9,000	
	Sold 600 shares of treasury stock at $60.			

Oct. 4	Cash	16,000		A = L + E
	Paid-In Capital from Sale of Treasury Stock	2,000		+ +
	Treasury Stock		18,000	
	Sold 400 shares of treasury stock at $40.			

[8] Another method that is infrequently used, called the *par value method*, is discussed in advanced accounting texts.

The October 4 entry in Exhibit 8 decreases paid-in capital by $2,000. Because Paid-In Capital from Sale of Treasury Stock has a credit balance of $9,000, the entire $2,000 was debited to Paid-In Capital from Sale of Treasury Stock. If the credit balance in Paid-In Capital from Sale of Treasury Stock on October 4 had been $1,500 instead of $9,000, Retained Earnings would have been debited for $500 ($2,000 − $1,500). This is because Paid-In Capital from Sale of Treasury Stock cannot have a debit balance.

No dividends (cash or stock) are paid on the shares of treasury stock. To do so would result in the corporation earning dividend revenue from itself.

Check Up Corner 12-3   Treasury Stock Transactions

The following transactions were completed by Grayson Inc. during the current fiscal year ended December 31:

Apr. 19   Reacquired 10,000 shares of its own $10 par common stock at $30 per share.
Aug. 30   Sold 6,000 of the reacquired shares at $36 per share.
Nov. 10   Sold 2,000 of the reacquired shares at $34 per share.

A. Journalize the transactions of April 19, August 30, and November 10.
B. What is the balance of Paid-In Capital from Sale of Treasury Stock on December 31 of the current year?

Solution:

Stock that a corporation has issued and then reacquired is called *treasury stock*.

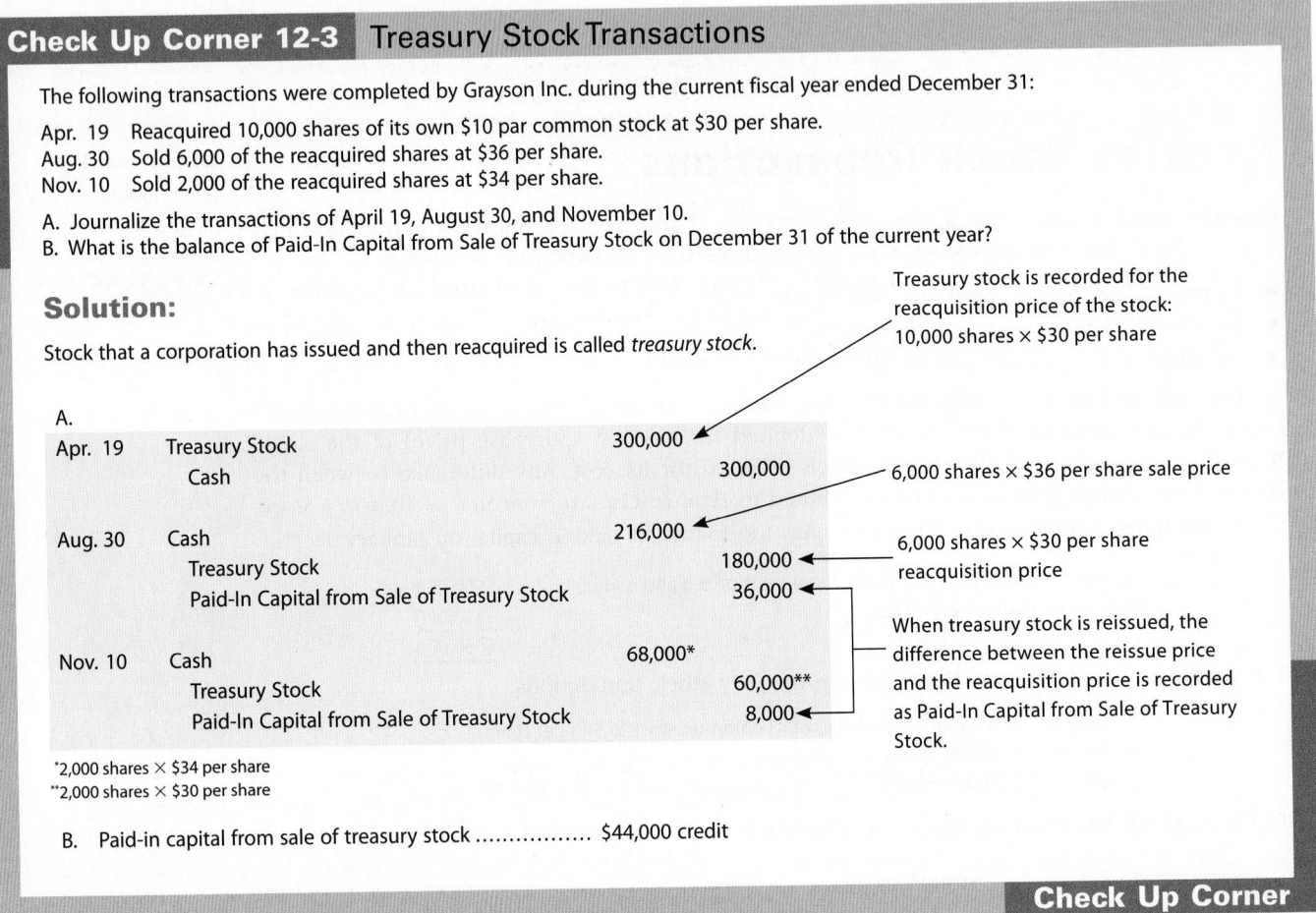

Treasury stock is recorded for the reacquisition price of the stock:
10,000 shares × $30 per share

A.

Apr. 19	Treasury Stock	300,000	
	Cash		300,000
Aug. 30	Cash	216,000	
	Treasury Stock		180,000
	Paid-In Capital from Sale of Treasury Stock		36,000
Nov. 10	Cash	68,000*	
	Treasury Stock		60,000**
	Paid-In Capital from Sale of Treasury Stock		8,000

6,000 shares × $36 per share sale price

6,000 shares × $30 per share reacquisition price

When treasury stock is reissued, the difference between the reissue price and the reacquisition price is recorded as Paid-In Capital from Sale of Treasury Stock.

*2,000 shares × $34 per share
**2,000 shares × $30 per share

B.   Paid-in capital from sale of treasury stock .... $44,000 credit

Check Up Corner

Why It Matters

Treasury Stock vs. Dividends

A company has two major ways to return cash to shareholders: cash dividends and stock repurchases. A shareholder preferring a current cash income may prefer to receive a steady cash dividend. A shareholder preferring share price appreciation may prefer stock repurchases. This is because when a company purchases treasury stock, the amount of shares outstanding will decline, and the

market value per share should increase. Another consideration is that cash dividends are currently taxed at 15%, while the gains on share price increases are tax-deferred until sold. A company may prefer returning cash through stock repurchases because it provides management greater flexibility in managing the company's cash flows. It is considered more difficult to decrease a cash dividend than it is to reduce share repurchases over time. So, overall, the answer to the question depends on circumstances. This is likely why many companies do both.

Reporting Stockholders' Equity

Objective 6
Describe and illustrate the reporting of stockholders' equity.

As with other sections of the balance sheet, alternative terms and formats may be used in reporting stockholders' equity. Also, changes in retained earnings and paid-in capital may be reported in separate statements or notes to the financial statements.

Stockholders' Equity on the Balance Sheet

Exhibit 9 shows two methods for reporting stockholders' equity for the December 31, 20Y7, balance sheet for Telex Inc.

- Method 1. Each class of stock is reported, followed by its related paid-in capital accounts. Retained earnings is then reported followed by a deduction for treasury stock.
- Method 2. The stock accounts are reported, followed by the paid-in capital reported as a single item, Additional paid-in capital. Retained earnings is then reported followed by a deduction for treasury stock.

Exhibit 9 Stockholders' Equity Section of a Balance Sheet

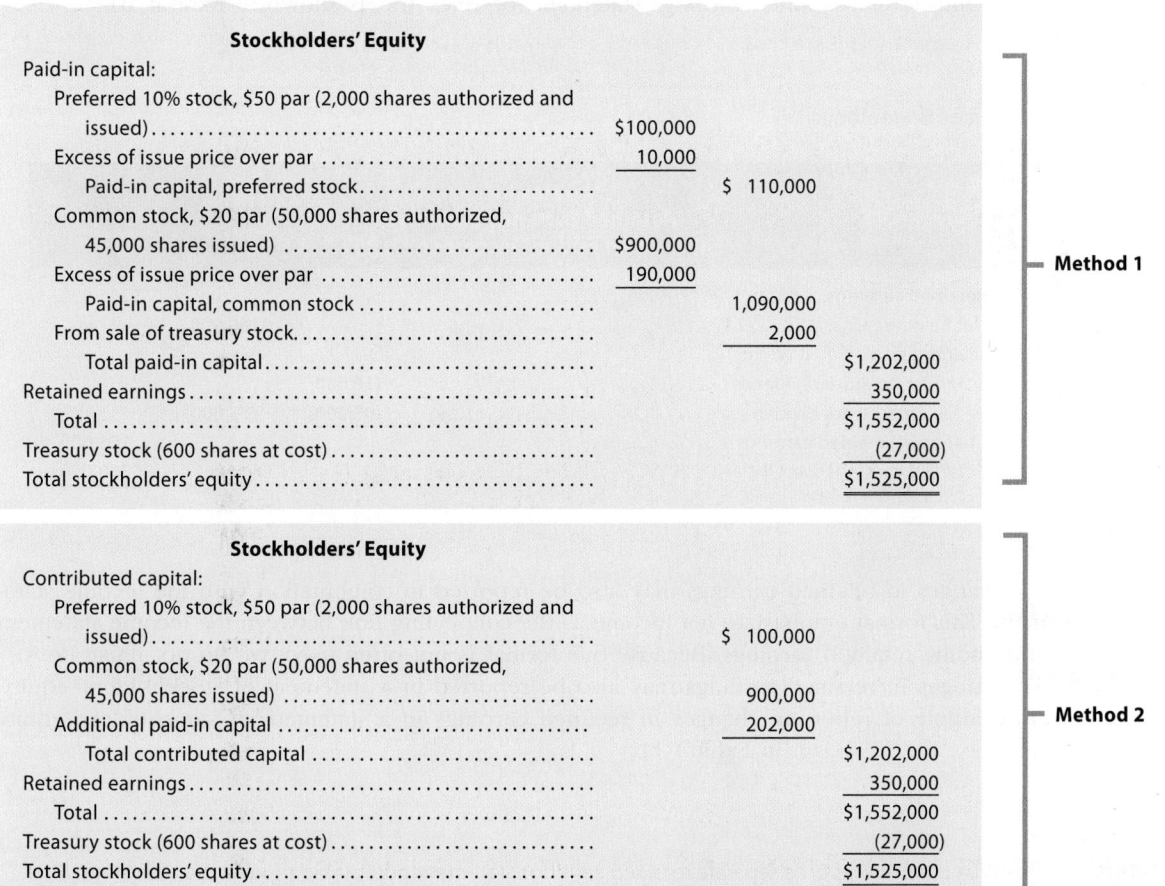

Telex Inc.
Balance Sheet
December 31, 20Y7

Stockholders' Equity

Paid-in capital:

Preferred 10% stock, $50 par (2,000 shares authorized and issued)	$100,000			
Excess of issue price over par	10,000			
Paid-in capital, preferred stock		$ 110,000		
Common stock, $20 par (50,000 shares authorized, 45,000 shares issued)	$900,000			
Excess of issue price over par	190,000			
Paid-in capital, common stock		1,090,000		
From sale of treasury stock		2,000		
Total paid-in capital			$1,202,000	
Retained earnings			350,000	
Total			$1,552,000	
Treasury stock (600 shares at cost)			(27,000)	
Total stockholders' equity			$1,525,000	

Method 1

Stockholders' Equity

Contributed capital:

Preferred 10% stock, $50 par (2,000 shares authorized and issued)	$ 100,000	
Common stock, $20 par (50,000 shares authorized, 45,000 shares issued)	900,000	
Additional paid-in capital	202,000	
Total contributed capital		$1,202,000
Retained earnings		350,000
Total		$1,552,000
Treasury stock (600 shares at cost)		(27,000)
Total stockholders' equity		$1,525,000

Method 2

Google has 671,664,000 shares of common stock outstanding as follows: Class A, 279,325,000 shares; Class B, 56,507,000 shares; and Class C, 335,832,000 shares.

Link to Google

Significant changes in stockholders' equity during a period may also be presented in a statement of stockholders' equity or in the notes to the financial statements. The statement of stockholders' equity is illustrated later in this section.

Relevant rights and privileges of the various classes of stock outstanding should also be reported.[9] Examples include dividend and liquidation preferences, conversion rights, and redemption rights. Such information may be disclosed on the face of the balance sheet or in the notes to the financial statements.

Reporting Retained Earnings

Changes in retained earnings may be reported using one of the following:

- Separate retained earnings statement
- Combined income and retained earnings statement
- Statement of stockholders' equity

Changes in retained earnings may be reported in a separate retained earnings statement. When a separate **retained earnings statement** is prepared, the beginning balance of retained earnings is reported. The net income is then added (or net loss is subtracted) and any dividends are subtracted to arrive at the ending retained earnings for the period.

Link to Google At the end of a recent year, **Google** reported retained earnings of $61,262,000,000.

To illustrate, a retained earnings statement for Telex Inc. is shown in Exhibit 10.

Exhibit 10 Retained Earnings Statement

Telex Inc. Retained Earnings Statement For the Year Ended December 31, 20Y7			
Retained earnings, January 1, 20Y7			$245,000
Net income		$180,000	
Dividends:			
Preferred stock dividends...............................	$(10,000)		
Common stock dividends..............................	(65,000)	(75,000)	
Change in retained earnings			105,000
Retained earnings, December 31, 20Y7....................			$350,000

Changes in retained earnings may also be reported in combination with the income statement. This format emphasizes net income as the connecting link between the income statement and ending retained earnings. Because this format is not often used, we do not illustrate it.

Changes in retained earnings may also be reported in a statement of stockholders' equity. An example of reporting changes in retained earnings in a statement of stockholders' equity for Telex Inc. is shown in Exhibit 11.

Link to Google **Google** does not report a separate retained earnings statement but instead reports changes in retained earnings in its statement of stockholders' equity.

[9] *FASB Accounting Standards Codification, Section 505-10-50.*

Restrictions The use of retained earnings for payment of dividends may be restricted by action of a corporation's board of directors. Such **restrictions**, sometimes called *appropriations*, remain part of the retained earnings.

Restrictions of retained earnings are classified as:

■ *Legal.* State laws may require a restriction of retained earnings.

> Example: States may restrict retained earnings by the amount of treasury stock purchased. In this way, legal capital cannot be used for dividends.

■ *Contractual.* A corporation may enter into contracts that require restrictions of retained earnings.

> Example: A bank loan may restrict retained earnings so that money for repaying the loan cannot be used for dividends.

■ *Discretionary.* A corporation's board of directors may restrict retained earnings voluntarily.

> Example: The board may restrict retained earnings and, thus, limit dividend distributions so that more money is available for expanding the business.

Restrictions of retained earnings must be disclosed in the financial statements. Such disclosures are usually included in the notes to the financial statements.

Prior Period Adjustments An error may arise from a mathematical mistake or from a mistake in applying accounting principles. Such errors may not be discovered within the same period in which they occur. In such cases, the effect of the error should not affect the current period's net income. Instead, the correction of the error, called a **prior period adjustment**, is reported in the retained earnings statement. Such corrections are reported as an adjustment to the beginning balance of retained earnings.[10]

Statement of Stockholders' Equity

When the only change in stockholders' equity is due to net income or net loss and dividends, a retained earnings statement is sufficient. However, when a corporation also has changes in stock and paid-in capital accounts, a **statement of stockholders' equity** is normally prepared.

A statement of stockholders' equity is normally prepared in a columnar format. Each column is a major stockholders' equity classification. Changes in each classification are then described in the left-hand column. Exhibit 11 illustrates a statement of stockholders' equity for Telex Inc.

Exhibit 11 Statement of Stockholders' Equity

Telex Inc.
Statement of Stockholders' Equity
For the Year Ended December 31, 20Y7

	Preferred Stock	Common Stock	Additional Paid-In Capital	Retained Earnings	Treasury Stock	Total
Balance, January 1, 20Y7	$100,000	$850,000	$177,000	$245,000	$(17,000)	$1,355,000
Net income				180,000		180,000
Dividends on preferred stock.				(10,000)		(10,000)
Dividends on common stock				(65,000)		(65,000)
Issuance of additional common stock. . . .		50,000	25,000			75,000
Purchase of treasury stock					(10,000)	(10,000)
Balance, December 31, 20Y7	$100,000	$900,000	$202,000	$350,000	$(27,000)	$1,525,000

[10] Prior period adjustments are illustrated in advanced accounting texts.

Link to Google   **Google** reports a separate statement of stockholders' equity.

International Connection

IFRS
IFRS for SMEs

In 2010, the International Accounting Standards Board (IASB) issued a set of accounting standards specifically designed for small- and medium-sized enterprises (SMEs) called International Financial Reporting Standards (IFRS) for SMEs. SMEs in the United States are private companies and such small corporations that they do not report to the Securities and Exchange Commission (SEC). IFRS for SMEs consist of only 230 pages, compared to 2,700 pages for full IFRS. These standards are designed to be cost effective for SMEs. Thus, IFRS for SMEs require fewer disclosures and contain no industry-specific standards or exceptions.

The American Institute of CPAs (AICPA) has accepted IFRS for SMEs as part of U.S. generally accepted accounting principles (GAAP) for private companies not reporting to the SEC. If users, such as bankers and investors, accept these financial statements, IFRS for SMEs may become popular in the United States.*

*Differences between U.S. GAAP and IFRS are further discussed and illustrated in Appendix C.

Mornin' Joe

Reporting Stockholders' Equity for Mornin' Joe

Mornin' Joe reports stockholders' equity in its balance sheet. Mornin' Joe also includes a retained earnings statement and statement of stockholders' equity in its financial statements.

The Stockholders' Equity section of Mornin' Joe's balance sheet as of December 31, 20Y6, follows:

Mornin' Joe
Balance Sheet
December 31, 20Y6

Stockholders' Equity

Paid-in capital:		
Preferred 10% stock, $50 par (6,000 shares authorized and issued)	$ 300,000	
Excess of issue price over par	50,000	
Paid-in capital, preferred stock		$ 350,000
Common stock, $20 par (50,000 shares authorized, 45,000 shares issued)	$ 900,000	
Excess of issue price over par	1,450,000	
Paid-in capital, common stock		2,350,000
Total paid-in capital		$2,700,000
Retained earnings		1,200,300
Total		$3,900,300
Treasury stock (1,000 shares at cost)		(46,000)
Total stockholders' equity		$3,854,300
Total liabilities and stockholders' equity		$6,169,700

Mornin' Joe's retained earnings statement for the year ended December 31, 20Y6, is as follows:

Mornin' Joe Retained Earnings Statement For the Year Ended December 31, 20Y6			
Retained earnings, January 1, 20Y6			$ 852,700
Net income		$421,600	
Dividends:			
Preferred stock	$(30,000)		
Common stock	(44,000)	(74,000)	
Change in retained earnings			347,600
Retained earnings, December 31, 20Y6			$1,200,300

The statement of stockholders' equity for Mornin' Joe follows:

	Preferred Stock	Common Stock	Additional Paid-In Capital	Retained Earnings	Treasury Stock	Total
Mornin' Joe Statement of Stockholders' Equity For the Year Ended December 31, 20Y6						
Balance, January 1, 20Y6	$300,000	$800,000	$1,325,000	$ 852,700	$(36,000)	$3,241,700
Net income				421,600		421,600
Dividends on preferred stock				(30,000)		(30,000)
Dividends on common stock				(44,000)		(44,000)
Issuance of additional common stock		100,000	175,000			275,000
Purchase of treasury stock					(10,000)	(10,000)
Balance, December 31, 20Y6	$300,000	$900,000	$1,500,000	$1,200,300	$(46,000)	$3,854,300

Analysis for Decision Making

Earnings per Share

Net income is often used by investors and creditors in evaluating a company's profitability. However, net income by itself is difficult to use in comparing companies of different sizes. Also, trends in net income may be difficult to evaluate if there have been significant changes in the company's stockholders' equity. One ratio used for analyzing profitability is the earnings per share of common stock outstanding during a period. This ratio is called **earnings per common share (EPS)**, or sometimes *basic earnings per share*.[11]

Corporations whose stock is traded in a public market must report earnings per common share on their income statements. Stockholders in these corporations measure the value of their shareholdings by the market price per share as quoted by a stock exchange. Generally, changes in the market price per share will be related to changes in the earnings per share of the stock. Thus, shareholders actively monitor the earnings per share because of this relationship.

Objective

Describe and illustrate the use of earnings per share in evaluating a company's profitability.

---

[11] For complex capital structures, including securities such as convertible bonds or executive stock options, earnings per share assuming dilution may also be reported.

Earnings per share is computed as follows:

$$\text{Earnings per Share} = \frac{\text{Net Income} - \text{Preferred Dividends}}{\text{Average Number of Common Shares Outstanding}}$$

Any preferred dividends are subtracted from net income because the numerator represents only those earnings available to the common shareholders.

To illustrate, the following data (in thousands, except per-share amounts) were taken from recent financial statements of **Google**:

	Recent Year	**Prior Year**
Net income.............................	$14,444,000	$12,920,000
Average number of common shares outstanding	675,935 shares	665,692 shares
Earnings per share......................	$21.37	$19.41
	($14,444,000 ÷ 675,935 shares)	($12,920,000 ÷ 665,692 shares)

Google had no preferred stock outstanding; thus, no preferred dividends were subtracted in computing earnings per share. As illustrated, Google's earnings per share increased from $19.41 in the prior year to $21.37 in the recent year. An increase in earnings per share is generally considered a favorable trend.

Make a Decision   Earnings per Share

Bank of America Corporation and **Wells Fargo & Company** are two large financial services companies. The following data (in millions) were taken from a recent year's financial statements for both companies:

	Bank of America	**Wells Fargo**
Net income	$ 4,833	$23,057
Preferred dividends	1,044	1,236
Average number of common shares outstanding	10,528	5,237

A. Compute the earnings per share for both companies. (Round to the nearest cent.)

B. Which company appears to be more profitable on an earnings-per-share basis?

C. Which company would you expect to have the larger quoted market price?

Solution

A.

$$\text{Earnings per Share} = \frac{\text{Net Income} - \text{Preferred Dividends}}{\text{Average Number of Common Shares Outstanding}}$$

Bank of America: $\dfrac{\$4,833 - \$1,044}{10,528} = \$0.36$

Wells Fargo: $\dfrac{\$23,057 - \$1,236}{5,237} = \$4.17$

B. Wells Fargo's earnings per share is $4.17, compared to Bank of America's earnings per share of $0.36. Wells Fargo is clearly more profitable than Bank of America on an earnings-per-share basis.

C. We would expect the market price of Wells Fargo to be higher than the market price of Bank of America based on the difference in earnings per share. The market price of a stock is determined by many influences, of which earnings per share is just one. Even so, given that Wells Fargo's earnings per share is more than ten times larger than Bank of America's, we would expect the market price to show a difference between the two companies. As of this writing, Bank of America's market price per share was $17.36, and Wells Fargo's market price per share was $57.30.

Make a Decision

Let's Review

Chapter Summary

1. Corporations have a separate legal existence, transferable units of stock, unlimited life, and limited stockholders' liability. The advantages and disadvantages of the corporate form are summarized in Exhibit 2. Costs incurred in organizing a corporation are debited to Organizational Expenses.

2. The main source of paid-in capital is from issuing common and preferred stock. Stock issued at par is recorded by debiting Cash and crediting the class of stock issued for its par amount. Stock issued for more than par is recorded by debiting Cash, crediting the class of stock for its par, and crediting Paid-In Capital in Excess of Par for the difference. When no-par stock is issued, the entire proceeds are credited to the stock account. No-par stock may be assigned a stated value per share, and the excess of the proceeds over the stated value may be credited to Paid-In Capital in Excess of Stated Value.

3. The entry to record a declaration of cash dividends debits Dividends and credits Dividends Payable. When a stock dividend is declared, Stock Dividends is debited for the fair value of the stock to be issued. Stock Dividends Distributable is credited for the par or stated value of the common stock to be issued. The difference between the fair value of the stock and its par or stated value is credited to Paid-In Capital in Excess of Par—Common Stock. When the stock is issued on the date of payment, Stock Dividends Distributable is debited and Common Stock is credited for the par or stated value of the stock issued.

4. When a corporation reduces the par or stated value of its common stock and issues a proportionate number of additional shares, a stock split has occurred. There are no changes in the balances of any accounts, and no entry is required for a stock split.

5. When a corporation buys its own stock, the cost method of accounting is normally used. Treasury Stock is debited for its cost, and Cash is credited. If the stock is resold, Treasury Stock is credited for its cost and any difference between the cost and the selling price is normally debited or credited to Paid-In Capital from Sale of Treasury Stock.

6. Two alternatives for reporting stockholders' equity are shown in Exhibit 9. Changes in retained earnings are reported in a retained earnings statement, as shown in Exhibit 10. Restrictions to retained earnings should be disclosed. Any prior period adjustments are reported on the retained earnings statement. Changes in stockholders' equity may be reported on a statement of stockholders' equity, as shown in Exhibit 11.

Key Terms

cash dividend (571)
common stock (566)
cumulative preferred stock (567)
discount (568)
earnings per common
   share (EPS) (581)
in arrears (567)
outstanding stock (565)

par value (565)
preferred stock (566)
premium (568)
prior period adjustment (579)
restrictions (579)
retained earnings statement (578)
statement of stockholders'
   equity (579)

stock (562)
stock dividend (572)
stock split (574)
stockholders (562)
treasury stock (575)

Practice

Multiple-Choice Questions

1. Which of the following is a disadvantage of the corporate form of organization?
   A. Limited liability
   B. Continuous life
   C. Owner is separate from management
   D. Ability to raise capital

2. Paid-in capital for a corporation may arise from which of the following sources?
   A. Issuing preferred stock
   B. Issuing common stock
   C. Selling the corporation's treasury stock
   D. All of the above

3. The Stockholders' Equity section of the balance sheet may include:
   A. common stock.
   B. stock dividends distributable.
   C. preferred stock.
   D. all of the above.

4. If a corporation reacquires its own stock, the stock is listed on the balance sheet in the:
   A. Current Assets section.
   B. Long-Term Liabilities section.
   C. Stockholders' Equity section.
   D. Investments section.

5. A corporation has issued 25,000 shares of $100 par common stock and holds 3,000 of these shares as treasury stock. If the corporation declares a $2 per share cash dividend, what amount will be recorded as cash dividends?
   A. $22,000
   B. $25,000
   C. $44,000
   D. $50,000

Answers provided after Problem. Need more practice? Find additional multiple-choice questions, exercises, and problems in CengageNOWv2.

Exercises

SHOW ME HOW

1. Dividends per share
Obj. 2

National Furniture Company has 25,000 shares of cumulative preferred 2% stock, $75 par and 200,000 shares of $10 par common stock. The following amounts were distributed as dividends:

Year 1	$25,000
Year 2	88,000
Year 3	95,500

Determine the dividends per share for preferred and common stock for each year.

SHOW ME HOW

2. Entries for issuing stock
Obj. 2

On August 26, Mountain Realty Inc. issued for cash 120,000 shares of no-par common stock (with a stated value of $5) at $8. On October 1, Mountain Realty issued at par value 40,000 shares of preferred 1% stock, $10 par for cash. On November 30, Mountain Realty issued for cash 18,000 shares of preferred 1% stock, $10 par at $13.

Journalize the entries to record the August 26, October 1, and November 30 transactions.

SHOW ME HOW

3. Entries for cash dividends
Obj. 3

The declaration, record, and payment dates in connection with a cash dividend of $710,000 on a corporation's common stock are June 15, August 10, and September 15. Journalize the entries required on each date.

SHOW ME HOW

4. Entries for stock dividends

Obj. 3

Olde Wine Corporation has 250,000 shares of $40 par common stock outstanding. On February 15, Olde Wine declared a 2% stock dividend to be issued May 2 to stockholders of record on March 27. The market price of the stock was $52 per share on February 15.

Journalize the entries required on February 15, March 27, and May 2.

SHOW ME HOW

5. Entries for treasury stock

Obj. 5

On January 31, Wilderness Resorts Inc. reacquired 22,500 shares of its common stock at $31 per share. On April 20, Wilderness Resorts sold 12,800 of the reacquired shares at $40 per share. On October 4, Wilderness Resorts sold the remaining shares at $28 per share.

Journalize the transactions of January 31, April 20, and October 4.

SHOW ME HOW

6. Reporting stockholders' equity

Obj. 6

Using the following accounts and balances, prepare the Stockholders' Equity section of the balance sheet. Two hundred fifty thousand shares of common stock are authorized, and 17,500 shares have been reacquired.

Common Stock, $60 par	$12,000,000
Paid-In Capital from Sale of Treasury Stock	320,000
Paid-In Capital in Excess of Par—Common Stock	3,200,000
Retained Earnings	18,500,000
Treasury Stock	1,137,500

SHOW ME HOW

7. Retained earnings statement

Obj. 6

Rockwell Inc. reported the following results for the month ended June 30:

Retained earnings, June 1	$3,900,000
Net income	714,000
Cash dividends declared	100,000
Stock dividends declared	50,000

Prepare a retained earnings statement for the month ended June 30.

Answers provided after Problem. Need more practice? Find additional multiple-choice questions, exercises, and problems in CengageNOWv2.

Problem

Altenburg Inc. is a lighting fixture wholesaler located in Arizona. During its current fiscal year, ended December 31, Altenburg completed the following selected transactions:

Feb. 3. Purchased 2,500 shares of its own common stock at $26, recording the stock at cost. (Prior to the purchase, there were 40,000 shares of $20 par common stock outstanding.)

May 1. Declared a semiannual dividend of $1 on the 10,000 shares of preferred stock and a $0.30 dividend on the common stock to stockholders of record on May 31, payable on June 15.

June 15. Paid the cash dividends.

Sept. 23. Sold 1,000 shares of treasury stock at $28, receiving cash.

Nov. 1. Declared semiannual dividends of $1 on the preferred stock and $0.30 on the common stock. In addition, a 5% common stock dividend was declared on the common stock outstanding, to be capitalized at the fair market value of the common stock, which is estimated at $30.

Dec. 1. Paid the cash dividends and issued the certificates for the common stock dividend.

Instructions

Journalize the entries to record the transactions for Altenburg Inc.

Need more practice? Find additional multiple-choice questions, exercises, and problems in CengageNOWv2.

Answers

Multiple-Choice Questions

1. **C** The separation of the owner from management (answer C) is a disadvantage of the corporate form of organization. This is because management may not always behave in the best interests of the owners. Limited liability (answer A), continuous life (answer B), and the ability to raise capital (answer D) are all advantages of the corporate form of organization.

2. **D** Paid-in capital is one of the two major subdivisions of the stockholders' equity of a corporation. It may result from many sources, including the issuance of preferred stock (answer A), the issuance of common stock (answer B), or the sale of a corporation's treasury stock (answer C).

3. **D** The Stockholders' Equity section of corporate balance sheets is divided into two principal subsections: (1) investments contributed by the stockholders and others and (2) net income retained in the business. Included as part of the investments by stockholders and others is the par of common stock (answer A), stock dividends distributable (answer B), and the par of preferred stock (answer C).

4. **C** Reacquired stock, known as treasury stock, should be listed in the Stockholders' Equity section (answer C) of the balance sheet. The price paid for the treasury stock is deducted from the total of all the stockholders' equity accounts.

5. **C** If a corporation that holds treasury stock declares a cash dividend, the dividends are not paid on the treasury shares. To do so would place the corporation in the position of earning income through dealing with itself. Thus, the corporation will record $44,000 (answer C) as cash dividends [(25,000 shares issued less 3,000 shares held as treasury stock) × $2 per share dividend].

Exercises

1.

	Year 1	Year 2	Year 3
Amount distributed	$25,000	$88,000	$95,500
Preferred dividend (25,000 shares)	25,000	50,000*	37,500
Common dividend (200,000 shares)	$ 0	$38,000	$58,000

*$12,500 + $37,500

Dividends per share:			
Preferred stock	$1.00	$2.00	$1.50
Common stock	None	$0.19	$0.29

2.

Aug. 26	Cash (120,000 shares × $8)	960,000	
	Common Stock (120,000 shares × $5)		600,000
	Paid-In Capital in Excess of Stated Value—		
	Common Stock [120,000 shares × ($8 – $5)]		360,000
Oct. 1	Cash	400,000	
	Preferred Stock (40,000 shares × $10)		400,000
Nov. 30	Cash (18,000 shares × $13)	234,000	
	Preferred Stock (18,000 shares × $10)		180,000
	Paid-In Capital in Excess of Par—		
	Preferred Stock [18,000 shares × ($13 – $10)]		54,000

3.

June 15	Cash Dividends	710,000	
	Cash Dividends Payable		710,000
Aug. 10	No entry required.		
Sept.15	Cash Dividends Payable	710,000	
	Cash		710,000

4.

Feb. 15	Stock Dividends (250,000 shares × 2% × $52)	260,000	
	Stock Dividends Distributable		
	(5,000 shares × $40)		200,000
	Paid-In Capital in Excess of Par—		
	Common Stock [$5,000 shares × ($52 – $40)]		60,000
Mar. 27	No entry required		
May 2	Stock Dividends Distributable	200,000	
	Common Stock		200,000

5.

Jan. 31	Treasury Stock (22,500 shares × $31)	697,500	
	Cash		697,500
Apr. 20	Cash (12,800 shares × $40)	512,000	
	Treasury Stock (12,800 shares × $31)		396,800
	Paid-In Capital from Sale of		
	Treasury Stock [12,800 shares × ($40 – $31)]		115,200
Oct. 4	Cash (9,700 shares × $28)	271,600	
	Paid-In Capital from Sale of		
	Treasury Stock [9,700 shares × ($31 – $28)]	29,100	
	Treasury Stock (9,700 shares × $31)		300,700

6.

Stockholders' Equity

Paid-in capital:

Common stock, $60 per (250,000 shares authorized, 200,000 shares issued)	$12,000,000	
Excess of issue price over par	3,200,000	
Paid-in capital, common stock		$15,200,000
From sale of treasury stock.		320,000
Total paid-in capital		$15,520,000
Retained earnings		18,500,000
Total.		$34,020,000
Treasury stock (17,500 shares at cost).		(1,137,500)
Total stockholders' equty		$32,882,500

7.

Rockwell Inc. Retained Earnings Statement For the Month Ended June 30		
Retained earnings, June 1......................		$3,900,000
Net income	$714,000	
Dividends	(150,000)	
Change in retained earnings...................		564,000
Retained earnings, June 30....................		$4,464,000

Need more help? Watch step-by-step videos of how to compute answers to these Exercises in CengageNOWv2.

Problem

Feb.	3	Treasury Stock	65,000	
		Cash		65,000
May	1	Cash Dividends	21,250	
		Cash Dividends Payable		21,250
		(10,000 × $1) + [(40,000 − 2,500) × $0.30].		
June	15	Cash Dividends Payable	21,250	
		Cash		21,250
Sept.	23	Cash	28,000	
		Treasury Stock		26,000
		Paid-In Capital from Sale of Treasury Stock		2,000
Nov.	1	Cash Dividends	21,550	
		Cash Dividends Payable		21,550
		(10,000 × $1) + [(40,000 − 1,500) × $0.30].		
	1	Stock Dividends	57,750*	
		Stock Dividends Distributable		38,500
		Paid-In Capital in Excess of		
		Par—Common Stock		19,250
		*(40,000 − 1,500) × 5% × $30.		
Dec.	1	Cash Dividends Payable	21,550	
		Stock Dividends Distributable	38,500	
		Cash		21,550
		Common Stock		38,500

Discussion Questions

1. Of two corporations organized at approximately the same time and engaged in competing businesses, one issued $80 par common stock, and the other issued $1 par common stock. Do the par designations provide any indication as to which stock is preferable as an investment? Explain.

2. A stockbroker advises a client to buy preferred stock, saying "With that type of stock, you will never have to worry about losing the dividends." Is the broker right?

3. A corporation with both preferred stock and common stock outstanding has a substantial credit balance in its retained earnings account at the beginning of the current fiscal year. Although net income for the current year is sufficient to pay the preferred dividend of $150,000 each quarter and a common dividend of $90,000 each quarter, the board of directors declares dividends only on the preferred stock. Suggest possible reasons for passing the dividends on the common stock.

4. An owner of 2,500 shares of Simmons Company common stock receives a stock dividend of 50 shares.

   A. What is the effect of the stock dividend on the stockholder's proportionate interest (equity) in the corporation?

   B. How does the total equity of 2,550 shares compare with the total equity of 2,500 shares before the stock dividend?

5. A. Where should a declared but unpaid cash dividend be reported on the balance sheet?

   B. Where should a declared but unissued stock dividend be reported on the balance sheet?

6. What is the primary purpose of a stock split?

7. A corporation reacquires 60,000 shares of its own $10 par common stock for $3,000,000, recording it at cost.

   A. What effect does this transaction have on revenue or expense of the period?

   B. What effect does it have on stockholders' equity?

8. The treasury stock in Discussion Question 7 is resold for $3,750,000.

   A. What is the effect on the corporation's revenue of the period?

   B. What is the effect on stockholders' equity?

9. What are the three classifications of restrictions of retained earnings, and how are such restrictions normally reported on the financial statements?

10. Indicate how prior period adjustments would be reported on the financial statements presented only for the current period.

Basic Exercises

SHOW ME HOW

BE 12-1   Dividends per share   Obj. 2

Zero Calories Company has 16,000 shares of cumulative preferred 1% stock, $40 par and 80,000 shares of $150 par common stock. The following amounts were distributed as dividends:

Year 1	$ 21,600
Year 2	4,000
Year 3	100,800

Determine the dividends per share for preferred and common stock for each year.

SHOW ME HOW

BE 12-2   Entries for issuing stock   Obj. 2

On January 22, Zentric Corporation issued for cash 180,000 shares of no-par common stock at $4. On February 14, Zentric issued at par value 44,000 shares of preferred 2% stock, $55 par for cash. On August 30, Zentric issued for cash 9,000 shares of preferred 2% stock, $55 par at $60.

Journalize the entries to record the January 22, February 14, and August 30 transactions.

SHOW ME HOW

BE 12-3   Entries for cash dividends   Obj. 3

The declaration, record, and payment dates in connection with a cash dividend of $335,000 on a corporation's common stock are October 1, November 7, and December 15. Journalize the entries required on each date.

SHOW ME HOW

BE 12-4 Entries for stock dividends

Obj. 3

Alpine Energy Corporation has 1,500,000 shares of $40 par common stock outstanding. On August 2, Alpine Energy declared a 4% stock dividend to be issued October 8 to stockholders of record on September 15. The market price of the stock was $70 per share on August 2.

Journalize the entries required on August 2, September 15, and October 8.

SHOW ME HOW

BE 12-5 Entries for treasury stock

Obj. 5

On May 27, Hydro Clothing Inc. reacquired 75,000 shares of its common stock at $8 per share. On August 3, Hydro Clothing sold 54,000 of the reacquired shares at $11 per share. On November 14, Hydro Clothing sold the remaining shares at $7 per share.

Journalize the transactions of May 27, August 3, and November 14.

SHOW ME HOW

BE 12-6 Reporting stockholders' equity

Obj. 6

Using the following accounts and balances, prepare the Stockholders' Equity section of the balance sheet. Five-hundred thousand shares of common stock are authorized, and 40,000 shares have been reacquired.

Common Stock, $120 par	$48,000,000
Paid-In Capital from Sale of Treasury Stock	4,500,000
Paid-In Capital in Excess of Par—Common Stock	6,400,000
Retained Earnings	63,680,000
Treasury Stock	5,200,000

SHOW ME HOW

BE 12-7 Retained earnings statement

Obj. 6

Noric Cruises Inc. reported the following results for the year ended October 31:

Retained earnings, October 1	$12,400,000
Net income	2,350,000
Cash dividends declared	175,000
Stock dividends declared	300,000

Prepare a retained earnings statement for the month ended October 31.

Exercises

✔ Preferred stock,
1st year: $0.45

SHOW ME HOW

EXCEL TEMPLATE

EX 12-1 Dividends per share

Obj. 2

Seventy-Two Inc., a developer of radiology equipment, has stock outstanding as follows: 80,000 shares of cumulative preferred 3% stock, $20 par and 400,000 shares of $25 par common. During its first four years of operations, the following amounts were distributed as dividends: first year, $36,000; second year, $72,000; third year, $80,000; fourth year, $100,000. Determine the dividends per share on each class of stock for each of the four years.

✔ Preferred stock,
1st year: $0.90

EX 12-2 Dividends per share

Obj. 2

Lightfoot Inc., a software development firm, has stock outstanding as follows: 40,000 shares of cumulative preferred 1% stock, $125 par and 100,000 shares of $150 par common. During its first four years of operations, the following amounts were distributed as dividends: first year, $36,000; second year, $58,000; third year, $75,000; fourth year, $124,000. Determine the dividends per share on each class of stock for each of the four years.

SHOW ME HOW

EX 12-3 Entries for issuing par stock

Obj. 2

On January 22, Jefferson County Rocks Inc., a marble contractor, issued for cash 180,000 shares of $20 par common stock at $23, and on February 27, it issued for cash 25,000 shares of preferred stock, $7 par at $9.

A. Journalize the entries for January 22 and February 27.

B. What is the total amount invested (total paid-in capital) by all stockholders as of February 27?

SHOW ME HOW

EX 12-4 Entries for issuing no-par stock   Obj. 2

On May 15, Helena Carpet Inc., a carpet wholesaler, issued for cash 750,000 shares of no-par common stock (with a stated value of $1.50) at $4, and on June 30, it issued for cash 17,500 shares of preferred stock, $50 par at $60.

A. Journalize the entries for May 15 and June 30, assuming that the common stock is to be credited with the stated value.

B. What is the total amount invested (total paid-in capital) by all stockholders as of June 30?

SHOW ME HOW

EX 12-5 Issuing stock for assets other than cash   Obj. 2

On November 23, Elder Lift Corporation, a wholesaler of hydraulic lifts, acquired land in exchange for 12,500 shares of $25 par common stock with a current market price of $38. Journalize the entry to record the transaction.

EX 12-6 Selected stock transactions   Obj. 2

Alpha Sounds Corp., an electric guitar retailer, was organized by Michele Kirby, Paul Glenn, and Gretchen Northway. The charter authorized 1,000,000 shares of common stock with a par of $1. The following transactions affecting stockholders' equity were completed during the first year of operations:

A. Issued 100,000 shares of stock at par to Paul Glenn for cash.

B. Issued 3,000 shares of stock at par to Michele Kirby for promotional services provided in connection with the organization of the corporation, and issued 45,000 shares of stock at par to Michele Kirby for cash.

C. Purchased land and a building from Gretchen Northway in exchange for stock issued at par. The building is mortgaged for $180,000 for 20 years at 6%, and there is accrued interest of $5,200 on the mortgage note at the time of the purchase. It is agreed that the land is to be priced at $60,000 and the building at $225,000 and that Gretchen Northway's equity will be exchanged for stock at par. The corporation agreed to assume responsibility for paying the mortgage note and the accrued interest.

Journalize the entries to record the transactions.

EX 12-7 Issuing stock   Obj. 2

Willow Creek Nursery, with an authorization of 75,000 shares of preferred stock and 200,000 shares of common stock, completed several transactions involving its stock on October 1, the first day of operations. The trial balance at the close of the day follows:

Cash	3,780,000	
Land	840,000	
Buildings	2,380,000	
Preferred 1% Stock, $80 par		2,800,000
Paid-In Capital in Excess of Par—Preferred Stock		420,000
Common Stock, $30 par		3,600,000
Paid-In Capital in Excess of Par—Common Stock		180,000
	7,000,000	7,000,000

All shares within each class of stock were sold at the same price. The preferred stock was issued in exchange for the land and buildings.

Journalize the two entries to record the transactions summarized in the trial balance.

SHOW ME HOW

EX 12-8   Issuing stock

Obj. 2

Professional Products Inc., a wholesaler of office products, was organized on February 5 of the current year, with an authorization of 50,000 shares of preferred 2% stock, $40 par and 1,000,000 shares of $8 par common stock. The following selected transactions were completed during the first year of operations:

Feb. 5.   Issued 600,000 shares of common stock at par for cash.

5.   Issued 1,500 shares of common stock at par to an attorney in payment of legal fees for organizing the corporation.

Apr. 9.   Issued 45,000 shares of common stock in exchange for land, buildings, and equipment with fair market prices of $100,000, $310,000, and $85,000 respectively.

June 14. Issued 30,000 shares of preferred stock at $53 for cash.

Journalize the transactions.

SHOW ME HOW

EX 12-9   Entries for cash dividends

Obj. 3

The declaration, record, and payment dates in connection with a cash dividend of $1,250,000 on a corporation's common stock are July 9, August 31, and October 1. Journalize the entries required on each date.

✔ B. (1) $42,000,000
(3) $131,550,000

SHOW ME HOW

EX 12-10   Entries for stock dividends

Obj. 3

Healthy Life Co. is an HMO for businesses in the Fresno area. The following account balances appear on Healthy Life's balance sheet: Common stock (3,000,000 shares authorized; 2,200,000 shares issued), $15 par, $33,000,000; Paid-in capital in excess of par—common stock, $9,000,000; and Retained earnings, $89,550,000. The board of directors declared a 5% stock dividend when the market price of the stock was $18 a share. Healthy Life reported no income or loss for the current year.

A. Journalize the entries to record (1) the declaration of the dividend, capitalizing an amount equal to market value, and (2) the issuance of the stock certificates.

B. Determine the following amounts before the stock dividend was declared: (1) total paid-in capital, (2) total retained earnings, and (3) total stockholders' equity.

C. Determine the following amounts after the stock dividend was declared and closing entries were recorded at the end of the year: (1) total paid-in capital, (2) total retained earnings, and (3) total stockholders' equity.

SHOW ME HOW

EX 12-11   Effect of stock split

Obj. 4

Willey's Grill & Restaurant Corporation wholesales ovens and ranges to restaurants throughout the Southwest. Willey's Grill & Restaurant, which had 325,000 shares of common stock outstanding, declared a 3-for-1 stock split.

A. What will be the number of shares outstanding after the split?

B. If the common stock had a market price of $450 per share before the stock split, what would be an approximate market price per share after the split?

EX 12-12   Effect of cash dividend and stock split

Obj. 3, 4

Indicate whether the following actions would (+) increase, (–) decrease, or (0) not affect Indigo Inc.'s total assets, liabilities, and stockholders' equity:

	Assets	Liabilities	Stockholders' Equity
A. Authorizing and issuing stock certificates in a stock split	_____	_____	_____
B. Declaring a stock dividend	_____	_____	_____
C. Issuing stock certificates for the stock dividend declared in (B)	_____	_____	_____
D. Declaring a cash dividend	_____	_____	_____
E. Paying the cash dividend declared in (D)	_____	_____	_____

EX 12-13 Selected dividend transactions, stock split

Obj. 3, 4

Selected transactions completed by Canyon Ferry Boating Corporation during the current fiscal year are as follows:

Jan. 8. Split the common stock 2 for 1 and reduced the par from $80 to $40 per share. After the split, there were 150,000 common shares outstanding.

Apr. 30. Declared semiannual dividends of $0.75 on 18,000 shares of preferred stock and $0.28 on the common stock payable on July 1.

July 1. Paid the cash dividends.

Oct. 31. Declared semiannual dividends of $0.75 on the preferred stock and $0.14 on the common stock (before the stock dividend). In addition, a 5% common stock dividend was declared on the common stock outstanding. The fair market value of the common stock is estimated at $52.

Dec. 31. Paid the cash dividends and issued the certificates for the common stock dividend.

Journalize the transactions.

EX 12-14 Treasury stock transactions

Obj. 5

✔ B. $170,000 credit

SHOW ME HOW

Mystic Lake Inc. bottles and distributes spring water. On July 9 of the current year, Mystic Lake reacquired 40,000 shares of its common stock at $44 per share. On September 22, Mystic Lake sold 30,000 of the reacquired shares at $50 per share. The remaining 10,000 shares were sold at $43 per share on November 23.

A. Journalize the transactions of July 9, September 22, and November 23.

B. What is the balance in Paid-In Capital from Sale of Treasury Stock on December 31 of the current year?

C. ▬▬▬▶ For what reasons might Mystic Lake Inc. have purchased the treasury stock?

EX 12-15 Treasury stock transactions

Obj. 5, 6

✔ B. $454,500 credit

SHOW ME HOW

SprayCo Inc. develops and produces spraying equipment for lawn maintenance and industrial uses. On March 9 of the current year, SprayCo reacquired 62,000 shares of its common stock at $51 per share. On June 9, 48,000 of the reacquired shares were sold at $60 per share, and on November 13, 7,500 of the reacquired shares were sold at $54.

A. Journalize the transactions of March 9, June 9, and November 13.

B. What is the balance in Paid-In Capital from Sale of Treasury Stock on December 31 of the current year?

C. What is the balance in Treasury Stock on December 31 of the current year?

D. How will the balance in Treasury Stock be reported on the balance sheet?

EX 12-16 Treasury stock transactions

Obj. 5, 6

✔ B. $55,500 credit

Biscayne Bay Water Inc. bottles and distributes spring water. On May 14 of the current year, Biscayne Bay Water reacquired 23,500 shares of its common stock at $75 per share. On September 6, Biscayne Bay Water sold 14,000 of the reacquired shares at $81 per share. The remaining 9,500 shares were sold at $72 per share on November 30.

A. Journalize the transactions of May 14, September 6, and November 30.

B. What is the balance in Paid-In Capital from Sale of Treasury Stock on December 31 of the current year?

C. Where will the balance in Paid-In Capital from Sale of Treasury Stock be reported on the balance sheet?

D. ▬▬▬▶ For what reasons might Biscayne Bay Water Inc. have purchased the treasury stock?

EX 12-17 Reporting paid-in capital

Obj. 6

✔ Total paid-in capital, $13,615,000

The following accounts and their balances were selected from the unadjusted trial balance of Point Loma Group Inc., a freight forwarder, at October 31, the end of the current fiscal year:

Common Stock, no par, $14 stated value	$ 4,480,000
Paid-In Capital from Sale of Treasury Stock	45,000
Paid-In Capital in Excess of Par—Preferred Stock	210,000
Paid-In Capital in Excess of Stated Value—Common Stock	480,000
Preferred 2% Stock, $120 par	8,400,000
Retained Earnings	39,500,000

Prepare the Paid-In Capital portion of the Stockholders' Equity section of the balance sheet using Method 1 of Exhibit 9. There are 375,000 shares of common stock authorized and 85,000 shares of preferred stock authorized.

EX 12-18 Stockholders' Equity section of balance sheet

Obj. 6

✔ Total stockholders' equity, $23,676,000

The following accounts and their balances appear in the ledger of Goodale Properties Inc. on June 30 of the current year:

Common Stock, $45 par	$ 3,060,000
Paid-In Capital from Sale of Treasury Stock	115,000
Paid-In Capital in Excess of Par—Common Stock	272,000
Retained Earnings	20,553,000
Treasury Stock	324,000

Prepare the Stockholders' Equity section of the balance sheet as of June 30. Eighty thousand shares of common stock are authorized, and 9,000 shares have been reacquired.

EX 12-19 Stockholders' Equity section of balance sheet

Obj. 6

✔ Total stockholders' equity, $89,100,000

Specialty Auto Racing Inc. retails racing products for BMWs, Porsches, and Ferraris. The following accounts and their balances appear in the ledger of Specialty Auto Racing on July 31, the end of the current year:

Common Stock, $36 par	$10,080,000
Paid-In Capital from Sale of Treasury Stock—Common	340,000
Paid-In Capital in Excess of Par—Common Stock	420,000
Paid-In Capital in Excess of Par—Preferred Stock	384,000
Preferred 1% Stock, $150 par	7,200,000
Retained Earnings	71,684,000
Treasury Stock—Common	1,008,000

Fifty thousand shares of preferred and 300,000 shares of common stock are authorized. There are 24,000 shares of common stock held as treasury stock.

Prepare the Stockholders' Equity section of the balance sheet as of July 31, the end of the current year, using Method 1 of Exhibit 9.

EX 12-20 Retained earnings statement

Obj. 6

✔ Retained earnings, December 31, $64,210,000

Sumter Pumps Corporation, a manufacturer of industrial pumps, reports the following results for the year ended December 31, 20Y3:

SHOW ME HOW

Retained earnings, January 1, 20Y3	$59,650,000
Net income	8,160,000
Cash dividends declared	1,000,000
Stock dividends declared	2,600,000

Prepare a retained earnings statement for the year ended December 31, 20Y3.

EX 12-21   Stockholders' Equity section of balance sheet   Obj. 6

✔ Corrected total
stockholders' equity,
$122,800,000

List the errors in the following Stockholders' Equity section of the balance sheet prepared as of the end of the current year:

Stockholders' Equity

Paid-in capital:		
Preferred 2% stock, $80 par (125,000 shares authorized and issued).......................................	$10,000,000	
Excess of issue price over par	500,000	
Paid-in capital, preferred stock.......................		$ 10,500,000
Retained earnings		96,700,000
Treasury stock (75,000 shares at cost)....................		1,755,000
Dividends payable......................................		430,000
Total paid-in capital.................................		$ 109,385,000
Common stock, $20 par (1,000,000 shares authorized, 825,000 shares issued)		17,655,000
Organizing costs		300,000
Total stockholders' equity.....................................		$127,340,000

EX 12-22   Statement of stockholders' equity   Obj. 6

✔ Total stockholders'
equity, Dec. 31,
$21,587,000

EXCEL TEMPLATE

The stockholders' equity T accounts of I-Cards Inc. for the year ended December 31, 20Y9, are as follows. Prepare a statement of stockholders' equity for the year ended December 31, 20Y9.

Common Stock

	Jan. 1	Balance	4,800,000
	Apr. 14	Issued	
		30,000 shares	1,200,000
	Dec. 31	Balance	6,000,000

Paid-In Capital in Excess of Par

	Jan. 1	Balance	960,000
	Apr. 14	Issued	
		30,000 shares	300,000
	Dec. 31	Balance	1,260,000

Treasury Stock

Aug. 7	Purchased	
	12,000 shares	552,000

Retained Earnings

Mar. 31	Dividend	69,000	Jan. 1	Balance	11,375,000
June 30	Dividend	69,000	Dec. 31	Closing	
Sept. 30	Dividend	69,000		(net income)	3,780,000
Dec. 31	Dividend	69,000	Dec. 31	Balance	14,879,000

Problems: Series A

PR 12-1A   Dividends on preferred and common stock   Obj. 2

✔ 1. Common
dividends in Year 3:
$20,000

Pecan Theatre Inc. owns and operates movie theaters throughout Florida and Georgia. Pecan Theatre has declared the following annual dividends over a six-year period: Year 1, $80,000; Year 2, $90,000; Year 3, $150,000; Year 4, $150,000; Year 5, $160,000; and Year 6, $180,000. During the entire period ended December 31 of each year, the outstanding stock of the company was composed of 250,000 shares of cumulative, preferred 2% stock, $20 par, and 500,000 shares of common stock, $15 par.

(Continued)

SHOW ME HOW   EXCEL TEMPLATE

Instructions

1. Determine the total dividends and the per-share dividends declared on each class of stock for each of the six years. There were no dividends in arrears at the beginning of Year 1. Summarize the data in tabular form, using the following column headings:

Year	Total Dividends	Preferred Dividends		Common Dividends	
		Total	Per Share	Total	Per Share
Year 1	$ 80,000				
Year 2	90,000				
Year 3	150,000				
Year 4	150,000				
Year 5	160,000				
Year 6	180,000				

2. Determine the average annual dividend per share for each class of stock for the six-year period.

3. Assuming a market price per share of $25.00 for the preferred stock and $17.50 for the common stock, determine the average annual percentage return on initial shareholders' investment, based on the average annual dividend per share (A) for preferred stock and (B) for common stock.

GENERAL LEDGER

PR 12-2A   Stock transactions for corporate expansion   Obj. 2

On December 1 of the current year, the following accounts and their balances appear in the ledger of Latte Corp., a coffee processor:

Preferred 2% Stock, $50 par (250,000 shares authorized, 80,000 shares issued)	$ 4,000,000
Paid-In Capital in Excess of Par—Preferred Stock	560,000
Common Stock, $35 par (1,000,000 shares authorized, 400,000 shares issued)	14,000,000
Paid-In Capital in Excess of Par—Common Stock	1,200,000
Retained Earnings.	180,000,000

At the annual stockholders' meeting on March 31, the board of directors presented a plan for modernizing and expanding plant operations at a cost of approximately $11,000,000. The plan provided (A) that a building, valued at $3,375,000, and the land on which it is located, valued at $1,500,000, be acquired in accordance with preliminary negotiations by the issuance of 125,000 shares of common stock, (B) that 40,000 shares of the unissued preferred stock be issued through an underwriter, and (C) that the corporation borrow $4,000,000. The plan was approved by the stockholders and accomplished by the following transactions:

May 11.   Issued 125,000 shares of common stock in exchange for land and a building, according to the plan.

  20.   Issued 40,000 shares of preferred stock, receiving $52 per share in cash.

  31.   Borrowed $4,000,000 from Laurel National, giving a 5% mortgage note.

Instructions

Journalize the entries to record the May transactions.

PR 12-3A   Selected stock transactions   Obj. 2, 3, 5

✔ F. Cash dividends, $328,500

The following selected accounts appear in the ledger of Parks Construction Inc. at the beginning of the current year:

SHOW ME HOW   GENERAL LEDGER

Preferred 2% Stock, $75 par (100,000 shares authorized, 80,000 shares issued)	$ 6,000,000
Paid-In Capital in Excess of Par—Preferred Stock.	420,000
Common Stock, $8 par (5,000,000 shares authorized, 3,000,000 shares issued)	24,000,000
Paid-In Capital in Excess of Par—Common Stock.	1,850,000
Retained Earnings	115,400,000

During the year, the corporation completed a number of transactions affecting the stockholders' equity. They are summarized as follows:

A. Issued 400,000 shares of common stock at $11, receiving cash.

B. Issued 5,000 shares of preferred 2% stock at $90.

C. Purchased 150,000 shares of treasury common for $10 per share.

D. Sold 80,000 shares of treasury common for $13 per share.

E. Sold 20,000 shares of treasury common for $9 per share.

F. Declared cash dividends of $1.50 per share on preferred stock and $0.06 per share on common stock.

G. Paid the cash dividends.

Instructions

Journalize the entries to record the transactions. Identify each entry by letter.

PR 12-4A Entries for selected corporate transactions

Obj. 2, 3, 4, 6

✔ 4. Total stockholders' equity, $44,436,200

EXCEL TEMPLATE   GENERAL LEDGER

Morrow Enterprises Inc. manufactures bathroom fixtures. Morrow Enterprises' stockholders' equity accounts, with balances on January 1, 20Y6, are as follows:

Common Stock, $20 stated value (500,000 shares authorized, 375,000 shares issued)	$ 7,500,000
Paid-In Capital in Excess of Stated Value—Common Stock	825,000
Retained Earnings	33,600,000
Treasury Stock (25,000 shares, at cost)	450,000

The following selected transactions occurred during the year:

Jan. 22. Paid cash dividends of $0.08 per share on the common stock. The dividend had been properly recorded when declared on December 1 of the preceding fiscal year for $28,000.

Apr. 10. Issued 75,000 shares of common stock for $24 per share.

June 6. Sold all of the treasury stock for $26 per share.

July 5. Declared a 4% stock dividend on common stock, to be capitalized at the market price of the stock, which is $25 per share.

Aug. 15. Issued shares of stock for the stock dividend declared on July 5.

Nov. 23. Purchased 30,000 shares of treasury stock for $19 per share.

Dec. 28. Declared a $0.10-per-share dividend on common stock.

31. Closed the credit balance of the income summary account, $1,125,000.

31. Closed the two dividends accounts to Retained Earnings.

Instructions

1. Enter the January 1 balances in T accounts for the stockholders' equity accounts listed. Also prepare T accounts for the following: Paid-In Capital from Sale of Treasury Stock; Stock Dividends Distributable; Stock Dividends; Cash Dividends.

2. Journalize the entries to record the transactions, and post to the eight selected accounts.

3. Prepare a retained earnings statement for the year ended December 31, 20Y6.

4. Prepare the Stockholders' Equity section of the December 31, 20Y6, balance sheet.

PR 12-5A Entries for selected corporate transactions

Obj. 2, 3, 4, 5

✔ Oct. 1, cash dividends, $202,800

GENERAL LEDGER

Selected transactions completed by Primo Discount Corporation during the current fiscal year are as follows:

Jan. 9. Split the common stock 3 for 1 and reduced the par from $75 to $25 per share. After the split, there were 1,200,000 common shares outstanding.

Feb. 28. Purchased 40,000 shares of the corporation's own common stock at $28, recording the stock at cost.

May 1. Declared semiannual dividends of $0.80 on 75,000 shares of preferred stock and $0.12 on the common stock to stockholders of record on June 1, payable on July 10.

July 10. Paid the cash dividends.

(Continued)

Sept. 7. Sold 30,000 shares of treasury stock at $34, receiving cash.

Oct. 1. Declared semiannual dividends of $0.80 on the preferred stock and $0.12 on the common stock (before the stock dividend). In addition, a 2% common stock dividend was declared on the common stock outstanding. The fair market value of the common stock is estimated at $36.

Dec. 1. Paid the cash dividends and issued the certificates for the common stock dividend.

Instructions

Journalize the transactions.

Problems: Series B

✔ 1. Common dividends in Year 3: $25,000

SHOW ME HOW   EXCEL TEMPLATE

PR 12-1B   Dividends on preferred and common stock   Obj. 2

Yosemite Bike Corp. manufactures mountain bikes and distributes them through retail outlets in California, Oregon, and Washington. Yosemite Bike has declared the following annual dividends over a six-year period ended December 31 of each year: Year 1, $24,000; Year 2, $10,000; Year 3, $126,000; Year 4, $100,000; Year 5, $125,000; and Year 6, $125,000. During the entire period, the outstanding stock of the company was composed of 25,000 shares of cumulative preferred 2% stock, $90 par, and 100,000 shares of common stock, $4 par.

Instructions

1. Determine the total dividends and the per-share dividends declared on each class of stock for each of the six years. There were no dividends in arrears at the beginning of Year 1. Summarize the data in tabular form, using the following column headings:

Year	Total Dividends	Preferred Dividends		Common Dividends	
		Total	Per Share	Total	Per Share
Year 1	$ 24,000				
Year 2	10,000				
Year 3	126,000				
Year 4	100,000				
Year 5	125,000				
Year 6	125,000				

2. Determine the average annual dividend per share for each class of stock for the six-year period.

3. Assuming a market price of $100 for the preferred stock and $5 for the common stock, determine the average annual percentage return on initial shareholders' investment, based on the average annual dividend per share (A) for preferred stock and (B) for common stock.

GENERAL LEDGER

PR 12-2B   Stock transaction for corporate expansion   Obj. 2

Pulsar Optics produces medical lasers for use in hospitals. The accounts and their balances appear in the ledger of Pulsar Optics on April 30 of the current year as follows:

Preferred 1% Stock, $120 par (300,000 shares authorized, 36,000 shares issued)	$ 4,320,000
Paid-In Capital in Excess of Par—Preferred Stock	180,000
Common Stock, $15 par (2,000,000 shares authorized, 1,400,000 shares issued)	21,000,000
Paid-In Capital in Excess of Par—Common Stock	3,500,000
Retained Earnings	78,000,000

At the annual stockholders' meeting on August 5, the board of directors presented a plan for modernizing and expanding plant operations at a cost of approximately $9,000,000. The plan provided (A) that the corporation borrow $1,500,000, (B) that 20,000 shares of the unissued preferred stock be issued through an underwriter, and (C) that a building, valued at

$4,150,000, and the land on which it is located, valued at $800,000, be acquired in accordance with preliminary negotiations by the issuance of 300,000 shares of common stock. The plan was approved by the stockholders and accomplished by the following transactions:

Oct. 9. Borrowed $1,500,000 from St. Peter City Bank, giving a 4% mortgage note.

17. Issued 20,000 shares of preferred stock, receiving $126 per share in cash.

28. Issued 300,000 shares of common stock in exchange for land and a building, according to the plan.

Instructions

Journalize the entries to record the October transactions.

PR 12-3B Selected stock transactions
Obj. 2, 3, 5

✔ F. Cash dividends,
$234,775

SHOW ME HOW

GENERAL LEDGER

Diamondback Welding & Fabrication Corporation sells and services pipe welding equipment in Illinois. The following selected accounts appear in the ledger of Diamondback Welding & Fabrication at the beginning of the current year:

Preferred 2% Stock, $80 par (100,000 shares authorized, 60,000 shares issued)	$ 4,800,000
Paid-In Capital in Excess of Par—Preferred Stock	210,000
Common Stock, $5 par (6,000,000 shares authorized, 3,150,000 shares issued)	15,750,000
Paid-In Capital in Excess of Par—Common Stock	1,400,000
Retained Earnings	52,840,000

During the year, the corporation completed a number of transactions affecting the stockholders' equity. They are summarized as follows:

A. Purchased 87,500 shares of treasury common for $8 per share.

B. Sold 55,000 shares of treasury common for $11 per share.

C. Issued 20,000 shares of preferred 2% stock at $84.

D. Issued 400,000 shares of common stock at $13, receiving cash.

E. Sold 18,000 shares of treasury common for $7.50 per share.

F. Declared cash dividends of $1.60 per share on preferred stock and $0.03 per share on common stock.

G. Paid the cash dividends.

Instructions

Journalize the entries to record the transactions. Identify each entry by letter.

PR 12-4B Entries for selected corporate transactions
Obj. 2, 3, 4, 6

✔ 4. Total
stockholders' equity,
$11,262,432

EXCEL TEMPLATE

GENERAL LEDGER

Nav-Go Enterprises Inc. produces aeronautical navigation equipment. Navo-Go Enterprises' stockholders' equity accounts, with balances on January 1, 20Y1, are as follows:

Common Stock, $5 stated value (900,000 shares authorized, 620,000 shares issued)	$3,100,000
Paid-In Capital in Excess of Stated Value—Common Stock............................	1,240,000
Retained Earnings	4,875,000
Treasury Stock (48,000 shares, at cost)	288,000

The following selected transactions occurred during the year:

Jan. 15. Paid cash dividends of $0.06 per share on the common stock. The dividend had been properly recorded when declared on December 1 of the preceding fiscal year for $34,320.

Mar. 15. Sold all of the treasury stock for $6.75 per share.

Apr. 13. Issued 200,000 shares of common stock for $8 per share.

June 14. Declared a 3% stock dividend on common stock, to be capitalized at the market price of the stock, which is $7.50 per share.

July 16. Issued stock for stock dividend declared on June 14.

Oct. 30. Purchased 50,000 shares of treasury stock for $6 per share.

Dec. 30. Declared an $0.08-per-share dividend on common stock.

31. Closed the credit balance of the income summary account, $775,000.

31. Closed the two dividends accounts to Retained Earnings.

(Continued)

Instructions

1. Enter the January 1 balances in T accounts for the stockholders' equity accounts listed. Also prepare T accounts for the following: Paid-In Capital from Sale of Treasury Stock; Stock Dividends Distributable; Stock Dividends; Cash Dividends.

2. Journalize the entries to record the transactions, and post to the eight selected accounts.

3. Prepare a retained earnings statement for the year ended December 31, 20Y1.

4. Prepare the Stockholders' Equity section of the December 31, 20Y1, balance sheet.

PR 12-5B   Entries for selected corporate transactions   Obj. 2, 3, 4, 5

✔ Sept. 1, Cash
dividends, $95,200

GENERAL LEDGER

West Yellowstone Outfitters Corporation manufactures and distributes leisure clothing. Selected transactions completed by West Yellowstone Outfitters during the current fiscal year are as follows:

Jan. 15.   Split the common stock 4 for 1 and reduced the par from $120 to $30 per share. After the split, there were 800,000 common shares outstanding.

Mar. 1.   Declared semiannual dividends of $0.25 on 100,000 shares of preferred stock and $0.07 on the 800,000 shares of $30 par common stock to stockholders of record on March 31, payable on April 30.

Apr. 30.   Paid the cash dividends.

May 31.   Purchased 60,000 shares of the corporation's own common stock at $32, recording the stock at cost.

Aug. 17.   Sold 40,000 shares of treasury stock at $38, receiving cash.

Sept. 1.   Declared semiannual dividends of $0.25 on the preferred stock and $0.09 on the common stock (before the stock dividend). In addition, a 1% common stock dividend was declared on the common stock outstanding, to be capitalized at the fair market value of the common stock, which is estimated at $40.

Oct. 31.   Paid the cash dividends and issued the certificates for the common stock dividend.

Instructions

Journalize the transactions.

Comprehensive Problem 4

✔ C. Total assets,
$13,500,000

GENERAL LEDGER

Selected transactions completed by Equinox Products Inc. during the fiscal year ended December 31, 20Y8, were as follows:

A.   Issued 15,000 shares of $20 par common stock at $30, receiving cash.

B.   Issued 4,000 shares of $80 par preferred 5% stock at $100, receiving cash.

C.   Issued $500,000 of 10-year, 5% bonds at 104, with interest payable semiannually.

D.   Declared a quarterly dividend of $0.50 per share on common stock and $1.00 per share on preferred stock. On the date of record, 100,000 shares of common stock were outstanding, no treasury shares were held, and 20,000 shares of preferred stock were outstanding.

E.   Paid the cash dividends declared in (D).

F.   Purchased 8,000 shares of treasury common stock at $33 per share.

G.   Declared a $1.00 quarterly cash dividend per share on preferred stock. On the date of record, 20,000 shares of preferred stock had been issued.

H.   Paid the cash dividends to the preferred stockholders.

I.   Sold, at $38 per share, 2,600 shares of treasury common stock purchased in (F).

J.   Recorded the payment of semiannual interest on the bonds issued in (C) and the amortization of the premium for six months. The amortization is determined using the straight-line method.

Instructions

1. Journalize the selected transactions.

2. After all of the transactions for the year ended December 31, 20Y8, had been posted [including the transactions recorded in part (1) and all adjusting entries], the data that follow were taken from the records of Equinox Products Inc.

Income statement data:

Advertising expense	$ 150,000
Cost of goods sold	3,700,000
Delivery expense	30,000
Depreciation expense—office buildings and equipment	30,000
Depreciation expense—store buildings and equipment	100,000
Income tax expense	140,500
Interest expense	21,000
Interest revenue	30,000
Miscellaneous administrative expense	7,500
Miscellaneous selling expense	14,000
Office rent expense	50,000
Office salaries expense	170,000
Office supplies expense	10,000
Sales	5,313,000
Sales commissions	185,000
Sales salaries expense	385,000
Store supplies expense	21,000

Retained earnings and balance sheet data:

Accounts payable	$ 194,300
Accounts receivable	545,000
Accumulated depreciation—office buildings and equipment	1,580,000
Accumulated depreciation—store buildings and equipment	4,126,000
Allowance for doubtful accounts	8,450
Bonds payable, 5%, due in 10 years	500,000
Cash	282,850
Common stock, $20 par (400,000 shares authorized; 100,000 shares issued, 94,600 outstanding)	2,000,000
Dividends:	
Cash dividends for common stock	155,120
Cash dividends for preferred stock	100,000
Goodwill	700,000
Income tax payable	44,000
Interest receivable	1,200
Inventory (December 31, 20Y8), at lower of cost (FIFO) or market	778,000
Office buildings and equipment	4,320,000
Paid-in capital from sale of treasury stock	13,000
Excess of issue price over par—common stock	886,800
Excess of issue price over par—preferred stock	150,000
Preferred 5% stock, $80 par (30,000 shares authorized; 20,000 shares issued)	1,600,000
Premium on bonds payable	19,000
Prepaid expenses	27,400
Retained earnings, January 1, 20Y8	8,197,220
Store buildings and equipment	12,560,000
Treasury stock (5,400 shares of common stock at cost of $33 per share)	178,200

A. Prepare a multiple-step income statement for the year ended December 31, 20Y8.

B. Prepare a retained earnings statement for the year ended December 31, 20Y8.

C. Prepare a balance sheet in report form as of December 31, 20Y8.

Analysis for Decision Making

REAL WORLD

ADM-1   Continuing Company Analysis—Amazon and Walmart: Earnings per share

Amazon.com, Inc. is one of the largest Internet retailers in the world. Walmart is the largest retailer in the United States. Amazon and Walmart compete in similar markets; however, Walmart sells through both traditional retail stores and the Internet, while Amazon sells only through the Internet. Earnings and common stock outstanding information was obtained from recent financial statements for both companies as follows (in millions):

	Amazon	Walmart
Net income (loss)	$(241)	$16,363
Average number of common shares outstanding	462	3,230

A. Determine the earnings per share for each company. Neither company had preferred stock outstanding. (Round to the nearest cent.)

B. Which company appears more profitable from an earnings-per-share perspective?

C. ━━━━▶ The market price of Amazon common stock was $437 per share at a time when Walmart's was $72 per share. How would you explain this difference in market price given the earnings per share computed in (A) for both companies?

REAL WORLD

ADM-2   Pacific Gas and Electric: Earnings per share

Pacific Gas and Electric Company is a large gas and electric utility operating in northern and central California. Three recent years of financial data for Pacific Gas and Electric are as follows (in millions):

	Year 3	Year 2	Year 1
Net income	$1,450	$828	$830
Preferred dividends	14	14	14
Average number of common shares outstanding	468	444	424

A. Determine the earnings per share for Years 1–3. (Round to the nearest cent.)

B. ━━━━▶ Interpret the trend in earnings per share using horizontal analysis for the three years in terms of the change in earnings and average shares outstanding.

REAL WORLD

ADM-3   Caterpillar: Earnings per share

Caterpillar Inc. is the world's leading manufacturer of construction and mining equipment. In addition, Birinyi Associates identified Caterpillar as one of the top five companies to repurchase their own shares in a recent year.[12] Three recent years of earnings and average common shares outstanding data for Caterpillar are as follows (in millions):

	Year 3	Year 2	Year 1
Net income	$3,695	$3,789	$5,681
Average number of common shares outstanding	617.2	645.2	652.6

A. Determine the earnings per share for Years 1–3. Caterpillar had no preferred stock outstanding. (Round to the nearest cent.)

B. ━━━━▶ Interpret the trend in earnings per share using horizontal analysis for the three years in terms of the change in earnings and average shares outstanding.

[12] Laura Lorenzetti, "5 Biggest Share Buybacks of 2014," *Fortune*, May 29, 2014 (online edition).

REAL WORLD

ADM-4 BB&T and Regions Financial: Earnings per share

BB&T Corporation and Regions Financial Corporation are large regional banking companies. The net income and average common shares outstanding for both companies were reported in recent financial reports as follows (in millions):

	BB&T	Regions Financial
Net income	$2,151	$1,090
Average number of common shares outstanding	718	1,375

In addition, BB&T had $2,603,000,000 in par value preferred stock outstanding during the period. The preferred stock had an average dividend rate of 5.7%. Regions Financial did not pay any preferred cash dividends.

A. Determine the preferred dividend for BB&T. (Round to the nearest million dollars.)
B. Determine the earnings per share for each company. (Round to the nearest cent.)
C. Which company appears more profitable from a total net income perspective?
D. Which company appears more profitable from an earnings per share perspective?
E. From a stockholder's perspective, is net income or earnings per share the better relative earnings measure between the two banks?

Take It Further

ETHICS

TIF 12-1 Ethics In Action

Tommy Gunn is a division manager for K-Cern Inc., a small pharmaceutical company. Tommy's division has been working on a new drug that has the potential to revolutionize the treatment of skin cancer. Once the drug is proven to be effective in clinical trials, it will be approved for sale by the government and patented by the company. Because of the potential market for this drug, it is highly likely that the company's revenues and net income will increase significantly when it is approved. Tommy recently saw an internal company memo indicating that the drug passed its final clinical trial and that the company has received government approval to sell the drug. The company will issue a press release announcing this news in the next two days, and this announcement is expected to result in a dramatic increase in the company's stock price. Tommy knows that there is "free money" to be made if he invests in the stock before the announcement is made. However, K-Cern has a strict policy against employee purchases of company stock outside of established employee stock purchase plans. To get around this rule, Tommy asks his father to purchase the stock for him. The next morning, Tommy's father purchases the stock with the understanding that he will split the profits with Tommy.

➤ Is Tommy behaving ethically? Why or why not?

REAL WORLD

TIF 12-2   Team Activity

In teams, select a public company that interests you. Obtain the company's most recent annual report on Form 10-K. The Form 10-K is a company's annually required filing with the Securities and Exchange Commission (SEC). It includes the company's financial statements and accompanying notes. The Form 10-K can be obtained either (A) from the investor relations section of the company's Web site or (B) by using the company search feature of the SEC's EDGAR database service found at www.sec.gov/edgar/searchedgar/companysearch.html.

Based on the information in the company's most recent annual report, determine the following:

1. Name of the corporation
2. State of incorporation
3. Nature of its operations
4. Total assets reported on the most recent balance sheet
5. Total liabilities reported on the most recent balance sheet
6. Total stockholders' equity reported on the most recent balance sheet
7. Total revenues reported on the most recent income statement
8. Net income reported on the most recent income statement
9. The number of shares of common stock authorized, issued, and outstanding
10. The par value per share of each class of stock
11. Market price of the stock outstanding
12. High and low price of the stock for the past year
13. Cash dividends paid for each share of stock during the past year

TIF 12-3   Communication

Motion Designs Inc. has paid quarterly cash dividends since 20Y7. These dividends have steadily increased from $0.05 per share to the latest dividend declaration of $0.50 per share. The board of directors would like to continue this trend and is hesitant to suspend or decrease the amount of quarterly dividends. Unfortunately, sales dropped sharply in the fourth quarter of 20Y8 due to worsening economic conditions and increased competition. As a result, the board is uncertain as to whether it should declare a dividend for the last quarter of 20Y8.

On October 1, 20Y8, Motion Designs Inc. borrowed $4,000,000 from Valley National Bank to use in modernizing its retail stores and to expand its product line in response to changes in its industry. The terms of the 10-year, 6% loan require Motion Designs to:

- Pay monthly interest on the last day of the month.
- Pay $400,000 of the principal each October 1, beginning in 20Y9.
- Maintain a current ratio (current assets ÷ current liabilities) of 2.
- Maintain a minimum balance (a compensating balance) of $100,000 in its Valley National Bank account.

On December 31, 20Y8, $1,000,000 of the $4,000,000 loan had been disbursed in modernization of the retail stores and in expansion of the product line. Motion Designs Inc.'s balance sheet as of December 31, 20Y8, follows:

Motion Designs Inc. Balance Sheet December 31, 20Y8			
Assets			
Current assets:			
Cash..		$ 250,000	
Marketable securities.........................		3,000,000	
Accounts reveivable..........................	$ 800,000		
Allowance for doubtful accounts	(50,000)		
Accounts receivable, net		750,000	
Inventory.....................................		2,980,000	
Prepaid expenses		20,000	
Total current assets			$ 7,000,000
Property, plant, and equipment:			
Land		$1,500,000	
Buildings	$ 5,050,000		
Accumulated depreciation—buildings............	(1,140,000)		
Buildings, book value		3,910,000	
Equipment....................................	$ 3,320,000		
Accumulated depreciation equipment	(730,000)		
Equipment, book value		2,590,000	
Total property, plant, and equipment....			8,000,000
Total assets			$15,000,000
Liabilities			
Current liabilities:			
Accounts payable............................	$ 1,590,000		
Notes payable (Valley National Bank).........	400,000		
Salaries payable.............................	10,000		
Total current liabilities		$2,000,000	
Long-term liabilities:			
Notes payable (Valley National Bank).........		3,600,000	
Total liabilities...................................			$ 5,600,000
Stockholders' Equity			
Paid-in capital:			
Common stock, $25 par (200,000 shares authorized, 180,000 shares issued).........	$ 4,500,000		
Excess of issue price over par................	270,000		
Total paid-in capital......................		$4,770,000	
Retained earnings...............................		4,630,000	
Total stockholders' equity......................			9,400,000
Total liabilities and stockholders' equity			$15,000,000

The board of directors is scheduled to meet January 10, 20Y9, to discuss the results of operations for 20Y8 and to consider the declaration of dividends for the fourth quarter of 20Y8. The chairman of the board, Lord Matt Cengage, has asked for your advice on the declaration of dividends.

➤ Write a brief memo to the chairman of the board, outlining the factors that the board should consider in deciding whether to declare a cash dividend.

Statement of Cash Flows

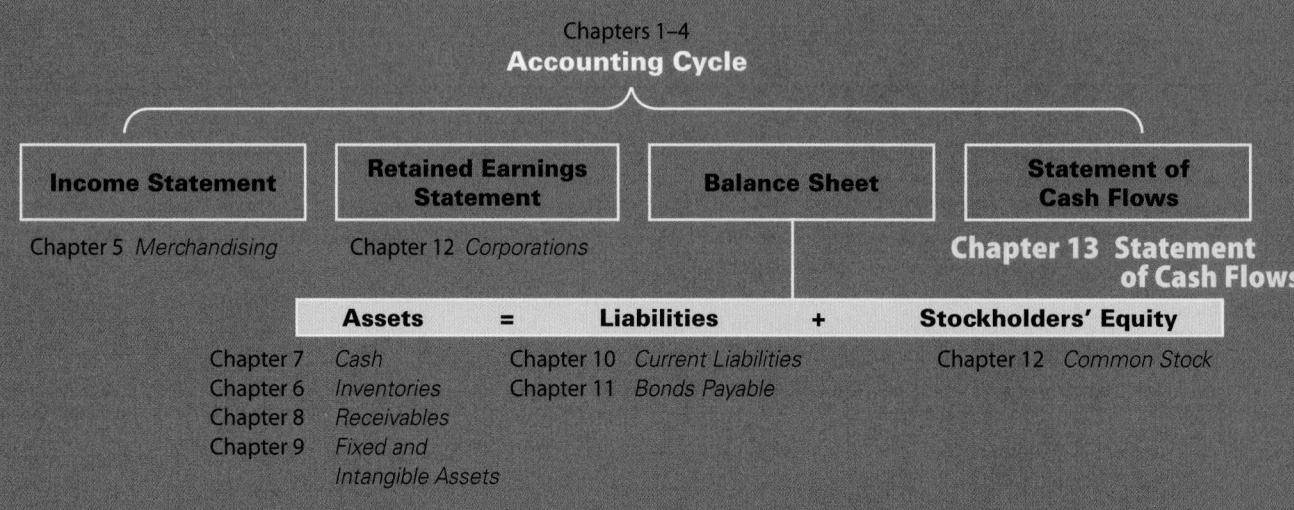

Chapters 1–4
Accounting Cycle

Income Statement	Retained Earnings Statement	Balance Sheet	Statement of Cash Flows

Chapter 5 *Merchandising*   Chapter 12 *Corporations*   **Chapter 13 Statement of Cash Flows**

Assets	=	Liabilities	+	Stockholders' Equity

Chapter 7   *Cash*   Chapter 10 *Current Liabilities*   Chapter 12   *Common Stock*
Chapter 6   *Inventories*   Chapter 11 *Bonds Payable*
Chapter 8   *Receivables*
Chapter 9   *Fixed and Intangible Assets*

Chapter 14
Financial Statement Analysis

Statement of Retained Earnings

Retained earnings, Jan. 1	$XXX
Net income	$ XXX
Dividends	(XXX)

Income Statement

Sales	$XXX
Cost of goods sold	XXX
Gross profit	$XXX
Operating expenses:	
Advertising expense	$XXX
Depreciation expense	XXX
Wages expense	XXX
Utilities expense	XXX
...	XXX
...	XXX
Total operating expenses	XXX
Income from operations	$XXX
Other revenue and expense	XXX
Net income	$XXX

Statement of Cash Flows

Cash flows from operating activities	$XXX
Cash flows from investing activities	XXX
Cash flows from financing activities	XXX
Change in cash	$XXX
Cash, January 1	XXX
Cash, December 31	$XXX

Cur...		
Ca...		
Ac...		
In...		
Property, plant and equipment	$XXX	
Intangible assets	XXX	
Total long-term assets		XXX
Total assets		$XXX
Liabilities:		
Current liabilities	$XXX	
Long-term liabilities	XXX	
Total liabilities		$XXX
Stockholders' equity:		
Retained earnings	$XXX	
Common stock	XXX	
Total stockholders' equity		XXX
Total liabilities and stockholders' equity		$XXX

National Beverage Corp.

Suppose you were to receive $100 from an event. Would it make a difference what the event was? Yes, it would! If you received $100 for your birthday, then it's a gift. If you received $100 as a result of working part time for a week, then it's the result of your effort. If you received $100 as a loan, then it's money that you will have to pay back in the future. If you received $100 as a result of selling your iPod, then it's the result of selling an asset. Thus, $100 received can be associated with different types of events, and these events have different meanings to you, and different implications for your future. You would much rather receive a $100 gift than take out a $100 loan. Likewise, company stakeholders view inflows and outflows of cash differently, depending on their source.

Companies are required to report information about the events causing a change in cash over a period of time. This information is reported on the statement of cash flows. One such company is **National Beverage**, which is an alternative beverage company, known for its innovative soft drinks, enhanced juices and waters, and fortified powders and supplements. You have probably seen the company's **Shasta** and **Faygo** soft drinks, or **LaCroix**, **Everfresh**, and **Crystal Bay** drinks at your local grocery or convenience store. As with any company, cash is important to National Beverage. Without cash, National Beverage would be unable to expand its brands, distribute its products, support extreme sports, or provide a return for its owners. Thus, its managers are concerned about the sources and uses of cash.

In previous chapters, we have used the income statement, balance sheet, statement of retained earnings, and other information to analyze the effects of management decisions on a business's financial position and operating performance. In this chapter, we focus on the events causing a change in cash by presenting the preparation and use of the statement of cash flows.

What's Covered

Statement of Cash Flows

Cash Flows	Operating Activities — Indirect Method	Investing Activities	Financing Activities	Reporting Cash Flows
■ Types of Cash Flows (Obj. 1) ■ Direct Method (Obj. 1) ■ Indirect Method (Obj. 1) ■ Noncash Transactions (Obj. 1)	■ Net Income (Obj. 2) ■ Noncash Expenses (Obj. 2) ■ Gains and Losses (Obj. 2) ■ Current Assets and Liabilities (Obj. 2)	■ Land (Obj. 3) ■ Buildings (Obj. 3)	■ Bonds Payable (Obj. 4) ■ Common Stock (Obj. 4) ■ Dividends and Dividends Payable (Obj. 4)	■ Preparing the Statement of Cash Flows (Obj. 5)

Learning Objectives

Obj. 1   Describe the cash flow activities reported on the statement of cash flows.

Obj. 2   Prepare the cash flows from operating activities section of the statement of cash flows using the indirect method.

Obj. 3   Prepare the cash flows from investing activities section of the statement of cash flows.

Obj. 4   Prepare the cash flows from financing activities section of the statement of cash flows.

Obj. 5   Prepare a statement of cash flows.

Analysis for Decision Making

Describe and illustrate the use of free cash flow in evaluating a company's cash flow.

Objective 1

Describe the cash flow activities reported on the statement of cash flows.

Reporting Cash Flows

The **statement of cash flows** reports a company's cash inflows and outflows for a period.[1] The statement of cash flows provides useful information about a company's ability to do the following:

■ Generate cash from operations
■ Maintain and expand its operating capacity
■ Meet its financial obligations
■ Pay dividends

The statement of cash flows is used by managers in evaluating past operations and in planning future investing and financing activities. It is also used by external users such as investors and creditors to assess a company's profit potential and ability to pay its debt and pay dividends.

The statement of cash flows reports three types of cash flow activities, as follows:

note:

The statement of cash flows reports cash flows from operating, investing, and financing activities.

1. **Cash flows from operating activities** are the cash flows from transactions that affect the net income of the company.

   Example: Purchase and sale of merchandise by a retailer.

2. **Cash flows from investing activities** are the cash flows from transactions that affect investments in the noncurrent assets of the company.

   Example: Purchase and sale of fixed assets, such as equipment and buildings.

3. **Cash flows from financing activities** are the cash flows from transactions that affect the debt and equity of the company.

   Example: Issuing or retiring equity and debt securities.

---

[1] As used in this chapter, *cash* refers to cash and cash equivalents. Examples of cash equivalents include short-term, highly liquid investments, such as money market accounts, bank certificates of deposit, and U.S. Treasury bills.

The cash flows are reported on the statement of cash flows as follows:

Cash flows from operating activities	$XXX
Cash flows from investing activities	XXX
Cash flows from financing activities	XXX
Change in cash	$XXX
Cash at the beginning of the period	XXX
Cash at the end of the period	$XXX

The ending cash on the statement of cash flows equals the cash reported on the company's balance sheet at the end of the year.

Exhibit 1 illustrates the sources (increases) and uses (decreases) of cash by each of the three cash flow activities. A *source* of cash causes the cash flow to increase and is called a *cash inflow*. A *use* of cash causes cash flow to decrease and is called *cash outflow*.

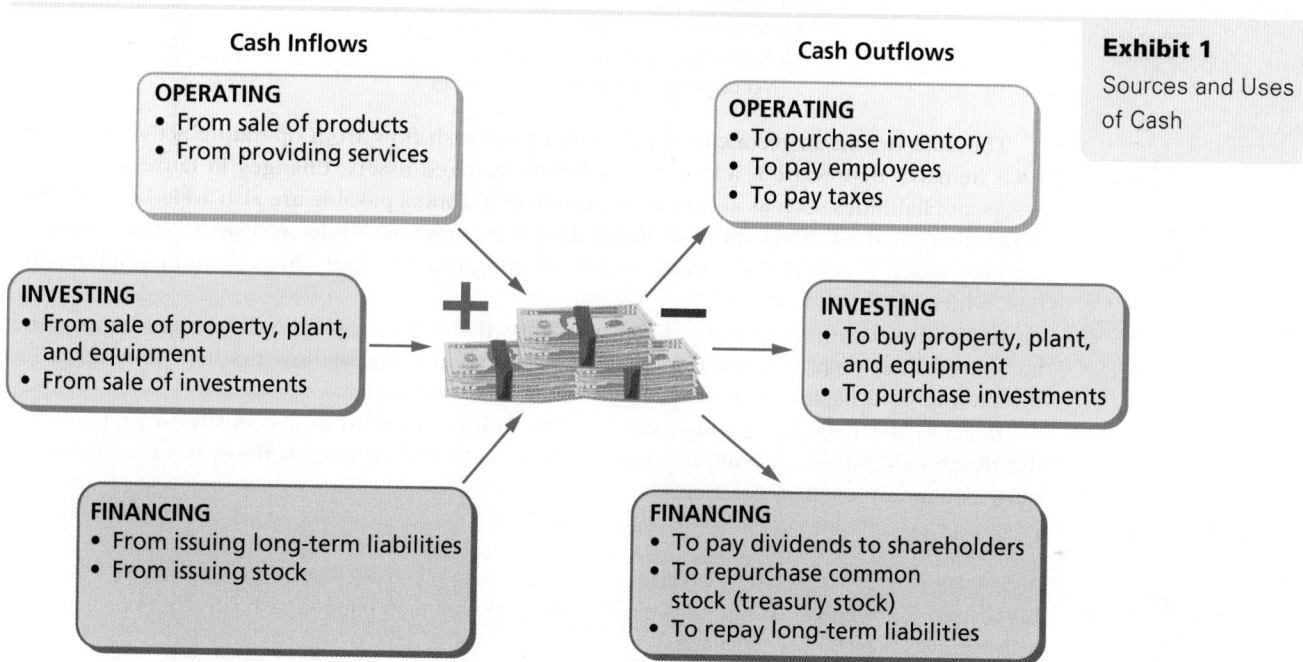

Exhibit 1

Sources and Uses of Cash

Cash Flows from Operating Activities

Cash flows from operating activities reports the cash inflows and outflows from a company's day-to-day operations. Companies may select one of two alternative methods for reporting cash flows from operating activities on the statement of cash flows:

- The direct method
- The indirect method

Both methods result in the same amount of cash flows from operating activities. They differ in the way they report cash flows from operating activities.

The Direct Method The **direct method** reports operating cash inflows (receipts) and cash outflows (payments) as follows:

Cash flows from operating activities:	
Cash received from customers	$ XXX
Cash payments for merchandise	(XXX)
Cash payments for operating expenses	(XXX)
Cash payments for interest	(XXX)
Cash payments for income taxes	(XXX)
Net cash flow from operating activities	$XXX

The primary operating cash inflow is cash received from customers. The primary operating cash outflows are cash payments for merchandise, operating expenses, interest, and income tax payments. The cash received from operating activities less the cash payments for operating activities is the net cash flow from operating activities.

The primary advantage of the direct method is that it *directly* reports cash receipts and cash payments on the statement of cash flows. Its primary disadvantage is that these data may not be readily available in the accounting records. Thus, the direct method is normally more costly to prepare and, as a result, is used infrequently in practice. For this reason, the direct method is described and illustrated in an appendix to this chapter.

The Indirect Method The **indirect method** reports cash flows from operating activities by beginning with net income and adjusting it for revenues and expenses that do not involve the receipt or payment of cash, as follows:

Cash flows from operating activities:	
Net income	$XXX
Adjustments to reconcile net income to net	
cash flow from operating activities	XXX
Net cash flow from operating activities	$XXX

The adjustments to reconcile net income to net cash flow from operating activities include such items as depreciation and gains or losses on fixed assets. Changes in current operating assets and liabilities such as accounts receivable or accounts payable are also added or deducted, depending on their effect on cash flows. In effect, these additions and deductions adjust net income, which is reported on an accrual accounting basis, to cash flows from operating activities, which is a cash basis.

A primary advantage of the indirect method is that it reconciles the differences between net income and net cash flow from operations. In doing so, it shows how net income is related to the ending cash balance that is reported on the balance sheet.

Because the data are readily available, the indirect method is less costly to prepare than the direct method. As a result, the indirect method of reporting cash flows from operations is most commonly used in practice.

Link to National Beverage

National Beverage Corp. uses the indirect method of reporting the cash flows from operating activities in its statement of cash flows.

Comparing the Direct and Indirect Methods Exhibit 2 illustrates the Cash Flows from Operating Activities section of the statement of cash flows for **NetSolutions**. Exhibit 2 shows the direct and indirect methods using the NetSolutions data from Chapter 1. As Exhibit 2 illustrates, both methods report the same amount of net cash flow from operating activities of $2,900.

Exhibit 2 Cash Flow from Operations: Direct and Indirect Methods—NetSolutions

Direct Method

Cash flows from operating activities:	
Cash received from customers.....................	$ 7,500
Cash payments for expenses	
and payments to creditors	(4,600)
Net cash flow from operating activities	$ 2,900

Indirect Method

Cash flows from operating activities:	
Net income	$3,050
Increase in accounts payable	400
Increase in supplies	(550)
Net cash flow from operating activities	$2,900

the same

Why It Matters

Cash Crunch!

The Wet Seal, Inc., a young women's clothing retailer, recently filed for bankruptcy protection. The cash flows from operating activities for the three years prior to bankruptcy (in thousands) follow:

	Year 3	Year 2	Year 1
Cash provided (used in) operating activities	$(17,589)	$(26,191)	$61,900

As can be seen, cash flows from operating activities trended into negative territory during the two years prior to the firm's bankruptcy. Thus, when cash flows from operating activities are negative, it can lead to financial distress.

Cash Flows from Investing Activities

Cash flows from investing activities show the cash inflows and outflows related to changes in a company's long-term assets. Cash flows from investing activities are reported on the statement of cash flows as follows:

Cash flows from investing activities:		
Cash inflows from investing activities	$ XXX	
Cash used for investing activities	(XXX)	
Net cash flow from investing activities		$XXX

Cash inflows from investing activities normally arise from selling fixed assets, investments, and intangible assets. Cash outflows normally include payments to purchase fixed assets, investments, and intangible assets.

For a recent year, **National Beverage** reported net cash used in investing activities of $9,725,000.

Link to National Beverage

Cash Flows from Financing Activities

Cash flows from financing activities show the cash inflows and outflows related to changes in a company's long-term liabilities and stockholders' equity. Cash flows from financing activities are reported on the statement of cash flows as follows:

Cash flows from financing activities:		
Cash inflows from financing activities	$ XXX	
Cash used for financing activities	(XXX)	
Net cash flow from financing activities		$XXX

Cash inflows from financing activities normally arise from issuing long-term debt or equity securities. For example, issuing bonds, notes payable, preferred stock, and common stock creates cash inflows from financing activities. Cash outflows from financing activities include paying cash dividends, repaying long-term debt, and acquiring treasury stock.

For a recent year, **National Beverage** reported net cash used in financing activities of $25,771,000.

Link to National Beverage

Why It Matters

Growing Pains

Twitter, Inc. is a global social media platform used for real-time self-expression and conversation within the limits of 140 character tweets. Twitter is a new, fast-growing company. The cash flows from operating, investing, and financing activities are summarized for its first three years as a public company (in thousands):

	Cash provided from (used in)			
	Operating activities	Investing activities	Financing activities	Net change for year
Year 1	$(27,935)	$ 49,443	$ (37,124)	$ (15,616)
Year 2	1,398	(1,306,066)	1,942,176	637,508
Year 3	81,796	(1,097,272)	1,691,722	676,246

One can see the significant improvement in Twitter's cash flows from operations from Year 1 to Year 3. This indicates that Twitter is succeeding as a new company and is able to provide cash from operations after only three years of operating as a public company. However, as a new company, Twitter must make significant investments in order to expand. This is clear in the trend in cash flows used in investing activities. Since the cash flows from operations are insufficient to fund this growth, the company must obtain cash from financing activities. We see significant sources of cash from stockholders in Year 2 and Year 3, which was used to expand and provide future flexibility.

Noncash Investing and Financing Activities

A company may enter into transactions involving investing and financing activities that do not *directly* affect cash. For example, a company may issue common stock to retire long-term debt. Although this transaction does not directly affect cash, it does eliminate future cash payments for interest and for paying the bonds when they mature. Because such transactions *indirectly* affect cash flows, they are reported in a separate section of the statement of cash flows. This section usually appears at the bottom of the statement of cash flows.

Format of the Statement of Cash Flows

The statement of cash flows presents the cash flows generated by, or used for, the three activities previously discussed: operating, investing, and financing. These three activities are always reported in the same order, as shown in Exhibit 3.

Exhibit 3

Order of Reporting Statement of Cash Flows

Rundell Inc.
Statement of Cash Flows
For the Year Ended 20Y8

Cash flows from operating activities		
(List of individual items, as illustrated in Exhibit 1)	$XXX	
Net cash flow from operating activities		$XXX
Cash flows from investing activities		
(List of individual items, as illustrated in Exhibit 1)	$XXX	
Net cash flow from (used for) investing activities		XXX
Cash flows from financing activities		
(List of individual items, as illustrated in Exhibit 1)	$XXX	
Net cash flow from (used for) financing activities		XXX
Change in cash		$XXX
Cash at the beginning of the period		XXX
Cash at the end of the period		$XXX
Noncash investing and financing activities		$XXX

No Cash Flow per Share

Cash flow per share is sometimes reported in the financial press. As reported, cash flow per share is normally computed as *cash flow from operations divided by the number of common shares outstanding*. However, such reporting may be misleading because of the following:

- Users may misinterpret cash flow per share as the per-share amount available for dividends. This would not be the case if the cash generated by operations is required for repaying loans or for reinvesting in the business.
- Users may misinterpret cash flow per share as equivalent to (or better than) earnings per share.

For these reasons, the financial statements, including the statement of cash flows, should not report cash flow per share.

Check Up Corner 13-1 | Classifications of Cash Flows

During its first month of operations, Templeton Company had the following cash transactions:

A. Issued 30,000 shares of common stock.
B. Purchased a new piece of equipment.
C. Sold merchandise to customers.
D. Paid employees' wages.
E. Paid a dividend.

Identify whether each of these transactions would be reported as an operating, investing, or financing activity on the statement of cash flows.

Solution:

A. Financing — Issued 30,000 shares of common stock.

B. Investing — Purchased a new piece of equipment.

C. Operating — Sold merchandise to customers.

D. Operating — Paid employees' wages.

E. Financing — Paid a dividend.

Operating activities show the cash inflows and outflows from a company's day-to-day operations.

Investing activities show the cash inflows and outflows related to changes in a company's long-term assets.

Financing activities show the cash inflows and outflows related to changes in a company's long-term liabilities and stockholders' equity.

Check Up Corner

Cash Flows from Operating Activities— The Indirect Method

Objective 2

Prepare the cash flows from operating activities section of the statement of cash flows using the indirect method.

The indirect method of reporting cash flows from operating activities uses the logic that a change in any balance sheet account (including cash) can be analyzed in terms of changes in the other balance sheet accounts. Thus, by analyzing changes in noncash balance sheet accounts, any change in the cash account can be *indirectly* determined.

To illustrate, the accounting equation can be solved for cash as follows:

$$\text{Assets} = \text{Liabilities} + \text{Stockholders' Equity}$$
$$\text{Cash} + \text{Noncash Assets} = \text{Liabilities} + \text{Stockholders' Equity}$$
$$\text{Cash} = \text{Liabilities} + \text{Stockholders' Equity} - \text{Noncash Assets}$$

Therefore, any change in the cash account can be determined by analyzing changes in the liability, stockholders' equity, and noncash asset accounts as follows:

Change in Cash = *Change* in Liabilities + *Change* in Stockholders' Equity − *Change* in Noncash Assets

Under the indirect method, there is no order in which the balance sheet accounts must be analyzed. However, net income (or net loss) is the first amount reported on the statement of cash flows. Because net income (or net loss) is a component of any change in Retained Earnings, the first account normally analyzed is Retained Earnings.

To illustrate the indirect method, the income statement and comparative balance sheets for **Rundell Inc.**, shown in Exhibit 4, are used. Ledger accounts and other data supporting the income statement and balance sheet are presented as needed.[2]

Exhibit 4

Income Statement and Comparative Balance Sheet

Rundell Inc.
Income Statement
For the Year Ended December 31, 20Y8

Sales		$1,180,000
Cost of goods sold		790,000
Gross profit		$ 390,000
Operating expenses:		
Depreciation expense	$ 7,000	
Other operating expenses	196,000	
Total operating expenses		203,000
Income from operations		$ 187,000
Other revenue and expense:		
Gain on sale of land	$ 12,000	
Interest expense	(8,000)	4,000
Income before income tax		$ 191,000
Income tax expense		83,000
Net income		$ 108,000

Rundell Inc.
Comparative Balance Sheet
December 31, 20Y8 and 20Y7

	20Y8	20Y7	Increase (Decrease)
Assets			
Cash	$ 97,500	$ 26,000	$ 71,500
Accounts receivable (net)	74,000	65,000	9,000
Inventories	172,000	180,000	(8,000)
Land	80,000	125,000	(45,000)
Building	260,000	200,000	60,000
Accumulated depreciation—building	(65,300)	(58,300)	(7,000)*
Total assets	$618,200	$537,700	$ 80,500
Liabilities			
Accounts payable (merchandise creditors)	$ 43,500	$ 46,700	$ (3,200)
Accrued expenses payable (operating expenses)	26,500	24,300	2,200
Income taxes payable	7,900	8,400	(500)
Dividends payable	14,000	10,000	4,000
Bonds payable	100,000	150,000	(50,000)
Total liabilities	$191,900	$239,400	$(47,000)
Stockholders' Equity			
Common stock, $2 par	$ 24,000	$ 16,000	$ 8,000
Paid-in capital in excess of par	120,000	80,000	40,000
Retained earnings	282,300	202,300	80,000
Total stockholders' equity	$426,300	$298,300	$128,000
Total liabilities and stockholders' equity	$618,200	$537,700	$ 80,500

*There is a $7,000 increase to Accumulated Depreciation—Building, which is a contra asset account. As a result, the $7,000 increase in this account must be subtracted in summing to the increase in total assets of $80,500.

[2] An appendix that discusses using a spreadsheet (work sheet) as an aid in assembling data for the statement of cash flows is presented at the end of this chapter. This appendix illustrates the use of this spreadsheet in reporting cash flows from operating activities using the indirect method.

Net Income

Rundell Inc.'s net income for 20Y8 is $108,000 as shown in the income statement in Exhibit 4. Since net income is closed to Retained Earnings, net income also helps explain the change in retained earnings during the year. The retained earnings account for Rundell is as follows:

Account Retained Earnings				Account No.	
				Balance	
Date	Item	Debit	Credit	Debit	Credit
20Y8					
Jan. 1	Balance				202,300
June 30	Dividends declared	14,000			188,300
Dec. 31	Net income		108,000		296,300
31	Dividends declared	14,000			282,300

The retained earnings account indicates that the $80,000 ($108,000 − $28,000) change resulted from net income of $108,000 and cash dividends of $28,000. The net income of $108,000 is the first amount reported in the Cash Flows from Operating Activities section. The impact of the dividends of $28,000 on cash flows will be included as part of financing activities.

Adjustments to Net Income

The net income of $108,000 reported by Rundell Inc. does not equal the cash flows from operating activities for the period. This is because net income is determined using the accrual method of accounting.

Under the accrual method of accounting, revenues and expenses are recorded at different times from when cash is received or paid. For example, merchandise may be sold on account and the cash received at a later date. Likewise, insurance premiums may be paid in the current period but expensed in a following period.

Thus, under the indirect method, adjustments to net income must be made to determine cash flows from operating activities. The typical adjustments to net income are shown in Exhibit 5.[3]

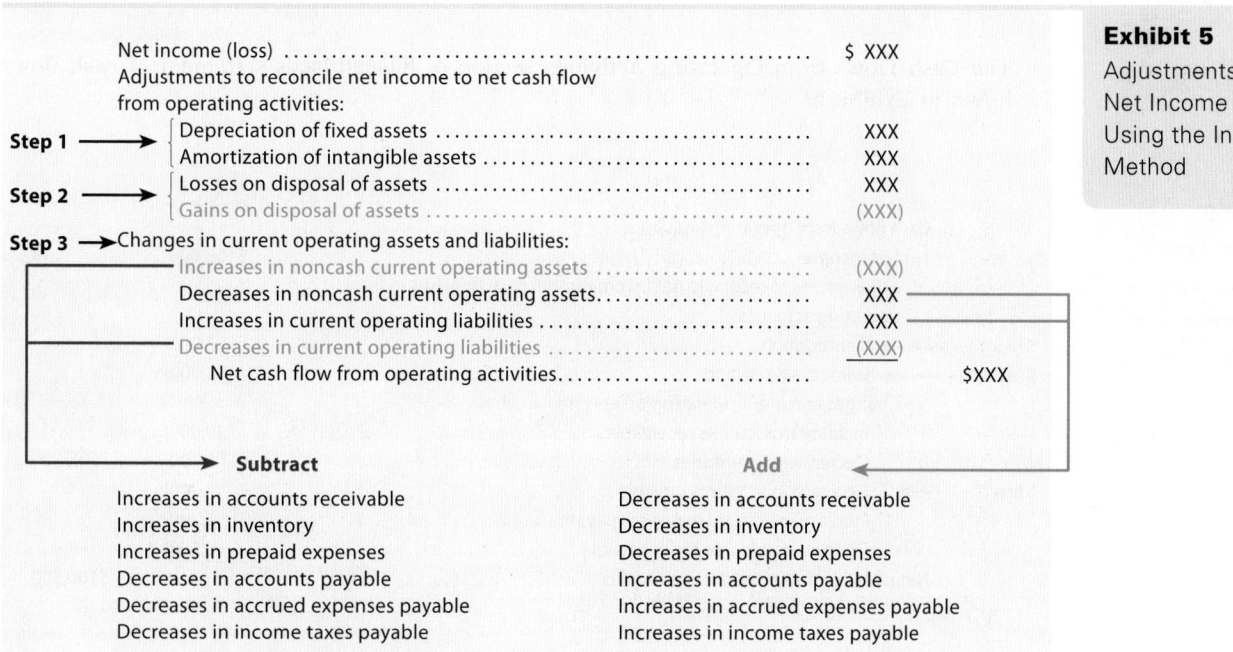

Exhibit 5
Adjustments to Net Income (Loss) Using the Indirect Method

[3] Other items that also require adjustments to net income to obtain cash flows from operating activities include amortization of bonds payable discounts (add), losses on debt retirement (add), amortization of bonds payable premiums (deduct), and gains on retirement of debt (deduct). These topics are covered in advanced accounting courses.

Net income is normally adjusted to cash flows from operating activities, using the following steps:

- Step 1. Expenses that do not affect cash are added. Such expenses decrease net income but do not involve cash payments.

  Example: Depreciation of fixed assets and amortization of intangible assets are added to net income.

- Step 2. Losses on the disposal of assets are added and gains on the disposal of assets are deducted. The disposal (sale) of assets is an investing activity rather than an operating activity. However, such losses and gains are reported as part of net income. As a result, any *losses* on disposal of assets are *added* back to net income. Likewise, any *gains* on disposal of assets are *deducted* from net income.

  Example: Land costing $100,000 is sold for $90,000. The loss of $10,000 is added back to net income.

- Step 3. Changes in current operating assets and liabilities are added or deducted as follows:

  - Increases in noncash current operating assets are deducted.
  - Decreases in noncash current operating assets are added.
  - Increases in current operating liabilities are added.
  - Decreases in current operating liabilities are deducted.

  Example: A sale of $10,000 on account increases sales, accounts receivable, and net income by $10,000. However, cash is not affected. Thus, the $10,000 increase in accounts receivable is deducted. Similar adjustments are required for the changes in the other current asset and liability accounts, such as inventory, prepaid expenses, accounts payable, accrued expenses payable, and income taxes payable, as shown in Exhibit 5.

Link to National Beverage   In a recent statement of cash flows, **National Beverage** reported changes in current asset and liability accounts for accounts receivable, inventories, prepaid assets, accounts payable, and accrued liabilities.

The Cash Flows from Operating Activities section of **Rundell Inc.**'s statement of cash flows is shown in Exhibit 6.

Exhibit 6
Net Cash Flow from Operating Activities—Indirect Method

Cash flows from operating activities:		
Net income		$108,000
Adjustments to reconcile net income to net cash flow from operating activities:		
Step 1 → Depreciation		7,000
Step 2 → Gain on sale of land		(12,000)
Changes in current operating assets and liabilities:		
Increase in accounts receivable.............................		(9,000)
Decrease in inventories		8,000
Step 3 → Decrease in accounts payable		(3,200)
Increase in accrued expenses payable		2,200
Decrease in income taxes payable		(500)
Net cash flow from operating activities		$100,500

Rundell's net income of $108,000 is converted to cash flows from operating activities of $100,500 as follows:

- Step 1. Add depreciation of $7,000.

    Analysis: The comparative balance sheet in Exhibit 4 indicates that Accumulated Depreciation—Building increased by $7,000. The following account indicates that depreciation for the year was $7,000 for the building:

Account Accumulated Depreciation—Building				Account No.	
				Balance	
Date	**Item**	**Debit**	**Credit**	**Debit**	**Credit**
20Y8					
Jan. 1	Balance				58,300
Dec. 31	Depreciation for year		7,000		65,300

- Step 2. Deduct the gain on the sale of land of $12,000.

    Analysis: The income statement in Exhibit 4 reports a gain of $12,000 from the sale of land. The proceeds, which include the gain, are reported in the Investing section of the statement of cash flows.[4] Thus, the gain of $12,000 is deducted from net income in determining cash flows from operating activities.

- Step 3. Add and deduct changes in current operating assets and liabilities excluding cash.

    Analysis: The increases and decreases in the current operating asset and current liability accounts excluding cash are as follows:

	December 31		**Increase**
Accounts	**20Y8**	**20Y7**	**(Decrease)**
Accounts Receivable (net)	$ 74,000	$ 65,000	$ 9,000
Inventories	172,000	180,000	(8,000)
Accounts Payable (merchandise creditors)	43,500	46,700	(3,200)
Accrued Expenses Payable (operating expenses)	26,500	24,300	2,200
Income Taxes Payable	7,900	8,400	(500)

Accounts receivable (net): The $9,000 increase is deducted from net income. This is because the $9,000 increase in accounts receivable indicates that sales on account were $9,000 more than the cash received from customers. Thus, sales (and net income) includes $9,000 that was not received in cash during the year.

Inventories: The $8,000 decrease is added to net income. This is because the $8,000 decrease in inventories indicates that the cost of goods *sold* exceeds the cost of the merchandise *purchased* during the year by $8,000. In other words, the cost of goods sold includes $8,000 of merchandise from inventory that was not purchased (used cash) during the year.

Accounts payable (merchandise creditors): The $3,200 decrease is deducted from net income. This is because a decrease in accounts payable indicates that the cash *payments* to merchandise creditors exceed the merchandise *purchased on account* by $3,200. Therefore, the cost of goods sold is $3,200 less than the cash paid to merchandise creditors during the year.

Accrued expenses payable (operating expenses): The $2,200 increase is added to net income. This is because an increase in accrued expenses payable indicates that operating expenses exceed the cash payments for operating expenses by $2,200. In other words, operating expenses reported on the income statement include $2,200 that did not require a cash outflow during the year.

Income taxes payable: The $500 decrease is deducted from net income. This is because a decrease in income taxes payable indicates that taxes paid exceed the amount of taxes incurred during the year by $500. In other words, the amount reported on the income statement for income tax expense is less than the amount paid by $500.

---

[4] The reporting of the proceeds (cash flows) from the sale of land as part of investing activities is discussed later in this chapter.

Check Up Corner 13-2   Cash Flows from Operating Activities

Omicron Inc. reported net income of $120,000 for 20Y2. In addition, the income statement reported $12,000 of depreciation expense and a $15,000 loss on the disposal of equipment. The current operating assets and liabilities from the company's comparative balance sheet are as follows:

	12/31/20Y2	12/31/20Y1	Increase (Decrease)
Accounts receivable	$18,240	$13,240	$ 5,000
Accounts payable	11,200	13,200	(2,000)

Prepare the Cash Flows from Operating Activities section of the statement of cash flows, using the indirect method.

Solution:

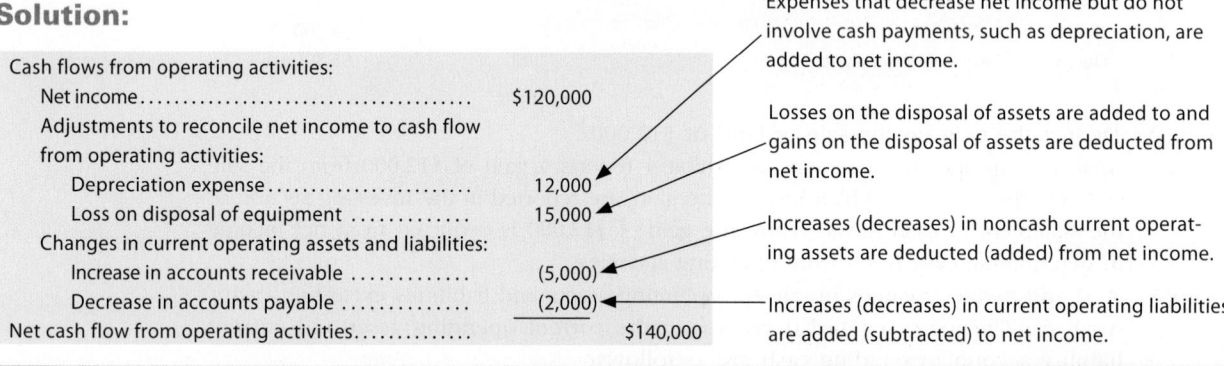

Cash flows from operating activities:

Net income.....................................	$120,000
Adjustments to reconcile net income to cash flow from operating activities:	
Depreciation expense........................	12,000
Loss on disposal of equipment	15,000
Changes in current operating assets and liabilities:	
Increase in accounts receivable	(5,000)
Decrease in accounts payable	(2,000)
Net cash flow from operating activities.............	$140,000

Expenses that decrease net income but do not involve cash payments, such as depreciation, are added to net income.

Losses on the disposal of assets are added to and gains on the disposal of assets are deducted from net income.

Increases (decreases) in noncash current operating assets are deducted (added) from net income.

Increases (decreases) in current operating liabilities are added (subtracted) to net income.

Check Up Corner

Objective 3

Prepare the cash flows from investing activities section of the statement of cash flows.

Cash Flows from Investing Activities

Cash flows from investing activities reports the cash inflows and outflows related to changes in a company's long-term assets. **Rundell Inc.**'s comparative balance sheet in Exhibit 4 lists land, building, and accumulated depreciation—building as long-term assets. Similar to preparing the Cash Flows from Operating Activities section, each change in each long-term asset account is analyzed for its effect on cash flows from investing activities.

Land

The $45,000 decline in the land account of **Rundell Inc.** was from two transactions, as follows:

Account Land						**Account No.**	
						Balance	
Date		**Item**	**Debit**	**Credit**	**Debit**	**Credit**	
20Y8							
Jan. 1		Balance			125,000		
June 8		Sold for $72,000 cash		60,000	65,000		
Oct. 12		Purchased for $15,000 cash	15,000		80,000		

The June 8 transaction is the sale of land with a cost of $60,000 for $72,000 in cash. The $72,000 proceeds from the sale are reported in the Investing Activities section as follows:

Cash flows from investing activities:

Cash received from sale of land $72,000

The proceeds of $72,000 include the $12,000 gain on the sale of land and the $60,000 cost (book value) of the land. As shown in Exhibit 6, the $12,000 gain in deducted from net income in the Cash Flows from Operating Activities section. This is so that the $12,000 cash inflow related to the gain is not included twice as a cash inflow.

The October 12 transaction is the purchase of land for cash of $15,000. This transaction is reported as an outflow of cash in the Investing Activities section as follows:

Cash flows from investing activities:

Cash paid for purchase of land .... $(15,000)

Building and Accumulated Depreciation—Building

The building account of **Rundell Inc.** increased by $60,000, and the accumulated depreciation—building account increased by $7,000, as follows:

Account Building				**Account No.**	
				Balance	
Date	**Item**	**Debit**	**Credit**	**Debit**	**Credit**
20Y8					
Jan. 1	Balance			200,000	
Dec. 27	Purchased for cash	60,000		260,000	

Account Accumulated Depreciation—Building				**Account No.**	
				Balance	
Date	**Item**	**Debit**	**Credit**	**Debit**	**Credit**
20Y8					
Jan. 1	Balance				58,300
Dec. 31	Depreciation for the year		7,000		65,300

The purchase of a building for cash of $60,000 is reported as an outflow of cash in the Investing Activities section as follows:

Cash flows from investing activities:

Cash paid for purchase of building .... $(60,000)

The credit in the accumulated depreciation—building account represents depreciation expense for the year. This depreciation expense of $7,000 on the building was added to net income in determining cash flows from operating activities, as reported in Exhibit 6.

In a recent statement of cash flows, **National Beverage** reported cash used for purchases of property, plant, and equipment of $11,630,000 and cash received for selling property, plant, and equipment of $1,905,000 resulting in net cash used for investing activities of $9,725,000.

Link to National Beverage

Check Up Corner 13-3   Cash Flows from Investing Activities

Mercury Inc. reported net income of $100,000 for 20Y2. In addition, the income statement reported $20,000 of depreciation expense and a $10,000 gain on the sale of land. The noncurrent assets from the company's comparative balance sheet are as follows:

	12/31/20Y2	12/31/20Y1	Increase (Decrease)
Land	$ 125,000	$ 225,000	$(100,000)
Equipment	500,000	400,000	100,000
Accumulated depreciation—equipment	(120,000)	(100,000)	20,000

There were no disposals of equipment, and all purchases of equipment were for cash. Prepare the Cash Flows from Investing Activities section of the statement of cash flows.

Solution:

Cash flows from investing activities:		
Cash received from sale of land................	$ 110,000	
Cash paid for purchase of equipment	(100,000)	
Net cash flow from investing activities		$10,000

Land was sold for $110,000 ($100,000 decrease in land account + $10,000 gain on the sale). This is the amount of cash received from the sale of land.

The increase in the balance of the equipment account comes from the purchase of equipment for cash.

Note: The increase in Accumulated Depreciation—Equipment is from 20Y2 depreciation expense, which is included in cash flows from operating activities.

Check Up Corner

Objective 4
Prepare the cash flows from financing activities section of the statement of cash flows.

Cash Flows from Financing Activities

Cash flows from financing activities reports the cash inflows and outflows related to changes in a company's long-term liabilities and stockholders' equity. **Rundell Inc.**'s comparative balance sheet in Exhibit 4 reports changes in bonds payable, common stock, and paid-in capital in excess of par. In addition, dividends payable has changed, which impacts retained earnings. Each change must be analyzed to determine its effect on cash flows from financing activities.

Bonds Payable

The bonds payable account of **Rundell Inc.** decreased by $50,000, as follows:

Account Bonds Payable				Account No.	
				Balance	
Date	Item	Debit	Credit	Debit	Credit
20Y8					
Jan. 1	Balance				150,000
June 1	Retired by payment of cash at face amount	50,000			100,000

This decrease is from retiring the bonds by a cash payment for their face amount. This cash outflow is reported in the Financing Activities section as follows:

Cash flows from financing activities:

Cash paid to retire bonds payable.................. $(50,000)

Common Stock

The common stock account of **Rundell Inc.** increased by $8,000, and the paid-in capital in excess of par—common stock account increased by $40,000, as follows:

Account Common Stock				Account No.	
				Balance	
Date	Item	Debit	Credit	Debit	Credit
20Y8					
Jan. 1	Balance				16,000
Nov. 1	4,000 shares issued for cash		8,000		24,000

Account *Paid-In Capital in Excess of Par—Common Stock*				Account No.	
				Balance	
Date	**Item**	**Debit**	**Credit**	**Debit**	**Credit**
20Y8					
Jan. 1	Balance				80,000
Nov. 1	4,000 shares issued for cash		40,000		120,000

These increases were from issuing 4,000 shares of common stock for $12 per share. This cash inflow is reported in the Financing Activities section as follows:

Cash flows from financing activities:

Cash received from sale of common stock $48,000

Dividends and Dividends Payable

The retained earnings account of **Rundell Inc.** indicates cash dividends of $28,000 were declared during the year. However, the following dividends payable account indicates that only $24,000 ($10,000 + $14,000) of dividends were paid during the year:

Account *Dividends Payable*				Account No.	
				Balance	
Date	**Item**	**Debit**	**Credit**	**Debit**	**Credit**
20Y8					
Jan. 1	Balance				10,000
10	Cash paid	10,000		—	—
June 30	Dividends declared		14,000		14,000
July 10	Cash paid	14,000		—	—
Dec. 31	Dividends declared		14,000		14,000

Cash dividends paid during the year can also be computed by adjusting the dividends declared during the year for the change in the dividends payable account as follows:

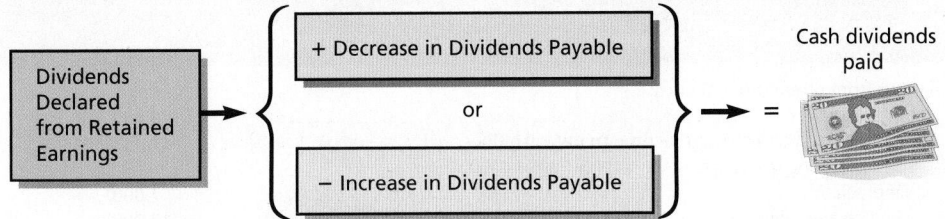

The cash dividends paid by Rundell Inc. during 20Y8 are $24,000, computed as follows:

Dividends declared ($14,000 + $14,000)	$28,000
Increase in Dividends Payable	(4,000)
Cash dividends paid	$24,000

Because dividend payments are a financing activity, the cash dividends paid of $24,000 are reported in the Financing Activities section of the statement of cash flows, as follows:

Cash flows from financing activities:

Cash paid for dividends . . . . $(24,000)

In a recent statement of cash flows, **National Beverage** reported cash used for dividends of $239,000; cash used for payment of debt of $20,000,000; and cash used for redeeming preferred stock of $6,000,000.

Link to National Beverage

Check Up Corner 13-4 Cash Flows from Financing Activities

Mohroman Inc. reported net income of $80,000 for 20Y2. The liability and equity accounts from the company's comparative balance sheet are as follows:

	12/31/20Y2	12/31/20Y1	Increase (Decrease)
Accounts payable	$ 42,680	$ 41,500	$ 1,180
Dividends payable	10,000	8,000	2,000
Bonds payable	210,000	300,000	(90,000)
Common stock, $10 par value	120,000	100,000	20,000
Excess of issue price over par value—common stock	300,000	200,000	100,000
Retained earnings	240,000	180,000	60,000

During the year, the company retired bonds payable at their face amount, declared dividends of $20,000, and issued 2,000 shares of common stock for $60 per share. Prepare the Cash Flows from Financing Activities section of the statement of cash flows.

Solution:

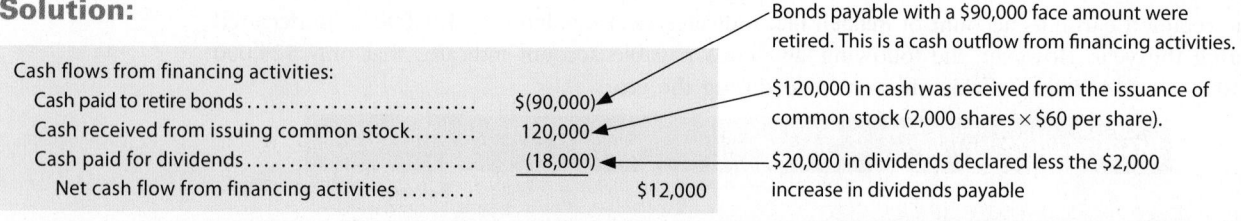

Cash flows from financing activities:		
Cash paid to retire bonds	$(90,000)	
Cash received from issuing common stock	120,000	
Cash paid for dividends	(18,000)	
Net cash flow from financing activities		$12,000

Bonds payable with a $90,000 face amount were retired. This is a cash outflow from financing activities.

$120,000 in cash was received from the issuance of common stock (2,000 shares × $60 per share).

$20,000 in dividends declared less the $2,000 increase in dividends payable

Check Up Corner

Objective 5

Prepare a statement of cash flows.

Preparing the Statement of Cash Flows

The statement of cash flows for **Rundell Inc.**, using the indirect method, is shown in Exhibit 7. The statement of cash flows indicates that cash increased by $71,500 during the year. The most significant increase in net cash flows ($100,500) was from operating activities.

Exhibit 7

Statement of Cash Flows—Indirect Method

Rundell Inc.
Statement of Cash Flows
For the Year Ended December 31, 20Y8

Cash flows from operating activities:		
Net income	$108,000	
Adjustments to reconcile net income to net cash flow from operating activities:		
Depreciation	7,000	
Gain on sale of land	(12,000)	
Changes in current operating assets and liabilities:		
Increase in accounts receivable	(9,000)	
Decrease in inventories	8,000	
Decrease in accounts payable	(3,200)	
Increase in accrued expenses payable	2,200	
Decrease in income taxes payable	(500)	
Net cash flow from operating activities		$100,500
Cash flows from investing activities:		
Cash received from sale of land	$ 72,000	
Cash paid for purchase of land	(15,000)	
Cash paid for purchase of building	(60,000)	
Net cash flow used for investing activities		(3,000)
Cash flows from financing activities:		
Cash received from sale of common stock	$ 48,000	
Cash paid to retire bonds payable	(50,000)	
Cash paid for dividends	(24,000)	
Net cash flow used for financing activities		(26,000)
Change in cash		$ 71,500
Cash at the beginning of the year		26,000
Cash at the end of the year		$ 97,500

The most significant use of cash ($26,000) was for financing activities. The ending balance of cash on December 31, 20Y8, is $97,500. This ending cash balance is also reported on the December 31, 20Y8, balance sheet shown in Exhibit 4.

In a recent statement of cash flows, National Beverage reported net cash provided by operating activities of $58,020,000; net cash used for investing activities of $9,725,000; net cash used for financing activities of $25,771,000 for a net increase in cash of $22,524,000 for the year.

Link to National Beverage

International Connection

IFRS
IFRS for Statement of Cash Flows

The statement of cash flows is required under International Financial Reporting Standards (IFRS). The statement of cash flows under IFRS is similar to that reported under U.S. GAAP in that the statement has separate sections for operating, investing, and financing activities. Like U.S. GAAP, IFRS also allow the use of either the indirect or direct method of reporting cash flows from operating activities. IFRS differ from U.S. GAAP in some minor areas, including:

- Interest paid can be reported as either an operating or a financing activity, while interest received can be reported as either an operating or an investing activity. In contrast, U.S. GAAP reports interest paid or received as an operating activity.
- Dividends paid can be reported as either an operating or a financing activity, while dividends received can be reported as either an operating or an investing activity. In contrast, U.S. GAAP reports dividends paid as a financing activity and dividends received as an operating activity.
- Cash flows to pay taxes are reported as a separate line in the operating activities, in contrast to U.S. GAAP, which does not require a separate line disclosure.

*IFRS are further discussed and illustrated in Appendix C.

Analysis for Decision Making

Free Cash Flow

A valuable tool for evaluating the profitability of a business is free cash flow. **Free cash flow** measures the operating cash flow available to a company after it purchases the property, plant, and equipment (PP&E) necessary to maintain its current operations. Since the investments in PP&E necessary to maintain current operations cannot often be determined from financial statements, analysts estimate this amount using the cash used to purchase PP&E, as shown in the statement of cash flows. Thus, free cash flow is computed as follows:

Objective
Describe and illustrate the use of free cash flow in evaluating a company's cash flow.

Cash flows from operating activities	XXX
Cash used to purchase property, plant, and equipment	(XXX)
Free cash flow	XXX

The free cash flow can be expressed as a percentage of sales in order to provide a relative measure that can be compared over time or to other companies. This ratio is computed as follows:

$$\text{Ratio of Free Cash Flow to Sales} = \frac{\text{Free Cash Flow}}{\text{Sales}}$$

Positive free cash flow is considered favorable. A company that has free cash flow is able to fund growth and acquisitions, retire debt, purchase treasury stock, and pay dividends. A company with no free cash flow may have limited financial flexibility, potentially leading to liquidity problems. As one analyst notes, "Free cash flow gives the company firepower to reduce debt and ultimately generate consistent, actual income."

To illustrate, information from the annual reports of **National Beverage** for three recent years is as follows (in thousands):

	Year 3	Year 2	Year 1
Cash flows from operating activities..........................	$ 58,020	$ 52,383	$ 40,264
Cash used to purchase property, plant, and equipment..........	11,630	12,124	9,693
Sales..	645,825	641,135	662,007

The free cash flow is computed for the three years as follows:

	Year 3	Year 2	Year 1
Cash flows from operating activities..........................	$ 58,020	$ 52,383	$40,264
Cash used to purchase property, plant, and equipment.........	(11,630)	(12,124)	(9,693)
Free cash flow	$ 46,390	$ 40,259	$30,571

As can be seen, free cash flow has increased across the three years. In Year 3, it is nearly 52% higher than in Year 1 [($46,390 − $30,571) ÷ $30,571]. The ratio of free cash flow to sales is as follows (rounded to one decimal place):

	Year 3	Year 2	Year 1
Ratio of free cash flow to sales	7.2%	6.3%	4.6%
	($46,390 ÷	($40,259 ÷	($30,571 ÷
	$645,825)	$641,135)	$662,007)

The ratio of free cash flow to sales has also increased across these three years, from 4.6% in Year 1 to 7.2% in Year 3, which is a 57% increase [(7.2% − 4.6%) ÷ 4.6%].

Make a Decision   Free Cash Flow

Financial information for **Apple Inc.** (a consumer electronics company), **The Coca-Cola Company** (a beverage company), and **Verizon Communications** (a telecommunications company) follows (in millions):

	Apple	Coca-Cola	Verizon
Sales..	$182,795	$45,998	$127,079
Cash flows from operating activities..........................	59,713	10,615	30,631
Cash used to purchase property, plant, and equipment..........	9,571	2,406	17,191

A.   Compute the free cash flow for each company.

B.   Compute the ratio of free cash flow to sales for each company. (Round to one decimal place.)

C.   Which company has the greatest free cash flow?

D.   How does Verizon differ from the other two companies?

Solution:

	Apple	Coca-Cola	Verizon
A. Cash flows from operating activities	$59,713	$10,615	$ 30,631
Cash used to purchase property, plant, and equipment	(9,571)	(2,406)	(17,191)
Free cash flow	$50,142	$ 8,209	$13,440

B.

	Apple	Coca-Cola	Verizon
Ratio of free cash flow to sales	27.4%	17.8%	10.6%
	($50,142 ÷	($8,209 ÷	($13,440 ÷
	$182,795)	$45,998)	$127,079)

C. Apple has the largest free cash flow. The ratio of free cash flow to sales is the best metric for comparing the three companies. In this comparison, the three companies, ranking from largest to smallest, are Apple, Coca-Cola, and Verizon. However, all three ratios would be considered acceptable.

D. Over 56% of Verizon's cash flows from operations are used to purchase PP&E ($17,191 ÷ $30,631), an amount much greater than the other two companies. Industries such as airlines, railroads, and telecommunications companies must invest heavily in new equipment to remain competitive. Such investments can significantly reduce free cash flow.

Make a Decision

Why It Matters

Twenty Years After

The S&P 500 is made of the 500 largest publicly traded companies in the United States. Deutsche Bank, one of the world's largest financial institutions, aggregated the free cash flow performance of today's S&P 500 companies and the S&P 500 companies from 20 years ago, as follows:

S&P 500 in aggregate (in billions, except ratio)	20 Years Ago	Currently
Free cash flow	$148	$958
Ratio of free cash flow to sales	6%	8%
Cash paid for dividends....................................	$58	$426
Cash paid for treasury stock purchases..................	30	475
Total..	$88	$901

As can be seen, the free cash flow has grown over six-fold while the ratio of free cash flow to sales has improved from 6% 20 years ago to 8% currently. Twenty years ago, $88 billion of free cash flow, or nearly 60% of free cash flow ($88 ÷ $148), was used to pay dividends and treasury stock. Currently, $901 billion of free cash flow, or 94% of free cash flow ($901 ÷ $958), is used to pay dividends and treasury stock. Compared to twenty years ago, companies are using a much greater portion of their free cash flow to return cash to stockholders. This suggests companies are seeing fewer opportunities for internal investment than 20 years ago.

Appendix 1 Spreadsheet (Work Sheet) for Statement of Cash Flows—The Indirect Method

A spreadsheet (work sheet) may be used in preparing the statement of cash flows. However, whether or not a spreadsheet (work sheet) is used, the concepts presented in this chapter are not affected.

The data for **Rundell Inc.**, presented in Exhibit 4, are used as a basis for illustrating the spreadsheet (work sheet) for the indirect method. The steps in preparing this spreadsheet (work sheet), shown in Exhibit 8, are as follows:

- Step 1. List the title of each balance sheet account in the Accounts column.
- Step 2. For each balance sheet account, enter its balance as of December 31, 20Y7, in the first column and its balance as of December 31, 20Y8, in the last column. Place the credit balances in parentheses.
- Step 3. Add the December 31, 20Y7 and 20Y8 column totals, which should total to zero.
- Step 4. Analyze the change during the year in each noncash account to determine its net increase (decrease) and classify the change as affecting cash flows from operating activities, investing activities, financing activities, or noncash investing and financing activities.

Exhibit 8   End-of-Period Spreadsheet (Work Sheet) for Statement of Cash Flows—Indirect Method

Step 2

	A	B	C	D	E	F	G
1		Rundell Inc.					
2		End-of-Period Spreadsheet (Work Sheet) for Statement of Cash Flows					
3		For the Year Ended December 31, 20Y8					
4	Accounts	Balance,		Transactions			Balance,
5		Dec. 31, 20Y7		Debit		Credit	Dec. 31, 20Y8
6	Cash	26,000	Ⓞ	71,500			97,500
7	Accounts receivable (net)	65,000	Ⓝ	9,000			74,000
8	Inventories	180,000			Ⓜ	8,000	172,000
9	Land	125,000	Ⓚ	15,000	Ⓛ	60,000	80,000
10	Building	200,000	Ⓙ	60,000			260,000
11	Accumulated depreciation—building	(58,300)			Ⓘ	7,000	(65,300)
12	Accounts payable (merchandise creditors)	(46,700)	Ⓗ	3,200			(43,500)
13	Accrued expenses payable (operating expenses)	(24,300)			Ⓖ	2,200	(26,500)
14	Income taxes payable	(8,400)	Ⓕ	500			(7,900)
15	Dividends payable	(10,000)			Ⓔ	4,000	(14,000)
16	Bonds payable	(150,000)	Ⓓ	50,000			(100,000)
17	Common stock	(16,000)			Ⓒ	8,000	(24,000)
18	Paid-in capital in excess of par	(80,000)			Ⓒ	40,000	(120,000)
19	Retained earnings	(202,300)	Ⓑ	28,000	Ⓐ	108,000	(282,300)
20	Totals Step 3 →	0		237,200		237,200	0 ← Step 3
21	Operating activities:						
22	Net income		Ⓐ	108,000			
23	Depreciation of building		Ⓘ	7,000			
24	Gain on sale of land				Ⓛ	12,000	
25	Increase in accounts receivable				Ⓝ	9,000	
26	Decrease in inventories		Ⓜ	8,000			
27	Decrease in accounts payable				Ⓗ	3,200	
28	Increase in accrued expenses payable		Ⓖ	2,200			
29	Decrease in income taxes payable				Ⓕ	500	
30	Investing activities:						
31	Sale of land		Ⓛ	72,000			
32	Purchase of land				Ⓚ	15,000	
33	Purchase of building				Ⓙ	60,000	
34	Financing activities:						
35	Issued common stock		Ⓒ	48,000			
36	Retired bonds payable				Ⓓ	50,000	
37	Declared cash dividends				Ⓑ	28,000	
38	Increase in dividends payable		Ⓔ	4,000			
39	Net increase in cash				Ⓞ	71,500	
40	Totals			249,200		249,200	
41							

Steps 4–7

- Step 5. Indicate the effect of the change on cash flows by making entries in the Transactions columns.
- Step 6. After all noncash accounts have been analyzed, enter the net increase (decrease) in cash during the period.
- Step 7. Add the Debit and Credit Transactions columns. The totals should be equal.

Analyzing Accounts

In analyzing the noncash accounts (Step 4), try to determine the type of cash flow activity (operating, investing, or financing) that led to the change in the account. As each noncash account is analyzed, an entry (Step 5) is made on the spreadsheet (work sheet) for the type of cash flow activity that caused the change. After all noncash accounts have been analyzed, an entry (Step 6) is made for the increase (decrease) in cash during the period.

The entries made on the spreadsheet are not posted to the ledger. They are only used in preparing and summarizing the data on the spreadsheet.

The order in which the accounts are analyzed is not important. However, it is more efficient to begin with Retained Earnings and proceed upward in the account listing.

Retained Earnings

The spreadsheet (work sheet) shows a Retained Earnings balance of $202,300 at December 31, 20Y7, and $282,300 at December 31, 20Y8. Thus, Retained Earnings increased $80,000 during the year. This increase is from the following:

- Net income of $108,000
- Declaring cash dividends of $28,000

To identify the cash flows from these activities, two entries are made on the spreadsheet.

The $108,000 is reported on the statement of cash flows as part of cash flows from operating activities. Thus, an entry is made in the Transactions columns on the spreadsheet, as follows:

(A)	Operating Activities—Net Income.	108,000	
	Retained Earnings		108,000

The preceding entry accounts for the net income portion of the change to Retained Earnings. It also identifies the cash flow in the bottom portion of the spreadsheet as related to operating activities.

The $28,000 of dividends is reported as a financing activity on the statement of cash flows. Thus, an entry is made in the Transactions columns on the spreadsheet, as follows:

(B)	Retained Earnings	28,000	
	Financing Activities—Declared Cash Dividends		28,000

The preceding entry accounts for the dividends portion of the change to Retained Earnings. It also identifies the cash flow in the bottom portion of the spreadsheet as related to financing activities. The $28,000 of declared dividends will be adjusted later for the actual amount of cash dividends paid during the year.

Other Accounts

The entries for the other noncash accounts are made in the spreadsheet in a manner similar to entries (A) and (B). A summary of these entries follows:

(C)	Financing Activities—Issued Common Stock.	48,000	
	Common Stock		8,000
	Paid-In Capital in Excess of Par—Common Stock		40,000
(D)	Bonds Payable.	50,000	
	Financing Activities—Retired Bonds Payable.		50,000
(E)	Financing Activities—Increase in Dividends Payable	4,000	
	Dividends Payable		4,000
(F)	Income Taxes Payable	500	
	Operating Activities—Decrease in Income Taxes Payable.		500
(G)	Operating Activities—Increase in Accrued Expenses Payable	2,200	
	Accrued Expenses Payable.		2,200
(H)	Accounts Payable.	3,200	
	Operating Activities—Decrease in Accounts Payable		3,200
(I)	Operating Activities—Depreciation of Building	7,000	
	Accumulated Depreciation—Building		7,000
(J)	Building.	60,000	
	Investing Activities—Purchase of Building		60,000

(K)	Land		15,000	
	Investing Activities—Purchase of Land.			15,000
(L)	Investing Activities—Sale of Land		72,000	
	Operating Activities—Gain on Sale of Land.			12,000
	Land			60,000
(M)	Operating Activities—Decrease in Inventories		8,000	
	Inventories			8,000
(N)	Accounts Receivable.		9,000	
	Operating Activities—Increase in Accounts Receivable			9,000
(O)	Cash		71,500	
	Net Increase in Cash.			71,500

After all the balance sheet accounts are analyzed and the entries made on the spreadsheet (work sheet), all the operating, investing, and financing activities are identified in the bottom portion of the spreadsheet. The accuracy of the entries is verified by totaling the Debit and Credit Transactions columns. The totals of the columns should be equal.

Preparing the Statement of Cash Flows

The statement of cash flows prepared from the spreadsheet is identical to the statement in Exhibit 7. The data for the three sections of the statement are obtained from the bottom portion of the spreadsheet.

Appendix 2 Preparing the Statement of Cash Flows—The Direct Method

The direct method reports cash flows from operating activities as follows:

Cash flows from operating activities:	
Cash received from customers	$ XXX
Cash payments for merchandise	(XXX)
Cash payments for operating expenses	(XXX)
Cash payments for interest	(XXX)
Cash payments for income taxes	(XXX)
Net cash flow from operating activities	$XXX

The Cash Flows from Investing and Financing Activities sections of the statement of cash flows are exactly the same under both the direct and indirect methods. The amount of net cash flow from operating activities is also the same, but the manner in which it is reported is different.

Under the direct method, the income statement is adjusted to cash flows from operating activities as shown in Exhibit 9.

Exhibit 9

Converting Income Statement to Cash Flows from Operating Activities Using the Direct Method

Income Statement	Adjusted to	Cash Flows from Operating Activities
Sales	→	Cash received from customers
Cost of goods sold	→	Cash payments for merchandise
Operating expenses:		
Depreciation expense*	n/a	n/a
Other operating expenses	→	Cash payments for operating expenses
Gain (loss) on sale of land**	n/a	n/a
Interest expense	→	Cash payments for interest
Income tax expense	→	Cash payments for income taxes
Net income	→	Net cash flow from operating activities

* Depreciation does not affect cash, thus, is not considered in the direct method.
** Gains (Losses) on sales of property, plant, and equipment are reported as part of investing activities.

As shown in Exhibit 9, depreciation expense is not adjusted or reported as part of cash flows from operating activities. This is because deprecation expense does not involve a cash outflow. The gain on the sale of the land is also not adjusted and is not reported as part of cash flows from operating activities. This is because the cash flow from operating activities is determined directly, rather than by reconciling net income. The cash proceeds from the sale of the land are reported as an investing activity.

To illustrate the direct method, the income statement and comparative balance sheet for **Rundell Inc.**, shown in Exhibit 4, are used.

Cash Received from Customers

The income statement (shown in Exhibit 4) of **Rundell Inc.** reports sales of $1,180,000. To determine the cash received from customers, the $1,180,000 is adjusted for any increase or decrease in accounts receivable. The adjustment is summarized in Exhibit 10.

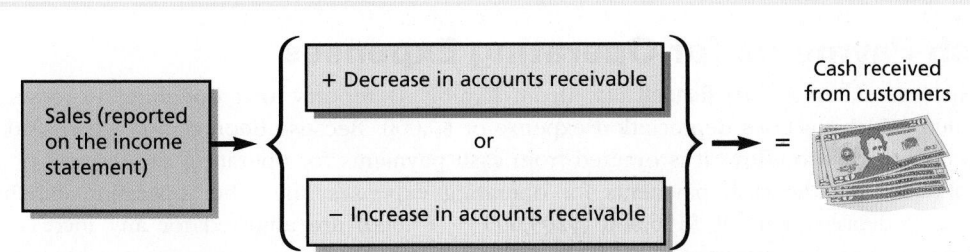

Exhibit 10
Determining the Cash Received from Customers

The cash received from customers is $1,171,000, computed as follows:

Sales	$1,180,000
Increase in accounts receivable	(9,000)
Cash received from customers	$1,171,000

The increase of $9,000 in accounts receivable (shown in Exhibit 4) during 20Y8 indicates that sales on account exceeded cash received from customers by $9,000. In other words, sales include $9,000 that did not result in a cash inflow during the year. Thus, $9,000 is deducted from sales to determine the cash received from customers.

Cash Payments for Merchandise

The income statement (shown in Exhibit 4) for **Rundell Inc.** reports cost of goods sold of $790,000. To determine the cash payments for merchandise, the $790,000 is adjusted for any increases or decreases in inventories and accounts payable. Assuming the accounts payable are owed to merchandise suppliers, the adjustment is summarized in Exhibit 11.

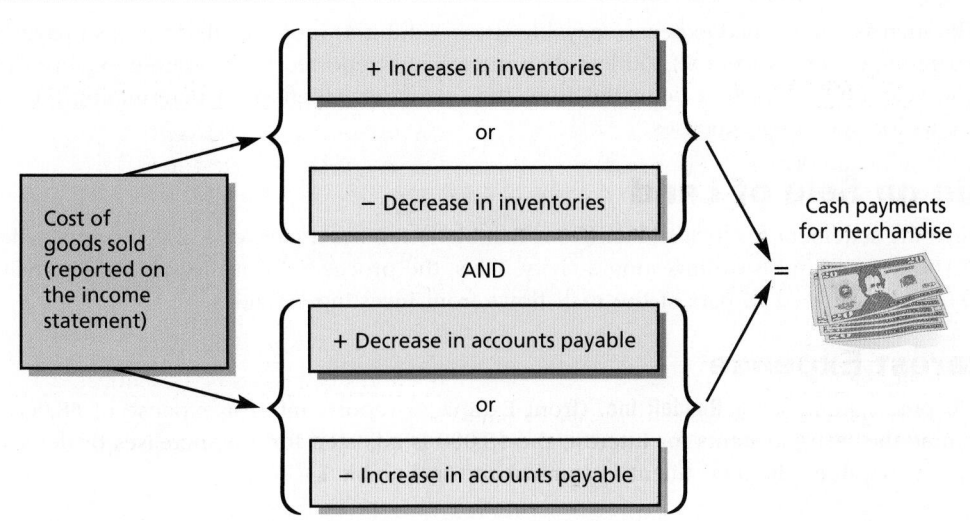

Exhibit 11
Determining the Cash Payments for Merchandise

The cash payments for merchandise are $785,200, computed as follows:

Cost of goods sold	$790,000
Decrease in inventories	(8,000)
Decrease in accounts payable	3,200
Cash payments for merchandise	$785,200

The $8,000 decrease in inventories (from Exhibit 4) indicates that the merchandise sold exceeded the cost of the merchandise purchased by $8,000. In other words, the cost of goods sold includes $8,000 of merchandise sold from inventory that did not require a cash outflow during the year. Thus, $8,000 is deducted from the cost of goods sold in determining the cash payments for merchandise.

The $3,200 decrease in accounts payable (from Exhibit 4) indicates that cash payments for merchandise were $3,200 more than the purchases on account during 20Y8. Therefore, $3,200 is added to the cost of goods sold in determining the cash payments for merchandise.

Cash Payments for Operating Expenses

The income statement for **Rundell Inc.** (from Exhibit 4) reports total operating expenses of $203,000, which includes depreciation expense of $7,000. Because depreciation expense does not require a cash outflow, it is omitted from cash payments for operating expenses.

To determine the cash payments for operating expenses, the other operating expenses (excluding depreciation) of $196,000 ($203,000 − $7,000) are adjusted for any increase or decrease in accrued expenses payable. Assuming that the accrued expenses payable are all operating expenses, this adjustment is summarized in Exhibit 12.

Exhibit 12

Determining the Cash Payments for Operating Expenses

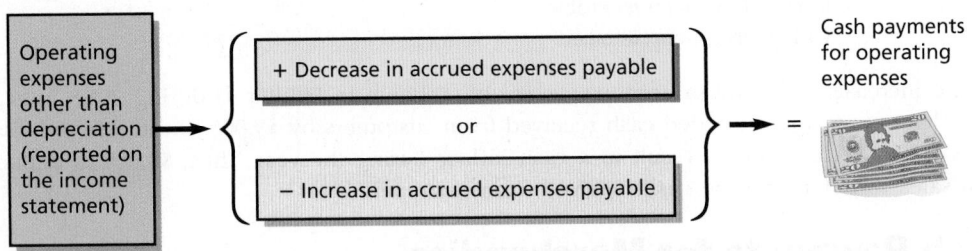

The cash payments for operating expenses are $193,800, computed as follows:

Operating expenses other than depreciation	$196,000
Increase in accrued expenses payable	(2,200)
Cash payments for operating expenses	$193,800

The increase in accrued expenses payable (from Exhibit 4) indicates that the cash payments for operating expenses were $2,200 less than the amount reported for operating expenses during the year. Thus, $2,200 is deducted from the operating expenses in determining the cash payments for operating expenses.

Gain on Sale of Land

The income statement for **Rundell Inc.** (from Exhibit 4) reports a gain of $12,000 on the sale of land. The sale of land is an investing activity. Thus, the proceeds from the sale, which include the gain, are reported as part of the cash flows from investing activities.

Interest Expense

The income statement for **Rundell Inc.** (from Exhibit 4) reports interest expense of $8,000. To determine the cash payments for interest, the $8,000 is adjusted for any increases or decreases in interest payable. The adjustment is summarized in Exhibit 13.

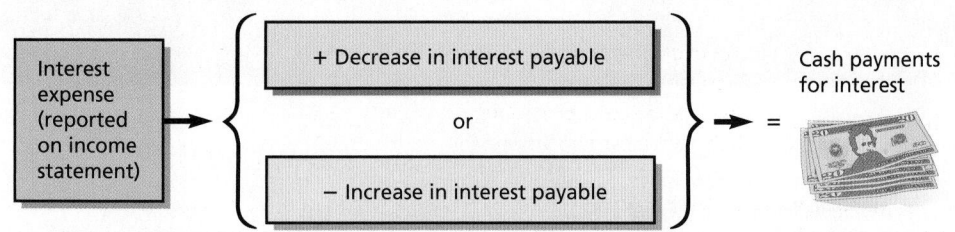

Exhibit 13
Determining the
Cash Payments for
Interest

The comparative balance sheet of Rundell in Exhibit 4 indicates no interest payable. This is because the interest expense on the bonds payable is paid on June 1 and December 31. Because there is no interest payable, no adjustment of the interest expense of $8,000 is necessary.

Cash Payments for Income Taxes

The income statement for **Rundell Inc.** (from Exhibit 4) reports income tax expense of $83,000. To determine the cash payments for income taxes, the $83,000 is adjusted for any increases or decreases in income taxes payable. The adjustment is summarized in Exhibit 14.

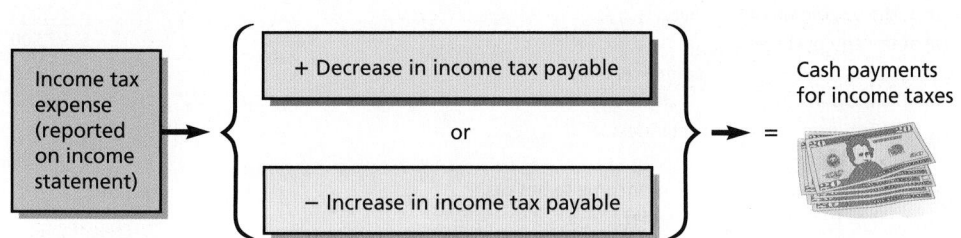

Exhibit 14
Determining the
Cash Payments for
Income Taxes

The cash payments for income taxes are $83,500, computed as follows:

Income tax expense	$83,000
Decrease in income taxes payable	500
Cash payments for income taxes	$83,500

The $500 decrease in income taxes payable (from Exhibit 4) indicates that the cash payments for income taxes were $500 more than the amount reported for income tax expense during 20Y8. Thus, $500 is added to the income tax expense in determining the cash payments for income taxes.

Reporting Cash Flows from Operating Activities—Direct Method

The statement of cash flows for **Rundell Inc.**, using the direct method for reporting cash flows from operating activities, is shown in Exhibit 15. The portions of the statement that differ from those prepared under the indirect method are highlighted.

Exhibit 15 also includes the separate schedule reconciling net income and net cash flow from operating activities. This schedule is included as part of the statement of cash flows when the direct method is used. This schedule is similar to the Cash Flows from Operating Activities section prepared under the indirect method.

Exhibit 15

Statement of Cash Flows—Direct Method

Rundell Inc.
Statement of Cash Flows
For the Year Ended December 31, 20Y8

Cash flows from operating activities:		
Cash received from customers	$1,171,000	
Cash payments for merchandise	(785,200)	
Cash payments for operating expenses	(193,800)	
Cash payments for interest	(8,000)	
Cash payments for income taxes	(83,500)	
Net cash flow from operating activities		$100,500
Cash flows from investing activities:		
Cash received from sale of land	$ 72,000	
Cash paid for purchase of land	(15,000)	
Cash paid for purchase of building	(60,000)	
Net cash flow used for investing activities		(3,000)
Cash flows from financing activities:		
Cash received from sale of common stock	$ 48,000	
Cash paid to retire bonds payable	(50,000)	
Cash paid for dividends	(24,000)	
Net cash flow used for financing activities		(26,000)
Change in cash		$ 71,500
Cash at the beginning of the year		26,000
Cash at the end of the year		$ 97,500
Schedule Reconciling Net Income with Cash		
Flows from Operating Activities:		
Cash flows from operating activities:		
Net income		$108,000
Adjustments to reconcile net income to net cash		
flow from operating activities:		
Depreciation		7,000
Gain on sale of land		(12,000)
Changes in current operating assets and liabilities:		
Increase in accounts receivable		(9,000)
Decrease in inventory		8,000
Decrease in accounts payable		(3,200)
Increase in accrued expenses payable		2,200
Decrease in income taxes payable		(500)
Net cash flow from operating activities		$100,500

Let's Review

Chapter Summary

1. The statement of cash flows reports cash receipts and cash payments by three types of activities: operating activities, investing activities, and financing activities. Cash flows from operating activities reports the cash inflows and outflows from a company's day-to-day operations. Cash flows from investing activities reports the cash inflows and outflows related to changes in a company's long-term assets. Cash flows from financing activities reports the cash inflows and outflows related to changes in a company's long-term liabilities and stockholders' equity. Investing and financing for a business may be affected by transactions that do not involve cash. The effect of such transactions should be reported in a separate schedule accompanying the statement of cash flows.

2. The indirect method reports cash flows from operating activities by adjusting net income for revenues and expenses that do not involve the receipt or payment of cash. Noncash expenses such as depreciation are added back to net income. Gains and losses on the disposal of assets are added to or deducted from net income. Changes in current operating assets and liabilities are added to or subtracted from net income, depending on their effect on cash.

3. Cash flows from investing activities are reported below cash flows from operating activities on the statement of cash flows. Cash flows from investing activities reports the cash inflows and outflows related to changes in a company's long-term assets.

4. Cash flows from financing activities are reported below cash flows from operating activities on the statement of cash flows. Cash flows from financing activities reports the cash inflows and outflows related to changes in a company's long-term liabilities and stockholders' equity.

5. The statement of cash flows reports cash flows from operating activities followed by cash flows from investing and financing activities. The result of adding the net cash flows from operating, investing, and financing activities is the net increase or decrease in cash for the period. Cash at the beginning of the year is added to determine the cash at the end of the period. This ending cash amount must agree with cash reported on the end-of-period balance sheet.

Key Terms

cash flow per share (613)
cash flows from financing
  activities (608)
cash flows from investing
  activities (608)

cash flows from operating
  activities (608)
direct method (609)
free cash flow (623)

indirect method (610)
statement of cash flows (608)

Practice

Multiple-Choice Questions

1. An example of a cash flow from an operating activity is:
   A. receipt of cash from the sale of stock.
   B. receipt of cash from the sale of bonds.
   C. payment of cash for dividends.
   D. receipt of cash from customers on account.

2. An example of a cash flow from an investing activity is:
   A. receipt of cash from the sale of equipment.
   B. receipt of cash from the sale of stock.
   C. payment of cash for dividends.
   D. payment of cash to acquire treasury stock.

3. An example of a cash flow from a financing activity is:
   A. receipt of cash from customers on account.
   B. receipt of cash from the sale of equipment.
   C. payment of cash for dividends.
   D. payment of cash to acquire land.

4. Which of the following methods of reporting cash flows from operating activities adjusts net income for revenues and expenses not involving the receipt or payment of cash?
   A. Direct method
   B. Purchase method
   C. Reciprocal method
   D. Indirect method

5. The net income reported on the income statement for the year was $55,000, and depreciation of fixed assets for the year was $22,000. The balances of the current asset and current liability accounts at the beginning and end of the year are as follows:

	End of Year	Beginning of Year
Cash	$ 65,000	$ 70,000
Accounts receivable	100,000	90,000
Inventories	145,000	150,000
Prepaid expenses	7,500	8,000
Accounts payable (merchandise creditors)	51,000	58,000

The total amount reported for cash flows from operating activities on the statement of cash flows using the indirect method is:
   A. $33,000.
   B. $55,000.
   C. $65,500.
   D. $77,000.

Answers provided after Problem. Need more practice? Find additional multiple-choice questions, exercises, and problems in CengageNOWv2.

Exercises

SHOW ME HOW

1. Classifying cash flows   Obj. 1

Identify whether each of the following would be reported as an operating, investing, or financing activity on the statement of cash flows:

A. Repurchase of common stock
B. Cash received from customers
C. Payment of accounts payable

D. Retirement of bonds payable
E. Purchase of equipment
F. Purchase of inventory for cash

SHOW ME HOW

2. Adjustments to net income—indirect method

Obj. 2

Pearl Corporation's accumulated depreciation—furniture account increased by $8,400, while $3,080 of patent amortization was recognized between balance sheet dates. There were no purchases or sales of depreciable or intangible assets during the year. In addition, the income statement showed a loss of $4,480 from the sale of land. Reconcile a net income of $120,400 to net cash flow from operating activities.

SHOW ME HOW

3. Changes in current operating assets and liabilities—indirect method

Obj. 2

Alpenrose Corporation's comparative balance sheet for current assets and liabilities was as follows:

	Dec. 31, Year 2	Dec. 31, Year 1
Accounts receivable	$27,000	$32,400
Inventory	18,000	15,480
Accounts payable	16,200	14,220
Dividends payable	49,500	53,100

Adjust net income of $207,000 for changes in operating assets and liabilities to arrive at net cash flow from operating activities.

SHOW ME HOW

4. Cash flows from operating activities—indirect method

Obj. 2

Pettygrove Inc. reported the following data:

Net income	$405,000
Depreciation expense	45,000
Gain on disposal of equipment	36,900
Decrease in accounts receivable	25,200
Decrease in accounts payable	6,480

Prepare the Cash Flows from Operating Activities section of the statement of cash flows, using the indirect method.

SHOW ME HOW

5. Land transactions on the statement of cash flows

Obj. 3

Milo Corporation purchased land for $540,000. Later in the year, the company sold a different piece of land with a book value of $270,000 for $180,000. How are the effects of these transactions reported on the statement of cash flows?

SHOW ME HOW

6. Common stock transactions on the statement of cash flows

Obj. 4

Wright Inc. received $1,200,000 from issuing shares of its common stock. During the year, Wright Inc. paid $500,000 to retire bonds and paid dividends of $250,000. How are the effects of these transactions reported on the statement of cash flows?

Answers provided after Problem. Need more practice? Find additional multiple-choice questions, exercises, and problems in CengageNOWv2.

Problem

The comparative balance sheet of Dowling Company for December 31, 20Y5 and 20Y4, is as follows:

	Dowling Company **Comparative Balance Sheet** **December 31, 20Y5 and 20Y4**	
	20Y5	**20Y4**
Assets		
Cash	$ 140,350	$ 95,900
Accounts receivable (net).....................................	95,300	102,300
Inventories	165,200	157,900
Prepaid expenses	6,240	5,860
Investments (long-term)	35,700	84,700
Land	75,000	90,000
Buildings...	375,000	260,000
Accumulated depreciation—buildings........................	(71,300)	(58,300)
Machinery and equipment......................................	428,300	428,300
Accumulated depreciation—machinery and equipment.........	(148,500)	(138,000)
Patents...	58,000	65,000
Total assets	$1,159,290	$1,093,660
Liabilities and Stockholders' Equity		
Accounts payable (merchandise creditors)	$ 43,500	$ 46,700
Accrued expenses payable (operating expenses)	14,000	12,500
Income taxes payable......................................	7,900	8,400
Dividends payable..	14,000	10,000
Mortgage note payable, due in 10 years......................	40,000	0
Bonds payable	150,000	250,000
Common stock, $30 par..	450,000	375,000
Excess of issue price over par—common stock	66,250	41,250
Retained earnings..	373,640	349,810
Total liabilities and stockholders' equity......................	$1,159,290	$1,093,660

The income statement for Dowling Company follows:

	Dowling Company **Income Statement** **For the Year Ended December 31, 20Y5**	
Sales		$1,100,000
Cost of goods sold		710,000
Gross profit...		$ 390,000
Operating expenses:		
Depreciation expense	$ 23,500	
Patent amortization.......................................	7,000	
Other operating expenses	196,000	
Total operating expenses............................		226,500
Income from operations		$ 163,500
Other revenue and expense:		
Gain on sale of investments...............................	$ 11,000	
Interest expense	(26,000)	(15,000)
Income before income tax		$ 148,500
Income tax expense		50,000
Net income		$ 98,500

An examination of the accounting records revealed the following additional information applicable to 20Y5:

A. Land costing $15,000 was sold for $15,000.

B. A mortgage note was issued for $40,000.

C. A building costing $115,000 was constructed.

D. 2,500 shares of common stock were issued at $40 in exchange for the bonds payable.

E. Cash dividends declared were $74,670.

Instructions

1. Prepare a statement of cash flows, using the indirect method of reporting cash flows from operating activities.

2. (*Appendix 2*) Prepare a statement of cash flows, using the direct method of reporting cash flows from operating activities.

Need more practice? Find additional multiple-choice questions, exercises, and problems in CengageNOWv2.

Answers

Multiple-Choice Questions

1. **D** Cash flows from operating activities affect transactions that enter into the determination of net income, such as the receipt of cash from customers on account (answer D). Receipts of cash from the sale of stock (answer A) and the sale of bonds (answer B) and payments of cash for dividends (answer C) are cash flows from financing activities.

2. **A** Cash flows from investing activities include receipts from the sale of noncurrent assets, such as equipment (answer A), and payments to acquire noncurrent assets. Receipts of cash from the sale of stock (answer B) and payments of cash for dividends (answer C) and to acquire treasury stock (answer D) are cash flows from financing activities.

3. **C** Payment of cash for dividends (answer C) is an example of a financing activity. The receipt of cash from customers on account (answer A) is an operating activity. The receipt of cash from the sale of equipment (answer B) and the payment of cash to acquire land (answer D) are examples of investing activities.

4. **D** The indirect method (answer D) reports cash flows from operating activities by beginning with net income and adjusting it for revenues and expenses not involving the receipt or payment of cash.

5. **C** The Cash Flows from Operating Activities section of the statement of cash flows would report net cash flow from operating activities of $65,500, determined as follows:

Cash flows from operating activities:		
Net income	$ 55,000	
Adjustments to reconcile net income to net cash flow from operating activities:		
Depreciation expense	22,000	
Changes in current operating assets and liabilities:		
Increase in accounts receivable............................	(10,000)	
Decrease in inventories......................................	5,000	
Decrease in prepaid expenses	500	
Decrease in accounts payable..............................	(7,000)	
Net cash flow from operating activities		$65,500

Exercises

1.

A. Financing	D. Financing
B. Operating	E. Investing
C. Operating	F. Operating

2.

Net income	$120,400
Adjustments to reconcile net income to net cash flow from operating activities:	
Depreciation	8,400
Amortization of patents.....................................	3,080
Loss from sale of land	4,480
Net cash flow from operating activities.....................	$136,360

3.

Net income	$207,000
Changes in current operating assets and liabilities:	
Decrease in accounts receivable	5,400
Increase in inventory..	(2,520)
Increase in accounts payable	1,980
Net cash flow from operating activities	$211,860

Note: The change in dividends payable impacts the cash paid for dividends, which is disclosed under financing activities.

4.

Cash flows from operating activities:	
Net income	$405,000
Adjustments to reconcile net income to net cash flow from operating activities:	
Depreciation	45,000
Gain on disposal of equipment	(36,900)
Changes in current operating assets and liabilities:	
Decrease in accounts receivable.............................	25,200
Decrease in accounts payable.................................	(6,480)
Net cash flow from operating activities...............	$431,820

5. The loss on the sale of land is added to net income in the Operating Activities section.

Loss on sale of land	$ 90,000

The purchase and sale of land is reported as part of cash flows from investing activities as follows:

Cash received from sale of land	$ 180,000
Cash paid for purchase of land	(540,000)

6.

Cash flows from financing activities:	
Cash received from issuing common stock	$1,200,000
Cash paid to retire bonds...	(500,000)
Cash paid for dividends	(250,000)
Net cash flows used for financing activities..........	$ 450,000

Need more help? Watch step-by-step videos of how to compute answers to these Exercises in CengageNOWv2.

Problem

1.

Dowling Company Statement of Cash Flows—Indirect Method For the Year Ended December 31, 20Y5		
Cash flows from operating activities:		
Net income		$ 98,500
Adjustments to reconcile net income to net cash flow from operating activities:		
Depreciation		23,500
Amortization of patents		7,000
Gain on sale of investments		(11,000)
Changes in current operating assets and liabilities:		
Decrease in accounts receivable		7,000
Increase in inventories		(7,300)
Increase in prepaid expenses		(380)
Decrease in accounts payable		(3,200)
Increase in accrued expenses payable		1,500
Decrease in income taxes payable		(500)
Net cash flow from operating activities		$115,120
Cash flows from investing activities:		
Cash received from sale of investments	$60,000[1]	
Cash received from sale of land	15,000	
Cash paid for construction of building	(115,000)	
Net cash flow used for investing activities		(40,000)
Cash flows from financing activities:		
Cash received from issuing mortgage note payable	$ 40,000	
Cash paid for dividends	(70,670)[2]	
Net cash flow used for financing activities		(30,670)
Change in cash		$ 44,450
Cash at the beginning of the year		95,900
Cash at the end of the year		$140,350

Schedule of Noncash Investing and Financing Activities:

Issued common stock to retire bonds payable	$100,000

[1] $60,000 = $11,000 gain + $49,000 (decrease in investments)
[2] $70,670 = $74,670 − $4,000 (increase in dividends)

2.

Dowling Company Statement of Cash Flows—Direct Method For the Year Ended December 31, 20Y5		
Cash flows from operating activities:		
Cash received from customers[1]		$1,107,000
Cash paid for merchandise[2]		(720,500)
Cash paid for operating expenses[3]		(194,880)
Cash paid for interest expense		(26,000)
Cash paid for income tax[4]		(50,500)
Net cash flow from operating activities		$115,120
Cash flows from investing activities:		
Cash received from sale of investments		$ 60,000[5]
Cash received from sale of land		15,000
Cash paid for construction of building		(115,000)
Net cash flow used for investing activities		(40,000)

(Continued)

Cash flows from financing activities:

Cash received from issuing mortgage note payable............	$ 40,000	
Cash paid for dividends[6].....................................	(70,670)	
Net cash flow used for financing activities		(30,670)
Change in cash..		$ 44,450
Cash at the beginning of the year.............................		95,900
Cash at the end of the year...................................		$140,350

Schedule of Noncash Investing and Financing Activities:

Issued common stock to retire bonds payable.................	$100,000

Schedule Reconciling Net Income with Cash Flows from
    Operating Activities[7]

Computations:

[1]$1,100,000 + $7,000 = $1,107,000

[2]$710,000 + $3,200 + $7,300 = $720,500

[3]$196,000 + $380 − $1,500 = $194,880

[4]$50,000 + $500 = $50,500

[5]$60,000 = $11,000 gain + $49,000 (decrease in investments)

[6]$74,670 + $10,000 − $14,000 = $70,670

[7]The content of this schedule is the same as the Operating Activities section of part (1) of this solution and is not reproduced here for the sake of brevity.

Discussion Questions

1. What is the principal disadvantage of the direct method of reporting cash flows from operating activities?

2. What are the major advantages of the indirect method of reporting cash flows from operating activities?

3. A corporation issued $2,000,000 of common stock in exchange for $2,000,000 of fixed assets. Where would this transaction be reported on the statement of cash flows?

4. A retail business, using the accrual method of accounting, owed merchandise creditors (accounts payable) $320,000 at the beginning of the year and $350,000 at the end of the year. How would the $30,000 increase be used to adjust net income in determining the amount of cash flows from operating activities by the indirect method? Explain.

5. If salaries payable was $100,000 at the beginning of the year and $75,000 at the end of the year, should the $25,000 decrease be added to or deducted from income to determine the amount of cash flows from operating activities by the indirect method? Explain.

6. A long-term investment in bonds with a cost of $500,000 was sold for $600,000 cash. (A) What was the gain or loss on the sale? (B) What was the effect of the transaction on cash flows? (C) How should the transaction be reported on the statement of cash flows if cash flows from operating activities are reported by the indirect method?

7. A corporation issued $2,000,000 of 20-year bonds for cash at 98. How would the transaction be reported on the statement of cash flows?

8. Fully depreciated equipment costing $50,000 was discarded. What was the effect of the transaction on cash flows if (A) $15,000 cash is received for the equipment, and (B) no cash is received for the equipment?

9. For the current year, Packers Company decided to switch from the indirect method to the direct method for reporting cash flows from operating activities on the statement of cash flows. Will the change cause the amount of net cash flow from operating activities to be larger, smaller, or the same as if the indirect method had been used? Explain.

10. Name five common major classes of operating cash receipts or operating cash payments presented on the statement of cash flows when the cash flows from operating activities are reported by the direct method.

Basic Exercises

SHOW ME HOW

BE 13-1 Classifying cash flows
Obj. 1

Identify whether each of the following would be reported as an operating, investing, or financing activity on the statement of cash flows:

A. Purchase of investments

B. Disposal of equipment

C. Payment for selling expenses

D. Collection of accounts receivable

E. Cash sales

F. Issuance of bonds payable

SHOW ME HOW

BE 13-2 Adjustments to net income—indirect method
Obj. 2

Ripley Corporation's accumulated depreciation—equipment account increased by $11,575 while $2,500 of patent amortization was recognized between balance sheet dates. There were no purchases or sales of depreciable or intangible assets during the year. In addition, the income statement showed a gain of $33,190 from the sale of investments. Reconcile a net income of $224,500 to net cash flow from operating activities.

SHOW ME HOW

BE 13-3 Changes in current operating assets and liabilities—indirect method
Obj. 2

Huluduey Corporation's comparative balance sheet for current assets and liabilities was as follows:

	Dec. 31, Year 2	Dec. 31, Year 1
Accounts receivable	$17,500	$12,500
Inventory	51,650	44,200
Accounts payable	8,480	5,100
Dividends payable	9,480	6,100

Adjust net income of $75,800 for changes in operating assets and liabilities to arrive at net cash flow from operating activities.

SHOW ME HOW

BE 13-4 Cash flows from operating activities—indirect method
Obj. 2

Staley Inc. reported the following data:

Net income	$396,200
Depreciation expense	61,250
Loss on disposal of equipment	27,600
Increase in accounts receivable	9,000
Increase in accounts payable	3,350

Prepare the Cash Flows from Operating Activities section of the statement of cash flows, using the indirect method.

SHOW ME HOW

BE 13-5 Land transactions on the statement of cash flows
Obj. 3

IZ Corporation purchased land for $400,000. Later in the year, the company sold a different piece of land with a book value of $200,000 for $240,000. How are the effects of these transactions reported on the statement of cash flows?

SHOW ME HOW

BE 13-6 Common stock transactions on the statement of cash flows
Obj. 4

Jones Industries received $800,000 from issuing shares of its common stock and $700,000 from issuing bonds. During the year, Jones Industries also paid dividends of $90,000. How are the effects of these transactions reported on the statement of cash flows?

SHOW ME HOW

Appendix 2
BE 13-7 Cash received from customers—direct method

Sales reported on the income statement were $112,000. The accounts receivable balance decreased $10,500 over the year. Determine the amount of cash received from customers.

SHOW ME HOW

Appendix 2
BE 13-8 Cash payments for merchandise—direct method

The cost of goods sold reported on the income statement was $240,000. The accounts payable balance increased $12,000, and the inventory balance increased by $19,200 over the year. Determine the amount of cash paid for merchandise.

Exercises

REAL WORLD

EX 13-1 Cash flows from operating activities—net loss
Obj. 1

United Continental Holdings, Inc., the parent company of **United Airlines**, reported a net *loss* of $723 million from operations. However, on its statement of cash flows, it reported $935 million of cash flows from operating activities.

➤ Explain this apparent contradiction between the loss and the positive cash flows.

EX 13-2 Effect of transactions on cash flows
Obj. 1

✔ A. Cash payment,
$411,000

State the effect (cash receipt or cash payment and amount) of each of the following transactions, considered individually, on cash flows:

A. Retired $400,000 of bonds, on which there was $3,000 of unamortized discount, for $411,000.

B. Sold 20,000 shares of $5 par common stock for $22 per share.

C. Sold equipment with a book value of $55,800 for $60,000.

D. Purchased land for $650,000 cash.

E. Purchased a building by paying $50,000 cash and issuing a $450,000 mortgage note payable.

F. Sold a new issue of $500,000 of bonds at 98.

G. Purchased 10,000 shares of $10 par common stock as treasury stock at $33.25 per share.

H. Paid dividends of $1.50 per share. There were 1,000,000 shares issued and 120,000 shares of treasury stock.

EX 13-3 Classifying cash flows
Obj. 1

Identify the type of cash flow activity for each of the following events (operating, investing, or financing):

A. Net income

B. Paid cash dividends

C. Issued common stock

D. Issued bonds

E. Redeemed bonds

F. Sold long-term investments

G. Purchased treasury stock

H. Sold equipment

I. Issued preferred stock

J. Purchased buildings

K. Purchased patents

EX 13-4 Cash flows from operating activities—indirect method   Obj. 2

Indicate whether each of the following would be added to or deducted from net income in determining net cash flow from operating activities by the indirect method:

A. Decrease in inventory

B. Increase in accounts receivable

C. Increase in accounts payable

D. Loss on retirement of long-term debt

E. Depreciation of fixed assets

F. Decrease in notes receivable due in 60 days from customers

G. Increase in salaries payable

H. Decrease in prepaid expenses

I. Amortization of patent

J. Increase in notes payable due in 120 days to vendors

K. Gain on disposal of fixed assets

EX 13-5 Cash flows from operating activities—indirect method   Obj. 1, 2

✔ Net cash flow from operating activities, $103,850

SHOW ME HOW

The net income reported on the income statement for the current year was $73,600. Depreciation recorded on store equipment for the year amounted to $27,400. Balances of the current asset and current liability accounts at the beginning and end of the year are as follows:

	End of Year	Beginning of Year
Cash	$23,500	$18,700
Accounts receivable (net)	56,000	48,000
Inventories	35,500	40,000
Prepaid expenses	4,750	7,000
Accounts payable (merchandise creditors)	21,800	16,800
Wages payable	4,900	5,800

A. Prepare the Cash Flows from Operating Activities section of the statement of cash flows, using the indirect method.

B. ▬▬▶ Briefly explain why net cash flow from operating activities is different than net income.

EX 13-6 Cash flows from operating activities—indirect method   Obj. 1, 2

✔ Net cash flow from operating activities, $260,850

SHOW ME HOW

The net income reported on the income statement for the current year was $185,000. Depreciation recorded on equipment and a building amounted to $96,000 for the year. Balances of the current asset and current liability accounts at the beginning and end of the year are as follows:

	End of Year	Beginning of Year
Cash	$ 75,900	$ 86,150
Accounts receivable (net)	84,550	90,000
Inventories	186,200	175,000
Prepaid expenses	3,600	4,500
Accounts payable (merchandise creditors)	91,500	110,000
Salaries payable	7,200	4,000

A. Prepare the Cash Flows from Operating Activities section of the statement of cash flows, using the indirect method.

B. ▬▬▶ If the direct method had been used, would the net cash flow from operating activities have been the same? Explain.

EX 13-7 Cash flows from operating activities—indirect method   Obj. 1, 2

✔ Net cash flow from operating activities, $525,410

SHOW ME HOW

The income statement disclosed the following items for the year:

Depreciation expense	$ 57,600
Gain on disposal of equipment	33,600
Net income	508,000

(Continued)

The changes in the current asset and liability accounts for the year are as follows:

	Increase (Decrease)
Accounts receivable	$ 8,960
Inventory	(5,120)
Prepaid insurance	(1,920)
Accounts payable	(6,080)
Income taxes payable	1,410
Dividends payable	2,200

A. Prepare the Cash Flows from Operating Activities section of the statement of cash flows, using the indirect method.

B. ▬▬▶ Briefly explain why net cash flow from operating activities is different than net income.

EX 13-8   Reporting changes in equipment on statement of cash flows   Obj. 3

An analysis of the general ledger accounts indicates that office equipment, which cost $202,500 and on which accumulated depreciation totaled $84,375 on the date of sale, was sold for $101,250 during the year. Using this information, indicate the items to be reported on the statement of cash flows.

EX 13-9   Reporting changes in equipment on statement of cash flows   Obj. 3

An analysis of the general ledger accounts indicates that delivery equipment, which cost $80,000 and on which accumulated depreciation totaled $36,000 on the date of sale, was sold for $37,200 during the year. Using this information, indicate the items to be reported on the statement of cash flows.

EX 13-10   Reporting land transactions on statement of cash flows   Obj. 3

On the basis of the details of the following fixed asset account, indicate the items to be reported on the statement of cash flows:

ACCOUNT *Land*   **ACCOUNT NO.**

					Balance	
Date		Item	Debit	Credit	Debit	Credit
Jan.	1	Balance			868,000	
Mar.	12	Purchased for cash	104,300		972,300	
Oct.	4	Sold for $95,550		63,840	908,460	

SHOW ME HOW

EX 13-11   Determining cash payments to stockholders   Obj. 4

The board of directors declared cash dividends totaling $1,200,000 during the current year. The comparative balance sheet indicates dividends payable of $250,000 at the beginning of the year and $100,000 at the end of the year. What was the amount of cash payments to stockholders during the year?

EX 13-12   Reporting stockholders' equity items on statement of cash flows   Obj. 4

On the basis of the following stockholders' equity accounts, indicate the items, exclusive of net income, to be reported on the statement of cash flows. There were no unpaid dividends at either the beginning or the end of the year.

ACCOUNT *Common Stock, $40 par*   ACCOUNT NO.

Date		Item	Debit	Credit	Balance Debit	Balance Credit
Jan.	1	Balance, 120,000 shares				4,800,000
Apr.	2	30,000 shares issued for cash		1,200,000		6,000,000
June	30	5% stock dividend		300,000		6,300,000

ACCOUNT *Paid-In Capital in Excess of Par—Common Stock*   ACCOUNT NO.

Date		Item	Debit	Credit	Balance Debit	Balance Credit
Jan.	1	Balance				360,000
Apr.	2	30,000 shares issued for cash		720,000		1,080,000
June	30	Stock dividend		150,000		1,230,000

ACCOUNT *Retained Earnings*   ACCOUNT NO.

Date		Item	Debit	Credit	Balance Debit	Balance Credit
Jan.	1	Balance				2,000,000
June	30	Stock dividend	450,000			1,550,000
Dec.	30	Cash dividend	315,000			1,235,000
	31	Net income		1,000,000		2,235,000

EX 13-13 Reporting land acquisition for cash and mortgage note on statement of cash flows   Obj. 3, 4

On the basis of the details of the following fixed asset account, indicate the items to be reported on the statement of cash flows:

ACCOUNT *Land*   ACCOUNT NO.

Date		Item	Debit	Credit	Balance Debit	Balance Credit
Jan.	1	Balance			156,000	
Feb.	10	Purchased for cash	246,000		402,000	
Nov.	20	Purchased with long-term mortgage note	324,000		726,000	

EX 13-14 Reporting issuance and retirement of long-term debt   Obj. 4

On the basis of the details of the following bonds payable and related discount accounts, indicate the items to be reported in the Financing Activities section of the statement of cash flows, assuming no gain or loss on retiring the bonds:

ACCOUNT *Bonds Payable*   ACCOUNT NO.

Date		Item	Debit	Credit	Balance Debit	Balance Credit
Jan.	1	Balance				750,000
	2	Retire bonds	150,000			600,000
June	30	Issue bonds		450,000		1,050,000

(Continued)

ACCOUNT *Discount on Bonds Payable*					ACCOUNT NO.		
						Balance	
Date		Item	Debit	Credit	Debit	Credit
Jan.	1	Balance			33,750	
	2	Retire bonds		12,000	21,750	
June	30	Issue bonds	30,000		51,750	
Dec.	31	Amortize discount		2,625	49,125	

EX 13-15   Determining net income from net cash flow from operating activities   Obj. 2, 3, 4

✔ Net income, $341,770

SHOW ME HOW

Curwen Inc. reported net cash flow from operating activities of $357,500 on its statement of cash flows for the year ended December 31. The following information was reported in the Cash Flows from Operating Activities section of the statement of cash flows, using the indirect method:

Decrease in income taxes payable	$ 7,700
Decrease in inventories	19,140
Depreciation	29,480
Gain on sale of investments	13,200
Increase in accounts payable	5,280
Increase in prepaid expenses	2,970
Increase in accounts receivable	14,300

A. Determine the net income reported by Curwen Inc. for the year ended December 31.

B. ▬▬▬▶ Briefly explain why Curwen's net income is different than net cash flow from operating activities.

EX 13-16   Cash flows from operating activities—indirect method   Obj. 2

✔ Net cash flow from operating activities, $58,020

EXCEL TEMPLATE   REAL WORLD

Selected data (in thousands) derived from the income statement and balance sheet of **National Beverage Corp.** for a recent year are as follows:

Income statement data:	
Net income	$49,311
Gain on disposal of property	1,188
Depreciation expense	11,580
Other items involving noncash expenses	1,383
Balance sheet data:	
Increase in accounts receivable	1,746
Decrease in inventory	990
Increase in prepaid expenses	605
Decrease in accounts payable	710
Decrease in accrued and other current liabilities	995

A. Prepare the Cash Flows from Operating Activities section of the statement of cash flows, using the indirect method for National Beverage Corp.

B. ▬▬▬▶ Interpret your results in part (A).

EX 13-17 Statement of cash flows—indirect method

Obj. 2, 3, 4, 5

✔ Net cash flow
from operating
activities, $38

SHOW ME HOW   EXCEL TEMPLATE

The comparative balance sheet of Olson-Jones Industries Inc. for December 31, 20Y2 and 20Y1, is as follows:

	Dec. 31, 20Y2	Dec. 31, 20Y1
Assets		
Cash	$183	$ 14
Accounts receivable (net)	55	49
Inventories	117	99
Land	250	330
Equipment	205	175
Accumulated depreciation—equipment	(68)	(42)
Total assets	$742	$625
Liabilities and Stockholders' Equity		
Accounts payable (merchandise creditors)	$ 51	$ 37
Dividends payable	5	—
Common stock, $1 par	125	80
Paid-in capital: Excess of issue price over par—common stock	85	70
Retained earnings	476	438
Total liabilities and stockholders' equity	$742	$625

The following additional information is taken from the records:

A. Land was sold for $120.

B. Equipment was acquired for cash.

C. There were no disposals of equipment during the year.

D. The common stock was issued for cash.

E. There was a $62 credit to Retained Earnings for net income.

F. There was a $24 debit to Retained Earnings for cash dividends declared.

A. Prepare a statement of cash flows, using the indirect method of presenting cash flows from operating activities.

B. ➤ Was Olson-Jones's net cash flow from operations more or less than net income? What is the source of this difference?

EX 13-18 Statement of cash flows—indirect method

Obj. 2, 3, 4, 5

List the errors you find in the following statement of cash flows. The cash balance at the beginning of the year was $240,000. All other amounts are correct, except the cash balance at the end of the year.

Shasta Inc.
Statement of Cash Flows
For the Year Ended December 31, 20Y9

Cash flows from operating activities:		
Net income	$ 360,000	
Adjustments to reconcile net income to net cash flow from operating activities:		
Depreciation	100,800	
Gain on sale of investments	17,280	
Changes in current operating assets and liabilities:		
Increase in accounts receivable	27,360	
Increase in inventories	(36,000)	
Increase in accounts payable	(3,600)	
Decrease in accrued expenses payable	(2,400)	
Net cash flow from operating activities		$ 463,440
Cash flows from investing activities:		
Cash received from sale of investments	$ 240,000	
Cash paid for purchase of land	(259,200)	
Cash paid for purchase of equipment	(432,000)	
Net cash flow used for investing activities		(415,200)

(Continued)

Cash flows from financing activities:

Cash received from sale of common stock.................	$ 312,000	
Cash paid for dividends.....................................	(132,000)	
Net cash flow from financing activities.................		180,000
Change in cash...		$ 47,760
Cash at the end of the year...................................		192,240
Cash at the beginning of the year...........................		$ 240,000

Appendix 2

EX 13-19 Cash flows from operating activities—direct method

✔ A. $801,900   The cash flows from operating activities are reported by the direct method on the statement of cash flows. Determine the following:

A. If sales for the current year were $753,500 and accounts receivable decreased by $48,400 during the year, what was the amount of cash received from customers?

B. If income tax expense for the current year was $50,600 and income tax payable decreased by $5,500 during the year, what was the amount of cash payments for income taxes?

C. ⬤▬▬▶ Briefly explain why the cash received from customers in (A) is different than sales.

Appendix 2

EX 13-20 Determining selected amounts for cash flows from operating activities—direct method

✔ A. $1,025,800   Selected data taken from the accounting records of Ginis Inc. for the current year ended December 31 are as follows:

	Balance, December 31	Balance, January 1
Accrued expenses payable (operating expenses)	$ 12,650	$ 14,030
Accounts payable (merchandise creditors)	96,140	105,800
Inventories	178,020	193,430
Prepaid expenses	7,360	8,970

During the current year, the cost of goods sold was $1,031,550, and the operating expenses other than depreciation were $179,400. The direct method is used for presenting the cash flows from operating activities on the statement of cash flows.

Determine the amount reported on the statement of cash flows for (A) cash payments for merchandise and (B) cash payments for operating expenses.

Appendix 2

EX 13-21 Cash flows from operating activities—direct method

✔ Net cash flow from operating activities, $96,040

The income statement of Booker T Industries Inc. for the current year ended June 30 is as follows:

Sales		$511,000
Cost of goods sold.......................................		290,500
Gross profit		$220,500
Operating expenses:		
Depreciation expense	$ 39,200	
Other operating expenses	105,000	
Total operating expenses		144,200
Income before income tax		$ 76,300
Income tax expense		21,700
Net income		$ 54,600

Changes in the balances of selected accounts from the beginning to the end of the current year are as follows:

	Increase (Decrease)
Accounts receivable (net)	$(11,760)
Inventories	3,920
Prepaid expenses	(3,780)
Accounts payable (merchandise creditors)	(7,980)
Accrued expenses payable (operating expenses)	1,260
Income tax payable	(2,660)

A. Prepare the Cash Flows from Operating Activities section of the statement of cash flows, using the direct method.

B. ━━━━▶ What does the direct method show about a company's cash flows from operating activities that is not shown using the indirect method?

Appendix 2

EX 13-22 Cash flows from operating activities—direct method

✔ Net cash flow from operating activities, $123,860

The income statement for Rhino Company for the current year ended June 30 and balances of selected accounts at the beginning and the end of the year are as follows:

Sales	$445,500
Cost of goods sold	154,000
Gross profit	$291,500
Operating expenses:	
Depreciation expense	$ 38,500
Other operating expenses	115,280
Total operating expenses	153,780
Income before income tax	$137,720
Income tax expense	39,600
Net income	$ 98,120

	End of Year	Beginning of Year
Accounts receivable (net)	$36,300	$31,240
Inventories	92,400	80,300
Prepaid expenses	14,520	15,840
Accounts payable (merchandise creditors)	67,540	62,700
Accrued expenses payable (operating expenses)	19,140	20,900
Income tax payable	4,400	4,400

Prepare the Cash Flows from Operating Activities section of the statement of cash flows, using the direct method.

Problems: Series A

PR 13-1A   Statement of cash flows—indirect method   Obj. 2, 3, 4, 5

The comparative balance sheet of Livers Inc. for December 31, 20Y3 and 20Y2, is shown as follows:

	Dec. 31, 20Y3	Dec. 31, 20Y2
Assets		
Cash	$ 155,000	$ 150,000
Accounts receivable (net)	450,000	400,000
Inventories	770,000	750,000
Investments	0	100,000
Land	500,000	0
Equipment	1,400,000	1,200,000
Accumulated depreciation—equipment	(600,000)	(500,000)
Total assets	$2,675,000	$2,100,000
Liabilities and Stockholders' Equity		
Accounts payable (merchandise creditors)	$ 340,000	$ 300,000
Accrued expenses payable (operating expenses)	45,000	50,000
Dividends payable	30,000	25,000
Common stock, $4 par	700,000	600,000
Paid-in capital: Excess of issue price over par—common stock	200,000	175,000
Retained earnings	1,360,000	950,000
Total liabilities and stockholders' equity	$2,675,000	$2,100,000

Additional data obtained from an examination of the accounts in the ledger for 20Y3 are as follows:

A. The investments were sold for $175,000 cash.

B. Equipment and land were acquired for cash.

C. There were no disposals of equipment during the year.

D. The common stock was issued for cash.

E. There was a $500,000 credit to Retained Earnings for net income.

F. There was a $90,000 debit to Retained Earnings for cash dividends declared.

Instructions

Prepare a statement of cash flows, using the indirect method of presenting cash flows from operating activities.

PR 13-2A   Statement of cash flows—indirect method   Obj. 2, 3, 4, 5

The comparative balance sheet of Yellow Dog Enterprises Inc. at December 31, 20Y8 and 20Y7, is as follows:

	Dec. 31, 20Y8	Dec. 31, 20Y7
Assets		
Cash	$ 80,000	$ 100,000
Accounts receivable (net)	275,000	300,000
Inventories	510,000	400,000
Prepaid expenses	15,000	10,000
Equipment	1,070,000	750,000
Accumulated depreciation—equipment	(200,000)	(160,000)
Total assets	$1,750,000	$1,400,000
Liabilities and Stockholders' Equity		
Accounts payable (merchandise creditors)	$ 100,000	$ 90,000
Mortgage note payable	0	400,000
Common stock, $10 par	600,000	200,000
Paid-in capital: Excess of issue price over par—common stock	300,000	100,000
Retained earnings	750,000	610,000
Total liabilities and stockholders' equity	$1,750,000	$1,400,000

Additional data obtained from the income statement and from an examination of the accounts in the ledger for 20Y8 are as follows:

A. Net income, $190,000.

B. Depreciation reported on the income statement, $115,000.

C. Equipment was purchased at a cost of $395,000 and fully depreciated equipment costing $75,000 was discarded, with no salvage realized.

D. The mortgage note payable was not due for six years, but the terms permitted earlier payment without penalty.

E. 40,000 shares of common stock were issued at $15 for cash.

F. Cash dividends declared and paid, $50,000.

Instructions

Prepare a statement of cash flows, using the indirect method of presenting cash flows from operating activities.

PR 13-3A   Statement of cash flows—indirect method   Obj. 2, 3, 4, 5

✔ Net cash flow used for operating activities, $(169,600)

EXCEL TEMPLATE

The comparative balance sheet of Whitman Co. at December 31, 20Y2 and 20Y1, is as follows:

	Dec. 31, 20Y2	Dec. 31, 20Y1
Assets		
Cash	$ 918,000	$ 964,800
Accounts receivable (net)	828,900	761,940
Inventories	1,268,460	1,162,980
Prepaid expenses	29,340	35,100
Land	315,900	479,700
Buildings	1,462,500	900,900
Accumulated depreciation—buildings.........................	(408,600)	(382,320)
Equipment...	512,280	454,680
Accumulated depreciation—equipment	(141,300)	(158,760)
Total assets	$4,785,480	$4,219,020
Liabilities and Stockholders' Equity		
Accounts payable (merchandise creditors)	$ 922,500	$ 958,320
Bonds payable	270,000	0
Common stock, $25 par.......................................	317,000	117,000
Paid-in capital: Excess of issue price over par—common stock	758,000	558,000
Retained earnings...	2,517,980	2,585,700
Total liabilities and stockholders' equity.......................	$4,785,480	$4,219,020

The noncurrent asset, noncurrent liability, and stockholders' equity accounts for 20Y2 are as follows:

ACCOUNT *Land*   **ACCOUNT NO.**

Date		Item	Debit	Credit	Balance Debit	Balance Credit
20Y2						
Jan.	1	Balance			479,700	
Apr.	20	Realized $151,200 cash from sale		163,800	315,900	

ACCOUNT *Buildings*   **ACCOUNT NO.**

Date		Item	Debit	Credit	Balance Debit	Balance Credit
20Y2						
Jan.	1	Balance			900,900	
Apr.	20	Acquired for cash	561,600		1,462,500	

(Continued)

ACCOUNT *Accumulated Depreciation—Buildings*   **ACCOUNT NO.**

Date		Item	Debit	Credit	Balance Debit	Balance Credit
20Y2						
Jan.	1	Balance				382,320
Dec.	31	Depreciation for year		26,280		408,600

ACCOUNT *Equipment*   **ACCOUNT NO.**

Date		Item	Debit	Credit	Balance Debit	Balance Credit
20Y2						
Jan.	1	Balance			454,680	
	26	Discarded, no salvage		46,800	407,880	
Aug.	11	Purchased for cash	104,400		512,280	

ACCOUNT *Accumulated Depreciation—Equipment*   **ACCOUNT NO.**

Date		Item	Debit	Credit	Balance Debit	Balance Credit
20Y2						
Jan.	1	Balance				158,760
	26	Equipment discarded	46,800			111,960
Dec.	31	Depreciation for year		29,340		141,300

ACCOUNT *Bonds Payable*   **ACCOUNT NO.**

Date		Item	Debit	Credit	Balance Debit	Balance Credit
20Y2						
May	1	Issued 20-year bonds		270,000		270,000

ACCOUNT *Common Stock, $25 par*   **ACCOUNT NO.**

Date		Item	Debit	Credit	Balance Debit	Balance Credit
20Y2						
Jan.	1	Balance				117,000
Dec.	7	Issued 8,000 shares of common stock for $50 per share		200,000		317,000

ACCOUNT *Paid-In Capital in Excess of Par—Common Stock*   **ACCOUNT NO.**

Date		Item	Debit	Credit	Balance Debit	Balance Credit
20Y2						
Jan.	1	Balance				558,000
Dec.	7	Issued 8,000 shares of common stock for $50 per share		200,000		758,000

ACCOUNT *Retained Earnings*   **ACCOUNT NO.**

Date		Item	Debit	Credit	Balance Debit	Balance Credit
20Y2						
Jan.	1	Balance				2,585,700
Dec.	31	Net loss	35,320			2,550,380
	31	Cash dividends	32,400			2,517,980

Instructions

Prepare a statement of cash flows, using the indirect method of presenting cash flows from operating activities.

Appendix 2

PR 13-4A Statement of cash flows—direct method

✔ Net cash flow from operating activities, $293,600

SHOW ME HOW   EXCEL TEMPLATE

GENERAL LEDGER

The comparative balance sheet of Canace Products Inc. for December 31, 20Y6 and 20Y5, is as follows:

	Dec. 31, 20Y6	Dec. 31, 20Y5
Assets		
Cash	$ 643,400	$ 679,400
Accounts receivable (net)	566,800	547,400
Inventories	1,011,000	982,800
Investments	0	240,000
Land	520,000	0
Equipment	880,000	680,000
Accumulated depreciation	(244,400)	(200,400)
Total assets	$3,376,800	$2,929,200
Liabilities and Stockholders' Equity		
Accounts payable (merchandise creditors)	$ 771,800	$ 748,400
Accrued expenses payable (operating expenses)	63,400	70,800
Dividends payable	8,800	6,400
Common stock, $2 par	56,000	32,000
Paid-in capital: Excess of issue price over par—common stock	408,000	192,000
Retained earnings	2,068,800	1,879,600
Total liabilities and stockholders' equity	$3,376,800	$2,929,200

The income statement for the year ended December 31, 20Y6, is as follows:

Sales		$5,980,000
Cost of goods sold		2,452,000
Gross profit		$3,528,000
Operating expenses:		
Depreciation expense	$ 44,000	
Other operating expenses	3,100,000	
Total operating expenses		3,144,000
Operating income		$ 384,000
Other expense:		
Loss on sale of investments		(64,000)
Income before income tax		$ 320,000
Income tax expense		102,800
Net income		$ 217,200

Additional data obtained from an examination of the accounts in the ledger for 20Y6 are as follows:

A. Equipment and land were acquired for cash.

B. There were no disposals of equipment during the year.

(Continued)

C. The investments were sold for $176,000 cash.

D. The common stock was issued for cash.

E. There was a $28,000 debit to Retained Earnings for cash dividends declared.

Instructions

Prepare a statement of cash flows, using the direct method of presenting cash flows from operating activities.

Appendix 2
PR 13-5A   Statement of cash flows—direct method applied to PR 13-1A

✔ Net cash flow from operating activities, $490,000

EXCEL TEMPLATE

The comparative balance sheet of Livers Inc. for December 31, 20Y3 and 20Y2, is as follows:

	Dec. 31, 20Y3	Dec. 31, 20Y2
Assets		
Cash	$ 155,000	$ 150,000
Accounts receivable (net)	450,000	400,000
Inventories	770,000	750,000
Investments	0	100,000
Land	500,000	0
Equipment	1,400,000	1,200,000
Accumulated depreciation—equipment	(600,000)	(500,000)
Total assets	$2,675,000	$2,100,000
Liabilities and Stockholders' Equity		
Accounts payable (merchandise creditors)	$ 340,000	$ 300,000
Accrued expenses payable (operating expenses)	45,000	50,000
Dividends payable	30,000	25,000
Common stock, $4 par	700,000	600,000
Paid-in capital: Excess of issue price over par—common stock	200,000	175,000
Retained earnings	1,360,000	950,000
Total liabilities and stockholders' equity	$2,675,000	$2,100,000

The income statement for the year ended December 31, 20Y3, is as follows:

Sales		$ 3,000,000
Cost of goods sold		1,400,000
Gross profit		$ 1,600,000
Operating expenses:		
Depreciation expense	$100,000	
Other operating expenses	950,000	
Total operating expenses		1,050,000
Operating income		$ 550,000
Other income:		
Gain on sale of investments		75,000
Income before income tax		$ 625,000
Income tax expense		125,000
Net income		$ 500,000

Additional data obtained from an examination of the accounts in the ledger for 20Y3 are as follows:

A. The investments were sold for $175,000 cash.

B. Equipment and land were acquired for cash.

C. There were no disposals of equipment during the year.

D. The common stock was issued for cash.

E. There was a $90,000 debit to Retained Earnings for cash dividends declared.

Instructions

Prepare a statement of cash flows, using the direct method of presenting cash flows from operating activities.

Problems: Series B

✔ Net cash flow from
operating activities,
$154,260

SHOW ME HOW   EXCEL TEMPLATE

PR 13-1B Statement of cash flows—indirect method

Obj. 2, 3, 4, 5

The comparative balance sheet of Merrick Equipment Co. for December 31, 20Y9 and 20Y8, is as follows:

	Dec. 31, 20Y9	Dec. 31, 20Y8
Assets		
Cash	$ 70,720	$ 47,940
Accounts receivable (net)	207,230	188,190
Inventories	298,520	289,850
Investments	0	102,000
Land	295,800	0
Equipment..	438,600	358,020
Accumulated depreciation—equipment	(99,110)	(84,320)
Total assets	$1,211,760	$901,680
Liabilities and Stockholders' Equity		
Accounts payable (merchandise creditors)	$ 205,700	$194,140
Accrued expenses payable (operating expenses)	30,600	26,860
Dividends payable..	25,500	20,400
Common stock, $1 par......................................	202,000	102,000
Paid-in capital: Excess of issue price over par—common stock	354,000	204,000
Retained earnings..	393,960	354,280
Total liabilities and stockholders' equity........................	$1,211,760	$901,680

Additional data obtained from an examination of the accounts in the ledger for 20Y9 are as follows:

A. Equipment and land were acquired for cash.

B. There were no disposals of equipment during the year.

C. The investments were sold for $91,800 cash.

D. The common stock was issued for cash.

E. There was a $141,680 credit to Retained Earnings for net income.

F. There was a $102,000 debit to Retained Earnings for cash dividends declared.

Instructions

Prepare a statement of cash flows, using the indirect method of presenting cash flows from operating activities.

✔ Net cash flow from
operating activities,
$561,400

SHOW ME HOW   EXCEL TEMPLATE

PR 13-2B Statement of cash flows—indirect method

Obj. 2, 3, 4, 5

The comparative balance sheet of Harris Industries Inc. at December 31, 20Y4 and 20Y3, is as follows:

	Dec. 31, 20Y4	Dec. 31, 20Y3
Assets		
Cash	$ 443,240	$ 360,920
Accounts receivable (net)	665,280	592,200
Inventories	887,880	1,022,560
Prepaid expenses	31,640	25,200
Land	302,400	302,400
Buildings	1,713,600	1,134,000
Accumulated depreciation—buildings.....................	(466,200)	(414,540)
Machinery and equipment.................................	781,200	781,200
Accumulated depreciation—machinery and equipment......	(214,200)	(191,520)
Patents...	106,960	112,000
Total assets	$4,251,800	$3,724,420

(Continued)

Liabilities and Stockholders' Equity

Accounts payable (merchandise creditors)	$ 837,480	$ 927,080
Dividends payable...	32,760	25,200
Salaries payable...	78,960	87,080
Mortgage note payable, due in nine years..................	224,000	0
Bonds payable	0	390,000
Common stock, $5 par......................................	200,400	50,400
Paid-in capital: Excess of issue price over par—common stock.......	366,000	126,000
Retained earnings...	2,512,200	2,118,660
Total liabilities and stockholders' equity....................	$4,251,800	$3,724,420

An examination of the income statement and the accounting records revealed the following additional information applicable to 20Y4:

A. Net income, $524,580.

B. Depreciation expense reported on the income statement: buildings, $51,660; machinery and equipment, $22,680.

C. Patent amortization reported on the income statement, $5,040.

D. A building was constructed for $579,600.

E. A mortgage note for $224,000 was issued for cash.

F. 30,000 shares of common stock were issued at $13 in exchange for the bonds payable.

G. Cash dividends declared, $131,040.

Instructions

Prepare a statement of cash flows, using the indirect method of presenting cash flows from operating activities.

PR 13-3B   Statement of cash flows—indirect method

Obj. 2, 3, 4, 5

✔ Net cash flow from operating activities, $162,800

EXCEL TEMPLATE

The comparative balance sheet of Coulson, Inc. at December 31, 20Y2 and 20Y1, is as follows:

	Dec. 31, 20Y2	Dec. 31, 20Y1
Assets		
Cash	$ 300,600	$ 337,800
Accounts receivable (net)	704,400	609,600
Inventories	918,600	865,800
Prepaid expenses	18,600	26,400
Land	990,000	1,386,000
Buildings	1,980,000	990,000
Accumulated depreciation—buildings....................	(397,200)	(366,000)
Equipment	660,600	529,800
Accumulated depreciation—equipment	(133,200)	(162,000)
Total assets	$5,042,400	$4,217,400
Liabilities and Stockholders' Equity		
Accounts payable (merchandise creditors)	$ 594,000	$ 631,200
Income taxes payable	26,400	21,600
Bonds payable	330,000	0
Common stock, $20 par....................................	320,000	180,000
Paid-in capital: Excess of issue price over par—common stock	950,000	810,000
Retained earnings.......................................	2,822,000	2,574,600
Total liabilities and stockholders' equity....................	$5,042,400	$4,217,400

The noncurrent asset, noncurrent liability, and stockholders' equity accounts for 20Y2 are as follows:

ACCOUNT *Land*   **ACCOUNT NO.**

Date		Item	Debit	Credit	Balance Debit	Balance Credit
20Y2						
Jan.	1	Balance			1,386,000	
Apr.	20	Realized $456,000 cash from sale		396,000	990,000	

ACCOUNT *Buildings*   **ACCOUNT NO.**

Date		Item	Debit	Credit	Balance Debit	Balance Credit
20Y2						
Jan.	1	Balance			990,000	
Apr.	20	Acquired for cash	990,000		1,980,000	

ACCOUNT *Accumulated Depreciation—Buildings*   **ACCOUNT NO.**

Date		Item	Debit	Credit	Balance Debit	Balance Credit
20Y2						
Jan.	1	Balance				366,000
Dec.	31	Depreciation for year		31,200		397,200

ACCOUNT *Equipment*   **ACCOUNT NO.**

Date		Item	Debit	Credit	Balance Debit	Balance Credit
20Y2						
Jan.	1	Balance			529,800	
	26	Discarded, no salvage		66,000	463,800	
Aug.	11	Purchased for cash	196,800		660,600	

ACCOUNT *Accumulated Depreciation—Equipment*   **ACCOUNT NO.**

Date		Item	Debit	Credit	Balance Debit	Balance Credit
20Y2						
Jan.	1	Balance				162,000
	26	Equipment discarded	66,000			96,000
Dec.	31	Depreciation for year		37,200		133,200

ACCOUNT *Bonds Payable*   **ACCOUNT NO.**

Date		Item	Debit	Credit	Balance Debit	Balance Credit
20Y2						
May	1	Issued 20-year bonds		330,000		330,000

(Continued)

ACCOUNT *Common Stock, $20 par*   **ACCOUNT NO.**

Date		Item	Debit	Credit	Balance Debit	Balance Credit
20Y2						
Jan.	1	Balance				180,000
Dec.	7	Issued 7,000 shares of common stock for $40 per share		140,000		320,000

ACCOUNT *Paid-In Capital in Excess of Par—Common Stock*   **ACCOUNT NO.**

Date		Item	Debit	Credit	Balance Debit	Balance Credit
20Y2						
Jan.	1	Balance				810,000
Dec.	7	Issued 7,000 shares of common stock for $40 per share		140,000		950,000

ACCOUNT *Retained Earnings*   **ACCOUNT NO.**

Date		Item	Debit	Credit	Balance Debit	Balance Credit
20Y2						
Jan.	1	Balance				2,574,600
Dec.	31	Net income		326,600		2,901,200
	31	Cash dividends	79,200			2,822,000

Instructions

Prepare a statement of cash flows, using the indirect method of presenting cash flows from operating activities.

Appendix 2

PR 13-4B   Statement of cash flows—direct method

✔ Net cash flow from operating activities, $509,220

The comparative balance sheet of Martinez Inc. for December 31, 20Y4 and 20Y3, is as follows:

SHOW ME HOW   EXCEL TEMPLATE

GENERAL LEDGER

	Dec. 31, 20Y4	Dec. 31, 20Y3
Assets		
Cash	$ 661,920	$ 683,100
Accounts receivable (net)	992,640	914,400
Inventories	1,394,400	1,363,800
Investments	0	432,000
Land	960,000	0
Equipment...	1,224,000	984,000
Accumulated depreciation—equipment	(481,500)	(368,400)
Total assets	$4,751,460	$4,008,900
Liabilities and Stockholders' Equity		
Accounts payable (merchandise creditors)	$1,080,000	$ 966,600
Accrued expenses payable (operating expenses)	67,800	79,200
Dividends payable.......................................	100,800	91,200
Common stock, $5 par	130,000	30,000
Paid-in capital: Excess of issue price over par—common stock	950,000	450,000
Retained earnings.......................................	2,422,860	2,391,900
Total liabilities and stockholders' equity...................	$4,751,460	$4,008,900

The income statement for the year ended December 31, 20Y3, is as follows:

Sales		$4,512,000
Cost of goods sold		2,352,000
Gross profit		$2,160,000
Operating expenses:		
Depreciation expense	$ 113,100	
Other operating expenses	1,344,840	
Total operating expenses		1,457,940
Operating income		$ 702,060
Other income:		
Gain on sale of investments		156,000
Income before income tax		$ 858,060
Income tax expense		299,100
Net income		$ 558,960

Additional data obtained from an examination of the accounts in the ledger for 20Y3 are as follows:

A. Equipment and land were acquired for cash.

B. There were no disposals of equipment during the year.

C. The investments were sold for $588,000 cash.

D. The common stock was issued for cash.

E. There was a $528,000 debit to Retained Earnings for cash dividends declared.

Instructions

Prepare a statement of cash flows, using the direct method of presenting cash flows from operating activities.

Appendix 2

PR 13-5B   Statement of cash flows—direct method applied to PR 13-1B

✔ Net cash flow from operating activities, $154,260

EXCEL TEMPLATE

The comparative balance sheet of Merrick Equipment Co. for Dec. 31, 20Y9 and 20Y8, is:

	Dec. 31, 20Y9	Dec. 31, 20Y8
Assets		
Cash	$ 70,720	$ 47,940
Accounts receivable (net)	207,230	188,190
Inventories	298,520	289,850
Investments	0	102,000
Land	295,800	0
Equipment	438,600	358,020
Accumulated depreciation—equipment	(99,110)	(84,320)
Total assets	$1,211,760	$ 901,680
Liabilities and Stockholders' Equity		
Accounts payable (merchandise creditors)	$ 205,700	$ 194,140
Accrued expenses payable (operating expenses)	30,600	26,860
Dividends payable	25,500	20,400
Common stock, $1 par	202,000	102,000
Paid-in capital: Excess of issue price over par—common stock	354,000	204,000
Retained earnings	393,960	354,280
Total liabilities and stockholders' equity	$1,211,760	$ 901,680

(Continued)

The income statement for the year ended December 31, 20Y9, is as follows:

Sales		$2,023,898
Cost of goods sold		1,245,476
Gross profit		$ 778,422
Operating expenses:		
Depreciation expense	$ 14,790	
Other operating expenses	517,299	
Total operating expenses		532,089
Operating income		$ 246,333
Other expenses:		
Loss on sale of investments		(10,200)
Income before income tax		$ 236,133
Income tax expense		94,453
Net income		$ 141,680

Additional data obtained from an examination of the accounts in the ledger for 20Y9 are as follows:

A. Equipment and land were acquired for cash.

B. There were no disposals of equipment during the year.

C. The investments were sold for $91,800 cash.

D. The common stock was issued for cash.

E. There was a $102,000 debit to Retained Earnings for cash dividends declared.

Instructions

Prepare a statement of cash flows, using the direct method of presenting cash flows from operating activities.

Analysis for Decision Making

REAL WORLD

ADM-1   Continuing Company Analysis—Amazon, Best Buy, and Walmart: Free cash flow

Amazon.com, Inc. is one of the largest Internet retailers in the world. Best Buy, Inc. is a leading retailer of consumer electronics and media products in the United States, while Walmart Stores, Inc. is the leading retailer in the United States. Amazon, Best Buy, and Walmart compete in similar markets. Best Buy and Walmart sell through both traditional retail stores and the Internet, while Amazon sells only through the Internet. Sales and cash flow information from recent annual reports for all three companies is as follows (in millions):

	Amazon	Best Buy	Walmart
Sales	$88,988	$40,339	$485,651
Cash flows from operating activities	6,842	1,935	28,564
Purchases of property, plant, and equipment	4,893	561	12,174

A. Determine the free cash flow for all three companies.

B. Compute the ratio of free cash flow to sales for all three companies. (Round percentages to one decimal place.)

C. ━━━━━ How does Amazon compare to the other two companies with respect to generating free cash flow?

REAL WORLD

ADM-2 RadioShack: Free cash flow

RadioShack Corporation is a consumer electronics retailer. Recently, the company declared bankruptcy to provide financial protection while attempting to reorganize its operations. Annual report information for the three most recent years prior to the bankruptcy are as follows (in millions):

	Year 3	Year 2	Year 1
Cash flows from operating activities	$ 36	$ (43)	$ 218
Cash used to purchase property, plant, and equipment	(42)	(68)	(82)
Sales	3,434	3,831	4,032

A. Determine the free cash flow.

B. Determine the ratio of free cash flow to sales. (Round percentages to one decimal place.)

C. ━━━► Did the free cash flow information indicate financial stress? Explain.

REAL WORLD

ADM-3 AT&T and Facebook: Free cash flow

AT&T Inc. is a leading global provider of telecommunication services. Facebook, Inc. is a major worldwide social media company. AT&T has a lengthy history and was founded by Alexander Graham Bell. Facebook has a short history and was founded by Mark Zuckerberg. Facebook uses telecommunication networks, like those of AT&T, to deliver social content to its users. Free cash flow and revenue information for both companies for three recent years is as follows (in millions):

AT&T
Information from the statement of cash flows:

	Year 3	Year 2	Year 1
Cash flows from operating activities	$ 31,338	$ 34,796	$ 39,176
Cash used to purchase property, plant, and equipment	(21,433)	(21,228)	(19,728)

Information from the income statement:

	Year 3	Year 2	Year 1
Revenue	$132,447	$128,752	$127,434

Facebook
Information from the statement of cash flows:

	Year 3	Year 2	Year 1
Cash flows from operating activities	$ 5,457	$ 4,222	$ 1,612
Cash used to purchase property, plant, and equipment	(1,831)	(1,362)	(1,235)

Information from the income statement:

	Year 3	Year 2	Year 1
Revenue	$12,466	$7,872	$5,089

A. Using total revenue, which company appears to be the larger at the end of Year 3?

B. Using total revenue, which company appears to be growing faster across the three years?

C. Compute the cash used to purchase property, plant, and equipment (PP&E) as a percent of the cash flows from operating activities for all three years for each company. (Round to nearest whole percent.)

D. ━━━► Using the computations in (C), which company appears to require more cash to purchase PP&E, and what impact does this have on free cash flow?

(Continued)

E. Compute the ratio of free cash flow to revenue for all three years for each company, and plot the data on a line chart with the years on the horizontal axis.

F. ━━━▶ Interpret the chart.

REAL WORLD

ADM-4   Priceline: Free cash flow

Priceline Group, Inc. is a leading provider of online travel reservation services, including brand names Priceline, KAYAK, and OpenTable. Selected cash flow information from the statement of cash flows for three recent years is as follows (in millions):

	Year 3	Year 2	Year 1
Net cash provided by operating activities	$ 2,914	$ 2,301	$ 1,786
Net cash used in investing activities	(2,349)	(2,162)	(1,563)
Net cash provided by (used in) financing activities	1,429	(404)	669
Additions to property, plant, and equipment	(132)	(84)	(55)
Repurchase common stock	(750)	(884)	(257)
Acquisitions and investments	(2,146)	(1,997)	(1,587)

A. Determine the net change in cash for each year.

B. Determine the free cash flow for each year.

C. ━━━▶ How is the free cash flow being used based on the data provided?

D. ━━━▶ Which is better for measuring the cash flow available for investment, dividends, debt repayments, and stock repurchases: the change in cash for the period or the free cash flow? Explain.

Take It Further

ETHICS

TIF 13-1   Ethics in Action

Head Donuts Inc. is a retailer of designer headphones, earphones, and hands-free audio devices. Polly Ester, the company president, is reviewing the company's financial statements after the close of the fiscal year and is troubled that earnings decreased by 10%. She shares her concerns with the company's chief accountant, Lucas Simmons, who points out that the drop in earnings was balanced by a 20% increase in cash flows, from operating activities. Polly is encouraged by the increase in cash flows from operating activities, but is worried that investors might miss this information because it is "buried" in the statement of cash flows. To make it easier for investors to find this information, she instructs Lucas to include an operating cash flow per share number on the face of the income statement, directly below earnings per share. While Lucas is concerned about using such an unconventional financial reporting tactic, he agrees to include the information on the income statement.

━━━▶ Is Lucas behaving in an ethical and professional manner? Explain your answer.

TIF 13-2 Team Activity

In teams, select a public company that interests you. Obtain the company's most recent annual report on Form 10-K. The Form 10-K is a company's annually required filing with the Securities and Exchange Commission (SEC). It includes the company's financial statements and accompanying notes. The Form 10-K can be obtained either (A) from the investor relations section of the company's Web site or (B) by using the company search feature of the SEC's EDGAR database service found at www.sec.gov/edgar/searchedgar/companysearch.html.

1. Based on the information in the company's most recent annual report, answer the following questions:

    A. What is the net cash flows from operating activities reported by the company at the end of the most recent year?

    B. What is the net cash flows from investing activities reported by the company at the end of the most recent year?

    C. What is the net cash flows from financing activities reported by the company at the end of the most recent year?

    D. What was the net increase (or decrease) in cash during the year?

2. ━━━▶ Evaluate the company's cash inflows and outflows.

TIF 13-3 Communication

Tidewater Inc., a retailer, provided the following financial information for its most recent fiscal year:

Net income	$ 945,000
Return on invested capital	8%
Cash flows from operating activities	(1,428,000)
Cash flows from investing activities	600,000
Cash flows from financing activities	900,000

The company's Cash Flows from Operating Activities Section is as follows:

Net income	$ 945,000
Depreciation	210,000
Increase in accounts receivable	(1,134,000)
Increase in inventory	(1,260,000)
Decrease in accounts payable	(189,000)
Net cash flow from operating activities	$(1,428,000)

An examination of the financial statements revealed the following additional information:

- Revenues increased during the year as a result of an aggressive marketing campaign aimed at increasing the number of new "Tidewater Card" credit card customers. This is the company's branded credit card, which can only be used at Tidewater stores. The credit card balances are accounts receivable on Tidewater's balance sheet.

- Some suppliers have made their merchandise available at a deep discount. As a result, the company purchased large quantities of these goods in an attempt to improve the company's profitability.

- In recent years, the company has struggled to pay its accounts payable on time. The company has improved on this during the past year and is nearly caught up on overdue payables balances.

- The company reported net losses in each of the two prior years.

━━━▶ Write a brief memo to your instructor evaluating the financial condition of Tidewater Inc.

14 Financial Statement Analysis

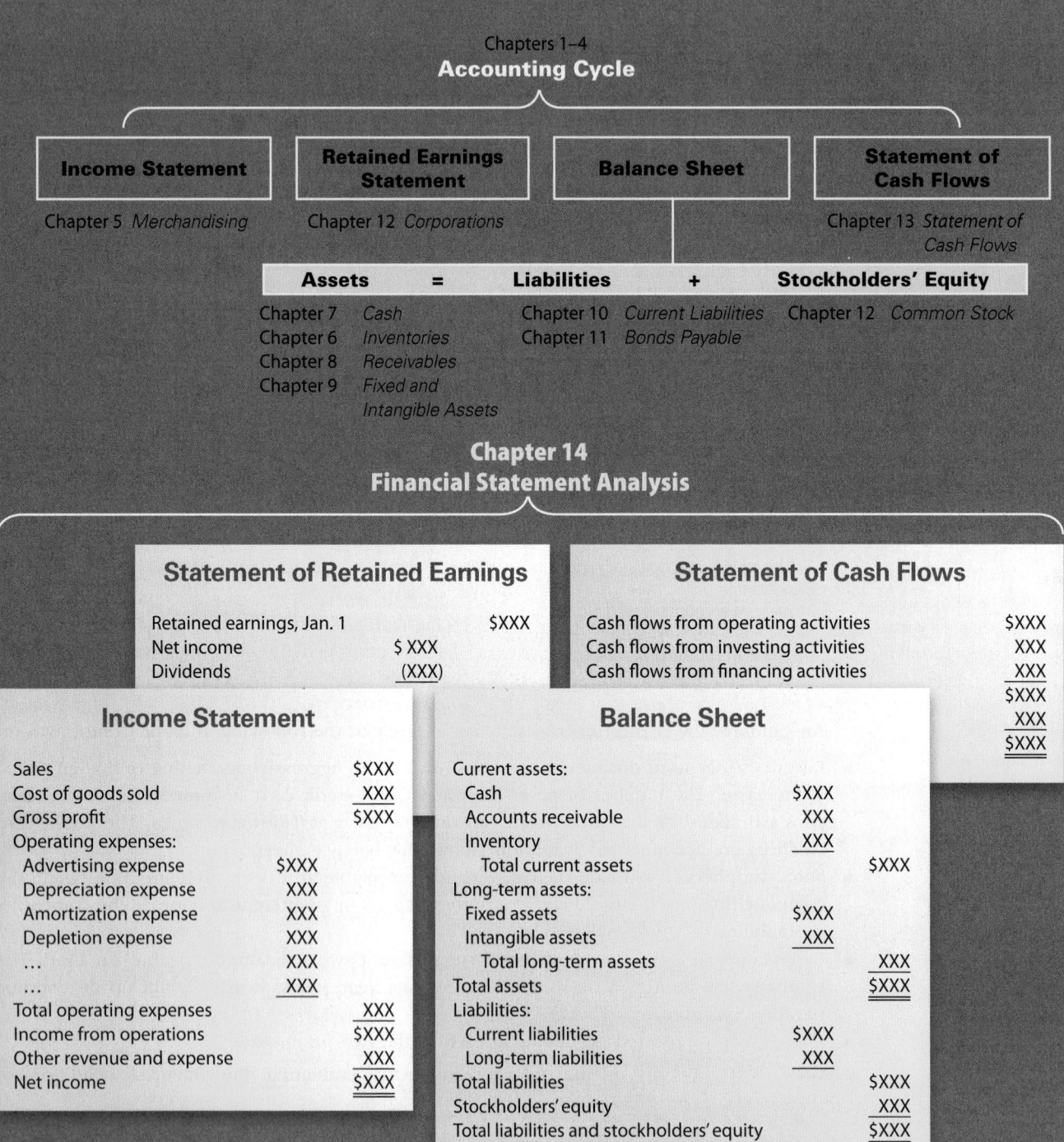

Nike, Inc.

"Just do it." These three words identify one of the most recognizable brands in the world, **Nike**. While this phrase inspires athletes to "compete and achieve their potential," it also defines the company.

Nike began in 1964 as a partnership between University of Oregon track coach Bill Bowerman and one of his former student-athletes, Phil Knight. The two began by selling shoes imported from Japan out of the back of Knight's car to athletes at track-and-field events. As sales grew, the company opened retail outlets, calling itself **Blue Ribbon Sports**. The company also began to develop its own shoes. In 1971, the company commissioned a graphic design student at Portland State University to develop the swoosh logo for a fee of $35. In 1978, the company changed its name to Nike, and in 1980, it sold its first shares of stock to the public.

Nike would have been a great company to invest in at the time. If you had invested in Nike's common stock back in 1990, you would have paid $5 per share. As of November 2015, Nike's stock was worth over $130 per share. Unfortunately, you can't invest using hindsight.

How can you select companies in which to invest? Like any significant purchase, you should do some research to guide your investment decision. If you were buying a car, for example, you might go to **Edmunds.com** to obtain reviews, ratings, prices, specifications, options, and fuel economies to evaluate different vehicles. In selecting companies in which to invest, you can use financial analysis to gain insight into a company's past performance and future prospects. This chapter describes and illustrates common financial data that can be analyzed to assist you in making investment decisions such as whether or not to invest in Nike's stock.

Source: www.nikebiz.com/.

Financial Statement Analysis

Analyzing and Interpreting Financial Statements	Analytical Methods	Analyzing			Understanding Corpoate Annual Reports
		Liquidity	**Solvency**	**Profitability**	
■ Value of Financial Statement Information (Obj. 1) ■ Techniques (Obj. 1)	■ Horizontal Analysis (Obj. 2) ■ Vertical Analysis (Obj. 2) ■ Common-Sized Statements (Obj. 2)	■ Current Position (Obj. 3) ■ Accounts Receivable (Obj. 3) ■ Inventory (Obj. 3)	■ Fixed Assets to Long-Term Liabilities (Obj. 4) ■ Liabilities to Stockholders' Equity (Obj. 4) ■ Times Interest Earned (Obj. 4)	■ Asset Turnover (Obj. 5) ■ Rates of Return (Obj. 5) ■ Earnings per Share (Obj. 5) ■ Price to Earnings (Obj. 5) ■ Dividend Measures (Obj. 5)	■ Management Discussion (Obj. 6) ■ Internal Control (Obj. 6) ■ Audit Report (Obj. 6)

Learning Objectives

Obj. 1 Describe the techniques and tools used to analyze financial statement information.

Obj. 2 Describe and illustrate basic financial statement analytical methods.

Obj. 3 Describe and illustrate how to use financial statement analysis to assess liquidity.

Obj. 4 Describe and illustrate how to use financial statement analysis to assess solvency.

Obj. 5 Describe and illustrate how to use financial statement analysis to assess profitability.

Obj. 6 Describe the contents of corporate annual reports.

Analysis for Decision Making

Describe and illustrate the use of financial statement analysis in evaluating potential stock price appreciation.

Objective 1

Describe the techniques and tools used to analyze financial statement information.

Analyzing and Interpreting Financial Statements

The objective of accounting is to provide relevant and timely information to support the decision-making needs of financial statement users. Bankers, creditors, and investors all rely on financial statements to provide insight into a company's financial condition and performance. This chapter discusses the value of financial statement information, techniques used to evaluate financial statements, and the impact of that information on decision making.

The Value of Financial Statement Information

General-purpose financial statements are distributed to a wide range of potential users, providing each group with valuable information about a company's economic performance and financial condition. Users typically evaluate this information along three dimensions: liquidity, solvency, and profitability.

Liquidity Short-term creditors such as banks and financial institutions are primarily concerned with whether a company will be able to repay short-term borrowings such as loans and notes. As such, they are most interested in evaluating a company's ability to convert assets into cash, which is called **liquidity**.

Solvency Long-term creditors, such as bondholders, loan money for long periods of time. Thus, they are interested in evaluating a company's ability to make its periodic interest payments and repay the face amount of debt at maturity, which is called **solvency**.

Profitability Investors, such as stockholders, are the owners of the company. They benefit from increases in the price of a company's shares and are interested in evaluating the potential for the price of the company's stock to increase. The price of a company's stock depends on a variety of factors, including the company's current and potential future earnings. As such, investors focus on evaluating a company's ability to generate earnings, which is called **profitability**.

Techniques for Analyzing Financial Statements

Financial statement users rely on the following techniques to analyze and interpret a company's financial performance and condition:

- **Analytical methods** examine changes in the amount and percentage of financial statement items within and across periods.
- **Ratios** express a financial statement item or set of financial statement items as a percentage of another financial statement item, in order to measure an important economic relationship as a single number.

Both analytical methods and ratios can be used to compare a company's financial performance over time or to another company.

- *Comparisons Over Time:* The comparison of a financial statement item or ratio with the same item or ratio from a prior period often helps the user identify trends in a company's economic performance, financial condition, liquidity, solvency, and profitability.
- *Comparisons Between Companies:* The comparison of a financial statement item or ratio to another company in the same industry can provide insight into a company's economic performance and financial condition relative to its competitors.

Analytical Methods

Objective 2

Describe and illustrate basic financial statement analytical methods.

Users analyze a company's financial statements using a variety of analytical methods. Three such methods are:

- Horizontal analysis
- Vertical analysis
- Common-sized statements

Horizontal Analysis

The analysis of increases and decreases in the amount and percentage of comparative financial statement items is called **horizontal analysis**. Each item on the most recent statement is compared with the same item on one or more earlier statements in terms of the following:

- *Amount* of increase or decrease
- *Percent* of increase or decrease

When comparing statements, the earlier statement is normally used as the base year for computing increases and decreases.

Exhibit 1 illustrates horizontal analysis for the December 31, 20Y6 and 20Y5 balance sheets of **Lincoln Company**. In Exhibit 1, the December 31, 20Y5, balance sheet (the earliest year presented) is used as the base year.

Exhibit 1 indicates that total assets decreased by $91,000 (7.4%), liabilities decreased by $133,000 (30.0%), and stockholders' equity increased by $42,000 (5.3%). Since the long-term investments account decreased by $82,500, it appears that most of the decrease in long-term liabilities of $100,000 was achieved through the sale of long-term investments.

Exhibit 1
Comparative
Balance Sheet—
Horizontal
Analysis

	Dec. 31, 20Y6	Dec. 31, 20Y5	Increase (Decrease) Amount	Percent
Lincoln Company				
Comparative Balance Sheet				
December 31, 20Y6 and 20Y5				
Assets				
Current assets..	$ 550,000	$ 533,000	$ 17,000	3.2%
Long-term investments.................................	95,000	177,500	(82,500)	(46.5%)
Property, plant, and equipment (net)	444,500	470,000	(25,500)	(5.4%)
Intangible assets	50,000	50,000	—	—
Total assets	$1,139,500	$1,230,500	$ (91,000)	(7.4%)
Liabilities				
Current liabilities.......................................	$ 210,000	$ 243,000	$ (33,000)	(13.6%)
Long-term liabilities	100,000	200,000	(100,000)	(50.0%)
Total liabilities	$ 310,000	$ 443,000	$(133,000)	(30.0%)
Stockholders' Equity				
Preferred 6% stock, $100 par	$ 150,000	$ 150,000	—	—
Common stock, $10 par.................................	500,000	500,000	—	—
Retained earnings......................................	179,500	137,500	$ 42,000	30.5%
Total stockholders' equity..............................	$ 829,500	$ 787,500	$ 42,000	5.3%
Total liabilities and stockholders' equity.................	$1,139,500	$1,230,500	$ (91,000)	(7.4%)

The balance sheets in Exhibit 1 may be expanded or supported by a separate schedule that includes the individual asset and liability accounts. For example, Exhibit 2 is a supporting schedule of Lincoln Company's current asset accounts.

Exhibit 2
Comparative
Schedule of
Current Assets—
Horizontal Analysis

	Dec. 31, 20Y6	Dec. 31, 20Y5	Increase (Decrease) Amount	Percent
Lincoln Company				
Comparative Schedule of Current Assets				
December 31, 20Y6 and 20Y5				
Cash	$ 90,500	$ 64,700	$ 25,800	39.9%
Temporary investments.....................................	75,000	60,000	15,000	25.0%
Accounts receivable, net....................................	115,000	120,000	(5,000)	(4.2%)
Inventories	264,000	283,000	(19,000)	(6.7%)
Prepaid expenses	5,500	5,300	200	3.8%
Total current assets..	$550,000	$533,000	$ 17,000	3.2%

Exhibit 2 indicates that while cash and temporary investments increased, accounts receivable and inventories decreased. The decrease in accounts receivable could be caused by improved collection policies, which would increase cash. The decrease in inventories could be caused by increased sales.

Exhibit 3 illustrates horizontal analysis for the 20Y6 and 20Y5 income statements of Lincoln Company. Exhibit 3 indicates an increase in sales of $298,000, or 24.8%. However, the percentage increase in sales of 24.8% was accompanied by an even greater percentage increase in the cost of goods sold of 27.2%. Thus, gross profit increased by only 19.7% rather than by the 24.8% increase in sales.

Exhibit 3 also indicates that selling expenses increased by 29.9%. Thus, the 24.8% increases in sales could have been caused by an advertising campaign, which increased selling expenses. Administrative expenses increased by only 6.8%, total operating expenses increased by 20.7%, and income from operations increased by 18.0%. Interest expense decreased by 50.0%. This decrease was probably caused by the 50.0% decrease in long-term liabilities (Exhibit 1). Overall, net income increased by 19.0%, a favorable result.

Lincoln Company Comparative Income Statement For the Years Ended December 31, 20Y6 and 20Y5			Increase (Decrease)	
	20Y6	**20Y5**	**Amount**	**Percent**
Sales	$1,498,000	$1,200,000	$298,000	24.8%
Cost of goods sold	1,043,000	820,000	223,000	27.2%
Gross profit	$ 455,000	$ 380,000	$ 75,000	19.7%
Selling expenses	$ 191,000	$ 147,000	$ 44,000	29.9%
Administrative expenses	104,000	97,400	6,600	6.8%
Total operating expenses	$ 295,000	$ 244,400	$ 50,600	20.7%
Income from operations	$ 160,000	$ 135,600	$ 24,400	18.0%
Other income	8,500	11,000	(2,500)	(22.7%)
	$ 168,500	$ 146,600	$ 21,900	14.9%
Other expense (interest)	6,000	12,000	(6,000)	(50.0%)
Income before income tax	$ 162,500	$ 134,600	$ 27,900	20.7%
Income tax expense	71,500	58,100	13,400	23.1%
Net income	$ 91,000	$ 76,500	$ 14,500	19.0%

Exhibit 3

Comparative Income Statement— Horizontal Analysis

Exhibit 4 illustrates horizontal analysis for the 20Y6 and 20Y5 retained earnings statements of **Lincoln Company**. Exhibit 4 indicates that retained earnings increased by 30.5% for the year. The increase is due to net income of $91,000 for the year, less dividends of $49,000.

Lincoln Company Comparative Retained Earnings Statement For the Years Ended December 31, 20Y6 and 20Y5			Increase (Decrease)	
	20Y6	**20Y5**	**Amount**	**Percent**
Retained earnings, January 1	$137,500	$100,000	$37,500	37.5%
Net income	91,000	76,500	14,500	19.0%
Total	$228,500	$176,500	$52,000	29.5%
Dividends:				
On preferred stock	$ 9,000	$ 9,000	—	—
On common stock	40,000	30,000	$10,000	33.3%
Total dividends	$ 49,000	$ 39,000	$10,000	25.6%
Retained earnings, December 31	$179,500	$137,500	$42,000	30.5%

Exhibit 4

Comparative Retained Earnings Statement— Horizontal Analysis

For a recent year, Nike's net income increased by 21.5%.

Link to Nike

Vertical Analysis

The percentage analysis of the relationship of each component in a financial statement to a total within the statement is called **vertical analysis**. Although vertical analysis is applied to a single statement, it may be applied on the same statement over time. This enhances the analysis by showing how the percentages of each item have changed over time.

In vertical analysis of the balance sheet, the percentages are computed as follows:

- Each asset item is stated as a percent of the total assets.
- Each liability and stockholders' equity item is stated as a percent of the total liabilities and stockholders' equity.

Exhibit 5 illustrates the vertical analysis of the December 31, 20Y6 and 20Y5 balance sheets of **Lincoln Company**. Exhibit 5 indicates that current assets have increased from 43.3% to 48.3% of total assets. Long-term investments decreased from 14.4% to 8.3% of total assets. Stockholders' equity increased from 64.0% to 72.8%, with a comparable decrease in liabilities.

Exhibit 5

Comparative Balance Sheet— Vertical Analysis

Lincoln Company
Comparative Balance Sheet
December 31, 20Y6 and 20Y5

	Dec. 31, 20Y6		Dec. 31, 20Y5	
	Amount	Percent	Amount	Percent
Assets				
Current assets..	$ 550,000	48.3%	$ 533,000	43.3%
Long-term investments...............................	95,000	8.3	177,500	14.4
Property, plant, and equipment (net)	444,500	39.0	470,000	38.2
Intangible assets	50,000	4.4	50,000	4.1
Total assets	$1,139,500	100.0%	$1,230,500	100.0%
Liabilities				
Current liabilities.....................................	$ 210,000	18.4%	$ 243,000	19.7%
Long-term liabilities..................................	100,000	8.8	200,000	16.3
Total liabilities	$ 310,000	27.2%	$ 443,000	36.0%
Stockholders' Equity				
Preferred 6% stock, $100 par	$ 150,000	13.2%	$ 150,000	12.2%
Common stock, $10 par...............................	500,000	43.9	500,000	40.6
Retained earnings....................................	179,500	15.7	137,500	11.2
Total stockholders' equity	$ 829,500	72.8%	$ 787,500	64.0%
Total liabilities and stockholders' equity..............	$1,139,500	100.0%	$1,230,500	100.0%

Link to Nike For a recent year, **Nike**'s current assets were 73.6% of total assets.

In a vertical analysis of the income statement, each item is stated as a percent of sales. Exhibit 6 illustrates the vertical analysis of the 20Y6 and 20Y5 income statements of **Lincoln Company**.

Exhibit 6

Comparative Income Statement—Vertical Analysis

Lincoln Company
Comparative Income Statement
For the Years Ended December 31, 20Y6 and 20Y5

	20Y6		20Y5	
	Amount	Percent	Amount	Percent
Sales	$1,498,000	100.0%	$1,200,000	100.0%
Cost of goods sold....................................	1,043,000	69.6	820,000	68.3
Gross profit..	$ 455,000	30.4%	$ 380,000	31.7%
Selling expenses	$ 191,000	12.8%	$ 147,000	12.3%
Administrative expenses..............................	104,000	6.9	97,400	8.1
Total operating expenses	$ 295,000	19.7%	$ 244,400	20.4%
Income from operations	$ 160,000	10.7%	$ 135,600	11.3%
Other income...	8,500	0.6	11,000	0.9
	$ 168,500	11.3%	$ 146,600	12.2%
Other expense (interest)..............................	6,000	0.4	12,000	1.0
Income before income tax	$ 162,500	10.9%	$ 134,600	11.2%
Income tax expense	71,500	4.8	58,100	4.8
Net income..	$ 91,000	6.1%	$ 76,500	6.4%

Exhibit 6 indicates a decrease in the gross profit rate from 31.7% in 20Y5 to 30.4% in 20Y6. Although this is only a 1.3 percentage point (31.7% – 30.4%) decrease, in dollars of potential gross profit, it represents a decrease of $19,474 (1.3% × $1,498,000) based on 20Y6 sales. Thus, a small percentage decrease can have a large dollar effect.

Common-Sized Statements

In a **common-sized statement**, all items are expressed as percentages, with no dollar amounts shown. Common-sized statements are often useful for comparing one company with another or for comparing a company with industry averages.

Exhibit 7 illustrates common-sized income statements for **Lincoln Company** and Madison Corporation. Exhibit 7 indicates that Lincoln has a slightly higher gross profit percentage (30.4%) than Madison (30.0%). However, Lincoln has a higher percentage of selling expenses (12.8%) and administrative expenses (6.9%) than does Madison (11.5% and 4.1%). As a result, the income from operations as a percentage of sales of Lincoln (10.7%) is less than that of Madison (14.4%).

	Lincoln Company	Madison Corporation	
Sales	100.0%	100.0%	
Cost of goods sold	69.6	70.0	
Gross profit	30.4%	30.0%	
Selling expenses	12.8%	11.5%	
Administrative expenses	6.9	4.1	
Total operating expenses	19.7%	15.6%	
Income from operations	10.7%	14.4%	
Other income	0.6	0.6	
	11.3%	15.0%	
Other expense (interest)	0.4	0.5	
Income before income tax	10.9%	14.5%	
Income tax expense	4.8	5.5	
Net income	6.1%	9.0%	

Exhibit 7

Common-Sized Income Statements

For a recent year, Nike's net income was 9.7% of sales.

Link to Nike

The unfavorable difference of 3.7 (14.4% – 10.7%) percentage points in income from operations would concern the managers and other stakeholders of Lincoln. The underlying causes of the difference should be investigated and possibly corrected. For example, Lincoln may decide to outsource some of its administrative duties so that its administrative expenses are more comparative to that of Madison.

Check Up Corner 14-1 Horizontal and Vertical Analyses

Select income statement data for Bukasy Company for two recent years ended December 31 are as follows:

	20Y2	20Y1
Sales	$2,200,000	$2,000,000
Cost of goods sold	1,337,500	1,250,000
Gross profit	$ 862,500	$ 750,000
Selling, general, and administrative expenses	440,000	400,000
Income from operations	$ 422,500	$ 350,000

Prepare horizontal and vertical analyses of Bukasy's income statement. (Round percentages to one decimal place.)

Solution:

Horizontal Analysis

			Increase (Decrease)	
	20Y2	20Y1	Amount	Percent
Sales	$2,200,000	$2,000,000	$200,000	10.0%
Cost of goods sold	1,337,500	1,250,000	87,500	7.0%
Gross profit	$ 862,500	$ 750,000	$112,500	15.0%
Selling, general, and administrative expenses	440,000	400,000	40,000	10.0%
Income from operations	$ 422,500	$ 350,000	$ 72,500	20.7%

Horizontal analysis shows increases and decreases in the amount and percentage of comparative financial statement items. The amount and percentage of each item on the most recent statement is compared with the same item on one or more earlier statements.

Vertical Analysis

	20Y2		20Y1	
	Amount	Percent	Amount	Percent
Sales	$2,200,000	100.0%	$2,000,000	100.0%
Cost of goods sold	1,337,500	60.8	1,250,000	62.5
Gross profit	$ 862,500	39.2%	$ 750,000	37.5%
Selling, general, and administrative expenses	440,000	20.0	400,000	20.0
Income from operations	$ 422,500	19.2%	$ 350,000	17.5%

Vertical analysis compares each component in a financial statement to a total within the statement. It can be applied to a single statement or to the same statement over time.

Check Up Corner

Objective 3
Describe and illustrate how to use financial statement analysis to assess liquidity.

Analyzing Liquidity

Liquidity analysis evaluates the ability of a company to convert current assets into cash. Banks and other short-term creditors rely heavily on liquidity analysis, because they are interested in evaluating a company's ability to repay loans and short-term notes. Exhibit 8 shows three categories of measures used to evaluate a company's liquidity. These ratios and measures focus upon a company's current position (current assets and liabilities), accounts receivable, and inventory.

Exhibit 8
Liquidity Ratios and Measures

Current Position Analysis	Accounts Receivable Analysis	Inventory Analysis
Working Capital	Accounts Receivable Turnover	Inventory Turnover
Current Ratio	Number of Days' Sales in Receivables	Number of Days' Sales in Inventory
Quick Ratio		

Current Position Analysis

Current position analysis evaluates a company's ability to pay its current liabilities. This information helps short-term creditors determine how quickly they will be repaid. This analysis includes:

- Working capital
- Current ratio
- Quick ratio

Working Capital A company's **working capital** is computed as follows:

Working Capital = Current Assets – Current Liabilities

To illustrate, the working capital for **Lincoln Company** for 20Y6 and 20Y5 is computed as follows:

	20Y6	20Y5
Current assets	$ 550,000	$ 533,000
Current liabilities	(210,000)	(243,000)
Working capital	$ 340,000	$ 290,000

The working capital is used to evaluate a company's ability to pay current liabilities. A company's working capital is often monitored monthly, quarterly, or yearly by creditors and other debtors. However, it is difficult to use working capital to compare companies of different sizes. For example, working capital of $250,000 may be adequate for a local sporting goods store, but it would be inadequate for **Nike**.

Current Ratio The **current ratio**, sometimes called the *working capital ratio*, is computed as follows:

$$\text{Current Ratio} = \frac{\text{Current Assets}}{\text{Current Liabilities}}$$

To illustrate, the current ratio for **Lincoln Company** is computed as follows:

	20Y6	20Y5
Current assets	$550,000	$533,000
Current liabilities	$210,000	$243,000
Current ratio	2.6 ($550,000 ÷ $210,000)	2.2 ($533,000 ÷ $243,000)

The current ratio is a more reliable indicator of a company's ability to pay its current liabilities than is working capital, and it is much easier to compare across companies. To illustrate, assume that as of December 31, 20Y6, the working capital of a competitor is much greater than Lincoln's $340,000, but its current ratio is only 1.3. Considering these facts alone, Lincoln is in a more favorable position to obtain short-term credit than the competitor because it has a higher current ratio.

For a recent five-year period, **Nike**'s average current ratio was 2.9.

Link to Nike

Quick Ratio One limitation of working capital and the current ratio is that they do not consider the types of current assets a company has and how easily they can be turned into cash. Because of this, two companies may have the same working capital and current ratios but differ significantly in their ability to pay their current liabilities.

To illustrate, the current assets and liabilities for **Lincoln Company** and Jefferson Company as of December 31, 20Y6, are as follows:

	Lincoln Company	Jefferson Company
Current assets:		
Cash	$ 90,500	$ 45,500
Temporary investments	75,000	25,000
Accounts receivable (net)	115,000	90,000
Inventories	264,000	380,000
Prepaid expenses	5,500	9,500
Total current assets	$ 550,000	$ 550,000
Current assets	$ 550,000	$ 550,000
Current liabilities	(210,000)	(210,000)
Working capital	$ 340,000	$ 340,000
Current ratio (Current assets ÷ Current liabilities)	2.6	2.6

Lincoln and Jefferson both have a working capital of $340,000 and current ratios of 2.6. Jefferson, however, has more of its current assets in inventories. These inventories must be sold and the receivables collected before all the current liabilities can be paid. This takes time. In addition, if the market for its product declines, Jefferson may have difficulty selling its inventory. This, in turn, could impair its ability to pay its current liabilities.

In contrast, Lincoln's current assets contain more cash, temporary investments, and accounts receivable, which can easily be converted to cash. Thus, Lincoln is in a stronger current position than Jefferson to pay its current liabilities.

A ratio that captures this difference and measures the "instant" debt-paying ability of a company is the **quick ratio**, sometimes called the *acid-test ratio*. The quick ratio is computed as follows:

$$\text{Quick Ratio} = \frac{\text{Quick Assets}}{\text{Current Liabilities}}$$

Quick assets are cash and other current assets that can be easily converted to cash. Quick assets normally include cash, temporary investments, and receivables but exclude inventories and prepaid assets.

To illustrate, the quick ratios for **Lincoln Company** and Jefferson Company are computed as follows:

	Lincoln Company	Jefferson Company
Quick assets:		
Cash	$ 90,500	$ 45,500
Temporary investments	75,000	25,000
Accounts receivable (net)	115,000	90,000
Total quick assets	$280,500	$160,500
Current liabilities	$210,000	$210,000
Quick ratio	1.3 ($280,500 ÷ $210,000)	0.8 ($160,500 ÷ $210,000)

Accounts Receivable Analysis

A company's ability to collect its accounts receivable is called **accounts receivable analysis**. It includes the computation and analysis of the following:

- Accounts receivable turnover
- Number of days' sales in receivables

Collecting accounts receivable as quickly as possible improves a company's liquidity. In addition, the cash collected from receivables may be used to improve or expand operations. Quick collection of receivables also reduces the risk of uncollectible accounts.

Accounts Receivable Turnover The **accounts receivable turnover** is computed as follows:

$$\text{Accounts Receivable Turnover} = \frac{\text{Sales}[1]}{\text{Average Accounts Receivable}}$$

[1] If known, *credit* sales should be used in the numerator. Because credit sales are not normally known by external users, we use sales in the numerator.

To illustrate, the accounts receivable turnover for **Lincoln Company** for 20Y6 and 20Y5 is computed as follows. Lincoln's accounts receivable balance at the beginning of 20Y5 is $140,000.

	20Y6	20Y5
Sales	$1,498,000	$1,200,000
Accounts receivable (net):		
Beginning of year	$ 120,000	$ 140,000
End of year	115,000	120,000
Total	$ 235,000	$ 260,000
Average accounts receivable	$117,500 ($235,000 ÷ 2)	$130,000 ($260,000 ÷ 2)
Accounts receivable turnover	12.7 ($1,498,000 ÷ $117,500)	9.2 ($1,200,000 ÷ $130,000)

The increase in Lincoln's accounts receivable turnover from 9.2 to 12.7 indicates that the collection of receivables has improved during 20Y6. This may be due to a change in how credit is granted, collection practices, or both.

For Lincoln, the average accounts receivable was computed using the accounts receivable balance at the beginning and the end of the year. When sales are seasonal and, thus, vary throughout the year, monthly balances of receivables are often used. Also, if sales on account include notes receivable as well as accounts receivable, notes and accounts receivable are normally combined for analysis.

Number of Days' Sales in Receivables The **number of days' sales in receivables** is computed as follows:

$$\text{Number of Days' Sales in Receivables} = \frac{\text{Average Accounts Receivable}}{\text{Average Daily Sales}}$$

where

$$\text{Average Daily Sales} = \frac{\text{Sales}}{365 \text{ days}}$$

To illustrate, the number of days' sales in receivables for **Lincoln Company** is computed as follows:

	20Y6	20Y5
Average accounts receivable	$117,500 ($235,000 ÷ 2)	$130,000 ($260,000 ÷ 2)
Average daily sales	$4,104 ($1,498,000 ÷ 365)	$3,288 ($1,200,000 ÷ 365)
Number of days' sales in receivables	28.6 ($117,500 ÷ $4,104)	39.5 ($130,000 ÷ $3,288)

The number of days' sales in receivables is an estimate of the time (in days) that the accounts receivable have been outstanding. The number of days' sales in receivables is often compared with a company's credit terms to evaluate the efficiency of the collection of receivables.

To illustrate, if Lincoln's credit terms are 2/10, n/30, then Lincoln was very *inefficient* in collecting receivables in 20Y5. In other words, receivables should have been collected in 30 days or less but were being collected in 39.5 days. Although collections improved during 20Y6 to 28.6 days, there is probably still room for improvement. On the other hand, if Lincoln's credit terms are n/45, then there is probably little room for improving collections.

Inventory Analysis

A company's ability to manage its inventory effectively is evaluated using **inventory analysis**. It includes the computation and analysis of the following:

- Inventory turnover
- Number of days' sales in inventory

Excess inventory decreases liquidity by tying up funds (cash) in inventory. In addition, excess inventory increases insurance expense, property taxes, storage costs, and other related expenses. These expenses further reduce funds that could be used elsewhere to improve or expand operations.

Excess inventory also increases the risk of losses because of price declines or obsolescence of the inventory. On the other hand, a company should keep enough inventory in stock so that it doesn't lose sales because of lack of inventory.

Inventory Turnover The **inventory turnover** is computed as follows:

$$\text{Inventory Turnover} = \frac{\text{Cost of Goods Sold}}{\text{Average Inventory}}$$

To illustrate, the inventory turnover for **Lincoln Company** for 20Y6 and 20Y5 is computed as follows. Lincoln's inventory balance at the beginning of 20Y5 is $311,000.

	20Y6	20Y5
Cost of goods sold	$1,043,000	$820,000
Inventories:		
Beginning of year	$ 283,000	$311,000
End of year	264,000	283,000
Total	$ 547,000	$594,000
Average inventory	$273,500 ($547,000 ÷ 2)	$297,000 ($594,000 ÷ 2)
Inventory turnover	3.8 ($1,043,000 ÷ $273,500)	2.8 ($820,000 ÷ $297,000)

The increase in Lincoln's inventory turnover from 2.8 to 3.8 indicates that the management of inventory has improved in 20Y6. The inventory turnover improved because of an increase in the cost of goods sold, which indicates more sales and a decrease in the average inventories.

What is considered a good inventory turnover varies by type of inventory, company, and industry. For example, grocery stores have a higher inventory turnover than jewelers or furniture stores. Likewise, within a grocery store, perishable foods have a higher turnover than the soaps and cleansers.

Link to Nike For a recent five-year period, Nike's average inventory turnover was 4.3.

Number of Days' Sales in Inventory The **number of days' sales in inventory** is computed as follows:

$$\text{Number of Days' Sales in Inventory} = \frac{\text{Average Inventory}}{\text{Average Daily Cost of Goods Sold}}$$

where

$$\text{Average Daily Cost of Goods Sold} = \frac{\text{Cost of Goods Sold}}{365 \text{ days}}$$

To illustrate, the number of days' sales in inventory for **Lincoln Company** is computed as follows:

	20Y6	20Y5
Average inventory	$273,500 ($547,000 ÷ 2)	$297,000 ($594,000 ÷ 2)
Average daily cost of goods sold	$2,858 ($1,043,000 ÷ 365)	$2,247 ($820,000 ÷ 365)
Number of days' sales in inventory	95.7 ($273,500 ÷ $2,858)	132.2 ($297,000 ÷ $2,247)

The number of days' sales in inventory is a rough measure of the length of time it takes to purchase, sell, and replace the inventory. Lincoln's number of days' sales in inventory improved from 132.2 days to 95.7 days during 20Y6. This is a major improvement in managing inventory.

Check Up Corner 14-2 | Liquidity Analysis

Select financial statement data for OM&M Inc. for two recent years follows:

	20Y2	20Y1
Select income statement information:		
Sales	$1,800,000	$1,740,000
Cost of goods sold	1,200,000	1,120,000
Select balance sheet information:		
Cash	$ 300,000	$ 290,000
Temporary investments	100,000	100,000
Accounts receivable (net)	200,000	160,000
Inventory	160,000	140,000
Accounts payable	400,000	350,000

Based on these data, calculate the following liquidity measures for 20Y2:

A. Current ratio
B. Quick ratio
C. Accounts receivable turnover
D. Inventory turnover

Solution:

A.

$$\text{Current Ratio} = \frac{\text{Current Assets}}{\text{Current Liabilities}} = \frac{\$300,000 + \$100,000 + \$200,000 + \$160,000}{\$400,000} = \frac{\$760,000}{\$400,000} = 1.9$$

The current ratio is used to evaluate a company's ability to pay current liabilities.

B.

$$\text{Quick Ratio} = \frac{\text{Quick Assets}}{\text{Current Liabilities}} = \frac{\$300,000 + \$100,000 + \$200,000}{\$400,000} = \frac{\$600,000}{\$400,000} = 1.5$$

The quick ratio measures the "instant" debt-paying ability of a company. Quick assets are cash and other current assets that can be easily converted to cash.

C.

$$\text{Accounts Receivable Turnover} = \frac{\text{Sales}}{\text{Average Accounts Receivable}} = \frac{\$1,800,000}{(\$200,000 + \$160,000) \div 2} = \frac{\$1,800,000}{\$180,000} = 10.0$$

Accounts receivable turnover measures the speed with which a company collects its accounts receivable.

D.

$$\text{Inventory Turnover} = \frac{\text{Cost of Goods Sold}}{\text{Average Inventory}} = \frac{\$1,200,000}{(\$160,000 + \$140,000) \div 2} = \frac{\$1,200,000}{\$150,000} = 8.0$$

Inventory turnover measures the number of times each year that a company sells its inventory.

Check Up Corner

Objective 4

Describe and illustrate how to use financial statement analysis to assess solvency.

Analyzing Solvency

Solvency analysis evaluates a company's ability to pay its long-term debts. Bondholders and other long-term creditors use solvency analysis to evaluate a company's ability to (i) repay the face amount of debt at maturity and (ii) make periodic interest payments. Three common solvency ratios are shown in Exhibit 9.

Exhibit 9

Solvency Ratios

Solvency Ratios		
Ratio of Fixed Assets to Long-Term Liabilities	Ratio of Liabilities to Stockholders' Equity	Times Interest Earned

Ratio of Fixed Assets to Long-Term Liabilities

Fixed assets are often pledged as security for long-term notes and bonds. The **ratio of fixed assets to long-term liabilities** provides a measure of how much fixed assets a company has to support its long-term debt. This measures a company's ability to repay the face amount of debt at maturity and is computed as follows:

$$\text{Ratio of Fixed Assets to Long-Term Liabilities} = \frac{\text{Fixed Assets (net)}}{\text{Long-Term Liabilities}}$$

To illustrate, the ratio of fixed assets to long-term liabilities for **Lincoln Company** is computed as follows:

	20Y6	20Y5
Fixed assets (net)	$444,500	$470,000
Long-term liabilities	$100,000	$200,000
Ratio of fixed assets to long-term liabilities	4.4 ($444,500 ÷ $100,000)	2.4 ($470,000 ÷ $200,000)

During 20Y6, Lincoln's ratio of fixed assets to long-term liabilities increased from 2.4 to 4.4. This increase was due primarily to Lincoln paying off one-half of its long-term liabilities in 20Y6.

Link to Nike 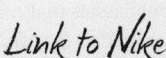   For a recent year, Nike's ratio of fixed assets to long-term liabilities was 1.0.

Ratio of Liabilities to Stockholders' Equity

The **ratio of liabilities to stockholders' equity** measures how much of the company is financed by debt and equity. It is computed as follows:

$$\text{Ratio of Liabilities to Stockholders' Equity} = \frac{\text{Total Liabilities}}{\text{Total Stockholders' Equity}}$$

To illustrate, the ratio of liabilities to stockholders' equity for **Lincoln Company** is computed as follows:

	20Y6	20Y5
Total liabilities	$310,000	$443,000
Total stockholders' equity	$829,500	$787,500
Ratio of liabilities to stockholders' equity	0.4 ($310,000 ÷ $829,500)	0.6 ($443,000 ÷ $787,500)

Lincoln's ratio of liabilities to stockholders' equity decreased from 0.6 to 0.4 during 20Y6. The lower ratio indicates that the proportion of Lincoln's liabilities and equity that is made up of liabilities is decreasing. This is an improvement and indicates that the margin of safety for Lincoln's creditors is improving.

For a recent five-year period, Nike's average ratio of liabilities to stockholders' equity was 0.6.

Link to Nike

Times Interest Earned

The **times interest earned**, sometimes called the *coverage ratio*, measures the risk that interest payments will not be made if earnings decrease. It is computed as follows:

$$\text{Times Interest Earned} = \frac{\text{Income Before Income Tax} + \text{Interest Expense}}{\text{Interest Expense}}$$

Interest expense is paid before income taxes. In other words, interest expense is deducted in determining taxable income and, thus, income tax. For this reason, income *before taxes* is used in computing the times interest earned.

The *higher* the ratio, the more likely interest payments will be paid if earnings decrease. To illustrate, the times interest earned for **Lincoln Company** is computed as follows:

	20Y6	**20Y5**
Income before income tax	$162,500	$134,600
Interest expense	6,000	12,000
Amount available to pay interest	$168,500	$146,600
Times interest earned	28.1 ($168,500 ÷ $6,000)	12.2 ($146,600 ÷ $12,000)

The times interest earned improved from 12.2 to 28.1 during 20Y6. The higher ratio indicates that the relationship between the amount of income available to pay interest and the amount of interest expense has improved. Lincoln has more than enough earnings (28 times) to make its interest payments.

For a recent year, Nike's times interest earned ratio was nine times higher than the industry average.

Link to Nike

Why It Matters

Liquidity Crunch

RadioShack Corporation, an electronics retailer, filed for bankruptcy protection. Information on the company's liquidity and solvency for the three years prior to bankruptcy follow:

	20Y3	**20Y2**	**20Y1**
Liquidity measures:			
Working capital (in thousands)	$748,400	$1,003,700	$1,176,700
Current ratio	2.3	2.0	2.9
Quick ratio	0.7	1.0	1.5
Solvency measures:			
Ratio of liabilities to stockholders' equity	6.7	2.8	1.9
Ratio of fixed assets to long-term liabilities	0.2	0.3	0.3

The data shows that the company's liquidity and solvency measures deteriorated in the years prior to the firm's bankruptcy. All three of the company's liquidity measures declined significantly during the three-year period, indicating a growing risk that the company would not be able to repay its current liabilities. The ratio of liabilities to stockholder's equity also increased significantly during this period, indicating that the company might not be able to repay its long-term debts. Finally, the ratio of fixed assets to long-term liabilities began to deteriorate in 20Y3, indicating that fewer assets would be available to secure the company's long-term liabilities.

Check Up Corner 14-3 | **Solvency Analysis**

The following are select balance sheet and income statement data for Wilton Strand Inc. for a recent year:

	Dec. 31, 20Y3
Assets	
Current assets	$ 560,000
Property, plant, and equipment (net)	1,400,000
Total assets	$1,960,000
Liabilities	
Current liabilities	$ 160,000
Long-term liabilities	400,000
Total liabilities	$ 560,000
Stockholders' Equity	
Common stock, $5 par	$ 200,000
Retained earnings	1,200,000
Total stockholders' equity	$1,400,000
Total liabilities and stockholders' equity	$1,960,000
Select income statement information:	
Interest expense	$ 100,000
Income before income tax	260,000

Based on these data, calculate the following solvency measures:

A. Ratio of fixed assets to long-term liabilities
B. Ratio of liabilities to stockholders' equity
C. Times interest earned

Solution:

A.

$$\text{Ratio of Fixed Assets to Long-Term Liabilities} = \frac{\text{Fixed Assets (net)}}{\text{Long-Term Liabilities}} = \frac{\$1,400,000}{\$400,000} = 3.5$$

Because fixed assets are often pledged as security for long-term notes and bonds, the ratio of fixed assets to long-term liabilities provides a measure of whether noteholders or bondholders will be paid.

B.

$$\text{Ratio of Liabilities to Stockholders' Equity} = \frac{\text{Total Liabilities}}{\text{Total Stockholders' Equity}} = \frac{\$560,000}{\$1,400,000} = 0.4$$

The ratio of liabilities to stockholders' equity measures how much of the company is financed by debt and equity.

C.

$$\text{Times Interest Earned} = \frac{\text{Income before Income Tax + Interest Expense}}{\text{Interest Expense}} = \frac{\$260,000 + \$100,000}{\$100,000} = \frac{\$360,000}{\$100,000} = 3.6$$

Times interest earned measures the risk that interest payments will not be made if earnings decrease.

Check Up Corner

Objective 5

Describe and illustrate how to use financial statement analysis to assess profitability.

Analyzing Profitability

Profitability analysis evaluates the ability of a company to generate future earnings. This ability depends on the relationship between the company's operating results and the assets the company has available for use in its operations. Thus, the relationship between income statement and balance sheet items are used to evaluate profitability.

Common profitability ratios are shown in Exhibit 10:

Profitability Ratios		
Asset Turnover	Return on Stockholders' Equity	Price-Earnings Ratio
Return on Total Assets	Return on Common Stockholders' Equity	Dividends per Share
	Earnings per Share on Common Stock	Dividend Yield

Exhibit 10
Profitability Ratios

Asset Turnover

The **asset turnover** ratio measures how effectively a company uses its assets. It is computed as follows:

$$\text{Asset Turnover} = \frac{\text{Sales}}{\text{Average Total Assets (excluding long-term investments)}}$$

Note that long-term investments are excluded in computing asset turnover. This is because long-term investments are unrelated to normal operations and sales.

To illustrate, the asset turnover for **Lincoln Company** is computed as follows. Total assets (excluding long-term investments) are $1,010,000 at the beginning of 20Y5.

	20Y6	20Y5
Sales	$1,498,000	$1,200,000
Total assets (excluding long-term investments):		
Beginning of year	$1,053,000*	$1,010,000
End of year	1,044,500**	1,053,000*
Total	$2,097,500	$2,063,000
Average total assets	$1,048,750 ($2,097,500 ÷ 2)	$1,031,500 ($2,063,000 ÷ 2)
Asset turnover	1.4 ($1,498,000 ÷ $1,048,750)	1.2 ($1,200,000 ÷ $1,031,500)

*($1,230,500 total assets – $177,500 long-term investments)
**($1,139,500 total assets – $95,000 long-term investments)

For Lincoln, the average total assets was computed using total assets (excluding long-term investments) at the beginning and end of the year. The average total assets could also be based on monthly or quarterly averages.

The asset turnover ratio indicates that Lincoln's use of its operating assets has improved in 20Y6. This was primarily due to the increase in sales in 20Y6.

Return on Total Assets

The **return on total assets** measures the profitability of total assets, without considering how the assets are financed. In other words, this rate is not affected by the portion of assets financed by creditors or stockholders. It is computed as follows:

$$\text{Return on Total Assets} = \frac{\text{Net Income} + \text{Interest Expense}}{\text{Average Total Assets}}$$

The return on total assets is computed by adding interest expense to net income. By adding interest expense to net income, the effect of whether the assets are financed by creditors (debt) or stockholders (equity) is eliminated. Because net income includes any income earned from long-term investments, the average total assets includes long-term investments as well as the net operating assets.

To illustrate, the return on total assets by **Lincoln Company** is computed as follows. Total assets are $1,187,500 at the beginning of 20Y5.

	20Y6	20Y5
Net income	$ 91,000	$ 76,500
Interest expense	6,000	12,000
	$ 97,000	$ 88,500
Total assets:		
Beginning of year	$1,230,500	$1,187,500
End of year	1,139,500	1,230,500
Total	$2,370,000	$2,418,000
Average total assets	$1,185,000 ($2,370,000 ÷ 2)	$1,209,000 ($2,418,000 ÷ 2)
Return on total assets	8.2% ($97,000 ÷ $1,185,000)	7.3% ($88,500 ÷ $1,209,000)

The return on total assets improved from 7.3% to 8.2% during 20Y6.

The *return on operating assets* is sometimes computed when there are large amounts of nonoperating income and expense. It is computed as follows:

$$\text{Return on Operating Assets} = \frac{\text{Income from Operations}}{\text{Average Operating Assets}}$$

Because Lincoln does not have a significant amount of nonoperating income and expense, the return on operating assets is not illustrated.

Return on Stockholders' Equity

The **return on stockholders' equity** measures the rate of income earned on the amount invested by the stockholders. It is computed as follows:

$$\text{Return on Stockholders' Equity} = \frac{\text{Net Income}}{\text{Average Total Stockholders' Equity}}$$

To illustrate, the return on stockholders' equity for **Lincoln Company** is computed as follows. Total stockholders' equity is $750,000 at the beginning of 20Y5.

	20Y6	20Y5
Net income	$ 91,000	$ 76,500
Total stockholders' equity:		
Beginning of year	$ 787,500	$ 750,000
End of year	829,500	787,500
Total	$1,617,000	$1,537,500
Average total stockholders' equity	$808,500 ($1,617,000 ÷ 2)	$768,750 ($1,537,500 ÷ 2)
Return on stockholders' equity	11.3% ($91,000 ÷ $808,500)	10.0% ($76,500 ÷ $768,750)

The return on stockholders' equity improved from 10.0% to 11.3% during 20Y6.

Leverage involves using debt to increase the return on an investment. The rate earned on stockholders' equity is normally higher than the return on total assets. This is because of the effect of leverage.

For **Lincoln Company**, the effect of leverage for 20Y6 is 3.1% and for 20Y5 is 2.7% computed as follows:

	20Y6	20Y5
Return on stockholders' equity	11.3%	10.0%
Return on total assets	(8.2)	(7.3)
Effect of leverage	3.1%	2.7%

Exhibit 11 shows the 20Y6 and 20Y5 effects of leverage for Lincoln.

Link to Nike   For a recent five-year period, **Nike**'s average return on stockholders' equity was 23.9%.

Why It Matters

Gearing for Profit

Another term for leverage is "financial gearing." **Exxon Mobil Corporation**, a worldwide-integrated energy company, is an example of a company that uses leverage for financial advantage. Exxon had a return on total assets of 9.35% for a recent year,

while its return on stockholders' equity was 18.7%. Thus, Exxon is "geared" 2:1 by using debt on its balance sheet. Exxon is very profitable, thus leverage is beneficial. In contrast, **Chesapeake Energy**, an oil and gas exploration company, had return on assets of –7.5% for a recent 12-month period, and return on stockholders' equity of –25%. In this case, the over 3:1 leverage (25% ÷ 7.5%) creates a financial disadvantage because the company is experiencing losses.

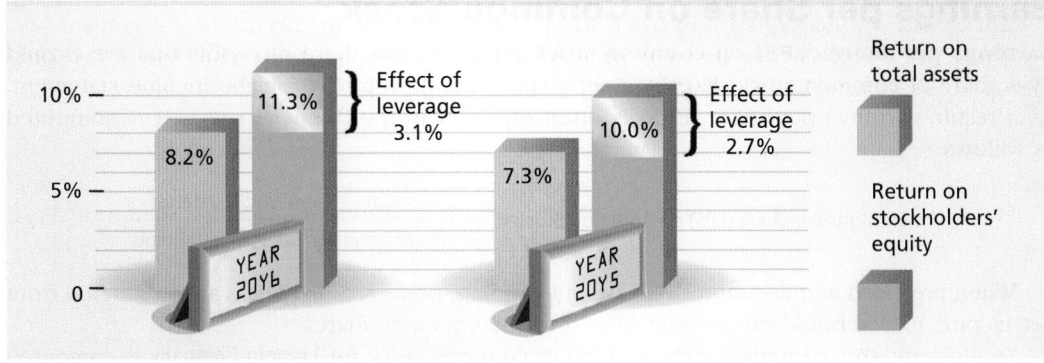

Exhibit 11
Effect of Leverage

Return on Common Stockholders' Equity

The **return on common stockholders' equity** measures the rate of profits earned on the amount invested by the common stockholders. It is computed as follows:

$$\frac{\text{Return on Common}}{\text{Stockholders' Equity}} = \frac{\text{Net Income} - \text{Preferred Dividends}}{\text{Average Common Stockholders' Equity}}$$

Because preferred stockholders rank ahead of the common stockholders in their claim on earnings, any preferred dividends are subtracted from net income in computing the return on common stockholders' equity.

Lincoln Company had $150,000 par value of 6% preferred stock outstanding on December 31, 20Y6 and 20Y5. Thus, preferred dividends of $9,000 ($150,000 × 6%) are deducted from net income. Lincoln's common stockholders' equity is determined as follows:

	December 31		
	20Y6	**20Y5**	**20Y4**
Common stock, $10 par	$500,000	$500,000	$500,000
Retained earnings	179,500	137,500	100,000
Common stockholders' equity	$679,500	$637,500	$600,000

The retained earnings on December 31, 20Y4, of $100,000 is the same as the retained earnings on January 1, 20Y5, as shown in Lincoln's retained earnings statement in Exhibit 4.

Using this information, the return on common stockholders' equity for Lincoln is computed as follows:

	20Y6	**20Y5**
Net income	$ 91,000	$ 76,500
Preferred dividends	(9,000)	(9,000)
Total	$ 82,000	$ 67,500
Common stockholders' equity:		
Beginning of year	$ 637,500	$ 600,000
End of year	679,500*	637,500**
Total	$1,317,000	$1,237,500
Average common stockholders' equity	$658,500 ($1,317,000 ÷ 2)	$618,750 ($1,237,500 ÷ 2)
Return on common stockholders' equity	12.5% ($82,000 ÷ $658,500)	10.9% ($67,500 ÷ $618,750)

*($829,500 total stockholders' equity – $150,000 preferred 6% stock)
**($787,500 total stockholders' equity – $150,000 preferred 6% stock)

Lincoln's return on common stockholders' equity improved from 10.9% to 12.5% in 20Y6. This return differs from Lincoln's returns on total assets and stockholders' equity, which follow:

	20Y6	20Y5
Return on total assets	8.2%	7.3%
Return on stockholders' equity	11.3%	10.0%
Return on common stockholders' equity	12.5%	10.9%

These returns differ because of leverage, as discussed in the preceding section.

Earnings per Share on Common Stock

Earnings per share (EPS) on common stock measures the share of profits that are earned by a share of common stock. Earnings per share must be reported on the income statement. As a result, earnings per share (EPS) is often reported in the financial press. It is computed as follows:

$$\text{Earnings per Share (EPS) on Common Stock} = \frac{\text{Net Income} - \text{Preferred Dividends}}{\text{Shares of Common Stock Outstanding}}$$

When preferred and common stock are outstanding, preferred dividends are subtracted from net income to determine the income related to the common shares.

To illustrate, the earnings per share (EPS) of common stock for **Lincoln Company** is computed as follows:

	20Y6	20Y5
Net income	$91,000	$76,500
Preferred dividends	(9,000)	(9,000)
Total	$82,000	$67,500
Shares of common stock outstanding	50,000	50,000
Earnings per share on common stock	$1.64 ($82,000 ÷ 50,000)	$1.35 ($67,500 ÷ 50,000)

Lincoln had $150,000 par value of 6% preferred stock outstanding on December 31, 20Y6 and 20Y5. Thus, preferred dividends of $9,000 ($150,000 × 6%) are deducted from net income in computing earnings per share on common stock.

Lincoln did not issue any additional shares of common stock in 20Y6. If Lincoln had issued additional shares in 20Y6, a weighted average of common shares outstanding during the year would have been used.

Lincoln's earnings per share (EPS) on common stock improved from $1.35 to $1.64 during 20Y6.

Lincoln has a simple capital structure with only common stock and preferred stock outstanding. Many corporations, however, have complex capital structures with various types of equity securities outstanding, such as convertible preferred stock, stock options, and stock warrants. In such cases, the possible effects of such securities on the shares of common stock outstanding are considered in reporting earnings per share. These possible effects are reported separately as *earnings per common share assuming dilution* or *diluted earnings per share*. This topic is described and illustrated in advanced accounting courses and textbooks.

Link to Nike   On a recent income statement, Nike reported net income of $2,693 million.

Price-Earnings Ratio

The **price-earnings (P/E) ratio** on common stock measures a company's future earnings prospects. It is often quoted in the financial press and is computed as follows:

$$\text{Price-Earnings (P/E) Ratio} = \frac{\text{Market Price per Share of Common Stock}}{\text{Earnings per Share on Common Stock}}$$

To illustrate, the price-earnings (P/E) ratio for **Lincoln Company** is computed as follows:

	20Y6	20Y5
Market price per share of common stock	$41.00	$27.00
Earnings per share on common stock	$1.64	$1.35
Price-earnings ratio on common stock	25 ($41 ÷ $1.64)	20 ($27 ÷ $1.35)

The price-earnings ratio improved from 20 to 25 during 20Y6. In other words, a share of common stock of Lincoln was selling for 20 times earnings per share at the end of 20Y5. At the end of 20Y6, the common stock was selling for 25 times earnings per share. This indicates that the market expects Lincoln to experience favorable earnings in the future.

Dividends per Share

Dividends per share measures the extent to which earnings are being distributed to common shareholders. It is computed as follows:

$$\text{Dividends per Share} = \frac{\text{Dividends on Common Stock}}{\text{Shares of Common Stock Outstanding}}$$

To illustrate, the dividends per share for **Lincoln Company** are computed as follows:

	20Y6	20Y5
Dividends on common stock	$40,000	$30,000
Shares of common stock outstanding	50,000	50,000
Dividends per share of common stock	$0.80 ($40,000 ÷ 50,000)	$0.60 ($30,000 ÷ 50,000)

The dividends per share of common stock increased from $0.60 to $0.80 during 20Y6.

Dividends per share are often reported with earnings per share. Comparing the two per-share amounts indicates the extent to which earnings are being retained for use in operations. To illustrate, the dividends and earnings per share for **Lincoln Company** are shown in Exhibit 12.

Exhibit 12
Dividends and Earnings per Share of Common Stock

Why It Matters

Investing for Yield

Companies that provide attractive dividend yields are often mature companies found in stable industries. Examples of such industries are public utilities and food. Coca Cola, Procter & Gamble, Kellogg's, Consolidated Edison, Southern Company, and General Mills all have attractive dividend yields in excess of 3%. Procter & Gamble has had 58 consecutive years of dividend payouts, and Kellogg's has not reduced its dividend for 56 years. The

stability of the food industry has allowed these companies to maintain dividends for many years. Growth companies, such as Google or Facebook, do not pay dividends, because they use their cash to grow the business. Investors in such growth companies expect to make their return from stock price appreciation, rather than dividends. Mark Cuban, billionaire, Shark Tank® investor, and owner of the Dallas Mavericks, stated, "I believe non-dividend stocks aren't much more than baseball cards. They are worth what you can convince someone to pay for it."

Quote source: Parker, Tim, "The Top Ten Dividend Quotes," *Dividend.com*, August 29, 2012.

Dividend Yield

The **dividend yield** on common stock measures the rate of return to common stockholders from cash dividends. It is of special interest to investors whose objective is to earn revenue (dividends) from their investment. It is computed as follows:

$$\text{Dividend Yield} = \frac{\text{Dividends per Share of Common Stock}}{\text{Market Price per Share of Common Stock}}$$

To illustrate, the dividend yield for **Lincoln Company** is computed as follows:

	20Y6	20Y5
Dividends per share of common stock	$0.80	$0.60
Market price per share of common stock	$41.00	$27.00
Dividend yield on common stock	2.0% ($0.80 ÷ $41)	2.2% ($0.60 ÷ $27)

The dividend yield declined slightly from 2.2% to 2.0% in 20Y6. This decline was primarily due to the increase in the market price of Lincoln's common stock.

Link to Nike For a recent five-year period, Nike's average dividend yield was 1.24%.

Check Up Corner 14-4 Profitability Analysis

The following data were taken from the financial statements of French Broad Steel Works Inc. for a recent year:

Shares of common stock outstanding	20,000
Sales	$2,400,000
Interest expense	40,000
Net income	250,000
Market price per share of common stock at year-end	120.00
Dividends per share of common stock	3.00
Average total assets (excluding long-term investments)	1,600,000
Average total assets	2,000,000
Average total stockholders' equity	1,000,000

Based on these data, determine the following profitability measures:

A. Asset turnover

B. Return on total assets

C. Return on stockholders' equity

D. Earnings per share

E. Price-earnings ratio

F. Dividend yield

Solution:

A.

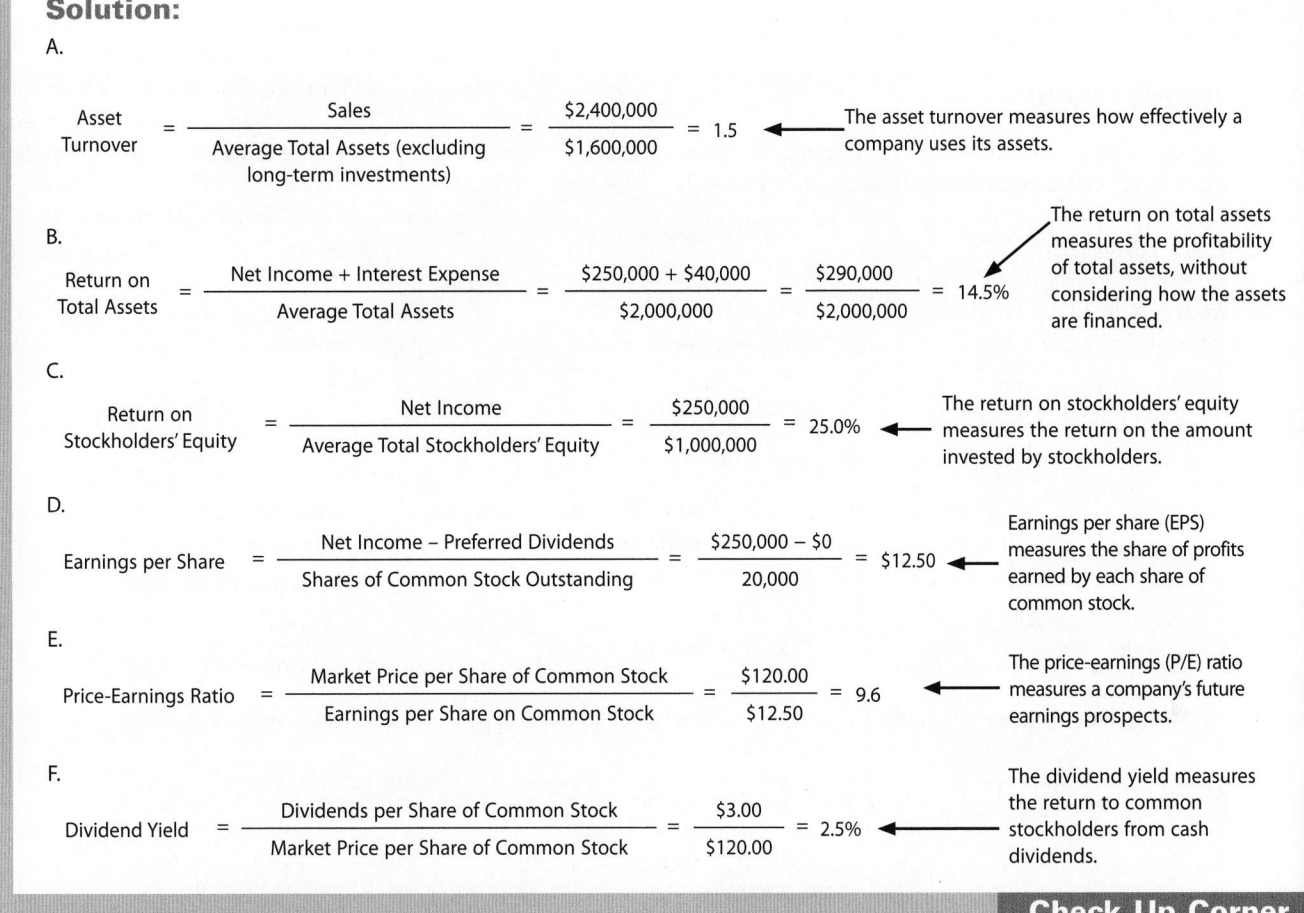

Asset Turnover $= \dfrac{\text{Sales}}{\text{Average Total Assets (excluding long-term investments)}} = \dfrac{\$2,400,000}{\$1,600,000} = 1.5$

The asset turnover measures how effectively a company uses its assets.

B.

Return on Total Assets $= \dfrac{\text{Net Income + Interest Expense}}{\text{Average Total Assets}} = \dfrac{\$250,000 + \$40,000}{\$2,000,000} = \dfrac{\$290,000}{\$2,000,000} = 14.5\%$

The return on total assets measures the profitability of total assets, without considering how the assets are financed.

C.

Return on Stockholders' Equity $= \dfrac{\text{Net Income}}{\text{Average Total Stockholders' Equity}} = \dfrac{\$250,000}{\$1,000,000} = 25.0\%$

The return on stockholders' equity measures the return on the amount invested by stockholders.

D.

Earnings per Share $= \dfrac{\text{Net Income – Preferred Dividends}}{\text{Shares of Common Stock Outstanding}} = \dfrac{\$250,000 – \$0}{20,000} = \$12.50$

Earnings per share (EPS) measures the share of profits earned by each share of common stock.

E.

Price-Earnings Ratio $= \dfrac{\text{Market Price per Share of Common Stock}}{\text{Earnings per Share on Common Stock}} = \dfrac{\$120.00}{\$12.50} = 9.6$

The price-earnings (P/E) ratio measures a company's future earnings prospects.

F.

Dividend Yield $= \dfrac{\text{Dividends per Share of Common Stock}}{\text{Market Price per Share of Common Stock}} = \dfrac{\$3.00}{\$120.00} = 2.5\%$

The dividend yield measures the return to common stockholders from cash dividends.

Check Up Corner

Summary of Analytical Measures

Exhibit 13 shows a summary of the solvency and profitability measures discussed in this chapter. The type of industry and the company's operations usually affect which measures are used. In many cases, additional measures are used for a specific industry. For example, airlines use *revenue per passenger mile* and *cost per available seat* as profitability measures. Likewise, hotels use *occupancy rates* as a profitability measure.

The analytical measures shown in Exhibit 13 are a useful starting point for analyzing a company's liquidity, solvency and profitability. However, they are not a substitute for sound judgment. The general economic and business environment should always be considered in analyzing a company's future prospects. In addition, any trends and interrelationships among the measures should be carefully studied.

Exhibit 13 Summary of Analytical Measures

Liquidity Measures

	Method of Computation	Use
Working Capital	Current Assets − Current Liabilities	Measures the company's ability to pay current liabilities.
Current Ratio	$\dfrac{\text{Current Assets}}{\text{Current Liabilities}}$	
Quick Ratio	$\dfrac{\text{Quick Assets}}{\text{Current Liabilities}}$	Measures the company's instant debt-paying ability.
Accounts Receivable Turnover	$\dfrac{\text{Sales}}{\text{Average Accounts Receivable}}$	Measures the company's efficiency in collecting receivables and in the management of credit .
Numbers of Days' Sales in Receivables	$\dfrac{\text{Average Accounts Receivable}}{\text{Average Daily Sales}}$	
Inventory Turnover	$\dfrac{\text{Cost of Goods Sold}}{\text{Average Inventory}}$	Measures the company's efficiency in managing inventory.
Number of Days' Sales in Inventory	$\dfrac{\text{Average Inventory}}{\text{Average Daily Cost of Goods Sold}}$	

Solvency Measures

	Method of Computation	Use
Ratio of Fixed Assets to Long-Term Liabilities	$\dfrac{\text{Fixed Assets (net)}}{\text{Long-Term Liabilities}}$	Measures the margin of safety available to long-term creditors.
Ratio of Liabilities to Stockholders' Equity	$\dfrac{\text{Total Liabilities}}{\text{Total Stockholders' Equity}}$	Measures how much of the company is financed by debt and equity.
Times Interest Earned	$\dfrac{\text{Income Before Income Tax + Interest Expense}}{\text{Interest Expense}}$	Measures the risk that interest payments will not be made if earnings decrease.

Profitability Measures

	Method of Computation	Use
Asset Turnover	$\dfrac{\text{Sales}}{\text{Average Total Assets (excluding long-term investments)}}$	Measures how effectively a company uses its assets.
Return on Total Assets	$\dfrac{\text{Net Income + Interest Expense}}{\text{Average Total Assets}}$	Measures the profitability of a company's assets.
Return on Stockholders' Equity	$\dfrac{\text{Net Income}}{\text{Average Total Stockholders' Equity}}$	Measures the profitability of the investment by stockholders.
Return on Common Stockholders' Equity	$\dfrac{\text{Net Income − Preferred Dividends}}{\text{Average Common Stockholders' Equity}}$	Measures the profitability of the investment by common stockholders.
Earnings per Share (EPS) on Common Stock	$\dfrac{\text{Net Income − Preferred Dividends}}{\text{Shares of Common Stock Outstanding}}$	
Price-Earnings (P/E) Ratio	$\dfrac{\text{Market Price per Share of Common Stock}}{\text{Earnings per Share on Common Stock}}$	Measures future earnings prospects, based on the relationship between market value of common stock and earnings.
Dividends per Share	$\dfrac{\text{Dividends on Common Stock}}{\text{Shares of Common Stock Outstanding}}$	Measures the extent to which earnings are being distributed to common stockholders.
Dividend Yield	$\dfrac{\text{Dividends per Share of Common Stock}}{\text{Market Price per Share of Common Stock}}$	Measures the rate of return to common stockholders in terms of dividends.

Corporate Annual Reports

Public corporations issue annual reports summarizing their operating activities for the past year and plans for the future. Such annual reports include the financial statements and the accompanying notes. In addition, annual reports normally include the following sections:

- Management discussion and analysis
- Report on internal control
- Report on fairness of the financial statements

Objective 6
Describe the contents of corporate annual reports.

IFRS
See Appendix C for more information.

Management Discussion and Analysis

Management's Discussion and Analysis (MD&A) is required in annual reports filed with the Securities and Exchange Commission. It includes management's analysis of current operations and its plans for the future. Typical items included in the MD&A are as follows:

- Management's analysis and explanations of any significant changes between the current and prior years' financial statements.
- Important accounting principles or policies that could affect interpretation of the financial statements, including the effect of changes in accounting principles or the adoption of new accounting principles.
- Management's assessment of the company's liquidity and the availability of capital to the company.
- Significant risk exposures that might affect the company.
- Any "off-balance-sheet" arrangements such as leases not included in the financial statements. Such arrangements are discussed in advanced accounting courses and textbooks.

Report on Internal Control

The Sarbanes-Oxley Act of 2002 requires a report on internal control by management. The report states management's responsibility for establishing and maintaining internal control. In addition, management's assessment of the effectiveness of internal controls over financial reporting is included in the report.

Sarbanes-Oxley also requires a public accounting firm to verify management's conclusions on internal control. Thus, two reports on internal control, one by management and one by a public accounting firm, are included in the annual report. In some situations, these may be combined into a single report on internal control.

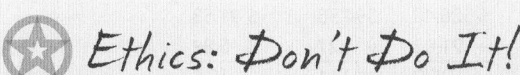 *Ethics: Don't Do It!*

Characteristics of Financial Statement Fraud

Each year the Association of Certified Fraud Examiners conducts a worldwide survey examining the characteristics of corporate fraud. The most recent study found that:

- 43.3% of frauds were detected by a tip from an employee or someone close to the company;
- Frauds committed by owners and executives tended to be much larger than those caused by employees;

- Most people who are caught committing fraud are first-time offenders with clean employment histories; and
- In 81% of the cases, the person committing the fraud displayed one or more behavioral red flags, such as living beyond their means, financial difficulties, and excessive control issues.

Fraud examiners can use these trends to help them narrow their focus when searching for fraud.

Source: *2012 Report to the Nations*, Association of Certified Fraud Examiners, 2012.

Report on Fairness of the Financial Statements

All publicly held corporations are required to have an independent audit (examination) of their financial statements. The Certified Public Accounting (CPA) firm that conducts the audit renders an opinion, called the *Report of Independent Registered Public Accounting Firm*, on the fairness of the statements.

An opinion stating that the financial statements present fairly the financial position, results of operations, and cash flows of the company is said to be an *unmodified opinion*, sometimes called a *clean opinion*. Any report other than an unmodified opinion raises a "red flag" for financial statement users and requires further investigation as to its cause. The types and nature of audit opinions are covered in more detail in advanced courses on auditing.

The annual report of Nike Inc. is shown in Appendix E. The Nike report includes the financial statements as well as the Management Discussion and Analysis, the Report on Internal Control, and the Report on Fairness of the Financial Statements.

Analysis for Decision Making

| Make a Decision | Price-Earnings Ratio and Dividend Yield |

Objective

Describe and illustrate the use of financial statement analysis in evaluating potential stock price appreciation.

The following table shows the stock price, earnings per share, and dividends per share for three companies for a recent year:

	Google	PepsiCo	Caterpillar
Market price of common stock at year-end	$526.40	$94.56	$91.53
Earnings per share	21.02	4.27	5.88
Dividends per share	0.00	2.53	2.70

A. For each company, determine the:
  - Price-earnings ratio (round to one decimal place)
  - Dividend yield (round to one decimal place)
B. Based on the information available, which company would you expect to have the best potential for future common stock price appreciation? Why?

Solution:

A.

	Google	PepsiCo	Caterpillar
Earnings per share	$ 21.02	$ 4.27	$ 5.88
Market price per share of common stock	$ 526.40	$94.56	$ 91.53
Earnings per share	÷ 21.02	÷ 4.27	÷ 5.88
Price-earnings ratio	25.0	22.1	15.6
Dividends per share	$ 0.00	$ 2.53	$ 2.70
Market price per share of common stock	÷526.40	÷94.56	÷91.53
Dividend yield	0.0%	2.7%	2.9%

B. Caterpillar has the largest dividend yield and strong earnings per share but has the lowest price-earnings ratio. Stock market participants seem to be skeptical about Caterpillar's future prospects and are discounting its stock price despite its relatively solid performance. Google pays no dividend and, thus, has no dividend yield. However, Google has the largest price-earnings ratio. Stock market participants are expecting a strong return on their investment from appreciation in Google's stock price. PepsiCo has the second highest price-earnings ratio, but has a lower dividend yield and earnings per share than Caterpillar. This suggests that the market expects PepsiCo's combination of earnings and dividends to improve in the coming years.

Make a Decision

Appendix 1 Unusual Items on the Income Statement

Generally accepted accounting principles require that unusual items be reported separately on the income statement. This is because such items do not occur frequently and are typically unrelated to current operations. Without separate reporting of these items, users of the financial statements might be misled about current and future operations.

Unusual items on the income statement are classified as one of the following:

- Affecting the *current period* income statement
- Affecting a *prior period* income statement

Unusual Items Affecting the Current Period's Income Statement

Discontinued operations are an unusual item that affects the current period's:

- Income statement presentation
- Earnings per share presentation

Discontinued operations are reported separately on the income statement for any period in which they occur.

Income Statement Presentation A company may discontinue a component of its operations by selling or abandoning the component's operations. For example, a retailer might decide to sell its product only online and, thus, discontinue selling its merchandise at its retail outlets (stores).

If the discontinued component is (1) the result of a strategic shift and (2) has a major effect on the entity's operations and financial results, any gain or loss on discontinued operations is reported on the income statement as a *Gain (or loss) from discontinued operations*. It is reported immediately following *Income from continuing operations*.

To illustrate, assume that Jones Corporation produces and sells electrical products, hardware supplies, and lawn equipment. Because of a lack of profits, Jones discontinues its electrical products operation and sells the remaining inventory and other assets at a loss of $100,000. Exhibit 14 illustrates the reporting of the loss on discontinued operations.[2]

Jones Corporation Income Statement For the Year Ended December 31, 20Y2	
Sales	$12,350,000
Cost of goods sold	5,800,000
Gross profit	$ 6,550,000
Selling and administrative expenses	5,240,000
Income from continuing operations before income tax	$ 1,310,000
Income tax expense	620,000
Income from continuing operations	$ 690,000
Loss on discontinued operations	100,000
Net income	$ 590,000

Exhibit 14

Unusual Items in the Income Statement

[2] The gain or loss on discontinued operations is reported net of any tax effects. To simplify, the tax effects are not specifically identified in Exhibit 14.

In addition, a note to the financial statements should describe the operations sold, including the date operations were discontinued, and details about the assets, liabilities, income, and expenses of the discontinued component.

Earnings per Share Earnings per common share should be reported separately for discontinued operations. To illustrate, a partial income statement for Jones Corporation is shown in Exhibit 15. The company has 200,000 shares of common stock outstanding.

Exhibit 15

Income Statement with Earnings per Share

Jones Corporation Income Statement For the Year Ended December 31, 20Y2	
Earnings per common share:	
Income from continuing operations..	$3.45
Loss on discontinued operations	0.50
Net income	$2.95

Exhibit 15 reports earnings per common share for income from continuing operations, discontinued operations. However, only earnings per share for income from continuing operations and net income are required by generally accepted accounting principles. The other per-share amounts may be presented in the notes to the financial statements.

Unusual Items Affecting the Prior Period's Income Statement

An unusual item may occur that affects a prior period's income statement. Two such items are as follows:

- Errors in applying generally accepted accounting principles
- Changes from one generally accepted accounting principle to another

If an error is discovered in a prior period's financial statement, the prior-period statement and all following statements are restated and thus corrected.

A company may change from one generally accepted accounting principle to another. In this case, the prior-period financial statements are restated as if the new accounting principle had always been used.[3]

For both of the preceding items, the current-period earnings are not affected. That is, only the earnings reported in prior periods are restated. However, because the prior earnings are restated, the beginning balance of Retained Earnings may also have to be restated. This, in turn, may cause the restatement of other balance sheet accounts. Illustrations of these types of adjustments and restatements are provided in advanced accounting courses.

Appendix 2 Fair Value and Comprehensive Income

In previous chapters, assets have been reported on the balance sheet using the cost basis. Many companies, however, acquire assets that are required by GAAP to be reported on the balance sheet at a different measurement basis called fair value. When a company reports assets at fair value, the financial reporting becomes complex. In the following sections, the concept of fair value and the financial statement effects of using fair value are introduced. A detailed discussion of these concepts is provided in intermediate and advanced accounting texts.

---

[3] Changes from one acceptable depreciation method to another acceptable depreciation method are an exception to this general rule and are to be treated prospectively as a change in estimate, as discussed in Chapter 9.

Fair Value

Fair value is the price that could be received for an asset if it were sold today. This differs from historical cost, in that the amount reported on the balance sheet changes each period to reflect the asset's fair (current) value at the balance sheet date. The change in an asset's fair value from one period to the next is recorded in the financial statements as either:

- a gain or loss on the income statement, or
- an increase or decrease in stockholders' equity reported as other comprehensive income.

Comprehensive Income

When a change in an asset's fair value is not recorded as a gain or loss on the income statement, it is recorded as an element of **other comprehensive income**.[4] These include changes in the fair value of certain investment securities, foreign currency exposures, and pension assets.

The elements of other comprehensive income are included in the computation of **comprehensive income**, which is defined as all changes in stockholders' equity during a period, except those resulting from dividends and stockholders' investments. Comprehensive income is determined by adding or subtracting *other comprehensive income* elements to (from) net income, as follows:

Net income	$XXX
Other comprehensive income	XXX
Comprehensive income	$XXX

Companies must report comprehensive income in the financial statements either:

- on the income statement, directly below net income, or
- in a separate statement of comprehensive income.

Reporting Comprehensive Income on the Income Statement Bart Company purchased investment securities during the year that had an increase of $2,600 in fair value. Because of the accounting methods selected by Bart, this increase in fair value is recorded as an element of other comprehensive income and is called an **unrealized gain**. If Bart elects to report other comprehensive income on the income statement, the elements of other comprehensive income are added to or subtracted from net income at the bottom of the income statement as follows:

Bart Company Income Statement For the Year Ended December 31, 20Y2	
Sales	$1,200,000
Cost of goods sold	960,000
Gross profit	$ 240,000
Operating expenses	144,500
Income from operations	$ 95,500
Income tax expense	36,290
Net income	$ 59,210
Other comprehensive income	2,600
Comprehensive income	$ 61,810

Reporting Comprehensive Income on the Statement of Comprehensive Income
As an alternative to reporting comprehensive income on the income statement, companies may elect to report comprehensive income on a separate statement of comprehensive income.

---

[4] Fair value accounting is discussed in greater detail in intermediate and advanced accounting texts. A primer on fair value accounting is also included in Appendix D.

This statement should immediately follow the income statement. Using the Bart Company example, the income statement and statement of comprehensive income would be presented as follows:

Bart Company	
Income Statement	
For the Year Ended December 31, 20Y2	
Sales	$1,200,000
Cost of goods sold	960,000
Gross profit	$ 240,000
Operating expenses	144,500
Income from operations	$ 95,500
Income tax expense	36,290
Net income	$ 59,210

Bart Company	
Statement of Comprehensive Income	
For the Year Ended December 31, 20Y2	
Net income	$59,210
Other comprehensive income	2,600
Comprehensive income	$61,810

Reporting Accumulated Other Comprehensive Income on the Balance Sheet

The *cumulative* effect of the elements of other comprehensive income is reported on the balance sheet as **accumulated other comprehensive income**.

Continuing the Bart Company example, the unrealized gain of $2,600 would be reported as accumulated other comprehensive income in the Stockholders' Equity section of the balance sheet, as follows:

Bart Company	
Balance Sheet	
December 31, 20Y2	
Stockholders' Equity	
Common stock	$ 20,000
Paid-in capital in excess of par	300,000
Retained earnings	250,000
Accumulated other comprehensive income	2,600
Total stockholders' equity	$572,600

Let's Review

Chapter Summary

1. The basic financial statements provide important information that users rely on to make economic decisions. Financial statement users typically evaluate this information along three dimensions: liquidity, solvency, and profitability. Two common techniques are used to analyze a company's financial performance and condition: analytical methods and ratios. Both analytical methods and ratios can be used to compare a company's financial performance over time or to another company.

2. Analytical methods are used to compare items on a current financial statement with related items on earlier statements or to examine relationships within a financial statement. Horizontal analysis is the analysis of percentage increases and decreases in related items in comparative financial statements. The analysis of the relationship of each component in a financial statement to a significant total within the statement is called vertical analysis. In a common-sized statement, all items are expressed as percentages with no dollar amounts shown.

3. Liquidity analysis evaluates a company's ability to convert current assets into cash. Short-term creditors use liquidity analysis to evaluate a company's ability to repay short-term debts by focusing on a company's current position, accounts receivable, and inventory. The measures and ratios used to evaluate a company's liquidity include: (1) working capital, (2) current ratio, (3) quick ratio, (4) accounts receivable turnover, (5) number of days' sales in receivables, (6) inventory turnover, and (7) number of days' sales in inventory.

4. Solvency analysis evaluates the ability of a company to pay its long-term debts. Long-term creditors use solvency analysis to evaluate a company's ability to make its periodic interest payments and repay the face amount of bonds at maturity. Solvency is normally assessed by examining (1) the ratio of fixed assets to long-term liabilities, (2) the ratio of liabilities to stockholders' equity, and (3) the times interest earned ratio.

5. Profitability analysis focuses on the relationship between operating results (income statement) and assets (balance sheet). Profitability analyses include (1) the asset turnover ratio, (2) the return on total assets, (3) the return on stockholders' equity, (4) the return on common stockholders' equity, (5) earnings per share on common stock, (6) the price-earnings ratio, (7) dividends per share, and (8) dividend yield.

6. Public corporations issue annual reports summarizing their operating activities for the past year and plans for the future. In addition to the financial statements and accompanying notes, annual reports include management discussion and analysis (MD&A), a report on internal control, and a report on fairness of the financial statements. Management discussion and analysis includes management's analysis of current operations and its plans for the future. The report on internal control states management's responsibility for establishing and maintaining internal controls. The report on fairness of the financial statements provides the CPA firm's opinion on whether the financial statements fairly present the financial position, results of operations, and cash flows of the company.

Key Terms

accounts receivable
analysis (674)

accounts receivable turnover (674)

accumulated other comprehensive
income (694)

analytical methods (667)

asset turnover (681)

common-sized statement (671)

comprehensive income (693)

current position analysis (673)

current ratio (673)

dividend yield (686)

dividends per share (685)

earnings per share (EPS)
on common stock (684)

fair value (693)

horizontal analysis (667)

inventory analysis (675)

inventory turnover (676)

leverage (682)

liquidity (666)

Management's Discussion and
Analysis (MD&A) (689)

number of days' sales in
inventory (676)

number of days' sales in
receivables (675)

other comprehensive income (693)

price-earnings (P/E) ratio (685)

profitability (667)

quick assets (674)

quick ratio (674)

ratio of fixed assets to long-term
liabilities (678)

ratio of liabilities to
stockholders' equity (678)

ratios (667)

return on common stockholders'
equity (683)

return on stockholders' equity (682)

return on total assets (681)

solvency (666)

times interest earned (679)

unrealized gain (693)

vertical analysis (669)

working capital (673)

Practice

Multiple-Choice Questions

1. What type of analysis is indicated by the following?

	Amount	Percent
Current assets	$100,000	20%
Property, plant, and equipment	400,000	80%
Total assets	$500,000	100%

   A. Vertical analysis
   B. Horizontal analysis
   C. Liquidity analysis
   D. Profitability analysis

2. The ability of a company to pay its debts is called:
   A. earnings per share.
   B. liquidity.
   C. profitability.
   D. solvency.

3. The ratio that measures how much of a company is financed by debt and equity is the:
   A. current ratio.
   B. ratio of fixed assets to long-term debt.
   C. ratio of liabilities to stockholders' equity.
   D. price-earnings ratio.

4. The ratio that measures the "instant" debt-paying ability of a firm, by focusing on current assets that can be easily converted to cash, is the:
   A. working capital.
   B. quick ratio.
   C. number of days' sales in inventory.
   D. ratio of fixed assets to long-term liabilities.

5. A measure useful in evaluating efficiency in the management of inventories is the:
   A. working capital.
   B. quick ratio.
   C. number of days' sales in inventory.
   D. ratio of fixed assets to long-term liabilities.

Answers provided after Problem. Need more practice? Find additional multiple-choice questions, exercises, and problems in CengageNOWv2.

Exercises

SHOW ME HOW

1. Horizontal analysis
Obj. 2

The comparative temporary investments and inventory balances of a company follow.

	Current Year	Previous Year
Temporary investments	$59,280	$52,000
Inventory	70,680	76,000

Based on this information, what is the amount and percentage of increase or decrease that would be shown on a balance sheet with horizontal analysis?

SHOW ME HOW

2. Vertical analysis
Obj. 2

Income statement information for Axiom Corporation follows:

Sales	$725,000
Cost of goods sold	391,500
Gross profit	333,500

Prepare a vertical analysis of the income statement for Axiom Corporation.

SHOW ME HOW

3. Current position analysis
Obj. 3

The following items are reported on a company's balance sheet:

Cash	$160,000
Marketable securities	75,000
Accounts receivable (net)	65,000
Inventory	140,000
Accounts payable	200,000

Determine (A) the current ratio and (B) the quick ratio. (Round to one decimal place.)

SHOW ME HOW

4. Accounts receivable analysis
Obj. 3

A company reports the following:

Sales	$832,000
Average accounts receivable (net)	80,000

Determine (A) the accounts receivable turnover and (B) the number of days' sales in receivables. (Round to one decimal place.)

SHOW ME HOW

5. Inventory analysis
Obj. 3

A company reports the following:

Cost of goods sold	$630,000
Average inventory	90,000

Determine (A) the inventory turnover and (B) the number of days' sales in inventory. (Round to one decimal place.)

SHOW ME HOW

6. Long-term solvency analysis
Obj. 4

The following information was taken from Kellman Company's balance sheet:

Fixed assets (net)	$ 960,000
Long-term liabilities	800,000
Total liabilities	1,000,000
Total stockholders' equity	625,000

Determine the company's (A) ratio of fixed assets to long-term liabilities and (B) ratio of liabilities to stockholders' equity. (Round to one decimal place.)

SHOW ME HOW

7. Times interest earned

Obj. 4

A company reports the following:

Income before income tax	$4,000,000
Interest expense	400,000

Determine the times interest earned ratio. (Round to one decimal place.)

SHOW ME HOW

8. Asset turnover

Obj. 5

A company reports the following:

Sales	$1,800,000
Average total assets (excluding long-term investments)	1,125,000

Determine the asset turnover ratio. (Round to one decimal place.)

SHOW ME HOW

9. Return on total assets

Obj. 5

A company reports the following income statement and balance sheet information for the current year:

Net income	$ 250,000
Interest expense	100,000
Average total assets	2,500,000

Determine the return on total assets. (Round to one decimal place.)

SHOW ME HOW

10. Common stockholders' profitability analysis

Obj. 5

A company reports the following:

Net income	$ 375,000
Preferred dividends	75,000
Average stockholders' equity	2,500,000
Average common stockholders' equity	1,875,000

Determine (A) the return on stockholders' equity and (B) the return on common stockholders' equity. (Round to one decimal place.)

SHOW ME HOW

11. Earnings per share and price-earnings ratio

Obj. 5

A company reports the following:

Net income	$185,000
Preferred dividends	$25,000
Shares of common stock outstanding	100,000
Market price per share of common stock	$20

A. Determine the company's earnings per share on common stock.

B. Determine the company's price-earnings ratio. (Round to one decimal place.)

Answers provided after Problem. Need more practice? Find additional multiple-choice questions, exercises, and problems in CengageNOWv2.

Problem

Rainbow Paint Co.'s comparative financial statements for the years ending December 31, 20Y9 and 20Y8, are as follows. The market price of Rainbow Paint's common stock was $25 on December 31, 20Y9, and $30 on December 31, 20Y8.

Rainbow Paint Co. Comparative Income Statement For the Years Ended December 31, 20Y9 and 20Y8		
	20Y9	**20Y8**
Sales	$5,000,000	$3,200,000
Cost of goods sold...	3,400,000	2,080,000
Gross profit	$1,600,000	$1,120,000
Selling expenses	$ 650,000	$ 464,000
Administrative expenses......................................	325,000	224,000
Total operating expenses	$ 975,000	$ 688,000
Income from operations	$ 625,000	$ 432,000
Other income..	25,000	19,200
	$ 650,000	$ 451,200
Other expense (interest)	105,000	64,000
Income before income tax	$ 545,000	$ 387,200
Income tax expense	300,000	176,000
Net income	$ 245,000	$ 211,200

Rainbow Paint Co. Comparative Retained Earnings Statement For the Years Ended December 31, 20Y9 and 20Y8		
	20Y9	**20Y8**
Retained earnings, January 1......................................	$723,000	$581,800
Net income	245,000	211,200
Total	$968,000	$793,000
Dividends:		
On preferred stock..	$ 40,000	$ 40,000
On common stock...	45,000	30,000
Total dividends...	$ 85,000	$ 70,000
Retained earnings, December 31	$883,000	$723,000

(Continued)

Rainbow Paint Co. **Comparative Balance Sheet** **December 31, 20Y9 and 20Y8**			
		20Y9	**20Y8**
Assets			
Current assets:			
Cash.....		$ 175,000	$ 125,000
Temporary investments.....		150,000	50,000
Accounts receivable (net).....		425,000	325,000
Inventories.....		720,000	480,000
Prepaid expenses.....		30,000	20,000
Total current assets.....		$1,500,000	$1,000,000
Long-term investments.....		250,000	225,000
Property, plant, and equipment (net).....		2,093,000	1,948,000
Total assets.....		$3,843,000	$3,173,000
Liabilities			
Current liabilities.....		$ 750,000	$ 650,000
Long-term liabilities:			
Mortgage note payable, 10%, due in five years.....		$ 410,000	—
Bonds payable, 8%, due in fifteen years.....		800,000	$ 800,000
Total long-term liabilities.....		$1,210,000	$ 800,000
Total liabilities.....		$1,960,000	$1,450,000
Stockholders' Equity			
Preferred 8% stock, $100 par.....		$ 500,000	$ 500,000
Common stock, $10 par.....		500,000	500,000
Retained earnings.....		883,000	723,000
Total stockholders' equity.....		$1,883,000	$1,723,000
Total liabilities and stockholders' equity.....		$3,843,000	$3,173,000

Instructions

Determine the following measures for 20Y9 (round percentages and ratios other than per-share amounts to one decimal place):

1. Working capital
2. Current ratio
3. Quick ratio
4. Accounts receivable turnover
5. Number of days' sales in receivables
6. Inventory turnover
7. Number of days' sales in inventory
8. Ratio of fixed assets to long-term liabilities
9. Ratio of liabilities to stockholders' equity
10. Times interest earned
11. Asset turnover
12. Return on total assets
13. Return on stockholders' equity
14. Return on common stockholders' equity
15. Earnings per share on common stock
16. Price-earnings ratio
17. Dividends per share
18. Dividend yield

Need more practice? Find additional multiple-choice questions, exercises, and problems in CengageNOWv2.

Answers

Multiple-Choice Questions

1. **A** Vertical analysis compares each component in a financial statement to a total within the statement. Horizontal analysis (answer B) compares the amount and percentage of each item on the most recent statement to the same item on an earlier statement. Liquidity analysis (answer C) evaluates the ability of a company to convert current assets into cash. Profitability analysis (answer D) focuses on the ability of a company to earn profits by examining the relationship between operating results and the resources available.

2. **D** Solvency is a company's ability to pay its debts. Earnings per share (answer A) measures the share of profits that are earned by a share of common stock. Liquidity (answer B) is the ability of a company to convert current assets into cash. Profitability (answer C) focuses on the ability of a company to earn profits by examining the relationship between operating results and the resources available.

3. **C** The ratio of liabilities to stockholders' equity measures the relationship between debt and equity, which measures how much of the company is financed with debt and equity. The current ratio (answer A) measures a company's ability to pay its current liabilities. The ratio of fixed assets to long-term liabilities (answer B) provides a measure of whether noteholders or bondholders will be paid. The price-earnings ratio (answer D) measures a company's future earnings prospects.

4. **B** The quick ratio measures the "instant" debt-paying ability of a company. Working capital (answer A) is the difference between current assets and current liabilities. The number of days' sales in inventory (answer C) is a measure of the length of time it takes to purchase, sell, and replace the inventory. The ratio of fixed assets to long-term liabilities (answer D) provides a measure of whether noteholders or bondholders will be paid.

5. **C** The number of days' sales in inventory is a measure of the length of time it takes to purchase, sell, and replace the inventory. Working capital (answer A) is the difference between current assets and current liabilities. The quick ratio (answer B) measures the "instant" debt-paying ability of a company. The ratio of fixed assets to long-term liabilities (answer D) provides a measure of whether noteholders or bondholders will be paid.

Exercises

1. Temporary investments.................... $7,280 increase ($59,280 – $52,000), or 14%

   Inventory .... $5,320 decrease ($70,680 – $76,000), or –7%

2.

	Amount	Percentage	
Sales...	$725,000	100%	($725,000 ÷ $725,000)
Cost of goods sold........................	391,500	54%	($391,500 ÷ $725,000)
Gross profit.................................	$333,500	46%	($333,500 ÷ $725,000)

3. A.   Current Ratio = Current Assets ÷ Current Liabilities

   = ($160,000 + $75,000 + $65,000 + $140,000) ÷ $200,000

   = 2.2

   B.   Quick Ratio = Quick Assets ÷ Current Liabilities

   = ($160,000 + $75,000 + $65,000) ÷ $200,000

   = 1.5

4. A.   Accounts Receivable Turnover = Sales ÷ Average Accounts Receivable

   = $832,000 ÷ $80,000
   = 10.4

(Continued)

B. Number of Days' Sales in Receivables = $\dfrac{\text{Average Accounts Receivable}}{\text{Average Daily Sales}}$

$$= \$80,000 \div (\$832,000 \div 365)$$

$$= \$80,000 \div \$2,279$$

$$= 35.1 \text{ days}$$

5. A. Inventory Turnover = Cost of Goods Sold ÷ Average Inventory

$$= \$630,000 \div \$90,000$$

$$= 7.0$$

B. Number of Days' Sales in Inventory = $\dfrac{\text{Average Inventory}}{\text{Average Daily Cost of Goods Sold}}$

$$= \$90,000 \div (\$630,000 \div 365)$$

$$= \$90,000 \div \$1,726$$

$$= 52.1 \text{ days}$$

6. A. Ratio of Fixed Assets to Long-Term Liabilities = $\dfrac{\text{Fixed Assets}}{\text{Long-Term Liabilities}}$

$$= \$960,000 \div \$800,000$$

$$= 1.2$$

B. Ratio of Liabilities to Stockholders' Equity = $\dfrac{\text{Total Liabilities}}{\text{Total Stockholders' Equity}}$

$$= \$1,000,000 \div \$625,000$$

$$= 1.6$$

7. Times Interest Earned = $\dfrac{\text{Income Before Income Tax + Interest Expense}}{\text{Interest Expense}}$

$$= \dfrac{\$4,000,000 + \$400,000}{\$400,000}$$

$$= 11.0$$

8. Asset Turnover = Sales ÷ Average Total Assets

$$= \$1,800,000 \div \$1,125,000$$

$$= 1.6$$

9. Return on Total Assets = $\dfrac{\text{Net Income + Interest Expense}}{\text{Average Total Assets}}$

$$= \dfrac{\$250,000 + \$100,000}{\$2,500,000}$$

$$= \dfrac{\$350,000}{\$2,500,000}$$

$$= 14.0\%$$

10. A. Return on Stockholders' Equity = $\dfrac{\text{Net Income}}{\text{Average Stockholders' Equity}}$

$$= \$375,000 \div \$2,500,000$$

$$= 15.0\%$$

B. Return on Common Stockholders' Equity = $\dfrac{\text{Net Income} - \text{Preferred Dividends}}{\text{Average Common Stockholders' Equity}}$

$$= \frac{\$375,000 - \$75,000}{\$1,875,000}$$

$$= 16.0\%$$

11. A. Earnings per Share on Common Stock = $\dfrac{\text{Net Income} - \text{Preferred Dividends}}{\text{Shares of Common Stock Outstanding}}$

$$= (\$185,000 - \$25,000) \div \$100,000$$

$$= \$1.60$$

B. Price-Earnings Ratio = $\dfrac{\text{Market Price per Share of Common Stock}}{\text{Earnings per Share on Common Stock}}$

$$= \$20.00 \div \$1.60$$

$$= 12.5$$

Need more help? Watch step-by-step videos of how to compute answers to these Exercises in CengageNOWv2.

Problem

(Ratios are rounded to one decimal place.)

1. Working capital: $750,000

$1,500,000 − $750,000

2. Current ratio: 2.0

$1,500,000 ÷ $750,000

3. Quick ratio: 1.0

$750,000 ÷ $750,000

4. Accounts receivable turnover: 13.3

$5,000,000 ÷ [($425,000 + $325,000) ÷ 2]

5. Number of days' sales in receivables: 27.4 days

$5,000,000 ÷ 365 days = $13,699

$375,000 ÷ $13,699

6. Inventory turnover: 5.7

$3,400,000 ÷ [($720,000 + $480,000) ÷ 2]

7. Number of days' sales in inventory: 64.4 days

$3,400,000 ÷ 365 days = $9,315

$600,000 ÷ $9,315

8. Ratio of fixed assets to long-term liabilities: 1.7

$2,093,000 ÷ $1,210,000

9. Ratio of liabilities to stockholders' equity: 1.0

$1,960,000 ÷ $1,883,000

10. Times interest earned: 6.2

($545,000 + $105,000) ÷ $105,000

11. Asset turnover: 1.5

$5,000,000 ÷ [($3,593,000 + $2,948,000) ÷ 2]

12. Return on total assets: 10.0%

($245,000 + $105,000) ÷ [($3,843,000 + $3,173,000) ÷ 2]

(Continued)

13. Return on stockholders' equity: 13.6%

$245,000 ÷ [($1,883,000 + $1,723,000) ÷ 2]

14. Return on common stockholders' equity: 15.7%

($245,000 − $40,000) ÷ [($1,383,000 + $1,223,000) ÷ 2]

15. Earnings per share on common stock: $4.10

($245,000 − $40,000) ÷ 50,000 shares

16. Price-earnings ratio: 6.1

$25 ÷ $4.10

17. Dividends per share: $0.90

$45,000 ÷ 50,000 shares

18. Dividend yield: 3.6%

$0.90 ÷ $25

Discussion Questions

1. Briefly explain the difference between liquidity, solvency, and profitability analysis.

2. What is the advantage of using comparative statements for financial analysis rather than statements for a single date or period?

3. A company's current year net income (after income tax) is 25% larger than that of the preceding year. Does this indicate improved operating performance? Why?

4. How would the current and quick ratios of a service business compare?

5. A. Why is a high inventory turnover considered to be a positive indicator?

   B. Is it possible to have a high inventory turnover and a high number of days' sales in inventory? Why?

6. What do the following data, taken from a comparative balance sheet, indicate about the company's ability to borrow additional long-term debt in the current year as compared to the preceding year?

	Current Year	Preceding Year
Fixed assets (net)	$1,260,000	$1,360,000
Total long-term liabilities	300,000	400,000

7. A. How does the rate earned on total assets differ from the rate earned on stockholders' equity?

   B. Which ratio is normally higher? Why?

8.  **Kroger**, a grocery store, recently had a price-earnings ratio of 13.7, while the average price-earnings ratio in the grocery store industry was 22.5. What might explain this difference?
REAL WORLD

9.  The dividend yield of **Suburban Propane** was 7.7% in a recent year, and the dividend yield of **Google** was 0% in the same year. What might explain the difference between these ratios?
REAL WORLD

10. Describe two reports provided by independent auditors in the annual report to shareholders.

Basic Exercises

SHOW ME HOW

BE 14-1 Horizontal analysis   Obj. 2

The comparative accounts payable and long-term debt balances for a company follow.

	Current Year	Previous Year
Accounts payable	$111,000	$100,000
Long-term debt	132,680	124,000

Based on this information, what is the amount and percentage of increase or decrease that would be shown on a balance sheet with horizontal analysis?

SHOW ME HOW

BE 14-2 Vertical analysis   Obj. 2

Income statement information for Einsworth Corporation follows:

Sales	$1,200,000
Cost of goods sold	780,000
Gross profit	420,000

Prepare a vertical analysis of the income statement for Einsworth Corporation. (Round percentages to one decimal place.)

SHOW ME HOW

BE 14-3 Current position analysis   Obj. 3

The following items are reported on a company's balance sheet:

Cash	$210,000
Marketable securities	120,000
Accounts receivable (net)	110,000
Inventory	160,000
Accounts payable	200,000

Determine (A) the current ratio and (B) the quick ratio. (Round to one decimal place.)

SHOW ME HOW

BE 14-4 Accounts receivable analysis   Obj. 3

A company reports the following:

Sales	$3,150,000
Average accounts receivable (net)	210,000

Determine (A) the accounts receivable turnover and (B) the number of days' sales in receivables. (Round to one decimal place.)

SHOW ME HOW

BE 14-5 Inventory analysis   Obj. 3

A company reports the following:

Cost of goods sold	$435,000
Average inventory	72,500

Determine (A) the inventory turnover and (B) the number of days' sales in inventory. (Round to one decimal place.)

SHOW ME HOW

BE 14-6 Long-term solvency analysis   Obj. 4

The following information was taken from Charu Company's balance sheet:

Fixed assets (net)	$860,000
Long-term liabilities	200,000
Total liabilities	600,000
Total stockholders' equity	250,000

Determine the company's (A) ratio of fixed assets to long-term liabilities and (B) ratio of liabilities to stockholders' equity. (Round to one decimal place.)

SHOW ME HOW

BE 14-7 Times interest earned   Obj. 4

A company reports the following:

Income before income tax	$8,000,000
Interest expense	500,000

Determine the number of times interest charges are earned. (Round to one decimal place.)

SHOW ME HOW

BE 14-8 Asset turnover   Obj. 5

A company reports the following:

Sales	$4,400,000
Average total assets (excluding long-term investments)	2,000,000

Determine the asset turnover ratio. (Round percentages to one decimal place.)

SHOW ME HOW

BE 14-9 Return on total assets   Obj. 5

A company reports the following income statement and balance sheet information for the current year:

Net income	$ 410,000
Interest expense	90,000
Average total assets	5,000,000

Determine the return on total assets. (Round percentages to one decimal place.)

SHOW ME HOW

BE 14-10 Common stockholders' profitability analysis   Obj. 5

A company reports the following:

Net income	$1,000,000
Preferred dividends	50,000
Average stockholders' equity	6,250,000
Average common stockholders' equity	3,800,000

Determine (A) the return on stockholders' equity and (B) the return on common stockholders' equity. (Round percentages to one decimal place.)

SHOW ME HOW

BE 14-11 Earnings per share and price-earnings ratio   Obj. 5

A company reports the following:

Net income	$410,000
Preferred dividends	$60,000
Shares of common stock outstanding	50,000
Market price per share of common stock	$84

A. Determine the company's earnings per share on common stock.

B. Determine the company's price-earnings ratio. (Round to one decimal place.)

Exercises

✔ A. Current year net
income: $360,000; 9%
of sales

SHOW ME HOW

EX 14-1 Vertical analysis of income statement   Obj. 2

Revenue and expense data for Innovation Quarter Inc. for two recent years are as follows:

	Current Year	Previous Year
Sales	$4,000,000	$3,600,000
Cost of goods sold	2,280,000	1,872,000
Selling expenses	600,000	648,000
Administrative expenses	520,000	360,000
Income tax expense	240,000	216,000

A. Prepare an income statement in comparative form, stating each item for both years as a percent of sales. (Round to the nearest whole percentage.)

B. ▬▬▬➤ Comment on the significant changes disclosed by the comparative income statement.

EX 14-2 Vertical analysis of income statement

Obj. 2

EXCEL TEMPLATE REAL WORLD

✔ A. Current fiscal year income from continuing operations, 13.0% of revenues

The following comparative income statement (in thousands of dollars) for two recent fiscal years was adapted from the annual report of **Speedway Motorsports, Inc.**, owner and operator of several major motor speedways, such as the Atlanta, Texas, and Las Vegas Motor Speedways.

	Current Year	Previous Year
Revenues:		
Admissions	$116,034	$130,239
Event-related revenue	151,562	163,621
NASCAR broadcasting revenue	192,662	185,394
Other operating revenue	29,902	26,951
Total revenues	$490,160	$506,205
Expenses and other:		
Direct expense of events	$101,402	$106,204
NASCAR purse and sanction fees	122,950	120,146
Other direct expenses	18,908	20,352
General and administrative	183,215	241,223
Total expenses and other	$426,475	$487,925
Income from continuing operations	$ 63,685	$ 18,280

A. Prepare a comparative income statement for these two years in vertical form, stating each item as a percent of revenues. (Round percentages to one decimal place.)

B. ➤ Comment on the significant changes.

EX 14-3 Common-sized income statement

Obj. 2

SHOW ME HOW

✔ A. Tannenhill net income: $120,000; 3.0% of sales

Revenue and expense data for the current calendar year for Tannenhill Company and for the electronics industry are as follows. Tannenhill's data are expressed in dollars. The electronics industry averages are expressed in percentages.

	Tannenhill Company	Electronics Industry Average
Sales	$4,000,000	100.0%
Cost of goods sold	2,120,000	60.0
Gross profit	$1,880,000	40.0%
Selling expenses	$1,080,000	24.0%
Administrative expenses	640,000	14.0
Total operating expenses	$1,720,000	38.0%
Operating income	$ 160,000	2.0%
Other income	120,000	3.0
	$ 280,000	5.0%
Other expense	80,000	2.0
Income before income tax	$ 200,000	3.0%
Income tax expense	80,000	2.0
Net income	$ 120,000	1.0%

A. Prepare a common-sized income statement comparing the results of operations for Tannenhill Company with the industry average. (Round to the nearest whole percentage.)

B. ➤ As far as the data permit, comment on significant relationships revealed by the comparisons.

EX 14-4 Vertical analysis of balance sheet

Obj. 2

Balance sheet data for Alvarez Company on December 31, the end of two recent fiscal years, follow:

	Current Year	Previous Year
Current assets	$2,500,000	$1,840,000
Property, plant, and equipment	5,600,000	6,072,000
Intangible assets	1,900,000	1,288,000
Current liabilities	2,000,000	1,380,000
Long-term liabilities	3,400,000	3,680,000
Common stock	920,000	920,000
Retained earnings	3,680,000	3,220,000

Prepare a comparative balance sheet for both years, stating each asset as a percent of total assets and each liability and stockholders' equity item as a percent of the total liabilities and stockholders' equity. (Round percentages to one decimal place.)

EX 14-5 Horizontal analysis of the income statement

Obj. 2

Income statement data for Winthrop Company for two recent years ended December 31 are as follows:

	Current Year	Previous Year
Sales	$2,280,000	$2,000,000
Cost of goods sold	1,960,000	1,750,000
Gross profit	$ 320,000	$ 250,000
Selling expenses	$ 156,500	$ 125,000
Administrative expenses	122,000	100,000
Total operating expenses	$ 278,500	$ 225,000
Income before income tax	$ 41,500	$ 25,000
Income tax expense	16,600	10,000
Net income	$ 24,900	$ 15,000

A. Prepare a comparative income statement with horizontal analysis, indicating the increase (decrease) for the current year when compared with the previous year. (Round percentages to one decimal place.)

B. ━━► What conclusions can be drawn from the horizontal analysis?

EX 14-6 Current position analysis

Obj. 3

The following data were taken from the balance sheet of Nilo Company at the end of two recent fiscal years:

	Current Year	Previous Year
Current assets:		
Cash	$ 414,000	$ 320,000
Marketable securities	496,800	336,000
Accounts and notes receivable (net)	619,200	464,000
Inventories	351,900	272,000
Prepaid expenses	188,100	208,000
Total current assets	$2,070,000	$1,600,000
Current liabilities:		
Accounts and notes payable (short-term)	$ 675,000	$ 600,000
Accrued liabilities	225,000	200,000
Total current liabilities	$ 900,000	$ 800,000

A. Determine for each year (1) the working capital, (2) the current ratio, and (3) the quick ratio. (Round ratios to one decimal place.)

B. ━━► What conclusions can be drawn from these data as to the company's ability to meet its currently maturing debts?

EX 14-7 Current position analysis
Obj. 3

✔ A. (1) Current year's current ratio, 1.1

REAL WORLD

PepsiCo, Inc., the parent company of Frito-Lay snack foods and Pepsi beverages, had the following current assets and current liabilities at the end of two recent years:

	Current Year (in millions)	Previous Year (in millions)
Cash and cash equivalents	$ 6,297	$ 4,067
Short-term investments, at cost	322	358
Accounts and notes receivable, net	7,041	6,912
Inventories	3,581	3,827
Prepaid expenses and other current assets	1,479	2,277
Short-term obligations	4,815	6,205
Accounts payable	12,274	11,949

A. Determine the (1) current ratio and (2) quick ratio for both years. (Round to one decimal place.)

B. ➤ What conclusions can you draw from these data about PepsiCo's liquidity?

EX 14-8 Current position analysis
Obj. 3

The bond indenture for the 10-year, 9% debenture bonds issued January 2, 20Y5, required working capital of $100,000, a current ratio of 1.5, and a quick ratio of 1.0 at the end of each calendar year until the bonds mature. At December 31, 20Y6, the three measures were computed as follows:

1.	Current assets:		
	Cash......................................	$102,000	
	Temporary investments	48,000	
	Accounts and notes receivable (net)..........	120,000	
	Inventories................................	36,000	
	Prepaid expenses...........................	24,000	
	Intangible assets	124,800	
	Property, plant, and equipment..............	55,200	
	Total current assets (net)		$510,000
	Current liabilities:		
	Accounts and short-term notes payable	$ 96,000	
	Accrued liabilities...........................	204,000	
	Total current liabilities		300,000
	Working capital		$210,000
2.	Current ratio	1.7	$510,000 ÷ $300,000
3.	Quick ratio.................................	1.2	$115,200 ÷ $ 96,000

A. List the errors in the determination of the three measures of current position analysis.

B. ➤ Is the company satisfying the terms of the bond indenture?

EX 14-9 Accounts receivable analysis
Obj. 3

✔ A. Accounts receivable turnover, 20Y3, 8.2

SHOW ME HOW

The following data are taken from the financial statements of Sigmon Inc. Terms of all sales are 2/10, n/45.

	20Y3	20Y2	20Y1
Accounts receivable, end of year	$ 725,000	$ 650,000	$600,000
Sales on account	5,637,500	4,687,500	

A. For 20Y2 and 20Y3, determine (1) the accounts receivable turnover and (2) the number of days' sales in receivables. (Round to the nearest dollar and one decimal place.)

B. ➤ What conclusions can be drawn from these data concerning accounts receivable and credit policies?

EX 14-10 Accounts receivable analysis

✔ A. 1. Lestrade, 7.0

Xavier Stores Company and Lestrade Stores Inc. are large retail department stores. Both companies offer credit to their customers through their own credit card operations. Information from the financial statements for both companies for two recent years is as follows (in millions):

	Xavier	Lestrade
Sales	$8,500,000	$4,585,000
Credit card receivables—beginning	820,000	600,000
Credit card receviables—ending	880,000	710,000

A. Determine the (1) accounts receivable turnover and (2) the number of days' sales in receivables for both companies. (Round to one decimal place.)

B. ➤ Compare the two companies with regard to their credit card policies.

EX 14-11 Inventory analysis

✔ A. Inventory turnover, current year, 9.0

SHOW ME HOW

The following data were extracted from the income statement of Keever Inc.:

	Current Year	Previous Year
Sales	$18,500,000	$20,000,000
Beginning inventories	940,000	860,000
Cost of goods sold	9,270,000	10,800,000
Ending inventories	1,120,000	940,000

A. Determine for each year (1) the inventory turnover and (2) the number of days' sales in inventory. (Round to the nearest dollar and one decimal place.)

B. ➤ What conclusions can be drawn from these data concerning the inventories?

EX 14-12 Inventory analysis

✔ A. QT inventory turnover, 32.1

QT, Inc. and Elppa Computers, Inc. compete with each other in the personal computer market. QT assembles computers to customer orders, building and delivering a computer within four days of a customer entering an order online. Elppa, on the other hand, builds computers for inventory prior to receiving an order. These computers are sold from inventory once an order is received. Selected financial information for both companies from recent financial statements follows (in millions):

	QT	Elppa
Sales	$56,940	$120,357
Cost of goods sold	44,754	92,385
Inventory, beginning of period	1,382	6,317
Inventory, end of period	1,404	7,490

A. Determine for both companies (1) the inventory turnover and (2) the number of days' sales in inventory. (Round to one decimal place.)

B. ➤ Interpret the inventory ratios in the context of both companies' operating strategies.

EX 14-13 Ratio of liabilities to stockholders' equity and number of times interest earned

✔ A. Ratio of liabilities to stockholders' equity, current year, 0.9

The following data were taken from the financial statements of Hunter Inc. for December 31 of two recent years:

	Current Year	Previous Year
Accounts payable	$ 924,000	$ 800,000
Current maturities of serial bonds payable	200,000	200,000
Serial bonds payable, 10%	1,000,000	1,200,000
Common stock, $10 par value	250,000	250,000
Paid-in capital in excess of par	1,250,000	1,250,000
Retained earnings	860,000	500,000

The income before income tax was $480,000 and $420,000 for the current and previous years, respectively.

A. Determine the ratio of liabilities to stockholders' equity at the end of each year. (Round to one decimal place.)

B. Determine the times interest earned ratio for both years. (Round to one decimal place.)

C. ▬▬▶ What conclusions can be drawn from these data as to the company's ability to meet its currently maturing debts?

EX 14-14   Ratio of liabilities to stockholders' equity and times interest earned   Obj. 4

Hasbro, Inc. and Mattel, Inc., are the two largest toy companies in North America. Condensed liabilities and stockholders' equity from a recent balance sheet are shown for each company as follows (in thousands):

	Hasbro	Mattel
Liabilities:		
Current liabilities	$ 960,435	$ 1,716,012
Long-term debt	1,396,421	1,100,000
Deferred liabilities	461,152	643,729
Total liabilities	$ 2,818,008	$ 3,459,741
Shareholders' equity:		
Common stock	$ 104,847	$ 441,369
Additional paid in capital	655,943	1,727,682
Retained earnings	3,354,545	3,515,181
Accumulated other comprehensive loss and other equity items	(72,307)	(464,486)
Treasury stock, at cost	(2,535,649)	(2,152,702)
Total stockholders' equity	$ 1,507,379	$ 3,067,044
Total liabilities and stockholders' equity	$ 4,325,387	$ 6,526,785

The income from operations and interest expense from the income statement for each company were as follows (in thousands):

	Hasbro	Mattel
Income from operations (before income tax)	$453,402	$945,045
Interest expense	117,403	88,835

A. Determine the ratio of liabilities to stockholders' equity for both companies. (Round to one decimal place.)

B. Determine the times interest earned ratio for both companies. (Round to one decimal place.)

C. ▬▬▶ Interpret the ratio differences between the two companies.

EX 14-15   Ratio of liabilities to stockholders' equity and ratio of fixed assets to long-term liabilities   Obj. 4

Recent balance sheet information for two companies in the food industry, Mondelez International, Inc. and The Hershey Company, is as follows (in thousands):

	Mondelez	Hershey
Net property, plant, and equipment	$10,010,000	$1,674,071
Current liabilities	14,873,000	1,471,110
Long-term debt	15,574,000	1,530,967
Other long-term liabilities	12,816,000	716,013
Stockholders' equity	32,215,000	1,036,749

A. Determine the ratio of liabilities to stockholders' equity for both companies. (Round to one decimal place.)

B. Determine the ratio of fixed assets to long-term liabilities for both companies. (Round to one decimal place.)

C. ▬▬▶ Interpret the ratio differences between the two companies.

EX 14-16 Asset turnover

Obj. 5

✔ A. YRC, 1.5

REAL WORLD

Three major segments of the transportation industry are motor carriers, such as **YRC Worldwide**; railroads, such as **Union Pacific**; and transportation logistics services, such as **C.H. Robinson Worldwide, Inc.** Recent financial statement information for these three companies follows (in thousands):

	YRC	Union Pacific	C.H. Robinson
Sales	$4,334,640	$16,965,000	$9,274,305
Average total assets	2,812,504	42,636,000	1,914,974

A. Determine the asset turnover for all three companies. (Round to one decimal place.)

B. ━━━ Assume that the asset turnover for each company represents their respective industry segment. Interpret the differences in the asset turnover in terms of the operating characteristics of each of the respective segments.

EX 14-17 Profitability ratios

Obj. 5

✔ A. return on total assets, 20Y7, 12.0%

SHOW ME HOW

The following selected data were taken from the financial statements of Vidahill Inc. for December 31, 20Y7, 20Y6, and 20Y5:

	20Y7	20Y6	20Y5
Total assets	$4,800,000	$4,400,000	$4,000,000
Notes payable (8% interest)	2,250,000	2,250,000	2,250,000
Common stock.....................................	250,000	250,000	250,000
Preferred 4% stock, $100 par (no change during year)	500,000	500,000	500,000
Retained earnings..................................	1,574,000	1,222,000	750,000

The 20Y7 net income was $372,000, and the 20Y6 net income was $492,000. No dividends on common stock were declared between 20Y5 and 20Y7. Preferred dividends were declared and paid in full in 20Y6 and 20Y7.

A. Determine the return on total assets, the rate earned on stockholders' equity, and the return on common stockholders' equity for the years 20Y6 and 20Y7. (Round percentages to one decimal place.)

B. ━━━ What conclusions can be drawn from these data as to the company's profitability?

EX 14-18 Profitability ratios

Obj. 5

✔A. Year 3 return on total assets, 12.2%

REAL WORLD

Ralph Lauren Corporation sells apparel through company-owned retail stores. Recent financial information for Ralph Lauren follows (in thousands):

	Fiscal Year 3	Fiscal Year 2	
Net income	$567,600	$479,500	
Interest expense	18,300	22,200	

	Fiscal Year 3	Fiscal Year 2	Fiscal Year 1
Total assets (at end of fiscal year)	$4,981,100	$4,648,900	$4,356,500
Total stockholders' equity (at end of fiscal year)	3,304,700	3,116,600	2,735,100

Assume the apparel industry average return on total assets is 8.0%, and the average rate earned on stockholders' equity is 10.0% for the year ended April 2, Year 3.

A. Determine the return on total assets for Ralph Lauren for fiscal Years 2 and 3. (Round percentages to one decimal place.)

B. Determine the return on stockholders' equity for Ralph Lauren for fiscal Years 2 and 3. (Round percentages to one decimal place.)

C. ━━━ Evaluate the two-year trend for the profitability ratios determined in (A) and (B).

D. ━━━ Evaluate Ralph Lauren's profit performance relative to the industry.

EX 14-19 Six measures of solvency or profitability

Obj. 4, 5

✔ C. Asset turnover, 4.2

The following data were taken from the financial statements of Gates Inc. for the current fiscal year.

Property, plant, and equipment (net)		$ 3,200,000
Liabilities:		
Current liabilities......................................	$1,000,000	
Note payable, 6%, due in 15 years	2,000,000	
Total liabilities		$ 3,000,000
Stockholders' equity:		
Preferred $10 stock, $100 par (no change during year) ...		$ 1,000,000
Common stock, $10 par (no change during year)		2,000,000
Retained earnings:		
Balance, beginning of year............................	$1,570,000	
Net income	930,000	$2,500,000
Preferred dividends	$ 100,000	
Common dividends	400,000	500,000
Balance, end of year.................................		2,000,000
Total stockholders' equity................................		$ 5,000,000
Sales		$18,900,000
Interest expense		$ 120,000

Assuming that long-term investments totaled $3,000,000 throughout the year and that total assets were $7,000,000 at the beginning of the current fiscal year, determine the following: (A) ratio of fixed assets to long-term liabilities, (B) ratio of liabilities to stockholders' equity, (C) asset turnover, (D) return on total assets, (E) return on stockholders' equity, and (F) return on common stockholders' equity. (Round ratios and percentages to one decimal place as appropriate.)

EX 14-20 Five measures of solvency or profitability

Obj. 4, 5

✔ C. Price-earnings ratio, 10.0

The balance sheet for Garcon Inc. at the end of the current fiscal year indicated the following:

Bonds payable, 8%	$5,000,000
Preferred $4 stock, $50 par	2,500,000
Common stock, $10 par	5,000,000

Income before income tax was $3,000,000, and income taxes were $1,200,000 for the current year. Cash dividends paid on common stock during the current year totaled $1,200,000. The common stock was selling for $32 per share at the end of the year. Determine each of the following: (A) times interest earned ratio (B) earnings per share on common stock, (C) price-earnings ratio, (D) dividends per share of common stock, and (E) dividend yield. (Round ratios and percentages to one decimal place, except for per-share amounts.)

EX 14-21 Earnings per share, price-earnings ratio, dividend yield

Obj. 5

✔ B. Price-earnings ratio, 15.0

The following information was taken from the financial statements of Tolbert Inc. for December 31 of the current fiscal year:

Common stock, $20 par (no change during the year)	$10,000,000
Preferred $4 stock, $40 par (no change during the year)	2,500,000

SHOW ME HOW

The net income was $1,750,000 and the declared dividends on the common stock were $1,125,000 for the current year. The market price of the common stock is $45 per share.

For the common stock, determine (A) the earnings per share, (B) the price-earnings ratio, (C) the dividends per share, and (D) the dividend yield. (Round ratios and percentages to one decimal place, except for per-share amounts.)

EX 14-22 Price-earnings ratio; dividend yield   Obj. 5

The table that follows shows the stock price, earnings per share, and dividends per share for three companies for a recent year:

	Price	Earnings per Share	Dividends per Share
Deere & Company	$ 86.20	$ 8.71	$2.04
Google	873.32	36.75	0.00
The Coca-Cola Company	39.79	1.97	1.02

A. Determine the price-earnings ratio and dividend yield for the three companies. (Round ratios and percentages to one decimal place as appropriate.)

B. ➡ Explain the differences in these ratios across the three companies.

Appendix 1

EX 14-23 Earnings per share, discontinued operations

The net income reported on the income statement of Cutler Co. was $4,000,000. There were 500,000 shares of $10 par common stock and 100,000 shares of $2 preferred stock outstanding throughout the current year. The income statement included a gain on discontinued operations of $400,000 after applicable income tax. Determine the per-share figures for common stock for (A) income before discontinued operations and (B) net income.

Appendix 1

EX 14-24 Income statement and earnings per share for discontinued operations

Apex Inc. reports the following for a recent year:

Income from continuing operations before income tax	$1,000,000
Loss from discontinued operations	$240,000*
Weighted average number of shares outstanding	20,000
Applicable tax rate	40%
*Net of any tax effect.	

A. Prepare a partial income statement for Apex Inc., beginning with income from continuing operations before income tax.

B. Determine the earnings per common share for Apex Inc., including per-share amounts for unusual items.

Appendix 1

EX 14-25 Unusual items

➡ Explain whether Colston Company correctly reported the following items in the financial statements:

A. In a recent year, the company discovered a clerical error in the prior year's accounting records. As a result, the reported net income for the previous year was overstated by $45,000. The company corrected this error by restating the prior-year financial statements.

B. In a recent year, the company voluntarily changed its method of accounting for long-term construction contracts from the percentage of completion method to the completed contract method. Both methods are acceptable under generally acceptable accounting principles. The cumulative effect of this change was reported as a separate component of income in the current period income statement.

Appendix 2

EX 14-26 Comprehensive Income

Anson Industries, Inc. reported the following information on its 20Y1 income statement:

Sales	$4,000,000
Cost of goods sold	2,300,000
Operating expenses	1,000,000
Income tax expense	280,000
Other comprehensive income	450,000

Prepare the following for Anson Industries, Inc.:

A. Income statement, including comprehensive income.

B. Income statement and a separate statement of comprehensive income.

Problems: Series A

PR 14-1A Horizontal analysis of income statement

Obj. 2

✔ 1. Sales, 12% increase

SHOW ME HOW

EXCEL TEMPLATE

GENERAL LEDGER

For 20Y2, McDade Company reported a decline in net income. At the end of the year, T. Burrows, the president, is presented with the following condensed comparative income statement:

McDade Company
Comparative Income Statement
For the Years Ended December 31, 20Y2 and 20Y1

	20Y2	20Y1
Sales	$16,800,000	$15,000,000
Cost of goods sold	11,500,000	10,000,000
Gross profit	$ 5,300,000	$ 5,000,000
Selling expenses	$ 1,770,000	$ 1,500,000
Administrative expenses	1,220,000	1,000,000
Total operating expenses	$ 2,990,000	$ 2,500,000
Income from operations	$ 2,310,000	$ 2,500,000
Other income	256,950	225,000
Income before income tax	$ 2,556,950	$ 2,725,000
Income tax expense	1,413,000	1,500,000
Net income	$ 1,153,950	$ 1,225,000

Instructions

1. Prepare a comparative income statement with horizontal analysis for the two-year period, using 20Y1 as the base year. (Round percentages to one decimal place.)

2. ▬▬▬▶ To the extent the data permit, comment on the significant relationships revealed by the horizontal analysis prepared in (1).

PR 14-2A Vertical analysis of income statement

Obj. 2

✔ 1. Net income, 20Y2, 10.0%

GENERAL LEDGER

EXCEL TEMPLATE

For 20Y2, Tri-Comic Company initiated a sales promotion campaign that included the expenditure of an additional $50,000 for advertising. At the end of the year, Lumi Neer, the president, is presented with the following condensed comparative income statement:

Tri-Comic Company
Comparative Income Statement
For the Years Ended December 31, 20Y2 and 20Y1

	20Y2	20Y1
Sales	$1,500,000	$1,250,000
Cost of goods sold	510,000	475,000
Gross profit	$ 990,000	$ 775,000
Selling expenses	$ 270,000	$ 200,000
Administrative expenses	180,000	156,250
Total operating expenses	$ 450,000	$ 356,250
Income from operations	$ 540,000	$ 418,750
Other income	60,000	50,000
Income before income tax	$ 600,000	$ 468,750
Income tax expense	450,000	375,000
Net income	$ 150,000	$ 93,750

(Continued)

Instructions

1. Prepare a comparative income statement for the two-year period, presenting an analysis of each item in relationship to sales for each of the years. (Round percentages to one decimal place.)

2. ━━━▶ To the extent the data permit, comment on the significant relationships revealed by the vertical analysis prepared in (1).

PR 14-3A   Effect of transactions on current position analysis   Obj. 3

✔ 2. C. Current ratio, 2.0

EXCEL TEMPLATE

Data pertaining to the current position of Forte Company follow:

Cash	$412,500
Marketable securities	187,500
Accounts and notes receivable (net)	300,000
Inventories	700,000
Prepaid expenses	50,000
Accounts payable	200,000
Notes payable (short-term)	250,000
Accrued expenses	300,000

Instructions

1. Compute (A) the working capital, (B) the current ratio, and (C) the quick ratio. (Round to one decimal place.)

2. List the following captions on a sheet of paper:

Transaction	Working Capital	Current Ratio	Quick Ratio

Compute the working capital, the current ratio, and the quick ratio after each of the following transactions, and record the results in the appropriate columns. *Consider each transaction separately* and assume that only that transaction affects the data given. (Round to one decimal place.)

A. Sold marketable securities at no gain or loss, $70,000.
B. Paid accounts payable, $125,000.
C. Purchased goods on account, $110,000.
D. Paid notes payable, $100,000.
E. Declared a cash dividend, $150,000.
F. Declared a common stock dividend on common stock, $50,000.
G. Borrowed cash from bank on a long-term note, $225,000.
H. Received cash on account, $125,000.
I. Issued additional shares of stock for cash, $600,000.
J. Paid cash for prepaid expenses, $10,000.

PR 14-4A   Measures of liquidity, solvency, and profitability   Obj. 3, 4, 5

✔ 5. Number of days' sales in receivables, 18.3

EXCEL TEMPLATE

The comparative financial statements of Marshall Inc. are as follows. The market price of Marshall common stock was $82.60 on December 31, 20Y2.

Marshall Inc.
Comparative Retained Earnings Statement
For the Years Ended December 31, 20Y2 and 20Y1

	20Y2	20Y1
Retained earnings, January 1	$3,704,000	$3,264,000
Net income	600,000	550,000
Total	$4,304,000	$3,814,000
Dividends:		
On preferred stock	$ 10,000	$ 10,000
On common stock	100,000	100,000
Total dividends	$ 110,000	$ 110,000
Retained earnings, December 31	$4,194,000	$3,704,000

Marshall Inc.
Comparative Income Statement
For the Years Ended December 31, 20Y2 and 20Y1

	20Y2	20Y1
Sales	$10,850,000	$10,000,000
Cost of goods sold	6,000,000	5,450,000
Gross profit	$ 4,850,000	$ 4,550,000
Selling expenses	$ 2,170,000	$ 2,000,000
Administrative expenses	1,627,500	1,500,000
Total operating expenses	$ 3,797,500	$ 3,500,000
Income from operations	$ 1,052,500	$ 1,050,000
Other income	99,500	20,000
	$ 1,152,000	$ 1,070,000
Other expense (interest)	132,000	120,000
Income before income tax	$ 1,020,000	$ 950,000
Income tax expense	420,000	400,000
Net income	$ 600,000	$ 550,000

Marshall Inc.
Comparative Balance Sheet
December 31, 20Y2 and 20Y1

	20Y2	20Y1
Assets		
Current assets:		
Cash	$1,050,000	$ 950,000
Marketable securities	301,000	420,000
Accounts receivable (net)	585,000	500,000
Inventories	420,000	380,000
Prepaid expenses	108,000	20,000
Total current assets	$ 2,464,000	$2,270,000
Long-term investments	800,000	800,000
Property, plant, and equipment (net)	5,760,000	5,184,000
Total assets	$ 9,024,000	$8,254,000
Liabilities		
Current liabilities	$ 880,000	$ 800,000
Long-term liabilities:		
Mortgage note payable, 6%,	$ 200,000	$ 0
Bonds payable, 4%,	3,000,000	3,000,000
Total long-term liabilities	$ 3,200,000	$3,000,000
Total liabilities	$ 4,080,000	$3,800,000
Stockholders' Equity		
Preferred 4% stock, $5 par	$ 250,000	$ 250,000
Common stock, $5 par	500,000	500,000
Retained earnings	4,194,000	3,704,000
Total stockholders' equity	$ 4,944,000	$4,454,000
Total liabilities and stockholders' equity	$ 9,024,000	$8,254,000

Instructions

Determine the following measures for 20Y2 (round to one decimal place, including percentages, except for per-share amounts):

1. Working capital
2. Current ratio
3. Quick ratio
4. Accounts receivable turnover
5. Number of days' sales in receivables
6. Inventory turnover
7. Number of days' sales in inventory
8. Ratio of fixed assets to long-term liabilities
9. Ratio of liabilities to stockholders' equity
10. Times interest earned

(Continued)

11. Asset turnover

12. Return on total assets

13. Return on stockholders' equity

14. Return on common stockholders' equity

15. Earnings per share on common stock

16. Price-earnings ratio

17. Dividends per share of common stock

18. Dividend yield

PR 14-5A   Solvency and profitability trend analysis

Obj. 4, 5

Addai Company has provided the following comparative information:

	20Y8	20Y7	20Y6	20Y5	20Y4
Net income	$ 273,406	$ 367,976	$ 631,176	$ 884,000	$ 800,000
Interest expense	616,047	572,003	528,165	495,000	440,000
Income tax expense	31,749	53,560	106,720	160,000	200,000
Total assets (ending balance)	4,417,178	4,124,350	3,732,443	3,338,500	2,750,000
Total stockholders' equity (ending balance)	3,706,557	3,433,152	3,065,176	2,434,000	1,550,000
Average total assets	4,270,764	3,928,396	3,535,472	3,044,250	2,475,000
Average total stockholders' equity	3,569,855	3,249,164	2,749,588	1,992,000	1,150,000

You have been asked to evaluate the historical performance of the company over the last five years.

Selected industry ratios have remained relatively steady at the following levels for the last five years:

	20Y4–20Y8
Return on total assets	28%
Return on stockholders' equity	18%
Times interest earned	2.7
Ratio of liabilities to stockholders' equity	0.4

Instructions

1. Prepare four line graphs with the ratio on the vertical axis and the years on the horizontal axis for the following four ratios (round to one decimal place):

    A. Return on total assets

    B. Return on stockholders' equity

    C. Times interest earned

    D. Ratio of liabilities to stockholders' equity

    Display both the company ratio and the industry benchmark on each graph. That is, each graph should have two lines.

2. ➤ Prepare an analysis of the graphs in (1).

Problems: Series B

✔ 1. Sales,
30.0% increase

PR 14-1B Horizontal analysis of income statement   Obj. 2

For 20Y2, Macklin Inc. reported a significant increase in net income. At the end of the year, John Mayer, the president, is presented with the following condensed comparative income statement:

Macklin Inc.
Comparative Income Statement
For the Years Ended December 31, 20Y2 and 20Y1

	20Y2	20Y1
Sales	$910,000	$700,000
Cost of goods sold	441,000	350,000
Gross profit	$469,000	$350,000
Selling expenses	$ 139,150	$115,000
Administrative expenses	99,450	85,000
Total operating expenses	$238,600	$200,000
Income from operations	$230,400	$150,000
Other income	65,000	50,000
Income before income tax	$295,400	$200,000
Income tax expense	65,000	50,000
Net income	$230,400	$150,000

Instructions

1. Prepare a comparative income statement with horizontal analysis for the two-year period, using 20Y1 as the base year. (Round percentages to one decimal place.)

2. ➥ To the extent the data permit, comment on the significant relationships revealed by the horizontal analysis prepared in (1).

✔ 1. Net income, 20Y1,
14.0%

PR 14-2B Vertical analysis of income statement   Obj. 2

For 20Y2, Fielder Industries Inc. initiated a sales promotion campaign that included the expenditure of an additional $40,000 for advertising. At the end of the year, Leif Grando, the president, is presented with the following condensed comparative income statement:

Fielder Industries Inc.
Comparative Income Statement
For the Years Ended December 31, 20Y2 and 20Y1

	20Y2	20Y1
Sales	$1,300,000	$1,180,000
Cost of goods sold	682,500	613,600
Gross profit	$ 617,500	$ 566,400
Selling expenses	$ 260,000	$ 188,800
Adminstrative expenses	169,000	177,000
Total operating expenses	$ 429,000	$ 365,800
Income from operations	$ 188,500	$ 200,600
Other income	78,000	70,800
Income before income tax	$ 266,500	$ 271,400
Income tax expense	117,000	106,200
Net income	$ 149,500	$ 165,200

Instructions

1. Prepare a comparative income statement for the two-year period, presenting an analysis of each item in relationship to sales for each of the years. (Round percentages to one decimal place.)

2. ➥ To the extent the data permit, comment on the significant relationships revealed by the vertical analysis prepared in (1).

PR 14-3B   Effect of transactions on current position analysis

Obj. 3

Data pertaining to the current position of Lucroy Industries Inc. follows:

Cash	$ 800,000
Marketable securities	550,000
Accounts and notes receivable (net)	850,000
Inventories	700,000
Prepaid expenses	300,000
Accounts payable	1,200,000
Notes payable (short-term)	700,000
Accrued expenses	100,000

Instructions

1. Compute (A) the working capital, (B) the current ratio, and (C) the quick ratio. (Round to one decimal place.)

2. List the following captions on a sheet of paper:

Transaction	Working Capital	Current Ratio	Quick Ratio

Compute the working capital, the current ratio, and the quick ratio after each of the following transactions, and record the results in the appropriate columns. *Consider each transaction separately* and assume that only that transaction affects the data given. (Round to one decimal place.)

A. Sold marketable securities at no gain or loss, $500,000.
B. Paid accounts payable, $287,500.
C. Purchased goods on account, $400,000.
D. Paid notes payable, $125,000.
E. Declared a cash dividend, $325,000.
F. Declared a common stock dividend on common stock, $150,000.
G. Borrowed cash from bank on a long-term note, $1,000,000.
H. Received cash on account, $75,000.
I. Issued additional shares of stock for cash, $2,000,000.
J. Paid cash for prepaid expenses, $200,000.

PR 14-4B   Measures of liquidity, solvency and profitability

Obj. 3, 4, 5

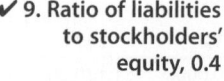

The comparative financial statements of Stargel Inc. are as follows. The market price of Stargel common stock was $119.70 on December 31, 20Y2.

Stargel Inc.
Comparative Retained Earnings Statement
For the Years Ended December 31, 20Y2 and 20Y1

	20Y2	20Y1
Retained earnings, January 1	$5,375,000	$4,545,000
Net income	900,000	925,000
Total	$6,275,000	$5,470,000
Dividends:		
On preferred stock	$ 45,000	$ 45,000
On common stock	50,000	50,000
Total dividends	$ 95,000	$ 95,000
Retained earnings, December 31	$6,180,000	$5,375,000

Stargel Inc.
Comparative Income Statement
For the Years Ended December 31, 20Y2 and 20Y1

	20Y2	20Y1
Sales	$10,000,000	$9,400,000
Cost of goods sold	5,350,000	4,950,000
Gross profit	$ 4,650,000	$4,450,000
Selling expenses	$ 2,000,000	$1,880,000
Administrative expenses	1,500,000	1,410,000
Total operating expenses	$ 3,500,000	$3,290,000
Income from operations	$ 1,150,000	$1,160,000
Other income	150,000	140,000
	$ 1,300,000	$1,300,000
Other expense (interest)	170,000	150,000
Income before income tax	$ 1,130,000	$1,150,000
Income tax expense	230,000	225,000
Net income	$ 900,000	$ 925,000

Stargel Inc.
Comparative Balance Sheet
December 31, 20Y2 and 20Y1

	20Y2	20Y1
Assets		
Current assets:		
Cash	$ 500,000	$ 400,000
Marketable securities	1,010,000	1,000,000
Accounts receivable (net)	740,000	510,000
Inventories	1,190,000	950,000
Prepaid expenses	250,000	229,000
Total current assets	$3,690,000	$3,089,000
Long-term investments	2,350,000	2,300,000
Property, plant, and equipment (net)	3,740,000	3,366,000
Total assets	$9,780,000	$8,755,000
Liabilities		
Current liabilities	$ 900,000	$ 880,000
Long-term liabilities:		
Mortgage note payable, 10%	$ 200,000	$ 0
Bonds payable, 10%	1,500,000	1,500,000
Total long-term liabilities	$1,700,000	$1,500,000
Total liabilities	$2,600,000	$2,380,000
Stockholders' Equity		
Preferred $0.90 stock, $10 par	$ 500,000	$ 500,000
Common stock, $5 par	500,000	500,000
Retained earnings	6,180,000	5,375,000
Total stockholders' equity	$7,180,000	$6,375,000
Total liabilities and stockholders' equity	$9,780,000	$8,755,000

Instructions

Determine the following measures for 20Y2 (round to one decimal place including percentages, except for per-share amounts):

1. Working capital
2. Current ratio
3. Quick ratio
4. Accounts receivable turnover
5. Number of days' sales in receivables
6. Inventory turnover

(Continued)

7. Number of days' sales in inventory
8. Ratio of fixed assets to long-term liabilities
9. Ratio of liabilities to stockholders' equity
10. Times interest earned
11. Asset turnover
12. Return on total assets
13. Return on stockholders' equity
14. Return on common stockholders' equity
15. Earnings per share on common stock
16. Price-earnings ratio
17. Dividends per share of common stock
18. Dividend yield

PR 14-5B   Solvency and profitability trend analysis   **Obj. 4, 5**

✔ 1.B. 20Y7, 32.9%   Crosby Company has provided the following comparative information:

	20Y8	20Y7	20Y6	20Y5	20Y4
Net income	$ 5,571,720	$ 3,714,480	$ 2,772,000	$ 1,848,000	$ 1,400,000
Interest expense	1,052,060	891,576	768,600	610,000	500,000
Income tax expense	1,225,572	845,222	640,320	441,600	320,000
Total assets (ending balance)	29,378,491	22,598,839	17,120,333	12,588,480	10,152,000
Total stockholders' equity (ending balance)	18,706,200	13,134,480	9,420,000	6,648,000	4,800,000
Average total assets	25,988,665	19,859,586	14,854,406	11,370,240	8,676,000
Average total stockholders' equity	15,920,340	11,277,240	8,034,000	5,724,000	4,100,000

You have been asked to evaluate the historical performance of the company over the last five years.

Selected industry ratios have remained relatively steady at the following levels for the last five years:

	20Y4–20Y8
Return on total assets	19%
Return on stockholders' equity	26%
Times interest earned	3.4
Ratio of liabilities to stockholders' equity	1.4

Instructions

1. Prepare four line graphs with the ratio on the vertical axis and the years on the horizontal axis for the following four ratios (round ratios and percentages to one decimal place):

   A. Return on total assets

   B. Return on stockholders' equity

   C. Times interest earned

   D. Ratio of liabilities to stockholders' equity

   Display both the company ratio and the industry benchmark on each graph. That is, each graph should have two lines.

2. ▬▬▬▶ Prepare an analysis of the graphs in (1).

Nike, Inc., Problem

Financial Statement Analysis

The financial statements for Nike, Inc., are presented in Appendix E at the end of the text. The following additional information is available (in thousands):

Accounts receivable at May 31, 2013	$ 3,117
Inventories at May 31, 2013	3,484
Total assets at May 31, 2013	17,545
Stockholders' equity at May 31, 2013	11,081

Instructions

1. Determine the following measures for the fiscal years ended May 31, 2015, and May 31, 2014. (Round ratios and percentages to one decimal place.)

   A. Working capital

   B. Current ratio

   C. Quick ratio

   D. Accounts receivable turnover

   E. Number of days' sales in receivables

   F. Inventory turnover

   G. Number of days' sales in inventory

   H. Ratio of liabilities to stockholders' equity

   I. Asset turnover

   J. Return on total assets, assuming interest expense is $28 million for the year ending May 31, 2015, and $24 million for the year ending May 31, 2014

   K. Return on common stockholders' equity

   L. Price-earnings ratio, assuming that the market price was $101.67 per share on May 29, 2015, and $76.91 per share on May 30, 2014

   M. Percentage relationship of net income to sales

2. ➤ What conclusions can be drawn from these analyses?

Analysis for Decision Making

REAL WORLD

ADM-1 Continuing Company Analysis—Amazon, Best Buy, and Walmart: Common-sized income statements

The condensed income statements through income from operations for Amazon.com, Inc., Best Buy, Inc., and Walmart Stores, Inc. for a recent fiscal year follow (in millions):

	Amazon	Best Buy	Walmart
Sales	$88,988	$40,339	$485,651
Cost of sales	62,752	31,292	365,086
Gross profit	$26,236	$ 9,047	$120,565
Selling, general, and administrative expenses	26,058	7,592	93,418
Operating expenses	0	5	0
Income from operations	$ 178	$ 1,450	$ 27,147

1. Prepare comparative common-sized income statements for each company. (Round percentages to one decimal place.)

2. ➤ Use the common-sized analysis to compare the financial performance of the three companies.

ADM-2   Deere: Profitability analysis

Deere & Company manufactures and distributes farm and construction machinery that it sells around the world. In addition to its manufacturing operations, Deere's credit division loans money to customers to finance the purchase of their farm and construction equipment.

The following information is available for three recent years (in millions except per-share amounts):

	Year 3	Year 2	Year 1
Net income (loss)	$3,064.7	$2,799.9	$1,865.0
Preferred dividends	$ 0.00	$ 0.00	$ 0.00
Interest expense	$ 782.8	$ 759.4	$ 811.4
Shares outstanding for computing earnings per share	397	417	424
Cash dividend per share	$ 1.79	$ 1.52	$ 1.16
Average total assets	$ 52,237	$ 45,737	$ 42,200
Average stockholders' equity	$ 6,821	$ 6,545	$ 5,555
Average stock price per share	$ 79.27	$ 80.48	$ 61.18

1. Calculate the following ratios for each year (round ratios and percentages to one decimal place, except for per-share amounts):

    A. Return on total assets

    B. Return on stockholders' equity

    C. Earnings per share

    D. Dividend yield

    E. Price-earnings ratio

2. ━━━▶ Based on these data, evaluate Deere's profitability.

ADM-3   Marriott and Hyatt: Solvency and profitability analysis

Marriott International, Inc., and **Hyatt Hotels Corporation** are two major owners and managers of lodging and resort properties in the United States. Abstracted income statement information for the two companies is as follows for a recent year (in millions):

	Marriott	Hyatt
Operating profit before other expenses and interest	$ 677	$ 39
Other income (expenses)	54	118
Interest expense	(180)	(54)
Income before income taxes	$ 551	$103
Income tax expense	93	37
Net income	$ 458	$ 66

Balance sheet information is as follows:

	Marriott	Hyatt
Total liabilities	$7,398	$2,125
Total stockholders' equity	1,585	5,118
Total liabilities and stockholders' equity	$8,983	$7,243

The average liabilities, average stockholders' equity, and average total assets are as follows:

	Marriott	Hyatt
Average total liabilities	$7,095	$2,132
Average total stockholders' equity	1,364	5,067
Average total assets	8,458	7,199

1. Determine the following ratios for both companies (round ratios and percentages to one decimal place):

    A. Return on total assets

    B. Return on stockholders' equity

    C. Times interest earned

    D. Ratio of total liabilities to stockholders' equity

2. ━━━▶ Based on the information in (1), analyze and compare the two companies' solvency and profitability.

Take It Further

ETHICS

TIF 14-1   Ethics in Action

Rodgers Industries Inc. completed its fiscal year on December 31. Near the end of the fiscal year, the company's internal audit department determined that an important internal control procedure had not been functioning properly. The head of internal audit, Dash Riprock, reported the internal control failure to the company's chief accountant, Todd Barleywine. Todd reported the failure to the company's chief financial officer, Josh McCoy. After discussing the issue, Josh instructed Todd not to inform the external auditors of the internal control failure and to fix the problem quietly after the end of the fiscal year. The external auditors did not discover the internal control failure during their audit. In March, after the audit was complete, the company released its annual report, including associated reports by management. As chief financial officer, Josh authorized the release of Management's Report on Internal Control, which stated that the management team believed that the company's internal controls were effective during the period covered by the annual report.

➤ Did Josh behave ethically in this situation? Explain your answer.

REAL WORLD

TIF 14-2   Team Activity

In teams, select a public company that interests you. Obtain the company's most recent annual report on Form 10-K. The Form 10-K is a company's annually required filing with the Securities and Exchange Commission (SEC). It includes the company's financial statements and accompanying notes. The Form 10-K can be obtained either (A) from the investor relations section of the company's Web site or (B) by using the company search feature of the SEC's EDGAR database service found at www.sec.gov/edgar/searchedgar/companysearch.html.

1. Based on the information in the company's annual report, compute the following for the most recent year (round ratios and percentages to one decimal place, except for per-share amounts):

    A. Liquidity analysis:
       (1) Working capital
       (2) Current ratio
       (3) Quick ratio
       (4) Accounts receivable turnover
       (5) Number of days' sales in receivables
       (6) Inventory turnover
       (7) Number of days' sales in inventory

    B. Solvency analysis:
       (1) Ratio of liabilities to stockholders' equity
       (2) Times interest earned

    C. Profitability analysis:
       (1) Asset turnover
       (2) Return on total assets
       (3) Return on stockholders' equity
       (4) Earnings per share
       (5) Price-earnings ratio

2. ➤ Evaluate the company's liquidity, solvency, and profitability.

TIF 14-3 Communication

The president of Freeman Industries Inc. made the following statement in the annual report to shareholders: "The founding family and majority shareholders of the company do not believe in using debt to finance future growth. The founding family learned from hard experience during Prohibition and the Great Depression that debt can cause loss of flexibility and eventual loss of corporate control. The company will not place itself at such risk again. As such, all future growth will be financed either by stock sales to the public or by internally generated resources."

━━━━▶ Write a brief memo to the company's president, Boss Freeman, outlining the errors in his logic.

Mornin' Joe

Financial Statements for Mornin' Joe

Financial Statements for Mornin' Joe International

Mornin' Joe

The financial statements of **Mornin' Joe** follow. Mornin' Joe is a fictitious coffeehouse chain featuring drip and espresso coffee in a café setting. The financial statements of Mornin' Joe are provided to illustrate the complete financial statements of a corporation, using the terms, formats, and reporting illustrated throughout this text. In addition, excerpts of the Mornin' Joe financial statements are used to illustrate the financial reporting presentation for the topics discussed in Chapters 6–12. Thus, you can refer to the complete financial statements in Exhibits 1, 2, 3, and 4 here or the excerpts in Chapters 6–12.

Exhibit 1
Income Statement for Mornin' Joe

Mornin' Joe Income Statement For the Year Ended December 31, 20Y6			
Sales...			$5,402,100
Cost of goods sold..............................			2,160,000
Gross profit.....................................			$3,242,100
Operating expenses			
Selling expenses:			
Wages expense.........................	$825,000		
Advertising expense....................	678,900		
Depreciation expense—buildings	124,300		
Miscellaneous selling expense............	26,500		
Total selling expenses		$1,654,700	
Administrative expenses:			
Office salaries expense...................	$325,000		
Rent expense	425,600		
Payroll tax expense	110,000		
Depreciation expense—office			
equipment............................	68,900		
Bad debt expense	14,000		
Amortization expense	10,500		
Total administrative expenses.........		954,000	
Total operating expenses			2,608,700
Income from operations.........................			$ 633,400
Other income and expense:			
Interest revenue..............................		$ 18,000	
Interest expense..............................		(136,000)	
Loss on disposal of fixed asset.................		(23,000)	
Unrealized gain on trading investments........		5,000**	
Equity income in AM Coffee...................		57,000**	(79,000)
Income before income taxes.....................			$ 554,400
Income tax expense.............................			132,800
Net income....................................			$ 421,600
Basic earnings per share*........................			$ 8.90

* Earnings per share = ($421,600 − $30,000) ÷ 44,000 shares issued and outstanding
** Discussed in Appendix D

Exhibit 2
Balance Sheet for
Mornin' Joe

Mornin' Joe
Balance Sheet
December 31, 20Y6

Assets

Current assets:			
Cash and cash equivalents		$ 235,000	
Trading investments (at cost)......................	$ 420,000*		
Valuation allowance for trading investments	45,000*		
Trading investments (at fair value)		465,000	
Accounts receivable	$ 305,000		
Allowance for doubtful accounts	(12,300)		
Accounts receivable, net		292,700	
Inventory—at lower of cost (first-in, first-out			
method) or net realizable value...............		120,000	
Prepaid insurance		24,000	
Total current assets			$1,136,700
Investments:			
Investment in AM Coffee (equity method)			565,000*
Property, plant, and equipment:			
Land		$1,850,000	
Buildings	$2,650,000		
Accumulated depreciation	(420,000)		
Buildings, book value		2,230,000	
Office equipment	$ 350,000		
Accumulated depreciation	(102,000)		
Office equipment, book value		248,000	
Total property, plant, and			
equipment, book value			4,328,000
Intangible assets:			
Patents			140,000
Total assets			$6,169,700

Liabilities

Current liabilities:			
Accounts payable		$ 133,000	
Notes payable (current portion)		200,000	
Salaries and wages payable		42,000	
Payroll taxes payable		16,400	
Interest payable................................		40,000	
Total current liabilities........................			$ 431,400
Long-term liabilities:			
Bonds payable, 8%, due in 10 years...............		$ 500,000	
Unamortized discount		(16,000)	$ 484,000
Notes payable			1,400,000
Total long-term liabilities			$1,884,000
Total liabilities.......................................			$2,315,400

Stockholders' Equity

Paid-in capital:			
Preferred 10% stock, $50 par (6,000 shares			
authorized and issued)......................		$ 300,000	
Excess of issue price over par.....................		50,000	
Paid-in capital, preferred stock................			$ 350,000
Common stock, $20 par (50,000 shares			
authorized, 45,000 shares issued)		$ 900,000	
Excess of issue price over par.....................		1,450,000	
Paid-in capital, common stock			2,350,000
Total paid-in capital			$2,700,000
Retained earnings			1,200,300
Total			$3,900,300
Treasury stock (1,000 shares at cost)..................			(46,000)
Total stockholders' equity			$3,854,300
Total liabilities and stockholders' equity			$6,169,700

* Discussed in Appendix D

Exhibit 3
Retained Earnings
Statement for
Mornin' Joe

Mornin' Joe Retained Earnings Statement For the Year Ended December 31, 20Y6			
Retained earnings, January 1, 20Y6....................			$ 852,700
Net income...		$421,600	
Dividends:			
Preferred stock..................................	$(30,000)		
Common stock...................................	(44,000)	(74,000)	
Change in retained earnings.........................			347,600
Retained earnings, December 31, 20Y6			$1,200,300

Exhibit 4   Statement of Stockholders' Equity for Mornin' Joe

Mornin' Joe Statement of Stockholders' Equity For the Year Ended December 31, 20Y6						
	Preferred Stock	Common Stock	Additional Paid-In Capital	Retained Earnings	Treasury Stock	Total
Balance, January 1, 20Y6...........................	$300,000	$800,000	$1,325,000	$ 852,700	$(36,000)	$3,241,700
Net income...				421,600		421,600
Dividends on preferred stock				(30,000)		(30,000)
Dividends on common stock........................				(44,000)		(44,000)
Issuance of additional common stock.............		100,000	175,000			275,000
Purchase of treasury stock..........................					(10,000)	(10,000)
Balance, December 31, 20Y6	$300,000	$900,000	$1,500,000	$1,200,300	$(46,000)	$3,854,300

Mornin' Joe is planning to expand operations to various places around the world. Financing for this expansion will come from foreign banks. While financial statements prepared under U.S. GAAP may be appropriate for U.S. operations, financial statements prepared for foreign bankers should be prepared using international accounting standards.

The European Union (EU) has developed accounting standards similar in structure to U.S. standards. Its accounting standards board is called the International Accounting Standards Board (IASB). The IASB issues accounting standards that are termed *International Financial Reporting Standards (IFRS)*. The intent of the IASB is to create a set of financial standards that can be used by public companies worldwide, not just in the EU.

Currently, the EU countries and more than 100 other countries around the world have adopted or are planning to adopt IFRS. As a result, there are efforts under way to converge U.S. GAAP with IFRS so as to harmonize accounting standards around the world.

Key Reporting Differences between IFRS and U.S. GAAP

The financial statements of **Mornin' Joe International** using IFRS are presented in Exhibits 5, 6, and 7. This illustration highlights reporting and terminology differences between IFRS and U.S. GAAP. Differences in recording transactions under IFRS and U.S. GAAP are discussed in Appendix C and in various International Connection boxes throughout the text.

The Mornin' Joe International financial statements in Exhibits 5, 6, and 7 are simplified and illustrate only portions of IFRS that are appropriate for introductory accounting. The financial statements are presented in euros (€) for demonstration purposes only. The euro is the standard currency of the European Union. The euro is translated at a 1:1 ratio from the dollar to simplify comparisons. Throughout the illustration, call-outs and end notes to each statement are used to highlight the differences between financial statements prepared under IFRS and under U.S. GAAP.

Statements of Comprehensive Income versus Income Statements

Exhibit 5 illustrates the statement of comprehensive income for **Mornin' Joe International** and shows key differences from the income statements prepared under U.S. GAAP.

Exhibit 5   Statement of Comprehensive Income for Mornin' Joe International

Title includes the word "Comprehensive."	

Mornin' Joe International
Statement of Comprehensive Income
For the Year Ended December 31, 20Y6

Sales*	€ 5,402,100
Cost of goods sold	(2,160,000)
Gross profit	€ 3,242,100
Selling expenses	(1,654,700)
Administrative expenses	(954,000)
Loss on disposal of fixed asset	(23,000)
Other income (expenses)	23,000
Share in profit (loss) of associates*	57,000
Operating profit	€ 690,400
Finance costs*	(136,000)
Profit before income tax	€ 554,400
Tax expense*	(132,800)
Profit for the year*	€ 421,600
Other comprehensive income	
Gain on revaluation of properties*	44,800
Total comprehensive income for the year, net of tax*	€ 466,400
Earnings per share basic* ((€421,600 − 30,000) ÷ 44,000 shares)	€ 9.58

*A required disclosure on the face of the statement of comprehensive income
** Discussed in Appendix D

Side annotations:
- This is a common term for an equity method investment.**
- The term "Finance costs" is used, rather than "Interest expense."
- The term "Profit for the year" is used, rather than "Net income."
- IFRS allows latitude on how statements are organized but does list minimum disclosure requirements that are less restrictive than required by the SEC. See Note 1.
- Expenses are organized by their nature. See Note 2.
- Diversity allowed with regard to subtotal definitions. See Note 3.
- Other comprehensive income is a required disclosure. See Note 4.

1. IFRS statements are often more summarized than U.S. GAAP statements. To compensate, IFRS requires specific disclosures on the face of the financial statements (denoted *) and additional disclosures in the footnotes to the financial statements. Because additions and subtractions are grouped together in sections of IFRS statements, parentheses are used to indicate subtractions.

2. Expenses in an IFRS income statement are classified by either their nature or function. The nature of an expense is how the expense would naturally be recorded in a journal entry reflecting the economic benefit received for that expense. Examples include salaries, depreciation, advertising, and utilities. The function of an expense identifies the purpose of the expense, such as a selling expense or an administrative expense. Mornin' Joe classifies by function.

3. IFRS provides flexibility with regard to line items, headings, and subtotals on the income statement. There is less flexibility under U.S. GAAP for public companies.

4. IFRS requires the reporting of other comprehensive income (see appendix to Chapter 14) either on the income statement (see Exhibit 5) or in a separate statement. U.S. GAAP has a similar disclosure treatment. For **Mornin' Joe International**, other comprehensive income consists of the restatement of café locations to fair value (see Note 6 for more details).

5. Under IFRS, there is no standard format for the balance sheet (statement of financial position, see Exhibit 6). A typical format for European Union companies is to begin the asset section of the balance sheet with noncurrent assets. This is followed by current assets listed in reverse order of liquidity. That is, the asset side of the balance sheet is reported in reverse order of liquidity from least liquid to most liquid. Listing noncurrent assets first emphasizes the going concern nature of the entity.

   The liability and owners' equity side of the balance sheet is also reported differently than under U.S. GAAP. Specifically, owners' equity is reported first followed by noncurrent liabilities and current liabilities. Listing equity first emphasizes the going concern nature of the entity and the long-term financial interest of the owners in the business.

6. Under IFRS, property, plant, and equipment (PP&E) may be measured at historical cost or fair value. If fair value is used, the revaluation must be for similar classifications of PP&E but need not be for all PP&E. This departs from U.S. GAAP, which requires PP&E to be measured at historical cost. **Mornin' Joe International** restated its Land and Buildings to fair value because the café sites have readily available real estate market prices. Land and buildings are included together because their fair values are not separable. The office equipment remains at historical cost because it does not have a readily available market price. The increase in fair value is recorded by reducing accumulated depreciation and recognizing the gain as other comprehensive income. This element of other comprehensive income is accumulated in stockholders' equity under the heading Property revaluation reserve.* This treatment is similar (with different titles) to the U.S. GAAP treatment of unrealized gains (losses) from available-for-sale securities. For Mornin' Joe International, there is an increase in the property revaluation reserve of €44,800. This amount is the only difference between Mornin' Joe's U.S. GAAP net income, total assets, and total stockholders' equity and Mornin' Joe International's IFRS total comprehensive income, total assets, and total stockholders' equity.

7. **Mornin' Joe International** recently acquired a coffee plantation. This is an example of a biological asset. IFRS requires separate reporting of biological assets (principally agricultural assets) at fair value.

8. U.S. GAAP allows companies to use LIFO for inventory valuation, while IFRS prohibits the use of LIFO.

9. Under IFRS, some elements of other comprehensive income and owners' equity are often aggregated under the term "reserves." In contrast, under U.S. GAAP, "reserve" is used to identify a liability. IFRS also does not require separate disclosure of treasury stock as does U.S. GAAP. Specifically, treasury stock may be reported as a reduction of a reserve, a reduction of a stock premium, or a separate item.

10. The term *provision* is used to denote a liability under IFRS, whereas this term often indicates an expense under U.S. GAAP. For example, *Provision for income taxes* means *Income tax expense* under U.S. GAAP, whereas it would mean *Income taxes payable* under IFRS.

11. Under U.S. GAAP, other comprehensive income items must be included as changes in accumulated other comprehensive income in the statement of changes in stockholders' equity (see Exhibit 7). IFRS allows for similar treatment, with wider latitude for terminology, such as *Property Revaluation Reserve* illustrated by the column title here. In this illustration, treasury stock is included as part of a reserve (Reserve for Own Shares). As discussed in Note 9, under U.S. GAAP the term *reserve* denotes a liability.

Statements of Financial Position versus Balance Sheets

Exhibit 6 illustrates the statement of financial position for Mornin' Joe International and shows key differences from the balance sheets prepared under U.S. GAAP.

Exhibit 6 Statement of Financial Position for Mornin' Joe International

---

Preferred title for the "Balance Sheet." →

Mornin' Joe International
Statement of Financial Position
December 31, 20Y6

Assets

Sub-classifications of PP&E may be valued at fair value. See Note 6.

Noncurrent assets

Property, plant, and equipment*			
Land and buildings at fair value	€4,180,000		
Accumulated depreciation	375,200	€3,804,800	
Office equipment at cost	€ 350,000		
Accumulated depreciation	102,000	248,000	
Biological assets at fair value*		320,000	
Patents at amortized cost*		140,000	
Investment in AM Coffee (equity method)* **		565,000	
Total noncurrent assets			€5,077,800

"Biological assets" are a required disclosure at fair value. See Note 7.

Reverse liquidity account order. See Note 5.

Current assets

Prepaid insurance	€ 24,000	
Inventory—at lower of cost (first-in, first-out) or realizable value*	120,000	
Accounts receivable (net of allowance for doubtful accounts)*	292,700	
Marketable securities	465,000	
Cash and cash equivalents*	235,000	
Total current assets		1,136,700
Total assets*		€6,214,500

Inventory valuation. See Note 8.

International terminology for "Trading investments." Same accounting treatment.**

Equity attributable to owners

Preferred 10% stock, €50 par (6,000 shares authorized and issued)*	€ 300,000	
Common stock, €20 par (50,000 shares authorized, 45,000 shares issued)*	900,000	
Share premium*	1,500,000	
Reserves*	(1,200)	
Retained earnings*	1,200,300	
Total equity attributable to owners*		€3,899,100

International terminology for "Excess of issue price over par."

Other comprehensive items and treasury stock. See Note 9.

Equities listed first, then liabilities. See Note 5.

Liabilities

Noncurrent liabilities*

Bonds payable, 8%, due in 10 years (net of discount)	€ 484,000	
Notes payable	1,400,000	
Total noncurrent liabilities		€1,884,000

Noncurrent liabilities listed prior to current liabilities.

Current liabilities

Accounts payable*	€ 133,000	
Loans*	200,000	
Employee provisions*	58,400	
Interest payable	40,000	
Total current liabilities		431,400
Total liabilities*		€2,315,400
Total equity and liabilities*		€6,214,500

Employee provisions are wages, salaries, and payroll taxes payable. See Note 10.

* Required disclosures. Footnotes provide additional subclassification detail.

** Discussed in Appendix D

Statements of Changes in Equity versus Statements of Stockholders' Equity

Exhibit 7 illustrates the statement of changes in equity for Mornin' Joe International and shows key differences from the statements of stockholders' equity prepared under U.S. GAAP.

Exhibit 7 Statement of Changes in Equity for Mornin' Joe International

Mornin' Joe International
Statement of Changes in Equity
For the Year Ended December 31, 20Y6

	Preferred Stock	Common Stock	Share Premium	Reserves Property Revaluation Reserve	Reserves Reserve for Own Shares	Retained Earnings	Total Equity Attributable to Owners
Balance, January 1, 20Y6........	€300,000	€800,000	€1,325,000	€ 0	€(36,000)	€ 852,700	€3,241,700
Profit for the year...............						421,600	421,600
Other comprehensive income							
Property revaluation (gain).......				44,800			44,800
Total comprehensive income ...				€44,800		€ 421,600	€ 466,400
Contributions by and distributions to owners							
Dividends on preferred stock.....						(30,000)	(30,000)
Dividends on common stock......						(44,000)	(44,000)
Issuance of additional common stock........................		100,000	175,000				275,000
Purchase of own shares..........					(10,000)		(10,000)
Total contributions by and distributions to owners.......	€ 0	€100,000	€ 175,000	€ 0	€(10,000)	€ (74,000)	€ 191,000
Balance, December 31, 20Y6.......	€300,000	€900,000	€1,500,000	€44,800	€(46,000)	€1,200,300	€3,899,100

"Reserves," see Notes 9 and 11.

Discussion Questions

1. Contrast U.S. GAAP financial statement terms with their differing IFRS terms.

2. What is the difference between classifying an expense by nature or function?

3. How is the term "provision" used differently under IFRS than under U.S. GAAP?

4. How does inventory valuation differ under IFRS compared to U.S. GAAP?

5. What is a "biological asset"?

6. What is the most significant IFRS departure from U.S. GAAP for valuing property, plant, and equipment?

7. What is a "share premium"?

8. How is the term "reserve" used under IFRS, and how does it differ from its meaning under U.S. GAAP?

9. How is treasury stock reported under IFRS? How does this differ from its treatment under U.S. GAAP?

IFRS

REAL WORLD

IFRS Activity 1

Unilever Group is a global company that markets a wide variety of products, including Lever® soap, Breyer's® ice cream, and Hellman's® mayonnaise. A recent income statement and statement of comprehensive income for the Dutch company, Unilever Group, follow:

Unilever Group Consolidated Income Statement For the Year Ended December 31 (in millions of euros)	
Turnover	€51,324
Operating profit	6,989
After (charging)/crediting:	
Non-core items	(73)
Net finance costs	(397)
Finance income	136
Finance costs	(526)
Pensions and similar obligations	(7)
Share of net profit/(loss) of joint ventures and associations	105
Other income from non-current investments	(14)
Profit before taxation	€ 6,683
Taxation	(1,735)
Net profit	€ 4,948
Earnings per share—basic	€ 1.58
Earnings per share—diluted	€ 1.54

Consolidated Statement of Comprehensive Income For the Year Ended December 31	
Fair value gains (losses), net of tax	€ (125)
Actuarial gains (losses) on pensions, net of tax	(644)
Currency retranslation gains (losses), net of tax	(316)
Net income (expense) recognized directly into equity	€(1,085)
Net profit	4,948
Total comprehensive income	€3,863

A. ▬▬▶ What do you think is meant by "turnover"?

B. ▬▬▶ How does Unilever's income statement presentation differ significantly from that of Mornin' Joe?

C. ▬▬▶ How is the total for net finance costs presented differently than would be typically found under U.S. GAAP?

IFRS Activity 2

The following is a recent consolidated statement of financial position on December 31 of a recent year for **LVMH**, a French company that markets the Louis Vuitton® and Moët Hennessy® brands:

LVMH Statement of Financial Position December 31 (in millions of euros)	
Assets	
Brands and other intangible assets—net	€11,510
Goodwill—net	7,806
Property, plant, and equipment—net	8,769
Investment in associates	163
Non-current available for sale financial assets	6,004
Other non-current assets	524
Deferred tax	881
Non-current assets	€35,657
Inventories	€ 8,080
Trade accounts receivable	1,985
Income taxes	201
Other current assets	1,811
Cash and cash equivalents	2,196
Current assets	€14,273
TOTAL ASSETS	€49,930
Liabilities and Equity	
Share capital	€ 152
Share premium	3,848
Treasury shares	(414)
Revaluation reserves	2,819
Other reserves	14,393
Cumulative translation adjustment	342
Net profit, group share	3,424
Equity, group share	€24,564
Minority interests	1,102
Total equity	€25,666
Long-term borrowings	€ 3,836
Provisions	1,530
Deferred tax	3,960
Other non-current liabilities	5,456
Total non-current liabilities	€14,782
Short-term borrowings	€ 2,976
Trade accounts payable	3,134
Income taxes payable	442
Provisions	335
Other current liabilities	2,595
Total current liabilities	€ 9,482
TOTAL LIABILITIES AND EQUITY	€49,930

A. ➤ Identify presentation differences between the balance sheet of LVMH and a balance sheet prepared under U.S. GAAP. Use the Mornin' Joe balance sheet (Exhibit 2) as an example of a U.S. GAAP balance sheet. (Ignore minority interests and cumulative translation adjustment.)

B. Compare the terms used in this balance sheet with the terms used by Mornin' Joe (Exhibit 2), using the table that follows:

LVMH Term	Mornin' Joe U.S. GAAP Term
Statement of financial position	
Share capital	
Share premium	
Other reserves	
Provisions	

C. ▬▬▶ What does the "Revaluation reserves" in the Equity section of the balance sheet represent?

IFRS Activity 3

Under U.S. GAAP, LIFO is an acceptable inventory method. Financial statement information for three companies that use LIFO follows. All table numbers are in millions of dollars.

	LIFO Inventory	FIFO Inventory (from notes)	Impact on Net Income from Using LIFO Rather than FIFO (from notes)	Total Current Assets	Net Income as Reported
Exxon	$9,852	$31,200	$317	$58,984	$30,460
Kroger	4,966	5,793	(57)	7,621	1,116
Ford Motor*	5,917	6,782	4	34,368	4,690

*Autos and trucks only

Assume these companies adopted IFRS, and thus were required to use FIFO rather than LIFO.

A. Prepare a table with the following columns:

(1)	(2)	(3)	(4)
FIFO less LIFO	IFRS Net Income	$\dfrac{\text{(FIFO less LIFO)}}{\text{Total Current Assets}}$	$\dfrac{\text{IFRS Net Income (Col. 2)}}{\text{Reported Net Income}}$

(1) Difference between FIFO and LIFO inventory valuation.

(2) Revised IFRS net income using FIFO.

(3) Difference between FIFO and LIFO inventory valuation as a percent of total current assets.

(4) Revised IFRS net income as a percent of the reported net income.

B. Complete the table for the three companies.

C. For which company would a change to IFRS for inventory valuation have the largest percentage impact on total current assets (Col. 3)?

D. For which company would a change to IFRS for inventory valuation have the largest percentage impact on net income (Col. 4)?

E. ▬▬▶ Why might Kroger have a negative impact on net income from using LIFO, while the other two companies have a positive impact on net income from using LIFO?

15 Introduction to Managerial Accounting

Gibson Guitars

Gibson guitars have been used by musical legends over the years, including B.B. King, Chet Atkins, Brian Wilson (Beach Boys), Jimmy Page (Led Zeppelin), Jackson Browne, John Fogerty, Jose Feliciano, Miranda Lambert, and Wynonna Judd. Known for its quality, **Gibson Guitars** celebrated its 120th anniversary in 2014.

Staying in business for 120 years requires a thorough understanding of how to manufacture high-quality guitars. In addition, it requires knowledge of how to account for the costs of making guitars. For example, Gibson needs cost information to answer the following questions:

- What should be the selling price of its guitars?
- How many guitars does it have to sell in a year to cover its costs and earn a profit?

- How many employees should the company have working on each stage of the manufacturing process?
- How would purchasing automated equipment affect the costs of its guitars?

This chapter introduces managerial accounting concepts that are useful in addressing these questions. This chapter begins by describing managerial accounting and its relationship to financial accounting. Following this overview, the management process is described along with the role of managerial accounting. Finally, characteristics of managerial accounting reports, managerial accounting terms, and uses of managerial accounting information are described and illustrated.

Source: http://www.gibson.com/Gibson/History.aspx

Introduction to Managerial Accounting

Role of Managerial Accounting	**Manufacturing Operations**	**Sustainability and Accounting**	**Manufacturing Financial Statements**
■ Differences with Financial Accounting (Obj. 1)	■ Nature of Manufacturing (Obj. 2)	■ Sustainability (Obj. 3)	■ Balance Sheet (Obj. 4)
■ Management Organization (Obj. 1)	■ Direct and Indirect Costs (Obj. 2)	■ Eco-Efficiency Measures (Obj. 3)	■ Income Statement (Obj. 4)
■ Management Process (Obj. 1)	■ Manufacturing Costs (Obj. 2)		
■ Uses of Managerial Accounting Information (Obj. 1)			

Learning Objectives

Obj. 1 Describe managerial accounting, including its differences with financial accounting, its place in the organization, and its uses.

Obj. 2 Describe and illustrate the nature of manufacturing operations, including different types and classifications of costs.

Obj. 3 Describe sustainable business activities and eco-efficiency measures.

Obj. 4 Describe and illustrate financial statements for a manufacturing business, including the balance sheet, statement of cost of goods manufactured, and income statement.

Analysis for Decision Making

Describe and measure utilization in evaluating performance for a service company.

Objective 1

Describe managerial accounting, including its differences with financial accounting, its place in the organization, and its uses.

Managerial Accounting

Managers make numerous decisions during the day-to-day operations of a business and in planning for the future. Managerial accounting provides much of the information used for these decisions.

Some examples of managerial accounting information along with the chapter in which it is described and illustrated follow:

- Classifying manufacturing and other costs and reporting them in the financial statements (Chapter 15)
- Determining the cost of manufacturing a product or providing a service (Chapters 16 and 17)
- Evaluating the impact of cost allocation and activity-based costing (Chapter 18)
- Estimating the behavior of costs for various levels of activity and assessing cost-volume-profit relationships (Chapter 19)
- Evaluating operating performance using cost behavior relationships (Chapter 20)
- Planning for the future by preparing budgets (Chapter 21)
- Evaluating manufacturing costs by comparing actual with expected results (Chapter 22)
- Evaluating decentralized operations by comparing actual and budgeted costs as well as computing various measures of profitability (Chapter 23)
- Evaluating special decision-making situations by comparing differential revenues and costs, pricing products, and managing bottlenecks (Chapter 24)
- Evaluating alternative proposals for long-term investments in fixed assets (Chapter 25)
- Planning operations using principles of lean manufacturing and activity analysis (Chapter 26)

Link to Gibson Guitars

Orville Gibson started producing guitars in 1894 in Kalamazoo, Michigan. He produced guitars and mandolins based upon the arch-top design of violins.

Differences Between Managerial and Financial Accounting

Accounting information is often classified into two types: financial and managerial. Exhibit 1 shows the relationship between financial accounting and managerial accounting.

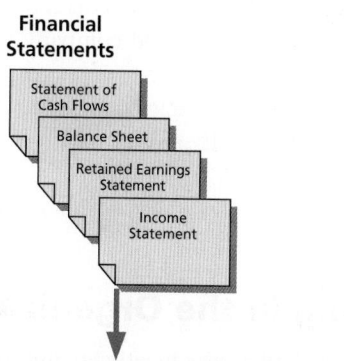
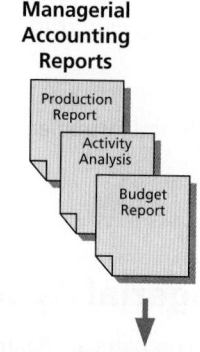

Exhibit 1 Financial Accounting and Managerial Accounting

	Financial Statements	**Managerial Accounting Reports**
Users of Information	External users and company management	Management
Nature of Information	Objective	Objective and subjective
Guidelines for Preparation	Prepared according to GAAP	Prepared according to management needs
Timeliness of Reporting	Prepared at fixed intervals	Prepared at fixed intervals and on an as-needed basis
Focus of Reporting	Company as a whole	Company as a whole or segment

Financial accounting information is reported at fixed intervals (monthly, quarterly, yearly) in general-purpose financial statements. These financial statements—the income statement, retained earnings statement, balance sheet, and statement of cash flows—are prepared according to generally accepted accounting principles (GAAP). These statements are used by external users such as the following:

- Shareholders
- Creditors
- Government agencies
- The general public

Gibson Mandolin-Guitar Mfg. Co., Ltd. was formed in 1902 in Kalamazoo, Michigan, with the support of five investors.

Link to Gibson Guitars

Managers of a company also use general-purpose financial statements. For example, in planning future operations, managers often begin by evaluating the current income statement and statement of cash flows.

Managerial accounting information is designed to meet the specific needs of a company's management. This information includes the following:

- Historical data, which provide *objective measures* of past operations
- Estimated data, which provide *subjective estimates* about future decisions

Management uses both types of information in directing daily operations, planning future operations, and developing business strategies.

Unlike the financial statements prepared in financial accounting, managerial accounting reports do *not* always have to be:

■ Prepared according to generally accepted accounting principles (GAAP). This is because *only* the company's management uses the information. Also, in many cases, GAAP are not relevant to the specific decision-making needs of management.

■ Prepared at fixed intervals (monthly, quarterly, yearly). Although some management reports are prepared at fixed intervals, most reports are prepared as management needs the information.

■ Prepared for the business as a whole. Most management reports are prepared for products, projects, sales territories, or other segments of the company.

Link to
Gibson Guitars

Chicago Musical Instrument Company purchased **Gibson** in 1944.

Managerial Accounting in the Organization

In most companies, departments or similar organizational units are assigned responsibilities for specific functions or activities. The operating structure of a company can be shown in an *organization chart*.

Exhibit 2 is a partial organization chart for **Callaway Golf Company**, the manufacturer and distributor of golf clubs, clothing, and other products.

Exhibit 2

Partial Organization Chart for Callaway Golf Company

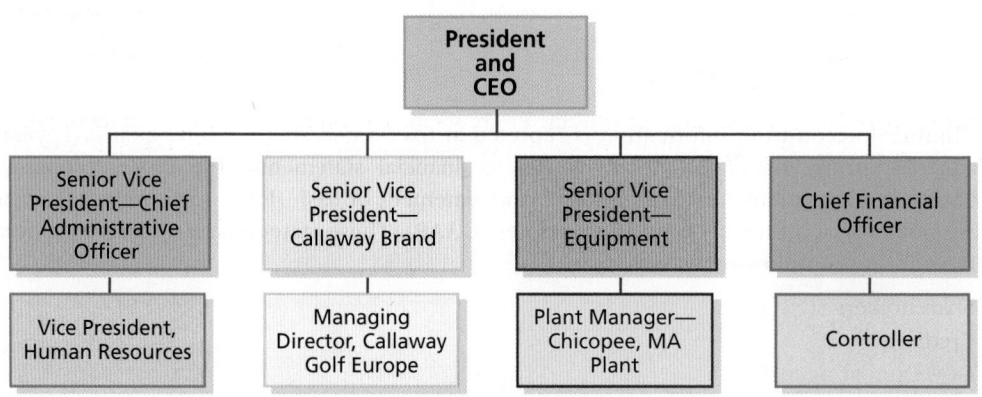

The departments in a company can be viewed as having either of the following:

■ Line responsibilities
■ Staff responsibilities

A **line department** is directly involved in providing goods or services to the customers of the company. For Callaway Golf (shown in Exhibit 2), the following occupy line positions:

■ Senior Vice President—Equipment
■ Plant Manager—Chicopee, MA Plant
■ Senior Vice President—Callaway Brand
■ Managing Director, Callaway Golf Europe

Individuals in these positions are responsible for manufacturing and selling Callaway's products.

A **staff department** provides services, assistance, and advice to the departments with line or other staff responsibilities. A staff department has no direct authority over a line department. For Callaway Golf (Exhibit 2), the following are staff positions:

- Senior Vice President—Chief Administrative Officer
- Vice President, Human Resources
- Chief Financial Officer
- Controller

In most companies, the **controller** is the chief management accountant. The controller's staff consists of a variety of other accountants who are responsible for specialized accounting functions such as the following:

- Systems and procedures
- General accounting
- Budgets and budget analysis
- Special reports and analysis
- Taxes
- Cost accounting

Experience in managerial accounting is often an excellent training ground for senior management positions. This is not surprising because accounting touches all phases of a company's operations.

One of **Gibson**'s most influential managers was Ted McCarty, who was the company president from 1950–1966. During this period, Gibson was known for its innovations. For example, in 1954, McCarty invented the tune-o-matic bridge with adjustable saddles.

Link to Gibson Guitars

The Management Process

As a staff department, managerial accounting supports management and the management process. The **management process** has the following five basic phases, as shown in Exhibit 3:

- Planning
- Directing
- Controlling
- Improving
- Decision making

Why It Matters

Line and Staff for Service Companies

The terms *line* and *staff* may also be applied to service organizations. Some examples follow:

Service Industry	Line	Staff
Airline	Crew, baggage handling, and gate staff	Information systems, accounting, human resources
Hotel	Housekeeping and reception staff	Maintenance, hotel manager, grounds
Hospital	Doctors, nurses, other caregivers	Admissions, records, billing
Banking	Tellers, loan officers, trust officers, and brokers	Branch manager, information systems
Telecommunications	Sales, customer service, and customer installation staff	Information systems, regional management, and network maintenance

As Exhibit 3 illustrates, the five phases interact with one another.

Exhibit 3
The Management
Process

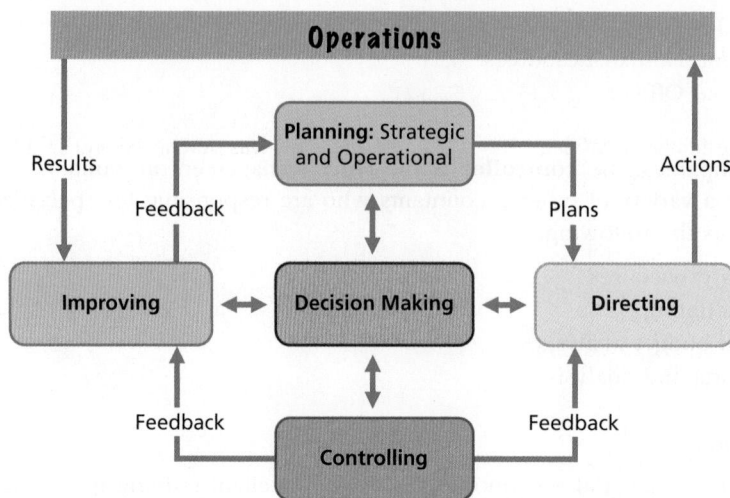

Planning Management uses **planning** in developing the company's **objectives (goals)** and translating these objectives into courses of action. For example, a company may set an objective to increase market share by 15% by introducing three new products. The actions to achieve this objective might be as follows:

- Increase the advertising budget
- Open a new sales territory
- Increase the research and development budget

Planning may be classified as follows:

- **Strategic planning**, which is developing long-term actions to achieve the company's objectives. These long-term actions are called **strategies**, which often involve periods of 5 to 10 years.
- **Operational planning**, which develops short-term actions for managing the day-to-day operations of the company.

Directing The process by which managers run day-to-day operations is called **directing**. An example of directing is a production supervisor's efforts to keep the production line moving without interruption (downtime). A credit manager's development of guidelines for assessing the ability of potential customers to pay their bills is also an example of directing.

Controlling Monitoring operating results and comparing actual results with the expected results is **controlling**. This **feedback** allows management to isolate areas for further investigation and possible remedial action. It may also lead to revising future plans. This philosophy of controlling by comparing actual and expected results is called **management by exception**.

Improving Feedback is also used by managers to support continuous process improvement. **Continuous process improvement** is the philosophy of continually improving employees, business processes, and products. The objective of continuous improvement is to eliminate the *source* of problems in a process. In this way, the right products (services) are delivered in the right quantities at the right time.

Decision Making Inherent in each of the preceding management processes is **decision making**. In managing a company, management must continually decide among alternative actions. For example, in directing operations, managers must decide on an operating structure, training procedures, and staffing of day-to-day operations.

Managerial accounting supports managers in all phases of the management process. For example, accounting reports comparing actual and expected operating results help managers plan and improve current operations. Such a report might compare the actual and expected costs of defective materials. If the cost of defective materials is unusually high, management might decide to change suppliers.

Gibson struggled financially from 1966–1986. The company was purchased and sold several times and experienced declining sales.

Link to
Gibson Guitars

 Ethics: Do It!

Environmental Managerial Accounting

Throughout the last decade, environmental issues have become an increasingly important part of the business environment for most companies. Companies and managers must now consider the environmental impact of their business decisions in the same way that they would consider other operational issues. To help managers make sound business decisions, the emerging field of environmental management accounting focuses on calculating the environmental-related costs of business decisions. Environmental managerial accountants evaluate a variety of issues such as the volume and level of emissions, the estimated costs of different levels of emissions, and the impact that environmental costs have on product cost. Managers use these results to consider clearly the environmental effects of their business decisions.

Uses of Managerial Accounting Information

As mentioned earlier, managerial accounting provides information and reports for managers to use in operating a business. Some examples of how managerial accounting could be used by a guitar manufacturer include the following:

- The cost of manufacturing each guitar could be used to determine its selling price.
- Comparing the costs of guitars over time can be used to monitor and control costs.
- Performance reports could be used to identify any large amounts of scrap or employee downtime. For example, large amounts of unusable wood (scrap) after the cutting process should be investigated to determine the underlying cause. Such scrap may be caused by saws that have not been properly maintained.
- A report could analyze the potential efficiencies and savings of purchasing a new computerized saw to speed up the production process.
- A report could analyze how many guitars need to be sold to cover operating costs and expenses. Such information could be used to set monthly selling targets and bonuses for sales personnel.

Why It Matters

Not According to Plan

There are times even the best of plans go awry. Sometimes plans are impacted by events outside of management control. For example, Hurricane Sandy ruined the beach and resort businesses along the New Jersey shore. Few management plans would be able to provide for such an extreme contingency. Force majeure (meaning "superior force") clauses in contracts can be used to nullify contracts when such events occur. Such clauses are used when the normal operating plans are disrupted by events beyond management control or expectation. For example, a hotel damaged by Hurricane Sandy under a force majeure clause would not be required to fulfill a contract to supply rooms for a convention. In other cases, events may be dramatic, but can be anticipated. An example was the dramatic decline in oil prices during the middle 2010s that reduced the oil revenue earned by U.S. shale oil producers. Many of these producers planned and then executed financial contracts, termed hedges, that earned money from lower oil prices, to partially offset revenue losses.

As the prior examples illustrate, managerial accounting information can be used for a variety of purposes. In the remaining chapters of this text, we examine these and other areas of managerial accounting.

Check Up Corner 15-1 Management Process

1. Indicate whether the following statements are true or false:
   A. Managerial accounting information is designed primarily to meet the needs of external users such as shareholders, creditors, and the general public.
   B. Managerial accounting reports must be prepared for the business as a whole.
   C. The Senior Vice President—Manufacturing would be considered a line position in a line department.

2. Three phases of the management process are planning, controlling, and improving. Match the following descriptions to the proper phase:

Phase of Management Process	Description
Planning	A. Monitoring the operating results and comparing the actual results with expected results
Controlling	B. Rejects solving problems with temporary solutions that fail to address the root cause of the problem
Improving	C. Used by management to develop the company's objectives

Solution:

1. A. False. The primary focus and design of managerial accounting information is to meet the specific needs of a company's management.
   B. False. Managerial accounting reports do not have to be prepared for the business as a whole. Most management reports are prepared for products, projects, sales territories, or other segments of the company.
   C. True. A line department is directly involved in providing goods or services to the customers of the company. A staff department provides services, assistance, and advice to other departments.

2. Planning: **C.** Used by management to develop the company's objectives

   Controlling: **A.** Monitoring the operating results and comparing the actual results with expected results

   Improving: **B.** Rejects solving problems with temporary solutions that fail to address the root cause of the problem

Check Up Corner

Objective 2

Describe and illustrate the nature of manufacturing operations, including different types and classifications of costs.

Manufacturing Operations

The operations of a business can be classified as service, merchandising, or manufacturing. The accounting for service and merchandising businesses has been described and illustrated in earlier chapters. For this reason, the remaining chapters of this text focus primarily on manufacturing businesses. Most of the managerial accounting concepts discussed, however, also apply to service and merchandising businesses.

Nature of Manufacturing

As a basis for illustration of manufacturing operations, a guitar manufacturer, **Legend Guitars**, is used. Exhibit 4 is an overview of Legend's guitar manufacturing operations.

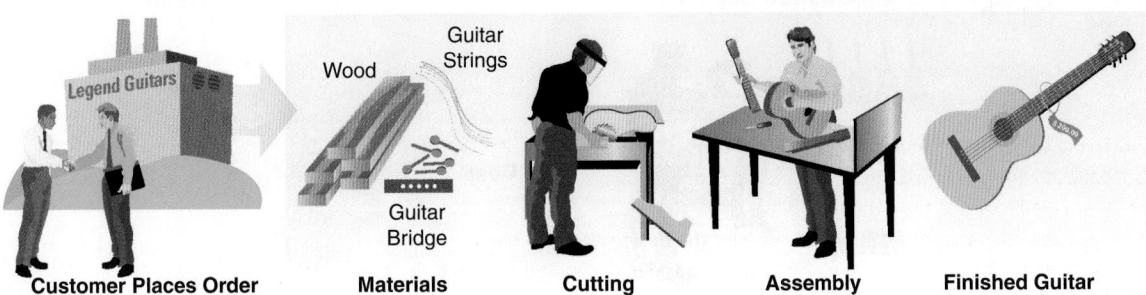

Exhibit 4 Guitar-Making Operations of Legend Guitars

Legend Guitars | Wood | Guitar Strings | Guitar Bridge

Customer Places Order — **Materials** — **Cutting** — **Assembly** — **Finished Guitar**

Legend's guitar-making process begins when a customer places an order for a guitar. Once the order is accepted, the manufacturing process begins by obtaining the necessary materials. An employee then cuts the body and neck of the guitar out of raw lumber. Once the wood is cut, the body and neck of the guitar are assembled. When the assembly is complete, the guitar is painted and finished.

Gibson provides tours of its Memphis guitar factory located at 145 Lt. George W. Lee Avenue.

Link to Gibson Guitars

Direct and Indirect Costs

A **cost** is a payment of cash or the commitment to pay cash in the future for the purpose of generating revenues. For example, cash (or credit) used to purchase equipment is the cost of the equipment. If equipment is purchased by exchanging assets other than cash, the current market value of the assets given up is the cost of the equipment purchased.

In managerial accounting, costs are classified according to the decision-making needs of management. For example, costs are often classified by their relationship to a segment of operations, called a **cost object**. A cost object may be a product, a sales territory, a department, or an activity, such as research and development. Costs identified with cost objects are either direct costs or indirect costs.

Direct costs are identified with and can be traced to a cost object. For example, as shown in Exhibit 5, the cost of wood (materials) used by **Legend Guitars** in manufacturing a guitar is a direct cost of the guitar.

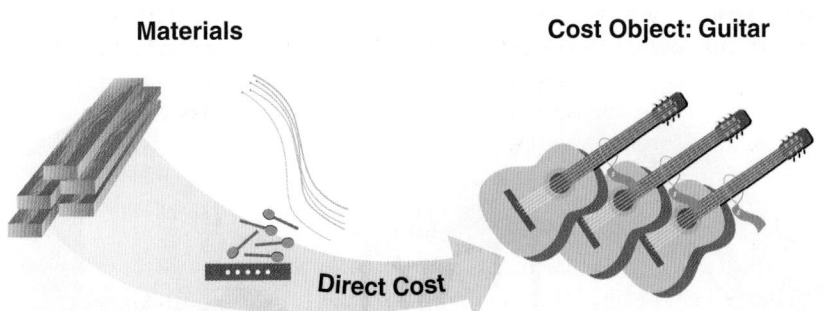

Materials | **Cost Object: Guitar**

Direct Cost

Exhibit 5

Direct Costs of Legend Guitars

Indirect costs cannot be identified with or traced to a cost object. For example, as shown in Exhibit 6, the salaries of the **Legend Guitars** production supervisors are indirect costs of producing a guitar. Although the production supervisors contribute to the production of a guitar, their salaries cannot be identified with or traced to any individual guitar.

Exhibit 6

Indirect Costs of
Legend Guitars

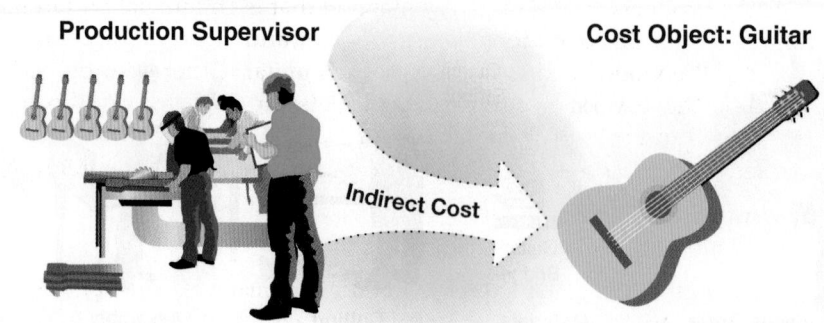

Depending on the cost object, a cost may be either a direct or an indirect cost. For example, the salaries of production supervisors are indirect costs when the cost object is an individual guitar. If, however, the cost object is **Legend Guitars**' overall production process, then the salaries of production supervisors are direct costs.

This process of classifying a cost as direct or indirect is illustrated in Exhibit 7.

Exhibit 7

Classifying Direct
and Indirect Costs

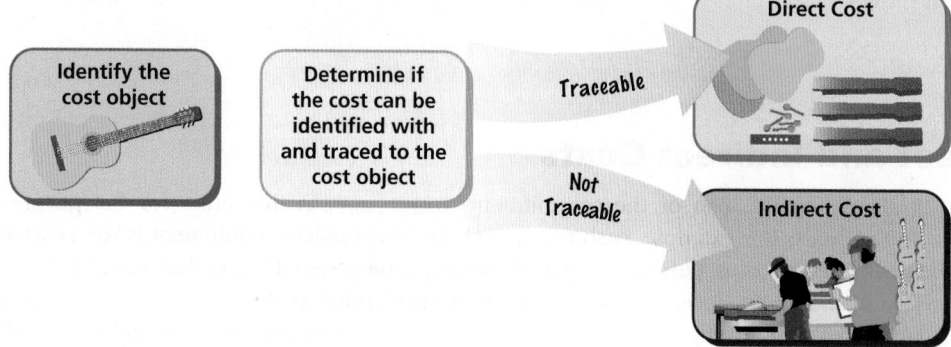

Manufacturing Costs

The cost of a manufactured product includes the cost of materials used in making the product. In addition, the cost of a manufactured product includes the cost of converting the materials into a finished product. For example, **Legend Guitars** uses employees and machines to convert wood (and other supplies) into finished guitars. Thus, as shown in Exhibit 8, the cost of a finished guitar (the cost object) includes the following:

- Direct materials cost
- Direct labor cost
- Factory overhead cost

Exhibit 8

Manufacturing
Costs of Legend
Guitars

Direct Materials   **Direct Labor**   **Factory Overhead**

Direct Materials Cost Manufactured products begin with raw materials that are converted into finished products. The cost of any material that is an integral part of the finished product is classified as a **direct materials cost**. For **Legend Guitars**, direct materials cost includes the cost of the wood used in producing each guitar. Other examples of direct materials costs include the cost of electronic components for a television, silicon wafers for microcomputer chips, and tires for an automobile.

To be classified as a direct materials cost, the cost must be *both* of the following:

■ An integral part of the finished product
■ A significant portion of the total cost of the product

For Legend, the cost of the guitar strings is not a direct materials cost. This is because the cost of guitar strings is an insignificant part of the total cost of each guitar. Instead, the cost of guitar strings is classified as a factory overhead cost, which is discussed later.

Direct Labor Cost Most manufacturing processes use employees to convert materials into finished products. The cost of employee wages that is an integral part of the finished product is classified as **direct labor cost**. For **Legend Guitars**, direct labor cost includes the wages of the employees who cut each guitar out of raw lumber and assemble it. Other examples of direct labor costs include mechanics' wages for repairing an automobile, machine operators' wages for manufacturing tools, and assemblers' wages for assembling a laptop computer.

Like a direct materials cost, a direct labor cost must meet *both* of the following criteria:

■ An integral part of the finished product
■ A significant portion of the total cost of the product

For Legend, the wages of the janitors who clean the factory are not a direct labor cost. This is because janitorial costs are not an integral part or a significant cost of each guitar. Instead, janitorial costs are classified as a factory overhead cost, which is discussed next.

Factory Overhead Cost Costs other than direct materials and direct labor that are incurred in the manufacturing process are combined and classified as **factory overhead cost**. Factory overhead is sometimes called **manufacturing overhead** or **factory burden**.

All factory overhead costs are indirect costs of the product. Some factory overhead costs include the following:

■ Heating and lighting the factory
■ Repairing and maintaining factory equipment
■ Property taxes on factory buildings and land
■ Insurance on factory buildings
■ Depreciation on factory plant and equipment

Factory overhead cost also includes materials and labor costs that do not enter directly into the finished product. Examples include the cost of oil used to lubricate machinery and the wages of janitorial and supervisory employees. Also, if the costs of direct materials or direct labor are not a significant portion of the total product cost, these costs may be classified as factory overhead costs.

Why It Matters

Overhead Costs

Defense contractors such as General Dynamics, Boeing, and Lockheed Martin sell products such as airplanes, ships, and military equipment to the U.S. Department of Defense. Building large products such as these requires a significant investment in facilities and tools, all of which are classified as factory overhead costs. As a result, factory overhead costs are a much larger portion of the cost of goods sold for defense contractors than they are in other industries. For example, a U.S. General Accounting Office study of six defense contractors found that overhead costs were almost one-third of the price of the final product. This is more than three times greater than the factory overhead costs for a laptop computer, which are typically about 10% of the price of the final product.

For **Legend Guitars**, the costs of guitar strings and janitorial wages are factory overhead costs. Additional factory overhead costs of making guitars are as follows:

- Sandpaper
- Buffing compound
- Glue
- Power (electricity) to run the machines
- Depreciation of the machines and building
- Salaries of production supervisors

Prime Costs and Conversion Costs Direct materials, direct labor, and factory overhead costs may be grouped together for analysis and reporting. Two such common groupings are as follows:

- **Prime costs**, which consist of direct materials and direct labor costs
- **Conversion costs**, which consist of direct labor and factory overhead costs

Conversion costs are the costs of converting the materials into a finished product. Direct labor is both a prime cost and a conversion cost, as shown in Exhibit 9.

Exhibit 9
Prime Costs and
Conversion Costs

Product Costs and Period Costs For financial reporting purposes, costs are classified as product costs or period costs.

- **Product costs** consist of manufacturing costs: direct materials, direct labor, and factory overhead.
- **Period costs** consist of selling and administrative expenses. *Selling expenses* are incurred in marketing the product and delivering the product to customers. *Administrative expenses* are incurred in managing the company and are not directly related to the manufacturing or selling functions.

Examples of product costs and period costs for **Legend Guitars** are presented in Exhibit 10.
To facilitate control, selling and administrative expenses may be reported by level of responsibility. For example, selling expenses may be reported by products, salespersons, departments, divisions, or territories. Likewise, administrative expenses may be reported by areas such as human resources, computer services, legal, accounting, or finance.

Why It Matters

Service Companies and Product Costs

Most service companies do not produce a product and, thus, do not have product costs. However, service companies may still have labor, materials, and overhead. Often, these costs are not associated with manufacturing product, but with serving customers. An example is a hospital. Caregivers provide care (similar to direct labor), drugs and health supplies are administered (similar to direct materials), and administrative salaries and utilities are paid (similar to factory overhead).

Exhibit 10   Examples of Product Costs and Period Costs—Legend Guitars

Product (Manufacturing) Costs

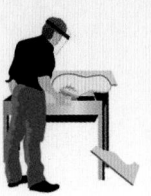

Direct Materials Cost
■ Wood used in neck and body

Direct Labor Cost
■ Wages of saw operator
■ Wages of employees who assemble the guitar

Factory Overhead
■ Guitar strings
■ Wages of janitor
■ Power to run the machines
■ Depreciation expense—factory building
■ Sandpaper and buffing materials
■ Glue used in assembly of the guitar
■ Salary of production supervisors

Period (Nonmanufacturing) Costs

Selling Expenses
■ Advertising expenses
■ Sales salaries expenses
■ Commissions expenses

Administrative Expenses
■ Office salaries expense
■ Office supplies expense
■ Depreciation expense—office building and equipment

The impact on the financial statements of product and period costs is summarized in Exhibit 11. As product costs are incurred, they are recorded and reported on the balance sheet as *inventory*. When the inventory is sold, the cost of the manufactured product sold is reported as *cost of goods sold* on the income statement. Period costs are reported as *expenses* on the income statement in the period in which they are incurred and, thus, never appear on the balance sheet.

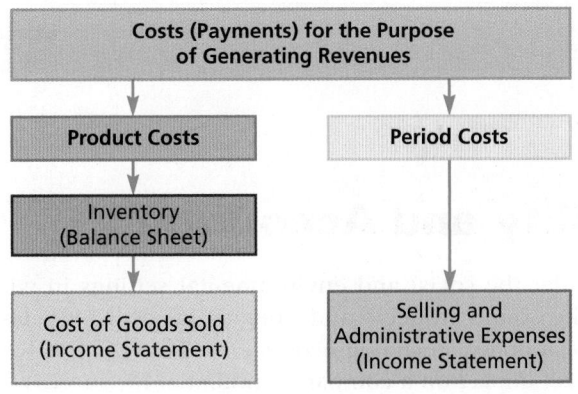

Exhibit 11

Product Costs, Period Costs, and the Financial Statements

In January 1986, guitar enthusiasts Henry Juszkiewicz and David Berryman purchased **Gibson**. Together they restored Gibson's reputation for innovation and quality. Under their leadership, Gibson began generating profits.

Link to Gibson Guitars

Check Up Corner 15-2 Manufacturing Operations

A partial list of the costs for MLB Mitt Company, a baseball glove manufacturer, is as follows:

A. Ink used to print a player's autograph
B. Salesperson's salary and commission
C. Padding material
D. Coolants for machines that sew the baseball gloves
E. Wages of assembly line employees
F. Cost of endorsement from a professional baseball player
G. Salary of manufacturing plant supervisor
H. Leather used to make the gloves
I. Office supplies used at company headquarters
J. Wages of office administrative staff

Using the following headings, classify each cost as a product cost or a period cost. In addition, identify product costs as:

- Direct materials, direct labor, or factory overhead, and
- Prime cost, conversion cost, or both.

	Product Cost					Period Cost
Item	Direct Materials	Direct Labor	Factory Overhead	Prime Cost	Conversion Cost	

Solution:

	Product Cost					Period Cost
Item	Direct Materials	Direct Labor	Factory Overhead	Prime Cost	Conversion Cost	
A.			X		X	
B.						X
C.	X			X		
D.			X		X	
E.		X		X	X	
F.						X
G.			X		X	
H.	X			X		
I.						X
J.						X

Check Up Corner

Objective 3

Describe sustainable business activities and eco-efficiency measures.

Sustainability and Accounting

Managers must consider the social and environmental settings in which a business operates, in order to make sound strategic and operational decisions. Issues such as population growth, resource scarcity, declining ecosystems, increasing urbanization, and climate change all have a direct impact on a company's potential for success. As a result, managers are using new management techniques and tools that consider these issues.

Sustainability

Sustainability is the practice of operating a business to maximize profits while attempting to preserve the environment, economy, and needs of future generations. Sustainability practices acknowledge that a company's long-term success requires the continued availability of natural resources and a productive social environment. Examples of sustainable business activities are provided in Exhibit 12.

Exhibit 12 Sustainable Business Activities

Category	Description	Example
Agriculture	Farming and ranching techniques that do not damage or disrupt the environment	Mixed farming, crop rotation, multiple cropping
Energy	Generating energy with little or no pollution	Wind turbines, solar power
Engineering and Construction	Designing and constructing buildings that are highly efficient in using natural resources, while minimizing pollution	Recycled building materials, high-efficiency heating and cooling systems, renewable energy generation
Transportation	Using transportation methods that result in little pollution and have a minimal impact on the environment	Expanded public transportation systems, green vehicles, biofuel-powered vehicles
Waste Minimization	Recycling and reuse practices that reduce the amount of waste disposed in landfills	Curbside recycling collection, composting, reusable products (e.g. water bottles)

Eco-Efficiency Measures in Managerial Accounting

Sustainability information can provide important feedback to guide a company's strategic and operational decision making. Managers can use this information to increase revenue, control costs, and allocate resources efficiently. **Eco-efficiency measures** are a form of managerial accounting information that helps managers evaluate the savings generated by using fewer natural resources in a company's operations. Examples of eco-efficiency measures are provided in Exhibit 13.

		Exhibit 13 Eco-Efficiency Measures
Energy Efficiency	Energy cost savings from replacing lighting fixtures in a production facility with energy-efficient lighting	
Material Use Efficiency	Materials cost savings from reducing the amount of product packaging materials	
Fuel Efficiency	Fuel cost savings from replacing gas-powered vehicles with hybrid or alternative energy-source vehicles	
Waste Efficiency	Waste removal cost savings from recycling and reusing waste and by-product materials	

Sustainability information can also benefit external financial statement users in their decision making. The risks and opportunities that a company faces are tied to the environment in which it operates and provide important insights into the potential for success. As such, external financial statement users may require sustainability information to evaluate investment and credit decisions. The **Sustainability Accounting Standards Board (SASB)** was organized in 2011 to develop accounting standards that help companies report decision-useful sustainability information to external financial statement users. While the SASB's standards are not required, they are designed to provide sustainability information that complements required financial statement information.

Financial Statements for a Manufacturing Business

Objective 4

Describe and illustrate financial statements for a manufacturing business, including the balance sheet, statement of cost of goods manufactured, and income statement.

The retained earnings and cash flow statements for a manufacturing business are similar to those for service and merchandising businesses. However, the balance sheet and income statement for a manufacturing business are more complex. This is because a manufacturer makes the products that it sells and, thus, must record and report product costs. The reporting of product costs primarily affects the balance sheet and the income statement.

Balance Sheet

A manufacturing business reports three types of inventory on its balance sheet as follows:

- **Materials inventory** (sometimes called raw materials inventory). This inventory consists of the costs of the direct and indirect materials that have not entered the manufacturing process.
  Examples for **Legend Guitars**: Wood, guitar strings, glue, sandpaper
- **Work in process inventory.** This inventory consists of the direct materials, direct labor, and factory overhead costs for products that have entered the manufacturing process, but are not yet completed (in process).
  Example for Legend: Unfinished (partially assembled) guitars
- **Finished goods inventory.** This inventory consists of completed (or finished) products that have not been sold.
  Example for Legend: Unsold guitars

Exhibit 14 illustrates the reporting of inventory on the balance sheet for a merchandising and a manufacturing business. MusicLand Stores, Inc., a retailer of musical instruments, reports only Inventory. In contrast, **Legend Guitars**, a manufacturer of guitars, reports Finished Goods, Work in Process, and Materials inventories. In both balance sheets, inventory is reported in the Current Assets section.

Exhibit 14

Balance Sheet Presentation of Inventory in Merchandising and Manufacturing Companies

MusicLand Stores, Inc.
Balance Sheet
December 31, 20Y8

Current assets:	
Cash..	$ 25,000
Accounts receivable (net)	85,000
Inventory..	142,000
Supplies...	10,000
Total current assets...	$262,000

Legend Guitars
Balance Sheet
December 31, 20Y8

Current assets:		
Cash..		$ 21,000
Accounts receivable (net)		120,000
Inventory:		
Direct materials....................................	$35,000	
Work in process....................................	24,000	
Finished goods......................................	62,500	
Total inventory..		121,500
Supplies...		2,000
Total current assets................................		$264,500

Income Statement

The income statements for merchandising and manufacturing businesses differ primarily in the reporting of the cost of goods (merchandise) *available for sale* and *sold* during the period. These differences are shown in Exhibit 15.

Merchandising Business			Manufacturing Business			
Income Statement			**Income Statement**			
Sales		$XXX	Sales			$XXX
Beginning inventory	$ XXX		Beginning finished goods inventory	$ XXX		
Net purchases	XXX		Cost of goods manufactured	XXX		
Inventory available for sale	$ XXX		Cost of finished goods available for sale	$ XXX		
Ending inventory	(XXX)		Ending finished goods inventory	(XXX)		
Cost of goods sold		XXX	Cost of goods sold			XXX
Gross profit		$XXX	Gross profit			$XXX

Exhibit 15
Income Statements for Merchandising and Manufacturing Businesses

As shown in Exhibit 15, a merchandising business determines its cost of goods sold by first adding its net purchases for the period to its beginning inventory. This determines inventory available for sale during the period. The ending inventory is then subtracted to determine the **cost of goods sold.**[1]

In contrast, a manufacturing business makes the products it sells using direct materials, direct labor, and factory overhead. As a result, a manufacturing business must determine its **cost of goods manufactured** during the period.

The cost of goods manufactured is determined by preparing a **statement of cost of goods manufactured.**[2] This statement summarizes the cost of goods manufactured during the period, as follows:

Statement of Cost of Goods Manufactured

Beginning work in process inventory...........			$ XXX
Direct materials:			
Beginning materials inventory..............	$ XXX		
Purchases................................	XXX		
Cost of materials available for use...........	$ XXX		
Ending materials inventory.................	(XXX)		
Cost of direct materials used		$XXX	
Direct labor		XXX	
Factory overhead.............................		XXX	
Total manufacturing costs incurred in period			XXX
Total manufacturing costs			$ XXX
Ending work in process inventory			(XXX)
Cost of goods manufactured			$ XXX

---

[1] To simplfy, we use the computation of cost of goods sold for periodic inventory systems.

[2] Chapters 16 and 17 describe and illustrate the use of job order and process cost systems. As will be illustrated, these systems do not require a statement of cost of goods manufactured.

To illustrate, the following data for **Legend Guitars** are used:

	Jan. 1, 20Y8	Dec. 31, 20Y8
Inventories:		
Materials..................................	$ 65,000	$ 35,000
Work in process	30,000	24,000
Finished goods............................	60,000	62,500
Total inventories..............................	$155,000	$121,500
Manufacturing costs incurred during 20Y8:		
Materials purchased.......................		$100,000
Direct labor		110,000
Factory overhead:		
Indirect labor..........................	$ 24,000	
Depreciation on factory equipment	10,000	
Factory supplies and utility costs	10,000	
Total factory overhead		44,000
Total		$254,000
Sales...		$366,000
Selling expenses..............................		20,000
Administrative expenses......................		15,000

The statement of cost of goods manufactured is prepared using the following three steps:

- Step 1. Determine the *cost of direct materials used* during the period.
- Step 2. Determine the *total manufacturing costs incurred* during the period.
- Step 3. Determine the *cost of goods manufactured* during the period.

Using the data for **Legend Guitars**, the cost of direct materials used, total manufacturing costs incurred, and cost of goods manufactured are computed as follows:

Step 1. The *cost of direct materials used* in production is determined as follows:

Materials inventory, January 1, 20Y8	$ 65,000
Purchases	100,000
Cost of materials available for use	$ 165,000
Materials inventory, December 31, 20Y8	(35,000)
Cost of direct materials used	$130,000

The January 1, 20Y8 (beginning), materials inventory of $65,000 is added to the cost of materials purchased of $100,000 to yield the $165,000 total cost of materials that are available for use during 20Y8. Deducting the December 31, 20Y8 (ending), materials inventory of $35,000 yields the $130,000 cost of direct materials used in production.

Step 2. The *total manufacturing costs incurred in 20Y8* are determined as follows:

Direct materials used in production (Step 1)	$130,000
Direct labor	110,000
Factory overhead	44,000
Total manufacturing costs incurred in 20Y8	$284,000

The total manufacturing costs incurred in 20Y8 of $284,000 are determined by adding the cost of direct materials used in production (Step 1), the direct labor cost, and the factory overhead costs.

Step 3. The *cost of goods manufactured* is determined as follows:

Work in process inventory, January 1, 20Y8	$ 30,000
Total manufacturing costs incurred (Step 2)	284,000
Total manufacturing costs incurred	$ 314,000
Work in process inventory, December 31, 20Y8	(24,000)
Cost of goods manufactured in 20Y8	$290,000

The cost of goods manufactured of $290,000 is determined by adding the total manufacturing costs incurred (Step 2) to the January 1, 20Y8 (beginning), work in process inventory of $30,000. This yields total manufacturing costs incurred of $314,000. The December 31, 20Y8 (ending), work in process inventory of $24,000 is then deducted to determine the cost of goods manufactured of $290,000.

The income statement and statement of cost of goods manufactured for **Legend Guitars** are shown in Exhibit 16.

Legend Guitars
Income Statement
For the Year Ended December 31, 20Y8

Sales		$366,000
Cost of goods sold:		
Finished goods inventory, January 1, 20Y8	$ 60,000	
Cost of goods manufactured	290,000	
Cost of finished goods available for sale	$350,000	
Finished goods inventory, December 31, 20Y8	(62,500)	
Cost of goods sold		287,500
Gross profit		$ 78,500
Operating expenses:		
Selling expenses	$ 20,000	
Administrative expenses	15,000	
Total operating expenses		35,000
Net income		$ 43,500

Legend Guitars
Statement of Cost of Goods Manufactured
For the Year Ended December 31, 20Y8

Work in process inventory, January 1, 20Y8			$ 30,000
Direct materials:			
Materials inventory, January 1, 20Y8	$ 65,000		
Purchases	100,000		
Cost of materials available for use	$165,000		
Materials inventory, December 31, 20Y8	(35,000)		
Cost of direct materials used		$130,000	
Direct labor		110,000	
Factory overhead:			
Indirect labor	$ 24,000		
Depreciation on factory equipment	10,000		
Factory supplies and utility costs	10,000		
Total factory overhead		44,000	
Total manufacturing costs incurred in 20Y8			284,000
Total manufacturing costs			$314,000
Work in process inventory, December 31, 20Y8			(24,000)
Cost of goods manufactured			$290,000

Exhibit 16
Manufacturing Company—Income Statement with Statement of Cost of Goods Manufactured

DYNAMIC
EXHIBIT

Exhibit 17 summarizes how manufacturing costs flow to the income statement and balance sheet of a manufacturing business.

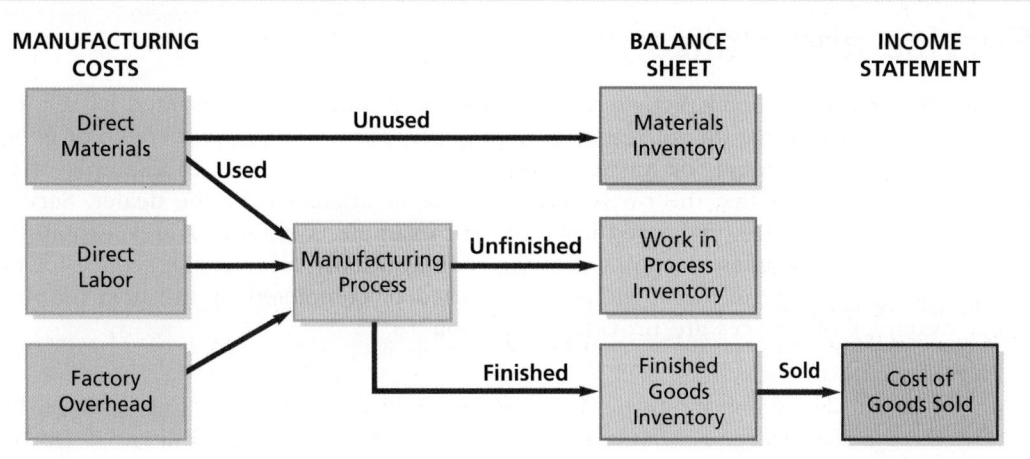

Exhibit 17
Flow of Manufacturing Costs

Check Up Corner 15-3 Manufacturing Financial Statements

The following information is available for January for MLB Mitt Company, a baseball glove manufacturer:

Cost of direct materials used in production	$25,000
Direct labor	35,000
Factory overhead	20,000
Work in process inventory, January 1	30,000
Work in process inventory, January 31	25,000
Finished goods inventory, January 1	15,000
Finished goods inventory, January 31	12,000

For January, determine (A) the cost of goods manufactured and (B) the cost of goods sold.

Solution:

The cost of goods manufactured is determined by adding the total manufacturing costs incurred to the beginning work in process inventory.

A.	Work in process inventory, January 1		$ 30,000
	Cost of direct materials used	$ 25,000	
	Direct labor	35,000	
	Factory overhead	20,000	
	Total manufacturing costs incurred in January		80,000
	Total manufacturing costs		$110,000
	Work in process inventory, January 31		(25,000)
	Cost of goods manufactured		$ 85,000
B.	Finished goods inventory, January 1		$ 15,000
	Cost of goods manufactured		85,000
	Cost of finished goods available for sale		$100,000
	Finished goods inventory, January 31		(12,000)
	Cost of goods sold		$ 88,000

The cost of goods manufactured is added to the beginning finished goods inventory to determine the finished goods available for sale.

Check Up Corner

Analysis for Decision Making

Objective
Describe and measure utilization in evaluating performance for a service company.

Service and Utilization

Nearly 80% of U.S. economic activity (gross domestic product) is represented by services. Services are activities that do not result in the transfer, possession, or ownership of goods. Services benefit a customer or an item under a customer's control. An example of the latter is an automobile that the owner brings in for maintenance by the dealer. Services cannot be stored and are often used instantly. For example, a hotel provides a room to a guest for a night. The guest does not own the room, but only receives the service for one night. Upon receiving the room, the service is used or completed by the next morning. Other examples of services are provided in Exhibit 18.

Service Industry	Service Example	Company Example
Utilities	Electric power generation	Consolidated Edison
Transportation	Overnight delivery	FedEx
Information	Social media	Facebook
Financial Services	Banking	Bank of America
Education	Higher education	University of Phoenix
Leisure and Hospitality	Entertainment	The Walt Disney Company
Health	General healthcare	Hospital Corporation of America
Personal Services	Fitness club	Life Time Fitness

Exhibit 18
Examples of Service Industries, Services, and Companies

Many of the principles discussed in this chapter for manufacturing companies can be applied to service companies. However, the unique characteristics of service companies also create some distinctions, as shown in Exhibit 19.

Manufacturing	Services
Uses materials, work in process, and finished goods inventory.	Inventory is often limited to supplies.
Uses both product and period costs.	Uses only period costs.
Uses cost of goods sold on the income statement.	May use cost of services on the income statement.
Manufacturing requires a physical production site.	Many services require a network that connects the service to the customer. Examples include telecommunications, banking, power distribution, distributed entertainment, and transportation.
Manufacturing overhead is an indirect cost in manufacturing products.	There is no manufacturing overhead; however, indirect costs are incurred in serving customers.
Labor is a direct cost to products.	Labor is not a direct cost to products, but may be a direct cost to customers. Examples are accountants in an accounting firm or doctors in a medical practice.
Materials are a direct cost to products.	Materials are often an indirect cost, but may be significant, such as fuel for transportation or utilities. In other cases, materials are not significant, such as financial, leisure, information, or education services.

Exhibit 19
Managerial Accounting Distinctions Between Manufacturing and Service Companies

Most of the distinctions in Exhibit 19 are caused by the nature of services. Service companies have no inventory or product costs. Managerial accounting in service companies is concerned with the economic use of people and fixed assets in serving customers.

The nature of services influences the performance measures used by management accountants. For example, the productive use of fixed assets is an important contributor to financial success for many service companies. This is because many service companies must build large networks or other fixed assets in order to deliver a service. For example, the cellular network of **Verizon Communications** is extremely costly and, thus, the use of the network is key to Verizon's financial success. Cruise lines (ships), utilities (power plants), railroads (track), hotels (buildings), hospitals (buildings), and educational services (buildings) also require costly fixed assets.

An important measure used in many service companies is utilization. **Utilization** measures the use of a fixed asset in serving customers relative to the asset's capacity. Higher utilization is considered favorable, while lower utilization is considered unfavorable. Different service industries will have different names and calculations used for measuring utilization. Some service industries, such as power generation, freight transportation, and telecommunications, measure utilization using complex formulas. However, other service industries use simpler methods to measure utilization. In the hotel industry, for example, utilization is measured by the *occupancy rate*, which is calculated as:

$$\text{Occupancy Rate} = \frac{\text{Guest Nights}}{\text{Available Room Nights}}$$

where,

Guest nights = number of guests × number of nights per visit (per time period)
Available room nights = number of available rooms × number of nights per time period

The number of guests is determined under single room occupancy, so that the number of guests is equal to the number of occupied rooms.

To illustrate, assume the EasyRest Hotel is a single hotel with 150 rooms. During the month of June, the hotel had 3,600 guests, each staying for a single night. The occupancy rate would be determined as follows:

$$\text{Occupancy Rate} = \frac{\text{Guest Nights}}{\text{Available Room Nights}}$$

$$= \frac{3,600 \text{ guest nights}}{150 \text{ rooms} \times 30 \text{ days}} = 80\%$$

The hotel was occupied to 80% of capacity, which would be considered favorable.

Make a Decision   Utilization

Comfort Plus, Inc. has a hotel with 300 rooms in a metropolitan city. Its main competitor, Connors Hotel, has a hotel with 350 rooms in the same city. The following operating data are available for April for the two hotels:

Comfort Plus		Connors	
Number of Guests	Nights per Visit	Number of Guests	Nights per Visit
3,680	1	4,390	1
1,100	2	700	2
500	3	800	3

A. Determine the guest nights for each hotel in April.
B. Determine the available room nights for each hotel in April.
C. Determine the occupancy rate for each hotel in April.
D. Which hotel has the better utilization of capacity in April?

Solution:

A. Comfort Plus:

Number of Guests		Nights per Visit		Guest Nights
3,680	×	1	=	3,680
1,100	×	2	=	2,200
500	×	3	=	1,500
Total guest nights				7,380

Connors:

Number of Guests		Nights per Visit		Guest Nights
4,390	×	1	=	4,390
700	×	2	=	1,400
800	×	3	=	2,400
Total guest nights				8,190

B. Comfort Plus: 300 rooms × 30 days = 9,000 available room nights for April
   Connors: 350 rooms × 30 days = 10,500 available room nights for April

C.

$$\text{Occupancy Rate} = \frac{\text{Guest Nights}}{\text{Available Room Nights}}$$

$$\text{Comfort Plus:} \quad \frac{7,380 \text{ guest nights}}{9,000 \text{ available room nights}} = 82\%$$

$$\text{Connors:} \quad \frac{8,190 \text{ guest nights}}{10,500 \text{ available room nights}} = 78\%$$

D. Comfort Plus has a better occupancy rate at 82% of capacity, compared to Connors' occupancy rate of 78%.

Make a Decision

Let's Review

Chapter Summary

1. Managerial accounting is a staff function that supports the management process by providing reports to aid management in planning, directing, controlling, improving, and decision making. This differs from financial accounting, which provides information to users outside of the organization. Managerial accounting reports are designed to meet the specific needs of management and aid management in planning long-term strategies and running the day-to-day operations. Managerial accounting provides a variety of information for decision making for use in operating a business.

2. Manufacturing companies use machinery and labor to convert materials into a finished product. A direct cost can be directly traced to a finished product, while an indirect cost cannot. The cost of a finished product is made up of three components: direct materials, direct labor, and factory overhead. These three manufacturing costs can be categorized into prime costs (direct materials and direct labor) or conversion costs (direct labor and factory overhead). Product costs consist of the elements of manufacturing cost—direct materials, direct labor, and factory overhead—while period costs consist of selling and administrative expenses.

3. To make sound strategic and operational decisions, managers must consider the social and environmental conditions in which their company operates. Sustainability is the practice of operating a business to maximize profits while attempting to preserve the environment, economy, and needs of future generations. Sustainability information provides important internal feedback that helps guide a company's strategic and operational decision making. This information also helps external financial statement users evaluate the risks and opportunities a company faces that are tied to the environment in which it operates.

4. The financial statements of manufacturing companies differ from those of merchandising companies. Manufacturing company balance sheets report three types of inventory: materials, work in process, and finished goods. The income statement of manufacturing companies reports the cost of goods sold, which is the total manufacturing cost of the goods sold. The income statement is supported by the statement of cost of goods manufactured, which provides the details of the cost of goods manufactured during the period.

Key Terms

continuous process improvement (746)
controller (745)
controlling (746)
conversion costs (752)
cost (749)
cost object (749)
cost of goods manufactured (757)
cost of goods sold (757)
decision making (746)
direct costs (749)
direct labor cost (751)
direct materials cost (751)
directing (746)
eco-efficiency measures (755)

factory burden (751)
factory overhead cost (751)
feedback (746)
financial accounting (743)
finished goods inventory (756)
indirect costs (749)
line department (744)
management by exception (746)
management process (745)
managerial accounting (743)
manufacturing overhead (751)
materials inventory (756)
objectives (goals) (746)
operational planning (746)
period costs (752)

planning (746)
prime costs (752)
product costs (752)
staff department (745)
statement of cost of goods manufactured (757)
strategic planning (746)
strategies (746)
sustainability (754)
Sustainability Accounting Standards Board (SASB) (755)
utilization (762)
work in process inventory (756)

Practice

Multiple-Choice Questions

1. Which of the following best describes the difference between financial and managerial accounting?
   A. Managerial accounting provides information to support decisions, while financial accounting does not.
   B. Managerial accounting is not restricted to generally accepted accounting principles, while financial accounting is restricted to GAAP.
   C. Managerial accounting does not result in financial reports, while financial accounting does result in financial reports.
   D. Managerial accounting is concerned solely with the future and does not record events from the past, while financial accounting records only events from past transactions.

2. Which of the following is *not* one of the five basic phases of the management process?
   A. Planning
   B. Controlling
   C. Decision making
   D. Operating

3. Which of the following is *not* considered a cost of manufacturing a product?
   A. Direct materials cost
   B. Factory overhead cost
   C. Sales salaries
   D. Direct labor cost

4. Which of the following costs would be included as part of the factory overhead costs of a microcomputer manufacturer?
   A. The cost of memory chips
   B. Depreciation of testing equipment
   C. Wages of microcomputer assemblers
   D. The cost of disk drives

5. For the month of May, Latter Company has beginning finished goods inventory of $50,000, ending finished goods inventory of $35,000, and cost of goods manufactured of $125,000. What is the cost of goods sold for May?
   A. $90,000
   B. $110,000
   C. $140,000
   D. $170,000

Answers provided after Problem. Need more practice? Find additional multiple-choice questions, exercises, and problems in CengageNOWv2.

Exercises

SHOW ME HOW

1. Management process   Obj. 1

Three phases of the management process are controlling, planning, and decision making. Match the following descriptions to the proper phase:

Phase of Management Process	Description
Controlling	A. Monitoring the operating results of implemented plans and comparing the actual results with expected results
Planning	
Decision making	B. Inherent in planning, directing, controlling, and improving
	C. Long-range courses of action

SHOW ME HOW

2. Direct materials, direct labor, and factory overhead   Obj. 2

Identify the following costs as direct materials (DM), direct labor (DL), or factory overhead (FO) for an automobile manufacturer:

A. Wages of employees that operate painting equipment

B. Wages of the plant manager

C. Steel

D. Oil used for assembly line machinery

SHOW ME HOW

3. Prime and conversion costs   Obj. 2

Identify the following costs as a prime cost (P), conversion cost (C), or both (B) for an automobile manufacturer:

A. Wages of employees that operate painting equipment

B. Wages of the plant manager

C. Steel

D. Oil used for assembly line machinery

SHOW ME HOW

4. Product and period costs   Obj. 2

Identify the following costs as a product cost or a period cost for an automobile manufacturer:

A. Steel

B. Wages of employees that operate painting equipment

C. Rent on office building

D. Sales staff salaries

5. Cost of goods sold, cost of goods manufactured   Obj. 4

Timbuk 3 Company has the following information for March:

Cost of direct materials used in production	$21,000
Direct labor	54,250
Factory overhead	35,000
Work in process inventory, March 1	87,500
Work in process inventory, March 31	92,750
Finished goods inventory, March 1	36,750
Finished goods inventory, March 31	42,000

For March, determine (A) the cost of goods manufactured and (B) the cost of goods sold.

Answers provided after Problem. Need more practice? Find additional multiple-choice questions, exercises, and problems in CengageNOWv2.

Problem

The following is a list of costs that were incurred in producing this textbook:

A. Insurance on the factory building and equipment

B. Salary of the vice president of finance

C. Hourly wages of printing press operators during production

D. Straight-line depreciation on the printing presses used to manufacture the text

E. Electricity used to run the presses during the printing of the text

F. Sales commissions paid to textbook representatives for each text sold

G. Paper on which the text is printed

H. Book covers used to bind the pages

I. Straight-line depreciation on an office building

J. Salaries of staff used to develop artwork for the text

K. Glue used to bind pages to cover

Instructions

With respect to the manufacture and sale of this text, classify each cost as either a product cost or a period cost. Indicate whether each product cost is a direct materials cost, a direct labor cost, or a factory overhead cost. Indicate whether each period cost is a selling expense or an administrative expense.

Need more practice? Find additional multiple-choice questions, exercises, and problems in CengageNOWv2.

Answers

Multiple-Choice Questions

1. **B** Managerial accounting is not restricted to generally accepted accounting principles, as is financial accounting (answer B). Both financial and managerial accounting support decision making (answer A). Financial accounting is mostly concerned with the decision making of external users, while managerial accounting supports decision making of management. Both financial and managerial accounting can result in financial reports (answer C). Managerial accounting reports are developed for internal use by managers at various levels in the organization. Both managerial and financial accounting record events from the past (answer D); however, managerial accounting can also include information about the future in the form of budgets and cash flow projections.

2. **D** The five basic phases of the management process are planning (answer A), directing (not listed), controlling (answer B), improving (not listed), and decision making (answer C). Operating (answer D) is not one of the five basic phases, but operations are the object of managers' attention.

3. **C** Sales salaries (answer C) is a selling expense and is not considered a cost of manufacturing a product. Direct materials cost (answer A), factory overhead cost (answer B), and direct labor cost (answer D) are costs of manufacturing a product.

4. **B** Depreciation of testing equipment (answer B) is included as part of the factory overhead costs of the microcomputer manufacturer. The cost of memory chips (answer A) and the cost of disk drives (answer D) are both considered a part of direct materials cost. The wages of microcomputer assemblers (answer C) are part of direct labor costs.

5. **C** Cost of goods sold is calculated as follows:

Beginning finished goods inventory	$ 50,000
Cost of goods manufactured	125,000
Ending finished goods inventory	(35,000)
Cost of goods sold	$140,000

Exercises

1. Controlling (A)
   Planning (C)
   Decision making (B)

2. A. DL
   B. FO
   C. DM
   D. FO

3. A. B
   B. C
   C. P
   D. C

4. A. Product cost
   B. Product cost
   C. Period cost
   D. Period cost

5. A.

Work in process inventory, March 1		$ 87,500
Cost of direct materials used in production	$21,000	
Direct labor	54,250	
Factory overhead	35,000	
Total manufacturing costs incurred in March		110,250
Total manufacturing costs		$197,750
Work in process inventory, March 31		(92,750)
Cost of goods manufactured		$105,000

   B.

Finished goods inventory, March 1	$ 36,750
Cost of goods manufactured	105,000
Cost of finished goods available for sale	$141,750
Finished goods inventory, March 31	(42,000)
Cost of goods sold	$ 99,750

Need more help? Watch step-by-step videos of how to compute answers to these Exercises in CengageNOWv2.

Problem

	Product Cost			Period Cost	
Cost	Direct Materials Cost	Direct Labor Cost	Factory Overhead Cost	Selling Expense	Administrative Expense
A.			X		
B.					X
C.		X			
D.			X		
E.			X		
F.				X	
G.	X				
H.	X				
I.					X
J.			X		
K.			X		

Discussion Questions

1. What are the major differences between managerial accounting and financial accounting?

2. A. Differentiate between a department with line responsibility and a department with staff responsibility.

   B. In an organization that has a Sales Department and a Personnel Department, among others, which of the two departments has (1) line responsibility and (2) staff responsibility?

3. What manufacturing cost term is used to describe the cost of materials that are an integral part of the manufactured end product?

4. Distinguish between prime costs and conversion costs.

5. What is the difference between a product cost and a period cost?

6. Name the three inventory accounts for a manufacturing business, and describe what each balance represents at the end of an accounting period.

7. In what order should the three inventories of a manufacturing business be presented on the balance sheet?

8. What are the three categories of manufacturing costs included in the cost of finished goods and the cost of work in process?

9. Describe sustainability and sustainable business practices.

10. How does the Cost of Goods Sold section of the income statement differ between merchandising and manufacturing companies?

Basic Exercises

SHOW ME HOW

BE 15-1   Management process   Obj. 1

Three phases of the management process are planning, directing, and controlling. Match the following descriptions to the proper phase:

Phase of Management Process	Description
Planning	A. Developing long-range courses of action to achieve goals
Directing	B. Isolating significant departures from plans for further investigation and possible remedial action; may lead to a revision of future plans
Controlling	C. Process by which managers, given their assigned levels of responsibilities, run day-to-day operations

SHOW ME HOW

BE 15-2 Direct materials, direct labor, and factory overhead

Obj. 2

Identify the following costs as direct materials (DM), direct labor (DL), or factory overhead (FO) for a magazine publisher:

A. Staples used to bind magazines

B. Wages of printing machine employees

C. Maintenance on printing machines

D. Paper used in the magazine

SHOW ME HOW

BE 15-3 Prime and conversion costs

Obj. 2

Identify the following costs as a prime cost (P), conversion cost (C), or both (B) for a magazine publisher:

A. Paper used for the magazine

B. Wages of printing machine employees

C. Glue used to bind magazine

D. Maintenance on printing machines

SHOW ME HOW

BE 15-4 Product and period costs

Obj. 2

Identify the following costs as a product cost or a period cost for a magazine publisher:

A. Sales salaries

B. Paper used for the magazine

C. Maintenance on printing machines

D. Depreciation expense—corporate headquarters

SHOW ME HOW

BE 15-5 Cost of goods sold, cost of goods manufactured

Obj. 4

Glenville Company has the following information for April:

Cost of direct materials used in production	$280,000
Direct labor	324,000
Factory overhead	188,900
Work in process inventory, April 1	72,300
Work in process inventory, April 30	76,600
Finished goods inventory, April 1	39,600
Finished goods inventory, April 30	41,200

For April, determine (A) the cost of goods manufactured and (B) the cost of goods sold.

Exercises

EX 15-1 Classifying costs as materials, labor, or factory overhead

Obj. 2

Indicate whether each of the following costs of an automobile manufacturer would be classified as direct materials cost, direct labor cost, or factory overhead cost:

A. Depreciation of robotic assembly line equipment

B. V8 automobile engine

C. Steering wheel

D. Wheels

E. Painting safety masks for employees working in the paint room

F. Salary of test driver

G. Glass used in the vehicle's windshield

H. Wages of assembly line worker

REAL WORLD

EX 15-2 Classifying costs as materials, labor, or factory overhead   Obj. 2

Indicate whether the following costs of **Procter & Gamble**, a maker of consumer products, would be classified as direct materials cost, direct labor cost, or factory overhead cost:

A. Plant manager salary for the Iowa City, Iowa, plant

B. Maintenance supplies

C. Salary of process engineers

D. Wages paid to Packaging Department employees in the Bear River City, Utah, paper products plant

E. Scents and fragrances used in making soaps and detergents

F. Wages of production line employees at the Pineville, Louisiana, soap and detergent plant

G. Depreciation on assembly line in the Mehoopany, Pennsylvania, paper products plant

H. Packaging materials

I. Resins for body wash products

J. Depreciation on the Auburn, Maine, manufacturing plant

REAL WORLD

EX 15-3 Classifying costs as factory overhead   Obj. 2

Which of the following items are properly classified as part of factory overhead for **Ford Motor Company**, a maker of heavy automobiles and trucks?

A. Plant manager's salary at Buffalo, New York, stamping plant, which manufactures auto and truck subassemblies

B. Depreciation on Flat Rock, Michigan, assembly plant

C. Dividends paid to shareholders

D. Machine lubricant used to maintain the assembly line at the Louisville, Kentucky, assembly plant

E. Leather to be used on vehicles that have leather interiors

F. Depreciation on mechanical robots used on the assembly line

G. Consultant fees for a study of production line efficiency

H. Dealership sales incentives

I. Vice president of human resources's salary

J. Property taxes on the Dearborn, Michigan, headquarters building

REAL WORLD

EX 15-4 Classifying costs as product or period costs   Obj. 2

For apparel manufacturer **Abercrombie & Fitch, Inc.**, classify each of the following costs as either a product cost or a period cost:

A. Research and development costs

B. Depreciation on sewing machines

C. Fabric used during production

D. Depreciation on office equipment

E. Advertising expenses

F. Repairs and maintenance costs for sewing machines

G. Salary of production quality control supervisor

H. Utility costs for office building

I. Sales commissions

J. Salaries of distribution center personnel

K. Wages of sewing machine operators

L. Factory janitorial supplies

M. Chief financial officer's salary

N. Travel costs of media relations employees

O. Factory supervisors' salaries

P. Oil used to lubricate sewing machines

Q. Property taxes on factory building and equipment

EX 15-5   Concepts and terminology

Obj. 1, 2, 4

From the choices presented in parentheses, choose the appropriate term for completing each of the following sentences:

A. Advertising costs are usually viewed as (period, product) costs.

B. Feedback is often used to (improve, direct) operations.

C. Payments of cash or the commitment to pay cash in the future for the purpose of generating revenues are (costs, expenses).

D. A product, sales territory, department, or activity to which costs are traced is called a (direct cost, cost object).

E. The balance sheet of a manufacturer would include an account for (cost of goods sold, work in process inventory).

F. Factory overhead costs combined with direct labor costs are called (prime, conversion) costs.

G. The implementation of automatic, robotic factory equipment normally (increases, decreases) the direct labor component of product costs.

EX 15-6   Concepts and terminology

Obj. 1, 2

From the choices presented in parentheses, choose the appropriate term for completing each of the following sentences:

A. The phase of the management process that uses process information to eliminate the source of problems in a process so that the process delivers the correct product in the correct quantities is called (directing, improving).

B. Direct labor costs combined with factory overhead costs are called (prime, conversion) costs.

C. The salaries of sales people are normally considered a (period, product) cost.

D. The plant manager's salary would be considered (direct, indirect) to the product.

E. Long-term plans are called (strategic, operational) plans.

F. Materials for use in production are called (supplies, materials inventory).

G. An example of factory overhead is (electricity used to run assembly line, CEO salary).

EX 15-7   Classifying costs in a service company

Obj. 2

A partial list of the costs for Wisconsin and Minnesota Railroad, a short hauler of freight, follows. Classify each cost as either indirect or direct. For purposes of classifying each cost, use the train as the cost object.

A. Cost to lease (rent) railroad cars

B. Cost of track and bed (ballast) replacement

C. Diesel fuel costs

D. Cost to lease (rent) train locomotives

E. Depreciation of terminal facilities

F. Maintenance costs of right of way, bridges, and buildings

G. Salaries of dispatching and communications personnel

H. Headquarters information technology support staff salaries

I. Safety training costs

J. Wages of train engineers

K. Wages of switch and classification yard personnel

L. Costs of accident cleanup

EX 15-8   Sustainability and Eco-Efficiency Measures

Obj. 3

Four types of eco-efficiency measures are identified below. Match the following descriptions to the proper eco-efficiency measures:

1. Energy Efficiency
2. Fuel Efficiency
3. Material Use Efficiency
4. Waste Efficiency

A. Cost savings from recycling and reusing waste and by-product materials

B. Cost savings from reducing the amount of product packaging materials

C. Cost savings from replacing lighting fixtures in a production facility with energy-efficient lighting

D. Cost savings from replacing gas-powered vehicles with hybrid or alternative energy-source vehicles

EX 15-9 Classifying costs

Obj. 2, 4

The following is a manufacturing cost report of Marching Ants Inc. Evaluate and correct this report.

Marching Ants Inc.
Manufacturing Costs
For the Quarter Ended June 30

Materials used in production (including $56,200 of indirect materials)	$ 607,500
Direct labor (including $84,400 maintenance salaries)........	562,500
Factory overhead:	
Supervisor salaries—plant	517,500
Heat, light, and power—plant............................	140,650
Sales salaries	348,750
Promotional expenses...................................	315,000
Insurance and property taxes—plant	151,900
Insurance and property taxes—corporate offices	219,400
Depreciation—plant and equipment	123,750
Depreciation—corporate offices	90,000
Total	$3,076,950

EX 15-10 Financial statements of a manufacturing firm

Obj. 4

✔ A. Net income,
$145,000

SHOW ME HOW

The following events took place for Digital Vibe Manufacturing Company during March, the first month of its operations as a producer of digital video monitors:

A. Purchased $168,500 of materials.

B. Used $149,250 of direct materials in production.

C. Incurred $360,000 of direct labor wages.

D. Incurred $120,000 of factory overhead.

E. Transferred $600,000 of work in process to finished goods.

F. Sold goods for $875,000.

G. Sold goods with a cost of $525,000.

H. Incurred $125,000 of selling expense.

I. Incurred $80,000 of administrative expense.

Using the information given, complete the following:

A. Prepare the March income statement for Digital Vibe Manufacturing Company.

B. Determine the inventory balances at the end of the first month of operations.

EX 15-11 Manufacturing company balance sheet

Obj. 4

SHOW ME HOW

Partial balance sheet data for Diesel Additives Company at August 31 are as follows:

Finished goods inventory	$ 89,400	Supplies	$ 13,800
Prepaid insurance	9,000	Materials inventory	26,800
Accounts receivable	348,200	Cash	167,500
Work in process inventory	61,100		

Prepare the Current Assets section of Diesel Additives Company's balance sheet at August 31.

EX 15-12 Cost of direct materials used in production for a manufacturing company

Obj. 4

SHOW ME HOW

Okaboji Manufacturing Company reported the following materials data for the month ending November 30:

Materials purchased	$490,900
Materials inventory, November 1	64,900
Materials inventory, November 30	81,300

Determine the cost of direct materials used in production by Okaboji during the month ended November 30.

EX 15-13   Cost of goods manufactured for a manufacturing company   Obj. 4

Two items are omitted from each of the following three lists of cost of goods manufactured statement data. Determine the amounts of the missing items, identifying them by letter.

Work in process inventory, August 1	$ 19,660	$ 41,650	(E)
Total manufacturing costs incurred during August	332,750	(C)	1,075,000
Total manufacturing costs	(A)	$515,770	$1,240,000
Work in process inventory, August 31	23,500	54,000	(F)
Cost of goods manufactured	(B)	(D)	$1,068,000

EX 15-14   Cost of goods manufactured for a manufacturing company   Obj. 4

The following information is available for Ethtridge Manufacturing Company for the month ending July 31:

Cost of direct materials used in production	$1,150,000
Direct labor	966,000
Work in process inventory, July 1	316,400
Work in process inventory, July 31	355,500
Total factory overhead	490,500

Determine Ethtridge's cost of goods manufactured for the month ended July 31.

EX 15-15   Income statement for a manufacturing company   Obj. 4

Two items are omitted from each of the following three lists of cost of goods sold data from a manufacturing company income statement. Determine the amounts of the missing items, identifying them by letter.

Finished goods inventory, June 1	$116,600	$ 38,880	(E)
Cost of goods manufactured	825,900	(C)	180,000
Cost of finished goods available for sale	(A)	$540,000	$1,100,000
Finished goods inventory, June 30	130,000	70,000	(F)
Cost of goods sold	(B)	(D)	$ 945,000

EX 15-16   Statement of cost of goods manufactured for a manufacturing company   Obj. 4

Cost data for Sandusky Manufacturing Company for the month ended January 31 are as follows:

Inventories	January 1	January 31
Materials	$180,000	$145,500
Work in process	334,600	290,700
Finished goods	675,000	715,000

Direct labor	$2,260,000
Materials purchased during January	1,375,000
Factory overhead incurred during January:	
Indirect labor	115,000
Machinery depreciation	90,000
Heat, light, and power	55,000
Supplies	18,500
Property taxes	10,000
Miscellaneous costs	33,100

A. Prepare a cost of goods manufactured statement for January.

B. Determine the cost of goods sold for January.

EX 15-17   Cost of goods sold, profit margin, and net income for a manufacturing company

Obj. 4

The following information is available for Bandera Manufacturing Company for the month ending January 31:

Cost of goods manufactured	$4,490,000
Selling expenses	530,000
Administrative expenses	340,000
Sales	6,600,000
Finished goods inventory, January 1	880,000
Finished goods inventory, January 31	775,000

For the month ended January 31, determine Bandera Manufacturing's (A) cost of goods sold, (B) gross profit, and (C) net income.

EX 15-18   Cost flow relationships

Obj. 4

The following information is available for the first month of operations of Bahadir Company, a manufacturer of mechanical pencils:

Sales	$792,000
Gross profit	462,000
Cost of goods manufactured	396,000
Indirect labor	171,600
Factory depreciation	26,400
Materials purchased	244,200
Total manufacturing costs for the period	455,400
Materials inventory, ending	33,000

Using the information given, determine the following missing amounts:

A. Cost of goods sold

B. Finished goods inventory at the end of the month

C. Direct materials cost

D. Direct labor cost

E. Work in process inventory at the end of the month

Problems: Series A

PR 15-1A   Classifying costs

Obj. 2

The following is a list of costs that were incurred in the production and sale of large commercial airplanes:

A. Salary of chief compliance officer of company

B. Power used by painting equipment

C. Instrument panel installed in the airplane cockpit

D. Annual bonus paid to the chief operating officer of the company

E. Turbo-charged airplane engine

F. Interior trim material used throughout the airplane cabin

G. Cost of normal scrap from production of airplane body

H. Hourly wages of employees that assemble the airplane

I. Salary of the Marketing Department personnel

J. Cost of paving the headquarters employee parking lot

K. Cost of electrical wiring throughout the airplane

L. Cost of electronic guidance system installed in the airplane cockpit

M. Salary of plant manager

N. Cost of miniature replicas of the airplane used to promote and market the airplane

O. Human Resources Department costs for the year

P. Metal used for producing the airplane body

Q. Annual fee to a celebrity to promote the aircraft

R. Hydraulic pumps used in the airplane's flight control system

S. Yearly cost of the maintenance contract for robotic equipment

T. Prebuilt leather seats installed in the first-class cabin

U. Depreciation on factory equipment

V. Special advertising campaign in *Aviation World* magazine

W. Oil to lubricate factory equipment

X. Masks for use by painters in painting the airplane body

Y. Decals for cockpit door, the cost of which is immaterial to the cost of the final product

Z. Salary of chief financial officer

Instructions

Classify each cost as either a product cost or a period cost. Indicate whether each product cost is a direct materials cost, a direct labor cost, or a factory overhead cost. Indicate whether each period cost is a selling expense or an administrative expense. Use the following tabular headings for your answer, placing an "X" in the appropriate column:

	Product Costs			Period Costs	
Cost	Direct Materials Cost	Direct Labor Cost	Factory Overhead Cost	Selling Expense	Administrative Expense

PR 15-2A   Classifying costs   Obj. 2

The following is a list of costs incurred by several businesses:

A. Cost of fabric used by clothing manufacturer

B. Maintenance and repair costs for factory equipment

C. Rent for a warehouse used to store work in process and finished products

D. Wages of production quality control personnel

E. Oil lubricants for factory plant and equipment

F. Depreciation of robot used to assemble a product

G. Travel costs of marketing executives to annual sales meeting

H. Depreciation of copying machines used by the Marketing Department

I. Fees charged by collection agency on past-due customer accounts

J. Electricity used to operate factory machinery

K. Maintenance costs for factory equipment

L. Pens, paper, and other supplies used by the Accounting Department in preparing various managerial reports

M. Charitable contribution to United Fund

N. Depreciation of microcomputers used in the factory to coordinate and monitor the production schedules

O. Fees paid to lawn service for office grounds upkeep

P. Cost of sewing machine needles used by a shirt manufacturer

Q. Cost of plastic for a telephone being manufactured

R. Telephone charges by president's office

S. Cost of 30-second television commercial

T. Surgeon's fee for heart bypass surgery

U. Depreciation of tools used in production

V. Wages of a machine operator on the production line

W. Salary of the vice president of manufacturing operations

X. Factory janitorial supplies

(Continued)

Instructions

Classify each of the preceding costs as a product cost or period cost. Indicate whether each product cost is a direct materials cost, a direct labor cost, or a factory overhead cost. Indicate whether each period cost is a selling expense or an administrative expense. Use the following tabular headings for preparing your answer, placing an "X" in the appropriate column:

	Product Costs			Period Costs	
Cost	Direct Materials Cost	Direct Labor Cost	Factory Overhead Cost	Selling Expense	Administrative Expense

PR 15-3A Cost classifications for a service company

Obj. 2

A partial list of Foothills Medical Center's costs follows:

A. Cost of patient meals

B. Nurses' salaries

C. Depreciation of X-ray equipment

D. Utility costs of the hospital

E. Salary of intensive care personnel

F. Cost of X-ray test

G. Operating room supplies used on patients (catheters, sutures, etc.)

H. Salary of the nutritionist

I. General maintenance of the hospital

J. Cost of new heart wing

K. Cost of drugs used for patients

L. Cost of advertising hospital services on television

M. Cost of improvements on the employee parking lot

N. Cost of intravenous solutions used for patients

O. Training costs for nurses

P. Cost of laundry services for operating room personnel

Q. Doctor's fee

R. Overtime incurred in the Patient Records Department due to a computer failure

S. Cost of blood tests

T. Cost of maintaining the staff and visitors' cafeteria

U. Depreciation on patient rooms

Instructions

1. What would be Foothills Medical Center's most logical definition for the final cost object?

2. Identify whether each of the costs is to be classified as direct or indirect. For purposes of classifying each cost as direct or indirect, use the patient as the cost object.

PR 15-4A Manufacturing income statement, statement of cost of goods manufactured

Obj. 4

✔ 1. B. Yakima Company, $1,330,000

EXCEL TEMPLATE

Several items are omitted from the income statement and cost of goods manufactured statement data for two different companies for the month of May:

	Rainier Company	Yakima Company
Materials inventory, May 1	$ 100,000	$ 48,200
Materials inventory, May 31	(A)	50,000
Materials purchased	950,000	710,000
Cost of direct materials used in production	938,500	(A)
Direct labor	2,860,000	(B)
Factory overhead	1,800,000	446,000
Total manufacturing costs incurred in May	(B)	2,484,200

	Rainier Company	Yakima Company
Total manufacturing costs	5,998,500	2,660,600
Work in process inventory, May 1	400,000	176,400
Work in process inventory, May 31	382,000	(C)
Cost of goods manufactured	(C)	2,491,500
Finished goods inventory, May 1	$ 615,000	$ 190,000
Finished goods inventory, May 31	596,500	(D)
Sales	9,220,000	4,550,000
Cost of goods sold	(D)	2,470,000
Gross profit	(E)	(E)
Operating expenses	1,000,000	(F)
Net income	(F)	1,500,000

Instructions

1. For both companies, determine the amounts of the missing items (A) through (F), identifying them by letter.

2. Prepare Yakima Company's statement of cost of goods manufactured for May.

3. Prepare Yakima Company's income statement for May.

PR 15-5A Statement of cost of goods manufactured and income statement for a manufacturing company

Obj. 4

✔ 1. Cost of goods manufactured, $1,989,250

The following information is available for Robstown Corporation for 20Y8:

SHOW ME HOW   EXCEL TEMPLATE

Inventories	January 1	December 31
Materials	$ 44,250	$31,700
Work in process	63,900	80,000
Finished goods	101,200	99,800

Advertising expense	$ 400,000
Depreciation expense—office equipment	30,000
Depreciation expense—factory equipment	80,000
Direct labor	1,100,000
Heat, light, and power—factory	53,300
Indirect labor	115,000
Materials purchased	556,600
Office salaries expense	318,000
Property taxes—factory	40,000
Property taxes—office building	25,000
Rent expense—factory	27,000
Sales	3,850,000
Sales salaries expense	200,000
Supplies—factory	9,500
Miscellaneous costs—factory	11,400

Instructions

1. Prepare the 20Y8 statement of cost of goods manufactured.

2. Prepare the 20Y8 income statement.

Problems: Series B

PR 15-1B   Classifying costs
Obj. 2

The following is a list of costs that were incurred in the production and sale of lawn mowers:

A.   Premiums on insurance policy for factory buildings

B.   Tires for lawn mowers

C.   Filter for spray gun used to paint the lawn mowers

D.   Paint used to coat the lawn mowers, the cost of which is immaterial to the cost of the final product

E.   Plastic for outside housing of lawn mowers

F.   Salary of factory supervisor

G.   Hourly wages of operators of robotic machinery used in production

H.   Engine oil used in mower engines prior to shipment

I.   Salary of vice president of marketing

J.   Property taxes on the factory building and equipment

K.   Cost of advertising in a national magazine

L.   Gasoline engines used for lawn mowers

M.   Electricity used to run the robotic machinery

N.   Straight-line depreciation on the robotic machinery used to manufacture the lawn mowers

O.   Salary of quality control supervisor who inspects each lawn mower before it is shipped

P.   Attorney fees for drafting a new lease for headquarters offices

Q.   Payroll taxes on hourly assembly line employees

R.   Telephone charges for company controller's office

S.   Steering wheels for lawn mowers

T.   Factory cafeteria cashier's wages

U.   Cash paid to outside firm for janitorial services for factory

V.   Maintenance costs for new robotic factory equipment, based on hours of usage

W.   Cost of boxes used in packaging lawn mowers

X.   License fees for use of patent for lawn mower blade, based on the number of lawn mowers produced

Y.   Steel used in producing the lawn mowers

Z.   Commissions paid to sales representatives, based on the number of lawn mowers sold

Instructions

Classify each cost as either a product cost or a period cost. Indicate whether each product cost is a direct materials cost, a direct labor cost, or a factory overhead cost. Indicate whether each period cost is a selling expense or an administrative expense. Use the following tabular headings for your answer, placing an "X" in the appropriate column:

	Product Costs			Period Costs	
Cost	Direct Materials Cost	Direct Labor Cost	Factory Overhead Cost	Selling Expense	Administrative Expense

---

PR 15-2B   Classifying costs
Obj. 2

The following is a list of costs incurred by several businesses:

A.   Salary of quality control supervisor

B.   Packing supplies for products sold. These supplies are a very small portion of the total cost of the product.

C.   Factory operating supplies

D.   Depreciation of factory equipment

E.   Hourly wages of warehouse laborers

F.   Wages of company controller's secretary

G.   Maintenance and repair costs for factory equipment

H. Paper used by commercial printer

I. Entertainment expenses for sales representatives

J. Protective glasses for factory machine operators

K. Sales commissions

L. Cost of hogs for meat processor

M. Cost of telephone operators for a toll-free hotline to help customers operate products

N. Hard drives for a microcomputer manufacturer

O. Lumber used by furniture manufacturer

P. Wages of a machine operator on the production line

Q. First-aid supplies for factory workers

R. Tires for an automobile manufacturer

S. Paper used by Computer Department in processing various managerial reports

T. Seed for grain farmer

U. Health insurance premiums paid for factory workers

V. Costs of operating a research laboratory

W. Costs for television advertisement

X. Executive bonus for vice president of marketing

Instructions

Classify each of the preceding costs as a product cost or period cost. Indicate whether each product cost is a direct materials cost, a direct labor cost, or a factory overhead cost. Indicate whether each period cost is a selling expense or an administrative expense. Use the following tabular headings for preparing your answer. Place an "X" in the appropriate column.

	Product Costs			Period Costs	
Cost	Direct Materials Cost	Direct Labor Cost	Factory Overhead Cost	Selling Expense	Administrative Expense

PR 15-3B Cost classifications for a service company
Obj. 2

A partial list of The Grand Hotel's costs follows:

A. Cost to mail a customer survey

B. Wages of convention setup employees

C. Pay-per-view movie rental costs (in rooms)

D. Cost of food

E. Cost of room mini-bar supplies

F. Training for hotel restaurant servers

G. Cost to paint lobby

H. Cost of laundering towels and bedding

I. Champagne for guests

J. Salary of the hotel manager

K. Depreciation of the hotel

L. Cost of valet parking

M. Wages of bellhops

N. Cost to replace lobby furniture

O. Cost of advertising in local newspaper

P. Wages of desk clerks

Q. Wages of maids

R. Cost of new carpeting

S. Guest room telephone costs for long-distance calls

T. Cost of soaps and shampoos for rooms

U. Utility cost

(Continued)

V. Wages of kitchen employees

W. General maintenance supplies

Instructions

1. What would be The Grand Hotel's most logical definition for the final cost object?

2. Identify whether each of the costs is to be classified as direct or indirect. For purposes of classifying each cost as direct or indirect, use the hotel guest as the cost object.

PR 15-4B Manufacturing income statement, statement of cost of goods manufactured

Obj. 4

✔ 1. C. On Company, $800,800

EXCEL TEMPLATE

Several items are omitted from the income statement and cost of goods manufactured statement data for two different companies for the month of December:

	On Company	Off Company
Materials inventory, December 1	$ 65,800	$ 195,300
Materials inventory, December 31	(A)	91,140
Materials purchased	282,800	(A)
Cost of direct materials used in production	317,800	(B)
Direct labor	387,800	577,220
Factory overhead	148,400	256,060
Total manufacturing costs incurred in December	(B)	1,519,000
Total manufacturing costs	973,000	1,727,320
Work in process inventory, December 1	119,000	208,320
Work in process inventory, December 31	172,200	(C)
Cost of goods manufactured	(C)	1,532,020
Finished goods inventory, December 1	224,000	269,080
Finished goods inventory, December 31	197,400	(D)
Sales	1,127,000	1,944,320
Cost of goods sold	(D)	1,545,040
Gross profit	(E)	(E)
Operating expenses	117,600	(F)
Net income	(F)	164,920

Instructions

1. For both companies, determine the amounts of the missing items (A) through (F), identifying them by letter.

2. Prepare On Company's statement of cost of goods manufactured for December.

3. Prepare On Company's income statement for December.

PR 15-5B Statement of cost of goods manufactured and income statement for a manufacturing company

Obj. 4

✔ 1. Cost of goods manufactured, $367,510

SHOW ME HOW   EXCEL TEMPLATE

The following information is available for Shanika Company for 20Y6:

Inventories	January 1	December 31
Materials	$ 77,350	$ 95,550
Work in process	109,200	96,200
Finished goods	113,750	100,100
Advertising expense		$ 68,250
Depreciation expense—office equipment		22,750
Depreciation expense—factory equipment		14,560
Direct labor		186,550
Heat, light, and power—factory		5,850
Indirect labor		23,660
Materials purchased		123,500

Inventories	January 1	December 31
Office salaries expense		77,350
Property taxes—factory		4,095
Property taxes—headquarters building		13,650
Rent expense—factory		6,825
Sales		864,500
Sales salaries expense		136,500
Supplies—factory		3,250
Miscellaneous costs—factory		4,420

Instructions

1. Prepare the 20Y6 statement of cost of goods manufactured.
2. Prepare the 20Y6 income statement.

Analysis for Decision Making

REAL WORLD

ADM-1   Hilton Hotels and Marriott International: Occupancy

A recent annual report of **Hilton Hotels** and **Marriott International** provided the following occupancy data for two recent years:

	Year 2	Year 1
Hilton Hotels	74.6%	72.2%
Marriott International	73.3%	71.3%

A. Is the occupancy trend favorable or unfavorable for Hilton Hotels?
B. Is the occupancy trend favorable or unfavorable for Marriott International?
C. Which company has the stronger occupancy?
D. ➤ What additional information would supplement occupancy in evaluating the performance of these two hotels?

ADM-2   Comparing occupancy for two hotels

Sunrise Suites and Nationwide Inns operate competing hotel chains across the region. Hotel capacity information for both hotels is as follows:

	Number of Hotels	Average Number of Rooms per Hotel
Sunrise Suites	120	90
Nationwide Inns	150	76

Information on the number of guests for each hotel and the average length of visit for June were as follows:

	Number of Guests	Average Length of Visit (in Nights)
Sunrise Suites	183,600	1.5
Nationwide Inns	228,000	1.2

A. Determine the guest nights for each hotel in June.
B. Determine the room nights for each hotel in June.
C. Determine the occupancy rate of each hotel in June.
D. ➤ Interpret the results in (C).

ADM-3   Occupancy for a hospital

The Valley Hospital measures the in-patient occupancy of the hospital by determining the number of patient days divided by the number of available bed days in the hospital for a time period. The following in-patient data are available for the months of April, May, and June:

	April	May	June
Admitted patients	1,440	1,860	2,250
Average length of stay per patient	4.0 days	3.5 days	3.0 days

The hospital has 200 rooms. One hundred rooms are private and have a single bed per room. The other hundred rooms are semi-private with two beds per room.

A. Determine the number of in-patient days for each month.

B. Determine the available bed days rate for each month.

C. Determine the occupancy rate for each month.

D. ▬▬▶ Interpret the results in (C).

ADM-4   Passenger load on a flight

Eastern Skies Airlines has three flights that depart from New York City and arrive in Chicago every day. The three flights are as follows:

Flight Number	Flight Departure Time	Flight Frequency
57	8:00 AM	7 days per week
85	10:00 AM	7 days per week
94	11:30 AM	7 days per week

Each flight uses a jet with a capacity of 180 seats. The airline measures the utilization of the aircraft by passenger load. Passenger load is the number of seats sold divided by the number of available seats on a flight for a time period. The following operating data are available for June:

Flight Number	Number of Seats Sold
57	5,130
85	2,592
94	2,376

A. Determine the available seat capacity for each flight number for June.

B. Determine the passenger load for each flight number for June.

C. ▬▬▶ What recommendations could you provide Eastern Skies based on the passenger load data?

Take It Further

ETHICS

TIF 15-1   Ethics in Action

Avett Manufacturing Company allows employees to purchase materials, such as metal and lumber, for personal use at a price equal to the company's cost. To purchase materials, an employee must complete a materials requisition form, which must then be approved by the employee's immediate supervisor. Brian Dadian, an assistant cost accountant, then charges the employee an amount based on Avett's net purchase cost.

Brian is in the process of replacing a deck on his home and has requisitioned lumber for personal use, which has been approved in accordance with company policy. In computing the cost of the lumber, Brian reviewed all the purchase invoices for the past year. He then used the lowest price to compute the amount due the company for the lumber.

The Institute of Management Accountants (IMA) is the professional organization for managerial accountants. The IMA has established four principles of ethical conduct for its members: honesty, fairness, objectivity, and responsibility. These principles are available at the IMA Web site: www.imanet.org.

➤ Using the IMA's four principles of ethical conduct, evaluate Brian's behavior. Has he acted in an ethical manner? Why?

REAL WORLD

TIF 15-2 Team Activity

In teams, visit a local restaurant. As you observe the operation, consider the costs associated with running the business. As a group, identify as many costs as you can and classify them according to the following table headings:

Cost	Direct Materials	Direct Labor	Overhead	Selling Expenses

TIF 15-3 Communication

Todd Johnson is the Vice President of Finance for Boz Zeppelin Industries Inc. At a recent finance meeting, Todd made the following statement: "The managers of a company should use the same information as the shareholders of the firm. When managers use the same information to guide their internal operations as shareholders use in evaluating their investments, the managers will be aligned with the stockholders' profit objectives."

➤ Prepare a one-half page memo to Todd discussing any concerns you might have with his statement.

Concepts and Principles

Chapter 15 *Introduction to Managerial Accounting*

Developing Information

COST SYSTEMS	COST BEHAVIOR
Chapter 16 *Job Order Costing*	**Chapter 19** *Cost-Volume-Profit Analysis*
Chapter 17 *Process Cost Systems*	
Chapter 18 *Activity-Based Costing*	

Decision Making

EVALUATING PERFORMANCE	COMPARING ALTERNATIVES
Chapter 20 *Variable Costing for Management Analysis*	**Chapter 24** *Differential Analysis and Product Pricing*
Chapter 21 *Budgeting*	**Chapter 25** *Capital Investment Analysis*
Chapter 22 *Evaluating Variances from Standard Costs*	**Chapter 26** *Lean Manufacturing*
Chapter 23 *Evaluating Decentralized Operations*	

ANTONIODIAZ/SHUTTERSTOCK.COM

Gibson Guitars

The selling price of a Gibson guitar ranges from less than $500 to over $11,000 for a Gibson 2015 Wes Montgomery electric guitar. These differences in selling prices reflect the quality of the materials and the craftsmanship required in making a guitar. In all cases, however, the selling price of a guitar must be greater than the cost of producing it. So, how does **Gibson** determine the cost of producing a guitar?

Costs associated with creating a guitar include materials such as wood and strings, the wages of employees who build the guitar, and factory overhead. To determine the purchase price of a guitar, Gibson identifies and records the costs that go into the guitar during each step of the manufacturing process. As the guitar moves through the production process, the costs of direct materials, direct labor, and factory overhead are recorded. When the guitar is complete, the costs that have been recorded are added up to determine the cost of the guitar. The company then prices the guitar to achieve a level of profit (or revenue greater than the cost of the guitar).

This chapter describes a job order cost accounting system that illustrates how costs could be recorded and accumulated in manufacturing a guitar. The chapter also describes how a job order cost system could be used by service businesses.

Source: http://www.gibson.com/Gibson/History.aspx

Job Order Costing

Cost Accounting Systems Overview	**Job Order Cost Systems for Manufacturing Businesses**	**Job Order Cost Systems for Service Businesses**
■ Job Order Cost Systems (Obj. 1)	■ Materials (Obj. 2)	■ Job Order Service Businesses (Obj. 3)
■ Process Cost Systems (Obj. 1)	■ Factory Labor (Obj. 2)	■ Flow of Costs (Obj. 3)
	■ Factory Overhead (Obj. 2)	
	■ Work in Process (Obj. 2)	
	■ Finished Goods (Obj. 2)	
	■ Sales and Cost of Goods Sold (Obj. 2)	
	■ Period Costs (Obj. 2)	

Learning Objectives

Obj. 1 Describe cost accounting systems used by manufacturing businesses.

Obj. 2 Describe and illustrate a job order cost accounting system for a manufacturing business.

Obj. 3 Describe job order cost accounting systems for service businesses.

Analysis for Decision Making

Describe the use of job order cost information for decision making.

Objective 1

Describe cost accounting systems used by manufacturing businesses.

Cost Accounting Systems Overview

Cost accounting systems measure, record, and report product costs. Managers use product costs for setting product prices, controlling operations, and developing financial statements.

The two main types of cost accounting systems for manufacturing operations are job order cost and process cost systems. Each system differs in how it accumulates and records costs.

Job Order Cost Systems

A **job order cost system** provides product costs for each quantity of product that is manufactured. Each quantity of product that is manufactured is called a *job*. Job order cost systems are often used by companies that manufacture custom products for customers or batches of similar products. For example, an apparel manufacturer, such as **Levi Strauss & Co.**, or a guitar manufacturer, such as **Gibson Guitars**, would use a job order cost system.

This chapter illustrates the job order cost system. As a basis for illustration, **Legend Guitars**, a manufacturer of guitars, is used. Exhibit 1 summarizes Legend Guitars' manufacturing operations.[1]

Process Cost Systems

A **process cost system** provides product costs for each manufacturing department or process. Process cost systems are often used by companies that manufacture units of a product that are indistinguishable from each other and are manufactured using a continuous production process. Examples would be oil refineries, paper producers, chemical processors, and food processors. The process cost system is illustrated in Chapter 17.

---

[1] Legend Guitars' manufacturing operation is described in more detail in Chapter 15.

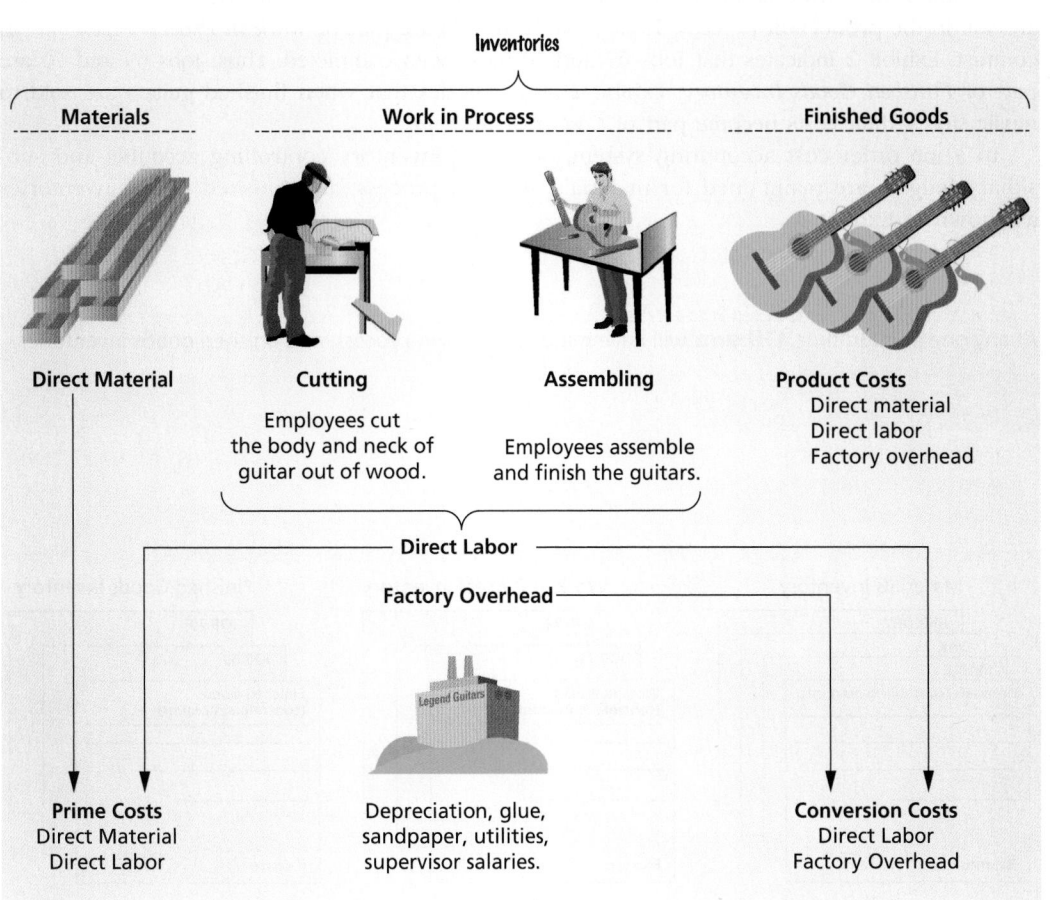

Exhibit 1
Summary of
Legend Guitars'
Manufacturing
Operations

Job Order Cost Systems for Manufacturing Businesses

A job order cost system records and summarizes manufacturing costs by jobs. The flow of manufacturing costs in a job order system is illustrated in Exhibit 2.

Objective 2
Describe and illustrate a job order cost accounting system for a manufacturing business.

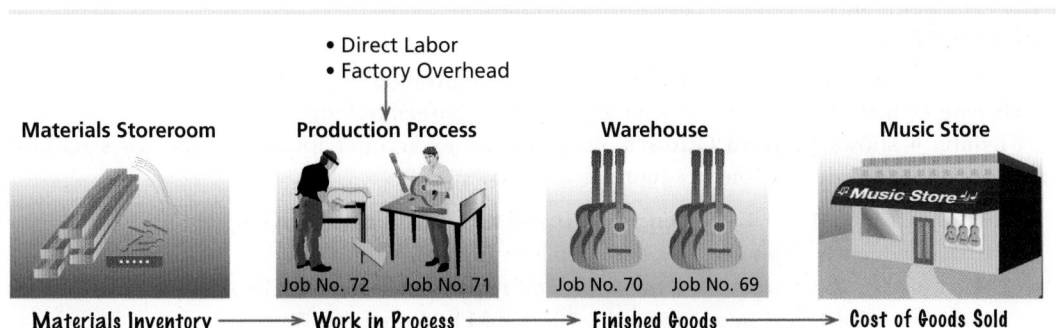

Exhibit 2
Flow of Manufacturing Costs

Exhibit 2 indicates that although the materials for Jobs 71 and 72 have been added, both jobs are still in the production process. Thus, Jobs 71 and 72 are part of *Work in Process Inventory*. In contrast, Exhibit 2 indicates that Jobs 69 and 70 have been completed. Thus, Jobs 69 and 70 are part of *Finished Goods Inventory*. Exhibit 2 also indicates that when finished guitars are sold to music stores, their costs become part of *Cost of Goods Sold*.

In a job order cost accounting system, perpetual inventory controlling accounts and subsidiary ledgers are maintained for materials, work in process, and finished goods inventories as shown in Exhibit 3.

Link to
Gibson Guitars

At any one point in time, **Gibson** will have materials, work in process, and finished goods inventories.

Exhibit 3

Inventory Ledger Accounts

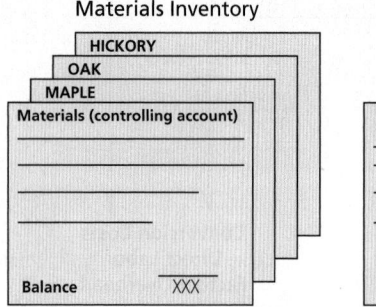
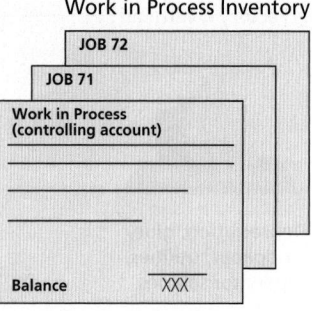
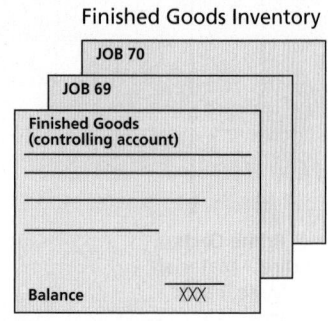

Why It Matters

3D Printing

3D printing is a technology that creates a three-dimensional product from an "additive" process. "Additive" means the product is built from plastic, metal, or other material that is built layer by successive layer until the final object is complete. The layers are very thin, allowing for extremely precise final specifications. The process is like printing on a piece of paper (which adds a layer of ink), but in three dimensions, hence the term 3D printing. The machines that add the thin material layers are computer controlled, so that the layers are added in exactly the right way to create the final product. 3D printers can manufacture very complex final products. 3D printing fits well within a job shop environment because the technology provides an economical way to create custom products.

Materials

The materials account in the general ledger is a controlling account. A separate account for each type of material is maintained in a subsidiary **materials ledger**.

Exhibit 4 shows **Legend Guitars**' materials ledger account for maple. Increases (debits) and decreases (credits) to the account are as follows:

- Increases (debits) are based on *receiving reports* such as Receiving Report No. 196 for $10,500, which is supported by the supplier's invoice.
- Decreases (credits) are based on *materials requisitions* such as Requisition No. 672 for $2,000 for Job 71 and Requisition No. 704 for $11,000 for Job 72.

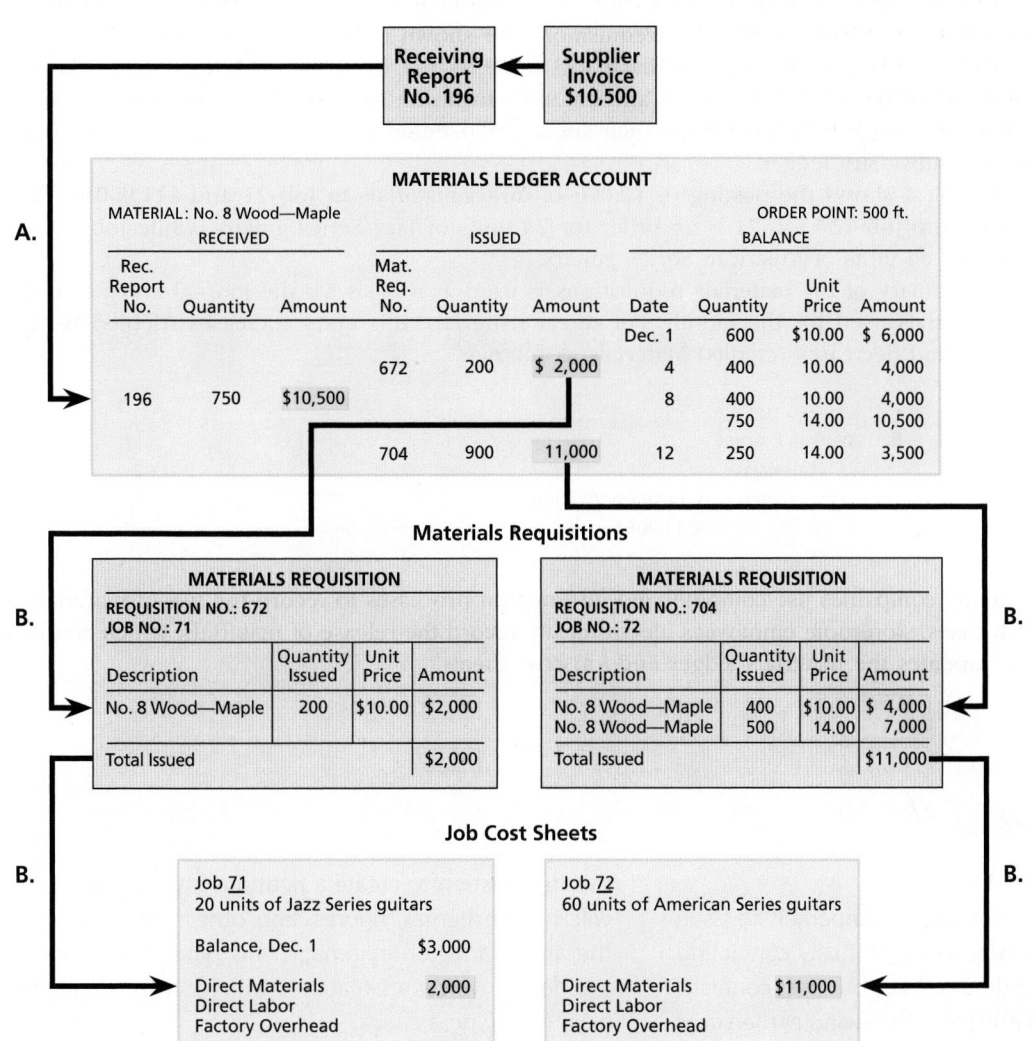

Gibson uses a variety of woods (direct materials) in making guitars, including cedar.

*Link to
Gibson Guitars*

A **receiving report** is prepared when materials that have been ordered are received and inspected. The quantity received and the condition of the materials are entered on the receiving report. When the supplier's invoice is received, it is compared to the receiving report. If there are no discrepancies, a journal entry is made to record the purchase. The journal entry to record the supplier's invoice related to Receiving Report No. 196 in Exhibit 4 is as follows:

A.	Materials	10,500	
	Accounts Payable		10,500
	Materials purchased during December.		

$A = L + E$
$+ \quad +$

The storeroom releases materials for use in manufacturing when a **materials requisition** is received. Examples of materials requisitions are shown in Exhibit 4.

The materials requisitions for each job serve as the basis for recording materials used. For direct materials, the quantities and amounts from the materials requisitions are posted to job cost sheets. **Job cost sheets**, which are also illustrated in Exhibit 4, make up the work in process subsidiary ledger.

Exhibit 4 shows the posting of $2,000 of direct materials to Job 71 and $11,000 of direct materials to Job 72.[2] Job 71 is an order for 20 units of Jazz Series guitars, while Job 72 is an order for 60 units of American Series guitars.

A summary of the materials requisitions is used as a basis for the journal entry recording the materials used for the month. For direct materials, this entry increases (debits) Work in Process and decreases (credits) Materials as follows:

A = L + E	B. Work in Process	13,000	
+ −	Materials		13,000
	Materials requisitioned to jobs		
	($2,000 + $11,000).		

Many companies use computerized information processes to record the use of materials. In such cases, storeroom employees electronically record the release of materials, which automatically updates the materials ledger and job cost sheets.

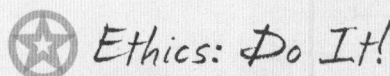 Ethics: Do It!

Phony Invoice Scams

A popular method for defrauding a company is to issue a phony invoice. The scam begins by initially contacting the target firm to discover details of key business contacts, business operations, and products. The swindler then uses this information to create a fictitious invoice. The invoice will include names, figures, and other details to give it the appearance of legitimacy. This type of scam can be avoided if invoices are matched with receiving documents prior to issuing a check.

Factory Labor

When employees report for work, they may use *electronic badges, clock cards,* or *in-and-out cards* to clock in. When employees work on an individual job, they use **time tickets** to record the amount of time they have worked on a specific job. Exhibit 5 illustrates time tickets for Jobs 71 and 72 at **Legend Guitars**.

Exhibit 5 shows that on December 13, 20Y8, D. McInnis spent six hours working on Job 71 at an hourly rate of $10 for a cost of $60 (6 hrs. × $10). Exhibit 5 also indicates that a total of 350 hours was spent by employees on Job 71 during December for a total cost of $3,500. This total direct labor cost of $3,500 is posted to the job cost sheet for Job 71, as shown in Exhibit 5.

Likewise, Exhibit 5 shows that on December 26, 20Y8, S. Andrews spent eight hours on Job 72 at an hourly rate of $15 for a cost of $120 (8 hrs. × $15). A total of 500 hours was spent by employees on Job 72 during December for a total cost of $7,500. This total direct labor cost of $7,500 is posted to the job cost sheet for Job 72, as shown in Exhibit 5.

---

[2] To simplify, Exhibit 4 and this chapter use the first-in, first-out cost flow method.

Exhibit 5

Labor Information and Cost Flows

DYNAMIC
EXHIBIT

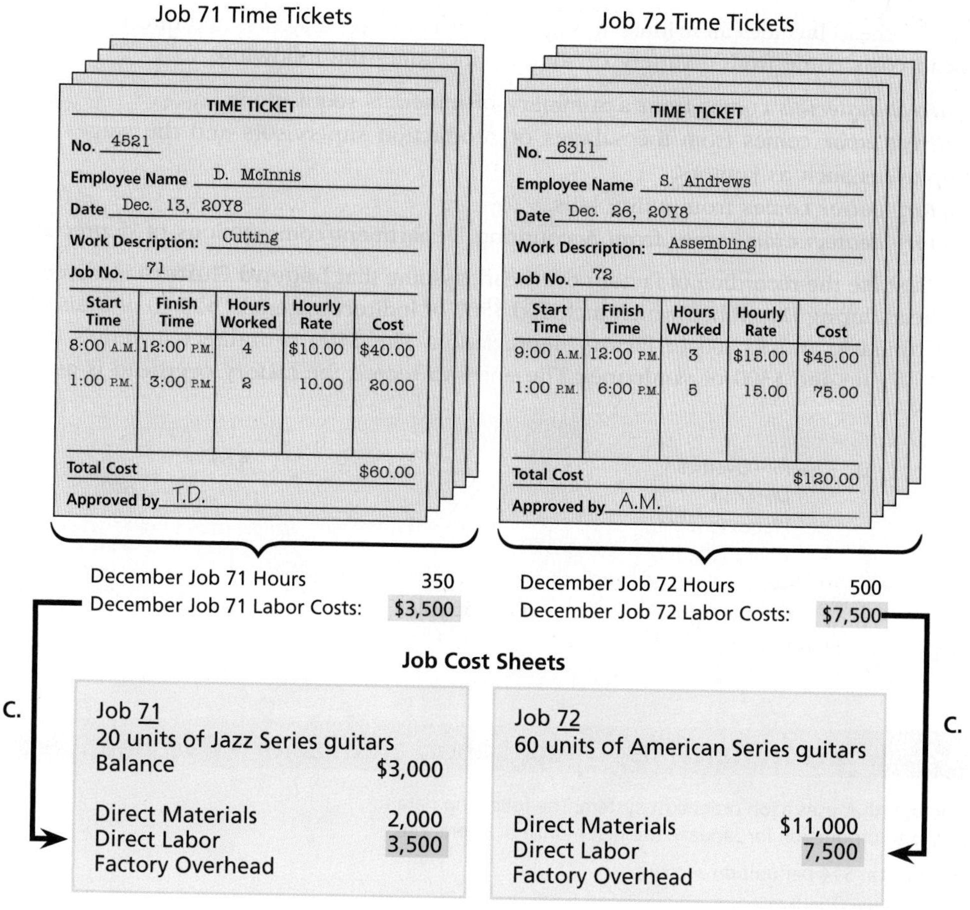

Job 71 Time Tickets

TIME TICKET

No. 4521

Employee Name   D. McInnis

Date   Dec. 13, 20Y8

Work Description: Cutting

Job No.   71

Start Time	Finish Time	Hours Worked	Hourly Rate	Cost
8:00 A.M.	12:00 P.M.	4	$10.00	$40.00
1:00 P.M.	3:00 P.M.	2	10.00	20.00

| Total Cost | | | | $60.00 |

Approved by   T.D.

Job 72 Time Tickets

TIME TICKET

No. 6311

Employee Name   S. Andrews

Date   Dec. 26, 20Y8

Work Description: Assembling

Job No.   72

Start Time	Finish Time	Hours Worked	Hourly Rate	Cost
9:00 A.M.	12:00 P.M.	3	$15.00	$45.00
1:00 P.M.	6:00 P.M.	5	15.00	75.00

| Total Cost | | | | $120.00 |

Approved by   A.M.

December Job 71 Hours   350
December Job 71 Labor Costs: $3,500

December Job 72 Hours   500
December Job 72 Labor Costs: $7,500

Job Cost Sheets

C.

Job 71
20 units of Jazz Series guitars
Balance $3,000

Direct Materials   2,000
Direct Labor   3,500
Factory Overhead

C.

Job 72
60 units of American Series guitars

Direct Materials $11,000
Direct Labor   7,500
Factory Overhead

A summary of the time tickets is used as the basis for the journal entry recording direct labor for the month. This entry increases (debits) Work in Process and increases (credits) Wages Payable, as follows:

C.	Work in Process	11,000	
	Wages Payable		11,000
	Factory labor used in production		
	of jobs ($3,500 + $7,500).		

A = L + E
+ +

As with direct materials, many businesses use computerized information processing to record direct labor. In such cases, employees may log their time directly into computer terminals at their workstations. In other cases, employees may be issued magnetic cards, much like credit cards, to log in and out of work assignments.

Link to Gibson Guitars

Gibson uses workers (factory labor) to perform a variety of tasks in making guitars, including cutting, matching wood grains, fitting braces, shaping and fitting necks, coloring, polishing, tuning, and inspecting.

Factory Overhead

Factory overhead includes all manufacturing costs except direct materials and direct labor. Factory overhead costs come from a variety of sources, including the following:

- *Indirect materials* comes from a summary of materials requisitions.
- *Indirect labor* comes from the salaries of production supervisors and the wages of other employees such as janitors.
- *Factory power* comes from utility bills.
- *Factory depreciation* comes from Accounting Department computations of depreciation.

To illustrate the recording of factory overhead, assume that **Legend Guitars** incurred $4,600 of overhead during December, which included $500 of indirect materials, $2,000 of indirect labor, $900 of utilities, and $1,200 of factory depreciation. The $500 of indirect materials consisted of $200 of glue and $300 of sandpaper. The entry to record the factory overhead is as follows:

D.	Factory Overhead	4,600	
	Materials		500
	Wages Payable		2,000
	Utilities Payable		900
	Accumulated Depreciation		1,200
	Factory overhead incurred in production.		

Check Up Corner 16-1   Direct Materials, Direct Labor, and Factory Overhead Costs

Grayson Company is a manufacturer that uses a job order cost system. The following data summarize the operations related to production for January, the first month of operations:

A. Purchased 400 units of materials at $14 per unit on account.

B. Requisitioned materials for production as follows:
- 200 units for Job 101 at $12 per unit.
- 300 units for Job 102 at $14 per unit.

C. Accumulated direct labor cost as follows:
- 700 hours of direct labor on Job 101 at $16 per hour.
- 600 hours of direct labor on Job 102 at $12 per hour.

D. Incurred factory overhead costs as follows: indirect materials, $800; indirect labor, $3,400; utilities cost, $1,600; and factory depreciation, $2,500.

Journalize the entries to record these transactions.

Solution:

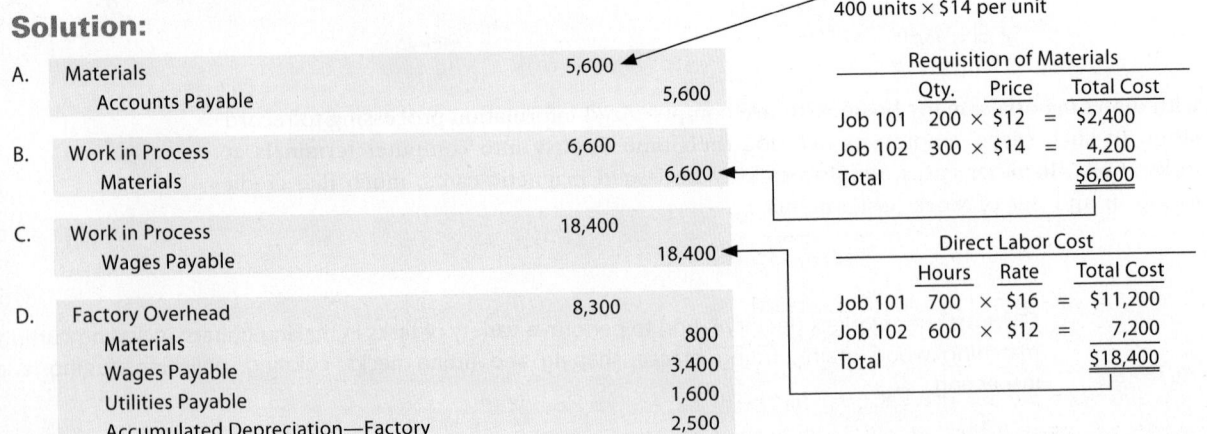

A.	Materials	5,600	
	Accounts Payable		5,600
B.	Work in Process	6,600	
	Materials		6,600
C.	Work in Process	18,400	
	Wages Payable		18,400
D.	Factory Overhead	8,300	
	Materials		800
	Wages Payable		3,400
	Utilities Payable		1,600
	Accumulated Depreciation—Factory		2,500

Purchase of Materials
400 units × $14 per unit

Requisition of Materials

	Qty.	Price		Total Cost
Job 101	200 × $12	=	$2,400
Job 102	300 × $14	=	4,200
Total			$6,600

Direct Labor Cost

	Hours	Rate		Total Cost
Job 101	700 × $16	=	$11,200
Job 102	600 × $12	=	7,200
Total			$18,400

Check Up Corner

Allocating Factory Overhead Factory overhead is different from direct labor and direct materials in that it is *indirectly* related to the jobs. That is, factory overhead costs cannot be identified with or traced to specific jobs. For this reason, factory overhead costs are allocated to jobs. The process by which factory overhead or other costs are assigned to a cost object, such as a job, is called **cost allocation**.

The factory overhead costs are *allocated* to jobs using a common measure related to each job. This measure is called an **activity base**, *allocation base*, or *activity driver*. The activity base used to allocate overhead should reflect the consumption or use of factory overhead costs. Three common activity bases used to allocate factory overhead costs are direct labor hours, direct labor cost, and machine hours.

Why It Matters

Advanced Robotics

Boston Consulting Group (BCG) believes the use of advanced robotics in manufacturing is about to take off. It estimates that by 2025, 25% of all tasks will be automated through robotics, driving a 10–30% increase in productivity. China, the United States, Japan, Germany, and South Korea will be the primary drivers of this trend. BCG anticipates significant use of advanced robotics will have a number of important impacts on manufacturing:

- Robotics reduces the need to move factories to low-labor cost countries to save costs.
- Robotics will reduce the size of manufacturing facilities, allowing for greater flexibility and a more regional focus.

- The economic costs of robotics will decline, opening up their broad use.
- The workforce will require new skills, such as programming and technical maintenance, to support robotic manufacturing. For example, **Shenzhen Everwin Precision Technology** recently announced plans to replace 90% of its 1,800 employees with advanced robotics in the near future. The remaining employees will be retrained to work with the robots.

Increasing use of robots will cause direct labor to go down, while factory overhead will increase. As a result, accurate factory overhead allocation will become increasingly important in these advanced manufacturing environments.

Source: Boston Consulting Group, "The Shifting Economics of Global Manufacturing: How a Takeoff in Advanced Robotics Will Power the Next Productivity Surge," February 2015.

Predetermined Factory Overhead Rate Factory overhead costs are normally allocated or *applied* to jobs using a **predetermined factory overhead rate**. The predetermined factory overhead rate is computed as follows:

$$\text{Predetermined Factory Overhead Rate} = \frac{\text{Estimated Total Factory Overhead Costs}}{\text{Estimated Activity Base}}$$

To illustrate, assume that **Legend Guitars** estimates the total factory overhead cost as $50,000 for the year and the activity base as 10,000 direct labor hours. The predetermined factory overhead rate of $5 per direct labor hour is computed as follows:

$$\text{Predetermined Factory Overhead Rate} = \frac{\$50,000}{10,000 \text{ direct labor hours}} = \$5 \text{ per direct labor hour}$$

As illustrated, the predetermined overhead rate is computed using *estimated* amounts at the beginning of the period. This is because managers need timely information on the product costs of each job. If a company waited until all overhead costs were known at the end of the period, the allocated factory overhead would be accurate, but not timely. Only through timely reporting can managers adjust manufacturing methods or product pricing.

Many companies are using a method for accumulating and allocating factory overhead costs. This method, called **activity-based costing**, uses a different overhead rate for each type of factory overhead activity, such as inspecting, moving, and machining. Activity-based costing is discussed and illustrated in Chapter 18.

Applying Factory Overhead to Work in Process **Legend Guitars** applies factory overhead using a rate of $5 per direct labor hour. The factory overhead applied to each job is recorded in the job cost sheets, as shown in Exhibit 6.

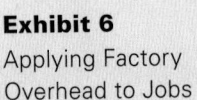

Exhibit 6
Applying Factory Overhead to Jobs

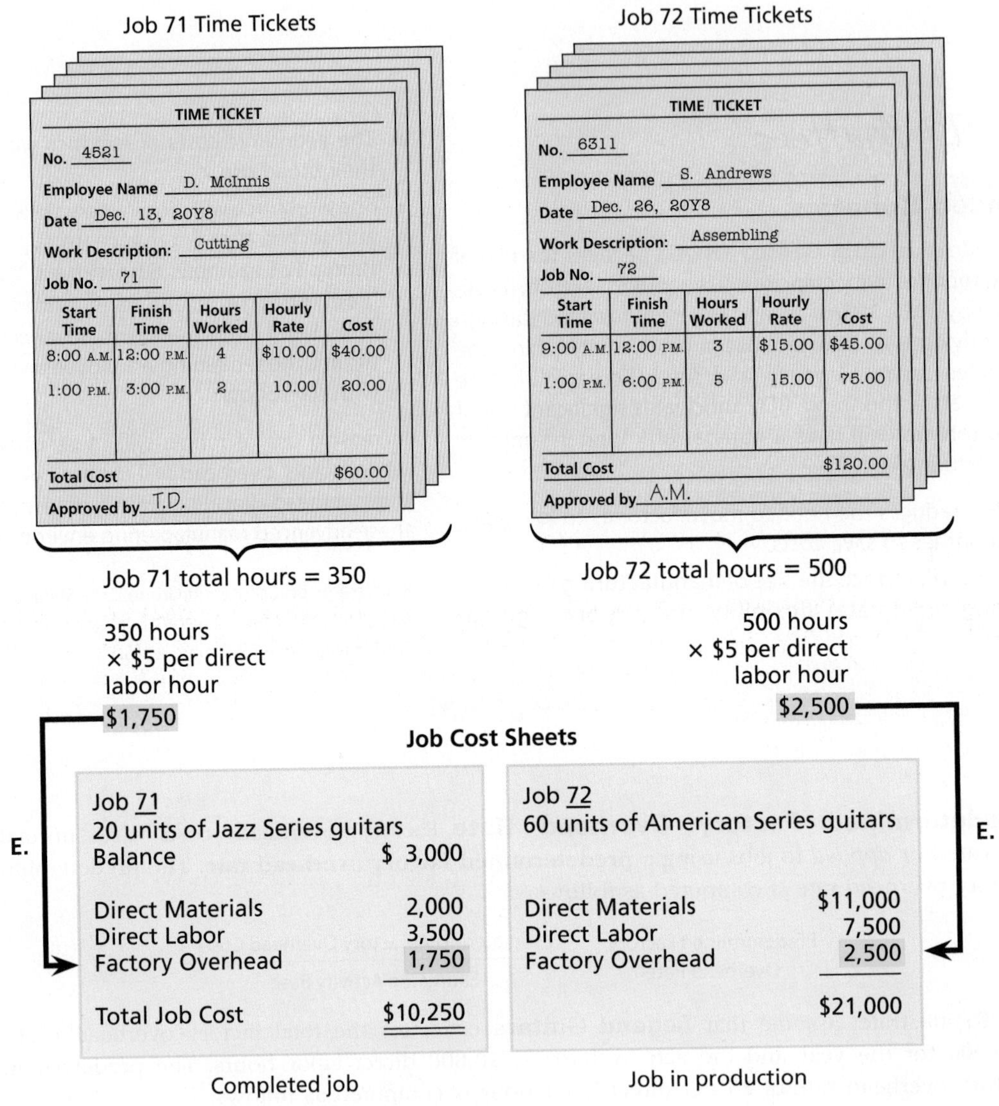

Job 71 Time Tickets

TIME TICKET

No. 4521
Employee Name D. McInnis
Date Dec. 13, 20Y8
Work Description: Cutting
Job No. 71

Start Time	Finish Time	Hours Worked	Hourly Rate	Cost
8:00 A.M.	12:00 P.M.	4	$10.00	$40.00
1:00 P.M.	3:00 P.M.	2	10.00	20.00

Total Cost $60.00
Approved by T.D.

Job 71 total hours = 350

350 hours
× $5 per direct labor hour
$1,750

Job 72 Time Tickets

TIME TICKET

No. 6311
Employee Name S. Andrews
Date Dec. 26, 20Y8
Work Description: Assembling
Job No. 72

Start Time	Finish Time	Hours Worked	Hourly Rate	Cost
9:00 A.M.	12:00 P.M.	3	$15.00	$45.00
1:00 P.M.	6:00 P.M.	5	15.00	75.00

Total Cost $120.00
Approved by A.M.

Job 72 total hours = 500

500 hours
× $5 per direct labor hour
$2,500

Job Cost Sheets

E.

Job 71
20 units of Jazz Series guitars
Balance .... $ 3,000

Direct Materials 2,000
Direct Labor 3,500
Factory Overhead 1,750

Total Job Cost $10,250

Completed job

E.

Job 72
60 units of American Series guitars

Direct Materials $11,000
Direct Labor 7,500
Factory Overhead 2,500

$21,000

Job in production

Exhibit 6 shows that 850 direct labor hours were used in Legend Guitars' December operations. Based on the time tickets, 350 hours can be traced to Job 71, and 500 hours can be traced to Job 72.

Using a factory overhead rate of $5 per direct labor hour, $4,250 of factory overhead is applied as follows:

	Direct Labor Hours	Factory Overhead Rate	Factory Overhead Applied
Job 71	350	$5	$1,750 (350 hrs. × $5)
Job 72	500	$5	2,500 (500 hrs. × $5)
Total	850		$4,250

As shown in Exhibit 6, the applied overhead is posted to each job cost sheet. Factory overhead of $1,750 is posted to Job 71, which results in a total product cost on December 31, 20Y8, of $10,250. Factory overhead of $2,500 is posted to Job 72, which results in a total product cost on December 31, 20Y8, of $21,000.

The journal entry to apply factory overhead increases (debits) Work in Process and decreases (credits) Factory Overhead. This journal entry to apply overhead to Jobs 71 and 72 is as follows:

E.	Work in Process	4,250	
	Factory Overhead		4,250
	Factory overhead applied to jobs according to the predetermined overhead rate (850 hrs. × $5).		

A = L + E
+ −

To summarize, the factory overhead account is:

- Increased (debited) for the *actual overhead* costs incurred, as shown for transaction (D).
- Decreased (credited) for the *applied overhead*, as shown for transaction (E).

The actual and applied overhead usually differ because the actual overhead costs are normally different from the estimated overhead costs. Depending on whether actual overhead is greater or less than applied overhead, the factory overhead account will either have a debit or credit ending balance as follows:

- If the applied overhead is *less than* the actual overhead incurred, the factory overhead account will have a debit balance. This debit balance is called **underapplied factory overhead** or *underabsorbed factory overhead*.
- If the applied overhead is *more than* the actual overhead incurred, the factory overhead account will have a credit balance. This credit balance is called **overapplied factory overhead** or *overabsorbed factory overhead*.

The factory overhead account for Legend Guitars, which follows, illustrates both underapplied and overapplied factory overhead. Specifically, the December 1, 20Y8, credit balance of $200 represents overapplied factory overhead. In contrast, the December 31, 20Y8, debit balance of $150 represents underapplied factory overhead.

Account *Factory Overhead*   *Account No.*

						Balance	
Date	Item	Post. Ref.	Debit	Credit	Debit	Credit
20Y8						
Dec. 1	Balance					200
31	Factory overhead cost incurred		4,600		4,400	
31	Factory overhead cost applied			4,250	150	

Underapplied balance
Overapplied balance

If the balance of factory overhead (either underapplied or overapplied) becomes large, the balance and related overhead rate should be investigated. For example, a large balance could be caused by changes in manufacturing methods. In this case, the factory overhead rate should be revised.

Gibson incurs a variety of overhead costs in making guitars, including depreciation on buildings and equipment.

Link to Gibson Guitars

Check Up Corner 16-2   Applying Overhead and Determining Job Cost

Grayson Company estimates that total factory overhead costs will be $100,000 for the year. Direct labor hours are estimated to be 25,000. The company had two completed jobs at the end of January, Jobs 101 and 102. Data on accumulated direct labor hours and units produced for these jobs are as follows:

	Direct Labor Hours	Units Produced
Job 101	700	500
Job 102	600	1,000

A. Using the information provided, determine:
1. The predetermined factory overhead rate using direct labor hours as the activity base.
2. The amount of factory overhead applied to Jobs 101 and 102 in January.

B. Prepare the journal entry to apply factory overhead to both jobs in January using the predetermined overhead rate from (A).

C. Using the information provided along with the job cost information from Check Up Corner 16-1, determine:
1. The balance on the job cost sheets for Jobs 101 and 102 at the end of the month.
2. The cost per unit for Jobs 101 and 102.

Solution:

A. 1.

$$\text{Predetermined Factory Overhead Rate} = \frac{\text{Estimated Total Factory Overhead Costs}}{\text{Estimated Activity Base}} = \frac{\$100,000}{25,000 \text{ direct labor hours}} = \$4.00 \text{ per direct labor hour}$$

A predetermined overhead rate is used to allocate overhead costs to individual jobs.

2.

	Direct Labor Hours		Factory Overhead Rate		Factory Overhead Applied
Job 101	700	×	$4.00	=	$2,800
Job 102	600	×	$4.00	=	2,400
Total					$5,200

The factory overhead cost applied to each job is recorded on the job cost sheet for each job.

B.

Work in Process	5,200	
Factory Overhead		5,200

C. 1.

	Job 101	Job 102
Direct materials	$ 2,400	$ 4,200
Direct labor	11,200	7,200
Factory overhead	2,800	2,400
Total costs	$16,400	$13,800

The direct materials cost and direct labor cost for each job were determined in Check Up Corner 16-1.

The total costs of each job are accumulated on the job cost sheet.

2. Cost per unit

	Job 101	Job 102
	$ 32.80	$ 13.80

$16,400 ÷ 500 units $13,800 ÷ 1,000 units

The total cost is divided by the number of units to determine the cost per unit.

Check Up Corner

Disposal of Factory Overhead Balance During the year, the balance in the factory overhead account is carried forward and reported as a deferred debit or credit on the monthly (interim) balance sheets. However, any balance in the factory overhead account should not be carried over to the next year. This is because any such balance applies only to operations of the current year.

If the estimates for computing the predetermined overhead rate are reasonably accurate, the ending balance of Factory Overhead should be relatively small. For this reason, the balance of Factory Overhead at the end of the year is disposed of by transferring it to the cost of goods sold account as follows:[3]

[3] An ending balance in the factory overhead account may also be allocated among the work in process, finished goods, and cost of goods sold accounts. This brings these accounts into agreement with the actual costs incurred. This approach is rarely used and is only required for large ending balances in the factory overhead account. For this reason, it will not be used in this text.

- If there is an ending debit balance (underapplied overhead) in the factory overhead account, it is disposed of by the entry that follows:

Cost of Goods Sold	XXX	
Factory Overhead		XXX
Transfer of underapplied		
overhead to cost of goods sold.		

- If there is an ending credit balance (overapplied overhead) in the factory overhead account, it is disposed of by the entry that follows:

Factory Overhead	XXX	
Cost of Goods Sold		XXX
Transfer of overapplied		
overhead to cost of goods sold.		

To illustrate, the journal entry to dispose of **Legend Guitars**' December 31, 20Y8, underapplied overhead balance of $150 is as follows:

F.	Cost of Goods Sold	150	
	Factory Overhead		150
	Closed underapplied factory		
	overhead to cost of goods sold.		

$A = L + E$
$-$ $- $ Exp

Work in Process

During the period, Work in Process is increased (debited) for the following:

- Direct materials cost
- Direct labor cost
- Applied factory overhead cost

To illustrate, the work in process account for **Legend Guitars** is shown in Exhibit 7. The balance of Work in Process on December 1, 20Y8 (beginning balance), was $3,000. As shown in Exhibit 7, this balance relates to Job 71, which was the only job in process on this date. During December, Work in Process was debited for the following:

- Direct materials cost of $13,000 [transaction (B)], based on materials requisitions.
- Direct labor cost of $11,000 [transaction (C)], based on time tickets.
- Applied factory overhead of $4,250 [transaction (E)], based on the predetermined overhead rate of $5 per direct labor hour.

The preceding Work in Process debits are supported by the postings to job cost sheets for Jobs 71 and 72, as shown in Exhibit 7.

During December, Job 71 was completed. Upon completion, the product costs (direct materials, direct labor, factory overhead) are totaled. This total is divided by the number of units produced to determine the cost per unit. Thus, the 20 Jazz Series guitars produced as Job 71 cost $512.50 ($10,250 ÷ 20) per guitar.

After completion, Job 71 is transferred from Work in Process to Finished Goods by the following entry:

G.	Finished Goods	10,250	
	Work in Process		10,250
	Job 71 completed in December.		

$A = L + E$
$+ -$

G.

Exhibit 7
Job Cost Sheets and the Work in Process Controlling Account

Job Cost Sheets

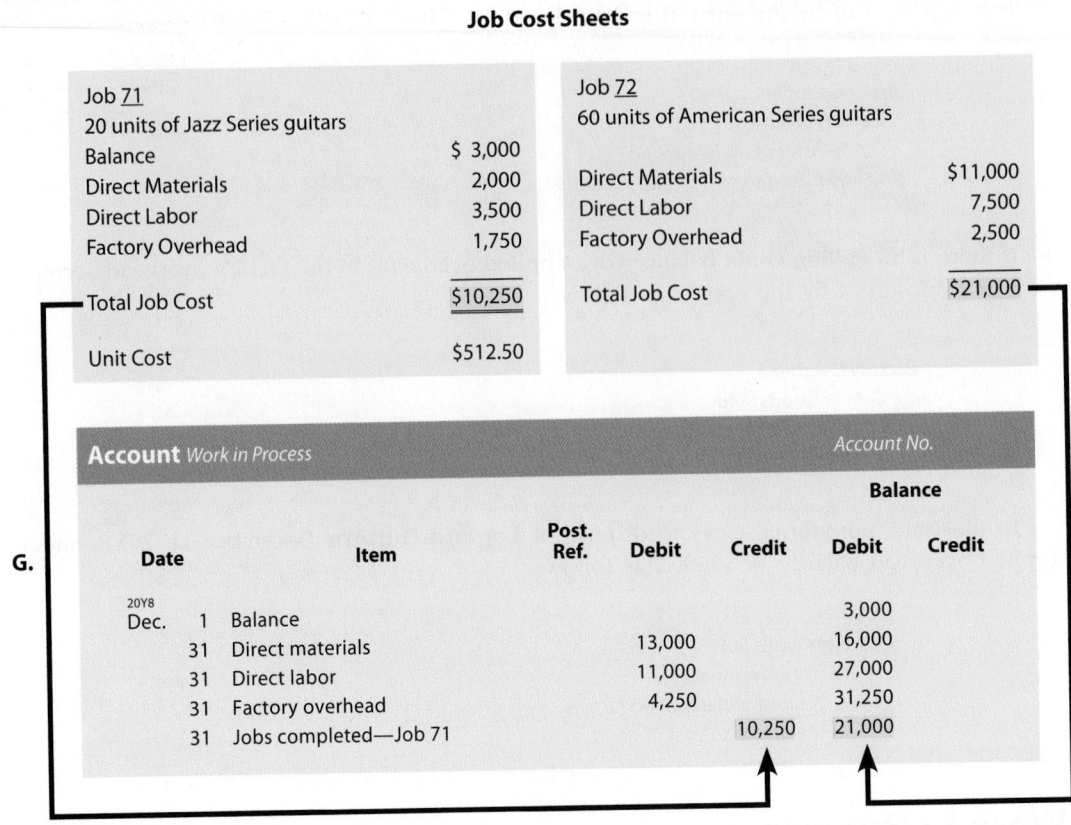

Job 71
20 units of Jazz Series guitars

Balance	$ 3,000
Direct Materials	2,000
Direct Labor	3,500
Factory Overhead	1,750
Total Job Cost	$10,250
Unit Cost	$512.50

Job 72
60 units of American Series guitars

Direct Materials	$11,000
Direct Labor	7,500
Factory Overhead	2,500
Total Job Cost	$21,000

Account *Work in Process*   *Account No.*

			Post. Ref.	Debit	Credit	Balance Debit	Balance Credit
Date		Item					
20Y8 Dec.	1	Balance				3,000	
	31	Direct materials		13,000		16,000	
	31	Direct labor		11,000		27,000	
	31	Factory overhead		4,250		31,250	
	31	Jobs completed—Job 71			10,250	21,000	

Job 72 was started in December but was not completed by December 31, 20Y8. Thus, Job 72 is still part of work in process on December 31, 20Y8. As shown in Exhibit 7, the balance of the job cost sheet for Job 72 ($21,000) is also the December 31, 20Y8, balance of Work in Process.

Finished Goods

The finished goods account is a controlling account for the subsidiary **finished goods ledger** or *stock ledger*. Each account in the finished goods ledger contains cost data for the units manufactured, units sold, and units on hand.

Exhibit 8 illustrates the finished goods ledger account for **Legend Guitars'** Jazz Series guitars. The exhibit indicates that there were 40 Jazz Series guitars on hand on December 1, 20Y8. During the month, 20 additional Jazz guitars were completed and transferred to Finished Goods from the completion of Job 71. In addition, the beginning inventory of 40 Jazz guitars was sold during the month.

Exhibit 8
Finished Goods Ledger Account

ITEM: *Jazz Series guitars*

Manufactured			Shipped			Balance			
Job Order No.	Quantity	Amount	Ship Order No.	Quantity	Amount	Date	Quantity	Amount	Unit Cost
						Dec. 1	40	$20,000	$500.00
			643	40	$20,000	9	—	—	—
71	20	$10,250				31	20	10,250	512.50

A virtual tour of **Gibson**'s Bozeman, Montana, manufacturing plant can be found at www2.gibson.com. The Bozeman plant makes acoustical guitars similar to those illustrated in this chapter. Acoustical guitars that do not require power or amps to produce sound are often used for folk and country music. Electric guitars are most often used for metal and rock music.

Link to Gibson Guitars

Sales and Cost of Goods Sold

During December, **Legend Guitars** sold 40 Jazz Series guitars for $850 each, generating total sales of $34,000 ($850 × 40 guitars). Exhibit 8 indicates that the cost of these guitars was $500 per guitar or a total cost of $20,000 ($500 × 40 guitars). The entries to record the sale and related cost of goods sold are as follows:

H.	Accounts Receivable	34,000		A = L + E
	Sales		34,000	+ + Rev
	Revenue received from guitars sold			
	on account.			

I.	Cost of Goods Sold	20,000		A = L + E
	Finished Goods		20,000	− − Exp
	Cost of 40 Jazz Series guitars sold.			

In a job order cost accounting system, the preparation of a statement of cost of goods manufactured, which was discussed in Chapter 15 is not necessary. This is because job order costing uses the perpetual inventory system and, thus, the cost of goods sold can be directly determined from the finished goods ledger as illustrated in Exhibit 8.

Period Costs

Period costs are used in generating revenue during the current period but are not involved in the manufacturing process. As discussed in Chapter 15, *period costs* are recorded as expenses of the current period as either selling or administrative expenses.

Selling expenses are incurred in marketing the product and delivering sold products to customers. Administrative expenses are incurred in managing the company but are not related to the manufacturing or selling functions. During December, **Legend Guitars** recorded the following selling and administrative expenses:

J.	Sales Salaries Expense	2,000		A = L + E
	Office Salaries Expense	1,500		+ − Exp
	Salaries Payable		3,500	
	Recorded December period costs.			

Why It Matters

Job Order Costing in Hollywood

A manufacturer uses a job order system to accumulate direct labor, direct material, and factory overhead costs by production job. In a similar way, Hollywood accumulates costs for a particular movie. However, rather than factory labor, a movie has the salaries of actors, directors, writers, and other creative and technical staff in making the movie. Rather than manufacturing materials, a movie will have scenery, costumes, props, and other materials in making the film. A movie will also have indirect costs associated with supervision, accounting, casting, and other costs that the studio shares with other movies. Such shared costs are allocated to each movie project using an overhead rate similar to that found in manufacturing. Work in process represents the costs accumulated while a movie is in production. A completed movie is treated similarly to finished goods inventory. Upon release, the accumulated costs will be expensed on the income statement as revenues from theatrical release, online streaming, cable, and DVDs are being earned.

Exhibit 9 Flow of Manufacturing Costs for Legend Guitars

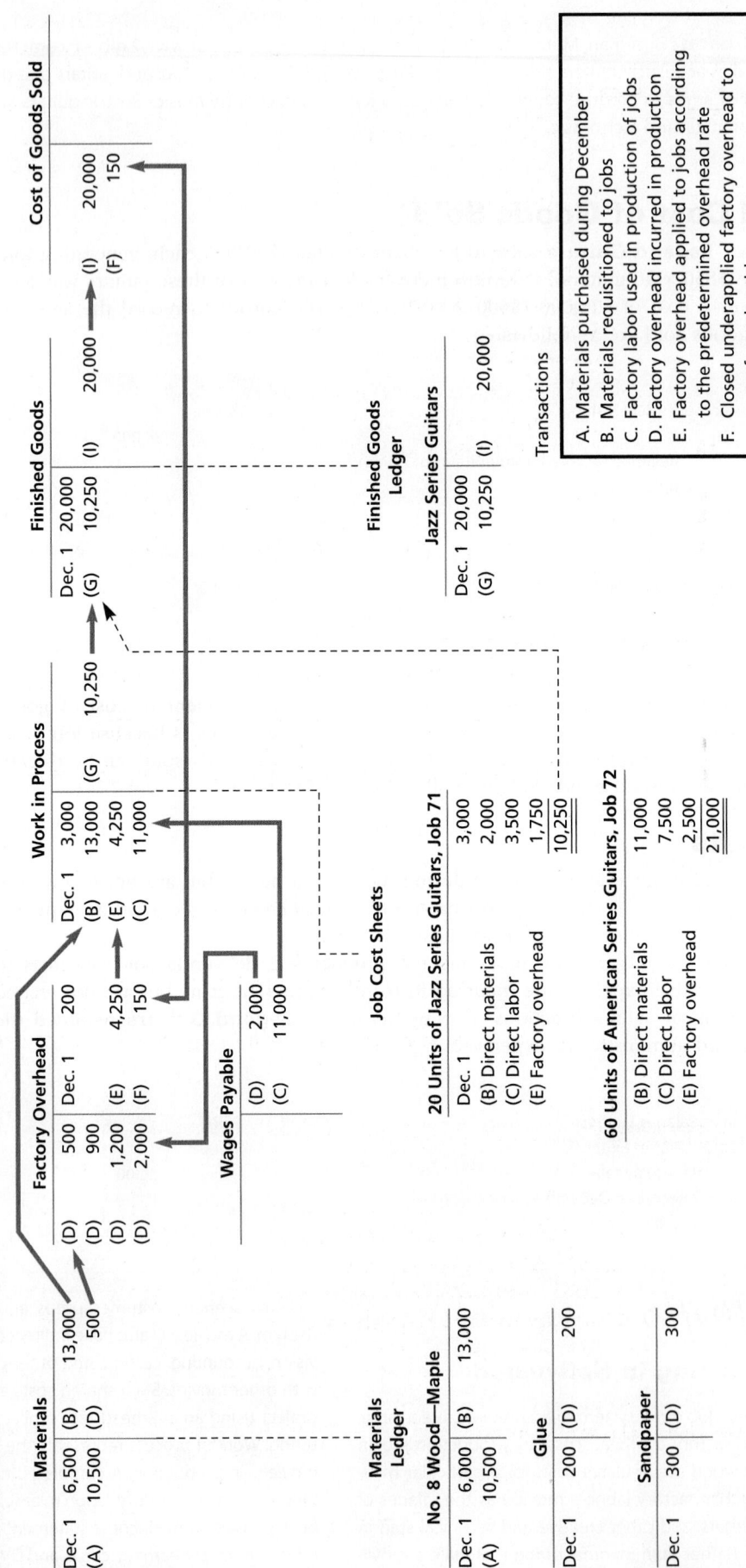

Summary of Cost Flows for Legend Guitars

Exhibit 9 shows the cost flows through the manufacturing accounts of **Legend Guitars** for December. In addition, summary details of the following subsidiary ledgers are shown:

- *Materials Ledger*—the subsidiary ledger for Materials.
- *Job Cost Sheets*—the subsidiary ledger for Work in Process.
- *Finished Goods Ledger*—the subsidiary ledger for Finished Goods.

Entries in the accounts shown in Exhibit 9 are identified by letters. These letters refer to the journal entries described and illustrated in the chapter. Entries (H) and (J) are not shown because they do not involve a flow of manufacturing costs.

As shown in Exhibit 9, the balances of Materials, Work in Process, and Finished Goods are supported by their subsidiary ledgers. These balances are as follows:

Controlling Account	Balance and Total of Related Subsidiary Ledger
Materials	$ 3,500
Work in Process	21,000
Finished Goods	10,250

The income statement for **Legend Guitars** is shown in Exhibit 10.

Exhibit 10

Income Statement of Legend Guitars

Legend Guitars
Income Statement
For the Month Ended December 31, 20Y8

Sales		$34,000
Cost of goods sold		20,150*
Gross profit		$13,850
Selling and administrative expenses:		
Sales salaries expense	$2,000	
Office salaries expense	1,500	
Total selling and administrative expenses		3,500
Income from operations		$10,350

*$20,150 = ($500 × 40 guitars) + $150 underapplied factory overhead

Job Order Cost Systems for Service Businesses

Objective 3

Describe job order cost accounting systems for service businesses.

A job order cost accounting system may be used by a service business. However, whether a service business uses a job order cost system depends upon the nature of the service provided to customers.

Types of Service Businesses

Hotels, taxis, newspapers, attorneys, accountants, and hospitals provide services to customers. All these businesses, however, would not use job order costing. For example, hotels, taxis, and newspapers would normally not use a job order cost system. In contrast, attorneys, accountants, and hospitals normally would use a job order system.

A service business using job order costing normally renders a service that is unique to each customer with related costs that vary significantly with each customer. For example, while hotels provide a service, the service is the same for each guest on any given night.

In contrast, an attorney or hospital provides a unique service for each client or patient. In addition, each client or patient incurs costs that are unique to them. For this reason, attorneys and hospitals normally use job order cost systems.[4] Other examples of service businesses using job order cost systems include advertising agencies, event planners, and car repair shops.

Flow of Costs in a Service Job Order Cost System

A service business using a job order cost system views each customer, client, or patient as a separate job for which costs are accumulated and reported.

Since a service is being provided, the primary product costs are normally direct labor and overhead. Any materials or supplies used in rendering services are usually insignificant. As a result, materials and supply costs are included as part of the overhead cost.

Like a manufacturing business, the direct labor and overhead costs of rendering services to clients are accumulated in a work in process account. Work in Process is supported by a cost ledger with a job cost sheet for each client.

When a job is completed and the client is billed, the costs are transferred to a cost of services account. Cost of Services is similar to the cost of goods sold account for a merchandising or manufacturing business. A finished goods account and related finished goods ledger are not necessary. This is because services cannot be inventoried and the revenues for the services are recorded upon completion.

In practice, other considerations unique to service businesses may need to be considered. For example, a service business may bill clients on a weekly or monthly basis rather than when a job is completed. In such cases, a portion of the costs related to each billing is transferred from the work in process account to the cost of services account. A service business may also bill clients for services in advance, which would be accounted for as deferred revenue until the services are completed.

The flow of costs through a service business using a job order cost accounting system is shown in Exhibit 11.

Exhibit 11   Flow of Costs Through a Service Business

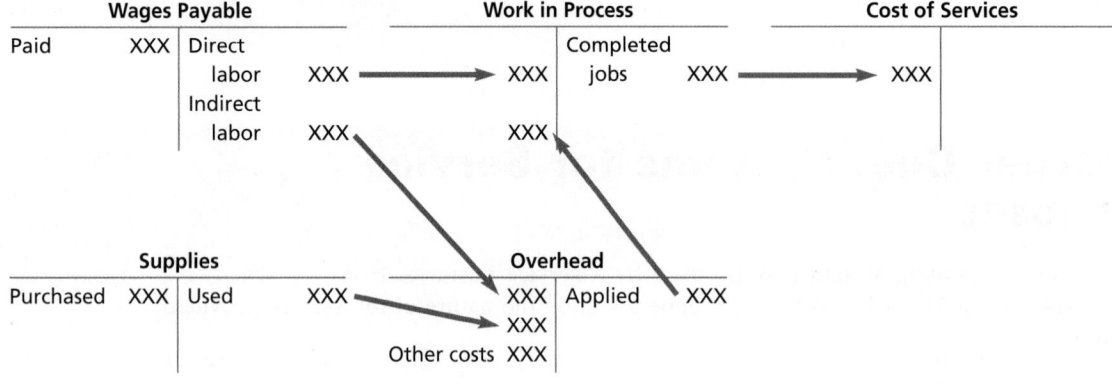

---

[4] Service businesses using job order cost systems normally require each customer, client, or patient to sign a contract that describes the nature of the service being rendered.

Check Up Corner 16-3 — Job Order Costing for a Service Business

The Mad-Fly Agency provides consulting services to a variety of clients across the country. The agency accumulates costs for each consulting project on the basis of direct labor costs and allocated overhead costs. Mad-Fly's estimated direct labor and overhead costs for the year are as follows:

Direct labor hours (professional staff)	20,000 hours
Hourly rate for professional staff	$180 per hour
Estimated total overhead costs	$1,200,000

Mad-Fly allocates overhead costs to individual jobs based on the total estimated direct labor hours of its professional services staff.

A. Determine Mad-Fly's estimated predetermined overhead rate for the year.

B. Mad-Fly started and completed a consulting job for MT Industries during the year (Job 402). The job required 200 direct labor hours from the agency's professional services staff. Determine the cost of the MT Industries job (Job 402).

Solution:

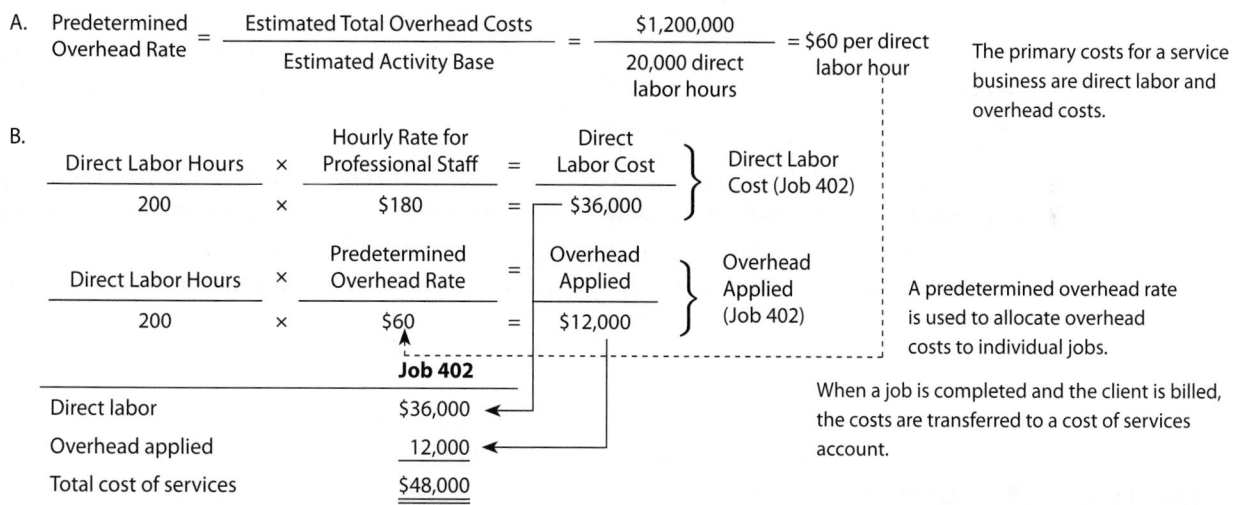

A. $\text{Predetermined Overhead Rate} = \dfrac{\text{Estimated Total Overhead Costs}}{\text{Estimated Activity Base}} = \dfrac{\$1,200,000}{20,000 \text{ direct labor hours}} = \$60 \text{ per direct labor hour}$

The primary costs for a service business are direct labor and overhead costs.

B.

Direct Labor Hours	×	Hourly Rate for Professional Staff	=	Direct Labor Cost	Direct Labor Cost (Job 402)
200	×	$180	=	$36,000	

Direct Labor Hours	×	Predetermined Overhead Rate	=	Overhead Applied	Overhead Applied (Job 402)
200	×	$60	=	$12,000	

A predetermined overhead rate is used to allocate overhead costs to individual jobs.

Job 402

Direct labor	$36,000
Overhead applied	12,000
Total cost of services	$48,000

When a job is completed and the client is billed, the costs are transferred to a cost of services account.

Check Up Corner

Analysis for Decision Making

Analyzing Job Costs

A job order cost accounting system accumulates and records product costs by jobs. The resulting total and unit product costs can be compared to similar jobs, compared over time, or compared to expected costs. In this way, a job order cost system can be used by managers for cost evaluation and control.

To illustrate, Exhibit 12 shows the direct materials used for Jobs 54 and 63 for **Legend Guitars**. The wood used in manufacturing guitars is measured in board feet. Because Jobs 54 and 63 produced the same type and number of guitars, the direct materials cost per unit should be about the same. However, the materials cost per guitar for Job 54 is $100, while for Job 63 it is $125. Thus, the materials costs are significantly more for Job 63.

The job cost sheets shown in Exhibit 12 can be analyzed for possible reasons for the increased materials cost for Job 63. Because the materials price did not change ($10 per board foot), the increased materials cost must be related to wood consumption.

Objective

Describe the use of job order cost information for decision making.

Exhibit 12

Comparing Data from Job Cost Sheets

Job 54
Item: 40 Jazz Series guitars

	Materials Quantity (board feet)	Materials Price	Materials Amount
Direct materials:			
No. 8 Wood—Maple	400	$10.00	$4,000
Direct materials per guitar			$ 100*
*$4,000 ÷ 40			

Job 63
Item: 40 Jazz Series guitars

	Materials Quantity (board feet)	Materials Price	Materials Amount
Direct materials:			
No. 8 Wood—Maple	500	$10.00	$5,000
Direct materials per guitar			$ 125*
*$5,000 ÷ 40			

Job 54 used 400 board feet to produce 40 guitars. In contrast, Job 63 used 500 board feet to produce the same number of guitars. Thus, the cause of the extra 100 board feet used for Job 63 should be investigated. Possible explanations could include the following:

- A new employee, who was not properly trained, cut the wood for Job 63. As a result, there was excess waste and scrap.
- The wood used for Job 63 was purchased from a new supplier. The wood was of poor quality, which created excessive waste and scrap.
- The cutting tools needed repair and were not properly maintained. As a result, the wood was miscut, which created excessive waste and scrap.
- The instructions attached to the job were incorrect. The wood was cut according to the instructions. The incorrect instructions were discovered later in assembly. As a result, the wood had to be recut and the initial cuttings scrapped.

Make a Decision   Analyzing Job Costs

Antolini Enterprises produces men's sports coats that are sold by popular department stores. Each retail order is treated as a job that accumulates materials, labor, and overhead costs for a batch of sports coats. Management has obtained data on the labor costs for four selected jobs over a six-month period. Each selected job represents a similar style and size of sports coat. The data are as follows:

	Count	Direct Labor Hours	Direct Labor Rate per Hour	Total Direct Labor Cost
Job 107	10	4.50	$14.00	$ 63.00
Job 125	14	7.00	14.00	98.00
Job 160	16	8.80	14.00	123.20
Job 192	8	3.20	16.00	51.20

A. Determine the direct labor cost per unit for each job.

B. Interpret the trend in per-unit labor cost.

C. Determine the direct labor hours per sports coat.

D. Interpret what may be happening with Job 192.

Solution:

A. Divide the total direct labor cost by the count to determine the direct labor cost per unit for each job:

	Total Direct Labor Cost	Count	Direct Labor Cost per Sports Coat
Job 107	$ 63.00	10	$6.30
Job 125	98.00	14	7.00
Job 160	123.20	16	7.70
Job 192	51.20	8	6.40

B. The direct labor cost per sports coat increased over the first three jobs, then declined with the last job. The increase for the first three jobs is not related to a change in the direct labor rate, which was the same for all three jobs. Thus, the increase in labor cost must be related to an increase in labor time to make the coats. This is confirmed in (C).

C. The direct labor hours per sports coat is determined by dividing the total direct labor hours by the count as follows:

	Direct Labor Hours	Count	Direct Labor Hours per Sports Coat
Job 107	4.50	10	0.45
Job 125	7.00	14	0.50
Job 160	8.80	16	0.55
Job 192	3.20	8	0.40

The direct labor hours per sports coat have increased over the first three jobs, which has led to the increased direct labor cost per coat noted in (B). Management would want to investigate why the direct labor hours per coat are increasing.

D. The direct labor rate for Job 192 increased from $14 to $16. This may be due to a raise in pay or the use of a more skilled and higher-paid employee. Regardless, the result was a significant drop in the direct labor hours per sports coat, down to 0.40 hours, which is the best of all the jobs. The net result of the higher efficiency, combined with the higher direct labor cost, was a direct labor cost per sports coat that was only ten cents higher than Job 107 and a significant improvement over Job 160.

Make a Decision

Let's Review

Chapter Summary

1. A cost accounting system accumulates product costs. The two primary cost accounting systems are the job order and the process cost systems. Job order cost systems accumulate costs for each quantity of product that passes through the factory. Process cost systems accumulate costs for each department or process within the factory.

2. A job order cost system accumulates costs for each quantity of product, or "job," that passes through the factory. Direct materials, direct labor, and factory overhead are accumulated on the job cost sheet, which is the subsidiary cost ledger for each job. Direct materials and direct labor are assigned to individual jobs, based on the quantity used. Factory overhead costs are assigned to each job, based on an activity base that reflects the use of factory overhead costs.

3. Job order cost accounting systems can be used by service businesses to plan and control operations. Because the product is a service, the focus is on direct labor and overhead costs. The costs of providing a service are accumulated in a work in process account and transferred to a cost of services account upon completion.

Key Terms

activity base (793)
activity-based costing (794)
cost accounting systems (786)
cost allocation (793)
finished goods ledger (798)
job cost sheets (790)

job order cost system (786)
materials ledger (788)
materials requisition (790)
overapplied factory overhead (795)
predetermined factory
   overhead rate (793)

process cost system (786)
receiving report (789)
time tickets (790)
underapplied factory
   overhead (795)

Practice

Multiple-Choice Questions

1. For which of the following would the job order cost system be appropriate?
   A. Antique furniture repair shop
   B. Rubber manufacturer
   C. Coal manufacturer
   D. Computer chip manufacturer

2. The journal entry to record the requisition of materials to the factory in a job order cost system is a debit to:
   A. Materials.
   B. Accounts Payable.
   C. Work in Process.
   D. Cost of Goods Sold.

3. Job order cost sheets accumulate all of the following costs except for:
   A. direct materials.
   B. indirect materials.
   C. direct labor.
   D. factory overhead applied.

4. A company estimated $420,000 of factory overhead cost and 16,000 direct labor hours for the period. During the period, a job was completed with $4,500 of direct materials and $3,000 of direct labor. The direct labor rate was $15 per hour. What is the factory overhead applied to this job?
   A. $2,100
   B. $5,250
   C. $78,750
   D. $420,000

5. If the factory overhead account has a credit balance, factory overhead is said to be:
   A. underapplied.
   B. overapplied.
   C. underabsorbed.
   D. in error.

Answers provided after Problem. Need more practice? Find additional multiple-choice questions, exercises, and problems in CengageNOWv2.

Exercises

SHOW ME HOW

1. Issuance of materials   Obj. 2

On April 6, Almerinda Company purchased on account 60,000 units of raw materials at $12 per unit. On April 21, raw materials were requisitioned for production as follows: 25,000 units for Job 50 at $10 per unit and 27,000 units for Job 51 at $12 per unit. Journalize the entry on April 6 to record the purchase and on April 21 to record the requisition from the materials storeroom.

SHOW ME HOW

2. Direct labor costs
Obj. 2

During April, Almerinda Company accumulated 20,000 hours of direct labor costs on Job 50 and 24,000 hours on Job 51. The total direct labor was incurred at a rate of $20 per direct labor hour for Job 50 and $22 per direct labor hour for Job 51. Journalize the entry to record the flow of labor costs into production during April.

SHOW ME HOW

3. Factory overhead costs
Obj. 2

During April, Almerinda Company incurred factory overhead costs as follows: indirect materials, $42,000; indirect labor, $90,000; utilities cost, $16,000; and factory depreciation, $54,000. Journalize the entry to record the factory overhead incurred during April.

SHOW ME HOW

4. Applying factory overhead
Obj. 2

Almerinda Company estimates that total factory overhead costs will be $1,750,000 for the year. Direct labor hours are estimated to be 500,000. For Almerinda Company, (A) determine the predetermined factory overhead rate using direct labor hours as the activity base, (B) determine the amount of factory overhead applied to Jobs 50 and 51 in April using the data on direct labor hours from Exercises 2 and 3, and (C) prepare the journal entry to apply factory overhead to both jobs in April according to the predetermined overhead rate.

SHOW ME HOW

5. Job costs
Obj. 2

At the end of April, Almerinda Company had completed Jobs 50 and 51. Job 50 is for 23,040 units, and Job 51 is for 26,000 units. Using the data from Exercises 1 through 4, determine (A) the balance on the job cost sheets for Jobs 50 and 51 at the end of April and (B) the cost per unit for Jobs 50 and 51 at the end of April.

SHOW ME HOW

6. Cost of goods sold
Obj. 2

Hosmer Company completed 312,000 units during the year at a cost of $7,800,000. The beginning finished goods inventory was 22,000 units at $440,000. Determine the cost of goods sold for 325,000 units, assuming a FIFO cost flow.

Answers provided after Problem. Need more practice? Find additional multiple-choice questions, exercises, and problems in CengageNOWv2.

Problem

Wildwing Entertainment Inc. is a manufacturer that uses a job order cost system. The following data summarize the operations related to production for March, the first month of operations:

A. Materials purchased on account, $15,500.

B. Materials requisitioned and labor used:

	Materials	Factory Labor
Job No. 100	$2,650	$1,770
Job No. 101	1,240	650
Job No. 102	980	420
Job No. 103	3,420	1,900
Job No. 104	1,000	500
Job No. 105	2,100	1,760
For general factory use	450	650

C. Factory overhead costs incurred on account, $2,700.

D. Depreciation of machinery, $1,750.

E. Factory overhead is applied at a rate of 70% of direct labor cost.

F. Jobs completed: Nos. 100, 101, 102, 104.

G. Jobs 100, 101, and 102 were shipped, and customers were billed for $8,100, $3,800, and $3,500, respectively.

Instructions

1. Journalize the entries to record these transactions.

2. Determine the account balances for Work in Process and Finished Goods.

3. Prepare a schedule of unfinished jobs to support the balance in the work in process account.

4. Prepare a schedule of completed jobs on hand to support the balance in the finished goods account.

Need more practice? Find additional multiple-choice questions, exercises, and problems in CengageNOWv2.

Answers

Multiple-Choice Questions

1. **A** Job order cost systems are best suited to businesses manufacturing special orders from customers, such as would be the case for a repair shop for antique furniture (answer A). A process cost system is best suited for manufacturers of similar units of products such as rubber manufacturers (answer B), coal manufacturers (answer C), and computer chip manufacturers (answer D).

2. **C** The journal entry to record the requisition of materials to the factory in a job order cost system is a debit to Work in Process and a credit to Materials.

3. **B** The job cost sheet accumulates the cost of direct materials (answer A), direct labor (answer C), and factory overhead applied (answer D). Indirect materials (answer B) are NOT accumulated on the job order cost sheets, but are included as part of factory overhead applied.

4. **B**

$$\text{Predetermined Factory Overhead Rate} = \frac{\text{Estimated Total Factory Overhead Costs}}{\text{Estimated Activity Base}}$$

$$\text{Predetermined Factory Overhead Rate} = \frac{\$420,000}{16,000 \text{ dlh}} = \$26.25$$

$$\text{Hours applied to the job:} = \frac{\$3,000}{\$15 \text{ per hour}} = 200 \text{ hours}$$

Factory overhead applied to the job: 200 hours × $26.25 = $5,250

5. **B** If the amount of factory overhead applied during a particular period exceeds the actual overhead costs, the factory overhead account will have a credit balance and is said to be overapplied (answer B) or overabsorbed. If the amount applied is less than the actual costs, the account will have a debit balance and is said to be underapplied (answer A) or underabsorbed (answer C). Since an "estimated" predetermined overhead rate is used to apply overhead, a credit balance does not necessarily represent an error (answer D).

Exercises

1.

Apr.	6	Materials	720,000	
		Accounts Payable		720,000
		$720,000 = 60,000 \times \$12.$		
	21	Work in Process*	574,000	
		Materials		574,000

* Job 50	$250,000 = 25,000 \times \$10$
Job 51	$\underline{324,000} = 27,000 \times \$12$
Total	$\underline{\$574,000}$

2.

Work in Process*	928,000	
Wages Payable		928,000

* Job 50	$400,000 = 20,000$ hours $\times \$20$
Job 51	$\underline{528,000} = 24,000$ hours $\times \$22$
Total	$\underline{\$928,000}$

3.

Factory Overhead	202,000	
Materials		42,000
Wages Payable		90,000
Utilities Payable		16,000
Accumulated Depreciation—Factory		54,000

4. A. $3.50 per direct labor hour = $1,750,000 \div 500,000$ direct labor hours

   B.
Job 50	$ 70,000 = 20,000$ hours $\times \$3.50$ per hour
Job 51	$\underline{84,000} = 24,000$ hours $\times \$3.50$ per hour
	$\underline{\$154,000}$

   C.

Work in Process	154,000	
Factory Overhead		154,000

5.

A.

	Job 50	Job 51
Direct materials	$250,000	$324,000
Direct labor	400,000	528,000
Factory overhead	70,000	84,000
Total costs	$720,000	$936,000

B. Job 50 $31.25 = $720,000 ÷ 23,040 units
   Job 51 $36.00 = $936,000 ÷ 26,000 units

6. $8,015,000 = $440,000 + (303,000 × $25)*

   *Cost per unit of goods produced during the year = $25 = $7,800,000 ÷ 312,000 units

Need more help? Watch step-by-step videos of how to compute answers to these Exercises in CengageNOWv2.

Problem

1. A.

Materials	15,500	
Accounts Payable		15,500

   B.

Work in Process	11,390	
Materials		11,390
Work in Process	7,000	
Wages Payable		7,000
Factory Overhead	1,100	
Materials		450
Wages Payable		650

   C.

Factory Overhead	2,700	
Accounts Payable		2,700

   D.

Factory Overhead	1,750	
Accumulated Depreciation—Machinery		1,750

   E.

Work in Process	4,900	
Factory Overhead (70% of $7,000)		4,900

   F.

Finished Goods	11,548	
Work in Process		11,548

Computation of the cost of jobs finished:

Job	Direct Materials	Direct Labor	Factory Overhead	Total
Job No. 100	$2,650	$1,770	$1,239	$ 5,659
Job No. 101	1,240	650	455	2,345
Job No. 102	980	420	294	1,694
Job No. 104	1,000	500	350	1,850
				$11,548

G.

Accounts Receivable	15,400	
Sales		15,400
Cost of Goods Sold	9,698	
Finished Goods		9,698

Cost of jobs sold computation:

Job No. 100	$5,659
Job No. 101	2,345
Job No. 102	1,694
	$9,698

2. Work in Process: $11,742 ($11,390 + $7,000 + $4,900 – $11,548)

Finished Goods: $1,850 ($11,548 – $9,698)

3.

Schedule of Unfinished Jobs

Job	Direct Materials	Direct Labor	Factory Overhead	Total
Job No. 103	$3,420	$1,900	$1,330	$ 6,650
Job No. 105	2,100	1,760	1,232	5,092
Balance of Work in Process, March 31				$11,742

4.

Schedule of Completed Jobs

Job No. 104:

Direct materials	$1,000
Direct labor	500
Factory overhead	350
Balance of Finished Goods, March 31	$1,850

Discussion Questions

1. A. Name two principal types of cost accounting systems.

   B. Which system provides for a separate record of each particular quantity of product that passes through the factory?

   C. Which system accumulates the costs for each department or process within the factory?

2. What kind of firm would use a job order cost system?

3. Which account is used in the job order cost system to accumulate direct materials, direct labor, and factory overhead applied to production costs for individual jobs?

4. What document is the source for (A) debiting the accounts in the materials ledger and (B) crediting the accounts in the materials ledger?

5. What is a job cost sheet?

6. What is the difference between a clock card and time ticket?

7. Discuss how the predetermined factory overhead rate can be used in job order cost accounting to assist management in pricing jobs.

8. A. How is a predetermined factory overhead rate calculated?

   B. Name three common bases used in calculating the rate.

9. A. What is (1) overapplied factory overhead and (2) underapplied factory overhead?

   B. If the factory overhead account has a debit balance, was factory overhead underapplied or overapplied?

   C. If the factory overhead account has a credit balance at the end of the first month of the fiscal year, where will the amount of this balance be reported on the interim balance sheet?

10. Describe how a job order cost system can be used for professional service businesses.

Basic Exercises

SHOW ME HOW

BE 16-1 Issuance of materials | Obj. 2

On May 7, Bergan Company purchased on account 10,000 units of raw materials at $8 per unit. During May, raw materials were requisitioned for production as follows: 7,500 units for Job 200 at $8 per unit and 1,480 units for Job 305 at $5 per unit. Journalize the entry on May 7 to record the purchase and on May 31 to record the requisition from the materials storeroom.

SHOW ME HOW

BE 16-2 Direct labor costs | Obj. 2

During May, Bergan Company accumulated 2,500 hours of direct labor costs on Job 200 and 3,000 hours on Job 305. The total direct labor was incurred at a rate of $28 per direct labor hour for Job 200 and $24 per direct labor hour for Job 305. Journalize the entry to record the flow of labor costs into production during May.

SHOW ME HOW

BE 16-3 Factory overhead costs | Obj. 2

During May, Bergan Company incurred factory overhead costs as follows: indirect materials, $8,800; indirect labor, $6,600; utilities cost, $4,800; and factory depreciation, $9,000. Journalize the entry to record the factory overhead incurred during May.

SHOW ME HOW

BE 16-4 Applying factory overhead | Obj. 2

Bergan Company estimates that total factory overhead costs will be $620,000 for the year. Direct labor hours are estimated to be 80,000. For Bergan Company, (A) determine the predetermined factory overhead rate using direct labor hours as the activity base, (B) determine the amount of factory overhead applied to Jobs 200 and 305 in May using the data on direct labor hours from BE 16-2, and (C) prepare the journal entry to apply factory overhead to both jobs in August according to the predetermined overhead rate.

SHOW ME HOW

BE 16-5 Job costs | Obj. 2

At the end of May, Bergan Company had completed Jobs 200 and 305. Job 200 is for 2,390 units, and Job 305 is for 2,053 units. Using the data from BE 16-1, BE 16-2, and BE 16-4, determine (A) the balance on the job cost sheets for Jobs 200 and 305 at the end of May, and (B) the cost per unit for Jobs 200 and 305 at the end of May.

SHOW ME HOW

BE 16-6 Cost of goods sold | Obj. 2

Pine Creek Company completed 200,000 units during the year at a cost of $3,000,000. The beginning finished goods inventory was 25,000 units at $310,000. Determine the cost of goods sold for 210,000 units, assuming a FIFO cost flow.

Exercises

EX 16-1 Transactions in a job order cost system | Obj. 2

Five selected transactions for the current month are indicated by letters in the following T accounts in a job order cost accounting system:

Materials		Work in Process	
(A)		(A)	(D)
		(B)	
		(C)	

Wages Payable		Finished Goods	
(B)		(D)	(E)

Factory Overhead		Cost of Goods Sold	
(A)	(C)	(E)	
(B)			

Describe each of the five transactions.

EX 16-2 Cost flow relationships

Obj. 2

✔ B. $4,425,000

SHOW ME HOW

The following information is available for the first year of operations of Engle Inc., a manufacturer of fabricating equipment:

Sales	$7,270,000
Gross profit	1,450,000
Indirect labor	330,000
Indirect materials	195,000
Other factory overhead	90,000
Materials purchased	5,100,000
Total manufacturing costs for the period	6,170,000
Materials inventory, end of period	480,000

Determine the following amounts:

A. Cost of goods sold

B. Direct materials cost

C. Direct labor cost

EX 16-3 Cost of materials issuances under the FIFO method

Obj. 2

✔ B. $2,280

EXCEL TEMPLATE

An incomplete subsidiary ledger of materials inventory for May is as follows:

RECEIVED			ISSUED			BALANCE			
Receiving Report Number	Quantity	Unit Price	Materials Requisition Number	Quantity	Amount	Date	Quantity	Unit Price	Amount
						May 1	285	$30.00	$8,550
40	130	$32.00				May 4	___	___	___
			91	365		May 10	___	___	___
44	110	38.00				May 21	___	___	___
			97	100		May 27	___	___	___

A. Complete the materials issuances and balances for the materials subsidiary ledger under FIFO.

B. Determine the materials inventory balance at the end of May.

C. Journalize the summary entry to transfer materials to work in process.

D. ━━━► Explain how the materials ledger might be used as an aid in maintaining inventory quantities on hand.

SHOW ME HOW

EX 16-4 Entry for issuing materials

Obj. 2

Materials issued for the current month are as follows:

Requisition No.	Material	Job No.	Amount
201	Aluminum	500	$88,700
202	Plastic	503	27,600
203	Rubber	504	3,650
204	Glue	Indirect	2,250
205	Steel	510	38,750

Journalize the entry to record the issuance of materials.

EX 16-5 Entries for materials

Obj. 2

✔ C. fabric, $35,500

SHOW ME HOW

GenX Furnishings Company manufactures designer furniture. GenX Furnishings uses a job order cost system. Balances on June 1 from the materials ledger are as follows:

Fabric	$40,500
Polyester filling	28,600
Lumber	62,400
Glue	6,550

The materials purchased during June are summarized from the receiving reports as follows:

Fabric	$440,000
Polyester filling	180,000
Lumber	360,000
Glue	40,000

Materials were requisitioned to individual jobs as follows:

	Fabric	Polyester Filling	Lumber	Glue	Total
Job 601	$205,000	$ 75,000	$120,000		$400,000
Job 602	110,000	36,000	88,000		234,000
Job 603	130,000	55,000	125,000		310,000
Factory overhead—indirect materials				$34,800	34,800
Total	$445,000	$166,000	$333,000	$34,800	$978,800

The glue is not a significant cost, so it is treated as indirect materials (factory overhead).

A. Journalize the entry to record the purchase of materials in June.

B. Journalize the entry to record the requisition of materials in June.

C. Determine the June 30 balances that would be shown in the materials ledger accounts.

EX 16-6 Entry for factory labor costs

Obj. 2

SHOW ME HOW

A summary of the time tickets for the current month follows:

Job No.	Amount	Job No.	Amount
100	$ 3,500	Indirect	$ 9,100
101	6,650	111	8,620
104	21,900	115	2,760
108	14,440	117	18,550

Journalize the entry to record the factory labor costs.

EX 16-7 Entry for factory labor costs
Obj. 2

The weekly time tickets indicate the following distribution of labor hours for three direct labor employees:

		Hours		
	Job 301	Job 302	Job 303	Process Improvement
Tom Couro	10	15	13	2
David Clancy	12	12	14	2
Jose Cano	11	13	15	1

The direct labor rate earned per hour by the three employees is as follows:

Tom Couro	$32
David Clancy	36
Jose Cano	28

The process improvement category includes training, quality improvement, and other indirect tasks.

A. Journalize the entry to record the factory labor costs for the week.

B. Assume that Jobs 301 and 302 were completed but not sold during the week and that Job 303 remained incomplete at the end of the week. How would the direct labor costs for all three jobs be reflected on the financial statements at the end of the week?

SHOW ME HOW

EX 16-8 Entries for direct labor and factory overhead
Obj. 2

Townsend Industries Inc. manufactures recreational vehicles. Townsend uses a job order cost system. The time tickets from November jobs are summarized as follows:

Job 11-101	$6,240
Job 11-102	9,000
Job 11-103	7,210
Job 11-104	6,750
Factory supervision	4,000

Factory overhead is applied to jobs on the basis of a predetermined overhead rate of $18 per direct labor hour. The direct labor rate is $40 per hour.

A. Journalize the entry to record the factory labor costs.

B. Journalize the entry to apply factory overhead to production for November.

✔ B. $40.80 per direct labor hour

SHOW ME HOW

EX 16-9 Factory overhead rates, entries, and account balance
Obj. 2

Sundance Solar Company operates two factories. The company applies factory overhead to jobs on the basis of machine hours in Factory 1 and on the basis of direct labor hours in Factory 2. Estimated factory overhead costs, direct labor hours, and machine hours are as follows:

	Factory 1	Factory 2
Estimated factory overhead cost for fiscal year beginning March 1	$12,900,000	$10,200,000
Estimated direct labor hours for year		250,000
Estimated machine hours for year	600,000	
Actual factory overhead costs for March	$12,990,000	$10,090,000
Actual direct labor hours for March		245,000
Actual machine hours for March	610,000	

A. Determine the factory overhead rate for Factory 1.

B. Determine the factory overhead rate for Factory 2.

C. Journalize the entries to apply factory overhead to production in each factory for March.

D. Determine the balances of the factory overhead accounts for each factory as of March 31, and indicate whether the amounts represent over- or underapplied factory overhead.

SHOW ME HOW

EX 16-10 Predetermined factory overhead rate

Obj. 2

Spring Street Engine Shop uses a job order cost system to determine the cost of performing engine repair work. Estimated costs and expenses for the coming period are as follows:

Engine parts	$ 875,000
Shop direct labor	660,000
Shop and repair equipment depreciation	44,500
Shop supervisor salaries	138,000
Shop property taxes	27,500
Shop supplies	10,000
Advertising expense	22,100
Administrative office salaries	73,500
Administrative office depreciation expense	8,600
Total costs and expenses	$1,859,200

The average shop direct labor rate is $30 per hour.

Determine the predetermined shop overhead rate per direct labor hour.

EX 16-11 Predetermined factory overhead rate

Obj. 2

✔ A. $290 per hour

SHOW ME HOW

Poehling Medical Center has a single operating room that is used by local physicians to perform surgical procedures. The cost of using the operating room is accumulated by each patient procedure and includes the direct materials costs (drugs and medical devices), physician surgical time, and operating room overhead. On January 1 of the current year, the annual operating room overhead is estimated to be:

Disposable supplies	$299,600
Depreciation expense	75,000
Utilities	32,000
Nurse salaries	278,500
Technician wages	126,900
Total operating room overhead	$812,000

The overhead costs will be assigned to procedures, based on the number of surgical room hours. Poehling Medical Center expects to use the operating room an average of eight hours per day, seven days per week. In addition, the operating room will be shut down two weeks per year for general repairs.

A. Determine the predetermined operating room overhead rate for the year.

B. Bill Harris had a five-hour procedure on January 22. How much operating room overhead would be charged to his procedure, using the rate determined in part (A)?

C. During January, the operating room was used 240 hours. The actual overhead costs incurred for January were $67,250. Determine the overhead under- or overapplied for the period.

EX 16-12 Entry for jobs completed; cost of unfinished jobs

Obj. 2

✔ B. $95,200

SHOW ME HOW

The following account appears in the ledger prior to recognizing the jobs completed in August:

Work in Process	
Balance, August 1	$ 60,000
Direct materials	325,000
Direct labor	462,000
Factory overhead	210,000

Jobs finished during August are summarized as follows:

Job 210	$197,800	Job 224	$160,000
Job 216	240,000	Job 230	364,000

A. Journalize the entry to record the jobs completed.

B. Determine the cost of the unfinished jobs at August 31.

EX 16-13 Entries for factory costs and jobs completed

Obj. 2

✔ D. $73,750

Old School Publishing Inc. began printing operations on January 1. Jobs 301 and 302 were completed during the month, and all costs applicable to them were recorded on the related cost sheets. Jobs 303 and 304 are still in process at the end of the month, and all applicable costs except factory overhead have been recorded on the related cost sheets. In addition to the materials and labor charged directly to the jobs, $8,000 of indirect materials and $12,400 of indirect labor were used during the month. The cost sheets for the four jobs entering production during the month are as follows, in summary form:

Job 301	
Direct materials	$10,000
Direct labor	8,000
Factory overhead	6,000
Total	$24,000

Job 302	
Direct materials	$20,000
Direct labor	17,000
Factory overhead	12,750
Total	$49,750

Job 303	
Direct materials	$24,000
Direct labor	18,000
Factory overhead	—

Job 304	
Direct materials	$14,000
Direct labor	12,000
Factory overhead	—

Journalize the summary entry to record each of the following operations for January (one entry for each operation):

A. Direct and indirect materials used.

B. Direct and indirect labor used.

C. Factory overhead applied to all four jobs (a single overhead rate is used based on direct labor cost).

D. Completion of Jobs 301 and 302.

EX 16-14 Financial statements of a manufacturing firm

Obj. 2

✔ A. Income from operations, $170,000

EXCEL TEMPLATE

The following events took place for Chi-Lite Inc. during June, the first month of operations as a producer of road bikes:

- Purchased $400,000 of materials.
- Used $343,750 of direct materials in production.
- Incurred $295,000 of direct labor wages.
- Applied factory overhead at a rate of 75% of direct labor cost.
- Transferred $815,000 of work in process to finished goods.
- Sold goods with a cost of $789,000.
- Sold goods for $1,400,000.
- Incurred $316,000 of selling expenses.
- Incurred $125,000 of administrative expenses.

A. Prepare the June income statement for Chi-Lite. Assume that Chi-Lite uses the perpetual inventory method.

B. Determine the inventory balances at the end of the first month of operations.

EX 16-15   Job order cost accounting for a service company   Obj. 3

✔ B. Underapplied, $5,530

The law firm of Furlan and Benson accumulates costs associated with individual cases, using a job order cost system. The following transactions occurred during July:

July 3.   Charged 175 hours of professional (lawyer) time to the Obsidian Co. breech of contract suit to prepare for the trial, at a rate of $150 per hour.

    10.   Reimbursed travel costs to employees for depositions related to the Obsidian case, $12,500.

    14.   Charged 260 hours of professional time for the Obsidian trial at a rate of $185 per hour.

    18.   Received invoice from consultants Wadsley and Harden for $30,000 for expert testimony related to the Obsidian trial.

    27.   Applied office overhead at a rate of $62 per professional hour charged to the Obsidian case.

    31.   Paid administrative and support salaries of $28,500 for the month.

    31.   Used office supplies for the month, $4,000.

    31.   Paid professional salaries of $74,350 for the month.

    31.   Billed Obsidian $172,500 for successful defense of the case.

A.   Provide the journal entries for each of these transactions.

B.   How much office overhead is over- or underapplied?

C.   Determine the gross profit on the Obsidian case, assuming that over- or underapplied office overhead is closed monthly to cost of services.

EX 16-16   Job order cost accounting for a service company   Obj. 3

✔ D. Dr. Cost of Services, $2,827,750

The Fly Company provides advertising services for clients across the nation. The Fly Company is presently working on four projects, each for a different client. The Fly Company accumulates costs for each account (client) on the basis of both direct costs and allocated indirect costs. The direct costs include the charged time of professional personnel and media purchases (air time and ad space). Overhead is allocated to each project as a percentage of media purchases. The predetermined overhead rate is 65% of media purchases.

On August 1, the four advertising projects had the following accumulated costs:

	August 1 Balances
Vault Bank	$270,000
Take Off Airlines	80,000
Sleepy Tired Hotels	210,000
Tastee Beverages	115,000
Total	$675,000

During August, The Fly Company incurred the following direct labor and media purchase costs related to preparing advertising for each of the four accounts:

	Direct Labor	Media Purchases
Vault Bank	$ 190,000	$ 710,000
Take Off Airlines	85,000	625,000
Sleepy Tired Hotels	372,000	455,000
Tastee Beverages	421,000	340,000
Total	$1,068,000	$2,130,000

At the end of August, both the Vault Bank and Take Off Airlines campaigns were completed. The costs of completed campaigns are debited to the cost of services account.

Journalize the summary entry to record each of the following for the month:

A.   Direct labor costs

B.   Media purchases

C.   Overhead applied

D.   Completion of Vault Bank and Take Off Airlines campaigns

Problems: Series A

SHOW ME HOW   GENERAL LEDGER

PR 16-1A   Entries for costs in a job order cost system   Obj. 2

Munson Co. uses a job order cost system. The following data summarize the operations related to production for July:

A.   Materials purchased on account, $225,750.

B.   Materials requisitioned, $217,600, of which $17,600 was for general factory use.

C.   Factory labor used, $680,000, of which $72,300 was indirect.

D.   Other costs incurred on account for factory overhead, $330,000; selling expenses, $180,000; and administrative expenses, $126,000.

E.   Prepaid expenses expired for factory overhead were $27,500; for selling expenses, $8,100; and for administrative expenses, $5,250.

F.   Depreciation of office building was $44,500; of office equipment, $16,800; and of factory equipment, $55,100.

G.   Factory overhead costs applied to jobs, $548,000.

H.   Jobs completed, $1,140,000.

I.   Cost of goods sold, $1,128,000.

Instructions

Journalize the entries to record the summarized operations.

PR 16-2A   Entries and schedules for unfinished jobs and completed jobs   Obj. 2

✔ 3. Work in Process balance, $11,840

Kurtz Fencing Inc. uses a job order cost system. The following data summarize the operations related to production for March, the first month of operations:

A.   Materials purchased on account, $45,000.

B.   Materials requisitioned and factory labor used:

Job	Materials	Factory Labor
301	$1,850	$2,500
302	3,150	7,220
303	2,200	5,350
304	1,800	2,400
305	4,230	6,225
306	1,770	2,900
For general factory use	1,200	5,000

C.   Factory overhead costs incurred on account, $1,800.

D.   Depreciation of machinery and equipment, $2,500.

E.   The factory overhead rate is $30 per machine hour. Machine hours used:

Job	Machine Hours
301	30
302	60
303	41
304	63
305	70
306	36
Total	300

(Continued)

F. Jobs completed: 301, 302, 303, and 305.

G. Jobs were shipped and customers were billed as follows: Job 301, $8,500; Job 302, $16,150; Job 303, $13,400.

Instructions

1. Journalize the entries to record the summarized operations.

2. Post the appropriate entries to T accounts for Work in Process and Finished Goods, using the identifying letters as transaction codes. Insert memo account balances as of the end of the month.

3. Prepare a schedule of unfinished jobs to support the balance in the work in process account.

4. Prepare a schedule of completed jobs on hand to support the balance in the finished goods account.

EXCEL TEMPLATE

PR 16-3A   Job order cost sheet
Obj. 2

Remnant Carpet Company sells and installs commercial carpeting for office buildings. Remnant Carpet Company uses a job order cost system. When a prospective customer asks for a price quote on a job, the estimated cost data are inserted on an unnumbered job cost sheet. If the offer is accepted, a number is assigned to the job, and the costs incurred are recorded in the usual manner on the job cost sheet. After the job is completed, reasons for the variances between the estimated and actual costs are noted on the sheet. The data are then available to management in evaluating the efficiency of operations and in preparing quotes on future jobs. On October 1, Remnant Carpet Company gave Jackson Consulting an estimate of $9,450 to carpet the consulting firm's newly leased office. The estimate was based on the following data:

Estimated direct materials:	
200 meters at $35 per meter	$7,000
Estimated direct labor:	
16 hours at $20 per hour	320
Estimated factory overhead (75% of direct labor cost)	240
Total estimated costs	$7,560
Markup (25% of production costs)	1,890
Total estimate	$9,450

On October 3, Jackson Consulting signed a purchase contract, and the delivery and installation were completed on October 10.

The related materials requisitions and time tickets are summarized as follows:

Materials Requisition No.	Description	Amount
112	140 meters at $35	$4,900
114	68 meters at $35	2,380

Time Ticket No.	Description	Amount
H10	10 hours at $20	$200
H11	10 hours at $20	200

Instructions

1. Complete that portion of the job order cost sheet that would be prepared when the estimate is given to the customer.

2. ➤ Record the costs incurred, and prepare a job order cost sheet. Comment on the reasons for the variances between actual costs and estimated costs. For this purpose, assume that the additional meters of material used in the job were spoiled, the factory overhead rate has proven to be satisfactory, and an inexperienced employee performed the work.

PR 16-4A   Analyzing manufacturing cost accounts   **Obj. 2**

✔ G. $751,870   Fire Rock Company manufactures designer paddle boards in a wide variety of sizes and styles.
The following incomplete ledger accounts refer to transactions that are summarized for June:

EXCEL TEMPLATE

Materials

| June | 1 | Balance | 82,500 | June 30 | Requisitions | (A) |
| | 30 | Purchases | 330,000 | | | |

Work in Process

June	1	Balance	(B)	June 30	Completed jobs	(F)
	30	Materials	(C)			
	30	Direct labor	(D)			
	30	Factory overhead applied	(E)			

Finished Goods

| June | 1 | Balance | 0 | June 30 | Cost of goods sold | (G) |
| | 30 | Completed jobs | (F) | | | |

Wages Payable

| | | | | June 30 | Wages incurred | 330,000 |

Factory Overhead

June	1	Balance	33,000	June 30	Factory overhead applied	(E)
	30	Indirect labor	(H)			
	30	Indirect materials	44,000			
	30	Other overhead	237,500			

In addition, the following information is available:

A. Materials and direct labor were applied to six jobs in June:

Job No.	Style	Quantity	Direct Materials	Direct Labor
201	T100	550	$ 55,000	$ 41,250
202	T200	1,100	93,500	71,500
203	T400	550	38,500	22,000
204	S200	660	82,500	69,300
205	T300	480	60,000	48,000
206	S100	380	22,000	12,400
Total		3,720	$351,500	$264,450

B. Factory overhead is applied to each job at a rate of 140% of direct labor cost.

C. The June 1 Work in Process balance consisted of two jobs, as follows:

Job No.	Style	Work in Process, June 1
201	T100	$16,500
202	T200	44,000
Total		$60,500

D. Customer jobs completed and units sold in June were as follows:

Job No.	Style	Completed in June	Units Sold in June
201	T100	X	440
202	T200	X	880
203	T400		0
204	S200	X	570
205	T300	X	420
206	S100		0

(Continued)

Instructions

1. Determine the missing amounts associated with each letter. Provide supporting calculations by completing a table with the following headings:

Job No.	Quantity	June 1 Work in Process	Direct Materials	Direct Labor	Factory Overhead	Total Cost	Unit Cost	Units Sold	Cost of Goods Sold

2. Determine the June 30 balances for each of the inventory accounts and factory overhead.

PR 16-5A   Flow of costs and income statement

Obj. 2

✔ 1. Income from operations, $432,000

EXCEL TEMPLATE

Ginocera Inc. is a designer, manufacturer, and distributor of custom gourmet kitchen knives. A new kitchen knife series called the Kitchen Ninja was released for production in early 20Y8. In January, the company spent $600,000 to develop a late-night advertising infomercial for the new product. During 20Y8, the company spent an additional $1,400,000 promoting the product through these infomercials, and $800,000 in legal costs. The knives were ready for manufacture on January 1, 20Y8.

Ginocera uses a job order cost system to accumulate costs associated with the Kitchen Ninja Knife. The unit direct materials cost for the knife is:

Hardened steel blanks (used for knife shaft and blade)	$4.00
Wood (for handle)	1.50
Packaging	0.50

The production process is straightforward. First, the hardened steel blanks, which are purchased directly from a raw material supplier, are stamped into a single piece of metal that includes both the blade and the shaft. The stamping machine requires one hour per 250 knives.

After the knife shafts are stamped, they are brought to an assembly area where an employee attaches the handle to the shaft and packs the knife into a decorative box. The direct labor cost is $0.50 per unit.

The knives are sold to stores. Each store is given promotional materials, such as posters and aisle displays. Promotional materials cost $60 per store. In addition, shipping costs average $0.20 per knife.

Total completed production was 1,200,000 units during the year. Other information is as follows:

Number of customers (stores)	60,000
Number of knives sold	1,120,000
Wholesale price (to store) per knife	$16

Factory overhead cost is applied to jobs at the rate of $800 per stamping machine hour after the knife blanks are stamped. There were an additional 25,000 stamped knives, handles, and cases in process and waiting to be assembled on December 31, 20Y8.

Instructions

1. Prepare an annual income statement for the Kitchen Ninja knife series, including supporting calculations, from the information provided.

2. Determine the balances in the work in process and finished goods inventories for the Kitchen Ninja knife series on December 31, 20Y8.

Problems: Series B

PR 16-1B   Entries for costs in a job order cost system

Obj. 2

SHOW ME HOW

GENERAL LEDGER

Royal Technology Company uses a job order cost system. The following data summarize the operations related to production for March:

A. Materials purchased on account, $770,000.

B. Materials requisitioned, $680,000, of which $75,800 was for general factory use.

C. Factory labor used, $756,000, of which $182,000 was indirect.

D. Other costs incurred on account for factory overhead, $245,000; selling expenses, $171,500; and administrative expenses, $110,600.

E. Prepaid expenses expired for factory overhead were $24,500; for selling expenses, $28,420; and for administrative expenses, $16,660.

F. Depreciation of factory equipment was $49,500; of office equipment, $61,800; and of office building, $14,900.

G. Factory overhead costs applied to jobs, $568,500.

H. Jobs completed, $1,500,000.

I. Cost of goods sold, $1,375,000.

Instruction
Journalize the entries to record the summarized operations.

PR 16-2B   Entries and schedules for unfinished jobs and completed jobs   Obj. 2

✔ 3. Work in Process
balance, $127,880

SHOW ME HOW   GENERAL LEDGER

Hildreth Company uses a job order cost system. The following data summarize the operations related to production for April, the first month of operations:

A. Materials purchased on account, $147,000.

B. Materials requisitioned and factory labor used:

Job No.	Materials	Factory Labor
101	$19,320	$19,500
102	23,100	28,140
103	13,440	14,000
104	38,200	36,500
105	18,050	15,540
106	18,000	18,700
For general factory use	9,000	20,160

C. Factory overhead costs incurred on account, $6,000.

D. Depreciation of machinery and equipment, $4,100.

E. The factory overhead rate is $40 per machine hour. Machine hours used:

Job	Machine Hours
101	154
102	160
103	126
104	238
105	160
106	174
Total	1,012

F. Jobs completed: 101, 102, 103, and 105.

G. Jobs were shipped and customers were billed as follows: Job 101, $62,900; Job 102, $80,700; Job 105, $45,500.

Instructions

1. Journalize the entries to record the summarized operations.

2. Post the appropriate entries to T accounts for Work in Process and Finished Goods, using the identifying letters as transaction codes. Insert memo account balances as of the end of the month.

3. Prepare a schedule of unfinished jobs to support the balance in the work in process account.

4. Prepare a schedule of completed jobs on hand to support the balance in the finished goods account.

EXCEL TEMPLATE

PR 16-3B   Job order cost sheet   Obj. 2

Stretch and Trim Carpet Company sells and installs commercial carpeting for office buildings. Stretch and Trim Carpet Company uses a job order cost system. When a prospective customer asks for a price quote on a job, the estimated cost data are inserted on an unnumbered job cost sheet. If the offer is accepted, a number is assigned to the job, and the costs incurred are recorded in the usual manner on the job cost sheet. After the job is completed, reasons for the variances between the estimated and actual costs are noted on the sheet. The data are then available to management in evaluating the efficiency of operations and in preparing quotes on future jobs. On May 9, Stretch and Trim gave Lunden Consulting an estimate

(Continued)

of $18,044 to carpet the consulting firm's newly leased office. The estimate was based on the following data:

Estimated direct materials:	
400 meters at $32 per meter	$12,800
Estimated direct labor:	
30 hours at $20 per hour..	600
Estimated factory overhead (80% of direct labor cost)................	480
Total estimated costs	$13,880
Markup (30% of production costs)..................................	4,164
Total estimate...	$18,044

On May 10, Lunden Consulting signed a purchase contract, and the carpet was delivered and installed on May 15.

The related materials requisitions and time tickets are summarized as follows:

Materials Requisition No.	Description	Amount
132	360 meters at $32	$11,520
134	50 meters at $32	1,600

Time Ticket No.	Description	Amount
H9	18 hours at $19	$342
H12	18 hours at $19	342

Instructions

1. Complete that portion of the job order cost sheet that would be prepared when the estimate is given to the customer. (Round factory overhead applied to the nearest dollar.)

2. ▬▬▶Record the costs incurred, and prepare a job order cost sheet. Comment on the reasons for the variances between actual costs and estimated costs. For this purpose, assume that the additional meters of material used in the job were spoiled, the factory overhead rate has proven to be satisfactory, and an inexperienced employee performed the work.

PR 16-4B Analyzing manufacturing cost accounts
Obj. 2

✔ G. $700,284

EXCEL TEMPLATE

Clapton Company manufactures custom guitars in a wide variety of styles. The following incomplete ledger accounts refer to transactions that are summarized for May:

Materials

May	1	Balance	105,600	May 31	Requisitions	(A)
	31	Purchases	500,000			

Work in Process

May	1	Balance	(B)	May 31	Completed jobs	(F)
	31	Materials	(C)			
	31	Direct labor	(D)			
	31	Factory overhead applied	(E)			

Finished Goods

May	1	Balance	0	May 31	Cost of goods sold	(G)
	31	Completed jobs	(F)			

Wages Payable

				May 31	Wages incurred	396,000

Factory Overhead

May	1	Balance	26,400	May 31	Factory overhead applied	(E)
	31	Indirect labor	(H)			
	31	Indirect materials	15,400			
	31	Other overhead	122,500			

In addition, the following information is available:

A. Materials and direct labor were applied to six jobs in May:

Job No.	Style	Quantity	Direct Materials	Direct Labor
101	AF1	330	$ 82,500	$ 59,400
102	AF3	380	105,400	72,600
103	AF2	500	132,000	110,000
104	VY1	400	66,000	39,600
105	VY2	660	118,800	66,000
106	AF4	330	66,000	30,800
	Total	2,600	$570,700	$378,400

B. Factory overhead is applied to each job at a rate of 50% of direct labor cost.

C. The May 1 Work in Process balance consisted of two jobs, as follows:

Job No.	Style	Work in Process, May 1
101	AF1	$26,400
102	AF3	46,000
Total		$72,400

D. Customer jobs completed and units sold in May were as follows:

Job No.	Style	Completed in May	Units Sold in May
101	AF1	X	264
102	AF3	X	360
103	AF2		0
104	VY1	X	384
105	VY2	X	530
106	AF4		0

Instructions

1. Determine the missing amounts associated with each letter. Provide supporting calculations by completing a table with the following headings:

Job No.	Quantity	May 1 Work in Process	Direct Materials	Direct Labor	Factory Overhead	Total Cost	Unit Cost	Units Sold	Cost of Goods Sold

2. Determine the May 31 balances for each of the inventory accounts and factory overhead.

PR 16-5B Flow of costs and income statement
Obj. 2

Technology Accessories Inc. is a designer, manufacturer, and distributor of accessories for consumer electronic products. Early in 20Y3, the company began production of a leather cover for tablet computers, called the iLeather. The cover is made of stitched leather with a velvet interior and fits snugly around most tablet computers. In January, $750,000 was spent on developing marketing and advertising materials. For the first six months of 20Y3, the company spent an additional $1,400,000 promoting the iLeather. The product was ready for manufacture on January 21, 20Y3.

Technology Accessories Inc. uses a job order cost system to accumulate costs for the iLeather. Direct materials unit costs for the iLeather are as follows:

Leather	$10.00
Velvet	5.00
Packaging	0.40
Total	$15.40

The actual production process for the iLeather is fairly straightforward. First, leather is brought to a cutting and stitching machine. The machine cuts the leather and stitches an exterior edge into the product. The machine requires one hour per 125 iLeathers.

After the iLeather is cut and stitched, it is brought to assembly, where assembly personnel affix the velvet interior and pack the iLeather for shipping. The direct labor cost for this work is $0.50 per unit.

(Continued)

The completed packages are then sold to retail outlets through a sales force. The sales force is compensated by a 20% commission on the wholesale price for all sales.

Total completed production was 500,000 units during the year. Other information is as follows:

Number of iLeather units sold in 20Y3	460,000
Wholesale price per unit	$40

Factory overhead cost is applied to jobs at the rate of $1,250 per machine hour. There were an additional 22,000 cut and stitched iLeathers waiting to be assembled on December 31, 20Y3.

Instructions

1. Prepare an annual income statement for the iLeather product, including supporting calculations, from the information provided.

2. Determine the balances in the finished goods and work in process inventories for the iLeather product on December 31, 20Y3.

Analysis for Decision Making

ADM-1 Graph job order costs over time

Alvarez Manufacturing Inc. is a job shop. The management of Alvarez Manufacturing Inc. uses the cost information from the job sheets to assess cost performance. Information on the total cost, product type, and quantity of items produced is as follows:

Date	Job No.	Product	Quantity	Amount
Jan. 2	1	TT	520	$16,120
Jan. 15	22	SS	1,610	20,125
Feb. 3	30	SS	1,420	25,560
Mar. 7	41	TT	670	15,075
Mar. 24	49	SLK	2,210	22,100
May 19	58	SLK	2,550	31,875
June 12	65	TT	620	10,540
Aug. 18	78	SLK	3,110	48,205
Sept. 2	82	SS	1,210	16,940
Nov. 14	92	TT	750	8,250
Dec. 12	98	SLK	2,700	52,650

A. Develop a graph for *each* product (three graphs), with Job Number (in date order) on the horizontal axis and Unit Cost on the vertical axis. Use this information to determine Alvarez Manufacturing Inc.'s cost performance over time for the three products.

B. ➤ What additional information would you require in order to investigate Alvarez Manufacturing Inc.'s cost performance more precisely?

ADM-2 Analyzing increase in job order costs

Raneri Trophies Inc. uses a job order cost system for determining the cost to manufacture award products (plaques and trophies). Among the company's products is an engraved plaque that is awarded to participants who complete a training program at a local business. The company sells the plaques to the local business for $80 each.

Each plaque has a brass plate engraved with the name of the participant. Engraving requires approximately 30 minutes per name. Improperly engraved names must be redone. The plate is screwed to a walnut backboard. This assembly takes approximately 15 minutes per unit. Improper assembly must be redone using a new walnut backboard.

During the first half of the year, Raneri had two separate plaque orders. The job cost sheets for the two separate jobs indicated the following information:

Job 101	May 4		
	Cost per Unit	**Units**	**Job Cost**
Direct materials:			
Wood	$20/unit	40 units	$ 800
Brass	15/unit	40 units	600
Engraving labor	20/hr.	20 hrs.	400
Assembly labor	30/hr.	10 hrs.	300
Factory overhead	10/hr.	30 hrs.	300
			$2,400
Plaques shipped			÷ 40
Cost per plaque			$ 60

Job 105	June 10		
	Cost per Unit	**Units**	**Job Cost**
Direct materials:			
Wood	$20/unit	34 units	$ 680
Brass	15/unit	34 units	510
Engraving labor	20/hr.	17 hrs.	340
Assembly labor	30/hr.	8.5 hrs.	255
Factory overhead	10/hr.	25.5 hrs.	255
			$2,040
Plaques shipped			÷ 30
Cost per plaque			$ 68

A. ➤ Why did the cost per plaque increase from $60 to $68?

B. ➤ What improvements would you recommend for Raneri Trophies Inc.?

ADM-3 Analyzing changes in job order direct material costs by product type

Brady Furniture Company manufactures wooden oak furniture. The company employs a job cost system to trace manufacturing costs to jobs. Each job represents a batch of furniture of the same type. Information regarding direct materials on selected jobs throughout the year is as follows:

Job No.	Date	Count	Style	Board Feet	Cost per Board Foot	Total Direct Materials Cost per Job
Job 102	Jan. 20	20	Dining tables	400	$5.00	$2,000
Job 106	Jan. 20	100	Coffee tables	1,000	5.00	5,000
Job 107	Jan. 20	50	Chairs	250	5.00	1,250
Job 203	Apr. 21	20	Dining tables	404	5.00	2,020
Job 205	Apr. 21	100	Coffee tables	990	5.00	4,950
Job 206	Apr. 21	52	Chairs	259	5.00	1,295
Job 289	July 20	20	Dining tables	448	6.00	2,688
Job 294	July 20	140	Coffee tables	1,414	6.00	8,484
Job 295	July 20	60	Chairs	312	6.00	1,872
Job 389	Oct. 18	22	Dining tables	517	6.00	3,102
Job 391	Oct. 18	160	Coffee tables	1,600	6.00	9,600
Job 392	Oct. 18	80	Chairs	400	6.00	2,400
Job 570	Dec. 11	25	Dining tables	615	6.00	3,690
Job 573	Dec. 11	180	Coffee tables	1,836	6.00	11,016
Job 574	Dec. 11	90	Chairs	450	6.00	2,700

(Continued)

Dining tables are the most difficult furniture item in Brady's catalog to manufacture. Thus, the most skilled employees are scheduled to make dining tables, unless they are required for other jobs.

A. Determine the material cost per unit for each job.

B. Use the January material cost per unit for each type of furniture as the base material cost. For each month and each type of furniture, determine the unit material cost as a percent of the base unit material cost. (Round percent to one decimal place.) Use the following table format:

	Jan.	Apr.	July	Oct.	Dec.
Dining tables	100%				
Coffee tables	100%				
Chairs	100%				

C. Develop a line chart of the percent of unit material cost to the base unit material cost. Place the months on the horizontal axis and use three lines for the three different types of furniture.

D. ━━━▶ Interpret the chart. What is happening to the dining tables?

Take It Further

ETHICS

TIF 16-1   Ethics in Action

TAC Industries Inc. sells heavy equipment to large corporations and federal, state, and local governments. Corporate sales are the result of a competitive bidding process, where TAC competes against other companies based on selling price. Sales to the government, however, are determined on a cost plus basis, where the selling price is determined by adding a fixed markup percentage to the total job cost.

Tandy Lane is the cost accountant for the Equipment Division of TAC Industries Inc. The division is under pressure from senior management to improve income from operations. As Tandy reviewed the division's job cost sheets, she realized that she could increase the division's income from operations by moving a portion of the direct labor hours that had been assigned to the job order cost sheets of corporate customers onto the job order costs sheets of government customers. She believed that this would create a "win–win" for the division by (1) reducing the cost of corporate jobs, and (2) increasing the cost of government jobs whose profit is based on a percentage of job cost. Tandy submitted this idea to her division manager, who was impressed by her creative solution for improving the division's profitability.

━━━▶ Is Tandy's plan ethical?

TIF 16-2   Team Activity

As an assistant cost accountant for Firewall Industries, you have been assigned to review the activity base for the predetermined factory overhead rate. The president, JoJo Gunn, is concerned about the wide fluctuation in the amount of over- or underapplied overhead in recent years.

An analysis of the company's operations and use of the current overhead rate (direct labor cost) has narrowed the possible alternative overhead bases to direct labor cost and machine hours. For the past five years, the following data have been gathered:

	Year 5	Year 4	Year 3	Year 2	Year 1
Actual overhead	$ 790,000	$ 870,000	$ 935,000	$ 845,000	$ 760,000
Applied overhead	777,000	882,000	924,000	840,000	777,000
(Over-) underapplied overhead	$ 13,000	$ (12,000)	$ 11,000	$ 5,000	$ (17,000)
Direct labor cost	$3,885,000	$4,410,000	$4,620,000	$4,200,000	$3,885,000
Machine hours	93,000	104,000	111,000	100,400	91,600

In teams:

A. Calculate a predetermined factory overhead rate for each alternative base, assuming that rates would have been determined using the total actual amount of factory overhead for the past five years to the total associated activity base for the same five-year period.

B. For each of the past five years, determine the over- or underapplied overhead, based on the two predetermined overhead rates developed in (A).

C. ━━━▶ Select a predetermined overhead rate that the company should use, and discuss the basis for your recommendation.

TIF 16-3 Communication

Carol Creedence, the plant manager of the Clearwater Company's Revival plant, has prepared the following graph of the unit costs from the job cost reports for the plant's highest volume product, Product CCR.

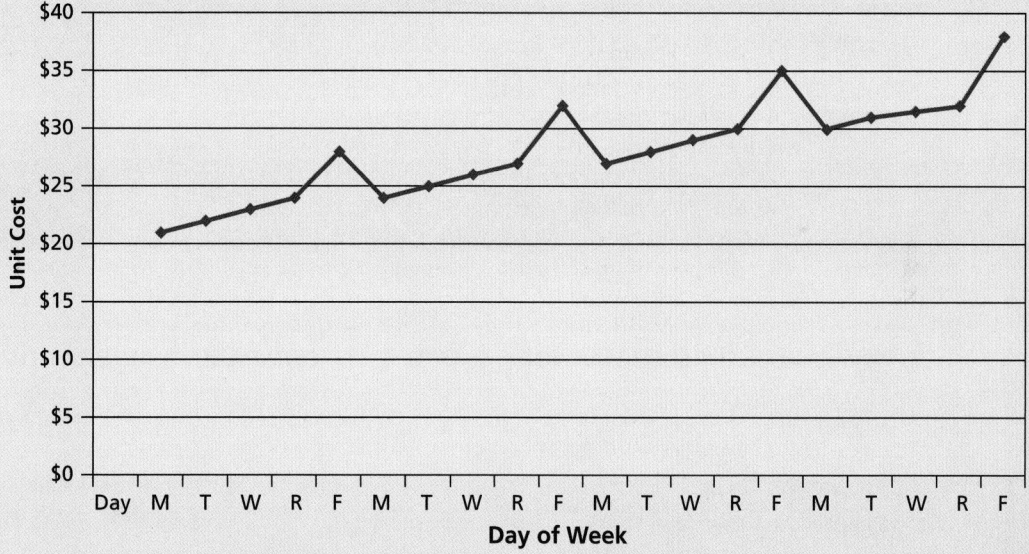

━━━▶ Carol is concerned about the erratic and increasing cost of Product CCR and has asked for your help. Prepare a one-half page memo to Carol, interpreting this graph and requesting any additional information that might be needed to explain this situation.

17 Process Cost Systems

Dreyer's Ice Cream

In making ice cream, an electric ice cream maker is used to mix ingredients, which include milk, cream, sugar, and flavoring. After the ingredients are added, the mixer is packed with ice and salt to cool the ingredients, and it is then turned on.

After mixing for half of the required time, would you have ice cream? Of course not, because the ice cream needs to mix longer to freeze. Now, assume that you ask the question:

What costs have I incurred so far in making ice cream?

The answer to this question requires knowing the cost of the ingredients and electricity. The ingredients are added at the beginning; thus, all the ingredient costs have been incurred. Because the mixing is only half complete, only 50% of the electricity cost has been incurred. Therefore, the answer to the preceding question is:

All the materials costs and half the electricity costs have been incurred.

These same cost concepts apply to larger ice cream processes like those of **Dreyer's Ice Cream** (a subsidiary of **Nestlé**), manufacturer of Dreyer's® and Edy's® ice cream. Dreyer's mixes ingredients in 3,000-gallon vats in much the same way you would with an electric ice cream maker. Dreyer's also records the costs of the ingredients, labor, and factory overhead used in making ice cream. These costs are used by managers for decisions such as setting prices and improving operations.

This chapter describes and illustrates process cost systems that are used by manufacturers such as Dreyer's. The principles of lean manufacturing are also described. Finally, the use of cost of production reports in decision making is discussed.

Source: www.dreyers.com

What's Covered

Process Cost Systems

Accounting for Process Manufacturers
- Compared to Job Order Cost Systems (Obj. 1)
- Cost Flows for Process Manufacturers (Obj. 1)

Cost of Production Report
- Units to Be Assigned Costs (Obj. 2)
- Equivalent Units (Obj. 2)
- Cost per Equivalent Unit (Obj. 2)
- Allocation of Costs (Obj. 2)
- Journalizing Costs (Obj. 3)
- Unit Cost Analysis (Obj. 4)

Lean Manufacturing
- Traditional Manufacturing Process (Obj. 5)
- Lean Manufacturing Process (Obj. 5)

Learning Objectives

Obj. 1 Describe process cost systems.

Obj. 2 Prepare a cost of production report.

Obj. 3 Journalize entries for transactions using a process cost system.

Obj. 4 Describe and illustrate the analysis of unit cost changes between periods.

Obj. 5 Compare lean manufacturing with traditional manufacturing processing.

Analysis for Decision Making

Describe and Illustrate the use of a cost of production report in evaluating a company's performance.

Objective 1
Describe process cost systems.

Accounting for Process Manufacturers

A **process manufacturer** produces products that are indistinguishable from each other using a continuous production process. For example, an oil refinery processes crude oil through a series of steps to produce a barrel of gasoline. One barrel of gasoline, the product, cannot be distinguished from another barrel. Other examples of process manufacturers include paper producers, chemical processors, aluminum smelters, and food processors.

The cost accounting system used by process manufacturers is called the **process cost system.** A process cost system records product costs for each manufacturing department or process.

In contrast, a job order manufacturer produces custom products for customers or batches of similar products. For example, a custom printer produces wedding invitations, graduation announcements, or other special print items that are tailored to the specifications of each customer. Each item manufactured is unique to itself. Other examples of job order manufacturers include furniture manufacturers, shipbuilders, and home builders.

As described and illustrated in Chapter 16, the cost accounting system used by job order manufacturers is called the *job order cost system*. A job order cost system records product costs for each job, using job cost sheets.

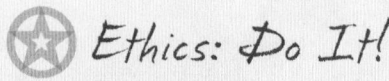
Ethics: Do It!

On Being Green

Process manufacturing often involves significant energy and material resources, which can be harmful to the environment. Thus, many process manufacturing companies, such as chemical, electronic, and metal processors, must address environmental issues. Companies such as **DuPont**, **Intel**, **Apple**, and **Alcoa** are at the forefront of providing environmental solutions for their products and processes.

For example, Apple provides free recycling programs for Macs®, iPhones®, and iPads®. Apple recovers more than 90% by weight of the original product in reusable components, glass, and plastic. You can even receive a free gift card for voluntarily recycling an older Apple product.

Source: www.apple.com.

Some examples of process and job order companies and their products are shown in Exhibit 1.

Process Manufacturing Companies		Job Order Companies	
Company	**Product**	**Company**	**Product**
PepsiCo	soft drinks	Disney	movies
Alcoa	aluminum	Nike	athletic shoes
Intel	computer chips	Nicklaus Design	golf courses
Apple	iPhone	Tennessee Heritage	log homes
Hershey	chocolate bars	DDB Worldwide	advertising

Exhibit 1

Examples of Process Cost and Job Order Companies

William Dreyer, an ice cream maker, and Joseph Edy, a candymaker, partnered to introduce **Dreyer's and Edy's Grand Ice Cream** in 1928. The ice cream was sold out of their ice cream parlor on Grand Avenue in Oakland, California.

Link to Dreyer's Ice Cream

Comparing Job Order and Process Cost Systems

Process and job order cost systems are similar in that each system:

■ Records and summarizes product costs.
■ Classifies product costs as direct materials, direct labor, and factory overhead.
■ Allocates factory overhead costs to products.
■ Uses a perpetual inventory system for materials, work in process, and finished goods.
■ Provides useful product cost information for decision making.

Process and job costing systems are different in several ways. As a basis for illustrating these differences, the cost systems for **Frozen Delight** and **Legend Guitars** are used.

Exhibit 2 illustrates the process cost system for Frozen Delight, an ice cream manufacturer. As a basis for comparison, Exhibit 2 also illustrates the job order cost system for Legend Guitars, a custom guitar manufacturer. Legend Guitars was described and illustrated in Chapters 15 and 16.

Exhibit 2 indicates that Frozen Delight manufactures ice cream, using two departments:

■ The Mixing Department mixes the ingredients, using large vats.
■ The Packaging Department puts the ice cream into cartons for shipping to customers.

Because each gallon of ice cream is similar, product costs are recorded in each department's work in process account. As shown in Exhibit 2, Frozen Delight accumulates (records) the cost of making ice cream in *work in process accounts* for the Mixing and Packaging departments.

The product costs of making a gallon of ice cream include:

■ *Direct materials costs,* which include milk, cream, sugar, and packing cartons. All materials costs are added at the beginning of the process for both the Mixing Department and the Packaging Department.
■ *Direct labor costs*, which are incurred by employees in each department who run the equipment and load and unload product.
■ *Factory overhead costs,* which include the utility costs (power) and depreciation on the equipment.

When the Mixing Department completes the mixing process, its product costs are transferred to the Packaging Department. When the Packaging Department completes its process, the product costs are transferred to Finished Goods. In this way, the cost of the product (a gallon of ice cream) accumulates across the entire production process.

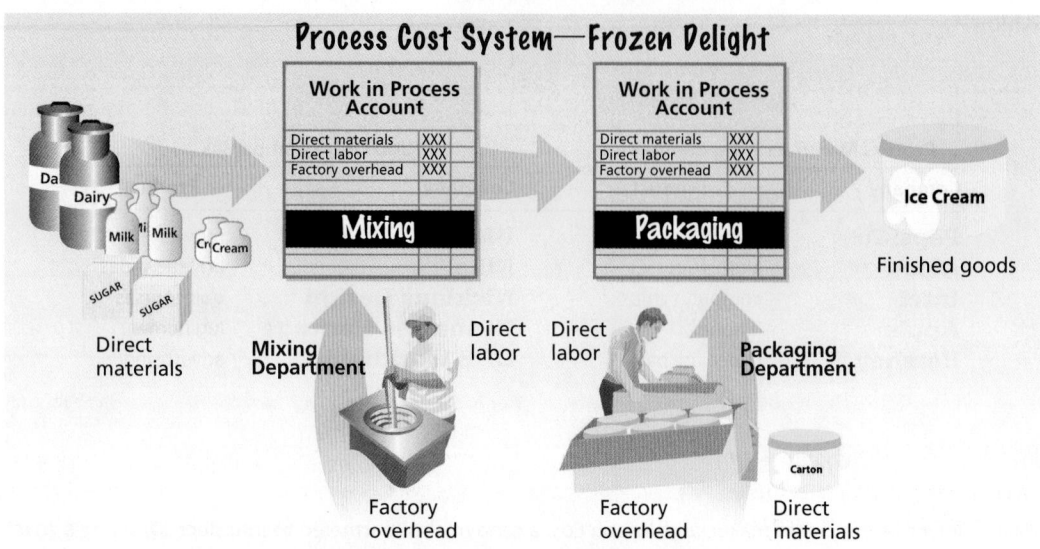

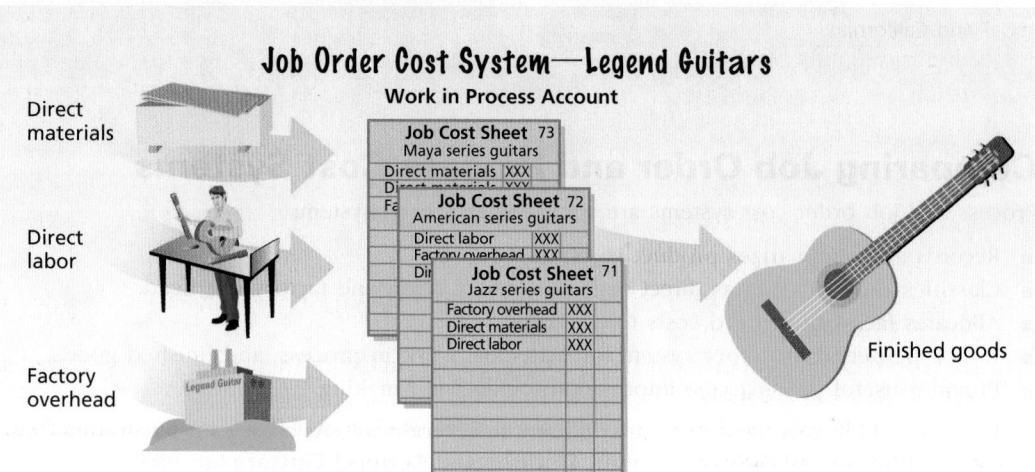

In contrast, Exhibit 2 shows that Legend Guitars accumulates (records) product costs by jobs, using a job cost sheet for each type of guitar. Thus, Legend Guitars uses just one work in process account. As each job is completed, its product costs are transferred to Finished Goods.

In a job order cost system, the work in process at the end of the period is the sum of the job cost sheets for partially completed jobs. In a process cost system, the work in process at the end of the period is the sum of the costs remaining in each department account at the end of the period.

Cost Flows for a Process Manufacturer

Exhibit 3 illustrates the *physical flow* of materials for **Frozen Delight**. Ice cream is made in a manufacturing plant in much the same way you would make it at home, except on a larger scale.

In the Mixing Department, direct materials in the form of milk, cream, and sugar are placed into a vat. An employee fills each vat, sets the cooling temperature, and sets the mix speed. The vat is cooled as the direct materials are being mixed by agitators (paddles). Factory overhead includes equipment depreciation and indirect materials.

Materials

Mixing Department

Packaging Department

Finished Goods Inventory

Freezer

Exhibit 3
Physical Flows for a Process Manufacturer

Dreyer's slow-churned ice cream uses a proprietary process that mixes nonfat milk slowly. This process, called low-temperature extrusion, allows ice cream to be made with one-third fewer calories and half the fat while tasting like normal ice cream.

Link to Dreyer's Ice Cream

In the Packaging Department, the ice cream is received from the Mixing Department in a form ready for packaging. The Packaging Department uses direct labor and factory overhead to package the ice cream into one-gallon containers. The ice cream is then transferred to finished goods, where it is frozen and stored in refrigerators prior to shipment to customers.

The *cost flows* in a process cost accounting system are similar to the *physical flow* of materials illustrated in Exhibit 3. The cost flows for **Frozen Delight** are illustrated in Exhibit 4 as follows:

A. The cost of materials purchased is recorded in the materials account.

B. The cost of direct materials used by the Mixing and Packaging departments is recorded in the work in process accounts for each department.

C. The cost of direct labor used by the Mixing and Packaging departments is recorded in work in process accounts for each department.

D. The cost of factory overhead incurred for indirect materials and other factory overhead such as depreciation is recorded in the factory overhead accounts for each department.

E. The factory overhead incurred in the Mixing and Packaging departments is applied to the work in process accounts for each department.

F. The cost of units completed in the Mixing Department is transferred to the Packaging Department.

G. The cost of units completed in the Packaging Department is transferred to Finished Goods.

H. The cost of units sold is transferred to Cost of Goods Sold.

As shown in Exhibit 4, the Mixing and Packaging departments have separate factory overhead accounts. The factory overhead costs incurred for indirect materials, depreciation, and other overhead are debited to each department's factory overhead account. The overhead is applied to work in process by debiting each department's work in process account and crediting the department's factory overhead account.

Exhibit 4 illustrates how the Mixing and Packaging departments have separate work in process accounts. Each work in process account is debited for direct materials, direct labor, and applied factory overhead. In addition, the work in process account for the Packaging Department is debited for the cost of the units transferred in from the Mixing Department. Each work in process account is credited for the cost of the units transferred to the next department.

Exhibit 4 shows that the finished goods account is debited for the cost of the units transferred from the Packaging Department. The finished goods account is credited for the cost of the units sold, which is debited to the cost of goods sold account.

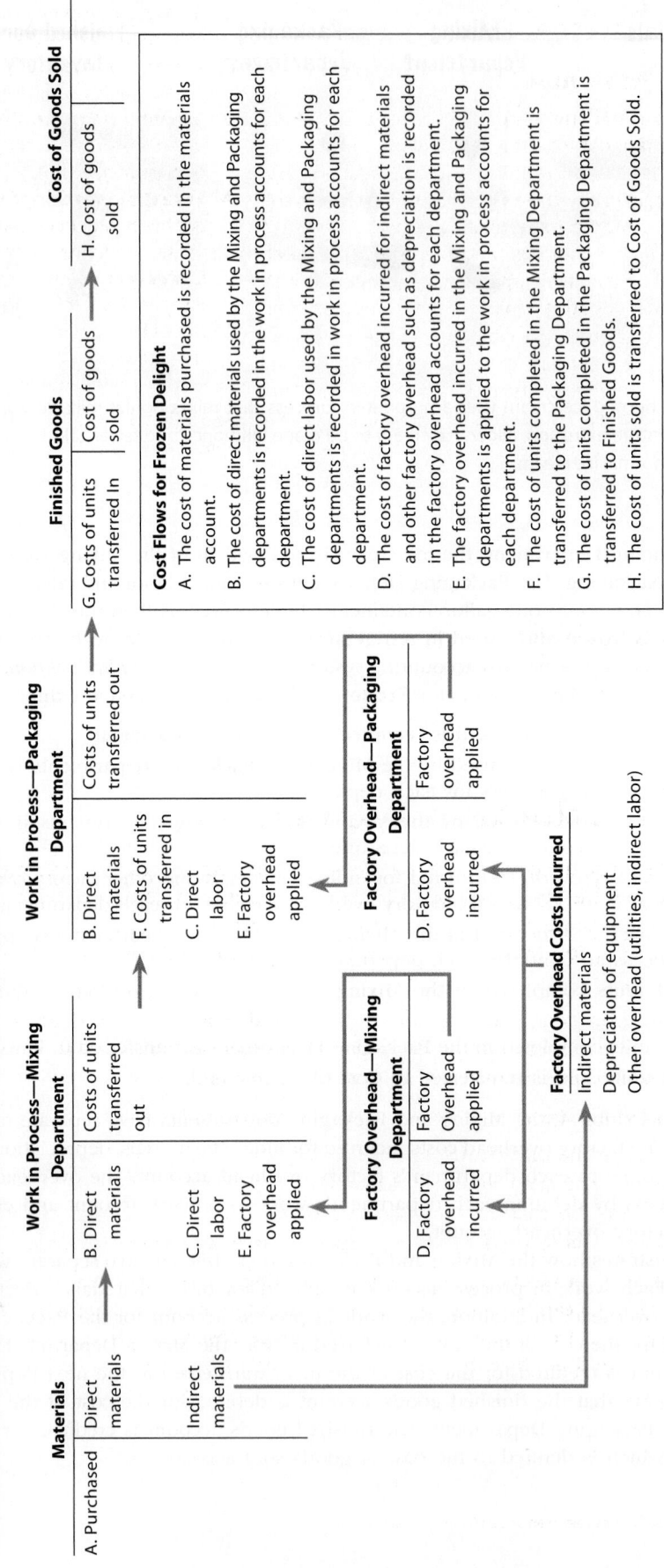

Exhibit 4 Cost Flows for a Process Manufacturer—Frozen Delight

Why It Matters

Sustainable Papermaking

We discussed social and environmental sustainability in the introductory managerial chapter. Processing companies involved with papermaking, refining, and chemical processing focus on sustainability because of their impact on the environment. For example, papermaking requires the use of large amounts of wood fiber (cellulous), energy, and water. Thus, papermakers are actively involved in sustainability efforts to reduce the negative environmental impacts from the use of these resources. To illustrate, International Paper Company provides an annual report to external stakeholders identifying its progress toward several sustainability objectives. A recent report identified six sustainability areas:

1. **Safety:** Improve worker health and safety, resulting in a 68% reduction in life-impacting injuries.
2. **Water use:** Identify and implement water conservation opportunities at each paper mill.
3. **Greenhouse gas emissions:** Reduce greenhouse gases by using renewable carbon-neutral biomass to meet over 70% of energy needs.
4. **Forest stewardship:** Implement sustainable forest management practices that provide a low-cost wood supply while simultaneously conserving primary forests.
5. **Ethics and compliance:** Train suppliers in the company's Supplier Code of Conduct.
6. **Stakeholder engagement:** Engage with communities, customers, and governments by participating in conferences, providing donations, and volunteering.

Source: *In Our Nature: Sustainability Year in Review 2014*, International Paper Company.

Dreyer's is currently a subsidiary of Nestlé, which produces Dreyer's ice cream at its Bakersfield, California plant.

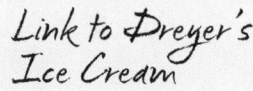
Link to Dreyer's Ice Cream

Cost of Production Report

Objective 2
Prepare a cost of production report.

In a process cost system, the cost of units transferred out of each processing department must be determined along with the cost of any partially completed units remaining in the department. The report that summarizes these costs is a cost of production report.

The **cost of production report** summarizes the production and cost data for a department as follows:

- The units the department is accountable for and the disposition of those units.
- The product costs incurred by the department and the allocation of those costs between completed (transferred out) and partially completed units.

A cost of production report is prepared using the following four steps:

- Step 1. Determine the units to be assigned costs.
- Step 2. Compute equivalent units of production.
- Step 3. Determine the cost per equivalent unit.
- Step 4. Allocate costs to units transferred out and partially completed units.

Preparing a cost of production report requires making a cost flow assumption. Like merchandise inventory, costs can be assumed to flow through the manufacturing process, using the first-in, first-out (FIFO), last in, first-out (LIFO), or average cost methods. Because the **first-in, first-out (FIFO) method** is often the same as the physical flow of units, the FIFO method is used in this chapter.[1]

---

[1] The average cost method is illustrated in an appendix to this chapter.

To illustrate, a cost of production report for the Mixing Department of **Frozen Delight** for July is prepared. The July data for the Mixing Department are as follows:

Inventory in process, July 1, 5,000 gallons:		
Direct materials cost, for 5,000 gallons	$5,000	
Conversion costs, for 5,000 gallons, 70% completed	1,225	
Total inventory in process, July 1		$ 6,225
Direct materials cost for July, 60,000 gallons		66,000
Direct labor cost for July		10,500
Factory overhead applied for July		7,275
Total production costs to account for		$90,000
Gallons transferred to Packaging in July (includes		
units in process on July 1), 62,000 gallons		?
Inventory in process, July 31, 3,000 gallons,		
25% completed as to conversion costs		?

By preparing a cost of production report, the cost of the gallons transferred to the Packaging Department in July and the ending work in process inventory in the Mixing Department are determined. These amounts are indicated by question marks (?).

Step 1: Determine the Units to Be Assigned Costs

The first step is to determine the units to be assigned costs. A unit can be any measure of completed production, such as tons, gallons, pounds, barrels, or cases. For **Frozen Delight**, a unit is a gallon of ice cream.

The Mixing Department is accountable for 65,000 gallons of direct materials during July, computed as follows:

Total units (gallons) charged to production:	
In process, July 1	5,000 gallons
Received from materials storage	60,000
Total units (gallons) accounted for	65,000 gallons

For July, the following three groups of units (gallons) are assigned costs:

- Group 1.   Units (gallons) in beginning work in process inventory on July 1.
- Group 2.   Units (gallons) started and completed during July.
- Group 3.   Units (gallons) in ending work in process inventory on July 31.

Exhibit 5 illustrates these groups of units (gallons) in the Mixing Department for July. The 5,000 gallons of beginning inventory were completed and transferred to the Packaging Department. During July, 60,000 gallons of material were started (entered into mixing). Of the 60,000 gallons started in July, 3,000 gallons were incomplete on July 31. Thus, 57,000 gallons (60,000 – 3,000) were started and completed in July.

The total units (gallons) to be assigned costs for July are summarized as follows:

Group 1	Inventory in process, July 1, completed in July	5,000 gallons
Group 2	Started and completed in July	57,000
	Transferred out to the Packaging Department in July	62,000 gallons
Group 3	Inventory in process, July 31	3,000
	Total units (gallons) to be assigned costs	65,000 gallons

The total gallons to be assigned costs (65,000) equal the total gallons accounted for (65,000) by the Mixing Department.

Step 2: Compute Equivalent Units of Production

Whole units are the number of units in production during a period, whether completed or not. **Equivalent units of production** are the portion of whole units that are complete with respect to materials or conversion (direct labor and factory overhead) costs.

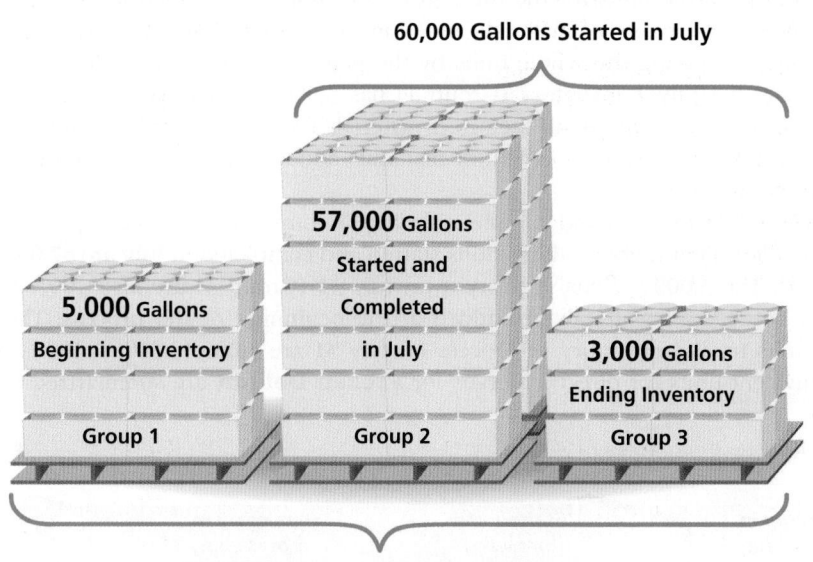

Exhibit 5
July Units to Be Costed—Mixing Department

60,000 Gallons Started in July

57,000 Gallons Started and Completed in July

5,000 Gallons Beginning Inventory

3,000 Gallons Ending Inventory

Group 1   Group 2   Group 3

65,000 Gallons to Be Assigned Costs

To illustrate, assume that a 1,000-gallon batch (vat) of ice cream at **Frozen Delight** is only 40% complete in the mixing process on May 31. Thus, the batch is only 40% complete as to conversion costs such as power. In this case, the whole units and equivalent units of production are as follows:

	Whole Units	Equivalent Units
Materials costs	1,000 gallons	1,000 gallons
Conversion costs	1,000 gallons	400 gallons (1,000 × 40%)

Because the materials costs are all added at the beginning of the process, the materials costs are 100% complete for the 1,000-gallon batch of ice cream. Thus, the whole units and equivalent units for materials costs are 1,000 gallons. However, because the batch is only 40% complete as to conversion costs, the equivalent units for conversion costs are 400 gallons.

Equivalent units for materials and conversion costs are usually determined separately as shown earlier. This is because materials and conversion costs normally enter production at different times and rates. In contrast, direct labor and factory overhead normally enter production at the same time and rate. For this reason, direct labor and factory overhead are combined as conversion costs in computing equivalent units.

Materials Equivalent Units To compute equivalent units for materials, it is necessary to know how materials are added during the manufacturing process. In the case of **Frozen Delight**, all the materials are added at the beginning of the mixing process. Thus, the equivalent units for materials in July are computed as follows:

		Whole Units	Percent Materials Added in July	Equivalent Units for Direct Materials
Group 1	Inventory in process, July 1	5,000	0%	0
Group 2	Started and completed in July (62,000 − 5,000)	57,000	100%	57,000
	Transferred out to Packaging Department in July	62,000	—	57,000
Group 3	Inventory in process, July 31	3,000	100%	3,000
	Total gallons to be assigned costs	65,000		60,000

As shown, the whole units for the three groups of units determined in Step 1 are listed in the first column. The percent of materials added in July is then listed. The equivalent units are determined by multiplying the whole units by the percent of materials added.

To illustrate, the July 1 inventory (Group 1) has 5,000 gallons of whole units, which are complete as to materials. That is, all the direct materials for the 5,000 gallons in process on July 1 were added in June. Thus, the percent of materials added in July is zero, and the equivalent units added in July are zero.

The 57,000 gallons started and completed in July (Group 2) are 100% complete as to materials. Thus, the equivalent units for the gallons started and completed in July are 57,000 (57,000 × 100%) gallons. The 3,000 gallons in process on July 31 (Group 3) are also 100% complete as to materials because all materials are added at the beginning of the process. Therefore, the equivalent units for the inventory in process on July 31 are 3,000 (3,000 × 100%) gallons.

The equivalent units for direct materials for **Frozen Delight** are summarized in Exhibit 6.

Exhibit 6

Direct Materials
Equivalent Units

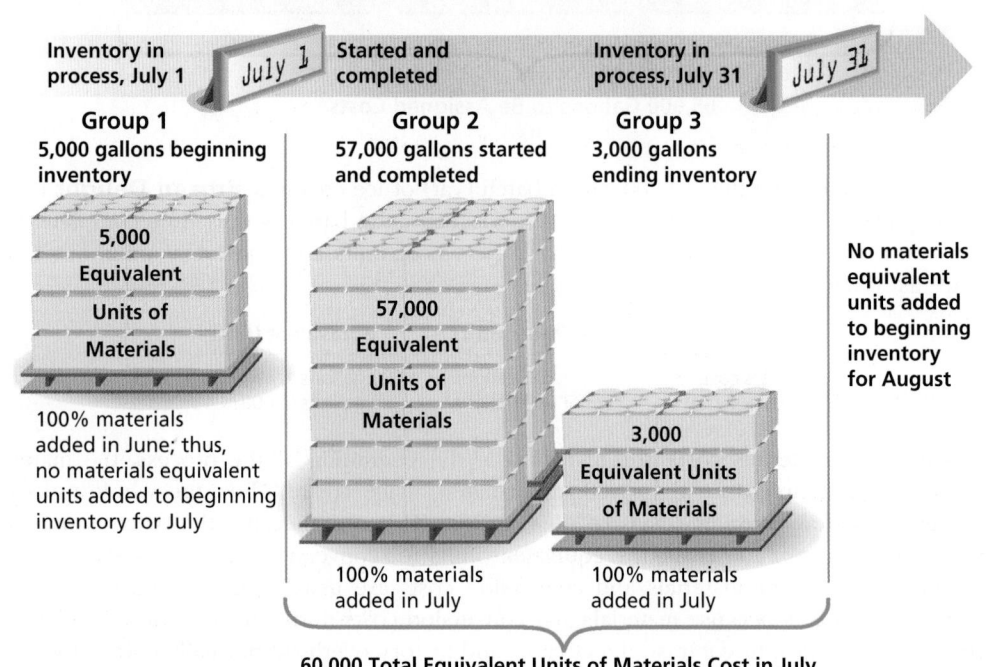

Conversion Equivalent Units To compute equivalent units for conversion costs, it is necessary to know how direct labor and factory overhead enter the manufacturing process. Direct labor, utilities, and equipment depreciation are often incurred uniformly during processing. For this reason, it is assumed that **Frozen Delight** incurs conversion costs evenly throughout its manufacturing process. Thus, the equivalent units for conversion costs in July are computed as follows:

		Whole Units	Percent Conversion Completed in July	Equivalent Units for Conversion
Group 1	Inventory in process, July 1 (70% completed).......	5,000	30%	1,500
Group 2	Started and completed in July (62,000 − 5,000)	57,000	100%	57,000
	Transferred out to Packaging			
	Department in July	62,000	—	58,500
Group 3	Inventory in process, July 31 (25% completed)......	3,000	25%	750
	Total gallons to be assigned costs	65,000		59,250

As shown, the whole units for the three groups of units determined in Step 1 are listed in the first column. The percent of conversion costs added in July is then listed. The equivalent units are determined by multiplying the whole units by the percent of conversion costs added.

To illustrate, the July 1 inventory has 5,000 gallons of whole units (Group 1), which are 70% complete as to conversion costs. During July, the remaining 30% (100% – 70%) of conversion costs was added. Therefore, the equivalent units of conversion costs added in July are 1,500 (5,000 × 30%) gallons.

The 57,000 gallons started and completed in July (Group 2) are 100% complete as to conversion costs. Thus, the equivalent units of conversion costs for the gallons started and completed in July are 57,000 (57,000 × 100%) gallons.

The 3,000 gallons in process on July 31 (Group 3) are 25% complete as to conversion costs. Hence, the equivalent units for the inventory in process on July 31 are 750 (3,000 × 25%) gallons.

The equivalent units for conversion costs for **Frozen Delight** are summarized in Exhibit 7.

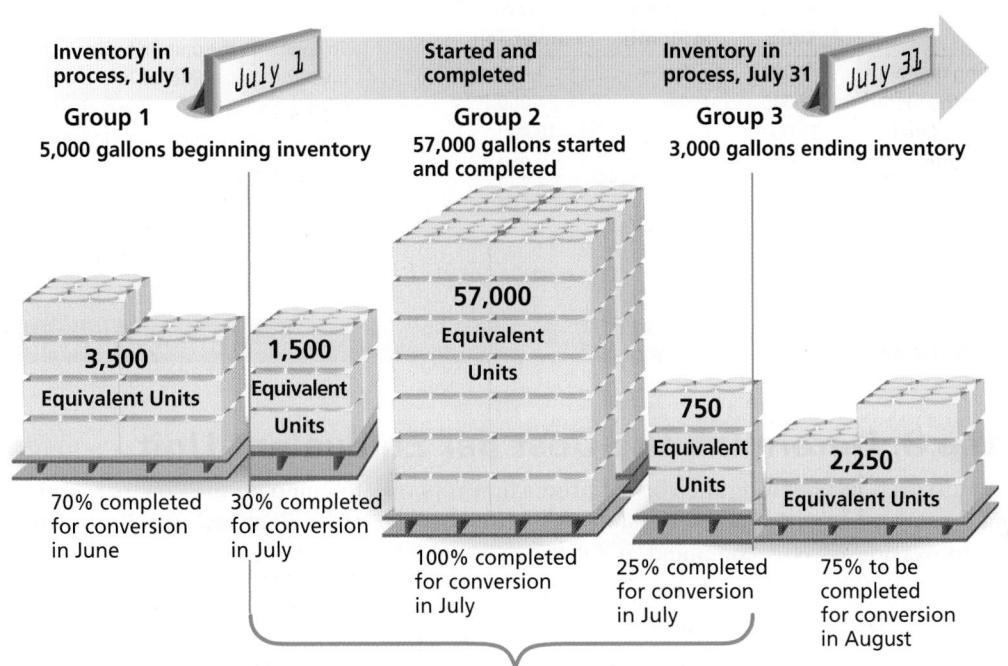

Exhibit 7

Conversion Equivalent Units

59,250 Total Equivalent Units of Conversion Costs in July

Check Up Corner 17-1 Equivalent Units

The Bottling Department of Rocky Springs Beverage Company had 2,000 liters in the beginning work in process (30% complete). During the month, 28,500 liters were started and 29,000 liters were completed. The ending work in process inventory was 1,500 liters (60% complete). Materials are added at the beginning of the process, while conversion costs are added evenly throughout the process.

A. How many units were started and completed during the month?

B. What are the total equivalent units for: (1) direct materials and (2) conversion costs?

Solution:

A. There are two ways to calculate the units started and completed.

	Units		Units
Completed (transferred out)	29,000	Started (during month)	28,500
Inventory in process, (beginning)	(2,000)	Inventory in process, (ending)	(1,500)
Started and completed	27,000	Started and completed	27,000

B.   1. Direct Materials

Whole units are the number of units in production.

Equivalent units are the portion of whole units that are complete for direct materials.

	Whole Units	Percent Materials Added in Month	Equivalent Units for Direct Materials
Inventory in process, beginning of month	2,000	0%	0
Started and completed during the month	27,000	100%	27,000
Transferred out of Bottling (completed)	29,000	—	27,000
Inventory in process, end of month	1,500	100%	1,500
Total units to be assigned costs	30,500		28,500

The equivalent units for beginning inventory is 0, because all (100%) of the materials were added at the beginning of the process, which occurred in the previous month.

Materials costs in ending inventory are 100% complete because all materials are added at the beginning of the process.

2. Conversion Costs

Equivalent units are the portion of whole units that are complete for conversion.

	Whole Units	Percent Conversion Completed in Month	Equivalent Units for Conversion
Inventory in process, beginning of month	2,000	70%	1,400
Started and completed during the month	27,000	100%	27,000
Transferred out of Bottling (completed)	29,000	—	28,400
Inventory in process, end of month	1,500	60%	900
Total units to be assigned costs	30,500		29,300

To complete the units in beginning inventory, an additional 70% of conversion costs (100% – 30% completed in prior month) must be added during the month.

Conversion costs in ending inventory are 60% complete because they are added evenly throughout the process during the current month.

Check Up Corner

Step 3: Determine the Cost per Equivalent Unit

The next step in preparing the cost of production report is to compute the cost per equivalent unit for direct materials and conversion costs. The **cost per equivalent unit** for direct materials and conversion costs is computed as follows:

$$\text{Direct Materials Cost per Equivalent Unit} = \frac{\text{Total Direct Materials Cost for the Period}}{\text{Total Equivalent Units of Direct Materials}}$$

$$\text{Conversion Cost per Equivalent Unit} = \frac{\text{Total Conversion Costs for the Period}}{\text{Total Equivalent Units of Conversion Costs}}$$

The July direct materials and conversion cost equivalent units for **Frozen Delight**'s Mixing Department from Step 2 are as follows:

		Equivalent Units	
		Direct Materials	Conversion
Group 1	Inventory in process, July 1	0	1,500
Group 2	Started and completed in July (62,000 – 5,000)	57,000	57,000
	Transferred out to Packaging Department in July	57,000	58,500
Group 3	Inventory in process, July 31	3,000	750
	Total gallons to be assigned costs	60,000	59,250

The direct materials and conversion costs incurred by Frozen Delight in July are as follows:

Direct materials		$66,000
Conversion costs:		
Direct labor..	$10,500	
Factory overhead	7,275	17,775
Total product costs incurred in July........................		$83,775

The direct materials and conversion costs per equivalent unit are $1.10 and $0.30 per gallon, respectively, computed as follows:

$$\text{Direct Materials Cost per Equivalent Unit} = \frac{\text{Total Direct Materials Cost for the Period}}{\text{Total Equivalent Units of Direct Materials}}$$

$$\text{Direct Materials Cost per Equivalent Unit} = \frac{\$66,000}{60,000 \text{ gallons}} = \$1.10 \text{ per gallon}$$

$$\text{Conversion Cost per Equivalent Unit} = \frac{\text{Total Conversion Costs for the Period}}{\text{Total Equivalent Units of Conversion Costs}}$$

$$\text{Conversion Cost per Equivalent Unit} = \frac{\$17,775}{59,250 \text{ gallons}} = \$0.30 \text{ per gallon}$$

The preceding costs per equivalent unit are used in Step 4 to allocate the direct materials and conversion costs to the completed and partially completed units.

Step 4: Allocate Costs to Units Transferred Out and Partially Completed Units

Product costs must be allocated to the units transferred out and the partially completed units on hand at the end of the period. The product costs are allocated using the costs per equivalent unit for materials and conversion costs that were computed in Step 3.

The total production costs to be assigned for **Frozen Delight** in July are $90,000, computed as follows:

Inventory in process, July 1, 5,000 gallons:		
Direct materials cost, for 5,000 gallons	$ 5,000	
Conversion costs, for 5,000 gallons, 70% completed	1,225	
Total inventory in process, July 1................................		$ 6,225
Direct materials cost for July, 60,000 gallons......................	$66,000	
Direct labor cost for July	10,500	
Factory overhead applied for July	7,275	
Costs incurred in July..		83,775
Total production costs to account for		$90,000

The units to be assigned these costs follow. The costs to be assigned these units are indicated by question marks (?).

		Whole Units	Total Cost
Group 1	Inventory in process, July 1, completed in July........	5,000 gallons	?
Group 2	Started and completed in July	57,000	?
	Transferred out to the Packaging		
	Department in July	62,000 gallons	?
Group 3	Inventory in process, July 31	3,000	?
	Total...	65,000 gallons	$90,000

Group 1: Inventory in Process on July 1 The 5,000 gallons of inventory in process on July 1 (Group 1) were completed and transferred out to the Packaging Department in July. The cost of these units of $6,675 is determined as follows:

	Direct Materials Costs	Conversion Costs	Total Costs
Inventory in process, July 1 balance.................			$6,225
Equivalent units for completing the			
July 1 in-process inventory	0	1,500	
Cost per equivalent unit	× $1.10	× $0.30	
Cost of completed July 1 in-process inventory........	0	$450	450
Cost of July 1 in-process inventory			
transferred to Packaging Department			$6,675

As shown, $6,225 of the cost of the July 1 in-process inventory of 5,000 gallons was carried over from June. This cost plus the cost of completing the 5,000 gallons in July was transferred to the Packaging Department during July. The cost of completing the 5,000 gallons during July is $450. The $450 represents the conversion costs necessary to complete the remaining 30% of the processing. There were no direct materials costs added in July because all the materials costs had been added in June. Thus, the cost of the 5,000 gallons in process on July 1 (Group 1) transferred to the Packaging Department is $6,675.

Group 2: Started and Completed The 57,000 units started and completed in July (Group 2) incurred all (100%) of their direct materials and conversion costs in July. Thus, the cost of the 57,000 gallons started and completed is $79,800, computed by multiplying 57,000 gallons by the costs per equivalent unit for materials and conversion costs as follows:

	Direct Materials Costs	Conversion Costs	Total Costs
Units started and completed in July..................	57,000 gallons	57,000 gallons	
Cost per equivalent unit	× $1.10	× $0.30	
Cost of the units started and completed in July.......	$62,700	$17,100	$79,800

The total cost of $86,475 transferred to the Packaging Department in July is the sum of the beginning inventory cost and the costs of the units started and completed in July, computed as follows:

Group 1	Cost of July 1 in-process inventory	$ 6,675
Group 2	Cost of the units started and completed in July	79,800
	Total costs transferred to Packaging Department in July	$86,475

Why It Matters

Fill 'Er Up

A study of the cost per gallon of unleaded gasoline in various parts of the country revealed the following:

Los Angeles	$3.71	Cleveland	$2.65
Chicago	3.58	Atlanta	2.49
Seattle	3.11	Boston	2.49
New York	2.87	St. Louis	2.42
Detroit	2.84	Austin	2.36
Omaha	2.66		

The cost per gallon ranged from a high of $3.71 in Los Angeles to a low of $2.36 in Austin, or a 57% difference. The price per barrel of oil was around $50 at the time of this study. Why would the price per gallon of gasoline be so different, when the price per barrel of oil, the basic material for making gasoline, is the same for everyone? Normally, the final price would be determined by the price of oil, the conversion cost of refining oil to gasoline, plus some additional amounts for distribution and profits. However, during this time period, refinery operations were shut down in parts of the country for repairs and overhauls. As a result, some regions were experiencing supply shortfalls that caused the price of gasoline to increase relative to those regions that remained well supplied. Refiners focus on minimizing downtime, so these types of disruptions do not occur.

Source: Alison Sider, "Refinery Woes Keep Pump Prices Up," *The Wall Street Journal,* August 24, 2015, p. A1.

Group 3: Inventory in Process on July 31 The 3,000 gallons in process on July 31 (Group 3) incurred all their direct materials costs and 25% of their conversion costs in July. The cost of these partially completed units of $3,525 is computed as follows:

	Direct Materials Costs	Conversion Costs	Total Costs
Equivalent units in ending inventory	3,000 gallons	750 gallons	
Cost per equivalent unit	× $1.10	× $0.30	
Cost of July 31 in-process inventory	$3,300	$225	$3,525

The 3,000 gallons in process on July 31 received all (100%) of their materials in July. Therefore, the direct materials cost incurred in July is $3,300 (3,000 × $1.10). The conversion costs of $225 represent the cost of the 750 (3,000 × 25%) equivalent gallons multiplied by the cost of $0.30 per equivalent unit for conversion costs. The sum of the direct materials cost ($3,300) and the conversion costs ($225) equals the total cost of the July 31 work in process inventory of $3,525 ($3,300 + $225).

To summarize, the total manufacturing costs for Frozen Delight in July were assigned as follows. In doing so, the question marks (?) for the costs to be assigned to units in Groups 1, 2, and 3 have been answered.

		Whole Units	Total Cost
Group 1	Inventory in process, July 1, completed in July	5,000 gallons	$ 6,675
Group 2	Started and completed in July	57,000	79,800
	Transferred out to the Packaging Department in July	62,000 gallons	$86,475
Group 3	Inventory in process, July 31	3,000	3,525
	Total.	65,000 gallons	$90,000

Dreyer's invented Rocky Road ice cream in 1929.

Link to Dreyer's Ice Cream

Preparing the Cost of Production Report

A cost of production report is prepared for each processing department at periodic intervals. The report summarizes the following production quantity and cost data:

- The units for which the department is accountable and the disposition of those units
- The production costs incurred by the department and the allocation of those costs between completed (transferred out) and partially completed units

Using Steps 1–4, the July cost of production report for **Frozen Delight**'s Mixing Department is shown in Exhibit 8. During July, the Mixing Department was accountable for 65,000 units (gallons). Of these units, 62,000 units were completed and transferred to the Packaging Department. The remaining 3,000 units are partially completed and are part of the in-process inventory as of July 31.

The Mixing Department was responsible for $90,000 of production costs during July. The cost of goods transferred to the Packaging Department in July was $86,475. The remaining cost of $3,525 is part of the in-process inventory as of July 31.

Exhibit 8   Cost of Production Report for Frozen Delight's Mixing Department—FIFO

	A	B	C	D	E
1		Frozen Delight			
2		Cost of Production Report—Mixing Department			
3		For the Month Ended July 31			
4					
5		Whole Units	Equivalent Units		
6	**UNITS**		Direct Materials	Conversion	
7	Units charged to production:				
8	Inventory in process, July 1	5,000			
9	Received from materials storeroom	60,000			
10	Total units accounted for by the Mixing Department	65,000			
11					
12	Units to be assigned costs:				
13	Inventory in process, July 1 (70% completed)	5,000	0	1,500	
14	Started and completed in July	57,000	57,000	57,000	
15	Transferred to Packaging Department in July	62,000	57,000	58,500	
16	Inventory in process, July 31 (25% completed)	3,000	3,000	750	
17	Total units to be assigned costs	65,000	60,000	59,250	
18					
19				Costs	
20	**COSTS**		Direct Materials	Conversion	Total
21					
22	Cost per equivalent unit:				
23	Total costs for July in Mixing Department		$ 66,000	$ 17,775	
24	Total equivalent units (from Step 2)		÷60,000	÷59,250	
25	Cost per equivalent unit		$ 1.10	$ 0.30	
26					
27	Costs assigned to production:				
28	Inventory in process, July 1				$ 6,225
29	Costs incurred in July				83,775[a]
30	Total costs accounted for by the Mixing Department				$90,000
31					
32					
33	Costs allocated to completed and partially				
34	completed units:				
35	Inventory in process, July 1—balance				$ 6,225
36	To complete inventory in process, July 1		$ 0 +	$ 450[b] =	450
37	Cost of completed July 1 work in process				$ 6,675
38	Started and completed in July		$ 62,700[c] +	$ 17,100[d] =	79,800
39	Transferred to Packaging Department in July				$86,475
40	Inventory in process, July 31		$ 3,300[e] +	$ 225[f] =	3,525
41	Total costs assigned by the Mixing Department				$90,000
42					

Step 1
Step 2
Step 3
Step 4

[a]$66,000 + $10,500 + $7,275 = $83,775   [b]1,500 units × $0.30 = $450   [c]57,000 units × $1.10 = $62,700   [d]57,000 units × $0.30 = $17,100
[e]3,000 units × $1.10 = $3,300   [f]750 units × $0.30 = $225

Check Up Corner 17-2 Cost per Equivalent Unit

The cost of direct materials transferred into the Bottling Department of Rocky Springs Beverage Company is $22,800. The conversion costs for the period in the Bottling Department are $8,790. The total equivalent units for direct materials and conversion costs are as follows:

	Equivalent Units (in liters)	
	Direct Materials	Conversion
Inventory in process, beginning of period	0	1,400
Started and completed during the period	27,000	27,000
Transferred out of Bottling (completed)	27,000	28,400
Inventory in process, end of period	1,500	900
Total units to be assigned costs	28,500	29,300

The beginning work in process inventory had a cost of $1,860.

A. Determine the cost per equivalent unit for: (1) direct materials and (2) conversion costs.

B. Determine the cost of units transferred out and the ending work in process inventory.

Note: The units transferred out and the equivalent units of production are computed in Check Up Corner 17-1.

Solution:

A. 1.

$$\frac{\text{Direct Materials Cost}}{\text{per Equivalent Unit}} = \frac{\text{Total Direct Materials Cost for the Period}}{\text{Total Equivalent Units of Direct Materials}}$$

$$\frac{\text{Direct Materials Cost}}{\text{per Equivalent Unit}} = \frac{\$22,800}{28,500 \text{ liters}} = \$0.80 \text{ per liter}$$

2.

$$\text{Conversion Cost per Equivalent Unit} = \frac{\text{Total Conversion Costs for the Period}}{\text{Total Equivalent Units of Conversion Costs}}$$

$$\text{Conversion Cost per Equivalent Unit} = \frac{\$8,790}{29,300 \text{ liters}} = \$0.30 \text{ per liter}$$

Costs per equivalent unit are used to allocate the direct materials and conversion costs to the completed and partially completed units in part B.

B.

Materials costs added during the current period

Conversion costs added during the current period

	Direct Materials Costs	Conversion Costs	Total Costs	
Inventory in process, beginning of period			$ 1,860	No materials cost is added during the current period for beginning inventory
To complete inventory in process, beginning of period	0	$ 420ᵃ	420	
Started and completed during the period	21,600ᵇ	$8,100ᶜ	29,700	
Transferred out of Bottling (completed)			$31,980	
Inventory in process, end of period	$ 1,200ᵈ	$ 270ᵉ	1,470	
Total costs assigned by the Bottling Department			$33,450	
Completed and transferred out of production			$31,980	
Inventory in process, ending			$ 1,470	

ᵃ$1,400 × $0.30 = $420 ᵇ$27,000 × $0.80 = $21,600 ᶜ$27,000 × $0.30 = $8,100 ᵈ$1,500 × $0.80 = $1,200
ᵉ$900 × $0.30 = $270

Journal Entries for a Process Cost System

The journal entries to record the cost flows and transactions for a process cost system are illustrated in this section. As a basis for illustration, the July transactions for **Frozen Delight** are used. To simplify, the entries are shown in summary form, even though many of the transactions would be recorded daily.

   A. Purchased materials, including milk, cream, sugar, packaging, and indirect materials on account, $88,000.

A = L + E
+   +

| A. | Materials | 88,000 | |
| | Accounts Payable | | 88,000 |

   B. The Mixing Department requisitioned milk, cream, and sugar, $66,000. This is the total amount from the original July data. Packaging materials of $8,000 were requisitioned by the Packaging Department. Indirect materials for the Mixing and Packaging departments were $4,125 and $3,000, respectively.

A = L + E
+ −

B.	Work in Process—Mixing	66,000	
	Work in Process—Packaging	8,000	
	Factory Overhead—Mixing	4,125	
	Factory Overhead—Packaging	3,000	
	Materials		81,125

   C. Incurred direct labor in the Mixing and Packaging departments of $10,500 and $12,000, respectively.

A = L + E
+   +

C.	Work in Process—Mixing	10,500	
	Work in Process—Packaging	12,000	
	Wages Payable		22,500

   D. Recognized equipment depreciation for the Mixing and Packaging departments of $3,350 and $1,000, respectively.

A = L + E
+ −

D.	Factory Overhead—Mixing	3,350	
	Factory Overhead—Packaging	1,000	
	Accumulated Depreciation—Equipment		4,350

   E. Applied factory overhead to Mixing and Packaging departments of $7,275 and $3,500, respectively.

A = L + E
+ −

E.	Work in Process—Mixing	7,275	
	Work in Process—Packaging	3,500	
	Factory Overhead—Mixing		7,275
	Factory Overhead—Packaging		3,500

F. Transferred costs of $86,475 from the Mixing Department to the Packaging Department per the cost of production report in Exhibit 8.

F.	Work in Process—Packaging	86,475		A = L + E
	Work in Process—Mixing		86,475	+ –

G. Transferred goods of $106,000 out of the Packaging Department to Finished Goods according to the Packaging Department cost of production report (not illustrated).

G.	Finished Goods—Ice Cream	106,000		A = L + E
	Work in Process—Packaging		106,000	+ –

H. Recorded the cost of goods sold out of the finished goods inventory of $107,000.

H.	Cost of Goods Sold	107,000		A = L + E
	Finished Goods—Ice Cream		107,000	– – Exp

Exhibit 9 shows the flow of costs for each transaction. The highlighted amounts in Exhibit 9 were determined from assigning the costs in the Mixing Department. These amounts were computed and are shown at the bottom of the cost of production report for the Mixing Department in Exhibit 8. Likewise, the amount transferred out of the Packaging Department to Finished Goods would have also been determined from a cost of production report for the Packaging Department.

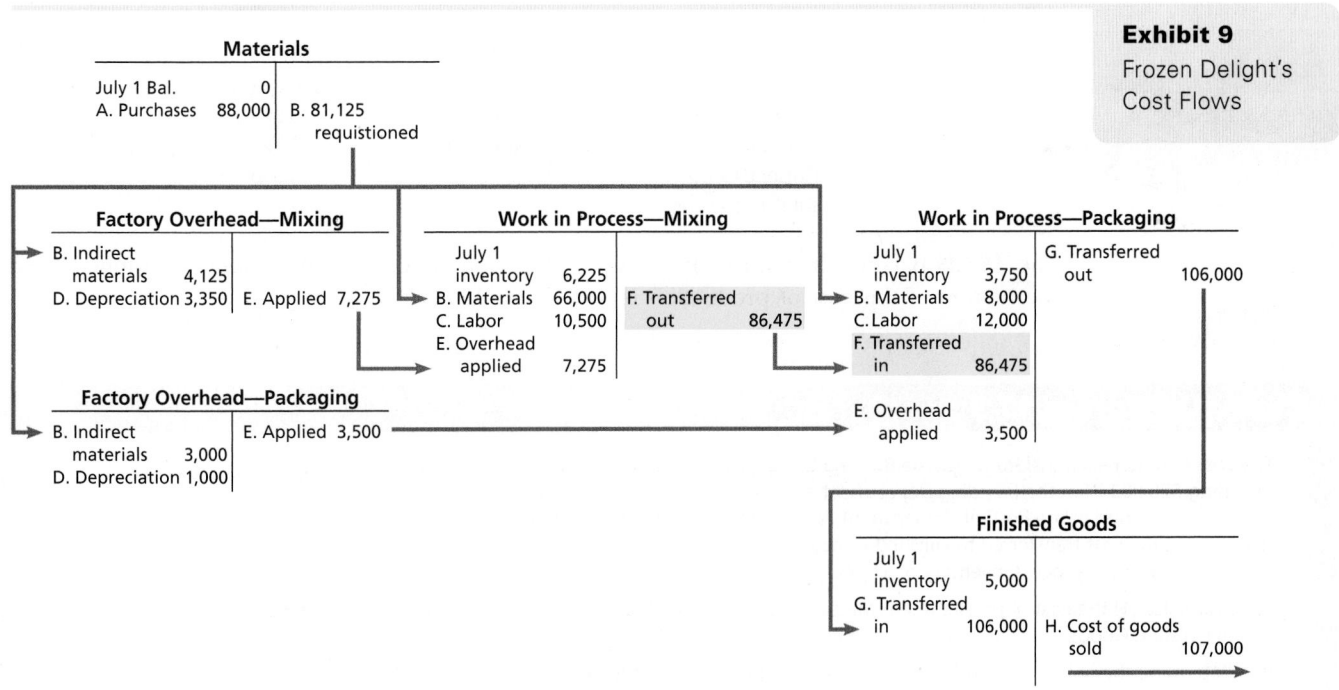

Exhibit 9
Frozen Delight's Cost Flows

Why It Matters

Process Costing for Services: Costing the Power Stack

Process costing can also be used in service businesses where the nature of the service is uniform across all units. Examples include electricity generation, wastewater treatment, and natural gas transmission. To illustrate, the unit of production in generating electricity is called a megawatt hour, where each megawatt hour is the same across all sources of generation.

Unlike product manufacturing, service companies often do not have inventory. For example, in generating electricity, the electricity cannot be stored. Thus, electric companies such as **Duke Energy Corporation** match the production of electricity to the demand in real time. Electric companies use what is termed the *power stack* to match power supply to demand by arranging generating facilities in order of cost per megawatt hour. The least-cost-per-megawatt-hour facilities satisfy initial demand at the bottom of the stack, while the highest-cost-per-megawatt-hour power sources are placed at

the top of the stack to satisfy peak loads, as illustrated in the following graph:

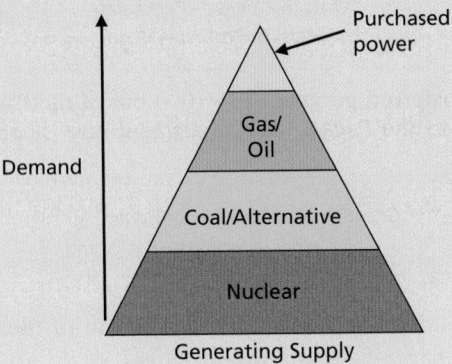

The cost per megawatt hour is determined using process costing by accumulating the conversion costs such as equipment depreciation, labor, and maintenance plus the cost of fuel for each facility. These costs are divided by the megawatt hours generated. Because there are no inventories, the additional complexity of equivalent units is avoided. The resulting cost per megawatt hour by facility is used to develop the power stack.

The ending inventories for Frozen Delight are reported on the July 31 balance sheet as follows:

Materials	$ 6,875
Work in Process—Mixing Department	3,525
Work in Process—Packaging Department	7,725
Finished Goods	4,000
Total inventories	$22,125

The $3,525 balance of Work in Process—Mixing Department is the amount determined from the bottom of the cost of production report in Exhibit 8.

Check Up Corner 17-3 | Process Costing Journal Entries

The cost of materials transferred into the Bottling Department of Rocky Springs Beverage Company is $22,800, including $20,000 from the Blending Department and $2,800 from the materials storeroom. The conversion costs for the period in the Bottling Department are $8,790 ($3,790 factory overhead applied and $5,000 direct labor). The total cost transferred to Finished Goods during the period is $31,980. The Bottling Department had a beginning work in process inventory of $1,860.

A. Journalize (1) the cost of transferred-in materials, (2) the conversion costs, and (3) the costs transferred out to Finished Goods.

B. Determine the balance of Work in Process—Bottling at the end of the period.

Note: The costs transferred out of the Bottling Department and the cost of the Bottling Department's ending inventory are computed in Check Up Corner 17-2.

Solution:

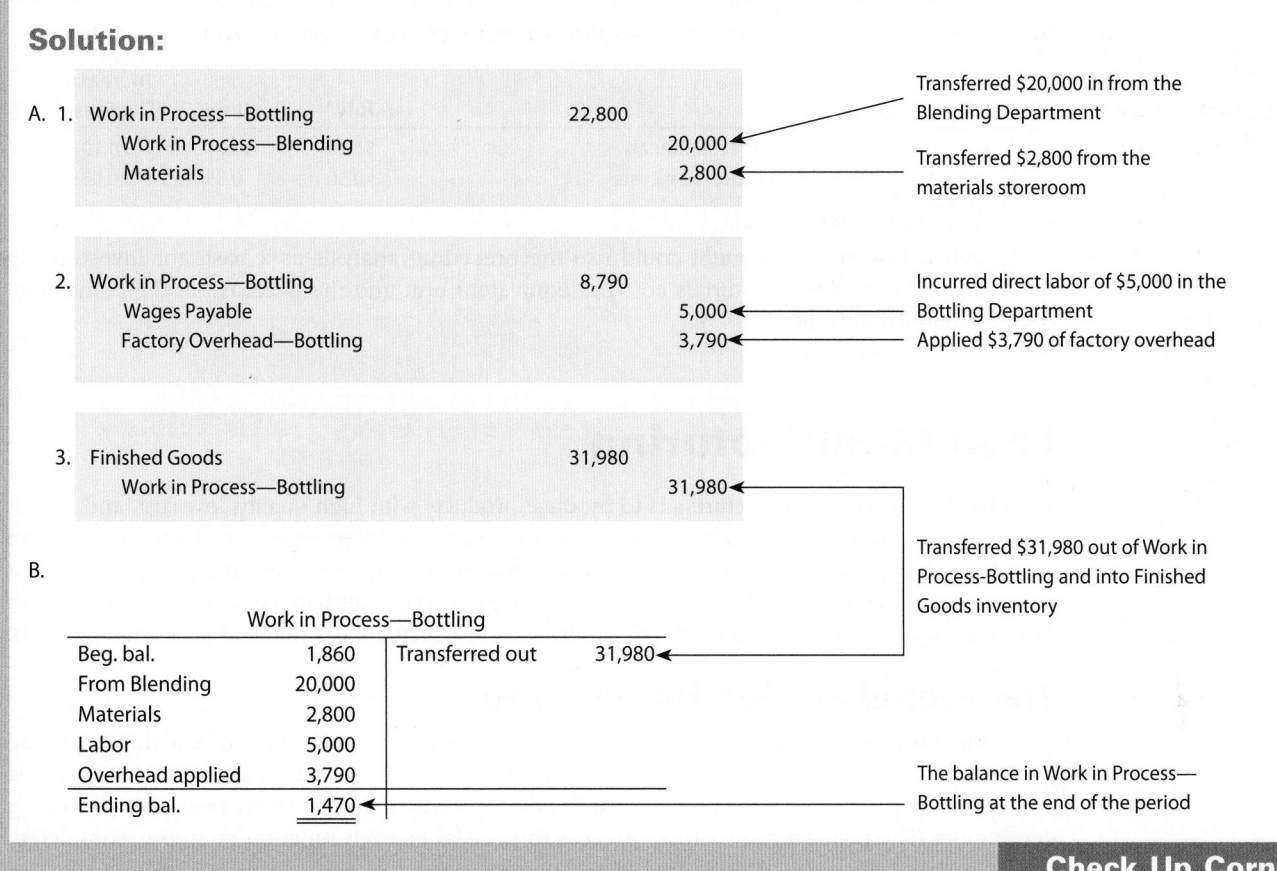

A. 1.
Work in Process—Bottling	22,800	
Work in Process—Blending		20,000
Materials		2,800

Transferred $20,000 in from the Blending Department

Transferred $2,800 from the materials storeroom

2.
Work in Process—Bottling	8,790	
Wages Payable		5,000
Factory Overhead—Bottling		3,790

Incurred direct labor of $5,000 in the Bottling Department

Applied $3,790 of factory overhead

3.
| Finished Goods | 31,980 | |
| Work in Process—Bottling | | 31,980 |

Transferred $31,980 out of Work in Process-Bottling and into Finished Goods inventory

B.

Work in Process—Bottling

Beg. bal.	1,860	Transferred out	31,980
From Blending	20,000		
Materials	2,800		
Labor	5,000		
Overhead applied	3,790		
Ending bal.	1,470		

The balance in Work in Process—Bottling at the end of the period

Check Up Corner

Using the Cost of Production Report

Objective 4
Describe and illustrate the analysis of unit cost changes between periods.

The cost of production report is often used by managers for analyzing the change in the conversion and direct materials cost per equivalent unit between periods. To illustrate, the cost of production report for **Frozen Delight** is used.

The cost of production report for the Mixing Department is shown in Exhibit 8. The cost per equivalent unit for June can be determined from the beginning inventory. The original Frozen Delight data indicate that the July 1 inventory in process of $6,225 consists of the following costs:

Direct materials cost, 5,000 gallons	$5,000
Conversion costs, 5,000 gallons, 70% completed	1,225
Total inventory in process, July 1	$6,225

Using the preceding data, the June costs per equivalent unit of materials and conversion costs can be determined as follows:

$$\text{Direct Materials Cost per Equivalent Unit} = \frac{\text{Total Direct Materials Cost for the Period}}{\text{Total Equivalent Units of Direct Materials}}$$

$$\text{Direct Materials Cost per Equivalent Unit} = \frac{\$5,000}{5,000 \text{ gallons}} = \$1.00 \text{ per gallon}$$

$$\text{Conversion Cost per Equivalent Unit} = \frac{\text{Total Conversion Costs for the Period}}{\text{Total Equivalent Units of Conversion Costs}}$$

$$\text{Conversion Cost per Equivalent Unit} = \frac{\$1,225}{(5,000 \times 70\%) \text{ gallons}} = \$0.35 \text{ per gallon}$$

In July, the cost per equivalent unit of materials increased by $0.10 per gallon, while the cost per equivalent unit for conversion costs decreased by $0.05 per gallon, computed as follows:

	July*	June	Increase (Decrease)
Cost per equivalent unit for direct materials	$1.10	$1.00	$ 0.10
Cost per equivalent unit for conversion costs	0.30	0.35	(0.05)

*From Exhibit 8

Frozen Delight's management could use the preceding analysis as a basis for investigating the increase in the direct materials cost per equivalent unit and the decrease in the conversion cost per equivalent unit.

Objective 5
Compare lean manufacturing with traditional manufacturing processing.

Lean Manufacturing

The objective of most manufacturers is to produce products with high quality, low cost, and instant availability. In attempting to achieve this objective, many manufacturers have implemented lean manufacturing (or just-in-time processing). **Lean manufacturing** is a management approach that produces products with high quality, low cost, fast response, and immediate availabililty. Lean manufacturing obtains efficiencies and flexibility by reorganizing the traditional production process.

Traditional Production Process

A traditional manufacturing process for a furniture manufacturer is shown in Exhibit 10. The product (chair) moves through seven processes. In each process, workers are assigned a specific job, which is performed repeatedly as unfinished products are received from the preceding department. The product moves from process to process as each function or step is completed.

Exhibit 10
Traditional Production Line

Furniture Manufacturer

Direct Materials — Work in Process — Finished Goods

Cutting Department · Drilling Department · Sanding Department · Staining Department · Varnishing Department · Upholstery Department · Assembly Department

For the furniture maker in Exhibit 10, the product (chair) moves through the following processes:

1. In the Cutting Department, the wood is cut to design specifications.
2. In the Drilling Department, the wood is drilled to design specifications.
3. In the Sanding Department, the wood is sanded.
4. In the Staining Department, the wood is stained.
5. In the Varnishing Department, varnish and other protective coatings are applied.
6. In the Upholstery Department, fabric and other materials are added.
7. In the Assembly Department, the product (chair) is assembled.

In the traditional production process, supervisors enter materials into manufacturing so as to keep all the manufacturing departments (processes) operating. Some departments, however, may process materials more rapidly than others. In addition, if one department stops because of machine breakdowns, for example, the preceding departments usually continue production in order to avoid idle time. In such cases, a buildup of work in process inventories results in some departments.

Lean Manufacturing

In lean manufacturing, processing functions are combined into work centers, sometimes called **manufacturing cells**. For example, the seven departments illustrated in Exhibit 10 might be reorganized into the following three work centers:

1. Work Center 1 performs the cutting, drilling, and sanding functions.
2. Work Center 2 performs the staining and varnishing functions.
3. Work Center 3 performs the upholstery and assembly functions.

The preceding lean manufacturing process is illustrated in Exhibit 11.

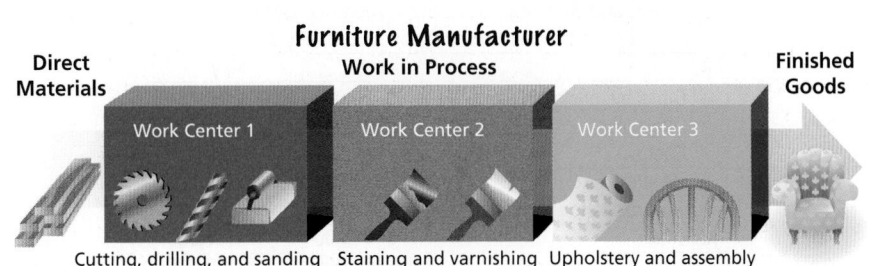

Furniture Manufacturer

Direct Materials — Work in Process — Finished Goods

Work Center 1 — Work Center 2 — Work Center 3

Cutting, drilling, and sanding   Staining and varnishing   Upholstery and assembly

Exhibit 11
Lean Production Line

In traditional manufacturing, a worker typically performs only one function. However, in lean manufacturing, work centers complete several functions. Thus, workers are often cross-trained to perform more than one function. Research has indicated that workers who perform several functions identify better with the end product. This creates pride in the product and improves quality and productivity.

The activities supporting the manufacturing process are called *service activities*. For example, repair and maintenance of manufacturing equipment are service activities. In lean manufacturing, service activities may be assigned to individual work centers, rather than to centralized service departments. For example, each work center may be assigned responsibility for the repair and maintenance of its machinery and equipment. This creates an environment in which workers gain a better understanding of the production process and their machinery. In turn, workers tend to take better care of the machinery, which decreases repairs and maintenance costs, reduces machine downtime, and improves product quality.

In lean manufacturing, the product is often placed on a movable carrier that is centrally located in the work center. After the workers in a work center have completed their activities with the product, the entire carrier and any additional materials are moved just in time to satisfy the demand or need of the next work center. In this sense, the product is said to be "pulled through." Each work center is connected to other work centers through information contained on a Kanban, which is a Japanese term for cards.

In summary, the primary objective of lean manufacturing is to increase the speed and quality, while reducing the cost of operations. This is achieved by eliminating waste and simplifying the production process. Lean manufacturing, including lean accounting and activity analysis, is further described and illustrated in Chapter 26.

Analysis for Decision Making

Analyzing Process Costs

Cost of production reports may be prepared showing more than direct materials and conversion costs. This greater detail can help managers isolate problems and seek opportunities for improvement.

To illustrate, the Blending Department of Holland Beverage Company prepared cost of production reports for April and May. Assume that the Blending Department had no beginning or ending work in process inventory in either month. That is, all units started were completed in each month. The cost of production reports showing multiple cost categories for April and May in the Blending Department are as follows:

	A	B	C
1	**Cost of Production Reports**		
2	**Holland Beverage Company—Blending Department**		
3	**For the Months Ended April 30 and May 31**		
4		**April**	**May**
5	Direct materials	$ 20,000	$ 40,600
6	Direct labor	15,000	29,400
7	Energy	8,000	20,000
8	Repairs	4,000	8,000
9	Tank cleaning	3,000	8,000
10	Total	$ 50,000	$106,000
11	Units completed	÷100,000	÷200,000
12	Cost per unit	$ 0.50	$ 0.53
13			

The reports indicate that total unit costs have increased in May from $0.50 to $0.53, or 6%. To determine the possible causes for this increase, the cost of production reports are restated in per-unit terms by dividing the costs by the number of units completed, as follows:

	A	B	C	D
1	**Blending Department**			
2	**Per-Unit Expense Comparisons**			
3		**April**	**May**	**% Change**
4	Direct materials	$0.200	$0.203	1.50%
5	Direct labor	0.150	0.147	−2.00%
6	Energy	0.080	0.100	25.00%
7	Repairs	0.040	0.040	0.00%
8	Tank cleaning	0.030	0.040	33.33%
9	Total	$0.500	$0.530	6.00%
10				

Both energy and tank cleaning per-unit costs have increased significantly in May. These increases should be further investigated. For example, the increase in energy may be due to the machines losing fuel efficiency. This could lead management to repair the machines. The tank cleaning costs could be investigated in a similar fashion.

Cost of production reports can also be used to compare the materials output quantity to the materials input quantity. Dividing the output quantities by the input quantities is termed the *yield* of a process. Often, there are materials losses from waste that will cause the materials output to be less than the materials input into the process. These materials losses can be investigated to improve the efficiency in using materials.

Make a Decision | Analyzing Process Costs

Dura-Conduit Corporation manufactures plastic conduit that is used in the cable industry. A conduit is a tube that encircles and protects the underground cable. In the process for making the plastic conduit, called *extrusion*, the melted plastic (*resin*) is pressed through a die to form a tube. Scrap is produced in this process.

Information from the cost of production reports for three months is as follows, assuming that inventory remains constant:

	May	June	July
Resin pounds input into the process	460,000	600,000	640,000
Price per pound	× $1.05	× $1.05	× $1.05
Plastic material costs	$483,000	$630,000	$672,000
Conversion costs	$ 90,000	$110,000	$112,000
Conduit output from the process (feet)	900,000	1,100,000	1,120,000

Assume that there is one-half pound of resin per foot of the finished product.

A. Determine the resin materials cost per foot of finished product for each month. (Round to the nearest whole cent.)

B. Determine the ratio of the number of resin pounds output in conduit by the number of pounds input into the process for each month. (Round percentages to one decimal place.)

C. Interpret the resin materials cost per foot for the three months. Use the information in (A.) and (B.) to explain what is happening.

D. Determine the conversion cost per foot of finished product for each month and interpret the result.

Solution:

A.

	May	June	July
Resin cost per foot	$0.54	$0.57	$0.60
	$483,000 ÷ 900,000 ft.	$630,000 ÷ 1,100,000 ft.	$672,000 ÷ 1,120,000 ft.

B. Pounds of resin:

	May	June	July
Conduit output (feet)	900,000	1,100,000	1,120,000
Pounds of resin per foot	× 0.5	× 0.5	× 0.5
Pounds of resin output	450,000	550,000	560,000

Ratio of output pounds to input pounds:

	May	June	July
Resin output pounds divided by input pounds	97.8%	91.7%	87.5%
	450,000 ÷ 460,000	550,000 ÷ 600,000	560,000 ÷ 640,000

C. The resin materials cost per foot of finished product is increasing over the three months, from $0.54 per foot in May to $0.60 per foot in July. This increased cost is not the result of a change in the price, which remained constant at $1.05 per pound. Rather, the increased cost is the result of the ratio of output pounds to input pounds deteriorating. Apparently, the level of scrap in the process is growing as fewer output pounds are being produced from input pounds.

D.

	May	June	July
Conversion cost per foot	$0.10	$0.10	$0.10
	$90,000 ÷ 900,000 ft.	$110,000 ÷ 1,100,000 ft.	$112,000 ÷ 1,120,000 ft.

The conversion cost per foot has remained constant and, thus, does not appear to need management attention.

Make a Decision

Appendix Average Cost Method

A cost flow assumption must be used as product costs flow through manufacturing processes. In this chapter, the first-in, first-out cost flow method was used for the Mixing Department of Frozen Delight. In this appendix, the average cost flow method is illustrated for **S&W Ice Cream Company (S&W)**.

Determining Costs Using the Average Cost Method

S&W's operations are similar to those of Frozen Delight. Like Frozen Delight, S&W mixes direct materials (milk, cream, sugar) in refrigerated vats and has two manufacturing departments, Mixing and Packaging.

The manufacturing data for the Mixing Department for July are as follows:

Inventory in process, July 1, 5,000 gallons (70% completed)...............	$ 6,200
Direct materials cost incurred in July, 60,000 gallons......................	66,000
Direct labor cost incurred in July...	10,500
Factory overhead applied in July..	6,405
Total production costs to account for	$89,105
Cost of goods transferred to Packaging in July (includes units in process on July 1), 62,000 gallons	?
Cost of work in process inventory, July 31, 3,000 gallons, 25% completed as to conversion costs...	?

Using the average cost method, the objective is to allocate the total costs of production of $89,105 to the following:

- The 62,000 gallons completed and transferred to the Packaging Department
- The 3,000 gallons in the July 31 (ending) work in process inventory

The preceding costs show two question marks. These amounts are determined by preparing a cost of production report, using the following four steps:

- Step 1. Determine the units to be assigned costs.
- Step 2. Compute equivalent units of production.
- Step 3. Determine the cost per equivalent unit.
- Step 4. Allocate costs to transferred out and partially completed units.

Under the average cost method, all production costs (materials and conversion costs) are combined together for determining equivalent units and cost per equivalent unit.

Step 1: Determine the Units to Be Assigned Costs The first step is to determine the units to be assigned costs. A unit can be any measure of completed production, such as tons, gallons, pounds, barrels, or cases. For **S&W**, a unit is a gallon of ice cream.

S&W's Mixing Department had 65,000 gallons of direct materials to account for during July, as shown here.

Total gallons to account for:

Inventory in process, July 1	5,000 gallons
Received from materials storeroom	60,000
Total units to account for by the Packaging Department	65,000 gallons

There are two groups of units to be assigned costs for the period.

Group 1	Units completed and transferred out
Group 2	Units in the July 31 (ending) work in process inventory

During July, the Mixing Department completed and transferred 62,000 gallons to the Packaging Department. Of the 60,000 gallons started in July, 57,000 (60,000 − 3,000) gallons were completed and transferred to the Packaging Department. Thus, the ending work in process inventory consists of 3,000 gallons.

The total units (gallons) to be assigned costs for S&W can be summarized as follows:

Group 1	Units transferred out to the Packaging Department in July	62,000 gallons
Group 2	Inventory in process, July 31	3,000
	Total gallons to be assigned costs.	65,000 gallons

The total units (gallons) to be assigned costs (65,000 gallons) equal the total units to account for (65,000 gallons).

Step 2: Compute Equivalent Units of Production S&W has 3,000 gallons of whole units in the work in process inventory for the Mixing Department on July 31. Because these units are 25% complete, the number of equivalent units in process in the Mixing Department on July 31 is 750 gallons (3,000 gallons × 25%). Because the units transferred to the Packaging Department have been completed, the whole units (62,000 gallons) transferred are the same as the equivalent units transferred.

The total equivalent units of production for the Mixing Department are determined by adding the equivalent units in the ending work in process inventory to the units transferred and completed during the period, computed as follows:

Equivalent units completed and transferred to the Packaging Department during July	62,000 gallons
Equivalent units in ending work in process, July 31	750
Total equivalent units	62,750 gallons

Step 3: Determine the Cost per Equivalent Unit Because materials and conversion costs are combined under the average cost method, the cost per equivalent unit is determined by dividing the total production costs by the total equivalent units of production as follows:

$$\text{Cost per Equivalent Unit} = \frac{\text{Total Production Costs}}{\text{Total Equivalent Units}} = \frac{\$89,105}{62,750 \text{ gallons}} = \$1.42$$

The cost per equivalent unit is used in Step 4 to allocate the production costs to the completed and partially completed units.

Step 4: Allocate Costs to Transferred Out and Partially Completed Units

The cost of transferred and partially completed units is determined by multiplying the cost per equivalent unit times the equivalent units of production. For **S&W**'s Mixing Department, these costs are determined as follows:

Group 1	Transferred out to the Packaging Department (62,000 gallons × $1.42)	$88,040
Group 2	Inventory in process, July 31 (3,000 gallons × 25% × $1.42).................	1,065
	Total production costs assigned	$89,105

The Cost of Production Report

The July cost of production report for **S&W**'s Mixing Department is shown in Exhibit 12. This cost of production report summarizes the following:

- The units for which the department is accountable and the disposition of those units
- The production costs incurred by the department and the allocation of those costs between completed and partially completed units

Exhibit 12

Cost of Production Report for S&W's Mixing Department— Average Cost

	A	B	C
1	S&W Ice Cream Company		
2	Cost of Production Report—Mixing Department		
3	For the Month Ended July 31		⟩ Step 1
4	**UNITS**		⟩ Step 2
5		Whole Units	Equivalent Units
6			of Production
7	Units charged to production:		
8	Inventory in process, July 1	5,000	
9	Received from materials storeroom	60,000	
10	Total units accounted for by the Mixing Department	65,000	
11			
12	Units to be assigned costs:		
13	Transferred to Packaging Department in July	62,000	62,000
14	Inventory in process, July 31 (25% completed)	3,000	750
15	Total units to be assigned costs	65,000	62,750
16			
17	**COSTS**		Costs
18			
19	Cost per equivalent unit:		
20	Total production costs for July in Mixing Department		$89,105
21	Total equivalent units (from Step 2)		÷62,750
22	Cost per equivalent unit		$ 1.42
23			
24	Costs assigned to production:		
25	Inventory in process, July 1		$ 6,200
26	Direct materials, direct labor, and factory overhead incurred in July		82,905
27	Total costs accounted for by the Mixing Department		$89,105
28			
29			
30	Costs allocated to completed and partially completed units:		
31	Transferred to Packaging Department in July (62,000 gallons × $1.42)		$88,040
32	Inventory in process, July 31 (3,000 gallons × 25% × $1.42)		1,065
33	Total costs assigned by the Mixing Department		$89,105
34			

Step 3 — rows 19–22

Step 4 — rows 30–33

Let's Review

Chapter Summary

1. The process cost system is best suited for industries that mass produce identical units of a product. Costs are charged to processing departments, rather than to jobs as with the job order cost system. These costs are transferred from one department to the next until production is completed.

2. A cost of production report summarizes the production and cost data for each processing department. The cost of production report is prepared by (1) determining the units to be assigned costs, (2) computing equivalent units of production, (3) determining the cost per equivalent unit, and (4) allocating costs to units transferred out and partially completed units.

3. Journal entries to record the cost flows and transactions for a process cost system include those for the purchase of material, usage of materials and direct labor, incurrence of overhead, application of overhead to departments, and transferring costs among departments and to finished goods. When goods are sold, their costs are transferred from finished goods to cost of goods sold.

4. The cost of production report is used for decision making by providing information for controlling and improving operations. Comparisons of equivalent costs per unit over time can be used to isolate increases or decreases in costs for further investigation.

5. Lean manufacturing focuses on producing products with high quality, low cost, and instant availability. It does this by combining processing functions into manufacturing cells (work centers) where cross-trained workers perform more than one function.

Key Terms

cost of production report (837)
cost per equivalent unit (842)
equivalent units of production (838)

first-in, first-out (FIFO) method (837)
lean manufacturing (852)
manufacturing cells (853)

process cost system (832)
process manufacturer (832)
whole units (838)

Practice

Multiple-Choice Questions

1. For which of the following businesses would the process cost system be most appropriate?
   A. Custom furniture manufacturer
   B. Commercial building contractor
   C. Crude oil refinery
   D. Automobile repair shop

2. There were 2,000 pounds in process at the beginning of the period in the Packing Department. Packing received 24,000 pounds from the Blending Department during the month, of which 3,000 pounds were in process at the end of the month. How many pounds were completed and transferred to finished goods from the Packing Department?
   A. 23,000
   B. 21,000
   C. 26,000
   D. 29,000

3. Information relating to production in Department A for May is as follows:

May	1	Balance, 1,000 units, ¾ completed	$22,150
	31	Direct materials, 5,000 units	75,000
	31	Direct labor	32,500
	31	Factory overhead	16,250

If 500 units were one-fourth completed at May 31, 5,500 units were completed during May, and the first-in, first-out method is used, what was the number of equivalent units of production with respect to conversion costs for May?

A. 4,500   C. 5,500
B. 4,875   D. 6,000

4. Based on the data presented in Question 3, what is the conversion cost per equivalent unit?

A. $10   C. $25
B. $15   D. $32

5. Information from the accounting system revealed the following:

	Day 1	Day 2	Day 3	Day 4	Day 5
Materials	$20,000	$18,000	$22,000	$20,000	$20,000
Electricity	2,500	3,000	3,500	4,000	4,700
Maintenance	4,000	3,750	3,400	3,000	2,800
Total costs	$26,500	$24,750	$28,900	$27,000	$27,500
Pounds produced	÷10,000	÷ 9,000	÷11,000	÷10,000	÷10,000
Cost per unit	$ 2.65	$ 2.75	$ 2.63	$ 2.70	$ 2.75

Which of the following statements best interprets this information?
A.   The total costs are out of control.
B.   The product costs have steadily increased because of higher electricity costs.
C.   Electricity costs have steadily increased because of lack of maintenance.
D.   The unit costs reveal a significant operating problem.

Answers provided after Problem. Need more practice? Find additional multiple-choice questions, exercises, and problems in CengageNOWv2.

Exercises

SHOW ME HOW

1. Job order versus process costing   Obj. 1

Which of the following industries would typically use job order costing, and which would typically use process costing?

Dentist	Movie studio
Gasoline refining	Paper manufacturing
Flour mill	Custom printing

SHOW ME HOW

2. Units to be assigned costs   Obj. 2

Lilac Skin Care Company consists of two departments, Blending and Filling. The Filling Department received 45,000 ounces from the Blending Department. During the period, the Filling Department completed 42,800 ounces, including 4,000 ounces of work in process at the beginning of the period. The ending work in process inventory was 6,200 ounces. How many ounces were started and completed during the period?

3. Equivalent units of materials cost
Obj. 2

The Filling Department of Lilac Skin Care Company had 4,000 ounces in beginning work in process inventory (70% complete). During the period, 42,800 ounces were completed. The ending work in process inventory was 6,200 ounces (40% complete). What are the total equivalent units for direct materials if materials are added at the beginning of the process?

4. Equivalent units of conversion costs
Obj. 2

The Filling Department of Lilac Skin Care had 4,000 ounces in beginning work in process inventory (70% complete). During the period, 42,800 ounces were completed. The ending work in process inventory was 6,200 ounces (40% complete). What are the total equivalent units for conversion costs?

5. Cost per equivalent unit
Obj. 2

The cost of direct materials transferred into the Filling Department of Lilac Skin Care Company is $20,250. The conversion cost for the period in the Filling Department is $6,372. The total equivalent units for direct materials and conversion are 45,000 ounces and 42,480 ounces, respectively. Determine the direct materials and conversion costs per equivalent unit.

6. Cost of units transferred out and ending work in process
Obj. 2

The costs per equivalent unit of direct materials and conversion in the Filling Department of Lilac Skin Care Company are $0.45 and $0.15, respectively. The equivalent units to be assigned costs are as follows:

	Equivalent Units	
	Direct Materials	Conversion
Inventory in process, beginning of period	0	1,200
Started and completed during the period	38,800	38,800
Transferred out of Filling (completed)	38,800	40,000
Inventory in process, end of period	6,200	2,480
Total units to be assigned costs	45,000	42,480

The beginning work in process inventory had a cost of $2,200. Determine the cost of completed and transferred-out production, the ending work in process inventory, and the total costs assigned by the Filling Department.

7. Process cost journal entries
Obj. 3

The cost of materials transferred into the Filling Department of Lilac Skin Care Company is $20,250, including $6,000 from the Blending Department and $14,250 from the materials storeroom. The conversion cost for the period in the Filling Department is $6,372 ($1,600 factory overhead applied and $4,772 direct labor). The total cost transferred to Finished Goods for the period was $25,660. The Filling Department had a beginning inventory of $2,200.

A. Journalize (1) the cost of transferred-in materials, (2) the conversion costs, and (3) the costs transferred out to Finished Goods.

B. Determine the balance of Work in Process—Filling at the end of the period.

8. Analyzing changes in unit costs
Obj. 4

The costs of energy consumed in producing good units in the Baking Department of Pan Company were $14,875 and $14,615 for June and July, respectively. The number of equivalent units produced in June and July was 42,500 pounds and 39,500 pounds, respectively. Evaluate the change in the cost of energy between the two months.

Answers provided after Problem. Need more practice? Find additional multiple-choice questions, exercises, and problems in CengageNOWv2.

Problem

Southern Aggregate Company manufactures concrete by a series of four processes. All materials are introduced in Crushing. From Crushing, the materials pass through Sifting, Baking, and Mixing, emerging as finished concrete. All inventories are costed by the first-in, first-out method.

The balances in the accounts Work in Process—Mixing and Finished Goods were as follows on May 1:

Inventory in Process—Mixing (2,000 units, ¼ completed)	$13,700
Finished Goods (1,800 units at $8.00 a unit)	14,400

The following costs were charged to Work in Process—Mixing during May:

Direct materials transferred from Baking: 15,200 units at	
$6.50 a unit	$98,800
Direct labor	17,200
Factory overhead	11,780

During May, 16,000 units of concrete were completed, and 15,800 units were sold. Inventories on May 31 were as follows:

Inventory in Process—Mixing (1,200 units, ½ completed)	
Finished Goods (2,000 units)	

Instructions

1. Prepare a cost of production report for the Mixing Department for the month of May.

2. Determine the cost of goods sold (indicate number of units and unit costs).

3. Determine the finished goods inventory, May 31.

Need more practice? Find additional multiple-choice questions, exercises, and problems in CengageNOWv2.

Answers

Multiple-Choice Questions

1. **C** The process cost system is most appropriate for a business where manufacturing is conducted by continuous operations and involves a series of uniform production processes, such as the processing of crude oil (answer C). The job order cost system is most appropriate for a business where the product is made to customers' specifications, such as custom furniture manufacturing (answer A), commercial building construction (answer B), or automobile repair shop (answer D).

2. **A** The total pounds transferred to finished goods (23,000) are the 2,000 in-process pounds at the beginning of the period plus the number of pounds started and completed during the month, 21,000 (24,000 − 3,000). Answer B incorrectly assumes that the beginning inventory is not transferred during the month. Answer C assumes that all 24,000 pounds started during the month are transferred to finished goods, instead of only the portion started and completed. Answer D incorrectly adds all the numbers together.

3. **B** The number of units that could have been produced from start to finish during a period is termed *equivalent units*. The 4,875 equivalent units (answer B) is determined as follows:

To process units in inventory on May 1 (1,000 × ¼)	250
To process units started and completed in May (5,500 units – 1,000 units)	4,500
To process units in inventory on May 31 (500 units × ¼)	125
Equivalent units of production in May	4,875

4. **A** The conversion costs (direct labor and factory overhead) totaling $48,750 are divided by the number of equivalent units (4,875) to determine the unit conversion cost of $10 (answer A).

5. **C** The electricity costs have increased, and maintenance costs have decreased. Answer C would be a reasonable explanation for these results. The total costs, materials costs, and costs per unit do not reveal any type of pattern over the time period. In fact, the materials costs have stayed at exactly $2.00 per pound over the time period. This demonstrates that aggregated numbers can sometimes hide underlying information that can be used to improve the process.

Exercises

1.

Dentist	Job order	Movie studio	Job order
Gasoline refining	Process	Paper manufacturing	Process
Flour mill	Process	Custom printing	Job order

2. 38,800 ounces started and completed (42,800 ounces completed – 4,000 ounces beginning WIP), or (45,000 ounces started – 6,200 ounces ending WIP)

3.

	Whole Units	Percent Materials Added in Period	Equivalent Units for Materials
Inventory in process, beginning of period...............	4,000	0%	0
Started and completed during the period...............	38,800*	100%	38,800
Transferred out of Filling (completed)....................	42,800		38,800
Inventory in process, end of period	6,200	100%	6,200
Total units to be assigned costs..........................	49,000		45,000

* 42,800 – 4,000

4.

	Whole Units	Percent Conversion Completed in Period	Equivalent Units for Conversion
Inventory in process, beginning of period...............	4,000	30%	1,200
Started and completed during the period...............	38,800*	100%	38,800
Transferred out of Filling (completed)....................	42,800		40,000
Inventory in process, end of period	6,200	40%	2,480
Total units to be assigned costs..........................	49,000		42,480

* 42,800 – 4,000

5.

$$\text{Equivalent units of direct materials: } \frac{\$20,250}{45,000} = \$0.45 \text{ per ounce}$$

$$\text{Equivalent units of conversion: } \frac{\$6,372}{42,480} = \$0.15 \text{ per ounce}$$

6.

	Direct Materials Costs		Conversion Costs	Total Costs
Inventory in process, balance.....................				$ 2,200
Inventory in process, beginning of period.........	0	+	180[a]	180
Cost of completed beginning work in process.....				$ 2,380
Started and completed during the period.........	17,460[b]	+	5,820[c]	23,280
Transferred out of Filling (completed).............				$25,660
Inventory in process, end of period	2,790[d]	+	372[e]	3,162
Total costs assigned by the Filling Department....				$28,822
Completed and transferred-out production.......	$25,660			
Inventory in process, ending	$3,162			

[a]$1,200 × $0.15 = $180 [b]$38,800 × $0.45 = $17,460 [c]$38,800 × $0.15 = $5,820
[d]$6,200 × $0.45 = $2,790 [e]$2,480 × $0.15 = $372

7. A.

Work in Process—Filling	20,250	
Work in Process—Blending		6,000
Materials		14,250
Work in Process—Filling	6,372	
Factory Overhead—Filling		1,600
Wages Payable		4,772
Finished Goods	25,660	
Work in Process—Filling		25,660

B. $3,162 ($2,200 + $20,250 + $6,372 − $25,660)

8.

$$\text{Energy cost per pound, June: } \frac{\$14,875}{42,500} = \$0.35$$

$$\text{Energy cost per pound, July: } \frac{\$14,615}{39,500} = \$0.37$$

The cost of energy has increased by 2 cents per pound between June and July, indicating inefficiency in the use of energy.

Need more help? Watch step-by-step videos of how to compute answers to these Exercises in CengageNOWv2.

Problem

1.

	A	B	C	D	E
1	Southern Aggregate Company				
2	Cost of Production Report—Mixing Department				
3	For the Month Ended May 31				
4			Equivalent Units		
5	**UNITS**	Whole Units	Direct Materials	Conversion	
6	Units charged to production:				
7	Inventory in process, May 1	2,000			
8	Received from Baking	15,200			
9	Total units accounted for by the Mixing Department	17,200			
10					
11	Units to be assigned costs:				
12	Inventory in process, May 1 (25% completed)	2,000	0	1,500	
13	Started and completed in May	14,000	14,000	14,000	
14	Transferred to finished goods in May	16,000	14,000	15,500	
15	Inventory in process, May 31 (50% completed)	1,200	1,200	600	
16	Total units to be assigned costs	17,200	15,200	16,100	
17					
18			Costs		
19	**COSTS**		Direct Materials	Conversion	Total
20	Cost per equivalent unit:				
21	Total costs for May in Mixing Department		$ 98,800	$ 28,980	
22	Total equivalent units (row 16)		÷ 15,200	÷ 16,100	
23	Cost per equivalent unit		$ 6.50	$ 1.80	
24					
25	Costs assigned to production:				
26	Inventory in process, May 1				$ 13,700
27	Costs incurred in May				127,780
28	Total costs accounted for by the Mixing Department				$141,480
29					
30	Costs allocated to completed and partially				
31	completed units:				
32	Inventory in process, May 1—balance				$ 13,700
33	To complete inventory in process, May 1		$ 0	$ 2,700ᵃ	2,700
34	Cost of completed May 1 work in process				$ 16,400
35	Started and completed in May		91,000ᵇ	25,200ᶜ	116,200
36	Transferred to finished goods in May				$132,600
37	Inventory in process, May 31		7,800ᵈ	1,080ᵉ	8,880
38	Total costs assigned by the Mixing Department				$141,480
39					

ᵃ1,500 × $1.80 = $2,700 ᵇ14,000 × $6.50 = $91,000 ᶜ14,000 × $1.80 = $25,200 ᵈ1,200 × $6.50 = $7,800
ᵉ600 × $1.80 = $1,080

2. Cost of goods sold:

1,800 units at $8.00	$ 14,400	(from finished goods beginning inventory)
2,000 units at $8.20*	16,400	(from inventory in process beginning inventory)
12,000 units at $8.30**	99,600	(from May production started and completed)
15,800 units	$130,400	

*($13,700 + $2,700) ÷ 2,000
**$116,200 ÷ 14,000

3. Finished goods inventory, May 31:

2,000 units at $8.30 $16,600

Discussion Questions

1. Which type of cost system, process or job order, would be best suited for each of the following: (A) TV assembler, (B) building contractor, (C) automobile repair shop, (D) paper manufacturer, (E) custom jewelry manufacturer? Give reasons for your answers.

2. In job order cost accounting, the three elements of manufacturing cost are charged directly to job orders. Why is it not necessary to charge manufacturing costs in process cost accounting to job orders?

3. In a job order cost system, direct labor and factory overhead applied are debited to individual jobs. How are these items treated in a process cost system and why?

4. Why is the cost per equivalent unit often determined separately for direct materials and conversion costs?

5. What is the purpose for determining the cost per equivalent unit?

6. Rameriz Company is a process manufacturer with two production departments, Blending and Filling. All direct materials are introduced in Blending from the materials store area. What is included in the cost transferred to Filling?

7. What is the most important purpose of the cost of production report?

8. How are cost of production reports used for controlling and improving operations?

9. How does lean manufacturing differ from the conventional manufacturing process?

Basic Exercises

SHOW ME HOW

BE 17-1 Job order versus process costing Obj. 1

Which of the following industries would typically use job order costing, and which would typically use process costing?

Steel manufactuirng	Computer chip manufacturing
Business consulting	Candy making
Web designer	Designer clothes manufacturing

SHOW ME HOW

BE 17-2 Units to be assigned costs Obj. 2

Oak Ridge Steel Company has two departments, Casting and Rolling. In the Rolling Department, ingots from the Casting Department are rolled into steel sheet. The Rolling Department received 2,400 tons from the Casting Department. During July, the Rolling Department completed 2,200 tons, including 300 tons of work in process on July 1. The ending work in process inventory on July 31 was 500 tons. How many tons were started and completed during July?

SHOW ME HOW

BE 17-3 Equivalent units of materials cost Obj. 2

The Rolling Department of Oak Ridge Steel Company had 300 tons in beginning work in process inventory (25% complete) on July 1. During July, 2,200 tons were completed. The ending work in process inventory on July 31 was 500 tons (40% complete). What are the total equivalent units for direct materials for July if materials are added at the beginning of the process?

SHOW ME HOW

BE 17-4 Equivalent units of conversion costs Obj. 2

The Rolling Department of Oak Ridge Steel Company had 300 tons in beginning work in process inventory (25% complete) on July 1. During July, 2,200 tons were completed. The ending work in process inventory on July 31 was 500 tons (40% complete). What are the total equivalent units for conversion costs?

SHOW ME HOW

BE 17-5 Cost per equivalent unit
Obj. 2

The cost of direct materials transferred into the Rolling Department of Oak Ridge Steel Company is $432,000. The conversion cost for the period in the Rolling Department is $144,150. The total equivalent units for direct materials and conversion are 2,400 tons and 2,325 tons, respectively. Determine the direct materials and conversion costs per equivalent unit.

SHOW ME HOW

BE 17-6 Cost of units transferred out and ending work in process
Obj. 2

The costs per equivalent unit of direct materials and conversion in the Rolling Department of Oak Ridge Steel Company are $180 and $62, respectively. The equivalent units to be assigned costs are as follows:

	Equivalent Units	
	Direct Materials	Conversion
Inventory in process, July 1	0	225
Started and completed during July	1,900	1,900
Transferred out of Rolling (completed)	1,900	2,125
Inventory in process, July 31	500	200
Total units to be assigned costs	2,400	2,325

The beginning work in process inventory on July 1 had a cost of $80,000. Determine the cost of completed and transferred-out production, the ending work in process inventory , and the total costs assigned by the Rolling Department..

SHOW ME HOW

BE 17-7 Process cost journal entries
Obj. 3

In July, the cost of materials transferred into the Rolling Department from the Casting Department of Oak Ridge Steel Company is $432,000. The conversion cost for the period in the Rolling Department is $144,150 ($54,700 factory overhead applied and $89,450 direct labor). The total cost transferred to Finished Goods for the period was $553,750. The Rolling Department had a beginning inventory of $80,000.

A. Journalize (1) the cost of transferred-in materials, (2) the conversion costs, and (3) the costs transferred out to Finished Goods.

B. Determine the balance of Work in Process—Rolling at the end of the period.

SHOW ME HOW

BE 17-8 Analyzing changes in unit costs
Obj. 4

The costs of materials consumed in producing good units in the Forming Department of Thomas Company were $76,000 and $77,350 for September and October, respectively. The number of equivalent units produced in September and October was 800 tons and 850 tons, respectively. Evaluate the change in the cost of materials between the two months.

Exercises

REAL WORLD

EX 17-1 Entries for materials cost flows in a process cost system
Obj. 1, 3

The Hershey Company manufactures chocolate confectionery products. The three largest raw materials are cocoa, sugar, and dehydrated milk. These raw materials first go into the Blending Department. The blended product is then sent to the Molding Department, where the bars of candy are formed. The candy is then sent to the Packing Department, where the bars are wrapped and boxed. The boxed candy is then sent to the distribution center, where it is eventually sold to food brokers and retailers.

(Continued)

Show the accounts debited and credited for each of the following business events:

A. Materials used by the Blending Department

B. Transfer of blended product to the Molding Department

C. Transfer of chocolate to the Packing Department

D. Transfer of boxed chocolate to the distribution center

E. Sale of boxed chocolate

REAL WORLD

EX 17-2 Flowchart of accounts related to service and processing departments Obj. 1

Alcoa Inc. is the world's largest producer of aluminum products. One product that Alcoa manufactures is aluminum sheet products for the aerospace industry. The entire output of the Smelting Department is transferred to the Rolling Department. Part of the fully processed goods from the Rolling Department are sold as rolled sheet, and the remainder of the goods are transferred to the Converting Department for further processing into sheared sheet.

Prepare a chart of the flow of costs from the processing department accounts into the finished goods accounts and then into the cost of goods sold account. The relevant accounts are as follows:

Cost of Goods Sold	Finished Goods—Rolled Sheet
Materials	Finished Goods—Sheared Sheet
Factory Overhead—Smelting Department	Work in Process—Smelting Department
Factory Overhead—Rolling Department	Work in Process—Rolling Department
Factory Overhead—Converting Department	Work in Process—Converting Department

---

SHOW ME HOW
REAL WORLD

EX 17-3 Entries for flow of factory costs for process cost system Obj. 1, 3

Domino Foods, Inc., manufactures a sugar product by a continuous process, involving three production departments—Refining, Sifting, and Packing. Assume that records indicate that direct materials, direct labor, and applied factory overhead for the first department, Refining, were $400,000, $150,000, and $100,000, respectively. Also, work in process in the Refining Department at the beginning of the period totaled $40,000, and work in process at the end of the period totaled $35,000.

Journalize the entries to record (A) the flow of costs into the Refining Department during the period for (1) direct materials, (2) direct labor, and (3) factory overhead, and (B) the transfer of production costs to the second department, Sifting.

EX 17-4 Factory overhead rate, entry for applying factory overhead, and Obj. 1, 3
factory overhead account balance

✔ A. 125%

The cost accountant for Kenner Beverage Co. estimated that total factory overhead cost for the Blending Department for the coming fiscal year beginning May 1 would be $3,000,000, and total direct labor costs would be $2,400,000. During May, the actual direct labor cost totaled $198,400, and factory overhead cost incurred totaled $253,200.

SHOW ME HOW

A. What is the predetermined factory overhead rate based on direct labor cost?

B. Journalize the entry to apply factory overhead to production for May.

C. What is the May 31 balance of the account Factory Overhead—Blending Department?

D. Does the balance in part (C) represent over- or underapplied factory overhead?

EX 17-5 Equivalent units of production Obj. 2

✔ Direct materials,
16,800 units

The Converting Department of Hopkinsville Company had 1,200 units in work in process at the beginning of the period, which were 25% complete. During the period, 16,000 units were completed and transferred to the Packing Department. There were 2,000 units in process at the end of the period, which were 40% complete. Direct materials are placed into the process at the beginning of production. Determine the number of equivalent units of production with respect to direct materials and conversion costs.

SHOW ME HOW

EX 17-6 Equivalent units of production

✔ A. Conversion, 96,720 units

SHOW ME HOW

Units of production data for the two departments of Pacific Cable and Wire Company for November of the current fiscal year are as follows:

	Drawing Department	Winding Department
Work in process, November 1	5,000 units, 40% completed	3,200 units, 80% completed
Completed and transferred to next processing department during November	95,000 units	95,100 units
Work in process, November 30	6,200 units, 60% completed	3,100 units, 15% completed

If all direct materials are placed in process at the beginning of production, determine the direct materials and conversion equivalent units of production for November for (A) the Drawing Department and (B) the Winding Department.

EX 17-7 Equivalent units of production

Obj. 2

✔ B. Conversion, 335,100

SHOW ME HOW

The following information concerns production in the Baking Department for March. All direct materials are placed in process at the beginning of production.

ACCOUNT *Work in Process—Baking Department*				ACCOUNT NO.	
				Balance	
Date	Item	Debit	Credit	Debit	Credit
Mar. 1	Bal., 18,000 units, ¼ completed			14,760	
31	Direct materials, 336,000 units	252,000		266,760	
31	Direct labor	40,000		306,760	
31	Factory overhead	60,530		367,290	
31	Goods finished, 330,000 units		346,410	20,880	
31	Bal. ? units, ⅔ completed			20,880	

A. Determine the number of units in work in process inventory at March 31.

B. Determine the equivalent units of production for direct materials and conversion costs in March.

EX 17-8 Costs per equivalent unit

Obj. 2, 4

✔ A. 2. Conversion cost per equivalent unit, $0.30

SHOW ME HOW

A. Based upon the data in Exercise 17-7, determine the following for March::

1. Direct materials cost per equivalent unit
2. Conversion cost per equivalent unit
3. Cost of the beginning work in process completed during March
4. Cost of units started and completed during March
5. Cost of the ending work in process

B. Assuming that the direct materials cost is the same for February and March, did the conversion cost per equivalent unit increase, decrease, or remain the same in March?

EX 17-9 Equivalent units of production

Obj. 2

REAL WORLD

Kellogg Company manufactures cold cereal products, such as *Frosted Flakes*. Assume that the inventory in process on March 1 for the Packing Department included 1,200 pounds of cereal in the packing machine hopper (enough for 800 24-oz. boxes) and 800 empty 24-oz. boxes held in the package carousel of the packing machine. During March, 65,400 boxes of 24-oz. cereal were packaged. Conversion costs are incurred when a box is filled with cereal. On March 31, the packing machine hopper held 900 pounds of cereal, and the package carousel held 600 empty 24-oz. (1½-pound) boxes. Assume that once a box is filled with cereal, it is immediately transferred to the finished goods warehouse.

(Continued)

Determine the equivalent units of production for cereal, boxes, and conversion costs for March. An equivalent unit is defined as "pounds" for cereal and "24-oz. boxes" for boxes and conversion costs.

EX 17-10   Costs per equivalent unit

Obj. 2

✔ C. $2.40

SHOW ME HOW

Georgia Products Inc. completed and transferred 89,000 particle board units of production from the Pressing Department. There was no beginning inventory in process in the department. The ending in-process inventory was 2,400 units, which were ⅗ complete as to conversion cost. All materials are added at the beginning of the process. Direct materials cost incurred was $219,360, direct labor cost incurred was $28,100, and factory overhead applied was $12,598.

Determine the following for the Pressing Department:

A. Total conversion cost

B. Conversion cost per equivalent unit

C. Direct materials cost per equivalent unit

EX 17-11   Equivalent units of production and related costs

Obj. 2

✔ A. 1,000 units

SHOW ME HOW   EXCEL TEMPLATE

The charges to Work in Process—Assembly Department for a period, together with information concerning production, are as follows. All direct materials are placed in process at the beginning of production.

Work in Process—Assembly Department			
Bal., 1,600 units, 35% completed	17,440	To Finished Goods, 29,600 units	?
Direct materials, 29,000 units @ $9.50	275,500		
Direct labor	84,600		
Factory overhead	39,258		
Bal. ? units, 45% completed	?		

Determine the following:

A. The number of units in work in process inventory at the end of the period

B. Equivalent units of production for direct materials and conversion

C. Costs per equivalent unit for direct materials and conversion

D. Cost of the units started and completed during the period

EX 17-12   Cost of units completed and in process

Obj. 2, 4

✔ A. 1. $21,808

A. Based on the data in Exercise 17-11, determine the following:

1. Cost of beginning work in process inventory completed this period

2. Cost of units transferred to finished goods during the period

3. Cost of ending work in process inventory

4. Cost per unit of the completed beginning work in process inventory, rounded to the nearest cent

B. ⬤▬▬▶ Did the production costs change from the preceding period? Explain.

C. Assuming that the direct materials cost per unit did not change from the preceding period, did the conversion costs per equivalent unit increase, decrease, or remain the same for the current period?

EX 17-13   Errors in equivalent unit computation

Obj. 2

Napco Refining Company processes gasoline. On June 1 of the current year, 6,400 units were ⅗ completed in the Blending Department. During June, 55,000 units entered the Blending Department from the Refining Department. During June, the units in process at the beginning of the month were completed. Of the 55,000 units entering the department, all were completed except 5,200 units that were ⅕ completed. The equivalent units for conversion costs for June for the Blending Department were computed as follows:

Equivalent units of production in June:	
To process units in inventory on June 1: 6,400 × ³/₅	3,840
To process units started and completed in June: 55,000 – 6,400	48,600
To process units in inventory on June 30: 5,200 × ¹/₅	1,040
Equivalent units of production	53,480

List the errors in the computation of equivalent units for conversion costs for the Blending Department for June.

EX 17-14   Cost per equivalent unit   Obj. 2

✔ A. 12,400 units

SHOW ME HOW

The following information concerns production in the Forging Department for November. All direct materials are placed into the process at the beginning of production, and conversion costs are incurred evenly throughout the process. The beginning inventory consists of $9,000 of direct materials.

ACCOUNT *Work in Process—Forging Department*   **ACCOUNT NO.**

Date		Item	Debit	Credit	Balance Debit	Balance Credit
Nov.	1	Bal., 900 units, 60% completed			10,566	
	30	Direct materials, 12,900 units	123,840		134,406	
	30	Direct labor	21,650		156,056	
	30	Factory overhead	16,870		172,926	
	30	Goods transferred, ? units		?	?	
	30	Bal., 1,400 units, 70% completed			?	

A. Determine the number of units transferred to the next department.

B. Determine the costs per equivalent unit of direct materials and conversion.

C. Determine the cost of units started and completed in November.

EX 17-15   Costs per equivalent unit and production costs   Obj. 2, 4

✔ A. $11,646

Based on the data in Exercise 17-14, determine the following:

A. Cost of beginning work in process inventory completed in November

B. Cost of units transferred to the next department during November

C. Cost of ending work in process inventory on November 30

D. Costs per equivalent unit of direct materials and conversion included in the November 1 beginning work in process

E. The November increase or decrease in costs per equivalent unit for direct materials and conversion from the previous month

---

EX 17-16   Cost of production report   Obj. 2, 4

✔ A. 4. $2,092

EXCEL TEMPLATE

The debits to Work in Process—Roasting Department for Morning Brew Coffee Company for August, together with information concerning production, are as follows:

Work in process, August 1, 700 pounds, 20% completed		$ 3,479*
*Direct materials (700 × $4.70)	$3,290	
Conversion (700 × 20% × $1.35)	189	
	$3,479	
Coffee beans added during August, 14,300 pounds		65,780
Conversion costs during August		21,942
Work in process, August 31, 400 pounds, 42% completed		?
Goods finished during August, 14,600 pounds		?

(Continued)

All direct materials are placed in process at the beginning of production.

A. Prepare a cost of production report, presenting the following computations:

1. Direct materials and conversion equivalent units of production for August

2. Direct materials and conversion costs per equivalent unit for August

3. Cost of goods finished during August

4. Cost of work in process at August 31

B. Compute and evaluate the change in cost per equivalent unit for direct materials and conversion from the previous month (July).

EX 17-17 Cost of production report Obj. 2, 4

✔ Conversion cost per equivalent unit, $5.10

The Cutting Department of Karachi Carpet Company provides the following data for January. Assume that all materials are added at the beginning of the process.

Work in process, January 1, 1,400 units, 75% completed		$ 22,960*
*Direct materials (1,400 × $12.65)	$17,710	
Conversion (1,400 × 75% × $5.00)	5,250	
	$22,960	
Materials added during January from Weaving Department, 58,000 units		$742,400
Direct labor for January		134,550
Factory overhead for January		151,611
Goods finished during January (includes goods in process, January 1), 56,200 units		—
Work in process, January 31, 3,200 units, 30% completed		—

A. Prepare a cost of production report for the Cutting Department.

B. Compute and evaluate the change in the costs per equivalent unit for direct materials and conversion from the previous month (December).

EX 17-18 Cost of production and journal entries Obj. 1, 2, 3, 4

✔ B. $29,760

AccuBlade Castings Inc. casts blades for turbine engines. Within the Casting Department, alloy is first melted in a crucible, then poured into molds to produce the castings. On May 1, there were 230 pounds of alloy in process, which were 60% complete as to conversion. The Work in Process balance for these 230 pounds was $32,844, determined as follows:

Direct materials (230 × $132)	$30,360
Conversion (230 × 60% × $18)	2,484
	$32,844

During May, the Casting Department was charged $350,000 for 2,500 pounds of alloy and $19,840 for direct labor. Factory overhead is applied to the department at a rate of 150% of direct labor. The department transferred out 2,530 pounds of finished castings to the Machining Department. The May 31 inventory in process was 44% complete as to conversion.

A. Prepare the following May journal entries for the Casting Department:

1. The materials charged to production

2. The conversion costs charged to production

3. The completed production transferred to the Machining Department

B. Determine the Work in Process—Casting Department May 31 balance.

C. Compute and evaluate the change in the costs per equivalent unit for direct materials and conversion from the previous month (April).

EX 17-19 Cost of production and journal entries

Obj. 1, 2, 3

✔ B. $14,319

Lighthouse Paper Company manufactures newsprint. The product is manufactured in two departments, Papermaking and Converting. Pulp is first placed into a vessel at the beginning of papermaking production. The following information concerns production in the Papermaking Department for March:

ACCOUNT *Work in Process—Papermaking Department*   **ACCOUNT NO.**

Date		Item	Debit	Credit	Balance Debit	Balance Credit
Mar.	1	Bal., 2,600 units, 35% completed			9,139	
	31	Direct materials, 105,000 units	330,750		339,889	
	31	Direct labor	40,560		380,449	
	31	Factory overhead	54,795		435,244	
	31	Goods transferred, 103,900 units		?	?	
	31	Bal., 3,700 units, 80% completed			?	

A. Prepare the following March journal entries for the Papermaking Department:

1. The materials charged to production
2. The conversion costs charged to production
3. The completed production transferred to the Converting Department

B. Determine the Work in Process—Papermaking Department March 31 balance.

EX 17-20 Process costing for a service company

Obj. 4

Madison Electric Company uses a fossil fuel (coal) plant for generating electricity. The facility can generate 900 megawatts (million watts) per hour. The plant operates 600 hours during March. Electricity is used as it is generated; thus, there are no inventories at the beginning or end of the period. The March conversion and fuel costs are as follows:

Conversion costs	$40,500,000
Fuel	10,800,000
Total	$51,300,000

Madison also has a wind farm that can generate 100 megawatts per hour. The wind farm receives sufficient wind to run 300 hours for March. The March conversion costs for the wind farm (mostly depreciation) are as follows:

Conversion costs	$2,700,000

A. Determine the cost per megawatt hour (MWh) for the fossil fuel plant and the wind farm to identify the lowest cost facility in March.

B. ▬▬▶ Why are equivalent units of production not needed in determining the cost per megawatt hour (MWh) for generating electricity?

C. ▬▬▶ What advantage does the fossil fuel plant have over the wind farm?

EX 17-21 Lean manufacturing

Obj. 5

The following are some quotes provided by a number of managers at Hawkeye Machining Company regarding the company's planned move toward a lean manufacturing system:

Director of Sales: I'm afraid we'll miss some sales if we don't keep a large stock of items on hand just in case demand increases. It only makes sense to me to keep large inventories in order to assure product availability for our customers.

Director of Purchasing: I'm very concerned about moving to a lean system for materials. What would happen if one of our suppliers were unable to make a shipment? A supplier could fall behind in production or have a quality problem. Without some safety stock in our materials, our whole plant would shut down.

(Continued)

Director of Manufacturing: If we go to lean manufacturing, I think our factory output will drop. We need in-process inventory in order to "smooth out" the inevitable problems that occur during manufacturing. For example, if a machine that is used to process a product breaks down, it would starve the next machine if I don't have in-process inventory between the two machines. If I have in-process inventory, then I can keep the next operation busy while I fix the broken machine. Thus, the in-process inventories give me a safety valve that I can use to keep things running when things go wrong.

➤ How would you respond to these managers?

Appendix
EX 17-22 Equivalent units of production: average cost method

✔ A. 17,000

The Converting Department of Tender Soft Tissue Company uses the average cost method and had 1,900 units in work in process that were 60% complete at the beginning of the period. During the period, 15,800 units were completed and transferred to the Packing Department. There were 1,200 units in process that were 30% complete at the end of the period.

A. Determine the number of whole units to be accounted for and to be assigned costs for the period.

B. Determine the number of equivalent units of production for the period.

Appendix
EX 17-23 Equivalent units of production: average cost method

✔ A. 12,100 units to be accounted for

Units of production data for the two departments of Atlantic Cable and Wire Company for July of the current fiscal year are as follows:

	Drawing Department	**Winding Department**
Work in process, July 1	500 units, 50% completed	350 units, 30% completed
Completed and transferred to next processing department during July	11,400 units	10,950 units
Work in process, July 31	700 units, 55% completed	800 units, 25% completed

Each department uses the average cost method.

A. Determine the number of whole units to be accounted for and to be assigned costs and the equivalent units of production for the Drawing Department.

B. Determine the number of whole units to be accounted for and to be assigned costs and the equivalent units of production for the Winding Department.

Appendix
EX 17-24 Equivalent units of production: average cost method

✔ A. 3,100

The following information concerns production in the Finishing Department for May. The Finishing Department uses the average cost method.

ACCOUNT *Work in Process—Finishing Department*   **ACCOUNT NO.**

Date		Item	Debit	Credit	Balance Debit	Balance Credit
May	1	Bal., 4,200 units, 70% completed			36,500	
	31	Direct materials, 23,600 units	125,800		162,300	
	31	Direct labor	75,400		237,700	
	31	Factory overhead	82,675		320,375	
	31	Goods transferred, 24,700 units		308,750	11,625	
	31	Bal., ? units, 30% completed			11,625	

A. Determine the number of units in work in process inventory at the end of the month.

B. Determine the number of whole units to be accounted for and to be assigned costs and the equivalent units of production for May.

Appendix

EX 17-25   Equivalent units of production and related costs

✔ B. 8,820 units

EXCEL TEMPLATE

The charges to Work in Process—Baking Department for a period as well as information concerning production are as follows. The Baking Department uses the average cost method, and all direct materials are placed in process during production.

Work in Process—Baking Department			
Bal., 900 units, 40% completed	2,466	To Finished Goods, 8,100 units	?
Direct materials, 8,400 units	34,500		
Direct labor	16,200		
Factory overhead	8,574		
Bal., 1,200 units, 60% completed	?		

Determine the following:

A. The number of whole units to be accounted for and to be assigned costs
B. The number of equivalent units of production
C. The cost per equivalent unit
D. The cost of units transferred to Finished Goods
E. The cost of units in ending Work in Process

Appendix

EX 17-26   Cost per equivalent unit: average cost method

✔ A. $26.00

The following information concerns production in the Forging Department for June. The Forging Department uses the average cost method.

ACCOUNT *Work in Process—Forging Department*   ACCOUNT NO.

Date		Item	Debit	Credit	Balance Debit	Balance Credit
June	1	Bal., 500 units, 40% completed			5,000	
	30	Direct materials, 3,700 units	49,200		54,200	
	30	Direct labor	25,200		79,400	
	30	Factory overhead	25,120		104,520	
	30	Goods transferred, 3,600 units		?	?	
	30	Bal., 600 units, 70% completed			?	

A. Determine the cost per equivalent unit.
B. Determine cost of units transferred to Finished Goods.
C. Determine the cost of units in ending Work in Process.

Appendix

EX 17-27   Cost of production report: average cost method

✔ Cost per equivalent unit, $3.60

The increases to Work in Process—Roasting Department for Highlands Coffee Company for May as well as information concerning production are as follows:

Work in process, May 1, 1,150 pounds, 40% completed	$ 1,700
Coffee beans added during May, 10,900 pounds	28,600
Conversion costs during May	12,504
Work in process, May 31, 800 pounds, 80% completed	—
Goods finished during May, 11,250 pounds	—

Prepare a cost of production report for May, using the average cost method.

Appendix

EX 17-28   Cost of production report: average cost method

✔ Cost per equivalent
unit, $9.00

EXCEL TEMPLATE

Prepare a cost of production report for the Cutting Department of Dalton Carpet Company for January. Use the average cost method with the following data:

Work in process, January 1, 3,400 units, 75% completed	$ 23,000
Materials added during January from Weaving Department, 64,000 units	366,200
Direct labor for January	105,100
Factory overhead for January	80,710
Goods finished during January (includes goods in process, January 1), 63,500 units	—
Work in process, January 31, 3,900 units, 10% completed	—

Problems: Series A

PR 17-1A   Entries for process cost system   Obj. 1, 3

✔ 2. Materials January
31 balance, $46,500

SHOW ME HOW

GENERAL LEDGER

Port Ormond Carpet Company manufactures carpets. Fiber is placed in process in the Spinning Department, where it is spun into yarn. The output of the Spinning Department is transferred to the Tufting Department, where carpet backing is added at the beginning of the process and the process is completed. On January 1, Port Ormond Carpet Company had the following inventories:

Finished Goods	$62,000
Work in Process—Spinning Department	35,000
Work in Process—Tufting Department	28,500
Materials	17,000

Departmental accounts are maintained for factory overhead, and both have zero balances on January 1.

Manufacturing operations for January are summarized as follows:

A. Materials purchased on account	$500,000
B. Materials requisitioned for use:	
Fiber—Spinning Department	$275,000
Carpet backing—Tufting Department	110,000
Indirect materials—Spinning Department	46,000
Indirect materials—Tufting Department	39,500
C. Labor used:	
Direct labor—Spinning Department	$185,000
Direct labor—Tufting Department	98,000
Indirect labor—Spinning Department	18,500
Indirect labor—Tufting Department	9,000
D. Depreciation charged on fixed assets:	
Spinning Department	$ 12,500
Tufting Department	8,500
E. Expired prepaid factory insurance:	
Spinning Department	$ 2,000
Tufting Department	1,000
F. Applied factory overhead:	
Spinning Department	$ 80,000
Tufting Department	55,000
G. Production costs transferred from Spinning Department to Tufting Department	$547,000
H. Production costs transferred from Tufting Department to Finished Goods	$807,200
I. Cost of goods sold during the period	$795,200

Instructions

1. Journalize the entries to record the operations, identifying each entry by letter.
2. Compute the January 31 balances of the inventory accounts.
3. Compute the January 31 balances of the factory overhead accounts.

PR 17-2A   Cost of production report   Obj. 2, 4

✔ 1. Conversion cost per equivalent unit, $0.76

EXCEL TEMPLATE

Hana Coffee Company roasts and packs coffee beans. The process begins by placing coffee beans into the Roasting Department. From the Roasting Department, coffee beans are then transferred to the Packing Department. The following is a partial work in process account of the Roasting Department at July 31:

	ACCOUNT *Work in Process—Roasting Department*				ACCOUNT NO.	
					Balance	
Date	Item	Debit	Credit	Debit	Credit
July 1	Bal., 30,000 units, 10% completed			121,800	
31	Direct materials, 155,000 units	620,000		741,800	
31	Direct labor	90,000		831,800	
31	Factory overhead	33,272		865,072	
31	Goods transferred, 149,000 units		?		
31	Bal., ? units, 45% completed			?	

Instructions

1. Prepare a cost of production report, and identify the missing amounts for Work in Process—Roasting Department.
2. Assuming that the July 1 work in process inventory includes $119,400 of direct materials, determine the increase or decrease in the cost per equivalent unit for direct materials and conversion between June and July.

PR 17-3A   Equivalent units and related costs; cost of production report;   Obj. 2, 3, 4
entries

✔ 2. Transferred to Packaging Dept., $40,183

EXCEL TEMPLATE

White Diamond Flour Company manufactures flour by a series of three processes, beginning with wheat grain being introduced in the Milling Department. From the Milling Department, the materials pass through the Sifting and Packaging departments, emerging as packaged refined flour.

The balance in the account Work in Process—Sifting Department was as follows on July 1:

Work in Process—Sifting Department (900 units, 3/5 completed):
Direct materials (900 × $2.05) $1,845
Conversion (900 × 3/5 × $0.40) 216
$2,061

The following costs were charged to Work in Process—Sifting Department during July:

Direct materials transferred from Milling Department:
15,700 units at $2.15 a unit $33,755
Direct labor 4,420
Factory overhead 2,708

During July, 15,500 units of flour were completed. Work in Process—Sifting Department on July 31 was 1,100 units, 4/5 completed.

Instructions

1. Prepare a cost of production report for the Sifting Department for July.
2. Journalize the entries for costs transferred from Milling to Sifting and the costs transferred from Sifting to Packaging.
3. Determine the increase or decrease in the cost per equivalent unit from June to July for direct materials and conversion costs.
4. ➤ Discuss the uses of the cost of production report and the results of part (3).

PR 17-4A   Work in process account data for two months; cost of production reports

Obj. 1, 2, 3, 4

✔ 1. C. Transferred to finished goods in April, $49,818

EXCEL TEMPLATE

Hearty Soup Co. uses a process cost system to record the costs of processing soup, which requires the cooking and filling processes. Materials are entered from the cooking process at the beginning of the filling process. The inventory of Work in Process—Filling on April 1 and debits to the account during April were as follows:

Bal., 800 units, 30% completed:	
Direct materials (800 × $4.30)	$ 3,440
Conversion (800 × 30% × $1.75)	420
	$ 3,860
From Cooking Department, 7,800 units	$34,320
Direct labor	8,562
Factory overhead	6,387

During April, 800 units in process on April 1 were completed, and of the 7,800 units entering the department, all were completed except 550 units that were 90% completed.

Charges to Work in Process—Filling for May were as follows:

From Cooking Department, 9,600 units	$44,160
Direct labor	12,042
Factory overhead	6,878

During May, the units in process at the beginning of the month were completed, and of the 9,600 units entering the department, all were completed except 300 units that were 35% completed.

Instructions

1. Enter the balance as of April 1, in a four-column account for Work in Process—Filling. Record the debits and the credits in the account for April. Construct a cost of production report, and present computations for determining (A) equivalent units of production for materials and conversion, (B) costs per equivalent unit, (C) cost of goods finished, differentiating between units started in the prior period and units started and finished in April, and (D) work in process inventory.

2. Provide the same information for May by recording the May transactions in the four-column work in process account. Construct a cost of production report, and present the May computations (A through D) listed in part (1).

3. ➡ Comment on the change in costs per equivalent unit for March through May for direct materials and conversion costs.

Appendix

PR 17-5A   Cost of production report: average cost method

✔ Cost per equivalent unit, $2.70

EXCEL TEMPLATE

Sunrise Coffee Company roasts and packs coffee beans. The process begins in the Roasting Department. From the Roasting Department, the coffee beans are transferred to the Packing Department. The following is a partial work in process account of the Roasting Department at December 31:

ACCOUNT *Work in Process—Roasting Department*   **ACCOUNT NO.**

	Date		Item	Debit	Credit	Balance Debit	Balance Credit
Dec.	1		Bal., 10,500 units, 75% completed			21,000	
	31		Direct materials, 210,400 units	246,800		267,800	
	31		Direct labor	135,700		403,500	
	31		Factory overhead	168,630		572,130	
	31		Goods transferred, 208,900 units		?	?	
	31		Bal., ? units, 25% completed			?	

Instructions

Prepare a cost of production report, using the average cost method, and identify the missing amounts for Work in Process—Roasting Department.

Problems: Series B

PR 17-1B   Entries for process cost system   Obj. 1, 3

✔ 2. Materials
July 31 balance, $11,390

SHOW ME HOW   GENERAL LEDGER

Preston & Grover Soap Company manufactures powdered detergent. Phosphate is placed in process in the Making Department, where it is turned into granulars. The output of Making is transferred to the Packing Department, where packaging is added at the beginning of the process. On July 1, Preston & Grover Soap Company had the following inventories:

Finished Goods	$13,500
Work in Process—Making	6,790
Work in Process—Packing	7,350
Materials	5,100

Departmental accounts are maintained for factory overhead, which both have zero balances on July 1.

Manufacturing operations for July are summarized as follows:

A. Materials purchased on account	$149,800
B. Materials requisitioned for use:	
Phosphate—Making Department	$105,700
Packaging—Packing Department	31,300
Indirect materials—Making Department	4,980
Indirect materials—Packing Department	1,530
C. Labor used:	
Direct labor—Making Department	$ 32,400
Direct labor—Packing Department	40,900
Indirect labor—Making Department	15,400
Indirect labor—Packing Department	18,300
D. Depreciation charged on fixed assets:	
Making Department	$ 10,700
Packing Department	7,900
E. Expired prepaid factory insurance:	
Making Department	$ 2,000
Packing Department	1,500
F. Applied factory overhead:	
Making Department	$ 32,570
Packing Department	30,050
G. Production costs transferred from Making Department to Packing Department	$166,790
H. Production costs transferred from Packing Department to Finished Goods	$263,400
I. Cost of goods sold during the period	$265,200

Instructions

1. Journalize the entries to record the operations, identifying each entry by letter.

2. Compute the July 31 balances of the inventory accounts.

3. Compute the July 31 balances of the factory overhead accounts.

PR 17-2B   Cost of production report   Obj. 2, 4

Bavarian Chocolate Company processes chocolate into candy bars. The process begins by placing direct materials (raw chocolate, milk, and sugar) into the Blending Department. All materials are placed into production at the beginning of the blending process. After blending, the milk chocolate is then transferred to the Molding Department, where the milk chocolate is formed into candy bars. The following is a partial work in process account of the Blending Department at October 31:

					Balance	
ACCOUNT *Work in Process—Blending Department*				**ACCOUNT NO.**		
Date	**Item**	**Debit**	**Credit**	**Debit**	**Credit**
Oct. 1	Bal., 2,300 units, ⅗ completed			46,368	
31	Direct materials, 26,000 units	429,000		475,368	
31	Direct labor	100,560		575,928	
31	Factory overhead	48,480		624,408	
31	Goods transferred, 25,700 units		?		
31	Bal., ? units, ⅕ completed			?	

Instructions

1. Prepare a cost of production report, and identify the missing amounts for Work in Process—Blending Department.

2. Assuming that the October 1 work in process inventory includes direct materials of $38,295, determine the increase or decrease in the cost per equivalent unit for direct materials and conversion between September and October.

PR 17-3B   Equivalent units and related costs; cost of production report;   Obj. 2, 3, 4
entries

Dover Chemical Company manufactures specialty chemicals by a series of three processes, all materials being introduced in the Distilling Department. From the Distilling Department, the materials pass through the Reaction and Filling departments, emerging as finished chemicals.

The balance in the account Work in Process—Filling was as follows on January 1:

Work in Process—Filling Department
(3,400 units, 60% completed):

Direct materials (3,400 × $9.58)	$32,572
Conversion (3,400 × 60% × $3.90)	7,956
	$40,528

The following costs were charged to Work in Process—Filling during January:

Direct materials transferred from Reaction	
Department: 52,300 units at $9.50 a unit	$496,850
Direct labor	101,560
Factory overhead	95,166

During January, 53,000 units of specialty chemicals were completed. Work in Process—Filling Department on January 31 was 2,700 units, 30% completed.

Instructions

1. Prepare a cost of production report for the Filling Department for January.

2. Journalize the entries for costs transferred from Reaction to Filling and the costs transferred from Filling to Finished Goods.

3. Determine the increase or decrease in the cost per equivalent unit from December to January for direct materials and conversion costs.

4. ▬▬▬▶ Discuss the uses of the cost of production report and the results of part (3).

PR 17-4B Work in process account data for two months; cost of production reports

Obj. 1, 2, 3, 4

✔ 1. C. Transferred to finished goods in September, $702,195

EXCEL TEMPLATE

Pittsburgh Aluminum Company uses a process cost system to record the costs of manufacturing rolled aluminum, which consists of the smelting and rolling processes. Materials are entered from smelting at the beginning of the rolling process. The inventory of Work in Process—Rolling on September 1 and debits to the account during September were as follows:

Bal., 2,600 units, ¼ completed:		
Direct materials (2,600 × $15.50)	$40,300	
Conversion (2,600 × ¼ × $8.50)	5,525	
	$45,825	
From Smelting Department, 28,900 units	$462,400	
Direct labor	158,920	
Factory overhead	101,402	

During September, 2,600 units in process on September 1 were completed, and of the 28,900 units entering the department, all were completed except 2,900 units that were ⅘ completed. Charges to Work in Process—Rolling for October were as follows:

From Smelting Department, 31,000 units	$511,500
Direct labor	162,850
Factory overhead	104,494

During October, the units in process at the beginning of the month were completed, and of the 31,000 units entering the department, all were completed except 2,000 units that were ⅖ completed.

Instructions

1. Enter the balance as of September 1 in a four-column account for Work in Process—Rolling. Record the debits and the credits in the account for September. Construct a cost of production report and present computations for determining (A) equivalent units of production for materials and conversion, (B) costs per equivalent unit, (C) cost of goods finished, differentiating between units started in the prior period and units started and finished in September, and (D) work in process inventory.

2. Provide the same information for October by recording the October transactions in the four-column work in process account. Construct a cost of production report, and present the October computations (A through D) listed in part (1).

3. ▬▬▶ Comment on the change in costs per equivalent unit for August through October for direct materials and conversion cost.

Appendix

PR 17-5B Cost of production report: average cost method

✔ Transferred to Packaging Dept., $54,000

EXCEL TEMPLATE

Blue Ribbon Flour Company manufactures flour by a series of three processes, beginning in the Milling Department. From the Milling Department, the materials pass through the Sifting and Packaging departments, emerging as packaged refined flour.

The balance in the account Work in Process—Sifting Department was as follows on May 1:

Work in Process—Sifting Department (1,500 units, 75% completed)	$3,400

The following costs were charged to Work in Process—Sifting Department during May:

Direct materials transferred from Milling Department: 18,300 units	$32,600
Direct labor	14,560
Factory overhead	7,490

During May, 18,000 units of flour were completed and transferred to finished goods. Work in Process—Sifting Department on May 31 was 1,800 units, 75% completed.

Instructions

Prepare a cost of production report for the Sifting Department for May, using the average cost method.

Analysis for Decision Making

EXCEL TEMPLATE

ADM-1 Analyzing process cost elements across product types

Mystic Bottling Company bottles popular beverages in the Bottling Department. The beverages are produced by blending concentrate with water and sugar. The concentrate is purchased from a concentrate producer. The concentrate producer sets higher prices for the more popular concentrate flavors. A simplified Bottling Department cost of production report separating the cost of bottling the four flavors follows:

A	B	C	D	E
	Orange	**Cola**	**Lemon-Lime**	**Root Beer**
2 Concentrate	$ 4,625	$129,000	$105,000	$ 7,600
3 Water	1,250	30,000	25,000	2,000
4 Sugar	3,000	72,000	60,000	4,800
5 Bottles	5,500	132,000	110,000	8,800
6 Flavor changeover	3,000	4,800	4,000	10,000
7 Conversion cost	1,750	24,000	20,000	2,800
8 Total cost transferred to finished goods	$19,125	$391,800	$324,000	$36,000
9 Number of cases	2,500	60,000	50,000	4,000
10				

Beginning and ending work in process inventories are negligible, so they are omitted from the cost of production report. The flavor changeover cost represents the cost of cleaning the bottling machines between production runs of different flavors. A production run of a new flavor is produced after a flavor changeover from the previous flavor. Higher-demand flavors are produced in larger production runs, while smaller-demand flavors are produced in smaller production runs.

▶ Prepare a memo to the production manager, analyzing this comparative cost information. In your memo, provide recommendations for further action, along with supporting schedules showing the total cost per case and cost per case by cost element. Round supporting calculations to the nearest cent.

ADM-2 Analyzing process cost elements over time

Pix Paper Inc. produces photographic paper for printing digital images. One of the processes for this operation is a coating (solvent spreading) operation, where chemicals are coated onto paper stock. There has been some concern about the cost performance of this operation. As a result, you have begun an investigation. You first discover that all materials and conversion prices have been stable for the last six months. Thus, increases in prices for inputs are not an explanation for increasing costs. However, you have discovered three possible problems from some of the operating personnel whose quotes follow:

Operator 1: "I've been keeping an eye on my operating room instruments. I feel as though our energy consumption is becoming less efficient."

Operator 2: "Every time the coating machine goes down, we produce waste on shutdown and subsequent startup. It seems like during the last half-year we have had more unscheduled machine shutdowns than in the past. Thus, I feel as though our yields must be dropping."

Operator 3: "My sense is that our coating costs are going up. It seems to me like we are spreading a thicker coating than we should. Perhaps the coating machine needs to be recalibrated."

The Coating Department had no beginning or ending inventories for any month during the study period. The following data from the cost of production report are made available:

A	B	C	D	E	F	G
1	January	February	March	April	May	June
2 Paper stock	$67,200	$63,840	$60,480	$64,512	$57,120	$53,760
3 Coating	$11,520	$11,856	$12,960	$15,667	$16,320	$18,432
4 Conversion cost (incl. energy)	$38,400	$36,480	$34,560	$36,864	$32,640	$30,720
5 Pounds input to the process	100,000	95,000	90,000	96,000	85,000	80,000
6 Pounds transferred out	96,000	91,200	86,400	92,160	81,600	76,800
7						

A. Prepare a table showing the paper cost per output pound, coating cost per output pound, conversion cost per output pound, and yield (pounds transferred out ÷ pounds input) for each month. Round costs to the nearest cent and yield to the nearest whole percent.

B. ━━━━▶ Interpret your table results.

ADM-3 Determining cost relationships

Midstate Containers Inc. manufactures cans for the canned food industry. The operations manager of a can manufacturing operation wants to conduct a cost study investigating the relationship of tin content in the material (can stock) to the energy cost for enameling the cans. The enameling was necessary to prepare the cans for labeling. A higher percentage of tin content in the can stock increases the cost of material. The operations manager believed that a higher tin content in the can stock would reduce the amount of energy used in enameling. During the analysis period, the amount of tin content in the steel can stock was increased for every month, from April to September. The following operating reports were available from the controller:

A	B	C	D	E	F	G
1	April	May	June	July	August	September
2 Materials	$ 14,000	$ 34,800	$ 33,000	$ 21,700	$ 28,800	$ 33,000
3 Energy	13,000	28,800	24,200	14,000	17,100	16,000
4 Total cost	$ 27,000	$ 63,600	$ 57,200	$ 35,700	$ 45,900	$ 49,000
5 Units produced	÷50,000	÷120,000	÷110,000	÷ 70,000	÷ 90,000	÷100,000
6 Cost per unit	$ 0.54	$ 0.53	$ 0.52	$ 0.51	$ 0.51	$ 0.49
7						

Differences in materials unit costs were entirely related to the amount of tin content. In addition, inventory changes are negligible and are ignored in the analysis.

━━━━▶ Interpret this information and report to the operations manager your recommendations with respect to tin content.

Take It Further

ETHICS

TIF 17-1 Ethics in Action

You are the Cookie division controller for Auntie M's Baked Goods Company. Auntie M recently introduced a new chocolate chip cookie brand called Full of Chips, which has more than twice as many chips as any other brand on the market. The brand has quickly become a huge market success, largely because of the number of chips in each cookie. As a result of the brand's success, the product manager who launched the Full of Chips brand has been promoted to division vice president. A new product manager, Brandon, has been brought in to replace the promoted manager.

At Auntie M's, product managers are evaluated on both the sales and profit margin of the products they manage. During his first week on the job, Brandon notices that the Full of Chips cookie uses a lot of chips, which increases the cost of the cookie. To improve the product's profitability, Brandon plans to reduce the amount of chips per cookie by 10%.

(Continued)

He believes that a 10% reduction in chips will not adversely affect sales, but will reduce cost and, hence, help him improve the profit margin. Brandon is focused on profit margins, because he knows that if he is able to increase the profitability of the Full of Chips brand, he will be in line for a big promotion.

To confirm this plan, Brandon has enlisted you to help evaluate it. After reviewing the cost of production reports segmented by cookie brand, you notice that there has been a continual drop in the materials costs for the Full of Chips brand since its launch. On further investigation, you discover that chip costs have declined because the previous product manager continually reduced the number of chips in each cookie. Both you and Brandon report to the division vice president, who was the original product manager for the Full of Chips brand who was responsible for reducing the chip count in prior periods.

1. ➤ Is this an ethical strategy for Brandon to pursue? What are the potential implications of this strategy?

2. ➤ What options might you, as the controller, consider taking in response to Brandon's plan?

REAL WORLD

TIF 17-2   Team Activity

The following categories represent typical process manufacturing industries:

- Beverages
- Chemicals
- Food
- Forest and paper products
- Metals
- Petroleum refining
- Pharmaceuticals
- Soap and cosmetics

In groups of two or three, identify one company for each category (following your instructor's specific instructions) and determine the following:

A. Typical products manufactured by the selected company, including brand names
B. Typical raw materials used by the selected company
C. Types of processes used by the selected company

Use annual reports, the Internet, or library resources in doing this activity.

TIF 17-3   Communication

Jamarcus Bradshaw, plant manager of Georgia Paper Company's papermaking mill, was looking over the cost of production reports for July and August for the Papermaking Department. The reports revealed the following:

	July	August
Pulp and chemicals.........................	$295,600	$304,100
Conversion cost............................	146,000	149,600
Total cost.................................	$441,600	$453,700
Number of tons...........................	÷ 1,200	÷ 1,130
Cost per ton..............................	$ 368	$ 401.50

Jamarcus was concerned about the increased cost per ton from the output of the department. As a result, he asked the plant controller to perform a study to help explain these results. The controller, Leann Brunswick, began the analysis by performing some interviews of key plant personnel in order to understand what the problem might be. Excerpts from an interview with Len Tyson, a paper machine operator, follow:

Len: We have two papermaking machines in the department. I have no data, but I think paper machine No. 1 is applying too much pulp and, thus, is wasting both conversion and materials resources. We haven't had repairs on paper machine No. 1 in a while. Maybe this is the problem.

Leann: How does too much pulp result in wasted resources?

Len: Well, you see, if too much pulp is applied, then we will waste pulp material. The customer will not pay for the extra product; we just use more material to make the product.. Also, when there is too much pulp, the machine must be slowed down in order to complete the drying process. This results in additional conversion costs.

Leann: Do you have any other suspicions?

Len: Well, as you know, we have two products—green paper and yellow paper. They are identical except for the color. The color is added to the papermaking process in the paper machine. I think that during August these two color papers have been behaving very differently. I don't have any data, but it just seems as though the amount of waste associated with the green paper has increased.

Leann: Why is this?

Len: I understand that there has been a change in specifications for the green paper, starting near the beginning of August. This change could be causing the machines to run poorly when making green paper. If this is the case, the cost per ton would increase for green paper.

Leann also asked for a database printout providing greater detail on August's operating results.

September 9   Requested by: Leann Brunswick
Papermaking Department—August detail

	A	B	C	D	E	F
1	Production					
2	Run	Paper		Material	Conversion	
3	Number	Machine	Color	Costs	Costs	Tons
4	1	1	Green	40,300	18,300	150
5	2	1	Yellow	41,700	21,200	140
6	3	1	Green	44,600	22,500	150
7	4	1	Yellow	36,100	18,100	120
8	5	2	Green	38,300	18,900	160
9	6	2	Yellow	33,900	15,200	140
10	7	2	Green	35,600	18,400	130
11	8	2	Yellow	33,600	17,000	140
12		Total		304,100	149,600	1,130
13						

➤ Prior to preparing a report, Leann resigned from Georgia Paper Company to start her own business. You have been asked to take the data that Leann collected, and write a memo to Jamarcus Bradshaw with a recommendation to management. Your memo should include analysis of the August data to determine whether the paper machine or the paper color explains the increase in the unit cost from July. Include any supporting schedules that are appropriate. Round any calculations to the nearest cent.

Concepts and Principles

Chapter 15 *Introduction to Managerial Accounting*

Developing Information

COST SYSTEMS	COST BEHAVIOR
Chapter 16 *Job Order Costing*	**Chapter 19** *Cost-Volume-Profit Analysis*
Chapter 17 *Process Cost Systems*	
Chapter 18 *Activity-Based Costing*	

Decision Making

EVALUATING PERFORMANCE	COMPARING ALTERNATIVES
Chapter 20 *Variable Costing for Management Analysis*	**Chapter 23** *Evaluating Decentralized Operations*
Chapter 21 *Budgeting*	**Chapter 24** *Differential Analysis and Product Pricing*
Chapter 22 *Evaluating Variances from Standard Costs*	**Chapter 25** *Capital Investment Analysis*
	Chapter 26 *Lean Manufacturing*

AP IMAGES/THE DAILY TIMES/LINDSAY PIERCE

Cold Stone Creamery

Have you ever had to request service repairs on an appliance at your home? The repair person may arrive and take five minutes to replace a part. Yet, the bill may indicate a minimum charge for more than five minutes of work.

Why might there be a minimum charge for a service call? The answer is that the service person must charge for the time and expense of coming to your house. In a sense, the bill reflects two elements of service: (1) the cost of coming to your house and (2) the cost of the repair. The first portion of the bill reflects the time required to "set up" the job. The second part of the bill reflects the cost of performing the repair. The setup charge will be the same, whether the repairs take five minutes or five hours. In contrast, the actual repair charge will vary with the time on the job.

Like the repair person, companies must be careful that the cost of their products and services accurately reflects the different activities involved in producing the product or service. Otherwise, the cost of products and services may be distorted and lead to improper management decisions.

To illustrate, **Cold Stone Creamery**, a chain of super premium ice cream shops, uses activity-based costing to determine the cost of its ice cream products, such as cones, mixings, cakes, frozen yogurt, smoothies, and sorbets. The costs of activities, such as scooping and mixing, are added to the cost of the ingredients to determine the total cost of each product. As stated by Cold Stone's president:

"... it only makes sense to have the price you pay for the product be reflective of the activities involved in making it for you."*

In this chapter, three different methods of allocating factory overhead to products are described and illustrated. In addition, product cost distortions resulting from improper factory overhead allocations are discussed. The chapter concludes by describing activity-based costing for selling and administrative expenses and its use in service businesses.

*Quote from "Experiencing Accounting Videos," Activity-Based Costing. © Cengage Learning, 2008.

Source: www.coldstonecreamery.com

What's Covered

Objective 1
Describe three methods used for allocating factory overhead costs to products.

Product Costing Allocation Methods

Determining the cost of a product is termed **product costing**. Product costs consist of direct materials, direct labor, and factory overhead. The direct materials and direct labor are direct costs that can be traced to the product. However, factory overhead includes indirect costs that must be allocated to the product as shown in Exhibit 1.

Exhibit 1
Allocation of Factory Overhead Costs

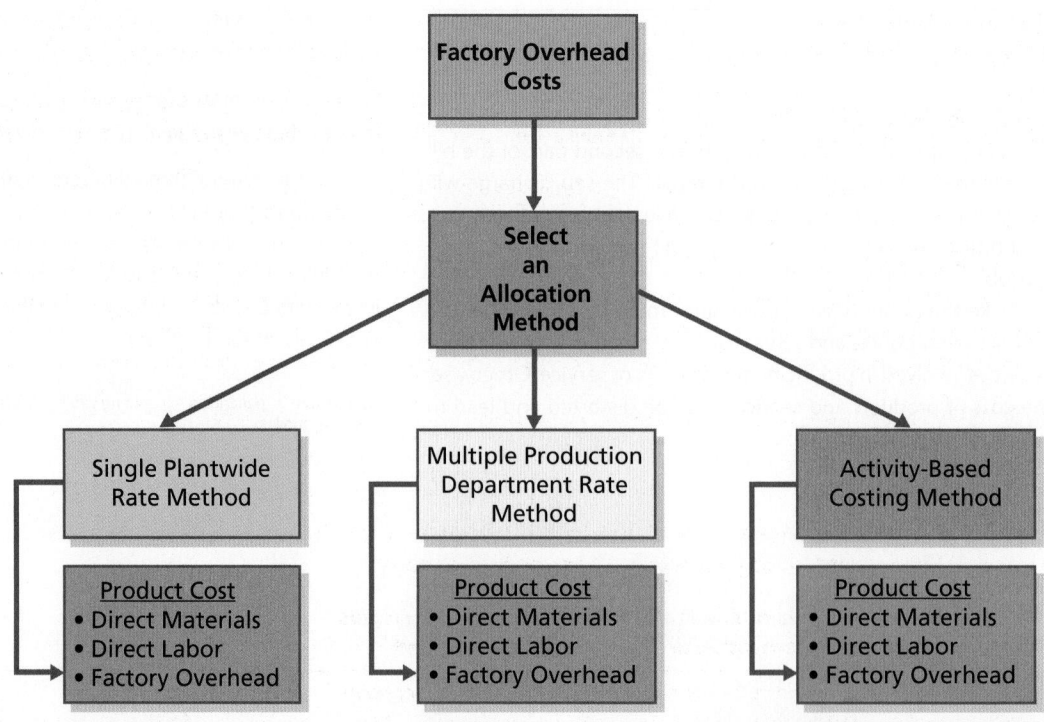

In Chapter 16, the allocation of factory overhead using a predetermined factory overhead rate was illustrated. The most common methods of allocating factory overhead using predetermined factory overhead rates are:

- Single plantwide factory overhead rate method
- Multiple production department factory overhead rate method
- Activity-based costing method

The choice of allocation method is important to managers because the allocation affects the product cost. Managers are concerned about the accuracy of product costs, which are used for decisions such as determining product mix, establishing product price, and determining whether to discontinue a product line.

The first **Cold Stone Creamery** was opened in Tempe, Arizona, by Donald and Susan Sutherland in 1988.

Link to Cold Stone Creamery

Single Plantwide Factory Overhead Rate Method

Objective 2
Illustrate the use of a single plantwide factory overhead rate for product costing.

A company may use a predetermined factory overhead rate to allocate factory overhead costs to products. Under the **single plantwide factory overhead rate method**, factory overhead costs are allocated to products using only one rate.

To illustrate, assume the following data for **Ruiz Company**, which manufactures snowmobiles and riding mowers in a single factory:

Total budgeted factory overhead costs for the year $1,600,000
Total budgeted direct labor hours (computed as follows). . . . . 20,000 hours

The total budgeted direct labor hours are computed as follows:

	Snowmobiles	**Riding Mowers**	**Total**
Planned production for the year.	1,000 units	1,000 units	
Direct labor hours per unit	× 10 hours	× 10 hours	
Budgeted direct labor hours	10,000 hours	10,000 hours	20,000 hours

Under the single plantwide factory overhead rate method, the $1,600,000 budgeted factory overhead is applied to all products by using one rate. This rate is computed as follows:

$$\frac{\text{Single Plantwide Factory}}{\text{Overhead Rate}} = \frac{\text{Total Budgeted Factory Overhead}}{\text{Total Budgeted Plantwide Allocation Base}}$$

The budgeted allocation base is a measure of operating activity in the factory. Common allocation bases would include direct labor hours, direct labor dollars, and machine hours. Ruiz allocates factory overhead using budgeted direct labor hours as the plantwide allocation base. Thus, Ruiz's single plantwide factory overhead rate is $80 per direct labor hour, computed as follows:

$$\text{Single Plantwide Factory Overhead Rate} = \frac{\$1,600,000}{20,000 \text{ direct labor hours}}$$

$$= \$80 \text{ per direct labor hour}$$

Ruiz uses the plantwide rate of $80 per direct labor hour to allocate factory overhead to snowmobiles and riding mowers, computed as follows:

	Single Plantwide Factory Overhead Rate	×	**Direct Labor Hours per Unit**	=	**Factory Overhead Cost per Unit**
Snowmobile	$80 per direct labor hour	×	10 direct labor hours	=	$800
Riding mower	$80 per direct labor hour	×	10 direct labor hours	=	$800

The factory overhead allocated to each product is $800. This is because each product uses the same number of direct labor hours.

The effects of Ruiz Company using the single plantwide factory overhead rate method are summarized in Exhibit 2.

Exhibit 2

Single Plantwide Factory Overhead Rate Method— Ruiz Company

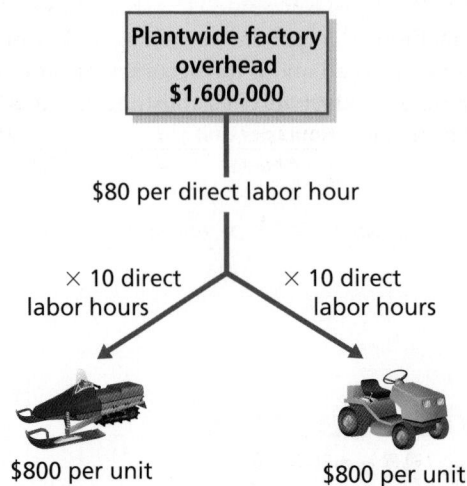

The primary advantage of using the single plantwide overhead rate method is that it is simple and inexpensive to use. However, the single plantwide rate assumes that the factory overhead costs are consumed in the same way by all products. For example, in the preceding illustration Ruiz assumes that factory overhead costs are consumed as each direct labor hour is incurred.

The preceding assumption may be valid for companies that manufacture one or a few products. However, if a company manufactures products that consume factory overhead costs in different ways, a single plantwide rate may not accurately allocate factory overhead costs to the products.

Link to Cold Stone Creamery   At **Cold Stone Creamery**, each serving of ice cream is blended on a frozen granite stone using a mixture of fruits, nuts, candy, cookies, and brownies. Each serving is unique to the customer and is called a "creation."

Check Up Corner 18-1   Single Plantwide Factory Overhead Rate

Lifestyle Furniture Company manufactures home furniture products. The total factory overhead for the company is budgeted at $600,000 for the year. The company manufactures two products: a computer desk and a designer table, each of which requires 4 direct labor hours (dlh) to make. Production for the year is budgeted for 5,000 units of each product.

Determine the:

A. Total number of budgeted direct labor hours for the year.

B. Single plantwide factory overhead rate.

C. Factory overhead allocated per unit for each product, using the single plantwide factory overhead rate.

Solution:

		Desks	Tables	Total
A.	Planned production for the year....	5,000 units	5,000 units	
	Direct labor hours per unit	× 4 hours	× 4 hours	
	Budgeted direct labor hours	20,000 hours	20,000 hours	40,000 hours

Lifestyle allocates factory overhead using budgeted direct labor hours.

The budgeted allocation base is a measure of operating activity in the factory.

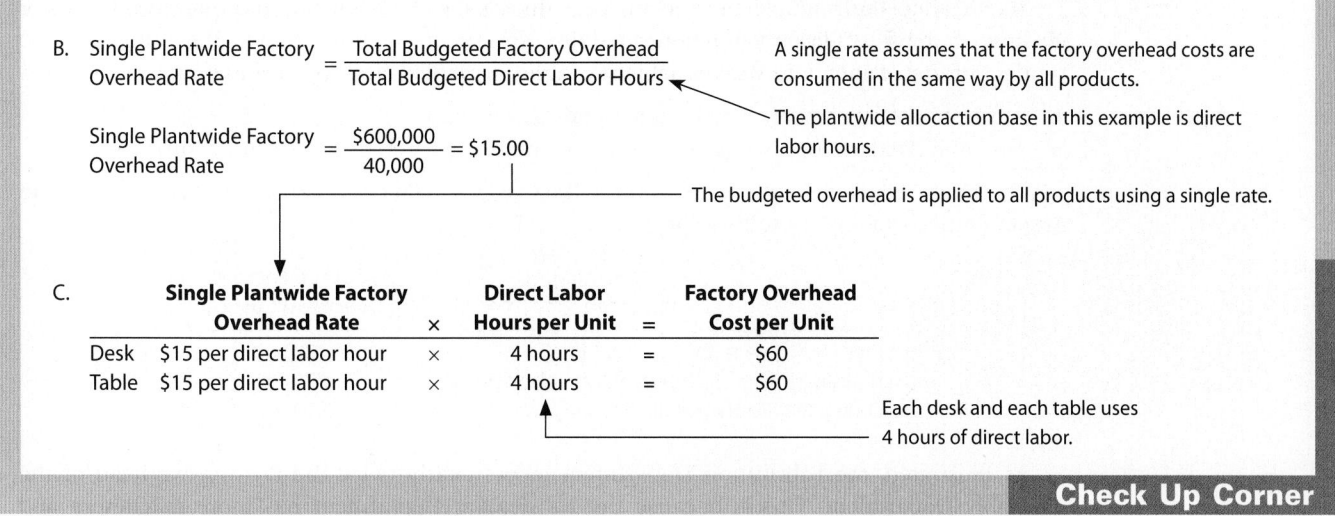

B. $\text{Single Plantwide Factory Overhead Rate} = \dfrac{\text{Total Budgeted Factory Overhead}}{\text{Total Budgeted Direct Labor Hours}}$

A single rate assumes that the factory overhead costs are consumed in the same way by all products.

The plantwide allocaction base in this example is direct labor hours.

$\text{Single Plantwide Factory Overhead Rate} = \dfrac{\$600,000}{40,000} = \$15.00$

The budgeted overhead is applied to all products using a single rate.

C.

Single Plantwide Factory Overhead Rate	×	Direct Labor Hours per Unit	=	Factory Overhead Cost per Unit
Desk	$15 per direct labor hour	×	4 hours	=	$60
Table	$15 per direct labor hour	×	4 hours	=	$60

Each desk and each table uses 4 hours of direct labor.

Check Up Corner

Multiple Production Department Factory Overhead Rate Method

Objective 3
Use multiple production department factory overhead rates for product costing.

When production departments *differ significantly* in their manufacturing processes, factory overhead costs are normally incurred differently in each department. In such cases, factory overhead costs may be more accurately allocated using multiple production department factory overhead rates.

The **multiple production department factory overhead rate method** uses different rates for each production department to allocate factory overhead costs to products. In contrast, the single plantwide rate method uses only one rate to allocate factory overhead costs. Exhibit 3 illustrates how these two methods differ.

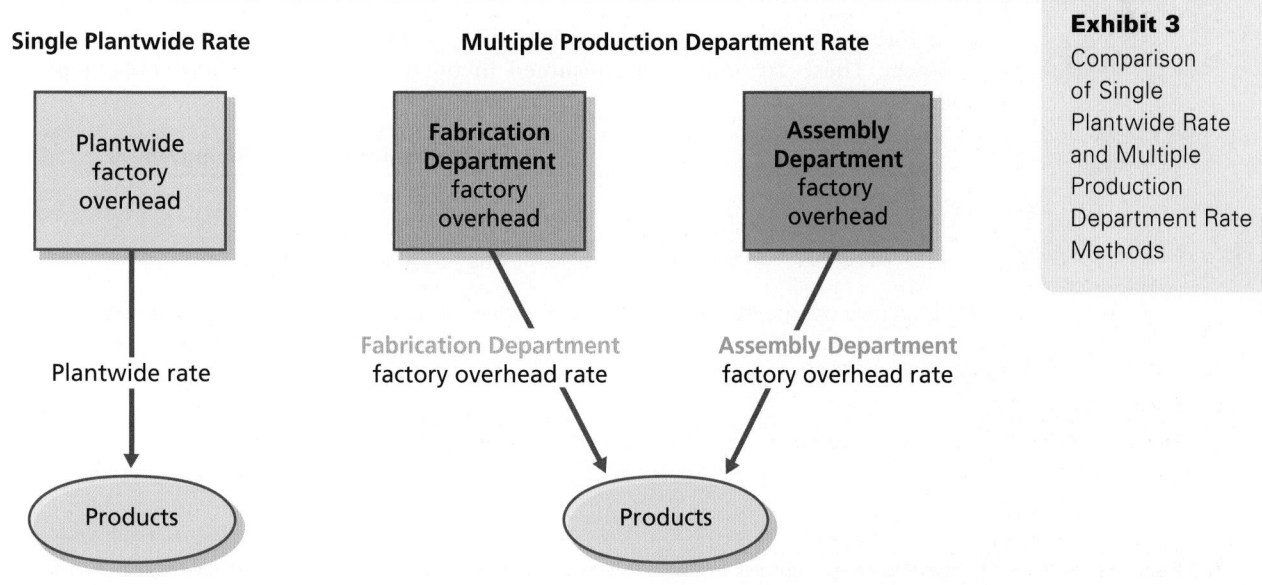

Single Plantwide Rate

Plantwide factory overhead

Plantwide rate

Products

Multiple Production Department Rate

Fabrication Department factory overhead

Assembly Department factory overhead

Fabrication Department factory overhead rate

Assembly Department factory overhead rate

Products

Exhibit 3
Comparison of Single Plantwide Rate and Multiple Production Department Rate Methods

To illustrate the multiple production department factory overhead rate method, the prior illustration for **Ruiz Company** is used. In doing so, assume that Ruiz uses the following two production departments in the manufacture of snowmobiles and riding mowers:

- Fabrication Department, which cuts metal to the shape of the product.
- Assembly Department, which manually assembles machined pieces into a final product.

The total budgeted factory overhead for Ruiz is $1,600,000 divided into the Fabrication and Assembly departments as follows:[1]

	Budgeted Factory Overhead Costs
Fabrication Department.............................	$1,030,000
Assembly Department	570,000
Total budgeted factory overhead costs	$1,600,000

As illustrated, the Fabrication Department incurs nearly twice the factory overhead of the Assembly Department. This is because the Fabrication Department has more machinery and equipment that uses more power, incurs more equipment depreciation, and uses more factory supplies.

Department Overhead Rates and Allocation

Each **production department factory overhead rate** is computed as follows:

$$\frac{\text{Production Department}}{\text{Factory Overhead Rate}} = \frac{\text{Budgeted Department Factory Overhead}}{\text{Budgeted Department Allocation Base}}$$

To illustrate, assume that **Ruiz Company** uses direct labor hours as the allocation base for the Fabrication and Assembly departments.[2] Each department uses 10,000 direct labor hours. Thus, the factory overhead rates are as follows:

$$\frac{\text{Fabrication Department}}{\text{Factory Overhead Rate}} = \frac{\$1,030,000}{10,000 \text{ direct labor hours}} = \$103 \text{ per direct labor hour}$$

$$\frac{\text{Assembly Department}}{\text{Factory Overhead Rate}} = \frac{\$570,000}{10,000 \text{ direct labor hours}} = \$57 \text{ per direct labor hour}$$

Ten direct labor hours are required for the manufacture of each snowmobile and riding mower. These 10 hours are consumed in the Fabrication and Assembly departments as follows:

	Snowmobile	Riding Mower
Fabrication Department	8 hours	2 hours
Assembly Department....................	2	8
Direct labor hours per unit.............	10 hours	10 hours

The factory overhead allocated to each snowmobile and riding mower is shown in Exhibit 4. As shown in Exhibit 4, each snowmobile is allocated $938 of total factory overhead costs. In contrast, each riding mower is allocated $662 of factory overhead costs.

---

[1] Factory overhead costs are assigned to production departments using methods discussed in advanced cost accounting textbooks.
[2] Departments need not use the same allocation base. The allocation base should be associated with the operating activity of the department.

Exhibit 4 Allocating Factory Overhead to Products—Ruiz Company

	Allocation Base Usage per Unit	×	Production Department Factory Overhead Rate	=	Allocated Factory Overhead per Unit of Product
Snowmobile					
Fabrication Department	8 direct labor hours	×	$103 per dlh	=	$824
Assembly Department	2 direct labor hours	×	$ 57 per dlh	=	114
Total factory overhead cost per snowmobile					$938
Riding mower					
Fabrication Department	2 direct labor hours	×	$103 per dlh	=	$206
Assembly Department	8 direct labor hours	×	$ 57 per dlh	=	456
Total factory overhead cost per riding mower					$662

Exhibit 5 summarizes the multiple production department rate allocation method for Ruiz. Exhibit 5 indicates that the Fabrication Department factory overhead rate is $103 per direct labor hour, while the Assembly Department rate is $57 per direct labor hour. Since the snowmobile uses more Fabrication Department direct labor hours than does the riding mower, the total overhead allocated to each snowmobile is $276 greater ($938–$662) than the amount allocated to each riding mower.

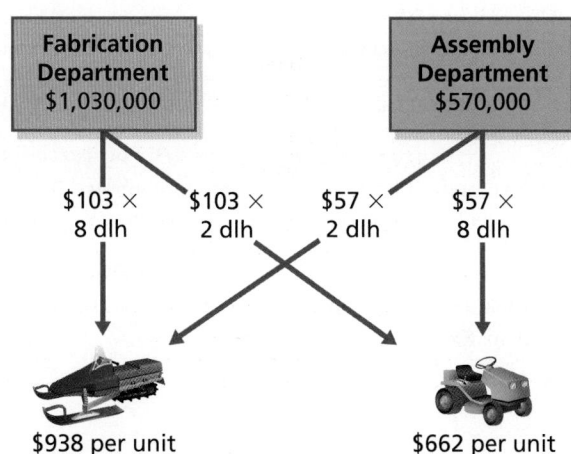

Exhibit 5
Multiple Production Department Rate Method—Ruiz Company

Distortion of Product Costs

The differences in **Ruiz Company's** factory overhead for each snowmobile and riding mower using the single plantwide and the multiple production department factory overhead rate methods are as follows:

	Factory Overhead Cost per Unit		
	Single Plantwide Method	Multiple Production Department Method	Difference
Snowmobile..............	$800	$938	$(138)
Riding mower.............	800	662	138

note:

The single plantwide factory overhead rate distorts product cost by averaging high and low factory overhead costs.

The single plantwide factory overhead rate distorts the product cost of both the snowmobile and riding mower. That is, the snowmobile is not allocated enough cost and, thus, is under-costed by $138. In contrast, the riding mower is allocated too much cost and is overcosted by $138 ($800–$662).

The preceding cost distortions are caused by averaging the differences between the high factory overhead costs in the Fabrication Department and the low factory overhead costs in the Assembly Department. Using the single plantwide rate, it is assumed that all factory overhead is directly related to a single allocation base for the entire plant. This assumption is not real-istic for Ruiz. Thus, using a single plantwide rate distorted the product costs of snowmobiles and riding mowers.

The following conditions indicate that a single plantwide factory overhead rate may cause product cost distortions:

■ **Condition 1:** *Differences in production department factory overhead rates.* Some departments have high rates, whereas others have low rates.

■ **Condition 2:** *Differences among products in the ratios of allocation base usage within a department and across departments.* Some products have a high ratio of allo-cation base usage within departments, whereas other products have a low ratio of allocation base usage within the same departments.

To illustrate, Condition 1 exists for Ruiz because the factory overhead rate for the Fabrica-tion Department is $103 per direct labor hour, whereas the rate for the Assembly Department is only $57 per direct labor hour. However, this condition by itself will not cause product cost distortions.

Condition 2 also exists for Ruiz. The snowmobile consumes 8 direct labor hours in the Fabrication Department, whereas the riding mower consumes only 2 direct labor hours. Thus, the ratio of allocation base usage is 4:1 in the Fabrication Department, computed as follows:[3]

$$\frac{\text{Ratio of Allocation Base Usage}}{\text{in the Fabrication Department}} = \frac{\text{Direct Labor Hours for snowmobiles}}{\text{Direct Labor Hours for riding mowers}} = \frac{8 \text{ hours}}{2 \text{ hours}} = 4{:}1$$

In contrast, the ratio of allocation base usage is 1:4 in the Assembly Department, computed as follows:

$$\frac{\text{Ratio of Allocation Base Usage}}{\text{in the Assembly Department}} = \frac{\text{Direct Labor Hours for snowmobiles}}{\text{Direct Labor Hours for riding mowers}} = \frac{2 \text{ hours}}{8 \text{ hours}} = 1{:}4$$

Because both conditions exist for Ruiz, the product costs from using the single plantwide factory overhead rate are distorted. The preceding conditions and the resulting product cost distortions are summarized in Exhibit 6.

[3] The numerator and denominator could be switched as long as the ratio is computed the same for each department. This is because the objective is to compare whether differences exist in the ratio of allocation base usage across products and departments.

Exhibit 6 Conditions for Product Cost Distortion—Ruiz Company

Fabrication Department	Assembly Department

Condition 1: Differences in production department factory overhead rates

$103 per direct labor hour

$57 per direct labor hour

Condition 2: Differences in the ratios of allocation base usage

8 direct labor hours

2 direct labor hours

2 direct labor hours

8 direct labor hours

Ratio of Allocation Base Usage = 4:1

Ratio of Allocation Base Usage = 1:4

Check Up Corner 18-2 | Multiple Production Department Factory Overhead Rates

The total factory overhead for Lifestyle Furniture Company is budgeted at $600,000 for the year, divided between two departments: Fabrication, $420,000, and Assembly, $180,000. Lifestyle manufactures two products: a computer desk and a designer table. Each desk requires 1 direct labor hour (dlh) in Fabrication and 3 direct labor hours in Assembly. Each table requires 3 direct labor hours in Fabrication and 1 direct labor hour in Assembly. Production for the year is budgeted for 5,000 units of each product.

Determine the:

A   Total number of budgeted direct labor hours for the year in each department.

B.   Departmental factory overhead rate for each department.

C.   Factory overhead allocated per unit for each product, using the departmental factory overhead rates.

Solution:

A.

	Direct Labor Hours per Unit	×	Number of Units	=	Toal Direct Labor Hours
Fabrication Department					
Desks	1 dlh	×	5,000	=	5,000
Tables	3 dlh	×	5,000	=	15,000
Total budgeted direct labor hours					20,000
Assembly Department					
Desks	3 dlh	×	5,000	=	15,000
Tables	1 dlh	×	5,000	=	5,000
Total budgeted direct labor hours					20,000

The budgeted allocation base is a measure of operating activity in each department.

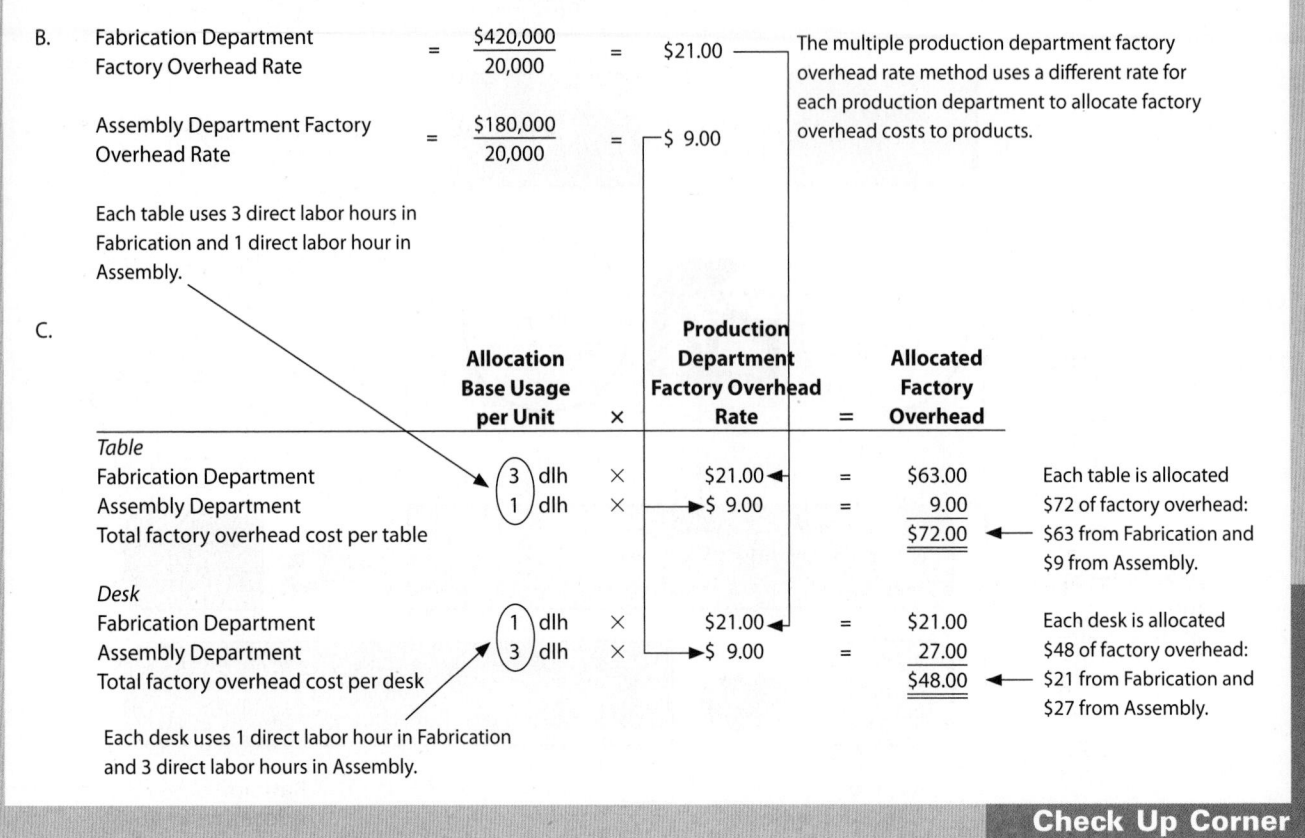

B.

$$\text{Fabrication Department Factory Overhead Rate} = \frac{\$420{,}000}{20{,}000} = \$21.00$$

$$\text{Assembly Department Factory Overhead Rate} = \frac{\$180{,}000}{20{,}000} = \$9.00$$

The multiple production department factory overhead rate method uses a different rate for each production department to allocate factory overhead costs to products.

Each table uses 3 direct labor hours in Fabrication and 1 direct labor hour in Assembly.

C.

	Allocation Base Usage per Unit	×	Production Department Factory Overhead Rate	=	Allocated Factory Overhead	
Table						
Fabrication Department	3 dlh	×	$21.00	=	$63.00	Each table is allocated
Assembly Department	1 dlh	×	$ 9.00	=	9.00	$72 of factory overhead:
Total factory overhead cost per table					$72.00	$63 from Fabrication and $9 from Assembly.
Desk						
Fabrication Department	1 dlh	×	$21.00	=	$21.00	Each desk is allocated
Assembly Department	3 dlh	×	$ 9.00	=	27.00	$48 of factory overhead:
Total factory overhead cost per desk					$48.00	$21 from Fabrication and $27 from Assembly.

Each desk uses 1 direct labor hour in Fabrication and 3 direct labor hours in Assembly.

Check Up Corner

Objective 4
Use activity-based costing for product costing.

Activity-Based Costing Method

As illustrated in the preceding section, product costs may be distorted when a single plantwide factory overhead rate is used. However, product costs may also be distorted when multiple production department factory overhead rates are used. Activity-based costing further reduces the possibility of product cost distortions.

The **activity-based costing (ABC) method** provides an alternative approach for allocating factory overhead that uses multiple factory overhead rates based on different activities. **Activities** are the types of work, or actions, involved in a manufacturing or service process. For example, the assembly, inspection, and engineering design functions are activities that might be used to allocate overhead.

Link to Cold Stone Creamery   **Cold Stone Creamery** uses the principles of activity-based costing.

Under activity-based costing, factory overhead costs are initially budgeted for activities, sometimes called *activity cost pools*, such as machine usage, inspections, moving, production setups, and engineering activities.[4] In contrast, when multiple production department factory overhead rates are used, factory overhead costs are first accounted for in production departments.

---

[4] The activity rate is based on budgeted activity costs. Activity-based budgeting and the reconciliation of budgeted activity costs to actual costs are topics covered in advanced texts.

Exhibit 7 illustrates how activity-based costing differs from the multiple production department method.

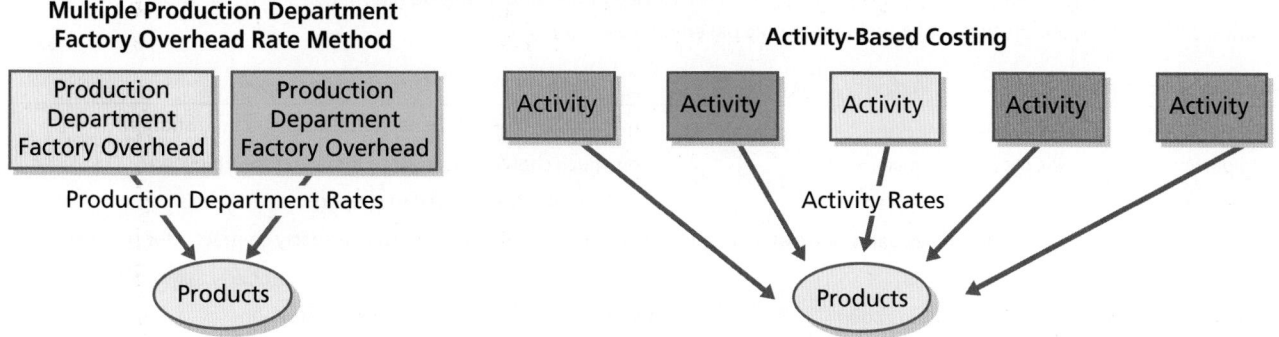

To illustrate the activity-based costing method, the prior illustration for **Ruiz Company** is used. Assume that the following activities have been identified for producing snowmobiles and riding mowers:

- *Fabrication*, which consists of cutting metal to shape the product. This activity is machine-intensive.
- *Assembly*, which consists of manually assembling machined pieces into a final product. This activity is labor-intensive.
- *Setup*, which consists of changing tooling in machines in preparation for making a new product. Each production run requires a **setup**.
- *Quality-control inspections*, which consist of inspecting the product for conformance to specifications. Inspection requires product tear down and reassembly.
- *Engineering changes*, which consist of processing changes in design or process specifications for a product. The document that initiates changing a product or process is called an **engineering change order (ECO)**.

Fabrication and assembly are now identified as *activities* rather than *departments*. As a result, the setup, quality-control inspections, and engineering change functions that were previously allocated to the Fabrication and Assembly departments are now classified as separate activities. The budgeted cost for each activity is as follows:

Activity	Budgeted Activity Cost
Fabrication	$ 530,000
Assembly...	70,000
Setup..	480,000
Quality-control inspections	312,000
Engineering changes	208,000
Total budgeted activity costs.....................................	$1,600,000

The costs for the fabrication and assembly activities are less than the costs shown in the preceding section where these activities were identified as production departments. This is because the costs of setup, quality-control inspections, and engineering changes, which total $1,000,000 ($480,000 + $312,000 + $208,000), have now been separated into their own activity cost pools.

Why It Matters

Activity-Based Costing in the Public Sector

Activity-based costing is used by some municipal, state, and federal entities to guide decision making. In these cases, the cost of activities are used to analyze the efficiency of services, set fees for services, and choose among alternative service providers. Examples of activities, activity costs, and decision making in the municipal environment are as follows:

Municipal Activity	Activity Cost	Decision Example
Voter registration	Cost per voter registered	How many people will be needed to staff voter registration?
Road plowing	Cost per lane mile	How much should be budgeted for winter road plowing?
Police protection	Cost per incident type	Is police overtime required to support incident levels?
Street repair	Cost per square yards of street repaired	How much should be paid to a third-party contractor for street repair?
Tax billing	Cost per tax bill	Is the Tax Department efficient in billing property taxes?
Immunization	Cost per immunization	What fee should be charged for immunization?

Source: *Costing Municipal Services*, Massachusetts Department of Revenue, Division of Local Services, March 2005.

Activity Rates

The budgeted activity costs are assigned to products using factory overhead rates for each activity. These rates are called **activity rates** because they are related to activities. Activity rates are computed as follows:

$$\text{Activity Rate} = \frac{\text{Budgeted Activity Cost}}{\text{Total Activity-Base Usage}}$$

note:

Activity rates are computed by dividing the budgeted activity cost pool by the total estimated activity-base usage.

The term **activity base**, rather than *allocation base*, is used because the base is related to an activity.

To illustrate, assume that snowmobiles are a new product for **Ruiz Company**, and engineers are still making minor design changes. Ruiz has produced riding mowers for many years. Activity-base usage for the two products is as follows:

	Snowmobile	Riding Mower
Estimated units of total production	1,000 units	1,000 units
Estimated setups	100 setups	20 setups
Quality-control inspections	100 inspections (10%)	4 inspections (0.4%)
Estimated engineering change orders...................	12 change orders	4 change orders

The number of direct labor hours used by each product is 10,000 hours, computed as follows:

	Direct Labor Hours per Unit	Number of Units of Production	Total Direct Labor Hours
Snowmobile:			
Fabrication Department..............	8 hours	1,000 units	8,000 hours
Assembly Department	2 hours	1,000 units	2,000 hours
Total...............................			10,000 hours
Riding Mower:			
Fabrication Department..............	2 hours	1,000 units	2,000 hours
Assembly Department	8 hours	1,000 units	8,000 hours
Total...............................			10,000 hours

Exhibit 8 summarizes the activity-base usage quantities for each product.

Exhibit 8 Activity Bases—Ruiz Company

			Activity-Base Usage		
Products	**Fabrication**	**Assembly**	**Setup**	**Quality-Control Inspections**	**Engineering Changes**
Snowmobile	8,000 dlh	2,000 dlh	100 setups	100 inspections	12 ECOs
Riding mower.	2,000	8,000	20	4	4
Total activity-base usage	10,000 dlh	10,000 dlh	120 setups	104 inspections	16 ECOs

The activity rates for Ruiz are shown in Exhibit 9.

Exhibit 9 Activity Rates—Ruiz Company

Activity	**Budgeted Activity Cost**	÷	**Total Activity-Base Usage**	=	**Activity Rate**
Fabrication	$530,000	÷	10,000 direct labor hours	=	$ 53 per direct labor hour
Assembly	$ 70,000	÷	10,000 direct labor hours	=	$ 7 per direct labor hour
Setup	$480,000	÷	120 setups	=	$ 4,000 per setup
Quality-control inspections	$312,000	÷	104 inspections	=	$ 3,000 per inspection
Engineering changes	$208,000	÷	16 engineering changes	=	$13,000 per engineering change order

Allocating Costs

Overhead costs of each activity are allocated to a product by multiplying the product's activity-base usage by the activity rate, as follows:

$$\text{Activity Overhead Allocated} = \text{Activity-Base Usage} \times \text{Activity Rate}$$

The estimated total factory overhead cost for a product is the sum of the product's individual activity allocations. The factory overhead cost per unit is computed by dividing the product's total factory overhead cost by the total units of estimated production, as follows:

$$\text{Factory Overhead Cost per Unit} = \frac{\text{Total Factory Overhead Cost}}{\text{Total Units of Estimated Production}}$$

These computations for Ruiz's snowmobile and riding mower are shown in Exhibit 10.

Exhibit 10   Activity-Based Product Cost Calculations

	A	B	C	D	E	F	G	H	I	J	K	L
1				Snowmobile						Riding Mower		
2		Activity-Base		Activity		Activity		Activity-Base		Activity		Activity
3	Activity	Usage	×	Rate	=	Cost		Usage	×	Rate	=	Cost
4												
5	Fabrication	8,000 dlh		$ 53 per dlh		$ 424,000		2,000 dlh		$ 53 per dlh		$106,000
6	Assembly	2,000 dlh		$ 7 per dlh		14,000		8,000 dlh		$ 7 per dlh		56,000
7	Setup	100 setups		$ 4,000 per setup		400,000		20 setups		$ 4,000 per setup		80,000
8	Quality-control											
9	inspections	100 inspections		$ 3,000 per insp.		300,000		4 inspections		$ 3,000 per insp.		12,000
10	Engineering											
11	changes	12 ECOs		$13,000 per ECO		156,000		4 ECOs		$13,000 per ECO		52,000
12	Total factory											
13	overhead cost					$1,294,000						$306,000
14	Estimated units											
15	of production					÷ 1,000						÷ 1,000
16	Factory overhead											
17	cost per unit					$ 1,294						$ 306
18												

The activity-based costing method for Ruiz is summarized in Exhibit 11.

Exhibit 11   Activity Bases—Ruiz Company

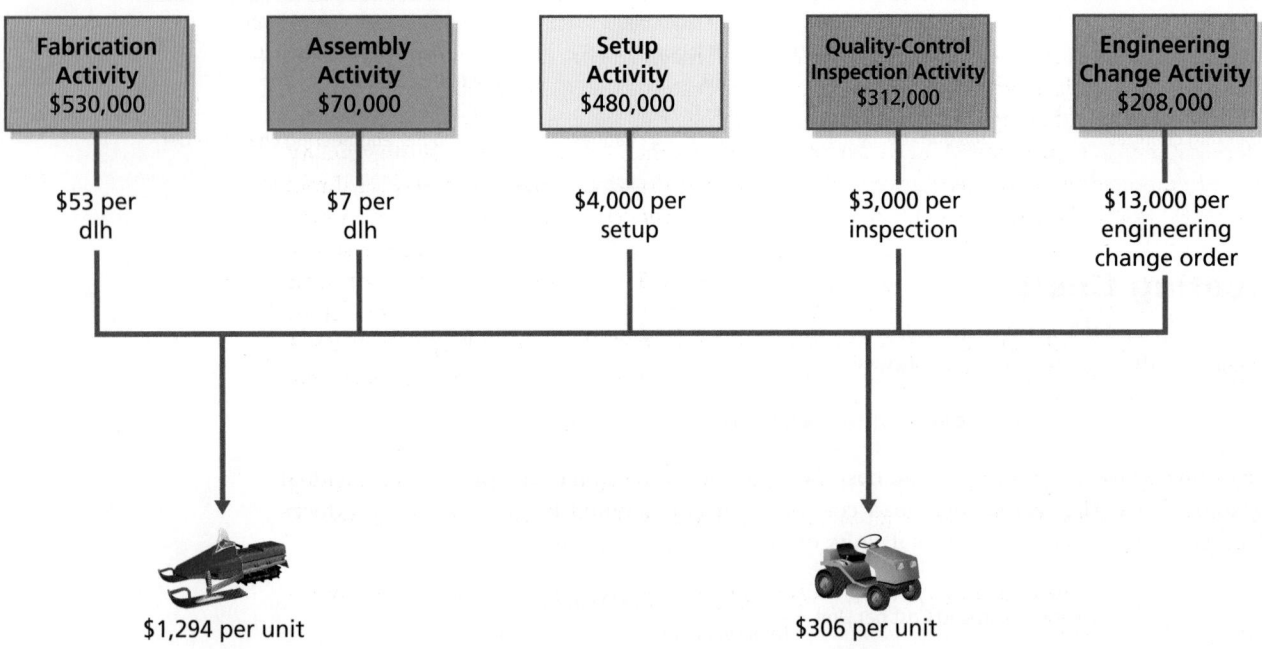

$1,294 per unit $306 per unit

Why It Matters

$600 Hammer

An old story is one of an ordinary hammer purchased under a government contract costing the government $600. This is actually not a story about waste, but a story about cost allocation

distortion. The actual story involves a hammer procured as part of a bundle of many different spare parts. When the engineering costs were allocated among the individual spare parts, every part was treated the same. Thus, a $15 hammer was allocated the same amount of relative engineering cost as were highly technical components. Thus, the hammer received as much relative overhead as did an engine. The allocation method did not trace engineering cost on the basis of engineering effort required by the product, but rather the cost was spread proportionally across all the products. In this way, the engine would end up under-allocated and the hammer over-allocated engineering cost. Today, this type of distortion is minimized through better cost allocation practices. This is accomplished through the Office of Federal Procurement

Policy Cost Accounting Standards Board, which operates as part of the U.S. government for purposes of prescribing standard cost accounting practices for U.S. government contracts.

Source: Sydney J. Freedberg, "The Myth of the $600 Hammer," *Government Executive*, December 7, 1998.

Distortion in Product Costs

The factory overhead costs per unit for Ruiz Company using the three allocation methods are shown in Exhibit 12.

Exhibit 12 Overhead Cost Allocation Methods: Ruiz Company

	Factory Overhead Cost per Unit— Three Cost Allocation Methods		
	Single Plantwide Rate	Multiple Production Department Rates	Activity-Based Costing
Snowmobile	$800	$938	$1,294
Riding mower	800	662	306

The activity-based costing method produces different factory overhead costs per unit (product costs) than the multiple department factory overhead rate method. This difference is caused by how the $1,000,000 of setup, quality control, and engineering change activities are allocated.

Under the multiple production department factory overhead rate method, setup, quality control, and engineering change costs were allocated using departmental rates based on direct labor hours. However, snowmobiles and riding mowers did *not* consume these *activities* in proportion to direct labor hours. That is, each snowmobile consumed a larger portion of the setup, quality-control inspection, and engineering change activities. This was true even though each product consumed 10,000 direct labor hours. As a result, activity-based costing allocated more of the cost of these activities to the snowmobile. Only under the activity-based approach were these differences reflected in the factory overhead cost allocations and thus in the product costs.

Dangers of Product Cost Distortion

If Ruiz Company used the $800 factory overhead cost allocation (single plantwide rate) instead of activity-based costing for pricing snowmobiles and riding mowers, the following would likely result:

- The snowmobile would be *underpriced* because its factory overhead cost would be understated by $494 ($1,294 − $800).
- The riding mower would be *overpriced* because its factory overhead cost would be overstated by $494 ($800 − $306).

As a result, Ruiz would likely lose sales of riding mowers because they are overpriced. In contrast, sales of snowmobiles would increase because they are underpriced. Due to these pricing errors, Ruiz might incorrectly decide to expand production of snowmobiles and discontinue making riding mowers.

If Ruiz uses the activity-based costing method, its product costs would be more accurate. Thus, Ruiz would have a better starting point for making proper pricing decisions. Although the product cost distortions are not as great, similar results would occur if Ruiz had used the multiple production department rate method.

Check Up Corner 18-3 | Activity-Based Costing

The total factory overhead for Lifestyle Furniture Company is budgeted at $600,000 for the year, divided among four activities: fabrication, $300,000; assembly, $120,000; setup, $100,000; and materials handling, $80,000. Lifestyle manufactures two designer furniture products: a wingback chair (chair) and a computer desk (desk). The activity-base usage quantities for each product by each activity are estimated as follows:

	Fabrication	Assembly	Setup	Materials Handling
Chair	5,000 dlh	15,000 dlh	30 setups	50 moves
Desk	15,000	5,000	220	350
Total activity-base usage	20,000 dlh	20,000 dlh	250 setups	400 moves

Production for the year is budgeted for 5,000 chairs and 5,000 desks.

Determine the:

A. Activity rate for each activity.

B. Activity-based factory overhead per unit for each product.

Solution:

A.

Fabrication	Assembly	Setup	Materials Handling
$300,000	$120,000	$100,000	$80,000
÷ 20,000 dlh	÷ 20,000 dlh	÷ 250 setups	÷ 400 moves
$ 15 per dlh	$ 6 per dlh	$ 400 per setup	$ 200 per move

The budgeted activity costs are assigned to products using a different rate for each activity.

$$\text{Activity Rate} = \frac{\text{Budgeted Activity Cost}}{\text{Total Activity-Base Usage}}$$

The activity rate for each department is multiplied by the department's activity-base usage for each product.

B.

	A	B	C	D	E	F	G	H	I	J	K	L
1				Chair						Desk		
2		Activity-Base		Activity		Activity		Activity-Base		Activity		Activity
3	Activity	Usage	×	Rate	=	Cost		Usage	×	Rate	=	Cost
4												
5	Fabrication	5,000 dlh		$ 15 per dlh		$ 75,000		15,000 dlh		$ 15 per dlh		$225,000
6	Assembly	15,000 dlh		$ 6 per dlh		90,000		5,000 dlh		$ 6 per dlh		30,000
7	Setup	30 setups		$400 per setup		12,000		220 setups		$400 per setup		88,000
8	Materials handling	50 moves		$200 per move		10,000		350 moves		$200 per move		70,000
9	Total factory overhead cost					$187,000						$413,000
10	Estimated units of											
11	production					÷ 5,000						÷ 5,000
12	Factory overhead											
13	cost per unit					$ 37.40						$ 82.60
14												

The factory overhead cost per unit is determined by dividing the factory overhead assigned to each product by the estimated number of units.

Check Up Corner

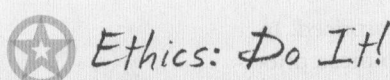 Ethics: Do It!

Fraud Against You and Me

The U.S. government makes a wide variety of purchases. Two of the largest are health care purchases under Medicare and military equipment. The purchase price for these and other items is often determined by the cost plus some profit. The cost is often the sum of direct costs plus allocated overhead. Due to the complexity of determining cost, government agencies review the amount charged for products and services. In the event of disagreement between the contractor and the government, the U.S.

government may sue the contractor under the False Claims Act, which provides for three times the government's damages plus civil penalties. The U.S. Department of Justice has recovered billions from the False Claims Act.

Most of the cases were the result of allegations by private citizens under the act's whistleblower provision.

Source: The False Claims Act Legal Center of the TAF Education Fund, www.taf.org.

Anyone can apply for and open a **Cold Stone Creamery** franchise. The company provides help in picking a location, constructing or leasing a building, and training employees. The initial franchise fee is $27,000, and it costs $250,000 to $400,000 to build and equip a store. The company receives a royalty fee of 6% and an advertising fee of 3% of gross sales.

Link to Cold Stone Creamery

Activity-Based Costing for Selling and Administrative Expenses

Objective 5
Use activity-based costing to allocate selling and administrative expenses to products.

Generally accepted accounting principles (GAAP) require that selling and administrative expenses be reported as period expenses on the income statement. However, selling and administrative expenses may be allocated to products for managerial decision making. For example, selling and administrative expenses may be allocated for analyzing product profitability.

One method of allocating selling and administrative expenses to the products is based on sales volumes. However, products may consume activities in ways that are unrelated to their sales volumes. When this occurs, activity-based costing may be a more accurate method of allocation.

To illustrate, assume that Abacus Company has two products, Ipso and Facto. Both products have the same total sales volume. However, Ipso and Facto consume selling and administrative activities differently, as shown in Exhibit 13.

Exhibit 13 Selling and Administrative Activity Product Differences

Selling and Administrative Activities	Ipso	Facto
Post-sale technical support	Product is easy for the customer to use.	Product requires specialized training in order for the customer to use it.
Order writing	Product requires no technical information from the customer.	Product requires detailed technical information from the customer.
Promotional support	Product requires no promotional effort.	Product requires extensive promotional effort.
Order entry	Product is purchased in large volumes per order.	Product is purchased in small volumes per order.
Customer return processing	Product has few customer returns.	Product has many customer returns.
Shipping document preparation	Product is shipped domestically.	Product is shipped internationally, requiring customs and export documents.
Shipping and handling	Product is not hazardous.	Product is hazardous, requiring specialized shipping and handling.
Field service	Product has few warranty claims.	Product has many warranty claims.

If Abacus's selling and administrative expenses are allocated on the basis of sales volumes, the same amount of expense would be allocated to Ipso and Facto. This is because Ipso and Facto have the same sales volume. However, as Exhibit 13 implies, such an allocation would be misleading.

The activity-based costing method can be used to allocate the selling and administrative activities to Ipso and Facto. Activity-based costing allocates selling and administrative expenses based on how each product consumes activities.

To illustrate, assume that Abacus's field warranty service activity has a budgeted cost of $150,000. Additionally, assume that 100 warranty claims are estimated for the period. Using warranty claims as an activity base, the warranty claim activity rate is $1,500, computed as follows:

$$\text{Activity Rate} = \frac{\text{Budgeted Activity Cost}}{\text{Total Activity-Base Usage}}$$

$$\text{Warranty Claim Activity Rate} = \frac{\text{Budgeted Warranty Claim Expenses}}{\text{Total Estimated Warranty Claims}}$$

$$= \frac{\$150,000}{100 \text{ claims}} = \$1,500 \text{ per warranty claim}$$

Assuming that Ipso had 10 warranty claims and Facto had 90 warranty claims, the field service activity expenses would be allocated to each product as follows:

Ipso: 10 warranty claims × $1,500 per warranty claim = $ 15,000
Facto: 90 warranty claims × $1,500 per warranty claim = $135,000

The remaining selling and administrative activities could be allocated to Ipso and Facto in a similar manner.

In some cases, selling and administrative expenses may be more related to *customer* behaviors than to differences in products. That is, some customers may demand more service and selling activities than other customers. In such cases, activity-based costing would allocate selling and administrative expenses to customers.

Objective 6
Use activity-based costing in a service business.

Activity-Based Costing in Service Businesses

Service companies need to determine the cost of their services so that they can make pricing, promoting, and other decisions. The use of single and multiple department overhead rate methods may lead to distortions similar to those of manufacturing firms. Thus, many service companies use activity-based costing for determining the cost of services.

To illustrate, assume that Hopewell Hospital uses activity-based costing to allocate hospital overhead to patients. Hopewell applies activity-based costing as follows:

- Step 1. Identifying activities.
- Step 2. Determining activity rates for each activity.
- Step 3. Allocating overhead costs to patients based upon activity-base usage.

Hopewell has identified the following activities:

- Admission
- Radiological testing
- Operating room
- Pathological testing
- Dietary and laundry

Each activity has an estimated patient activity-base usage. Based on the budgeted costs for each activity and related estimated activity-base usage, the activity rates shown in Exhibit 14 were developed.

Exhibit 14 Activity-Based Costing Method—Hopewell Hospital

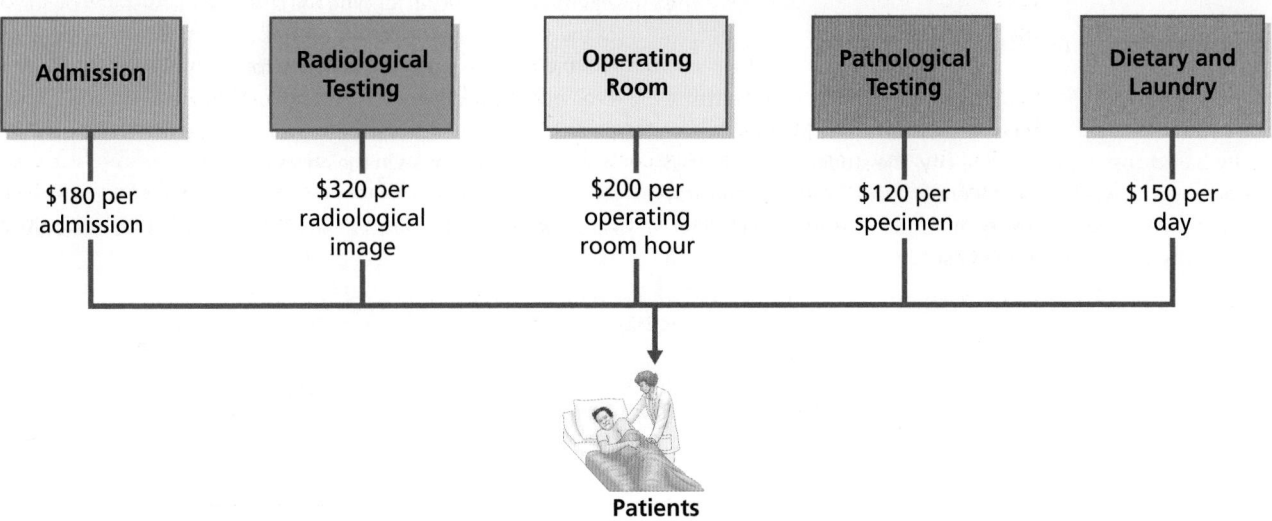

Patients

To illustrate, assume the following data for radiological testing:

Budgeted costs.....................................	$960,000
Total estimated activity-base usage	3,000 images

The activity rate of $320 per radiological image is computed as follows:

$$\text{Activity Rate} = \frac{\text{Budgeted Activity Cost}}{\text{Total Activity-Base Usage}}$$

$$\text{Radiological Testing Activity Rate} = \frac{\text{Budgeted Radiological Testing Costs}}{\text{Total Estimated Images}}$$

$$= \frac{\$960,000}{3,000 \text{ images}} = \$320 \text{ per image}$$

The activity rates for the other activities are determined in a similar manner. These activity rates along with the patient activity-base usage are used to allocate costs to patients as follows:

$$\text{Activity Cost Allocated to Patient} = \text{Patient Activity-Base Usage} \times \text{Activity Rate}$$

To illustrate, assume that Mia Wilson was a patient of the hospital. The hospital overhead services (activities) performed for Mia Wilson were as follows:

	Patient (Mia Wilson) Activity-Base Usage
Admission....................................	1 admission
Radiological testing...........................	2 images
Operating room...............................	4 hours
Pathological testing...........................	1 specimen
Dietary and laundry...........................	7 days

Based on the preceding services (activities), the Hopewell Hospital overhead costs allocated to Mia Wilson total $2,790, as computed in Exhibit 15.

Exhibit 15

Hopewell Hospital Overhead Costs Allocated to Mia Wilson

	A	B	C	D	E	F
1	Patient Name: Mia Wilson					
2		Activity-Base		Activity		Activity
3	Activity	Usage	×	Rate	=	Cost
4						
5	Admission	1 admission		$180 per admission		$ 180
6	Radiological testing	2 images		$320 per image		640
7	Operating room	4 hours		$200 per hour		800
8	Pathological testing	1 specimen		$120 per specimen		120
9	Dietary and laundry	7 days		$150 per day		1,050
10	Total					$2,790
11						

The patient activity costs can be combined with the direct costs, such as drugs and supplies. These costs and the related revenues can be reported for each patient in a patient (customer) profitability report. A partial patient profitability report for Hopewell is shown in Exhibit 16.

Exhibit 16

Customer Profitability Report—Hopewell Hospital

Hopewell Hospital
Patient (Customer) Profitability Report
For the Period Ending December 31

	Adcock, Aesha	Birini, Sergey	Diaz, Mateo	Wilson, Mia
Revenues	$9,500	$21,400	$5,050	$3,300
Patient costs:				
Drugs and supplies	$ 400	$ 1,000	$ 300	$ 200
Admission	180	180	180	180
Radiological testing	1,280	2,560	1,280	640
Operating room	2,400	6,400	1,600	800
Pathological testing	240	600	120	120
Dietary and laundry	4,200	14,700	1,050	1,050
Total patient costs	$8,700	$25,440	$4,530	$2,990
Income from operations	$ 800	$ (4,040)	$ 520	$ 310

Exhibit 16 can be used by hospital administrators for decisions on pricing or services. For example, there was a large loss on services provided to Sergey Birini. Investigation might reveal that some of the services provided to Birini were not reimbursed by insurance. As a result, Hopewell might lobby the insurance company to reimburse these services or request higher insurance reimbursement on other services.

Check Up Corner 18-4 Activity-Based Costing for a Service Business

Metro University uses activity-based costing to assign indirect costs to academic departments, using four activities. The activity base, budgeted activity cost, and estimated activity-base usage for each activity are identified below.

Activity	Activity Base	Budgeted Activity Cost	Activity-Base Usage
Academic support	Number of departments	$ 400,000	40 departments (dept.)
Facilities	Square feet	1,800,000	200,000 square feet (sq. ft.)
Instruction	Number of course sections	2,000,000	1,000 sections (sec.)
Student services	Number of students	360,000	4,500 students (stdt.)

The activity-base usage associated with the Chemistry Department and History Department is as follows:

	Academic Support	Facilities	Instruction	Student Services
Chemistry	1 department	9,000 square feet	15 sections	80 students
History	1 department	3,200 square feet	30 sections	175 students

Determine the:

A. Activity rate for each activity.

B. Total activity cost for the Chemistry Department and the History Department.

Solution:

A.

Academic Support	Facilities	Instruction	Student Services
$400,000	$1,800,000	$2,000,000	$360,000
÷ 40 dept.	÷ 200,000 sq. ft.	÷ 1,000 sec.	÷ 4,500 stdt.
$ 10,000 per dept.	$ 9 per sq. ft.	$ 2,000 per sec.	$ 80 per stdt.

The budgeted activity costs are assigned to departments using a different rate for each activity. These rates are called activity rates.

$$\text{Activity Rate} = \frac{\text{Budgeted Activity Cost}}{\text{Total Activity-Base Usage}}$$

Activity rates for each activity are multiplied by the activity-base usage in each department.

B.

	Chemistry Department				History Department			
Activity	Activity-Base Usage	×	Activity Rate	= Activity Cost	Activity-Base Usage	×	Activity Rate	= Activity Cost
Academic support	1 dept.	×	$10,000 per dept. =	$ 10,000	1 dept.	×	$10,000 per dept. =	$ 10,000
Facilities	9,000 sq. ft.	×	$9 per sq. ft. =	81,000	3,200 sq. ft.	×	$9 per sq. ft. =	28,800
Instruction	15 sec.	×	$2,000 per sec. =	30,000	30 sec.	×	$2,000 per sec. =	60,000
Student services	80 stdt.	×	$80 per stdt. =	6,400	175 stdt.	×	$80 per stdt. =	14,000
Total activity cost				$127,400				$112,800

The total activity cost assigned to each department

Check Up Corner

Analysis for Decision Making

Using ABC Product Cost Information to Reduce Costs

Activity-based costing (ABC) can be used to improve the cost of a product. For example, Lee Corporation assembles LCD monitors. The following activity information is available for its 40-inch monitor:

Activity	Activity-Base Usage (hrs. per unit)	×	Activity Rate per Hour	=	Activity Cost
Assembly	0.80		$14		$11.20
Setup	0.30		20		6.00
Production control	0.15		32		4.80
Materials control	0.10		32		3.20
Moving	0.40		12		4.80
Testing	0.25		24		6.00
Activity cost per unit					$36.00

All of the activity cost is related to labor. The activity information can be used to isolate cost improvement opportunities. Management is seeking to remove $3.00 of activity cost from the product in order to remain price competitive. The activity cost reduction can be accomplished in two basic ways:

1. Improve operations so that the activity-base usage per unit is either reduced or eliminated.
2. Change the classification of employees doing an activity and thereby decrease the activity rate. Higher-classified employees are more expensive but more skilled than lower-classified employees.

Assume the process was improved so that the setup activity required one-third less time to complete per unit. In addition, the moving distance was cut in half. Would these improvements be sufficient to remove $3.00 of activity cost from the product? The activity information under the improvements would be as follows:

Activity	Activity-Base Usage (hrs. per unit)	×	Activity Rate per Hour	=	Activity Cost
Assembly	0.80		$14		$11.20
Setup	0.20		20		4.00
Production control	0.15		32		4.80
Materials control	0.10		32		3.20
Moving	0.20		12		2.40
Testing	0.25		24		6.00
Activity cost per unit					$31.60

The shaded areas show the improvements. Setup was reduced from 0.3 hours to 0.2 hours. The moving distance was cut from 0.4 hours to 0.2 hours. These changes reduced the activity cost of each monitor from $36.00 to $31.60, or $4.40, thus exceeding the $3.00 target.

Make a Decision Using ABC Product Cost Information to Reduce Costs

Life Force Fitness, Inc. assembles and sells treadmills. Activity-based product information for each treadmill is as follows:

Activity	Activity-Base Usage (hrs. per unit)	×	Activity Rate per Hour	=	Activity Cost
Motor assembly	1.50		$20		$30.00
Final assembly	1.00		18		18.00
Testing	0.25		22		5.50
Rework	0.40		22		8.80
Moving	0.20		15		3.00
Activity cost per unit					$65.30

All of the activity costs are related to labor. Management must remove $2.00 of activity cost from the product in order to remain competitive.

Rework involves disassembling and repairing a unit that fails testing. Not all units require rework, but the average is 0.40 hours per unit. Presently, the testing is done on the completed assembly; but much of the rework has been related to motors to test the motor independently, prior to assembling it into the final treadmill. Thus, motor assembly issues can be diagnosed and solved without having to disassemble the complete treadmill. This change will reduce the average rework per unit by one-quarter.

A. Determine the new activity cost per unit under the rework improvement scenario.

B. If management had the choice of doing the rework improvement in (A) or cutting the moving activity in half by improving the product flow, which decision should be implemented? Why?

Solution:

A. The average rework per unit will be improved by one-quarter, or 25%. Thus, the new average rework time will be reduced from 0.40 to 0.30 hours [0.40 × (1 – 0.25)].

Activity	Activity-Base Usage (hrs. per unit)	×	Activity Rate per Hour	=	Activity Cost
Motor assembly	1.50		$20		$30.00
Final assembly	1.00		18		18.00
Testing	0.25		22		5.50
Rework	0.30		22		6.60
Moving	0.20		15		3.00
Activity cost per unit					$63.10

B. The rework improvement reduces the cost per unit by $2.20 ($65.30 – $63.10), which meets management's $2.00 per unit cost improvement objective. Halving the moving activity would reduce the moving activity cost by $1.50 per unit (0.10 hours × $15 per hour), which is $0.70 less than the rework improvement ($2.20 – $1.50). Thus, management should select the rework improvement project.

Make a Decision

Let's Review

Chapter Summary

1. Three cost allocation methods used for determining product costs are the (1) single plant-wide factory overhead rate method, (2) multiple production department rate method, and (3) activity-based costing method.

2. A single plantwide factory overhead rate can be used to allocate all plant overhead to all products. The single plantwide factory overhead rate is simple to apply, but can lead to product cost distortions.

3. Product costing using multiple production department factory overhead rates requires identifying the factory overhead by each production department. Using these rates can result in greater accuracy than using single plantwide factory overhead rates when: (A) There are significant differences in the factory overhead rates across different production departments. (B) The products require different ratios of allocation-base usage in each production department.

4. Activity-based costing requires factory overhead to be budgeted to activities. The budgeted activity costs are allocated to products by multiplying activity rates by the activity-base quantity consumed for each product. Activity-based costing is more accurate when products consume activities in proportions unrelated to plantwide or departmental allocation bases.

5. Selling and administrative expenses can be allocated to products for management profit reporting, using activity-based costing. Activity-based costing would be preferred when the products use selling and administrative activities in ratios that are unrelated to their sales volumes.

6. Activity-based costing may be applied in service businesses to determine the cost of individual services offered. Service costs are determined by multiplying activity rates by the activity-base quantities consumed by the customer.

Key Terms

activities (896)
activity base (898)
activity rates (898)
activity-based costing
   (ABC) method (896)

engineering change order
   (ECO) (897)
multiple production department
   factory overhead rate
   method (891)
product costing (888)

production department
   factory overhead rate (892)
setup (897)
single plantwide factory
   overhead rate method (889)

Practice

Multiple-Choice Questions

1. Which of the following statements is most accurate?
   A. The single plantwide factory overhead rate method will usually provide management with accurate product costs.
   B. Activity-based costing can be used by management to determine accurate profitability for each product.
   C. The multiple production department factory overhead rate method will usually result in more product cost distortion than the single plantwide factory overhead rate method.
   D. Generally accepted accounting principles require activity-based costing methods for inventory valuation.

2. San Madeo Company had the following factory overhead costs:

Power	$120,000
Indirect labor	60,000
Equipment depreciation	500,000

The factory budgeted to work 20,000 direct labor hours in the upcoming period. San Madeo uses a single plantwide factory overhead rate based on direct labor hours. What is the overhead cost per unit associated with Product M, if Product M uses 6 direct labor hours per unit in the factory?

A. $34
B. $54
C. $204
D. $150

3. Which of the following activity bases would best be used to allocate setup activity to products?

A. Number of inspections
B. Direct labor hours
C. Direct machine hours
D. Number of production runs

4. Production Department 1 (PD1) and Production Department 2 (PD2) had factory overhead budgets of $26,000 and $48,000, respectively. Each department was budgeted for 5,000 direct labor hours of production activity. Product T required 5 direct labor hours in PD1 and 2 direct labor hours in PD2. What is the factory overhead cost associated with Product T, assuming that factory overhead is allocated using the multiple production rate method?

A. $26.00
B. $40.40
C. $45.20
D. $58.40

5. The following activity rates are associated with moving rail cars by train: $4 per gross ton mile; $50 per rail car switch; $200 per rail car. A train with 20 rail cars traveled 100 miles. Each rail car carried 10 tons of product. Each rail car was switched two times. What is the total cost of moving this train?

A. $5,400
B. $10,000
C. $44,100
D. $86,000

Answers provided after Problem. Need more practice? Find additional multiple-choice questions, exercises, and problems in CengageNOWv2.

Exercises

SHOW ME HOW

1. Single plantwide factory overhead rate
Obj. 2

The total factory overhead for Diva-nation Inc. is budgeted for the year at $180,000. Diva-nation manufactures two types of men's pants: jeans and khakis. The jeans and khakis each require 0.10 direct labor hour for manufacture. Each product is budgeted for 20,000 units of production for the year. Determine (A) the total number of budgeted direct labor hours for the year, (B) the single plantwide factory overhead rate, and (C) the factory overhead allocated per unit for each product using the single plantwide factory overhead rate.

SHOW ME HOW

2. Multiple production department factory overhead rates
Obj. 3

The total factory overhead for Diva-nation is budgeted for the year at $180,000, divided into two departments: Cutting, $60,000, and Sewing, $120,000. Diva-nation manufactures two types of men's pants: jeans and khakis. The jeans require 0.04 direct labor hour in Cutting and 0.06 direct labor hour in Sewing. The khakis require 0.06 direct labor hour in Cutting and 0.04 direct labor hour in Sewing. Each product is budgeted for 20,000 units of production for the year. Determine (A) the total number of budgeted direct labor hours for the year in each department, (B) the departmental factory overhead rates for both departments, and (C) the factory overhead allocated per unit for each product using the department factory overhead allocation rates.

SHOW ME HOW

3. Activity-based costing: factory overhead costs

Obj. 4

The total factory overhead for Diva-nation is budgeted for the year at $180,000, divided into four activities: cutting, $18,000; sewing, $36,000; setup, $96,000; and inspection, $30,000. Diva-nation manufactures two types of men's pants: jeans and khakis. The activity-base usage quantities for each product by each activity are as follows:

	Cutting	Sewing	Setup	Inspection
Jeans	800 dlh	1,200 dlh	1,400 setups	3,000 inspections
Khakis	1,200	800	1,000	2,000
	2,000 dlh	2,000 dlh	2,400 setups	5,000 inspections

Each product is budgeted for 20,000 units of production for the year. Determine (A) the activity rates for each activity and (B) the activity-based factory overhead per unit for each product.

SHOW ME HOW

4. Activity-based costing: selling and administrative expenses

Obj. 5

Fancy Feet Company manufactures and sells shoes. Fancy Feet uses activity-based costing to determine the cost of the sales order processing and the shipping activity. The sales order processing activity has an activity rate of $12 per sales order, and the shipping activity has an activity rate of $20 per shipment. Fancy Feet sold 27,500 units of walking shoes, which consisted of 5,000 orders and 1,400 shipments. Determine (A) the total activity cost and (B) the per-unit sales order processing and shipping activity cost for walking shoes.

SHOW ME HOW

5. Activity-based costing for a service business

Obj. 6

Draper Bank uses activity-based costing to determine the cost of servicing customers. There are three activity pools: teller transaction processing, check processing, and ATM transaction processing. The activity rates associated with each activity pool are $3.50 per teller transaction, $0.12 per canceled check, and $0.10 per ATM transaction. Draper Bank had 12 teller transactions, 100 canceled checks, and 20 ATM transactions during the month. Determine the total monthly activity-based cost for Draper Bank during the month.

Answers provided after Problem. Need more practice? Find additional multiple-choice questions, exercises, and problems in CengageNOWv2.

Problem

Hammer Company plans to use activity-based costing to determine its product costs. It presently uses a single plantwide factory overhead rate for allocating factory overhead to products, based on direct labor hours. The total factory overhead cost is as follows:

Department	Factory Overhead
Production Support....................................	$1,225,000
Production (factory overhead only)....................	175,000
Total cost...	$1,400,000

The company determined that it performed four major activities in the Production Support Department. These activities, along with their budgeted activity costs, are as follows:

Production Support Activities	Budgeted Activity Cost
Setup..	$ 428,750
Production control....................................	245,000
Quality control......................................	183,750
Materials management	367,500
Total	$1,225,000

Hammer estimated the following activity-base usage and units produced for each of its three products:

Products	Number of Units	Direct Labor Hrs.	Setups	Production Orders	Inspections	Material Requisitions
LCD TV..................	10,000	25,000	80	80	35	320
Tablet...................	2,000	10,000	40	40	40	400
Smartphone.............	50,000	140,000	5	5	0	30
Total cost	62,000	175,000	125	125	75	750

Instructions

1. Determine the factory overhead cost per unit for the LCD TV, tablet, and smartphone under the single plantwide factory overhead rate method. Use direct labor hours as the activity base.

2. Determine the factory overhead cost per unit for the LCD TV, tablet, and smartphone under activity-based costing. (Round to two decimal places.)

3. Which method provides more accurate product costing? Why?

Need more practice? Find additional multiple-choice questions, exercises, and problems in CengageNOWv2.

Answers

Multiple-Choice Questions

1. **B** Activity-based costing provides accurate product costs, which can be used for strategic product profitability analysis. The single plantwide factory overhead rate method (answer A) can distort the individual product costs under a variety of reasonable conditions. The multiple production department factory overhead rate method will lead to less (not more) distortion than the single plantwide factory overhead rate method (answer C). Generally accepted accounting principles do not require activity-based costing methods for inventory valuation (answer D).

2. **C** The single plantwide factory overhead rate is $34 per hour (answer A), determined as $680,000 ÷ 20,000 hours. This rate is multiplied by 6 direct labor hours per unit of Product M to determine the correct overhead per unit of $204 (answer C). The total overhead should be used in the numerator in determining the overhead rate, not just power and indirect labor (answer B) or equipment depreciation (answer D).

3. **D** The number of production runs best relates the activity cost of setup to the products. Number of inspections (answer A), direct labor hours (answer B), and direct machine hours (answer C) will likely have very little logical association with the costs incurred in setting up production runs.

4. **C** PD1 rate: $26,000 ÷ 5,000 dlh = $5.20 per dlh
   PD2 rate: $48,000 ÷ 5,000 dlh = $9.60 per dlh
   Product T: (5 dlh × $5.20) + (2 dlh × $9.60) = $45.20

5. **D** (100 miles × 20 cars × 10 tons × $4) + ($200 × 20 cars) + (20 cars × 2 switches × $50)
   = $80,000 + $4,000 + $2,000 = $86,000

Exercises

1.

A. Jeans: 20,000 units × 0.10 direct labor hour = 2,000 direct labor hours
   Khakis: 20,000 units × 0.10 direct labor hour = <u>2,000</u>
   <u>4,000</u> direct labor hours

B. Single plantwide factory overhead rate: $180,000 ÷ 4,000 dlh = $45 per dlh

C. Jeans: $45 per direct labor hour × 0.10 dlh per unit = $4.50 per unit
   Khakis: $45 per direct labor hour × 0.10 dlh per unit = $4.50 per unit

2.

A. Cutting: (20,000 jeans × 0.04 dlh) + (20,000 khakis × 0.06 dlh)
       = 2,000 direct labor hours
   Sewing: (20,000 jeans × 0.06 dlh) + (20,000 khakis × 0.04 dlh)
       = 2,000 direct labor hours

B. Cutting Department rate: $60,000 ÷ 2,000 dlh = $30 per dlh
   Sewing Department rate: $120,000 ÷ 2,000 dlh = $60 per dlh

C. Jeans: Cutting Department 0.04 dlh × $30 = $1.20
            Sewing Department 0.06 dlh × $60 =   <u>3.60</u>
            Total factory overhead per pair of jeans   <u>$4.80</u>

   Khakis: Cutting Department 0.06 dlh × $30 = $1.80
            Sewing Department 0.04 dlh × $60 =   <u>2.40</u>
            Total factory overhead per pair of khakis   <u>$4.20</u>

3.

A. Cutting: $18,000 ÷ 2,000 direct labor hours = $9.00 per dlh
   Sewing: $36,000 ÷ 2,000 direct labor hours = $18.00 per dlh
   Setup: $96,000 ÷ 2,400 setups = $40.00 per setup
   Inspection: $30,000 ÷ 5,000 inspections = $6.00 per inspection

B.

	Jeans				Khakis		
Activity	**Activity-Base Usage** ×	**Activity Rate** =	**Activity Cost**	**Activity-Base Usage** ×	**Activity Rate** =	**Activity Cost**
Cutting	800 dlh	$ 9.00 per dlh	$ 7,200	1,200 dlh	$ 9.00 per dlh	$10,800
Sewing	1,200 dlh	$18.00 per dlh	21,600	800 dlh	$18.00 per dlh	14,400
Setup	1,400 setups	$40.00 per setup	56,000	1,000 setups	$40.00 per setup	40,000
Inspections	3,000 insp.	$ 6.00 per insp.	18,000	2,000 insp.	$ 6.00 per insp.	12,000
Total			$102,800			$77,200
÷ Budgeted items			÷ 20,000			÷20,000
Factory overhead per unit			$ 5.14			$ 3.86

4.

A. Sales order processing activity: 5,000 orders × $12 per order = $60,000
   Shipping activity: 1,400 shipments × $20 per shipment =   <u>28,000</u>
   Total activity cost   <u>$88,000</u>

B. $3.20 per unit ($88,000 ÷ 27,500 units)

5.

Teller transaction processing	$42.00	(12 transactions × $3.50)
Check processing	12.00	(100 checks × $0.12)
ATM transaction processing	<u>2.00</u>	(20 transactions × $0.10)
Total activity cost	<u>$56.00</u>	

Need more help? Watch step-by-step videos of how to compute answers to these Exercises in CengageNOWv2.

Problem

1. Single Plantwide Factory Overhead Rate $= \dfrac{\$1,400,000}{175,000 \text{ direct labor hours}}$

$= \$8$ per direct labor hour

Factory overhead cost per unit:

	LCD TV	Tablet	Smartphone
Number of direct labor hours....................	25,000	10,000	140,000
Single plantwide factory overhead rate..........	× $8 per dlh	× $8 per dlh	× $ 8 per dlh
Total factory overhead	$ 200,000	$ 80,000	$ 1,120,000
Number of units	÷ 10,000	÷ 2,000	÷ 50,000
Factory overhead cost per unit	$ 20.00	$ 40.00	$ 22.40

2. Under activity-based costing, an activity rate must be determined for each activity pool:

Activity	Budgeted Activity Cost	÷	Total Activity-Base Usage	=	Activity Rate
Setup......................	$428,750	÷	125 setups	=	$3,430 per setup
Production control.........	$245,000	÷	125 production orders	=	$1,960 per production order
Quality control.............	$183,750	÷	75 inspections	=	$2,450 per inspection
Materials management	$367,500	÷	750 requisitions	=	$ 490 per requisition
Production	$175,000	÷	175,000 direct labor hours	=	$ 1 per direct labor hour

These activity rates can be used to determine the activity-based factory overhead cost per unit as follows:

LCD TV

Activity	Activity-Base Usage	×	Activity Rate	=	Activity Cost
Setup	80 setups	×	$3,430	=	$274,400
Production control..........	80 production orders	×	1,960	=	156,800
Quality control..............	35 inspections	×	2,450	=	85,750
Materials management	320 requisitions	×	490	=	156,800
Production	25,000 direct labor hrs.	×	1	=	25,000
Total factory overhead					$698,750
Unit volume					÷ 10,000
Factory overhead cost per unit...............					$ 69.88

Tablet

Activity	Activity-Base Usage	×	Activity Rate	=	Activity Cost
Setup	40 setups	×	$3,430	=	$137,200
Production control..........	40 production orders	×	1,960	=	78,400
Quality control..............	40 inspections	×	2,450	=	98,000
Materials management	400 requisitions	×	490	=	196,000
Production	10,000 direct labor hrs.	×	1	=	10,000
Total factory overhead					$519,600
Unit volume					÷ 2,000
Factory overhead cost per unit...............					$ 259.80

Smartphone

Activity	Activity-Base Usage	×	Activity Rate	=	Activity Cost
Setup	5 setups	×	$3,430	=	$ 17,150
Production control...........	5 production orders	×	1,960	=	9,800
Quality control...............	0 inspections	×	2,450	=	0
Materials management	30 requisitions	×	490	=	14,700
Production	140,000 direct labor hrs.	×	1	=	140,000
Total factory overhead					$181,650
Unit volume					÷ 50,000
Factory overhead cost per unit..............					$ 3.63

3. Activity-based costing is more accurate, compared to the single plantwide factory overhead rate method. Activity-based costing properly shows that the smartphone is actually less expensive to make, while the other two products are more expensive to make. The reason is that the single plantwide factory overhead rate method fails to account for activity costs correctly. The setup, production control, quality control, and materials management activities are all performed on products in amounts that are proportionately different than their volumes. For example, the tablet requires many of these activities relative to its actual unit volume. The tablet requires 40 setups over a volume of 2,000 units (average production run size = 50 units), while the smartphone has only 5 setups over 50,000 units (average production run size = 10,000 units). Thus, the tablet requires greater support costs relative to the smartphone.

   The smartphone requires minimum activity support because it is scheduled in large batches and requires no inspections (has high quality) and few requisitions. The other two products exhibit the opposite characteristics.

Discussion Questions

1. Why would management be concerned about the accuracy of product costs?

2. Why would a manufacturing company with multiple production departments still prefer to use a single plantwide overhead rate?

3. How do the multiple production department and the single plantwide factory overhead rate methods differ?

4. Under what two conditions would the multiple production department factory overhead rate method provide more accurate product costs than the single plantwide factory overhead rate method?

5. How does activity-based costing differ from the multiple production department factory overhead rate method?

6. Shipping, selling, marketing, sales order processing, return processing, and advertising activities can be related to products by using activity-based costing. Would allocating these activities to products for financial statement reporting be acceptable according to GAAP?

7. What would happen to net income if the activities noted in Discussion Question 6 were allocated to products for financial statement reporting and the inventory increased?

8. Under what circumstances might the activity-based costing method provide more accurate product costs than the multiple production department factory overhead rate method?

9. When might activity-based costing be preferred over using a relative amount of product sales in allocating selling and administrative expenses to products?

10. How can activity-based costing be used in service companies?

Basic Exercises

SHOW ME HOW

BE 18-1 Single plantwide factory overhead rate   Obj. 2

The total factory overhead for Bardot Marine Company is budgeted for the year at $600,000. Bardot Marine manufactures two types of boats: speedboats and bass boats. The speedboat and bass boat each require 12 direct labor hours for manufacture. Each product is budgeted for 250 units of production for the year. Determine (A) the total number of budgeted direct labor hours for the year, (B) the single plantwide factory overhead rate, and (C) the factory overhead allocated per unit for each product using the single plantwide factory overhead rate.

SHOW ME HOW

BE 18-2 Multiple production department factory overhead rates   Obj. 3

The total factory overhead for Bardot Marine Company is budgeted for the year at $600,000 divided into two departments: Fabrication, $420,000, and Assembly, $180,000. Bardot Marine manufactures two types of boats: speedboats and bass boats. The speedboats require 8 direct labor hours in Fabrication and 4 direct labor hours in Assembly. The bass boats require 4 direct labor hours in Fabrication and 8 direct labor hours in Assembly. Each product is budgeted for 250 units of production for the year. Determine (A) the total number of budgeted direct labor hours for the year in each department, (B) the departmental factory overhead rates for both departments, and (C) the factory overhead allocated per unit for each product using the department factory overhead allocation rates.

SHOW ME HOW

BE 18-3 Activity-based costing: factory overhead costs   Obj. 4

The total factory overhead for Bardot Marine Company is budgeted for the year at $600,000, divided into four activities: fabrication, $204,000; assembly, $105,000; setup, $156,000; and inspection, $135,000. Bardot Marine manufactures two types of boats: speedboats and bass boats. The activity-base usage quantities for each product by each activity are as follows:

	Fabrication	Assembly	Setup	Inspection
Speedboat	2,000 dlh	1,000 dlh	300 setups	1,100 inspections
Bass boat	1,000	2,000	100	400
	3,000 dlh	3,000 dlh	400 setups	1,500 inspections

Each product is budgeted for 250 units of production for the year. Determine (A) the activity rates for each activity and (B) the activity-based factory overhead per unit for each product.

SHOW ME HOW

BE 18-4 Activity-based costing: selling and administrative expenses   Obj. 5

Jungle Junior Company manufactures and sells outdoor play equipment. Jungle Junior uses activity-based costing to determine the cost of the sales order processing and the customer return activity. The sales order processing activity has an activity rate of $20 per sales order, and the customer return activity has an activity rate of $100 per return. Jungle Junior sold 2,500 swing sets, which consisted of 750 orders and 80 returns. Determine (A) the total and (B) the per-unit sales order processing and customer return activity cost for swing sets.

SHOW ME HOW

BE 18-5 Activity-based costing for a service business   Obj. 6

Sterling Hotel uses activity-based costing to determine the cost of servicing customers. There are three activity pools: guest check-in, room cleaning, and meal service. The activity rates associated with each activity pool are $8 per guest check-in, $25 per room cleaning, and $4 per served meal (not including food). Ginny Campbell visited the hotel for a three-night stay. Campbell had three meals in the hotel during her visit. Determine the total activity-based cost for Campbell's visit.

Exercises

EX 18-1   Single plantwide factory overhead rate   Obj. 2

Nixon Machine Parts Inc.'s Fabrication Department incurred $560,000 of factory overhead cost in producing gears and sprockets. The two products consumed a total of 8,000 direct machine hours. Of that amount, sprockets consumed 5,150 direct machine hours.

Determine the total amount of factory overhead that should be allocated to sprockets using machine hours as the allocation base.

EX 18-2   Single plantwide factory overhead rate   Obj. 2

✔ A. $380 per direct labor hour

Mozart Music Inc. makes three musical instruments: trumpets, tubas, and trombones. The budgeted factory overhead cost is $3,469,400. Factory overhead is allocated to the three products on the basis of direct labor hours. The products have the following budgeted production volume and direct labor hours per unit:

	Budgeted Production Volume	Direct Labor Hours per Unit
Trumpets	4,000 units	1.2
Tubas	1,200	0.9
Trombones	2,500	1.3

A.   Determine the single plantwide factory overhead rate.

B.   Use the factory overhead rate in (A) to determine the amount of total and per-unit factory overhead allocated to each of the three products.

EX 18-3   Single plantwide factory overhead rate   Obj. 2

✔ A. $60 per processing hour

Salty Sensations Snacks Company manufactures three types of snack foods: tortilla chips, potato chips, and pretzels. The company has budgeted the following costs for the upcoming period:

Factory depreciation	$ 31,360
Indirect labor	78,400
Factory electricity	7,840
Indirect materials	35,400
Selling expenses	25,000
Administrative expenses	18,000
Total costs	$196,000

Factory overhead is allocated to the three products on the basis of processing hours. The products had the following production budget and processing hours per case:

	Budgeted Volume (Cases)	Processing Hours per Case
Tortilla chips	4,000	0.20
Potato chips	5,000	0.15
Pretzels	2,500	0.40
Total	11,500	

A.   Determine the single plantwide factory overhead rate.

B.   Use the factory overhead rate in (A) to determine the amount of total and per-case factory overhead allocated to each of the three products under generally accepted accounting principles.

EX 18-4 Product costs and product profitability reports, using a single plantwide factory overhead rate

Obj. 2

Elliott Engines Inc. produces three products—pistons, valves, and cams—for the heavy equipment industry. Elliott Engines has a very simple production process and product line and uses a single plantwide factory overhead rate to allocate overhead to the three products. The factory overhead rate is based on direct labor hours. Information about the three products for 20Y2 is as follows:

	Budgeted Volume (Units)	Direct Labor Hours per Unit	Price per Unit	Direct Materials per Unit
Pistons	5,000	0.50	$45	$ 8
Valves	12,500	0.30	17	3
Cams	1,500	0.20	60	40

The estimated direct labor rate is $30 per direct labor hour. Beginning and ending inventories are negligible and are, thus, assumed to be zero. The budgeted factory overhead for Elliott Engines is $163,750.

A. Determine the plantwide factory overhead rate.

B. Determine the factory overhead and direct labor cost per unit for each product.

C. Use the information provided to construct a budgeted gross profit report by product line for the year ended December 31, 20Y2. Include the gross profit as a percent of sales in the last line of your report, rounded to one decimal place.

D. ➤ What does the report in (C) indicate to you?

EX 18-5 Multiple production department factory overhead rate method

Obj. 3

Performance Gloves, Inc. produces three sizes of sports gloves: small, medium, and large. A glove pattern is first stenciled onto leather in the Pattern Department. The stenciled patterns are then sent to the Cut and Sew Department, where the glove is cut and sewed together. Performance Gloves uses the multiple production department factory overhead rate method of allocating factory overhead costs. Its factory overhead costs were budgeted as follows:

Pattern Department overhead	$ 216,000
Cut and Sew Department overhead	960,000
Total	$1,176,000

The direct labor estimated for each production department was as follows:

Pattern Department	36,000 direct labor hours
Cut and Sew Department	60,000
Total	96,000 direct labor hours

Direct labor hours are used to allocate the production department overhead to the products. The direct labor hours per unit for each product for each production department were obtained from the engineering records as follows:

Production Departments	Small Glove	Medium Glove	Large Glove
Pattern Department	0.20	0.24	0.30
Cut and Sew Department	0.50	0.60	0.72
Direct labor hours per unit	0.70	0.84	1.02

A. Determine the two production department factory overhead rates.

B. Use the two production department factory overhead rates to determine the factory overhead per unit for each product.

EX 18-6 Single plantwide and multiple production department factory overhead rate methods and product cost distortion

Obj. 2, 3

✔ B. Residential
motor, $330 per unit

Pineapple Motor Company manufactures two types of specialty electric motors, a commercial motor and a residential motor, through two production departments, Assembly and Testing. Presently, the company uses a single plantwide factory overhead rate for allocating factory overhead to the two products. However, management is considering using the multiple production department factory overhead rate method. The following factory overhead was budgeted for Pineapple:

Assembly Department	$240,000
Testing Department	750,000
Total	$990,000

Direct machine hours were estimated as follows:

Assembly Department	3,000 hours
Testing Department	6,000
Total	9,000 hours

In addition, the direct machine hours (dmh) used to produce a unit of each product in each department were determined from engineering records, as follows:

	Commercial	Residential
Assembly Department	1.5 dmh	1.0 dmh
Testing Department	3.0	2.0
Total machine hours per unit	4.5 dmh	3.0 dmh

A. Determine the per-unit factory overhead allocated to the commercial and residential motors under the single plantwide factory overhead rate method, using direct machine hours as the allocation base.

B. Determine the per-unit factory overhead allocated to the commercial and residential motors under the multiple production department factory overhead rate method, using direct machine hours as the allocation base for each department.

C. ✏️ Recommend to management a product costing approach, based on your analyses in (A) and (B). Support your recommendation.

EX 18-7 Single plantwide and multiple production department factory overhead rate methods and product cost distortion

Obj. 2, 3

✔ B. Diesel engine,
$370 per unit

The management of Firebolt Industries Inc. manufactures gasoline and diesel engines through two production departments, Fabrication and Assembly. Management needs accurate product cost information in order to guide product strategy. Presently, the company uses a single plantwide factory overhead rate for allocating factory overhead to the two products. However, management is considering the multiple production department factory overhead rate method. The following factory overhead was budgeted for Firebolt:

Fabrication Department factory overhead	$550,000
Assembly Department factory overhead	250,000
Total	$800,000

Direct labor hours were estimated as follows:

Fabrication Department	5,000 hours
Assembly Department	5,000
Total	10,000 hours

In addition, the direct labor hours (dlh) used to produce a unit of each product in each department were determined from engineering records, as follows:

Production Departments	Gasoline Engine	Diesel Engine
Fabrication Department	3.0 dlh	2.0 dlh
Assembly Department	2.0	3.0
Direct labor hours per unit	5.0 dlh	5.0 dlh

A. Determine the per-unit factory overhead allocated to the gasoline and diesel engines under the single plantwide factory overhead rate method, using direct labor hours as the activity base.

B. Determine the per-unit factory overhead allocated to the gasoline and diesel engines under the multiple production department factory overhead rate method, using direct labor hours as the activity base for each department.

C. ━━━━▶ Recommend to management a product costing approach, based on your analyses in (A) and (B). Support your recommendation.

EX 18-8 Identifying activity bases in an activity-based cost system
Obj. 4

Select Foods Inc. uses activity-based costing to determine product costs. For each activity listed in the left column, match an appropriate activity base from the right column. You may use items in the activity-base list more than once or not at all.

Activity	Activity Base
Accounting reports	Engineering change orders
Customer return processing	Kilowatt hours used
Electric power	Number of accounting reports
Human resources	Number of customers
Inventory control	Number of customer orders
Invoice and collecting	Number of customer returns
Machine depreciation	Number of employees
Materials handling	Number of inspections
Order shipping	Number of inventory transactions
Payroll	Number of machine hours
Production control	Number of material moves
Production setup	Number of payroll checks processed
Purchasing	Number of production orders
Quality control	Number of purchase orders
Sales order processing	Number of sales orders
	Number of setups

EX 18-9 Product costs using activity rates
Obj. 4

✔ B. $405,000

Nozama.com Inc. sells consumer electronics over the Internet. For the next period, the budgeted cost of the sales order processing activity is $540,000 and 60,000 sales orders are estimated to be processed.

A. Determine the activity rate of the sales order processing activity.

B. Determine the amount of sales order processing cost that Nozama.com would receive if it had 45,000 sales orders.

EX 18-10 Product costs using activity rates
Obj. 4

✔ Treadmill activity cost per unit, $82.10

EXCEL TEMPLATE

Atlas Enterprises Inc. manufactures elliptical exercise machines and treadmills. The products are produced in its Fabrication and Assembly production departments. In addition to production activities, several other activities are required to produce the two products. These activities and their associated activity rates are as follows:

Activity	Activity Rate
Fabrication	$28 per machine hour
Assembly	$20 per direct labor hour
Setup	$75 per setup
Inspecting	$30 per inspection
Production scheduling	$12 per production order
Purchasing	$ 8 per purchase order

(Continued)

The activity-base usage quantities and units produced for each product were as follows:

Activity Base	Elliptical Machines	Treadmill
Machine hours	700	600
Direct labor hours	182	64
Setups	20	15
Inspections	10	16
Production orders	30	20
Purchase orders	56	75
Units produced	400	250

Use the activity rate and usage information to calculate the total activity cost and activity cost per unit for each product.

EX 18-11   Activity rates and product costs using activity-based costing   Obj. 4

✔ B. Dining room lighting fixtures, $167.40 per unit

EXCEL TEMPLATE

Garfield Inc. manufactures entry and dining room lighting fixtures. Five activities are used in manufacturing the fixtures. These activities and their associated budgeted activity costs and activity bases are as follows:

Activity	Budgeted Activity Cost	Activity Base
Casting	$560,000	Machine hours
Assembly	75,000	Direct labor hours
Inspecting	30,000	Number of inspections
Setup	18,750	Number of setups
Materials handling	14,000	Number of loads

Corporate records were obtained to estimate the amount of activity to be used by the two products. The estimated activity-base usage quantities and units produced follow:

Activity Base	Entry	Dining	Total
Machine hours	7,500	12,500	20,000
Direct labor hours	2,000	3,000	5,000
Number of inspections	500	250	750
Number of setups	150	100	250
Number of loads	400	300	700
Units produced	5,000	2,500	7,500

A. Determine the activity rate for each activity.

B. Use the activity rates in (A) to determine the total and per-unit activity costs associated with each product.

EX 18-12   Activity cost pools, activity rates, and product costs using   Obj. 4
activity-based costing

✔ B. Ovens, $93.80 per unit

EXCEL TEMPLATE

Caldwell Home Appliances Inc. is estimating the activity cost associated with producing ovens and refrigerators. The indirect labor can be traced into four separate activity pools, based on time records provided by the employees. The budgeted activity cost and activity-base information are provided as follows:

Activity	Activity Pool Cost	Activity Base
Procurement	$ 12,600	Number of purchase orders
Scheduling	90,000	Number of production orders
Materials handling	11,000	Number of moves
Product development	50,000	Number of engineering changes
Total cost	$163,600	

The estimated activity-base usage and unit information for two product lines was determined as follows:

	Number of Purchase Orders	Number of Production Orders	Number of Moves	Number of Engineering Change Orders	Units
Ovens	400	800	300	80	1,000
Refrigerators	300	400	200	120	500
Totals	700	1,200	500	200	1,500

A. Determine the activity rate for each activity cost pool.

B. Determine the activity-based cost per unit of each product.

EX 18-13 Activity-based costing and product cost distortion   Obj. 2, 4

✔ C. Cell phones,
$1.68 per unit

EXCEL TEMPLATE

Digital Storage Concept Inc. is considering a change to activity-based product costing. The company produces two products, cell phones and tablet PCs, in a single production department. The production department is estimated to require 3,750 direct labor hours. The total indirect labor is budgeted to be $375,000.

Time records from indirect labor employees revealed that they spent 40% of their time setting up production runs and 60% of their time supporting actual production.

The following information about cell phones and tablet PCs was determined from the corporate records:

	Number of Setups	Direct Labor Hours	Units
Cell phones	600	1,875	93,750
Tablet PCs	1,400	1,875	93,750
Total	2,000	3,750	187,500

A. Determine the indirect labor cost per unit allocated to cell phones and tablet PCs under a single plantwide factory overhead rate system using the direct labor hours as the allocation base.

B. Determine the budgeted activity costs and activity rates for the indirect labor under activity-based costing. Assume two activities—one for setup and the other for production support.

C. Determine the activity cost per unit for indirect labor allocated to each product under activity-based costing.

D. ▬▬▶ Why are the per-unit allocated costs in (A) different from the per-unit activity cost assigned to the products in (C)?

EX 18-14 Multiple production department factory overhead rate method   Obj. 3

✔ B. Blender, $18.20
per unit

EXCEL TEMPLATE

Four Finger Appliance Company manufactures small kitchen appliances. The product line consists of blenders and toaster ovens. Four Finger Appliance presently uses the multiple production department factory overhead rate method. The factory overhead is as follows:

Assembly Department	$186,000
Test and Pack Department	120,000
Total	$306,000

The direct labor information for the production of 7,500 units of each product is as follows:

	Assembly Department	Test and Pack Department
Blender	750 dlh	2,250 dlh
Toaster oven	2,250	750
Total	3,000 dlh	3,000 dlh

(Continued)

Four Finger Appliance used direct labor hours to allocate production department factory overhead to products.

A.   Determine the two production department factory overhead rates.

B.   Determine the total factory overhead and the factory overhead per unit allocated to each product.

EX 18-15   Activity-based costing and product cost distortion   Obj. 4

✔ B. Blender, $23.60 per unit

EXCEL TEMPLATE

The management of Four Finger Appliance Company in Exercise 14 has asked you to use activity-based costing instead of direct labor hours to allocate factory overhead costs to the two products. You have determined that $81,000 of factory overhead from each of the production departments can be associated with setup activity ($162,000 in total). Company records indicate that blenders required 135 setups, while the toaster ovens required only 45 setups. Each product has a production volume of 7,500 units.

A.   Determine the three activity rates (assembly, test and pack, and setup).

B.   Determine the total factory overhead and factory overhead per unit allocated to each product using the activity rates in (A).

EX 18-16   Single plantwide rate and activity-based costing   Obj. 2, 4

✔ A. Low, Col. C, 93.5%

EXCEL TEMPLATE   REAL WORLD

Whirlpool Corporation conducted an activity-based costing study of its Evansville, Indiana, plant in order to identify its most profitable products. Assume that we select three representative refrigerators (out of 333): one low-, one medium-, and one high-volume refrigerator. Additionally, we assume the following activity-base information for each of the three refrigerators:

Three Representative Refrigerators	Number of Machine Hours	Number of Setups	Number of Sales Orders	Number of Units
Refrigerator—Low Volume	24	14	38	160
Refrigerator—Medium Volume	225	13	88	1,500
Refrigerator—High Volume	900	9	120	6,000

Prior to conducting the study, the factory overhead allocation was based on a single machine hour rate. The machine hour rate was $200 per hour. After conducting the activity-based costing study, assume that three activities were used to allocate the factory overhead. The new activity rate information is assumed to be as follows:

	Machining Activity	Setup Activity	Sales Order Processing Activity
Activity rate	$160	$240	$55

A.   Complete the following table, using the single machine hour rate to determine the per-unit factory overhead for each refrigerator (Column A) and the three activity-based rates to determine the activity-based factory overhead per unit (Column B). Finally, compute the percent change in per-unit allocation from the single to activity-based rate methods (Column C). (Round per-unit overhead to two decimal places and percents to one decimal place.)

Product Volume Class	Column A Single Rate Overhead Allocation per Unit	Column B ABC Overhead Allocation per Unit	Column C Percent Change in Allocation (Col. B – Col. A)/Col. A
Low			
Medium			
High			

B.   Why is the traditional overhead rate per machine hour greater under the single rate method than under the activity-based method?

C.   ━━━▶ Interpret Column C in your table from part (A).

EX 18-17 Evaluating selling and administrative cost allocations

Obj. 5

Gordon Gecco Furniture Company has two major product lines with the following characteristics:

- Commercial office furniture: Few large orders, little advertising support, shipments in full truckloads, and low handling complexity
- Home office furniture: Many small orders, large advertising support, shipments in partial truckloads, and high handling complexity

The company produced the following profitability report for management:

Gordon Gecco Furniture Company
Product Profitability Report
For the Year Ended December 31

	Commercial Office Furniture	Home Office Furniture	Total
Revenue	$5,600,000	$2,800,000	$8,400,000
Cost of goods sold	2,100,000	980,000	3,080,000
Gross profit	$3,500,000	$1,820,000	$5,320,000
Selling and administrative expenses	1,680,000	840,000	2,520,000
Income from operations	$1,820,000	$ 980,000	$2,800,000

The selling and administrative expenses are allocated to the products on the basis of relative sales dollars.

➤ Evaluate the accuracy of this report and recommend an alternative approach.

EX 18-18 Construct and interpret a product profitability report, allocating selling and administrative expenses

Obj. 5

✔ B. Generators operating profit-to-sales, 24.29%

SHOW ME HOW

Naper Inc. manufactures power equipment. Naper has two primary products—generators and air compressors. The following report was prepared by the controller for Naper's senior marketing management for the year ended December 31:

	Generators	Air Compressors	Total
Revenue	$4,200,000	$3,000,000	$7,200,000
Cost of goods sold	2,940,000	2,100,000	5,040,000
Gross profit	$1,260,000	$ 900,000	$2,160,000
Selling and administrative expenses			610,000
Income from operations			$1,550,000

The marketing management team was concerned that the selling and administrative expenses were not traced to the products. Marketing management believed that some products consumed larger amounts of selling and administrative expense than did other products. To verify this, the controller was asked to prepare a complete product profitability report, using activity-based costing.

The controller determined that selling and administrative expenses consisted of two activities: sales order processing and post-sale customer service. The controller was able to determine the activity base and activity rate for each activity, as follows:

Activity	Activity Base	Activity Rate
Sales order processing	Sales orders	$ 65 per sales order
Post-sale customer service	Service requests	$200 per customer service request

The controller determined the following activity-base usage information about each product:

	Generators	Air Compressors
Number of sales orders	3,000	4,000
Number of service requests	225	550

(Continued)

A. Determine the activity cost of each product for sales order processing and post-sale customer service activities.

B. Use the information in (A) to prepare a complete product profitability report dated for the year ended December 31. Compute the gross profit to sales and the income from operations to sales percentages for each product. (Round to two decimal places.)

C. ➤ Interpret the product profitability report. How should management respond to the report?

EX 18-19 Activity-based costing and customer profitability

Obj. 5

✔ A. Customer 1, Income from operations after customer service activities, $34,075

SHOW ME HOW

Schneider Electric manufactures power distribution equipment for commercial customers, such as hospitals and manufacturers. Activity-based costing was used to determine customer profitability. Customer service activities were assigned to individual customers, using the following assumed customer service activities, activity base, and activity rate:

Customer Service Activity	Activity Base	Activity Rate
Bid preparation	Number of bid requests	$400 per request
Shipment	Number of shipments	$ 80 per shipment
Support standard items	Number of standard items ordered	$ 25 per std. item
Support nonstandard items	Number of nonstandard items ordered	$150 per nonstd. item

Assume that the company had the following gross profit information for three representative customers:

	Customer 1	Customer 2	Customer 3
Revenue	$120,000	$200,000	$160,000
Cost of goods sold	76,800	110,000	83,200
Gross profit	$ 43,200	$ 90,000	$ 76,800
Gross profit as a percent of sales	36%	45%	48%

The administrative records indicated that the activity-base usage quantities for each customer were as follows:

Activity Base	Customer 1	Customer 2	Customer 3
Number of bid requests	14	38	55
Number of shipments	30	60	48
Number of standard items ordered	15	30	50
Number of nonstandard items ordered	5	70	80

A. Prepare a customer profitability report dated for the year ended December 31, 20Y8, showing (1) the income from operations after customer service activities, (2) the gross profit as a percent of sales, and (3) the income from operations after customer service activities as a percent of sales. Prepare the report with a column for each customer. Round percentages to the nearest whole percent.

B. ➤ Interpret the report in part (A).

EX 18-20 Activity-based costing for a service company

Obj. 6

✔ A. Patient Umit, $6,025

EXCEL TEMPLATE

Crosswinds Hospital plans to use activity-based costing to assign hospital indirect costs to the care of patients. The hospital has identified the following activities and activity rates for the hospital indirect costs:

Activity	Activity Rate
Room and meals	$ 240 per day
Radiology	$ 215 per image
Pharmacy	$ 50 per physician order
Chemistry lab	$ 80 per test
Operating room	$1,000 per operating room hour

The activity usage information associated with the two patients is as follows:

	Abel Putin	Cheryl Umit
Number of days	6 days	4 days
Number of images	4 images	3 images
Number of physician orders	6 orders	2 orders
Number of tests	5 tests	4 tests
Number of operating room hours	8 hours	4 hours

A. Determine the activity cost associated with each patient.

B. ━━▶ Why is the total activity cost different for the two patients?

✔ A. Auto, Income from operations, $820,380

SHOW ME HOW

EXCEL TEMPLATE

EX 18-21 Activity-based costing for a service company

Obj. 5, 6

Safety First Insurance Company carries three major lines of insurance: auto, workers' compensation, and homeowners. The company has prepared the following report:

Safety First Insurance Company
Product Profitability Report
For the Year Ended December 31

	Auto	Workers' Compensation	Homeowners
Premium revenue	$5,750,000	$6,240,000	$8,160,000
Estimated claims	4,312,500	4,680,000	6,120,000
Underwriting income	$1,437,500	$1,560,000	$2,040,000
Underwriting income as a percent of premium revenue	25%	25%	25%

Management is concerned that the administrative expenses may make some of the insurance lines unprofitable. However, the administrative expenses have not been allocated to the insurance lines. The controller has suggested that the administrative expenses could be assigned to the insurance lines using activity-based costing. The administrative expenses are comprised of five activities. The activities and their rates are as follows:

Activity	Activity Rates
New policy processing	$120 per new policy
Cancellation processing	$175 per cancellation
Claim audits	$320 per claim audit
Claim disbursements processing	$104 per disbursement
Premium collection processing	$ 24 per premium collected

Activity-base usage data for each line of insurance were retrieved from the corporate records as follows:

	Auto	Workers' Compensation	Homeowners
Number of new policies	1,320	1,500	4,080
Number of canceled policies	480	240	2,160
Number of audited claims	385	120	960
Number of claim disbursements	480	216	840
Number of premiums collected	8,400	1,800	15,000

A. Complete the product profitability report through the administrative activities. Determine the income from operations as a percent of premium revenue, rounded to the nearest whole percent.

B. ━━▶ Interpret the report.

Problems: Series A

PR 18-1A Single plantwide factory overhead rate
Obj. 2

✔ 1. B. $48 per machine hour

Orange County Chrome Company manufactures three chrome-plated products—automobile bumpers, valve covers, and wheels. These products are manufactured in two production departments (Stamping and Plating). The factory overhead for Orange County Chrome is $220,800.

The three products consume both machine hours and direct labor hours in the two production departments as follows:

	Direct Labor Hours	Machine Hours
Stamping Department		
Automobile bumpers	560	800
Valve covers	300	560
Wheels	340	600
	1,200	1,960
Plating Department		
Automobile bumpers	170	1,170
Valve covers	180	710
Wheels	175	760
	525	2,640
Total	1,725	4,600

Instructions

1. Determine the single plantwide factory overhead rate, using each of the following allocation bases: (A) direct labor hours and (B) machine hours.

2. Determine the product factory overhead costs, using (A) the direct labor hour plantwide factory overhead rate and (B) the machine hour plantwide factory overhead rate.

PR 18-2A Multiple production department factory overhead rates
Obj. 3

✔ 2. Wheels, $63,040

The management of Orange County Chrome Company, described in Problem 1A, now plans to use the multiple production department factory overhead rate method. The total factory overhead associated with each department is as follows:

Stamping Department	$115,200
Plating Department	105,600
Total	$220,800

Instructions

1. Determine the multiple production department factory overhead rates, using direct labor hours for the Stamping Department and machine hours for the Plating Department.

2. Determine the product factory overhead costs, using the multiple production department rates in (1).

PR 18-3A Activity-based and department rate product costing and product cost distortions
Obj. 3, 4

✔ 2. Snowboards, $390,000 and $65

EXCEL TEMPLATE

Black and Blue Sports Inc. manufactures two products: snowboards and skis. The factory overhead incurred is as follows:

Indirect labor	$507,000
Cutting Department	156,000
Finishing Department	192,000
Total	$855,000

The activity base associated with the two production departments is direct labor hours. The indirect labor can be assigned to two different activities as follows:

Activity	Budgeted Activity Cost	Activity Base
Production control	$237,000	Number of production runs
Materials handling	270,000	Number of moves
Total	$507,000	

The activity-base usage quantities and units produced for the two products follow:

	Number of Production Runs	Number of Moves	Direct Labor Hours—Cutting	Direct Labor Hours—Finishing	Units Produced
Snowboards	430	5,000	4,000	2,000	6,000
Skis	70	2,500	2,000	4,000	6,000
Total	500	7,500	6,000	6,000	12,000

Instructions

1. Determine the factory overhead rates under the multiple production department rate method. Assume that indirect labor is associated with the production departments, so that the total factory overhead is $315,000 and $540,000 for the Cutting and Finishing departments, respectively.

2. Determine the total and per-unit factory overhead costs allocated to each product, using the multiple production department overhead rates in (1).

3. Determine the activity rates, assuming that the indirect labor is associated with activities rather than with the production departments.

4. Determine the total and per-unit cost assigned to each product under activity-based costing.

5. ▬▬▶ Explain the difference in the per-unit overhead allocated to each product under the multiple production department factory overhead rate and activity-based costing methods.

PR 18-4A   Activity-based product costing
Obj. 4

✔ 2. Alpha total activity cost, $160,450

EXCEL TEMPLATE

Mello Manufacturing Company is a diversified manufacturer that manufactures three products (Alpha, Beta, and Omega) in a continuous production process. Senior management has asked the controller to conduct an activity-based costing study. The controller identified the amount of factory overhead required by the critical activities of the organization as follows:

Activity	Activity Cost Pool
Production	$259,200
Setup	55,000
Material handling	9,750
Inspection	60,000
Product engineering	123,200
Total	$507,150

The activity bases identified for each activity are as follows:

Activity	Activity Base
Production	Machine hours
Setup	Number of setups
Material handling	Number of parts
Inspection	Number of inspection hours
Product engineering	Number of engineering hours

(Continued)

The activity-base usage quantities and units produced for the three products were determined from corporate records and are as follows:

	Machine Hours	Number of Setups	Number of Parts	Number of Inspection Hours	Number of Engineering Hours	Units
Alpha	1,440	75	65	400	125	1,800
Beta	1,080	165	80	300	175	1,350
Omega	720	310	180	500	140	900
Total	3,240	550	325	1,200	440	4,050

Each product requires 40 minutes per unit of machine time.

Instructions

1. Determine the activity rate for each activity.

2. Determine the total and per-unit activity cost for all three products. Round to nearest cent.

3. ➤ Why aren't the activity unit costs equal across all three products since they require the same machine time per unit?

PR 18-5A Allocating selling and administrative expenses using activity-based costing

Obj. 5

✔ 3. The Martin Group loss from operations, ($11,300)

SHOW ME HOW

EXCEL TEMPLATE

Arctic Air Inc. manufactures cooling units for commercial buildings. The price and cost of goods sold for each unit are as follows:

Price	$60,000 per unit
Cost of goods sold	28,000
Gross profit	$32,000 per unit

In addition, the company incurs selling and administrative expenses of $226,250. The company wishes to assign these costs to its three major customers, Gough Industries, Breen Inc., and The Martin Group. These expenses are related to three major nonmanufacturing activities: customer service, project bidding, and engineering support. The engineering support is in the form of engineering changes that are placed by the customer to change the design of a product. The budgeted activity costs and activity bases associated with these activities are:

Activity	Budgeted Activity Cost	Activity Base
Customer service	$ 31,500	Number of service requests
Project bidding	74,000	Number of bids
Engineering support	120,750	Number of customer design changes
Total costs	$226,250	

Activity-base usage and unit volume information for the three customers is as follows:

	Gough Industries	Breen Inc.	The Martin Group	Total
Number of service requests	36	28	116	180
Number of bids	50	40	95	185
Number of customer design changes	18	35	108	161
Unit volume	30	16	4	50

Instructions

1. Determine the activity rates for each of the three nonmanufacturing activity pools.

2. Determine the activity costs allocated to the three customers, using the activity rates in (1).

3. Construct customer profitability reports for the three customers, dated for the year ended December 31, using the activity costs in (2). The reports should disclose the gross profit and income from operations associated with each customer.

4. ➤ Provide recommendations to management, based on the profitability reports in (3).

EXCEL TEMPLATE

✔ 3. Procedure B
excess, $597,700

PR 18-6A Product costing and decision analysis for a service company   Obj. 6

Pleasant Stay Medical Inc. wishes to determine its product costs. Pleasant Stay offers a variety of medical procedures (operations) that are considered its "products." The overhead has been separated into three major activities. The annual estimated activity costs and activity bases follow:

Activity	Budgeted Activity Cost	Activity Base
Scheduling and admitting	$ 432,000	Number of patients
Housekeeping	4,212,000	Number of patient days
Nursing	5,376,000	Weighted care unit
Total costs	$10,020,000	

Total "patient days" are determined by multiplying the number of patients by the average length of stay in the hospital. A weighted care unit (wcu) is a measure of nursing effort used to care for patients. There were 192,000 weighted care units estimated for the year. In addition, Pleasant Stay estimated 6,000 patients and 27,000 patient days for the year. (The average patient is expected to have a a little more than a four-day stay in the hospital.)

During a portion of the year, Pleasant Stay collected patient information for three selected procedures, as follows:

	Activity-Base Usage
Procedure A	
Number of patients	280
Average length of stay	× 6 days
Patient days	1,680
Weighted care units	19,200
Procedure B	
Number of patients	650
Average length of stay	× 5 days
Patient days	3,250
Weighted care units	6,000
Procedure C	
Number of patients	1,200
Average length of stay	× 4 days
Patient days	4,800
Weighted care units	24,000

Private insurance reimburses the hospital for these activities at a fixed daily rate of $406 per patient day for all three procedures.

Instructions

1. Determine the activity rates.
2. Determine the activity cost for each procedure.
3. Determine the excess or deficiency of reimbursements to activity cost.
4. ➤ Interpret your results.

Problems: Series B

PR 18-1B   Single plantwide factory overhead rate   Obj. 2

✔ 1. B. $111 per
machine hour

Spotted Cow Dairy Company manufactures three products—whole milk, skim milk, and cream—in two production departments, Blending and Packing. The factory overhead for Spotted Cow Dairy is $299,700.

The three products consume both machine hours and direct labor hours in the two production departments as follows:

	Direct Labor Hours	Machine Hours
Blending Department		
Whole milk	260	650
Skim milk	245	710
Cream	215	260
	720	1,620
Packing Department		
Whole milk	470	500
Skim milk	300	415
Cream	130	165
	900	1,080
Total	1,620	2,700

Instructions

1. Determine the single plantwide factory overhead rate, using each of the following allocation bases: (A) direct labor hours and (B) machine hours.

2. Determine the product factory overhead costs, using (A) the direct labor hour plantwide factory overhead rate and (B) the machine hour plantwide factory overhead rate.

PR 18-2B   Multiple production department factory overhead rates   Obj. 3

✔ 2. Cream, $46,150

The management of Spotted Cow Dairy Company, described in Problem 1B, now plans to use the multiple production department factory overhead rate method. The total factory overhead associated with each department is as follows:

Blending Department	$178,200
Packing Department	121,500
Total	$299,700

Instructions

1. Determine the multiple production department factory overhead rates, using machine hours for the Blending Department and direct labor hours for the Packing Department.

2. Determine the product factory overhead costs, using the multiple production department rates in (1).

PR 18-3B   Activity-based department rate product costing and product cost   Obj. 3, 4
distortions

✔ 4. Loudspeakers,
$465,430 and $66.49

Big Sound Inc. manufactures two products: receivers and loudspeakers. The factory overhead incurred is as follows:

EXCEL TEMPLATE

Indirect labor	$400,400
Subassembly Department	198,800
Final Assembly Department	114,800
Total	$714,000

The activity base associated with the two production departments is direct labor hours. The indirect labor can be assigned to two different activities as follows:

Activity	Budgeted Activity Cost	Activity Base
Setup	$138,600	Number of setups
Quality control	261,800	Number of inspections
Total	$400,400	

The activity-base usage quantities and units produced for the two products follow:

	Number of Setups	Number of Inspections	Direct Labor Hours— Subassembly	Direct Labor Hours— Final Assembly	Units Produced
Receivers	80	450	875	525	7,000
Loudspeakers	320	1,750	525	875	7,000
Total	400	2,200	1,400	1,400	14,000

Instructions

1. Determine the factory overhead rates under the multiple production department rate method. Assume that indirect labor is associated with the production departments, so that the total factory overhead is $420,000 and $294,000 for the Subassembly and Final Assembly departments, respectively.

2. Determine the total and per-unit factory overhead costs allocated to each product, using the multiple production department overhead rates in (1).

3. Determine the activity rates, assuming that the indirect labor is associated with activities rather than with the production departments.

4. Determine the total and per-unit cost assigned to each product under activity-based costing.

5. ▬▬▶ Explain the difference in the per-unit overhead allocated to each product under the multiple production department factory overhead rate and activity-based costing methods.

PR 18-4B Activity-based product costing
Obj. 4

✔ 2. Brown sugar total activity cost, $293,600

EXCEL TEMPLATE

Sweet Sugar Company manufactures three products (white sugar, brown sugar, and powdered sugar) in a continuous production process. Senior management has asked the controller to conduct an activity-based costing study. The controller identified the amount of factory overhead required by the critical activities of the organization as follows:

Activity	Budgeted Activity Cost
Production	$500,000
Setup	144,000
Inspection	44,000
Shipping	115,000
Customer service	84,000
Total	$887,000

The activity bases identified for each activity are as follows:

Activity	Activity Base
Production	Machine hours
Setup	Number of setups
Inspection	Number of inspections
Shipping	Number of customer orders
Customer service	Number of customer service requests

(Continued)

The activity-base usage quantities and units produced for the three products were determined from corporate records and are as follows:

	Machine Hours	Number of Setups	Number of Inspections	Number of Customer Orders	Customer Service Requests	Units
White sugar	5,000	85	220	1,150	60	10,000
Brown sugar	2,500	170	330	2,600	350	5,000
Powdered sugar	2,500	195	550	2,000	190	5,000
Total	10,000	450	1,100	5,750	600	20,000

Each product requires 0.5 machine hour per unit.

Instructions

1. Determine the activity rate for each activity.

2. Determine the total and per-unit activity cost for all three products. (Round to nearest cent.)

3. ➤ Why aren't the activity unit costs equal across all three products since they require the same machine time per unit?

PR 18-5B   Allocating selling and administrative expenses using   **Obj. 5**
activity-based costing

✔ 3. Supply Universe, income from operations, $283,820

Shrute Inc. manufactures office copiers, which are sold to retailers. The price and cost of goods sold for each copier are as follows:

Price	$1,110 per unit
Cost of goods sold	682
Gross profit	$ 428 per unit

SHOW ME HOW   EXCEL TEMPLATE

In addition, the company incurs selling and administrative expenses of $414,030. The company wishes to assign these costs to its three major retail customers, The Warehouse, Kosmo Co., and Supply Universe. These expenses are related to its three major nonmanufacturing activities: customer service, sales order processing, and advertising support. The advertising support is in the form of advertisements that are placed by Shrute Inc. to support the retailer's sale of Shrute copiers to consumers. The budgeted activity costs and activity bases associated with these activities are:

Activity	Budgeted Activity Cost	Activity Base
Customer service	$ 76,860	Number of service requests
Sales order processing	25,920	Number of sales orders
Advertising support	311,250	Number of ads placed
Total activity cost	$414,030	

Activity-base usage and unit volume information for the three customers is as follows:

	The Warehouse	Kosmo Co.	Supply Universe	Total
Number of service requests	62	340	25	427
Number of sales orders	300	640	140	1,080
Number of ads placed	25	180	44	249
Unit volume	810	810	810	2,430

Instructions

1. Determine the activity rates for each of the three nonmanufacturing activities.

2. Determine the activity costs allocated to the three customers, using the activity rates in (1).

3. Construct customer profitability reports for the three customers, dated for the year ended December 31, using the activity costs in (2). The reports should disclose the gross profit and income from operations associated with each customer.

4. ➤ Provide recommendations to management, based on the profitability reports in (3).

PR 18-6B Product costing and decision analysis for a service company   Obj. 6

✔ 3. Flight 102 income from operations, $4,415

EXCEL TEMPLATE

Blue Star Airline provides passenger airline service, using small jets. The airline connects four major cities: Charlotte, Pittsburgh, Detroit, and San Francisco. The company expects to fly 170,000 miles during a month. The following costs are budgeted for a month:

Fuel	$2,120,000
Ground personnel	788,500
Crew salaries	850,000
Depreciation	430,000
Total costs	$4,188,500

Blue Star management wishes to assign these costs to individual flights in order to gauge the profitability of its service offerings. The following activity bases were identified with the budgeted costs:

Airline Cost	Activity Base
Fuel, crew, and depreciation costs	Number of miles flown
Ground personnel	Number of arrivals and departures at an airport

The size of the company's ground operation in each city is determined by the size of the workforce. The following monthly data are available from corporate records for each terminal operation:

Terminal City	Ground Personnel Cost	Number of Arrivals/Departures
Charlotte	$256,000	320
Pittsburgh	97,500	130
Detroit	129,000	150
San Francisco	306,000	340
Total	$788,500	940

Three recent representative flights have been selected for the profitability study. Their characteristics are as follows:

	Description	Miles Flown	Number of Passengers	Ticket Price per Passenger
Flight 101	Charlotte to San Francisco	2,000	80	$695.00
Flight 102	Detroit to Charlotte	800	50	441.50
Flight 103	Charlotte to Pittsburgh	400	20	382.00

Instructions

1. Determine the fuel, crew, and depreciation cost per mile flown.

2. Determine the cost per arrival or departure by terminal city.

3. Use the information in (1) and (2) to construct a profitability report for the three flights. Each flight has a single arrival and departure to its origin and destination city pairs.

Analysis for Decision Making

ADM-1 Activity-based product cost improvement

Gourmet Master, Inc. uses activity-based costing to determine the cost of its stainless steel ovens. Activity-based product cost information is as follows:

Activity	Activity-Base Usage (hrs. per unit)	×	Activity Rate per Hour	=	Activity Cost
Fabrication	0.75		$24.00		$18.00
Assembly	1.50		20.00		30.00
Inspection	0.30		25.00		7.50
Moving	0.25		12.00		3.00
Total activity cost per unit					$58.50

These activities only include the labor portion of the cost. Fabrication is the cutting and shaping of metal to be used in the assembly of the ovens. If the metal is not fabricated properly, additional time is required during final assembly to trim and adjust the metal pieces to fit properly. This has been a problem in Assembly. Management proposes improvements in Fabrication requiring the fabrication work to be done slower, but more accurately. As a result, the time in fabrication will increase to an hour per unit. However, because of the additional care, the parts are expected to fit better during assembly, thus reducing assembly time to 1.10 hours per unit.

A. Determine the revised activity-based cost per unit under the new fabrication plan.

B. Does this plan reduce the activity cost per unit of the oven?

ADM-2 Labor classification trade-off

Skidmore Electronics manufactures consumer electronic products. The company has three assembly labor classifications, S-1, S-2, and S-3. The three classifications are paid $15, $18, and $22 per hour, respectively. The assembly activity for a new smartphone is as follows:

Activity	Activity-Base Usage (hrs. per unit)	×	Activity Rate per Hour (S-2)	=	Activity Cost
Assembly	0.40		$18.00		$7.20

A product engineer proposes using a higher-rated employee to perform the assembly on the new phone. His analysis has shown that an S-3 employee can perform the assembly in 0.35 hour per unit.

A. Determine the Assembly activity cost using the S-3 labor classification.

B. ━━━━▶ Is the product engineer's proposal supported?

ADM-3 Production run size and activity improvement

Littlejohn, Inc. manufactures machined parts for the automotive industry. The activity cost associated with Part XX-10 is as follows:

Activity	Activity-Base Usage	×	Activity Rate	=	Activity Cost
Fabrication	250 dlh		$80 per dlh		$20,000
Setup	10 setups		$80 per setup		800
Production control	10 prod. runs		$30 per prod. run		300
Moving	10 moves		$25 per move		250
Total activity cost per unit					$21,350
Estimated units of production					÷ 500
Activity cost per unit					$ 42.70

Each unit requires 30 minutes of fabrication direct labor. Moreover, Part XX-10 is manufactured in production run sizes of 50 units. Each production run is set up, scheduled (production control), and moved as a batch of 50 units. Management is considering improvements in the setup, production control, and moving activities in order to cut the production run sizes by half. As a result, the number of setups, production runs, and moves will double from 10 to 20. Such improvements are expected to speed the company's ability to respond to customer orders.

- Setup is reengineered so that it takes 60% of the original cost per setup.
- Production control software will allow production control effort and cost per production run to decline by 60%.
- Moving distance was reduced by 40%, thus reducing the cost per move by the same amount.

A. Determine the revised activity cost per unit under the proposed changes.
B. Did these improvements reduce the activity cost per unit?
C. What cost per unit for setup would be required for the solution in (A) to equal the base solution?

ADM-4 Hospital activity-based costing analysis

Lancaster County Hospital uses activity-based costing to determine the cost of serving patients. The hospital identified common treatments and developed the activity-based cost per patient by treatment. The activities and activity rates for a patient receiving coronary bypass surgery are as follows:

Activity	Activity Rate
Admission	$ 150 per admission
Operating room	$3,000 per hour
Nursing	$ 50 per nursing care unit
Discharge	$ 100 per discharge

Nursing care units are measures of time and effort to perform nursing duties, such as providing IV care, checking vital signs, and administering drugs. It is determined that there are an average of 10 nursing care units per patient-day in the hospital for a coronary bypass. The average bypass patient is in the hospital for 6 days. The bypass procedure requires an average of 3 hours of operating room time.

A. Determine the activity cost per patient for the coronary bypass treatment.
B. Assume the hospital was able to make improvements such that the average length of stay in the hospital for the bypass was reduced from 6 days to 5 days. Further assume that additional improvements in medical technology reduced the operating room time for a bypass to 2½ hours. Determine the activity cost per patient for the coronary bypass treatment under these revised conditions. What is the cost improvement?

Take It Further

TIF 18-1 Ethics in Action

ETHICS

The controller of Tri Con Global Systems Inc. has developed a new costing system that traces the cost of activities to products. The new system is able to measure post-manufacturing activities, such as selling, promotional, and distribution activities, and allocate these activities to products in a manner that provides a more complete view of the company's product costs. This system produces better strategic information about the relative profitability of product lines.

In the course of implementing the new costing system, the controller realized that the company's current period GAAP net income would increase significantly if the new product cost information were used for inventory valuation on the financial statements. The controller

(Continued)

has been under intense pressure to improve the company's net income, and this would be an easy and effective way for her to help meet the company's short-term net income goals. As a result, she has decided to use the new costing system to determine GAAP net income.

1. ➤ Why does the company's net income increase when the new costing system is applied?

2. ➤ Is the controller acting ethically by using the new costing system for GAAP net income? Explain your answer.

REAL WORLD

TIF 18-2 Team Activity

In teams, select a company from one of the following industries: banking, food service, manufacturing, or retail. For this company:

A. Identify the primary activities that the company must perform to provide its product or service.

B. Identify an activity base for each of these activities.

TIF 18-3 Communication

The controller of New Wave Sounds Inc. prepared the following product profitability report for management, using activity-based costing methods for allocating both the factory overhead and the marketing expenses. As such, the controller has confidence in the accuracy of this report.

	Home Theater Speakers	Wireless Speakers	Wireless Headphones	Total
Sales	$ 1,500,000	$1,200,000	$900,000	$3,600,000
Cost of goods sold	1,050,000	720,000	810,000	2,580,000
Gross profit	$ 450,000	$ 480,000	$ 90,000	$1,020,000
Marketing expenses	600,000	120,000	72,000	792,000
Income from operations	$ (150,000)	$ 360,000	$ 18,000	$ 228,000

In addition, the controller interviewed the vice president of marketing, who provided the following insight into the company's three products:

- The home theater speakers are an older product that is highly recognized in the marketplace.
- The wireless speakers are a new product that was just recently launched.
- The wireless headphones are a new technology that has no competition in the marketplace, and it is hoped that they will become an important future addition to the company's product portfolio. Initial indications are that the product is well received by customers.

The controller believes that the manufacturing costs for all three products are in line with expectations.

Based on the information provided:

1. Calculate the ratio of gross profit to sales and the ratio of income from operations to sales for each product.

2. ➤ Write a brief (one page) memo using the product profitability report and the calculations in (1) to make recommendations to management with respect to strategies for the three products.

Concepts and Principles

Chapter 15 *Introduction to Managerial Accounting*

Developing Information

COST SYSTEMS	COST BEHAVIOR
Chapter 16 *Job Order Costing* **Chapter 17** *Process Cost Systems* **Chapter 18** *Activity-Based Costing*	**Chapter 19** *Cost-Volume-Profit Analysis*

Decision Making

EVALUATING PERFORMANCE	COMPARING ALTERNATIVES
Chapter 20 *Variable Costing for Management Analysis* **Chapter 21** *Budgeting* **Chapter 22** *Evaluating Variances from Standard Costs*	**Chapter 23** *Evaluating Decentralized Operations* **Chapter 24** *Differential Analysis and Product Pricing* **Chapter 25** *Capital Investment Analysis* **Chapter 26** *Lean Manufacturing*

Ford Motor Company

Making a profit isn't easy for U.S. auto manufacturers like **Ford Motor Company**. The cost of materials, labor, equipment, and advertising makes it very expensive to produce cars and trucks.

How many cars does Ford need to produce and sell to break even? The answer depends on the relationship between Ford's sales revenue and costs. Some of Ford's costs, like direct labor and materials, will change in direct proportion to the number of vehicles that are built. Other costs, such as the costs of manufacturing equipment, are fixed and do not change with the number of vehicles that are produced. Ford will break even when it generates enough sales revenue to cover both its fixed and variable costs.

During the depths of the 2009 recession, Ford renegotiated labor contracts with its employees. These renegotiations reduced the direct labor cost incurred to build each car, which lowered the number of cars that the company needed to sell to break even by 45%.

As with Ford, understanding how costs behave, and the relationship between costs, profits, and volume, is important for all businesses. This chapter discusses commonly used methods for classifying costs according to how they change and techniques for determining how many units must be sold for a company to break even. Techniques that management can use to evaluate costs in order to make sound business decisions are also discussed.

Source: J. Booton, "Moody's Upgrades Ford's Credit Rating, Returns Blue Oval Trademark," *Fox Business,* May 22, 2012.

What's Covered

Cost-Volume-Profit Analysis

Cost Behavior
- Variable Costs (Obj. 1)
- Fixed Costs (Obj. 1)
- Mixed Costs (Obj. 1)

Cost-Volume-Profit Relationships
- Contribution Margin (Obj. 2)
- Contribution Margin Ratio (Obj. 2)
- Unit Contribution Margin (Obj. 2)

Cost-Volume-Profit Analysis
- Break-Even Point (Obj. 3)
- Target Profit (Obj. 3)
- Cost-Volume-Profit Chart (Obj. 4)
- Profit-Volume Chart (Obj. 4)
- Assumptions (Obj. 4)

Special Relationships and Analyses
- Sales Mix (Obj. 5)
- Operating Leverage (Obj. 5)
- Margin of Safety (Obj. 5)

Learning Objectives

Obj. 1 Classify costs as variable costs, fixed costs, or mixed costs.

Obj. 2 Compute the contribution margin, the contribution margin ratio, and the unit contribution margin.

Obj. 3 Determine the break-even point and sales necessary to achieve a target profit.

Obj. 4 Using a cost-volume-profit chart and a profit-volume chart, determine the break-even point and sales necessary to achieve a target profit.

Obj. 5 Compute the break-even point for a company selling more than one product, the operating leverage, and the margin of safety.

Analysis for Decision Making

Describe and Illustrate the use of cost-volume-profit analysis for decision making in a service business.

Objective 1

Classify costs as variable costs, fixed costs, or mixed costs.

Cost Behavior

Cost behavior is the manner in which a cost changes as a related activity changes. The behavior of costs is useful to managers for a variety of reasons. For example, knowing how costs behave allows managers to predict profits as sales and production volumes change. Knowing how costs behave is also useful for estimating costs, which affects a variety of decisions such as whether to replace a machine.

Understanding the behavior of a cost depends on the following:

- Identifying the activities that cause the cost to change. These activities are called **activity bases** (or *activity drivers*).
- Specifying the range of activity over which the changes in the cost are of interest. This range of activity is called the **relevant range**.

To illustrate, assume that a hospital is concerned about planning and controlling patient food costs. A good activity base is the number of patients who *stay* overnight in the hospital. The number of patients who are *treated* is not as good an activity base because some patients are outpatients and, thus, do not consume food. Once an activity base is identified, food costs can then be analyzed over the range of the number of patients who normally stay in the hospital (the relevant range).

Costs are normally classified as variable costs, fixed costs, or mixed costs.

Link to Ford Motor Company

The first vehicle built by Henry Ford in 1896 was a Quadricycle that consisted of four bicycle wheels powered by a four-horsepower engine. The first Ford Model A was sold by **Ford Motor Company** in 1903. In 1908, the Ford Model T was introduced, which had sales of 15 million before its production was halted in 1927.

Source: www.corporate.ford.com

Variable Costs

Variable costs are costs that vary in proportion to changes in the activity base. When the activity base is units produced, direct materials and direct labor costs are normally classified as variable costs.

To illustrate, assume that Jason Sound Inc. produces stereo systems. The parts for the stereo systems are purchased from suppliers for $10 per unit and are assembled by Jason Sound. For Model JS-12, the direct materials costs for the relevant range of 5,000 to 30,000 units of production are as follows:

Number of Units of Model JS-12 Produced	Direct Materials Cost per Unit	Total Direct Materials Cost
5,000 units	$10	$ 50,000
10,000	10	100,000
15,000	10	150,000
20,000	10	200,000
25,000	10	250,000
30,000	10	300,000

As shown, variable costs have the following characteristics:

- *Cost per unit* remains the same regardless of changes in the activity base. For Jason Sound, units produced is the activity base. For Model JS-12, the cost per unit is $10.
- *Total cost* changes in proportion to changes in the activity base. For Model JS-12, the direct materials cost for 10,000 units ($100,000) is twice the direct materials cost for 5,000 units ($50,000).

Exhibit 1 illustrates how the variable costs for direct materials for Model JS-12 behave in total and on a per-unit basis as production changes.

Exhibit 1 Variable Cost Graphs

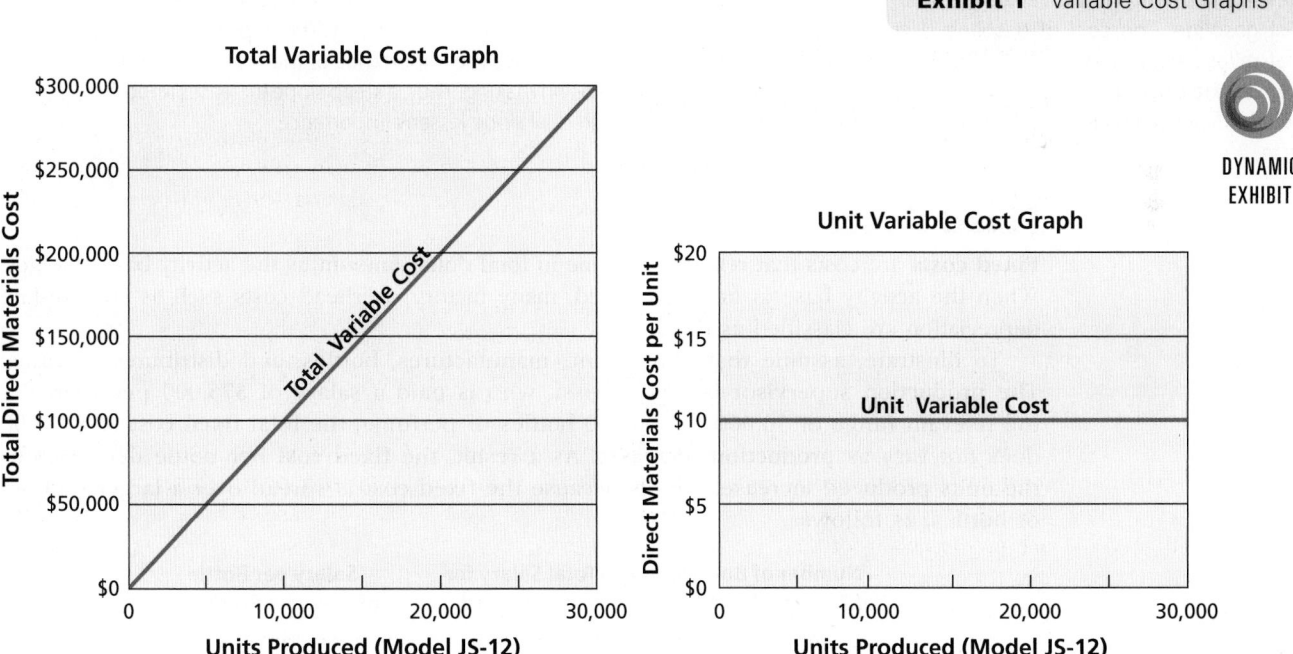

DYNAMIC
EXHIBIT

Some examples of variable costs and their related activity bases for various types of businesses are shown in Exhibit 2.

Exhibit 2

Variable Costs and Their Activity Bases

Type of Business	Cost	Activity Base
University	Instructor salaries	Number of classes
Passenger airline	Fuel	Number of miles flown
Manufacturing	Direct materials	Number of units produced
Hospital	Nurse wages	Number of patients
Hotel	Housekeeping wages	Number of guests
Bank	Teller wages	Number of banking transactions

Link to Ford Motor Company

Changing emission, fuel economy, and safety standards increase the variable cost of each vehicle manufactured by **Ford Motor Company**.

Why It Matters

Variable Cost for Home and Business

Variable costs are important to our individual lives. For example, an important variable cost for many of us is the cost of gasoline. The cost of gasoline is variable to the number of miles driven and the gas efficiency of our vehicles. Thus, when the price of gasoline increases, the demand for smaller, fuel-efficient vehicles rises. Moreover, during periods of high gasoline prices, there is an incentive to drive less, even to the point of living closer to work or school. When the cost of gasoline falls, fuel efficiency and driving preferences become less important. This is seen with the slope of the variable cost line on the total variable cost graph. The slope is the variable cost per unit, as was shown in Exhibit 1. The slope of the variable cost line will influence the importance of the underlying activity base for decision making. Thus, a steep slope increases importance, while a gradual slope lessens importance.

Fixed Costs

Fixed costs are costs that remain the same in total dollar amount as the activity base changes. When the activity base is units produced, many factory overhead costs such as straight-line depreciation are classified as fixed costs.

To illustrate, assume that Minton Inc. manufactures, bottles, and distributes perfume. The production supervisor is Jane Sovissi, who is paid a salary of $75,000 per year. For the relevant range of 50,000 to 300,000 bottles of perfume, the total fixed cost of $75,000 does not vary as production increases. As a result, the fixed cost per bottle decreases as the units produced increase. This is because the fixed cost is spread over a larger number of bottles, as follows:

Number of Bottles of Perfume Produced	Total Salary for Jane Sovissi	Salary per Bottle of Perfume Produced
50,000 bottles	$75,000	$1.500
100,000	75,000	0.750
150,000	75,000	0.500
200,000	75,000	0.375
250,000	75,000	0.300
300,000	75,000	0.250

As shown, fixed costs have the following characteristics:

- *Cost per unit* decreases as the activity level increases and increases as the activity level decreases. For Jane Sovissi's salary, the cost per unit decreased from $1.50 for 50,000 bottles produced to $0.25 for 300,000 bottles produced.
- *Total cost* remains the same regardless of changes in the activity base. Jane Sovissi's salary of $75,000 remained the same regardless of whether 50,000 bottles or 300,000 bottles were produced.

Exhibit 3 illustrates how Jane Sovissi's salary (fixed cost) behaves in total and on a per-unit basis as production changes.

A high proportion of **Ford Motor Company**'s costs are fixed in nature.
Source: Ford Motor Company, Form 10-K for Year Ended December 31, 2014.

Link to Ford Motor Company

Exhibit 3 Fixed Cost Graphs

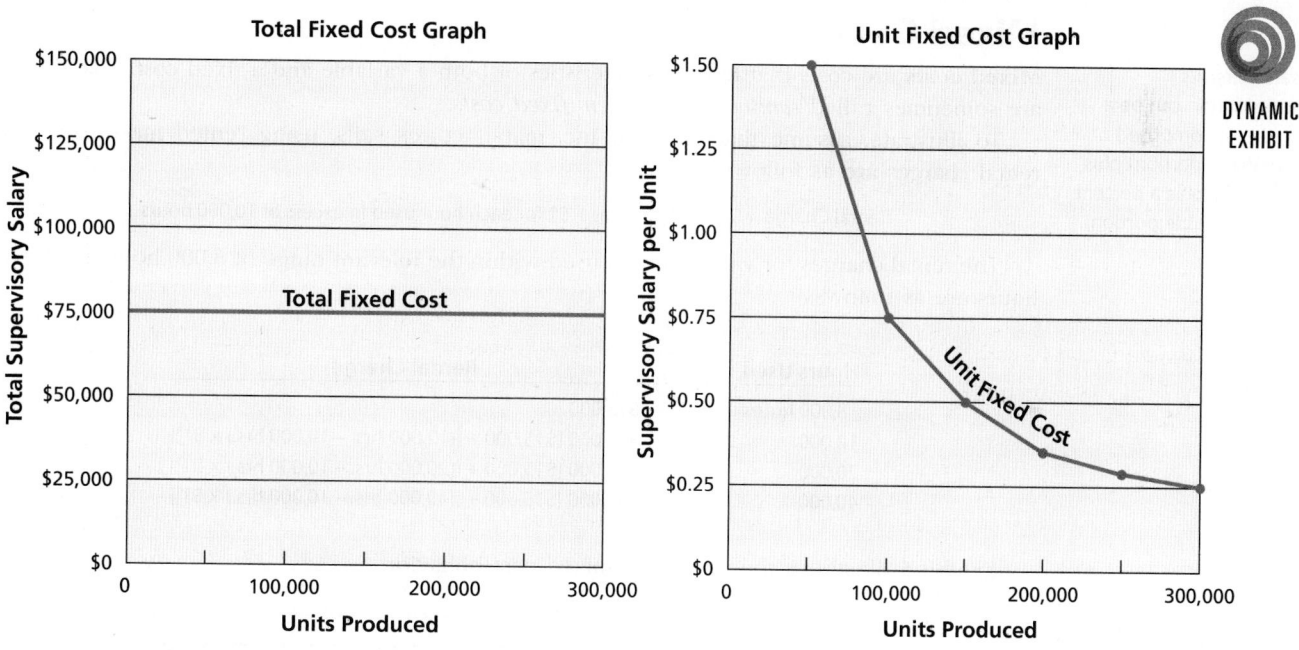

DYNAMIC EXHIBIT

Some examples of fixed costs and their related activity bases for various types of businesses are shown in Exhibit 4.

Type of Business	Fixed Cost	Activity Base
University	Building (straight-line) depreciation	Number of students
Passenger airline	Airplane (straight-line) depreciation	Number of miles flown
Manufacturing	Plant manager salary	Number of units produced
Hospital	Property insurance	Number of patients
Hotel	Property taxes	Number of guests
Bank	Branch manager salary	Number of customer accounts

Exhibit 4

Fixed Costs and Their Activity Bases

Why It Matters

Booking Fees

A major fixed cost for a concert promoter is the booking fee for the act. The booking fee is the amount to be paid to the act for a single show at a venue. **Degy Entertainment**, a booking agency, provided a list of asking prices for several popular acts. The following is a sampling from the list.

Taylor Swift	$1,000,000+
Justin Timberlake	$1,000,000+
Rihanna	$500K–$750K
Katy Perry	$500K
Keith Urban	$400K–$600K
Maroon 5	$400K–$600K

Kanye West	$400K–$600K
Carrie Underwood	$400K–$500K
Alicia Keys	$350k–$500K
Bruno Mars	$200K–$400K
Pitbull	$200K–$300K
Ke$ha	$150K–$200K
The Script	$125K–$175K

The promoter must cover these fixed costs with ticket revenues; thus, the size of the booking fee is necessarily related to the popularity of the act represented by the number of potential tickets sold and the ticket price.

Source: Zachery Crockett, "How Much Does It Cost to Book Your Favorite Band?" *Priceconomics.com*, May 16, 2014.

Mixed Costs

note:

A salesperson's compensation can be a mixed cost comprised of a salary (fixed portion) plus a commission as a percent of sales (variable portion).

Mixed costs are costs that have characteristics of both a variable and a fixed cost. Mixed costs are sometimes called *semivariable* or *semifixed costs*.

To illustrate, assume that Simpson Inc. manufactures sails, using rented machinery. The rental charges are as follows:

Rental Charge = $15,000 per year + $1 for each hour used in excess of 10,000 hours

The rental charges for various hours used within the relevant range of 8,000 hours to 40,000 hours are as follows:

Hours Used	Rental Charge
8,000 hours	$15,000
12,000	$17,000 {$15,000 + [(12,000 hrs. – 10,000 hrs.) × $1]}
20,000	$25,000 {$15,000 + [(20,000 hrs. – 10,000 hrs.) × $1]}
40,000	$45,000 {$15,000 + [(40,000 hrs. – 10,000 hrs.) × $1]}

Exhibit 5 illustrates the preceding mixed cost behavior.

Exhibit 5
Mixed Costs

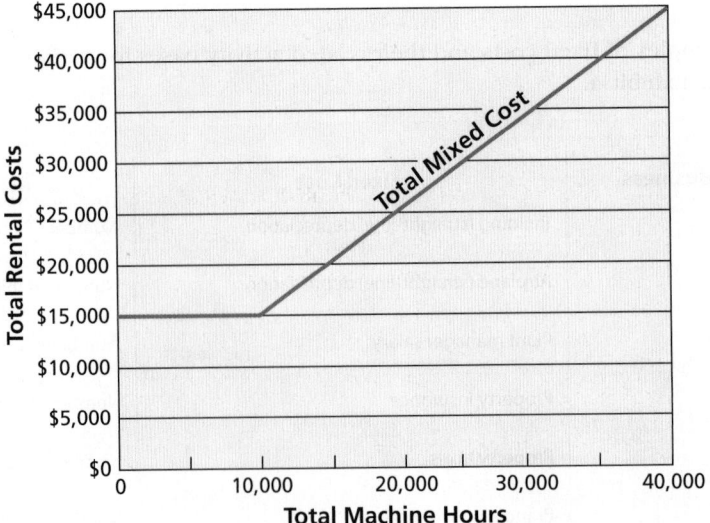

For purposes of analysis, mixed costs are usually separated into their fixed and variable components. The **high-low method** is a cost estimation method that may be used for this purpose.[1] The high-low method uses the highest and lowest activity levels and their related costs to estimate the variable cost per unit and the fixed cost.

To illustrate, assume that the Equipment Maintenance Department of Kason Inc. incurred the following costs during the past five months:

	Units Produced	Total Cost
June	1,000 units	$45,550
July	1,500	52,000
August	2,100	61,500
September	1,800	57,500
October	750	41,250

The number of units produced is the activity base, and the relevant range is the units produced between June and October. For Kason, the difference between the units produced and the total costs at the highest and lowest levels of production are as follows:

	Units Produced	Total Cost
Highest level	2,100 units	$61,500
Lowest level	750	41,250
Difference	1,350 units	$20,250

The total fixed cost does not change with changes in production. Thus, the $20,250 difference in the total cost is the change in the total variable cost. Dividing this difference of $20,250 by the difference in production is an estimate of the variable cost per unit. For Kason, this estimate is $15, computed as follows:

$$\text{Variable Cost per Unit} = \frac{\text{Difference in Total Cost}}{\text{Difference in Units Produced}}$$

$$= \frac{\$20,250}{1,350 \text{ units}} = \$15 \text{ per unit}$$

The fixed cost is estimated by subtracting the total variable costs from the total costs for the units produced, as follows:

$$\text{Fixed Cost} = \text{Total Costs} - (\text{Variable Cost per Unit} \times \text{Units Produced})$$

The fixed cost is the same at the highest and the lowest levels of production, as follows for Kason:

Highest level (2,100 units):

$$\begin{aligned}\text{Fixed Cost} &= \text{Total Costs} - (\text{Variable Cost per Unit} \times \text{Units Produced})\\ &= \$61,500 - (\$15 \times 2,100 \text{ units})\\ &= \$61,500 - \$31,500\\ &= \$30,000\end{aligned}$$

Lowest level (750 units):

$$\begin{aligned}\text{Fixed Cost} &= \text{Total Costs} - (\text{Variable Cost per Unit} \times \text{Units Produced})\\ &= \$41,250 - (\$15 \times 750 \text{ units})\\ &= \$41,250 - \$11,250\\ &= \$30,000\end{aligned}$$

[1] Other methods of estimating costs, such as the scattergraph method and the least squares method, are discussed in cost accounting textbooks.

Using the variable cost per unit and the fixed cost, the total equipment maintenance cost for Kason can be computed for various levels of production as follows:

$$\text{Total Cost} = (\text{Variable Cost per Unit} \times \text{Units Produced}) + \text{Fixed Costs}$$
$$= (\$15 \times \text{Units Produced}) + \$30,000$$

To illustrate, the estimated total cost of 2,000 units of production is $60,000, computed as follows:

$$\text{Total Cost} = (\$15 \times \text{Units Produced}) + \$30,000$$
$$= (\$15 \times 2,000 \text{ units}) + \$30,000$$
$$= \$30,000 + \$30,000$$
$$= \$60,000$$

Link to Ford Motor Company   **Ford Motor Company** entered into a collective bargaining agreement with the United Auto Workers union that provides for lump-sum payments in lieu of general wage increases. This has the effect of making wages more like a mixed cost.

Summary of Cost Behavior Concepts

The cost behavior of variable costs and fixed costs is summarized in Exhibit 6.

Exhibit 6
Variable and Fixed Cost Behavior

Cost	EFFECT OF CHANGING ACTIVITY LEVEL	
	Total Amount	**Per-Unit Amount**
Variable	Increases and decreases proportionately with activity level.	Remains the same regardless of activity level.
Fixed	Remains the same regardless of activity level.	Increases and decreases inversely with activity level.

Mixed costs contain a fixed cost component that is incurred even if nothing is produced. For analysis, the fixed and variable cost components of mixed costs are separated using the high-low method.

Exhibit 7 provides some examples of variable, fixed, and mixed costs for the activity base of *units produced*.

Exhibit 7
Variable, Fixed, and Mixed Costs

Variable Costs	Fixed Costs	Mixed Costs
■ Direct materials	■ Straight-line depreciation	■ Quality Control Department salaries
■ Direct labor	■ Property taxes	■ Purchasing Department salaries
■ Electricity expense	■ Production supervisor salaries	■ Maintenance expenses
■ Supplies	■ Insurance expense	■ Warehouse expenses

One method of reporting variable and fixed costs is called **variable costing** or *direct costing*. Under variable costing, only the variable manufacturing costs (direct materials, direct labor, and variable factory overhead) are included in the product cost. The fixed factory overhead is treated as an expense of the period in which it is incurred. Variable costing is described and illustrated in the appendix to this chapter.

Check Up Corner 19-1 | Cost Behavior

O&W Metal Company makes designer emblems for luxury vehicles. Each emblem is handcrafted out of titanium to the customer's design specifications. O&W's artisans are paid an hourly wage and work between 30 and 60 hours a week. O&W uses the straight-line method of depreciation. To ensure that each emblem conforms to the customer's specifications, O&W has each emblem inspected by an independent company. The inspection company charges a set price per month, plus an additional amount for each item inspected. After inspection, each emblem is shipped in a crush-resistant shipping container.

A. Which of O&W's costs (titanium, artisan wages, equipment depreciation, inspection, shipping containers) is a mixed cost?

B. Data on total mixed costs and total production for O&W's last five months of operations follow:

	Units Produced	Total Cost
August	1,000 units	$ 80,000
September	1,200	86,000
October	1,600	98,000
November	2,500	125,000
December	2,200	116,000

Using the high-low method, determine the (1) variable cost per unit and (2) total fixed costs.

C. O&W estimates that it will produce 2,000 units during January. Using your answer to (B), estimate the (1) total variable costs and (2) fixed cost per unit for January.

Solution:

A. The inspection cost is a mixed cost because it includes a fixed cost (the set price per month) and a variable cost (an amount based on the number of items inspected).

B. 1.

	Total Cost	Units Produced
Highest level (November)	$125,000	2,500
Lowest level (August)	80,000	1,000
Difference	$ 45,000	1,500

Mixed costs have characteristics of both variable and fixed costs.

The high-low method separates mixed costs into their fixed and variable components.

$$\text{Variable Cost per Unit} = \frac{\text{Difference in Total Cost}}{\text{Difference in Units Produced}}$$

The variable cost per unit is determined by dividing the difference between the highest and lowest cost by the difference between the highest and lowest activity level.

$$= \frac{\$45,000}{1,500} = \$30.00 \text{ per unit}$$

2. Fixed Costs = Total Costs − (Variable Cost per Unit × Units Produced)

The variable cost per unit is constant at all activity levels.

Highest level (2,500 units):

Fixed Costs = $125,000 − ($30 × 2,500 units)
= $125,000 − $75,000
= $50,000

Lowest level (1,000 units):

Fixed Costs = $80,000 − ($30 × 1,000 units)
= $80,000 − $30,000
= $50,000

The total fixed costs calculated are the same, using either the high or low activity level.

C. 1. Total Variable Costs = $30 per unit × 2,000 units = $60,000

2. Fixed Cost per Unit = Total Fixed Costs ÷ Units Produced
= $50,000 ÷ 2,000 units
= $25.00

Total variable costs increase as the activity level increases.

The fixed cost per unit decreases as the activity level increases.

Check Up Corner

Cost-Volume-Profit Relationships

Cost-volume-profit analysis is the examination of the relationships among selling prices, sales and production volume, costs, expenses, and profits. Cost-volume-profit analysis is useful for managerial decision making. Some of the ways cost-volume-profit analysis may be used include the following:

- Analyzing the effects of changes in selling prices on profits
- Analyzing the effects of changes in costs on profits
- Analyzing the effects of changes in volume on profits
- Setting selling prices
- Selecting the mix of products to sell
- Choosing among marketing strategies

Contribution Margin

Contribution margin is especially useful because it provides insight into the profit potential of a company. **Contribution margin** is the excess of sales over variable costs, computed as follows:

$$\text{Contribution Margin} = \text{Sales} - \text{Variable Costs}$$

To illustrate, assume the following data for Lambert Inc.:

Sales	50,000 units
Sales price per unit	$20 per unit
Variable cost per unit	$12 per unit
Fixed costs	$300,000

Exhibit 8 illustrates an income statement for Lambert prepared in a contribution margin format.

Exhibit 8

Contribution Margin Income Statement Format

Sales (50,000 units × $20)	$1,000,000
Variable costs (50,000 units × $12)	600,000
Contribution margin (50,000 units × $8)	$ 400,000
Fixed costs	300,000
Income from operations	$ 100,000

Lambert's contribution margin of $400,000 is available to cover the fixed costs of $300,000. Once the fixed costs are covered, any additional contribution margin increases income from operations.

Contribution Margin Ratio

Contribution margin can also be expressed as a percentage. The **contribution margin ratio**, sometimes called the *profit-volume ratio*, indicates the percentage of each sales dollar available to cover fixed costs and to provide income from operations. The contribution margin ratio is computed as follows:

$$\text{Contribution Margin Ratio} = \frac{\text{Contribution Margin}}{\text{Sales}}$$

The contribution margin ratio is 40% for Lambert Inc., computed as follows:

$$\text{Contribution Margin Ratio} = \frac{\$400,000}{\$1,000,000} = 40\%$$

The contribution margin ratio is most useful when the increase or decrease in sales volume is measured in sales *dollars*. In this case, the change in sales dollars multiplied by the contribution margin ratio equals the change in income from operations, computed as follows:

Change in Income from Operations = Change in Sales Dollars × Contribution Margin Ratio

To illustrate, if Lambert adds $80,000 in sales from the sale of an additional 4,000 units, its income from operations will increase by $32,000, computed as follows:

Change in Income from Operations = Change in Sales Dollars × Contribution Margin Ratio
Change in Income from Operations = $80,000 × 40% = $32,000

The preceding analysis is confirmed by Lambert's contribution margin income statement that follows:

Sales (54,000 units × $20)	$1,080,000
Variable costs (54,000 units × $12)	648,000*
Contribution margin (54,000 units × $8)	$ 432,000**
Fixed costs	300,000
Income from operations	$ 132,000

*$1,080,000 × 60%
**$1,080,000 × 40%

Income from operations increased from $100,000 to $132,000 when sales increased from $1,000,000 to $1,080,000. Variable costs as a percentage of sales are equal to 100% minus the contribution margin ratio. Thus, in the preceding income statement, the variable costs are 60% (100% – 40%) of sales, or $648,000 ($1,080,000 × 60%). The total contribution margin, $432,000, can also be computed directly by multiplying the total sales by the contribution margin ratio ($1,080,000 × 40%).

In the preceding analysis, factors other than sales volume, such as variable cost per unit and sales price, are assumed to remain constant. If such factors change, their effect must also be considered.

The contribution margin ratio is also useful in developing business strategies. For example, assume that a company has a high contribution margin ratio and is producing below 100% of capacity. In this case, a large increase in income from operations can be expected from an increase in sales volume. Therefore, the company might consider implementing a special sales campaign to increase sales. In contrast, a company with a small contribution margin ratio will probably want to give more attention to reducing costs before attempting to promote sales.

Unit Contribution Margin

The unit contribution margin is also useful for analyzing the profit potential of proposed decisions. The **unit contribution margin** is computed as follows:

Unit Contribution Margin = Sales Price per Unit – Variable Cost per Unit

To illustrate, if Lambert Inc.'s unit selling price is $20 and its variable cost per unit is $12, the unit contribution margin is $8, computed as follows:

Unit Contribution Margin = Sales Price per Unit – Variable Cost per Unit
Unit Contribution Margin = $20 – $12 = $8

The unit contribution margin is most useful when the increase or decrease in sales volume is measured in sales *units* (quantities). In this case, the change in sales volume (units) multiplied by the unit contribution margin equals the change in income from operations, computed as follows:

Change in Income from Operations = Change in Sales Units × Unit Contribution Margin

To illustrate, assume that Lambert's sales could be increased by 15,000 units, from 50,000 units to 65,000 units. Lambert's income from operations would increase by $120,000 (15,000 units × $8), computed as follows:

Change in Income from Operations = Change in Sales Units × Unit Contribution Margin
Change in Income from Operations = 15,000 units × $8 = $120,000

The preceding analysis is confirmed by Lambert's contribution margin income statement that follows, which shows that income increased to $220,000 when 65,000 units are sold. The income statement in Exhibit 8 indicates income of $100,000 when 50,000 units are sold. Thus, selling an additional 15,000 units increases income by $120,000 ($220,000 – $100,000).

Sales (65,000 units × $20)	$1,300,000
Variable costs (65,000 units × $12)	780,000
Contribution margin (65,000 units × $8)	$ 520,000
Fixed costs	300,000
Income from operations	$ 220,000

Unit contribution margin analysis is useful information for managers. For example, in the preceding illustration, Lambert could spend up to $120,000 for special advertising or other product promotions to increase sales by 15,000 units and still increase income by $100,000, the $220,000 increase in sales minus the $120,000 cost of special advertising.

Check Up Corner 19-2   Contribution Margin

Toussant Company sells 20,000 units at $120 per unit. Variable costs are $90 per unit, and fixed costs are $250,000.

A. Prepare an income statement for Toussant in contribution margin format.
B. Determine Toussant's (1) contribution margin ratio and (2) unit contribution margin.
C. How much would income from operations change if Toussant's sales increased by 3,000 units?

Solution:

A.

Sales	$2,400,000	← 20,000 units × $120 sales price per unit
Variable costs	1,800,000	← 20,000 units × $90 variable cost per unit
Contribution margin	$ 600,000	← Contribution margin is the excess of sales over variable costs.
Fixed costs	250,000	← Toussant's contribution margin is available to cover its fixed costs of $250,000.
Income from operations	$ 350,000	

Once fixed costs are covered, increases in contribution margin directly increase income from operations.

B. 1. $\text{Contribution Margin Ratio} = \dfrac{\text{Contribution Margin}}{\text{Sales}}$

$\text{Contribution Margin Ratio} = \dfrac{\$600,000}{\$2,400,000} = 25\%$ ← The contribution margin ratio indicates the percentage of each sales dollar available to cover fixed costs and provide income from operations.

2. $\text{Unit Contribution Margin} = \dfrac{\text{Sales Price}}{\text{per Unit}} - \dfrac{\text{Variable Cost}}{\text{per Unit}}$

The unit contribution margin measures the dollar amount of contribution margin generated from each unit sold.

Unit Contribution Margin = $120 – $90
= $30

Both the contribution margin ratio and unit contribution margin can be used to determine how changes in sales volume (units) impact income from operations.

C. *Using Contribution Margin Ratio:*

Change in sales dollars	$360,000	← 3,000 unit increase × $120 selling price per unit
Contribution margin ratio	× 25%
Change in income from operations	$ 90,000

Using Unit Contribution Margin:

Change in sales units	3,000
Unit contribution margin	× $30
Change in income from operations	$ 90,000

Both methods yield the same result.

Mathematical Approach to Cost-Volume-Profit Analysis

Objective 3
Determine the break-even point and sales necessary to achieve a target profit.

The mathematical approach to cost-volume-profit analysis uses equations to determine the following:

- Sales necessary to break even
- Sales necessary to make a target or desired profit

Break-Even Point

The **break-even point** is the level of operations at which a company's revenues and expenses are equal, as shown in Exhibit 9. At break-even, a company reports neither income nor a loss from operations.

$$\text{Revenues} = \text{Costs}$$

Break-Even Point

Exhibit 9
Break-Even Point

The break-even point in *sales units* is computed as follows:

$$\text{Break-Even Sales (units)} = \frac{\text{Fixed Costs}}{\text{Unit Contribution Margin}}$$

To illustrate, assume the following data for Baker Corporation:

Fixed costs	$90,000
Unit selling price	$25
Unit variable cost	15
Unit contribution margin	$10

The break-even point for Baker is 9,000 units, computed as follows:

$$\text{Break-Even Sales (units)} = \frac{\text{Fixed Costs}}{\text{Unit Contribution Margin}} = \frac{\$90,000}{\$10} = 9,000 \text{ units}$$

The following income statement for Baker verifies the break-even point of 9,000 units:

Sales (9,000 units × $25)	$225,000
Variable costs (9,000 units × $15)	135,000
Contribution margin	$ 90,000
Fixed costs	90,000
Income from operations	$ 0

As shown in Baker's income statement, the break-even point is $225,000 (9,000 units × $25) of sales. The break-even point in *sales dollars* can be determined directly as follows:

$$\text{Break-Even Sales (dollars)} = \frac{\text{Fixed Costs}}{\text{Contribution Margin Ratio}}$$

The contribution margin ratio can be computed using the unit contribution margin and unit selling price as follows:

$$\text{Contribution Margin Ratio} = \frac{\text{Unit Contribution Margin}}{\text{Unit Selling Price}}$$

The contribution margin ratio for Baker is 40%, computed as follows:

$$\text{Contribution Margin Ratio} = \frac{\text{Unit Contribution Margin}}{\text{Unit Selling Price}} = \frac{\$10}{\$25} = 40\%$$

Thus, the break-even sales dollars for Baker of $225,000 can be computed directly as follows:

$$\text{Break-Even Sales (dollars)} = \frac{\text{Fixed Costs}}{\text{Contribution Margin Ratio}} = \frac{\$90,000}{40\%} = \$225,000$$

The break-even point is affected by changes in the fixed costs, unit variable costs, and unit selling price.

Link to Ford Motor Company   **Ford Motor Company** reported that its 2014 operations in the Middle East and Africa were at break-even.

Source: Ford Motor Company, Form 10-K for Year Ended December 31, 2014.

Effect of Changes in Fixed Costs   Fixed costs do not change in total with changes in the level of activity. However, fixed costs may change because of other factors such as advertising campaigns, changes in property tax rates, or changes in factory supervisors' salaries.

Changes in fixed costs affect the break-even point as follows:

- Increases in fixed costs increase the break-even point.
- Decreases in fixed costs decrease the break-even point.

This relationship is illustrated in Exhibit 10.

Exhibit 10

Effect of Change in Fixed Costs on Break-Even Point

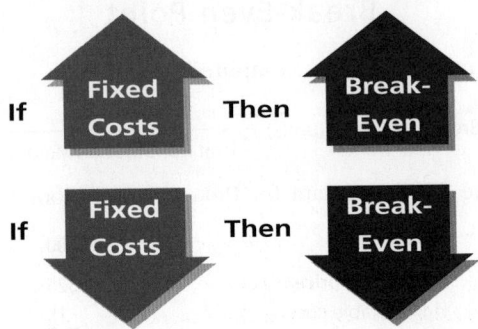

To illustrate, assume that Bishop Co. is evaluating a proposal to budget an additional $100,000 for advertising. The data for Bishop follow:

	Current	Proposed
Unit selling price	$90	$90
Unit variable cost	70	70
Unit contribution margin	$20	$20
Fixed costs	$600,000	$700,000

Bishop's break-even point *before* the additional advertising expense of $100,000 is 30,000 units, computed as follows:

$$\text{Break-Even Sales (units)} = \frac{\text{Fixed Costs}}{\text{Unit Contribution Margin}} = \frac{\$600,000}{\$20} = 30,000 \text{ units}$$

Bishop's break-even point *after* the additional advertising expense of $100,000 is 35,000 units, computed as follows:

$$\text{Break-Even Sales (units)} = \frac{\text{Fixed Costs}}{\text{Unit Contribution Margin}} = \frac{\$700,000}{\$20} = 35,000 \text{ units}$$

As shown for Bishop, the $100,000 increase in advertising (fixed costs) requires an additional 5,000 units (35,000 − 30,000) of sales to break even.[2] In other words, an increase in sales of

[2] The increase of 5,000 units can also be computed by dividing the increase in fixed costs of $100,000 by the unit contribution margin, $20, as follows: 5,000 units = $100,000 ÷ $20.

Why It Matters

Airline Industry Break-Even

Airlines measure revenues and costs by available seat miles. An available seat mile is one seat (empty or filled) flying one mile. Thus, the average revenue earned per available seat mile is termed the RASM, and the average cost per available seat mile is termed the CASM. The operating break-even occurs when the RASM equals the CASM. Since airlines have high aircraft fixed costs, filling passenger seats is an important contributor to exceeding break-even. This is measured by the average proportion of seats filled across all flights, which is termed the load factor. In addition, important variable costs such as labor and fuel impact the break-even performance. Thus, airlines monitor employee productivity and fuel costs to maintain

profitability. The RASM, CASM, and load factor for a recent year for major airlines are as follows:

	American Airlines	United Airlines	Delta Air Lines	Southwest Airlines	US Airways
RASM	$0.129	$0.124	$0.132	$0.135	$0.125
CASM	0.082	0.079	0.089	0.075	0.077
RASM – CASM	$0.047	$0.045	$0.043	$0.060	$0.048
Load factor	82%	84%	85%	82%	83%

As can be seen, all the major airlines are operating above their break-even points, with Southwest Airlines demonstrating the best profit performance by these metrics. The load factors are all more than 80%, indicating that the airlines are using their aircraft efficiently.

Source: MIT Airline Data Project.

5,000 units is required in order to generate an additional $100,000 of total contribution margin (5,000 units × $20) to cover the increased fixed costs.

Effect of Changes in Unit Variable Costs Unit variable costs do not change with changes in the level of activity. However, unit variable costs may be affected by other factors such as changes in the cost per unit of direct materials, changes in the wage rate for direct labor, or changes in the sales commission paid to salespeople.

Changes in unit variable costs affect the break-even point as follows:

- Increases in unit variable costs increase the break-even point.
- Decreases in unit variable costs decrease the break-even point.

This relationship is illustrated in Exhibit 11.

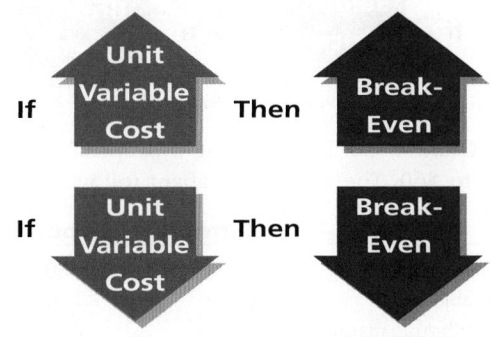

Exhibit 11

Effect of Change in Unit Variable Cost on Break-Even Point

To illustrate, assume that Park Co. is evaluating a proposal to pay an additional 2% commission on sales to its salespeople as an incentive to increase sales. The data for Park follow:

	Current	Proposed
Unit selling price	$250	$250
Unit variable cost	145	150*
Unit contribution margin	$105	$100
Fixed costs	$840,000	$840,000

*$150 = $145 + (2% × $250 unit selling price)

Park's break-even point *before* the additional 2% commission is 8,000 units, computed as follows:

$$\text{Break-Even Sales (units)} = \frac{\text{Fixed Costs}}{\text{Unit Contribution Margin}} = \frac{\$840,000}{\$105} = 8,000 \text{ units}$$

If the 2% sales commission proposal is adopted, unit variable costs will increase by $5 ($250 × 2%), from $145 to $150 per unit. This increase in unit variable costs will decrease the unit contribution margin from $105 to $100 ($250 − $150). Thus, Park's break-even point *after* the additional 2% commission is 8,400 units, computed as follows:

$$\text{Break-Even Sales (units)} = \frac{\text{Fixed Costs}}{\text{Unit Contribution Margin}} = \frac{\$840,000}{\$100} = 8,400 \text{ units}$$

As shown for Park, an additional 400 units of sales will be required in order to break even. This is because if 8,000 units are sold, the new unit contribution margin of $100 provides only $800,000 (8,000 units × $100) of contribution margin. Thus, $40,000 more contribution margin is necessary to cover the total fixed costs of $840,000. This additional $40,000 of contribution margin is provided by selling 400 more units (400 units × $100).

Effect of Changes in Unit Selling Price Changes in the unit selling price affect the unit contribution margin and, thus, the break-even point. Specifically, changes in the unit selling price affect the break-even point as follows:

- Increases in the unit selling price decrease the break-even point.
- Decreases in the unit selling price increase the break-even point.

This relationship is illustrated in Exhibit 12.

<table>
<tr><td>

Exhibit 12

Effect of Change in Unit Selling Price on Break-Even Point

</td><td>

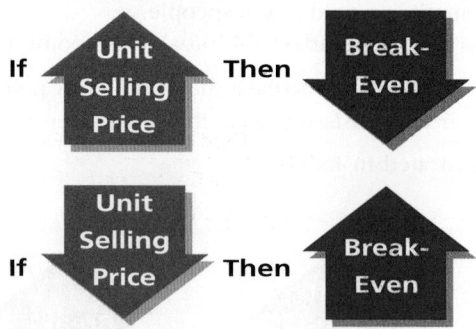

</td></tr>
</table>

To illustrate, assume that Graham Co. is evaluating a proposal to increase the unit selling price of its product from $50 to $60. The data for Graham follow:

	Current	Proposed
Unit selling price	$50	$60
Unit variable cost	30	30
Unit contribution margin	$20	$30
Fixed costs	$600,000	$600,000

Graham's break-even point *before* the price increase is 30,000 units, computed as follows:

$$\text{Break-Even Sales (units)} = \frac{\text{Fixed Costs}}{\text{Unit Contribution Margin}} = \frac{\$600,000}{\$20} = 30,000 \text{ units}$$

The increase of $10 per unit in the selling price increases the unit contribution margin by $10. Thus, Graham's break-even point *after* the price increase is 20,000 units, computed as follows:

$$\text{Break-Even Sales (units)} = \frac{\text{Fixed Costs}}{\text{Unit Contribution Margin}} = \frac{\$600,000}{\$30} = 20,000 \text{ units}$$

As shown for Graham, the price increase of $10 increased the unit contribution margin by $10, which decreased the break-even point by 10,000 units (30,000 units – 20,000 units).

Summary of Effects of Changes on Break-Even Point The break-even point in sales changes in the same direction as changes in the variable cost per unit and fixed costs. In contrast, the break-even point in sales changes in the opposite direction as changes in the unit selling price. These changes on the break-even point in sales are summarized in Exhibit 13.

Type of Change	Direction of Change	Effect of Change on Break-Even Sales
Fixed cost	↑ ↓	↑ ↓
Unit variable cost	↑ ↓	↑ ↓
Unit selling price	↑ ↓	↓ ↑

Exhibit 13
Effects of Changes in Selling Price and Costs on Break-Even Point

Target Profit

At the break-even point, sales and costs are exactly equal. However, the goal of most companies is to make a profit.

By modifying the break-even equation, the sales required to earn a target or desired amount of profit may be computed. For this purpose, target profit is added to the break-even equation, as follows:

$$\text{Sales (units)} = \frac{\text{Fixed Costs} + \text{Target Profit}}{\text{Unit Contribution Margin}}$$

To illustrate, assume the following data for Waltham Co.:

Fixed costs	$200,000
Target profit	100,000
Unit selling price	$75
Unit variable cost	45
Unit contribution margin	$30

The sales necessary for Waltham to earn the target profit of $100,000 would be 10,000 units, computed as follows:

$$\text{Sales (units)} = \frac{\text{Fixed Costs} + \text{Target Profit}}{\text{Unit Contribution Margin}} = \frac{\$200,000 + \$100,000}{\$30} = 10,000 \text{ units}$$

The following income statement for Waltham verifies this computation:

Sales (10,000 units × $75)	$750,000
Variable costs (10,000 units × $45)	450,000
Contribution margin (10,000 units × $30)	$300,000
Fixed costs	200,000
Income from operations	$100,000 ← Target profit

As shown in the income statement for Waltham, sales of $750,000 (10,000 units × $75) are necessary to earn the target profit of $100,000. The sales of $750,000 needed to earn the target profit of $100,000 can be computed directly using the contribution margin ratio as follows:

$$\text{Contribution Margin Ratio} = \frac{\text{Unit Contribution Margin}}{\text{Unit Selling Price}} = \frac{\$30}{\$75} = 40\%$$

$$\text{Sales (dollars)} = \frac{\text{Fixed Costs} + \text{Target Profit}}{\text{Contribution Margin Ratio}}$$

$$= \frac{\$200,000 + \$100,000}{40\%} = \frac{\$300,000}{40\%} = \$750,000$$

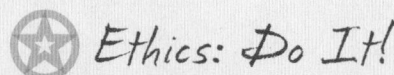 Ethics: Do It!

Orphan Drugs

Each year, pharmaceutical companies develop new drugs that cure a variety of physical conditions. In order to be profitable, drug companies must sell enough of a product at a reasonable price to exceed break-even. Break-even points, however, create a problem for drugs, called "orphan drugs," targeted at rare diseases. These drugs are typically expensive to develop and have low sales volumes, making it impossible to achieve break-even. To ensure that orphan drugs are not overlooked, Congress passed the Orphan Drug Act, which provides incentives for pharmaceutical companies to develop drugs for rare diseases that might not generate enough sales to reach break-even. The program has been a great success. Since 1982, more than 200 orphan drugs have come to market, including **Jacobus Pharmaceutical Company Inc.**'s drug for the treatment of tuberculosis and **Novartis International AG**'s drug for the treatment of Paget's disease.

Objective 4
Using a cost-volume-profit chart and a profit-volume chart, determine the break-even point and sales necessary to achieve a target profit.

Graphic Approach to Cost-Volume-Profit Analysis

Cost-volume-profit analysis can be presented graphically as well as in equation form. Many managers prefer the graphic form because the operating profit or loss for different levels can be easily seen.

Cost-Volume-Profit (Break-Even) Chart

A **cost-volume-profit chart**, sometimes called a *break-even chart*, graphically shows sales, costs, and the related profit or loss for various levels of units sold. It assists in understanding the relationship among sales, costs, and operating profit or loss.

To illustrate, the cost-volume-profit chart in Exhibit 14 is based on the following data for Munoz Co.:

Total fixed costs	$100,000
Unit selling price	$50
Unit variable cost	30
Unit contribution margin	$20

The cost-volume-profit chart in Exhibit 14 is constructed using the following steps:

- Step 1. Volume in units of sales is indicated along the horizontal axis. The range of volume shown is the relevant range in which the company expects to operate. Dollar amounts of total sales and total costs are indicated along the vertical axis.
- Step 2. A total sales line is plotted by connecting the point at zero on the left corner of the graph to a second point on the chart. The second point is determined by multiplying

the maximum number of units in the relevant range, which is found on the far right of the horizontal axis, by the unit sales price. A line is then drawn through both of these points. This is the total sales line. For Munoz, the maximum number of units in the relevant range is 10,000. The second point on the line is determined by multiplying the 10,000 units by the $50 unit selling price to get the second point for the total sales line of $500,000 (10,000 units × $50). The sales line is drawn upward to the right from zero through the $500,000 point at the end of the relevant range.

- Step 3. A total cost line is plotted by beginning with total fixed costs on the vertical axis. A second point is determined by multiplying the maximum number of units in the relevant range, which is found on the far right of the horizontal axis, by the unit variable costs and adding the total fixed costs. A line is then drawn through both of these points. This is the total cost line. For Munoz, the maximum number of units in the relevant range is 10,000. The second point on the line is determined by multiplying the 10,000 units by the $30 unit variable cost and then adding the $100,000 total fixed costs to get the second point for the total estimated costs of $400,000 [(10,000 units × $30) + $100,000]. The cost line is drawn upward to the right from $100,000 on the vertical axis through the $400,000 point at the end of the relevant range.

- Step 4. The break-even point is the intersection point of the total sales and total cost lines. A vertical dotted line drawn downward at the intersection point indicates the units of sales at the break-even point. A horizontal dotted line drawn to the left at the intersection point indicates the sales dollars and costs at the break-even point.

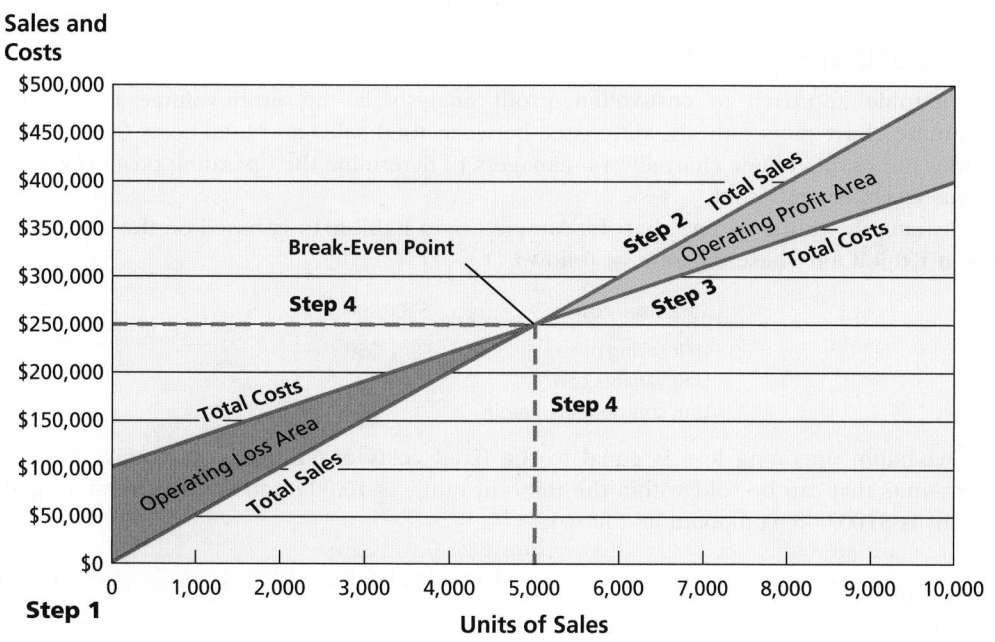

Exhibit 14

Cost-Volume-Profit Chart

In Exhibit 14, the break-even point for Munoz is $250,000 of sales, which represents sales of 5,000 units. Operating profits will be earned when sales levels are to the right of the break-even point (*operating profit area*). Operating losses will be incurred when sales levels are to the left of the break-even point (*operating loss area*).

Changes in the unit selling price, total fixed costs, and unit variable costs can be analyzed by using a cost-volume-profit chart. Using the data in Exhibit 14, assume that Munoz is evaluating a proposal to reduce fixed costs by $20,000. In this case, the total fixed costs would be $80,000 ($100,000 − $20,000).

Under this scenario, the total sales line is not changed, but the total cost line will change. As shown in Exhibit 15, the total cost line is redrawn, starting at the $80,000 point (total fixed costs) on the vertical axis. The second point is determined by multiplying the maximum number of units in the relevant range, which is found on the far right of the horizontal axis, by the unit variable costs and adding the fixed costs. For Munoz, this is the total estimated cost for 10,000 units, which is $380,000 [(10,000 units × $30) + $80,000]. The cost line is drawn upward to the right from $80,000 on the vertical axis through the $380,000 point. The revised cost-volume-profit chart in Exhibit 15 indicates that the break-even point for Munoz decreases to $200,000 and 4,000 units of sales.

| **Exhibit 15** Revised Cost-Volume-Profit Chart | 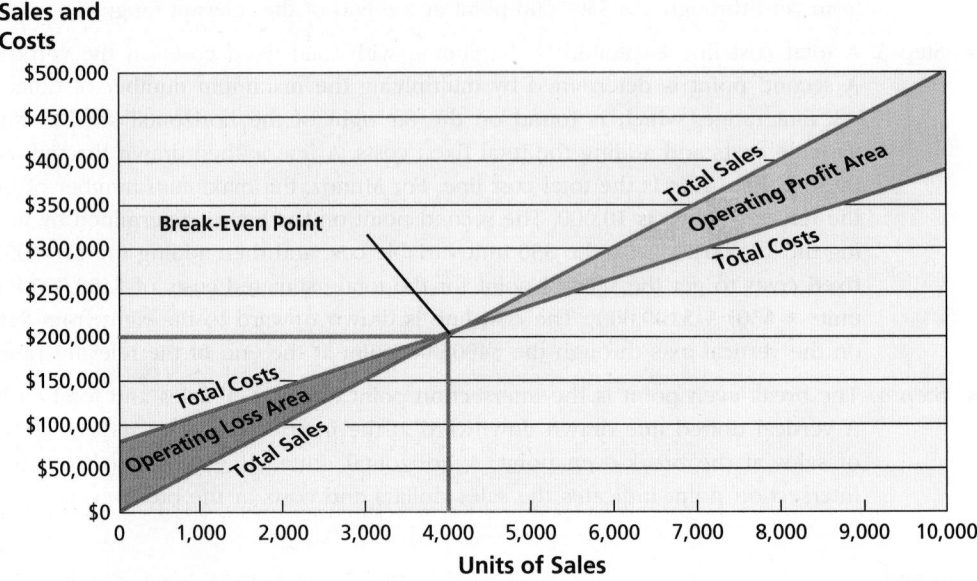 |

Profit-Volume Chart

Another graphic approach to cost-volume-profit analysis is the profit-volume chart. The **profit-volume chart** plots only the difference between total sales and total costs (or profits). In this way, the profit-volume chart allows managers to determine the operating profit (or loss) for various levels of units sold.

To illustrate, the profit-volume chart for Munoz Co. in Exhibit 16 is based on the same data as used in Exhibit 14. These data are as follows:

Total fixed costs	$100,000
Unit selling price	$50
Unit variable cost	30
Unit contribution margin	$20

The maximum operating loss is equal to the fixed costs of $100,000. Assuming that the maximum units that can be sold within the relevant range is 10,000 units, the maximum operating profit is $100,000, computed as follows:

Sales (10,000 units × $50)	$500,000
Variable costs (10,000 units × $30)	300,000
Contribution margin (10,000 units × $20).	$200,000
Fixed costs	100,000
Operating profit.	$100,000 ◄— Maximum profit

The profit-volume chart in Exhibit 16 is constructed using the following steps:

- Step 1. Volume in units of sales is indicated along the horizontal axis. The range of volume shown is the relevant range in which the company expects to operate. In Exhibit 16, the maximum units of sales is 10,000 units. Dollar amounts indicating operating profits and losses are shown along the vertical axis.
- Step 2. A point representing the maximum operating loss is plotted on the vertical axis at the left. This loss is equal to the total fixed costs at the zero level of sales. Thus, the maximum operating loss is equal to the fixed costs of $100,000.

- Step 3. A point representing the maximum operating profit within the relevant range is plotted on the right. Assuming that the maximum unit sales within the relevant range is 10,000 units, the maximum operating profit is $100,000.

- Step 4. A diagonal profit line is drawn connecting the maximum operating loss point with the maximum operating profit point.

- Step 5. The profit line intersects the horizontal zero operating profit line at the break-even point in units of sales. The area indicating an operating profit is identified to the right of the intersection, and the area indicating an operating loss is identified to the left of the intersection.

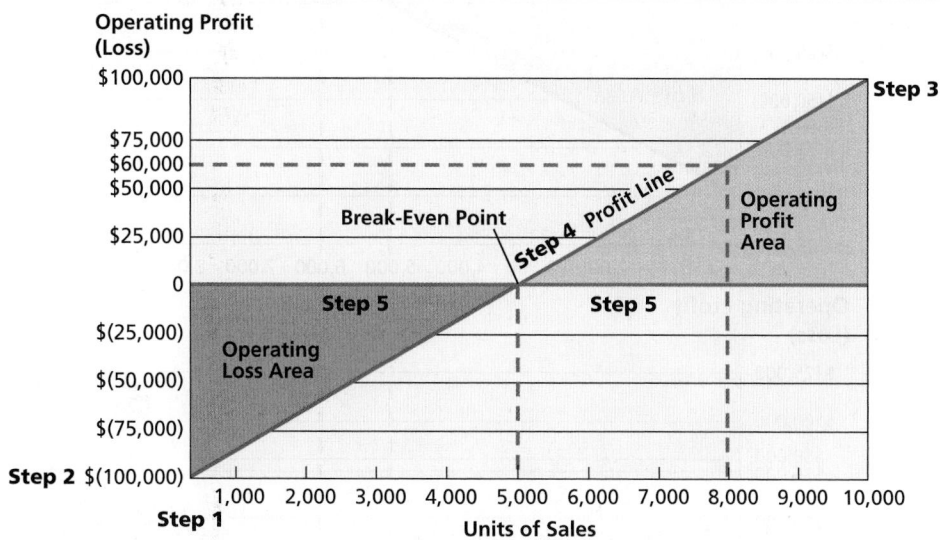

Exhibit 16

Profit-Volume Chart

In Exhibit 16, the break-even point for Munoz is 5,000 units of sales, which is equal to total sales of $250,000 (5,000 units × $50). Operating profit will be earned when sales levels are to the right of the break-even point (*operating profit area*). Operating losses will be incurred when sales levels are to the left of the break-even point (*operating loss area*). For example, at sales of 8,000 units, an operating profit of $60,000 will be earned, as shown in Exhibit 16.

The effect of changes in the unit selling price, total fixed costs, and unit variable costs on profit can be analyzed using a profit-volume chart. Using the data in Exhibit 16, consider the effect that a $20,000 increase in fixed costs will have on profit. In this case, the total fixed costs will increase to $120,000 ($100,000 + $20,000), and the maximum operating loss will also increase to $120,000. At the maximum sales of 10,000 units, the maximum operating profit would be $80,000, computed as follows:

Sales (10,000 units × $50)	$500,000
Variable costs (10,000 units × $30)	300,000
Contribution margin (10,000 units × $20).....................	$200,000
Fixed costs	120,000
Operating profit...	$ 80,000

← Revised maximum profit

A revised profit-volume chart is constructed by plotting the maximum operating loss and maximum operating profit points and drawing the revised profit line. The original and the revised profit-volume charts for Munoz are shown in Exhibit 17.

The revised profit-volume chart indicates that the break-even point for Munoz is 6,000 units of sales. This is equal to total sales of $300,000 (6,000 units × $50). The operating loss area of the chart has increased, while the operating profit area has decreased.

Use of Computers in Cost-Volume-Profit Analysis

With computers, the graphic approach and the mathematical approach to cost-volume-profit analysis are easy to use. Managers can vary assumptions regarding selling prices, costs, and

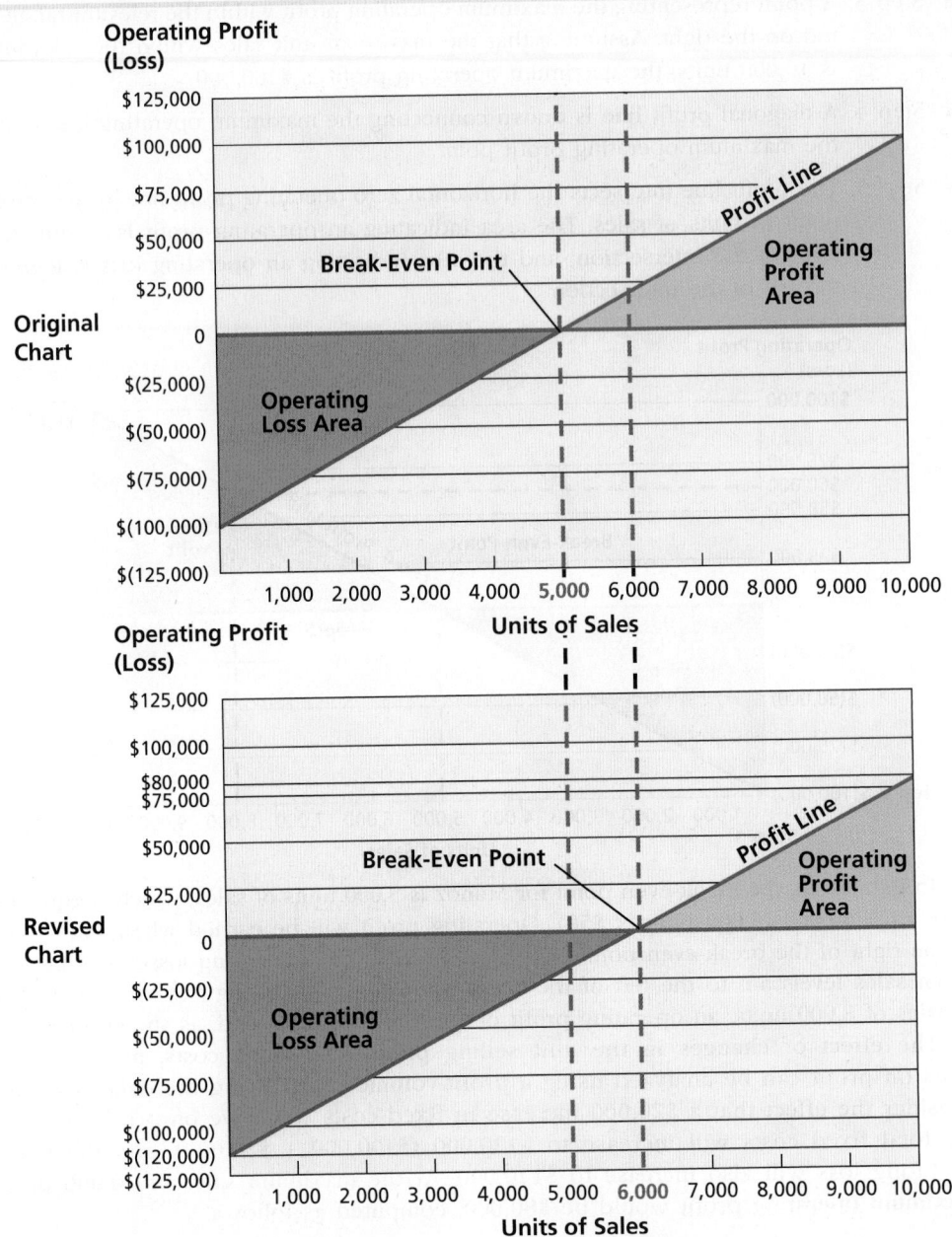

volume and can observe the effects of each change on the break-even point and profit. Such an analysis is called a *"what if"* analysis or *sensitivity* analysis.

Assumptions of Cost-Volume-Profit Analysis

Cost-volume-profit analysis depends on several assumptions. The primary assumptions are as follows:

- Total sales and total costs can be represented by straight lines.
- Within the relevant range of operating activity, the efficiency of operations does not change.
- Costs can be divided into fixed and variable components.
- The sales mix is constant.
- There is no change in the inventory quantities during the period.

These assumptions simplify cost-volume-profit analysis. Because they are often valid for the relevant range of operations, cost-volume-profit analysis is useful for decision making.[3]

---

[3] The impact of violating these assumptions is discussed in advanced accounting texts.

Check Up Corner 19-3   Break-Even Sales and Target Profit

DeHan Company, a sporting goods manufacturer, sells binoculars for $140 per unit. The variable cost is $100 per unit, while the fixed costs are $1,200,000.

A. Compute:

1. The anticipated break-even sales (units) for binoculars.
2. The sales (units) for binoculars required to realize target income from operations of $400,000.

B. Construct a cost-volume-profit chart for the anticipated break-even sales for binoculars.

Solution:

A. 1.

$$\text{Break-Even Sales (units)} = \frac{\text{Fixed Costs}}{\text{Unit Contribution Margin}}$$

Unit selling price	$140
Unit variable cost	100
Unit contribution margin	$ 40

$$\text{Break-Even Sales (units)} = \frac{\$1,200,000}{\$40}$$

$$= 30,000 \text{ units}$$

The break-even point is the level of operations at which a company's revenues and expenses are equal.

A company's revenues will equal costs when:
(Unit contribution margin × Units sold) = Fixed costs

Sales (30,000 units × $140)	$4,200,000
Variable costs (30,000 units × $100)	3,000,000
Contribution margin (30,000 units × $40)	$1,200,000
Fixed costs	1,200,000
Income from operations	$ 0

2.

$$\text{Sales (units)} = \frac{\text{Fixed Costs + Target Profit}}{\text{Unit Contribution Margin}}$$

$$\text{Sales (units)} = \frac{\$1,200,000 + \$400,000}{\$40}$$

$$= 40,000 \text{ units}$$

The sales required to earn a target or desired amount of profit may be computed by adding the amount of the target profit to fixed costs in the numerator of the break-even equation.

Sales (40,000 units × $140)	$5,600,000
Variable costs (40,000 units × $100)	4,000,000
Contribution margin (40,000 units × $40)	$1,600,000
Fixed costs	1,200,000
Income from operations	$ 400,000

B.

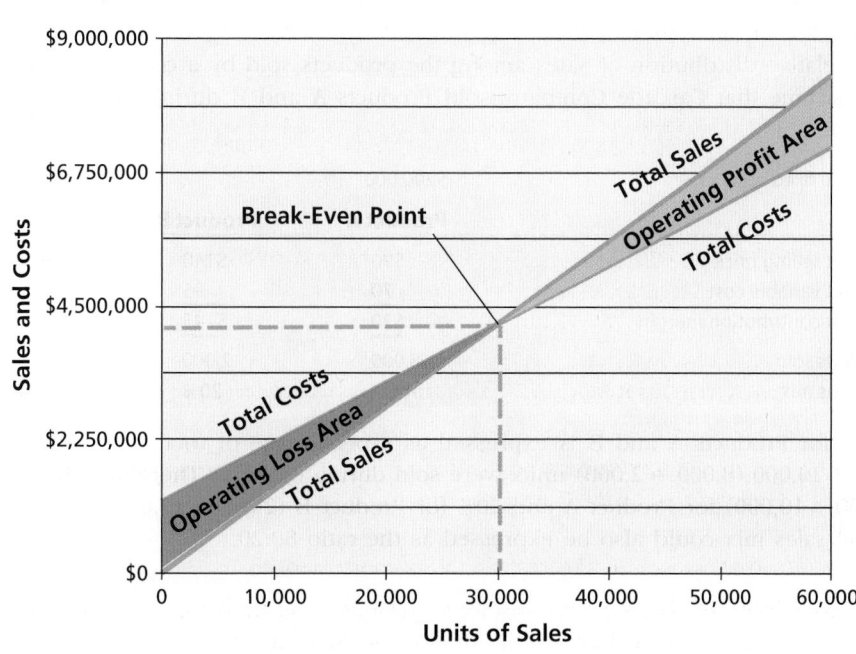

Why It Matters

Profit, Loss, and Break-Even in Major League Baseball

Major League Baseball is a tough game and a tough business. Ticket prices (unit selling price), player salaries and stadium fees (fixed costs), game day personnel (variable costs), and attendance (volume) converge to make it difficult for teams to make a profit, or at least break even. So, which major league baseball team was the most profitable in 2013? Well, it wasn't the World Champion Boston Red Sox. Nor was it the star-studded New York Yankees. Then, it had to be the recently turned around Los Angeles Angels, right? Not even close. It was actually the worst team in baseball—the Houston Astros.

Just how profitable were the Astros? They earned $99 million in 2013, which was more than the combined 2013 profits of the six most recent World Series champions. How could the team with the worst record in baseball since 2005 have one of the most

profitable years in baseball history? By paying careful attention to costs and volume. Between 2011 and 2013, the Astros cut their player payroll from $56 million to less than $13 million. That's right, all of the players on the Houston Astros baseball team, combined, made less in 2013 than Alex Rodriguez (New York Yankees), Cliff Lee (Philadelphia Phillies), Prince Fielder (Detroit Tigers), and Tim Lincecum (San Francisco Giants) made individually. While attendance at Astros games has dropped by around 20% since 2011, the cost reductions from reduced player salaries have far outpaced the drop in attendance, making the 2013 Astros the most profitable team in baseball history. While no one likes losing baseball games, the Houston Astros have shown that focusing on the relationship between cost and volume can yield a hefty profit, even when they aren't winning.

Source: D. Alexander, "2013 Houston Astros: Baseball's Worst Team Is the Most Profitable in History," *Forbes*, August 26, 2013.

Objective 5

Compute the break-even point for a company selling more than one product, the operating leverage, and the margin of safety.

Special Cost-Volume-Profit Relationships

Cost-volume-profit analysis can also be used when a company sells several products with different costs and prices. In addition, operating leverage and the margin of safety are useful in analyzing cost-volume-profit relationships.

Sales Mix Considerations

Many companies sell more than one product at different selling prices. In addition, the products normally have different unit variable costs and, thus, different unit contribution margins. In such cases, break-even analysis can still be performed by considering the sales mix. The **sales mix** is the relative distribution of sales among the products sold by a company.

To illustrate, assume that Cascade Company sold Products A and B during the past year, as follows:

Total fixed costs	$200,000	
	Product A	**Product B**
Unit selling price	$90	$140
Unit variable cost....................	70	95
Unit contribution margin	$20	$ 45
Units sold	8,000	2,000
Sales mix..........................	80%	20%

The sales mix for Products A and B is expressed as a percentage of total units sold. For Cascade, a total of 10,000 (8,000 + 2,000) units were sold during the year. Therefore, the sales mix is 80% (8,000 ÷ 10,000) for Product A and 20% for Product B (2,000 ÷ 10,000), as shown in Exhibit 18. The sales mix could also be expressed as the ratio 80:20.

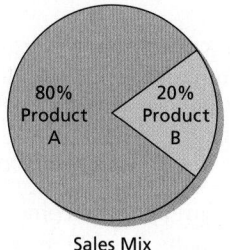

Exhibit 18
Multiple Product
Sales Mix

For break-even analysis, it is useful to think of Products A and B as components of one overall enterprise product called E. The unit selling price of E equals the sum of the unit selling prices of each product multiplied by its sales mix percentage. Likewise, the unit variable cost and unit contribution margin of E equal the sum of the unit variable costs and unit contribution margins of each product multiplied by its sales mix percentage.

For Cascade, the unit selling price, unit variable cost, and unit contribution margin for E are computed as follows:

Product E	Product A	Product B
Unit selling price of E	$100 = ($90 × 0.8)	+ ($140 × 0.2)
Unit variable cost of E	75 = ($70 × 0.8)	+ ($95 × 0.2)
Unit contribution margin of E	$ 25 = ($20 × 0.8)	+ ($45 × 0.2)

Cascade has total fixed costs of $200,000. The break-even point of 8,000 units of E can be determined as follows using the unit selling price, unit variable cost, and unit contribution margin of E:

$$\text{Break-Even Sales (units) for E} = \frac{\text{Fixed Costs}}{\text{Unit Contribution Margin}} = \frac{\$200,000}{\$25} = 8,000 \text{ units}$$

Because the sales mix for Products A and B is 80% and 20% respectively, the break-even quantity of A is 6,400 units (8,000 units × 80%) and B is 1,600 units (8,000 units × 20%) which is verified in Exhibit 19.

	Product A	Product B	Total
Sales:			
6,400 units × $90	$576,000		$576,000
1,600 units × $140		$224,000	224,000
Total sales	$576,000	$224,000	$800,000
Variable costs:			
6,400 units × $70	$448,000		$448,000
1,600 units × $95		$152,000	152,000
Total variable costs	$448,000	$152,000	$600,000
Contribution margin	$128,000	$ 72,000	$200,000
Fixed costs			200,000
Income from operations			$ 0

← Break-even point

Exhibit 19
Break-Even Sales:
Multiple Products

The effects of changes in the sales mix on the break-even point can be determined by assuming a different sales mix. The break-even point of E can then be recomputed.

The sales mix of Ford and Lincoln vehicles sold has a major impact on Ford Motor Company's overall profitability.

Link to Ford Motor Company

Operating Leverage

The relationship between a company's contribution margin and income from operations is measured by **operating leverage**. A company's operating leverage is computed as follows:

$$\text{Operating Leverage} = \frac{\text{Contribution Margin}}{\text{Income from Operations}}$$

The difference between contribution margin and income from operations is fixed costs. Thus, companies with high fixed costs will normally have high operating leverage. Examples of such companies include airline and automotive companies, like **Ford Motor Company**. Low operating leverage is normal for companies that are labor intensive, such as professional service companies, which have low fixed costs.

To illustrate operating leverage, assume the following data for Jones Inc. and Wilson Inc.:

	Jones Inc.	Wilson Inc.
Sales...	$400,000	$400,000
Variable costs	300,000	300,000
Contribution margin......................................	$100,000	$100,000
Fixed costs	80,000	50,000
Income from operations	$ 20,000	$ 50,000

As shown, Jones and Wilson have the same sales, the same variable costs, and the same contribution margin. However, Jones has larger fixed costs than Wilson and, thus, a higher operating leverage. The operating leverage for each company is computed as follows:

Jones Inc.

$$\text{Operating Leverage} = \frac{\text{Contribution Margin}}{\text{Income from Operations}} = \frac{\$100,000}{\$20,000} = 5$$

Wilson Inc.

$$\text{Operating Leverage} = \frac{\text{Contribution Margin}}{\text{Income from Operations}} = \frac{\$100,000}{\$50,000} = 2$$

Operating leverage can be used to measure the impact of changes in sales on income from operations. Using operating leverage, the effect of changes in sales on income from operations is computed as follows:

$$\frac{\text{Percent Change in}}{\text{Income from Operations}} = \frac{\text{Percent Change in}}{\text{Sales}} \times \frac{\text{Operating}}{\text{Leverage}}$$

To illustrate, assume that sales increased by 10%, or $40,000 ($400,000 × 10%), for Jones and Wilson. The percent increase in income from operations for Jones and Wilson is computed as follows:

Jones Inc.

$$\frac{\text{Percent Change in}}{\text{Income from Operations}} = \frac{\text{Percent Change in}}{\text{Sales}} \times \frac{\text{Operating}}{\text{Leverage}}$$

$$= 10\% \times 5 = 50\%$$

Wilson Inc.

$$\frac{\text{Percent Change in}}{\text{Income from Operations}} = \frac{\text{Percent Change in}}{\text{Sales}} \times \frac{\text{Operating}}{\text{Leverage}}$$

$$= 10\% \times 2 = 20\%$$

As shown, Jones's income from operations increases by 50%, while Wilson's income from operations increases by only 20%. The validity of this analysis is shown in the following income statements for Jones and Wilson based on the 10% increase in sales:

	Jones Inc.	Wilson Inc.
Sales	$440,000	$440,000
Variable costs	330,000	330,000
Contribution margin	$110,000	$110,000
Fixed costs	80,000	50,000
Income from operations	$ 30,000	$ 60,000

The preceding income statements indicate that Jones's income from operations increased from $20,000 to $30,000, a 50% increase ($10,000 ÷ $20,000). In contrast, Wilson's income from operations increased from $50,000 to $60,000, a 20% increase ($10,000 ÷ $50,000).

Because even a small increase in sales will generate a large percentage increase in income from operations, Jones might consider ways to increase sales. Such actions could include special advertising or sales promotions. In contrast, Wilson might consider ways to increase operating leverage by reducing variable costs.

The impact of a change in sales on income from operations for companies with high and low operating leverage is summarized in Exhibit 20.

Operating Leverage	Percentage Impact on Income from Operations from a Change in Sales
High	Large
Low	Small

Exhibit 20
Effect of Operating Leverage on Income from Operations

Ford Motor Company has a high proportion of fixed costs with the result that small changes in units sold can significantly affect its overall profitability.
Source: Ford Motor Company, Form 10-K for Year Ended December 31, 2014.

Link to Ford Motor Company

Margin of Safety

The **margin of safety** indicates the possible decrease in sales that may occur before an operating loss results. Thus, if the margin of safety is low, even a small decline in sales revenue may result in an operating loss.

The margin of safety may be expressed in the following ways:

- Dollars of sales
- Units of sales
- Percent of current sales

To illustrate, assume the following data:

Sales	$250,000
Sales at the break-even point	200,000
Unit selling price	25

The margin of safety in dollars of sales is $50,000 ($250,000 – $200,000). The margin of safety in units is 2,000 units ($50,000 ÷ $25). The margin of safety expressed as a percent of current sales is 20%, computed as follows:

$$\text{Margin of Safety} = \frac{\text{Sales} - \text{Sales at Break-Even Point}}{\text{Sales}}$$

$$= \frac{\$250,000 - \$200,000}{\$250,000} = \frac{\$50,000}{\$250,000} = 20\%$$

Therefore, the current sales may decline $50,000, 2,000 units, or 20% before an operating loss occurs.

Check Up Corner 19-4 **Special Cost-Volume-Profit Relationships**

Blueberry Inc., a consumer electronics company, manufactures and sells two products, smartphones and tablet computers. The unit selling price, unit variable cost, and sales mix for each product are as follows:

Products	Unit Selling Price	Unit Variable Cost	Sales Mix
Smartphone	$650	$560	60%
Tablet	550	475	40%

The company's fixed costs are $4,200,000.
A. How many units of each product would be sold at the break-even point?
B. Assume Blueberry sells 37,500 smartphones and 25,000 tablets during a recent year. Compute the company's (1) operating leverage and (2) margin of safety.

Solution:

A.

Product E		Smartphone	Tablet
Unit selling price of E	$610 =	($650 × 0.6) +	($550 × 0.4)
Unit variable cost of E	526 =	($560 × 0.6) +	($475 × 0.4)
Unit contribution margin of E	$ 84 =	($90 × 0.6) +	($75 × 0.4)

$$\text{Break-Even Sales of E (units)} = \frac{\text{Fixed Costs}}{\text{Unit Contribution Margin}}$$

$$\text{Break-Even Sales of E (units)} = \frac{\$4,200,000}{\$84}$$

$$= 50,000 \text{ units}$$

	Smartphones	Tablets
Break-even sales of E (units)	50,000	50,000
Sales mix	× 60%	× 40%
Break-even sales of product	30,000	20,000

In break-even analysis for multiple products, it is useful to think of the individual product as components of one overall product called product E.

The unit selling price of E equals the sum of the unit selling price of each product multiplied by its sales mix percentage.

The unit variable cost of E equals the sum of the unit variable cost of each product multiplied by its sales mix percentage.

The break-even number of units of E is determined by dividing the company's total fixed costs by the unit contribution margin of E.

The break-even quantity of each product is determined by multiplying the sales mix percentage of each product by the break-even units of product E.

B. 1.

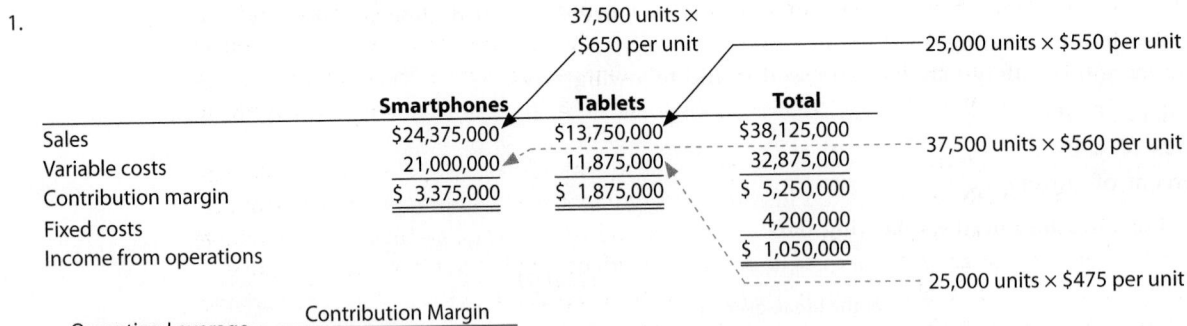

	Smartphones	Tablets	Total
Sales	$24,375,000	$13,750,000	$38,125,000
Variable costs	21,000,000	11,875,000	32,875,000
Contribution margin	$ 3,375,000	$ 1,875,000	$ 5,250,000
Fixed costs			4,200,000
Income from operations			$ 1,050,000

37,500 units × $650 per unit
25,000 units × $550 per unit
37,500 units × $560 per unit
25,000 units × $475 per unit

$$\text{Operating Leverage} = \frac{\text{Contribution Margin}}{\text{Income from Operations}}$$

$$\text{Operating Leverage} = \frac{\$5,250,000}{\$1,050,000}$$

$$= 5.0$$

The relationship between a company's contribution margin and income from operations is called operating leverage.

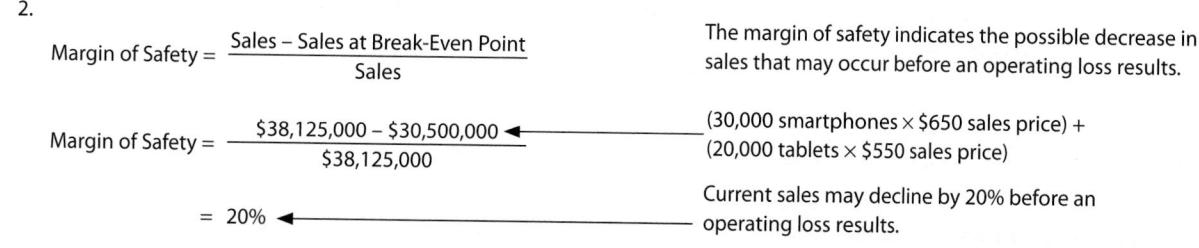

2.

$$\text{Margin of Safety} = \frac{\text{Sales} - \text{Sales at Break-Even Point}}{\text{Sales}}$$

The margin of safety indicates the possible decrease in sales that may occur before an operating loss results.

$$\text{Margin of Safety} = \frac{\$38,125,000 - \$30,500,000}{\$38,125,000}$$

(30,000 smartphones × $650 sales price) + (20,000 tablets × $550 sales price)

= 20%

Current sales may decline by 20% before an operating loss results.

Check Up Corner

Analysis for Decision Making

Cost-Volume-Profit Analysis for Service Companies

Objective
Describe and illustrate the use of cost-volume-profit analysis for decision making in a service business.

The break-even point is as relevant in a service company as it is in a manufacturing company. Services are delivered to customers, such as patients, or to other items, such as invested funds. Thus, cost-volume-profit relationships in a service company are measured with respect to customers and activities, rather than units of product. Examples are as follows:

Service	Break-Even Analysis
Education	Break-even number of students per course
Air transportation	Break-even number of passengers per flight
Health care	Break-even number of patients per outpatient facility
Hotel	Break-even number of guests per time period (day, month, etc.)
Freight transportation	Break-even number of tons per train
Theme park	Break-even number of guests per time period (day, month, etc.)
Financial services	Break-even number of invested funds (dollars) under management
Subscription services	Break-even number of subscribers

Break-even analysis for a service company involves identifying the correct unit of analysis and the correct measure of activity for that unit. For example, the unit of analysis for an educational institution could be a course, a major, a college, or the university as a whole. For a specific course, the measure of activity would be the number of students enrolled in the course. Each student is the same in his or her demand for course-level services. Thus, a break-even analysis would discover the number of students required for the course to break even.

At other units of analysis, the measure of activity may change. For example, the break-even for a college would likely be measured in number of student credit hours, not number of students. Not all students are equal in their demand for college services, because some students are part-time and some are full-time. However, each student credit hour is nearly the same.

Moreover, the unit of analysis can influence whether costs are defined as fixed or variable. For example, the instructor's salary is a fixed cost for a specific course, but can be a variable cost to the number of sections taught at the college level.

To illustrate, consider the break-even number of students for a noncredit course in pottery. The course tuition is $500.

The costs consist of the following:

Variable costs per student:
Pottery supplies .... $ 300
Enrollment costs 20

Fixed costs for the course:
Instructor's salary $3,000
Rental cost of the classroom 1,500

The break-even point is computed as follows:

$$\text{Break-Even Sales (units)} = \frac{\text{Fixed Costs}}{\text{Unit Contribution Margin}}$$

$$\text{Break-Even Sales (units)} = \frac{\$4,500}{\$500 - \$320} = 25 \text{ students}$$

Thus, the course would need to enroll 25 students to break even.

Make a Decision — Cost-Volume-Profit Analysis for Service Companies

An airline is considering a new flight between Atlanta and Los Angeles. The average fare per seat for the flight is $760. The costs associated with the flight are as follows:

Fixed costs for the flight:
Crew salaries .... $ 5,000
Operating costs 50,000
Aircraft depreciation 25,000
Total $80,000

Variable costs per passenger:
Passenger check-in .... $ 20
Operating costs 100
Total $120

The airline estimates that the flight will sell 175 seats.

A. Determine the break-even number of passengers per flight.
B. Based on your answer in (A), should the airline add this flight to its schedule?
C. How much profit should each flight produce?
D. What additional issues might the airline consider in this decision?

Solution:

A.

$$\text{Break-Even Sales (units)} = \frac{\text{Fixed Costs}}{\text{Unit Contribution Margin}}$$

$$\text{Break-Even Sales (units)} = \frac{\$80,000}{\$760 - \$120} = 125 \text{ passengers}$$

B. The airline should consider adding the flight. The number of passengers (175) is well above the break-even number of passengers for the flight (125).

C. Each flight should cover fixed costs and produce a contribution margin for 50 additional passengers above break-even. Thus, the profit for the flight would be computed as:

$$(175 \text{ passengers} - 125 \text{ passengers}) \times (\$760 - \$120) = \$32,000$$

D. First, the airline should consider the impact of the new flight on other flights to Los Angeles. That is, the airline should determine whether the seats sold on the new flight are truly incremental seats for the airline, or whether passengers are shifting from one of the airline's other flights to this new flight. Second, the airline should consider the impact of the new flight on system load. For example, is there sufficient gate, runway, maintenance, and baggage handling capacity to support the additional flight? If not, the fixed costs of adding the flight could be much higher than $80,000.

Make a Decision

Let's Review

Chapter Summary

1. Variable costs vary in proportion to changes in the level of activity. Fixed costs remain the same in total dollar amount as the level of activity changes. Mixed costs are comprised of both fixed and variable costs.

2. Contribution margin is the excess of sales revenue over variable costs and can be expressed as a ratio (contribution margin ratio) or a dollar amount (unit contribution margin).

3. The break-even point is the point at which a business's revenues exactly equal costs. The mathematical approach to cost-volume-profit analysis uses the unit contribution margin concept and mathematical equations to determine the break-even point and the volume necessary to achieve a target profit.

4. Graphical methods can be used to determine the break-even point and the volume necessary to achieve a target profit. A cost-volume-profit chart focuses on the relationship among costs, sales, and operating profit or loss. The profit-volume chart focuses on profits rather than on revenues and costs.

5. Cost-volume-profit relationships can be used for analyzing the effects of sales mix on the break-even point and profits. Operating leverage can be used to analyze the effects of changes in sales on income from operations. The margin of safety indicates how much sales must decrease before an operating loss occurs.

Key Terms

activity bases (drivers) (942)
break-even point (953)
contribution margin (950)
contribution margin ratio (950)
cost behavior (942)
cost-volume-profit
   analysis (950)

cost-volume-profit chart (958)
fixed costs (944)
high-low method (947)
margin of safety (967)
mixed costs (946)
operating leverage (966)

profit-volume chart (960)
relevant range (942)
sales mix (964)
unit contribution margin (951)
variable costing (948)
variable costs (943)

Practice

Multiple-Choice Questions

1. Which of the following statements describes variable costs?
   A. Costs that vary on a per-unit basis as the level of activity changes
   B. Costs that vary in total in direct proportion to changes in the level of activity
   C. Costs that remain the same in total dollar amount as the level of activity changes
   D. Costs that vary on a per-unit basis, but remain the same in total as the level of activity changes

2. If sales are $500,000, variable costs are $200,000, and fixed costs are $240,000, what is the contribution margin ratio?
   A. 40%
   B. 48%
   C. 52%
   D. 60%

3. If the unit selling price is $16, the unit variable cost is $12, and fixed costs are $160,000, what is the break-even sales (units)?
   A. 5,714 units
   B. 10,000 units
   C. 13,333 units
   D. 40,000 units

4. Based on the data presented in Question 3, how many units of sales would be required to realize income from operations of $20,000?
   A. 11,250 units
   B. 5,000 units
   C. 40,000 units
   D. 45,000 units

5. Based on the following operating data, what is the operating leverage?

Sales	$600,000
Variable costs	240,000
Contribution margin	$360,000
Fixed costs	160,000
Income from operations	$200,000

   A. 0.8
   B. 1.2
   C. 1.8
   D. 4.0

Answers provided after Problem. Need more practice? Find additional multiple-choice questions, exercises, and problems in CengageNOWv2.

Exercises

SHOW ME HOW

1. High-low method   Obj. 1

The manufacturing costs of Lightfoot Industries for three months of the year follow:

	Total Costs	Units Produced
January	$640,000	30,000 units
February	900,000	40,000
March	350,000	12,500

Using the high-low method, determine (A) the variable cost per unit and (B) the total fixed cost.

SHOW ME HOW

2. Contribution margin   Obj. 2

Michigan Company sells 10,000 units at $100 per unit. Variable costs are $75 per unit, and fixed costs are $125,000. Determine (A) the contribution margin ratio, (B) the unit contribution margin, and (C) income from operations.

SHOW ME HOW

3. Break-even point   Obj. 3

Santana sells a product for $115 per unit. The variable cost is $75 per unit, while fixed costs are $65,000. Determine (A) the break-even point in sales units and (B) the break-even point if the selling price were increased to $125 per unit.

SHOW ME HOW

4. Target profit   Obj. 3

Versa Inc. sells a product for $100 per unit. The variable cost is $75 per unit, and fixed costs are $45,000. Determine (A) the break-even point in sales units and (B) the sales units required for the company to achieve a target profit of $25,000.

SHOW ME HOW

5. Sales mix and break-even analysis   Obj. 5

Wide Open Industries Inc. has fixed costs of $475,000. The unit selling price, variable cost per unit, and contribution margin per unit for the company's two products follow:

Product	Selling Price	Variable Cost per Unit	Contribution Margin per Unit
AA	$145	$105	$40
BB	110	75	35

The sales mix for products AA and BB is 60% and 40%, respectively. Determine the break-even point in units of AA and BB.

SHOW ME HOW

6. Operating leverage   Obj. 5

SungSam Enterprises reports the following data:

Sales	$340,000
Variable costs	180,000
Contribution margin	$160,000
Fixed costs	80,000
Income from operations	$ 80,000

Determine SungSam Enterprises's operating leverage.

SHOW ME HOW

7. Margin of safety   Obj. 5

Melton Inc. has sales of $1,750,000, and the break-even point in sales dollars is $875,000. Determine the company's margin of safety as a percent of current sales.

Answers provided after Problem. Need more practice? Find additional multiple-choice questions, exercises, and problems in CengageNOWv2.

Problem

Wyatt Inc. expects to maintain the same inventories at the end of the year as at the beginning of the year. The estimated fixed costs for the year are $288,000, and the estimated variable costs per unit are $14. It is expected that 60,000 units will be sold at a price of $20 per unit. Maximum sales within the relevant range are 70,000 units.

Instructions

1. What is (A) the contribution margin ratio and (B) the unit contribution margin?

2. Determine the break-even point in units.

3. Construct a cost-volume-profit chart, indicating the break-even point.

4. Construct a profit-volume chart, indicating the break-even point.

5. What is the margin of safety?

Need more practice? Find additional multiple-choice questions, exercises, and problems in CengageNOWv2.

Answers

Multiple-Choice Questions

1. **B** Variable costs vary in total in direct proportion to changes in the level of activity (answer B). Costs that vary on a per-unit basis as the level of activity changes (answer A) or remain constant in total dollar amount as the level of activity changes (answer C), or both (answer D), are fixed costs.

2. **D** The contribution margin ratio indicates the percentage of each sales dollar available to cover the fixed costs and provide income from operations and is determined as follows:

$$\text{Contribution Margin Ratio} = \frac{\text{Sales} - \text{Variable Costs}}{\text{Sales}}$$

$$\text{Contribution Margin Ratio} = \frac{\$500,000 - \$200,000}{\$500,000}$$

$$= 60\%$$

3. **D** The break-even sales of 40,000 units (answer D) is computed as follows:

$$\text{Break-Even Sales (units)} = \frac{\text{Fixed Costs}}{\text{Unit Contribution Margin}}$$

$$\text{Break-Even Sales (units)} = \frac{\$160,000}{\$4} = 40,000 \text{ units}$$

4. **D** Sales of 45,000 (answer D) units are required to realize income from operations of $20,000, computed as follows:

$$\text{Sales (units)} = \frac{\text{Fixed Costs} + \text{Target Profit}}{\text{Unit Contribution Margin}}$$

$$\text{Sales (units)} = \frac{\$160,000 + \$20,000}{\$4} = 45,000 \text{ units}$$

5. **C** The operating leverage is 1.8 (answer C), computed as follows:

$$\text{Operating Leverage} = \frac{\text{Contribution Margin}}{\text{Income from Operations}}$$

$$\text{Operating Leverage} = \frac{\$360,000}{\$200,000} = 1.8$$

Exercises

1.

    A. $20 per unit = ($900,000 − $350,000) ÷ (40,000 units − 12,500 units)

    B. $100,000 = $900,000 − ($20 × 40,000 units), or $350,000 − ($20 × 12,500 units)

2.

    A. 25.0% = ($100 − $75) ÷ $100, or ($1,000,000 − $750,000) ÷ $1,000,000

    B. $25 per unit = $100 − $75

    C.

Sales	$1,000,000	(10,000 units × $100 per unit)
Variable costs	750,000	(10,000 units × $75 per unit)
Contribution margin	$ 250,000	(10,000 units × $25 per unit)
Fixed costs	125,000	
Income from operations	$ 125,000	

3.

    A. 1,625 units = $65,000 ÷ ($115 − $75)

    B. 1,300 units = $65,000 ÷ ($125 − $75)

4.

    A. 1,800 units = $45,000 ÷ ($100 − $75)

    B. 2,800 units = ($45,000 + $25,000) ÷ ($100 − $75)

5.

Unit selling price of E: [($145 × 0.60) + ($110 × 0.40)] = $131.00

Unit variable cost of E: [($105 × 0.60) + ($75 × 0.40)] = 93.00

Unit contribution margin of E = $ 38.00

Break-Even Sales (units) = $475,000 ÷ $38.00 = 12,500 units

Break-Even Sales (units) for AA = 12,500 units of E × 60% = 7,500 units of Product AA

Break-Even Sales (units) for BB = 12,500 units of E × 40% = 5,000 units of Product BB

6.

$$\text{Operating Leverage} = \frac{\text{Contribution Margin}}{\text{Income from Operations}} = \frac{\$160,000}{\$80,000} = 2$$

7.

$$\text{Margin of Safety} = \frac{\text{Sales − Sales at Break-Even Point}}{\text{Sales}}$$

$$= (\$1,750,000 − \$875,000) ÷ \$1,750,000 = 50\%$$

Need more help? Watch step-by-step videos of how to compute answers to these Exercises in CengageNOWv2.

Problem

1. A. Contribution Margin Ratio $= \dfrac{\text{Sales − Variable Costs}}{\text{Sales}}$

$$= \frac{(60,000 \text{ units} × \$20) − (60,000 \text{ units} × \$14)}{(60,000 \text{ units} × \$20)}$$

$$= \frac{\$1,200,000 − \$840,000}{\$1,200,000} = \frac{\$360,000}{\$1,200,000}$$

$$= 30\%$$

    B. Unit Contribution Margin = Unit Selling Price − Unit Variable Costs

$$= \$20 − \$14 = \$6$$

2. Break-Even Sales (units) = $\dfrac{\text{Fixed Costs}}{\text{Unit Contribution Margin}}$

$$= \frac{\$288{,}000}{\$6} = 48{,}000 \text{ units}$$

3. **Sales and Costs**

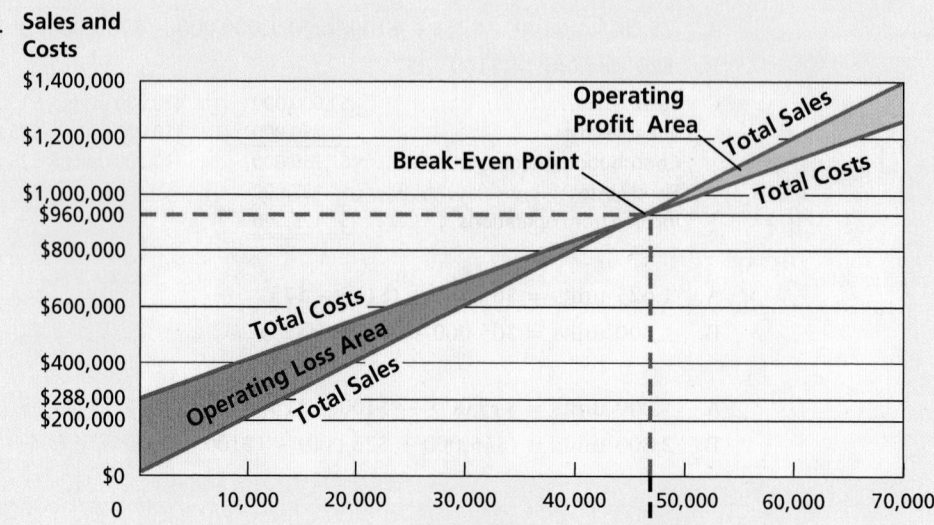

4. **Operating Profit (Loss)**

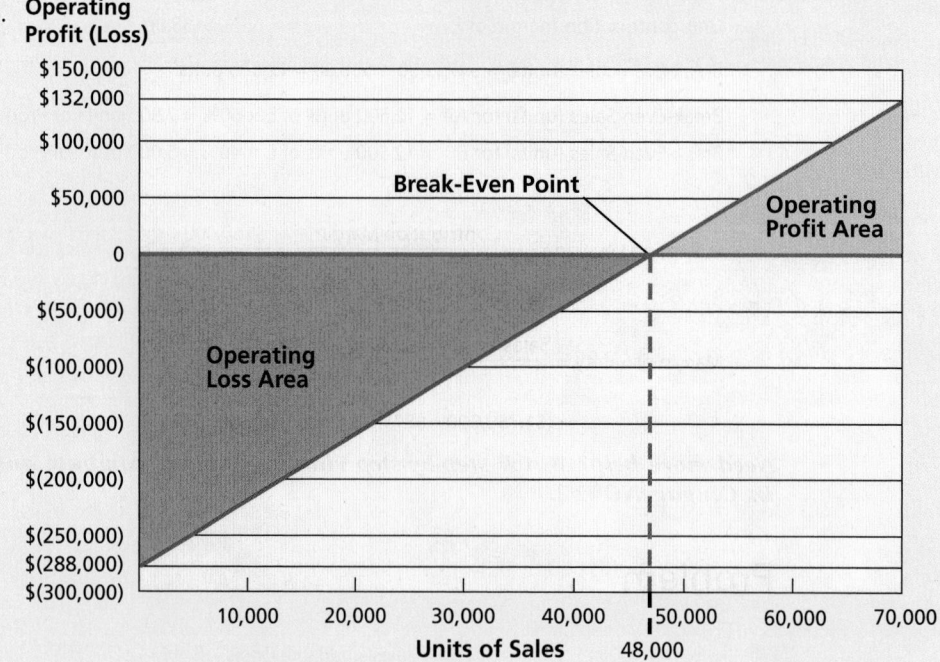

5. Margin of safety:

Expected sales (60,000 units × $20)	$1,200,000
Break-even point (48,000 units × $20)	960,000
Margin of safety	$ 240,000

or

Margin of Safety (units) = $\dfrac{\text{Margin of Safety (dollars)}}{\text{Unit Selling Price}}$

$$= \frac{\$240{,}000}{\$20} = 12{,}000 \text{ units}$$

or

$$\text{Margin of Safety} = \frac{\text{Sales} - \text{Sales at Break-Even Point}}{\text{Sales}}$$

$$= \frac{\$240,000}{\$1,200,000} = 20\%$$

Discussion Questions

1. Describe how total variable costs and unit variable costs behave with changes in the level of activity.

2. Which of the following costs would be classified as variable and which would be classified as fixed, if units produced is the activity base?

   A. Direct materials costs
   B. Electricity costs of $0.35 per kilowatt-hour

3. Describe how total fixed costs and unit fixed costs behave with changes in the level of activity.

4. In applying the high-low method of cost estimation to mixed costs, how is the total fixed cost estimated?

5. If fixed costs increase, what would be the impact on the (A) contribution margin? (B) income from operations?

6. An examination of the accounting records of Clowney Company disclosed a high contribution margin ratio and production at a level below maximum capacity. Based on this information, suggest a likely means of improving income from operations. Explain.

7. If the unit cost of direct materials is decreased, what effect will this change have on the break-even point?

8. Both Austin Company and Hill Company had the same unit sales, total costs, and income from operations for the current fiscal year; yet, Austin Company had a lower break-even point than Hill Company. Explain the reason for this difference in break-even points.

9. How does the sales mix affect the calculation of the break-even point?

10. What does operating leverage measure, and how is it computed?

Basic Exercises

SHOW ME HOW

BE 19-1   High-low method   **Obj. 1**

The manufacturing costs of Ackerman Industries for the first three months of the year follow:

	Total Costs	Units Produced
January	$1,900,000	20,000 units
February	2,250,000	27,000
March	2,400,000	30,000

Using the high-low method, determine (A) the variable cost per unit and (B) the total fixed cost.

SHOW ME HOW

BE 19-2   Contribution margin   **Obj. 2**

Lanning Company sells 160,000 units at $45 per unit. Variable costs are $27 per unit, and fixed costs are $975,000. Determine (A) the contribution margin ratio, (B) the unit contribution margin, and (C) income from operations.

SHOW ME HOW

BE 19-3   Break-even point   **Obj. 3**

Bigelow Inc. sells a product for $1,200 per unit. The variable cost is $816 per unit, while fixed costs are $3,120,000. Determine (A) the break-even point in sales units and (B) the break-even point if the selling price were increased to $1,232 per unit.

SHOW ME HOW

BE 19-4 Target profit   Obj. 3

Ramirez Company sells a product for $80 per unit. The variable cost is $60 per unit, and fixed costs are $4,850,000. Determine (A) the break-even point in sales units and (B) the sales units required for the company to achieve a target profit of $500,000.

SHOW ME HOW

BE 19-5 Sales mix and break-even analysis   Obj. 5

Hughes Company has fixed costs of $3,565,000. The unit selling price, variable cost per unit, and contribution margin per unit for the company's two products follow:

Product	Selling Price	Variable Cost per Unit	Contribution Margin per Unit
Model 94	$1,600	$960	$640
Model 81	1,000	800	200

The sales mix for products Model 94 and Model 81 is 25% and 75%, respectively. Determine the break-even point in units of Model 94 and Model 81.

SHOW ME HOW

BE 19-6 Operating leverage   Obj. 5

Taft Co. reports the following data:

Sales	$875,000
Variable costs	425,000
Contribution margin	$450,000
Fixed costs	150,000
Income from operations	$300,000

Determine Taft Co.'s operating leverage.

SHOW ME HOW

BE 19-7 Margin of safety   Obj. 5

Liu Company has sales of $48,500,000, and the break-even point in sales dollars is $31,040,000. Determine the company's margin of safety as a percent of current sales.

Exercises

EX 19-1 Classify costs   Obj. 1

Following is a list of various costs incurred in producing replacement automobile parts. With respect to the production and sale of these auto parts, classify each cost as either variable, fixed, or mixed.

1. Oil used in manufacturing equipment
2. Plastic
3. Property taxes, $165,000 per year on factory building and equipment
4. Salary of plant manager
5. Cost of labor for hourly workers
6. Packaging
7. Factory cleaning costs, $6,000 per month
8. Metal
9. Rent on warehouse, $10,000 per month plus $25 per square foot of storage used
10. Property insurance premiums, $3,600 per month plus $0.01 for each dollar of property over $1,200,000
11. Straight-line depreciation on the production equipment
12. Hourly wages of machine operators
13. Electricity costs, $0.20 per kilowatt-hour
14. Computer chip (purchased from a vendor)
15. Pension cost, $1.00 per employee hour on the job

EX 19-2 Identify cost graphs

Obj. 1

The following cost graphs illustrate various types of cost behavior:

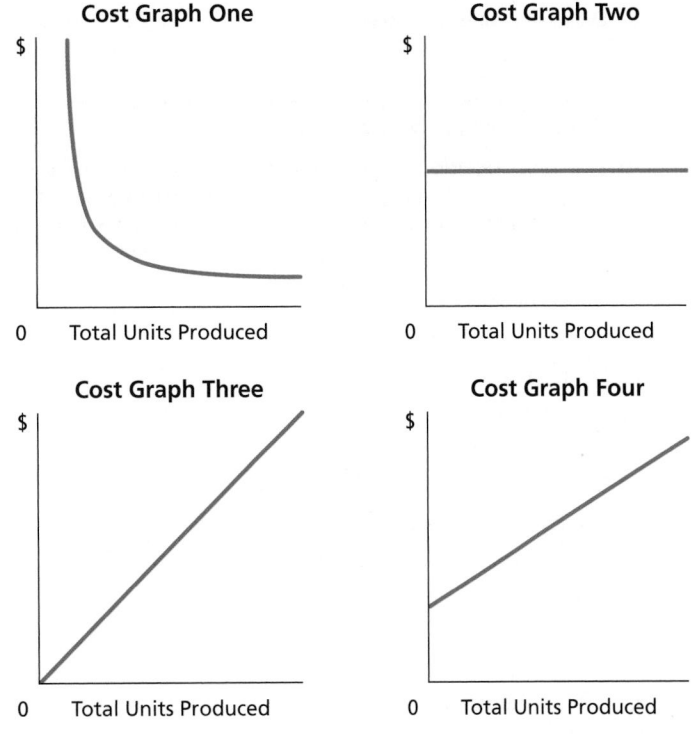

Cost Graph One

$ | Total Units Produced

0

Cost Graph Two

$ | Total Units Produced

0

Cost Graph Three

$ | Total Units Produced

0

Cost Graph Four

$ | Total Units Produced

0

For each of the following costs, identify the cost graph that best illustrates its cost behavior as the number of units produced increases:

A. Total direct materials cost

B. Electricity costs of $1,000 per month plus $0.10 per kilowatt-hour

C. Per-unit cost of straight-line depreciation on factory equipment

D. Salary of quality control supervisor, $20,000 per month

E. Per-unit direct labor cost

EX 19-3 Identify activity bases

Obj. 1

For a major university, match each cost in the following table with the activity base most appropriate to it. An activity base may be used more than once or not used at all.

Cost:	Activity Base:
1. Financial aid office salaries	A. Number of enrollment applications
2. Office supplies	B. Number of students
3. Instructor salaries	C. Student credit hours
4. Housing personnel wages	D. Number of enrolled students and alumni
5. Employee wages for maintaining student records	E. Number of financial aid applications
6. Admissions office salaries	F. Number of students living on campus

---

EX 19-4 Identify activity bases

Obj. 1

From the following list of activity bases for an automobile dealership, select the base that would be most appropriate for each of these costs: (1) preparation costs (cleaning, oil, and gasoline costs) for each car received, (2) salespersons' commission of 5% of the sales price for each car sold, and (3) administrative costs for ordering cars.

A. Number of cars sold

B. Dollar amount of cars ordered

C. Number of cars ordered

(Continued)

D. Number of cars on hand

E. Number of cars received

F. Dollar amount of cars sold

G. Dollar amount of cars received

H. Dollar amount of cars on hand

REAL WORLD

EX 19-5   Identify fixed and variable costs

Obj. 1

Intuit Inc. develops and sells software products for the personal finance market, including popular titles such as Quickbooks® and TurboTax®. Classify each of the following costs and expenses for this company as either variable or fixed to the number of units produced and sold:

A. Packaging costs

B. Sales commissions

C. Property taxes on general offices

D. Shipping expenses

E. Straight-line depreciation of computer equipment

F. President's salary

G. Salaries of software developers

H. Salaries of human resources personnel

I. Wages of telephone order assistants

J. Costs of providing online support

K. Users' guides

✔ A. $30.00

SHOW ME HOW

EX 19-6   Relevant range and fixed and variable costs

Obj. 1

Vogel Inc. manufactures memory chips for electronic toys within a relevant range of 25,000 to 100,000 memory chips per year. Within this range, the following partially completed manufacturing cost schedule has been prepared:

Memory chips produced..............	45,000	60,000	75,000
Total costs:			
Total variable costs	$ 1,350,000	(D)	(J)
Total fixed costs	810,000	(E)	(K)
Total costs.........................	$2,160,000	(F)	(L)
Cost per unit:			
Variable cost per unit	(A)	(G)	(M)
Fixed cost per unit..................	(B)	(H)	(N)
Total cost per unit	(C)	(I)	(O)

Complete the cost schedule, identifying each cost by the appropriate letter (A) through (O).

✔ A. $175.50 per unit variable cost

SHOW ME HOW   EXCEL TEMPLATE

EX 19-7   High-low method

Obj. 1

Ziegler Inc. has decided to use the high-low method to estimate the total cost and the fixed and variable cost components of the total cost. The data for various levels of production are as follows:

Units Produced	Total Costs
80,000	$25,100,000
92,000	27,206,000
120,000	32,120,000

A. Determine the variable cost per unit and the total fixed cost.

B. Based on part (A), estimate the total cost for 115,000 units of production.

EX 19-8   High-low method for a service company

Obj. 1

✔ Fixed cost, $600,000

SHOW ME HOW

Boston Railroad decided to use the high-low method and operating data from the past six months to estimate the fixed and variable components of transportation costs. The activity base used by Boston Railroad is a measure of railroad operating activity, termed "gross-ton miles," which is the total number of tons multiplied by the miles moved.

	Transportation Costs	Gross-Ton Miles
January	$1,776,000	560,000
February	2,700,000	1,000,000
March	1,650,000	500,000
April	1,860,000	600,000
May	1,440,000	400,000
June	1,566,000	460,000

Determine the variable cost per gross-ton mile and the total fixed cost.

EX 19-9   Contribution margin ratio

Obj. 2

✔ A. 41%

SHOW ME HOW

A. Young Company budgets sales of $112,900,000, fixed costs of $25,000,000, and variable costs of $66,611,000. What is the contribution margin ratio for Young Company?

B. If the contribution margin ratio for Martinez Company is 40%, sales were $34,800,000, and fixed costs were $1,500,000, what was the income from operations?

EX 19-10   Contribution margin and contribution margin ratio

Obj. 2

✔ B. 34.6%

SHOW ME HOW   REAL WORLD

For a recent year, **McDonald's** company-owned restaurants had the following sales and expenses (in millions):

Sales	$18,169.3
Food and packaging	$ 6,129.7
Payroll	4,756.0
Occupancy (rent, depreciation, etc.)	4,402.6
General, selling, and administrative expenses	2,487.9
	$17,776.2
Income from operations	$ 393.1

Assume that the variable costs consist of food and packaging, payroll, and 40% of the general, selling, and administrative expenses.

A. What is McDonald's contribution margin? Round to the nearest tenth of a million (one decimal place).

B. What is McDonald's contribution margin ratio? Round to one decimal place.

C. How much would income from operations increase if same-store sales increased by $500 million for the coming year, with no change in the contribution margin ratio or fixed costs? Round your answer to the nearest tenth of a million (one decimal place).

EX 19-11   Break-even sales and sales to realize income from operations

Obj. 3

✔ B. 128,500 units

SHOW ME HOW

For the current year ended October 31, Friedman Company expects fixed costs of $14,300,000, a unit variable cost of $250, and a unit selling price of $380.

A. Compute the anticipated break-even sales (units).

B. Compute the sales (units) required to realize income from operations of $2,405,000.

EX 19-12   Break-even sales   Obj. 3

Anheuser-Busch InBev Companies, Inc., reported the following operating information for a recent year (in millions):

Sales	$47,063
Cost of goods sold	$18,756
Selling, general, and administration	12,999
	$31,755
Income from operations	$15,308*

*Before special items

In addition, assume that Anheuser-Busch InBev sold 400 million barrels of beer during the year. Assume that variable costs were 75% of the cost of goods sold and 50% of selling, general, and administration expenses. Assume that the remaining costs are fixed. For the following year, assume that Anheuser-Busch InBev expects pricing, variable costs per barrel, and fixed costs to remain constant, except that new distribution and general office facilities are expected to increase fixed costs by $300 million.

A. Compute the break-even number of barrels for the current year. (*Note:* For the selling price per barrel and variable costs per barrel, round to the nearest cent. Round to one decimal place in millions of barrels.)

B. Compute the anticipated break-even number of barrels for the following year. (Round to one decimal place in millions of barrels.)

EX 19-13   Break-even sales   Obj. 3

Currently, the unit selling price of a product is $1,500, the unit variable cost is $1,200, and the total fixed costs are $4,500,000. A proposal is being evaluated to increase the unit selling price to $1,600.

A. Compute the current break-even sales (units).

B. Compute the anticipated break-even sales (units), assuming that the unit selling price is increased and all costs remain constant.

EX 19-14   Break-even analysis   Obj. 3

The Junior League of Yadkinville, California, collected recipes from members and published a cookbook entitled *Food for Everyone.* The book will sell for $18 per copy. The chairwoman of the cookbook development committee estimated that the club needed to sell 2,000 books to break even on its $4,000 investment. What is the variable cost per unit assumed in the Junior League's analysis?

EX 19-15   Break-even analysis   Obj. 3

Media outlets such as **ESPN** and **FOX Sports** often have Web sites that provide in-depth coverage of news and events. Portions of these Web sites are restricted to members who pay a monthly subscription to gain access to exclusive news and commentary. These Web sites typically offer a free trial period to introduce viewers to the Web site. Assume that during a recent fiscal year, ESPN.com spent $4,200,000 on a promotional campaign for the ESPN.com Web site that offered two free months of service for new subscribers. In addition, assume the following information:

Number of months an average new customer stays with the service (including the two free months)	14 months
Revenue per month per customer subscription	$10.00
Variable cost per month per customer subscription	$5.00

Determine the number of new customer accounts needed to break even on the cost of the promotional campaign. In forming your answer, (1) treat the cost of the promotional campaign as a fixed cost, and (2) treat the revenue less variable cost per account for the subscription period as the unit contribution margin.

EXCEL TEMPLATE

REAL WORLD

EX 19-16 Break-even analysis for a service company

Obj. 3

Sprint Nextel is one of the largest digital wireless service providers in the United States. In a recent year, it had approximately 32.5 million direct subscribers (accounts) that generated revenue of $35,345 million. Costs and expenses for the year were as follows (in millions):

Cost of revenue	$20,841
Selling, general, and administrative expenses	9,765
Depreciation	2,239

Assume that 70% of the cost of revenue and 30% of the selling, general, and administrative expenses are variable to the number of direct subscribers (accounts).

A. What is Sprint Nextel's break-even number of accounts, using the data and assumptions given? Round units (accounts) and per-account amounts to one decimal place.

B. How much revenue per account would be sufficient for Sprint Nextel to break even if the number of accounts remained constant?

EX 19-17 Cost-volume-profit chart

Obj. 4

✔ B. $1,500,000

For the coming year, Loudermilk Inc. anticipates fixed costs of $600,000, a unit variable cost of $75, and a unit selling price of $125. The maximum sales within the relevant range are $2,500,000.

A. Construct a cost-volume-profit chart.

B. Estimate the break-even sales (dollars) by using the cost-volume-profit chart constructed in part (A).

C. ➤What is the main advantage of presenting the cost-volume-profit analysis in graphic form rather than equation form?

EX 19-18 Profit-volume chart

Obj. 4

✔ B. $400,000

Using the data for Loudermilk Inc. in Exercise 17, (A) determine the maximum possible operating loss, (B) compute the maximum possible operating profit, (C) construct a profit-volume chart, and (D) estimate the break-even sales (units) by using the profit-volume chart constructed in part (C).

EX 19-19 Break-even chart

Obj. 4

Name the following chart, and identify the items represented by the letters (A) through (F):

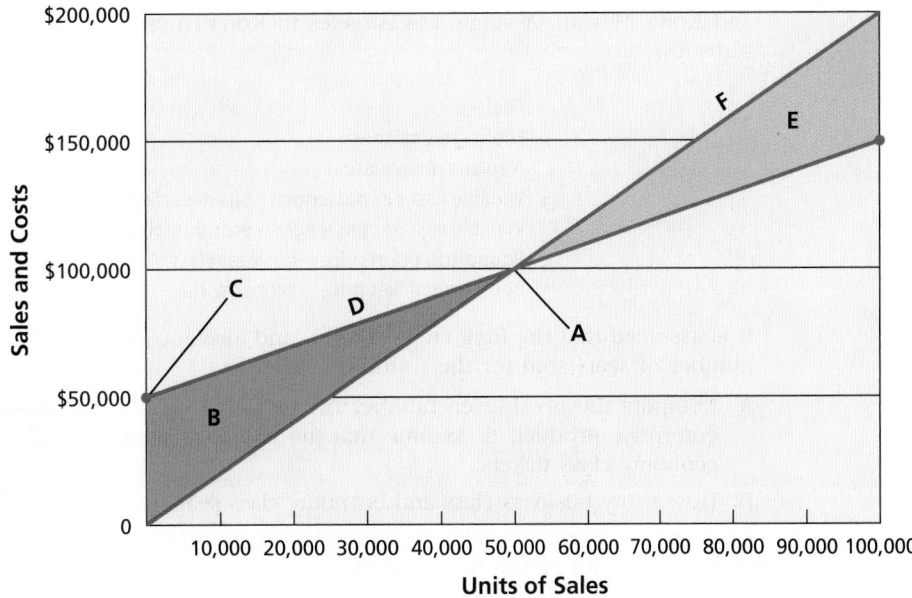

EX 19-20   Break-even chart   Obj. 4

Name the following chart, and identify the items represented by the letters (A) through (F):

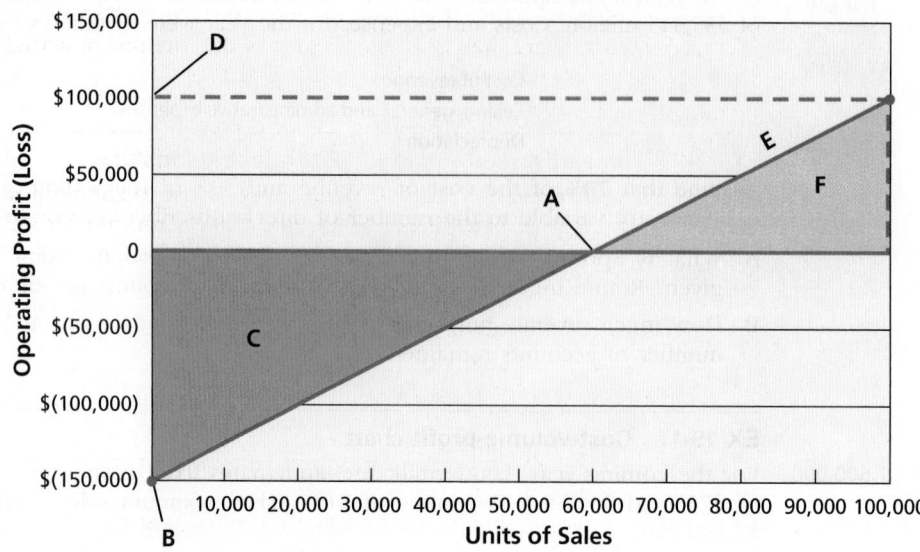

EX 19-21   Sales mix and break-even sales   Obj. 5

✔ A. 15,500 units

SHOW ME HOW

Dragon Sports Inc. manufactures and sells two products, baseball bats and baseball gloves. The fixed costs are $620,000, and the sales mix is 40% bats and 60% gloves. The unit selling price and the unit variable cost for each product are as follows:

Products	Unit Selling Price	Unit Variable Cost
Bats	$ 90	$50
Gloves	105	65

A. Compute the break-even sales (units) for the overall enterprise product, E.

B. How many units of each product, baseball bats and baseball gloves, would be sold at the break-even point?

EX 19-22   Break-even sales and sales mix for a service company   Obj. 5

✔ A. 60 seats

Zero Turbulence Airline provides air transportation services between Los Angeles, California, and Kona, Hawaii. A single Los Angeles to Kona round-trip flight has the following operating statistics:

Fuel	$7,000
Flight crew salaries	3,200
Airplane depreciation	3,480
Variable cost per passenger—business class	140
Variable cost per passenger—economy class	120
Round-trip ticket price—business class	800
Round-trip ticket price—economy class	300

It is assumed that the fuel, crew salaries, and airplane depreciation are fixed, regardless of the number of seats sold for the round-trip flight.

A. Compute the break-even number of seats sold on a single round-trip flight for the overall enterprise product, E. Assume that the overall product mix is 10% business class and 90% economy class tickets.

B. How many business class and economy class seats would be sold at the break-even point?

EX 19-23   Margin of safety

Obj. 5

A. If Canace Company, with a break-even point at $960,000 of sales, has actual sales of $1,200,000, what is the margin of safety expressed (1) in dollars and (2) as a percentage of sales?

B. If the margin of safety for Canace Company was 20%, fixed costs were $1,875,000, and variable costs were 80% of sales, what was the amount of actual sales (dollars)? (*Hint:* Determine the break-even in sales dollars first.)

EX 19-24   Break-even and margin of safety relationships

Obj. 5

At a recent staff meeting, the management of Boost Technologies Inc. was considering discontinuing the Rocket Man line of electronic games from the product line. The chief financial analyst reported the following current monthly data for the Rocket Man:

Units of sales	420,000
Break-even units	472,500
Margin of safety in units	29,400

➤ For what reason would you question the validity of these data?

EX 19-25   Operating leverage

Obj. 5

Beck Inc. and Bryant Inc. have the following operating data:

	Beck Inc.	Bryant Inc.
Sales	$1,250,000	$2,000,000
Variable costs	750,000	1,250,000
Contribution margin	$ 500,000	$ 750,000
Fixed costs	400,000	450,000
Income from operations	$ 100,000	$ 300,000

A. Compute the operating leverage for Beck Inc. and Bryant Inc.

B. How much would income from operations increase for each company if the sales of each increased by 20%?

C. ➤ Why is there a difference in the increase in income from operations for the two companies? Explain.

Problems: Series A

PR 19-1A   Classify costs

Obj. 1

Seymour Clothing Co. manufactures a variety of clothing types for distribution to several major retail chains. The following costs are incurred in the production and sale of blue jeans:

A. Shipping boxes used to ship orders

B. Consulting fee of $200,000 paid to industry specialist for marketing advice

C. Straight-line depreciation on sewing machines

D. Salesperson's salary, $10,000 plus 2% of the total sales

E. Fabric

F. Dye

G. Thread

H. Salary of designers

I. Brass buttons

J. Legal fees paid to attorneys in defense of the company in a patent infringement suit, $50,000 plus $87 per hour

K. Insurance premiums on property, plant, and equipment, $70,000 per year plus $5 per $30,000 of insured value over $8,000,000

(Continued)

L. Rental costs of warehouse, $5,000 per month plus $4 per square foot of storage used

M. Supplies

N. Leather for patches identifying the brand on individual pieces of apparel

O. Rent on plant equipment, $50,000 per year

P. Salary of production vice president

Q. Janitorial services, $2,200 per month

R. Wages of machine operators

S. Electricity costs of $0.10 per kilowatt-hour

T. Property taxes on property, plant, and equipment

Instructions

Classify the preceding costs as either fixed, variable, or mixed. Use the following tabular headings and place an X in the appropriate column. Identify each cost by letter in the cost column.

Cost	Fixed Cost	Variable Cost	Mixed Cost

PR 19-2A   Break-even sales under present and proposed conditions   Obj. 2, 3

✔ 2. B. $50

SHOW ME HOW

Darby Company, operating at full capacity, sold 500,000 units at a price of $94 per unit during the current year. Its income statement is as follows:

Sales	$ 47,000,000
Cost of goods sold	25,000,000
Gross profit	$ 22,000,000
Expenses:	
Selling expenses............. $4,000,000	
Administrative expenses...... 3,000,000	
Total expenses	7,000,000
Income from operations	$15,000,000

The division of costs between variable and fixed is as follows:

	Variable	Fixed
Cost of goods sold	70%	30%
Selling expenses	75%	25%
Administrative expenses	50%	50%

Management is considering a plant expansion program for the following year that will permit an increase of $3,760,000 in yearly sales. The expansion will increase fixed costs by $1,800,000 but will not affect the relationship between sales and variable costs.

Instructions

1. Determine the total variable costs and the total fixed costs for the current year.

2. Determine (A) the unit variable cost and (B) the unit contribution margin for the current year.

3. Compute the break-even sales (units) for the current year.

4. Compute the break-even sales (units) under the proposed program for the following year.

5. Determine the amount of sales (units) that would be necessary under the proposed program to realize the $15,000,000 of income from operations that was earned in the current year.

6. Determine the maximum income from operations possible with the expanded plant.

7. If the proposal is accepted and sales remain at the current level, what will the income or loss from operations be for the following year?

8. ▬▬▬▶ Based on the data given, would you recommend accepting the proposal? Explain.

PR 19-3A   Break-even sales and cost-volume-profit chart

Obj. 3, 4

✔ 1. 12,000 units   For the coming year, Cleves Company anticipates a unit selling price of $100, a unit variable cost of $60, and fixed costs of $480,000.

Instructions

1. Compute the anticipated break-even sales (units).

2. Compute the sales (units) required to realize a target profit of $240,000.

3. Construct a cost-volume-profit chart, assuming maximum sales of 20,000 units within the relevant range.

4. Determine the probable income (loss) from operations if sales total 16,000 units.

PR 19-4A   Break-even sales and cost-volume-profit chart

Obj. 3, 4

✔ 1. 1,000 units   Last year, Hever Inc. had sales of $500,000, based on a unit selling price of $250. The variable cost per unit was $175, and fixed costs were $75,000. The maximum sales within Hever Inc.'s relevant range are 2,500 units. Hever Inc. is considering a proposal to spend an additional $33,750 on billboard advertising during the current year in an attempt to increase sales and utilize unused capacity.

Instructions

1. Construct a cost-volume-profit chart indicating the break-even sales for last year. Verify your answer, using the break-even equation.

2. Using the cost-volume-profit chart prepared in part (1), determine (A) the income from operations for last year and (B) the maximum income from operations that could have been realized during the year. Verify your answers using the mathematical approach to cost-volume-profit analysis.

3. Construct a cost-volume-profit chart indicating the break-even sales for the current year, assuming that a noncancellable contract is signed for the additional billboard advertising. No changes are expected in the unit selling price or other costs. Verify your answer, using the break-even equation.

4. Using the cost-volume-profit chart prepared in part (3), determine (A) the income from operations if sales total 2,000 units and (B) the maximum income from operations that could be realized during the year. Verify your answers using the mathematical approach to cost-volume-profit analysis.

PR 19-5A   Sales mix and break-even sales

Obj. 5

✔ 1. 4,030 units   Data related to the expected sales of laptops and tablets for Tech Products Inc. for the current year, which is typical of recent years, are as follows:

Products	Unit Selling Price	Unit Variable Cost	Sales Mix
Laptops	$1,600	$800	40%
Tablets	850	350	60%

The estimated fixed costs for the current year are $2,498,600.

Instructions

1. Determine the estimated units of sales of the overall (total) product, E, necessary to reach the break-even point for the current year.

2. Based on the break-even sales (units) in part (1), determine the unit sales of both laptops and tablets for the current year.

3. ➤ Assume that the sales mix was 50% laptops and 50% tablets. Compare the break-even point with that in part (1). Why is it so different?

PR 19-6A   Contribution margin, break-even sales, cost-volume-profit chart,   Obj. 2, 3, 4, 5
margin of safety, and operating leverage

✔ 2. 25%

EXCEL TEMPLATE

Wolsey Industries Inc. expects to maintain the same inventories at the end of 20Y3 as at the beginning of the year. The total of all production costs for the year is therefore assumed to be equal to the cost of goods sold. With this in mind, the various department heads were asked to submit estimates of the costs for their departments during the year. A summary report of these estimates is as follows:

	Estimated Fixed Cost	Estimated Variable Cost (per unit sold)
Production costs:		
Direct materials.............................	—	$ 46
Direct labor	—	40
Factory overhead...........................	$200,000	20
Selling expenses:		
Sales salaries and commissions..............	110,000	8
Advertising.................................	40,000	—
Travel	12,000	—
Miscellaneous selling expense	7,600	1
Administrative expenses:		
Office and officers' salaries	132,000	—
Supplies....................................	10,000	4
Miscellaneous administrative expense	13,400	1
Total..	$525,000	$120

It is expected that 21,875 units will be sold at a price of $160 a unit. Maximum sales within the relevant range are 27,000 units.

Instructions

1. Prepare an estimated income statement for 20Y3.

2. What is the expected contribution margin ratio?

3. Determine the break-even sales in units and dollars.

4. Construct a cost-volume-profit chart indicating the break-even sales.

5. What is the expected margin of safety in dollars and as a percentage of sales?

6. Determine the operating leverage.

Problems: Series B

PR 19-1B   Classify costs   Obj. 1

Cromwell Furniture Company manufactures sofas for distribution to several major retail chains. The following costs are incurred in the production and sale of sofas:

A. Fabric for sofa coverings

B. Wood for framing the sofas

C. Legal fees paid to attorneys in defense of the company in a patent infringement suit, $25,000 plus $160 per hour

D. Salary of production supervisor

E. Cartons used to ship sofas

F. Rent on experimental equipment, $50 for every sofa produced

G. Straight-line depreciation on factory equipment

H. Rental costs of warehouse, $30,000 per month

I. Property taxes on property, plant, and equipment

J. Insurance premiums on property, plant, and equipment, $25,000 per year plus $25 per $25,000 of insured value over $16,000,000

K. Springs for seat cushions

L. Consulting fee of $120,000 paid to efficiency specialists

M. Electricity costs of $0.13 per kilowatt-hour

N. Salesperson's salary, $80,000 plus 4% of the selling price of each sofa sold

O. Foam rubber for cushion fillings

P. Janitorial supplies, $2,500 per month

Q. Employer's FICA taxes on controller's salary of $180,000

R. Salary of designers

S. Wages of sewing machine operators

T. Sewing supplies

Instructions

Classify the preceding costs as either fixed, variable, or mixed. Use the following tabular headings and place an X in the appropriate column. Identify each cost by letter in the cost column.

Cost	Fixed Cost	Variable Cost	Mixed Cost

PR 19-2B Break-even sales under present and proposed conditions Obj. 2, 3

✔ 3. 29,375 units

Howard Industries Inc., operating at full capacity, sold 64,000 units at a price of $45 per unit during the current year. Its income statement is as follows:

SHOW ME HOW

Sales	$2,880,000
Cost of goods sold	1,400,000
Gross profit	$1,480,000
Expenses:	
Selling expenses $400,000	
Administrative expenses........... 387,500	
Total expenses...................	787,500
Income from operations	$ 692,500

The division of costs between variable and fixed is as follows:

	Variable	Fixed
Cost of goods sold	75%	25%
Selling expenses	60%	40%
Administrative expenses	80%	20%

Management is considering a plant expansion program for the following year that will permit an increase of $900,000 in yearly sales. The expansion will increase fixed costs by $212,500 but will not affect the relationship between sales and variable costs.

Instructions

1. Determine the total fixed costs and the total variable costs for the current year.

2. Determine (A) the unit variable cost and (B) the unit contribution margin for the current year.

3. Compute the break-even sales (units) for the current year.

4. Compute the break-even sales (units) under the proposed program for the following year.

5. Determine the amount of sales (units) that would be necessary under the proposed program to realize the $692,500 of income from operations that was earned in the current year.

6. Determine the maximum income from operations possible with the expanded plant.

7. If the proposal is accepted and sales remain at the current level, what will the income or loss from operations be for the following year?

8. ━━━▶ Based on the data given, would you recommend accepting the proposal? Explain.

PR 19-3B   Break-even sales and cost-volume-profit chart

Obj. 3, 4

✔ 1. 20,000 units For the coming year, Culpeper Products Inc. anticipates a unit selling price of $150, a unit variable cost of $110, and fixed costs of $800,000.

Instructions

1. Compute the anticipated break-even sales (units).

2. Compute the sales (units) required to realize income from operations of $300,000.

3. Construct a cost-volume-profit chart, assuming maximum sales of 40,000 units within the relevant range.

4. Determine the probable income (loss) from operations if sales total 32,000 units.

PR 19-4B   Break-even sales and cost-volume-profit chart

Obj. 3, 4

✔ 1. 3,000 units Last year, Parr Co. had sales of $900,000, based on a unit selling price of $200. The variable cost per unit was $125, and fixed costs were $225,000. The maximum sales within Parr Co.'s relevant range are 7,500 units. Parr Co. is considering a proposal to spend an additional $112,500 on billboard advertising during the current year in an attempt to increase sales and utilize unused capacity.

Instructions

1. Construct a cost-volume-profit chart indicating the break-even sales for last year. Verify your answer, using the break-even equation.

2. Using the cost-volume-profit chart prepared in part (1), determine (A) the income from operations for last year and (B) the maximum income from operations that could have been realized during the year. Verify your answers using the mathematical approach to cost-volume-profit analysis.

3. Construct a cost-volume-profit chart indicating the break-even sales for the current year, assuming that a noncancellable contract is signed for the additional billboard advertising. No changes are expected in the selling price or other costs. Verify your answer, using the break-even equation.

4. Using the cost-volume-profit chart prepared in part (3), determine (A) the income from operations if sales total 6,000 units and (B) the maximum income from operations that could be realized during the year. Verify your answers using the mathematical approach to cost-volume-profit analysis.

PR 19-5B   Sales mix and break-even sales

Obj. 5

✔ 1. 4,500 units Data related to the expected sales of two types of frozen pizzas for Norfolk Frozen Foods Inc. for the current year, which is typical of recent years, are as follows:

Products	Unit Selling Price	Unit Variable Cost	Sales Mix
12" Pizza	$12	$3	30%
16" Pizza	15	4	70%

The estimated fixed costs for the current year are $46,800.

Instructions

1. Determine the estimated units of sales of the overall enterprise product, E, necessary to reach the break-even point for the current year.

2. Based on the break-even sales (units) in part (1), determine the unit sales of both the 12" pizza and 16" pizza for the current year.

3. ━━━▶ Assume that the sales mix was 50% 12" pizza and 50% 16" pizza. Compare the break-even point with that in part (1). Why is it so different?

**PR 19-6B   Contribution margin, break-even sales, cost-volume-profit chart,   Obj. 2, 3, 4, 5
margin of safety, and operating leverage**

✔ 3. 8,000 units

EXCEL TEMPLATE

Belmain Co. expects to maintain the same inventories at the end of 20Y7 as at the beginning of the year. The total of all production costs for the year is therefore assumed to be equal to the cost of goods sold. With this in mind, the various department heads were asked to submit estimates of the costs for their departments during the year. A summary report of these estimates is as follows:

	Estimated Fixed Cost	Estimated Variable Cost (per unit sold)
Production costs:		
Direct materials	—	$50.00
Direct labor.....................................	—	30.00
Factory overhead	$ 350,000	6.00
Selling expenses:		
Sales salaries and commissions..................	340,000	4.00
Advertising....................................	116,000	—
Travel	4,000	—
Miscellaneous selling expense	2,300	1.00
Administrative expenses:		
Office and officers' salaries.....................	325,000	—
Supplies.......................................	6,000	4.00
Miscellaneous administrative expense...........	8,700	1.00
Total	$1,152,000	$96.00

It is expected that 12,000 units will be sold at a price of $240 a unit. Maximum sales within the relevant range are 18,000 units.

Instructions

1. Prepare an estimated income statement for 20Y7.

2. What is the expected contribution margin ratio?

3. Determine the break-even sales in units and dollars.

4. Construct a cost-volume-profit chart indicating the break-even sales.

5. What is the expected margin of safety in dollars and as a percentage of sales? (Round to one decimal place.)

6. Determine the operating leverage.

Analysis for Decision Making

ADM-1   Break-even number of passengers for a cruise

Ocean Escape Cruise Lines has a boat with a capacity of 1,200 passengers. An eight-day ocean cruise involves the following costs:

Crew	$240,000
Fuel	60,000
Fixed operating costs	800,000

The variable costs per passenger for the eight-day cruise include the following:

Meals	$900
Variable operating costs	400

(Continued)

The price of the cruise is $2,400 per passenger.

A. Determine the break-even number of passengers for the eight-day cruise.

B. Assume 900 passengers booked the cruise. What would be the profit or loss for the cruise?

C. Assume the cruise was booked to capacity. What would be the profit or loss for the cruise?

D. ➤ If the cruise cannot book enough passengers to break even, how might the cruise line respond?

ADM-2 Break-even subscribers for a video service

Star Stream is a subscription-based video streaming service. Subscribers pay $120 per year for the service. Star Stream licenses and develops content for its subscribers. In addition, Star Stream leases servers to hold this content. These costs are not variable to the number of subscribers, but must be incurred regardless of the subscriber base. In addition, Star Stream compensates telecommunication companies for bandwidth so that Star Stream customers receive fast streaming services. These costs are variable to the number of subscribers. These and other costs are as follows:

Server lease costs per year	$ 100,000,000
Content costs per year	2,000,000,000
Fixed operating costs per year	900,000,000
Bandwidth costs per subscriber per year	15
Variable operating costs per subscriber per year	25

A. Determine the break-even number of subscribers.

B. Assume Star Stream planned to increase available programming and thus increase the annual content costs to $2,600,000,000. What impact would this change have on the break-even number of subscribers?

C. Assume the same content cost scenario in (B). How much would the annual subscription need to change in order to maintain the same break-even as in (A)?

ADM-3 Break-even number of guests for a theme park

MusicLand Theme Park has an average daily admission price of $60 per guest. The following financial data are available for analysis:

Daily operating fixed costs	$750,000
Variable daily operating cost per guest	24
Average daily concession revenue per guest	30
Average daily variable cost of concession items per guest	16

Additional operating data indicate that the park averages 24,000 daily guests during the weekdays and 40,000 average daily guests on Saturdays and Sundays.

A. Determine the break-even number of guests per day at the theme park.

B. How much profit does MusicLand earn on an average weekday?

C. How much profit does MusicLand earn on an average weekend day?

D. Determine the revised break-even if the daily fixed costs increased to $1,000,000.

E. Would the theme park still remain profitable for an average weekday under the scenario in (D)?

Take It Further

ETHICS

TIF 19-1 Ethics in Action

Edward Seymour is a financial consultant to Cornish Inc., a real estate syndicate. Cornish finances and develops commercial real estate (office buildings) projects. The completed projects are then sold as limited partnership interests to individual investors. The syndicate makes a profit on the sale of these partnership interests. Edward provides financial information for prospective investors in a document called the offering "prospectus." This document discusses the financial and legal details of the limited partnership investment.

One of the company's current projects is called JEDI 2, and has the syndicate borrowing money from a local bank to build a commercial office building. The interest rate on the loan is 6.5% for the first four years. After four years, the interest rate jumps to 15% for the remaining 20 years of the loan. The interest expense is one of the major costs of this project and significantly affects the number of renters needed for the project to break even. In the prospectus, Edward has prominently reported that the break-even occupancy for the first four years is 65%. This is the amount of office space that must be leased to cover the interest and general upkeep costs during the first four years. The 65% break-even point is very low compared to similar projects and thus communicates a low risk to potential investors. Edward uses the 65% break-even rate as a major marketing tool in selling the limited partnership interests. Buried in the fine print of the prospectus is additional information that would allow an astute investor to determine that the break-even occupancy jumps to 95% after the fourth year when the interest rate on the loan increases to 15%. Edward believes prospective investors are adequately informed of the investment's risk.

➤ Is Edward behaving ethically? Explain your answer.

REAL WORLD

TIF 19-2 Team Activity

Break-even analysis is an important tool for managing any business, including colleges and universities. In a group, identify three areas where break-even analysis might be used at your college or university. For each area, identify the revenues, variable costs, and fixed costs.

TIF 19-3 Communication

Sun Airlines is a commercial airline that targets business and non-business travelers. In recent months, the airline has been unprofitable. The company has break-even sales volume of 75% of capacity, which is significantly higher than the industry average of 65%. Sun's CEO, Neil Armstrong, is concerned about the recent string of losses and is considering a strategic plan that could reduce the break-even sales volume by increasing ticket prices. He has asked for your help in evaluating this plan.

➤ Write a brief memo to Neil Armstrong evaluating this strategy.

Concepts and Principles

Chapter 15 *Introduction to Managerial Accounting*

Developing Information

COST SYSTEMS	COST BEHAVIOR
Chapter 16 *Job Order Costing*	**Chapter 19** *Cost-Volume-Profit Analysis*
Chapter 17 *Process Cost Systems*	
Chapter 18 *Activity-Based Costing*	

Decision Making

EVALUATING PERFORMANCE	COMPARING ALTERNATIVES
Chapter 20 *Variable Costing for Management Analysis*	**Chapter 23** *Evaluating Decentralized Operations*
Chapter 21 *Budgeting*	**Chapter 24** *Differential Analysis and Product Pricing*
Chapter 22 *Evaluating Variances from Standard Costs*	**Chapter 25** *Capital Investment Analysis*
	Chapter 26 *Lean Manufacturing*

Adobe Systems Incorporated

Assume that you have three different options for a summer job. How would you evaluate these options? Naturally there are many things to consider, including how much you could earn from each job.

Determining how much you could earn from each job may not be as simple as comparing the wage rate per hour. For example, a job as an office clerk at a local company pays $8 per hour. A job delivering pizza pays $10 per hour (including estimated tips), although you must use your own transportation. Another job working in a beach resort over 500 miles away from your home pays $8 per hour. All three jobs offer 40 hours per week for the whole summer. If these options were ranked according to their pay per hour, the pizza delivery job would be the most attractive. However, the costs associated with each job must also be evaluated. For example, the office job may require that you pay for downtown parking and purchase office clothes. The pizza delivery job will require you to pay for gas and maintenance for your car. The resort job will require you to move to the resort city and incur additional living costs. Only by considering the costs for each job will you be able to determine which job will provide you with the most income.

Just as you should evaluate the relative income of various choices, a business also evaluates the income earned from its choices. Important choices include the products offered and the geographical regions to be served.

A company will often evaluate the profitability of products and regions. For example, **Adobe Systems Incorporated**, one of the largest software companies in the world, determines the income earned from its various product lines, such as Acrobat®, Photoshop®, Premiere®, and Dreamweaver® software. Adobe uses this information to establish product line pricing, as well as sales, support, and development effort. Likewise, Adobe evaluates the income earned in the geographic regions it serves, such as the United States, Europe, and Asia. Again, such information aids management in managing revenue and expenses within the regions.

In this chapter, how businesses measure profitability using absorption costing and variable costing is discussed. After illustrating and comparing these concepts, how businesses use them for controlling costs, pricing products, planning production, analyzing market segments, and analyzing contribution margins is described and illustrated.

Variable Costing for Management Analysis

Income Under Absorption and Variable Costing	**Using Absorption and Variable Costing**	**Variable Costing for Service Businesses**
■ Absorption Costing (Obj. 1)	■ Controlling Costs (Obj. 3)	■ Reporting Income (Obj. 6)
■ Variable Costing (Obj. 1)	■ Pricing Products (Obj. 3)	■ Analyzing Segments (Obj. 6)
■ Effects of Inventory (Obj. 1)	■ Planning Production (Obj. 3)	■ Analyzing Contribution Margin (Obj. 6)
■ Analyzing Income (Obj. 2)	■ Analyzing Market Segments (Obj. 4)	
	■ Contribution Margin Analysis (Obj. 5)	

Learning Objectives

Obj. 1 Describe and illustrate reporting income from operations under absorption and variable costing.

Obj. 2 Describe and illustrate the effects of absorption and variable costing on analyzing income from operations.

Obj. 3 Describe management's use of absorption and variable costing.

Obj. 4 Use variable costing for analyzing market segments, including product, territories, and salespersons segments.

Obj. 5 Use variable costing for analyzing and explaining changes in contribution margin as a result of quantity and price factors.

Obj. 6 Describe and illustrate contribution margin analysis for service businesses.

Analysis for Decision Making

Describe and illustrate the use of segment analysis and earnings before interest, taxes, depreciation, and amortization (EBITDA) in evaluating a company's performance.

Objective 1
Describe and illustrate reporting income from operations under absorption and variable costing.

Income from Operations: Absorption and Variable Costing

Income from operations is one of the most important items reported by a company. Depending on the decision-making needs of management, income from operations can be determined using absorption or variable costing.

Absorption Costing

Absorption costing is required under generally accepted accounting principles for financial statements distributed to external users. Under absorption costing, the cost of goods manufactured includes direct materials, direct labor, and factory overhead costs. Both fixed and variable factory costs are included as part of factory overhead. In the financial statements, these costs are included in the cost of goods sold (income statement) and inventory (balance sheet).

The reporting of income from operations under absorption costing is as follows:

Sales	$XXX
Cost of goods sold	XXX
Gross profit	$XXX
Selling and administrative expenses	XXX
Income from operations	$XXX

The income statements illustrated in the preceding chapters of this text have used absorption costing.

Adobe Systems uses absorption costing for its annual financial statements filed with the Securities and Exchange Commission.

Link to Adobe Systems

Variable Costing

For internal use in decision making, managers often use variable costing. Under **variable costing**, sometimes called *direct costing*, the cost of goods manufactured includes only variable manufacturing costs. Thus, the cost of goods manufactured consists of the following:

■ Direct materials
■ Direct labor
■ *Variable* factory overhead

Under variable costing, *fixed* factory overhead costs are not a part of the cost of goods manufactured. Instead, fixed factory overhead costs are treated as a period expense. Exhibit 1 illustrates the differences between absorption costing and variable costing.

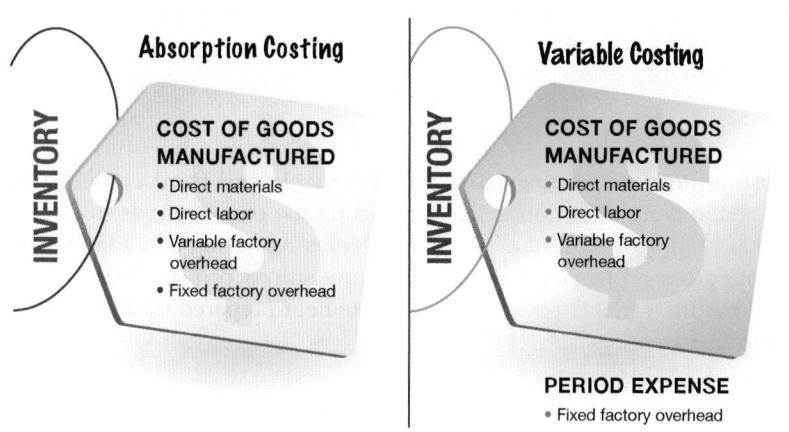

Exhibit 1
Absorption Costing Versus Variable Costing

The reporting of income from operations under variable costing is as follows:

Sales..		$XXX
Variable cost of goods sold		XXX
Manufacturing margin		$XXX
Variable selling and administrative expenses		XXX
Contribution margin.....................................		$XXX
Fixed costs:		
Fixed manufacturing costs...........................	$XXX	
Fixed selling and administrative expenses	XXX	
Total fixed costs.....................................		XXX
Income from operations		$XXX

Manufacturing margin is the excess of sales over variable cost of goods sold:

Manufacturing Margin = Sales – Variable Cost of Goods Sold

Variable cost of goods sold consists of direct materials, direct labor, and variable factory overhead for the units sold. **Contribution margin** is the excess of manufacturing margin over variable selling and administrative expenses:

Contribution Margin = Manufacturing Margin – Variable Selling and Administrative Expenses

Subtracting fixed costs from contribution margin yields *income from operations*:

Income from Operations = Contribution Margin – Fixed Costs

To illustrate variable costing and absorption costing, assume that Martinez Co. manufactures 15,000 units, which are sold at a price of $50. The related costs and expenses for Martinez are as follows:

	Total Cost	Number of Units	Unit Cost
Manufacturing costs:			
Variable...	$375,000	15,000	$25
Fixed	150,000	15,000	10
Total	$525,000		$35
Selling and administrative expenses:			
Variable...	$ 75,000	15,000	$ 5
Fixed	50,000		
Total	$125,000		

Exhibit 2 shows the absorption costing income statement prepared for Martinez. The computations are shown in parentheses.

Exhibit 2
Absorption Costing Income Statement

Sales (15,000 × $50)...	$750,000
Cost of goods sold (15,000 × $35)...	525,000
Gross profit...	$225,000
Selling and administrative expenses ($75,000 + $50,000).............................	125,000
Income from operations	$100,000

Absorption costing does not distinguish between variable and fixed costs. All manufacturing costs are included in the cost of goods sold. Deducting the cost of goods sold of $525,000 from sales of $750,000 yields gross profit of $225,000. Deducting selling and administrative expenses of $125,000 from gross profit yields income from operations of $100,000.

Exhibit 3 shows the variable costing income statement prepared for Martinez. The computations are shown in parentheses.

Exhibit 3
Variable Costing Income Statement

Sales (15,000 × $50)		$750,000
Variable cost of goods sold (15,000 × $25)...............................		375,000
Manufacturing margin...		$375,000
Variable selling and administrative expenses (15,000 × $5)............		75,000
Contribution margin...		$300,000
Fixed costs:		
Fixed manufacturing costs	$150,000	
Fixed selling and administrative expenses	50,000	
Total fixed costs		200,000
Income from operations		$100,000

note:
The variable costing income statement includes only variable manufacturing costs in the cost of goods sold.

Variable costing income reports variable costs separately from fixed costs. Deducting the variable cost of goods sold of $375,000 from sales of $750,000 yields the manufacturing margin of $375,000. Deducting variable selling and administrative expenses of $75,000 from the manufacturing margin yields the contribution margin of $300,000. Deducting fixed costs of $200,000 from the contribution margin yields income from operations of $100,000.

The contribution margin reported in Exhibit 3 is the same as that used in Chapter 19. That is, the contribution margin is sales less variable costs and expenses. The only difference is that Exhibit 3 reports manufacturing margin before deducting variable selling and administrative expenses.

Effects of Inventory

Income from operations will vary between absorption and variable costing, depending upon whether there is any change in inventory. The effects of inventory on income from operations are illustrated for the following:

- Units manufactured equal units sold, resulting in no change in inventory.
- Units manufactured exceed units sold, resulting in an increase in inventory.
- Units manufactured are less than units sold, resulting in a decrease in inventory.

Units Manufactured Equal Units Sold In Exhibits 2 and 3, Martinez manufactured and sold 15,000 units. Thus, the variable and absorption costing income statements reported the same income from operations of $100,000. When the number of units manufactured equals the number of units sold, income from operations will be the same under both methods.

Units Manufactured Exceed Units Sold When units manufactured exceed the units sold, the variable costing income from operations will be *less* than it is for absorption costing. To illustrate, assume that only 12,000 units of the 15,000 units Martinez manufactured were sold.

Exhibit 4 shows the absorption and variable costing income statements when units manufactured exceed units sold.

Variable Costing Income Statement		
Sales (12,000 × $50)		$600,000
Variable cost of goods sold:		
Variable cost of goods manufactured (15,000 × $25)	$ 375,000	
Ending inventory (3,000 × $25)	(75,000)	
Total variable cost of goods sold		300,000
Manufacturing margin		$300,000
Variable selling and administrative expenses (12,000 × $5)		60,000
Contribution margin		$240,000
Fixed costs:		
Fixed manufacturing costs	$ 150,000	
Fixed selling and administrative expenses	50,000	
Total fixed costs		200,000
Income from operations		$ 40,000
Absorption Costing Income Statement		
Sales (12,000 × $50)		$600,000
Cost of goods sold:		
Cost of goods manufactured (15,000 × $35)	$ 525,000	
Ending inventory (3,000 × $35)	(105,000)	
Total cost of goods sold		420,000
Gross profit		$180,000
Selling and administrative expenses [(12,000 × $5) + $50,000]		110,000
Income from operations		$ 70,000

Exhibit 4
Units Manufactured Exceed Units Sold

Exhibit 4 shows a $30,000 ($70,000 − $40,000) difference in income from operations. This difference is due to the fixed manufacturing costs. All of the $150,000 of fixed manufacturing costs is included as a period expense in the variable costing statement. However, the 3,000 units of ending inventory in the absorption costing statement include $30,000 (3,000 units × $10) of fixed manufacturing costs. By being included in inventory, this $30,000 is thus excluded from the cost of goods sold. Thus, the absorption costing income from operations is $30,000 higher than the income from operations for variable costing.

Units Manufactured Less Than Units Sold When the units manufactured are less than the number of units sold, the variable costing income from operations will be *greater* than that of absorption costing. To illustrate, assume that beginning inventory, units manufactured, and units sold for Martinez were as follows:

Beginning inventory......................................	5,000 units
Units manufactured during current period	10,000 units
Units sold during current period at $50 per unit	15,000 units

Martinez's manufacturing costs and selling and administrative expenses are as follows:

	Total Cost	Number of Units	Unit Cost
Beginning inventory (5,000 units):			
Manufacturing costs:			
Variable	$125,000	5,000	$25
Fixed..	50,000	5,000	10
Total	$175,000		$35
Current period (10,000 units):			
Manufacturing costs:			
Variable	$250,000	10,000	$25
Fixed..	150,000	10,000	15
Total	$400,000		$40
Selling and administrative expenses:			
Variable	$ 75,000	15,000	$ 5
Fixed..	50,000		
Total	$125,000		

Exhibit 5 shows the absorption and variable costing income statements for Martinez when units manufactured are less than units sold.

Exhibit 5 Units Manufactured Are Less Than Units Sold	**Absorption Costing Income Statement**		
	Sales (15,000 × $50)		$750,000
	Cost of goods sold:		
	Beginning inventory (5,000 × $35)...	$175,000	
	Cost of goods manufactured (10,000 × $40).....................................	400,000	
	Total cost of goods sold		575,000
	Gross profit..		$175,000
	Selling and administrative expenses ($75,000 + $50,000)		125,000
	Income from operations		$ 50,000
	Variable Costing Income Statement		
	Sales (15,000 × $50)		$750,000
	Variable cost of goods sold:		
	Beginning inventory (5,000 × $25)...	$125,000	
	Variable cost of goods manufactured (10,000 × $25).............................	250,000	
	Total variable cost of goods sold...		375,000
	Manufacturing margin...		$375,000
	Variable selling and administrative expenses (15,000 × $5)........................		75,000
	Contribution margin...		$300,000
	Fixed costs:		
	Fixed manufacturing costs	$150,000	
	Fixed selling and administrative expenses......................................	50,000	
	Total fixed costs...		200,000
	Income from operations		$100,000

Exhibit 5 shows a $50,000 ($100,000 − $50,000) difference in income from operations. This difference is due to the fixed manufacturing costs. The beginning inventory under absorption costing includes $50,000 (5,000 units × $10) of fixed manufacturing costs incurred in the preceding period. By being included in the beginning inventory, this $50,000 is included in the cost of goods sold for the current period. Under variable costing, this $50,000 was included as an expense in an income statement of a prior period. Thus, the variable costing income from operations is $50,000 higher than the income from operations for absorption costing.

The preceding effects of inventory on income from operations reported under absorption and variable costing are summarized in Exhibit 6.

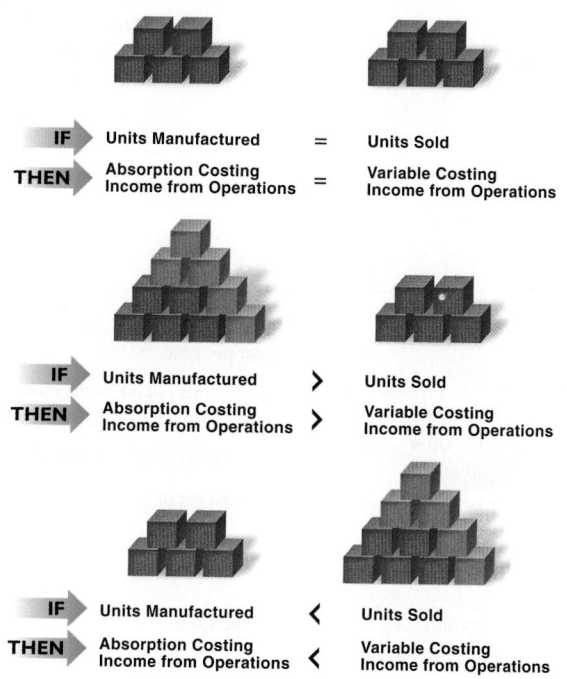

IF Units Manufactured = Units Sold	**Exhibit 6**
THEN Absorption Costing Income from Operations = Variable Costing Income from Operations	Effects of Inventory on Absorption and Variable Costing

IF Units Manufactured > Units Sold

THEN Absorption Costing Income from Operations > Variable Costing Income from Operations

IF Units Manufactured < Units Sold

THEN Absorption Costing Income from Operations < Variable Costing Income from Operations

Adobe Systems outsources its purchasing, production, inventory, and fulfillment activities to third parties in the United States.   *Link to*
Adobe Systems

Source: Adobe Systems Incorporated, Form 10-K for the Fiscal Year Ended November 27, 2015.

Check Up Corner 20-1   Absorption and Variable Costing Income Statements

Walsh Company manufactured 30,000 units during July. There were no units in inventory on July 1. Information on costs and expenses for July is as follows:

	Total Cost	Number of Units	Unit Cost
Manufacturing costs:			
Variable	$660,000	30,000	$22.00
Fixed	300,000	30,000	10.00
Total...	$960,000		
Selling and administrative expenses:			
Variable	$200,000		
Fixed	160,000		
Total...	$360,000		

If the company sells 25,000 units at $75 (units manufactured exceed units sold), prepare an income statement for July using:

A. Absorption costing
B. Variable costing

Solution:

A.

Under absorption costing, both fixed and variable manufacturing costs are included in cost of goods sold and in inventory.

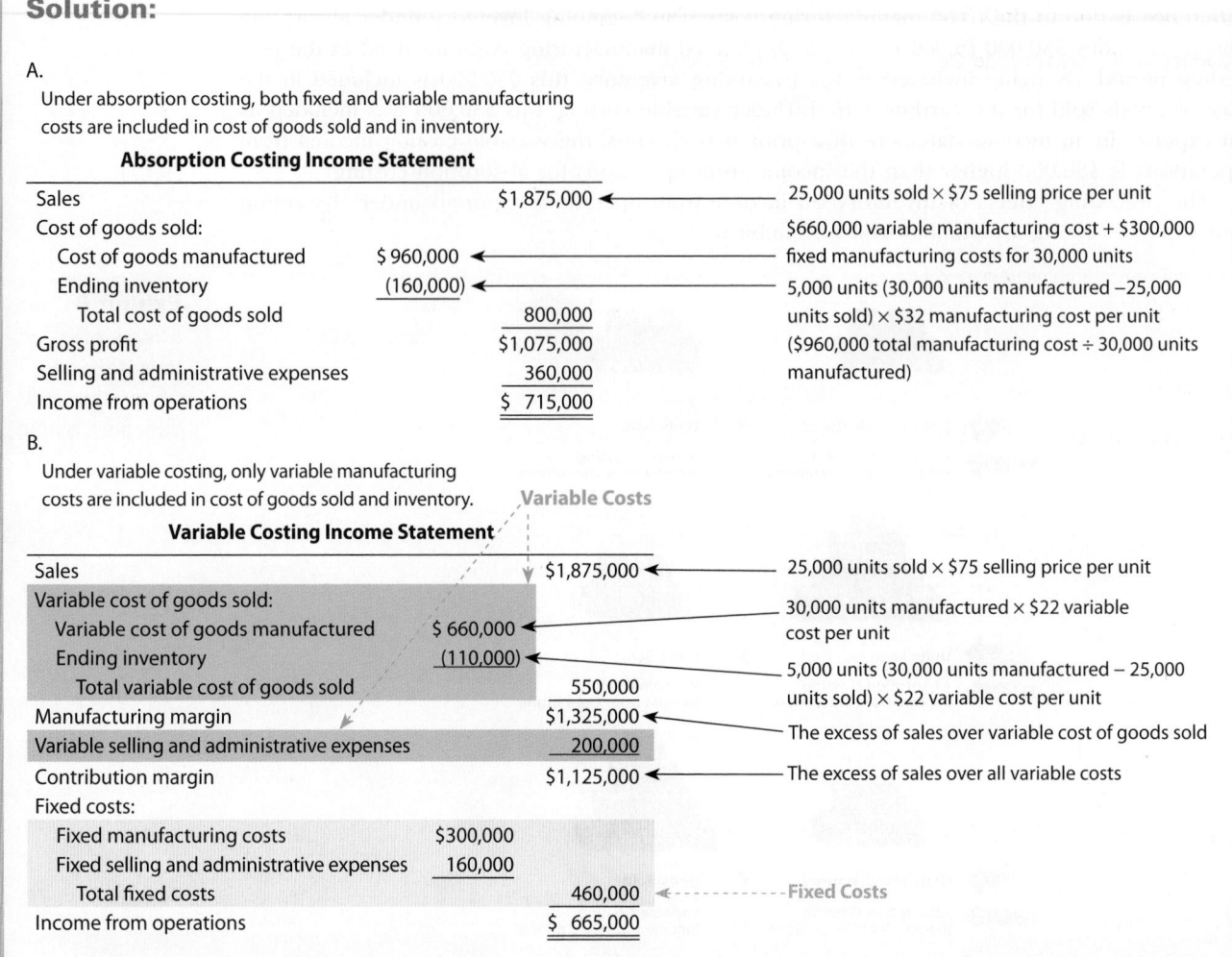

Absorption Costing Income Statement

Sales		$1,875,000
Cost of goods sold:		
Cost of goods manufactured	$ 960,000	
Ending inventory	(160,000)	
Total cost of goods sold		800,000
Gross profit		$1,075,000
Selling and administrative expenses		360,000
Income from operations		$ 715,000

25,000 units sold × $75 selling price per unit

$660,000 variable manufacturing cost + $300,000 fixed manufacturing costs for 30,000 units

5,000 units (30,000 units manufactured −25,000 units sold) × $32 manufacturing cost per unit ($960,000 total manufacturing cost ÷ 30,000 units manufactured)

B.

Under variable costing, only variable manufacturing costs are included in cost of goods sold and inventory.

Variable Costs

Variable Costing Income Statement

Sales		$1,875,000
Variable cost of goods sold:		
Variable cost of goods manufactured	$ 660,000	
Ending inventory	(110,000)	
Total variable cost of goods sold		550,000
Manufacturing margin		$1,325,000
Variable selling and administrative expenses		200,000
Contribution margin		$1,125,000
Fixed costs:		
Fixed manufacturing costs	$300,000	
Fixed selling and administrative expenses	160,000	
Total fixed costs		460,000
Income from operations		$ 665,000

25,000 units sold × $75 selling price per unit

30,000 units manufactured × $22 variable cost per unit

5,000 units (30,000 units manufactured − 25,000 units sold) × $22 variable cost per unit

The excess of sales over variable cost of goods sold

The excess of sales over all variable costs

Fixed Costs

Check Up Corner

Objective 2

Describe and illustrate the effects of absorption and variable costing on analyzing income from operations.

Analyzing Income Using Absorption and Variable Costing

Whenever the units manufactured differ from the units sold, finished goods inventory is affected. When the units manufactured are greater than the units sold, finished goods inventory increases. Under absorption costing, a portion of this increase is related to the allocation of fixed manufacturing overhead to ending inventory. As a result, increases or decreases in income from operations can be due to changes in inventory levels. In analyzing income from operations, such increases and decreases could be misinterpreted as operating efficiencies or inefficiencies.

To illustrate, assume that Frand Manufacturing Company has no beginning inventory and sales are estimated to be 20,000 units at $75 per unit. Also, assume that sales will not change if more than 20,000 units are manufactured.

Frand's management is evaluating whether to manufacture 20,000 units (Proposal 1) or 25,000 units (Proposal 2). The costs and expenses related to each proposal follow.

Proposal 1: 20,000 Units to Be Manufactured and Sold

	Total Cost	Number of Units	Unit Cost
Manufacturing costs:			
Variable...	$ 700,000	20,000	$35
Fixed	400,000	20,000	20*
Total	$1,100,000		$55
Selling and administrative expenses:			
Variable...	$ 100,000	20,000	$ 5
Fixed	100,000		
Total	$ 200,000		

*$400,000 ÷ 20,000 units

Proposal 2: 25,000 Units to Be Manufactured and 20,000 Units to Be Sold

	Total Cost	Number of Units	Unit Cost
Manufacturing costs:			
Variable...	$ 875,000	25,000	$35
Fixed	400,000	25,000	16*
Total	$1,275,000		$51
Selling and administrative expenses:			
Variable...	$ 100,000	20,000	$ 5
Fixed	100,000		
Total	$ 200,000		

*$400,000 ÷ 25,000 units

The absorption costing income statements for each proposal are shown in Exhibit 7.

Frand Manufacturing Company **Absorption Costing Income Statements**		
	Proposal 1 **20,000 Units** **Manufactured**	**Proposal 2** **25,000 Units** **Manufactured**
Sales (20,000 units × $75)...	$1,500,000	$1,500,000
Cost of goods sold:		
Cost of goods manufactured:		
(20,000 units × $55)	$1,100,000	
(25,000 units × $51)		$1,275,000
Ending inventory:		
(5,000 units × $51)...		(255,000)
Total cost of goods sold	$1,100,000	$1,020,000
Gross profit..	$ 400,000	$ 480,000
Selling and administrative expenses:		
($100,000 + $100,000)...	200,000	200,000
Income from operations	$ 200,000	$ 280,000

Exhibit 7
Absorption Costing Income Statements for Two Production Levels

Exhibit 7 shows that if Frand manufactures 25,000 units, sells 20,000 units, and adds the 5,000 units to finished goods inventory (Proposal 2), income from operations will be $280,000. In contrast, if Frand manufactures and sells 20,000 units (Proposal 1), income from operations will be $200,000. In other words, Frand can increase income from operations by $80,000 ($280,000 − $200,000) by simply increasing finished goods inventory by 5,000 units.

The $80,000 increase in income from operations under Proposal 2 is caused by the allocation of the fixed manufacturing costs of $400,000 over a greater number of units manufactured. Specifically, an increase in production from 20,000 units to 25,000 units means that the fixed manufacturing cost per unit decreases from $20 ($400,000 ÷ 20,000 units) to $16 ($400,000 ÷ 25,000 units). Thus, the cost of goods sold when 25,000 units are manufactured is $4 per unit less, or $80,000 less in total (20,000 units sold × $4). Since the cost of goods sold is less, income from operations is $80,000 more when 25,000 units rather than 20,000 units are manufactured.

Managers should be careful in analyzing income from operations under absorption costing when finished goods inventory changes. Increases in income from operations may be created by simply increasing finished goods inventory. Thus, managers could misinterpret such increases (or decreases) in income from operations as due to changes in sales volume, prices, or costs.

Link to
Adobe Systems

In a recent absorption costing income statement, **Adobe Systems** reported (in millions) total revenue of $4,147, cost of revenue of $622, gross revenue of $3,525, operating expenses of $3,112, and operating income of $413.

Under variable costing, income from operations is $200,000, regardless of whether 20,000 units or 25,000 units are manufactured. This is because no fixed manufacturing costs are allocated to the units manufactured. Instead, all fixed manufacturing costs are treated as a period expense.

To illustrate, Exhibit 8 shows the variable costing income statements for Frand for the production of 20,000 units, 25,000 units, and 30,000 units. In each case, the income from operations is $200,000.

Exhibit 8
Variable
Costing Income
Statements for
Three Production
Levels

	Frand Manufacturing Company Variable Costing Income Statements		
	20,000 Units Manufactured	**25,000 Units Manufactured**	**30,000 Units Manufactured**
Sales (20,000 units × $75).................	$1,500,000	$1,500,000	$1,500,000
Variable cost of goods sold:			
Variable cost of goods manufactured:			
(20,000 units × $35)	$ 700,000		
(25,000 units × $35)		$ 875,000	
(30,000 units × $35)			$1,050,000
Ending inventory:			
(0 units × $35).......................	0		
(5,000 units × $35)...................		(175,000)	
(10,000 units × $35)			(350,000)
Total variable cost of goods sold.........	$ 700,000	$ 700,000	$ 700,000
Manufacturing margin.....................	$ 800,000	$ 800,000	$ 800,000
Variable selling and administrative			
expenses	100,000	100,000	100,000
Contribution margin.......................	$ 700,000	$ 700,000	$ 700,000
Fixed costs:			
Fixed manufacturing costs	$ 400,000	$ 400,000	$ 400,000
Fixed selling and administrative			
expenses	100,000	100,000	100,000
Total fixed costs.........................	$ 500,000	$ 500,000	$ 500,000
Income from operations	$ 200,000	$ 200,000	$ 200,000

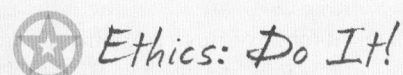 *Ethics: Do It!*

Taking an "Absorption Hit"

Aligning production to demand is a critical decision in business. Managers must not allow the temporary benefits of excess production through higher absorption of fixed costs to guide their decisions. Likewise, if demand falls, production should be dropped and inventory liquidated to match the new demand level, even though earnings will be penalized. The following interchange provides an example of an appropriate response to lowered demand for H.J. Heinz Company:

Analyst's question: *It seems.…that you're guiding to a little bit of a drop in performance between 3Q (third Quarter) and 4Q (fourth Quarter).…if so, maybe you could walk us through some of the drivers of that relative softness.*

Heinz executive's response: *No, I think, frankly, we're really pleased with the performance in the business.… We're also aggressively taking out inventory in the fourth quarter. And as you know, as you reduce inventory, you take an absorption hit. You're pulling basically fixed costs off the balance sheet into the P&L and there's a hit associated with that, but we think that's the right thing to do, to pull inventory out and to drive cash flow. So now, we feel very good about the business and feel very good about the fact that we're taking it to the middle of the range and taking up the bottom end of our guidance.*

Management operating with integrity will seek the tangible benefits of reducing inventory, even though there may be an adverse impact on published financial statements caused by absorption costing.

Source of question and response from http://seekingalpha.com/ article/375151-h-j-heinz-management-discusses-q3-2012-results-earnings-call-transcript?page=6&p=qanda. Accessed February 2012.

As shown, absorption costing may encourage managers to produce inventory. This is because producing inventory absorbs fixed manufacturing costs, which increases income from operations. However, producing inventory leads to higher handling, storage, financing, and obsolescence costs. For this reason, many accountants believe that variable costing should be used by management for evaluating operating performance.

Check Up Corner 20-2	Absorption and Variable Costing with Different Levels of Production

Third Street Manufacturing Company has no beginning inventory, and sales are estimated to be 30,000 units at $100 per unit. Third Street's management is evaluating whether to manufacture 30,000 units (Proposal 1) or 40,000 units (Proposal 2). Sales will not change if more than 30,000 units are manufactured. The costs and expenses for each proposal follow:

	Proposal 1: 30,000 Units Manufactured			**Proposal 2:** 40,000 Units Manufactured		
	Total Cost	Number of Units	Unit Cost	Total Cost	Number of Units	Unit Cost
Manufacturing costs:						
Variable	$1,200,000	30,000	$40	$1,600,000	40,000	$40
Fixed	600,000	30,000	$20	600,000	40,000	$15
Total................................	$1,800,000			$2,200,000		
Selling and administrative expenses:						
Variable	$ 210,000	30,000	$ 7	$ 210,000	30,000	$ 7
Fixed	140,000			140,000		
Total................................	$ 350,000			$ 350,000		

A. Prepare an estimated income statement, comparing operating results if 30,000 and 40,000 units are manufactured in (1) the absorption costing format and (2) the variable costing format.
B. What is the reason for the difference in income from operations reported for the two levels of production by the absorption costing income statement?

Solution:

A. (1)

Absorption Costing Income Statements

	Proposal 1: 30,000 Units Manufactured	Proposal 2: 40,000 Units Manufactured	
Sales (30,000 units × $100)	$3,000,000	$3,000,000	
Cost of goods sold:			
Cost of goods manufactured	$1,800,000	$2,200,000	(30,000 units produced × $40 variable manufacturing cost per unit) + $600,000 fixed cost
Ending inventory	—	(550,000)	(40,000 units produced × $40 variable manufacturing cost per unit) + $600,000 fixed cost
Total cost of goods sold	$1,800,000	$1,650,000	10,000 units (40,000 produced – 30,000 sold) × $55 per unit ($2,200,000 ÷ 40,000 units)
Gross profit	$1,200,000	$1,350,000	
Selling and administrative expenses	350,000	350,000	(30,000 units sold × $7 variable selling cost per unit) + $140,000
Income from operations	$ 850,000	$1,000,000	

(2)

Variable Costing Income Statements

	Proposal 1: 30,000 Units Manufactured	Proposal 2: 40,000 Units Manufactured	
Sales (30,000 units × $100)	$3,000,000	$3,000,000	
Variable cost of goods sold:			
Variable cost of goods manufactured	$1,200,000	$1,600,000	30,000 units produced × $40 variable manufacturing cost per unit
Ending inventory	—	(400,000)	40,000 units produced × $40 variable manufacturing cost per unit
Total variable cost of goods sold	$1,200,000	$1,200,000	10,000 units (40,000 produced – 30,000 sold) × $40 variable cost per unit
Manufacturing margin	$1,800,000	$1,800,000	
Variable selling and administrative expenses	210,000	210,000	30,000 units sold × $7 variable selling cost per unit
Contribution margin	$1,590,000	$1,590,000	
Fixed costs:			
Fixed manufacturing costs	$ 600,000	$ 600,000	◄---- Fixed Costs
Fixed selling and administrative expenses	140,000	140,000	
Total fixed costs	$ 740,000	$ 740,000	
Income from operations	$ 850,000	$ 850,000	

B. The difference (in A.) is caused by including $150,000 fixed manufacturing costs (10,000 units × $15 fixed manufacturing cost per unit) in the ending inventory, which decreases the cost of goods sold and increases the income from operations by $150,000.

Check Up Corner

Objective 3

Describe management's use of absorption and variable costing.

Using Absorption and Variable Costing

Each decision-making situation should be carefully analyzed in deciding whether absorption or variable costing reporting would be more useful. As a basis for discussion, the use of absorption and variable costing in the following decision-making situations is described:

- Controlling costs
- Pricing products
- Planning production
- Analyzing contribution margins
- Analyzing market segments

The role of accounting reports in these decision-making situations is shown in Exhibit 9.

Absorption Costing and Variable Costing

Accounting Report

Management

Decisions

Controlling Costs Pricing Products Planning Production Analyzing Contribution Margins Analyzing Market Segments

Actual vs. Planned

Exhibit 9
Accounting Reports and Management Decisions

Controlling Costs

All costs are controllable in the long run by someone within a business. However, not all costs are controllable at the same level of management. For example, plant supervisors control the use of direct materials in their departments. They have no control, though, over insurance costs related to the property, plant, and equipment.

For a level of management, **controllable costs** are costs that can be influenced (increased or decreased) by management at that level. **Noncontrollable costs** are costs that another level of management controls. This distinction is useful for reporting costs to those responsible for their control.

Variable manufacturing costs are controlled by operating management. In contrast, fixed manufacturing overhead costs such as the salaries of production supervisors are normally controlled at a higher level of management. Likewise, control of the variable and fixed operating expenses usually involves different levels of management. Since fixed costs and expenses are reported separately under variable costing, variable costing reports are normally more useful than absorption costing reports for controlling costs.

Pricing Products

Many factors enter into determining the selling price of a product. However, the cost of making the product is significant in all pricing decisions.

In the short run, fixed costs cannot be avoided. Thus, the selling price of a product should at least be equal to the variable costs of making and selling it. Any price above this minimum selling price contributes to covering fixed costs and generating income. Since variable costing reports variable and fixed costs and expenses separately, it is often more useful than absorption costing for setting short-run prices.

In the long run, a company must set its selling price high enough to cover all costs and expenses (variable and fixed) and generate income. Since absorption costing includes fixed and variable costs in the cost of manufacturing a product, absorption costing is often more useful than variable costing for setting long-term prices.

Planning Production

In the short run, planning production is limited to existing capacity. In many cases, operating decisions must be made quickly before opportunities are lost.

To illustrate, a company with seasonal demand for its products may have an opportunity to obtain an off-season order that will not interfere with its current production schedule. The relevant factors for such a short-run decision are the additional revenues and the additional variable costs associated with the order. If the revenues from the order exceed the related variable costs, the order will increase contribution margin and, thus, increase the company's income from operations. Since variable costing reports contribution margin, it is often more useful than absorption costing in such cases.

In the long run, planning production can include expanding existing capacity. Thus, when analyzing and evaluating long-run sales and operating decisions, absorption costing, which considers fixed and variable costs, is often more useful.

Analyzing Contribution Margins

For planning and control purposes, managers often compare planned and actual contribution margins. For example, an increase in the price of fuel could have a significant impact on the planned contribution margins of an airline. The use of variable costing as a basis for such analyses is described and illustrated later in this chapter.

Analyzing Market Segments

Market analysis determines the profit contributed by the market segments of a company. A **market segment** is a portion of a company that can be analyzed using sales, costs, and expenses to determine its profitability. Examples of market segments include sales territories, products, salespersons, and customers. Variable costing as an aid in decision making regarding market segments is discussed next.

Analyzing Market Segments

Companies can report income for internal decision making using either absorption or variable costing. Absorption costing is often used for long-term analysis of market segments. Variable costing is often used for short-term analysis of market segments. In this section, segment profitability reporting using variable costing is described and illustrated.

Most companies prepare variable costing reports for each product. These reports are often used for product pricing and deciding whether to discontinue a product. In addition, variable costing reports may be prepared for geographic areas, customers, distribution channels, or salespersons. A distribution channel is the method for selling a product to a customer.

To illustrate analysis of market segments using variable costing, the following data for the month ending March 31 for Camelot Fragrance Company are used:

Camelot Fragrance Company
Sales and Production Data
For the Month Ended March 31

	Northern Territory	Southern Territory	Total
Sales:			
Gwenevere	$60,000	$30,000	$ 90,000
Lancelot	20,000	50,000	70,000
Total territory sales	$80,000	$80,000	$160,000
Variable production costs:			
Gwenevere (12% of sales)	$ 7,200	$ 3,600	$ 10,800
Lancelot (12% of sales)	2,400	6,000	8,400
Total variable production cost by territory	$ 9,600	$ 9,600	$ 19,200
Promotion costs:			
Gwenevere (variable at 30% of sales)	$18,000	$ 9,000	$ 27,000
Lancelot (variable at 20% of sales)	4,000	10,000	14,000
Total promotion cost by territory	$22,000	$19,000	$ 41,000
Sales commissions:			
Gwenevere (variable at 20% of sales)	$12,000	$ 6,000	$ 18,000
Lancelot (variable at 10% of sales)	2,000	5,000	7,000
Total sales commissions by territory	$14,000	$11,000	$ 25,000

Camelot Fragrance manufactures and sells the Gwenevere perfume for women and the Lancelot cologne for men. To simplify, no inventories are assumed to exist at the beginning or end of March.

Why It Matters

Business Segments

A business segment represents a component of business that earns revenues and incurs expenses and whose performance is evaluated by management. Business segments can be determined along different dimensions, such as the nature of products and services, geographic region, class of customer, or methods for distributing products or providing services. Examples from a sampling of companies follow:

Company	Segment Type	Segments
Amazon	Geographic	North America, Germany, Japan, UK, Other International
Apple	Product	iPhone, iPad, Mac, Services, Other Products
Boeing	Product	Commercial Airplanes, Military Aircraft, Network and Space Systems, Global Services and Support, Boeing Capital
Comcast	Distribution channel	Cable Communications, Cable Networks, Broadcast TV, Filmed Entertainment, Theme Parks
Deere and Co.	Customer application	Agriculture and Turf, Construction and Forestry
Intel	Customer	Hewlett-Packard, Dell Inc., Lenovo Group Limited
McDonald's	Geographic	United States, Europe, APMEA (Asia-Pacific, Middle East, and Africa), Other Countries
Procter & Gamble	Product	Beauty, Grooming, Health Care, Fabric and Home Care
Skechers	Distribution channel	Domestic Wholesale, International Wholesale, Retail, E-commerce

Sales Territory Profitability Analysis

An income statement presenting the contribution margin by sales territories is often used in evaluating past performance and in directing future sales efforts. Sales territory profitability analysis may lead management to do the following:

- Reduce costs in lower-profit sales territories
- Increase sales efforts in higher-profit territories

To illustrate sales territory profitability analysis, Exhibit 10 shows the contribution margin for the Northern and Southern territories of Camelot Fragrance Company. As Exhibit 10 indicates, the Northern Territory is generating $34,400 of contribution margin, while the Southern Territory is generating $40,400 of contribution margin.

Exhibit 10

Contribution Margin by Sales Territory Report

Camelot Fragrance Company Contribution Margin by Sales Territory For the Month Ended March 31				
		Northern Territory		**Southern Territory**
Sales		$80,000		$80,000
Variable cost of goods sold		9,600		9,600
Manufacturing margin		$70,400		$70,400
Variable selling expenses:				
Promotion costs	$22,000		$19,000	
Sales commissions	14,000		11,000	
Total variable selling expenses		36,000		30,000
Contribution margin		$34,400		$40,400
Contribution margin ratio.........................		43%		50.5%

In addition to the contribution margin, the contribution margin ratio for each territory is shown in Exhibit 10. The contribution margin ratio is computed as follows:

$$\text{Contribution Margin Ratio} = \frac{\text{Contribution Margin}}{\text{Sales}}$$

Exhibit 10 indicates that the Northern Territory has a contribution margin ratio of 43% ($34,400 ÷ $80,000). In contrast, the Southern Territory has a contribution margin ratio of 50.5% ($40,400 ÷ $80,000).

The difference in profit of the Northern and Southern territories is due to the difference in sales mix between the territories. **Sales mix**, sometimes referred to as *product mix*, is the relative amount of sales among the various products. The sales mix is computed by dividing the sales of each product by the total sales of each territory. Sales mix of the Northern and Southern territories is as follows:

Product	Northern Territory		Southern Territory	
	Sales	**Sales Mix**	**Sales**	**Sales Mix**
Gwenevere	$60,000	75%	$30,000	37.5%
Lancelot	20,000	25	50,000	62.5
Total	$80,000	100%	$80,000	100.0%

As shown, 62.5% of the Southern Territory's sales are sales of Lancelot. Since the Southern Territory's contribution margin ($40,400) is higher (as shown in Exhibit 10) than that of the Northern Territory ($34,400), Lancelot must be more profitable than Gwenevere. To verify this, product profitability analysis is performed.

Product Profitability Analysis

A company should focus its sales efforts on products that will provide the maximum total contribution margin. In doing so, product profitability analysis is often used by management in making decisions regarding product sales and promotional efforts.

To illustrate product profitability analysis, Exhibit 11 shows the contribution margin by product for Camelot Fragrance Company.

Camelot Fragrance Company Contribution Margin by Product Line For the Month Ended March 31				
		Gwenevere		**Lancelot**
Sales		$90,000		$70,000
Variable cost of goods sold		10,800		8,400
Manufacturing margin		$79,200		$61,600
Variable selling expenses:				
Promotion costs	$27,000		$14,000	
Sales commissions	18,000		7,000	
Total variable selling expenses		45,000		21,000
Contribution margin		$34,200		$40,600
Contribution margin ratio		38%		58%

Exhibit 11
Contribution Margin by Product Line Report

Exhibit 11 indicates that Lancelot's contribution margin ratio (58%) is greater than Gwenevere's (38%). Lancelot's higher contribution margin ratio is a result of its lower promotion and sales commissions costs. Thus, management should consider the following:

- Emphasizing Lancelot in its marketing plans
- Reducing Gwenevere's promotion and sales commissions costs
- Increasing the price of Gwenevere

Link to Adobe Systems

Adobe Systems recently reported the following data (in millions) for its three segments:

	Digital Media	**Digital Marketing**	**Print and Publishing**
Revenue	$2,603	$1,355	$188
Cost of revenue	149	464	9
Gross profit	$2,454	$ 891	$179

Source: Adobe Systems Incorporated, Form 10-K for the Fiscal Year Ended November 27, 2015.

Salesperson Profitability Analysis

A salesperson profitability report is useful in evaluating sales performance. Such a report normally includes total sales, variable cost of goods sold, variable selling expenses, contribution margin, and contribution margin ratio for each salesperson.

Exhibit 12 illustrates such a salesperson profitability report for three salespersons in the Northern Territory of Camelot Fragrance Company. The exhibit indicates that Beth Williams produced the greatest contribution margin ($15,200), but had the lowest contribution margin ratio (38%). Beth sold $40,000 of product, which is twice as much product as the other two salespersons. However, Beth sold only Gwenevere, which has the lowest contribution margin ratio (from Exhibit 11). The other two salespersons sold equal amounts of Gwenevere and Lancelot. As a result, Inez Rodriguez and Deshawn Thomas had higher contribution margin ratios because they sold more Lancelot. The Northern Territory manager could use this report to encourage Inez and Deshawn to sell more total product, while encouraging Beth to sell more Lancelot.

Exhibit 12

Contribution Margin by Salesperson Report

	Camelot Fragrance Company Contribution Margin by Salesperson—Northern Territory For the Month Ended March 31			
	Inez Rodriguez	Deshawn Thomas	Beth Williams	Northern Territory— Total
Sales	$20,000	$20,000	$40,000	$80,000
Variable cost of goods sold	2,400	2,400	4,800	9,600
Manufacturing margin	$17,600	$17,600	$35,200	$70,400
Variable selling expenses:				
Promotion costs........................	$ 5,000	$ 5,000	$12,000	$22,000
Sales commissions	3,000	3,000	8,000	14,000
Total variable selling expenses	$ 8,000	$ 8,000	$20,000	$36,000
Contribution margin......................	$ 9,600	$ 9,600	$15,200	$34,400
Contribution margin ratio.................	48%	48%	38%	43%
Sales mix (% Lancelot sales)	50%	50%	0%	25%

Other factors should also be considered in evaluating salespersons' performance. For example, sales growth rates, years of experience, customer service, territory size, and actual performance compared to budgeted performance may also be important.

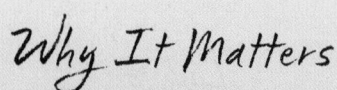

Chipotle Contribution Margin per Restaurant

Chipotle Mexican Grill's annual report identifies revenues and costs for its company-owned stores. We assume that food, beverage, packaging, and labor are variable and that occupancy (rent expense) and other expenses are fixed. By dividing the totals provided in the annual report by the number of stores (1,783), a contribution margin and income from operations can be constructed for an average restaurant as follows (in thousands):

Sales...		$2,304
Variable restaurant expenses:		
Food, beverage, and packaging...........	$797	
Labor.....................................	507	
Total variable restaurant operating costs		1,304
Contribution margin........................		$ 1,000
Occupancy and other expenses.............		373
Income from operations		$ 627

As can be seen, the average Chipotle restaurant is very profitable. Chipotle can use this information for pricing products; evaluating the sensitivity of store profitability to changes in sales volume, prices, and costs; and analyzing profitability by geographic segment by aggregating individual store data.

Source: Chipotle 10-K Annual Report to the SEC, February 2015.

Check Up Corner 20-3	Contribution Margin by Segment

Vintage Apparel Company manufactures and sells two styles of baseball jerseys, the Retro and the New Age. These jerseys are sold in two regions, East and West. Information about the two jerseys and sales in the two regions is as follows:

	Retro	New Age
Sales price	$100	$120
Variable cost of goods sold per unit	75	90
Manufacturing margin per unit	$ 25	$ 30
Variable selling expense per unit	17	18
Contribution margin per unit	$ 8	$ 12

	Units Sold	
	East Region	West Region
Retro	10,000	6,000
New Age	0	5,000

Prepare a contribution margin by sales territory report. Calculate the contribution margin ratio for each territory.

Solution:

- - - - - - - - - 10,000 units of Retro × $100 sales price

	East Region	West Region
Sales	$1,000,000	$1,200,000
Variable cost of goods sold	750,000	900,000
Manufacturing margin	$ 250,000	$ 300,000
Variable selling expenses	170,000	192,000
Contribution margin	$ 80,000	$ 108,000
Contribution margin ratio	8%	9%

(6,000 units of Retro × $100 sales price) +
(5,000 units of New Age × $120 sales price)

(6,000 units of Retro × $75 variable cost per unit) +
(5,000 units of New Age × $90 variable cost per unit)

(6,000 units of Retro × $17 variable selling expense per unit)
+ (5,000 units of New Age × $18 variable selling expense per unit)

10,000 units of Retro × $75 variable cost per unit

10,000 units of Retro × $17 variable selling expense per unit

Check Up Corner

Contribution Margin Analysis

Objective 5

Use variable costing for analyzing and explaining changes in contribution margin as a result of quantity and price factors.

Managers often use contribution margin in planning and controlling operations. In doing so, managers use contribution margin analysis. **Contribution margin analysis** focuses on explaining the differences between planned and actual contribution margins.

Contribution margin is defined as sales less variable costs. Thus, a difference between the planned and actual contribution margin may be caused by an increase or a decrease in:

- Sales
- Variable costs

An increase or a decrease in sales or variable costs may in turn be due to an increase or a decrease in the:

- Number of units sold
- Unit sales price or unit cost

The effects of the preceding factors on sales or variable costs may be stated as follows:

- **Quantity factor:** The effect of a difference in the number of units sold, assuming no change in unit sales price or unit cost. The *sales quantity factor* and the *variable cost quantity factor* are computed as follows:

Sales Quantity Factor = (Actual Units Sold − Planned Units of Sales) × Planned Sales Price

Variable Cost Quantity Factor = (Planned Units of Sales − Actual Units Sold) × Planned Unit Cost

The preceding factors are computed so that a positive amount increases contribution margin and a negative amount decreases contribution margin.

- **Unit price factor** or *unit cost factor*: The effect of a difference in unit sales price or unit cost on the number of units sold. The unit price factor and unit cost factor are computed as follows:

  Unit Price Factor = (Actual Selling Price per Unit – Planned Selling Price per Unit) × Actual Units Sold

  Unit Cost Factor = (Planned Cost per Unit – Actual Cost per Unit) × Actual Units Sold

The preceding factors are computed so that a positive amount increases contribution margin and a negative amount decreases contribution margin.

The effects of the preceding factors on contribution margin are summarized in Exhibit 13.

Exhibit 13
Contribution
Margin Analysis

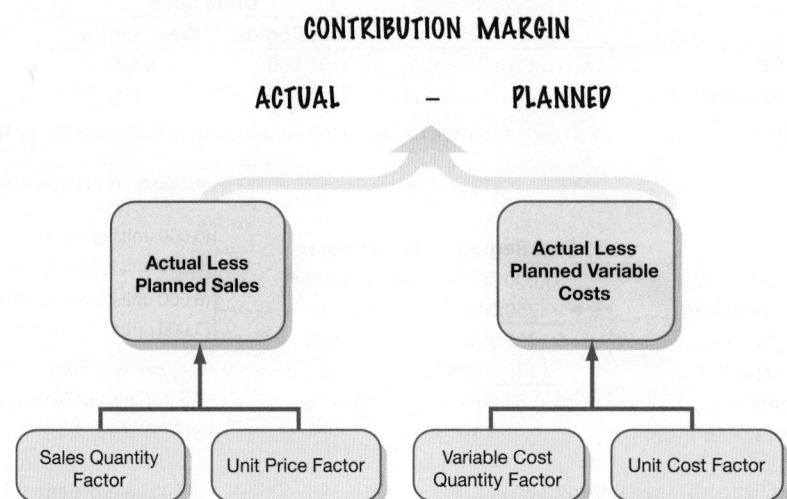

To illustrate, the following data for the year ended December 31, for Noble Inc., which sells a single product, are used:[1]

	Actual	Planned
Sales	$937,500	$800,000
Variable cost of goods sold	$425,000	$350,000
Variable selling and administrative expenses	162,500	125,000
Total	$587,500	$475,000
Contribution margin	$350,000	$325,000
Number of units sold	125,000	100,000
Per unit:		
Sales price	$7.50	$8.00
Variable cost of goods sold	3.40	3.50
Variable selling and administrative expenses	1.30	1.25

Exhibit 14 shows the contribution margin analysis report for Noble Inc. for the year ended December 31. The exhibit indicates that the favorable difference of $25,000 ($350,000 – $325,000) between the actual and planned contribution margins was due in large part to an increase in the quantity sold (sales quantity factor) of $200,000. This $200,000 increase was partially offset by a decrease in the unit sales price (unit price factor) of $62,500 and an increase in the amount of variable costs of $112,500 ($75,000 + $37,500).

[1] To simplify, it is assumed that Noble Inc. sells a single product. The analysis would be more complex, but the principles would be the same, if more than one product were sold.

Noble Inc. Contribution Margin Analysis For the Year Ended December 31		
Planned contribution margin		$325,000
Effect of changes in sales:		
Sales quantity factor [(125,000 units – 100,000 units) × $8.00]	$200,000	
Unit price factor [($7.50 – $8.00) × 125,000 units]	(62,500)	
Total effect of changes in sales		137,500
Effect of changes in variable cost of goods sold:		
Variable cost quantity factor [(100,000 units – 125,000 units) × $3.50]	$ (87,500)	
Unit cost factor [($3.50 – $3.40) × 125,000 units]	12,500	
Total effect of changes in variable cost of goods sold		(75,000)
Effect of changes in selling and administrative expenses:		
Variable cost quantity factor [(100,000 units – 125,000 units) × $1.25]	$ (31,250)	
Unit cost factor [($1.25 – $1.30) × 125,000 units]	(6,250)	
Total effect of changes in selling and administrative expenses		(37,500)
Actual contribution margin		$350,000

Exhibit 14

Contribution Margin Analysis Report

The contribution margin analysis reports are useful to management in evaluating past performance and in planning future operations. For example, the impact of the $0.50 reduction in the unit sales price by Noble Inc. on the number of units sold and on the total sales for the year is useful information in determining whether further price reductions might be desirable.

The contribution margin analysis report also highlights the impact of changes in unit variable costs and expenses. For example, the $0.05 increase in the unit variable selling and administrative expenses might be a result of increased advertising expenditures. If so, the increase in the number of units sold could be attributed to both the $0.50 price reduction and the increased advertising.

Check Up Corner 20-4   Contribution Margin Analysis

H-TECH Industries Inc. manufactures only one product. In an attempt to increase sales and improve the contribution margin, the company decreased the sales price of the product and pursued an aggressive marketing campaign. The marketing campaign increased variable selling and administrative expenses.

The following data have been gathered from the accounting records for the year ended December 31:

	Actual	Planned
Sales	$3,360,000	$2,100,000
Variable cost of goods sold	$1,776,000	$1,050,000
Variable selling and administrative expenses	552,000	280,000
Total variable costs	$2,328,000	$1,330,000
Contribution margin	$1,032,000	$ 770,000
Number of units sold	24,000	14,000
Per unit:		
Sales price	$140	$150
Variable cost of goods sold	74	75
Variable selling and administrative expenses	23	20

Prepare a contribution margin analysis report for the year ended December 31.

Solution:

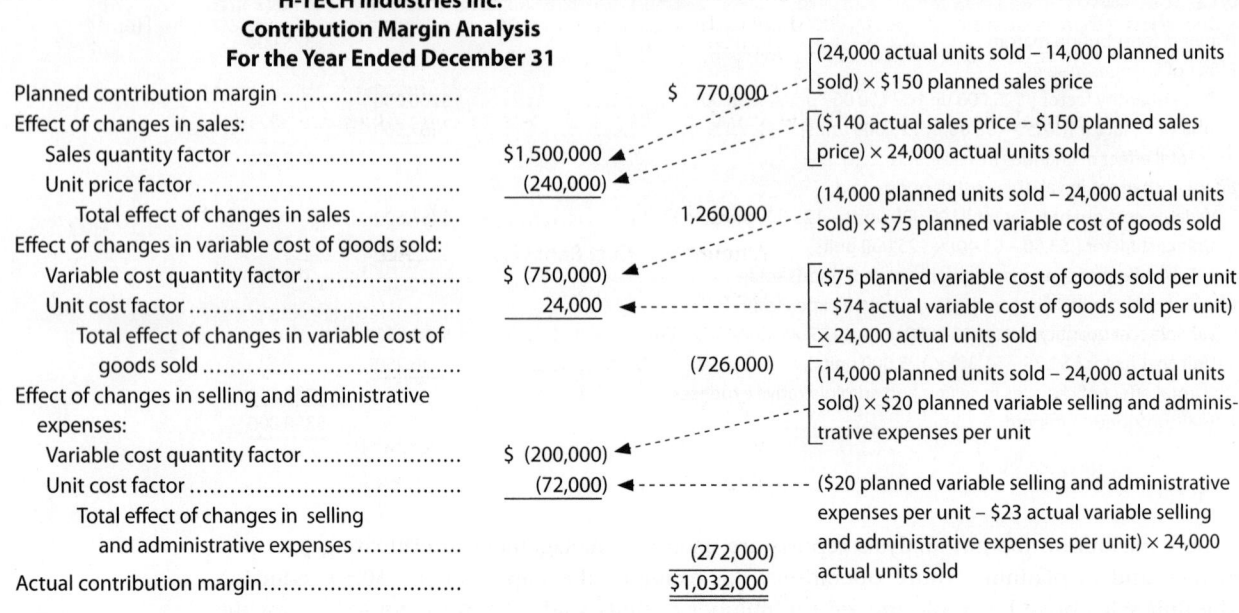

H-TECH Industries Inc.
Contribution Margin Analysis
For the Year Ended December 31

Planned contribution margin		$ 770,000
Effect of changes in sales:		
Sales quantity factor	$1,500,000	
Unit price factor	(240,000)	
Total effect of changes in sales		1,260,000
Effect of changes in variable cost of goods sold:		
Variable cost quantity factor.......................	$ (750,000)	
Unit cost factor	24,000	
Total effect of changes in variable cost of goods sold		(726,000)
Effect of changes in selling and administrative expenses:		
Variable cost quantity factor.......................	$ (200,000)	
Unit cost factor	(72,000)	
Total effect of changes in selling and administrative expenses		(272,000)
Actual contribution margin.............................		$1,032,000

Right-side annotations:

- (24,000 actual units sold – 14,000 planned units sold) × $150 planned sales price
- ($140 actual sales price – $150 planned sales price) × 24,000 actual units sold
- (14,000 planned units sold – 24,000 actual units sold) × $75 planned variable cost of goods sold
- ($75 planned variable cost of goods sold per unit – $74 actual variable cost of goods sold per unit) × 24,000 actual units sold
- (14,000 planned units sold – 24,000 actual units sold) × $20 planned variable selling and administrative expenses per unit
- ($20 planned variable selling and administrative expenses per unit – $23 actual variable selling and administrative expenses per unit) × 24,000 actual units sold

Check Up Corner

Why It Matters

Eastman Revenue Price and Volume Effects

Eastman Chemical Company is a global specialty chemical company. Eastman began as a division of Eastman Kodak, producing chemicals for Kodak's photographic processes. Eastman explains the changes in its revenues for each of its major segments by providing information on volume (quantity) and price effects. The disclosure for the Additives and Function Products Segment is as follows (in millions):

	2014	2013	Amount Change	% Change
Sales	$1,821	$1,719	$102	6%
Volume effect			82	5%
Price effect			20	1%

This analysis shows that the sales increase (6%) between 2013 and 2014 was mostly caused by increasing sales volume (5%), rather than increasing price (1%). Thus, Eastman is growing its business in this segment without sacrificing price.

Source: Eastman Chemical Company 10-K Annual Report to the SEC, February 2015.

Objective 6

Describe and illustrate contribution margin analysis for service businesses.

Variable Costing for Service Businesses

Variable costing and the use of variable costing for manufacturing firms have been discussed earlier in this chapter. Service companies also use variable costing, contribution margin analysis, and segment analysis.

Reporting Income

Unlike a manufacturing company, a service company does not make or sell a product. Thus, service companies do not have inventory. Since service companies have no inventory, they do not use absorption costing to allocate fixed costs. In addition, variable costing reports of service companies do not report a manufacturing margin.

To illustrate variable costing for a service company, Blue Skies Airlines Inc., which operates as a small commercial airline, is used. The variable and fixed costs of Blue Skies are shown in Exhibit 15.

Cost	Amount	Cost Behavior	Activity Base
Depreciation expense	$3,600,000	Fixed	
Food and beverage service expense..............	444,000	Variable	Number of passengers
Fuel expense.....................................	4,080,000	Variable	Number of miles flown
Rental expense...................................	800,000	Fixed	
Selling expense	3,256,000	Variable	Number of passengers
Wages expense...................................	6,120,000	Variable	Number of miles flown

Exhibit 15

Costs of Blue Skies Airlines Inc.

As discussed in Chapter 19, a cost is classified as a fixed or variable cost according to how it changes relative to an activity base. A common activity for a manufacturing firm is the number of units produced. In contrast, most service companies use several activity bases.

To illustrate, Blue Skies uses the activity base *number of passengers* for food and beverage service and selling expenses. Blue Skies uses *number of miles flown* for fuel and wage expenses.

The variable costing income statement for Blue Skies, assuming revenue of $19,238,000, is shown in Exhibit 16.

Blue Skies Airlines Inc. Variable Costing Income Statement For the Month Ended April 30		
Revenue		$19,238,000
Variable costs:		
Fuel expense	$4,080,000	
Wages expense	6,120,000	
Food and beverage service expense.........................	444,000	
Selling expense...	3,256,000	
Total variable costs.......................................		13,900,000
Contribution margin...		$ 5,338,000
Fixed costs:		
Depreciation expense.......................................	$3,600,000	
Rental expense	800,000	
Total fixed costs		4,400,000
Income from operations		$ 938,000

Exhibit 16

Variable Costing Income Statement for a Service Company

Unlike a manufacturing company, Exhibit 16 does not report cost of goods sold, inventory, or manufacturing margin. However, as shown in Exhibit 16, contribution margin is reported separately from income from operations.

Analyzing Segments

A contribution margin report for service companies can be used to analyze and evaluate market segments. Typical segments for various service companies are shown in Exhibit 17.

Exhibit 17   Service Industry Market Segments

Service Industry	Market Segments
Electric power	Regions, customer types (industrial, consumer)
Banking	Customer types (commercial, retail), products (loans, savings accounts)
Airlines	Products (passengers, cargo), routes
Railroads	Products (commodity type), routes
Hotels	Hotel properties
Telecommunications	Customer type (commercial, retail), service type (voice, data)
Health care	Procedure, payment type (Medicare, insured)

To illustrate, a contribution margin report segmented by route is used for Blue Skies Airlines Inc. In preparing the report, the following data for April are used:

	Chicago/Atlanta	Atlanta/LA	LA/Chicago
Average ticket price per passenger	$400	$1,075	$805
Total passengers served................................	16,000	7,000	6,600
Total miles flown..	56,000	88,000	60,000

The variable costs per unit are as follows:

Fuel	$ 20 per mile
Wages	30 per mile
Food and beverage service	15 per passenger
Selling	110 per passenger

A contribution margin report for Blue Skies is shown in Exhibit 18. The report is segmented by the routes (city pairs) flown.

Exhibit 18

Contribution Margin by Segment Report for a Service Company

Blue Skies Airlines Inc. Contribution Margin by Route For the Month Ended April 30				
	Chicago/ Atlanta	Atlanta/ Los Angeles	Los Angeles/ Chicago	Total
Revenue				
(Ticket price × No. of passengers)	$ 6,400,000	$ 7,525,000	$ 5,313,000	$19,238,000
Aircraft fuel				
($20 × No. of miles flown)	(1,120,000)	(1,760,000)	(1,200,000)	(4,080,000)
Wages and benefits				
($30 × No. of miles flown)	(1,680,000)	(2,640,000)	(1,800,000)	(6,120,000)
Food and beverage service				
($15 × No. of passengers)	(240,000)	(105,000)	(99,000)	(444,000)
Selling expenses				
($110 × No. of passengers)	(1,760,000)	(770,000)	(726,000)	(3,256,000)
Contribution margin......................	$ 1,600,000	$ 2,250,000	$ 1,488,000	$ 5,338,000
Contribution margin ratio* (rounded)	25%	30%	28%	28%

*Contribution Margin/Revenue

Exhibit 18 indicates that the Chicago/Atlanta route has the lowest contribution margin ratio of 25%. In contrast, the Atlanta/Los Angeles route has the highest contribution margin ratio of 30%.

Analyzing Contribution Margin

Blue Skies Airlines Inc. is also used to illustrate contribution margin analysis. Specifically, assume that Blue Skies decides to try to improve the contribution margin of its Chicago/Atlanta route during May by decreasing ticket prices. Thus, Blue Skies decreases the ticket price from $400 to $380 beginning May 1. As a result, the number of tickets sold (passengers) increased from 16,000 to 20,000. However, the cost per mile also increased during May from $20 to $22 due to increasing fuel prices.

The actual and planned results for the Chicago/Atlanta route during May follow. The planned amounts are based on the April results without considering the price change or cost per mile increase. The highlighted numbers indicate changes during May.

	Chicago/Atlanta Route	
	Actual, May	Planned, May
Revenue	$7,600,000	$6,400,000
Variable expenses:		
Aircraft fuel	$1,232,000	$1,120,000
Wages	1,680,000	1,680,000
Food and beverage service	300,000	240,000
Selling expenses	2,200,000	1,760,000
Total variable expenses	$5,412,000	$4,800,000
Contribution margin	$2,188,000	$1,600,000
Contribution margin ratio	29%	25%
Number of miles flown	56,000	56,000
Number of passengers flown	20,000	16,000
Per unit:		
Ticket price	$380	$400
Aircraft fuel expense	22	20
Wages expense	30	30
Food and beverage service expense	15	15
Selling expense	110	110

Using the preceding data, a contribution margin analysis report can be prepared for the Chicago/Atlanta route for May as shown in Exhibit 19. Since the planned and actual wages and benefits expense are the same ($1,680,000), its quantity and unit cost factors are not included in Exhibit 19.

Exhibit 19

Contribution Margin Analysis Report—Service Company

Blue Skies Airlines Inc. Contribution Margin Analysis Chicago/Atlanta Route For the Month Ended May 31		
Planned contribution margin		$1,600,000
Effect of changes in revenue:		
Revenue quantity factor [(20,000 pass. – 16,000 pass.) × $400]	$1,600,000	
Unit price factor [($380 – $400) × 20,000 passengers]	(400,000)	
Total effect of changes in revenue		1,200,000
Effect of changes in fuel cost:		
Variable cost quantity factor [(56,000 miles – 56,000 miles) × $20]	$ 0	
Unit cost factor [($20 – $22) × 56,000 miles]	(112,000)	
Total effect of changes in fuel costs		(112,000)
Effect of changes in food and beverage expenses:		
Variable cost quantity factor [(16,000 pass. – 20,000 pass.) × $15]	$ (60,000)	
Unit cost factor [($15 – $15) × 20,000 passengers]	0	
Total effect of changes in food and beverage expenses.		(60,000)
Effect of changes in selling expenses:		
Variable cost quantity factor [(16,000 pass. – 20,000 pass.) × $110]	$ (440,000)	
Unit cost factor [($110 – $110) × 20,000 passengers]	0	
Total effect of changes in selling expenses		(440,000)
Actual contribution margin		$2,188,000

Exhibit 19 indicates that the price decrease generated an additional $1,200,000 in revenue. This consists of $1,600,000 from an increased number of passengers (revenue quantity factor) and a $400,000 revenue reduction from the decrease in ticket price (unit price factor).

The increased fuel costs (by $2 per mile) reduced the contribution margin by $112,000 (unit cost factor). The increased number of passengers also increased the food and beverage service expenses by $60,000 and the selling expenses by $440,000 (variable cost quantity factors). The net increase in contribution margin is $588,000 ($2,188,000 – $1,600,000).

Analysis for Decision Making

Segment Analysis and Earnings Before Interest, Taxes, Depreciation, and Amortization (EBITDA)

Objective

Describe and illustrate the use of segment analysis and Earnings Before Interest, Taxes, Depreciation, and Amortization (EBITDA) in evaluating a company's performance.

The financial statements of public companies include footnote disclosure of selected segment information. This information can be used to identify strengths and weaknesses among segments.

To illustrate, **Amazon.com, Inc.** reports two Web site segments, North America and International. The sales, operating income, and depreciation expense are segment disclosures in Amazon's financial statement footnotes and are shown as follows for a recent year (in millions):

	North America	**International**
Sales	$55,469	$33,519
Segment operating income	2,105	(297)
Depreciation and amortization expense	2,701	915

North American sales are approximately 62% [$55,469 ÷ ($55,469 + $33,519)] of the total sales, and International sales are 38% of total sales. Thus, the International segment, while smaller than North America, is still significant.

Operating income is often expressed by adding back depreciation and amortization expense. This amount is termed earnings before interest, taxes, depreciation, and amortization, or **EBITDA**.[2] EBITDA removes a significant fixed and noncash cost from the operating income number and may approximate the contribution margin. As a result, EBITDA may be used by managers for decision making, either in addition to contribution margin or as a substitute.

The EBITDA as a percent of sales, termed EBITDA margin, can be compared between Amazon's two segments as follows:

	North America	International
Segment operating income (EBIT)	$2,105	$(297)
Depreciation and amortization expense	2,701	915
Operating income before depreciation and amortization expense (EBITDA)	$4,806	$ 618
EBITDA as a percent of sales	8.7%	1.8%
	($4,806 ÷ $55,469)	($618 ÷ $33,519)

North America has an EBITDA of 8.7% of sales, while the International segment has an EBITDA of only 1.8% of sales. This performance difference is likely the result of more established recognition in North America. There also may be greater competition in international markets, such as from Alibaba in China. As Amazon grows its international business, these margins may improve.

[2] Recall that operating income is already determined prior to deducting interest and tax expense, and is often termed earnings before interest and taxes (EBIT).

Make a Decision   Segment Analysis and EBITDA

Comcast Corporation is a global media and entertainment company with operations divided into five major segments:

- Cable Communications (XFINITY)
- Cable Networks (USA Network, Syfy, E!, CNBC, others)
- Broadcast Television (NBC)
- Filmed Entertainment (Universal Pictures)
- Theme Parks (Universal)

Revenue, operating income, and depreciation and amortization information for these segments for a recent year are as follows (in millions):

	Revenue	Operating Income	Depreciation and Amortization
Cable Communications	$44,140	$18,112	$6,422
Cable Networks	9,563	3,589	748
Broadcast Television	8,542	734	127
Filmed Entertainment	5,008	711	21
Theme Parks	2,623	1,168	273
Total	$69,876	$24,314	$7,591

A. Prepare a vertical analysis of the segment revenues to total revenues. (Round to nearest whole percent.)
B. Which segment contributes most to total revenues?
C. Compute (1) EBITDA and (2) EBITDA as a percent of revenue for each segment. (Round to nearest whole percent.)
D. Evaluate segment EBITDA as a percent of revenue.
E. What might management do to increase performance in the segments with the lowest EBITDA?

Solution:

A.

	Revenue	Revenue as a Percent of Total Revenues
Cable Communications	$44,140	63%
Cable Networks	9,563	14%
Broadcast Television	8,542	12%
Filmed Entertainment	5,008	7%
Theme Parks	2,623	4%
Total	$69,876	100%

B. The Cable Communications segment has the largest revenue as a percent (63%) of total revenues. This segment provides more revenue than do all the other remaining segments combined.

C. 1. and 2.

	Revenue	Operating Income	Depreciation and Amortization	(1) EBITDA*	(2) EBITDA as a Percent of Revenue
Cable Communications	$44,140	$18,112	$6,422	$24,534	56%
Cable Networks	9,563	3,589	748	4,337	45%
Broadcast Television	8,542	734	127	861	10%
Filmed Entertainment	5,008	711	21	732	15%
Theme Parks	2,623	1,168	273	1,441	55%
Total	$69,876	$24,314	$7,591	$31,905	

*EBITDA = Operating Income + Deprecation and Amortization

D. The Cable Communications segment provides the greatest EBITDA as a percent of revenues (56%). Both the Cable Networks and Theme Parks segments are close behind at 45% and 55%, respectively. All three segments appear very profitable. The remaining two segments, Broadcast Television and Filmed Entertainment, are less profitable but acceptable.

E. Broadcast Television and Filmed Entertainment performance is highly contingent upon audience responses to TV shows and films. Management needs to build content development processes that maximize the audience appeal of TV shows and films.

Make a Decision

Let's Review

Chapter Summary

1. Under absorption costing, the cost of goods manufactured is comprised of all direct materials, direct labor, and factory overhead costs (both fixed and variable). Under variable costing, the cost of goods manufactured is composed of only variable costs: direct materials, direct labor, and variable factory overhead costs. Fixed factory overhead costs are considered a period expense.

   The variable costing income statement is structured differently than a traditional absorption costing income statement. Sales less variable cost of goods sold is presented as manufacturing margin. Manufacturing margin less variable selling and administrative expenses is presented as contribution margin. Contribution margin less fixed costs is presented as income from operations.

2. Management should be aware of the effects of changes in inventory levels on income from operations reported under variable costing and absorption costing. If absorption costing is used, managers could misinterpret increases or decreases in income from operations due to changes in inventory levels to be the result of operating efficiencies or inefficiencies.

3. Variable costing is especially useful at the operating level of management because the amount of variable manufacturing costs is controllable at this level. The fixed factory overhead costs are ordinarily controllable by a higher level of management.

   In the short run, variable costing may be useful in establishing the selling price of a product. This price should be at least equal to the variable costs of making and selling the product. In the long run, however, absorption costing is useful in establishing selling prices because all costs must be covered and a reasonable amount of operating income earned.

4. Variable costing can support management decision making in analyzing and evaluating market segments, such as territories, products, salespersons, and customers. Contribution margin reports by segment can be used by managers to support price decisions, evaluate cost changes, and plan volume changes.

5. Contribution margin analysis is the systematic examination of differences between planned and actual contribution margins. These differences can be caused by an increase/decrease in the amount of sales or variable costs, which can be caused by changes in the amount of units sold, unit sales price, or unit cost.

6. Service businesses will not have inventories, manufacturing margin, or cost of goods sold. Service firms can prepare variable costing income statements and contribution margin reports for market segments. In addition, service firms can use contribution margin analysis to plan and control operations.

Key Terms

absorption costing (996)
contribution margin (997)
contribution margin analysis (1013)
controllable costs (1007)
EBITDA (1021)

manufacturing margin (997)
market segment (1008)
noncontrollable costs (1007)
quantity factor (1013)
sales mix (1010)

unit price (cost) factor (1014)
variable cost of goods sold (997)
variable costing (997)

Practice

Multiple-Choice Questions

1. Sales were $750,000, the variable cost of goods sold was $400,000, the variable selling and administrative expenses were $90,000, and fixed costs were $200,000. The contribution margin was:
   A. $60,000.
   B. $260,000.
   C. $350,000.
   D. none of the above.

2. During the year in which the number of units manufactured exceeded the number of units sold, the income from operations reported under the absorption costing concept would be:
   A. larger than the income from operations reported under the variable costing concept.
   B. smaller than the income from operations reported under the variable costing concept.
   C. the same as the income from operations reported under the variable costing concept.
   D. none of the above.

3. The beginning inventory consists of 6,000 units, all of which are sold during the period. The beginning inventory fixed costs are $20 per unit, and the variable costs per unit are $90 per unit. What is the difference in income from operations between variable and absorption costing?
   A. Variable costing income from operations is $540,000 less than under absorption costing.
   B. Variable costing income from operations is $600,000 greater than under absorption costing.
   C. Variable costing income from operations is $120,000 less than under absorption costing.
   D. Variable costing income from operations is $120,000 greater than under absorption costing.

4. Variable costs are $70 per unit and fixed costs are $150,000. Sales are estimated to be 10,000 units. How much would absorption costing income from operations differ between a plan to produce 10,000 units and 12,000 units?
   A. $150,000 greater for 12,000 units
   B. $150,000 less for 12,000 units
   C. $25,000 greater for 12,000 units
   D. $25,000 less for 12,000 units

5. If actual sales totaled $800,000 for the current year (80,000 units at $10 each) and planned sales were $765,000 (85,000 units at $9 each), the difference between actual and planned sales due to the quantity factor is:
   A. a $50,000 increase.
   B. a $325,000 increase.
   C. a $45,000 decrease.
   D. none of the above.

Answers provided after Problem. Need more practice? Find additional multiple-choice questions, exercises, and problems in CengageNOWv2.

Exercises

SHOW ME HOW

---

1. Variable costing   Obj. 1

Light Company has the following information for January:

Sales	$648,000
Variable cost of goods sold	233,200
Fixed manufacturing costs	155,500
Variable selling and administrative expenses	51,800
Fixed selling and administrative expenses	36,800

Determine (A) the manufacturing margin, (B) the contribution margin, and (C) income from operations for Light Company for the month of January.

SHOW ME HOW

2. Variable costing—production exceeds sales

Obj. 1

Fixed manufacturing costs are $60 per unit, and variable manufacturing costs are $150 per unit. Production was 453,000 units, while sales were 426,000 units. Determine (A) whether variable costing income from operations is less than or greater than absorption costing income from operations, and (B) the difference in variable costing and absorption costing income from operations.

SHOW ME HOW

3. Variable costing—sales exceed production

Obj. 1

The beginning inventory is 11,600 units. All of the units that were manufactured during the period and 11,600 units of the beginning inventory were sold. The beginning inventory fixed manufacturing costs are $32 per unit, and variable manufacturing costs are $72 per unit. Determine (A) whether variable costing income from operations is less than or greater than absorption costing income from operations, and (B) the difference in variable costing and absorption costing income from operations.

SHOW ME HOW

4. Analyzing income under absorption and variable costing

Obj. 2

Variable manufacturing costs are $13 per unit, and fixed manufacturing costs are $75,000. Sales are estimated to be 12,000 units.

A. How much would absorption costing income from operations differ between a plan to produce 12,000 units and a plan to produce 15,000 units?

B. How much would variable costing income from operations differ between the two production plans?

SHOW ME HOW

5. Contribution margin by segment

Obj. 4

The following information is for Olivio Coaster Bikes Inc.:

	North	South
Sales volume (units):		
Red Dream	50,000	66,000
Blue Marauder	112,000	140,000
Sales price:		
Red Dream	$480	$500
Blue Marauder	$560	$600
Variable cost per unit:		
Red Dream	$248	$248
Blue Marauder	$260	$260

Determine the contribution margin for (A) Red Dream and (B) North Region.

SHOW ME HOW

6. Contribution margin analysis

Obj. 5

The actual price for a product was $28 per unit, while the planned price was $25 per unit. The volume decreased by 20,000 units to 410,000 actual total units. Determine (A) the sales quantity factor and (B) the unit price factor for sales.

Answers provided after Problem. Need more practice? Find additional multiple-choice questions, exercises, and problems in CengageNOWv2.

Problem

During the current period, McLaughlin Company sold 60,000 units of product at $30 per unit. At the beginning of the period, there were 10,000 units in inventory and McLaughlin Company manufactured 50,000 units during the period. The manufacturing costs and selling and administrative expenses were as follows:

	Total Cost	Number of Units	Unit Cost
Beginning inventory:			
Direct materials	$ 67,000	10,000	$ 6.70
Direct labor	155,000	10,000	15.50
Variable factory overhead	18,000	10,000	1.80
Fixed factory overhead	20,000	10,000	2.00
Total	$ 260,000		$26.00
Current period costs:			
Direct materials	$ 350,000	50,000	$ 7.00
Direct labor	810,000	50,000	16.20
Variable factory overhead	90,000	50,000	1.80
Fixed factory overhead	100,000	50,000	2.00
Total	$1,350,000		$27.00
Selling and administrative expenses:			
Variable	$ 65,000		
Fixed	45,000		
Total	$ 110,000		

Instructions

1. Prepare an income statement based on the absorption costing concept.

2. Prepare an income statement based on the variable costing concept.

3. Give the reason for the difference in the amount of income from operations in parts (1) and (2).

Need more practice? Find additional multiple-choice questions, exercises, and problems in CengageNOWv2.

Answers

Multiple-Choice Questions

1. **B** The contribution margin of $260,000 (answer B) is determined by deducting all the variable costs ($400,000 + $90,000) from sales ($750,000).

2. **A** In a period in which the number of units manufactured exceeds the number of units sold, the income from operations under the absorption costing concept is larger than the income from operations reported under the variable costing concept (answer A). This is because a proportion of the fixed manufacturing costs are deferred when the absorption costing concept is used. This deferment has the effect of excluding a portion of the fixed manufacturing costs from the current cost of goods sold.

3. **D** (6,000 units × $20 per unit) Answer A incorrectly computes the difference in income from operations using the variable cost per unit. Answer B incorrectly computes the difference in income from operations using the total cost per unit. Answer C is incorrect because variable costing income from operations will be greater than absorption costing income from operations when units manufactured is less than units sold.

4. **C** [2,000 units × ($150,000 ÷ 12,000)] Answers A and B incorrectly compute the difference in income from operations using variable cost per unit. When production exceeds sales, absorption costing will include fixed costs in the ending inventory, which causes costs of goods sold to decline and income from operations to increase. Thus, income from operations would not decline (answer D) for a production level of 12,000 units.

5. **C** The $45,000 decrease (answer C) attributed to the quantity factor is determined as follows:

Decrease in number of units sold	5,000
Planned unit sales price..	× $9
Quantity factor decrease	$45,000

The difference between planned and actual sales can be attributed to a unit price factor. The unit price factor can be determined as follows:

Actual number of units sold	80,000
Increase in unit sales price	× $1
Price factor increase	$80,000

The increase of $80,000 attributed to the price factor less the decrease of $45,000 attributed to the quantity factor accounts for the $35,000 increase in total sales.

Exercises

1.
   A. $414,800 = $648,000 − $233,200
   B. $363,000 = $414,800 − $51,800
   C. $170,700 = $363,000 − $155,500 − $36,800

2.
   A. Variable costing income from operations is less than absorption costing income from operations because the units manufactured are greater than the units sold.
   B. $1,620,000 ($60 per unit × 27,000 units)

3.
   A. Variable costing income from operations is greater than absorption costing income from operations because the units manufactured are less than the units sold.
   B. $371,200 ($32 per unit × 11,600 units)

4.
   A. $15,000 greater in producing 15,000 units. 12,000 units × ($6.25* − $5.00**), or [3,000 units × ($75,000 ÷ 15,000 units)].
      * $75,000 ÷ 12,000 units
      ** $75,000 ÷ 15,000 units
   B. There would be no difference in variable costing income from operations.

5.
   A. $28,232,000 = [50,000 units × ($480 − $248)] + [66,000 units × ($500 − $248)]
   B. $45,200,000 = [50,000 units × ($480 − $248)] + [112,000 units × ($560 − $260)]

6.
   A. $500,000 decrease in sales = 20,000 units × $25 per unit
   B. $1,230,000 increase in sales = ($28 − $25) × 410,000 units

Need more help? Watch step-by-step videos of how to compute answers to these Exercises in CengageNOWv2.

Problem

1.

Absorption Costing Income Statement		
Sales (60,000 × $30)		$1,800,000
Cost of goods sold:		
Beginning inventory (10,000 × $26)	$ 260,000	
Cost of goods manufactured (50,000 × $27)	1,350,000	
Total cost of goods sold		1,610,000
Gross profit		$ 190,000
Selling and administrative expenses ($65,000 + $45,000)		110,000
Income from operations		$ 80,000

2.

Variable Costing Income Statement		
Sales (60,000 × $30)		$1,800,000
Variable cost of goods sold:		
Beginning inventory (10,000 × $24)	$ 240,000	
Variable cost of goods manufactured (50,000 × $25)	1,250,000	
Total variable cost of goods sold		1,490,000
Manufacturing margin		$ 310,000
Variable selling and administrative expenses		65,000
Contribution margin		$ 245,000
Fixed costs:		
Fixed manufacturing costs	$ 100,000	
Fixed selling and administrative expenses	45,000	
Total fixed costs		145,000
Income from operations		$ 100,000

3. The difference of $20,000 ($100,000 – $80,000) in the amount of income from operations is attributable to the different treatment of the fixed manufacturing costs. The beginning inventory in the absorption costing income statement includes $20,000 (10,000 units × $2) of fixed manufacturing costs incurred in the preceding period. This $20,000 was included as an expense in a variable costing income statement of a prior period. Therefore, none of it is included as an expense in the current period variable costing income statement.

Discussion Questions

1. What types of costs are customarily included in the cost of manufactured products under (A) the absorption costing concept and (B) the variable costing concept?

2. Which type of manufacturing cost (direct materials, direct labor, variable factory overhead, fixed factory overhead) is included in the cost of goods manufactured under the absorption costing concept but is excluded from the cost of goods manufactured under the variable costing concept?

3. Which of the following costs would be included in the cost of a manufactured product according to the variable costing concept: (A) rent on factory building, (B) direct materials, (C) property taxes on factory building, (D) electricity purchased to operate factory equipment, (E) salary of factory supervisor, (F) depreciation on factory building, (G) direct labor?

4. In the variable costing income statement, how are the fixed manufacturing costs reported, and how are the fixed selling and administrative expenses reported?

5. Since all costs of operating a business are controllable, what is the significance of the term *noncontrollable cost*?

6. Discuss how financial data prepared on the basis of variable costing can assist management in the development of short-run pricing policies.

7. Why might management analyze product profitability?

8. Explain why rewarding sales personnel on the basis of total sales might not be in the best interests of a business whose goal is to maximize profits.

9. Discuss the two factors affecting both sales and variable costs to which a change in contribution margin can be attributed.

10. How is the quantity factor for an increase or a decrease in the amount of sales computed in using contribution margin analysis?

11. Explain why service companies use different activity bases than manufacturing companies to classify costs as fixed or variable.

Basic Exercises

SHOW ME HOW

BE 20-1 Variable costing

Obj. 1

Marley Company has the following information for March:

Sales	$912,000
Variable cost of goods sold	474,000
Fixed manufacturing costs	82,000
Variable selling and administrative expenses	238,100
Fixed selling and administrative expenses	54,700

Determine (A) the manufacturing margin, (B) the contribution margin, and (C) income from operations for Marley Company for the month of March.

SHOW ME HOW

BE 20-2 Variable costing—production exceeds sales

Obj. 1

Fixed manufacturing costs are $44 per unit, and variable manufacturing costs are $100 per unit. Production was 67,200 units, while sales were 50,400 units. Determine (A) whether variable costing income from operations is less than or greater than absorption costing income from operations, and (B) the difference in variable costing and absorption costing income from operations.

SHOW ME HOW

BE 20-3 Variable costing—sales exceed production

Obj. 1

The beginning inventory is 52,800 units. All of the units that were manufactured during the period and 52,800 units of the beginning inventory were sold. The beginning inventory fixed manufacturing costs are $14.70 per unit, and variable manufacturing costs are $30 per unit. Determine (A) whether variable costing income from operations is less than or greater than absorption costing income from operations, and (B) the difference in variable costing and absorption costing income from operations.

SHOW ME HOW

BE 20-4 Analyzing income under absorption and variable costing

Obj. 2

Variable manufacturing costs are $126 per unit, and fixed manufacturing costs are $157,500. Sales are estimated to be 10,000 units.

A. How much would absorption costing income from operations differ between a plan to produce 10,000 units and a plan to produce 15,000 units?

B. How much would variable costing income from operations differ between the two production plans?

SHOW ME HOW

BE 20-5 Contribution margin by segment   Obj. 4

The following information is for LaPlanche Industries Inc.:

	East	West
Sales volume (units):		
Product XX	45,000	38,000
Product YY	60,000	50,000
Sales price:		
Product XX	$700	$660
Product YY	$728	$720
Variable cost per unit:		
Product XX	$336	$336
Product YY	$360	$360

Determine the contribution margin for (A) Product YY and (B) West Region.

SHOW ME HOW

BE 20-6 Contribution margin analysis   Obj. 5

The actual variable cost of goods sold for a product was $140 per unit, while the planned variable cost of goods sold was $136 per unit. The volume increased by 2,400 units to 14,000 actual total units. Determine (A) the variable cost quantity factor and (B) the unit cost factor for variable cost of goods sold.

Exercises

EX 20-1   Inventory valuation under absorption costing and variable costing   Obj. 1

✔ B. Inventory, $780,800

At the end of the first year of operations, 6,400 units remained in the finished goods inventory. The unit manufacturing costs during the year were as follows:

Direct materials	$75
Direct labor	35
Fixed factory overhead	15
Variable factory overhead	12

Determine the cost of the finished goods inventory reported on the balance sheet under (A) the absorption costing concept and (B) the variable costing concept.

EX 20-2   Income statements under absorption costing and variable costing   Obj. 1

✔ A. Income from operations, $128,000

Shawnee Motors Inc. assembles and sells snowmobile engines. The company began operations on August 1 and operated at 100% of capacity during the first month. The following data summarize the results for August:

SHOW ME HOW

Sales (2,000 units)		$600,000
Production costs (2,400 units):		
Direct materials	$300,000	
Direct labor	115,200	
Variable factory overhead	43,200	
Fixed factory overhead	21,600	480,000
Selling and administrative expenses:		
Variable selling and administrative expenses	$ 50,000	
Fixed selling and administrative expenses	22,000	72,000

A. Prepare an income statement according to the absorption costing concept.

B. Prepare an income statement according to the variable costing concept.

C. ━━━▶ What is the reason for the difference in the amount of income from operations reported in (A) and (B)?

EX 20-3 Income statements under absorption costing and variable costing   Obj. 1

✔ B. Income from operations, $18,522,000

SHOW ME HOW

Joplin Industries Inc. manufactures and sells high-quality sporting goods equipment under its highly recognizable J-Sports logo. The company began operations on May 1 and operated at 100% of capacity (270,000 units) during the first month, creating an ending inventory of 24,000 units. During June, the company produced 246,000 garments during the month but sold 270,000 units at $300 per unit. The June manufacturing costs and selling and administrative expenses were as follows:

	Number of Units	Unit Cost	Total Cost
Manufacturing costs in June 1 beginning inventory:			
Variable...	24,000	$150.00	$ 3,600,000
Fixed	24,000	32.80	787,200
Total		$182.80	$ 4,387,200
Manufacturing costs in June:			
Variable...	246,000	$150.00	$36,900,000
Fixed	246,000	36.00	8,856,000
Total		$186.00	$45,756,000
Selling and administrative expenses in June:			
Variable	270,000	$ 45.00	$12,150,000
Fixed	270,000	3.60	972,000
Total		$ 48.60	$13,122,000

A. Prepare an income statement according to the absorption costing concept for June.

B. Prepare an income statement according to the variable costing concept for June.

C. ▬▬▶ What is the reason for the difference in the amount of income from operations reported in (A) and (B)?

EX 20-4 Cost of goods manufactured, using variable costing and absorption costing   Obj. 1

✔ B. Unit cost of goods manufactured, $275

On December 31, the end of the first year of operations, Frankenreiter Inc. manufactured 25,600 units and sold 24,000 units. The following income statement was prepared, based on the variable costing concept:

Frankenreiter Inc.
Variable Costing Income Statement
For the Year Ended December 31, 20Y1

Sales...		$9,600,000
Variable cost of goods sold:		
Variable cost of goods manufactured	$5,376,000	
Inventory, December 31.......................................	(336,000)	
Total variable cost of goods sold.............................		5,040,000
Manufacturing margin..		$4,560,000
Total variable selling and administrative expenses..................		1,150,000
Contribution margin...		$3,410,000
Fixed costs:		
Fixed manufacturing costs	$1,664,000	
Fixed selling and administrative expenses......................	890,000	
Total fixed costs...		2,554,000
Income from operations		$ 856,000

Determine the unit cost of goods manufactured, based on (A) the variable costing concept and (B) the absorption costing concept.

EX 20-5   Variable costing income statement

✔ Income from
operations, $720,000

SHOW ME HOW

Obj. 1

On November 30, the end of the first month of operations, Weatherford Company prepared the following income statement, based on the absorption costing concept:

Weatherford Company
Absorption Costing Income Statement
For the Month Ended November 30

Sales (104,000 units)		$5,200,000
Cost of goods sold:		
Cost of goods manufactured (120,000 units)	$4,560,000	
Inventory, November 30 (16,000 units)	(608,000)	
Total cost of goods sold		3,952,000
Gross profit		$1,248,000
Selling and administrative expenses		400,000
Income from operations		$ 848,000

If the fixed manufacturing costs were $960,000 and the fixed selling and administrative expenses were $280,000, prepare an income statement according to the variable costing concept.

EX 20-6   Absorption costing income statement

✔ Income from
operations,
$17,025,000

SHOW ME HOW

Obj. 1

On March 31, the end of the first month of operations, Sullivan Equipment Company prepared the following income statement, based on the variable costing concept:

Sullivan Equipment Company
Variable Costing Income Statement
For the Month Ended March 31

Sales (264,000 units)		$66,000,000
Variable cost of goods sold:		
Variable cost of goods manufactured	$45,000,000	
Inventory, March 31 (36,000 units)	(5,400,000)	
Total variable cost of goods sold		39,600,000
Manufacturing margin		$26,400,000
Variable selling and administrative expenses		2,400,000
Contribution margin		$24,000,000
Fixed costs:		
Fixed manufacturing costs	$ 7,500,000	
Fixed selling and administrative expenses	375,000	
Total fixed costs		7,875,000
Income from operations		$16,125,000

Prepare an income statement under absorption costing.

EX 20-7   Variable costing income statement

✔ A. Income from
operations,
$15,288

REAL WORLD

Obj. 1

The following data were adapted from a recent income statement of **Procter & Gamble Company**:

	(in millions)
Sales	$83,062
Operating costs:	
Cost of products sold	$42,460
Marketing, administrative, and other expenses	25,314
Total operating costs	$67,774
Income from operations	$15,288

Assume that the variable amount of each category of operating costs is as follows:

	(in millions)
Cost of products sold	$23,778
Marketing, administrative, and other expenses	10,125

A. Based on the data given, prepare a variable costing income statement for Procter & Gamble Company, assuming that the company maintained constant inventory levels during the period.

B. ▬▬▬▶ If Procter & Gamble reduced its inventories during the period, what impact would that have on the income from operations determined under absorption costing?

EX 20-8   Estimated income statements, using absorption and variable costing   Obj. 1, 2

✔ A. 1. Income from operations, $1,069,000 (50,000 units)

SHOW ME HOW

Prior to the first month of operations ending October 31, Marshall Inc. estimated the following operating results:

Sales (40,000 × $90)	$3,600,000
Manufacturing costs (40,000 units):	
Direct materials	1,440,000
Direct labor	480,000
Variable factory overhead	240,000
Fixed factory overhead	120,000
Fixed selling and administrative expenses.	75,000
Variable selling and administrative expenses.	200,000

The company is evaluating a proposal to manufacture 50,000 units instead of 40,000 units, thus creating an ending inventory of 10,000 units. Manufacturing the additional units will not change sales, unit variable factory overhead costs, total fixed factory overhead cost, or total selling and administrative expenses.

A. Prepare an estimated income statement, comparing operating results if 40,000 and 50,000 units are manufactured in (1) the absorption costing format and (2) the variable costing format.

B. ▬▬▬▶ What is the reason for the difference in income from operations reported for the two levels of production by the absorption costing income statement?

EX 20-9   Variable and absorption costing   Obj. 1

✔ A. Contribution margin, $6,263

Ansara Company had the following abbreviated income statement for the year ended December 31, 20Y2:

	(in millions)
Sales	$18,769
Cost of goods sold	$15,471
Selling, administrative, and other expenses	2,049
Total expenses	$17,520
Income from operations	$ 1,249

Assume that there were $3,860 million fixed manufacturing costs and $1,170 million fixed selling, administrative, and other costs for the year.

The finished goods inventories at the beginning and end of the year from the balance sheet were as follows:

January 1	$2,354 million
December 31	$2,408 million

Assume that 30% of the beginning and ending inventory consists of fixed costs. Assume work in process and materials inventory were unchanged during the period.

A. Prepare an income statement according to the variable costing concept for Ansara Company for 20Y2. (Round numbers to nearest million.)

B. ▬▬▬▶ Explain the difference between the amount of income from operations reported under the absorption costing and variable costing concepts. (Round numbers to nearest million.)

EX 20-10   Variable and absorption costing—three products

Obj. 2, 3

✔ B. Cross Training
Shoes, income
from operations,
$348,000

Winslow Inc. manufactures and sells three types of shoes. The income statements prepared under the absorption costing method for the three shoes are as follows:

Winslow Inc.
Product Income Statements—Absorption Costing
For the Year Ended December 31, 20Y1

	Cross Training Shoes	Golf Shoes	Running Shoes
Revenues	$5,800,000	$6,900,000	$4,200,000
Cost of goods sold	3,016,000	3,381,000	2,814,000
Gross profit	$2,784,000	$3,519,000	$1,386,000
Selling and administrative expenses	2,436,000	2,484,000	2,142,000
Income from operations	$ 348,000	$1,035,000	$ (756,000)

In addition, you have determined the following information with respect to allocated fixed costs:

	Cross Training Shoes	Golf Shoes	Running Shoes
Fixed costs:			
Cost of goods sold	$928,000	$897,000	$798,000
Selling and administrative expenses	696,000	828,000	588,000

These fixed costs are used to support all three product lines and will not change with the elimination of any one product. In addition, you have determined that the effects of inventory may be ignored.

The management of the company has deemed the profit performance of the running shoe line as unacceptable. As a result, it has decided to eliminate the running shoe line. Management does not expect to be able to increase sales in the other two lines. However, as a result of eliminating the running shoe line, management expects the profits of the company to increase by $756,000.

A. ━━━▶ Do you agree with management's decision and conclusions? Explain your answer.

B. Prepare a variable costing income statement for the three products.

C. ━━━▶ Use the report in (B) to determine the profit impact of eliminating the running shoe line, assuming no other changes.

EX 20-11   Change in sales mix and contribution margin

Obj. 4

Head Pops Inc. manufactures two models of solar-powered, noise-canceling headphones: Sun Sound and Ear Bling models. The company is operating at less than full capacity. Market research indicates that 28,000 additional Sun Sound and 30,000 additional Ear Bling headphones could be sold. The income from operations by unit of product is as follows:

	Sun Sound Headphones	Ear Bling Headphones
Sales price	$140.00	$125.00
Variable cost of goods sold	78.40	70.00
Manufacturing margin	$ 61.60	$ 55.00
Variable selling and administrative expenses	28.00	25.00
Contribution margin	$ 33.60	$ 30.00
Fixed manufacturing costs	14.00	12.50
Income from operations	$ 19.60	$ 17.50

Prepare an analysis indicating the increase or decrease in total profitability if 28,000 additional Sun Sound and 30,000 additional Ear Bling headphones are produced and sold, assuming that there is sufficient capacity for the additional production.

EX 20-12 Product profitability analysis   **Obj. 4**

✔ A. Desert Dragon
contribution margin,
$4,583,250

PowerTrain Sports Inc. manufactures and sells two styles of All Terrain Vehicles (ATVs), the Mountain Monster and Desert Dragon, from a single manufacturing facility. The manufacturing facility operates at 100% of capacity. The following per-unit information is available for the two products:

	Mountain Monster	Desert Dragon
Sales price	$5,400	$5,250
Variable cost of goods sold	3,285	3,400
Manufacturing margin	$2,115	$1,850
Variable selling expenses	1,035	905
Contribution margin..................	$1,080	$ 945
Fixed expenses........................	485	310
Income from operations	$ 595	$ 635

In addition, the following sales unit volume information for the period is as follows:

	Mountain Monster	Desert Dragon
Sales unit volume	5,000	4,850

A. Prepare a contribution margin by product report. Calculate the contribution margin ratio for each.

B. ▬▬▶ What advice would you give to the management of PowerTrain Sports Inc. regarding the relative profitability of the two products?

EX 20-13 Territory and product profitability analysis   **Obj. 4**

✔ A. East Coast
contribution margin,
$640,000

Coast to Coast Surfboards Inc. manufactures and sells two styles of surfboards, Atlantic Wave and Pacific Pounder. These surfboards are sold in two regions, East Coast and West Coast. Information about the two surfboards is as follows:

	Atlantic Wave	Pacific Pounder
Sales price	$200	$120
Variable cost of goods sold per unit........	150	90
Manufacturing margin per unit	$ 50	$ 30
Variable selling expense per unit..........	34	16
Contribution margin per unit..............	$ 16	$ 14

The sales unit volume for the sales territories and products for the period is as follows:

	East Coast	West Coast
Atlantic Wave	40,000	25,000
Pacific Pounder	0	25,000

A. Prepare a contribution margin by sales territory report. Calculate the contribution margin ratio for each territory as a whole percent, rounded to two decimal places.

B. ▬▬▶ What advice would you give to the management of Coast to Coast Surfboards regarding the relative profitability of the two territories?

EX 20-14 Sales territory and salesperson profitability analysis Obj. 4

Havasu Off-Road Inc. manufactures and sells a variety of commercial vehicles in the Northeast and Southwest regions. There are two salespersons assigned to each territory. Higher commission rates go to the most experienced salespersons. The following sales statistics are available for each salesperson:

| | Northeast | | Southwest | |
	Rene	Steve	Colleen	Paul
Average per unit:				
Sales price	$15,500	$16,000	$14,000	$18,000
Variable cost of goods sold	$9,300	$8,000	$8,400	$9,000
Commission rate	8%	12%	10%	8%
Units sold	36	24	40	60
Manufacturing margin ratio	40%	50%	40%	50%

A. 1. Prepare a contribution margin by salesperson report. Calculate the contribution margin ratio for each salesperson.

    2. ▸ Interpret the report.

B. 1. Prepare a contribution margin by territory report. Calculate the contribution margin for each territory as a percent, rounded to one decimal place.

    2. ▸ Interpret the report.

EX 20-15 Segment profitability analysis Obj. 4

The marketing segment sales for **Caterpillar, Inc.**, for a year follow:

Caterpillar, Inc.
Machinery and Engines Marketing Segment Sales
(in millions)

	Building Construction Products	Cat Japan	Core Components	Earth-moving	Electric Power	Excavation	Large Power Systems	Logistics	Marine & Petroleum Power	Mining	Turbines
Sales	$2,217	$1,225	$1,234	$5,045	$2,847	$4,562	$2,885	$659	$2,132	$3,975	$3,321

In addition, assume the following information:

	Building Construction Products	Cat Japan	Core Components	Earth-moving	Electric Power	Excavation	Large Power Systems	Logistics	Marine & Petroleum Power	Mining	Turbines
Variable cost of goods sold as a percent of sales	45%	55%	49%	51%	54%	52%	53%	50%	50%	52%	48%
Dealer commissions as a percent of sales	9%	11%	8%	8%	10%	6%	5%	10%	9%	7%	9%
Variable promotion expenses (in millions)	310	120	150	600	200	600	300	75	270	480	400

A. Use the sales information and the additional assumed information to prepare a contribution margin by segment report. Round to two decimal places. In addition, calculate the contribution margin ratio for each segment as a percentage, rounded to one decimal place.

B. Prepare a table showing the manufacturing margin, dealer commissions, and variable promotion expenses as a percent of sales for each segment. (Round whole percents to one decimal place.)

C. ▸ Use the information in (A) and (B) to interpret the segment performance.

EX 20-16 Segment contribution margin analysis

Obj. 4, 6

✔ A. Turner, 60%

REAL WORLD

The operating revenues of the three largest business segments for **Time Warner, Inc.**, for a recent year follow. Each segment includes a number of businesses, examples of which are indicated in parentheses.

Time Warner, Inc.
Segment Revenues
(in millions)

Turner (cable networks and digital media)	$10,596
Home Box Office (pay television)	5,615
Warner Bros. (films, television, and videos)	12,993

Assume that the variable costs as a percent of sales for each segment are as follows:

Turner	40%
Home Box Office	35%
Warner Bros.	25%

A. Determine the contribution margin (round to whole millions) and contribution margin ratio (round to whole percents) for each segment from the information given.

B. Does the segment with the highest contribution margin in (A) mean that it is the most profitable segment with the highest operating income?

EX 20-17 Contribution margin analysis—sales

Obj. 5

✔ A. Sales quantity factor, $121,875

EXCEL TEMPLATE

Select Audio Inc. sells electronic equipment. Management decided early in the year to reduce the price of the speakers in order to increase sales volume. As a result, for the year ended December 31, the sales increased by $31,875 from the planned level of $1,048,125. The following information is available from the accounting records for the year ended December 31.

	Actual	Planned	Increase or (Decrease)
Sales	$1,080,000	$1,048,125	$31,875
Number of units sold	36,000	32,250	3,750
Sales price	$30.00	$32.50	$(2.50)
Variable cost per unit	$10.00	$10.00	$0

A. Prepare an analysis of the sales quantity and unit price factors.

B. ▬▬▬▶ Did the price decrease generate sufficient volume to result in a net increase in contribution margin if the actual variable cost per unit was $10, as planned?

EX 20-18 Contribution margin analysis—sales

Obj. 5

✔ Sales quantity factor, $(600,000)

EXCEL TEMPLATE

The following data for Romero Products Inc. are available:

For the Year Ended December 31	Actual	Planned	Difference— Increase or (Decrease)
Sales	$8,360,000	$8,200,000	$ 160,000
Variable costs:			
Variable cost of goods sold	$3,496,000	$3,280,000	$ 216,000
Variable selling and administrative expenses. . . .	760,000	902,000	(142,000)
Total variable costs.	$4,256,000	$4,182,000	$ 74,000
Contribution margin.	$4,104,000	$4,018,000	$ 86,000
Number of units sold	38,000	41,000	
Per unit:			
Sales price	$220	$200	
Variable cost of goods sold	92	80	
Variable selling and administrative expenses. . . .	20	22	

Prepare an analysis of the sales quantity and unit price factors.

✔ Variable
cost of goods
sold quantity
factor, EXCEL TEMPLATE
$240,000

EX 20-19 Contribution margin analysis—variable costs

Obj. 5

Based on the data in Exercise 18 prepare a contribution margin analysis of the variable costs for Romero Products Inc. for the year ended December 31.

✔ A. Contribution
margin, Atlanta/
Baltimore, $(29,291)

EX 20-20 Variable costing income statement for a service company

Obj. 4, 6

East Coast Railroad Company transports commodities among three routes (city-pairs): Atlanta/Baltimore, Baltimore/Pittsburgh, and Pittsburgh/Atlanta. Significant costs, their cost behavior, and activity rates for April are as follows:

Cost	Amount	Cost Behavior	Activity Rate
Labor costs for loading and unloading railcars	$ 175,582	Variable	$46.00 per railcar
Fuel costs	460,226	Variable	12.40 per train-mile
Train crew labor costs	267,228	Variable	7.20 per train-mile
Switchyard labor costs	118,327	Variable	31.00 per railcar
Track and equipment depreciation	194,400	Fixed	
Maintenance	129,600	Fixed	
	$1,345,363		

Operating statistics from the management information system reveal the following for April:

	Atlanta/ Baltimore	Baltimore/ Pittsburgh	Pittsburgh/ Atlanta	Total
Number of train-miles	12,835	10,200	14,080	37,115
Number of railcars	425	2,160	1,232	3,817
Revenue per railcar	$600	$275	$440	

A. Prepare a contribution margin by route report for East Coast Railroad Company for the month of April. Calculate the contribution margin ratio in whole percents, rounded to one decimal place.

B. ━━━━▶ Evaluate the route performance of the railroad using the report in (A).

✔ A. East Coast
contribution
margin, $44,534

EXCEL TEMPLATE

EX 20-21 Contribution margin reporting and analysis for a service company

Obj. 5, 6

The management of East Coast Railroad Company introduced in Exercise 20 improved the profitability of the Atlanta/Baltimore route in May by reducing the price of a railcar from $600 to $500. This price reduction increased the demand for rail services. Thus, the number of railcars increased by 275 railcars to a total of 700 railcars. This was accomplished by increasing the size of each train but not the number of trains. Thus, the number of train-miles was unchanged. All the activity rates remained unchanged.

A. Prepare a contribution margin report for the Atlanta/Baltimore route for May. Calculate the contribution margin ratio in percentage terms to one decimal place.

B. Prepare a contribution margin analysis to evaluate management's actions in May. Assume that the May planned quantity, price, and unit cost were the same as April.

✔ A. Contribution
margin, $2,147,700

EXCEL TEMPLATE

EX 20-22 Variable costing income statement and contribution margin analysis for a service company

Obj. 5, 6

The actual and planned data for Underwater University for the Fall term were as follows:

	Actual	Planned
Enrollment	4,500	4,125
Tuition per credit hour	$120	$135
Credit hours	60,450	43,200
Registration, records, and marketing cost per enrolled student	$275	$275
Instructional costs per credit hour	$64	$60
Depreciation on classrooms and equipment	$825,600	$825,600

Registration, records, and marketing costs vary by the number of enrolled students, while instructional costs vary by the number of credit hours. Depreciation is a fixed cost.

A. Prepare a variable costing income statement showing the contribution margin and income from operations for the Fall term.

B. Prepare a contribution margin analysis report comparing planned with actual performance for the Fall term.

Problems: Series A

PR 20-1A   Absorption and variable costing income statements   Obj. 1, 2

✔ 2. Income from operations, $868,000

SHOW ME HOW

During the first month of operations ended August 31, Kodiak Fridgeration Company manufactured 80,000 mini refrigerators, of which 72,000 were sold. Operating data for the month are summarized as follows:

Sales		$10,800,000
Manufacturing costs:		
Direct materials	$ 6,400,000	
Direct labor	1,600,000	
Variable manufacturing cost	1,280,000	
Fixed manufacturing cost	320,000	9,600,000
Selling and administrative expenses:		
Variable	$1,080,000	
Fixed	180,000	1,260,000

Instructions

1. Prepare an income statement based on the absorption costing concept.

2. Prepare an income statement based on the variable costing concept.

3. ➤ Explain the reason for the difference in the amount of income from operations reported in (1) and (2).

PR 20-2A   Income statements under absorption costing and variable costing   Obj. 1, 2

✔ 2. Contribution margin, $92,800

The demand for solvent, one of numerous products manufactured by RZM Industries Inc., has dropped sharply because of recent competition from a similar product. The company's chemists are currently completing tests of various new formulas, and it is anticipated that the manufacture of a superior product can be started on June 1, one month in the future. No changes will be needed in the present production facilities to manufacture the new product because only the mixture of the various materials will be changed.

The controller has been asked by the president of the company for advice on whether to continue production during May or to suspend the manufacture of solvent until June 1. The controller has assembled the following pertinent data:

RZM Industries Inc.
Income Statement—Solvent
For the Month Ended April 30

Sales (4,000 units)	$500,000
Cost of goods sold	424,000
Gross profit	$ 76,000
Selling and administrative expenses	102,000
Loss from operations	$ (26,000)

(Continued)

The production costs and selling and administrative expenses, based on production of 4,000 units in April, are as follows:

Direct materials	$45 per unit
Direct labor	20 per unit
Variable manufacturing cost	16 per unit
Variable selling and administrative expenses	15 per unit
Fixed manufacturing cost	$100,000 for April
Fixed selling and administrative expenses	42,000 for April

Sales for May are expected to drop about 20% below those of the preceding month. No significant changes are anticipated in the fixed costs or variable costs per unit. No extra costs will be incurred in discontinuing operations in the portion of the plant associated with solvent. The inventory of solvent at the beginning and end of May is expected to be inconsequential.

Instructions

1. Prepare an estimated income statement in absorption costing form for May for solvent, assuming that production continues during the month.

2. Prepare an estimated income statement in variable costing form for May for solvent, assuming that production continues during the month.

3. What would be the estimated loss in income from operations if the solvent production were temporarily suspended for May?

4. ➤ What advice should the controller give to management?

PR 20-3A   Absorption and variable costing income statements for two months and analysis

Obj. 1, 2

✔ 1. B. Income from operations, $847,000

SHOW ME HOW

During the first month of operations ended July 31, Western Creations Company produced 80,000 designer cowboy hats, of which 72,000 were sold. Operating data for the month are summarized as follows:

Sales		$4,320,000
Manufacturing costs:		
Direct materials	$1,600,000	
Direct labor	1,440,000	
Variable manufacturing cost	240,000	
Fixed manufacturing cost	320,000	3,600,000
Selling and administrative expenses:		
Variable	$ 144,000	
Fixed	25,000	169,000

During August, Western Creations produced 64,000 designer cowboy hats and sold 72,000 cowboy hats. Operating data for August are summarized as follows:

Sales		$4,320,000
Manufacturing costs:		
Direct materials	$1,280,000	
Direct labor	1,152,000	
Variable manufacturing cost	192,000	
Fixed manufacturing cost	320,000	2,944,000
Selling and administrative expenses:		
Variable	$ 144,000	
Fixed	25,000	169,000

Instructions

1. Using the absorption costing concept, prepare income statements for (A) July and (B) August.

2. Using the variable costing concept, prepare income statements for (A) July and (B) August.

3. A. ➤ Explain the reason for the differences in the amount of income from operations in (1) and (2) for July.

   B. ➤ Explain the reason for the differences in the amount of income from operations in (1) and (2) for August.

4. ➤ Based on your answers to (1) and (2), did Western Creations Company operate more profitably in July or in August? Explain.

PR 20-4A Salespersons' report and analysis
Obj. 4

✔ 1. Dix contribution margin ratio, 44.0%

Walthman Industries Inc. employs seven salespersons to sell and distribute its product throughout the state. Data taken from reports received from the salespersons during the year ended December 31 are as follows:

Salesperson	Total Sales	Variable Cost of Goods Sold	Variable Selling Expenses
Case	$610,000	$268,400	$109,800
Dix	603,000	241,200	96,480
Johnson	588,000	305,760	105,840
LaFave	586,000	281,280	123,060
Orcas	616,000	221,760	86,240
Sussman	620,000	310,000	124,000
Willbond	592,000	272,320	88,800

Instructions

1. Prepare a table indicating contribution margin, variable cost of goods sold as a percent of sales, variable selling expenses as a percent of sales, and contribution margin ratio by salesperson. (Round whole percent to one digit after decimal point.)

2. ➤ Which salesperson generated the highest contribution margin ratio for the year and why?

3. ➤ Briefly list factors other than contribution margin that should be considered in evaluating the performance of salespersons.

PR 20-5A   Segment variable costing income statement and effect on income of change in operations
Obj. 4

✔ 1. Contribution margin, Size S, $235,520

EXCEL TEMPLATE

Valdespin Company manufactures three sizes of camping tents—small (S), medium (M), and large (L). The income statement has consistently indicated a net loss for the M size, and management is considering three proposals: (1) continue Size M, (2) discontinue Size M and reduce total output accordingly, or (3) discontinue Size M and conduct an advertising campaign to expand the sales of Size S so that the entire plant capacity can continue to be used.

If Proposal 2 is selected and Size M is discontinued and production curtailed, the annual fixed production costs and fixed operating expenses could be reduced by $46,080 and $32,240, respectively. If Proposal 3 is selected, it is anticipated that an additional annual expenditure of $34,560 for the rental of additional warehouse space would yield an additional 130% in Size S sales volume. It is also assumed that the increased production of Size S would utilize the plant facilities released by the discontinuance of Size M.

(Continued)

The sales and costs have been relatively stable over the past few years, and they are expected to remain so for the foreseeable future. The income statement for the past year ended June 30, 20Y9, is as follows:

	Size			
	S	**M**	**L**	**Total**
Sales	$668,000	$737,300	$ 956,160	$2,361,460
Cost of goods sold:				
Variable costs	$300,000	$357,120	$437,760	$1,094,880
Fixed costs	74,880	138,250	172,800	385,930
Total cost of goods sold	$374,880	$495,370	$ 610,560	$1,480,810
Gross profit	$293,120	$241,930	$ 345,600	$ 880,650
Operating expenses:				
Variable expenses	$132,480	$155,500	$ 195,840	$ 483,820
Fixed expenses	92,160	103,680	115,200	311,040
Total operating expenses	$224,640	$ 259,180	$ 311,040	$ 794,860
Income from operations	$ 68,480	$ (17,250)	$ 34,560	$ 85,790

Instructions

1. Prepare an income statement for the past year in the variable costing format. Use the following headings:

Size			
S	M	L	Total

   Data for each style should be reported through contribution margin. The fixed costs should be deducted from the total contribution margin, as reported in the "Total" column, to determine income from operations.

2. Based on the income statement prepared in (1) and the other data presented, determine the amount by which total annual income from operations would be reduced below its present level if Proposal 2 is accepted.

3. Prepare an income statement in the variable costing format, indicating the projected annual income from operations if Proposal 3 is accepted. Use the following headings:

Size		
S	L	Total

   Data for each style should be reported through contribution margin. The fixed costs should be deducted from the total contribution margin as reported in the "Total" column. For purposes of this problem, the expenditure of $34,560 for the rental of additional warehouse space can be added to the fixed operating expenses.

4. ━━━━━▶ By how much would total annual income increase above its present level if Proposal 3 is accepted? Explain.

PR 20-6A   Contribution margin analysis   **Obj. 5**

1. Sales quantity
factor, $(2,200,000)

EXCEL TEMPLATE

Farr Industries Inc. manufactures only one product. For the year ended December 31, the contribution margin increased by $560,000 from the planned level of $5,200,000. The president of Farr Industries Inc. has expressed concern about such a small increase in contribution margin and has requested a follow-up report.

The following data have been gathered from the accounting records for the year ended December 31:

	Actual	Planned	Difference—Increase (Decrease)
Sales	$30,000,000	$28,600,000	$1,400,000
Variable costs:			
Variable cost of goods sold	$21,600,000	$21,450,000	$ 150,000
Variable selling and administrative expenses	2,640,000	1,950,000	690,000
Total variable costs	$24,240,000	$23,400,000	$ 840,000
Contribution margin	$ 5,760,000	$ 5,200,000	$ 560,000
Number of units sold	120,000	130,000	
Per unit:			
Sales price	$250	$220	
Variable cost of goods sold	180	165	
Variable selling and administrative expenses	22	15	

Instructions

1. Prepare a contribution margin analysis report for the year ended December 31.

2. ➤ At a meeting of the board of directors on January 30, the president, after reviewing the contribution margin analysis report, made the following comment:

It looks as if the price increase of $30 had the effect of increasing sales. However, this was a trade-off since sales volume decreased. Also, variable cost of goods sold per unit increased by $15 more than planned. The variable selling and administrative expenses appear out of control. They increased by $7 per unit more than was planned, which is an increase of over 47% more than was planned. Let's look into these expenses and get them under control! Also, let's consider increasing the sales price to $275 and continue this favorable trade-off between higher price and lower volume.

Do you agree with the president's comment? Explain.

Problems: Series B

✔ 2. Contribution margin, $666,000

SHOW ME HOW

PR 20-1B Absorption and variable costing income statements Obj. 1, 2

During the first month of operations ended July 31, YoSan Inc. manufactured 2,400 flat panel televisions, of which 2,000 were sold. Operating data for the month are summarized as follows:

Sales		$2,150,000
Manufacturing costs:		
Direct materials	$960,000	
Direct labor	420,000	
Variable manufacturing cost	156,000	
Fixed manufacturing cost	288,000	1,824,000
Selling and administrative expenses:		
Variable	$204,000	
Fixed	96,000	300,000

Instructions

1. Prepare an income statement based on the absorption costing concept.

2. Prepare an income statement based on the variable costing concept.

3. ➤ Explain the reason for the difference in the amount of income from operations reported in (1) and (2).

PR 20-2B Income statements under absorption costing and variable costing   Obj. 1, 2

✔ 2. Contribution
margin, $960,000

The demand for aloe vera hand lotion, one of numerous products manufactured by Smooth Skin Care Products Inc., has dropped sharply because of recent competition from a similar product. The company's chemists are currently completing tests of various new formulas, and it is anticipated that the manufacture of a superior product can be started on December 1, one month in the future. No changes will be needed in the present production facilities to manufacture the new product because only the mixture of the various materials will be changed.

The controller has been asked by the president of the company for advice on whether to continue production during November or to suspend the manufacture of aloe vera hand lotion until December 1. The controller has assembled the following pertinent data:

Smooth Skin Care Products Inc.
Income Statement—Aloe Vera Hand Lotion
For the Month Ended October 31

Sales (400,000 units)	$32,000,000
Cost of goods sold	28,330,000
Gross profit	$ 3,670,000
Selling and administrative expenses	4,270,000
Loss from operations	$ (600,000)

The production costs and selling and administrative expenses, based on production of 400,000 units in October, are as follows:

Direct materials	$15 per unit
Direct labor	17 per unit
Variable manufacturing cost	35 per unit
Variable selling and administrative expenses	10 per unit
Fixed manufacturing cost	$1,530,000 for October
Fixed selling and administrative expenses	270,000 for October

Sales for November are expected to drop about 20% below those of the preceding month. No significant changes are anticipated in the fixed costs or variable costs per unit. No extra costs will be incurred in discontinuing operations in the portion of the plant associated with aloe vera hand lotion. The inventory of aloe vera hand lotion at the beginning and end of November is expected to be inconsequential.

Instructions

1. Prepare an estimated income statement in absorption costing form for November for aloe vera hand lotion, assuming that production continues during the month.

2. Prepare an estimated income statement in variable costing form for November for aloe vera hand lotion, assuming that production continues during the month.

3. What would be the estimated loss in income from operations if the aloe vera hand lotion production were temporarily suspended for November?

4. ◖▬▬▶ What advice should the controller give to management?

PR 20-3B Absorption and variable costing income statements for   Obj. 1, 2
two months and analysis

✔ 2. A.
Manufacturing
margin, $37,440

SHOW ME HOW

During the first month of operations ended July 31, Head Gear Inc. manufactured 6,400 hats, of which 5,200 were sold. Operating data for the month are summarized as follows:

Sales		$104,000
Manufacturing costs:		
Direct materials	$47,360	
Direct labor	22,400	
Variable manufacturing cost	12,160	
Fixed manufacturing cost	15,360	97,280
Selling and administrative expenses:		
Variable	$10,920	
Fixed	5,200	16,120

During August, Head Gear Inc. manufactured 4,000 hats and sold 5,200 hats. Operating data for August are summarized as follows:

Sales		$104,000
Manufacturing costs:		
Direct materials	$29,600	
Direct labor	14,000	
Variable manufacturing cost	7,600	
Fixed manufacturing cost	15,360	66,560
Selling and administrative expenses:		
Variable	$10,920	
Fixed	5,200	16,120

Instructions

1. Using the absorption costing concept, prepare income statements for (A) July and (B) August.

2. Using the variable costing concept, prepare income statements for (A) July and (B) August.

3. A. ➤ Explain the reason for the differences in the amount of income from operations in (1) and (2) for July.

   B. ➤ Explain the reason for the differences in the amount of income from operations in (1) and (2) for August.

4. ➤ Based on your answers to (1) and (2), did Head Gear Inc. operate more profitably in July or in August? Explain.

PR 20-4B Salespersons' report and analysis Obj. 4

✔ 1. Crowell contribution margin ratio, 44.0%

Pachec Inc. employs seven salespersons to sell and distribute its product throughout the state. Data taken from reports received from the salespersons during the year ended June 30 are as follows:

Salesperson	Total Sales	Variable Cost of Goods Sold	Variable Selling Expenses
Asarenka	$437,500	$196,875	$ 83,125
Crowell	570,000	228,000	91,200
Dempster	675,000	310,500	141,750
MacLean	587,500	246,750	123,375
Ortiz	525,000	215,250	126,000
Sullivan	587,500	246,750	99,875
Williams	575,000	253,000	115,000

Instructions

1. Prepare a table indicating contribution margin, variable cost of goods sold as a percent of sales, variable selling expenses as a percent of sales, and contribution margin ratio by salesperson.

2. ➤ Which salesperson generated the highest contribution margin ratio for the year and why?

3. ➤ Briefly list factors other than contribution margin that should be considered in evaluating the performance of salespersons.

PR 20-5B Variable costing income statement and effect on income of change in operations Obj. 4

✔ 3. Income from operations, $106,820

EXCEL TEMPLATE

Kimbrell Inc. manufactures three sizes of utility tables—small (S), medium (M), and large (L). The income statement has consistently indicated a net loss for the M size, and management is considering three proposals: (1) continue Size M, (2) discontinue Size M and reduce total output accordingly, or (3) discontinue Size M and conduct an advertising campaign to expand the sales of Size S so that the entire plant capacity can continue to be used.

(Continued)

If Proposal 2 is selected and Size M is discontinued and production curtailed, the annual fixed production costs and fixed operating expenses could be reduced by $142,500 and $28,350, respectively. If Proposal 3 is selected, it is anticipated that an additional annual expenditure of $85,050 for the salary of an assistant brand manager (classified as a fixed operating expense) would yield an additional 130% in Size S sales volume. It is also assumed that the increased production of Size S would utilize the plant facilities released by the discontinuance of Size M.

The sales and costs have been relatively stable over the past few years, and they are expected to remain so for the foreseeable future. The income statement for the past year ended December 31, 20Y8, is as follows:

| | Size | | | |
	S	M	L	Total
Sales	$990,000	$1,087,500	$945,000	$3,022,500
Cost of goods sold:				
Variable costs	$538,500	$718,500	$567,000	$1,824,000
Fixed costs	241,000	288,000	250,000	779,000
Total cost of goods sold	$779,500	$1,006,500	$817,000	$2,603,000
Gross profit	$210,500	$81,000	$128,000	$419,500
Less operating expenses:				
Variable expenses	$118,100	$108,750	$85,050	$311,900
Fixed expenses	32,125	42,525	14,250	88,900
Total operating expenses	$150,225	$151,275	$99,300	$400,800
Income from operations	$60,275	$(70,275)	$28,700	$18,700

Instructions

1. Prepare an income statement for the past year in the variable costing format. Use the following headings:

Size		
S	M	L	Total

   Data for each style should be reported through contribution margin. The fixed costs should be deducted from the total contribution margin, as reported in the "Total" column, to determine income from operations.

2. Based on the income statement prepared in (1) and the other data presented above, determine the amount by which total annual income from operations would be reduced below its present level if Proposal 2 is accepted.

3. Prepare an income statement in the variable costing format, indicating the projected annual income from operations if Proposal 3 is accepted. Use the following headings:

Size	
S	L	Total

   Data for each style should be reported through contribution margin. The fixed costs should be deducted from the total contribution margin as reported in the "Total" column. For purposes of this problem, the additional expenditure of $85,050 for the assistant brand manager's salary can be added to the fixed operating expenses.

4. ⬤━━▶ By how much would total annual income increase above its present level if Proposal 3 is accepted? Explain.

PR 20-6B Contribution margin analysis

Obj. 5

✔ 1. Sales quantity factor, $310,500

EXCEL TEMPLATE

Mathews Company manufactures only one product. For the year ended December 31, the contribution margin decreased by $126,000 from the planned level of $540,000. The president of Mathews Company has expressed some concern about this decrease and has requested a follow-up report.

The following data have been gathered from the accounting records for the year ended December 31:

	Actual	Planned	Difference—Increase or (Decrease)
Sales	$2,277,000	$2,070,000	$ 207,000
Variable costs:			
Variable cost of goods sold	$1,035,000	$ 990,000	$ 45,000
Variable selling and administrative expenses	828,000	540,000	288,000
Total variable costs	$1,863,000	$1,530,000	$ 333,000
Contribution margin	$ 414,000	$ 540,000	$(126,000)
Number of units sold	34,500	30,000	
Per unit:			
Sales price	$66	$69	
Variable cost of goods sold	30	33	
Variable selling and administrative expenses	24	18	

Instructions

1. Prepare a contribution margin analysis report for the year ended December 31.

2. ➤ At a meeting of the board of directors on January 30, the president, after reviewing the contribution margin analysis report, made the following comment:

   It looks as if the price decrease of $3.00 had the effect of increasing sales. However, we lost control over the variable cost of goods sold and variable selling and administrative expenses. Let's look into these expenses and get them under control! Also, let's consider decreasing the sales price to $60 to increase sales further.

   Do you agree with the president's comment? Explain.

Analysis for Decision Making

REAL WORLD

ADM-1 Yum! Brands: Segment sales and EBITDA analysis

Yum! Brands, Inc. is a worldwide operator and franchisor of fast food restaurants, under the familiar brands of KFC, Pizza Hut, and Taco Bell. Segment revenues, operating income, and depreciation and amortization expense for Yum!'s operating segments are provided for a recent year as follows (in millions):

	Sales	Operating Income	Depreciation and Amortization Expense
China	$6,934	$713	$411
KFC	3,193	708	187
Pizza Hut	1,148	295	39
Taco Bell	1,863	480	83
India	141	(9)	10

Yum!'s segments include the three restaurant brands plus two emerging regional segments, China and India. In China and India, all three restaurant brands are combined into the regional reporting.

A. Prepare a vertical analysis of the sales as a percent of total sales for the five segments. (Round percentages to the nearest whole percent.) Which segment has the greatest percentage of total sales?

B. Determine the earnings before interest, taxes, depreciation, and amortization (EBITDA) for the five segments.

(Continued)

C.   Determine the EBITDA as a percent of sales (EBITDA margin) for the five segments. (Round percentages to the nearest whole percent.)

D.   ━━━▶ Interpret the analysis in (C).

REAL WORLD

ADM-2   Walt Disney: Segment revenue analysis

The Walt Disney Company is a leading worldwide entertainment company. Disney operates five business segments. These segments and some of their larger businesses are:

- Media Networks: ABC Network, ESPN, Disney Channel, and A&E
- Parks and Resorts: Walt Disney World Resort, Disneyland, and International Disney Resorts
- Studio Entertainment: Walt Disney Pictures, Pixar, Marvel, and Lucasfilm
- Consumer Products: licensing of Disney characters, publishing, and retail stores
- Interactive: video games

Recent comparative revenues for the five segments are as follows (in millions):

	Year 3	Year 1
Media Networks	$21,152	$19,436
Parks and Resorts	15,099	12,920
Studio Entertainment	7,278	5,825
Consumer Products	3,985	3,252
Interactive	1,299	845
Total	$48,813	$42,278

A.   Prepare a vertical analysis of the segment sales to total sales for Year 1 and Year 3. (Round percentages to nearest whole percent.)

B.   Using the analysis in (A), has the relative segment sales changed between Year 1 and Year 3?

C.   Prepare a horizontal analysis of the segment sales between Year 1 and Year 3. (Round percentages to nearest whole percent.)

D.   ━━━▶ Interpret the horizontal segment sales analysis in (C).

REAL WORLD

ADM-3   Apple Inc.: Segment revenue analysis

Segment disclosure by **Apple Inc.** provides sales information for its major product lines for three recent years as follows (in millions):

	Year 3	Year 2	Year 1
iPhone	$101,991	$ 91,279	$ 78,692
iPad	30,283	31,980	30,945
Mac	24,079	21,483	23,221
iPod	2,286	4,411	5,615
iTunes, Software, and Services	18,063	16,051	12,890
Accessories	6,093	5,706	5,145
Total sales	$182,795	$170,910	$156,508

A.   Which product had the greatest percentage of Year 3 sales? Which product had the least percentage of Year 3 sales? (Round to nearest whole percent.)

B.   Which product grew the most in sales, in percentage terms, using Year 1 as the base year? (Round to nearest whole percent.)

ADM-4   LVMH: Group segment sales and EBITDA analysis

LVMH Group is a French domiciled company known for Dior, Givenchy, Louis Vuitton, and many other fashion brands. LVMH's operating segment revenues, operating income, and depreciation and amortization expenses for a recent year are as follows (in millions of euros):

	Wine and Spirits	Fashion and Leather Goods	Perfumes and Cosmetics	Watches and Jewelry	Selective Retailing
Sales	€3,973	€10,828	€3,916	€2,782	€ 312
Operating income	1,147	3,189	415	283	(162)
Depreciation and amortization expense	119	555	149	171	41

A. Prepare a vertical analysis of the segment sales to total sales. (Round to nearest whole percent.)
B. Interpret the vertical analysis in (A).
C. Compute (1) EBITDA and (2) EBITDA as a percent of sales (EBITDA margin) for each segment. (Round to nearest whole percent.)
D. Prepare a column bar chart of the EBITDA as a percent of sales for the segments in descending order.
E.  Interpret the chart in (D).

Take It Further

TIF 20-1   Ethics in Action

The Southern Division manager of Texcaliber Inc. is growing concerned that the division will not be able to meet its current period income objectives. The division uses absorption costing for internal profit reporting and had an appropriate level of inventory at the beginning of the period. The division manager knows that he can boost profits by increasing production at the end of the period. The increased production will allocate fixed costs over a greater number of units, reducing cost of goods sold and increasing earnings. Unfortunately, it is unlikely that additional production will be sold, resulting in a large ending inventory balance.

The division manager has come to Aston Melon, the divisional controller, to determine exactly how much additional production is needed to increase net income enough to meet the division's profit objectives. Aston analyzes the data and determines that the division will need to increase inventory by 30% in order to absorb enough fixed costs to meet the division's income objective. Aston reports this information to the division manager.

Is Aston acting ethically?

TIF 20-2   Team Activity

BendOR, Inc. manufactures control panels for the electronics industry and has just completed its first year of operations. The following discussion took place between the controller, Gordon Merrick, and the company president, Matt McCray:

Matt: I've been looking over our first year's performance by quarters. Our earnings have been increasing each quarter, even though our sales have been flat and our prices and costs have not changed. Why is this?

Gordon: Our actual sales have stayed even throughout the year, but we've been increasing the utilization of our factory every quarter. By keeping our factory utilization high, we will keep our costs down by allocating the fixed plant costs over a greater number of units. Naturally, this causes our cost per unit to be lower than it would be otherwise.

Matt: Yes, but what good is this if we are unable to sell everything that we make? Our inventory is also increasing.

Gordon: This is true. However, our unit costs are lower because of the additional production. When these lower costs are matched against sales, it has a positive impact on our earnings.

Matt: Are you saying that we are able to create additional earnings merely by building inventory? Can this be true?

Gordon: Well, I've never thought about it quite that way. . . but I guess so.

Matt: And another thing. What will happen if we begin to reduce our production in order to liquidate the inventory? Don't tell me our earnings will go down even though our production effort drops!

Gordon: Well. . .

Matt: There must be a better way. I'd like our quarterly income statements to reflect what's really going on. I don't want our income reports to reward building inventory and penalize reducing inventory.

Gordon: I'm not sure what I can do—we have to follow generally accepted accounting principles.

In teams:

A. Discuss why reporting income under generally accepted accounting principles "rewards" building inventory and "penalizes" reducing inventory.

B. Discuss what advice you would give to Gordon in responding to Matt's concern about the present method of accounting.

Be prepared to discuss your answers in class.

TIF 20-3   Communication

Bon Jager Inc. manufactures and sells medical devices used in cardiovascular surgery. The sales team consists of two salespeople, Dean and Martin. A contribution margin report by salesperson was prepared as follows:

Bon Jager Inc. Contribution Margin by Salesperson	Dean	Martin
Sales..	$400,000	$480,000
Variable cost of goods sold...	184,000	264,000
Manufacturing margin	$216,000	$216,000
Variable selling expenses:		
Variable promotion expenses..	$ 72,000	$ 43,200
Variable sales commission expenses	56,000	67,200
Total variable selling expenses.....................................	$128,000	$110,400
Contribution margin..	$ 88,000	$105,600
Manufacturing margin as a percent of sales (manufacturing margin ratio)...	54%	45%
Contribution margin ratio..	22%	22%

> Write a brief memo to Anna Berenson, the Vice President of Marketing, evaluating the performance of the company's salespeople and providing recommendations on how the salespeople could improve profitability.

Concepts and Principles

Chapter 15 *Introduction to Managerial Accounting*

Developing Information

COST SYSTEMS	**COST BEHAVIOR**
Chapter 16 *Job Order Costing*	**Chapter 19** *Cost-Volume-Profit Analysis*
Chapter 17 *Process Cost Systems*	
Chapter 18 *Activity-Based Costing*	

Decision Making

EVALUATING PERFORMANCE	**COMPARING ALTERNATIVES**
Chapter 20 *Variable Costing for Management Analysis*	**Chapter 23** *Evaluating Decentralized Operations*
Chapter 21 *Budgeting*	**Chapter 24** *Differential Analysis and Product Pricing*
Chapter 22 *Evaluating Variances from Standard Costs*	**Chapter 25** *Capital Investment Analysis*
	Chapter 26 *Lean Manufacturing*

Hendrick Motorsports

You may have financial goals for your life. To achieve these goals, it is necessary to plan for future expenses. For example, you may consider taking a part-time job to save money for school expenses for the coming school year. How much money would you need to earn and save in order to pay these expenses? One way to find an answer to this question would be to prepare a budget. A budget would show an estimate of your expenses associated with school, such as tuition, fees, and books. In addition, you would have expenses for day-to-day living, such as rent, food, and clothing. You might also have expenses for travel and entertainment. Once the school year begins, you can use the budget as a tool for guiding your spending priorities during the year.

The budget is used in businesses in much the same way it can be used in personal life. For example, **Hendrick Motorsports**, featuring drivers Dale Earnhardt, Jr., Jeff Gordon, and Jimmie Johnson, uses budget information to remain one of the most valuable racing teams in NASCAR. Hendrick uses budgets to keep revenues greater than expenses. For example, Hendrick plans revenues from car sponsorships and winnings. Primary and secondary sponsorships (car decals) can provide as much as 70% of the revenues for a typical race team. Costs include salaries, engines, tires, cars, travel, and research and development. In addition, star drivers such as Dale Earnhardt, Jr. can earn as much as $28 million in salary, winnings, and endorsements. Overall, Hendrick is estimated to earn $179 million in revenues and $16.6 million in operating income from its four race teams. The budget provides the company with a "game plan" for the year. In this chapter, you will see how budgets can be used for financial planning and control.

Sources: Kurt Badenhausen, "Hendrick Motorsports Tops List of Nascar's Most Valuable Teams," *Forbes*, March 13, 2013. Bob Pockrass, "NASCAR's highest-paid drivers make their money from a variety of sources," *Sporting News*, December 4, 2012. Ed Hilton, "Under the Hood at Hendrick Motorsports," *Chicago Tribune*, July 13, 2007. www.hendrickmotorsports.com.

What's Covered

Learning Objectives

Obj. 1 Describe budgeting, its objectives, and its impact on human behavior.

Obj. 2 Describe the basic elements of the budget process, the two major types of budgeting, and the use of computers in budgeting.

Obj. 3 Describe the master budget for a manufacturing company.

Obj. 4 Prepare the basic operating budgets for a manufacturing company.

Obj. 5 Prepare financial budgets for a manufacturing company.

Analysis for Decision Making

Describe and Illustrate the use of staffing budgets for nonmanufacturing businesses.

Objective 1

Describe budgeting, its objectives, and its impact on human behavior.

Nature and Objectives of Budgeting

Budgets play an important role for organizations of all sizes and forms. For example, budgets are used in managing the operations of government agencies, churches, hospitals, and other nonprofit organizations. Individuals and families also use budgeting in managing their financial affairs. This chapter describes and illustrates budgeting for a manufacturing company.

Link to Hendrick Motorsports

Hendrick Motorsports holds a record of 11 NASCAR Sprint Cup Series Championships won by the following drivers: 6 by Jimmie Johnson, 4 by Jeff Gordon, and 1 by Terry Labonte.

Objectives of Budgeting

Budgeting involves (1) establishing specific goals, (2) executing plans to achieve the goals, and (3) periodically comparing actual results with the goals. In doing so, budgeting affects the following managerial functions:

- Planning
- Directing
- Controlling

The relationships of these activities are illustrated in Exhibit 1.

Planning involves setting goals to guide decisions and help motivate employees. The planning process often identifies where operations can be improved.

Directing involves decisions and actions to achieve budgeted goals. A budgetary unit of a company is called a **responsibility center**. Each responsibility center is led by a manager who has the authority and responsibility for achieving the center's budgeted goals.

Exhibit 1 Planning, Directing, and Controlling

Controlling involves comparing actual performance against the budgeted goals. Such comparisons provide feedback to managers and employees about their performance. If necessary, responsibility centers can use such feedback to adjust their activities in the future.

Human Behavior and Budgeting

Human behavior problems can arise in the budgeting process in the following situations:

■ Budgeted goals are set too tight, which are very hard or impossible to achieve.
■ Budgeted goals are set too loose, which are very easy to achieve.
■ Budgeted goals conflict with the objectives of the company and employees.

These behavior problems are illustrated in Exhibit 2.

Exhibit 2
Human Behavior Problems in Budgeting

Setting Budget Goals Too Tightly Employees and managers may become discouraged if budgeted goals are set too high. That is, if budgeted goals are viewed as unrealistic or unachievable, the budget may have a negative effect on the ability of the company to achieve its goals.

Reasonable, attainable goals are more likely to motivate employees and managers. For this reason, it is important for employees and managers to be involved in the budgeting process. Involving employees in the budgeting process provides them with a sense of control and, thus, more of a commitment in meeting budgeted goals.

Setting Budget Goals Too Loosely Although it is desirable to establish attainable goals, it is undesirable to plan budget goals that are too easy. Such budget "padding" is termed **budgetary slack**. Managers may plan slack in their budgets to provide a "cushion" for unexpected events. However, slack budgets may create inefficiency by reducing the budgetary incentive to trim spending.

Setting Conflicting Budget Goals Goal conflict occurs when the employees' or managers' self-interest differs from the company's objectives or goals. To illustrate, assume that the sales department manager is given an increased sales goal and as a result accepts customers who are poor credit risks. Thus, while the sales department might meet sales goals, the overall firm may suffer reduced profitability from bad debts.

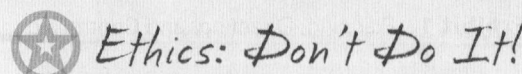

⚝ Ethics: Don't Do It!

Budget Games

The budgeting system is designed to plan and control a business. However, it is common for the budget to be "gamed" by its participants. For example, managers may pad their budgets with excess resources. In this way, the managers have additional resources for unexpected events during the period. If the budget is being used to establish the incentive plan, then sales managers have incentives to understate the sales potential of a territory to ensure hitting their quotas. Other times, managers engage in "land grabbing," which occurs when they overstate the sales potential of a territory to guarantee access to resources. If managers believe that unspent resources will not roll over to future periods, then they may be encouraged to "spend it or lose it," causing wasteful expenditures. These types of problems can be partially overcome by separating the budget into planning and incentive components. This is why many organizations have two budget processes, one for resource planning and another, more challenging budget for motivating managers.

Objective 2

Describe the basic elements of the budget process, the two major types of budgeting, and the use of computers in budgeting.

Budgeting Systems

Budgeting systems vary among companies and industries. For example, the budget system used by **Ford Motor Company** differs from that used by **Delta Air Lines**. However, the basic budgeting concepts discussed in this section apply to all types of businesses and organizations.

The budgetary period for operating activities normally includes the fiscal year of a company. A year is short enough that future operations can be estimated fairly accurately, yet long enough that the future can be viewed in a broad context. However, for control purposes, annual budgets are usually subdivided into shorter time periods, such as quarters of the year, months, or weeks.

Link to Hendrick Motorsports

Rick Hendrick uses budgeting in **Hendrick Motorsports** as well as the **Hendrick Automotive Group**. The Hendrick Automotive Group is the largest privately held dealership group in the United States with 120 retail franchises.

A variation of fiscal-year budgeting, called **continuous budgeting**, maintains a 12-month projection into the future. The 12-month budget is continually revised by replacing the data for the month just ended with the budget data for the same month in the next year. A continuous budget is illustrated in Exhibit 3.

Exhibit 3 Continuous Budgeting

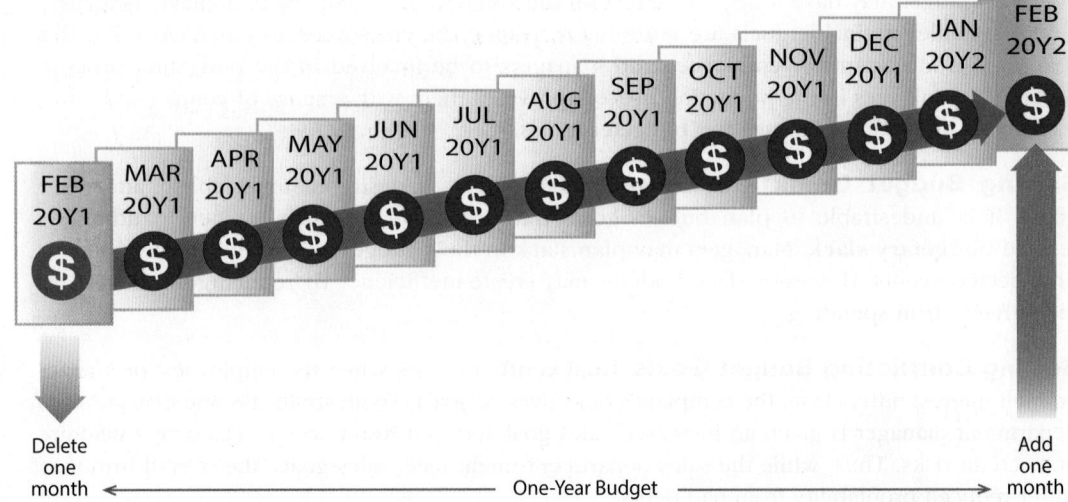

Developing an annual budget usually begins several months prior to the end of the current year. This responsibility is normally assigned to a budget committee. Such a committee often consists of the budget director, the controller, the treasurer, the production manager, and the sales manager. The budget process is monitored and summarized by the Accounting Department, which reports to the committee.

There are several methods of developing budget estimates. One method, called **zero-based budgeting**, requires managers to estimate sales, production, and other operating data as though operations are being started for the first time. This approach has the benefit of taking a fresh view of operations each year. A more common approach is to start with last year's budget and revise it for actual results and expected changes for the coming year. Two major budgets using this approach are the static budget and the flexible budget.

Static Budget

A **static budget** shows the expected results of a responsibility center for only one activity level. Once the budget has been determined, it is not changed, even if the activity changes. Static budgeting is used by many service companies and governmental entities and for some functions of manufacturing companies, such as purchasing, engineering, and accounting.

To illustrate, the static budget for the Assembly Department of Colter Manufacturing Company is shown in Exhibit 4.

	A	B
1	Colter Manufacturing Company	
2	Assembly Department Budget	
3	For the Year Ending July 31, 20Y8	
4	Direct labor	$40,000
5	Electric power	5,000
6	Supervisor salaries	15,000
7	Total department costs	$60,000
8		

Exhibit 4
Static Budget

A disadvantage of static budgets is that they do not adjust for changes in activity levels. For example, assume that the Assembly Department of Colter Manufacturing spent $70,800 for the year ended July 31, 20Y8. Thus, the Assembly Department spent $10,800 ($70,800 – $60,000), or 18% ($10,800 ÷ $60,000) more than budgeted. Is this good news or bad news?

The first reaction is that this is bad news and the Assembly Department was inefficient in spending more than budgeted. However, assume that the Assembly Department's budget was based on plans to assemble 8,000 units during the year. If 10,000 units were actually assembled, the additional $10,800 spent in excess of budget might be good news. That is, the Assembly Department assembled 25% (2,000 units ÷ 8,000 units) more than planned for only 18% more cost. In this case, a static budget may not be useful for controlling costs.

Why It Matters

Film Budgeting

Service businesses, like film and entertainment, use budgets as a roadmap to control expenses. In film production, the budget is a valuable tool to manage the tension between creative expression and cost.

The film budget is a static budget that can be divided into three major categories:

- above the line
- below the line
- post-production costs

The *above the line* costs include costs attributed to creative talent, such as the lead cast's and director's salaries and script fees. The *below the line* costs include the remaining costs to create the film, including location, costume, and prop rentals; permits; and other production costs. The *post-production costs* include the costs to complete the film, including editing, sound, and special effects. Marketing has a separate budget.

The total cost of the film is influenced by many decisions, including the cost of story rights, location, star quality of creative talent, union representation of the production crew, music, and special effects. Even a low-budget indie (independent) documentary could easily have a budget of more than $1 million. In contrast, a special effect-laden Hollywood film could have a budget in excess of $200 million.

Flexible Budget

note:
Flexible budgets show expected results for several activity levels.

Unlike static budgets, **flexible budgets** show the expected results of a responsibility center for several activity levels. A flexible budget is, in effect, a series of static budgets for different levels of activity.

To illustrate, a flexible budget for the Assembly Department of Colter Manufacturing Company is shown in Exhibit 5.

Exhibit 5
Flexible Budget

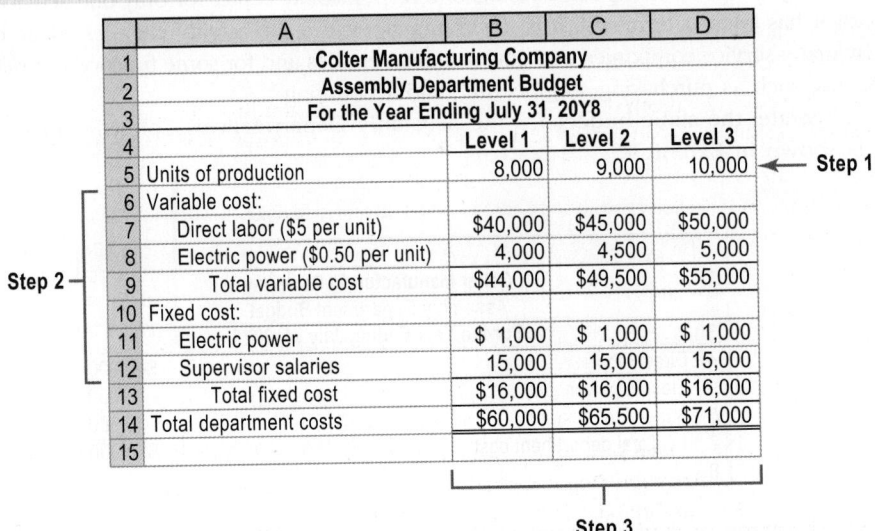

	A	B	C	D
1	Colter Manufacturing Company			
2	Assembly Department Budget			
3	For the Year Ending July 31, 20Y8			
4		Level 1	Level 2	Level 3
5	Units of production	8,000	9,000	10,000
6	Variable cost:			
7	Direct labor ($5 per unit)	$40,000	$45,000	$50,000
8	Electric power ($0.50 per unit)	4,000	4,500	5,000
9	Total variable cost	$44,000	$49,500	$55,000
10	Fixed cost:			
11	Electric power	$ 1,000	$ 1,000	$ 1,000
12	Supervisor salaries	15,000	15,000	15,000
13	Total fixed cost	$16,000	$16,000	$16,000
14	Total department costs	$60,000	$65,500	$71,000
15				

Step 1 ← Level 1, Level 2, Level 3 (row 4), Units of production (row 5)

Step 2 (rows 6–12)

Step 3

A flexible budget is constructed as follows:

- Step 1. Identify the relevant activity levels. The relevant levels of activity could be expressed in units, machine hours, direct labor hours, or some other activity base. In Exhibit 5, the levels of activity are 8,000, 9,000, and 10,000 units of production.
- Step 2. Identify the fixed and variable cost components of the costs being budgeted. In Exhibit 5, the electric power cost is separated into its fixed cost ($1,000 per year) and variable cost ($0.50 per unit). The direct labor is a variable cost, and the supervisor salaries are all fixed costs.
- Step 3. Prepare the budget for each activity level by multiplying the variable cost per unit by the activity level and then adding the monthly fixed cost.

With a flexible budget, actual costs can be compared to the budgeted costs for actual activity. To illustrate, assume that the Assembly Department spent $70,800 to produce 10,000 units. Exhibit 5 indicates that the Assembly Department was *under* budget by $200 ($71,000 − $70,800).

Under the static budget in Exhibit 4, the Assembly Department was $10,800 *over* budget. This comparison is illustrated in Exhibit 6.

The flexible budget for the Assembly Department is much more accurate and useful than the static budget. This is because the flexible budget adjusts for changes in the level of activity. Flexible budgets can be used in service businesses when the variable costs can be associated to an activity. For example, hospital room expenses are related to number of patients, or transportation fuel costs are related to number of miles.

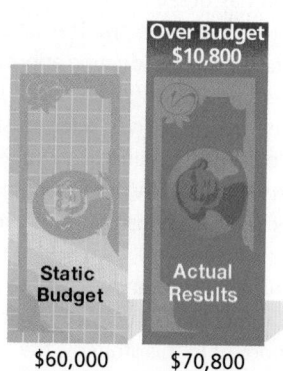
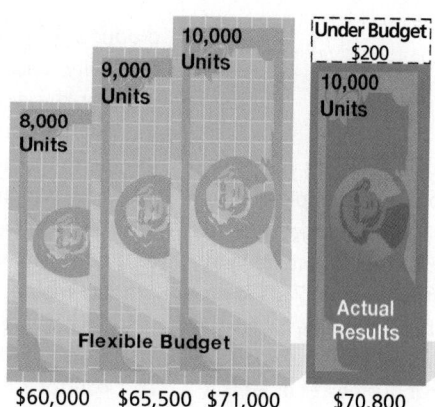

Exhibit 6
Static and Flexible
Budgets

Static Budget	Actual Results
$60,000	$70,800

Over Budget $10,800

Flexible Budget			Actual Results
$60,000	$65,500	$71,000	$70,800

8,000 Units / 9,000 Units / 10,000 Units / Under Budget $200 / 10,000 Units

Check Up Corner 21-1   Flexible Budget

O-wen Snowboard Company designs and manufactures snowboards. The boards are assembled in the company's Assembly Department in Colorado. Information for the Assembly Department is as follows:

Depreciation	$4,500 per month
Direct labor hours per unit produced	0.5 hours per board
Supervisor salaries	$22,000 per month
Utilities	$1 per direct labor hour plus $1,500 per month
Wages	$20 per hour

Prepare a flexible budget for the Assembly Department for 3,000, 4,000, and 5,000 boards in August 20Y1.

Solution:

Variable costs change with the level of activity

O-wen Snowboard Company
Assembly Department Budget
For the Month Ending August 31, 20Y1

Units of production	3,000	4,000	5,000
Variable costs:			
Direct labor	$30,000	$40,000	$50,000
Utilities	1,500	2,000	2,500
Total variable costs	$31,500	$42,000	$52,500
Fixed costs:			
Depreciation	$ 4,500	$ 4,500	$ 4,500
Supervisor salaries	22,000	22,000	22,000
Utilities	1,500	1,500	1,500
Total fixed costs	$28,000	$28,000	$28,000
Total department costs	$59,500	$70,000	$80,500

Flexible budgets show the expected results of a responsibility center for several activity levels.

3,000 units × 0.5 hour per unit × $20 per hour
4,000 units × 0.5 hour per unit × $20 per hour
5,000 units × 0.5 hour per unit × $20 per hour

The variable utility cost is equal to the activity level (# of units) × 0.5 direct labor hour × $1 per direct labor hour

Fixed costs remain constant across all activity levels.

Total estimated costs change with the level of activity.

Check Up Corner

Computerized Budgeting Systems

In developing budgets, companies use a variety of computerized approaches. Two of the most popular computerized approaches use:

- Spreadsheet software such as Microsoft Excel
- Integrated budget and planning (B&P) software systems

Why It Matters

Build Versus Harvest

Budgeting systems are not "one size fits all" solutions but must adapt to the underlying business conditions. For example, a business can adopt either a build strategy or a harvest strategy. A *build* strategy is one where the business is designing, launching, and growing new products and markets. Apple Inc.'s iPad® is an example of a product managed under a build strategy. A *harvest* strategy is often employed for business units with mature products enjoying high market share in low-growth industries. H.J. Heinz Company's ketchup and P&G's *Ivory* soap are examples of such

products. A build strategy often has greater uncertainty, unpredictability, and change than a harvest strategy. The difference between these strategies implies different budgeting approaches.

The build strategy should employ a budget approach that is flexible to the uncertainty of the business. Thus, budgets should adapt to changing conditions by allowing periodic revisions and flexible targets. The budget serves as a short-term planning tool to guide management in executing an uncertain and evolving product market strategy.

In a harvest strategy, the business is often much more stable and is managed to maximize profitability and cash flow. Because cost control is much more important in this strategy, the budget is used to restrict the actions of managers.

Spreadsheets ease budget preparation by summarizing budget information in linked spreadsheets across the organization. In addition, the impact of proposed changes in various assumptions or operating alternatives can be analyzed on a spreadsheet.

B&P software systems use the Web (Intranet) to link thousands of employees together during the budget process. Employees can input budget data onto Web pages that are integrated and summarized throughout the company. In this way, a company can quickly and consistently integrate top-level strategies and goals to lower-level operational goals.

Objective 3

Describe the master budget for a manufacturing company.

Master Budget

The **master budget** is an integrated set of operating and financial budgets for a period of time. Most companies prepare a master budget on a yearly basis. Exhibit 7 shows that the operating budgets can be used to prepare a budgeted income statement, while the financial budgets provide information for a budgeted balance sheet.

Exhibit 7

Master Budget for a Manufacturing Company

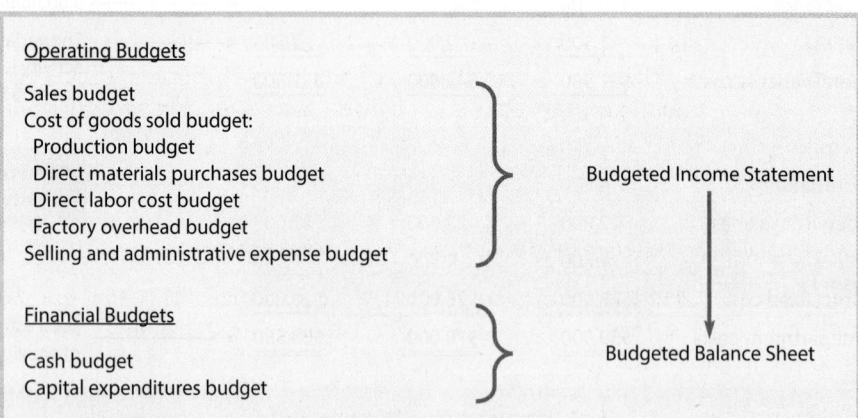

Operating Budgets

Sales budget
Cost of goods sold budget:
  Production budget
  Direct materials purchases budget
  Direct labor cost budget
  Factory overhead budget
Selling and administrative expense budget

    } Budgeted Income Statement

Financial Budgets

Cash budget
Capital expenditures budget

    } Budgeted Balance Sheet

The master budget begins with preparing the operating budgets, which form the budgeted income statement. Exhibit 8 shows the relationships among the operating budgets leading to an income statement budget.

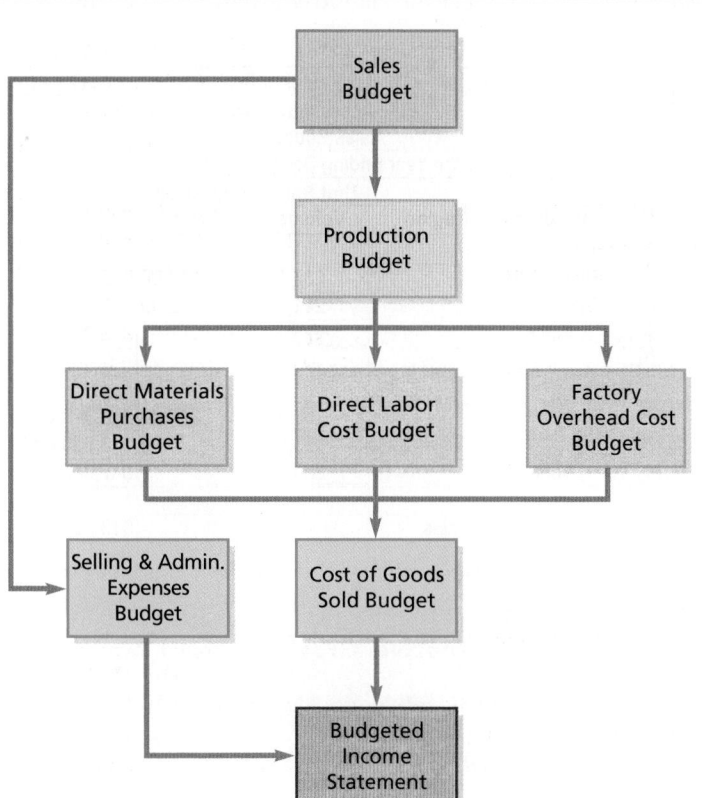

Exhibit 8
Operating Budgets

Operating Budgets

Objective 4
Prepare the basic operating budgets for a manufacturing company.

The integrated operating budgets that support the income statement budget are illustrated for **Elite Accessories Inc.**, a small manufacturing company of personal accessories.

Sales Budget

The **sales budget** begins by estimating the quantity of sales. The prior year's sales are often used as a starting point. These sales quantities are then revised for such factors as planned advertising and promotion, projected pricing changes, and expected industry and general economic conditions.

Once sales quantities are estimated, the budgeted sales revenue can be determined as follows:

Budgeted Revenue = Expected Sales Volume × Expected Unit Sales Price

To illustrate, **Elite Accessories Inc.** manufactures wallets and handbags that are sold in two regions, the East and West regions. Elite Accessories estimates the following sales volumes and prices for 20Y1:

	East Region Sales Volume	West Region Sales Volume	Unit Selling Price
Wallets	287,000	241,000	$12
Handbags	156,400	123,600	25

Exhibit 9 illustrates the sales budget for Elite Accessories based on the preceding data.

Exhibit 9

Sales Budget

	A	B	C	D
1	Elite Accessories Inc.			
2	Sales Budget			
3	For the Year Ending December 31, 20Y1			
4		Unit Sales	Unit Selling	
5	Product and Region	Volume	Price	Total Sales
6	Wallet:			
7	East	287,000	$12.00	$ 3,444,000
8	West	241,000	12.00	2,892,000
9	Total	528,000		$ 6,336,000
10				
11	Handbag:			
12	East	156,400	$25.00	$ 3,910,000
13	West	123,600	25.00	3,090,000
14	Total	280,000		$ 7,000,000
15				
16	Total revenue from sales			$13,336,000
17				

Link to Hendrick Motorsports In a recent year, **Hendrick Automotive Group** generated over $7 billion of revenue across 13 states.

Production Budget

The production budget should be integrated with the sales budget to ensure that production and sales are kept in balance during the year. The **production budget** estimates the number of units to be manufactured to meet budgeted sales and desired inventory levels.

The budgeted units to be produced are determined as follows:

Expected units to be sold	XXX units
Desired units in ending inventory	XXX
Estimated units in beginning inventory	(XXX)
Total units to be produced	XXX units

Elite Accessories Inc. expects the following inventories of wallets and handbags:

	Estimated Inventory, January 1, 20Y1	Desired Inventory, December 31, 20Y1
Wallets	88,000	80,000
Handbags	48,000	60,000

Exhibit 10 illustrates the production budget for Elite Accessories.

Exhibit 10

Production Budget

	A	B	C
1	Elite Accessories Inc.		
2	Production Budget		
3	For the Year Ending December 31, 20Y1		
4		Units	
5		Wallet	Handbag
6	Expected units to be sold (from Exhibit 9)	528,000	280,000
7	Desired ending inventory, December 31, 20Y1	80,000	60,000
8	Total units available	608,000	340,000
9	Estimated beginning inventory, January 1, 20Y1	(88,000)	(48,000)
10	Total units to be produced	520,000	292,000
11			

Direct Materials Purchases Budget

The direct materials purchases budget should be integrated with the production budget to ensure that production is not interrupted during the year. The **direct materials purchases budget** estimates the quantities of direct materials to be purchased to support budgeted production and desired inventory levels and can be developed in three steps.

Step 1 Determine the budgeted direct material required for production, which is computed as follows:

Budgeted Direct Material = Budgeted Production Volume × Direct Material Quantity
Required for Production   (from Exhibit 10)   Expected per Unit

To illustrate, **Elite Accessories Inc.** uses leather and lining in producing wallets and handbags. The quantity of direct materials expected to be used for each unit of product is as follows:

	Wallet	Handbag
Leather	0.30 sq. yd. per unit	1.25 sq. yds. per unit
Lining	0.10 sq. yd. per unit	0.50 sq. yd. per unit

For the wallet, the direct material required for production is computed as follows:

Leather: 520,000 units × 0.30 sq. yd. per unit = 156,000 sq. yds.
Lining: 520,000 units × 0.10 sq. yd. per unit = 52,000 sq. yds.

For the handbag, the direct material required for production is computed as follows:

Leather: 292,000 units × 1.25 sq. yds. per unit = 365,000 sq. yds.
Lining: 292,000 units × 0.50 sq. yd. per unit = 146,000 sq. yds.

Step 2 The budgeted material required for production is adjusted for beginning and ending inventories to determine the direct materials to be purchased for each material, as follows:

Materials required for production (Step 1)	XXX
Desired ending materials inventory	XXX
Estimated beginning materials inventory	(XXX)
Direct material quantity to be purchased	XXX

Step 3 The budgeted direct materials to be purchased is computed as follows:

Budgeted Direct Material = Direct Material Quantity to Be Purchased × Unit Price
to Be Purchased   (Step 2)

Complete Direct Materials Purchases Budget The following inventory and unit price information for **Elite Accessories Inc.** is expected:

	Estimated Direct Materials Inventory, January 1, 20Y1	Desired Direct Materials Inventory, December 31, 20Y1
Leather	18,000 sq. yds.	20,000 sq. yds.
Lining	15,000 sq. yds.	12,000 sq. yds.

The estimated price per square yard of leather and lining during 20Y1 follows:

	Price per Square Yard
Leather	$4.50
Lining	1.20

Exhibit 11 illustrates the complete direct materials purchases budget for Elite Accessories by combining all three steps into a single schedule.

Exhibit 11

Direct Materials
Purchases Budget

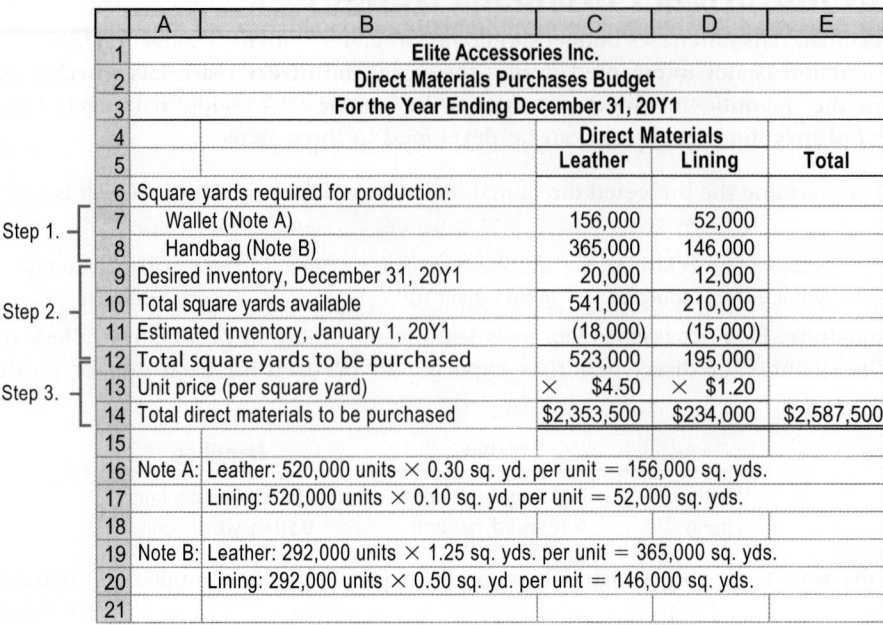

	A	B	C	D	E
1		Elite Accessories Inc.			
2		Direct Materials Purchases Budget			
3		For the Year Ending December 31, 20Y1			
4			Direct Materials		
5			Leather	Lining	Total
6	Square yards required for production:				
7	Wallet (Note A)		156,000	52,000	
8	Handbag (Note B)		365,000	146,000	
9	Desired inventory, December 31, 20Y1		20,000	12,000	
10	Total square yards available		541,000	210,000	
11	Estimated inventory, January 1, 20Y1		(18,000)	(15,000)	
12	Total square yards to be purchased		523,000	195,000	
13	Unit price (per square yard)		× $4.50	× $1.20	
14	Total direct materials to be purchased		$2,353,500	$234,000	$2,587,500
15					
16	Note A:	Leather: 520,000 units × 0.30 sq. yd. per unit = 156,000 sq. yds.			
17		Lining: 520,000 units × 0.10 sq. yd. per unit = 52,000 sq. yds.			
18					
19	Note B:	Leather: 292,000 units × 1.25 sq. yds. per unit = 365,000 sq. yds.			
20		Lining: 292,000 units × 0.50 sq. yd. per unit = 146,000 sq. yds.			
21					

Step 1. — rows 7, 8
Step 2. — rows 9–12
Step 3. — rows 13, 14

The timing of the direct materials purchases should be coordinated between the purchasing and production departments so that production is not interrupted.

Link to Hendrick Motorsports   **Hendrick Motorsports** uses sheet metal in building its race cars. "Used" sections of sheet metal (from crashed cars) can be purchased from its online store.

Direct Labor Cost Budget

The **direct labor cost budget** estimates the direct labor hours and related cost needed to support budgeted production. Production managers study work methods to provide estimates used in preparing the direct labor cost budget.

The direct labor cost budget for each department is determined in two steps, as follows.

Step 1 Determine the budgeted direct labor hours required for production, which is computed as follows:

Budgeted Direct Labor = Budgeted Production Volume × Direct Labor Hours Expected
Hours Required for   (from Exhibit 10)   per Unit
Production

To illustrate, **Elite Accessories Inc.**'s production managers estimate the following direct labor hours are needed to produce a wallet and handbag:

	Wallet	**Handbag**
Cutting Department	0.10 hr. per unit	0.15 hr. per unit
Sewing Department	0.25 hr. per unit	0.40 hr. per unit

Thus, for the wallet, the budgeted direct labor hours required for production is computed as follows:

Cutting: 520,000 units × 0.10 hr. per unit = 52,000 direct labor hours
Sewing: 520,000 units × 0.25 hr. per unit = 130,000 direct labor hours

For the handbag, the budgeted direct labor hours required for production is computed as follows:

Cutting: 292,000 units × 0.15 hr. per unit = 43,800 direct labor hours
Sewing: 292,000 units × 0.40 hr. per unit = 116,800 direct labor hours

Step 2 Determine the total direct labor cost as follows:

Direct Labor Cost = Direct Labor Required for Production (Step 1) × Hourly Rate

The estimated direct labor hourly rates for the Cutting and Sewing departments for **Elite Accessories Inc.** during 20Y1 follow:

	Hourly Rate
Cutting Department	$12
Sewing Department	15

Complete Direct Labor Cost Budget Exhibit 12 illustrates the direct labor cost budget by combining both steps for **Elite Accessories Inc.**

	A	B	C	D	E
1		Elite Accessories Inc.			
2		Direct Labor Cost Budget			
3		For the Year Ending December 31, 20Y1			
4			Cutting	Sewing	Total
5	Hours required for production:				
6	Wallet (Note A)		52,000	130,000	
7	Handbag (Note B)		43,800	116,800	
8	Total		95,800	246,800	
9	Hourly rate		× $12	× $15	
10	Total direct labor cost		$1,149,600	$3,702,000	$4,851,600
11					
12	Note A:	Cutting Department: 520,000 units × 0.10 hr. per unit = 52,000 hrs.			
13		Sewing Department: 520,000 units × 0.25 hr. per unit = 130,000 hrs.			
14					
15	Note B:	Cutting Department: 292,000 units × 0.15 hr. per unit = 43,800 hrs.			
16		Sewing Department: 292,000 units × 0.40 hr. per unit = 116,800 hrs.			
17					

Step 1. (rows 6–8)
Step 2. (rows 9–10)

Exhibit 12
Direct Labor
Cost Budget

The direct labor needs should be coordinated between the production and personnel departments so that there will be enough labor available for production.

Hendrick Motorports offers an internship program for college students who want to experience and learn the operations of a NASCAR team.

Link to Hendrick Motorsports

Factory Overhead Cost Budget

The **factory overhead cost budget** estimates the cost for each item of factory overhead needed to support budgeted production.

Exhibit 13 illustrates the factory overhead cost budget for **Elite Accessories Inc.**

Exhibit 13

Factory Overhead
Cost Budget

	A	B
1	Elite Accessories Inc.	
2	Factory Overhead Cost Budget	
3	For the Year Ending December 31, 20Y1	
4	Indirect factory wages	$ 732,800
5	Supervisor salaries	360,000
6	Power and light	306,000
7	Depreciation of plant and equipment	288,000
8	Indirect materials	182,800
9	Maintenance	140,280
10	Insurance and property taxes	79,200
11	Total factory overhead cost	$2,089,080
12		

The factory overhead cost budget shown in Exhibit 13 may be supported by departmental schedules. Such schedules normally separate factory overhead costs into fixed and variable costs to better enable department managers to monitor and evaluate costs during the year.

The factory overhead cost budget should be integrated with the production budget to ensure that production is not interrupted during the year.

Cost of Goods Sold Budget

The **cost of goods sold budget** is prepared by integrating the following budgets:

- Direct materials purchases budget (Exhibit 11)
- Direct labor cost budget (Exhibit 12)
- Factory overhead cost budget (Exhibit 13)

In addition, the estimated and desired inventories for direct materials, work in process, and finished goods must be integrated into the cost of goods sold budget.

Elite Accessories Inc. expects the following direct materials, work in process, and finished goods inventories:

	Estimated Inventory, January 1, 20Y1	Desired Inventory, December 31, 20Y1
Direct materials:		
Leather	$ 81,000 (18,000 sq. yds. × $4.50)	$ 90,000 (20,000 sq. yds. × $4.50)
Lining	18,000 (15,000 sq. yds. × $1.20)	14,400 (12,000 sq. yds. × $1.20)
Total direct materials	$ 99,000	$ 104,400
Work in process	$ 214,400	$ 220,000
Finished goods	$1,095,600	$1,565,000

The cost of goods sold budget for Elite Accessories in Exhibit 14 indicates that total manufacturing costs of $9,522,780 are budgeted to be incurred in 20Y1. Of this total, $2,582,100 is budgeted for direct materials, $4,851,600 is budgeted for direct labor, and $2,089,080 is budgeted for factory overhead. After considering work in process inventories, the total budgeted cost of goods manufactured and transferred to finished goods during 20Y1 is $9,517,180. Based on expected sales, the budgeted cost of goods sold is $9,047,780.

Cost of Goods
Sold Budget

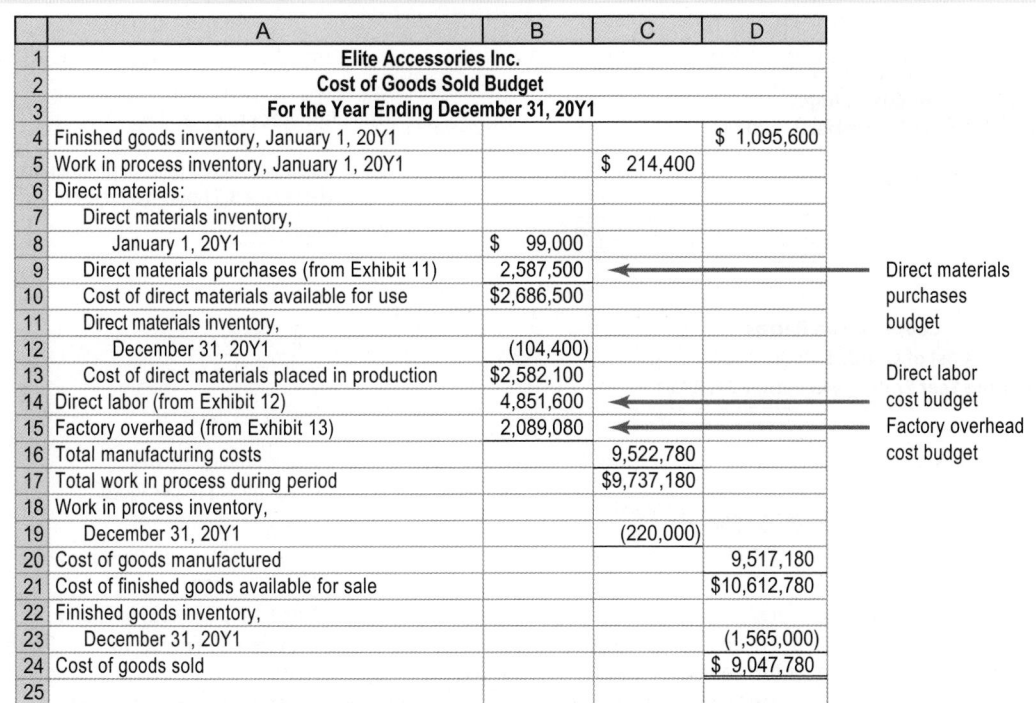

DYNAMIC
EXHIBIT

Direct materials
purchases
budget

Direct labor
cost budget

Factory overhead
cost budget

	A	B	C	D
1	Elite Accessories Inc.			
2	Cost of Goods Sold Budget			
3	For the Year Ending December 31, 20Y1			
4	Finished goods inventory, January 1, 20Y1			$ 1,095,600
5	Work in process inventory, January 1, 20Y1		$ 214,400	
6	Direct materials:			
7	Direct materials inventory,			
8	January 1, 20Y1	$ 99,000		
9	Direct materials purchases (from Exhibit 11)	2,587,500		
10	Cost of direct materials available for use	$2,686,500		
11	Direct materials inventory,			
12	December 31, 20Y1	(104,400)		
13	Cost of direct materials placed in production	$2,582,100		
14	Direct labor (from Exhibit 12)	4,851,600		
15	Factory overhead (from Exhibit 13)	2,089,080		
16	Total manufacturing costs		9,522,780	
17	Total work in process during period		$9,737,180	
18	Work in process inventory,			
19	December 31, 20Y1		(220,000)	
20	Cost of goods manufactured			9,517,180
21	Cost of finished goods available for sale			$10,612,780
22	Finished goods inventory,			
23	December 31, 20Y1			(1,565,000)
24	Cost of goods sold			$ 9,047,780
25				

Check Up Corner 21-2 **Direct Materials, Direct Labor, and Cost of Goods Sold Budget**

Cooperstown Retros makes replica major league baseball jerseys that match those worn in the 1950s. The company budgeted production of 15,000 jerseys in 20Y1. Each jersey requires 1.5 square yards of wool fabric. Wool fabric costs $14 per square yard. Each jersey requires cutting and assembly. Assume that 3.5 hours are required to cut and assemble each jersey. Labor costs are estimated at $20 per hour. Factory overhead was budgeted for $210,000.

Estimated January 1 and desired December 31 inventories are as follows:

	Direct Materials:		
	Wool Fabric	**Work-In-Process**	**Finished Goods**
Estimated inventory, January 1, 20Y1	2,250 sq. yds.	$20,000	$200,000
Desired inventory, December 31, 20Y1	2,340 sq. yds.	$24,500	$230,000

Prepare (A) a direct materials purchases budget, (B) a direct labor cost budget, and (C) a cost of goods sold budget for Cooperstown for the year ending December 31, 20Y1.

Solution:

A.

Cooperstown Retros
Direct Materials Purchases Budget
For the Year Ending December 31, 20Y1

Square yards of material required for production	22,500
Desired ending inventory, December 31	2,340
Total square yards available	24,840
Estimated beginning inventory, January 1	(2,250)
Total square yards to be purchased	22,590
Unit price (per square yard)	× $14
Total direct materials to be purchased	$316,260

15,000 expected units of production (jerseys) × 1.5 square yards per jersey

Estimated quantity of direct materials to be purchased to support budgeted production and meet desired inventory levels

B.

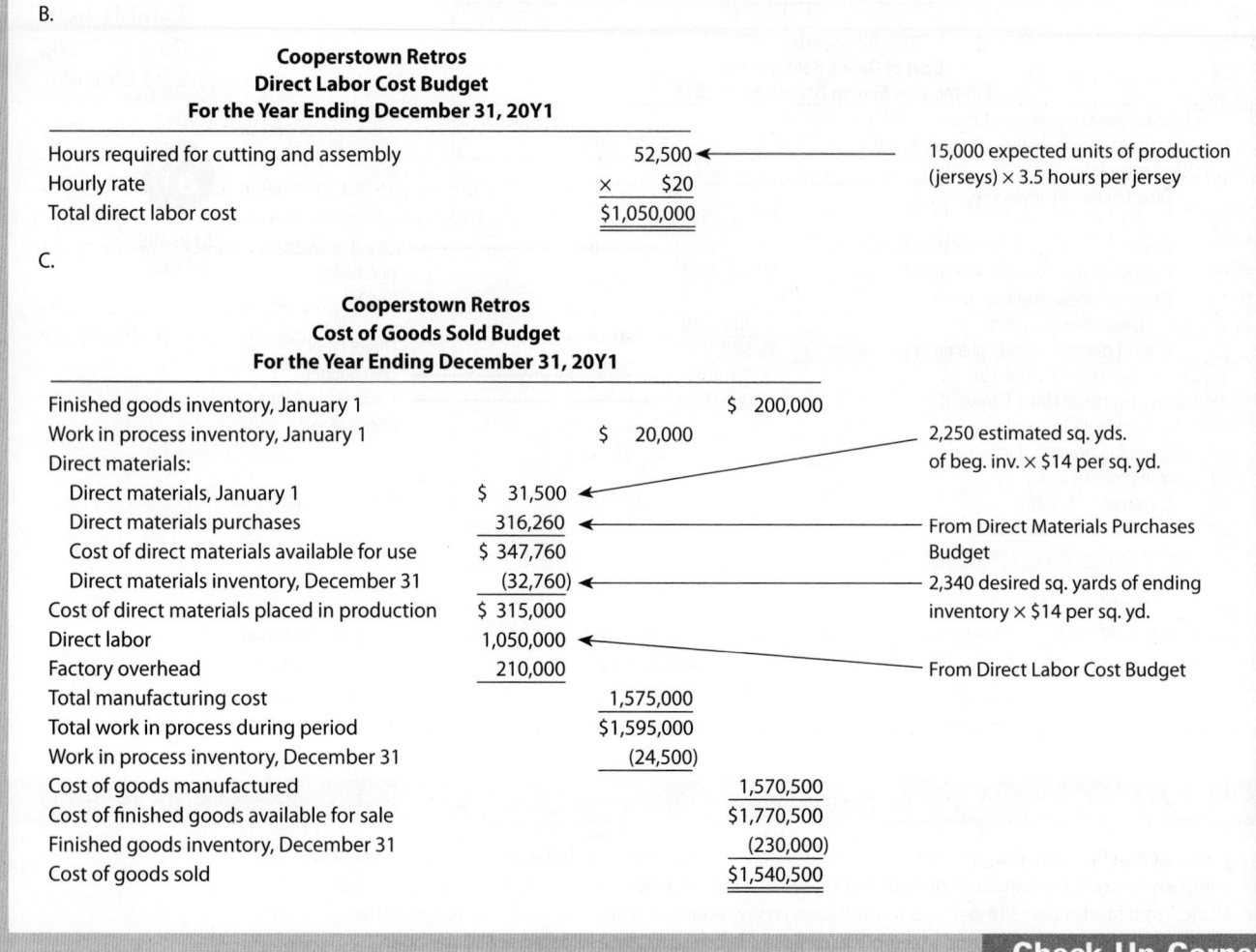

Cooperstown Retros
Direct Labor Cost Budget
For the Year Ending December 31, 20Y1

Hours required for cutting and assembly	52,500 ←
Hourly rate	× $20
Total direct labor cost	$1,050,000

15,000 expected units of production (jerseys) × 3.5 hours per jersey

C.

Cooperstown Retros
Cost of Goods Sold Budget
For the Year Ending December 31, 20Y1

Finished goods inventory, January 1			$ 200,000
Work in process inventory, January 1		$ 20,000	
Direct materials:			
Direct materials, January 1	$ 31,500 ←		
Direct materials purchases	316,260 ←		
Cost of direct materials available for use	$ 347,760		
Direct materials inventory, December 31	(32,760) ←		
Cost of direct materials placed in production	$ 315,000		
Direct labor	1,050,000 ←		
Factory overhead	210,000		
Total manufacturing cost		1,575,000	
Total work in process during period		$1,595,000	
Work in process inventory, December 31		(24,500)	
Cost of goods manufactured			1,570,500
Cost of finished goods available for sale			$1,770,500
Finished goods inventory, December 31			(230,000)
Cost of goods sold			$1,540,500

2,250 estimated sq. yds. of beg. inv. × $14 per sq. yd.

From Direct Materials Purchases Budget

2,340 desired sq. yards of ending inventory × $14 per sq. yd.

From Direct Labor Cost Budget

Check Up Corner

Selling and Administrative Expenses Budget

The sales budget is often used as the starting point for the selling and administrative expenses budget. For example, a budgeted increase in sales may require more advertising expenses.

Exhibit 15 illustrates the selling and administrative expenses budget for **Elite Accessories Inc.**

Exhibit 15

Selling and Administrative Expenses Budget

	A	B	C
1	Elite Accessories Inc.		
2	Selling and Administrative Expenses Budget		
3	For the Year Ending December 31, 20Y1		
4	Selling expenses:		
5	Sales salaries expense	$715,000	
6	Advertising expense	360,000	
7	Travel expense	115,000	
8	Total selling expenses		$1,190,000
9	Administrative expenses:		
10	Officers' salaries expense	$360,000	
11	Office salaries expense	258,000	
12	Office rent expense	34,500	
13	Office supplies expense	17,500	
14	Miscellaneous administrative expenses	25,000	
15	Total administrative expenses		695,000
16	Total selling and administrative expenses		$1,885,000
17			

Why It Matters

Mad Men

The advertising budget can be one of the largest selling and administrative expenses for a business. The top 200 leading national advertisers accounted for 51% of all advertising dollars for all businesses combined. Of this amount, 68.5% went toward video broadcast advertising, 7.2% for Internet display ads, and 24.3% for print and radio. The top five spenders according to *Advertising Age* were:

Company	U.S. Advertising Spending
Procter & Gamble	$4.6 billion
AT&T	3.3 billion
General Motors	3.1 billion
Comcast	3.0 billion
Verizon	2.5 billion

The advertising budget is segmented between "measured" and "unmeasured" media. Measured media are tracked to determine the number of impressions an ad is receiving due to audience, viewership, or readership counts. Unmeasured media are not counted for impressions, and include promotions, direct marketing, and coupons.

A major trend is allocating ad budget dollars toward digital strategies, such as search, social, video, and mobile. These strategies are believed to be more efficient and effective than TV or print. For Colgate-Palmolive, digital went from 2% of the advertising budget in 2006 to 13% in 2014, with expectations of growing to 25%.

Source: Bradley Johnson, "Big Spenders on a Budget: What the Top 200 U.S. Advertisers Are Doing to Spend Smarter," *Advertising Age*, July 5, 2015.

The selling and administrative expenses budget shown in Exhibit 15 is normally supported by departmental schedules. For example, an advertising expense schedule for the Marketing Department could include the advertising media to be used (newspaper, direct mail, television), quantities (column inches, number of pieces, minutes), and related costs per unit.

Budgeted Income Statement

The budgeted income statement for **Elite Accessories Inc.** in Exhibit 16 is prepared by integrating the following budgets:

- Sales budget (Exhibit 9)
- Cost of goods sold budget (Exhibit 14)
- Selling and administrative expenses budget (Exhibit 15)

In addition, estimates of other income, other expense, and income tax are also integrated into the budgeted income statement.

This budget summarizes the budgeted operating activities of the company. In doing so, the budgeted income statement allows management to assess the effects of estimated sales, costs, and expenses on profits for the year.

Exhibit 16

Budgeted Income Statement

	A	B	C	
1	Elite Accessories Inc.			
2	Budgeted Income Statement			
3	For the Year Ending December 31, 20Y1			
4	Revenue from sales (from Exhibit 9)		$13,336,000	← Sales budget
5	Cost of goods sold (from Exhibit 14)		9,047,780	← Cost of goods sold budget
6				
7	Gross profit		$ 4,288,220	
8	Selling and administrative expenses:			
9	Selling expenses (from Exhibit 15)	$1,190,000		Selling and administrative expenses budget
10	Administrative expenses (from Exhibit 15)	695,000		
11	Total selling and administrative expenses		1,885,000	
12	Income from operations		$ 2,403,220	
13	Other revenue and expense:			
14	Interest revenue	$ 98,000		
15	Interest expense	90,000	8,000	
16	Income before income tax		$ 2,411,220	
17	Income tax		600,000	
18	Net income		$ 1,811,220	
19				

Link to Hendrick Motorsports   **Hendrick Motorsports** is located in Concord, North Carolina, one mile from the Charlotte Motor Speedway. Visitors are welcome, and tours are provided at no charge during the week.

Objective 5

Prepare financial budgets for a manufacturing company.

Financial Budgets

While the operating budgets reflect the operating activities of the company, the financial budgets reflect the financing and investing activities. In this section, the following financial budgets are described and illustrated:

- Cash budget
- Capital expenditures budget

Cash Budget

note:

The cash budget presents the expected receipts and payments of cash for a period of time.

The **cash budget** estimates the expected receipts (inflows) and payments (outflows) of cash for a period of time. The cash budget is integrated with the various operating budgets. In addition, the capital expenditures budget, dividends, and equity or long-term debt financing plans of the company affect the cash budget.

To illustrate, a monthly cash budget for January, February, and March 20Y1 for **Elite Accessories Inc.** is prepared. The preparation of the cash budget begins by estimating cash receipts.

Estimated Cash Receipts The primary source of estimated cash receipts is from cash sales and collections on account. In addition, cash receipts may be obtained from plans to issue equity or debt financing as well as other sources such as interest revenue.

To estimate cash receipts from cash sales and collections on account, a *schedule of collections from sales* is prepared. To illustrate, the following data for **Elite Accessories Inc.** are used:

	January	February	March
Sales:			
Budgeted sales....................................	$1,080,000	$1,240,000	$970,000
Accounts receivable:			
Accounts receivable January 1, 20Y1	$480,000		
Receipts from sales on account:			
From prior month's sales on account	40%		
From current month's sales on account	60		
	100%		

The budgeted cash collected for any month is the sum of the cash collected from previous month's sales and the cash collected from current month's sales. To illustrate, the cash collected in February is 40% of cash collected on sales in January ($1,080,000 × 40%) added to 60% of cash collected on sales in February ($1,240,000 × 60%), shown as follows:

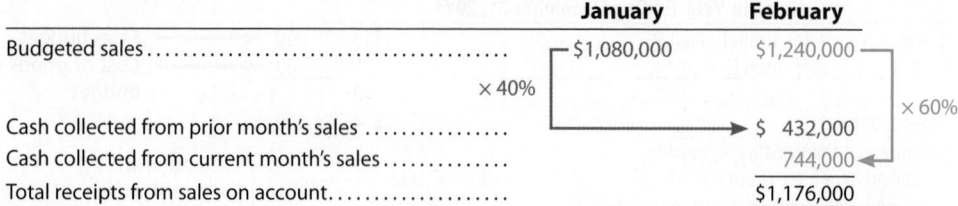

	January	February
Budgeted sales......................................	$1,080,000	$1,240,000
Cash collected from prior month's sales		$ 432,000
Cash collected from current month's sales.............		744,000
Total receipts from sales on account...................		$1,176,000

Using the preceding data, Exhibit 17 shows the schedule of collections from sales for Elite Accessories for all three months. To simplify, it is assumed that all accounts receivable are collected and there are no cash sales.

	A	B	C	D	E
1		Elite Accessories Inc.			
2		Schedule of Collections from Sales			
3		For the Three Months Ending March 31, 20Y1			
4			January	February	March
5	Cash collected from prior month's sales—Note A		$ 480,000	$ 432,000	$ 496,000
6	Cash collected from current month's sales—Note B		648,000	744,000	582,000
7	Total receipts from sales on account		$1,128,000	$1,176,000	$1,078,000
8					
9	Note A:	$480,000, given as January 1, 20Y1, Accounts Receivable balance			
10		$432,000 = $1,080,000 × 40%			
11		$496,000 = $1,240,000 × 40%			
12					
13	Note B:	$648,000 = $1,080,000 × 60%			
14		$744,000 = $1,240,000 × 60%			
15		$582,000 = $970,000 × 60%			
16					

Exhibit 17

Schedule of Collections from Sales

Estimated Cash Payments Estimated cash payments must be budgeted for operating costs and expenses such as manufacturing costs, selling expenses, and administrative expenses. In addition, estimated cash payments may be planned for capital expenditures, dividends, interest payments, or long-term debt payments.

To estimate cash payments for manufacturing costs, a *schedule of payments for manufacturing costs* is prepared. To illustrate, the following data for **Elite Accessories Inc.** are used:

	January	February	March
Manufacturing costs:			
Budgeted manufacturing costs	$840,000	$780,000	$812,000
Depreciation on machines included			
in manufacturing costs.................................	24,000	24,000	24,000
Accounts payable:			
Accounts payable, January 1, 20Y1	$190,000		
Payments of manufacturing costs on account:			
From prior month's manufacturing costs	25%		
From current month's manufacturing costs.................	75		
	100%		

Depreciation on machines is included in budgeted manufacturing costs but does not require a cash outlay. Thus, depreciation is deducted (not included) in determining monthly budgeted cash payments. In addition, manufacturing costs incurred in one month may be paid in the following month. To illustrate, the cash paid in February is 25% of manufacturing costs (less depreciation) in January [($840,000 – $24,000) × 25%] added to 75% of cash paid on manufacturing costs (less depreciation) in February [($780,000 – $24,000) × 75%], computed as follows:

		January	February
Budgeted manufacturing costs		$840,000	$780,000
Depreciation on machines		(24,000)	(24,000)
Manufacturing costs (less depreciation)		$816,000	$756,000
	× 25%		
Payments of prior month's manufacturing			
costs (less depreciation)			$204,000
Payments of current month's manufacturing			
costs (less depreciation)			567,000
Total payments			$771,000

× 75%

Using the preceding data, Exhibit 18 shows the schedule of payments for manufacturing costs for Elite Accessories for all three months.

Exhibit 18

Schedule of
Payments for
Manufacturing
Costs

	A	B	C	D	E
1		Elite Accessories Inc.			
2		Schedule of Payments for Manufacturing Costs			
3		For the Three Months Ending March 31, 20Y1			
4			January	February	March
5	Payments of prior month's manufacturing costs				
6	{[25% × previous month's manufacturing costs				
7	(less depreciation)]—Note A}		$190,000	$204,000	$189,000
8	Payments of current month's manufacturing costs				
9	{[75% × current month's manufacturing costs				
10	(less depreciation)]—Note B}		612,000	567,000	591,000
11	Total payments		$802,000	$771,000	$780,000
12					
13	Note A: $190,000, given as January 1, 20Y1, Accounts Payable balance				
14	$204,000 = ($840,000 − $24,000) × 25%				
15	$189,000 = ($780,000 − $24,000) × 25%				
16					
17	Note B: $612,000 = ($840,000 − $24,000) × 75%				
18	$567,000 = ($780,000 − $24,000) × 75%				
19	$591,000 = ($812,000 − $24,000) × 75%				
20					

Completing the Cash Budget The cash budget is structured for a budget period as follows:

Budget Period:

Estimated cash receipts
Less estimated cash payments
Cash increase (decrease)
Plus cash balance at the beginning of the month
Cash balance at the end of the month ⟶ Becomes the beginning balance for the next period
Less minimum cash balance
Excess (deficiency)

The budgeted balance at the end of the period is determined by adding the net increase (decrease) for the period to the beginning cash balance. The ending balance is compared to a minimum cash balance to support operations as determined by management. Any difference between the ending balance and the minimum cash balance represents an excess or deficiency that may require management action.

To illustrate, assume the following additional data for **Elite Accessories Inc.**:

Cash balance on January 1, 20Y1	$225,000
Quarterly taxes paid on March 31, 20Y1	150,000
Quarterly interest expense paid on January 10, 20Y1	22,500
Quarterly interest revenue received on March 21, 20Y1	24,500
Sewing equipment purchased in February 20Y1	274,000
Selling and administrative expenses (paid in month incurred):	

January	February	March
$160,000	$165,000	$145,000

The cash budget for Elite Accessories is shown in Exhibit 19.

The estimated cash receipts include the total receipts from sales on account (Exhibit 17). The estimated cash payments include the cash payments from manufacturing costs (Exhibit 18). Other receipts and payments are provided by the additional information. Additionally, assume the minimum cash balance is $340,000.

Exhibit 19

Cash Budget

	A	B	C	D	
1	Elite Accessories Inc.				
2	Cash Budget				
3	For the Three Months Ending March 31,20Y1				
4		January	February	March	
5	Estimated cash receipts from:				
6	Collections of accounts receivable				
7	(from Exhibit 17)	$1,128,000	$1,176,000	$1,078,000	← Schedule of
8	Interest revenue			24,500	collections
9	Total cash receipts	$1,128,000	$1,176,000	$1,102,500	from sales
10	Less estimated cash payments for:				
11	Manufacturing costs (from Exhibit 18)	$ 802,000	$ 771,000	$ 780,000	← Schedule of
12	Selling and administrative expenses	160,000	165,000	145,000	payments for
13	Capital additions (sewing equipment)		274,000		manufacturing
14	Interest expense	22,500			costs
15	Income taxes			150,000	
16	Total cash payments	$ 984,500	$1,210,000	$1,075,000	
17	Cash increase (decrease)	$ 143,500	$ (34,000)	$ 27,500	
18	Cash balance at beginning of month	225,000	368,500	334,500	
19	Plus cash balance at end of month	$ 368,500	$ 334,500	$ 362,000	
20	Less minimum cash balance	340,000	340,000	340,000	
21	Excess (deficiency)	$ 28,500	$ (5,500)	$ 22,000	
22					

Exhibit 19 indicates that Elite Accessories expects a cash excess at the end of January of $28,500. This excess could be invested in temporary income-producing securities such as U.S. Treasury bills or notes. In contrast, the estimated cash deficiency at the end of February of $5,500 might require Elite Accessories to borrow cash from its bank.

Check Up Corner 21-3   Cash Budget

Quincy Company has both cash and credit customers. The company expects that 40% of total monthly sales will be collected in cash in the month of sale, and the remaining 60% will be collected in the month following the month of sale. The Accounts Receivable balance on January 1 is $97,500, all of which is expected to be collected during January. Projected sales for the first three months of the year are as follows:

January	$190,000
February	200,000
March	210,000

Projected manufacturing costs and selling and administrative expenses for the first three months of the year are as follows:

	Manufacturing Costs	Selling & Administrative Expenses
January	$110,000	$72,000
February	134,000	70,000
March	160,000	75,000

Manufacturing costs include depreciation, insurance, and property taxes, which represent $18,000 of the estimated monthly manufacturing costs. The annual insurance premium was paid on December 31 of the prior year, and property taxes for the year will be paid in June. Sixty percent of the remainder of manufacturing costs are expected to be paid in the month in which they are incurred, with the balance to be paid in the following month. The Accounts Payable balance on January 1, which consisted entirely of unpaid manufacturing costs from December, is $36,700. All selling and administrative expenses are paid in cash in the period in which they are incurred. The cash balance on January 1 was $26,000, and management desires to maintain a minimum cash balance of $20,000.

Prepare:

A. A schedule of collections from sales.
B. A schedule of cash payments for manufacturing costs.
C. A cash budget.

Solution:

A.

Quincy Company
Schedule of Collections from Sales
For the Three Months Ending March 31

	January	February	March
Cash collections from prior month's sales	$ 97,500	$114,000	$120,000
Cash collections from current month's sales	76,000	80,000	84,000
Total cash collections from sales	$173,500	$194,000	$204,000

January 1 accounts receivable balance

60% × January sales

40% × March sales

B.

Quincy Company
Schedule of Payments for Manufacturing Costs
For the Three Months Ending March 31

	January	February	March
Payment of prior month's costs	$36,700	$ 36,800	$ 46,400
Payment of current month's costs	55,200	69,600	85,200
Total manufacturing cost cash payments	$91,900	$106,400	$131,600

January 1 accounts payable balance

40% × January manufacturing costs excluding depreciation, insurance, and property taxes ($100,000 – $18,000)

60% × March manufacturing costs excluding depreciation, insurance, and property taxes ($142,000 – $18,000)

60% × February manufacturing costs excluding depreciation, insurance, and property taxes ($134,000 – $18,000)

C.

Quincy Company
Cash Budget
For the Three Months Ending March 31

	January	February	March
Estimated cash receipts	$173,500	$194,000	$204,000
Less estimated cash payments for:			
Manufacturing costs	$ 91,900	$106,400	$131,600
Selling and administrative expenses	72,000	70,000	75,000
Total cash payments	$163,900	$176,400	$206,600
Cash increase (decrease)	$ 9,600	$ 17,600	$ (2,600)
Plus cash balance at beginning of month	26,000	35,600	53,200
Cash balance at end of month	$ 35,600	$ 53,200	$ 50,600
Less minimum cash balance	20,000	20,000	20,000
Excess (deficiency)	$ 15,600	$ 33,200	$ 30,600

From Schedule of Cash Collections in Part A

From Schedule of Cash Payments in Part B

Check Up Corner

Capital Expenditures Budget

The **capital expenditures budget** summarizes plans for acquiring fixed assets. Such expenditures are necessary as machinery and other fixed assets wear out or become obsolete. In addition, purchasing additional fixed assets may be necessary to meet increasing demand for the company's product.

To illustrate, a five-year capital expenditures budget for **Elite Accessories Inc.** is shown in Exhibit 20.

Exhibit 20
Capital
Expenditures
Budget

	A	B	C	D	E	F
1	Elite Accessories Inc.					
2	Capital Expenditures Budget					
3	For the Five Years Ending December 31, 20Y5					
4	Item	20Y1	20Y2	20Y3	20Y4	20Y5
5	Machinery—Cutting Department	$400,000			$280,000	$360,000
6	Machinery—Sewing Department	274,000	$260,000	$560,000	200,000	
7	Office equipment		90,000			60,000
8	Total	$674,000	$350,000	$560,000	$480,000	$420,000
9						

As shown in Exhibit 20, capital expenditures budgets are often prepared for five to ten years into the future. This is necessary because fixed assets often must be ordered years in advance. Likewise, it could take years to construct new buildings or other production facilities.

The capital expenditures budget should be integrated with the operating and financing budgets. For example, depreciation of new manufacturing equipment affects the factory overhead cost budget. The plans for financing the capital expenditures also affect the cash budget.

Budgeted Balance Sheet

The budgeted balance sheet is prepared based on the operating and financial budgets of the master budget. The budgeted balance sheet is dated as of the end of the budget period and is similar to a normal balance sheet except that estimated amounts are used. For this reason, a budgeted balance sheet for Elite Accessories Inc. is not illustrated.

Analysis for Decision Making

Nonmanufacturing Staffing Levels

Objective

Describe and illustrate the use of staffing budgets for nonmanufacturing businesses.

The budgeting illustrated in this chapter is similar to budgeting used for nonmanufacturing businesses. However, many nonmanufacturing businesses often do not have direct materials purchases budgets, direct labor cost budgets, or factory overhead cost budgets. Thus, the budgeted income statement is simplified in many nonmanufacturing settings.

A primary budget in nonmanufacturing businesses is the labor, or staffing, budget. This budget, which is highly flexible to service demands, is used to manage staffing levels. For example, a theme park will have greater staffing in the summer vacation months than in the fall months. Likewise, a retailer will have greater staffing during the holidays than on typical weekdays.

To illustrate, Concord Hotel operates a hotel in a business district. The hotel has 150 rooms that average 120 guests per night during the weekdays and 50 guests per night during the weekend. The housekeeping staff is able to clean 10 rooms per employee. The number of housekeepers required for an average weekday and weekend is determined as follows:

	Weekday	Weekend
Number of guests per day	120	50
Rooms per housekeeper	÷ 10	÷ 10
Number of housekeepers per day	12	5

If each housekeeper is paid $15 per hour for an eight-hour shift per day, the annual budget for the staff is as follows:

	Weekday	Weekend	Total
Number of housekeepers per day	12	5	
Hours per shift	× 8	× 8	
Days per year	× 260*	× 104**	
Number of hours per year	24,960	4,160	
Rate per hour	× $15	× $15	
Housekeeping staff annual budget	$374,400	$62,400	$436,800

* 52 weeks × 5 days

** 52 weeks × 2 days

The budget can be used to plan and manage the staffing of the hotel. For example, if a wedding were booked for the weekend, the budgeted increase in staffing could be compared with the increased revenue from the wedding to verify the profit plan.

Make a Decision | Nonmanufacturing Staffing Levels

Johnson Stores is planning its staffing for the upcoming holiday season. From past history, the store determines that it needs one additional sales clerk for each $12,000 in daily sales. The average daily sales is anticipated to increase by $96,000 from Black Friday until Christmas Eve, or 27 shopping days. Each additional sales clerk will work an eight-hour shift and will be paid $14 per hour.

A. Determine the amount to budget for additional sales clerks for the holiday season.
B. If Johnson Stores has an average 40% gross profit on sales, should it add the staff suggested by your answer in A? That is, is it profitable to staff for the increased sales in A?

Solution:

A.

Average daily revenue	$96,000
Revenue per clerk	÷12,000
Number of additional sales clerks	8
Hours per day per clerk	× 8
Number of hours per day	64
Number of shopping days	× 27
Number of hours	1,728
Rate per hour	× $14
Holiday staff budget for additional clerks	$24,192

B.

Johnson Stores should add the staff because it will be profitable.

Increase in daily revenue	$ 96,000
Gross profit percentage	× 40%
Increase in daily gross profit	$ 38,400
Number of shopping days	× 27
Additional gross profit	$1,036,800
Staff budget increase [from (A)]	(24,192)
Additional profit	$1,012,608

Make a Decision

Let's Review

Chapter Summary

1. Budgeting involves (1) establishing plans (planning), (2) directing operations (directing), and (3) evaluating performance (controlling). In addition, budgets should be established to avoid human behavior problems.

2. The budget estimates received by the budget committee should be carefully studied, analyzed, revised, and integrated. The static and flexible budgets are two major budgeting approaches. Computers can be used to make the budget process more efficient and organizationally integrated.

3. The master budget is an integrated set of operating and financial budgets for a period of time. The operating budgets are prepared and integrated into a budgeted income statement. The financial budgets are prepared and integrated into a budgeted balance sheet.

4. The basic operating budgets are the sales budget, production budget, direct materials purchases budget, direct labor cost budget, factory overhead cost budget, cost of goods sold budget, and selling and administrative expenses budget. These budgets are the basis for preparing a budgeted income statement.

5. The cash budget and capital expenditures budget are financial budgets showing the investing and financing activities of the firm. These budgets are the basis for preparing a budgeted balance sheet.

Key Terms

budgetary slack (1055)
budgets (1054)
capital expenditures budget (1074)
cash budget (1070)
continuous budgeting (1056)
cost of goods sold budget (1066)

direct labor cost budget (1064)
direct materials purchases
   budget (1063)
factory overhead cost budget (1066)
flexible budgets (1058)
goal conflict (1055)

master budget (1060)
production budget (1062)
responsibility center (1054)
sales budget (1061)
static budget (1057)
zero-based budgeting (1057)

Practice

Multiple-Choice Questions

1. A tight budget may create:
   A. budgetary slack.
   B. discouragement.
   C. a flexible budget.
   D. a "spend it or lose it" mentality.

2. The first step of the budget process is to:
   A. plan.
   B. direct.
   C. control.
   D. analyze feedback.

3. Static budgets are often used by:
   A. production departments.
   B. administrative departments.
   C. responsibility centers.
   D. capital projects.

4. The total estimated sales for the coming year is 250,000 units. The estimated inventory at the beginning of the year is 22,500 units, and the desired inventory at the end of the year is 30,000 units. The total production indicated in the production budget is:

A. 242,500 units. C. 280,000 units.
B. 257,500 units. D. 302,500 units.

5. Dixon Company expects $650,000 of credit sales in March and $800,000 of credit sales in April. Dixon historically collects 70% of its sales in the month of sale and 30% in the following month. How much cash does Dixon expect to collect in April?

A. $800,000 C. $755,000
B. $560,000 D. $1,015,000

Answers provided after Problem. Need more practice? Find additional multiple-choice questions, exercises, and problems in CengageNOWv2.

Exercises

SHOW ME HOW

1. Flexible budgeting Obj. 2

At the beginning of the period, the Assembly Department budgeted direct labor of $112,000 and property tax of $12,000 for 7,000 hours of production. The department actually completed 7,500 hours of production. Determine the budget for the department, assuming that it uses flexible budgeting.

SHOW ME HOW

2. Production budget Obj. 4

MyLife Chronicles Inc. projected sales of 240,000 diaries for the year. The estimated January 1 inventory is 19,900 units, and the desired December 31 inventory is 18,800 units. What is the budgeted production (in units) for the year?

SHOW ME HOW

3. Direct materials purchases budget Obj. 4

MyLife Chronicles Inc. budgeted production of 238,900 diaries for the year. Paper is required to produce a diary. Assume five square yards of paper are required for each diary. The estimated January 1 paper inventory is 32,400 square yards. The desired December 31 paper inventory is 30,800 square yards. If paper costs $0.30 per square yard, determine the direct materials purchases budget for the year.

SHOW ME HOW

4. Direct labor cost budget Obj. 4

MyLife Chronicles Inc. budgeted production of 238,900 diaries for the year. Each diary requires assembly. Assume that six minutes are required to assemble each diary. If assembly labor costs $12 per hour, determine the direct labor cost budget for the year.

SHOW ME HOW

5. Cost of goods sold budget Obj. 4

Prepare a cost of goods sold budget for MyLife Chronicles Inc. using the information in Exercises 3 and 4. Assume the estimated inventories on January 1 for finished goods and work in process were $25,000 and $19,000, respectively. Also assume the desired inventories on December 31 for finished goods and work in process were $31,500 and $16,700, respectively. Factory overhead was budgeted at $197,100.

SHOW ME HOW

6. Cash budget Obj. 5

MyLife Chronicles Inc. collects 30% of its sales on account in the month of the sale and 70% in the month following the sale. If sales on account are budgeted to be $170,000 for June and $200,000 for July, what are the budgeted cash receipts from sales on account for July?

Answers provided after Problem. Need more practice? Find additional multiple-choice questions, exercises, and problems in CengageNOWv2.

Problem

Selected information concerning sales and production for Cabot Co. for July are summarized as follows:

A. Estimated sales:

Product K:	40,000 units at $30 per unit	
Product L:	20,000 units at $65 per unit	

B. Estimated inventories, July 1:

Material A:	4,000 lbs.	Product K:	3,000 units at $17 per unit	$ 51,000
Material B:	3,500 lbs.	Product L:	2,700 units at $35 per unit	94,500
		Total		$145,500

There were no work in process inventories estimated for July.

C. Desired inventories at July 31:

Material A:	3,000 lbs.	Product K:	2,500 units at $17 per unit	$ 42,500
Material B:	2,500 lbs.	Product L:	2,000 units at $35 per unit	70,000
		Total		$112,500

There were no work in process inventories desired for July 31.

D. Direct materials used in production:

	Product K	Product L
Material A:	0.7 lb. per unit	3.5 lbs. per unit
Material B:	1.2 lbs. per unit	1.8 lbs. per unit

E. Unit costs for direct materials:

Material A:	$4.00 per lb.
Material B:	$2.00 per lb.

F. Direct labor requirements:

	Department 1	Department 2
Product K	0.4 hr. per unit	0.15 hr. per unit
Product L	0.6 hr. per unit	0.25 hr. per unit

G.

	Department 1	Department 2
Direct labor rate	$12 per hr.	$16 per hr.

H. Estimated factory overhead costs for July:

Indirect factory wages	$200,000
Depreciation of plant and equipment	40,000
Power and light	25,000
Indirect materials	34,000
Total	$299,000

Instructions

1. Prepare a sales budget for July.
2. Prepare a production budget for July.
3. Prepare a direct materials purchases budget for July.
4. Prepare a direct labor cost budget for July.
5. Prepare a cost of goods sold budget for July.

Need more practice? Find additional multiple-choice questions, exercises, and problems in CengageNOWv2.

Answers

Multiple-Choice Questions

1. **B** Individuals can be discouraged with budgets that appear too tight or unobtainable. Flexible budgeting (answer C) provides a series of budgets for varying rates of activity and thereby builds into the budgeting system the effect of fluctuations in the level of activity. Budgetary slack (answer A) comes from a loose budget, not a tight budget. A "spend it or lose it" mentality (answer D) is often associated with loose budgets.

2. **A** The first step of the budget process is to develop a plan. Once plans are established, management may direct actions (answer B). The results of actions can be controlled (answer C) by comparing them to the plan. This feedback (answer D) can be used by management to change plans or redirect actions.

3. **B** Administrative departments (answer B), such as Purchasing or Human Resources, will often use static budgeting. Production departments (answer A) frequently use flexible budgets. Responsibility centers (answer C) can use either static or flexible budgeting. Capital expenditures budgets are used to plan capital projects (answer D).

4. **B** The total production indicated in the production budget is 257,500 units (answer B), which is computed as follows:

Sales	250,000 units
Desired ending inventory	30,000 units
Total	280,000 units
Estimated beginning inventory	(22,500) units
Total production	257,500 units

5. **C** Dixon expects to collect 70% of April sales ($560,000) plus 30% of the March sales ($195,000) in April, for a total of $755,000 (answer C). Answer A is 100% of April sales. Answer B is 70% of April sales. Answer D adds 70% of both March and April sales.

Exercises

1.

Variable cost:	
Direct labor (7,500 hours × $16* per hour)	$120,000
Fixed cost:	
Property tax	12,000
Total department costs	$132,000

* $112,000 ÷ 7,000 hours

2.

MyLife Chronicles Inc.
Production Budget
For the Year Ending December 31

Expected units to be sold	240,000
Desired ending inventory, December 31	18,800
Total units available	258,800
Estimated beginning inventory, January 1..................	(19,900)
Total units to be produced	238,900

3.

MyLife Chronicles Inc.
Direct Materials Purchases Budget
For the Year Ending December 31

Square yards required for production:	
Diaries (238,900 × 5 sq. yds.)	1,194,500
Desired ending inventory, December 31	30,800
Total square yards available	1,225,300
Estimated beginning inventory, January 1.................	(32,400)
Total square yards to be purchased	1,192,900
Unit price (per sq. yd.)	× $0.30
Total direct materials to be purchased	$ 357,870

4.

MyLife Chronicles Inc.
Direct Labor Cost Budget
For the Year Ending December 31

Hours required for assembly:	
Diaries (238,900 × 6 min.)	1,433,400 min.
Convert minutes to hours	÷ 60 min.
Assembly hours	23,890 hrs.
Hourly rate	× $12
Total direct labor cost	$ 286,680

5.

MyLife Chronicles Inc.
Cost of Goods Sold Budget
For the Year Ending December 31

Finished goods inventory, January 1			$ 25,000
Work in process inventory, January 1		$ 19,000	
Direct materials:			
Direct materials inventory, January 1 (32,400 × $0.30).	$ 9,720		
Direct materials purchases	357,870		
Cost of direct materials available for use	$367,590		
Less direct materials inventory, December 31			
(30,800 × $0.30)	(9,240)		
Cost of direct materials placed in production	$358,350		
Direct labor	286,680		
Factory overhead	197,100		
Total manufacturing costs		842,130	
Total work in process during period		$861,130	
Work in process inventory, December 31		(16,700)	
Cost of goods manufactured			844,430
Cost of finished goods available for sale			$869,430
Finished goods inventory, December 31			(31,500)
Cost of goods sold			$837,930

6.

	July
Collections from June sales (70% × $170,000)	$119,000
Collections from July sales (30% × $200,000)	60,000
Total receipts from sales on account	$179,000

Need more help? Watch step-by-step videos of how to compute answers to these Exercises in CengageNOWv2.

Problem

1.

	A	B	C	D
1		Cabot Co.		
2		Sales Budget		
3		For the Month Ending July 31		
4	Product	Unit Sales Volume	Unit Selling Price	Total Sales
5	Product K	40,000	$30.00	$1,200,000
6	Product L	20,000	65.00	1,300,000
7	Total revenue from sales			$2,500,000
8				

2.

	A	B	C
1	Cabot Co.		
2	Production Budget		
3	For the Month Ending July 31		
4		Units	
5		Product K	Product L
6	Sales	40,000	20,000
7	Desired inventories at July 31	2,500	2,000
8	Total units available	42,500	22,000
9	Estimated inventories, July 1	(3,000)	(2,700)
10	Total units to be produced	39,500	19,300
11			

3.

	A	B	C	D	E	F	G
1	Cabot Co.						
2	Direct Materials Purchases Budget						
3	For the Month Ending July 31						
4			Direct Materials				
5			Material A		Material B		Total
6	Units required for production:						
7	Product K (39,500 × lbs. per unit)		27,650	lbs.*	47,400	lbs.*	
8	Product L (19,300 × lbs. per unit)		67,550	**	34,740	**	
9	Desired units of inventory, July 31		3,000		2,500		
10	Total		98,200	lbs.	84,640	lbs.	
11	Estimated units of inventory, July 1		(4,000)		(3,500)		
12	Total units to be purchased		94,200	lbs.	81,140	lbs.	
13	Unit price		× $4.00		× $2.00		
14	Total direct materials to be purchased		$376,800		$162,280		$539,080
15							
16	*27,650 = 39,500 × 0.7 47,400 = 39,500 × 1.2						
17	**67,550 = 19,300 × 3.5 34,740 = 19,300 × 1.8						
18							

4.

	A	B	C	D	E	F	G
1	Cabot Co.						
2	Direct Labor Cost Budget						
3	For the Month Ending July 31						
4			Department 1		Department 2		Total
5	Hours required for production:						
6	Product K (39,500 × hrs. per unit)		15,800	*	5,925	*	
7	Product L (19,300 × hrs. per unit)		11,580	**	4,825	**	
8	Total		27,380		10,750		
9	Hourly rate		× $12		× $16		
10	Total direct labor cost		$328,560		$172,000		$500,560
11							
12	*15,800 = 39,500 × 0.4 5,925 = 39,500 × 0.15						
13	**11,580 = 19,300 × 0.6 4,825 = 19,300 × 0.25						
14							

5.

	A	B	C	D
1	Cabot Co.			
2	Cost of Goods Sold Budget			
3	For the Month Ending July 31			
4	Finished goods inventory, July 1			$ 145,500
5	Direct materials:			
6	Direct materials inventory, July 1 (Note A)		$ 23,000	
7	Direct materials purchases		539,080	
8	Cost of direct materials available for use		$562,080	
9	Direct materials inventory, July 31 (Note B)		(17,000)	
10	Cost of direct materials placed in production		$545,080	
11	Direct labor		500,560	
12	Factory overhead		299,000	
13	Cost of goods manufactured			1,344,640
14	Cost of finished goods available for sale			$1,490,140
15	Finished goods inventory, July 31			(112,500)
16	Cost of goods sold			$1,377,640
17				
18	Note A:			
19	Material A 4,000 lbs. at $4.00 per lb.	$16,000		
20	Material B 3,500 lbs. at $2.00 per lb.	7,000		
21	Direct materials inventory, July 1	$23,000		
22				
23	Note B:			
24	Material A 3,000 lbs. at $4.00 per lb.	$12,000		
25	Material B 2,500 lbs. at $2.00 per lb.	5,000		
26	Direct materials inventory, July 31	$17,000		
27				

Discussion Questions

1. What are the three major objectives of budgeting?

2. Briefly describe the type of human behavior problems that might arise if budget goals are set too tightly.

3. What behavioral problems are associated with setting a budget too loosely?

4. What behavioral problems are associated with establishing conflicting goals within the budget?

5. Under what circumstances would a static budget be appropriate?

6. How do computerized budgeting systems aid firms in the budgeting process?

7. Why should the production requirements set forth in the production budget be carefully coordinated with the sales budget?

8. Why should the timing of direct materials purchases be closely coordinated with the production budget?

9. A. Discuss the purpose of the cash budget.
   B. If the cash for the first quarter of the fiscal year indicates excess cash at the end of each of the first two months, how might the excess cash be used?

10. Give an example of how the capital expenditures budget affects other operating budgets.

Basic Exercises

SHOW ME HOW

BE 21-1 Flexible budgeting

Obj. 2

At the beginning of the period, the Fabricating Department budgeted direct labor of $33,600 and equipment depreciation of $5,000 for 1,200 hours of production. The department actually completed 1,300 hours of production. Determine the budget for the department, assuming that it uses flexible budgeting.

SHOW ME HOW

BE 21-2 Production budget

Obj. 4

Pasadena Candle Inc. projected sales of 800,000 candles for the year. The estimated January 1 inventory is 35,000 units, and the desired December 31 inventory is 20,000 units. What is the budgeted production (in units) for the year?

SHOW ME HOW

BE 21-3 Direct materials purchases budget

Obj. 4

Pasadena Candle Inc. budgeted production of 785,000 candles for the year. Wax is required to produce a candle. Assume 10 ounces of wax is required for each candle. The estimated January 1 wax inventory is 16,000 pounds. The desired December 31 wax inventory is 12,500 pounds. If candle wax costs $1.24 per pound, determine the direct materials purchases budget for the year.

SHOW ME HOW

BE 21-4 Direct labor cost budget

Obj. 4

Pasadena Candle Inc. budgeted production of 785,000 candles for the year. Each candle requires molding. Assume that six minutes are required to mold each candle. If molding labor costs $18 per hour, determine the direct labor cost budget for the year.

SHOW ME HOW

BE 21-5 Cost of goods sold budget

Obj. 4

Prepare a cost of goods sold budget for Pasadena Candle Inc. using the information in Basic Exercises 3 and 4. Assume the estimated inventories on January 1 for finished goods and work in process were $200,000 and $41,250, respectively. Also assume the desired inventories on December 31 for finished goods and work in process were $120,000 and $28,500, respectively. Factory overhead was budgeted at $300,000.

SHOW ME HOW

BE 21-6 Cash budget

Obj. 5

Pasadena Candle Inc. pays 40% of its purchases on account in the month of the purchase and 60% in the month following the purchase. If purchases are budgeted to be $40,000 for August and $36,000 for September, what are the budgeted cash payments for purchases on account for September?

Exercises

✔ A. December 31 cash
balance, $3,150

SHOW ME HOW

EXCEL TEMPLATE

EX 21-1 Personal budget

Obj. 2, 5

At the beginning of the school year, Priscilla Wescott decided to prepare a cash budget for the months of September, October, November, and December. The budget must plan for enough cash on December 31 to pay the spring semester tuition, which is the same as the fall tuition. The following information relates to the budget:

Cash balance, September 1 (from a summer job).....................	$6,000
Purchase season football tickets in September......................	150
Additional entertainment for each month...........................	250
Pay fall semester tuition in September	3,500
Pay rent at the beginning of each month...........................	450
Pay for food each month...	400
Pay apartment deposit on September 2 (to be returned December 15)	450
Part-time job earnings each month (net of taxes)	1,300

A. Prepare a cash budget for September, October, November, and December.

B. Are the four monthly budgets that are presented prepared as static budgets or flexible budgets?

C. ━━━▶ What are the budget implications for Priscilla Wescott?

EX 21-2 Flexible budget for selling and administrative expenses for a service company

Obj. 2, 4

 Total selling and administrative expenses at $400,000 sales, $332,500

SHOW ME HOW   EXCEL TEMPLATE

Cloud Productivity Inc. uses flexible budgets that are based on the following data:

Sales commissions	14% of sales
Advertising expense.......................................	18% of sales
Miscellaneous administrative expense	$6,500 per month plus 12% of sales
Office salaries expense	$28,000 per month
Customer support expenses................................	$12,000 per month plus 20% of sales
Research and development expense........................	$30,000 per month

Prepare a flexible selling and administrative expenses budget for March for sales volumes of $400,000, $500,000, and $600,000.

EX 21-3 Static budget versus flexible budget

Obj. 2, 4

 B. Excess of actual cost over budget for March, $45,750

SHOW ME HOW   EXCEL TEMPLATE

The production supervisor of the Machining Department for Niland Company agreed to the following monthly static budget for the upcoming year:

Niland Company
Machining Department
Monthly Production Budget

Wages...	$1,125,000
Utilities...	90,000
Depreciation..	50,000
Total	$1,265,000

The actual amount spent and the actual units produced in the first three months in the Machining Department were as follows:

	Amount Spent	Units Produced
January	$1,100,000	80,000
February	1,200,000	90,000
March	1,250,000	95,000

The Machining Department supervisor has been very pleased with this performance because actual expenditures for January–March have been significantly less than the monthly static budget of $1,265,000. However, the plant manager believes that the budget should not remain fixed for every month but should "flex" or adjust to the volume of work that is produced

(Continued)

in the Machining Department. Additional budget information for the Machining Department is as follows:

Wages per hour	$15.00
Utility cost per direct labor hour	$1.20
Direct labor hours per unit	0.75
Planned monthly unit production	100,000

A. Prepare a flexible budget for the actual units produced for January, February, and March in the Machining Department. Assume depreciation is a fixed cost.

B. Compare the flexible budget with the actual expenditures for the first three months. What does this comparison suggest?

EX 21-4   Flexible budget for Assembly Department
Obj. 2

✔ Total department cost at 25,000 units, $386,250

SHOW ME HOW   EXCEL TEMPLATE

REAL WORLD

Steelcase Inc. is one of the largest manufacturers of office furniture in the United States. In Grand Rapids, Michigan, it assembles filing cabinets in an Assembly Department. Assume the following information for the Assembly Department:

Direct labor per filing cabinet	15 minutes
Supervisor salaries	$200,000 per month
Depreciation	$30,000 per month
Direct labor rate	$25 per hour

Prepare a flexible budget for 25,000, 40,000, and 55,000 filing cabinets for the month of March in the Assembly Department, similar to Exhibit 5.

EX 21-5   Production budget
Obj. 4

✔ Bath scale total units to be produced, 144,500 units

SHOW ME HOW

Weightless Inc. produces a Bath and Gym version of its popular electronic scale. The anticipated unit sales for the scales by sales region are as follows:

	Bath Scale	Gym Scale
East Region unit sales	55,000	30,000
West Region unit sales	95,000	60,000
Total	150,000	90,000

The finished goods inventory estimated for October 1, for the Bath and Gym scale models is 18,000 and 10,000 units, respectively. The desired finished goods inventory for October 31 for the Bath and Gym scale models is 12,500 and 8,000 units, respectively.

Prepare a production budget for the Bath and Gym scales for the month ended October 31.

EX 21-6   Sales and production budgets
Obj. 4

✔ B. Model Rumble total production, 25,750 units

SHOW ME HOW   EXCEL TEMPLATE

Sonic Inc. manufactures two models of speakers, Rumble and Thunder. Based on the following production and sales data for June, prepare (A) a sales budget and (B) a production budget:

	Rumble	Thunder
Estimated inventory (units), June 1	750	300
Desired inventory (units), June 30	500	250
Expected sales volume (units):		
Midwest Region	12,000	3,500
South Region	14,000	4,000
Unit sales price	$60	$90

EX 21-7   Professional fees earned budget for a service company
Obj. 4

✔ Total professional fees earned, $10,270,000

Rollins and Cohen, CPAs, offer three types of services to clients: auditing, tax, and small business accounting. Based on experience and projected growth, the following billable hours have been estimated for the year ending December 31, 20Y8:

	Billable Hours
Audit Department:	
Staff..	22,400
Partners...	7,900
Tax Department:	
Staff..	13,200
Partners...	5,500
Small Business Accounting Department:	
Staff..	3,000
Partners...	600

The average billing rate for staff is $150 per hour, and the average billing rate for partners is $320 per hour. Prepare a professional fees earned budget for Rollins and Cohen, CPAs, for the year ending December 31, 20Y8, using the following column headings and showing the estimated professional fees by type of service rendered:

Billable Hours	Hourly Rate	Total Revenue

✔ Staff total labor cost, $1,737,000

EX 21-8 Professional labor cost budget for a service company   Obj. 4

Based on the data in Exercise 7 and assuming that the average compensation per hour for staff is $45 and for partners is $140, prepare a professional labor cost budget for each department for Rollins and Cohen, CPAs, for the year ending December 31, 20Y8. Use the following column headings:

Staff	Partners

✔ Total cheese purchases, $35,448

SHOW ME HOW   EXCEL TEMPLATE

EX 21-9 Direct materials purchases budget   Obj. 4

Romano's Frozen Pizza Inc. has determined from its production budget the following estimated production volumes for 12" and 16" frozen pizzas for September:

	Units	
	12" Pizza	16" Pizza
Budgeted production volume	5,300	8,900

There are three direct materials used in producing the two types of pizza. The quantities of direct materials expected to be used for each pizza are as follows:

	12" Pizza	16" Pizza
Direct materials:		
Dough	0.70 lb. per unit	1.50 lbs. per unit
Tomato	0.40	0.70
Cheese	0.60	1.30

In addition, Romano's has determined the following information about each material:

	Dough	Tomato	Cheese
Estimated inventory, September 1	520 lbs.	200 lbs.	295 lbs.
Desired inventory, September 30	580 lbs.	185 lbs.	315 lbs.
Price per pound	$0.80	$1.60	$2.40

Prepare September's direct materials purchases budget for Romano's Frozen Pizza Inc.

✔ Concentrate budgeted purchases, $47,400

REAL WORLD

EX 21-10 Direct materials purchases budget   Obj. 4

Coca-Cola Enterprises is the largest bottler of Coca-Cola® in Western Europe. The company purchases Coke® and Sprite® concentrate from **The Coca-Cola Company**, dilutes and mixes the concentrate with carbonated water, and then fills the blended beverage into cans or plastic

(Continued)

two-liter bottles. Assume that the estimated production for Coke and Sprite two-liter bottles at the Wakefield, UK, bottling plant is as follows for the month of May:

Coke	153,000 two-liter bottles
Sprite	86,500 two-liter bottles

In addition, assume that the concentrate costs $75 per pound for both Coke and Sprite and is used at a rate of 0.15 pound per 100 liters of carbonated water in blending Coke and 0.10 pound per 100 liters of carbonated water in blending Sprite. Assume that two liters of carbonated water are used for each two-liter bottle of finished product. Assume further that two-liter bottles cost $0.08 per bottle and carbonated water costs $0.06 per liter.

Prepare a direct materials purchases budget for May, assuming inventories are ignored, because there are no changes between beginning and ending inventories for concentrate, bottles, and carbonated water.

✔ Total steel belt purchases, $291,200

EXCEL TEMPLATE

EX 21-11 Direct materials purchases budget

Obj. 4

Anticipated sales for Safety Grip Company were 42,000 passenger car tires and 19,000 truck tires. Rubber and steel belts are used in producing passenger car and truck tires as follows:

	Passenger Car	Truck
Rubber	35 lbs. per unit	78 lbs. per unit
Steel belts	5 lbs. per unit	8 lbs. per unit

The purchase prices of rubber and steel are $1.20 and $0.80 per pound, respectively. The desired ending inventories of rubber and steel belts are 40,000 and 10,000 pounds, respectively. The estimated beginning inventories for rubber and steel belts are 46,000 and 8,000 pounds, respectively.

Prepare a direct materials purchases budget for Safety Grip Company for the year ended December 31, 20Y9.

✔ Total direct labor cost, Assembly, $31,080

EX 21-12 Direct labor cost budget

Obj. 4

Ace Racket Company manufactures two types of tennis rackets, the Junior and Pro Striker models. The production budget for July for the two rackets is as follows:

	Junior	Pro Striker
Production budget	1,500 units	6,200 units

Both rackets are produced in two departments, Forming and Assembly. The direct labor hours required for each racket are estimated as follows:

	Forming Department	Assembly Department
Junior	0.16 hr. per unit	0.24 hr. per unit
Pro Striker	0.20 hr. per unit	0.30 hr. per unit

The direct labor rate for each department is as follows:

Forming Department	$18 per hour
Assembly Department	$14 per hour

Prepare the direct labor cost budget for July.

✔ A. Total production of 501 Jeans, 53,300

EXCEL TEMPLATE

REAL WORLD

EX 21-13 Production and direct labor cost budgets

Obj. 4

Levi Strauss & Co. manufactures slacks and jeans under a variety of brand names, such as Dockers® and 501 Jeans®. Slacks and jeans are assembled by a variety of different sewing operations. Assume that the sales budget for Dockers and 501 Jeans shows estimated sales of

23,600 and 53,100 pairs, respectively, for May. The finished goods inventory is assumed as follows:

	Dockers	501 Jeans
May 1 estimated inventory	670	1,660
May 31 desired inventory	420	1,860

Assume the following direct labor data per 10 pairs of Dockers and 501 Jeans for four different sewing operations:

	Direct Labor per 10 Pairs	
	Dockers	**501 Jeans**
Inseam	18 minutes	9 minutes
Outerseam	20	14
Pockets	6	9
Zipper	12	6
Total	56 minutes	38 minutes

A. Prepare a production budget for May. Prepare the budget in two columns: Dockers® and 501 Jeans®.

B. Prepare the May direct labor cost budget for the four sewing operations, assuming a $13 wage per hour for the inseam and outerseam sewing operations and a $15 wage per hour for the pocket and zipper sewing operations. Prepare the direct labor cost budget in four columns: inseam, outerseam, pockets, and zipper.

EX 21-14 Factory overhead cost budget

Obj. 4

✔ Total variable factory overhead costs, $268,000

EXCEL TEMPLATE

Sweet Tooth Candy Company budgeted the following costs for anticipated production for August:

Advertising expenses	$232,000	Production supervisor wages	$135,000
Manufacturing supplies	14,000	Production control wages	32,000
Power and light	48,000	Executive officer salaries	310,000
Sales commissions	298,000	Materials management wages	39,000
Factory insurance	30,000	Factory depreciation	22,000

Prepare a factory overhead cost budget, separating variable and fixed costs. Assume that factory insurance and depreciation are the only fixed factory costs.

EX 21-15 Cost of goods sold budget

Obj. 4

✔ Cost of goods sold, $3,788,100

EXCEL TEMPLATE

Delaware Chemical Company uses oil to produce two types of plastic products, P1 and P2. Delaware budgeted 35,000 barrels of oil for purchase in June for $90 per barrel. Direct labor budgeted in the chemical process was $240,000 for June. Factory overhead was budgeted at $400,000 during June. The inventories on June 1 were estimated to be:

Oil	$15,200
P1	8,300
P2	8,600
Work in process	12,900

The desired inventories on June 30 were:

Oil	$16,100
P1	9,400
P2	7,900
Work in process	13,500

Use the preceding information to prepare a cost of goods sold budget for June.

EX 21-16 Cost of goods sold budget

Obj. 4

✔ Cost of goods sold,
$488,360

The controller of MingWare Ceramics Inc. wishes to prepare a cost of goods sold budget for September. The controller assembled the following information for constructing the cost of goods sold budget:

Direct materials:	Enamel	Paint	Porcelain	Total
Total direct materials purchases budgeted for September	$36,780	$6,130	$145,500	$188,410
Estimated inventory, September 1	1,240	950	4,250	6,440
Desired inventory, September 30	1,890	1,070	5,870	8,830

Direct labor cost:	Kiln Department	Decorating Department	Total
Total direct labor cost budgeted for September	$47,900	$145,700	$193,600

Finished goods inventories:	Dish	Bowl	Figurine	Total
Estimated inventory, September 1	$5,780	$3,080	$2,640	$11,500
Desired inventory, September 30	3,710	2,670	3,290	9,670

Work in process inventories:	
Estimated inventory, September 1	$3,400
Desired inventory, September 30	1,990

Budgeted factory overhead costs for September:	
Indirect factory wages	$ 81,900
Depreciation of plant and equipment	14,300
Power and light	5,200
Indirect materials	4,100
Total	$105,500

Use the preceding information to prepare a cost of goods sold budget for September.

EX 21-17 Schedule of cash collections of accounts receivable

Obj. 5

✔ Total cash collected in
July, $163,050

SHOW ME HOW   EXCEL TEMPLATE

Pet Place Supplies Inc., a pet wholesale supplier, was organized on May 1. Projected sales for each of the first three months of operations are as follows:

May	$134,000
June	155,000
July	169,000

All sales are on account. Sixty-five percent of sales are expected to be collected in the month of the sale, 30% in the month following the sale, and the remainder in the second month following the sale.

Prepare a schedule indicating cash collections from sales for May, June, and July.

EX 21-18 Schedule of cash collections of accounts receivable

Obj. 5

✔ Total cash collected in
October, $62,550

OfficeMart Inc. has "cash and carry" customers and credit customers. OfficeMart estimates that 25% of monthly sales are to cash customers, while the remaining sales are to credit customers. Of the credit customers, 30% pay their accounts in the month of sale, while the remaining 70% pay their accounts in the month following the month of sale. Projected sales for the next three months are as follows:

October	$58,000
November	65,000
December	72,000

The Accounts Receivable balance on September 30 was $35,000.

Prepare a schedule of cash collections from sales for October, November, and December.

EX 21-19   Schedule of cash payments for a service company

Obj. 5

✔ Total cash payments in May, $58,490

Horizon Financial Inc. was organized on February 28. Projected selling and administrative expenses for each of the first three months of operations are as follows:

March	$52,400
April	64,200
May	68,900

Depreciation, insurance, and property taxes represent $9,000 of the estimated monthly expenses. The annual insurance premium was paid on February 28, and property taxes for the year will be paid in June. Seventy percent of the remainder of the expenses are expected to be paid in the month in which they are incurred, with the balance to be paid in the following month.

Prepare a schedule of cash payments for selling and administrative expenses for March, April, and May.

EX 21-20   Schedule of cash payments for a service company

Obj. 5

✔ Total cash payments in March, $113,740

EXCEL TEMPLATE

EastGate Physical Therapy Inc. is planning its cash payments for operations for the first quarter (January–March). The Accrued Expenses Payable balance on January 1 is $15,000. The budgeted expenses for the next three months are as follows:

	January	February	March
Salaries	$56,900	$ 68,100	$ 72,200
Utilities	2,400	2,600	2,500
Other operating expenses	32,300	41,500	44,700
Total	$91,600	$112,200	$119,400

Other operating expenses include $3,000 of monthly depreciation expense and $500 of monthly insurance expense that was prepaid for the year on May 1 of the previous year. Of the remaining expenses, 70% are paid in the month in which they are incurred, with the remainder paid in the following month. The Accrued Expenses Payable balance on January 1 relates to the expenses incurred in December.

Prepare a schedule of cash payments for operations for January, February, and March.

EX 21-21   Capital expenditures budget

Obj. 5

✔ Total capital expenditures in 20Y6, $4,000,000

EXCEL TEMPLATE

On January 1, 20Y6, the controller of Omicron Inc. is planning capital expenditures for the years 20Y6–20Y9. The following interviews helped the controller collect the necessary information for the capital expenditures budget:

Director of Facilities: A construction contract was signed in late 20Y5 for the construction of a new factory building at a contract cost of $10,000,000. The construction is scheduled to begin in 20Y6 and be completed in 20Y9.

Vice President of Manufacturing: Once the new factory building is finished, we plan to purchase $1.5 million in equipment in late 20Y7. I expect that an additional $200,000 will be needed early in the following year (20Y8) to test and install the equipment before we can begin production. If sales continue to grow, I expect we'll need to invest another $1,000,000 in equipment in 20Y9.

Chief Operating Officer: We have really been growing lately. I wouldn't be surprised if we need to expand the size of our new factory building in 20Y9 by at least 35%. Fortunately, we expect inflation to have minimal impact on construction costs over the next four years. Additionally, I would expect the cost of the expansion to be proportional to the size of the expansion.

Director of Information Systems: We need to upgrade our information systems to wireless network technology. It doesn't make sense to do this until after the new factory building is completed and producing product. During 20Y8, once the factory is up and running, we should equip the whole facility with wireless technology. I think it would cost us $800,000 today to install the technology. However, prices have been dropping by 25% per year, so it should be less expensive at a later date.

Chief Financial Officer: I am excited about our long-term prospects. My only short-term concern is managing our cash flow while we expend the $4,000,000 of construction costs in 20Y6 and $6,000,000 in 20Y7 on the portion of the new factory building scheduled to be completed in 20Y9.

Use this interview information to prepare a capital expenditures budget for Omicron Inc. for the years 20Y6–20Y9.

Problems: Series A

✔ 3. Total revenue from sales, $878,403

EXCEL TEMPLATE

PR 21-1A Forecast sales volume and sales budget   Obj. 4

For 20Y8, Raphael Frame Company prepared the sales budget that follows.

At the end of December 20Y8, the following unit sales data were reported for the year:

	Unit Sales	
	8" × 10" Frame	12" × 16" Frame
East	8,755	3,686
Central	6,510	3,090
West	12,348	5,616

Raphael Frame Company
Sales Budget
For the Year Ending December 31, 20Y8

Product and Area	Unit Sales Volume	Unit Selling Price	Total Sales
8" × 10" Frame:			
East.............................	8,500	$16	$136,000
Central..........................	6,200	16	99,200
West	12,600	16	201,600
Total	27,300		$436,800
12" × 16" Frame:			
East.............................	3,800	$30	$114,000
Central..........................	3,000	30	90,000
West	5,400	30	162,000
Total	12,200		$366,000
Total revenue from sales			$802,800

For the year ending December 31, 20Y9, unit sales are expected to follow the patterns established during the year ending December 31, 20Y8. The unit selling price for the 8" × 10" frame is expected to increase to $17 and the unit selling price for the 12" × 16" frame is expected to increase to $32, effective January 1, 20Y9.

Instructions

1. Compute the increase or decrease of actual unit sales for the year ended December 31, 20Y8, over budget. Place your answers in a columnar table with the following format:

	Unit Sales, Year Ended 20Y8		Increase (Decrease) Actual Over Budget	
	Budget	Actual Sales	Amount	Percent
8" × 10" Frame:				
East.............................				
Central..........................				
West				
12" × 16" Frame:				
East.............................				
Central..........................				
West				

2. Assuming that the increase or decrease in actual sales to budget indicated in part (1) is to continue in 20Y9, compute the unit sales volume to be used for preparing the sales budget for the year ending December 31, 20Y9. Place your answers in a columnar table similar to that in part (1) but with the following column heads. Round budgeted units to the nearest unit.

20Y8 Actual Units	Percentage Increase (Decrease)	20Y9 Budgeted Units (rounded)

3. Prepare a sales budget for the year ending December 31, 20Y9.

✔ 3. Total direct materials purchases, $771,490

PR 21-2A Sales, production, direct materials purchases, and direct labor cost budgets Obj. 4

The budget director of Gourmet Grill Company requests estimates of sales, production, and other operating data from the various administrative units every month. Selected information concerning sales and production for July is summarized as follows:

A. Estimated sales for July by sales territory:

Maine:

Backyard Chef...	310 units at $700 per unit
Master Chef	150 units at $1,200 per unit

Vermont:

Backyard Chef...	240 units at $750 per unit
Master Chef	110 units at $1,300 per unit

New Hampshire:

Backyard Chef...	360 units at $750 per unit
Master Chef	180 units at $1,400 per unit

B. Estimated inventories at July 1:

Direct materials:		Finished products:	
Grates.........................	290 units	Backyard Chef	30 units
Stainless steel.................	1,500 lbs.	Master Chef..............	32 units
Burner subassemblies	170 units		
Shelves......................	340 units		

C. Desired inventories at July 31:

Direct materials:		Finished products:	
Grates.........................	340 units	Backyard Chef	40 units
Stainless steel.................	1,800 lbs.	Master Chef..............	22 units
Burner subassemblies	155 units		
Shelves......................	315 units		

D. Direct materials used in production:

In manufacture of Backyard Chef:

Grates..	3 units per unit of product
Stainless steel...	24 lbs. per unit of product
Burner subassemblies	2 units per unit of product
Shelves...	4 units per unit of product

In manufacture of Master Chef:

Grates..	6 units per unit of product
Stainless steel...	42 lbs. per unit of product
Burner subassemblies	4 units per unit of product
Shelves...	5 units per unit of product

E. Anticipated purchase price for direct materials:

Grates.....................	$15 per unit	Burner subassemblies	$110 per unit
Stainless steel..............	$6 per lb.	Shelves......................	$10 per unit

F. Direct labor requirements:

Backyard Chef:

Stamping Department.......................................	0.50 hr. at $17 per hr.
Forming Department..	0.60 hr. at $15 per hr.
Assembly Department.......................................	1.00 hr. at $14 per hr.

Master Chef:

Stamping Department.......................................	0.60 hr. at $17 per hr.
Forming Department..	0.80 hr. at $15 per hr.
Assembly Department.......................................	1.50 hrs. at $14 per hr.

(Continued)

Instructions

1. Prepare a sales budget for July.
2. Prepare a production budget for July.
3. Prepare a direct materials purchases budget for July.
4. Prepare a direct labor cost budget for July.

PR 21-3A   Budgeted income statement and supporting budgets   Obj. 4

✔ 4. Total direct labor cost in Fabrication Dept., $29,216

EXCEL TEMPLATE

The budget director of Feathered Friends Inc., with the assistance of the controller, treasurer, production manager, and sales manager, has gathered the following data for use in developing the budgeted income statement for December:

A. Estimated sales for December:

Bird house .... 3,200 units at $50 per unit
Bird feeder .... 3,000 units at $70 per unit

B. Estimated inventories at December 1:

Direct materials:
Wood .... 200 ft.
Plastic........ 240 lbs.

Finished products:
Bird house....... 320 units at $27 per unit
Bird feeder....... 270 units at $40 per unit

C. Desired inventories at December 31:

Direct materials:
Wood .... 220 ft.
Plastic........ 200 lbs.

Finished products:
Bird house....... 290 units at $27 per unit
Bird feeder....... 250 units at $41 per unit

D. Direct materials used in production:

In manufacture of Bird House:
Wood .... 0.80 ft. per unit of product
Plastic........... 0.50 lb. per unit of product

In manufacture of Bird Feeder:
Wood .... 1.20 ft. per unit of product
Plastic........... 0.75 lb. per unit of product

E. Anticipated cost of purchases and beginning and ending inventory of direct materials:

Wood .... $7.00 per ft.   Plastic........... $1.00 per lb.

F. Direct labor requirements:

Bird House:
Fabrication Department .... 0.20 hr. at $16 per hr.
Assembly Department.. 0.30 hr. at $12 per hr.
Bird Feeder:
Fabrication Department .... 0.40 hr. at $16 per hr.
Assembly Department.. 0.35 hr. at $12 per hr.

G. Estimated factory overhead costs for December:

Indirect factory wages	$75,000	Power and light	$6,000
Depreciation of plant and equipment	23,000	Insurance and property tax	5,000

H. Estimated operating expenses for December:

Sales salaries expense	$70,000
Advertising expense	18,000
Office salaries expense	21,000
Depreciation expense—office equipment	600
Telephone expense—selling	550
Telephone expense—administrative	250
Travel expense—selling	4,000
Office supplies expense	200
Miscellaneous administrative expense	400

I. Estimated other income and expense for December:

Interest revenue	$200
Interest expense	122

J. Estimated tax rate: 30%

Instructions

1. Prepare a sales budget for December.

2. Prepare a production budget for December.

3. Prepare a direct materials purchases budget for December.

4. Prepare a direct labor cost budget for December.

5. Prepare a factory overhead cost budget for December.

6. Prepare a cost of goods sold budget for December. Work in process at the beginning of December is estimated to be $29,000, and work in process at the end of December is estimated to be $35,400.

7. Prepare a selling and administrative expenses budget for December.

8. Prepare a budgeted income statement for December.

PR 21-4A   Cash budget

Obj. 5

✔ 1. November
deficiency, $8,500

The controller of Bridgeport Housewares Inc. instructs you to prepare a monthly cash budget for the next three months. You are presented with the following budget information:

SHOW ME HOW

EXCEL TEMPLATE

	September	October	November
Sales	$250,000	$300,000	$315,000
Manufacturing costs	150,000	180,000	185,000
Selling and administrative expenses	42,000	48,000	51,000
Capital expenditures			200,000

The company expects to sell about 10% of its merchandise for cash. Of sales on account, 70% are expected to be collected in the month following the sale and the remainder the following month (second month following sale). Depreciation, insurance, and property tax expense represent $50,000 of the estimated monthly manufacturing costs. The annual insurance premium is paid in January, and the annual property taxes are paid in December. Of the remainder of the manufacturing costs, 80% are expected to be paid in the month in which they are incurred and the balance in the following month.

Current assets as of September 1 include cash of $40,000, marketable securities of $75,000, and accounts receivable of $300,000 ($60,000 from July sales and $240,000 from August sales). Sales on account for July and August were $200,000 and $240,000, respectively. Current liabilities as of September 1 include $40,000 of accounts payable incurred in August for manufacturing costs. All selling and administrative expenses are paid in cash in the period they are incurred. An estimated income tax payment of $55,000 will be made in October. Bridgeport's regular quarterly dividend of $25,000 is expected to be declared in October and paid in November. Management desires to maintain a minimum cash balance of $50,000.

Instructions

1. Prepare a monthly cash budget and supporting schedules for September, October, and November.

2. ➤ On the basis of the cash budget prepared in part (1), what recommendation should be made to the controller?

PR 21-5A Budgeted income statement and balance sheet Obj. 4, 5

✔ 1. Budgeted net income, $96,600

EXCEL TEMPLATE

As a preliminary to requesting budget estimates of sales, costs, and expenses for the fiscal year beginning January 1, 20Y9, the following tentative trial balance as of December 31, 20Y8, is prepared by the Accounting Department of Regina Soap Co.:

Cash	$ 85,000	
Accounts Receivable	125,600	
Finished Goods	69,300	
Work in Process	32,500	
Materials	48,900	
Prepaid Expenses	2,600	
Plant and Equipment	325,000	
Accumulated Depreciation—Plant and Equipment		$156,200
Accounts Payable		62,000
Common Stock, $10 par		180,000
Retained Earnings		290,700
	$688,900	$688,900

Factory output and sales for 20Y9 are expected to total 200,000 units of product, which are to be sold at $5.00 per unit. The quantities and costs of the inventories at December 31, 20Y9, are expected to remain unchanged from the balances at the beginning of the year.

Budget estimates of manufacturing costs and operating expenses for the year are summarized as follows:

	Estimated Costs and Expenses	
	Fixed (Total for Year)	Variable (Per Unit Sold)
Cost of goods manufactured and sold:		
Direct materials	—	$1.10
Direct labor	—	0.65
Factory overhead:		
Depreciation of plant and equipment	$40,000	—
Other factory overhead	12,000	0.40
Selling expenses:		
Sales salaries and commissions	46,000	0.45
Advertising	64,000	—
Miscellaneous selling expense	6,000	0.25
Administrative expenses:		
Office and officers salaries	72,400	0.12
Supplies	5,000	0.10
Miscellaneous administrative expense	4,000	0.05

Balances of accounts receivable, prepaid expenses, and accounts payable at the end of the year are not expected to differ significantly from the beginning balances. Federal income tax of $30,000 on 20Y9 taxable income will be paid during 20Y9. Regular quarterly cash dividends of $0.15 per share are expected to be declared and paid in March, June, September, and December on 18,000 shares of common stock outstanding. It is anticipated that fixed assets will be purchased for $75,000 cash in May.

Instructions

1. Prepare a budgeted income statement for 20Y9.

2. Prepare a budgeted balance sheet as of December 31, 20Y9, with supporting calculations.

Problems: Series B

✔ 3. Total revenue from sales, $2,148,950

EXCEL TEMPLATE

PR 21-1B   Forecast sales volume and sales budget   Obj. 4

Sentinel Systems Inc. prepared the following sales budget for 20Y8:

Sentinel Systems Inc.
Sales Budget
For the Year Ending December 31, 20Y8

Product and Area	Unit Sales Volume	Unit Selling Price	Total Sales
Home Alert System:			
United States	1,700	$200	$ 340,000
Europe	580	200	116,000
Asia	450	200	90,000
Total	2,730		$ 546,000
Business Alert System:			
United States	980	$750	$ 735,000
Europe	350	750	262,500
Asia	240	750	180,000
Total	1,570		$1,177,500
Total revenue from sales			$1,723,500

At the end of December 20Y8, the following unit sales data were reported for the year:

	Unit Sales	
	Home Alert System	Business Alert System
United States	1,734	1,078
Europe	609	329
Asia	432	252

For the year ending December 31, 20Y9, unit sales are expected to follow the patterns established during the year ending December 31, 20Y8. The unit selling price for the Home Alert System is expected to increase to $250, and the unit selling price for the Business Alert System is expected to be increased to $820, effective January 1, 20Y9.

Instructions

1. Compute the increase or decrease of actual unit sales for the year ended December 31, 20Y8, over budget. Place your answers in a columnar table with the following format:

	Unit Sales, Year Ended 20Y8		Increase (Decrease) Actual Over Budget	
	Budget	Actual Sales	Amount	Percent
Home Alert System:				
United States				
Europe				
Asia				
Business Alert System:				
United States				
Europe				
Asia				

(Continued)

2. Assuming that the increase or decrease in actual sales to budget indicated in part (1) is to continue in 20Y9, compute the unit sales volume to be used for preparing the sales budget for the year ending December 31, 20Y9. Place your answers in a columnar table similar to that in part (1) but with the following column heads. Round budgeted units to the nearest unit.

20Y8 Actual Units	Percentage Increase (Decrease)	20Y9 Budgeted Units (rounded)

3. Prepare a sales budget for the year ending December 31, 20Y9.

PR 21-2B   Sales, production, direct materials purchases, and direct labor cost budgets   Obj. 4

✔ 3. Total direct materials purchases, $987,478

EXCEL TEMPLATE

The budget director of Royal Furniture Company requests estimates of sales, production, and other operating data from the various administrative units every month. Selected information concerning sales and production for February is summarized as follows:

A. Estimated sales of King and Prince chairs for February by sales territory:

Northern Domestic:

King... 610 units at $780 per unit
Prince.. 750 units at $550 per unit

Southern Domestic:

King... 340 units at $780 per unit
Prince.. 440 units at $550 per unit

International:

King... 360 units at $850 per unit
Prince.. 290 units at $600 per unit

B. Estimated inventories at February 1:

Direct materials:		Finished products:	
Fabric	420 sq. yds.	King	90 units
Wood	580 linear ft.	Prince	25 units
Filler	250 cu. ft.		
Springs	660 units		

C. Desired inventories at February 28:

Direct materials:		Finished products:	
Fabric	390 sq. yds.	King	80 units
Wood	650 linear ft.	Prince	35 units
Filler	300 cu. ft.		
Springs	540 units		

D. Direct materials used in production:

In manufacture of King:

Fabric.. 6.0 sq. yds. per unit of product
Wood... 38 linear ft. per unit of product
Filler... 4.2 cu. ft. per unit of product
Springs... 16 units per unit of product

In manufacture of Prince:

Fabric.. 4.0 sq. yds. per unit of product
Wood... 26 linear ft. per unit of product
Filler... 3.4 cu. ft. per unit of product
Springs... 12 units per unit of product

E. Anticipated purchase price for direct materials:

Fabric	$12.00 per sq. yd.	Filler	$3.00 per cu. ft.
Wood	7.00 per linear ft.	Springs	4.50 per unit

F. Direct labor requirements:

King:

Framing Department..	1.2 hrs. at $12 per hr.
Cutting Department...	0.5 hr. at $14 per hr.
Upholstery Department.......................................	0.8 hr. at $15 per hr.

Prince:

Framing Department..	1.0 hr. at $12 per hr.
Cutting Department...	0.4 hr. at $14 per hr.
Upholstery Department.......................................	0.6 hr. at $15 per hr.

Instructions

1. Prepare a sales budget for February.

2. Prepare a production budget for February.

3. Prepare a direct materials purchases budget for February.

4. Prepare a direct labor cost budget for February.

✔ 4. Total direct labor
cost in Assembly Dept.,
$171,766

EXCEL TEMPLATE

PR 21-3B Budgeted income statement and supporting budgets   Obj. 4

The budget director of Gold Medal Athletic Co., with the assistance of the controller, treasurer, production manager, and sales manager, has gathered the following data for use in developing the budgeted income statement for March:

A. Estimated sales for March:

Batting helmet............................	1,200 units at $40 per unit
Football helmet	6,500 units at $160 per unit

B. Estimated inventories at March 1:

Direct materials:		Finished products:	
Plastic.............	90 lbs.	Batting helmet........	40 units at $25 per unit
Foam lining........	80 lbs.	Football helmet	240 units at $77 per unit

C. Desired inventories at March 31:

Direct materials:		Finished products:	
Plastic.............	50 lbs.	Batting helmet........	50 units at $25 per unit
Foam lining........	65 lbs.	Football helmet	220 units at $78 per unit

D. Direct materials used in production:

In manufacture of batting helmet:

Plastic..................................	1.2 lbs. per unit of product
Foam lining..............................	0.5 lb. per unit of product

In manufacture of football helmet:

Plastic..................................	3.5 lbs. per unit of product
Foam lining..............................	1.5 lbs. per unit of product

E. Anticipated cost of purchases and beginning and ending inventory of direct materials:

Plastic....................................	$6 per lb.
Foam lining................................	$4 per lb.

F. Direct labor requirements:

Batting helmet:

Molding Department.....................	0.2 hr. at $20 per hr.
Assembly Department....................	0.5 hr. at $14 per hr.

Football helmet:

Molding Department.....................	0.5 hr. at $20 per hr.
Assembly Department....................	1.8 hrs. at $14 per hr.

(Continued)

G. Estimated factory overhead costs for March:

Indirect factory wages	$86,000	Power and light	$4,000
Depreciation of plant and equipment	12,000	Insurance and property tax	2,300

H. Estimated operating expenses for March:

Sales salaries expense	$184,300
Advertising expense	87,200
Office salaries expense	32,400
Depreciation expense—office equipment	3,800
Telephone expense—selling	5,800
Telephone expense—administrative	1,200
Travel expense—selling	9,000
Office supplies expense	1,100
Miscellaneous administrative expense	1,000

I. Estimated other income and expense for March:

Interest revenue	$940
Interest expense	872

J. Estimated tax rate: 30%

Instructions

1. Prepare a sales budget for March.
2. Prepare a production budget for March.
3. Prepare a direct materials purchases budget for March.
4. Prepare a direct labor cost budget for March.
5. Prepare a factory overhead cost budget for March.
6. Prepare a cost of goods sold budget for March. Work in process at the beginning of March is estimated to be $15,300, and work in process at the end of March is desired to be $14,800.
7. Prepare a selling and administrative expenses budget for March.
8. Prepare a budgeted income statement for March.

PR 21-4B   Cash budget   **Obj. 5**

✔ 1. August
deficiency, $9,000

SHOW ME HOW   EXCEL TEMPLATE

The controller of Mercury Shoes Inc. instructs you to prepare a monthly cash budget for the next three months. You are presented with the following budget information:

	June	July	August
Sales	$160,000	$185,000	$200,000
Manufacturing costs	66,000	82,000	105,000
Selling and administrative expenses	40,000	46,000	51,000
Capital expenditures	—	—	120,000

The company expects to sell about 10% of its merchandise for cash. Of sales on account, 60% are expected to be collected in the month following the sale and the remainder the following month (second month after sale). Depreciation, insurance, and property tax expense represent $12,000 of the estimated monthly manufacturing costs. The annual insurance premium is paid in February, and the annual property taxes are paid in November. Of the remainder of the manufacturing costs, 80% are expected to be paid in the month in which they are incurred and the balance in the following month.

Current assets as of June 1 include cash of $42,000, marketable securities of $25,000, and accounts receivable of $198,000 ($150,000 from May sales and $48,000 from April sales). Sales on account in April and May were $120,000 and $150,000, respectively. Current liabilities as of June 1 include $13,000 of accounts payable incurred in May for manufacturing costs. All selling and administrative expenses are paid in cash in the period they are incurred. An estimated income tax payment of $24,000 will be made in July. Mercury Shoes' regular quarterly dividend of $15,000 is expected to be declared in July and paid in August. Management desires to maintain a minimum cash balance of $40,000.

Instructions

1. Prepare a monthly cash budget and supporting schedules for June, July, and August.

2. ➤ On the basis of the cash budget prepared in part (1), what recommendation should be made to the controller?

PR 21-5B   Budgeted income statement and balance sheet   Obj. 4, 5

✔ 1. Budgeted net income, $114,660

EXCEL TEMPLATE

As a preliminary to requesting budget estimates of sales, costs, and expenses for the fiscal year beginning January 1, 20Y9, the following tentative trial balance as of December 31, 20Y8, is prepared by the Accounting Department of Mesa Publishing Co.:

Cash	$ 26,000	
Accounts Receivable..	23,800	
Finished Goods	16,900	
Work in Process	4,200	
Materials	6,400	
Prepaid Expenses	600	
Plant and Equipment	82,000	
Accumulated Depreciation—Plant and Equipment.................		$ 32,000
Accounts Payable		14,800
Common Stock, $1.50 par....................................		30,000
Retained Earnings...		83,100
	$159,900	$159,900

Factory output and sales for 20Y9 are expected to total 3,800 units of product, which are to be sold at $120 per unit. The quantities and costs of the inventories at December 31, 20Y9, are expected to remain unchanged from the balances at the beginning of the year.

Budget estimates of manufacturing costs and operating expenses for the year are summarized as follows:

	Estimated Costs and Expenses	
	Fixed (Total for Year)	**Variable (Per Unit Sold)**
Cost of goods manufactured and sold:		
Direct materials	—	$30.00
Direct labor..	—	8.40
Factory overhead:		
Depreciation of plant and equipment..................	$ 4,000	—
Other factory overhead..............................	1,400	4.80
Selling expenses:		
Sales salaries and commissions.........................	12,800	13.50
Advertising	13,200	—
Miscellaneous selling expense	1,000	2.50
Administrative expenses:		
Office and officers salaries	7,800	7.00
Supplies...	500	1.20
Miscellaneous administrative expense	400	2.40

Balances of accounts receivable, prepaid expenses, and accounts payable at the end of the year are not expected to differ significantly from the beginning balances. Federal income tax of $35,000 on 20Y9 taxable income will be paid during 20Y9. Regular quarterly cash dividends of $0.20 per share are expected to be declared and paid in March, June, September, and December on 20,000 shares of common stock outstanding. It is anticipated that fixed assets will be purchased for $22,000 cash in May.

Instructions

1. Prepare a budgeted income statement for 20Y9.

2. Prepare a budgeted balance sheet as of December 31, 20Y9, with supporting calculations.

Analysis for Decision Making

ADM-1 Nursing staff budget

Mercy Hospital staffs its medical/surgical floors with nurses depending on the number of patients assigned to the floor and the severity of their condition. The index used to capture nurse effort is termed a relative value unit, or RVU. For example, taking vital signs for a single patient may be equal to one RVU. RVU's are then summed to estimate the total RVU requirements for the floor. From this, the nursing staff budget is determined.

The medical/surgical floor is scheduled to have 25 patients for each day of the coming seven-day week. Some patients will require more nursing effort than others, depending on the severity of their conditions or their ages. The following table summarizes the expected RVU requirements for the patients:

Number of Patients	RVUs per Day
5	20
8	25
10	30
2	40

A nurse earns $180 per day and is able to perform 40 RVUs per day.

A. Determine the total number of RVUs expected per day for the coming week.

B. Determine the total weekly nurse budget for the coming week.

ADM-2 Parking lot staff budget

Adventure Park is a large theme park. Staffing for the theme park involves many different labor classifications, one of which is the parking lot staff. The parking lot staff collects parking fees, provides directions, and operates trams. The staff size is a function of the number of daily vehicles. Adventure Park has determined from historical experience that a staff member is needed for every 200 vehicles.

Adventure Park estimates staff for both school days and nonschool days. Nonschool days are higher attendance days than school days. The number of expected vehicles for each day is as follows:

	School Days	Nonschool Days
Number of vehicles per day	3,000	8,000
Number of days per year	165	200

Parking fees are $10 per vehicle. Each parking lot employee is paid $110 per day.

A. Determine the annual parking lot staff budget for school days, nonschool days, and total.

B. Determine the parking revenue for school days, nonschool days, and total.

C. If depreciation expense and other expenses for running the parking lot were estimated to be $2 million per year, determine the parking lot's budgeted profit.

ADM-3 Housekeeping staff budget

Ambassador Suites Inc. operates a downtown hotel property that has 300 rooms. On average, 80% of Ambassador Suites' rooms are occupied on weekdays, and 40% are occupied during the weekend. The manager has asked you to develop a budget for the housekeeping and restaurant staff for weekdays and weekends. You have determined that the housekeeping staff requires 30 minutes to clean each occupied room. The housekeeping staff is paid $14 per hour. The house-keeping labor cost is fully variable to the number of occupied rooms. The restaurant has six full-time staff on duty to staff the restaurant for breakfast and lunch (eight hours), regardless of occupancy. However, for every 60 occupied rooms, an additional person is brought in to work in the restaurant for breakfast and lunch (eight hours). The restaurant staff is paid $12 per hour.

Prepare two columns, labeled as weekday and weekend day.

A. Determine the number of rooms occupied for an average weekday and weekend day.

B. Determine the housekeeping staff budget for an average weekday and weekend day.

C. Determine the restaurant staff budget for an average weekday and weekend day.

D. Determine the total staff budget for an average weekday and weekend day.

Take It Further

TIF 21-1 Ethics in Action

The director of marketing for Starr Computer Co., Megan Hewitt, had the following discussion with the company controller, Cam Morley, on July 26 of the current year:

Megan: Cam, it looks like I'm going to spend much less than indicated on my July budget.

Cam: I'm glad to hear it.

Megan: Well, I'm not so sure it's good news. I'm concerned that the president will see that I'm under budget and reduce my budget in the future. The only reason that I look good is that we've delayed an advertising campaign. Once the campaign hits in September, I'm sure my actual expenditures will go up. You see, we are also having our sales convention in September. Having the advertising campaign and the convention at the same time is going to kill my September numbers.

Cam: I don't think that's anything to worry about. We all expect some variation in actual spending month to month. What's really important is staying within the budgeted targets for the year. Does that look as if it's going to be a problem?

Megan: I don't think so, but just the same, I'd like to be on the safe side.

Cam: What do you mean?

Megan: Well, this is what I'd like to do. I want to pay the convention-related costs in advance this month. I'll pay the hotel for room and convention space and purchase the airline tickets in advance. In this way, I can charge all these expenditures to July's budget. This would cause my actual expenses to come close to budget for July. Moreover, when the big advertising campaign hits in September, I won't have to worry about expenditures for the convention on my September budget as well. The convention costs will already be paid. Thus, my September expenses should be pretty close to budget.

Cam: I can't tell you when to make your convention purchases, but I'm not too sure that September items should be expensed in July's budget.

Megan: What's the problem? It looks like "no harm, no foul" to me. I can't see that there's anything wrong with this—it's just smart management.

➤ How should Cam Morley respond to Megan Hewitt's request to expense the advanced payments for convention-related costs against July's budget?

TIF 21-2 Team Activity

In teams, find the home page of a state that interests you. The home page will be of the form *www.statename.gov*. For example, the state of Tennessee can be found at www.tennessee.gov. At the home page site, search for annual budget information.

1. What are the budgeted sources of revenue and their percentage breakdown?
2. What are the major categories of budgeted expenditures (or appropriations) and their percentage breakdown?
3. Is the projected budget in balance?

TIF 21-3 Communication

The city of Milton has an annual budget cycle that begins on July 1 and ends on June 30. At the beginning of each budget year, an annual budget is established for each department. The annual budget is divided equally among the 12 months to provide a constant monthly static budget. On June 30, all unspent budgeted monies for the budget year from the various city departments must be "returned" to the General Fund. Thus, if department heads fail to use their budget by year-end, they will lose it. A budget analyst prepared a chart of the difference between the monthly actual and budgeted amounts for all departments in a recent fiscal year. The chart was as follows:

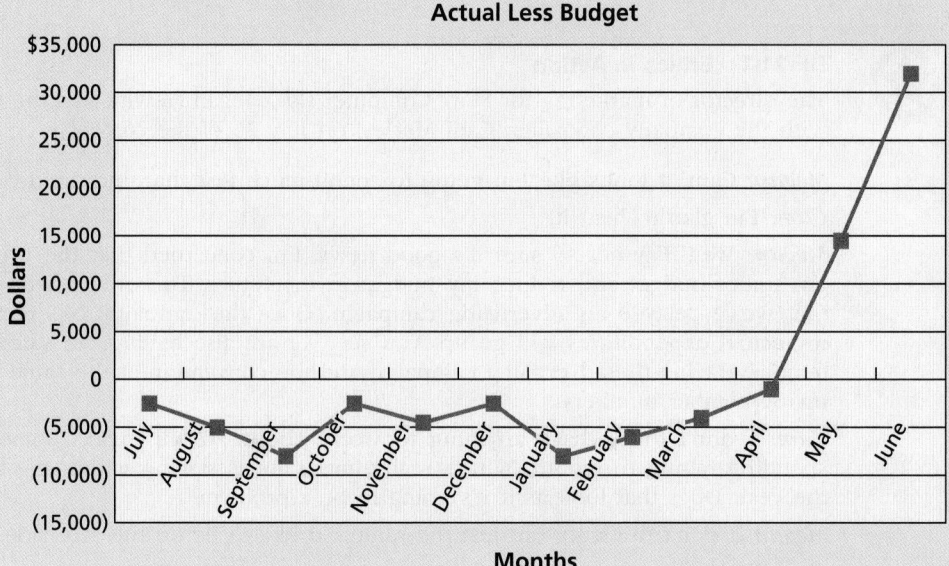

Write a memo to Stacy Poindexter, the city manager, interpreting the chart and suggesting improvements to the budgeting system.

Concepts and Principles

Chapter 15 *Introduction to Managerial Accounting*

Developing Information

COST SYSTEMS	COST BEHAVIOR
Chapter 16 *Job Order Costing*	**Chapter 19** *Cost-Volume-Profit Analysis*
Chapter 17 *Process Cost Systems*	
Chapter 18 *Activity-Based Costing*	

Decision Making

EVALUATING PERFORMANCE	COMPARING ALTERNATIVES
Chapter 20 *Variable Costing for Management Analysis*	**Chapter 23** *Evaluating Decentralized Operations*
Chapter 21 *Budgeting*	**Chapter 24** *Differential Analysis and Product Pricing*
Chapter 22 *Evaluating Variances from Standard Costs*	**Chapter 25** *Capital Investment Analysis*
	Chapter 26 *Lean Manufacturing*

1959-2000

BMW Group

When you play a sport, you are evaluated with respect to how well you perform compared to a standard or to a competitor. In bowling, for example, your score is compared to a perfect score of 300 or to the scores of your competitors. In this class, you are compared to performance standards. These standards are often described in terms of letter grades, which provide a measure of how well you achieved the class objectives. In your job, you are also evaluated according to performance standards.

Just as your class performance is evaluated, managers are evaluated according to goals and plans. For example, BMW Group uses manufacturing standards at its automobile assembly plants to guide performance. The Mini Cooper, a BMW Group car, is manufactured in a modern facility in Oxford, England. There are a number of performance targets used in this plant.

For example, the bodyshell is welded by more than 250 robots so as to be two to three times stiffer than rival cars. In addition, the bodyshell dimensions are tested to the accuracy of the width of a human hair. Such performance standards are not surprising given the automotive racing background of John W. Cooper, the designer of the original Mini Cooper.

If you want to get a view of the BMW manufacturing process, go to the BMW Web site, search the phrase "How an automobile is born," and click on the Production link.

Performance is often measured as the difference between actual results and planned results. In this chapter, we will discuss and illustrate the ways in which business performance is evaluated.

Source: www.bmwgroup.com

What's Covered

Evaluating Variances from Standard Costs

Standards
- Setting Standards (Obj. 1)
- Types of Standards (Obj. 1)
- Reviewing and Revising Standards (Obj. 1)

Variance Analysis
- Budget Performance Report (Obj. 2)
- Direct Materials Variances (Obj. 3)
- Direct Labor Variances (Obj. 3)
- Factory Overhead Variances (Obj. 4)

Recording Variances
- Journalizing Variances (Obj. 5)
- Variances in the Income Statement (Obj. 5)
- Nonfinancial Performance Measures (Obj. 6)

Learning Objectives

Obj. 1 Describe the types of standards and how they are established.

Obj. 2 Describe and illustrate how standards are used in budgeting.

Obj. 3 Compute and interpret direct materials and direct labor variances.

Obj. 4 Compute and interpret factory overhead controllable and volume variances.

Obj. 5 Describe and illustrate the recording and reporting of standards and variances.

Obj. 6 Describe and illustrate nonfinancial performance measures.

Analysis for Decision Making

Describe and Illustrate the use of the direct labor time variance in evaluating staff performance in a service setting.

Objective 1

Describe the types of standards and how they are established.

Standards

Standards are performance goals. Manufacturing companies normally use **standard cost** for each of the three following product costs:

- Direct materials
- Direct labor
- Factory overhead

Accounting systems that use standards for product costs are called **standard cost systems**. Standard cost systems enable management to determine the following:

- How much a product *should* cost (standard cost)
- How much it *does* cost (actual cost)

When actual costs are compared with standard costs, the exceptions or cost variances are reported. This reporting by the *principle of exceptions* allows management to focus on correcting the cost variances.

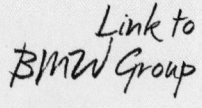 **BMW** began in Germany in the early 1900s as a manufacturer of airplane engines. The BMW emblem, which was first used in 1917, represents a rotating airplane propeller with the white and blue state colors of Bavaria.

Setting Standards

The standard-setting process normally requires the joint efforts of accountants, engineers, and other management personnel. The accountant converts the results of judgments and process studies into dollars and cents. Engineers with the aid of operation managers identify the materials, labor, and machine requirements needed to produce the product. For example, engineers estimate direct materials by studying the product specifications and estimating normal spoilage. Time and motion studies may be used to determine the direct labor required for each manufacturing operation. Engineering studies may also be used to determine standards for factory overhead, such as the amount of power needed to operate machinery.

Types of Standards

Standards imply an acceptable level of production efficiency. One of the major objectives in setting standards is to motivate employees to achieve efficient operations.

Ideal standards, or *theoretical standards*, are standards that can be achieved only under perfect operating conditions, such as no idle time, no machine breakdowns, and no materials spoilage. Such standards may have a negative impact on performance because they may be viewed by employees as unrealistic.

Currently attainable standards, sometimes called *normal standards*, are standards that can be attained with reasonable effort. Such standards, which are used by most companies, allow for normal production difficulties and mistakes. When reasonable standards are used, employees focus more on cost and are more likely to put forth their best efforts.

An example from the game of golf illustrates the distinction between ideal and normal standards. In golf, *par* is an ideal standard for most players. Each player's USGA (United States Golf Association) handicap is the player's normal standard. The motivation of average players is to beat their handicaps because beating par is unrealistic for most players.

Reviewing and Revising Standards

Standard costs should be periodically reviewed to ensure that they reflect current operating conditions. Standards should not be revised, however, just because they differ from actual costs. For example, the direct labor standard would not be revised just because employees are unable to meet properly set standards. On the other hand, standards should be revised when prices, product designs, labor rates, or manufacturing methods change.

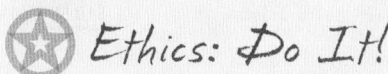 Ethics: Do It!

Company Reputation: The Best of the Best

Harris Interactive annually ranks American corporations in terms of reputation. The ranking is based on how respondents rate corporations on 20 attributes in six major areas. The six areas are emotional appeal, products and services, financial performance, workplace environment, social responsibility, and vision and leadership. The five highest (best) ranked companies in a recent survey were **Amazon.com**, **Apple Inc.**, **The Walt Disney Company**, **Google**, and **Johnson & Johnson**.

Criticisms of Standard Costs

Some criticisms of using standard costs for performance evaluation include the following:

- Standards limit operating improvements by discouraging improvement beyond the standard.
- Standards are too difficult to maintain in a dynamic manufacturing environment, resulting in "stale standards."
- Standards can cause employees to lose sight of the larger objectives of the organization by focusing only on efficiency improvement.
- Standards can cause employees to unduly focus on their own operations to the possible harm of other operations that rely on them.

Regardless of these criticisms, standards are used widely. In addition, standard costs are only one part of the performance evaluation system used by most companies. As discussed in this chapter, other nonfinancial performance measures are often used to supplement standard costs, with the result that many of the preceding criticisms are overcome.

In addition to BMW, Mini Cooper, and Rolls-Royce automobiles, **BMW Group** manufactures motorcycles.

Link to BMW Group

Budgetary Performance Evaluation

As discussed in Chapter 21, the master budget assists a company in planning, directing, and controlling performance. The control function, or budgetary performance evaluation, compares the actual performance against the budget.

To illustrate, **Western Rider Inc.**, a manufacturer of blue jeans, uses standard costs in its budgets. The standards for direct materials, direct labor, and factory overhead are separated into the following two components:

- Standard price
- Standard quantity

The standard cost per unit for direct materials, direct labor, and factory overhead is computed as follows:

$$\text{Standard Cost per Unit} = \text{Standard Price} \times \text{Standard Quantity}$$

Western Rider's standard costs per unit for its XL jeans are shown in Exhibit 1.

Exhibit 1
Standard Cost for XL Jeans

Manufacturing Costs	Standard Price	×	Standard Quantity per Pair	=	Standard Cost per Pair of XL Jeans
Direct materials	$5.00 per sq. yd.		1.5 sq. yds.		$ 7.50
Direct labor	$9.00 per hr.		0.80 hr. per pair		7.20
Factory overhead	$6.00 per hr.		0.80 hr. per pair		4.80
Total standard cost per pair					$19.50

As shown in Exhibit 1, the standard cost per pair of XL jeans is $19.50, which consists of $7.50 for direct materials, $7.20 for direct labor, and $4.80 for factory overhead.

The standard price and standard quantity are separated for each product cost. For example, Exhibit 1 indicates that for each pair of XL jeans, the standard price for direct materials is $5.00 per square yard and the standard quantity is 1.5 square yards. The standard price and quantity are separated because the department responsible for their control is normally different. For example, the direct materials price per square yard is controlled by the Purchasing Department, and the direct materials quantity per pair is controlled by the Production Department.

As illustrated in Chapter 21, the master budget is prepared based on planned sales and production. The budgeted costs for materials purchases, direct labor, and factory overhead are determined by multiplying their standard costs per unit by the planned level of production. Budgeted (standard) costs are then compared to actual costs during the year for control purposes.

Budget Performance Report

The differences between actual and standard costs are called **cost variances**. A **favorable cost variance** occurs when the actual cost is less than the standard cost. An **unfavorable cost variance** occurs when the actual cost exceeds the standard cost. These cost variances are illustrated in Exhibit 2.

Exhibit 2
Cost Variances

Favorable Cost Variance	Unfavorable Cost Variance
Actual cost < Standard cost at actual volumes	Actual cost > Standard cost at actual volumes

The report that summarizes actual costs, standard costs, and the differences for the units produced is called a **budget performance report**. To illustrate, assume that **Western Rider Inc.** produced the following pairs of jeans during June:

XL jeans produced and sold	5,000 pairs
Actual costs incurred in June:	
Direct materials	$ 40,150
Direct labor	38,500
Factory overhead	22,400
Total costs incurred	$101,050

Exhibit 3 illustrates the budget performance report for June for Western Rider.

Exhibit 3
Budget
Performance
Report

Western Rider Inc.
Budget Performance Report
For the Month Ended June 30

Manufacturing Costs	Actual Costs	Standard Cost at Actual Volume (5,000 pairs of XL Jeans)*	Cost Variance— (Favorable) Unfavorable
Direct materials....................................	$ 40,150	$37,500	$ 2,650
Direct labor	38,500	36,000	2,500
Factory overhead	22,400	24,000	(1,600)
Total manufacturing costs.....................	$101,050	$97,500	$ 3,550

*5,000 pairs × $7.50 per pair = $37,500
5,000 pairs × $7.20 per pair = $36,000
5,000 pairs × $4.80 per pair = $24,000

The budget performance report shown in Exhibit 3 is based on the actual units produced in June of 5,000 XL jeans. Even though 6,000 XL jeans might have been *planned* for production, the budget performance report is based on *actual* production.

Manufacturing Cost Variances

The **total manufacturing cost variance** is the difference between total standard costs and total actual cost for the units produced. As shown in Exhibit 3, the total manufacturing cost unfavorable variance is $3,550, which consists of an unfavorable direct materials cost variance of $2,650, an unfavorable direct labor cost variance of $2,500, and a favorable factory overhead cost variance of $1,600.

For control purposes, each product cost variance is separated into two additional variances as shown in Exhibit 4.

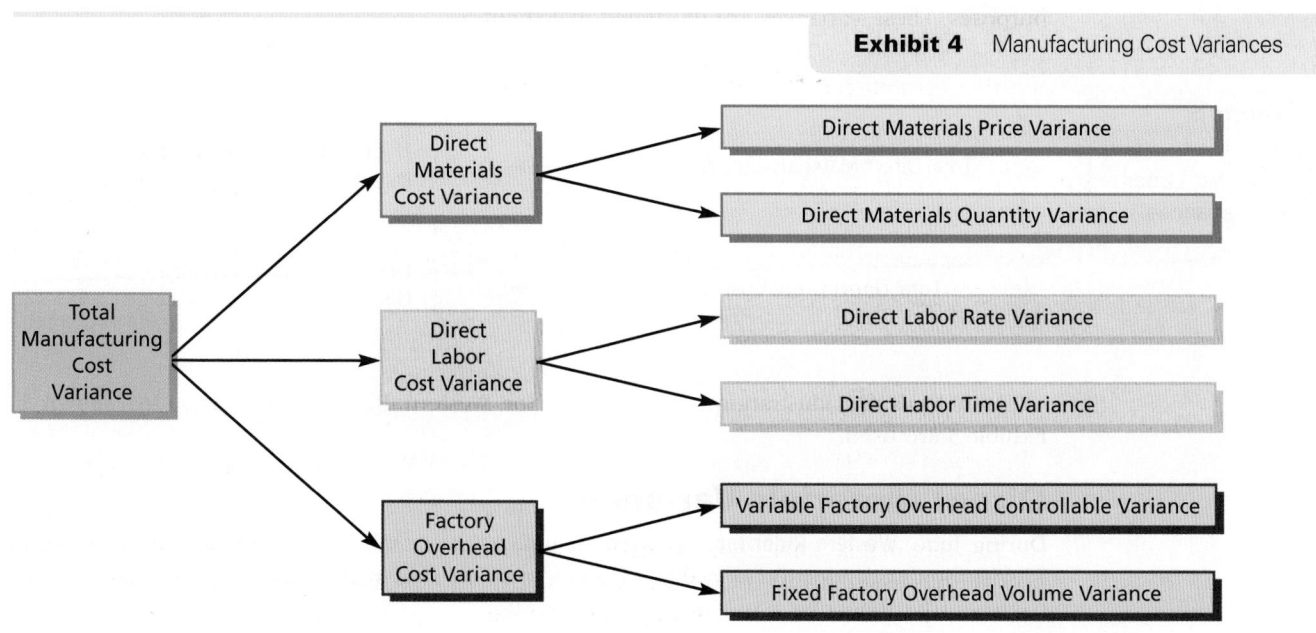

Exhibit 4   Manufacturing Cost Variances

The total direct materials variance is separated into a *price* variance and a *quantity* variance. This is because standard and actual direct materials costs are computed as follows:

Actual Direct Materials Cost	=	Actual Price	× Actual Quantity
Standard Direct Materials Cost	=	Standard Price	× Standard Quantity
Direct Materials Cost Variance	=	Price Difference	+ Quantity Difference

Thus, the actual and standard direct materials costs may differ because of a price difference (variance), a quantity difference (variance), or both.

Likewise, the total direct labor variance is separated into a *rate* variance and a *time* variance. This is because standard and actual direct labor costs are computed as follows:

Actual Direct Labor Cost	=	Actual Rate	× Actual Time
Standard Direct Labor Cost	=	Standard Rate	× Standard Time
Direct Labor Cost Variance	=	Rate Difference	+ Time Difference

Therefore, the actual and standard direct labor costs may differ because of a rate difference (variance), a time difference (variance), or both.

The total factory overhead variance is separated into a *controllable* variance and a *volume* variance. Because factory overhead has fixed and variable cost elements, it uses different variances than direct materials and direct labor, which are variable costs.

In the next sections, the price and quantity variances for direct materials, the rate and time variances for direct labor, and the controllable and volume variances for factory overhead are further described and illustrated.

Link to *BMW Group*

BMW's Spartanburg, South Carolina plant employs 8,000 workers in its 6 million-square-foot facility where it manufactures X3 and X5 SUVs. Visitors may tour the manufacturing plant and company museum.

Objective 3
Compute and interpret direct materials and direct labor variances.

Direct Materials and Direct Labor Variances

As indicated in the prior section, the total direct materials and direct labor variances are separated into the direct materials cost and direct labor cost variances for analysis and control purposes. These variances are illustrated in Exhibit 5.

Exhibit 5
Direct Materials and Direct Labor Cost Variances

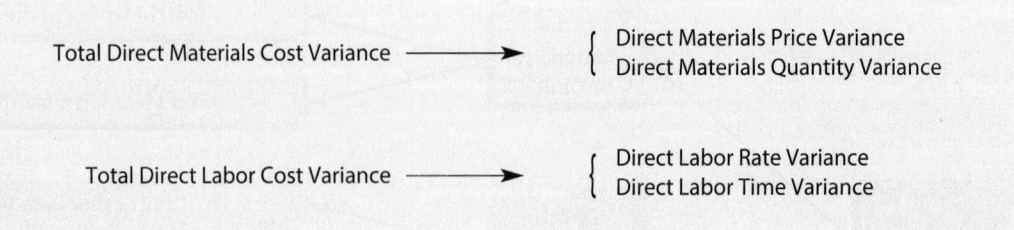

As a basis for illustration, the variances for Western Rider's June operations shown in Exhibit 3 are used.

Direct Materials Variances

During June, **Western Rider Inc.** reported an unfavorable total direct materials cost variance of $2,650 for the production of 5,000 XL style jeans, as shown in Exhibit 3. This variance was based on the following actual and standard costs:

Actual costs	$40,150
Standard costs	37,500
Total direct materials cost variance	$ 2,650

The actual costs incurred of $40,150 consist of the following:

$$\text{Actual Direct Materials Cost} = \text{Actual Price} \times \text{Actual Quantity}$$
$$= (\$5.50 \text{ per sq. yd.}) \times (7{,}300 \text{ sq. yds.})$$
$$= \$40{,}150$$

The standard costs of $37,500 consist of the following:

$$\text{Standard Direct Materials Cost} = \text{Standard Price} \times \text{Standard Quantity}$$
$$= \$5.00 \text{ per sq. yd.} \times 7{,}500 \text{ sq. yds.}$$
$$= \$37{,}500$$

The standard price of $5.00 per square yard is taken from Exhibit 1. In addition, Exhibit 1 indicates that 1.5 square yards is the standard quantity of materials for producing one pair of XL jeans. Thus, 7,500 (5,000 × 1.5) square yards is the standard quantity of materials for producing 5,000 pairs of XL jeans.

Comparing the actual and standard cost computations indicates that the total direct materials unfavorable cost variance of $2,650 is caused by the following:

- A price per square yard of $0.50 ($5.50 – $5.00) more than standard
- A quantity usage of 200 square yards (7,300 sq. yds. – 7,500 sq. yds.) less than standard

The impact of these differences from standard is reported and analyzed as a direct materials *price* variance and direct materials *quantity* variance.

Direct Materials Price Variance The **direct materials price variance** is computed as follows:

$$\text{Direct Materials Price Variance} = (\text{Actual Price} - \text{Standard Price}) \times \text{Actual Quantity}$$

If the actual price per unit exceeds the standard price per unit, the variance is unfavorable. This positive amount (unfavorable variance) can be thought of as increasing costs (a debit). If the actual price per unit is less than the standard price per unit, the variance is favorable. This negative amount (favorable variance) can be thought of as decreasing costs (a credit).

To illustrate, the direct materials price variance for **Western Rider Inc.** for June is $3,650 (unfavorable), computed as follows:[1]

$$\text{Direct Materials Price Variance} = (\text{Actual Price} - \text{Standard Price}) \times \text{Actual Quantity}$$
$$= (\$5.50 - \$5.00) \times 7{,}300 \text{ sq. yds.}$$
$$= \$3{,}650 \text{ Unfavorable Variance}$$

Direct Materials Quantity Variance The **direct materials quantity variance** is computed as follows:

$$\text{Direct Materials Quantity Variance} = (\text{Actual Quantity} - \text{Standard Quantity}) \times \text{Standard Price}$$

If the actual quantity for the units produced exceeds the standard quantity, the variance is unfavorable. This positive amount (unfavorable variance) can be thought of as increasing costs (a debit). If the actual quantity for the units produced is less than the standard quantity, the variance is favorable. This negative amount (favorable variance) can be thought of as decreasing costs (a credit).

To illustrate, the direct materials quantity variance for **Western Rider Inc.** for June is $1,000 (favorable), computed as follows:

$$\text{Direct Materials Quantity Variance} = (\text{Actual Quantity} - \text{Standard Quantity}) \times \text{Standard Price}$$
$$= (7{,}300 \text{ sq. yds.} - 7{,}500 \text{ sq. yds.}) \times \$5.00$$
$$= \$(1{,}000) \text{ Favorable Variance}$$

Steel and aluminium are pressed into doors and side panels in BMW's stamping facility.

Link to BMW Group

[1] To simplify, it is assumed that there is no change in the beginning and ending materials inventories. Thus, the amount of materials budgeted for production equals the amount purchased.

Direct Materials Variance Relationships The relationship among the *total* direct materials cost variance, the direct materials *price* variance, and the direct materials *quantity* variance is shown in Exhibit 6.

Reporting Direct Materials Variances The direct materials quantity variances should be reported to the manager responsible for the variance. For example, an unfavorable quantity variance might be caused by either of the following:

- Equipment that has not been properly maintained
- Low-quality (inferior) direct materials

Exhibit 6
Direct Materials
Variance
Relationships

DYNAMIC
EXHIBIT

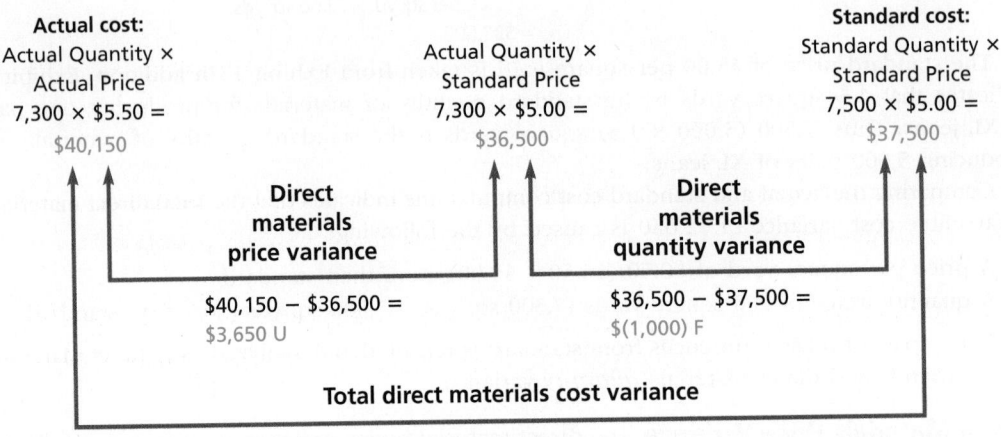

In the first case, the Operating Department responsible for maintaining the equipment should be held responsible for the variance. In the second case, the Purchasing Department should be held responsible.

Not all variances are controllable. For example, an unfavorable materials price variance might be due to market-wide price increases. In this case, there is nothing the Purchasing Department might have done to avoid the unfavorable variance. On the other hand, if materials of the same quality could have been purchased from another supplier at the standard price, the variance was controllable.

Direct Labor Variances

During June, **Western Rider Inc.** reported an unfavorable total direct labor cost variance of $2,500 for the production of 5,000 XL style jeans, as shown in Exhibit 3. This variance was based on the following actual and standard costs:

Actual costs	$38,500
Standard costs	36,000
Total direct labor cost variance	$ 2,500

The actual costs incurred of $38,500 consist of the following:

Actual Direct Labor Cost = Actual Rate per Hour × Actual Time
= $10.00 per hr. × 3,850 hrs.
= $38,500

The standard costs of $36,000 consist of the following:

Standard Direct Labor Cost = Standard Rate per Hour × Standard Time
= $9.00 per hr. × 4,000 hrs.
= $36,000

The standard rate of $9.00 per direct labor hour is taken from Exhibit 1. In addition, Exhibit 1 indicates that 0.80 hour is the standard time required for producing one pair of XL jeans. Thus, 4,000 (5,000 units × 0.80 hr.) direct labor hours is the standard for producing 5,000 pairs of XL jeans.

Comparing the actual and standard cost computations indicates that the total direct labor unfavorable cost variance of $2,500 is caused by the following:

- A rate of $1.00 per hour ($10.00 – $9.00) more than standard
- A quantity of 150 hours (4,000 hrs. – 3,850 hrs.) less than standard

The impact of these differences from standard is reported and analyzed as a direct labor *rate* variance and a direct labor *time* variance.

The camshafts of **BMW**'s engines are manufactured using computer-controlled machine tools to a precision of one hundredth of a human hair. Workers are primarily used to adjust the machine tools.

Link to BMW Group

Direct Labor Rate Variance The **direct labor rate variance** is computed as follows:

Direct Labor Rate Variance = (Actual Rate per Hour – Standard Rate per Hour) × Actual Hours

If the actual rate per hour exceeds the standard rate per hour, the variance is unfavorable. This positive amount (unfavorable variance) can be thought of as increasing costs (a debit). If the actual rate per hour is less than the standard rate per hour, the variance is favorable. This negative amount (favorable variance) can be thought of as decreasing costs (a credit).

To illustrate, the direct labor rate variance for **Western Rider Inc.** in June is $3,850 (unfavorable), computed as follows:

Direct Labor Rate Variance = (Actual Rate per Hour – Standard Rate per Hour) × Actual Hours
= ($10.00 – $9.00) × 3,850 hours
= $3,850 Unfavorable Variance

Direct Labor Time Variance The **direct labor time variance** is computed as follows:

Direct Labor Time Variance = (Actual Direct Labor Hours – Standard Direct Labor Hours)
× Standard Rate per Hour

If the actual direct labor hours for the units produced exceed the standard direct labor hours, the variance is unfavorable. This positive amount (unfavorable variance) can be thought of as increasing costs (a debit). If the actual direct labor hours for the units produced are less than the standard direct labor hours, the variance is favorable. This negative amount (favorable variance) can be thought of as decreasing costs (a credit).

To illustrate, the direct labor time variance for **Western Rider Inc.** for June is $1,350 (favorable) computed as follows:

Direct Labor Time Variance = (Actual Direct Labor Hours – Standard Direct Labor Hours)
× Standard Rate per Hour
= (3,850 hours – 4,000 direct labor hours) × $9.00
= $(1,350) Favorable Variance

Direct Labor Variance Relationships The relationship among the *total* direct labor cost variance, the direct labor *rate* variance, and the direct labor *time* variance is shown in Exhibit 7.

Exhibit 7
Direct Labor
Variance
Relationships

**DYNAMIC
EXHIBIT**

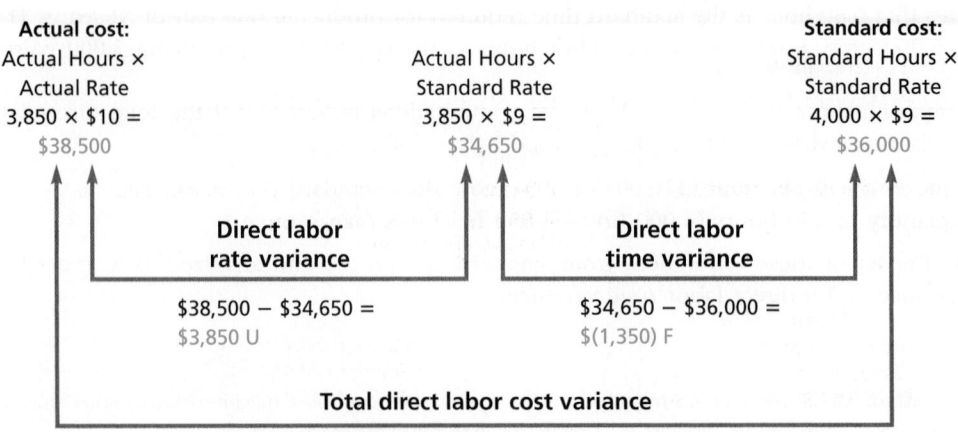

Reporting Direct Labor Variances Production supervisors are normally responsible for controlling direct labor cost. For example, an investigation could reveal the following causes for unfavorable rate and time variances:

- An unfavorable rate variance may be caused by the improper scheduling and use of employees. In such cases, skilled, highly paid employees may be used in jobs that are normally performed by unskilled, lower-paid employees. In this case, the unfavorable rate variance should be reported to the managers who schedule work assignments.
- An unfavorable time variance may be caused by a shortage of skilled employees. In such cases, there may be an abnormally high turnover rate among skilled employees. In this case, production supervisors with high turnover rates should be questioned as to why their employees are quitting.

Direct Labor Standards for Nonmanufacturing Activities Direct labor time standards can also be developed for use in administrative, selling, and service activities. This is most appropriate when the activity involves a repetitive task that produces a common output. In these cases, the use of standards is similar to that for a manufactured product.

To illustrate, standards could be developed for customer service personnel who process sales orders. A standard time for processing a sales order (the output) could be developed and used to control sales order processing costs. Similar standards could be developed for computer help desk operators, nurses, and insurance application processors.

When labor-related activities are not repetitive, direct labor time standards are less commonly used. For example, the time spent by a senior executive or the work of a research and development scientist would not normally be controlled using time standards.

Check Up Corner 22-1 Direct Materials and Direct Labor Cost Variances

Menounos Manufacturing Co. uses standard costs in its budgets. Standard costs and actual costs for direct materials and direct labor for the manufacture of 3,000 units during 20Y6 were as follows:

	Standard Costs	Actual Costs
Direct materials	18,000 lbs. at $4.50 per lb.	18,500 lbs. at $4.35 per lb.
Direct labor	7,500 hours at $12.00 per hr.	7,420 hours at $12.30 per hr.

Each unit requires 2.5 hours of direct labor.

Determine:
A. The direct materials price variance, direct materials quantity variance, and total direct materials cost variance. Present your answer using the format shown in Exhibit 6.
B. The direct labor rate variance, direct labor time variance, and total direct labor cost variance. Present your answer using the format shown in Exhibit 7.

Solution:

A. Direct Materials Variances

Direct Materials Price Variance = (Actual Price − Standard Price) × Actual Quantity
    = ($4.35 − $4.50) × 18,500 lbs.
    = $(2,775) Favorable Variance

Direct Materials Quantity Variance = (Actual Quantity − Standard Quantity) × Standard Price
    = (18,500 lbs. − 18,000 lbs.) × $4.50
    = $2,250 Unfavorable Variance

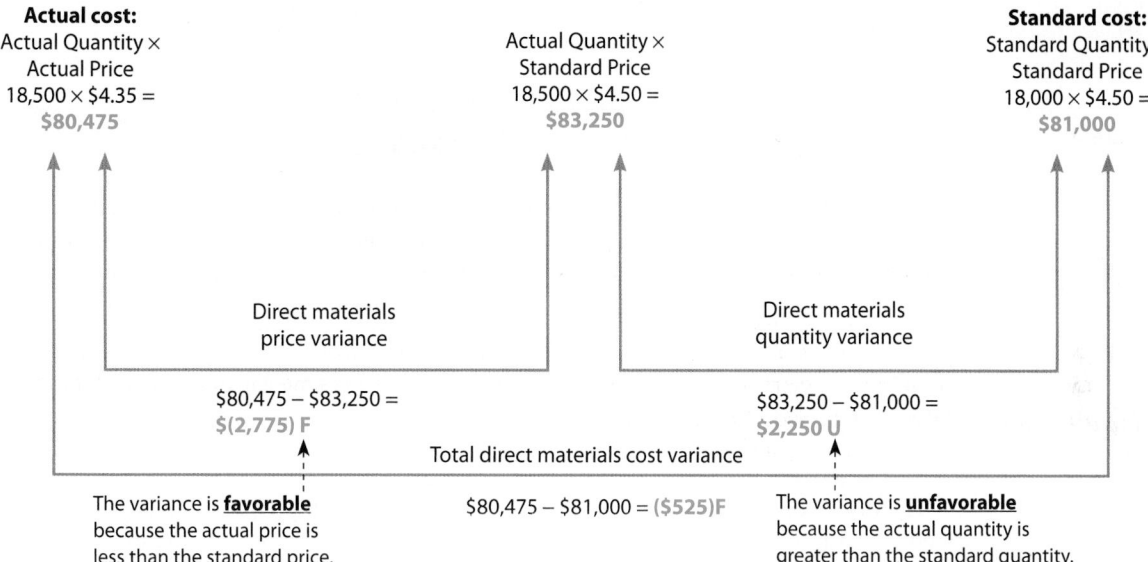

Actual cost:
Actual Quantity ×
Actual Price
18,500 × $4.35 =
$80,475

Actual Quantity ×
Standard Price
18,500 × $4.50 =
$83,250

Standard cost:
Standard Quantity ×
Standard Price
18,000 × $4.50 =
$81,000

Direct materials
price variance

Direct materials
quantity variance

$80,475 − $83,250 =
$(2,775) F

$83,250 − $81,000 =
$2,250 U

Total direct materials cost variance

$80,475 − $81,000 = ($525)F

The variance is **favorable**
because the actual price is
less than the standard price.

The variance is **unfavorable**
because the actual quantity is
greater than the standard quantity.

B. Direct Labor Variances

Direct Labor Rate Variance = (Actual Rate per Hour − Standard Rate per Hour) × Actual Hours
    = ($12.30 − $12.00) × 7,420 hours
    = $2,226 Unfavorable Variance

Direct Labor Time Variance = (Actual Direct Labor Hours − Standard Direct Labor Hours) × Standard Rate per Hour
    = (7,420 hours − 7,500 direct labor hours) × $12.00
    = $(960) Favorable Variance

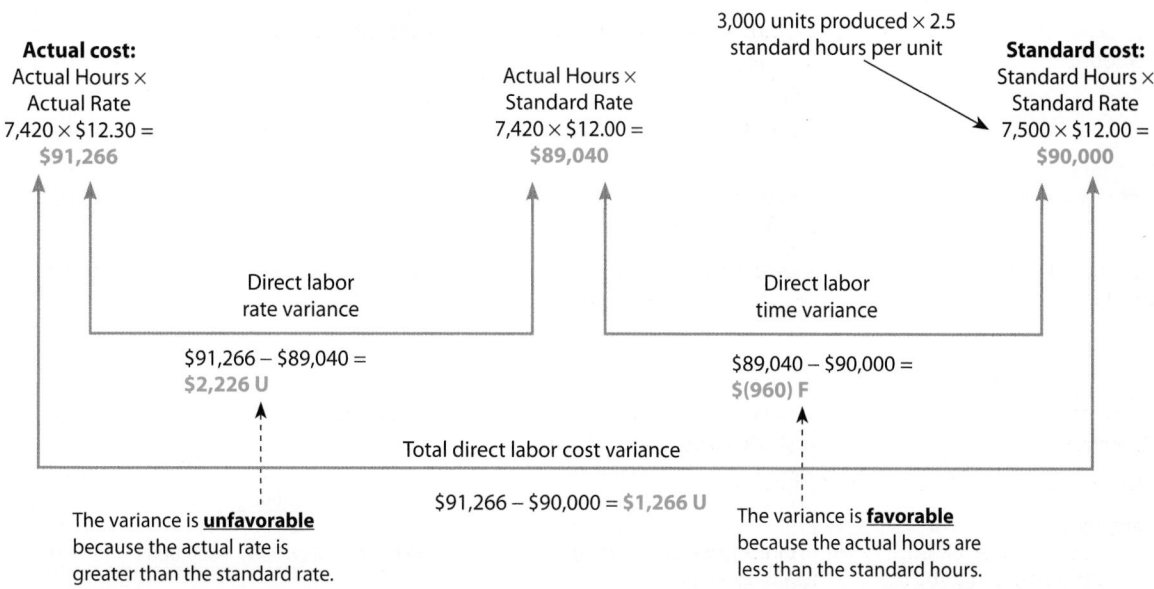

Actual cost:
Actual Hours ×
Actual Rate
7,420 × $12.30 =
$91,266

Actual Hours ×
Standard Rate
7,420 × $12.00 =
$89,040

3,000 units produced × 2.5
standard hours per unit

Standard cost:
Standard Hours ×
Standard Rate
7,500 × $12.00 =
$90,000

Direct labor
rate variance

Direct labor
time variance

$91,266 − $89,040 =
$2,226 U

$89,040 − $90,000 =
$(960) F

Total direct labor cost variance

$91,266 − $90,000 = $1,266 U

The variance is **unfavorable**
because the actual rate is
greater than the standard rate.

The variance is **favorable**
because the actual hours are
less than the standard hours.

Check Up Corner

Why It Matters

Standard Costing in the Restaurant Industry

Many restaurants use standard costs to manage their business. Food costs are typically the largest expense for a restaurant. As a result, many restaurants use food quantity standards to control food costs by establishing the amount of food that is served to a customer. For example, Red Lobster restaurants, a division of **Darden Restuarants, Inc.**, establishes food quantity

standards for the number of shrimp, scallops, or clams on a seafood plate.

The second-largest cost to most restaurants is labor cost. Many restaurants base their labor cost standards on the labor cost percentage, which is the ratio of total labor cost to total sales. This ratio helps the restaurants of Darden Restaurants, Inc., including Olive Garden and Red Lobster, control and monitor labor costs. Focusing on this metric has paid off recently, as labor cost has dropped and earnings have increased as a percent of sales.

Source: N. Irwin, "What Olive Garden and Red Lobster tell us about the economy," *The Washington Post*, September 21, 2012.

Objective 4

Compute and interpret factory overhead controllable and volume variances.

Factory Overhead Variances

Factory overhead costs are analyzed differently than direct labor and direct materials costs. This is because factory overhead costs have fixed and variable cost elements. For example, indirect materials and factory supplies normally behave as a variable cost as units produced change. In contrast, straight-line plant depreciation on factory machinery is a fixed cost.

Link to BMW Group

The **BMW Group** has significant overhead costs due to its investment in robotic and other state-of-the art technology, machinery, and facilities.

Factory overhead costs are budgeted and controlled by separating factory overhead into fixed and variable components. Doing so allows the preparation of flexible budgets and the analysis of factory overhead controllable and volume variances.

The Factory Overhead Flexible Budget

The preparation of a flexible budget was described and illustrated in Chapter 21. Exhibit 8 illustrates a flexible factory overhead budget for **Western Rider Inc.** for June.

Exhibit 8

Factory Overhead Cost Budget Indicating Standard Factory Overhead Rate

	A	B	C	D	E
1	Western Rider Inc.				
2	Factory Overhead Cost Budget				
3	For the Month Ending June 30				
4	Percent of normal capacity	80%	90%	100%	110%
5	Units produced	5,000	5,625	6,250	6,875
6	Direct labor hours (0.80 hr. per unit)	4,000	4,500	5,000	5,500
7	Budgeted factory overhead:				
8	Variable costs:				
9	Indirect factory wages	$ 8,000	$ 9,000	$10,000	$11,000
10	Power and light	4,000	4,500	5,000	5,500
11	Indirect materials	2,400	2,700	3,000	3,300
12	Total variable cost	$14,400	$16,200	$18,000	$19,800
13	Fixed costs:				
14	Supervisory salaries	$ 5,500	$ 5,500	$ 5,500	$ 5,500
15	Depreciation of plant				
16	and equipment	4,500	4,500	4,500	4,500
17	Insurance and property taxes	2,000	2,000	2,000	2,000
18	Total fixed cost	$12,000	$12,000	$12,000	$12,000
19	Total factory overhead cost	$26,400	$28,200	$30,000	$31,800
20					
21	Factory overhead rate per direct labor hour, $30,000 ÷ 5,000 hours = $6.00				
22					

Exhibit 8 indicates that the budgeted factory overhead rate for Western Rider is $6.00, computed as follows:

$$\text{Factory Overhead Rate} = \frac{\text{Budgeted Factory Overhead at Normal Capacity}}{\text{Normal Productive Capacity}}$$

$$= \frac{\$30,000}{5,000 \text{ direct labor hrs.}} = \$6.00 \text{ per direct labor hr.}$$

The normal productive capacity is expressed in terms of an activity base such as direct labor hours, direct labor cost, or machine hours. For Western Rider, 100% of normal capacity is 5,000 direct labor hours. The budgeted factory overhead cost at 100% of normal capacity is $30,000, which consists of variable overhead of $18,000 and fixed overhead of $12,000.

For analysis purposes, the budgeted factory overhead rate is subdivided into a variable factory overhead rate and a fixed factory overhead rate. For Western Rider, the variable overhead rate is $3.60 per direct labor hour, and the fixed overhead rate is $2.40 per direct labor hour, computed as follows:

$$\text{Variable Factory Overhead Rate} = \frac{\text{Budgeted Variable Overhead at Normal Capacity}}{\text{Normal Productive Capacity}}$$

$$= \frac{\$18,000}{5,000 \text{ direct labor hrs.}} = \$3.60 \text{ per direct labor hr.}$$

$$\text{Fixed Factory Overhead Rate} = \frac{\text{Budgeted Fixed Overhead at Normal Capacity}}{\text{Normal Productive Capacity}}$$

$$= \frac{\$12,000}{5,000 \text{ direct labor hrs.}} = \$2.40 \text{ per direct labor hr.}$$

To summarize, the budgeted factory overhead rates for Western Rider Inc. are as follows:

Variable factory overhead rate	$3.60
Fixed factory overhead rate	2.40
Total factory overhead rate	$6.00

As mentioned previously, factory overhead variances can be separated into a controllable variance and a volume variance as discussed in the next sections.

Variable Factory Overhead Controllable Variance

The variable factory overhead **controllable variance** is the difference between the actual variable overhead costs and the budgeted variable overhead for actual production. It is computed as follows:

$$\frac{\text{Variable Factory Overhead}}{\text{Controllable Variance}} = \frac{\text{Actual}}{\text{Variable Factory Overhead}} - \frac{\text{Budgeted}}{\text{Variable Factory Overhead}}$$

If the actual variable overhead is less than the budgeted variable overhead, the variance is favorable. If the actual variable overhead exceeds the budgeted variable overhead, the variance is unfavorable.

The **budgeted variable factory overhead** is the standard variable overhead for the *actual* units produced. It is computed as follows:

$$\text{Budgeted Variable Factory Overhead} = \text{Standard Hours for Actual Units Produced} \times \text{Variable Factory Overhead Rate}$$

To illustrate, the budgeted variable overhead for **Western Rider Inc.** for June, when 5,000 units of XL jeans were produced, is $14,400, computed as follows:

$$\text{Budgeted Variable Factory Overhead} = \text{Standard Hours for Actual Units Produced} \times \text{Variable Factory Overhead Rate}$$
$$= 4,000 \text{ direct labor hrs.} \times \$3.60$$
$$= \$14,400$$

The preceding computation is based on the fact that Western Rider produced 5,000 XL jeans, which requires a standard of 4,000 (5,000 units × 0.8 hr.) direct labor hours. The variable factory overhead rate of $3.60 was computed earlier. Thus, the budgeted variable factory overhead is $14,400 (4,000 direct labor hrs. × $3.60).

During June, assume that Western Rider incurred the following actual factory overhead costs:

	Actual Costs in June
Variable factory overhead	$10,400
Fixed factory overhead	12,000
Total actual factory overhead	$22,400

Based on the actual variable factory overhead incurred in June, the variable factory overhead controllable variance is a $4,000 favorable variance, computed as follows:

$$\begin{aligned} \text{Variable Factory Overhead} &= \text{Actual} - \text{Budgeted} \\ \text{Controllable Variance} &\quad \text{Variable Factory Overhead} \quad \text{Variable Factory Overhead} \\ &= \$10,400 - \$14,400 \\ &= \$(4,000) \text{ Favorable Variance} \end{aligned}$$

The variable factory overhead controllable variance indicates the ability to keep the factory overhead costs within the budget limits. Because variable factory overhead costs are normally controllable at the department level, responsibility for controlling this variance usually rests with department supervisors.

Fixed Factory Overhead Volume Variance

Western Rider's budgeted factory overhead is based on a 100% normal capacity of 5,000 direct labor hours, as shown in Exhibit 8. This is the expected capacity that management believes will be used under normal business conditions. Exhibit 8 indicates that the 5,000 direct labor hours is less than the total available capacity of 110%, which is 5,500 direct labor hours.

The fixed factory overhead **volume variance** is the difference between the budgeted fixed overhead at 100% of normal capacity and the standard fixed overhead for the actual units produced. It is computed as follows:

$$\begin{aligned} \text{Fixed Factory} \\ \text{Overhead} \\ \text{Volume Variance} \end{aligned} = \left(\begin{aligned} \text{Standard Hours} &\quad \text{Standard Hours for} \\ \text{for 100\% of} &\quad - \quad \text{Actual Units} \\ \text{Normal Capacity} &\quad \text{Produced} \end{aligned} \right) \times \begin{aligned} \text{Fixed Factory} \\ \text{Overhead Rate} \end{aligned}$$

The volume variance measures the use of fixed overhead resources (plant and equipment). The interpretation of an unfavorable and a favorable fixed factory overhead volume variance is as follows:

- *Unfavorable* fixed factory overhead volume variance. The actual units produced is *less than* 100% of normal capacity; thus, the company used its fixed overhead resources (plant and equipment) less than would be expected under normal operating conditions.
- *Favorable* fixed factory overhead volume variance. The actual units produced is *more than* 100% of normal capacity; thus, the company used its fixed overhead resources (plant and equipment) more than would be expected under normal operating conditions.

To illustrate, the fixed factory overhead volume variance for **Western Rider Inc.** is a $2,400 unfavorable variance, computed as follows:

$$\begin{aligned} \text{Fixed Factory} \\ \text{Overhead} \\ \text{Volume Variance} \end{aligned} = \left(\begin{aligned} \text{Standard Hours} &\quad \text{Standard Hours for} \\ \text{for 100\% of} &\quad - \quad \text{Actual Units} \\ \text{Normal Capacity} &\quad \text{Produced} \end{aligned} \right) \times \begin{aligned} \text{Fixed Factory} \\ \text{Overhead Rate} \end{aligned}$$

$$= \left(\begin{aligned} 5,000 \text{ direct} &\quad 4,000 \text{ direct} \\ \text{labor hrs.} &\quad - \quad \text{labor hrs.} \end{aligned} \right) \times \$2.40$$

$$= \$2,400 \text{ Unfavorable Variance}$$

Because Western Rider produced 5,000 XL jeans during June, the standard for the actual units produced is 4,000 (5,000 units × 0.80) direct labor hours. This is 1,000 hours less than the 5,000 standard hours of normal capacity. The fixed overhead rate of $2.40 was computed earlier. Thus, the unfavorable fixed factory overhead volume variance is $2,400 (1,000 direct labor hrs. × $2.40).

Exhibit 9 illustrates graphically the fixed factory overhead volume variance for **Western Rider Inc.** The budgeted fixed overhead does not change and is $12,000 at all levels of production. At 100% of normal capacity (5,000 direct labor hours), the standard fixed overhead line intersects the budgeted fixed costs line. For production levels *more than* 100% of normal capacity (5,000 direct labor hours), the volume variance is *favorable*. For production levels *less than* 100% of normal capacity (5,000 direct labor hours), the volume variance is *unfavorable*.

Exhibit 9 indicates that Western Rider's fixed factory overhead volume variance is unfavorable in June because the actual production is 4,000 direct labor hours, or 80% of normal volume. The unfavorable volume variance of $2,400 can be viewed as the cost of the unused capacity (1,000 direct labor hours).

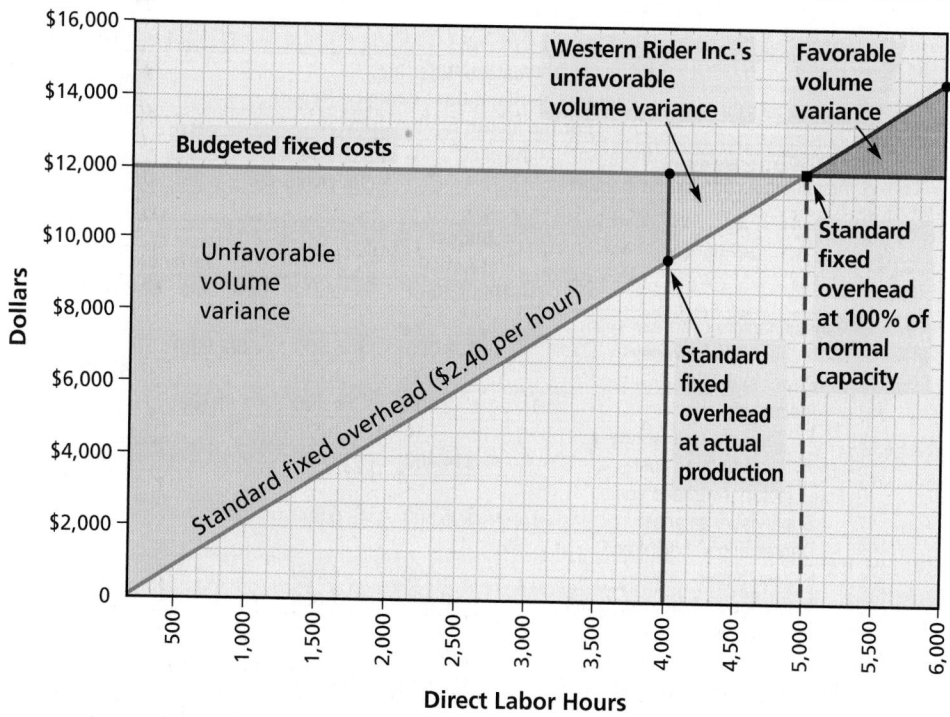

Exhibit 9

Graph of Fixed Overhead Volume Variance

An unfavorable volume variance may be due to factors such as the following:

- Failure to maintain an even flow of work
- Machine breakdowns
- Work stoppages caused by lack of materials or skilled labor
- Lack of enough sales orders to keep the factory operating at normal capacity

Management should determine the causes of the unfavorable variance and consider taking corrective action. For example, a volume variance caused by an uneven flow of work could be remedied by changing operating procedures. Lack of sales orders may be corrected through increased advertising.

Favorable volume variances may not always be desirable. For example, in an attempt to create a favorable volume variance, manufacturing managers might run the factory above the normal capacity. However, if the additional production cannot be sold, it must be stored as inventory, which would incur storage costs.

Reporting Factory Overhead Variances

The total factory overhead cost variance can also be determined as the sum of the variable factory overhead controllable and fixed factory overhead volume variances, computed as follows for **Western Rider Inc.**:

Variable factory overhead controllable variance	$(4,000) Favorable Variance
Fixed factory overhead volume variance	2,400 Unfavorable Variance
Total factory overhead cost variance	$(1,600) Favorable Variance

A **factory overhead cost variance report** is useful to management in controlling factory overhead costs. Budgeted and actual costs for variable and fixed factory overhead along with the related controllable and volume variances are reported by each cost element.

Exhibit 10 illustrates a factory overhead cost variance report for Western Rider Inc. for June.

Exhibit 10

Factory Overhead Cost Variance Report

	A	B	C	D	E
1		Western Rider Inc.				
2		Factory Overhead Cost Variance Report				
3		For the Month Ending June 30				
4	Productive capacity for the month (100% of normal)	5,000 hours			
5	Actual production for the month	4,000 hours			
6						
7		**Budget**			**Variances**	
8		**(at Actual**				
9		**Production)**	**Actual**	**Favorable**	**Unfavorable**
10	Variable factory overhead costs:				
11	Indirect factory wages	$ 8,000	$ 5,100	$(2,900)	
12	Power and light	4,000	4,200		$ 200
13	Indirect materials	2,400	1,100	(1,300)	
14	Total variable factory				
15	overhead cost	$14,400	$10,400		
16	Fixed factory overhead costs:				
17	Supervisory salaries	$ 5,500	$ 5,500		
18	Depreciation of plant and				
19	equipment	4,500	4,500		
20	Insurance and property taxes	2,000	2,000		
21	Total fixed factory				
22	overhead cost	$12,000	$12,000		
23	Total factory overhead cost	$26,400	$22,400		
24	Total controllable variances			$(4,200)	$ 200
25					
26					
27	Net controllable variance—favorable [$(4,200) favorable + $200] unfavorable				$(4,000)
28	Volume variance—unfavorable:				
29	Capacity not used at the standard rate for fixed				
30	factory overhead—1,000 × $2.40				2,400
31	Total factory overhead cost variance—favorable				$(1,600)
32					

Why It Matters

Standard Costing in Action: Expanding Brewing Operations

U.S. west coast craft brewers Sierra Nevada (CA) and New Belgium (CO) recently announced plans to expand their brewing operations to the Asheville, North Carolina, area. Both companies considered the standard cost of their product when making the decision to expand, and in selecting Asheville as their east coast location. The standard price of direct materials includes the cost of shipping direct materials to the manufacturers' place of business. The Asheville location was desirable when considering these costs.

In addition, New Belgium projected that its Fort Collins, Colorado, brewery would reach maximum capacity in three to five years. While operating at 100% capacity creates a favorable overhead volume variance, any demand in excess of 100% capacity will result in lost sales. Thus, New Belgium felt that adding a new brewery prior to reaching 100% capacity at Fort Collins was supported. In both cases, standard costing was used to support the expansion and location decisions.

Sources: H. Dornbusch, "The Case for Low Mileage Beer," *Brewers Association.org*; J. McCurry, "Hops City: Beer Culture Comes to a Head in the Asheville Region," *Site Selection*, July 2012; J. Shikes, "New Belgium, Maker of Fat Tire, Plans a Second Brewery on the East Coast," *Denver Westward*, May 19, 2011.

Factory Overhead Account

The applied factory overhead for **Western Rider Inc.** for the 5,000 XL jeans produced in June is $24,000, computed as follows:

Applied Factory Overhead = Standard Hours for Actual Units Produced × Total Factory Overhead Rate
= (5,000 jeans × 0.80 direct labor hr. per pair of jeans) × $6.00
= 4,000 direct labor hrs. × $6.00 = $24,000

The total actual factory overhead for Western Rider, as shown in Exhibit 10, was $22,400. Thus, the total factory overhead cost variance for Western Rider for June is a $1,600 favorable variance, computed as follows:

$$\frac{\text{Total Factory Overhead}}{\text{Cost Variance}} = \text{Actual Factory Overhead} - \text{Applied Factory Overhead}$$

$$= \$22,400 - \$24,000 = \$(1,600) \text{ Favorable Variance}$$

At the end of the period, the factory overhead account normally has a balance. A debit balance in Factory Overhead represents underapplied overhead. Underapplied overhead occurs when actual factory overhead costs exceed the applied factory overhead. A credit balance in Factory Overhead represents overapplied overhead. Overapplied overhead occurs when actual factory overhead costs are less than the applied factory overhead.

The difference between the actual factory overhead and the applied factory overhead is the total factory overhead cost variance. Thus, underapplied and overapplied factory overhead account balances represent the following total factory overhead cost variances:

- *Underapplied* Factory Overhead = *Unfavorable* Total Factory Overhead Cost Variance
- *Overapplied* Factory Overhead = *Favorable* Total Factory Overhead Cost Variance

The factory overhead account for **Western Rider Inc.** for the month ending June 30 is as follows:

Factory Overhead

Actual factory overhead ($10,400 + $12,000)	22,400	24,000	Applied factory overhead (4,000 hrs. × $6.00 per hr.)
		Bal., June 30 1,600	Overapplied factory overhead

The $1,600 overapplied factory overhead account balance and the favorable total factory overhead cost variance shown in Exhibit 10 are the same.

The variable factory overhead controllable variance and the volume variance can be computed by comparing the factory overhead account with the budgeted total overhead for the actual level produced, as shown in Exhibit 11.

The controllable and volume variances are determined as follows:

- The difference between the actual overhead incurred and the budgeted overhead is the *controllable* variance.
- The difference between the applied overhead and the budgeted overhead is the *volume* variance.

If the actual factory overhead exceeds (is less than) the budgeted factory overhead, the controllable variance is unfavorable (favorable). In contrast, if the applied factory overhead is less than (exceeds) the budgeted factory overhead, the volume variance is unfavorable (favorable).

Exhibit 11 Factory Overhead Variances

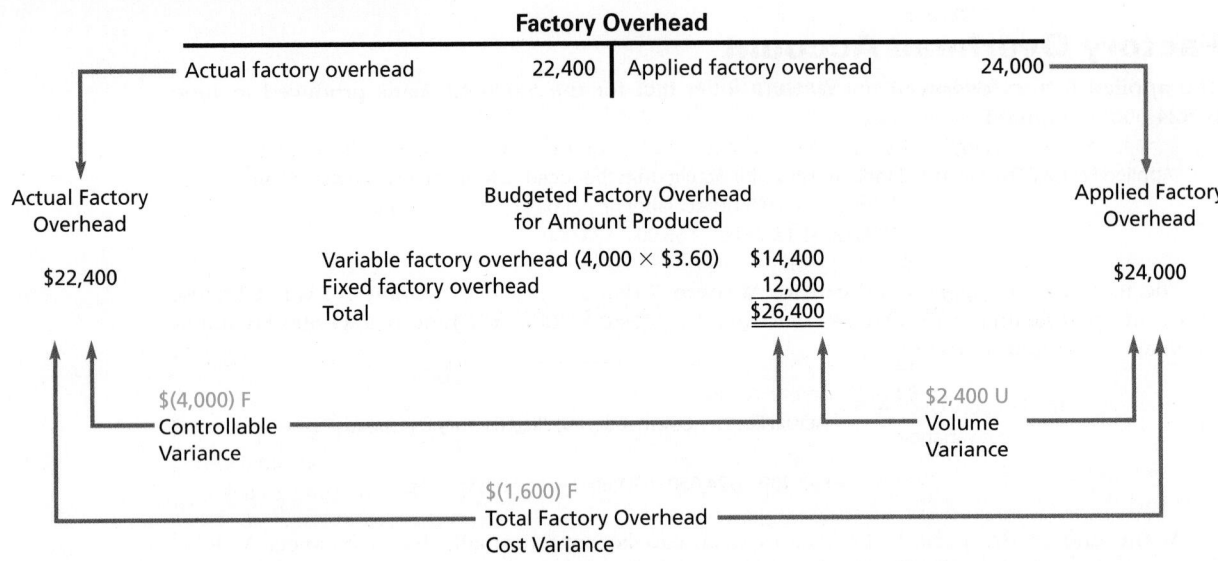

Check Up Corner 22-2 — Factory Overhead Cost Variances

Menounos Manufacturing Co. uses standard costs in its budgets. Standard costs and actual costs for direct labor and factory overhead for the manufacture of 3,000 units during 20Y6 were as follows:

	Standard Costs	**Actual Costs**
Direct labor	7,500 hours at $12.00 per hour	7,420 hours at $12.30 per hour
Factory overhead	Rates per direct labor hr., based on 100% of normal capacity of 8,000 direct labor hrs.:	
	Variable cost, $2.20	$16,850 variable cost
	Fixed cost, $0.90	$7,200 fixed cost

Each unit requires 2.5 hours of direct labor.

Determine the:

A. Variable factory overhead controllable variance,

B. Fixed factory overhead volume variance, and

C. Total factory overhead cost variance.

Solution:

A.

$$\begin{array}{rcl} \text{Variable Factory Overhead} \\ \text{Controllable Variance} \end{array} = \begin{array}{c}\text{Actual} \\ \text{Variable Factory Overhead}\end{array} - \begin{array}{c}\text{Budgeted} \\ \text{Variable Factory Overhead}\end{array}$$

$$= \$16,850 - \$16,500 \longleftarrow$$

$$= \$350 \text{ Unfavorable Variance}$$

Budgeted Variable Factory Overhead = Standard Hours for Actual Units Produced
× Variable Factory Overhead Rate

= 7,500 direct labor hrs. × $2.20

= $16,500 ———

B.

$$\begin{array}{c}\text{Fixed Factory} \\ \text{Overhead} \\ \text{Volume Variance}\end{array} = \left(\begin{array}{c}\text{Standard Hours} \\ \text{for 100\% of} \\ \text{Normal Capacity}\end{array} - \begin{array}{c}\text{Standard Hours for} \\ \text{Actual Units} \\ \text{Produced}\end{array}\right) \times \begin{array}{c}\text{Fixed Factory} \\ \text{Overhead Rate}\end{array}$$

$$= \left(\begin{array}{c}\text{8,000 direct} \\ \text{labor hrs.}\end{array} - \begin{array}{c}\text{7,500 direct} \\ \text{labor hrs.}\end{array}\right) \times \$0.90$$

$$= \$450 \text{ Unfavorable Variance}$$

C.

Applied Factory Overhead = Standard Hours for Actual Units Produced × Total Factory Overhead Rate

= (3,000 units × 2.5 direct labor hrs. per unit) × ($2.20 variable cost per hour
+ $0.90 fixed cost per hour)

= 7,500 direct labor hrs. × $3.10

= $23,250 ———

$$\begin{array}{c}\text{Total Factory Overhead} \\ \text{Cost Variance}\end{array} = \text{Actual Factory Overhead} - \text{Applied Factory Overhead}$$

$$= \$24,050 - \$23,250 \longleftarrow$$

$$= 800 \text{ Unfavorable Variance}$$

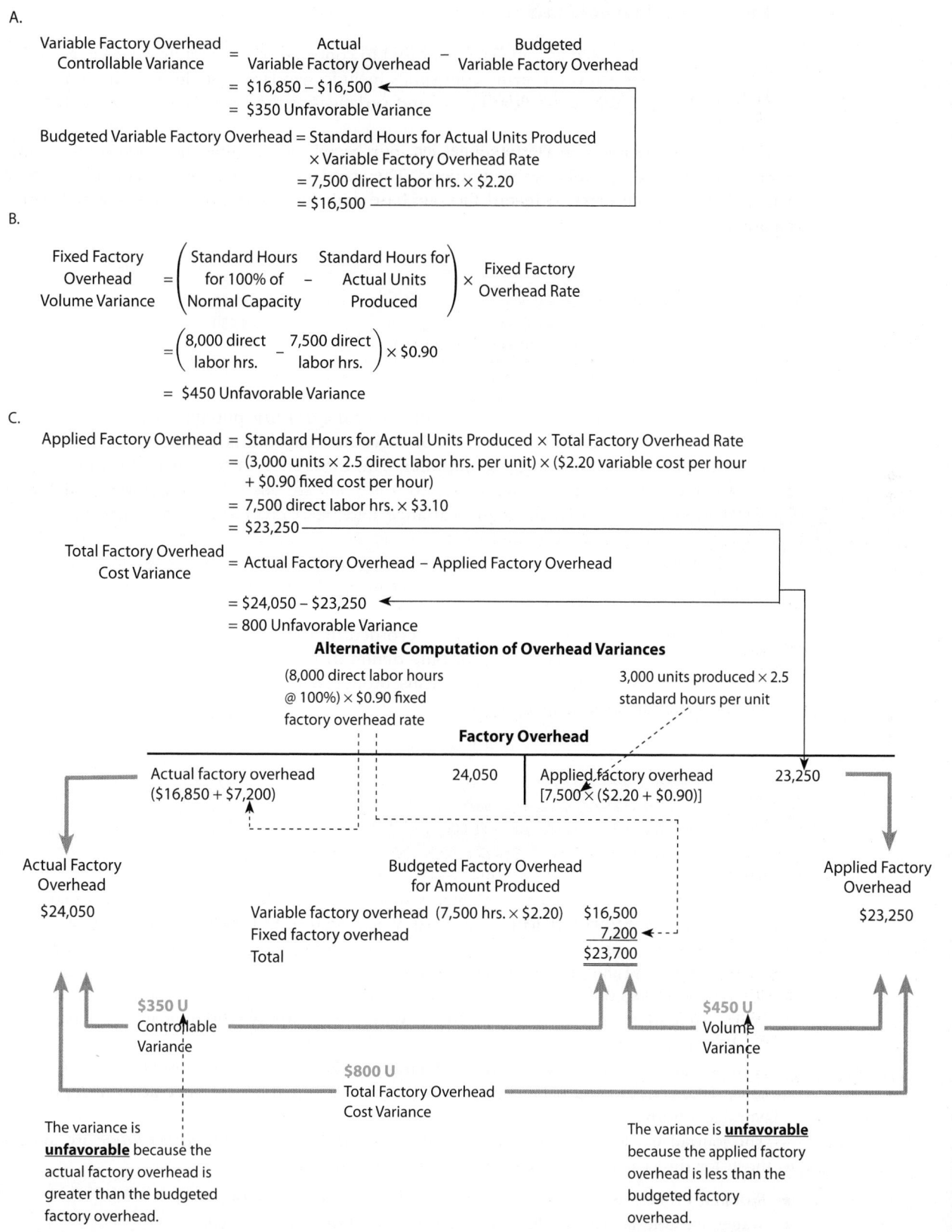

Alternative Computation of Overhead Variances

Objective 5

Describe and illustrate the recording and reporting of standards and variances.

Recording and Reporting Variances from Standards

Standard costs may be used as a management tool to control costs separately from the accounts in the general ledger. However, many companies include standard costs in their accounts. One method for doing so records standard costs and variances at the same time the actual product costs are recorded.

To illustrate, assume that **Western Rider Inc.** purchased, on account, the 7,300 square yards of blue denim used at $5.50 per square yard. The standard price for direct materials is $5.00 per square yard. The entry to record the purchase and the unfavorable direct materials price variance is as follows:

Materials (7,300 sq. yds. × $5.00)	36,500	
Direct Materials Price Variance	3,650	
Accounts Payable (7,300 sq. yds. × $5.50)		40,150

The materials account is debited for the *actual quantity* purchased at the *standard price*, $36,500 (7,300 square yards × $5.00). Accounts Payable is credited for the $40,150 actual cost and the amount due the supplier. The difference of $3,650 is the unfavorable direct materials price variance [($5.50 – $5.00) × 7,300 sq. yds.]. It is recorded by debiting Direct Materials Price Variance. If the variance had been favorable, Direct Materials Price Variance would have been credited for the variance.

A debit balance in the direct materials price variance account represents an unfavorable variance. Likewise, a credit balance in the direct materials price variance account represents a favorable variance.

The direct materials quantity variance is recorded in a similar manner. For example, **Western Rider Inc.** used 7,300 square yards of blue denim to produce 5,000 pairs of XL jeans. The standard quantity of denim for the 5,000 jeans produced is 7,500 square yards. The entry to record the materials used is as follows:

Work in Process (7,500 sq. yds. × $5.00)	37,500	
Direct Materials Quantity Variance		1,000
Materials (7,300 sq. yds. × $5.00)		36,500

Work in Process is debited for $37,500, which is the standard cost of the direct materials required to produce 5,000 XL jeans (7,500 sq. yds. × $5.00). Materials is credited for $36,500, which is the actual quantity of materials used at the standard price (7,300 sq. yds. × $5.00). The difference of $1,000 is the favorable direct materials quantity variance [(7,300 sq. yds. – 7,500 sq. yds.) × $5.00]. It is recorded by crediting Direct Materials Quantity Variance. If the variance had been unfavorable, Direct Materials Quantity Variance would have been debited for the variance.

A debit balance in the direct materials quantity variance account represents an unfavorable variance. Likewise, a credit balance in the direct materials quantity variance account represents a favorable variance.

The journal entries to record the standard costs and variances for *direct labor* are similar to those for direct materials. These entries are summarized as follows:

- Work in Process is debited for the standard cost of direct labor.
- Wages Payable is credited for the actual direct labor cost incurred.

■ Direct Labor Rate Variance is debited for an unfavorable variance and credited for a favorable variance.

■ Direct Labor Time Variance is debited for an unfavorable variance and credited for a favorable variance.

As illustrated in the prior section, the factory overhead account already incorporates standard costs and variances into its journal entries. That is, Factory Overhead is debited for actual factory overhead and credited for applied (standard) factory overhead. The ending balance of factory overhead (overapplied or underapplied) is the total factory overhead cost variance. By comparing the actual factory overhead with the budgeted factory overhead, the controllable variance can be determined. By comparing the budgeted factory overhead with the applied factory overhead, the volume variance can be determined.

When goods are completed, Finished Goods is debited and Work in Process is credited for the standard cost of the product transferred.

At the end of the period, the balances of each of the variance accounts indicate the net favorable or unfavorable variance for the period. These variances may be reported in an income statement prepared for management's use.

Exhibit 12 is an example of an income statement for **Western Rider Inc.** that includes variances. In Exhibit 12, a sales price of $28 per pair of jeans, selling expenses of $14,500, and administrative expenses of $11,225 are assumed.

Exhibit 12
Variance from Standards in Income Statement

Western Rider Inc.
Income Statement
For the Month Ended June 30

	Favorable	Unfavorable	
Sales			$140,000[1]
Cost of goods sold—at standard			97,500[2]
Gross profit—at standard			$ 42,500
Variances from standard cost:			
Direct materials price		$ 3,650	
Direct materials quantity	$(1,000)		
Direct labor rate		3,850	
Direct labor time	(1,350)		
Factory overhead controllable	(4,000)		
Factory overhead volume		2,400	
Net variance from standard cost—unfavorable			3,550
Gross profit			$ 38,950
Operating expenses:			
Selling expenses		$14,500	
Administrative expenses		11,225	
Total operating expenses			25,725
Income before income tax			$ 13,225

[1]5,000 × $28
[2]$37,500 + $36,000 + $24,000 (from Exhibit 3), or 5,000 × $19.50 (from Exhibit 1)

The income statement shown in Exhibit 12 is for internal use by management. That is, variances are not reported to external users. Thus, the variances shown in Exhibit 12 must be transferred to other accounts in preparing an income statement for external users.

In preparing an income statement for external users, the balances of the variance accounts are normally transferred to Cost of Goods Sold. However, if the variances are significant or if many of the products manufactured are still in inventory, the variances should be allocated to Work in Process, Finished Goods, and Cost of Goods Sold. Such an allocation, in effect, converts these account balances from standard cost to actual cost.

Check Up Corner 22-3 | Income Statement with Variances

Using the variance data for Menounos Manufacturing Co. in Check Up Corners 22-1 (pp. 1116–1117) and 22-2 (pp. 1124–1125), prepare an income statement through gross profit for the year ended December 31, 20Y6. Assume the company sold 3,000 units at $100 per unit.

Solution:

Menounos Manufacturing Co.
Income Statement Through Gross Profit
For the Year Ended December 31, 20Y6

3,000 units sold × $100
selling price per unit

Sales..		$300,000
Cost of goods sold—at standard		194,250
Gross profit—at standard........................		$105,750

	Favorable	**Unfavorable**
Variances from standard cost:		
Direct materials price	$(2,775)	
Direct materials quantity........................		$2,250
Direct labor rate		2,226
Direct labor time	(960)	
Factory overhead controllable		350
Factory overhead volume.......................		450
Net variance from standard cost—unfavorable		1,541
Gross profit....................................		$104,209

From Check Up Corner 22-1

From Check Up Corner 22-2

Direct materials at standard	$ 81,000
Direct labor cost at standard (3,000 units × 2.5 standard hours per unit × $12 standard rate per hour)	90,000
Factory overhead at standard (3,000 units × 2.5 standard hours per unit × $3.10 standard rate per hour)	23,250
Cost of goods sold at standard	$194,250

Check Up Corner

Objective 6

Describe and illustrate nonfinancial performance measures.

Nonfinancial Performance Measures

Many companies supplement standard costs and variances from standards with nonfinancial performance measures. A **nonfinancial performance measure** expresses performance in a measure other than dollars. For example, airlines use on-time performance, percent of bags lost, and number of customer complaints as nonfinancial performance measures. Such measures are often used to evaluate the time, quality, or quantity of a business activity.

Link to BMW Group

The **BMW Group** uses a variety of nonfinancial performance measures for its vehicles and its manufacturing operations, including energy consumption, water consumption, carbon dioxide emissions, percent of women in its workforce, average days of training per employee, and accident frequency.

Using financial and nonfinancial performance measures aids managers and employees in considering multiple performance objectives. Such measures often bring additional perspectives, such as quality of work, to evaluating performance. Some examples of nonfinancial performance measures are shown in Exhibit 13.

- Inventory turnover
- Percent on-time delivery
- Elapsed time between a customer order and product delivery
- Customer preference rankings compared to competitors
- Response time to a service call
- Time to develop new products
- Employee satisfaction
- Number of customer complaints

Exhibit 13
Nonfinancial Performance Measures

Nonfinancial measures are often linked to either the inputs or outputs of an activity or process. A **process** is a sequence of activities for performing a task. The relationship between an activity or a process and its inputs and outputs is shown in Exhibit 14.

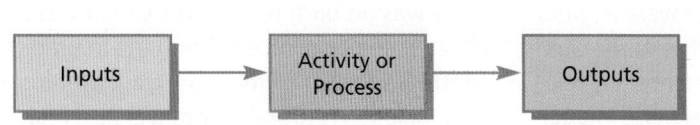

Exhibit 14
Relationship Between a Process and Its Inputs and Outputs

To illustrate, the counter service activity of a fast-food restaurant is used. The inputs/outputs for providing counter service at a fast-food restaurant are shown in Exhibit 15.

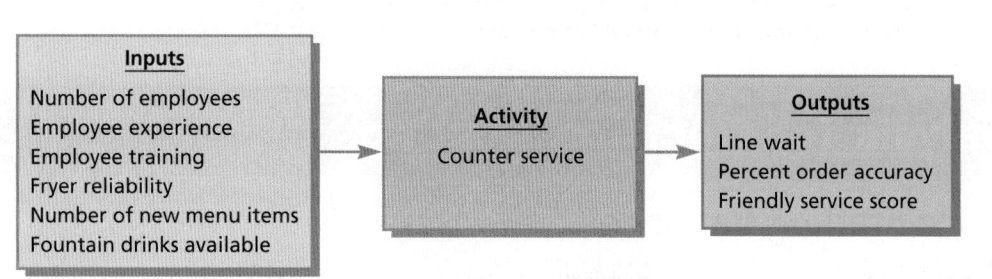

Exhibit 15
Inputs/Outputs for a Fast-Food Restaurant

The customer service outputs of the counter service activity include the following:

- Line wait for the customer
- Percent order accuracy in serving the customer
- Friendly service experience for the customer

Some of the inputs that impact the customer service outputs include the following:

- Number of employees
- Employee experience
- Employee training
- Fryer (and other cooking equipment) reliability
- Number of new menu items
- Fountain drink availability

A fast-food restaurant can develop a set of linked nonfinancial performance measures across inputs and outputs. The output measures tell management how the activity is performing, such as keeping the line wait to a minimum. The input measures are used to improve the output measures. For example, if the customer line wait is too long, then improving employee training or hiring more employees could improve the output (decrease customer line wait).

Link to BMW Group

The **BMW Group** assesses its suppliers using a BMW sustainablity standard that measures compliance with human rights, labor, and social issues.

Why It Matters

The Lesson of Moneyball

The book and movie, *Moneyball*, showed how the **Oakland A's** baseball organization built a winning team by using player performance measures that were aligned to winning games. At that time, the front office of the Oakland A's baseball organization analyzed the statistical relationship between various measures of player performance and scoring runs. It discovered "on-base percentage," an unlikely and underutilized measure, as the dominant predictor of scoring runs. The on-base percentage is the number of times a player gets on base as a percentage of total at-bats. Prior to this, baseball organizations relied on the manager's intuitive assessment of a player's performance. Oftentimes, this intuition poorly predicted a player's contribution to team success. In addition, the focus was on batting average, which was statistically less effective than on-base percentage in predicting a player's contribution to scoring runs and winning games. Thus, the Oakland A's looked for players that had high on-base percentages and built a winning team out of players the rest of the league overlooked. The lesson for business is that performance measures should be highly aligned to strategic objectives so that high performance on the measure will lead to high performance toward the organization's larger goals.

Analysis for Decision Making

Objective

Describe and illustrate the use of the direct labor time variance in evaluating staff performance in a service setting.

Service Staffing Variances

As we stated earlier in this chapter, standards can be used in nonmanufacturing settings where the tasks are repetitive in nature. Standards are used in hotels, hospitals, restaurants, transportation services, banks, retail stores, professional services, software development, automotive services, and many other service settings.

To illustrate, Marion Hotel uses labor standards to control the costs of the housekeeping staff. From historical information, the hotel expects a housekeeping employee to clean a room in 42 minutes. An occupied room for one night is termed a "guest room night." In addition, housekeeping employees are paid $13 per hour. Information for a recent week follows:

Number of guest room nights	1,050
Number of housekeeping staff hours	840

The guest room nights can be translated into standard staff hours as follows:

Number of guest room nights	1,050
Multiplied by standard hours per room (42 min. ÷ 60 min.)	× 0.70
Standard housekeeping staff hours	735

The direct labor time variance can be calculated as:

Direct Labor Time Variance = (Actual Staff Hours – Standard Staff Hours) × Standard Rate per Hour
= (840 hrs. – 735 hrs.) × $13 per hour
= $1,365 Unfavorable

The actual staff hours were greater than the standard hours, causing an unfavorable staff time variance. Management can investigate the causes of the variance, which may include overscheduling staff, insufficient staff training, difficult room cleaning situations, and staff inefficiency.

Make a Decision   Service Staffing Variances

Advent Software uses standards to manage the cost of the programming staff. There are two programmer levels, Level 1 and Level 2. Level 1 programmers normally work on the easier projects. Level 1 and Level 2 programmers are paid $25 and $35 per hour, respectively. It has been determined from experience that Level 2 programmers can complete 50 lines of code per hour. If a Level 1 programmer is assigned to a Level 2 task, the programming work will be slower than the Level 2 time standard, but will be accomplished at a lower labor rate.

During a recent week, a Level 2 project was assigned to a Level 1 programmer. The programmer worked 40 hours and completed 1,400 lines of code.

A. Determine the direct labor time variance for this worker.
B. Determine the direct labor rate variance for this worker.
C. Using the information in (A) and (B), is it more cost effective to use a Level 1 worker or a Level 2 worker on a Level 2 project?

Solution:
A. Standard hours for coding:

Lines of code	1,400
Level 2 standard lines per hour	÷ 50
Standard hours at Level 2 coding standard	28

Direct Labor Time Variance = (Actual Staff Hours – Standard Staff Hours) × Standard Rate per Hour
= (40 hrs. – 28 hrs.) × $35 per hour
= $420 Unfavorable

Note that the standard rate per hour is set at the Level 2 rate for this Level 2 project. We are comparing the Level 1 performance to the Level 2 standard.

The Level 1 programmer is not as efficient as a Level 2 programmer on a Level 2 project. Therefore, there is an unfavorable labor time variance.

B. Direct Labor Rate Variance = (Actual Rate per Hour – Standard Rate per Hour) × Actual Hours
= ($25 – $35) × 40 hrs.
= $(400) Favorable

The Level 1 programmer has a lower labor rate than the Level 2 programmer. Thus, there is a favorable direct labor rate variance.

C. The amount of the unfavorable time variance is greater than the amount of the favorable rate variance. Thus, this analysis suggests that it is not cost effective to use a Level 1 programmer on a Level 2 project. The Level 1 programmer's lower cost per hour does not make up for the slower coding performance.

Make a Decision

Let's Review

Chapter Summary

1. Standards represent performance goals that can be compared to actual results in evaluating performance. Standards should be established so that they are neither too high nor too low, but are attainable.

2. Budgets are prepared by multiplying the standard cost per unit by the planned production. To measure performance, the standard cost per unit is multiplied by the actual number of units produced, and the actual results are compared with the standard cost at actual volumes (cost variance).

3. The direct materials cost variance can be separated into direct materials price and quantity variances. The direct labor cost variance can be separated into direct labor rate and time variances.

4. The factory overhead cost variance can be separated into a variable factory overhead controllable variance and a fixed factory overhead volume variance.

5. Standard costs and variances can be recorded in the accounts at the same time the manufacturing costs are recorded in the accounts. Work in Process is debited at standard. Under a standard cost system, the cost of goods sold will be reported at standard cost. Manufacturing variances can be disclosed on the income statement to adjust the gross profit at standard to the actual gross profit.

6. Many companies use a combination of financial and nonfinancial measures in order for multiple perspectives to be incorporated in evaluating performance. Nonfinancial measures are often used in conjunction with the inputs or outputs of a process or an activity.

Key Terms

budget performance report (1110)

budgeted variable factory overhead (1119)

controllable variance (1119)

cost variances (1110)

currently attainable standards (1109)

direct labor rate variance (1115)

direct labor time variance (1115)

direct materials price variance (1113)

direct materials quantity variance (1113)

factory overhead cost variance report (1122)

favorable cost variance (1110)

ideal standards (1109)

nonfinancial performance measure (1128)

process (1129)

standard cost (1108)

standard cost systems (1108)

standards (1108)

total manufacturing cost variance (1111)

unfavorable cost variance (1110)

volume variance (1120)

Practice

Multiple-Choice Questions

1. The actual and standard direct materials costs for producing a specified quantity of product are as follows:

Actual:	51,000 lbs. at $5.05	$257,550
Standard:	50,000 lbs. at $5.00	$250,000

The direct materials price variance is:

A. $50 unfavorable.

B. $2,500 unfavorable.

C. $2,550 unfavorable.

D. $7,550 unfavorable.

2. Bower Company produced 4,000 units of product. Each unit requires 0.5 standard hour. The standard labor rate is $12 per hour. Actual direct labor for the period was $22,000 (2,200 hrs. × $10 per hr.). The direct labor time variance is:
   A. 200 hours unfavorable.   C. $4,000 favorable.
   B. $2,000 unfavorable.   D. $2,400 unfavorable.

3. The actual and standard factory overhead costs for producing a specified quantity of product are as follows:

Actual: Variable factory overhead	$72,500	
Fixed factory overhead	40,000	$112,500
Standard: 19,000 hrs. at $6		
($4 variable and $2 fixed)		114,000

   If 1,000 hours were unused, the fixed factory overhead volume variance would be:
   A. $1,500 favorable.   C. $4,000 unfavorable.
   B. $2,000 unfavorable.   D. $6,000 unfavorable.

4. Ramathan Company produced 6,000 units of Product Y, which is 80% of capacity. Each unit required 0.25 standard machine hour for production. The standard variable factory overhead rate is $5 per machine hour. The actual variable factory overhead incurred during the period was $8,000. The variable factory overhead controllable variance is:
   A. $500 favorable.   C. $1,875 favorable.
   B. $500 unfavorable.   D. $1,875 unfavorable.

5. Applegate Company has a normal budgeted capacity of 200 machine hours. Applegate produced 600 units. Each unit requires a standard 0.2 machine hour to complete. The standard fixed factory overhead is $12 per hour, determined at normal capacity. The fixed factory overhead volume variance is:
   A. $4,800 unfavorable.   C. $960 favorable.
   B. $4,800 favorable.   D. $960 unfavorable.

Answers provided after Problem. Need more practice? Find additional multiple-choice questions, exercises, and problems in CengageNOWv2.

Exercises

1. Direct materials variances   Obj. 3

SHOW ME HOW

Lo-bed Company produces a product that requires 2 standard gallons per unit. The standard price is $20.00 per gallon. If 4,000 units required 8,200 gallons, which were purchased at $19.75 per gallon, what is the direct materials (A) price variance, (B) quantity variance, and (C) total cost variance.

2. Direct labor variances   Obj. 3

SHOW ME HOW

Lo-bed Company produces a product that requires 4 standard direct labor hours per unit at a standard hourly rate of $28.00 per hour. If 4,000 units required 16,750 direct labor hours at an hourly rate of $28.40 per hour, what is the direct labor (A) rate variance, (B) time variance, and (C) total cost variance.

3. Factory overhead controllable variance   Obj. 4

SHOW ME HOW

Lo-bed Company produced 4,000 units of product that required 4 standard hours per unit. The standard variable overhead cost per unit is $3.00 per hour. The actual variable factory overhead was $51,240. Determine the variable factory overhead controllable variance.

4. Factory overhead volume variance   Obj. 4

SHOW ME HOW

Lo-bed Company produced 4,000 units of product that required 4 standard hours per unit. The standard fixed overhead cost per unit is $1.20 per hour at 16,400 hours, which is 100% of normal capacity. Determine the fixed factory overhead volume variance.

SHOW ME HOW

5. Standard cost journal entries

Obj. 5

Lo-bed Company produced 4,000 units that require 2 standard gallons per unit at $20.00 standard price per gallon. The company actually used 8,200 gallons in production. Journalize the entry to record the standard direct materials used in production.

SHOW ME HOW

6. Income statement with variances

Obj. 5

Prepare an income statement for Lo-bed Company for the month ending March 31. Prepare the income statement through gross profit using the variance data from Exercises 1, 2, 3, and 4. Assume Lo-bed sold 4,000 units at $250 per unit.

SHOW ME HOW

7. Activity inputs and outputs

Obj. 6

The following are inputs and outputs to the copying process of a copy shop:

Number of employee errors
Number of times paper supply runs out
Copy machine downtime (broken)
Number of pages copied per hour
Number of customer complaints
Percent jobs done on time

Identify whether each is an input or output to the copying process.

Answers provided after Problem. Need more practice? Find additional multiple-choice questions, exercises, and problems in CengageNOWv2.

Problem

Hawley Inc. manufactures designer iPod cases for national distribution. The standard costs for the manufacture of designer iPod cases were as follows:

	Standard Costs	Actual Costs
Direct materials	1,500 lbs. at $35	1,600 lbs. at $32
Direct labor	4,800 hrs. at $11	4,500 hrs. at $11.80
Factory overhead	Rates per labor hour, based on 100% of normal capacity of 5,500 labor hrs.:	
	Variable cost, $2.40	$12,300 variable cost
	Fixed cost, $3.50	$19,250 fixed cost

Instructions

1. Determine the direct materials price variance, direct materials quantity variance, and total direct materials cost variance for the designer iPod cases.

2. Determine the direct labor rate variance, direct labor time variance, and total direct labor cost variance for the designer iPod cases.

3. Determine the variable factory overhead controllable variance, fixed factory overhead volume variance, and total factory overhead cost variance for the designer iPod cases.

Need more practice? Find additional multiple-choice questions, exercises, and problems in CengageNOWv2.

Answers

Multiple-Choice Questions

1. **C** The unfavorable direct materials price variance of $2,550 is determined as follows:

Actual price	$ 5.05 per lb.
Standard price	5.00
Price variance	$0.05 per lb.
Actual lbs.	× 51,000 lbs.
Price variance—unfavorable	$ 2,550

2. **D** The unfavorable direct labor time variance of $2,400 is determined as follows:

Actual direct labor time	2,200 hrs.
Standard direct labor time	2,000 hrs.*
Direct labor time variance	200 hrs.
Standard direct labor rate	× $12
Direct labor time variance—unfavorable	$2,400

*4,000 units × 0.5 hr.

3. **B** The unfavorable factory overhead volume variance of $2,000 is determined as follows:

Productive capacity not used	1,000 hrs.
Standard fixed factory overhead cost rate	× $2
Factory overhead volume variance—unfavorable	$2,000

4. **B** The controllable variable factory overhead variance is determined as follows:

Actual variable overhead	$ 8,000
Budgeted variable overhead at actual volume	(7,500)*
Controllable variance—unfavorable	$ 500

*6,000 units × 0.25 hr. = 1,500 hours;
1,500 hrs. × $5 per hr. = $7,500

5. **D** The fixed factory overhead volume variance can be determined as follows:

Practical capacity	200 machine hrs.
Actual production in standard hours	120 machine hrs.*
Idle capacity	80 machine hrs.
Standard fixed factory overhead rate	×$12
Volume variance—unfavorable	$960

*600 units × 0.2 machine hr. = 120 machine hrs.

Exercises

1. A. Direct materials price variance (favorable) $(2,050)   [($19.75 – $20.00) × 8,200 gal.]

   B. Direct materials quantity variance (unfavorable) $4,000   [(8,200 gal. – 8,000 gal.) × $20.00]

   C. Direct materials total cost variance (unfavorable) $1,950   [$(2,050) + $4,000] or
                                                 [($19.75 × 8,200 gal.) – ($20.00 × 8,000 gal.)]
                                                   = $161,950 – $160,000

2. A. Direct labor rate variance (unfavorable) $6,700   [($28.40 – $28.00) × 16,750 hrs.]

   B. Direct labor time variance (unfavorable) $21,000   [(16,750 hrs. – 16,000 hrs.) × $28.00]

   C. Direct labor total cost variance (unfavorable) $27,700   ($6,700 + $21,000) or
                                                 [($28.40 × 16,750 hrs.) – ($28.00 × 16,000 hrs.)]
                                                   = $475,700 – $448,000

3. Variable Factory Overhead Controllable Variance = $51,240 – [$3.00 × (4,000 units × 4 hrs.)]

                                         = $51,240 – $48,000

                                         = $3,240 Unfavorable

4. $480 Unfavorable = $1.20 × [16,400 hrs. – (4,000 units × 4 hrs.)]

5.

Work in Process (8,000* gal. × $20.00)	160,000	
Direct Materials Quantity Variance**	4,000	
Materials (8,200 gal. × $20.00)		164,000

*4,000 units × 2 standard gal. per unit
**[(8,200 gal. – 8,000 gal.) × $20.00]

6.

Lo-bed Company
Income Statement Through Gross Profit
For the Month Ended March 31

Sales (4,000 units × $250)		$ 1,000,000
Cost of goods sold—at standard*		675,200
Gross profit—at standard		$ 324,800

	Favorable	Unfavorable	
Variances from standard cost:			
Direct materials price (Exercise 1)	$(2,050)		
Direct materials quantity (Exercise 1)		$ 4,000	
Direct labor rate (Exercise 2)		6,700	
Direct labor time (Exercise 2)		21,000	
Factory overhead controllable (Exercise 3)		3,240	
Factory overhead volume (Exercise 4)		480	
Net variance from standard cost—unfavorable			33,370
Gross profit			$ 291,430
*Direct materials (4,000 units × 2 gal. × $20.00)			$160,000
Direct labor (4,000 units × 4 hrs. × $28.00)			448,000
Factory overhead [4,000 units × 4 hrs. × ($3.00 + $1.20)]			67,200
Cost of goods sold at standard			$675,200

7.

Number of employee errors	Input
Number of times paper supply runs out	Input
Copy machine downtime (broken)	Input
Number of pages copied per hour	Output
Number of customer complaints	Output
Percent jobs done on time	Output

Need more help? Watch step-by-step videos of how to compute answers to these Exercises in CengageNOWv2.

Problem

1.

Direct Materials Cost Variance

Price variance:
Direct Materials Price Variance = (Actual Price – Standard Price) × Actual Quantity
= ($32 per lb. – $35 per lb.) × 1,600 lbs.
= $(4,800) Favorable Variance

Quantity variance:
Direct Materials Quantity Variance = (Actual Quantity – Standard Quantity) × Standard Price
= (1,600 lbs. – 1,500 lbs.) × $35 per lb.
= $3,500 Unfavorable Variance

Total direct materials cost variance:
Direct Materials Cost Variance = Direct Materials Quantity Variance + Direct Materials Price Variance
= $3,500 + $(4,800)
= $(1,300) Favorable Variance

2.

Direct Labor Cost Variance

Rate variance:

Direct Labor Rate Variance = (Actual Rate per Hour – Standard Rate per Hour) × Actual Hours
= ($11.80 – $11.00) × 4,500 hrs.
= $3,600 Unfavorable Variance

Time variance:

Direct Labor Time Variance = (Actual Direct Labor Hours – Standard Direct Labor Hours) ×
Standard Rate per Hour
= (4,500 hrs. – 4,800 hrs.) × $11.00 per hour
= $(3,300) Favorable Variance

Total direct labor cost variance:

Direct Labor Cost Variance = Direct Labor Time Variance + Direct Labor Rate Variance
= $(3,300) + $3,600
= $300 Unfavorable Variance

3.

Factory Overhead Cost Variance

Variable factory overhead controllable variance:

Variable Factory Overhead Controllable Variance = Actual Variable Factory Overhead – Budgeted Variable Factory Overhead
= $12,300 – $11,520*
= $780 Unfavorable Variance

*4,800 hrs. × $2.40 per hour

Fixed factory overhead volume variance:

Fixed Factory Overhead Volume Variance = $\left(\begin{array}{c}\text{Standard Hours for 100\%} \\ \text{of Normal Capacity}\end{array} - \begin{array}{c}\text{Standard Hours for} \\ \text{Actual Units Produced}\end{array}\right) \times \begin{array}{c}\text{Fixed Factory} \\ \text{Overhead Rate}\end{array}$
= (5,500 hrs. – 4,800 hrs.) × $3.50 per hr.
= $2,450 Unfavorable Variance

Total factory overhead cost variance:

Factory Overhead Cost Variance = Variable Factory Overhead Controllable Variance + Fixed Factory Overhead Volume Variance
= $780 + $2,450
= $3,230 Unfavorable Variance

Alternative Computation of Overhead Variances

Factory Overhead			
Actual costs	31,550	Applied costs	28,320
($12,300 + $19,250)		[4,800 × ($2.40 + $3.50)]	
Balance (underapplied)	3,230		

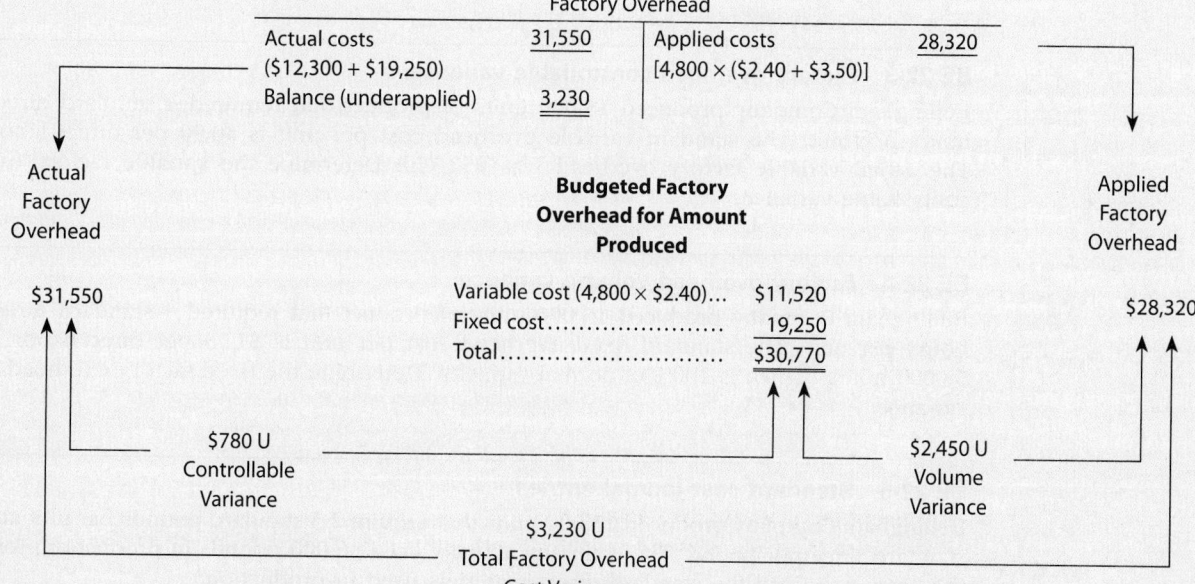

	Budgeted Factory Overhead for Amount Produced	
Actual Factory Overhead		Applied Factory Overhead
$31,550	Variable cost (4,800 × $2.40)... $11,520	$28,320
	Fixed cost 19,250	
	Total $30,770	

$780 U Controllable Variance

$2,450 U Volume Variance

$3,230 U Total Factory Overhead Cost Variance

Discussion Questions

1. What are the basic objectives in the use of standard costs?

2. What is meant by reporting by the "principle of exceptions," as the term is used in reference to cost control?

3. What are the two variances between the actual cost and the standard cost for direct materials?

4. The materials cost variance report for Nickols Inc. indicates a large favorable materials price variance and a significant unfavorable materials quantity variance. What might have caused these offsetting variances?

5. A. What are the two variances between the actual cost and the standard cost for direct labor?

   B. Who generally has control over the direct labor cost variances?

6. A new assistant controller recently was heard to remark: "All the assembly workers in this plant are covered by union contracts, so there should be no labor variances." Was the controller's remark correct? Discuss.

7. Would the use of standards be appropriate in a non-manufacturing setting, such as a fast-food restaurant?

8. A. Describe the two variances between the actual costs and the standard costs for factory overhead.

   B. What is a factory overhead cost variance report?

9. If variances are recorded in the accounts at the time the manufacturing costs are incurred, what does a debit balance in Direct Materials Price Variance represent?

10. Briefly explain why firms might use nonfinancial performance measures.

Basic Exercises

SHOW ME HOW

BE 22-1 Direct materials variances
Obj. 3

Bellingham Company produces a product that requires 2.5 standard pounds per unit. The standard price is $3.75 per pound. If 15,000 units used 36,000 pounds, which were purchased at $4.00 per pound, what is the direct materials (A) price variance, (B) quantity variance, and (C) cost variance?

SHOW ME HOW

BE 22-2 Direct labor variances
Obj. 3

Bellingham Company produces a product that requires 4 standard direct labor hours per unit at a standard hourly rate of $20 per hour. If 15,000 units used 61,800 hours at an hourly rate of $19.85 per hour, what is the direct labor (A) rate variance, (B) time variance, and (C) cost variance?

SHOW ME HOW

BE 22-3 Factory overhead controllable variance
Obj. 4

Bellingham Company produced 15,000 units of product that required 4 standard direct labor hours per unit. The standard variable overhead cost per unit is $0.90 per direct labor hour. The actual variable factory overhead was $52,770. Determine the variable factory overhead controllable variance.

SHOW ME HOW

BE 22-4 Factory overhead volume variance
Obj. 4

Bellingham Company produced 15,000 units of product that required 4 standard direct labor hours per unit. The standard fixed overhead cost per unit is $1.15 per direct labor hour at 58,000 hours, which is 100% of normal capacity. Determine the fixed factory overhead volume variance.

SHOW ME HOW

BE 22-5 Standard cost journal entries
Obj. 5

Bellingham Company produced 15,000 units that require 2.5 standard pounds per unit at a $3.75 standard price per pound. The company actually used 36,000 pounds in production. Journalize the entry to record the standard direct materials used in production.

BE 22-6 Income statement with variances   **Obj. 5**

Prepare an income statement through gross profit for Bellingham Company for the month ending March 31 using the variance data from Brief Exercises 1, 2, 3, and 4. Assume Bellingham sold 15,000 units at $172 per unit.

BE 22-7 Activity inputs and outputs   **Obj. 6**

The following are inputs and outputs to the cooking process of a restaurant:

Number of times ingredients are missing
Number of customer complaints
Number of hours kitchen equipment is down for repairs
Number of server order mistakes
Percent of meals prepared on time
Number of unexpected cook absences

Identify whether each is an input or output to the cooking process.

Exercises

EX 22-1 Standard direct materials cost per unit   **Obj. 2**

Roanoke Company produces chocolate bars. The primary materials used in producing chocolate bars are cocoa, sugar, and milk. The standard costs for a batch of chocolate (5,200 bars) are as follows:

Ingredient	Quantity	Price
Cocoa	400 lbs.	$1.25 per lb.
Sugar	80 lbs.	$0.40 per lb.
Milk	120 gal.	$2.50 per gal.

Determine the standard direct materials cost per bar of chocolate.

EX 22-2 Standard product cost   **Obj. 2**

Sana Rosa Furniture Company manufactures designer home furniture. Sana Rosa uses a standard cost system. The direct labor, direct materials, and factory overhead standards for an unfinished dining room table are as follows:

Direct labor:	standard rate	$18.00 per hr.
	standard time per unit	3.5 hrs.
Direct materials (oak):	standard price	$15.00 per bd. ft.
	standard quantity	26 bd. ft.
Variable factory overhead:	standard rate	$4.20 per direct labor hr.
Fixed factory overhead:	standard rate	$1.80 per direct labor hr.

A. Determine the standard cost per dining room table.

B. ▬▬▬▶ Why would Sana Rosa Furniture Company use a standard cost system?

EX 22-3 Budget performance report   **Obj. 2**

✔ B. Direct labor cost variance, $(580) F

Genie in a Bottle Company (GBC) manufactures plastic two-liter bottles for the beverage industry. The cost standards per 100 two-liter bottles are as follows:

Cost Category	Standard Cost per 100 Two-Liter Bottles
Direct labor	$ 2.00
Direct materials	9.10
Factory overhead	0.55
Total	$11.65

(Continued)

At the beginning of July, GBC management planned to produce 400,000 bottles. The actual number of bottles produced for July was 406,000 bottles. The actual costs for July of the current year were as follows:

Cost Category	Actual Cost for the Month Ended July 31
Direct labor	$ 7,540
Direct materials	35,750
Factory overhead	2,680
Total	$45,970

A. Prepare the July manufacturing standard cost budget (direct labor, direct materials, and factory overhead) for GBC, assuming planned production.

B. Prepare a budget performance report for manufacturing costs, showing the total cost variances for direct materials, direct labor, and factory overhead for July.

C. ➤ Interpret the budget performance report.

EX 22-4 Direct materials variances
✔ A. Price variance, $7,250 U

Obj. 3

The following data relate to the direct materials cost for the production of 10,000 automobile tires:

Actual:	145,000 lbs. at $2.80 per lb.
Standard:	150,000 lbs. at $2.75 per lb.

SHOW ME HOW

A. Determine the direct materials price variance, direct materials quantity variance, and total direct materials cost variance.

B. ➤ To whom should the variances be reported for analysis and control?

EX 22-5 Direct materials variances

Obj. 3

✔ Quantity variance, $300 U

Silicone Engine Inc. produces wrist-worn tablet computers. The company uses Thin Film Crystal (TFC) LCD displays for its products. Each tablet uses one display. The company produced 580 tablets during December. However, due to LCD defects, the company actually used 600 LCD displays during December. Each display has a standard cost of $15.00. Six hundred LCD displays were purchased for December production at a cost of $8,550.

SHOW ME HOW

Determine the price variance, quantity variance, and total direct materials cost variance for December.

SHOW ME HOW

EX 22-6 Standard direct materials cost per unit from variance data

Obj. 2, 3

The following data relating to direct materials cost for October of the current year are taken from the records of Good Clean Fun Inc., a manufacturer of organic toys:

Quantity of direct materials used	3,000 lbs.
Actual unit price of direct materials	$5.50 per lb.
Units of finished product manufactured	1,400 units
Standard direct materials per unit of finished product	2 lbs.
Direct materials quantity variance—unfavorable	$1,000
Direct materials price variance—unfavorable	$1,500

Determine the standard direct materials cost per unit of finished product, assuming that there was no inventory of work in process at either the beginning or the end of the month.

EX 22-7 Standard product cost, direct materials variance

Obj. 2, 3

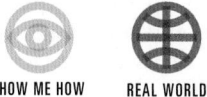

✔ A. $1.25 per lb.

SHOW ME HOW   REAL WORLD

H.J. Heinz Company uses standards to control its materials costs. Assume that a batch of ketchup (3,128 pounds) has the following standards:

	Standard Quantity	Standard Price
Whole tomatoes	4,000 lbs.	$ 0.60 per lb.
Vinegar	260 gal.	2.25 per gal.
Corn syrup	25 gal.	28.00 per gal.
Salt	100 lbs.	2.25 per lb.

The actual materials in a batch may vary from the standard due to tomato characteristics. Assume that the actual quantities of materials for batch K-111 were as follows:

4,250 lbs. of tomatoes
275 gal. of vinegar
22 gal. of corn syrup
90 lbs. of salt

A. Determine the standard unit materials cost per pound for a standard batch.

B. Determine the direct materials quantity variance for batch K-111. Round your answer to the nearest cent.

EX 22-8 Direct labor variances

Obj. 3

✔ A. Rate variance, $(4,225) F

SHOW ME HOW

The following data relate to labor cost for production of 20,000 cellular telephones:

Actual:	8,450 hrs. at $22.50
Standard:	8,400 hrs. at $23.00

A. Determine the direct labor rate variance, direct labor time variance, and total direct labor cost variance.

B. ▬▬▶ Discuss what might have caused these variances.

EX 22-9 Direct labor variances

Obj. 3, 5

✔ A. Time variance, $(5,600) F

SHOW ME HOW

La Batre Bicycle Company manufactures commuter bicycles from recycled materials. The following data for July of the current year are available:

Quantity of direct labor used	5,050 hrs.
Actual rate for direct labor	$16.80 per hr.
Bicycles completed in April	1,000 bicycles
Standard direct labor per bicycle	5.4 hrs.
Standard rate for direct labor	$16.00 per hr.

A. Determine the direct labor rate variance, direct labor time variance, and total direct labor cost variance.

B. How much direct labor should be debited to Work in Process?

EX 22-10 Direct labor variances

Obj. 3

✔ A. Cutting Department rate variance, $(638) F

Greeson Clothes Company produced 25,000 units during June of the current year. The Cutting Department used 6,380 direct labor hours at an actual rate of $10.90 per hour. The Sewing Department used 9,875 direct labor hours at an actual rate of $11.12 per hour. Assume there were no work in process inventories in either department at the beginning or end of the month. The standard labor rate is $11.00. The standard labor time for the Cutting and Sewing departments is 0.25 hour and 0.4 hour per unit, respectively.

A. Determine the direct labor rate, direct labor time, and total direct labor cost variance for the (1) Cutting Department and (2) Sewing Department.

B. ▬▬▶ Interpret your results.

EX 22-11   Direct labor variances for a service company

Obj. 3

✔ A. Direct labor rate variance, $(12) F

SHOW ME HOW

Hit-n-Run Food Trucks, Inc. owns and operates food trucks (mobile kitchens) throughout the west coast. The company's employees have varying wage levels depending on their experience and length of time with the company. Employees work 8-hour shifts and are assigned to a truck each day based on labor needs to support the daily menu. One of its trucks, Jose O'Brien's Mobile Fiesta, specializes in Irish-Mexican fusion cuisine. The truck offers a single menu item that changes daily. On November 11, the truck prepared 200 of its most popular item, the Irish Breakfast Enchilada. The following data are available for that day:

Quantity of direct labor used (3 employees, working 8-hour shifts)	24 hrs.
Actual rate for direct labor	$15.00 per hr.
Standard direct labor per meal	0.1 hr.
Standard rate for direct labor	$15.50 per hr.

A. Determine the direct labor rate variance, direct labor time variance, and total direct labor cost variance.

B. Discuss what might have caused these variances.

EX 22-12   Direct materials and direct labor variances

Obj. 3

✔ Direct materials quantity variance, $1,100 U

SHOW ME HOW

At the beginning of June, Bezco Toy Company budgeted 5,000 toy action figures to be manufactured in June at standard direct materials and direct labor costs as follows:

Direct materials	$50,000
Direct labor	36,000
Total	$86,000

The standard materials price is $4.00 per pound. The standard direct labor rate is $18.00 per hour. At the end of June, the actual direct materials and direct labor costs were as follows:

Actual direct materials	$49,600
Actual direct labor	34,020
Total	$83,620

There were no direct materials price or direct labor rate variances for June. In addition, assume no changes in the direct materials inventory balances in June. Bezco Toy Company actually produced 4,850 units during June.

Determine the direct materials quantity and direct labor time variances.

EX 22-13   Flexible overhead budget

Obj. 4

✔ Total factory overhead, 22,000 hrs., $443,600

Leno Manufacturing Company prepared the following factory overhead cost budget for the Press Department for October of the current year, during which it expected to require 20,000 hours of productive capacity in the department:

Variable overhead costs:		
Indirect factory labor	$180,000	
Power and light	12,000	
Indirect materials	64,000	
Total variable overhead cost		$256,000
Fixed overhead costs:		
Supervisory salaries	$ 80,000	
Depreciation of plant and equipment	50,000	
Insurance and property taxes	32,000	
Total fixed overhead cost		162,000
Total factory overhead cost		$418,000

Assuming that the estimated costs for November are the same as for October, prepare a flexible factory overhead cost budget for the Press Department for November for 18,000, 20,000, and 22,000 hours of production.

EX 22-14 Flexible overhead budget

Obj. 4

✔ B. $94,500

Wiki Wiki Company has determined that the variable overhead rate is $4.50 per direct labor hour in the Fabrication Department. The normal production capacity for the Fabrication Department is 10,000 hours for the month. Fixed costs are budgeted at $60,000 for the month.

A. Prepare a monthly factory overhead flexible budget for 9,000, 10,000, and 11,000 hours of production.

B. How much overhead would be applied to production if 9,000 hours were used in the department during the month?

EX 22-15 Factory overhead cost variances

Obj. 4

✔ Volume variance, $6,000 U

The following data relate to factory overhead cost for the production of 10,000 computers:

Actual:	Variable factory overhead	$262,000
	Fixed factory overhead	90,000
Standard:	14,000 hrs. at $25	350,000

If productive capacity of 100% was 15,000 hours and the total factory overhead cost budgeted at the level of 14,000 standard hours was $356,000, determine the variable factory overhead controllable variance, fixed factory overhead volume variance, and total factory overhead cost variance. The fixed factory overhead rate was $6.00 per hour.

EX 22-16 Factory overhead cost variances

Obj. 4

✔ A. $(13,000) F

EXCEL TEMPLATE

Blumen Textiles Corporation began April with a budget for 90,000 hours of production in the Weaving Department. The department has a full capacity of 100,000 hours under normal business conditions. The budgeted overhead at the planned volumes at the beginning of April was as follows:

Variable overhead	$540,000
Fixed overhead	240,000
Total	$780,000

The actual factory overhead was $782,000 for April. The actual fixed factory overhead was as budgeted. During April, the Weaving Department had standard hours at actual production volume of 92,500 hours.

A. Determine the variable factory overhead controllable variance.

B. Determine the fixed factory overhead volume variance.

EX 22-17 Factory overhead variance corrections

Obj. 4

The data related to Shunda Enterprises Inc.'s factory overhead cost for the production of 100,000 units of product are as follows:

Actual:	Variable factory overhead	$458,000
	Fixed factory overhead	494,000
Standard:	132,000 hrs. at $7.30 ($3.50 for variable factory overhead)	963,600

Productive capacity at 100% of normal was 130,000 hours, and the factory overhead cost budgeted at the level of 132,000 standard hours was $956,000. Based on these data, the chief cost accountant prepared the following variance analysis:

Variable factory overhead controllable variance:		
Actual variable factory overhead cost incurred	$458,000	
Budgeted variable factory overhead for 132,000 hours	462,000	
Variance—favorable		$ (4,000)
Fixed factory overhead volume variance:		
Normal productive capacity at 100%	130,000 hrs.	
Standard for amount produced	132,000	

(Continued)

Productive capacity not used	2,000 hrs.
Standard variable factory overhead rate	× $7.30
Variance—unfavorable	14,600
Total factory overhead cost variance—unfavorable	$10,600

Identify the errors in the factory overhead cost variance analysis.

EX 22-18   Factory overhead cost variance report   Obj. 4

✔ Net controllable variance, $900 U

EXCEL TEMPLATE

Tannin Products Inc. prepared the following factory overhead cost budget for the Trim Department for July of the current year, during which it expected to use 20,000 hours for production:

Variable overhead costs:		
Indirect factory labor	$46,000	
Power and light	12,000	
Indirect materials	20,000	
Total variable overhead cost		$ 78,000
Fixed overhead costs:		
Supervisory salaries	$54,500	
Depreciation of plant and equipment	40,000	
Insurance and property taxes	35,500	
Total fixed overhead cost		130,000
Total factory overhead cost		$208,000

Tannin has available 25,000 hours of monthly productive capacity in the Trim Department under normal business conditions. During July, the Trim Department actually used 22,000 hours for production. The actual fixed costs were as budgeted. The actual variable overhead for July was as follows:

Actual variable factory overhead costs:	
Indirect factory labor	$49,700
Power and light	13,000
Indirect materials	24,000
Total variable cost	$86,700

Construct a factory overhead cost variance report for the Trim Department for July.

EX 22-19   Recording standards in accounts   Obj. 5

Cioffi Manufacturing Company incorporates standards in its accounts and identifies variances at the time the manufacturing costs are incurred. Journalize the entries to record the following transactions:

A. Purchased 2,450 units of copper tubing on account at $52.00 per unit. The standard price is $48.50 per unit.

B. Used 1,900 units of copper tubing in the process of manufacturing 200 air conditioners. Ten units of copper tubing are required, at standard, to produce one air conditioner.

EX 22-20   Recording standards in accounts   Obj. 5

The Assembly Department produced 5,000 units of product during March. Each unit required 2.20 standard direct labor hours. There were 11,500 actual hours used in the Assembly Department during March at an actual rate of $17.60 per hour. The standard direct labor rate is $18.00 per hour. Assuming direct labor for a month is paid on the fifth day of the following month, journalize the direct labor in the Assembly Department on March 31.

EX 22-21   Income statement indicating standard cost variances   Obj. 5

✔ Income before income tax, $85,900

The following data were taken from the records of Griggs Company for December:

Administrative expenses	$100,800
Cost of goods sold (at standard)	550,000
Direct materials price variance—unfavorable	1,680
Direct materials quantity variance—favorable	(560)

Direct labor rate variance—favorable	(1,120)
Direct labor time variance—unfavorable	490
Variable factory overhead controllable variance—favorable	(210)
Fixed factory overhead volume variance—unfavorable	3,080
Interest expense	2,940
Sales	868,000
Selling expenses	125,000

Prepare an income statement for presentation to management.

EX 22-22 Nonfinancial performance measures   Obj. 6

Diamond Inc. is an Internet retailer of woodworking equipment. Customers order woodworking equipment from the company, using an online catalog. The company processes these orders and delivers the requested product from its warehouse. The company wants to provide customers with an excellent purchase experience in order to expand the business through favorable word-of-mouth advertising and to drive repeat business. To help monitor performance, the company developed a set of performance measures for its order placement and delivery process:

> Average computer response time to customer "clicks"
> Dollar amount of returned goods
> Elapsed time between customer order and product delivery
> Maintenance dollars divided by hardware investment
> Number of customer complaints divided by the number of orders
> Number of misfilled orders divided by the number of orders
> Number of orders per warehouse employee
> Number of page faults or errors due to software programming errors
> Number of software fixes per week
> Server (computer) downtime
> Training dollars per programmer

A. For each performance measure, identify it as either an input or output measure related to the "order placement and delivery" process.

B. ➤ Provide an explanation for each performance measure.

EX 22-23 Nonfinancial performance measures   Obj. 6

Alpha University wishes to monitor the efficiency and quality of its course registration process.

A. Identify three input and three output measures for this process.

B. ➤ Why would Alpha University use nonfinancial measures for monitoring this process?

Problems: Series A

PR 22-1A Direct materials and direct labor variance analysis   Obj. 2, 3

✔ C. Direct labor time variance, $600 U

SHOW ME HOW

Abbeville Fixture Company manufactures faucets in a small manufacturing facility. The faucets are made from brass. Manufacturing has 90 employees. Each employee presently provides 36 hours of labor per week. Information about a production week is as follows:

Standard wage per hr.	$15.00
Standard labor time per faucet	40 min.
Standard number of lbs. of brass	3 lbs.
Standard price per lb. of brass	$2.40
Actual price per lb. of brass	$2.50
Actual lbs. of brass used during the week	14,350 lbs.
Number of faucets produced during the week	4,800
Actual wage per hr.	$14.40
Actual hrs. for the week (90 employees × 36 hours)	3,240

(Continued)

Instructions

Determine (A) the standard cost per unit for direct materials and direct labor; (B) the direct materials price variance, direct materials quantity variance, and total direct materials cost variance; and (C) the direct labor rate variance, direct labor time variance, and total direct labor cost variance.

PR 22-2A Flexible budgeting and variance analysis

Obj. 1, 2, 3

✔ 1. A. Direct materials quantity variance, $(625) F

EXCEL TEMPLATE

I Love My Chocolate Company makes dark chocolate and light chocolate. Both products require cocoa and sugar. The following planning information has been made available:

	Standard Amount per Case		
	Dark Chocolate	Light Chocolate	Standard Price per Pound
Cocoa	12 lbs.	8 lbs.	$7.25
Sugar	10 lbs.	14 lbs.	1.40
Standard labor time	0.50 hr.	0.60 hr.	

	Dark Chocolate	Light Chocolate
Planned production	4,700 cases	11,000 cases
Standard labor rate	$15.50 per hr.	$15.50 per hr.

I Love My Chocolate Company does not expect there to be any beginning or ending inventories of cocoa or sugar. At the end of the budget year, I Love My Chocolate Company had the following actual results:

	Dark Chocolate	Light Chocolate
Actual production (cases)	5,000	10,000

	Actual Price per Pound	Actual Pounds Purchased and Used
Cocoa	$7.33	140,300
Sugar	1.35	188,000

	Actual Labor Rate	Actual Labor Hours Used
Dark chocolate	$15.25 per hr.	2,360
Light chocolate	15.80 per hr.	6,120

Instructions

1. Prepare the following variance analyses for both chocolates and the total, based on the actual results and production levels at the end of the budget year:

   A. Direct materials price, quantity, and total variance.

   B. Direct labor rate, time, and total variance.

2. ▬▬▶ Why are the standard amounts in part (1) based on the actual production for the year instead of the planned production for the year?

PR 22-3A Direct materials, direct labor, and factory overhead cost variance analysis

Obj. 3, 4

✔ C. Controllable variance, $(4,800) F

EXCEL TEMPLATE

Mackinaw Inc. processes a base chemical into plastic. Standard costs and actual costs for direct materials, direct labor, and factory overhead incurred for the manufacture of 40,000 units of product were as follows:

	Standard Costs	Actual Costs
Direct materials	120,000 lbs. at $3.20 per lb.	118,500 lbs. at $3.25 per lb.
Direct labor	12,000 hrs. at $24.40 per hr.	11,700 hrs. at $25.00 per hr.
Factory overhead	Rates per direct labor hr., based on 100% of normal capacity of 15,000 direct labor hrs.:	
	Variable cost, $8.00	$91,200 variable cost
	Fixed cost, $10.00	$150,000 fixed cost

Each unit requires 0.3 hour of direct labor.

Instructions

Determine (A) the direct materials price variance, direct materials quantity variance, and total direct materials cost variance; (B) the direct labor rate variance, direct labor time variance, and total direct labor cost variance; and (C) the variable factory overhead controllable variance, fixed factory overhead volume variance, and total factory overhead cost variance.

PR 22-4A   Factory overhead cost variance report   Obj. 4

✔ Controllable
variance, $770 U

EXCEL TEMPLATE   GENERAL LEDGER

Tiger Equipment Inc., a manufacturer of construction equipment, prepared the following factory overhead cost budget for the Welding Department for May of the current year. The company expected to operate the department at 100% of normal capacity of 8,400 hours.

Variable costs:		
Indirect factory wages	$30,240	
Power and light	20,160	
Indirect materials	16,800	
Total variable cost		$ 67,200
Fixed costs:		
Supervisory salaries	$20,000	
Depreciation of plant and equipment	36,200	
Insurance and property taxes	15,200	
Total fixed cost		71,400
Total factory overhead cost		$138,600

During May, the department operated at 8,860 hours, and the factory overhead costs incurred were indirect factory wages, $32,400; power and light, $21,000; indirect materials, $18,250; supervisory salaries, $20,000; depreciation of plant and equipment, $36,200; and insurance and property taxes, $15,200.

Instructions

Prepare a factory overhead cost variance report for May. To be useful for cost control, the budgeted amounts should be based on 8,860 hours.

PR 22-5A   Standards for nonmanufacturing expenses   Obj. 3, 6

✔ 3. $1,600 U

CodeHead Software Inc. does software development. One important activity in software development is writing software code. The manager of the WordPro Development Team determined that the average software programmer could write 25 lines of code in an hour. The plan for the first week in May called for 4,650 lines of code to be written on the WordPro product. The WordPro Team has five programmers. Each programmer is hired from an employment firm that requires temporary employees to be hired for a minimum of a 40-hour week. Programmers are paid $32.00 per hour. The manager offered a bonus if the team could generate more lines for the week, without overtime. Due to a project emergency, the programmers wrote more code in the first week of May than planned. The actual amount of code written in the first week of May was 5,650 lines, without overtime. As a result, the bonus caused the average programmer's hourly rate to increase to $40.00 per hour during the first week in May.

Instructions

1. If the team generated 4,650 lines of code according to the original plan, what would have been the labor time variance?

2. What was the actual labor time variance as a result of generating 5,650 lines of code?

3. What was the labor rate variance as a result of the bonus?

4. ▬▬▶ Are there any performance-related issues that the labor time and rate variances fail to consider? Explain.

5. The manager is trying to determine if a better decision would have been to hire a temporary programmer to meet the higher programming demand in the first week of May, rather than paying out the bonus. If another employee was hired from the employment firm, what would have been the labor time variance in the first week?

6. ▬▬▶ Which decision is better, paying the bonus or hiring another programmer?

Problems: Series B

PR 22-1B   Direct materials and direct labor variance analysis   Obj. 2, 3

Lenni Clothing Co. manufactures clothing in a small manufacturing facility. Manufacturing has 25 employees. Each employee presently provides 40 hours of productive labor per week. Information about a production week is as follows:

Standard wage per hr.	$12.00
Standard labor time per unit	12 min.
Standard number of yds. of fabric per unit	5.0 yds.
Standard price per yd. of fabric	$5.00
Actual price per yd. of fabric	$5.10
Actual yds. of fabric used during the week	26,200 yds.
Number of units produced during the week	5,220
Actual wage per hr.	$11.80
Actual hrs. for the week	1,000 hrs.

Instructions

Determine (A) the standard cost per unit for direct materials and direct labor; (B) the price variance, quantity variance, and total direct materials cost variance; and (C) the rate variance, time variance, and total direct labor cost variance.

PR 22-2B   Flexible budgeting and variance analysis   Obj. 1, 2, 3

I'm Really Cold Coat Company makes women's and men's coats. Both products require filler and lining material. The following planning information has been made available:

	Standard Amount per Unit		
	Women's Coats	Men's Coats	Standard Price per Unit
Filler	4.0 lbs.	5.20 lbs.	$2.00 per lb.
Liner	7.00 yds.	9.40 yds.	8.00 per yd.
Standard labor time	0.40 hr.	0.50 hr.	

	Women's Coats	Men's Coats
Planned production	5,000 units	6,200 units
Standard labor rate	$14.00 per hr.	$13.00 per hr.

I'm Really Cold Coat Company does not expect there to be any beginning or ending inventories of filler and lining material. At the end of the budget year, I'm Really Cold Coat Company experienced the following actual results:

	Women's Coats	Men's Coats
Actual production	4,400	5,800

	Actual Price per Unit	Actual Quantity Purchased and Used
Filler	$1.90 per lb.	48,000
Liner	8.20 per yd.	85,100

	Actual Labor Rate	Actual Labor Hours Used
Women's coats	$14.10 per hr.	1,825
Men's coats	13.30 per hr.	2,800

The expected beginning inventory and desired ending inventory were realized.

Instructions

1. Prepare the following variance analyses for both coats and the total, based on the actual results and production levels at the end of the budget year:

   A. Direct materials price, quantity, and total variance.

   B. Direct labor rate, time, and total variance.

2. ━━━━▶ Why are the standard amounts in part (1) based on the actual production at the end of the year instead of the planned production at the beginning of the year?

PR 22-3B Direct materials, direct labor, and factory overhead cost variance analysis

Obj. 3, 4

✔ A. Direct materials price variance, $10,100 U

EXCEL TEMPLATE

Road Gripper Tire Co. manufactures automobile tires. Standard costs and actual costs for direct materials, direct labor, and factory overhead incurred for the manufacture of 4,160 tires were as follows:

	Standard Costs	Actual Costs
Direct materials	100,000 lbs. at $6.40	101,000 lbs. at $6.50
Direct labor	2,080 hrs. at $15.75	2,000 hrs. at $15.40
Factory overhead	Rates per direct labor hr., based on 100% of normal capacity of 2,000 direct labor hrs.:	
	Variable cost, $4.00	$8,200 variable cost
	Fixed cost, $6.00	$12,000 fixed cost

Each tire requires 0.5 hour of direct labor.

Instructions

Determine (A) the direct materials price variance, direct materials quantity variance, and total direct materials cost variance; (B) the direct labor rate variance, direct labor time variance, and total direct labor cost variance; and (C) the variable factory overhead controllable variance, fixed factory overhead volume variance, and total factory overhead cost variance.

PR 22-4B Factory overhead cost variance report

Obj. 4

✔ Controllable variance, $(1,450) F

EXCEL TEMPLATE GENERAL LEDGER

Feeling Better Medical Inc., a manufacturer of disposable medical supplies, prepared the following factory overhead cost budget for the Assembly Department for October of the current year. The company expected to operate the department at 100% of normal capacity of 30,000 hours.

Variable costs:		
Indirect factory wages	$247,500	
Power and light	189,000	
Indirect materials	52,500	
Total variable cost		$489,000
Fixed costs:		
Supervisory salaries	$126,000	
Depreciation of plant and equipment	70,000	
Insurance and property taxes	44,000	
Total fixed cost		240,000
Total factory overhead cost		$729,000

During October, the department operated at 28,500 hours, and the factory overhead costs incurred were indirect factory wages, $234,000; power and light, $178,500; indirect materials, $50,600; supervisory salaries, $126,000; depreciation of plant and equipment, $70,000; and insurance and property taxes, $44,000.

Instructions

Prepare a factory overhead cost variance report for October. To be useful for cost control, the budgeted amounts should be based on 28,500 hours.

PR 22-5B   Standards for nonmanufacturing expenses for a service company   Obj. 3, 6

✔ 2. $(161) F

The Radiology Department provides imaging services for Emergency Medical Center. One important activity in the Radiology Department is transcribing digitally recorded analyses of images into a written report. The manager of the Radiology Department determined that the average transcriptionist could type 700 lines of a report in an hour. The plan for the first week in May called for 81,900 typed lines to be written. The Radiology Department has three transcriptionists. Each transcriptionist is hired from an employment firm that requires temporary employees to be hired for a minimum of a 40-hour week. Transcriptionists are paid $23.00 per hour. The manager offered a bonus if the department could type more lines for the week, without overtime. Due to high service demands, the transcriptionists typed more lines in the first week of May than planned. The actual amount of lines typed in the first week of May was 88,900 lines, without overtime. As a result, the bonus caused the average transcriptionist hourly rate to increase to $30.00 per hour during the first week in May.

Instructions

1. If the department typed 81,900 lines according to the original plan, what would have been the labor time variance?

2. What was the labor time variance as a result of typing 88,900 lines?

3. What was the labor rate variance as a result of the bonus?

4. The manager is trying to determine if a better decision would have been to hire a temporary transcriptionist to meet the higher typing demands in the first week of May, rather than paying out the bonus. If another employee was hired from the employment firm, what would have been the labor time variance in the first week?

5. ➡ Which decision is better, paying the bonus or hiring another transcriptionist?

6. ➡ Are there any performance-related issues that the labor time and rate variances fail to consider? Explain.

Comprehensive Problem 5

Genuine Spice Inc. began operations on January 1 of the current year. The company produces 8-ounce bottles of hand and body lotion called *Eternal Beauty*. The lotion is sold wholesale in 12-bottle cases for $100 per case. There is a selling commission of $20 per case. The January direct materials, direct labor, and factory overhead costs are as follows:

DIRECT MATERIALS

	Cost Behavior	Units per Case	Cost per Unit	Direct Materials Cost per Case
Cream base	Variable	100 ozs.	$0.02	$ 2.00
Natural oils	Variable	30 ozs.	0.30	9.00
Bottle (8-oz.)	Variable	12 bottles	0.50	6.00
				$17.00

DIRECT LABOR

Department	Cost Behavior	Time per Case	Labor Rate per Hour	Direct Labor Cost per Case
Mixing	Variable	20 min.	$18.00	$6.00
Filling	Variable	5	14.40	1.20
		25 min.		$7.20

FACTORY OVERHEAD

	Cost Behavior	Total Cost
Utilities	Mixed	$ 600
Facility lease	Fixed	14,000
Equipment depreciation	Fixed	4,300
Supplies	Fixed	660
		$19,560

Part A—Break-Even Analysis

✔ 2. $55.60

The management of Genuine Spice Inc. wishes to determine the number of cases required to break even per month. The utilities cost, which is part of factory overhead, is a mixed cost. The following information was gathered from the first six months of operation regarding this cost:

Month	Case Production	Utility Total Cost
January	500	$600
February	800	660
March	1,200	740
April	1,100	720
May	950	690
June	1,025	705

Instructions

1. Determine the fixed and variable portions of the utility cost using the high-low method.
2. Determine the contribution margin per case.
3. Determine the fixed costs per month, including the utility fixed cost from part (1).
4. Determine the break-even number of cases per month.

Part B—August Budgets

✔ 6. Bottles purchased, $8,070

During July of the current year, the management of Genuine Spice Inc. asked the controller to prepare August manufacturing and income statement budgets. Demand was expected to be 1,500 cases at $100 per case for August. Inventory planning information is provided as follows:

Finished Goods Inventory:

	Cases	Cost
Estimated finished goods inventory, August 1	300	$12,000
Desired finished goods inventory, August 31	175	7,000

Materials Inventory:

	Cream Base (ozs.)	Oils (ozs.)	Bottles (bottles)
Estimated materials inventory, August 1	250	290	600
Desired materials inventory, August 31	1,000	360	240

There was negligible work in process inventory assumed for either the beginning or end of the month; thus, none was assumed. In addition, there was no change in the cost per unit or estimated units per case operating data from January.

Instructions

5. Prepare the August production budget.
6. Prepare the August direct materials purchases budget.
7. Prepare the August direct labor budget. Round the hours required for production to the nearest hour.
8. Prepare the August factory overhead budget.
9. Prepare the August budgeted income statement, including selling expenses.

Part C—August Variance Analysis

✔ 11. Filling Dept. direct labor time variance, $216 U

✔ 12. $5 U

During September of the current year, the controller was asked to perform variance analyses for August. The January operating data provided the standard prices, rates, times, and quantities

(Continued)

per case. There were 1,500 actual cases produced during August, which was 250 more cases than planned at the beginning of the month. Actual data for August were as follows:

	Actual Direct Materials Price per Unit	Actual Direct Materials Quantity per Case
Cream base	$0.016 per oz.	102 ozs.
Natural oils	$0.32 per oz.	31 ozs.
Bottle (8-oz.)	$0.42 per bottle	12.5 bottles

	Actual Direct Labor Rate	Actual Direct Labor Time per Case
Mixing	$18.20	19.50 min.
Filling	14.00	5.60 min.

Actual variable overhead	$305.00
Normal volume	1,600 cases

The prices of the materials were different than standard due to fluctuations in market prices. The standard quantity of materials used per case was an ideal standard. The Mixing Department used a higher grade labor classification during the month, thus causing the actual labor rate to exceed standard. The Filling Department used a lower grade labor classification during the month, thus causing the actual labor rate to be less than standard.

Instructions

10. Determine and interpret the direct materials price and quantity variances for the three materials.

11. Determine and interpret the direct labor rate and time variances for the two departments. Round hours to the nearest hour.

12. Determine and interpret the factory overhead controllable variance.

13. Determine and interpret the factory overhead volume variance.

14. Why are the standard direct labor and direct materials costs in the calculations for parts (10) and (11) based on the actual 1,500-case production volume rather than the planned 1,250 cases of production used in the budgets for parts (6) and (7)?

Analysis for Decision Making

ADM-1 Admissions time variance

Valley Hospital began using standards to evaluate its Admissions Department. The standard was broken into two types of admissions as follows:

Type of Admission	Standard Time to Complete Admission Record
Unscheduled	30 min.
Scheduled	15 min.

The unscheduled admission took longer because name, address, and insurance information needed to be determined and verified at the time of admission. Information was collected on scheduled admissions prior to admitting the patient, thus requiring less time in admissions.

The Admissions Department employs four full-time people for 40 hours per week at $15 per hour. For the most recent week, the department handled 140 unscheduled and 340 scheduled admissions.

A. How much was actually spent on labor for the week?

B. What are the standard hours for the actual volume of work for the week?

C. Compute the direct labor time variance, and report how well the department performed for the week.

D. ▬▬▬► What are some factors that may cause an unfavorable direct labor time variance for the Admissions Department?

REAL WORLD

ADM-2 United States Postal Service: Mail sorting time variance

One of the operations in the United States Postal Service is a mechanical mail sorting operation. In this operation, handwritten letter mail is sorted at a rate of 1.5 letters per second. An operator sitting at a keyboard mechanically sorts the letter from a three-digit code. The manager of the mechanical sorting operation wishes to determine the number of temporary employees to hire for December. The manager estimates that there will be an additional 24,192,000 pieces of mail in December, due to the upcoming holiday season.

Assume that the sorting operators are temporary employees. The union contract requires that temporary employees be hired for one month at a time. Each temporary employee is hired to work 160 hours in the month.

A. How many temporary employees should the manager hire for December?

B. If each temporary employee earns a standard $17 per hour, what would be the direct labor time variance if the actual number of additional letters sorted in December was 23,895,000?

ADM-3 Direct labor time variance

Maywood City Police uses variance analysis to monitor police staffing. The following table identifies three common police activities, the standard time to perform each activity, and their actual frequency to establish the expected cost to serve these activities.

Police Activity	Standard Hours per Activity	Actual Activities for Year	Total Employee Hours
Theft	0.60	7,000	4,200
Arrest	1.50	18,000	27,000
Patrol activities	0.30	9,000	2,700
			33,900

The police are paid $25 per hour.

The actual amount of hours per activity for the year were as follows:

Police Activity	Actual Hours per Activity
Theft	0.75
Arrest	2.00
Patrol activities	0.40

A. Determine the total budgeted cost to perform the three police activities.

B. Determine the total actual cost to perform the three police activities.

C. Determine the direct labor time variance.

D. ▬▬▬► What does the time variance suggest?

Take It Further

ETHICS

TIF 22-1   Ethics in Action

Dash Riprock is a cost analyst with Safe Insurance Company. Safe is applying standards to its claims payment operations. Claims payment is a repetitive operation that could be evaluated with standards. Dash used time and motion studies to identify an ideal standard of 36 claims processed per hour. The Claims Processing Department manager, Henry Tudor, has rejected this standard and has argued that the standard should be 30 claims processed per hour. Henry and Dash were unable to agree, so they decided to discuss this matter openly at a joint meeting with the Vice President of Operations, who would arbitrate a final decision. Prior to the meeting, Dash wrote the following memo to the Vice President:

To: Anne Boleyn, Vice President of Operations

From: Dash Riprock

Re: Standards in the Claims Processing Department

> As you know, Henry and I are scheduled to meet with you to discuss our disagreement about the appropriate standards for the Claims Processing Department. I have conducted time and motion studies and have determined that the ideal standard is 36 claims processed per hour. Henry argues that 30 claims processed per hour would be more appropriate. I believe he is trying to "pad" the budget with some slack. I'm not sure what he is trying to get away with, but I believe a tight standard will drive efficiency up in his area. I hope you will agree when we meet with you next week.

 Discuss the ethical and professional issues in this situation.

REAL WORLD

TIF 22-2   Team Activity

Many city and county governments realize that an entity can only control what it measures. As a result, many municipal governments are introducing nonfinancial performance measures to help improve municipal services. In a group, use the Google search engine to perform a search for "municipal government performance measurement." Google will provide a list of Internet sites that outline various city efforts in using nonfinancial performance measures.

 As a group, report on the types of measures used by one of the cities from the search.

TIF 22-3   Communication

The senior management of Tungston Company has proposed the following three performance measures for the company:

1. Net income as a percent of stockholders' equity

2. Revenue growth

3. Employee satisfaction

Management believes these three measures combine both financial and nonfinancial measures and are thus superior to using only financial measures.

 Write a brief memo to David Tungston, the company president, providing suggestions on how to improve the company's performance measurement system.

Concepts and Principles

Chapter 15 *Introduction to Managerial Accounting*

Developing Information

COST SYSTEMS	COST BEHAVIOR

Chapter 16 *Job Order Costing*

Chapter 17 *Process Cost Systems*

Chapter 18 *Activity-Based Costing*

Chapter 19 *Cost-Volume-Profit Analysis*

Decision Making

EVALUATING PERFORMANCE	COMPARING ALTERNATIVES

Chapter 20 *Variable Costing for Management Analysis*

Chapter 21 *Budgeting*

Chapter 22 *Evaluating Variances from Standard Costs*

Chapter 23 *Evaluating Decentralized Operations*

Chapter 24 *Differential Analysis and Product Pricing*

Chapter 25 *Capital Investment Analysis*

Chapter 26 *Lean Manufacturing*

Caterpillar Inc.

Have you ever wondered why large retail stores like **Macy's**, **JCPenney**, and **Sears** are divided into departments? Organizing into departments allows retailers to provide products and expertise in specialized areas while offering a wide range of products. Departments also allow companies to assign responsibility for financial performance. This information can be used to make product decisions, evaluate operations, and guide company strategy. Strong departmental performance might be attributable to a good department manager, while weak departmental performance may be the result of a product mix that has low customer appeal. By tracking departmental performance, companies can identify and reward excellent performance and take corrective action in departments that are performing poorly.

Like retailers, most businesses organize into operational units, such as divisions and departments. For example, **Caterpillar Inc.** manufactures a variety of equipment and machinery and is organized into a number of different segments, including Construction Industries, Resource Industries, Energy & Transportation, and Financial Products. The Construction Industries segment manufactures construction equipment such as tractors, dump trucks, and loaders. The Resource Industries segment makes equipment for the mining industry, such as off-highway and mining trucks. The Energy & Transportation segment manufactures equipment that is used to generate power, such as engines and turbines for power plants and railroads. The Financial Products segment provides financing for Caterpillar products to customers and dealers.

Managers at Caterpillar Inc. are responsible for running their business segment. Each segment is evaluated on segment profit, which excludes certain expense items from the calculation of profit that are not within the control of the business segment. The company uses segment profit to determine how to allocate resources between business segments and to plan and control the company's operations.

In this chapter, the role of accounting in assisting managers in planning and controlling organizational units, such as departments, divisions, and stores, is described and illustrated.

Source: www.caterpillar.com

What's Covered

Evaluating Decentralized Operations

Decentralized Operations
- Advantages (Obj. 1)
- Disadvantages (Obj. 1)

Responsibilty Accounting
- Cost Centers (Obj. 2)
- Profit Centers (Obj. 3)
- Investment Centers (Obj. 4)
- Balanced Scorecard (Obj. 4)

Transfer Pricing
- Market Price Approach (Obj. 5)
- Negotiated Price Approach (Obj. 5)
- Cost Price Approach (Obj. 5)

Learning Objectives

Obj. 1 Describe the advantages and disadvantages of decentralized operations.

Obj. 2 Prepare a responsibility accounting report for a cost center.

Obj. 3 Prepare responsibility accounting reports for a profit center.

Obj. 4 Compute and interpret the return on investment, the residual income, and the balanced scorecard for an investment center.

Obj. 5 Describe and illustrate how the market price, negotiated price, and cost price approaches to transfer pricing may be used by decentralized segments of a business.

Analysis for Decision Making

Describe and Illustrate the use of profit margin, investment turnover, and ROI in evaluating whether a company should expand through franchised or owner-operated stores.

Objective 1

Describe the advantages and disadvantages of decentralized operations.

Centralized and Decentralized Operations

In a *centralized* company, all major planning and operating decisions are made by top management. For example, a one-person, owner–manager-operated company is centralized because all plans and decisions are made by one person. In a small owner–manager-operated business, centralization may be desirable. This is because the owner–manager's close supervision ensures that the business will be operated in the way the owner–manager wishes.

In a *decentralized* company, managers of separate divisions or units are delegated operating responsibility. The division (unit) managers are responsible for planning and controlling the operations of their divisions. Divisions are often structured around products, customers, or regions.

The proper amount of decentralization for a company depends on the company's unique circumstances. For example, in some companies, division managers have authority over all operations, including fixed asset purchases. In other companies, division managers have authority over profits but not fixed asset purchases.

Advantages of Decentralization

For large companies, it is difficult for top management to:

- Maintain daily contact with all operations, and
- Maintain operating expertise in all product lines and services

In such cases, delegating authority to managers closest to the operations usually results in better decisions. These managers often anticipate and react to operating data more quickly than could top management. These managers can also focus their attention on becoming "experts" in their area of operation.

Decentralized operations provide excellent training for managers. Delegating responsibility allows managers to develop managerial experience early in their careers. This helps a company retain managers, some of whom may be later promoted to top management positions.

Managers of decentralized operations often work closely with customers. As a result, they tend to identify with customers and, thus, are often more creative in suggesting operating and product improvements. This helps create good customer relations.

Caterpillar uses a decentralized network of over a thousand dealers to sell its products.

Link to Caterpillar

Disadvantages of Decentralization

A primary disadvantage of decentralized operations is that decisions made by one manager may negatively affect the profits of the company. For example, managers of divisions whose products compete with one another might start a price war that decreases the profits of both divisions and, thus, the overall company.

Another disadvantage of decentralized operations is that assets and expenses may be duplicated across divisions. For example, each manager of a product line might have a separate sales force and office support staff.

The advantages and disadvantages of decentralization are summarized in Exhibit 1.

Advantages of Decentralization

- Allows managers closest to the operations to make decisions
- Provides excellent training for managers
- Allows managers to become experts in their area of operation
- Helps retain managers
- Improves creativity and customer relations

Disadvantages of Decentralization

- Decisions made by managers may negatively affect the profits of the company
- Duplicates assets and expenses

Exhibit 1

Advantages and Disadvantages of Decentralized Operations

Responsibility Accounting

In a decentralized business, accounting assists managers in evaluating and controlling their areas of responsibility, called *responsibility centers*. **Responsibility accounting** is the process of measuring and reporting operating data by responsibility center.

Why It Matters

Dover Corporation: Many Pieces, One Picture

Dover Corporation has grown over 45 years by acquiring more than 100 different manufacturing companies within a variety of industries. Dover uses a highly decentralized operating strategy. For example, of Dover's 30,000 employees, only about 50 employees staff the headquarters. Thus, almost all of the employees work within the 100 operating companies. The primary benefit of this approach is giving the operating companies room to respond to threats and opportunities without the bureaucratic hindrance of a centralized structure. As a result, the operating company presidents have unusual levels of autonomy. As stated by the company, "Dover company presidents set the direction of their own companies, make their own decisions, and nurture and grow their own organizations." The presidents are evaluated using metrics similar to those discussed in this chapter to keep the businesses aligned to the performance objectives of the overall organization.

Source: Dover Corporation Web Site, Dover's Culture and Operating Philosophy.

Three types of responsibility centers are as follows:

- *Cost centers,* which have responsibility over costs
- *Profit centers,* which have responsibility over revenues and costs
- *Investment centers,* which have responsibility over revenues, costs, and investment in assets

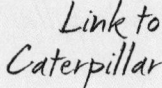

Link to Caterpillar **Caterpillar**'s corporate headquarters are located in Peoria, Illinois.

Objective 2

Prepare a responsibility accounting report for a cost center.

Responsibility Accounting for Cost Centers

A **cost center** manager has responsibility for controlling costs. For example, the supervisor of the Power Department has responsibility for the costs of providing power. A cost center manager does not make decisions concerning sales or the amount of fixed assets invested in the center.

Cost centers may vary in size from a small department to an entire manufacturing plant. In addition, cost centers may exist within other cost centers. For example, an entire university or college could be viewed as a cost center, and each college and department within the university could also be a cost center, as shown in Exhibit 2.

Exhibit 2

Cost Centers in a University

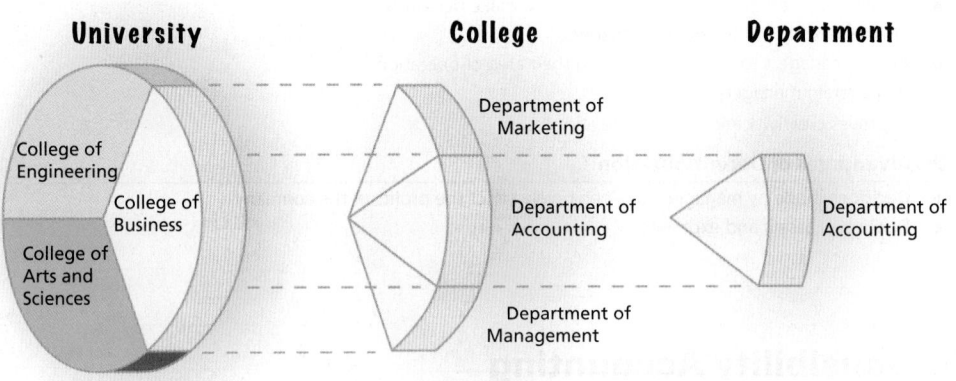

Responsibility accounting for cost centers focuses on the controlling and reporting of costs. Budget performance reports that report budgeted and actual costs are normally prepared for each cost center.

Link to Caterpillar **Caterpillar**'s "Corporate Services" group performs support services for its operating segments and is organized as a cost center.

Exhibit 3 illustrates budget performance reports for the following cost centers:

- Vice President, Production
- Manager, Plant A
- Supervisor, Department 1—Plant A

Exhibit 3 shows how cost centers are often linked together within a company. For example, the budget performance report for Department 1—Plant A supports the report for Plant A, which supports the report for the vice president of production.

Exhibit 3 Responsibility Accounting Reports for Cost Centers

Budget Performance Report
Vice President, Production
For the Month Ended October 31

	Budget	Actual	Over Budget	Under Budget
Administration	$ 19,500	$ 19,700	$ 200	
Plant A	467,475	470,330	2,855	
Plant B	395,225	394,300		$925
	$882,200	$884,330	$3,055	$925

Budget Performance Report
Manager, Plant A
For the Month Ended October 31

	Budget	Actual	Over Budget	Under Budget
Administration	$ 17,500	$ 17,350		$150
Department 1	109,725	111,280	$1,555	
Department 2	190,500	192,600	2,100	
Department 3	149,750	149,100		650
	$467,475	$470,330	$3,655	$800

Budget Performance Report
Supervisor, Department 1—Plant A
For the Month Ended October 31

	Budget	Actual	Over Budget	Under Budget
Factory wages	$ 58,100	$ 58,000		$100
Materials	32,500	34,225	$1,725	
Supervisory salaries	6,400	6,400		
Power and light	5,750	5,690		60
Depreciation of plant and equipment	4,000	4,000		
Maintenance	2,000	1,990		10
Insurance and property taxes	975	975		
	$109,725	$111,280	$1,725	$170

Vice President Production

Plant A   Plant B

Manager Plant A

Dept. 1   Dept. 2   Dept. 3

Supervisor Dept. 1

The reports in Exhibit 3 show the budgeted costs and actual costs along with the differences. Each difference is classified as either *over* budget or *under* budget. Such reports allow cost center managers to focus on areas of significant differences.

For example, the supervisor for Department 1 of Plant A can focus on why the materials cost was over budget. The supervisor might discover that excess materials were scrapped. This could be due to such factors as machine malfunctions, improperly trained employees, or low-quality materials.

As shown in Exhibit 3, responsibility accounting reports are usually more summarized for higher levels of management. For example, the budget performance report for the manager of Plant A shows only administration and departmental data. This report enables the plant manager to identify the departments responsible for major differences. Likewise, the report for the vice president of production summarizes the cost data for each plant.

Check Up Corner 23-1   Cost Center Responsibility Measures

Delinco Tech Inc. manufactures corrosion-resistant water pumps and fluid meters. Its Commercial Products Division is organized as a cost center. The division's budget for the month ended July 31, 20Y1, is as follows (in thousands):

Materials	$140,000
Factory wages	77,000
Supervisor salaries	15,500
Utilities	8,700
Depreciation of plant equipment	9,000
Maintenance	3,200
Insurance	750
Property taxes	800
	$254,950

During July, actual costs incurred in the Commercial Products Division were as follows:

Materials	$152,000
Factory wages	77,800
Supervisor salaries	15,500
Utilities	8,560
Depreciation of plant equipment	9,000
Maintenance	3,025
Insurance	750
Property taxes	820
	$267,455

Prepare a budget performance report for the director of the Commercial Products Division for July.

Solution:

The report shows the budgeted costs and actual costs along with the differences.

The report allows cost center managers to focus on areas of significant differences.

Budget Performance Report Director, Commercial Products Division For the Month Ended July 31, 20Y1				
	Budget	**Actual**	**Over Budget**	**Under Budget**
Materials..	$140,000	$152,000	$12,000	
Factory wages	77,000	77,800	800	
Supervisor salaries..........................	15,500	15,500		
Utilities...	8,700	8,560		$140
Depreciation of plant equipment.....	9,000	9,000		
Maintenance	3,200	3,025		175
Insurance...	750	750		
Property taxes	800	820	20	
	$254,950	$267,455	$12,820	$315

Each difference is classified as *over* budget or *under* budget.

Responsibility Accounting for Profit Centers

Objective 3

Prepare responsibility accounting reports for a profit center.

A **profit center** manager has the responsibility and authority for making decisions that affect revenues and costs and, thus, profits. Profit centers may be divisions, departments, or products.

The manager of a profit center does not make decisions concerning the fixed assets invested in the center. However, profit centers are an excellent training assignment for new managers.

Responsibility accounting for profit centers focuses on reporting revenues, expenses, and income from operations. Thus, responsibility accounting reports for profit centers take the form of income statements.

The profit center income statement should include only revenues and expenses that are controlled by the manager. **Controllable revenues** are revenues earned by the profit center. **Controllable expenses** are costs that can be influenced (controlled) by the decisions of profit center managers.

Service Department Charges

The controllable expenses of profit centers include *direct operating expenses* such as sales salaries and utility expenses. In addition, a profit center may incur expenses provided by internal centralized *service departments*. Examples of such service departments include the following:

- Research and Development
- Legal
- Telecommunications
- Information and Computer Systems
- Facilities Management
- Purchasing
- Advertising
- Payroll Accounting
- Transportation
- Human Resources

Caterpillar's research and development is conducted at its Tech Center in Mossville, Illinois.

Link to Caterpillar

Service department charges are *indirect* expenses to a profit center. They are similar to the expenses that would be incurred if the profit center purchased the services from outside the company. A profit center manager has control over service department expenses if the manager is free to choose how much service is used. In such cases, **service department charges** are allocated to profit centers based on the usage of the service by each profit center.

To illustrate, Nova Entertainment Group (NEG), a diversified entertainment company, is used. NEG has the following two operating divisions organized as profit centers:

- Theme Park Division
- Movie Production Division

The revenues and direct operating expenses for the two divisions follow. The operating expenses consist of direct expenses, such as the wages and salaries of a division's employees.

	Theme Park Division	Movie Production Division
Revenues	$6,000,000	$2,500,000
Operating expenses	2,495,000	405,000

NEG's service departments and the expenses they incurred for the year ended December 31, 20Y8, are as follows:

Purchasing	$400,000
Payroll Accounting	255,000
Legal	250,000
Total	$905,000

An activity base for each service department is used to charge service department expenses to the Theme Park and Movie Production divisions. The activity base for each service department is a measure of the services performed. For NEG, the service department activity bases are as follows:

Department	Activity Base
Purchasing	Number of purchase requisitions
Payroll Accounting	Number of payroll checks
Legal	Number of billed hours

The use of services by the Theme Park and Movie Production divisions is as follows:

	Service Usage		
Division	**Purchasing**	**Payroll Accounting**	**Legal**
Theme Park	25,000 purchase requisitions	12,000 payroll checks	100 billed hrs.
Movie Production	15,000	3,000	900
Total	40,000 purchase requisitions	15,000 payroll checks	1,000 billed hrs.

The rates at which services are charged to each division are called *service department charge rates*. These rates are computed as follows:

$$\text{Service Department Charge Rate} = \frac{\text{Service Department Expense}}{\text{Total Service Department Usage}}$$

NEG's service department charge rates are computed as follows:

$$\text{Purchasing Charge Rate} = \frac{\$400,000}{40,000 \text{ purchase requisitions}} = \$10 \text{ per purchase requisition}$$

$$\text{Payroll Charge Rate} = \frac{\$255,000}{15,000 \text{ payroll checks}} = \$17 \text{ per payroll check}$$

$$\text{Legal Charge Rate} = \frac{\$250,000}{1,000 \text{ billed hrs.}} = \$250 \text{ per hr.}$$

The services used by each division are multiplied by the service department charge rates to determine the service charges for each division, computed as follows:

$$\text{Service Department Charge} = \text{Service Usage} \times \text{Service Department Charge Rate}$$

Exhibit 4 illustrates the service department charges and related computations for NEG's Theme Park and Movie Production divisions.

The differences in the service department charges between the two divisions can be explained by the nature of their operations and, thus, usage of services. For example, the Theme Park Division employs many part-time employees who are paid weekly. As a result, the Theme Park Division requires 12,000 payroll checks and incurs a $204,000 payroll service department charge (12,000 × $17). In contrast, the Movie Production Division has more permanent employees who are paid monthly. Thus, the Movie Production Division requires only 3,000 payroll checks and incurs a payroll service department charge of $51,000 (3,000 × $17).

Nova Entertainment Group Service Department Charges to NEG Divisions For the Year Ended December 31, 20Y8		
Service Department	**Theme Park Division**	**Movie Production Division**
Purchasing (Note A)	$250,000	$150,000
Payroll Accounting (Note B)	204,000	51,000
Legal (Note C)..	25,000	225,000
Total service department charges	$479,000	$426,000

Note A:

25,000 purchase requisitions × $10 per purchase requisition = $250,000

15,000 purchase requisitions × $10 per purchase requisition = $150,000

Note B:

12,000 payroll checks × $17 per check = $204,000

3,000 payroll checks × $17 per check = $51,000

Note C:

100 hours × $250 per hour = $25,000

900 hours × $250 per hour = $225,000

Exhibit 4

Service Department Charges to NEG Divisions

Profit Center Reporting

The divisional income statements for NEG are shown in Exhibit 5.

Nova Entertainment Group Divisional Income Statements For the Year Ended December 31, 20Y8		
	Theme Park Division	**Movie Production Division**
Revenues*..	$6,000,000	$2,500,000
Operating expenses	2,495,000	405,000
Income from operations before service department charges...............................	$3,505,000	$2,095,000
Service department charges:		
Purchasing...	$ 250,000	$ 150,000
Payroll Accounting	204,000	51,000
Legal	25,000	225,000
Total service department charges	$ 479,000	$ 426,000
Income from operations	$3,026,000	$1,669,000

*For a profit center that sells products, the income statement would show: Sales – Cost of goods sold = Gross profit. The operating expenses would be deducted from the gross profit to get the income from operations before service department charges.

Exhibit 5

Divisional Income Statements—NEG

In evaluating the profit center manager, the income from operations should be compared over time to a budget. However, it should not be compared across profit centers because the profit centers are usually different in terms of size, products, and customers.

Check Up Corner 23-2   Profit Center Responsibility Reporting

Johnson Company has two divisions, East and West, that operate as profit centers. Sales, cost of goods sold, and selling expenses for the two divisions for the year ended December 31 are as follows:

	East Division	West Division
Sales	$3,000,000	$8,000,000
Cost of goods sold	1,650,000	4,200,000
Selling expenses	850,000	1,850,000

In addition, the company has two service departments, Legal and Tech Support.

The service department expenses for the year ended December 31 are as follows:

Legal Department	Tech Support Department
$350,000	$250,000

The Legal Department costs are charged to user divisions based on the number of hours of service, and the Tech Support Department costs are charged to user divisions based on the number of computers. The usage of service by the two divisions is as follows:

	Legal	Tech Support
East Division	500 hours	80 computers
West Division	1,500	120
Total	2,000 hours	200 computers

Prepare income statements for the year ended December 31, showing income from operations for the two divisions. Use two column headings: East and West.

Solution:

Johnson Company
Divisional Income Statements
For the Year Ended December 31

	East	West	
Sales	$3,000,000	$8,000,000	
Cost of goods sold	1,650,000	4,200,000	
Gross profit	$1,350,000	$3,800,000	
Selling expenses	850,000	1,850,000	
Income from operations before service departments charges	$ 500,000	$1,950,000	
Service department charges:			
Legal	$ 87,500	$ 262,500	← 500 hours × $175 per hour* 1,500 hours × $175 per hour*
Tech Support	100,000	150,000	← 120 computers × $1,250 per computer**
Total service department charges	$ 187,500	$ 412,500	
Income from operations	$ 312,500	$1,537,500	

80 computers × $1,250 per computer**

$$*\text{Legal Department Rate} = \frac{\$350,000}{2,000 \text{ hours}} = \$175 \text{ per hour of service}$$

$$**\text{Tech Support Department Rate} = \frac{\$250,000}{200 \text{ computers}} = \$1,250 \text{ per computer}$$

Responsibility Accounting for Investment Centers

Objective 4
Compute and interpret the return on investment, the residual income, and the balanced scorecard for an investment center.

An **investment center** manager has the responsibility and the authority to make decisions that affect not only costs and revenues but also the assets invested in the center. Investment centers are often used in diversified companies organized by divisions. In such cases, the divisional manager has authority similar to that of a chief operating officer or president of a company.

Caterpillar has four group presidents that are responsible for the operations of each of its four major segments: Construction, Resource, Energy & Transportation, and Financial Products. A fifth group president is responsible for three smaller operating segments.

Link to Caterpillar

Because investment center managers have responsibility for revenues and expenses, *income from operations* is part of investment center reporting. In addition, because the manager has responsibility for the assets invested in the center, the following two additional measures of performance are used:

- Return on investment
- Residual income

To illustrate, DataLink Inc., a cellular phone company with three regional divisions, is used. Condensed divisional income statements for the Northern, Central, and Southern divisions of DataLink are shown in Exhibit 6.

DataLink Inc. Divisional Income Statements For the Year Ended December 31, 20Y8			
	Northern Division	**Central Division**	**Southern Division**
Revenues	$560,000	$672,000	$750,000
Operating expenses.................................	336,000	470,400	562,500
Income from operations before service department charges	$224,000	$201,600	$187,500
Service department charges..........................	154,000	117,600	112,500
Income from operations.............................	$ 70,000	$ 84,000	$ 75,000

Exhibit 6
Divisional Income Statements— DataLink Inc.

Using only income from operations, the Central Division is the most profitable division. However, income from operations does not reflect the amount of assets invested in each center. For example, the Central Division could have twice as many assets as the Northern Division. For this reason, performance measures that consider the amount of invested assets, such as the return on investment and residual income, are used.

Return on Investment

Because investment center managers control the amount of assets invested in their centers, they should be evaluated based on the use of these assets. One measure that considers the amount of assets invested is the **return on investment (ROI)** or *return on assets*. It is computed as follows:

$$\text{Return on Investment (ROI)} = \frac{\text{Income from Operations}}{\text{Invested Assets}}$$

The return on investment is useful because the three factors subject to control by divisional managers (revenues, expenses, and invested assets) are considered. The higher the return on investment, the better the division is using its assets to generate income. In effect, the return on investment measures the income (return) on each dollar invested. As a result, the return on investment can be used as a common basis for comparing divisions with each other.

To illustrate, the invested assets of DataLink's three divisions are as follows:

	Invested Assets
Northern Division	$350,000
Central Division	700,000
Southern Division	500,000

Using the income from operations for each division shown in Exhibit 6, the return on investment for each division is computed as follows:

Northern Division:

$$\text{Return on Investment} = \frac{\text{Income from Operations}}{\text{Invested Assets}} = \frac{\$70,000}{\$350,000} = 20\%$$

Central Division:

$$\text{Return on Investment} = \frac{\text{Income from Operations}}{\text{Invested Assets}} = \frac{\$84,000}{\$700,000} = 12\%$$

Southern Division:

$$\text{Return on Investment} = \frac{\text{Income from Operations}}{\text{Invested Assets}} = \frac{\$75,000}{\$500,000} = 15\%$$

Although the Central Division generated the largest income from operations, its return on investment (12%) is the lowest. Hence, relative to the assets invested, the Central Division is the least profitable division. In comparison, the return on investment of the Northern Division is 20%, and the Southern Division is 15%.

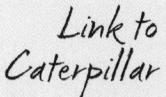

Based upon recent financial statements, the return on investment for each of **Caterpillar**'s four segments was as follows:

Construction	**Resource**	**Energy & Transportation**	**Financial Products**
35.2%	(1.0)%	37.9%	2.4%

To analyze differences in the return on investment across divisions, the **DuPont formula** for the return on investment is often used.[1] The DuPont formula views the return on investment as the product of the following two factors:

- **Profit margin**, which is the ratio of income from operations to sales.
- **Investment turnover**, which is the ratio of sales to invested assets.

[1] The DuPont formula was created by a financial executive of E. I. du Pont de Nemours and Company in 1919.

Using the DuPont formula, the return on investment is expressed as follows:

$$\text{Return on Investment} = \text{Profit Margin} \times \text{Investment Turnover}$$

$$\text{Return on Investment} = \frac{\text{Income from Operations}}{\text{Sales}} \times \frac{\text{Sales}}{\text{Invested Assets}}$$

The DuPont formula is useful in evaluating divisions. This is because the profit margin and the investment turnover reflect the following underlying operating relationships of each division:

- Profit margin indicates *operating profitability* by computing the profit earned on each sales dollar.
- Investment turnover indicates *operating efficiency* by computing the number of sales dollars generated by each dollar of invested assets.

If a division's profit margin increases, and all other factors remain the same, the division's return on investment will increase. For example, a division might add more profitable products to its sales mix and, thus, increase its operating profit, profit margin, and return on investment.

If a division's investment turnover increases, and all other factors remain the same, the division's return on investment will increase. For example, a division might attempt to increase sales through special sales promotions and thus increase operating efficiency, investment turnover, and return on investment.

The return on investment, profit margin, and investment turnover operate in relationship to one another. Specifically, more income can be earned by either increasing the investment turnover, increasing the profit margin, or both.

Using the DuPont formula yields the same return on investment for each of DataLink's divisions, computed as follows:

$$\text{Return on Investment} = \frac{\text{Income from Operations}}{\text{Sales}} \times \frac{\text{Sales}}{\text{Invested Assets}}$$

Northern Division:

$$\text{Return on Investment} = \frac{\$70,000}{\$560,000} \times \frac{\$560,000}{\$350,000} = 12.5\% \times 1.6 = 20\%$$

Central Division:

$$\text{Return on Investment} = \frac{\$84,000}{\$672,000} \times \frac{\$672,000}{\$700,000} = 12.5\% \times 0.96 = 12\%$$

Southern Division:

$$\text{Return on Investment} = \frac{\$75,000}{\$750,000} \times \frac{\$750,000}{\$500,000} = 10\% \times 1.5 = 15\%$$

The Northern and Central divisions have the same profit margins of 12.5%. However, the Northern Division's investment turnover of 1.6 is larger than that of the Central Division's turnover of 0.96. By using its invested assets more efficiently, the Northern Division's return on investment of 20% is 8 percentage points higher than the Central Division's return on investment of 12%.

The Southern Division's profit margin of 10% and investment turnover of 1.5 are lower than those of the Northern Division. The product of these factors results in a return on investment of 15% for the Southern Division, compared to 20% for the Northern Division.

Even though the Southern Division's profit margin is lower than the Central Division's, its higher turnover of 1.5 results in a return on investment of 15%, which is greater than the Central Division's return on investment of 12%.

Link to Caterpillar

Based upon recent financial statements, the profit margin, investment turnover, and return on investment (ROI) for each of **Caterpillar**'s four segments were as follows:

	Construction	Resource	Energy & Transportation	Financial Products
Profit margin	11.5%	(1.1)%	16.4%	26.3%
Investment turnover	3.06	0.92	2.31	0.09
ROI	35.2%	(1.0)%	37.9%	2.4%

To increase the return on investment, the profit margin and investment turnover for a division may be analyzed. For example, assume that the Northern Division is in a highly competitive industry in which the profit margin cannot be easily increased. As a result, the division manager might focus on increasing the investment turnover.

To illustrate, assume that the revenues of the Northern Division could be increased by $56,000 through increasing operating expenses, such as advertising, to $385,000. The Northern Division's income from operations will increase from $70,000 to $77,000, computed as follows:

Revenues ($560,000 + $56,000)	$616,000
Operating expenses	385,000
Income from operations before service department charges	$231,000
Service department charges	154,000
Income from operations	$ 77,000

The return on investment for the Northern Division, using the DuPont formula, is recomputed as follows:

$$\text{Return on Investment} = \frac{\$77,000}{\$616,000} \times \frac{\$616,000}{\$350,000} = 12.5\% \times 1.76 = 22\%$$

Although the Northern Division's profit margin remains the same (12.5%), the investment turnover has increased from 1.6 to 1.76, an increase of 10% (0.16 ÷ 1.6). The 10% increase in investment turnover increases the return on investment by 10% (from 20% to 22%).

The return on investment is also useful in deciding where to invest additional assets or expand operations. For example, DataLink should give priority to expanding operations in the Northern Division because it earns the highest return on investment. In other words, an investment in the Northern Division will return 20 cents (20%) on each dollar invested. In contrast, investments in the Central and Southern divisions will earn only 12 cents and 15 cents, respectively, per dollar invested.

A disadvantage of the return on investment as a performance measure is that it may lead divisional managers to reject new investments that could be profitable for the company as a whole. To illustrate, assume the following returns on investment for the Northern Division of DataLink:

Current return on investment	20%
Minimum acceptable return on investment set by top management	10%
Expected return on investment for new project	14%

If the manager of the Northern Division invests in the new project, the Northern Division's overall return on investment will decrease from 20% due to averaging. Thus, the division manager might decide to reject the project, even though the new project's expected return on investment of 14% exceeds DataLink's minimum acceptable return on investment of 10%.

Why It Matters

Coca-Cola Company: Go West Young Man

A major decision early in the history of Coca-Cola was to expand outside of the United States to the rest of the world. As a result, Coca-Cola is known today the world over. What is revealing is how this decision has impacted the revenues and profitability of Coca-Cola across its international and North American segments. The following table shows the percent of revenues and percent of income from operations from the international and North American geographic segments.

	Revenues	Income from Operations
International segments	35.4%	94.3%
North American segment	49.2	28.5
Other (bottling companies, headquarters)	15.4	(22.8)
Total	100%	100%

The first column shows that the international segments provide over 35% of the revenues, while North America provides over 49% of the revenues, as the United States is a large market for Coca-Cola products. However, the income from operations tells a different story. More than 94% of Coca-Cola's profitability comes from international segments. Given the revenue segmentation, this suggests that the international profit margins must be much higher than the North American profit margin. Indeed this is the case, as can be seen in the following table:

	Profit Margin
International average	52.5%
North America	11.4%
Overall average	19.7%

The average profit margin for all the international segments is over four times as large as the North American segment. These results speak to the heart of the Coca-Cola marketing strategy. In international markets, Coca-Cola is able to charge relatively higher prices due to high demand and less competition as compared to the North American market.

Source: The Coca-Cola Company, Form 10-K for the Fiscal Year ended December 31, 2015.

Residual Income

Residual income is useful in overcoming some of the disadvantages of the return on investment. **Residual income** is the excess of income from operations over a minimum acceptable income from operations, as shown in Exhibit 7.

Income from operations	$XXX
Minimum acceptable income from operations as a percent of invested assets	XXX
Residual income	$XXX

Exhibit 7
Residual Income

The minimum acceptable income from operations is computed by multiplying the company minimum return on investment by the invested assets. The minimum rate is set by top management, based on such factors as the cost of financing.

To illustrate, assume that DataLink Inc. has established 10% as the minimum acceptable return on investment for divisional assets. The residual incomes for the three divisions are shown in Exhibit 8.

	Northern Division	Central Division	Southern Division
Income from operations	$70,000	$84,000	$75,000
Minimum acceptable income from operations as a percent of invested assets:			
$350,000 × 10%	35,000		
$700,000 × 10%		70,000	
$500,000 × 10%			50,000
Residual income	$35,000	$14,000	$25,000

Exhibit 8
Residual Income—
DataLink, Inc.

As shown in Exhibit 8, the Northern Division has more residual income ($35,000) than the other divisions, even though it has the least amount of income from operations ($70,000). This is because the invested assets are less for the Northern Division than for the other divisions.

The major advantage of residual income as a performance measure is that it considers the minimum acceptable return on investment, invested assets, and the income from operations for each division. In doing so, residual income encourages division managers to maximize income from operations in excess of the minimum. This provides an incentive to accept any project that is expected to have a return on investment in excess of the minimum.

To illustrate, assume the following returns on investment for the Northern Division of DataLink:

Current return on investment	20%
Minimum acceptable return on investment	
set by top management	10%
Expected return on investment for new project	14%

If the manager of the Northern Division is evaluated on new projects using only the return on investment, the division manager might decide to reject the new project. This is because investing in the new project will decrease Northern's current return on investment of 20%. While this helps the division maintain its high ROI, it hurts the company as a whole because the expected return on investment of 14% exceeds DataLink's minimum acceptable return on investment of 10%.

In contrast, if the manager of the Northern Division is evaluated using residual income, the new project would probably be accepted because it will increase the Northern Division's residual income. In this way, residual income supports both divisional and overall company objectives.

Check Up Corner 23-3   Investment Center Performance Measures

Yummy Foods Company is a diversified company with three divisions organized as investment centers. Condensed data taken from the records of the three divisions for the year ended December 31 are as follows:

	Snack Goods	Canned Foods	Frozen Foods
Revenues	$784,000	$940,800	$1,050,000
Operating expenses	470,400	700,000	562,500
Income from operations before service			
department charges	$313,600	$240,800	$ 487,500
Service department charges	219,520	99,680	382,500
Income from operations	$ 94,080	$141,120	$ 105,000
Invested assets	$448,000	$940,800	$ 750,000

A. Using the DuPont formula, for return on investment compute the profit margin, investment turnover, and return on investment for each division.

B. Determine the residual income for each division, assuming a minimum acceptable return on investment is 14%.

Solution:

A.

	Return on Investment	=	Profit Margin	×	Investment Turnover
Snack Goods Division	21.0%	=	12.0%	×	1.75
Canned Foods Division	15.0%	=	15.0%	×	1.00
Frozen Foods Division	14.0%	=	10.0%	×	1.40

> The Snack Goods Division has the highest return on investment.

Profit Margin

	Snack Goods	Canned Foods	Frozen Foods
Income from operations	$ 94,080	$141,120	$ 105,000
Sales	÷784,000	÷940,800	÷1,050,000
Profit margin	12.0%	15.0%	10.0%

> The Canned Foods Division has the highest income from operations.

Investment Turnover

	Snack Goods	Canned Foods	Frozen Foods
Sales	$784,000	$940,800	$1,050,000
Invested assets	÷448,000	÷940,800	÷750,000
Investment turnover	1.75	1.00	1.40

B.

	Residual Income	=	Income from Operations	−	Minimum Acceptable Income from Operations
Snack Goods Division	$31,360	=	$94,080	−	$62,720
Canned Foods Division	$9,408	=	$141,120	−	$131,712
Frozen Foods Division	$0	=	$105,000	−	$105,000

> The Snack Goods Division has the highest residual income.

	Snack Goods	Canned Foods	Frozen Foods
Invested assets	$448,000	$940,800	$750,000
Minimum acceptable return	× 14%	× 14%	× 14%
Minimum acceptable income from operations	$ 62,720	$131,712	$105,000

Check Up Corner

The Balanced Scorecard[2]

The **balanced scorecard** is a set of multiple performance measures for a company. In addition to financial performance, a balanced scorecard normally includes performance measures for customer service, innovation and learning, and internal processes, as shown in Exhibit 9.

Exhibit 9

The Balanced Scorecard

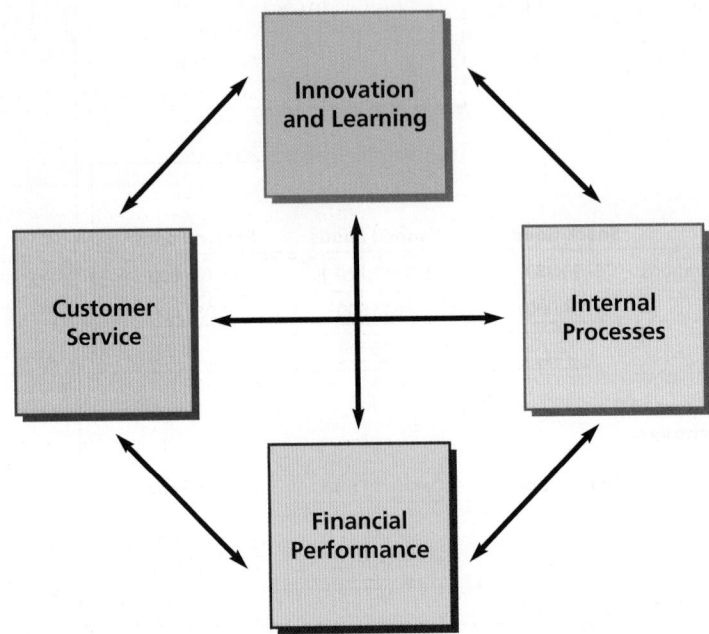

Performance measures for learning and innovation often revolve around a company's research and development efforts. For example, the number of new products developed during a year and the time it takes to bring new products to the market are performance measures for innovation. Performance measures for learning could include the number of employee training sessions and the number of employees who are cross-trained in several skills.

Performance measures for customer service include the number of customer complaints and the number of repeat customers. Customer surveys can also be used to gather measures of customer satisfaction with the company as compared to competitors.

Performance measures for internal processes include the length of time it takes to manufacture a product. The amount of scrap and waste is a measure of the efficiency of a company's manufacturing processes. The number of customer returns is a performance measure of both the manufacturing and sales ordering processes.

All companies will use financial performance measures. Some financial performance measures have been discussed earlier in this chapter and include income from operations, return on investment, and residual income.

The balanced scorecard attempts to identify the underlying nonfinancial drivers, or causes, of financial performance related to innovation and learning, customer service, and internal processes. In this way, the financial performance may be improved. For example, customer satisfaction is often measured by the number of repeat customers. By increasing the number of repeat customers, sales and income from operations can be increased.

Link to Caterpillar   **Caterpillar**'s Financial Products segment's performance is measured by interest coverage and leverage ratios as well as its credit rating and timeliness of financial reporting.

---

[2] The balanced scorecard was developed by R. S. Kaplan and D. P. Norton and explained in *The Balanced Scorecard: Translating Strategy into Action* (Cambridge: Harvard Business School Press, 1996).

Some common performance measures used in the balanced scorecard approach are shown in Exhibit 10.

Innovation and Learning
■ Number of new products
■ Number of new patents
■ Number of cross-trained employees
■ Number of training hours
■ Number of ethics violations
■ Employee turnover

Internal Processes
■ Waste and scrap
■ Time to manufacture products
■ Number of defects
■ Number of rejected sales orders
■ Number of stockouts
■ Labor utilization

Customer Service
■ Number of repeat customers
■ Customer brand recognition
■ Delivery time to customer
■ Customer satisfaction
■ Number of sales returns
■ Customer complaints

Financial Performance
■ Sales
■ Income from operations
■ Return on investment
■ Profit margin and investment turnover
■ Residual income
■ Actual versus budgeted (standard) costs

Exhibit 10
Balanced Scorecard Performance Measures

Why It Matters

Turning Around Charles Schwab

Customer service is a key component to any balanced scorecard, and it is a particularly critical component in service industries. Since 2003, Bain & Company consulting has helped companies improve customer service by focusing on a customer loyalty metric called the *Net Promoter Score*. This metric, when used as part of a balanced scorecard, evaluates customer service by assessing how likely a customer is to recommend the company to others.

Charles Schwab Corporation is a full-service financial advisory firm that was founded in 1973. In 2004, the company was struggling. Although Schwab had been built on delivering exceptional customer service, the company had lost its way. When customers were surveyed, they gave Schwab a negative

35% Net Promoter Score, indicating that more customers wanted to see the company fail than would be willing to promote the company to others.

In response, Schwab enlisted Bain to help improve its customer experience and customer loyalty. Bain helped Schwab develop and implement a Client Promoter System that focused on embedding the Client Promoter Score deep within the company's values and core strategy. As Schwab CEO Walt Bettinger describes, "If you serve clients in the way that you would like to be served, they are going to want to do more business with you." The results were significant. By 2008, the company's stock price had more than doubled, and in 2010, Schwab received a Net Promoter Score of 46%, the highest in its sector.

Source: "Schwab Earns Highest Customer Loyalty Ranking Among Brokerage & Investment Firms in Satmetrix Net Promoter's 2010 Industry Report," *BusinessWire*, March 25, 2010. "Seeing the world through the client's eyes," Bain & Company, *www.netpromotersystem.com/videos/trailblazer-video/charles-schwab.aspx*

Transfer Pricing

When divisions transfer products or render services to each other, a **transfer price** is used to charge for the products or services.[3] Because transfer prices will affect a division's financial performance, setting a transfer price is a sensitive matter for the managers of both the selling and buying divisions.

Three common approaches to setting transfer prices are as follows:

- Market price approach
- Negotiated price approach
- Cost price approach

Objective 5
Describe and illustrate how the market price, negotiated price, and cost price approaches to transfer pricing may be used by decentralized segments of a business.

Transfer prices may be used for cost, profit, or investment centers. The objective of setting a transfer price is to motivate managers to behave in a manner that will increase the overall company income. As will be illustrated, however, transfer prices may be misused in such a way that overall company income suffers.

Link to Caterpillar

In recent financial statements, Caterpillar reported $2,346 million of revenues among its four segments.

Transfer prices can be set as low as the variable cost per unit or as high as the market price. Often, transfer prices are negotiated at some point between variable cost per unit and market price. Exhibit 11 shows the possible range of transfer prices.

Exhibit 11
Commonly Used Transfer Prices

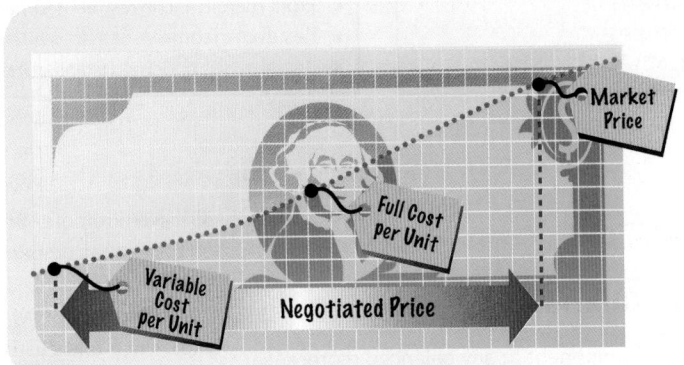

To illustrate, Wilson Company, a packaged snack food company with no service departments, is used. Wilson has two operating divisions (Eastern and Western) that are organized as investment centers. Condensed income statements for Wilson, assuming no transfers between divisions, are shown in Exhibit 12.

Exhibit 12
Income Statements—No Transfers Between Divisions

Wilson Company Income Statements For the Year Ended December 31, 20Y1			
	Eastern Division	**Western Division**	**Total Company**
Sales:			
50,000 units × $20 per unit	$1,000,000		$1,000,000
20,000 units × $40 per unit		$800,000	800,000
Total sales			$1,800,000
Expenses:			
Variable:			
50,000 units × $10 per unit	$ 500,000		$ 500,000
20,000 units × $30* per unit		$600,000	600,000
Fixed	300,000	100,000	400,000
Total expenses	$ 800,000	$700,000	$1,500,000
Income from operations	$ 200,000	$100,000	$ 300,000

*$20 of the $30 per unit represents materials costs, and the remaining $10 per unit represents other variable conversion expenses incurred within the Western Division.

---

[3] The discussion in this chapter highlights the essential concepts of transfer pricing. In-depth discussion of transfer pricing can be found in advanced texts.

Market Price Approach

Using the **market price approach**, the transfer price is the price at which the product or service transferred could be sold to outside buyers. If an outside market exists for the product or service transferred, the current market price may be a proper transfer price.

Transfer Price = Market Price

To illustrate, assume that materials used by Wilson in producing snack food in the Western Division are currently purchased from an outside supplier at $20 per unit. The same materials are produced by the Eastern Division. The Eastern Division is operating at full capacity of 50,000 units and can sell all it produces to either the Western Division or to outside buyers.

A transfer price of $20 per unit (the market price) has no effect on the Eastern Division's income or total company income. The Eastern Division will earn revenues of $20 per unit on all its production and sales, regardless of who buys its product.

Likewise, the Western Division will pay $20 per unit for materials (the market price). Thus, the use of the market price as the transfer price has no effect on the Western Division's income or total company income.

In this situation, the use of the market price as the transfer price is proper. The condensed divisional income statements for Wilson would be the same as shown in Exhibit 12.

Negotiated Price Approach

If unused or excess capacity exists in the supplying division (the Eastern Division), and the transfer price is equal to the market price, total company profit may not be maximized. This is because the manager of the Western Division will be indifferent toward purchasing materials from the Eastern Division or from outside suppliers. That is, in both cases the Western Division manager pays $20 per unit (the market price). As a result, the Western Division may purchase the materials from outside suppliers.

If, however, the Western Division purchases the materials from the Eastern Division, the difference between the market price of $20 and the variable costs of the Eastern Division of $10 per unit (from Exhibit 12) can cover fixed costs and contribute to overall company profits. Thus, the Western Division manager should be encouraged to purchase the materials from the Eastern Division.

The **negotiated price approach** allows the managers to agree (negotiate) among themselves on a transfer price. The only constraint is that the transfer price be less than the market price but greater than the supplying division's variable costs per unit, as follows:

Variable Costs per Unit < Transfer Price < Market Price

To illustrate, assume that instead of a capacity of 50,000 units, the Eastern Division's capacity is 70,000 units. In addition, assume that the Eastern Division can continue to sell only 50,000 units to outside buyers.

A transfer price less than $20 would encourage the manager of the Western Division to purchase from the Eastern Division. This is because the Western Division is currently purchasing its materials from outside suppliers at a cost of $20 per unit. Thus, its materials cost would decrease, and its income from operations would increase.

At the same time, a transfer price above the Eastern Division's variable costs per unit of $10 would encourage the manager of the Eastern Division to supply materials to the Western Division. In doing so, the Eastern Division's income from operations would also increase.

Exhibit 13 illustrates the divisional and company income statements, assuming that the Eastern and Western division managers agree to a transfer price of $15.

The Eastern Division increases its sales by $300,000 (20,000 units × $15 per unit) to $1,300,000. As a result, the Eastern Division's income from operations increases by $100,000 ($300,000 sales − $200,000 variable costs) to $300,000, as shown in Exhibit 13.

Exhibit 13

Income Statements—Negotiated Transfer Price

DYNAMIC EXHIBIT

	Wilson Company Income Statements For the Year Ended December 31, 20Y1		
	Eastern Division	Western Division	Total Company
Sales:			
50,000 units × $20 per unit...............	$1,000,000		$1,000,000
20,000 units × $15 per unit...............	300,000		300,000
20,000 units × $40 per unit...............		$800,000	800,000
Total sales........................	$1,300,000	$800,000	$2,100,000
Expenses:			
Variable:			
70,000 units × $10 per unit............	$ 700,000		$ 700,000
20,000 units × $25* per unit..........		$500,000	500,000
Fixed................................	300,000	100,000	400,000
Total expenses....................	$1,000,000	$600,000	$1,600,000
Income from operations..............	$ 300,000	$200,000	$ 500,000

*$10 of the $25 represents variable conversion expenses incurred solely within the Western Division, and $15 per unit represents the transfer price per unit from the Eastern Division.

The increase of $100,000 in the Eastern Division's income can also be computed as follows:

$$\text{Increase in Eastern (Supplying) Division's Income from Operations} = (\text{Transfer Price} - \text{Variable Cost per Unit}) \times \text{Units Transferred}$$

$$= (\$15 - \$10) \times 20,000 \text{ units} = \$100,000$$

The Western Division's materials cost decreases by $5 per unit ($20 – $15) for a total of $100,000 (20,000 units × $5 per unit). Thus, the Western Division's income from operations increases by $100,000 to $200,000, as shown in Exhibit 13.

The increase of $100,000 in the Western Division's income can also be computed as follows:

$$\text{Increase in Western (Purchasing) Division's Income from Operations} = (\text{Market Price} - \text{Transfer Price}) \times \text{Units Transferred}$$

$$= (\$20 - \$15) \times 20,000 \text{ units} = \$100,000$$

Comparing Exhibits 12 and 13 shows that Wilson's income from operations increased by $200,000, computed as follows:

	Income from Operations		
	No Units Transferred (Exhibit 12)	20,000 Units Transferred at $15 per Unit (Exhibit 13)	Increase (Decrease)
Eastern Division	$200,000	$300,000	$100,000
Western Division	100,000	200,000	100,000
Wilson Company	$300,000	$500,000	$200,000

In the preceding illustration, any negotiated transfer price between $10 and $20 is acceptable, as shown in the following formula:

$$\text{Variable Costs per Unit} < \text{Transfer Price} < \text{Market Price}$$
$$\$10 < \text{Transfer Price} < \$20$$

Any transfer price within this range will increase the overall income from operations for Wilson by $200,000. However, the increases in the Eastern and Western divisions' income from operations will vary depending on the transfer price.

To illustrate, a transfer price of $16 would increase the Eastern Division's income from operations by $120,000, computed as follows:

$$\text{Increase in Eastern (Supplying) Division's Income from Operations} = (\text{Transfer Price} - \text{Variable Cost per Unit}) \times \text{Units Transferred}$$

$$= (\$16 - \$10) \times 20{,}000 \text{ units} = \$120{,}000$$

A transfer price of $16 would increase the Western Division's income from operations by $80,000, computed as follows:

$$\text{Increase in Western (Purchasing) Division's Income from Operations} = (\text{Market Price} - \text{Transfer Price}) \times \text{Units Transferred}$$

$$= (\$20 - \$16) \times 20{,}000 \text{ units} = \$80{,}000$$

With a transfer price of $16, Wilson Company's income from operations still increases by $200,000, which consists of the Eastern Division's increase of $120,000 plus the Western Division's increase of $80,000.

As shown, a negotiated price provides each division manager with an incentive to negotiate the transfer of materials. At the same time, the overall company's income from operations will also increase. However, the negotiated approach only applies when the supplying division has excess capacity. In other words, the supplying division cannot sell all its production to outside buyers at the market price.

Check Up Corner 23-4   Transfer Pricing

The materials used by the South Division of Eagle Company are currently purchased from outside suppliers at $30 per unit. These same materials are produced by Eagle's North Division. Income from operations assuming no transfers between divisions is $1,200,000 for the North Division and $1,360,000 for the South Division.

The North Division has unused capacity and can produce the materials needed by the South Division at a variable cost of $15 per unit. The two divisions have recently negotiated a transfer price of $22 per unit for 30,000 units.

Based on the agreed upon transfer price, with no reduction in the North Division's current sales:
   A. How much would the North Division's income from operations increase?
   B. How much would the South Division's income from operations increase?
   C. How much would Eagle Company's income from operations increase?

Solution:

A.

$$\text{Increase in North (Supplying) Division's Income from Operations} = (\text{Transfer Price} - \text{Variable Cost per Unit}) \times \text{Units Transferred}$$

$$= (\$22 - \$15) \times 30{,}000 \text{ units} = \$210{,}000$$

B.

$$\text{Increase in South (Purchasing) Division's Income from Operations} = (\text{Market Price} - \text{Transfer Price}) \times \text{Units Transferred}$$

$$= (\$30 - \$22) \times 30{,}000 \text{ units} = \$240{,}000$$

C.

	Income from Operations		
	No Units Transferred	**30,000 Units Transferred**	**Increase (Decrease)**
North Division	$1,200,000	$1,410,000	$210,000
South Division	1,360,000	1,600,000	240,000
Eagle Company	$2,560,000	$3,010,000	$450,000

Eagle company's income from operations will increase by $450,000; the sum of the income increases for the North Division ($210,000) and the South Division ($240,000).

Check Up Corner

Cost Price Approach

Under the **cost price approach**, cost is used to set transfer prices. A variety of costs may be used in this approach, including the following:

- Total product cost per unit
- Variable product cost per unit

If total product cost per unit is used, direct materials, direct labor, and factory overhead are included in the transfer price. If variable product cost per unit is used, the fixed factory overhead cost is excluded from the transfer price.

Actual costs or standard (budgeted) costs may be used in applying the cost price approach. If actual costs are used, inefficiencies of the producing (supplying) division are transferred to the purchasing division. Thus, there is little incentive for the producing (supplying) division to control costs. For this reason, most companies use standard costs in the cost price approach. In this way, differences between actual and standard costs remain with the producing (supplying) division for cost control purposes.

The cost price approach is most often used when the responsibility centers are organized as cost centers. When the responsibility centers are organized as profit or investment centers, the cost price approach is normally not used.

For example, using the cost price approach when the supplying division is organized as a profit center ignores the supplying division manager's responsibility for earning profits. In this case, using the cost price approach prevents the supplying division from reporting any profit (revenues – costs) on the units transferred. As a result, the division manager has little incentive to transfer units to another division, even though it may be in the best interests of the company.

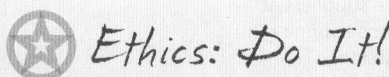 Ethics: Do It!

The Ethics of Transfer Prices

Transfer prices allow large multinational companies to minimize taxes by shifting taxable income from countries with high tax rates to countries with low taxes. For example, a British company will pay U.S. taxes on income from its U.S. division, and British taxes on income from its British division. Because this company can set its own transfer price, it can minimize its overall tax bill by setting a high transfer price when transferring goods to the United States. This increases cost of goods sold for the highly taxed U.S. division and increases sales for the lesser taxed British division. The overall result is a lower tax bill for the multinational company as a whole. In recent years, government tax authorities like the Internal Revenue Service (IRS) have become concerned with tax avoidance through transfer price manipulation. In response, many countries now have guidelines for setting transfer prices that assure that transfer prices are not subject to manipulation for tax purposes.

Source: L. Eden and L. M. Smith, "The Ethics of Transfer Pricing," unpublished working paper, Texas A&M University, 2011.

Analysis for Decision Making

Franchise Operations

Objective

Describe and illustrate the use of profit margin, investment turnover, and ROI in evaluating whether a company should expand through franchised or owner-operated stores.

Franchising is a popular method of expanding a brand, concept, product, or service offering. The franchisor is the entity that provides the franchise, while the franchisee is the entity that pays for the franchise. Under a franchise agreement, the franchisee pays a fee for the right to sell the franchised product or service. The franchise fee is often expressed as a percent of revenues earned by the franchisee. In addition, the franchisee invests in the property and equipment to deliver the franchised product or service. The franchisor often provides support in start-up, advertising, management development, business systems, and supplier relationships.

The benefits to a franchisee are instant access to a recognized brand, established customer base, and working business systems. The main benefit to the franchisor is an ability to expand the brand without investing significantly in property and equipment.

From the franchisor's perspective, the return on investment for franchised operations should be increased by the low investment. Thus, the DuPont formula should show a healthy profit margin combined with a high investment turnover. To illustrate, **Hilton Worldwide Holdings, Inc.** has both company-operated and franchised hotel operations. In a recent year, Hilton had 144 company-operated hotels and 4,178 franchised hotels around the world. Clearly, Hilton emphasizes franchised operations. Segment disclosures with some assumptions regarding owned and franchised operations are as follows (in millions):

	Company-Operated	Franchised
Revenues	$4,239	$1,401
Operating expenses	3,252	0
General and administrative expenses*		491
Property, plant, and equipment**	8,123	903

*Assume all the general and administrative expenses support franchised operations, since less than 3% of hotel properties are company-operated.

** Total property, plant, and equipment is $9,026. Assume 10% of total property, plant, and equipment support administrative (franchised) operations, while the remaining 90% consist of owned hotel properties.

The return on investment (ROI) using the DuPont formula for both segments is as follows:

$$\text{Return on Investment} = \text{Profit Margin} \times \text{Investment Turnover}$$

$$\text{Return on Investment} = \frac{\text{Income from Operations}}{\text{Revenues}} \times \frac{\text{Revenues}}{\text{Invested Assets}}$$

Company-Operated Hotels:

$$\text{Return on Investment} = \frac{\$987^*}{\$4,239} \times \frac{\$4,239}{\$8,123}$$

$$= 23\% \times 0.52$$
$$= 12\% \text{ (rounded)}$$

Franchised Hotels:

$$\text{Return on Investment} = \frac{\$910^{**}}{\$1,401} \times \frac{\$1,401}{\$903}$$

$$= 65\% \times 1.55$$
$$= 101\% \text{ (rounded)}$$

$$^*\$4,239 - \$3,252$$
$$^{**}\$1,401 - \$491$$

Under these assumptions, franchised hotels provide a superior ROI compared to company-operated hotels. The superior performance is caused by both a stronger profit margin and a higher investment turnover. The ROI will often favor franchised operations in this way. This is likely the reason for Hilton's decision to emphasize franchised operations.

Make a Decision | **Franchise Operations**

Kelly Kitchens operates both franchised and company-operated restaurants under the brand name Kelly Kitchens. Income from operations, sales, and invested assets for both segments are provided as follows:

	Company-Operated	Franchised
Income from operations	$ 180,000	$192,000
Sales	600,000	240,000
Invested assets	1,500,000	150,000

A. Determine the profit margin for company-operated and franchised restaurants. (Round to the nearest whole percent.)
B. Determine the investment turnover for company-operated and franchised restaurants. (Round to two decimal places.)
C. Use the DuPont formula to determine the return on investment for company-operated and franchised restaurants.
D. Kelly Kitchens is expanding to the Midwest. How would you advise management regarding the use of company-operated versus franchised restaurants in the expansion?

Solution:

A. Profit Margin = $\dfrac{\text{Income from Operations}}{\text{Sales}}$

Company-Operated: $\dfrac{\$180,000}{\$600,000} = 30\%$

Franchised: $\dfrac{\$192,000}{\$240,000} = 80\%$

B. Investment Turnover = $\dfrac{\text{Sales}}{\text{Invested Assets}}$

Company-Operated: $\dfrac{\$600,000}{\$1,500,000} = 0.40$

Franchised: $\dfrac{\$240,000}{\$150,000} = 1.60$

C. Return on Investment (ROI) = Profit Margin × Investment Turnover
Company-Operated: 30% × 0.40 = 12%
Franchised: 80% × 1.60 = 128%

D. The profit margin, investment turnover, and ROI favor franchised over company-operated restaurants. Thus, from a financial perspective, franchising appears to be a more favorable route for expanding into the Midwest. In addition, Kelly may be able to expand faster using franchisees rather than using its own funds for constructing restaurants. Kelly Kitchens may view company-operated restaurants as a way to protect the brand and control the customer experience. However, franchise agreements can be designed to provide for quality control and consistency of customer experience. Thus, Kelly can still protect the brand while expanding through franchisees.

Make a Decision

Let's Review

Chapter Summary

1. In a centralized business, all major planning and operating decisions are made by top management. In a decentralized business, these responsibilities are delegated to unit managers. Decentralization may be more effective because operational decisions are made by the managers closest to the operations.

2. Cost centers limit the responsibility and authority of managers to decisions related to the costs of their unit. The primary tools for planning and controlling are budgets and budget performance reports.

3. In a profit center, managers have the responsibility and authority to make decisions that affect both revenues and costs. Responsibility reports for a profit center usually show income from operations for the unit.

4. In an investment center, the unit manager has the responsibility and authority to make decisions that affect the unit's revenues, expenses, and assets invested in the center. Three measures are commonly used to assess investment center performance: return on investment (ROI), residual income, and the balanced scorecard. These measures are often used to compare investment center performance.

5. When divisions within a company transfer products or provide services to each other, a transfer price is used to charge for the products or services. Transfer prices should be set so that the overall company income is increased when goods are transferred between divisions. One of three approaches is typically used to establish transfer prices: market price, negotiated price, or cost price.

Key Terms

balanced scorecard (1174)
controllable expenses (1163)
controllable revenues (1163)
cost center (1160)
cost price approach (1180)
DuPont formula (1168)

investment center (1167)
investment turnover (1168)
market price approach (1177)
negotiated price approach (1177)
profit center (1163)
profit margin (1168)

residual income (1171)
responsibility accounting (1159)
return on investment (ROI) (1168)
service department charges (1163)
transfer price (1175)

Practice

Multiple-Choice Questions

1. When the manager has the responsibility and authority to make decisions that affect costs and revenues but no responsibility for or authority over assets invested in the department, the department is called a(n):
   A. cost center.
   B. profit center.
   C. investment center.
   D. service department.

2. The Accounts Payable Department has expenses of $600,000 and makes 150,000 payments to the various vendors who provide products and services to the divisions. Division A has income from operations of $900,000 before service department charges and requires 60,000 payments to vendors. If the Accounts Payable Department is treated as a service department, what is Division A's income from operations?
   A. $300,000   C. $660,000
   B. $900,000   D. $540,000

3. Division A of Kern Co. has sales of $350,000, cost of goods sold of $200,000, operating expenses of $30,000, and invested assets of $600,000. What is the return on investment for Division A?
   A. 20%   C. 33%
   B. 25%   D. 40%

4. Division L of Liddy Co. has a return on investment of 24% and an investment turnover of 1.6. What is the profit margin?
   A. 6%   C. 24%
   B. 15%   D. 38%

5. Which approach to transfer pricing uses the price at which the product or service transferred could be sold to outside buyers?
   A. Cost price approach   C. Market price approach
   B. Negotiated price approach   D. Standard cost approach

Answers provided after Problem. Need more practice? Find additional multiple-choice questions, exercises, and problems in CengageNOWv2.

Exercises

SHOW ME HOW

1. Budgetary performance for cost center   Obj. 2

Caroline Company's costs were over budget by $319,000. The company is divided into West and East regions. The East Region's costs were under budget by $47,500. Determine the amount that the West Region's costs were over or under budget.

SHOW ME HOW

2. Service department charges   Obj. 3

The centralized employee travel department of Camtro Company has expenses of $528,000. The department has serviced a total of 6,000 travel reservations for the period. The Southeast Division has made 2,400 reservations during the period, and the Pacific Northwest Division has made 3,600 reservations. How much should each division be charged for travel services?

SHOW ME HOW

3. Income from operations for profit center   Obj. 3

Using the data for Camtro Company from Exercise 2 along with the following data, determine the divisional income from operations for the Southeast and Pacific Northwest divisions:

	Southeast Division	Pacific Northwest Division
Sales	$1,155,000	$1,204,000
Cost of goods sold	590,800	658,000
Selling expenses	231,000	252,000

SHOW ME HOW

4. Profit margin, investment turnover, and ROI   Obj. 4

Cash Company has income from operations of $112,500, invested assets of $750,000, and sales of $1,875,000. Use the DuPont formula to compute the return on investment and show (A) the profit margin, (B) the investment turnover, and (C) the return on investment.

SHOW ME HOW

5. Residual income

Obj. 4

The Consumer Division of Hernandez Company has income from operations of $90,000 and assets of $450,000. The minimum acceptable return on assets is 10%. What is the residual income for the division?

SHOW ME HOW

6. Transfer pricing

Obj. 5

The materials used by the North Division of Horton Company are currently purchased from outside suppliers at $60 per unit. These same materials are produced by Horton's South Division. The South Division can produce the materials needed by the North Division at a variable cost of $42 per unit. The division is currently producing 200,000 units and has capacity of 250,000 units. The two divisions have recently negotiated a transfer price of $52 per unit for 30,000 units. By how much will each division's income increase as a result of this transfer?

Answers provided after Problem. Need more practice? Find additional multiple-choice questions, exercises, and problems in CengageNOWv2.

Problem

Quinn Company has two divisions, Domestic and International. Invested assets and condensed income statement data for each division for the year ended December 31, 20Y9, are as follows:

	Domestic Division	International Division
Revenues	$675,000	$480,000
Operating expenses	450,000	372,400
Service department charges	90,000	50,000
Invested assets	600,000	384,000

Instructions

1. Prepare condensed income statements for the past year for each division.

2. Using the DuPont formula, determine the profit margin, investment turnover, and return on investment for each division.

3. If management's minimum acceptable return on investment is 10%, determine the residual income for each division.

Need more practice? Find additional multiple-choice questions, exercises, and problems in CengageNOWv2.

Answers

Multiple-Choice Questions

1. **B** The manager of a profit center (answer B) has responsibility for and authority over costs and revenues. If the manager has responsibility for only costs, the department is called a cost center (answer A). If the responsibility and authority extend to the investment in assets as well as costs and revenues, it is called an investment center (answer C). A service department (answer D) provides services to other departments. A service department could be a cost center, a profit center, or an investment center.

2. **C** $600,000 ÷ 150,000 = $4 per payment. Division A anticipates 60,000 payments or $240,000 (60,000 × $4) in service department charges from the Accounts Payable Department. Income from operations is thus $900,000 − $240,000, or $660,000. Answer A assumes that all service department overhead is assigned to Division A, which would be incorrect, since Division A does not use all of the Accounts Payable service. Answer B incorrectly assumes that there are no service department charges from Accounts Payable. Answer D incorrectly determines the Accounts Payable transfer rate from Division A's income from operations.

3. **A** The return on investment for Division A is 20% (answer A), computed as follows:

$$\text{Return on Investment} = \frac{\text{Income from Operations}}{\text{Invested Assets}}$$

$$= \frac{\$350,000 - \$200,000 - \$30,000}{\$600,000} = 20\%$$

4. **B** The profit margin for Division L of Liddy Co. is 15% (answer B), computed as follows:

$$\text{Return on Investment} = \text{Profit Margin} \times \text{Investment Turnover}$$

$$24\% = \text{Profit Margin} \times 1.6$$

$$15\% = \text{Profit Margin}$$

5. **C** The market price approach (answer C) to transfer pricing uses the price at which the product or service transferred could be sold to outside buyers. The cost price approach (answer A) uses cost as the basis for setting transfer prices. The negotiated price approach (answer B) allows managers of decentralized units to agree (negotiate) among themselves as to the proper transfer price. The standard cost approach (answer D) is a version of the cost price approach that uses standard costs in setting transfer prices.

Exercises

1. $366,500 over budget ($319,000 + $47,500)

2. <u>Southeast Division Service Charge for Travel Department:</u>
   $211,200 = 2,400 billed reservations × ($528,000 ÷ 6,000 reservations)

   <u>Pacific Northwest Division Service Charge for Travel Department:</u>
   $316,800 = 3,600 billed reservations × ($528,000 ÷ 6,000 reservations)

3.

	Southeast Division	Pacific Northwest Division
Sales	$1,155,000	$1,204,000
Cost of goods sold	590,800	658,000
Gross profit	$ 564,200	$ 546,000
Selling expenses	231,000	252,000
Income from operations before service department charges	$ 333,200	$ 294,000
Service department charges	211,200	316,800
Income from operations	$ 122,000	$ (22,800)

4. A. Profit Margin = $112,500 ÷ $1,875,000 = 6.0%
   B. Investment Turnover = $1,875,000 ÷ $750,000 = 2.5
   C. Return on Investment = 6.0% × 2.5 = 15.0%

5.

Income from operations	$90,000
Minimum acceptable income from operations as a percent of assets ($450,000 × 10%)	45,000
Residual income	$45,000

6. Increase in South (Supplying) Division's Income from Operations = (Transfer Price – Variable Cost per Unit) × Units Transferred

   = ($52 – $42) × 30,000 units = $300,000

   Increase in North (Purchasing) Division's Income from Operations = (Market Price – Transfer Price) × Units Transferred

   = ($60 – $52) × 30,000 units = $240,000

Need more help? Watch step-by-step videos of how to compute answers to these Exercises in CengageNOWv2.

Problem

1.

	Domestic Division	**International Division**
Quinn Company		
Divisional Income Statements		
For the Year Ended December 31, 20Y9		
Revenues	$675,000	$480,000
Operating expenses	450,000	372,400
Income from operations before		
service department charges....................	$225,000	$107,600
Service department charges	90,000	50,000
Income from operations	$135,000	$ 57,600

2. Return on Investment = Profit Margin × Investment Turnover

$$\text{Return on Investment} = \frac{\text{Income from Operations}}{\text{Sales}} \times \frac{\text{Sales}}{\text{Invested Assets}}$$

$$\text{Domestic Division: ROI} = \frac{\$135,000}{\$675,000} \times \frac{\$675,000}{\$600,000}$$

$$= 20\% \times 1.125$$

$$= 22.5\%$$

$$\text{International Division: ROI} = \frac{\$57,600}{\$480,000} \times \frac{\$480,000}{\$384,000}$$

$$= 12\% \times 1.25$$

$$= 15\%$$

3. Domestic Division: $75,000 [$135,000 − (10% × $600,000)]
   International Division: $19,200 [$57,600 − (10% × $384,000)]

Discussion Questions

1. Differentiate between centralized and decentralized operations.

2. Differentiate between a profit center and an investment center.

3. **Weyerhaeuser** developed a system that assigns service department expenses to user divisions on the basis of actual services consumed by the division. Here are **REAL WORLD** a number of Weyerhaeuser's activities in its central Financial Services Department:

   - Payroll
   - Accounts payable
   - Accounts receivable
   - Database administration—report preparation

   For each activity, identify an activity base that could be used to charge user divisions for service.

4. What is the major shortcoming of using income from operations as a performance measure for investment centers?

5. In a decentralized company in which the divisions are organized as investment centers, how could a division be considered the least profitable even though it earned the largest amount of income from operations?

6. How does using the return on investment facilitate comparability between divisions of decentralized companies?

7. Why would a firm use a balanced scorecard in evaluating divisional performance?

8. What is the objective of transfer pricing?

9. When is the negotiated price approach preferred over the market price approach in setting transfer prices?

10. When using the negotiated price approach to transfer pricing, within what range should the transfer price be established?

Basic Exercises

SHOW ME HOW

BE 23-1   Budgetary performance for cost center   Obj. 2

Vinton Company's costs were under budget by $36,000. The company is divided into North and South regions. The North Region's costs were over budget by $45,000. Determine the amount that the South Region's costs were over or under budget.

SHOW ME HOW

BE 23-2   Service department charges   Obj. 3

The centralized computer technology department of Hardy Company has expenses of $320,000. The department has provided a total of 4,000 hours of service for the period. The Retail Division has used 2,750 hours of computer technology service during the period, and the Commercial Division has used 1,250 hours of computer technology service. How much should each division be charged for computer technology department services?

SHOW ME HOW

BE 23-3   Income from operations for profit center   Obj. 3

Using the data for Hardy Company from Brief Exercise 2 along with the following data, determine the divisional income from operations for the Retail Division and the Commercial Division:

	Retail Division	Commercial Division
Sales	$2,150,000	$1,200,000
Cost of goods sold	1,300,000	800,000
Selling expenses	150,000	175,000

SHOW ME HOW

BE 23-4   Profit margin, investment turnover, and ROI   Obj. 4

Briggs Company has income from operations of $36,000, invested assets of $180,000, and sales of $720,000. Use the DuPont formula to compute the return on investment and show (A) the profit margin, (B) the investment turnover, and (C) the return on investment.

SHOW ME HOW

BE 23-5   Residual income   Obj. 4

The Commercial Division of Galena Company has income from operations of $12,680,000 and assets of $74,500,000. The minimum acceptable return on assets is 12%. What is the residual income for the division?

SHOW ME HOW

BE 23-6   Transfer pricing   Obj. 5

The materials used by the Multinomah Division of Isbister Company are currently purchased from outside suppliers at $90 per unit. These same materials are produced by the Pembroke Division. The Pembroke Division can produce the materials needed by the Multinomah Division at a variable cost of $75 per unit. The division is currently producing 120,000 units and has capacity of 150,000 units. The two divisions have recently negotiated a transfer price of $82 per unit for 15,000 units. By how much will each division's income increase as a result of this transfer?

Exercises

✔ A. (C) $22,950

SHOW ME HOW

EX 23-1 Budget performance reports for cost centers   Obj. 2

Partially completed budget performance reports for Garland Company, a manufacturer of light duty motors, follow:

Garland Company
Budget Performance Report—Vice President, Production
For the Month Ended November 30

Plant	Budget	Actual	Over Budget	Under Budget
Eastern Region	$2,300,000	$2,287,900		$ (12,100)
Central Region	3,000,000	2,988,400		(11,600)
Western Region	(G)	(H)	$ (I)	
	$ (J)	$ (K)	$ (L)	$ (23,700)

Garland Company
Budget Performance Report—Manager, Western Region Plant
For the Month Ended November 30

Department	Budget	Actual	Over Budget	Under Budget
Chip Fabrication	$ (A)	$ (B)	$ (C)	
Electronic Assembly	700,000	703,200	3,200	
Final Assembly	525,000	516,600		$(8,400)
	$ (D)	$ (E)	$ (F)	$(8,400)

Garland Company
Budget Performance Report—Supervisor, Chip Fabrication
For the Month Ended November 30

Cost	Budget	Actual	Over Budget	Under Budget
Factory wages	$ 82,000	$ 95,500	$13,500	
Materials	120,000	115,300		$(4,700)
Power and light	45,000	49,950	4,950	
Maintenance	28,000	37,200	9,200	
	$275,000	$297,950	$27,650	$(4,700)

A. Complete the budget performance reports by determining the correct amounts for the lettered spaces.

B. ━━▶ Compose a memo to Cassandra Reid, vice president of production for Garland Company, explaining the performance of the production division for November.

EX 23-2 Divisional income statements   Obj. 3

✔ Commercial
Division income from
operations, $179,890

The following data were summarized from the accounting records for Jersey Coast Construction Company for the year ended June 30, 20Y8:

Cost of goods sold:		Service department charges:	
Commercial Division	$912,250	Commercial Division	$112,560
Residential Division	423,675	Residential Division	67,830
Administrative expenses:		Sales:	
Commercial Division	$149,800	Commercial Division	$1,354,500
Residential Division	128,625	Residential Division	743,780

Prepare divisional income statements for Jersey Coast Construction Company.

EX 23-3 Service department charges and activity bases

Obj. 3

For each of the following service departments, identify an activity base that could be used for charging the expense to the profit center:

A. Legal
B. Duplication services
C. Electronic data processing
D. Central purchasing
E. Telecommunications
F. Accounts receivable

EX 23-4 Activity bases for service department charges

Obj. 3

✔ C. 2

For each of the following service departments, select the activity base listed that is most appropriate for charging service expenses to responsible units:

Service Department		Activity Base
A. Accounts Receivable	1.	Number of conference attendees
B. Central Purchasing	2.	Number of computers
C. Computer Support	3.	Number of employees trained
D. Conferences	4.	Number of cell phone minutes used
E. Employee Travel	5.	Number of purchase requisitions
F. Payroll Accounting	6.	Number of sales invoices
G. Telecommunications	7.	Number of payroll checks
H. Training	8.	Number of travel claims

EX 23-5 Service department charges

Obj. 3

✔ B. Residential payroll, $32,640

SHOW ME HOW

In divisional income statements prepared for Demopolis Company, the Payroll Department costs are charged back to user divisions on the basis of the number of payroll distributions, and the Purchasing Department costs are charged back on the basis of the number of purchase requisitions. The Payroll Department had expenses of $64,560, and the Purchasing Department had expenses of $40,000 for the year. The following annual data for Residential, Commercial, and Government Contract divisions were obtained from corporate records:

	Residential	Commercial	Government Contract
Sales	$2,000,000	$3,250,000	$2,900,000
Number of employees:			
Weekly payroll (52 weeks per year)	400	250	150
Monthly payroll	80	30	10
Number of purchase requisitions per year	7,500	3,000	2,000

A. Determine the total amount of payroll checks and purchase requisitions processed per year by the company and each division.

B. Using the activity base information in (A), determine the annual amount of payroll and purchasing costs charged back to the Residential, Commercial, and Government Contract divisions from payroll and purchasing services.

C. ▬▬▬▶ Why does the Residential Division have a larger service department charge than the other two divisions, even though its sales are lower?

EX 23-6 Service department charges and activity bases

Obj. 3

✔ B. Help desk, $93,600

Middler Corporation, a manufacturer of electronics and communications systems, uses a service department charge system to charge profit centers with Computing and Communications Services (CCS) service department costs. The following table identifies an abbreviated list of service categories and activity bases used by the CCS department. The table also includes some assumed cost and activity base quantity information for each service for October.

CCS Service Category	Activity Base	Budgeted Cost	Budgeted Activity Base Quantity
Help desk	Number of calls	$160,000	3,200
Network center	Number of devices monitored	735,000	9,800
Electronic mail	Number of user accounts	100,000	10,000
Smartphone support	Number of smartphones issued	124,600	8,900

One of the profit centers for Middler Corporation is the Communication Systems (COMM) sector. Assume the following information for the COMM sector:

- The sector has 5,200 employees, of whom 25% are office employees.
- All the office employees have been issued a smartphone, and 96% of them have a computer on the network.
- One hundred percent of the employees with a computer also have an e-mail account.
- The average number of help desk calls for October was 1.5 calls per individual with a computer.
- There are 600 additional printers, servers, and peripherals on the network beyond the personal computers.

A. Determine the service charge rate for the four CCS service categories for October.

B. Determine the charges to the COMM sector for the four CCS service categories for October.

✔ Commercial income from operations, $1,261,260

SHOW ME HOW   EXCEL TEMPLATE

EX 23-7 Divisional income statements with service department charges   Obj. 3

Yozamba Technology has two divisions, Consumer and Commercial, and two corporate service departments, Tech Support and Purchasing. The corporate expenses for the year ended December 31, 20Y7, are as follows:

Tech Support Department	$ 516,000
Purchasing Department	89,600
Other corporate administrative expenses	560,000
Total corporate expense	$1,165,600

The other corporate administrative expenses include officers' salaries and other expenses required by the corporation. The Tech Support Department charges the divisions for services rendered, based on the number of computers in the department, and the Purchasing Department charges divisions for services, based on the number of purchase orders for each department. The usage of service by the two divisions is as follows:

	Tech Support	Purchasing
Consumer Division	375 computers	1,960 purchase orders
Commercial Division	225	3,640
Total	600 computers	5,600 purchase orders

The service department charges of the Tech Support Department and the Purchasing Department are considered controllable by the divisions. Corporate administrative expenses are not considered controllable by the divisions. The revenues, cost of goods sold, and operating expenses for the two divisions are as follows:

	Consumer	Commercial
Revenues	$7,430,000	$6,184,000
Cost of goods sold	4,123,000	3,125,000
Operating expenses	1,465,000	1,546,000

Prepare the divisional income statements for the two divisions.

EX 23-8   Corrections to service department charges for a service company   Obj. 3

✔ B. Income from operations, Cargo Division, $84,400

Wild Sun Airlines Inc. has two divisions organized as profit centers, the Passenger Division and the Cargo Division. The following divisional income statements were prepared:

Wild Sun Airlines Inc.
Divisional Income Statements
For the Year Ended December 31, 20Y9

	Passenger Division	Cargo Division
Revenues	$3,025,000	$3,025,000
Operating expenses	2,450,000	2,736,000
Income from operations before service department charges	$ 575,000	$ 289,000
Service department charges:		
Training	$ 125,000	$ 125,000
Flight scheduling	108,000	108,000
Reservations	151,200	151,200
Total service department charges	384,200	384,200
Income from operations	$ 190,800	$ (95,200)

The service department charge rate for the service department costs was based on revenues. Because the revenues of the two divisions were the same, the service department charges to each division were also the same.

The following additional information is available:

	Passenger Division	Cargo Division	Total
Number of personnel trained	350	150	500
Number of flights	800	1,200	2,000
Number of reservations requested	20,000	0	20,000

A. ▬▬▬▶ Does the income from operations for the two divisions accurately measure performance? Explain.

B. Correct the divisional income statements, using the activity bases provided in revising the service department charges.

EX 23-9   Profit center responsibility reporting   Obj. 3

✔ Income from operations, Summer Sports Division, $1,499,400

XSport Sporting Goods Co. operates two divisions—the Winter Sports Division and the Summer Sports Division. The following income and expense accounts were provided from the trial balance as of December 31, 20Y9, the end of the fiscal year, after all adjustments, including those for inventories, were recorded and posted:

SHOW ME HOW   EXCEL TEMPLATE

Sales—Winter Sports Division	$10,500,000
Sales—Summer Sports Division	13,600,000
Cost of Goods Sold—Winter Sports Division	6,300,000
Cost of Goods Sold—Summer Sports Division	7,888,000
Sales Expense—Winter Sports Division	1,680,000
Sales Expense—Summer Sports Division	1,904,000
Administrative Expense—Winter Sports Division	1,050,000
Administrative Expense—Summer Sports Division	1,210,400
Advertising Expense	482,000
Transportation Expense	240,000
Accounts Receivable Collection Expense	120,500
Warehouse Expense	1,200,000

The bases to be used in allocating expenses, together with other essential information, are as follows:

A. Advertising expense—incurred at headquarters, charged back to divisions on the basis of usage: Winter Sports Division, $216,900; Summer Sports Division, $265,100.

B. Transportation expense—charged back to divisions at a charge rate of $8.00 per bill of lading: Winter Sports Division, 14,400 bills of lading; Summer Sports Division, 15,600 bills of lading.

C. Accounts receivable collection expense—incurred at headquarters, charged back to divisions at a charge rate of $5.00 per invoice: Winter Sports Division, 9,640 sales invoices; Summer Sports Division, 14,460 sales invoices.

D. Warehouse expense—charged back to divisions on the basis of floor space used in storing division products: Winter Sports Division, 94,000 square feet; Summer Sports Division, 106,000 square feet.

Prepare a divisional income statement with two column headings: Winter Sports Division and Summer Sports Division. Provide supporting calculations for service department charges.

EX 23-10   Return on investment   Obj. 4

✔ A. Retail, 18%

SHOW ME HOW

The income from operations and the amount of invested assets in each division of Beck Industries are as follows:

	Income from Operations	Invested Assets
Retail Division	$5,400,000	$30,000,000
Commercial Division	6,250,000	25,000,000
Internet Division	1,800,000	12,000,000

A. Compute the return on investment for each division.

B. Which division is the most profitable per dollar invested?

EX 23-11   Residual income   Obj. 4

✔ A. Retail Division, $2,700,000

SHOW ME HOW

Based on the data in Exercise 10 assume that management has established a 9% minimum acceptable return for invested assets.

A. Determine the residual income for each division.

B. Which division has the most residual income?

EX 23-12   Determining missing items in return on investment computation   Obj. 4

✔ D. 3.00

One item is omitted from each of the following computations of the return on investment:

Return on Investment	=	Profit Margin	×	Investment Turnover
13.2%	=	6%	×	(A)
(B)	=	10%	×	1.80
10.5%	=	(C)	×	1.50
15%	=	5%	×	(D)
(E)	=	12%	×	1.10

Determine the missing items, identifying each by the appropriate letter.

EX 23-13   Profit margin, investment turnover, and return on investment   Obj. 4

✔ A. ROI, 24%

SHOW ME HOW

The condensed income statement for the Consumer Products Division of Fargo Industries Inc. is as follows (assuming no service department charges):

Sales	$82,500,000
Cost of goods sold	53,625,000
Gross profit	$28,875,000
Administrative expenses	15,675,000
Income from operations	$13,200,000

(Continued)

The manager of the Consumer Products Division is considering ways to increase the return on investment.

A. Using the DuPont formula for return on investment, determine the profit margin, investment turnover, and return on investment of the Consumer Products Division, assuming that $55,000,000 of assets have been invested in the Consumer Products Division.

B. If expenses could be reduced by $1,650,000 without decreasing sales, what would be the impact on the profit margin, investment turnover, and return on investment for the Consumer Products Division?

EX 23-14   Return on investment   Obj. 4

✔ A. Media Networks ROI, 24.6%

The Walt Disney Company has four profitable business segments, described as follows:

- **Media Networks:** Television and radio
- **Parks and Resorts:** Resorts, including Disneyland
- **Studio Entertainment:** Motion pictures, musical recordings, and stage plays
- **Consumer Products:** Character merchandising, Disney stores, books, and magazines

REAL WORLD

Disney recently reported sector income from operations, revenue, and invested assets (in millions) as follows:

	Income from Operations	Revenue	Invested Assets
Media Networks	$7,321	$21,152	$29,887
Parks and Resorts	2,663	15,099	23,335
Studio Entertainment	1,549	6,988	15,155
Consumer Products	1,356	4,274	7,526

A. Use the DuPont formula to determine the return on investment for the four Disney sectors. (Round percentages to one decimal place and investment turnover to two decimal places.)

B. ▬▬▶ How do the four sectors differ in their profit margin, investment turnover, and return on investment?

EX 23-15   Determining missing items in return and residual income computations   Obj. 4

✔ C. $46,250

Data for Uberto Company are presented in the following table of returns on investment and residual incomes:

Invested Assets	Income from Operations	Return on Investment	Minimum Return on Investment	Minimum Acceptable Income from Operations	Residual Income
$925,000	$185,000	(A)	15%	(B)	(C)
$775,000	(D)	(E)	(F)	$93,000	$23,250
$450,000	(G)	18%	(H)	$58,500	(I)
$610,000	$97,600	(J)	12%	(K)	(L)

Determine the missing items, identifying each item by the appropriate letter.

EX 23-16   Determining missing items from computations   Obj. 4

✔ A. (E) $300,000

Data for the North, South, East, and West divisions of Free Bird Company are as follows:

	Sales	Income from Operations	Invested Assets	Return on Investment	Profit Margin	Investment Turnover
North	$860,000	(A)	(B)	17.5%	7.0%	(C)
South	(D)	$51,300	(E)	(F)	4.5%	3.8
East	$1,020,000	(G)	$680,000	15.0%	(H)	(I)
West	$1,120,000	$89,600	$560,000	(J)	(K)	(L)

A. Determine the missing items, identifying each by the letters (A) through (L). (Round percentages and investment turnover to one decimal place.)

B. Determine the residual income for each division, assuming that the minimum acceptable return on investment established by management is 12%.

C. Which division is the most profitable in terms of (1) return on investment and (2) residual income?

REAL WORLD

EX 23-17 Balanced scorecard for a service company   Obj. 4

American Express Company is a major financial services company, noted for its American Express® card. Some of the performance measures used by the company in its balanced scorecard follow:

Average card member spending	Number of Internet features
Cards in force	Number of merchant signings
Earnings growth	Number of new card launches
Hours of credit consultant training	Return on equity
Investment in information technology	Revenue growth
Number of card choices	

For each measure, identify whether the measure best fits the innovation, customer, internal process, or financial dimension of the balanced scorecard.

EX 23-18 Building a balanced scorecard   Obj. 4

Hit-n-Run Inc. owns and operates 10 food trucks (mobile kitchens) throughout metropolitan Los Angeles. Each food truck has a different food theme, such as Irish-Mexican fusion, traditional Mexican street food, Ethiopian cuisine, and Lebanese-Italian fusion. The company was founded three years ago by Juanita O'Brien when she opened a single food truck with a unique menu. As her business has grown, she has become concerned about her ability to manage and control the business. O'Brien describes how the company was built, its key success factors, and its recent growth.

"I built the company from the ground up. In the beginning it was just me. I drove the truck, set the menu, bought the ingredients, prepared the meals, served the meals, cleaned the kitchen, and maintained the equipment. I made unique meals from quality ingredients, and didn't serve anything that wasn't perfect. I changed my location daily and notified customers of my location via Twitter.

As my customer base grew, I hired employees to help me in the truck. Then one day I realized that I had a formula that could be expanded to multiple trucks. Before I knew it, I had 10 trucks and was hiring people to do everything that I used to do by myself. Now, I work with my team to build the menu, set daily locations for the trucks, and manage the operations of the business.

My business model is based on providing the highest quality street food and charging more for it than other trucks. You won't get the cheapest meal at one of my trucks, but you will get the best. The superior quality allows me to price my meals a little bit higher than the other trucks. My employees are critical to my success. I pay them a better wage than they could make on other food trucks, and I expect more from them. I rely on them to maintain the quality that I established when I opened my first truck.

Things are going great, but I'm feeling overwhelmed. So far, the growth in sales has led to a growth in profitability—but I'm getting nervous. If quality starts to fall off, my brand value erodes, and that could affect the prices that I charge for my meals and the success of my business."

Create balanced scorecard measures for Hit-n-Run Inc. Identify whether these measures best fit the innovation, customer, internal process, or financial dimension of the balanced scorecard.

EX 23-19   Decision on transfer pricing   Obj. 5

✔ A. $3,000,000

Materials used by the Instrument Division of XPort Industries are currently purchased from outside suppliers at a cost of $210 per unit. However, the same materials are available from the Components Division. The Components Division has unused capacity and can produce the materials needed by the Instrument Division at a variable cost of $160 per unit.

A. If a transfer price of $180 per unit is established and 60,000 units of materials are transferred, with no reduction in the Components Division's current sales, how much would XPort Industries' total income from operations increase?

B. How much would the Instrument Division's income from operations increase?

C. How much would the Components Division's income from operations increase?

EX 23-20   Decision on transfer pricing   Obj. 5

✔ B. $1,200,000

Based on XPort Industries' data in Exercise 19, assume that a transfer price of $190 has been established and that 60,000 units of materials are transferred, with no reduction in the Components Division's current sales.

A. How much would XPort Industries' total income from operations increase?

B. How much would the Instrument Division's income from operations increase?

C. How much would the Components Division's income from operations increase?

D. ▬▬▬► If the negotiated price approach is used, what would be the range of acceptable transfer prices and why?

Problems: Series A

PR 23-1A   Budget performance report for a cost center   Obj. 2

Valotic Tech Inc. sells electronics over the Internet. The Consumer Products Division is organized as a cost center. The budget for the Consumer Products Division for the month ended January 31 is as follows:

Customer service salaries	$ 546,840
Insurance and property taxes	114,660
Distribution salaries	872,340
Marketing salaries	1,028,370
Engineer salaries	836,850
Warehouse wages	586,110
Equipment depreciation	183,792
Total	$4,168,962

During January, the costs incurred in the Consumer Products Division were as follows:

Customer service salaries	$ 602,350
Insurance and property taxes	110,240
Distribution salaries	861,200
Marketing salaries	1,085,230
Engineer salaries	820,008
Warehouse wages	562,632
Equipment depreciation	183,610
Total	$4,225,270

Instructions

1. Prepare a budget performance report for the director of the Consumer Products Division for the month of January.

2. ▬▬▬► For which costs might the director be expected to request supplemental reports?

✔ 1. Income from operations, West Division, $341,650

SHOW ME HOW   EXCEL TEMPLATE

PR 23-2A Profit center responsibility reporting for a service company   Obj. 3

Red Line Railroad Inc. has three regional divisions organized as profit centers. The chief executive officer (CEO) evaluates divisional performance, using income from operations as a percent of revenues. The following quarterly income and expense accounts were provided from the trial balance as of December 31:

Revenues—East	$1,400,000
Revenues—West	2,000,000
Revenues—Central	3,200,000
Operating Expenses—East	800,000
Operating Expenses—West	1,350,000
Operating Expenses—Central	1,900,000
Corporate Expenses—Shareholder Relations	300,000
Corporate Expenses—Customer Support	320,000
Corporate Expenses—Legal	500,000
General Corporate Officers' Salaries	1,200,000

The company operates three service departments: Shareholder Relations, Customer Support, and Legal. The Shareholder Relations Department conducts a variety of services for shareholders of the company. The Customer Support Department is the company's point of contact for new service, complaints, and requests for repair. The department believes that the number of customer contacts is an activity base for this work. The Legal Department provides legal services for division management. The department believes that the number of hours billed is an activity base for this work. The following additional information has been gathered:

	East	West	Central
Number of customer contacts	1,500	2,800	5,700
Number of hours billed	750	1,750	1,500

Instructions

1. Prepare quarterly income statements showing income from operations for the three divisions. Use three column headings: East, West, and Central.

2. Identify the most successful division according to the profit margin. (Round to the nearest whole percent.)

3. ➡ Provide a recommendation to the CEO for a better method for evaluating the performance of the divisions. In your recommendation, identify the major weakness of the present method.

PR 23-3A Divisional income statements and return on investment analysis   Obj. 4

✔ 2. Cereal Division ROI, 10.0%

EXCEL TEMPLATE

The Crunchy Granola Company is a diversified food company that specializes in all natural foods. The company has three operating divisions organized as investment centers. Condensed data taken from the records of the three divisions for the year ended June 30, 20Y7, are as follows:

	Cereal Division	Snack Cake Division	Retail Bakeries Division
Sales	$25,000,000	$8,000,000	$9,750,000
Cost of goods sold	16,670,000	5,575,000	6,795,000
Operating expenses	7,330,000	1,945,000	2,272,500
Invested assets	10,000,000	4,000,000	6,500,000

The management of The Crunchy Granola Company is evaluating each division as a basis for planning a future expansion of operations.

Instructions

1. Prepare condensed divisional income statements for the three divisions, assuming that there were no service department charges.

2. Using the DuPont formula for return on investment, compute the profit margin, investment turnover, and return on investment for each division. (Round percentages and the investment turnover to one decimal place.)

3. ➡ If available funds permit the expansion of operations of only one division, which of the divisions would you recommend for expansion, based on parts (1) and (2)? Explain.

PR 23-4A Effect of proposals on divisional performance

Obj. 4

✔ 1. ROI, 16.8%

EXCEL TEMPLATE

A condensed income statement for the Commercial Division of Maxell Manufacturing Inc. for the year ended December 31, 20Y9, is as follows:

Sales	$3,500,000
Cost of goods sold	2,480,000
Gross profit	$1,020,000
Operating expenses	600,000
Income from operations	$ 420,000
Invested assets	$2,500,000

Assume that the Commercial Division received no charges from service departments. The president of Maxell Manufacturing has indicated that the division's return on a $2,500,000 investment must be increased to at least 21% by the end of the next year if operations are to continue. The division manager is considering the following three proposals:

Proposal 1: Transfer equipment with a book value of $312,500 to other divisions at no gain or loss and lease similar equipment. The annual lease payments would exceed the amount of depreciation expense on the old equipment by $105,000. This increase in expense would be included as part of the cost of goods sold. Sales would remain unchanged.

Proposal 2: Purchase new and more efficient machining equipment and thereby reduce the cost of goods sold by $560,000 after considering the effects of depreciation expense on the new equipment. Sales would remain unchanged, and the old equipment, which has no remaining book value, would be scrapped at no gain or loss. The new equipment would increase invested assets by an additional $1,875,000 for the year.

Proposal 3: Reduce invested assets by discontinuing a product line. This action would eliminate sales of $595,000, reduce cost of goods sold by $406,700, and reduce operating expenses by $175,000. Assets of $1,338,000 would be transferred to other divisions at no gain or loss.

Instructions

1. Using the DuPont formula for return on investment, determine the profit margin, investment turnover, and return on investment for the Commercial Division for the past year.

2. Prepare condensed estimated income statements and compute the invested assets for each proposal.

3. Using the DuPont formula for return on investment, determine the profit margin, investment turnover, and return on investment for each proposal. (Round the investment turnover and return on investment to one decimal place.)

4. Which of the three proposals would meet the required 21% return on investment?

5. If the Commercial Division were in an industry where the profit margin could not be increased, how much would the investment turnover have to increase to meet the president's required 21% return on investment?

PR 23-5A Divisional performance analysis and evaluation

Obj. 4

✔ 2. Business
Division ROI, 23.0%

SHOW ME HOW   EXCEL TEMPLATE

The vice president of operations of Recycling Industries is evaluating the performance of two divisions organized as investment centers. Invested assets and condensed income statement data for the past year for each division are as follows:

	Business Division	Consumer Division
Sales	$42,800,000	$56,000,000
Cost of goods sold	23,500,000	30,500,000
Operating expenses	11,424,800	14,300,000
Invested assets	34,240,000	70,000,000

Instructions

1. Prepare condensed divisional income statements for the year ended December 31, 20Y8, assuming that there were no service department charges.

2. Using the DuPont formula for return on investment, determine the profit margin, investment turnover, and return on investment for each division. (Round percentages to one decimal place and the investment turnover to two decimal places.)

3. If management desires a minimum acceptable return on investment of 10%, determine the residual income for each division.

4. ━━━▶ Discuss the evaluation of the two divisions, using the performance measures determined in parts (1), (2), and (3).

PR 23-6A Transfer pricing

Obj. 5

EXCEL TEMPLATE

✔ 3. Total income from operations, $1,759,680

Garcon Inc. manufactures electronic products, with two operating divisions, Consumer and Commercial. Condensed divisional income statements, which involve no intracompany transfers and which include a breakdown of expenses into variable and fixed components, are as follows:

Garcon Inc.
Divisional Income Statements
For the Year Ended December 31, 20Y2

	Consumer Division	Commercial Division	Total
Sales:			
14,400 units × $144 per unit	$2,073,600		$2,073,600
21,600 units × $275 per unit		$5,940,000	5,940,000
Total sales	$2,073,600	$5,940,000	$8,013,600
Expenses:			
Variable:			
14,400 units × $104 per unit	$1,497,600		$1,497,600
21,600 units × $193* per unit		$4,168,800	4,168,800
Fixed	200,000	520,000	720,000
Total expenses	$1,697,600	$4,688,800	$6,386,400
Income from operations	$ 376,000	$1,251,200	$1,627,200

*$150 of the $193 per unit represents materials costs, and the remaining $43 per unit represents other variable conversion expenses incurred within the Commercial Division.

The Consumer Division is presently producing 14,400 units out of a total capacity of 17,280 units. Materials used in producing the Commercial Division's product are currently purchased from outside suppliers at a price of $150 per unit. The Consumer Division is able to produce the materials used by the Commercial Division. Except for the possible transfer of materials between divisions, no changes are expected in sales and expenses.

Instructions

1. ━━━▶ Would the market price of $150 per unit be an appropriate transfer price for Garcon Inc.? Explain.

2. ━━━▶ If the Commercial Division purchases 2,880 units from the Consumer Division, rather than externally, at a negotiated transfer price of $115 per unit, how much would the income from operations of each division and the total company income from operations increase?

3. Prepare condensed divisional income statements for Garcon Inc. based on the data in part (2).

4. ━━━▶ If a transfer price of $126 per unit is negotiated, how much would the income from operations of each division and the total company income from operations increase?

5. A. ━━━▶ What is the range of possible negotiated transfer prices that would be acceptable for Garcon Inc.?

   B. Assuming that the managers of the two divisions cannot agree on a transfer price, what price would you suggest as the transfer price?

Problems: Series B

EXCEL TEMPLATE

PR 23-1B Budget performance report for a cost center

Obj. 2

The Eastern District of Adelson Inc. is organized as a cost center. The budget for the Eastern District of Adelson Inc. for the month ended December 31 is as follows:

Sales salaries	$ 819,840
System administration salaries	448,152
Customer service salaries	152,600
Billing salaries	98,760
Maintenance	271,104
Depreciation of plant and equipment	92,232
Insurance and property taxes	41,280
Total	$1,923,968

During December, the costs incurred in the Eastern District were as follows:

Sales salaries	$ 818,880
System administration salaries	447,720
Customer service salaries	183,120
Billing salaries	98,100
Maintenance	273,000
Depreciation of plant and equipment	92,232
Insurance and property taxes	41,400
Total	$1,954,452

Instructions

1. Prepare a budget performance report for the manager of the Eastern District of Adelson for the month of December.

2. ▬▬▬▶ For which costs might the manager be expected to request supplemental reports?

PR 23-2B Profit center responsibility reporting for a service company

Obj. 3

✔ 1. Income from operations, West Region, $820,800

SHOW ME HOW   EXCEL TEMPLATE

Thomas Railroad Company organizes its three divisions, the North (N), South (S), and West (W) regions, as profit centers. The chief executive officer (CEO) evaluates divisional performance, using income from operations as a percent of revenues. The following quarterly income and expense accounts were provided from the trial balance as of December 31:

Revenues—N Region	$3,780,000
Revenues—S Region	5,673,000
Revenues—W Region	5,130,000
Operating Expenses—N Region	2,678,500
Operating Expenses—S Region	4,494,890
Operating Expenses—W Region	3,770,050
Corporate Expenses—Dispatching	182,000
Corporate Expenses—Equipment Management	1,200,000
Corporate Expenses—Treasurer's	734,000
General Corporate Officers' Salaries	1,380,000

The company operates three service departments: the Dispatching Department, the Equipment Management Department, and the Treasurer's Department. The Dispatching Department manages the scheduling and releasing of completed trains. The Equipment Management Department manages the railroad cars inventories. It makes sure the right freight cars are at the right place at the right time. The Treasurer's Department conducts a variety of services for the company as a whole. The following additional information has been gathered:

	North	South	West
Number of scheduled trains	650	1,105	845
Number of railroad cars in inventory	6,000	8,400	9,600

Instructions

1. Prepare quarterly income statements showing income from operations for the three regions. Use three column headings: North, South, and West.

2. Identify the most successful region according to the profit margin.

3. ━━━➤ Provide a recommendation to the CEO for a better method for evaluating the performance of the regions. In your recommendation, identify the major weakness of the present method.

PR 23-3B   Divisional income statements and return on investment analysis   Obj. 4

✔ 2. Mutual Fund Division, ROI, 22.4%

E.F. Lynch Company is a diversified investment company with three operating divisions organized as investment centers. Condensed data taken from the records of the three divisions for the year ended June 30, 20Y8, are as follows:

	Mutual Fund Division	Electronic Brokerage Division	Investment Banking Division
Fee revenue	$4,140,000	$3,360,000	$4,560,000
Operating expenses	2,980,800	3,091,200	3,739,200
Invested assets	5,175,000	1,120,000	3,800,000

The management of E.F. Lynch Company is evaluating each division as a basis for planning a future expansion of operations.

Instructions

1. Prepare condensed divisional income statements for the three divisions, assuming that there were no service department charges.

2. Using the DuPont formula for return on investment, compute the profit margin, investment turnover, and return on investment for each division. (Round percentages and the investment turnover to one decimal place.)

3. ━━━➤ If available funds permit the expansion of operations of only one division, which of the divisions would you recommend for expansion, based on parts (1) and (2)? Explain.

PR 23-4B   Effect of proposals on divisional performance   Obj. 4

✔ 3. Proposal 3 ROI, 16.0%

A condensed income statement for the Electronics Division of Gihbli Industries Inc. for the year ended December 31, 20Y9, is as follows:

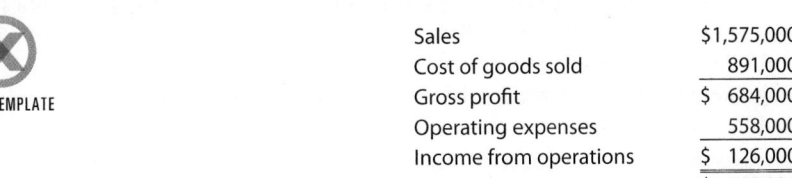

Sales	$1,575,000
Cost of goods sold	891,000
Gross profit	$ 684,000
Operating expenses	558,000
Income from operations	$ 126,000
Invested assets	$1,050,000

Assume that the Electronics Division received no charges from service departments.

The president of Gihbli Industries Inc. has indicated that the division's return on a $1,050,000 investment must be increased to at least 20% by the end of the next year if operations are to continue. The division manager is considering the following three proposals:

Proposal 1: Transfer equipment with a book value of $300,000 to other divisions at no gain or loss and lease similar equipment. The annual lease payments would be less than the amount of depreciation expense on the old equipment by $31,400. This decrease in expense would be included as part of the cost of goods sold. Sales would remain unchanged.

Proposal 2: Reduce invested assets by discontinuing a product line. This action would eliminate sales of $180,000, reduce cost of goods sold by $119,550, and reduce operating expenses by $60,000. Assets of $112,500 would be transferred to other divisions at no gain or loss.

(Continued)

Proposal 3: Purchase new and more efficient machinery and thereby reduce the cost of goods sold by $189,000 after considering the effects of depreciation expense on the new equipment. Sales would remain unchanged, and the old machinery, which has no remaining book value, would be scrapped at no gain or loss. The new machinery would increase invested assets by $918,750 for the year.

Instructions

1. Using the DuPont formula for return on investment, determine the profit margin, investment turnover, and return on investment for the Electronics Division for the past year. (Round percentages and investment turnover to one decimal place.)

2. Prepare condensed estimated income statements and compute the invested assets for each proposal.

3. Using the DuPont formula for return on investment, determine the profit margin, investment turnover, and return on investment for each proposal. (Round percentages and investment turnover to one decimal place.)

4. Which of the three proposals would meet the required 20% return on investment?

5. If the Electronics Division were in an industry where the profit margin could not be increased, how much would the investment turnover have to increase to meet the president's required 20% return on investment? (Round to one decimal place.)

PR 23-5B   Divisional performance analysis and evaluation   Obj. 4

✔ 2. Road Bike Division ROI, 12.0%

SHOW ME HOW   EXCEL TEMPLATE

The vice president of operations of Free Ride Bike Company is evaluating the performance of two divisions organized as investment centers. Invested assets and condensed income statement data for the past year for each division are as follows:

	Road Bike Division	Mountain Bike Division
Sales	$1,728,000	$1,760,000
Cost of goods sold	1,380,000	1,400,000
Operating expenses	175,200	236,800
Invested assets	1,440,000	800,000

Instructions

1. Prepare condensed divisional income statements for the year ended December 31, 20Y7, assuming that there were no service department charges.

2. Using the DuPont formula for return on investment, determine the profit margin, investment turnover, and return on investment for each division. (Round percentages and the investment turnover to one decimal place.)

3. If management's minimum acceptable return on investment is 10%, determine the residual income for each division.

4. ▬▬▶ Discuss the evaluation of the two divisions, using the performance measures determined in parts (1), (2), and (3).

PR 23-6B   Transfer pricing   Obj. 5

✔ 3. Navigational Systems Division, $179,410

EXCEL TEMPLATE

Exoplex Industries Inc. is a diversified aerospace company, including two operating divisions, Semiconductors and Navigational Systems. Condensed divisional income statements, which involve no intracompany transfers and include a breakdown of expenses into variable and fixed components, are as follows:

Exoplex Industries Inc.
Divisional Income Statements
For the Year Ended December 31, 20Y8

	Semiconductors Division	Navigational Systems Division	Total
Sales:			
2,240 units × $396 per unit	$887,040		$ 887,040
3,675 units × $590 per unit		$2,168,250	2,168,250
Total sales	$887,040	$2,168,250	$3,055,290
Expenses:			
Variable:			
2,240 units × $232 per unit	$519,680		$ 519,680
3,675 units × $472* per unit		$1,734,600	1,734,600
Fixed	220,000	325,000	545,000
Total expenses	$739,680	$2,059,600	$2,799,280
Income from operations	$147,360	$ 108,650	$ 256,010

*$432 of the $472 per unit represents materials costs, and the remaining $40 per unit represents other variable conversion expenses incurred within the Navigational Systems Division.

The Semiconductors Division is presently producing 2,240 units out of a total capacity of 2,820 units. Materials used in producing the Navigational Systems Division's product are currently purchased from outside suppliers at a price of $432 per unit. The Semiconductors Division is able to produce the components used by the Navigational Systems Division. Except for the possible transfer of materials between divisions, no changes are expected in sales and expenses.

Instructions

1. ➤ Would the market price of $432 per unit be an appropriate transfer price for Exoplex Industries Inc.? Explain.

2. ➤ If the Navigational Systems Division purchases 580 units from the Semiconductors Division, rather than externally, at a negotiated transfer price of $310 per unit, how much would the income from operations of each division and total company income from operations increase?

3. Prepare condensed divisional income statements for Exoplex Industries Inc. based on the data in part (2).

4. ➤ If a transfer price of $340 per unit is negotiated, how much would the income from operations of each division and total company income from operations increase?

5. A. ➤ What is the range of possible negotiated transfer prices that would be acceptable for Exoplex Industries Inc.?

   B. Assuming that the managers of the two divisions cannot agree on a transfer price, what price would you suggest as the transfer price?

Analysis for Decision Making

REAL WORLD

ADM-1 GNC: Franchise segment return on investment

GNC Holdings Inc. is a leading retailer of health and nutrition products, which are sold through both company-operated (3,500 outlets) and franchised retail (3,200 outlets) stores. In addition, GNC manufactures many of the products that it sells through its company-operated and franchised channels. As such, GNC's operating segments are Retail, Franchise, and Manufacturing. The Retail segment is made up of company-operated stores, and the Franchise segment is made up of franchised stores. Recent financial information from these segments is as follows (in millions):

	Retail	Franchise	Manufacturing
Sales	$1,939	$433	$486
Income from operations	349	157	90
Invested assets	1,573	512	407

A. Determine the profit margin for each segment. (Round percentages to one decimal place.)

B. ━━━━▶ Why might the profit margin of the Franchise segment be larger than the other two segments?

C. Determine the investment turnover for each segment. (Round to one decimal place.)

D. Use the DuPont formula to determine the return on investment for each segment. (Round percentages to one decimal place.)

E. What is the source of revenues for the Manufacturing segment? What are the revenue reporting considerations for sales to company-operated stores?

REAL WORLD

ADM-2 Domino's Pizza: Franchise segment return on investment

Domino's Pizza, Inc. is the second-largest pizza chain in the world. In the United States, Domino's has 377 company-owned restaurants and 4,690 franchised restaurants. In addition, Domino's has a supply chain that manufactures and delivers dough and other food products to all the domestic restaurants. Franchisees are required to purchase food products from the Domino's supply chain as part of their franchise agreement. Thus, in the United States, Domino's has three segments: Company-Owned Restaurants, Franchised Restaurants, and Supply Chain. Operating data for these three segments in the United States are as follows (in millions):

	Company-Owned Restaurants	Franchised Restaurants	Supply Chain
Sales	$348	$230	$1,262
Cost of sales	267		1,132
General and administrative expenses*	25	125	100
Invested assets**	32	30	146

*Allocation to segments assumed
**Allocation between Company-Owned and Franchised assumed

A. Determine the income from operations for each segment.

B. Determine the profit margin for each segment. (Round percentages to one decimal place.)

C. Determine the investment turnover for each segment. (Round to one decimal place.)

D. Use the DuPont formula to determine the return on investment for each segment. (Round to nearest whole percent.)

E. ━━━━▶ Explain Domino's business model and how it is related to ROI in each segment.

ADM-3   H&R Block: Franchise segment return on investment

H&R Block Inc. provides tax preparation services throughout the United States and other parts of the world. These services are provided through company-owned and franchised operations. The total number of U.S. offices that are company-owned and franchised for a recent year is as follows:

	Company-Owned	Franchised	Total
H&R Block Offices (U.S.)	6,365	3,921	10,286

Recent financial information provided by H&R Block for its company-owned and franchised operations is as follows (in millions):

	Company-Owned	Franchised
Revenues	$2,651	
Franchise fees		$335
Cost of services	1,630	
Property, plant, and equipment	2,979	

In addition, H&R Block had $653 million in selling, general, and administrative expenses. These expenses support both company-owned and franchised operations. For example, H&R Block advertising supports both segments. H&R Block had an additional $1,537 million in unallocated property, plant, and equipment. These fixed assets are not associated with its tax service offices, but represent other assets, such as those used at its general headquarters.

A. Allocate the selling, general, and administrative expenses to the company-owned and franchised operations based on the relative number of offices in each segment. (Round to the nearest million.)

B. Allocate the unallocated property, plant, and equipment to the company-owned and franchised operations based on the relative number of offices in each segment. (Round to the nearest million.)

C. Determine the income from operations for each segment, including the allocated selling, general, and administrative expenses from (A).

D. Determine the profit margin for each segment. (Round percentages to one decimal place.)

E. Determine the investment turnover for each segment, including the allocated property, plant, and equipment from (B). (Round to two decimal places.)

F. Use the DuPont formula to determine the return on investment for each segment. (Round percentages to one decimal place.)

G. ▬▬▶ What financial variables would impact an H&R Block franchisee's ROI as compared to variables impacting a non-franchised independent tax preparation business?

Take It Further

ETHICS

TIF 23-1 Ethics in Action

Sembotix Company has several divisions including a Semiconductor Division that sells semiconductors to both internal and external customers. The company's X-ray Division uses semiconductors as a component in its final product and is evaluating whether to purchase them from the Semiconductor Division or from an external supplier. The market price for semiconductors is $100 per 100 semiconductors. Dave Bryant is the controller of the X-ray Division, and Howard Hillman is the controller of the Semiconductor Division. The following conversation took place between Dave and Howard:

Dave: I hear you are having problems selling semiconductors out of your division. Maybe I can help.

Howard: You've got that right. We're producing and selling at about 90% of our capacity to outsiders. Last year, we were selling 100% of capacity. Would it be possible for your division to pick up some of our excess capacity? After all, we are part of the same company.

Dave: What kind of price could you give me?

Howard: Well, you know as well as I that we are under strict profit responsibility in our divisions, so I would expect to get market price, $100 for 100 semiconductors.

Dave: I'm not so sure we can swing that. I was expecting a price break from a "sister" division.

Howard: Hey, I can only take this "sister" stuff so far. If I give you a price break, our profits will fall from last year's levels. I don't think I could explain that. I'm sorry, but I must remain firm—market price. After all, it's only fair—that's what you would have to pay from an external supplier.

Dave: Fair or not, I think we'll pass. Sorry we couldn't have helped.

━━━▶ Is Dave behaving unethically by trying to force the Semiconductor Division into a price break? Comment on Howard's reactions.

REAL WORLD

TIF 23-2 Team Activity

In teams, visit the Web site of a company that uses the balanced scorecard to evaluate the company's performance. Identify the performance measures used by the company on its balanced scorecard. For each measure, identify whether the measure best fits the innovation, customer, internal process, or financial dimension of the balanced scorecard.

TIF 23-3 Communication

The Norse Division of Gridiron Concepts Inc. experienced significant revenue and profit growth from 20Y4 to 20Y6 as shown in the following divisional income statements:

Gridiron Concepts Inc.
Divisional Income Statements, Norse Division
For the Three Years Ended December 31, 20Y6

	20Y4	20Y5	20Y6
Sales	$1,470,000	$2,100,000	$2,450,000
Cost of goods sold	1,064,000	1,498,000	1,680,000
Gross profit	$ 406,000	$ 602,000	$ 770,000
Operating expenses	185,500	224,000	231,000
Income from operations	$ 220,500	$ 378,000	$ 539,000
Invested assets	$ 735,000	$ 1,500,000	$3,500,000

There are no service department charges, and the division operates as an investment center that must maintain a 15% return on invested assets.

━━━▶ Determine the profit margin, investment turnover, and return on investment for the Norse Division for 20Y4–20Y6. Based on your calculations, write a brief memo to the president of Gridiron Concepts Inc., Knute Holz, evaluating the division's performance.

24 Differential Analysis and Product Pricing

Concepts and Principles

Chapter 15 *Introduction to Managerial Accounting*

Developing Information

COST SYSTEMS	COST BEHAVIOR

Chapter 16 *Job Order Costing*

Chapter 17 *Process Cost Systems*

Chapter 18 *Activity-Based Costing*

Chapter 19 *Cost-Volume-Profit Analysis*

Decision Making

EVALUATING PERFORMANCE	COMPARING ALTERNATIVES

Chapter 20 *Variable Costing for Management Analysis*

Chapter 21 *Budgeting*

Chapter 22 *Evaluating Variances from Standard Costs*

Chapter 23 *Evaluating Decentralized Operations*

Chapter 24 *Differential Analysis and Product Pricing*

Chapter 25 *Capital Investment Analysis*

Chapter 26 *Lean Manufacturing*

Facebook, Inc.

Many of the decisions that you make depend on comparing the estimated costs of alternatives. The payoff from such comparisons is described in the following report from a University of Michigan study:

Richard Nisbett and two colleagues quizzed Michigan faculty members and university seniors on such questions as how often they walk out on a bad movie, refuse to finish a bad meal, start over on a weak term paper, or abandon a research project that no longer looks promising. They believe that people who cut their losses this way are following sound economic rules: calculating the net benefits of alternative courses of action, writing off past costs that can't be recovered, and weighing the opportunity to use future time and effort more profitably elsewhere.

Among students, those who have learned to use cost-benefit analysis frequently are apt to have far better grades than their Scholastic Aptitude Test scores would have predicted. Again, the more economics courses the students have, the more likely they are to apply cost-benefit analysis outside the classroom.

Dr. Nisbett concedes that for many Americans, cost-benefit rules often appear to conflict with such traditional principles as "never give up" and "waste not, want not."

Managers must also evaluate the costs and benefits of alternative actions. Facebook, the largest social networking site in the world, was cofounded by Mark Zuckerberg in 2004. Since then, it has grown to more than 1 billion users and made Zuckerberg a multibillionaire. Such growth involves decisions about where to expand. For example, expanding the site to new languages and countries involves software programming, marketing, and computer hardware costs. The benefits include adding new users to Facebook.

Analysis of the benefits and costs might lead Facebook to expand in some languages before others. For example, such an analysis might lead Facebook to expand in Swedish before it expands in Tok Pisin (the language of Papua New Guinea).

In this chapter, differential analysis, which reports the effects of decisions on total revenues and costs, is discussed. Practical approaches to setting product prices are also described and illustrated. Finally, how production bottlenecks influence pricing and other decisions is also discussed.

Source: Alan L. Otten, "Economic Perspective Produces Steady Yields," from People Patterns, *The Wall Street Journal*, March 31,1992, p. B1.

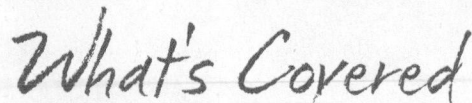

Differential Analysis and Product Pricing

Differential Analysis
- Lease or Sell (Obj. 1)
- Discontinue a Segment or Product (Obj. 1)
- Make or Buy (Obj. 1)
- Replace Equipment (Obj. 1)
- Process or Sell (Obj. 1)
- Accept Business at a Special Price (Obj. 1)

Normal Product Pricing
- Product Cost Method (Obj. 2)
- Target Costing (Obj. 2)

Managing Production Bottlenecks
- Contribution Margin Analysis (Obj. 3)
- Pricing Implications (Obj. 3)

Learning Objectives

Obj. 1 Prepare differential analysis reports for a variety of managerial decisions.

Obj. 2 Determine the selling price of a product, using the product cost method.

Obj. 3 Describe and illustrate the managing of manufacturing bottlenecks.

Analysis for Decision Making

Describe and illustrate the use of yield pricing for a service business.

Objective 1

Prepare differential analysis reports for a variety of managerial decisions.

Differential Analysis

Managerial decision making involves choosing between alternative courses of action. A commonly used decision-making process used in business is differential analysis. **Differential analysis**, sometimes called *incremental analysis*, analyzes differential revenues and costs in order to determine the differential impact on income of two alternative courses of action.

Differential revenue is the amount of increase or decrease in revenue that is expected from a course of action compared to an alternative. **Differential cost** is the amount of increase or decrease in cost that is expected from a course of action as compared to an alternative. **Differential income (loss)** is the difference between the differential revenue and differential costs. Differential income indicates that a decision is expected to increase income, while a differential loss indicates the decision is expected to decrease income.

Link to Facebook   **Facebook**'s purchase of **WhatsApp** in 2014 was estimated to yield differential income.

To illustrate, assume that on July 11 Bryant Restaurants is deciding whether to replace some of its customer seating (tables) with a salad bar. Exhibit 1 illustrates differential analysis for this decision.

Differential Analysis
Tables (Alternative 1) or Salad Bar (Alternative 2)
July 11

	Tables (Alternative 1)	Salad Bar (Alternative 2)	Differential Effect on Income (Alternative 2)
Revenues............................	$100,000	$120,000	$20,000
Costs.................................	–60,000	–65,000	–5,000
Income (loss)	$ 40,000	$ 55,000	$15,000

Exhibit 1
Differential Analysis—Bryant Restaurants

The differential analysis is prepared in three columns, where positive amounts indicate the effect is to increase income and negative amounts indicate the effect is to decrease income. The first column is the revenues, costs, and income for maintaining floor space for tables (Alternative 1). The second column is the revenues, costs, and income for using that floor space for a salad bar (Alternative 2). The third column is the difference between the revenues, costs, and income of one alternative over the other.

In Exhibit 1, the salad bar is being considered over retaining the existing tables. Thus, Column 3 in Exhibit 1 is expressed in terms of Alternative 2 (salad bar) over Alternative 1 (tables).

In Exhibit 1, the differential revenue of a salad bar over tables is $20,000 ($120,000 – $100,000). Because the increased revenue would increase income, it is entered as a positive $20,000 in the Differential Effect on Income column. The differential cost of a salad bar over tables is $5,000 ($65,000 – $60,000). Because the increased costs will decrease income, it is entered as a negative $5,000 in the Differential Effect on Income column.

The differential income (loss) of a salad bar over tables of $15,000 is determined by subtracting the differential costs from the differential revenues in the Differential Effect on Income column. Thus, installing a salad bar increases income by $15,000.

The preceding differential revenue, costs, and income can also be determined using the following formulas:

$$\text{Differential Revenue} = \text{Revenue (Alt. 2)} - \text{Revenue (Alt. 1)}$$
$$= \$120,000 - \$100,000 = \$20,000$$

$$\text{Differential Costs} = \text{Costs (Alt. 2)} - \text{Costs (Alt. 1)}$$
$$= -\$65,000 - (-\$60,000) = -\$5,000$$

$$\text{Differential Income (Loss)} = \text{Income (Alt. 2)} - \text{Income (Alt. 1)}$$
$$= \$55,000 - \$40,000 = \$15,000$$

Based upon the differential analysis shown in Exhibit 1, Bryant Restaurants should decide to replace some of its tables with a salad bar. Doing so will increase its income by $15,000.

Over time, Bryant Restaurants should review its decision based upon actual revenues and costs. If the actual revenues and costs differ significantly from those shown in Exhibit 2, another differential analysis should be performed.

In this chapter, differential analysis is illustrated for the following common decisions:

- Leasing or selling equipment
- Discontinuing an unprofitable segment
- Manufacturing or purchasing a needed part
- Replacing fixed assets
- Selling a product or processing further
- Accepting additional business at a special price

Lease or Sell

Management may lease or sell a piece of equipment that is no longer needed. This may occur when a company changes its manufacturing process and can no longer use the equipment in the manufacturing process. In making a decision, differential analysis can be used.

To illustrate, assume that on June 22 of the current year, Marcus Company is considering leasing or disposing of the following equipment:

Cost of equipment	$ 200,000
Accumulated depreciation	(120,000)
Book value	$ 80,000
Lease (Alternative 1):	
Total revenue for five-year lease	$ 160,000
Total estimated repair, insurance, and	
property tax expenses during life of lease	35,000
Residual value at end of fifth year of lease	0
Sell (Alternative 2):	
Sales price	$ 100,000
Commission on sales	6%

Exhibit 2 shows the differential analysis of whether to lease (Alternative 1) or sell (Alternative 2) the equipment.

Exhibit 2
Differential Analysis—Lease or Sell Equipment

Differential Analysis
Lease Equipment (Alternative 1) or Sell Equipment (Alternative 2)
June 22

	Lease Equipment (Alternative 1)	Sell Equipment (Alternative 2)	Differential Effect on Income (Alternative 2)
Revenues.....................	$160,000	$100,000	–$60,000
Costs.........................	–35,000	–6,000	29,000
Income (loss)	$125,000	$ 94,000	–$31,000

If the equipment is sold, differential revenues will decrease by $60,000, differential costs will decrease by $29,000, and the differential effect on income is a decrease of $31,000. Thus, the decision should be to lease the equipment.

Exhibit 2 includes only the differential revenues and differential costs associated with the lease-or-sell decision. The $80,000 book value ($200,000 − $120,000) of the equipment is a *sunk cost* and is not considered in the differential analysis. **Sunk costs** are costs that have been incurred in the past, cannot be recouped, and are not relevant to future decisions. That is, the $80,000 is not affected regardless of which decision is made. For example, if the $80,000 were included in Exhibit 2, the costs for each alternative would both increase by $80,000, but the differential effect on income of −$31,000 would remain unchanged.

To simplify, the following factors were not considered in Exhibit 2:

- Differential revenue from investing funds
- Differential income tax

Differential revenue, such as interest revenue, could arise from investing the cash created by the two alternatives. Differential income tax could also arise from differences in income. These factors are discussed in Chapter 25.

Discontinue a Segment or Product

A product, department, branch, territory, or other segment of a business may be generating losses. As a result, management may consider discontinuing (eliminating) the product or segment. In such cases, it may be erroneously assumed that the total company income will increase by eliminating the operating loss.

Discontinuing the product or segment usually eliminates all of the product's or segment's variable costs. Such costs include direct materials, direct labor, variable factory overhead, and sales commissions. However, fixed costs such as depreciation, insurance, and property taxes may not be eliminated. Thus, it is possible for total company income to decrease rather than increase if the unprofitable product or segment is discontinued.

To illustrate, the income statement for Battle Creek Cereal Co. is shown in Exhibit 3. As shown in Exhibit 3, Bran Flakes incurred an operating loss of $11,000. Because Bran Flakes has incurred annual losses for several years, management is considering discontinuing it.

Exhibit 3

Income (Loss) by Product

Battle Creek Cereal Co.
Condensed Income Statement
For the Year Ended August 31, 20Y8

	Corn Flakes	Toasted Oats	Bran Flakes	Total Company
Sales...	$500,000	$400,000	$100,000	$1,000,000
Cost of goods sold:				
Variable costs................................	$220,000	$200,000	$ 60,000	$ 480,000
Fixed costs	120,000	80,000	20,000	220,000
Total cost of goods sold...................	$340,000	$280,000	$ 80,000	$ 700,000
Gross profit.....................................	$160,000	$120,000	$ 20,000	$ 300,000
Operating expenses:				
Variable expenses............................	$ 95,000	$ 60,000	$ 25,000	$ 180,000
Fixed expenses................................	25,000	20,000	6,000	51,000
Total operating expenses	$120,000	$ 80,000	$ 31,000	$ 231,000
Income (loss) from operations....................	$ 40,000	$ 40,000	$ (11,000)	$ 69,000

However, the differential analysis dated September 29, 20Y8, in Exhibit 4 indicates that discontinuing Bran Flakes (Alternative 2) actually decreases operating income by $15,000, even though it incurs a net loss of $11,000. This is because discontinuing Bran Flakes has no effect on fixed costs and expenses.

Exhibit 4 only considers the short-term (one-year) effects of discontinuing Bran Flakes. When discontinuing a product or segment, long-term effects should also be considered. For example, employee morale and productivity might suffer if employees have to be laid off or relocated.

Differential Analysis
Continue Bran Flakes (Alternative 1) or Discontinue Bran Flakes (Alternative 2)
September 29, 20Y8

	Continue Bran Flakes (Alternative 1)	Discontinue Bran Flakes (Alternative 2)	Differential Effect on Income (Alternative 2)
Revenues.............................	$100,000	$ 0	−$100,000
Costs:			
Variable	−$ 85,000	$ 0	$ 85,000
Fixed.............................	−26,000	−26,000	0
Income (loss).........................	−$ 11,000	−$26,000	−$ 15,000

Link to Facebook **Facebook** reports its financial results by geographic area (United States and Rest of the World), but does not have separate business segments.

Make or Buy

Companies often manufacture products made up of components that are assembled into a final product. For example, an automobile manufacturer assembles tires, radios, motors, interior seats, transmissions, and other parts into a finished automobile. In such cases, the manufacturer must decide whether to make a part or purchase it from a supplier.

Differential analysis can be used to decide whether to make or buy a part. The analysis is similar whether management is considering making a part that is currently being purchased or purchasing a part that is currently being made.

To illustrate, assume that an automobile manufacturer has been purchasing instrument panels for $240 a unit. The factory is currently operating at 80% of capacity, and no major increase in production is expected in the near future. The cost per unit of manufacturing an instrument panel internally is estimated on February 15 as follows:

Direct materials	$ 80
Direct labor	80
Variable factory overhead	52
Fixed factory overhead	68
Total cost per unit	$280

If the make price of $280 is simply compared with the buy price of $240, the decision is to buy the instrument panel. However, if unused capacity could be used in manufacturing the part, only the variable factory overhead costs would increase.

The differential analysis for this make (Alternative 1) or buy (Alternative 2) decision is shown in Exhibit 5. The first line shows that there is no revenue earned in this decision, since the component is not sold but used in production. The remaining lines show the cost per unit under each alternative. The fixed factory overhead cannot be eliminated by purchasing the panels. Thus, both alternatives include the fixed factory overhead. The differential analysis indicates there is a loss of $28 per unit from buying the instrument panels. Thus, the instrument panels should be manufactured.

Exhibit 5

Differential Analysis—Make or Buy Instrument Panels

Differential Analysis
Make (Alternative 1) or Buy (Alternative 2) Panels
February 15

	Make Panels (Alternative 1)	Buy Panels (Alternative 2)	Differential Effect on Income (Alternative 2)
Sales price...............................	$ 0	$ 0	$ 0
Unit costs:			
Purchase price..........................	0	–240	–240
Direct materials........................	–80	0	80
Direct labor	–80	0	80
Variable factory overhead...............	–52	0	52
Fixed factory overhead	–68	–68	0
Income (loss)	–$280	–$308	–$ 28

Other factors should also be considered in the analysis. For example, productive capacity used to make the instrument panel would not be available for other production. The decision may also affect the future business relationship with the instrument panel supplier. For example, if the supplier provides other parts, the company's decision to make instrument panels might jeopardize the timely delivery of other parts.

Rather than develop its own virtual reality technology, Facebook purchased Oculus VR, LLC, a privately held company, in 2014.

Link to Facebook

Replace Equipment

The usefulness of a fixed asset may decrease before it is worn out. For example, old equipment may no longer be as efficient as new equipment.

Differential analysis can be used for decisions to replace fixed assets such as equipment and machinery. The analysis normally focuses on the costs of continuing to use the old equipment versus replacing the equipment. The book value of the old equipment is a sunk cost and, thus, is irrelevant.

To illustrate, assume that on November 28 of the current year, a business is considering replacing an old machine with a new machine:

Old Machine:	
Book value	$100,000
Estimated annual variable manufacturing costs	225,000
Estimated selling price	25,000
Estimated remaining useful life	5 years
New Machine:	
Purchase price of new machine	$250,000
Estimated annual variable manufacturing costs	150,000
Estimated residual value	0
Estimated useful life	5 years

The differential analysis for whether to continue with the old machine (Alternative 1) or replace the old machine with a new machine (Alternative 2) is shown in Exhibit 6.

Exhibit 6

Differential
Analysis—Continue
with or Replace
Old Equipment

	Differential Analysis Continue with (Alternative 1) or Replace (Alternative 2) Machine November 28		
	Continue with Old Machine (Alternative 1)	**Replace Old Machine (Alternative 2)**	**Differential Effect on Income (Alternative 2)**
Revenues:			
Proceeds from sale of old machine	$ 0	$ 25,000	$ 25,000
Costs:			
Purchase price.............................	$ 0	–$ 250,000	–$250,000
Variable manufacturing costs (5 years)	–1,125,000	–750,000	375,000
Income (loss)	–$1,125,000	–$ 975,000	$150,000

As shown in Exhibit 6, there is five-year differential effect on income of $150,000 (or $30,000 per year) from replacing the machine. Thus, the decision should be to purchase the new machine and sell the old machine.

Other factors are often important in equipment replacement decisions. For example, differences between the remaining useful life of the old equipment and the estimated life of the new equipment could exist. In addition, the new equipment might improve the overall quality of the product and, thus, increase sales.

The time value of money and other uses for the cash needed to purchase the new equipment could also affect the decision to replace equipment.[1] The revenue that is forgone from an alternative use of an asset, such as cash, is called an **opportunity cost**. Although the opportunity cost is not recorded in the accounting records, it is useful in analyzing alternative courses of action.

Process or Sell

During manufacturing, a product normally progresses through various stages or processes. In some cases, a product can be sold at an intermediate stage of production, or it can be processed further and then sold.

Differential analysis can be used to decide whether to sell a product at an intermediate stage or to process it further. In doing so, the differential revenues and costs from further processing are compared. The costs of producing the intermediate product do not change, regardless of whether the intermediate product is sold or processed further.

To illustrate, assume that a business produces kerosene as an intermediate product as follows:

Kerosene:	
Batch size	4,000 gallons
Cost of producing kerosene	$2,400 per batch
Selling price	$2.50 per gallon

---

[1] The time value of money in purchasing equipment (capital assets) is discussed in Chapter 25.

The kerosene can be processed further to yield gasoline as follows:

Gasoline:	
Input batch size	4,000 gallons
Less evaporation (20%)	(800) (4,000 × 20%)
Output batch size	3,200 gallons
Cost of producing gasoline	$3,050 per batch
Selling price	$3.50 per gallon

Exhibit 7 shows the differential analysis dated October 1 for whether to sell kerosene (Alternative 1) or process it further into gasoline (Alternative 2).

As shown in Exhibit 7, there is additional income of $550 per batch from further processing the kerosene into gasoline. Therefore, the decision should be to process the kerosene further into gasoline.

Differential Analysis
Sell Kerosene (Alternative 1) or Process into Gasoline (Alternative 2)
October 1

	Sell Kerosene (Alternative 1)	Process into Gasoline (Alternative 2)	Differential Effect on Income (Alternative 2)
Revenues................................	$10,000*	$11,200**	$1,200
Costs	–2,400	–3,050	–650
Income (loss)	$ 7,600	$ 8,150	$ 550

*4,000 gallons × $2.50
**(4,000 gallons – 800 gallons) × $3.50

Exhibit 7
Differential Analysis—Sell Kerosene or Process into Gasoline

Facebook provides advertising and other services to its customers and does not manufacture a product.

Link to Facebook

Accept Business at a Special Price

A company may be offered the opportunity to sell its products at prices other than normal prices. For example, an exporter may offer to sell a company's products overseas at special discount prices.

Differential analysis can be used to decide whether to accept additional business at a special price. The differential revenue from accepting the additional business is compared to the differential costs of producing and delivering the product to the customer.

The differential costs of accepting additional business depend on whether the company is operating at less than capacity. If the company is operating at less than full capacity, then the additional production does not increase fixed manufacturing costs. However, selling and administrative expenses may change because of the additional business.

To illustrate, assume that B-Ball Inc. manufactures basketballs as follows:

Monthly productive capacity	12,500 basketballs
Current monthly sales	10,000 basketballs
Normal (domestic) selling price	$30.00 per basketball
Manufacturing costs:	
Variable costs	$12.50 per basketball
Fixed costs	7.50
Total manufacturing costs	$20.00 per basketball

On March 10 of the current year, B-Ball Inc. received an offer from an exporter for 5,000 basketballs at $18 each. Production can be spread over three months without interfering with normal production or incurring overtime costs. Pricing policies in the domestic market will not be affected.

As shown in Exhibit 8, a differential analysis on whether to reject the order (Alternative 1) or accept the order (Alternative 2) shows that the special order should be accepted. The special business is accepted even though the sales price of $18 per unit is less than the manufacturing cost of $20 per unit because the fixed costs are not affected by the decision and are, thus, omitted from the analysis.

Exhibit 8

Differential Analysis—Accept Business at a Special Price

	Differential Analysis Reject Order (Alternative 1) or Accept Order (Alternative 2) March 10		
	Reject Order (Alternative 1)	**Accept Order (Alternative 2)**	**Differential Effect on Income (Alternative 2)**
Revenues....................................	$0	$90,000*	$90,000
Costs:			
Variable manufacturing costs..............	0	−62,500**	−62,500
Income (loss)................................	$0	$27,500	$27,500

*5,000 units × $18
**5,000 units × $12.50 variable cost per unit

Proposals to sell products at special prices often require additional considerations. For example, special prices in one geographic area may result in price reductions in other areas, with the result that total company sales revenues decrease. Manufacturers must also conform to the Robinson-Patman Act, which prohibits price discrimination within the United States unless price differences can be justified by different costs.

Why It Matters

60% Off!

Priceline.com was founded in the late 1990s and has become a successful survivor of the Internet revolution. Priceline offers deep discounts of up to 60% for travel services, such as hotels and flights. How does it work? For hotel services, Priceline has arrangements with hotels to provide deeply discounted rooms. These rooms are resold to customers on Priceline's Web site. Why do hotels provide rooms at such a large discount? If the hotel has unused rooms, the variable cost of an incremental guest is low relative to the fixed cost of the room. During low occupancy times, any price greater than the variable cost of providing the room can add to the profitability of the hotel. Thus, hotels view Priceline as an additional source of profit from filling unused rooms during low demand periods.

Check Up Corner 24-1 Differential Analysis

For the three cases below, prepare a differential analysis.

Case A (Discontinue a Segment): Product K has revenue of $65,000, variable cost of goods sold of $50,000, variable selling expenses of $12,000, and fixed costs of $25,000, creating a loss from operations of $22,000.

Required: Prepare a differential analysis dated February 22 to determine whether Product K should be continued (Alternative 1) or discontinued (Alternative 2), assuming fixed costs are unaffected by the decision.

Case B (Make vs. Buy): A company manufactures a subcomponent of a product for $80 per unit, including fixed costs of $25 per unit. The subcomponent could be purchased from an outside supplier for $60 per unit, plus $5 per unit freight.

Required: Prepare a differential analysis dated November 2 to determine whether the company should make (Alternative 1) or buy (Alternative 2) the subcomponent, assuming fixed costs are unaffected by the decision.

Case C (Sell or Process Further): Product T is produced for $2.50 per gallon. Product T can be sold without additional processing for $3.50 per gallon, or processed further into Product V at an additional total cost of $0.70 per gallon. Product V can be sold for $4.00 per gallon.

Required: Prepare a differential analysis dated April 8 to determine whether to sell Product T (Alternative 1) or process it further into Product V (Alternative 2).

Solution:

Case A (Discontinue a Segment):

Differential Analysis
Continue K (Alternative 1) or Discontinue K (Alternative 2)
February 22

	Continue Product K (Alternative 1)	Discontinue Product K (Alternative 2)	Differential Effect on Income (Alternative 2)
Revenues	$65,000	$ 0	–$65,000
Costs:			
Variable	–$62,000*	$ 0	$62,000
Fixed	– 25,000	– 25,000	0
Total costs	–$87,000	–$25,000	$62,000
Income (loss)	–$22,000	–$25,000	–$ 3,000

*$50,000 Variable cost of goods sold + $12,000 Variable selling expenses

If Product K is discontinued, revenues and variable costs will be zero.

If Product K is discontinued, fixed costs remain at $25,000.

The effect on income of discontinuing Product K is the difference between the income from discontinuing Product K and the income from continuing Product K.

Discontinuing Product K (Alternative 2) decreases operating income by $3,000. As a result, Product K should **not** be discontinued.

Case B (Make vs. Buy):

There are no differential revenues in this case.

Differential Analysis
Make Subcomponent (Alternative 1) or Buy Subcomponent (Alternative 2)
November 2

	Make Subcomponent (Alternative 1)	Buy Subcomponent (Alternative 2)	Differential Effect on Income (Alternative 2)
Sales price	$ 0	$ 0	$ 0
Unit costs:			
Purchase price	0	−60	−60
Freight	0	−5	−5
Variable costs ($80 − $25)	−55	0	55
Fixed factory overhead	−25	−25	0
Income (loss)	−$80	−$90	−$10

Variable costs to purchase, which are the differential costs of Alternative 2.

Differential income is the difference between the variable costs to purchase (differential cost of Alternative 2) and the variable costs to manufacture (differential cost of Alternative 1).

Variable cost to manufacture, which is the differential cost of Alternative 1.

Fixed factory overhead costs cannot be eliminated if the subcomponent is purchased.

The differential cost of buying the component ($65 per unit) is $10 per unit more than the differential cost of making the subcomponent ($55 per unit). Therefore, the subcomponent should be manufactured.

Case C (Sell or Process Further):

Differential revenue from processing Product T (Alternative 1) into Product V (Alternative 2).

Differential Analysis
Sell Product T (Alternative 1) or Process Further into Product V (Alternative 2)
April 8

	Sell Product T (Alternative 1)	Process Further into Product V (Alternative 2)	Differential Effect on Income (Alternative 2)
Revenues, per unit	$3.50	$4.00	$0.50
Costs, per unit	−2.50	−3.20*	−0.70
Income (loss), per unit	$1.00	$0.80	−$0.20

*$2.50 + $0.70

Differential costs from processing Product T (Alternative 1) further into Product V (Alternative 2).

Product V can be sold for $4.00 ($0.50 more than Product T).

It costs a total of $3.20 to make Product V ($2.50 to produce Product T and an additional $0.70 to process Product T into Product V).

Processing Product T further into Product V reduces income by $0.20 per unit. Therefore, Product T should **not** be processed further into Product V.

Check Up Corner

Setting Normal Product Selling Prices

Objective 2

Determine the selling price of a product, using the product cost method.

The *normal* selling price is the target selling price to be achieved in the long term. The normal selling price must be set high enough to cover all costs and expenses (fixed and variable) and provide a reasonable profit. Otherwise, the business will not survive.

In contrast, in deciding whether to accept additional business at a special price, only differential costs are considered. Any price greater than the differential costs will increase profits in the short term. However, in the long term, products are sold at normal prices rather than special prices.

Managers can use one of two market methods to determine selling price:

- Demand-based method
- Competition-based method

The **demand-based method** sets the price according to the demand for the product. If there is high demand for the product, then the price is set high. Likewise, if there is a low demand for the product, then the price is set low.

The **competition-based method** sets the price according to the price offered by competitors. For example, if a competitor reduces the price, then management adjusts the price to meet the competition. The market-based pricing approaches are discussed in greater detail in marketing courses.

Facebook's prices are affected by its competitors such as **Google**.

Link to Facebook

Managers can use one of three cost-plus methods to determine the selling price:

- Product cost method
- Total cost method
- Variable cost method

The product cost method is illustrated in this section. The total cost and variable cost methods are illustrated in the appendix to this chapter.

Facebook generates advertising revenue based upon the number of clicks, impressions displayed, or number of actions taken by people. Facebook establishes prices for its customers for each of these options.

Link to Facebook

Why It Matters

Dynamic Pricing

Hotels and airlines were the first to dynamically adjust prices based on real-time demand. Thus, hotel rates and airfares were less expensive on the weekend than on busier weekdays. Dynamic pricing has since migrated into many other areas of product and service delivery. **Uber**'s cab fares adjust dynamically to ride demand. A ride during rush hour is more expensive than one in the middle of the day. The **Indianapolis Zoo** began dynamic pricing admission tickets so that cold, rainy days had an admission price as low as $8, while pleasant summer days had an admission price as high as $30. Prior to dynamic pricing,

the zoo charged $18 for every admission. Since introducing dynamic pricing, revenues have increased by 12%. A seven-mile stretch of highway around Dallas can vary tolls from $0.90 to $4.50 depending on traffic patterns. **SeaWorld Entertainment** dynamically prices admissions based on daily demand. **Kohl's** now employs electronic price tags that can remotely adjust prices for hours, rather than days, depending upon real-time foot traffic and demand. Most **Major League Baseball** teams dynamically price admission tickets. It would seem dynamic pricing is here to stay, as information technology allows companies greater visibility to demand.

Source: Nicas, Jack, "The Price You Pay Depends on the Time and Day," *The Wall Street Journal*, December 14, 2015, p. B1.

Cost-Plus Methods

Cost-plus methods determine the normal selling price by estimating a cost amount per unit and adding a markup, computed as follows:

$$\text{Normal Selling Price} = \text{Cost Amount per Unit} + \text{Markup}$$

Management determines the markup based on the desired profit for the product. The markup must be sufficient to earn the desired profit plus cover any costs and expenses that are not included in the cost amount.

Product Cost Method

Under the **product cost method**, the costs of manufacturing the product, termed the *product costs*, are included in the cost amount per unit to which the markup is added. Estimated selling expenses, administrative expenses, and desired profit are included in the markup. The markup per unit is added to the product cost per unit to determine the normal selling price as shown in Exhibit 9.

Exhibit 9
Product Cost Method

The product cost method is applied using the following steps:

- Step 1. Estimate the total product cost as follows:

Product costs:	
Direct materials	$XXX
Direct labor	XXX
Factory overhead	XXX
Total product cost	$XXX

- Step 2. Estimate the total selling and administrative expenses.
- Step 3. Divide the total product cost by the number of units expected to be produced and sold to determine the total product cost per unit, computed as follows:

$$\text{Product Cost per Unit} = \frac{\text{Total Product Cost}}{\text{Estimated Units Produced and Sold}}$$

■ Step 4. Compute the markup percentage as follows:

$$\text{Markup Percentage} = \frac{\text{Desired Profit} + \text{Total Selling and Administrative Expenses}}{\text{Total Product Cost}}$$

The numerator of the markup percentage is the desired profit plus the total selling and administrative expenses. These expenses must be included in the markup percentage because they are not included in the cost amount to which the markup is added.

The desired profit is normally computed based on a return on assets as follows:

$$\text{Desired Profit} = \text{Desired Return} \times \text{Total Assets}$$

■ Step 5. Determine the markup per unit by multiplying the markup percentage times the product cost per unit as follows:

$$\text{Markup per Unit} = \text{Markup Percentage} \times \text{Product Cost per Unit}$$

■ Step 6. Determine the normal selling price by adding the markup per unit to the product cost per unit as follows:

Product cost per unit	$XXX
Markup per unit	XXX
Normal selling price per unit	$XXX

Illustration

The product cost method is illustrated for determining the price of calculators produced by **Digital Solutions Inc.** Assume the following data for 100,000 calculators that Digital Solutions Inc. expects to produce and sell during the current year:

Manufacturing costs:	
Direct materials ($3.00 × 100,000)	$ 300,000
Direct labor ($10.00 × 100,000)	1,000,000
Factory overhead	200,000
Total product (manufacturing) costs	$1,500,000
Selling and administrative expenses	170,000
Total cost	$1,670,000
Total assets	$ 800,000
Desired return	20%

The normal selling price of $18.30 is determined under the product cost method as follows:

■ Step 1. Total product cost: $1,500,000
■ Step 2. Total selling and administrative expenses: $170,000
■ Step 3. Total product cost per unit: $15.00

$$\text{Total Cost per Unit} = \frac{\text{Total Product Cost}}{\text{Estimated Units Produced and Sold}} = \frac{\$1,500,000}{100,000 \text{ units}} = \$15.00 \text{ per unit}$$

■ Step 4. Markup percentage: 22%

$$\text{Desired Profit} = \text{Desired Return} \times \text{Total Assets} = 20\% \times \$800,000 = \$160,000$$

$$\text{Markup Percentage} = \frac{\text{Desired Profit} + \text{Total Selling and Administrative Expenses}}{\text{Total Product (Manufacturing) Costs}}$$

$$= \frac{\$160,000 + \$170,000}{\$1,500,000} = \frac{\$330,000}{\$1,500,000} = 22\%$$

■ Step 5. Markup per unit: $3.30

$$\text{Markup per Unit} = \text{Markup Percentage} \times \text{Product Cost per Unit}$$
$$= 22\% \times \$15.00 = \$3.30 \text{ per unit}$$

■ Step 6.   Normal selling price: $18.30

Total product cost per unit	$15.00
Markup per unit	3.30
Normal selling price per unit	$18.30

Product cost estimates, rather than actual costs, may be used in computing the markup. Management should be careful, however, when using estimated or standard costs in applying the cost-plus approach. Specifically, estimates should be based on normal (attainable) operating levels and not theoretical (ideal) levels of performance. In product pricing, the use of estimates based on ideal operating performance could lead to setting product prices too low.

Target Costing Method

Target costing is a method of setting prices that combines market-based pricing with a cost-reduction emphasis. Under target costing, a future selling price is anticipated, using the demand or competition-based methods. The target cost is then determined by subtracting a desired profit from the expected selling price, computed as follows:

Target Cost = Expected Selling Price − Desired Profit

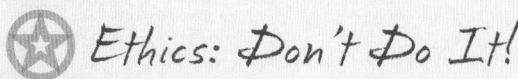 Ethics: Don't Do It!

Price Fixing

Federal law prevents companies competing in similar markets from sharing cost and price information, or what is commonly termed "price fixing." For example, the Federal Trade Commission (FTC) brought a suit against U-Haul for releasing company-wide memorandums to its managers telling them to encourage competitors to match U-Haul price increases. Commenting on the case, the chairman of the FTC stated, "It's a bedrock principle that you can't conspire with your competitors to fix prices, and shouldn't even try."

Source: Edward Wyatt, "U-Haul to Settle with Trade Agency in Case on Truck Rental Price-Fixing," *The New York Times*, June 10, 2010, p. B3.

Target costing tries to reduce costs as shown in Exhibit 10. The bar at the left in Exhibit 10 shows the actual cost and profit that can be earned during the current period. The bar at the right shows that the market price is expected to decline in the future. The target cost is estimated as the difference between the expected market price and the desired profit.

The target cost is normally less than the current cost. Thus, managers must try to reduce costs from the design and manufacture of the product. The planned cost reduction is sometimes referred to as the cost drift. Costs can be reduced in a variety of ways such as the following:

■ Simplifying the design
■ Reducing the cost of direct materials
■ Reducing the direct labor costs
■ Eliminating waste

Target costing is especially useful in highly competitive markets such as the market for personal computers. Such markets require continual product cost reductions to remain competitive.

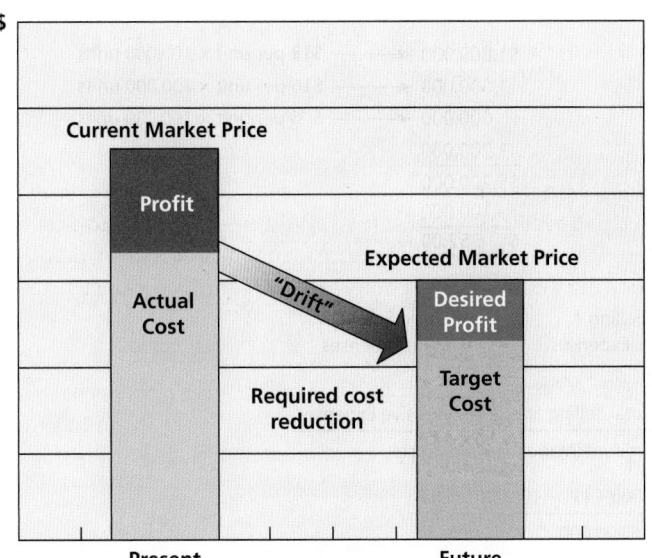

Exhibit 10
Target Cost
Method

Check Up Corner 24-2   Setting Product Selling Prices

SMB Company recently began production of a new product, Q, which required an investment of $2,500,000 in assets. The costs of producing and selling 100,000 units of Product Q are estimated as follows:

Variable costs:	
Direct materials	$18 per unit
Direct labor	16
Factory overhead	6
Selling and administrative expenses	4
Total variable costs	$44 per unit
Fixed costs:	
Factory overhead	$1,200,000
Selling and administrative expenses	600,000

Using the cost-plus approach to product pricing, a 12% return on invested assets is required.

A. Determine the amount of desired profit from the production and sale of Product Q.

B. Using the product cost method, determine (1) the cost per unit, (2) the markup percentage, and (3) the selling price.

C. If the market price for a similar product is estimated at $61, compute the reduction in manufacturing cost per unit needed to maintain (1) the desired profit [from part (A)] and (2) the existing selling and administrative expenses under target costing.

Solution:

A.	Invested assets	$2,500,000
	Required return	× 12%
	Desired profit	$ 300,000

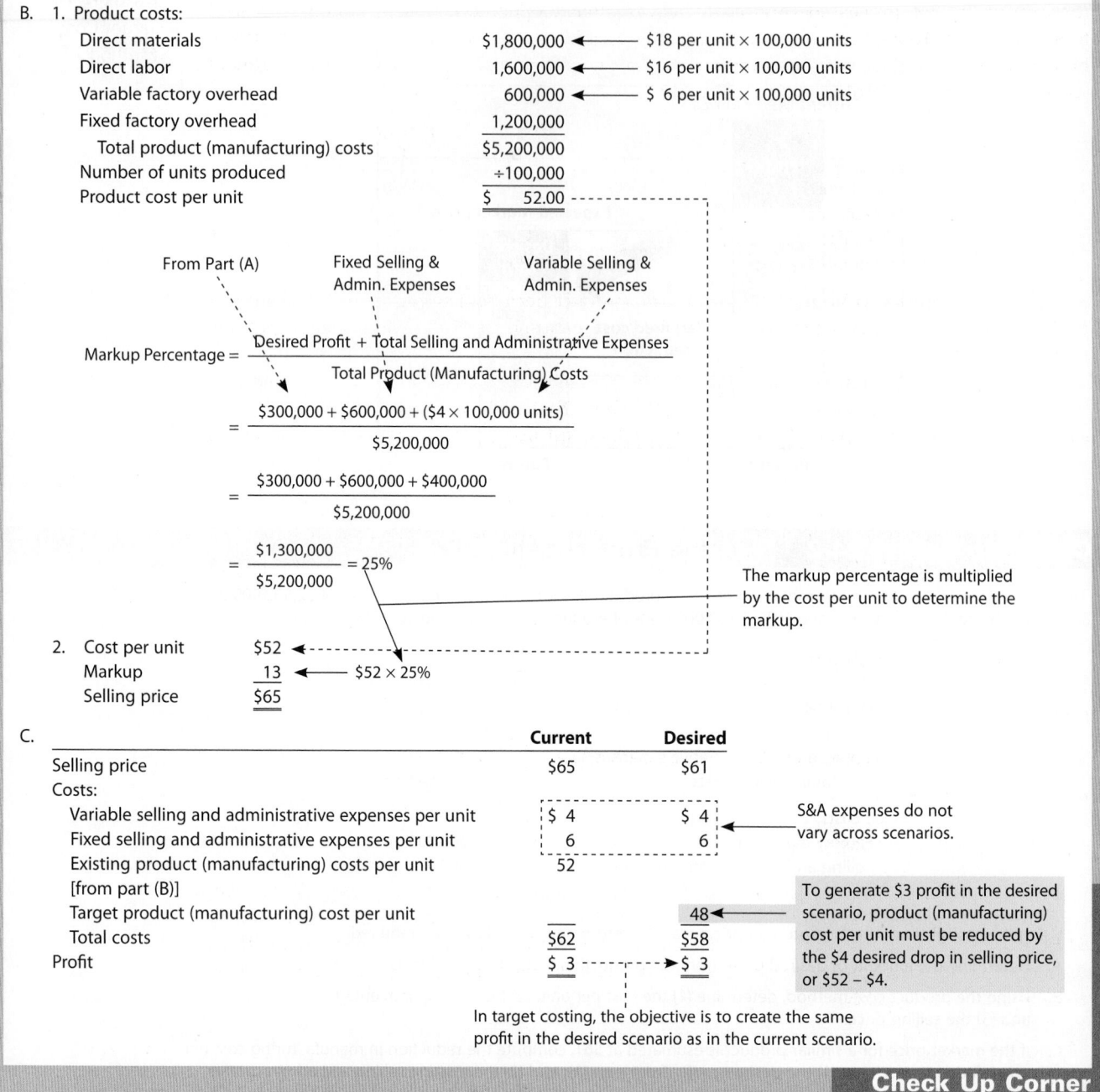

B. 1. Product costs:

Direct materials	$1,800,000	← $18 per unit × 100,000 units
Direct labor	1,600,000	← $16 per unit × 100,000 units
Variable factory overhead	600,000	← $ 6 per unit × 100,000 units
Fixed factory overhead	1,200,000	
Total product (manufacturing) costs	$5,200,000	
Number of units produced	÷100,000	
Product cost per unit	$ 52.00	

From Part (A)   Fixed Selling & Admin. Expenses   Variable Selling & Admin. Expenses

$$\text{Markup Percentage} = \frac{\text{Desired Profit} + \text{Total Selling and Administrative Expenses}}{\text{Total Product (Manufacturing) Costs}}$$

$$= \frac{\$300,000 + \$600,000 + (\$4 \times 100,000 \text{ units})}{\$5,200,000}$$

$$= \frac{\$300,000 + \$600,000 + \$400,000}{\$5,200,000}$$

$$= \frac{\$1,300,000}{\$5,200,000} = 25\%$$

The markup percentage is multiplied by the cost per unit to determine the markup.

2.
Cost per unit	$52 ←
Markup	13 ← $52 × 25%
Selling price	$65

C.

	Current	Desired	
Selling price	$65	$61	
Costs:			
Variable selling and administrative expenses per unit	$ 4	$ 4	S&A expenses do not vary across scenarios.
Fixed selling and administrative expenses per unit	6	6	
Existing product (manufacturing) costs per unit [from part (B)]	52		
Target product (manufacturing) cost per unit		48 ←	To generate $3 profit in the desired scenario, product (manufacturing) cost per unit must be reduced by the $4 desired drop in selling price, or $52 – $4.
Total costs	$62	$58	
Profit	$ 3	$ 3	

In target costing, the objective is to create the same profit in the desired scenario as in the current scenario.

Check Up Corner

Objective 3

Describe and illustrate the managing of manufacturing bottlenecks.

Production Bottlenecks

A **production bottleneck** (or *constraint*) is a point in the manufacturing process where the demand for the company's product exceeds the ability to produce the product. The **theory of constraints (TOC)** is a manufacturing strategy that focuses on reducing the influence of bottlenecks on production processes.

Managing Bottlenecks

When a company has a production bottleneck in its production process, it should attempt to maximize its profits, subject to the production bottleneck. In doing so, the unit contribution margin of each product per production bottleneck constraint is used.

To illustrate, assume that PrideCraft Tool Company makes three products: A, B, and C. All three products are processed through a heat treatment operation, which hardens the steel tools. PrideCraft Tool's heat treatment process is operating at full capacity and is a production bottleneck. The product unit contribution margin and the number of hours of heat treatment used by each type of tool are as follows:

	Product A	Product B	Product C
Unit selling price	$130	$140	$160
Unit variable cost	40	40	40
Unit contribution margin	$ 90	$100	$120
Heat treatment hours per unit	1 hr.	4 hrs.	8 hrs.

Product C appears to be the most profitable product because its unit contribution margin of $120 is the greatest. However, the unit contribution margin can be misleading in a production bottleneck operation.

In a production bottleneck operation, the best measure of profitability is the unit contribution margin per bottleneck constraint. For PrideCraft Tool, the bottleneck constraint is heat treatment process hours. Therefore, the unit contribution margin per bottleneck constraint is expressed as follows:

$$\text{Unit Contribution Margin per Production Bottleneck Hour} = \frac{\text{Unit Contribution Margin}}{\text{Heat Treatment Hours per Unit}}$$

The unit contribution per bottleneck hour for each of the products produced by PrideCraft Tool is computed as follows:

Product A

$$\text{Unit Contribution Margin per Bottleneck Hour} = \frac{\$90}{1 \text{ hr.}} = \$90 \text{ per hr.}$$

Product B

$$\text{Unit Contribution Margin per Bottleneck Hour} = \frac{\$100}{4 \text{ hrs.}} = \$25 \text{ per hr.}$$

Product C

$$\text{Unit Contribution Margin per Bottleneck Hour} = \frac{\$120}{8 \text{ hrs.}} = \$15 \text{ per hr.}$$

Product A produces the highest unit contribution margin per bottleneck hour (heat treatment) of $90 per hour. In contrast, Product C has the largest contribution margin per unit of $120 but has the smallest unit contribution margin per bottleneck hour of $15 per hour. Thus, Product A is the most profitable product per bottleneck hour and is the one that should be emphasized in the market.

Pricing Bottleneck Products

In the preceding illustration, Product A is the most profitable product per bottleneck hour. As a result, if one product is to be produced, it should be Product A. But, what about Products B and C?

Customers may expect a combination of products from a company. For example, even though Product A is the most profitable, PrideCraft Tool's customers may also want Products B and C. In these situations, Products B and C should be comparably priced to Product A or the production process for the other products should be adjusted so that they consume less of the bottleneck.

To illustrate, if the price of Product C were increased to $720 ($90 × 8 hrs.), Product C would produce a unit contribution margin of $90 per hour. Alternatively, the manufacturing process for Product C could be adjusted to reduce its consumption of the bottleneck.

Analysis for Decision Making

Objective

Describe and illustrate the use of yield pricing for a service business.

Yield Pricing in Service Businesses

Service businesses, compared to manufacturing or retail businesses, often have larger fixed costs because they require significant property, plant, and equipment to deliver the service. Examples include airlines, railroads, hotels, universities, and utility companies. Due to the large fixed costs, many service companies have a low variable cost per unit. For example, the additional variable cost of an additional guest in a hotel is small relative to the total cost of the service. High-fixed-cost service businesses often charge different prices to different customers, depending upon their utilization of fixed capacity. During periods when the demand on fixed capacity is high, prices are higher. During periods when the demand for fixed capacity is low, prices are lower. For example, a hotel with frequent business guests will charge lower prices during the weekend, when demand for rooms is lower, than on weekdays when demand for rooms is higher.

In addition, high-capacity-cost service businesses will offer attractive prices to customers who reserve a portion of fixed capacity early and will penalize customers for reserving a portion of fixed capacity late. It is more difficult for a business to manage scheduled capacity if everyone tries to schedule at the last minute. This is why booking a flight early provides better pricing than booking late. These practices are termed "yield pricing" and are common in many high-fixed-cost service businesses.

Yield pricing is a type of "accepting business at a special price" differential analysis. To illustrate, Alpine Airline provides flight services between Atlanta and Dallas. Assume an analysis reveals the following fixed and variable costs for a flight:

	Fixed Costs per Flight	**Variable Costs per Passenger**
Plane depreciation	$10,400	
Crew salaries	1,000	
Fuel	3,000	$12
Ground salaries	2,000	8
Airport fees	2,000	
Passenger services		15
Total	$18,400	$35

Alpine's the variable cost per passenger is not large. This is because many of the costs do not vary by changing the number of seats sold on a flight. For example, the number of crew-members per flight is fixed and does not vary to the seats sold on a flight.

Assume the plane has a capacity of 200 seats, of which 170 have been sold at an average ticket price of $150. The contribution margin for each passenger is as follows:

$$\text{Contribution Margin per Passenger} = \text{Ticket Price} - \text{Variable Cost per Passenger}$$
$$= \$150 - \$35$$
$$= \$115$$

The break-even number of seats per flight is:

$$\text{Break-Even Seats per Flight} = \frac{\text{Fixed Costs per Flight}}{\text{Contribution Margin per Passenger}}$$

$$= \frac{\$18,400}{\$115}$$

$$= 160 \text{ seats}$$

Thus, each flight is earning a profit, since the actual seats sold (170) exceed the break-even number of seats (160).

To attract customers to its 30 unsold seats, Alpine offers a 50% discounted ticket for standby passengers. Assuming 10 standby passengers purchase the discounted ticket, Alpine will have additional income based on the contribution margin of these seats, determined as follows:

Discounted ticket price (50% × $150)	$ 75
Variable cost per passenger	35
Contribution margin per standby passenger	$ 40
Number of standby passengers per flight	× 10
Income from standby passengers per flight	$400

Make a Decision — Yield Pricing in Service Businesses

Pacific Airways provides air travel services between Los Angeles and Seattle. Cost information per flight is as follows:

	Fixed Costs per Flight	Variable Costs per Passenger
Plane depreciation	$ 9,500	
Crew salaries	900	
Fuel	2,500	$18
Ground salaries	1,100	12
Airport fees	2,100	
Passenger services		10
Total	$16,100	$40

Each flight has a capacity of 150 seats, with an average of 125 seats sold per flight at an average ticket price of $180. Assume Pacific Airways is considering a new service that would provide tickets at half price. Passengers would need to fly standby to receive the discount, but would be provided a flight for a given day of travel. An analysis revealed that an average of 8 existing passengers would use the new discounted tickets for travel. In addition, 15 new passengers would be attracted to the offer.

A. Determine the contribution margin per passenger for the full-priced ticket.

B. Determine the break-even number of seats sold per flight.

C. Determine the contribution margin per passenger for discounted tickets.

D. Should Pacific Airways offer the discounted ticket plan? Answer the question by computing the incremental contribution margin per flight for the plan.

Solution:

A. Contribution Margin per Passenger = Ticket Price – Variable Costs per Passenger

$$= \$180 - \$40$$

$$= \$140$$

B. Break-Even Seats per Flight $= \dfrac{\text{Fixed Costs per Flight}}{\text{Contribution Margin per Passenger}}$

$$= \dfrac{\$16,100}{\$140}$$

$$= 115 \text{ seats}$$

C. Contribution Margin per Passenger = Discounted Ticket Price – Variable Costs per Passenger

$$= \$90 - \$40$$

$$= \$50$$

D. Lost contribution margin from customers who switch tickets: 8 × $140 = $1,120

   Gained contribution margin from discount customers: (8 + 15) × $50 = $1,150

   Incremental contribution per flight from the discounted ticket plan: $1,150 − $1,120 = $30

   The new ticket plan will produce a positive contribution margin per flight and should be implemented based on these assumptions.

   The same answer can be determined from a differential analysis table, as follows:

Differential Analysis
Continue with No Change (Alternative A) or Execute the Discount Plan (Alternative B)

	No Change (Alternative 1)	Discount Plan (Alternative 2)	Differential Effect on Income (Alternative 2)
Revenues per flight[1]	$22,500	$23,130	$630
Costs per flight:			
Plane depreciation	−$ 9,500	−$ 9,500	0
Crew salaries	−900	−900	0
Fuel[2]	−4,750	−5,020	−$270
Ground salaries[3]	−2,600	−2,780	−180
Airport fees	−2,100	−2,100	0
Passenger services[4]	−1,250	−1,400	−150
Income per flight	$ 1,400	$ 1,430	$ 30

[1]Revenues:
No change revenues: $180 × 125 seats

Discount plan revenues:

	Ticket Price	No. of Tickets	Revenue
Full price	$180	117*	$21,060
Discount price	90	23**	2,070
Total		140	$23,130

*125 − 8

**15 + 8

[2] Fuel:
No change: $2,500 + ($18 × 125 seats)
Discount Plan: $2,500 + ($18 × 140 seats)

[3] Ground salaries:
No change: $1,100 + ($12 × 125 seats)
Discount Plan: $1,100 + ($12 × 140 seats)

[4] Passenger services:
No change: $10 × 125 seats
Discount plan: $10 × 140 seats

Make a Decision

Appendix Total and Variable Cost Methods to Setting Normal Price

Recall from the chapter that cost-plus methods determine the normal selling price by estimating a cost amount per unit and adding a markup, as follows:

Normal Selling Price = Cost Amount per Unit + Markup

Management determines the markup based on the desired profit for the product. The markup should be sufficient to earn the desired profit plus cover any cost and expenses that are not included in the cost amount. The product cost method was discussed in the chapter, and the total and variable cost methods are discussed in this appendix.

Total Cost Method

As shown in Exhibit 11, under the **total cost method**, manufacturing cost plus the selling and administrative expenses are included in the total cost per unit. The markup per unit is then computed and added to the total cost per unit to determine the normal selling price.

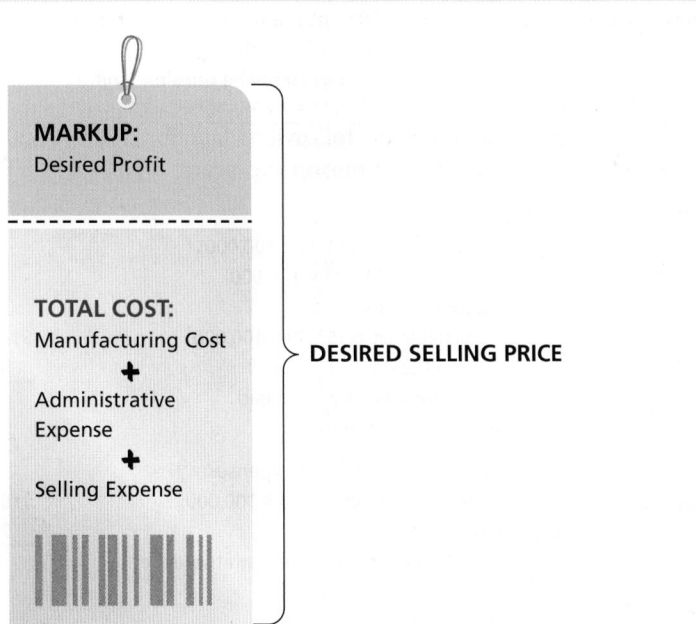

Exhibit 11
Total Cost Method

The total cost method is applied using the following steps:

- Step 1. Estimate the total manufacturing cost as follows:

Manufacturing costs:	
Direct materials	$XXX
Direct labor	XXX
Factory overhead	XXX
Total manufacturing cost	$XXX

- Step 2. Estimate the total selling and administrative expenses.
- Step 3. Estimate the total cost as follows:

Total manufacturing costs	$XXX
Selling and administrative expenses	XXX
Total cost	$XXX

- Step 4. Divide the total cost by the number of units expected to be produced and sold to determine the total cost per unit, as follows:

$$\text{Total Cost per Unit} = \frac{\text{Total Cost}}{\text{Estimated Units Produced and Sold}}$$

- Step 5. Compute the markup percentage as follows:

$$\text{Markup Percentage} = \frac{\text{Desired Profit}}{\text{Total Cost}}$$

The desired profit is normally computed based on a return on assets as follows:

$$\text{Desired Profit} = \text{Desired Return} \times \text{Total Assets}$$

■ Step 6. Determine the markup per unit by multiplying the markup percentage times the total cost per unit as follows:

$$\text{Markup per Unit} = \text{Markup Percentage} \times \text{Total Cost per Unit}$$

■ Step 7. Determine the normal selling price by adding the markup per unit to the total cost per unit as follows:

Total cost per unit	$XXX
Markup per unit	XXX
Normal selling price per unit	$XXX

To illustrate, assume the following data for 100,000 calculators that **Digital Solutions Inc.** expects to produce and sell during the year:

Manufacturing costs:		
Direct materials ($3.00 × 100,000)		$ 300,000
Direct labor ($10.00 × 100,000)		1,000,000
Factory overhead:		
Variable costs ($1.50 × 100,000)	$150,000	
Fixed costs	50,000	
Total factory overhead		200,000
Total manufacturing cost		$1,500,000
Selling and administrative expenses:		
Variable expenses ($1.50 × 100,000)	$150,000	
Fixed costs	20,000	
Total selling and administrative expenses		170,000
Total cost		$1,670,000
Desired return		20%
Total assets		$ 800,000

Using the total cost method, the normal selling price of $18.30 is determined as follows:

■ Step 1. Total manufacturing cost: $1,500,000
■ Step 2. Total selling and administrative expenses: $170,000
■ Step 3. Total cost: $1,670,000
■ Step 4. Total cost per unit: $16.70

$$\text{Total Cost per Unit} = \frac{\text{Total Cost}}{\text{Estimated Units Produced and Sold}} = \frac{\$1,670,000}{100,000 \text{ units}} = \$16.70 \text{ per unit}$$

■ Step 5. Markup percentage: 9.6% (rounded)

$$\text{Desired Profit} = \text{Desired Return} \times \text{Total Assets} = 20\% \times \$800,000 = \$160,000$$

$$\text{Markup Percentage} = \frac{\text{Desired Profit}}{\text{Total Cost}} = \frac{\$160,000}{\$1,670,000} = 9.6\% \text{ (rounded)}$$

■ Step 6. Markup per unit: $1.60

$$\text{Markup per Unit} = \text{Markup Percentage} \times \text{Total Cost per Unit}$$
$$= 9.6\% \times \$16.70 = \$1.60 \text{ per unit (rounded)}$$

■ Step 7. Normal selling price: $18.30

Total cost per unit	$16.70
Markup per unit	1.60
Normal selling price per unit	$18.30

The ability of the selling price of $18.30 to generate the desired profit of $160,000 is illustrated by the income statement that follows:

Digital Solutions Inc.
Income Statement
For the Year Ended December 31, 20Y8

Sales (100,000 units × $18.30).....................................		$1,830,000
Expenses:		
Variable (100,000 units × $16.00)	$1,600,000	
Fixed ($50,000 + $20,000)	70,000	
Total expenses...		1,670,000
Income from operations		$ 160,000

The total cost method is often used by contractors who sell products to government agencies. This is because in many cases government contractors are required by law to be reimbursed for their products on a total-cost-plus-profit basis.

Variable Cost Method

As shown in Exhibit 12, under the **variable cost method**, only variable costs are included in the cost amount per unit to which the markup is added. All variable manufacturing costs, as well as variable selling and administrative expenses, are included in the cost amount. Fixed manufacturing costs, fixed selling and administrative expenses, and desired profit are included in the markup. The markup per unit is then added to the variable cost per unit to determine the normal selling price.

The variable cost method is applied using the following steps:

■ Step 1. Estimate the total variable product cost as follows:

Variable product costs:	
Direct materials	$XXX
Direct labor	XXX
Variable factory overhead	XXX
Total variable product cost	$XXX

Exhibit 12
Variable Cost
Method

MARKUP:
Total Fixed Costs
+
Desired Profit

VARIABLE
COST:
Variable
Manufacturing Cost
+
Variable
Administrative and
Selling Expenses

> DESIRED SELLING PRICE

- Step 2. Estimate the total variable selling and administrative expenses.
- Step 3. Determine the total variable cost as follows:

Total variable product cost	$XXX
Total variable selling and administrative expenses	XXX
Total variable cost	$XXX

- Step 4. Compute the variable cost per unit as follows:

$$\text{Variable Cost per Unit} = \frac{\text{Total Variable Cost}}{\text{Estimated Units Produced and Sold}}$$

- Step 5. Compute the markup percentage as follows:

$$\text{Markup Percentage} = \frac{\text{Desired Profit} + \text{Total Fixed Costs and Expenses}}{\text{Total Variable Cost}}$$

The numerator of the markup percentage is the desired profit plus the total fixed costs (fixed factory overhead) and expenses (selling and administrative). These fixed costs and expenses must be included in the markup percentage because they are not included in the cost amount to which the markup is added.

As illustrated for the total and product cost methods, the desired profit is normally computed based on a return on assets as follows:

$$\text{Desired Profit} = \text{Desired Return} \times \text{Total Assets}$$

- Step 6. Determine the markup per unit by multiplying the markup percentage times the variable cost per unit as follows:

$$\text{Markup per Unit} = \text{Markup Percentage} \times \text{Variable Cost per Unit}$$

- Step 7. Determine the normal selling price by adding the markup per unit to the variable cost per unit as follows:

Variable cost per unit	$XXX
Markup per unit	XXX
Normal selling price per unit	$XXX

To illustrate, assume the same data for the production and sale of 100,000 calculators by **Digital Solutions Inc.** as in the preceding example. The normal selling price of $18.30 is determined under the variable cost method as follows:

- Step 1. Total variable product cost: $1,450,000

Variable product costs:	
Direct materials ($3.00 × 100,000)	$ 300,000
Direct labor ($10.00 × 100,000)	1,000,000
Variable factory overhead ($1.50 × 100,000)	150,000
Total variable product cost	$1,450,000

- Step 2. Total variable selling and administrative expenses: $150,000 ($1.50 × 100,000)
- Step 3. Total variable cost: $1,600,000 ($1,450,000 + $150,000)
- Step 4. Variable cost per unit: $16.00

$$\text{Variable Cost per Unit} = \frac{\text{Total Variable Cost}}{\text{Estimated Units Produced and Sold}} = \frac{\$1,600,000}{100,000 \text{ units}} = \$16.00 \text{ per unit}$$

- Step 5. Markup percentage: 14.4% (rounded)

$$\text{Desired Profit} = \text{Desired Return} \times \text{Total Assets} = 20\% \times \$800,000 = \$160,000$$

$$\text{Markup Percentage} = \frac{\text{Desired Profit} + \text{Total Fixed Costs and Expenses}}{\text{Total Variable Cost}}$$

$$= \frac{\$160,000 + \$50,000 + \$20,000}{\$1,600,000} = \frac{\$230,000}{\$1,600,000}$$

$$= 14.4\% \text{ (rounded)}$$

■ Step 6. Markup per unit: $2.30

Markup per Unit = Markup Percentage × Variable Cost per Unit
= 14.4% × $16.00 = $2.30 per unit (rounded)

■ Step 7. Normal selling price: $18.30

Variable cost per unit	$16.00
Markup per unit	2.30
Normal selling price per unit	$18.30

Let's Review

Chapter Summary

1. Differential analyses for various decisions are illustrated in the chapter. Each analysis focuses on the differential effects of revenues and expenses on income (loss) for alternative courses of action.

2. The three cost methods commonly used in applying the cost-plus approach to product pricing are the product cost, total cost (appendix), and variable cost (appendix) methods. Target costing combines market-based methods with a cost-reduction emphasis.

3. Managing a production bottleneck focuses on the relative profitability of a product given the bottleneck. This profitability is measured by dividing the product's unit contribution margin by the bottleneck hours per unit.

Key Terms

competition-based method (1221)
cost-plus methods (1222)
demand-based method (1221)
differential analysis (1210)
differential cost (1210)

differential income (loss) (1210)
differential revenue (1210)
opportunity cost (1216)
product cost method (1222)
production bottleneck (1226)

sunk costs (1212)
target costing (1224)
theory of constraints (TOC) (1226)
total cost method (1231)
variable cost method (1233)

Practice

Multiple-Choice Questions

1. Johnston Company is considering discontinuing a product. The costs of the product consist of $20,000 fixed costs and $15,000 variable costs. The variable operating expenses related to the product total $4,000. What is the differential cost of discontinuing the product?
   A. $19,000
   B. $15,000
   C. $35,000
   D. $39,000

2. Madden Company is considering disposing of equipment that was originally purchased for $200,000 and has $150,000 accumulated depreciation to date. The same equipment would cost $310,000 to replace. What is the sunk cost?
   A. $50,000
   B. $150,000
   C. $200,000
   D. $310,000

3. Hancock Inc. is considering spending $100,000 for a new grinding machine. This amount could be invested to yield a 12% return. What is the opportunity cost?
   A. $112,000
   B. $88,000
   C. $12,000
   D. $100,000

4. Which method of setting normal product selling prices includes administrative and selling expenses in the markup that is added to the cost amount?
   A. Target costing method
   B. Demand-based method
   C. Product cost method
   D. Competition-based method

5. Twitchell Industries produces three products. All of the products use a furnace operation, which is a production bottleneck. The following data are available:

	Product 1	Product 2	Product 3
Unit volume—May	1,000	1,500	1,000
Per-unit data:			
Sales price	$35	$33	$29
Variable cost	15	15	15
Contribution margin	$20	$18	$14
Furnace hours	4 hrs.	3 hrs.	2 hrs.

Which product is most profitable and should be emphasized in June's advertising campaign?
   A. Product 1
   B. Product 2
   C. Product 3
   D. The products are equally profitable.

Answers provided after Problem. Need more practice? Find additional multiple-choice questions, exercises, and problems in CengageNOWv2.

Exercises

1. Lease or sell
Obj. 1

Claxon Company owns a machine with a cost of $305,000 and accumulated depreciation of $65,000 that can be sold for $262,000, less a 5% sales commission. Alternatively, the machine can be leased by Claxon Company for three years for a total of $272,000, at the end of which there is no residual value. In addition, the repair, insurance, and property tax expense that would be incurred by Claxon Company on the machine would total $21,600 over the three years. Prepare a differential analysis on January 12 as to whether Claxon Company should lease (Alternative 1) or sell (Alternative 2) the machine.

2. Discontinue a segment
Obj. 1

Product TS-20 has revenue of $102,000, variable cost of goods sold of $52,500, variable selling expenses of $21,500, and fixed costs of $35,000, creating a loss from operations of $7,000. Prepare a differential analysis as of September 12 to determine if Product TS-20 should be continued (Alternative 1) or discontinued (Alternative 2), assuming fixed costs are unaffected by the decision.

3. Make or buy
Obj. 1

A restaurant bakes its own bread for a cost of $165 per unit (100 loaves), including fixed costs of $43 per unit. A proposal is offered to purchase bread from an outside source for $110 per unit, plus $15 per unit for delivery. Prepare a differential analysis dated August 16 to determine whether the company should make (Alternative 1) or buy (Alternative 2) the bread, assuming fixed costs are unaffected by the decision.

SHOW ME HOW

4. Replace equipment

Obj. 1

A machine with a book value of $126,000 has an estimated six-year life. A proposal is offered to sell the old machine for $84,000 and replace it with a new machine at a cost of $145,000. The new machine has a six-year life with no residual value. The new machine would reduce annual direct labor costs from $55,000 to $43,000. Prepare a differential analysis dated February 18 on whether to continue with the old machine (Alternative 1) or replace the machine (Alternative 2).

SHOW ME HOW

5. Process or sell

Obj. 1

Product T is produced for $5.90 per pound. Product T can be sold without additional processing for $7.10 per pound, or processed further into Product U at an additional cost of $0.74 per pound. Product U can be sold for $8.00 per pound. Prepare a differential analysis dated August 2 on whether to sell Product T (Alternative 1) or process further into Product U (Alternative 2).

SHOW ME HOW

6. Accept business at special price

Obj. 1

Product R is normally sold for $52 per unit. A special price of $42 is offered for the export market. The variable production cost is $30 per unit. An additional export tariff of 30% of revenue must be paid for all export products. Assume there is sufficient capacity for the special order. Prepare a differential analysis dated October 23 on whether to reject (Alternative 1) or accept (Alternative 2) the special order.

SHOW ME HOW

7. Product cost markup percentage

Obj. 2

Magna Lighting Inc. produces and sells lighting fixtures. An entry light has a total cost of $125 per unit, of which $80 is product cost and $45 is selling and administrative expenses. In addition, the total cost of $125 is made up of $90 variable cost and $35 fixed cost. The desired profit is $55 per unit. Determine the markup percentage on product cost.

SHOW ME HOW

8. Bottleneck profit

Obj. 3

Product A has a unit contribution margin of $24. Product B has a unit contribution margin of $30. Product A requires four testing hours, while Product B requires six testing hours. Determine the most profitable product, assuming the testing is a bottleneck constraint.

Answers provided after Problem. Need more practice? Find additional multiple-choice questions, exercises, and problems in CengageNOWv2.

Problem

Inez Company recently began production of a new product, a digital clock, which required the investment of $1,600,000 in assets. The costs of producing and selling 80,000 units of the digital clock are estimated as follows:

Variable costs:	
Direct materials	$10.00 per unit
Direct labor	6.00
Factory overhead	4.00
Selling and administrative expenses	5.00
Total variable costs	$25.00 per unit
Fixed costs:	
Factory overhead	$800,000
Selling and administrative expenses	400,000

Inez Company is currently considering establishing a selling price for the digital clock. The president of Inez Company has decided to use the cost-plus approach to product pricing and has indicated that the digital clock must earn a 10% return on invested assets.

Instructions

1. Determine the amount of desired profit from the production and sale of the digital clock.

2. Assuming that the product cost method is used, determine (A) the cost amount per unit, (B) the markup percentage, and (C) the selling price of the digital clock.

3. Under what conditions should Inez Company consider using activity-based costing rather than a single factory overhead allocation rate in allocating factory overhead to the digital clock?

4. Assume the market price for similar digital clocks was estimated at $38. Compute the reduction in manufacturing cost per unit needed to maintain the desired profit and existing selling and administrative expenses under target costing.

5. Assume that for the current year, the selling price of the digital clock was $42 per unit. To date, 60,000 units have been produced and sold, and analysis of the domestic market indicates that 15,000 additional units are expected to be sold during the remainder of the year. On August 7, Inez Company received an offer from Wong Inc. for 4,000 units of the digital clock at $28 each. Wong Inc. will market the units in Korea under its own brand name, and no selling and administrative expenses associated with the sale will be incurred by Inez Company. The additional business is not expected to affect the domestic sales of the digital clock, and the additional units could be produced during the current year, using existing capacity. Prepare a differential analysis dated August 7 to determine whether to reject (Alternative 1) or accept (Alternative 2) the special order from Wong.

Need more practice? Find additional multiple-choice questions, exercises, and problems in CengageNOWv2.

Answers

Multiple-Choice Questions

1. **A** Differential cost is the amount of increase or decrease in cost that is expected from a particular course of action compared with an alternative. For Johnston Company, the differential cost is $19,000 (answer A). This is the total of the variable product cost ($15,000) and the variable operating expenses ($4,000), which would not be incurred if the product is discontinued.

2. **A** A sunk cost is not affected by later decisions. For Madden Company, the sunk cost is the $50,000 (answer A) book value of the equipment, which is equal to the original cost of $200,000 (answer C) less the accumulated depreciation of $150,000 (answer B). The original cost of the equipment of $200,000 (answer C) is the sunk cost immediately after the equipment was purchased. However, the sunk cost as of the date of the decision is the remaining book value of the equipment. The replacement cost of $310,000 (answer D) is not a sunk cost since it would be incurred in the future.

3. **C** The amount of income that could have been earned from the best available alternative to a proposed use of cash is the opportunity cost. For Hancock Inc., the opportunity cost is 12% times $100,000, or $12,000 (answer C).

4. **C** The product cost method (answer C) includes administrative and selling expenses in the markup that is added to the product cost amount. The target costing method (answer A) anticipates a future selling price and then determines the target cost by subtracting the desired markup (profit). The demand-based method (answer B) sets the price based upon the demand for the product. The competition-based method (answer D) sets the price based upon that offered by competitors.

5. **C** Product 3 has the highest unit contribution margin per bottleneck hour of $7 ($14 ÷ 2 hrs.). Product 1 (answer A) has the largest contribution margin per unit of $20, but the lowest unit contribution margin per bottleneck hour of $5 ($20 ÷ 4 hrs.) so it is the least profitable product in the constrained environment. Product 2 (answer B) has the highest total profitability in May of $27,000 (1,500 units × $18), but this does not suggest that it has the highest profit potential. Product 2's unit contribution margin per bottleneck hour of $6 ($18 ÷ 3 hrs.) is between Products 1 and 3. Answer D is not true since the products have different profit potential in terms of their unit contribution margin per bottleneck hour.

Exercises

1.

Differential Analysis
Lease (Alt. 1) or Sell (Alt. 2) Machine
January 12

	Lease Machine (Alternative 1)	Sell Machine (Alternative 2)	Differential Effect on Income (Alternative 2)
Revenues	$272,000	$262,000	–$10,000
Costs	–21,600	–13,100*	8,500
Income (loss)	$250,400	$248,900	–$ 1,500

*$262,000 × 5%

Claxon Company should lease the machine.

2.

Differential Analysis
Continue (Alt. 1) or Discontinue (Alt. 2) Product TS-20
September 12

	Continue Product TS-20 (Alternative 1)	Discontinue Product TS-20 (Alternative 2)	Differential Effect on Income (Alternative 2)
Revenue	$102,000	$ 0	–$102,000
Costs:			
Variable cost of goods sold	–52,500	0	52,500
Variable selling and admin. expenses	–21,500	0	21,500
Fixed costs	–35,000	–35,000	0
Income (loss)	–$ 7,000	–$35,000	–$ 28,000

Product TS-20 should be continued.

3.

Differential Analysis
Make (Alt. 1) or Buy (Alt. 2) Bread
August 16

	Make Bread (Alternative 1)	Buy Bread (Alternative 2)	Differential Effect on Income (Alternative 2)
Sales price	$ 0	$ 0	$ 0
Unit costs:			
Purchase price	0	–110	–110
Delivery	0	–15	–15
Variable costs ($165 – $43)	–122	0	122
Fixed factory overhead	–43	–43	0
Income (loss)	–$165	–$168	–$ 3

The company should make the bread.

4.

Differential Analysis
Continue with (Alt. 1) or Replace (Alt. 2) Old Machine
February 18

	Continue with Old Machine (Alternative 1)	Replace Old Machine (Alternative 2)	Differential Effect on Income (Alternative 2)
Revenues:			
Proceeds from sale of old machine	$ 0	$ 84,000	$ 84,000
Costs:			
Purchase price	0	–145,000	–145,000
Direct labor (6 years)	–330,000[1]	–258,000[2]	72,000
Income (loss)	–$330,000	–$319,000	$ 11,000

[1]$55,000 × 6 years

[2]$43,000 × 6 years

The company should replace the old machine.

5.
Differential Analysis
Sell Product T (Alt. 1) or Process Further into Product U (Alt. 2)
August 2

	Sell Product T (Alternative 1)	Process Further into Product U (Alternative 2)	Differential Effect on Income (Alternative 2)
Revenues, per unit	$7.10	$8.00	$0.90
Costs, per unit	−5.90	−6.64*	−0.74
Income (loss), per unit	$1.20	$1.36	$0.16

*$5.90 + $0.74

The company should process further into Product U.

6.
Differential Analysis
Reject Order (Alt. 1) or Accept Order (Alt. 2)
October 23

	Reject Order (Alternative 1)	Accept Order (Alternative 2)	Differential Effect on Income (Alternative 2)
Revenues, per unit	$0.00	$42.00	$42.00
Costs:			
Variable manufacturing costs, per unit	0.00	−30.00	−30.00
Export tariff, per unit	0.00	−12.60*	−12.60
Income (loss), per unit	$0.00	−$ 0.60	−$ 0.60

*$42.00 × 30%

The company should not accept the special order.

7. Markup Percentage on Product Cost $= \dfrac{\text{Desired Profit} + \text{Total Selling and Administrative Expenses}}{\text{Total Product Cost}}$

$$= \dfrac{\$55 + \$45}{\$80^*} = 125\%$$

*$125 − $45

8.

	Product A	Product B
Unit contribution margin	$24	$30
Testing hours per unit	÷ 4	÷ 6
Unit contribution margin per production bottleneck hour	$ 6	$ 5

Product A is the most profitable in using bottleneck resources.

Need more help? Watch step-by-step videos of how to compute answers to these Exercises in CengageNOWv2.

Problem

1. $160,000 ($1,600,000 × 10%)

2. A. Total manufacturing costs:

Variable ($20 × 80,000 units)	$1,600,000
Fixed factory overhead	800,000
Total	$2,400,000

Cost amount per unit: $2,400,000 ÷ 80,000 units = $30.00

B. Markup Percentage = $\dfrac{\text{Desired Profit} + \text{Total Selling and Administrative Expenses}}{\text{Total Product Cost}}$

$$= \frac{\$160,000 + \$400,000 + (\$5 \times 80,000 \text{ units})}{\$2,400,000}$$

$$= \frac{\$160,000 + \$400,000 + \$400,000}{\$2,400,000}$$

$$= \frac{\$960,000}{\$2,400,000} = 40\%$$

C.
Cost amount per unit	$30.00
Markup ($30 × 40%)	12.00
Selling price	$42.00

3. Inez should consider using activity-based costing for factory overhead allocation when the product and manufacturing operations are complex. For example, if the digital clock was introduced as one among many different consumer digital products, then it is likely these products will consume factory activities in different ways. If this is combined with complex manufacturing and manufacturing support processes, then it is likely a single overhead allocation rate will lead to distorted factory overhead allocation. Specifically, the digital clock is a new product. Thus, it is likely that it will consume more factory overhead than existing stable and mature products. In this case, a single rate would result in the digital clock being undercosted compared to results using activity-based rates for factory overhead allocation.

4.
Current selling price	$42
Expected selling price	−38
Required reduction in manufacturing cost to maintain same profit	$ 4

Revised revenue and cost figures:

	Current	Desired
Selling price	$42	$38
Costs:		
Variable selling and administrative expenses per unit	$ 5	$ 5
Fixed selling and administrative expenses per unit ($400,000 ÷ 80,000 units)	5	5
Existing manufacturing cost per unit [part (2)]	30	
Target manufacturing cost per unit ($30 – $4)		26
Total costs	$40	$36
Profit	$ 2	$ 2

5.
Differential Analysis—Wong Inc. Special Order
Reject (Alternative 1) or Accept (Alternative 2) Order
August 7

	Reject Order (Alternative 1)	Accept Order (Alternative 2)	Differential Effect on Income (Alternative 2)
Revenues	$0	$112,000*	$112,000
Costs:			
Variable manufacturing costs	0	−80,000**	−80,000
Income (loss)	$0	$ 32,000	$ 32,000

*4,000 units × $28 per unit
**4,000 units × $20 per unit

The proposal should be accepted.

Discussion Questions

1. Explain the meaning of (A) differential revenue, (B) differential cost, and (C) differential income.

2. A company could sell a building for $250,000 or lease it for $2,500 per month. What would need to be considered in determining if the lease option would be preferred?

3. A chemical company has a commodity-grade and premium-grade product. Why might the company elect to process the commodity-grade product further to the premium-grade product?

4. A company accepts incremental business at a special price that exceeds the variable cost. What other issues must the company consider in deciding whether to accept the business?

5. A company fabricates a component at a cost of $6.00. A supplier offers to supply the same component for $5.50. Under what circumstances is it reasonable to purchase from the supplier?

6. Many fast-food restaurant chains, such as **McDonald's**, will occasionally discontinue restaurants in their system. What are some financial considerations in deciding to eliminate a store?

7. In the long run, the normal selling price must be set high enough to cover what factors?

8. Although the cost-plus approach to product pricing may be used by management as a general guideline, what are some examples of other factors that managers should also consider in setting product prices?

9. How does the target cost method differ from cost-plus approaches?

10. What is the appropriate measure of a product's value when a firm is operating under production bottlenecks?

Basic Exercises

BE 24-1 Lease or sell   Obj. 1

McFadden Company owns equipment with a cost of $475,000 and accumulated depreciation of $280,000 that can be sold for $175,000, less a 7% sales commission. Alternatively, McFadden Company can lease the equipment for four years for a total of $180,000, at the end of which there is no residual value. In addition, the repair, insurance, and property tax expense that would be incurred by McFadden Company on the equipment would total $35,500 over the four-year lease. Prepare a differential analysis on February 18 as to whether McFadden Company should lease (Alternative 1) or sell (Alternative 2) the equipment.

BE 24-2 Discontinue a segment   Obj. 1

Product AG52 has revenue of $748,000, variable cost of goods sold of $640,000, variable selling expenses of $90,000, and fixed costs of $50,000, creating a loss from operations of $32,000. Prepare a differential analysis as of October 7 to determine if Product AG52 should be continued (Alternative 1) or discontinued (Alternative 2), assuming fixed costs are unaffected by the decision.

BE 24-3 Make or buy   Obj. 1

A company manufactures various-sized plastic bottles for its medicinal product. The manufacturing cost for small bottles is $75 per unit (100 bottles), including fixed costs of $28 per unit. A proposal is offered to purchase small bottles from an outside source for $40 per unit, plus $4 per unit for freight. Prepare a differential analysis dated July 31 to determine whether the company should make (Alternative 1) or buy (Alternative 2) the bottles, assuming fixed costs are unaffected by the decision.

SHOW ME HOW

BE 24-4 Replace equipment
Obj. 1

A machine with a book value of $80,000 has an estimated five-year life. A proposal is offered to sell the old machine for $50,500 and replace it with a new machine at a cost of $75,000. The new machine has a five-year life with no residual value. The new machine would reduce annual direct labor costs from $11,200 to $7,400. Prepare a differential analysis dated April 11 on whether to continue with the old machine (Alternative 1) or replace the old machine (Alternative 2).

SHOW ME HOW

BE 24-5 Process or sell
Obj. 1

Product J19 is produced for $11 per gallon. Product J19 can be sold without additional processing for $18 per gallon, or processed further into Product R33 at an additional cost of $7 per gallon. Product R33 can be sold for $24 per gallon. Prepare a differential analysis dated April 30 on whether to sell Product J19 (Alternative 1) or process further into Product R33 (Alternative 2).

SHOW ME HOW

BE 24-6 Accept business at special price
Obj. 1

Product A is normally sold for $9.60 per unit. A special price of $7.20 is offered for the export market. The variable production cost is $5.00 per unit. An additional export tariff of 15% of revenue must be paid for all export products. Assume there is sufficient capacity for the special order. Prepare a differential analysis dated March 16 on whether to reject (Alternative 1) or accept (Alternative 2) the special order.

SHOW ME HOW

BE 24-7 Product cost markup percentage
Obj. 2

Green Thumb Garden Tools Inc. produces and sells home and garden tools and equipment. A lawnmower has a total cost of $230 per unit, of which $160 is product cost and $70 is selling and administrative expenses. In addition, the total cost of $230 is made up of $120 variable cost and $110 fixed cost. The desired profit is $58 per unit. Determine the markup percentage on product cost.

SHOW ME HOW

BE 24-8 Bottleneck profit
Obj. 3

Product K has a unit contribution margin of $120. Product L has a unit contribution margin of $100. Product K requires five furnace hours, while Product L requires four furnace hours. Determine the most profitable product, assuming the furnace is a bottleneck constraint.

Exercises

EX 24-1 Differential analysis for a lease or sell decision
Obj. 1

✔ A. Differential income from selling, $5,400

SHOW ME HOW

Granite Construction Company is considering selling excess machinery with a book value of $175,000 (original cost of $315,000 less accumulated depreciation of $140,000) for $180,000, less a 5% brokerage commission. Alternatively, the machinery can be leased for a total of $200,000 for four years, after which it is expected to have no residual value. During the period of the lease, Granite Construction Company's costs of repairs, insurance, and property tax expenses are expected to be $34,400.

A. Prepare a differential analysis, dated November 7 to determine whether Granite should lease (Alternative 1) or sell (Alternative 2) the machinery.

B. ▬▬▶ On the basis of the data presented, would it be advisable to lease or sell the machinery? Explain.

EX 24-2 Differential analysis for a lease or buy decision
Obj. 1

Sloan Corporation is considering new equipment. The equipment can be purchased from an overseas supplier for $125,500. The freight and installation costs for the equipment are $1,600. If purchased, annual repairs and maintenance are estimated to be $2,500 per year over the five-year useful life of the equipment. Alternatively, Sloan can lease the equipment from a domestic supplier for $30,000 per year for five years, with no additional costs. Prepare a differential analysis dated December 3 to determine whether Sloan should lease (Alternative 1) or purchase (Alternative 2) the equipment. *Hint:* This is a "lease or *buy*" decision, which must be analyzed from the perspective of the equipment user, as opposed to the equipment owner.

✔ A. Differential loss, –$1,275,000

EX 24-3 Differential analysis for a discontinued product
Obj. 1

A condensed income statement by product line for Healthy Beverage Inc. indicated the following for Fruit Cola for the past year:

Sales	$12,750,000
Cost of goods sold	8,500,000
Gross profit	$ 4,250,000
Operating expenses	6,000,000
Loss from operations	$ (1,750,000)

It is estimated that 25% of the cost of goods sold represents fixed factory overhead costs and that 15% of the operating expenses are fixed. Because Fruit Cola is only one of many products, the fixed costs will not be materially affected if the product is discontinued.

A. Prepare a differential analysis dated January 5 to determine whether Fruit Cola should be continued (Alternative 1) or discontinued (Alternative 2).

B. ━━━▶ Should Fruit Cola be retained? Explain.

✔ A. Alternative 1 loss, $2,200

EX 24-4 Differential analysis for a discontinued product
Obj. 1

The condensed product-line income statement for Dish N' Dat Company for the month of March is as follows:

Dish N' Dat Company
Product-Line Income Statement
For the Month Ended March 31

	Bowls	Plates	Cups
Sales	$71,000	$105,700	$31,300
Cost of goods sold	32,600	42,300	16,800
Gross profit	$38,400	$ 63,400	$14,500
Selling and administrative expenses	27,400	42,800	16,700
Income from operations	$11,000	$ 20,600	$ (2,200)

Fixed costs are 15% of the cost of goods sold and 40% of the selling and administrative expenses. Dish N' Dat assumes that fixed costs would not be materially affected if the Cups line were discontinued.

A. Prepare a differential analysis dated March 31 to determine if Cups should be continued (Alternative 1) or discontinued (Alternative 2).

B. ━━━▶ Should the Cups line be retained? Explain.

EX 24-5 Segment analysis for a service company
Obj. 1

Charles Schwab Corporation is one of the more innovative brokerage and financial service companies in the United States. The company recently provided information about its major business segments as follows (in millions):

	Investor Services	Advisor Services
Revenues	$4,647	$1,360
Income from operations	1,673	459
Depreciation	154	45

A. ▬▬▶ How does a brokerage company like Schwab define the Investor Services and Advisor Services segments? Use the Internet to develop your answer.

B. Provide a specific example of a variable and fixed cost in the Investor Services segment.

C. Estimate the contribution margin for each segment, assuming depreciation represents the majority of fixed costs.

D. If Schwab decided to sell its Advisor Services accounts to another company, estimate how much operating income would decline.

EX 24-6 Decision to discontinue a product
Obj. 1

▬▬▶ On the basis of the following data, the general manager of Featherweight Shoes Inc. decided to discontinue Children's Shoes because it reduced income from operations by $17,000. What is the flaw in this decision, if it is assumed fixed costs would not be materially affected by the discontinuance?

Featherweight Shoes Inc.
Product-Line Income Statement
For the Year Ended April 30, 20Y8

	Children's Shoes	Men's Shoes	Women's Shoes	Total
Sales	$235,000	$300,000	$500,000	$1,035,000
Costs of goods sold:				
Variable costs	$130,000	$150,000	$220,000	$ 500,000
Fixed costs	41,000	60,000	120,000	221,000
Total cost of goods sold	$171,000	$210,000	$340,000	$ 721,000
Gross profit	$ 64,000	$ 90,000	$160,000	$ 314,000
Selling and adminstrative expenses:				
Variable selling and admin. expenses	$ 46,000	$ 45,000	$ 95,000	$ 186,000
Fixed selling and admin. expenses	35,000	20,000	25,000	80,000
Total selling and admin. expenses	$ 81,000	$ 65,000	$120,000	$ 266,000
Income (loss) from operations	$ (17,000)	$ 25,000	$ 40,000	$ 48,000

EX 24-7 Make-or-buy decision
Obj. 1

✔ A. Differential loss from buying, −$3.00 per case

SHOW ME HOW   EXCEL TEMPLATE

Fremont Computer Company has been purchasing carrying cases for its portable computers at a purchase price of $40 per unit. The company, which is currently operating below full capacity, charges factory overhead to production at the rate of 25% of direct labor cost. The unit costs to produce comparable carrying cases are expected to be as follows:

Direct materials	$16
Direct labor	20
Factory overhead (25% of direct labor)	5
Total cost per unit	$41

If Fremont Computer Company manufactures the carrying cases, fixed factory overhead costs will not increase and variable factory overhead costs associated with the cases are expected to be 5% of the direct labor costs.

A. Prepare a differential analysis dated September 30 to determine whether the company should make (Alternative 1) or buy (Alternative 2) the carrying case.

B. ▬▬▶ On the basis of the data presented, would it be advisable to make the carrying cases or to continue buying them? Explain.

EX 24-8 Make-or-buy decision for a service company
Obj. 1

EXCEL TEMPLATE

The Theater Arts Guild of Dallas (TAG-D) employs five people in its Publication Department. These people lay out pages for pamphlets, brochures, magazines, and other publications for the TAG-D productions. The pages are delivered to an outside company for printing. The company is considering an outside publication service for the layout work. The outside service

(Continued)

is quoting a price of $13 per layout page. The budget for the Publication Department for the current year is as follows:

Salaries	$224,000
Benefits	36,000
Supplies	21,000
Office expenses	39,000
Office depreciation	28,000
Computer depreciation	24,000
Total	$372,000

The department expects to lay out 24,000 pages for the current year. The Publication Department office space and equipment would be used for future administrative needs, if the department's function were purchased from the outside.

A. Prepare a differential analysis dated February 22 to determine whether TAG-D should lay out pages internally (Alternative 1) or purchase layout services from the outside (Alternative 2).

B. ━━━ On the basis of your analysis in part (A), should the page layout work be purchased from an outside company? Explain.

C. ━━━ What additional considerations might factor into the decision making?

SHOW ME HOW

EX 24-9 Machine replacement decision

Obj. 1

A company is considering replacing an old piece of machinery, which cost $600,000 and has $350,000 of accumulated depreciation to date, with a new machine that has a purchase price of $545,000. The old machine could be sold for $231,000. The annual variable production costs associated with the old machine are estimated to be $61,000 per year for eight years. The annual variable production costs for the new machine are estimated to be $19,000 per year for eight years.

A. Prepare a differential analysis dated September 13 to determine whether to continue with (Alternative 1) or replace (Alternative 2) the old machine.

B. What is the sunk cost in this situation?

✔ A. Differential loss, −$2,500

EXCEL TEMPLATE

EX 24-10 Differential analysis for machine replacement

Obj. 1

Kim Kwon Digital Components Company assembles circuit boards by using a manually operated machine to insert electronic components. The original cost of the machine is $60,000, the accumulated depreciation is $24,000, its remaining useful life is five years, and its residual value is negligible. On May 4 of the current year, a proposal was made to replace the present manufacturing procedure with a fully automatic machine that has a purchase price of $180,000. The automatic machine has an estimated useful life of five years and no significant residual value. For use in evaluating the proposal, the accountant accumulated the following annual data on present and proposed operations:

	Present Operations	Proposed Operations
Sales	$205,000	$205,000
Direct materials	$ 72,000	$ 72,000
Direct labor	51,000	—
Power and maintenance	5,000	18,000
Taxes, insurance, etc.	1,500	4,000
Selling and administrative expenses	45,000	45,000
Total expenses	$174,500	$139,000

A. Prepare a differential analysis dated May 4 to determine whether to continue with (Alternative 1) or replace (Alternative 2) the old machine. Prepare the analysis over the useful life of the new machine.

B. Based only on the data presented, should the proposal be accepted?

C. ━━━ What are some of the other factors that should be considered before a final decision is made?

SHOW ME HOW

EX 24-11 Sell or process further   Obj. 1

Calgary Lumber Company incurs a cost of $315 per hundred board feet (hbf) in processing certain "rough-cut" lumber, which it sells for $440 per hbf. An alternative is to produce a "finished cut" at a total processing cost of $465 per hbf, which can be sold for $600 per hbf. Prepare a differential analysis dated March 15 on whether to sell rough-cut lumber (Alternative 1) or process further into finished-cut lumber (Alternative 2).

EXCEL TEMPLATE

EX 24-12 Sell or process further   Obj. 1

Rise N' Shine Coffee Company produces Columbian coffee in batches of 6,000 pounds. The standard quantity of materials required in the process is 6,000 pounds, which cost $5.50 per pound. Columbian coffee can be sold without further processing for $9.22 per pound. Columbian coffee can also be processed further to yield Decaf Columbian, which can be sold for $11.88 per pound. The processing into Decaf Columbian requires additional processing costs of $10,230 per batch. The additional processing will also cause a 5% loss of product due to evaporation.

A. Prepare a differential analysis dated October 6 on whether to sell regular Columbian (Alternative 1) or process further into Decaf Columbian (Alternative 2).

B. ━━━▶ Should Rise N' Shine sell Columbian coffee or process further and sell Decaf Columbian? Explain.

C. Determine the price of Decaf Columbian that would cause neither an advantage nor a disadvantage for processing further and selling Decaf Columbian.

EX 24-13 Decision on accepting additional business   Obj. 1

✔ A. Differential income, $54,000

Homestead Jeans Co. has an annual plant capacity of 65,000 units, and current production is 45,000 units. Monthly fixed costs are $54,000, and variable costs are $29 per unit. The present selling price is $42 per unit. On November 12 of the current year, the company received an offer from Dawkins Company for 18,000 units of the product at $32 each. Dawkins Company will market the units in a foreign country under its own brand name. The additional business is not expected to affect the domestic selling price or quantity of sales of Homestead Jeans Co.

A. Prepare a differential analysis dated November 12 on whether to reject (Alternative 1) or accept (Alternative 2) the Dawkins order.

B. ━━━▶ Briefly explain the reason why accepting this additional business will increase operating income.

C. What is the minimum price per unit that would produce a positive contribution margin?

EX 24-14 Accepting business at a special price   Obj. 1

Portable Power Company expects to operate at 80% of productive capacity during July. The total manufacturing costs for July for the production of 25,000 batteries are budgeted as follows:

Direct materials	$162,500
Direct labor	70,000
Variable factory overhead	30,000
Fixed factory overhead	112,500
Total manufacturing costs	$375,000

The company has an opportunity to submit a bid for 2,500 batteries to be delivered by July 31 to a government agency. If the contract is obtained, it is anticipated that the additional activity will not interfere with normal production during July or increase the selling or administrative expenses. What is the unit cost below which Portable Power Company should not go in bidding on the government contract?

EX 24-15   Decision on accepting additional business   Obj. 1

✔ **A. Differential revenues, $15,000,000**

SHOW ME HOW   EXCEL TEMPLATE

Talladega Tire and Rubber Company has capacity to produce 500,000 tires. Talladega presently produces and sells 400,000 tires for the North American market at a price of $200 per tire. Talladega is evaluating a special order from a European automobile company, Autobahn Motors. Autobahn is offering to buy 100,000 tires for $150 per tire. Talladega's accounting system indicates that the total cost per tire is as follows:

Direct materials	$ 75
Direct labor	20
Factory overhead (70% variable)	30
Selling and administrative expenses (60% variable)	18
Total	$143

Talladega pays a selling commission equal to 3% of the selling price on North American orders, which is included in the variable portion of the selling and administrative expenses. However, this special order would not have a sales commission. If the order was accepted, the tires would be shipped overseas for an additional shipping cost of $3 per tire. In addition, Autobahn has made the order conditional on receiving European safety certification. Talladega estimates that this certification would cost $400,000.

A. Prepare a differential analysis dated July 31 on whether to reject (Alternative 1) or accept (Alternative 2) the special order from Autobahn Motors.

B. What is the minimum price per unit that would be financially acceptable to Talladega?

EX 24-16   Product cost method of product pricing   Obj. 2

✔ **B. $40.00**

SHOW ME HOW

La Femme Accessories Inc. produces women's handbags. The cost of producing 800 handbags is as follows:

Direct materials	$18,000
Direct labor	8,500
Factory overhead	5,500
Total manufacturing cost	$32,000

The selling and administrative expenses are $17,000. The management desires a profit equal to 22% of invested assets of $250,000.

A. Determine the amount of desired profit from the production and sale of 800 handbags.

B. Determine the product cost per unit for the production of 800 handbags.

C. Determine the product cost markup percentage for handbags.

D. Determine the selling price of handbags.

EX 24-17   Product cost method of product costing   Obj. 2

✔ **D. $325**

Smart Stream Inc. uses the product cost method of applying the cost-plus approach to product pricing. The costs of producing and selling 10,000 cell phones are as follows:

Variable costs per unit:		Fixed costs:	
Direct materials	$150	Factory overhead	$350,000
Direct labor	25	Selling and admin. exp.	140,000
Factory overhead	40		
Selling and administrative expenses	25		
Total variable cost per unit	$240		

Smart Stream desires a profit equal to a 30% return on invested assets of $1,200,000.

A. Determine the amount of desired profit from the production and sale of 10,000 cell phones.

B. Determine the product cost per unit for the production of 10,000 cell phones.

C. Determine the product cost markup percentage for cell phones.

D. Determine the selling price of cell phones.

REAL WORLD

EX 24-18 Target costing
Obj. 2

Toyota Motor Corporation uses target costing. Assume that Toyota marketing personnel estimate that the competitive selling price for the Camry in the upcoming model year will need to be $27,000. Assume further that the Camry's total unit cost for the upcoming model year is estimated to be $22,500 and that Toyota requires a 20% profit margin on selling price (which is equivalent to a 25% markup on total cost).

A. What price will Toyota establish for the Camry for the upcoming model year?

B. ━━━▶ What impact will target costing have on Toyota, given the assumed information?

EX 24-19 Target costing
Obj. 2

✔ B. $30

Instant Image Inc. manufactures color laser printers. Model J20 presently sells for $460 and has a product cost of $230, as follows:

Direct materials	$175
Direct labor	40
Factory overhead	15
Total	$230

It is estimated that the competitive selling price for color laser printers of this type will drop to $400 next year. Instant Image has established a target cost to maintain its historical markup percentage on product cost. Engineers have provided the following cost-reduction ideas:

1. Purchase a plastic printer cover with snap-on assembly, rather than with screws. This will reduce the amount of direct labor by 15 minutes per unit.

2. Add an inspection step that will add six minutes per unit of direct labor but reduce the materials cost by $20 per unit.

3. Decrease the cycle time of the injection molding machine from four minutes to three minutes per part. Forty percent of the direct labor and 48% of the factory overhead are related to running injection molding machines.

The direct labor rate is $30 per hour.

A. Determine the target cost for Model J20, assuming that the historical markup on product cost and selling price are maintained.

B. Determine the required cost reduction.

C. Evaluate the three engineering improvements together to determine if the required cost reduction (drift) can be achieved.

EX 24-20 Product decisions under bottlenecked operations
Obj. 3

Mill Metals Inc. has three grades of metal product, Type 5, Type 10, and Type 20. Financial data for the three grades are as follows:

	Type 5	Type 10	Type 20
Revenues	$43,000	$49,000	$56,500
Variable cost	$34,000	$28,000	$26,500
Fixed cost	8,000	8,000	8,000
Total cost	$42,000	$36,000	$34,500
Income from operations	$ 1,000	$13,000	$22,000
Number of units	÷ 5,000	÷ 5,000	÷ 5,000
Income from operations per unit	$ 0.20	$ 2.60	$ 4.40

(Continued)

Mill's operations require all three grades to be melted in a furnace before being formed. The furnace runs 24 hours a day, 7 days a week, and is a production bottleneck. The furnace hours required per unit of each product are as follows:

Type 5:	6 hours
Type 10:	6 hours
Type 20:	12 hours

The Marketing Department is considering a new marketing and sales campaign.

Which product should be emphasized in the marketing and sales campaign in order to maximize profitability?

EX 24-21   Product decisions under bottlenecked operations   **Obj. 3**

✔ A. Total income from operations, $269,000

Youngstown Glass Company manufactures three types of safety plate glass: large, medium, and small. All three products have high demand. Thus, Youngstown Glass is able to sell all the safety glass that it can make. The production process includes an autoclave operation, which is a pressurized heat treatment. The autoclave is a production bottleneck. Total fixed costs are $85,000 for the company as a whole. In addition, the following information is available about the three products:

	Large	Medium	Small
Unit selling price	$184	$160	$100
Unit variable cost	130	120	76
Unit contribution margin	$ 54	$ 40	$ 24
Autoclave hours per unit	3	2	1
Total process hours per unit	5	4	2
Budgeted units of production	3,000	3,000	3,000

A. Determine the contribution margin by glass type and the total company income from operations for the budgeted units of production.

B. Prepare an analysis showing which product is the most profitable per bottleneck hour.

Appendix

EX 24-22   Total cost method of product pricing

✔ B. 12.46%

Based on the data presented in Exercise 17, assume that Smart Stream Inc. uses the total cost method of applying the cost-plus approach to product pricing.

A. Determine the total costs and the total cost amount per unit for the production and sale of 10,000 cellular phones.

B. Determine the total cost markup percentage (rounded to two decimal places) for cellular phones.

C. Determine the selling price of cellular phones. (Round markup to the nearest dollar.)

Appendix

EX 24-23   Variable cost method of product pricing

✔ B. 35.42%

Based on the data presented in Exercise 17, assume that Smart Stream Inc. uses the variable cost method of applying the cost-plus approach to product pricing.

A. Determine the variable costs and the variable cost amount per unit for the production and sale of 10,000 cellular phones.

B. Determine the variable cost markup percentage (rounded to two decimal places) for cellular phones.

C. Determine the selling price of cellular phones. (Round markup to the nearest dollar.)

Problems: Series A

PR 24-1A   Differential analysis involving opportunity costs   **Obj. 1**

✔ 3. $1,450,000

EXCEL TEMPLATE

On August 1, Rantoul Stores Inc. is considering leasing a building and purchasing the necessary equipment to operate a retail store. Alternatively, the company could use the funds to invest in $1,000,000 of 4% U.S. Treasury bonds that mature in 15 years. The bonds could be purchased at face value. The following data have been assembled:

Cost of store equipment	$1,000,000
Life of store equipment	15 years
Estimated residual value of store equipment	$50,000
Yearly costs to operate the store, excluding depreciation of store equipment	$200,000
Yearly expected revenues—years 1–6	$300,000
Yearly expected revenues—years 7–15	$400,000

Instructions

1. Prepare a differential analysis as of August 1 presenting the proposed operation of the store for the 15 years (Alternative 1) as compared with investing in U.S. Treasury bonds (Alternative 2).

2. Based on the results disclosed by the differential analysis, should the proposal be accepted?

3. If the proposal is accepted, what would be the total estimated income from operations of the store for the 15 years?

EXCEL TEMPLATE

PR 24-2A   Differential analysis for machine replacement proposal   **Obj. 1**

Lexigraphic Printing Company is considering replacing a machine that has been used in its factory for four years. Relevant data associated with the operations of the old machine and the new machine, neither of which has any estimated residual value, are as follows:

Old Machine	
Cost of machine, 10-year life	$89,000
Annual depreciation (straight-line)	8,900
Annual manufacturing costs, excluding depreciation	23,600
Annual nonmanufacturing operating expenses	6,100
Annual revenue	74,200
Current estimated selling price of machine	29,700

New Machine	
Purchase price of machine, six-year life	$119,700
Annual depreciation (straight-line)	19,950
Estimated annual manufacturing costs, excluding depreciation	6,900

Annual nonmanufacturing operating expenses and revenue are not expected to be affected by purchase of the new machine.

Instructions

1. Prepare a differential analysis as of April 30 comparing operations using the present machine (Alternative 1) with operations using the new machine (Alternative 2). The analysis should indicate the total differential income that would result over the six-year period if the new machine is acquired.

2. ▬▬▬▶ List other factors that should be considered before a final decision is reached.

PR 24-3A   Differential analysis for sales promotion proposal   Obj. 1

Kankakee Cosmetics Company is planning a one-month campaign for December to promote sales of one of its two cosmetics products. A total of $150,000 has been budgeted for advertising, contests, redeemable coupons, and other promotional activities. The following data have been assembled for their possible usefulness in deciding which of the products to select for the campaign:

	Moisturizer	Perfume
Unit selling price	$35	$55
Unit production costs:		
Direct materials	$12	$20
Direct labor	8	10
Variable factory overhead	3	6
Fixed factory overhead	2	6
Total unit production costs	$25	$42
Unit variable selling expenses	2	3
Unit fixed selling expenses	2	8
Total unit costs	$29	$53
Operating income per unit	$ 6	$ 2

No increase in facilities would be necessary to produce and sell the increased output. It is anticipated that 40,000 additional units of moisturizer or 30,000 additional units of perfume could be sold from the campaign without changing the unit selling price of either product.

Instructions

1. Prepare a differential analysis as of November 2 to determine whether to promote moisturizer (Alternative 1) or perfume (Alternative 2).

2. ▬▬▶ The sales manager had tentatively decided to promote moisturizer estimating that operating income would be increased by $50,000 ($5 operating income per unit for 40,000 units, less promotion expenses of $150,000). The manager also believed that the selection of perfume would reduce operating income by $90,000 ($2 operating income per unit for 30,000 units, less promotion expenses of $150,000). State briefly your reasons for supporting or opposing the tentative decision.

PR 24-4A   Differential analysis for further processing   Obj. 1

✔ 1. Raw sugar
income, $23,800

The management of Dominican Sugar Company is considering whether to process further raw sugar into refined sugar. Refined sugar can be sold for $2.20 per pound, and raw sugar can be sold without further processing for $1.40 per pound. Raw sugar is produced in batches of 42,000 pounds by processing 100,000 pounds of sugar cane, which costs $0.35 per pound of cane. Refined sugar will require additional processing costs of $0.50 per pound of raw sugar, and 1.25 pounds of raw sugar will produce 1 pound of refined sugar.

Instructions

1. Prepare a differential analysis as of March 24 to determine whether to sell raw sugar (Alternative 1) or process further into refined sugar (Alternative 2).

2. ▬▬▶ Briefly report your recommendations.

Appendix

PR 24-5A   Product pricing using the cost-plus approach methods; differential analysis for accepting additional business

Obj. 1, 2

✔ 2. B. Markup percentage, 44%

Crystal Displays Inc. recently began production of a new product, flat panel displays, which required the investment of $1,500,000 in assets. The costs of producing and selling 5,000 units of flat panel displays are estimated as follows:

Variable costs per unit:		Fixed costs:	
Direct materials	$120	Factory overhead	$250,000
Direct labor	30	Selling and administrative expenses	150,000
Factory overhead	50		
Selling and administrative expenses	35		
Total variable cost per unit	$235		

Crystal Displays Inc. is currently considering establishing a selling price for flat panel displays. The president of Crystal Displays has decided to use the cost-plus approach to product pricing and has indicated that the displays must earn a 15% return on invested assets.

Instructions

1. Determine the amount of desired profit from the production and sale of flat panel displays.

2. Assuming that the product cost method is used, determine (A) the cost amount per unit, (B) the markup percentage, and (C) the selling price of flat panel displays.

3. (*Appendix*) Assuming that the total cost method is used, determine (A) the cost amount per unit, (B) the markup percentage (rounded to two decimal places), and (C) the selling price of flat panel displays. (Round markup to nearest whole dollar.)

4. (*Appendix*) Assuming that the variable cost method is used, determine (A) the cost amount per unit, (B) the markup percentage (rounded to two decimal places), and (C) the selling price of flat panel displays. (Round markup to nearest whole dollar.)

5. ➤ Comment on any additional considerations that could influence establishing the selling price for flat panel displays.

6. Assume that as of August 1, 3,000 units of flat panel displays have been produced and sold during the current year. Analysis of the domestic market indicates that 2,000 additional units are expected to be sold during the remainder of the year at the normal product price determined under the product cost method. On August 3, Crystal Displays Inc. received an offer from Maple Leaf Visual Inc. for 800 units of flat panel displays at $225 each. Maple Leaf Visual Inc. will market the units in Canada under its own brand name, and no variable selling and administrative expenses associated with the sale will be incurred by Crystal Displays Inc. The additional business is not expected to affect the domestic sales of flat panel displays, and the additional units could be produced using existing factory, selling, and administrative capacity.

A. Prepare a differential analysis of the proposed sale to Maple Leaf Visual Inc.

B. Based on the differential analysis in part (A), should the proposal be accepted?

PR 24-6A   Product pricing and profit analysis with bottleneck operations

Obj. 3

✔ 1. High Grade, $10

EXCEL TEMPLATE

Hercules Steel Company produces three grades of steel: high, good, and regular grade. Each of these products (grades) has high demand in the market, and Hercules is able to sell as much as it can produce of all three. The furnace operation is a bottleneck in the process and is running at 100% of capacity. Hercules wants to improve steel operation profitability. The variable conversion cost is $15 per process hour. The fixed cost is $200,000. In addition, the cost analyst was able to determine the following information about the three products:

	High Grade	Good Grade	Regular Grade
Budgeted units produced	5,000	5,000	5,000
Total process hours per unit	12	11	10
Furnace hours per unit	4	3	2.5
Unit selling price	$280	$270	$250
Direct materials cost per unit	$90	$84	$80

(*Continued*)

The furnace operation is part of the total process for each of these three products. Thus, for example, 4.0 of the 12.0 hours required to process High Grade steel are associated with the furnace.

Instructions

1. Determine the unit contribution margin for each product.

2. Provide an analysis to determine the relative product profitability, assuming that the furnace is a bottleneck.

Problems: Series B

EXCEL TEMPLATE

✔ 3. $525,000

PR 24-1B Differential analysis involving opportunity costs

Obj. 1

On July 1, Coastal Distribution Company is considering leasing a building and buying the necessary equipment to operate a public warehouse. Alternatively, the company could use the funds to invest in $740,000 of 5% U.S. Treasury bonds that mature in 14 years. The bonds could be purchased at face value. The following data have been assembled:

Cost of equipment	$740,000
Life of equipment	14 years
Estimated residual value of equipment	$75,000
Yearly costs to operate the warehouse, excluding depreciation of equipment	$175,000
Yearly expected revenues—years 1–7	$280,000
Yearly expected revenues—years 8–14	$240,000

Instructions

1. Prepare a differential analysis as of July 1 presenting the proposed operation of the warehouse for the 14 years (Alternative 1) as compared with investing in U.S. Treasury bonds (Alternative 2).

2. Based on the results disclosed by the differential analysis, should the proposal be accepted?

3. If the proposal is accepted, what is the total estimated income from operations of the warehouse for the 14 years?

EXCEL TEMPLATE

PR 24-2B Differential analysis for machine replacement proposal

Obj. 1

Flint Tooling Company is considering replacing a machine that has been used in its factory for two years. Relevant data associated with the operations of the old machine and the new machine, neither of which has any estimated residual value, are as follows:

Old Machine	
Cost of machine, eight-year life	$38,000
Annual depreciation (straight-line)	4,750
Annual manufacturing costs, excluding depreciation	12,400
Annual nonmanufacturing operating expenses	2,700
Annual revenue	32,400
Current estimated selling price of the machine	12,900

New Machine	
Cost of machine, six-year life	$57,000
Annual depreciation (straight-line)	9,500
Estimated annual manufacturing costs, exclusive of depreciation	3,400

Annual nonmanufacturing operating expenses and revenue are not expected to be affected by purchase of the new machine.

Instructions

1. Prepare a differential analysis as of November 8 comparing operations using the present machine (Alternative 1) with operations using the new machine (Alternative 2). The analysis should indicate the differential income that would result over the six-year period if the new machine is acquired.

2. ➤ List other factors that should be considered before a final decision is reached.

PR 24-3B Differential analysis for sales promotion proposal Obj. 1

✔ 1. Differential revenues, $105,000

SHOW ME HOW EXCEL TEMPLATE

Sole Mates Inc. is planning a one-month campaign for July to promote sales of one of its two shoe products. A total of $100,000 has been budgeted for advertising, contests, redeemable coupons, and other promotional activities. The following data have been assembled for their possible usefulness in deciding which of the products to select for the campaign:

	Tennis Shoes	Walking Shoes
Unit selling price	$85	$100
Unit production costs:		
Direct materials	$19	$ 32
Direct labor	8	12
Variable factory overhead	7	5
Fixed factory overhead	16	11
Total unit production costs	$50	$ 60
Unit variable selling expenses	6	10
Unit fixed selling expenses	20	15
Total unit costs	$76	$ 85
Operating income per unit	$ 9	$ 15

No increase in facilities would be necessary to produce and sell the increased output. It is anticipated that 7,000 additional units of tennis shoes or 7,000 additional units of walking shoes could be sold without changing the unit selling price of either product.

Instructions

1. Prepare a differential analysis as of June 19 to determine whether to promote tennis shoes (Alternative 1) or walking shoes (Alternative 2).

2. ➤ The sales manager had tentatively decided to promote walking shoes, estimating that operating income would be increased by $5,000 ($15 operating income per unit for 7,000 units, less promotion expenses of $100,000). The manager also believed that the selection of tennis shoes would reduce operating income by $37,000 ($9 operating income per unit for 7,000 units, less promotion expenses of $100,000). State briefly your reasons for supporting or opposing the tentative decision.

PR 24-4B Differential analysis for further processing Obj. 1

✔ 1. Ingot income, $35,500

The management of International Aluminum Co. is considering whether to process aluminum ingot further into rolled aluminum. Rolled aluminum can be sold for $2,200 per ton, and ingot can be sold without further processing for $1,100 per ton. Ingot is produced in batches of 80 tons by smelting 500 tons of bauxite, which costs $105 per ton of bauxite. Rolled aluminum will require additional processing costs of $620 per ton of ingot, and 1.25 tons of ingot will produce 1 ton of rolled aluminum (due to trim losses).

Instructions

1. Prepare a differential analysis as of February 5 to determine whether to sell aluminum ingot (Alternative 1) or process further into rolled aluminum (Alternative 2).

2. ➤ Briefly report your recommendations.

Appendix

PR 24-5B   Product pricing using the cost-plus approach methods;   Obj. 1, 2
differential analysis for accepting additional business

✔ 2. B. Markup
percentage, 30%

Night Glow Inc. recently began production of a new product, the halogen light, which required the investment of $600,000 in assets. The costs of producing and selling 10,000 halogen lights are estimated as follows:

Variable costs per unit:		Fixed costs:	
Direct materials	$32	Factory overhead	$180,000
Direct labor	12	Selling and administrative expenses	80,000
Factory overhead	8		
Selling and administrative expenses	7		
Total variable cost per unit	$59		

Night Glow Inc. is currently considering establishing a selling price for the halogen light. The president of Night Glow Inc. has decided to use the cost-plus approach to product pricing and has indicated that the halogen light must earn a 10% return on invested assets.

Instructions

1. Determine the amount of desired profit from the production and sale of the halogen light.

2. Assuming that the product cost method is used, determine (A) the cost amount per unit, (B) the markup percentage, and (C) the selling price of the halogen light.

3. (*Appendix*) Assuming that the total cost method is used, determine (A) the cost amount per unit, (B) the markup percentage (rounded to two decimal places), and (C) the selling price of the halogen light. (Round markup to the nearest whole dollar.)

4. (*Appendix*) Assuming that the variable cost method is used, determine (A) the cost amount per unit, (B) the markup percentage (rounded to two decimal places), and (C) the selling price of the halogen light. (Round markup to nearest whole dollar.)

5. ▬▬▶ Comment on any additional considerations that could influence establishing the selling price for the halogen light.

6. Assume that as of September 1, 7,000 units of halogen light have been produced and sold during the current year. Analysis of the domestic market indicates that 3,000 additional units of the halogen light are expected to be sold during the remainder of the year at the normal product price determined under the product cost method. On September 5, Night Glow Inc. received an offer from Tokyo Lighting Inc. for 1,600 units of the halogen light at $57 each. Tokyo Lighting Inc. will market the units in Japan under its own brand name, and no variable selling and administrative expenses associated with the sale will be incurred by Night Glow Inc. The additional business is not expected to affect the domestic sales of the halogen light, and the additional units could be produced using existing productive, selling, and administrative capacity.

   A. Prepare a differential analysis of the proposed sale to Tokyo Lighting Inc.

   B. Based on the differential analysis in part (A), should the proposal be accepted?

PR 24-6B   Product pricing and profit analysis with bottleneck operations   Obj. 3

✔ 1. Ethylene, $15

EXCEL TEMPLATE

Wilmington Chemical Company produces three products: ethylene, butane, and ester. Each of these products has high demand in the market, and Wilmington Chemical is able to sell as much as it can produce of all three. The reaction operation is a bottleneck in the process and is running at 100% of capacity. Wilmington wants to improve chemical operation profitability. The variable conversion cost is $10 per process hour. The fixed cost is $400,000. In addition, the cost analyst was able to determine the following information about the three products:

	Ethylene	Butane	Ester
Budgeted units produced	9,000	9,000	9,000
Total process hours per unit	4.0	4.0	3.0
Reactor hours per unit	1.5	1.0	0.5
Unit selling price	$170	$155	$130
Direct materials cost per unit	$115	$88	$85

The reaction operation is part of the total process for each of these three products. Thus, for example, 1.5 of the 4.0 hours required to process ethylene is associated with the reactor.

Instructions

1. Determine the unit contribution margin for each product.
2. Provide an analysis to determine the relative product profitabilities, assuming that the reactor is a bottleneck.

Analysis for Decision Making

ADM-1 Service yield pricing and differential analysis

Cityscape Hotels has 200 rooms available in a major metropolitan city. The hotel is able to attract business customers during the weekdays and leisure customers during the weekend. However, the leisure customers on weekends occupy fewer rooms than do business customers on weekdays. Thus, Cityscape plans to provide special weekend pricing to attract additional leisure customers. A hotel room is priced at $180 per room night. The cost of a hotel room night includes the following:

	Cost Per Room Night (at normal occupancy)
Housekeeping service	$ 23
Utilities	7
Amenities	3
Hotel depreciation	55
Hotel staff (excluding housekeeping)	42
Total	$130

The special weekend price is proposed for $120 per room night. At this price, it is anticipated that average occupancy for the weekend (Friday, Saturday, and Sunday) will increase from 30% to 50% of available rooms.

A. What is the contribution margin for a room night under the normal pricing if only the hotel depreciation and hotel staff (excluding housekeeping) are assumed fixed for all occupancy levels?

B. Determine the contribution margin for a room night under the proposed weekend pricing.

C. Prepare a differential analysis showing the differential income for an average weekend between the existing (Alternative 1) and discount (Alternative 2) price plan.

D. ➤ Should management accept the proposed weekend pricing plan? Explain.

ADM-2 Service yield pricing

Valley Power Company uses natural gas to create steam to spin turbines to generate electricity. The costs of the power plant, including depreciation, taxes, and insurance, are fixed to generating electricity. The costs of operating personnel, maintenance, and fuel are variable to generating electricity. The fixed and variable costs are expressed in terms of costs per megawatt hour. A megawatt is 1 million watts generated per hour. A kilowatt is one thousand watts generated per hour. The fixed and variable costs per megawatt hour for Valley Power Company are:

Fixed cost per megawatt hour	$ 50
Variable cost per megawatt hour	80
Total cost per megawatt hour	$130

Valley Power Company runs gas turbines at 85% of capacity during the day and at 40% of capacity during the night. Daytime is considered peak demand time, while night is considered off-peak time. Industrial customers are charged $0.15 per kilowatt-hour, regardless of time of use. A new industrial customer is contracting for service from Valley Power. The new customer has

(Continued)

the ability to move production to the night shift, and thereby shift electricity demand to the night hours. However, to accomplish this, the new customer expects a discounted price per kilowatt-hour.

A. Determine the operating income per megawatt hour for industrial customers.

B. Determine the contribution margin per megawatt hour for industrial customers.

C. What is the lowest price per kilowatt-hour that Valley Power could offer for off-peak power and maintain a positive contribution margin?

D. ━━━━━▶ What are some other implications in offering a discounted off-peak price to the new customer?

ADM-3 Service yield pricing and differential analysis

Atlantis Cruise Lines offers luxury, one-week cruise packages in the Greek Aegean Sea. The ship has a capacity for 1,200 people. Atlantis averages 1,000 passengers per cruise. The price per passenger is $6,000. Costs associated with a cruise are as follows:

Variable costs per cruise:	
Crew to serve passengers	$1,200,000
Food	1,500,000
Amenity and excursion	400,000
Total variable cost per cruise	$3,100,000
Fixed costs per cruise:	
Crew to run ship	$1,500,000
Depreciation expense	120,000
Fuel	50,000
Total fixed cost per cruise	$1,670,000

Atlantis proposes an early booking program to help increase the number of passengers per cruise. Under the proposed early booking program, the first 300 passengers to book a cruise will receive a $1,500 discount off the normal price for the cruise. Atlantis expects this program to increase the number of passengers from 1,000 to 1,180 per cruise. The proposed booking program will be launched with $15,000 of advertising per cruise.

A. Determine the income from operations for a cruise.

B. Determine the variable cost per passenger for each variable cost item.

C. Determine the contribution margin per passenger.

D. Prepare a differential analysis showing the differential income per cruise between the existing plan (Alternative 1) and the proposed early booking program (Alternative 2). Is the new booking program financially acceptable?

Take It Further

ETHICS

TIF 24-1 Ethics in Action

Aaron McKinney is a cost accountant for Majik Systems Inc. Martin Dodd, Vice President of Marketing, has asked Aaron to meet with representatives of Majik Systems' major competitor to discuss product cost data. Martin indicates that the sharing of these data will enable Majik Systems to determine a fair and equitable price for its products.

━━━━▶ Would it be ethical for Aaron to attend the meeting and share the relevant cost data? Explain your answer.

REAL WORLD

TIF 24-2 Team Activity

Product pricing and product costs vary significantly depending on company and industry. Three such companies, their industries, and an associated product are:

Company	Industry	Product
Delta Air Lines	Air travel	Airline tickets
Amazon	Internet retailing	Various consumer products
Dell Inc.	Computer manufacturer	Computers

In teams of three, assign each person in your group to one of the companies listed above. Go to the company's Web site and determine the following:

1. A product (or service) description
2. Based on your responses to part (1) along with the description of the company's business, identify the potential costs that are required to sell the product selected in part (1), and categorize them as fixed or variable.

TIF 24-3 Communication

The following conversation took place between Juanita Jackson, Vice President of Marketing, and Les Miles, Controller of Diamond Computer Company:

Juanita: I am really excited about our new computer coming out. I think it will be a real market success.

Les: I'm really glad you think so. I know that our success will be determined by our price. If our price is too high, our competitors will be the ones with the market success.

Juanita: Don't worry about it. We'll just mark our product cost up by 25%, and it will all work out. I know we'll make money at those markups. By the way, what does the estimated product cost look like?

Les: Well, there's the rub. The product cost looks as if it's going to come in at around $1,200. With a 25% markup, that will give us a selling price of $1,500.

Juanita: I see your concern. That's a little high. Our research indicates that computer prices are dropping and that this type of computer should be selling for around $1,250 when we release it to the market.

Les: I'm not sure what to do.

Juanita: Let me see if I can help. How much of the $1,200 is fixed cost?

Les: About $200.

Juanita: There you go. The fixed cost is sunk. We don't need to consider it in our pricing decision. If we reduce the product cost by $200, the new price with a 25% markup would be right at $1,250. Boy, I was really worried for a minute there. I knew something wasn't right.

━━━━▶ Write a brief memo from Les Miles to Juanita Jackson (1) responding to her solution to the pricing problem, and (2) explaining how target costing could be used to solve the problem.

Concepts and Principles

Chapter 15 *Introduction to Managerial Accounting*

Developing Information

COST SYSTEMS	COST BEHAVIOR
Chapter 16 *Job Order Costing* **Chapter 17** *Process Cost Systems* **Chapter 18** *Activity-Based Costing*	**Chapter 19** *Cost-Volume-Profit Analysis*

Decision Making

EVALUATING PERFORMANCE	COMPARING ALTERNATIVES
Chapter 20 *Variable Costing for Management Analysis* **Chapter 21** *Budgeting* **Chapter 22** *Evaluating Variances from Standard Costs*	**Chapter 23** *Evaluating Decentralized Operations* **Chapter 24** *Differential Analysis and Product Pricing* **Chapter 25** *Capital Investment Analysis* **Chapter 26** *Lean Manufacturing*

Vail Resorts, Inc.

Why are you paying tuition, studying this text, and spending time and money on a higher education? Most people believe that the money and time spent now will return them more earnings in the future. That is, the cost of higher education is an investment in your future earning ability. How would you know if this investment is worth it?

One method would be for you to compare the cost of a higher education against the estimated increase in your future earning power. The bigger the difference between your expected future earnings and the cost of your education, the better the investment. A business also evaluates its investments in fixed assets by comparing the initial cost of the investment to its future earnings and cash flows.

For example, **Vail Resorts, Inc.**, is one of the largest ski resort owner-operators in the world. It is known for its Vail,

Breckenridge, and Keystone ski resorts, among others. A ski resort requires significant investments in property and equipment. Thus, Vail Resorts routinely makes major investments in new or improved amenities, lodging, retail, lifts, snowmaking and grooming equipment, and technology infrastructure. These investments are evaluated by their ability to enhance cash flows.

In this chapter, the methods used to make investment decisions, which may involve thousands, millions, or even billions of dollars, are described and illustrated. The similarities and differences among the most commonly used methods of evaluating investment proposals, as well as the benefits of each method, are emphasized. Factors that can complicate the analysis are also discussed.

What's Covered

Capital Investment Analysis

Capital Investments	**Methods Not Using Present Values**	**Methods Using Present Values**	**Additional Considerations**
■ Nature (Obj. 1)	■ Average Rate of Return Method (Obj. 2)	■ Present Value Concepts (Obj. 3)	■ Complicating Factors (Obj. 4)
■ Importance (Obj. 1)	■ Cash Payback Method (Obj. 2)	■ Net Present Value Method (Obj. 3)	■ Capital Rationing (Obj. 5)
■ Evaluation Methods (Obj. 1)		■ Internal Rate of Return Method (Obj. 3)	

Learning Objectives

Obj. 1 Describe the nature and importance of capital investment analysis.

Obj. 2 Evaluate capital investment proposals, using the average rate of return and cash payback methods.

Obj. 3 Evaluate capital investment proposals, using the net present value and internal rate of return methods.

Obj. 4 Describe factors that complicate capital investment analysis.

Obj. 5 Describe and diagram the capital rationing process.

Analysis for Decision Making

Describe and illustrate the use of capital investment analysis in evaluating a sustainability investment.

Objective 1

Describe the nature and importance of capital investment analysis.

Nature of Capital Investment Analysis

Companies use capital investment analysis to evaluate long-term investments. **Capital investment analysis** (or *capital budgeting*) is the process by which management plans, evaluates, and controls investments in fixed assets. Capital investments use funds and affect operations for many years and must earn a reasonable rate of return. Thus, capital investment decisions are some of the most important decisions that management makes.

Capital investment evaluation methods can be grouped into the following categories:

Methods That Do Not Use Present Values

■ Average rate of return method
■ Cash payback method

Methods That Use Present Values

■ Net present value method
■ Internal rate of return method

The two methods that use present values consider the time value of money. The **time value of money concept** recognizes that a dollar today is worth more than a dollar tomorrow because today's dollar can earn interest.

Link to Vail Resorts

In 2014, **Vail Resorts, Inc.**, purchased the Park City Mountain Resort and ski area in Park City, Utah, for $182.5 million.

Why It Matters

Business Use of Investment Analysis Methods

A survey of chief financial officers of large U.S. companies reported their use of the four investment methods as follows:

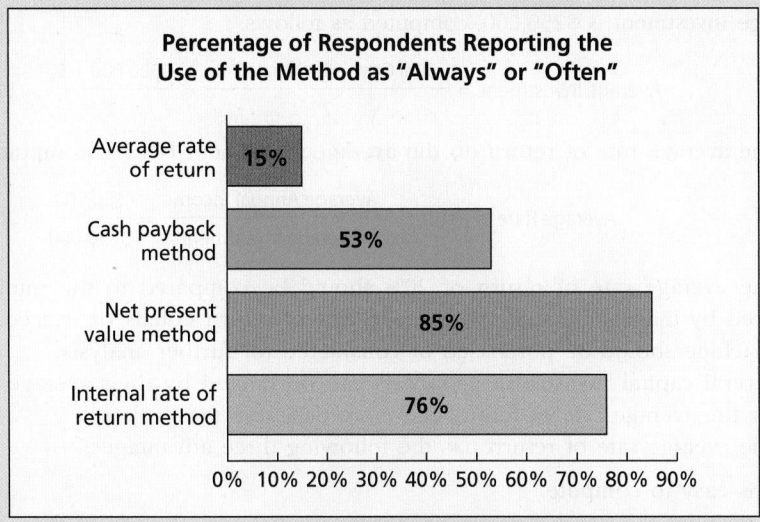

Source: Patricia A. Ryan and Glenn P. Ryan, "Capital Budgeting Practice of the Fortune 1000: How Have Things Changed?" *Journal of Business and Management* (Winter 2002).

Methods Not Using Present Values

Objective 2
Evaluate capital investment proposals, using the average rate of return and cash payback methods.

The methods not using present values are often useful in evaluating capital investment proposals that have relatively short useful lives. In such cases, the timing of the cash flows (the time value of money) is less important.

Because the methods not using present values are easy to use, they are often used to screen proposals. Minimum standards for accepting proposals are set, and proposals not meeting these standards are dropped. If a proposal meets the minimum standards, it may be subject to further analysis using the present value methods.

Average Rate of Return Method

The **average rate of return**, sometimes called the *accounting rate of return*, measures the average income as a percent of the average investment. The average rate of return is computed as follows:

$$\text{Average Rate of Return} = \frac{\text{Average Annual Income}}{\text{Average Investment}}$$

In the preceding equation, the numerator is the average of the annual income expected to be earned from the investment over its life, after deducting depreciation. The denominator is the average investment (book value) over the life of the investment. Assuming straight-line depreciation, the average investment is computed as follows:

$$\text{Average Investment} = \frac{\text{Initial Cost} + \text{Residual Value}}{2}$$

To illustrate, assume that management is evaluating the purchase of a new machine as follows:

Cost of new machine	$500,000
Residual value	0
Expected total income from machine	200,000
Expected useful life	4 years

The average annual income expected from the machine is $50,000 ($200,000 ÷ 4 years). The average investment is $250,000, computed as follows:

$$\text{Average Investment} = \frac{\text{Initial Cost} + \text{Residual Value}}{2} = \frac{\$500,000 + \$0}{2} = \$250,000$$

The average rate of return on the average investment is 20%, computed as follows:

$$\text{Average Rate of Return} = \frac{\text{Average Annual Income}}{\text{Average Investment}} = \frac{\$50,000}{\$250,000} = 20\%$$

The average rate of return of 20% should be compared to the minimum rate of return required by management. If the average rate of return equals or exceeds the minimum rate, the machine should be purchased or considered for further analysis.

Several capital investment proposals can be ranked by their average rates of return. The higher the average rate of return, the more desirable the proposal.

The average rate of return has the following three advantages:

- It is easy to compute.
- It includes the entire amount of income earned over the life of the proposal.
- It emphasizes accounting income, which is often used by investors and creditors in evaluating management performance.

The average rate of return has the following two disadvantages:

- It does not directly consider the expected cash flows from the proposal.
- It does not directly consider the timing of the expected cash flows.

Link to Vail Resorts

Vail Resorts' average rate of return on its property, plant, and equipment is slightly more than 10%.

Cash Payback Method

A capital investment uses cash and must return cash in the future to be successful. The expected period of time between the date of an investment and the recovery in cash of the amount invested is the **cash payback period**.

When annual net cash inflows are equal, the cash payback period is computed as follows:

$$\text{Cash Payback Period} = \frac{\text{Initial Cost}}{\text{Annual Net Cash Inflow}}$$

To illustrate, assume that management is evaluating the purchase of the following new machine:

Cost of new machine	$200,000
Cash revenues from machine per year	50,000
Expenses of machine per year,	
including depreciation	30,000
Depreciation per year	20,000

To simplify, the revenues and expenses other than depreciation are assumed to be in cash. Hence, the net cash inflow per year from use of the machine is as follows:

Net cash flow per year:	
Cash revenues from machine	$ 50,000
Cash expenses of machine	(10,000)*
Net cash inflow per year	$ 40,000
*Expenses of machine, including depreciation	$ 30,000
Depreciation expense	(20,000)
Cash expenses of machine	$ 10,000

The time required for the net cash flow to equal the cost of the new machine is the payback period. Thus, the cash payback period for the investment is five years, computed as follows:

$$\text{Cash Payback Period} = \frac{\text{Initial Cost}}{\text{Annual Net Cash Inflow}} = \frac{\$200,000}{\$40,000} = 5 \text{ years}$$

In the preceding illustration, the annual net cash inflows are equal ($40,000 per year). When the annual net cash inflows are not equal, the cash payback period is determined by adding the annual net cash inflows until the cumulative total equals the initial cost of the proposed investment.

To illustrate, assume that a proposed investment has an initial cost of $400,000. The annual and cumulative net cash inflows over the proposal's six-year life are as follows:

Year	Net Cash Flow	Cumulative Net Cash Flow
1	$ 60,000	$ 60,000
2	80,000	140,000
3	105,000	245,000
4	155,000	400,000
5	100,000	500,000
6	90,000	590,000

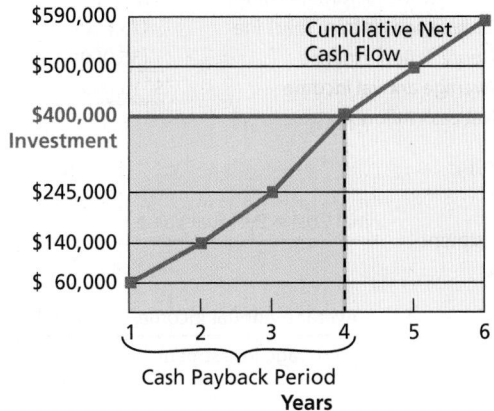

The cumulative net cash flow at the end of Year 4 equals the initial cost of the investment, $400,000. Thus, the payback period is four years.

If the initial cost of the proposed investment had been $450,000, the cash payback period would occur during Year 5. Because $100,000 of net cash flow is expected during Year 5, the additional $50,000 to increase the cumulative total to $450,000 occurs halfway through the year ($50,000 ÷ $100,000). Thus, the cash payback period would be 4½ years.[1]

A short cash payback period is desirable. This is because the sooner cash is recovered, the sooner it can be reinvested in other projects. In addition, there is less chance of losses from changing economic or business conditions. A short cash payback period is also desirable for quickly repaying any debt used to purchase the investment.

The cash payback method has the following two advantages:

- It is simple to use and understand.
- It analyzes cash flows.

The cash payback method has the following two disadvantages:

- It ignores cash flows occurring after the payback period.
- It does not use present value concepts in valuing cash flows occurring in different periods.

[1] Unless otherwise stated, net cash inflows are received uniformly throughout the year.

Link to
Vail Resorts

The ski operations are seasonal in nature and typically run from mid-November to mid-April. To increase cash flows, **Vail Resorts** promotes nonski activities in the summer months, including sightseeing, mountain biking, and zip tours.

Check Up Corner 25-1   Capital Investment Analysis Not Using Present Value

Tyme Manufacturing Inc. is evaluating a capital investment proposal for a new machine. The new machine has a cost of $230,000, an expected useful life of six years, and a residual value of $20,000. Information on expected annual revenues and expenses associated with the machine is as follows:

Revenue from machine	$125,000
Expenses of machine, other than depreciation	75,000
Depreciation expense	35,000

All revenues and expenses are in cash, except for depreciation expense. Determine the following:

A.   The average rate of return, and

B.   The cash payback period.

Solution:

	Average Annual	
	Income	**Cash Flow**
Cash revenues from machine	$125,000	$125,000
Cash expenses from machine	(75,000)	(75,000)
Depreciation expense	(35,000)	- - - - - - - -
Average annual income	$ 15,000	
Net cash inflow per year		$ 50,000

Depreciation is not included in determining cash flow because it is a noncash expense.

A.   Average Rate of Return:

$$\text{Average Investment} = \frac{\text{Initial Cost} + \text{Residual Value}}{2} = \frac{\$230,000 + \$20,000}{2} = \$125,000$$

$$\text{Average Rate of Return} = \frac{\text{Average Annual Income}}{\text{Average Investment}} = \frac{\$15,000}{\$125,000} = 12\%$$

B.   Cash Payback Period:

$$\text{Cash Payback Period} = \frac{\text{Initial Cost}}{\text{Annual Net Cash Inflow}} = \frac{\$230,000}{\$50,000} = 4.6 \text{ years}$$

Check Up Corner

Objective 3

Evaluate capital investment proposals, using the net present value and internal rate of return methods.

Methods Using Present Values

An investment in fixed assets may be viewed as purchasing a series of net cash flows over a period of time. The timing of when the net cash flows will be received is important in determining the value of a proposed investment.

Present value methods use the amount and timing of the net cash flows in evaluating an investment. The two methods of evaluating capital investments using present values are as follows:

■   Net present value method
■   Internal rate of return method

Present Value Concepts

Both the net present value and the internal rate of return methods use the following two **present value concepts**:

- Present value of an amount
- Present value of an annuity

Present Value of an Amount If you were given the choice, would you prefer to receive $1 now or $1 three years from now? You should prefer to receive $1 now, because you could invest the $1 and earn interest for three years. As a result, the amount you would have after three years would be greater than $1.

To illustrate, assume that you have $1 to invest as follows:

Amount to be invested	$1
Period to be invested	3 years
Interest rate	12%

After one year, the $1 earns interest of $0.12 ($1 × 12%) and, thus, will grow to $1.12 ($1 × 1.12). In the second year, the $1.12 earns 12% interest of $0.134 ($1.12 × 12%) and, thus, will grow to $1.254 ($1.12 × 1.12) by the end of the second year. This process of interest earning interest is called *compounding*. By the end of the third year, your $1 investment will grow to $1.404 as shown in Exhibit 1.

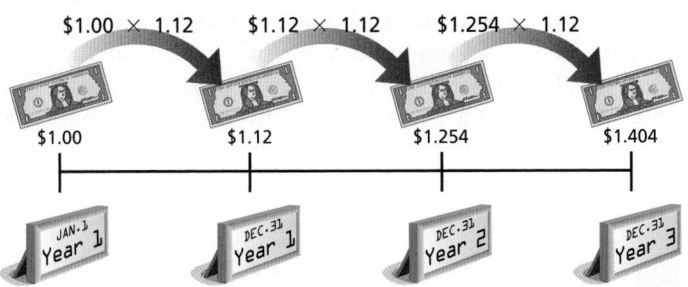

Exhibit 1

Compound Amount of $1 for Three Periods at 12%

On January 1, Year 1, what is the present value of $1.404 to be received on December 31, Year 3? This is a present value question. The answer can be determined with the aid of a present value of $1 table. For example, the partial table in Exhibit 2 indicates that the present value of $1 to be received in three years with earnings compounded at the rate of 12% per year is 0.712.[2]

Exhibit 2

Partial Present Value of $1 Table

Present Value of $1 at Compound Interest					
Year	**6%**	**10%**	**12%**	**15%**	**20%**
1	0.943	0.909	0.893	0.870	0.833
2	0.890	0.826	0.797	0.756	0.694
3	0.840	0.751	0.712	0.658	0.579
4	0.792	0.683	0.636	0.572	0.482
5	0.747	0.621	0.567	0.497	0.402
6	0.705	0.564	0.507	0.432	0.335
7	0.665	0.513	0.452	0.376	0.279
8	0.627	0.467	0.404	0.327	0.233
9	0.592	0.424	0.361	0.284	0.194
10	0.558	0.386	0.322	0.247	0.162

[2] The present value factors in the table are rounded to three decimal places. More complete tables of present values are in Appendix A.

Multiplying 0.712 by $1.404 yields $1 as follows:

	Present Value	Amount to Be Received in 3 Years		Present Value Factor for $1 to Be Received in 3 Years (from Exhibit 2)
	$1 =	$1.404	×	0.712

That is, the present value of $1.404 to be received in three years using a compound interest rate of 12% is $1, as shown in Exhibit 3.

Exhibit 3

Present Value of an Amount of $1.404

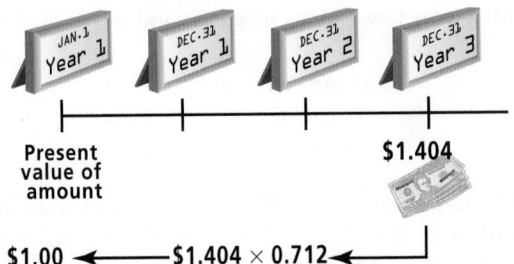

Present Value of an Annuity An **annuity** is a series of equal net cash flows at fixed time intervals. Annuities are very common in business. Cash payments for monthly rent, salaries, and bond interest are all examples of annuities. The **present value of an annuity** is the amount of cash needed today to yield a series of equal net cash flows at fixed time intervals in the future.

To illustrate, the present value of a $100 annuity for five periods at 12% could be determined by using the present value factors in Exhibit 2. Each $100 net cash flow could be multiplied by the present value of $1 at a 12% factor for the appropriate period and summed to determine a present value of $360.50, as shown in Exhibit 4.

Exhibit 4

Present Value of a $100 Amount for Five Consecutive Periods

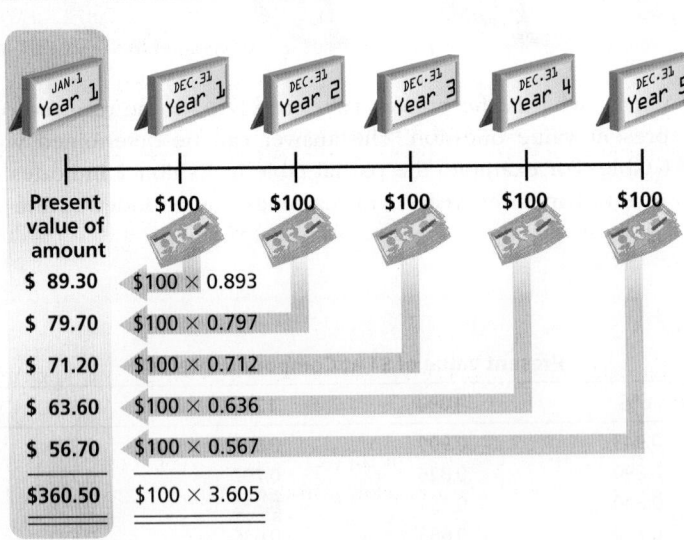

Using a present value of an annuity table is a simpler approach. Exhibit 5 is a partial table of present value annuity factors.[3]

---

[3] The present value factors in the table are rounded to three decimal places. More complete tables of present values are in Appendix A.

Exhibit 5
Partial Present
Value of an
Annuity Table

Present Value of an Annuity of $1 at Compound Interest

Year	6%	10%	12%	15%	20%
1	0.943	0.909	0.893	0.870	0.833
2	1.833	1.736	1.690	1.626	1.528
3	2.673	2.487	2.402	2.283	2.106
4	3.465	3.170	3.037	2.855	2.589
5	4.212	3.791	3.605	3.353	2.991
6	4.917	4.355	4.111	3.785	3.326
7	5.582	4.868	4.564	4.160	3.605
8	6.210	5.335	4.968	4.487	3.837
9	6.802	5.759	5.328	4.772	4.031
10	7.360	6.145	5.650	5.019	4.192

The present value factors in the table shown in Exhibit 5 are the sum of the present value of $1 factors in Exhibit 2 for the number of annuity periods. Thus, 3.605 in the annuity table (Exhibit 5) is the sum of the five present value of $1 factors at 12% from Exhibit 2, computed as follows:

	Present Value Factor for $1 (Exhibit 2)
Present value factor for $1 for 1 year @12%	0.893
Present value factor for $1 for 2 years @12%	0.797
Present value factor for $1 for 3 years @12%	0.712
Present value factor for $1 for 4 years @12%	0.636
Present value factor for $1 for 5 years @12%	0.567
Present value factor for an annuity of $1 for 5 years (from Exhibit 5)	3.605

Multiplying $100 by 3.605 yields $360.50 as follows:

Present Value		Amount to Be Received Annually for 5 Years		Present Value Factor for an Annuity of $1 to Be Received for 5 Years (Exhibit 5)
$360.50	=	$100	×	3.605

Thus, $360.50 is the same amount that was determined in the preceding illustration by five successive multiplications.

Net Present Value Method and Index

The net present value method and present value index are often used in combination, as we illustrate in this section.

Net Present Value Method The **net present value method** compares the amount to be invested with the present value of the net cash inflows. It is sometimes called the *discounted cash flow method*.

The interest rate (return) used in net present value analysis is the company's minimum desired rate of return. This rate, sometimes termed the *hurdle rate*, is based on such factors as the purpose of the investment and the cost of obtaining funds for the investment. If the present value of the cash inflows equals or exceeds the amount to be invested, the proposal is desirable.

note:

The net present value method compares an investment's initial cash outflow with the present value of its cash inflows.

To illustrate, assume the following data for a proposed investment in new equipment:

Cost of new equipment	$200,000
Expected useful life	5 years
Minimum desired rate of return	10%
Expected cash flows to be received each year:	
Year 1	$ 70,000
Year 2	60,000
Year 3	50,000
Year 4	40,000
Year 5	40,000
Total expected cash flows	$260,000

The present value of the net cash flow for each year is computed by multiplying the net cash flow for the year by the present value factor of $1 for that year, as follows:

Year	Present Value of $1 at 10%	×	Net Cash Flow	=	Present Value of Net Cash Flow
1	0.909		$ 70,000		$ 63,630
2	0.826		60,000		49,560
3	0.751		50,000		37,550
4	0.683		40,000		27,320
5	0.621		40,000		24,840
Total			$260,000		$ 202,900
Amount to be invested					(200,000)
Net present value					$ 2,900

The preceding computations are also graphically illustrated in Exhibit 6.

Exhibit 6

Present Value of Equipment Cash Flows

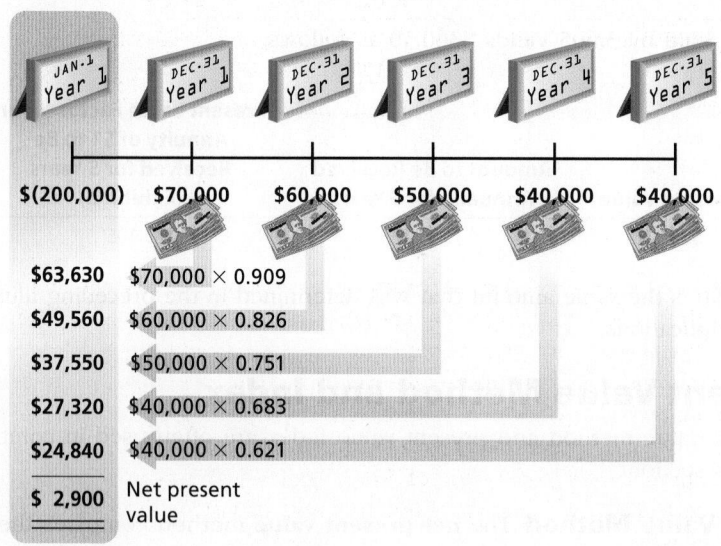

The net present value of $2,900 indicates that the purchase of the new equipment is expected to recover the investment and provide more than the minimum rate of return of 10%. Thus, the purchase of the new equipment is desirable.

The net present value method has the following three advantages:

- It considers the cash flows of the investment.
- It considers the time value of money.
- It can rank projects with equal lives, using the present value index.

The net present value method has the following two disadvantages:

■ It has more complex computations than methods that don't use present value.
■ It assumes the cash flows can be reinvested at the minimum desired rate of return, which may not be valid.

Vail Resorts uses present values in determining the value of assets and liabilities acquired in business acquisitions.

Source: Vail Resorts, Inc., *Form 10-K for the Fiscal Year Ended July 31, 2015.*

Link to Vail Resorts

Present Value Index When capital investment funds are limited and the proposals involve different investments, a ranking of the proposals can be prepared by using a present value index. The **present value index** is computed as follows:

$$\text{Present Value Index} = \frac{\text{Total Present Value of Net Cash Flow}}{\text{Amount to Be Invested}}$$

The present value index for the investment in the preceding illustration is 1.0145, computed as follows:

$$\text{Present Value Index} = \frac{\$202,900}{\$200,000} = 1.0145$$

Assume that a company is considering three proposals. The net present value and the present value index for each proposal are as follows:

	Proposal A	Proposal B	Proposal C
Total present value of net cash flow	$ 107,000	$ 86,400	$ 86,400
Amount to be invested	(100,000)	(80,000)	(90,000)
Net present value	$ 7,000	$ 6,400	$ (3,600)
Present value index:			
Proposal A ($107,000 ÷ $100,000)	1.07		
Proposal B ($86,400 ÷ $80,000)		1.08	
Proposal C ($86,400 ÷ $90,000)			0.96

A project will have a present value index greater than 1 when the net present value is positive. This is the case for Proposals A and B. When the net present value is negative, the present value index will be less than 1, as is the case for Proposal C.

Although Proposal A has the largest net present value, the present value indices indicate that it is not as desirable as Proposal B. That is, Proposal B returns $1.08 present value per dollar invested, whereas Proposal A returns only $1.07. Proposal B requires an investment of $80,000, compared to an investment of $100,000 for Proposal A. The possible use of the $20,000 difference between Proposals A and B investments should also be considered before making a final decision.

Internal Rate of Return Method

The **internal rate of return (IRR) method** uses present value concepts to compute the rate of return from a capital investment proposal based on its expected net cash flows. This method, sometimes called the *time-adjusted rate of return method*, starts with the proposal's net cash flows and works backward to estimate the proposal's expected rate of return.

To illustrate, assume that management is evaluating the following proposal to purchase new equipment:

Cost of new equipment	$33,530
Yearly expected cash flows to be received	$10,000
Expected life	5 years
Minimum desired rate of return	12%

The present value of the net cash flows, using the present value of an annuity table in Exhibit 5, is $2,520, as shown in Exhibit 7.

Exhibit 7

Net Present Value Analysis at 12%

Annual net cash flow (at the end of each of five years)	$10,000
Present value factor for an annuity of $1 at 12% for five years (Exhibit 5)	× 3.605
Present value of annual net cash flows	$36,050
Amount to be invested	(33,530)
Net present value	$ 2,520

In Exhibit 7, the $36,050 present value of the cash inflows, based on a 12% rate of return, is greater than the $33,530 to be invested. Thus, the internal rate of return must be greater than 12%. Through trial and error, the rate of return equating the $33,530 cost of the investment with the present value of the net cash flows can be determined to be 15%, as shown in Exhibit 8.

Exhibit 8

Present Value of an Annuity at the Internal Rate of Return Rate

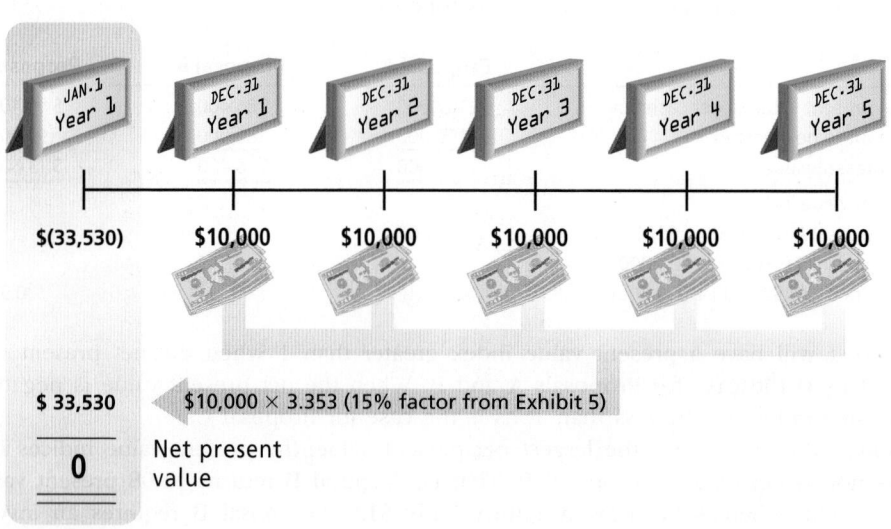

When equal annual net cash flows are expected from a proposal, as in the preceding example, the internal rate of return can be determined as follows:[4]

- Step 1. Determine a present value factor for an annuity of $1 as follows:

$$\text{Present Value Factor for an Annuity of \$1} = \frac{\text{Amount to Be Invested}}{\text{Equal Annual Net Cash Flows}}$$

[4] To simplify, equal annual net cash flows are assumed. If the net cash flows are not equal, spreadsheet software can be used to determine the rate of return.

- Step 2. Locate the present value factor determined in Step 1 in the present value of an annuity of $1 table (Exhibit 5) as follows:
  - A. Locate the number of years of expected useful life of the investment in the Year column.
  - B. Proceed horizontally across the table until you find the present value factor computed in Step 1.
- Step 3. Identify the internal rate of return by the heading of the column in which the present value factor in Step 2 is located.

To illustrate, assume that management is evaluating the following proposal to purchase new equipment:

Cost of new equipment	$97,360
Yearly expected cash flows to be received	$20,000
Expected useful life	7 years

The present value factor for an annuity of $1 is 4.868, computed as follows:

$$\text{Present Value Factor for an Annuity of } \$1 = \frac{\text{Amount to Be Invested}}{\text{Equal Annual Net Cash Flows}}$$

$$= \frac{\$97,360}{\$20,000} = 4.868$$

Using the partial present value of an annuity of $1 table shown in Exhibit 9 and a period of seven years, the factor 4.868 is related to 10%. Thus, the internal rate of return for this proposal is 10%.

Present Value of an Annuity of $1 at Compound Interest

Year	6%	Step 3 10%	12%
1	0.943	0.909	0.893
2	1.833	1.736	1.690
3	2.673	2.487	2.402
4	3.465	3.170	3.037
5	4.212	3.791	3.605
6	4.917	**Step 2(b)** 4.355	4.111
Step 2(a) 7	5.582	→ 4.868	4.564
8	6.210	5.335	4.968
9	6.802	5.759	5.328
10	7.360	6.145	5.650

Step 1: Determine present value factor for an annuity of $1 $= \dfrac{\$97,360}{\$20,000} = 4.868$

Exhibit 9

Partial Present Value of an Annuity Table

If the minimum acceptable rate of return is 10%, then the proposal is considered acceptable. Several proposals can be ranked by their internal rates of return. The proposal with the highest rate is the most desirable.

The internal rate of return method has the following three advantages:

- It considers the cash flows of the investment.
- It considers the time value of money.
- It ranks proposals based upon the cash flows over their complete useful life, even if the project lives are not the same.

The internal rate of return method has the following two disadvantages:

- It has complex computations, requiring a computer if the periodic cash flows are not equal.
- It assumes the cash received from a proposal can be reinvested at the internal rate of return, which may not be valid.

Check Up Corner 25-2   **Net Present Value and Internal Rate of Return Analyses**

The management of Broncial Industries Inc. is considering a capital investment project. The net cash flows expected from the project are $50,000 a year for seven years. The project requires an investment of $243,400, and no residual value is expected.

Determine:

A. The net present value for the project, using a minimum rate of return of 6% and the present value of an annuity table appearing in this chapter (Exhibit 5).

B. The present value index. (Round to two decimal places.)

C. The internal rate of return for the project by (1) computing a present value factor for an annuity of $1 and (2) using the present value of an annuity table appearing in this chapter (Exhibit 5).

Solution:

A. & B.

	Net Present Value	**Present Value Index**
Annual net cash flows	$ 50,000	$ 50,000
Present value factor for an annuity of $1 at 6% for 7 periods	× 5.582	× 5.582
Total present value of net cash flows	$ 279,100	$279,100
Amount to be invested	(243,400)	÷243,400
A. Net present value	$ 35,700	
B. Present value index		1.15 (rounded)

The project has a positive net present value, which is also indicated by the present value index, which is greater than 1.00.

C.

$$\text{Present Value Factor for an Annuity of \$1} = \frac{\text{Amount to Be Invested}}{\text{Equal Annual Net Cash Flows}}$$

$$= \frac{\$243,400}{\$50,000} = 4.868$$

Internal rate of return = 10%

The internal rate of return is the rate of return that equates the present value of equal annual net cash flows to the amount to be invested.

Present Value of an Annuity of $1 at Compound Interest					
Year	**6%**	**10%**	**12%**	**15%**	**20%**
1	0.943	0.909	0.893	0.870	0.833
2	1.833	1.736	1.690	1.626	1.528
3	2.673	2.487	2.402	2.283	2.106
4	3.465	3.170	3.037	2.855	2.589
5	4.212	3.791	3.605	3.353	2.991
6	4.917	4.355	4.111	3.785	3.326
7	5.582	4.868	4.564	4.160	3.605
8	6.210	5.335	4.968	4.487	3.837
9	6.802	5.759	5.328	4.772	4.031
10	7.360	6.145	5.650	5.019	4.192

Check Up Corner

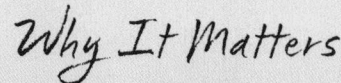

Panera Bread Store Rate of Return

Panera Bread owns, operates, and franchises bakery-cafes throughout the United States. A recent annual report to the Securities and Exchange Commission (SEC Form 10-K) allowed the following information to be determined about an average company-owned store:

Operating profit	$ 405,000
Depreciation	115,000
Investment book value	1,500,000

Assume that the operating profit and depreciation will remain unchanged for the next 15 years. Assume operating profit plus depreciation approximates annual net cash flows and that the investment residual value will be zero. The average rate of return on a company-owned store is:

$$\frac{\$405,000}{\$1,500,000 \div 2} = 54\%$$

The internal rate of return is calculated by first determining the present value of an annuity of $1:

$$\begin{array}{c} \text{Present Value} \\ \text{of an Annuity of \$1} \end{array} = \frac{\$1,500,000}{\$405,000 + \$115,000} = 2.88$$

For a period of five years, this factor implies an internal rate of return of more than 20% (from Exhibit 5). However, if we more realistically assumed these cash flows for 15 years, Panera's company-owned stores generate an estimated internal rate of return of approximately 34% (from a spreadsheet calculation). Clearly, both investment evaluation methods indicate a highly successful business.

Source: Panera Bread, *Form 10-K for the Fiscal Year Ended December 25, 2015.*

Factors That Complicate Capital Investment Analysis

Objective 4
Describe factors that complicate capital investment analysis.

Four widely used methods of evaluating capital investment proposals have been described and illustrated in this chapter. In practice, additional factors such as the following may impact capital investment decisions:

- Income tax
- Proposals with unequal lives
- Leasing versus purchasing
- Uncertainty
- Changes in price levels
- Qualitative factors

Income Tax

The impact of income taxes on capital investment decisions can be material. For example, in determining depreciation for federal income tax purposes, useful lives that are much shorter than the actual useful lives are often used. Also, depreciation for tax purposes often differs from depreciation for financial statement purposes. As a result, the timing of the cash flows for income taxes can have a significant impact on capital investment analysis.[5]

Unequal Proposal Lives

The prior capital investment illustrations assumed that the alternative proposals had the same useful lives. In practice, however, proposals often have different lives.

To illustrate, assume that a company is considering purchasing a new truck or a new computer network. The data for each proposal follow:

	Truck	Computer Network
Cost	$100,000	$100,000
Minimum desired rate of return	10%	10%
Expected useful life	8 years	5 years

---

[5] The impact of taxes on capital investment analysis is covered in advanced accounting textbooks.

Yearly expected cash flows to be received:

Year 1	$ 30,000	$ 30,000
Year 2	30,000	30,000
Year 3	25,000	30,000
Year 4	20,000	30,000
Year 5	15,000	35,000
Year 6	15,000	0
Year 7	10,000	0
Year 8	10,000	0
Total	$155,000	$155,000

The expected cash flows and net present value for each proposal are shown in Exhibit 10. Because of the unequal useful lives, however, the net present values in Exhibit 10 are not comparable.

To make the proposals comparable, the useful lives are adjusted to end at the same time. In this illustration, this is done by assuming that the truck will be sold at the end of five years. The selling price (residual value) of the truck at the end of five years is estimated and included in the cash inflows. Both proposals will then cover five years; thus, the net present value analyses will be comparable.

Exhibit 10   Net Present Value Analysis—Unequal Lives of Proposals

	A	B	C	D
1		Truck		
2		Present	Net	Present
3		Value of	Cash	Value of
4	Year	$1 at 10%	Flow	Net Cash Flow
5	1	0.909	$ 30,000	$ 27,270
6	2	0.826	30,000	24,780
7	3	0.751	25,000	18,775
8	4	0.683	20,000	13,660
9	5	0.621	15,000	9,315
10	6	0.564	15,000	8,460
11	7	0.513	10,000	5,130
12	8	0.467	10,000	4,670
13	Total		$155,000	$112,060
14				
15	Amount to be invested			(100,000)
16	Net present value			$ 12,060
17				

	A	B	C	D
1		Computer Network		
2		Present	Net	Present
3		Value of	Cash	Value of
4	Year	$1 at 10%	Flow	Net Cash Flow
5	1	0.909	$ 30,000	$ 27,270
6	2	0.826	30,000	24,780
7	3	0.751	30,000	22,530
8	4	0.683	30,000	20,490
9	5	0.621	35,000	21,735
10	Total		$155,000	$116,805
11				
12	Amount to be invested			(100,000)
13	Net present value			$ 16,805
14				

Cannot be compared (unequal lives)

Exhibit 11

Net Present Value Analysis— Equalized Lives of Proposals

	A	B	C	D
1		Truck—Revised to 5-Year Life		
2		Present	Net	Present
3		Value of	Cash	Value of
4	Year	$1 at 10%	Flow	Net Cash Flow
5	1	0.909	$ 30,000	$ 27,270
6	2	0.826	30,000	24,780
7	3	0.751	25,000	18,775
8	4	0.683	20,000	13,660
9	5	0.621	15,000	9,315
10	5 (Residual value)	0.621	40,000	24,840
11	Total		$160,000	$118,640
12				
13	Amount to be invested			(100,000)
14	Net present value			$ 18,640
15				

Truck Net Present Value Greater than Computer Network Net Present Value by $1,835

Compared (equal lives)

To illustrate, assume that the truck's estimated selling price (residual value) at the end of Year 5 is $40,000. Exhibit 11 shows the truck's revised present value analysis assuming a five-year life.

As shown in Exhibit 11, the net present value for the truck exceeds the net present value for the computer network by $1,835 ($18,640 – $16,805). Thus, the truck is the more attractive of the two proposals.

Check Up Corner 25-3 | Net Present Value—Unequal Lives

Acme Company is evaluating two projects with unequal lives. Project 1 requires an original investment of $50,000. The project will yield cash flows of $12,000 per year for five years. Project 1 could be sold at the end of five years for a price of $30,000. Project 2 has a net present value of $8,900 over a five-year life.

A. Determine the net present value of Project 1 over a five-year life, with residual value, assuming a minimum rate of return of 12%.

B. Which project provides the greater net present value?

Solution:

A.

Present value of $12,000 per year at 12% for 5 years	$ 43,260 ←	[$12,000 × 3.605 (Exhibit 5, 12%, 5 years)]
Present value of $30,000 at 12% at the end of 5 years	17,010 ←	[$30,000 × 0.567 (Exhibit 2, 12%, 5 years)]
Total present value of Project 1	$ 60,270	
Total cost of Project 1	(50,000)	
Net present value of Project 1	$ 10,270	

B. **Project 1.** Project 1 has a net present value of $10,270, which is greater than the net present value of Project 2, $8,900.

Check Up Corner

Lease Versus Capital Investment

Leasing fixed assets is common in many industries. For example, hospitals often lease medical equipment. Some advantages of leasing a fixed asset include the following:

- The company has use of the fixed asset without spending large amounts of cash to purchase the asset.
- The company eliminates the risk of owning an obsolete asset.
- The company may deduct the annual lease payments for income tax purposes.

A disadvantage of leasing a fixed asset is that it is normally more costly than purchasing the asset. This is because the lessor (owner of the asset) includes in the rental price not only the costs of owning the asset, but also a profit.

The methods of evaluating capital investment proposals illustrated in this chapter can also be used to decide whether to lease or purchase a fixed asset.

Uncertainty

All capital investment analyses rely on factors that are uncertain. For example, estimates of revenues, expenses, and cash flows are uncertain. This is especially true for long-term capital investments. Errors in one or more of the estimates could lead to incorrect decisions. Methods that consider the impact of uncertainty on capital investment analysis are discussed in advanced accounting and finance textbooks.

Why It Matters

If You Build It, They Will Come

A business model describes how an organization delivers products or services to make a profit. Many service companies use what is termed a *network business model*. A network business model connects people and businesses with each other or to a centralized service. Examples of network service businesses include telecommunication, transportation, power and natural gas distribution, cable, satellite, and Internet companies. Network businesses often require significant investment in physical assets in order to create the network. Often, this is described as a *Field of Dreams strategy* (from the movie of that name) because the network can only generate revenue once it is largely built. For example, a cell phone company draws value from having many cell towers linking many callers together. A critical mass of cell towers must be pre-built in order to establish the business. This is risky. As a result, network businesses carefully evaluate capital investments prior to building networks.

Changes in Price Levels

Price levels normally change as the economy improves or deteriorates. General price levels often increase in a rapidly growing economy, which is called **inflation**. During such periods, the rate of return on an investment should exceed the rising price level. If this is not the case, the cash returned on the investment will be less than expected.

Price levels may also change for foreign investments. This occurs as currency exchange rates change. **Currency exchange rates** are the rates at which currency in another country can be exchanged for U.S. dollars.

If the amount of local dollars that can be exchanged for one U.S. dollar increases, then the local currency is said to be weakening to the dollar. When a company has an investment in another country where the local currency is weakening, the return on the investment, as expressed in U.S. dollars, is adversely impacted. This is because the expected amount of local currency returned on the investment would purchase fewer U.S. dollars.[6]

[6] Further discussion on accounting for foreign currency transactions is available on the companion Web site at www.cengagebrain.com.

Qualitative Considerations

Some benefits of capital investments are qualitative in nature and cannot be estimated in dollar terms. However, if a company does not consider qualitative considerations, an acceptable investment proposal could be rejected.

Some examples of qualitative considerations that may influence capital investment analysis include the investment proposal's impact on the following:

- Product quality
- Manufacturing flexibility
- Employee morale
- Manufacturing productivity
- Market (strategic) opportunities

Many qualitative factors may be as important as, if not more important than, quantitative factors.

The mission of **Vail Resorts** is to provide exceptional guest experiences at each of its resorts.

Source: Vail Resorts, Inc., *Form 10-K for the Fiscal Year Ended July 31, 2015.*

Link to Vail Resorts

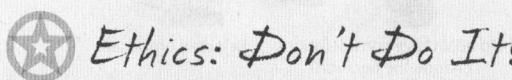 **Ethics: Don't Do It!**

Assumption Fudging

The results of any capital budgeting analysis depend on many subjective estimates, such as the cash flows, discount rate, time period, and total investment amount. The results of the analysis should be used to either support or reject a project. Capital budgeting should not be used to justify an assumed net present value. That is, the analyst should not work backwards, filling in assumed numbers that will produce the desired net present value. Such a reverse approach reduces the credibility of the entire process.

Capital Rationing

Objective 5
Describe and diagram the capital rationing process.

Capital rationing is the process by which management allocates funds among competing capital investment proposals. In this process, management often uses a combination of the methods described in this chapter.

Exhibit 12 illustrates the capital rationing decision process. Alternative proposals are initially screened by establishing minimum standards, using the cash payback and the average rate of return methods. The proposals that survive this screening are further analyzed, using the net present value and internal rate of return methods.

Qualitative factors related to each proposal should also be considered throughout the capital rationing process. For example, new equipment might improve the quality of the product and, thus, increase consumer satisfaction and sales.

At the end of the capital rationing process, accepted proposals are ranked and compared with the funds available. Proposals that are selected for funding are included in the capital expenditures budget. Unfunded proposals may be reconsidered if funds later become available.

Exhibit 12

Capital Rationing
Decision Process

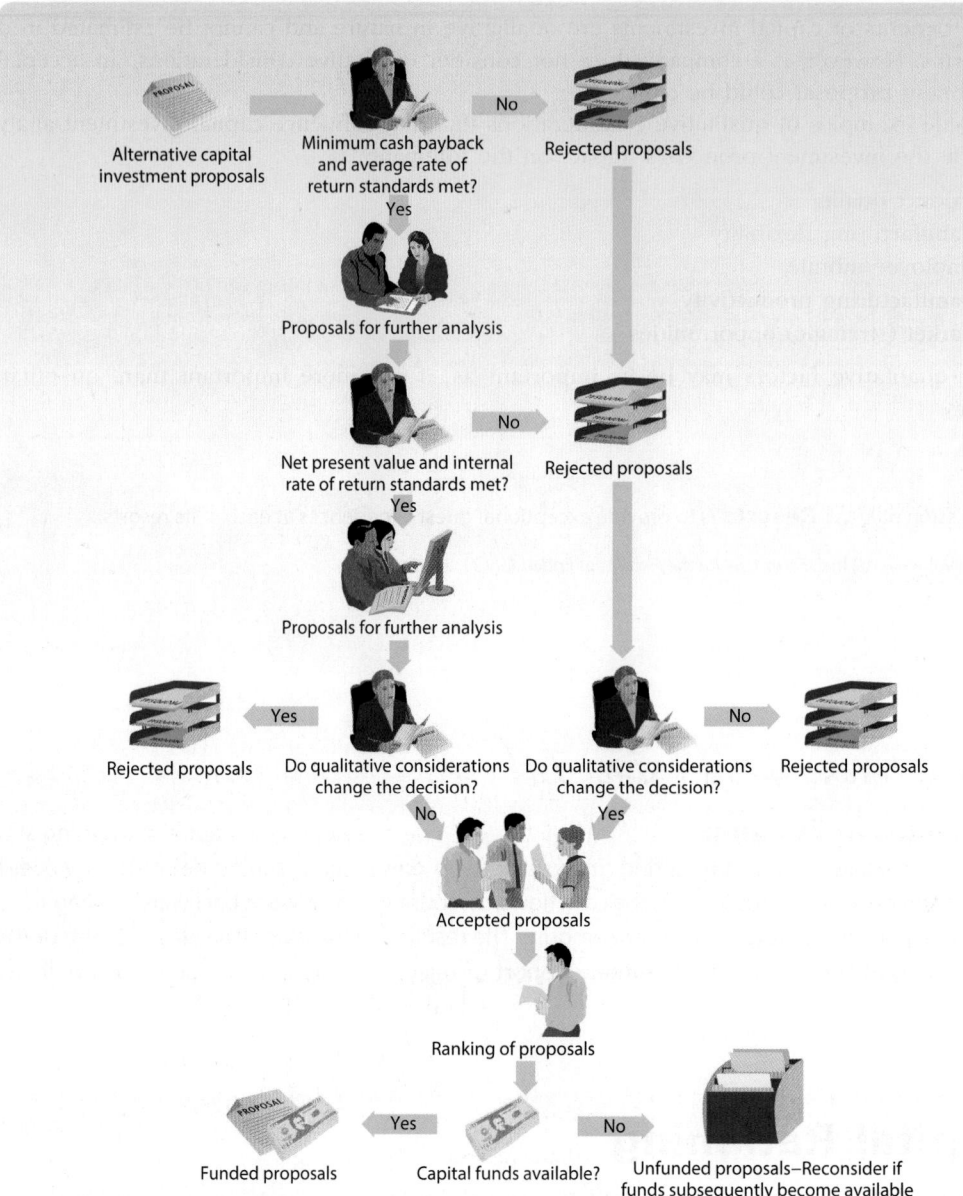

Alternative capital investment proposals

Minimum cash payback and average rate of return standards met?

No → Rejected proposals

Yes

Proposals for further analysis

Net present value and internal rate of return standards met?

No → Rejected proposals

Yes

Proposals for further analysis

Yes ← Do qualitative considerations change the decision?

Rejected proposals

Do qualitative considerations change the decision? → No → Rejected proposals

No

Yes

Accepted proposals

Ranking of proposals

Funded proposals ← Yes

Capital funds available?

No → Unfunded proposals—Reconsider if funds subsequently become available

Analysis for Decision Making

Capital Investment for Sustainability

Objective
Describe and illustrate the use of capital investment analysis in evaluating a sustainability investment.

In Chapter 15, we defined sustainability as the practice of operating a business to maximize profits while attempting to preserve the environment, economy, and needs of future generations. Sustainability practices often require capital investments in order to establish these priorities. Some examples are listed in Exhibit 13.

Sustainability Objective	Capital Investment Example
Minimize resource waste and environmental degradation	Invest in land, soil, and water reclamation projects for a mining company.
Develop new sustainable markets	Invest in equipment to produce an environmentally safe cleaning product for a consumer products company.
Reduce litigation risks	Invest in wastewater recycling to avoid river contamination and potential legal liability for a papermaking company.
Maintain an attractive and safe working environment	Invest in an employee wellness and fitness center to attract and retain high-performance employees for a software company.

Exhibit 13
Examples of Sustainability Capital Investments

Often, sustainability investments can be analyzed using methods described in this chapter. An example would be manufacturing equipment for the new environmentally safe cleaning product listed in Exhibit 13. In contrast, the benefits of some sustainability investments may be difficult to measure and, thus, must be evaluated qualitatively. An example might be the wellness and fitness center for employees listed in Exhibit 13. In addition, sustainability investments may be legally mandated and, thus, are justified more by the requirements of the law than by their immediate economic benefits. Examples might be the land, soil, and water reclamation projects and the wastewater recycling project listed in Exhibit 13.

To illustrate a capital investment analysis, Carpenter Company proposes to install solar panels to satisfy a portion of its power requirements for its manufacturing plant. The solar panels investment cost is $150,000. The solar panels operating and maintenance cost is expected to be $20,000 per year. The plant uses an average of 3,000 kilowatt-hours (kwh) per day for 250 sunny days per year. A kilowatt-hour is the use of 1,000 watts per hour and is a standard measure of electricity consumption. The solar panels replace metered electricity from the power company that costs Carpenter $0.12 per kwh. The solar panels are expected to last 10 years with no salvage value.

Annual cost savings:

Kilowatt-hours per day	3,000 kwh
Number of sunny operating days	× 250 days
Kilowatt-hours per year	750,000 kwh
Metered electricity cost per kwh	× $0.12 per kwh
Total metered cost savings	$ 90,000
Annual solar panel operating cost	(20,000)
Net annual savings	$ 70,000

The net present value of the project, assuming a minimum rate of return of 10%, is (use Exhibit 5):

Annual net cash flow savings from installing solar panels	$ 70,000
Present value factor for an annuity of $1 at 10% for 10 periods	× 6.145
Present value of annual savings (rounded)	$ 430,150
Amount to be invested	(150,000)
Net present value	$ 280,150

The net present value is positive; thus, the proposal is supported by the analysis.

Make a Decision   Capital Investment for Sustainability

Den-Tex Company is evaluating a proposal to replace its HID (high intensity discharge) lighting with LED (light emitting diode) lighting throughout its warehouse. LED lighting consumes less power and lasts longer than HID lighting for similar performance. The following information was developed:

HID watt hour consumption per fixture	500 watts per hr.
LED watt hour consumption per fixture	300 watts per hr.
Number of fixtures	700
Lifetime investment cost (in present value terms) to replace each HID fixture with LED	$500
Operating hours per day	10
Operating days per year	300
Metered utility rate per kilowatt-hour (kwh)*	$0.11

*Note a kilowatt-hour equals 1,000 watts per hour.

A. Determine the investment cost for replacing the 700 fixtures.

B. Determine the annual utility cost savings from employing the new energy solution.

C. Should the proposal be accepted? Evaluate the proposal using net present value, assuming a 15-year life and 8% minimum rate of return.

Solution:

A.
Lifetime cost to replace each HID fixture with LED	$ 500
Number of fixtures	× 700
Investment cost	$350,000

B.
HID kilowatt-hour consumption per fixture	0.5*
LED kilowatt-hour consumption per fixture	(0.3)
Kilowatt-hour savings per fixture	0.2
Number of operating hours per day	× 10
Number of operating days per year	× 300
Number of fixtures	× 700
Kilowatt-hour savings per year	420,000
Metered utility rate per kwh	× $0.11
Annual utility cost savings	$ 46,200

* 500 watts ÷ 1,000 watts = 0.5 kilowatts

C.
Annual net cash flow savings from installing LED	$ 46,200
Present value factor for an annuity of $1 at 8% for 15 periods (Appendix A)	× 8.55948
Present value of annual savings (rounded)	$ 395,448
Amount to be invested	(350,000)
Net present value	$ 45,448

The net present value is positive; thus, the proposal should be accepted.

Let's Review

Chapter Summary

1. Capital investment analysis is the process by which management plans, evaluates, and controls investments involving fixed assets. Capital investment analysis is important to a business because such investments affect profitability for a long period of time.

2. The average rate of return method measures the expected profitability of an investment in fixed assets. The expected period of time that will pass between the date of an investment and the complete recovery in cash (or equivalent) of the amount invested is the cash payback period.

3. The net present value method computes the net present value of the cash inflows expected from a proposal and compares the result to the amount to be invested. The internal rate of return method uses present values to compute the rate of return from the net cash flows expected from capital investment proposals.

4. Factors that may complicate capital investment analysis include the impact of income tax, unequal lives of alternative proposals, leasing, uncertainty, changes in price levels, and qualitative considerations.

5. Capital rationing refers to the process by which management allocates available investment funds among competing capital investment proposals. A diagram of the capital rationing process appears in Exhibit 12.

Key Terms

annuity (1268)
average rate of return (1263)
capital investment analysis (1262)
capital rationing (1279)
cash payback period (1264)

currency exchange rate (1278)
inflation (1278)
internal rate of return (IRR) method (1271)
net present value method (1269)

present value concepts (1267)
present value index (1271)
present value of an annuity (1268)
time value of money concept (1262)

Practice

Multiple-Choice Questions

1. Methods of evaluating capital investment proposals that ignore present value include:
   A. average rate of return.
   B. cash payback.
   C. both A and B.
   D. neither A nor B.

2. Management is considering a $100,000 investment in a project with a five-year life and no residual value. If the total income from the project is expected to be $60,000 and straight-line depreciation is used, the average rate of return is:
   A. 12%.
   B. 24%.
   C. 60%.
   D. 75%.

3. The expected period of time that will elapse between the date of a capital investment and the complete recovery of the amount of cash invested is called the:
   A. average rate of return period.   C. net present value period.
   B. cash payback period.   D. internal rate of return period.

4. A project that will cost $120,000 is estimated to generate cash flows of $25,000 per year for eight years. What is the net present value of the project, assuming an 11% required rate of return? (Use the present value tables in Appendix A.)
   A. $(38,214)   C. $55,180
   B. $8,653   D. $75,000

5. A project is estimated to generate cash flows of $40,000 per year for 10 years. The cost of the project is $226,009. What is the internal rate of return for this project?
   A. 8%   C. 12%
   B. 10%   D. 14%

Answers provided after Problem. Need more practice? Find additional multiple-choice questions, exercises, and problems in CengageNOWv2.

Exercises

SHOW ME HOW

1. Average rate of return   Obj. 2
Determine the average rate of return for a project that is estimated to yield total income of $170,000 over five years, has a cost of $320,000, and has a $20,000 residual value.

SHOW ME HOW

2. Cash payback period   Obj. 2
A project has estimated annual net cash flows of $118,600. It is estimated to cost $616,720. Determine the cash payback period. (Round to one decimal place.)

SHOW ME HOW

3. Net present value   Obj. 3
A project has estimated annual net cash flows of $6,800 for five years and is estimated to cost $23,125. Assume a minimum acceptable rate of return of 12%. Using Exhibit 5, determine (1) the net present value of the project and (2) the present value index, rounded to two decimal places.

SHOW ME HOW

4. Internal rate of return   Obj. 3
A project is estimated to cost $104,328 and provide annual net cash flows of $21,000 for eight years. Determine the internal rate of return for this project, using Exhibit 5.

SHOW ME HOW

5. Net present value—unequal lives   Obj. 4
Project A requires an original investment of $32,600. The project will yield cash flows of $7,000 per year for nine years. Project B has a calculated net present value of $3,500 over a six-year life. Project A could be sold at the end of six years for a price of $15,000. (A) Determine the net present value of Project A over a six-year life, with residual value, assuming a minimum rate of return of 12%. (B) Which project provides the greatest net present value?

Answers provided after Problem. Need more practice? Find additional multiple-choice questions, exercises, and problems in CengageNOWv2.

Problem

The capital investment committee of Hopewell Company is currently considering two investments. The estimated income from operations and net cash flows expected from each investment are as follows:

	Truck		Equipment	
Year	Income from Operations	Net Cash Flow	Income from Operations	Net Cash Flow
1	$ 6,000	$ 22,000	$13,000	$ 29,000
2	9,000	25,000	10,000	26,000
3	10,000	26,000	8,000	24,000
4	8,000	24,000	8,000	24,000
5	11,000	27,000	3,000	19,000
	$44,000	$124,000	$42,000	$122,000

Each investment requires $80,000. Straight-line depreciation will be used, and no residual value is expected. The committee has selected a rate of 15% for purposes of the net present value analysis.

Instructions

1. Compute the following:

    A. The average rate of return for each investment.

    B. The net present value for each investment. Use the present value of $1 table appearing in this chapter (Exhibit 2).

2. Why is the net present value of the equipment greater than the truck, even though its average rate of return is less?

3. Prepare a summary for the capital investment committee, advising it on the relative merits of the two investments.

Need more practice? Find additional multiple-choice questions, exercises, and problems in CengageNOWv2.

Answers

Multiple-Choice Questions

1. **C** Methods of evaluating capital investment proposals that ignore the time value of money include the average rate of return method (answer A) and the cash payback method (answer B).

2. **B** The average rate of return is 24% (answer B), determined by dividing the expected average annual earnings by the average investment, as follows:

$$\frac{\$60,000 \div 5}{(\$100,000 + \$0) \div 2} = 24\%$$

3. **B** Of the four methods of analyzing proposals for capital investments, the cash payback period (answer B) refers to the expected period of time required to recover the amount of cash to be invested. The average rate of return (answer A) is a measure of the anticipated profitability of a proposal. The net present value method (answer C) reduces the expected future net cash flows originating from a proposal to their present values. The internal rate of return method (answer D) uses present value concepts to compute the rate of return from the net cash flows expected from the investment.

4. **B** The net present value is determined as follows:

Present value of $25,000 for 8 years at 11% ($25,000 × 5.14612)	$ 128,653
Project cost	(120,000)
Net present value	$ 8,653

5. **C** The internal rate of return for this project is determined by solving for the present value of an annuity factor that when multiplied by $40,000 will equal $226,009. By division, the factor is:

$$\frac{\$226,009}{\$40,000} = 5.65022$$

In Appendix A on pp. A-5 and A-6, scan along the n = 10 years row until finding the 5.65022 factor. The column for this factor is 12%.

Exercises

1. Estimate average annual income $34,000 ($170,000 ÷ 5 years)
   Average investment $170,000 [($320,000 + $20,000) ÷ 2]
   Average rate of return   20% ($34,000 ÷ $170,000)

2. 5.2 years ($616,720 ÷ $118,600)

3. A. $1,389   [($6,800 × 3.605) − $23,125]

   B.   1.06   ($24,514 ÷ $23,125)

4. 12%   [($104,328 ÷ $21,000) = 4.968, the present value of an annuity factor for eight periods at 12%, from Exhibit 5]

5. A.

Present value of $7,000 per year at 12% for 6 years*	$ 28,777
Present value of $15,000 at 12% at the end of 6 years**	7,605
Total present value of Project A	$ 36,382
Total cost of Project A	(32,600)
Net present value of Project A	$ 3,782

   *[$7,000 × 4.111 (Exhibit 5, 12%, 6 years)]

   **[$15,000 × 0.507 (Exhibit 2, 12%, 6 years)]

   B.   Project A. Project A's net present value of $3,782 is more than the net present value of Project B, $3,500.

Need more help? Watch step-by-step videos of how to compute answers to these Exercises in CengageNOWv2.

Problem

1. A.   Average rate of return for the truck:

$$\frac{\$44,000 \div 5}{(\$80,000 + \$0) \div 2} = 22\%$$

   Average rate of return for the equipment:

$$\frac{\$42,000 \div 5}{(\$80,000 + \$0) \div 2} = 21\%$$

B. Net present value analysis:

Year	Present Value Factor for $1 at 15%	Net Cash Flow Truck	Net Cash Flow Equipment	Present Value of Net Cash Flow Truck	Present Value of Net Cash Flow Equipment
1	0.870	$ 22,000	$ 29,000	$ 19,140	$ 25,230
2	0.756	25,000	26,000	18,900	19,656
3	0.658	26,000	24,000	17,108	15,792
4	0.572	24,000	24,000	13,728	13,728
5	0.497	27,000	19,000	13,419	9,443
Total		$124,000	$122,000	$ 82,295	$ 83,849
Amount to be invested				(80,000)	(80,000)
Net present value				$ 2,295	$ 3,849

2. The equipment has a lower average rate of return than the truck because the equipment's total income from operations for the five years is $42,000, which is $2,000 less than the truck's. Even so, the net present value of the equipment is greater than that of the truck because the equipment has higher cash flows in the early years.

3. Both investments exceed the selected rate established for the net present value analysis. The truck has a higher average rate of return, but the equipment offers a larger net present value. Thus, if only one of the two investments can be accepted, the equipment would be the more attractive.

Discussion Questions

1. What are the principal objections to the use of the average rate of return method in evaluating capital investment proposals?

2. Discuss the principal limitations of the cash payback method for evaluating capital investment proposals.

3. Why would the average rate of return differ from the internal rate of return on the same project?

4. Your boss has suggested that a one-year payback period is the same as a 100% average rate of return. Do you agree?

5. Why would the cash payback method understate the attractiveness of a project with a large residual value?

6. Why would the use of the cash payback period for analyzing the financial performance of theatrical releases from a motion picture production studio be supported over the net present value method?

7. A net present value analysis used to evaluate a proposed equipment acquisition indicated a $7,900 net present value. What is the meaning of the $7,900 as it relates to the desirability of the proposal?

8. Two projects have an identical net present value of $9,000. Are both projects equal in desirability?

9. What are the major disadvantages of the use of the net present value method of analyzing capital investment proposals?

10. What are the major disadvantages of the use of the internal rate of return method of analyzing capital investment proposals?

11. What are the major advantages of leasing a fixed asset rather than purchasing it?

12. Give an example of a qualitative factor that should be considered in a capital investment analysis related to acquiring automated factory equipment.

Basic Exercises

SHOW ME HOW

BE 25-1   Average rate of return   Obj. 2

Determine the average rate of return for a project that is estimated to yield total income of $170,000 over five years, has a cost of $320,000, and has a $20,000 residual value.

SHOW ME HOW

BE 25-2   Cash payback period   Obj. 2

A project has estimated annual net cash flows of $36,500. It is estimated to cost $222,650. Determine the cash payback period. (Round to one decimal place.)

SHOW ME HOW

BE 25-3   Net present value   Obj. 3

A project has estimated annual net cash flows of $70,000 for four years and is estimated to cost $190,000. Assume a minimum acceptable rate of return of 10%. Using Exhibit 5, determine (A) the net present value of the project and (B) the present value index, rounded to two decimal places.

SHOW ME HOW

BE 25-4   Internal rate of return   Obj. 3

A project is estimated to cost $463,565 and provide annual net cash flows of $115,000 for nine years. Determine the internal rate of return for this project, using Exhibit 5.

SHOW ME HOW

BE 25-5   Net present value—unequal lives   Obj. 4

Project 1 requires an original investment of $125,000. The project will yield cash flows of $50,000 per year for 10 years. Project 2 has a calculated net present value of $135,000 over an eight-year life. Project 1 could be sold at the end of eight years for a price of $8,000. (A) Determine the net present value of Project 1 over an eight-year life, with residual value, assuming a minimum rate of return of 12%. (B) Which project provides the greatest net present value?

Exercises

EX 25-1   Average rate of return   Obj. 2

✔ 3D Printer, 16%

The following data are accumulated by Lone Peak Inc. in evaluating two competing capital investment proposals:

SHOW ME HOW

	3D Printer	Truck
Amount of investment	$40,000	$50,000
Useful life	7 years	10 years
Estimated residual value	$3,000	$6,000
Estimated total income over the useful life	$24,080	$36,400

Determine the expected average rate of return for each proposal.

EX 25-2   Average rate of return—cost savings   Obj. 2

Midwest Fabricators Inc. is considering an investment in equipment that will replace direct labor. The equipment has a cost of $132,000 with a $16,000 residual value and a 10-year life. The equipment will replace one employee who has an average wage of $34,000 per year. In addition, the equipment will have operating and energy costs of $5,380 per year.

Determine the average rate of return on the equipment, giving effect to straight-line depreciation on the investment.

EX 25-3 Average rate of return—new product

Obj. 2

✔ Average annual income, $405,000

SHOW ME HOW

Galactic Inc. is considering an investment in new equipment that will be used to manufacture a smartphone. The phone is expected to generate additional annual sales of 6,000 units at $250 per unit. The equipment has a cost of $850,000, residual value of $50,000, and an eight-year life. The equipment can only be used to manufacture the phone. The cost to manufacture the phone follows:

Cost per unit:	
Direct labor	$ 15.00
Direct materials	134.00
Factory overhead (including depreciation)	33.50
Total cost per unit	$182.50

Determine the average rate of return on the equipment.

EX 25-4 Calculate cash flows

Obj. 2

✔ Year 1: $(168,500)

SHOW ME HOW

Nature's Way Inc. is planning to invest in new manufacturing equipment to make a new garden tool. The new garden tool is expected to generate additional annual sales of 2,500 units at $60 each. The new manufacturing equipment will cost $227,000 and is expected to have a 10-year life and $17,000 residual value. Selling expenses related to the new product are expected to be 5% of sales revenue. The cost to manufacture the product includes the following on a per-unit basis:

Direct labor	$ 8.00
Direct materials	22.00
Fixed factory overhead—depreciation	8.40
Variable factory overhead	3.60
Total	$42.00

Determine the net cash flows for the first year of the project, Years 2–9, and for the last year of the project.

EX 25-5 Cash payback period for a service company

Obj. 2

✔ Location 1: 4.5 years

SHOW ME HOW

Chinook Industries Inc. is evaluating two capital investment proposals for a retail outlet, each requiring an investment of $900,000 and each with an eight-year life and expected total net cash flows of $1,000,000. Location 1 is expected to provide equal annual net cash flows of $200,000, and Location 2 is expected to have the following unequal annual net cash flows:

Year 1	$300,000		Year 5	$50,000
Year 2	220,000		Year 6	50,000
Year 3	180,000		Year 7	30,000
Year 4	150,000		Year 8	20,000

Determine the cash payback period for both location proposals.

EX 25-6 Cash payback method

Obj. 2

EXCEL TEMPLATE

Lily Products Company is considering an investment in one of two new product lines. The investment required for either product line is $540,000. The net cash flows associated with each product are as follows:

Year	Liquid Soap	Body Lotion
1	$170,000	$ 90,000
2	150,000	90,000
3	120,000	90,000
4	100,000	90,000
5	70,000	90,000
6	40,000	90,000
7	40,000	90,000
8	30,000	90,000
Total	$720,000	$720,000

(Continued)

A. Recommend a product offering to Lily Products Company, based on the cash payback period for each product line.

B. ━━━➤ Why is one product line preferred over the other, even though they both have the same total net cash flows through eight periods?

EX 25-7 Net present value method

Obj. 3

✔ A. NPV, $24,520

SHOW ME HOW

The following data are accumulated by Geddes Company in evaluating the purchase of $150,000 of equipment, having a four-year useful life:

	Net Income	Net Cash Flow
Year 1	$42,500	$80,000
Year 2	27,500	65,000
Year 3	12,500	50,000
Year 4	2,500	40,000

A. Assuming that the desired rate of return is 15%, determine the net present value for the proposal. Use the table of the present value of $1 appearing in Exhibit 2 of this chapter.

B. ━━━➤ Would management be likely to look with favor on the proposal? Explain.

EX 25-8 Net present value method for a service company

Obj. 3

✔ A. 20Y1, $13,000

AM Express Inc. is considering the purchase of an additional delivery vehicle for $55,000 on January 1, 20Y1. The truck is expected to have a five-year life with an expected residual value of $15,000 at the end of five years. The expected additional revenues from the added delivery capacity are anticipated to be $58,000 per year for each of the next five years. A driver will cost $42,000 in 20Y1, with an expected annual salary increase of $1,000 for each year thereafter. The annual operating costs for the truck are estimated to be $3,000 per year.

A. Determine the expected annual net cash flows from the delivery truck investment for 20Y1–20Y5.

B. Calculate the net present value of the investment, assuming that the minimum desired rate of return is 12%. Use the present value of $1 table appearing in Exhibit 2 of this chapter.

C. ━━━➤ Is the additional truck a good investment based on your analysis? Explain.

EX 25-9 Net present value method—annuity for a service company

Obj. 3

✔ B. $8 million

SHOW ME HOW

Welcome Inn Hotels is considering the construction of a new hotel for $90 million. The expected life of the hotel is 30 years, with no residual value. The hotel is expected to earn revenues of $26 million per year. Total expenses, including depreciation, are expected to be $15 million per year. Welcome Inn management has set a minimum acceptable rate of return of 14%.

A. Determine the equal annual net cash flows from operating the hotel.

B. Calculate the net present value of the new hotel, using the present value of an annuity of $1 table found in Appendix A. (Round to the nearest million dollars.)

C. ━━━➤ Does your analysis support construction of the new hotel? Explain.

EX 25-10 Net present value method—annuity

Obj. 3

✔ A. $46,000

Briggs Excavation Company is planning an investment of $132,000 for a bulldozer. The bulldozer is expected to operate for 1,500 hours per year for five years. Customers will be charged $110 per hour for bulldozer work. The bulldozer operator costs $28 per hour in wages and benefits. The bulldozer is expected to require annual maintenance costing $8,000. The bulldozer uses fuel that is expected to cost $46 per hour of bulldozer operation.

A. Determine the equal annual net cash flows from operating the bulldozer.

B. Determine the net present value of the investment, assuming that the desired rate of return is 10%. Use the present value of an annuity of $1 table in the chapter (Exhibit 5). (Round to the nearest dollar.)

C. ━━━➤ Should Briggs invest in the bulldozer, based on this analysis? Explain.

D. Determine the number of operating hours such that the present value of cash flows equals the amount to be invested. (Round all calculations to whole numbers.)

EX 25-11 Net present value method for a service company Obj. 3

✔ A. $157,600,000

REAL WORLD

Carnival Corporation has recently placed into service some of the largest cruise ships in the world. One of these ships, the *Carnival Breeze*, can hold up to 3,600 passengers, and it can cost $750 million to build. Assume the following additional information:

- There will be 330 cruise days per year operated at a full capacity of 3,600 passengers.
- The variable expenses per passenger are estimated to be $140 per cruise day.
- The revenue per passenger is expected to be $340 per cruise day.
- The fixed expenses for running the ship, other than depreciation, are estimated to be $80,000,000 per year.
- The ship has a service life of 10 years, with a residual value of $140,000,000 at the end of 10 years.

A. Determine the annual net cash flow from operating the cruise ship.

B. Determine the net present value of this investment, assuming a 12% minimum rate of return. Use the present value tables (Exhibit 2 and Exhibit 5) provided in the chapter in determining your answer.

EX 25-12 Present value index Obj. 3

✔ Ft. Collins, 0.98

Dip N' Dunk Doughnuts has computed the net present value for capital expenditure at two locations. Relevant data related to the computation are as follows:

	Ft. Collins	Boulder
Total present value of net cash flow	$ 607,600	$ 624,000
Amount to be invested	(620,000)	(600,000)
Net present value	$(12,400)	$ 24,000

A. Determine the present value index for each proposal.

B. ━━━▶ Which location does your analysis support? Explain.

EX 25-13 Net present value method and present value index Obj. 3

✔ B. Packing machine, 1.55

Diamond & Turf Inc. is considering an investment in one of two machines. The sewing machine will increase productivity from sewing 150 baseballs per hour to sewing 290 per hour. The contribution margin per unit is $0.32 per baseball. Assume that any increased production of baseballs can be sold. The second machine is an automatic packing machine for the golf ball line. The packing machine will reduce packing labor cost. The labor cost saved is equivalent to $21 per hour. The sewing machine will cost $260,000, have an eight-year life, and will operate for 1,800 hours per year. The packing machine will cost $85,000, have an eight-year life, and will operate for 1,400 hours per year. Diamond & Turf seeks a minimum rate of return of 15% on its investments.

A. Determine the net present value for the two machines. Use the present value of an annuity of $1 table in the chapter (Exhibit 5). (Round to the nearest dollar.)

B. Determine the present value index for the two machines. (Round to two decimal places.)

C. ━━━▶ If Diamond & Turf has sufficient funds for only one of the machines and qualitative factors are equal between the two machines, in which machine should it invest? Explain.

EX 25-14 Average rate of return, cash payback period, net present value method for a service company Obj. 2, 3

✔ B. 4 years

SHOW ME HOW

Spanish Peaks Railroad Inc. is considering acquiring equipment at a cost of $1,250,000. The equipment has an estimated life of eight years and no residual value. It is expected to provide yearly net cash flows of $312,500. The company's minimum desired rate of return for net present value analysis is 12%.

Compute the following:

A. The average rate of return, giving effect to straight-line depreciation on the investment.

B. The cash payback period.

C. The net present value. Use the present value of an annuity of $1 table appearing in this chapter (Exhibit 5).

EX 25-15 Cash payback period, net present value analysis, and qualitative considerations Obj. 2, 3, 4

✔ A. 4 years

The plant manager of Shenzhen Electronics Company is considering the purchase of new automated assembly equipment. The new equipment will cost $1,400,000. The manager believes that the new investment will result in direct labor savings of $350,000 per year for 10 years.

A. What is the payback period on this project?

B. What is the net present value, assuming a 10% rate of return? Use the present value of an annuity of $1 table in Exhibit 5.

C. ▬▬▶ What else should the manager consider in the analysis?

EX 25-16 Internal rate of return method Obj. 3

✔ A. 3.785

SHOW ME HOW

The internal rate of return method is used by Testerman Construction Co. in analyzing a capital expenditure proposal that involves an investment of $113,550 and annual net cash flows of $30,000 for each of the six years of its useful life.

A. Determine a present value factor for an annuity of $1, which can be used in determining the internal rate of return.

B. Using the factor determined in part (A) and the present value of an annuity of $1 table appearing in this chapter (Exhibit 5), determine the internal rate of return for the proposal.

REAL WORLD

EX 25-17 Internal rate of return method for a service company Obj. 3, 4

Park City Mountain Resort, a Utah ski resort, announced a $415 million expansion of lodging properties, lifts, and terrain. Assume that this investment is estimated to produce $99 million in equal annual cash flows for each of the first 10 years of the project life.

A. Determine the expected internal rate of return of this project for 10 years, using the present value of an annuity of $1 table found in Exhibit 5.

B. ▬▬▶ What are some uncertainties that could reduce the internal rate of return of this project?

EX 25-18 Internal rate of return method—two projects Obj. 3

✔ A. Delivery truck, 15%

Munch N' Crunch Snack Company is considering two possible investments: a delivery truck or a bagging machine. The delivery truck would cost $43,056 and could be used to deliver an additional 95,000 bags of pretzels per year. Each bag of pretzels can be sold for a contribution margin of $0.45. The delivery truck operating expenses, excluding depreciation, are $1.35 per mile for 24,000 miles per year. The bagging machine would replace an old bagging machine, and its net investment cost would be $61,614. The new machine would require three fewer hours of direct labor per day. Direct labor is $18 per hour. There are 250 operating days in the year. Both the truck and the bagging machine are estimated to have seven-year lives. The minimum rate of return is 13%. However, Munch N' Crunch has funds to invest in only one of the projects.

A. Compute the internal rate of return for each investment. Use the present value of an annuity of $1 table appearing in this chapter (Exhibit 5).

B. ▬▬▶ Provide a memo to management, with a recommendation.

EX 25-19 **Net present value method and internal rate of return method for a service company** Obj. 3

✔ A. ($12,845)

Buckeye Healthcare Corp. is proposing to spend $186,725 on an eight-year project that has estimated net cash flows of $35,000 for each of the eight years.

A. Compute the net present value, using a rate of return of 12%. Use the present value of an annuity of $1 table in the chapter (Exhibit 5).

B. ▬▬▬▶ Based on the analysis prepared in part (A), is the internal rate of return (1) more than 12%, (2) 12%, or (3) less than 12%? Explain.

C. Determine the internal rate of return by computing a present value factor for an annuity of $1 and using the present value of an annuity of $1 table presented in the text (Exhibit 5).

EX 25-20 **Identify error in capital investment analysis calculations** Obj. 3

Artscape Inc. is considering the purchase of automated machinery that is expected to have a useful life of five years and no residual value. The average rate of return on the average investment has been computed to be 20%, and the cash payback period was computed to be 5.5 years.

▬▬▬▶ Do you see any reason to question the validity of the data presented? Explain.

EX 25-21 **Net present value—unequal lives** Obj. 3, 4

✔ Net present value, Processing mill, $196,220

EXCEL TEMPLATE

Bunker Hill Mining Company has two competing proposals: a processing mill and an electric shovel. Both pieces of equipment have an initial investment of $750,000. The net cash flows estimated for the two proposals are as follows:

	Net Cash Flow	
Year	Processing Mill	Electric Shovel
1	$310,000	$330,000
2	260,000	325,000
3	260,000	325,000
4	260,000	320,000
5	180,000	
6	130,000	
7	120,000	
8	120,000	

The estimated residual value of the processing mill at the end of Year 4 is $280,000.

Determine which equipment should be favored, comparing the net present values of the two proposals and assuming a minimum rate of return of 15%. Use the present value tables presented in this chapter (Exhibit 2).

EX 25-22 **Net present value—unequal lives** Obj. 3, 4

✔ Net present value, blending equipment, $6,344

Daisy's Creamery Inc. is considering one of two investment options. Option 1 is a $75,000 investment in new blending equipment that is expected to produce equal annual cash flows of $19,000 for each of seven years. Option 2 is a $90,000 investment in a new computer system that is expected to produce equal annual cash flows of $27,000 for each of five years. The residual value of the blending equipment at the end of the fifth year is estimated to be $15,000. The computer system has no expected residual value at the end of the fifth year.

Assume there is sufficient capital to fund only one of the projects. Determine which project should be selected, computing the (A) net present values and (B) present value indices of the two projects. Assume a minimum rate of return of 10%. Round the present value index to two decimal places. Use the present value tables presented in this chapter (Exhibits 2 and 5).

Problems: Series A

PR 25-1A **Average rate of return method, net present value method, and analysis for a service company**

Obj. 2, 3

✔ 1. A. 30.0%

SHOW ME HOW   EXCEL TEMPLATE

The capital investment committee of Arches Landscaping Company is considering two capital investments. The estimated income from operations and net cash flows from each investment are as follows:

	Front-End Loader		Greenhouse	
Year	Income from Operations	Net Cash Flow	Income from Operations	Net Cash Flow
1	$25,000	$ 40,000	$11,250	$ 26,250
2	20,000	35,000	11,250	26,250
3	7,000	22,000	11,250	26,250
4	3,000	18,000	11,250	26,250
5	1,250	16,250	11,250	26,250
Total	$56,250	$131,250	$56,250	$131,250

Each project requires an investment of $75,000. Straight-line depreciation will be used, and no residual value is expected. The committee has selected a rate of 12% for purposes of the net present value analysis.

Instructions

1. Compute the following:

   A. The average rate of return for each investment.

   B. The net present value for each investment. Use the present value of $1 table appearing in this chapter (Exhibit 2). (Round present values to the nearest dollar.)

2. ➤ Prepare a brief report for the capital investment committee, advising it on the relative merits of the two investments.

PR 25-2A **Cash payback period, net present value method, and analysis**

Obj. 2, 3

✔ 1. B. Plant expansion, $305,040

EXCEL TEMPLATE

Elite Apparel Inc. is considering two investment projects. The estimated net cash flows from each project are as follows:

Year	Plant Expansion	Retail Store Expansion
1	$ 450,000	$ 500,000
2	450,000	400,000
3	340,000	350,000
4	280,000	250,000
5	180,000	200,000
Total	$1,700,000	$1,700,000

Each project requires an investment of $900,000. A rate of 15% has been selected for the net present value analysis.

Instructions

1. Compute the following for each product:

   A. Cash payback period.

   B. The net present value. Use the present value of $1 table appearing in this chapter (Exhibit 2).

2. ➤ Prepare a brief report advising management on the relative merits of each project.

PR 25-3A Net present value method, present value index, and analysis for a service company

Obj. 3

✔ 2. Computer Network, 1.20

EXCEL TEMPLATE

Continental Railroad Company is evaluating three capital investment proposals by using the net present value method. Relevant data related to the proposals are summarized as follows:

	Maintenance Equipment	Ramp Facilities	Computer Network
Amount to be invested	$8,000,000	$20,000,000	$9,000,000
Annual net cash flows:			
Year 1	4,000,000	12,000,000	6,000,000
Year 2	3,500,000	10,000,000	5,000,000
Year 3	2,500,000	9,000,000	4,000,000

Instructions

1. Assuming that the desired rate of return is 20%, prepare a net present value analysis for each proposal. Use the present value of $1 table appearing in this chapter (Exhibit 2).

2. Determine a present value index for each proposal. (Round to two decimal places.)

3. ━━━━▶ Which proposal offers the largest amount of present value per dollar of investment? Explain.

PR 25-4A Net present value method, internal rate of return method, and analysis for a service company

Obj. 3

✔ 1. A. Wind turbines, $82,600

The management of Advanced Alternative Power Inc. is considering two capital investment projects. The estimated net cash flows from each project are as follows:

Year	Wind Turbines	Biofuel Equipment
1	$280,000	$300,000
2	280,000	300,000
3	280,000	300,000
4	280,000	300,000

The wind turbines require an investment of $887,600, while the biofuel equipment requires an investment of $911,100. No residual value is expected from either project.

Instructions

1. Compute the following for each project:

   A. The net present value. Use a rate of 6% and the present value of an annuity of $1 table appearing in this chapter (Exhibit 5).

   B. A present value index. (Round to two decimal places.)

2. Determine the internal rate of return for each project by (A) computing a present value factor for an annuity of $1 and (B) using the present value of an annuity of $1 table appearing in this chapter (Exhibit 5).

3. ━━━━▶ What advantage does the internal rate of return method have over the net present value method in comparing projects?

PR 25-5A Alternative capital investments

Obj. 3, 4

✔ 1. Servers, $11,105

EXCEL TEMPLATE

The investment committee of Sentry Insurance Co. is evaluating two projects, office expansion and upgrade to computer servers. The projects have different useful lives, but each requires an investment of $490,000. The estimated net cash flows from each project are as follows:

	Net Cash Flows	
Year	Office Expansion	Servers
1	$125,000	$165,000
2	125,000	165,000
3	125,000	165,000
4	125,000	165,000
5	125,000	
6	125,000	

(Continued)

The committee has selected a rate of 12% for purposes of net present value analysis. It also estimates that the residual value at the end of each project's useful life is $0, but at the end of the fourth year, the office expansion's residual value would be $180,000.

Instructions

1. For each project, compute the net present value. Use the present value of an annuity of $1 table appearing in this chapter (Exhibit 5). (Ignore the unequal lives of the projects.)

2. For each project, compute the net present value, assuming that the office expansion is adjusted to a four-year life for purposes of analysis. Use the present value of $1 table appearing in this chapter (Exhibit 2).

3. ➤ Prepare a report to the investment committee, providing your advice on the relative merits of the two projects.

PR 25-6A Capital rationing decision for a service company involving four proposals   Obj. 2, 3, 5

✔ 5. Proposal C, 1.57

EXCEL TEMPLATE

Renaissance Capital Group is considering allocating a limited amount of capital investment funds among four proposals. The amount of proposed investment, estimated income from operations, and net cash flow for each proposal are as follows:

	Investment	Year	Income from Operations	Net Cash Flow
Proposal A:	$680,000	1	$ 64,000	$ 200,000
		2	64,000	200,000
		3	64,000	200,000
		4	24,000	160,000
		5	24,000	160,000
			$240,000	$ 920,000
Proposal B:	$320,000	1	$ 26,000	$ 90,000
		2	26,000	90,000
		3	6,000	70,000
		4	6,000	70,000
		5	(44,000)	20,000
			$ 20,000	$340,000
Proposal C:	$108,000	1	$ 33,400	$ 55,000
		2	31,400	53,000
		3	28,400	50,000
		4	25,400	47,000
		5	23,400	45,000
			$142,000	$ 250,000
Proposal D:	$400,000	1	$100,000	$ 180,000
		2	100,000	180,000
		3	80,000	160,000
		4	20,000	100,000
		5	0	80,000
			$300,000	$700,000

The company's capital rationing policy requires a maximum cash payback period of three years. In addition, a minimum average rate of return of 12% is required on all projects. If the preceding standards are met, the net present value method and present value indexes are used to rank the remaining proposals.

Instructions

1. Compute the cash payback period for each of the four proposals.

2. Giving effect to straight-line depreciation on the investments and assuming no estimated residual value, compute the average rate of return for each of the four proposals. (Round to one decimal place.)

3. Using the following format, summarize the results of your computations in parts (1) and (2). By placing the calculated amounts in the first two columns on the left and by placing a check mark in the appropriate column to the right, indicate which proposals should be accepted for further analysis and which should be rejected.

Proposal	Cash Payback Period	Average Rate of Return	Accept for Further Analysis	Reject
A				
B				
C				
D				

4. For the proposals accepted for further analysis in part (3), compute the net present value. Use a rate of 15% and the present value of $1 table appearing in this chapter (Exhibit 2).

5. Compute the present value index for each of the proposals in part (4). (Round to two decimal places.)

6. Rank the proposals from most attractive to least attractive, based on the present values of net cash flows computed in part (4).

7. Rank the proposals from most attractive to least attractive, based on the present value indexes computed in part (5).

8. ━━━▶ Based on the analyses, comment on the relative attractiveness of the proposals ranked in parts (6) and (7).

Problems: Series B

PR 25-1B Average rate of return method, net present value method, and analysis for a service company

Obj. 2, 3

✔ 1. A. 18.7%

SHOW ME HOW   EXCEL TEMPLATE

The capital investment committee of Ellis Transport and Storage Inc. is considering two investment projects. The estimated income from operations and net cash flows from each investment are as follows:

Year	Warehouse Income from Operations	Warehouse Net Cash Flow	Tracking Technology Income from Operations	Tracking Technology Net Cash Flow
1	$ 61,400	$135,000	$ 34,400	$108,000
2	51,400	125,000	34,400	108,000
3	36,400	110,000	34,400	108,000
4	26,400	100,000	34,400	108,000
5	(3,600)	70,000	34,400	108,000
Total	$172,000	$540,000	$172,000	$540,000

Each project requires an investment of $368,000. Straight-line depreciation will be used, and no residual value is expected. The committee has selected a rate of 15% for purposes of the net present value analysis.

Instructions

1. Compute the following:

   A. The average rate of return for each investment. (Round to one decimal place.)

   B. The net present value for each investment. Use the present value of $1 table appearing in this chapter (Exhibit 2). (Round present values to the nearest dollar.)

2. ━━━▶ Prepare a brief report for the capital investment committee, advising it on the relative merits of the two projects.

PR 25-2B Cash payback period, net present value method, and analysis for a service company

Obj. 2, 3

✔ 1. B. *Pro Gamer,* $49,465

EXCEL TEMPLATE

Social Circle Publications Inc. is considering two new magazine products. The estimated net cash flows from each product are as follows:

Year	Sound Cellar	Pro Gamer
1	$ 65,000	$ 70,000
2	60,000	55,000
3	25,000	35,000
4	25,000	30,000
5	45,000	30,000
Total	$220,000	$220,000

Each product requires an investment of $125,000. A rate of 10% has been selected for the net present value analysis.

Instructions

1. Compute the following for each product:

   A. Cash payback period.

   B. The net present value. Use the present value of $1 table appearing in this chapter (Exhibit 2).

2. ▬▬▶ Prepare a brief report advising management on the relative merits of each of the two products.

PR 25-3B Net present value method, present value index, and analysis for a service company

Obj. 3

✔ 2. Branch office expansion, 0.95

EXCEL TEMPLATE

First United Bank Inc. is evaluating three capital investment projects by using the net present value method. Relevant data related to the projects are summarized as follows:

	Branch Office Expansion	Computer System Upgrade	ATM Kiosk Expansion
Amount to be invested	$420,000	$350,000	$520,000
Annual net cash flows:			
Year 1	200,000	190,000	275,000
Year 2	160,000	180,000	250,000
Year 3	160,000	170,000	250,000

Instructions

1. Assuming that the desired rate of return is 15%, prepare a net present value analysis for each project. Use the present value of $1 table appearing in this chapter (Exhibit 2).

2. Determine a present value index for each project. (Round to two decimal places.)

3. ▬▬▶ Which project offers the largest amount of present value per dollar of investment? Explain.

PR 25-4B Net present value method, internal rate of return method, and analysis for a service company

Obj. 3

✔ 1. A. *After Hours* $100,800

The management of Style Networks Inc. is considering two TV show projects. The estimated net cash flows from each project are as follows:

Year	After Hours	Sun Fun
1	$320,000	$290,000
2	320,000	290,000
3	320,000	290,000
4	320,000	290,000

After Hours requires an investment of $913,600, while *Sun Fun* requires an investment of $880,730. No residual value is expected from either project.

Instructions
1. Compute the following for each project:
   A. The net present value. Use a rate of 10% and the present value of an annuity of $1 table appearing in this chapter (Exhibit 5).
   B. A present value index. (Round to two decimal places.)
2. Determine the internal rate of return for each project by (A) computing a present value factor for an annuity of $1 and (B) using the present value of an annuity of $1 table appearing in this chapter (Exhibit 5).
3. ➤ What advantage does the internal rate of return method have over the net present value method in comparing projects?

PR 25-5B Alternative capital investments
Obj. 3, 4

✔ 1. Topeka, $135,600

EXCEL TEMPLATE

The investment committee of Auntie M's Restaurants Inc. is evaluating two restaurant sites. The sites have different useful lives, but each requires an investment of $900,000. The estimated net cash flows from each site are as follows:

	Net Cash Flows	
Year	Wichita	Topeka
1	$310,000	$400,000
2	310,000	400,000
3	310,000	400,000
4	310,000	400,000
5	310,000	
6	310,000	

The committee has selected a rate of 20% for purposes of net present value analysis. It also estimates that the residual value at the end of each restaurant's useful life is $0, but at the end of the fourth year, Wichita's residual value would be $500,000.

Instructions
1. For each site, compute the net present value. Use the present value of an annuity of $1 table appearing in this chapter (Exhibit 5). (Ignore the unequal lives of the projects.)
2. For each site, compute the net present value, assuming that Wichita is adjusted to a four-year life for purposes of analysis. Use the present value of $1 table appearing in this chapter (Exhibit 2).
3. ➤ Prepare a report to the investment committee, providing your advice on the relative merits of the two sites.

PR 25-6B Capital rationing decision for a service company involving four proposals
Obj. 2, 3, 5

✔ 5. Proposal B, 1.13

EXCEL TEMPLATE

Clearcast Communications Inc. is considering allocating a limited amount of capital investment funds among four proposals. The amount of proposed investment, estimated income from operations, and net cash flow for each proposal are as follows:

	Investment	Year	Income from Operations	Net Cash Flow
Proposal A:	$450,000	1	$ 30,000	$120,000
		2	30,000	120,000
		3	20,000	110,000
		4	10,000	100,000
		5	(30,000)	60,000
			$ 60,000	$510,000
Proposal B:	$200,000	1	$ 60,000	$100,000
		2	40,000	80,000
		3	20,000	60,000
		4	(10,000)	30,000
		5	(20,000)	20,000
			$ 90,000	$290,000

(Continued)

	Investment	Year	Income from Operations	Net Cash Flow
Proposal C:	$320,000	1	$ 36,000	$100,000
		2	26,000	90,000
		3	26,000	90,000
		4	16,000	80,000
		5	16,000	80,000
			$120,000	$440,000
Proposal D:	$540,000	1	$ 92,000	$200,000
		2	72,000	180,000
		3	52,000	160,000
		4	12,000	120,000
		5	(8,000)	100,000
			$220,000	$760,000

The company's capital rationing policy requires a maximum cash payback period of three years. In addition, a minimum average rate of return of 12% is required on all projects. If the preceding standards are met, the net present value method and present value indexes are used to rank the remaining proposals.

Instructions

1. Compute the cash payback period for each of the four proposals.

2. Giving effect to straight-line depreciation on the investments and assuming no estimated residual value, compute the average rate of return for each of the four proposals. (Round to one decimal place.)

3. Using the following format, summarize the results of your computations in parts (1) and (2). By placing the calculated amounts in the first two columns on the left and by placing a check mark in the appropriate column to the right, indicate which proposals should be accepted for further analysis and which should be rejected.

Proposal	Cash Payback Period	Average Rate of Return	Accept for Further Analysis	Reject
A				
B				
C				
D				

4. For the proposals accepted for further analysis in part (3), compute the net present value. Use a rate of 12% and the present value of $1 table appearing in this chapter (Exhibit 2).

5. Compute the present value index for each of the proposals in part (4). (Round to two decimal places.)

6. Rank the proposals from most attractive to least attractive, based on the present values of net cash flows computed in part (4).

7. Rank the proposals from most attractive to least attractive, based on the present value indexes computed in part (5).

8. Based on the analyses, comment on the relative attractiveness of the proposals ranked in parts (6) and (7).

Analysis for Decision Making

ADM-1 Wind turbine capital investment analysis

Central Plains Power Company is considering an investment in wind farm technology to reduce its use of natural gas. Initial installation costs are expected to be $1,200 per kilowatt-hour of capacity. The wind turbine has a capacity of generating 2 megawatts per hour. A kilowatt-hour is 1,000 watts generated per hour and a megawatt hour is 1,000 kilowatts generated per hour.

Annual operating information related to the wind turbine project was developed as follows:

Wind capacity factor	25%*
Operating cost per wind turbine megawatt hour	$10
Variable operating, fuel, and maintenance costs per natural gas megawatt hour	$95
Days per year	365

*A factor that measures the reduction from full capacity due to the variability of wind

A. Determine the initial investment cost of the wind turbine.

B. Determine the annual cost savings from the wind turbine in replacing natural gas generation. (Round to the nearest dollar.)

C. Determine the net present value of the project assuming a 15-year life and 12% minimum rate of return. (Use the present value tables in Appendix A.)

ADM-2 Paper reclaim capital investment analysis

The Victor Paper Company manufactures paper products from pulp. The process creates paper scrap from paper trim, off-grade, and machine errors. Presently, the scrap paper is discarded in a landfill. Management is considering a proposal for a scrap paper reclamation system. The system is designed so that paper is discarded in vacuum collection points located throughout the plant. The vacuum system would be attached to a reclaim process that would digest the scrap paper, turning it back into pulp, and then blending the reclaimed product back into the papermaking process with virgin (new) pulp. The blended stream is termed "blended pulp." It has been determined that the quality of the final product is not adversely impacted by using blended pulp versus using 100% virgin pulp. In addition, the cost of the reclaimed pulp is considered "free" to the blended stream, and causes the amount of virgin pulp used in the blended stream to be less than would be otherwise. These factors reduce the cost of the blended stream. Some information involving this proposal is as follows:

Reclaim system investment cost	$40,000,000
Annual operating cost of reclaim system	$500,000
Cost of virgin pulp	$600 per ton
Cost of blended pulp	$560 per ton
Finished processing volume	1,200 tons per day
Operating days per year	360

A. Determine the annual cost savings from using blended pulp.

B. Prepare a capital investment analysis using net present value to determine if the reclamation system is justified. Assume a 10-year life and 8% minimum rate of return. (Use the present value tables in Appendix A. Round present value calculations to the nearest dollar.)

ADM-3 Tire design capital investment analysis

AutoSource, Inc. designs and manufactures tires for automobiles. The company's strategy is to design products that incorporate the full environmental impact of the product over its life cycle. This includes designing tires for ease of recycling and fuel efficiency.

The technical team has determined that the tires manufactured with a silica blend will reduce road resistance. Thus, silica-blended tires will be significantly more fuel-efficient for the consumer without compromising tire life. To produce the silica-blended tires, AutoSource will need to invest $5,000,000 in new equipment. It is expected that the new tire will be attractive

(Continued)

to consumers and will result in increased tire sales. However, sales of conventional tires will be reduced as a result of the new silica-blended tires. To evaluate the project, the sales prices and costs of silica-blended and conventional tires are given as follows:

	Silica-Blended Tires	Conventional Tires
Sales price per tire	$160	$140
Material cost per tire	80	70
Variable manufacturing cost per tire	15	12

It is anticipated that there will be 80,000 silica-blended tires sold annually, while the sales of conventional tires will be reduced by 70,000 tires annually.

A. Determine the annual contribution margin for manufacturing and selling the silica-blended tires.

B. Determine the annual cash flows of manufacturing and selling silica-blended tires, incorporating the impact of lost sales from conventional tires.

C. Prepare a net present value analysis of the silica equipment investment assuming an eight-year life and 12% minimum rate of return. (Use the present value tables in Appendix A. Round to the nearest dollar.)

D. ▬▬▬▶ AutoSource is also concerned with the cost of recycling tires. What questions must the company consider for recycling silica-blended tires?

Take It Further

ETHICS

TIF 25-1 Ethics in Action

Danielle Hastings was recently hired as a cost analyst by CareNet Medical Supplies Inc. One of Danielle's first assignments was to perform a net present value analysis for a new warehouse. Danielle performed the analysis and calculated a present value index of 0.75. The plant manager, Jerrod Moore, is very intent on purchasing the warehouse because he believes that more storage space is needed. Jerrod asks Danielle into his office and the following conversation takes place:

Jerrod: Danielle, you're new here, aren't you?

Danielle: Yes, I am.

Jerrod: Well, Danielle, I'm not at all pleased with the capital investment analysis that you performed on this new warehouse. I need that warehouse for my production. If I don't get it, where am I going to place our output?

Danielle: Well, we need to get product into our customers' hands.

Jerrod: I agree, and we need a warehouse to do that.

Danielle: My analysis does not support constructing a new warehouse. The numbers don't lie; the warehouse does not meet our investment return targets. In fact, it seems to me that purchasing a warehouse does not add much value to the business. We need to be producing product to satisfy customer orders, not to fill a warehouse.

Jerrod: The headquarters people will not allow me to build the warehouse if the numbers don't add up. You know as well as I that many assumptions go into your net present value analysis. Why don't you relax some of your assumptions so that the financial savings will offset the cost?

Danielle: I'm willing to discuss my assumptions with you. Maybe I overlooked something.

Jerrod: Good. Here's what I want you to do. I see in your analysis that you don't project greater sales as a result of the warehouse. It seems to me that if we can store more goods, then we will have more to sell. Thus, logically, a larger warehouse translates into more sales. If you incorporate this into your analysis, I think you'll see that the numbers will work out. Why don't you work it through and come back with a new analysis. I'm really counting on you on this one. Let's get off to a good start together and see if we can get this project accepted.

▬▬▬▶ What is your advice to Danielle?

REAL WORLD

TIF 25-2 Team Activity

Divide your team into two groups. In one group, find a local business, such as a copy shop that rents time on desktop computers for an hourly rate. Determine the hourly rate. In the other group, determine the price of a mid-range desktop computer at www.dell.com. Combine this information from the two groups and perform a capital budgeting analysis. Assume that one student will use the computer for 40 hours per semester for the next three years. Also assume that the minimum rate of return is 10%. Use the interest tables in Appendix A in performing your analysis. [*Hint:* Use the appropriate present value of an annuity of $1 factor for 5% compounded for six semiannual periods (periods = 6).]

➤ Does your analysis support the student purchasing the computer?

TIF 25-3 Communication

Global Electronics Inc. invested $1,000,000 to build a plant in a foreign country. The labor and materials used in production are purchased locally. The plant expansion was estimated to produce an internal rate of return of 20% in U.S. dollar terms. Due to a currency crisis, the currency exchange rate between the local currency and the U.S. dollar doubled from two local units per U.S. dollar to four local units per U.S. dollar.

➤ Write a brief memo to the Chief Financial Officer, Tom Greene, explaining the impact that the currency exchange rate change would have on the project's internal rate of return if (1) the plant produced and sold product in the local economy only, and (2) the plant produced all product locally and exported all product to the United States for sale.

Concepts and Principles

Chapter 15 *Introduction to Managerial Accounting*

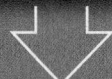

Developing Information

COST SYSTEMS	COST BEHAVIOR
Chapter 16 *Job Order Costing*	**Chapter 19** *Cost-Volume-Profit Analysis*
Chapter 17 *Process Cost Systems*	
Chapter 18 *Activity-Based Costing*	

Decision Making

EVALUATING PERFORMANCE	COMPARING ALTERNATIVES
Chapter 20 *Variable Costing for Management Analysis*	**Chapter 23** *Evaluating Decentralized Operations*
Chapter 21 *Budgeting*	**Chapter 24** *Differential Analysis and Product Pricing*
Chapter 22 *Evaluating Variances from Standard Costs*	**Chapter 25** *Capital Investment Analysis*
	Chapter 26 *Lean Manufacturing and Activity Analysis*

Precor Incorporated

When you order the salad bar at the local restaurant, you are able to serve yourself at your own pace. There is no waiting for the waitress to take the order or for the cook to prepare the meal. You are able to move directly to the salad bar and select from various offerings. You might wish to have salad with lettuce, cole slaw, bacon bits, croutons, and salad dressing. The offerings are arranged in a row so that you can build your salad as you move down the salad bar.

Many manufacturers are producing products in much the same way that the salad bar is designed to satisfy each customer's needs. Like customers at the salad bar, products move through a production process as they are built for each customer. Such a process eliminates many sources of waste, which is why it is called *lean*.

Using lean practices can improve performance. For example, when **Precor**, a manufacturer of fitness equipment, used lean principles, it improved its manufacturing operations and achieved the following results:

- Increased on-time shipments from near 40% to above 90%.
- Decreased direct labor costs by 30%.
- Reduced the number of suppliers from 3,000 to under 250.
- Reduced inventory by 40%.
- Reduced warranty claims by almost 60%.

In this chapter, lean practices are described and illustrated. The chapter concludes by describing and illustrating the accounting for quality costs and activity analysis.

What's Covered

Lean Manufacturing and Activity Analysis

Principles of Lean Manufacturing
- Reducing Inventory (Obj. 1)
- Reducing Lead Times (Obj. 1)
- Reducing Setup Time (Obj. 1)
- Product-Oriented Layout (Obj. 1)
- Employee Involvement (Obj. 1)
- Pull Manufacturing (Obj. 1)
- Zero Defects (Obj. 1)
- Supply Chain Management (Obj. 1)

Accounting for Lean Manufacturing
- Fewer Transactions (Obj. 2)
- Combined Accounts (Obj. 2)
- Nonfinancial Performance Measures (Obj. 2)
- Direct Tracing of Overhead (Obj. 2)

Activity Analysis
- Costs of Quality (Obj. 3)
- Quality Activity Analysis (Obj. 3)
- Value-Added Activity Analysis (Obj. 3)
- Process Activity Analysis (Obj. 3)

Learning Objectives

Obj. 1 Describe lean manufacturing practices.

Obj. 2 Describe the implications of lean manufacturing on the accounting system.

Obj. 3 Describe and illustrate activity analysis for improving operations.

Analysis for Decision Making

Describe and illustrate the use of lean principles and activity analysis in a service or administrative setting.

Objective 1
Describe lean manufacturing practices.

Lean Principles

The **lean enterprise** is a business that produces products or services with high quality, low cost, fast response, and immediate availability. **Lean manufacturing**, sometimes called *just-in-time processing (JIT)*, accomplishes these objectives in a manufacturing setting. Both manufacturing and nonmanufacturing businesses use **lean principles** to accomplish these service and cost objectives. However, these principles will be discussed within the context of lean manufacturing. Lean manufacturing principles are listed and contrasted with traditional manufacturing principles in Exhibit 1.

Exhibit 1 Lean versus Traditional Manufacturing Principles

Issue	Lean Manufacturing	Traditional Manufacturing
Inventory	Reduces inventory.	Increases inventory to protect against process problems.
Lead time	Reduces lead time.	Increases lead time to protect against uncertainty.
Setup time	Reduces setup time.	Disregards setup time as an improvement priority.
Production layout	Emphasizes product-oriented layout.	Emphasizes process-oriented layout.
Role of the employee	Emphasizes team-oriented employee involvement.	Emphasizes work of individuals, following manager instructions.
Production scheduling policy	Emphasizes pull manufacturing.	Emphasizes push manufacturing.
Quality	Emphasizes zero defects.	Tolerates defects.
Suppliers and customers	Emphasizes supply chain management.	Treats suppliers and customers as "arm's-length," independent entities.

Link to Precor **Precor** was established in 1980 when the company began selling a rowing machine that supported the natural movement of the human body. Precor is currently owned by Amer Sports Corporation.

Reducing Inventory

Lean manufacturing views inventory as wasteful and unnecessary, and thus emphasizes reducing or eliminating inventory.

Under traditional manufacturing, inventory often hides underlying production problems. For example, if machine breakdowns occur, work in process inventories can be used to keep production running in other departments while the machines are being repaired. Likewise, inventories can be used to hide problems caused by a shortage of trained employees, unreliable suppliers, or poor product quality.

In contrast, lean manufacturing solves and removes production problems. In this way, raw materials, work in process, and finished goods inventories are reduced or eliminated.

The role of inventory in manufacturing can be illustrated using a river, as shown in Exhibit 2. Inventory is the water in a river. The rocks at the bottom of the river are production problems. When the water level (inventory) is high, the rocks (production problems) at the bottom of the river are hidden. As the water level (inventory) drops, the rocks (production problems) become visible, one by one. Lean manufacturing reduces the water level (inventory), exposes the rocks (production problems), and removes the rocks so that the river can flow smoothly.

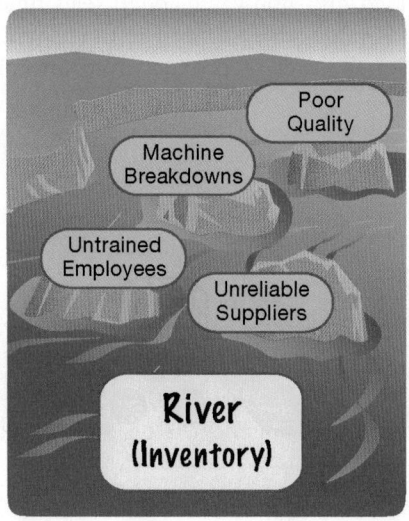

Exhibit 2
Inventory's Role in Manufacturing

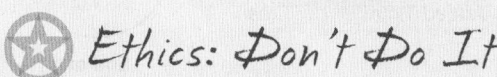

The Inventory Shift

Some managers take a shortcut to reducing inventory by shifting inventory to their suppliers. With this tactic, the hard work of improving processes is avoided. Enlightened managers realize that such tactics often have short-lived savings. Suppliers will eventually increase their prices to compensate for the additional inventory holding costs, thus resulting in no savings. Therefore, shifting a problem doesn't eliminate a problem.

Reducing Lead Times

Lead time, sometimes called *throughput time*, measures the time interval between when a product enters production (started) and when it is completed (finished). That is, lead time measures how long it takes to manufacture a product. To illustrate, in Exhibit 3, if a product enters production at 1:00 P.M. and is completed at 5:00 P.M., the lead time is four hours.

Exhibit 3
Lead Time

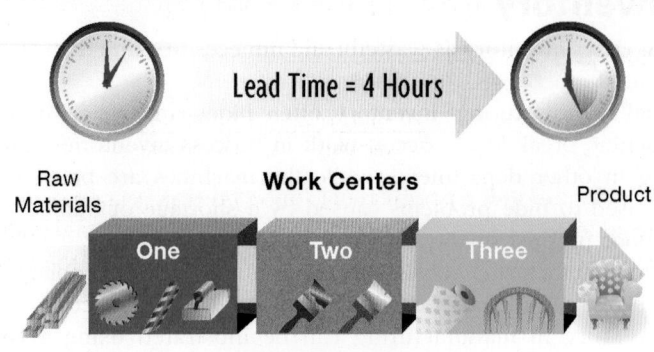

Production Process

The lead time can be classified as one of the following:

- **Value-added lead time**, which is the time spent in converting raw materials into a finished unit of product
- **Non-value-added lead time**, which is the time spent while the unit of product is waiting to enter the next production process or is moved from one process to another

Exhibit 4 illustrates value-added and non-value-added lead time. The time spent drilling and packing the unit of product is value-added time. The time spent waiting to enter the next process or the time spent moving the unit of product from one process to another is non-value-added time.

Exhibit 4   Components of Lead Time

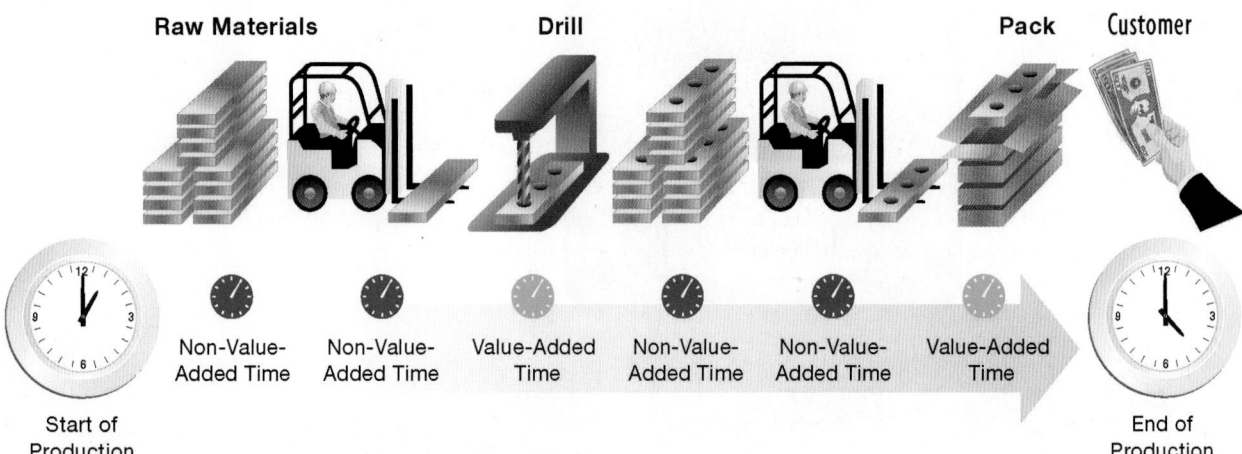

The **value-added ratio** is computed as follows:

$$\text{Value-Added Ratio} = \frac{\text{Value-Added Lead Time}}{\text{Total Lead Time}}$$

To illustrate, assume that the lead time to manufacture a unit of product is as follows (value-added times are highlighted):

Move raw materials to machining	5 minutes
Machining	35
Move time to assembly	10
Assembly	20
Move time to packing	15
Wait time for packing	30
Packing	10
Total lead time	125 minutes

The value-added ratio for the preceding product is 52%, computed as follows:

$$\text{Value-Added Ratio} = \frac{\text{Value-Added Lead Time}}{\text{Total Lead Time}}$$

$$= \frac{(35 + 20 + 10)\text{ minutes}}{125\text{ minutes}} = \frac{65\text{ minutes}}{125\text{ minutes}} = 52\%$$

A low value-added ratio indicates a poor manufacturing process. A good manufacturing process will reduce non-value-added lead time to a minimum and thus have a high value-added ratio.

Lean manufacturing reduces or eliminates non-value-added time. In contrast, traditional manufacturing processes may have a value-added ratio as small as 5%.

Reducing Setup Time

A *setup* is the effort spent preparing an operation or process for production. A **batch size** is the amount of production in units of product that is produced after a setup. If setups are long and costly, the batch size for the related production run is normally large. Large batch sizes allow setup costs to be spread over more units and, thus, reduce the cost per unit. However, large batch sizes increase inventory and lead time.

Exhibit 5 shows the relationship between setup times and lead time.

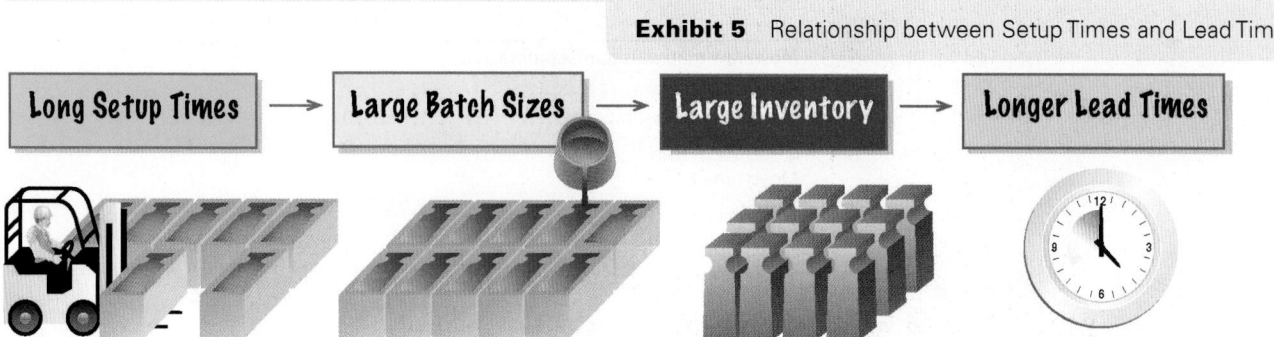

Exhibit 5 Relationship between Setup Times and Lead Time

To help understand the relationship of batch sizes to lead time, consider a group of 10 friends purchasing a ticket at a single-window ticket counter as shown in Exhibit 6.

Exhibit 6
Batch Size and
Lead Time

The friends are traveling together, so they are like a "batch" of production. If each friend takes one minute to purchase a ticket, the other nine friends are either waiting in line, or waiting for the remaining friends to finish. Thus, it takes 10 minutes for all of the friends to receive tickets as a group, but it took only one minute for any one friend to actually buy a ticket.

The amount of time each friend is waiting is called within-batch wait time. The total within-batch wait time is computed as follows:

Total Within-Batch Wait Time = (Value-Added Time) × (Batch Size − 1)

In this example, the value-added time is the 1 minute to purchase a ticket. So the total within-batch wait time is 9 minutes, computed as follows:

$$\text{Total Within-Batch Wait Time} = 1 \text{ minute} \times (10 - 1) = 9 \text{ minutes}$$

The value added ratio is 10%, computed as follows:

$$\text{Value-Added Ratio} = \frac{\text{Value-Added Lead Time}}{\text{Total Lead Time}}$$

$$= \frac{1 \text{ minute}}{10 \text{ minutes}} = 10\%$$

Now consider someone buying a ticket without a group of friends present. A single person would only take one minute to buy the ticket, with no waiting for friends. In this case, the lead-time drops down to one minute, or simply the time to purchase the ticket, and the value-added ratio is 100%.

Lean manufacturing emphasizes decreasing setup times in order to reduce the batch size, whereas traditional manufacturing does not treat setup improvement as an important priority. By reducing batch sizes, work in process inventory and within-batch wait time decrease, thus reducing total lead-time and increasing the value-added ratio.

To illustrate in a manufacturing setting, assume that Automotive Components Inc. manufactures engine starters as follows (value-added times are highlighted):

	Processing Time per Unit
Move raw materials to Machining..........	5 minutes
Machining	7
Move time to Assembly	10
Assembly	9
Move time to Testing	10
Testing	8
Total	49 minutes
Batch size	40 units

The total lead time is 985 minutes, computed as follows:

Value-added time (7 + 9 + 8)	24 minutes
Move time (5 + 10 + 10)	25
Total within-batch wait time	936*
Total time	985 minutes

*Total Within-Batch Wait Time = (Value-Added Time) × (Batch Size – 1)
= (7 + 9 + 8) minutes × (40 – 1) = 24 minutes × 39
= 936 minutes

Of the total lead time of 985 minutes, 24 minutes is value-added time and 961 minutes (985 – 24) is non-value-added time. The total non-value-added time of 961 minutes can also be determined as the sum of the total within-batch time of 936 minutes plus the move time of 25 minutes.

Based on the preceding data, the value-added ratio is approximately 2.4%, computed as follows:

$$\text{Value-Added Ratio} = \frac{\text{Value-Added Lead Time}}{\text{Total Lead Time}}$$

$$= \frac{(7 + 9 + 8) \text{ minutes}}{985 \text{ minutes}} = \frac{24 \text{ minutes}}{985 \text{ minutes}} = 2.4\% \text{ (rounded)}$$

Thus, the non-value-added time for Automotive Components Inc. is approximately 97.6% (100% – 2.4%).

Automotive Components can increase its value-added ratio by reducing setups so that the batch size is one unit, called *one-piece flow.* Automotive Components could also move the Machining, Assembly, and Testing activities closer to each other so that the move time could be reduced. With these changes, Automotive Components' value-added ratio would increase.

Why It Matters

P&G's "Pit Stops"

What do **Procter & Gamble (P&G)** and **Formula One** racing have in common? P&G answered this question by realizing that Formula One racing pit stops could teach the company how to more quickly change over from one sized package to another on its packing lines. As a result, P&G videotaped actual Formula One pit stops to identify the principles for conducting a fast setup, as follows:

- Position the tools near their point of use on the line prior to stopping the line, to reduce time going back and forth to the tool room.

- Arrange the tools in the exact order of work, so that no time is wasted looking for a tool.
- Have each employee perform a very specific task during the setup.
- Design the workflow so that employees don't interfere with each other.
- Have each employee in position at the moment the line is stopped.
- Train each employee, and practice, practice, practice.
- Put a stop watch on the setup process.
- Plot improvements over time on a visible chart.

As a result of these changes, P&G was able to reduce packline setup time from several hours to 20 minutes. This decrease allowed the company to reduce lead time and to improve the cost performance of the Packing Department.

Emphasizing Product-Oriented Layout

Manufacturing processes can be organized around a product, which is called a **product-oriented layout** (or *product cells*). Alternatively, manufacturing processes can be organized around a process, which is called a **process-oriented layout**.

Lean manufacturing normally organizes manufacturing around products rather than processes. Organizing work around products reduces:

- Moving materials and products between processes
- Work in process inventory
- Lead time
- Production costs

In addition, a product-oriented layout improves coordination among the various work activities, or operations, of the facility.

Emphasizing Employee Involvement

Traditional manufacturing often values direct labor employees only for their manual labor, whereas lean manufacturing values labor for contributions beyond labor tasks, using employee involvement. **Employee involvement** is a management approach that grants employees the responsibility and authority to make decisions about operations. Employee involvement is often applied in lean manufacturing by organizing employees into *product cells*. Within each product cell, employees are organized as teams where the employees are cross-trained to perform any operation within the product cell.

To illustrate, employees learn how to operate several different machines within their product cell. In addition, team members are trained to perform functions traditionally performed by centralized service departments. For example, product cell employees may perform their own equipment maintenance, quality control, housekeeping, and improvement studies.

Precor encourages a collaborative, innovative environment for its employees. Precor believes that its employees are its #1 asset.

Link to Precor

Emphasizing Pull Manufacturing

Pull manufacturing (or *make to order*) is an important lean practice. In pull manufacturing, products are manufactured only as they are needed by the customer. Products can be thought of as being pulled through the manufacturing process. In other words, the status of the next operation determines when products are moved or produced. If the next operation is busy, production stops so that work in process does not pile up in front of the busy operation. When the next operation is ready, the product is moved to that operation.

A system used in pull manufacturing is *kanban*, which is Japanese for "cards." Electronic cards or containers signal production quantities to be filled by the preceding operation. The cards link the customer's order for a product back through each stage of production. In other words, when a consumer orders a product, a kanban card triggers the manufacture of the product.

In contrast, the traditional approach to manufacturing is based on estimated customer demand. This principle is called **push manufacturing** (or make to stock). In push manufacturing, products are manufactured according to a production schedule that is based upon estimated sales. The schedule "pushes" product into inventory before customer orders are received. As a result, push manufacturers normally have more inventory than pull manufacturers.

Emphasizing Zero Defects

Lean manufacturing attempts to eliminate poor quality. Poor quality creates:

- Scrap
- Rework, which is fixing product made wrong the first time
- Disruption in the production process
- Dissatisfied customers
- Warranty costs and expenses

One way to improve product quality and manufacturing processes is Six Sigma. **Six Sigma** was developed by Motorola Corporation and consists of five steps: define, measure, analyze, improve, and control (DMAIC).[1] Since its development, Six Sigma has been adopted by thousands of organizations worldwide.

Emphasizing Supply Chain Management

Supply chain management coordinates and controls the flow of materials, services, information, and finances with suppliers, manufacturers, and customers. Supply chain management partners with suppliers using long-term agreements. These agreements ensure that products are delivered with the right quality, at the right cost, at the right time.

To enhance the interchange of information between suppliers and customers, supply chain management often uses:

- **Electronic data interchange (EDI)**, which uses computers to electronically communicate orders, relay information, and make or receive payments from one organization to another
- **Radio frequency identification devices (RFID)**, which are electronic tags (chips) placed on or embedded within products that can be read by radio waves that allow instant monitoring of product location
- **Enterprise resource planning (ERP)** systems, which are used to plan and control internal and supply chain operations

Why It Matters

Lean Manufacturing in Action

- Yamaha manufactures musical instruments such as trumpets, horns, saxophones, clarinets, and flutes using **product-oriented layouts**.
- Sony uses **employee involvement** to organize employees into small, four-person teams to completely assemble a camcorder, doing everything from soldering to testing. This team-based approach reduces assembly time from 70 minutes to 15 minutes per camcorder.

- Kenney Manufacturing Company, a manufacturer of window shades, estimated that 50% of its window shade process was non-value-added. By using **pull manufacturing** and changing the line layout, it was able to reduce inventory by 82% and lead time by 84%.
- Motorola has claimed over $17 billion in savings from **Six Sigma**.
- Hyundia/Kia Motors Group will use 20 million RFID tags annually to track automotive parts from its suppliers, providing greater **supply chain** transparency and flexibility.

[1] The term "Six Sigma" refers to a statistical property where a process has less than 3.4 defects per one million items.

Check Up Corner 26-1   Lean Concepts and Lead Time Analysis

I. Lean Concepts

Match the following lean concepts with the appropriate description.

Concept	Description
1. Batch	A. Measures the time interval between when a product enters production and when it is completed.
2. Lead time	
3. Product-oriented layout	B. Manufacturing process that reduces (1) moving materials and products between processes, (2) work-in process inventory, (3) lead time, and (4) production costs.
4. Pull manufacturing	
5. Setup time	C. The effort spent preparing an operation or process for production.
	D. Products are manufactured only as they are needed by the customer.
	E. The amount of production in units of product that is produced after setup.

II. Lead Time Analysis

The Helping Hands Company manufactures designer gloves. Gloves are manufactured in 50-glove batch sizes, and cut and assembled by the company's workforce. The cutting time is 4 minutes per glove. The assembly time is 6 minutes per glove. It takes 12 minutes to move a batch of gloves from cutting to assembly.

A. For this process, compute (1) the value-added lead time, (2) the non-value-added lead time, and (3) total lead time.
B. Compute the value-added ratio. (Round to one decimal place.)

Solution:

I.

1. E
2. A
3. B
4. D
5. C

II.

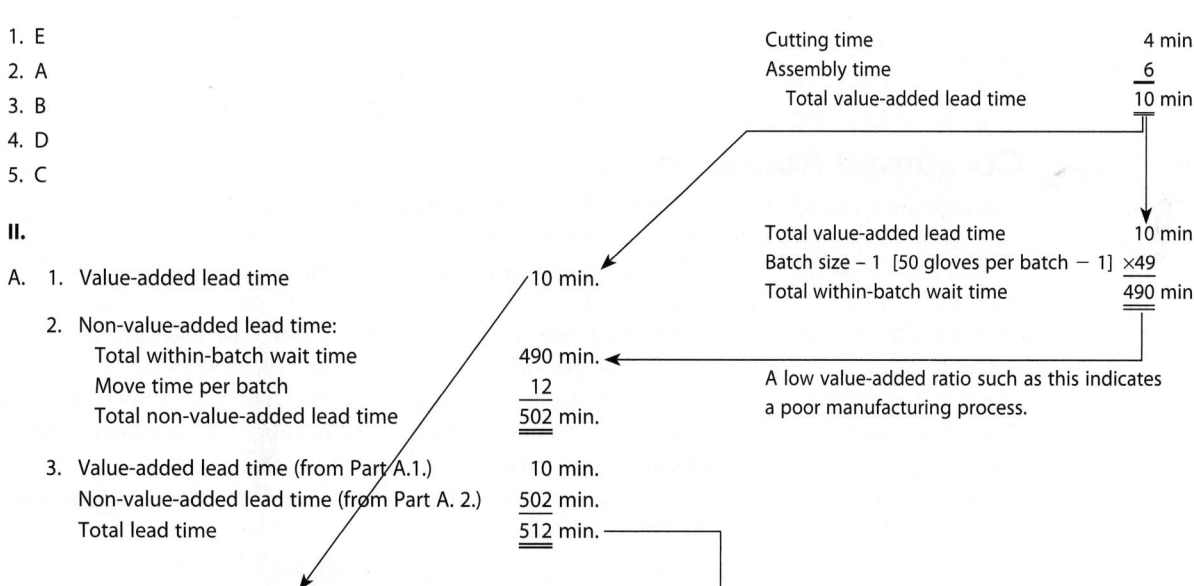

Cutting time		4 min.
Assembly time		6
Total value-added lead time		10 min.

Total value-added lead time		10 min.
Batch size – 1 [50 gloves per batch – 1]	×49	
Total within-batch wait time		490 min.

A. 1. Value-added lead time   10 min.

   2. Non-value-added lead time:
     Total within-batch wait time   490 min.
     Move time per batch   12
     Total non-value-added lead time   502 min.

A low value-added ratio such as this indicates a poor manufacturing process.

   3. Value-added lead time (from Part A.1.)   10 min.
     Non-value-added lead time (from Part A. 2.)   502 min.
     Total lead time   512 min.

B. Value-added ratio: $\dfrac{10 \text{ min.}}{512 \text{ min.}} = 2.0\%$ (rounded)

Objective 2

Describe the implications of lean manufacturing on the accounting system.

Lean Accounting

In lean manufacturing, the accounting system reflects the lean philosophy. Such systems are called **lean accounting**, and have the following characteristics:

- *Fewer transactions.* There are fewer transactions to record, thus simplifying the accounting system.
- *Combined accounts.* All in-process work is combined with raw materials to form a new account, **Raw and In Process (RIP) Inventory**. Direct labor is also combined with other costs to form a new account titled **Conversion Costs**.
- *Nonfinancial performance measures.* Nonfinancial performance measures are emphasized.
- *Direct tracing of overhead.* Indirect labor is directly assigned to product cells; thus, less factory overhead is allocated to products.

Fewer Transactions

The traditional process cost accounting system accumulates product costs by department. These costs are transferred from department to department as the product is manufactured. Thus, materials are recorded into and out of work in process inventories as the product moves through the factory.

The recording of product costs by departments facilitates the control of costs. However, this requires that many transactions and costs be recorded and reported. This adds cost and complexity to the cost accounting system.

In lean manufacturing, there is less need for cost control. This is because lower inventory levels make problems more visible. That is, managers don't need accounting reports to indicate problems because any problems become immediately known.

The lean accounting system uses **backflush accounting**. Backflush accounting simplifies the accounting system by eliminating the accumulation and transfer of product costs by departments, but instead pulls material and conversion costs directly to finished goods. Thus, efficiency is gained by not transferring costs through intermediate departmental work in process accounts.

Combined Accounts

Materials are received directly by the product cells and enter immediately into production. Thus, there is no central materials inventory location (warehouse) or a materials account. Instead, lean accounting debits all materials and conversion costs to an account titled *Raw and In Process Inventory.* Doing so combines materials and work in process costs into one account.

Lean manufacturing often does not use a separate direct labor cost classification. This is because the employees in product cells perform many tasks. Some of these tasks could be classified as direct, such as performing operations, and some as indirect, such as performing repairs. Thus, labor cost (direct and indirect) is combined with other product cell overhead costs and recorded in an account titled *Conversion Costs.*

To illustrate, assume the following data for Anderson Metal Fabricators, a manufacturer of metal covers for electronic test equipment:

Budgeted conversion cost $2,400,000
Planned hours of production . . . .   1,920 hours

The cell conversion cost rate is determined as follows:

$$\text{Cell Conversion Cost Rate} = \frac{\text{Budgeted Conversion Cost}}{\text{Planned Hours of Production}}$$

$$= \frac{\$2,400,000}{1,920 \text{ hours}} = \$1,250 \text{ per hour}$$

The cell conversion rate is similar to a predetermined factory overhead rate, except that it includes all conversion costs in the numerator.

Assume that Anderson Metal's cover product cell is expected to require 0.02 hour of manufacturing time per unit. Thus, the conversion cost for the cover is $25 per unit, computed as follows:

Conversion Cost for Cover = Manufacturing Time × Cell Conversion Cost Rate

= 0.02 hour × $1,250 = $25 per unit

The recording of selected lean accounting transactions for Anderson Metal Fabricators for April is illustrated in Exhibit 7.

Exhibit 7 Transactions Using Lean Accounting—Anderson Metal Fabricators

Transaction	Journal Entry	Comment
	Raw and In Process Inventory .... 120,000 　Accounts Payable .... 120,000 　　To record materials purchases.	Note that the materials purchased are debited to the combined account, Raw and In Process Inventory. A separate materials account is not used, because materials are received directly in the product cells, rather than in an inventory location.
Conversion costs are applied to 8,000 covers at a rate of $25 per cover.	Raw and In Process Inventory .... 200,000 　Conversion Costs.................... 200,000 　　To record applied conversion 　　costs of the medium-cover line.	The raw and in process inventory account is used to accumulate the applied cell conversion costs during the period. The credit to Conversion Costs is similar to the treatment of applied factory overhead.
All 8,000 covers were completed in the cell. The raw and in process inventory account is reduced by the $15 per unit materials cost and the $25 per unit conversion cost.	Finished Goods Inventory.............. 320,000 　Raw and In Process Inventory .... 320,000 　　To transfer the cost of completed 　　units to finished goods.	Materials ($15 × 8,000 units) .... $120,000 Conversion ($25 × 8,000 units) .... 200,000 　Total .... $320,000 After the cost of the completed units is transferred from the raw and in process inventory account, the account's balance is zero. There are no units left in process within the cell.[2] This is a backflush transaction.
Of the 8,000 units completed, 7,800 were sold and shipped to customers at $70 per unit, leaving 200 finished units in stock. Thus, the finished goods inventory account has a balance of $8,000 (200 × $40).	Accounts Receivable................... 546,000 　Sales.............................. 546,000 　　To record sales. Cost of Goods Sold .... 312,000 　Finished Goods Inventory .... 312,000 　　To record cost of goods sold.	Units sold .... 7,800 Conversion and materials 　cost per unit .... × $40 Transferred to Cost of Goods Sold $312,000

[2] The actual conversion cost per unit may be different from the budgeted conversion cost per unit due to cell inefficiency, improvements in processing methods, or excess scrap. These deviations from the budgeted cost can be accounted for as cost variances, as illustrated in more advanced texts.

Check Up Corner 26-2 　Lean Accounting

The budgeted conversion costs for a lean cell are $142,500 for 1,900 production hours. Each unit produced by the cell requires 10 minutes of cell process time. During the month, 1,050 units are manufactured in the cell. The estimated materials cost is $46 per unit. Journalize entries for the following:

A. Materials are purchased to produce 1,100 units.
B. Conversion costs are applied to 1,050 units of production.
C. The cell completes 1,030 units, which are placed into finished goods.

Solution:

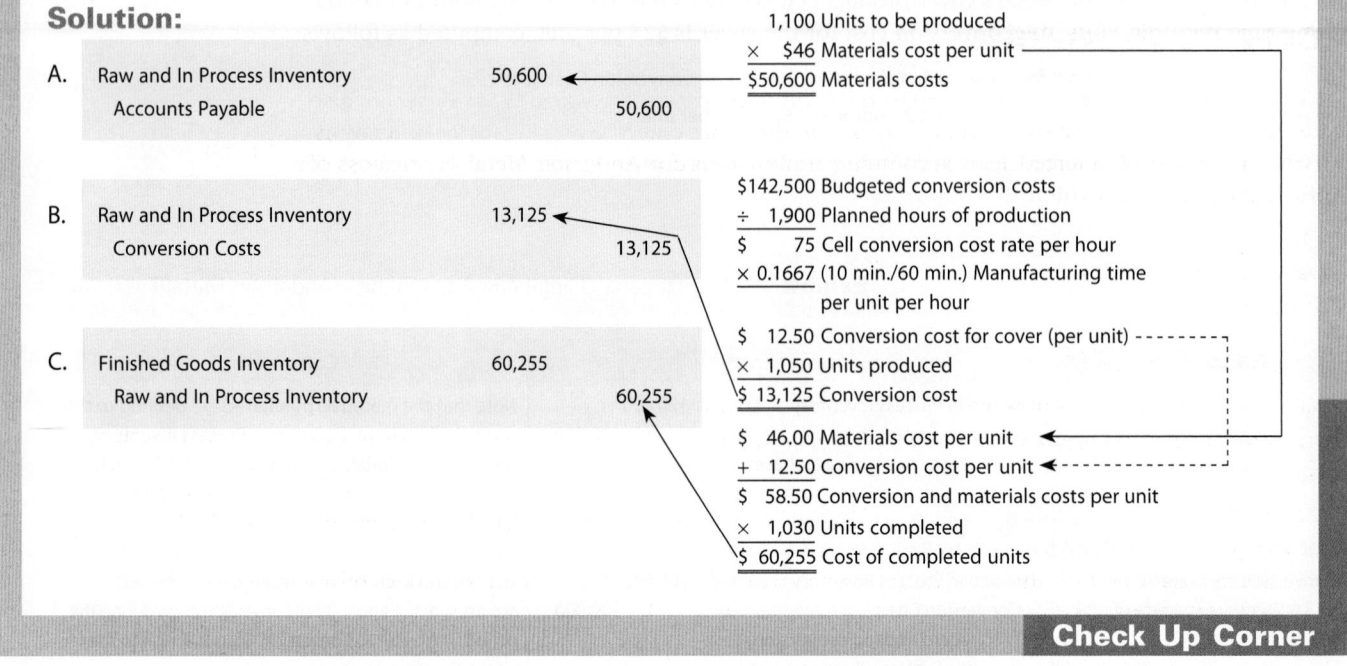

A.

Raw and In Process Inventory	50,600	
Accounts Payable		50,600

B.

Raw and In Process Inventory	13,125	
Conversion Costs		13,125

C.

Finished Goods Inventory	60,255	
Raw and In Process Inventory		60,255

1,100	Units to be produced
× $46	Materials cost per unit
$50,600	Materials costs

$142,500	Budgeted conversion costs
÷ 1,900	Planned hours of production
$ 75	Cell conversion cost rate per hour
× 0.1667	(10 min./60 min.) Manufacturing time per unit per hour
$ 12.50	Conversion cost for cover (per unit)
× 1,050	Units produced
$ 13,125	Conversion cost

$ 46.00	Materials cost per unit
+ 12.50	Conversion cost per unit
$ 58.50	Conversion and materials costs per unit
× 1,030	Units completed
$ 60,255	Cost of completed units

Check Up Corner

Nonfinancial Performance Measures

Lean manufacturing normally uses nonfinancial measures to help guide short-term operating performance. A **nonfinancial measure** is operating information not stated in dollar terms. Examples of nonfinancial measures of performance include:

- Lead time
- Value-added ratio
- Setup time
- Number of production line stops
- Number of units scrapped
- Deviations from scheduled production
- Number of failed inspections

Most companies use a combination of financial and nonfinancial operating measures, which are often referred to as *key performance indicators* (or *KPIs*). Nonfinancial measures are often available more quickly than financial measures. Thus, nonfinancial measures are often used for day-to-day operating decisions that require quick feedback. In contrast, traditional financial accounting measures are often used for longer-term operating decisions.

Direct Tracing of Overhead

In lean manufacturing, many indirect tasks are assigned to a product cell. For example, maintenance department personnel may be assigned to a product cell and cross-trained to perform other operations. Thus, the salary of maintenance personnel can be traced directly to the product cell and, thus, to the product.

In traditional manufacturing, maintenance personnel are part of the maintenance department. The cost of the maintenance department is then allocated to products based on predetermined factory overhead rates. Such allocations are not necessary when maintenance personnel are assigned directly to a product cell.

Activity Analysis

In Chapter 18, we discussed activity-based costing for product costing. Activities can also be used to support operational improvement in the lean enterprise using activity analysis. **Activity analysis** determines the cost of activities for the purpose of determining the cost of the following:

- Quality
- Value-added activities
- Processes

Costs of Quality

Competition encourages businesses to emphasize high-quality products, services, and processes. In doing so, businesses incur **costs of quality**, as illustrated in Exhibit 8. These costs of quality can be classified as follows:

- **Prevention costs**, which are costs of preventing defects before or during the manufacture of the product or delivery of services

    Examples: Costs of engineering good product design, controlling vendor quality, training equipment operators, maintaining equipment

- **Appraisal costs**, which are costs of activities that detect, measure, evaluate, and inspect products and processes to ensure that they meet customer needs

    Examples: Costs of inspecting and testing products

- **Internal failure costs**, which are costs associated with defects discovered before the product is delivered to the consumer

    Examples: Cost of scrap and rework

- **External failure costs**, which are costs incurred after defective products have been delivered to consumers

    Examples: Cost of recalls and warranty work

Exhibit 8 Costs of Quality

Costs of Controlling Quality — Prevention Costs, Appraisal Costs
Costs of Failing to Control Quality — Internal Failure Costs, External Failure Costs

Prevention and appraisal costs can be thought of as costs of controlling quality *before* any products are known to be defective. Internal and external failure costs can be thought of as the cost of controlling quality *after* products have become defective. Internal and external failure costs also can be thought of as the costs of "failing to control quality" through prevention and appraisal efforts.

Prevention and appraisal costs are incurred *before* the product is manufactured or delivered to the customer. Prevention costs are incurred in an attempt to permanently improve product quality. In contrast, appraisal costs are incurred in an attempt to limit the amount of defective products that "slip out the door."

Internal and external failure costs are incurred *after* the defective products have been discovered. In addition to costs of scrap and rework, internal failure costs may be incurred for lost equipment time because of rework and the costs of carrying additional inventory used for reworking. In addition to costs of recall and warranty work, external failure costs include the loss of customer goodwill. Although the loss of customer goodwill is difficult to measure, it may be the largest and most important quality control cost.

Link to Precor   **Precor** provides training and workout videos on how to use its equipment.

The relationship between the costs of quality is shown in Exhibit 9. The graph in Exhibit 9 indicates that as prevention and appraisal costs (blue line) increase, the percent of good units increases. In contrast, as internal and external failure costs (green line) decrease, the percent of good units increases. Total quality costs (red line) is the sum of the prevention/appraisal costs and internal/external failure costs.

Exhibit 9

The Relationship between the Costs of Quality

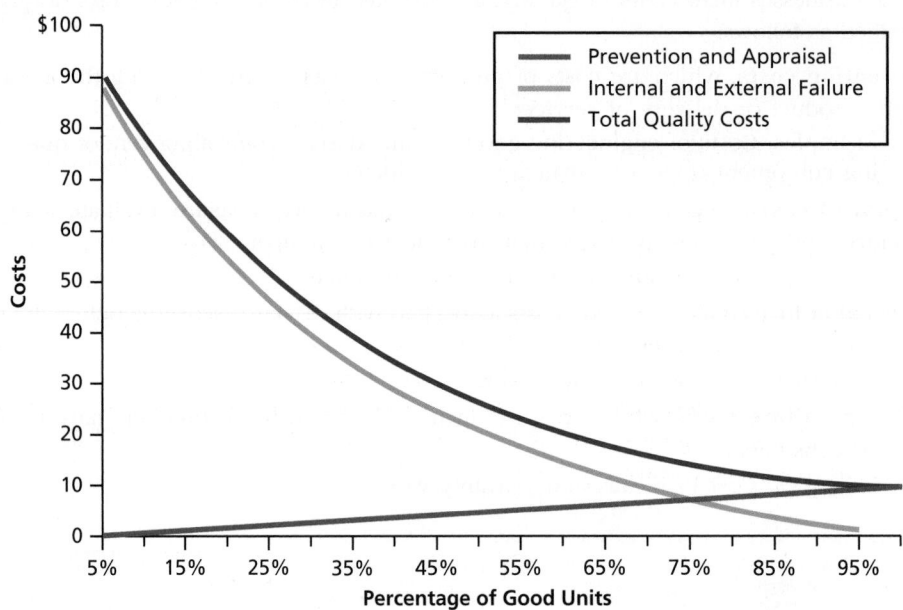

The optimal level of quality (percent of good units) is the one that minimizes the total quality costs. At this point, prevention and appraisal costs are balanced against internal and external failure costs. Exhibit 9 indicates that the optimal level of quality occurs at (or near) 100% quality. This is because prevention and appraisal costs grow moderately as quality increases. However, the costs of internal and external failure drop dramatically as quality increases.

Why It Matters

External Failure Costs: Lululemon Stretched Thin

Lululemon Athletica Inc. experienced a significant product recall in 2013 because its women's black luon pants produced a visible level of "sheerness," which was deemed unacceptable to its customers. It was discovered that the material purchased for the product failed to meet its technical specifications. As a result, 17% of the pants were recalled and returned to the manufacturer, resulting in rework, allowances, and nearly $60 million in lost revenues.

Source: E. Tovar, "Cost of Quality: Case Study of Lululemon Recall 2013," *Prezi.com,* February 14, 2014.

Quality Activity Analysis

An activity analysis of quality quantifies the costs of quality in dollar terms. To illustrate, the quality control activities, activity costs, and quality cost classifications for Gifford Company, a consumer electronics company, are shown in Exhibit 10.

Quality Control Activities	Activity Cost	Quality Cost Classification
Design engineering	$ 55,000	Prevention
Disposing of rejected materials	160,000	Internal Failure
Finished goods inspection	140,000	Appraisal
Materials inspection	70,000	Appraisal
Preventive maintenance	80,000	Prevention
Processing returned materials	150,000	External Failure
Disposing of scrap	195,000	Internal Failure
Assessing vendor quality	45,000	Prevention
Rework	380,000	Internal Failure
Warranty work	225,000	External Failure
Total activity cost	$1,500,000	

Exhibit 10
Quality Control Activity Analysis— Gifford Company

Pareto Chart of Quality Costs One method of reporting quality cost information is using a Pareto chart. A **Pareto chart** is a bar chart that shows the totals of an attribute for a number of categories. The categories are ranked and shown left to right, so that the largest total attribute is on the left and the smallest total is on the right.

To illustrate, Exhibit 11 is a Pareto chart for the quality control activities in Exhibit 10. In Exhibit 11, the vertical axis is dollars, which represents quality control costs. The horizontal axis represents activity categories, which are the 10 quality control cost activities. The 10 quality control cost categories are ranked from the one with the largest total on the left to the one with the smallest total on the right. Thus, the largest bar on the left is rework costs ($380,000), the second bar is warranty work ($225,000), and so on.

The Pareto chart gives managers a quick visual tool for identifying the most important quality control cost categories. Exhibit 11 indicates that Gifford Company should focus efforts on reducing rework and warranty costs.

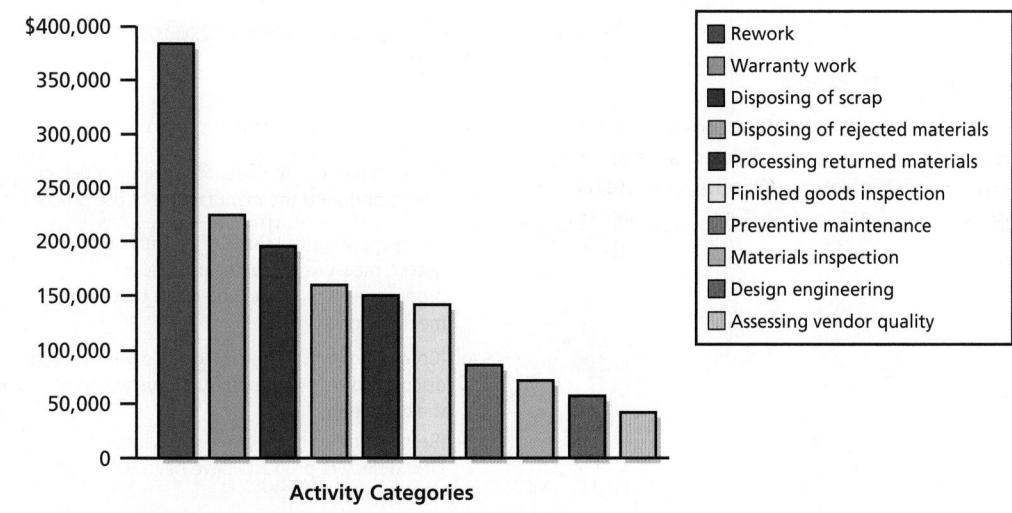

Exhibit 11
Pareto Chart of Quality Costs

Cost of Quality Report The costs of quality also can be summarized in a cost of quality report. A **cost of quality report** normally reports the following:

- Total activity cost for each quality cost classification
- Percent of total quality costs associated with each classification
- Percent of each quality cost classification to sales

Exhibit 12 is a cost of quality report for Gifford Company, based on assumed sales of $5,000,000. Exhibit 12 indicates that only 12% of the total quality cost is the cost of preventing quality problems, while 14% is the cost of appraisal activities. Thus, prevention and appraisal costs make up only 26% of the total quality control costs. In contrast, 74% (49% + 25%) of the quality control costs are incurred for internal (49%) and external failure (25%) costs. In addition, internal and external failure costs are 22.2% (14.7% + 7.5%) of sales.

Exhibit 12 implies that Gifford Company is not spending enough on prevention and appraisal activities. By spending more on prevention and appraisal, internal and external failure costs will decrease, as was shown in Exhibit 9.

Exhibit 12
Cost of Quality Report—Gifford Company

Gifford Company
Cost of Quality Report

Quality Cost Classification	Quality Cost	Percent of Total Quality Cost	Percent of Total Sales
Prevention	$ 180,000	12%	3.6%
Appraisal	210,000	14	4.2
Internal failure	735,000	49	14.7
External failure	375,000	25	7.5
Total	$1,500,000	100%	30.0%

Check Up Corner 26-3 Cost of Quality Report

A quality control activity analysis indicated the following four activity costs of an administrative department:

Verifying the accuracy of a form	$ 50,000
Responding to customer complaints	100,000
Correcting errors in forms	75,000
Redesigning forms to reduce errors	25,000
Total	$250,000

Sales are $2,000,000. Prepare a cost of quality report.

Associated activity cost ÷ $250,000

Solution:

Associated activity cost ÷ $2,000,000

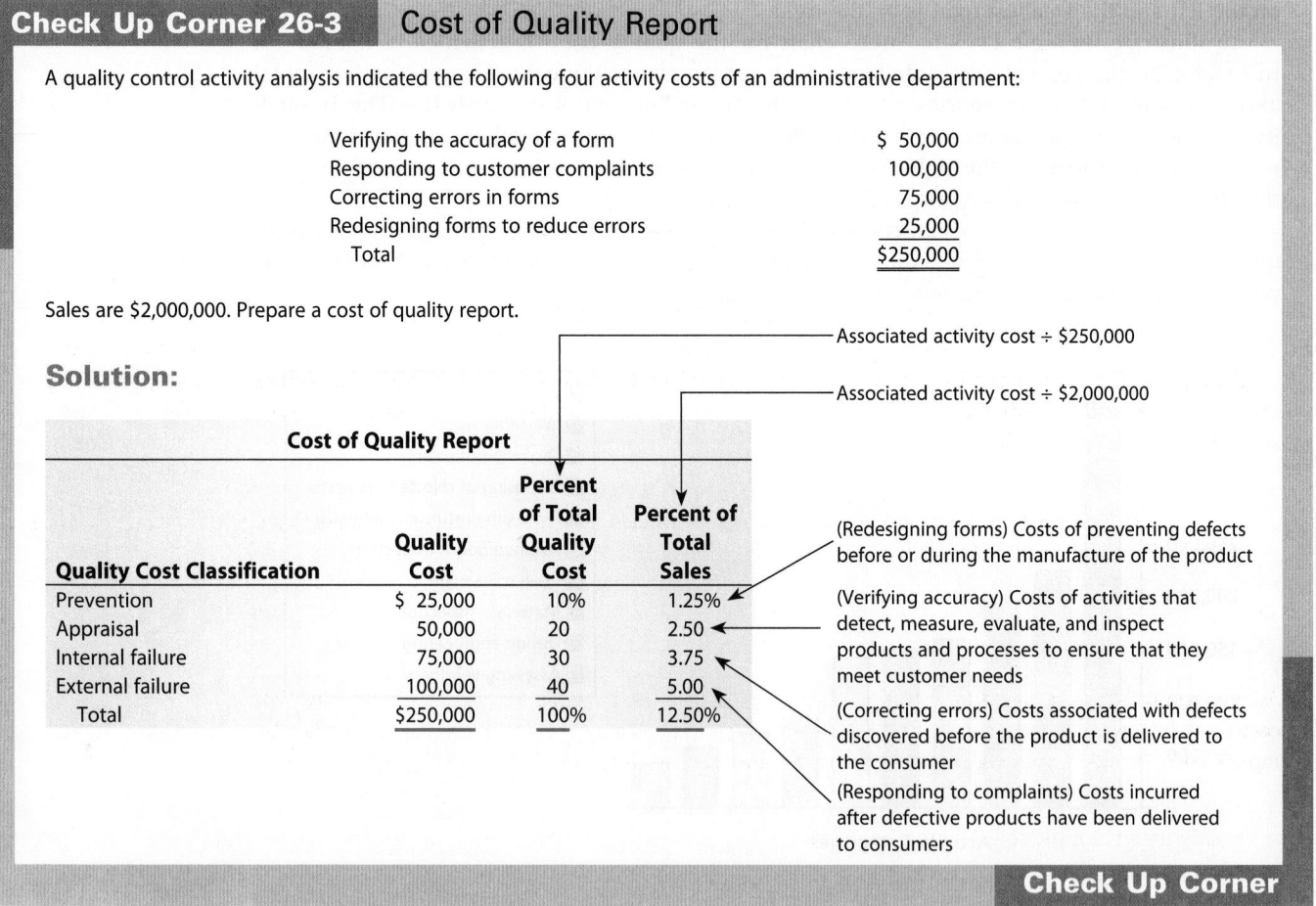

Cost of Quality Report

Quality Cost Classification	Quality Cost	Percent of Total Quality Cost	Percent of Total Sales	
Prevention	$ 25,000	10%	1.25%	(Redesigning forms) Costs of preventing defects before or during the manufacture of the product
Appraisal	50,000	20	2.50	(Verifying accuracy) Costs of activities that detect, measure, evaluate, and inspect products and processes to ensure that they meet customer needs
Internal failure	75,000	30	3.75	
External failure	100,000	40	5.00	(Correcting errors) Costs associated with defects discovered before the product is delivered to the consumer
Total	$250,000	100%	12.50%	(Responding to complaints) Costs incurred after defective products have been delivered to consumers

Check Up Corner

Value-Added Activity Analysis

In the preceding section, the quality control activities of Gifford Company were classified as prevention, appraisal, internal failure, and external failure activities. Activities also may be classified as follows:

- Value-added
- Non-value-added

A **value-added activity** is one that is necessary to meet customer requirements. A **non-value-added activity** is *not* required by the customer but occurs because of mistakes, errors, omissions, and process failures.

To illustrate, Exhibit 13 shows the value-added and non-value-added classification for the quality control activities for Gifford Company.[3] This exhibit also reveals that internal and external failure costs are classified as non-value-added. In contrast, prevention and appraisal costs are classified as value-added.[4]

A summary of the value-added and non-value-added activities follows. The summary expresses value-added and non-value-added costs as a percent of total costs.

Quality Control Activities	Activity Cost	Classification
Design engineering	$ 55,000	Value-added
Disposing of rejected materials	160,000	Non-value-added
Finished goods inspection	140,000	Value-added
Materials inspection	70,000	Value-added
Preventive maintenance	80,000	Value-added
Processing returned materials	150,000	Non-value-added
Disposing of scrap	195,000	Non-value-added
Assessing vendor quality	45,000	Value-added
Rework	380,000	Non-value-added
Warranty work	225,000	Non-value-added
Total activity cost	$1,500,000	

Exhibit 13
Value-Added/
Non-Value-Added
Quality Control
Activities

Classification	Amount	Percent
Value-added	$ 390,000	26%
Non-value-added	1,110,000	74
Total	$1,500,000	100%

The preceding summary indicates that 74% of Gifford Company's quality control activities are non-value-added. This should motivate Gifford Company to make improvements to reduce non-value-added activities.

Innovation and product improvement are value-added activities. Precor holds numerous patents for treadmills, bikes, and elliptical products.

Link to Precor

Process Activity Analysis

Activity analysis can be used to evaluate business processes. A **process** is a series of activities that converts an input into an output. In other words, a process is a set of activities linked together by inputs and outputs. Common business processes include the following:

- Procurement
- Product development
- Manufacturing
- Distribution
- Sales order fulfillment

Exhibit 14 shows a sales order fulfillment process for Masters Company. This process converts a customer order (the input) into a product received by the customer (the output).

---

[3] We use the quality control activities for illustrating the value-added and non-value-added activities in this section. However, a value-added/non-value-added activity analysis can be done for any activity in a business, not just quality control activities.

[4] Some believe that appraisal costs are non-value-added. They argue that if the product had been made correctly, then no inspection would be required. We take a less strict view and assume that appraisal costs are value-added.

Exhibit 14 Sales Order Fulfillment Process

*Operators driving forklifts receive a list of orders, drive to stacking locations within the warehouse, pick the orders, and then transport them back to an area to prepare for shipment.

Exhibit 14 indicates that Masters Company's sales order fulfillment process has the following four activities:

- Customer credit check
- Order entered into computer system
- Order picked from warehouse
- Order shipped

A process activity analysis can be used to determine the cost of the preceding activities. To illustrate, assume that a process activity analysis determines that the cost of the four activities is as follows:

Sales Order Fulfillment Activities	Activity Cost	Percent of Total Process Cost
Customer credit check	$14,400	18%
Order entered into computer system	9,600	12
Order picked from warehouse	36,000	45
Order shipped	20,000	25
Total sales order fulfillment process cost	$80,000	100%

If 10,000 sales orders are filled during the current period, the per-unit process cost is $8 per order ($80,000 ÷ 10,000 orders).

Management can use process activity analysis to improve a process. To illustrate, assume that Masters Company sets a cost improvement target of $6 per order. A $2 reduction per order ($8 – $6) requires improving efficiency or eliminating unnecessary activities.

Masters Company determines that only *new* customers need to have a credit check. If this change is made, it is estimated that only 25% of sales orders would require credit checks. In addition, by revising the warehouse product layout, it is estimated that the cost of picking orders can be reduced by 35%.

Assuming that 10,000 orders will be filled, the cost savings from these two improvements are as follows:

Sales Order Fulfillment Activities	Activity Cost Prior to Improvement	Activity Cost After Improvement	Activity Cost Savings
Customer credit check	$14,400	$ 3,600*	$10,800
Order entered in computer system	9,600	9,600	0
Order picked from warehouse	36,000	23,400**	12,600
Order shipped	20,000	20,000	0
Total sales order fulfillment process cost...............	$80,000	$56,600	$23,400
Cost per order (total cost divided by 10,000 orders)	$8.00	$5.66	

*$14,400 × 25%
**$36,000 – ($36,000 × 35%)

As illustrated, the activity changes generate a savings of $23,400.[5] In addition, the cost per order is reduced to $5.66, which is less than the $6.00 per order targeted cost.[6]

[5] This analysis assumes that the activity costs are variable to the inputs and outputs of the process. While this is likely true for processes primarily using labor, such as a sales order fulfillment process, other types of processes may have significant fixed costs that would not change with changes of inputs and outputs.

[6] Process activity analysis also can be integrated into a company's budgeting system using flexible budgets. Process activity analysis used in this way is discussed in advanced texts.

Analysis for Decision Making

Lean Performance for Nonmanufacturing

Objective

Describe and illustrate the use of lean principles and activity analysis in a service or administrative setting.

All of the lean principles and activity analyses discussed for a manufacturer can be adapted to service businesses or administrative processes. Examples of service businesses that use lean principles include hospitals, banks, insurance companies, and hotels. For service businesses, the "product" is normally the customer. Thus, for example, a hospital would measure the length of time to admit a patient in evaluating its admissions process.

Examples of administrative processes that use lean principles include processing insurance applications, product designs, and sales orders. For administrative processes, the "product" is often information. Thus, for example, a product design department would measure how long it takes to process a product design modification.

To illustrate, the customer service department of Municipal Water Services, Inc. resolves residential water problems. To determine how to improve its customer service, the department would measure its resolution response time. Resolution response time data are as follows:

	Average Response Time
First contact	0.5 hour
Service scheduling	0.5 hour
Wait for service	17.0 hours
Service	2.0 hours
Total resolution time	20.0 hours

The total lead time from the customer's first contact to final resolution is 20 hours. Of this time, 17 hours represent the customer waiting for the service. This represents 85% (17 hrs. ÷ 20 hrs.) non-value-added lead time in this process, or a 15% value-added ratio. Process improvement should focus on reducing the amount of time a customer waits for service. Improving scheduling or adding resources to the process could reduce wait time.

Make a Decision   Lean Performance for Nonmanufacturing

Northern Highlands Hospital is evaluating its admissions process by measuring the time elapsed between patient check-in and arrival in the clinical area. The present process involves a patient checking in at a centralized area and providing information to an admissions specialist. After being admitted, the patient is escorted from the admissions area to the appropriate clinical area in the hospital. Average lead time information is as follows:

	Average Lead Time
Wait in line at check-in window	15 min.
Check in (one check-in service line)	5
Wait in check-in area for admissions desk	30
Give information at admissions desk (one desk)	10
Wait for escort in check-in area	15
Go with escort to clinical area	5
Total lead time to arrive at clinical area	80 min.

The hospital staffs one person at check-in and one person at the admissions desk. There is one dedicated escort.

A. Determine the non-value-added lead time in this process.
B. Determine the value-added ratio of this process.
C. Identify some areas where the hospital could make improvements to increase the value-added ratio of this process.

Solution:

A.

	Average Lead Time
Wait in line at check-in desk	15 min.
Wait in check-in area for admissions desk	30
Wait for escort in check-in area	15
Total non-value-added lead time to arrive at clinical area	60 min.

B. Value-Added Ratio $= \dfrac{\text{Value–Added Lead Time}}{\text{Total Lead Time}}$

$$= \dfrac{20 \text{ min.}^*}{80 \text{ min.}} = 25\%$$

*20 min. = 80 min. – 60 min.

C. The non-value-added lead time is related to waiting between each process element. Adding resources to the process during the busier times of the day can reduce the waiting. The check-in window could be expanded to multiple service lines, and the admissions desk could be expanded to multiple desks. This would reduce the waiting time between these activities. Adding more escorts could reduce the amount of time waiting to be escorted to a clinical area. A more radical approach would be to provide patients access to an admissions Web site prior to arriving at the hospital. In this way, admissions information could be input by the patient prior to coming to the hospital. In this scenario, the patient would check in and be escorted directly to a clinical area, because admissions information would have been captured previously. A complete redesign could decentralize the check-in process and make it part of the clinical areas. In this way, the patient could just go directly to the appropriate clinical area to check in. Combining preadmission with decentralized check-in at the clinical areas would virtually eliminate the existing process.

Make a Decision

Let's Review

Chapter Summary

1. Lean manufacturing emphasizes reduced lead time, a product-oriented production layout, a team-oriented work environment, setup time reduction, pull manufacturing, high quality, and supplier and customer partnering in order to improve the supply chain.

2. Under lean manufacturing, the lean accounting system will have fewer transactions, will combine the materials and work in process accounts, and will account for direct labor as a part of cell conversion cost. Lean accounting will use nonfinancial reporting measures and result in more direct tracing of factory overhead to product cells.

3. Companies use activity analysis to identify the costs of quality, which include prevention, appraisal, internal failure, and external failure costs. The quality cost activities may be reported on a Pareto chart or quality cost report. An alternative method for categorizing activities is by value-added and non-value-added classifications. An activity analysis also can be used to improve the cost of processes.

Key Terms

activity analysis (1317)
appraisal costs (1317)
backflush accounting (1314)
batch size (1309)
Conversion Costs (1314)
cost of quality report (1319)
costs of quality (1317)
electronic data interchange (EDI) (1312)
employee involvement (1311)
enterprise resource planning (ERP) (1312)
external failure costs (1317)

internal failure costs (1317)
lead time (1307)
lean accounting (1314)
lean enterprise (1306)
lean manufacturing (1306)
lean principles (1306)
nonfinancial measure (1316)
non-value-added activity (1321)
non-value-added lead time (1308)
Pareto chart (1319)
prevention costs (1317)
process (1321)

process-oriented layout (1311)
product-oriented layout (1311)
pull manufacturing (1311)
push manufacturing (1312)
radio frequency identification devices (RFID) (1312)
Raw and In Process (RIP) Inventory (1314)
Six Sigma (1312)
supply chain management (1312)
value-added activity (1321)
value-added lead time (1308)
value-added ratio (1308)

Practice

Multiple-Choice Questions

1. Which of the following is **not** a characteristic of the lean manufacturing philosophy?
   A. Product-oriented layout
   B. Push manufacturing (make to stock)
   C. Short lead times
   D. Reducing setup time as a critical improvement priority

2. Accounting for lean manufacturing is best described as:
   A. more complex.
   B. focused on direct labor.
   C. providing detailed variance reports.
   D. providing less transaction control.

3. A product cell for Dynah Company has budgeted conversion costs of $420,000 for the year. The cell is planned to be available 2,100 hours for production. Each unit requires $12.50 of materials cost. The cell started and completed 700 units. The cell process time for the product is 15 minutes per unit. What is the cost to be debited to Finished Goods for the period?
   A. $8,750
   B. $35,000
   C. $43,750
   D. $140,000

4. In-process inspection activities are an example of what type of quality cost?
   A. Prevention
   B. Appraisal
   C. Internal failure
   D. External failure

5. A Pareto chart is used to display:
   A. a ranking of attribute totals, by category, in the form of a bar chart.
   B. important trends in the form of a line chart.
   C. percentage information in the form of a pie chart.
   D. a listing of attribute totals, by category, in a table.

Answers provided after Problem. Need more practice? Find additional multiple-choice questions, exercises, and problems in CengageNOWv2.

Exercises

SHOW ME HOW

1. Lead time
Obj. 1

The Swift Mountain Ski Company manufactures skis in the finishing and assembly process. Skis are manufactured in 30-ski batch sizes. The finishing time is 14 minutes per ski. The assembly time is 10 minutes per ski. It takes 8 minutes to move a batch of skis from finishing to assembly.

A. Compute the value-added, non-value-added, and total lead time of this process.

B. Compute the value-added ratio. (Round to one decimal place.)

SHOW ME HOW

2. Lean features
Obj. 1

Which of the following are features of a lean manufacturing system?

A. Production pace matches demand

B. Centralized work in process inventory locations

C. Push scheduling

D. Receive raw materials directly to manufacturing cells

SHOW ME HOW

3. Lean accounting
Obj. 2

The annual budgeted conversion costs for a lean cell are $663,000 for 1,950 production hours. Each unit produced by the cell requires 15 minutes of cell process time. During the month, 665 units are manufactured in the cell. The estimated materials costs are $160 per unit. Journalize entries for the following:

A. Materials are purchased to produce 700 units.

B. Conversion costs are applied to 665 units of production.

C. The cell completes 650 units, which are placed into finished goods.

SHOW ME HOW

4. Cost of quality report
Obj. 3

A quality control activity analysis indicated the following four activity costs of a manufacturing department:

Rework	$ 39,000
Inspecting incoming raw materials	51,000
Warranty work	27,000
Process improvement effort	183,000
Total	$300,000

Sales are $1,000,000. Prepare a cost of quality report. (Round percentages to one decimal place.)

SHOW ME HOW

5. Process activity analysis
Obj. 3

Lexter Company incurred an activity cost of $180,000 for inspecting 25,000 units of production. Management determined that the inspecting objectives could be met without inspecting every unit. Therefore, rather than inspecting 25,000 units of production, the inspection activity was limited to 40% of the production. Determine the inspection activity cost per unit on 25,000 units of total production both before and after the improvement.

Answers provided after Problem. Need more practice? Find additional multiple-choice questions, exercises, and problems in CengageNOWv2.

Problem

Krisco Company operates under the lean philosophy. As such, it has a production cell for its microwave ovens. The conversion cost for 2,400 hours of production is budgeted for the year at $4,800,000.

During January, 2,000 microwave ovens were started and completed. Each oven requires 6 minutes of cell processing time. The materials cost for each oven is $100.

Instructions

Use lean accounting to:

1. Determine the budgeted cell conversion cost per hour.
2. Determine the manufacturing cost per unit.
3. Journalize the entry to record the costs charged to the production cell in January.
4. Journalize the entry to record the costs transferred to finished goods.

Need more practice? Find additional multiple-choice questions, exercises, and problems in CengageNOWv2.

Answers

Multiple-Choice Questions

1. **B** The lean manufacturing philosophy embraces a product-oriented layout (answer A), making lead times short (answer C), and reducing setup times (answer D). Pull manufacturing, the opposite of push manufacturing (answer B), is also a lean manufacturing principle.

2. **D** Accounting in a lean manufacturing environment should not be complex (answer A), should not focus on direct labor (answer B) because it is combined with other conversion costs, and should not provide detailed variance reporting (answer C) because of higher reliance on nonfinancial performance measures. However, the lean manufacturing environment will have fewer transaction control features than the traditional system (answer D).

3. **C** $420,000 ÷ 2,100 hours = $200 per hour

   $200 per hour × 0.25 per hour = $50 per unit

   700 units × ($50 + $12.50) = $43,750

4. **B** Appraisal costs (answer B) are the cost of inspecting and testing activities, which include detecting, measuring, evaluating, and auditing products and processes. Prevention (answer A) activities are incurred to prevent defects from occurring during the design and delivery of products or services. Internal failure costs (answer C) are associated with defects that are discovered by the organization before the product or service is delivered to the customer. External failure costs (answer D) are costs incurred after defective units or services have been delivered to customers.

5. **A** A Pareto chart is a bar chart that ranks attribute totals by category (answer A). A line chart (answer B), a pie chart (answer C), and a table listing (answer D) are other ways of displaying information, but they are not Pareto charts.

Exercises

1. A. Value-added lead time .... 24 min. (14 min. + 10 min.)

   Non-value-added lead time:

   Total within-batch wait time .... 696 (14 min. + 10 min.) × (30 − 1)

   Move time .... $\underline{8}$

   Total lead time .... $\underline{728}$ min.

   B. Value-added ratio: $\dfrac{24 \text{ min}}{728 \text{ min.}} = 3.3\%$

2. A. Production pace matches demand

   D. Receive raw materials directly to manufacturing cells

3. A. Raw and In Process Inventory*   112,000
      Accounts Payable   112,000

   *$160 per unit × 700 units

   B. Raw and In Process Inventory*   56,525
      Conversion Costs   56,525

   *[($663,000 ÷ 1,950 hours) × (15 min. ÷ 60 min.)]
   = $85 per unit; $85 × 665 units = $56,525

   C. Finished Goods Inventory*   159,250
      Raw and In Process Inventory   159,250

   *($160 + $85) × 650 units

4.

Cost of Quality Report

Quality Cost Classification	Quality Cost	Percent of Total Quality Cost	Percent of Total Sales
Prevention	$183,000	61%	18.3%
Appraisal.................................	51,000	17	5.1
Internal failure...........................	39,000	13	3.9
External failure	27,000	9	2.7
Total..................................	$300,000	100%	30.0%

5. Inspection activity before improvement .... $180,000 ÷ 25,000 units = $7.20 per unit
   Inspection activity after improvement:
      Revised inspection cost.....................   (40% × 25,000 units) × $7.20 per unit = $72,000
      Revised inspection cost per unit .... $72,000 ÷ 25,000 units = $2.88 per unit

Need more help? Watch step-by-step videos of how to compute answers to these Exercises in CengageNOWv2.

Problem

1. Budgeted Cell Conversion Cost Rate = $\dfrac{\$4,800,000}{2,400 \text{ hours}}$ = $2,000 per cell hour

2. Materials $100 per unit
   Conversion cost [($2,000 per hour ÷ 60 min.) × 6 min.]   200
      Total $300 per unit

3.
   Raw and In Process Inventory   200,000
      Accounts Payable   200,000
         To record materials costs.
            (2,000 units × $100 per unit)

   Raw and In Process Inventory   400,000
      Conversion Costs   400,000
         To record conversion costs.
            (2,000 units × $200 per unit)

4.
   Finished Goods (2,000 × $300 per unit)   600,000
      Raw and In Process Inventory   600,000
         To record finished production.

Discussion Questions

1. What is the benefit of the lean philosophy?

2. What are some examples of non-value-added lead time?

3. Why is a product-oriented layout preferred by lean manufacturers over a process-oriented layout?

4. How is setup time related to lead time?

5. Why do lean manufacturers favor pull or "make to order" manufacturing?

6. Why would a lean manufacturer strive to produce zero defects?

7. How is supply chain management different from traditional supplier and customer relationships?

8. Why does lean accounting result in fewer transactions?

9. Why do lean manufacturers use a "raw and in process inventory" account, rather than separately reporting materials and work in process?

10. Why is the direct labor cost category eliminated in many lean manufacturing environments?

11. How does a Pareto chart assist management?

12. What is the benefit of identifying non-value-added activities?

13. In what ways can the cost of a process be improved?

Basic Exercises

SHOW ME HOW

BE 26-1 Lead time
Obj. 1

Rough Riders Inc. manufactures jeans in the cutting and sewing process. Jeans are manufactured in 50-jean batch sizes. The cutting time is 6 minutes per jean. The sewing time is 15 minutes per jean. It takes 5 minutes to move a batch of jeans from cutting to sewing.

A. Compute the value-added, non-value-added, and total lead time of this process.

B. Compute the value-added ratio. (Round to one decimal place.)

SHOW ME HOW

BE 26-2 Lean features
Obj. 1

Which of the following are features of a lean manufacturing system?

A. Centralized maintenance areas

B. Smaller batch sizes

C. Employee involvement

D. Less wasted movement of material and people

SHOW ME HOW

BE 26-3 Lean accounting
Obj. 2

The annual budgeted conversion costs for a lean cell are $180,000 for 2,000 production hours. Each unit produced by the cell requires 18 minutes of cell process time. During the month, 550 units are manufactured in the cell. The estimated materials costs are $32 per unit. Journalize the following entries for the month:

A. Materials are purchased to produce 600 units.

B. Conversion costs are applied to 550 units of production.

C. The cell completes 500 units, which are placed into finished goods.

SHOW ME HOW

BE 26-4 Cost of quality report
Obj. 3

A quality control activity analysis indicated the following four activity costs of a hotel:

Inspecting cleanliness of rooms	$175,000
Processing lost customer reservations	40,000
Rework incorrectly prepared room service meal	20,000
Employee training	265,000
Total	$500,000

Sales are $4,000,000. Prepare a cost of quality report. (Round percentage to one decimal.)

BE 26-5 Process activity analysis Obj. 3

Roen Company incurred an activity cost of $105,600 for inspecting 40,000 units of production. Management determined that the inspecting objectives could be met without inspecting every unit. Therefore, rather than inspecting 40,000 units of production, the inspection activity was limited to a random selection of 5,000 units out of the 40,000 units of production. Determine the inspection activity cost per unit on 40,000 units of total production both before and after the improvement.

Exercises

EX 26-1 Lean principles Obj. 1

The chief executive officer (CEO) of Platnum Inc. has just returned from a management seminar describing the benefits of the lean philosophy. The CEO issued the following statement after returning from the conference:

This company will become a lean manufacturing company. Presently, we have too much inventory. To become lean, we need to eliminate the excess inventory. Therefore, I want all employees to begin reducing inventories until we make products "just in time." Thank you for your cooperation.

 How would you respond to the CEO's statement?

EX 26-2 Lean as a strategy Obj. 1

The American textile industry has moved much of its operations offshore in the pursuit of lower labor costs. Textile imports have risen from 2% of all textile production in the early 1960s to over 70%. Offshore manufacturers make long runs of standard mass-market apparel items. These are then brought to the United States in container ships, requiring significant time between original order and delivery. As a result, retail customers must accurately forecast market demands for imported apparel items.

 Assuming that you work for a U.S.-based textile company, how would you recommend responding to the low-cost imports?

EX 26-3 Lean principles Obj. 1

Active Apparel Company manufactures various styles of men's casual wear. Shirts are cut and assembled by a workforce that is paid by piece rate. This means that they are paid according to the amount of work completed during a period of time. To illustrate, if the piece rate is $0.15 per sleeve assembled, and the worker assembles 700 sleeves during the day, then the worker would be paid $105 (700 × $0.15) for the day's work.

The company is considering adopting a lean manufacturing philosophy by organizing work cells around various types of products and employing pull manufacturing. However, no change is expected in the compensation policy. On this point, the manufacturing manager stated the following:

"Piecework compensation provides an incentive to work fast. Without it, the workers will just goof off and expect a full day's pay. We can't pay straight hourly wages—at least not in this industry."

 How would you respond to the manufacturing manager's comments?

EX 26-4 Lead time analysis Obj. 1

Palm Pals Inc. manufactures toy stuffed animals. The direct labor time required to cut, sew, and stuff a toy is 12 minutes per unit. The company makes two types of stuffed toys—a lion and a bear. The lion is assembled in lot sizes of 40 units per batch, while the bear is assembled in lot sizes of 5 units per batch. Since each product has direct labor time of 12 minutes per unit, management has determined that the lead time for each product is 12 minutes.

 Is management correct? What are the lead times for each product?

EX 26-5 Reduce setup time

Obj. 1

Hammond Inc. has analyzed the setup time on its computer-controlled lathe. The setup requires changing the type of fixture that holds a part. The average setup time has been 135 minutes, consisting of the following steps:

Turn off machine and remove fixture from lathe	10 minutes
Go to tool room with fixture	15
Record replacement of fixture to tool room	18
Return to lathe	20
Clean lathe	15
Return to tool room	20
Record withdrawal of new fixture from tool room	12
Return to lathe	15
Install new fixture and turn on machine	10
Total setup time	135 minutes

A. ➤ Why should management be concerned about improving setup time?

B. ➤ What do you recommend to Hammond Inc. for improving setup time?

C. How much time would be required for a setup, using your suggestion in (B)?

EX 26-6 Calculate lead time

Obj. 1

Value-added, 12 minutes

EXCEL TEMPLATE

Flint Fabricators Inc. machines metal parts for the automotive industry. Under the traditional manufacturing approach, the parts are machined through two processes: milling and finishing. Parts are produced in batch sizes of 30 parts. A part requires 5 minutes in milling and 7 minutes in finishing. The move time between the two operations for a complete batch is 5 minutes.

Under the lean philosophy, the part is produced in a cell that includes both the milling and finishing operations. The operating time is unchanged; however, the batch size is reduced to 4 parts and the move time is eliminated.

Determine the value-added, non-value-added, and total lead times, and the value-added ratio under the traditional and lean manufacturing methods. (Round percentages to one decimal place.)

EX 26-7 Calculate lead time

Obj. 1

✔ B. Non-value-added, 50 minutes

EXCEL TEMPLATE

Williams Optical Inc. is considering a new lean product cell. The present manufacturing approach produces a product in four separate steps. The production batch sizes are 45 units. The process time for each step is as follows:

Process Step 1	5 minutes
Process Step 2	8 minutes
Process Step 3	4 minutes
Process Step 4	3 minutes

The time required to move each batch between steps is 5 minutes. In addition, the time to move raw materials to Process Step 1 is also 5 minutes, and the time to move completed units from Process Step 4 to finished goods inventory is 5 minutes.

The new lean layout will allow the company to reduce the batch sizes from 45 units to 3 units. The time required to move each batch between steps and the inventory locations will be reduced to 2 minutes. The processing time in each step will stay the same.

Determine the value-added, non-value-added, and total lead times, and the value-added ratio under the (A) present and (B) proposed production approaches. (Round percentages to one decimal place.)

REAL WORLD

EX 26-8 Suppy chain management

Obj. 1

The following is an excerpt from an article discussing supplier relationships with the Big Three North American automakers.

"The Big Three select suppliers on the basis of lowest price and annual price reductions," said Neil De Koker, president of the Original Equipment Suppliers Association. "They look globally for the lowest parts prices from the lowest cost countries," De Koker said. "There is little trust and respect. Collaboration is missing." Japanese auto makers want long-term supplier relationships. They select suppliers as a person would a mate. The Big Three are quick to beat down prices with methods such as electronic auctions or rebidding work to a competitor. The Japanese are equally tough on price but are committed to maintaining supplier continuity. "They work with you to arrive at a competitive price, and they are willing to pay because they want long-term partnering," said Carl Code, a vice president at **Ernie Green Industries**. "They [**Honda** and **Toyota**] want suppliers to make enough money to stay in business, grow, and bring them innovation." The Big Three's supply chain model is not much different from the one set by Henry Ford. In 1913, he set up the system of independent supplier firms operating at arm's length on short-term contracts. One consequence of the Big Three's low-price-at-all-costs mentality is that suppliers are reluctant to offer them their cutting-edge technology out of fear the contract will be resourced before the research and development costs are recouped.

Source: Robert Sherefkin and Amy Wilson, "Suppliers Prefer Japanese Business Model," *Rubber & Plastics News*, March 17, 2003, Vol. 24, No. 11.

A. ➤ Contrast the Japanese supply chain model with that of the Big Three.

B. ➤ Why might a supplier prefer the Japanese model?

C. ➤ What benefits might accrue to the Big Three by adopting the Japanese supply chain practices?

REAL WORLD

EX 26-9 Employee involvement

Obj. 1

Quickie Designs Inc. uses teams in the manufacture of lightweight wheelchairs. Two features of its team approach are team hiring and peer reviews. Under team hiring, the team recruits, interviews, and hires new team members from within the organization. Using peer reviews, the team evaluates each member of the team with regard to quality, knowledge, teamwork, goal performance, attendance, and safety. These reviews provide feedback to the team member for improvement.

➤ How do these two team approaches differ from using managers to hire and evaluate employees?

EX 26-10 Lean principles for a restaurant

Obj. 1

The management of Grill Rite Burger fast-food franchise wants to provide hamburgers quickly to customers. It has been using a process by which precooked hamburgers are prepared and placed under hot lamps. These hamburgers are then sold to customers. In this process, every customer receives the same type of hamburger and dressing (ketchup, onions, mustard). If a customer wants something different, then a "special order" must be cooked to the customer's requirements. This requires the customer to wait several minutes, which often slows down the service line. Grill Rite has been receiving more and more special orders from customers, which has been slowing service down considerably.

A. ➤ Is the Grill Rite service delivery system best described as a push or pull system? Explain.

B. ➤ How might you use lean principles to provide customers quick service, yet still allow them to custom order their burgers?

EX 26-11 Accounting issues in a lean environment

Obj. 2

Pinnacle Technologies has recently implemented a lean manufacturing approach. A production manager has approached the controller with the following comments:

I am very upset with our accounting system now that we have implemented our new lean manufacturing methods. It seems as if all I'm doing is paperwork. Our product is moving so fast through the manufacturing process that the paperwork can hardly keep up. For example, it just doesn't make sense to me to fill out daily labor reports. The employees are assigned to complete cells, performing many different tasks. I can't keep up with direct labor reports on each individual task. I thought we were trying to eliminate waste. Yet the information requirements of the accounting system are slowing us down and adding to overall lead time. Moreover, I'm still getting my monthly variance reports. I don't think that these are necessary. I have nonfinancial performance measures that are more timely than these reports. Besides, the employees don't really understand accounting variances. How about giving some information that I can really use?

➤ What accounting system changes would you suggest in light of the production department manager's criticisms?

EX 26-12 Lean accounting

Obj. 2

✔ B. $105

SHOW ME HOW

Westgate Inc. uses a lean manufacturing strategy to manufacture DVR (digital video recorder) players. The company manufactures DVR players through a single product cell. The budgeted conversion cost for the year is $600,000 for 2,000 production hours. Each unit requires 21 minutes of cell process time. During March, 500 DVR players were manufactured in the cell. The materials cost per unit is $60. The following summary transactions took place during March:

1. Materials were purchased for March production.
2. Conversion costs were applied to production.
3. 500 DVR players were assembled and placed in finished goods.
4. 480 DVR players were sold for $240 per unit.

A. Determine the budgeted cell conversion cost per hour.
B. Determine the budgeted cell conversion cost per unit.
C. Journalize the summary transactions (1)–(4) for March.

EX 26-13 Lean accounting

Obj. 2

✔ A. $140

SHOW ME HOW

Modern Lighting Inc. manufactures lighting fixtures, using lean manufacturing methods. Style Omega has a materials cost per unit of $16. The budgeted conversion cost for the year is $308,000 for 2,200 production hours. A unit of Style Omega requires 18 minutes of cell production time. The following transactions took place during June:

1. Materials were acquired to assemble 620 Style Omega units for June.
2. Conversion costs were applied to 620 Style Omega units of production.
3. 600 units of Style Omega were completed in June.
4. 580 units of Style Omega were sold in June for $100 per unit.

A. Determine the budgeted cell conversion cost per hour.
B. Determine the budgeted cell conversion cost per unit.
C. Journalize the summary transactions (1)–(4) for June.

EX 26-14 Lean accounting

Obj. 2

✔ B. Finished goods, $7,300

SHOW ME HOW

Vintage Audio Inc. manufactures audio speakers. Each speaker requires $48 per unit of direct materials. The speaker manufacturing assembly cell includes the following estimated costs for the period:

Speaker assembly cell, estimated costs:	
Labor	$30,000
Depreciation	12,000
Supplies	6,000
Power	2,000
Total cell costs for the period	$50,000

The operating plan calls for 800 operating hours for the period. Each speaker requires 24 minutes of cell process time. The unit selling price for each speaker is $90. During the period, the following transactions occurred:

1. Purchased materials to produce 2,000 speaker units.
2. Applied conversion costs to production of 1,800 speaker units.

(Continued)

3. Completed and transferred 1,700 speaker units to finished goods.

4. Sold 1,600 speaker units.

There were no inventories at the beginning of the period.

A. Journalize the summary transactions (1)–(4) for the period.

B. Determine the ending balance of Raw and In Process Inventory and Finished Goods Inventory.

EX 26-15 Pareto chart   Obj. 3

Meagher Solutions Inc. manufactures memory chips for personal computers. An activity analysis was conducted, and the following activity costs were identified with the manufacture and sale of memory chips:

Activities	Activity Cost
Correct shipment errors	$ 150,000
Disposing of scrap	95,000
Emergency equipment maintenance	125,000
Employee training	50,000
Final inspection	80,000
Inspecting incoming materials	60,000
Preventive equipment maintenance	40,000
Processing customer returns	90,000
Scrap reporting	45,000
Supplier development	15,000
Warranty claims	250,000
Total	$1,000,000

Prepare a Pareto chart of these activities.

EX 26-16 Cost of quality report   Obj. 3

✔ B. Appraisal, 14.0% of total quality cost

A. Using the information in Exercise 15, identify the cost of quality classification for each activity.

B. Prepare of cost of quality report. Assume sales for the period were $4,000,000. (Round percentages to one decimal place.)

C. 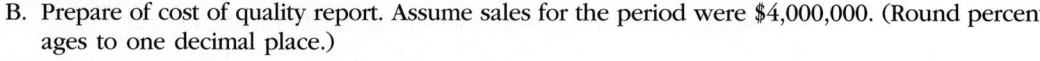 Interpret the cost of quality report.

SHOW ME HOW

EX 26-17 Pareto chart for a service company   Obj. 1, 3

Three Rivers Inc. provides cable TV and Internet service to the local community. The activities and activity costs of Three Rivers are identified as follows:

Activities	Activity Cost
Billing error correction	$ 60,000
Cable signal testing	140,000
Reinstalling service (installed incorrectly the first time)	40,000
Repairing satellite equipment	50,000
Repairing underground cable connections to the customer	25,000
Replacing old technology cable with higher quality cable	175,000
Replacing old technology signal switches with higher quality switches	150,000
Responding to customer home repair requests	30,000
Training employees	80,000
Total	$750,000

Prepare a Pareto chart of these activities.

EX 26-18   Cost of quality and value-added/non-value-added reports for a service company

Obj. 1, 3

SHOW ME HOW   EXCEL TEMPLATE

A. Using the information in Exercise 17, identify the cost of quality classification for each activity and whether the activity is value-added or non-value-added.

B. Prepare a cost of quality report. Assume that sales are $3,000,000. (Round percentages to one decimal place.)

C. Prepare a value-added/non-value-added analysis.

D. ➤ Interpret the information in (B) and (C).

EX 26-19   Process activity analysis

Obj. 3

The Brite Beverage Company bottles soft drinks into aluminum cans. The manufacturing process consists of three activities:

1. **Mixing:** water, sugar, and beverage concentrate are mixed.

2. **Filling:** mixed beverage is filled into 12-oz. cans.

3. **Packaging:** properly filled cans are boxed into cardboard "fridge packs."

The activity costs associated with these activities for the period are as follows:

Mixing	$216,000
Filling	168,000
Packaging	96,000
Total	$480,000

The activity costs do not include materials costs, which are ignored for this analysis. Each can is expected to contain 12 ounces of beverage. Thus, after being filled, each can is automatically weighed. If a can is too light, it is rejected, or "kicked," from the filling line prior to being packaged. The primary cause of kicks is heat expansion. With heat expansion, the beverage overflows during filling, resulting in underweight cans.

This process begins by mixing and filling 6,300,000 cans during the period, of which only 6,000,000 cans are actually packaged. Three hundred thousand cans are rejected due to underweight kicks.

A process improvement team has determined that cooling the cans prior to filling them will reduce the amount of overflows due to expansion. After this improvement, the number of kicks is expected to decline from 300,000 cans to 63,000 cans, thus increasing the number of filled cans to 6,237,000 [6,000,000 + (300,000 − 63,000)].

A. Determine the total activity cost per packaged can under present operations.

B. Determine the amount of increased packaging activity costs from the expected improvements.

C. Determine the expected total activity cost per packaged can after improvements. (Round to three decimal places.)

EX 26-20   Process activity analysis for a service company

Obj. 1, 3

SHOW ME HOW   EXCEL TEMPLATE

Statewide Insurance Company has a process for making payments on insurance claims as follows:

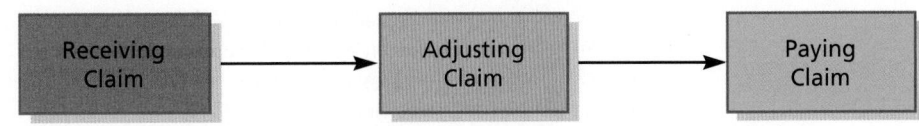

An activity analysis revealed that the cost of these activities was as follows:

Receiving claim	$ 120,000
Adjusting claim	260,000
Paying claim	120,000
Total	$ 500,000

(Continued)

This process includes only the cost of processing the claim payments, not the actual amount of the claim payments. The adjusting activity involves verifying and estimating the amount of the claim and is variable to the number of claims adjusted.

The process received, adjusted, and paid 2,000 claims during the period. All claims were treated identically in this process.

To improve the cost of this process, management has determined that claims should be segregated into two categories. Claims under $1,000 and claims greater than $1,000: claims under $1,000 would not be adjusted but would be accepted upon the insured's evidence of claim. Claims above $1,000 would be adjusted. It is estimated that 80% of the claims are under $1,000 and would thus be paid without adjustment. It is also estimated that the additional effort to segregate claims would add 10% to the "receiving claim" activity cost.

A. Develop a table showing the percent of individual activity cost to the total process cost.

B. Determine the average total process cost per claim payment, assuming 2,000 total claims.

C. Prepare a table showing the changes in the activity costs as a result of the changes proposed by management. Show columns of activity cost prior to improvement, after improvement, and savings.

D. Estimate the average cost per claim payment, assuming that the changes proposed by management are enacted for 2,000 total claims.

EX 26-21   Process activity analysis   Obj. 1, 3

✔ B. $20 per payment

EXCEL TEMPLATE

The procurement process for Omni Wholesale Company includes a series of activities that transforms a materials requisition into a vendor check. The process begins with a request for materials. The requesting department prepares and sends a materials request form to the Purchasing Department. The Purchasing Department then places a request for a quote to vendors. Vendors prepare bids in response to the request for a quote. A vendor is selected based on the lowest bid. A purchase order to the low-bid vendor is prepared. The vendor delivers the materials to the company, whereupon a receiving ticket is prepared. Payment to the vendor is authorized if the materials request form, receiving ticket, and vendor invoice are in agreement. These three documents fail to agree 40% of the time, initiating effort to reconcile the differences. Once the three documents agree, a check is issued. The process can be diagrammed as follows:

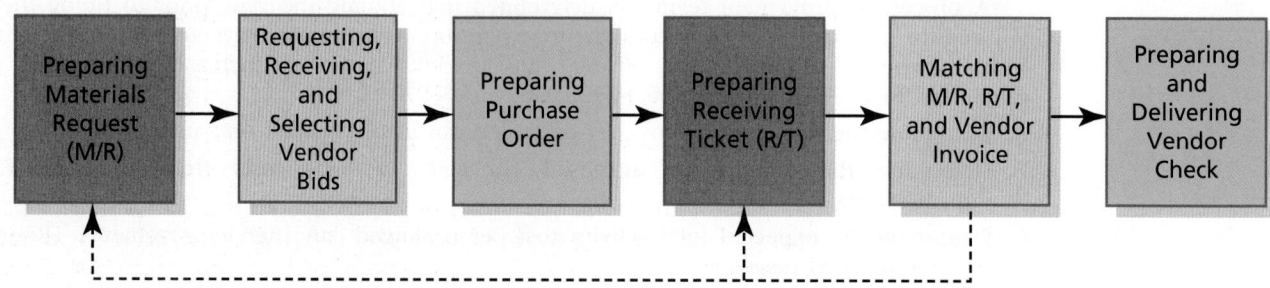

Correcting Reconciliation Differences

An activity analysis indicated the following activity costs with this process:

Preparing materials request	$ 36,000
Requesting, receiving, and selecting vendor bids	100,000
Preparing purchase order	20,000
Preparing receiving ticket	24,000
Matching M/R, R/T, and invoice	48,000
Correcting reconciliation differences	140,000
Preparing and delivering vendor payment	32,000
Total process activity cost	$400,000

On average, the process handles 20,000 individual requests for materials that result in 20,000 individual payments to vendors.

Management proposes to improve this process in two ways. First, the Purchasing Department will develop a preapproved vendor list for which orders can be placed without a request for quote. It is expected that this will reduce the cost of requesting and receiving vendor bids by 75%. Second, additional training and standardization will be provided to reduce errors introduced into the materials requisition form and receiving tickets. It is expected that this will reduce the number of reconciliation differences from 40% to 10%, over an average of 20,000 payments.

A. Develop a table showing the percent of individual activity cost to the total process cost.

B. Determine the average total process cost per vendor payment, assuming 20,000 payments.

C. Prepare a table showing the improvements in the activity costs as a result of the changes proposed by management. Show columns of activity cost prior to improvement, after improvement, and savings.

D. Estimate the average cost per vendor payment, assuming that the changes proposed by management are enacted for 20,000 total payments.

Problems: Series A

PR 26-1A   Lean principles

Obj. 1

3. Average inventory for quarter, 22,500 lbs.

Soft Glow, Inc. manufactures light bulbs. Its purchasing policy requires that the purchasing agents place each quarter's purchasing requirements out for bid. This is because the Purchasing Department is evaluated solely by its ability to get the lowest purchase prices. The lowest bidder receives the order for the next quarter (90 working days).

To make its bulb products, Soft Glow requires 45,000 pounds of glass per quarter. Soft Glow received two glass bids for the third quarter, as follows:

- *Mid-States Glass Company*: $28.00 per pound of glass. Delivery schedule: 45,000 (500 lbs. × 90 days) pounds at the beginning of July to last for 3 months.

- *Cleveland Glass Company*: $28.20 per pound of glass. Delivery schedule: 500 pounds per working day (90 days in the quarter).

Soft Glow accepted Mid-States Glass Company's bid because it was the low-cost bid.

Instructions

1. ➡ Comment on Soft Glow's purchasing policy.

2. ➡ What are the additional (hidden) costs, beyond price, of Mid-States Glass Company's bid? Why weren't these costs considered?

3. Considering only inventory financing costs, what is the additional cost per pound of Mid-States Glass Company's bid if the annual cost of money is 10%? (*Hint:* Determine the average value of glass inventory held for the quarter and multiply by the quarterly interest charge, then divide by the number of pounds.)

PR 26-2A   Lead time

Obj. 1

✔ **1. Total wait time, 1,741 minutes**

EXCEL TEMPLATE

Sound Tek Inc. manufactures electronic stereo equipment. The manufacturing process includes printed circuit (PC) board assembly, final assembly, testing, and shipping. In the PC board assembly operation, a number of individuals are responsible for assembling electronic components into printed circuit boards. Each operator is responsible for soldering components according to a given set of instructions. Operators work on batches of 45 printed circuit boards. Each board requires 5 minutes of board assembly time. After each batch is completed, the operator moves the assembled boards to the final assembly area. This move takes 10 minutes to complete.

The final assembly for each stereo unit requires 15 minutes and is also done in batches of 45 units. A batch of 45 stereos is moved into the test building, which is across the street. The move takes 20 minutes. Before conducting the test, the test equipment must be set up for the particular stereo model. The test setup requires 25 minutes. The units wait while the setup is performed. In the final test, the 45-unit batch is tested one at a time. Each test requires 9 minutes. The completed batch, after all testing, is sent to shipping for packaging and final shipment to customers. A complete batch of 45 units is sent from testing to shipping. The Shipping Department

(Continued)

is located next to testing. Thus, there is no move time between these two operations. Packaging and labeling requires 10 minutes per unit.

Instructions

1. Determine the amount of value-added and non-value-added lead time and the value-added ratio in this process for an average stereo unit in a batch of 45 units. (Round percentages to one decimal place.) Categorize the non-value-added time into wait and move time.

2. ▬▬▬▶ How could this process be improved so as to reduce the amount of waste?

PR 26-3A   Lean accounting   **Obj. 2**

✔ 4. Raw and In Process Inventory, $22,400

SHOW ME HOW   EXCEL TEMPLATE

Dashboard Inc. manufactures and assembles automobile instrument panels for both eCar Motors and Greenville Motors. The process consists of a lean product cell for each customer's instrument assembly. The data that follow concern only the eCar lean cell.

For the year, Dashboard Inc. budgeted the following costs for the eCar production cell:

Conversion Cost Categories	Budget
Labor	$ 800,000
Supplies	275,000
Utilities	325,000
Total	$1,400,000

Dashboard Inc. plans 2,000 hours of production for the eCar cell for the year. The materials cost is $240 per instrument assembly. Each assembly requires 24 minutes of cell assembly time. There was no April 1 inventory for either Raw and In Process Inventory or Finished Goods Inventory.

The following summary events took place in the eCar cell during April:

A. Electronic parts and wiring were purchased to produce 450 instrument assemblies in April.

B. Conversion costs were applied for the production of 400 units in April.

C. 380 units were started, completed, and transferred to finished goods in April.

D. 350 units were shipped to customers at a price of $800 per unit.

Instructions

1. Determine the budgeted cell conversion cost per hour.

2. Determine the budgeted cell conversion cost per unit.

3. Journalize the summary transactions (A) through (D).

4. Determine the ending balance in Raw and In Process Inventory and Finished Goods Inventory.

5. ▬▬▬▶ How does the accounting in a lean environment differ from traditional accounting?

PR 26-4A   Pareto chart and cost of quality report for a service company   **Obj. 1, 3**

✔ 4. Non-value-added, 61%

EXCEL TEMPLATE

The administrator of Hope Hospital has been asked to perform an activity analysis of the emergency room (ER). The ER activities include cost of quality and other patient care activities. The lab tests and transportation are hospital services external to the ER for determining external failure costs. The result of the activity analysis is summarized as follows:

Activities	Activity Cost
Patient registration	$ 6,400
Verifying patient information	9,600
Assigning patients	12,800
Searching/waiting for doctor	8,000
Doctor exam	4,800
Waiting for transport	17,600
Transporting patients	16,000
Verifying lab orders	14,400
Searching for equipment	8,000
Incorrect labs	12,800
Lab tests	17,600
Counting supplies	19,200

Looking for supplies	8,000
Staff training	4,800
Total	$160,000

Instructions

1. Prepare a Pareto chart of the ER activities.

2. Classify the activities into prevention, appraisal, internal failure, external failure, and other patient care activities. Classify the activities into value-added and non-value-added activities.

3. Use the activity cost information to determine the percentages of total ER costs that are prevention, appraisal, internal failure, external failure, and other patient care activities.

4. Determine the percentages of the total ER costs that are value-added and non-value-added.

5. ▬▬▶ Interpret the information.

Problems: Series B

PR 26-1B Lean principles
Obj. 1

3. Average frames in inventory, 2,250

HD Hogg Motorcycle Company manufactures a variety of motorcycles. Hogg's purchasing policy requires that the purchasing agents place each quarter's purchasing requirements out for bid. This is because the Purchasing Department is evaluated solely by its ability to get the lowest purchase prices. The lowest cost bidder receives the order for the next quarter (90 days). To make its motorcycles, Hogg requires 4,500 frames per quarter. Hogg received two frame bids for the third quarter, as follows:

- *Famous Frames, Inc.*: $301 per frame. Delivery schedule: 50 frames per working day (90 days in the quarter).
- *Iron Horse Frames Inc.*: $300 per frame. Delivery schedule: 4,500 (50 frames × 90 days) frames at the beginning of July to last for three months.

Hogg accepted Iron Horse Frames Inc.'s bid because it was the low-cost bid.

Instructions

1. ▬▬▶ Comment on Hogg's purchasing policy.

2. ▬▬▶ What are the additional (hidden) costs, beyond price, of Iron Horse Frames Inc.'s bid? Why weren't these costs considered?

3. Considering only inventory financing costs, what is the additional cost per frame of Iron Horse Frames Inc.'s bid if the annual cost of money is 12%? (*Hint:* Determine the average value of frame inventory held for the quarter and multiply by the quarterly interest charge, then divide by the number of frames.)

PR 26-2B Lead time
Obj. 1

✔ *1. Total wait time, 2,010 minutes*

EXCEL TEMPLATE

Master Chef Appliance Company manufactures home kitchen appliances. The manufacturing process includes stamping, final assembly, testing, and shipping. In the stamping operation, a number of individuals are responsible for stamping the steel outer surface of the appliance. The stamping operation is set up prior to each run. A run of 40 stampings is completed after each setup. A setup requires 60 minutes. The parts wait for the setup to be completed before stamping begins. Each stamping requires 5 minutes of operating time. After each batch is completed, the operator moves the stamped covers to the final assembly area. This move takes 10 minutes to complete.

The final assembly for each appliance unit requires 22 minutes and is also done in batches of 40 appliance units. The batch of 40 appliance units is moved into the test building, which is across the street. The move takes 25 minutes. In the final test, the 40-unit batch is tested one at a time. Each test requires 8 minutes. The completed units are sent to shipping for packaging and final shipment to customers. A complete batch of 40 units is sent from testing to shipping. The Shipping Department is located next to testing. Thus, there is no move time between these two operations. Packaging and shipment labeling requires 15 minutes per unit.

(Continued)

Instructions

1. Determine the amount of value-added and non-value-added lead time and the value-added ratio in this process for an average kitchen appliance in a batch of 40 units. (Round percentages to one decimal place.) Categorize the non-value-added time into wait and move time.

2. ➤ How could this process be improved so as to reduce the amount of waste?

PR 26-3B   Lean accounting Obj. 2

✔ 4. Raw and In Process Inventory, $9,700

SHOW ME HOW   EXCEL TEMPLATE

Com-Tel Inc. manufactures and assembles two models of smartphones—the Tiger Model and the Lion Model. The process consists of a lean cell for each product. The data that follow concern only the Lion Model lean cell.

For the year, Com-Tel Inc. budgeted these costs for the Lion Model production cell:

Conversion Cost Categories	Budget
Labor	$122,000
Supplies	49,000
Utilities	18,000
Total	$189,000

Com-Tel plans 2,100 hours of production for the Lion Model cell for the year. The materials cost is $185 per unit. Each assembly requires 12 minutes of cell assembly time. There was no May 1 inventory for either Raw and In Process Inventory or Finished Goods Inventory.

The following summary events took place in the Lion Model cell during May:

A. Electronic parts were purchased to produce 900 Lion Model assemblies in May.

B. Conversion costs were applied for 875 units of production in May.

C. 850 units were completed and transferred to finished goods in May.

D. 800 units were shipped to customers at a price of $500 per unit.

Instructions

1. Determine the budgeted cell conversion cost per hour.

2. Determine the budgeted cell conversion cost per unit.

3. Journalize the summary transactions (A) through (D).

4. Determine the ending balance in Raw and In Process Inventory and Finished Goods Inventory.

5. ➤ How does the accounting in a lean environment differ from traditional accounting?

PR 26-4B   Pareto chart and cost of quality report for a manufacturing company Obj. 3

✔ 4. Non-value-added, 35%

The president of Mission Inc. has been concerned about the growth in costs over the last several years. The president asked the controller to perform an activity analysis to gain a better insight into these costs. The activity analysis revealed the following:

Activities	Activity Cost
Correcting invoice errors	$ 7,500
Disposing of incoming materials with poor quality	15,000
Disposing of scrap	27,500
Expediting late production	22,500
Final inspection	20,000
Inspecting incoming materials	5,000
Inspecting work in process	25,000
Preventive machine maintenance	15,000
Producing product	97,500
Responding to customer quality complaints	15,000
Total	$250,000

The production process is complicated by quality problems, requiring the production manager to expedite production and dispose of scrap.

Instructions

1. Prepare a Pareto chart of the company activities.

2. Classify the activities into prevention, appraisal, internal failure, external failure, and not costs of quality (producing product). Classify the activities into value-added and non-value-added activities.

3. Use the activity cost information to determine the percentages of total costs that are prevention, appraisal, internal failure, external failure, and not costs of quality.

4. Determine the percentages of total costs that are value-added and non-value-added.

5. ▬▬▬▶ Interpret the information.

Analysis for Decision Making

ADM-1 Lead time reduction for an insurance company

Shield Insurance Company takes 10 days to make payments on insurance claims. Claims are processed through three departments: Data Input, Claims Audit, and Claims Adjustment. The three departments are located in different buildings, approximately one hour apart from each other. Claims are processed in batches of 100. Each batch of 100 claims moves through the three departments on a wheeled cart. Management is concerned about customer dissatisfaction caused by the long lead time for claim payments.

▬▬▬▶ How might this process be changed so that the lead time is reduced significantly?

ADM-2 Turn around time in an operating room of a hospital

Turn around time (TAT) is a measure of the length of time from the end of one surgery in an operating room to the beginning of the next surgery. Improving TAT improves the operating room efficiency by allowing more surgeries to be performed per day. TAT involves:

- sterilizing the operating room.
- setting up equipment and supplies for the next patient.
- preparing the next patient for surgery.

The average times associated with TAT activities were determined as follows:

Sterilization	15 min.
Equipment and supply setup	10
Patient preparation	15
Total TAT	40 min.

Each activity is performed in the operating room sequentially so that the total TAT averages 40 minutes. A process improvement team determined that the TAT could be improved by moving some of this activity outside of the operating room, thus allowing these activities to be done simultaneously. Sterilization must be done in the operating room, so this activity was not changed. However, equipment and supplies were prepared in a room outside of the operating room while sterilization was proceeding. The equipment and supplies were placed on a rolling cart, and then rolled into the operating room and staged for the next surgery. In addition, the improvement team determined the patient could be prepared outside of the operating room by using a small room for patient preparation. When the operating room was ready, the patient could be rolled in on a rolling bed and staged for the procedure. As a result of these changes, the total equipment and supply setup only consumed 2 minutes in the operating room, while the total patient preparation only consumed 3 minutes in the operating room.

(Continued)

A. Determine the revised TAT of the new process.

B. What is the ratio of TAT improvement between the old and new processes?

C. If the average surgical time took 40 minutes, how many additional surgeries could be performed in an eight-hour day as a result of the new process?

ADM-3   Lead time in a doctor's office

Marcus Simmons caught the flu and needed to see the doctor. Simmons called to set up an appointment and was told to come in at 1:00 P.M. Simmons arrived at the doctor's office promptly at 1:00 P.M. The waiting room had five other people in it. Patients were admitted from the waiting room in FIFO (first-in, first-out) order at a rate of 5 minutes per patient. After waiting until his turn, a nurse finally invited Simmons to an examining room. Once in the examining room, Simmons waited another 5 minutes before a nurse arrived to take some basic readings (temperature, blood pressure). The nurse needed 10 minutes to collect this clinical information. After the nurse left, Simmons waited 30 additional minutes before the doctor arrived. The doctor diagnosed the flu and provided a prescription for antibiotics, which took 5 minutes. Before leaving the doctor's office, Simmons waited 10 minutes at the business office to pay for the office visit.

Simmons spent 5 minutes walking next door to fill the prescription at the pharmacy. There were four people in front of Simmons, each person requiring 5 minutes to fill and purchase a prescription. Simmons arrived home 15 minutes after paying for his prescription.

A. What time does Simmons arrive home?

B. How much of the total elapsed time from 1:00 P.M. until when Simmons arrived home was non-value-added time?

C. What is the value-added ratio? (Round percentage to one decimal place.)

D. Why does the doctor require patients to wait so long for service?

Take It Further

TIF 26-1   Ethics in Action

In August, Lannister Company introduced a new performance measurement system in manufacturing operations. One of the new performance measures is lead time, which is determined by tagging a random sample of items with a log sheet throughout the month. The log sheets recorded the time that the sample items started production and the time that they ended production, as well as all steps in between. At the end of the month, the controller collected the log sheets and calculated the average lead time of the tagged products. This number was reported to central management and was used to evaluate the performance of the plant manager. Because of the poor lead time results reported for August, the plant was under extreme pressure to reduce lead time in September.

The following memo was intercepted by the controller.

Date: September 3

To: Hourly Employees

From: Plant Manager

During last month, you may have noticed that some of the products were tagged with a log sheet. This sheet records the time that a product enters production and the time that it leaves production. The difference between these two times is termed the "lead time." Our plant is evaluated on improving lead time. From now on, I ask all of you to keep an eye out for the tagged items. When you see a tagged item, it is to receive special attention. Work on that item first, and then immediately move it to the next operation. Under no circumstances should tagged items wait on any other work that you have. Naturally, report accurate information. I insist that you record the correct times on the log sheet as the product goes through your operations.

➤ How should the controller respond to this discovery?

REAL WORLD

TIF 26-2 Team Activity

In groups of two to four people, visit a sit-down restaurant and do a lead time study. If more than one group chooses to visit the same restaurant, choose different times for your visits. Note the time when you walk in the door of the restaurant and the time when you walk out the door after you have eaten. The difference between these two times is the total lead time of your restaurant experience. While in the restaurant, determine the time spent on non-value-added time, such as wait time, and the time spent on value-added eating time. Note the various activities and the time required to perform each activity during your visit to the restaurant.

➤ Compare your analyses, identifying possible reasons for differences in the times recorded by teams that visited the same restaurant.

TIF 26-3 Communication

Ethan Fromme, the Chief Financial Officer of Maximal Inc., has asked for your help in interpreting the company's operating performance. He has provided you with the following three performance graphs for the most recent fiscal year.

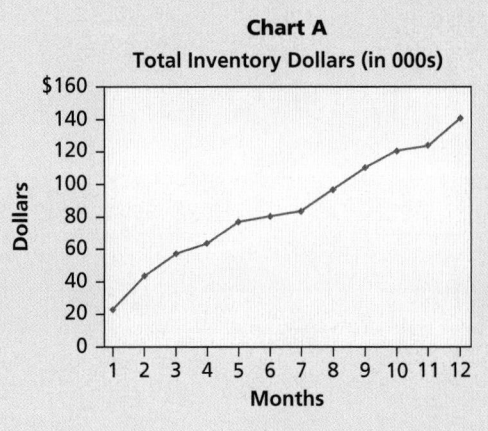

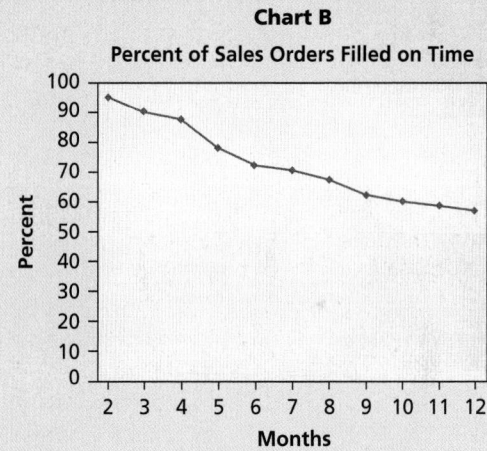

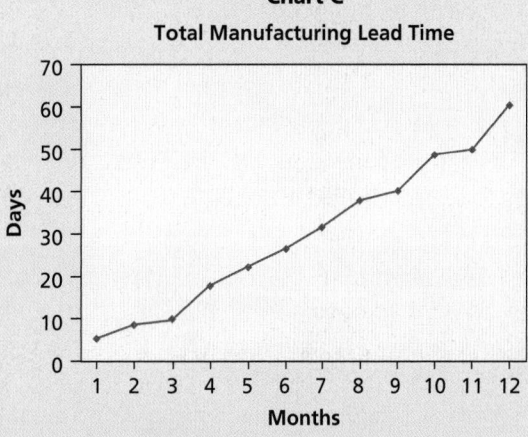

➤ Based on the information in these graphs, write a brief memo to Mr. Fromme, evaluating the company's ability to produce high-quality products at a low cost with a fast response time and immediate availability.

Appendices

Interest Tables

Present Value of $1 at Compound Interest Due in *n* Periods

Periods	4.0%	4.5%	5%	5.5%	6%	6.5%	7%
1	0.96154	0.95694	0.95238	0.94787	0.94340	0.93897	0.93458
2	0.92456	0.91573	0.90703	0.89845	0.89000	0.88166	0.87344
3	0.88900	0.87630	0.86384	0.85161	0.83962	0.82785	0.81630
4	0.85480	0.83856	0.82270	0.80722	0.79209	0.77732	0.76290
5	0.82193	0.80245	0.78353	0.76513	0.74726	0.72988	0.71299
6	0.79031	0.76790	0.74622	0.72525	0.70496	0.68533	0.66634
7	0.75992	0.73483	0.71068	0.68744	0.66506	0.64351	0.62275
8	0.73069	0.70319	0.67684	0.65160	0.62741	0.60423	0.58201
9	0.70259	0.67290	0.64461	0.61763	0.59190	0.56735	0.54393
10	0.67556	0.64393	0.61391	0.58543	0.55839	0.53273	0.50835
11	0.64958	0.61620	0.58468	0.55491	0.52679	0.50021	0.47509
12	0.62460	0.58966	0.55684	0.52598	0.49697	0.46968	0.44401
13	0.60057	0.56427	0.53032	0.49856	0.46884	0.44102	0.41496
14	0.57748	0.53997	0.50507	0.47257	0.44230	0.41410	0.38782
15	0.55526	0.51672	0.48102	0.44793	0.41727	0.38883	0.36245
16	0.53391	0.49447	0.45811	0.42458	0.39365	0.36510	0.33873
17	0.51337	0.47318	0.43630	0.40245	0.37136	0.34281	0.31657
18	0.49363	0.45280	0.41552	0.38147	0.35034	0.32189	0.29586
19	0.47464	0.43330	0.39573	0.36158	0.33051	0.30224	0.27651
20	0.45639	0.41464	0.37689	0.34273	0.31180	0.28380	0.25842
21	0.43883	0.39679	0.35894	0.32486	0.29416	0.26648	0.24151
22	0.42196	0.37970	0.34185	0.30793	0.27751	0.25021	0.22571
23	0.40573	0.36335	0.32557	0.29187	0.26180	0.23494	0.21095
24	0.39012	0.34770	0.31007	0.27666	0.24698	0.22060	0.19715
25	0.37512	0.33273	0.29530	0.26223	0.23300	0.20714	0.18425
26	0.36069	0.31840	0.28124	0.24856	0.21981	0.19450	0.17220
27	0.34682	0.30469	0.26785	0.23560	0.20737	0.18263	0.16093
28	0.33348	0.29157	0.25509	0.22332	0.19563	0.17148	0.15040
29	0.32065	0.27902	0.24295	0.21168	0.18456	0.16101	0.14056
30	0.30832	0.26700	0.23138	0.20064	0.17411	0.15119	0.13137
31	0.29646	0.25550	0.22036	0.19018	0.16425	0.14196	0.12277
32	0.28506	0.24450	0.20987	0.18027	0.15496	0.13329	0.11474
33	0.27409	0.23397	0.19987	0.17087	0.14619	0.12516	0.10723
34	0.26355	0.22390	0.19035	0.16196	0.13791	0.11752	0.10022
35	0.25342	0.21425	0.18129	0.15352	0.13011	0.11035	0.09366
40	0.20829	0.17193	0.14205	0.11746	0.09722	0.08054	0.06678
45	0.17120	0.13796	0.11130	0.08988	0.07265	0.05879	0.04761
50	0.14071	0.11071	0.08720	0.06877	0.05429	0.04291	0.03395

Present Value of $1 at Compound Interest Due in *n* Periods

Periods	8%	9%	10%	11%	12%	13%	14%
1	0.92593	0.91743	0.90909	0.90090	0.89286	0.88496	0.87719
2	0.85734	0.84168	0.82645	0.81162	0.79719	0.78315	0.76947
3	0.79383	0.77218	0.75131	0.73119	0.71178	0.69305	0.67497
4	0.73503	0.70843	0.68301	0.65873	0.63552	0.61332	0.59208
5	0.68058	0.64993	0.62092	0.59345	0.56743	0.54276	0.51937
6	0.63017	0.59627	0.56447	0.53464	0.50663	0.48032	0.45559
7	0.58349	0.54703	0.51316	0.48166	0.45235	0.42506	0.39964
8	0.54027	0.50187	0.46651	0.43393	0.40388	0.37616	0.35056
9	0.50025	0.46043	0.42410	0.39092	0.36061	0.33288	0.30751
10	0.46319	0.42241	0.38554	0.35218	0.32197	0.29459	0.26974
11	0.42888	0.38753	0.35049	0.31728	0.28748	0.26070	0.23662
12	0.39711	0.35553	0.31863	0.28584	0.25668	0.23071	0.20756
13	0.36770	0.32618	0.28966	0.25751	0.22917	0.20416	0.18207
14	0.34046	0.29925	0.26333	0.23199	0.20462	0.18068	0.15971
15	0.31524	0.27454	0.23939	0.20900	0.18270	0.15989	0.14010
16	0.29189	0.25187	0.21763	0.18829	0.16312	0.14150	0.12289
17	0.27027	0.23107	0.19784	0.16963	0.14564	0.12522	0.10780
18	0.25025	0.21199	0.17986	0.15282	0.13004	0.11081	0.09456
19	0.23171	0.19449	0.16351	0.13768	0.11611	0.09806	0.08295
20	0.21455	0.17843	0.14864	0.12403	0.10367	0.08678	0.07276
21	0.19866	0.16370	0.13513	0.11174	0.09256	0.07680	0.06383
22	0.18394	0.15018	0.12285	0.10067	0.08264	0.06796	0.05599
23	0.17032	0.13778	0.11168	0.09069	0.07379	0.06014	0.04911
24	0.15770	0.12640	0.10153	0.08170	0.06588	0.05323	0.04308
25	0.14602	0.11597	0.09230	0.07361	0.05882	0.04710	0.03779
26	0.13520	0.10639	0.08391	0.06631	0.05252	0.04168	0.03315
27	0.12519	0.09761	0.07628	0.05974	0.04689	0.03689	0.02908
28	0.11591	0.08955	0.06934	0.05382	0.04187	0.03264	0.02551
29	0.10733	0.08215	0.06304	0.04849	0.03738	0.02889	0.02237
30	0.09938	0.07537	0.05731	0.04368	0.03338	0.02557	0.01963
31	0.09202	0.06915	0.05210	0.03935	0.02980	0.02262	0.01722
32	0.08520	0.06344	0.04736	0.03545	0.02661	0.02002	0.01510
33	0.07889	0.05820	0.04306	0.03194	0.02376	0.01772	0.01325
34	0.07305	0.05339	0.03914	0.02878	0.02121	0.01568	0.01162
35	0.06763	0.04899	0.03558	0.02592	0.01894	0.01388	0.01019
40	0.04603	0.03184	0.02209	0.01538	0.01075	0.00753	0.00529
45	0.03133	0.02069	0.01372	0.00913	0.00610	0.00409	0.00275
50	0.02132	0.01345	0.00852	0.00542	0.00346	0.00222	0.00143

Present Value of Ordinary Annuity of $1 per Period

Periods	4.0%	4.5%	5%	5.5%	6%	6.5%	7%
1	0.96154	0.95694	0.95238	0.94787	0.94340	0.93897	0.93458
2	1.88609	1.87267	1.85941	1.84632	1.83339	1.82063	1.80802
3	2.77509	2.74896	2.72325	2.69793	2.67301	2.64848	2.62432
4	3.62990	3.58753	3.54595	3.50515	3.46511	3.42580	3.38721
5	4.45182	4.38998	4.32948	4.27028	4.21236	4.15568	4.10020
6	5.24214	5.15787	5.07569	4.99553	4.91732	4.84101	4.76654
7	6.00205	5.89270	5.78637	5.68297	5.58238	5.48452	5.38929
8	6.73274	6.59589	6.46321	6.33457	6.20979	6.08875	5.97130
9	7.43533	7.26879	7.10782	6.95220	6.80169	6.65610	6.51523
10	8.11090	7.91272	7.72173	7.53763	7.36009	7.18883	7.02358
11	8.76048	8.52892	8.30641	8.09254	7.88687	7.68904	7.49867
12	9.38507	9.11858	8.86325	8.61852	8.38384	8.15873	7.94269
13	9.98565	9.68285	9.39357	9.11708	8.85268	8.59974	8.35765
14	10.56312	10.22283	9.89864	9.58965	9.29498	9.01384	8.74547
15	11.11839	10.73955	10.37966	10.03758	9.71225	9.40267	9.10791
16	11.65230	11.23402	10.83777	10.46216	10.10590	9.76776	9.44665
17	12.16567	11.70719	11.27407	10.86461	10.47726	10.11058	9.76322
18	12.65930	12.15999	11.68959	11.24607	10.82760	10.43247	10.05909
19	13.13394	12.59329	12.08532	11.60765	11.15812	10.73471	10.33560
20	13.59033	13.00794	12.46221	11.95038	11.46992	11.01851	10.59401
21	14.02916	13.40472	12.82115	12.27524	11.76408	11.28498	10.83553
22	14.45112	13.78442	13.16300	12.58317	12.04158	11.53520	11.06124
23	14.85684	14.14777	13.48857	12.87504	12.30338	11.77014	11.27219
24	15.24696	14.49548	13.79864	13.15170	12.55036	11.99074	11.46933
25	15.62208	14.82821	14.09394	13.41393	12.78336	12.19788	11.65358
26	15.98277	15.14661	14.37519	13.66250	13.00317	12.39237	11.82578
27	16.32959	15.45130	14.64303	13.89810	13.21053	12.57500	11.98671
28	16.66306	15.74287	14.89813	14.12142	13.40616	12.74648	12.13711
29	16.98371	16.02189	15.14107	14.33310	13.59072	12.90749	12.27767
30	17.29203	16.28889	15.37245	14.53375	13.76483	13.05868	12.40904
31	17.58849	16.54439	15.59281	14.72393	13.92909	13.20063	12.53181
32	17.87355	16.78889	15.80268	14.90420	14.08404	13.33393	12.64656
33	18.14765	17.02286	16.00255	15.07507	14.23023	13.45909	12.75379
34	18.41120	17.24676	16.19290	15.23703	14.36814	13.57661	12.85401
35	18.66461	17.46101	16.37419	15.39055	14.49825	13.68696	12.94767
40	19.79277	18.40158	17.15909	16.04612	15.04630	14.14553	13.33171
45	20.72004	19.15635	17.77407	16.54773	15.45583	14.48023	13.60552
50	21.48218	19.76201	18.25593	16.93152	15.76186	14.72452	13.80075

Present Value of Ordinary Annuity of $1 per Period

Periods	8%	9%	10%	11%	12%	13%	14%
1	0.92593	0.91743	0.90909	0.90090	0.89286	0.88496	0.87719
2	1.78326	1.75911	1.73554	1.71252	1.69005	1.66810	1.64666
3	2.57710	2.53129	2.48685	2.44371	2.40183	2.36115	2.32163
4	3.31213	3.23972	3.16987	3.10245	3.03735	2.97447	2.91371
5	3.99271	3.88965	3.79079	3.69590	3.60478	3.51723	3.43308
6	4.62288	4.48592	4.35526	4.23054	4.11141	3.99755	3.88867
7	5.20637	5.03295	4.86842	4.71220	4.56376	4.42261	4.28830
8	5.74664	5.53482	5.33493	5.14612	4.96764	4.79677	4.63886
9	6.24689	5.99525	5.75902	5.53705	5.32825	5.13166	4.94637
10	6.71008	6.41766	6.14457	5.88923	5.65022	5.42624	5.21612
11	7.13896	6.80519	6.49506	6.20652	5.93770	5.68694	5.45273
12	7.53608	7.16073	6.81369	6.49236	6.19437	5.91765	5.66029
13	7.90378	7.48690	7.10336	6.74987	6.42355	6.12181	5.84236
14	8.22424	7.78615	7.36669	6.96187	6.62817	6.30249	6.00207
15	8.55948	8.06069	7.60608	7.19087	6.81086	6.46238	6.14217
16	8.85137	8.31256	7.82371	7.37916	6.97399	6.60388	6.26506
17	9.12164	8.54363	8.02155	7.54879	7.11963	6.72909	6.37286
18	9.37189	8.75563	8.20141	7.70162	7.24967	6.83991	6.46742
19	9.60360	8.95011	8.36492	7.83929	7.36578	6.93797	6.55037
20	9.81815	9.12855	8.51356	7.96333	7.46944	7.02475	6.62313
21	10.01680	9.29224	8.64869	8.07507	7.56200	7.10155	6.68696
22	10.20074	9.44243	8.77154	8.17574	7.64465	7.16951	6.74294
23	10.37106	9.58021	8.88322	8.26643	7.71843	7.22966	6.79206
24	10.52876	9.70661	8.98474	8.34814	7.78432	7.28288	6.83514
25	10.67478	9.82258	9.07704	8.42174	7.84314	7.32998	6.87293
26	10.80998	9.92897	9.16095	8.48806	7.89566	7.37167	6.90608
27	10.93516	10.02658	9.23722	8.54780	7.94255	7.40856	6.93515
28	11.05108	10.11613	9.30657	8.60162	7.98442	7.44120	6.96066
29	11.15841	10.19828	9.36961	8.65011	8.02181	7.47009	6.98304
30	11.25778	10.27365	9.42691	8.69379	8.05518	7.49565	7.00266
31	11.34980	10.34280	9.47901	8.73315	8.08499	7.51828	7.01988
32	11.43500	10.40624	9.52638	8.76860	8.11159	7.53830	7.03498
33	11.51389	10.46444	9.56943	8.80054	8.13535	7.55602	7.04823
34	11.58693	10.51784	9.60857	8.82932	8.15656	7.57170	7.05985
35	11.65457	10.56682	9.64416	8.85524	8.17550	7.58557	7.07005
40	11.92461	10.75736	9.77905	8.95105	8.24378	7.63438	7.10504
45	12.10840	10.88120	9.86281	9.00791	8.28252	7.66086	7.12322
50	12.23348	10.96168	9.91481	9.04165	8.30450	7.67524	7.13266

Revenue Recognition

Companies recognize revenue when services have been performed or products have been delivered to customers. For example, when **McDonald's** sells a hamburger, the revenue is earned when the hamburger is delivered to the customer. In this example, revenue recognition is simple because the hamburger is delivered and cash is received at a single point in time.

Revenue recognition is more complex, however, when a transaction includes several items that are sold together, items that are delivered over time, or items whose prices depend upon future events. To address these more complex transactions, the Financial Accounting Standards Board (FASB) issued a new accounting standard in May 2014.[1] The new Standard uses a five-step method for determining when revenue should be recognized. The five steps are as follows:

- Step 1. *Identify the contract with the customer.* The new Standard treats every revenue transaction as a contract. A contract is an agreement by the seller to provide a good or service in exchange for payment from the buyer. A contract may be verbal and implicit, such as the purchase of a **McDonald's** hamburger, or written and explicit, such as a cell phone contract.
- Step 2. *Identify the separate performance obligations in the contract.* Every contract requires the seller and buyer to perform. For example, when you purchase a **McDonald's** hamburger, you (the buyer) perform by paying and McDonald's (the seller) performs by delivering a hamburger. When you purchase a cell phone from **Verizon**, the transaction is more complex. You perform by paying cash or charging your credit card and signing a written contract. Verizon performs by delivering you the phone and promising to provide you cellular service in the future. In this case, Verizon has two performance obligations: (1) to provide the phone and (2) to provide cellular service in the future.
- Step 3. *Determine the transaction price.* The transaction price is the amount the seller is entitled to receive in exchange for the goods and services they have provided. In the case of the **McDonald's** hamburger, the transaction price is the amount paid for the hamburger. In the case of **Verizon**, the transaction price must be estimated for the phone (the first performance obligation) and cellular service (the second performance obligation).
- Step 4. *Allocate the transaction price to the separate performance obligations.* Since the sale of a **McDonald's** hamburger involves the sale of a single item that is immediately delivered, the entire transaction price is allocated to the hamburger. In more complex transactions, such as a **Verizon** cellular service contract, the revenue received from the customer must be allocated among the performance obligations. This allocation is often based on the stand-alone (separate) price of each good or service. For example, Verizon should allocate the revenue from the customer between the phone (first performance obligation) and the commitment to provide cellular service (second performance obligation).
- Step 5. *Recognize revenue when each separate performance obligation is satisfied.* The seller should recognize (record) revenue as each performance obligation is satisfied. In the case of **McDonald's**, the performance obligation is satisfied when the clerk delivers the hamburger to the customer. At this point, the control of the hamburger has passed to the customer. In the case of **Verizon**, it satisfies its first performance obligation when it delivers you the phone. Verizon satisfies its second performance obligation over time by providing you cellular service. Thus, Verizon should record a portion of the total revenue at the time you sign the contract and receive your phone and the remaining revenue over the period cellular service is provided.

[1] Accounting Standards Update, *Revenue from Contracts with Customers (Topic 606)*, Financial Accounting Standards Board, May 2014, Norwalk, CT.

To illustrate, assume that on March 1, Chandler Evans upgrades (replaces) his cell phone with Star Cellular at no cost by signing a two-year agreement. The new agreement cannot be cancelled and requires a payment of $90 per month. The cell phone selected by Evans cost Star Cellular $250.

The five-step method for recognizing revenue from this transaction would be applied as follows:

- **Step 1.** *Identify the contract with the customer.* The contract with Chandler Evans is the two-year cellular service agreement that includes delivery of a new cell phone.
- **Step 2.** *Identify the separate performance obligations in the contract.* Star Cellular has two separate performance obligations under this contract. First, Star Cellular must deliver a new cell phone at the time that Evans signs the service agreement. Second, Star Cellular must provide Evans with cell service for two years.
- **Step 3.** *Determine the transaction price.* The transaction price is the total amount Star Cellular will receive over the contract period. In this case, Star Cellular will receive $2,160 ($90 × 24 months) over the contract period.[2]
- **Step 4.** *Allocate the transaction price to the separate performance obligations.* If Star Cellular sold the cell phone and cell service separately, the individual prices would be as follows:

Cell phone (sold separately)	$ 600
Cell service for two years	3,000
Total price if sold separately	$3,600

The transaction price is allocated to each performance obligation based upon what each obligation would sell for separately as a stand-alone product. To illustrate, the cell phone is allocated $360 of the transaction price of $2,160, computed as follows:

$$\text{Cell Phone} = \text{Transaction Price} \times \frac{\text{Price of Cell Phone Sold Separately}}{\text{Total Price of Cell Phone and Cell Service Sold Separately}}$$

$$= \$2,160 \times \frac{\$600}{\$3,600} = \$360$$

The cell service is allocated $1,800 of the transaction price of $2,160, computed as follows:

$$\text{Cell Service} = \text{Transaction Price} \times \frac{\text{Price of Cell Service Sold Separately}}{\text{Total Price of Cell Phone and Cell Service Sold Separately}}$$

$$= \$2,160 \times \frac{\$3,000}{\$3,600} = \$1,800$$

- **Step 5.** *Recognize revenue when each separate performance obligation is satisfied.* The $360 of revenue assigned to the cell phone is recognized when the customer signs the service agreement and receives the phone. At this point, the first performance obligation has been satisfied by Star Cellular and the control of the phone has passed to the customer. The journal entry to record revenue on March 1 is as follows:

Mar. 1	Accounts Receivable—Chandler Evans	360	
	Sales		360
1	Cost of Goods Sold	250	
	Inventory		250

---

[2] An interest component may need to be considered in long-term contracts. To simplify, we ignore interest.

The $1,800 of cell service revenue is recognized as the performance obligation is satisfied over the two-year term of the contract. For example, $75 ($1,800 ÷ 24 months) of service revenue would be recorded each month. The journal entry to record the service revenue for March is as follows:

Mar. 31	Cash	90	
	Accounts Receivable ($360 ÷ 24 months)		15
	Cell Service Revenue ($1,800 ÷ 24 months)		75

The preceding journal entries illustrate how over the life of the two-year contract the total revenue from the contract of $2,160 is divided between the sale of the cell phone ($360 of revenue) and providing of cell service ($1,800 of revenue). In addition, the journal entries illustrate when revenue from the phone and service is recorded.

Exhibit 1 summarizes the division of revenue and its recording over the two-year contract.

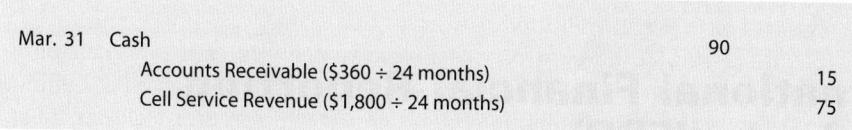

Exhibit 1 Recording Revenue over Two-Year Contract

Recording Revenue over Two-Year Contract

	Signing of Contract									Total Revenue over Two-Year Contract
	Mar. 1	Mar. 31	Apr. 30	Dec. 31	Jan. 31	Dec. 31	Jan. 31	Feb. 28		
Sale of Phone	$360									$ 360
Cell Service		$75	$75	$75	$75	$75	$75	$75		1,800
	Total Revenue of $1,110 [$360 + ($75 × 10 months)]				Total Revenue of $900 ($75 × 12 months)		Total Revenue of $150 ($75 × 2 months)			$2,160
	Year 1				**Year 2**		**Year 3**			Year 1: $1,110 Year 2: 900 Year 3: 150

Appendix C

International Financial Reporting Standards (IFRS)

IFRS

The Need for Global Accounting Standards

As discussed in Chapter 1, the Financial Accounting Standards Board (FASB) establishes generally accepted accounting principles (GAAP) for public companies in the United States. Of course, there is a world beyond the borders of the United States. In recent years, the removal of trade barriers and the growth in cross-border equity and debt issuances have led to a dramatic increase in international commerce. As a result, often companies are reporting financial results to users outside of the United States.

Historically, accounting standards have varied considerably across countries. These variances have been driven by cultural, legal, and political differences and resulted in financial statements that were not easily comparable and difficult to interpret. These differences caused problems for companies in Europe and Asia, where local economies have become increasingly tied to international commerce.

A common set of International Financial Reporting Standards (IFRS) has begun to emerge to reduce cross-country differences in accounting standards. While much of the world has migrated to IFRS, the United States has not. Because of the size of the United States and its significant role in world commerce, U.S. GAAP still has a global impact. As a result, there are currently two major accounting standard-setting efforts in the world, U.S. GAAP and IFRS. These two sets of accounting standards add cost and complexity for companies operating internationally.

Overview of IFRS

International Financial Reporting Standards are designed to meet the financial reporting needs of an increasingly global business environment.

What Is IFRS? International Financial Reporting Standards are a set of global accounting standards developed by an international standard-setting body called the International Accounting Standards Board (IASB). Like the Financial Accounting Standards Board, the IASB is an independent entity that establishes accounting rules. Unlike the FASB, the IASB does not establish accounting rules for any specific country. Rather, it develops accounting rules that can be used by a variety of countries, with the goal of developing a single set of global accounting standards.

Who Uses IFRS? IFRS applies to companies that issue publicly traded debt or equity securities, called **public companies**, in countries that have adopted IFRS as their accounting standards. For example, public companies in the European Union (EU) are required to prepare financial statements using IFRS. The 140 countries and jurisdictions that have adopted or permit the use of IFRS for financial reporting are shown in Exhibit 1.

Exhibit 1
IFRS Adopters

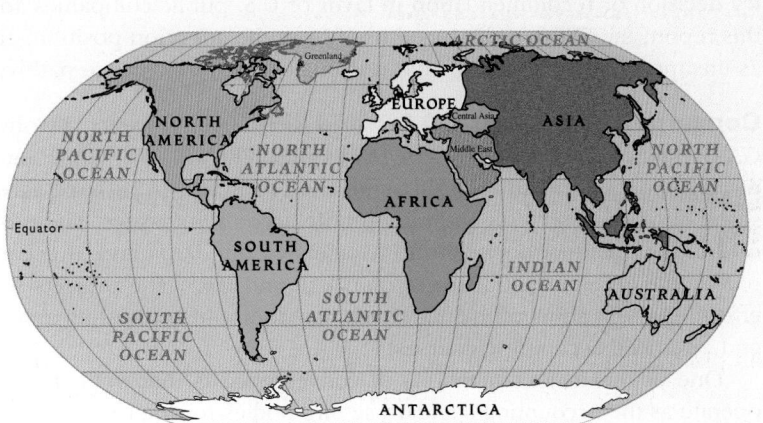

Afghanistan	Bulgaria	Ghana	Liechtenstein	Palestine	Sweden
Albania	Cambodia	Greece	Lithuania	Panama	Switzerland
Angola	Canada	Grenada	Luxembourg	Paraguay	Syria
Anguilla	Cayman Islands	Guatemala	Macao	Peru	Taiwan
Antigua and Barbuda	Chile	Guinea-Bissau	Macedonia	Philippines	Tanzania
Argentina	China	Guyana	Madagascar	Poland	Thailand
Armenia	Colombia	Honduras	Malaysia	Portugal	Trinidad and Tobago
Australia	Costa Rica	Hong Kong	Maldives	Romania	Turkey
Austria	Croatia	Hungary	Malta	Russia	Uganda
Azerbaijan	Cyprus	Iceland	Mauritius	Rwanda	Ukraine
Bahamas	Czech Republic	India	Mexico	Saint Lucia	United Arab Emirates
Bahrain	Denmark	Indonesia	Moldova	Saudi Arabia	United Kingdom
Bangladesh	Dominica	Iraq	Mongolia	Serbia	United States
Barbados	Dominican Republic	Ireland	Montserrat	Sierra Leone	Uruguay
Belarus	Ecuador	Israel	Myanmar	Singapore	Uzbekistan
Belgium	Egypt	Italy	Nepal	Slovakia	Venezuela
Belize	El Salvador	Jamaica	Netherlands	Slovenia	Vietnam
Bermuda	Estonia	Japan	New Zealand	South Africa	Yemen
Bhutan	European Union	Jordan	Nicaragua	Spain	Zambia
Bolivia	Fiji	Kenya	Niger	Sri Lanka	Zimbabwe
Bosnia and Herzegovina	Finland	Korea (South)	Nigeria	St Kitts and Nevis	
Botswana	France	Kosovo	Norway	St Vincent and the Grenadines	
Brazil	Georgia	Latvia	Oman	Suriname	
Brunei	Germany	Lesotho	Pakistan	Swaziland	

Source: *Financial Reporting Standards for the World Economy*, IFRS, June 2015.

U.S. GAAP and IFRS: The Road Forward

The United States has not formally adopted IFRS for U.S. companies. The wide acceptance being gained by IFRS around the world, however, has placed considerable pressure on the United States to align U.S. GAAP with IFRS. There are two possible paths that the United States could take to achieve this: (1) adoption of IFRS by the U.S. Securities and Exchange Commission or (2) convergence of U.S. GAAP and IFRS. These two options are briefly discussed in this section.

Adoption of IFRS by the SEC The U.S. Securities and Exchange Commission (SEC) is the U.S. governmental agency that has authority over the accounting and financial disclosures for U.S. public companies. Only the SEC has the authority to adopt IFRS for U.S. public companies. After considerable deliberation over a period of nearly five years, the SEC published a Final

Report on the issues surrounding IFRS adoption.[1] Notably, this report did not include a final policy decision or recommendation in favor of U.S. public companies adopting IFRS. Indeed, since this report, the SEC has distanced itself from the adoption position, and it is now acknowledged as unsupported. This leaves what remains of the convergence pathway.

Convergence of U.S. GAAP and IFRS Convergence involves aligning IFRS and U.S. GAAP one topic at a time, by slowly merging IFRS and U.S. GAAP into two broadly uniform sets of accounting standards. To this end, the FASB and IASB have agreed to work together on a select number of difficult and high-profile accounting issues. These issues frame a large portion of the disagreement between the two sets of standards and, if accomplished, will significantly reduce the differences between U.S. GAAP and IFRS. The projects selected for the convergence effort represent some of the more technical topics in accounting and are covered in intermediate and advanced accounting courses.

One of the major limitations of convergence is that both the FASB and IASB continue to operate as the accounting standard-setting bodies for their respective jurisdictions. As such, convergence would not result in a single set of global accounting standards. Only those standards that go through the joint FASB–IASB standard-setting process would be released as uniform. Standards that do not go through a joint standard-setting process may create inconsistencies between U.S. GAAP and IFRS.

Differences Between U.S. GAAP and IFRS

U.S. GAAP and IFRS differ both in their approach to standard setting, as well as their financial statement presentation and recording of transactions.

Rules-Based Versus Principles Approach to Standard Setting U.S. GAAP is considered to be a "rules-based" approach to accounting standard setting. The accounting standards provide detailed and specific rules on the accounting for business transactions. There are few exceptions or varying interpretations of the accounting for a business event. This structure is consistent with the U.S. legal and regulatory system, reflecting the social and economic values of the United States.

In contrast, IFRS is designed to meet the needs of many countries. Differences in legal, political, and economic systems create different needs for and uses of financial information in different countries. For example, Germany needs a financial reporting system that reflects the central role of banks in its financial system, while the Netherlands needs a financial reporting system that reflects the significant role of outside equity in its financial system.

To accommodate economic, legal, and social diversity, IFRS must be broad enough to capture these differences while still presenting comparable financial statements. Under IFRS, there is greater opportunity for different interpretations of the accounting treatment of a business event across different business entities. To support this, IFRS often has more extensive disclosures that support alternative assumptions. Thus, IFRS provides more latitude for professional judgment than typically found in comparable U.S. GAAP. Many countries find this feature attractive in reducing regulatory costs associated with using and auditing financial reports. This "principles-based" approach presents one of the most significant challenges to adopting IFRS in the United States.

Technical Differences Between IFRS and U.S. GAAP Although U.S. GAAP is similar to IFRS, differences arise in the presentation format, balance sheet valuations, and technical accounting procedures. The Mornin' Joe International financial statements presented after Chapter 14 highlight the financial statement format, presentation, and recording differences between U.S. GAAP and IFRS. A more comprehensive summary of the key differences between U.S. GAAP and IFRS that are relevant to an introductory accounting course is provided in Exhibit 2.

---

[1] Work Plan for the Consideration of Incorporating International Financial Accounting Standards into the Financial Reporting System for U.S. Issuers: Final Staff Report, U.S. Securities Exchange Commission, July 13, 2012.

Exhibit 2 Comparison of Accounting for Selected Items Under U.S. GAAP and IFRS

	U.S. GAAP	IFRS	Text Reference
General:			
Financial statement titles	Balance Sheet Statement of Stockholders' Equity Statement of Cash Flows	Statement of Financial Position Statement of Changes in Equity Statement of Cash Flows	General
Financial periods presented	Public companies must present two years of comparative information for income statement, statement of stockholders' equity, and statement of cash flows	One year of comparative information must be presented	General
Conceptual basis for standard setting	"Rules-based" approach	"Principles-based" approach	General
Internal control requirements	Sarbanes-Oxley Act (SOX) Section 404		Ch 7
Balance Sheet:	***Balance Sheet***	***Statement of Financial Position***	
Terminology differences	"Payable" "Stockholders' Equity" "Net Income (Loss)"	"Provision" "Capital and Reserves" "Profit or (Loss)"	Ch 10 Ch 12 General
Inventory—LIFO	LIFO allowed	LIFO prohibited	Ch 6
Inventory—valuation	Reversal of lower-of-cost-or-market write-downs not allowed	Reversal of write-downs allowed	Ch 6
Long-lived assets	May NOT be revalued to fair value	May be revalued to fair value on a regular basis	Ch 9

(Continued)

Exhibit 2   Comparison of Accounting for Selected Items Under U.S. GAAP and IFRS (Continued)

	U.S. GAAP	IFRS	Text Reference
Land held for investment	Treated as held for use or sale, and recorded at historical cost	May be accounted for on a historical cost basis or on a fair value basis with changes in fair value recognized through profit and loss	Ch 9
Property, plant, and equipment—valuation	Historical cost	May select between historical cost or revalued amount (a form of fair value)	Ch 9
	If impaired, impairment loss may NOT be reversed in future periods	If impaired, impairment loss may be reversed in future periods	Ch 9
Cost of major overhaul (Capital and revenue expenditures)	Different treatment for ordinary repairs and maintenance, asset improvement, extraordinary repairs	Typically included as part of the cost of the asset or asset component if future economic benefit is probable and can be reliably measured	Ch 9
Intangible assets—valuation	Acquisition cost, unless impaired	Fair value permitted if the intangible asset trades in an active market	Ch 9
Intangible assets—impairment loss reversal	Prohibited	Prohibited for goodwill but allowed for other intangible assets	Ch 9
Income Statement:	***Income Statement***	***Statement of Comprehensive Income***	
Classification of expenses on income statement	Public companies must present expenses on the income statement by function (e.g., cost of goods sold, selling, administrative)	Expenses may be presented based either by function (e.g., cost of goods sold, selling) or by the nature of expense (e.g., wages expense, interest expense)	Chs 3, 4, 5
Statement of Cash Flows:	***Statement of Cash Flows***	***Statement of Cash Flows***	
Classification of interest paid or received	Treated as an operating activity	Interest paid may be treated as either an operating or a financing activity; interest received may be treated as an operating or investing activity	Ch. 13
Classification of dividend paid or received	Dividend paid treated as a financing activity, dividend received treated as an operating activity	Dividend paid may be treated as either an operating or a financing activity; dividend received may be treated as an operating or investing activity	Ch. 13

Discussion Questions

1. Briefly discuss why global accounting standards are needed in today's business environment.

2. What are International Financial Reporting Standards? Who uses these accounting standards?

3. What body is responsible for setting International Financial Reporting Standards?

4. Briefly discuss the differences between (A) adoption of IFRS by the U.S. Securities and Exchange Commission and (B) convergence of U.S. GAAP with IFRS.

5. Briefly discuss the difference between (A) a "rules-based" approach to accounting standard setting and (B) a "principles-based" approach to accounting standard setting.

6. How is property, plant, and equipment measured on the balance sheet under IFRS? How does this differ from the way property, plant, and equipment is measured on the balance sheet under U.S. GAAP?

7. What inventory costing methods are allowed under IFRS? How does this differ from the treatment under U.S. GAAP?

Appendix D

Investments

Most companies generate cash from their operations. This cash can be used for the following purposes:

- Investing in current operations
- Investing in temporary investments to earn additional revenue
- Investing in long-term investments in stock of other companies for strategic reasons

Cash is often used to support the current operating activities of a company. For example, cash may be used to replace worn-out equipment or to purchase new, more efficient, and productive equipment. In addition, cash may be reinvested in the company to expand its current operations. For example, a retailer based in the northwest United States might decide to expand by opening stores in the Midwest.

A company may temporarily have excess cash that is not needed for use in its current operations. This is often the case when a company has a seasonal operating cycle. For example, a significant portion of the annual merchandise sales of a retailer occurs during the fall holiday season. As a result, retailers often experience a large increase in cash during this period, which is not needed until the spring buying season.

Instead of letting excess cash remain idle in a checking account, most companies invest their excess cash in temporary investments. In doing so, companies invest in securities such as:

- **Debt securities**, which are notes and bonds that pay interest and have a fixed maturity date.
- **Equity securities**, which are preferred and common stocks that represent ownership in a company and do not have a fixed maturity date.

Investments in debt and equity securities, termed **investments** or *temporary investments*, are reported in the current assets section of the balance sheet.

The primary objective of investing in temporary investments is to:

- earn interest revenue.
- receive dividends.
- realize gains from increases in the market price of the securities.

A company may invest cash in the debt or equity of another company as a long-term investment. Long-term investments may be held for the same investment objectives as temporary investments. However, long-term investments often involve the purchase of a significant portion of the stock of another company. Such investments usually have a strategic purpose, such as reduction of costs or expansion into new markets.

Debt Investments at Cost

Debt securities include notes and bonds issued by corporations and governmental organizations. Most companies invest excess cash in bonds as investments to earn interest revenue.

Many bond investments[1] are recorded at cost.[2] Typical transactions for bond investments include the following:

- Purchase of bonds
- Interest revenue
- Sale of bonds

---

[1] Debt investments may also include installment notes and short-term notes. The accounting for these debt investments is covered in intermediate and advanced accounting courses.

[2] When bond investments are recorded at cost, they are called held-to-maturity investments. This section provides an overview of held-to-maturity investments. These investments are covered in more detail in intermediate and advanced accounting courses.

Purchase of Bonds

The purchase of bonds is recorded by debiting an investments account for the cost of acquiring the bonds. This cost includes any fees charged by a broker in acquiring the bonds. If bonds are purchased between interest dates, the buyer must also pay the seller any accrued interest since the last interest payment date. Any accrued interest is debited to an interest receivable account rather than to the investment account.

To illustrate, assume that Homer Company purchases $18,000 of bonds at their face amount on March 17, 20Y3, plus accrued interest. The bonds have an interest rate of 6%, payable on July 31 and January 31.

The entry to record the purchase of the bonds is as follows:

20Y3			
Mar. 17	Investments—Bonds	18,000	
	Interest Receivable	135	
	Cash		18,135
	Purchased $18,000, 6% U.S. Treasury bonds.		

Because Homer Company purchased the bonds on March 17, it is also purchasing the accrued interest for 45 days (January 31 to March 17), as shown in Exhibit 1. The accrued interest of $135 is computed as follows:[3]

$$\text{Accrued Interest} = \$18,000 \times 6\% \times (45 \div 360) = \$135$$

The accrued interest is recorded by debiting Interest Receivable for $135. Investments is debited for the purchase price of the bonds of $18,000.

Interest Revenue

On July 31, Homer Company receives a semiannual interest payment of $540 ($18,000 × 6% × ½). The $540 interest includes the $135 accrued interest that Homer purchased with the bonds on March 17. Thus, Homer has earned $405 ($540 − $135) of interest revenue since the purchase date, as shown in Exhibit 1.

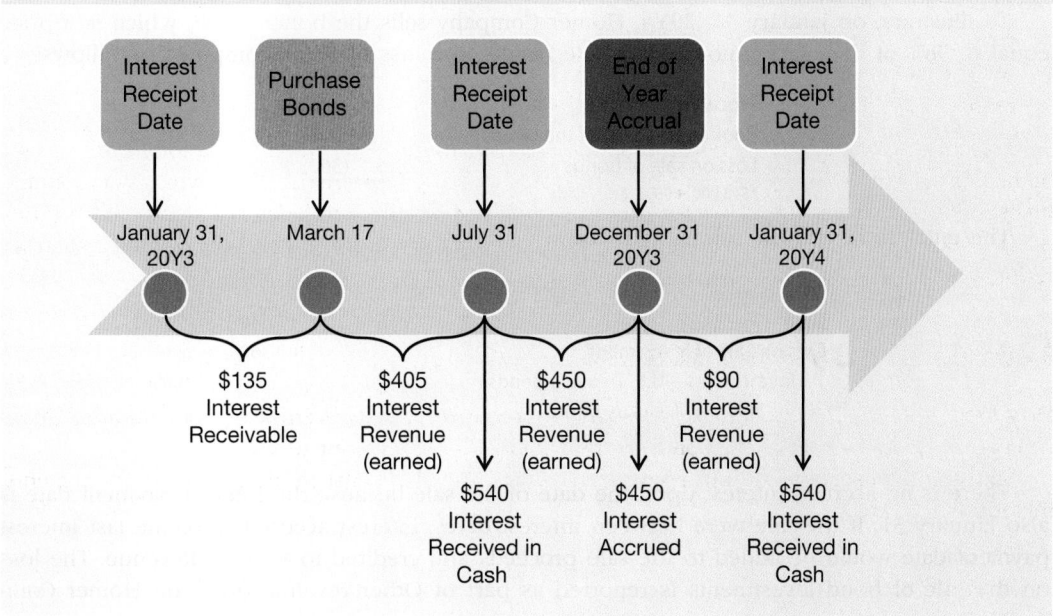

Exhibit 1

Interest Timeline

---

[3] To simplify, a 360-day year is used to compute interest.

The receipt of the interest on July 31 is recorded as follows:

20Y3			
July 31	Cash	540	
	Interest Receivable		135
	Interest Revenue		405
	Received semiannual interest.		

Homer Company's accounting period ends on December 31. Thus, an adjusting entry must be made to accrue interest for five months (August 1 to December 31) of $450 ($18,000 $\times$ 6% $\times$ 5/12), as shown in Exhibit 1. The adjusting entry to record the accrued interest is as follows:

20Y3			
Dec. 31	Interest Receivable	450	
	Interest Revenue		450
	Accrued 5 months of interest.		

For the year ended December 31, 20Y3, Homer Company would report Interest Revenue of $855 ($405 + $450) as part of Other revenue on its income statement.

The receipt of the semiannual interest of $540 on January 31, 20Y4, is recorded as follows:

20Y4			
Jan. 31	Cash	540	
	Interest Revenue		90
	Interest Receivable		450
	Received semiannual interest.		

Sale of Bonds

The sale of bond investments normally results in a gain or loss. If the proceeds from the sale exceed the balance of the investment account, then a gain is recorded. If the proceeds are less than the balance of the investment account, a loss is recorded.

To illustrate, on January 31, 20Y4, Homer Company sells the bonds at 98, which is a price equal to 98% of their face amount. The sale results in a loss of $360, computed as follows:

Proceeds from sale	$ 17,640*
Book value (cost) of the bonds	(18,000)
Loss on sale of bonds	$ (360)
*$18,000 × 98%	

The entry to record the sale is as follows:

20Y4			
Jan. 31	Cash	17,640	
	Loss on Sale of Investment	360	
	Investments—U.S. Treasury Bonds		18,000
	Sold U.S. Treasury bonds.		

There is no accrued interest upon the date of the sale because the interest payment date is also January 31. If the sale were between interest dates, interest accrued since the last interest payment date would be added to the sale proceeds and credited to Interest Revenue. The loss on the sale of bond investments is reported as part of Other revenue (loss) on Homer Company's income statement.

Equity Investments

A company may invest in the preferred or common stock of another company. The company investing in another company's stock is the **investor**. The company whose stock is purchased is the **investee**.

The percent of the investee's outstanding stock purchased by the investor determines the degree of control that the investor has over the investee. This, in turn, determines the accounting method used for the stock investment, as shown in Exhibit 2.

Percent of Outstanding Stock Owned by Investor	Degree of Control of Investor over Investee	Accounting Method
Less than 20%	No control	Cost method
Between 20% and 50%	Significant influence	Equity method
Greater than 50%	Control	Consolidation

Exhibit 2
Stock Investments

Cost Method: Less Than 20% Ownership

If the investor purchases less than 20% of the outstanding stock of the investee, the investor is considered to have no control over the investee. In this case, it is assumed that the investor purchased the stock primarily to earn dividends or to realize gains on price increases of the stock.

Investments of less than 20% of the investee's outstanding stock are accounted for using the **cost method**. Under the cost method, entries are recorded for the following:

- Purchase of stock
- Receipt of dividends
- Sale of stock

Purchase of Stock The purchase of stock is recorded at its cost. To illustrate, assume that on May 1, Bart Company purchases 2,000 shares of Lisa Company common stock at $49.90 per share plus a broker fee of $200. The entry to record the purchase of the stock is as follows:

May 1	Investments—Lisa Company Stock	100,000	
	Cash		100,000
	Purchased 2,000 shares of Lisa Company common stock [($49.90 × 2,000 shares) + $200].		

Receipt of Dividends On July 31, Bart Company receives a dividend of $0.40 per share from Lisa Company. The entry to record the receipt of the dividend is as follows:

July 31	Cash	800	
	Dividend Revenue		800
	Received dividend on Lisa Company common stock (2,000 shares × $0.40).		

Dividend Revenue is reported as part of Other revenue on Bart Company's income statement.

Sale of Stock The sale of a stock investment normally results in a gain or loss. A gain is recorded if the proceeds from the sale exceed the balance of the investment account. A loss is recorded if the proceeds from the sale are less than the balance of the investment account.

To illustrate, on September 1, Bart Company sells 1,500 shares of Lisa Company stock for $54.50 per share, less a $160 commission. The sale results in a gain of $6,590, computed as follows:

Proceeds from sale	$ 81,590*
Book value (cost) of the stock	(75,000)**
Gain on sale	$ 6,590

*($54.50 × 1,500 shares) − $160
**($100,000 ÷ 2,000 shares) × 1,500 shares

The entry to record the sale is as follows:

Sept. 1	Cash	81,590	
	Gain on Sale of Investments		6,590
	Investments—Lisa Company Stock		75,000
	Sold 1,500 shares of Lisa Company common stock.		

The gain on the sale of investments is reported as part of Other revenue on Bart Company's income statement.

Equity Method: Between 20%–50% Ownership

If a company (investor) purchases between 20% and 50% of the outstanding stock of another company (investee), the investor is considered to have a *significant influence* over the investee. Investments of between 20% and 50% of the investee's outstanding stock are accounted for using the **equity method**.

Under the equity method, a stock investment is recorded at its initial cost. However, the investor's share of the investee's operating results and dividends are also recorded in the investment account as follows:

- *Net Income:* The investor records its share of the net income of the investee as an increase (debit) in the investment account. Its share of any net loss is recorded as a decrease (credit) in the investment account.
- *Dividends:* The investor's share of cash dividends received from the investee are recorded as decreases (credits) to the investment account.

Purchase of Stock To illustrate, assume that Simpson Inc. purchased its 40% interest in Flanders Corporation's common stock on January 2, 20Y7, for $350,000. The entry to record the purchase is as follows:

20Y7			
Jan. 2	Investment in Flanders Corporation Stock	350,000	
	Cash		350,000
	Purchased 40% of Flanders Corporation stock.		

Recording Investee Net Income For the year ended December 31, 20Y7, Flanders Corporation reported net income of $105,000. Under the equity method, Simpson Inc. (the investor) records its share of Flanders net income, as follows:

20Y7			
Dec. 31	Investment in Flanders Corporation Stock	42,000	
	Income of Flanders Corporation		42,000
	Recorded 40% share of Flanders Corporation net income, $105,000 × 40%.		

Income of Flanders Corporation is reported on Simpson Inc.'s income statement separately or as part of Other Revenue. If Flanders had a loss during the period, the loss would be recorded as a debit to Loss of Flanders Corporation and a credit to the investment account.

Recording Investee Dividends During the year, Flanders Corporation declared and paid cash dividends of $45,000. Under the equity method, Simpson Inc. (the investor) records its share of Flanders dividends as follows:

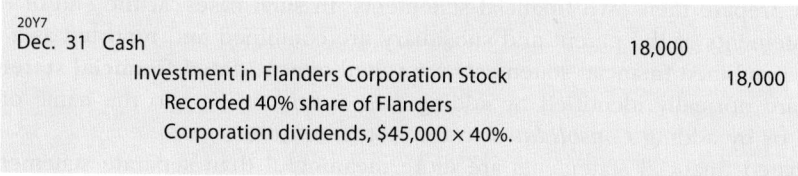

20Y7			
Dec. 31	Cash	18,000	
	Investment in Flanders Corporation Stock		18,000
	Recorded 40% share of Flanders		
	Corporation dividends, $45,000 × 40%.		

The effect of recording 40% of Flanders Corporation's net income and dividends is to increase the investment account by $24,000 ($42,000 − $18,000). Thus, Investment in Flanders Corporation Stock increases from $350,000 to $374,000, as shown in Exhibit 3.

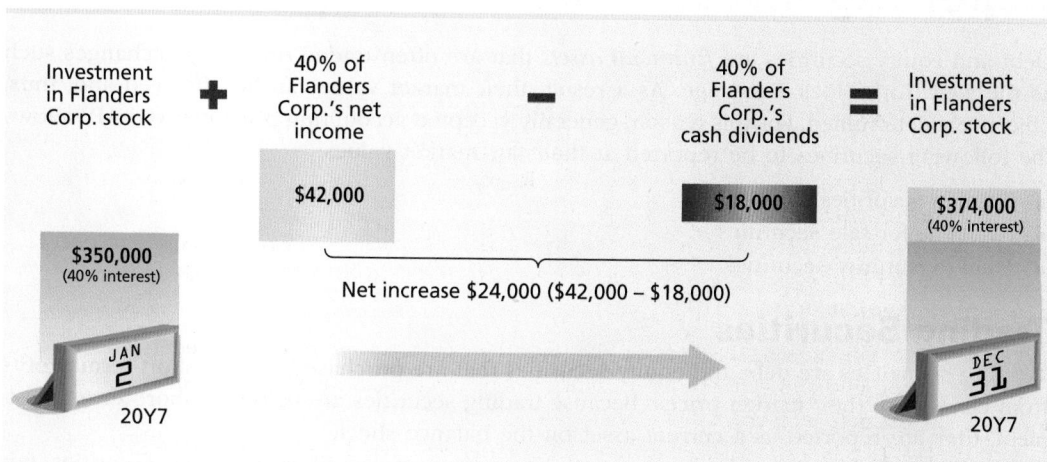

Exhibit 3
Investment and Dividends

Investments accounted for under the equity method are classified on the balance sheet as noncurrent assets.

Sale of Stock Under the equity method, a gain or loss is normally recorded from the sale of an investment. A gain is recorded if the proceeds exceed the balance of the investment account. A loss is recorded if the proceeds are less than the balance of the investment account.

To illlustrate, if Simpson Inc. sold Flanders Corporation's stock on January 1, 20Y8, for $400,000, a gain of $26,000 would be reported, computed as follows:

Proceeds from sale	$ 400,000
Book value of stock investment	(374,000)
Gain on sale	$ 26,000

The entry to record the sale is as follows:

20Y8			
Jan. 1	Cash	400,000	
	Investment in Flanders Corporation Stock		374,000
	Gain on Sale of Flanders Corporation Stock		26,000
	Sold Flanders Corporation stock.		

Consolidation: More Than 50% Ownership

If the investor purchases more than 50% of the outstanding stock of the investee, the investor is considered to have *control* over the investee. The purchase of more than 50% ownership of the investee's stock is termed a **business combination**. The corporation owning all or a majority of the voting stock of another corporation is called a **parent company**. The corporation that is controlled is called the **subsidiary company**.

Parent and subsidiary corporations normally continue to maintain separate accounting records and prepare their own financial statements. In such cases, at the end of the year, the financial statements of the parent and subsidiary are combined and reported as a single company. These combined financial statements are called **consolidated financial statements**. Such statements are normally identified by adding *and Subsidiary(ies)* to the name of the parent corporation or by adding *Consolidated* to the statement title.

Consolidated financial statements are more meaningful than separate statements for each corporation. This is because the parent company, in substance, controls the subsidiaries. The accounting for business combinations, including preparing consolidated financial statements, is described and illustrated in advanced accounting courses and textbooks.

Reporting Investments

Debt and equity securities are *financial assets* that are often traded on public exchanges such as the New York Stock Exchange. As a result, their market value can be observed and, thus, objectively determined. For this reason, generally accepted accounting principles (GAAP) allows the following securities to be reported at their fair market values:

- Trading securities
- Available-for-sale securities
- Held-to-maturity securities

Trading Securities

Trading securities are debt and equity securities that are purchased to earn short-term profits from changes in their market prices. Because trading securities are held as a short-term investment, they are reported as a current asset on the balance sheet.

Trading securities are valued as a portfolio (group) of securities using the securities' fair values. **Fair value** is the market price that the company would receive for a security if it were sold. A change in the fair value of the portfolio (group) of trading securities is recognized in net income as an **unrealized gain or loss** for the period.

To illustrate, assume Maggie Company purchased a portfolio of trading securities during 20Y1. On December 31, 20Y1, the cost and fair values of the securities were as follows:

Name	Number of Shares	Total Cost	Total Fair Value
Armour Company	400	$ 5,000	$ 7,200
Maven, Inc.	500	11,000	7,500
Polaris Co.	200	8,000	10,600
Total		$24,000	$25,300

The portfolio of trading securities is reported on the balance sheet as a current asset with a fair value of $25,300. An adjusting entry is necessary to record the increase in the fair value of $1,300 ($25,300 – $24,000). In order to maintain a record of the original cost of the securities, a valuation account, called *Valuation Allowance for Trading Investments*, is debited for $1,300, and Unrealized Gain on Trading Investments is credited for $1,300.[4] The adjusting entry on December 31, 20Y1, to record the fair value of the portfolio of trading securities is as follows:

---

[4] We assume that the valuation allowance account has a beginning balance of zero to simplify our illustrations.

20Y1			
Dec. 31	Valuation Allowance for Trading Investments	1,300	
	Unrealized Gain on Trading Investments		1,300
	To record increase in fair value of		
	trading securities.		

Unrealized Gain on Trading Investments is reported on the income statement. Depending on its significance, it may be reported separately or as Other revenue on the income statement. The valuation allowance is reported on the December 31, 20Y1, balance sheet as follows:

Maggie Company
Balance Sheet (selected items)
December 31, 20Y1

Current assets:		
Cash..		$120,000
Trading investments (at cost)...............................	$24,000	
Valuation allowance for trading investments	1,300	
Trading investments (at fair value)		25,300

If the fair value of the portfolio of trading securities was less than the cost, then the adjustment would debit Unrealized Loss on Trading Investments and credit Valuation Allowance for Trading Investments for the difference. Unrealized Loss on Trading Investments would be reported on the income statement as Other expenses. Valuation Allowance for Trading Investments would be shown on the balance sheet as a *deduction* from Trading Investments (at cost).

Over time, the valuation allowance account is adjusted to reflect the difference between the cost and the fair value of the portfolio. Thus, increases in the valuation allowance account from the beginning of the period will result in an adjustment to record an unrealized gain, similar to the preceding journal entry. Likewise, decreases in the valuation allowance account from the beginning of the period will result in an adjustment to record an unrealized loss.

Available-for-Sale Securities

Available-for-sale securities are debt and equity securities that are recorded at fair value but are not classified as trading securities. Changes in their fair values are not reported on the income statement, but are reported directly in stockholders' equity.

To illustrate, assume that Maggie Company purchased the three securities during 20Y1 as available-for-sale securities instead of trading securities. On December 31, 20Y1, the cost and fair values of the securities were as follows:

Name	Number of Shares	Total Cost	Total Fair Value
Armour Company	400	$ 5,000	$ 7,200
Maven, Inc.	500	11,000	7,500
Polaris Co.	200	8,000	10,600
Total		$24,000	$25,300

The portfolio of available-for-sale securities is reported at its fair value of $25,300. An adjusting entry is necessary to record the increase in fair value of $1,300 ($25,300 – $24,000). In order to maintain a record of the original cost of the securities, a valuation account, called

Valuation Allowance for Available-for-Sale Investments, is debited for $1,300. This account is similar to the valuation account used for trading securities.

Unlike trading securities, the December 31, 20Y1, adjusting entry credits a stockholders' equity account instead of an income statement account. The $1,300 increase in fair value is credited to Unrealized Gain (Loss) on Available-for-Sale Investments.

The adjusting entry on December 31, 20Y1, to record the fair value of the available-for-sale securities is as follows:

20Y1			
Dec. 31	Valuation Allowance for Available-for-Sale Investments	1,300	
	Unrealized Gain (Loss) on Available-for-Sale Investments		1,300
	To record increase in fair value of available-for-sale investments.		

A credit balance in Unrealized Gain (Loss) on Available-for-Sale Investments is added to stockholders' equity, while a debit balance is subtracted from stockholders' equity.

The valuation allowance and the unrealized gain are reported on the December 31, 20Y1, balance sheet as follows:

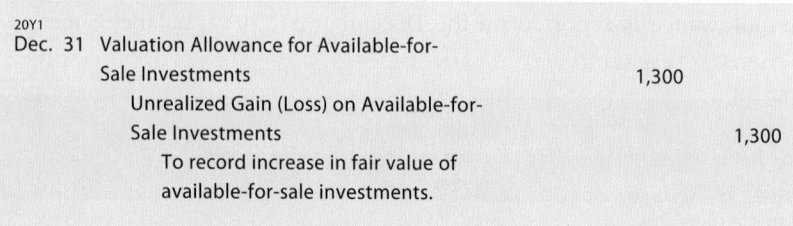

Maggie Company
Balance Sheet
December 31, 20Y1

Current assets:		
Cash...		$120,000
Available-for-sale investments (at cost)............................	$24,000	
Valuation allowance for available-for-sale investments	1,300	
Available-for-sale investments (at fair value)..................		25,300

Stockholders' Equity

Common stock..	$ 10,000
Paid-in capital in excess of par...	150,000
Retained earnings...	250,000
Unrealized gain (loss) on available-for-sale investments...................	1,300
Total stockholders' equity..	$411,300

Equal

As shown, Unrealized Gain (Loss) on Available-for-Sale Investments is reported as an addition to stockholders' equity. In future years, the cumulative effects of unrealized gains and losses are reported in this account.

If the fair value was less than the cost, then the adjustment would debit Unrealized Gain (Loss) on Available-for-Sale Investments and credit Valuation Allowance for Available-for-Sale Investments for the difference. Unrealized Gain (Loss) on Available-for-Sale Investments would be reported in the stockholders' equity section as a negative item. Valuation Allowance for Available-for-Sale Investments would be shown on the balance sheet as a deduction from available-for-sale investments (at cost).

Over time, the valuation allowance account is adjusted to reflect the difference between the cost and the fair value of the portfolio. Thus, increases in the valuation allowance from the beginning of the period will result in an adjustment to record an increase in the valuation and unrealized gain (loss) accounts, similar to the journal entry illustrated earlier. Likewise, decreases in the valuation allowance from the beginning of the period will result in an adjustment to record decreases in the valuation and unrealized gain (loss) accounts.

Held-to-Maturity Securities

Held-to-maturity securities are debt investments, such as notes or bonds, that a company intends to hold until their maturity date. Held-to-maturity securities are primarily purchased to earn interest revenue.

If a held-to-maturity security will mature within a year, it is reported as a current asset on the balance sheet. Held-to-maturity securities maturing beyond a year are reported as noncurrent assets.

Only securities with maturity dates, such as corporate notes and bonds, are classified as held-to-maturity securities. Equity securities are not held-to-maturity securities because they have no maturity date.

Held-to-maturity bond investments are recorded at their cost, as illustrated earlier in this appendix. If the interest rate on the bonds differs from the market rate of interest, the bonds may be purchased at a premium or discount. In such cases, the premium or discount is amortized over the life of the bonds as an increase (discount) or decrease (premium) to the investment account.

Held-to-maturity bond investments are reported on the balance sheet at their amortized cost. The accounting for held-to-maturity investments, including premium and discount amortization, is described in advanced accounting texts.

Summary

Exhibit 4 summarizes the valuation and balance sheet reporting of trading, available-for-sale, and held-to-maturity securities.

	Trading Securities	Available-for-Sale Securities	Held-to-Maturity Securities	
Valued at:	Fair value	Fair value	Amortized cost	**Exhibit 4**
Changes in valuation are reported as:	Unrealized gain or loss on the income statement as Other Revenue (loss).	Accumulated unrealized gain or loss in stockholders' equity on the balance sheet.	Not applicable. Reported at cost.	Summary of Valuing and Reporting of Investments
Reported on the balance sheet as:	Cost of investments plus or minus valuation allowance.	Cost of investments plus or minus valuation allowance.	Amortized cost of investment.	
Classified on balance sheet as:	A current asset.	Either a current or noncurrent asset, depending on management's intent.	Either a current or noncurrent asset, depending on remaining term to maturity.	

Exercises

SHOW ME HOW

EX D-1   Bond investment transactions

Journalize the entries to record the following selected bond investment transactions for Starks Products:

A. Purchased for cash $120,000 of Iceline, Inc. 5% bonds at 100 plus accrued interest of $1,000.

B. Received first semiannual interest payment.

C. Sold $60,000 of the bonds at 101 plus accrued interest of $500.

SHOW ME HOW

EX D-2   Entries for investment in bonds, interest, and sale of bonds

Parilo Company acquired $170,000 of Makofske Co., 5% bonds on May 1, 20Y5, at their face amount. Interest is paid semiannually on May 1 and November 1. On November 1, 20Y5, Parilo sold $50,000 of the bonds for 96.

Journalize the entries to record the following:

A. The initial acquisition of the bonds on May 1.

B. The semiannual interest received on November 1.

C. The sale of the bonds on November 1.

D. The accrual of $1,000 interest on December 31, 20Y5.

SHOW ME HOW

EX D-3   Entries for investments in bonds, interest, and sale of bonds

Kalyagin Investments acquired $220,000 of Jerris Corp., 7% bonds at their face amount on October 1, 20Y2. The bonds pay interest on October 1 and April 1. On April 1, 20Y3, Kalyagin sold $80,000 of Jerris bonds at 103.

Journalize the entries to record the following:

A. The initial acquisition of the Jerris Corp. bonds on October 1, 20Y2.

B. The adjusting entry for three months of accrued interest earned on the Jerris Corp. bonds on December 31, 20Y2.

C. The receipt of semiannual interest on April 1, 20Y3.

D. The sale of $80,000 of Jerris Corp. bonds on April 1, 20Y3, at 103.

SHOW ME HOW

EX D-4   Stock investment transactions

On September 12, 2,000 shares of Aspen Company were acquired at a price of $50 per share plus a $200 brokerage commission. On October 15, a $0.50-per-share dividend was received on the Aspen stock. On November 10, 1,200 shares of the Aspen stock were sold for $42 per share less a $150 brokerage commission. Journalize the entries to record the original purchase, the dividend, and the sale under the cost method.

SHOW ME HOW

EX D-5   Entries for stock investments, dividends, and sale of stock

Seamus Industries Inc. buys and sells investments as part of its ongoing cash management. The following investment transactions were completed during the year:

Feb. 24.   Acquired 1,000 shares of Tett Co. stock for $85 per share plus a $150 brokerage commission.

May 16.   Acquired 2,500 shares of Issacson Co. stock for $36 per share plus a $100 commission.

July 14.   Sold 400 shares of Tett Co. stock for $100 per share less a $75 brokerage commission.

Aug. 12.   Sold 750 shares of Issacson Co. stock for $32.50 per share less an $80 brokerage commission.

Oct. 31.   Received dividends of $0.40 per share on Tett Co. stock.

Journalize the entries for these transactions.

EX D-6 Equity method

On January 2, Yorkshire Company acquired 40% of the outstanding stock of Fain Company for $500,000. For the year ended December 31, Fain earned income of $140,000 and paid dividends of $50,000. Journalize the entries for Yorkshire Company for the purchase of the stock, the share of Fain income, and the dividends received from Fain Company.

SHOW ME HOW

EX D-7 Equity method for stock investment

On January 4, 20Y6, Spandella Company purchased 175,000 shares of Filington Company direct-ly from one of the founders for a price of $30 per share. Filington has 500,000 shares outstand-ing, including the Spandella shares. On July 2, 20Y6, Filington paid $620,000 in total dividends to its shareholders. On December 31, 20Y6, Filington reported a net income of $1,050,000 for the year. Spandella uses the equity method in accounting for its investment in Filington.

A. Journalize the Spandella Inc. entries for the transactions involving its investment in Filington Company during 20Y6.

B. Determine the December 31, 20Y6, balance of the investment in Filington Company stock account.

✔ B. $5,400,500

EXCEL TEMPLATE   SHOW ME HOW

EX D-8 Valuing trading securities at fair value

On January 1, 20Y9, Valuation Allowance for Trading Investments had a zero balance. On December 31, 20Y9, the cost of the trading securities portfolio was $41,500, and the fair value was $46,300. Journalize the December 31, 20Y9, adjusting journal entry to record the unrealized gain or loss on trading investments.

SHOW ME HOW

EX D-9 Fair value journal entries, trading investments

The investments of Charger Inc. include a single investment: 14,500 shares of Raiders Inc. com-mon stock purchased on February 24, 20Y1, for $38 per share including brokerage commission. These shares were classified as trading securities. As of the December 31, 20Y1, balance sheet date, the share price had increased to $42 per share.

A. Journalize the entries to acquire the investment on February 24, and record the adjustment to fair value on December 31, 20Y1.

B. How is the unrealized gain or loss for trading investments reported on the financial statements?

SHOW ME HOW

EX D-10 Fair value journal entries, trading investments

Jets Bancorp Inc. purchased a portfolio of trading securities during 20Y3. The cost and fair value of this portfolio on December 31, 20Y3, was as follows:

Name	Number of Shares	Total Cost	Total Fair Value
Dolphins Inc.	1,400	$28,000	$30,800
Marino Company	1,200	30,000	27,600
Namath Company	800	28,000	26,400
Total		$86,000	$84,800

Journalize the entry to record the adjustment of the trading security portfolio to fair value on December 31, 20Y3.

SHOW ME HOW

EX D-11 Valuing available-for-sale securities at fair value

On January 1, 20Y5, Valuation Allowance for Available-for-Sale Investments had a zero bal-ance. On December 31, 20Y5, the cost of the available-for-sale securities was $24,260, and the fair value was $26,350. Journalize the adjusting entry to record the unrealized gain or loss on available-for-sale investments on December 31, 20Y5.

SHOW ME HOW

EX D-12   Fair value journal entries, available-for-sale investments

The investments of Steelers Inc. include a single investment: 33,100 shares of Bengals Inc. common stock purchased on September 12, 20Y7, for $13 per share including brokerage commission. These shares were classified as available-for-sale securities. As of the December 31, 20Y7, balance sheet date, the share price declined to $11 per share.

A. Journalize the entries to acquire the investment on September 12 and record the adjustment to fair value on December 31, 20Y7.

B. How is the unrealized gain or loss for available-for-sale investments disclosed on the financial statements?

EXCEL TEMPLATE

EX D-13   Fair value journal entries, available-for-sale investments

Storm, Inc. purchased the following available-for-sale securities during 20Y9, its first year of operations:

Name	Number of Shares	Cost
Dust Devil, Inc.	1,900	$ 81,700
Gale Co.	850	68,000
Whirlwind Co.	2,850	114,000
Total		$263,700

The market price per share for the available-for-sale security portfolio on December 31, 20Y9, was as follows:

	Market Price per Share, Dec. 31, 20Y9
Dust Devil, Inc.	$40
Gale Co.	75
Whirlwind Co.	42

A. Journalize the entry to adjust the available-for-sale security portfolio to fair value on December 31, 20Y9.

B. ➤ Describe the income statement impact from the December 31, 20Y9, journal entry.

EX D-14   Balance sheet presentation of available-for-sale investments

During 20Y8, its first year of operations, Galileo Company purchased two available-for-sale investments as follows:

Security	Shares Purchased	Cost
Hawking Inc.	900	$44,000
Pavlov Co.	1,780	38,000

Assume that as of December 31, 20Y8, the Hawking Inc. stock had a market value of $50 per share, and the Pavlov Co. stock had a market value of $24 per share. Galileo Company had net income of $300,000 and paid no dividends for the year ended December 31, 20Y8. All of the available-for-sale investments are classified as current assets.

A. Prepare the current assets section of the balance sheet presentation for the available-for-sale investments.

B. Prepare the stockholders' equity section of the balance sheet to reflect the earnings and unrealized gain (loss) for the available-for-sale investments.

Appendix E

Nike Inc., Form 10-K for the Fiscal Year Ended May 31, 2015

UNITED STATES
SECURITIES AND EXCHANGE COMMISSION
Washington, D.C. 20549

FORM 10-K

(Mark One)

☑ ANNUAL REPORT PURSUANT TO SECTION 13 OR 15(D) OF THE SECURITIES EXCHANGE ACT OF 1934
FOR THE FISCAL YEAR ENDED MAY 31, 2015

OR

☐ TRANSITION REPORT PURSUANT TO SECTION 13 OR 15(D) OF THE SECURITIES EXCHANGE ACT OF 1934
FOR THE TRANSITION PERIOD FROM   TO   .

Commission File No. 1-10635

NIKE, Inc.

(Exact name of Registrant as specified in its charter)

OREGON	**93-0584541**
(State or other jurisdiction of incorporation)	*(IRS Employer Identification No.)*
One Bowerman Drive, Beaverton, Oregon	**97005-6453**
(Address of principal executive offices)	*(Zip Code)*

(503) 671-6453
(Registrant's Telephone Number, Including Area Code)

SECURITIES REGISTERED PURSUANT TO SECTION 12(B) OF THE ACT:	
Class B Common Stock	**New York Stock Exchange**
(Title of Each Class)	*(Name of Each Exchange on Which Registered)*

SECURITIES REGISTERED PURSUANT TO SECTION 12(G) OF THE ACT:
NONE

Indicate by check mark:	YES	NO
• if the registrant is a well-known seasoned issuer, as defined in Rule 405 of the Securities Act.	☑	☐
• if the registrant is not required to file reports pursuant to Section 13 or Section 15(d) of the Act.	☐	☑
• whether the Registrant (1) has filed all reports required to be filed by Section 13 or 15(d) of the Securities Exchange Act of 1934 during the preceding 12 months (or for such shorter period that the Registrant was required to file such reports), and (2) has been subject to such filing requirements for the past 90 days.	☑	☐
• whether the registrant has submitted electronically and posted on its corporate Website, if any, every Interactive Data File required to be submitted and posted pursuant to Rule 405 of Regulation S-T (§232.405 of this chapter) during the preceding 12 months (or for such shorter period that the registrant was required to submit and post such files).	☑	☐

• if disclosure of delinquent filers pursuant to Item 405 of Regulation S-K (§229.405 of this chapter) is not contained herein, and will not be contained, to the best of Registrant's knowledge, in definitive proxy or information statements incorporated by reference in Part III of this Form 10-K or any amendment to this Form 10-K.	☑

• whether the Registrant is a large accelerated filer, an accelerated filer, a non-accelerated filer, or a smaller reporting company. See the definitions of "large accelerated filer," "accelerated filer" and "smaller reporting company" in Rule 12b-2 of the Exchange Act.

Large accelerated filer ☑   Accelerated filer ☐   Non-accelerated filer ☐   Smaller reporting company ☐

	YES	NO
• whether the registrant is a shell company (as defined in Rule 12b-2 of the Act).	☐	☑

As of November 30, 2014, the aggregate market values of the Registrant's Common Stock held by non-affiliates were:

Class A	$ 4,394,312,083
Class B	67,997,995,244
	$72,392,307,327

As of July 17, 2015, the number of shares of the Registrant's Common Stock outstanding were:

Class A	177,457,876
Class B	677,893,713
	855,351,589

DOCUMENTS INCORPORATED BY REFERENCE:

Parts of Registrant's Proxy Statement for the Annual Meeting of Shareholders to be held on September 17, 2015 are incorporated by reference into Part III of this Report.

ITEM 8.   Financial Statements and Supplementary Data

Management of NIKE, Inc. is responsible for the information and representations contained in this report. The financial statements have been prepared in conformity with the generally accepted accounting principles we considered appropriate in the circumstances and include some amounts based on our best estimates and judgments. Other financial information in this report is consistent with these financial statements.

Our accounting systems include controls designed to reasonably assure assets are safeguarded from unauthorized use or disposition and provide for the preparation of financial statements in conformity with generally accepted accounting principles. These systems are supplemented by the selection and training of qualified financial personnel and an organizational structure providing for appropriate segregation of duties.

An internal Corporate Audit department reviews the results of its work with the Audit Committee of the Board of Directors, presently consisting of four outside directors. The Audit Committee is responsible for the appointment of the independent registered public accounting firm and reviews, with the independent registered public accounting firm, management and the internal audit staff, the scope and the results of the annual examination, the effectiveness of the accounting control system and other matters relating to the financial affairs of NIKE as the Audit Committee deems appropriate. The independent registered public accounting firm and the internal auditors have full access to the Committee, with and without the presence of management, to discuss any appropriate matters.

Management's Annual Report on Internal Control Over Financial Reporting

Management is responsible for establishing and maintaining adequate internal control over financial reporting, as such term is defined in Rule 13(a)-15(f) and Rule 15(d)-15(f) of the Securities Exchange Act of 1934, as amended. Internal control over financial reporting is a process designed to provide reasonable assurance regarding the reliability of financial reporting and the preparation of the financial statements for external purposes in accordance with generally accepted accounting principles in the United States of America. Internal control over financial reporting includes those policies and procedures that: (i) pertain to the maintenance of records that, in reasonable detail, accurately and fairly reflect the transactions and dispositions of assets of the Company; (ii) provide reasonable assurance that transactions are recorded as necessary to permit preparation of financial statements in accordance with generally accepted accounting principles, and that receipts and expenditures of the Company are being made only in accordance with authorizations of our management and directors; and (iii) provide reasonable assurance regarding prevention or timely detection of unauthorized acquisition, use or disposition of assets of the Company that could have a material effect on the financial statements.

While "reasonable assurance" is a high level of assurance, it does not mean absolute assurance. Because of its inherent limitations, internal control over financial reporting may not prevent or detect every misstatement and instance of fraud. Controls are susceptible to manipulation, especially in instances of fraud caused by the collusion of two or more people, including our senior management. Also, projections of any evaluation of effectiveness to future periods are subject to the risk that controls may become inadequate because of changes in conditions, or that the degree of compliance with the policies or procedures may deteriorate.

Under the supervision and with the participation of our Chief Executive Officer and Chief Financial Officer, our management conducted an evaluation of the effectiveness of our internal control over financial reporting based upon the framework in *Internal Control — Integrated Framework (2013)* issued by the Committee of Sponsoring Organizations of the Treadway Commission (COSO). Based on the results of our evaluation, our management concluded that our internal control over financial reporting was effective as of May 31, 2015.

PricewaterhouseCoopers LLP, an independent registered public accounting firm, has audited (1) the Consolidated Financial Statements and (2) the effectiveness of our internal control over financial reporting as of May 31, 2015, as stated in their report herein.

Mark G. Parker
President and Chief Executive Officer

Donald W. Blair
Chief Financial Officer

Report of Independent Registered Public Accounting Firm

To the Board of Directors and Shareholders of NIKE, Inc.:

In our opinion, the consolidated financial statements listed in the index appearing under Item 15(a)(1) present fairly, in all material respects, the financial position of NIKE, Inc. and its subsidiaries at May 31, 2015 and 2014, and the results of their operations and their cash flows for each of the three years in the period ended May 31, 2015 in conformity with accounting principles generally accepted in the United States of America. In addition, in our opinion, the financial statement schedule listed in the index appearing under Item 15(a)(2) presents fairly, in all material respects, the information set forth therein when read in conjunction with the related consolidated financial statements. Also in our opinion, the Company maintained, in all material respects, effective internal control over financial reporting as of May 31, 2015, based on criteria established in *Internal Control — Integrated Framework (2013)* issued by the Committee of Sponsoring Organizations of the Treadway Commission (COSO). The Company's management is responsible for these financial statements and financial statement schedule, for maintaining effective internal control over financial reporting and for its assessment of the effectiveness of internal control over financial reporting, included in Management's Annual Report on Internal Control Over Financial Reporting appearing under Item 8. Our responsibility is to express opinions on these financial statements, on the financial statement schedule and on the Company's internal control over financial reporting based on our integrated audits. We conducted our audits in accordance with the standards of the Public Company Accounting Oversight Board (United States). Those standards require that we plan and perform the audits to obtain reasonable assurance about whether the financial statements are free of material misstatement and whether effective internal control over financial reporting was maintained in all material respects. Our audits of the financial statements included examining, on a test basis, evidence supporting the amounts and disclosures in the financial statements, assessing the accounting principles used and significant estimates made by management and evaluating the overall financial statement presentation. Our audit of internal control over financial reporting included obtaining an understanding of internal control over financial reporting, assessing the risk that a material weakness exists and testing and evaluating the design and operating effectiveness of internal control based on the assessed risk. Our audits also included performing such other procedures as we considered necessary in the circumstances. We believe that our audits provide a reasonable basis for our opinions.

A company's internal control over financial reporting is a process designed to provide reasonable assurance regarding the reliability of financial reporting and the preparation of financial statements for external purposes in accordance with generally accepted accounting principles. A company's internal control over financial reporting includes those policies and procedures that (i) pertain to the maintenance of records that, in reasonable detail, accurately and fairly reflect the transactions and dispositions of the assets of the Company; (ii) provide reasonable assurance that transactions are recorded as necessary to permit preparation of financial statements in accordance with generally accepted accounting principles, and that receipts and expenditures of the Company are being made only in accordance with authorizations of management and directors of the Company; and (iii) provide reasonable assurance regarding prevention or timely detection of unauthorized acquisition, use, or disposition of the Company's assets that could have a material effect on the financial statements.

Because of its inherent limitations, internal control over financial reporting may not prevent or detect misstatements. Also, projections of any evaluation of effectiveness to future periods are subject to the risk that controls may become inadequate because of changes in conditions, or that the degree of compliance with the policies or procedures may deteriorate.

/s/ PRICEWATERHOUSECOOPERS LLP

Portland, Oregon
July 23, 2015

NIKE, Inc. Consolidated Statements of Income

		Year Ended May 31,	
(In millions, except per share data)	2015	2014	2013
Income from continuing operations:			
Revenues	$ 30,601	$ 27,799	$ 25,313
Cost of sales	16,534	15,353	14,279
Gross profit	14,067	12,446	11,034
Demand creation expense	3,213	3,031	2,745
Operating overhead expense	6,679	5,735	5,051
Total selling and administrative expense	9,892	8,766	7,796
Interest expense (income), net (Notes 6, 7 and 8)	28	33	(3)
Other (income) expense, net (Note 17)	(58)	103	(15)
Income before income taxes	4,205	3,544	3,256
Income tax expense (Note 9)	932	851	805
NET INCOME FROM CONTINUING OPERATIONS	**3,273**	**2,693**	**2,451**
NET INCOME FROM DISCONTINUED OPERATIONS	**—**	**—**	**21**
NET INCOME	**$ 3,273**	**$ 2,693**	**$ 2,472**
Earnings per common share from continuing operations:			
Basic (Notes 1 and 12)	$ 3.80	$ 3.05	$ 2.74
Diluted (Notes 1 and 12)	$ 3.70	$ 2.97	$ 2.68
Earnings per common share from discontinued operations:			
Basic (Notes 1 and 12)	$ —	$ —	$ 0.02
Diluted (Notes 1 and 12)	$ —	$ —	$ 0.02
Dividends declared per common share	$ 1.08	$ 0.93	$ 0.81

The accompanying Notes to the Consolidated Financial Statements are an integral part of this statement.

NIKE, Inc. Consolidated Statements of Comprehensive Income

		Year Ended May 31,		
(In millions)		2015	2014	2013
Net income	$	3,273 $	2,693 $	2,472
Other comprehensive income (loss), net of tax:				
Change in net foreign currency translation adjustment[1]		(20)	(32)	38
Change in net gains (losses) on cash flow hedges[2]		1,188	(161)	12
Change in net gains (losses) on other[3]		(7)	4	(8)
Change in release of cumulative translation loss related to Umbro[4]		—	—	83
Total other comprehensive income (loss), net of tax		1,161	(189)	125
TOTAL COMPREHENSIVE INCOME	$	4,434 $	2,504 $	2,597

(1) Net of tax benefit (expense) of $0 million, $0 million and $(13) million, respectively.

(2) Net of tax benefit (expense) of $(31) million, $18 million and $(22) million, respectively.

(3) Net of tax benefit (expense) of $0 million, $0 million and $1 million, respectively.

(4) Net of tax benefit (expense) of $0 million, $0 million and $47 million, respectively.

The accompanying Notes to the Consolidated Financial Statements are an integral part of this statement.

NIKE, Inc. Consolidated Balance Sheets

	May 31,	
(In millions)	2015	2014
ASSETS		
Current assets:		
Cash and equivalents (Note 6)	$ 3,852	$ 2,220
Short-term investments (Note 6)	2,072	2,922
Accounts receivable, net (Note 1)	3,358	3,434
Inventories (Notes 1 and 2)	4,337	3,947
Deferred income taxes (Note 9)	389	355
Prepaid expenses and other current assets (Notes 6 and 17)	1,968	818
Total current assets	15,976	13,696
Property, plant and equipment, net (Note 3)	3,011	2,834
Identifiable intangible assets, net (Note 4)	281	282
Goodwill (Note 4)	131	131
Deferred income taxes and other assets (Notes 6, 9 and 17)	2,201	1,651
TOTAL ASSETS	$ 21,600	$ 18,594
LIABILITIES AND SHAREHOLDERS' EQUITY		
Current liabilities:		
Current portion of long-term debt (Note 8)	$ 107	$ 7
Notes payable (Note 7)	74	167
Accounts payable (Note 7)	2,131	1,930
Accrued liabilities (Notes 5, 6 and 17)	3,951	2,491
Income taxes payable (Note 9)	71	432
Total current liabilities	6,334	5,027
Long-term debt (Note 8)	1,079	1,199
Deferred income taxes and other liabilities (Notes 6, 9, 13 and 17)	1,480	1,544
Commitments and contingencies (Note 16)		
Redeemable preferred stock (Note 10)	—	—
Shareholders' equity:		
Common stock at stated value (Note 11):		
Class A convertible — 178 and 178 shares outstanding	—	—
Class B — 679 and 692 shares outstanding	3	3
Capital in excess of stated value	6,773	5,865
Accumulated other comprehensive income (Note 14)	1,246	85
Retained earnings	4,685	4,871
Total shareholders' equity	12,707	10,824
TOTAL LIABILITIES AND SHAREHOLDERS' EQUITY	$ 21,600	$ 18,594

The accompanying Notes to the Consolidated Financial Statements are an integral part of this statement.

NIKE, Inc. Consolidated Statements of Cash Flows

(In millions)		Year Ended May 31,		
		2015	2014	2013
Cash provided by operations:				
Net income	$	3,273 $	2,693 $	2,472
Income charges (credits) not affecting cash:				
Depreciation		606	518	438
Deferred income taxes		(113)	(11)	20
Stock-based compensation (Note 11)		191	177	174
Amortization and other		43	68	64
Net foreign currency adjustments		424	56	66
Net gain on divestitures		—	—	(124)
Changes in certain working capital components and other assets and liabilities:				
(Increase) decrease in accounts receivable		(216)	(298)	142
(Increase) in inventories		(621)	(505)	(219)
(Increase) in prepaid expenses and other current assets		(144)	(210)	(28)
Increase in accounts payable, accrued liabilities and income taxes payable		1,237	525	27
Cash provided by operations		4,680	3,013	3,032
Cash used by investing activities:				
Purchases of short-term investments		(4,936)	(5,386)	(4,133)
Maturities of short-term investments		3,655	3,932	1,663
Sales of short-term investments		2,216	1,126	1,330
Investments in reverse repurchase agreements		(150)	—	—
Additions to property, plant and equipment		(963)	(880)	(598)
Disposals of property, plant and equipment		3	3	14
Proceeds from divestitures		—	—	786
(Increase) in other assets, net of other liabilities		—	(2)	(2)
Cash used by investing activities		(175)	(1,207)	(940)
Cash used by financing activities:				
Net proceeds from long-term debt issuance		—	—	986
Long-term debt payments, including current portion		(7)	(60)	(49)
(Decrease) increase in notes payable		(63)	75	10
Payments on capital lease obligations		(19)	(17)	—
Proceeds from exercise of stock options and other stock issuances		514	383	313
Excess tax benefits from share-based payment arrangements		218	132	72
Repurchase of common stock		(2,534)	(2,628)	(1,674)
Dividends — common and preferred		(899)	(799)	(703)
Cash used by financing activities		(2,790)	(2,914)	(1,045)
Effect of exchange rate changes on cash and equivalents		(83)	(9)	36
Net increase (decrease) in cash and equivalents		1,632	(1,117)	1,083
Cash and equivalents, beginning of year		2,220	3,337	2,254
CASH AND EQUIVALENTS, END OF YEAR	$	3,852 $	2,220 $	3,337
Supplemental disclosure of cash flow information:				
Cash paid during the year for:				
Interest, net of capitalized interest	$	53 $	53 $	20
Income taxes		1,262	856	702
Non-cash additions to property, plant and equipment		206	167	137
Dividends declared and not paid		240	209	188

The accompanying Notes to the Consolidated Financial Statements are an integral part of this statement.

NIKE, Inc. Consolidated Statements of Shareholders' Equity

(In millions, except per share data)	Common Stock Class A Shares	Class A Amount	Common Stock Class B Shares	Class B Amount	Capital in Excess of Stated Value	Accumulated Other Comprehensive Income	Retained Earnings	Total
Balance at May 31, 2012	180	$ —	736	$ 3	$ 4,641	$ 149	$ 5,526	$ 10,319
Stock options exercised			10		322			322
Conversion to Class B Common Stock	(2)		2					—
Repurchase of Class B Common Stock			(34)		(10)		(1,647)	(1,657)
Dividends on common stock ($0.81 per share)							(727)	(727)
Issuance of shares to employees			2		65			65
Stock-based compensation (Note 11)					174			174
Forfeiture of shares from employees			—		(8)		(4)	(12)
Net income							2,472	2,472
Other comprehensive income (loss)						125		125
Balance at May 31, 2013	178	$ —	716	$ 3	$ 5,184	$ 274	$ 5,620	$ 11,081
Stock options exercised			11		445			445
Repurchase of Class B Common Stock			(37)		(11)		(2,617)	(2,628)
Dividends on common stock ($0.93 per share)							(821)	(821)
Issuance of shares to employees			2		78			78
Stock-based compensation (Note 11)					177			177
Forfeiture of shares from employees			—		(8)		(4)	(12)
Net income							2,693	2,693
Other comprehensive income (loss)						(189)		(189)
Balance at May 31, 2014	178	$ —	692	$ 3	$ 5,865	$ 85	$ 4,871	$ 10,824
Stock options exercised			14		639			639
Repurchase of Class B Common Stock			(29)		(9)		(2,525)	(2,534)
Dividends on common stock ($1.08 per share)							(931)	(931)
Issuance of shares to employees			2		92			92
Stock-based compensation (Note 11)					191			191
Forfeiture of shares from employees			—		(5)		(3)	(8)
Net income							3,273	3,273
Other comprehensive income (loss)						1,161		1,161
Balance at May 31, 2015	178	$ —	679	$ 3	$ 6,773	$ 1,246	$ 4,685	$ 12,707

The accompanying Notes to the Consolidated Financial Statements are an integral part of this statement.

Notes to Consolidated Financial Statements

NOTE 1 — Summary of Significant Accounting Policies

Description of Business

NIKE, Inc. is a worldwide leader in the design, development and worldwide marketing and selling of athletic footwear, apparel, equipment, accessories and services. NIKE, Inc. portfolio brands include the NIKE Brand, Jordan Brand, Hurley and Converse. The NIKE Brand is focused on performance athletic footwear, apparel, equipment, accessories and services across a wide range of sport categories, amplified with sport-inspired sportswear products carrying the Swoosh trademark as well as other NIKE Brand trademarks. The Jordan Brand is focused on athletic and casual footwear, apparel and accessories, using the Jumpman trademark. Sales of Jordan Brand products are included within the NIKE Brand Basketball category. The Hurley brand is focused on surf and action sports and youth lifestyle footwear, apparel and accessories, using the Hurley trademark. Sales of Hurley brand products are included within the NIKE Brand Action Sports category. Converse designs, distributes, markets and sells casual sneakers, apparel and accessories under the Converse, Chuck Taylor, All Star, One Star, Star Chevron and Jack Purcell trademarks. In some markets outside the U.S., these trademarks are licensed to third parties who design, distribute, market and sell similar products. Operating results of the Converse brand are reported on a stand-alone basis.

Basis of Consolidation

The Consolidated Financial Statements include the accounts of NIKE, Inc. and its subsidiaries (the "Company"). All significant intercompany transactions and balances have been eliminated.

The Company completed the sale of Cole Haan during the third quarter ended February 28, 2013 and completed the sale of Umbro during the second quarter ended November 30, 2012. As a result, the Company reports the operating results of Cole Haan and Umbro in the Net income from discontinued operations line in the Consolidated Statements of Income for all applicable periods presented. There were no assets or liabilities of discontinued operations as of May 31, 2015 and May 31, 2014 (refer to Note 15 — Discontinued Operations). Unless otherwise indicated, the disclosures accompanying the Consolidated Financial Statements reflect the Company's continuing operations.

On November 15, 2012, the Company announced a two-for-one split of both NIKE Class A and Class B Common shares. The stock split was a 100 percent stock dividend payable on December 24, 2012 to shareholders of record at the close of business on December 10, 2012. Common stock began trading at the split-adjusted price on December 26, 2012. All share numbers and per share amounts presented reflect the stock split.

Reclassifications

Certain prior year amounts have been reclassified to conform to fiscal 2015 presentation.

Revisions

During the third quarter of fiscal 2015, management determined it had incorrectly reflected unrealized gains and losses from re-measurement of non-functional currency intercompany balances between certain of its foreign wholly-owned subsidiaries in its Consolidated Statements of Cash Flows. These unrealized gains and losses should have been classified as non-cash reconciling items from Net income to Cash provided by operations, but were instead reported on the Effect of exchange rate changes on cash and equivalents line of the Consolidated Statements of Cash Flows. This resulted in an understatement of Cash provided by operations reported on the Consolidated Statements of Cash Flows for certain prior periods; there was no impact for any period to Net increase (decrease) in cash and equivalents reported on the Consolidated Statements of Cash Flows, or Cash and equivalents reported on the Consolidated Statements of Cash Flows and Balance Sheets. The Company assessed the materiality of the misclassifications on prior periods' financial statements in accordance with SEC Staff Accounting Bulletin ("SAB") No. 99, Materiality, codified in Accounting Standards Codification ("ASC") 250, Presentation of Financial Statements, and concluded that these misstatements were not material to any prior annual or interim periods. Accordingly, in accordance with ASC 250 (SAB No. 108, Considering the Effects of Prior Year Misstatements when Quantifying Misstatements in Current Year Financial Statements), the amounts have been revised in the applicable Consolidated Statements of Cash Flows. For the three and six months ended August 31, 2014 and November 30, 2014 of fiscal 2015, the revisions increased Cash provided by operations and decreased Effect of exchange rate changes on cash and equivalents by $95 million and $312 million, respectively. For the fiscal years ended May 31, 2014 and 2013, the revisions increased Cash provided by operations and decreased Effect of exchange rate changes on cash and equivalents by $10 million and $64 million, respectively. These amounts have been reflected in the applicable tables below. As part of the revision to the Consolidated Statements of Cash Flows, the Company has updated its presentation to separately report Net foreign currency adjustments, which was previously included within Amortization and other.

The following are selected line items from the Company's Unaudited Condensed Consolidated Statements of Cash Flows illustrating the effect of these corrections:

NIKE, Inc. Unaudited Condensed Consolidated Statements of Cash Flows

(In millions)	Three Months Ended August 31, 2014			Six Months Ended November 30, 2014		
	As Reported	Adjustment	As Revised	As Reported	Adjustment	As Revised
Cash provided by operations:						
Net income	$ 962	$ —	$ 962	$ 1,617	$ —	$ 1,617
Income charges (credits) not affecting cash:						
Amortization and other	(34)	42	8	(54)	69	15
Net foreign currency adjustments	—	53	53	—	243	243
Cash provided by operations	588	95	683	1,235	312	1,547
Effect of exchange rate changes on cash and equivalents	97	(95)	2	288	(312)	(24)
Net increase (decrease) in cash and equivalents	83	—	83	53	—	53
Cash and equivalents, beginning of period	2,220	—	2,220	2,220	—	2,220
CASH AND EQUIVALENTS, END OF PERIOD	$ 2,303	$ —	$ 2,303	$ 2,273	$ —	$ 2,273

The following are selected line items from the Company's Consolidated Statements of Cash Flows illustrating the effect of these corrections on the amounts previously reported in the Company's fiscal 2014 Annual Report on Form 10-K:

| | NIKE, Inc. Consolidated Statements of Cash Flows | | | | | |
| | Year Ended May 31, 2014 | | | Year Ended May 31, 2013 | | |
(In millions)	As Reported	Adjustment	As Revised	As Reported	Adjustment	As Revised
Cash provided by operations:						
Net income	$ 2,693 $	—	$ 2,693	$ 2,472 $	—	$ 2,472
Income charges (credits) not affecting cash:						
Amortization and other	114	(46)	68	66	(2)	64
Net foreign currency adjustments	—	56	56	—	66	66
Cash provided by operations	3,003	10	3,013	2,968	64	3,032
Effect of exchange rate changes on cash and equivalents	1	(10)	(9)	100	(64)	36
Net increase (decrease) in cash and equivalents	(1,117)	—	(1,117)	1,083	—	1,083
Cash and equivalents, beginning of year	3,337	—	3,337	2,254	—	2,254
CASH AND EQUIVALENTS, END OF YEAR	$ 2,220 $	—	$ 2,220	$ 3,337 $	—	$ 3,337

Recognition of Revenues

Wholesale revenues are recognized when title and the risks and rewards of ownership have passed to the customer, based on the terms of sale. This occurs upon shipment or upon receipt by the customer depending on the country of the sale and the agreement with the customer. Retail store revenues are recorded at the time of sale and online store revenues are recorded upon delivery to the customer. Provisions for post-invoice sales discounts, returns and miscellaneous claims from customers are estimated and recorded as a reduction to revenue at the time of sale. Post-invoice sales discounts consist of contractual programs with certain customers or discretionary discounts that are expected to be granted to certain customers at a later date. Estimates of discretionary discounts, returns and claims are based on historical rates, specific identification of outstanding claims and outstanding returns not yet received from customers and estimated discounts, returns and claims expected, but not yet finalized with customers. As of May 31, 2015 and 2014, the Company's reserve balances for post-invoice sales discounts, returns and miscellaneous claims were $724 million and $610 million, respectively.

Cost of Sales

Cost of sales consists primarily of inventory costs, as well as warehousing costs (including the cost of warehouse labor), third-party royalties, certain foreign currency hedge gains and losses and research, design and development costs.

Shipping and Handling Costs

Outbound shipping and handling costs are expensed as incurred and included in *Cost of sales*.

Operating Overhead Expense

Operating overhead expense consists primarily of payroll and benefit related costs, rent, depreciation and amortization, professional services and meetings and travel.

Demand Creation Expense

Demand creation expense consists of advertising and promotion costs, including costs of endorsement contracts, television, digital and print advertising, brand events and retail brand presentation. Advertising production costs are expensed the first time an advertisement is run. Advertising communication costs are expensed when the advertisement appears. Costs related to brand events are expensed when the event occurs. Costs related to retail brand presentation are expensed when the presentation is completed and delivered.

A significant amount of the Company's promotional expenses result from payments under endorsement contracts. Accounting for endorsement payments is based upon specific contract provisions. Generally, endorsement payments are expensed on a straight-line basis over the term of the contract after giving recognition to periodic performance compliance provisions of the contracts. Prepayments made under contracts are included in *Prepaid expenses and other current assets* or *Deferred income taxes and other assets* depending on the period to which the prepayment applies.

Certain contracts provide for contingent payments to endorsers based upon specific achievements in their sports (e.g., winning a championship). The Company records demand creation expense for these amounts when the endorser achieves the specific goal.

Certain contracts provide for variable payments based upon endorsers maintaining a level of performance in their sport over an extended period of time (e.g., maintaining a specified ranking in a sport for a year). When the Company determines payments are probable, the amounts are reported in demand creation expense ratably over the contract period based on our best estimate of the endorser's performance. In these instances, to the extent that actual payments to the endorser differ from the Company's estimate due to changes in the endorser's performance, increased or decreased demand creation expense may be recorded in a future period.

Certain contracts provide for royalty payments to endorsers based upon a predetermined percent of sales of particular products. The Company expenses these payments in *Cost of sales* as the related sales occur. In certain contracts, the Company offers minimum guaranteed royalty payments. For contracts for which the Company estimates it will not meet the minimum guaranteed amount of royalty fees through sales of product, the Company records the amount of the guaranteed payment in excess of that earned through sales of product in *Demand creation expense* uniformly over the guarantee period.

Through cooperative advertising programs, the Company reimburses retail customers for certain costs of advertising the Company's products. The Company records these costs in *Demand creation expense* at the point in time when it is obligated to its customers for the costs. This obligation may arise prior to the related advertisement being run.

Total advertising and promotion expenses were $3,213 million, $3,031 million and $2,745 million for the years ended May 31, 2015, 2014 and 2013, respectively. Prepaid advertising and promotion expenses totaled $455 million and $516 million at May 31, 2015 and 2014, respectively, and were recorded in *Prepaid expenses and other current assets* and *Deferred income taxes and other assets* depending on the period to which the prepayment applies.

Cash and Equivalents

Cash and equivalents represent cash and short-term, highly liquid investments, including commercial paper, U.S. Treasury, U.S. Agency, money market funds, time deposits and corporate debt securities with maturities of 90 days or less at the date of purchase.

Short-Term Investments

Short-term investments consist of highly liquid investments, including commercial paper, U.S. Treasury, U.S. Agency and corporate debt securities, with maturities over 90 days at the date of purchase. Debt securities that the Company has the ability and positive intent to hold to maturity are carried at amortized cost. At May 31, 2015 and 2014, the Company did not hold any short-term investments that were classified as trading or held-to-maturity.

At May 31, 2015 and 2014, *Short-term investments* consisted of available-for-sale securities. Available-for-sale securities are recorded at fair value with unrealized gains and losses reported, net of tax, in *Other comprehensive income*, unless unrealized losses are determined to be other than temporary. Realized gains and losses on the sale of securities are determined by specific identification. The Company considers all available-for-sale securities, including those with maturity dates beyond 12 months, as available to support current operational liquidity needs and therefore classifies all securities with maturity dates beyond 90 days at the date of purchase as current assets within *Short-term investments* on the Consolidated Balance Sheets.

Refer to Note 6 — Fair Value Measurements for more information on the Company's short-term investments.

Allowance for Uncollectible Accounts Receivable

Accounts receivable consists primarily of amounts receivable from customers. The Company makes ongoing estimates relating to the collectability of its accounts receivable and maintains an allowance for estimated losses resulting from the inability of its customers to make required payments. In determining the amount of the allowance, the Company considers historical levels of credit losses and makes judgments about the creditworthiness of significant customers based on ongoing credit evaluations. Accounts receivable with anticipated collection dates greater than 12 months from the balance sheet date and related allowances are considered non-current and recorded in *Deferred income taxes and other assets*. The allowance for uncollectible accounts receivable was $78 million and $78 million at May 31, 2015 and 2014, respectively, of which $24 million and $37 million, respectively, was classified as long-term and recorded in *Deferred income taxes and other assets*.

Inventory Valuation

Inventories are stated at lower of cost or market and valued on either an average or specific identification cost basis. For inventories in transit that represent direct shipments to customers, the related inventory and cost of sales are recognized on a specific identification basis. Inventory costs primarily consist of product cost from the Company's suppliers, as well as inbound freight, import duties, taxes, insurance and logistics and other handling fees.

Property, Plant and Equipment and Depreciation

Property, plant and equipment are recorded at cost. Depreciation is determined on a straight-line basis for buildings and leasehold improvements over 2 to 40 years and for machinery and equipment over 2 to 15 years.

Depreciation and amortization of assets used in manufacturing, warehousing and product distribution are recorded in *Cost of sales*. Depreciation and amortization of other assets are recorded in *Total selling and administrative expense*.

Software Development Costs

Internal Use Software. Expenditures for major software purchases and software developed for internal use are capitalized and amortized over a 2 to 10 year period on a straight-line basis. The Company's policy provides for the capitalization of external direct costs of materials and services associated with developing or obtaining internal use computer software. In addition, the Company also capitalizes certain payroll and payroll-related costs for employees who are directly associated with internal use computer software projects. The amount of capitalizable payroll costs with respect to these employees is limited to the time directly spent on such projects. Costs associated with preliminary project stage activities, training, maintenance and all other post-implementation stage activities are expensed as incurred.

Computer Software to be Sold, Leased or Otherwise Marketed. Development costs of computer software to be sold, leased or otherwise marketed as an integral part of a product are subject to capitalization beginning when a product's technological feasibility has been established and ending when a product is available for general release to customers. In most instances, the Company's products are released soon after technological feasibility has been established. Therefore, software development costs incurred subsequent to achievement of technological feasibility are usually not significant, and generally most software development costs have been expensed as incurred.

Impairment of Long-Lived Assets

The Company reviews the carrying value of long-lived assets or asset groups to be used in operations whenever events or changes in circumstances indicate that the carrying amount of the assets might not be recoverable. Factors that would necessitate an impairment assessment include a significant adverse change in the extent or manner in which an asset is used, a significant adverse change in legal factors or the business climate that could affect the value of the asset or a significant decline in the observable market value of an asset, among others. If such facts indicate a potential impairment, the Company would assess the recoverability of an asset group by determining if the carrying value of the asset group exceeds the sum of the projected undiscounted cash flows expected to result from the use and eventual disposition of the assets over the remaining economic life of the primary asset in the asset group. If the recoverability test indicates that the carrying value of the asset group is not recoverable, the Company will estimate the fair value of the asset group using appropriate valuation methodologies, which would typically include an estimate of discounted cash flows. Any impairment would be measured as the difference between the asset group's carrying amount and its estimated fair value.

Goodwill and Indefinite-Lived Intangible Assets

The Company performs annual impairment tests on goodwill and intangible assets with indefinite lives in the fourth quarter of each fiscal year, or when events occur or circumstances change that would, more likely than not, reduce the fair value of a reporting unit or an intangible asset with an indefinite life below its carrying value. Events or changes in circumstances that may trigger interim impairment reviews include significant changes in business climate, operating results, planned investments in the reporting unit, planned divestitures or an expectation that the carrying amount may not be recoverable, among other factors. The Company may first assess qualitative factors to determine whether it is more likely than not that the fair value of a reporting unit is less than its carrying amount. If, after assessing the totality of events and circumstances, the Company determines that it is more likely than not that the fair value of the reporting unit is greater than its carrying amount, the two-step impairment test is unnecessary. The two-step impairment test first requires the Company to estimate the fair value of its reporting units. If the carrying value of a reporting unit exceeds its fair value, the goodwill of that reporting unit is potentially impaired and the Company proceeds to step two of the impairment analysis. In step two of the analysis, the Company measures and records an impairment loss equal to the excess of the carrying value of the reporting unit's goodwill over its implied fair value, if any.

The Company generally bases its measurement of the fair value of a reporting unit on a blended analysis of the present value of future discounted cash flows and the market valuation approach. The discounted cash flows model indicates the fair value of the reporting unit based on the present value of the cash flows that the Company expects the reporting unit to generate in the future. The Company's significant estimates in the discounted cash flows model include: its weighted average cost of capital; long-term rate of growth and profitability of the reporting unit's business; and working capital effects. The market valuation approach indicates the fair value of the business based on a comparison of the reporting unit to comparable publicly traded companies in similar lines of business. Significant estimates in the market valuation approach model include identifying similar companies with comparable business factors such as size, growth, profitability, risk and return on investment and assessing comparable revenue and operating income multiples in estimating the fair value of the reporting unit.

Indefinite-lived intangible assets primarily consist of acquired trade names and trademarks. The Company may first perform a qualitative assessment to determine whether it is more likely than not that an indefinite-lived intangible asset is impaired. If, after assessing the totality of events and circumstances, the Company determines that it is more likely than not that the indefinite-lived intangible asset is not impaired, no quantitative fair value measurement is necessary. If a quantitative fair value measurement calculation is required for these intangible assets, the Company utilizes the relief-from-royalty method. This method assumes that trade names and trademarks have value to the extent that their owner is relieved of the obligation to pay royalties for the benefits received from them. This method requires the Company to estimate the future revenue for the related brands, the appropriate royalty rate and the weighted average cost of capital.

Operating Leases

The Company leases retail store space, certain distribution and warehouse facilities, office space and other non-real estate assets under operating leases. Operating lease agreements may contain rent escalation clauses, rent holidays or certain landlord incentives, including tenant improvement allowances. Rent expense for non-cancelable operating leases with scheduled rent increases or landlord incentives are recognized on a straight-line basis over the lease term, beginning with the effective lease commencement date, which is generally the date in which the Company takes possession of or controls the physical use of the property. Certain leases also provide for contingent rents, which are determined as a percent of sales in excess of specified levels. A contingent rent liability is recognized together with the corresponding rent expense when specified levels have been achieved or when the Company determines that achieving the specified levels during the period is probable.

Fair Value Measurements

The Company measures certain financial assets and liabilities at fair value on a recurring basis, including derivatives and available-for-sale securities. Fair value is the price the Company would receive to sell an asset or pay to transfer a liability in an orderly transaction with a market participant at the measurement date. The Company uses a three-level hierarchy established by the Financial Accounting Standards Board ("FASB") that prioritizes fair value measurements based on the types of inputs used for the various valuation techniques (market approach, income approach and cost approach).

The levels of hierarchy are described below:

- Level 1: Quoted prices in active markets for identical assets or liabilities.

- Level 2: Inputs other than quoted prices that are observable for the asset or liability, either directly or indirectly; these include quoted prices for similar assets or liabilities in active markets and quoted prices for identical or similar assets or liabilities in markets that are not active.

- Level 3: Unobservable inputs for which there is little or no market data available, which require the reporting entity to develop its own assumptions.

The Company's assessment of the significance of a particular input to the fair value measurement in its entirety requires judgment and considers factors specific to the asset or liability. Financial assets and liabilities are classified in their entirety based on the most conservative level of input that is significant to the fair value measurement.

Pricing vendors are utilized for certain Level 1 and Level 2 investments. These vendors either provide a quoted market price in an active market or use observable inputs without applying significant adjustments in their pricing. Observable inputs include broker quotes, interest rates and yield curves observable at commonly quoted intervals, volatilities and credit risks. The fair value of derivative contracts is determined using observable market inputs such as the daily market foreign currency rates, forward pricing curves, currency volatilities, currency correlations and interest rates and considers nonperformance risk of the Company and that of its counterparties.

The Company's fair value processes include controls that are designed to ensure appropriate fair values are recorded. These controls include a comparison of fair values to another independent pricing vendor.

Refer to Note 6 — Fair Value Measurements for additional information.

Foreign Currency Translation and Foreign Currency Transactions

Adjustments resulting from translating foreign functional currency financial statements into U.S. Dollars are included in the foreign currency translation adjustment, a component of *Accumulated other comprehensive income* in *Total shareholders' equity*.

The Company's global subsidiaries have various assets and liabilities, primarily receivables and payables, which are denominated in currencies other than their functional currency. These balance sheet items are subject to re-measurement, the impact of which is recorded in *Other (income) expense, net*, within the Consolidated Statements of Income.

Accounting for Derivatives and Hedging Activities

The Company uses derivative financial instruments to reduce its exposure to changes in foreign currency exchange rates and interest rates. All derivatives are recorded at fair value on the Consolidated Balance Sheets and changes in the fair value of derivative financial instruments are either recognized in *Accumulated other comprehensive income* (a component of *Total shareholders' equity*), *Long-term debt* or *Net income* depending on the nature of the underlying exposure, whether the derivative is formally designated as a hedge and, if designated, the extent to which the hedge is effective. The Company classifies the cash flows at settlement from derivatives in the same category as the cash flows from the related hedged items. For undesignated hedges and designated cash flow hedges, this is primarily within the *Cash provided by operations* component of the Consolidated Statements of Cash Flows. For designated net investment hedges, this is within the *Cash used by investing activities* component of the Consolidated Statement of Cash Flows. For the Company's fair value hedges, which are interest rate swaps used to mitigate the change in fair value of its fixed-rate debt attributable to changes in interest rates, the related cash flows from periodic interest payments are reflected within the *Cash provided by operations* component of the Consolidated Statements of Cash Flows. Refer to Note 17 — Risk Management and Derivatives for more information on the Company's risk management program and derivatives.

Stock-Based Compensation

The Company estimates the fair value of options and stock appreciation rights granted under the NIKE, Inc. 1990 Stock Incentive Plan (the "1990 Plan") and employees' purchase rights under the Employee Stock Purchase Plans ("ESPPs") using the Black-Scholes option pricing model. The Company recognizes this fair value, net of estimated forfeitures, as *Operating overhead expense* in the Consolidated Statements of Income over the vesting period using the straight-line method.

Refer to Note 11 — Common Stock and Stock-Based Compensation for more information on the Company's stock programs.

Income Taxes

The Company accounts for income taxes using the asset and liability method. This approach requires the recognition of deferred tax assets and liabilities for the expected future tax consequences of temporary differences between the carrying amounts and the tax basis of assets and liabilities. The Company records a valuation allowance to reduce deferred tax assets to the amount management believes is more likely than not to be realized. United States income taxes are provided currently on financial statement earnings of non-U.S. subsidiaries that are expected to be repatriated. The Company determines annually the amount of undistributed non-U.S. earnings to invest indefinitely in its non-U.S. operations.

The Company recognizes a tax benefit from uncertain tax positions in the financial statements only when it is more likely than not that the position will be sustained upon examination by relevant tax authorities. The Company recognizes interest and penalties related to income tax matters in *Income tax expense*.

Refer to Note 9 — Income Taxes for further discussion.

Earnings Per Share

Basic earnings per common share is calculated by dividing *Net income* by the weighted average number of common shares outstanding during the year. Diluted earnings per common share is calculated by adjusting weighted average outstanding shares, assuming conversion of all potentially dilutive stock options and awards.

Refer to Note 12 — Earnings Per Share for further discussion.

Management Estimates

The preparation of financial statements in conformity with generally accepted accounting principles requires management to make estimates, including estimates relating to assumptions that affect the reported amounts of assets and liabilities and disclosure of contingent assets and liabilities at the date of financial statements and the reported amounts of revenues and expenses during the reporting period. Actual results could differ from these estimates.

Recently Adopted Accounting Standards

In July 2013, the FASB issued an accounting standards update intended to provide guidance on the presentation of unrecognized tax benefits, reflecting the manner in which an entity would settle, at the reporting date, any additional income taxes that would result from the disallowance of a tax position when net operating loss carryforwards, similar tax losses or tax credit carryforwards exist. This accounting standard was effective for the Company beginning June 1, 2014 and early adoption was permitted. Management early adopted this guidance and the adoption did not have a material impact on the Company's consolidated financial position or results of operations.

In July 2012, the FASB issued an accounting standards update intended to simplify how an entity tests indefinite-lived intangible assets other than goodwill for impairment by providing entities with an option to perform a qualitative assessment to determine whether further impairment testing is necessary. This accounting standards update was effective for the Company beginning June 1, 2013. The adoption of this standard did not have a material impact on the Company's consolidated financial position or results of operations.

In December 2011, the FASB issued guidance enhancing disclosure requirements surrounding the nature of an entity's right to offset and related arrangements associated with its financial instruments and derivative instruments. This new guidance requires companies to disclose both gross and net information about instruments and transactions eligible for offset in the statement of financial position and instruments and transactions subject to master netting arrangements. This new guidance was effective for the Company beginning June 1, 2013. As this guidance only requires expanded disclosures, the adoption had no impact on the Company's consolidated financial position or results of operations.

Recently Issued Accounting Standards

In May 2014, the FASB issued an accounting standards update that replaces existing revenue recognition guidance. The updated guidance requires companies to recognize revenue in a way that depicts the transfer of promised goods or services to customers in an amount that reflects the consideration to which the entity expects to be entitled in exchange for those goods or services. In addition, the new standard requires that reporting companies disclose the nature, amount, timing and uncertainty of revenue and cash flows arising from contracts with customers. Based on the FASB's decision in July 2015 to defer the effective date and to allow more flexibility with implementation, the Company anticipates the new standard will be effective for the Company beginning June 1, 2018. The new standard is required to be applied retrospectively to each prior reporting period presented or retrospectively with the cumulative effect of initially applying it recognized at the date of initial application. The Company has not yet selected a transition method and is currently evaluating the effect the guidance will have on the Consolidated Financial Statements.

NOTE 2 — Inventories

Inventory balances of $4,337 million and $3,947 million at May 31, 2015 and 2014, respectively, were substantially all finished goods.

NOTE 3 — Property, Plant and Equipment

Property, plant and equipment, net included the following:

(In millions)	As of May 31, 2015	As of May 31, 2014
Land	$ 273	$ 270
Buildings	1,250	1,261
Machinery, equipment and internal-use software	3,329	3,376
Leasehold improvements	1,150	1,066
Construction in process	350	247
Total property, plant and equipment, gross	6,352	6,220
Less accumulated depreciation	3,341	3,386
TOTAL PROPERTY, PLANT AND EQUIPMENT, NET	**$ 3,011**	**$ 2,834**

Capitalized interest was not material for the years ended May 31, 2015, 2014 and 2013. The Company had $5 million and $74 million in capital lease obligations as of May 31, 2015 and May 31, 2014, respectively, included in machinery, equipment and internal-use software. During the fiscal year ended May 31, 2015, the Company restructured the terms of certain capital leases, which now qualify as operating leases.

NOTE 4 — Identifiable Intangible Assets and Goodwill

Identifiable intangible assets, net consists of indefinite-lived trademarks, which are not subject to amortization, and acquired trademarks and other intangible assets, which are subject to amortization. At May 31, 2015 and 2014, indefinite-lived trademarks were $281 million and $282 million, respectively. Acquired trademarks and other intangible assets at May 31, 2015 and 2014 were $17 million and $39 million, respectively, and were fully amortized at the end of both periods. *Goodwill* was $131 million at May 31, 2015 and 2014 of which $65 million and $64 million were included in the Converse segment in the respective periods. The remaining amounts were included in Global Brand Divisions for segment reporting purposes. There were no accumulated impairment balances for goodwill as of either period end.

NOTE 5 — Accrued Liabilities

Accrued liabilities included the following:

(In millions)	As of May 31, 2015	As of May 31, 2014
Compensation and benefits, excluding taxes	$ 997	$ 782
Collateral received from counterparties to hedging instruments	968	—
Endorsement compensation	388	328
Dividends payable	240	209
Import and logistics costs	207	127
Taxes other than income taxes	174	204
Fair value of derivatives	162	85
Advertising and marketing	117	133
Other[1]	698	623
TOTAL ACCRUED LIABILITIES	**$ 3,951**	**$ 2,491**

(1) Other consists of various accrued expenses with no individual item accounting for more than 5% of the total Accrued liabilities balance at May 31, 2015 and 2014.

NOTE 6 — Fair Value Measurements

The following tables present information about the Company's financial assets and liabilities measured at fair value on a recurring basis as of May 31, 2015 and 2014 and indicate the fair value hierarchy of the valuation techniques utilized by the Company to determine such fair value. Refer to Note 1 — Summary of Significant Accounting Policies for additional detail regarding the Company's fair value measurement methodology.

	As of May 31, 2015			
(In millions)	Assets at Fair Value	Cash and Cash Equivalents	Short-term Investments	Other Long-term Assets
Cash	$ 615	$ 615	$ —	$ —
Level 1:				
U.S. Treasury securities	869	225	644	—
Level 2:				
Time deposits	684	684	—	—
U.S. Agency securities	976	110	866	—
Commercial paper and bonds	914	352	562	—
Money market funds	1,866	1,866	—	—
Total level 2	4,440	3,012	1,428	—
Level 3:				
Non-marketable preferred stock	8	—	—	8
TOTAL	$ 5,932	$ 3,852	$ 2,072	$ 8

	As of May 31, 2014			
(In millions)	Assets at Fair Value	Cash and Cash Equivalents	Short-term Investments	Other Long-term Assets
Cash	$ 780	$ 780	$ —	$ —
Level 1:				
U.S. Treasury securities	1,137	151	986	—
Level 2:				
Time deposits	227	227	—	—
U.S. Agency securities	1,027	25	1,002	—
Commercial paper and bonds	959	25	934	—
Money market funds	1,012	1,012	—	—
Total level 2	3,225	1,289	1,936	—
Level 3:				
Non-marketable preferred stock	7	—	—	7
TOTAL	$ 5,149	$ 2,220	$ 2,922	$ 7

The Company elects to record the gross assets and liabilities of its derivative financial instruments on the Consolidated Balance Sheets. The Company's derivative financial instruments are subject to master netting arrangements that allow for the offset of assets and liabilities in the event of default or early termination of the contract. Any amounts of cash collateral received related to these instruments associated with the Company's credit-related contingent features are recorded in *Cash and equivalents* and *Accrued liabilities*, the latter of which would further offset against the Company's derivative asset balance (refer to Note 17 — Risk Management and Derivatives). Cash collateral received related to the Company's credit related contingent features is presented in the *Cash provided by operations* component of the Consolidated Statement of Cash Flows. Any amounts of non-cash collateral received, such as securities, are not recorded on the Consolidated Balance Sheets pursuant to the accounting standards for non-cash collateral received.

The following tables present information about the Company's derivative assets and liabilities measured at fair value on a recurring basis as of May 31, 2015 and May 31, 2014, and indicate the level in the fair value hierarchy in which the Company classifies the fair value measurement.

	As of May 31, 2015					
	Derivative Assets			Derivative Liabilities		
(In millions)	Assets at Fair Value	Other Current Assets	Other Long-term Assets	Liabilities at Fair Value	Accrued Liabilities	Other Long-term Liabilities
Level 2:						
Foreign exchange forwards and options[1]	$ 1,554	$ 1,034	$ 520	$ 164	$ 160	$ 4
Embedded derivatives	7	2	5	11	2	9
Interest rate swaps[2]	78	78	—	—	—	—
TOTAL	$ 1,639	$ 1,114	$ 525	$ 175	$ 162	$ 13

(1) If the foreign exchange derivative instruments had been netted in the Consolidated Balance Sheets, the asset and liability positions each would have been reduced by $161 million as of May 31, 2015. As of that date, the Company had received $900 million of cash collateral and $74 million of securities from various counterparties related to these foreign exchange derivative instruments. No amount of collateral was posted on the Company's derivative liability balance as of May 31, 2015.

(2) As of May 31, 2015, the Company had received $68 million of cash collateral related to its interest rate swaps.

| (In millions) | As of May 31, 2014 | | | | | |
| | Derivative Assets | | | Derivative Liabilities | | |
	Assets at Fair Value	Other Current Assets	Other Long-term Assets	Liabilities at Fair Value	Accrued Liabilities	Other Long-term Liabilities
Level 2:						
Foreign exchange forwards and options[1]	$ 127	$ 101	$ 26	$ 85	$ 84	$ 1
Interest rate swaps	6	—	6	—	—	—
TOTAL	**$ 133**	**$ 101**	**$ 32**	**$ 85**	**$ 84**	**$ 1**

(1)   If the foreign exchange derivative financial instruments had been netted in the Consolidated Balance Sheets, the asset and liability positions each would have been reduced by $63 million as of May 31, 2014. No amounts of collateral were received or posted on the Company's derivative assets and liabilities as of May 31, 2014.

Available-for-sale securities comprise investments in U.S. Treasury and Agency securities, money market funds, corporate commercial paper and bonds. These securities are valued using market prices on both active markets (Level 1) and less active markets (Level 2). The gross realized gains and losses on sales of available-for-sale securities were immaterial for the fiscal years ended May 31, 2015 and 2014. Unrealized gains and losses on available-for-sale securities included in *Other comprehensive income* were immaterial as of May 31, 2015 and 2014.

The Company regularly reviews its available-for-sale securities for other-than-temporary impairment. For the years ended May 31, 2015 and 2014, the Company did not consider its securities to be other-than-temporarily impaired and accordingly, did not recognize any impairment losses.

As of May 31, 2015, the Company held $1,808 million of available-for-sale securities with maturity dates within one year and $264 million with maturity dates over one year and less than five years within *Short-term investments* on the Consolidated Balance Sheets.

Included in *Interest expense (income), net* was interest income related to the Company's available-for-sale securities of $6 million, $5 million and $4 million for the years ended May 31, 2015, 2014 and 2013, respectively.

The Company's Level 3 assets comprise investments in certain non-marketable preferred stock. These Level 3 investments are an immaterial portion of the Company's portfolio. Changes in Level 3 investment assets were immaterial during the years ended May 31, 2015 and 2014.

Derivative financial instruments include foreign exchange forwards and options, embedded derivatives and interest rate swaps. Refer to Note 17 — Risk Management and Derivatives for additional detail.

No transfers among the levels within the fair value hierarchy occurred during the years ended May 31, 2015 or 2014.

As of May 31, 2015 and 2014, the Company had no assets or liabilities that were required to be measured at fair value on a non-recurring basis.

For fair value information regarding *Notes payable* and *Long-term debt*, refer to Note 7 — Short-Term Borrowings and Credit Lines and Note 8 — Long-Term Debt.

At May 31, 2015, the Company had $150 million of outstanding receivables related to its investments in reverse repurchase agreements recorded within *Prepaid expenses and other current assets* on the Consolidated Balance Sheet. The carrying amount of these agreements approximates their fair value based upon observable inputs other than quoted prices (Level 2). The reverse repurchase agreements are fully collateralized.

NOTE 7 — Short-Term Borrowings and Credit Lines

Notes payable and interest-bearing accounts payable to Sojitz Corporation of America ("Sojitz America") as of May 31, 2015 and 2014 are summarized below:

| (Dollars in millions) | As of May 31, | | | |
| | 2015 | | 2014 | |
	Borrowings	Interest Rate	Borrowings	Interest Rate
Notes payable:				
U.S. operations	$ —	0.00%[1]	$ —	0.00%[1]
Non-U.S. operations	74	12.39%[1]	167	10.04%[1]
TOTAL NOTES PAYABLE	**$ 74**		**$ 167**	
Interest-bearing accounts payable:				
Sojitz America	$ 78	0.98%	$ 60	0.94%

(1)   Weighted average interest rate includes non-interest bearing overdrafts.

The carrying amounts reflected in the Consolidated Balance Sheets for *Notes payable* approximate fair value.

The Company purchases through Sojitz America certain NIKE Brand products it acquires from non-U.S. suppliers. These purchases are for products sold in certain countries in the Company's Emerging Markets geographic operating segment and Canada, excluding products produced and sold in the same country. Accounts payable to Sojitz America are generally due up to 60 days after shipment of goods from the foreign port. The interest rate on such accounts payable is the 60-day London Interbank Offered Rate ("LIBOR") as of the beginning of the month of the invoice date, plus 0.75%.

As of May 31, 2015 and 2014, the Company had no amounts outstanding under its commercial paper program.

On November 1, 2011, the Company entered into a committed credit facility agreement with a syndicate of banks which provides for up to $1 billion of borrowings with the option to increase borrowings to $1.5 billion with lender approval. Following an extension agreement on September 17, 2013 between the Company and the syndicate of banks, the facility matures November 1, 2017. Based on the Company's current long-term senior unsecured debt ratings of AA- and A1 from Standard and Poor's Corporation and Moody's Investor Services, respectively, the interest rate charged on any outstanding borrowings would be the prevailing LIBOR plus 0.445%. The facility fee is 0.055% of the total commitment. Under this committed credit facility, the Company must maintain, among other things, certain minimum specified financial ratios with which the Company was in compliance at May 31, 2015. No amounts were outstanding under this facility as of May 31, 2015 or 2014.

NOTE 8 — Long-Term Debt

Long-term debt, net of unamortized premiums and discounts and swap fair value adjustments, comprises the following:

Scheduled Maturity (Dollars and Yen in millions)	Original Principal	Interest Rate	Interest Payments	Book Value Outstanding As of May 31,	
				2015	2014
Corporate Bond Payables:[4]					
October 15, 2015[1]	$ 100	5.15%	Semi-Annually	$ 101	$ 108
May 1, 2023[5]	$ 500	2.25%	Semi-Annually	499	499
May 1, 2043[5]	$ 500	3.63%	Semi-Annually	499	499
Promissory Notes:					
April 1, 2017[2]	$ 40	6.20%	Monthly	39	39
January 1, 2018[2]	$ 19	6.79%	Monthly	19	19
Japanese Yen Notes:					
August 20, 2001 through November 20, 2020[3]	¥ 9,000	2.60%	Quarterly	20	29
August 20, 2001 through November 20, 2020[3]	¥ 4,000	2.00%	Quarterly	9	13
Total				1,186	1,206
Less current maturities				107	7
TOTAL LONG-TERM DEBT				**$ 1,079**	**$ 1,199**

(1)   *The Company has entered into interest rate swap agreements whereby the Company receives fixed interest payments at the same rate as the note and pays variable interest payments based on the six-month LIBOR plus a spread. The swaps have the same notional amount and maturity date as the corresponding note. At May 31, 2015, the interest rates payable on these swap agreements ranged from approximately 0.3% to 0.5%.*

(2)   *The Company assumed a total of $59 million in bonds payable as part of its agreement to purchase certain Corporate properties; this was treated as a non-cash financing transaction. The property serves as collateral for the debt. The purchase of these properties was accounted for as a business combination where the total consideration of $85 million was allocated to the land and buildings acquired; no other tangible or intangible assets or liabilities resulted from the purchase. The bonds mature in 2017 and 2018 and the Company does not have the ability to re-negotiate the terms of the debt agreements and would incur significant financial penalties if the notes were paid-off prior to maturity.*

(3)   *NIKE Logistics YK assumed a total of ¥13.0 billion in loans as part of its agreement to purchase a distribution center in Japan, which serves as collateral for the loans. These loans mature in equal quarterly installments during the period August 20, 2001 through November 20, 2020.*

(4)   *These senior unsecured obligations rank equally with the Company's other unsecured and unsubordinated indebtedness.*

(5)   *The bonds are redeemable at the Company's option prior to February 1, 2023 and November 1, 2042, respectively, at a price equal to the greater of (i) 100% of the aggregate principal amount of the notes to be redeemed, and (ii) the sum of the present values of the remaining scheduled payments, plus in each case, accrued and unpaid interest. Subsequent to February 1, 2023 and November 1, 2042, respectively, the bonds also feature a par call provision, which allows for the bonds to be redeemed at a price equal to 100% of the aggregate principal amount of the notes being redeemed, plus accrued and unpaid interest.*

The scheduled maturity of *Long-term debt* in each of the years ending May 31, 2016 through 2020 are $106 million, $44 million, $24 million, $6 million and $6 million, respectively, at face value.

The fair value of the Company's *Long-term debt*, including the current portion, was approximately $1,160 million at May 31, 2015 and $1,154 million at May 31, 2014. The fair value of *Long-term debt* is estimated based upon quoted prices of similar instruments (level 2).

NOTE 9 — Income Taxes

Income before income taxes is as follows:

(In millions)	Year Ended May 31,		
	2015	2014	2013
Income before income taxes:			
United States	$ 1,967	$ 3,066	$ 1,231
Foreign	2,238	478	2,025
TOTAL INCOME BEFORE INCOME TAXES	**$ 4,205**	**$ 3,544**	**$ 3,256**

The provision for income taxes is as follows:

(In millions)	Year Ended May 31, 2015	Year Ended May 31, 2014	Year Ended May 31, 2013
Current:			
United States			
Federal	$ 596	$ 259	$ 378
State	80	104	79
Foreign	369	499	442
Total	1,045	862	899
Deferred:			
United States			
Federal	(66)	19	(4)
State	(11)	(3)	(4)
Foreign	(36)	(27)	(86)
Total	(113)	(11)	(94)
TOTAL INCOME TAX EXPENSE	$ 932	$ 851	$ 805

A reconciliation from the U.S. statutory federal income tax rate to the effective income tax rate is as follows:

	Year Ended May 31, 2015	Year Ended May 31, 2014	Year Ended May 31, 2013
Federal income tax rate	35.0%	35.0%	35.0%
State taxes, net of federal benefit	0.9%	1.8%	1.4%
Foreign earnings	-15.7%	2.2%	-11.8%
Deferred charge	0.9%	-14.6%	0.0%
Other, net	1.1%	-0.4%	0.1%
EFFECTIVE INCOME TAX RATE	**22.2%**	**24.0%**	**24.7%**

The effective tax rate from continuing operations for the year ended May 31, 2015 was 180 basis points lower than the effective tax rate from continuing operations for the year ended May 31, 2014 primarily due to the favorable resolution of audits in several jurisdictions.

The effective tax rate from continuing operations for the year ended May 31, 2014 was 70 basis points lower than the effective tax rate from continuing operations for the year ended May 31, 2013 primarily due to an increase in the amount of earnings from lower tax rate jurisdictions.

During the fourth quarter of the fiscal year ended May 31, 2014, the Company reached a resolution with the IRS on a U.S. Unilateral Advanced Pricing Agreement that covers intercompany transfer pricing for fiscal years 2011 through 2020. This agreement resulted in an increase in the effective tax rate due to a reduction in the Company's permanently reinvested foreign earnings, which was partially offset by a reduction in previously unrecognized tax benefits. It also resulted in a decrease in the effective tax rate due to the recognition of a deferred tax charge. The net result of the agreement did not have a material impact on the Company's effective income tax rate in fiscal 2014.

Deferred tax assets and (liabilities) comprise the following:

(In millions)	As of May 31, 2015	As of May 31, 2014
Deferred tax assets:		
Allowance for doubtful accounts	$ 11	$ 11
Inventories	59	49
Sales return reserves	143	113
Deferred compensation	258	211
Stock-based compensation	179	162
Reserves and accrued liabilities	92	95
Net operating loss carry-forwards	10	16
Undistributed earnings of foreign subsidiaries	149	194
Other	76	51
Total deferred tax assets	977	902
Valuation allowance	(9)	(9)
Total deferred tax assets after valuation allowance	968	893
Deferred tax liabilities:		
Property, plant and equipment	(220)	(237)
Intangibles	(93)	(94)
Other	(38)	(2)
Total deferred tax liability	(351)	(333)
NET DEFERRED TAX ASSET	$ 617	$ 560

The following is a reconciliation of the changes in the gross balance of unrecognized tax benefits:

	As of May 31,		
(In millions)	2015	2014	2013
Unrecognized tax benefits, beginning of the period	$ 506	$ 447	$ 285
Gross increases related to prior period tax positions[1]	32	814	77
Gross decreases related to prior period tax positions[1]	(123)	(166)	(3)
Gross increases related to current period tax positions	82	125	130
Gross decreases related to current period tax positions	(9)	(30)	(9)
Settlements[1]	(27)	(676)	—
Lapse of statute of limitations	(10)	(4)	(21)
Changes due to currency translation	(13)	(4)	(12)
UNRECOGNIZED TAX BENEFITS, END OF THE PERIOD	$ 438	$ 506	$ 447

(1)   During the fourth quarter of the fiscal year ended May 31, 2014, the Company reached a resolution with the IRS on a U.S. Unilateral Advanced Pricing Agreement that covers intercompany transfer pricing for fiscal years 2011 through 2020. As a result, the Company recorded a gross increase in unrecognized tax benefits related to prior period tax positions, a gross decrease in unrecognized tax benefits related to prior period tax positions and a settlement. The net impact of these items resulted in a decrease to unrecognized tax benefits.

As of May 31, 2015, total gross unrecognized tax benefits, excluding related interest and penalties, were $438 million, $260 million of which would affect the Company's effective tax rate if recognized in future periods.

The Company recognizes interest and penalties related to income tax matters in *Income tax expense*. The liability for payment of interest and penalties decreased $3 million during the year ended May 31, 2015, and increased $55 million and $4 million during the years ended May 31, 2014 and 2013, respectively. As of May 31, 2015 and 2014, accrued interest and penalties related to uncertain tax positions were $164 million and $167 million, respectively (excluding federal benefit).

The Company incurs tax liabilities primarily in the United States, China and the Netherlands, as well as various state and other foreign jurisdictions. The Company is currently under audit by the U.S. Internal Revenue Service (IRS) for the 2012 through 2014 tax years. The Company has closed all U.S. federal income tax matters through fiscal 2011, with the exception of the validation of foreign tax credits utilized. As previously disclosed, the Company received a statutory notice of deficiency for fiscal 2011 proposing an increase in tax of $31 million, subject to interest, related to the foreign tax credit matter. This notice also reported a decrease in foreign tax credit carryovers for fiscal 2010 and 2011. The Company has contested this deficiency notice by filing a petition with the U.S Tax Court in April 2015. The Company does not expect the outcome of this matter to have a material impact on the financial statements. No payments on the assessment would be required until the dispute is definitively resolved. Based on the information currently available, the Company does not anticipate a significant increase or decrease to its unrecognized tax benefits for this matter within the next 12 months.

The Company's major foreign jurisdictions, China, the Netherlands and Brazil, have concluded substantially all income tax matters through calendar 2005, fiscal 2009 and calendar 2008, respectively. Although the timing of resolution of audits is not certain, the Company evaluates all domestic and foreign audit issues in the aggregate, along with the expiration of applicable statutes of limitations, and estimates that it is reasonably possible the total gross unrecognized tax benefits could decrease by up to $63 million within the next 12 months.

The Company provides for U.S. income taxes on the undistributed earnings of foreign subsidiaries unless they are considered indefinitely reinvested outside the United States. At May 31, 2015, the indefinitely reinvested earnings in foreign subsidiaries upon which United States income taxes have not been provided were approximately $8.3 billion. If these undistributed earnings were repatriated to the United States, or if the shares of the relevant foreign subsidiaries were sold or otherwise transferred, they would generate foreign tax credits that would reduce the federal tax liability associated with the foreign dividend or the otherwise taxable transaction. Assuming a full utilization of the foreign tax credits, the potential net deferred tax liability associated with these temporary differences of undistributed earnings would be approximately $2.7 billion at May 31, 2015.

A portion of the Company's foreign operations are benefiting from a tax holiday, which is set to expire in 2021. This tax holiday may be extended when certain conditions are met or may be terminated early if certain conditions are not met. The impact of this tax holiday decreased foreign taxes by $174 million, $138 million and $108 million for the fiscal years ended May 31, 2015, 2014 and 2013, respectively. The benefit of the tax holiday on diluted earnings per common share was $0.20, $0.15 and $0.12 for the fiscal years ended May 31, 2015, 2014 and 2013, respectively.

Deferred tax assets at May 31, 2015 and 2014 were reduced by a valuation allowance relating to tax benefits of certain subsidiaries with operating losses. There was no net change in the valuation allowance for the year ended May 31, 2015 compared to a net increase of $4 million and a net decrease of $22 million for the years ended May 31, 2014 and 2013, respectively.

The Company has available domestic and foreign loss carry-forwards of $36 million at May 31, 2015. Such losses will expire as follows:

	Year Ending May 31,						
(In millions)	2016	2017	2018	2019	2020-2035	Indefinite	Total
Net operating losses	$ —	$ —	$ 4	$ 1	$ 17	$ 14	$ 36

During the years ended May 31, 2015, 2014 and 2013, income tax benefits attributable to employee stock-based compensation transactions of $224 million, $135 million and $76 million, respectively, were allocated to *Total shareholders' equity*.

NOTE 10 — Redeemable Preferred Stock

Sojitz America is the sole owner of the Company's authorized redeemable preferred stock, $1 par value, which is redeemable at the option of Sojitz America or the Company at par value aggregating $0.3 million. A cumulative dividend of $0.10 per share is payable annually on May 31 and no dividends may be declared or paid on the common stock of the Company unless dividends on the redeemable preferred stock have been declared and paid in full. There have been no changes in the redeemable preferred stock in the three years ended May 31, 2015, 2014 and 2013. As the holder of the redeemable preferred stock, Sojitz America does not have general voting rights, but does have the right to vote as a separate class on the sale of all or substantially all of the assets of the Company and its subsidiaries, on merger, consolidation, liquidation or dissolution of the Company or on the sale or assignment of the NIKE trademark for athletic footwear sold in the United States. The redeemable preferred stock has been fully issued to Sojitz America and is not blank check preferred stock. The Company's articles of incorporation do not permit the issuance of additional preferred stock.

NOTE 11 — Common Stock and Stock-Based Compensation

The authorized number of shares of Class A Common Stock, no par value, and Class B Common Stock, no par value, are 200 million and 1,200 million, respectively. Each share of Class A Common Stock is convertible into one share of Class B Common Stock. Voting rights of Class B Common Stock are limited in certain circumstances with respect to the election of directors. There are no differences in the dividend and liquidation preferences or participation rights of the Class A and Class B common shareholders.

In 1990, the Board of Directors adopted, and the shareholders approved, the NIKE, Inc. 1990 Stock Incentive Plan (the "1990 Plan"). The 1990 Plan, as amended, provides for the issuance of up to 326 million previously unissued shares of Class B Common Stock in connection with stock options and other awards granted under the plan. The 1990 Plan authorizes the grant of non-statutory stock options, incentive stock options, stock appreciation rights, restricted stock, restricted stock units and performance-based awards. The exercise price for stock options and stock appreciation rights may not be less than the fair market value of the underlying shares on the date of grant. A committee of the Board of Directors administers the 1990 Plan. The committee has the authority to determine the employees to whom awards will be made, the amount of the awards and the other terms and conditions of the awards. Substantially all stock option grants outstanding under the 1990 Plan were granted in the first quarter of each fiscal year, vest ratably over four years and expire 10 years from the date of grant.

The following table summarizes the Company's total stock-based compensation expense recognized in *Operating overhead expense*:

(In millions)	Year Ended May 31,		
	2015	2014	2013
Stock options[1]	$ 136	$ 125	$ 123
ESPPs	24	22	19
Restricted stock	31	30	32
TOTAL STOCK-BASED COMPENSATION EXPENSE	$ 191	$ 177	$ 174

(1) *Expense for stock options includes the expense associated with stock appreciation rights. Accelerated stock option expense is recorded for employees eligible for accelerated stock option vesting upon retirement. Accelerated stock option expense for the years ended May 31, 2015, 2014 and 2013 was $19 million, $15 million and $22 million, respectively.*

As of May 31, 2015, the Company had $180 million of unrecognized compensation costs from stock options, net of estimated forfeitures, to be recognized in *Operating overhead expense* over a weighted average period of 1.9 years.

The weighted average fair value per share of the options granted during the years ended May 31, 2015, 2014 and 2013, as computed using the Black-Scholes pricing model, was $16.95, $14.89 and $12.71, respectively. The weighted average assumptions used to estimate these fair values are as follows:

	Year Ended May 31,		
	2015	2014	2013
Dividend yield	1.2%	1.3%	1.5%
Expected volatility	23.6%	27.9%	35.0%
Weighted average expected life (in years)	5.8	5.3	5.3
Risk-free interest rate	1.7%	1.3%	0.6%

The Company estimates the expected volatility based on the implied volatility in market traded options on the Company's common stock with a term greater than one year, along with other factors. The weighted average expected life of options is based on an analysis of historical and expected future exercise patterns. The interest rate is based on the U.S. Treasury (constant maturity) risk-free rate in effect at the date of grant for periods corresponding with the expected term of the options.

The following summarizes the stock option transactions under the plan discussed above:

	Shares[1]	Weighted Average Option Price
	(In millions)	
Options outstanding May 31, 2012	64.3	$ 30.59
Exercised	(9.9)	24.70
Forfeited	(1.3)	40.14
Granted	14.6	46.55
Options outstanding May 31, 2013	67.7	$ 34.72
Exercised	(11.0)	28.29
Forfeited	(1.3)	48.33
Granted	8.1	63.54
Options outstanding May 31, 2014	63.5	$ 39.28
Exercised	(13.6)	30.78
Forfeited	(1.0)	59.02
Granted	9.2	77.68
Options outstanding May 31, 2015	58.1	$ 47.00
Options exercisable at May 31,		
2013	35.9	$ 27.70
2014	37.0	31.42
2015	34.3	36.53

(1)   *Includes stock appreciation rights transactions.*

The weighted average contractual life remaining for options outstanding and options exercisable at May 31, 2015 was 6.0 years and 4.7 years, respectively. The aggregate intrinsic value for options outstanding and exercisable at May 31, 2015 was $3,178 million and $2,235 million, respectively. The aggregate intrinsic value was the amount by which the market value of the underlying stock exceeded the exercise price of the options. The total intrinsic value of the options exercised during the years ended May 31, 2015, 2014 and 2013 was $795 million, $474 million and $293 million, respectively.

In addition to the 1990 Plan, the Company gives employees the right to purchase shares at a discount to the market price under employee stock purchase plans ("ESPPs"). Employees are eligible to participate through payroll deductions of up to 10% of their compensation. At the end of each six-month offering period, shares are purchased by the participants at 85% of the lower of the fair market value at the beginning or the end of the offering period. Employees purchased 1.4 million, 1.4 million and 1.6 million shares during each of the three years ended May 31, 2015, 2014 and 2013, respectively.

From time to time, the Company grants restricted stock and restricted stock units to key employees under the 1990 Plan. The number of shares underlying such awards granted to employees during the years ended May 31, 2015, 2014 and 2013 were 0.3 million, 0.3 million and 1.6 million, respectively, with weighted average values per share of $79.38, $63.89 and $46.86, respectively. Recipients of restricted stock are entitled to cash dividends and to vote their respective shares throughout the period of restriction. Recipients of restricted stock units are entitled to dividend equivalent cash payments upon vesting. The value of all grants of restricted stock and restricted stock units was established by the market price on the date of grant. During the years ended May 31, 2015, 2014 and 2013, the aggregate fair value of restricted stock and restricted stock units vested was $20 million, $28 million and $25 million, respectively, determined as of the date of vesting. As of May 31, 2015, the Company had $48 million of unrecognized compensation costs from restricted stock units to be recognized in *Operating overhead expense* over a weighted average period of 1.5 years.

NOTE 12 — Earnings Per Share

The following is a reconciliation from Basic earnings per common share to Diluted earnings per common share. The computation of Diluted earnings per common share omitted options to purchase an additional 0.1 million, 0.1 million and 0.1 million shares of common stock outstanding for the years ended May 31, 2015, 2014 and 2013, respectively, because the options were anti-dilutive.

	Year Ended May 31,		
(In millions, except per share data)	**2015**	**2014**	**2013**
Determination of shares:			
Weighted average common shares outstanding	861.7	883.4	897.3
Assumed conversion of dilutive stock options and awards	22.7	22.4	19.1
DILUTED WEIGHTED AVERAGE COMMON SHARES OUTSTANDING	**884.4**	**905.8**	**916.4**
Earnings per common share from continuing operations:			
Basic	$ 3.80	$ 3.05	$ 2.74
Diluted	$ 3.70	$ 2.97	$ 2.68
Earnings per common share from discontinued operations:			
Basic	$ —	$ —	$ 0.02
Diluted	$ —	$ —	$ 0.02
Basic earnings per common share for NIKE, Inc.	$ 3.80	$ 3.05	$ 2.76
Diluted earnings per common share for NIKE, Inc.	$ 3.70	$ 2.97	$ 2.70

NOTE 13 — Benefit Plans

The Company has a qualified 401(k) Savings and Profit Sharing Plan to which all U.S. employees who work at least 1,000 hours in a year are able to participate. The Company matches a portion of employee contributions. Company contributions to the savings plan were $58 million, $51 million and $46 million for the years ended May 31, 2015, 2014 and 2013, respectively, and are included in *Operating overhead expense*. The terms of the plan also allow for annual discretionary profit sharing contributions to the accounts of eligible employees by the Company as determined by the Board of Directors. Contributions of $58 million, $49 million and $47 million were made to the plan and are included in *Operating overhead expense* for the years ended May 31, 2015, 2014 and 2013, respectively.

The Company also has a Long-Term Incentive Plan ("LTIP") that was adopted by the Board of Directors and approved by shareholders in September 1997 and later amended in fiscal 2007. The Company recognized $68 million, $46 million and $50 million of *Operating overhead expense* related to cash awards

under the LTIP during the years ended May 31, 2015, 2014 and 2013, respectively.

The Company allows certain highly compensated employees and non-employee directors of the Company to defer compensation under a nonqualified deferred compensation plan. Deferred compensation plan liabilities were $443 million and $390 million at May 31, 2015 and 2014, respectively, and primarily classified as long-term in *Deferred income taxes and other liabilities*.

The Company has pension plans in various countries worldwide. The pension plans are only available to local employees and are generally government mandated. The liability related to the unfunded pension liabilities of the plans was $98 million and $100 million at May 31, 2015 and May 31, 2014, respectively, which was primarily classified as long-term in *Deferred income taxes and other liabilities*.

NOTE 14 — Accumulated Other Comprehensive Income

The changes in *Accumulated other comprehensive income*, net of tax, were as follows:

(In millions)	Foreign Currency Translation Adjustment[1]	Cash Flow Hedges	Net Investment Hedges[1]	Other	Total
Balance at May 31, 2014	$ 9	$ 32	$ 95	$ (51)	$ 85
Other comprehensive gains (losses) before reclassifications[2]	(20)	1,447	—	33	1,460
Reclassifications to net income of previously deferred (gains) losses[3]	—	(259)	—	(40)	(299)
Other comprehensive income (loss)	(20)	1,188	—	(7)	1,161
Balance at May 31, 2015	$ (11)	$ 1,220	$ 95	$ (58)	$ 1,246

(1) The accumulated foreign currency translation adjustment and net investment hedge gains/losses related to an investment in a foreign subsidiary are reclassified to Net income upon sale or upon complete or substantially complete liquidation of the respective entity.

(2) Net of tax benefit (expense) of $ 0 million, $ (33) million, $ 0 million, $ 0 million and $ (33) million, respectively.

(3) Net of tax (benefit) expense of $ 0 million, $ 2 million, $ 0 million, $ 0 million and $ 2 million, respectively.

(In millions)	Foreign Currency Translation Adjustment[1]	Cash Flow Hedges	Net Investment Hedges[1]	Other	Total
Balance at May 31, 2013	$ 41	$ 193	$ 95	$ (55)	$ 274
Other comprehensive gains (losses) before reclassifications[2]	(32)	(134)	—	—	(166)
Reclassifications to net income of previously deferred (gains) losses[3]	—	(27)	—	4	(23)
Other comprehensive income (loss)	(32)	(161)	—	4	(189)
Balance at May 31, 2014	$ 9	$ 32	$ 95	$ (51)	$ 85

(1) The accumulated foreign currency translation adjustment and net investment hedge gains/losses related to an investment in a foreign subsidiary are reclassified to Net income upon sale or upon complete or substantially complete liquidation of the respective entity.

(2) Net of tax benefit (expense) of $ 0 million, $ 9 million, $ 0 million, $ 0 million and $ 9 million, respectively.

(3) Net of tax (benefit) expense of $ 0 million, $ 9 million, $ 0 million, $ 0 million and $ 9 million respectively.

The following table summarizes the reclassifications from *Accumulated other comprehensive income* to the Consolidated Statements of Income:

(In millions)	Amount of Gain (Loss) Reclassified from Accumulated Other Comprehensive Income into Income Year Ended May 31, 2015	2014	Location of Gain (Loss) Reclassified from Accumulated Other Comprehensive Income into Income
Gains (losses) on cash flow hedges:			
Foreign exchange forwards and options	$ (95)	$ 14	Revenues
Foreign exchange forwards and options	220	12	Cost of sales
Foreign exchange forwards and options	—	—	Total selling and administrative expense
Foreign exchange forwards and options	136	10	Other (income) expense, net
Total before tax	261	36	
Tax expense	(2)	(9)	
Gain, net of tax	**259**	**27**	
Gains (losses) on other	40	(4)	Other (income) expense, net
Total before tax	40	(4)	
Tax expense	—	—	
Gain (loss), net of tax	**40**	**(4)**	
Total net gain reclassified for the period	**$ 299**	**$ 23**	

Refer to Note 17 — Risk Management and Derivatives for more information on the Company's risk management program and derivatives.

NOTE 15 — Discontinued Operations

During the year ended May 31, 2013, the Company divested of Umbro and Cole Haan, allowing it to focus its resources on driving growth in the NIKE, Jordan, Converse and Hurley brands.

On February 1, 2013, the Company completed the sale of Cole Haan to Apax Partners for an agreed upon purchase price of $570 million and received at closing $561 million, net of $9 million of purchase price adjustments. The transaction resulted in a gain on sale of $231 million, net of $137 million in

Income tax expense; this gain is included in the *Net income from discontinued operations* line item on the Consolidated Statements of Income. There were no adjustments to these recorded amounts as of May 31, 2015. Beginning November 30, 2012, the Company classified the Cole Haan disposal group as held-for-sale and presented the results of Cole Haan's operations in the *Net income from discontinued operations* line item on the Consolidated Statements of Income. From this date until the sale, the assets and liabilities of Cole Haan were recorded in the *Assets of discontinued operations* and

Liabilities of discontinued operations line items on the Consolidated Balance Sheets, respectively. Previously, these amounts were reported in the Company's operating segment presentation as "Other Businesses."

Under the sale agreement, the Company agreed to provide certain transition services to Cole Haan for an expected period of 3 to 9 months from the date of sale. These services were essentially complete as of May 31, 2013 and the Company has had no significant involvement with Cole Haan beyond the transition services. The Company has also licensed NIKE proprietary Air and Lunar technologies to Cole Haan for a transition period. The continuing cash flows related to these items are not significant to Cole Haan. Additionally, preexisting guarantees of certain Cole Haan lease payments remained in place after the sale; the maximum exposure under the guarantees is $23 million at May 31, 2015. The fair value of the guarantees is not material.

On November 30, 2012, the Company completed the sale of certain assets of Umbro to Iconix Brand Group ("Iconix") for $225 million. The Umbro disposal group was classified as held-for-sale as of November 30, 2012 and the results of Umbro's operations are presented in the *Net income from discontinued operations* line item on the Consolidated Statements of Income. The liabilities of Umbro were recorded in the *Liabilities of discontinued operations* line items on the Consolidated Balance Sheets. Previously, these amounts were reported in the Company's operating segment presentation as "Other Businesses." Upon meeting the held-for-sale criteria, the Company recorded a loss of $107 million, net of tax, on the sale of Umbro and the loss is included in the *Net income from discontinued operations* line item on the Consolidated Statements of Income. The loss on sale was calculated as the net sales price less Umbro assets of $248 million, including intangibles, goodwill and fixed assets, other miscellaneous charges of $22 million and the release of the associated cumulative translation adjustment of $129 million. The tax benefit on the loss was $67 million. There were no adjustments to these recorded amounts as of May 31, 2015.

Summarized results of the Company's discontinued operations are as follows:

		Year Ended May 31,	
(In millions)	2015	2014	2013
Revenues	$ —	$ —	$ 523
Income before income taxes	—	—	108
Income tax expense	—	—	87
NET INCOME FROM DISCONTINUED OPERATIONS	$ —	$ —	$ 21

There were no assets or liabilities of discontinued operations as of May 31, 2015 and May 31, 2014.

NOTE 16 — Commitments and Contingencies

The Company leases space for certain of its offices, warehouses and retail stores under leases expiring from 1 to 19 years after May 31, 2015. Rent expense was $594 million, $533 million and $482 million for the years ended May 31, 2015, 2014 and 2013, respectively. Amounts of minimum future annual commitments under non-cancelable operating and capital leases are as follows (in millions):

	2016	2017	2018	2019	2020	Thereafter	Total
Operating leases	$ 447	$ 423	$ 371	$ 311	$ 268	$ 1,154	$ 2,974
Capital leases	$ 2	$ 2	$ 1	$ —	$ —	$ —	$ 5

As of May 31, 2015 and 2014, the Company had letters of credit outstanding totaling $165 million and $135 million, respectively. These letters of credit were generally issued for the purchase of inventory and guarantees of the Company's performance under certain self-insurance and other programs.

In connection with various contracts and agreements, the Company provides routine indemnification relating to the enforceability of intellectual property rights, coverage for legal issues that arise and other items where the Company is acting as the guarantor. Currently, the Company has several such agreements in place. However, based on the Company's historical experience and the estimated probability of future loss, the Company has

determined that the fair value of such indemnification is not material to the Company's financial position or results of operations.

In the ordinary course of its business, the Company is involved in various legal proceedings involving contractual and employment relationships, product liability claims, trademark rights and a variety of other matters. While the Company cannot predict the outcome of its pending legal matters with certainty, the Company does not believe any currently identified claim, proceeding or litigation, either individually or in aggregate, will have a material impact on the Company's results of operations, financial position or cash flows.

NOTE 17 — Risk Management and Derivatives

The Company is exposed to global market risks, including the effect of changes in foreign currency exchange rates and interest rates, and uses derivatives to manage financial exposures that occur in the normal course of business. The Company does not hold or issue derivatives for trading or speculative purposes.

The Company may elect to designate certain derivatives as hedging instruments under the accounting standards for derivatives and hedging. The Company formally documents all relationships between designated hedging instruments and hedged items as well as its risk management objectives and

strategies for undertaking hedge transactions. This process includes linking all derivatives designated as hedges to either recognized assets or liabilities or forecasted transactions.

The majority of derivatives outstanding as of May 31, 2015 are designated as foreign currency cash flow hedges primarily for Euro/U.S. Dollar, British Pound/Euro and Japanese Yen/U.S. Dollar currency pairs. All derivatives are recognized on the Consolidated Balance Sheets at fair value and classified based on the instrument's maturity date.

The following table presents the fair values of derivative instruments included within the Consolidated Balance Sheets as of May 31, 2015 and 2014:

(In millions)		Asset Derivatives				Liability Derivatives		
	Balance Sheet Location	2015	2014		Balance Sheet Location	2015	2014
Derivatives formally designated as hedging instruments:								
Foreign exchange forwards and options	Prepaid expenses and other current assets	$ 825	$ 76		Accrued liabilities	$ 140	$ 57
Interest rate swaps	Prepaid expenses and other current assets	78	—		Accrued liabilities	—	—
Foreign exchange forwards and options	Deferred income taxes and other assets	520	26		Deferred income taxes and other liabilities	4	1
Interest rate swaps	Deferred income taxes and other assets	—	6		Deferred income taxes and other liabilities	—	—
Total derivatives formally designated as hedging instruments		1,423	108			144	58
Derivatives not designated as hedging instruments:								
Foreign exchange forwards and options	Prepaid expenses and other current assets	209	25		Accrued liabilities	20	27
Embedded derivatives	Prepaid expenses and other current assets	2	—		Accrued liabilities	2	—
Embedded derivatives	Deferred income taxes and other assets	5	—		Deferred income taxes and other liabilities	9	—
Total derivatives not designated as hedging instruments		216	25			31	27
TOTAL DERIVATIVES		**$ 1,639**	**$ 133**			**$ 175**	**$ 85**

The following tables present the amounts affecting the Consolidated Statements of Income for years ended May 31, 2015, 2014 and 2013:

(In millions)	Amount of Gain (Loss) Recognized in Other Comprehensive Income on Derivatives[1]				Amount of Gain (Loss) Reclassified From Accumulated Other Comprehensive Income into Income[1]			
	Year Ended May 31,			Location of Gain (Loss) Reclassified From Accumulated Other Comprehensive Income Into Income[1]	Year Ended May 31,		
	2015	2014	2013		2015	2014	2013
Derivatives designated as cash flow hedges:							
Foreign exchange forwards and options	$ (202)	$ (48)	$ 42	Revenues	$ (95)	$ 14	$ (19)
Foreign exchange forwards and options	1,109	(78)	67	Cost of sales	220	12	113
Foreign exchange forwards and options	—	4	(3)	Total selling and administrative expense	—	—	2
Foreign exchange forwards and options	497	(21)	33	Other (income) expense, net	136	10	9
Interest rate swaps	76	—	—	Interest expense (income), net	—	—	—
Total designated cash flow hedges	$1,480	$(143)	$ 139		$261	$ 36	$105
Derivatives designated as net investment hedges:							
Foreign exchange forwards and options	$ —	$ —	$ —	Other (income) expense, net	$ —	$ —	$ —

(1) For the years ended May 31, 2015, 2014 and 2013, the amounts recorded in Other (income) expense, net as a result of hedge ineffectiveness and the discontinuance of cash flow hedges because the forecasted transactions were no longer probable of occurring were immaterial.

(In millions)	Amount of Gain (Loss) Recognized in Income on Derivatives			Location of Gain (Loss) Recognized in Income on Derivatives
	Year Ended May 31,			
	2015	2014	2013	
Derivatives designated as fair value hedges:				
Interest rate swaps[1]	$ 5	$ 5	$ 5	Interest expense (income), net
Derivatives not designated as hedging instruments:				
Foreign exchange forwards and options	$ 611	$ (75)	$ 51	Other (income) expense, net
Embedded derivatives	$ (1)	$ (1)	$ (4)	Other (income) expense, net

(1) All interest rate swaps designated as fair value hedges meet the shortcut method requirements under the accounting standards for derivatives and hedging. Accordingly, changes in the fair values of the interest rate swaps are considered to exactly offset changes in the fair value of the underlying long-term debt. Refer to "Fair Value Hedges" in this note for additional detail.

Refer to Note 6 — Fair Value Measurements for a description of how the above financial instruments are valued and Note 14 — Accumulated Other Comprehensive Income and the Consolidated Statements of Shareholders' Equity for additional information on changes in *Other comprehensive income* for the years ended May 31, 2015, 2014 and 2013.

Cash Flow Hedges

The purpose of the Company's foreign exchange risk management program is to lessen both the positive and negative effects of currency fluctuations on the Company's consolidated results of operations, financial position and cash flows. Foreign currency exposures that the Company may elect to hedge in this manner include product cost exposures, non-functional currency denominated external and intercompany revenues, selling and administrative expenses, investments in U.S. Dollar-denominated available-for-sale debt securities and certain other intercompany transactions.

Product cost exposures are primarily generated through non-functional currency denominated product purchases and the foreign currency adjustment program described below. NIKE entities primarily purchase products in two ways: (1) Certain NIKE entities, including those supporting the Company's North America, Greater China, Japan and European geographies, purchase product from the NIKE Trading Company ("NTC"), a wholly owned sourcing hub that buys NIKE branded products from third party factories, predominantly in U.S. Dollars. The NTC, whose functional currency is the U.S. Dollar, then sells the products to NIKE entities in their respective functional currencies. When the NTC sells to a NIKE entity with a different functional currency, the result is a foreign currency exposure for the NTC. (2) Other NIKE entities purchase product directly from third party factories in U.S. Dollars. These purchases generate a foreign currency exposure for those NIKE entities with a functional currency other than the U.S. Dollar.

The Company operates a foreign currency adjustment program with certain factories. The program is designed to more effectively manage foreign currency risk by assuming certain of the factories' foreign currency exposures, some of which are natural offsets to the Company's existing foreign currency exposures. Under this program, the Company's payments to these factories are adjusted for rate fluctuations in the basket of currencies ("factory currency exposure index") in which the labor, materials and overhead costs incurred by the factories in the production of NIKE branded products ("factory input costs") are denominated. For the portion of the indices denominated in the local or functional currency of the factory, the Company may elect to place formally designated cash flow hedges. For all currencies within the indices, excluding the U.S. Dollar and the local or functional currency of the factory, an embedded derivative contract is created upon the factory's acceptance of NIKE's purchase order. Embedded derivative contracts are separated from the related purchase order, and their accounting treatment is described further below.

The Company's policy permits the utilization of derivatives to reduce its foreign currency exposures where internal netting or other strategies cannot be effectively employed. Typically the Company may enter into hedge contracts starting up to 12 to 24 months in advance of the forecasted transaction and may place incremental hedges up to 100% of the exposure by the time the forecasted transaction occurs. The total notional amount of outstanding foreign currency derivatives designated as cash flow hedges was $14.4 billion as of May 31, 2015.

During the year ended May 31, 2015, the Company entered into a series of forward-starting interest rate swap agreements with a total notional amount of $1 billion. These instruments were designated as cash flow hedges of the variability in the expected cash outflows of interest payments on future debt due to changes in benchmark interest rates.

All changes in fair value of derivatives designated as cash flow hedges, excluding any ineffective portion, are recorded in *Other comprehensive income* until *Net income* is affected by the variability of cash flows of the hedged transaction. In most cases, amounts recorded in *Other comprehensive income* will be released to *Net income* in periods following the maturity of the related derivative, rather than at maturity. Effective hedge results are classified within the Consolidated Statements of Income in the same manner as the underlying exposure, with the results of hedges of non-functional currency denominated revenues and product cost exposures, excluding embedded derivatives as described below, recorded in *Revenues* or *Cost of sales*, when the underlying hedged transaction affects consolidated *Net income*. Results of hedges of selling and administrative expense are recorded together with those costs when the related expense is recorded. Amounts recorded in *Other comprehensive income* related to forward-starting interest rate swaps will be released through *Interest expense (income), net* over the term of the issued debt. Results of hedges of anticipated purchases and sales of U.S. Dollar-denominated available-for-sale securities are recorded in *Other (income) expense, net* when the securities are sold. Results of hedges of certain anticipated intercompany transactions are recorded in *Other (income) expense, net* when the transaction occurs. The Company classifies the cash flows at settlement from these designated cash flow hedge derivatives in the same category as the cash flows from the related hedged items, primarily within the *Cash provided by operations* component of the Consolidated Statements of Cash Flows.

Premiums paid on options are initially recorded as deferred charges. The Company assesses the effectiveness of options based on the total cash flows method and records total changes in the options' fair value to *Other comprehensive income* to the degree they are effective.

The Company formally assesses, both at a hedge's inception and on an ongoing basis, whether the derivatives that are used in the hedging transaction have been highly effective in offsetting changes in the cash flows of hedged items and whether those derivatives may be expected to remain highly effective in future periods. Effectiveness for cash flow hedges is assessed based on changes in forward rates. Ineffectiveness was immaterial for the years ended May 31, 2015, 2014 and 2013.

The Company discontinues hedge accounting prospectively when: (1) it determines that the derivative is no longer highly effective in offsetting changes in the cash flows of a hedged item (including hedged items such as firm commitments or forecasted transactions); (2) the derivative expires or is sold, terminated or exercised; (3) it is no longer probable that the forecasted transaction will occur; or (4) management determines that designating the derivative as a hedging instrument is no longer appropriate.

When the Company discontinues hedge accounting because it is no longer probable that the forecasted transaction will occur in the originally expected period, but is expected to occur within an additional two-month period of time thereafter, the gain or loss on the derivative remains in *Accumulated other comprehensive income* and is reclassified to *Net income* when the forecasted transaction affects consolidated *Net income*. However, if it is probable that a forecasted transaction will not occur by the end of the originally specified time period or within an additional two-month period of time thereafter, the gains and losses that were accumulated in *Other comprehensive income* will be recognized immediately in *Other (income) expense, net*. In all situations in which hedge accounting is discontinued and the derivative remains outstanding, the Company will carry the derivative at its fair value on the Consolidated Balance Sheets, recognizing future changes in the fair value in *Other (income) expense, net*. For the years ended May 31, 2015, 2014 and 2013, the amounts recorded in *Other (income) expense, net* as a result of the discontinuance of cash flow hedging because the forecasted transaction was no longer probable of occurring were immaterial.

As of May 31, 2015, $685 million of deferred net gains (net of tax) on both outstanding and matured derivatives accumulated in *Other comprehensive income* are expected to be reclassified to *Net income* during the next 12 months concurrent with the underlying hedged transactions also being recorded in *Net income*. Actual amounts ultimately reclassified to *Net income* are dependent on the exchange rates in effect when derivative contracts that are currently outstanding mature. As of May 31, 2015, the maximum term over which the Company is hedging exposures to the variability of cash flows for its forecasted transactions was 36 months.

Fair Value Hedges

The Company is also exposed to the risk of changes in the fair value of certain fixed-rate debt attributable to changes in interest rates. Derivatives currently used by the Company to hedge this risk are receive-fixed, pay-variable interest rate swaps. All interest rate swaps designated as fair value hedges of the related long-term debt meet the shortcut method requirements under the accounting standards for derivatives and hedging. Accordingly, changes in the fair values of the interest rate swaps are considered to exactly offset changes in the fair value of the underlying long-term debt. The cash flows associated with the Company's fair value hedges are periodic interest payments while the swaps are outstanding, which are reflected within the *Cash provided by operations* component of the Consolidated Statements of Cash Flows. The Company recorded no ineffectiveness from its interest rate swaps designated as fair value hedges for the years ended May 31, 2015, 2014 or 2013. As of May 31, 2015, interest rate swaps designated as fair value hedges had a total notional amount of $100 million.

Net Investment Hedges

The Company has, in the past, hedged and may, in the future, hedge the risk of variability in foreign-currency-denominated net investments in wholly-owned international operations. All changes in fair value of the derivatives designated as net investment hedges, except ineffective portions, are reported as a component of *Other comprehensive income* along with the foreign currency translation adjustments on those investments. The Company classifies the cash flows at settlement of its net investment hedges within the *Cash used by investing activities* component of the Consolidated Statement of Cash Flows. The Company assesses hedge effectiveness based on changes in forward rates. The Company recorded no ineffectiveness from its net investment hedges for the years ended May 31, 2015, 2014 or 2013. The Company had no outstanding net investment hedges as of May 31, 2015.

Undesignated Derivative Instruments

The Company may elect to enter into foreign exchange forwards to mitigate the change in fair value of specific assets and liabilities on the balance sheet and/or the embedded derivative contracts explained below. These forwards are not designated as hedging instruments under the accounting standards for derivatives and hedging. Accordingly, these undesignated instruments are recorded at fair value as a derivative asset or liability on the Consolidated Balance Sheets with their corresponding change in fair value recognized in *Other (income) expense, net*, together with the re-measurement gain or loss from the hedged balance sheet position or embedded derivative contract. The Company classifies the cash flows at settlement from undesignated instruments within the *Cash provided by operations* component of the Consolidated Statements of Cash Flows. The total notional amount of outstanding undesignated derivative instruments was $4.4 billion as of May 31, 2015.

Embedded Derivatives

As part of the foreign currency adjustment program described above, an embedded derivative contract is created upon the factory's acceptance of NIKE's purchase order for currencies within the factory currency exposure indices that are neither the U.S. Dollar nor the local or functional currency of the factory. Embedded derivative contracts are treated as foreign currency forward contracts that are bifurcated from the related purchase order and

recorded at fair value as a derivative asset or liability on the Consolidated Balance Sheets with their corresponding change in fair value recognized in *Other (income) expense, net*, from the date a purchase order is accepted by a factory through the date the purchase price is no longer subject to foreign currency fluctuations.

In addition, the Company has entered into certain other contractual agreements which have payments that are indexed to currencies that are not the functional currency of either substantial party to the contracts. These payment terms expose NIKE to variability in foreign exchange rates and create embedded derivative contracts that must be bifurcated from the related contract and recorded at fair value as derivative assets or liabilities on the Consolidated Balance Sheets with their corresponding changes in fair value recognized in *Other (income) expense, net* until each payment is settled.

At May 31, 2015, the notional amount of all embedded derivatives outstanding was approximately $205 million.

Credit Risk

The Company is exposed to credit-related losses in the event of nonperformance by counterparties to hedging instruments. The counterparties to all derivative transactions are major financial institutions with investment grade credit ratings. However, this does not eliminate the Company's exposure to credit risk with these institutions. This credit risk is limited to the unrealized gains in such contracts should any of these counterparties fail to perform as contracted. To manage this risk, the Company has established strict counterparty credit guidelines that are continually monitored.

The Company's derivative contracts contain credit risk related contingent features designed to protect against significant deterioration in counterparties' creditworthiness and their ultimate ability to settle outstanding derivative contracts in the normal course of business. The Company's bilateral credit related contingent features generally require the owing entity, either the Company or the derivative counterparty, to post collateral for the portion of the fair value in excess of $50 million should the fair value of outstanding derivatives per counterparty be greater than $50 million. Additionally, a certain level of decline in credit rating of either the Company or the counterparty could also trigger collateral requirements. As of May 31, 2015, the Company was in compliance with all credit risk related contingent features and had derivative instruments with credit risk related contingent features in a net liability position of $4 million. Accordingly, the Company was not required to post any collateral as a result of these contingent features. Further, as of May 31, 2015, the Company had received $968 million of cash collateral and $74 million of securities from various counterparties to its derivative contracts (refer to Note 6 — Fair Value Measurements). Given the considerations described above, the Company considers the impact of the risk of counterparty default to be immaterial.

NOTE 18 — Operating Segments and Related Information

The Company's operating segments are evidence of the structure of the Company's internal organization. The NIKE Brand segments are defined by geographic regions for operations participating in NIKE Brand sales activity.

Each NIKE Brand geographic segment operates predominantly in one industry: the design, development, marketing and selling of athletic footwear, apparel and equipment. The Company's reportable operating segments for the NIKE Brand are: North America, Western Europe, Central & Eastern Europe, Greater China, Japan and Emerging Markets, and include results for the NIKE, Jordan and Hurley brands. The Company's NIKE Brand Direct to Consumer operations are managed within each geographic operating segment. Converse is also a reportable segment for NIKE, Inc., and operates in one industry: the design, marketing, licensing and selling of casual sneakers, apparel and accessories.

Global Brand Divisions is included within the NIKE Brand for presentation purposes to align with the way management views the Company. Global

Brand Divisions primarily represent NIKE Brand licensing businesses that are not part of a geographic operating segment, and demand creation, operating overhead and product creation and design expenses that are centrally managed for the NIKE Brand.

Corporate consists largely of unallocated general and administrative expenses, including expenses associated with centrally managed departments; depreciation and amortization related to the Company's headquarters; unallocated insurance, benefit and compensation programs, including stock-based compensation; and certain foreign currency gains and losses, including certain hedge gains and losses.

The primary financial measure used by the Company to evaluate performance of individual operating segments is earnings before interest and taxes (commonly referred to as "EBIT"), which represents *Net income* before *Interest expense (income), net* and *Income tax expense* in the Consolidated Statements of Income. Reconciling items for EBIT represent corporate expense items that are not allocated to the operating segments for management reporting.

As part of the Company's centrally managed foreign exchange risk management program, standard foreign currency rates are assigned twice per year to each NIKE Brand entity in the Company's geographic operating segments and to Converse. These rates are set approximately nine months in advance of the future selling season based on average market spot rates in the calendar month preceding the date they are established. *Inventories* and *Cost of sales* for geographic operating segments and Converse reflect use of these standard rates to record non-functional currency product purchases in the entity's functional currency. Differences between assigned standard foreign currency rates and actual market rates are included in Corporate, together with foreign currency hedge gains and losses generated from the Company's centrally managed foreign exchange risk management program and other conversion gains and losses.

Accounts receivable, net, Inventories and *Property, plant and equipment, net* for operating segments are regularly reviewed by management and are therefore provided below. Additions to long-lived assets as presented in the following table represent capital expenditures.

Certain prior year amounts have been reclassified to conform to fiscal 2015 presentation.

		Year Ended May 31,			
(In millions)		2015		2014	2013
REVENUES					
North America	$	13,740	$	12,299 $	11,158
Western Europe		5,709		4,979	4,193
Central & Eastern Europe		1,417		1,387	1,229
Greater China		3,067		2,602	2,478
Japan		755		771	876
Emerging Markets		3,898		3,949	3,832
Global Brand Divisions		115		125	115
Total NIKE Brand		28,701		26,112	23,881
Converse		1,982		1,684	1,449
Corporate		(82)		3	(17)
TOTAL NIKE CONSOLIDATED REVENUES	$	30,601	$	27,799 $	25,313
EARNINGS BEFORE INTEREST AND TAXES					
North America	$	3,645	$	3,077 $	2,639
Western Europe		1,277		855	643
Central & Eastern Europe		247		279	234
Greater China		993		816	813
Japan		100		131	139
Emerging Markets		818		952	985
Global Brand Divisions		(2,263)		(1,993)	(1,716)
Total NIKE Brand		4,817		4,117	3,737
Converse		517		496	425
Corporate		(1,101)		(1,036)	(909)
Total NIKE Consolidated Earnings Before Interest and Taxes		4,233		3,577	3,253
Interest expense (income), net		28		33	(3)
TOTAL NIKE CONSOLIDATED EARNINGS BEFORE TAXES	$	4,205	$	3,544 $	3,256
ADDITIONS TO LONG-LIVED ASSETS					
North America	$	208	$	240 $	132
Western Europe		216		120	75
Central & Eastern Europe		20		19	22
Greater China		69		63	52
Japan		15		9	7
Emerging Markets		37		55	50
Global Brand Divisions		225		225	270
Total NIKE Brand		790		731	608
Converse		69		30	20
Corporate		144		161	153
TOTAL ADDITIONS TO LONG-LIVED ASSETS	$	1,003	$	922 $	781
DEPRECIATION					
North America	$	121	$	109 $	92
Western Europe		75		71	68
Central & Eastern Europe		12		11	9
Greater China		46		38	32
Japan		22		19	22
Emerging Markets		27		25	20
Global Brand Divisions		210		175	122
Total NIKE Brand		513		448	365
Converse		18		16	15
Corporate		75		54	38
TOTAL DEPRECIATION	$	606	$	518 $	418

(In millions)	As of May 31,	
	2015	2014
ACCOUNTS RECEIVABLE, NET		
North America	$ 1,737	$ 1,505
Western Europe	344	341
Central & Eastern Europe	242	280
Greater China	84	68
Japan	134	162
Emerging Markets	461	819
Global Brand Divisions	88	71
Total NIKE Brand	3,090	3,246
Converse	258	171
Corporate	10	17
TOTAL ACCOUNTS RECEIVABLE, NET	$ 3,358	$ 3,434
INVENTORIES		
North America	$ 2,207	$ 1,758
Western Europe	699	711
Central & Eastern Europe	169	271
Greater China	249	221
Japan	94	94
Emerging Markets	528	633
Global Brand Divisions	32	18
Total NIKE Brand	3,978	3,706
Converse	237	261
Corporate	122	(20)
TOTAL INVENTORIES	$ 4,337	$ 3,947
PROPERTY, PLANT AND EQUIPMENT, NET		
North America	$ 632	$ 545
Western Europe	451	384
Central & Eastern Europe	47	51
Greater China	254	232
Japan	205	258
Emerging Markets	103	115
Global Brand Divisions	484	537
Total NIKE Brand	2,176	2,122
Converse	122	70
Corporate	713	642
TOTAL PROPERTY, PLANT AND EQUIPMENT, NET	$ 3,011	$ 2,834

Revenues by Major Product Lines

Revenues to external customers for NIKE Brand products are attributable to sales of footwear, apparel and equipment. Other revenues to external customers consist primarily of sales by Converse.

(In millions)	Year Ended May 31,		
	2015	2014	2013
Footwear	$ 18,318	$ 16,208	$ 14,635
Apparel	8,636	8,109	7,491
Equipment	1,632	1,670	1,640
Other	2,015	1,812	1,547
TOTAL NIKE CONSOLIDATED REVENUES	$ 30,601	$ 27,799	$ 25,313

Revenues and Long-Lived Assets by Geographic Area

After allocation of revenues for Global Brand Divisions, Converse and Corporate to geographical areas based on the location where the sales originated, revenues by geographical area are essentially the same as reported above under operating segments with the exception of the United States. Revenues derived in the United States were $14,180 million, $12,711 million and $11,385 million for the years ended May 31, 2015, 2014 and 2013, respectively. The Company's largest concentrations of long-lived assets primarily consist of the Company's world headquarters and distribution facilities in the United States and distribution facilities in Japan, Belgium and China. Long-lived assets attributable to operations in the United States, which are primarily composed of net property, plant &

equipment, were $1,877 million and $1,652 million at May 31, 2015 and 2014, respectively. Long-lived assets attributable to operations in Japan were $205 million and $258 million at May 31, 2015 and 2014, respectively. Long-lived assets attributable to operations in Belgium were $234 million and $175 million at May 31, 2015 and 2014, respectively. Long-lived assets attributable to operations in China were $267 million and $234 million at May 31, 2015 and 2014, respectively.

Major Customers

No customer accounted for 10% or more of the Company's net revenues during the years ended May 31, 2015, 2014 and 2013.

Glossary

A

absorption costing The reporting of the costs of manufactured products, normally direct materials, direct labor, and factory overhead, as product costs. (Ch. 20)

accelerated depreciation method A depreciation method that provides for a higher depreciation amount in the first year of the asset's use, followed by a gradually declining amount of depreciation. (Ch. 9)

account An accounting form that is used to record the increases and decreases in each financial statement item. (Ch. 2)

account payable The liability created by a purchase on account. (Ch. 1)

account receivable A claim against the customer created by selling merchandise or services on credit. (Chs. 1, 2, 8)

accounting An information system that provides reports to users about the economic activities and condition of a business. (Ch. 1)

accounting assumptions Assumptions that provide the framework upon which accounting standards are constructed. (Ch. 1)

accounting cycle The process that begins with analyzing and journalizing transactions and ends with the post-closing trial balance. (Ch. 4)

accounting equation Assets = Liabilities + Stockholder's Equity. (Ch. 1)

accounting principles Principles that provide the framework upon which accounting standards are constructed. (Ch. 1)

accounting standards The rules that determine the accounting for individual business transactions. (Ch. 1)

accounts payable subsidiary ledger The subsidiary ledger containing the individual accounts with creditors (suppliers). (Ch. 5)

accounts receivable analysis A company's ability to collect its accounts receivable. (Ch. 14)

accounts receivable subsidiary ledger The subsidiary ledger containing the individual accounts with customers. (Ch. 5)

accounts receivable turnover The relationship between sales and accounts receivable, computed by dividing sales by the average accounts receivable; measures how frequently during the year the accounts receivable are being converted to cash. (Chs. 8, 14)

accrual An accrual occurs when revenue has been earned or an expense has been incurred but has not been recorded. (Ch. 3)

accrual basis of accounting Under this basis of accounting, revenues and expenses are reported in the income statement in the period in which they are earned or incurred. (Ch. 3)

Accumulated Depreciation The contra asset account credited when recording the depreciation of a fixed asset. (Ch. 3)

accumulated other comprehensive income The cumulative effects of other comprehensive income items reported separately in the Stockholders' Equity section of the balance sheet. (Ch. 14)

activities The types of work, or actions, involved in a manufacturing or service process. (Ch. 18)

activity analysis The study of employee effort and other business records to determine the cost of activities. (Ch. 26)

activity base (driver) A measure of activity that is related to changes in cost. Used in analyzing and classifying cost behavior. Activity bases are also used in the denominator in calculating the predetermined factory overhead rate to assign overhead costs to cost objects. (Chs. 16, 18, 19)

activity rate The estimated activity cost divided by estimated activity-base usage. (Ch. 18)

activity-based costing (ABC) A cost allocation method that identifies activities causing the incurrence of costs and allocates these costs to products (or other cost objects), based on activity drivers (bases). (Chs. 16, 18)

adjusted trial balance The trial balance prepared after all the adjusting entries have been posted. (Ch. 3)

adjusting entries The journal entries that bring the accounts up to date at the end of the accounting period. (Ch. 3)

adjusting process An analysis and updating of the accounts when financial statements are prepared. (Ch. 3)

administrative expenses (general expenses) Expenses incurred in the administration or general operations of the business. (Ch. 5)

aging the receivables The process of analyzing the accounts receivable and classifying them according to various age groupings, with the due date being the base point for determining age. (Ch. 8)

Allowance for Doubtful Accounts The contra asset account for accounts receivable. (Ch. 8)

allowance method The method of accounting for uncollectible accounts that provides an expense for uncollectible receivables in advance of their write-off. (Ch. 8)

amortization The periodic transfer of the cost of an intangible asset to expense. (Chs. 9, 11)

analytical methods Methods that examine changes in the amount and percentage of financial statement items within and across periods. (Ch. 14)

annuity A series of equal cash flows at fixed intervals. (Chs. 11, 25)

appraisal costs Costs to detect, measure, evaluate, and inspect products and processes to ensure that they conform to customer requirements and performance standards. (Ch. 26)

arm's-length transactions Transactions between two independent parties. (Ch. 1)

asset turnover ratio A ratio that measures how effectively a business is using its assets to generate sales, computed as sales divided by average total assets. (Chs. 5, 14)

assets The resources owned by a business. (Chs. 1, 2)

average rate of return A method of evaluating capital investment proposals that focuses on the expected profitability of the investment. (Ch. 25)

B

backflush accounting Simplification of the accounting system by eliminating accumulation and transfer of costs as products move through production. (Ch. 26)

bad debt expense The operating expense incurred because of the failure to collect receivables. (Ch. 8)

balance of the account The amount of the difference between the debits and the credits that have been entered into an account. (Ch. 2)

balance sheet A list of the assets, liabilities, and stockholders' equity as of a specific date, usually at the close of the last day of a month or a year. (Ch. 1)

balanced scorecard A performance evaluation approach that incorporates multiple performance dimensions by combining financial and nonfinancial measures. (Ch. 23)

bank reconciliation The analysis that details the items responsible for the difference between the cash balance reported in the bank statement and the balance of the cash account in the ledger. (Ch. 7)

bank statement A summary of all transactions mailed to the depositor or made available online by the bank each month. (Ch. 7)

batch size The amount of production in units of product that is produced after a setup. (Ch. 26)

bond A form of an interest-bearing note used by corporations to borrow on a long-term basis. (Ch. 11)

bond indenture The contract between a corporation issuing bonds and the bondholders. (Ch. 11)

book value The cost of a fixed asset minus accumulated depreciation on the asset. (Ch. 9)

book value of the asset (or net book value) The difference between the cost of a fixed asset and its accumulated depreciation. (Ch. 3)

boot The amount a buyer owes a seller when a fixed asset is traded in on a similar asset. (Ch. 9)

break-even point The level of business operations at which revenues and expired costs are equal. (Ch. 18)

budget An accounting device used to plan and control resources of operational departments and divisions. (Ch. 21)

budget performance report A report comparing actual results with budget figures. (Ch. 22)

budgetary slack Excess resources set within a budget to provide for uncertain events. (Ch. 21)

budgeted variable factory overhead The standard variable overhead for the actual units produced. (Ch. 22)

business An organization in which basic resources (inputs), such as materials and labor, are assembled and processed to provide goods or services (outputs) to customers. (Ch. 1)

business entity assumption A concept of accounting that limits the economic data in the accounting system to data related directly to the activities of the business. (Ch. 1)

business transaction An economic event or condition that directly changes an entity's financial condition or directly affects its results of operations. (Ch. 1)

C

capital expenditures The costs of acquiring fixed assets, adding to a fixed asset, improving a fixed asset, or extending a fixed asset's useful life. (Ch. 9)

capital expenditures budget The budget summarizing future plans for acquiring plant facilities and equipment. (Ch. 21)

capital investment analysis The process by which management plans, evaluates, and controls long-term capital investments involving property, plant, and equipment. (Ch. 25)

capital rationing The process by which management plans, evaluates, and controls long-term capital investments involving fixed assets. (Ch. 25)

carrying amount The balance of the bonds payable account (face amount of the bonds) less any unamortized discount or plus any unamortized premium. (Ch. 11)

cash Coins, currency (paper money), checks, money orders, and money on deposit that is available for unrestricted withdrawal from banks and other financial institutions. (Ch. 7)

cash basis of accounting Under this basis of accounting, revenues and expenses are reported on the income statement in the period in which cash is received or paid. (Ch. 3)

cash budget A budget of estimated cash receipts and payments. (Ch. 21)

cash dividend A cash distribution of earnings by a corporation to its shareholders. (Ch. 12)

cash equivalents Highly liquid investments that are usually reported with cash on the balance sheet. (Ch. 7)

cash flow per share Normally computed as cash flow from operations per share. (Ch. 13)

cash flows from financing activities The section of the statement of cash flows that reports cash flows from transactions affecting the equity and debt of the business. (Ch. 13)

cash flows from investing activities The section of the statement of cash flows that reports cash flows from transactions affecting investments in noncurrent assets. (Ch. 13)

cash flows from operating activities The section of the statement of cash flows that reports the cash transactions affecting the determination of net income. (Ch. 13)

cash payback period The expected period of time between the date of an investment and the recovery in cash of the amount invested. (Ch. 25)

cash refund An amount paid by the seller to the buyer for merchandise that is defective, is damaged during shipment, or does not meet the buyer's expectations. (Ch. 5)

cash short and over account An account which has recorded errors in cash sales or errors in making change causing the amount of actual cash on hand to differ from the beginning amount of cash plus the cash sales for the day. (Ch. 7)

Certified Public Accountant (CPA) Public accountants who have met a state's education, experience, and examination requirements. (Ch. 1)

chart of accounts A list of the accounts in the ledger. (Ch. 2)

clearing account Another name for the income summary account because it has the effect of clearing the revenue and expense accounts of their balances. (Ch. 4)

closing entries The entries that transfer the balances of the revenue, expense, and dividends accounts to the retained earnings account. (Ch. 4)

closing process The transfer process of converting temporary account balances to zero by transferring the revenue and expense account balances to Income Summary, transferring the income summary account balance to the retained earnings account, and transferring the dividends account to the retained earnings account. (Ch. 4)

closing the books The process of transferring temporary account balances to permanent accounts at the end of the accounting period. (Ch. 4)

common stock The stock outstanding when a corporation has issued only one class of stock. (Chs. 1, 2, 12)

common-sized statement A financial statement in which all items are expressed only in relative terms. (Ch. 14)

compensating balance A requirement by some banks requiring depositors to maintain minimum cash balances in their bank accounts. (Ch. 7)

comprehensive income All changes in stockholders' equity during a period, except those resulting from dividends and stockholders' investments. (Ch. 14)

consigned inventory Merchandise that is shipped by manufacturers to retailers who act as the manufacturer's selling agent. (Ch. 6)

consignee The name for the retailer in a consigned inventory arrangement. (Ch. 6)

consignor The name for the manufacturer in a consigned inventory arrangement. (Ch. 6)

contingent liabilities Liabilities that may arise from past transactions if certain events occur in the future. (Ch. 10)

continuous budgeting A method of budgeting that provides for maintaining a 12-month projection into the future. (Ch. 21)

continuous process improvement A management approach that is part of the overall total quality management philosophy. The approach requires all employees to constantly improve processes of which they are a part or for which they have managerial responsibility. (Ch. 15)

contra accounts (or contra asset accounts) An account offset against another account. (Ch. 3)

contract rate The periodic interest to be paid on the bonds that is identified in the bond indenture; expressed as a percentage of the face amount of the bond. (Ch. 11)

contribution margin The excess of sales over variable costs. (Chs. 19, 20)

contribution margin analysis The systematic examination of the differences between planned and actual contribution margins. (Ch. 20)

contribution margin ratio The percentage of each sales dollar that is available to cover the fixed costs and provide an operating income. (Ch. 19)

control environment The overall attitude of management and employees about the importance of controls. (Ch. 7)

controllable costs Costs that can be influenced (increased, decreased, or eliminated) by someone such as a manager or factory worker. (Ch. 20)

controllable expenses Costs that can be influenced by the decisions of a manager. (Ch. 23)

controllable revenues Revenues earned by the profit center. (Ch. 23)

controllable variance The difference between the actual amount of variable factory overhead cost incurred and the amount of variable factory overhead budgeted for the standard product. (Ch. 22)

controller The chief management accountant of a division or other segment of a business. (Ch. 15)

controlling A phase in the management process that consists of monitoring the operating results of implemented plans and comparing the actual results with the expected results. (Ch. 15)

controlling account The account in the general ledger that summarizes the balances of the accounts in a subsidiary ledger. (Ch. 5)

conversion costs The combination of direct labor and factory overhead costs. (Chs. 15, 26)

copyright An exclusive right to publish and sell a literary, artistic, or musical composition. (Ch. 9)

corporation A business organized under state or federal statutes as a separate legal entity. (Ch. 1)

correcting journal entry An entry that is prepared when an error has already been journalized and posted. (Ch. 2)

cost A payment of cash (or a commitment to pay cash in the future) for the purpose of generating revenues. (Ch. 15)

cost accounting systems Systems that measure, record, and report product costs. (Ch. 16)

cost allocation The process of assigning indirect cost to a cost object, such as a job. (Ch. 16)

cost behavior The manner in which a cost changes in relation to its activity base (driver). (Ch. 19)

cost center A decentralized unit in which the department or division manager has responsibility for the control of costs incurred and the authority to make decisions that affect these costs. (Ch. 23)

cost object The object or segment of operations to which costs are related for management's use, such as a product or department. (Ch. 15)

cost of goods manufactured The total cost of making and finishing a product. (Ch. 15)

cost of goods sold The cost of finished goods available for sale minus the ending finished goods inventory. (Chs. 5, 15)

cost of goods sold budget A budget of the estimated direct materials, direct labor, and factory overhead consumed by sold products. (Ch. 21)

cost of production report A report prepared periodically by a processing department, summarizing (1) the units for which the department is accountable and the disposition of those units and (2) the costs incurred by the department and the allocation of those costs between completed and incomplete production. (Ch. 17)

cost of quality report A report summarizing the costs, percent of total, and percent of sales by appraisal, prevention, internal failure, and external failure cost of quality categories. (Ch. 26)

cost per equivalent unit The rate used to allocate costs between completed and partially completed production. (Ch. 17)

cost price approach An approach to transfer pricing that uses cost as the basis for setting the transfer price. (Ch. 23)

cost principle Recording an item at its initial transaction price, also called the historical cost principle. (Ch. 1)

cost variance The difference between actual cost and the flexible budget at actual volumes. (Ch. 22)

costs of quality The cost associated with controlling quality (prevention and appraisal) and failing to control quality (internal and external failure). (Ch. 26)

cost-volume-profit analysis The systematic examination of the relationships among selling prices, volume of sales and production, costs, expenses, and profits. (Ch. 19)

cost-volume-profit chart A chart that graphically shows sales, costs, and the related profit or loss for various levels of units sold. (Ch. 19)

credit Amount entered on the right side of an account. (Ch. 2)

credit memorandum (credit memo) A form used by a seller to inform the buyer of the amount the seller proposes to credit to the account receivable due from the buyer. (Ch. 5)

credit period The amount of time the buyer is allowed in which to pay the seller. (Ch. 5)

credit terms Terms for payment on account by the buyer to the seller. (Ch. 5)

cumulative preferred stock Stock that has a right to receive regular dividends that were not declared (paid) in prior years. (Ch. 12)

currency exchange rate The rate at which currency in another country can be exchanged for local currency. (Ch. 25)

current assets Cash and other assets that are expected to be converted to cash or sold or used up, usually within one year or less, through the normal operations of the business. (Ch. 4)

current liabilities Liabilities that will be due within a short time (usually one year or less) and that are to be paid out of current assets. (Ch. 4)

current position analysis A company's ability to pay its current liabilities. (Ch. 14)

current ratio A financial ratio that is computed by dividing current assets by current liabilities. (Chs. 4, 14)

currently attainable standards Standards that represent levels of operation that can be attained with reasonable effort. (Ch. 22)

customer allowances Returns to the seller by the customer or reductions from the initial selling price due to defective or damaged merchandise or goods that did not meet the customer's expectations. (Ch. 5)

customer discounts A variety of discounts offered by the seller as incentive for the customer to act in a way benefiting the seller. (Ch. 5)

customer refunds payable A liability account for estimated refunds and allowances that will be paid or granted customers in the future. (Ch. 5)

D

days' cash on hand A calculation that measures how long a company could survive if its sources of revenue were to decline significantly. (Ch. 7)

debit Amount entered on the left side of an account. (Ch. 2)

debit memorandum (debit memo) A form used by a buyer to inform the seller of the amount the buyer proposes to debit to the account payable due the seller. (Ch. 5)

decision making A component inherent in the other management processes of planning, directing, controlling, and improving. (Ch. 15)

deferral A deferral occurs when cash related to a future revenue or expense has been initially recorded as a liability or an asset. (Ch. 3)

defined benefit plan A pension plan that promises employees a fixed annual pension benefit at retirement, based on years of service, age, and compensation levels. (Ch. 10)

defined contribution plan A pension plan that requires a fixed amount of money to be invested on the employee's behalf during the employee's working years. (Ch. 10)

depletion expense An expense account that includes the cost of natural resources as they are harvested and mined and then sold. (Ch. 9)

depreciable cost The difference between a fixed asset's initial cost and its residual value. (Ch. 9)

depreciate To lose usefulness as all fixed assets except land do. (Ch. 3)

depreciation The systematic periodic transfer of the cost of a fixed asset to an expense account during its expected useful life. (Chs. 3, 9)

depreciation expense The portion of the cost of a fixed asset that is recorded as an expense each year of its useful life. (Ch. 3)

differential analysis The area of accounting concerned with the effect of alternative courses of action on revenues and costs. (Ch. 24)

differential cost The amount of increase or decrease in cost expected from a particular course of action compared with an alternative. (Ch. 24)

differential income (loss) The difference between the differential revenue and the differential costs. (Ch. 24)

differential revenue The amount of increase or decrease in revenue expected from a particular course of action as compared with an alternative. (Ch. 24)

direct costs Costs that can be traced directly to a cost object. (Ch. 15)

direct labor cost The wages of factory workers who are directly involved in converting materials into a finished product. (Ch. 15)

direct labor cost budget Budget that estimates direct labor hours and related cost needed to support budgeted production. (Ch. 21)

direct labor rate variance The cost associated with the difference between the actual rate and the standard rate paid for direct labor multiplied by the actual direct labor hours used in producing a commodity. (Ch. 22)

direct labor time variance The cost associated with the difference between the actual hours and the standard hours of direct labor spent producing a commodity multiplied by the standard direct labor rate per hour. (Ch. 22)

direct materials cost The cost of materials that are an integral part of the finished product. (Ch. 15)

direct materials price variance The cost associated with the difference between the actual price and the standard price of direct materials multiplied by the actual quantity of direct materials used in producing a commodity. (Ch. 22)

direct materials purchases budget A budget that uses the production budget as a starting point to budget materials purchases. (Ch. 21)

direct materials quantity variance The cost associated with the difference between the actual quantity and the standard quantity of direct materials used in producing a commodity multiplied by the standard direct material price. (Ch. 22)

direct method A method of reporting the cash flows from operating activities as the difference between the operating cash receipts and the operating cash payments. (Ch. 13)

direct write-off method The method of accounting for uncollectible accounts that recognizes the expense only when accounts are judged to be worthless. (Ch. 8)

directing The process by which managers, given their assigned level of responsibilities, run day-to-day operations. (Ch. 15)

discount The interest deducted from the maturity value of a note or the excess of the face amount of bonds over their issue price. (Chs. 11, 12)

dishonored note receivable A note that the maker fails to pay on the due date. (Ch. 8)

dividend yield A ratio, computed by dividing the annual dividends paid per share of common stock by the market price per share at a specific date, that indicates the rate of return to stockholders in terms of cash dividend distributions. (Ch. 14)

dividends Distribution of a corporation's earnings to stockholders. (Chs. 1, 2)

dividends per share Measures the extent to which earnings are being distributed to common shareholders. (Ch. 14)

double-declining-balance method A method of depreciation that provides periodic depreciation expense based on the declining book value of a fixed asset over its estimated life. (Ch. 9)

double-entry accounting system A system of accounting for recording transactions, based on recording increases and decreases in accounts so that debits equal credits. (Ch. 2)

DuPont formula An expanded expression of return on investment determined by multiplying the profit margin by the investment turnover. (Ch. 23)

E

earnings The amount by which revenues exceed expenses. (Ch. 1)

earnings per common share (EPS) Net income per share of common stock outstanding during a period. (Ch. 12)

earnings per share (EPS) on common stock The profitability ratio of net income available to common shareholders to the number of common shares outstanding. (Ch. 14)

EBITDA Term for earnings before interest, taxes, depreciation, and amortization; operating income expressed by adding back depreciation and amortization expense. (Ch. 20)

eco-efficiency measures Measures that help managers evaluate the savings generated by using fewer natural resources in a company's operations. (Ch. 15)

effective rate of interest The market rate of interest at the time bonds are issued. (Ch. 11)

electronic data interchange (EDI) An information technology that allows different business organizations to use computers to communicate orders, relay information, and make or receive payments. (Ch. 26)

electronic funds transfer (EFT) A system in which computers rather than paper (money, checks, etc.) are used to effect cash transactions. (Ch. 7)

elements of internal control The control environment, risk assessment, control procedures, information and communication, and monitoring. (Ch. 7)

employee fraud The intentional act of deceiving an employer for personal gain. (Ch. 7)

employee involvement A philosophy that grants employees the responsibility and authority to make their own decisions about their operations. (Ch. 26)

engineering change order (ECO) The document that initiates changing a product or process. (Ch. 18)

enterprise resource planning (ERP) An integrated business and information system used by companies to plan and control both internal and supply chain operations. (Ch. 26)

equity The rights of owners. (Ch. 1)

equivalent units of production The number of production units that could have been completed within a given accounting period, given the resources consumed. (Ch. 17)

estimated returns inventory A current asset that is reported on the balance sheet after inventory. (Ch. 5)

ethics Moral principles that guide the conduct of individuals. (Ch. 1)

expected useful life The estimated length of time a fixed asset will be used in normal operations. (Ch. 9)

expense recognition principle A principle, sometimes called the matching principle, that requires expenses to be recorded in the same period as the related revenue. (Chs. 1, 3)

expenses Assets used up or services consumed in the process of generating revenues. (Chs. 1, 2)

external failure costs The costs incurred after defective units or services have been delivered to consumers. (Ch. 26)

F

face amount An amount at which bonds sell if the market rate equals the contract rate. (Ch. 11)

factory burden Another term for manufacturing overhead or factory overhead. (Ch. 15)

factory overhead cost All of the costs of producing a product except for direct materials and direct labor. (Ch. 15)

factory overhead cost budget Budget that estimates the cost for each item of factory overhead needed to support budgeted production. (Ch. 21)

factory overhead cost variance report Reports budgeted and actual costs for variable and fixed factory overhead along with the related controllable and volume variances. (Ch. 22)

fair value The price that would be received for selling an asset or paying off a liability, often the market price for an equity or debt security. (Ch. 14)

faithful representation A characteristic of financial reports that pertains to information accurately reflecting an entity's economic activity or condition. (Ch. 1)

favorable cost variance A variance that occurs when the actual cost is less than standard cost. (Ch. 22)

feedback Measures provided to operational employees or managers on the performance of subunits of the organization. These measures are used by employees to adjust a process or a behavior to achieve goals. See management by exception. (Ch. 15)

fees earned Revenue from providing services. (Ch. 1)

FICA tax Federal Insurance Contributions Act tax used to finance federal programs for retirees, survivors, and disability insurance (social security) and health insurance for senior citizens (Medicare). (Ch. 10)

financial accounting The branch of accounting that is concerned with recording transactions using generally accepted accounting principles (GAAP) for a business or other economic unit and with a periodic preparation of various statements from such records. (Chs. 1, 15)

Financial Accounting Standards Board (FASB) The authoritative body that has the primary responsibility for developing accounting principles. (Ch. 1)

financial statements Financial reports that summarize the effects of events on a business. (Ch. 1)

finished goods inventory The direct materials costs, direct labor costs, and factory overhead costs of finished products that have not been sold. (Ch. 15)

finished goods ledger The subsidiary ledger that contains the individual accounts for each kind of commodity or product produced. (Ch. 16)

first-in, first-out (FIFO) inventory cost flow method The method of inventory costing based on the assumption that the costs of merchandise sold should be charged against revenue in the order in which the costs were incurred. (Chs. 6, 17)

fiscal year The annual accounting period adopted by a business. (Ch. 4)

fixed asset turnover ratio The number of dollars of sales that are generated from each dollar of average fixed assets during the year, computed by dividing sales by average book value of fixed assets. (Ch. 9)

fixed assets (or plant assets) Long-term or relatively permanent tangible assets such as equipment, machinery, and buildings that are used in the normal business operations and that depreciate over time. (Chs. 3, 4, 9)

fixed costs Costs that tend to remain the same in amount, regardless of variations in the level of activity. (Ch. 19)

flexible budget A budget that adjusts for varying rates of activity. (Ch. 21)

FOB (free on board) destination Freight terms in which the seller pays the transportation costs from the shipping point to the final destination. (Ch. 5)

FOB (free on board) shipping point Freight terms in which the buyer pays the transportation costs from the shipping point to the final destination. (Ch. 5)

free cash flow The amount of operating cash flow remaining after replacing current productive capacity. (Ch. 13)

fringe benefits Benefits provided to employees in addition to wages and salaries. (Ch. 10)

future value The value of an asset or cash at a specified date in the future that is equivalent in value to a specified sum today. (Ch. 11)

G

general ledger The primary ledger, when used in conjunction with subsidiary ledgers, that contains all of the balance sheet and income statement accounts. (Ch. 5)

general-purpose financial statements A type of financial accounting report that is distributed to external users. The term "general purpose" refers to the wide range of decision-making needs that the reports are designed to serve. (Ch. 1)

generally accepted accounting principles (GAAP) Generally accepted guidelines for the preparation of financial statements. (Ch. 1)

goal conflict A condition that occurs when individual objectives conflict with organizational objectives. (Ch. 21)

going concern assumption An assumption that requires that financial reports be prepared assuming that the entity will continue operating into the future. (Ch. 1)

goodwill An intangible asset that is created from such favorable factors as location, product quality, reputation, and managerial skill. (Ch. 9)

gross pay The total earnings of an employee for a payroll period. (Ch. 10)

gross profit Sales minus the cost of merchandise sold. (Ch. 5)

gross profit method A method of estimating inventory cost that is based on the relationship of gross profit to sales. (Ch. 6)

H

high-low method A technique that uses the highest and lowest total costs as a basis for estimating the variable cost per unit and the fixed cost component of a mixed cost. (Ch. 19)

historical cost principle Recording an item at its initial transaction price. (Ch. 1)

horizontal analysis Financial analysis that compares an item in a current statement with the same item in prior statements. (Chs. 2, 14)

I

ideal standards Standards that can be achieved only under perfect operating conditions, such as no idle time, no machine breakdowns, and no materials spoilage; also called theoretical standards. (Ch. 22)

in arrears Cumulative preferred stock dividends that have not been paid in prior years are said to be in arrears. (Ch. 12)

income from operations (operating income) Revenues less operating expenses and service department charges for a profit or an investment center. (Ch. 5)

income statement A summary of the revenue and expenses for a specific period of time, such as a month or a year. (Ch. 1)

Income Summary An account to which the revenue and expense account balances are transferred at the end of a period. (Ch. 4)

indirect costs Costs that cannot be traced directly to a cost object. (Ch. 15)

indirect method A method of reporting the cash flows from operating activities as the net income from operations adjusted for all deferrals of past cash receipts and payments and all accruals of expected future cash receipts and payments. (Ch. 13)

inflation A period when prices in general are rising and the purchasing power of money is declining. (Ch. 25)

initial cost The purchase price of a fixed asset plus all costs to obtain and ready it for use. (Ch. 9)

installment note A debt that requires the borrower to make equal periodic payments to the lender for the term of the note. (Ch. 10)

intangible assets Long-term assets that are useful in the operations of a business, are not held for sale, and are without physical qualities. (Ch. 9)

interest revenue Money received for interest. (Ch. 1)

internal control The policies and procedures used to safeguard assets, ensure accurate business information, and ensure compliance with laws and regulations. (Ch. 7)

internal failure costs The costs associated with defects that are discovered by the organization before the product or service is delivered to the consumer. (Ch. 26)

internal rate of return (IRR) method A method of analysis of proposed capital investments that uses present value concepts to compute the rate of return from the net cash flows expected from the investment. (Ch. 25)

International Accounting Standards Board (IASB) An organization that issues International Financial Reporting Standards for many countries outside the United States. (Ch. 1)

inventory Merchandise on hand (not sold) at the end of an accounting period. (Ch. 5)

inventory analysis A company's ability to manage its inventory effectively. (Ch. 14)

inventory shrinkage (inventory shortage) The amount by which the merchandise for sale, as indicated by the balance of the merchandise inventory account, is larger than the total amount of merchandise counted during the physical inventory. (Ch. 5)

inventory subsidiary ledger A ledger containing individual accounts with a common characteristic. (Ch. 5)

inventory turnover The relationship between the volume of goods sold and inventory, computed by dividing the cost of goods sold by the average inventory. (Chs. 6, 14)

investment center A decentralized unit in which the manager has the responsibility and authority to make decisions that affect not only costs and revenues but also the fixed assets available to the center. (Ch. 23)

investment turnover A component of the rate of return on investment, computed as the ratio of sales to invested assets. (Ch. 23)

invoice The bill that the seller sends to the buyer. (Ch. 5)

J

job cost sheet An account in the work in process subsidiary ledger in which the costs charged to a particular job order are recorded. (Ch. 16)

job order cost system A type of cost accounting system that provides for a separate record of the cost of each particular quantity of product that passes through the factory. (Ch. 16)

journal The initial record in which the effects of a transaction are recorded. (Ch. 2)

journal entry The form of recording a transaction in a journal. (Ch. 2)

journalizing The process of recording a transaction in the journal. (Ch. 2)

L

last-in, first-out (LIFO) inventory cost flow method A method of inventory costing based on the assumption that the most recent merchandise inventory costs should be charged against revenue. (Ch. 6)

lead time The elapsed time between starting a unit of product into the beginning of a process and its completion. (Ch. 26)

lean accounting An accounting system characterized by fewer transactions, combined accounts, nonfinancial performance measures, and direct tracing of overhead. (Ch. 26)

lean enterprise A business that produces products or services with high quality, low cost, fast response, and immediate availability using lean principles. (Ch. 26)

lean manufacturing (or just-in-time manufacturing) A manufacturing enterprise that uses lean principles. (Chs. 17, 26)

lean principles Principles associated with the lean enterprise that include reducing inventory, reducing lead time, reducing setup time, product-/customer-oriented layouts, employee involvement, pull scheduling, zero defects, and supply chain management. (Ch. 26)

ledger A group of accounts for a business. (Ch. 2)

leverage Using debt to increase the return on an investment. (Ch. 14)

liabilities The rights of creditors that represent debts of the business. (Chs. 1, 2)

limited liability company (LLC) A business form consisting of one or more persons or entities filing an operating agreement with a state to conduct business with limited liability to the owners, yet treated as a partnership for tax purposes. (Ch. 1)

line department A unit that is directly involved in the basic objectives of an organization. (Ch. 15)

liquidity The ability to convert assets into cash. (Chs. 4, 14)

long-term liabilities Liabilities that usually will not be due for more than one year. (Ch. 4)

lower-of-cost-or-market (LCM) method A method of valuing inventory that reports the inventory at the lower of its cost or current market value (replacement cost). (Ch. 6)

M

management (or managerial) accounting The branch of accounting that uses both historical and estimated data in providing information that management uses in conducting daily operations, in planning future operations, and in developing overall business strategies. (Ch. 1)

management by exception The philosophy of managing which involves monitoring the operating results of implemented plans and comparing the expected results with the actual results. This feedback allows management to isolate significant variations for further investigation and possible remedial action. (Ch. 15)

management process The five basic management functions of (1) planning, (2) directing, (3) controlling, (4) improving, and (5) decision making. (Ch. 15)

Management's Discussion and Analysis (MD&A) An annual report disclosure that provides management's analysis of the results of operations and financial condition. (Ch. 14)

managerial accounting Type of accounting that deals with information designed to meet the specific needs of a company's management. (Ch. 15)

manufacturing business A type of business that changes basic inputs into products that are sold to individual customers. (Ch. 1)

manufacturing cells A grouping of processes where employees are cross-trained to perform more than one function. (Ch. 17)

manufacturing margin Sales less variable cost of goods sold. (Ch. 20)

manufacturing overhead Costs, other than direct materials and direct labor costs, that are incurred in the manufacturing process. (Ch. 15)

margin of safety Indicates the possible decrease in sales that may occur before an operating loss results. (Ch. 19)

market price approach An approach to transfer pricing that uses the price at which the product or service transferred could be sold to outside buyers as the transfer price. (Ch. 23)

market rate of interest The rate determined from sales and purchases of similar bonds. (Ch. 11)

market segment A portion of business that can be assigned to a manager for profit responsibility. (Ch. 20)

master budget The comprehensive budget plan linking all the individual budgets related to sales, cost of goods sold, operating expenses, projects, capital expenditures, and cash. (Ch. 21)

matching principle A concept of accounting in which expenses are matched with the revenue generated during a period by those expenses. (Ch. 3)

materials inventory The cost of materials that have not yet entered into the manufacturing process. (Ch. 15)

materials ledger The subsidiary ledger containing the individual accounts for each type of material. (Ch. 16)

materials requisition The form or electronic transmission used by a manufacturing department to authorize materials issuances from the storeroom. (Ch. 16)

maturity value The amount that is due at the maturity or due date of a note. (Ch. 8)

measurement principle A principle that determines the amount that will be recorded and reported. (Ch. 1)

merchandising business A type of business that purchases products from other businesses and sells them to customers. (Ch. 1)

mixed costs Costs with both variable and fixed characteristics, sometimes called semivariable or semifixed costs. (Ch. 19)

monetary unit assumption An assumption that requires that financial reports be expressed in a single monetary unit, or currency. (Ch. 1)

multiple production department factory overhead rate method A method that allocated factory overhead to product by using factory overhead rates for each production department. (Ch. 18)

multiple-step income statement A form of income statement that contains several sections, subsections, and subtotals. (Ch. 5)

N

natural business year A fiscal year that ends when business activities have reached the lowest point in an annual operating cycle. (Ch. 4)

negotiated price approach An approach to transfer pricing that allows managers of decentralized units to agree (negotiate) among themselves as to the transfer price. (Ch. 23)

net income (or net profit) The amount by which revenues exceed expenses. (Ch. 1)

net loss The amount by which expenses exceed revenues. (Ch. 1)

net pay Gross pay less payroll deductions; the amount the employer is obligated to pay the employee. (Ch. 10)

net present value method A method of analysis of proposed capital investments that subtracts the amount to be invested from the present value of the cash flows expected from the investments. (Ch. 25)

net realizable value The estimated selling price of an item of inventory less any direct costs of disposal, such as sales commissions. (Chs. 6, 8)

noncontrollable cost Cost that cannot be influenced (increased, decreased, or eliminated) by someone such as a manager or factory worker. (Ch. 20)

nonfinancial measure A performance measure that has not been stated in dollar terms. (Ch. 26)

nonfinancial performance measure A performance measure expressed in units rather than dollars. (Ch. 22)

non-value-added activity The cost of activities that are perceived as unnecessary from the customer's perspective and are thus candidates for elimination. (Ch. 26)

non-value-added lead time The time that units wait in inventories, move unnecessarily, and wait during machine breakdowns. (Ch. 26)

normal balance of an account The normal balance of an account can be either a debit or a credit depending on whether increases in the account are recorded as debits or credits. (Ch. 2)

notes receivable A customer's written promise to pay an amount and possibly interest at an agreed-upon rate. (Chs. 4, 8)

number of days' sales in inventory The relationship between the volume of sales and inventory, computed by dividing the average inventory by the average daily cost of goods sold. (Chs. 6, 14)

number of days' sales in receivables The relationship between sales and accounts receivable, computed by dividing average accounts receivable by average daily sales. (Chs. 8, 14)

O

objectives (goals) Developed in the planning stage, these reflect the direction and desired outcomes of certain courses of action. (Ch. 15)

operating cycle The process by which a company spends cash, generates revenues, and receives cash either at the time the revenues are generated or later by collecting an accounts receivable. (Ch. 5)

operating leverage A measure of the relative mix of a business's variable costs and fixed costs, computed as contribution margin divided by income from operations. (Ch. 19)

operational planning The development of short-term plans to achieve goals identified in a business's strategic plan. Sometimes called tactical planning. (Ch. 15)

opportunity cost The amount of income forgone from an alternative to a proposed use of cash or its equivalent. (Ch. 24)

other comprehensive income Specified items that are reported separately from net income, including foreign currency items, pension liability adjustments, and unrealized gains and losses on investments. (Ch. 14)

other expense Expenses that cannot be traced directly to operations. (Ch. 5)

other revenue Revenue from sources other than the primary operating activity of a business. (Ch. 5)

outstanding stock The stock in the hands of stockholders. (Ch. 12)

overapplied factory overhead The amount of factory overhead applied in excess of the actual factory overhead costs incurred for production during a period. (Ch. 16)

owner's equity The owner's right to the assets of the business. (Ch. 1)

P

par value A dollar amount assigned to each share of stock. (Ch. 12)

Pareto chart A bar chart that shows the totals of a particular attribute for a number of categories, ranked left to right from the largest to smallest totals. (Ch. 26)

partnership An unincorporated business form consisting of two or more persons conducting business as co-owners for profit. (Ch. 1)

patents Exclusive rights to produce and sell goods with one or more unique features. (Ch. 9)

payroll The total amount paid to employees for a certain period. (Ch. 10)

pension A cash payment to retired employees. (Ch. 10)

period costs Those costs that are used up in generating revenue during the current period and that are not involved in manufacturing a product, such as selling, general, and administrative expenses. (Ch. 15)

periodic inventory system The inventory system in which the inventory records do not show the amount available for sale or sold during the period. (Ch. 5)

perpetual inventory system The inventory system in which each purchase and sale of merchandise is recorded in an inventory account. (Ch. 5)

petty cash fund A special cash fund to pay relatively small amounts. (Ch. 7)

physical inventory A detailed listing of merchandise on hand. (Chs. 5, 6)

planning A phase of the management process whereby objectives are outlined and courses of action determined. (Ch. 15)

posting The process of transferring the debits and credits from the journal entries to the accounts. (Ch. 2)

predetermined factory overhead rate The rate used to apply factory overhead costs to the goods manufactured. The rate is determined by dividing the budgeted overhead cost by the estimated activity usage at the beginning of the fiscal period. (Ch. 16)

preferred stock A class of stock with preferential rights over common stock. (Ch. 12)

premium The excess of the issue price of a stock over its par value or the excess of the issue price of bonds over their face amount. (Chs. 11, 12)

prepaid expenses Items such as supplies that will be used in the business in the future. (Chs. 1, 3)

present value The value of an asset or cash at present that is equivalent in value to a specified sum in the future. (Ch. 11)

present value concept Cash to be received (or paid) in the future is not the equivalent of the same amount of money received at an earlier date. (Ch. 25)

present value index An index computed by dividing the total present value of the net cash flow to be received from a proposed capital investment by the amount to be invested. (Ch. 25)

present value of an annuity The sum of the present values of a series of equal cash flows to be received at fixed intervals. (Chs. 11, 25)

prevention costs Costs incurred to prevent defects from occurring during the design and delivery of products or services. (Ch. 26)

price-earnings (P/E) ratio The ratio of the market price per share of common stock, at a specific date, to the annual earnings per share. (Ch. 14)

prime costs The combination of direct materials and direct labor costs. (Ch. 15)

prior period adjustments Corrections of material errors related to a prior period or periods, excluded from the determination of net income. (Ch. 12)

private accounting The field of accounting whereby accountants are employed by a business firm or a not-for-profit organization. (Ch. 1)

process A sequence of activities linked together for performing a particular task. (Chs. 22, 26)

process cost system A type of cost system that accumulates costs for each of the various departments within a manufacturing facility. (Chs. 16, 17)

process manufacturer A manufacturer that uses large machines to process a continuous flow of raw materials through various stages of completion into a finished state. (Ch. 17)

process-oriented layout Organizing work in a plant or administrative function around processes (tasks). (Ch. 26)

product cost method A concept used in applying the cost-plus approach to product pricing in which only the costs of manufacturing the product, termed the product cost, are included in the cost amount to which the markup is added. (Ch. 24)

product costing Determining the cost of a product. (Ch. 18)

product costs The three components of manufacturing cost: direct materials, direct labor, and factory overhead costs. (Ch. 15)

production bottleneck A condition that occurs when product demand exceeds production capacity. (Ch. 24)

production budget A budget of estimated unit production. (Ch. 21)

production department factory overhead rates Rates determined by dividing the budgeted production department factory overhead by the budgeted allocation base for each department. (Ch. 18)

product-oriented layout Organizing work in a plant or administrative function around products; sometimes referred to as product cells. (Ch. 26)

profit The difference between the amounts received from customers for goods or services provided and the amounts paid for the inputs used to provide the goods or services. (Ch. 1)

profit center A decentralized unit in which the manager has the responsibility and the authority to make decisions that affect both costs and revenues (and thus profits). (Ch. 23)

profit margin A component of the rate of return on investment, computed as the ratio of income from operations to sales. (Ch. 23)

profit-volume chart A chart used to assist management in understanding the relationship between profit and volume. (Ch. 19)

profitability The ability of a firm to earn income. (Ch. 14)

property, plant, and equipment A section of the balance sheet that includes equipment, machinery, buildings, and land. (Ch. 4)

proprietorship A business owned by one individual. (Ch. 1)

public accounting The field of accounting where accountants and their staff provide services on a fee basis. (Ch. 1)

pull manufacturing A just-in-time method wherein customer orders trigger the release of finished goods, which triggers production, which triggers release of materials from suppliers. (Ch. 26)

Public Company Accounting Oversight Board (PCAOB) A new oversight body for the accounting profession that was established by the Sarbanes-Oxley Act. (Ch. 1)

purchase order The purchase order authorizes the purchase of the inventory from an approved vendor. (Ch. 6)

purchases discounts Discounts taken by the buyer for early payment of an invoice. (Ch. 5)

purchases returns and allowances From the buyer's perspective, returned merchandise or an adjustment for defective merchandise. (Ch. 5)

push manufacturing Materials are released into production and work in process is released into finished goods in anticipation of future sales. (Ch. 26)

Q

quantity factor The effect of a difference in the number of units sold, assuming no change in unit sales price or unit cost. (Ch. 20)

quick assets Cash and other current assets that can be quickly converted to cash, such as marketable securities and receivables. (Chs. 10, 14)

quick ratio A financial ratio that measures the ability to pay current liabilities with quick assets (cash, marketable securities, accounts receivable). (Chs. 10, 14)

R

radio frequency identification devices (RFID) Electronic tags (chips) placed on or embedded within products that can be read by radio waves that allow instant monitoring of product location. (Ch. 26)

ratio of fixed assets to long-term liabilities A leverage ratio that measures the margin of safety of long-term creditors, calculated as the net fixed assets divided by the long-term liabilities. (Ch. 14)

ratio of liabilities to stockholders' equity A comprehensive leverage ratio that measures the relationship of the claims of creditors to stockholders' equity. (Chs. 1, 14)

ratio of sales to assets Ratio that measures how effectively a company uses its assets, computed as sales divided by average total assets. (Ch. 15)

ratios A number that expresses a financial statement item or set of financial statement items as a percentage of another financial item, in order to measure an important economic relationship as a single number. (Ch. 14)

Raw and In Process (RIP) Inventory The capitalized cost of direct materials purchases, labor, and overhead charged to the production cell. (Ch. 26)

real (permanent) accounts Term for balance sheet accounts because they are relatively permanent and carried forward from year to year. (Ch. 4)

receivables All money claims against other entities, including people, companies, and other organizations. (Ch. 8)

receiving report The form or electronic transmission used by the receiving personnel to indicate that materials have been received and inspected. (Chs. 6, 16)

relevant A characteristic of financial reports that pertains to information having the potential to impact decision making. (Ch. 1)

relevant range The range of activity over which changes in cost are of interest to management. (Ch. 19)

rent revenue Money received for rent. (Ch. 1)

report form The form of balance sheet with the Liabilities and Stockholders' Equity sections presented below the Assets section. (Ch. 1)

residual income The excess of divisional income from operations over a "minimum" acceptable income from operations. (Ch. 23)

residual value The estimated value of a fixed asset at the end of its useful life. (Ch. 9)

responsibility accounting The process of measuring and reporting operating data by areas of responsibility. (Ch. 23)

responsibility center An organizational unit for which a manager is assigned responsibility over costs, revenues, or assets. (Ch. 21)

restrictions Amounts of retained earnings that have been limited for use as dividends. (Ch. 12)

retail inventory method A method of estimating inventory cost that is based on the relationship of gross profit to sales. (Ch. 6)

retained earnings Net income retained in a corporation. (Chs. 1, 2)

retained earnings statement A summary of the changes in the retained earnings that have occurred during a specific period of time, such as a month or a year. (Chs. 1, 12)

return on common stockholders' equity The rate of profits earned on the amount invested by the common stockholders. (Ch. 14)

return on investment (ROI) A measure that considers the amount of assets invested, computed as income from operations divided by invested assets. (Ch. 23)

return on total assets The profitability of total assets, without considering how the assets are financed. (Ch. 14)

revenue expenditures Costs that benefit only the current period or costs incurred for normal maintenance and repairs of fixed assets. (Ch. 9)

revenue recognition The process of recording revenues. (Ch. 3)

revenue recognition concept The concept that supports recording revenues when services have been performed or products delivered to customers. (Ch. 3)

revenue recognition principle A principle that determine when revenue is recorded in the accounting records. (Ch. 1)

revenues Increases in assets and stockholders' equity from performing services or delivering products to customers. (Chs. 1, 2)

reversing entries Journal entries that are recorded on the first day of the next period that are the exact opposite of the related adjusting entry from the last day of the prior period. (Ch. 4)

rules of debit and credit In the double-entry accounting system, specific rules for recording debits and credits based on the type of account. (Ch. 2)

S

sales The total amount charged customers for merchandise sold, including cash sales and sales on account. (Chs. 1, 5)

sales budget One of the major elements of the income statement budget that indicates the quantity of estimated sales and the expected unit selling price. (Ch. 21)

sales discounts From the seller's perspective, discounts that a seller may offer the buyer for early payment. (Ch. 5)

sales mix The relative distribution of sales among the various products available for sale. (Chs. 19, 20)

Sarbanes-Oxley Act (SOX) An act passed by Congress to restore public confidence and trust in the financial statements of companies. (Chs. 1, 7)

Securities and Exchange Commission (SEC) An agency of the U.S. government that has authority over the accounting and financial disclosures for companies whose shares of ownership (stock) are traded and sold to the public. (Ch. 1)

selling expenses Expenses that are incurred directly in the selling of merchandise. (Ch. 5)

service business A business providing services rather than products to customers. (Ch. 1)

service department charges The costs of services provided by an internal service department and transferred to a responsibility center. (Ch. 23)

setup An overhead activity that consists of changing tooling in machines in preparation for making a new product. (Ch. 18)

single plantwide factory overhead rate method A method that allocates all factory overhead to products by using a single factory overhead rate. (Ch. 18)

single-step income statement A form of income statement in which the total of all expenses is deducted from the total of all revenues in one step. (Ch. 5)

Six Sigma A quality improvement process developed by Motorola Corporation consisting of five steps: define, measure, analyze, improve, and control (DMAIC). (Ch. 26)

slide An error in which the entire number is moved one or more spaces to the right or the left, such as writing $542.00 as $54.20 or $5,420.00. (Ch. 2)

solvency The ability of a firm to pay its debts as they come due. (Chs. 4, 14)

special journals Journals designed to be used for recording a single type of transaction. (Ch. 5)

special-purpose funds Cash funds used for a special business need. (Ch. 7)

specific identification inventory cost flow method Inventory method in which the unit sold is identified with a specific purchase. (Ch. 6)

staff department A unit that provides services, assistance, and advice to the departments with line or other staff responsibilities. (Ch. 15)

standard cost A detailed estimate of what a product should cost. (Ch. 22)

standard cost systems Accounting systems that use standards for each element of manufacturing cost entering into the finished product. (Ch. 22)

standards Performance goals, often relating to how much a product should cost. (Ch. 22)

statement of cash flows A summary of the cash receipts and cash payments for a specific period of time, such as a month or a year. (Chs. 1, 13)

statement of cost of goods manufactured The income statement of manufacturing companies. (Ch. 15)

statement of stockholders' equity A summary of the changes in the stockholders' equity in a corporation that have occurred during a specific period of time. (Ch. 12)

static budget A budget that does not adjust to changes in activity levels. (Ch. 21)

stock Shares of ownership of a corporation. (Ch. 12)

stock dividend A distribution of shares of stock to stockholders. (Ch. 12)

stock split A reduction in the par or stated value of a common stock and the issuance of a proportionate number of additional shares. (Ch. 12)

stockholders The owners of a corporation. (Ch. 12)

stockholders' equity The stockholders' right to the assets of the business. (Chs. 1, 2)

straight-line method A method of depreciation that provides for equal periodic depreciation expense over the estimated life of a fixed asset. (Chs. 9, 11)

strategic planning The development of a long-range course of action to achieve business goals. (Ch. 15)

strategies The means by which business goals and objectives will be achieved. (Ch. 15)

subsidiary inventory ledger The subsidiary ledger containing individual accounts for items of inventory. (Ch. 6)

subsidiary ledger A ledger containing individual accounts with a common characteristic. (Ch. 5)

sunk cost A cost that is not affected by subsequent decisions. (Ch. 24)

supply chain management The coordination and control of materials, services, information, and finances as they move in a process from supplier, through the manufacturer, wholesaler, and retailer to the consumer. (Ch. 26)

sustainability The practice of operating a business to maximize profits while attempting to preserve the environment, economy, and needs of future generations. (Ch. 15)

Sustainability Accounting Standards Board (SASB) A board that was organized in 2011 to develop accounting standards that help companies report decision-useful sustainability information to external financial statement users. (Ch. 15)

T

T account The simplest form of an account. (Ch. 2)

target costing The target cost is determined by subtracting a desired profit from a market method determined price. The resulting target cost is used to motivate cost improvements in design and manufacture. (Ch. 24)

temporary (nominal) accounts Accounts that report amounts for only one period. (Ch. 4)

theory of constraints (TOC) A manufacturing strategy that attempts to remove the influence of bottlenecks (constraints) on a process. (Ch. 24)

time period assumption An assumption that allows a company to report its economic activities on a regular basis for a specific period of time. (Ch. 1)

time tickets The form on which the amount of time spent by each employee and the labor cost incurred for each individual job, or for factory overhead, are recorded. (Ch. 16)

time value of money concept The concept that an amount of money invested today will earn income. (Ch. 25)

times interest earned A ratio that computes the number of times interest payments could be paid out of current-period earnings. (Chs. 11, 14)

total cost method A concept used in applying the cost-plus approach to product pricing in which all the costs of manufacturing the product plus the selling and administrative expenses are included in the cost amount to which the markup is added. (Ch. 24)

total manufacturing cost variance The difference between total standard costs and total actual costs for units produced. (Ch. 22)

trade discounts Discounts from the list prices in published catalogs or special discounts offered to certain classes of buyers. (Ch. 5)

trade-in allowance The amount a seller allows a buyer for a fixed asset that is traded in for a similar asset. (Ch. 9)

trademark A name, term, or symbol used to identify a business and its products. (Ch. 9)

trading securities Securities that management intends to actively trade for profit. (Ch. 13)

transfer price The price charged one decentralized unit by another for the goods or services provided. (Ch. 23)

transposition An error in which the order of the digits is changed, such as writing $542 as $452 or $524. (Ch. 2)

treasury stock Stock that a corporation has once issued and then reacquires. (Ch. 12)

trial balance A summary listing of the titles and balances of accounts in the ledger. (Ch. 2)

U

unadjusted trial balance A summary listing of the titles and balances of accounts in the ledger prior to the posting of adjusting entries. (Ch. 2)

underapplied factory overhead The amount of actual factory overhead in excess of the factory overhead applied to production during a period. (Ch. 16)

unearned revenue The liability created by receiving revenue in advance. (Chs. 2, 3)

unfavorable cost variance A variance that occurs when the actual cost exceeds the standard cost. (Ch. 22)

unit contribution margin The dollars available from each unit of sales to cover fixed costs and provide operating profits. (Ch. 19)

unit price (cost) factor The effect of a difference in unit sales price or unit cost on the number of units sold. (Ch. 20)

units-of-activity method A method of depreciation that provides for depreciation expense based on the expected productive capacity of a fixed asset. (Ch. 9)

unrealized gain Changes in the fair value of equity or debt securities for a period. (Ch. 14)

utilization A measure of the use of a fixed asset in serving customers relative to the asset's capacity. (Ch. 15)

V

value-added activity The cost of activities that are needed to meet customer requirements. (Ch. 26)

value-added lead time The time required to manufacture a unit of product or other output. (Ch. 26)

value-added ratio The ratio of the value-added lead time to the total lead time. (Ch. 26)

variable cost method A concept used in applying the cost-plus approach to product pricing in which only the variable costs are included in the cost amount to which the markup is added. (Ch. 24)

variable cost of goods sold Consists of direct materials, direct labor, and variable factory overhead for the units sold. (Ch. 20)

variable costing The concept that considers the cost of products manufactured to be composed only of those manufacturing costs that increase or decrease as the volume of production rises or falls (direct materials, direct labor, and variable factory overhead). (Chs. 19, 20)

variable costs Costs that vary in total dollar amount as the level of activity changes. (Ch. 19)

vertical analysis An analysis that compares each item in a current statement with a total amount within the same statement. (Chs. 3, 14)

volume variance The difference between the budgeted fixed overhead at 100% of normal capacity and the standard fixed overhead for the actual production achieved during the period. (Ch. 22)

voucher A special form for recording relevant data about a liability and the details of its payment. (Ch. 7)

voucher system A set of procedures for authorizing and recording liabilities and cash payments. (Ch. 7)

W

weighted average inventory cost flow method A method of inventory costing in which the cost of the units sold and in ending inventory is a weighted average of the purchase costs. (Ch. 6)

whole units The number of units in production during a period, whether completed or not. (Ch. 17)

work in process inventory The direct materials costs, the direct labor costs, and the applied factory overhead costs that have entered into the manufacturing process but are associated with products that have not been finished. (Ch. 15)

working capital The excess of the current assets of a business over its current liabilities. (Chs. 4, 14)

Z

zero-based budgeting A concept of budgeting that requires all levels of management to start from zero and estimate budget data as if there had been no previous activities in their units. (Ch. 21)

Index

The Basics

Accounting Equation:

Assets = Liabilities + Stockholders' Equity

T Account:

Account Title	
Left side	Right side
debit	credit

Rules of Debit and Credit:

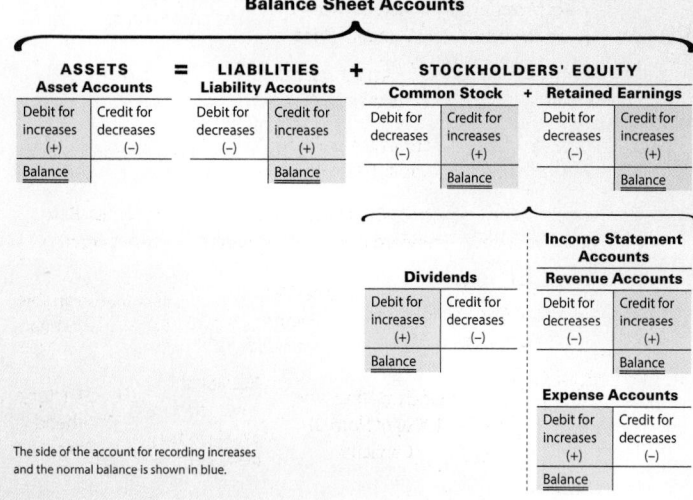

Balance Sheet Accounts

The side of the account for recording increases and the normal balance is shown in blue.

Accounting Cycle:

1. Transactions are analyzed and recorded in the journal.
2. Transactions are posted to the ledger.
3. An unadjusted trial balance is prepared.
4. Adjustment data are assembled and analyzed.
5. An optional end-of-period spreadsheet is prepared.
6. Adjusting entries are journalized and posted to the ledger.
7. An adjusted trial balance is prepared.
8. Financial statements are prepared.
9. Closing entries are journalized and posted to the ledger.
10. A post-closing trial balance is prepared.

Types of Adjusting Entries:

- Accrued revenue (accrued asset)
- Accrued expense (accrued liability)
- Unearned revenue (deferred revenue)
- Prepaid expense (deferred expense)
- Depreciation expense

Each entry will always affect both a balance sheet account and an income statement account.

Analyzing and Journalizing Transactions

1. Carefully read the description of the transaction to determine whether an asset, liability, common stock, retained earnings, revenue, expense, or dividends account is affected.
2. For each account affected by the transaction, determine whether the account increases or decreases.
3. Determine whether each increase or decrease should be recorded as a debit or a credit, following the rules of debit and credit.
4. Record the transaction using a journal entry.
5. Periodically post journal entries to the accounts in the ledger.
6. Prepare an unadjusted trial balance at the end of the period.

Financial Statements:

- **Income statement:** A summary of the revenue and expenses of a business entity for a specific period of time, such as a month or a year.
- **Retained earnings statement:** A summary of the changes in the retained earnings of a business entity that have occurred during a specific period of time, such as a month or a year.
- **Balance sheet:** A list of the assets, liabilities, and stockholders' equity of a business entity as of a specific date, usually at the close of the last day of a month or a year.
- **Statement of cash flows:** A summary of the cash receipts and cash payments of a business entity for a specific period of time, such as a month or a year.

Closing Entries:

1. Revenue account balances are transferred to an account called Income Summary.
2. Expense account balances are transferred to an account called Income Summary.
3. The balance of Income Summary (net income or net loss) is transferred to Retained Earnings.
4. The balance of the dividends account is transferred to Retained Earnings.

Shipping Terms:

	FOB Shipping Point	FOB Destination
Ownership (title) passes to buyer when merchandise is..................	delivered to freight carrier	delivered to buyer
Freight costs are paid by.........................	buyer	seller

Format for Bank Reconciliation:

Cash balance according to bank statement		$XXX
Add: Additions by company not on bank statement	$XXX	
Bank errors	XXX	XXX
		$XXX
Deduct: Deductions by company not on bank statement	$XXX	
Bank errors	XXX	XXX
Adjusted balance		$XXX

Cash balance according to company's records		$XXX
Add: Additions by bank not recorded by company	$XXX	
Company errors	XXX	XXX
		$XXX
Deduct: Deductions by bank not recorded by company	$XXX	
Company errors	XXX	XXX
Adjusted balance		$XXX

Inventory Costing Methods:

- First-in, First-out (FIFO)
- Last-in, First-out (LIFO)
- Average Cost

Interest Computations:

$$\text{Interest} = \text{Face Amount (or Principal)} \times \text{Rate} \times \text{Time}$$

Methods of Determining Annual Depreciation:

Straight-Line: $\dfrac{\text{Cost} - \text{Estimated Residual Value}}{\text{Estimated Life}}$

Double-Declining-Balance: Rate* × Book Value at Beginning of Period

*Rate is commonly twice the straight-line rate (1 ÷ Estimated Life).

Units-of-Activity Method:

Depreciation per Unit $= \dfrac{\text{Cost} - \text{Residual Value}}{\text{Total Estimated Units of Activity}}$

Depreciation Expense = Depreciation per Unit × Units of Activity for Period

Adjustments to Net Income (Loss) Using the Indirect Method:

	Increase (Decrease)
Net income (loss)	$ XXX
Adjustments to reconcile net income to net cash flow from operating activities:	
Depreciation of fixed assets	XXX
Amortization of intangible assets	XXX
Losses on disposal of assets	XXX
Gains on disposal of assets	(XXX)
Changes in current operating assets and liabilities:	
Increases in noncash current operating assets	(XXX)
Decreases in noncash current operating assets	XXX
Increases in current operating liabilities	XXX
Decreases in current operating liabilities	(XXX)
Net cash flow from operating activities	$ XXX
	or
	$(XXX)

Contribution Margin Ratio $= \dfrac{\text{Sales} - \text{Variable Costs}}{\text{Sales}}$

Break-Even Sales (Units) $= \dfrac{\text{Fixed Costs}}{\text{Unit Contribution Margin}}$

Sales (Units) $= \dfrac{\text{Fixed Costs} + \text{Target Profit}}{\text{Unit Contribution Margin}}$

Margin of Safety $= \dfrac{\text{Sales} - \text{Sales at Break-Even Point}}{\text{Sales}}$

Operating Leverage $= \dfrac{\text{Contribution Margin}}{\text{Income from Operations}}$

Variances:

$$\text{Direct Materials Price Variance} = \left(\begin{array}{c}\text{Actual Price} - \\ \text{Standard Price}\end{array}\right) \times \text{Actual Quantity}$$

$$\text{Direct Materials Quantity Variance} = \left(\begin{array}{c}\text{Actual Quantity} - \\ \text{Standard Quantity}\end{array}\right) \times \begin{array}{c}\text{Standard} \\ \text{Price}\end{array}$$

$$\text{Direct Labor Rate Variance} = \left(\begin{array}{c}\text{Actual Rate per Hour} - \\ \text{Standard Rate per Hour}\end{array}\right) \times \text{Actual Hours}$$

$$\text{Direct Labor Time Variance} = \left(\begin{array}{c}\text{Actual Direct Labor Hours} - \\ \text{Standard Direct Labor Hours}\end{array}\right) \times \begin{array}{c}\text{Standard Rate} \\ \text{per Hour}\end{array}$$

$$\begin{array}{c}\text{Variable Factory} \\ \text{Overhead Controllable} \\ \text{Variance}\end{array} = \begin{array}{c}\text{Actual Variable} \\ \text{Factory} \\ \text{Overhead}\end{array} - \begin{array}{c}\text{Budgeted Variable} \\ \text{Factory Overhead}\end{array}$$

$$\begin{array}{c}\text{Fixed Factory} \\ \text{Overhead} \\ \text{Volume} \\ \text{Variance}\end{array} = \left(\begin{array}{c}\text{Standard Hours for} \\ \text{100\% of Normal} \\ \text{Capacity}\end{array} - \begin{array}{c}\text{Standard} \\ \text{Hours for} \\ \text{Actual Units} \\ \text{Produced}\end{array}\right) \times \begin{array}{c}\text{Fixed Factory} \\ \text{Overhead} \\ \text{Rate}\end{array}$$

Return on Investment (ROI) $= \dfrac{\text{Income from Operations}}{\text{Invested Assets}}$

Alternative ROI Computation:

$$\text{ROI} = \dfrac{\text{Income from Operations}}{\text{Sales}} \times \dfrac{\text{Sales}}{\text{Invested Assets}}$$

Capital Investment Analysis Methods:

Methods That Ignore Present Values:

- Average Rate of Return Method
- Cash Payback Method

Methods That Use Present Values:

- Net Present Value Method
- Internal Rate of Return Method

Average Rate of Return $= \dfrac{\text{Estimated Average Annual Income}}{\text{Average Investment}}$

Present Value Index $= \dfrac{\text{Total Present Value of Net Cash Flow}}{\text{Amount to Be Invested}}$

Present Value Factor for an Annuity of $1 $= \dfrac{\text{Amount to Be Invested}}{\text{Equal Annual Net Cash Flows}}$

Abbreviations and Acronyms Commonly Used in Business and Accounting

AAA	American Accounting Association
ABC	Activity-based costing
AICPA	American Institute of Certified Public Accountants
B2B	Business-to-business
B2C	Business-to-consumer
CFO	Chief Financial Officer
CMA	Certified Management Accountant
COGM	Cost of goods manufactured
COGS	Cost of goods sold
CPA	Certified Public Accountant
Cr.	Credit
CVP	Cost-volume-profit
Dr.	Debit
EFT	Electronic funds transfer
EPS	Earnings per share
ERP	Enterprise resource planning
FASB	Financial Accounting Standards Board
FICA tax	Federal Insurance Contributions Act tax
FIFO	First-in, first-out
FOB	Free on board
FUTA	Federal unemployment compensation tax
GAAP	Generally accepted accounting principles
IASB	International Accounting Standards Board
IFRS	International Financial Reporting Standards
IMA	Institute of Management Accountants
IRC	Internal Revenue Code
IRR	Internal rate of return
IRS	Internal Revenue Service
JIT	Just-in-time
LIFO	Last-in, first-out
LCM	Lower of cost or market
MACRS	Modified Accelerated Cost Recovery System
MD&A	Management's Discussion and Analysis
n/30	Net 30
n/eom	Net, end-of-month
NPV	Net present value
NSF	Not sufficient funds
P/E Ratio	Price-earnings ratio
POS	Point of sale
ROI	Return on investment
R&D	Research and development
SCM	Supply chain management
SEC	Securities and Exchange Commission
SOX	Sarbanes-Oxley Act
TQC	Total quality control
W-4	Employee's Withholding Allowance Certificate
WIP	Work in process

Classification of Accounts

Account Title	Account Classification	Normal Balance	Financial Statement
Accounts Payable	Current liability	Credit	Balance sheet
Accounts Receivable	Current asset	Debit	Balance sheet
Accumulated Depletion	Contra fixed asset	Credit	Balance sheet
Accumulated Depreciation	Contra fixed asset	Credit	Balance sheet
Advertising Expense	Operating expense	Debit	Income statement
Allowance for Doubtful Accounts	Contra current asset	Credit	Balance sheet
Amortization Expense	Operating expense	Debit	Income statement
Bonds Payable	Long-term liability	Credit	Balance sheet
Building	Fixed asset	Debit	Balance sheet
Cash	Current asset	Debit	Balance sheet
Cash Dividends	Stockholders' equity	Debit	Retained earnings statement
Cash Dividends Payable	Current liability	Credit	Balance sheet
Common Stock	Stockholders' equity	Credit	Balance sheet
Cost of Goods Sold	Cost of goods sold	Debit	Income statement
Customer Refunds Payable	Current liability	Credit	Balance sheet
Delivery Expense	Operating expense	Debit	Income statement
Depletion Expense	Operating expense	Debit	Income statement
Discount on Bonds Payable	Long-term liability	Debit	Balance sheet
Dividend Revenue	Other income	Credit	Income statement
Dividends	Stockholders' equity	Debit	Retained earnings statement
Employees Federal Income Tax Payable	Current liability	Credit	Balance sheet
Equipment	Fixed asset	Debit	Balance sheet
Estimated Returns Inventory	Current asset	Debit	Balance sheet
Factory Overhead (Overapplied)	Deferred credit	Credit	Balance sheet (interim)
Factory Overhead (Underapplied)	Deferred debit	Debit	Balance sheet (interim)
Federal Income Tax Payable	Current liability	Credit	Balance sheet
Federal Unemployment Tax Payable	Current liability	Credit	Balance sheet
Finished Goods	Current asset	Debit	Balance sheet
Freight In	Cost of goods sold	Debit	Income statement
Freight Out	Operating expense	Debit	Income statement
Gain on Disposal of Fixed Assets	Other income	Credit	Income statement
Gain on Redemption of Bonds	Other income	Credit	Income statement
Gain on Sale of Investments	Other income	Credit	Income statement
Goodwill	Intangible asset	Debit	Balance sheet
Income Tax Expense	Income tax	Debit	Income statement
Income Tax Payable	Current liability	Credit	Balance sheet
Insurance Expense	Operating expense	Debit	Income statement
Interest Expense	Other expense	Debit	Income statement
Interest Receivable	Current asset	Debit	Balance sheet
Interest Revenue	Other income	Credit	Income statement
Inventory	Current asset/Cost of goods sold	Debit	Balance sheet/Income statement
Investment in Bonds	Investment	Debit	Balance sheet
Investment in Stocks	Investment	Debit	Balance sheet
Investment in Subsidiary	Investment	Debit	Balance sheet
Land	Fixed asset	Debit	Balance sheet
Loss on Disposal of Fixed Assets	Other expense	Debit	Income statement
Loss on Redemption of Bonds	Other expense	Debit	Income statement

Account Title	Account Classification	Normal Balance	Financial Statement
Loss on Sale of Investments	Other expense	Debit	Income statement
Marketable Securities	Current asset	Debit	Balance sheet
Materials	Current asset	Debit	Balance sheet
Medicare Tax Payable	Current liability	Credit	Balance sheet
Notes Payable	Current liability/Long-term liability	Credit	Balance sheet
Notes Receivable	Current asset/Investment	Debit	Balance sheet
Patents	Intangible asset	Debit	Balance sheet
Paid-In Capital from Sale of Treasury Stock	Stockholders' equity	Credit	Balance sheet
Paid-In Capital in Excess of Par (Stated Value)	Stockholders' equity	Credit	Balance sheet
Payroll Tax Expense	Operating expense	Debit	Income statement
Pension Expense	Operating expense	Debit	Income statement
Petty Cash	Current asset	Debit	Balance sheet
Preferred Stock	Stockholders' equity	Credit	Balance sheet
Premium on Bonds Payable	Long-term liability	Credit	Balance sheet
Prepaid Insurance	Current asset	Debit	Balance sheet
Prepaid Rent	Current asset	Debit	Balance sheet
Purchases	Cost of goods sold	Debit	Income statement
Purchases Discounts	Cost of goods sold	Credit	Income statement
Purchases Returns and Allowances	Cost of goods sold	Credit	Income statement
Rent Expense	Operating expense	Debit	Income statement
Rent Revenue	Other income	Credit	Income statement
Retained Earnings	Stockholders' equity	Credit	Balance sheet/Retained earnings statement
Salaries Expense	Operating expense	Debit	Income statement
Salaries Payable	Current liability	Credit	Balance sheet
Sales Tax Payable	Current liability	Credit	Balance sheet
Social Security Tax Payable	Current liability	Credit	Balance sheet
State Unemployment Tax Payable	Current liability	Credit	Balance sheet
Stock Dividends	Stockholders' equity	Debit	Retained earnings statement
Stock Dividends Distributable	Stockholders' equity	Credit	Balance sheet
Supplies	Current asset	Debit	Balance sheet
Supplies Expense	Operating expense	Debit	Income statement
Treasury Stock	Stockholders' equity	Debit	Balance sheet
Uncollectible Accounts Expense	Operating expense	Debit	Income statement
Unearned Rent	Current liability	Credit	Balance sheet
Utilities Expense	Operating expense	Debit	Income statement
Vacation Pay Expense	Operating expense	Debit	Income statement
Vacation Pay Payable	Current liability/Long-term liability	Credit	Balance sheet
Work in Process	Current asset	Debit	Balance sheet

Abbreviations and Acronyms Commonly Used in Business and Accounting

AAA	American Accounting Association
ABC	Activity-based costing
AICPA	American Institute of Certified Public Accountants
B2B	Business-to-business
B2C	Business-to-consumer
CFO	Chief Financial Officer
CMA	Certified Management Accountant
COGM	Cost of goods manufactured
COGS	Cost of goods sold
CPA	Certified Public Accountant
Cr.	Credit
CVP	Cost-volume-profit
Dr.	Debit
EFT	Electronic funds transfer
EPS	Earnings per share
ERP	Enterprise resource planning
FASB	Financial Accounting Standards Board
FICA tax	Federal Insurance Contributions Act tax
FIFO	First-in, first-out
FOB	Free on board
FUTA	Federal unemployment compensation tax
GAAP	Generally accepted accounting principles
IASB	International Accounting Standards Board
IFRS	International Financial Reporting Standards
IMA	Institute of Management Accountants
IRC	Internal Revenue Code
IRR	Internal rate of return
IRS	Internal Revenue Service
JIT	Just-in-time
LIFO	Last-in, first-out
LCM	Lower of cost or market
MACRS	Modified Accelerated Cost Recovery System
MD&A	Management's Discussion and Analysis
n/30	Net 30
n/eom	Net, end-of-month
NPV	Net present value
NSF	Not sufficient funds
P/E Ratio	Price-earnings ratio
POS	Point of sale
ROI	Return on investment
R&D	Research and development
SCM	Supply chain management
SEC	Securities and Exchange Commission
SOX	Sarbanes-Oxley Act
TQC	Total quality control
W-4	Employee's Withholding Allowance Certificate
WIP	Work in process

Classification of Accounts

Account Title	Account Classification	Normal Balance	Financial Statement
Accounts Payable	Current liability	Credit	Balance sheet
Accounts Receivable	Current asset	Debit	Balance sheet
Accumulated Depletion	Contra fixed asset	Credit	Balance sheet
Accumulated Depreciation	Contra fixed asset	Credit	Balance sheet
Advertising Expense	Operating expense	Debit	Income statement
Allowance for Doubtful Accounts	Contra current asset	Credit	Balance sheet
Amortization Expense	Operating expense	Debit	Income statement
Bonds Payable	Long-term liability	Credit	Balance sheet
Building	Fixed asset	Debit	Balance sheet
Cash	Current asset	Debit	Balance sheet
Cash Dividends	Stockholders' equity	Debit	Retained earnings statement
Cash Dividends Payable	Current liability	Credit	Balance sheet
Common Stock	Stockholders' equity	Credit	Balance sheet
Cost of Goods Sold	Cost of goods sold	Debit	Income statement
Customer Refunds Payable	Current liability	Credit	Balance sheet
Delivery Expense	Operating expense	Debit	Income statement
Depletion Expense	Operating expense	Debit	Income statement
Discount on Bonds Payable	Long-term liability	Debit	Balance sheet
Dividend Revenue	Other income	Credit	Income statement
Dividends	Stockholders' equity	Debit	Retained earnings statement
Employees Federal Income Tax Payable	Current liability	Credit	Balance sheet
Equipment	Fixed asset	Debit	Balance sheet
Estimated Returns Inventory	Current asset	Debit	Balance sheet
Factory Overhead (Overapplied)	Deferred credit	Credit	Balance sheet (interim)
Factory Overhead (Underapplied)	Deferred debit	Debit	Balance sheet (interim)
Federal Income Tax Payable	Current liability	Credit	Balance sheet
Federal Unemployment Tax Payable	Current liability	Credit	Balance sheet
Finished Goods	Current asset	Debit	Balance sheet
Freight In	Cost of goods sold	Debit	Income statement
Freight Out	Operating expense	Debit	Income statement
Gain on Disposal of Fixed Assets	Other income	Credit	Income statement
Gain on Redemption of Bonds	Other income	Credit	Income statement
Gain on Sale of Investments	Other income	Credit	Income statement
Goodwill	Intangible asset	Debit	Balance sheet
Income Tax Expense	Income tax	Debit	Income statement
Income Tax Payable	Current liability	Credit	Balance sheet
Insurance Expense	Operating expense	Debit	Income statement
Interest Expense	Other expense	Debit	Income statement
Interest Receivable	Current asset	Debit	Balance sheet
Interest Revenue	Other income	Credit	Income statement
Inventory	Current asset/Cost of goods sold	Debit	Balance sheet/Income statement
Investment in Bonds	Investment	Debit	Balance sheet
Investment in Stocks	Investment	Debit	Balance sheet
Investment in Subsidiary	Investment	Debit	Balance sheet
Land	Fixed asset	Debit	Balance sheet
Loss on Disposal of Fixed Assets	Other expense	Debit	Income statement
Loss on Redemption of Bonds	Other expense	Debit	Income statement